KEY TO

🛏 Children welcome (from age shown in brackets, if specified)

P Off-street car parking (number of places shown in brackets)

✂ No smoking

📺 Television (either in every room or in a TV lounge)

🐕 Pets accepted (by prior arrangement)

✗ Evening meal available (by prior arrangement)

Ⓥ Special diets catered for (by prior arrangement - please check with owner to see if your particular requirements are catered for)

▥ Central heating throughout

GW00708305

independently, ᵃ ⸺
user travelling with assistance; 3 means
accessible to person with limited mobility able to walk a few paces/up maximum three steps

❄ Christmas breaks a speciality

☕ Coffee/tea making facilities

cc Credit cards accepted

Use the **National Grid** reference with Ordnance Survey maps and any atlas that uses the British National Grid. The letters refer to a 100 kilometre grid square. The first two numbers refer to a North/South grid line and the last two numbers refer to an East/West grid line. The grid reference indicates their intersection point.

The **location heading** – every hamlet, village, town and city listed in this directory is represented on the local county map at the head of each section.

Local pubs – these are the names of nearby pubs that serve food in the evening, as suggested by local B&Bs.

Penny Hassett

PH2096 ◀ *Cat & Fiddle, The Bull*

The Old Rectory, Main Street,
Penny Hassett, Borchester, Borsetshire,
BC2 3QT.
C18th former rectory, lovely garden. Convenient for countryside and Borchester.
Open: All Year
Grades: ETC 3 Diamond
01676 512480 Mrs Grundy
Fax: 01676 512481
oldrectory@aol.com
D: £18.00-£20.00 **S:** £20.00-£23.00
Beds: 1F 1D 1T **Baths:** 1 En 1 Pr 1 Sh
🛏 P (5) ✂ 📺 ✗ ▥ Ⓥ ❄ ☕ ♿ cc

D: **Price range** *per person* sharing in a *double room*.
S: **Price range** for a single person in a room.

Bedrooms
F = Family
D = Double
T = Twin
S = Single

Bathrooms
En = Ensuite
Pr = Private
Sh = Shared

Grades – The English Tourism Council (**ETC**) grades B&Bs for quality in Diamonds (**1 Diamond** to **5 Diamond**, highest) and hotels in Stars (**1 Star** to **5 Star**). The Jersey Tourist Board (**JTB**) uses the same system. Scottish and Welsh Tourist Board (**STB** and **WTB**) grades have two parts: the Star rating is for quality (**1 Star** to **5 Star**, highest), the other part designates the type of establishment, e.g. B&B, Guest House (**GH**), Country House (**CH**) etc. Isle of Man Tourist Board (**IOMTB**) grades have two parts: the range of facilities provided is represented by 'Listed' to 1 through 5 Crowns (**Cr**); there is also a general quality grading such as Approved (**Approv**) or Commended (**Comm**). The Guernsey Tourist Board (**GTB**) rates B&Bs for quality as Grade A (higher) or B. Ask at Tourist Information Centres for further information on these systems. The Automobile Association (**AA**) and Royal Automobile Club (**RAC**) both use, throughout the British–Irish Isles, the same system of Diamonds and Stars as the English Tourism Council.

Currency Converter

Here is a quick dollar/sterling conversion table for our American readers, based on rates as we went to press in November 2000 ($10 = £7.01 or £10 = $14.27). On these terms, the average starting double rate per person per night in this book is $27.

$20 = £14.02

$30 = £21.03

$40 = £28.04

$50 = £35.06

£15 = $21.41

£20 = $28.55

£25 = $35.68

£30 = $42.82

Please note: while it may be fine in some States to make advance bookings with several B&Bs for the same date, only to choose the final one later, it is certainly not acceptable practice in Britain. Owners who suffer at the hands of 'double-bookers' in this way are entitled to sue for compensation.

BRITAIN BED & BREAKFAST 2001

Publisher **Tim Stilwell**

Editor **Martin Dowling**

SKY HOTEL (140).
Columbia Hotel,
Lancaster Gate
PADDINGTON
020 7402 0021.
2nd July.

STILWELL

Publishing Ltd

Distributed in Great Britain, Ireland and the Commonwealth by Orca Book Services,
Stanley House, 3 Fleets Lane, Poole, Dorset BH15 3AJ (Tel: 01202 665432); and in the USA
by Seven Hills Distributors, 49 Central Avenue, Cincinatti, OH 45202 (Tel: 513 381 3881).
Available from all good bookshops.

ISBN 1-900861-22-4

Published by Stilwell Publishing Ltd,
59 Charlotte Road, Shoreditch, London, EC2A 3QW.
Tel: 020 7739 7179.

Publisher: Tim Stilwell
Editor: Martin Dowling
Design and Maps: Space Design and Production Services Ltd
Front Cover Design: Crush Design Associates

Front Cover: Triscombe Farm, Wheddon Cross, Somerset is on page 306 of this directory.

Printed in France by Aubin Imprimeur, Poitiers.

Contents

Introduction

This directory is really very straightforward. It sets out simply to list as many B&Bs in as many places in Britain as possible, so that wherever you go, you know there is one nearby. The book was actually born of frustration. My wife and I walked a long distance footpath over several weekends in the summer of 1991. As neither of us are born to camping or wished to stay in expensive hotels, we decided on B&Bs for our overnight stays. We encountered a problem straightaway. One could not find good value bed and breakfast accommodation along the route without going to a lot of trouble. Local libraries, directory enquiries, six different Tourist Information Centres and a large pile of brochures yielded nothing but a hotchpotch of B&B addresses, most of them miles out of our way. We abandoned the research and did the walk in one-day stretches, high-tailing it back to our London home each evening on the train. The memory stayed with us, however.

Earlier on that year I had needed to visit the National Exhibition Centre outside Birmingham, while working for a large publishing company. My colleagues and I had wished to stay in the area together and at short notice. Our office was typical of the times – the recession was in full swing and our budget did not stretch far. We asked for the local Tourist Information Centre's brochure, but it did not help us much – it arrived three days later, had no map and consisted mostly of hotels outside our price range. A 2-mile trek to the local reference library to trawl through the Birmingham Yellow Pages yielded a list of local guest house telephone numbers. There was no way of knowing the kind of facilities they had or how much they cost – it was like blind man's buff. We were lucky. We got what we wanted after 20 calls – bed and breakfast in a thriving Coleshill pub, five miles from the Centre. We had booked it unseen, though, on the landlord's word only – an uninformed decision. In their small way, both experiences illustrated the need for a book such as *Stilwell's Britain: Bed & Breakfast*.

As the recession grew worse, I lost my job with the large publishing company. A year later, I set up a small publishing company myself and our first project was this directory. It has been rather successful. The reason must be that over the years many others have found themselves in similar straits – stuck for somewhere to stay overnight. For lack of information, they missed out on the good value offered by B&Bs. This is therefore a book to save the reader time and money: it suits anyone who wishes to plan a trip in Britain, who appreciates good value and who is open to ideas. The directory is quite deliberately not a guidebook. Its aim is that of any directory in any field: to be comprehensive, to offer the widest choice. By this definition, *Stilwell's Britain: Bed & Breakfast* outstrips any guidebook

– we publish by far and away the largest number of B&Bs listed anywhere in this country. What we do not do is make up the reader's mind for them. There are plenty of other B&B books that push their particular premises as 'exclusive' or 'special'. We think that a simple glance over the salient details on any page and the reader will be his or her own guide.

We have two kinds of reader in mind. The first knows exactly where to go but not where to stay. The nearest B&B is the best solution; a quick look at the right county map gives the answer. The other reader is not so sure where to go. As they browse the pages, the short ten-word descriptions provide good ideas.

All information here has been supplied by the B&B owners themselves. All are bona fide B&Bs; 99% are on the books of the local Tourist Information Centre. We should make it clear that inclusion in these pages does not imply personal recommendation. We have not visited them all individually; all we have done is write to them. The directory lists over 7,500 entries in over 4,000 locations throughout Britain. The vast majority were included because they offered B&B for under £27.50 per person per night (in fact the average starting double rate per person per night in this book is £19.00).

Owners were canvassed in the summer of 2000 and responded by the end of October. They were asked to provide their range of rates per person per night for 2001. The rates are thus forecasts and are in any case always subject to seasonal fluctuation in demand. Some information may, of course, be out of date already. Grades may go up or down, or be removed altogether. British Telecom may alter exchange numbers. Proprietors may decide to sell up and move out of the business altogether. This is why the directory has to be a yearbook; in general, though, the information published here will be accurate, pertinent and useful for many a year. The pink highlight boxes are advertisements – the B&B has paid for some extra wordage and for their entry to stand out from the page a little more.

The main aim has been to provide details that are concise and easy to understand. The only symbols used are some conventional tourist symbols. There are some abbreviations, but it should be clear what they stand for without having to refer to the keys on the first and last pages. The grades are perhaps more difficult – each inspecting organisation has its own classification system with its own definition of merit. Once again, though, the reader will soon pick out the exceptional establishments – many have high grades from each organisation. The general rule is that more facilities mean higher prices. Do not be misled into thinking that an ungraded establishment is inferior. Many B&B owners are locally registered but never apply for a grade or do not wish to pay for one. They thrive on business from guests who return again and again because the hospitality is excellent. My advice is: ring around. A simple telephone call and some judicious questions will give you an impression of your host very effectively. If you write to a B&B for more details, it is a good idea to enclose a stamped, addressed envelope for a quick reply. The largest number of British B&Bs is now laid out before you - the greatest choice available in the market. We think that your tastes and preferences will do the rest.

We have deliberately arranged the book by administrative county in alphabetical order (unless this would disrupt a perceived sequence such as East, North, South and West Yorkshire). There is an exception to prove the rule – County Durham appears perversely under D, as most people look for it under this heading. Merseyside is merged into the adjacent Greater Manchester section. South, West and Mid-Glamorgan appear together under the heading of 'The Glamorgans'. We also hope to delight the hearts of many who show pride in their native or adopted counties. The Conservative government legislated to rename administrative counties and to revise many local government boundaries, as from April 1996. Out went many of the 1974 creations of the Heath government – Avon, Cleveland, Hereford & Worcester, Humberside, Dyfed, Clwyd, Gwynedd, Strathclyde, Grampian, Central and Tayside. In came older and more loved names, such as Argyll & Bute or Pembrokeshire. While this has undoubtedly served to make many people happier (hatred of the 1974 names was quite intense), it has proved rather a headache for travel book publishers. We are still stuck for a better name for North West Wales – Caernarfonshire & Merionethshire is horribly long and Aberconwy & Colwyn is as obscure as the Gwynedd it half replaces. Many of the new Scottish regions are too small to merit their own chapter and so we have merged them into neighbouring regions - hence 'Lothian & Falkirk' or 'Stirling & the Trossachs' (which includes Clackmannanshire). The Glasgow chapter mixes six new unitary authorities. The same goes for much of our Glamorgan and Monmouthshire chapters. We offer our commiserations to the aggrieved inhabitants of Powys, for they missed out on the reorganisation by a whisker. Those in Rutland now have a chapter to themselves. The reason for the reorganisation was to provide 'unitary' as opposed to 'two-tier' authorities. This, presumably, will cost the tax payer less. In perusing the map the dispassionate observer finds other, more cynical reasons. The major boundary changes occurred along the Clyde and in the Welsh Valleys and seem calculated to help to neuter power in traditional Labour heartlands. Other long-sought name changes must provide a welcome fillip for shire Tories, whose power has recently been on the wane. In the end, the savings to be made in running these new unitary authorities will, hopefully, outweigh the general confusion caused to the average tourist. There is a pig in the sky outside my window.

Another feature of the book is that we insist on using the proper postal address. Many entries thus carry a county name different from the one they are listed under or show a 'post town' that is some miles from the village. These oddities arise from the Royal Mail's distribution system. They should not, under any circumstances, be used as a directional guide. In one case the village of Durness in North Western Scotland is 69 miles from Lairg, its quoted 'post town' – not a journey to make in error. Used on a letter though, it does speed the mail up. If you need directions to a B&B (especially if you are travelling at night), the best solution is to telephone the owner and ask the way.

The county maps are intended to act as a general reference. They present only the locations of each entry in the directory. For a more accurate idea of the location of a B&B, use the six-figure National Grid Reference published under each location's name. Used in tandem with an Ordnance Survey map (such as the excellent Landranger series) or any atlas that uses the National Grid, these numbers provide first-class route-planning references. The pubs that appear beneath each location heading are included on the recommendation of B&Bs themselves. The tankard symbol shows that they are local pubs where one can get a decent evening meal at a reasonable price.

Throughout the book you will find boxes offering peremptory advice to readers. These may seem of little consequence; some, we have been told, can annoy. We are sorry to tread upon delicate sensibilities, but the boxes fill up odd bits of space and neaten the page. Those that request courtesy and care for the customs of your hosts need no apology, however. Opening one's home to strangers, albeit for payment, requires a leap of faith for most people; B&B owners are no exceptions. We simply ask everyone to observe the usual house rules. In this way, other guests will continue to meet with a welcome when they, too, pass through.

The Publisher
Stoke Newington, November 2000.

SHETLAND ISLANDS

ISLES OF ORKNEY

WESTERN ISLES

Wick

Stornoway

GREAT BRITAIN

Inverness

Aberdeen

SCOTLAND

Fort William

Glasgow

EDINBURGH

Newcastle upon Tyne

Durham

NORTHERN

IRELAND

ISLE OF MAN

Kendal

York

Manchester

REPUBLIC
OF
IRELAND

Liverpool

Norwich

Birmingham

Aberystwyth

ENGLAND

WALES

CARDIFF

Bristol

LONDON

Dover

Portsmouth

Exeter

Plymouth

ISLE OF WIGHT

ISLES OF SCILLY

CHANNEL ISLANDS

FRANCE

England & Wales – *Regions*

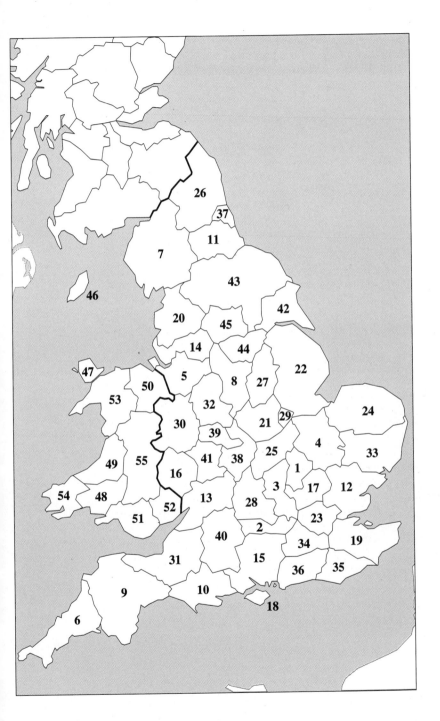

Scotland – *Regions*

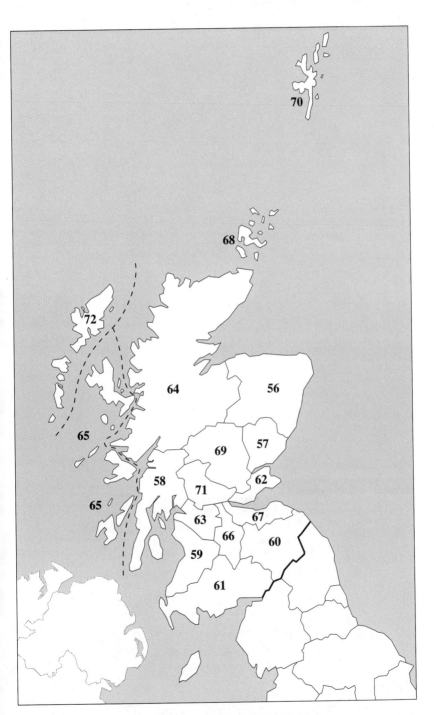

Channel Islands

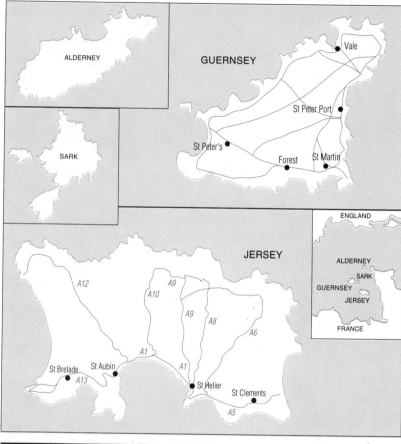

Tourist Information Centre

States Office, Queen Elizabeth II Street, **Alderney**, Guernsey, GY9 3TB, 01481 822994.

The Airport, La Villiaze, **Forest**, Guernsey, GY8 0DS, 01481 37267.

Crown Pier, **St Peter Port**, Guernsey, GY1 2LG, 01481 723552.

Administration Office, **Herm**, Guernsey, 01481 700334.

Liberation Square, **St Helier**, Jersey, JE1 1BB, 01534 500777.

Sark, Guernsey, GY9 0SB, 01481 832345.

B&B owners may vary rates - be sure to check when booking

▼ ALDERNEY

Alderney

🏶 *Harbour Lights, Rose & Crown, Maria's Hall, Albert Inn*

L'Haras, *Newtown Road, Alderney, Guernsey, C.I., GY9 3XP.*
Quiet, family-run guest house, close to harbour and town.
Open: All Year
01481 823174 (also fax)
Mrs Jansen
lharas@internet.alderney.gg
D: £18.00–£26.00 **S:** £18.00–£24.00
Beds: 1D 2T 2S **Baths:** 2 En 1 Sh
🛇 (10) 📺 🛒 🏥

Simerock, *Les Venelles, Alderney, Guernsey, C.I., GY9 3TW.*
Family run, centrally situated to town and other amenities.
Open: All Year
01481 823645 Mrs Lowe
simerock.guests@virgin.net
D: £18.00–£38.00
S: £20.00–£45.00
Beds: 3F 2T 1D
Baths: 2 En 2 Sh
🛇 🅿 (10) 📺 ✕ 🛒 Ⓥ ✻ 🏥 ♿

St Annes Guest House, *Alderney, C.I., GY9 3TB.*
Period style secluded garden, ideally situated for beaches, cliff paths.
Open: All Year
01481 823145 Miss Murdoch
Fax: 01481 824858
D: £22.00–£26.00
S: £22.00–£30.00
Beds: 1F 1T 1S 1D
Baths: 1 En 1 Sh
🛇 📺 🏨 ✕ 🛒 Ⓥ ✻ 🏥

▼ GUERNSEY

Forest

🏚 *The Venture Inn, Deerhound Inn*

Mon Plaisir Guest House, *Route de Farras, Forest, Guernsey, C.I., GY8 0DY.*
Delightful Guernsey farmhouse with garden. Excellent base to explore island.
Open: All Year **Grades:** AA 3 Diamond
01481 264498 Mrs Torode
Fax: 01481 263493
info@mon-plaisir.com
D: £18.00–£26.00 **S:** fr £23.00
Beds: 3D 2T **Baths:** 5 En
🛏 (3) 🅿 (8) ⊬ 📺 🛏 🍴 cc

Tudor Lodge Deer Farm, *Forest Road, Forest, Guernsey, C.I., GY8 0AU.*
Guest house with unique atmosphere; old fashioned home-cooked breakfast.
Open: Easter to Sep
01481 37849 Mrs Gallienne
Fax: 01481 35662
D: £27.50–£30.00 **S:** £35.00
Beds: 2F 1D 2T **Baths:** 5 En
🛏 (12) 🅿 (12) ⊬ 📺 🛏 🍴

St Martin

🏚 *Queens Hotel*

Rosewood, *La Grand Rue, St Martin, Guernsey, Channel Islands, GY4 6RU.*
Centrally situated in St Martins village - homely guest house, large garden.
Open: Easter to Oct
Grades: ETC Grade B Commended
01481 238329 Mr Sinkinson
Fax: 01481 239457
D: £16.00–£20.00 **S:** £19.00–£23.00
Beds: 1F 2D 2T 1S **Baths:** 2 Sh
🛏 (3) 🅿 (8) ⊬ 📺 ✕ 🛏 🍴

St Peter Port

🏚 *Moore's Hotel, Mamma Rosa, Absolute End, La Collinette Hotel, Simple Ireland, Rosie Jacques*

Grisnoir, *Les Graves, St Peter Port, Guernsey, Channel Islands, GY1 1RW.*
Friendly, family run guest house - comfortable beds and good food!
Open: All Year
01481 727267 Mrs Goodlass
Fax: 01481 730661
goodlass@guernsey.net
D: £14.50–£20.00 **S:** £14.50–£23.00
Beds: 2F 1D 5T 2S **Baths:** 3 Sh
🛏 ⊬ 📺 ✕ 🛏 🍴

Foresters Arms, *St Georges Esplanade, St Peter Port, Guernsey, Channel Islands, GY1 2BQ.*
Old Guernsey pub with character and friendly atmosphere. Overlooks sea.
Open: All Year (not Xmas/New Year)
01481 723583 (also fax)
Mrs Hillion
D: £20.00–£25.00 **S:** £20.00–£25.00
Beds: 2F 1T 1D **Baths:** En
📺 ✕ 🛏 🍴

Planning a longer stay? Always ask for any special rates

Marine Hotel, *Well Road, St Peter Port, Guernsey, C.I., GY1 1WS.*
Highly recommended, friendly, comfortable hotel, 25 metres from sea.
Open: All Year
01481 724978 Mrs Clegg
Fax: 01481 711729
D: £16.00–£24.95 **S:** £16.00–£26.95
Beds: 3F 4D 3T 1S **Baths:** 11 En
🛏 📺 🛏 🍴 🍴 🚿

St Peter's

🏚 *Deerhound Inn*

Les Guilberts Farm, *Route de la Palloterie, St Peter's, Guernsey, C.I., GY7 9AR.*
Traditional Guernsey farmhouse near cliff walks, direct bus route, town, South Coast.
Open: All Year
01481 263890 Fax: 01481 266165
D: £18.00–£23.00
S: £20.00–£35.00
Beds: 1D 1T **Baths:** 2 En
🛏 (3) 🅿 (10) ⊬ 📺 🛏 🍴 cc

Vale

L'Ancresse View Guest House, *La Garenne, Vale, Guernsey, C.I., GY3 5SQ.*
Bordering L'Ancresse Golf Course. Main bus route to St Peter Port.
Open: All Year
01481 243963 (also fax)
Mr Peacegood
lancresse@hotmail.com
D: £12.00–£18.50
S: £12.00–£18.50
Beds: 1F 2D 1T
🛏 📺 🐴 🛏 🍴

▼ JERSEY

St Aubin

🏚 *Old Court House, Tenbys Bar*

Peterborough House, *Rue du Crocquet, High Street, St Aubin, Jersey, C.I., JE3 8BZ.*
C17th house, personally run, conservation area, some rooms sea view.
Open: Mar to Oct
Grades: ETC 3 Diamond, AA 3 Diamond
01534 741568 Mr & Mrs Cabral
Fax: 01534 746787
fernando@localdial.com
D: £17.25–£28.25
S: £22.25–£33.25
Beds: 1F 4D 5T 4S **Baths:** 12 En 1 Sh
🛏 (12) ⊬ 📺 🛏 🍴 cc

Panorama, *Rue du Crocquet, St Aubin, Jersey, C.I., JE3 8BZ.*
Gold merit award guest house. Exceptional standards, food, service, accommodation.
Open: Easter to Oct
Grades: ETC 3 Diamond, AA 4 Diamond
01534 742429 Fax: 01534 745940
D: £24.00–£46.00 **S:** £24.00–£72.00
Beds: 12T 2D 3S **Baths:** 17 En
🛏 (12) ⊬ 📺 🛏 🍴

St Brelade

🏚 *Goose on the Green*

Lyndhurst, *Route de la Haule, St Brelade, Jersey, C.I., JE3 8BA.*
Overlooking the golden sands of St Aubin's Bay. Superb food. **Open:** All Year
Grades: ETC 2 Diamond
01534 720317 Fax: 01534 613776
D: £15.50–£25.50 **S:** £25.50–£35.50
Beds: 4F 4D 3T **Baths:** 11 Pr
🛏 (6) 📺 🛏 🍴 cc

Au Caprice, *Route de la Haule, St Brelade, Jersey, C.I., JE3 8BA.*
Small friendly establishment situated opposite a large safe sandy beach.
Open: April-Dec
Grades: ETC 2 Diamond
01534 722083 Ms Monpetit
Fax: 01534 280058
aucaprice@jerseymail.co.uk
D: £18.50–£28.00 **S:** £20.00–£29.00
Beds: 2F 6D 4T **Baths:** 12 En
🛏 (2) 🅿 (20) ⊬ 📺 ✕ 🛏 🍴 ✳ 🍴 cc

St Clement

🏚 *Le Hocq Inn, Seymour Inn*

Rocqueberg View, *Rue de Samares, St Clement, Jersey, JE2 6LS.*
Comfortable friendly quiet house in convenient quiet location near beach.
Open: All Year
Grades: ETC 2 Diamond
01534 852642 L & S Monks
Fax: 01534 851694
D: £15.00–£20.00 **S:** £15.00–£46.00
Beds: 2F 5D 2T **Baths:** 9 En
🛏 🅿 (9) 📺 ✕ 🛏 🍴 🚿

St Helier

🏚 *Harvest Barn, The Admiral, The Ramsbottom, Tipsy Toad, Earl Grey*

Millbrook House, *Rue de Trachy, Millbrook, St Helier, Jersey, C.I., JE2 3JN.*
Open: Apr to Oct
Grades: AA 4 Diamond
01534 733036 Mr Pirouet
Fax: 01534 724317
D: £31.00–£36.50 **S:** £31.00–£36.50
Beds: 5F 10D 9T 3S **Baths:** 27 En
🛏 🅿 (20) 📺 ✕ 🍴
Where the air is clear, Millbrook house offers peace, quiet and character. Exceptional park and gardens with views of the sea. A good table and extensive wine list.

Bromley Guest House, *7 Winchester Street, St Helier, Jersey, C.I., JE2 4TH.*
Open: All Year
Grades: ETC 2 Diamond
01534 725045 Mrs Schillaci
Fax: 01534 769712
113555.1035@compuserve.com
D: £15.00–£20.00 **S:** £29.00–£44.00
Beds: 1F 3D 3T 2S **Baths:** 7 En 2 Sh
🛏 ⊬ 📺 🛏 🍴 🍴 cc
Jersey town guesthouse, open all year. Double/twin/family rooms all ensuite, single rooms basic only. Colour TV , tea/coffee facilities. Situated only 3-4 minutes from shopping area and all amenities. Travel can be arranged from England, Scotland and Ireland.

Glenroyd, *26 Cleveland Road, St Helier, Jersey, C.I., JE2 4PB.*
Comfortable Victorian family-run guest house, 10 minutes town, 1 minute beach.
Open: All Year (not Xmas)
01534 731578 Mr Hill
Fax: 01534 617367
D: £15.00–£27.00 **S:** £16.00–£27.00
Beds: 1F 4D 2T 2S **Baths:** 7 En 2 Sh
cc

Shandene, *St Aubins Road, St Helier, Jersey, C.I., JE2 3SF.*
No smoking, sea views, en suite, tv, tea/coffee. Own beach close.
Open: All Year
01534 720386 Mrs Jayes
Fax: 01534 723760
D: £16.00–£23.00
S: £16.00–£23.00
Beds: 2F 6D 4T 2S **Baths:** 8 En 1 Sh
(5) **cc**

La Sirene, *23 Clarendon Road, St Helier, Jersey, C.I., JE2 3YS.*
Close to town. Very popular holiday choice. Recommended by Which?.
Open: All Year
01534 723364 Mr Hitchmough
Fax: 01534 509727
D: £16.00–£23.00 **S:** £16.00–£23.00
Beds: 1F 4D 2T 2S **Baths:** All Pr
(5)

Almorah, *Almorah Crescent, St Helier, Jersey, C.I., JE2 3GU.*
Small family-run hotel in an elevated position overlooking the town of St Helier.
Open: Easter to Oct
01534 721648 Fax: 01534 509724
hammond@ic24.net
D: £24.00–£32.00
S: £39.00–£47.00
Beds: 3F 9D 2T **Baths:** 14 En

▼ SARK

Sark

Aval du Crust

Les Quatre Vents Guest House, *Les Quatre Vents, Sark, Guernsey, C.I., GY9 0SE.*
Family owned modern guest house, centrally situated with good sea views.
Open: Jan to Oct
01481 832247 Mrs Godwin
Fax: 01481 832332
D: £22.00–£24.00 **S:** £22.00–£24.00
Beds: 1F 1D 1T 1S **Baths:** 2 En 2 Pr
(1)

B&B owners may vary rates - be sure to check when booking

Bedfordshire

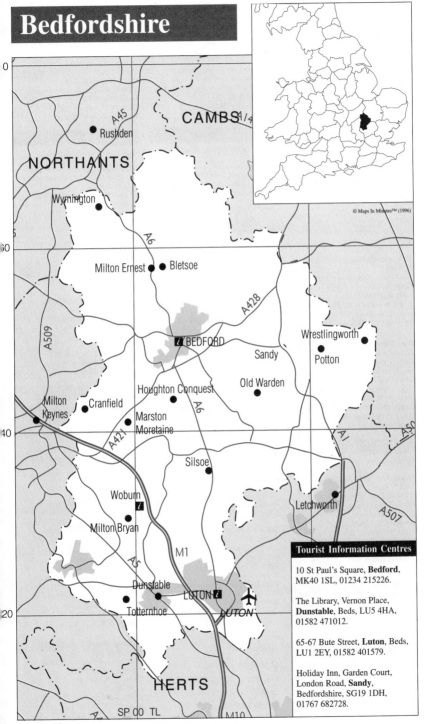

© Maps In Minutes™ (1996)

National Grid References are for villages, towns and cities – not for individual houses

Bedford

TL0549   ⚑ *Embankment Hotel, Blue Bell, Castle, Park Hotel*

Bedford Oak House, 33 Shakespear Road, Bedford, Beds, MK40 2DX.
Open: All Year (not Xmas/New Year)
01234 266972 Mr Kemp
bkemp@easynet.co.uk
D: £22.00–£24.00 **S:** £31.00–£35.00
Beds: 1D 2T 1S **Baths:** 4 En
🛏 (8) 🅿 (15) ⌿ 📺 🛏, 🛢
Newly refurbished Victorian house close to town centre, comfortable accommodation with ensuite and tea/coffee facilities, private off street parking.

20 Haylands Way, Bedford, Beds, MK41 9BU.
Family home 1 mile from town centre.
Open: All Year
01234 353272 Mrs Franklin
D: £15.00–£16.00 **S:** £15.00–£16.00
Beds: 1T 1S **Baths:** 1 En 1 Sh
🛏 (5) 🅿 (1) ⌿ 📺 🛏, 🛢

Park View, 11 Shaftesbury Avenue, Bedford, MK40 3SA.
Central, riverside, quiet Edwardian house overlooks park and Bedford embankment.
Open: All Year (not Xmas)
01234 341376 Ms Sedgwick
D: £17.50–£20.00 **S:** £17.50–£20.00
Beds: 1T 2S **Baths:** 1 En 1 Sh
🛏 ⌿ 📺 🛏, 🛢 🛢

Bletsoe

TL0357   ⚑ *Fox & Hounds*

North End Farm, Riseley Road, Bletsoe, Bedford, MK44 1QT.
A beautiful barn conversion in quiet countryside on a farm.
Open: All Year
Grades: ETC 4 Diamond
01234 781320 (also fax)
Mr & Mrs Forster
D: £25.00–£50.00 **S:** £25.00–£30.00
Beds: 4T **Baths:** 4 En
🛏 (5) 🅿 (20) ⌿ 📺 🛏 🛏, 🛢 cc

Cranfield

SP9542   ⚑ *Two Brewers*

The Queen Hotel, 40 Dartmouth Road, Olney, Buckinghamshire, MK46 4BH.
Enchanting Victorian house in bustling market town.
Open: All Year
Grades: AA 3 Diamond
01234 711924 Mrs Elsmore
Fax: 01234 711924
D: £27.50–£29.00 **S:** £42.00–£44.50
Beds: 3T 4D 2S **Baths:** 7 En 1 Sh
🅿 (9) ⌿ 📺 🛏, 🛢 cc

Dunstable

TL0121   ⚑ *Sugar Loaf*

Regent House Guest House, 79a High Street North, Dunstable, Beds, LU6 1JF.
Dunstable town centre, close to M1
Open: All Year
01582 660196 Mr Woodhouse
D: £17.00 **S:** £20.00
Beds: 5T 5S 1F **Baths:** 4 En
🛏 🅿 (6) 📺 🛏 🛏, 🛢 🛢

Luton

TL0921   ⚑ *Wigmore Arms, O'Shea's*

Stockwood Hotel, 41-43 Stockwood Crescent, Luton, Beds, LU1 3SS.
Tudor-style town centre premises, near M1, airport, golf course.
Open: All Year (not Xmas)
01582 721000 Mr Blanchard
D: fr £20.00 **S:** fr £25.00
Beds: 1F 2D 6T 9S **Baths:** 4 Pr 3 Sh
🛏 🅿 (14) 📺 ✕ 🛏

Belzayne, 70 Lalleford Road, Luton, Beds, LU2 9JH.
Modern semi, close to London bus stop.
Old fashioned hospitality.
Open: All Year (not Xmas)
01582 736591 (also fax)
Mrs Bell
D: £12.00–£14.00 **S:** fr £18.00
Beds: 1F 2T **Baths:** 2 Sh
🛏 (7) 🅿 (5) 🛏, 🛢

Marston Moretaine

SP9941   ⚑ *Bell*

The Coach House, The Old Rectory, Marston Moretaine, Bedford, MK43 0NF.
Listed building fully modernised in 5 acres of mature gardens.
Open: All Year (not Xmas)
01234 767794 (also fax)
G S Lake
isla.lake@uk.uumail.com
D: £19.50 **S:** £30.00
Beds: 1T 4D 1S **Baths:** 6 En
🛏 🅿 (20) 📺 🛏, 🛢 🛢 cc

Milton Bryan

SP9730   ⚑ *Red Lion*

Town Farm, Milton Bryan, Milton Keynes, Bucks, MK17 9HS.
Quiet, secluded farmhouse, good views, easy access Woburn and M1.
Open: All Year (not Xmas)
Grades: ETC 4 Diamond
01525 210001 Mrs Harris
D: £20.00 **S:** £23.00
Beds: 2T **Baths:** 2 En
🛏 (12) 🅿 (4) ⌿ 📺 🛏, 🛢 🛢

RATES

D = Price range per person sharing in a double room

S = Price range for a single room

Milton Ernest

TL0156   ⚑ *The Swan*

Church Barn, Churchgreen, Milton Ernest, Bedford, MK44 1RH.
Quiet country converted stone barn. Gardens. Open views. Medieval church.
Open: All Year (not Xmas)
01234 824097 (also fax) Mrs Robson
D: £15.00 **S:** £15.00
Beds: 2T 1S **Baths:** 1 En 1 Sh
🛏 🅿 (15) 📺 🛏 ✕ 🛏, 🛢 🛢

Old Warden

TL1343   ⚑ *Hare & Hounds*

Old Warden Guest House, Shop & Post Office, Old Warden, Biggleswade, Beds, SG18 9HQ.
Centre of quiet, picturesque village.
Open: All Year
Grades: ETC 3 Diamond
01767 627201 Mr Bruton
D: £21.00 **S:** £25.00–£27.00
Beds: 2D 1T **Baths:** 3 En
🛏 🅿 (5) 🛏 🛏, 🛢 🛢 ఄ cc

Potton

TL2248   ⚑ *Rose & Crown*

Rose & Crown, Market Square, Potton, Sandy, Beds, SG19 2NP.
Former C17th coaching inn. Home cooked food and real ales.
Open: All Year
01767 260221
D: £23.50–£28.50 **S:** fr £40.00
Beds: 2F 4D 4T **Baths:** 10 En
🛏 🅿 ⌿ 📺 ✕ 🛏, 🛢 🛢 cc

Sandy

TL1748   ⚑ *Chequers, Royal Oak, King's Arms, Hare & Hounds, The Bell*

Highfield Farm, Great North Road, Sandy, Beds, SG19 2AQ.
Wonderfully comfortable farmhouse in delightful grounds. Ample safe parking.
Open: All Year
Grades: ETC 5 Diamond
01767 682332 Mrs Codd
Fax: 01767 692503
margaret@highfield.farm.co.uk
D: £25.00–£30.00 **S:** £25.00–£45.00
Beds: 2F 2D 2T **Baths:** 3 En 1 Pr 1 Sh
🛏 🅿 (10) ⌿ 📺 🛏 🛏, 🛢 🛢 cc

The Pantiles, 6 Swaden Everton Road, Sandy, Beds, SG19 2DA.
Converted barn in wooded valley overlooking acre lawned gardens.
Open: All Year
01767 680668 enjaperonius@aol.com
D: £25.00 **S:** £30.00–£35.00
Beds: 1F 1T 1D **Baths:** 3 En
🛏 🅿 ⌿ 📺 🛏 🛏, 🛢 🛢

Fairlawn Hotel, 70 Bedford Road, Sandy, Beds, SG19 1EP.
Small and friendly. Easy access A1 and mainline railway station.
Open: All Year (not Xmas)
01767 680336
D: £23.00–£26.00 **S:** £23.00–£26.00
Beds: 1F 2D 2T 3S **Baths:** 2 Pr 1 Sh
🛏 🅿 (16) 📺 🛏 ✕ 🛏, 🛢 🛢

Orchard Cottage, *1 High Street,*
Wrestlingworth, Sandy, Beds, SG19 2EW.
Charming C16th thatched cottage with
modern extension, formerly village bakery.
Open: All Year (not Xmas)
Grades: ETC 3 Diamond
01767 631355 Mrs Strong
D: £20.00 **S:** £23.00
Beds: 1D 1T 2S **Baths:** 2 Sh
🛪 🅿 (4) ⌿ ⅲ Ⅴ ₤

Silsoe

TL0836 🍺 *Old George*

The Old George Hotel, *High Street,*
Silsoe, Bedford, Beds., MK45 4EP.
Old coaching inn. Village location, large
garden, famous fish restaurant.
Open: All Year (not Xmas)
Grades: AA 2 Diamond
01525 860218 J C Bridge
D: £24.00–£35.00
S: £35.00–£39.00
Beds: 5D 1T 1S
Baths: 2 En 2 Sh
🛪 🅿 (50) ⌿ ⅲ ㌤ ✕ ⅲ Ⅴ ₤ cc

Totternhoe

SP9821 🍺 *Old Farm Inn, Cross Keys*

Country Cottage, *5 Brightwell Avenue,*
Totternhoe, Dunstable, Beds, LU6 1QT.
Quiet village house in countryside with
views of Dunstable Downs.
Open: All Year (not Xmas)
01582 601287 (also fax)
Mrs Mardell
D: £25.00 **S:** £25.00
Beds: 1T 1D 1S **Baths:** 2 En 1Shared
🛪 🅿 (3) ⌿ ㌤ ⅲ Ⅴ ₤

Woburn

SP9433 🍺 *Black Horse, Royal Oak*

11 George Street, *Woburn, Milton*
Keynes, Bucks, MK17 9PX.
Small, cosy, personally run, Grade II
Listed cottage. Very near Woburn Abbey.
Open: All Year
01525 290405 (also fax) Mrs Tough
D: £15.00–£20.00 **S:** £15.00–£20.00
Beds: 1D 2T 1S 4F **Baths:** 3 Sh
🛪 ⌿ ㌤ ⅲ ₤ ⅊

Wrestlingworth

TL2547 🍺 *Chequers*

Orchard Cottage, *1 High Street,*
Wrestlingworth, Sandy, Beds, SG19 2EW.
Charming C16th thatched cottage with
modern extension, formerly village bakery.
Open: All Year (not Xmas)
Grades: ETC 3 Diamond
01767 631355 Mrs Strong
D: £20.00 **S:** £23.00
Beds: 1D 1T 2S **Baths:** 2 Sh
🛪 🅿 (4) ⌿ ⅲ Ⅴ ₤

Wymington

SP9563

The Old Rectory, *45 Rushden Road,*
Wymington, Rushden, Northants,
NN10 9LN.
A Victorian rectory set in 5.5 acres of
private grounds. A warm welcome
guaranteed. **Open:** All Year
01933 314486 Mrs Denton
Fax: 01933 411266
D: £18.50–£21.00 **S:** £17.50–£22.00
Beds: 2F 4D 2T 2S **Baths:** 6 En
🛪 🅿 (20) ⌿ Ⅴ ✕ ⅲ Ⅴ ₤ ⅊

Berkshire

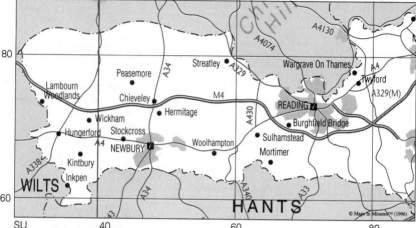

SU   40   60   80

Burghfield Bridge

SU6870   ◀ *The Cunningham*

Boathouse, Kennet House, Burghfield Bridge, Reading, Berks, RG30 3RA.
Luxury houseboat on Kennet & Avon Canal, accommodation only.
Open: All Year
0118 957 1060 Mrs Ogden
D: £15.00 **S:** £15.00
Beds: 2D
🛇 🅿 (3) ⚡ 📺 🕿 🛏.

Chieveley

SU4773   ◀ *Red Lion*

The Old Farmhouse, Downend Lane, Chieveley, Newbury, Berks, RG20 8TN.
Old farmhouse in large gardens. Accommodation in ground floor annexe.
Open: All Year
Grades: ETC 3 Diamond
01635 248361 Mrs Pallett
palletts@aol.com
D: £25.00–£26.00 **S:** £30.00
Beds: 1F **Baths:** 1 En
🛇 🅿 (4) ⚡ 📺 🛒 🍽 & ♿

19 Heathfields, Chieveley, Newbury, Berks, RG20 8TW.
Modern house in quiet development, attractive garden. Near shop, pub.
Open: Feb to Dec
Grades: ETC 3 Diamond
01635 248179 Mrs Wood
Fax: 01635 248799
ingeandco@aol.com
D: £22.50–£25.00 **S:** £22.50–£25.00
Beds: 1D 1T **Baths:** 1 Sh
🛇 🅿 (3) ⚡ 📺 🛒 🍽 & ♿

Cookham Dean

SU8684   ◀ *Chequers*

Cartlands Cottage, King's Lane, Cookham Dean, Maidenhead, Berks, SL6 9AY.
Self-contained guest room in garden. Rural, very quiet. **Open:** All Year
01628 482196 Mr & Mrs Parkes
D: £22.00–£25.00 **S:** £23.50–£26.00
Beds: 1F **Baths:** 1 Pr
🛇 🅿 (2) 📺 🛏 🅥 ♿

Hermitage

SU5173   ◀ *The Red Lion, The Bunk*

The Granary, Hermitage, Thatcham, Berks, RG18 9SD.
Charming converted barn with large garden in pretty rural hamlet.
Open: All Year (not Xmas/New Year)
01635 200249 Mr & Mrs De Lisle-Bush
Fax: 01635 200249
D: £20.00–£22.50 **S:** £22.00–£25.00
Beds: 2T 1S **Baths:** 1 Sh
🛇 (12) 🅿 (3) ⚡ 📺 🛒 🍽 & ♿

B&B owners may vary rates - be sure to check when booking

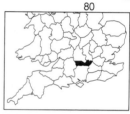

Hungerford

SU3368   ◀ *Just Williams, John O'Gaunt, Plume Of Feathers*

Wilton House, 33 High Street, Hungerford, Berks, RG17 0NF.
Elegant ensuite bedrooms in classic, historic English town house predating 1450. **Open:** All Year (not Xmas)
Grades: ETC 4 Diamond
01488 684228 Mrs Welfare
Fax: 01488 685037 welfares@hotmail.com
D: £25.00–£27.50 **S:** £35.00–£38.00
Beds: 1D 1T **Baths:** 2 En
🛇 (8) 🅿 (3) ⚡ 📺 🛏 🅥 ♿

Alderborne, 33 Bourne Vale, Hungerford, Berkshire, RG17 0LL.
Modern detached family house overlooking open country. Walking distance to shops.
Open: All Year (not Xmas)
01488 683228 Mr & Mrs Honeybone
honeybones@hungerford.co.uk
D: £17.50–£18.50 **S:** £17.50–£22.50
Beds: 2T 1S **Baths:** 1 Pr 1 Sh
🛇 (5) 🅿 (3) ⚡ 📺 🛏 🅥 ♿

Wasing, 35 Sanden Close, Hungerford, Berkshire, RG17 0LA.
Warm welcome to the home of ex farmers. 3 miles M4. **Open:** All Year (not Xmas)
01488 684127 Mrs Smalley
D: £17.00–£17.00 **S:** £17.00–£18.00
Beds: 1D 1T 1S **Baths:** 1 En 1 Sh
🛇 🅿 📺 🛏 ♿

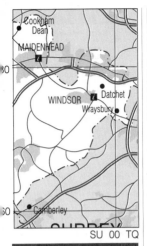

SU 00 TQ

Inkpen

SU3764

Beacon House, Bell Lane, Upper Green, Inkpen, Hungerford, Berks, RG17 9QJ.
Visit our 1930s country home on Berks/Wilts/Hants border. Lovely countryside.
Open: All Year **Grades:** AA 3 Diamond
01488 668640 Mr & Mrs Cave
l.g.cave@classicfm.net
D: fr £22.00 **S:** fr £22.00
Beds: 1T 2S **Baths:** 2 Sh
🛏 🅿 (6) 📺 ♒ ✕ 🃏 🎥 ♣ 🎱

Kintbury

SU3866 🍺 Crown & Garter

The Forbury, Crossways, Kintbury, Hungerford, Berks, RG17 9SU.
Extended C17th cottage. Lovely position facing south, overlooking own woodlands. **Open:** All Year (not Xmas)
01488 658377 Mr Cubitt
D: £22.50–£27.50 **S:** £22.50–£25.00
Beds: 1F **Baths:** 1 Pr 1 Sh
🛏 🅿 (10) 📺 🃏 ✕ 🎥 🎥 🎱

Lambourn Woodlands

SU3175 🍺 Hare and Hound

Lodge Down, Lambourn , Hungerford, Berks, RG17 7BJ.
Open: All Year
Grades: ETC 2 Crown
01672 540304 (also fax) Mrs Cook
D: fr £22.50 **S:** fr £30.00
Beds: 1F 2D 2T **Baths:** 3 En
🛏 🅿 (6) 📺 🎥 🎱
Magnificent house with spacious rooms and extensive garden with woodland and crosscountry course in the grounds overlooking horse training gallops and wonderful views of the Downs,looking towards the Ridgeway, the centre of Dick Francis country.

Maidenhead

SU8781 🍺 Boulter's Lock Inn, Thames Hotel, Kingswood Hotel, Windsor Castle, Pond House, Hare & Hounds

Sheephouse Manor, Sheephouse Road, Maidenhead, Berks, SL6 8HJ.
Charming C16th farmhouse, with health suite and jacuzzi. beautiful grounds.
Open: All Year (not Xmas)
Grades: ETC 3 Diamond
01628 776902 Mrs Street **Fax: 01628 625138**
info@sheephousemanor.co.uk
D: £28.00–£30.00 **S:** £40.00–£45.00
Beds: 1D 1T 3S **Baths:** 5 En
🛏 🅿 (7) 📺 🃏 🎥 🎥 🎱 🆑 cc

Laburnham Guest House, 31 Laburnham Road, Maidenhead, Berks, SL6 4DB.
Fine Edwardian house, near town centre, station and M4 motorway.
Open: All Year (not Xmas)
01628 676748 (also fax) Mrs Stevens
rdgs@waitrose.com
D: £23.00–£25.00 **S:** £35.00–£40.00
Beds: 1F 2D 1T 1S **Baths:** 5 En
🛏 🅿 (5) 📺 🎥 🎥 🎱

Clifton Guest House, 21 Craufurd Rise, Maidenhead, Berks, SL6 7LR.
Family-run guest house. 10 mins from town centre. Easy access London M4/M25/M40. **Open:** All Year
Grades: ETC 3 Diamond, RAC 3 Diamond
01628 623572 (also fax) Mr Arora
clifton@aroram.freeserve.co.uk
D: £45.00–£60.00
Beds: 2F 5D 5T 3S **Baths:** 8 En 1 Pr 4 Sh
🛏 🅿 ✕ 🎥 🎥 ♣ 🎱 🆑 cc

Mortimer

SU6564 🍺 Red Lion

35 The Avenue, Mortimer, Reading, Berks, RG7 3QU.
Large garden, quiet location, Mortimer Station 1 mile, rural location.
Open: All Year
0118 933 3166 Mrs Keast
D: fr £20.00 **S:** fr £20.00
Beds: 3F 2D 1S **Baths:** 1 En 1 Sh
🛏 (2) 🅿 (8) 📺 🃏 ✕ 🎥 🎥 ♣ 🎱 🎱

Newbury

SU4767 🍺 Lord Lyon, Red Lion, Gun Inn

The Old Farmhouse, Downend Lane, Chieveley, Newbury, Berks, RG20 8TN.
Old farmhouse in large gardens. Accommodation in ground floor annexe.
Open: All Year **Grades:** ETC 3 Diamond
01635 248361 Mrs Pallett
palletts@aol.com
D: £25.00–£26.00 **S:** £30.00
Beds: 1F **Baths:** 1 En
🛏 🅿 (4) 🎥 🎥 🎱 🎱

15 Shaw Road, Newbury, Berks, RG14 1HG.
Late Georgian terraced house near town centre, rail and canal. **Open:** All Year
01635 44962 Mrs Curtis
D: £17.00–£18.00 **S:** £17.00–£18.00
Beds: 1D, 1T **Baths:** 1 Sh
🛏 🅿 🎥 🎥 🎥 🎱

Laurel House, 157 Andover Road, Newbury, RG14 6NB.
A warm welcome awaits you in our delightful Georgian house.
Open: All Year (not Xmas)
01635 35931 Mr & Mrs Dixon
D: fr £18.00 **S:** fr £18.00
Beds: 1D 1T **Baths:** 1 Sh
🅿 (2) 🎥 📺 🎥 🎥 🎱

Peasemore

SU4576 🍺 Fox and Hounds

Peasemore House, Peasemore, Newbury, Berks, RG20 7JH.
Open: All Year (not Xmas/New Year)
01635 248505 (also fax) Mrs Brown
D: £25.00 **S:** £25.00–£30.00
Beds: 1T 1D **Baths:** 2 En
🛏 🅿 🎥 🃏 🎥 🎱
Traditional family farmhouse with beautiful gardens set in arable downland. Peaceful village only 4 miles J13 M4/A34. Excellent walking/ riding. Spacious comfortable accommodation. Wonderful breakfasts with home-made produce.

Reading

SU7173 🍺 Clifton Arms, Horse & Jockey, Unicorn, Red Lion, Grouse & Claret, Rose & Thistle, Sweeney & Todd, Queen's Head

Greystoke Guest House, 10 Greystoke Road, Caversham, Reading, Berks, RG4 5EL.
Private home in quiet road, TV & tea/coffee making in lounge.
Open: All Year (not Xmas)
Grades: ETC 3 Diamond
0118 947 5784 Mrs Tyler
D: £25.00–£30.00 **S:** £28.00–£35.00
Beds: 1D 2S **Baths:** 1 Sh
🅿 (3) 🎥 📺 🎥 🎱

St Hilda's, 24 Castle Crescent, Reading, Berkshire, RG1 6AG.
Quiet Victorian home near town centre, all rooms have colour TVs & fridges.
Open: All Year
Grades: ETC 1 Crown
0118 961 0329 Mr & Mrs Hubbard
Fax: 0118 954 2585
D: £19.00–£24.00 **S:** £20.00–£27.00
Beds: 3F 2T **Baths:** 3 Sh
🛏 (1) 🅿 🎥 📺 🃏 🎥 🎥 🎱

Dittisham Guest House, 63 Tilehurst Road, Reading, Berks, RG30 2JL.
Quiet central location in a restored Edwardian home. High standards at sensible prices. **Open:** All Year
Grades: ETC 3 Diamond
0118 956 9483 Mr Harding
D: £20.00–£27.50 **S:** £26.00–£35.00
Beds: 2D 1T 2S **Baths:** 3 En 2 Sh
🛏 🅿 🎥 🃏 🎥 🎱 cc

Pennyford House, Peppard, Henley-on-Thames, Oxon, RG9 5JE.
Family home with dogs. Happy atmosphere. Nice garden. Local interests.
Open: All Year **Grades:** ETC 2 Crowns
01491 628272 (also fax)
Mrs Howden-Ferme
D: £25.00–£35.00 **S:** £30.00–£35.00
Beds: 1T 3D 1S **Baths:** 4 En 1 Pr
🛏 🅿 (10) 🎥 📺 🃏 🎥 🎱

Abadair House, *46 Redlands Road, Reading, Berks, RG1 5HE.*
Family run guest house close to railway and town centre.
Open: All Year **Grades:** ETC 2 Diamond
0118 986 3792 (also fax) Mrs Clifford
abadair@globalnet.co.uk
D: fr £30.00 **S:** £30.00–£35.00
Beds: 3T 6S **Baths:** 8 En 1 Sh
🛏 🅿 (6) ⊬ 📺 🕇 🎹 🔳 👤

Stockcross

SU4368   🍺 *Lord Lyon*

79 Glebe Lane, *Stockcross, Newbury, Berks, RG19 8AD.*
Spacious detached Edwardian house. Easy reach of Chievely Interchange/ Newbury. **Open:** All Year
01488 608561 Mr & Mrs Tipple
D: £25.00 **S:** £25.00
Beds: 1F 1T **Baths:** 1 Sh
🛏 🅿 (5) ⊬ 📺 🕇 🎹 👤

Streatley

SU5980   🍺 *The Bull, Catherine Wheel*

Pennyfield, *The Coombe, Streatley, Reading, Berkshire, RG8 9QT.*
Pretty village house with attractive terraced garden. Friendly welcoming hosts.
Open: All Year (not Xmas/New Year)
Grades: ETC 4 Diamond
01491 872048 (also fax)
mandrvanstone@hotmail.com
D: £22.50–£25.00 **S:** £22.50–£25.00
Beds: 1T 2D **Baths:** 2 En 1 Sh
🅿 (4) ⊬ 📺 🎹 🔳 👤

Sulhamstead

SU6368

The Old Manor, *Whitehouse Manor, Sulhamstead, Reading, Berks, RG7 4EA.*
Open: All Year (not Xmas/New Year)
Grades: ETC 5 Diamond, AA 5 Diamond
0118 983 2423 Fax: 0118 983 6262
D: £35.00 **S:** £25.00–£35.00
Beds: 2D **Baths:** 2 En
🅿 (4) ⊬ 📺 ✕ 🎹
C17th manor house with very large and beautiful beamed bedrooms. Every modern convenience in ensuite bathrooms. Elegance and tranquillity, superb meals for discerning guest.

Twyford

SU7975   🍺 *Queen Victoria, La Fontana, Waggon & Horse, The Bull*

Somewhere To Stay, *c/o Loddon Acres, Bath Road, Twyford, Reading, Berks, RG10 9RU.*
Open: All Year **Grades:** ETC 4 Diamond
0118 934 5880 (also fax) R Fisher
D: £24.50–£29.00 **S:** £35.00–£45.00
Beds: 1F 1D 1T 1S **Baths:** 3 En 1 Pr
🛏 🅿 (6) ⊬ 📺 🕇 🎹 👤
Self-contained, modern, detached accommodation with kitchenette and sauna. Situated next to owners house in beautiful river fronted 2 acre garden, tennis/canoes available. Rooms en suite, tastefully decorated with colour TV, tea/coffee, easy access to Reading, Windsor, Maidenhead and Heathrow.

Copper Beeches, *Bath Road, Kiln Green, Twyford, Reading, Berks, RG10 9UT.*
Quiet house in large gardens with tennis court, warm welcome.
Open: All Year
0118 940 2929 (also fax)
Mrs Gorecki
D: £22.50–£25.00 **S:** £28.00–£35.00
Beds: 3F 4T 1D 1S **Baths:** 1 En 3 Sh
🛏 (3) 🅿 (14) 📺 🎹 👤

Chesham House, *79 Wargrave Road, Twyford, Reading, Berks, RG10 9PE.*
Windsor 20 minutes by car or rail, to London 30 minutes.
Open: Mar to Dec
0118 932 0428 Mr & Mrs Ferguson
D: £30.00–£50.00 **S:** fr £27.50
Beds: 1D 1T **Baths:** 2 En
🛏 (7) 🅿 (3) 📺 🎹 👤

The Hermitage, *63 London Road, Twyford, Reading, Berks, RG10 9EJ.*
Elegant period house, village centre, close mainline railway, London 40 mins.
Open: All Year (not Xmas)
0118 934 0004 (also fax)
Mrs Barker
bookings@hermitage-twyford.co.uk
D: £26.00–£30.00 **S:** £35.00–£48.00
Beds: 2D 3T **Baths:** 3 En 1 Sh
🅿 (6) ⊬ 📺 🎹 🔳 👤

Wargrave-on-Thames

SU7978   🍺 *The Bull, The Queen Victoria*

Windy Brow, *204 Victoria Road, Wargrave-on-Thames, Reading, Berks, RG10 8AJ.*
Victorian detached house, close M4/M40, 1 mile A4, 6 miles Reading and Maidenhead.
Open: All Year (not Xmas/New Year)
Grades: ETC 4 Diamond
0118 940 3336 Mrs Carver
Fax: 0118 401 1260
heathcar@aol.com
D: £25.00–£30.00
S: £32.00–£45.00
Beds: 1D 2T 2S **Baths:** 1 En 2 Sh
🛏 🅿 (5) ⊬ 📺 🕇 🎹 🔳 👤 ♿

Wickham

SU3971   🍺 *Five Bells*

St Swithin's B & B, *3 St Swithin's Close, Wickham, Newbury, Berks, RG20 8HJ.*
A warm welcome awaits you in this home in outstanding countryside.
Open: All Year
01488 657566 Mrs Edwards
Fax: 0870 1693325
r.edwards@iee.org
D: £20.00–£25.00
S: £25.00–£28.00
Beds: 1T 1S **Baths:** 1 Pr
🛏 🅿 (2) ⊬ 📺 🎹 🔳 👤

All details shown are as supplied by B&B owners in Autumn 2000

Windsor

SU9676   🍺 *The Mitre, Bexley Arms, The Trooper, Nags Head, The Queen, Windsor Lad, George Inn, Vansitart Arms,Crow's Nest, Red Lion, White Horse, Hungry Horse*

Jean's, *1 Stovell Road, Windsor, Berks, SL4 5JB.*
Open: All Year
Grades: ETC 2 Diamond
01753 852055 Ms Sumner
Fax: 01753 842932
jeanlsumner@aol.com
D: £22.50–£25.00 **S:** £40.00
Beds: 1D 1T **Baths:** 1 En
🅿 (2) ⊬ 📺 🕇 🎹 🔳 👤 ♿
Quiet comfortable self-contained ground floor flat comprising 2 ensuite bedrooms which share a large lounge. 100 yds river and leisure centre, 7 mins' walk to castle, town centre and railway stations, 4 mins to buses.

Langton House, *46 Alma Road, Windsor, Berks, SL4 3HA.*
Victorian house, quiet tree-lined road, 5 minutes walk to town and castle.
Open: All Year (not Xmas)
01753 858299 Mrs Fogg
bookings@langtonhouse.co.uk
D: £30.00–£32.50 **S:** fr £50.00
Beds: 2D 1T **Baths:** 2 En 1 Pr
🅿 (2) ⊬ 📺 🎹 👤

62 Queen's Road, *Windsor, Berks, SL4 3BH.*
Excellent reputation, quiet, convenient, ground floor rooms. Largest family room available.
Open: All Year
01753 866036 (also fax)
Mrs Hughes
D: £20.00–£25.00 **S:** £30.00–£35.00
Beds: 1F 1T **Baths:** 2 Pr
🛏 🅿 (1) ⊬ 📺 🎹 🔳 👤 ♿ 3

Elansey, *65 Clifton Rise, Windsor, Berks, SL4 5SX.*
Modern, quiet, comfortable house. Garden, patio, excellent breakfasts, highly recommended.
Open: All Year (not Xmas)
01753 864438 Mrs Forbutt
D: £20.00–£25.00 **S:** £20.00–£26.00
Beds: 1D 1T 1S **Baths:** 1 En 1 Sh
🅿 (3) ⊬ 📺 🎹 👤

The Andrews, *77 Whitehorse Road, Windsor, Berks, SL4 4PG.*
Modern, comfortable private house.
Open: All Year (not Xmas)
01753 866803 Mrs Andrews
D: £18.00–£20.00 **S:** £23.00–£25.00
Beds: 1D 2T **Baths:** 2 Sh
🛏 (5) 🅿 (3) ⊬ 📺 🎹

Chasela, *30 Convent Road, Windsor, Berks, SL4 3RB.*
Modern semi-detached near M4, M40, M25. Castle 1 mile and Legoland.
Open: All Year
Grades: ETC 3 Diamond
01753 860410 Mrs Williams
D: £22.00–£24.00 **S:** £22.00–£24.00
Beds: 1T 1S **Baths:** 1 Sh
🛏 (12) 🅿 (5) ⊬ 📺 🎹 👤

The Laurells, 22 Dedworth Road, Windsor, Berks, SL4 5AY.
Pretty Victorian house 3/4 mile town centre. Heathrow 20 minutes.
Open: All Year (not Xmas)
01753 855821 Mrs Joyce
D: fr £20.00 **S:** fr £25.00
Beds: 2T
🛏 (5) ⅍ 📺 🐕 🛏 Ⓥ 🛗

Honeysuckle Cottage, 61 Fairfield Approach, Wraysbury, Staines, TW19 5DR.
Picturesque cottage in the historic Thames-side village of Wraysbury, excellent country pubs.
Open: All Year (not Xmas)
Grades: ETC 4 Diamond
01784 482519 Mrs Vogel
Fax: 01784 482305
B&B@berks.force9.co.uk
D: £22.50–£27.50 **S:** £30.00–£40.00
Beds: 2F 1D 1T 1S **Baths:** 4 En 1 Pr
🛏 (3) 🅿 (8) ⅍ 📺 🛏 Ⓥ 🛗 cc

Please respect a B&B's wishes regarding children, animals and smoking

---

RATES
D = Price range per person sharing in a double room
S = Price range for a single room

2 Benning Close, St Leonards Park, Windsor, Berks, SL4 4YS.
A modern detached house set in a quiet residential area.
Open: All Year (not Xmas/New Year)
01753 852294 Mrs Hume
D: £20.00 **S:** £25.00
Beds: 1F 1D 1S
🛏 🅿 (2) ⅍ 📺 🛏 Ⓥ 🛗 ♿

12 Parsonage Lane, Windsor, Berks, SL4 5EN.
Tastefully furnished detached private house. Quiet location. Parking. Lovely gardens.
Open: All Year
01753 868052 (also fax)
Mr & Mrs Riddle
D: £25.00–£35.00 **S:** £32.00–£35.00
Beds: 1D 1S **Baths:** 1 Sh
🛏 🅿 (4) ⅍ 📺 🐕 🛏 🛗

Woolhampton

SU5766 🍺 Rowbarge Inn, Angel Inn

Bridge Cottage, Station Road, Woolhampton, Reading, Berks, RG7 5SF.
Beautiful 300- year- old riverside home with secluded cottage garden.
Open: All Year (not Xmas)
01189 713138 Mrs Thornely
Fax: 01189 714331
D: £26.00 **S:** fr £24.00
Beds: 1D 1T 3S **Baths:** 2 En 1 Sh
🛏 🅿 📺 🛏 🛗

Wraysbury

TQ0073 🍺 George Inn

Honeysuckle Cottage, 61 Fairfield Approach, Wraysbury, Staines, TW19 5DR.
Picturesque cottage in the historic Thames-side village of Wraysbury, excellent country pubs.
Open: All Year (not Xmas)
Grades: ETC 4 Diamond
01784 482519 Mrs Vogel
Fax: 01784 482305
B&B@berks.force9.co.uk
D: £22.50–£27.50 **S:** £30.00–£40.00
Beds: 2F 1D 1T 1S **Baths:** 4 En 1 Pr
🛏 (3) 🅿 (8) ⅍ 📺 🛏 Ⓥ 🛗 ♿ cc

Bristol

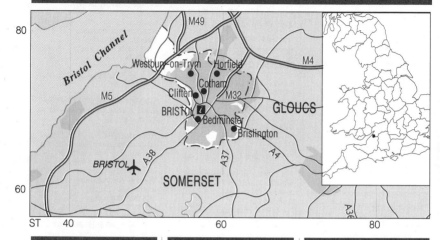

Bedminster

ST5771

Maison George, 10 Greville Road, Southville, Bristol, BS3 1LL.
Large Victorian town house within walking distance of city centre.
Open: All Year
Grades: ETC 2 Diamond
0117 963 9416 Mr Evans
Fax: 0117 953 5760
D: £20.00–£30.00 **S:** £20.00–£30.00
Beds: 1F 1D 2T 1S **Baths:** 2 Sh
🛏 🍴 📺 🐾 🛗 ⚓

Brislington

ST6170

Kingston House, 101 Hardenhuish Road, Brislington, Bristol, BS4 3SR.
Kingston House B&B is situated in a quiet residential area.
Open: All Year
Grades: ETC 2 Diamond
0117 971 2456
Ms Small
D: £22.50–£45.00
S: £24.00–£80.00
Beds: 1T 1D 1S
Baths: 1 En 1 Pr 1 Sh
🅿 (1) 🍴 📺 🛗 Ⓥ ⚓

Clifton

ST5674

Downs View Guest House, 38 Upper Belgrave Road, Clifton, Bristol, BS8 2XN.
Centrally situated. Overlooking Durdham Down. Near Zoo and Clifton Suspension Bridge.
Open: All Year (not Xmas)
Grades: ETC 3 Diamond
0117 973 7046 Ms Cox
Fax: 0117 973 8169
D: £22.50–£27.50 **S:** £30.00–£35.00
Beds: 2F 4D 3T 6S **Baths:** 7 En 2 Sh
🛏 📺 🐾 🛗 Ⓥ ⚓

Cotham

ST5874

Arches Hotel, 132 Cotham Brow, Cotham, Bristol, BS6 6AE.
Friendly, non-smoking city centre hotel, close to shops and restaurants.
Open: All Year (not Xmas)
Grades: ETC 3 Diamond
0117 924 7398 (also fax) Mr Lambert
ml@arches-hotel.co.uk
D: £21.50–£25.50 **S:** £24.50–£37.00
Beds: 3F 2D 1T 3S **Baths:** 4 En 2 Sh
🛏 (6) 🍴 📺 🐾 🛗 Ⓥ ⚓ cc

Horfield

ST5976

Norfolk Guest House, 577 Gloucester Road, Horfield, Bristol, BS7 0BW.
Pleasant Victorian house overlooking parklands and shops. Bus stop 100 yards.
Open: All Year
Grades: ETC 3 Diamond
0117 951 3191 (also fax)
Mr Thomas
D: £38.00–£45.00
S: £20.00–£25.00
Beds: 2D 1T **Baths:** 1 En 1 Pr
🛏 🍴 ✕ 🛗 ⚓

Westbury-on-Trym

ST5677

18 Charlton Road, Westbury-on-Trym, Bristol, BS10 6NG.
Comfortable quiet house in leafy suburb of Bristol. Non smoking.
Open: All Year (not Xmas/New Year)
Grades: ETC 1 Diamond
0117 950 0490
Mrs Duggan
D: £18.00 **S:** £18.00
Beds: 1D 1T 1S
Baths: 1 Sh
🛏 🅿 🍴 📺 🛗 Ⓥ ⚓

Buckinghamshire

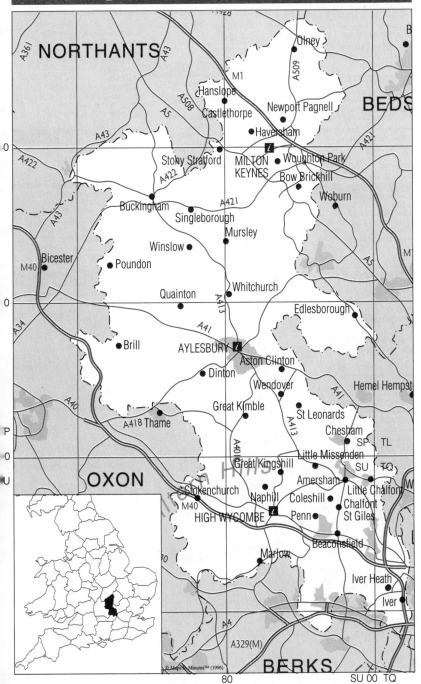

Tourist Information Centre

London Road, **Amersham**, Buckinghamshire, HP7 0HA, 01494 729492 (Easter to Oct).

County Hall, Walton Street, **Aylesbury**, Bucks, HP20 1UA, 01296 330559 (Easter to Oct).

The Old Gaol Museum, Market Hill, **Buckingham**, Bucks, MK18 1EW, 01280 823020.

6 Cornmarket, **High Wycombe**, Bucks, HP11 2BW, 01494 421892.

Court Garden Leisure Complex, Pound Lane, **Marlow**, Bucks, SL7 2AE, 01628 483597 (Easter to Oct).

Food Hall, 411 Secklow Gate East, **Milton Keynes**, Bucks, MK9 3NE, 01908 558300.

The Clock Tower, **Wendover**, Bucks, HP22 6DU, 01296 696759.

Amersham

SU9698   🍺 *King's Head, The Swan, The Griffin, The Plough, Boot & Slipper*

The Vicarage, 70 Sycamore Road, Amersham, Bucks, HP6 5DR.
Spacious, delightful home. Quiet garden. Station to London 3 minute walk.
Open: All Year (not Xmas/New Year)
01494 729993 Mrs Roderick
Fax: 01494 727553
philip.roderick@ukonline.co.uk
D: £24.00 **S:** £27.00–£30.00
Beds: 1T 1S
🅿 (6) ⊬ 📺 🛏 📖 Ⅴ ⚲

Glory Farm Cottage, Fagnall Lane, Winchmore Hill, Amersham, Bucks, HP7 0PQ.
Friendly, comfortable beamed countryside cottage. Convenient - pubs, underground, M40/M25.
Open: All Year (not Xmas)
Grades: ETC 4 Diamond
01494 727598 Mrs Olliver
frangfc@aol.com
D: £28.00–£31.00 **S:** £36.00–£40.00
Beds: 1D 1T **Baths:** 1 En 1 Sh
🐾 🅿 (2) ⊬ 📺 📖 Ⅴ ⚲

Aston Clinton

SP8712   🍺 *Rising Sun*

B&B at 103, 103 London Road, Aston Clinton, Aylesbury, Bucks, HP22 5LD.
Superior, comfortable B&B, centrally located for business/tourists. French & German spoken.
Open: All Year
01296 631313 Mr & Mrs Taylor
Fax: 01296 631616
D: £20.00–£24.00 **S:** £30.00–£35.00
Beds: 1D 2T **Baths:** 2 En 1 Sh
🐾 (8) 🅿 (6) ⊬ 📺 📖 Ⅴ ✻ ⚲ �&ᴄ cc

BATHROOMS

Pr - Private

Sh - Shared

En - Ensuite

RATES

D = Price range per person sharing in a double room

S = Price range for a single room

Aylesbury

SP8113   🍺 *5 Bells, Rising Sun, Red Lion*

62 Bierton Road, Aylesbury, Bucks, HP20 1EJ.
Comfortable Victorian house, family home. Ten minutes from town centre.
Open: All Year (not Xmas/New Year)
01296 427980 Mrs Canover
davidcanover@yahoo.co.uk
S: fr £15.00
Beds: 2S **Baths:** 1 Sh
⊬ 📺 📖 Ⅴ

331 Tring Road, Aylesbury, Bucks, HP20 1PJ.
High quality accommodation, spacious, en suite. Easy parking. Close Aylesbury. Facilities.
Open: All Year
Grades: ETC 4 Diamond
01296 424012 Mrs Mason
D: £25.00–£27.00 **S:** £26.00–£35.00
Beds: 1T 1S **Baths:** 1 En 1 Pr
🅿 (2) ⊬ 📺 📖 ⚲

The Seasons, 9 Ballard Close, Aylesbury, Bucks, HP21 9UY.
Friendly quiet quality home close to NT and Chilterns. Ideal business or pleasure.
Open: All Year (not Xmas)
01296 484465 Mrs Ion
D: £20.00–£25.00 **S:** £20.00–£25.00
Beds: 1D 1T 1S **Baths:** 2 Sh
🐾 (10) 🅿 (6) ⊬ 📺 📖 Ⅴ ⚲

Beaconsfield

SU9390   🍺 *Charles Dickens*

Beacon House, 113 Maxwell Road, Beaconsfield, Bucks, HP9 1RF.
Extended family house, use of gardens. Easy access London and Windsor.
Open: All Year
Grades: ETC 3 Diamond
01494 672923 (also fax)
Mr Dickinson
ben.dickinson@tesco.net
D: £19.00–£22.00 **S:** £27.00–£38.00
Beds: 1D 1T 2S **Baths:** 2 En 1 Sh
🐾 (6) 🅿 (5) ⊬ 📺 📖 Ⅴ ⚲

Bletchley

SP8534   🍺 *The Enigma*

The Townhouse, 3 Westfield Road, Bletchley, Milton Keynes, Bucks, MK2 2RR.
Comfortable town house, centre of Bletchley, close to station and Milton Keynes.
Open: All Year (not Xmas)
01908 368713 (also fax)
Mrs Friedman
D: £25.00–£28.00 **S:** £28.00
Beds: 1T 3S **Baths:** 1 En 1 Sh
🐾 ⊬ 📺 📖 ⚲

Bow Brickhill

SP9034

Plough House, Church Road, Bow Brickhill, Milton Keynes, Bucks, MK17 9LH.
Georgian house, adjoining Woburn estates, woodland, 5 miles Milton Keynes.
Open: All Year
Grades: ETC Listed
01908 372097 (also fax)
Mrs Drabble
D: £25.00–£30.00
S: £25.00–£30.00
Beds: 1D 1S **Baths:** 1 Sh
🐾 (10) 🅿 (2) 📺 🛏 🗙 📖 Ⅴ ⚲

Brill

SP6513   🍺 *The Pheasant*

Poletrees Farm, Ludgershall Road, Brill, Aylesbury, Bucks, HP18 9TZ.
Historical oak-beamed farmhouse with lovely garden for guests to sit in.
Open: All Year
Grades: ETC 3 Diamond
01844 238276 (also fax)
Mrs Cooper
D: £26.00–£30.00 **S:** £30.00
Beds: 1F 2D 1T **Baths:** 1 En 1 Sh
🐾 🅿 (50) ⊬ 📺 🗙 📖 Ⅴ ⚲ ᴅ&

Buckingham

SP6933   🍺 *Bull & Butcher, Wheatsheaf, Queens Head, White Hart*

Folly Farm, Padbury, Buckingham, Bucks, MK18 2HS.
Open: All Year (not Xmas)
Grades: ETC 3 Diamond
01296 712413 Mrs Webb
Fax: 01296 714923
D: £20.00–£25.00
S: £22.50–£25.00
Beds: 3D **Baths:** 3 En
🐾 (6) ⊬ 📺 🗙 📖 Ⅴ ⚲
Substantial Victorian farmhouse set in open countryside along A413 between market towns of Buckingham and Winslow. Ensuite rooms, evening meal available on request.

The White Cottage, Verney Junction, Buckingham, MK18 2JZ.
Lovely country house in small hamlet. Super breakfasts, log fires. Plants for sale.
Open: 1 Jan to 23 Dec
Grades: ETC 2 Diamond
01296 714416 Mrs Gilchrist
D: £20.00
S: £20.00
Beds: 2D 1S **Baths:** 1 Sh
🅿 (3) ⊬ 📺 🗙 📖 Ⅴ ⚲

The Hall Farm, Lillingstone Lovell, Buckingham, Bucks, MK18 5BL.
Spacious farmhouse, rural setting M1, M40, Intercity railway within easy reach.
Open: All Year (not Xmas)
01280 860665 (also fax)
Mrs Culley
D: fr £18.00
S: fr £18.00
Beds: 1D 2T **Baths:** 3 Pr 1 Sh
🐾 🅿 (6) 📺 ⚲

River View, *97 Fishers Field,*
Buckingham, MK18 1SF.
Elegant riverside town house. Convenient
for town centre, Stowe, Claydon
Open: All Year
01280 821265 (also fax)
Mrs Dunnington
D: £19.00–£21.00 **S:** £25.00–£27.00
Beds: 1T 1D **Baths:** 2 Pr
🅿 (2) ⊬ 📺 ▥.

5 Bristle Hill, *Buckingham,*
Buckinghamshire, MK18 1EZ.
Restored C18th cottage in conservation
area. Convenient Stowe and Silverstone.
Open: All Year
Grades: ETC 3 Diamond
01280 814426 Mrs Seeby
D: £25.00–£27.50 **S:** £25.00–£27.50
Beds: 1T **Baths:** 1 En
🐾 (5) ⊬ 📺 ▥. ₤

Castlethorpe

SP7944 🍺 *Carrington Arms, Navigation Inn*

Milford Leys Farm, *Castlethorpe,*
Milton Keynes, Bucks, MK19 7HH.
Comfortable family farmhouse, working
farm.
Open: All Year
01908 510153 Mrs Frost
D: £17.50–£20.00 **S:** £17.50–£20.00
Beds: 1F 1D 1T **Baths:** 2 Sh
🐾 🅿 (4) 📺 ▥. ₤

Manor Farm House, *South Street,*
Castlethorpe, Milton Keynes, Bucks, MK19
7EL.
Lovely Grade II Listed farmhouse within
easy reach of M1 and Central Milton
Keynes.
Open: All Year (not Xmas)
01908 510216 Mrs Tate
D: £22.50–£27.50 **S:** £25.00–£32.50
Beds: 1F 1D 2T **Baths:** 2 Pr 2 Sh
🅿 (6) ⊬ 📺 ⊺ ▥. Ⓥ ₤

Chalfont St Giles

SU9893 🍺 *White Hart, Pheasant Inn*

The Shieling, *81 Bottrells Lane,*
Chalfont St Giles, Bucks, HP8 4EH.
Detached bungalow. Lovely gardens,
close Heathrow, Windsor, underground,
British Rail.
Open: All Year (not Xmas)
Grades: AA 4 Diamond
01494 872147 Mrs Morris
Fax: 01494 871431
dimorrisshieling@talk21.com
D: £22.50–£25.00 **S:** £27.50–£35.00
Beds: 2D 1T **Baths:** 2 En 1 Pr
🐾 🅿 (6) 📺 ▥. ₤

Gorelands Corner, *Gorelands Lane,*
Chalfont St Giles, Bucks, HP8 4HQ.
Family house set in large garden. Easy
access to motorway.
Open: All Year
Grades: ETC 3 Diamond
01494 872689 (also fax)
Mrs Bickford
bickfordcsg@compuserve.com
D: fr £25.00 **S:** fr £25.00
Beds: 1D 1S **Baths:** 1 En 1 Pr
🅿 (3) ⊬ 📺 ▥. Ⓥ ₤

Chesham

SP9601 🍺 *Wetherspoon, Queens Head*

May Tree House, S: *32 Hampden*
Avenue, Chesham, Bucks., HP5 2HL.
Open: Feb to Nov
01494 784019 A Bartle
Fax: 01494 776896
D: £28.00 **S:** £34.00
Beds: 2T 2S **Baths:** 4 En
🅿 (3) ⊬ 📺 ▥. Ⓥ ₤
High standard maintained in comfortable
family home. Quiet location 10 mins' walk
to underground Metropolitan line and all
amenities. Courtesy car to station, pick
up-drop off Heathrow, Gatwick. Day
excursion with pub lunch to out of the
way places.

49 Lowndes Avenue, *Chesham,*
Bucks, HP5 2HH.
House located in Chiltern Hills. Good
walking and old pubs.
Open: All Year (not Xmas/New Year)
Grades: ETC 2 Diamond
01494 792647 Mrs Orme
D: £30.00–£50.00 **S:** £25.00
Beds: 1T **Baths:** 1 En
🐾 (8) 🅿 (1) ⊬ 📺 ⊺ ▥. ₤

Coleshill

SU9595 🍺 *Red Lion*

Pond Cottage, *Village Road, Coleshill,*
Amersham, Bucks, HP7 0LH.
Delightful beamed C17th Listed cottage
in peaceful Chiltern village.
Open: All Year
Grades: ETC 4 Diamond
01494 728177 Mrs Wayland
Fax: 01494 729168
pondcott@msn.com
D: £22.50–£27.50 **S:** £35.00–£45.00
Beds: 1F 3D/T 1S **Baths:** 1 En 2 Pr 1 Sh
🐾 🅿 (5) ⊬ 📺 ▥. ₤

Dinton

SP7610 🍺 *Seven Stars*

Wallace Farm, *Dinton, Aylesbury,*
Bucks, HP17 8UF.
Wallace Farm is a small family farm
located in peaceful and charming village.
Open: All Year
01296 748660 Mrs Cook
Fax: 01296 748851
jackiecook@wallacefarm.freeserve.co.uk
D: £22.00–£23.00 **S:** £30.00
Beds: 1D 2T **Baths:** 3 Pr
🐾 🅿 (5) 📺 ▥. ₤

Edlesborough

SP9719 🍺 *The Golden Rule*

Ridgeway End, *5 Ivinghoe Way,*
Edlesborough, Dunstable, Beds, LU6 2EL.
Pretty bungalow in private road,
surrounded by fields and views of the
Chiltern Hills.
Open: All Year (not Xmas)
01525 220405 (also fax)
Mrs Lloyd
D: £20.00–£22.00 **S:** £22.00–£24.00
Beds: 1D 1T **Baths:** 1 En
🐾 (2) 🅿 (3) ⊬ 📺 ▥. ₤

RATES

D = Price range per person
sharing in a double room
S = Price range for a
single room

Great Kimble

SP8205

The Swan, *Grave Lane, Great Kimble,*
Aylesbury, HP17 9TR.
Friendly Real Ale country Inn close to
historic Ridgeway walk.
Open: All Year
01844 275288
Mr Woolnough
Fax: 01494 837312
D: £25.00–£35.00
S: £35.00–£45.00
Beds: 1F 2T 1D **Baths:** 4 En
🐾 🅿 (25) 📺 ⊺ ✕ ▥. Ⓥ ₤ cc

Great Kingshill

SU8798 🍺 *Pole Cat, Red Lion*

Hatches Farm, *Hatches Lane, Great*
Kingshill, High Wycombe, Bucks, HP15 6DS.
Quiet, comfortable farmhouse. Rooms
overlooking garden. Easy reach of
Oxford/Windsor.
Open: All Year (not Xmas)
Grades: ETC 2 Diamond
01494 713125 Mrs Davies
Fax: 01494 714666
D: £16.00–£17.50 **S:** £20.00
Beds: 1D 1T **Baths:** 1 Sh
🐾 (12) 🅿 (6) ▥.

Hanslope

SP8046

Woad Farm, *Tathall End, Hanslope,*
Milton Keynes, Bucks, MK19 7NE.
Situated on edge of village, large garden,
tennis court. Milton Keynes &
Northampton accessible.
Open: All Year
Grades: ETC 3 Diamond
01908 510985 (also fax)
Mr & Mrs Stacey
mail@srahstacey.freeserve.co.uk
D: £22.00–£24.00 **S:** £22.00–£25.00
Beds: 2D 1T **Baths:** 3 Sh
🐾 🅿 ⊬ 📺 ⊺ ✕ ▥. Ⓥ ₤

Haversham

SP8243 🍺 *Greyhound*

The Bungalow, *The Crescent,*
Haversham, Milton Keynes, Bucks.,
MK19 7AW.
Village location within six minutes drive
from central Milton Keynes.
Open: All Year
01908 311883
D: £18.00–£20.00
S: £18.00–£20.00
Beds: 2F 1T 1S
🅿 (2) 📺 ▥. ₤

High Wycombe

SU8693   ⚑ *Masons Arms, Falcon*

Harfa House, *Station Road, High Wycombe, Bucks, HP13 6AD.*
Open: All Year
01494 529671 (also fax)
Mrs Foster-Brown
irena@freenetname.co.uk
D: £15.00–£20.00 **S:** £15.00–£25.00
Beds: 1T 2S **Baths:** 1 Sh
🅿 📺 🕮 ♿
Private, self-contained annexe to Victorian house. Comfortable, pleasant rooms with own fridge and microwave. Convenient for town centre, bus and railway stations. 30 minutes to London. Excellent location for touring lovely English countryside, Marlow, Oxford, Henley, Windsor. Good pubs and restaurants nearby.

Wayside House, *2 Hampden Road, High Wycombe, Bucks, HP13 6SX.*
Spacious 1920s house of character. Quiet location 5 minutes from town centre.
Open: All Year
01494 528463
Mrs Rifkin
D: £18.00–£20.00 **S:** £20.00–£25.00
Beds: 1F 1T **Baths:** 1 Sh
🐾 🅿 (2) 📺 🕮 Ⅴ ♿

Iver Heath

TQ0282   ⚑ *Crooked Billet, Black Horse*

Oaklands, *Bangors Road South, Iver Heath, Bucks, SL10 0BB.*
Large family house convenient for Heathrow, Windsor, Uxbridge and Slough.
Open: All Year (not Xmas/New Year)
01753 653005
Mrs Fowler
Fax: 01753 653003
D: £20.00 **S:** £20.00–£25.00
Beds: 1F 2T 1D 1S
Baths: 1 En 2 Sh
🅿 (4) ♨ 📺 🕮 ♿

Little Chalfont

SU9997   ⚑ *Ivy House*

Holmdale, *Cokes Lane, Little Chalfont, Amersham, HP8 4TX.*
Comfortable cottage in the Chilterns; easy access to London on trains.
Open: All Year
Grades: ETC 4 Diamond
01494 762527 Fax: 01494 764701
judy@holmdalebb.freeserve.co.uk
D: £30.00–£35.00 **S:** £40.00–£45.00
Beds: 1D/F 1T 1S
Baths: 3 En
🐾 🅿 (2) ♨ 📺 🕮 Ⅴ ♿

BATHROOMS

Pr - Private

Sh - Shared

En - Ensuite

Little Missenden

SU9299   ⚑ *Red Lion*

Herons Mead, *Little Missenden, Amersham, BUcks., HP7 0RA.*
Victorian house in picturesque village; lovely views, good walking country.
Open: All Year (not Xmas)
01494 862086 (also fax)
Mrs Powell
D: £22.00–£25.00 **S:** £22.00–£25.00
Beds: 1D 1T **Baths:** 1 En 1 Sh
🐾 🅿 (1) ♨ 📺 🕮 Ⅴ

Marlow

SU8586   ⚑ *Hare & Hounds, Three Horseshoes, Osbourne Arms, Clayton Arms, Royal Oak*

Merrie Hollow, *Seymour Court Hill, Marlow, Bucks, SL7 3DE.*
Open: All Year
Grades: ETC 3 Diamond
01628 485663 (also fax)
Mr Wells
D: £20.00–£25.00 **S:** £25.00–£35.00
Beds: 1D 1T **Baths:** 1 Sh
🐾 🅿 (4) ♨ 📺 🍴 ✕ 🕮 Ⅴ ♿
Secluded quiet country cottage in large garden 150 yds off B482 Marlow to Stokenchurch road, easy access to M4 & M25, 35 mins from Heathrow & Oxford, private off-road car parking.

Sneppen House, *Henley Road, Marlow, Bucks, SL7 2DF.*
Within walking distance of town centre and river. Breakfast menu choice. Pub food nearby.
Open: All Year **Grades:** ETC 4 Diamond
01628 485227 Mr Norris
D: £22.50 **S:** £30.00
Beds: 1D 1T **Baths:** 1 Sh
🐾 🅿 (2) 🅿 (3) 📺 🕮 ♿

Acha Pani, *Bovingdon Green, Marlow, Bucks, SL7 2JL.*
Quiet location, easy access Thames Foothpath, Chilterns, Windsor, London, Heathrow.
Open: All Year **Grades:** ETC 2 Diamond
01628 483435 (also fax)
Mrs Cowling
D: £17.00–£18.00 **S:** £17.00–£18.00
Beds: 1D 1T 1S **Baths:** 1 En 1 Sh
🐾 (10) 🅿 (3) 🕮 🍴 ✕ 🕮 Ⅴ ♿

Sunnyside, *Munday Dean, Marlow, Bucks, SL7 3BU.*
Comfortable, friendly, family home in Area of Outstanding Natural Beauty.
Open: All Year
01628 485701 Mrs O'Connor
ruthandtom@tinyworld.co.uk
D: £17.50 **S:** £20.00
Beds: 2D 1T **Baths:** 1 Sh
🐾 🅿 (5) ♨ 📺 ♿

29 Oaktree Road, *Marlow, Bucks, SL7 3ED.*
Friendly and efficiently run Bed & Breakfast. Convenient M4, M48 and M25.
Open: All Year (not Xmas)
01628 472145 Mr Lasenby
D: £25.00–£27.50 **S:** £28.00–£30.00
Beds: 5F 2T **Baths:** 1 En
🅿 (2) ♨ 📺 🍴 🕮 ♿

All details shown are as supplied by B&B owners in Autumn 2000

Milton Keynes

SP8636   ⚑ *Navigation Inn, Ye Olde Swan, Suffolk Punch*

Rovers Return, *49 Langcliffe Drive, Milton Keynes, Bucks, MK13 7LA.*
Open: All Year (not Xmas/New Year)
01908 310465 E Levins
D: £20.00–£25.00 **S:** £23.00–£25.00
Beds: 1T 1S 1D **Baths:** 2 Sh
🐾 (10) ♨ 📺 🕮 Ⅴ ♿
Warm welcoming modern chalet type house situated in tree lined courtyard adjacent to Redway Cycle Track. One mile from Milton Keynes city centre, bus and railway stations. Convenient for hockey stadium, theatre district, Xscape Snow Dome, night clubs, bars and restaurants.

Kingfishers, *9 Rylstone Close, Heelands, Milton Keynes, Bucks, MK13 7QT.*
Modern luxurious house. Near central Milton Keynes and station.
Open: All Year
Grades: ETC 3 Diamond
01908 310231 Mrs Botterill
Fax: 01908 318601
sheila-derek@m-keynes.freeserve.co.uk
D: £20.00 **S:** £23.00–£28.00
Beds: 1F 1D 1S
Baths: 2 En 1 Pr
🐾 (2) 🅿 (4) 📺 🍴 ✕ 🕮 ♿

Mursley

SP8128   ⚑ *Green Man, The Swan*

Richmond Hill Farm, *Stewkley Lane, Mursley, Milton Keynes, Bucks, MK17 0JD.*
Spacious, bedrooms overlook landscaped gardens. Tranquil setting. Woburn Abbey, Waddesdon Man, Silverstone.
Open: All Year
01296 720385 (also fax)
Mrs Oldham
D: £22.50–£25.00 **S:** £25.00–£27.00
Beds: 2T **Baths:** 1 Sh
🐾 🅿 (10) ♨ 📺 🍴 🕮 ♿

Naphill

SU8596   ⚑ *The Black Lion*

Woodpeckers, *244 Main Road, Naphill, High Wycombe, Bucks, HP14 4CX.*
Open: All Year
01494 563728 Mrs Brand
angela.brand@virgin.net
D: £23.50–£25.00 **S:** £25.00
Beds: 1T 1D 1S
Baths: 2 En 1 Pr
🐾 🅿 (4) 📺 🍴 🕮 ♿
In the heart of the Chiltern Hills. Close proximity to London, Windsor, Heathrow, Oxford. Good public transport links. Wonderful walks and scenery with place of historic interest nearby. Available as self-catering unit (4-6 people, prices on request).

Newport Pagnell

SP8743   *White Hart, Cock Inn, The Swan, The Dolphin*

The Clitheroes, 5 Walnut Close, Newport Pagnell, Bucks, MK16 8JH.
Homely atmosphere, comfortable rooms, full English breakfast, off road parking.
Open: All Year (not Xmas)
Grades: ETC 2 Diamond
01908 611643 (also fax)
D: £17.50–£20.00 **S:** £20.00–£22.00
Beds: 2T 2S **Baths:** 2 Sh
  (5) 📺 🛋 📶

Olney

SP8851   *Two Brewers*

Colchester House, 26 High Street, Olney, Bucks, MK46 4BB.
Georgian town house in market town near pubs and restaurants.
Open: All Year (not Xmas)
01234 712602 Fax: 01234 240564
blenkinsops@compuserve.com
D: £25.00 **S:** £25.00
Beds: 2D 1T **Baths:** 2 En 1 Sh
🅿 (4) 📺 🛋 📶

Penn

SU9293   *Hit Or Miss*

Little Penn Farmhouse, Penn Bottom, Penn, High Wycombe, Bucks, HP10 8PJ.
Character family house with beautiful garden surrounded by picturesque countryside.
Open: All Year (not Xmas)
Grades: ETC 4 Diamond
01494 813439 Mrs Harris
Fax: 01494 817740
sally@saundersharris.co.uk
D: fr £24.00 **S:** fr £34.00
Beds: 1D **Baths:** 1 En
🅿 (4) 📺 🛋 📶

Poundon

SP6425   *Sow & Pigs*

Manor Farm, Poundon, Bicester, Oxon, OX6 0BB.
Extremely comfortable and welcoming. Delicious breakfasts and lovely surroundings.
Open: All Year (not Xmas)
Grades: ETC 3 Diamond
01869 277212 Mrs Collett
Fax: 01869 277166
D: £20.00–£25.00 **S:** £25.00–£30.00
Beds: 1F 1D 1S **Baths:** 2 Sh
  (10) 📺 🛋 📶

Quainton

SP7419   *George and Dragon*

Woodlands Farmhouse, Edgcott Road, Quainton, Aylesbury, Bucks, HP22 4DE.
C18th farmhouse offering peaceful accommodation in 11 acres of ground.
Open: All Year
Grades: ETC 3 Diamond
01296 770225 Mrs Creed
D: £25.00–£30.00 **S:** £25.00–£30.00
Beds: 1f 2T 1D **Baths:** 4 En
  (10) 📺 🛋 📶

Singleborough

SP7632   *Swan*

Laurel Farm, Singleborough, Milton Keynes, Bucks, MK17 0RF.
Part C16th large farmhouse in very quiet hamlet. Guest rooms overlook gardens.
Open: All Year (not Xmas)
01296 712282 Mrs Crawford
D: £18.00 **S:** £20.00
Beds: 2T 1S **Baths:** 1 Sh
  🅿 (4) 📺 🛋 📶

St Leonards

SP9006   *Old Swan*

Field Cottage, St Leonards, Tring, Herts, HP23 6NS.
Open: All Year (not Xmas/New Year)
Grades: ETC 4 Diamond, Silver Award
01494 837602 Mr & Mrs Jepson
D: £25.00–£30.00 **S:** £25.00–£35.00
Beds: 1D 1T 1S
  (12) 🅿 (4) 📺 🛋 📶
A warm welcome awaits you at this pretty secluded cottage near the Ridgeway and convenient for Wendover, Chesham and Great Missenden. High standard of accommodation with guests lounge, cottage garden and breakfast in flower filled conservatory overlooking open fields and woodland.

Stokenchurch

SU7695   *Blue Flag*

Gibbons Farm, Bigmore Lane, Stokenchurch, High Wycombe, Bucks, HP14 3UR.
Open: All Year
01494 482385 Mrs McKelvey
Fax: 01494 485400
D: £25.00–£30.00 **S:** £25.00–£30.00
Beds: 2F 1D 1T 4S **Baths:** 6 En 1 Sh
  🅿 (20) 📺 🛋 📶
Traditional farm offering accommodation in converted barn. Set in courtyard surrounded by open countryside, this family-run B&B offers a warm and friendly welcome with Marlow and Oxford within half-hour drive, situated within 5 mins of M40, London is easily accessible.

Stony Stratford

SP7940   *Bull, Cock*

Fegans View, 119 High Street, Stony Stratford, Milton Keynes, Bucks, MK11 1AT.
C18th comfortable town house near local amenities.
Open: All Year
Grades: ETC 3 Diamond
01908 562128 Mrs Levitt
D: £18.00–£19.00 **S:** £22.00–£25.00
Beds: 3T 1S **Baths:** 1 En 2 Sh
  (1) 🅿 (5) 📺 📶

BATHROOMS

Pr - Private

Sh - Shared

En - Ensuite

Wendover

SP8608   *Red Lion*

46 Lionel Avenue, Wendover, Aylesbury, Bucks, HP22 6LP.
Family home. Lounge, conservatory, garden. English/vegetarian breakfasts. Tea/coffee always available.
Open: All Year (not Xmas/New Year)
Grades: ETC 3 Diamond
01296 623426 Mr & Mrs MacDonald
D: £22.00 **S:** £24.00
Beds: 1T 2S **Baths:** 1 Sh
  🅿 (3) 📺 🛋 📶

Whitchurch

SP8020   *White Swan, White Horse*

3 Little London, Whitchurch, Aylesbury, Bucks, HP22 4LE.
Quiet location near Waddesdon Manor; 1 hour London, Stratford.
Open: All Year (not Xmas)
01296 641409 Mrs Gurr
D: £20.00 **S:** £20.00
Beds: 1D 1T 1S **Baths:** 2 Sh
🅿 (3) 📺 🛋

Winslow

SP7627   *Old Thatch, The Bell*

Tuckey Farm, Winslow, Buckingham, Bucks, MK18 3ND.
C18th farmhouse, convenient for Stowe, Waddesdon Manor, Claydon House, Silverstone.
Open: All Year (not Xmas)
01296 713208 Mrs Haynes
D: fr £20.00 **S:** fr £20.00
Beds: 1T 2S **Baths:** 1 Sh
  (5) 🅿 (4) 📺 🛋

The Congregational Church, 15 Horn Street, Winslow, Buckingham, MK18 3AP.
Victorian church turned into fascinating home in old town centre.
Open: All Year
Grades: ETC 3 Diamond
01296 715717 (also fax)
Mrs Hood
D: £22.50 **S:** £25.00
Beds: 1D 1T 1S **Baths:** 2 Sh
📺 🛋 📶

Woughton Park

SP8737   *Ye Olde Swan*

Vignoble, 2 Medland, Woughton Park, Milton Keynes, Bucks, MK6 3BH.
Quiet, secluded, comfortable private house.
Open: All Year
01908 666804 Fax: 01908 666626
101532.627@compuserve.com
D: £25.00–£37.00 **S:** £25.00–£27.00
Beds: 4F 1D 1T **Baths:** 3 En 1 Pr 2 Sh
  (7) 🅿 (3) 📺 🛋 📶

Cambridgeshire

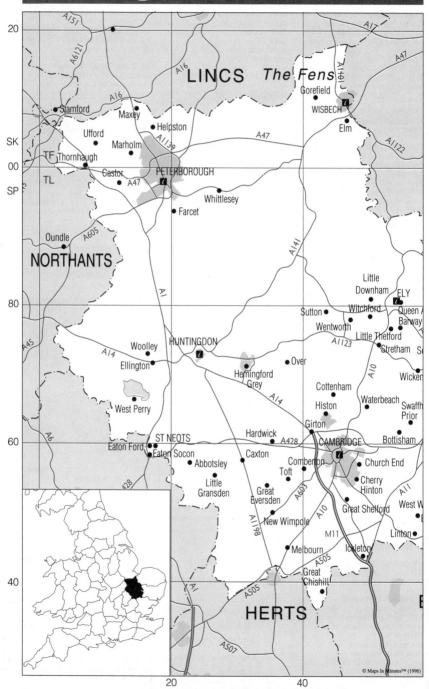

© Maps In Minutes™ (1996)

Tourist Information Centres

Wheeler Street, **Cambridge**, Cambs, CB2 3QB, 01223 322640.

Oliver Cromwell's House, 29 St Mary's Street, **Ely**, Cambs, CB7 4HF, 01353 662062.

The Library, Princes Street, **Huntingdon**, Cambs, PE18 6PH, 01480 388588.

45 Bridge Street, **Peterborough**, Cambs, PE1 1HA, 01733 452336.

District Library, Ely Place, **Wisbech**, Cambs, PE13 1EU, 01945 583263.

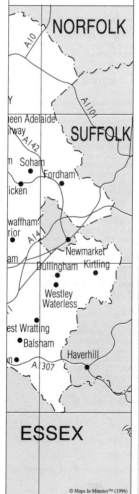

© Maps In Minutes™ (1996)

Abbotsley

TL2256   Eight Bells, Jolly Abbot

Rectory Farm , High Street, Abbotsley, St Neots, Cambs, PE19 6UE.
Open: All Year (not Xmas)
01767 677282 (also fax)
Mr Hipwell
D: £20.00 **S:** £20.00
Beds: 1D 2T 1S **Baths:** 1 Sh
Quiet Victorian farmhouse large gardens and ample private parking short stroll from centre of picturesque village with local pubs serving good food. Local countryside walks. Cambridge Bedford Huntingdon 30 mins drive, London 1 hour by train from St. Neots.

Balsham

TL5849

The Garden End, 10 West Wratting Road, Balsham, Cambridge, CB1 6DX.
Self-contained ground floor suite - children / pets welcome all year.
Open: All Year
01223 894021 (also fax)
Mrs Greenaway
D: £18.00 **S:** fr £20.00
Beds: 1F **Baths:** 1 En 1 Pr

Barway

TL5375   Fish & Duck, Popes Corner

The Manor House, Barway, Ely, Cambs, CB7 5UB.
Rural location near Ely and Newmarket. Generous breakfast. Large garden.
Open: All Year (not Xmas/New Year)
07968 654640 Mr & Mrs Rose
boxer1@dialstart.net
D: £20.00 **S:** £25.00
Beds: 1T 1D
Baths: 1 En 1 Pr

Bottisham

TL5460   White Swan, Wheatsheaf

27 Beechwood Avenue, Bottisham, Cambridge, CB5 9BG.
Modern house backing farmland near Cambridge city and Newmarket racecourse.
Open: All Year (not Xmas)
01223 811493 Mrs Knight
Fax: 0870 1312396
mike.knight@home.cam.net.uk
D: £22.50–£25.00
S: £22.50–£25.00
Beds: 1D 2T 1S **Baths:** 1 Sh

RATES

D = Price range per person sharing in a double room

S = Price range for a single room

Cambridge

SO7403   Milton Arms, Haymakers, Master Mariner, George Inn, Black Bull, Granta Inn, Coach & Horses, Green Man, Robin Hood, Clarendon Arms, Free Press, Red Lion, Old Crown, Travellers Rest, White Horse, The Grapes, Old Spring, The Volunteer, Browns, Live & Let Live, The Rock, Cambridge Blue, Crown

Hamden Guest House, 89 High Street, Cherry Hinton, Cambridge, CB1 9LU.
Open: All Year
Grades: AA 3 Diamond
01223 413263 Mr Casciano
Fax: 01223 245960
D: £22.50–£25.00 **S:** £28.00–£32.00
Beds: 1F 2D 1T 1S **Baths:** 5 En
High standard of bed & breakfast accommodation. All rooms with ensuite shower. Situated on the outskirts of Cambridge, short distance from city centre, approx. 2 miles. Frequent bus service. Private car park. Local shops, pubs, restaurants within walking distance.

Carolina Bed & Breakfast, 148 Perne Road, Cambridge, CB1 3NX.
Open: All Year
01223 247015 (also fax)
Mrs Amabile
carolina.amabile@tesco.net
D: £20.00–£30.00 **S:** fr £25.00
Beds: 1D 1T **Baths:** 2 En
Comfortable home offering a warm and friendly service. Easy access from and to M11 and A14, within easy distance of city centre, railway station, bus station, Addenbrookes Hospital, Cambridge Airport, golf club and colleges. Long stay discount. Credit cards accepted.

Victoria B&B, 57 Arbury Road, Cambridge, CB4 2JB.
Open: All Year
Grades: ETC 4 Diamond
01223 350086 (also fax)
Mrs Fasano
vicmaria@globalnet.co.uk
D: £17.50–£25.00 **S:** £20.00–£35.00
Beds: 1F 1D 1T **Baths:** 1 En 1 Pr 1 Sh
Victorian house - all rooms have TV, tea and coffee making facilities, ensuite private or shared facilities ideally situated for city centre, colleges and river Cam easy access to A14 and M11. Special rates for long term bookings available.

Home From Home, 39 Milton Road, Cambridge, Cambs, CB4 1XA.
Open: All Year
Grades: ETC 4 Diamond, AA
01223 323555 Mrs Fasano
Fax: 01223 563509
homefromhome@tesco.net
D: £25.00–£30.00 **S:** £40.00–£45.00
Beds: 4D 2T **Baths:** 5 En 1 Pr
Very comfortable, spacious family guest house. Ideally located for river, colleges, city centre, A14 and M11. All rooms with own facilities providing home from home hospitality and excellent breakfasts. Also available, four ETC graded self-catering apartments.

Tudor Cottage, *292 Histon Road,*
Cambridge, CB4 3HF.
Open: All Year
01223 565212 Mrs Celentano
Fax: 01223 565660
lucia/celetano@tesco.net
D: £19.00–£25.00 **S:** £25.00–£30.00
Beds: 1D 1S **Baths:** 1 En 1 Sh
ॐ ₽ (4) ⊬ ⊡ ▥ ▣ ⚲ &
Comfortable friendly Tudor style cottage
situated within walking distance of city
centre & colleges. Ensuite or shared
facilities, central heating, colour TV,
tea/coffee making facilities, excellent
food & friendly personal service, off street
parking easy access to A14/M11.

53 Eltisley Avenue, *Newnham,*
Cambridge, CB3 9JQ.
Open: All Year (not Xmas)
01223 560466 Mrs Dathan
D: £21.00–£22.00 **S:** £22.00–£24.00
Beds: 1D 1S **Baths:** 1 Sh
ॐ ⊬ ⊡ ▥ ▣ ⚲
Comfortable Edwardian family home in
quiet area close to city centre, university
departments, colleges and footpath to
Grantchester. Tariff includes full English
breakfast if required. Wash basin/shaver
point in all rooms. Easy access, Exit 12
M11.

Dykelands Guest House, *157*
Mowbray Road, Cambridge, CB1 7SP.
Open: All Year
Grades: ETC 3 Diamond, AA 3 Diamond
01223 244300 Ms Tweddell
Fax: 01223 566746
dykelands@fsbdial.co.uk
D: £18.50–£24.00 **S:** £25.00–£30.00
Beds: 3F 3D 2T 1S **Baths:** 7 En 1 Sh
ॐ ₽ (6) ⊬ ⊡ ⊀ ▥ ▣ ⚲
Lovely detached guest house on south
side of city. Easy access from M11 and
A14, yet only 1.75 miles from historic
city centre. Private parking. Spacious,
well furnished, comfortable rooms,
2 on ground floor, most ensuite. Good
breakfasts.

El Shaddai, *41 Warkworth Street,*
Cambridge, Cambs, CB1 1EG.
Centrally located, within a ten minute
walk to College, shops and other social
amenities.
Open: All Year
01223 327978 Mrs Droy
Fax: 01223 501024
pauline@droy.freeserve.co.uk
D: £20.00–£22.50 **S:** £23.00–£25.00
Beds: 1F 1D 2T 1S **Baths:** 1 Sh
ॐ ⊬ ⊡ ▥ ▣ ⚲

Cristinas Guest House, *47 St*
Andrew's Road, Cambridge, CB4 1DH.
Quiet location, 15 minutes' walk from city
centre. Hairdryers. Radio alarm clocks.
Open: All Year (not Xmas)
Grades: ETC 3 Diamond, AA 3 Diamond
01223 365855 Mrs Celentano
Fax: 01223 365855
Cristinas.guesthouse@ntlworld.com
D: £25.00–£28.00
S: fr £37.00
Beds: 1F 4D 4T **Baths:** 7 En 2 Sh
ॐ ₽ (8) ⊡ ▥ ⚲ & 2

Ashtrees Guest House, *128 Perne*
Road, Cambridge, Cambs, CB1 3RR.
Comfortable suburban residence with
garden. Good bus to city centre.
Open: Jan to Jan
Grades: ETC 3 Diamond RAC 3 Diamond
01223 411233 (also fax)
Mrs Hill
D: £19.50–£22.00 **S:** £20.00–£38.00
Beds: 1F 3D 1T 2S **Baths:** 3 En 1 Sh
ॐ ₽ (6) ⊬ ⊡ ✕ ▥ ⚲ cc

70 Girton Road, *Cambridge, CB3 0LN.*
Lovely outlook opposite college playing
fields, golf and tennis nearby. Parking.
Open: All Year
01223 276277 Mrs Barnes
D: fr £16.00 **S:** fr £17.00
Beds: 1D 1T 2S
ॐ (6) ₽ (2) ⊬ ⊡ ▥ ▣ ⚲

Cam Guest House, *17 Elizabeth Way,*
Cambridge, CB4 1DD.
Open: All Year (not Xmas/New Year)
Grades: ETC 3 Diamond
01223 354512 Fax: 01223 353164
camguesthouse@btinternet.com
D: £21.00–£30.00 **S:** £30.00
Beds: 3F 3D 4S **Baths:** 2 En 3 Sh
ॐ ₽ (5) ⊬ ⊡ ▥ ▣ ⚲
Situated near the river Cam, 15 minutes
walk to city centre, 5 minute walk to the
Grafton shopping centre. Some room ensuite, one with Jacuzzi. Tea and coffee
making facilities in all rooms. Extensive
breakfast menu available.

145 Gwydir Street, *Cambridge,*
Cambs, CB1 2LJ.
Terraced Victorian house near town
centre and sports facilities.
Open: All Year (not Xmas/New Year)
01223 356615 (also fax)
Mrs Sanders
marysand@waitrose.com
D: £20.00–£22.00 **S:** fr £20.00
Beds: 1T **Baths:** 1 Sh
⊬ ▥ ▣ ⚲

3 Dean Drive, *Holbrook Road,*
Cambridge, CB1 4SW.
A beautiful, quiet house. 30 minute walk
from city centre.
Open: All Year
Grades: ETC 3 Diamond
01223 210404 Mrs Dennett
carol.dennett@btinternet.com
D: £22.50 **S:** £28.00
Beds: 1D 1T **Baths:** 1 Pr
ॐ (3) ₽ (6) ⊬ ⊡ ▥ ▣ ⚲

Oakley Lodge, *627-631 Newmarket*
Road, Cambridge, CB5 8PA.
Approx 1.5 miles city centre, equally
suitable for individuals, families and
groups.
Open: All Year (not Xmas)
01223 241398 Fax: 01223 506783
oakleylodge@talk21.com
D: £18.00–£25.00
S: £20.00–£45.00
Beds: 4F 6D 6T 6S
Baths: 10 En 4 Sh
ॐ ₽ (25) ⊡ ⊀ ✕ ▥ ⚲ cc

The Ark, *30 St Matthews Street,*
Cambridge, CB1 2LT.
Centrally situated. Rail/coach stations,
cinema, restaurants, shops nearby.
Landlady speaks
German/Spanish/French.
Open: All Year (not Xmas/New Year)
01223 311130 Alexander Bartow Wylie
bartow.wylie@iscs.org.uk
D: £18.00–£22.00
Beds: 1T 1D **Baths:** 1 Sh
ॐ (10) ⊬ ▣ ⚲

Double Two, *22 St Margarets Road,*
Cambridge, CB3 0LT.
Convenient A14, M11 in quiet cul-de-sac,
2 km from city centre.
Open: All Year (not Xmas)
01223 276103 (also fax)
Mrs Noble
carol.noble@dtn.ntl.com
D: £21.00–£23.00 **S:** £32.00–£36.00
Beds: 1D 2T **Baths:** 2 En 1 Sh
ॐ ₽ (2) ⊬ ⊡ ⊀ ▥ ▣ ⚲

Old College House, *39 Trumpington*
Street, Cambridge, CB2 1QY.
Old town centre college house.
Open: All Year (not Xmas)
01223 355439 Mrs Rowell
D: £24.00 **S:** £24.00–£26.00
Beds: 1T 4S **Baths:** 2 Sh
ॐ (6) ₽ (1) ⊬ ⊡ ▣ ⚲

Arbury Lodge, *82 Arbury Road,*
Cambridge, CB4 2JE.
Comfortable furnished family run guest
house situated approx 1.5 m north of city
centre.
Open: All Year (not Xmas)
01223 364319 Mrs Celentano
Fax: 01223 566988
arburylodge@dtn.ntl.com
D: £21.00–£60.00 **S:** fr £22.00
Beds: 1F 2D 1T 1S **Baths:** 3 En 1 Sh
ॐ ₽ (8) ⊬ ⊡ ▥ ⚲

Aviemore Guest House, *310 Cherry*
Hinton Road, Cambridge, CB1 4AU.
Comfortable friendly family-run guest
house. Good breakfast, private parking.
Open: All Year (not Xmas)
01223 410956 Mrs Gawthrop
D: £20.00–£25.00 **S:** £25.00–£40.00
Beds: 1F 3D 2T 4S **Baths:** 6 En 1 Pr 2 Sh
ॐ (3) ₽ (9) ⊬ ⊡ ▥ ▣ ⚲ cc

A & B Guesthouse, *124 Tenison Road,*
Cambridge, CB1 2DP.
Victorian house situated very close to
station and town centre.
Open: All Year
01223 315702 Mr Williams
Fax: 01223 576702
abguest@hotmail.com
D: £20.00–£22.00 **S:** £22.00–£35.00
Beds: 3F 5D 2T 3S **Baths:** 3 En 7 Pr 3 Sh
ॐ ₽ (8) ⊡ ⊀ ✕ ▥ ▣ ⚲ cc

All details shown are as
supplied by B&B owners in
Autumn 2000

Castor

TL1297 ❦ *Fitzwilliam Arms*

Cobnut Cottage, 45 Peterborough Road, Castor, Peterborough, PE5 7AX.
Open: All Year
01733 380745 (also fax) Mrs Huckle
huckle.cobnut@talk21.com
D: £20.00–£24.00 **S:** £26.00–£30.00
Beds: 1F 1T 2D **Baths:** 2 En 1 Sh
⌖ (4) ▣ (6) ⌀ �📺 ⌖ ▥ 🍴
Listed stone house close to Cathedral city of Peterborough and Historic Stamford. Near country park for walking, cycling, fishing, sailing, golf,self catering cottage sleeps four available (weekly lets), all in 2/3 acre mature garden with summer house for guests use.

Cherry Hinton

TL4855 ❦ *Robin Hood, Red Lion, Sitar*

Hamden Guest House, 89 High Street, Cherry Hinton, Cambridge, CB1 9LU.
High standard of bed & breakfast accommodation. All rooms with ensuite shower. **Open:** All Year
Grades: AA 3 Diamond
01223 413263 Mr Casciano
Fax: 01223 245960
D: £22.50–£25.00 **S:** £28.00–£32.00
Beds: 1F 2D 1T 1S **Baths:** 5 En
⌖ (10) ▣ (7) ⌀ 📺 ▥ 🍴 cc

Comberton

TL3856 ❦ *Three Horseshoes, White Horse*

White Horse Cottage, 28 West Street, Comberton, Cambridge, CB3 7DS.
Restored C17th cottage near Cambridge. Pretty garden, many local attractions.
Open: All Year
01223 262914 Mrs Wright
D: £20.00–£22.50 **S:** £25.00–£30.00
Beds: 1F 1D **Baths:** 1 En 1 Sh
⌖ ▣ (3) ⌀ 📺 ▥ ▩ 🍴

Cottenham

TL4467

Denmark House, 58 Denmark Road, Cottenham, Cambridge, CB4 4QS.
Delightful detached residence in village 6 miles from Cambridge.
Open: All Year
01954 251060 Mrs Whittaker
Fax: 01954 251629
Denmark.House@tesco.net
D: fr £23.00
Beds: 2D 1T **Baths:** All En
⌖ ▣ (3) ⌀ ▥ ▩ 🍴

Dullingham

TL6257

The Old School, Dullingham, Newmarket, Suffolk, CB8 9XF.
Attractive conversion, spacious rooms, delightful village, nearby pub serves food.
Open: All Year
01638 507813 Mrs Andrews
Fax: 01638 507022
gill.andrews@premeirhoildays.co.uk
D: £23.00–£25.00
Beds: 1D **Baths:** 1 En
⌖ ▣ (2) ⌀ ▥ ▩ 🍴

Eaton Ford

TL1759 ❦ *Waggon & Horses*

Home From Home, 1 Laxton Close, Eaton Ford, St Neots, Cambs, PE19 3AR.
Friendly family house, tea/coffee served. ten minutes walk town.
Open: All Year
01480 383677 Mrs Francis-Macrae
Fax: 01480 383677
gillmacrae@cheerful.com
D: £20.00–£22.00 **S:** £16.00–£18.00
Beds: 1D 1S **Baths:** 1 Sh
⌖ ▣ (2) ⌀ 📺 ⌖ 🍴

Eaton Socon

TL1758

North Laurels House, 206 Great North Road, Eaton Socon, St Neots, Cambs, PE19 8EF.
Comfortable and well presented Georgian family home.
Open: All Year
01480 385086 jeffval@supanet.net
D: £20.00–£28.00 **S:** £20.00–£28.00
Beds: 1F 1T 1S **Baths:** 1 En 1 Sh
⌖ ▣ (3) ⌀ 📺 ▥ ▩ 🍴

Ellington

TL1671 ❦ *Brewers Fayre*

Grove Cottage, Malting Lane, Ellington, Huntingdon, PE28 0AA.
Peaceful, relaxing, self-contained suite in charming comfortable period cottage.
Open: All Year
01480 890167 (also fax)
Mr Silver
hr73@dial.pipex.com
D: £20.00–£22.50
S: £27.50–£30.00
Beds: 1D **Baths:** 1 En
⌖ ▣ (2) ⌀ ▥ 🍴

Elm

TF4606 ❦ *Blacksmiths Arms*

Elm Manor, Main Road, Elm, Wisbech, Cambs, PE14 0AG.
Charles II manor house. Beams, inglenooks, four posters, gardens, adjacent to local inn.
Open: All Year (not Xmas)
01945 861069 (also fax)
sandynye.co.uk
D: £20.00–£22.50 **S:** £30.00–£40.00
Beds: 1D 1T **Baths:** 1 En 1 Pr
⌖ (8) ▣ (2) ⌀ 📺 ▥ 🍴

Ely

TL5480 ❦ *The Crown, Red Lion, High Flyer, Old Boathouse, Cutter Inn, Stagecoach, Maids Head*

Greenways, Prickwillow Road, Queen Adelaide, Ely, Cambs, CB7 4TZ.
Comfortable ground floor accommodation, 1 mile cathedral city of Ely. **Open:** All Year
01353 666706 Mr Dunlop-Hill
D: £21.00–£26.00 **S:** fr £26.00
Beds: 1F 1D 1T 1S **Baths:** 4 En
⌖ ▣ (6) 📺 ⌖ ▥ 🍴 &

Bridge House, Green End, Stretham, Ely, Cambs, CB6 3LF.
Period farmhouse, river frontage, in 13 acres. Relaxed atmosphere, wildlife in profusion.
Open: All Year (not Xmas)
01353 649212 Mr & Mrs Whitmore
D: £20.00–£25.00 **S:** £25.00–£35.00
Beds: 2F 1D 2T **Baths:** 3 En 1 Pr
⌖ ▣ (6) ⌀ 📺 ⌖ ▥ ▩ 🍴 &

82 Broad Street, Ely, Cambs, CB7 4BE.
Comfortable rooms, central Ely. Near station, cathedral & river.
Open: All Year (not Xmas)
01353 667609 Mr & Mrs Hull
Fax: 01353 667005
D: £15.00–£18.00 **S:** fr £20.00
Beds: 1F 1T 1S **Baths:** 1 En 1 Pr 1 Sh
⌖ ▣ 📺 ⌖ ▩ 🍴

Cathedral House, 17 St Mary's Street, Ely, Cambs, CB7 4ER.
Grade II Listed house, in shadow of cathedral, close to museums, restaurants, shops **Open:** All Year (not Xmas)
Grades: ETC 4 Diamond, Silver Award
01353 662124 (also fax)
Mr & Mrs Farndale
farndale@cathedralhouse.co.uk
D: £25.00–£30.00 **S:** £35.00–£45.00
Beds: 1F 1D 1T **Baths:** 3 En
⌖ ▣ (4) ⌀ 📺 ▥ ▩ 🍴

Ivy Cottage, 1 Holt Fen, Little Thetford, Ely, Cambs, CB6 3HB.
Quiet village 200 year old cottage set in large garden. **Open:** All Year
01353 649328 Mrs Badcock
miriam@holtfen.f9.co.uk
S: £18.00–£20.00
Beds: 2S **Baths:** 1 Sh
▣ (2) ⌀ ▥ 🍴

84 Broad Street, Ely, Cambs, CB7 4BE.
Renovated cottage, courtyard garden. Near river, cathedral and station.
Open: All Year
01353 666862 Mrs Collins
D: £16.00 **S:** £18.00
Beds: 1F 1D **Baths:** 1 Sh
⌖ ⌀ ▥ × ▩ ▥ 🍴

The Nyton Hotel, 7 Barton Road, Ely, Cambs, CB7 4HZ.
Residential family hotel, lovely situation, close city centre and cathedral.
Open: All Year
01353 662459 Mr Setchell
Fax: 01353 666217
D: £25.00–£30.00 **S:** £35.00–£40.00
Beds: 3F 3D 2T 2S **Baths:** 10 En
⌖ ▣ (26) ⌀ 📺 ⌖ × ▥ ▩ 🍴 & cc

Annesdale Lodge, 8 Annesdale, Ely, Cambs, CB7 4BN.
Riverside home from home accommodation near railway station. Great views. **Open:** All Year
01353 667533 Mr Drage
Fax: 01353 667005
D: £16.00–£22.50 **S:** £25.00–£35.00
Beds: 1D 1T **Baths:** 2 Pr
⌖ ▣ (1) ⌀ 📺 ⌖ ▥ 🍴

Sycamore House, 91 Cambridge Road, Ely, Cambs, CB7 4HX.
Newly renovated Edwardian family home set in acre of mature gardens.
Open: All Year (not Xmas)
01353 662139 Mrs Webster
D: £22.00–£25.00 **S:** £28.00–£30.00
Beds: 2D 2T **Baths:** 3 En 1 Pr
🅿 (8) ⅋ 📺 🎹 🛢 ♨

Farcet
TL2094   🍺 *Duck and Drake*

Red House Farm, Broadway, Farcet, Peterborough, PE7 3AZ.
Situated close to A1 and city centre with lovely views. **Open:** All Year
Grades: ETC 3 Diamond
01733 243129 (also fax)
gill.emberson@totalise.co.uk
D: £18.00–£20.00 **S:** £18.00–£20.00
Beds: 2T 1D
🐾 🅿 (6) ⅋ 📺 🎹 ✕ 🛢 Ⅴ ♨

Fordham
TL6270   🍺 *The Crown, White Pheasant, The Chequers*

Homelands, 1 Carter Street, Fordham, Ely, Cambs, CB7 5NG.
Comfort in a private house. Rooms of character. Garden and private parking.
Open: All Year (not Xmas)
01638 720363 Mrs Bycroft
D: £22.00–£25.00 **S:** £22.00–£25.00
Beds: 1F 1D 1T **Baths:** 2 En
🐾 🅿 (4) ⅋ 📺 🎹 🛢 Ⅴ ♨

Queensberry, 196 Carter Street, Fordham, Ely, Suffolk, CB7 5JU.
Country house comfort. First village off A14 Newmarket to Ely road.
Open: All Year
01638 720916 Mr & Mrs Roper
Fax: 01638 720233
D: £20.00 **S:** £25.00
Beds: 1D 1T 1S **Baths:** 1 En 1 Pr 1 Sh
🐾 🅿 (12) ⅋ 📺 🎹 🛢 Ⅴ ✿ ♨ ♿

Girton
TL4261

Finches, 144 Thorton Road, Girton, Cambridge, CB3 0ND.
A friendly welcome to our home, beautiful new ensuite rooms.
Open: All Year (not Xmas)
Grades: ETC 4 Diamond
01223 276653 Mr & Mrs Green
liz.green.b-b@talk21.com
D: £30.00–£50.00 **S:** £30.00–£50.00
Beds: 1D 2T
🐾 🅿 (4) ⅋ 📺 🛢 Ⅴ ♨

Gorefield
TF4211

Maison De La Chien, 35 Churchill Road, Gorefield, Wisbech, Cambs, PE13 4NA.
Quiet village location overlooking farmland on the beautiful Cambridgeshire fens. **Open:** All Year
01945 870789 (also fax) Mrs Barnard
hols-maisonchien@faxvia.net
D: £15.00 **S:** £15.00
Beds: 1D 1T **Baths:** 1 Sh
🅿 (2) ⅋ 📺 🎹 ✕ 🛢 Ⅴ ♨

Grantchester
TL4355   🍺 *Green Man, Rupert Brook, Red Lion*

Honeysuckle Cottage, 38 High Street, Grantchester, Cambridge, CB3 8PL.
Grantchester is a beauty spot, the home of politician Geoffrey Archer.
Open: All Year
01223 845850 Mr & Mrs Salt
D: fr £38.00 **S:** fr £38.00
Beds: 3F 3D 3T 3S **Baths:** 3 En
🐾 🅿 (20) ⅋ 📺 ✕ 🛢 Ⅴ ♨

Great Chishill
TL4238   🍺 *The Pleasant*

Hall Farm, Great Chishill, Royston, Cambridgeshire, SG8 8SH.
Open: All Year
Grades: ETC 4 Diamond
01763 838263 (also fax)
Mrs Wiseman
D: £20.00–£30.00 **S:** £30.00–£35.00
Beds: 1F 1T 1D **Baths:** 1 En 1 Sh
🐾 🅿 (4) ⅋ 📺 Ⅴ ♨
Beautiful Manor house in secluded gardens on the edge of this pretty hilltop village 11 miles south of Cambridge, wonderful views and footpaths. Duxford Air Museum 4 miles. Good local food. Working Arable farm. Comfortable new beds.

Great Eversden
TL3653   🍺 *The Hoops*

The Moat House, Great Eversden, Cambridge, CB3 7HN.
Welcoming period family home. Easy access Cambridge and East Anglia.
Open: All Year (not Xmas)
01223 262836 Mr Webster
Fax: 01223 262979
websterassociates@breathemail.net
D: £22.50 **S:** £22.50
Beds: 1T 1S **Baths:** 1 Pr
🐾 🅿 (4) ⅋ 📺 🎹 🛢 ♨

Great Shelford
TL4652   🍺 *The Rose*

Norfolk House, 2 Tunwells Lane, Great Shelford, Cambridge, Cambs, CB2 5LJ.
Elegant Victorian residence retaining original character plus 21st century comforts.
Open: All Year (not Xmas/New Year)
01223 840287 Mrs Diver
D: £18.50–£22.50 **S:** £25.00–£30.00
Beds: 2T 1D **Baths:** 1 En 1 Sh
🐾 (10) 🅿 (2) ⅋ 📺 🛢 ♨

National Grid References are
for villages, towns and cities –
not for individual houses

Hardwick
TL3759   🍺 *Blue Lion*

Wallis Farm, 98 Main Street, Hardwick, Cambridge, CB3 7QU.
Open: All Year
Grades: ETC 4 Diamond
01954 210347 Mrs Sadler
Fax: 01954 210988
wallisfarm@mcmail.com
D: £22.50–£30.00 **S:** £35.00–£40.00
Beds: 1F 2D 3T **Baths:** 6 En
🐾 🅿 (8) ⅋ 📺 🎹 🛢 Ⅴ ♨ ♿
Quiet location close to city of Cambridge. 4 ensuite rooms in converted barn with exposed beams decorated to high standard. Large gardens leading to meadows and woodland.

Helpston
TF1205   🍺 *Exeter Arms*

Helpston House, Helpston, Peterborough, Cambs, PE6 7DX.
Grade II Listed stone manor house set in beautiful grounds, dating back to 1090.
Open: All Year
Grades: ETC 4 Diamond
01733 252190 Mrs Orton
Fax: 01733 253853
orton.helpstonhouse@btinternet.com
D: £17.50–£20.00 **S:** £22.00–£25.00
Beds: 1F 1D 1S **Baths:** 1 En 1 Sh
🐾 🅿 (6) ⅋ 📺 ✕ 🛢 Ⅴ ♨

Blue Wisteria House, Church Lane, Helpston, Peterborough, Cambs, PE6 7DT.
Old Listed cottage. Easy reach Peterborough, business park, showground, Stamford, Bourne.
Open: All Year
01733 252272 Mr Hammond
D: £22.00 **S:** £25.00–£30.00
Beds: 1D 2T **Baths:** 1 En 1 Sh
🐾 🅿 (3) ⅋ 📺 🛢 Ⅴ ♨

Hemingford Grey
TL2970   🍺 *Axe & Compass*

Willow Guest House, 45 High Street, Hemingford Grey, Huntingdon, Cambs, PE18 9BJ.
Large comfortable quiet guest house in pretty riverside village.
Open: All Year
01480 494748 Mr Webster
Fax: 01480 464456
D: £21.00–£24.00 **S:** £28.00–£35.00
Beds: 2F 2D 2T 1S **Baths:** 7 En
🐾 🅿 (12) ⅋ 📺 🛢 ♨

Histon
TL4363   🍺 *Boot, William IV*

Wynwyck, 55 Narrow Lane, Histon, Cambridge, CB4 9HD.
Comfortable peaceful ideal for Cambridge, Ely, Newmarket, Duxford, Museum and East Anglia.
Open: All Year (not Xmas)
01223 232496 (also fax)
Mrs Torrens
D: £23.00–£30.00 **S:** £30.00–£35.00
Beds: 1F 1D 2T **Baths:** 2 En 1 Sh
🐾 🅿 (4) ⅋ 📺 🛢 Ⅴ ♨

Huntingdon

TL2472   🍺 *Victoria Inn*

Braywood House, *27 St Peters Road, Huntingdon, Cambs, PE18 7AA.*
Built 1828, governor's house of Huntingdon Gaol. Full fire certificate.
Open: All Year (not Xmas)
01480 459782 (also fax)
Mrs Knapp
D: £25.00 **S:** £25.00–£30.00
Beds: 2F 3D 2T 3S **Baths:** 8 En 2 Pr
🛇 🄿 (10) 📺 🍴 📓 🖤 ♿

Ickleton

TL4843   🍺 *Red Lion*

New Inn House, *10 Brookhampton Street, Ickleton, Duxford, Cambs, CB10 1SP.*
Open: All Year (not Xmas)
01799 530463 Mrs Fletcher
Fax: 01799 531499
jpinternational@nascr.net
D: £15.00–£19.00 **S:** £25.00–£30.00
Beds: 1D 1T **Baths:** 1 Sh
🛇 (5) 🄿 (6) 🖍 📺 📓 ♿
Traditional beamed property combining comfortable modern facilities with historic charm. Luxury guest shower room. Good breakfasts. Small rural village, 3 miles Duxford Imperial War Museum. Handy for Cambridge and Saffron Walden. 2 miles M11.

Kirtling

TL6858   🍺 *Rain Deer*

Hill Farm Guest House, *Kirtling, Newmarket, Suffolk, CB8 9HQ.*
Open: All Year
Grades: ETC 3 Diamond, AA 3 Diamond
01638 730253 (also fax)
Mrs Benley
D: £25.00–£50.00 **S:** £25.00
Beds: 1D 1T 1S **Baths:** 2 En 1 Pr
🄿 (5) 📺 🍴 ✕ 📓 🖤 ♿
Delightful farm house in rural setting.

Linton

TL5646   🍺 *Crown, Dog & Duck*

Cantilena, *4 Harefield Rise, Linton, Cambridge, CB1 6LS.*
Spacious bungalow, quiet cul-de-sac, edge of historic village. Cambridge, 9 miles.
Open: All Year
01223 892988 (also fax)
Mr & Mrs Clarkson
D: £18.00–£20.00 **S:** £18.00–£25.00
Beds: 1F 1D 1T **Baths:** 1 Sh
🛇 🄿 (3) 🖍 📺 📓 🖤 ♿

Linton Heights, *36 Wheatsheaf Way, Linton, Cambridge, Cambs, CB1 6XB.*
Comfortable, friendly home, sharing lounge, convenient Duxford, Cambridge, Newmarket, Saffron Walden, Bury.
Open: All Year (not Xmas)
01223 892516 Mr & Mrs Peake
D: £17.00–£20.00 **S:** £17.00–£20.00
Beds: 1T 1S **Baths:** 1 Sh
🛇 (6) 🄿 (2) 🖍 📺 📓 🖤 ♿

Little Downham

TL5283   🍺 *Plough, Anchor*

Bury House, *11 Main Street, Little Downham, Ely, Cambs, CB6 2ST.*
Grade II Listed ex -farmhouse large comfortable bedrooms in friendly home.
Open: All Year (not Xmas)
01353 698766 Mrs Ambrose
D: £18.00 **S:** fr £18.00
Beds: 1F 2T **Baths:** 2 Sh
🛇 🄿 (2) 🖍 📺 📓 🖤 ♿

Little Gransden

TL2754   🍺 *Golden Miller, The Cock*

Elms Farm, *52 Main Road, Little Gransden, Sandy, Beds, SG19 3DL.*
Farm house, quiet, picturesque gardens and village. Central to many attractions
Open: All Year (not Xmas)
01767 677459 Mrs Bygraves
joan@elmsfarmct.freeserve.co.uk
D: £20.00–£25.00 **S:** £25.00–£30.00
Beds: 1F 1D 1T 1S **Baths:** 1 En 1 Pr 1 Sh
🛇 🄿 (10) 🖍 📺 🖤 ♿

Little Thetford

TL5276

Ivy Cottage, *1 Holt Fen, Little Thetford, Ely, Cambs, CB6 3HB.*
Quiet village 200 year old cottage set in large garden.
Open: All Year
01353 649328 Mrs Badcock
miriam@holtfen.f9.co.uk
S: £18.00–£20.00
Beds: 2S **Baths:** 1 Sh
🄿 (2) 🖍 📺 📓 ♿

Marholm

TF1402   🍺 *Fitzwilliam Arms*

Ancient Marholm Farm, *Woodcroft Road, Marholm, Peterborough, Cambs, PE6 7HU.*
Ancient farmhouse with oak beams, stone walls, set in peaceful and pastoral surroundings.
Open: All Year
01733 262824 Mrs Scott
D: £20.00–£35.00 **S:** £20.00–£35.00
Beds: 3F 1T 1S 1D **Baths:** 1 Sh
🛇 🄿 (20) 📺 🍴 📓 ♿

Maxey

TF1208   🍺 *Golden Pheasant*

Abbey House & Coach House, *West End Road, Maxey, Peterborough, Cambridgeshire, PE6 9EJ.*
Grade II Listed, dating from 1190, quiet village location.
Open: All Year (not Xmas)
01778 344642
Mr & Mrs Fitton
abbeyhouse@maxey1.freeserve.co.uk
D: £24.50–£29.50
S: £30.00–£40.00
Beds: 2F 4D 3T 1S **Baths:** 10 En
🄿 (12) 🖍 📺 📓 ♿

Melbourn

TL3844   🍺 *The Star, Black Horse, The Chequers*

The Carlings, *Melbourn, Royston, SG8 6DX.*
Luxurious rooms in delightful secluded setting. Separate entrance, conservatory gardens.
Open: All Year (not Xmas)
01763 260686 Mrs Howard
Fax: 01763 261988
D: £22.00 **S:** £30.00–£35.00
Beds: 1D 1T **Baths:** 2 En
🛇 🄿 (3) 🖍 📺 🍴 📓 🖤 ♿

New Wimpole

TL3449   🍺 *Royal Oak, The Plough*
Red Lion

Foxhounds, *71 Cambridge Road, Wimpole, Royston, Herts, SG8 5QD.*
Wimpole Hall (NT) nearby. Comfortable family home, large garden.
Open: All Year (not Xmas)
Grades: ETC 3 Diamond
01223 207344 Mrs Parker
D: £20.00 **S:** £20.00
Beds: 2T 1S **Baths:** 2 Sh
🛇 🄿 (3) 🖍 📺 ✕ 📓 🖤 ♿

Over

TL3770   🍺 *The Exhibition*

Charter Cottage, *Horseware, Church End, Over, Cambridge, CB4 5NX.*
Peaceful country cottage close to Cambridge, Ely & St Ives.
Open: All Year
01954 230056 Mr & Mrs Warren
Fax: 01954 232300
charter.cottage@talk21.com
D: fr £16.00 **S:** £20.00
Beds: 1D 1T **Baths:** 1 Sh
🛇 (3) 🄿 (6) 🖍 📺 🍴 📓 ♿

Peterborough

TL1999   🍺 *Cherry Tree, Exeter Arms, Barnyards, Botolph Arms, Fitzwilliam Arms*

Aragon House, *75/77 London Road, Peterborough, Cambs, PE2 9BS.*
Comfortable, friendly, easy parking and close to city centre.
Open: All Year (not Xmas)
Grades: ETC 3 Diamond
01733 563718 (also fax)
Mr & Mrs Spence
aragon@fsbdial.co.uk
D: £19.00–£22.00 **S:** £20.00–£30.00
Beds: 1F 3D 2T 6S **Baths:** 3 En 2 Sh
🛇 🄿 (8) 🖍 📺 🍴 📓 🖤 ♿ cc

Montana, *15 Fletton Avenue, Peterborough, Cambs, PE2 8AX.*
Clean, friendly, family-run. Close city centre. Traditional breakfasts.
Open: All Year (not Xmas)
Grades: ETC 3 Diamond
01733 567917 (also fax)
Mr & Mrs Atkins
D: £17.00–£20.00 **S:** £19.00–£25.00
Beds: 1D 2T 4S **Baths:** 2 Sh
🄿 (6) 🖍 📺 🍴 📓 ♿

Rose-Marie, 14 Eastfield Road, Peterborough, Cambs, PE1 4AN.
The Rose Marie is a family-run guest house close to city centre.
Open: All Year
01733 557548 Mr Doyle
Fax: 01733 764801
D: £15.00–£18.00 **S:** £18.00–£20.00
Beds: 1F 2D 1T 2S **Baths:** 1 Sh
🛏 📺 �🏠 🛁 Ⅴ ⚓

Ancient Marholm Farm, Woodcroft Road, Marholm, Peterborough, Cambs, PE6 7HU.
Ancient farmhouse with oak beams, stone walls, set in peaceful and pastoral surroundings. **Open:** All Year
01733 262824 Mrs Scott
D: £ **S:** £20.00–£35.00
Beds: 3F 1T 1S 1D **Baths:** 1 Sh
🛏 🅿 (20) 📺 �🏠 🛁 Ⅴ ⚓

Queen Adelaide

TL5580   🍺 Highflyer

Greenways, Prickwillow Road, Queen Adelaide, Ely, Cambs, CB7 4TZ.
Comfortable ground floor accommodation, 1 mile cathedral city of Ely.
Open: All Year
01353 666706 Mr Dunlop-Hill
D: £21.00–£26.00 **S:** fr £26.00
Beds: 1F 1D 1T 1S **Baths:** 4 En
🛏 🅿 (6) 📺 �🏠 🛁 ⚓ ⚓

Soham

TL5973   🍺 Fountain, Cherry Tree

Greenbank, 111 Brook Street, Soham, Ely, Cambs, CB7 5AE.
Open: All Year (not Xmas/New Year)
01353 720929 Mrs Rump
D: £16.00 **S:** £16.00
Beds: 1T 1D **Baths:** 1 Sh
🛏 (3) 🅿 (2) �️ 📺 ⏰ 🛁 Ⅴ ⚓ cc
Pleasant bungalow in a quiet street, convenient for Newmarket, Ely or Cambridge. 3 miles from nature reserve at Wicken Fen. Favoured area for fishing and bird watching.

The Fountain, 1 Churchgate Street, Soham, Ely, Cambs, CB7 5DS.
Offering excellent quality food and good value accommodation.
Open: All Year
01353 720374 Mr Hall Smith
Fax: 01353 722103
jhs@thefountain.co.uk
D: £18.00–£20.00 **S:** £25.50–£27.50
Beds: 5T **Baths:** 3 En 2 Sh
🛏 🅿 (30) 📺 ⏰ ✕ 🛁 Ⅴ ⚓ cc

St Neots

TL1860   🍺 Chequers

North Laurels House, 206 Great North Road, Eaton Socon, St Neots, Cambs, PE19 8EF.
Comfortable and well presented Georgian family home.
Open: All Year
01480 385086 jeffval@supanet.net
D: £20.00–£28.00 **S:** £20.00–£28.00
Beds: 1F 1T 1S **Baths:** 1 En 1 Sh
🛏 🅿 (3) ✏ 📺 🛁 Ⅴ ⚓

The Ferns, Berkley Street, Eynesbury, St Neots, Huntingdon, Cambs, PE19 2NE.
Welcoming family home in picturesque C18th former farmhouse.
Open: All Year (not Xmas)
01480 213884 Mrs Raggatt
D: £17.00–£19.00 **S:** £19.00–£21.00
Beds: 1F 1D **Baths:** 1 En 1 Sh
🛏 🅿 (2) ✏ 📺 ⏰ 🛁 Ⅴ ⚓

Stretham

TL5074   🍺 Red Lion, Maids Head

The Red Lion, 47 High Street, Stretham, Ely, Cambs, CB6 3JQ.
Open: All Year (not Xmas)
Grades: ETC 3 Diamond, AA 3 Diamond
01353 648132 Mrs Hayes
Fax: 01353 648327
D: £21.90 **S:** £32.75–£37.95
Beds: 3F 5D 2T 2S **Baths:** 12 En
🛏 🅿 (18) 📺 ⏰ ✕ 🛁 ⚓ cc
A C18th inn centrally situated for touring or business. 4 miles from Ely, 14 miles Newmarket, 12 miles Cambridge, 30 miles from Stansted Airport. Close to major motorways, M11, A14, A428 and A. Conservatory restaurant for guests.

Bridge House, Green End, Stretham, Ely, Cambs, CB6 3LF.
Period farmhouse, river frontage, in 13 acres. Relaxed atmosphere, wildlife in profusion.
Open: All Year (not Xmas)
01353 649212 Mr & Mrs Whitmore
D: £20.00–£25.00 **S:** £25.00–£35.00
Beds: 2F 1D 2T **Baths:** 3 En 1 Pr
🛏 🅿 (6) ✏ 📺 ⏰ 🛁 Ⅴ ⚓ ♿

Sutton (Ely)

TL4479   🍺 The Chequers

2 Eastwood Close, Sutton, Ely, Cambs, CB6 2RH.
Quiet modern house in Fenland village, C13th church opposite the close.
Open: All Year (not Xmas)
01353 778423 Mrs Monk
aemonk@callnet.uk.com
D: £18.00 **S:** £18.00
Beds: 1D 1T 1S **Baths:** 2 Sh
🛏 🅿 (2) ✏ 📺 🛁 ⚓

Swaffham Prior

TL5663   🍺 Red Lion

Sterling Farm, Health Road, Swaffham Prior, Cambridge, CB5 0LA.
Convenient for visiting Newmarket, Cambridge and Ely. Anglesea Abbey 3 miles.
Open: All Year (not Xmas)
Grades: ETC 3 Diamond
01638 741431 Mrs Harris
D: £20.00–£25.00 **S:** £20.00–£25.00
Beds: 1D 1T 1S **Baths:** 1 Sh
🛏 🅿 (8) ✏ 📺 🛁 ⚓

B&B owners may vary rates - be sure to check when booking

Thornhaugh

TF0700   🍺 The Papermills

Sacrewell Lodge Farm, Thornhaugh, Peterborough, PE8 6HJ.
Farmhouse in quiet location surrounded by attractive gardens and farmland.
Open: All Year (not Xmas)
01780 782277 Mrs Armitage
D: £18.00–£20.00 **S:** £15.00–£18.00
Beds: 1D 1T 1S **Baths:** 1 En 1 Sh
🅿 (10) ✏ 📺 🛁 ⚓

Toft

TL3655   🍺 Blue Lion

Meadowview, 3 Brookside, Toft, Cambridge, CB3 7RJ.
Large family house with modern comforts on the edge of a small village.
Open: All Year (not Xmas)
01223 263395 (also fax)
Mrs McVey
medoview@aol.com
D: £20.00–£22.00 **S:** £25.00–£30.00
Beds: 2D 1T **Baths:** 2 En 1 Pr
🛏 🅿 (6) ✏ 📺 🛁 ⚓

Ufford

TF0904

Ufford Farm, Ufford, Stamford, PE9 3BP.
Open: All Year
01780 740220 (also fax)
Mrs Vergette
vergette@ufford1.freeserve.co.uk
D: £25.00–£30.00 **S:** £25.00–£30.00
Beds: 1T 1S **Baths:** 1 Sh
🛏 (3) 🅿 (4) ✏ 📺 ✕ 🛁 Ⅴ ⚓
C18th farmhouse, comfortably furnished, with open fires on edge of a peaceful village. A working farm, with the Torpel Way crossing the farm. Large garden with Gazebo and pond.

Waterbeach

TL4964   🍺 White Horse

Goose Hall Farm, Ely Road, Waterbeach, Cambridge, CB5 9PG.
Open: All Year (not Xmas)
01223 860235 (also fax)
Mrs Lock
D: £19.00–£21.00 **S:** £30.00–£35.00
Beds: 1F 1D 1T **Baths:** 2 En 1 Pr
🛏 (5) 🅿 (8) 📺 🛁 Ⅴ ⚓
Modern farmhouse on 13 acres surrounded by high hedgerows enclosing meadows, a deer run and a half acre lake. Comfortable ensuite private bathrooms and hearty breakfasts. 4 miles from Cambridge. TV, tea, coffee, guest lounge, gardens.

92 Bannold Road, Waterbeach, Cambridge, CB5 9LQ.
Tiny garden Listed in NGS and featured on Channel 4.
Open: All Year
01223 863661 Mr & Mrs Guy
rguy@richardguy.screaming.net
D: £20.00–£25.00 **S:** £20.00–£25.00
Beds: 1T **Baths:** 1 En
🅿 (1) ✏ 📺 🛁 ⚓

RATES

D = Price range per person sharing in a double room
S = Price range for a single room

Wentworth

TL4777

Desiderata, *44 Main Street, Wentworth, Ely, Cambs, CB6 3QG.*
Large modern house in quiet country lane; ideal disabled.
Open: All Year
01353 776131 Mrs Graham
chips.1@virgin.net
D: £15.00 **S:** fr £20.00
Beds: 1D 2T **Baths:** 1 Sh
🛏 🅿 (6) 📺 🛋 🖂 ✿ 🖈 ⟐

West Perry

TL1566　🍺 *Wheatsheaf*

38 West Perry, *West Perry, Huntingdon, Cambs, PE28 0BX.*
Victorian country cottage, peaceful, interesting Garden. Close Grafham water reservoir.
Open: All Year
01480 810225
Mrs Hickling
D: £17.00–£22.00 **S:** £17.00–£22.00
Beds: 2T 1S **Baths:** 1 Sh
🛏 (13) 🅿 (3) ⟐ 📺 🛋 🖂 ⟐

West Wratting

TL5951　🍺 *The Chesnut*

The Old Bakery, *West Wratting, Cambridge, CB1 5LU.*
Period cottage situated in quiet village with nice garden.
Open: All Year
01223 290492
Mr & Mrs Denny
Fax: 01223 290845
ddtractors@zoom.co.uk
D: £22.50 **S:** £22.50
Beds: 2T 3D **Baths:** 1 En 1 Pr
🛏 🅿 (2) 📺 🛋 ⟐

Westley Waterless

TL6256　🍺 *Kings Head*

Westley House, *Westley Waterless, Newmarket, Suffolk, CB8 0RQ.*
C18th Georgian country home in quiet rural area 5 miles from Newmarket.
Open: All Year
01638 508112 Mrs Galpin
Fax: 01638 508113
westlyhs@aol.com
D: £22.50–£24.00 **S:** £24.00–£25.00
Beds: 2T 2S **Baths:** 2 Sh
🛏 (4) 🅿 (6) 📺 🍴 🗙 🛋 📺

Whittlesey

TL2797　🍺 *Mortons Fork*

Cobwebs Guest House, *21 The Delph, Whittlesey, Peterborough, Cambs, PE7 1QH.*
Close to diving centre, fishing, lakes East of England showground.
Open: All Year (not Xmas)
01733 350960 Mrs Ekins
D: £15.00–£20.00 **S:** £15.00–£20.00
Beds: 1F 5T **Baths:** 1 Pr 2 Sh
🅿 (4) 📺 🍴 🗙 🛋 ⟐ ⟐

Wicken

TL5670　🍺 *Maids Head*

The Old School, *48 North Street, Wicken, Ely, Cambs, CB7 5XW.*
Tastefully renovated Edwardian village school, with tearoom, gifts, Bygones shop.
Open: All Year (not Xmas/New Year)
01353 720526 Mrs Wright
wicken.oldschool@btinternet.com
D: £20.00–£24.00 **S:** £25.00–£30.00
Beds: 1F 1D **Baths:** 1 En 1 Pr
🛏 🅿 ⟐ 📺 🛋 📺 ⟐

Wisbech

TF4609　🍺 *Blackfriars, Red Lion*

Marmion House Hotel, *11 Lynn Road, Wisbech, Cambs, PE13 3DD.*
Georgian town house hotel located in the capital of the Fens.
Open: All Year (not Xmas)
Grades: ETC 3 Diamond
01945 582822 Mrs Lilley
Fax: 01945 475889
D: £18.00–£22.00 **S:** £20.00–£26.00
Beds: 20F 10D 2T 6S
Baths: 18 En 1 Pr 2 Sh
🛏 🅿 📺 🛋 ⟐ **cc**

Ravenscourt, *138 Lynn Road, Wisbech, Cambs, PE13 3DP.*
Quality accommodation, friendly atmosphere, well situated for business or holiday.
Open: All Year (not Xmas/New Year)
Grades: ETC Welcome Host Listed
01945 585052 (also fax)
Mr Parish
ravenscourt@rya-online.net
D: fr £16.00 **S:** £17.50–£20.00
Beds: 1F 2D 1T **Baths:** 4 Pr
🛏 🅿 (3) ⟐ 📺 🛋 📺 ⟐

Algethi Guest House, *136 Lynn Road, Wisbech, Cambs, PE13 3DP.*
Friendly family-run guest house near town centre and river.
Open: All Year
01945 582278 Mrs McManus
Fax: 01945 466456
D: £15.00–£17.50 **S:** £15.00–£17.50
Beds: 2F 1D 2S **Baths:** 2 Pr
🛏 🅿 (3) 📺 🍴 🗙 🛋 📺 ⟐

Witchford

TL5078　🍺 *Shoulder of Mutton*

17 Common Road, *Witchford, Ely, Cambs, CB6 2HY.*
Detached house and garden opposite village common.
Open: All Year (not Xmas/New Year)
01353 663918 R J Westell
rjwest@elyfl.freeserve.co.uk
D: £20.00 **S:** £20.00
Beds: 1T 1D 1S **Baths:** 1 Sh
🅿 (1) ⟐ 📺 🛋 ⟐

Clare Farm House, *Main Street, Witchford, Ely, Cambs, CB6 2HQ.*
Large, modern house, convenient for Ely. Warm & friendly.
Open: All Year
01353 664135 Mrs Seymour
D: £20.00–£30.00 **S:** £20.00–£30.00
Beds: 1F 1T 2S **Baths:** 1 En 1 Sh
🛏 (7) 🅿 (10) 📺 🛋 📺 ⟐

BEDROOMS
F - Family
D - Double
T - Twin
S - Single

Cheshire

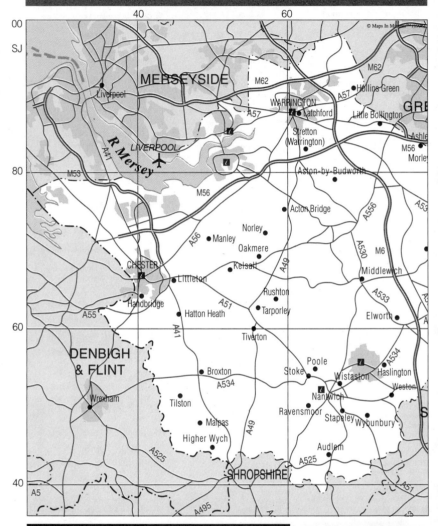

Tourist Information Centres

Town Hall, Northgate Street, **Chester**, CH1 2HJ, 01244 402111.

Chester Railway Station, Station Road, **Chester**, CH1 3NT, 01244 322220.

Town Hall, High Street, **Congleton**, Cheshire, CW12 1BN, 01260 271095.

Council Offices, Toft Road, **Knutsford**, Cheshire, WA16 6TA, 01565 632611.

Macclesfield Town Hall, **Macclesfield**, Cheshire, SK10 1DX, 01625 504114.

Beam Street, **Nantwich**, Cheshire, CW5 5LY, 01270 610983.

57-61 Church Street, **Runcorn**, Cheshire, WA7 1LG, 01928 576776.

21 Rylands Street, **Warrington**, Cheshire, WA1 1EJ, 01925 442180.

Acton Bridge

SJ5975 • *Maypole, Hazel Pear*

Manor Farm, *Cliff Road, Acton Bridge, Northwich, Cheshire, CW8 3QP.*
Peaceful, elegantly furnished traditional country house. Large garden and views.
Open: All Year (not Xmas)
Grades: ETC 4 Diamond
01606 853181
Mrs Campbell
D: £20.00–£25.00
S: £20.00–£25.00
Beds: 1F 1T 1S
Baths: 1 En 2 Pr
🛇 (1) 🅿 (10) ⊬ 📺 🛏 🏠 Ⓥ ᵻ

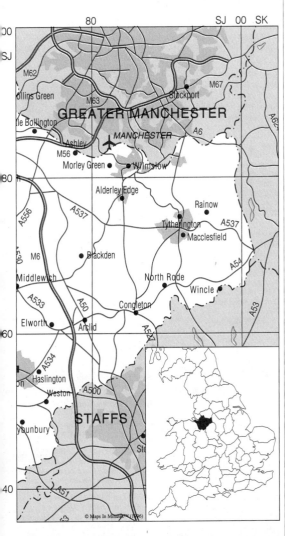

Ashley

SJ7784 ⚐ *The Greyhound*

Birtles Farm, Ashley, Altrincham, Cheshire, WA14 3QH.
Open: All Year
Grades: ETC 4 Diamond
0161 928 0458 (also fax)
Mrs Norbury
birtlesl@supanet.com
D: £22.00–£23.00 **S:** £25.00–£26.00
Beds: 1F 1T 1D **Baths:** 2 En 1 Pr
🛇 🅿 (10) ⥅ 🖻 📺 🛏 ✕ Ⅲ. 🖲. Ⅴ 🌣 🔥
A warm welcome awaits you at our delightful riverside farmhouse. The spacious bedrooms are beautifully decorated and include every comfort. Peaceful yet close to the motorway network and Manchester airport. No smoking. Easy to get to - hard to leave.

Tanyard Farm, Castle Mill Lane, Ashley, Altrincham, Cheshire, WA15 0QT.
Large attractive timbered farmhouse.
Open: All Year (not Xmas/New Year)
0161 928 1009 (also fax)
Mrs Jackson
D: £20.00–£25.00 **S:** £25.00–£30.00
Beds: 1T 1D 1S
🛇 (10) 📺 Ⅲ. 🔥

Aston-by-Budworth

SJ6976 ⚐ *The Red Lion*

Clock Cottage, Hield Lane, Aston-by-Budworth, Northwich, Cheshire, CW9 6LP.
Lovely C17th thatched country cottage, beautiful country garden, wooded countryside.
Open: All Year (not Xmas)
01606 891271 Mrs Tanner-Betts
D: £17.50–£20.00 **S:** £17.50–£20.00
Beds: 1T 2S **Baths:** 1 Sh
🛇 (2) 🅿 (4) ⥅ 📺 Ⅲ. 🔥

Audlem

SJ6643 ⚐ *Lord Cumbermere*

Little Heath Farm, Audlem, Crewe, Cheshire, CW3 0HE.
Warm traditionally furnished oak beamed farmhouse in canal side village of Audlem.
Open: All Year (not Xmas/New Year)
Grades: AA 3 Diamond
01270 811324 (also fax)
Mrs Bennion
D: £18.00–£24.00 **S:** £22.00–£26.00
Beds: 1D 1T 1F **Baths:** 1 Pr 1 En
🛇 🅿 (3) ⥅ 📺 🛏 ✕ Ⅲ. Ⅴ 🔥

Blackden

SJ7870 ⚐ *The Crown*

Bridge Farm, Blackden, Jodrell Bank, Crewe, Cheshire, CW4 8BX.
Beautiful farmhouse, spectacular situation by Jodrell Bank telescope. M6 3 miles.
Open: All Year
01477 571202 Ms Massey
pmassey648@aol.com
D: £20.00–£22.00 **S:** £19.00–£22.00
Beds: 1D 1T 2S **Baths:** 1 En 1 Sh
🛇 🅿 (6) 📺 🛏 Ⅲ. Ⅴ 🌣 🔥 & 2

Alderley Edge

SJ8478 ⚐ Prospect House Hotel, Oakwood, Bird In Hand, Frozen Mop, Plough & Flail, Kings Arms

Trafford House Farm, Beswicks Lane, Row of Trees, Alderley Edge, Wilmslow, Cheshire, SK9 7SN.
Trafford House Farm is situated in quiet rural location, but with easy access
Open: All Year
01625 582160 Mr & Mrs Blackmore
Fax: 01625 584968
D: £15.00 **S:** £20.00
Beds: 1F 1T 1S **Baths:** 2 Sh
🛇 🅿 (10) ⥅ 📺 🛏 ✕ Ⅲ. 🔥

Arclid

SJ7862 ⚐ *New Inn*

Yew Tree Farm, Love Lane, Betchton, Sandbach, Cheshire, CW11 4TD.
Open plan bungalow - panoramic views - many local attractions - close to J17 M6.
Open: All Year
01477 500382
Mrs Hollinshead
D: £19.00–£24.00
S: £20.00–£24.00
Beds: 1F 1D
Baths: 1 En 1 Pr
🛇 (5) 🅿 (10) 📺 Ⅲ. Ⅴ 🔥

Broxton

SJ4754   ⏺ *Frog Manor*

Frogg Manor Hotel, *Fullers Moor,*
Nantwich Road, Broxton, Chester, CH3 9JH.
Not far from the madding crowd, a
superb Georgian manor house.
Open: All Year
01829 782629
D: £45.00–£72.50 **S:** £60.00–£100.00
Beds: 6D **Baths:** 6 En
⏚ (4) ▣ (40) � ▣ ħ ✕ ▥ ⓥ ⚲ cc

Chester

SJ4066   ⏺ *Bromfield Arms, Faulkner Arms,*
Spinning Wheel, Chester Bells, Plough, Red Lion,
King's Head, Eversley Hotel, Royal Oak, Swan Inn,
Wetherspoons, Cavendish, Glynne Arms, Miller's
Kitchen, Town Crier, Halfway House, Watergates,
Benson's, Chester Court

Dee Heights Guest House, *23 City*
Walls, Chester, CH1 1SB.
Open: All Year
01244 350386 Mrs Willis
D: £20.00–£24.00 **S:** £30.00–£35.00
Beds: 1D **Baths:** 1 Pr
ỵ ▣ ▥ ⓥ ⚲
A charming riverside house situated on
the Roman walls overlooking the River
Dee and Old Dee Bridge. Fresh flowers
and magnificent river views. Studio bedsitting room with French window opening
onto south facing balcony. Three minutes
from city centre.

Aplas Guest House, *106 Brook Street,*
Chester, Cheshire, CH1 3DU.
Open: All Year
01244 312401 Mr Aplas
D: £13.00–£17.50
Beds: 1F 4D 2T **Baths:** 5 En, 2 Sh
⏚ (3) ▣ (7) ▣ ▥ ⚲
We are a family run guest house, under the
personal supervision of Patricia and
Michael Aplas. We are ideally located for
historic Chester. 10 minutes walk to city
centre, 5 minutes walk to railway/bus
station. Parking and room only rates
available.

Grosvenor Place Guest House, *2-4*
Grosvenor Place, Chester, CH1 2DE.
City centre guest house; proprietor: Alma
Wood.
Open: All Year (not Xmas)
01244 324455 Mrs Wood
Fax: 01244 400225
D: £18.00–£22.00 **S:** £20.00–£25.00
Beds: 2F 3D 2T 3S **Baths:** 4 En 2 Sh
⏚ ▣ ▣ ▥ ⓥ ⚲ cc

Oakenholt Farm, *Chester Road, Flint,*
Flintshire, CH6 5SU.
Set in a beautiful location, convenient for
touring Chester, North Wales and
Liverpool.
Open: All Year
Grades: ETC 2 Star
01352 733264 Mrs Hulme
jenny@oakenholt.freeserve.co.uk
D: £20.00–£22.00 **S:** £25.00–£27.00
Beds: 1F 1D 1T 1S **Baths:** 4 En
⏚ ▣ ỵ ▣ ħ ✕ ▥ ⚲

Firbank, *64 Tarvin Road, Littleton,*
Chester, CH3 7DF.
Traditional Victorian house, warm
welcome, extensive gardens, two miles
Chester.
Open: All Year (not Xmas)
01244 335644 Mrs Shambler
Fax: 01244 332068
firbank.bedandbreakfast@btinternet.com
D: £20.00–£27.50 **S:** £25.00–£30.00
Beds: 1D 1T **Baths:** 2 En
▣ (2) ▣ ▥ ⚲

Stone Villa, *3 Stone Place, Hoole,*
Chester, CH2 3NR.
A haven of quiet relaxation with
individual attention and warm hospitality.
Open: All Year (not Xmas)
Grades: RAC 4 Diamond, Sparkling
Diamond Award
01244 345014 Mr Pow
adam@stonevilla.freeserve.co.uk
D: £25.00–£28.00 **S:** £25.00–£32.00
Beds: 1F 6D 2T 1S **Baths:** 9 En 1 Pr
⏚ ▣ (10) ỵ ▣ ħ ▥ ⚲ ৬ cc

Castle House, *23 Castle Street,*
Chester, CH1 2DS.
Pre-1580 Tudor house, plus Georgian
front (1738).
Open: All Year
Grades: ETC 3 Diamond
01244 350354 Mr Marl
D: £24.00–£25.00 **S:** £38.00
Beds: 1F 1D 1T 2S **Baths:** 3 En 1 Sh
⏚ ▣ ▣ ħ ▥ ⚲ cc

Green Cottage, *Higher Kinnerton,*
Chester, CH4 9BZ.
Open: All Year
Grades: ETC 3 Star
01244 660137 Mrs Milner
D: fr £19.00 **S:** £23.00–£24.00
Beds: 1D 1T **Baths:** 1 Pr
⏚ ▣ ỵ ▣ ▥ ⓥ ⚲
6 miles from historic Chester, relaxing
atmosphere, good food, in a Welsh rural
setting.

Homeleigh, *14 Hough Green, Chester,*
CH4 8JG.
Family-run Victorian house, 10 minutes
walk from city centre.
Open: All Year (not Xmas)
Grades: ETC 3 Diamond
01244 676761 Mr & Mrs Smith
Fax: 01244 679977
D: £18.00–£20.00 **S:** £20.00–£22.00
Beds: 1F 4D 2T 2S **Baths:** 9 En
⏚ ▣ (10) ▣ ħ ▥ ⓥ ⚲ cc

Buckingham House, *38 Hough*
Green, Chester, Cheshire, CH4 8JQ.
Well appointed rooms. Near city centre
and race course. Excellent value.
Open: All Year
Grades: ETC 3 Diamond
01244 678885 (also fax)
Ms Langmead
zoe.langmead@virgin.net
D: £17.00–£23.00 **S:** £22.00–£38.00
Beds: 3F 1D **Baths:** 4 En
⏚ ▣ (8) ▣ ħ ▥ ⚲

Ba Ba Guest House, *65 Hoole Road,*
Hoole, Chester, Cheshire, CH2 3NJ.
Family run B&B in Victorian town house,
birthplace of Leonard Cheshire.
Open: All Year (not Xmas/New Year)
01244 315047 Mrs Smith
Fax: 01244 315046
reservations@babaguesthouse.freeserve.
co.uk
D: £20.00–£25.00 **S:** £25.00–£30.00
Beds: 3F 2D/T **Baths:** 4 En 1 Pr
⏚ ▣ (5) ỵ ▣ ▥ ⓥ ⚲ cc

Mitchells Of Chester, *Green Gables*
House, 28 Hough Green, Chester,
Cheshire, CH4 8JQ.
Victorian residence with tall ceilings,
sweeping staircase and antique furniture.
Open: All Year (not Xmas)
Grades: ETC 4 Diamond Sliver Award
01244 679004 Mrs Mitchell
Fax: 01244 659567
mitoches@dialstart.net
D: £24.00–£28.00 **S:** £30.00–£40.00
Beds: 1F 1D 1T 1S **Baths:** 7 En
⏚ ▣ (5) ỵ ▣ ▥ ⓥ ⚲ cc

Laurels, *14 Selkirk Road, Curzon Park,*
Chester, CH4 8AH.
Lovely family home near racecourse; best
residential area, very quiet.
Open: All Year (not Xmas)
01244 679682 Mrs Roberts
howell@ellisroberts.freeserve.co.uk
D: £18.50–£19.50 **S:** £18.50–£19.50
Beds: 1F 2D 1T 1S **Baths:** 1 En 1 Pr
⏚ ▣ (3) ▣ ▥ ⓥ ⚲

Devonia, *33-35 Hoole Road, Chester,*
CH2 3NH.
Large Victorian family-run guest house.
Same owner for 35 years.
Open: All Year
01244 322236 Fax: 01244 401511
D: £17.50–£20.00 **S:** £25.00–£30.00
Beds: 4F 2D 2T 2S **Baths:** 1 En 3 Sh
⏚ ▣ (20) ỵ ▣ ħ ▥ ⓥ ✤ ⚲

Congleton

SJ8663   ⏺ *Lamb Inn, Bull's Head Hotel, Brown*
Cow Inn, Edgerton Arms, Brownlow Inn

The Lamb Inn, *3 Blake Street,*
Congleton, Cheshire, CW12 4DS.
Central location convenient for Cheshire
country houses and attractions.
Open: All Year
01260 272731 Mr Kelly
john.kelly5@tesco.net
D: £16.00–£20.00 **S:** £18.00–£24.00
Beds: 1F 2D 2T 1S **Baths:** 3 En 3 Sh
⏚ ▣ (40) ▣ ħ ▥ ⓥ ⚲

8 Cloud View, *Congleton, Cheshire,*
CW12 3TP.
Lovely family home, edge of countryside,
good views.
Open: All Year (not Xmas)
01260 276048 Mrs Stewart
D: £18.00–£20.00 **S:** £19.00–£20.00
Beds: 1D 1S **Baths:** 1 En 1 Sh
⏚ ▣ (1) ỵ ▣ ✕ ▥ ⓥ ⚲

Cuttleford Farm, *Newcastle Road, Astbury, Congleton, Cheshire, CW12 4SD.*
16th Century farmhouse - working farm close to National Trust House.
Open: All Year **Grades:** ETC 2 Cr
01260 272499 Mrs Downs
D: £20.00–£25.00
Beds: 2D 1T **Baths:** 1 En 1 Sh
⛺ 🅿 ⛷ 📺 🐾 🛍 ♿

Loachbrook Farm, *Sandbach Road, Congleton, Cheshire, CW12 4TE.*
C17th working farm close to M6 and many attractions.
Open: All Year (not Xmas)
01260 273318 Mrs Dale
D: £17.50–£19.00 **S:** £18.50–£20.00
Beds: 1D 1T 1S **Baths:** 1 Sh
⛺ (5) 🅿 (4) ⛷ 📺 🛍 ♿

Elworth

SJ7461 🍺 *Fox Inn*

Poplar Mount Guest House, *2 Station Road, Elworth, Sandbach, Cheshire, CW11 9JG.*
Friendly family-run guest house, convenient for M6 motorway.
Open: All Year
Grades: AA 3 Diamond, RAC 3 Diamond
01270 761268 (also fax) Mrs McDonald
D: £20.00 **S:** £20.00–£28.00
Beds: 2F 3D 1T 2S **Baths:** 4 En 1 Sh
⛺ 🅿 (9) 📺 ✕ 🛍 ♿ cc

Handbridge

SJ4065 🍺 *Cross Keys*

Eaton House, *36 Eaton Road, Handbridge, Chester, CH4 7EY.*
Victorian town house within close walking distance of city centre.
Open: All Year (not Xmas/New Year)
01244 680349 Fax: 01244 659021
grahamd@aol.com
D: £19.00–£24.00 **S:** £20.00–£24.00
Beds: 1F 1D
⛺ (8) 🅿 (3) ⛷ 📺 🛍 📶 ♿ cc

Haslington

SJ7355

Ferndale House, *Gutterscroft, Haslington, Crewe, Cheshire, CW1 5RJ.*
Victorian home, large rooms, excellent food, secure parking, convenient M6.
Open: All Year **01270 584048** L M Docherty
ferndalehouse@tinyworld.co.uk
D: £20.00–£23.50 **S:** £20.00
⛺ 🅿 (7) ⛷ 📺 ✕ 🛍 📶 ♿

Hatton Heath

SJ4561 🍺 *Grosvenor Arms*

Golborne Manor, *Platts Lane, Hatton Heath, Chester, Cheshire, CH3 9AN.*
Beautifully decorated 19th century manor house with glorious views and garden.
Open: All Year **Grades:** ETC 4 Diamond
01829 770310 Mrs Ikin
Fax: 01829 770370
ann.ikin@golbornemanor.co.uk
D: £58.00–£68.00 **S:** £28.00–£38.00
Beds: 1F 1T 1D **Baths:** 3 En
⛺ 🅿 (6) ⛷ 📺 🛍 📶 ♿

Higher Wych

SJ4943 🍺 *Redbrook Hunting Lodge*

Mill House, *Higher Wych, Malpas, Cheshire, SY14 7JR.*
Modernised mill house, peaceful valley.
Convenient for Chester, Shrewsbury, Llangollen.
Open: Jan to Nov
Grades: ETC 3 Star
01948 780362 Mrs Smith
Fax: 01948 780566
chris_smith@videoactive.co.uk
D: fr £20.00 **S:** fr £20.00
Beds: 1D 1T **Baths:** 1 En 1 Sh
⛺ 🅿 (4) 📺 ✕ 🛍 📶 ♿

Hollins Green

SJ6991

Brook Farm, *Manchester Road, Rixton, Hollins Green, Warrington, Cheshire, WA3 6HX.*
Situated in semi-rural location, close to M6, M62, M56 and Manchester Airport.
Open: All Year
0161 775 6053
D: £18.00–£22.00 **S:** £22.00–£26.00
Beds: 2D 2T 2S **Baths:** 3 En 1 Sh
🅿 (20) 📺 🐾 🛍 ♿

Kelsall

SJ5268 🍺 *Morris Dancer, The Boot*

Northwood Hall, *Dog Lane, Kelsall, Tarporley, Cheshire, CW6 0RP.*
Elegant Victorian farmhouse with cobblestone courtyard. All rooms traditionally appointed.
Open: All Year (not Xmas)
01829 752569 Mr & Mrs Nock
Fax: 01829 751157
D: £21.50–£23.50 **S:** fr £27.50
Beds: 2D **Baths:** 2 En
⛺ 🅿 (6) ⛷ 📺 🛍 ♿

Latchford

SJ6187

The Maples Private Hotel, *11 Longdin Street, Latchford, WA4 1PJ.*
Family run hotel. Close village/town.
Good access motorways. Friendly welcome.
Open: All Year (not Xmas/New Year)
01925 637752 S M Savory
D: £15.00–£30.00 **S:** £10.00–£20.00
Beds: 1F 3T 2D 2S **Baths:** 2 En 1 Pr 1 Sh
⛺ 🅿 📺 🛍 ♿

Little Bollington

SJ7286 🍺 *Stamford Arms*

Bollington Hall Farm, *Park Lane, Little Bollington, Altrincham, Cheshire, WA14 4TJ.*
Close to Manchester & Dunham Massey Hall, Talton Hall, Trans-Pennine trail and motorway network
Open: All Year (not Xmas/New Year)
0161 928 1760 Mrs Owen
D: fr £18.00 **S:** fr £18.00
Beds: 1F 1D **Baths:** 1 Sh
🅿 (10) 📺 🛍 📶 ♿

Littleton

SJ4466 🍺 *The Plough*

Firbank, *64 Tarvin Road, Littleton, Chester, CH3 7DF.*
Traditional Victorian house, warm welcome, extensive gardens, two miles Chester.
Open: All Year (not Xmas)
01244 335644 Mrs Shambler
Fax: 01244 332068
firbank.bedandbreakfast@btinternet.com
D: £20.00–£27.50 **S:** £25.00–£30.00
Beds: 1D 1T **Baths:** 2 En
🅿 (2) 📺 🛍 ♿

Macclesfield

SJ9173

Penrose Guest House, *56 Birtles Road, Whirley, Macclesfield, Cheshire, SK10 3JQ.*
Central for Wilmslow, Prestbury, Macclesfield. Close intercity trains, motorway, airport.
Open: All Year
01625 615323 Fax: 01625 432284
info@PenroseGuestHouse.co.uk
D: fr £20.00 **S:** fr £20.00
Beds: 1T 2S
⛺ (4) 🅿 (6) ⛷ 📺 🛍 ♿

Malpas

SJ4847

Farm Ground Cottage, *Edge, Malpas, Cheshire, SY14 8LE.*
Peaceful, comfortable Victorian Cottage in rural surroundings. Excellent touring base.
Open: All Year (not Xmas)
01948 820333 D: £19.50–£21.00 **S:** £20.00–£22.00
Beds: 1D **Baths:** 1 Pr
🅿 (2) ⛷ 📺 🐾 ✕ 🛍 📶 ♿

Manley

SJ5071 🍺 *The Goshawk, White Lion*

Rangeway Bank Farm, *Manley, Warrington, Cheshire, WA6 9EF.*
Friendly traditional farmhouse in quiet countryside adjacent to Delamere Forest.
Open: All Year (not Xmas)
01928 740236 J Challoner
Fax: 01928 740703
D: £20.00–£25.00 **S:** £22.00–£25.00
Beds: 1F 1D 1T **Baths:** 2 En 1 Sh
⛺ 🅿 (6) ⛷ 📺 🐾 🛍 📶 ♿

Middlewich

SJ7066 🍺 *Big Lock, Narrow Boat*

Sandhurst Lodge, *69 Chester Road, Middlewich, Cheshire, CW10 9EW.*
Charming Edwardian residence close to M6 and Manchester Airport.
Open: All Year (not Xmas)
01606 834125 Mrs Fair
Fax: 01606 833753
D: £22.00–£24.00 **S:** £22.00–£30.00
Beds: 2F 5D 1T **Baths:** 8 En
⛺ 🅿 (8) 📺 🛍 📶 ♿

Morley Green

SJ8281

Oversley, Altrincham Road, Morley Green, Wilmslow, Cheshire, SK9 4LT.
Beautiful country house situated close to Manchester Airport and motorway.
Open: All Year
01625 535551 Fax: 01625 531510
D: £19.50–£27.50 **S:** £35.00–£49.50
Beds: 1F 3D 3T **Baths:** 7 En
🛇 🅿 ⅍ 📺 ✕ 🏯 📖 Ⅵ ৬ cc

Nantwich

SJ6452   🍺 Barbridge Inn, Vine Inn, Red Cow, Railway Hotel, Royal Oak

Lea Farm, Wrinehill Road, Wybunbury, Nantwich, Cheshire, CW5 7HS.
Charming farmhouse set in landscaped gardens where peacocks roam.
Open: All Year (not Xmas)
Grades: AA 3 Diamond
01270 841429 (also fax)
Mrs Callwood
D: fr £18.00 **S:** fr £21.00
Beds: 1F 1D 1T **Baths:** 2 Pr 1 Sh
🛇 🅿 (22) 📺 🏯 ✕ Ⅵ ⅃

The Red Cow, 51 Beam Street, Nantwich, Cheshire, CW5 5NF.
Grade I Listed building serving award winning food.
Open: All Year
01270 628581 Ms Casson
Fax: 01270 620550
D: fr £19.50 **S:** £19.50
Beds: 1D 2T **Baths:** 1 Sh
🛇 🅿 (9) ⅍ 📺 🏯 ✕ 🏯 Ⅵ ⅃ ৬ cc

The Railway Hotel, Pillory Street, Nantwich, Cheshire, CW5 5SS.
Historic 1890 building, on the edge of beautiful Nantwich town.
Open: All Year
01270 623482 J Hobson
jhobson@freeuk.com
D: £25.00 **S:** £30.00–£40.00
Beds: 2F 1T 1S **Baths:** 4 En
🛇 🅿 📺 🏯 ✕ 📖 ⅃ cc

Henhull Hall, Welshman's Lane, Nantwich, Cheshire, CW5 6AD.
Hearty breakfasts and a special welcome awaits you at our beautiful farmhouse.
Open: All Year (not Xmas)
01270 624158 Mr & Mrs Percival
D: £25.00–£27.50 **S:** £25.00–£27.50
Beds: 1D 1T 1S **Baths:** 1 En 1 Sh
🛇 🅿 (4) ⅍ 📺 📖 ⅃

Norley

SJ5672   🍺 Carriers Inn

Wicken Tree Farm, Blakemere Lane, Norley, Warrington, Cheshire, WA6 6NW.
High quality self-catering accommodation and B&B, surrounded by Delamere Forest.
Open: All Year
01928 788355 Mr Appleton
ches@williamj99.freeserve.co.uk
D: £23.50–£25.00 **S:** £23.50–£31.00
Beds: 1F 5D 7T 3S **Baths:** 6 En 1 Pr 2 Sh
🛇 🅿 (14) ⅍ 📺 🏯 📖 Ⅵ ⅃ ৬

North Rode

SJ8866   🍺 Robin Hood

Yew Tree Farm, North Rode, Congleton, Cheshire, CW12 2PF.
Cosy farmhouse in wooded parkland, traditional home-made meals.
Open: All Year
Grades: ETC 4 Diamond
01260 223569 Mrs Kidd
Fax: 01260 223328
kiddyewtreefarm@netscapeonline.co.uk
D: fr £19.00 **S:** fr £19.00
Beds: 1D 2T **Baths:** 1 En 1 Sh
🛇 🅿 (10) ⅍ 📺 ✕ 📖 Ⅵ ⅃

Oakmere

SJ5769   🍺 Fourways Inn

Springfield Guest House, Chester Road, Oakmere, Northwich, Cheshire, CW8 2HB.
Quality accommodation in attractive guest house.
Open: All Year
01606 882538 Mrs Mulholland
D: £17.50–£22.50 **S:** £19.00–£23.00
Beds: 1F 2D 1T 3S **Baths:** 2 Pr 1 Sh
🛇 🅿 (8) 📖

Poole

SJ6455   🍺 Boot & Slipper, Royal Oak

Poole Bank Farm, Poole, Nantwich, Cheshire, CW5 6AL.
Charming C17th timbered farmhouse, surrounded by picturesque dairy farmland.
Open: All Year
01270 625169 Ms Hocknell
D: £18.00–£22.00 **S:** £20.00–£24.00
Beds: 1D 1T 1F **Baths:** 1 Pr 2 Sh
🛇 🅿 (10) 📺 Ⅵ ⅃

Rainow

SJ9576   🍺 Rising Sun, Robin Hood

The Tower House, Tower Hill, Rainow, Macclesfield, Cheshire, SK10 5TX.
Luxury accommodation in carefully restored C16th farmhouse. Superb breakfasts.
Open: All Year
01625 438022 (also fax)
Mrs Buckley
D: £25.00 **S:** £25.00–£35.00
Beds: 2T 1S
Baths: 1 Pr
🛇 🅿 (4) ⅍ 📺 📖 ⅃

Ravensmoor

SJ6250   🍺 Farmers Arms

Pujols, Barracks Lane, Ravensmoor, Nantwich, Cheshire, CW5 8PR.
Quiet location, easy reach M6, railways, north Wales, Peak District.
Open: All Year
01270 626528
D: £12.00–£15.00 **S:** £15.00–£18.00
Beds: 1T 1D **Baths:** 1 Sh
🅿 (2) ⅍ 📖 ⅃

Rushton

SJ5863   🍺 Red Lion

Hill House Farm, The Hall Lane, Rushton, Tarporley, Cheshire, CW6 9AU.
Beautiful Victorian former farmhouse, comfortable accommodation, 1.5 miles from Oulton Park.
Open: All Year (not Xmas/New Year)
Grades: ETC 3 Diamond
01829 732238 Mrs Rayner
rayner@hillhousefarm.fsnet.co.uk
D: fr £22.00 **S:** fr £25.00
Beds: 1F 1T 1D **Baths:** 2 En 1 Pr
🛇 🅿 (10) ⅍ 📺 📖 ⅃

Stapeley

SJ6749   🍺 Globe

York Cottage, 82 Broad Lane, Stapeley, Nantwich, Cheshire, CW5 7QL.
Comfortable detached rural cottage, with garden, 2 miles from Nantwich.
Open: All Year
01270 629829 Mrs Orford
Fax: 01270 625404
D: £18.00–£20.00 **S:** £18.00–£22.00
Beds: 2D 1F **Baths:** 1 Sh
🛇 🅿 (3) ⅍ 📺 🏯 📖 Ⅵ ✤ ⅃

Stoke

SJ6552   🍺 Barbridge Inn

Stoke Grange Farm, Chester Road, Stoke, Nantwich, Cheshire, CW5 6BT.
Picturesque garden views, canalside farmhouse. Welcoming. Excellent breakfast. Pets corner. SC available.
Open: All Year
01270 625525 (also fax)
Mrs West
D: £22.50–£25.00 **S:** £25.00–£30.00
Beds: 1D 2T **Baths:** 3 En
🛇 🅿 (10) 📺 📖 Ⅵ ⅃

Stretton (Warrington)

SJ6182   🍺 Cat & Lion, Stretton Fox

The School House, Stretton Road, Stretton, Warrington, Cheshire, WA4 4NT.
Old headmaster's school house (1835). Now an upmarket B&B - semi-rural location.
Open: All Year (not Xmas/New Year)
01925 730826 D: £22.50 **S:** £35.00
Beds: 4F 1T 3D **Baths:** 4 En

Tarporley

SJ5462   🍺 Red Lion

Hill House Farm, The Hall Lane, Rushton, Tarporley, Cheshire, CW6 9AU.
Beautiful Victorian former farmhouse, comfortable accommodation, 1.5 miles from Oulton Park.
Open: All Year (not Xmas/New Year)
Grades: ETC 3 Diamond
01829 732238
Mrs Rayner
rayner@hillhousefarm.fsnet.co.uk
D: fr £22.00 **S:** fr £25.00
Beds: 1F 1T 1D **Baths:** 2 En 1 Pr
🛇 🅿 (10) ⅍ 📺 🏯 📖 ⅃

Foresters Arms, *92 High Street, Tarporley, Cheshire, CW6 0AX.*
A traditional country Inn offering fine ales and comfortable rooms.
Open: All Year (not Xmas/New Year)
Grades: ETC 3 Diamond
01829 733151 Fax: 01829 730020
D: £18.00–£22.50 **S:** £18.00–£22.50
Beds: 4T 1D **Baths:** 1 En 1 Sh
(10) (20) cc

Tilston

SJ4551 *Carden Arms*

Tilston Lodge, *Tilston, Malpas, Cheshire, SY14 7DR.*
Handsome country house with spacious grounds. luxuriously equipped quiet bedrooms.
Open: All Year (not Xmas/New Year)
Grades: AA 5 Diamond
01829 250223 Mrs Ritchie
Fax: 01829 250223
D: £33.00–£35.00 **S:** £43.00–£45.00
Beds: 1T 1D **Baths:** 2 En
(10)

Tiverton

SJ5460 *Red Lion*

The Gables, *Tiverton, Tarporley, Cheshire, CW6 9NH.*
Beautiful country cottage set amidst almost 1/2 acre of gardens.
Open: All Year
01829 733028 Mr Wilson
Fax: 01829 733399
D: £17.50–£19.00 **S:** £25.00–£35.00
Beds: 3D **Baths:** 1 Sh
(8)

Tytherington

SJ9175 *Cock & Pheasant*

Moorhayes House Hotel, *27 Manchester Road, Tytherington, Macclesfield, Cheshire, SK10 2JJ.*
Warm welcome comfortable home, attractive garden, 0.5 mile from Macclesfield.
Open: All Year (not Xmas)
01625 433228 (also fax) Helen Wood
helen@moorhayeshouse.freeserve.co.uk
D: £24.00–£29.00 **S:** £28.00–£45.00
Beds: 1F 4D 2T 1S **Baths:** 7 En 1 Sh
(14) cc

Warrington

SJ6088 *Paddington House Hotel, Donattelo*

Braemar Guest House, *274 Manchester Road, Woolston, Warrington, WA1 4PS.*
Large family house on A57 1/2 mile from J21 on M6. **Open:** All Year
01925 491683 Mr Freeman
Fax: 01925 816666
D: £20.00–£25.00 **S:** £22.00–£27.50
Beds: 2S **Baths:** 1 Sh
(5)

The Cottage Guest House, *37 Tanners Lane, Warrington, Cheshire, WA2 7NL.*
Open: All Year (not Xmas/New Year)
01925 631524 Mr & Mrs Ramsdale
Fax: 01925 445400
j.h.@3pigeons.fsnet.co.uk
D: £16.00–£18.00 **S:** £20.00–£22.00
Beds: 3T 1S **Baths:** 2 En 2 Sh
(6)
Side street location, homely atmosphere, comfortable beds. 3 minutes to town centre. Handy for visiting places of interest with the motorway network only 10 mins away.

The Hollies, *1 Long Lane, Orford, Warrington, Cheshire, WA2 8PT.*
Open: All Year (not Xmas/New Year)
01925 635416 (also fax)
Mrs Brown
D: £17.50–£20.00 **S:** £20.00–£22.00
Beds: 1F 2T 1D **Baths:** 1 Sh
(5) (8)
Small and friendly. New bathroom and beds this year. Great cooked breakfasts including vegetarian option. Just off M62 Manchester/ Liverpool airport 20 minutes away.

New House Farm, *Hatton Lane, Stretton, Warrington, Cheshire, WA4 4BZ.*
Fields surround cottages 1 mile, M56, J10, 3 miles M6, j21.
Open: All Year
01925 730567 Mrs Delooze
newhousefarmcottage@talk21.com
D: £18.00–£20.00 **S:** £18.00–£20.00
Beds: 1D 2T 1S **Baths:** 1 En 1 Pr 1 Sh
(30)

10 Hanover Street, *Warrington, Cheshire, WA1 1LZ.*
Town centre location. Train, bus 5 minutes walk. Victorian building quiet part.
Open: All Year
01925 418914 (also fax)
Mrs Harrington
harringtonhouse@hotmail.com
D: £17.50–£23.50 **S:** £21.50–£22.50
Beds: 1F 1D 2T 1S **Baths:** 2 Sh
(5)

Weston (Crewe)

SJ7352 *White Lion Inn*

Snape Farm, *Snape Lane, Weston, Crewe, Cheshire, CW2 5NB.*
Warm comfortable Victorian farmhouse in quiet location near Junction 16 M6.
Open: All Year (not Xmas)
01270 820208 (also fax)
Mrs Williamson
D: £18.00–£20.00 **S:** £20.00–£28.00
Beds: 3F 1D 2T **Baths:** 1 En 1 Pr 1 Sh
(6)

National Grid References are for villages, towns and cities – not for individual houses

Wilmslow

SJ8480 *Bulls Head, Wagon & Horses*

The Grange, *Clay Lane, Handforth, Wilmslow, Cheshire, SK9 3NR.*
Set in rural surroundings but close to all amenities and public transport.
Open: All Year
01625 523653 Mrs Godlee
Fax: 01625 530140
alisongodlee@lineone.net
D: £20.00 **S:** £30.00
Beds: 3F 1T 2S **Baths:** 3 En
(6)

Wincle

SJ9566 *Ship Inn*

Hill Top Farm, *Wincle, Macclesfield, Cheshire, SK11 0QH.*
Peaceful, comfortable farmhouse accommodation, set in beautiful countryside. Lovely walks.
Open: All Year (not Xmas)
01260 227257 Mrs Brocklehurst
D: £18.00–£20.00 **S:** £20.00–£22.00
Beds: 2T 1D **Baths:** 2 En 1 Pr
(4)

Wistaston

SJ6853 *Woodside, Manor*

Greenfields, *518 Crewe Road, Wistaston, Crewe, Cheshire, CW2 6PS.*
Non-smoking, pleasant residential area. Midway Crewe - Nantwich. Parking available.
Open: All Year (not Xmas/New Year)
01270 569325 Mrs Gildea
D: £18.00–£19.00 **S:** £18.00–£19.00
Beds: 1T 2S **Baths:** 1 Sh
(4)

Wybunbury

SJ6949 *Swan*

Lea Farm, *Wrinehill Road, Wybunbury, Nantwich, Cheshire, CW5 7HS.*
Charming farmhouse set in landscaped gardens where peacocks roam.
Open: All Year (not Xmas)
Grades: AA 3 Diamond
01270 841429 (also fax)
Mrs Callwood
D: fr £18.00 **S:** fr £21.00
Beds: 1F 1D 1T **Baths:** 2 Pr 1 Sh
(22)

Cornwall

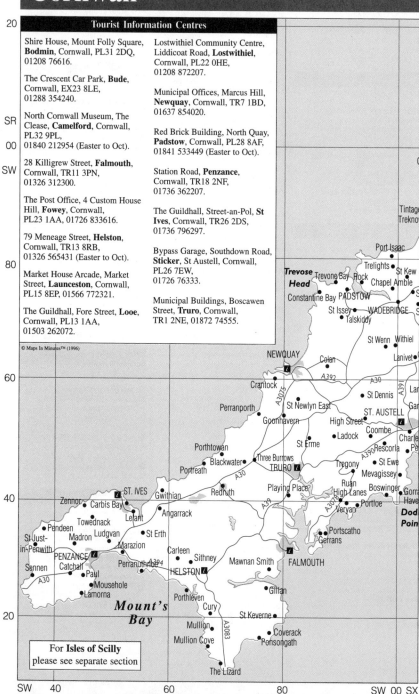

Tourist Information Centres

Shire House, Mount Folly Square, **Bodmin**, Cornwall, PL31 2DQ, 01208 76616.

The Crescent Car Park, **Bude**, Cornwall, EX23 8LE, 01288 354240.

North Cornwall Museum, The Clease, **Camelford**, Cornwall, PL32 9PL, 01840 212954 (Easter to Oct).

28 Killigrew Street, **Falmouth**, Cornwall, TR11 3PN, 01326 312300.

The Post Office, 4 Custom House Hill, **Fowey**, Cornwall, PL23 1AA, 01726 833616.

79 Meneage Street, **Helston**, Cornwall, TR13 8RB, 01326 565431 (Easter to Oct).

Market House Arcade, Market Street, **Launceston**, Cornwall, PL15 8EP, 01566 772321.

The Guildhall, Fore Street, **Looe**, Cornwall, PL13 1AA, 01503 262072.

Lostwithiel Community Centre, Liddicoat Road, **Lostwithiel**, Cornwall, PL22 0HE, 01208 872207.

Municipal Offices, Marcus Hill, **Newquay**, Cornwall, TR7 1BD, 01637 854020.

Red Brick Building, North Quay, **Padstow**, Cornwall, PL28 8AF, 01841 533449 (Easter to Oct).

Station Road, **Penzance**, Cornwall, TR18 2NF, 01736 362207.

The Guildhall, Street-an-Pol, **St Ives**, Cornwall, TR26 2DS, 01736 796297.

Bypass Garage, Southdown Road, **Sticker**, St Austell, Cornwall, PL26 7EW, 01726 76333.

Municipal Buildings, Boscawen Street, **Truro**, Cornwall, TR1 2NE, 01872 74555.

© Maps In Minutes™ (1996)

For **Isles of Scilly**
please see separate section

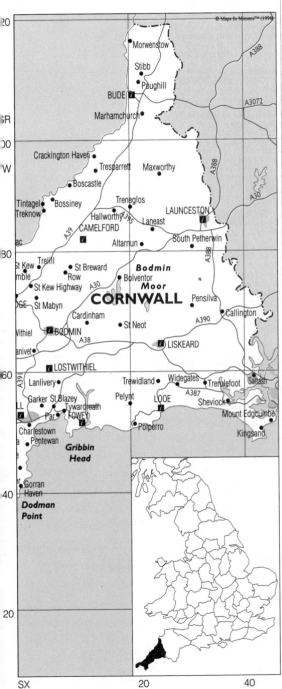

© Maps In Minutes™ (1996)

Altarnun

SX2281 ◀ *Rising Sun*

Casa Moor Lodge, *Five Lanes, Altarnun, Launceston, Cornwall, PL15 7RX.*
Refurbished Victorian house; licensed, central for touring Cornwall and Devon.
Open: Mar to Oct
01566 86070 Mr Appleyard
Fax: 01566 86767
bappleyard@aol.com
D: £16.00–£19.00 **S:** £18.50–£21.50
Beds: 2F 2D 1T **Baths:** 3 En 1 Sh
⛺ ₽ (10) ▣ ⛏ ✕ ▥ ▣ ⚓ cc

Angarrack

SW5838 ◀ *Angarrack Inn*

Byways, *22 Steamers Hill, Angarrack, Hayle, Cornwall, TR27 5JB.*
Informal family-run guest house in pretty village. Beach 2 miles. **Open:** Mar to Oct
01736 753463 Mrs Pooley
bywaysbb@lineone.net
D: £13.00–£16.00 **S:** £13.00–£25.00
Beds: 2D 1T **Baths:** 3 En
₽ (3) ⛥ ▣ ✕ ▥ ▣ ⚓

Blackwater

SW7346 ◀ *Fox & Hounds, Chiverton Arms, Victoria Inn, Three Milestone*

Rock Cottage, *Blackwater, Truro, Cornwall, TR4 8EU.*
C18th beamed cob cottage. Haven for non-smokers. Full central heating.
Open: All Year (not Xmas/New Year)
Grades: ETC 4 Diamond, AA 4 Diamond
01872 560252 (also fax) Mrs Wakeling
rockcottage@yahoo.com
D: £22.00–£24.00 **S:** £26.00–£28.00
Beds: 2D 1T **Baths:** 3 En
₽ (3) ⛥ ▣ ▥ ⚓ cc

Bodmin

SX0667 ◀ *Borough Arms, Halfway House, St Benet's Abbey, Crown Inn, Lanivet Arms, Hole In The Wall, Weavers*

Bokiddick Farm, *Lanivet, Bodmin, Cornwall, PL30 5HP.*
Open: All Year (not Xmas)
Grades: ETC 5 Diamond, Gold Award
01208 831481 (also fax) Mrs Hugo
Rob.hugo@farming.co.uk
D: £21.00–£23.00 **S:** £25.00–£30.00
Beds: 1F 2D **Baths:** 3 En
⛺ (5) ₽ (4) ⛥ ▣ ▥ ⚓
Georgian farmhouse, oak beams, wood panelling, magnificent views, peaceful location. Central for touring all Cornwall. Close to National Trust, Lanhydrock House and Eden Project. Delicious farmhouse breakfasts cooked on Aga. Working dairy farm, many lovely walks from our doorstep.

High Cross Farm, *Lanivet, Bodmin, Cornwall, PL30 5JR.*
Traditional farmhouse c.1890 in geographical centre of Cornwall. Local for beaches & moor.
Open: All Year (not Xmas)
01208 831341 D: fr £14.00 **S:** fr £20.00
Beds: 1F 1D 1T **Baths:** 1 Sh
⛺ ₽ (6) ⛥ ▣ ✕ ▥ ▣ ⚓

Bolventor

SX1876

Jamaica Inn, *Bolventor, Launceston, Cornwall, PL15 7TS.*
Relax in comfort and experience Daphne du Maurier's Bodmin Moor.
Open: All Year (not Xmas)
01566 86250 Fax: 01566 86177
jamaicainn@eclipse.co.uk
D: £30.00–£38.00 **S:** £38.00
Beds: 5D 1T **Baths:** 6 En
🛏 🅿 📺 ✕ 🏞 🖳 Ⓥ 🛂 cc

Boscastle

SX1090 ⊞ *Napoleon Inn, Cobweb Inn, Wellington Hotel, Olde Manor House, Tolcarne House*

The Old Coach House, *Tintagel Road, Boscastle, Cornwall, PL35 0AS.*
Open: All Year
Grades: ETC 4 Diamond, AA 4 Diamond
01840 250398 Mrs & Mrs Parsons
Fax: 01840 250346
parsons@old-coach.demon.co.uk
D: £19.00–£22.00 **S:** £25.00–£36.00
Beds: 3F 4D 1T **Baths:** 8 En
🛏 🅿 (9) ⅍ 📺 🏞 🖳 Ⓥ 🛂 ⅙ cc
300-year-old coach house which guarantees a warm, helpful and friendly welcome. In an Area of Outstanding Natural Beauty. A centre for coastal and woodland walks. Close to unspoilt National Trust harbour. All rooms en suite. Parking.

Pencarmol, *The Harbour, Boscastle, Cornwall, PL35 0HA.*
Open: Feb to Oct
01840 250435 Mrs Murphy
enquiries@pencarmol.co.uk
D: £20.00–£22.50 **S:** £25.00–£30.00
Beds: 1F 2D **Baths:** 3 En
🅿 (3) ⅍ 📺 🖳 Ⓥ 🛂
Pencarmol is a 300-year-old Listed house dramatically situated overlooking Boscastle Harbour. Comfortable bedrooms, all enjoying harbour views. Beautiful cliff garden adjacent coastal path. Full English or vegetarian breakfast. A warm welcome is assured from congenial hosts.

Tolcarne House Hotel & Restaurant, *Tintagel Road, Boscastle, Cornwall, PL35 0AS.*
Victorian character house with spectacular views and large grounds.
Open: Mar to Nov
Grades: ETC 4 Diamond
01840 250654 (also fax) Mr & Mrs Crown
crowntolhouse@eclipse.co.uk
D: £25.00–£32.00 **S:** £30.00–£32.00
Beds: 1F 2T 4D 2S **Baths:** 9 En
🛏 (10) 🅿 (12) 📺 🏞 ✕ 🖳 Ⓥ 🛂 cc

Bottreaux House Hotel, *Boscastle, Cornwall, PL35 0BG.*
High quality Silver Award B&B accommodation. Free video of hotel.
Open: All Year
Grades: ETC 2 Star , Silver Award
01840 250231 Mr Mee
Fax: 01840 250170 bothotel@dircon.co.uk
D: £16.00–£30.00 **S:** £20.00–£30.00
Beds: 5D 2T **Baths:** 7 En
🛏 (10) 🅿 (9) ⅍ 📺 🏞 ✕ 🖳 Ⓥ 🛂 cc

The Wellington Hotel, *The Harbour, Boscastle, Cornwall, PL35 0AQ.*
Historic C16th Anglo/French restaurant & freehouse pub. Log fires and beams.
Open: All Year
01840 250202 Mrs Tobutt
vtobutt@enterprise.net
D: £29.00–£38.00 **S:** £32.00–£44.00
Beds: 11D 2T 4S **Baths:** 16 En 1 Pr
🛏 (7) 🅿 (20) 📺 🏞 ✕ 🖳 Ⓥ 🛂 🛎 cc

Bossiney

SX0688 ⊞ *Tintagel Arms, Cornishman, Mill House, Willapark Manor Hotel*

The Old Borough House, *Bossiney, Tintagel, Cornwall, PL34 0AY.*
Traditional C16th Cornish house close to coastal path, luxury bedrooms.
Open: All Year (not Xmas)
01840 770475 (also fax) Mrs Bryant
borough@fsbdial.co.uk
D: £25.00–£30.00 **S:** £35.00
Beds: 3D 1T **Baths:** 3 En 1 Pr
🛏 (12) 🅿 (10) ⅍ 📺 ✕ 🖳 Ⓥ ⅙ cc

Boswinger

SW9840

The Granary, *Boswinger, Gorran, St Austell, Cornwall, PL26 6LL.*
Comfortable bedrooms. Scrumptious breakfasts/suppers. Spectacular sea views. Warm welcome. **Open:** All Year
01726 844381 S Chubb
hoildays@
thegranaryboswinger.freeserve.co.uk
D: £16.00–£19.00 **S:** £18.00–£22.00
Beds: 2D 1T **Baths:** 2 Pr 1 Sh
🛏 🅿 (3) 📺 ✕ 🖳 Ⓥ 🛂

Bude

SS2106 ⊞ *Crooklets, Sportsman, Preston Gate, Bencoolen Inn, Inn On The Green, Falcon Inn, Kings Arms*

Sunrise Guest House, *6 Burn View, Bude, Cornwall, EX23 8BY.*
Open: Feb to Nov **Grades:** ETC 4 Diamond
01288 353214 Mr Masters
D: £18.00–£23.00 **S:** £18.00–£25.00
Beds: 1F 3D 1T 1S **Baths:** 6 En
🛏 (3) 🅿 (2) ⅍ 📺 🖳 Ⓥ ⅙
'The general standards are high and many of the features are delightful. The hospitality of the owners and the cleanliness experienced count for a lot.' (English Tourist Board Assessment) Come see for yourselves! Centrally located. All rooms en suite.

St Merryn, *Coastview, Bude, Cornwall, EX23 8AG.*
Open: All Year
01288 352058 Miss Abbot
Fax: 01288 359050
st.merryn@ukonline.co.uk
D: £14.00–£16.00 **S:** £20.00–£25.00
Beds: 1F 1D 1T 1S **Baths:** 2 Sh
🛏 🅿 (4) ⅍ 📺 🏞 🖳 ⅙ ⅙
A large dormer bungalow with good sized ground floor bedrooms each having vanity unit with hot/cold water, colour TV with remote and tea/coffee making facilities situated on A3072 approximately 500 yards from A39 Atlantic highway, off-road parking.

Lower Northcott Farm, *Poughill, Bude, Cornwall, EX23 7EL.*
Georgian farmhouse with outstanding views. Ideal for walking/touring holiday.
Open: All Year
Grades: ETC 3 Diamond, AA 3 Diamond
01288 352350 Mrs Trewin
Fax: 01288 352712
sally@coast-countryside.co.uk
D: £20.00–£22.00 **S:** £20.00–£25.00
Beds: 1F 2D 1T 1S **Baths:** 4 En 1 Pr
🛏 🅿 (4) ⅍ 📺 🏞 🖳 Ⓥ 🛂

Laundry Cottage, *Higher Wharf, Bude, Cornwall, EX23 8LW.*
Open: All Year (not Xmas)
01288 353560 Mrs Noakes
D: £17.00–£21.00 **S:** £17.00–£21.00
Beds: 1D 1T **Baths:** 1 Sh 1 Pr
🛏 🅿 (2) 📺 🖳 Ⓥ 🛂
Grade II Listed cottage in two acres of garden on historic Bude canal. Secluded yet only a few minutes' walk from town centre, restaurants, coastal path, beach, cycle routes etc. Rooms overlook garden and canal. Quiet, many extras, private parking.

Link's Side Guest House, *Burn View, Bude, Cornwall, EX23 8BY.*
Victoria house town centre, beaches, path, overlooking golf course.
Open: All Year **Grades:** ETC 4 Diamond
01288 352410 Mr & Mrs Dockrill
linksidebude@north-cornwall.co.uk
D: £16.00–£21.00 **S:** £16.00–£21.00
Beds: 1F 4D 1T 1S **Baths:** 5 En 1 Sh
🛏 ⅍ 📺 🏞 🖳 🛂 ⅙

Marhamrise Guest House, *50 Kings Hill, Bude, Cornwall, EX23 8QH.*
Beautiful views. Gardens. Ground floor bedrooms. Plenty good home cooking.
Open: May to Sept
01288 354713 Mrs Thornton
D: £15.00–£17.00 **S:** £15.00–£18.00
Beds: 1F 2D 1S **Baths:** 1 En 2 Sh
🛏 (3) 🅿 (5) 📺 ✕ 🖳 🛂 ⅙

Meadow View, *Kings Hill Close, Bude, Cornwall, EX23 8RR.*
A large house 400 yds from canal. Room overlooks garden and fields.
Open: All Year
01288 355095 Mrs Shepherd
D: £15.00–£16.00 **S:** £15.00–£16.00
Beds: 1D **Baths:** 1 Pr
⅍ 🖳 Ⓥ 🛂

Raetor, *Stratton Road, Bude, Cornwall, EX23 8AQ.*
Modern detached house situated on the main road. Bude one mile. **Open:** All Year
01288 354128 M Barnard
D: £15.00 **S:** £15.00
Beds: 1D 1T 1S **Baths:** 1 Sh
🅿 (2) 📺 🖳 🛂

Kisauni, *4 Downs View, Bude, Cornwall, EX23 8RF.*
Bright, airy Victorian house. 2 minutes beach. Romantic four poster bed. Home cooking. **Open:** All Year (not Xmas)
01288 352653 Mrs Kimpton
D: £14.00–£16.00 **S:** £14.00–£16.00
Beds: 2F 1D 1T 1S **Baths:** 3 En 3 Sh
🛏 🅿 (5) 📺 🏞 ✕ Ⓥ 🛂 ⅙

Callington

SX3669 ◀ *Coachmakers' Arms, Who'd Have Thought It*

Dozmary, *Tors View Close, Tavistock Road, Callington, Cornwall, PL17 7DY.*
Spacious dormer bungalow in quiet cul-de-sac near town centre.
Open: All Year (not Xmas)
Grades: ETC 3 Diamond, AA 3 Diamond
01579 383677 Mrs Wills
dozmarybb@aol.com
D: £16.00–£17.00 **S:** £19.00–£20.00
Beds: 1F 1D 1T **Baths:** 2 En 1 Pr
🛇 ₽ (4) ⊬ ⓣⓥ Ⅲ. Ⓥ ♨

Dupath Farm, *Callington, Cornwall, PL17 8AD.*
Large rooms on working farm beside Dupath Well (Ancient Monument).
Open: All Year
01579 382197 Mrs Coombe
D: fr £17.00 **S:** fr £17.00
Beds: 1F 1D **Baths:** 2 En
🛇 ₽ (4) ⊬ ⓣⓥ Ⓥ ♨

Camelford

SX1083 ◀ *Masons' Arms, Darlington Inn, Bridge, Osiers*

Masons Arms, *Market Place, Camelford, Cornwall, PL32 9PD.*
C18th public house in the centre of Camelford. **Open:** All Year
01840 213309 Mr Connolly
D: £17.50 **S:** £17.50
Beds: 1F 2D 1T 1S **Baths:** 2 Sh
🛇 ₽ (2) ⓣⓥ ⊁ Ⅲ. Ⓥ ♨

Trenarth, *Victoria Road, Camelford, Cornwall, PL32.*
Friendly comfortable country home, open views. **Open:** All Year
01840 213295 Mrs Hopkins
ann@di-ren.demon.co.uk
D: £15.00–£17.00 **S:** £15.00–£17.00
Beds: 1F 1D 1S **Baths:** 1 En 1 Sh
🛇 (2) ₽ (4) ⊬ ⓣⓥ ⓣ Ⅲ. Ⓥ ♨ ♿

Carbis Bay

SW5238 ◀ *Cornish Arms, Badger Inn*

Chy-An-Gwedhen, *St Ives Road, Carbis Bay, St Ives, Cornwall, TR26 3JW.*
'Haven for non-smokers'. Chy-An-Gwedhen offers a warm and relaxed atmosphere. **Open:** All Year (not Xmas)
01736 798684 M Hart
gwedhen@btinternet.com
D: £20.00–£25.00 **S:** £25.00–£28.00
Beds: 4D 1T **Baths:** 5 En
₽ (7) ⊬ ⓣⓥ ⊁ Ⅲ. Ⓥ ♨ cc

Cardinham

SX1268 ◀ *London Inn, Hole In The Wall, Blisland Inn*

The Stables, *Cardinham, Bodmin, Cornwall, PL30 4EG.*
Peaceful location on the edge of Bodmin Moor. Ideal area for walking and cycling.
Open: All Year **01208 821316** Mr Moseley
gerald@stablebarns.freeserve.co.uk
D: £16.00–£19.00 **S:** £16.00–£25.00
Beds: 3T 1D 1S **Baths:** 2 En 2 Pr 1 Sh
🛇 (4) ₽ (4) ⊬ ⓣⓥ ⊁ Ⅲ. Ⓥ ♨ ♨

The Old School House, *Averys Green, Cardinham, Bodmin, Cornwall, PL30 4EA.*
Pretty Victorian schoolhouse in rural location. Traditional B&B.
Open: All Year (not Xmas/New Year)
01208 821303 Mrs Pidcock
libby@pidcock18.freeserve.co.uk
D: £15.00–£17.50 **S:** £15.00–£17.50
Beds: 2D
₽ (2) ⊬ ⓣⓥ ⓣ Ⅲ. Ⓥ ♨

Carleen

SW6130 ◀ *Queen's Arms*

Primrose Cottage, *Poldown Camping Park, Carleen, Helston, Cornwall, TR13 9NN.*
Open: Jun to Sep
01326 574560 (also fax)
Mr Couturier
primrose@poldown.co.uk
D: £16.00 **S:** £20.00
Beds: 2D **Baths:** 1 Sh
🛇 ₽ (2) ⓣⓥ ⓣ Ⅲ. ♨
Nestled in wooded countryside away from the road, a charming cottage with pretty rooms with hot and cold, TV, tea-making facilities. Full English breakfast. Gardens available to the guests. A centrally located base to which you will enjoy returning.

Catchall

SW4228 ◀ *Jolly Eater*

Coth A Noweth, *Catchall, Penzance, Cornwall, TR19 6AQ.*
Detached house; stream borders large garden. Convenient for Penwith's attractions.
Open: Easter to Sep
Grades: AA 2 Diamond
01736 810572 Mrs Craigue
D: £15.00–£17.00 **S:** fr £15.00
Beds: 2F 1D 1T **Baths:** 1 Sh
🛇 ₽ (7) ⓣⓥ Ⅲ. Ⓥ ♨

Chapel Amble ○

SW9975

Kivells, *Chapel Amble, Wadebridge, PL27 6EP.*
Comfortable, attractive house and gardens set amid peaceful countryside.
Open: Easter to Oct
01208 841755 Mr & Mrs Hosegood
info@kivellsbandb.co.uk
D: £20.00–£24.00 **S:** £20.00–£26.00
Beds: 1T 2D **Baths:** 1 En 1 Sh
🛇 (12) ₽ (5) ⊬ ⓣⓥ Ⅲ. ♨

Charlestown

SX0351 ◀ *Rashleigh Arms, Pier House Hotel*

Ardenconnel, *179 Charlestown Road, Charlestown, St Austell, Cornwall, PL25 3NN.*
Beautiful Victorian house situated in the unchanged C18th port of Charlestown.
Open: All Year
01726 75469 Mr Callis
ardenconnel@bun.com
D: £18.00–£21.00 **S:** £26.00–£29.00
Beds: 1F 1T 1D **Baths:** 1 En 1 Pr
🛇 ₽ (2) ⊬ ⓣⓥ Ⅲ. Ⓥ ♨

Colan

SW8661 ◀ *Two Clomes*

Colan Barton Farmhouse, *Colan, Newquay, Cornwall, TR8 4NB.*
C17th Farmhouse set in stunning countryside. Very warm welcome.
Open: April to September
Grades: AA 4 Diamond
01637 874395 Mrs Machan-Weaver
Fax: 01637 881388
D: £16.00–£24.00 **S:** £21.00–£29.00
Beds: 3F 1T 1D **Baths:** 1 En 1 Pr
🛇 ₽ (6) ⊬ ⓣⓥ Ⅲ. ♨

Constantine Bay

SW8574 ◀ *Trevose Golf Club, Treyarnon Bay Hotel*

Chyloweth, *Constantine Bay, Padstow, Cornwall, PL28 8JQ.*
Quiet location close to sandy beaches and Trevose Golf Club. **Open:** All Year
01841 521012 R & S Vivian
rogervivian@netscapeonline.co.uk
D: £20.00–£25.00 **S:** £25.00–£27.50
Beds: 1T 1D **Baths:** 2 En
🛇 ₽ (2) ⊬ ⓣⓥ Ⅲ. Ⓥ ♨

Coombe (St Austell)

SW9552

Selsey House, *Coombe, St Stephen, St Austell, Cornwall, PL26 7LL.*
Family-run guest house in quiet rural setting, situated in mid Cornwall.
Open: All Year
01726 882401 Mr Bracken
D: £17.50–£25.00 **S:** £17.50–£28.00
Beds: 1D 2T 1S **Baths:** 1 En 1 Sh
🛇 ₽ (5) ⊬ ⓣⓥ ⊁ Ⅲ. Ⓥ

Coverack

SW7818 ◀ *Paris Hotel*

Wych Elm, *Ponsongath, Helston, Cornwall, TR12 6SQ.*
Idyllic quiet setting close secluded Lankidden Cove. Backwoodsmen's bliss!
Open: All Year (not Xmas)
01326 280576 Mrs Whitaker
D: £18.00 **S:** £20.00
Beds: 1T **Baths:** 1 En
🛇 (8) ₽ (2) ⊬ ⓣⓥ ⊁ Ⅲ. Ⓥ

Crackington Haven

SX1496 ◀ *Coombe Barton Inn*

Venn Park Farm, *Crackington Haven, Bude, Cornwall, EX23 0LB.*
Open: All Year
01840 230159 (also fax)
Ms Wilson
D: £18.00–£20.00 **S:** £20.00–£22.00
Beds: 1F 2D **Baths:** 2 En 1 Pr
🛇 ₽ ⊬ ⓣⓥ ⓣ ⊁ Ⅲ. Ⓥ ♨ ♨
Relaxation opportunity. Modernised farmhouse with extensive sea, countryside views. Ensuite, family bedrooms, colour TV. Coastal/ Moorland walks, fishing, golfing & cycling easily accessible. Participation farm/ natural environmental tasks arrangeable. Close picturesque Boscastle/Crackington Beach. Traditionally cooked food, Vegetarian option.

Hallagather, Crackington Haven, Bude, Cornwall, EX23 0LA.
Ancient farmhouse, warm, welcoming. Substantial buffet style breakfast. Spectacular scenery.
Open: Feb to Nov
Grades: ETC 4 Diamond, AA 4 Diamond
01840 230 276 Mrs Anthony
Fax: 01840 230 449
D: £17.50–£24.00 **S:** £18.00–£26.00
Beds: 1F 1D 1S **Baths:** 4 En
⌂ (11) ▣ (6) ⅙ ▣ ⊬ ▥ ▤ ♨

Crantock

SW7960 ◁ Albion, Bowgie

Carden Cottage, Halwyn Hill, Crantock, Newquay, Cornwall, TR8 5RR.
Open: All Year (not Xmas/New Year)
01637 830806 Mr Clark
D: fr £20.00 **S:** fr £20.00
Beds: 1T 2D **Baths:** 3 En
⌂ (10) ▣ (4) ⅙ ▣ ▥ ♨
A beautiful place with king-size beds, tea & coffee, soap and towels and a full English breakfast, situated in the heart of the village, with two pubs, a church and a few minutes walks from a lovely sandy beach.

Cury

SW6721 ◁ Old Mill Wheel Inn, Black Swan, Hazlephron Inn

Tregaddra Farmhouse, Cury, Helston, Cornwall, TR12 7BB.
Farmhouse B&B quiet, peaceful, set in Area of Outstanding Natural Beauty.
Open: All Year (not Xmas)
Grades: ETC 4 Diamond
01326 240235 (also fax)
Mrs Lugg
D: £20.00–£25.00 **S:** £20.00–£25.00
Beds: 2F 4D 1T **Baths:** 6 En 1 Pr
⌂ ▣ (10) ⅙ ▣ ⊠ ▥ ♨ cc

Falmouth

SW8032 ◁ Seaview Inn, Quayside Inn, Cross Keys, Falmouth Hotel, Chain Locker, Norway Inn, Pandora Inn, Bosanneth Hotel, Warehouse Bistro, Laughing Pirate

Trevu House Hotel, 45 Melvill Road, Falmouth, Cornwall, TR11 4DG.
Open: All year (not Xmas)
01326 312852 Mrs Eustice
Fax: 01326 318631
elaine.eddy@lineone.net
D: £17.50–£21.50 **S:** £17.50–£21.50
Beds: 1F 2D 3T 3S **Baths:** 9 En
⌂ (5) ▣ ⅙ ▣ ⊠ ▥ ▤ ♨
Small select, non-smoking hotel. Superb for town, Princess Pavilion and beautiful gardens. Sandy beaches, coastal walks and some of the finest scenery in Cornwall. All en-suite rooms some with 6' wide beds. Ground-floor bedroom.

BATHROOMS
Pr - Private
Sh - Shared
En - Ensuite

Melvill House Hotel, 52 Melvill Road, Falmouth, Cornwall, TR11 4DQ.
Open: All Year (not Xmas)
Grades: AA 4 Diamond
01326 316645 Mr & Mrs Crawford
Fax: 01326 211608
crawfords@crawfords.eurobell.co.uk
D: £19.00–£24.50 **S:** £19.00–£25.00
Beds: 2F 3D 2T **Baths:** 7 En
⌂ ▣ (9) ⅙ ▣ ⊠ ▥ ▤ ♨ cc
Friendly hotel run by Franco-Scottish couple. It has spacious, comfortable and attractive rooms with views of the sea and harbour. Excellent home cooking, table licence, special diets catered for. Lots of ideas for trips and visits for all ages.

Beachwalk House, 39 Castle Drive, Falmouth, Cornwall, TR11 4NF.
Fabulous views, seafront position, overlooks Falmouth Bay, beaches and castle. **Open:** All Year (not Xmas)
01326 319841 Mr & Mrs Clarke
D: £18.00–£20.00 **S:** £20.00–£25.00
Beds: 3D 1T **Baths:** 4 En
⌂ ▣ (4) ▣ ▥ ♨

20 Dracaena Avenue, Falmouth, Cornwall, TR11 2EQ.
Friendly, comfortable, homely Victorian house.
Open: Easter to Oct
01326 211784 Mr Blowers
D: fr £16.00 **S:** fr £18.00
Beds: 1D 2T
⌂ ▣ (3) ▥ ♨

Rosemullion Hotel, Gyllyngvase Hill, Falmouth, Cornwall, TR11 4DF.
Imposing Tudor-style building with balcony rooms, sea view, king-size beds and town centre.
Open: All Year
Grades: AA 4 Diamond
01326 314690 Mrs Jones
Fax: 01326 210098
D: £21.50–£26.00 **S:** £24.50–£26.00
Beds: 3T 9D 1S **Baths:** 1 En 2 Pr
▣ ⅙ ▥ ▤ ♨

Ambleside Guest House, 9 Marlborough Road, Falmouth, Cornwall, TR11 3LP.
Victorian guest house. Relaxed & friendly.
Open: All Year
01326 319630 Mr Walker
D: fr £18.00 **S:** fr £18.00
Beds: 1F 2D 1T 1S **Baths:** 1 Sh
⌂ ▣ ▥ ♨

Dolvean Hotel, 50 Melvill Road, Falmouth, Cornwall, TR11 4DQ.
Open: All Year (not Xmas)
Grades: AA 4 Diamond
01326 313658 Mrs Crocker
Fax: 01326 313995
reservations@dolvean.freeserve.co.uk
D: £23.00–£27.00 **S:** £25.00–£30.00
Beds: 1F 6D 3T 2S **Baths:** 12 En
⌂ (12) ▣ (12) ⅙ ▣ ▥ ♨ cc
The Dolvean is a traditional Victorian hotel with old fashioned standards of care and courtesy. However, whilst retaining the charm and dignity of yesterday, The Dolvean offers you a warm welcome, today's modern amenities, and just a touch of luxury.

Castleton Guest House, 68 Killigrew Street, Falmouth, Cornwall, TR11 3PR.
Convenient to town centre and all local attractions.
Open: All Year (not Xmas/New Year)
Grades: ETC Listed, Approv
01326 311072 Mr & Mrs Davies
Fax: 01326 317613
castleton@falmouthbandb.co.uk
D: £16.00–£20.00 **S:** £20.00
Beds: 2D 3T **Baths:** 4 En
⌂ (4) ▣ ▥ ▥ ♨

The Grove Hotel, Grove Place, Falmouth, Cornwall, TR11 4AU.
Harbourside Georgian hotel, friendly atmosphere. Central for all local amenities.
Open: All Year (not Xmas)
01326 319577 Mrs Cumins
janet@hillgate.demon.co.uk
D: £22.00–£24.00 **S:** £22.00–£24.00
Beds: 2F 2D 6T 2S **Baths:** 13 En 2 Sh
⌂ ▣ ⊠ ▥ ♨ cc

Fowey

SX1251 ◁ Fowey Galleon, Polruan Galleon, Old Ferry Inn, The Ship, Safe Harbour

Safe Harbour Hotel, Lostwithiel Road, Fowey, Cornwall, PL23 1BD.
Friendly inn, river views, car parking, quiet lounge bar, full menu available.
Open: All Year
01726 833379 **D:** £21.00–£25.00 **S:** £25.00
Beds: 2F 2D 1T **Baths:** 5 En
⌂ ▣ (8) ⅙ ▣ ▥ ⊠ ▥ ♨

St Keverne, 4 Daglands Road, Fowey, Cornwall, PL23 1JL.
Comfortable Edwardian house close to town centre, with river views
Open: All Year (not Xmas/New Year)
01726 833164 Mrs Eardley
carol@stkeverne1.fsnet.co.uk
D: £20.00 **S:** £20.00
Beds: 2D **Baths:** 2 En
▣ (1) ⅙ ▣ ▥ ▥ ▤ ♨

Coombe Farm, Coombe, Fowey, Cornwall, PL23 1HW.
Charming farmhouse overlooking walled garden, serving cream teas. Sea views.
Open: All Year
01726 833123 Mrs Paull
D: £15.50–£22.50 **S:** £17.50–£25.00
Beds: 1D 1T **Baths:** 1 En
⌂ ▣ ▥ ♨

Carnethic House, Lambs Barn, Fowey, Cornwall, PL23 1HQ.
Regency house, 2 acres mature gardens. Parking. Family run.
Open: Feb to Nov
Grades: ETC 4 Diamond, AA 4 Diamond
01726 833336 Mr Hogg
Fax: 01726 833296
carnethic@btinternet.com
D: £25.00–£35.00 **S:** £40.00–£50.00
Beds: 1F 5D 2T **Baths:** 7 En 1 Sh
⌂ ▣ ▣ ⊠ ▥ ▤ ♨ cc

Planning a longer stay? Always ask for any special rates

Garker

SX0454   *Britannia Inn*

Restineas Cottage, Garker, St Austell, Cornwall, PL26 8YA.
Country cottage set in two acre garden and grounds. Peaceful surroundings.
Open: All Year (not Xmas/New Year)
01726 812171 (also fax)
Mrs Sampson
D: £20.00–£25.00 **S:** £30.00–£35.00
Beds: 1D **Baths:** 1 Pr
🏠 (1) 🗲 📺 ✕ 🖳 ♨

Gerrans

SW8735   *Royal Standard, Plume of Feathers*

Harberton House, Churchtown Road, Gerrans, Portscatho, Truro, Cornwall, TR2 5DZ.
Large traditionally-built family home with excellent views.
Open: Easter to Oct
01872 580598 Mr & Mrs Davis
Fax: 01872 580789
D: £19.00 **S:** £19.00
Beds: 1D 1T **Baths:** 2 Sh
🏠 📌 (6) 🗲 📺 🖳 ♨

Gillan

SW7824   *New Inn*

Porthvean, Gillan, Manaccan, Helston, Cornwall, TR12 6HL.
Specially suitable for walkers on SW Coastal Path, view of Gillan Creek and Helford.
Open: All Year (not Xmas)
01326 231204 Mrs Whale
D: £15.00 **S:** £15.00
Beds: 1T **Baths:** 1 Pr
📌 (3) 🗲 📌 🖳 ♨

Goonhavern

SW7853   *Smugglers Dew Inn*

September Lodge, Wheal Hope Goonhavern, Truro, Cornwall, TR4 9QJ.
Modern house with countryside views. Ideally situated for touring Cornwall.
Open: All Year (not Xmas/New Year)
Grades: ETC 3 Diamond
01872 571435 (also fax)
Mr Philipps
jc.septlodge@virgin.net
D: £20.00 **S:** £25.00–£28.00
Beds: 1F 1D
Baths: 2 En
🏠 📌 (10) 🗲 📺 📌 🖳 📺 ♨

Gorran Haven

SX0041   *Barleysheaf, Llawnroc Inn*

Homestead, 34 Chute Lane, Gorran Haven, St Austell, Cornwall, PL26 6NU.
Cottage/ beach 100m/ overlooking garden/ parking/ easy reach Heligon/ Eden.
Open: All Year
01726 842567 Mr & Mrs Smith
D: £25.00 **S:** £50.00
Beds: 1T 1D **Baths:** 2 Pr
📌 🗲 🖳

Grampound

SW9348   *The Dolphin*

Perran House, Grampound, Truro, Cornwall, TR2 4RS.
Open: All Year
Grades: ETC 3 Diamond, AA 3 Diamond
01726 882066 Mr Diboll
D: £17.00–£18.00 **S:** £15.00–£16.00
Beds: 3D 1T 2S **Baths:** 3 En 1 Sh
🏠 📌 (8) 🗲 📺 🖳 📺 ♨
Delightful C17th cottage in the pretty village of Grampound within a conservation area. Centrally located for touring, visiting the many nearby gardens including The Lost Gardens of Heligan and The Eden Project, also within easy reach of the coastal footpaths.

Gwithian

SW5841   *Pendarves Arms*

Nanterrow Farm, Gwithian, Hayle, Cornwall, TR27 5BP.
Open: All Year (not Xmas)
01209 712282 Mrs Davies
jamesdavies2@hotmail.com
D: £16.00–£18.00 **S:** £16.00–£20.00
Beds: 1F 1D 1S **Baths:** 2 Sh
🏠 📌 (4) 📺 📌 📺
Come and enjoy a relaxing stay on our traditional working farm situated in a quiet traffic-free valley 1.5 miles from St Ives Bay. 3 miles of sandy beaches; good area for coastal walks; many other local attractions. Good farmhouse fare.

Calize Country House, Prosper Hill, Gwithian, Hayle, Cornwall, TR27 5BW.
Country house overlooking sea. Rural location near beautiful beaches/countryside.
Open: All Year **Grades:** AA 3 Diamond
01736 753268 (also fax) Mrs Bailey
penny.bailey@talk21.com
D: £16.00–£19.00 **S:** £15.50–£19.00
Beds: 3D 2T **Baths:** 3 En 1 Sh
🏠 (10) 📌 (5) 🗲 📺 📌 🖳 ♨

Hallworthy

SX1887

Wilsey Down Hotel, Hallworthy, Camelford, Cornwall, PL32 9SH.
Warm welcome, friendly hotel, views over Bodmin Moor, near to coast.
Open: All Year **01840 261205** J Bremdon
D: £18.00–£24.00 **S:** £15.00–£18.00
Beds: 1F 2T 2D **Baths:** 2 En 1 Pr 1 Sh
🏠 📌 (50) 📺 ✕ ♨ cc

Helston

SW6627   *Gweek Inn, Wheal Dream, Ship Inn, New Inn, Red Lion*

Lyndale Guest House, Greenbank, Meneage Road, Helston, Cornwall, TR13 8JA.
Pretty cottage style guest house. Central for touring/ walking coastal footpath.
Open: All Year **Grades:** ETC 3 Diamond
01326 561082 Mrs Tucker
Fax: 01326 565813
enquiries@lyndale1.freeserve.co.uk
D: £16.50–£20.50 **S:** £23.00–£26.00
Beds: 1F 3D 2T 1S **Baths:** 3 En 1 Sh
🏠 📌 (6) 📺 📌 ✕ 🖳 📺 ♨ cc

Mandeley Guest House, Clodgey Lane, Helston, Cornwall, TR13 8PJ.
Luxurious B&B accommodation central for touring West Cornwall.
Open: All Year
Grades: ETC 3 Diamond
01326 572550 Mr Johns
D: £17.00–£20.00 **S:** £23.00–£25.00
Beds: 1F 1D 1T **Baths:** 1 En 1 Pr
🏠 📌 (4) 📺 📺 🖳 ♨

Landsrow House, 4 Cross Street, Helston, Cornwall, TR13 8NQ.
Period residence with walled garden in historic town near coast.
Open: All Year
01326 572261 Mrs Rowlands
D: £18.00–£21.00 **S:** £18.00–£21.00
Beds: 1F 1T 2D **Baths:** 1 En 1 Sh
🏠 (5) 📌 (4) 📺 🖳 ♨

High Street

SW9653   *Rashleigh Inn, Hewas Inn*

Manor Farm, High Street, Burngullow, St Austell, Cornwall, PL26 7TQ.
Beautiful Grade II Listed manor house. Eden Project, Heligan 6 miles.
Open: All Year (not Xmas/New Year)
01726 72242 (also fax)
S Manuell
suzannemanuell@tinyworld.co.uk
D: £21.00–£22.00 **S:** £25.00–£30.00
Beds: 1F 1D **Baths:** 2 En
🏠 📌 (10) 🗲 📺 🖳 📺 ♨

Kingsand

SX4350   *Halfway House, Rising Sun*

Cliff House, Devon Port Hill, Kingsand, Torpoint, Cornwall, PL10 1NT.
Listed comfortable house. Sea and country views. Great wholefood cookery.
Open: All Year
01752 823110 Mrs Heasman
Fax: 01752 822595
info@cliffhse.abel.co.uk
D: £21.00–£25.00 **S:** £25.00–£35.00
Beds: 3F 2D **Baths:** 3 En 3 Pr
🏠 📌 (3) 🗲 📺 ✕ 🖳 📺 ✳ ♨

Clarendon, Garrett Street, Cawsand, Kingsand, Torpoint, Cornwall, PL10 1PD.
Cornish fishing village. Close to Mount Edgecombe Park. Resident chef.
Open: All Year (not Xmas/New Year)
01752 823460 Mrs Goodwright
D: £16.00–£18.00 **S:** £16.00–£18.00
Beds: 1D 1T 1S **Baths:** 1 Sh
🏠 (5) 🖳

Algoma, The Green, Kingsand, Cawsand Bay, Cornwall, PL10 1NH.
Family run guest house in picturesque, unspoilt village overlooking Plymouth Sound.
Open: All Year (not Xmas/New Year)
01752 822706 Mr Ogilvie
alan@aogilvie.freeserve.co.uk
D: £20.00 **S:** £20.00–£40.00
Beds: 1F 1D
Baths: 2 En
🏠 📺 🖳 📺 ♨

Ladock

SW8950   🍺 *Falmouth Arms*

Swallows Court, Treworyan, Ladock, Truro, Cornwall, TR2 4QD.
Beautifully converted stone barn, peaceful location, delicious breakfasts, friendly atmosphere. **Open:** March to Sept **Grades:** ETC 3 Diamond
01726 883488 Mrs Harvey
D: £19.00–£22.00 **S:** £22.00–£25.00
🛏 🄿 ⅍ 📺 🛏 🕭

Lamorna

SW4425   🍺 *Lamorna Hotel*

Tremeneth Hotel, Lamorna, Penzance, Cornwall, TR19 6XL.
Set in the heart of a wooded valley.
Open: Easter to Oct
01736 731367 (also fax) J J Rowley
D: £22.00–£26.00 **S:** £18.00–£20.00
Beds: 3D 1T 1S 1F **Baths:** 5 En 1 Sh
🛏 (2) 🄿 (8) 📺 🛏 ✕ 🛏 🕭 ❀ 🕭

Laneast

SX2284   🍺 *Wilsey Down*

Stitch Park, Laneast, Launceston, Cornwall, PL15 8PN.
Situated close to Bodmin Moor with magnificent views towards Dartmoor.
Open: All Year
01566 86687 Mrs Handford
D: £16.50–£18.00 **S:** £16.50–£18.00
Beds: 1T 1D **Baths:** 2 En
🄿 (6) ⅍ 📺 ✕ 🛏 🕭 🕭

Lanivet

SX0364   🍺 *Borough Arms, Halfway House, St Benet's Abbey, Crown Inn, Lanivet Arms, Welcome Stranger*

Bokiddick Farm, Lanivet, Bodmin, Cornwall, PL30 5HP.
Georgian farmhouse, oak beams, wood panelling, magnificent views, peaceful location. **Open:** All Year (not Xmas)
Grades: ETC 5 Diamond, Gold Award
01208 831481 (also fax) Mrs Hugo
Rob.hugo@farming.co.uk
D: £21.00–£23.00 **S:** £25.00–£30.00
Beds: 1F 2D **Baths:** 3 En
🛏 (5) 🄿 (4) ⅍ 📺 🛏 🕭

High Cross Farm, Lanivet, Bodmin, Cornwall, PL30 5JR.
Traditional farmhouse c.1890 in geographical centre of Cornwall.
Open: All Year (not Xmas)
01208 831341 D: fr £14.00 **S:** fr £20.00
Beds: 1F 1D 1T **Baths:** 1 Sh
🛏 🄿 (6) ⅍ 📺 ✕ 🛏 🕭

Tremeere Manor, Lanivet, Bodmin, Cornwall, PL30 5BG.
Spacious farmhouse in lovely surroundings. Easy access coasts and moors.
Open: Feb to Nov
01208 831513 Mrs Oliver
Fax: 01208 832417
oliver.tremeere.manor@farming.co.uk
D: £15.00–£20.00 **S:** £16.00–£20.00
Beds: 2D 1T **Baths:** 1 En 1 Sh
🛏 🄿 (6) ⅍ 📺 🛏 🕭

Rosehill Cottage, Lanivet, Bodmin, Cornwall, PL30 5HZ.
Beautiful old farmhouse built 1702, centrally situated in lovely countryside.
Open: All Year (not Xmas)
01208 831965
tonytrives@rosehillcottage.freeserve.co.uk
D: £16.00–£20.00
Beds: 1F 2D 1T **Baths:** 3 En 1 Pr
🛏 (6) 🄿 (4) ⅍ 📺 🛏 🕭

Lower Woon Farm, Lanivet, Bodmin, Cornwall, PL30 5JE.
Easy access from main routes, bus, set in countryside.
Open: All Year
01208 831756 (also fax)
D: £16.00 **S:** £16.00
Beds: 1D 1T **Baths:** 1 Pr
🛏 🄿 📺 ✕ 🛏 📺 🕭

Lanlivery

SX0759   🍺 *Crown Inn, Royal Oak*

Higher Pennant, Lanlivery, Bodmin, PL30 5DD.
Friendly, relaxed, rural accommodation. Ideal family break with horse-riding available.
Open: All Year
01208 873252 Mr Chester
dave@higherpennant.freeserve.co.uk
D: £20.00 **S:** £20.00–£30.00
Beds: 1F 1D 1S **Baths:** 2 En 1 Pr
🛏 🄿 📺 🛏 ✕ 🛏 📺 ❀ 🕭

Longfield House, Lanlivery, Bodmin, Cornwall, PL30 5BT.
Quiet family house. Panoramic countryside views. 4 miles Eden Project.
Open: All Year (not Xmas/New Year)
01208 873439 Mrs Haley
D: £20.00 **S:** £30.00
Beds: 1F 2D **Baths:** 3 En
🛏 🄿 ⅍ 📺 ✕ 🛏 🕭 &

Poltip Cottage, Lanlivery, Bodmin, Cornwall, PL30 5BX.
Picturesque cottage and gardens. Central for exploring both Cornish coasts.
Open: All Year
01208 872715 Mrs Bromley-Fox
D: £20.00–£25.00
Beds: 1D **Baths:** 1 Pr
🄿 (2) ⅍ 🛏 📺 🕭

Launceston

SX3384   🍺 *Country Man, Elliott Arms, White Hart, Westgate Inn, Three Steps to Heaven*

Landrayne Manor, Coads Green, Launceston, Cornwall, PL15 7LZ.
Open: All Year
Grades: ETC Cornwall Tourist Board
01566 782528 Mrs Loe
loe@landreyne.fsnet.co.uk
D: £24.00–£28.00 **S:** £24.00–£34.00
Beds: 1T 2D 1S **Baths:** 2 En 1 Pr
🛏 🄿 ✕ 🛏 📺 ❀ 🕭
A superb country property providing extremely comfortable accommodation in Cornwall's rural heart. The house is full of character, charm and an atmosphere of tranquillity. Fine food is a speciality and a memorable part of any stay. A beautiful spot.

11 Castle Street, Launceston, Cornwall, PL15 8BA.
Georgian St. Town facilities. Castle views. Gourmet breakfasts. Parking. Period Furnishings.
Open: Easter to October
01566 773873 Mrs Bowles
D: £17.50–£25.00 **S:** £20.00–£25.00
Beds: 2T 1D **Baths:** 1 En 1 Sh
⅍ 📺 🛏 🕭

Oakside, South Petherwin, Launceston, Cornwall, PL15 7LJ.
Open: Easter to Nov
01566 86733 Mrs Crossman
D: £16.00–£20.00 **S:** £16.00–£20.00
Beds: 1F 1D 1T **Baths:** 1 En 1 Sh
🛏 (2) 🄿 (4) ⅍ 📺 🛏 🕭
Panoramic views of Bodmin Moor and a warm welcome awaits. Farm bungalow nestling peacefully in beautiful surroundings 1 min from A30 trunk road, Exeter, M5. Ideal touring base for Cornwall. English breakfasts speciality, attractively furnished, well equipped rooms, many legendary land marks nearby.

Bradbridge Farm, Boyton, Launceston, Cornwall, PL15 9RL.
On Devon/ Cornwall border, fishing, walks, wildlife, golf, riding, beach nearby.
Open: Easter to Oct
01409 271264 Mrs Strout
D: fr £16.00 **S:** fr £16.00
Beds: 1D 1T 1S
🛏 🄿 ⅍ 📺 🛏 ✕ 🛏 🕭

Trethorne Leisure Farm, Kennards House, Launceston, Cornwall, PL15 8QE.
Open: All Year (not Xmas)
Grades: ETC 3 Diamond
01566 86324 Mrs Davey
Fax: 01566 86981
trethorneleisure@eclipse.co.uk
D: £21.00–£22.00 **S:** £20.00–£22.00
Beds: 3F 2D 1T **Baths:** 6 Pr
🛏 🄿 (20) 📺 🛏 ✕ 🛏 📺 🕭
Warm, friendly farmhouse accommodation which overlooks our 18-hole golf course. Free access to activities, roller blading, animals and leisure farm. Tenpin bowling, restaurant, bar and conference facilities.

Tregerrie, Trebursye Road, Launceston, Cornwall, PL15 7EL.
Welcoming, modern farmhouse overlooking Launceston. Ideal for touring Devon, Cornwall.
Open: Mar to Nov
01566 775884 Mrs Cobbledick
D: £16.50–£20.00 **S:** £18.00–£22.00
Beds: 2D **Baths:** 1 En 1 Pr
🛏 🄿 (4) 📺 🛏 📺 🕭

The Cottages, 21 St Stephens Hill, Launceston, Cornwall, PL15 8HN.
Comfortable, welcoming cottage. Ideal base for touring Devon and Cornwall.
Open: All Year
01566 776691 Mrs Kean
D: £15.00–£17.00 **S:** £15.00–£17.00
Beds: 1F 1D 1T 1S **Baths:** 1 Sh
🛏 ⅍ 📺 🛏 ✕ 🛏 📺 ❀ 🕭

Planning a longer stay? Always ask for any special rates

The Old Vicarage, Treneglos, Launceston, Cornwall, PL15 8UQ.
Renowned for hospitals and excellent food. Highest standards throughout.
Open: March to Nov
Grades: ETC 4 Diamond, Silver Award
01566 781351 (also fax) Mrs Fancourt
maggie@fancourt.freeserve.co.uk
D: £25.00 **S:** £25.00
Beds: 2D 1S **Baths:** 2 En
🛏 (2) 🅿 (10) ⚲ 🍽 × 🎴 🖤

West Down End, Pipers Pool, Launceston, Cornwall, PL15 8QG.
Family farmhouse accommodation easy access to coast and moors.
Open: Easter to Oct
01566 86613 Mrs Bloye
peterb5@breathemail.net
D: £16.00–£20.00
Beds: 1F 1D **Baths:** 1 En 1 Pr
🛏 🅿 (3) ⚲ 🎴 × 🖤

Lelant

SW5437 🍺 Badger Inn

Hindon Hall, Lelant, St Ives, Cornwall, TR26 3EN.
Open: All Year (not Xmas/New Year)
01736 753046 (also fax)
Ms O'Sullivan
hindonhall@talk21.com
D: £23.00–£30.00 **S:** £34.00–£38.00
Beds: 4D **Baths:** 4 En
🅿 (10) ⚲ 🎴 🎴 🖤
A delightful setting in a conservation area village. Lovely Edwardian house overlooking RSPB, has luxurious double rooms with lots of extras, super breakfasts and small bar. Nearby beaches, cycle hire, golf, gardens, galleries. Ideal base for touring West Cornwall.

Liskeard

SX2564 🍺 Fountain Hotel, Caradon Inn, Cheesewring Hotel, Old Stag, Spicers

Elnor Guest House, 1 Russell Street, Liskeard, Cornwall, PL14 4BP.
Many nearby attractions, good local restaurants. Lovely scenery, station near.
Open: Jan to Dec
Grades: ETC 3 Diamond, AA 3 Diamond
01579 342472 Mr Slocombe & Mrs G G M Slocombe
Fax: 01579 345673
D: £19.00–£22.00 **S:** £19.00–£22.00
Beds: 1F 2D 2T 4S **Baths:** 7 En 1 Sh
🛏 🅿 (8) 🎴 × 🎴 🖤

Hyvue House, Barras Cross, Liskeard, Cornwall, PL14 6BN.
Family-run exclusively for non-smokers on outskirts of town overlooking Bodmin Moor.
Open: All Year
Grades: ETC 3 Diamond
01579 348175 Mrs Demmer
D: £17.50–£22.00 **S:** £20.00
Beds: 2D 1T **Baths:** 3 En 3 Pr
🛏 (5) 🅿 (6) ⚲ 🎴 🖤

Looe

SX2553 🍺 Harbour Moon, Salutation Arms, Jolly Sailors, Harbour Moon, The Ship, Ye Olde Salvation Inne, Killarney Hotel, Tom Sawyers Inn, Dagger

The Beach House, Marine Drive, Looe, Cornwall, PL13 2DH.
Open: All Year
01503 262598 **Fax:** 01503 262298
enquires@thebeachhouse.uk.com
D: £20.00–£28.00 **S:** £25.00–£38.00
Beds: 2T 3D **Baths:** 4 En 1 Pr
🛏 (12) 🅿 (5) ⚲ 🎴 🎴 🖤 cc
On the sea front / SW coastal path, we enjoy uninterrupted views of Looe Bay. Ideally placed for boating, fishing, diving, rambling or bird watching, we aim to offer quality, comfort, stunning sea views, delicious breakfasts and a very special welcome.

Tidal Court, 3 Church Street, Looe, Cornwall, PL13 2EX.
Open: All Year (not Xmas)
01503 263695 Mrs Hocking
D: £16.00–£21.00 **S:** £16.00–£25.00
Beds: 3F 1D 1T 1S **Baths:** 5 En 1 Pr
🛏 🅿 (3) 🎴 🎴 🖤
Tidal court is situated in floral award-winning street just 50 yards from harbour central for coast and woodland walks. Various boating activities and shoreline safaris.

Schooner Point Guest House, 1 Trelawney Terrace, Polperro Road, Looe, Cornwall, PL13 2AG.
Family guest house, river views, close to centre and beach. **Open:** Jan to Nov
01503 262670 Mr & Mrs Neaves
melv.neaves@tinyworld.co.uk
D: £14.00–£20.00 **S:** £14.00–£17.00
Beds: 1F 3D 2S **Baths:** 2 En 1 Sh
🛏 🅿 (2) 🎴 🎴 🖤

Marwinthy Guest House, East Cliff, Looe, Cornwall, PL13 1DE.
Small friendly guest house, on coastal footpath overlooking beach. In Which? Guide. **Open:** All Year
01503 264382 E Mawby
eddie.mawby@tinyonline.co.uk
D: fr £17.00 **S:** fr £17.00
Beds: 2F 2D 1T **Baths:** 2 Pr 1 Sh
🛏 (4) 🎴 🎴 🎴 🖤

Sea Haze, Polperro Road, Looe, PL13 2JS.
Country/ sea views friendly family, award winning garden, good food.
Open: All Year (not Xmas)
01503 262708 (also fax)
Mr & Mrs Dearsley
dearsley@tinyonline.co.uk
D: £17.00–£20.00 **S:** £17.00–£20.00
Beds: 1F 4D 1T **Baths:** 1 En 2 Sh
🛏 (2) 🅿 (7) ⚲ 🎴 🎴 🖤 🐕 3

Treveria Farm, Widegates, Looe, Cornwall, PL13 1QR.
Delightful manor Offering luxurious accommodation in spacious and elegant rooms. **Open:** Easter to Oct
01503 240237 (also fax) Mrs Kitto
D: £20.00–£25.00 **S:** £25.00–£30.00
Beds: 2D 1T **Baths:** 3 Pr
🅿 (3) ⚲ 🎴 🎴 🖤

Sea Breeze Guest House, Lower Chapel Street, Looe, Cornwall, PL13 1AT.
In Old Looe, close to beach, harbour, restaurants and shops.
Open: All Year (not Xmas)
01503 263131 Mr Jenkin
Fax: 01503 263131
johnjenkin@sbgh.freeserve.co.uk
D: £16.00–£21.00 **S:** £16.00–£20.00
Beds: 4D 1T **Baths:** 3 Pr 1 Sh
🛏 🅿 (2) 🎴 🎴 🎴 🖤 cc

Westcliff Hotel, Hannafore Road, Looe, Cornwall, PL13 2DE.
A family run hotel where a friendly welcome awaits you.
Open: March to Nov
01503 262500 Mr & Mrs Petrie
D: £15.00–£17.00 **S:** £15.00–£17.00
Beds: 4F 2D 4T 2S **Baths:** 4 Sh
🛏 (6) ⚲ 🎴 🎴 × 🎴 🖤

Kantara Guest House, 7 Trelawney Terrace, Looe, Cornwall, PL13 2AG.
Comfortable family-run guest house convenient for harbour, beach and town.
Open: All Year
01503 262093 Mr & Mrs Storer
D: £14.00–£16.00 **S:** £14.00–£16.00
Beds: 3F 4D 2T 3S **Baths:** 4 Sh
🛏 🅿 (1) 🎴 🎴 × 🖤 cc

Bucklawren Farm, St Martin, Looe, Cornwall, PL13 1NZ.
Beautiful farmhouse in the countryside beside the sea.
Open: Mar to Oct
Grades: ETC 4 Diamond, Silver Award
01503 240738 Mrs Henly
Fax: 01503 240481
bucklawren@compuserve.com
D: £22.00–£25.00 **S:** £27.00–£30.00
Beds: 2F 2T 2D **Baths:** 6 En
🛏 (5) 🅿 (6) 🎴 × 🎴 🖤 🚿 cc

Trevanion Hotel, Hannafore Road, Looe, Cornwall, PL13 2DE.
Turn of century residence, overlooking river, beach, harbour. 20 m headland.
Open: All Year
Grades: ETC 3 Diamond
01503 262003 Mr Fildes
Fax: 01503 265408
hotel@looecornwall.co.uk
D: £17.00–£26.50 **S:** £19.00–£28.50
Beds: 2F 6D 2S
Baths: 10 En
🛏 🅿 (5) 🎴 🎴 × 🎴 🖤 ✳ cc

Lostwithiel

SX1059 🍺 Ship Inn, Earl of Chatham

Treview House, Redlake, Lostwithiel, Cornwall, PL22 0ND.
Charming country house set amidst woodlands. Ideal location for visiting Eden Project.
Open: All Year (not Xmas/New Year)
01208 872664 (also fax)
Mrs Phipps
sue@treview.freeserve.co.uk
D: £18.00–£25.00 **S:** £22.00–£25.00
Beds: 1T 1D 1S
Baths: 2 En 1 Pr
🅿 (4) ⚲ 🎴 🎴 🖤

Benthams, Grenville Road, Lostwithiel, Cornwall, *PL22 0RA.*
Large house in 2 acres; central for all of Cornwall.
Open: All Year
01208 872472 Mrs Sanders
sanders.benthams@virgin.net
D: £18.00–£20.00 **S:** £20.00–£22.00
Beds: 2D 1T 1S **Baths:** 1 Pr 1 Sh
🛇 🅿 (6) ⅏ ⅏ ⅏ 🐾

Ludgvan

SW5033   ◫ White Hart

Menwidden Farm, Ludgvan, Penzance, Cornwall, *TR20 8BN.*
Comfortable farmhouse, centrally situated in peaceful countryside. Friendly welcome guaranteed.
Open: Easter to Oct
Grades: ETC 3 Diamond
01736 740415 Mrs Quick
D: £16.50–£20.00 **S:** £16.50–£20.00
Beds: 3D 1T 1S **Baths:** 1 En 2 Sh
🛇 🅿 (8) ⅏ 🐾 ✕ ⅏ 🐾

Madron

SW4432   ◫ King William IV

Tregoddick House, Madron, Penzance, Cornwall, *TR20 8SS.*
Charming house in small village, close to all amenities.
Open: All Year (not Xmas)
01736 362643 Mrs Scoble
Fax: 01736 332920
D: £17.00–£18.00 **S:** £17.00–£18.00
Beds: 2T **Baths:** 2 Pr
🛇 (2) 🅿 (2) ⅏ ⅏ ⅏ 🐾

Marazion

SW5130

Chymorvah Private Hotel,
Marazion, Cornwall, *TR17 0DQ.*
Cheerful, coastal Victorian family house. Comfortable ensuite rooms, good breakfasts.
Open: All Year (not Xmas)
01736 710497 Mrs Bull
Fax: 01736 710508
D: £26.00–£30.50 **S:** £26.00–£30.50
Beds: 9F 5D 3T 1S **Baths:** 9 En 1 Sh
🛇 🅿 (12) ⅏ ✕ ⅏ ⅏ 🐾 cc

Marhamchurch

SS2203   ◫ Bullers Arms

Hilton Farm House, Marhamchurch, Bude, Cornwall, *EX23 0HE.*
Open: All Year
01288 361521 (also fax)
Mr & Mrs Goodman
ian@hiltonfarmhouse.freeserve.co.uk
D: £16.00–£25.00 **S:** £20.00–£24.00
Beds: 1F 1D 1S **Baths:** 2 En 1 Pr
🛇 🅿 (18) ⅏ 🐾 ⅏ ⅏ 🐾 🐾
C16th Hilton Farmhouse is set in 25 acres with panoramic views of countryside and sea, heated swimming pool (80f) and jacuzzi for guests' use only.
Pub/restaurant ten minutes walk. Ideal location for making the most of Devon and Cornwall.

Floraldene, Marhamchurch, Bude, Cornwall, *EX23 0HE.*
Lovely and peaceful character cottage in picturesque village of Marhamchurch.
Open: All Year (not Xmas)
01288 361118 Mrs Sibley
D: £12.00–£16.00 **S:** £16.00–£18.00
Beds: 2D 1T **Baths:** 1 En
🛇 🅿 (2) ⅏ ⅏ 🐾

Mawnan Smith

SW7728   ◫ Red Lion Inn, Ferry Boat Inn

Carwinion Vean, Grove Hill, Mawnan Smith, Falmouth, Cornwall, *TR11 5ER.*
Lovely country house near beautiful Helford River, gardens, coastal footpaths and beaches.
Open: All Year (not Xmas)
01326 250513 Mrs Spike
D: £20.00–£23.00 **S:** £20.00–£25.00
Beds: 1F 3D 2T **Baths:** 2 En 2 Sh
🛇 (5) 🅿 (6) ⅏ 🐾 ⅏ ⅏ 🐾

The White House, 28 Castle View Park, Mawnan Smith, Falmouth, Cornwall, *TR11 5HB.*
Friendly family guest house near village centre and easy access from coast.
Open: All Year
01326 250768 Mrs Grant
D: £18.00–£20.00 **S:** £20.00–£25.00
Beds: 1F 1D 1T 1S **Baths:** 1 En 1 Sh
🛇 🅿 (2) ⅏ ✕ ⅏ ⅏ 🐾

Maxworthy

SX2592   ◫ Treetops

Wheatley Farm, Maxworthy, Launceston, Cornwall, *PL15 8LY.*
Country farmhouse. Superb food, near coast, every comfort. Perfect holiday.
Open: Easter to Oct
01566 781232 (also fax)
Mrs Griffin
wheatley@farming.co.uk
D: £18.00–£23.00 **S:** £23.00–£25.00
Beds: 1F 3D 1T **Baths:** 5 En
🛇 🅿 (5) ⅏ ⅏ ⅏ ⅏ cc

Mevagissey

SX0145

Mevagissey House, Vicarage Hill, Mevagissey, St Austell, *PL26 6SZ.*
Peaceful Georgian house in three acres, close to Eden Project.
Open: March to October
01726 842427 Mrs Dodds
Fax: 01726 844327
D: £20.00–£25.00 **S:** £30.00–£35.00
Beds: 1F 1T 1D **Baths:** 3 En
🛇 🅿 (8) ⅏ 🐾 ⅏ 🐾

Kerryanna, Valley Road, Mevagissey, St Austell, Cornwall, *PL26 6RZ.*
Stunning position overlooking village close to Heligan and Eden.
Open: Easter to Oct
Grades: ETC 4 Diamond, AA 4 Diamond
01726 843558 (also fax)
Mr Hennah
linda.hennah@talk21.com
D: £24.00–£27.00
Beds: 1F 1T 4D **Baths:** 6 En
🛇 (5) 🅿 (6) ⅏ ✕ ⅏ 🐾 cc

Morwenstow

SS2015   ◫ London, New Inn

Meadow Park, Lee Barton, Morwenstow, Bude, Cornwall, *EX23 9ST.*
Superb views on family farm. Traditional farmhouse cooking, friendly atmosphere.
Open: Mar to Nov
01288 331499 Mrs Hobbs
D: £16.50–£17.50 **S:** £16.50–£18.00
Beds: 1F 1D 1S **Baths:** 1 Pr
🛇 🅿 (4) ⅏ ✕ ⅏ ⅏ 🐾

East Woolley Farm, Woolley, Bude, Cornwall, *EX23 9PP.*
Peaceful dairy farm, barn conversion rooms. Breakfast in farmhouse.
Open: All Year
Grades: ETC 3 Diamond
01288 331525 (also fax)
Mrs Dauncey
D: £19.00–£22.00 **S:** £24.00–£27.00
Beds: 3D **Baths:** 3 En
🛇 🅿 (4) ⅏ ⅏ ⅏ 🐾

Mount Edgcumbe

SX4552

Friary Manor Hotel, Maker Heights, Mount Edgcumbe, Millbrook, Torpoint, Cornwall, *PL10 1JB.*
C17th former Vicarage. Close to sea and smugglers villages.
Open: All Year
Grades: ETC 3 Cr, Comm
01752 822112 Mr & Mrs Bartlett
Fax: 01752 822804
106220.3641@compuserve.com
D: £22.50–£29.00 **S:** £35.00–£41.50
Beds: 3F 3D 3T 2S **Baths:** 6 En 1 Pr
🛇 🅿 (25) ⅏ 🐾 ✕ ⅏ ⅏ 🐾 cc

Mousehole

SW4626

Carn Du Hotel, Mousehole, Penzance, Cornwall, *TR19 6SS.*
Peaceful comfortable hotel. Superb views, food, accommodation overlooking Mounts Bay. **Open:** All Year
01736 731233 (also fax) Mr Field
D: £25.00–£35.00 **S:** £35.00–£45.00
Beds: 4D 3T **Baths:** 6 En 1 Pr
🛇 🅿 (12) ⅏ ✕ ⅏ ⅏ 🐾 cc

Mullion

SW6719   ◫ Old Inn, Mounts Bay Inn, Black Swan, Hazlephron Inn

Meaver Farm, Mullion, Helston, Cornwall, *TR12 7DN.*
Open: All Year
Grades: ETC 4 Diamond, Silver Award
01326 240128 J Stanland
Fax: 01326 240011 spinthree@aol.com
D: £22.50–£25.00 **S:** £25.00–£30.00
Beds: 1T 2D **Baths:** 3 En
🅿 (3) ⅏ ⅏ 🐾 🐾
300 year old former farmhouse in quiet valley on beautiful Lizard Peninsula. Spectacular coastline and romantic Helford River nearby. Exposed beams, log fire, luxury bathrooms, Aga breakfasts. A warm welcome awaits you. Come and unwind - let Cornwall work its magic - wonderful any time of year.

Campden House, *The Commons, Mullion, Helston, Cornwall, TR12 7HZ.*
One acre of gardens. Home-grown vegetables when in season.
Open: All Year (not Xmas) Mr & Mrs Hyde
D: £15.50–£16.50 **S:** £15.50–£16.50
Beds: 2F 5D 1T 2S **Baths:** 2 Sh
⌂ **P** (9) 📺 🍴 ✕ Ⓥ ♨

Tregaddra Farmhouse, *Cury, Helston, Cornwall, TR12 7BB.*
Open: All Year (not Xmas)
Grades: ETC 4 Diamond
01326 240235 (also fax)
Mrs Lugg
D: £20.00–£25.00 **S:** £20.00–£25.00
Beds: 2F 4D 1T **Baths:** 6 En 1 Pr
⌂ **P** (10) ⅄ 📺 ✕ Ⓥ ♨ **cc**
Farmhouse B&B quiet, peaceful, set in Area of Outstanding Natural Beauty. Coastal path just 3 miles. Ensuite bedrooms with television. Magnificent views, tennis court, swimming pool, open log fires, Aga cooking and relaxed family atmosphere. Groups welcome.

Mullion Cove

SW6617 🍺 *Ridgeback Hotel*

Criggan Mill, *Mullion Cove, Helston, Cornwall, TR12 7EU.*
Timber Lodges 200 yards from fishing harbour and coastal footpath.
Open: Easter to Oct
01326 240496 Mr Bolton
Fax: 0870 1640549
info@criggan-mill.co.uk
D: £17.00–£22.00 **S:** £20.00–£25.00
Beds: 5F 6D 4T **Baths:** 3 En
⌂ (1) **P** 📺 🍴 ✕ ♨ **cc**

Newquay

SW8161 🍺 *The Fort, Godolphin Arms, Red Lion, Olde Dolphin,Chy An Mor Inn, Great Western*

Chichester Guest House, *14 Bay View Terrace, Newquay, Cornwall, TR7 2LR.*
Good coffee, we provide walking, mineral collecting and archaeology weeks.
Open: Mar to Nov
Grades: ETC 3 Diamond
01637 874216 Miss Harper
sheila.harper@virgin.net
D: £16.50 **S:** £16.50
Beds: 2F 2D 2T 1S **Baths:** 2 Sh
⌂ (2) **P** (6) ✕ Ⅲ ♨

The Croft Hotel, *37 Mount Wise, Newquay, Cornwall, TR7 2BL.*
Ideally situated close to beaches, pubs and clubs, coach and rail stations.
Open: All Year (not Xmas)
01637 871520 L Duffin
D: £14.00–£25.00 **S:** £20.00–£40.00
Beds: 4F 2T 2D **Baths:** 4 En 2 Pr 1 Sh
⌂ **P** ⅄ 📺 ✕ Ⅲ Ⓥ ♨ **cc**

Alicia, *136 Henver Road, Newquay, Cornwall, TR7 3EQ.*
Guaranteed to take your breath away. Soaring Cliffs, sheltered Coves.
Open: All Year
01637 874328 Mrs Limer
D: £15.00–£25.00 **S:** £20.00–£27.50
Beds: 2F 2D 1T 1S **Baths:** 2 En 3 Sh
⌂ **P** (6) ⅄ 📺 🍴 ✕ Ⅲ Ⓥ ♨

Pengilley, *12 Trebarwith Crescent, Newquay, Cornwall, TR7 1DX.*
Open: All Year
01637 872039 jan@pengilley-guesthouse.com
D: £15.00–£23.00 **S:** £15.00–£25.00
Beds: 2F 2D 1T 1S **Baths:** 4 En 2 Sh
⌂ (5) 📺 Ⅲ ✕ Ⓥ ♨
A friendly atmosphere awaits you at Pengilley, one minute from town, beach, close to shops and Newquay's famous nightlife and restaurants. For those wishing to try surfing, an introduction to Newquay's coolest surf school - West Coast Surfari.

Cotehele Lodge, *84 Tower Road, Newquay, Cornwall, TR7 1LY.*
Close to all beaches. Also town centre. Car park. Ensuite rooms.
Open: All Year (not Xmas)
01637 873421 Mrs Drysdale
D: £16.00–£22.00 **S:** £25.00–£35.00
Beds: 2F 4D **Baths:** 4 En 2 Sh
⌂ (4) ⅄ 📺 ✕ Ⅲ Ⓥ ♨

Padstow

SW9175 🍺 *Golden Lion, Old Customs House, London Inn, Ring of Bells*

Trevorrick Farm, *St Issey, Wadebridge, Cornwall, PL27 7QH.*
Near Camel Trail and Padstow, centrally situated in North Cornwall for touring.
Open: All Year (not Xmas)
Grades: ETC 3 Diamond
01841 540574 (also fax) Mr Mealing
D: £18.00–£25.00 **S:** £27.00–£36.00
Beds: 1F 1D 1T **Baths:** 3 En
⌂ **P** (6) ⅄ 📺 🍴 Ⅲ Ⓥ ♨ **cc**

Hemingford House, *21 Grenville Road, Padstow, Cornwall, PL28 8EX.*
Comfortable relaxed style. Hearty breakfast. 10 minutes walk to harbour. Welcome. **Open:** All Year
01841 532806 (also fax) Mr Tamblin
peter@ptamblin.freeserve.co.uk
D: £22.50–£27.50 **S:** £25.00–£30.00
Beds: 1T 2D **Baths:** 1 En 1 Pr 1 Sh
⌂ (12) **P** (1) ⅄ 📺 🍴 Ⅲ Ⓥ ♨

Mother Ivey Cottage, *Trevose Head, Padstow, Cornwall, PL28 8SL.*
Open: Easter to Oct
01841 520329 (also fax)
Mrs Woosnam Mills
woosnammills@compuserve.com
D: fr £22.50 **S:** fr £25.00
Beds: 2T **Baths:** 2 En
⌂ (6) **P** 📺 🍴 ✕ Ⓥ ♨
Traditionally-built Cornish clifftop house with stunning sea views, overlooking Trevose Head with a beach below. The area is renowned for swimming, fishing, surfing and walking. A championship golf course - Trevose - is nearby. The Cornwall Coastal Path is adjacent.

Khandalla, *Sarahs Lane, Padstow, Cornwall, PL28 8EL.*
Traditional bed and breakfast in elegant surroundings with estuary views.
Open: All Year 01841 532961 Mrs Hair
lisahair@khandalla.freeserve.co.uk
D: £20.00–£25.00 **S:** £30.00–£40.00
Beds: 1D 1S **Baths:** 2 En 1 Sh
⌂ **P** (3) ⅄ 📺 🍴 Ⅲ Ⓥ ✽ ♨

Althea Library B&B, *27 High Street, Padstow, Cornwall, PL28 8BB.*
Converted library, short walk from harbour, old part of town.
Open: All Year (not Xmas)
Grades: ETC 4 Diamond, Silver Award
01841 532717
D: £24.00–£30.00 **S:** £27.00–£60.00
Beds: 2D 1T **Baths:** 3 En
P (3) ⅄ 📺 Ⅲ Ⓥ ♨ **cc**

Par

SX0753

Hidden Valley Gardens, *Treesmill, Par, Cornwall, PL24 2TU.*
Secluded location. Near Eden Project and Fowey, in own grounds.
Open: All Year
01208 873225
D: £20.00–£22.00 **S:** £22.00–£24.00
Beds: 2D **Baths:** 2 En
P (7) ⅄ Ⅲ ♨

Paul

SW4527 🍺 *Kings Arms*

Kerris Farm, *Paul, Penzance, Cornwall, TR19 6UY.*
Peaceful dairy farm, rural views, central to Minack Theatre, St Ives.
Open: Easter to Oct
01736 731309
susangiles@btconnect.com
D: £15.00–£20.00 **S:** £16.00–£18.00
Beds: 1F 1D 1T **Baths:** 1 En 1 Sh
⌂ **P** (4) 📺 ✕ Ⓥ ♨

Pelynt

SX2055 🍺 *Jubilee Inn*

Talehay, *Tremaine, Pelynt, Looe, Cornwall, PL13 2LT.*
Open: All year
01503 220252 (also fax)
Mr & Mrs Brumpton
pr.brumpton@ukonline.co.uk
D: £20.00–£23.00 **S:** £30.00
Beds: 1F 1D 1T **Baths:** 3 En
⌂ **P** (12) ⅄ 📺 🍴 Ⅲ Ⓥ ♨
Charming C17th former farmstead. Large ensuite rooms with beautiful views. A quiet haven with countryside/coastal walks nearby. Delicious breakfasts served with our own free range eggs and home-made marmalade. An ideal comfortable base for exploring the delights of Cornwall.

Pendeen

SW3834 🍺 *North Inn*

The Old Count House, *Boscaswell Downs, Pendeen, Penzance, Cornwall, TR19 7ED.*
Old granite house in quiet village, on the dramatic North Coast.
Open: Easter to Oct
01736 788058
Mrs Dymond
D: £16.00–£18.00
S: £16.00–£18.00
Beds: 2D **Baths:** 1 Sh
⌂ (2) **P** (4) 📺 Ⅲ Ⓥ ♨

Quiddles, Boscaswell Downs, Pendeen, Penzance, Cornwall, TR19 7DW.
Beautiful 200-year-old granite house, 1 mile from North Coast Path.
Open: All year (not Xmas)
01736 787278 Ms Bailey
D: £12.00–£19.00 **S:** £12.00–£19.00
Beds: 1F 1D 1T **Baths:** 1 En 1 Sh
🛇 P (6) 🖵 ✕ Ⓥ ⚓

Manor Farm, Pendeen, Penzance, Cornwall, TR19 7ED.
A rare opportunity to visit a beautiful Grade I Listed building on Granite Coast.
Open: All Year
01736 788753 (also fax)
Ms Davey
D: £18.00–£20.00
Beds: 1F 3D 1T **Baths:** 1 En 1 Pr 1 Sh
🛇 P 🖵 ✝ 🏛 Ⓥ ⚓

Pensilva

SX2969

Wheal Tor Hotel, Caradon Hill, Pensilva, Liskeard, Cornwall, PL14 5PJ.
Highest inn in Cornwall. Set in rugged Bodmin moor location.
Open: All Year
01579 362281 Mr & Mrs Chapman
Fax: 01579 363401
pdc@whealtorhotel.freeserve.co.uk
D: £22.50–£27.50 **S:** £30.00–£32.50
Beds: 1F 2T 3D **Baths:** 4 En 2 Sh
🖵 ✝ 🏛 Ⓥ ⚓ & cc

Pentewan

SX0147 ⚓ *Ship Inn*

Piskey Cove, The Square, Pentewan, St Austell, Cornwall, PL26 6DA.
Open: All Year (not Xmas/New Year)
01726 843781 (also fax) Ms Avery
gillian@averya.freeserve.co.uk
D: £22.50–£35.00 **S:** £22.50–£30.00
Beds: 1F 2T 3D **Baths:** 3 En 1 Pr
🛇 P (1) 🖵 ✝ ✕ Ⓥ ⚓ cc
Close to 'The Eden Project' and Heligan Gardens. Family run and situated in peaceful, pretty coastal village. Ideal base for cosy winter, refreshing spring, British summer and beautiful autumn breaks, to visit Cornwall's sites. Complimentary and sports therapy in house.

Penzance

SW4630 ⚓ *Bosun's Locker, Turk's Head, The Coalstreamer, Dolphin & Neptune, The Lugger, Union Hotel, White Hart, Admiral Benbow, Mounts Bay, Olde Bush Inn, Tarbert Hotel, Long Boat, Yacht Inn*

Lynwood Guest House, 41 Morrab Road, Penzance, Cornwall, TR18 4EX.
Open: All Year
Grades: RAC 3 Diamond
01736 365871 (also fax) Mrs Stacey
Lynwoodpz@aol.com
D: £13.50–£17.50 **S:** £12.50–£16.50
Beds: 6F 2D 2T 2S **Baths:** 4 En 2 Pr 2 Sh
🛇 (5) 🖵 ✝ 🏛 Ⓥ ⚓ cc
Family-run Victorian guest house. Internationally recommended for good food, cleanliness. Close to all amenities. Ideally situated for visiting Land's End and St Michael's Mount.

Glencree Private Hotel, 2 Mennaye Road, Penzance, Cornwall, TR18 4NG.
Open: Mar to Oct **Grades:** ETC 3 Diamond
01736 362026 (also fax) Mr Hodgetts
D: £16.00–£20.00 **S:** £19.00–£22.00
Beds: 2F 4D 1T 2S **Baths:** 7 En 2 Sh
🛇 (5) 🖵 ✝ ✕ 🏛 Ⓥ ⚓ cc
A charming Victorian house in a quiet road 100 yards off seafront. Spacious rooms, some with sea views and some with four poster beds. Highly recommended for its comfort, cleanliness, excellent food & friendly personal service. Town centre 10 minutes walk.

Chy an Gof Guest House, 10 Regent Terrace, Penzance, Cornwall, TR18 4DW.
Listed Regency house overlooking Penzance promenade and the lovely Mount's Bay **Open:** All Year
01736 332361 (also fax)
Mr & Mrs Schofield
scholfield@callnetuk.com
D: £22.00 **S:** £22.00
Beds: 2T 2S **Baths:** 4 En
P (4) 🖵 🏛 Ⓥ ⚓

Carnson House Private Hotel, East Terrace, Market Jew Street, Penzance, Cornwall, TR18 2TD.
Centrally located, friendly, small hotel near station and harbour. **Open:** All Year
01736 365589 Mr & Mrs Smyth
Fax: 01736 365594
carnson@netcomuk.co.uk
D: £24.00–£24.50 **S:** fr £20.00
Beds: 3D 2T 2S **Baths:** 2 Pr 1 Sh
🛇 (12) 🖵 🖵 Ⓥ ⚓

Mount Royal Hotel, Chyandour Cliff, Penzance, Cornwall, TR18 3LQ.
Small family-run hotel facing the sea & overlooking the entrance of Penzance harbour.
Open: March-Oct
Grades: AA 3 Diamond, RAC 3 Diamond
01736 362233 (also fax) Mr Cox
mountroyal@talk21.com
D: £22.50–£27.50 **S:** £25.00–£27.50
Beds: 3F 3D 2T **Baths:** 5 En 2 Sh
🛇 (1) 🖵 (10) 🖵 🖵 🏛 Ⓥ ⚓

Pendennis Hotel, Alexandra Road, Penzance, Cornwall, TR18.
Victorian licensed hotel built in 1830 in a quiet tree lined residential area.
Open: All Year
Grades: AA 3 Diamond
01736 363823 (also fax)
Mrs Cook
ray@pendennishotel.compuserve.net
D: £15.00–£22.00 **S:** £15.00–£22.00
Beds: 5F 2D **Baths:** 7 En 1 Sh
🛇 🖵 ✝ ✕ 🏛 Ⓥ ⚓ cc

Woodstock Guest House, 29 Morrab Road, Penzance, Cornwall, TR18 4EZ.
Central Penzance. Ideal for touring and visiting the Lands End Peninsula.
Open: All Year
Grades: ETC 3 Diamond, RAC 3 Diamond
01736 369049 (also fax)
Mr & Mrs Hopkins
woodstocp@aol.com
D: £14.00–£20.00 **S:** £14.00–£20.00
Beds: 1F 2T 3D 2S **Baths:** 4 En 1 Pr 1 Sh
🛇 P 🖵 🖵 ✝ 🏛 Ⓥ ✳ ⚓ & cc

Trewella Guest House, 18 Mennaye Road, Penzance, Cornwall, TR18 4NG.
Large Victorian house. Recommended for good food. Ideal touring centre.
Open: Mar to Oct
01736 363818 Mr & Mrs Glenn
D: £18.00–£19.00 **S:** £16.00–£23.00
Beds: 2F 4D 2S **Baths:** 6 En 1 Sh
🛇 (5) 🖵 ✕ 🏛 ⚓

Kimberley House, 10 Morrab Road, Penzance, Cornwall, TR18 4EZ.
Convenient bus and railway station. Minutes walk town and seafront.
Open: Feb to Dec
Grades: AA 3 Diamond
01736 362727 Mr & Mrs Bashford
D: £15.00–£21.00 **S:** £15.00–£18.00
Beds: 2F 2D 3T 1S **Baths:** 3 En 2 Pr 3 Sh
🛇 (5) P (3) 🖵 🏛 Ⓥ ⚓

Penalva Guest House, Alexandra Road, Penzance, Cornwall, TR18 4LZ.
Victorian guest house walking distance from sea front and town centre.
Open: All Year
Grades: AA 3 Diamond
01736 369060 (also fax) Mrs Buswell
D: £15.00–£22.00 **S:** £15.00–£22.00
Beds: 1F 2D 1T 1S **Baths:** 4 En 1 Pr
🛇 (5) 🖵 🏛 Ⓥ ⚓

Menwidden Farm, Ludgvan, Penzance, Cornwall, TR20 8BN.
Comfortable farmhouse, centrally situated in peaceful countryside. Friendly welcome guaranteed.
Open: Easter to Oct
Grades: ETC 3 Diamond
01736 740415 Mrs Quick
D: £16.50–£20.00 **S:** £16.50–£20.00
Beds: 3D 1T 1S **Baths:** 1 En 2 Sh
🛇 P (8) 🖵 ✝ ✕ ⚓

Tarbert Hotel, Clarence Street, Penzance, Cornwall, TR18 2NU.
Georgian house with an atmosphere of quality, character and charm.
Open: Feb to Dec
Grades: AA 2 Star, RAC 2 Star
01736 363758 Mrs Evans
Fax: 01736 331336
reception@tarbert-hotel.co.uk
D: £26.00–£38.00 **S:** £30.00–£38.00
Beds: 2F 7D 1T 2S
🛇 P (4) 🖵 ✕ 🏛 Ⓥ ⚓ cc

Boscreeg Guest House, 10 Mennaye Road, Penzance, Cornwall, TR18 4NG.
Family run guest house, good food, warm welcome, friendly atmosphere.
Open: All Year
01736 364067 Mrs Davies
boscreeg@yahoo.com
D: £16.00–£20.00 **S:** £18.00–£22.00
Beds: 1F 1T 1S 2D
🛇 🖵 ✝ ✕ Ⓥ ⚓

Ocean View, Chayndour Cliffe, Penzance, Cornwall, TR18 3LQ.
Charming, comfortable seafront guest house.
Open: All Year (not Xmas)
01736 351770 Mr Mayes
D: £13.00–£18.00 **S:** fr £18.00
Beds: 2D 1T **Baths:** 2 Sh
🛇 P (3) 🖵 🏛 Ⓥ ⚓ &

Keigwin Hotel, *Alexandra Road, Penzance, Cornwall, TR18 4LZ.*
Eat and sleep smoke-free. Comfortable family-run guest house, ensuite and standard rooms available.
Open: All Year
01736 363930 Mr & Mrs Flint
D: £15.00–£23.00 **S:** £15.00–£19.00
Beds: 2F 2D 2T 2S **Baths:** 5 En 3 Sh
🛏 ⅍ 📺 ✕ 🔟 🗓 ⚓ **cc**

Perranporth

SW7554 ⚭ *Bolingey Inn, Seinner's Arms, Waterfront Bar, Tywarnhayle Inn*

Tremore, *Liskey Hill Crescent, Perranporth, Cornwall, TR6 0HP.*
Open: All Year (not Xmas)
01872 573537 (also fax) Ms Crofts
tremore@totalise.co.uk
D: £19.00–£22.00 **S:** £20.00–£25.00
Beds: 3D 1T 1S **Baths:** 3 En 2 Sh
🛏 (11) 🅿 (6) ⅍ 📺 🔟 🗓 ⚓
A warm welcome awaits in our well-established and highly recommended guest house. Totally non-smoking. Special diets catered for . Off-road parking. Ideal for touring. Excellent value. Try us, you won't be disappointed.

Chy an Kerensa, *Cliff Road, Perranporth, Cornwall, TR6 0DR.*
Panoramic coastal views from lounge, bar/dining room and ensuite bedrooms. 200 metres beach.
Open: All Year
Grades: ETC 3 Diamond
01872 572470 Mrs Woodcock
D: £17.00–£24.00 **S:** £17.00–£24.00
Beds: 3F 2D 2T 2S **Baths:** 6 En 2 Sh
🛏 🅿 (4) 📺 ⅍ 🔟 🗓 ⚓

Perranuthnoe

SW5329 ⚭ *Victoria Inn*

Ednovean House, *Perranuthnoe, Penzance, Cornwall, TR20 9LZ.*
Open: All Year (not Xmas/New Year)
Grades: AA 3 Diamond
01736 711071 Mr & Mrs Whittington
D: £20.00–£27.00 **S:** £24.00–£25.00
Beds: 2T 4D 2S **Baths:** 6 En 2 Sh
🛏 (7) 🅿 (10) 📺 ⅍ 🔟 ✱ ⚓ **cc**
Beautiful 180 year old country house standing standing above Perranuthnoe village in one acre of lovely gardens. Surrounded by farmland. Stunning views across Mounts Bay, overlooking St. Michael's Mount and beyond to Penzance, Newlyn and Mousehole. Putting green and licensed bar.

Playing Place

SW8141 ⚭ *Punch Bowl And Ladle Inn*

Clestwyth, *20 Penhalls Way, Playing Place, Truro, Cornwall, TR3 6EX.*
Attractive house, tastefully furnished, peaceful mature gardens, ideal sightseeing location.
Open: All Year
Grades: ETC Approv
01872 864120 Mr Mallinson
mallinson@clestwyth.freeserve.co.uk
D: £17.50–£19.50 **S:** £21.00–£25.00
Beds: 1T 1D **Baths:** 1 En 1 Sh
🅿 (4) ⅍ 📺 🔟 🗓 ⚓

Polperro

SX2050 ⚭ *Old Mill House, Three Pilchards, Penryn House, Crumplehorn Inn*

Crumplehorn Inn, *Polperro, Cornwall, PL13 2RJ.*
Inn & watermill in quaint Cornish fishing village. B&B, S/C, 2-8.
Open: All Year
01503 272348 Andrew & Joanne Taylor
host@crumplehorn-inn.co.uk
D: £22.50–£32.50 **S:** £27.50–£60.00
Beds: 4F 3T 3D **Baths:** 10 Pr
🛏 🅿 📺 ⅍ ✕ 🔟 🗓 ✱ ⚓ **cc**

Little Tregue, *Langreek Road, Polperro, Cornwall, PL13 2PR.*
Pretty country cottage near sea and village, tranquil surroundings, great breakfasts.
Open: All Year (not Xmas/New Year)
01503 272758 (also fax)
Ms Kellaway
little-tregue@cornwall-online.co.uk
D: £15.00–£20.00 **S:** £15.00–£30.00
Beds: 1F 1T **Baths:** 2 En 1 Sh
🛏 🅿 (30) 📺 🔟 🗓 ⚓

Penryn House Hotel, *The Coombes, Polperro, Looe, Cornwall, PL13 2RQ.*
Charming Victorian hotel in village centre close to path and harbour.
Open: All Year
01503 272157 Ms Kay
Fax: 01503 273055
D: £24.00–£30.00 **S:** £32.00–£38.00
Beds: 9D 1T **Baths:** 10 En
🛏 🅿 (16) 📺 ⅍ ✕ 🔟 🗓 ⚓ **cc**

Chyavallon, *Landaviddy Lane, Polperro, Looe, Cornwall, PL13 2RT.*
Situated in central village with views towards the harbour and sea.
Open: All Year (not Xmas)
01503 272788 D: £17.00–£19.50 **S:** £20.00–£30.00
Beds: 2D 1T **Baths:** 3 En
🛏 🅿 (3) 🔟 ⅍ 🔟 🗓 ⚓

Ponsongath

SW7517

Wych Elm, *Ponsongath, Helston, Cornwall, TR12 6SQ.*
Idyllic quiet setting close secluded Lankidden Cove. Backwoodsmen's bliss!
Open: All Year (not Xmas)
01326 280576 Mrs Whitaker
D: £18.00 **S:** £20.00
Beds: 1T **Baths:** 1 En
🛏 (8) 🅿 (2) ⅍ 📺 ⅍ ✕ 🔟 🗓

Port Isaac

SW9980 ⚭ *Port Gaverne Hotel*

Bay Hotel, *1 The Terrace, Port Isaac, Cornwall, PL29 3SG.*
Small, friendly Victorian hotel overlooking bay with wonderful views.
Open: All Year
01208 880380 Mr Hawkes & J Burns
jacki-burns@talk21
D: £22.00–£29.50 **S:** £20.00–£28.00
Beds: 9F 2T 1D 6 S **Baths:** 8 En 1 Pr 1 Sh
🛏 🅿 (9) 📺 ⅍ 🔟 🗓 ⚓

Fairholme, *30 Trewetha Lane, Port Isaac, Cornwall, PL26 3RW.*
Beautiful house in historic picturesque fishing village, near coastal paths.
Open: All Year (not Xmas/New Year)
01208 880397 Mrs Von-Lintzgy
Fax: 01208 880198
paulworden@ukgateway.net
D: £17.00–£20.00 **S:** £20.00–£25.00
Beds: 2F 3D 1T **Baths:** 2 Pr 2 Sh
🛏 🅿 (6) 📺 ⅍ ✕ 🔟 🗓 ⚓

Porthleven

SW6225 ⚭ *Atlantic Inn, Ship Inn, Harbour Inn*

Seefar, *Peverell Terrace, Porthleven, Helston, Cornwall, TR13 9DZ.*
Traditional Cornish Victorian mine captain's house, overlooking sea.
Open: Mar to Nov
Grades: ETC 3 Diamond
01326 573778 Mr & Mrs Hallam
seefar@talk21.com
D: £16.00–£21.00 **S:** £15.00–£16.00
Beds: 2D 1T 1S **Baths:** 2 En 1 Pr 1 Sh
🛏 🅿 (1) ⅍ 📺 ⅍ 🔟 🗓 ⚓

Greystones, *40 West End, Porthleven, Helston, Cornwall, TR13 9JL.*
Overlooking sea. Close, harbour/beach/shops/restaurants/pubs. Dogs welcome.
Open: All Year (not Xmas)
01326 565583 (also fax) Mrs Woodward
D: £15.00–£20.00 **S:** £20.00–£25.00
Beds: 1F 1D 1S **Baths:** 1 Sh
🛏 📺 ⅍ 🗓 ⚓

Pentre House, *Peverell Terrace, Porthleven, Helston, Cornwall, TR13 9DZ.*
Spectacular sea views, delightful village, home-baked bread. Highly recommended.
Open: Easter to Oct
01326 574493 Mrs Cookson
pentre@eurobell.co.uk
D: £16.50–£17.50
Beds: 1D 1T 2S **Baths:** 1 Sh
🛏 📺 ⅍ 🔟 🗓 ⚓

Porthtowan

SW6847 ⚭ *Commodore Inn*

Buzby View, *Forthvean Road, Porthtowan, Truro, Cornwall, TR4 8AY.*
Large, modern, detached, dormer bungalow set in beautiful secluded gardens.
Open: Easter to Oct
01209 891178 (also fax) Mrs Parkinson
buzbyview@freenet.co.uk
D: fr £18.00 **S:** fr £18.00
Beds: 2D 1T 1S **Baths:** 1 Sh
🛏 (12) 🅿 (6) ⅍ 📺 🔟 🗓

Portloe

SW9339

Pine Cottage, *Portloe, Truro, Cornwall, TR2 5QU.*
Friendly welcome, peaceful fishing village, fish restaurant, home cooking.
Open: Easter to Oct
01872 501385
Mrs Holdsworth
D: £22.00 **S:** £22.00
Beds: 1D 1T **Baths:** 1 En 1 Pr
⅍ ✕ 📺

Portreath

SW6545   🍺 *Bassett Arms, Waterfront Inn, Portreath Arms*

Fountain Springs, Glenfeadon House, Portreath, Redruth, Cornwall, TR16 4JU.
Listed Georgian house. Peaceful valley. Gardens, aviary, wooded/cliff walks.
Open: Feb to Dec
01209 842650 (also fax)
A Keast
D: £18.50–£20.00 **S:** £20.00–£25.00
Beds: 3F 1D 2T 1S **Baths:** 5 En 1 Sh
🛏 🅿 (12) ⅟ 📺 🖳 🛆 ♿

Cliff House, The Square, Portreath, Redruth, Cornwall, TR16 4LB.
200-year-old whitewashed cottage; clean and comfortable.
Open: All Year (not Xmas)
01209 842008 Mrs Healan
D: £17.50–£20.00 **S:** £20.00–£25.00
Beds: 1D 1T 2S **Baths:** 2 En 2 Pr
🛏 (7) 🅿 (4) 📺 🖳 🛆

Bensons, 1 The Hillside, Portreath, Redruth, Cornwall, TR16 4LL.
Beautiful accommodation - panoramic sea views - quiet, warm, friendly and comfortable.
Open: Easter to Sept
Grades: AA 4 Diamond
01209 842534 Mr & Mrs Smythe
Fax: 01209 843578
D: £20.00 **S:** £25.00
Beds: 2D 2S **Baths:** 4 En
🛏 🅿 (6) ⅟ 📺 🖳 🛆

Portscatho

SW8735   🍺 *Plume of Feathers, The Boat House*

Hillside House, 8 The Square, Portscatho, Truro, Cornwall, TR2 5HW.
Open: All Year
01872 580526 Mrs Hart
Fax: 01872 580527
D: £17.50–£20.00
S: £17.50–£20.00
Beds: 1F 2D 1T
Baths: 1 Pr 2 Sh
🛏 🅿 (2) 📺 🍴 🖳 🛒 🛆
Charming Georgian house in centre of unspoilt picturesque fishing village. Beaches, harbour, coastal path only yards away. Comfortable bedrooms, loads of hot water, excellent Aga cooking. Children, dogs and walkers welcome. Those choosing to visit will find a special place.

Poughill

SS2207   🍺 *Preston Gate*

Lower Northcott Farm, Poughill, Bude, Cornwall, EX23 7EL.
Georgian farmhouse with outstanding views. Ideal for walking/touring holiday.
Open: All Year
Grades: ETC 3 Diamond, AA 3 Diamond
01288 352350 Mrs Trewin
Fax: 01288 352712
sally@coast-countryside.co.uk
D: £20.00–£22.00 **S:** £20.00–£25.00
Beds: 1F 2D 1T 1S **Baths:** 4 En 1 Pr
🛏 🅿 (4) ⅟ 📺 🍴 🛒 🖳 🛆

Redruth

SW6942   🍺 *Lanner Inn*

Lyndhurst Guest House, 80 Agar Road, Redruth, Cornwall, TR15 3NB.
Comfortable spacious house, friendly welcome. Close to Cornish History and beaches.
Open: All Year
Grades: RAC 2 Diamond
01209 215146 M Smith-Potter
Fax: 01209 313625
sales@lyndhurst-guesthouse.net
D: £18.00–£20.00 **S:** £16.00–£20.00
Beds: 1F 1D 3S **Baths:** 4 En 1 Sh
🛏 🅿 (6) 📺 ✕ 🖳 🛆 ♿

Lansdowne House, 42 Clinton Road, Redruth, Cornwall, TR15 2QE.
Architecturally interesting house with castellated tower and spire. 5 minute shops/rail/coach.
Open: All Year
01209 216002 (also fax)
Mrs Kilpatrick
D: £18.00–£25.00 **S:** £18.00–£25.00
Beds: 2F 2D 2T 2S **Baths:** 2 En 2 Sh
🛏 🅿 (6) ⅟ 📺 ✕ 🖳 ♿ 🛆

Rescorla

SW9848   🍺 *Bugle Inn*

Yazumez, Rescorla, St Austell, Cornwall, PL26 8YT.
Dormer bungalow near Eden Project, beaches, moors, countryside. Central location.
Open: All Year
01726 852043 (also fax)
D: £15.00 **S:** £15.00
Beds: 1F 2D **Baths:** 2 En 1 Pr
🛏 🅿 (3) 📺 🍴 ✕ 🖳 ♿ 🛆

Rock

SW9476   🍺 *Roskarnon House*

Silvermead, Rock, Wadebridge, Cornwall, PL27 6LB.
Open: All Year
Grades: ETC 3 Diamond, AA 3 Diamond
01208 862425 Mrs Martin
Fax: 01208 862919
D: £20.00–£26.00
S: £20.00–£45.00
Beds: 2F 3D 2T 2S
Baths: 6 En 1 Sh
🛏 🅿 (9) 📺 🍴 ✕ 🖳 ♿ 🛆
Ten-bedroom family-run guest house overlooking Camel Estuary, adjoining St Enodoc golf courses. 2 minutes' walk to beach, sailing club. Most rooms ensuite. Licensed.

Roskarnon House Hotel, Rock, Wadebridge, Cornwall, PL27 6LD.
Edwardian hotel, overlooking estuary, 100 metres from ferry to Padstow.
Open: Mar to Oct
Grades: ETC 3 Diamond, AA 3 Diamond, RAC 3 Diamond
01208 862785 Mr Veall
D: £25.00–£35.00 **S:** £30.00–£40.00
Beds: 2F 4D 4T 2S
Baths: 10 En 1 Sh
🛏 (5) 🅿 (14) ⅟ 📺 🍴 ✕ 🖳 ♿ 🛆 ♿

Tzitzikama Lodge,

Rock Road, Rock, Wadebridge, Cornwall, PL27 6NP.
Stylish accommodation near the Camel Estuary and the North Cornish coast.
Open: All Year (not Xmas)
01208 862839 Mr Cox & Alison Jones
tzitzikama.stilwell@btinternet.com
D: £22.00–£27.00 **S:** £32.00–£37.00
Beds: 1F 1D 1T **Baths:** 3 En
🛏 🅿 ⅟ 📺 🍴 🖳 🛆 cc

Row

SX0976

Tarny Guest House, Row, St Breward, Bodmin, Cornwall, PL30 4LW.
Warm welcome, large luxury rooms, magnificent views, acres of private gardens with woodside waterfalls.
Open: All Year (not Xmas)
01208 850583 Mrs Turner
D: £17.00–£22.00 **S:** £18.00–£25.00
Beds: 2F 1D 1T **Baths:** 2 En 1 Sh
🛏 🅿 (8) ⅟ 📺 🖳 🛆

Ruan High Lanes

SW9039   🍺 *King's Head, Roseland Inn*

Trenona Farm, Ruan High Lanes, Truro, Cornwall, TR2 5JS.
Victorian farmhouse on mixed working farm. Enjoy our Cornish hospitality.
Open: March to Oct
01872 501339 (also fax) Mrs Carbis
pcarbis@compuserve.com
D: £15.00–£20.00 **S:** £15.00–£20.00
Beds: 4F **Baths:** 2 En 2 Sh
🛏 🅿 (6) ⅟ 📺 🍴 🖳 🛆

Saltash

SX4259   🍺 *Boatman Inn, Notter Inn*

The Old Cottage, Barkers Hill, St Stephens, Saltash, Cornwall, PL12 4QA.
Charming old beamed cottage, hearty breakfasts. **Open:** All Year (not Xmas)
01752 845260 Mrs Plant
roger.plant@virgin.net
D: £14.50 **S:** £14.50
Beds: 1D 2S **Baths:** 1 Sh
🛏 🅿 (2) ⅟ 🖳 🛆

Mill Park House, Pill, Saltash, Cornwall, PL12 6LQ.
Non-working farmhouse, country setting, Cornwall Tourist Board registered.
Open: All Year (not Xmas)
01752 843234 Mrs Wadge
mikedebkatem@yahoo.co.uk
D: £15.00 **S:** £16.00
Beds: 1F 1T **Baths:** 1 Sh
🛏 🅿 (2) 🖳 🛆

Sennen

SW3525   🍺 *Sunny Bank*

Sunny Bank Hotel, Seaview Hill, Sennen, Lands End, Penzance, Cornwall, TR19 7AR.
Comfortable detached hotel, close beaches, Minack Theatre, good food, licensed. **Open:** Jan to Nov
01736 871278 Mr & Mrs Comber
D: £15.00–£20.00 **S:** £15.00–£25.00
Beds: 2F 5D 2T 2S **Baths:** 2 Sh
🛏 🅿 (15) 📺 ✕ 🖳 🛆 🛆

Sheviock

SX3755 ◀ *Finnygook Inn*

Sheviock Barton, *Sheviock, Torpoint, Cornwall, PL11 3EH.*
Beautifully restored 300-year-old farmhouse. Guests' sitting room.
Open: all year (not Xmas)
01503 230793 (also fax)
Mr Johnson
thebarton@sheviock.freeserve.co.uk
D: £20.00 **S:** £25.00
Beds: 1F 2D **Baths:** 2 En 1 Pr
🛏 🅿 (10) ⅍ 📺 🛏 🛲 Ⅴ ♨

Sithney

SW6328

Parc-An-Ithan, *Sithney, Helston, Cornwall, TR13 0RN.*
Quiet, country hotel in 3/4 acre garden. Beautiful rural views.
Open: Feb to Nov
01326 572565 (also fax)
Mr Channing
parc@dircon.co.uk
D: £20.00–£23.00 **S:** £20.00–£25.00
Beds: 1F 4D 1T **Baths:** 6 En
🛏 🅿 (14) 📺 ✕ 🛲 Ⅴ ♨ ♨

South Petherwin

SX3181 ◀ *Elliott Arms*

Oakside, *South Petherwin, Launceston, Cornwall, PL15 7LJ.*
Panoramic views of Bodmin Moor and a warm welcome awaits. Farm bungalow.
Open: Easter to Nov
01566 86733 Mrs Crossman
D: £16.00–£20.00 **S:** £16.00–£20.00
Beds: 1F 1D 1T **Baths:** 1 En 1 Sh
🛏 (2) 🅿 (4) ⅍ 📺 🛲 ♨ ♿

St Austell

SX0252 ◀ *Britannia Inn, Polgooth Inn, Western Inn*

Restineas Cottage, *Garker, St Austell, Cornwall, PL26 8YA.*
Open: All Year (not Xmas/New Year)
01726 812171 (also fax)
Mrs Sampson
D: £20.00–£25.00 **S:** £30.00–£35.00
Beds: 1D **Baths:** 1 Pr
🅿 (1) ⅍ 📺 ✕ 🛲 ♨
Country cottage set in two acre garden and grounds. Peaceful surroundings. Only two miles to main road for access to South Cornwall coast and within fifteen minutes walking distance to new 'Eden Project' via Cornish Way Cycle/Foot Path. Private lounge.

Crossways, *6 Cromwell Road, St Austell, Cornwall, PL25 4PS.*
Beaches, golf, Heligan, Eden Project, coastal walks nearby. Contractor welcome.
Open: All Year
01726 71436 Mrs Nancarrow
Fax: 01726 66877
D: £16.00–£25.00 **S:** £22.00–£26.00
Beds: 2F 2D 1T 1S **Baths:** 1 En 1 Sh
🅿 ⅍ 📺 🛲 ♨

Cornerways Guest House,
Penwinnick Road, St Austell, Cornwall, PL25 5DS.
Cornerways stands in its own grounds surrounded by garden/ large car park.
Open: All Year
01726 61579 B J Edwards
Fax: 01726 66871
nwsurveys@aol.com
D: £16.50–£19.00 **S:** £16.50–£22.50
Beds: 1F 1T 1S **Baths:** 2 En 1Shared
🅿 (10) 📺 🛏 🛲 Ⅴ ♨

Poltarrow Farm, *St Mewan, St Austell, Cornwall, PL26 7DR.*
Open: All Year (not Xmas/New Year)
01726 67111 (also fax)
Mrs Nancarrow
enquire@poltarrow.co.uk
D: £23.00–£29.00 **S:** £28.00–£30.00
Beds: 1F 3D 1T **Baths:** 4 En 1 Pr
🛏 🅿 (10) 📺 🛲 Ⅴ ♨ cc
The charming farmhouse at Poltarrow, with pretty ensuite rooms, delicious breakfast and all year indoor swimming pool. Can be the perfect place to stay any time of year. Secluded, yet central for beaches, gardens and the exciting Eden Project.

St Blazey

SX0655

Nanscawen Manor House, *Prideaux Road, St Blazey, Par, Cornwall, PL24 2SR.*
Lovely Georgian home; peaceful countryside. 3 ensuite bedrooms, swimming pool.
Open: All Year
Grades: AA 5 Diamond
01726 814488 (also fax)
Mr & Mrs Martin
keith@nanscawen.com
D: £25.00–£42.00
S: £45.00–£57.00
Beds: 2D 1T **Baths:** 3 En
🛏 (12) 🅿 (8) ⅍ 📺 🛲 Ⅴ ♨ cc

St Breward

SX0977 ◀ *The Old Inn*

Treswallock Farm, *St Breward, Bodmin, Cornwall, PL30 4PL.*
Beef and sheep farm on peaceful location of Bodmin Moor.
Open: May to Oct
01208 850255 (also fax)
D: £17.50 **S:** £18.00
Beds: 1D 1S **Baths:** 1 Sh
🛏 🅿 ⅍ 📺 🛏 🛲 ♨

St Dennis

SW9558

Boscawen Hotel, *Foe Street, St Dennis, St Austell, Cornwall, PL26 8AD.*
Easy access north and south coast, near Cornwall's Eden Project.
Open: All Year
01726 822275
K Mason
D: £17.50–£25.00 **S:** £15.00–£20.00
Beds: 1F 1T 1D 1S **Baths:** 1 En 2 Sh
🅿 ⅍ 📺 🛏 ✕ 🛲 Ⅴ ♨

St Erme

SW8449 ◀ *Wheel Inn*

Trevispian Vean Farm Guest House, *St Erme, Truro, Cornwall, TR4 9BL.*
300 year old working farm - family run - lovely views of Cornish countryside.
Open: Feb to Nov
Grades: ETC 4 Diamond, AA 4 Diamond, RAC 4 Diamond
01872 279514 Mr & Mrs Dymond
Fax: 01872 263730
D: £18.50 **S:** £24.00
Beds: 2F 5D 2T **Baths:** 9 Pr
🛏 🅿 (12) ⅍ 📺 Ⅴ ♨

St Erth

SW5535 ◀ *Star Inn*

Lanuthnoe Barns, *St Erth Hill, St Erth, Hayle, Cornwall, TR27 6HX.*
Picturesque converted barn, peaceful village location yet 1.5 miles to sea.
Open: All Year
01736 755529 Mrs Crutchfield
D: £18.00
Beds: 1F 1D **Baths:** 1 Pr
🛏 🅿 (4) 📺 🛏 ✕ 🛲 ♨ ♨ ♿

St Ewe

SW9746 ◀ *Crown Inn*

Corran Farm, *St Ewe, St Austell, Cornwall, PL26 6ER.*
Quality B&B in open countryside, adjoining Heligan Gardens. Eden nearby.
Open: All Year (not Xmas)
01726 842159 Mrs Lobb
terryandkathy@corranfarm.fsnet.co.uk
D: £17.00–£19.00 **S:** £20.00–£22.00
Beds: 1T 1D **Baths:** 1 En 1 Pr
🛏 🅿 (4) ⅍ 📺 🛲 Ⅴ ♨

St Issey

SW9271 ◀ *Ring of Bells*

Trevorrick Farm, *St Issey, Wadebridge, Cornwall, PL27 7QH.*
Near Camel Trail and Padstow, centrally situated in North Cornwall for touring.
Open: All Year (not Xmas)
Grades: ETC 3 Diamond
01841 540574 (also fax)
Mr Mealing
D: £18.00–£25.00 **S:** £27.00–£36.00
Beds: 1F 1D 1T **Baths:** 3 En
🛏 🅿 (6) ⅍ 📺 🛏 🛲 Ⅴ ♨ cc

St Ives

SW5140 ◀ *Sheaf of Wheat, Stennack, Sloop Inn, Castle, Golden Lion, Queen's Arms, Croft, Cornish Arms, Union Inn*

Rivendell, *7 Porthminster Terrace, St Ives, Cornwall, TR26 2DQ.*
Open: All Year
01736 794923 Ms Walker
D: £16.00–£25.00 **S:** £16.00–£21.00
Beds: 1F 4D 1T 1S **Baths:** 3 En 1 Sh
🛏 🅿 (6) ⅍ 📺 ✕ 🛲 Ⅴ ♨ ♨
Highly recommended family-run guest house. Superb sea views from many rooms. Close to town, beaches, bus and rail stations. Friendly hospitality, excellent food. As featured in the TV drama 'Wycliffe'.

Whitewaves, *4 Sea View, St Ives, Cornwall, TR26 2DH.*
Small, warm, friendly, family-run non-smoking guest house in quiet private road.
Open: All Year (not Xmas)
01736 796595 (also fax)
Mrs Webb
jan@whitewaves.in2home.co.uk
D: £14.00–£20.00 **S:** £14.00–£20.00
Beds: 1F 3D 1T 2S **Baths:** 3 Sh
🛇 🅿 ⅍ 📺 🛒 Ⓥ ⚓

Carlill, *9 Porthminster Terrace, St Ives, Cornwall, TR26 2DQ.*
Friendly, comfortable, licensed, family-run guest house. Good food. Highly recommended.
Open: 27/12/99 to 23/12/00
01736 796738 Mrs Bowden
Lynne@lgpa9.freeserve.co.uk
D: £16.00–£23.00 **S:** £18.00–£22.00
Beds: 2F 2D 2T 1S **Baths:** 1 En 2 Pr 2 Sh
🛇 (5) 🅿 (6) ⅍ 📺 🛒 ➍ 🛒 Ⓥ ⚓

Chy-An-Creet Hotel, *The Stennack, St Ives, Cornwall, TR26 2HA.*
Warm welcome, relaxing home comfort, excellent touring and walking base.
Open: Jan to Nov
Grades: ETC 3 Diamond, AA 3 Diamond
01736 796559 (also fax)
Mr & Mrs Tremelling
judith@chy.co.uk
D: £20.00–£27.00 **S:** £20.00–£27.00
Beds: 2F 4D 2T 1S **Baths:** 9 En
🛇 🅿 (10) 📺 ➍ ✕ 🛒 Ⓥ ♿ **cc**

Downlong Cottage Guest House, *95 Back Road East, St Ives, Cornwall, TR26 1PF.*
Open: All Year (not Xmas)
01736 798107
D: £15.00–£21.00 **S:** £16.00–£20.00
Beds: 1F 4D 1T **Baths:** 4 En 1 Sh
🛇 (11) 📺 🛒
Ideally situated in the heart of Downlong, the old fishing quarter of picturesque St Ives, Downlong Cottage is only minutes away from the harbour and beaches. St Ives is famous for its artists and galleries including the Tate.

The Anchorage, *5 Bunkers Hill, St Ives, Cornwall, TR26 1LJ.*
Harbour location, cobbled street, 1 minute walk to Tate Gallery.
Open: All Year
Grades: ETC 4 Diamond
01736 797135 (also fax)
Mrs Brown
james@theanchoragebb.fsnet.co.uk
D: £20.00–£25.00 **S:** £20.00–£25.00
Beds: 1F 1T 3D 1S **Baths:** 4 En 1 Sh
🛇 (1) ⅍ 📺 🛒 Ⓥ ⚓ **cc**

Making Waves Vegan Guest House, *3 Richmond Place, St Ives, Cornwall, TR26 1JN.*
Eco-renovated Victorian house. 100% animal-free, organic. Relaxed, friendly, sea views.
Open: Easter to Oct
01736 793895 S Money
D: £18.50–£25.00 **S:** £22.00
Beds: 1F 1T 1D **Baths:** 2 Sh
🛇 🅿 (1) ⅍ 📺 ✕ 🛒 Ⓥ ⚓

Kynance, *The Warren, St Ives, Cornwall, TR26 2EA.*
Former Tin- miners cottage. Beach/harbour location. Railway/bus stations 100 yards. **Open:** Mar to Nov
Grades: AA 4 Diamond
01736 796636 Mr & Mrs Norris
D: £21.00–£25.00 **S:** fr £20.00
Beds: 4D 1T 1F **Baths:** 5 En 1 Pr
🛇 (7) 🅿 (4) ⅍ 📺 🛒 Ⓥ ⚓ **cc**

St Just-in-Penwith

* SW3631   ◗ The Wellington

Boscean Country Hotel, *St Just-in-Penwith, Penzance, Cornwall, TR19 7QP.*
Open: All Year (not Xmas)
Grades: ETC 3 Diamond
01736 788748 (also fax)
Mr & Mrs Wilson
boscean@aol.com
D: £22.00 **S:** £27.00
Beds: 3F 4D 5T **Baths:** 12 En
🛇 🅿 (15) 📺 🛒 🛒 Ⓥ ⚓ **cc**
A warm & hospitable welcome awaits you at Boscean - a magnificent country house in three acres of private walled garden, set amidst some the most dramatic scenery in West Cornwall. Home cooking, using fresh local and home-grown produce.

Bosavern House, *St Just-in-Penwith, Penzance, Cornwall, TR19 7RD.*
Pleasant C17th Cornish manor house. Delightful grounds. Warm welcome awaits.
Open: All Year (not Xmas)
Grades: ETC 3 Diamond
01736 788301 (also fax)
Mr Collinson
marcol@bosavern.u-net.com
D: £19.00–£26.00 **S:** £19.00–£26.00
Beds: 3F 2D 2T 1S **Baths:** 7 En 1 Pr
🛇 🅿 (15) ⅍ 📺 ➍ 🛒 Ⓥ ⚓ **3 cc**

Boswedden House Hotel, *Cape Cornwall, St Just-in-Penwith, Penzance, Cornwall, TR19 7NJ.*
Spacious Georgian mansion. Quiet country setting. Large garden, warm welcome.
Open: All Year **Grades:** ETC 3 Diamond
01736 788733 (also fax) Miss Griffiths
relax@boswedden.org.uk
D: £20.00–£25.00 **S:** £20.00–£30.00
Beds: 1F 2D 3T 2S **Baths:** 8 En
🛇 🅿 ⅍ 📺 ➍ 🛒 Ⓥ ⚓ **cc**

St Keverne

SW7921   ◗ White Hart, Three Tuns

Trevinock, *St Keverne, Helston, Cornwall, TR12 6QP.*
Open: Easter to Oct
01326 280498 Mrs Kelly
D: £18.00–£22.00 **S:** £18.00–£22.00
Beds: 2D 2S **Baths:** 1 En 1 Sh
🛇 🅿 (5) ⅍ 📺 ➍ ✕ 🛒 Ⓥ ⚓
Excellent food and accommodation. Ideally situated in a very lovely and unspoilt part of Cornwall. Near to Helford River, beaches and places of interest. All rooms of high standard, overlooking colourful gardens. Ample off road parking. Ensuite available. Near coastal footpath.

▬▬▬▬▬▬▬▬▬
Planning a longer stay? Always ask for any special rates
──────────────

Tregoning Lea, *Laddenvean, St Keverne, Heltson, Cornwall, TR12 6QE.*
New bungalow in quiet valley setting close to village amenities.
Open: All Year (not Xmas/New Year)
01326 280947 (also fax) Mr & Mrs Perry
D: £17.00–£19.00 **S:** £18.00–£25.00
Beds: 1T 1D 2T **Baths:** 1 En 1 Pr
🛇 (10) 🅿 (6) ⅍ 📺 🛒

St Kew

SX0177   ◗ St Kew Inn

Tregellist Farm, *Tregellist, St Kew, Bodmin, Cornwall, PL30 3HG.*
Tregellist Farm set in beautiful countryside with splendid views. Close to Camel Trail.
Open: All Year (not Xmas/New Year)
Grades: ETC 3 Diamond
01208 880537 Mrs Cleave
Fax: 01208 881017
D: £20.00–£24.00 **S:** £24.00–£26.00
Beds: 1F 1D 1T **Baths:** 3 En
🛇 🅿 (6) 📺 ✕ 🛒 Ⓥ ⚓

St Kew Highway

SX0375   ◗ Red Lion, The Maltsters, St Kew Inn, St Mabyn Inn

Porchester House, *St Kew Highway, Bodmin, Cornwall, PL30 3ED.*
In rural village, secluded detached house with large conservatory/aviary.
Open: All Year (not Xmas)
01208 841725 Mr Ashley
D: £25.00
Beds: 1D 1T **Baths:** 1 En 1 Pr
🅿 (4) ⅍ 📺 ➍ ✕ 🛒 ⚓

St Mabyn

SX0473   ◗ St Mabyn Inn

Cles Kernyk, *Wadebridge Road, St Mabyn, Bodmin, Cornwall, PL30 3BH.*
Relax in quiet North Cornwall village. Handy for beaches/moors.
Open: All Year (not Xmas)
01208 841258 Mr & Mrs Jago
sue@mabyn.freeserve.co.uk
D: £15.00–£20.00 **S:** £15.00–£20.00
Beds: 1F 1D 1S **Baths:** 1 Sh
🛇 🅿 (3) 📺 ⚓

St Neot

SX1867   ◗ London Inn

Lampen Farm, *St Neot, Liskeard, Cornwall, PL14 6PB.*
Open: All Year
01579 320284
D: £17.00–£22.00 **S:** £20.00–£25.00
Beds: 1F 1T 1D **Baths:** 2 En 1 Pr
🛇 🅿 (4) ⅍ 📺 🛒 Ⓥ ⚓
Delightful, spacious 16th century farmhouse in a tranquil setting on the edge of Bodmin Moor. Only a few minutes walk from the charming village of St Neot with its beautiful church-popular Inn. Ideal location for walking/touring.

National Grid References are
for villages, towns and cities –
not for individual houses

Dye Cottage, *St Neot, Liskeard,
Cornwall, PL14 6NG.*
Charming C17th cottage, oak beams,
flagstone floors, lovely gardens by river.
Open: All Year (not Xmas)
01579 321394 S M Williams
Fax: 0870 169 2029
dyecott@lineone.net
D: £16.00–£16.50 **S:** £16.50
Beds: 1D 2S **Baths:** 1 Sh
🛏 🅿 (1) ½ 📺 🐾 🛋 Ⅴ 🛁

St Newlyn East
SW8256   🍺 *The Pheasant*

Trewerry Mill, *Trerice, St Newlyn East,
Newquay, Cornwall, TR8 5GS.*
Picturesque C17th watermill in peaceful
riverside gardens, 4m from coast.
Open: Feb to Nov
01872 510345 (also fax)
D & T Clark
trewerry.mill@which.net
D: £20.00–£24.00 **S:** £20.00–£24.00
Beds: 1F 2D 1T 2S **Baths:** 3 En 3 Sh
🛏 (7) 🅿 (12) ½ 📺 🐾 🛋 🛁

St Wenn
SW9665

Tregolls Farm, *St Wenn, Bodmin,
Cornwall, PL30 5PG.*
Open: All Year (not Xmas)
Grades: ETC 3 Diamond
01208 812154 Mrs Hawkey
D: £14.00–£17.00 **S:** £15.50–£17.00
Beds: 2D 1T 1S **Baths:** 1 En 1 Sh
🛏 🅿 (10) ½ 📺 ✕ 🛋 Ⅴ 🛁
Tregolls is a Grade II Listed building, on a
beef and sheep farm in mid Cornwall. We
have a farm trail which links up to the
Saints Way Footpath. Convenient for
visiting Padstow, Lanhydrock House,
Heligan Garden and The Eden Project.

Old School House, *St Wenn, Bodmin,
Cornwall, PL30 5PS.*
A tranquil upland hamlet, yet within easy
reach of both coasts.
Open: All Year (not Xmas)
01726 890010
D: £17.00–£19.00 **S:** £17.00–£22.00
Beds: 1D 1T **Baths:** 1 En 1 Pr
🅿 ½ 📺 ✕ 🛋 Ⅴ 🛁

Stibb
SS2210   🍺 *London Inn*

Strands, *Stibb, Bude, Cornwall, EX23 9HW.*
Modern house within 1 acre approx in
rural hamlet. Extensive country views.
Open: All Year
01288 353514 Mrs Dutstan
D: £15.00 **S:** £20.00
Beds: 1F 2D **Baths:** 2 En 1 Sh
🛏 🅿 (3) 📺 ✕ 🛋 🛁 ♿

Talskiddy
SW9165

Pennatillie Farm, *Talskiddy, St Columb
Major, TR9 6EF.*
Secluded delightful 450 acre dairy farm.
Excellent accommodation and food.
Open: All Year
01637 880280 (also fax)
Mrs Colgrove
D: £16.00–£18.00 **S:** £16.00–£18.00
Beds: 3D **Baths:** 3 En
🛏 🅿 📺 ✕ 🛋 🛁

The Lizard
SW7012   🍺 *Top House*

Parc Brawse House, *Penmenner
Road, The Lizard, Helston, Cornwall, TR12
7NR.*
Old Cornish house with extensive sea
views and secluded garden.
Open: All Year
01326 290466 (also fax)
Mrs Brookes
lindabrookes@cwcom.net
D: £16.50–£23.00 **S:** £16.50–£29.00
Beds: 1F 1T 4D 1S **Baths:** 4 Pr 2 Sh
🛏 🅿 (7) 📺 🐾 ✕ 🛋 Ⅴ ❋ 🛁 ♿ cc

The Most Southerly House, *Lizard
Point, The Lizard, Helston, Cornwall,
TR12 7NU.*
England's most southerly house.
Magnificent location on coastal path.
Open: All Year (not Xmas/New Year)
01326 290300 (also fax)
Mrs Sowden
D: £18.00–£20.00 **S:** £20.00
Beds: 1T 1D 1S **Baths:** 1 Sh
🛏 (7) 🅿 (4) ½ 📺 🛋 🛁

Three Burrows
SW7447   🍺 *Victoria Inn, Miners Arms*

Lands Vue Country House, *Lands
Vue, Three Burrows, Truro, Cornwall,
TR4 8JA.*
Special welcome for all our guests at a
peaceful country home.
Open: All Year (not Xmas)
Grades: AA 4 Diamond
01872 560242
Mrs Hutchings
Fax: 01872 560950
D: £20.00–£24.00 **S:** £25.00–£32.00
Beds: 1D 2T **Baths:** 3 En
🛏 (12) 🅿 (4) ½ 📺 🛋 Ⅴ 🛁

Tintagel
SX0588   🍺 *Tintagel Arms, The Cornishman, Mill
House*

Tintagel Arms Hotel, *Fore Street,
Tintagel, Cornwall, PL34 0DB.*
Open: All Year
Grades: AA 4 Diamond
01840 770780 Mr Hunter
D: £20.00–£25.00 **S:** £25.00–£30.00
Beds: 1F 4D 2T **Baths:** 7 En
🛏 🅿 (8) 📺 Ⅴ 🛋 Ⅴ 🛁 cc
200 year old stone building built on site of
Chapel of St Dennis (1400 AD).

BATHROOMS
Pr - Private
Sh - Shared
En - Ensuite

Bosayne Guest House, *Atlantic
Road, Tintagel, Cornwall, PL34 0DE.*
Warm, friendly family-run guest house
with sea views, serving a great breakfast.
Open: All Year
01840 770514
Mr Clark
clark@clarky100.freeserve.co.uk
D: £16.00–£20.00
S: £16.00–£18.00
Beds: 2F 3D 1T 3S **Baths:** 4 En 3 Sh
🛏 ½ 📺 🛋 Ⅴ 🛁 ♿

Pendrin House, *Atlantic Road,
Tintagel, Cornwall, PL34 0DE.*
Beautiful Victorian house close to many
amenities, castle and beaches.
Open: March to Nov
Grades: ETC 3 Diamond
01840 770560 (also fax)
Mrs Howe
pendrin@tesco.net
D: £16.00–£19.00 **S:** £16.00
Beds: 2F 2D 4D 1S
Baths: 3 En 3 Sh
🛏 🅿 (5) ½ 📺 🐾 ✕ 🛋 Ⅴ 🛁 ♿

Grange Cottage, *Tintagel, Cornwall,
PL34 0AX.*
Peaceful traditional stone cottage. Close
Tintagel Castle, cliff walks, beach.
Open: Easter to Nov
01840 770487
Mrs Jones
D: £18.00–£25.00 **S:** £18.00
Beds: 1T 1D 1S **Baths:** 1 En 1 Sh
🛏 (4) 🅿 (4) ½ 📺 🛋 Ⅴ 🛁

Bossiney Cottage, *Tintagel, Cornwall,
PL34 0AY.*
Character cottage, carefully restored.
Good touring base, close coastal
footpath.
Open: All Year (not Xmas)
01840 770327
D: £16.00 **S:** £16.00–£20.00
Beds: 1F 2D **Baths:** 1 Sh
🛏 (3) 🅿 (4) ½ 📺 Ⅴ 🛋 Ⅴ

Towednack
SW4838   🍺 *Engine Inn*

Chytodden Farm, *Towednack, St Ives,
Cornwall, TR26 3AT.*
Comfortable accommodation in peaceful
surroundings, good food, car essential.
Open: Easter to Octq
01736 795029
Mr & Mrs Hollow
D: £15.00 **S:** £15.00
Beds: 1F 1D **Baths:** 1 Sh
🅿 🛁

Planning a longer stay? Always
ask for any special rates

Lynwood House, Tregony, Truro,
Cornwall, TR2 5RU.
Very comfortable accommodation with
attractive gardens, rural location, warm
hospitality.
Open: All Year (not Xmas)
01872 530371 Mrs Pedler
D: £16.00–£17.00 **S:** fr £16.00
Beds: 2D 1T
🐕 (5) ⓟ (4) ⚡ 📺 🛁 ☕

Treknow

SX0586   🍴 Millhouse Inn, Port William

Challoch Guest House, Treknow,
Tintagel, Cornwall, PL34 0EN.
Small friendly guest house, superb views,
near beautiful surfing beach.
Open: Easter to Oct
01840 770273 Mrs May
D: £17.00–£19.00 **S:** £19.00–£20.00
Beds: 2D 1T
🐕 📺 🍴 ☕

Hillscroft, Treknow, Tintagel, Cornwall,
PL34 0EN.
Scenic views across Trebarwith Valley.
Use of garden and summer house.
Open: All Year (not Xmas/New Year)
01840 770551 Mrs Nutt
pat@bascastle.fsnet.co.uk
D: £16.00–£20.00 **S:** £16.00–£20.00
Beds: 1T 2D **Baths:** 2 En 1 Sh
🐕 (8) ⓟ (6) 📺 🍴 🛁 ☕

Atlantic View Hotel, Treknow,
Tintagel, Cornwall, PL34 0E.
Victorian house, glorious position, set 300
yards from cliff top.
Open: Feb to Dec.
Grades: ETC 2 Star
01840 770221 Fax: 01840 770995
atlantic-view@eclipse.co.uk
D: £28.00–£32.00 **S:** £32.00
Beds: 2F 1T 6D **Baths:** 9 En
🐕 ⓟ (10) 📺 🍴 ✕ 🛁 ☕ 💳 CC

Trelights

SW9979

Long Cross Hotel, Trelights, Port
Isaac, Cornwall, PL29 3TF.
Character country house hotel, with
unique Victorian garden and free house
tavern.
Open: All Year (not Xmas)
01208 880243 Mr & Mrs Crawford
D: £18.00–£25.00 **S:** £24.00–£30.00
Beds: 2F 1T 9D **Baths:** 12 En

Trelill

SX0477   🍴 White Hart

Trevorrian Farm, Trelill, Bodmin,
Cornwall, PL30 3HZ.
Dairy farm. Near Port Isaac. Wonderful
views over peaceful countryside.
Open: Easter to Oct
01208 850434 (also fax)
Mrs Kingdon
D: £20.00–£25.00 **S:** £30.00
Beds: 2D **Baths:** 1 En 1 Sh
ⓟ (4) ⚡ ✕ 🛁 ☕

Treneglos

SX2088   🍴 Eliot Arms

The Old Vicarage, Treneglos,
Launceston, Cornwall, PL15 8UQ.
Renowned for hospitals and excellent
food. Highest standards throughout.
Open: March to Nov
Grades: ETC 4 Diamond, Silver Award
01566 781351 (also fax)
Mrs Fancourt
maggie@fancourt.freeserve.co.uk
D: £25.00 **S:** £25.00
Beds: 2D 1S **Baths:** 2 En
🐕 (2) ⓟ (10) ⚡ 📺 ✕ 🛁 ☕ ☕

Trerulefoot

SX3258   🍴 White Hart

Catchfrench Farm, Trerulefoot,
Saltash, Cornwall, PL12 5BY.
Relaxing farmhouse surrounded by
beautiful countryside easy access to A38.
Open: Mar to Oct
01503 240203 Mrs Gillbard
D: £17.00–£19.00 **S:** £17.00–£19.00
Beds: 1F 1D 1S **Baths:** 1 En 1 Sh
🐕 ⓟ 📺 🛁 ☕

Tresparrett

SX1491   🍴 Manor House

Oaklands, Tresparrett, Boscastle,
Cornwall, PL32 9SX.
Open: Easter to Sept
Grades: ETC Cornwall Tourist Board
01840 261302 Mrs Routly
D: £16.00–£19.00 **S:** £16.00–£20.00
Beds: 1T 2D **Baths:** 1 En 1 Sh
🐕 (11) ⓟ (4) ⚡ 📺 🛁 ☕
2 miles north of picturesque Boscastle, 6
miles historic Tintagel. Superb, quiet,
spacious ground floor accommodation,
panoramic country views, near splendid
coastal footpath, ideal touring centre,
Moors, Beaches, serving hearty
breakfasts, guest TV lounge, short
breaks, warm welcome.

Trevone Bay

SW8876   🍴 Well Parc Hotel

Well Parc Hotel, Trevone Bay,
Padstow, Cornwall, PL28 8QN.
Family run hotel and inn very close to
beaches, two miles from Padstow.
Open: All Year (not Xmas)
01841 520318 Mrs Mills
D: £20.00–£28.00 **S:** £20.00–£28.00
Beds: 4F 4D 1T 1S **Baths:** 7 En 3 Sh
🐕 ⓟ 📺 ✕ 🛁 ☕

Trewidland

SX2559

Linden Cottage, Trewidland, Liskeard,
PL14 4SS.
Charming C18th cottage with superior
furnished ensuite bedrooms. Tranquil
hamlet, beautiful wooded Looe Valley.
Open: All Year (not Xmas)
01503 240856 (also fax) Mr Faulkner
D: £18.00–£20.00 **S:** £20.00
Beds: 2D 1T **Baths:** 3 En
🐕 ⓟ (3) ⚡ 📺 ✕ 🛁 ☕ CC

Truro

SW8244   🍴 Fox & Hounds, Victoria Inn, Dansell
Arms, Inn, The Threemile Stone, Miners Arms,
Wheel Inn, County Arms, Chiverton Arms, William IV

Rock Cottage, Blackwater, Truro,
Cornwall, TR4 8EU.
Open: All Year (not Xmas/New Year)
Grades: ETC 4 Diamond, AA 4 Diamond
01872 560252 (also fax)
Mrs Wakeling
rockcottage@yahoo.com
D: £22.00–£24.00 **S:** £26.00–£28.00
Beds: 2D 1T **Baths:** 3 En
ⓟ ⚡ 📺 🛁 ☕ CC
C18th beamed cob cottage. Haven for
non-smokers. Full central heating.
Bedrooms with colour television, radio,
beverage tray, hairdryer. Sitting/TV room.
Cosy dining room. Village location 6
miles Truro, 3 miles ocean. Delightful
gardens. MasterCard/Visa/Delta/Switch.

Lands Vue Country House, Lands
Vue, Three Burrows, Truro, Cornwall,
TR4 8JA.
Open: All Year (not Xmas)
Grades: AA 4 Diamond
01872 560242 Mrs Hutchings
Fax: 01872 560950
D: £20.00–£24.00 **S:** £25.00–£32.00
Beds: 1D 2T **Baths:** 3 En
🐕 (12) ⓟ (4) ⚡ 📺 🛁 ☕ ☕
Special welcome for all our guests at a
peaceful country home where you will
find friendly atmosphere, lovely ensuite
bedrooms, open fires, central location.
Highly recommended by many of our
guests who return year after year.

**Trevispian Vean Farm Guest
House,** St Erme, Truro, Cornwall, TR4 9BL.
300 year old working farm - family run -
lovely views of Cornish countryside.
Open: Feb to Nov
Grades: ETC 4 Diamond, AA 4 Diamond,
RAC 4 Diamond
01872 279514
Mr & Mrs Dymond
Fax: 01872 263730
D: £18.50 **S:** £24.00
Beds: 2F 5D 2T **Baths:** 9 Pr
🐕 ⓟ (12) ⚡ 📺 ☕ ☕

Patmos, 8 Burley Close, Truro, Cornwall,
TR1 2EP.
Beautiful friendly home, close to centre.
River view. Excellent breakfast.
Open: All Year
01872 278018 Mrs Ankers
b.ankers@fdn.co.uk
D: £16.00–£38.00 **S:** £16.00–£20.00
Beds: 1D 1T **Baths:** 1 En 1 Pr
🐕 (5) ⚡ 📺 🛁 ☕ ☕

4 Upper Lemon Villas, Lemon Street,
Truro, Cornwall, TR1 2PD.
Georgian family house. Warm, friendly. 3
min walk to city centre and cathedral.
Open: All Year
01872 277000
Mrs Trudgian
D: £20.00–£22.00 **S:** £21.00–£23.00
Beds: 2T 1S
🐕 ⓟ ⚡ 📺 🍴 🛁 ☕ ☕

Tywardreath

SX0854   ⚓ *Ship Inn*

Polbrean House, *Woodland Avenue, Tywardreath, Par, Cornwall, PL24 2PL.*
Lovely Victorian family home, comfortable bedrooms with four poster beds. **Open:** All Year (not Xmas)
01726 812530 Mrs Ball
D: £17.50 **S:** £25.00
Beds: 2D 1S **Baths:** 1 Sh
🛏 🅿 (4) ⅟ 📺 ▥ Ⅴ 🌢

Veryan

SW9139   ⚓ *New Inn*

The New Inn, *Veryan, Truro, Cornwall, TR2 5QA.*
Open: All Year (not Xmas)
01872 501362 Mr Gayton
Fax: 01872 501078
jack@veryan44.freeserve.co.uk
D: £22.50 **S:** £22.50–£32.50
Beds: 1D 1T 1S **Baths:** 2 En 1 Sh
📺 ✕ ▥ Ⅴ 🌢 cc
The inn is based on a pair of C16th cottages. The single bar is welcoming and unspoilt. Situated in a beautiful village close by safe bathing beaches. Renowned locally for a high standard of catering.

Wadebridge

SW9872   ⚓ *Earl of St Vincent, The Ship*

Little Pound, *Bodieve, Wadebridge, Cornwall, PL27 6EG.*
Quiet hamlet, terraced gardens to stream, close to Camel Trail.
Open: All Year (not Xmas)
01208 814449 Mrs Crook
D: £16.00–£20.00 **S:** £16.00–£22.00
Beds: 1D 1T 1S **Baths:** 1 En 1 Sh
🛏 (3) 🅿 (4) ⅟ 📺 ▥ 🌢

Trevanion House, *Trevanion Road, Wadebridge, Cornwall, PL27 7JY.*
C18th house, casual bookings welcome, specialist holidays for adults with learning disability.
Open: All Year
01208 814903 Mrs Todd
Fax: 01208 816268
trevanion@dial.pipex.com
D: £19.00–£21.00 **S:** £20.00–£22.00
Beds: 10T 5S **Baths:** 13 Pr 2 Sh
🛏 (5) 🅿 (8) ⅟ 📺 ✕ ▥ Ⅴ 🌢 🌢 ♿

Widegates

SX2857   ⚓ *Copley Arms, Globe Inn, Snooty Fox*

Treveria Farm, *Widegates, Looe, Cornwall, PL13 1QR.*
Delightful manor Offering luxurious accommodation in spacious and elegant rooms. **Open:** Easter to Oct
01503 240237 (also fax) Mrs Kitto
D: £20.00–£22.00 **S:** £25.00–£30.00
Beds: 2D 1T **Baths:** 3 Pr
🅿 (3) ⅟ 📺 ▥ Ⅴ 🌢

Withiel

SW9965   ⚓ *Quarryman Inn*

Tregawne, *Withiel, Bodmin, Cornwall, PL30 5NR.*
Open: All Year
01208 831552 Mr Jackson
Fax: 01208 832122
D: £25.00–£35.50 **S:** £35.00–£47.50
Beds: 1F 1T 1D
🛏 🅿 📺 ⊁ ✕ ▥ Ⅴ 🌢 🌢 cc
Tregawne an C18th farmhouse lovingly restored and situated on the beautiful Ruthern Valley, on 8 acres of grounds running down to the river and woodlands. Bedrooms are large & elegant. Beaches, golf, Rick Stein's restaurant 20 mins, Eden Project 15 mins. Walking & cycling.

Zennor

SW4538   ⚓ *Tinners' Arms, Gurnard's Head*

Rosmorva, *Boswednack, Zennor, St Ives, Cornwall, TR26 3DD.*
Lovely views from garden. Superb walking on cliffs and moorland.
Open: All Year
01736 796722 Ms Hamlett
D: £16.50–£17.50 **S:** £16.50–£17.50
Beds: 1F 1D 1S **Baths:** 1 Sh, 1 En
🛏 (4) 🅿 (3) ⅟ ▥ 🌢

Boswednack Manor, *Zennor, St Ives, Cornwall, TR26 3DD.*
Peaceful, vegetarian, non-smoking. Organic gardens, superb views, sea sunsets. **Open:** Easter to Oct
01736 794183 Mrs Gynn
D: £17.00–£22.00 **S:** £18.00–£23.00
Beds: 1F 2D 1T 1S **Baths:** 2 En 1 Sh
🛏 🅿 (6) ⅟ Ⅴ 🌢

Trewey Farm, *Zennor, St Ives, Cornwall, TR26 3DA.*
Working farm. Peaceful attractive surroundings. Warm welcome, excellent food.
Open: Feb to Nov
01736 796936 Mrs Mann
D: £18.00–£21.00
S: £19.00–£21.00
Beds: 2F 2D 1T 1S **Baths:** 1 Sh
🛏 🅿 (6) 📺 ⊁ Ⅴ 🌢 cc

RATES

D = Price range per person sharing in a double room
S = Price range for a single room

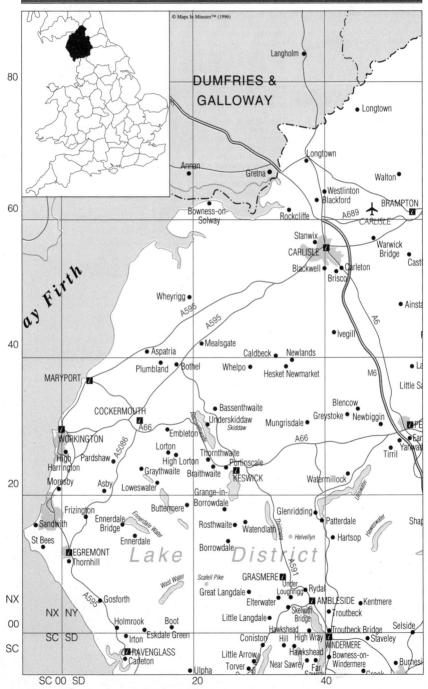

Cumbria

© Maps In Minutes™ (1996)

DUMFRIES & GALLOWAY

Langholm

Longtown

Annan

Gretna

Longtown

Walton

Westlinton
Blackford

BRAMPTON

Bowness-on-Solway

Rockcliffe

CARLISLE

A689

Stanwix

Warwick
Bridge

CARLISLE

Cast

Blackwell

Carleton

Brisco

Wheyrigg

A596

Ainsta

A595

A6

Ivegill

Aspatria

Mealsgate

Caldbeck

Newlands

Plumbland

Bothel

Whelpo

Hesket Newmarket

M6

MARYPORT

Blencow

La

Little Sa

COCKERMOUTH

A66

Bassenthwaite

Underskiddaw

Skiddaw

Mungrisdale

Greystoke

Newbiggin

PE

Embleton

Lorton

High Lorton

Thornthwaite

Portinscale

A66

San

Tirril

Yanwa

WORKINGTON

A5086

High
Harrington

Pardshaw

Graythwaite

Braithwaite

KESWICK

Watermillock

Ulswater

Moresby

Asby

Loweswater

Grange-in-Borrowdale

Glenridding

Frizington

Buttermere

Rosthwaite

Watendlath

Helvellyn

Patterdale

Hartsop

Haweswater

Shap

Sandwith

Ennerdale
Bridge

Ennerdale Water

St Bees

Ennerdale

Borrowdale

Thirlmere

EGREMONT

Lake

District

Thornhill

Scafell Pike

A591

GRASMERE

Wast Water

Great Langdale

Under
Loughrigg

Rydal

NX

NY

Elterwater

Skelwith
Bridge

AMBLESIDE

Kentmere

Gosforth

Little Langdale

Troutbeck

Selside

Holmrook

Boot

Hawkshead

High Wray

Troutbeck Bridge

Staveley

00

Irton

Eskdale Green

Coniston

Hill

SC

SD

WINDERMERE

SC

RAVENGLASS

Carleton

Little Arrow

Hawkshead

Bowness-on-Windermere

Burnesi

Ulpha

Torver

Near Sawrey

Far
Sawrey

Creek

| SC 00 SD | 20 | 40 |

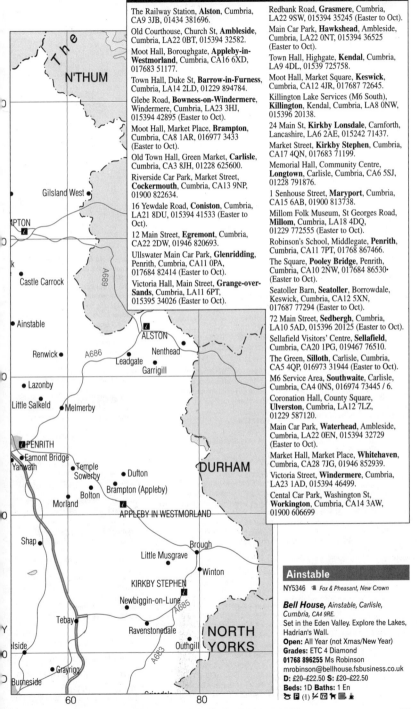

The Railway Station, **Alston**, Cumbria, CA9 3JB, 01434 381696.

Old Courthouse, Church St, **Ambleside**, Cumbria, LA22 0BT, 015394 32582.

Moot Hall, Boroughgate, **Appleby-in-Westmorland**, Cumbria, CA16 6XD, 017683 51177.

Town Hall, Duke St, **Barrow-in-Furness**, Cumbria, LA14 2LD, 01229 894784.

Glebe Road, **Bowness-on-Windermere**, Windermere, Cumbria, LA23 3HJ, 015394 42895 (Easter to Oct).

Moot Hall, Market Place, **Brampton**, Cumbria, CA8 1AR, 016977 3433 (Easter to Oct).

Old Town Hall, Green Market, **Carlisle**, Cumbria, CA3 8JH, 01228 625600.

Riverside Car Park, Market Street, **Cockermouth**, Cumbria, CA13 9NP, 01900 822634.

16 Yewdale Road, **Coniston**, Cumbria, LA21 8DU, 015394 41533 (Easter to Oct).

12 Main Street, **Egremont**, Cumbria, CA22 2DW, 01946 820693.

Ullswater Main Car Park, **Glenridding**, Penrith, Cumbria, CA11 0PA, 017684 82414 (Easter to Oct).

Victoria Hall, Main Street, **Grange-over-Sands**, Cumbria, LA11 6PT, 015395 34026 (Easter to Oct).

Redbank Road, **Grasmere**, Cumbria, LA22 9SW, 015394 35245 (Easter to Oct).

Main Car Park, **Hawkshead**, Ambleside, Cumbria, LA22 0NT, 015394 36525 (Easter to Oct).

Town Hall, Highgate, **Kendal**, Cumbria, LA9 4DL, 01539 725758.

Moot Hall, Market Square, **Keswick**, Cumbria, CA12 4JR, 017687 72645.

Killington Lake Services (M6 South), **Killington**, Kendal, Cumbria, LA8 0NW, 015396 20138.

24 Main St, **Kirkby Lonsdale**, Carnforth, Lancashire, LA6 2AE, 015242 71437.

Market Street, **Kirkby Stephen**, Cumbria, CA17 4QN, 017683 71199.

Memorial Hall, Community Centre, **Longtown**, Carlisle, Cumbria, CA6 5SJ, 01228 791876.

1 Senhouse Street, **Maryport**, Cumbria, CA15 6AB, 01900 813738.

Millom Folk Museum, St Georges Road, **Millom**, Cumbria, LA18 4DQ, 01229 772555 (Easter to Oct).

Robinson's School, Middlegate, **Penrith**, Cumbria, CA11 7PT, 01768 867466.

The Square, **Pooley Bridge**, Penrith, Cumbria, CA10 2NW, 017684 86530· (Easter to Oct).

Seatoller Barn, **Seatoller**, Borrowdale, Keswick, Cumbria, CA12 5XN, 017687 77294 (Easter to Oct).

72 Main Street, **Sedbergh**, Cumbria, LA10 5AD, 015396 20125 (Easter to Oct).

Sellafield Visitors' Centre, **Sellafield**, Cumbria, CA20 1PG, 019467 76510.

The Green, **Silloth**, Carlisle, Cumbria, CA5 4QP, 016973 31944 (Easter to Oct).

M6 Service Area, **Southwaite**, Carlisle, Cumbria, CA4 0NS, 016974 73445 / 6.

Coronation Hall, County Square, **Ulverston**, Cumbria, LA12 7LZ, 01229 587120.

Main Car Park, **Waterhead**, Ambleside, Cumbria, LA22 0EN, 015394 32729 (Easter to Oct).

Market Hall, Market Place, **Whitehaven**, Cumbria, CA28 7JG, 01946 852939.

Victoria Street, **Windermere**, Cumbria, LA23 1AD, 015394 46499.

Cental Car Park, Washington St, **Workington**, Cumbria, CA14 3AW, 01900 606699

Ainstable

NY5346   🍺 Fox & Pheasant, New Crown

Bell House, Ainstable, Carlisle, Cumbria, CA4 9RE.
Set in the Eden Valley. Explore the Lakes, Hadrian's Wall.
Open: All Year (not Xmas/New Year)
Grades: ETC 4 Diamond
01768 896255 Ms Robinson
mrobinson@bellhouse.fsbusiness.co.uk
D: £20–£22.50 **S:** £20–£22.50
Beds: 1D **Baths:** 1 En
🛇 🄿 (1) ⊬ 📺 🍴 🛏 ⬛, ⚴

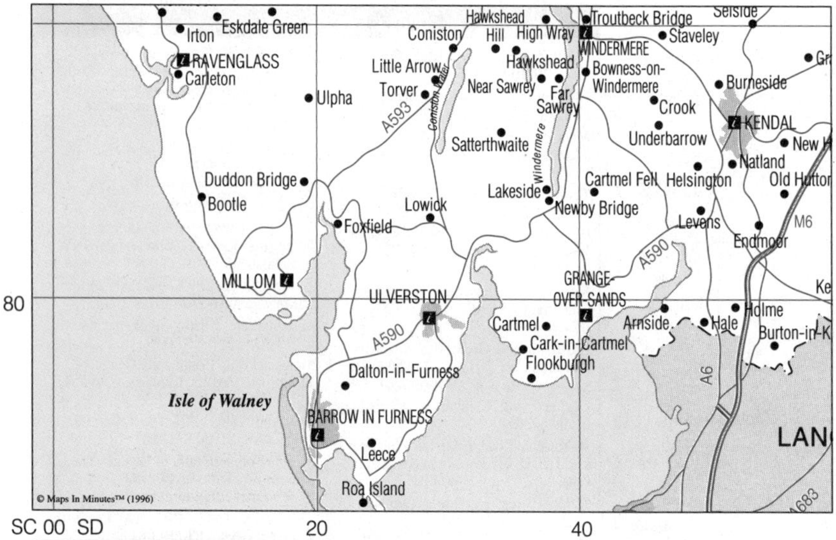

Alston

NY7146 *Blue Bell Inn, Angel Inn, Turks Head, Crown*

Nentholme, *The Butts, Alston, Cumbria, CA9 3JQ.*
Quiet location, 1 min walk to town. C2C and walkers welcome. **Open:** All Year
01434 381523 (also fax) Mrs Thompson
nentholme@mcmail.com
D: £17–£20 **S:** £22–£25
Beds: 2F 3D 3T 1S **Baths:** 2 En 1 Sh
(6)

Ambleside

NY3704 *White Lion, The Unicorn, Queen's Head, Drunken Duck Inn, Outgate Inn, Lucy's, Traveller's Rest*

The Old Vicarage, *Vicarage Road, Ambleside, Cumbria, LA22 9DH.*
Open: All Year **Grades:** ETC 4 diamonds
015394 33364 Mrs Burt
Fax: 015394 34734
the.old.vicarage@kencomp.net
D: £25–£30 **S:** £30–£40
Beds: 2F 6D 2T **Baths:** 10 En
(15)
Quality bed & breakfast accommodation in a peaceful location in central Ambleside. Large car park. Pets welcome. All bedrooms are well-appointed and have multi-channel TV, hairdryers, radio alarm, mini fridge, kettle, private bath/shower and WC.

Borwick Lodge, *Hawkshead, Ambleside, Cumbria, LA22 0PU.*
Open: All Year
Grades: ETC 4 Diamond, Silver
015394 36332 (also fax) Mr & Mrs Haskell
borwicklodge@talk21.com
D: £25–£36 **S:** fr £35
Beds: 1F 4D 1T **Baths:** All En
(8) (8)
Award-winning 'accommodation of the highest standards'. A rather special C17th country house+.

Rothay House, *Rothay Road, Ambleside, Cumbria, LA22 2EE.*
Quality establishment, professional care, first class breakfast. Private car park.
Open: Feb to Dec
015394 32434
email@rothay-house.fsnet.co.uk
D: £21–£26 **S:** £30–£35
Beds: 1F 1T 4D **Baths:** 6 En
(2) (9) **cc**

Fisherbeck Cottage, *Lake Road, Low Fold, Ambleside, Cumbria, LA22 0DN.*
Lovely stone-built cottage, own gardens. Quiet location near village.
Open: All Year
015394 33353
Mrs Dawson
D: £15–£16 **S:** £15–£16
Beds: 2D 1T 1S **Baths:** 1 Sh

Fern Cottage, *6 Waterhead Terrace, Ambleside, Cumbria, LA22 0HA.*
Homely Lakeland stone terraced cottage, two minutes from Lake Windermere.
Open: All Year (not Xmas)
Grades: ETC 3 Diamond
015394 33007
S M Rushby
D: £15–£17 **S:** £18–£20
Beds: 2D 1T **Baths:** 1 Sh
(4)

Cowrie Creek, *5 Stockghyll Brow, Ambleside, Cumbria, LA22 0QZ.*
Small B&B, quiet location, 5 mins centre, 2 mins waterfalls.
Open: May to Oct
015394 33732
sally@cowrie.freeserve.co.uk
D: £20–£28 **S:** £25–£40
Beds: 2D 1T **Baths:** 2 En 1 Pr
(3)

Rowanfield Country House, *Kirkstone Road, Ambleside, Cumbria, LA22 9ET.*
Idyllic, quiet location. Central Lakeland. Breathtaking views, beautiful house.
Open: Mar to Dec
Grades: ETC 5 Diamond, AA 5 Diamond , RAC 5 Diamond
015394 33686 Mrs Butcher
Fax: 015394 31569
mail@rowanfield.com
D: £31–£45 **S:** £52–£65
Beds: 1F 5D 1T **Baths:** 7 En
(8) (9) **cc**

Appleby-in-Westmorland

NY6820 *Royal Oak, Crown & Cushion*

Limnerslease, *Bongate, Appleby-in-Westmorland, Cumbria, CA16 6UE.*
Family-run guest house 10 mins town centre. Lovely golf course & many walks.
Open: All Year (not Xmas)
017683 51578 Mrs Coward
D: £17
Beds: 2D 1T **Baths:** 1 Pr 1 Sh
(13) (3)

Wemyss House, *48 Boroughgate, Appleby-in-Westmorland, Cumbria, CA16 6XG.*
Georgian house in small country town.
Open: Easter to Oct
017683 51494 Mrs Hirst
nickhirst@aol.com
D: £17 **S:** £17
Beds: 1D 1T 1S **Baths:** 2 Sh
(2)

All details shown are as supplied by B&B owners in Autumn 2000

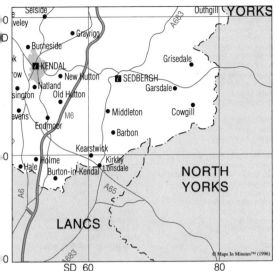

Arnside

SD4578 🍺 *The Albion*

Willowfield Hotel, *The Promenade, Arnside, Carnforth, Lancs, LA5 0AD.*
Non-smoking family-run hotel in superb estuary-side location. **Open:** All Year
Grades: ETC 4 Diamond, AA 4 Diamond, RAC 4 Diamond
01524 761354 Mr Kerr
kerr@willowfield.net.1.co.uk
D: £26–£28 **S:** £25–£42
Beds: 2F 3D 3T 2S **Baths:** 8 En 1 Pr 2 Sh
🛇 🅿 (8) 🍴 📺 ✗ 🎱 Ⓥ ♨ cc

Aspatria

NY1441 🍺 *The Bush, Lakeside Inn*

Castlemont, *Aspatria, Carlisle, Cumbria, CA7 2JU.*
Castlemont is a large Victorian family residence in 2 acres of garden.
Open: All Year
016973 20205
Mr & Mrs Lines
castlemont@tesco.net
D: £19–£23 **S:** £22–£26
Beds: 1F 1D 1T **Baths:** 1 En 2 Sh
🛇 🅿 🍴 📺 🎱 Ⓥ ♨ cc

Barbon

SD6282 🍺 *Barbon Inn*

Kemps Hill, *Moorthwaite Lane, Barbon, Kirkby Lonsdale, Carnforth, LA6 .*
Ideally situated between the Lake District and Yorkshire Dales.
Open: All Year
015242 76233
Fax: 015242 76544
info@kempshil.co.uk
D: £20 **S:** £30
Beds: 2D **Baths:** 2 En
🅿 🍴 📺 🛏 ✗ 🎱 Ⓥ ♨

Barrow-in-Furness

SD1969 🍺 *Brown Cow*

Glen Garth Hotel, *359 Abbey Road, Barrow-in-Furness, Cumbria, LA13 9JY.*
Open: All Year
01229 825374 Fax: 01229 811744
D: £27.45–£34.95 **S:** £49.90–£59.90
Beds: 2F 1T 5D 7S **Baths:** 15 En
🛇 🅿 (15) 🍴 📺 ✗ 🎱 Ⓥ ♨ cc
Beautiful Victorian Mansion with friendly service. All rooms well appointed, ensuite with satellite television. popular restaurant serving A La Carte and Bistro menus daily. comfortable relaxing lounge. Occasions and parties catered for. Perfect wedding venue and pretty lawn and gazebo for photos.

Bassenthwaite

NY2332 🍺 *Sun Inn*

Parkergate, *Bassenthwaite, Keswick, Cumbria, CA12 4QG.*
Wonderful views of mountains and lake. Cosy. Tranquil and relaxing.
Open: All year (not Xmas)
017687 76376 Mr & Mrs Phillips
Fax: 017687 76911
phillips@parkergate.freeserve.co.uk
D: £18–£25 **S:** £25–£30
Beds: 1F 2D 1T **Baths:** 3 En 1 Pr
🛇 (5) 🅿 (4) 🍴 📺 🛏 ✗ 🎱 Ⓥ ♨

Bassenthwaite Hall Farm,
Bassenthwaite, Keswick, Cumbria, CA12 4QP.
Charming olde worlde, farmhouse – excellent accommodation. by a stream with ducks! **Open:** All year
017687 76393 (also fax)
Mrs Trafford
D: £16–£20 **S:** £25–£30
Beds: 1D 1T **Baths:** 2 Sh
🛇 (10) 🅿 (4) 🍴 📺 🎱 Ⓥ ♨

Chapel Farm, *Bassenthwaite Lake, Bassenthwaite, Keswick, Cumbria, CA12 4QH.*
Working family farm, friendly accommodation, good home cooking.
Open: All Year
017687 76495 Mrs Fell
D: £15–£17 **S:** £15–£17
Beds: 1T 1D **Baths:** 1 Sh
🛇 🅿 (3) 📺 🛏 ✗ Ⓥ

Mirkholme Farm, *Bassenthwaite, Keswick, Cumbria, CA12 4QX.*
Near the Cumbrian Way on the back 'o' Skiddaw. Friendly.
Open: All Year
016973 71333 Mrs Todd
mirkholme@talk21.com
D: £16–£17 **S:** £16–£17
Beds: 1F 1D **Baths:** 1 Sh
🛇 🅿 📺 🛏 ✗ Ⓥ ♨ 👶

Willow Cottage, *Bassenthwaite, Keswick, Cumbria, CA12 4QP.*
Peaceful village location, log fires, stencilling, patchwork, beams, flagged floors. **Open:** All Year (not Xmas)
017687 76440 Mrs Beaty
D: £20–£22.50 **S:** £25–£30
Beds: 1D 1T **Baths:** 2 En
🅿 (2) 🍴 🎱 Ⓥ ♨

Blackford

NY3962 🍺 *Crown & Thistle, Coach & Horses, Golden Fleece*

Gill Farm, *Blackford, Carlisle, Cumbria, CA6 4EL.*
Welcome to our C18th farmhouse on working farm, set in quiet peaceful countryside. **Open:** All Year
01228 675326 Mrs Nicholson
D: £17.50–£21 **S:** £18–£20
Beds: 1F 1D 1T **Baths:** 2 Sh
🛇 🅿 (7) 📺 🛏 🎱 Ⓥ ♨ 👶

Blackwell

NY4053 🍺 *Black Lion, Old Tote, White Quey*

Blackwell Farm, *Lowry Street, Blackwell, Carlisle, Cumbria, CA2 4SH.*
Warm and comfortable family farm close to M6 junction 42.
Open: All Year (not Xmas)
Grades: AA 3 Diamond
01228 524073 Ms Westmorland
blackwellfarm@ukf.net
D: £18 **S:** £20 **Beds:** 1F 1D
🛇 🅿 (4) 📺 🛏 🎱 Ⓥ ♨

Bolton

NY6323

Glebe House, *Bolton, Appleby in Westmorland, Cumbria, CA16 6AW.*
Former C17th farmhouse, quiet location, comfortable rooms, hearty breakfast.
Open: All Year (not Xmas)
017683 61125 Mrs Cotton
derick.cotton@btinternet.com
D: £15–£20 **S:** £15–£20
Beds: 2D 1T **Baths:** 1 En 1 Sh
🛇 🅿 (8) 🍴 📺 🛏 ✗ 🎱 Ⓥ ♨ 3

Boot

NY1701

Dale View, *Boot, Eskdale, Holmrook, Cumbria, CA19 1TG.*
Comfortable Edwardian house, beautiful views. **Open:** All Year (not Xmas)
019467 23236 Mr & Mrs Gray
D: £17–£20 **S:** £17–£20
Beds: 2D 1T 1S **Baths:** 1 Sh
🐾 ⅍ 📺 Ⅵ

Bootle

SD1188

The Stables, *Bootle, Millom, Cumbria, LA19 5TJ.*
Spacious accommodation, lovely views, two rivers, mountains, fells. Home-cooking. **Open:** All Year
01229 718644 Mrs Light
D: £16–£18.50 **S:** £17.50–£25
Beds: 1F 2D **Baths:** 2 En 1 Sh
🐾 📖 (6) 📺 🛏 ✕ 📖 Ⅵ 🔥

Borrowdale

NY2417 ⬛ *Black Lion, Langstrath, Dog & Gun, Riverside*

Greenbank Country House Hotel, *Borrowdale, Keswick, Cumbria, CA12 5UY.*
Open: Feb to Xmas Eve & New Year
Grades: ETC 4 Diamond, Silver Award, AA 4 Diamond, RAC 4 Diamond, Sparkling
017687 77215 Mrs Wood
D: £28–£34 **S:** £30–£42
Beds: 1F 2T 7D **Baths:** 10 En
🐾 (2) 📖 (15) 📺 ✕ 📖 Ⅵ 🔥 cc
Greenbank is quietly situated in the heart of Borrowdale. Superb walking area and lovely views. 10 ensuite bedrooms with tea & coffee-making facilities etc. Two lounges with log fires. Excellent cuisine and warm welcome.

Ashness Cottage, *Borrowdale, Keswick, Cumbria, CA12 5UN.*
Cosy cottage, in pleasant grounds, near Ashness Bridge, overlooking Derwent Water. **Open:** All Year (not Xmas)
017687 77244 Mrs Hamilton-Wright
D: £15–£16 **S:** fr £16
Beds: 1D 1T **Baths:** 1 Sh
🐾 (10) 📖 (2) ⅍ 📺 📖 🔥

Mary Mount, *Country House Hotel, Borrowdale, Keswick, Cumbria, CA12 5UU.*
Country house in gardens and woodlands on shores of Derwent Water.
Open: All Year **Grades:** ETC 2 Star
017687 77223 Mrs Mawdsley
marymount@bigfoot.com
D: £27–£32 **S:** £27–£32
Beds: 3F 6T 4D 1S **Baths:** 14 En
🐾 📖 (25) 📺 🛏 ✕ 📖 Ⅵ 🔥 🔥 ⅙ cc

Hollows Farm, *Grange-in-Borrowdale, Keswick, Cumbria, CA12 5UQ.*
Comfortably furnished C17th farmhouse, working farm in beautiful location.
Open: Feb to Dec
017687 77298 Mrs Fearon
D: £17–£21
Beds: 3D **Baths:** 2 En 1 Pr
🐾 📖 (3) ⅍ 📺 📖 Ⅵ 🔥

Derwent House, *Borrowdale, Keswick, Cumbria, CA12 5UY.*
Family-run guest house with beautiful Fell views from bedrooms.
Open: Feb to Dec
017687 77658 T Lopez
Fax: 017687 77217
derwenthse@aol.com
D: £19–£25 **S:** £23–£25
Beds: 1F 5D 3T 1S **Baths:** 6 En 1 Sh
🐾 (5) 📖 (15) ⅍ 📺 ✕ 📖 Ⅵ 🔥

Bothel

NY1838 ⬛ *Greyhound Inn*

Bothel Parks Farm, *Bothel, Carlisle, Cumbria, CA5 2HX.*
Comfortable farmhouse on working farm near lakes and Scottish borders.
Open: Easter to Oct
016973 20567 Mrs Bowe
D: fr £15 **S:** fr £16
Beds: 1F 1D **Baths:** 1 Sh
🐾 (6) ⅍ 📺 Ⅵ 🔥

Bowness-on-Solway

NY2262 ⬛ *Kings Arms*

Maia Lodge, *Bowness-on-Solway, Wigton, Cumbria, CA7 5BH.*
Panoramic views of Solway Firth and Scottish Borders. End of Hadrian's Wall.
Open: All Year (not Xmas)
Grades: ETC 3 Diamond
016973 51955 Mrs Chettle
D: £17–£20 **S:** £20
Beds: 1F 1D 1T **Baths:** 2 Sh
🐾 (5) 📖 (4) ⅍ 📺 ✕ 📖 🔥

The Old Rectory, *Bowness-on-Solway, Carlisle, Cumbria, CA75AF.*
Fully ensuite old rectory at end of Hadrian's Wall.
Open: All Year (not Xmas)
Grades: ETC 4 Diamond
016973 51055 Mr & Mrs Knowles
www.wallsend.net
wallsend@btinternet.com
D: £20–£25 **S:** £20–£25
Beds: 1F 2D 1S **Baths:** 4 En
🐾 (5) 📖 (6) ⅍ 📺 🛏 ✕ 📖 🔥

Bowness-on-Windermere

SD4097 ⬛ *Royal Oak, Hole In Twall, Brown Horse, Sun Inn, Jacksons, The Mariners , Village Inn*

The Fairfield, *Brantfell Road, Bowness-on-Windermere, Windermere, Cumbria, LA23 3AE.*
Open: Feb to Oct
Grades: ETC 4 Diamond, AA 4 Diamond, RAC 4 Diamond
015394 46565 (also fax)
Mr & Mrs Hood
Ray&barb@the-fairfield.co.uk
D: fr £25 **S:** fr £34
Beds: 2F 5D 1T 1S **Baths:** 8 En 1 Pr
🐾 📖 (12) ⅍ 📺 📖 Ⅵ 🔥
Small friendly family-run hotel in Bowness at the end of the Dales Way. Ensuite rooms with colour TVs. Leisure facilities. Ideal venue to end your walk. Private car park. Genuine hospitality in a homely atmosphere.

Lingwood, *Birkett Hill, Bowness-on-Windermere, Windermere, Cumbria, LA23 3EZ.*
Friendly, comfortable, family guest house within 400 yards of lake.
Open: All Year
Grades: ETC 3 Diamond
015394 44680 Mr & Mrs Atkinson
enquiries@lingwood-guesthouse.co.uk
D: £19–£30 **S:** £19–£30
Beds: 2F 3D 1T **Baths:** 4 En 2 Pr
🐾 📖 (6) 📺 📖 Ⅵ 🔥

Virginia Cottage, *Kendal Road, Bowness-on-Windermere, Windermere, Cumbria, LA23 3EJ.*
C19th house set in heart of village. Friendly welcome assured.
Open: All Year
Grades: ETC 3 Diamond, AA 3 Diamond
015394 44891 Mr Tyler
Fax: 015394 44855
paul-deb@
virginia-cottage.freeserve.co.uk
D: £18–£36 **S:** £20–£30
Beds: 1F 1T 8D 1S **Baths:** 9 En 2 Pr
🐾 (9) ⅍ 📺 🛏 📖 Ⅵ 🔥 🔥 cc

Elim House, *Bisky Howe Road, Bowness-on-Windermere, Windermere, Cumbria, LA23 2JP.*
Warm, friendly and peaceful family-run guest house with award winning garden.
Open: All Year
Grades: AA 3 Diamond
015394 42021
lakedistrict@elimhouse.freeserve.co.uk
D: £16–£50 **S:** £20–£50
Beds: 2F 11D 2T **Baths:** 7 En 2 Sh
🐾 (7) 📖 (6) 📺 🛏 📖 Ⅵ 🔥 🔥

Rosemount, *Lake Road, Bowness-on-Windermere, Windermere, Cumbria, LA23 2EQ.*
Open: All Year
Grades: ETC 3 Diamond, AA 3 Diamond
015394 43739 Mr Thomas
Fax: 015394 48978
rosemt3739@aol.com
D: £20–£30 **S:** £20–£30
Beds: 3F 10D 1T 3S **Baths:** 15 En 2 Pr
🐾 📖 (12) ⅍ 📺 📖 Ⅵ 🔥 cc
Firm comfortable beds and breakfasts worth getting up for at this impressive Victorian guest house with elegant public rooms. Between Windermere and Bowness, yet seconds from a wood where the loudest thing you'll hear is a stream seeking the lake.

Annisgarth House, *2 Annisgarth, Bowness-on-Windermere, Windermere, Cumbria, LA23 2HF.*
Views of lake and mountains. Private parking. Quiet location.
Open: Mar to Dec
015394 44049 (also fax)
Mrs Erwig
D: £16–£22 **S:** £21–£27
Beds: 1T 1D **Baths:** 1 En 1 Sh
🐾 📖 (3) 📺 🛏 📖 🔥

Please respect a B&B's wishes regarding children, animals and smoking

Langthwaite, *Crook Road, Ferry View, Bowness-on-Windermere, Windermere, Cumbria, LA23 3JB.*
Beautiful bungalow. Luxurious, quiet accommodation, breakfast in conservatory, warm welcome.
Open: Feb to Nov **Grades:** AA 4 Diamond
015394 43329 Mr Newham
howard.t.newham@amserve.net
D: £20–£26 **S:** £30–£40
Beds: 2D 1T **Baths:** 3 En
🅿 (4) ⌦ ⊞ ▥ ▦ ⅏ ♨

Thornleigh, *Thornbarrow Road, Bowness-on-Windermere, Windermere, Cumbria, LA23 2EW.*
Friendly licensed guest house. Excellent home cooking and a warm welcome.
Open: All Year (not Xmas/New Year)
Grades: ETC 3 Diamond
015394 44203 Mrs Grant
D: £16–£26 **S:** £16–£26
Beds: 1T 3D 1F 1S **Baths:** 4 En 2 Sh
🅧 🅿 (3) ⌦ ⊞ ♈ ✕ ▥ ▦ ⅏ ♨ ▴ cc

Bay House Lake View, *Guest House, Fallbarrow Road, Bowness-on-Windermere, Windermere, Cumbria, LA23 3DJ.*
Informal, fun & friendly. Close to all amenities. Vegetarians catered for.
Open: All Year
015394 43383 Mrs Large
D: £17.50–£35 **S:** £22.50–£30
Beds: 5D 1T **Baths:** 2 Sh
🅧 🅿 (4) ⊞ ♈ ✕ ▥ ▦ ⅏ ♨ ▴ cc

Langdale View Guest House, *114 Craig Walk, Helm Road, Bowness-on-Windermere, Windermere, Cumbria, LA23 3AX.*
Enjoy this quiet location, warm welcome good food, private parking.
Open: All Year (not Xmas)
015394 44076 **D:** £17–£25 **S:** £20–£25
Beds: 1F 2D 1T 1S **Baths:** 3 En 2 Pr
🅧 (2) 🅿 (5) ⌦ ⊞ ▥ ✕ ▦ ⅏ ♨

Lowfell, *Ferney Green, Bowness-on-Windermere, Windermere, Cumbria, LA23 3ES.*
Close Lake Windermere, in heart of English Lake District.
Open: All Year (not Xmas)
015394 45612 S & L Broughton
Fax: 015394 48411
louise@lakes-pages.co.uk
D: £25
Beds: 1F 1T 1D **Baths:** 3 En
🅧 🅿 (6) ⌦ ⊞ ▦ ⅏ ♨

Elim Lodge, *Bisky Howe Road, Bowness-on-Windermere , Windermere, Cumbria, LA23 2JP.*
Comfortable family-run guest house with a lovely garden and private parking.
Open: All Year
015394 47299 Mrs Mickelfield
elimlodge@lakedistrict.freeserve.co.uk
D: £16–£28 **S:** £16–£28
Beds: 2F 2D 1T 1S **Baths:** 3 En 2 Sh
🅧 🅿 (6) ⊞ ♈ ✕ ▥ ▦ ⅏ ♨

B&B owners may vary rates - be sure to check when booking

All details shown are as supplied by B&B owners in Autumn 2000

NY2323 ⬧ *Royal Oak, Middle Ruddings Hotel, Coledale Inn*

Coledale Inn, *Braithwaite, Keswick, Cumbria, CA12 5TN.*
Georgian inn with spectacular mountain views. Situated in peaceful countryside village.
Open: All Year
Grades: ETC 3 Diamond
017687 78272 Mr Mawdsley
D: £22–£30 **S:** £17–£25
Beds: 5F 1T 5D 1S **Baths:** 12 En
🅧 🅿 (15) ⊞ ▥ ♈ ✕ ▦ ⅏ ♨ ❋ ▴ ㋭ cc

Cottage In The Wood Hotel, *Whinlatter Pass, Braithwaite, Keswick, Cumbria, CA12 5TW.*
Superb location in the Whinlatter Forest Park. Wonderful views.
Open: Mar to Nov
017687 78409 Mrs Littlefair
Fax: 017687 78064
cottage@lake-district.net
D: £25–£33 **S:** £25–£47
Beds: 3F 3D 1T **Baths:** 7 En
🅧 🅿 (15) ⌦ ⊞ ▥ ♈ ✕ ▦ ⅏ ♨ ▴ ㋭ cc

NY6723 ⬧ *New Inn, Drove Inn, White Lion*

Sunray, *Brampton (Appleby), Appleby-in-Westmorland, Cumbria, CA16 6JS.*
Modern bungalow. Guest rooms overlook Pennines, comfortable, welcoming, good breakfast.
Open: Easter to Oct
017683 52905 Mrs Tinkler
D: £15–£20 **S:** £18–£20
Beds: 2D **Baths:** 1 En

NY4251 ⬧ *Crown Inn, Plough, Black Lion, White Lion, Quay, Carrow House*

Crossroads House, *Brisco, Carlisle, Cumbria, CA4 0QZ.*
Charming country house with a Roman well. High standards. Excellent breakfasts.
Open: All Year (not Xmas/New Year)
01228 528994 Mr & Mrs Wilson
Fax: 01228 528994
D: £20–£22 **S:** £18–£20
Beds: 1F 1T 2D 1S **Baths:** 1 En 2 Sh
🅧 🅿 (6) ⌦ ⊞ ✕ ▦ ⅏ ♨

Staggs Cottage, *Brisco, Carlisle, CA4 0QS.*
Converted barn. Open views. Close Carlisle, Hadrian's Wall, Northern Lakes.
Open: All Year (not Xmas)
Grades: ETC 4 Diamond
01228 547419 Mrs Gray
D: £18–£27 **S:** £19–£28
Beds: 2T **Baths:** 1 En 1 Pr
🅧 🅿 ⌦ ⊞ ▦ ⅏ ♨

NY7914 ⬧ *Golden Fleece*

Riverview, *Brough, Kirkby Stephen, Cumbria, CA17 4BZ.*
Friendly welcome, clean, comfortable attractive bedrooms, quiet location, great breakfasts.
Open: All Year (not Xmas)
017683 41894 (also fax)
Mrs Holmes
D: £15–£18 **S:** £15–£18
Beds: 1F 1D 1S **Baths:** 1 En 1 Sh
🅧 🅿 (3) ⌦ ⊞ ▦ ⅏ ♨ ▴

SD5095

Gateside House Farm, *Windermere Road, Burneside, Kendal, Cumbria, LA9 5SE.*
Gateside farm is a working dairy and sheep farm.
Open: All Year
Grades: ETC 3 Diamond
015397 22036 (also fax)
Mrs Ellis
D: £18–£23 **S:** £18–£23
Beds: 1F 3D 1T **Baths:** 3 En 2 Sh
🅧 🅿 (5) ⊞ ♈ ✕ ▦ ⅏ ♨

SD5376 ⬧ *Kings Arms*

Coat Green Farm, *Burton-in-Kendal, Carnforth, Lancs, LA6 1JG.*
Comfortable farmhouse accommodation on a working farm. Quiet rural location.
Open: Easter to Nov
01524 781535 (also fax)
Mrs Duckett
D: £16–£18 **S:** £18
Beds: 1F 1D 1S **Baths:** 1 Sh
🅧 🅿 ⌦ ⊞ ▥ ▦ ⅏ ♨

NY1717 ⬧ *Bridge Hotel, Fish Hotel*

Trevene, *Buttermere, Cockermouth, Cumbria, CA13 9XA.*
Peaceful house surrounded by ideal walking country, close to lakes.
Open: All Year (not Xmas)
017687 70210 (also fax)
Mrs Knight
roland@trevene.fsbusiness.co.uk
D: £18 **S:** £18
Beds: 1F 1D 1T **Baths:** 1 Sh
🅧 (6) 🅿 (3) ⌦ ⊞ ♈ ▦ ♨

Dalegarth, *Buttermere, Cockermouth, Cumbria, CA13 9XA.*
Large Swiss chalet-style house with grounds extending to lake shore.
Open: Apr to Oct
017687 70233 Mr Parker
D: £15–£24 **S:** £20–£30
Beds: 1F 4D 4T **Baths:** 4 En 2 Sh
🅧 (3) 🅿 (20) ♈ ▥ ❋ ▴ ㋭

National Grid References are for villages, towns and cities – not for individual houses

Caldbeck

NY3239   Oddfellow Arm

The Briars, *Friar Row, Caldbeck, Wigton, Cumbria, CA7 8DS.*
In Caldbeck village, right on Cumbria Way. 2 mins' walk pub.
Open: All Year (not Xmas)
Grades: ETC 3 Diamond
016974 78633 Mrs Coulthard
D: £18.50–£20 **S:** £18.50–£20
Beds: 1D 1T 1S **Baths:** 1 En 1 Sh
🅿 (4) ⅏ 📺 🐾 🛏 Ⅷ ₤

Cark-in-Cartmel

SD3676   Engine Inn

Eeabank House, *123 Station Road, Cark-in-Cartmel, Grange-over-Sands, Cumbria, LA11 7NY.*
C17th coaching house inn, licensed bar, log fires, Old England is here.
Open: All Year
015395 58156 (also fax) Mr Reece
D: £16.50–£24 **S:** £16.50–£24
Beds: 2D 1T **Baths:** 2 En 1 Pr
📺 🐾 ✕ 🛏 Ⅷ ₤

Carleton (Carlisle)

NY4252

Country House B&B, *High Scalesceugh House, High Scalesceugh, Carleton, Carlisle, Cumbria, CA4 0BT.*
Lovely country house with picturesque surroundings. Cosy bedrooms with a fantastic view. **Open:** All year
016974 73381 Mr & Mrs Walters
D: £18–£20 **S:** £15–£16
Beds: 1D 1T 1S **Baths:** 1 En 1 Sh
🛏 🅿 (8) 📺 🛏 ❋ ₤

Carleton (Holmrook)

SD0898   Horse & Groom

Coachman's Cottage, *Carleton Hall, Carleton, Holmrook, Cumbria, CA19 1YX.*
Converted coach house, oak beams, good food, warm welcome.
Open: All Year (not Xmas)
019467 24369 Mrs Marshall
D: £16–£20 **S:** £16–£20
Beds: 3F 1D 1S **Baths:** 1 En 2 Sh
🛏 🅿 (5) ⅏ 📺 🛏 Ⅷ ₤

Carlisle

NY3955   Metal Bridge Inn, The Beehive, Mary's Pantry, Crown & Thistle, Coach & Horses, Golden Fleece, Black Lion

Howard Lodge, *90 Warwick Road, Carlisle, Cumbria, CA1 1JU.*
Open: All Year
Grades: ETC 4 Diamond, AA 3 Diamond
01228 529842 Mr Hendrie
D: £15–£25 **S:** £20–£30
Beds: 2F 1D 2T 1S **Baths:** 6 En 1 Sh
🛏 🅿 (6) 📺 🛏 ✕ 🛏 Ⅷ ₤
Friendly family-run guest house in comfortable Victorian town house in conservation area. Spacious rooms all fully ensuite with satellite TV, welcome tray, hairdryer and clock radio. Large breakfasts. 5 minutes' walk from station and city centre. Evening meals by prior arrangement. Private car park.

Craighead, *6 Hartington Place, Carlisle, Cumbria, CA1 1HL.*
Open: All Year (not Xmas)
Grades: ETC 3 Diamond
01228 596767 Mrs Smith
D: fr £17 **S:** fr £16
Beds: 1F 2D 1T 1S **Baths:** 1 En 2 Sh
🛏 📺 🛏 Ⅷ Ⅵ ₤
You will receive a warm welcome at Craighead, a Grade II Listed spacious Victorian town house with comfortable rooms and original features. CTV, tea/coffee tray in all rooms. Minutes' walk to city centre bus and rail stations and all amenities. Friendly personal service.

Gill Farm, *Blackford, Carlisle, Cumbria, CA6 4EL.*
Open: All Year
01228 675326 Mrs Nicholson
D: £17.50–£21 **S:** £18–£20
Beds: 1F 1D 1T **Baths:** 1 En 2 Sh
🛏 🅿 (7) 📺 🛏 🛏 Ⅷ ❋ ₤
Welcome to our C18th farmhouse on working farm, set in quiet peaceful countryside only 5 minutes from M6 (J44). Good touring situation for Hadrian's Wall, Scottish Borders and Lake District. Ideal stopover to and from Scotland. Large garden and beautiful scenery.

Angus Hotel & Almonds Bistro, *14 Scotland Road, Stanwix, Carlisle, Cumbria, CA3 9DG.*
Open: All Year
Grades: AA 4 Diamond
01228 523546 Mr Webster
Fax: 01228 531895
angus@hadrians-wall.fsnet.co.uk
D: £20–£27 **S:** £26–£42
Beds: 4F 3D 4T 3S **Baths:** 11 En 3 Sh
🛏 🅿 (6) 📺 🛏 ✕ 🛏 Ⅷ ₤ cc
Victorian town house, foundations on Hadrian's Wall. Excellent food, Les Routiers Awards, local cheeses, home baked bread. Genuine warm welcome from owners. Licensed, draught beer, lounge, meeting room, internet cafe, direct dial telephones, secure garaging. Group rates for cyclists available.

Cherry Grove, *87 Petteril Street, Carlisle, Cumbria, CA1 2AW.*
Lovely red brick building close to golf club and town.
Open: All Year
Grades: AA 3 Diamond
01228 541942 Mr & Mrs Houghton
petteril87@aol.com
D: £17.50–£20 **S:** £20–£30
Beds: 3F 2D **Baths:** 5 En
🛏 🅿 (3) ⅏ 📺 🛏 Ⅷ Ⅵ ₤

Avondale, *3 St Aidans Road, Carlisle, Cumbria, CA1 1LT.*
Attractive comfortable Edwardian house. Quiet central position convenient M6 J43.
Open: All Year (not Xmas)
Grades: ETC 4 Diamond
01228 523012 (also fax)
Mr & Mrs Hayes
beeanbee@hotmail.com
D: £20 **S:** £20–£40
Beds: 1D 2T **Baths:** 1 En 1 Pr
🛏 🅿 (3) ⅏ 📺 ✕ 🛏 Ⅷ ₤

Dalroc, *411 Warwick Road, Carlisle, Cumbria, CA1 2RZ.*
Small friendly house. Midway city centre and M6 motorway.
Open: All Year (not Xmas/New Year)
01228 542805 Mrs Irving
D: £16 **S:** £16
Beds: 1F 1D 1S
🛏 (7) 🅿 📺 ✕ 🛏 ₤

Chatsworth Guest House, *22 Chatsworth Square, Carlisle, Cumbria, CA1 1HF.*
City centre Grade II Listed building, close to all amenities.
Open: All Year (not Xmas)
Grades: ETC 3 Diamond
01228 524023 (also fax)
Mrs Mackin
D: £19–£22 **S:** £25
Beds: 1F 1D 2T 1S **Baths:** 5 En
🛏 🅿 (2) ⅏ 📺 Ⅷ ₤

Kingstown Hotel, *246 Kingstown Road, Carlisle, CA3 0DE.*
Open: All Year
Grades: AA 3 Diamond
01228 515292 (also fax)
Mrs Marshall
D: fr £23.50 **S:** £35–£40
Beds: 1F 4D 2T **Baths:** 7 En
🛏 🅿 (14) 📺 🛏 ✕ 🛏 Ⅷ ₤ ₤ Ⅰ cc
Just off the M6 (Jct. 44) we are a licensed hotel providing high-quality accommodation. You will find a friendly and relaxed atmosphere, freshly-prepared cuisine and fine wine at reasonable prices. A good base to explore Cumbria, Northumbria, Lake District, Scotland

Corner House Hotel & Bar, *4 Grey Street, Carlisle, CA1 2JP.*
Open: All Year
Grades: ETC 3 Diamond
01228 533239 Mrs Anderson
Fax: 01228 546628
D: £17.50–£22 **S:** £20–£30
Beds: 3F 4D 4T 3S **Baths:** All En
🛏 📺 🛏 ✕ 🛏 Ⅷ ❋ ₤ Ⅰ cc
Refurbished family run hotel. All rooms ensuite, colour TV, phones, tea/coffee, radio, toiletries etc. Cosy bar, Sky TV lounge, games room, easy access city centre, bus/train. Base for golf, walking, cycling, touring the Lakes, Roman Wall, Carlisle/ Settle line etc.

Ashleigh House, *46 Victoria Place, Carlisle, Cumbria, CA1 1EX.*
Beautifully decorated town house. Two minutes from city centre.
Open: All Year (not Xmas/New Year)
Grades: ETC 4 Diamond
01228 521631 Mr Davies
D: £19–£22.50 **S:** £25–£30
Beds: 3F 1T 2D 1S **Baths:** 7 En
🛏 (5) 📺 🛏 Ⅷ ₤ cc

Cornerways Guest House, *107 Warwick Road, Carlisle, Cumbria, CA1 1EA.*
Large Victorian town house.
Open: All Year (not Xmas)
Grades: ETC 4 Diamond
01228 521733 Mrs Fisher
D: £14–£18 **S:** £16–£18
Beds: 2F 1D 4T 3S **Baths:** 3 En 2 Sh
🛏 🅿 (4) 📺 🛏 🛏 Ⅷ Ⅵ ₤

Courtfield Guest House, 169
Warwick Road, Carlisle, Cumbria, CA1 1LP.
Short walk to historic city centre. Close to
M6, J43.
Open: All Year (not Xmas)
Grades: ETC 4 Diamond
01228 522767 Mrs Dawes
D: £18–£22 **S:** fr £25
Beds: 1F 2D 2T **Baths:** 5 En
� 🅿 (4) ⊬ ⚐ ▥ Ⅵ ♨

East View Guest House, 110 *Warwick
Road, Carlisle, Cumbria, CA1 1JU.*
10 minutes' walking distance from city
centre, railway station and restaurants.
Open: All Year (not Xmas)
Grades: ETC 3 Diamond, AA 3 Diamond,
RAC 3 Diamond
01228 522112 (also fax)
Mrs Glease
D: £18–£20 **S:** £20–£25
Beds: 3F 2D 1T 1S **Baths:** 7 En
� 🅿 (4) ⊬ ⚐ ▥ Ⅵ ♨

Cambro House, 173 *Warwick Road,
Carlisle, Cumbria, CA1 1LP.*
Open: All Year
Grades: AA 3 Diamond
01228 543094 (also fax)
Mr & Mrs Mawson
cambrohouse@amserve.net
D: £17–£20 **S:** £20–£25
Beds: 2D 1T **Baths:** 3 En
🅿 (2) ⊬ ⚐ ▥ ♨
Guests can expect warm hospitality and
friendly service at this attractively
decorated and well-maintained guest
house. Each ensuite bedroom includes
TV, clock, radio, hairdryer and welcome
tray. Private off-road parking available,
non-smoking, close to golf course.

Crossroads House, *Brisco, Carlisle,
Cumbria, CA4 0QZ.*
Charming country house with a Roman
well. High standards. Excellent
breakfasts.
Open: All Year (not Xmas/New Year)
01228 528994
Mr & Mrs Wilson
Fax: 01228528994
D: £20–£22 **S:** £18–£20
Beds: 1F 1T 2D 1S **Baths:** 1 En 2 Sh
🌼 🅿 (6) ⊬ ⚐ ✕ ▥ Ⅵ ♨

Cartmel

SD3878 🍺 *Caverdish Arms, Royal Oak, Kings
Arms*

Bank Court Cottage, *The Square,
Cartmel, Grange-over-Sands, Cumbria,
LA11 6QB.*
Open: All Year (not Xmas)
Grades: ETC 3 Diamond
015395 36593 (also fax)
Mrs Lawson
D: £18.50–£25 **S:** fr £18.50
Beds: 1D 1T **Baths:** 1 Sh
🌼 ⊬ ⚐ ✕ ⚐ ▥ Ⅵ ♨
We offer a warm welcome to our pretty
character cottage in a quiet courtyard off
the village square. Beams, log fires, home
grown vegetables and fruit, free range
eggs from our own hens. Lovely views of
Cartmel Park and racecourse.

Cartmel Fell

SD4187 🍺 *Masons Arms, The Hare and
Hounds*

Lightwood Farmhouse, *Cartmel Fell,
Grange-over-Sands, Cumbria, LA11 6NP.*
Open: All Year (not Xmas)
015395 31454 (also fax)
Ms Cervetti
D: £24–£28 **S:** £30–£35
Beds: 2F 2D 2T **Baths:** 6 En
🌼 🅿 (8) ⊬ ⚐ ✕ ▥ ♨ cc
Dating back to 1656, Lightwood has many
original features, 2 acres of gardens.
extensive views. All rooms ensuite,
tastefully decorated, with tea-making
facilities. Excellent home cooking. Two
and a half miles from southern end of
Lake Windermere.

Castle Carrock

NY5455 🍺 *The Bluebell*

Gelt Hall Farm, *Castle Carrock,
Carlisle, Cumbria, CA4 9LT.*
Near Hadrian's Wall, Scottish border,
Gretna Green. Scenic walks all around,
looks onto Pennines. **Open:** All Year
Grades: AA 3 Diamond
01228 670260 Ms Robinson
D: £15–£16.50 **S:** £16–£17
Beds: 1F 1D 1T **Baths:** 2 Sh
🌼 🅿 ⊬ ⚐ ⚐ ▥ ❋

Catlowdy

NY4576

Liddel Lodge, *Penton, Catlowdy,
Carlisle, Cumbria, CA6 5QN .*
Old Hunting Lodge with large gardens.
All rooms have panoramic views of Liddel
valley. **Open:** All Year
01228 577335 G H Casson
D: £18–£20 **S:** £18–£20
Beds: 1D 1T 1S **Baths:** 2 En
🌼 🅿 (6) ⊬ ⚐ ✕ ▥ Ⅵ ♨

Cockermouth

NY1230 🍺 *Black Bull, Brown Cow, Bitter End,
Old Post House, Shepherds Hotel*

The Rook Guest House, 9
*Castlegate, Cockermouth, Cumbria,
CA13 9EU.*
Cosy C17th town house. Spiral staircase.
Convenient for all amenities.
Open: All Year (not Xmas)
01900 828496 Mrs Waters
D: £16–£18 **S:** £20
Beds: 2D 1T **Baths:** 1 En 1 Pr 1 Sh
🌼 (5) ⊬ ⚐ ▥ Ⅵ ♨

Shepherds Hotel, *Egremont Road,
Cockermouth, Cumbria, CA13 0QX.*
Modern hotel with views towards Lake
District, close to gem town of
Cockermouth and bustling Keswick.
Excellent hot and cold food available all
day. Attached to visitors centre and large
gift shop. Ideal for touring on business or
pleasure. **Open:** All Year (not Xmas)
01900 822673 (also fax)
E A Campbell
D: £18.75–£20 **S:** £37.50–£40
Beds: 4D 9T **Baths:** 13 En
🌼 🅿 (99) ⚐ ⚐ ✕ ▥ Ⅵ ♨ ⚐ cc

Albany House, *Wordsworth Terrace,
Cockermouth, Cumbria, CA13 9AH.*
Beautiful Victorian guest house, stripped
pine doors and a warm welcome.
Open: All Year
01900 825630 Mr Nichol
albany@eletrotest.org
D: £16 **S:** £16
Beds: 1F 2D 2T 2S **Baths:** 1 Pr 1 Sh
🌼 ⊬ ⚐ ⚐ ⚐ ▥ Ⅵ ♨

Benson Court Cottage, 10 *St Helen's
Street, Cockermouth, Cumbria, CA13 9HX.*
Town centre 1727 cottage. Commercial/
tourist guests welcome. Generous
breakfasts.
Open: All Year
01900 822303 Mrs Townley
D: £15–£20 **S:** £15–£22
Beds: 1F 1D
🌼 (6) ⊬ ⚐ ▥ Ⅵ ♨

Coniston

SD3097 🍺 *Sun, Crown, Wilson Arms, Church
House Inn, Yewdale, Swan, Ship Inn*

Kirkbeck House, *Lake Road, Coniston,
Cumbria, LA21 8EW.*
Open: All Year
015394 41358 Mrs Potter
ann@kirkbeck.co.uk
D: £16 **S:** £18
Beds: 1F 1D 1T
🌼 🅿 (3) ⚐ ▥ Ⅵ ♨
Long established family run bed and
breakfast offering a warm friendly
atmosphere. Comfortable bedrooms with
pleasant views, good food, attractive
garden and private parking. Situated in
the quiet area of Coniston Village. Within
walking distance of all amenities.

Thwaite Cottage, *Waterhead,
Coniston, Cumbria, LA21 8AJ.*
Beautiful C17th cottage. Peaceful
location near head of Coniston Water.
Open: All Year (not Xmas)
Grades: ETC 3 Diamond
015394 41367 Mrs Aldridge
m@thwaitcot.freeserve.co.uk
D: £21–£24
Beds: 2D 1T **Baths:** 1 En 2 Pr
🌼 🅿 (3) ⊬ ⚐ ▥ Ⅵ ♨

Crown Hotel, *Coniston, Cumbria,
LA21 8EA.*
Situated in the picturesque village of
Coniston within easy reach of the famous
lake. **Open:** All Year (not Xmas)
Grades: ETC 2 Diamond RAC 2 Diamond
015394 41243 Mr Tiidus
Fax: 015394 41804
enntiidus@crownhotel.freeserve.co.uk
D: £25–£35 **S:** £30–£40
Beds: 8D 6T **Baths:** 12 En 1 Sh
🌼 🅿 (20) ⚐ ✕ ▥ Ⅵ ♨ cc

Oaklands, *Yewdale Road, Coniston,
Cumbria, LA21 8DX.*
Beautiful spacious lakeland house, near
village centre, private parking.
Open: All Year (not Xmas/New Year)
015394 41245 (also fax)
Mrs Myers
D: £20–£25 **S:** £20–£25
Beds: 1T 2D **Baths:** 1 En 1 Sh
🅿 (4) ⊬ ⚐ ▥ Ⅵ ♨

Waverley, Lake Road, Coniston,
Cumbria, *LA21 8EW.*
Clean and friendly, excellent value. Large
Victorian house.
Open: All Year (not Xmas)
015394 41127 (also fax)
Mrs Graham
D: fr £16 **S:** fr £16
Beds: 1F 1D 1T **Baths:** 1 Pr 2 Sh
🛇 **P** (3) ⅍ 📺 ★ 🏬 ⅣⅤ ♨

Lakeland House, Tilberthwaite
Avenue, Coniston, Cumbria, *LA21 8ED.*
Friendly, family-run, village centre,
lounge/log fire, groups welcome.
Open: All Year (not Xmas)
Grades: ETC 3 Diamond
015394 41303 Mrs Holland
lakelandhouse_coniston@hotmail.com
D: £16–£35 **S:** £16–£35
Beds: 5F 2D 1T 1S **Baths:** 3 En 3 Sh
🛇 📺 ★ 🏬 Ⅴ ♨ cc

Knipe Ground Farm, (East of Lake),
Coniston, Cumbria, *LA21 8AE.*
Comfortable, peaceful C16th farmhouse
in fields overlooking woodland, lake,
mountains.
Open: All Year (not Xmas)
015394 41221 Mrs Dutton
D: £16–£20 **S:** £16–£18
Beds: 2D 2S **Baths:** 1 Sh
🛇 (8) **P** (2) ⅍ 📺 Ⅴ ♨

Sunny Brae Cottage, Hawes Bank,
Coniston, Cumbria, *LA21 8AP.*
Quality B&B in traditional whitewashed
cottage on outskirts of village.
Open: All Year
015394 41654 Mr Beacock
Fax: 015394 41532
D: £18–£30 **S:** £18–£30
Beds: 2D 2T 1S **Baths:** 4 En 1 Pr
🛇 **P** (4) ⅍ 📺 ★ 🏬 Ⅴ ✿ ♨ &

Cowgill

SD7587   🍺 Sportsman Inn, George & Dragon

The Sportsman's Inn, Cowgill, Dent,
Sedbergh, Cumbria, *LA10 5RG.*
Family owned freehouse 1670, scenic
location, rooms overlooking River Dee.
Open: All Year
015396 25282 Mr & Mrs Martin
ronmartin@bun.com
D: £17.50–£23.50 **S:** £17.50–£23.50
Beds: 1F 2D 3T **Baths:** 3 Sh
🛇 **P** (10) ★ ✕ 🏬 Ⅴ ♨

Scow Cottage, Cowgill, Dent,
Sedbergh, Cumbria, *LA10 5RN.*
Attractive and comfortable 250-year-old
Dales farmhouse, set in beautiful
countryside.
Open: All Year
015396 25445 Mrs Ferguson
D: £16–£17 **S:** £19–£25
Beds: 1D 1T **Baths:** 1 Sh
🛇 (12) **P** (4) ⅍ ★ ✕ 🏬 Ⅴ

All details shown are as
supplied by B&B owners in
Autumn 2000

Crook

SD4695   🍺 Brown Horse Inn

Mitchelland Farm Bungalow,
Crook, Kendal, Cumbria, *LA8 8LL.*
Wheelchair accessible spacious working
farm bungalow. Wonderful views near
Windermere.
Open: All Year
015394 47421 Mr Higham
D: £22–£26 **S:** £25–£30
Beds: 1T 1D **Baths:** 1 En 1 Pr
🛇 **P** (5) ⅍ 📺 ★ 🏬 Ⅴ ♨ &

Crosby Ravensworth

NY6215   🍺 Butchers Arms

Low Row Farm, Crosby Ravensworth,
Penrith, Cumbria, *CA10 3JJ.*
Large farmhouse on working farm, all
rooms bright and comfortable.
Open: All Year (not Xmas)
01931 715238 D: fr £16.50 **S:** fr £18.50
Beds: 1F 1D 1T **Baths:** 2 Sh
P (8) 📺 ★ ✕ 🏬 Ⅴ ♨ cc

Dalton-in-Furness

SD2374   🍺 Black Dog Inn

Black Dog Inn, Holmes Green,
Broughton Road, Dalton-in-Furness,
Cumbria, *LA15 8JP.*
A cosy, beamed coaching inn with open
fires, a friendly atmosphere.
Open: All Year
01229 462561 Mr Taylor
Fax: 01229 468036
jack@blackdoginn.freeserve.co.uk
D: £15–£17.50 **S:** £12.50–£20
Beds: 3D 3S **Baths:** 3 En 2 Pr 1 Sh
🛇 (1) **P** (30) ⅍ 📺 ★ ✕ Ⅴ ♨ cc

Dent

SD7086   🍺 George & Dragon, Sun Inn,
Sportsmans Inn

Rash House, Dent Foot, Dent,
Sedbergh, Cumbria, *LA10 5SU.*
Charming C18th farmhouse situated in
picturesque Dentdale.
Open: All Year (not Xmas)
015396 20113 (also fax)
Mrs Hunter
D: £16–£18 **S:** £18–£20
Beds: 1F 1D **Baths:** 1 Sh
🛇 **P** (2) 📺 ★ ✕ 🏬 Ⅴ ♨

Garda View Guest House, Dent,
Sedbergh, Cumbria, *LA10 5QL.*
Village centre, friendly family house.
Hearty breakfasts, walking information
available. **Open:** All Year (not Xmas)
015396 25209 Mrs Smith
dentstores@cwcom.net
D: £17 **S:** £17
Beds: 2D 1T 1S **Baths:** 1 Sh
🛇 **P** (2) 📺 ★ Ⅴ ♨

Stone Close Tea Shop, Main Street,
Dent, Sedbergh, Cumbria, *LA10 5QL.*
C17th oak beamed tea shop with log
fires. **Open:** Feb to Dec
015396 25231 Mr Rushton
D: £17–£25 **S:** £19.50–£49
Beds: 1F 2D 1S **Baths:** 1 En 1 Sh
🛇 **P** (4) ⅍ 📺 ★ ✕ 🏬 Ⅴ ♨ cc

Planning a longer stay? Always
ask for any special rates

Smithy Fold, Whernside Manor, Dent,
Sedbergh, Cumbria, *LA10 5RE.*
Small C18th country house.
Open: All Year (not Xmas)
015396 25368
Mrs Cheetham
D: £17.50 **S:** £17.50
Beds: 1F 1D 1T **Baths:** 1 Sh
🛇 (4) **P** (6) 📺 ★ ✕ 🏬 Ⅴ ♨

Little Oak, Helmside View, Dent,
Sedbergh, Cumbria, *LA10 5QY.*
Oak-beamed studio for two, warm
welcome, pretty, unspoilt village.
Open: All Year (not Xmas)
015396 25330 Mr & Mrs Priestley
D: £18 **S:** fr £18
Beds: 1D
⅍ 📺 ♨

Syke Fold, Dent, Sedbergh, Cumbria,
LA10 5RE.
Peaceful country hose with stunning
views. Quiet location 1.5 miles east of
cobbled Dent.
Open: Feb to Nov
015396 25486
Mrs Newsham
D: £21.50–£23 **S:** £21.50–£23
Beds: 1F 1D **Baths:** 2 En
🛇 **P** (2) ⅍ 📺 ★ ✕ Ⅴ cc

The White House, Dent, Sedbergh,
Cumbria, *LA10 5QR.*
House in picturesque Dales village. Quiet
location, garden, superb walking.
Open: Easter to Oct
015396 25041
Mrs Allen
WhiteHouseDent@lineone.net
D: £17–£18 **S:** £17–£18
Beds: 1D 1T 1S **Baths:** 2 Sh
P (2) ⅍ 📺 🏬 Ⅴ ♨

Duddon Bridge

SD1988   🍺 High Cross Inn

The Dower House, High Duddon,
Duddon Bridge, Broughton in Furness,
Cumbria, *LA20 6ET.*
Delightful Victorian country house
offering a warm and friendly welcome.
Comfortable bedrooms.
Open: All Year (not Xmas/New Year)
01229 716279 (also fax)
Mrs Nichols
D: £20–£25 **S:** £25–£27
Beds: 1F 2D 1T 1S **Baths:** 1 En 3 Pr
🛇 **P** (8) 📺 ✕ 🏬 Ⅴ ♨ cc

RATES
D = Price range per person
sharing in a double room
S = Price range for a
single room

Sycamore House, *Dufton, Appleby-in-Westmorland, Cumbria, CA16 6DB.*
Listed cottage, cosy living room, close to pub and shop.
Open: Easter to Dec
017683 51296 Mrs O'Halloran
o_halloran@hotmail.com
D: £18–£20 **S:** £17–£20
Beds: 1D 1T 2S **Baths:** 1 En 1 Sh
🛇 **P** (2) 📺 ♒ 🎂 🕭

Eamont Bridge

NY5228 🍺 *Beehive Inn*

River View, *6 Lowther Glen, Eamont Bridge, Penrith, Cumbria, CA10 2BP.*
Beautiful riverside bungalow near Lake Ullswater. Comfortable beds, good breakfasts.
Open: All Year
01768 864405 Mrs O'Neil
D: £18–£22 **S:** £20–£22
Beds: 1T 2D 2S **Baths:** 1 En
🛇 **P** (4) 📺 🎂 🕭 🖑 🕭 ♿

Egremont

NY0110 🍺 *White Mare, Oddfellows*

Ghyll Farm Guest House, *Egremont, Cumbria, CA22 2UA.*
Open: All Year (not Xmas)
01946 822256 Mrs Holliday
D: £14 **S:** £14
Beds: 2T 2S **Baths:** 2 Sh
🛇 **P** (6) 📺 🎂 🕭
Comfortable clean friendly farmhouse. Good breakfast, private off-road parking. Try a fishing holiday on River Irt at Holmrook and catch salmon and sea trout. Reasonable rates while the men fish, the ladies can visit our beautiful lakes etc.

Far Head of Haile, *Haile, Egremont, CA22 2PE.*
Explore the quieter Western lakes, mountains and coast. Between Ennerdale and Wastwater.
Open: All Year
01946 841205 Mr Greening
D: £15–£18.50 **S:** £15.50–£21
Beds: 1F 2D 5S **Baths:** 1 En 3 Sh
🛇 **P** (12) 🕭 📺 🎂 🕭

Elterwater

NY3204 🍺 *Britannia Inn*

Britannia Inn, *Elterwater, Langdale, Ambleside, Cumbria, LA22 9HP.*
Traditional Lakeland inn overlooking village green. Cosy bars with log fires.
Open: All Year (not Xmas)
Grades: ETC 1 Star
015394 37210 J A Fry
Fax: 015394 37311
info@britinn.co.uk
D: £24–£39 **S:** £24–£30
Beds: 9D 3T **Baths:** 9 En 3 Sh
🛇 **P** (10) 📺 ♒ ✕ 🎂 🖑 🕭 cc

Please respect a B&B's wishes regarding children, animals and smoking

---

Embleton

NY1630 🍺 *Wheatsheaf Inn*

Orchard House, *Embleton, Cockermouth, Cumbria, CA13 9XP.*
Detached Edwardian country house with 3/4 acre garden. Mountain views.
Open: All Year
017687 76347 (also fax)
Mrs Newton
barbaraorchardhouse@yahoo.co.uk
D: £18–£20 **S:** £20–£25
Beds: 2D **Baths:** 2 En
🛇 (7) **P** (8) ♒ 📺 ♒ 🎂 🖑 🕭

Lambfoot House, *Embleton, Cockermouth, Cumbria, CA13 9XL.*
Relax in elegant and spacious ensuite rooms, lounge or conservatory.
Open: All Year
017687 76424
Mr & Mrs Holden
Fax: 017687 76721
lambfoot@lake-district.net
D: £22–£23 **S:** £22–£23
Beds: 1D 1T 1S **Baths:** 3 En
P (5) ♒ 📺 🎂 🖑 🕭 cc

Endmoor

SD5385

Summerlands Tower, *Summerlands, Endmoor, Kendal, Cumbria, LA8 0ED.*
Victorian country house with fine rooms and gardens. 3 miles from M6, J36.
Open: Easter to Nov
015395 61081 (also fax)
Mr & Mrs Green
m_green@virgin.net
D: £24–£29.50 **S:** £29–£34050
Beds: 2T 1D **Baths:** 1 En 1 Pr
🛇 (12) **P** (3) ♒ 📺 🎂 🕭

Ennerdale Bridge

NY0715 🍺 *Fox & Hounds, Shepherds Arms*

The Old Vicarage, *Ennerdale Bridge, Cleator, Cumbria, CA23 3AG.*
Charming old former vicarage with spectacular views of Ennerdale Fells.
Open: All Year (not Xmas)
01946 861107
Mrs Lake
D: £18 **S:** £18
Beds: 1F 2D 1T 1S **Baths:** 3 Sh
🛇 **P** (6) 📺 ♒ 🎂 🖑 🕭

The Shepherds Arms Hotel, *Ennerdale Bridge, Cleator, Cumbria, CA23 3AR.*
Small friendly hotel in the Lake District National Park which has been completely refurbished.
Open: All Year
Grades: ETC 2 Star
01946 861249 (also fax)
Mr Stanfield
enquiries@shepherdsarmshotel.co.uk
D: £28 **S:** £30–£35
Beds: 1F 3D 3T 1S **Baths:** 6 En 2 Pr
🛇 **P** (6) 📺 ♒ 🎂 🖑 🕭 cc

Eskdale Green

NY1400 🍺 *King George IV, Bower House Inn*

The Ferns, *Eskdale Green, Holmrook, Cumbria, CA19 1UA.*
Homely accommodation in large Victorian residence. Near lakes and mountains.
Open: All Year
019467 23217 (also fax)
Mr & Mrs Prestwood
ferns@eskdale-green.demon.co.uk
D: £18–£25 **S:** £22–£25
Beds: 2D 1T **Baths:** 1 En 2 Sh
🛇 **P** (4) ♒ 📺 🎂 🖑 🕭

Far Sawrey

SD3895 🍺 *Sawrey Hotel, Tower Bank Arms*

Sawrey Hotel, *Far Sawrey, Ambleside, Cumbria, LA22 0LQ.*
C18th century country inn. Log fires. Bar in old stables.
Open: All Year (not Xmas)
Grades: ETC 2 Star, RAC 2 Star
015394 43425 (also fax)
Mr Brayshaw
D: £29.50 **S:** £29.50
Beds: 3F 8D 5T 2S **Baths:** 18 Pr 1 Sh
🛇 **P** (30) 📺 ♒ ✕ 🎂 🖑 🕭 cc

West Vale Country Guest House, *Far Sawrey, Ambleside, Cumbria, LA22 0LQ.*
Peaceful, private, family-run accommodation overlooking open countryside. Home cooking.
Open: Mar to Oct
015394 42817 Mrs Forbes
D: £25–£26 **S:** £28–£29
Beds: 1F 3D 2T **Baths:** 6 En
🛇 (7) **P** (8) ♒ ✕ 🎂 🖑 🕭

Flookburgh

SD3675 🍺 *Rose & Crown*

Fieldhead Farm House, *Flookburgh, Grange-over-Sands, Cumbria, LA11 7LN.*
A C17th farmhouse on edge of ancient fishing village.
Open: All Year
015395 58651 **D:** £17–£20 **S:** £17–£20
Beds: 2D 1S 1T 1F **Baths:** 1 Sh
🛇 **P** (3) ♒ 📺 ✕ 🎂 🖑 🕭

Foxfield

SD2185 🍺 *Prince of Wales*

Woodhouse, *Foxfield, Broughton-in-Furness, Cumbria, LA20 6BT.*
Charming C17th farmhouse, superb views, 3 acres of private grounds.
Open: All Year
01229 716086 Mrs Corkill
Fax: 01229 716644
D: £19–£22 **S:** £30
Beds: 1F 1D **Baths:** 2 En
🛇 **P** 📺 ♒ ✕ 🎂 🖑 🕭 ♒ cc

All details shown are as supplied by B&B owners in Autumn 2000

Frizington

NY0317

14 Lingley Fields, *Frizington, Cumbria, CA26 3RU.*
Village, House set in cottage-style Garden, Choice of breakfast.
Open: All Year
01946 811779 Mrs Hall
D: £16–£20 **S:** £16–£20
Beds: 1F 1T **Baths:** 1 En 1 Sh
🛏 🅿 ⫫ ✕ 🎟 📺 ⚓

Garrigill

NY7441   ◁ *George & Dragon*

Ivy House, *Garrigill, Alston, Cumbria, CA9 3DU.*
C17th converted farmhouse. Comfortable, friendly atmosphere. Picturesque North Pennines village. **Open:** All Year
01434 382501 Mrs Humble
Fax: 01434 382660
ivyhousebb@aol.com
D: £17–£19.50 **S:** £26–£29
Beds: 2F 1T **Baths:** 3 En
🛏 🅿 (10) ⫫ 📺 ✕ 🎟 📺 ⚓

Garsdale

SD7389   ◁ *Dalesman, Red Lion, Bull Hotel*

Farfield Country Guest House, *Garsdale Road, Garsdale, Sedbergh, Cumbria, LA10 5JN.*
Quietly located amongst some of the finest walking country in the Yorkshire Dales. **Open:** All Year
015396 20537 Mr & Mrs Wilson
hi@farfield-house.co.uk
D: £19–£24 **S:** £20–£21
Beds: 1F 4D 1T 1S **Baths:** 4 En 1 Pr 2 Sh
🛏 🅿 (12) ⫫ 📺 🎟 📺 ⚓

Gilsland West

NY6266   ◁ *Samson Inn*

The Hill on the Wall, *Gilsland, Brampton, Cumbria, CA8 7DA.*
Open: All Year **Grades:** ETC 4 Diamond
016977 47214 (also fax) Mr Swan
thehill@hadrians-wall.demon.co.uk
D: £20–£22 **S:** £25–£27
Beds: 2D 1T **Baths:** 3 En
🛏 🅿 ⫫ 📺 🎟 ✕ 🎟 📺 ⚓
Fascinating Listed C16th 'fortified farmhouse' overlooking Hadrian's Wall and the Irthing Valley. An area rich in Roman and Border history in an outstanding landscape and an ideal location for walking 'The Wall', where we provide routes, accommodation and transportation.

Glenridding

NY3816   ◁ *Traveller's Rest, White Lion*

Grisedale Lodge, *Grisedale Bridge, Patterdale, Penrith, Cumbria, CA11 0PJ.*
Quietly situated, comfortable accommodation. **Open:** All Year (not Xmas/New Year)
017684 82084 Mrs Martin **Fax: 017684 82327**
D: £17–£25 **S:** £21–£25
Beds: 1D 2T **Baths:** 2 Sh
🛏 (11) 🅿 (3) ⫫ 📺 🎟 🎟 📺 ⚓

Gosforth

NY0603

Longacre Country Guest House, *Santon Bridge Road, Gosforth, Seascale, Cumbria, CA20 1JA.*
Detached house, village edge, 15 minutes drive. Excellent countryside, mountain walking.
Open: All Year
019467 25328 Mrs Moorhouse
D: £17–£19 **S:** £17–£21
Beds: 1D 1F 1S **Baths:** 1 Sh
🛏 🅿 (3) 📺 🎟 🎟 📺 ⚓

Grange-in-Borrowdale

NY2517   ◁ *Swinside Inn, Riverside Inn, Mary Mount*

Grayrigg, *Grange-in-Borrowdale, Keswick, Cumbria, CA12 5UQ.*
Open: All Year (not Xmas)
017687 77607 Mrs Figg
D: £19–£22 **S:** £19–£30
Beds: 1F 1D 1T **Baths:** 2 En 1 Pr
🛏 🅿 (4) ⫫ 📺 🎟 🎟 📺 ⚓
Situated just below Peace How at foot of Maiden Moor, in a quiet location on the outskirts of Grange Village. Grayrigg is a comfortable and friendly house, often described as being 'home from home'. A warm welcome awaits you.

Grange-over-Sands

SD4077   ◁ *Lindale Inn, Commodore Hotel, Kents Bank Hotel, Hard Crag Hotel*

Grangeways, *6 Morecambe Bank, Grange-over-Sands, Cumbria, LA11 6DX.*
Quiet location overlooking Morecambe Bay. Ideal base for Lake District.
Open: Easter to Nov
015395 35329 (also fax)
Mr & Mrs Campbell
marymartin@lineone.net
D: £18–£20 **S:** £18–£20
Beds: 1F 1D 1T 1S
Baths: 1 Sh
🛏 (6) 🅿 (2) ⫫ 📺 🎟 ✕ 🎟 📺 ⚓

Cartmel Fell, *High Tarn Green, Grange-over-Sands, Cumbria, LA11 6NE.*
Warm welcome in quiet country setting,ideal for touring, walking and cycling.
Open: All Year (not Xmas)
015395 52314 (also fax)
D: £18–£22
Beds: 1F 1D **Baths:** 1 En
🛏 🅿 📺 🎟 ✕ 🎟 ⚓

The Laurels B&B, *Berriedale Terrace, Lindale Road, Grange-over-Sands, Cumbria, LA11 6ER.*
Relax and enjoy the friendly atmosphere of our elegant Victorian villa.
Open: All Year
015395 35919 (also fax)
gml@thelaurels71.freeserve.co.uk
D: £20–£25 **S:** £25–£27
Beds: 2T 1D
Baths: 3 En
🅿 (3) 📺 🎟 ✕ 🎟 📺 ⚓

Grasmere

NY3307   ◁ *Traveller's Rest, Rowan Tree, Red Lion, Tweedies Bistro*

Oak Lodge, *Easedale Road, Grasmere, Ambleside, Cumbria, LA22 9QJ.*
Quiet location with open views of the Easedale Valley.
Open: Feb to Dec
015394 35527 Mrs Dixon
D: £22–£26 **S:** fr £30
Beds: 2D 1T **Baths:** 3 En
🛏 (10) 🅿 (3) ⫫ 📺 🎟 📺 ⚓

Titteringdales, *Pye Lane, Grasmere, Ambleside, Cumbria, LA22 9RQ.*
Quietly situated guest house with character, in the village of Grasmere.
Open: All Year (not Xmas/New Year)
015394 35439 (also fax)
Mr Scott
titteringdales@grasmere.net
D: £18.50–£25
Beds: 6D 1T 7F **Baths:** 6 En 1 Pr
🛏 (12) 🅿 (7) ⫫ 📺 🎟 📺 ⚓ 🅲🅲

Grayrigg

SD5797

Punchbowl House, *Grayrigg, Kendal, Cumbria, LA8 9BU.*
Spacious and comfortable former Victorian farmhouse in the centre of the village.
Open: Mar to Dec
Grades: ETC 4 Diamond, Silver Award
01539 824345 (also fax) Mrs Johnson
D: £20–£25 **S:** £20–£40
Beds: 2D 1T **Baths:** 1 En 1 Sh
🅿 (4) ⫫ 📺 ✕ 🎟 📺 ⚓

Graythwaite

NY1123

Low Graythwaite Hall, *Graythwaite, Ulverston, Cumbria, LA12 8AZ.*
Historic statesman's house, old panelling, fine furnishings, open log fires.
Open: 1st Feb to 2nd Jan
Grades: ETC 4 Diamond
015395 31676 (also fax)
D: £22–£30 **S:** £25–£30
Beds: 1F 1T 1D **Baths:** 2 En
🛏 🅿 (20) 🎟 ✕ 🎟 📺 ⚓

Great Langdale

NY3006   ◁ *New Dungeon*

The New Dungeon Ghyll Hotel, *Great Langdale, Ambleside, Cumbria, LA22 9JY.*
Amidst Lakeland's dramatic fells at the head of the famed Langdale Valley.
Open: All Year
015394 37213 enquiries@dungeon-ghyll.com
D: £30–£36 **S:** £40–£46
Beds: 13D 7T **Baths:** 20 En
🛏 🅿 📺 🎟 ✕ 🎟 📺 ⚓ ✳ ⚓ 🅲🅲

Please respect a B&B's wishes regarding children, animals and smoking

Planning a longer stay? Always ask for any special rates

Greystoke

NY4430 🍺 *Clickham Inn, Boot & Shoe*

Orchard Cottage, *Church Road, Greystoke, Penrith, Cumbria, CA11 0TW.*
Comfortable peaceful bedrooms overlooking gardens. M6 junction 40 just 4 1/2 miles.
Open: All Year
017684 83264 Mrs Theakston
Fax: 017684 80015
D: fr £22 **S:** fr £22
Beds: 1F 1D **Baths:** 1 En 1 Pr
☺ **P** (3) ☰ 📺 📷 **V** 🚿 🚹

Lattendales Farm, *Greystoke, Penrith, Cumbria, CA11 0UE.*
Comfortable farmhouse in pleasant quiet village.
Open: Mar to Oct
017684 83474 Mrs Ashburner
D: £16–£17 **S:** £17–£18
Beds: 2D 1T **Baths:** 1 Sh
☺ (1) **P** (5) 📺 📷 🚹

Grisedale

SD7792 🍺 *Moorcock*

Aldershaw, *Grisedale, Sedbergh, Cumbria, LA10 5PS.*
Superb Daleside renovated farmhouse, oak-beamed. Delicious food.
Open: All Year (not Xmas)
Grades: ETC 2 Diamond
015396 21211 Mr & Mrs Robinson
D: £17.50–£25 **S:** £20–£27
Beds: 1D 1T 1S **Baths:** 1 En 1 Sh
☺ **P** (3) 📺 📷 ✕ 🚹 **V** 🚹

Hale

SD5078 🍺 *Kings Arms*

Yewdale, *Hale, Milnthorpe, Cumbria, LA7 7BL.*
Open: All Year (not Xmas)
015395 62457 Mrs Westworth
t.westworth@virgin.net
D: £22.50–£25 **S:** £18–£22.50
Beds: 1D 2T 1S **Baths:** 1 En 2 Sh
☺ **P** (4) 📺 📷 🚹 🚹
Situated in quiet hamlet, commanding elevated position, private house in AONB, beautiful 180-degree views Lakeland fells and Howgills, 20 mins' drive Windermere and Lakes, Lancaster, Kirkby Lonsdale, gateway to Yorkshire Dales, estuary with cross bay walks, fascinating tidal bore, A6, 5 miles north from M6 (J35).

Hartsop

NY4013 🍺 *Brotherswater Inn*

Patterdale, *Fellside, Hartsop, Patterdale, Penrith, Cumbria, CA11 0NZ.*
C17th stone built farmhouse, close to lakes and High Mountains.
Open: All Year (not Xmas/New Year)
017684 82532 Mrs Knight
D: £16–£18 **S:** £20–£24
Beds: 2T **Baths:** 1 Sh
☺ **P** (2) 📺 📷 🚹 🚹

Hawkshead

SD3597 🍺 *Drunken Duck, Outgate Inn, Queen's Head, Red Lion, Tower Bank Arms*

Borwick Lodge, *Hawkshead, Ambleside, Cumbria, LA22 0PU.*
Award-winning 'accommodation of the highest standards'. A rather special C17th country house+.
Open: All Year
Grades: ETC 4 Diamond, Silver
015394 36332 (also fax)
Mr & Mrs Haskell
borwicklodge@talk21.com
D: £25–£36 **S:** fr £35
Beds: 1F 4D 1T **Baths:** All En
☺ (8) **P** (8) 📺 📷 **V** 🚹

Beechmount, *Near Sawrey, Hawkshead, Ambleside, Cumbria, LA22 0JZ.*
Open: All Year
Grades: ETC 3 Diamond, AA 3 Diamond
015394 36356 Mrs Siddall
D: £20–£22 **S:** £25–£30
Beds: 3D **Baths:** 3 Pr
☺ **P** (3) 📺 📷 🚹 **V** 🚹
Beechmount is a charming, spacious country house situated in Beatrix Potter's picturesque village near Sawrey with its Olde Worlde Inn. Delightful appointed bedrooms with superb lake/country views. Relaxed friendly atmosphere. Delicious breakfasts. Excellent value. Coloured brochure available.

Violet Bank, *Hawkshead, Ambleside, Cumbria, LA22 0PL.*
Beautifully situated farmhouse of charm and character nestling beside a quiet country lane. **Open:** All Year (not Xmas)
015394 36222 Mrs Penrice
D: £20
Beds: 2D **Baths:** 1 Sh
P (8) 📺 📷 **V**

Hawkshead Hill

SD3398 🍺 *Drunken Duck*

Yewfield Vegetarian Guest House, *Hawkshead Hill, Ambleside, LA22 0PR.*
Open: Feb to mid Nov
Grades: ETC 4 Diamond
015394 36765 Mr Hook
D: £20–£33 **S:** £25–£33
Beds: 1T 2D **Baths:** 3 En
☺ (9) **P** (6) 📺 📷 🚹 **cc**
A peaceful retreat in 30 acres grounds, this impressive Gothic house looks over the Vale of Esthwaite and the Fells beyond, and is ideally situated for walking in the Lakeland Fells and enjoying this exquisite region.

Helsington

SD5090 🍺 *The Kendal arms*

Helsington Laithes Manor, *Helsington, Kendal, Cumbria, LA9 5RJ.*
Historic Listed Manor House in 3 acre grounds,5 minutes M6 J36.
Open: All Year (not Xmas/New Year)
01539 741253 Fax: 01539 741346
themanor@helsington.uk.com
D: £20–£25 **S:** £25–£30
Beds: 1F 1D 3D **Baths:** 2 En 1 Pr
☺ (5) **P** (5) 📺 📷 **V**

Hesket Newmarket

NY3338

Newlands Grange, *Hesket Newmarket, Caldbeck, Wigton, Cumbria, CA7 8HP.*
Comfortable, oak beamed farmhouse offering all home cooking. All welcome.
Open: All Year (not Xmas)
016974 78676 Mrs Studholme
D: £16.50–£19.50 **S:** £16.50–£19.50
Beds: 1F 1D 1T 1S **Baths:** 1 En 1 Sh
☺ **P** 📺 📷 ✕ 🚹 🚹

High Harrington

NY0025 🍺 *Galoping Horse*

Riversleigh Guest House, *39 Primrose Terrace, High Harrington, Workington, Cumbria, CA14 5PS.*
Riverside house overlooking gardens, 5 mins from station and marina.
Open: All Year
01946 830267 Mrs Davies
D: £15–£20 **S:** £15–£20
Beds: 1F 1T 1D **Baths:** 2 En 1 Pr
☺ (5) **P** (8) 📺 📷 **V**

High Lorton

NY1625 🍺 *Wheatsheaf Inn*

Owl Brook, *Whinlatter Pass, High Lorton, Cockermouth, Cumbria, CA13 9TX.*
Green slate bungalow, designed by owners. Pine ceilings. Oak floors.
Open: All Year
01900 85333 Mrs Roberts
D: £16.50–£17.50 **S:** £16.50–£17.50
Beds: 3D **Baths:** 1 Sh
☺ (0) **P** (2) 📺 📷 ✕ 🚹 **V** 🚿 🚹

High Wray

SD3799 🍺 *Queen's Head, Outgate Inn, Drunken Duck*

Tock How Farm, *High Wray, Ambleside, Cumbria, LA22 0JF.*
Traditional farmhouse overlooking to Lake Windermere and the surrounding Fells.
Open: All Year **Grades:** ETC 3 Diamond
015394 36106 Mrs Irvine
D: £19.50–£23 **S:** £21–£25
Beds: 1F 1D **Baths:** En
☺ **P** (4) 📺 📷 **V** 🚹

Holme

SD5279 🍺 *Smithy Inn*

Marwin House, *Duke Street, Holme, Carnforth, Cumbria, LA6 1PY.*
Gateway to Lake District, Yorkshire Dales. M6 (J36) 5 minutes.
Open: All Year
Grades: ETC 2 Diamond
01524 781144 (also fax)
D: £16–£18 **S:** £17–£19
Beds: 1F 1T **Baths:** 1 Sh
☺ **P** (3) 📺 📷 **V** 🚹

B&B owners may vary rates - be sure to check when booking

Holmrook

SD0799   ◖ *Lulwidge Arms, Bridge Inn*

Hill Farm, Holmrook, Cumbria, CA19
1UG.
Working farm; beautiful views
overlooking River Irt and Wasdale Fells.
Open: All Year (not Xmas)
019467 24217 Mrs Leak
D: fr £14 **S:** fr £14
Beds: 2F 1D **Baths:** 2 Sh
📺 🅿 📺 🏠 🔟 🍴

Irton

NY1000   ◖ *Santon Bridge Inn, Ratty Arms*

Cookson Place Farm, Irton,
Holmrook, Cumbria, CA19 1YQ.
Working farm. Quiet area within easy
reach of Wasdale, Eskdale.
Open: All Year (not Xmas)
019467 24286
Mrs Crayston
D: £13–£14 **S:** £14
Beds: 1F 1T **Baths:** 1 Sh
🅿 ⊬ 📺 🔟 🍴 ✳ 🚼

Ivegill

NY4143   ◖ *White Quay, Crown Inn*

Streethead Farm, Ivegill, Carlisle,
Cumbria, CA4 0NG.
Distant hills, real fires, home-baking,
convenient for Lakes or Scotland.
Open: All Year (not Xmas)
016974 73327 (also fax)
Mrs Wilson
D: £20–£22 **S:** £22–£25
Beds: 2D **Baths:** 2 En
📺 (7) 🅿 (2) 📺 🔟 🍴

Croft End Hurst, Ivegill, Carlisle,
Cumbria, CA4 0NL.
Rural bungalow situated midway
between J41/42 of M6.
Open: All Year
Grades: ETC 3 Diamond
017684 84362 Mrs Nichol
D: £17–£19 **S:** fr £17
Beds: 1D 1T **Baths:** 1 Sh
📺 (1) 🅿 (4) ⊬ 📺 🔟 🍴 🚼 &

Kearstwick

SD6080   ◖ *Courtyard, Snooty Fox, Orange Tree*

Kearstwick House, Kearstwick ,
Kirkby Lonsdale, Carnforth, LA6 2EA.
Elegant Edwardian Country House on
edge of historic Kirkby Lonsdale.
Open: All Year (not Xmas/New Year)
015242 72398
D: £20–£22.50 **S:** £25–£30
Beds: 1T 1D **Baths:** 1 Pr 1 Sh
📺 (12) 🅿 (3) 📺 🏠 🍴 🔟 🍴

BEDROOMS
F - Family
D - Double
T - Twin
S - Single

Kendal

SD5192   ◖ *Blue Bell, Gilpin Bridge, Hare &
Hounds, Stricklands Arms, Kendal Arms,
Station,Castle, Plough, Union, Ye Olde Fleece,
Wheatsheaf, Castle Inn, Punch Bowl, Moon,
Watermill, Brown Horse, Gateway Hotel*

Sonata, 19 Burnside Road, Kendal,
Cumbria, LA9 4RL.
Open: All Year
Grades: ETC 3 Diamond
015397 32290 Mr Wilkinson
chriswilkinson@sonataguesthouse.freese
rve.co.uk
D: £22 **S:** £30
Beds: 1F 2D 1T **Baths:** 4 En
📺 🔟 🍴 🔟 🍴 cc
Friendly, family-run, Georgian, terraced
guest house with comfortable, ensuite
bedrooms containing radio, alarm, colour
TV, complimentary beverage facilities,
hairdryer and independently controlled
central heating. Shopping centres 3 mins
walk, Windermere 10 mins drive.

Bridge House, 65 Castle Street,
Kendal, Cumbria, LA9 7AD.
Open: All Year
Grades: ETC 4 Diamond
015397 22041 Mrs Brindley
D: £18–£25 **S:** £20–£30
Beds: 1D 1T **Baths:** 1 En 1 Sh
📺 ⊬ 📺 🔟 🍴
Beautiful Georgian Listed building a
short walk from Kendal castle and the
River Kent. Home made bread and
preserves a speciality. Complimentary
Kendal mint cake for our visitors. A lovely
private garden for guests' use. A warm
and friendly welcome.

Punchbowl House, Grayrigg, Kendal,
Cumbria, LA8 9BU.
Spacious and comfortable former
Victorian farmhouse in the centre of the
village.
Open: Mar to Dec
Grades: ETC 4 Diamond, Silver Award
01539 824345 (also fax)
Mrs Johnson
D: £20–£25 **S:** £20–£40
Beds: 2D 1T **Baths:** 1 En 1 Sh
🅿 (4) ⊬ 📺 ✕ 🔟 🍴

Sundial House, 51 Milnthorpe Road,
Kendal, Cumbria, LA9 5QG.
Quality guest house comfortable rooms
car park excellent breakfast.
Open: All Year (not Xmas)
01539 724468 Mr & Mrs Richardson
Fax: 01539 736900
D: £17.50–£25 **S:** £18.50–£22.50
Beds: 1F 1D 1T 1S **Baths:** 1 En 2 Sh
📺 🅿 (8) 📺 🏠 🔟 🍴 🔟

Birslack Grange, Hutton Lane, Levens,
Kendal, Cumbria, LA8 8PA.
Converted farm buildings in rural setting
overlooking the scenic Lyth Valley.
Open: All Year (not Xmas)
015395 60989 Mrs Carrington-Birch
birslackgrange@msn.com
D: £18–£20 **S:** £22–£25
Beds: 1F 1D 2T 2S **Baths:** 4 En 2 Sh
📺 (3) 🅿 (6) ⊬ 📺 🏠 ✕ 🔟 🍴 🚼 &

Higher House Farm, Oxenholme

Higher House Farm, Oxenholme
Lane, Natland, Kendal, Cumbria, LA9 7QH.
Tranquil Lakeland village, C17th
farmhouse.
Open: All Year (not Xmas)
Grades: ETC 4 Diamond, Silver Award,
AA 4 Diamond
015395 61177 Mrs Sunter
Fax: 015395 61520
D: £24.50–£27.50 **S:** £29.50–£32.50
Beds: 2D 1T **Baths:** 3 En
📺 (12) 🅿 (9) ⊬ 📺 🔟 🍴

Hillside Guest House, 4 Beast
Banks, Kendal, Cumbria, LA9 4JW.
Large Victorian guest house, town centre.
Ideal for Lake District and Yorkshire
Dales.
Open: Mar to Nov
Grades: ETC 3 Diamond
015397 22836 Mrs Denison
D: £18–£21 **S:** £18–£22
Beds: 3D 1T 3S **Baths:** 5 En 4 Pr 1 Sh
📺 (4) 🅿 (4) 📺 🔟 🍴 🔟

Fairways, 102 Windermere Road,
Kendal, Cumbria, LA9 5EZ.
Victorian guest house, ensuite rooms. TV,
tea/coffee. Lovely views.
Open: All Year
Grades: ETC 3 Diamond
015397 25564 Mrs Paylor
mp@fairwaysl.fsnet.co.uk
D: £18–£20 **S:** £20–£25
Beds: 1F 2D 1S **Baths:** 3 En 1 Pr
📺 (2) 🅿 (4) ⊬ 📺 🔟 🍴 🚼 🍴

Highgate Hotel, 128 Highgate, Kendal,
Cumbria, LA9 4HE.
Grade II* Listed town centre B&B. Private
car park. Built 1769.
Open: All Year (not Xmas/New Year)
01539 724229 (also fax)
Mr Dawson
highgatehotel@kendal-hotels
D: £21.50–£23.50 **S:** £27–£29
Beds: 1F 4D 2T 3S **Baths:** 10 En
📺 🅿 (10) ⊬ 📺 🔟 🍴 cc

Airethwaite House, 1 Airethwaite,
Horncop Lane, Kendal, Cumbria, LA9 4SP.
Unspoilt Victorian guesthouse with
spacious rooms, many original features
and antique furniture.
Open: All Year
01539 730435 Mrs Dean
D: £20–£25 **S:** £25
Beds: 3D/T **Baths:** 3 En
📺 🅿 (3) ⊬ 📺 🔟 🍴

Magic Hills House, 123 Appleby
Road, Kendal, Cumbria, LA9 6HF.
Open: All Year (not Xmas)
01539 736248 C.K Moseley
ckm@ukgateway.net
D: £18.50–£22.50 **S:** £21–£27
Beds: 2D 1T **Baths:** 1 En 1 Pr 1 Sh
📺 (12) ⊬ 📺 🔟 🍴
Late Victorian family house, comfortably
furnished and tastefully decorated. 10
minutes walk to centre. Convenient for
Lakes, Yorkshire Dales and Dales Way.
Conservatory for relaxing. Generous
home-cooked breakfast. Rural views.
Personally run by Christine and Richard
Moseley.

Mitchelland House, Off Crook Road,
Kendal, Cumbria, LA8 8LL.
Delightful country location, only 5
minutes Lake Windermere and all
attractions. **Open:** All Year (not Xmas)
Grades: ETC 4 Diamond
015394 48589
marie.mitchelland@talk21.com
D: £18–£24 **S:** £21–£26
Beds: 1F 1D 1T **Baths:** 1 En 1 Sh
🛇 🅿 (10) 📺 🏇 🎀 🖵 Ⅴ ♨

Meadow Croft Country Hotel, Ings,
Staveley, Kendal, Cumbria, LA8 9PY.
Superior ensuite accommodation in
village hotel, 2 miles from Windermere.
Open: Easter to Dec
01539 821171 Mr Cross
D: £24–£28 **S:** £30–£38
Beds: 3F 3D 2T **Baths:** 7 En 1 Pr
🛇 🅿 (10) 📺 🗙 🖵 Ⅴ ♨

Winlea, 88 Windermere Road, Kendal,
Cumbria, LA9 5EZ.
Friendly Victorian guest house lovely
views 10 minutes walk town centre.
Open: All Year (not Xmas)
015397 23177 Mrs Ellison
D: £18–£20
Beds: 1F 2D 1T **Baths:** 2 En
🛇 (8) 🅿 (4) 🗲 📺 🏇 🖵 Ⅴ ♨

7 Thorny Hills, Kendal, Cumbria,
LA9 7AL.
Listed building in a peaceful location
near the town centre.
Open: Jan to Nov **Grades:** ETC 3 Diamonds
015397 20207 Mrs Jowett
martyn.jowett@btinternet.com
D: £21 **S:** £24
Beds: 2D 1T **Baths:** 2 En 1 Pr
🛇 🗲 📺 🗙 🖵 Ⅴ ♨

Summerlands Tower, Summerlands,
Endmoor, Kendal, Cumbria, LA8 0ED.
Victorian country house with fine rooms
and gardens. 3 miles from M6, J36.
Open: Easter to Nov
015395 61081 (also fax) Mr & Mrs Green
m_.green@virgin.net
D: £24–£29.50 **S:** £29–£34.50
Beds: 2T 1D **Baths:** 1 En 1 Pr
🛇 (12) 🅿 (3) 🗲 📺 🖵 Ⅴ ♨

Garnette House Farm, Burneside,
Kendal, Cumbria, LA9 5SF.
C15th farmhouse on edge of Burneside
Village & 10 mins from Windermere.
Open: All Year (not Xmas)
015397 24542 (also fax) Mrs Beaty
D: £16–£21
Beds: 2F 3D 1T **Baths:** 4 En 2 Sh
🛇 🅿 (6) 📺 🖵 Ⅴ ♨

Kentmere

NY4504

Maggs Howe, Kentmere, Kendal,
Cumbria, LA8 9JP.
Detached former farmhouse in beautiful,
quiet, unspoilt cul-de-sac valley.
Open: All Year (not Xmas)
Grades: ETC 3 Dimaond
01539 821689 Mrs Hevey
D: £18–£20 **S:** £18–£20
Beds: 1F 1D 1T **Baths:** 1 En 1 Sh
🛇 🅿 (6) 📺 🏇 🗙 Ⅴ ♨

Keswick

NY2623 🍴 Packhorse, Packhouse Covet, Sun
Inn, Four In Hand, Twa Dogs, Chaucer House,
George Hotel, Kitchin's Cellar Bar, Skiddaw Hotel,
Dog & Gun, Golden Lion, Farmers Arms, Pheasant,
Bank, Wild Strawberry

Spooney Green, Spooney Green Lane,
Keswick, Cumbria, CA12 4PJ.
Open: All Year
017687 72601 Ms Wallace
spooneygreen@beeb.net
D: £20–£25 **S:** £25–£40
Beds: 1T 1D **Baths:** 1 En 1 Pr
🛇 🅿 (5) 🗲 📺 🏇 🗙 🖵 Ⅴ ♨
Only 15 minutes' walk into Keswick yet
on the foothills of Skiddaw, Spooney
Green provides a relaxing country retreat.
All rooms have extensive views of the
western fells. The Large wildlife Garden
includes Woodland wetland and flower
meadow.

Chaucer House Hotel, Derwentwater
Place, Keswick, Cumbria, CA12 4DR.
Open: Feb to Dec
Grades: RAC 2 Star
017687 72318 Mr Pechartscheck
Fax: 017687 75551
enquiries@chaucer-house.demon.co.uk
D: £30–£40 **S:** £30–£40
Beds: 4F 9D 12T 8S **Baths:** 29 En 4 Pr
🛇 🅿 📺 🏇 🗙 🖵 Ⅴ ♨ ᵫ cc
Lakeland hospitality at its best. Quiet
setting, surrounded by spectacular
mountains. Close to Theatre, Market
place and Lake. Renowned for a relaxed
informal atmosphere and excellent
freshly prepared food. Friendly,
professional staff always available to help
you enjoy your stay, plan tours and walks.

Sunnyside Guest House, 25 Southey
Street, Keswick, Cumbria, CA12 4EF.
Open: All Year (not Xmas)
Grades: ETC 4 Diamond, AA 4 Diamond,
RAC 4 Diamond
017687 72446 Mr & Mrs Newton
Fax: 017687 74447
raynewton@survey.u-net.com
D: fr £19 **S:** fr £24
Beds: 1F 4D 1T 1S **Baths:** 5 En 2 Sh
🛇 🅿 (7) 🗲 📺 🏇 🖵 ♨
This recently refurbished Victorian
building is situated just five minutes walk
from the town centre and ten minutes
walk from the lake, yet provides quiet and
comfortable accommodation throughout.
Relaxing guest lounge with views of
Skiddaw.

Brookfield, Penrith Road, Keswick,
Cumbria, CA12 4LJ.
Open: All Year
017687 72867 Mr Gregory
ronnie.sally@talk21.com
D: £16–£20 **S:** £16–£20
Beds: 2F 2D **Baths:** 4 En
🛇 🅿 🗲 📺 🏇 🗙 🖵 Ⅴ ♨
A warm welcome awaits you at this
family run Victorian guest house. Walking
distance to the historic stone circle.
Ample street parking. Some rooms with a
view of Latrigg. Local information books
and videos. Walking boots welcome.
Family discounts.

Watendlath, 15 Acorn Street, Keswick,
Cumbria, CA12 4EA.
Open: All Year
Grades: ETC 3 Diamond
017687 74165 D: £17–£20
Beds: 2F 2D **Baths:** 3 En 1 Sh
🛇 📺 🖵 Ⅴ ♨
Just a few mins from Keswick town
centre, Watendlath is a quiet and relaxed
retreat. Renowned for its superb traditional English breakfasts.
The attractive rooms have everything to
make your holiday a home-from-home
experience.

Berkeley Guest House, The Heads,
Keswick, Cumbria, CA12 5ER.
Open: Jan to Dec
Grades: ETC 4 Diamond
017687 74222 Mrs Crompton
berkeley@tesco.net
D: £17–£24 **S:** £20
Beds: 1F 2D 1T 1S **Baths:** 3 En 2 Sh
🛇 (3) 🗲 📺 🖵 Ⅴ ♨
Friendly relaxed guest house with superb
mountain views from each comfortable
room. Situated on a quiet road on the
edge of town, close to the lake, an ideal
base for walking or water sports.
Delicious breakfast choice and warm
welcome assured.

Claremont House, Chestnut Hill,
Keswick, Cumbria, CA12 4LT.
Open: Easter to Nov
Grades: AA 4 Diamond
017687 72089 Peter & Jackie Werfel
claremont@netscapeonline.co.uk
D: £21–£25
Beds: 3D 1T **Baths:** 4 En
🛇 (12) 🅿 (5) 🗲 📺 🖵 Ⅴ ♨
Claremont House, built about 150 years
ago as a lodge house to the Fieldside
estate, stands elevated about one mile
from Keswick centre. Fine
accommodation in pleasant
surroundings, all tastes catered for with
our substantial breakfasts.

Badgers Wood Guest House, 30
Stanger Street, Keswick, Cumbria,
CA12 5JU.
All rooms have mountain views in this
outstanding guest house.
Open: All Year (not Xmas)
Grades: ETC 4 Diamond, AA 4 Diamond
017687 72621 Ms Godfrey
enquiries@badgers-wood.co.uk
D: £18–£22 **S:** fr £18
Beds: 3D 1T 2S **Baths:** 4 En 1 Sh
🗲 📺 🖵 Ⅴ ♨

Lairbeck Hotel, Vicarage Hill, Keswick,
Cumbria, CA12 5QB.
Secluded setting, superb mountain views.
Spacious parking. No single
supplements.
Open: Mar to Jan
Grades: ETC 2 Star, Silver Award, AA 2
Star, RAC 2 Star
017687 73373 Mr Coy
Fax: 017687 73144
swell@lairbeckhotel-keswick.co.uk
D: £30–£38 **S:** £30–£38
Beds: 1F 8D 1T 4S **Baths:** 14 En
🛇 (5) 🅿 (16) 🗲 📺 🗙 🖵 Ⅴ ✴ ♨

Lynwood House, 35 Helvellyn Street, Keswick, Cumbria, CA12 4EP.
Victorian-style with modern comforts. Traditional or home-made organic breakfasts.
Open: All Year
Grades: ETC 4 Diamond, Silver
017687 72398 Mr Picken
lynwoodho@aol.com
D: £17–£20.50 **S:** £18.50–£23
Beds: 1F 2D 1S **Baths:** 1 En
🛇 (3) ⊬ 📺 🛍 🖳 🛦

The Paddock Guest House,
Wordsworth Street, Keswick, Cumbria, CA12 4HU.
Delightful 1800's residence. Close to town, lake, parks and Fells.
Open: All Year (not Xmas)
Grades: ETC 4 Diamond
017687 72510 D: £19–£21 **S:** £25–£40
Beds: 1F 1T 4D **Baths:** All En
🛇 📭 (5) ⊬ 📺 🛏 🛍 🖳 🛦 cc

Clarence House, 14 Eskin Street, Keswick, Cumbria, CA12 4DQ.
Lovely detached Victorian house, excellent ensuite accommodation. Cleanliness guaranteed. No smoking.
Open: All Year (not Xmas)
017687 73186 Mr & Mrs Robertson
Fax: 017687 72317
clarenceho@aol.com
D: £20–£28 **S:** £20–£28
Beds: 1F 4D 3T 1S **Baths:** 8 Pr
🛇 (5) ⊬ 📺 🛍 🛦

Glendale Guest House, 7 Eskin Street, Keswick, Cumbria, CA12 4DH.
Victorian House, Mountain views, Close to the Town and lake.
Open: All Year
017687 73562 Mr Lankester
D: £16–£20 **S:** £16–£20
Beds: 1F 2T 2D 1S **Baths:** 3 En 2 Sh
🛇 ⊬ 📺 🛍 🖳 🛦

Hawcliffe House, 30 Eskin Street, Keswick, Cumbria, CA12 4DG.
Warm welcome assured. Short walk to lake and town centre.
Open: All Year
017687 73250 D McConnell
D: £16–£18 **S:** £16–£18
Beds: 1T 2D 2S **Baths:** 2 Sh
⊬ 📺 🛏 🛍 🛦

Long Close Farm, Underskiddaw, Keswick, Cumbria, CA12 4QD.
Period farmhouse enjoying exceptional views over mountains and Bassenthwaite Lake. **Open:** All Year
017687 72851 (also fax)
Mrs Evers & Mr Barnes
D: £17–£25 **S:** £20–£25
Beds: 1D 2T **Baths:** 1 En 1 Sh
🛇 📭 📺 🛍 🖳 🛦

Tamara Guest House, 10 Stanger Street, Keswick, Cumbria, CA12 5JU.
Cosy house, minute walk from town centre with private parking.
Open: All Year
017687 72913 Miss Dussoye
D: £16–£18 **S:** £16–£18
Beds: 1T 3D **Baths:** 1 Sh
🛇 📭 (4) ⊬ 📺 ✕ 🛍 🖳 ✿ 🛦

High Hill Farm, High Hill, Keswick, Cumbria, CA12 5NY.
Modernised former farmhouse, special breaks, available all year, lovely views.
Open: All Year **Grades:** ETC Member
017687 74793 Ms Davies
D: £18–£19
Beds: 2D 1T **Baths:** 3 En
📭 (3) ⊬ 📺 🛍 🖳 🛦

The Queens Hotel, Main Street, Keswick, Cumbria, CA12 5JF.
Comfortable, traditional Lake District hotel. **Open:** All Year (not Xmas)
Grades: ETC 3 Star, RAC 3 Star
017687 73333 Fax: 017687 71144
book@queenshotel.co.uk
D: £30–£44 **S:** £30–£44
Beds: 10F 20D 5S **Baths:** 35 En
🛇 📭 📺 ✕ 🛍 🖳 🛦 cc

Dalkeith House, 1 Leonards Street, Keswick, Cumbria, CA12 4EJ.
Clean, comfortable and friendly accommodation. Quiet area close to town.
Open: All Year (not Xmas/New Year)
017687 72696 (also fax)
Mr & Mrs Marsden
Fmarsden@aol.com
D: £18–£22 **S:** £18–£22
Beds: 4D 1T 1S 1F **Baths:** 4 En 3 Sh
🛇 ⊬ 📺 🛍 🖳 🛦

Century House, 17 Church Street, Keswick, Cumbria, CA12 4DT.
Warm, friendly guesthouse - The house of many returns.
Open: All Year (not Xmas/New Year)
017687 72843 (also fax)
S North
centuryhouse@tinyonline.co.uk
D: £17.50–£19.50 **S:** £17.50–£19.50
Beds: 1F 1T 3D **Baths:** 4 En 1 Pr
🛇 ⊬ 📺 🛍 🖳 🛦

Derwentdale Guest Hotel, 8 Blencathra Street, Keswick, Cumbria, CA12 4HP.
Friendly, family-run guest house close to lake and parks. **Open:** All Year
Grades: ETC 3 Diamond
017687 74187 (also fax) Mrs Riding
D: £17.50–£21 **S:** £17.50–£18
Beds: 3D 1T 2S **Baths:** 2 En 3 Pr
🛇 ⊬ 📺 ✕ 🛍 🖳 ✿ 🛦

Greenside, 48 St John Street, Keswick, Cumbria, CA12 5AG.
Listed building in conservation area. Views, vegetarian and snack making facilities.
Open: All Year
017687 74491 Mrs Dalkins
D: £15–£17 **S:** £25–£30
Beds: 1D 1T **Baths:** 2 En
🛇 (12) 📭 (2) ⊬ 📺 🛍 🖳 🛦

Sandon Guest House, 13 Southey Street, Keswick, Cumbria, CA12 4EG.
Victorian guest house conveniently situated close to lake and theatre.
Open: All Year (not Xmas)
Grades: ETC 3 diamond
017687 73648 D: £18–£21 **S:** £18–£21
Beds: 2T 2D 2S **Baths:** 4 En 1 Sh
🛇 ⊬ 📺 ✕ 🛍 🛦

Cumbria House, 1 Derwentwater Place, Ambleside Road, Keswick, Cumbria, CA12 4DR.
Ideal base for a Lakeland holiday - quiet, 3 minutes from centre of Keswick.
Open: Feb to Nov
017687 73171 (also fax)
Mr Colam
cumbriah@globalnet.co.uk
D: £18–£23.50 **S:** £18–£23.50
Beds: 1F 3D 2T 3S **Baths:** 4 En 2 Sh
🛇 📭 (7) ⊬ 🛏 ✕ 🛍 🖳 🛦

Kirkby Lonsdale

SD6178   🍺 Kings Arms, Sun Inn, Lunesdale Arms, Swan Inn, Orange Tree, Snooty Fox

Wyck House, 4 Main Street, Kirkby Lonsdale, Carnforth, Lancs, LA6 2AE.
A Victorian town house situated 50 yards from the market square.
Open: All Year (except 2 weeks)
015242 71953 (also fax)
Pat & Brian Bradley
wyckhouse@studioarts.co.uk
D: £20–£22.50 **S:** £18.50–£30
Beds: 1F 1T 2D 2S **Baths:** 3 En 1 Sh
🛇 📭 (3) ⊬ 📺 🛍 🛦

Tossbeck Farm, Middleton, Carnforth, Lancashire, LA6 2LZ.
Open: Easter to Oct
015242 76214 D: £17–£19 **S:** £22–£25
Beds: 1F 1D **Baths:** 1 En 1 Pr
🛇 📭 (2) ⊬ 📺 🛍 🛦
A friendly welcome awaits you at Tossbeck, mixed farm in unspoilt Lune Valley.

9 Mill Brow House, Kirkby Lonsdale, Carnforth, Lancs, LA6 2AT.
Wonderful views of river, shops/pubs nearby, holiday apartment available.
Open: Easter to Oct
015242 71615 (also fax)
Mrs Nicholson
D: £18–£21 **S:** £20–£25
Beds: 1D 1T **Baths:** 2 Sh
🛇 📭 (2) ⊬ 🛍 🛦

Kirkby Stephen

NY7708   🍺 King's Arms, Old Forge, Pennine Hotel

The Old Coach House, Faraday Road, Kirkby Stephen, Cumbria, CA17 4QL.
Quiet comfortable c18th coach house close to town centre.
Open: All Year
017683 71582 Mrs Rome
D: £17–£19 **S:** £17–£22
Beds: 1D 1T 1S **Baths:** 1 En 1 Sh
🛇 (5) ⊬ 📺 🛍 🖳 🛦

Cold Keld Guided Walking Holidays, Fell End, Kirkby Stephen, Cumbria, CA17 4LN.
Guided walking holidays. Delectable dining. Suit all abilities. Singles welcome.
Open: All Year (not Xmas/New Year)
015396 23273 (also fax)
Mr & Mrs Trimmer
D: £20–£30 **S:** £20–£30
Beds: 1F 3D 1T 2S **Baths:** 7 En
🛇 📭 (12) ⊬ 📺 🛏 🛍 🖳 🛦

Lyndhurst, *46 South Road, Kirkby Stephen, Cumbria, CA17 4SN.*
A warm welcome to a delightful Victorian home. Lovely breakfast.
Open: All Year (not Xmas/New Year)
017683 71448 Mrs Bell
D: £16–£20 **S:** £20–£22.50
Beds: 1D 2T **Baths:** 1 Pr 1 Sh
🛇 🅿 (3) 🗇 📺 🛪 🎟 Ⅴ

Lockholme, *48 South Road, Kirkby Stephen, Cumbria, CA17 4SN.*
Friendly Victorian home with antique furnishings and king sized beds.
Open: All Year (not Xmas)
017683 71321 Mrs Graham
D: £16–£18 **S:** £16–£22
Beds: 1F 1T 1D 1S **Baths:** 2 En 1 Sh
🛇 🅿 (4) 🗇 📺 🛪 🎟 Ⅴ

Lakeside

SD3787

The Knoll Country Guest House, *Lakeside, Newby Bridge, Ulverston, Cumbria, LA12 8AU.*
Open: All Year
Grades: ETC 4 Diamond
015395 31347 Mr Rushton
info@theknoll.co.uk
D: £20–£30 **S:** £40
Beds: 2F 5D 1T **Baths:** 8 En
🛇 🅿 (9) 🗇 📺 🛪 🗙 🎟 Ⅴ ⚹ ♿ cc
The Knoll - a delightful Victorian house, set amidst peaceful wooded countryside at the South end of Lake Windermere, offering a relaxed nights sleep and hearty breakfast. Only 5 minuets walk from main attractions, an ideal base for relaxing or exploring.

Lazonby

NY5439 🍺 *Midland hotel, Joiners Arms*

Harlea, *Lazonby, Penrith, Cumbria, CA10 1BX.*
Open: All Year (not Xmas/New Year)
01768 897055 Mrs Blaylock
harlea.eden@ukgateway.net
D: £20–£21 **S:** £25
🛇 (11) 🅿 🗇 📺 🛪 🎟 Ⅴ
Refurbished 19th Century Coach House with panoramic views of the Pennines and Eden Valley. Overlooks the famous Carlisle/Settle Railway line. Ideal for walkers, twitchers, rail enthusiasts and those seeking peace and quiet in comfort and style.

Leadgate

NY7043 🍺 *Angel Inn*

Brownside House, *Leadgate, Alston, Cumbria, CA9 3EL.*
Open: All Year
Grades: ETC 3 Diamond
01434 382169 (also fax) Mrs Le Marie
brownside_hse@hotmail.com
D: £18 **S:** £18
Beds: 1D 2T 1S **Baths:** 1 Sh
🛇 🅿 (4) 🗇 📺 🛪 🗙 🎟 Ⅴ ⚹ cc
A warm welcome awaits you at this peaceful house set in the country with superb views. Situated in the unspoilt North Pennines near Alston. Ideal centre for visiting Hadrian's Wall, Lake District, Northumberland.

Leece

SD2469

Winander, *Leece, Ulverston, Cumbria, LA12 0QP.*
Converted barn in quiet village location in Lake District Peninsula.
Open: All Year (not Xmas)
01229 822353 Mr Cockshott
D: £18–£23 **S:** £21–£26
Beds: 1T 1D **Baths:** 1 Pr 1 Sh
🛇 (5) 🅿 (3) 🗇 📺 🗙 🎟 Ⅴ ⚹

Levens

SD4886 🍺 *Blue Bell, Gilpin Bridge, Hare & Hounds, Stricklands Arms, Kendal Arms, The Station, The Castle, The Plough, The Union, Ye Olde Fleece, The Wheatsheaf, Castle Inn, Punch Bowl, The Moon, The Watermill, Brown Horse*

Glen Robin, *Church Road, Levens, Kendal, Cumbria, LA8 8PS.*
Beautiful house with lovely views, delicious breakfasts, peace and quiet.
Open: All Year (not Xmas)
015395 60369 (also fax)
D: £16–£20 **S:** £16–£20
Beds: 1D 1T 1S **Baths:** 1 Sh
🛇 (3) 🅿 (3) 🗇 📺 🎟 Ⅴ ⚹

Little Arrow

SD2895 🍺 *Church House Inn, Wilson Arms*

Browside, *Little Arrow, Coniston, Cumbria, LA21 8AU.*
Panoramic views across Coniston Water to Brantwood, Grisdale Forest and Ambleside Fells. **Open:** Feb to Nov
Grades: AA 4 Diamond
015394 41162 Mrs Dugdale
D: £18–£22 **S:** £20–£25
Beds: 1T 1D **Baths:** 2 En
🛇 🅿 🗇 📺 🎟 Ⅴ ⚹

Little Langdale

NY3103 🍺 *Three Shire Inn*

Wilson Place Farm, *Little Langdale, Ambleside, Cumbria, LA22 9NY.*
Cosy relaxing farmhouse in quiet valley, excellent scenery, lovely walks.
Open: All Year
015394 37269 **D:** £17–£18 **S:** £20–£21
Beds: 2D **Baths:** 1 Sh
🛇 🅿 (2) 🎟 Ⅴ ⚹

Little Musgrave

NY7513

Smithfield Barn, *Little Musgrave, Kirkby Stephen, Cumbria, CA17 4PG.*
Modern barn conversion. Tranquil setting. beautiful views over unspoilt countryside.
Open: All Year
017683 41002 E Hodgson
D: £19 **S:** £19
Beds: 2D **Baths:** 1 En 1 Pr
🛇 🅿 🗇 📺 🛪 🗙 🎟 Ⅴ ⚹

National Grid References are for villages, towns and cities – not for individual houses

Little Salkeld

NY5636 🍺 *Shepher's Inn*

Bank house Farm and Stables, *Bankhouse, Little Salkeld, Penrith, Cumbria, CA10 1NN.*
Converted barns on stable yard. Village location in Eden Valley. **Open:** All Year
01768 881257 **D:** £20–£30 **S:** £25–£30
Beds: 3F 3T 3D **Baths:** 6 En 3 Sh
🛇 🅿 (20) 📺 🛪 🎟 Ⅴ ⚹ ♿

Longtown

NY3868 🍺 *Crossways Inn, Graham Arms*

Briar Lea House, *Brampton Road, Longtown, Carlisle, Cumbria, CA6 5TN.*
A substantial country house in 1.75 acres of attractive grounds.
Open: All Year (not Xmas)
Grades: ETC 4 Diamond
01228 791538 (also fax) Mr Gildert
D: £19.50–£25 **S:** £25–£30
Beds: 2D 1T **Baths:** 3 En
🛇 🅿 (10) 🗇 📺 🛪 🗙 🎟 Ⅴ ⚹ ♿

Orchard House, *Blackbank, Longtown, Carlisle, Cumbria, CA6 5LQ.*
Spacious, tastefully furnished accommodation. Quiet wooded location near Gretna Green. **Open:** All Year (not Xmas) **Grades:** ETC 4 Diamond
01461 338596 Mrs Payne
orchard.gretna@virgin.net
D: £20–£22.50
Beds: 1D 1T **Baths:** 2 En
🛇 🅿 (4) 🗇 📺 🎟 Ⅴ ⚹

Lorton

NY1525 🍺 *The Wheatsheaf*

The Old Vicarage, *Church Lane, Lorton, Cockermouth, Cumbria, CA13 9UN.*
Elegant Victorian country house with stunning views, wooded grounds, log fires. **Open:** All Year (not Xmas)
Grades: AA 4 Diamond
01900 85656 (also fax) Mr Humphreys
enquiries@oldvicarage.co.uk
D: £22–£32 **S:** £22–£30
Beds: 5D 3T **Baths:** 8 En
🛇 🅿 (10) 🗇 📺 🗙 🎟 Ⅴ ⚹ cc

Cragg End Farm, *Rogerscale, Lorton Vale, Cockermouth, Cumbria, CA13 0RG.*
Beautiful views, ideal situation for walking. Quiet, working, family farm.
Open: All Year
01900 85658 Mrs Steel
D: £20–£18 **S:** fr £20
Beds: 1F 1D 2T **Baths:** 3 Sh
🛇 🅿 🗇 📺 🛪 🗙 Ⅴ

Loweswater

NY1420 🍺 *Wheatsheaf, Kirkstile*

Askhill Farm, *Loweswater, Cockermouth, Cumbria, CA13 0SU.*
Beef and sheep rearing farm, quiet valley, Loweswater. Ideal country walking area.
Open: Easter to Oct
Grades: ETC 3 Diamond
01946 861640 Mrs Vickers
D: £18–£20 **S:** £19–£21
Beds: 1F 1D **Baths:** 1 Sh
🛇 🅿 (3) 🗇 📺 🛪 🗙 🎟 Ⅴ ⚹

Brook Farm, *Loweswater,
Cockermouth, Cumbria, CA13 0RP.*
Comfortable, quiet, working farmhouse.
Good food, open fire, pretty garden.
Open: May to Nov
01900 85606 (also fax)
Mrs Hayton
D: £20–£21 **S:** £20–£21
Beds: 1F 1D **Baths:** 1 Sh
🛇 🄿 (3) ⠧ 📺 ➤ ✕ 🛊

Lowick

SD2986   🍺 *Red Lion*

Garth Row, *Lowick Green, Lowick,
Ulverston, Cumbria, LA12 8EB.*
Traditional Lakeland house; warm
welcome; super, peaceful setting; quality
accommodation.
Open: All Year (not Xmas/New Year)
Grades: ETC 3 Diamond
01229 885633
Mrs Wickens
b&b@garthrow.freeserve.co.uk
D: £18–£20 **S:** £23–£25
Beds: 1F 1D **Baths:** 1 Sh
🛇 🄿 (4) ⠧ 📺 ➤ 🛆 📵 🖵

Maryport

NY0336   🍺 *Retreat Hotel*

The Retreat Hotel, *Birkby, Maryport,
Cumbria, CA15 6RG.*
Former Victorian sea captain's residence
with large walled garden to rear.
Open: All Year (not Xmas)
01900 814056
Mr & Mrs Geissler
D: £23.50–£26 **S:** £33.50–£38.50
Beds: 2D 1T **Baths:** 3 En
🄿 (12) 📺 ✕ 📵 🖵 🛆 cc

Mealsgate

NY2041   🍺 *Kilsey Hotel, Oddfellows*

Appletree House, *Mealsgate, Wigton,
Cumbria, CA7 1JP.*
Open: All Year (not Xmas)
016973 71200
Mrs Exley
D: £18 **S:** £18
Beds: 1D 1T **Baths:** 1 Sh
🛇 🄿 (3) ⠧ 📺 📵
Modernised police house in rural
surroundings, open views, not
overlooked, close to many places of
interest; all rooms overlook countryside
and gardens, comfortable beds, good
English breakfast, private-off road
parking, on A595 between Carlisle and
Cockermouth.

Melmerby

NY6137   🍺 *Shepherds Inn*

Gale Hall Farm, *Melmerby, Penrith,
Cumbria, CA10 1HN.*
Large comfortable farmhouse near
Pennines and Lake District.
Open: Jun to Nov
01768 881254 Mrs Toppin
D: £15 **S:** £15
Beds: 1F 1T 1S **Baths:** 1 Sh
🛇 🄿 (3) 📺 ➤ 🖵

Middleton

SD6286   🍺 *Swan Inn*

Tossbeck Farm, *Middleton, Carnforth,
Lancashire, LA6 2LZ.*
A friendly welcome awaits you at
Tossbeck, mixed farm in unspoilt Lune
Valley.
Open: Easter to Oct
015242 76214 D: £17–£19 **S:** £22–£25
Beds: 1F 1D **Baths:** 1 En 1 Pr
🛇 🄿 (2) ⠧ 📺 ➤ 🖵 🛆

Moresby

NX9921   🍺 *Moresby Hall, Howgate Inn*

Moresby Hall, *Moresby, Whitehaven,
Cumbria, CA28 6PJ.*
Open: All Year
01946 696317 Mrs Saxon
Fax: 01946 692666
saxon@moresbyhall.co.uk
D: £22.50–£32.50 **S:** £25–£35
Beds: 1F 1T 2D **Baths:** 2 En 2 Pr
🛇 (10) 🄿 (6) ⠧ 📺 ✕ 📵 🖵 ✳ 🛆 cc
A Grade I Listed character building.
Spacious and well equipped rooms.
Semi-rural location and 2 acres of walled
gardens. Lakes, fells, cultural & tourist
locations. Delicious food in an elegant
setting. Licensed. A warm welcome to
our relaxing family home.

Morland

NY5923   🍺 *Crown Inn, Eden Vale Inn*

Mill Beck Cottage, *Water Street,
Morland, Penrith, Cumbria, CA10 3AY.*
Traditional riverside cottage, unspoilt
village & countryside, comfortable rooms,
good beds.
Open: All Year (not Xmas/New Year)
01931 714567
Mrs Jackson
Fax: 01931 714567
D: £19–£21 **S:** £21–£23
Beds: 1T 1D **Baths:** 1 Pr
🛇 (12) ⠧ 📺 ✕ 📵 🖵 🛆

Hill Top Guest House, *Morland,
Penrith, Cumbria, CA10 3AX.*
Fine Georgian house in picturesque
village elegant rooms, superb views.
Open: All Year
01931 714561 liz@hilltophouse.co.uk
D: £25–£30 **S:** £30–£35
Beds: 3F 1T 2D **Baths:** 3 En
🛇 (7) 🄿 (6) 📺 ✕ 📵 🖵 🛆

Mungrisdale

NY3630

Near Howe Hotel, *Mungrisdale,
Penrith, Cumbria, CA11 0SH.*
Small hotel in beautiful area. Warm
welcome awaits you.
Open: All Year (not Xmas)
Grades: ETC 3 Diamond
017687 79678 (also fax)
Mrs Weightman
D: £19–£23 **S:** £22–£23
Beds: 3F 3D 1D **Baths:** 5 En 2 Sh
🛇 🄿 (20) ⠧ ✕ 📵 🖵 🛆

Natland

SD5289   🍺 *Punch Bowl, Station Inn*

Higher House Farm, *Oxenholme
Lane, Natland, Kendal, Cumbria, LA9 7QH.*
Tranquil Lakeland village, C17th
farmhouse. **Open:** All Year (not Xmas)
Grades: ETC 4 Diamond, Silver Award,
AA 4 Diamond
015395 61177 Mrs Sunter
Fax: 015395 61520
D: £24.50–£27.50 **S:** £29.50–£32.50
Beds: 2D 1T **Baths:** 3 En
🛇 (12) 🄿 (9) ⠧ 📵 🖵 🛆

Near Sawrey

SD3795   🍺 *Tower Bank Arms*

High Green Gate Guest House,
*Near Sawrey, Ambleside, Cumbria,
LA22 0LF.*
Converted farmhouse in Beatrix Potter's
village countryside, farm position.
Open: Apr to Oct
Grades: ETC 3 Diamond, AA 3 Diamond,
RAC 3 Diamond
015394 36296 Miss Fletcher
D: £23–£26 **S:** fr £23
Beds: 4F 1D **Baths:** 3 Pr 1 Sh
🛇 🄿 (7) 📵 ➤ ✕ 📵 🖵 🛆

Esthwaite How Farm, *Near Sawrey,
Ambleside, Cumbria, LA22 0LB.*
Friendly farmhouse overlooking lake and
fields. Beatrix Potter's house in village.
Open: All Year (not Xmas)
015394 36450 D: £15 **S:** £15
Beds: 2D 1T **Baths:** 1 Sh
🄿 (3) 📺 ➤ ✕ 📵 🖵 🛆

Nenthead

NY7843   🍺 *Miners Arms*

The Miners Arms, *Nenthead, Alston,
Cumbria, CA9 3PF.*
Friendly family pub. Real ales, real food,
real fires. **Open:** All Year
01434 381427 Miss Clark
D: £15 **S:** £15
Beds: 2F 2D 2T 2S
🛇 🄿 ⠧ 📺 ➤ 📵 🖵 🛆 cc

Mill Cottage Bunkhouse, *Nenthead,
Alston, Cumbria, CA9 3PD.*
Open: All Year
01434 382771
administration.office@virgin.net
D: £12 **S:** £12
Beds: 2F
🛇 🄿 (4) ⠧ ✕ 📵 🖵 🛆
Bunkhouse in spectacular landscape,
part of Nenthead Mines heritage site.

New Hutton

SD5691   🍺 *Station Inn*

Cragg Farm, *New Hutton, Kendal,
Cumbria, LA8 0BA.*
Comfortable C17th farmhouse, working
farm. Quiet, rural location 3 miles M6
(J37).
Open: Mar to Nov
015397 21760 Mrs Knowles
D: £16–£17 **S:** £16.50–£17
Beds: 1F 1D **Baths:** 1 Sh
🛇 🄿 (3) ⠧ 📺 📵 🖵 🛆

Newbiggin (Stainton)

NY4629   Clickham

Tymparon Hall, Newbiggin , Penrith, Cumbria, CA11 0HS.
Secluded farmhouse. 3/4 mile A66 close M6 J40 and Lake Ullswater.
Open: Feb to Nov
Grades: RAC 4 Diamond
017684 83236 Ms Taylor
margaret@pearson.freeserve.co.uk
D: £21–£25 **S:** £21–£25
Beds: 1F 1D 1T **Baths:** 2 En 1 Pr
🛇 🅿 ⌿ 📺 🛉 ✕ 🎱 🖤 ⚓

Newbiggin-on-Lune

NY7005   Kings Head

Tranna Hill, Newbiggin-on-Lune, Kirkby Stephen, Cumbria, CA17 4NY.
Fantastic views, good food, warm welcome, excellent for walking.
Open: Easter to Oct
015396 23227 Mrs Boustead
brendatrannahill@hotmail.com
D: £17–£18 **S:** £20
Beds: 1D 1T **Baths:** 1 En 1 Pr
🛇 🅿 (4) ⌿ 📺 ✕ 🎱 ⚓

Newby Bridge

SD3786   Swan Hotel, Anglers Arms, Cavendish Arms, Boaters, Rusland Pool

Alloa Guest House, Newby Bridge, Cumbria, LA12 8LZ.
Open: All Year (not Xmas/New Year)
015395 30391 (also fax)
D: £20–£25 **S:** £25–£30
Beds: 1F 1T 1D **Baths:** 2 En 1 Pr
🛇 (2) 🅿 (10) ⌿ 📺 ✕ 🎱 ⚓
Secluded luxury bungalow with all amenities. Excellent home cooking. Ample parking. Superb lake views. Ideal touring/ walking centre for Southern Lakes. One acre grounds. Warm hospitality assured, special breaks available, ring for a colour brochure.

Lyndhurst Country House, Newby Bridge, Ulverston, Cumbria, LA12 8ND.
Warm welcome for walkers, cyclists, vegetarian/vegans. Bird watchers' paradise.
Open: Easter to November
015395 31245 Mr & Mrs Evans
lyndhurst@gofree.co.uk
D: £19–£24
Beds: 1T 2D **Baths:** 3 En
🛇 🅿 (3) ⌿ 📺 ✕ 🎱 🖤 ⚓

Miller Beck, Newby Bridge, Ulverston, Cumbria, LA12 8NE.
Open: All Year (not Xmas)
015395 31329 E I Foster
D: £22.50–£25 **S:** £30–£35
Beds: 1D 1T 1S **Baths:** 2 En
🛇 (8) 🅿 (10) ⌿ 📺 🛉 🎱 🖤 ⚓
Typical Lakeland house from 1920, backing onto Lake Windermere. Warm welcome, comfortable beds, good breakfast. Plenty of off road parking, even for boat and car trailers. Restaurants within 500 yards, plus 3 pubs within 2 miles. Good location.

Hill Crest, Backbarrow, Newby Bridge, Ulverston, Cumbria, LA12 8PL.
Traditional Lakeland house, magnificent views, country location - quality accommodation, homely.
Open: All Year (not Xmas)
Grades: AA 4 Diamond
015395 31766 Mrs Jenkinson
Fax: 015395 31986
D: £20–£25 **S:** £25–£32
Beds: 1F 3D 1T **Baths:** 2 En 1 Pr
🛇 🅿 (3) ⌿ 📺 ✕ 🎱 🖤 ⚓

Old Barn Farm, Fiddler Hall, Lake Windermere, Newby Bridge, Ulverston, Cumbria, LA12 8NQ.
Beautiful C17th house, large gardens, views, quiet. Lake Windermere nearby.
Open: All Year (not Xmas)
015395 31842 (also fax)
Mrs Winton
D: £20–£25 **S:** £25–£30
Beds: 1F 1D 1T **Baths:** 3 En
🛇 🅿 (4) ⌿ 📺 🎱 🖤 ⚓

Newlands

NY2420   Coledale Inn, Swinside Inn

Uzzicar Farm, Newlands, Keswick, Cumbria, CA12 5TS.
Clean, cosy, comfortable farmhouse with character; situated in idyllic surroundings.
Open: All Year (not Xmas)
Grades: ETC 3 Diamond
017687 78367
Mrs Simpson
D: £17–£19 **S:** £20
Beds: 1D 1F **Baths:** 1 Sh
🛇 🅿 ⌿ 🎱 🖤 ⚓

Swinside Farm, Newlands, Keswick, Cumbria, CA12 5UE.
Comfortable, modernised farmhouse. Superb scenery and walking, excellent breakfasts offered.
Open: All Year
017687 78363 Mr Bright
D: £22.50 **S:** fr £30
Beds: 2D 1T **Baths:** 3 En
🅿 📺 🎱 🖤 🖤

Old Hutton

SD5688   Kings Arms, Royal Hotel, Station Inn

Blaven, Middleshaw Head Barn, Old Hutton, Kendal, Cumbria, LA8 0LZ.
Open: All Year
01539 734894
Mrs Beale & Mr Green
Fax: 01539 727447
blaven@greenarrow.demon.co.uk
D: £25–£32 **S:** £28–£42
Beds: 1S 1T 1F **Baths:** 1 En 1 Pr
🛇 🅿 (4) ⌿ 📺 🛉 ✕ 🎱 🖤 ✻ ⚓ **cc**
Peaceful, hilly location. Lovely stream side Lakeland house, very convenient for Junc 36/37 M6. Station - 5 minute taxi ride. Windermere 20 mins. Excellent for touring Lakes and Dales. Superb gourmet cooking by owners Jan & Barry. Complimentary aperitifs. Memorable dinners.

Outhgill

NY7801

Faraday Cottage, Outhgill, Kirkby Stephen, Cumbria, CA17 4JU.
Historic cottage. Heart of Mallerstang Valley, walkers paradise.
Open: All Year (not Xmas/New Year)
017683 72351 Mrs Porter
D: £15 **S:** £15
Beds: 1T 1D **Baths:** 1 Sh
🛇 🅿 (2) ⌿ 📺 🛉 ✕ 🎱 🖤 ⚓

Pardshaw

NY0924   Old Posting House

Brow Howe, Pardshaw, Cockermouth, Cumbria, CA13 0SP.
Attractive cottage with large garden perfectly situated for Lakes, Fells and coast.
Open: All Year
01900 827780 Mr Fielden
brow.howe@virgin.net
D: £19 **S:** £19
Beds: 1D 1T **Baths:** 1 Sh
🛇 (5) 🅿 (2) ⌿ 📺 🎱 🖤 ⚓

Sunny Corner, Pardshaw, Cockermouth, Cumbria, CA13 0SP.
This luxurious former hostelry nestling in lovely North Western Lake District.
Open: All Year
01900 826380 (also fax)
Ms Hill
D: £23–£27
Beds: 2D **Baths:** 2 En
🅿 (2) ⌿ 📺 🎱 🖤

Patterdale

NY3915

Greenbank Farm, Patterdale, Penrith, Cumbria, CA11 0NR.
C16th converted comfortable farmhouse.
Open: All Year (not Xmas)
017684 82292 Mrs Iredale
D: fr £14 **S:** fr £14
Beds: 1F 1T **Baths:** 1 Sh
🛇 (1) 🅿 (4) ⌿ 📺 ✕ 🎱 🖤 ⚓

Penrith

NY5130   Royal Hotel, Lowther Arms, Glen Cottage, Dog & Duck, Gloucester Arms, Cross Keys, Agricultural Hotel, Beacon Bank, Herdwick Inn, Beehive Inn

Norcroft Guest House, Graham Street, Penrith, Cumbria, CA11 9LQ.
Open: All Year
Grades: ETC 3 Diamond RAC 4 Diamond, Welcome Award
01768 862365 (also fax)
Mrs Jackson
D: £19.50–£21.50 **S:** fr £21.50
Beds: 2F 2D 4T 1S **Baths:** 9 En
🛇 🅿 (9) ⌿ 📺 🎱 🖤 ⚓ **1 cc**
Charming Victorian house with relaxed friendly atmosphere ideal centre or stop over (M6 junction 40 just 10 mins away) for English lakes or Scottish borders. Enjoy our hearty Cumbria food or 5 mins' walk to town centre for alternatives. Ample private parking.

Blue Swallow, *11 Victoria Road, Penrith, Cumbria, CA11 8HR.*
Victorian town house situated in lovely market town of Penrith.
Open: All Year (not Xmas)
Grades: ETC 3 Diamond
01768 866335 (also fax) Mrs Hughes
D: £17–£20 **S:** £22–£27
Beds: 1F 2D 2T **Baths:** 3 En 1 Sh
☺ **P** (5) �📺 🛏 ▥ **V** ⅙

Brooklands Guest House, *2 Portland Place, Penrith, Cumbria, CA11 7QN.*
Open: All Year
01768 863395 Fax: 01768 864895
D: £18–£22.50 **S:** £20–£22
Beds: 1F 2S 3D/T **Baths:** 2 Sh, 3 En
☺ **P** (1) �📺 🛏 ▥ **V** ⅙
A fine Victorian town house just 100 m, from the Town centre, built in 1874 retaining many of the original features, with spacious rooms tastefully decorated to a very high standard. Home from Home comforts a very friendly atmosphere awaits you.

Albany House, *5 Portland Place, Penrith, Cumbria, CA11 7QN.*
Friendly, comfortable Victorian house, good breakfast, town centre M6 5 minutes. **Open:** All Year
Grades: ETC 3 Diamond
01768 863072 (also fax) Mrs Blundell
D: £17.50–£25 **S:** £20–£27.50
Beds: 4F 1D **Baths:** 2 En 1 Sh
☺ **P** (1) �📺 ▥ **V** ⅙

Grosvenor House, *3 Lonsdale Terrace, Meeting House Lane, Penrith, Cumbria, CA11 7TS.*
Large comfortable town house convenient for lakes and fells.
Open: Easter to Nov
01768 863813 Mrs Fitzpatrick
D: £14–£18 **S:** £20
Beds: 1D 2T **Baths:** 1 Sh
☺ ⅙ �📺 🛏 **V**

Makalolo, *Barco Avenue, Penrith, Cumbria, CA11 8LU.*
Spacious modern house, beamed lounge, conservatory, views of Lakeland hills.
Local Authority Approved. **Open:** All Year
01768 891519 Mr Dawson
D: £17–£20 **S:** £25–£28
Beds: 1T 1D **Baths:** 1 En 1 Pr
P (6) ⅙ �📺 ✕ ▥ **V** ⅙

Caledonia Guest House, *8 Victoria Road, Penrith, Cumbria, CA11 8HR.*
Comfortable family-run Victorian house close to all amenities. **Open:** All Year
01768 864482 Mrs Land
D: £18–£20 **S:** £25–£30
Beds: 1F 2D 3T **Baths:** 4 En 2 Pr
☺ **P** (5) ⅙ �📺 ▥ **V** ⅙

The White House, *94 Lowther Street, Penrith, Cumbria, CA11 7UW.*
Lovely renovated Victorian home, ensuite facilities, splendid breakfast, friendly atmosphere. **Open:** All Year
01768 892106 huit-lansbury@msn.com
D: £20–£24 **S:** £25–£30
Beds: 1T 1D **Baths:** 2 En
☺ ⅙ �📺 ▥ **V** ⅙

Keepers Cottage, *Brougham, Penrith, Cumbria, CA10 2DE.*
Beamed period cottage in rural setting. Heated indoor swimming pool.
Open: All Year
Grades: ETC 3 Diamond
01768 865280 (also fax)
stay@keeperscottage.co.uk
D: £20–£24.50 **S:** £24.50–£30
Beds: 1F 1T 1D **Baths:** 3 En
P (4) ⅙ �📺 🛏 ▥ **V** ⅙

Roundthorn Country House, *Beacon Edge, Penrith, Cumbria, CA11 8SJ.*
Beautiful Georgian mansion with spectacular views of the surrounding area.
Open: All Year
Grades: ETC 4 Diamond, Silver
01768 863952 G Carruthers
Fax: 01768 864100
enquiries@roundthorn.co.uk
D: £25–£31.50 **S:** £37.50–£45
Beds: 1F 1T 8D **Baths:** 10 En
☺ **P** ⅙ �📺 🛏 ✕ ▥ **V** ⅙ **CC**

The Friarage, *Friargate, Penrith, Cumbria, CA11 7XR.*
Clean, comfortable historical house, town centre. Ideal North/South, East/West travellers.
Open: Mar to Oct
01768 863635 (also fax) Mrs Clark
D: £15–£20 **S:** £17–£18
Beds: 1F 1D 1T 1S **Baths:** 1 En 2 Sh
☺ **P** (3) ⅙ �📺 ▥ **V** ⅙

Beacon Bank Hotel, *Beacon Edge, Penrith, Cumbria, CA11 7BD.*
Beacon Bank is a beautiful Victorian house in an acre of landscaped gardens.
Open: All Year
01768 862633 Mrs Black
beaconbank.hotel@virgin.net
D: £25–£30 **S:** £35
Beds: 2F 4D 2T **Baths:** 8 En
☺ **P** (10) ⅙ �📺 ✕ ▥ **CC**

Cumrew, *Graham Street, Penrith, Cumbria, CA11 9LG.*
Home from home B&B 5 minutes' walk from town centre.
Open: Mar to Oct
01768 867923 (also fax)
Mrs Ablewhite
D: £15–£16 **S:** £15–£16
Beds: 1D 1S **Baths:** 1 Sh
☺ (5) **P** (1) ⅙ �📺 ▥ **V** ⅙

NY1439   🍺 Horse and Jockey Pub

Chapel House, *Plumbland, Aspatria, Carlisle, Cumbria, CA5 2HA.*
Open: All Year (not Xmas/New Year)
01697 321480 Mr & Mrs Wells
dennis.wells@talk21.com
D: £17.50 **S:** £17.50
Beds: 1T 1D **Baths:** 2 En
☺ **P** (3) ⅙ �📺 🛏 ▥ ⅙
Well located between Keswick, Cockermouth and the Solway Coast with excellent access to the Lake District National Park. Our emphasis is on quality and personal attention. We serve a freshly cooked full Cumbrian breakfast to start your day.

NY2523   🍺 Farmers Arms, Swinside Inn

Skiddaw Croft, *Portinscale, Keswick, Cumbria, CA12 5RD.*
Open: All Year
017687 72321 (also fax) J Downer
skiddawcroft@talk21.com
D: £20–£25 **S:** £20–£25
Beds: 1F 1T 2D 2S **Baths:** 4 En 1 Sh
☺ **P** (6) ⅙ �📺 🛏 ▥ **V** ⅙
Comfortable & friendly B&B in charming village. Easy walk to Keswick (15 mins) Splendid lake & mountain views. Health & hearty breakfasts. Vegetarians welcome. Good base for hill & water sports (marina 5 mins).

Rickerby Grange, *Portinscale, Keswick, Cumbria, CA12 5RH.*
Set within own garden, private parking. In the pretty village of Portinscale.
Open: All Year
Grades: ETC 4 Diamond, AA 4 Diamond, RAC 4 Diamond, Sparkling
017687 72344 Mrs Bradley
val@ricor.demon.co.uk
D: £28–£30 **S:** £28–£30
Beds: 3F 9D 2S **Baths:** 14 En
☺ (5) **P** (14) ⅙ �📺 🛏 ✕ ▥ **V** ⚘ ⅙

Thirnbeck Guest House, *Portinscale, Keswick, Cumbria, CA12 5RD.*
Comfortable Georgian guest house with fine views over Derwent water.
Open: All Year (not Xmas)
Grades: AA 3 Diamond
017687 72869 Martin & Lynn Savage
mls@thirnbeck.fsnet.co.uk
D: £23 **S:** £23
Beds: 4D 1T 1S **Baths:** 5 En 1 Pr
☺ (4) **P** (4) ⅙ �📺 🛏 ▥ **V** ⅙

SD0896   🍺 Ratty Arms, Brown Cow

Muncaster Country Guest House, *Ravenglass, Cumbria, CA18 1RD.*
Open: Mar to Oct
Grades: RAC 3 Diamond
01229 717693 (also fax)
Mr Putnam
D: £20–£24 **S:** £22–£28
Beds: 1F 3D 2T 3S **Baths:** 2 En 2 Sh
☺ (1) **P** (16) ⅙ �📺 🛏 ▥ **V** ⅙ & ⅙
A very comfortable and welcoming country guest house adjoining Muncaster estate and open countryside. Easy access to miniature railway, Eskdale and Wasdale. Walkers welcome. Children and dogs accepted. Hearty breakfasts.

NY7203   🍺 Black Swan, Kings Head

Bowber Head, *Ravenstonedale, Kirkby Stephen, Cumbria, CA17 4NL.*
C17th farmhouse, open views, centre for classic coach tours.
Open: All Year
015396 23254 (also fax)
Mr Hamer
hols@cumbriaclassiccoaches.co.uk
D: £20–£22 **S:** £20–£22
Beds: 1F 2D 2T **Baths:** 1 En 2 Pr
☺ **P** (6) ⅙ �📺 🛏 ✕ ▥ **V** ⅙ & ⅙

Renwick

NY5943

Scalehouse Farm, Scalehouses, Renwick, Penrith, Cumbria, CA10 1JY.
Old farmhouse with period features, open fires and beams, tastefully renovated.
Open: All Year (not Xmas)
01768 896493 (also fax)
D: £14–£18 **S:** £16–£20
Beds: 2D 1T **Baths:** 1 Pr 1 Sh
🛇 🅿 (6) 🔌 🎺 🖭 ✕ 🎦 🖤 ₤

Roa Island

SD2364 🍺 The Clarkes Arms

Villa Marina, Roa Island, Barrow-in-Furness, Cumbria, LA13 0QL.
Victorian Gentleman's residence situated on Morecambe Bay.
Open: All Year (not Xmas/New Year)
01229 822520
Mrs Allen
D: £15–£20 **S:** £20–£25
Beds: 1F 2T **Baths:** 1 En 1 Sh
🛇 🅿 (4) 🔌 🖭 🎺 🎦 🖤 ₤

Rockcliffe

NY3561 🍺 Metal Bridge Inn

Metal Bridge House, Metal Bridge, Rockcliffe, Carlisle, Cumbria, CA6 4HG.
In country, close to M6/A74, quality accommodation, friendly welcome.
Open: All Year (not Xmas)
01228 674695
Mr Rae
D: £16–£18 **S:** £20–£22
Beds: 1D 2T **Baths:** 1 Sh
🛇 🅿 (6) 🔌 🎺 🎦 ₤

Rosthwaite (Borrowdale)

NY2514 🍺 Langstrath Inn, Royal Oak,Scafell Hotel, Riverside Bar

Royal Oak Hotel, Rosthwaite, Keswick, Cumbria, CA12 5XB.
Open: All Year
Grades: ETC 1 Star
017687 77214 (also fax) Mr Dowie
royaloakhotel@ukgateway.net
D: fr £26 **S:** fr £25
Beds: 6F 5D 2T 2S **Baths:** 12 En 3 Sh
🛇 🅿 (15) 🖭 🎺 ✕ 🎦 🖤 ₤
A traditional family-run walkers' hotel in the heart of beautiful Borrowdale. Come and enjoy our friendly service, cosy bar, open fire and good home cooking. Brochure, tariffs and special breaks available.

The How, Rosthwaite, Keswick, Cumbria, CA12 5BX.
Open: Mar to Nov
017687 77692 **D:** £19–£20.50 **S:** £22–£23
Beds: 1T 2D **Baths:** 2 Sh
🅿 (4) 🖭 🎺 🎦 ₤
Rosthwaite is in the beautiful Borrowdale Valley about six miles from Keswick. Fell and riverside walking. Country house in well kept garden. Comfortable lounge with television, log fire when required. Breakfast room. Superb views.

Yew Craggs, Rosthwaite, Borrowdale, Keswick, Cumbria, CA12 5XB.
Central Borrowdale, spectacular views, car park, riverside location (by the bridge).
Open: Mar to Nov
017687 77260 Mr & Mrs Crofts
yewcraggs@aol.com
D: £17–£21 **S:** fr £25
Beds: 2F 3D **Baths:** 1 Sh
🛇 (6) 🅿 (6) 🔌

Gillercombe, Stonethwaite Road End, Rosthwaite, Borrowdale, Keswick, Cumbria, CA12 5XG.
Comfortable, homely, clean and good views.
Open: Feb to Nov
017687 77602 Mrs Dunkley
D: £18 **S:** £18
Beds: 2D 2T 1S
🅿 (5) 🔌 🎦

Rydal

NY3606

Nab Cottage, Rydal, Grasmere, Cumbria, LA22 9SD.
Idyllic situation in the heart of the Lakes overlooking Rydal Water, surrounded by mountains.
Open: All Year
015394 35311 Fax: 015394 35493
ell@nab.dial.lakesnet.co.uk
D: £20–£22 **S:** £20–£40
Beds: 1F 3D 2T 1S **Baths:** 3 En 1 Sh
🛇 🅿 (10) 🖭 🎺 ✕ 🎦 ₤

Sandwith

NX9614 🍺 Lowther Arms

The Old Granary, Spout Howse, Sandwith, Whitehaven, Cumbria, CA28 9UG.
Tastefully converted barn on C2C route and Coast to Coast path.
Open: All Year
01946 692097 Mrs Buchanan
D: fr £17 **S:** fr £16
Beds: 1F 1D 1T **Baths:** 2 En
🛇 🅿 (2) 🎺 🖤 ₤

Satterthwaite

SD3392 🍺 Eagles Head

Force Mill Farm, Satterthwaite, Ulverston, Cumbria, LA12 8LQ.
17th Century riverside farmhouse, near Grizedale forest, lakes and fells.
Open: All Year
01229 860205 (also fax)
D: £20 **S:** £20–£25
Beds: 1F 1T 2D **Baths:** 4 En
🛇 🅿 (6) 🔌 🖭 🎺 🎦 🖤 ₤

Pepper House, Satterthwaite, Ulverston, Cumbria, LA12 8LS.
C16th former farmhouse, tranquil valley, views, log fires, great cooking.
Open: All Year (not Xmas)
01229 860206 (also fax)
Mr Townsend
frances.townsend@virgin.net
D: £23.50 **S:** £27.50
Beds: 2D 1T **Baths:** 3 En
🛇 (8) 🅿 (4) 🔌 🖭 🎺 ✕ 🎦 🖤 ₤

Sedbergh

SD6592 🍺 Dalesman Inn, Cross Keys, Red Lion, Bull Hotel

Stable Antiques, 15 Back Lane, Sedbergh, Cumbria, LA10 5AQ.
C18th wheelwright's cottage with wonderful views of Howgill Fells.
Open: All Year
Grades: ETC 2 Diamond
015396 20251 Miss Thurlby
D: £18–£19 **S:** £18–£19
Beds: 1D 1T **Baths:** 1 Sh
🛇 (10) 🖭 🎺 🎦 🖤 ₤ cc

Holmecroft, Station Road, Sedbergh, Cumbria, LA10 5DW.
Recommended by 'Which' Good Bed and Breakfast Guide.
Open: All Year (not Xmas)
Grades: ETC 3 Diamond
015396 20754 (also fax)
Mrs Sharrocks
ssharrocks@breathemail.net
D: £19 **S:** £19
Beds: 1D 1T 1S **Baths:** 1 Sh
🛇 🅿 (6) 🔌 🖭 🎦 🖤 ₤

Sun Lea, Joss Lane, Sedbergh, Cumbria, LA10 5AS.
Large Victorian family house near town centre run by walkers.
Open: All Year (not Xmas/New Year)
015396 20828 Mr & Mrs Ramsden
pat@josslane.freeserve.co.uk
D: £18–£20 **S:** £18–£20
Beds: 2D 1T **Baths:** 2 En 1 Sh
🛇 🅿 (3) 🔌 🖭 🎦 🖤 ₤

Marshall House, Main Street, Sedbergh, Cumbria, LA10 5BL.
Which? recommended Dales town house situated under the magnificent Howgill Fells. **Open:** All Year (not Xmas)
015396 21053 Mrs Kerry
D: £22–£27 **S:** £35–£45
Beds: 1D 2T **Baths:** 2 En 1 Pr
🛇 (12) 🅿 (5) 🖭 🎦 🖤 ₤ ♿

Selside

SD5399 🍺 Plough Inn

Hollowgate, Selside, Kendal, Cumbria, LA8 9LG.
C16th comfortable farmhouse.
Open: Easter to Oct
Grades: ETC 3 Diamond
01539 823258 Mrs Knowles
hollowgate@talk21.com
D: £17–£17.50 **S:** £17–£17.50
Beds: 2D 1S
🛇 🅿 (3) 🖭 ✕ 🎦 🖤 ₤

Shap

NY5615 🍺 Bulls Head, The Greyhound, The Crown

Fell House, Shap, Penrith, Cumbria, CA10 3NY.
Spacious Victorian house convenient for Lakes and Dales. **Open:** All Year
01931 716343 Mr & Mrs Smith
johnsmith@fellhouse.freeserve.co.uk
D: £16.50–£20 **S:** £18.50–£24
Beds: 3F 1D 1T **Baths:** 1 En 2 Sh
🛇 🅿 🔌 🖭 🎺 🎦 🖤 ₤

Brookfield, Shap, Penrith, Cumbria, CA10 3PZ.
Renowned for good food, comfort and personal attention. Ensuite, licensed.
Open: All Year (not Xmas/New Year)
Grades: AA 4 Diamond
01931 716397 (also fax)
Mrs Brunskill
D: £19–£23 **S:** £19–£25
Beds: 3F 5D 3T 1S **Baths:** 4 En 4 Pr 1 Sh
🛇 ⓟ (20) 𝌆 ⊡ ✕ ⊞ Ⓥ ⸙

1 The Rockery, Shap, Penrith, Cumbria, CA10 3LY.
C18th coaching inn.
Open: All Year (not Xmas)
01931 716340 Mrs Hicks
D: fr £18 **S:** fr £18
Beds: 1F 1D 1T **Baths:** 2 Sh
🛇 ⓟ (4) 𝌆 ⊡ ⊞ Ⓥ ⸙

Skelwith Bridge

NY3403   🍴 *The Talbot*

Greenbank, Skelwith Bridge, Ambleside, Cumbria, LA22 9NW.
Comfortable, friendly B & B in superb central lakes location.
Open: Feb to Nov
Grades: ETC 4 Diamond, Silver
015394 33236 Mr Green
greenbank@bigwig.net
D: £22–£25 **S:** £32–£35
Beds: 2D 1T **Baths:** 3 En
🛇 (8) ⓟ (5) 𝌆 ⊡ ⊞ Ⓥ ⸙

St Bees

NX9711   🍴 *Queens Head, Manor House, Oddfellows*

Tomlin Guest House, 1 Tomlin House, St Bees, Cumbria, CA27 0EN.
Comfortable Victorian house convenient to beach and St Bees Head.
Open: All Year (not Xmas)
01946 822284 Mrs Whitehead
Fax: 01946 824243
id.whitehead@which.net
D: £15–£18 **S:** £18
Beds: 1F 2D 1T **Baths:** 2 En 2 Sh
🛇 ⓟ (2) 𝌆 ⊡ ⊞ Ⓥ ⸙

Stonehouse Farm, Main Street, St Bees, Cumbria, CA27 0DE.
Modern Georgian farmhouse in centre of village, next to railway station.
Open: All Year (not Xmas)
Grades: ETC 3 Diamond
01946 822224 Mrs Smith
D: £16–£20 **S:** £20
Beds: 1F 2D 2T 1S **Baths:** 4 En 1 Sh
🛇 ⓟ (20) ⊡ 🐾 ⊞ Ⓥ ⸙

Fairladies Barn Guest House, Main Street, St Bees, CA27 0AD.
Large converted barn located in centre of seaside village.
Open: All Year
01946 822718 Mrs Carr
D: £16 **S:** £16
Beds: 6D 2T 1S **Baths:** 3 En 2 Sh
🛇 ⓟ (10) ⊡ ⊞ Ⓥ ⸙

Stanwix

NY3957   🍴 *Cumbria Park Hotel*

No. 1, 1 Etterby Street, Stanwix, Carlisle, Cumbria, CA3 9JB.
Homely accommodation in easy reach of Hadrians Wall & Scotland lakes.
Open: All Year (not Xmas/New Year)
Grades: ETC 3 Diamond
01228 547285 Ms Nixon
D: £17–£20 **S:** £17–£20
Beds: 1D 2S
🛇 (4) ⓟ (1) 𝌆 ⊡ ✕ ⊞ Ⓥ ⸙

Staveley

SD4698   🍴 *Railway Inn, Duke William, Eagle & Child*

Stock Bridge Farm, Staveley, Kendal, Cumbria, LA8 9LP.
Modernised comfortable C17th farmhouse in picturesque village close to Lakes. **Open:** Mar to Oct
01539 821580 Mrs Fishwick
D: £16.50–£17.50 **S:** £16.50–£17.50
Beds: 1F 4D 1T 1S **Baths:** 1 Sh
🛇 ⓟ (6) ⊡ 🐾 ⊞ Ⓥ

Heywood, Kentmere Road, Staveley, Kendal, Cumbria, LA8 9JF.
Peaceful spacious bungalow in hamlet with views of Kentmere Valley.
Open: Feb to Nov **01539 821198**
D: £18–£20 **S:** £20
Beds: 1D **Baths:** 1 En
ⓟ (1) 𝌆 ⊞ ⸙

The Old Vicarage, Brow Lane, Staveley, Kendal, Cumbria, LA8 9PH.
Peaceful retreat with panoramic views in national park. Overlooking village. Midway Kendal/Windermere.
Open: All Year
01539 822432 Mrs Ellwood
Fax: 01539 822375
jellwood@globalnet.co.uk
D: £17–£20 **S:** £20–£25
Beds: 1F 2D 1T **Baths:** 1 En 2 Pr
ⓟ (4) 𝌆 ⊡ ⊞ Ⓥ ⸙

Tebay

NY6104   🍴 *Cross Keys*

Primrose Cottage, Orton Road, Tebay, Penrith, Cumbria, CA10 3TL.
Adjacent M6 junction 38. 4 poster bed, jacuzzi hathroom, rural village with pub.
Open: All Year **Grades:** ETC 4 Diamond
015396 24791 Mrs Jones
D: £20–£25 **S:** £20–£30
Beds: 2D 1T **Baths:** 1 En 2 Pr
🛇 ⓟ (6) ⊡ 🐾 ✕ ⊞ Ⓥ ⸙

Temple Sowerby

NY6127   🍴 *Kings Arms*

Skygarth Farm, Temple Sowerby, Penrith, CA10 1SS.
Traditional family-run farm, warm welcome assured. 500 yards from A66.
Open: Easter to Nov
017683 61300 (also fax) Mrs Robinson
enquire@skygarth.co.uk
D: £17 **S:** £17
Beds: 2F 1S **Baths:** 1 Sh
🛇 ⓟ (4) ⊡ ✕ ⊞ ⸙

Thornhill

NY0108   🍴 *Royal Oak*

The Old Vicarage Guest House, Thornhill, Egremont, Cumbria, CA22 2NY.
C19th vicarage of character, within easy reach fells & lakes.
Open: All Year (not Xmas)
Grades: ETC 3 Diamond
01946 841577 Mrs Graham
D: £15–£17 **S:** £15–£17
Beds: 3F **Baths:** 2 Sh
🛇 ⓟ (6) ⊡ 🐾 ⊞ Ⓥ ⸙

Thornthwaite

NY2225

Thwaite Howe Hotel, Thornthwaite, Keswick, Cumbria, CA12 5SA.
Open: Mar to Oct
Grades: ETC 2 Star, AA 2 Star, RAC 2 Star
017687 78281 Mr & Mrs Marshall
D: £28–£35 **S:** £48–£58
Beds: 5D 3T 1F 1S **Baths:** 8 En
🛇 (12) ⓟ (10) ⊡ 𝌆 ✕ ⊞ Ⓥ ⸙ cc
Beautiful small country house hotel backing on to Thornthwaite Forest with views over Derwent Valley to Skiddaw, Dod and Latrigg mountains. Midway between Bassenthwaite lake and Derwent Water. Tranquil and romantic atmosphere. Good food and excellent rooms.

Tirril

NY5026   🍴 *Queens Head*

The Queens Head Inn, Tirril, Penrith, Cumbria, CA10 2JF.
C1719, once owned by Wordsworth, own brewery, food awards.
Open: All Year (not Xmas)
Grades: ETC 2 Diamond
01768 863219 Fax: 01768 863243
bookings@queensheadinn.co.uk
D: £22.50–£25 **S:** £30–£35
Beds: 1F 5D 1T **Baths:** 4 En 1 Pr 1 Sh
🛇 ⓟ (40) ⊡ ✕ ⊞ Ⓥ ⸙ cc

April Cottage, Margote Cross, Tirril, Penrith, Cumbria, CA10 2LN.
Large bungalow situated on B5320 just outside village of Tirril.
Open: All Year (not Xmas)
017684 86277 H Threlked
D: £20–£23 **S:** fr £25
Beds: 1D 1T **Baths:** 1 En 1 Sh
🛇 ⓟ (4) 𝌆 ⊡ 🐾 ✕ ⊞ ⸙ ♿

Torver

SD2894   🍴 *Church House Inn*

The Coach House, Torver, Coniston, Cumbria, LA21 8AY.
Tranquil country house in beautiful surroundings at the foot of Coniston Old man.
Open: Mar to Nov
015394 41592 Mrs Newport
Fax: 015394 41092
brigg.house@virgin.net
D: £20–£22
Beds: 2D 1T **Baths:** 3 En
🛇 (8) ⓟ (4) 𝌆 ⊡ 🐾 ⊞ Ⓥ ⸙

Troutbeck Bridge

NY3900 🍴 *Sun, Queens Head*

High View, Sun Hill Lane, Troutbeck
Bridge, Windermere, Cumbria, LA23 1HJ.
Elevated bungalow enjoying panoramic
views. Centrally located for all attractions.
Open: All Year
Grades: ETC 4 Diamond
015934 44618 Mrs Ramsay
sbenson@talk21.com
D: £19.50–£24 **S:** £19.50–£24
Beds: 1F 1D **Baths:** 2 En
🐾 🅿 ⅙ 📺 🛏 🎵 🚭

Corner Cottage Guest House, Old
Hall Road, Troutbeck Bridge, Windermere,
Cumbria, LA23 1HF.
Secluded gardens, all rooms ensuite,
family atmosphere, generous breakfasts.
Open: All Year
Grades: AA 4 Diamond
015394 48226 (also fax)
D: £20–£25 **S:** £22–£27
Beds: 2F 2D **Baths:** 4 En
🐾 🅿 (9) 📺 ✕ 🛏 ✿ 🚿 ⅙ cc

Troutbeck (Penrith)

NY3826 🍴 *Mortal Man, Queen's Head The
Sportsmans Inn, Troutbeck Inn, White Horse Inn,
Herdwick Inn*

Greenah Crag Farm, Troutbeck,
Penrith, Cumbria, CA11 0SQ.
Open: Feb to Nov
017684 83233 D: £16.50–£23 **S:** £20–£25
Beds: 2D 1T **Baths:** 2 En 1 Sh
🐾 🅿 ⅙ 📺 🛏 🎵 🚭
Warm welcome in old farmhouse, oak-
beamed dining room, guest sitting room
with wood burner and TV, quiet, secluded
yet accessible location - Keswick 10m,
Penrith/Motorway 8m, Ullswater 6m, ideal
centre for Lakes, Eden Valley, Hadrian's
Wall, Carlisle and Borders.

Troutbeck (Windermere)

NY4002 🍴 *Mortal Man, Queen's Head The
Sportsmans Inn*

Yew Grove, Troutbeck, Windermere,
Cumbria, LA23 1PG.
Comfortable C18th stone house, beautiful
village, valley and mountain views.
Open: All Year (not Xmas)
015394 33304 Mr Pratt
D: £20–£24 **S:** £22–£23
Beds: 1F 1D 1T 1S **Baths:** 1 En 1 Pr 1 Sh
🐾 🅿 (3) ⅙ 📺 🛏 🎵 🚭

Ulpha

SD1993 🍴 *Newfield Inn*

Oak Bank, Ulpha, Duddon Valley,
Broughton in Furness, Cumbria, LA20 6DZ.
Victorian house in peaceful valley, relax
indoors or ramble.
Open: All Year (not Xmas)
Grades: ETC 2 Diamond
01229 716393 Mrs Batten
D: £20 **S:** £22
Beds: 2D 1T **Baths:** 3 Sh
🐾 🅿 (8) 📺 🎵 🚭

Ulverston

SD2878 🍴 *Rose & Crown, Pier Castle, Farmers
Arms*

Sefton House , Queen Street,
Ulverston, Cumbria, LA12 7AF.
Georgian town house in the busy market
town of Ulverston.
Open: All Year (not Xmas)
01229 582190 Mrs Glaister
Fax: 01229 581773
romo@seftonhouse.co.uk
D: £20–£22.50 **S:** £27.50–£30
Beds: 1F 1D 1S 1T **Baths:** 4 En
🐾 🅿 (15) 📺 🛏 🎵 cc

Rock House, 1 Alexander Road,
Ulverston, Cumbria, LA12 0DE.
Large family rooms. Convenient to
Railway/ Bus station/ Town centre.
Open: March to October
Grades: ETC 4 Diamond
01229 586879 Mr Ramsay
D: £20 **S:** £20
Beds: 3F 1S **Baths:** 1 Sh
🐾 ⅙ 📺 ✕ 🛏 🎵 🚭

Under Loughrigg

NY3404 🍴 *White Lion*

Foxghyll, Lake Road, Under Loughrigg,
Ambleside, Cumbria, LA22 9LL.
Large country house. 2 acre garden, 4
poster bed, spa bath, parking.
Open: All Year
Grades: ETC 4 Diamond
015394 33292 Mrs Mann
foxghyll@hotmail.com
D: £23.50–£27 **S:** £23.50–£27
Beds: 1D 2T **Baths:** 3 En
🐾 (5) 🅿 (7) 📺 🛏 🎵 🚭

Underbarrow

SD4692 🍴 *Punch Bowl*

Tranthwaite Hall, Underbarrow,
Kendal, Cumbria, LA8 8HG.
Tranthwaite Hall is something special
dating back to C11th. Excellent
accommodation.
Open: All Year
Grades: ETC 4 Diamond
015395 68285 Mrs Swindlehurst
tranthwaitehall@hotmail.com
D: £22–£25 **S:** £25–£30
Beds: 1F 1D **Baths:** 2 En
🐾 🅿 (4) ⅙ 📺 🛏 🎵 🚭

Underskiddaw

NY2328 🍴 *Sun Inn*

Long Close Farm, Underskiddaw,
Keswick, Cumbria, CA12 4QD.
Period farmhouse enjoying exceptional
views over mountains and Bassenthwaite
Lake.
Open: All Year
017687 72851 (also fax)
Mrs Evers & Mr Barnes
D: £17–£25 **S:** £20–£25
Beds: 1F 1D **Baths:** 1 En 1 Sh
🐾 🅿 📺 🛏 🎵 🚭

Walton

NY5264 🍴 *Stag, Centurion, Lane End Inn*

High Rigg Farm, Walton, Brampton,
Cumbria, CA8 2AZ.
Open: All Year (not Xmas)
Grades: ETC 3 Diamond
016977 2117 Mrs Mounsey
D: £16–£18 **S:** fr £18
Beds: 2F **Baths:** 1 Pr 1 Sh
🐾 🅿 (4) ⅙ 📺 🛏 🎵 🚭
A warm welcome to our Listed beautiful
Georgian farmhouse with breath taking
views of the Pennines & Lake District
hills. Comfortable spacious
accommodation, excellent food, much
home produced. A working dairy sheep
farm. Good parking. Central for visits to
Roman Wall/Lakes.

Low Rigg Farm, Walton, Brampton,
Cumbria, CA8 2DX.
Comfortable accommodation on a
working farm in beautiful Hadrian's Wall
country. Excellent home cooking.
Open: All Year (not Xmas)
016977 3233 Mrs Thompson
lowridge@lineone.net
D: £15–£18 **S:** £18–£20
Beds: 1F **Baths:** 1 Sh
🐾 🅿 (6) 📺 🛏 ✕ 🎵 🚭

Warwick Bridge

NY4756 🍴 *Lane End Inn*

Brookside B&B, Warwick Bridge,
Carlisle, Cumbria, CA4 8RE.
Delightful sandstone Listed building.
Original miller's house, homely
atmosphere, comfortable beds.
Open: All Year (not Xmas)
Grades: ETC 4 Diamond
01228 560250 D Wearing
brookside@contactme.co.uk
D: £17–£20 **S:** £20–£24
Beds: 2D 1T **Baths:** 1 En 1 Sh
🐾 🅿 (3) 📺 🛏 🎵 🚭

Troutbeck Cottage, Warwick Bridge,
Carlisle, Cumbria, CA4 8RN.
Detached house in rural setting next to
Troutbeck Stream.
Open: All Year
01228 561929
Mrs Fraser
D: £16–£20 **S:** £16–£25
Baths: 2 En 1 Sh
🐾 🅿 (5) ⅙ 📺 🛏 🎵 🚭

Watendlath

NY2716

Fold Head Farm, Watendlath, Keswick,
Cumbria, CA12 5UN.
Comfortable friendly accommodation on
working farm in beautiful unspoiled
Valley.
Open: March to November
017687 77255 Mrs Richardson
D: £17–£18 **S:** £17–£18
Beds: 1F 2D **Baths:** 1 Sh
🐾 🅿 📺 🛏 ✕ 🎵 🚭

Watermillock

NY4422   🍺 *Herdwick Inn, Brackenrigg Inn, Horse and Farrier*

Land End Country Lodge,
Watermillock, Ullswater, Penrith, Cumbria, CA11 0NB.
Converted farmhouse. Idyllic location. 7 acre grounds with lakes, gardens, wildlife.
Open: All Year
Grades: ETC 3 Diamond
017684 86438 Miss Holmes
Fax: 017684 86959
D: £28–£31 **S:** £30–£32
Beds: 4D 2T 3S **Baths:** 9 En
🐕 🅿 (15) 📺 🎞 💷 ♨ 🏊 ♿

Mellfell House Farm, *Watermillock, Penrith, Cumbria, CA11 0LS.*
Beautiful old farmhouse high above Ullswater, log fires, relaxed atmosphere.
Open: All Year (not Xmas)
017684 86295 (also fax)
Mrs Goddard
D: £13.50–£17.50 **S:** £13.50–£20
Beds: 1F 1D 1T **Baths:** 2 Sh
🐕 🅿 (6) 💷 📺 🎞 💷

Waterside House, *Watermillock on Ullswater, Penrith, Cumbria, CA11 0JH.*
Beautiful old house set on Lake Ullswater's glorious shores.
Open: All Year
017684 86038 Mrs Jenner
suzij@waterside.demon.co.uk
D: fr £33 **S:** fr £33
Beds: 1F 4D 1T 1S **Baths:** 4 Pr 2 Sh
🐕 🅿 (10) 💷 📺 🎞 💷 ♿

Rampsbeck Lodge on Ullswater,
Watermillock on Ullswater, Penrith, Cumbria, CA11 0LP.
Unique lake side property set in 2 acres of garden, private jetty.
Open: All Year
017684 86647 Mrs Windle
D: £22.50–£30 **S:** £45–£55
Beds: 2D 1T 1S 1F **Baths:** 1 En 1 Sh
🐕 🅿 (6) 📺 🎞 💷 ♨ 🏊 ♿

Westlinton

NY3964

Lynebank, *Westlinton, Carlisle, Cumbria, CA6 6AA.*
Family-run, excellent food, ideal stop for England/Scotland journey.
Open: All Year
Grades: ETC 4 Diamond
01228 792820 (also fax)
Mrs Butler
info@lynebank.co.uk
D: £18–£22 **S:** £20–£24
Beds: 2F 3D 1T 3S **Baths:** 9 En
🐕 🅿 (15) 📺 🎞 💷 🏊 cc

BEDROOMS
F - Family
D - Double
T - Twin
S - Single

Whelpo

NY3039

Swaledale Watch, *Whelpo, Caldbeck, Wigton, Cumbria, CA7 8HQ.*
Enjoy great comfort, excellent home cooking, warm friendly farmhouse welcome. **Open:** All Year (not Xmas)
016974 78409 (also fax)
Mrs Savage
nan.savage@talk21.com
D: £17.50–£20.50 **S:** £18.50–£25
Beds: 2F 2D 1T **Baths:** 4 En 1 Pr
🐕 🅿 (10) 💷 📺 🎞 💷

Wheyrigg

NY1948

Wheyrigg Hall, *Wheyrigg, Wigton, Cumbria, CA7 0DH.*
Former farm situated on the Solway plain, with views to Scotland & Skiddaw.
Open: All Year
016973 61242 Fax: 016973 61020
D: £20–£25 **S:** £30–£36
Beds: 1F 3D 8T
🐕 🅿 📺 🎞 💷 cc

Windermere

SD4198   🍺 *Brown Horse, The Lamplighter, Grey Walls Inn, Elleray Hotel, Queen's, Village Inn, Chase, Waverley*

Kenilworth Guest House, *Holly Road, Windermere, Cumbria, LA23 2AF.*
Open: All Year
015394 44004 Mr Roberts
Fax: 015394 46554
D: fr £16 **S:** fr £16
Beds: 1F 2T 2D 1S **Baths:** 3 En 3 Sh
🐕 🅿 (3) 💷 📺 🎞 💷 ♨
Comfortable Victorian house, two minutes centre Windermere. Convenient centre for exploring all Lakeland's beautiful scenery. Memorable breakfast. Helpful friendly hosts. Free transport to/from station.

Braemount House, *Sunny Bank Road, Windermere, Cumbria, LA23 2EN.*
Open: All Year (not Xmas)
Grades: ETC 4 Diamond
015394 45967 (also fax)
braemount.house@virgin.net
D: £23–£27 **S:** £23–£27
Beds: 3F 2D 1T **Baths:** 6 En
🐕 🅿 (6) 💷 📺 🎞 💷 cc
Our guest book reads 'immaculate accommodation and lots of extras not normally available', 'excellent, especially breakfast in bed', 'great once again', 'wonderful', 'lovely room, brilliant hospitality, yummy breakfast', 'we will be back' and many more. Why not come and read it?

BATHROOMS
Pr - Private
Sh - Shared
En - Ensuite

Heatherbank, *13 Birch Street, Windermere, Cumbria, LA23 1EG.*
Open: All Year (not Xmas)
Grades: ETC 3 Diamond
015394 46503 (also fax)
Mrs Houghton
heatherbank@btinternet.com
D: £19–£27 **S:** £20–£30
Beds: 3D 2T **Baths:** 5 En
🅿 (4) 💷 📺 🎞 💷 cc
Heatherbank is a quiet, comfortable, non-smoking, Lakeland stone guest house. Situated in the centre of Windermere village, it is within 5 mins walk of the rail/bus station. Heatherbank is noted for its superb English breakfast.

Villa Lodge, *Cross Street, Windermere, Cumbria, LA23 1AE.*
Open: All Year
Grades: ETC 4 Diamond, AA 4 Diamond
015394 43318 (also fax)
Mr Rooney
rooneym@btconnect.com
D: £22–£35 **S:** £22–£30
Beds: 5D 1T 2S **Baths:** 8 En
🐕 🅿 (8) 💷 📺 🎞 🎞 💷 ♨ 🏊 cc
Warm welcome, extremely comfortable and traditional accommodation in peaceful area overlooking Windermere village, yet two minutes from bus/ rail stations. All bedrooms are ensuite. English breakfast a speciality in delightful dining room. An excellent base for exploring the Lake District.

Meadfoot, *New Road, Windermere, Cumbria, LA23 2LA.*
Detached house, large garden, patio and summerhouse. Warm welcome assured.
Open: Feb to Nov
Grades: ETC 4 Diamond
015394 42610 T Shaw
Fax: 015394 45280
enquiries@meadfoot-guesthouse.co.uk
D: £20–£27 **S:** £22.50–£27
Beds: 1F 3D 2T 1S **Baths:** 7 En
🐕 🅿 (7) 💷 📺 🎞 💷 ♿

Firgarth, *Ambleside Road, Windermere, Cumbria, LA23 1EU.*
Comfortable Victorian country house, fine views, opposite riding stables.
Open: All Year
Grades: ETC 3 Diamond, AA 3 Diamond
015394 46974 Mr & Mrs Lucking
Fax: 015394 42384
D: £17.50–£21 **S:** £17.50–£24
Beds: 1F 3D 1T 1S **Baths:** 8 Pr
🐕 🅿 (9) 🎞 🎞 💷 cc

Holly Lodge Guest House, *6 College Road, Windermere, Cumbria, LA23 1BX.*
Family-run centrally situated traditional Lakeland guest house. Good English breakfasts.
Open: All Year (not Xmas)
Grades: ETC 3 Diamond, AA 3 Diamond
015394 43873 (also fax)
Mr Priestley
D: £18–£27 **S:** £18–£27
Beds: 2F 5D 3T 1S **Baths:** 6 En 2 Sh
🐕 🅿 (7) 📺 🎞 💷

Westbury House, 27 Broad Street, Windermere, Cumbria, *LA23 2AB.*
Victorian house, centre of Windermere. Near lake, shops, trains. Lovely food.
Open: All Year
Grades: ETC 3 Diamond
015394 46839 Mrs Baker
Fax: 015394 42784
westhouse@commundo.net
D: £14–£23 **S:** £16–£30
Beds: 2F 3D 1T **Baths:** 4 En 1 Sh
⛄ (2) 🅿 (5) 📺 🍴 📖 🆅 🍷 cc

Ivy Bank, Holly Road, Windermere, Cumbria, *LA23 2AF.*
Pretty Victorian stone built home offering comfortable and attractive accommodation.
Open: All Year (not Xmas/New Year)
Grades: ETC 4 Diamond
015394 42601 Mr Clothier
ivybank@clara.co.uk
D: £18–£25
Beds: 1F 1T 3D **Baths:** 5 En
⛄ 🅿 (6) 📺 🍴 📖 🆅 🍷 cc

The Buzzards, off Thornbarrow Road, Windermere, Cumbria, *LA23 2DF.*
Bungalow with mountain views. Ideal centre for cycling, walking, sailing.
Open: All Year (not Xmas)
015394 42271 M Whelan
davidwhelan@ukgateway.net
D: £14.50–£19.50 **S:** £14.50–£19.50
Beds: 1D 1S **Baths:** 1 Sh
🅿 (6) 📺 📖 🆅 🍷

Autumn Leaves Guest House, 29 Broad Street, Windermere, Cumbria, *LA23 2AB.*
Victorian house, five minutes from station, one minute from centre.
Open: All Year
Grades: ETC 3 Diamond
015394 48410 **D:** £14–£24 **S:** £14–£20
Beds: 1F 1T 3D 1S **Baths:** 3 En 1 Sh
⛄ 📺 🍴 ✕ 📖 🆅 🍷 cc

Aspen Cottage, 6 Havelock Road, Windermere, Cumbria, *LA23 1EH.*
Stone built cottage. Ten minute walk to lake Windermere.
Open: All Year
015394 43946 Mrs Walsh
D: £15–£17 **S:** £16–£18
Beds: 1F 2D **Baths:** 2 Sh
⛄ 🅿 (2) 📺 🍴 📖 🆅

Westbourne, Biskey Howe Road, Windermere, Cumbria, *LA23 2JR.*
Situated below picturesque Biskley Howe view point. 2 minutes off the Dales Way.
Open: All Year (not Xmas)
Grades: ETC 4 Diamond
015394 43625 (also fax)
Mr Wright
westbourne@btinternet.com
D: £20–£50 **S:** £28–£38
Beds: 2F 7D 2T 1S **Baths:** 9 En
⛄ 🅿 (11) 📺 🍴 ✕ 📖 🆅 🍷 cc

Planning a longer stay? Always ask for any special rates

Chestnuts Cottage, Princes Road, Windermere, Cumbria, *LA23 2DD.*
Chestnuts offers hotel accommodation at guest house prices.
Open: All Year
Grades: ETC 4 Diamond
015394 46999 Mr Reed
chestnuts@chestnuts92.freeserve.co.uk
D: £22.50–£45
Beds: 6D **Baths:** 4 Pr 1 Sh
⛄ 🅿 (6) 📺 🍴 📖 🆅 cc

Broadlands Guest House, 19 Broad Street, Windermere, Cumbria, *LA23 2AB.*
Small family run guest house near village centre. ideal touring base.
Open: All Year (not Xmas)
Grades: AA 3 Diamond
015394 46532 Mrs Pearson
Fax: 015394 48474
broadlands@clara.co.uk
D: £19–£25
Beds: 1F 1T 2D **Baths:** 4 En
⛄ 📺 🍴 📖 🆅 cc

Lingmoor, 7 High Street, Windermere, Cumbria, *LA23 1AF.*
Excellent value. Small family-run guest house, very close to all local amenities.
Open: All Year
015394 44947 Mr Hill
D: £12–£20 **S:** £12–£20
Beds: 1F 4D 2T 1S **Baths:** 2 En 2 Sh
⛄ 📺 📖 🆅 🍷

Cambridge House, 9 Oak Street, Windermere, Cumbria, *LA23 1EN.*
A traditional Lakeland stone guest house situated in Windermere village centre.
Open: All Year (not Xmas)
015394 43846 Mr Fear
mbdfear@aol.com
D: £16–£20
Beds: 1F 5D **Baths:** 6 En
⛄ (5) 📺 📖 🆅 cc

Eastbourne Hotel, Biskey Howe Road, Windermere, Cumbria, *LA23 2JR.*
Located below Biskey Howe Viewpoint and close to Lake and all amenities.
Open: Feb to Dec
015394 43525 Mr Whitfield
Fax: 015394 43338
eastbourne@lakes-pages.co.uk
D: £19–£30 **S:** £27–£35
Beds: 1F 5D 1T 1S **Baths:** 7 En 1 Pr
⛄ (5) 🅿 (6) 📺 📖 🆅 cc

Kays Cottage, 7 Broad Street, Windermere, Cumbria, *LA23 2AB.*
Small guest house, comfortable ensuite rooms, conveniently situated, generous breakfast. **Open:** Feb to Nov
015394 44146 Ms Richardson
terriss@globalnet.co.uk
D: £15–£22 **S:** £22–£30
Beds: 1F 3D **Baths:** 4 En
⛄ (4) 📺 📖 🆅 cc

Upper Oakmere Guest House, 3 Upper Oak Street, Windermere, Cumbria, *LA23 2LB.*
Ideal location. Friendly atmosphere, home cooking, 100 yards Main Street.
Open: All Year
015394 45649 **D:** £12–£18 **S:** £12–£18
Beds: 1F 3D 2T **Baths:** 2 En 1 Sh
⛄ 🅿 (2) 📺 🍴 ✕ 📖 🆅 🍷

Many rates vary according to season – the lowest are shown here

Glencree Private Hotel, Lake Road, Windermere, Cumbria, *LA23 2EQ.*
A very warm welcome awaits you at this recently refurbished traditional Lakeland house.
Open: All Year
015394 45822 Mrs Butterworth
h.butterworth@btinternet.com
D: £20–£30 **S:** £25–£40
Beds: 1F 5D **Baths:** 6 En
⛄ (5) 🅿 (5) 📺 🍴 ✕ 📖 🆅 🍷 🍴 cc

Clifton House, 28 Ellerthwaite Road, Windermere, Cumbria, *LA23 2AH.*
Friendly guest house. All ensuite with TV. Non-smoking.
Open: All Year
015394 44968 **D:** £15–£25 **S:** £15–£30
Beds: 1F 2D 1T 1S **Baths:** 5 En
⛄ (6) 📺 🆅 🍷

Winton

NY7811 🍺 *Bay Horse Inn*

South View Farm, Winton, Kirkby Stephen, Cumbria, *CA17 4HS.*
Lovely farmhouse situated in quiet village, easy access to the Lakes and Dales. **Open:** All Year
017683 71120 Mrs Marston
D: £15 **S:** £15
Beds: 1F 1D 1S
⛄ 🅿 (2) 📺 🍴 ✕ 🆅 🍷

Workington

NX9927 🍺 *Ye Old Sportsman*

Fernleigh House, 15 High Seaton, Workington, Cumbria, *CA14 1PE.*
Georgian house, lovely Garden, warm and friendly welcome, Excellent Breakfasts.
Open: All Year
01900 605811 Ms Bewsher
D: £17–£45 **S:** £17
Beds: 1F 2T 1S
⛄ 🅿 📺 📖 🆅 🍷 🍴

Silverdale, 17 Banklands, Workington, Cumbria, *CA14 3EL.*
Large Victorian private house. Near start C2C cycleway and lakes.
Open: All Year (not Xmas)
01900 61887 Mrs Hardy
D: £11–£13.50 **S:** £12.50–£15
Beds: 2T 2S **Baths:** 2 Sh
⛄ 📺 🍴 📖 🆅 🍷

Yanwath

NY5128 🍺 *Yanwath Gate Inn*

Yanwath Gate Farm, Yanwath, Penrith, Cumbria, *CA10 2LF.*
Comfortable C17th farmhouse, good food, near a pub.
Open: All Year
01768 864459 Mr & Mrs Donnelly
D: £17–£20 **S:** £17–£20
Beds: 1F 1D **Baths:** 2 En
⛄ 🅿 (9) 📺 📖 🆅

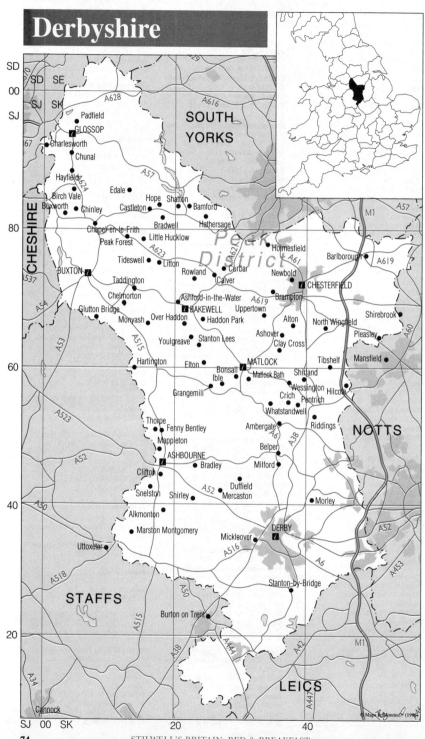

Derbyshire

Tourist Information Centres

13 Market Place, **Ashbourne**, Derbyshire, DE6 1EU, 01335 343666.

Old Market Hall, Bridge Street, **Bakewell**, Derbyshire, DE4 1DS, 01629 813227.

The Crescent, **Buxton**, Derbyshire, SK17 6BQ, 01298 25106.

Peacock Information Centre, Low Pavement, **Chesterfield**, Derbyshire, S40 1PB, 01246 345777.

Assembly Rooms, Market Place, **Derby**, DE1 3AH, 01332 255802.

The Gatehouse, Victoria Street, **Glossop**, Derbyshire, SK13 8HT, 01457 855920.

The Pavilion, **Matlock Bath**, Matlock, Derbyshire, DE4 3NR, 01629 55082.

Town Hall, Market Place, **Ripley**, Derbyshire, DE4 3BT, 01773 841488.

Alkmonton

SK1838

Dairy House Farm, Alkmonton, Longford, Ashbourne, Derbyshire, DE6 3DG.
Open: All Year
Grades: AA 4 Diamond, RAC 4 Diamond, Warm Welcome
01335 330359 (also fax)
Mrs Harris
andy@dairyhousefarm.force9.co.uk
D: £25 **S:** £23–£45
Beds: 1T 4S **Baths:** 4 En 1 Pr
⭐ (16) 🅿 (8) ⅃ �📺 ✕ ▦ 🆅 ♨
Old farmhouse; warm welcome, comfortable rooms, guests' own lounges and dining room. Lovely walled garden, good food, farmhouse fare, residential licence, peaceful location and 18 acre stock grazing farm close to many old houses: Chatsworth, Calke Abbey and Alton Towers.

Alsop en le Dale

SK1655

Dove Top Farm, Coldeaton, Alsop en le Dale, Ashbourne, Derbyshire, DE6 1QR.
Open: Easter to Sept
01335 310472
Mrs Wainwright
D: £18 **S:** £20
Beds: 1F 1D
Baths: 2 En
⭐ 🅿 📺 ✕ ▦ 🆅 ♨
Friendly welcome to our peaceful working farm. Good breakfasts. Spacious rooms overlooking large gardens. Beautiful Derbyshire countryside with views over River Dove and surrounding Dales within the grounds. Ideal for walking, cycling and trekking.

Alton

SK3664 🍺 *Blacksmiths Arms, Royal Oak, Talbot Inn*

Fernlea Guest House, Cedar Hill, Alton, Stoke-on-Trent, Staffs, ST10 4BH.
Stone country guest house 5 mins Alton Towers. Families most welcome.
Open: Mar to Nov **Grades:** ETC 3 Diamond
01538 702327 (also fax) Mrs Nother
D: £16.50–£20 **S:** £25–£30
Beds: 2F 1D **Baths:** 3 En
⭐ 🅿 (3) 📺 🍴 ▦ 🆅 ♨

Yoxal Cottage, Malt House Road, Alton, Stoke-on-Trent, Staffs, ST10 4AG.
Pretty old red brick cottage, cosy rooms and hearty breakfast. **Open:** Easter to Nov
Grades: ETC 3 Diamond
01538 702537 Mrs Rowlinson
D: £17.50 **S:** £20
Beds: 1F **Baths:** 1 En
⭐ ⅃ 📺 ▦ 🆅 ♨

Ambergate

SK3451 🍺 *Lord Nelson Bullbridge*

Lawn Farm, Whitewells Lane, Holly Lane, Ambergate, Belper, Derbyshire, DE56 2DN.
Comfortable farmhouse accommodation on working farm; quiet rural location.
Open: Easter to Oct
01773 852352 Mrs Oulton
carol.oulton@farming.co.uk
D: £17.50–£22.50 **S:** £20–£30
Beds: 1F 1D **Baths:** 1 En 1 Sh
⭐ 🅿 (4) ⅃ 📺 ♨

Ashbourne

SK1846 🍺 *Beresford Arms, Coach & Horses, Royal Oak, Smith's Tavern, White Hart, Ye Olde Vaults*

Dove House, Bridge Hill, Mayfield, Ashbourne, Derbyshire, DE6 2HN.
Large detached Victorian house close to Peak District and Alton Towers.
Open: All Year (not Xmas/New Year)
Grades: ETC 4 Diamond
01335 343329 Mrs Green
D: fr £20 **S:** fr £28
Beds: 1D **Baths:** 1 En
🅿 (1) 📺 ✕ ▦ 🆅 ♨

Hurtswood, Sandybrook, Ashbourne, Derbyshire, DE6 2AQ.
Comfortable rooms, excellent breakfasts, superb views, extensive off-road parking.
Open: All Year (not Xmas) **Grades:** ETC 3 Diamond **01335 342031**
Mrs Hadley & Mrs S Loveridge
Fax: 01335 347467 gl.hurtswood@virgin.net
D: fr £20 **S:** £23–£25
Beds: 1F 3D 1T 2S **Baths:** All En
⭐ 🅿 ⅃ 📺 ▦ 🆅 ♨

Compton House, 27-31 Compton, Ashbourne, Derbyshire, DE6 1BX.
Originally three terraced cottages, lovely garden, warm welcome, safe parking.
Open: All Year
Grades: ETC 3 Diamond, AA 3 Diamond
01335 343100 Mrs Maher
Fax: 01335 348100
D: £19–£23 **S:** £20–£25
Beds: 1F 3D 1T **Baths:** 4 En
⭐ 🅿 (6) 📺 🍴 ✕ 🆅 ♨

Beresford Arms Hotel, Station Road, Ashbourne, Derbyshire, DE6 1AA.
12 bedroom family hotel situated close to Alton Towers.
Open: All Year
Grades: AA 2 Star
01335 300035 Miss Cadman
D: £25–£30 **S:** £30–£40
Beds: 5F 5D 2T **Baths:** 12 En
⭐ 🅿 (20) 📺 🍴 ✕ ▦ 🆅 ♨ ♨ cc

Ashford-in-the-Water

SK1969 🍺 *Bulls Head*

Gritstone House, Greaves Lane, Ashford-in-the-Water, Bakewell, Derbyshire, DE45 1QH.
Open: All Year (not Xmas)
Grades: ETC 4 Diamond, Silver Award
01629 813563 (also fax)
Mrs Lindsay
D: £20–£25 **S:** fr £30
Beds: 2D 1T **Baths:** 1 En 1 Sh
⅃ 📺 ▦ 🆅 ♨
Very comfortable Georgian house located in beautiful conservation village in Peak District National Park near to Bakewell, Chatsworth and Haddon and choice dining out and other facilities useful touring centre for Derbyshire and Staffordshire Moorlands.

Rowdale, Ashford-in-the-Water, Bakewell, Derbyshire, DE45 1NX.
C17th Listed farmhouse, friendly, comfortable, relaxed, large gardens, generous breakfasts.
Open: All Year (not New Year)
Grades: RAC 3 Diamond, Silver Award, Welcome Host
01629 640260 Mrs Mills
info@rowdale.co.uk
D: £20–£25 **S:** £25–£27.50
Beds: 3F 1T 2D **Baths:** 2 En 1 Pr 1 Sh
⭐ 🅿 (20) 📺 🍴 ▦ 🆅 ♨

Chy-An-Dour, Vicarage Lane, Ashford-in-the-Water, Bakewell, Derbyshire, DE45 1QL.
Quality accommodation. Quiet position overlooking picturesque village. Friendly welcome.
Open: All Year (not Xmas)
Grades: ETC 4 Diamond
01629 813162 Mrs Rowland
D: £23–£27 **S:** £30–£35
Beds: 2D 1T **Baths:** 3 En
⭐ (6) 🅿 (4) ⅃ 📺 🍴 ▦ ♿ cc

Woodland View, John Bank Lane, Ashford-in-the-Water, Bakewell, Derbyshire, DE45 1PY.
Renovated farmhouse set in 4 acres. 10 minutes walk to village.
Open: All Year (not Xmas)
Grades: ETC 3 Diamond
01629 813008 (also fax)
Neil Ellis
woodview@neilellis.free-online.co.uk
D: £18–£22
Beds: 2D **Baths:** 1 En 1 Pr
🅿 (4) 📺 🍴 ▦ ♨

Planning a longer stay? Always ask for any special rates

Ashover

SK3463   ◀ *Black Swan, Red Lion*

Old School Farm, *Uppertown,
Ashover, Chesterfield, Derbyshire, S45 0JF.*
Spacious, comfortable, working farm,
home from home, peaceful and friendly.
Open: Easter to Oct
Grades: ETC 4 Diamond RAC 4 Diamond
01246 590813 Mrs Wooton
D: fr £22 **S:** fr £22
Beds: 2F 1D 1T 1S **Baths:** 3 En 1 Pr 1 Sh
⌂ ▣ (6) �📺 ▥ ♨

Bakewell

SK2168   ◀ *Castle Inn, Peacock Hotel, The
Wheatsheaf, Red Lion, The Manners, Devonshire
Arms, Aitch's, Bridge*

Bene-Dorme, *The Avenue, Bakewell,
Derbyshire, DE45 1EQ.*
A friendly welcome in our traditional built
house in quiet cul-de-sac.
Open: All Year (not Xmas)
Grades: AA 4 Diamond
01629 813292 Mrs Twigg
Fax: 01629 814208
judithtwigg@callnetuk.com
D: £21–£23 **S:** fr £33
Beds: 2D 1T **Baths:** 3 En
▣ (4) ⌀ 📺 ▥ ▥ ♨

Croft Cottages, *Coombs Road,
Bakewell, Derbyshire, DE45 1AQ.*
Open: All Year
Grades: AA 4 Diamond
01629 814101 Mr & Mrs Weatherley
Fax: 01629 815083
croftco@btinternet.com
D: £23–£30 **S:** £25–£35
Beds: 1F 2D 1T **Baths:** 3 En 1 Pr
⌂ 📺 ♔ ▥ ▥ ♨
Your dream accommodation - lovely
C17th cottage within old fashioned
walled garden; peaceful riverside
location, town centre two minute stroll.
Celebrate special occasions or simply
unwind. Splendid choice of breakfast;
charming rooms, plus luxurious suite in
delightfully converted barn - personal
hospitality assured.

Wye Close, *5 Granby Croft , Bakewell,
Derbyshire, DE45 1ET.*
Edwardian house in quiet location in the
centre of Bakewell.
Open: All Year (not Xmas/New Year)
Grades: ETC 3 Diamond
01629 813702 (also fax)
Ms Wilson
h.wilson@talk21.com
D: £18–£19 **S:** £20
Beds: 1T 1D **Baths:** 1 Sh
▣ (34) ⌀ 📺 ▥ ▥ ♨

Haddon Park Farm, *Bakewell,
Derbyshire, DE45 1ND.*
Farmhouse two miles Bakewell, close to
Chatsworth and Haddon Hall.
Open: May to Oct
01629 814854 Mrs Cooper
D: £20–£25 **S:** £25
Beds: 1D 1T **Baths:** 1 Pr 1 Sh
▣ (2) ⌀ 📺 ♨

Easthorpe, *Buxton Road, Bakewell,
Derbyshire, DE45 1DA .*
A gothic style family home ideal for
walkers near Chatsworth.
Open: All Year (not Xmas)
Grades: ETC 4 Diamond
01629 814929 M Peters
D: £20–£24 **S:** £28–£32
Beds: 1F 1T 1D **Baths:** 3 En
⌂ ▣ (2) ⌀ 📺 ♔ ▥ ▥ ♨

Loughrigg, *Burton Close Drive,
Bakewell, Derbyshire, DE45 1BG.*
Extensive landscaped gardens, magnificent
views, splendid walking, peaceful.
Breakfast menu. **Open:** All Year (not Xmas)
Grades: ETC 4 Diamond Silver Award
01629 813173 Mrs Morris
john@bakewell55.freeserve.co.uk
D: £20–£25 **S:** £25–£30
Beds: 2D **Baths:** 1 En 1 Pr
⌂ (10) ▣ (2) ⌀ 📺 ♔ ▥ ▥ ♨ ♿ ♨

1 Coach House Mews, *Bagshaw Hill,
Bakewell, Derbyshire, DE45 1DL.*
Quiet courtyard location - near town
centre. lovely views. Excellent breakfasts.
Open: All Year (not Xmas/New Year)
01629 814847 (also fax) Mrs Northin
nonthin@crosswinds.net
D: £23–£25 **S:** £30–£35
Beds: 1T **Baths:** 1 Pr
▣ (1) ⌀ 📺 ▥ ▥ ♨

Holly House, *The Avenue, Bakewell,
Derbyshire, DE45 1EQ.*
Victorian house in quiet cul-de-sac.
Chatsworth House, Haddon Hall, town,
restaurants, pubs nearby.
Open: All Year (not Xmas/New Year)
Grades: AA 3 Diamond
01629 813207 Mrs Wright
D: £22–£25 **S:** £30
Beds: 2D 1T **Baths:** 2 En 1 Pr
⌂ (10) ▣ (3) ⌀ 📺 ♔ ▥ ▥ ♨

Haddon House Farm, *Haddon Hall
Estate, Bakewell, Derbyshire, DE45 1BN.*
Sink into our gorgeous beds - 'a slice of
Heaven', with far-reaching views.
Open: All Year
01629 814024 Mrs Nichols
Fax: 01629 812759
info@haddon-house.co.uk
D: £30–£37.50 **S:** £35–£40
Beds: 1D 1T **Baths:** 2 En
⌂ (5) ▣ (2) ⌀ 📺 ▥ ▥ ♨ ♿

Bamford

SK2083   ◀ *Anglers' Rest*

Pioneer House, *Station Road,
Bamford, Hope Valley, Derbyshire, S33 0BN.*
Open: All Year **Grades:** ETC 4 Diamond
01433 650638 Mrs Treacher
Pioneerhouse@yahoo.co.uk
D: £20–£22
Beds: 2D 1T **Baths:** 3 En
▣ (3) ⌀ 📺 ▥ ▥ ♨
We offer a relaxing and friendly
atmosphere in our comfortable
Edwardian home. our beautifully
decorated, spacious bedrooms are
ensuite, with colour television and
beverage tray. Enjoy our hearty breakfast
before exploring the stunning Peak
District and the nearby Derbyshire Dales.

Barlborough

SK4777   ◀ *Rose & Crown Royal Oak*

Stone Croft, *15 Church Street,
Barlborough, Chesterfield, Derbyshire,
S43 4ER.*
A grade II house built in 1670. Full of
charm. **Open:** All Year
Grades: ETC 3 Diamond
01246 810974 Mrs Widdowson
D: £16–£18 **S:** £18–£20
Beds: 1F **Baths:** 1 En
⌂ ▣ (6) ⌀ 📺 ♔ ✗ ▥ ▥ ♨

Belper

SK3547   ◀ *Hanging Gate, The Bluebell, The
Railway, Cross Keys, Fishermans Rest, Bulls Head,
Talbot*

Chevin Green Farm, *Chevin Road,
Belper, Derbyshire, DE56 2UN.*
Open: All Year (not Xmas)
Grades: ETC 4 Diamond, AA 4 Diamond
01773 822328 Mr Postles
spostles@globalnet.co.uk
D: £20–£23 **S:** £23–£26
Beds: 1F 3D 2T **Baths:** 6 En
⌂ ▣ (10) ⌀ 📺 ▥ ▥ ♨ cc
Farmhouse set in 38 acres, in picturesque
hillside scenery (the Chevin) looking
across Derwent Valley. Ensuite rooms,
guests' own lounge and dining room,
generous breakfasts, peace and
tranquillity. Central for all Derbyshire and
its attractions.

The Cedars, *Field Lane, Belper,
Derbyshire, DE56 1DD.*
Luxury B&B in an 1828 Grade II Listed
Nailmaster's mansion.
Open: All Year **Grades:** ETC 4 Diamond
01773 824157 Mr & Mrs Wayne
Fax: 01773 825573
cedars@derbyshire-holidays.com
D: £20–£22 **S:** £25
Beds: 2F 1T **Baths:** 2 En 1 Pr 1 Sh
⌂ ▣ (6) ⌀ 📺 ▥ ♨

Birch Vale

SK0186   ◀ *Waltzing Weasel*

Spinney Cottage B&B, *Spinner
Bottom, Birch Vale, High Peak, SK22 1BL.*
Tastefully furnished country home,
excellent walking and biking area, 1 miles
Hayfield. **Open:** All Year (not Xmas)
Grades: ETC 4 Diamond
01663 743230 D: £20–£22 **S:** £20–£25
Beds: 1D 1T 1S **Baths:** 2 En 1 Pr
⌂ ⌀ 📺 ▥ ♨

Bonsall

SK2758   ◀ *Kings Head*

Town Head Farmhouse, *70 High
Street, Bonsall, Matlock, Derbyshire,
DE4 2AR.*
Converted friendly C18th farmhouse set
in peaceful pretty village.
Open: All Year
Grades: ETC 4 Diamond, Silver Award
01629 823762 Mrs Cordin
townhead70@hotmail.com
D: £20–£22 **S:** £24–£30
Beds: 3D 2T **Baths:** 5 En
⌂ ▣ (6) 📺 ▥ ♨

Sycamore House, *Bonsall, Matlock, Derbyshire, DE4 2AR.*
Attractive C18th stone house overlooking rolling hills. Village situation. Ideal base Derbyshire.
Open: All Year
01629 823903 (also fax)
Mr & Mrs Sanders
D: £23–£26 **S:** £35–£40
Beds: 1F 2D 2T 1S **Baths:** 4 En 2 Pr
🛏 🅿 (7) ⊁ 🖵 📺 ✕ 🃏 🆅 ✿ ♨

Bradley

SK2246 🍺 *Jinglers Inn, Fox & Hounds, Saracen's Head, Shoulder of Mutton*

Yeldersley Old Hall Farm, *Yeldersley Lane, Bradley, Ashbourne, Derbyshire, DE6 1PH.*
Relax and unwind in peaceful surroundings at our Grade II Listed farmhouse.
Open: Easter to Nov
Grades: ETC 4 Diamond
01335 344504 (also fax)
Mrs Hinds
janethindsfarm@yahoo.co.uk
D: £20–£25 **S:** £25–£26
Beds: 2D 1T **Baths:** 2 En 1 Pr
🅿 (7) ⊁ 🖵 📺 ♨

Jinglers Inn Fox & Hound, *Belper Road, Bradley, Ashbourne, Derbyshire, DE6 3EN.*
The pub with two names - The Jinglers on one side, Fox & Hounds on other.
Open: All Year
01335 370855 (also fax)
Mrs Catlin
jinglers@gdc.globalnet.co.uk
D: £20–£22.50 **S:** £22.50–£25
Beds: 1F 1D 3T 1S **Baths:** 2 En 2 Pr 2 Sh
🛏 🅿 (50) 📺 🃏 ✕ 🃏 🆅 ♨ ♿

Bradwell

SK1781 🍺 *Bowling Green, Valley Lodge, Bulls Head*

Stoney Ridge, *Granby Road, Bradwell, Hope Valley, S33 9HU.*
Open: All Year
Grades: ETC 4 Diamond, Silver Award, AA 4 Diamond
01433 620538 Mrs Plant
Fax: 01433 623154
stoneyridge@aol.com
D: £28 **S:** £31
Beds: 3D 1T **Baths:** 3 En 1 Pr
🛏 (10) 🅿 (4) 📺 🃏 🃏 🆅 ✿ ♨ cc
Our lovely home is set in the beautiful Peak District. Enjoy a swim in our heated indoor pool followed by breakfast on the balcony.

Ashbrook, *Brookside, Bradwell, Hope Valley, S33 9HF.*
Idyllic peaceful location lovely gardens with fish pond, stunning views.
Open: All Year (not Xmas)
Grades: ETC 3 Diamond
01433 620803 J Maskrey
D: £19–£25 **S:** £20–£25
Beds: 2D 1T **Baths:** 2 Sh
🅿 (2) 🖵 📺 🃏 🆅 ♨

Brampton

SK3670 🍺 *Brampton Manor*

Brampton Guest House, *75 Old Road, Brampton, Chesterfield, Derbyshire, S40 2QU.*
Victorian house on quiet cul-de-sac close to Chatsworth. **Open:** All Year
01246 276533 Mr Thompson
Fax: 01246 211636
guesthouse@oldroadbrampton.freeserve.co.uk
D: £14–£16 **S:** £14–£18.50
Beds: 2F 1D 1S **Baths:** 3 Pr 1 Sh
🛏 🅿 (4) 📺 ✕ 🃏 🆅 ♨

Buxton

SK0573 🍺 *King's Head, Railway Hotel, Devonshire Arms, Old Clubhouse, Duke Of York, The Burbage, Robin Hood, London Road Inn, Sun Inn, Old Hall Hotel, Cockeral Bar*

Grosvenor House Hotel, *1 Broad Walk, Buxton, Derbyshire, SK17 6JE.*
Open: All Year
Grades: ETC 4 Diamond, AA 4 Diamond
01298 72439 (also fax)
Mr & Mrs Fairbairn
D: £25–£37.50 **S:** £45–£50
Beds: 2F 5D 1T **Baths:** 8 En
🛏 (8) ⊁ 🖵 🃏 ♨
Idyllically set in the heart of historic spa town, overlooking Pavilion Gardens/Opera house. Bedrooms ensuite, non-smoking, hearty full English breakfast. Ideal centre for exploring Peak District and Derbyshire Dales. Within easy walking distance of numerous pubs and restaurants. Which? Recommended.

Compton House Guest House, *4 Compton Road, Buxton, Derbyshire, SK17 9DN.*
Warm & friendly atmosphere. Comfortable rooms, good food, excellent value.
Open: All Year
Grades: ETC 3 Diamond
01298 26926 (also fax)
Mr Hesp
D: £16–£20 **S:** £20–£30
Beds: 2F 2D 1T 1S **Baths:** 4 En 1 Sh
🛏 📺 ✕ 🃏 🆅 ♨

The Victorian Guest House, *3a Broad Walk, Buxton, Derbyshire, SK17 6JE.*
Unique quiet elegant home, refurbished 1999, overlooking Pavilion Gardens/Opera House.
Open: All Year
Grades: ETC 5 Diamond, Gold
01298 78759 Mrs Whiston
Fax: 01298 74732
buxvic@x-stream.co.uk
D: £25–£32.50 **S:** fr £35
Beds: 2F 5D 2T **Baths:** 9 En
🛏 🅿 (10) ⊁ 🖵 🃏 🆅 ♨

Templeton Guest House, *Compton Road, Buxton, Derbyshire, SK17 9DN.*
Family-run licensed guest house superbly situated for exploring Peak District.
Open: All Year
01298 25275 G Spicer
D: £18.50–£20 **S:** £21.50–£24
Beds: 2D 1T **Baths:** All En
🛏 🅿 (6) 📺 ✕ 🃏 🆅 ♨

The Old Manse Private Hotel, *6 Clifton Road, Silverlands, Buxton, Derbyshire, SK17 6QL.*
Quietly situated Victorian hotel. Delicious food. Warm welcome. Friendly atmosphere
Open: All Year
Grades: ETC 3 Diamond, AA 3 Diamond
01298 25638 (also fax)
P A Cotton
old_manse@yahoo.co.uk
D: £18–£25 **S:** £18–£25
Beds: 2F 4D 2S **Baths:** 4 En 2 Sh
🛏 🅿 (3) 📺 🃏 🃏 🆅 ✿ ♨ cc

Buxton Wheelhouse Hotel, *19 College Road, Buxton, Derbyshire, SK17 9DZ.*
Elegant Victorian establishment. Refurbished spacious bedrooms. Central. Warm welcome, excellent value.
Open: All Year (not Xmas)
Grades: ETC 4 Diamond, Silver Award, AA 4 Diamond
01298 24869 (also fax)
Ms Thompson Price
lyndsie@buxton-wheelhouse.com
D: £22–£27 **S:** £27–£35
Beds: 3F 3D 2T 1S **Baths:** 9 En
🅿 (10) ⊁ 🖵 🃏 ♨ cc

Ford Side House, *125 Lightwood Road, Buxton, Derbyshire, SK17 6RW.*
Peaceful elegant Edwardian house for non-smokers. Premier residential area.
Open: Easter to Oct
Grades: ETC 4 Diamond, Silver
01298 72842 Mr & Mrs Roberts
D: £19–£20 **S:** £25–£30
Beds: 3D 1T **Baths:** 3 En
🛏 (10) 🅿 (3) ⊁ 🖵 🃏 ✕ 🃏 🆅 ♨

Barms Farm, *Fairfield, Buxton, Derbyshire, SK17 7HW.*
Sparkling gold taps. Romantic beds. Quality, comfort and cleanliness assured.
Open: All Year (not Xmas/New Year)
Grades: ETC 4 Diamond
01298 77723 Mrs Naden
Fax: 01298 78692
info@peakpracticegolf.co.uk
D: £23–£25 **S:** £35–£45
Beds: 3D **Baths:** 3 En
🛏 (10) 🅿 (3) ⊁ 🖵 🃏 🆅 ♨ cc

Clifton Guest House, *2 Clifton Road, Silverlands, Buxton, Derbyshire, SK17 6QL.*
Clifton house - Family-run Victorian guest house situated close to town centre.
Open: All Year (not Xmas/New Year)
Grades: ETC Listed, Comm
01298 71671 Mrs Lowe
D: £16 **S:** £16
Beds: 2T 2S **Baths:** 1 Sh
⊁ 🖵 🃏 ♨

Oldfield Guest House, *8 Macclesfield Road, Buxton, Derbyshire, SK17 9AH.*
Elegant detached house set back in a large garden.
Open: All Year
Grades: ETC 4 Diamond
01298 24371 Mr Oldfield
bookings@oldfieldhouses.freeserve.co.uk
D: £22–£25 **S:** £32
Beds: 1F 1D 1T **Baths:** 3 En
🛏 🅿 (5) ⊁ 🖵 🃏 🆅 ♨

Hilldeen, *97 Dale Road, Buxton, Derbyshire, SK17 6PD.*
Family-run business, established 15 yrs. Pavilion, gardens, opera house 10 mins walk.
Open: All Year (not Xmas)
01298 23015 Mr Taylor
D: £17.50–£18.50 **S:** £18–£20
Beds: 1F 1T 1S **Baths:** 2 En 1 Pr
ⓢ🅿📺🕭🏠♿

Hawthorn Farm Guest House, *Fairfield Road, Buxton, Derbyshire, SK17 7ED.*
Well established guest house for over 40 years full English breakfast.
Open: Easter to Oct
01298 23230 Mr Smith
D: £22–£26 **S:** £20–£23
Beds: 4F 2D 2T **Baths:** 5 En 2 Sh
ⓢ🅿(12)📺🕭🏠♿

Lynstone, *3 Grange Road, Buxton, Derbyshire, SK17 6NH.*
Quiet; off-street parking. Substantial breakfasts, clean, good base for touring.
Open: All Year (not Xmas)
01298 77043 Mrs Beresford
lynstone@talk21.com
D: £16–£17 **S:** £20–£22
Beds: 2F 2D 2T **Baths:** 2 Sh
ⓢ(3)🅿(3)📺🏠♿

Westlands, *Bishops Lane, St Johns Road, Buxton, Derbyshire, SK17 6UN.*
Westlands is a beautiful Edwardian guest hose close to theatre, golf, course & walking areas. **Open:** All Year
01298 23242 D: £17–£18 **S:** £22
Beds: 1D 1T 1S **Baths:** 1 Sh
ⓢ(5)🅿(3)📺🏠♿

Grendon, *Bishops Lane, Buxton, Derbyshire, SK17 6UN.*
A beautifully appointed guest house set in lovely gardens with stunning hill views. **Open:** All Year
01298 78831 Mrs Parker
D: £21–£25 **S:** £30–£40
Beds: 2D 1T **Baths:** 3 En
ⓢ(11)🅿(6)📺🕭✕🏠♿cc

Buxworth

SK0382   ◀ *Cross Keys Inn*

Cote Bank Farm, *Buxworth, High Peak, Derbyshire, SK23 7NR*
Welcoming family home in peaceful countryside,stunning views, hearty breakfasts.
Open: Mar to Dec
01663 750566 (also fax)
Mrs Broadhurst
cotebank@btinternet.com
D: £22–£28 **S:** £22–£28
Beds: 2D 1T **Baths:** 3 En
ⓢ(10)🅿(3)📺♿

RATES

D = Price range per person sharing in a double room
S = Price range for a single room

Calver

SK2374   ◀ *Derwent Water Arms*

Hydrangea Cottage, *Hall Fold, Main Street, Calver, Hope Valley, S32 3XL.*
Luxurious accommodation, beautiful garden and views. Quiet location near Chatsworth.
Open: All Year (not Xmas)
Grades: ETC 4 Diamond
01433 630760 Mrs Hall
D: £25 **S:** £50
Beds: 1D **Baths:** 1 Pr
🅿(1)♿📺🏠♿

Castleton

SK1582   ◀ *George Hotel, Castle Hotel*

Cryer House, *Castleton, Hope Valley, S33 8WG.*
C17th rectory with cottage garden; views of church and castle.
Open: All Year (not Xmas)
Grades: ETC 3 Diamond
01433 620244 Mrs Skelton
FleeSkel@aol.com
D: £21–£23.50 **S:** £30
Beds: 1F 1D **Baths:** 1 En 1 Pr
ⓢ📺🏠♿

Bray Cottage, *Market Place, Castleton, Hope Valley, S33 8WQ.*
Charming C18th cottage, excellent accommodation, hearty breakfast, very friendly atmosphere.
Open: All Year (not Xmas)
01433 621532 Mrs Heard
D: £21 **S:** £23
Beds: 2D **Baths:** 1 En 1 Pr
ⓢ🅿(1)♿📺🕭🏠♿

Hillside House, *Pindale Road, Castleton, Hope Valley, S33 8WU.*
Peaceful location, panoramic views, hearty breakfasts. Clean, spacious family house.
Open: All Year (not Xmas)
Grades: ETC 4 Diamond
01433 620244 (also fax)
Mrs Webster
D: £22.50–£24
Beds: 2D **Baths:** 2 En
🅿(3)♿📺♿

Dunscar Farm, *Castleton, Hope Valley, S33 8WA.*
Delightful farm house set at the foot of Mam Tor.
Open: All Year
Grades: ETC 4 Diamond
01433 620483 Mrs Glennerster
D: £20–£22 **S:** £25–£32
Beds: 1F 3D 2T **Baths:** All En
ⓢ(6)🅿(5)♿📺♿

Bargate Cottage, *Market Place, Castleton, Hope Valley, Derbyshire, S33 8WQ.*
Quiet and comfortable C17th cottage, located just above village green.
Open: All Year (not Xmas)
01433 620201 Mrs Saxon
Fax: 01433 621739
D: £21.50–£23.50 **S:** £39–£37
Beds: 2D 1T **Baths:** 3 Pr
🅿(4)♿📺🏠♿

Chapel-en-le-Frith

SK0680   ◀ *Beehive, Lamb Inn*

Potting Shed, *Bank Hall, Chapel-en-le-Frith, High Peak, Derbyshire, SK23 9UB.*
Open: All Year (not Xmas/New Year)
Grades: ETC 4 Diamond
01298 812656 Mr Ashton
D: £22.50–£25 **S:** £35–£40
Beds: 2D **Baths:** 2 En
🅿(3)♿📺🏠♿
Unusual stone converted potting shed. Enchanted walled 1 acre secret garden. Designated outstanding landscape area. Breakfast in plant lovers conservatory, gorgeous views, oak beams, antique furniture. Ground floor room with courtyard garden. Fancy bantams, wildlife, orchard. Features in National Gardens Book.

Slack Hall Farm, *Castleton Road, Chapel-en-le-Frith, High Peak, SK23 6QS.*
17th Century Farmhouse on family run working farm, comfortable friendly accommodation.
Open: All Year (not Xmas/New Year)
01298 812845 Mrs Hayward
D: £18–£19
Beds: 1F 1D **Baths:** 1 En 1 Pr
ⓢ🅿(2)♿📺🏠♿

Charlesworth

SK0093   ◀ *George & Dragon*

Brentwood, *120 Glossop Road, Charlesworth, Glossop, Derbyshire, SK13 5HB.*
A Christian guest house. Dormer bungalow, exceptional garden.
Open: All Year (not Xmas)
01457 869001 Mrs Ehlinger
D: £20 **S:** £20
Beds: 1D 1T 1S **Baths:** 2 En 1 Pr
ⓢ🅿(6)♿📺🕭🏠♿⚓

Chelmorton

SK1169   ◀ *Church Inn*

Shallow Grange, *Chelmorton, Buxton, Derbyshire, SK17 9SG.*
Fantastic views, accommodation perfect location in Peak District.
Open: All Year
Grades: ETC 5 Diamond, Gold Award
01298 23578
Ms Holland
Fax: 01298 78242
holland@shallowgrangefarm.freeserve.co.uk
D: £23–£30 **S:** £25–£60
Beds: 2F 1T 2D **Baths:** 5 En
ⓢ(5)🅿♿📺🏠♿⚓

Chesterfield

SK3871   ⚫ *Highfield Hotel, The Rutland, Heathcotes*

Abbeydale Hotel, *Cross Street, Chesterfield, Derbyshire, S40 4TD.*
Comfortable, friendly, Victorian town hotel in a quiet location. Clean, bright, well-appointed ensuite rooms.
Open: All Year
Grades: ETC 2 Star, AA 2 Star
01246 277849 Mrs Harper
Fax: 01246 558223
elaine@abbey66.freeserve.co.uk
D: £25–£30 **S:** £39–£43
Beds: 1F 5D 1T 4S **Baths:** 11 En
🛇 (1) 🄿 (14) 📺 🛏 ✕ 📖 Ⅴ 🔥 🕹 3 **cc**

Anis Louise Guest House, *34 Clarence Road, Chesterfield, Derbyshire, S40 1LN.*
Town centre location. Convenient for local cafes, restaurants and amenities.
Open: All Year
Grades: ETC 3 Diamond, AA 3 Diamond
01246 235412 Mr Connell
neil@anislouise.co.uk
D: £18–£19.50 **S:** fr £21
Beds: 1F 2D 1T 1S **Baths:** All En
🛇 (8) 🄿 (5) ⅃ 📺 📖 🔥

Locksley, *21 Tennyson Avenue, Chesterfield, Derbyshire, S40 4SN.*
Comfortable friendly atmosphere; pleasant location near town centre.
Open: All Year (not Xmas)
Grades: ETC 2 Diamond
01246 273332 Mrs Parker
D: £15 **S:** £17
Beds: 1D 1T/S **Baths:** 1 Sh

Abigails Guest House, *62 Brockwell Lane, Chesterfield, Derbyshire, S40 4EE.*
Breakfast served in the conservatory overlooking Chesterfield and surrounding moorlands.
Open: All Year
01246 279391 Ms Rodgers
D: £21 **S:** £26
Beds: 3D 2T 2S **Baths:** 7 En
🛇 🄿 📺 🛏 📖 Ⅴ 🔥

Clarendon Guest House, *32 Clarence Road, West Bars, Chesterfield, Derbyshire, S40 1LN.*
Victorian town house near town centre, theatre, leisure centre, special diets.
Open: All Year
01246 235004 D: £15–£17.50 **S:** £15–£17.50
Beds: 1D 2T 2S **Baths:** 4 En 1 Pr
🛇 🄿 (2) ⅃ 🛏 ✕ 📖 ❋

Chinley

SK0482   ⚫ *Crown & Mitre, Squirrels Hotel, Cross Keys Inn*

Craigside, *4 Buxton Road, Chinley, High Peak, SK23 6DJ.*
Warm welcome, small, clean, comfortable. Good walking and cycling location.
Open: All Year (not Xmas)
01663 750604 Mrs Cameron
D: £16–£20 **S:** £16–£20
Beds: 1D 1T 1S **Baths:** 1 Sh
🛇 🄿 (2) 📺 🛏 📖 Ⅴ 🔥

Mosley House Farm, *Maynestone Road, Chinley, High Peak, SK23 6AH.*
Family farm in Peak District, offering comfort and hospitality. Ensuite facilities.
Open: All Year (not Xmas/New Year)
Grades: ETC 3 Diamond
01663 750240 (also fax)
Mrs Goddard
D: £19–£20 **S:** £20–£22
Beds: 1F 2D **Baths:** 1 En 1 Pr
🛇 🄿 (4) 📺 📖 Ⅴ 🔥

Chunal

SK0491   ⚫ *Grouse Inn*

Stanley Farm, *Chunal, Glossop, Derbyshire, SK13 9JY.*
Beautiful country house in wonderful location offers friendly welcome.
Open: All Year
01457 863727 Mrs Brown
D: £20 **S:** £20–£25
Beds: 1F 1D 1T **Baths:** 1 En 1 Sh
🛇 🄿 (20) ⅃ 📺 ✕ 📖 Ⅴ 🔥

Clay Cross

SK3963   ⚫ *Cannon Bar*

Ashview Lodge, *171 High Street, Clay Cross, Chesterfield, Derbyshire, S45 9DZ.*
Overlooking beautiful country views. Many attractions for town and country.
Open: All Year
Grades: AA 3 Diamond
01246 860992 Mrs Morley
D: £15–£17.50 **S:** £15–£17.50
Beds: 4T 1D 2S **Baths:** 2 Sh
🛇 (5) 🄿 (7) 📺 ✕ 📖 🔥

Clifton

SK1644   ⚫ *Cock Inn, Royal Oak*

Stone Cottage, *Green Lane, Clifton, Ashbourne, Derbyshire, DE6 1BX.*
Charming cottage in quiet village of Clifton, 1 mile Georgian market town of Ashbourne.
Open: All Year
01335 343377 Mrs Whittle
Fax: 01335 347117
awhittle@tinyonline.co.uk
D: £20–£28 **S:** £22–£30
Beds: 1F 1D 1T **Baths:** 3 Pr
🛇 🄿 (4) 📺 🛏 ✕ 📖 Ⅴ 🔥

Crich

SK3554   ⚫ *Derwent Arms, Jovial Dutchman*

Clovelly Guest House, *Roe's Lane, Crich, Matlock, Derbyshire, DE4 5DH.*
Friendly family home near to tramway museum and local attractions.
Open: All Year
Grades: ETC 2 Diamond
01773 852295 Mrs Lester
D: £18 **S:** £14
Beds: 1D 1S
🛇 🄿 (3) 📺 🛏 ✕ 📖 Ⅴ ❋ 🔥

All details shown are as supplied by B&B owners in Autumn 2000

Avista, *Penrose, Sandy Lane, Crich, Matlock, Derbyshire, DE4 5DE.*
Beautiful cottage in private grounds, magnificent views, quiet and relaxing.
Open: All Year
Grades: ETC 4 Diamond, Silver Award
01773 852625 Mr & Mrs Bendon
keith@avista.freeserve.co.uk
D: £14–£21 **S:** £18–£25
Beds: 4D 3T 7S **Baths:** 6 En 1 Sh
🄿 (10) ⅃ 📺 📖 Ⅴ 🔥 **cc**

Curbar

SK2574   ⚫ *Bridge Inn*

Bridgend, *Dukes Drive, Curbar, Calver, Hope Valley, S32 3YP.*
Quiet bungalow near village shops and pub, 3 miles from Chatsworth.
Open: All Year
Grades: ETC 4 Diamond
01433 630226 Mrs Hunt
D: £18–£20 **S:** £20–£25
Beds: 1D 1T **Baths:** 1 Sh
🛇 🄿 ⅃ 📺 🛏 📖 Ⅴ 🔥 🕹

Derby

SK3535   ⚫ *Wetherspoons, Babington Arms*

Hill House Hotel, *294 Burton Road, Derby, DE23 6AD.*
Open: All Year (not Xmas/New Year)
Grades: ETC 3 Crowns
01332 361523 (also fax)
Ms Fearn
D: £17.50–£20 **S:** £20–£22.50
Beds: 1F 2D 3T 4S **Baths:** 3 Pr
🛇 (1) 🄿 (10) 📺 🛏 📖 Ⅴ 🔥
Newly refurbished 10 bedroom hotel near city centre, exceptional value.

Plews Guest House, *51-53 Uttoxeter New Road, Derby, DE22 3NL.*
Small family-run guest house close to the city centre.
Open: All Year (not Xmas/New Year)
01332 344325 Mr Plews
D: £13 **S:** £13
Beds: 2F 2T 7S **Baths:** 1 Sh
🛇 🄿 (6) 📺 ✕ 📖 🔥

Chuckles Guest House, *48 Crompton Street, Derby, DE1 1NX.*
Tastefully decorated city centre house, convenient for all local amenities.
Open: All Year
01332 367193 Mr Fraser
ianfraser@chuckleguesthouse.freeserve.c
o.uk
D: £15–£18 **S:** £17–£20
Beds: 1D 1T 2S **Baths:** 1 Sh
🛇 📺 🛏 📖 Ⅴ 🔥

Edale

SK1285   ⚫ *Nags Head, Rambler Inn, Cheshire Cheese, Poachers' Arms*

The Old Parsonage, *Grindsbrook, Edale, Hope Valley, S33 7ZD.*
Secluded C17th house & garden. Walk straight into the hills.
Open: Mar to Oct
01433 670232 Mrs Beney
D: £15–£15.50 **S:** £15–£15.50
Beds: 1D 1T 1S **Baths:** 1 Sh
🛇 🄿 (1) ⅃ 📖 🔥

RATES

D = Price range per person sharing in a double room
S = Price range for a single room

Mam Tor House, Grindsbrook, Edale, Hope Valley, Derbyshire, S33 7ZA.
Edwardian family home, 2 minutes from start of Pennine way.
Open: All Year
01433 670253 Mrs Jackson
D: £17.50 **S:** £17.50
Beds: 1F 2T
🛇 🅿 (4) 📺 ⊁ 📺 🖾 ⅋ & &

Brookfield, Edale, Hope Valley, S33 7ZL.
Peaceful, high-quality accommodation, outstanding views, excellent food and beds.
Open: Easter to Oct
Grades: ETC 2 Diamond
01433 670227 Mrs Chapman
D: fr £18 **S:** fr £20
Beds: 1D 1T **Baths:** 1 Sh
🅿 (3) ⊁ 📺 📺 🖾 ⅋

Stonecroft, Grindsbrook, Edale, Hope Valley, S33 7ZA.
Luxury country house accommodation in spectacular situation amongst Derbyshire Hills.
Open: All Year (not Xmas)
Grades: ETC 4 Diamond, Silver Award
01433 670262 (also fax) Mrs Reid
D: £26–£29 **S:** £36–£39
Beds: 2D **Baths:** 1 En 1 Pr
🛇 (12) 🅿 (2) ⊁ 📺 ✕ 📺 🖾 ⅋ cc

Elton

SK2261   ◖ Bowling Green

Elton Guest House, Moor Lane, Elton, Matlock, Derbyshire, DE4 2DA.
Beautiful house, peaceful village, 4 posters. Convenient Alton Towers. As featured in 'Peak Practice'.
Open: All Year (not Xmas)
01629 650217 Mr Hirst
D: £20–£22
Beds: 1F 1D 1T **Baths:** 3 Pr
🛇 🅿 (4) ⊁ ✕ 🖾 ✲ cc

Fenny Bentley

SK1750   ◖ Coach and Horses

Cairn Grove, Ashes Lane, Fenny Bentley, Ashbourne, Derbyshire, DE6 1LD.
Open: All Year
Grades: ETC 4 Diamond
01335 350538 Mrs Wheeldon
keith.wheeldon@virgin.net
D: £18–£25 **S:** £22–£27
Beds: 1T 2D **Baths:** 2 En 1 Pr
🛇 🅿 (6) ⊁ 📺 ⊁ 📺 🖾 🖾 ⅋
Spacious limestone house in 1 acre grove. Cherry tree drive to pleasant aspect overlooking Fenny Bentley within the Peak National Park. Convenient for Buxton, Chatsworth, Haddon, White Peak, Alton Towers, and local to Ashbourne, Dovedale, Carsington Water and the Tissington Trail.

Glossop

SK0492   ◖ Royal Oak, Grouse Inn

Kings Clough Head Farm, Monks Road, Glossop, Derbyshire, SK13 6ED.
Open: All Year (not Xmas)
01457 862668 Mrs Keegan
patricia@keeganp.freeserve.co.uk
D: £17 **S:** £17
Beds: 1T, 1D, 1S **Baths:** 1 Sh
🛇 🅿 (4) 📺 ⊁ 📺 🖾 ⅋
An C18th stone farmhouse in the Peak National Park offers panoramic views and comfortable accommodation, set in a peaceful secluded countryside ideal for walking and riding, half hour from Buxton and Manchester.

Glutton Bridge

SK0866

Dowall Hall Farm, Glutton Bridge, Buxton, Derbyshire, SK17 0RW.
Open: All Year (not Xmas/New Year)
01298 83297 D: £16–£20 **S:** £17–£20
Beds: 1F 1D **Baths:** 1 En 1 Pr
🛇 🅿 ⊁ 📺 ✕ 🖾 🖾 ⅋
A warm welcome awaits you at our C17th farmhouse, situated in our secluded valley amongst some of Derbyshire's most beautiful countryside, we have 300 acres for you to explore and enjoy on our working Dairy and sheep farm.

Grangemill

SK2457   ◖ Hollybush Grange Mill, Bowling Green

Avondale Farm, Grangemill, Matlock, Derbyshire, DE4 4HT.
Quality B&B in tastefully converted barn. Ground floor level. Close Chatsworth.
Open: All Year (not Xmas)
Grades: ETC 4 Diamond, Silver
01629 650820 Mrs Wragg
avondale@tinyworld.co.uk
D: £22.50–£26 **S:** fr £36
Beds: 1T **Baths:** 1 En
🅿 (1) ⊁ 📺 🖾 🖾 ⅋

Middle Hills Farm, Grangemill, Matlock, Derbyshire, DE4 4HY.
Comfortable farmhouse. Magnificent views, walking, cycling, watersports, Chatsworth, Dovedale nearby.
Open: All Year (not Xmas)
01629 650368 (also fax)
Mrs Lomas
l.lomas@btinternet.com
D: £20–£22 **S:** £25–£30
Beds: 2F 1T **Baths:** 3 En
🛇 🅿 (6) 📺 📺 🖾 ⅋

Haddon Park

SK2367   ◖ Devonshire Arms

Haddon Park Farm, Bakewell, Derbyshire, DE45 1ND.
Farmhouse two miles Bakewell, close to Chatsworth and Haddon Hall.
Open: May to Oct
01629 814854 Mrs Cooper
D: £20–£22 **S:** £25
Beds: 1D 1T **Baths:** 1 Pr 1 Sh
🅿 (2) ⊁ 📺 ⅋

Hartington

SK1260   ◖ Manifold Inn, Hulme Ende, The Greyhound, Devonshire Arms

Wolfscote Grange Farm, Hartington, Buxton, Derbyshire, SK17 0AX.
Open: All Year (not Xmas)
Grades: ETC 4 Diamond
01298 84342 (also fax)
Mrs Gibbs
wolfscote@btinternet.com
D: fr £25
Beds: 1F 1D 1T **Baths:** 2 En 1 Pr
🛇 🅿 📺 ⊁ ✕ 🖾 🖾 ⅋
'A more beautiful setting would be hard to find' Wolfscote farmhouse steeped in history (dating to the Doomsday Book) nestles on the edge of the Dove Valley. Full of 'Olde Worlde' touches (all ensuite). 'Wake to the birds singing and beautiful Dovedale on the doorstep'.

Bank House, Hartington, Buxton, Derbyshire, SK17 0AL.
Central village location, excellent walking, cycling. Near many attractions, 15 miles to Alton Towers.
Open: All Year (not Xmas)
Grades: AA 2 Diamond
01298 84465 Mrs Harrison
D: £18–£25 **S:** £20–£25
Beds: 1F 2D 1T 1S **Baths:** 3 En 2 Sh
🛇 🅿 (2) 📺 ✕ 🖾 🖾 ⅋

Hathersage

SK2381   ◖ The George, The Plough, Scotsman's Pack

Cannon Croft, Cannonfields , Hathersage, Hope Valley, Derbyshire, S32 1AG.
Open: All Year
Grades: ETC 4 Diamonds, Silver Award
01433 650005 (also fax)
Mrs Oates
soates@cannoncroft.fsbusiness.co.uk
D: £20–£22 **S:** £25–£40
Beds: 1T 2D
Baths: 3 En
🛇 (12) 🅿 (5) ⊁ 📺 🖾 🖾 ⅋
Stunning panoramic views of Hope Valley from conservatory, beautiful garden, private off-road parking. Extensive breakfast menu. Rooms have TV, hospitality tray & many extras. Climbing/walking for all abilities. Nearby visit Chatsworth, Haddon, Hardwick, Sheffield. Try our 'Sundancer' eggs.

Hillfoot Farm, Castleton Road, Hathersage, Hope Valley, Derbyshire, S32 1EG.
Originally 16th Century Inn and toll house on the old jaggers pack horse route.
Open: All Year
Grades: ETC 4 Diamond, AA 4 Diamond
01433 651673
Mrs Wilcockson
lorna@wilcockson0.fsnet.co.uk
D: £20–£25 **S:** £25–£50
Beds: 2D 2T **Baths:** 4 En
🛇 🅿 (10) ⊁ 📺 🖾 🖾 ⅋ ✲

Polly's B&B, *Moorview Cottage, Cannonfields, Jaggers Lane, Hathersage, Hope Valley, S32 1AG.*
Open: All Year
Grades: AA 4 Diamond
01433 650110 P Fisher
D: £19–£23 **S:** £25–£28
Beds: 2D 1T **Baths:** 3 En
❄ (4) **P** (3) ⌿ ⊡ ⊩ ▥ Ⓥ ✿ ♨
Warm and friendly first class accommodation in quiet location offering a very imaginative breakfast menu, famous mumbled eggs. Ideal base for walking, cycling and climbing. Stanage Edge close by. Your stay is made very special at this homely guest house.

Moorgate, *Castleton Road, Hathersage, Hope Valley, S32 1EH.*
Fringe of Hathersage in Peak National Park - touring, walking, climbing.
Open: All Year
Grades: AA 3 Diamond
01433 650293 Mrs Veevers
D: £16 **S:** £19
Beds: 1D 1T 1S **Baths:** 1 Sh
❄ **P** (3) ⌿ ⊡ ▥ Ⓥ ♨

The Mount, *Castleton Road, Hathersage, Hope Valley, Derbyshire, S32 1AH.*
Victorian house with large rooms, centrally positioned in attractive village.
Open: All Year (not Xmas/New Year)
Grades: AA 3 Diamond
01433 650388 (also fax)
Mrs Ward
ward.themount@btinternet.com
D: £20 **S:** £20–£25
Beds: 1D 1T 1F **Baths:** 2 Sh
❄ **P** (6) ⌿ ⊡ ⊩ ▥ Ⓥ ♨

Hayfield

SK0386 🍺 *Lantern Pike, The Grouse, Pack Horse*

Shudehill, *Hayfield, High Peak, SK22 2EP.*
Private suite, c1700 farmhouse, charming village, great pubs, wonderful walks.
Open: All Year (not Xmas)
01663 742784 Leslie Sadleir
Fax: 07971 046755
D: £25 **S:** £27
Beds: 1T **Baths:** 1 Pr
P (1) ⌿ ⊡ ▥ ♨

Hilcote

SK4457 🍺 *Robin Hood*

Hillcote Hall, *Hilcote Lane, Hilcote, Alfreton, Derbyshire, DE55 5HR.*
Listed country house with easy access to M1 and Derbyshire.
Open: Mar to Nov
Grades: ETC 2 Diamond
01773 812608 Mrs Doncaster
D: fr £18 **S:** fr £20
Beds: 1F 1D
❄ **P** (4) ⌿ ⊡ Ⓥ ♨

Planning a longer stay? Always ask for any special rates

Holmesfield

SK3277 🍺 *Trout Inn*

Cordwell House, *Cordwell Lane, Millthorpe, Holmesfield, Dronfield, Derbyshire, S18 7WH.*
C17th cottage on the edge of the peak district.
Open: All Year (not Xmas)
0114 289 0271 Mr Eshelby
D: £19 **S:** £28
Beds: 1T **Baths:** 1 Pr
⌿ ⊡ ⊩ ▥ Ⓥ ♨

Hope

SK1683 🍺 *Cheshire Cheese, Woodruffe Arms, Bowling Green*

The Woodroffe Arms Hotel, *1 Castleton Road, Hope, Hope Valley, Derbyshire, S33 6SB.*
Open: All Year **Grades:** ETC 3 Diamond
01433 620351 Mr Thompson
Fax: 01433 623465
tanya.thomson@online.net
D: £27–£29.50 **S:** £35–£39
Beds: 1T 2D **Baths:** 3 En
❄ **P** (20) ⌿ ⊡ ✕ ▥ Ⓥ ✿ ♨ cc
Situated in Hope in heart of the Peak District, superb ensuite accommodation. Open fire, warm friendly atmosphere, 4 case ales, local attractions include; Castleton, Chatsworth House and Bakewell. The Inn is run by a very experienced management team.

Round Meadow Barn, *Parsons Lane, Hope , Hope Valley, Derbyshire, S33 6RA.*
Open: All Year **Grades:** AA 3 Diamond
01433 621347 Fax: 01433 621347
rmbarn@bigfoot.com
D: £20–£23 **S:** £25–£28
Beds: 1F 1T **Baths:** 2 Sh
❄ **P** (12) ⌿ ⊡ ⊩ Ⓥ ♨
A recently converted barn with magnificent views all round. Ideal for walking, hang gliding, rock climbing, mountain biking etc. Places of interest; Chatsworth House and Gardens, Haddon Hall, Bakewell and the caverns at Castleton. Also the plague village of Eyam.

Underleigh, *Edale Road, Hope, Hope Valley, S33 6RF.*
A stunning, tranquil setting in the heart of magnificent walking country.
Open: All Year (not Xmas/New Year)
Grades: ETC 5 Diamond, AA 5 Diamond
01433 621372 Mrs Singleton
Fax: 01433 621324
underleigh.house@btinternet.com
D: £27.50–£33 **S:** £33–£46
Beds: 4D 2T **Baths:** 6 En
❄ (12) **P** (6) ⌿ ⊡ ✕ ▥ Ⓥ ✿ ♨ cc

Old Blacksmith's Cottage, *18 Castleton Road, Hope, Hope Valley, S33 6RD.*
Oak beamed cottage, friendly atmosphere, home baking, patchwork/walking holidays.
Open: All Year (not Xmas)
01433 621407 (also fax) Mr Lane
judith@woodbinecafe.freeserve.co.uk
D: £19–£22.50 **S:** £25–£30
Beds: 1D 5T **Baths:** 4 En 1 Sh
❄ **P** (6) ⌿ ⊡ ✕ ▥ Ⓥ ♨

Mill Farm, *Edale Road, Hope, Hope Valley, Derbyshire, S33 6ZF.*
Traditional farmhouse home, exposed beams, log fires, delightful gardens, village setting.
Open: All Year (not Xmas)
01433 621181 (also fax)
D: £20–£22 **S:** £27.50
Beds: 1D 2T **Baths:** 2 Sh
❄ **P** (4) ⌿ ⊡ ▥ Ⓥ ♨

Little Hucklow

SK1678

Ye Olde Bull's Head, *Little Hucklow, Tideswell, Buxton, Derbyshire, SK17 8RT.*
Unspoilt 12th century inn with cosy log fires and panoramic views.
Open: All Year
Grades: AA 2 Diamond
01298 871097 (also fax)
Mr Denton
accom@yeoldebullshead.freeserve.co.uk
D: £25–£30 **S:** £30–£60
Beds: 2D **Baths:** 2 En
❄ **P** ⌿ ⊡ ✕ ▥ Ⓥ ✿ ♨ ♿ cc

Litton

SK1675 🍺 *George Hotel, Red Lion*

Beacon House, *Litton, Buxton, Derbyshire, SK17 8QP.*
Farm smallholding overlooking Tansley Dale. Quietly situated, walks from the door.
Open: Feb to Nov
Grades: ETC 3 Diamond
01298 871752
Mrs Parsons
D: £19–£21
Beds: 2D **Baths:** 2 En
P (4) ⌿ ⊡ ⊩ ▥ Ⓥ ♨

Laurel House, *The Green, Litton, Buxton, Derbyshire, SK17 8QP.*
Victorian house in centre of village. Lovely walks, maps available if tempted.
Open: Mar to Nov
Grades: ETC 4 Diamond
01298 871971
Ms Harris
D: £16–£22
Beds: 1D 1T **Baths:** 1 En 1 Pr
❄ ⌿ ⊡ ⊩ ▥ ♨

Mapleton

SK1647 🍺 *Royal Oak*

Little Park Farm, *Mapleton, Ashbourne, Derbyshire, DE6 2BR.*
Enjoy the peace & quiet, also the beautiful views of the Dove Valley & wildlife.
Open: Easter to Oct
01335 350341
Mrs Harrison
D: £17–£18
Beds: 1D 1T **Baths:** 1 Sh
❄ **P** ⌿ ⊡ ▥ ♨

All details shown are as supplied by B&B owners in Autumn 2000

National Grid References are for villages, towns and cities – not for individual houses

Marston Montgomery

SK1337 ⚑ Crown Inn

Waldley Manor, Marston Montgomery, Doveridge, Ashbourne, Derbyshire, DE6 5LR.
Relax in this C16th manor farmhouse. Quiet location, access to commuter roads.
Open: All Year (not Xmas/New Year)
01889 590287 Ms Whitfield
D: £20–£25 **S:** £20–£25
Beds: 1F 1D **Baths:** 2 En
🛇 🅿 📺 📖 Ⅴ ♨

Matlock

SK3060 ⚑ Crown, Boat, Duke William, Red Lion, J D Wetherspoon, Gate Hotel, Plough, Tavern At Tansley, Kings Head, Strand

Norden House, Chesterfield Road, Two Dales, Matlock, Derbyshire, DE4 2EZ.
Converted barn, village outskirts. Friendly, cosy accommodation, pub nearby. Tasty home cooking.
Open: All Year (not Xmas)
Grades: ETC 4 Diamond
01629 732074 Mrs Pope
Fax: 01629 735805
david.a.pope@talk21.com
D: £20–£26 **S:** £37–£40
Beds: 2D **Baths:** 2 En
🛇 🅿 (2) ⚡ 📺 🐾 ✕ 📖 Ⅴ ♨

Edgemount, 16 Edge Road, Matlock, Derbyshire, DE4 3NH.
Quality accommodation. Quiet, picturesque central position. Near rail/bus station. (Comfort assured).
Open: All Year (not Xmas)
Grades: ETC 2 Diamond
01629 584787 Mrs Allen
D: £17–£20 **S:** £17–£20
Beds: 1D 1T 1S **Baths:** 1 Sh 2 Toilets
🛇 (5) 🅿 (2) ⚡ 📺 🐾 📖 Ⅴ ♨

Bank House, 12 Snitterton Road, Matlock, Derbyshire, DE4 3LZ.
Beamed C17th stone cottage with double/family converted stable suite.
Open: All Year
Grades: ETC 5 Diamond, Silver
01629 56101 (also fax) Mrs Donnell
D: £20–£23 **S:** £23
Beds: 1F 1D **Baths:** 1 En 1 Pr
🛇 🅿 (2) ⚡ 📖 Ⅴ ♨

Riverbank House, Derwent Avenue, Matlock, Derbyshire, DE4 3LX.
Victorian house nestling on the banks of the River Derwent.
Open: All Year (not Xmas/New Year)
Grades: ETC 4 Diamond
01629 582593 Mr & Mrs Newberry
Fax: 01629 580885
bookings@riverbankhouse.co.uk
D: £22.50–£30 **S:** £25–£30
Beds: 2F 1T 2D **Baths:** 6 En
🛇 🅿 ⚡ 📺 ✕ 📖 Ⅴ ♨

Kensington Villa, 84 Dale Road, Matlock, Derbyshire, DE4 3LU.
Warm welcome, comfortable accommodation, substantial breakfast, central for touring area.
Open: All Year (not Xmas)
Grades: AA 3 Diamond
01629 57627 Mrs Gorman
bill.gorman@virginnet.co.uk
D: £20 **S:** £20
Beds: 2D 1T **Baths:** 1 Sh
🛇 🅿 (3) ⚡ 📺 📖 Ⅴ ♨

Glendon, Knowleston Place, Matlock, Derbyshire, DE4 3BU.
Conveniently situated, well-equipped accommodation in a relaxed atmosphere.
Open: Jan to Nov
Grades: AA 4 Diamond
01629 584732 Mrs Elliott
D: £19–£23 **S:** fr £23
Beds: 1F 2D 1T **Baths:** 2 En 2 Sh
🛇 (3) 🅿 (5) ⚡ 📺 📖 Ⅴ ♨

Victoria House, 65 Wellington Street, Matlock, Derbyshire, DE4 3GS.
Victorian family house with panoramic views over Matlock.
Open: All Year **Grades:** AA 3 Diamond
01629 55862 Mrs Stevenson
amsmatlock@hotmail.com
D: fr £20 **S:** fr £30
Beds: 1F 1T 1D **Baths:** 1 Sh
🛇 🅿 (2) ⚡ 📺 ✕ 📖 Ⅴ ♣ ♨

Bradvilla, 26 Chesterfield Road, Matlock, Derbyshire, DE4 3DQ.
House is Victorian, fine views and gardens. friendly family atmosphere.
Open: All Year (not Xmas/New Year)
Grades: AA 3 Diamond
01629 57147 Mrs Saunders
Fax: 01629 583021
D: £18–£22 **S:** £22
Beds: 2F 1S **Baths:** 1 Pr 1 En
🛇 🅿 (4) ⚡ 📺 📖 ♨

Tuckers Guest House, 48 Dale Road, Matlock, Derbyshire, DE4 3NB.
Spacious, relaxed Victorian home, close to station, helpful hosts, pets most welcome. **Open:** All Year (not Xmas)
01629 583018 Mrs Martin
D: £18.50 **S:** £23
Beds: 1F 1D 1T **Baths:** 1 Sh
🛇 (3) 🅿 (2) 📺 🐾 📖 Ⅴ ♨

Matlock Bath

SK2958 ⚑ Midland Hotel

Old Museum Guest House, 170-172 South Parade, Matlock Bath, Matlock, Derbyshire, DE4 3NR.
Open: All Year (not Xmas)
Grades: ETC 3 Diamond
01629 57783 (also fax)
Mr & Mrs Bailey
lindsayandstewartbailey@tinyworld.co.uk
D: £15 **S:** £20
Beds: 1F 2D **Baths:** 3 En
🛇 📺 ✕ 📖 Ⅴ ♨
Friendly family-run guest house; ensuite double rooms with four-poster beds, residents' lounge with superb views over river. Extensive menu in restaurant. Situated within easy reach of all local attractions.

Ashdale Guest House, 92 North Parade, Matlock Bath, Matlock, Derbyshire, DE4 3NS.
Listed Victorian villa, central Matlock Bath. Level walking to station etc.
Open: All Year
Grades: ETC 2 Dimaond
01629 57826 Mrs Lomas
ashdale@matlockbath.fsnt.co.uk
D: £22–£25 **S:** £25–£28
Beds: 2F 1T 1D **Baths:** 4 En
🛇 🅿 (4) ⚡ 📺 ✕ 📖 Ⅴ ♨

Sunnybank Guest House, Clifton Road, Matlock Bath, Matlock, Derbyshire, DE4 3PW.
Spacious Victorian residence offering peace and comfort in wonderful location.
Open: All Year (not Xmas)
Grades: ETC 4 Diamond, Silver
01629 584621 Mr & Mrs Ward
sunward@lineone.net
D: £20–£33 **S:** £20–£30
Beds: 1F 2D 1T 1S **Baths:** 4 En 1 Pr
⚡ 📺 ✕ 📖 Ⅴ ♨

Mercaston

SK2643 ⚑ Cock Inn

Mercaston Hall, Mercaston, Ashbourne, Derbyshire, DE6 3BL.
A warm welcome in comfortable historic farmhouse set in peaceful attractive countryside.
Open: All Year (not Xmas)
Grades: AA 4 Diamond
01335 360263 Mrs Haddon
Fax: 01335 361399
Mercastonhall@btinternet.com
D: £20–£22.50 **S:** £25–£28
Beds: 2D 1T **Baths:** 2 En 1 Pr
🛇 (8) 🅿 (6) 📺 🐾 📖 Ⅴ ♨

Mickleover

SK3033 ⚑ Blue Bell

Bonehill Farm, Etwall Road, Mickleover, Derby, DE3 5DN.
Comfortable Georgian farmhouse in countryside, 3 miles from centre of Derby.
Open: All Year
Grades: ETC 3 Diamond
01332 513553 Mrs Dicken
D: £20–£25 **S:** £20–£25
Beds: 2T 1S **Baths:** 2 En 2 Sh
🛇 🅿 (6) 📺 🐾 📖 Ⅴ ♨

Milford

SK3545 ⚑ Strutt Arms

The Milford Inn and Restaurant, The Bridge, Milford, Belper, Derbyshire, DE56 0RR.
Riverside location, traditional home cooked food. Warm and friendly atmosphere.
Open: All Year
01332 840842 P & J Brailsford
D: £15–£20 **S:** £20–£25
Beds: 2T 1S **Baths:** 3 En
🛇 (14) 🅿 (10) 📺 ✕ 📖 Ⅴ ♣ ♨ cc

Planning a longer stay? Always ask for any special rates

Please respect a B&B's wishes regarding children, animals and smoking

Strutt Arms Hotel, *Milford, Belper, Derbyshire, DE56 1QH.*
Lovely old coach inn family-run hotel famous for high quality low priced meals.
Open: All Year
01332 840240 Fax: 01332 841758
D: fr £17.50 **S:** fr £21
Beds: 1F 2D 3T 4S **Baths:** 2 En 7 Sh
🛇 🏿 🎰 🗙 🛒 💷 🛱

Monyash

SK1566 *Bull's Head, Cock & Pullet, Queen's Arms*

Rowson Farm, *Monyash, Bakewell, Derbyshire, DE45 1JH.*
Open: All Year
01629 813521 Mr Mycock
gm@rowson99.freeserve.co.uk
D: £20–£25 **S:** £15–£25
🛇 🏿 (10) 🗲 🎰 🎀 🛒 💷 🛱
Rowson Farm dates from the late 1700s, has been farmed traditionally for generations, and has many acres of ancient hay meadows. Delicious Aga-cooked Breakfasts are served daily. Clean and comfortable accommodation awaits you (ask about our drive and hike service).

Sheldon House, *Chapel Street, Monyash, Bakewell, Derbyshire, DE45 1JJ.*
Recently renovated Grade II Listed house - a warm welcome awaits you.
Open: All Year (not Xmas)
Grades: ETC 4 Diamond
01629 813067 (also fax) Mr & Mrs Tyler
sheldonhouse@lineone.net
D: £20–£22 **S:** £30–£32
Beds: 3D **Baths:** 3 En
🛇 (10) 🏿 (2) 🗲 🎰 🛒 💷 🛱

Sunnyside, *Handley Lane, off Chapel St, Monyash, Bakewell, Derbys, DE45 1JJ.*
Traditional stone house in quiet lane in village. Lovely views.
Open: All Year (not Xmas)
01629 813981 (also fax)
Mrs Slater
D: £18.50–£20 **S:** £20–£23
Beds: 1D **Baths:** 1 En
🛇 🏿 (1) 🗲 🎰 🎀 🛒 🛱

Morley

SK3940 *Rose & Crown*

Alambie, *189 Main Road, Morley, Ilkeston, Derbyshire, DE7 6DG.*
Warm welcome. Good food. Comfy beds. Spotlessly clean. Ensuite rooms.
Open: All Year
Grades: ETC 3 Diamond
01332 780349 (also fax)
Mrs Green-Armytage
alambie@beeb.net
D: £20–£25
Beds: 1F 2D 1T **Baths:** 4 En
🛇 🏿 (5) 🗲 🎰 🗙 🛒 🛱

Newbold

SK3672

Buckinghams Hotel, *85-87 Newbold Road, Newbold, Chesterfield, Derbyshire, S41 7PU.*
Open: All Year
01246 201041 Fax: 01246 550059
info@buckinghams-table.com
D: £26–£38 **S:** £26–£38
Beds: 2F 3T 3D 6S **Baths:** 2 En 9 Pr
🛇 🏿 (5) 🎰 🗙 🛒 💷 🛱 **cc**
A pair of Victorian houses which have been sympathetically converted into this smart, comfortable and relaxed hotel in Newbold, a residential part of Chesterfield. Nick and Tina Buckingham are well known for their warm and friendly hotel with superlative food.

North Wingfield

SK4165 *Blue Bell*

South View, *95 Church Lane, North Wingfield, Chesterfield, Derbyshire, S42 5HR.*
Peaceful farmhouse, 3 miles from M1 junction 29 easy to find.
Open: All Year
Grades: ETC 3 Diamond
01246 850091 Mrs Hopkinson
D: £17.50 **S:** £17
Beds: 1D 1T 1S **Baths:** 1 Sh
🛇 (10) 🏿 (4) 🗲 🎰 🛒 🛱

Over Haddon

SK2066 *Lathkil Hotel*

Mandale House, *Haddon Grove, Over Haddon, Bakewell, Derbyshire, DE45 1JF.*
Peaceful farmhouse near Lathkilldale. Good breakfasts, packed lunches available.
Open: Mar to Nov
Grades: ETC 4 Diamond
01629 812416 Mrs Finney
julia.finney@virgin.net
D: £19–£22 **S:** £21–£25
Beds: 2D 1T **Baths:** 3 En
🛇 (5) 🏿 (4) 🗲 🎰 🛒 💷 🛱 ♿

Padfield

SK0296

The Peels Arms, *Temple Street, Padfield, Hyde, Cheshire, SK14 7ET.*
Country inn, oak beams, log fires, real ale, fine foods. Manchester/Sheffield 40 minutes.
Open: All Year
Grades: ETC 3 Diamond
01457 852719 Mrs Murray
Fax: 01457 850536
peels@talk21.com
D: £20–£25 **S:** £25
Beds: 3D 2T **Baths:** 3 En 1 Sh
🛇 🏿 (20) 🎰 🎀 🗙 🛒 💷 🛱 **cc**

All details shown are as supplied by B&B owners in Autumn 2000

Peak Forest

SK1179 *Devonshire Arms*

Dam Dale Farm, *Peak Forest, Buxton, Derbyshire, SK17 8EF.*
Working farm, homely, comfortable atmosphere, wonderful views, hearty breakfast, secure parking.
Open: Feb to Nov
01298 24104 Mrs Fletcher
D: £18–£20 **S:** £25
Beds: 1D 1T **Baths:** 2 Sh
🛇 (9) 🏿 (6) 🗲 🎰 💷 🛱

Devonshire Arms, *Hernstone Lane, Peak Forest, Buxton, Derbyshire, SK17 8EJ.*
C17th former coaching inn in the heart of the Peak District.
Open: All Year
01298 23875 Mrs Clough
D: £21 **S:** £28.50
Beds: 4D 1T **Baths:** 5 En
🛇 🏿 (40) 🎰 🎀 🗙 🛒 💷 🛱 **cc**

Pentrich

SK3952 *Anchor, Devonshire Arms*

Coney Grey Farm, *Chesterfield Road, Pentrich, Ripley, Derbyshire, DE5 3RF.*
Beautiful farmhouse with panoramic views. Ripley, Alfreton and Crich nearby.
Open: All Year (not Xmas/New Year)
Grades: ETC 1 Diamond
01773 833179 D: £14–£15 **S:** £15
Beds: 1T 1D **Baths:** 1 Sh
🛇 (6) 🏿 (4) 🎰 🛒 🛱

Pleasley

SK5064 *Ye Olde Plough*

Appleby Guesthouse, *Chesterfield Road, Pleasley, Mansfield, Notts, NG19 7PF.*
Large Victorian guest house.
Open: All Year (not Xmas)
01623 810508 Mrs Simpson
D: £18 **S:** £18
Beds: 1F 3D 4T 2S **Baths:** 3 En 2 Pr
🛇 🏿 (10) 🗲 🎰 🛒 💷 🛱 **cc**

Riddings

SK4252 *Swan and Salmon*

1 Peveril Drive, *Riddings, Alfreton, Derbyshire, DE55 4AP.*
Self-contained bungalow accommodation with private bathroom, lounge and parking. **Open:** All Year
01773 607712 Mrs Brown
D: £15 **S:** £20
Beds: 1D **Baths:** 1 Pr
🛇 🏿 (3) 🎰 🎀 🛒 💷 🛱 ♿

Rowland

SK2172 *Eyre Arms*

Rowland Cottage, *Rowland, Great Longstone, Bakewell, Derbyshire, DE45 1NR.*
Hamlet C17th cottage, near Chatsworth, traffic free, quiet relaxing, comfortable.
Open: All Year
01629 640365 (also fax) Mrs Scott
jgarde7@aol.com
D: £17.50–£22.50 **S:** £20–£22.50
Beds: 1F 1T **Baths:** 1 Pr 1 Sh
🛇 🏿 (3) 🗲 🎰 🎀 🛒 💷 🛱 ♿

Holly Cottage, Rowland, Bakewell, Derbyshire, DE45 1NR.
Most attractive comfortable old-lime-stone cottage in peaceful beautiful countryside. **Open:** Jan to Oct
01629 640624 Mrs Everard
D: £21–£22 **S:** £25–£26
Beds: 1D 1T **Baths:** 1 Sh
🛇 🅿 (4) ⅙ 📺 🕇 🛋 🆅 🔱

Shatton

SK1982 ⬟ Woodroffe Arms, Plough Inn, Yorkshire Bridge

The White House, Shatton, Bamford, Hope Valley, S33 0BG.
Friendly, comfortable, private country house, lovely views, close to amenities.
Open: All Year (not Xmas)
Grades: AA 3 Diamond
01433 651487 (also fax)
Mrs Middleton
D: £17.50–£20 **S:** £17.50–£20
Beds: 1D 1T 2S **Baths:** 2 Sh
🛇 🅿 (4) 📺 🕇 🛋 🆅 🔱

Shirebrook

SK5267

Old School Guest House, Main Street, Shirebrook, Mansfield, Derbyshire, NG20 8DL.
Converted C19th school in Midlands. Market, town situated conveniently.
Open: All Year
01623 744610 Mrs Miles
D: fr £18 **S:** fr £18
Beds: 2F 1D 1T 1S **Baths:** 5 En
🛇 🅿 (12) ⅙ 📺 ✕ 🆅 🔱

Shirland

SK4058 ⬟ Greyhound Inn

Park Lane Farm, Park Lane, Shirland, Alfreton, Derbyshire, DE55 6AX.
Open: All Year
Grades: ETC 4 Diamond
01773 831880 D: £22.50–£25 **S:** £25
Beds: 2F 2D 2T
🛇 🅿 (8) 📺 🛋 🔱
Early C18th farmhouse, situated on the borders of the Peak National Park, all rooms ensuite, easy reach of M1, close to Chatsworth, Haddon, Hardwick Hall, Bakewell, etc. A warm welcome to all.

Shirley

SK2141 ⬟ Saracens Head

Shirley Hall Farm, Shirley, Brailsford, Ashbourne, Derbyshire, DE6 3AS.
Open: All Year
Grades: ETC 4 Diamond
01335 360346 (also fax) Mrs Foster
sylviafoster@shirleyhallfarm.com
D: £21–£25 **S:** £23–£27
Beds: 1F 1T 1D **Baths:** 2 En 1 Pr
🛇 (6) 🅿 (6) ⅙ 📺 🛋 🆅 🔱
Enjoy the peacefulness of our lovely old farmhouse set in large lawned gardens a few minutes walk from Shirley Village, four miles from Ashbourne. Superb breakfasts with home-made bread and preserves, locally made sausages. Evening meals at our village pub. Free coarse fishing on farm.

Snelston

SK1543 ⬟ Cock Inn

Sidesmill Farm, Snelston, Ashbourne, Derbyshire, DE6 2GQ.
Comfortable farmhouse accommodation on working farm. C18th stone-built house overlooks pretty garden.
Open: Easter to Nov
01335 342710 Ms Brandrick
D: £18–£20 **S:** £25
Beds: 1D 1T **Baths:** 1 En 1 Pr
🛇 (10) 🅿 (2) 📺 🛋 🔱

Stanton by Bridge

SK3727 ⬟ Hardindge Arms

Ivy House Farm, Stanton by Bridge, Derby, DE73 1HT.
Open: March-Oct
Grades: ETC 4 Diamond
01332 863152 (also fax)
Mrs Kidd
mary@guesthouse.fsbusiness.co.uk
D: £20–£25 **S:** fr £25
Beds: 4D 2T **Baths:** 6 En
🛇 🅿 (9) ⅙ 📺 🕇 🛋 🆅 🔱 ♿ 3
These purpose-built B&B chalets are in this small quiet village, but close to lots of interesting things - Donington Park racing, Calke Abbey, Alton Towers, Twycross Zoo, Swadlincote ski slopes, the National Forest.

Stanton Lees

SK2563 ⬟ Bowling Green Inn

Woodside, Stanton Lees, Matlock, Derbyshire, DE4 2LQ.
Open: All Year
Grades: AA 4 Diamond
01629 734320 Mrs Potter
D: £18–£24
Beds: 1F 1D 1T **Baths:** 3 En
⅙ 📺 🛋 🔱
Panoramic views from house in picturesque Peak District hamlet. Landscaped garden home to many birds. Nearby Bakewell/Chatsworth House/Stanton Moor. Peak Rail in valley below. Spring water on tap. Your comfort and enjoyment our speciality. Required: a hearty appetite.

Taddington

SK1470

Ade House, Taddington, Buxton, Derbyshire, SK17 9TY.
Find peace, home baking, organic produce, good walks and a warm welcome. **Open:** All Year (not Xmas)
Grades: ETC 4 Diamond
01298 85203 Mrs Elkington
D: £20 **S:** £20
Beds: 1F 1T 3S **Baths:** 2 Sh
🛇 🅿 (4) ⅙ 📺 🕇 ✕ 🛋 🆅 🔱

BATHROOMS

Pr - Private

Sh - Shared

En - Ensuite

B&B owners may vary rates - be sure to check when booking

Thorpe

SK1550

Jasmine Cottage, Thorpe, Ashbourne, Derbyshire, DE6 2AW.
Picturesque spacious stone cottage near Dovedale. Warm, comfortable with good food.
Open: All Year
01335 350465 Mrs Round
D: £20–£25 **S:** £25
Beds: 1D 1T
🅿 (4) ⅙ 📺 ✕ 🛋 🔱

The Old Orchard, Thorpe, Ashbourne, Derbyshire, DE6 2AW.
Quietly situated limestone home with colourful gardens. Ample car parking.
Open: All Year
01335 350410 (also fax)
Mrs Challinor
D: £18–£20 **S:** £18–£20
Beds: 2D, 2S **Baths:** 2 En, 1 Pr
🅿 📺 🛋 🆅 🔱

Tibshelf

SK4360 ⬟ Royal Oak

Rosvern House, High Street, Tibshelf, Alfreton, Derbyshire, DE55 6AX.
Friendly, homely atmosphere. Comfortable rooms, convenient for business travellers/tourists.
Open: All Year
Grades: ETC 4 Diamond
01773 874800 Mrs Byard
byard.tibshelf@lineone.net
D: £16–£18 **S:** £17–£18
Beds: 1F 1D
🛇 🅿 (2) ⅙ 📺 🛋 🔱

Tideswell

SK1575 ⬟ The Star

Poppies, Bank Square, Tideswell, Buxton, Derbyshire, SK17 8LA.
Central for many Peak activities and other attractions, friendly.
Open: Mar to Dec
01298 871083 Mrs Pinnegar
poptidza@dialstart.net
D: £17–£21.50 **S:** £17–£21.50
Beds: 1F 1D 1T **Baths:** 1 En 1 Sh
🛇 ⅙ 📺 🕇 ✕ 🛋 🆅 🔱 ♿ cc

Uppertown

SK3264 ⬟ Black Swan, Red Lion

Old School Farm, Uppertown, Ashover, Chesterfield, Derbyshire, S45 0JF.
Spacious, comfortable, working farm, home from home, peaceful and friendly.
Open: Easter to Oct
Grades: ETC 4 Diamond, RAC 4 Diamond
01246 590813 Mrs Wooton
D: fr £22 **S:** fr £22
Beds: 2F 1D 1T 1S **Baths:** 3 En 1 Pr 1 Sh
🛇 🅿 (6) 📺 🛋 🔱

Wessington

SK3757 · *Three Horseshoes, Horse & Jockey, Peacock*

Crich Lane Farm, *Moorwood Moor Lane, Wessington, Alfreton, Derbyshire, DE55 6DU.*
C17th farmhouse. Peaceful surroundings, friendly atmosphere.
Open: All Year (not Xmas)
Grades: ETC 4 Diamond
01773 835186 Mrs Green
D: £20–£25 **S:** £20–£25
Beds: 2F 3D 2T 1S **Baths:** 5 En 1 Pr 1 Sh
🛏 🅿 (8) ⊬ 📺 🕭 🎟 🖳 🖂 ᕀ

Oaktree Farm, *Matlock Road, Oakerthorpe, Wessington, Alfreton, Derbyshire, DE55 7NA.*
Modern stone farmhouse. Coarse fishing free to residents. Sky TV.
Open: All Year (not Xmas/New Year)
Grades: AA 3 Diamond
01773 832957 Mrs Prince
oaktree_farm@talk21.com
D: £21–£25 **S:** £23–£27
Beds: 2D 1T **Baths:** 3 En
🛏 🅿 (10) ⊬ 📺 🕭 ✕ 🕭 🖳 🖂

All details shown are as supplied by B&B owners in Autumn 2000

Whatstandwell

SK3354 · *Homesford Cottage Inn, Derwent Hotel*

Robin Hood Cottage, *Robin Hood, Whatstandwell, Matlock, Derbyshire, DE4 5HF.*
Detached 17th Century country cottage within one acre overlooking Derwent Valley.
Open: All Year (not Xmas/New Year)
01773 856238 Mrs Hitchcock
D: £19.50–£22.50 **S:** £21–£39.50
Beds: 2D 1T 1S **Baths:** 1 En 1 Sh
🛏 🅿 (4) ⊬ 📺 ✕ 🕭 🖂

Youlgreave

SK2164 · *Bull's Head, George Hotel, Farmyard Inn*

Bulls Head Hotel, *Fountain Square, Church Street, Youlgreave, Bakewell, Derbyshire, DE45 1UR.*
Open: All Year
01629 636307 Mrs Atkinson
D: £15–£20 **S:** £20
Beds: 2F 2T 3D **Baths:** 1 En 1 Sh
🛏 (5) 🅿 📺 ✕ 🕭 🖳 🖂 cc
A Grade II Listed building with lots of charm and a friendly welcome. Lying between two beautiful Dales the Lathkill and Bradford. Great area for walking and touring the close by Chatsworth house, Haddon Hall and Market towns of Bakewell, Buxton, Chesterfield.

National Grid References are for villages, towns and cities – not for individual houses

The Old Bakery, *Church Street, Youlgreave, Bakewell, Derbyshire, DE45 1UR.*
Two bedroom guest wing or tasteful barn conversion for two.
Open: All Year
Grades: ETC 3 Diamond
01629 636887 Ms Croasdell
croasdell@oldbakeryoulgrave.freeserve.co.uk
D: £16–£27 **S:** fr £18
Beds: 1D 2T **Baths:** 1 En 1 Sh
🛏 🅿 (1) ⊬ 📺 🕭 🖳 🖂 ❋ 🖂

Bankside Cottage, *Youlgreave, Bakewell, Derbyshire, DE45 1WD.*
Open: All Year
Grades: ETC 2 Diamond
01629 636689 Mr Blackburn
D: £16.50 **S:** £16.50
Beds: 1D 1T **Baths:** 1 Sh
🛏 ⊬ 📺 🕭 🖳 🖂
Large stone cottage, unique off-road position, terrace garden overlooks secluded Bradford Dale, guest lounge. Relaxed friendly atmosphere. A house full of art and books.

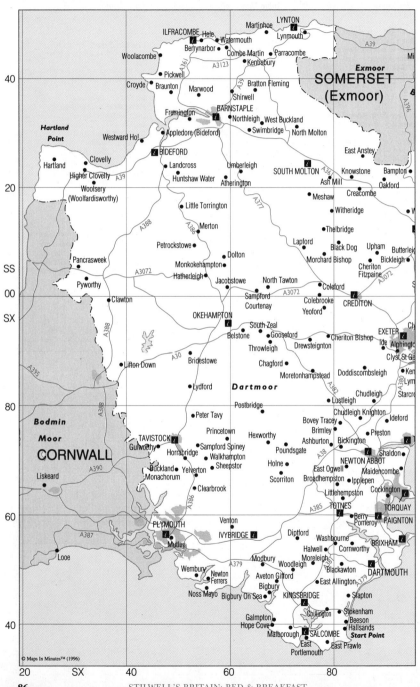

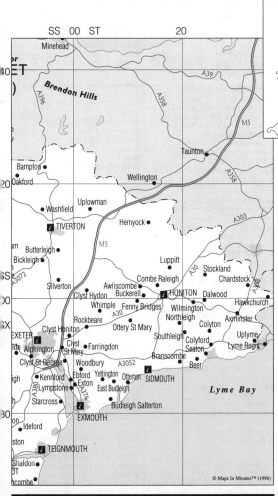

SS 00 ST   20

Minehead

Brendon Hills

A396

A39

A358

M5

Taunton

Bampton

Oakford

Wellington

Washfield

Uplowman

A358

A303

TIVERTON

Hemyock

M5

Butterleigh

Bickleigh

A3072

Luppitt

Silverton

Awliscombe

Combe Raleigh

Stockland

Chardstock

Clyst Hydon

Buckerell

HONITON

Dalwood

A30

Whimple

Fenny Bridges

Wilmington

Hawkchurch

Rockbeare

Northleigh

Axminster

EXETER

Clyst Honiton

Ottery St Mary

Colyton

Alphington

Clyst

Farringdon

Southleigh

Colyford

Uplyme

St Mary

Seaton

Lyme Regis

Clyst St George

Woodbury

A3052

Branscombe

Beer

Kennford

Ebford

Yettington

Otterton

SIDMOUTH

Lympstone

Exton

Starcross

East Budleigh

Lyme Bay

Budleigh Salterton

EXMOUTH

Ideford

TEIGNMOUTH

Shaldon

© Maps In Minutes™ (1996)

Tourist Information Centres

The Old Courthouse, Church Street, **Axminster**, Devon, EX13 5AQ, 01297 34386 (Easter to Oct).

North Devon Library, Tuly Street, **Barnstaple**, Devon, EX31 1TY, 08706 085531.

The Pill, The Quay, **Bideford**, Devon, EX39 2QQ, 01237 477676.

Caen Street Car Park, **Braunton**, Devon, EX33 1AA, 01271 816400 (Easter to Oct).

The Old Market House, The Quay, **Brixham**, Devon, TQ5 8TB, 01803 852861.

Fore Street, **Budleigh Salterton**, Devon, EX9 6NG, 01395 445275.

Cross Street, **Combe Martin**, Devon, EX34 0DN, 01271 883319 (Easter to Oct).

Plymouth Discovery Centre, **Crabtree**, Plymouth, Devon, PL3 6RN, 01752 266030 / 266031.

Market Street Car Park, Market Street, **Crediton**, Devon, EX17 2BN, 01363 772006 (Easter to Oct).

Engine House, Mayors Avenue, **Dartmouth**, Devon, TQ6 9YY, 01803 834224.

The Lawn, **Dawlish**, Devon, EX7 9AW, 01626 863589.

Civic Centre, Paris Street, **Exeter**, Devon, EX1 1JJ, 01392 72434.

Exeter Services, Sandygate (M5), **Exeter**, Devon, EX2 7NJ, 01392 437581.

Alexandra Terrace, **Exmouth**, Devon, EX8 1NZ, 01395 222299.

Dowell Street Car Park, **Honiton**, Devon, EX14 8LT, 01404 43716 (Easter to Oct).

The Promenade, **Ilfracombe**, Devon, EX34 9BX, 01271 863001.

Leonards Road, **Ivybridge**, Devon, PL21 0SL, 01752 897035.

The Quay, **Kingsbridge**, Devon, TQ7 1HS, 01548 853195.

Town Hall, Lee Road, **Lynton**, Devon, EX35 6BT, 01598 752225.

Poundwell Meadow Car Park, **Modbury**, Ivybridge, Devon, PL21 0QL, 01548 830159 (Easter to Oct).

6 Bridge House, Courtenay Street, **Newton Abbot**, Devon, TQ12 4QS, 01626 67494.

3 West Street, **Okehampton**, Devon, EX20 1HQ, 01837 53020 (Easter to Oct).

10b Broad Street, **Ottery St Mary**, Devon, EX11 1BZ, 01404 813964 (Easter to Oct).

The Esplanade, **Paignton**, Devon, TQ4 6BN, 01803 558383.

Island House, 9 The Barbican, **Plymouth**, Devon, PL1 2LS, 01752 264849.

Council Hall, Market Street, **Salcombe**, Devon, TQ8 8DE, 01548 842736 (Easter to Oct).

Tiverton Services, M5, Junction 27, **Sampford Peverell**, Tiverton, Devon, EX16 7SB, 08706 085531 (Easter to Oct).

The Esplanade, **Seaton**, Devon, EX12 2QQ, 01297 21660.

Harn Lane, **Sidmouth**, Devon, EX10 8XR, 01395 516441.

1 East Street, **South Molton**, Devon, EX36 3BU, 01769 574122 (Easter to Oct).

Town Hall, Bedford Square, **Tavistock**, Devon, PL19 0AE,   01822 612938 (Easter to Oct).

The Den, Sea Front, **Teignmouth**, Devon, TQ14 8BE, 01626 779769.

Phoenix Lane, **Tiverton**, Devon, EX16 6LU, 01884 255827.

Vaughan Parade, **Torquay**, Devon, TQ2 5JG, 01803 297428.

The Plains, **Totnes**, Devon, TQ9 5EJ, 01803 863168.

Red Barn Cafe Car Park, Barton Road, **Woolacombe**, Devon, EX34 7BT, 01271 870553 (Easter to Oct)

Alphington

SX9189   🏚 *New Inn*

The Old Mill, *Mill Lane, Alphington, Exeter, Devon, EX2 8SG.*
Historical premises in quiet area. full farm breakfast. Recommended for 26 years.
Open: All Year
01392 259977 Mrs Marchant
D: £10.50–£13.50 **S:** £10.50–£15
Beds: 2F 1D 1T 1S **Baths:** 1 Pr 1 Sh
🛏 🄿 (8) ⊬ 📺 🎂 🖤 ⓥ 🎓 &

Appledore (Bideford)

SS4630   🏚 *Seagate Hotel*

The Seagate Hotel, *The Quay, Appledore, Bideford, Devon, EX39 1QS.*
C17th riverside inn. Quaint fishing village on Torridge Estuary.
Open: All Year
01237 472589 (also fax)
Mr & Mrs Gent
D: £25–£35 **S:** £29–£35
Beds: 1F 5D 1T **Baths:** 7 Pr
🛏 🄿 (10) 📺 🎂 🗙 🖤 ⓥ 🎓 cc

Ash Mill

SS7823

Kerscott Farm, *Ash Mill, South Molton, Devon, EX36 4QG.*
Peacefully quiet rural retreat. Working Exmoor beef/sheep farm mentioned in Domesday Book (1086).
Open: All Year (not Xmas)
01769 550262 Mrs Sampson
D: £20 **S:** £25
Beds: 2D 1T **Baths:** 3 En
🄿 (6) ⊬ 📺 🗙 🖤 🎓

Ashburton

SX7570   🏚 *Dartbridge Inn, Abbey Inn*

Rosary Mount House, *Ashburton, Newton Abbot, Devon, TQ13 7JL.*
Open: All Year (not Xmas/New Year)
Grades: AA 3 Diamond
01364 653900 Mr Stone
Fax: 01364 653821
annette@rosarymount.co.uk
D: £17.50–£20 **S:** £20–£40
Beds: 2D 1T **Baths:** 2 Sh
🛏 (8) 🄿 (6) ⊬ 📺 🖤 🎓
A luxuriously furnished Country House (circa 1857) standing in its own landscaped gardens, nesting at Dartmoor's edge just inside the National Country Park, Rosary Mount is ideal for exploring the Moors.

Atherington

SS5922

The Village Shop and Tea Rooms, *The Square, Atherington, Umberleigh, Devon, EX37 9HY.*
C17th building in pretty North Devon village. Friendly comfortable atmosphere.
Open: All Year (not Xmas/New Year)
01769 560248 Mr & Mrs Hart
D: £18 **S:** £18
Beds: 1T 1D **Baths:** 1 Sh
🛏 ⊬ 📺 🎂 🗙 🎓

National Grid References are for villages, towns and cities – not for individual houses

---

Aveton Gifford

SX6947   🏚 *Sloop Inn, Church House Inn*

Marsh Mills, *Aveton Gifford, Kingsbridge, Devon, TQ7 4JW.*
Mill house, pond, stream, gardens, orchard, small farm. Friendly animals.
Open: All Year (not Xmas/New Year)
01548 550549 (also fax)
Mrs Newsham
newsham@marshmills.co.uk
D: £18–£22 **S:** £18–£22
Beds: 2T 2D 1S **Baths:** 2 En 1 Sh 1 Pr
🛏 (6) 🄿 (6) ⊬ 🎂 🎂 🎓

Court Barton Farmhouse, *Aveton Gifford, Kingsbridge, Devon, TQ7 4LE.*
Delightful C16th farmhouse in colourful gardens. You'll love our scrumptious breakfasts. **Open:** All Year (not Xmas)
01548 550312 Mrs Balkwill
Fax: 01548 550128
jill@courtbarton.co.uk
D: £22–£30 **S:** £24–£35
Beds: 2F 2D 2T 1S **Baths:** 6 En 1 Sh
🛏 🄿 (10) 📺 🎂 ⓥ 🎓

Awliscombe

ST1301   🏚 *Awliscombe Inn, Otter Inn*

Wessington Farm, *Awliscombe, Honiton, Devon, EX14 0NU.*
Elegant late Victorian stone farmhouse in designated Area of Outstanding Natural Beauty. **Open:** All Year
Grades: ETC 4 Diamond, Silver
01404 42280 Mrs Summers
Fax: 01404 45271
b&b@eastdevon.com
D: £20–£25 **S:** £20–£40
Beds: 1D 2T **Baths:** 2 En 1 Pr
🛏 🄿 (10) ⊬ 📺 🎂 ⓥ 🎓

Threshays, *Awliscombe, Honiton, Devon, EX14 3QB.*
Tastefully converted cob barn on non-working farm. Lovely views.
Open: All Year
01404 43551 (also fax) Mrs Gillingham
D: £16 **S:** £16
Beds: 1F 1D **Baths:** 1 Sh
🛏 🄿 (6) ⊬ 📺 🎂 ⓥ

Axminster

SY2998   🏚 *Hunters Lodge, George*

Millbrook Farmhouse, *Chard Road, Axminster, Devon, EX13 5EG.*
Open: All Year (not Xmas)
01297 35351 Ms Gay **Fax: 01297 35739**
D: £20 **S:** £–£25
Beds: 1D 1T **Baths:** 1 En 1 Pr
🛏 🄿 (3) ⊬ 📺 🗙 🎂 ⓥ 🎓
Millbrook Farmhouse is a Grade II Listed building in rural surroundings on the edge of Axminster. All rooms have an olde worlde charm with all modern comforts, including satellite TV in all bedrooms. Non-smoking establishment.

Mount House, *Lyme Road, Axminster, Devon, EX13 5BL.*
Large regency family house. Warm welcome, good food, lovely countryside.
Open: All Year
01297 34630 Mrs Morrison
D: £16–£18 **S:** £16–£20
Beds: 2F 1D **Baths:** 2 En 1 Sh
🛏 🄿 📺 🎂 🗙 🖤 ⓥ 🎓

Coaxdon Farm, *Smallridge, Coaxdon, Axminster, Devon, EX13 7LP.*
Peace and tranquillity set in 14 acres with indoor pool.
Open: All Year (not Xmas/New Year)
Grades: ETC 4 Diamond
01297 35540 N & D Ray
D: £22–£34
Beds: 2F 1D **Baths:** 2 En
🛏 🄿 (20) ⊬ 📺 🎂 ⓥ 🎓 &

Highridge Guest House, *Lyme Road, Axminster, Devon, EX13 5BQ.*
Cosy accommodation, pretty gardens, ponds with wild fowl.
Open: All Year (not Xmas)
01297 34037 Mrs Putt
D: £16.50 **S:** fr £16.50
Beds: 1F 1T 1S **Baths:** 1 Sh
📺 🎂 🗙 🖤 ⓥ 🎓

Bampton

SS9522   🏚 *Masons Arms, Seahorse*

Manor Mill House, *Bampton, Devon, EX16 9LP.*
Welcoming C17th home in historic Bampton. Ideal base, close to Exmoor.
Open: All Year
Grades: ETC 4 Diamond, Silver Award
01398 332211 Mrs Ayres
Fax: 01398 332009
stay@manormill.demon.co.uk
D: £21–£24
Beds: 2D 1T **Baths:** 3 En
🄿 (20) ⊬ 📺 🎂 ⓥ 🎓

Harton Farm, *Oakford, Tiverton, Devon, EX16 9HH.*
Peaceful farmhouse. Home grown additive free meat, vegetables. Friendly animals.
Open: All Year (not Xmas/New Year)
Grades: ETC 3 Diamond
01398 351209 (also fax)
Mrs Head
harton@eclipse.co.uk
D: £16–£17 **S:** £16–£17
Beds: 1F 1T **Baths:** 1 Sh
🛏 (4) 🄿 (2) 📺 🎂 🗙 ⓥ 🎓

Barnstaple

SS5633   🏚 *Windsor Arms, Williams Arms, Rolle Quay Inn, North Country Inn, Pyne Arms, Ring O'Bells, Chichester Arms*

Crossways, *Braunton Road, Barnstaple, Devon, EX31 1JY.*
Detached house - town & Tarka Trail 150 yards, bicycle hire.
Open: All Year
01271 379120 Mr & Mrs Tysn
D: fr £15 **S:** fr £17
Beds: 1F 1D 1T **Baths:** 2 Pr 1 Sh
🛏 🄿 (6) ⊬ 📺 🗙 🎂 🎓

Mount Sandford, Landkey Road, Barnstaple, Devon, EX32 0HL.
Georgian house in 1.5 acres gardens. 2 double, 1 twin, all ensuite.
Open: All Year (not Xmas)
01271 342354 Mrs White
D: £18–£22 **S:** fr £20
Beds: 1F 1D 1T **Baths:** 3 En
🛏 (3) 🅿 (3) 🏷 📺 🖾 📶 ♿

Beer

SY2289 🍺 Anchor Inn, Dolphin

Bay View Guest House, Fore Street, Beer, Seaton, Devon, EX12 3EE.
Seafront location, coastal views, large comfortable rooms and great breakfasts!
Open: Easter to Nov
Grades: AA 3 Diamond
01297 20489 Mr & Mrs Oswald
D: fr £15.50 **S:** fr £15.50
Beds: 1F 1T 4D 2S **Baths:** 3 En 1 Pr 4 Sh
🛏 📺 🍴 🖾 ♿

Garlands, Stovar Long Lane, Beer, Seaton, Devon, EX12 3EA.
Edwardian character house in an acre of ground - superb views sea and Devon countryside. **Open:** All Year (not Xmas)
01297 20958 Ms Harding
Fax: 01297 23869
nigelharding1@compuserve.com
D: £20–£22.50 **S:** £30–£33
Beds: 2F 2D 1T 1S **Baths:** 6 En
🛏 🅿 (10) 📺 🍴 🖾 ♿ cc

Pamber House, Clapps Lane, Beer, Seaton, Devon, EX12 3HD.
Set in idyllic fishing village. Quiet positions, 2 minutes' walk from village and beach. **Open:** All Year
01297 20722 (also fax) Mrs Cummins
D: fr £21 **S:** fr £28
Beds: 1F 2D **Baths:** 3 Pr
🛏 (7) 🅿 (3) 🏷 📺 🖾 ♿

Beeson

SX8140 🍺 Cricket Inn

Marybank House, Beeson, Kingsbridge, Devon, TQ7 2HW.
Open: May to Oct
01548 580531
B.M Honeywill
D: £18.50–£25 **S:** £18.50–£28
Beds: 1T 2D **Baths:** 1 En 1 Pr
🛏 🅿 (2) 🏷 📺 🍴 📶 ♿
Beautifully located Victorian country house, have delicious breakfasts whilst enjoying sea views.

Belstone

SX6293 🍺 Tors Inn

Moorlands House, Belstone, Okehampton, Devon, EX20 1QZ.
Open: All Year
01837 840549 Mr Weaver
D: £18–£20 **S:** £20–£25
Beds: 2T 2D **Baths:** 1 En 1 Pr 1 Sh
🛏 🅿 (6) 📺 🍴 🖾 ♿
Beautifully situated on the edge of unspoilt Dartmoor village with superb Moorland views. Direct access to Moor for excellent walking/ riding/ cycling. Five minutes walk to friendly village pub for good home cooked food. Ideal base for touring Devon/ Cornwall.

Moor Hall, Belstone, Okehampton, Devon, EX20 1QZ.
Glorious views, unspoilt peaceful village. Dartmoor is our front garden.
Open: Easter to Oct
01837 840604 Mrs Wood
D: £18–£20 **S:** £20
Beds: 2D 1T **Baths:** 2 En 1 Pr
🛏 (13) 🅿 (2) 🏷 📺 🖾 📶 ♿

Berry Pomeroy

SX8261 🍺 Pig & Whistle, Kingsbridge Inn

Berry Farm, Berry Pomeroy, Totnes, Devon, TQ9 6LG.
Welcome, spacious, clean and comfortable. Ideal for coast and moors.
Open: All Year
01803 863231 Mrs Nicholls
D: £17–£18 **S:** £17–£20
Beds: 1F 1D 1T **Baths:** 1 En 1 Sh
🛏 (3) 🅿 (4) 🏷 📺 ✗ 📶 ♿

Berrynarbor

SS5646 🍺 Old Goose, Globe Inn, Miss Muffits

Tower Cottage, Berrynarbor, Ilfracombe, Devon, EX34 9SE.
Charming Cottage with beautiful garden in 'Best kept village Berrynarbor'.
Open: All Year (not Xmas/New Year)
01271 883408
tombartlettbooks@berrynarbor.fsnet.co.uk
D: £18–£22 **S:** £25
Beds: 1F 1D **Baths:** 2 En
🛏 🅿 🏷 📺 🖾 ♿

Langleigh House, Berrynarbor, Ilfracombe, Devon, EX34 9SG.
Set in delightful North Devon. Lovely gardens with stream, barbecue area.
Open: All Year (not Xmas)
01271 883410 Mr & Mrs Pierpoint
Fax: 01271 882396
D: £17.50–£24.50 **S:** £23.50–£24.50
Beds: 1F 3D 1T **Baths:** 5 En 2 Pr
🛏 🅿 (6) 🏷 📺 🍴 🖾 ♿ cc

Sloley Farm, Castle Hill, Berrynarbor, Ilfracombe, Devon, EX34 9SX.
Enjoy the peace of Berrynarbor, a quintessential English village, from our superb ensuite rooms.
Open: All Year (not Xmas)
01271 883032
Mrs Mountain & Mr & Mrs J Boxall
Fax: 01271 882675
D: £18–£25 **S:** £18–£25
Beds: 2D 1T **Baths:** 3 En
🅿 (10) 🏷 📺 🖾 📶 ♿ ♿

Bickington (Newton Abbot)

SX7972 🍺 Dartmoor Halfway House, Toby Jug

Chipley Farm, Bickington, Newton Abbot, Devon, TQ12 6JW.
A delightful modern farmhouse nestling into the southern slope of a beautiful Devon valley. **Open:** All Year
01626 821486 (also fax) Mrs Westcott
louisachipleyfarm@callnetuk.com
D: £20–£25 **S:** £25–£40
Beds: 1F 1D 1T **Baths:** 1 En 2 Sh
🛏 🅿 (6) 🏷 📺 ✗ 🖾 📶 ♿

Bickleigh (Tiverton)

SS9407 🍺 Fishermans Cot, The Trout

The Old Post Office, Bickleigh, Tiverton, Devon, EX16 8RH.
Open: All Year
01884 855731 Mr Latchem
Fax: 0700 0783845
bickleighpostoffice@asgardltd.co.uk
D: £20–£25 **S:** £20
Beds: 1D 1T 1S **Baths:** 2 En 1 Pr 1 Sh
🛏 🅿 🏷 🍴 ✗ 🖾 📶 ♿ ♿
Stay somewhere special. Home from Home our guests say. Trained nurse proprietor available. Visit Exeter, Dartmoor the coast Exmoor beautiful Dunster and Bickleigh castle national trust houses 20 minutes drive. We offer light convalesence, rest relaxation, superb quality accommodation, good valve.

Bickleigh Cottage Hotel, Bickleigh Bridge, Bickleigh, Tiverton, Devon, EX16 8RS.
C17th riverside hotel, thatched, family-run for 65 yrs.
Open: Easter to Oct
01884 855230 Mr Cochrane
D: £22.50–£25 **S:** £25–£30
Beds: 5D 3T 1S **Baths:** 7 En 2 Pr
🛏 (14) 🅿 (10) 🏷 📺 ✗ 🖾 ♿ cc

Willow Grove House, The Orchard, Bickleigh, Tiverton, Devon, EX16 8RD.
Bickleigh by the River Exe. Thatched village, waterside restaurant in walking distance. **Open:** All Year
01884 855263 Mrs Lock
D: £20–£22 **S:** £17.50–£20
Beds: 1D 1T 1S **Baths:** 2 En 1 Pr
🛏 (5) 🅿 (3) 📺 🖾 📶 ♿

East Barton, Bickleigh, Tiverton, Devon, EX16 8HD.
Picturesque Exe Valley location. Luxury ensuite accommodation in unique character farmhouse. **Open:** All Year
01884 855244
pam.jim@eastbarton.demon.co.uk
D: £18.50–£23 **S:** £22.50–£25
Beds: 2D 1T
🛏 🅿 (10) 🏷 📺 🖾 📶 ♿ ♿

Bideford

SS4526 🍺 Tanton's Hotel, Farmers Arms, Crab & Ale, Royal Hotel, Swan Inn, Joiners' Arms, Hunters' Inn, Sunset Hotel

Sunset Hotel, Landcross, Bideford, Devon, EX39 5JA.
Open: Easter to Nov
Grades: ETC 3 Diamond, AA 3 Diamond
01237 472962 Mrs Lamb
bellcraig@eidosnet.co.uk
D: £27–£30 **S:** £25–£36
Beds: 2F 2D 2T **Baths:** 4 En
🅿 (8) 🏷 📺 ✗ 🖾 📶 ♿ cc
Small country Hotel. Peaceful location overlooking spectacular scenery and Tarka Trail. 11/2 miles from Bideford town. Highly recommended quality accommodation. All ensuites- CTV and beverages. Superb food, everything home-made, special diets catered for. Licensed. Private parking. Non smoking establishment.

B&B owners may vary rates - be sure to check when booking

The Mount Hotel, *Northdown Road, Bideford, Devon, EX39 3LP.*
Open: Jan to Dec
Grades: AA 4 Diamond
01237 473748 Mr & Mrs Laugharne
themount@4unet.co.uk
D: £23–£25 **S:** £25–£33
Beds: 1F 3D 1T 2S **Baths:** 7 En
⌂ ⅋ (4) ⌖ ⊡ ▥ ♨ ⚘ **cc**
Charming Georgian licensed guest house only 5 minutes' walk to town centre, private lounge for guests' use, all rooms ensuite, attractive garden, car parking for guests. Convenient for touring N Devon coastline, Clovelly, Lundy, Exmoor and Dartmoor. No smoking.

Bigbury
SX6646 ⌕ *The Royal Oak*

Lincombe, *Bigbury, Kingsbridge, Devon, TQ7 4BD.*
Superb rural setting. Views, Garden, Terrace, Pond and warm welcome.
Open: All Year (not Xmas/New Year)
01548 810426 Ms Phelan
tuphelan@clara.co.uk
D: £20–£25 **S:** £20–£25
Beds: 1F 1T 1D **Baths:** 3 En
⌂ ⅋ ⌖ ⊡ ♨ ▥ ⊻ ♨

Bigbury on Sea
SX6544

Folly Foot, *Challaborough, Bigbury On Sea, Kingsbridge, TQ7 4JB.*
50m sandy beach/ South West Way. Friendly welcome, bungalow.
Open: Feb-Oct
01548 810036 D: £20–£26 **S:** £20–£25
Beds: 1F 2D 1S **Baths:** 2 En 1 Sh
⌂ (6) ⅋ (6) ⌖ ⊡ ▥ ♨

Black Dog
SS8009 ⌕ *Black Dog Inn*

Oaklands, *Black Dog, Crediton, Devon, EX17 4RQ.*
Friendly accommodation in peaceful countryside, central for coast and moors.
Open: All Year
01884 860645 Mrs Bradford
Fax: 01884 861030
D: £18–£20 **S:** £20–£22
Beds: 1F 1D 1T **Baths:** 2 En 1 Pr
⌂ ⅋ (6) ⊡ ▥ ⊻ ♨

Lower Brownstone Farm, *Black Dog, Crediton, Devon, EX17 4QE.*
Peaceful Georgian farmhouse. Lawns, ponds, birds, farm animals, artwork.
Open: All Year
01363 877256 Mrs Wedlake
D: £12.50–£15 **S:** £12–£15
Beds: 3D **Baths:** 2 Sh
⌂ ⅋ (10) ⌖ ⊡ ♨ ✗ ⊻

Blackawton
SX8050 ⌕ *Normandy Arms, George Inn, Forces Tavern*

Seven Gates Farm, *Blackawton, Totnes, Devon, TQ9 7AJ.*
Farm bungalow, lovely country views, near golf, Woodland Country Park.
Open: Easter to Oct
01803 712339 Mrs Dayment
D: £15–£16.50 **S:** £16.50–£17.50
Beds: 1F 1D **Baths:** 1 Sh
⌂ (2) ⅋ (2) ⌖ ⊡ ♨ ▥ ⊻ ♨ ⚘

Woodside Cottage, *Blackawton, Totnes, Devon, TQ9 7BL.*
Fine old C18th house. Quiet, peaceful, yet only 4 miles from Dartmouth.
Open: Mar to Oct
01803 712375 Mrs Clark
Fax: 01803 712605
b&b@woodside-cottage.demon.co.uk
D: £20–£25 **S:** £27–£33
Beds: 3D 1T **Baths:** 3 En
⌂ (12) ⅋ (6) ⌖ ⊡ ▥ ⊻ ♨

Bovey Tracey
SX8178 ⌕ *Cleave Inn, White Hart Hotel, Clay Cutters*

Front House Lodge, *East Street, Bovey Tracey, Newton Abbot, Devon, TQ13 9EL.*
Delightful 16th century house, edge of Dartmoor. Antiques, atmosphere. Delicious breakfasts.
Open: All Year (not Xmas)
Grades: AA 5 Diamond
01626 832202 (also fax)
fronthouselodge@yahoo.co.uk
D: £22.50–£25 **S:** £25–£30
Beds: 1F 3D 2T
⅋ (6) ⌖ ⊡ ✗ ▥ ⊻ ♨ **cc**

Whitstone Farm, *Bovey Tracey, TQ13 9NA.*
Restored farmhouse, luxury accommodation overlooking Dartmoor, beautiful grounds, bountiful breakfasts.
Open: All Year
01626 832258 (also fax)
Mrs Bunn
D: £25–£27.50 **S:** £35–£38.50
Beds: 1D 1T 1S **Baths:** 3 En
⅋ (4) ⌖ ⊡ ✗ ▥ ⊻ ♨

Branscombe
SY1988 ⌕ *Masons Arms, Fountain Head*

Hole Mill, *Branscombe, Seaton, Devon, EX12 3BX.*
Open: All Year
01297 680314 Mr & Mrs Hart
D: £17.50–£21 **S:** £25–£34
Beds: 2D 1T **Baths:** 2 Sh
⌂ (6) ⅋ (6) ⌖ ⊡ ♨ ▥ ⊻ ♨
Old converted watermill providing comfortable accommodation in style of yesteryear. Beams, brass beds, inglenook lounge, garden, stream. No rush, no town noises - just peace/relaxation. Featured in 'Which? The Good Bed & Breakfast Guide' & 'Staying Off the Beaten Track'.

The Chapel House, *Branscombe, Seaton, Devon, EX12 3AY.*
Converted chapel, just behind the cliffs, with spectacular outlook over NT wooded valley. **Open:** All Year
01297 680520 Mr & Mrs Van den Broeck
D: £18–£20 **S:** £25
Beds: 1F 2D **Baths:** 2 Sh
⌂ (6) ⅋ (3) ⌖ ⊡ ♨ ♨ ▥

Bratton Fleming
SS6437 ⌕ *Black Venus*

Haxton Down Farm, *Bratton Fleming, Barnstaple, Devon, EX32 7JL.*
Peaceful working farm in central position. Warm welcome, good food.
Open: Easter to Nov
01598 710275 Mrs Burge
ron-steph@buckgrove.freeserve.co.uk
D: £17–£20 **S:** £18–£20
Beds: 1F 1D **Baths:** 2 En
⌂ ⅋ (3) ⊡ ♨ ✗ ▥ ⊻ ♨

Braunton
SS4936 ⌕ *Agricultural Inn*

St Merryn, *Higher Park Road, Braunton, Devon, EX33 2LG.*
Open: Jan to Dec
01271 813805 Mrs Bradford
Fax: 01271 812097
willieb@argonet.co.uk
D: £20–£22 **S:** £20–£22
Beds: 1F 1T 1D **Baths:** 1 En 2 Pr
⌂ ⅋ (5) ⌖ ⊡ ♨ ✗ ▥ ⊻ ♨
Beautiful 1930's home set in delightful large garden. Tranquil setting with excellent parking and within easy walking distance of village. Excellent beaches and golf courses within a short drive.

Pixie Dell, *1 Willand Rd, Braunton, N. Devon, EX33 1AX.*
Large chalet bungalow and garden. Warm welcome assured.
Open: All Year (not Xmas)
01271 812233 Mrs Dale
D: £18 **S:** £18–£20
Beds: 1D 2T 1S **Baths:** 2 Sh
⌂ ⅋ (4) ⌖ ⊡ ♨ ▥ ♨ ⚘

Bridestowe
SX5189 ⌕ *White Hart*

The White Hart Inn, *Fore Street, Bridestowe, Okehampton, Devon, EX20 4EL.*
C17th country inn, close to Dartmoor. Same owners for 39 years.
Open: All Year **Grades:** ETC 3 Diamond
01837 861318 (also fax) Mr Owen
whihartinn@aol.com
D: £23.75 **S:** £29.95
Beds: 2D **Baths:** 2 En
⅋ (20) ⊡ ⊻ ♨ **cc**

Week Farm, *Bridestowe, Okehampton, Devon, EX20 4HZ.*
C17th farmhouse home-from-home, guests returning annually.
Open: All Year (not Xmas)
01837 861221 (also fax) Ms Hockridge
email.weekfarm@biscuits.win-uk.net
D: £23–£24 **S:** £23–£24
Beds: 2F 3D **Baths:** 5 En
⌂ ⅋ ⌖ ⊡ ♨ ✗ ▥ ⊻ ♨ ⚘ **3 cc**

Brimley

SX8077 🍴 *Rock Inn*

Corbyns Brimley, *Higher Brimley, Bovey Tracey, Newton Abbot, TQ13 9JT.*
Within Dartmoor National Park, picturesque C16th former longhouse with beams and inglenooks.
Open: All Year (not Xmas)
01626 833332 Mrs White
D: £24–£25 **S:** £38
Beds: 2T **Baths:** 1 Pr 1 Sh
🄿 (6) ⊁ 📺 Ⅴ ♨

Brixham

SX9255 🍴 *The Vigilance, Smugglers Haunt Hotel, Blue Anchor, Berry Head Hotel, Weary Ploughman*

Smugglers Haunt Hotel & Restaurant, *Church Hill, Brixham, Devon, TQ5 8HH.*
Open: All Year
Grades: AA 1 Star
01803 853050 Mr Hudson
enquiries@
smugglershaunt-hotel-devon.co.uk
D: £24–£27 **S:** fr £29
Beds: 4F 7D 4T 1S **Baths:** 16 En
🄲 📺 � ✕ 🔲 ♨ ✿ ♨
Friendly, private 300-year-old hotel. Up to 100 main course meals. Pets and children welcome. From 1st October-1st February (not Xmas period) 3 nights for the cost of 2.

Richmond House Hotel, *Higher Manor Road, Brixham, Devon, TQ5 8HA.*
Comfortable Victorian house with spacious rooms and a homely atmosphere.
Open: Feb to Dec
Grades: ETC 3 Diamond, AA 3 Diamond
01803 882391 (also fax)
Mr Hayhurst
D: £16–£24
Beds: 2F 4D **Baths:** 5 En 1 Pr
🄲 🄿 (6) ⊁ 📺 🔲 ♨ cc

Westbury, *51 New Road, Brixham, TQ5 8NL.*
Charming Georgian house, short level walk from shops and harbour.
Open: All Year
01803 851684 (also fax)
ann.burt@lineone.net
D: £16–£23 **S:** £16–£23
Beds: 4F 2D **Baths:** 4 En 1 Sh
🄲 (6) 🄿 ⊁ 📺 Ⅴ ♨

Mimosa Guest House, *75 New Road, Brixham, Devon, TQ5 8NL.*
Spacious, well-furnished Georgian house close to harbour and town centre.
Open: All Year (not Xmas)
01803 855719 Mr Kershaw
D: £15–£17 **S:** £15–£17
Beds: 2D 1T 1S **Baths:** 1 En 2 Pr
🄲 (5) 🄿 (3) 📺 🔲 Ⅴ ♨

All details shown are as supplied by B&B owners in Autumn 2000

Broadhempston

SX8066 🍴 *Coppa Dolla, Monk's Retreat*

Manor Farm, *Broadhempston, Totnes, Devon, TQ9 6BD.*
Elegant Georgian farmhouse set in peaceful rural village, surrounded by 7 acres green fields.
Open: All Year (not Xmas)
01803 813260 (also fax)
clappfamily@shines.swis.net
D: £24–£26 **S:** £24–£26
Beds: 1D 1T **Baths:** 1 En 1 Pr
🄲 (12) 🄿 (4) ⊁ 📺 � 🔲 Ⅴ ♨

Buckerell

ST1200 🍴 *Greyhound Inn, Otter Inn*

Broadlands, *Buckerell, Honiton , Devon, EX14 3EP.*
Open: All Year
01404 850894 Mrs Pratt
D: £20–£25 **S:** £25–£30
Beds: 2T 1D **Baths:** 2 En 1 Pr
🄲 🄿 (3) ⊁ 📺 🔲 ♨
Charming house surrounded by country views. Approx. 2 miles from Honiton. Convenient for Exeter and South Coast. Enjoy total relaxation on the terrace and savour the panoramic views. A warm welcome awaits you offering excellent Bed and Breakfast with comfortable accommodation.

Splatthayes, *Buckerell, Honiton, Devon, EX14 0ER.*
Exquisite food & aromatherapy or reflexology in peaceful thatched village house.
Open: All Year (not Xmas)
01404 850464 (also fax)
Ms Dalton
mandy.dalton@ukgateway.net
D: £22 **S:** £22
Beds: 2F 1D 1T **Baths:** 1 En 1 Sh
🄲 (9) 🄿 (6) ⊁ 📺 ✕ 🔲 Ⅴ ♨ ♿

Buckland Monachorum

SX4968

Uppaton Country Guest House, *Coppicetown Road, Buckland Monachorum, Yelverton, Devon, PL20 7LL.*
Beautiful Victorian mansion between Tavistock & Plymouth on the edge of Dartmoor National Park.
Open: All Year
01822 855511 Mr & Dr McQueen
D: £20–£25 **S:** £20–£25
Beds: 1F 2D 2T 1S **Baths:** 3 En 2 Sh
🄲 🄿 ⊁ 📺 � ✕ 🔲 Ⅴ ♨ ♨

Budleigh Salterton

SY0682 🍴 *Salterton Arms*

Chapter House, *6 Westbourne Terrace, Budleigh Salterton, Devon, EX9 6BR.*
Budleigh Salterton self-catering ensuite family room with own sitting room.
Open: All Year
01395 444100 Ms Simmons
D: £20–£25 **S:** fr £20
Beds: 1F **Baths:** 1 En
🄲 (1) ⊁ 📺 � 🔲 ✿ ♨

Long Range Hotel, *Budleigh Salterton, Devon, EX9 6HS.*
A haven of peace and tranquillity, close to sea and countryside.
Open: All Year **Grades:** AA 4 Diamond
01395 443321 Mr & Mrs Morton
Fax: 01395 445220
D: £37.50–£49.50 **S:** £25–£30
Beds: 1F 3D 2T 1S **Baths:** 6 En 1 Pr
🄲 🄿 (7) ⊁ 📺 🔲 Ⅴ ♨ ♨ cc

Rosehill, *West Hill Lane, Budleigh Salterton, Devon, EX9 6BO.*
This unique property oozes relaxation - rooms spacious, garden Victorian, ambience restful. **Open:** All Year
01395 444031 (also fax) Mr Taylor
rosehill@bnbrelaxed.demon.co.uk
D: £20–£27.50 **S:** £20–£27.50
Beds: 1F 2D 1T 1S **Baths:** 4 En 1 Pr
🄲 🄿 (4) 📺 � 🔲 ♨ cc

Butterleigh

SS9708 🍴 *Butterleigh Inn*

Sunnyside Farmhouse, *Butterleigh, Cullompton, Devon, EX15 1PP.*
Sunnyside is set amongst 100 acres of glorious mid-Devon countryside. Convenient for Tiverton & Cullompton.
Open: All Year (not Xmas)
01884 855322 Mrs Hill
D: £17.50–£20 **S:** fr £20
Beds: 2F 3D 2T **Baths:** 3 En
🄲 🄿 📺 � ✕ ♨

Cadbury

SS9104 🍴 *The Bell, Thorverton Arms*

Beers Farm, *Cadbury, Exeter, Devon, EX5 5PY.*
Comfortable farmhouse in beautiful countryside overlooking peaceful valley. Attractive gardens. **Open:** All Year
01884 855426 Mrs Holmes
beersfarm@cs.com
D: £18 **S:** £18
Beds: 1F 1D **Baths:** 2 En
🄲 🄿 (6) ⊁ 📺 ♨

Chagford

SX7087 🍴 *Three Crowns, Ring O' Bells, Bullers Arms, Sandy Park Inn*

St Johns West, *Chagford, Newton Abbot, Devon, TQ13 8HJ.*
Tranquil setting, warm welcome, comfortable beds, sumptuous breakfasts.
Open: All Year
01647 432468 Mr & Mrs West
D: £22.50 **S:** £25–£27.50
Beds: 3T **Baths:** 3 En
🄲 (12) 🄿 (5) ⊁ 📺 � ✕ 🔲 Ⅴ ♨

Glendarah House, *Lower Street, Chagford, Newton Abbot, Devon, TQ13 8BZ.*
Spacious Victorian house peaceful location. Five minutes' walk from village centre. **Open:** All Year (not Xmas)
Grades: ETC 4 Diamond, Silver, AA 4 Diamond
01647 433270 Mr & Mrs Croxen
Fax: 01647 433483
enquiries@glendarah-house.co.uk
D: £26–£29 **S:** £26–£29
Beds: 3D 3T 1S **Baths:** 7 En
🄲 (10) 🄿 (7) ⊁ 📺 � 🔲 ♨ cc

Lawn House, 24 Mill Street, Chagford,
Newton Abbot, Devon, TQ13 7AW.
Friendly B&B. C18th thatched house, near
centre Chagford.
Open: All Year
01647 433329 Mrs Law
D: £20–£24 **S:** £25–£40
Beds: 1F 1D **Baths:** 1 En 1 Pr
⌂ (8) ⊬ ⊡ ⅋ Ⅲ. Ⅵ ♨

Ring O'Bells, 44 The Square, Chagford,
Newton Abbot, Devon, TQ13 8AH.
Right on the square of historic Dartmoor
Stannary town.
Open: All Year
01647 432466 Ms Pool
D: fr £22.50 **S:** £20–£30
Beds: 2D 1T 1S **Baths:** 2 En 1 Sh
⌂ (10) ⊬ ⊡ ⅋ ✕ Ⅲ. Ⅵ ♨

Chardstock

ST3004   ⌐ *The George*

Barn Owls Cottage, Chardstock,
Axminster, Devon, EX13 7BY.
Quality stone cottage. On edge of village
overlooking beautiful country views.
Open: Mar to Oct
01460 220475 (also fax)
Mrs Hafner
D: £17–£22 **S:** £15
Beds: 2D **Baths:** 1 En 1 Pr
🅿 (3) ⊬ ⊡ Ⅲ. ♨

Cheriton Bishop

SX7793   ⌐ *Old Thatch Inn*

Lewdon Farm, Medland Lane, Cheriton
Bishop, Exeter, Devon, EX6 6HF.
Listed character house in three acres.
Views of Dartmoor.
Open: All Year (not Xmas)
01647 24283 (office) Mr Dodgeon
Fax: 01647 24283
dodgydavid@compuserve.com
D: £18–£20 **S:** £18–£20
Beds: 1D **Baths:** 1 En
⌂ (2) 🅿 (3) ⊬ ⊡ Ⅲ. Ⅵ ♨

Cheriton Fitzpaine

SS8606

Jellicoe's, Higher Holn, Upham,
Cheriton Fitzpaine, Crediton, Devon,
EX17 4HN.
Peaceful cottage and garden. Beautiful
landscape. Convenient position.
Exceptional food.
Open: All Year (not Xmas)
01363 866165 (also fax)
Mr Jellicoe
jellicoes@higherholn.freeserve.co.uk
D: fr £22 **S:** fr £22
Beds: 1F 2D 1T **Baths:** 3 En
⌂ 🅿 (4) ⊬ ⊡ ✕ Ⅲ. Ⅵ ♨

Hayne Farm, Cheriton Fitzpaine,
Crediton, Devon, EX17 4HR.
Guest are welcome to our C17th working
beef and sheep farm.
Open: All Year (not Xmas)
01363 866392 Mrs Reed
D: £15–£16 **S:** £15–£18
Beds: 2D 1T **Baths:** 1 Sh
⌂ 🅿 (10) ⊡ ✕ Ⅲ. Ⅵ ♨

Chillington

SX7942   ⌐ *Church House Inn, Chilllington Inn,
Open Arms*

Coleridge, Chillington, Kingsbridge,
Devon, TQ7 2JG.
Georgian farmhouse on working farm
near Torcross and Slapton Sands.
Open: May to Oct
01548 580274 Mrs Darke
D: £18 **S:** £18
Beds: 2T 1D **Baths:** 1 Pr 1 Sh
⌂ 🅿 (2) ⊬ ⊡ ♨

Chudleigh

SX8679   ⌐ *The Manor*

Huxbear Barton, Teign Valley,
Chudleigh, Newton Abbot, Devon,
TQ13 0NY.
Spacious luxury barn conversion.
Extensive grounds, pond, stream. Rural
views. **Open:** All Year
01626 852670 Mrs Thomas
D: £21–£23.50 **S:** £25–£30
Beds: 1T 1D 1S **Baths:** 1 En 1 Pr
⌂ (12) 🅿 (6) ⊬ ⊡ Ⅲ. ♨

Chudleigh Knighton

SX8477   ⌐ *Claycutters Arms*

Church House, Chudleigh Knighton,
Newton Abbot, Devon, TQ13 0HE.
Elegant Georgian home near Dartmoor,
Exeter, seaside and several NT properties.
Open: All Year (not Xmas)
01626 852123 (also fax) Mr Brandon
brandon@churchhouse100.freeserve.co.uk
D: £19–£21 **S:** £22–£25
Beds: 2D 1T **Baths:** 2 En 1 Sh
⌂ (10) 🅿 (3) ⊬ ⊡ Ⅲ. Ⅵ ♨

Clawton

SX3599

Churchtown House, Clawton,
Holsworthy, Devon, EX22 6PS.
An elegant part-Georgian C17th
farmhouse with a friendly atmosphere.
Open: All Year
01409 271467 Mrs Farrow
farrow@churchtown100.freeserve.co.uk
D: £16–£18 **S:** fr £16
Beds: 1F 1D 1T **Baths:** 1 En 1 Sh
⌂ 🅿 (6) ✕ Ⅲ. ♨

Clearbrook

SX5265   ⌐ *Skylark Inn*

Sunbeam House, Clearbrook,
Yelverton, Devon, PL20 6JD.
Open: All Year (not Xmas)
01822 853871 Ms Newberry
Fax: 01822 855672
christine.newberry@lineone.net
D: £17.50 **S:** £20
Beds: 1D 1T **Baths:** 2 Sh
⌂ 🅿 (6) ⊬ ⊡ Ⅲ. Ⅵ ♨
Direct access to Dartmoor. Large double
fronted family house offering peace and
tranquillity. Good-sized bay-windowed
double bedrooms overlooking Dartmoor.
Friendly welcome, hearty country
breakfast. Close to local pub for evening
meals. Ideal for walking, cycling, fishing,
golf.

Clovelly

SS3225   ⌐ *New Inn, Farmers Arms, Red Lion*

The Old Smithy, Slerra Hill, Clovelly,
Bideford, Devon, EX39 5ST.
Cottage - converted C17th blacksmith's
forge. Large rooms, warm welcome.
Open: All Year (not Xmas)
01237 431202 Mrs Vanstone
D: £16.50–£20.50
Beds: 2F 1D **Baths:** 1 En 1 Pr 1 Sh
⌂ 🅿 (4) ⊬ ⊡ Ⅲ. Ⅵ ♨

Boat House Cottage, 148 Slerra Hill,
Clovelly, Bideford, Devon, EX39 5ST.
Delightful C17th cottage. Sea views.
Comfortable rooms, warm welcome
Open: Jan to Dec
01237 431209 Mrs May
D: £15–£16 **S:** £17–£18
Beds: 1F 1D 1T **Baths:** 1 En 1 Sh
⌂ (3) 🅿 (3) ⊬ ⊡ ⅋ ✕ Ⅲ. Ⅵ ♨ cc

New Inn Hotel, Clovelly, Bideford,
Devon, EX39 4TQ.
Beautifully restored inn. Heart of
peaceful heritage village. Sea views.
Open: All Year
Grades: ETC 3 Crown, AA 2 Star
01237 431303 Mr Murphy
Fax: 01237 431636
newinn@clovelly.co.uk
D: £34.25–£42.25 **S:** £34.25–£57.25
Beds: 7D 1S **Baths:** 8 En
⌂ 🅿 (200) ⊡ ⅋ ✕ Ⅲ. Ⅵ ♨ cc

Clyst Honiton

SX9893

Holbrook Farm, Clyst Honiton, Exeter,
Devon, EX5 2HR.
Delightful rooms with beautiful countryside views (own entrance, unrestricted
access). Tasty breakfasts, fresh produce.
Open: All Year **Grades:** AA 4 Diamond
01392 367000 Mrs Glanvill
heatherglanvill@holbrookfarm.co.uk
D: £19–£21 **S:** £18–£25
Beds: 1F 1D 1T **Baths:** 3 En
⌂ 🅿 (4) ⊬ ⊡ Ⅲ. Ⅵ ♨ ⅋

Clyst Hydon

ST0301

Town Tenement Farm, Clyst Hydon,
Cullompton, Devon, EX15 2NB.
16th Century farmhouse in quiet village,
comfortable stop for good food.
Open: All Year (not Xmas)
01884 277230 Ms Coleman
D: £16
Beds: 1D 1T 1F **Baths:** 1 En 1 Sh
🅿 ⅋ Ⅲ. cc

Clyst St George

SX9888   ⌐ *George & Dragon*

Marianne Pool Farm, Clyst St
George, Exeter, Devon, EX3 0NZ.
Devon longhouse, peaceful setting but
near to Exeter and coast. 2 miles M5
(J30). **Open:** Mar to Nov
01392 874939 Mrs Bragg
D: £17–£19 **S:** £18–£20
Beds: 1F 1T **Baths:** 1 En 1 Sh
⌂ 🅿 (2) ⊡ ⅋ Ⅵ ♨

BEDROOMS

F - Family
D - Double
T - Twin
S - Single

Clyst St Mary

SX9791 🍺 *The Diggers' Rest, White House*

Old Mill House, *Oil Mill Lane, Clyst St Mary, Exeter, Devon, EX5 1AG.*
Welcoming and very comfortable ensuite accommodation. Close to M5 Junction 30.
Open: All Year
01392 877733 Mrs Moore
Fax: 01392 461278
oldmillhouse@aol.com
D: £23–£25 **S:** £27–£30
Beds: 2D 1T
🛏 🅿 (5) ⅍ 🗹 🎀 🛢 ♨

Cockington

SX8963

Fairmount House Hotel, *Herbert Road, Cockington, Torquay, Devon, TQ2 6RW.*
Open: Mar to Oct
Grades: ETC 4 Diamond
01803 605446 (also fax)
Mr Richards
D: £25–£35.50 **S:** £25–£35.50
Beds: 2F 2T 4D 2S **Baths:** 8 En
🛏 (12) 🅿 (9) 🗹 🎀 ✕ 🛢 ♨ ♿ cc
Fairmount House Hotel , somewhere special. Unhurried English breakfast, quiet undisturbed nights, feel completely at home at small hotel in peaceful setting. Away from the busy sea front and near Cockington Village and Country Park. Fairmount offers quality, comfort and genuine friendly service.

Colebrooke

SS7700 🍺 *New Inn, Mare & Foal*

The Oyster, *Colebrooke, Crediton, Devon, EX17 5JQ.*
Peaceful, homely, modern, spacious bungalow in beautiful mid-Devon. Tea/coffee facilities and TV.
Open: All Year
01363 84576 Mrs Hockridge
D: £17 **S:** £17
Beds: 2D 1T **Baths:** 1 En 2 Pr
🛏 🅿 🗹 🎀 🛢 ♨ ♿ 1

Coleford

SS7701 🍺 *New Inn*

Butsford Barton, *Coleford, Crediton, Devon, EX17 5DH.*
Modern spacious farmhouse in beautiful mid-Devon countryside.
Open: Easter to Oct
01363 84353 Mrs Hockridge
D: £17–£18 **S:** £17–£18
Beds: 1F 1D 1T **Baths:** 1 Sh
🅿 ⅍ 🗹 ♨ ♨

Colyford

SY2592 🍺 *Wheelwright, White Hart*

Horriford Farm, *Holyford Lane, Colyford, Colyton, Devon, EX24 6HW.*
Open: All Year (not Xmas)
01297 552316 Mr & Mrs Pady
horriford@aol.com
D: £20–£21 **S:** £18
Beds: 1D 1T 2S **Baths:** 2 En 1 Pr
🛏 🅿 (3) ⅍ 🗹 🛢 ⍗
Attractive C16th farmhouse in quiet valley at end of Devon lane, close to coast near Devon/Dorset border. Guest rooms overlooking attractive garden. Excellent centre for exploring east Devon & west Dorset. Working farm with Devon cattle, sheep and alpacas.

Colyton

SY2493 🍺 *Kingfisher, Wheelwright*

Bonehayne Farm, *Colyton, Devon, EX24 6SG.*
Clean/tidy working farm. Glorious views, walks, fishing, coast 10 mins.
Open: All Year
01404 871416 Mrs Gould
thisfarm33@netscapeonline.co.uk
D: £16–£18 **S:** £18–£20
Beds: 1F 1D **Baths:** 1 Pr
🛏 🅿 ⅍ 🗹 🛢 ♨

The Toll House, *Umborne Bridge, Colyton, Devon, EX24 6EY.*
Attractive private toll house on quiet edge of this historic town.
Open: All Year (not Xmas)
01297 553739 D: £17.50–£20 **S:** £17.50–£20
Beds: 1D 1T 1S
🅿 (2) ⅍ 🗹 🛢 ⍗ ♨

Combe Martin

SS5846 🍺 *Dolphin Inn, Focsle Inn, Royal Marine*

Royal Marine, *Seaside, Combe Martin, Ilfracombe, EX34 0AW.*
Award winning pub with five superbly appointed ensuite rooms, cooked food, sea views. **Open:** All Year
01271 882470 Mr Lethaby
Fax: 01271 889080
D: £20–£25 **S:** £20–£25
Beds: 5F **Baths:** 5 En
🛏 🅿 🗹 🛢 ⍗ ♨ cc

Crimond, *King Street, Combe Martin, Ilfracombe, EX34 0BS.*
Friendly comfortable Victorian house. Hearty English breakfast. Close to sea.
Open: All Year (not Xmas)
01271 882348 Mr Parkes
Fax: 01271 882348
D: fr £17 **S:** fr £17
Beds: 1F 1D 1T 1S **Baths:** 1 Sh 4 En
🛏 ⅍ 🗹 🎀 🛢 ♨

Hillview Guest House, *Woodlands, Combe Martin, Ilfracombe, Devon, EX34 0AT.*
Beautifully situated Edwardian house. Quiet position offering comfort and cleanliness. **Open:** Easter to Oct
01271 882331 Mrs Bosley
hillviewgh@appleonline.net
D: £16–£18.50 **S:** £18–£20.50
Beds: 2D 1T **Baths:** 2 En 1 Pr
🅿 (6) ⅍ 🗹 🛢 ⍗ ♨

Glendower, *King Street, Combe Martin, Ilfracombe, Devon, EX33 2AL.*
Close to South West Coastal Path and seaside. **Open:** Easter to Nov
01271 883449 Mr & Mrs Barry
frankjbarry@netscapeonline.co.uk
D: £13–£14 **S:** £16–£18
Beds: 2D 1S **Baths:** 2 En 1 Sh
🛏 (1) 🅿 (3) 🗹 🎀 ⍗ ♨

Combe Raleigh

ST1502 🍺 *Otter Inn, Red Cow*

Pulshays, *Windgate Hill, Combe Raleigh, Honiton, Devon, EX14 0UJ.*
C17th thatched house nestling in a secluded hillside overlooking Honiton.
Open: All Year (not Xmas)
01404 891326 (also fax) Mrs Turrell
moiraturrell@cwcom.net
D: £18–£20 **S:** £16–£20
Beds: 1D 2S **Baths:** 1 Pr
🛏 (10) 🅿 (2) 🗹 🛢

Cornworthy

SX8255 🍺 *The Hunters Lodge*

Black Ness Cottage, *East Cornworthy, Cornworthy, Totnes, Devon, TQ9 7HQ.*
Delightful cottage, extensive gardens, idyllic rural situation, midway Totnes/Dartmouth.
Open: All Year (not Xmas)
01803 722467 Mrs Bryant
Fax: 01803 722209
bryaj@yahoo.com
D: £16–£20 **S:** £16–£20
Beds: 1D 1T **Baths:** 1 Sh
🛏 (8) 🅿 (4) ⅍ 🗹 🛢 ⍗ ♨

Cotleigh

ST2001

Barn Park Farm, *Stockland Hill, Cotleigh, Honiton, Devon, EX14 9JA.*
Farmhouse, full of character, home from home atmosphere in 140 acres of picturesque countryside.
Open: All Year (not Xmas)
01404 861297 (also fax) Mrs Boyland
D: £16–£20 **S:** £20
Beds: 2F **Baths:** 2 En
🛏 🅿 🗹 🎀 ✕ ⍗ ♨

Creacombe

SS8219

Creacombe Parsonage, *Parsonage Cross, Creacombe, Rackenford, Tiverton, Devon, EX16 8EL.*
Open: All Year
01884 881441 Mrs Poole
Fax: 01884 881551
creaky.parson@dial.pipex.com
D: fr £18 **S:** fr £18
Beds: 1F 2T **Baths:** 1 Sh 1 En
🛏 🅿 ⅍ 🗹 🎀 ✕ 🛢 ⍗ ✻ cc
C17th farmhouse in open countryside, views of Dartmoor. Ideal spot to rest, or explore Exmoor & N Devon. We enjoy catering for those with special dietary requirements. Organised walking breaks, craft workshops. BARN CAMPING for groups. All rooms own washing facilities, 1 with WC.

Crediton

SS8300 🍺 *Lamb, Red Lion, Three Little Pigs*

Creedy Manor, *Long Barn, Crediton, Devon, EX17 4AB.*
Victorian farmhouse, picturesque peaceful comfort. Town 0.50 mile. Also self-catering apartments.
Open: All Year
01363 772684 (also fax) Mrs Turner
creedymanor@eclipse.co.uk
D: £18–£25 **S:** £19.50
Beds: 1D 1T 1F **Baths:** 3 En
🐕 🅿 (6) ⚡ 📺 🛏 📖 Ⅴ ✉ ⓒ

Taw Vale, *2 Taw Vale, Crediton, Devon, EX17 3BU.*
Open: All Year
01363 777879 (also fax) Mrs Whitby
D: £17–£19 **S:** £18–£22
Beds: 1F 1D 1T **Baths:** 2 En 1 Pr
🐕 🅿 (3) ⚡ 📺 ✕ 📖 Ⅴ ♦
Listed Georgian-style family home on edge of Crediton. Ideal touring base for Dartmoor, Exmoor and both coasts. Easy access to Exeter and beyond, via bus and train. 6 National Trust properties within 30 minutes. Choice of Aga-cooked breakfasts.

Libbetts Cottage, *Church Street, Crediton, Devon, EX17 2AQ.*
A great taste of Devon in lovely olde worlde cottage. **Open:** All Year
01363 772709 Mrs Venn
D: £22 **S:** £25
🐕 (6) 🅿 (2) ⚡ 📺 ✕ 📖 Ⅴ ✿ ⚘

North Hollacombe Farm, *Crediton, Devon, EX17 5BS.*
Farmhouse in beautiful secluded valley views to Dartmoor. 1.5 miles Crediton.
Open: All Year
01363 84243 Ms Searle
D: fr £17 **S:** fr £20
Beds: 1D 1S **Baths:** 2 Sh
🐕 🅿 (6) 📺 ✕ Ⅴ ⚘

Fircroft, *George Hill, Crediton, Devon, EX17 2DS.*
No expense has been spared transforming this stunning 1914 home.
Open: All Year
01363 774224 R Belcher
D: £19–£21 **S:** £25–£27.50
Beds: 2F **Baths:** 2 En
🐕 🅿 (6) ⚡ 📺 🛏 📖 ⚘

Croyde

SS4439 🍺 *Manor, Thatched Barn Inn*

Moorsands, *Moor Lane, Croyde Bay, Braunton, Devon, EX33 1NP.*
Open: All Year **Grades:** ETC 3 Diamond
01271 890781 Mr & Mrs Davis
D: £20–£26 **S:** £20–£26
Beds: 1F 1T 2D 1S **Baths:** 5 En
🐕 🅿 (6) ⚡ 📖 ⚘
Originally a Victorian coastguard station with stunning views, Moorsands offers short walks to beach, village and local facilities. Come and surf, ride, cycle etc. or simply relax with our comfortable ensuite rooms, guest lounge, beautiful surroundings and superb breakfasts.

Oamaru, *Down End, Croyde, Braunton, Devon, EX33 1QE.*
400m from top surfing beach and village. Relaxed friendly atmosphere.
Open: All Year
01271 890765 Mr & Mrs Jenkins
philcroyde@hotmail.com
D: £17.50–£25 **S:** £17.50–£25
Beds: 1F 1D **Baths:** 1 En 1 Pr
🐕 🅿 (6) ⚡ 📺 📖 Ⅴ ✉ ⓒ

West Winds Guest House, *Moor Lane, Croyde Bay, Croyde, Braunton, Devon, EX33 1PA.*
Stunning waters' edge location with views over Croyde Beach.
Open: Mar to Nov
Grades: ETC 4 Diamond, AA 4 Diamond
01271 890489 (also fax)
Mr & Mrs Gedling
chris@croydewestwinds.freeserve.co.uk
D: £26–£31 **S:** £26–£31
Beds: 3D 2T **Baths:** 3 Pr 2 Sh
🐕 🅿 (6) ⚡ 📺 ✕ 📖 Ⅴ ⚘

Chapel Farm, *Hobbs Hill, Croyde, Braunton, Devon, EX33 1NE.*
C16th thatched farmhouse, 10 minutes to beach.
Open: Easter to Nov
01271 890429 Mrs Windsor
D: £18–£26 **S:** £18–£30
Beds: 1F 2D **Baths:** 3 En
🐕 🅿 (6) ⚡ 📺 📖 Ⅴ ✉ ⓒ

Dalwood

ST2400 🍺 *Tuckers' Arms*

The Tuckers Arms, *Dalwood, Axminster, Devon, EX13 7EG.*
A beautiful C12th inn set in a delightful village beside the Cory Brook.
Open: All Year
01404 881342 Mr Beck
D: £22.50–£27.50 **S:** £25–£35
Beds: 1F 2D 3T **Baths:** 6 En
🐕 🅿 📖 ✕ 📖 Ⅴ ⚘ ♦

The Quest, *4 Danes Hill, Dalwood, Axminster, Devon, EX13 7EH.*
Private house, large peaceful garden with picturesque views over countryside.
Open: All Year (not Xmas)
01404 881586 D: £17.50–£20 **S:** £25
Beds: 1F 1T **Baths:** 1 Sh
🐕 🅿 (2) ⚡ 📺 📖 ⚘

Dartmouth

SX8751 🍺 *Seven Stars, Searle Arms, Windjammer, Cherub, Royal Castle, Norton Park Forces Tavern, Sportsmans' Arms*

Greenswood Farm, *Greenswood Lane, Dartmouth, Devon, TQ6 0LY.*
Open: All Year
01803 712100 Mrs Baron
D: £18–£25 **S:** £20–£25
Beds: 1F 1T 1D **Baths:** 1 En 1 Pr 1 Sh
🐕 (12) 🅿 (8) ⚡ 📺 ✕ 📖 ⚘
A 15th century Devon longhouse set in its own secluded valley, with large sub-tropical gardens. A haven for wildlife. Only 4 miles to Dartmouth, Start Bay and Slapton Ley nature reserve. 2 miles to Dartmouth golf and country club.

The Cedars, *79 Victoria Road, Dartmouth, Devon, TQ6 9RX.*
The Cedars, level location, near town centre, friendly welcome.
Open: All Year (not Xmas)
01803 834421 Mrs Greene
D: £18–£19 **S:** £18–£20
Beds: 2F 1D 2T 1S **Baths:** 1 Sh
🐕 📺 📖 ⚘

Valley House, *46 Victoria Road, Dartmouth, Devon, TQ6 9DZ.*
Comfortable, small friendly guest house.
Open: Feb to Dec
01803 834045 Mr & Mrs Ellis
D: £21–£25 **S:** £25–£30
Beds: 2D 2T **Baths:** 4 En
🅿 (4) ⚡ 📺 📖 ⚘

Campbells B & B, *5 Mount Boone, Dartmouth, Devon, TQ6 9PB.*
Luxury bedrooms with fabulous views. flexible breakfasts with home baking.
Open: All Year (not Xmas)
01803 833438 (also fax)
D: £27.50 **S:** £35–£55
Beds: 2D **Baths:** 2 En
🅿 (2) ⚡ 📺 ✕ 📖 Ⅴ ⚘

Sunnybanks, *1 Vicarage Hill, Dartmouth, Devon, TQ6 9EW.*
Friendly atmosphere. Excellent breakfasts and just minutes from the River Dart.
Open: All Year
Grades: ETC 3 Diamond
01803 832766 (also fax)
sue@sunnybanks.com
D: £21–£25 **S:** £20–£30
Beds: 2F 2T 5D 1S **Baths:** 8 En 1 Pr 1 Sh
🐕 🅿 (2) 📺 🛏 ✕ 📖 Ⅴ ⚘

Brenec House, *73 South Ford Road, Dartmouth, Devon, TQ6 9QT.*
Five minutes walk to river front and town centre.
Open: All Year
01803 834788 Mr & Mrs Culley
D: £16–£17 **S:** £16–£17
Beds: 2D 1S **Baths:** 1 Sh
🐕 🅿 📺 📖 Ⅴ ⚘

Boringdon House, *1 Church Road, Dartmouth, Devon, TQ6 9HQ.*
Welcoming Georgian house overlooking Dartmoor and River Dart and Sea.
Open: All Year
01803 832235 Mr Green
boringdonhouse@talk21.com
D: fr £22.50 **S:** fr £38
Beds: 1D 2T **Baths:** 3 En
🅿 (3) ⚡ 📺 📖 Ⅴ ⚘

Browns Norton Farm, *Dartmouth, Devon, TQ6 0ND.*
Charming C17th farmhouse with sloping ceilings, modern bathroom shower etc.
Open: All Year (not Xmas/New Year)
01803 712321 Mrs Bond
D: £15–£20 **S:** fr £12.50
Beds: 1T 1D 1S **Baths:** 1 Sh
🐕 🅿 ⚡ 📺 ⚘

Planning a longer stay? Always ask for any special rates

Victoria Cote, *105 Victoria Road, Dartmouth, Devon, TQ6 9DY.*
Detached, comfortable, Victorian house 5 minutes' stroll from town centre.
Open: All Year (not Xmas)
01803 832997 Mr Fell
D: £22–£25 **S:** £25–£28
Beds: 2D 1T **Baths:** 3 En
🛇 🅿 (4) 🗇 ⓣ ⚹ ✕ 🏢 Ⓥ ⚘

Diptford

SX7256

Charford Manor, *Diptford, Totnes, Devon, TQ9 7LT.*
Friendly, family run restaurant with rooms in beautiful south countryside.
Open: All Year (not Xmas/New Year)
01364 73111
Mr & Mrs Trott
Fax: 01364 72214
D: £17.50–£25 **S:** £30–£40
Beds: 1F 2D **Baths:** 2 En 1 Pr
🛇 🅿 🗇 ✕ ⚘ cc

Doddiscombsleigh

SX8586   The Nobody Inn

Whitemoor Farm, *Doddiscombsleigh, Exeter, Devon, EX6 7PU.*
Open: All Year (not Xmas)
01647 252423
D: £17.50–£18.50 **S:** £19
Beds: 4F 1D 1T 2S **Baths:** 1 Sh
🛇 🅿 (4) ⅀ 🗇 ⓣ ✕ 🏢 Ⓥ ⚘
C16th thatched farmhouse with oak beams, central heating, Home produce.

Dolton

SS5712   Royal Oak, Ye Olde Inn

Robin Cottage, *Church Street, Dolton, Winkleigh, Devon, EX19 8QE.*
Open: All Year
01805 804430
S Newman
D: £18–£20 **S:** £18–£20
Beds: 1T 1S **Baths:** 1 En 1 Sh
🛇 (12) ⅀ 🗇 ⚘
Modernised cottage situated near church in attractive Devon village, near RHS Rosemoor Garden. Warm welcome. Quiet, comfortable accommodation and excellent breakfasts. Ideal centre for touring, exploring coast, Dartmoor/Exmoor. Good stopover when visiting Cornwall. Walkers also welcome. Tarka Trail nearby.

Drewsteignton

SX7390   Old Inn, Drewe Arms, Anglers' Rest

The Old Inn Restaurant & Guest House, *The Square, Drewsteignton, Exeter, Devon, EX6 6QR.*
Comfortable former C18th inn in village square. Fishing, superb walks, 3 nights less 10%.
Open: All Year
01647 281276 (also fax)
Mr & Mrs Gribble
D: £22.50–£27.50 **S:** £30–£35
Beds: 1F 2D 1T **Baths:** 2 En 1 Pr 1 Sh
🛇 (3) 🅿 (3) 🗇 ⓣ ✕ Ⓥ ⚘

East Fingle Farm, *Drewsteignton, Exeter, Devon, EX6 6NJ.*
Devon farm longhouse, beautiful views, friendly farm animals, warm welcome. Children half-price.
Open: All Year
01647 281639 Mrs Cordy
D: £18–£21 **S:** £18–£21
Beds: 2D 1T **Baths:** 2 En 1 Sh
🛇 🅿 (10) 🗇 ✕ Ⓥ ⚘

East Allington

SX7648   Sir Walter Raleigh, Rolle Arms, Old Inn, Fortescue Arms

Tor Cottage, *The Mounts, East Allington, Totnes, Devon, TQ9 7QJ.*
Warm welcome. Beautiful country views, central location, superb breakfasts.
Open: All Year
01548 521316 (also fax)
Mr Larner
john@torcottage.freeserve.co.uk
D: £14–£19 **S:** £14–£19
Beds: 2F **Baths:** 2 En 1 Pr
🛇 (2) 🅿 (5) ⅀ 🗇 ✕ 🏢 Ⓥ ⚘

The Fortescue Arms, *East Allington, Totnes, Devon, TQ9 7RA.*
Delightful Devon Inn with superb restaurant - CAMRA recommended real ales.
Open: All Year (not Xmas/New Year)
Grades: ETC 3 Diamond
01548 521215 Mr Gledhill
steve_trish@talk21.com
D: £17.50–£22.50 **S:** £22.50–£30
Beds: 3D 1T **Baths:** 2 En 2 Sh
🅿 (10) ⅀ 🗇 ⓣ ✕ 🏢 Ⓥ ⚘ cc

East Anstey

SS8626

Threadneedle, *East Anstey, Tiverton, Devon, EX16 9JH.*
Built in the style of a Devon Longhouse, set in three acres, close Dulverton.
Open: All Year
Grades: ETC 3 Diamond
01398 341598 Mr & Mrs Webb
D: £23–£25 **S:** £23–£25
Beds: 1D 1T **Baths:** 2 En
🛇 🅿 (10) ⅀ 🗇 ⓣ 🏢 Ⓥ ⚘

East Budleigh

SY0684   Rolle Arms, Sir Walter Raleigh

Wynards Farm, *East Budleigh, Budleigh Salterton, Devon, EX9 7DQ.*
Open: Easter to October
01395 443417 (also fax)
Mrs Smith
jsmith17@talk21.com
D: £18–£20 **S:** £20–£25
Beds: 1F 1D 1T **Baths:** 2 Sh
🛇 (1) 🅿 (3) ⅀ 🗇 🏢 Ⓥ ⚘
Farmhouse Bed and Breakfast on a working farm in the heart of the Raleigh Country. Ideal for relaxing and walking only two miles from the coast. Situated in centre of Village close to Pubs and shop. Full English Breakfast.

BEDROOMS
F - Family
D - Double
T - Twin
S - Single

East Ogwell

SX8370   Jolly Sailor Inn

Milton Farm, *East Ogwell, Newton Abbot, Devon, TQ12 6AT.*
Bungalow in picturesque village - 7 miles Torbay - golf 3 miles.
Open: Mar to Nov
01626 354988 D: £16.50–£18 **S:** £18–£20
Beds: 1T 1D **Baths:** 1 Sh
🛇 🅿 (3) ⅀ 🗇 🏢

East Portlemouth

SX7438   Pigs Nose

Meadow Barn, *East Portlemouth, Salcombe, Devon, TQ8 8PN.*
Quiet, comfortable private accommodation in idyllic coastal and countryside location.
Open: All Year (not Xmas)
01548 843085 Mr & Mrs Griffiths
dcgriffiths@portables1.ngfl.gov.uk
D: £20–£24 **S:** £20–£24
Beds: 1D 1T **Baths:** 1 Sh
🛇 (7) 🅿 (4) ⅀ 🗇 ✕ 🏢 Ⓥ ⚘

East Prawle

SX7836   Freebooter, Pig's Nose

Stures Court, *East Prawle, Kingsbridge, Devon, TQ7 2BY.*
C17th thatched cottage with C21st comfort. Highly commended by guests.
Open: All Year
01548 511261 Miss Benson
D: £18–£20 **S:** £19–£21
Beds: 2D 2S **Baths:** 1 Sh
🛇 (7) ⅀ 🏢 Ⓥ ⚘

Ebford

SX9887   St George & Dragon, Diggers Rest

Ebford Court, *Ebford, Exeter, Devon, EX3 0RA.*
C15th peaceful thatched farmhouse. Close to sea and moors.
Open: All Year (not Xmas)
01392 875353 Mrs Howard
Fax: 01392 876776
D: £17–£19 **S:** £17–£19
Beds: 1D 1T 1S **Baths:** 1 Sh
🛇 (8) 🅿 (7) ⅀ 🗇 ⓣ 🏢 Ⓥ ⚘

Little Holt, *Ebford Lane, Ebford, Exeter, Devon, EX3 0QX.*
C18th coaching cottage, quiet hamlet, tranquil gardens: roses, honeysuckle, jasmine, pond and woodlands.
Open: May to Oct
01392 876945 (also fax)
Ms Schoenburg
D: £16–£20 **S:** £18–£22
Beds: 1D **Baths:** 1 En
⅀ 🗇 ⚘

Exeter

SX9192 ✈ *Mill-on-the-Exe, Papermakers, Chaucer's Inn, Seven Stars, New Inn, Red House Hotel, Jolly Porter, Micawbers Inn, Imperial, George & Dragon, Digger's Rest, Puffing Billy, White Hart, Gissons Arms, White Horse, Twisted Oak*

Montgomery House, *144 Fore Street, Exeter, Devon, EX4 3AN.*
Open: All Year
01392 424086 0113/@fsmail.net
D: £24–£28 **S:** £32–£38
Beds: 2T 2D **Baths:** 4 En
🗔 ♻ ▸ cc
Very large well furnished quiet rooms in city centre, close cathedral, shops and quay. Ideal for weekend break. For business person, the Crown courts, the business district and Marsh Barton Industrial Estate. Within a few minutes walking distance, a host of good restaurants, pubs and clubs.

St David's Guest House, *89 St David's Hill, Exeter, Devon, EX4 4DW.*
Stations and city 10 mins walk. Good selection restaurants nearby.
Open: All Year
01392 434737 (also fax)
Mr & Mrs Morris
D: £15–£17.50 **S:** £15–£25
Beds: 1F 2D 2T 1S **Baths:** 4 En 1 Sh
🚲 ♻ (4) 🗔 🐴 ♻ 🍸 ♻

Tanglewood, *Little Silver Lane, Matford, Exeter, Devon, EX2 8XZ.*
Open: Apr to Oct
01392 832556 Mrs Perks
D: £15–£16 **S:** £16–£17
Beds: 1F 1D 1T **Baths:** 1 Sh
♻ (8) 🗔 ✕ ♻ 🍸 ♻
Pleasantly situated bungalow in own grounds with rural views. Off-road parking. Enroute ideal base for touring Cornwall, Devon, Dorset. Near Matford Business Park. Many attractions locally. Evening meals optional.

Marianne Pool Farm, *Clyst St George, Exeter, Devon, EX3 0NZ.*
Devon longhouse, peaceful setting but near to Exeter and coast. 2 miles M5 (J30).
Open: Mar to Nov
01392 874939 Mrs Bragg
D: £17–£19 **S:** £18–£20
Beds: 1F 1T **Baths:** 1 En 1 Sh
🚲 ♻ (2) 🗔 🐴 ♻ ♻

The Grange, *Stoke Hill, Exeter, Devon, EX4 7JH.*
Country house in private grounds wooded location overlooking Exeter, surrounding countryside.
Open: All Year
Grades: ETC 4 Diamond
01392 259723 Mr Dudley
dudleythegrange@aol.com
D: £17–£20 **S:** £21–£24
Beds: 4D **Baths:** 4 En
🚲 ♻ (8) 🗔 ♻

Ebford Court, *Ebford, Exeter, Devon, EX3 0RA.*
C15th peaceful thatched farmhouse. Close to sea and moors.
Open: All Year (not Xmas)
01392 875353 Mrs Howard
Fax: 01392 876776
D: £17–£19 **S:** £17–£19
Beds: 1D 1T 1S **Baths:** 1 Sh
🚲 (8) ♻ (7) 🗔 🐴 ♻ 🍸 ♻

Holbrook Farm, *Clyst Honiton, Exeter, Devon, EX5 2HR.*
Delightful rooms with beautiful countryside views (own entrance, unrestricted access). Tasty breakfasts, fresh produce.
Open: All Year **Grades:** AA 4 Diamond
01392 367000 Mrs Glanvill
heatherglanvill@holbrookfarm.co.uk
D: £19–£21 **S:** £18–£25
Beds: 1F 1D 1T **Baths:** 3 En
🚲 ♻ (4) 🗔 🐴 ♻ 🍸 ♻ ♻ ♿

Dunmore Hotel, *22 Blackall Road, Exeter, Devon, EX4 4HE.*
Close to city centre, coach and railway stations and university.
Open: All Year
Grades: AA 2 Diamond
01392 431643 (also fax)
Mr & Mrs Gilderthorp
dunmorehtl@aol.com
D: £17–£20 **S:** £20–£25
Beds: 3F 2D 1T 1S **Baths:** 4 En 3 Sh
🚲 🗔 ✕ ♻ 🍸 ♻ cc

The Old Mill, *Mill Lane, Alphington, Exeter, Devon, EX2 8SG.*
Historical premises in quiet area. full farm breakfast. Recommended for 26 years.
Open: All Year
01392 259977 Mrs Marchant
D: £10.50–£13.50 **S:** £10.50–£15
Beds: 2F 1D 1T 1S **Baths:** 1 Pr 1 Sh
🚲 ♻ (8) 🗔 ♻ 🍸 ♻ ♿

Hotel Maurice, *5 Bystock Terrace, Exeter, Devon, EX4 4HY.*
Town house in quiet Georgian square in the heart of the city.
Open: All Year (not Xmas)
01392 213079 Mr Wenley
hotel.maurice@eclipse.co.uk
D: £16–£18 **S:** £20
Beds: 1F 3D 2T 2S **Baths:** 8 En
🚲 (3) ♻ (1) 🗔 ♻ ♻ cc

2 Deanery Place, *Exeter, Devon, EX1 1HU.*
Dating from C14th, looking out onto Cathedral, Secluded from passing noise & traffic.
Open: All Year
01392 490081 Mrs Somers
D: £26.50–£29.50 **S:** £23–£24
Beds: 2D 1S **Baths:** 2 En 1 Sh

All details shown are as supplied by B&B owners in Autumn 2000

Killarney Guest House, *Alphington Street, Exeter, Devon, EX2 8AT.*
Adjacent to leisure centre, River Exe, close to city centre.
Open: All Year (not Xmas/New Year)
01392 276932 Mrs Flint
Fax: 01392 499330
bob.flint@virgin.net
D: £16–£18 **S:** £17–£19
Beds: 2F 2T 1D 3S **Baths:** 3 Sh
🚲 ♻ 🗔 🐴 ♻ 🍸 ♻

Park View Hotel, *8 Howell Road, Exeter, Devon, EX4 4LG.*
Family-run, overlooking park, near city centre, stations and university.
Open: All Year (not Xmas/New Year)
Grades: ETC 3 Diamond, AA 3 Diamond, RAC 3 Diamond
01392 271772 Mrs Batho
philbatho@parkviewhotel.freeserve.co.uk
D: £19–£25 **S:** £22–£35
Beds: 2F 8D 3T 1S **Baths:** 9 En 3 Pr 1 Sh
🚲 ♻ (6) 🐴 ♻ ♻ ♿ cc

Crossmead, *Barley Lane, Dunsford Hill, Exeter, Devon, EX4 1TF.*
Comfortable bedrooms within beautiful landscaped grounds of attractive Victorian house.
Open: All Year (not Xmas)
01392 273703 Mrs Snow
Fax: 01392 422594
crossmead@exeter.ac.uk
D: £15.95–£47 **S:** £15.95–£47
Beds: 33D 15T 39S **Baths:** 52 En 30 Sh
🚲 ♻ 🗔 ♻ ♻ cc

Raffles, *11 Blackall Road, Exeter, EX4 4HD.*
Attractive Victorian town house close to city centre.
Open: All Year
01392 270200 Mr Hyde
rafflesthtl@btinternet.com
D: £24–£25 **S:** £34–£35
Beds: 1F 2D 2T 2S **Baths:** 7 En
🚲 ♻ (4) 🗔 🐴 ✕ ♻ 🍸 ♻ cc

Exmouth

SY0081 ✈ *Redwing Inn, Deer Leap Inn, Ship Inn, Nutwell Inn, Carlton Lodge, The Grove, Beachcomber Inn*

Hope Cottage, *The Strand, Lympstone, Exmouth, Devon, EX8 5JS.*
C15th cottage in beautiful village on Exe estuary (Mr & Mrs Clarke).
Open: All Year
01395 268349 Mr Clarke
D: £17.50 **S:** £17.50
Beds: 3D 1T **Baths:** 1 En 1 Sh
♻ 🍸 ♻

Sea Breeze, *42 Victoria Road, Exmouth, Devon, EX8 1DW.*
Small friendly guest house close to beach river and town.
Open: All Year
01395 224888 Mrs Bane
D: £16–£22 **S:** £16–£22
Beds: 2F 1D 1S **Baths:** 4 En
🚲 ♻ 🗔 ♻ ❄ ♻

Aslema, *61 St Andrews Road, Exmouth, Devon, EX8 1AS.*
Charming long established guest house 200 yards from Exmouth sea front.
Open: Feb to Nov
01395 270731 Mrs Stevens
D: £17 **S:** £17
Beds: 2D 1T **Baths:** 3 En
⌂ (8) **P** (2) ⊠ ✕ ▥ 🏃

Sandrevin, *59 Salterton Road, Exmouth, Devon, EX8 2EQ.*
Large Victorian house, ensuite bedrooms. Exe estuary views. Car park.
Open: All Year (not Xmas)
01395 266898 Mr & Mrs Cooper
bernardcooper@sandrevin.freeserve.co.uk
D: £18–£23 **S:** £21–£26
⌂ **P** (5) ✗ 🏃 ▥ 🏃

30 Withycombe Road, *Exmouth, Devon, EX8 1TG.*
Large Victorian house which is close to shops. Seafront 20 min walk away.
Open: Easter to Oct
01395 277025 Mrs Shobbrook
D: fr £15 **S:** fr £15
Beds: 1F 1D 1S **Baths:** 1 Sh
⌂ (6) **P** (2) ⊠ 🏃 ✕ 🏃

No 37, *37 Salterton Road, Exmouth, Devon, EX8 2ED.*
Warm and welcoming period house a few minutes from seafront and town.
Open: Apr to Oct
01395 279381 (also fax) Mrs Blunt
D: £16–£20 **S:** £16–£30
Beds: 1F 1D **Baths:** 1 En 1 Pr
⌂ **P** (2) ⊠ ▥ 🏃

Exton

SX9886 ⁂ *Puffing Billy, Nutwell Lodge*

Chatfield, *Exmouth Road, Exton, Exeter, Devon, EX3 0PQ.*
Edwardian house near Topsham, coast, motorway. Large garden. Comfortable rooms.
Open: All Year (not Xmas/New Year)
01392 874135
chatfield@exton.freeserve.co.uk
D: £18–£22 **S:** £20–£25
Beds: 1F 1T 2D **Baths:** 2 En 1 Sh
⌂ **P** (8) ✗ ⊠ ▥ 🏃

Farringdon

SY0191 ⁂ *White Horse*

Wood Barton, *Farringdon, Exeter, Devon, EX5 2HY.*
Attractive farmhouse with countryside views. Breakfast cooked on Aga. Ideal Exeter, coast and moors.
Open: All Year (not Xmas)
01395 233407 Mrs Bolt
D: £21 **S:** £25
Beds: 1F 1D 1T **Baths:** 3 En
⌂ **P** (6) ✗ ⊠ ▥ 🏃

B&B owners may vary rates - be sure to check when booking

Fenny Bridges

SY1198 ⁂ *Greyhound, Otter Inn*

Little Ash Farm, *Fenny Bridges, Honiton, Devon, EX14 0BL.*
Warm welcome at comfortable farmhouse. Large peaceful garden, mini golf.
Open: All Year (not Xmas)
01404 850271 Mrs Reid
D: £14–£18.50 **S:** £14–£18
Beds: 1F 1T 1S **Baths:** 1 En 2 Sh
⌂ **P** (4) ✗ ⊠ ▥ 🏃 🏃

Skinners Ash Farm, *Fenny Bridges, Honiton, Devon, EX14 3BH.*
Old farmhouse. Scrumptious food, pony rides, collect your own eggs, lovely garden/views.
Open: All Year
Grades: ETC 3 Diamond
01404 850231 (also fax)
Mrs Godfrey
D: £18–£19
Beds: 1F 1D **Baths:** 1 Pr
⌂ **P** (7) ✗ ⊠ 🏃 ✕ 🏃 ❀ 🏃

Fremington

SS5132 ⁂ *New Inn, Boat House*

Lower Yelland Farm, *Yelland Road, Fremington, Barnstaple, Devon, EX31 3EN.*
Open: All Year (not Xmas/New Year)
01271 860101 (also fax) Mr Day
D: £20 **S:** £20
Beds: 1T 2D **Baths:** 3 En
⌂ **P** (6) ⊠ 🏃 ▥ 🏃
North Devon Coast beautifully situated period house on Taw Estuary. Ideal touring centre, Instow beach/marina approximately 1 mile, Bideford, Barnstaple 4.50 miles. Several golf courses in the vicinity. Adjacent to bird sanctuary. Private off road parking.

Galmpton (Salcombe)

SX6840 ⁂ *Hope & Anchor*

Rose Cottage, *Galmpton, Kingsbridge, Devon, TQ7 3EU.*
C17th thatched, Listed cottage. Under 1 mile , Hope Cove beaches, coastal path, close Salcombe. **Open:** All Year (not Xmas)
01548 561953 (also fax) Mrs Daly
D: £18–£23 **S:** £28
Beds: 2D 1T **Baths:** 3 En
✗ ⊠ ▥ 🏃 🏃

Gooseford

SX6791 ⁂ *Post Inn*

Fairhaven Farm, *Gooseford, Whiddon Down, Okehampton, Devon, EX20 2QH.*
Open: All Year (not Xmas/New Year)
Grades: ETC 3 Diamond
01647 231261 Mrs Scott
D: £20–£24 **S:** £20–£24
Beds: 1F 1D **Baths:** 1 En 1 Sh
⌂ **P** (4) ⊠ 🏃 ✕ 🏃
Our farmhouse has magnificent views of patchwork fields with rising hills of Dartmoor beyond. This sturdy farmhouse with active farm, gardens and pond offers you quiet and comfort. Easy reach north and south coast, Castle Drogo. 1/4 mile A30 dual carriageway.

Gulworthy

SX4572 ⁂ *Harvest Home*

Broadacre, *Gulworthy, Tavistock, PL19 8HX.*
Near to Dartmoor, cottage-style bungalow set in large garden for your use.
Open: All Year (not Xmas)
01822 832470 D: £16–£18 **S:** £18–£20
Beds: 1D 1T **Baths:** 1 Sh
⌂ **P** (2) ⊠ ▥ 🏃

Hallsands

SX8138 ⁂ *Cricket Inn*

Widget, *Hallsands, Kingsbridge, Devon, TQ7 2EX.*
Open: All Year (not Xmas)
01548 511110 Mrs Wolstenholme
D: £20–£25 **S:** £20–£25
Beds: 2D 1T **Baths:** 1 En 1 Pr
⌂ **P** (4) ✗ ⊠ ▥ 🏃
A brand new bungalow 50 yards from the beach and coastal path in a wonderful peaceful area for relaxing or using as a base for the beautiful South Hams. A warm welcome, lovely accommodation and unbeatable breakfast await you. No pets.

Halwell

SX7753 ⁂ *New Inn*

Orchard House, *Horner, Halwell, Totnes, Devon, TQ9 7LB.*
Beautiful country house beneath cider orchard. Luxury throughout. Large garden.
Open: Mar to Nov
01548 821448 D: £20 **S:** £30
Beds: 1F 1D 1T **Baths:** 3 En
⌂ (3) **P** (5) ✗ ⊠ ▥ 🏃 🏃

Hartland

SS2624 ⁂ *Hartland Quay Hotel, Manor Inn*

West Titchberry Farm, *Hartland, Bideford, Devon, EX39 6AU.*
Typical Devon long house on traditional family run coastal stock farm.
Open: All Year (not Xmas)
01237 441287 (also fax)
Mrs Heard
D: £17–£18 **S:** £17–£18
Beds: 1F 1D 1T **Baths:** 2 Sh
⌂ **P** ⊠ ✕ ▥ 🏃 🏃

Hatherleigh

SS5404

Pressland Country House Hotel, *Hatherleigh, Okehampton, Devon, EX20 3LW.*
Open: Mar to Nov
Grades: AA 5 Diamond
01837 810871 Fax: 01837 810303
accom@presslandhouse.co.uk
D: £20–£32 **S:** £28–£36
Beds: 2T 3D **Baths:** 4 En 1 Pr
⌂ (12) **P** (6) ✗ ⊠ ✕ ▥ 🏃 🏃 cc
Delightful and spacious Victorian house set in 1.5 acres of landscaped garden, with glorious views of Dartmoor and surrounding countryside. The family-run hotel is licensed and there is a large, comfortable lounge, separate bar and a restaurant of growing repute.

Hawkchurch

ST3300 🍺 Tytherleigh Arms

Castle House, Hawkchurch, Axminster, Devon, EX13 5UA.
Open: All Year (not Xmas/New Year)
01297 678291 Mrs Lewis
D: £18–£20 **S:** £18–£20
Beds: 1T 2D **Baths:** 1 En 1 Pr 1 Sh
🛇 🅿 (4) ⅄ 📺 🎔 🛢 🕏
Comfortable Grade II Listed house set in 2 acres of beautiful gardens with delightful country views; within easy reach of the Dorset/Devon coastline and the picturesque town of Lyme Regis only 6 miles away.

Hele (Ilfracombe)

SS5347 🍺 Hele Bay hotel, Ye Olde Globe

Moles Farmhouse, Old Berrynarbor Road, Hele, Ilfracombe, Devon, EX34 9RB.
Beautifully restored former farmhouse, situated in picturesque Hele Valley, near Ilfracombe. **Open:** All Year
01271 862099 (also fax) Ms Grindlay
wendy@molesfarmhouse.freeserve.co.uk
D: £17–£20
Beds: 1F 1T 1D **Baths:** 2 En 1 Sh
🛇 🅿 (4) ⅄ 📺 🛢 🕏

Hemyock

ST1313 🍺 Catherine Wheel Hemyock

Orchard Lea 78, 78 Culmstock Road, Hemyock, Cullompton, Devon, EX15 3RN.
Good touring centre, ground floor accommodation, peaceful family home with panoramic views.
Open: All Year (not Xmas)
01823 680057 (also fax) Mrs Sworn
D: £15–£17 **S:** £15–£17
Beds: 1D 2T **Baths:** 1 Pr 2 Sh
🛇 🅿 (3) ⅄ 📺 ✕ 🛢 🕏 🛢 🕏

Hexworthy

SX6572 🍺 Forest Inn

The Forest Inn, Hexworthy, Princetown, Devon, PL20 6SD.
Open: Feb to Dec
Grades: ETC 3 Diamond
01364 631211 Mr Selwood
Fax: 01364 631515
forestinn@hotmail.com
D: £20–£29.50 **S:** £25–£33
Beds: 5D 3T 2S **Baths:** 7 En 3 Pr
🅿 (30) 📺 🎔 🛢 🕏 cc
A country inn in the middle of Dartmoor, it is ideal for walking, fishing, riding, or just relaxing. Home-made food can be enjoyed in the restaurant, bar or round the fire in the lounge. Dogs and muddy boots welcome.

Higher Clovelly

SS3124 🍺 Farmers Arms, Hart Inn, New Inn, Red Lion

Dyke Green Farm, Higher Clovelly, Bideford, Devon, EX39 5RU.
Beautiful converted barn, every comfort.
Open: All Year (not Xmas)
01237 431699 (also fax) Mrs Johns
D: fr £15.50 **S:** fr £18.50
Beds: 2D 1T **Baths:** 2 Pr 1 Sh
🛇 🅿 (6) ⅄ 📺 🎔 🛢 🕏

Fuchsia Cottage, Burscott Lane, Higher Clovelly, Bideford, Devon, EX39 5RR.
Situated in a quiet lane, beautiful coastal and countryside views.
Open: All Year (not Xmas/New Year)
Grades: ETC 3 Diamond, AA 3 Diamond
01237 431398 Mrs Curtis
tomsuecurtis.fuchiacot@currantbun.com
D: £18.50 **S:** fr £16
Beds: 1F 1D 1S **Baths:** 2 En 1 Sh
🛇 🅿 (3) ⅄ 📺 🎔 🛢 🕏

Holne

SX7069 🍺 Church House Inn, Tradesman's Arms

Chase Gate Farm, Holne, Newton Abbot, Devon, TQ13 7RX.
Comfortable, friendly farmhouse with lovely views and well-equipped rooms.
Open: All Year
01364 631261 Mr & Mrs Higman
D: £17.50–£20 **S:** £17.50–£20
Beds: 1F 2D 1T **Baths:** 2 En 1 Pr 1 Sh
🛇 🅿 📺 🎔 🛢 🕏

Mill Leat Farm, Holne, Ashburton, Newton Abbot, Devon, TQ13 7RZ.
C18th Farmhouse offering great food, set off the beaten track.
Open: All Year (not Xmas)
Grades: ETC 3 Diamond
01364 631283 (also fax) Mrs Cleave
D: £17–£19 **S:** £19–£20
Beds: 2F **Baths:** 1 En 1 Pr
🛇 📺 🎔 ✕ 🛢 🕏

Hazelwood, Holne, Newton Abbot, Devon, TQ13 7SJ.
Friendly home from home welcome with panoramic views of Devon.
Open: Easter to October
01364 631235 Mrs Mortimore
D: £18.50–£19 **S:** £18.50–£19
Beds: 2D 1S
🛇 🅿 (3) ⅄ 📺 🎔 ✕ 🛢 🕏

Honiton

ST1600 🍺 Awliscombe Inn, Otter Inn

Wessington Farm, Awliscombe, Honiton, Devon, EX14 0NU.
Open: All Year
Grades: ETC 4 Diamond, Silver
01404 42280 Mrs Summers
Fax: 01404 45271
b&b@eastdevon.com
D: £20 £25 **S:** £20–£40
Beds: 1D 2T **Baths:** 2 En 1 Pr
🛇 🅿 (10) ⅄ 📺 🛢 🕏
Elegant late Victorian stone farmhouse in designated Area of Outstanding Natural Beauty. Aga English breakfast served in stylish dining room with superb views overlooking open countryside. Honiton, centre of antiques and lace 1 mile, historic Exeter 16 miles, picturesque east Devon coast 20 minutes.

Threshays, Awliscombe, Honiton, Devon, EX14 3QB.
Tastefully converted cob barn on non-working farm. Lovely views.
Open: All Year
01404 43551 (also fax) Mrs Gillingham
D: £16 **S:** £16
Beds: 1F 1D **Baths:** 1 Sh
🛇 🅿 (6) ⅄ 📺 🛢 🕏

Hope Cove

SX6739 🍺 Hope & Anchor, Sand Pebbles

Hope Cove Hotel, Hope Cove, Kingsbridge, Devon, TQ7 3HH.
On coastal path. Spectacular sea views to Eddystone Lighthouse.
Open: Easter to Oct
Grades: RAC 3 Diamond
01548 561233 (also fax) Mr Clarke
D: £23.50–£28.50 **S:** £33.50–£38.50
Beds: 2T 5D **Baths:** 7 En
🛇 (6) 🅿 (12) 📺 ✕ 🛢 🕏 🛢 cc

Cove Cottage, Hope Cove, Kingsbridge, Devon, TQ7 3HG.
Detached cottage 100 yds from sea.
Open: Easter to Oct
01548 561446 Mrs Guymer
D: £13–£16 **S:** fr £13.50
Beds: 1D 1T 1S **Baths:** 1 Sh
🛇 🅿 (3) ⅄ 📺 🎔 🛢 🕏

Horrabridge

SX5169 🍺 Leaping Salmon, London Inn

Overcombe Hotel, Old Station Road, Horrabridge, Yelverton, Devon, PL20 7RA.
Enjoy beautiful views across the Walkham Valley towards High Tor.
Open: All Year
01822 853501 GH & G Wright
D: £22–£22.50 **S:** £22–£28
Beds: 2F 5D 3T 1S **Baths:** 10 Pr 1 Sh
🛇 🅿 (10) 📺 🎔 ✕ 🛢 🕏 🛢 🕏

The Old Mine House, Sortridge, Horrabridge, Yelverton, Devon, PL20 7UA.
Peaceful grounds. Dartmoor views. Woods, pond, chickens. Distinctive house.
Open: All Year (not Xmas/New Year)
01822 855586 (also fax)
Ian Robinson
D: £15–£20 **S:** £15–£20
Beds: 3F 3T 1D **Baths:** 3 Pr
🛇 🅿 (20) ⅄ 📺 🎔 ✕ 🛢 🕏 🛢 🕏

Huntshaw Water

SS5023 🍺 Hunters Inn

The Roundhouse, Guscott, Huntshaw Water, Torrington, Devon, EX38 7HE.
Splendid roundhouse amidst beautiful peaceful countryside betwixt sea and moors. **Open:** All Year
01271 858626 Mrs Smith
D: £17.50–£20 **S:** £17.50–£20
Beds: 1F 2D **Baths:** 1 En 3 Pr
🛇 🅿 (6) ⅄ 📺 🎔 ✕ 🛢 🕏 🛢 🕏

Ide

SX9090 🍺 Huntsman Inn, Twisted Oak

Drakes Farm House, Ide, Exeter, Devon, EX2 9RQ.
C15th farmhouse, quiet, village 2 miles, M5 and Exeter city centre.
Open: All Year
01392 256814 (also fax)
Mrs Easterbrook
drakesfarmhouse@hotmail.com
D: £17.50–£20 **S:** £20–£30
Beds: 1F 2D 1T **Baths:** 2 En 1 Pr 1 Sh
🛇 🅿 (4) ⅄ 📺 🛢 🕏 🛢 cc

Ideford

SX8977   🍺 *Elizabethan Inn*

Higher Rixdale Farm, *Ideford, Newton Abbot, TQ13 0BW.*
Open: Feb to Nov
01626 866232 D: £15–£17 **S:** £15–£17
Beds: 1T 2D 1S **Baths:** 2 Sh
🛏 (2) 🄿 (8) 📺 🍴 🖳 🌢
The farm is situated near Teignmouth, set in secluded surrounding visitors can enjoy lovely walks around the farm. A warm welcome is assured, cider is made, and offered free to guests. Dartmoor, and safe beaches near by.

Ilfracombe

SS5147   🍺 *Williams Arms, Agricultural Inn, Cider Apple, Crown, Sherbourne Lodge, Hele Bay, Ye Old Globe*

Cairn House Hotel, *43 St Brannocks Road, Ilfracombe, Devon, EX34 8EH.*
Open: All Year (not Xmas/New Year)
Grades: ETC 1 Star, RAC 1 Star
01271 863911 (also fax)
Mrs Tupper
D: £18–£21.50 **S:** £18–£21.50
Beds: 3F 6D 1S **Baths:** 10 En
🛏 🄿 📺 🍴 ✕ 🖳 🌢 cc
The Cairn House Hotel is a beautiful Victorian hotel delightfully situated in its own grounds with extensive views over town, sea and surrounding countryside. There is a comfortable lounge/bar to relax in before or after your evening meal.

Beechwood Hotel, *Torrs Park, Ilfracombe, Devon, EX34 8AZ.*
Open: Mar to Oct
Grades: ETC 2 Star
01271 863800 (also fax)
P Burridge
info@beechwoodhotel.co.uk
D: £22–£25 **S:** £22–£25
Beds: 2T 5D **Baths:** 7 En
🄿 (8) ⅏ 📺 ✕ 🖳 🌢 cc
Peacefully situated non-smoking Victorian mansion, own woods bordering spectacular National Trust lands and coast path. Superb views over town and countryside to sea. Just 10 minutes walk to harbour and town. Spacious well appointed guest rooms, good food. Licensed. Parking.

Lyncott Guest House, *56 St Brannock's Road, Ilfracombe, Devon, EX34 8EQ.*
Open: All Year
Grades: ETC 4 Diamond
01271 862425 (also fax)
Mr & Mrs Holdsworth
davidh@correo.com
D: £18–£21 **S:** fr £18
Beds: 2F 3D 1S **Baths:** 6 En
🛏 🄿 (5) ⅏ 📺 🖳 🌢
Join David and Marianna in their charming, lovingly refurbished Victorian house pleasantly situated near lovely Bicclescombe Park. Relax in elegant, smoke-free surroundings. Enjoy delightful, spacious, individually designed ensuite bedrooms and sample their scrumptious home-made fare.

Moles Farmhouse, *Old Berrynarbor Road, Hele, Ilfracombe, Devon, EX34 9RB.*
Open: All Year
01271 862099 (also fax) Ms Grindlay
wendy@molesfarmhouse.freeserve.co.uk
D: £17–£20
Beds: 1F 1T 1D **Baths:** 2 En 1 Sh
🛏 🄿 (4) ⅏ 📺 🍴 🖳 🌢
Beautifully restored former farmhouse, situated in picturesque Hele Valley, near Ilfracombe. Close to coastal path and Tarka Trail, it's an ideal base for touring the delights of North Devon. Come and sample our 'home from home' relaxed atmosphere and comfortable accommodation.

Strathmore Hotel, *57 St Brannock's Road, Ilfracombe, Devon, EX34 8EQ.*
Open: All Year
Grades: ETC 4 Diamond, AA 4 Diamond, RAC 4 Diamond
01271 862248 Mr Smith
Fax: 01271 862243
D: £20–£28 **S:** £25–£33
Beds: 1F 5D 1T 1S **Baths:** 8 Pr
🛏 🄿 (7) ⅏ 📺 🍴 🖳 🌢 ❋ 🌢 cc
Delightful Victorian Hotel near to Ilfracombe town centre, Bicclescombe Park, Cairn Nature Reserve and glorious beaches. All rooms are ensuite with colour TV and hospitality trays. We offer varied and delicious menus. All meals are freshly prepared on the premises.

Combe Lodge Hotel, *Chambercombe Park, Ilfracombe, Devon, EX34 9QW.*
Open: All Year (not Xmas)
Quiet position, overlooking harbour, ideal for walking, cycling, golf holidays.
01271 864518 Mr & Mrs Wileman
D: £16.50–£18.50 **S:** £20.50–£22.50
Beds: 2F 4D 2S **Baths:** 4 En 1 Pr 1 Sh
🛏 (1) 🄿 (8) ⅏ 📺 🍴 🖳 📺 🌢 cc

Varley House, *Chambercombe Park, Ilfracombe, Devon, EX34 9QW.*
Period house with attractive ensuite accommodation, close to coastal walks.
Open: Easter to Oct
01271 863927
Mrs S O'Sullivan & Mr D Small
Fax: 01271 879299
info@varleyhouse.freeserve.co.uk
D: £24–£25 **S:** £23–£24
Beds: 2F 4D 1T 1S **Baths:** 7 En 1 Pr
🛏 (5) 🄿 (7) ⅏ 🍴 ✕ 🖳 🌢 cc

Westwell Hall, *Torrs Park, Ilfracombe, Devon, EX34 8AZ.*
Elegant Victorian gentleman's residence in own grounds - superb views.
Open: All Year
01271 862792 (also fax) Mr & Mrs Lomas
westwellhall.ilfracombe@currantbun.com
D: £22–£24 **S:** £22–£24
Beds: 7D 2T 1S **Baths:** 10 En
🛏 🄿 📺 🍴 ✕ 🖳 🌢 cc

Harcourt Hotel, *Fore Street, Ilfracombe, Devon, EX34 9DS.*
Friendly licensed hotel ensuite rooms TV tea coffee, sea views.
Open: All Year
01271 862931 Mr Doorbar
D: £17–£24 **S:** £17–£24
Beds: 3F 4D 1T 2S **Baths:** 8 En 2 Sh
🛏 🄿 (4) 📺 🍴 ✕ 🖳 🌢

Sherborne Lodge Hotel, *Torrs Park, Ilfracombe, Devon, EX34 8AY.*
Friendly, fully-licensed family hotel providing good food, wine, comfortable accommodation.
Open: All Year
01271 862297 Mr & Mrs Millington
Fax: 01271 865520
113121.222@compuserve.com
D: £15.50–£21.50 **S:** £15.50–£21.50
Beds: 1F 8D 2T 1S
🛏 🄿 (10) 📺 🍴 ✕ 🖳 📺 🌢 cc

Ipplepen

SX8366

June Cottage, *Dornafield Road, Ipplepen, Newton Abbot, Devon, TQ12 5SH.*
Very comfortable 250 year old cottage - Quiet, village edge location.
Open: All Year
Grades: ETC 3 Diamond, RAC 3 Diamond
01803 813081 Mr & Mrs Bell
D: £19–£22 **S:** £19–£25
Beds: 1T 2D **Baths:** 1 En 1 Sh
🄿 (1) ⅏ ✕ 🖳 📺 🌢

Ivybridge

SX6356   🍺 *The Sportsman Ivybridge*

The Toll House, *Exeter Road, Ivybridge, Devon, PL21 0DE.*
1850s house with attractive gardens overlooked by Dartmoor.
Open: All Year
01752 893522 Mrs Hancox
info@thetollhouse.co.uk
D: £18 **S:** £25
Beds: 2T 1S **Baths:** 3 En
🛏 🄿 (5) ⅏ 📺 🖳 📺 🌢

Jacobstowe

SS5801

Higher Cadham Farm, *Jacobstowe, Okehampton, Devon, EX20 3RB.*
Superb farmhouse accommodation with country walks. Hearty farmhouse food.
Open: All Year (not Xmas)
Grades: ETC 4 Diamond, AA 4 Diamond
01837 851647 Mrs King
Fax: 01837 851410
D: £18.50–£25 **S:** £18.50–£25
Beds: 3F 2D 3T 1S **Baths:** 5 En 1 Sh
🛏 (1) 🄿 (10) 📺 🍴 ✕ 🖳 📺 🌢 ♿ cc

Kennford

SX9186   🍺 *Gissons Arms*

Kerswell Grange Country House, *Old Dawlish Road, Kennford, Exeter, Devon, EX6 7LR.*
Deluxe accommodation in lovely country house, idyllic setting in 70 acres.
Open: All Year (not Xmas)
01392 833660 Mrs Forrest
Fax: 01392 833601
forrest@kerswellgrange.telme.com
D: £22.50–£25 **S:** £28–£30
Beds: 3D 1T **Baths:** 4 En
🛏 (9) 🄿 (6) ⅏ 📺 🖳 📺 🌢

Kentisbury

SS6243   Pyne Arms, Old Station Inn

Kentisbury Mill, Kentisbury, Barnstaple, Devon, EX31 4NF.
Secluded house, 2 acre garden, close to sea and Exmoor.
Open: All Year (not Xmas/New Year)
01271 883545 Mr Denham
denham@kenmill.fsnet.co.uk
D: £15 **S:** £17.50
Beds: 1T 3D

Kingsbridge

SX7344   Church House Inn

Ashleigh House, Ashleigh Road, Kingsbridge, Devon, TQ7 1HB.
Licensed Victorian guest house. Spacious accommodation, good food in friendly atmosphere.
Open: All Year
Grades: ETC 3 Diamond, AA 3 Diamond
01548 852893 reception@ashleigh-house.co.uk
D: £19–£25 **S:** £24–£35
Beds: 1F 5D 2T **Baths:** 4 En 2 Sh

Centry Farm, Kingsbridge, Devon, TQ7 2HF.
Centry is located in a peaceful secluded valley one mile from Kingsbridge.
Open: Easter to Oct
01548 852037 Mrs Lidstone
pamlidstone@yahoo.co.uk
D: £19.50–£22 **S:** £25–£35
Beds: 1D 1T **Baths:** 2 En

Knowstone

SS8223

West Bowden Farm, Knowstone, South Molton, Devon, EX36 4RP.
West Bowden is a working farm quietly situated just north of the A361.
Open: All Year
Grades: ETC 3 Diamond
01398 341224 Mrs Bray
D: £19–£22 **S:** £19–£25
Beds: 2F 2T 4D 1S **Baths:** 5 En 1 Sh

Landcross

SS4623

Sunset Hotel, Landcross, Bideford, Devon, EX39 5JA.
Small country Hotel. Peaceful location overlooking spectacular scenery and Tarka Trail.
Open: Easter to Nov
Grades: ETC 3 Diamond, AA 3 Diamond
01237 472962 Mrs Lamb
bellcraig@eidosnet.co.uk
D: £27–£30 **S:** £36–£40
Beds: 2F 2D 2T **Baths:** 4 En

Lapford

SS7308   Malt Scoop Inn, Yeovale Inn

Parsonage Farm, Lapford, Crediton, Devon, EX17 6LX.
Working farm in mid Devon. Central for visiting Devon.
Open: All Year
01363 83784 Mrs John
D: £12–£18 **S:** £14–£20
Beds: 1F 1D

Lifton Down

SX3785

Heale Farmhouse, Heale, Lifton Down, Lifton, Devon, PL15 9QX.
Lovely listed farmhouse in tranquil river valley we offer a gourmet organic vegetarian cuisine.
Open: All Year
01566 784869 (also fax)
J & J Edgley
D: £17.50–£18.50 **S:** £18.50
Beds: 1F 2D **Baths:** 1 En 2 Pr

Little Torrington

SS4916

Smytham Manor, Little Torrington, Torrington, Devon, EX38 8PU.
C17th manor house. beautiful tranquil grounds. Outdoor heated pool.
Open: All Year (not Xmas/New Year)
01805 622110
Mrs Crowe
D: £20–£30 **S:** £24–£36
Beds: 4D 3T **Baths:** 5 En 1 Sh

Littlehempston

SX8162   Sea Trout, Tally Ho

Buckyette Farm, Littlehempston, Totnes, Devon, TQ9 6ND.
Glorious views, friendly welcome, cotton sheets, home-made bread and marmalade. **Open:** Mar to Oct
01803 762638 (also fax) Mrs Miller
D: £19–£23 **S:** £23–£25
Beds: 4F 1D 1T **Baths:** 6 En

Post Cottage, Littlehempston, Totnes, Devon, TQ9 6L.
C16th thatched cottage in hamlet two miles from Elizabethan market town of Totnes.
Open: All Year (not Xmas)
01803 868192 Mr & Mrs Galton-Fenzi
D: fr £19.50 **S:** £19.50
Beds: 1D 1T 1S **Baths:** 1 Pr 1 Sh

RATES

D = Price range per person sharing in a double room
S = Price range for a single room

Luppitt

ST1606

Jacks House, Luppitt, Honiton, Devon, EX14 4SR.
Open: All Year (not Xmas/New Year)
01404 891341 Mrs Krestovnikoff
D: £18.50–£25 **S:** £25
Beds: 1F 1T
Jacks house a charming stone house, surrounded by large gardens, in the Blackdown Hills. Only ten minutes from Honiton, and half an hour from the seaside. Ideal for walking, cycling, visiting historic houses, wild life parks, sailing and riding.

Lustleigh

SX7881   Cleave Inn

Brookside, Lustleigh, Newton Abbot, Devon, TQ13 9TJ.
Beautiful granite house with history dating back to C15th in picturesque village.
Open: All Year
01647 277310 Mr & Mrs Halsey
D: £20 **S:** £25
Beds: 2D 1T **Baths:** 1 Sh

Lydford

SX5184   Dartmoor Inn

Moor View House, Vale Down, Lydford, Okehampton, Devon, EX20 4BB.
Licensed Victorian country house, edge Dartmoor. Outskirts of Lydford, ideal touring Devon & Cornwall.
Open: All Year
Grades: AA 5 Diamond, RAC 5 Diamond
01822 820220 (also fax)
Mr Sharples
D: £25–£36 **S:** £30–£45
Beds: 3D 1T **Baths:** 4 Pr

Lympstone

SX9984   Saddlers Arms, Swan Inn, Redwing Inn, Puffing Billy, White Hart

Gulliford Farm, Lympstone, Exmouth, Devon, EX8 5AQ.
Lovely C16th farmhouse. Garden, swimming pool, large rooms.
Open: All Year (not Xmas)
01392 873067 (also fax)
Mrs Hallett
D: £20–£25 **S:** £20–£25
Beds: 2F 1T 1S **Baths:** 1 En

Hope Cottage, The Strand, Lympstone, Exmouth, Devon, EX8 5JS.
C15th cottage in beautiful village on Exe estuary (Mr & Mrs Clarke).
Open: All Year
01395 268349 Mr Clarke
D: £17.50 **S:** £17.50
Beds: 3D 1T **Baths:** 1 En 1 Sh

Lynmouth

SS7249   🍺 *Riverside Cottages, Village Inn*

Glenville House, *2 Tors Road, Lynmouth, Devon, EX35 6ET.*
Open: Feb to Nov **Grades:** AA 4 Diamond
01598 752202 Mr & Mrs Francis
D: £22–£26 **S:** £22–£30
Beds: 4D 1T 1S **Baths:** 3 En 1 Pr 2 Sh
🐲 (12) 🖾 📺 🛋 🏌
Idyllic riverside setting. Delightful
Victorian house full of character and
charm. Licensed. Tastefully decorated
bedrooms. Picturesque harbour, village
and unique Cliff Railway nestled amidst
wooded valley. Magnificent Exmoor
scenery, spectacular coastline and
beautiful walks. Peaceful, tranquil,
romantic - a very special place.

Tregonwell Riverside Guest House, *1 Tors Road, Lynmouth, Devon, EX35 6ET.*
Open: All Year (not Xmas)
Grades: ETC 3 Diamond, AA 3 Diamond
01598 753369 Mrs Parker
D: £22–£27 **S:** £22–£25
Beds: 2F 5D 1T 1S **Baths:** 5 En 1 Pr 3 Sh
🐲 🅿 (7) ⚡ 🖾 📺 🐾 🛋 🏌
Award-winning, romantic, elegant
riverside (former sea captain's) stone-
built house, snuggled amidst waterfalls,
cascades, wooded valleys, soaring cliff
tops, lonely beaches, enchanting
harbourside 'Olde Worlde' smugglers'
village. Shelley, Wordsworth, Coleridge
stayed here. 'England's Switzerland'.
Pretty bedrooms, dramatic views.
Garaged parkings.

Lynton

SS7149   🍺 *Rising Sun Inn, Staghunters Inn, Ye Olde Cottage Inn, Royal Castle, Sandrock*

The Turret, *33 Lee Road, Lynton, Devon, EX35 6BS.*
Open: All Year **Grades:** ETC 3 Diamond
01598 753284 (also fax)
Mrs Wayman
D: £18–£23 **S:** fr £25
Beds: 5D 1T **Baths:** 4 En 1Sh
🐲 (12) 📺 ✕ 🛋 📺 ⚡ cc
Step back in time and experience old
world hospitality. Built in 1898, the charm
of our hotel will relax and welcome you.
Beautiful ensuite bedrooms, enhanced
with all the modern facilities. Evening
meals served in cosy dining room.
Vegetarian and special dietary needs
catered for.

The Denes Guest House, *Longmead, Lynton, Devon, EX35 6DQ.*
Open: All Year
Grades: ETC 3 Diamond
01598 753573 Mr McGowan
j.e.mcgowan@btinternet.com
D: £16–£22.50 **S:** £16–£22.50
Beds: 3F 2D **Baths:** 2 En 1 Pr 2 Sh
🐲 🅿 (5) ⚡ 📺 ✕ 📺 ❋ ⚡ cc
A warm friendly greeting awaits you at
The Denes, with its Edwardian charm.
Comfortable accommodation and home
cooked food, evening meals served in our
licensed dining room. Ideal base to
explore Exmoor on the South West
Coastal Path. An Exmoor paths partner.

Victoria Lodge, *Lee Road, Lynton, Devon, EX35 6BP.*
Awarded B&B of the Year for S.W.
England by South West Tourism.
Open: Feb to Nov
Grades: AA 5 Diamond
01598 753203 (also fax)
Mr & Mrs Bennett
info@victorialodge.co.uk
D: £26–£36 **S:** £35–£54
Beds: 1F 7D 1T **Baths:** 9 En
🐲 🅿 (7) ⚡ 📺 ✕ 🛋 📺 ⚡ cc

Lynhurst Hotel, *Lynton, Devon, EX35 6AX.*
Character Victorian residence situated in
gardens/woodland overlooking Lynmouth
Bay.
Open: All Year
Grades: AA 4 Diamond
01598 752241 (also fax)
Mr Townsend
enq@thelynhurst.co.uk
D: £22–£30 **S:** £25–£28
Beds: 2F 5D 1T 1S **Baths:** 7 En
🐲 (1) 🅿 (2) 📺 ✕ 🛋 📺 ⚡ cc

Gable Lodge, *Lee Road, Lynton, Devon, EX35 6BS.*
Large Victorian house with views along
the East Lyn valley.
Open: Easter to Oct
01598 752367 (also fax)
Mr & Mrs Bowman
donbowman@compuserve.com
D: £18.50–£19.50 **S:** £18.50–£19.50
Beds: 1F 5D **Baths:** 5 En 1 Sh
🐲 🅿 (8) ⚡ 📺 🐾 🛋 📺 ⚡ cc

Croft House Hotel, *Lydiate Lane, Lynton, Devon, EX35 6HE.*
Croft house nestling in the old village,
built 1828 for a sea captain.
Open: All Year (not Xmas)
01598 752391 (also fax)
Mrs Johnson
D: £17–£27 **S:** £20–£30
Beds: 5D 2T **Baths:** 6 En 1 Pr
⚡ 📺 🐾 ✕ 🛋 ⚡ cc

Malborough

SX7039   🍺 *Old Inn*

Quill View, *Well Hill Close, Malborough, Kingsbridge, Devon, TQ7 3SS.*
Very quiet village position with views and
patios, super lounge.
Open: All Year (not Xmas)
01548 562085 willwrite@tesco.net
D: £16–£20 **S:** £19–£23
Beds: 1D 1T **Baths:** 1 En 1 Pr
🐲 (7) 🅿 (2) ⚡ 📺 🐾 🛋 📺

Martinhoe

SS6648   🍺 *Hunters Inn, Fox & Goose*

Mannacott Farm, *Martinhoe, Parracombe, Barnstaple, Devon, EX31 4QS.*
In area of outstanding natural scenery.
Ideal for walkers, bird watchers. Near
coast.
Open: Apr to mid-Oct
01598 763227 Mrs Dallyn
D: £15–£16 **S:** £16–£17
Beds: 1D 1T 1S **Baths:** 1 Sh
🅿 (2) ⚡ 📺 🛋 📺

Marwood

SS5437   🍺 *New Ring O' Bells*

Lee House, *Marwood, Barnstaple, Devon, EX31 4DZ.*
Family-run Elizabethan manor house.
Wonderful views, secluded grounds.
Open: Apr to Oct
01271 374345 Mrs Darling
D: £20–£22 **S:** £20–£22
Beds: 1T 2D **Baths:** 3 En
🐲 (14) 🅿 (8) ⚡ 📺 🐾 🛋 📺

Merton

SS5212   🍺 *Bull & Dragon*

Richmond House, *New Road (A386), Merton, Okehampton, Devon, EX20 3EG.*
Open: All Year
01805 603258 Mrs Wickett
D: £15 **S:** £15
Beds: 3F 1T 2D **Baths:** 1 Sh
🐲 (5) 🅿 (4) 📺 🐾 ✕ ⚡ cc
Country house within easy reach of beach,
moors, gardens, Tarka Trail. Evening meal
optional. H.C. in all bedrooms.

Meshaw

SS7519

Bournebridge Farm, *Meshaw, South Molton, Devon, EX36 4NL.*
Traditional warm welcome on small
working farm; peaceful, rural setting,
easy access from A361.
Open: All Year (not Xmas)
01884 860002 Mrs Teesdale
D: £17.50–£20 **S:** £17.50–£20
Beds: 1F 1D 1T **Baths:** 1 En 1 Sh
🐲 🅿 📺 🐾 ✕ 🛋 📺 ⚡

Modbury

SX6551   🍺 *Exeter Inn*

Orchard Cottage, *Palm Cross Green, Modbury, Ivybridge, Devon, PL21 0QZ.*
Double ensuite garden room in private
cottage. Views over Modbury.
Open: All Year
01548 830633 Mrs Ewen
Beds: 1D **Baths:** 1 En
D: £22.50 **S:** £27.50
🅿 ⚡ 📺 🛋 📺 ⚡

Little Orcheton Farm, *Modbury, Ivybridge, Devon, PL21 0TF.*
Working farm on estate, spectacular
natural beauty. 3 miles Wembury Beach,
coastal walks, Dartmoor.
Open: Easter to Nov
01548 830515 Mr & Mrs Doidge
D: £16–£20 **S:** £16–£20
Beds: 3F 1D 1T **Baths:** 2 En 1 Pr
🐲 🅿 ⚡ 📺 🐾 ✕ 🛋 ⚡

Monkokehampton

SS5805   🍺 *Duke Of York*

Seldon Farm, *Monkokehampton, Winkleigh, Devon, EX19 8RY.*
Charming C17th farmhouse in beautiful,
tranquil, rural setting. **Open:** Easter to
Oct. **Grades:** ETC 2 Diamond
01837 810312 Mrs Case
D: £20 **S:** £23
Beds: 1F 2D **Baths:** 1 En 1 Pr 1 Sh
🐲 🅿 📺 🐾 ⚡

Morchard Bishop

SS7607   London Inn, White Hart

Oldborough Fishing Retreat,
Morchard Bishop, Crediton, Devon, EX17
6JQ.
Lakeside rural retreat. 40 minutes drive
M5 J27. Nice place for Exeter city break.
Open: All Year (not Xmas/New Year)
01363 877437 Mrs Wilshaw
fishingretreat@eclipse.co.uk
D: £16–£17 **S:** £16–£17
Beds: 1F 1T **Baths:** 1 Sh
🛏 🅿 (10) ⊬ 📺 🔭 ✕ ⬛ 🏃 CC

Moreleigh

SX7652   The New Inn

Island Farm, Moreleigh, Totnes, Devon,
TQ9 7SH.
Situated in the heart of South Hams.
Panoramic views of countryside.
Open: All Year (not Xmas/New Year)
01548 821441 Mrs Finch
D: £20–£22 **S:** £20–£22
Beds: 1F 1T 2D **Baths:** 2 En 1 Pr
🛏 🅿 (4) 📺 ✕ ⬛ 🏃

Moretonhampstead

SX7586   The Bell, London Inn, White Hart,
Plymouth Inn

Great Wooston Farm,
Moretonhampstead, Newton Abbot,
Devon, TQ13 8QA.
Open: All Year (not Xmas)
Grades: ETC 4 Diamond, AA 4 Diamond
01647 440367 (also fax) Mrs Cuming
D: £20–£22 **S:** £20–£25
Beds: 2D 1T **Baths:** 2 En 1 Pr
🛏 (8) 🅿 (3) ⊬ 📺 ⬛ 🏃 CC
High above the Teign Valley in Dartmoor
National Park, this delightful farmhouse
is a peaceful haven with views across the
moors. All bedrooms are prettily
decorated; 2 ensuite, 1 with private
bathroom, 1 with four-poster bed. Every
facility included in this quality
accommodation.

Little Wooston Farm,
Moretonhampstead, Newton Abbot,
Devon, TQ13 8QA.
Working farm in beautiful countryside.
Ideally situated for walking. Quiet
location. **Open:** All Year
Grades: ETC 3 Diamond
01647 440551 (also fax)
Mrs Cuming
D: £15–£16 **S:** £15–£16
Beds: 1F 1D 1S **Baths:** 1 Sh
🛏 🅿 (4) ⊬ 📺 🔭 ✕ ⬛ 🏃

Great Sloncombe Farm,
Moretonhampstead, Newton Abbot,
Devon, TQ13 8QF.
C13th Dartmoor farmhouse, everything
provided for an enjoyable stay.
Open: All Year
Grades: ETC 4 Diamond, Silver, AA 4
Diamond
01647 440595 (also fax)
Mrs Merchant
D: £23–£24 **S:** £30
Beds: 2D 1T **Baths:** 3 En
🛏 (8) 🅿 (3) 📺 🔭 ✕ ⬛ 🏃

Yarningale, Exeter Road,
Moretonhampstead, Newton Abbot,
Devon, TQ13 8QA.
Secluded rural property, with absolutely
stunning Dartmoor views.
Open: All Year
Grades: ETC 3 Diamond
01647 440560 (also fax)
Mrs Radcliffe
sally.radcliffe@virgin.net
D: £19–£22 **S:** £20–£25
Beds: 1F 1D **Baths:** 1 En 1 Pr
🛏 🅿 (3) ⊬ 🔭 🔭 ✕ ⬛ 📺 🏃 ⚘ 🏃

Newton Abbot

SX8671   Bickley Mill

Bulleigh Park Farm, Ipplepen,
Newton Abbot, Devon, TQ12 5UA.
Beautiful farmhouse and surroundings.
Complimentary tea/coffee with
homemade cakes.
Open: All Year (not Xmas/New Year)
01803 872254 (also fax)
Angela Dallyn
D: £15–£21 **S:** £18–£25
Beds: 1F 1D 1S **Baths:** 1 En 1 Pr
🛏 🅿 (6) 📺 🔭 📺 🏃 ⅅ

Newton Ferrers

SX5448   Dartmoor Inn, Dolphin Inn, Swan
Inn, Ship Inn

Crown Yealm, Bridgend Hill, Newton
Ferrers, Plymouth, Devon, PL8 1AW.
Beautiful riverside country house. All
guest rooms overlook garden to water's
edge.
Open: All Year
01752 872365 (also fax)
Mrs Johnson
D: £17–£24 **S:** £21–£30
Beds: 1F 1D 1T **Baths:** 2 En 1 Sh
🛏 🅿 (7) 📺 🔭 ⬛ 🏃

Wood Cottage, Bridgend, Newton
Ferrers, Plymouth, Devon, PL8 1AW.
Welcoming, modernised cottage,
overlooking end of Yealm Estuary and
farmland.
Open: All Year
01752 872372 Mrs Cross
jillx@wdcott.freeserve.co.uk
D: £17.50–£20 **S:** £20–£22.50
Beds: 1T 1D **Baths:** 1 En 1 Sh
🛏 🅿 (2) 📺 🔭 ✕ ⬛ 📺 🏃

North Molton

SS7329   Politemore Arms, Miners Arms

Middle Poole, North Molton, South
Molton, Devon, EX36 3HL.
Fifteenth century thatched cottage.
Wealth of Olde Worlde charm - a rare
find.
Open: All Year
01598 740206 (also fax)
Mrs Procter
D: £15–£18 **S:** £15–£18
Beds: 1D 1T **Baths:** 1 En 1 Pr
🛏 (10) 🅿 (2) ⊬ 📺 🔭 ✕ ⬛ 🏃

Planning a longer stay? Always

ask for any special rates

North Tawton

SS6601

Kayden House Hotel, High Street,
North Tawton, Devon, EX20 2HF.
Devon Heartland, ideal for Moors and
Coasts. Warm welcome assured.
Open: All Year
01837 82242 Ms Waldron
D: fr £20 **S:** fr £26
Beds: 1F 2T 2D 2S **Baths:** 5 En 2 Pr
🛏 📺 🔭 ⬛ 📺 🏃 CC

Northleigh (Honiton)

SY1996

Smallicombe Farm, Northleigh,
Colyton, Devon, EX24 6BU.
Open: All Year
Grades: ETC 4 Diamond
01404 831310 Mrs Todd
Fax: 01404 831431
maggie_todd@yahoo.com
D: £20–£23.50 **S:** £25
Beds: 1F 1D 1T **Baths:** 3 En
🛏 (10) ⊬ 📺 ✕ ⬛ 📺 🏃 ⅅ 3
Relax in old world charm, idyllic rural
setting with only the sights and sounds
of the countryside. Meet our prize-
winning Berkshire pigs. Explore this
unspoilt corner of Devon with its
stunning coastline. Featured in Guide to
Good Food in the West Country.

Sunnyacre, Rockerhayne Farm,
Northleigh, Colyton, Devon, EX24 6DA.
Bungalow on working farm in beautiful
scenic countryside close to coast.
Open: All Year (not Xmas)
01404 871422 N Rich
D: £15–£20 **S:** £15–£20
Beds: 1F 1D 1T **Baths:** 1 Sh
🛏 🅿 (4) 📺 ✕ ⬛ 📺

Noss Mayo

SX5447   Old Ship Inn, Swan Inn

Rowden House, Stoke Road, Noss
Mayo, Plymouth, Devon, PL8 1JG.
Victorian farmhouse with lovely garden in
peaceful rural setting.
Open: All Year (not Xmas)
01752 872153 Mrs Hill
tifhil@globalnet.co.uk
D: £20 **S:** £20
Beds: 1F 2T **Baths:** 2 Pr
🛏 🅿 (6) 📺 🔭 ⬛ 📺 🏃

Oakford

SS9021   Masons Arms, Higher Western

Harton Farm, Oakford, Tiverton, Devon,
EX16 9HH.
Peaceful farmhouse. Home grown
additive free meat, vegetables. Friendly
animals.
Open: All Year (not Xmas/New Year)
Grades: ETC 3 Diamond
01398 351209 (also fax)
Mrs Head
harton@eclipse.co.uk
D: £16–£17 **S:** £16–£17
Beds: 1F 1T **Baths:** 1 Sh
🛏 (4) 🅿 (2) 📺 🔭 ✕ 📺 🏃

The Old Rectory, Holme Place, Oakford, Tiverton, Devon, EX16 9EW.
Close Exmoor elegant accommodation and vineyard in tranquil beautiful location.
Open: All Year (not Xmas)
Grades: AA 4 Diamond
01398 351486 (also fax) Mrs Rostron
prot@oakford57.freeserve.co.uk
D: £18.50–£22 **Baths:** 1 En 1 Sh
P (3) ⊬ TV ✕ ▥ V ♨

Red Deer House, Oakford, Tiverton, Devon, EX16 9JE.
Old coaching inn overlooking open countryside noted for personal service.
Open: All Year (not Xmas)
01398 351286 Mrs Lester
D: £15–£17 **S:** £15–£17
Beds: 1D 2T **Baths:** 3 En
ఆ (8) P (3) ⊬ TV ▥ ♨

Newhouse Farm, Oakford, Tiverton, Devon, EX16 9JE.
Home-baked bread, comfort, warm hospitality, relaxation guaranteed.
Open: All Year (not Xmas)
01398 351347 Mrs Boldry
D: £19–£22.50 **S:** £25
Beds: 1D 1T **Baths:** 2 En
ఆ (10) P (2) ⊬ TV ✕ ▥ V ♨

Okehampton

SX5895 ⬧ Oxenham Arms, River Inn, Tors Hotel, New Inn, Taw River, Sticklepath, Cellars, Plume Of Feathers

North Lake, Exeter Road, Okehampton, Devon, EX20 1QH .
Open: All Year (not Xmas)
Grades: ETC 3 Diamond
01837 53100 Mrs Jones
D: fr £20 **S:** fr £23
Beds: 2D 1T **Baths:** 2 En 1 Pr
ఆ (6) P (10) ⊬ TV ✝ ▥ V ♨
Set in large grounds with panoramic views across Dartmoor. Tastefully furnished, good food, with a personal friendly touch; come and go as you please. Superb walking and riding base, stunning scenery and cascading rivers.

Heathfield House, Klondyke Road, Okehampton, Devon, EX20 1EW.
Open: Feb to Dec
Grades: AA 4 Diamond
01837 54211 (also fax) Mr & Mrs Gibbins
Tim@tgibbins.freeserve.co.uk
D: £17–£30 **S:** £30–£35
Beds: 1F 2D 1T **Baths:** 4 En
ఆ (8) ⊬ TV ✝ ✕ ▥ V ♨ cc
Situated high on north face of Dartmoor, tucked away & private, although only 10 mins from market town of Okehampton. Chef owner, direct access Dartmoor, spectacular views. Fine food and wine. Heated outdoor pool. Residential pottery courses. Christmas breaks.

Southey Farm, Sampford Courtenay, Okehampton, Devon, EX20 2TE.
Comfortable farmhouse overlooking gardens and fields, close to Dartmoor.
Open: All Year (not Xmas/New Year)
01837 82446 Mr & Mrs Townsend Green
TG@southeyfarm.freeserve.co.uk
D: £15 **S:** £15
Beds: 1T 1S/T **Baths:** 2 Pr
ఆ P (4) TV ✝ ▥ ♨

Arnley House, 7 Oaklands Park, Okehampton, Devon, EX20 1LN.
Modern luxury house, warm welcome, discount for 3 days plus.
Open: Jan to Nov
Grades: ETC DTA Approved
01837 53311 Ms Masereeuw
beryl@masereeuw.fsnet.co.uk
D: £23.50 **S:** £23.50
Beds: 1D **Baths:** 1 En
P (1) ⊬ TV ▥ ♨

Otterton

SY0885 ⬧ Kings Arms

Ropers Cottage, Ropers Lane, Otterton, Budleigh Salterton, Devon, EX9 7JF.
C17th cottage in picturesque village, near river and coastal path.
Open: Easter to Oct
01395 568826 Mrs Earl
Fax: 01395 568206
D: £18–£18.50 **S:** £18–£18.50
Beds: 1T 1S **Baths:** 2 En
ఆ (1) P (2) ⊬ TV ▥ ♨

Ottery St Mary

SY1095

Holly Ridge , West Hill, Ottery St Mary, Devon, EX11 1UX.
Open: All Year
01404 812776 (also fax) Mr Abel
HollyRidge@aol.com
D: £18–£26 **S:** £18–£26
Beds: 1F 2D **Baths:** 1 En 1 Sh
ఆ (12) P (8) ⊬ TV ✝ ✕ ▥ V ♨ ♨ &
Holly Ridge is on the edge of the peaceful village of West Hill, near Ottery St. Mary, in an area of outstanding natural beauty. All our guest rooms enjoy panoramic views across the Exe valley and Dartmoor.

Normandy House Hotel and Bistro, 5 Cornhill, Ottery St Mary, Devon, EX11 1DW.
Georgian town house opposite beautiful C14th church. Peaceful and relaxing.
Open: All Year (not Xmas/New Year)
Grades: ETC 4 Diamond Silver Award, AA 4 Diamond
01404 811088 Fax: 01404 811023
D: £24.75–£27.50 **S:** £29.95
Beds: 1T 3D 1S **Baths:** 5 En
ఆ (6) TV ✕ ▥ V ♨ cc

Paignton

SX8960 ⬧ Inn On The Quay, Harbour Lights, Inn On The Green, Talk Of The Town, Esplanade

South Sands Hotel, Alta Vista Road, Paignton, Devon, TQ4 6BZ.
Open: Mar to Oct
Grades: ETC 2 Star
01803 557231 Mr Cahill
D: £20–£25 **S:** £20–£25
Beds: 7F 4D 6T 2S **Baths:** 17 En 2 Pr
ఆ P (17) TV ✝ ✕ ▥ V ♨ ♨ & cc
South-facing, licensed family-run hotel in peaceful location overlooking beach/park. Close to harbour/amenities. Huge help-yourself buffet-style breakfast. Outstanding value for money. All rooms ensuite with television, telephone, teamakers, most with king size beds.

Cherwood Hotel, 26 Garfield Road, Paignton, TQ4 6AX.
Open: All Year
Grades: ETC 4 Diamond
01803 556515 J Alderson
Fax: 01803 555126
james-pauline@cherwood-hotel.co.uk
D: £16–£20 **S:** £16–£20
Beds: 3F 3D 2T 1S **Baths:** 9 En
ఆ P (4) TV ✝ ✕ ▥ V ♨ ♨ cc
All ensuite, licensed bar, prestigious 4 diamond etc. award. Quality assured. Ideal position by central seafront/ pier, close to town. CTVs, beverage trays, radio alarms, ceiling fans, hairdryers, complimentary toiletries. Luxury 4 poster rooms available. Satisfaction guaranteed.

Hotel Fiesta, 2 Kernou Road, Paignton, TQ4 6BA.
Open: All Year
Grades: ETC 3 Diamond
01803 521862 (also fax)
Mr Hawker
hotelfiesta@alk21.com
D: £16–£20 **S:** £22–£26
Beds: 2F 5D 1T 2S **Baths:** 7 En 3 Sh
ఆ P ▥ ♨ ♨ & cc
An attractive seaside property close to Paignton's clean beaches, pier, crazy golf, sea fishing, Dartmouth Steam Railway and our new multiplex cinema with restaurant and children's area. Also plenty of night life for all ages. Ideal for short breaks throughout the year.

Park View Guest House, 19 Garfield Road, Paignton, Devon, TQ4 6AX.
Small friendly guest house - short level stroll town and sea front.
Open: All Year (not Xmas/New Year)
01803 528521 D: £13–£16 **S:** £13–£16
Beds: 3F 1D **Baths:** 1 Sh
ఆ P TV ✝ ✕ ▥ V ♨

Sundale Hotel, 10 Queens Road, Paignton, Devon, TQ4 6AT.
Quiet family run hotel, close to all amenities, highly recommended.
Open: All Year
01803 557431 Mr McDermott
D: £14.50–£17.50 **S:** £14.50–£17.50
Beds: 2F 2T 3D 1S **Baths:** 4 En 1 Sh
ఆ ⊬ TV ✝ ✕ ▥ V ♨ ♨

Channel View Hotel, 8 Marine Parade, Paignton, Devon, TQ3 2NU.
Sea front level east, access to all areas, amazing views.
Open: All Year
Grades: AA 3 Diamond
01803 522432 D: £25–£30 **S:** £25–£30
Beds: 3F 6D 2T 2S **Baths:** 13 En
ఆ P (10) TV ✕ ▥ V ♨ ♨ cc

Adelphi Hotel, 14 Queens Road, Paignton, Devon, TQ4 6AT.
Only 200 yards level walks - Beach,train, coach/ bus stations.
Open: All Year
01803 558022 Mr Elnor
D: £14–£18 **S:** £20–£25
Beds: 2F 3D 4T 2S **Baths:** 5 En 2 Sh
ఆ (1) TV ✝ ✕ ▥ V ♨ ♨

Bayview Hotel, 6 Cleveland Road, Paignton, TQ4 6EN.
Friendly family-run hotel, licensed, ideal location near town harbour.
Open: All Year (not Xmas)
01803 557400 bayview@eurodrell.co.uk
D: £12–£18 **S:** £12–£18
Beds: 3F 2D 2T 1S **Baths:** 3 En 2 Sh
⌂ 🅿 (9) 🍴 ✕ 🖳 Ⅴ 🏃

Birchwood House Hotel, 33 St Andrews Road, Paignton, Devon, TQ4 6HA.
Licensed family-run hotel close to beaches and all facilities.
Open: Easter to Nov
Grades: ETC 4 Diamond
01803 551323 Fax: 01803 401301
yates3048@aol.com
D: £20–£24 **S:** £20–£24
Beds: 3F 3T 5D 1S **Baths:** 12 En
⌂ (5) 🅿 (8) 🖵 🍴 ✕ 🖳 Ⅴ 🏃 cc

Mandalay Hotel, Cleveland Road, Paignton, Devon, TQ4 6EN.
Comfortable family-run licensed hotel.
Open: All Year
01803 525653 Mr & Mrs Davis
Fax: 01803 525193
mandalayhotel@btconnect.com
D: £16–£20 **S:** £16–£20
Beds: 2F 6D 2T **Baths:** 5 En 1 Pr 3 Sh
⌂ 🅿 (10) 🖵 🍴 ✕ 🖳 Ⅴ ❋ 🏃 cc

SS2906

The Barton, Pancrasweek, Holsworthy, Devon, EX22 7JT.
Working farm. Peaceful position. Easy reach coast, moors, famous Clovelly.
Open: Easter to Oct
01288 381315 Mrs Chant
D: £20 **S:** £20
Beds: 2D 1T **Baths:** 3 En
🅿 ✂ 🖵 ✕ 🏃

SS6644

'Tranquillity Voley', Parracombe, Barnstaple, Devon, EX31 4PG.
Tranquillity just for two. Relax in ground-floor accommodation, surrounded by superb views.
Open: All Year (not Xmas)
01598 763385 Mrs Brown
tranquility@mailandnews.com
D: £17–£20 **S:** £17–£20
Beds: 1D **Baths:** 1 Pr
🅿 (4) ✂ 🖵 ✕ 🏃

SX5177 🍴 Peter Tavy Inn

Churchtown, Peter Tavy, Tavistock, Devon, PL19 9NP.
Detached Victorian house standing in own large quiet garden.
Open: All Year (not Xmas)
01822 810477 Mrs Lane
lane@swcg.co.uk
D: £17–£18 **S:** £17–£18
Beds: 2D 1S **Baths:** 1 En 1 Sh
⌂ (10) 🅿 (6) 🖵 🍴 🖳 Ⅴ 🏃

SS5109 🍴 The Laurels Inn

Aish Villa, Petrockstowe, Okehampton, Devon, EX20 3HL.
Peaceful location, superb views, ideal for visiting Dartmoor, Exmoor, coast.
Open: All Year
01837 810581 Ms Gordon
gillandtonygordon@compuserve.com
D: £17 **S:** £17
Beds: 1F 1T 1D **Baths:** 1 Sh
⌂ 🅿 (4) ✂ 🖵 🖳 Ⅴ 🏃 ♿

SS4641 🍴 Rock Inn, Thatched Barn

Meadow Cottage, Pickwell, Georgeham, Braunton, Devon, EX33 1LA.
Open: All Year
01271 890938 (also fax)
Mrs Holmes
rpholmes@talk21.com
D: fr £20 **S:** fr £20
Beds: 1D 1S **Baths:** 1 Pr
⌂ 🅿 (3) ✂ 🖵 🖳 Ⅴ
Meadow Cottage is in the tranquil setting of Pickwell. Off the beaten track with panoramic views of patchwork fields to the sea, close to the coastal path and beaches of Woolacombe, Putsborough and Croyde and the championship golf course, Saunton.

SX4756 🍴 West Hoe, Brown Bear, Odd Wheel, Eddystone Inn, The Walrus, Sippers, The Yardarm, Frog & Frigate, Waterfront, Notte Inn

Mountbatten Hotel, 52 Exmouth Road, Stoke, Plymouth, Devon, PL1 4QH.
Open: All Year
Grades: ETC 3 Diamond
01752 563843 Mr Hendy
Fax: 01752 606014
D: £23–£25 **S:** £20–£27
Beds: 3F 6D 2T 4S **Baths:** 7 En 2 Sh
⌂ 🅿 (4) 🖵 🍴 ✕ 🖳 🏃 cc
Small licensed Victorian hotel overlooking parkland with river views. Quiet cul de sac. Close city centre/ferryport. Good access Cornwall. Walking distance Naval base, Royal Fleet Club, FE College. Secure parking. Well appointed rooms. Tea/coffee, CTVs, telephones. Credit cards accepted.

Bay Cottage, 150 Church Road, Wembury, Plymouth, Devon, PL9 0HR.
Open: All Year (not Xmas)
Grades: ETC 3 Diamond
01752 862559 (also fax)
Mrs Farrington
TheFairies@aol.com
D: £26–£29 **S:** £25–£35
Beds: 2D 2T 1S **Baths:** 3 En 2 Sh
⌂ 🅿 (2) ✂ 🖵 🍴 🖳 Ⅴ 🏃
Victorian cottage by the sea, surrounded by National Trust land.

Please respect a B&B's wishes regarding children, animals and smoking

Planning a longer stay? Always ask for any special rates

The Old Pier Guest House, 20 Radford Road, West Hoe, Plymouth, Devon, PL1 3BY.
Convenient for ferry, Barbican, city centre, sea front. Offers exceptional value.
Open: All Year (not Xmas/New Year)
Grades: ETC 3 Diamond
01752 268468 Mrs Jones
enquiries@oldpier.co.uk
D: £15–£19 **S:** £16–£25
Beds: 1F 2T 3D 1S
⌂ (10) ✂ 🖵 🖳 Ⅴ 🏃 cc

Teviot Guest House, 20 North Road East, Plymouth, Devon, PL4 6AS.
Excellent Bed & Breakfast in central location for non-smokers.
Open: All Year (not Xmas)
Grades: ETC 4 Diamond, Silver Award
01752 262656 Mrs Fisher
Fax: 01752 251660
teviotGH@BTinternet.com
D: £18–£30 **S:** £18–£30
Beds: 2F 2D 1T 1S **Baths:** 2 En 3 Pr 1 Sh
⌂ (7) 🅿 (2) ✂ 🖵 🖳 Ⅴ 🏃 cc

The Elizabethan Guest House, 223 Citadel Road, The Hoe, Plymouth, Devon, PL1 2NG.
Central location. Close to Hoe, harbour, Barbican and city centre.
Open: All Year
01752 661672 (also fax)
D: £14–£20 **S:** £18–£22
Beds: 1F 4D 2T **Baths:** 1 En 2 Sh
⌂ 🅿 (3) 🖵 🖳 Ⅴ 🏃 ♿ cc

Caraneal, 12-14 Pier Street, The Hoe, Plymouth, Devon, PL1 3BS.
Friendly, family run. Close to city centre, seafront, continental ferry port.
Open: All Year **Grades:** AA 3 Diamond
01752 663589 Mrs Crosland
Fax: 01752 212871
D: £19–£22.50 **S:** £25–£30
Beds: 1F 6D 1T 1S **Baths:** 9 En
⌂ 🅿 (2) 🖵 ✕ 🖳 Ⅴ 🏃 cc

Sunray Hotel, 3/5 Alfred Street, The Hoe, Plymouth, Devon, PL1 2RP.
Centrally located, convenient for theatre, shops, Barbican and National Aquarium.
Open: All Year (not Xmas/New Year)
01752 669113 Mr Sutton
Fax: 01752 268969
D: £23–£26 **S:** £28–£35
Beds: 6F 4D 5T 3S **Baths:** 16 En 2 Pr
🅿 (6) 🖵 🖳 🏃

Olivers Hotel & Restaurant, 33 Sutherland Road, Plymouth, Devon, PL4 6BN.
Welcoming, restful Victorian hotel convenient for City, Sea and Moors.
Open: All Year
Grades: RAC 4 diamond
01752 663923 Mrs Purser
Fax: 01752 262295
D: £22.50–£25 **S:** £20–£30
Beds: 1F 2D 1T 2S **Baths:** 4 En 1 Sh
⌂ (11) 🅿 (2) 🖵 ✕ 🖳 Ⅴ 🏃 cc

Georgian House Hotel, *51 Citadel Road, The Hoe, Plymouth, PL1 3AU.*
Family-run hotel in central location near all Plymouth's amenities.
Open: Feb to Dec **Grades:** AA 3 Diamond
01752 663237
georgianhousehotel@msn.com
D: £19–£22 **S:** £22–£29
Beds: 6D 2T 2S **Baths:** 10 En
⌂ 乡 ⊠ ▦ ⊠ ⚊ cc

Osmond Guest House, *42 Pier Street, West Hoe, Plymouth, Devon, PL1 3BT.*
Seafront Edwardian house. Walking distance to all attractions. Courtesy pick-up from stations. **Open:** All Year
01752 229705 Mrs Richards
Fax: 01752 269655
D: £16–£20 **S:** £17–£25
Beds: 3D 2T 1S **Baths:** 4 En
▣ (2) 乡 ⊠ ▦ ⚊ ⚬

Hotspur Guest House, *108 North Road East, Plymouth, Devon, PL4 6AW.*
Victorian property, adjacent city centre; bus/rail stations, historic Barbican, Hoe, seafronts. **Open:** All Year (not Xmas)
01752 663928 J Taylor
Fax: 01752 261493
info@hotspur.co.uk
D: £16–£17 **S:** £16.50–£17.50
Beds: 2F 1D 2T 3S
⌂ ⊠ ⌇ ✕ ▦ ⊠ ⚊ cc

Postbridge

SX6579 ⚑ *Warren House Inn, East Dart Hotel*

Hartyland, *Postbridge, Yelverton, Devon, PL20 6SZ.*
Large, warm, comfortable Dartmoor house, direct access to open moorland.
Open: All Year (not Xmas)
01822 880210 Mr & Mrs Bishop
Fax: 01822 880384
andybishop@compuserve.com
D: £20–£25 **S:** £20–£25
Beds: 1F 3T 1S **Baths:** 2 Sh
⌂ ▣ (6) ⊠ ⌇ ✕ ▦ ⊠ ⚊

Poundsgate

SX7072 ⚑ *Tavistock Inn*

New Cott Farm, *Poundsgate, Newton Abbot, Devon, TQ13 7PD.*
Lovely walking in Dartmoor National Park. Good food, beds, welcoming + peaceful. **Open:** All Year
Grades: ETC 4 Diamond
01364 631421 Mrs Phipps
newcott@ruralink.co.uk
D: £20–£22
Beds: 1F 2D 1T **Baths:** 3 En 1 Pr
⌂ (5) ▣ (4) 乡 ⊠ ⌇ ▦ ⊠ ⚬

Preston

SX8574

Sampsons Farm Hotel, *Preston, Newton Abbot, Devon, TQ12 3PP.*
C14th longhouse and converted stables. Quiet location. Luxury ensuite.
Open: All Year
01626 354913 (also fax) Mr Bell
info@sampsonsfarm.com
D: £22.50–£40 **S:** fr £25
Beds: 2F 2T **Baths:** 6 En
⌂ ▣ (15) ⊠ ⌇ ✕ ▦ ⊠ ✿ ⚊ ⚬ 2 cc

Princetown

SX5873

Brimpts Farm, *Princetown, Yelverton, Devon, PL20 6SG.*
Beautiful converted granite barn within stunning peaceful Dartmoor National Park.
Open: All Year (not Xmas)
Grades: AA 3 Diamond
01364 631250 G Cross
Fax: 01364 631450
brimpts@hotmail.com
D: £15–£17.50 **S:** £20
Beds: 1F 3D 6T **Baths:** 10 En
⌂ ▣ (40) 乡 ⊠ ⌇ ✕ ▦ ⊠ ⚊ ⚬ cc

Pyworthy

SS3103 ⚑ *Molesworth Arms*

Leworthy Farm, *Pyworthy, Holsworthy, Devon, EX22 6SJ.*
Open: All Year
01409 259469 Mrs Jennings
D: £22–£25 **S:** £30–£40
Beds: 1F 1T 2D **Baths:** 3 En 1 Pr
⌂ ▣ (8) 乡 ⊠ ✕ ⚊
North Cornish Coast 20 minutes. Georgian farmhouse in tranquil, unspoilt location. Lawned gardens, orchard, wildlife haven and fishing lake. Fresh flowers, pretty bone china, fresh milk, hearty breakfasts. Homely atmosphere. Peaceful lounge. Exquisitely decorated with pictures, plates and china throughout.

Little Knowle Farm, *Pyworthy, Holsworthy, Devon, EX22 6JY.*
Friendly relaxed farmhouse, home cooking, children welcome.
Open: Easter to Oct
01409 254642 Mrs Aston
D: £16–£17.50 **S:** £16–£17.50
Beds: 1D 1T **Baths:** 1 Sh
⌂ ▣ (3) ⊠ ✕ ⊠ ⚊

Rockbeare

SY0294 ⚑ *Jack In The Green*

Forth, *Marsh Green, Rockbeare, Exeter, Devon, EX5 2EX.*
Rural location. 6 miles M5, 8 miles Exeter, Honiton, Sidmouth, Exmouth.
Open: All Year (not Xmas)
01404 822694 Mrs Smith
D: £16–£17 **S:** £16–£17
Beds: 1T 1S **Baths:** 1 Sh
▣ (4) 乡 ⊠ ▦ ⊠ ⚊

Salcombe

SX7339 ⚑ *Victoria Inn, Fortescue Inn, Kings Arms*

Motherhill Farm, *Salcombe, Devon, TQ8 8NB.*
Peaceful and homely Victorian farmhouse on a mixed working farm.
Open: Easter to Oct
01548 842552 (also fax)
Mrs Weymouth
djw@dweymouth.fsnet.co.uk
D: £17–£19 **S:** £17–£19
Beds: 1F/D 1T 1S **Baths:** 1 Sh
⌂ (7) ▣ (6) 乡 ⊠ ⚊

Torre View Hotel, *Devon Road, Salcombe, Devon, TQ8 8HJ.*
Small licensed non-smoking hotel, same owners for 15 years. Sea views. Town easy reach.
Open: Mar to Oct.
Grades: ETC 4 Diamond, RAC 4 Diamond
01548 842633 (also fax)
Mrs Bouttle
bouttle@torreview.eurobell.co.uk
D: £27.50–£30 **S:** £30–£34
Beds: 1F 4D 2T 1S **Baths:** 8 Pr
⌂ (4) ▣ (5) 乡 ⊠ ✕ ▦ ⚊ ⚬ cc

Limericks, *Raleigh Road, Salcombe, Devon, TQ8 8AY.*
Devon-style double-fronted detached family house with TV lounge.
Open: All Year (not Xmas)
01548 842350 Mr & Mrs Collins
D: £17–£20 **S:** £17–£25
Beds: 2D 1T **Baths:** 2 En 1 Sh
⌂ (10) ▣ (4) 乡 ⊠ ▦ ⚊

Rocarno, *Grenville Road, Salcombe, Devon, TQ8 8BJ.*
Estuary views, television, ensuite, beverage trays, heating, friendly welcome.
Open: All Year (not Xmas)
01548 842732 Mr & Mrs Petty-Brown
rocarno@cs.com
D: £17.50–£19.50 **S:** £20–£30
Beds: 1D 1T **Baths:** 2 En
⌂ (4) 乡 ⊠ ⌇ ✕ ▦ ⊠ ⚊

Trennels Hotel, *Herbert Road, Salcombe, Devon, TQ8 8HR.*
A former sea captain's house close to town centre, local sandy beaches, NT properties.
Open: Mar to Oct
01548 842500
trennels_hotel@btinternet.com
D: £22–£26
Beds: 5D **Baths:** 5 En
⌂ (4) ▣ (5) 乡 ⊠ ▦ ⊠ ⚊

Sampford Courtenay

SS6301 ⚑ *New Inn, Railway*

West Trecott Farm, *Sampford Courtenay, Okehampton, Devon, EX20 2TD.*
Open: May to Oct
01837 82569 Mrs Horn
D: £15 **S:** £15
Beds: 3D **Baths:** 2 En 1 Sh
⌂ (2) ▣ (6) 乡 ⊠ ⌇ ⚊
Early 15th Century farmhouse situated in the heart of Devon countryside close to Dartmoor National Park. Farmhouse breakfast, private off road parking. Pleasant surroundings.

Southey Farm, *Sampford Courtenay, Okehampton, Devon, EX20 2TE.*
Comfortable farmhouse overlooking gardens and fields, close to Dartmoor.
Open: All Year (not Xmas/New Year)
01837 82446 Mr & Mrs Townsend Green
TG@southeyfarm.freeserve.co.uk
D: £15 **S:** £15
Beds: 1T 1S/T **Baths:** 2 Pr
⌂ (4) ▣ (4) ⊠ ⌇ ▦ ⚊

Sampford Spiney

SX5372   London Inn

Withill Farm, Sampford Spiney, Yelverton, Devon, PL20 6LN.
Open: All Year
01822 853992 (also fax)
Mrs Kitchen
D: £18–£21 **S:** £19–£23
Beds: 1D 2T **Baths:** 1 En 1 Sh
⏱ 🅿 (6) 📺 ⛷ ✗ 📖 🎵 ⚓
West Dartmoor. Relax at our friendly, small working farm in an secluded setting, surrounded by woods, a tumbling brook, moorland and granite tors. Ideal for walking, riding, cycling, central for visiting Devon & Cornwall.

Scorriton

SX7068   Tradesman's Arms, Dartbridge Inn, Abbey Inn

The Tradesmans Arms, Scorriton, Buckfastleigh, Devon, TQ11 0JB.
Open: All Year (not Xmas/New Year)
01364 631206 Mr Lunday
john.lunday@virgin,net
D: £25 **S:** £25
Beds: 2D **Baths:** 1 Sh
🅿 (20) ⛷ 📺 ⛷ ✗ 📖 ⚓
Warm friendly village pub within Dartmoor National Park set in beautiful Devon lanes within superb country views. No pool table, No juke box, no gambling machines. Real ales, malt whiskies and impromptu musical gatherings. Bring your own instrument.

Seaton

SY2490   Harbour Inn, Ship Inn, Rossini's, The Terrace

The Harbour House, 1 Trevelyan Road, Seaton, Devon, EX12 2NL.
Spacious and comfortable harbourside house, directly on SW Coast Path.
Open: March to Nov
01297 21797 Linda & Roger Sandbrook
D: £20 **S:** £25
Beds: 1T 1D **Baths:** 2 En
⏱ 🅿 (5) 📺 ⛷ 📖 ⚓

The Kettle Restaurant, 15 Fore Street, Seaton, Devon, EX12 2LE.
Close to shops, sea front. Comfortable, friendly & great food.
Open: All Year (not Xmas)
01297 20428 Mr Wallis
thekettleson@seatondevon.freeserve.co.uk
D: £17–£22 **S:** £19–£25
Beds: 1T 1D **Baths:** 2 Pr
⏱ 🅿 (2) ⛷ 📺 ⛷ ✗ 📖 🎵 ⚓

Beaumont, Castle Hill, Seaton, Devon, EX12 2QW.
Beautiful sea front house with spectacular sea and cliff views.
Open: All Year (not Xmas/New Year)
Grades: ETC 3 Diamond
01297 20832 Mrs Hill
tony@lymebay.demon.co.uk
D: £23–£25 **S:** £25
Beds: 2F 3D **Baths:** 5 En
⏱ 🅿 (5) 📺 ⛷ ✗ 📖 🎵 ⚓

Tors Guest House, 55 Harbour Road, Seaton, Devon, EX12 2LX.
Comfort, conviviality, good food. You know it's what you want.
Open: All Year
01297 20531 Mrs Webber
D: £20 **S:** £20
Beds: 4D 1T 1S **Baths:** 2 En 2 Sh
⏱ (15) 🅿 (5) 📺 📖 🎵 ⚓

Shaldon

SX9372   Bull, White Horse, Blacksmiths' Arms, Clifford Inn, Shipwrights

Virginia Cottage, Brook Lane, Shaldon, Teignmouth, Devon, TQ14 0HL.
Early C17th house in one acre garden near sea. Ample parking.
Open: All Year
01626 872634 (also fax)
Mr & Mrs Britton
D: £24–£25 **S:** £30–£35
Beds: 2D 1T **Baths:** 2 En 1 Pr
⏱ (9) 🅿 (4) ⛷ 📺 📖 🎵 ⚓

Ringmore House, Brook Lane, Shaldon, Teignmouth, Devon, TQ14 0AJ.
Open: All Year (not Xmas/New Year)
01626 873323 Mr & Mrs Scull
Fax: 01626 873353
hscull@aol.com
D: £25–£35 **S:** £30–£40
Beds: 3D 1T **Baths:** 2 Pr 1 En
⏱ (9) 🅿 (10) ⛷ 📺 ✗ 📖 ⚓
Beautiful old house and cottage set in ancient gardens full of exotic and unusual plants. Ten metres from Teign Estuary, in easy walking distance of village centre. Lovely decor, home-made bread and Aga cooking. Morning tea in bed!

Sheepstor

SX5567   The Royal Oak

Burrator House, Sheepstor, Yelverton, Devon, PL20 2PF.
Secluded historic country house. Guest rooms overlook lake and gardens. Dartmoor Tourist Association Member.
Open: All Year (not Xmas)
01822 855669 (also fax)
Mr Flint
burratorhouse@compuserve.com
D: £25–£27.50 **S:** £35–£37.50
Beds: 3D 1T 1S **Baths:** 3 En 1 Pr
⏱ (8) 🅿 (12) ⛷ 📺 ⛷ ✗ 📖 ⚓ cc

Shirwell

SS5937   Pyne Arms, Muddisford Inn

Waytown Farm, Shirwell, Barnstaple, Devon, EX31 4JN.
Comfortable C17th spacious farmhouse with superb views, 3 miles from Barnstaple.
Open: All Year (not Xmas)
Grades: ETC 4 Diamond
01271 850396 (also fax)
Mrs Kingdon
hazel@waytown.enterprise-plc.com
D: £20–£22 **S:** £18.50–£20
Beds: 2F 1T 1S **Baths:** 3 En 1 Sh
⏱ 🅿 📺 ✗ 📖 ⚓

The Spinney Country Guest House, Shirwell, Barnstaple, Devon, EX31 4JR.
Comfortable former rectory. Chef/proprietor. Dining-room, conservatory, Exmoor views. **Open:** All Year (not Xmas)
01271 850282 Mrs Pelling
D: £17–£21 **S:** £17–£21
Beds: 2F 1D 1T 1S **Baths:** 2 En 2 Sh
⏱ 🅿 (7) ⛷ 📺 ⛷ ✗ 📖 🎵 ⚓

6 Youlston Close, Shirwell, Barnstaple, Devon, EX31 4JW.
Chalet bungalow, panoramic views, Exmoor to Dartmoor, private road parking. **Open:** Easter to Oct
01271 850347 Mr Bushnell
jebushn@netcomuk.co.uk
D: £15–£17 **S:** £15–£17
Beds: 2D **Baths:** 1 En 1 Pr
🅿 (2) ⛷ 📺 📖 🎵 ⚓

Sidmouth

SY1287   Anchor, Balfour Arms, Blue Ball, Bowd Inn, Black Bull, Kings Arms, Tudor Rose, Old Ship

Barrington Villa Guest House, Salcombe Road, Sidmouth, Devon, EX10 8PU.
Open: Jan to Nov **Grades:** ETC 3 Diamond
01395 514252 Mr & Mrs Carr
D: £14.50–£19 **S:** £18–£23.50
Beds: 3D 2T 3S **Baths:** 4 En 4 Sh
⏱ 🅿 (10) 📺 ⛷ ✗ 📖 🎵 ⚓
A charming Regency Gothic Villa, set in beautiful gardens on the bank of the River Sid in the heart of glorious East Devon.

Ryton Guest House, 52-54 Winslade Road, Sidmouth, Devon, EX10 9EX.
Open: Mar to Nov
Grades: ETC 2 Crowns, AA 3 Diamond
01395 513981 Mr & Mrs Bradnam
D: £20–£22 **S:** £20–£24
Beds: 4F 3D 1T 2S **Baths:** 8 En 2 Sh
⏱ 🅿 ⛷ 📺 ⛷ ✗ 📖 🎵 ⚓
An attractive double fronted house in central location 2 minutes walk from river location, bright bedrooms, cosy lounge, smart dining room, home cooked evening meals, friendly hosts, home from home.

Kyneton Cottage, 87 Alexandria Road, Sidmouth, Devon, EX10 9HG.
Quiet guest house, comfortable beds, good breakfast. Beautiful garden.
Open: All Year (not Xmas/New Year)
Grades: ETC 4 Diamond Silver Award
01395 513213 (also fax) Mrs Peirson
june@kyneton.freeserve.co.uk
D: £18–£23 **S:** £18–£23
Beds: 1T 1D **Baths:** 2 En
⏱ 🅿 (6) ⛷ 📺 📖 ⚓

Woodlands Hotel, Station Rd, Sidmouth, Devon, EX10 8HG.
16th Century building. All modern conveniences in the heart of Sidmouth.
Open: All Year **Grades:** ETC 2 Star
01395 513120 (also fax)
info@woodlands-hotel.com
D: £20–£44 **S:** £24–£42
Beds: 3F 8T 8D 5S **Baths:** 24 En
⏱ 🅿 (20) 📺 ⛷ ✗ 📖 🎵 ⚓ 🐾 ⚓ & cc

Avalon, *Vicarage Road, Sidmouth, Devon, EX10 8UQ.*
Elegant town house, backing onto river and National Trust park.
Open: All Year (not Xmas)
01395 513443 Mrs Young
janetyoungavalon@aol.com
D: £20–£27.50 **S:** £30–£35
Beds: 4D 1T **Baths:** 5 En
⛱ (5) 🅿 (5) ⊬ 📺 ✕ 🏛 🖾 ⓥ ♨

Sidling Field, *105 Peaslands Road, Sidmouth, Devon, EX10 8XE.*
Large bungalow on outskirts of town quiet location.
Open: Jan to Nov
01395 513859 Mrs Shenfield
su1889@eclipse.co.uk
D: £17–£18 **S:** £20–£25
Beds: 1D 1T **Baths:** 1 Sh
⛱ (8) 🅿 (3) 🍴 ♨ 🏛 ♨

Cheriton Guest House, *Vicarage Road, Sidmouth, Devon, EX10 8UQ.*
Private garden for guest use to banks of River Sid.
Open: All Year
01395 513810 (also fax)
Mrs Lee
D: £18–£22 **S:** £18–£22
Beds: 2F 4D 2T 2S **Baths:** 10 En
⛱ 🅿 (10) ⊬ 🏛 🍴 ✕ 🏛 🖾 ⓥ ♨ ⅙

Bramley Lodge, *Vicarage Road, Sidmouth, Devon, EX10 8UQ.*
Open: All Year
01395 515710 Mr & Mrs Haslam
haslam@bramleylodge.fsnet.co.uk
D: £18–£25 **S:** £18–£25
Beds: 1F 1T 2D 3S
Baths: 3 En 1 Sh
⛱ 🅿 (6) ⊬ 📺 🍴 ✕ 🏛 🖾 ⓥ ✲ ♨ ⅙ ⅖
A family owned and run guest house in a town house only a half-mile level walk, via shops, to the sea front. Explore Sidmouth on foot. Residents garden backing onto the River Sid and Byes Parkland.

Burnthouse Farm, *Sidmouth, Devon, EX10 0NL.*
Farmhouse Bed & Breakfast on a working farm, set in the beautiful Otter Valley, with plenty of good walks. A warm welcome awaits you.
Open: Easter to Oct
01395 568304
Mrs Hill
D: £16–£18
Beds: 1F 1T **Baths:** 1 Sh
⛱ 🅿 (3) ⊬ 📺 ♨

Canterbury Guest House, *Salcombe Road, Sidmouth, Devon, EX10 8PR.*
Georgian house adjacent to NT. parkland and the River Sid.
Open: All Year
Grades: ETC 3 Diamond
01395 513373 Mr & Mrs Penaluna
cgh@eclipse.co.uk
D: £16–£32 **S:** £16–£21.50
Beds: 3F 3D 2T **Baths:** 7 Pr 1 Sh
⛱ 🅿 (6) ⊬ 📺 🍴 ✕ 🏛 🖾 ⓥ ✲ ♨ ⅖ ⅙ cc

Lynstead, *Lynstead Vicarage Road, Sidmouth, Devon, EX10 8UQ.*
Cosy guest house backing on to 'The Byes' NT park.
Open: All Year
Grades: ETC 4 Diamond
01395 514635 Mr & Mrs Mair
lynstead@aol.com
D: £20–£22 **S:** £20–£30
Beds: 2F 2D 1T 1S **Baths:** 4 En 1 Sh
⛱ 🅿 (8) ⊬ 📺 ✕ 🏛 🖾 ⓥ ♨

Berwick Guest House, *Salcombe Road, Sidmouth, Devon, EX10 8PX.*
Ideally situated to charming town, unspoilt sea front and coastal path.
Open: Mar to Nov
Grades: ETC 4 Diamond
01395 513621 Mrs Tingley
D: £17–£24 **S:** £22–£27
Beds: 2F 2T 3D **Baths:** 6 En 1 Sh
⛱ (7) 🅿 (7) ⊬ 📺 ✕ 🏛 ♨

Pinn Barton Farm, *Peak Hill, Sidmouth, Devon, EX10 0NN.*
Comfortable farmhouse on working farm.
Open: All Year
Grades: ETC 4 Diamond
01395 514004 (also fax)
Mrs Sage
Betty@PimmBartonFarm.co.uk
D: £20–£22 **S:** fr £25
Beds: 1F 1D 1T **Baths:** 3 En
⛱ (3) 🅿 (6) 📺 🍴 🏛 🖾 ♨

Silverton

SS9502 🍺 *Ruffwell Inn*

Hayne House, *Silverton, Exeter, Devon, EX5 4HE.*
Georgian farmhouse, peacefully situated, overlooking farm and woods. Relax in style. **Open:** Apr to Oct
Grades: ETC 3 Diamond
01392 860725 (also fax) Mrs Kelly
haynehouse@ukonline.co.uk
D: £16–£20 **S:** £16–£20
Beds: 1F 1T **Baths:** 2 Pr
⛱ 🅿 ⊬ 📺 ♨

Slapton

SX8245 🍺 *Queens' Arms, Tower Inn*

Start House, *Start, Slapton, Kingsbridge, Devon, TQ7 2QD.*
Open: All Year (not Xmas)
01548 580254 Mrs Ashby
D: fr £22 **S:** fr £20
Beds: 2D 1T 1S **Baths:** 2 Pr 1 Sh
⛱ 🅿 (4) ⊬ 📺 🍴 ✕ 🏛 🖾 ⓥ ♨
Comfortable Georgian house. Situated in quiet hamlet 1 mile from Slapton Ley. All bedrooms overlook a beautiful valley with Slapton and the sea at the end. Large interesting garden. Ideal for wildlife and walking. Traditional or vegetarian breakfast.

Old Walls, *Slapton, Kingsbridge, Devon, TQ7 2QN.*
Listed C18th house in beautiful village near sea, Nature Reserve.
Open: All Year
01548 580516 Mrs Mercer
D: £17–£20 **S:** £22–£25
Beds: 2F 1T **Baths:** 1 En 1 Pr 1 Sh
⛱ ⊬ 📺 🏛 🖾 ⓥ ♨

B&B owners may vary rates - be sure to check when booking

South Molton

SS7125 🍺 *Castle Inn, Stags Head Inn, Mill Inn, Stumbles Hotel, Politemore Arms, Miners Arms*

Stumbles Hotel & Restaurant, *131-134 East Street, South Molton, Devon, EX36 3BU.*
Acclaimed restaurant, quiet rooms, large beds, in-town hotel.
Open: All Year
01769 574145 M J Potter
Fax: 01769 572558
info@stumbles.co.uk
D: £22.50–£30 **S:** £35–£40
Beds: 1F 4T 5D **Baths:** 10 En
⛱ 🅿 (15) 📺 🍴 ✕ 🏛 ⓥ ♨ ⅙ cc

West Down Guest House, *Whitechapel, South Molton, Devon, EX36 3EQ.*
Be spoilt in tranquil, outstanding setting, 35 acres: family-run.
Open: All Year
Grades: ETC 4 Diamond
01769 550373 Mrs Savery
Fax: 01769 550839
westdown@zetnet.co.uk
D: £22–£24 **S:** £27–£29
Beds: 1F 1D 1T **Baths:** 3 En
⛱ 🅿 (10) 📺 ✕ 🏛 🖾 ♨

The Mill Inn, *Bish Mill, South Molton, Devon, EX36 3QF.*
500m from A361 in glorious scenic Devon. CAMRA Good Beer Guide listed.
Open: All Year
01769 550944 W J Trebilcock
millinn@lineone.net
D: £18 **S:** £18
Beds: 1D 1T **Baths:** 1 Sh
⛱ 🅿 (13) 📺 ✕ 🏛 🖾 ⓥ ♨

South Zeal

SX6593 🍺 *Oxenham Arms*

The Oxenham Arms, *South Zeal, Okehampton, Devon, EX20 2JT.*
Ancient C12th inn in centre of rural village in Dartmoor National Park.
Open: All Year
01837 840244 Mr & Mrs Henry
Fax: 01837 840791
jhenry1928@aol.com
D: £30 **S:** £40–£45
Beds: 2F 3D 3T **Baths:** 7 En
⛱ 🅿 (8) 📺 🍴 ✕ 🏛 ⓥ ✲ ♨ cc

Southleigh

SY2093 🍺 *Hare & Hounds Inn*

South Bank, *Southleigh, Colyton, Devon, EX24 6JB.*
Sunny house, beautiful garden, lovely views, relaxing walking/bird watching.
Open: All Year (not Xmas/New Year)
01404 871251 Mrs Connor
D: £14–£15 **S:** £14–£15
Beds: 2D **Baths:** 1 Sh
⛱ (10) 🅿 (4) ⊬ 📺 🍴 ✕ 🏛 🖾 ⓥ ♨

Starcross

SX9781   ⚓ *Anchor Inn, Ship Inn, Courtenay Arms, Welcome Inn*

The Croft Guest House, *Cockwood Harbour, Starcross, Exeter, Devon, EX6 8QY.*
Open: All Year (not Xmas)
Grades: ETC 3 Diamond
01626 890282 Mr Stewart
Fax: 01626 891768
D: £16–£22 **S:** £20–£25
Beds: 2F 3D 4T 1S **Baths:** 7 En
🛇 🅿 (8) 🖭 🛏 🗙 🛌 🔌 🐾 ♿
Set in an acre of secluded gardens overlooking Cockwood Harbour and River Exe. Convenient for Powderham Castle and Dawlish Warren Nature Reserve. 2 mins walk to 2 of Devon's finest seafood pub/restaurants, discount card for our guests.

Stile Farm, *Starcross, Exeter, Devon, EX6 8PD.*
Country location, close to Powderham Castle and Exe Estuary.
Open: Easter to Nov
01626 890268 (also fax)
Mrs Williams
D: £16–£20 **S:** £20–£36
Beds: 1D 2T **Baths:** 1 En 1 Sh
🛇 🅿 (4) 🗙 🖭 🔽 🐾

The Old Vicarage, *Starcross, Exeter, Devon, EX6 8PX.*
Character, comfort, charm. Ideal location, Exe estuary south of Exeter.
Open: All Year
01626 890206 Mr & Mrs Hayes
D: £17.50–£22 **S:** £23–£26
Beds: 3D 2T **Baths:** 3 En
🅿 (5) 🖭 🛌 🐾

Stockland

ST2404   ⚓ *King's Arms*

The Kings Arms Inn, *Stockland, Honiton, Devon, EX14 9BS.*
C16th inn set in beautiful Devon countryside.
Open: All Year (not Xmas)
01404 881361 Fax: 01404 881732
reserve@kingsarms.net
D: fr £25 **S:** fr £30
Beds: 2D 1T **Baths:** 3 En
🛇 🅿 (40) 🖭 🛏 🗙 🛌 🔽 🐾 cc

Brindley Fold Guest House, *Shorebottom, Stockland, Honiton, Devon, EX14 9DQ.*
Beautiful wooded stream, comfortable country house, wildlife, ramblings, very peaceful.
Open: All Year
01404 881774 Mr Brewer
D: £15 **S:** £15
Beds: 1D 1T 1S **Baths:** 1 Sh
🛇 🅿 (4) 🖭 🗙 🛌 🐾

National Grid References are for villages, towns and cities – not for individual houses

Stokenham

SX8042   ⚓ *Church House Inn, Tradesman Arms*

Brookfield, *Stokenham, Kingsbridge, Devon, TQ7 2SL.*
Comfortable sunny detached house in the beautiful South Hams.
Open: All Year
Grades: ETC 3 Diamond
01548 580615 (also fax)
Mrs Heath
heath@brookfield37.freeserve.co.uk
D: £20 **S:** £25
Beds: 1T 1D **Baths:** 2 En
🅿 (2) 🗙 🖭 🔽 🐾 🔌

Harcroft, *Kiln Lane, Stokenham, Kingsbridge, TQ7 2SQ.*
Quiet bungalow, sea and country views, beautiful garden, warm welcome.
Open: All Year
01548 580612 Mr & Mrs Grainger
D: £17.50–£18.50 **S:** £17.50–£19.50
Beds: 2D 1T **Baths:** 2 En 1 Pr
🛇 🅿 (4) 🗙 🖭 🛌 🐾

Swimbridge

SS6129   ⚓ *Jack Russell*

Lower Mearson Farm, *Swimbridge, Barnstaple, Devon, EX32 0QH.*
300-year-old farmhouse situated in 12 acres of gardens and woodland.
Open: All Year (not Xmas)
01271 830702 Mrs Trimnell
lowermearson@hotmail.com
D: £18–£22 **S:** £18–£25
Beds: 1D 1T 1S **Baths:** 2 En 1 Pr
🛇 (3) 🅿 (2) 🗙 🖭 🛌 🐾

Tavistock

SX4874   ⚓ *Blacksmiths' Arms, Cornish Arms, Peter Tavy Inn, Montery Jacks, Chip Shop Inn, Carpenters Arms, Ordulph Arms, Dartmoor Inn*

Acorn Cottage, *Heathfield, Tavistock, Devon, PL19 0LQ.*
Open: All Year
Grades: ETC 4 Diamond
01822 810038 Mrs Powell-Thomas
viv@acorncot.fsnet.co.uk
D: £15–£20 **S:** £20–£30
Beds: 1D 2T **Baths:** 3 En 1 Pr
🛇 (6) 🅿 (20) 🗙 🖭 🛏 🛌 🐾
C17th Grade II Listed, many original features retained. Peaceful, rural location, beautiful views, just 3 miles from Tavistock on the Chillaton road. Quality accommodation near Lydford Gorge and Brentor medieval church. Central to many activities. Also self catering accommodation available.

Bracken B & B, *36 Plymouth Road, Tavistock, Devon, PL19 8BU.*
Comfortable Victorian town house. Adjacent Dartmoor National Park. Warm welcome.
Open: All Year
01822 613914 Ms Spartley
niklin@supanet.com
D: £16–£20 **S:** £20–£30
Beds: 1T 3D **Baths:** 1 En 1 Pr 1 Sh
🛇 (5) 🅿 (4) 🗙 🖭 🛌 🔽 🐾 ♿

Mount Tavy Cottage, *Tavistock, Devon, PL19 9JL.*
Stone cottage in ten acres, own walled garden, close to Dartmoor.
Open: All Year
01822 614253 Mr Moule
D: £20–£22.50 **S:** £18–£22.50
Beds: 2D 1S **Baths:** 2 Pr
🛇 🅿 (6) 🗙 🖭 🛏 🗙 🛌 🔽 🐾

Westward, *15 Plymouth Road, Tavistock, Devon, PL19 8AU.*
Listed Victorian house. Charming wall garden bounded by Tavistock Canal.
Open: All Year
Grades: ETC 2 Cr, Comm
01822 612094 Ms Parkin
D: £16–£20 **S:** £16–£18
Beds: 1F 1S **Baths:** 1 En 1 Sh
🛇 🅿 (3) 🖭 🛏 🛌 🔽 🐾

Kingfisher Cottage, *Mount Tavy Road, Vigo Bridge, Tavistock, Devon, PL19 9JB.*
Riverside accommodation in characterful cottage near town and beautiful Dartmoor.
Open: All Year
01822 613801 Mrs Toland
D: £16–£21 **S:** £16–£35
Beds: 2D 1T **Baths:** 1 En
🛇 🅿 (5) 🗙 🖭 🛏 🛌 🔽 🐾

Hele Farm, *Tavistock, Devon, PL19 8PA.*
Comfortable accommodation at fully organic dairy farm dated 1780.
Open: Apr to Oct
01822 833084
Mrs Steer
D: £18–£20 **S:** £20–£25
Beds: 1D 1T **Baths:** 2 Pr
🛇 🅿 (3) 🗙 🖭 🛏 🛌 🐾

Teignmouth

SX9473   ⚓ *The Endeavour, London Hotel, Trade Winds, New Quay Inn, Drakes Hotel, Ship Inn, The Elizabethan*

The Bay Hotel, *Sea Front, Teignmouth, Devon, TQ14 8BL.*
Open: All Year
01626 774123 Mrs Dumont
Fax: 01626 777794
D: £23–£26 **S:** £23–£26
Beds: 4F 6T 6D 2S
Baths: 18 En
🛇 🅿 (14) 🗙 🛌 🔽 🐾 🔌 cc
Overlooking the sea, previously the summer house of the Earl of Devon of nearby Powderham Castle. Ideal central stop over for seeing South Devon, Dartmoor, South Hams, Torbay, Exeter – all only half hour away. Only 4 miles from express way A38. Superb golf courses around.

Beachley Guest House, *3 Brunswick Street, Teignmouth, Devon, TQ14 8AE.*
One minute to sea front and shops. Level position.
Open: All Year (not Xmas)
01626 774249 D: fr £16 **S:** fr £17
Beds: 3F 1D 1T 1S **Baths:** 2 Sh
🛇 🖭 🗙 🛌 🔽 🐾

Higher Holcombe, *Holcombe, Devon Road, Teignmouth, TQ14 9NU.*
A scrumptious breakfast while overlooking panoramic sea and moorland views. **Open:** All Year
01626 777144 Mrs Smith
D: £17.50–£19 **S:** £20–£22
Beds: 2F 1D **Baths:** 3 En
🅿 ⽊ 📺 🛏 🗓 ♿

Meran House, *Third Drive, Landscore Road, Teignmouth, Devon, TQ14 9JT.*
Lovely Victorian house, quiet area lounge and garden, homely atmosphere.
Open: All Year (not Xmas)
01626 778828 Mrs Hughes
D: £16–£19 **S:** £20–£23
Beds: 3D **Baths:** 3 En
🅿 (5) ⽊ 📺 🗓 🛏

Valentine Guest House, *1 Glendaragh Road, Teignmouth, Devon, TQ14 8PH.*
Refurbished in 1999. near town, beach, rail, coach stations. Some rooms beautiful sea views. **Open:** all year (not Xmas) **01626 772316 (also fax)**
D: £15–£18.50 **S:** £15–£18.50
Beds: 2D 1T **Baths:** 3 En
⽊ 📺 🗓 🛏

Thelbridge

SS7911 🍺 *Thelbridge Cross Inn*

Hele Barton, *Thelbridge Cross, Thelbridge, Black Dog, Crediton, Devon, EX17 4QJ.*
Lovely thatched farmhouse, family atmosphere, many recommendations, brochure. **Open:** All Year (not Xmas)
01884 860278 (also fax) Mrs Gillbard
gillbard@eclipse.co.uk
D: £15–£20 **S:** £16–£20
Beds: 1D 2T **Baths:** 1 En 1 Sh
🛏 🅿 (6) 📺 🛏

Throwleigh

SX6690 🍺 *Three Crowns, Ring Of Bells*

Throwleigh Manor, *Throwleigh, Okehampton, Devon, EX20 2JF.*
Beautiful country house in idyllic, peaceful 12-acre grounds within National Park. **Open:** All Year (not Xmas)
01647 231630 (also fax)
Mr & Mrs Smitheram
D: £20–£26 **S:** £28–£38
Beds: 1F 1D 1S **Baths:** 1 En 2 Pr
🛏 🅿 (10) ⽊ 📺 🗓 🛏

Tiverton

SS9512 🍺 *Exeter Inn, Twyford Inn, Trout Inn, Seahorse, Anchor, White Ball*

Lodgehill Farm Hotel, *Tiverton, Devon, EX16 5PA.*
Good parking, tranquil setting on A396, 1 mile south of Tiverton, with Dartmoor, Exmoor. **Open:** All Year
Grades: ETC 3 Diamond, AA 3 Diamond, RAC 3 Diamond
01884 251200 Mr & Mrs Reader
Fax: 01884 242090
lodgehill@dial.pipex.com
D: £23–£27.50 **S:** £25–£29.50
Beds: 2F 2D 3S **Baths:** 9 En
🅿 (12) 📺 🛏 ✕ 🗓 🛏 ❄ 🛏 cc

Angel Guest House, *13 St Peter Street, Tiverton, Devon, EX16 6NU.*
Town centre. Georgian house, large cycle shed, ideal touring centre.
Open: All Year
01884 253392 Mr & Mrs Evans
Fax: 01884 251154
cerimar@globalnet.co.uk
D: £16–£18 **S:** £16–£18
Beds: 2F 3D 1T 1S **Baths:** 3 Pr 2 Sh
🛏 🅿 (4) 📺 🗓 🗓 🛏

Hill Cottage, *Cove, Tiverton, Devon, EX16 7RN.*
Stress-free and calming countryside location. The silence is deafening.
Open: All Year (not Xmas)
01884 256978 Mrs Harris
bnbnbio@talk21.com
D: £20 **S:** £20–£25
Beds: 1D 1T **Baths:** 1 Sh
🅿 (4) ⽊ 📺 ✕ 🗓 🛏

Torquay

SX9165 🍺 *Ansteys Cove, Chelston Manor, Devon Arms, Landsdowne, London Inn, Drum Tun, Harbourside, Black Tulip*

Heathcliff House Hotel, *16 Newton Road, Torquay, TQ2 5BZ.*
Open: All Year (not Xmas)
01803 211580 (also fax)
Mr & Mrs Sanders
hhhtorquay@btclick.com
D: £15–£20 **S:** fr £20
Beds: 2F 8D **Baths:** 10 En
🛏 🅿 (10) 📺 ✕ 🗓 🛏 cc
Whether taking your main holiday, having a weekend away, touring Devon, visiting friends or on business, this family hotel offers great value B&B. Built in 1860s, the Heathcliff, once a vicarage, now features in the official Torquay Agatha Christie trail.

Devon Court Hotel, *24 Croft Road, Torquay, Devon, TQ2 5UE.*
Open: All Year
Grades: AA 3 Diamond, RAC 3 Diamond
01803 293603 Fax: 01803 213660
info@devoncourt.co.uk
D: £15–£25 **S:** £22.50–£32.50
Beds: 4F 8D 2T **Baths:** 10 En 6 Pr
🛏 🅿 (14) ⽊ 📺 🛏 ✕ 🗓 🛏 🛏 cc
Family-run Victorian hotel in the heart of Torquay. Few minutes' walk to beach, shops, Riviera, leisure centre, licensed bar, lounge overlooking outdoor heated pool & palm lined patio. Warm & friendly, home baking, cream teas, etc. Remote control colour TV in room.

Aries House, *1 Morgan Avenue, Torquay, Devon, TQ2 5RP.*
Central Victorian town house near bus/coach/train stations, shops, beachs, clubs.
Open: All Year (not Xmas/New Year)
01803 215655 Mr & Mrs Sherry
sherry-arieshouse@hotmail.com
D: £11–£20 **S:** £11–£20
Beds: 2F 2T 1D 1S **Baths:** 2 En 2 Sh
🛏 🅿 (0) 🅿 (1) ⽊ 📺 ✕ 🗓 🛏

Swiss Court, *68 Vane Hill Road, Torquay, Devon, TQ1 2BZ.*
Blissfully quiet location, sea views, yet near harbour and town.
Open: All Year (not Xmas)
01803 215564 Mr Davies
D: £16–£20 **S:** £16–£20
Beds: 1F 2D 5S **Baths:** 6 En 1 Sh
🛏 (6) 🅿 (8) 📺 🛏 🗓 🛏 ♿

Treander Guest House, *10 Morgan Avenue, Torquay, Devon, TQ2 5RS.*
Stag and Hen parties welcome. Central all amenities. Access all times.
Open: All Year
01803 296906 B Hurren
D: £13.50–£17.50 **S:** £13.50–£17.50
Beds: 3F 4T 4D 1S **Baths:** 2 En, 1 Pr 2 Sh
🛏 🅿 (4) 📺 🛏 ✕ 🗓 ❄ 🛏

Palm Tree House, *93 Avenue Road, Torquay, Devon, TQ2 5LH.*
Small, friendly, relaxed guest house. Home from home. Good breakfast.
Open: All Year (not Xmas/New Year)
01803 299141 Ms Barnett
D: £15–£17 **S:** £15–£17
Beds: 2T 4D **Baths:** 1 Sh
🛏 (3) 🅿 (3) ✕ 🗓 🛏

Brampton Court Hotel, *St Luke's Road South, Torquay, Devon, TQ2 2NZ.*
Panoramic views of Torbay, close to town, beach and conference centre.
Open: All Year
Grades: ETC 4 Diamond
01803 294237 Mr & Mrs Markham
Fax: 01803 211842
stay@bramptoncourt.co.uk
D: £22–£28 **S:** £27–£33
Beds: 6F 4T 8D 2S **Baths:** 20 En
🛏 🅿 (14) ⽊ 📺 ✕ 🗓 🗓 ❄ 🛏 cc

Chester Court Hotel, *30 Cleveland Road, Torquay, Devon, TQ2 5BE.*
Comfortable ensuite accommodation. Midweek bookings and short breaks. Pleasant gardens.
Open: All Year
Grades: ETC 3 Diamond
01803 294565 (also fax)
Mrs Morris
D: £16–£20 **S:** £16–£33
Beds: 3F 2T 4D 1S **Baths:** 9 En, 1 Sh
🛏 🅿 (10) ⽊ 📺 ✕ 🗓 🛏 cc

Chesterfield Hotel, *62 Belgrave Road, Torquay, Devon, TQ2 5HY.*
A warm and friendly welcome awaits you. Close to all amenities.
Open: All Year (not Xmas)
Grades: ETC 4 Diamond, AA 4 Diamond
01803 292318 J Daglish
Fax: 01803 293676
D: £16–£25 **S:** £16–£20
Beds: 3F 4D 3T 1S **Baths:** 10 En 1 Sh
🛏 🅿 📺 ✕ 🗓 🛏 cc

Tower Hall Hotel, *Solsbro Road, Torquay, TQ2 6PF.*
Victorian villa, sea views, near seafront, romantic atmosphere. Licensed. Short breaks. **Open:** Easter to Oct
01803 605292 Mr Butler
D: £16–£20 **S:** £16–£20
Beds: 2F 4D 2T 2S **Baths:** 7 En 2 Sh
🛏 🅿 (6) 📺 🛏 ✕ 🗓 🗓 🛏

Exmouth View Hotel, St Albans
Road, Torquay, Devon, TQ1 3LG.
Friendly family-run hotel just yards from
stunning Babbacombe Downs.
Open: All Year
01803 327307 Mr Browne
Fax: 01803 329967
relax@exmouth-view.co.uk
D: £16–£25 **S:** £20–£30
Beds: 8F 8D 5T 1S **Baths:** 22 En
⚡ 🄿 (20) 📺 🎞 🖤 ♨ & cc

Sandpiper Lodge Hotel, 96 Avenue
Road, Torquay, TQ2 5LF.
Guests keep returning, loving our homely
atmosphere and hearty breakfasts.
Open: All Year
01803 293293 D: £15–£22 **S:** £13–£20
Beds: 2F 4D 1S **Baths:** 7 En
⚡ 🄿 (7) 🖤 📺 🍴 🎞 ♨ cc

Maple Lodge, 36 Ash Hill Road,
Torquay, Devon, TQ1 3JD.
Quality award winning guest house.
Panoramic views over town and Torbay.
Open: All Year
Grades: ETC 3 Diamond
01803 297391 Mr Allen
D: £16–£22 **S:** £16–£22
Beds: 2F 3D 1T 1S **Baths:** 6 En 1 Pr
⚡ (2) 🄿 (4) 🖤 📺 × 🎞 🖤 ♨

Howard Court Hotel, 31 St Efrides
Road, Torquay, TQ2 5SG.
Friendly licensed hotel. Close to beach
and town. Secured Parking.
Open: All Year
01803 295494 K Lorimer
D: £13–£18 **S:** £15–£22
Beds: 2F 3T 5D 1S **Baths:** 2 Sh
⚡ 🄿 (6) 📺 🍴 × 🎞 🖤 ♨ cc

Knowle Court Hotel, Kents Road
Wellswood, Torquay, TQ1 2NN.
Peaceful location near beaches, town,
good bus service.
Open: All Year
Grades: AA 4 Diamond
01803 297076 Mr Baderay
Fax: 01803 292980
D: £20–£30 **S:** £20–£30
Beds: 3F 4D 1T 1S **Baths:** 9 En
⚡ 🄿 (5) 🖤 × 🎞 🖤 ♨ cc

Garlieston Hotel, Bridge Road,
Torquay, Devon, TQ2 5BA.
Small friendly family run private hotel.
Central for all amenities.
Open: All Year
Grades: ETC 3 Diamond, AA 3 Diamond
01803 294050 Mr & Mrs Ridewood
garleistonhotel@jridewood.fsnet.co.uk
D: £13–£18 **S:** £13–£18
Beds: 2F 2D 1S **Baths:** 3 En 2 Pr
⚡ 📺 × 🎞 🖤 ♨ cc

Cranborne Hotel, 58 Belgrave Road,
Torquay, Devon, TQ2 5HY.
In excellent situation, close to town
centre shop and Riviera centre.
Open: All Year (not Xmas)
Grades: ETC 5 Diamonds
01803 298046 (also fax)
Mrs Dawkins
D: £20–£30 **S:** £25–£50
Beds: 3F 8D **Baths:** 11 En
⚡ (2) 🄿 (8) 📺 × 🎞 🖤 ♨ cc

Craig Court Hotel, 10 Ash Hill Road,
Torquay, Devon, TQ1 3HZ.
A Victorian villa close to town centre and
all amenities.
Open: All Year (not Xmas)
Grades: AA 3 Diamond, RAC 3 Diamond
01803 294400
Mrs Box
Fax: 01803 212525
info@craigcourthotel.co.uk
D: £20.50–£23.50 **S:** £20.50–£23.50
Beds: 4F 1T 3D 2S **Baths:** 10 En
⚡ 🄿 (6) 🖤 📺 × 🍴 🎞 ♨ ♨ & 2

Shirley Hotel, Braddons Hill Road
East, Torquay, Devon, TQ1 1HF.
Elegant detached Victorian villa in quiet
location, yet close to harbour.
Open: All Year (not Xmas)
01803 293016 Mrs Stephens
D: £16–£25 **S:** £16–£25
Beds: 9D 2T 2S **Baths:** 11 En 1 Sh
⚡ (12) 🄿 (8) 📺 🎞 ♨ cc

Carysfort, 13 Warren Road, Torquay,
Devon, TQ2 5TQ.
Ideally situated near town centre,
beaches, harbour and night life.
Open: All Year
01803 294160 Mr Tanner
etanner@talk21.com
D: £16–£20 **S:** £17–£20
Beds: 2F 2D 2T 1S **Baths:** 4 En 2 Sh
⚡ (1) 🄿 (3) 📺 🍴 🎞 ♨

Wilsbrook, 77 Avenue Road, Torquay,
Devon, TQ2 5LL.
Attractive Victorian house, short walk to
beach, town, Riviera centre.
Open: All Year (not Xmas)
01803 298413 Mr Brook
D: fr £14 **S:** fr £13
Beds: 1F 2D 1T 1S **Baths:** 3 En 1 Sh
⚡ (3) 🄿 (6) 🖤 📺 🎞 🖤 ♨ cc

SX8060 🍺 Kingsbridge Inn, Royal Seven Stars,
Smugglers Inn, Steam Packet Inn

Royal Seven Stars Hotel, The
Plains, Totnes, Devon, TQ9 5DD.
1660 town centre former coaching inn
near River Dart; restaurant.
Open: All Year
Grades: ETC 2 Star, AA 2 Star, RAC 2
Star
01803 862125 R Baron
D: £31–£46.50 **S:** £49–£59
Beds: 2F 10D 3T 1S **Baths:** 14 En 2 Pr
⚡ 🄿 (20) 📺 🍴 × 🎞 🖤 ♨ cc

3 Plymouth Road, Totnes, Devon,
TQ9 5PH.
Top of town Georgian house, near station,
restaurants and shops.
Open: Mar to Nov
01803 866917 Ms Fenwick
D: £16–£18 **S:** £18–£20
Beds: 1D 2T **Baths:** 1 En 1 Sh
⚡ (6) 🖤 📺 🍴 🎞 ♨

All details shown are as
supplied by B&B owners in
Autumn 2000

Planning a longer stay? Always
ask for any special rates

Acacias, 7 Cherry Cross, Totnes, TQ9 5EU.
Peaceful fieldside house. Panoramic
views. Convenient. Eco-friendly, organic
breakfasts available.
Open: All Year
01803 867306 (also fax)
Ms Parkinson
seventhheaven7cc@hotline.com
D: £17–£24 **S:** £17–£25
Beds: 1F 1D **Baths:** 1 En 1 Pr
⚡ (6) 🄿 (1) 🖤 📺 🎞 🖤 ♨

Great Court Farm, Weston Lane,
Totnes, Devon, TQ9 6LB.
Victorian farmhouse, spacious
comfortable rooms, delicious home
cooking, friendly atmosphere.
Open: All Year
01803 862326 (also fax)
Mrs Hooper
D: fr £17 **S:** fr £18
Beds: 1F 2D 1T **Baths:** 1 En 2 Sh
⚡ (5) 🄿 (4) 🖤 × 🎞 🖤 ♨

SS6123 🍺 The Bell, Rising Sun

The Gables Guest House, On-the-
Bridge, Umberleigh, Devon, EX37 9AB.
Open: Feb to Dec
01769 560461 Mr Pring
D: £18.50–£22.50 **S:** £18.50–£22.50
Beds: 1T 1D 1S **Baths:** 3 En
🄿 (4) 📺 🖤 🖤 ♨
Offering a warm and friendly personal
service, situated in the picturesque Taw
Valley, facing the River Taw, famous for
its salmon and sea trout (fishing can be
arranged). Also featuring a 118 year old
grapevine in our conservatory tea room.

SS8808

Jellicoe's, Higher Holn, Upham,
Cheriton Fitzpaine, Crediton, Devon, EX17
4HN.
Peaceful cottage and garden. Beautiful
landscape. Convenient position.
Exceptional food.
Open: All Year (not Xmas)
01363 866165 (also fax)
Mr Jellicoe
jellicoes@higherholn.freeserve.co.uk
D: fr £22 **S:** fr £22
Beds: 1F 2D 1T **Baths:** 3 En
⚡ 🄿 (4) 🖤 📺 🖤 ♨

ST0115 🍺 Globe

Hill Farm, Uplowman, Tiverton, Devon,
EX16 7PE.
15th century Devon longhouse quiet
working farm. Tennis court games room.
Open: All Year
01884 820388 M Branton
D: £17–£18 **S:** £17–£18
Beds: 3D 1S
⚡ 🄿 (6) 📺 🍴 🎞 ♨

Uplyme

SY3293 *Pilot Boat*

Lydwell House, *Lyme Road , Uplyme, Lyme Regis, Dorset, DT7 3TJ.*
A pre-Victorian house set within 0.75 acre of Victorian gardens.
Open: All Year
Grades: ETC 3 Diamond
01297 443522 Mr Brittain
D: £23–£27 **S:** £23–£27
Beds: 2F 1D 1T 1S **Baths:** 5 En
⛫ 🅿 (7) ⅌ 📺 ✕ 🍴 📺 ₤ cc

Hill Barn, *Gore Lane, Uplyme, Lyme Regis, Dorset, DT7 3RJ.*
Beautifully converted stone barn, surrounded by countryside, only 1 mile Lyme Regis.
Open: All Year (not Xmas)
Grades: ETC 4 Diamond
01297 445185 (also fax)
Mrs Wyon-Brown
jwb@lymeregis-accommodation.com
D: £18–£20 **S:** fr £18
Beds: 1F 1D 1T **Baths:** 2 Sh
⛫ 🅿 ⅌ 📺 ✕ 🍴 📺 ₤ ♿

Venton

SX5956 *New Country Inn*

Flora House, *Venton, Sparkwell, Plymouth, PL7 5DR.*
Warm welcome, overlooking Dartmoor, home produce when available, morn/eve. drinks.
Open: All Year (not Xmas/New Year)
01752 837239 Mrs Laid
D: £17.50–£18.50 **S:** £17.50–£18.50
Beds: 1D 1T **Baths:** 1 Sh
⛫ 🅿 (2) ⅌ 📺 🍴 ✕

Walkhampton

SX5369

Town Farm, *Walkhampton, Yelverton, Devon, PL20 6JX.*
Open: All Year
01822 855145 Mr & Mrs Morley
Fax: 01822 852180
crmorley@town-farm.com
D: fr £20 **S:** fr £25
Beds: 1T 1D **Baths:** 2 En
⛫ 🅿 (2) ⅌ 📺 ✕ 🍴 📺 ₤
Self contained accommodation in recently refurbished Listed barn. Attractive courtyard location. Breakfast in main house. Centre of moorland village. Excellent base for exploring Dartmoor on foot & by car. Close to historic Plymouth & the market town of Tavistock both connected to Sir Francis Drake. Personally guided tours.

RATES

D = Price range per person sharing in a double room
S = Price range for a single room

B&B owners may vary rates - be sure to check when booking

Washbourne

SX7954 *Durant Arms, Hunters Lodge*

Penny Rowden, *Washbourne, Dartmouth, Totnes, Devon, TQ9 7DN.*
Open: All Year (not Xmas)
Grades: ETC 4 Diamond
01803 712485 (also fax) Mrs Parsons
ap@pennyrowden.freeserve.co.uk
D: £20–£25 **S:** £20–£25
Beds: 1F 2D 1T 1S **Baths:** 5 En
⛫ (8) 🅿 (10) 📺 🍴 ✕ 🍴 📺 ₤
200-year-old farmhouse nestling in a tranquil valley with 11 acres of conserved pastures and woods; e/m available, all meals served in beamed dining room with log fire. Ideally situated for spectacular South Devon coastline and moors.

Washfield

SS9315

The Mill, *Lower Washfield, Washfield, Tiverton, Devon, EX16 9PD.*
Relax, unwind, enjoy the peace and tranquillity of our idyllic riverside location. **Open:** All Year
01884 255297 (also fax) Mrs Arnold
D: £17–£19 **S:** £18–£22
Beds: 1F 1T 2D **Baths:** 4 En
⛫ 🅿 (8) 📺 ✕ 📺 ₤

Watermouth

SS5547

The Old Sawmill Inn, *Watermouth, Ilfracombe, Devon, EX34 9SX.*
Pub with stream through garden. Summer entertainment.
Open: All Year (not Xmas/New Year)
01271 882259 K Rudd
D: £20 **S:** £20–£40
Beds: 4D **Baths:** 4 En
⛫ 🅿 (30) 📺 ✕ 🍴 📺 ₤ cc

Wembury

SX5248 *Odd Wheel, Eddystone Inn*

Bay Cottage, *150 Church Road, Wembury, Plymouth, Devon, PL9 0HR.*
Victorian cottage by the sea, surrounded by National Trust land.
Open: All Year (not Xmas)
Grades: ETC 3 Diamond
01752 862559 (also fax) Mrs Farrington
TheFairies@aol.com
D: £26–£29 **S:** £25–£35
Beds: 2D 2T 1S **Baths:** 3 En 2 Sh
⛫ 🅿 (2) ⅌ 📺 🍴 🍴 📺 ₤

Willowhayes, Near Post Office, *Ford Road, Wembury, Plymouth, Devon, PL9 0JA.*
Comfortable house, sea/country views.
Open: All Year (not Xmas/New Year)
01752 862581 Mrs Mills
D: £12.50–£17.50 **S:** £15–£25
Beds: 1S 2D 1T **Baths:** 1 En 1 Sh
⛫ 🅿 (4) ⅌ 📺 🍴 🍴 📺 ₤

West Anstey

SS8527

Jubilee House, *Highaton Farm, West Anstey, South Molton, Devon, EX36 3PJ.*
Open: All Year
Grades: ETC 4 Diamond
01398 341312 Mrs Denton
Fax: 01398 341323
denton@exmoorholiday.co.uk
D: £19.50–£22.50 **S:** £19.50
Beds: 2D 3S **Baths:** 2 Sh
⛫ 🅿 (4) ⅌ 📺 🍴 ✕ 🍴 📺 ♿ ₤
Elegant farmhouse, close edge Exmoor National Park, situated on Two Moors Way. Peaceful surroundings, easily accessible, great atmosphere. Large lounge (with log fire), dining room available for guests, local produce/home preserves. Bill is an international chef. Patio/BBQ/badminton areas, therapeutic hot tub spa.

West Buckland

SS6531

Huxtable Farm, *West Buckland, Barnstaple, Devon, EX32 0SR.*
Medieval farmhouse (1520) in secluded countryside. Tennis court and sauna.
Open: Feb to Nov
Grades: ETC 4 Diamond
01598 760254 (also fax)
Mrs Payne
jackie@huxhilton.enterprise-plc.com
D: £24–£25 **S:** £35
Beds: 2F 3D 1T **Baths:** 5 En 1 Pr
⛫ 🅿 (10) ⅌ 📺 ✕ 🍴 📺 ₤ cc

Westward Ho!

SS4329 *The Waterfront, The Elizabethan, Pig On The Hill, Village Inn, Country Cousins*

Eversley, *1 Youngaton Road, Westward Ho!, Bideford, Devon, EX39 1HU.*
Victorian gentleman's residence. Superb accommodation. Sea views, beach 2 mins.
Open: All Year
Grades: ETC 4 Diamond
01237 471603 Mr Sharratt
D: £18–£20 **S:** £24–£29
Beds: 1F 1D 1T **Baths:** 1 En 1 Sh
⛫ 🅿 (3) 📺 🍴 🍴 📺 ₤

Brockenhurst, *11 Atlantic Way, Westward Ho!, Bideford, Devon, EX39 1HX.*
Comfortable, detached house. Views of Lundy Island and vast beach.
Open: All Year (not Xmas)
Grades: ETC 3 Diamond
01237 423346 (also fax)
Mrs Snowball
D: £22.50–£25 **S:** £27–£30
Beds: 2D 1T **Baths:** 3 En
🅿 (4) 📺 🍴 🍴 📺 ₤

Mayfield, *Avon Lane, Westward Ho!, Bideford, Devon, EX39 1LR.*
Victorian house close to beach. Sea views, full English breakfast.
Open: All Year (not Xmas/New Year)
01237 477128 Mrs Clegg
D: fr £14 **S:** fr £14
Beds: 2D 1T 1S **Baths:** 2 Sh
⛫ 🅿 (1) ⅌ 📺 🍴 📺 ₤

Four Winds, *Cornborough Road, Westward Ho!, Bideford, Devon, EX39 1AA.*
Beautiful Edwardian house 0.75 mile from beach and coastal footpath.
Open: All Year
01237 421741 Mr Evers
D: £18–£20 **S:** £18–£20
Beds: 1F 2T **Baths:** 3 Pr
🛇 🅿 🗢 📺 🐾 🛆 🕭 🕭 &

Whimple

SY0497 🍺 *Hungry Fox, New Inn, New Fountain, Red Lion, Thirsty Farmer*

Busy Bee, *Mellifera, Church Road, Whimple, Exeter, Devon, EX5 2TF.*
Friendly, lovely views, bungalow. Ideal for coast, city or Airport.
Open: All Year
01404 823019 (also fax)
Mr & Mrs Janaway
bandb.busybee@virgin.net
D: £18–£19 **S:** £21–£22
Beds: 1T 2D **Baths:** 3 En
🛇 (5) 🅿 (6) 🗢 📺 🕭 🕭

The Jays, *The Square, Whimple, Exeter, Devon, EX5 2SL.*
16th century village square cottage. ideal for Dartmoor and coast.
Open: All Year (not Xmas/New Year)
01404 823614 J & J Discombe
Fax: 01404 823629
jaydiscombe@supanet.com
D: £17–£18.50 **S:** £17.50–£20
Beds: 1T 2D 1S **Baths:** 1 Sh
🗢 📺 🕭 🕭

Keepers Lodge, *Strete Raleigh, Whimple, Exeter, Devon, EX5 2PS.*
Delightful country position, with fields overlooking the Exe Valley to Dartmoor.
Open: All Year (not Xmas/New Year)
01404 822980 Mrs Rudham
D: £15–£18 **S:** £15–£18
Beds: 1F 1D 1T 1S
🛇 🅿 🗢 📺 🐾 🗙 🕭 🕭 &

Wilmington

ST2000 🍺 *Home Farm*

The Crest Guest House, *Moorcox Lane, Wilmington, Honiton, Devon, EX14 9JU.*
The Crest - a modern chalet style house nestling in the picturesque Unborne valley.
Open: All Year
Grades: AA 3 Diamond
01404 831419 Mrs Kidwell
D: £19–£21 **S:** £26–£27
Beds: 1F 1D 1T
🛇 🅿 (8) 📺 🐾 🕭 🕭 & &

The Old Forge, *Wilmington, Honiton, Devon, EX14 9JR.*
A warm welcome guaranteed at charming C17th thatched cottage between Honiton & Axminster.
Open: All Year
01404 831297 Mr Hudson
oldforge.wilmington@tesco.net
D: £19 **S:** £21–£25
Beds: 1T 2D **Baths:** 1 En 1 Sh
🛇 🅿 (4) 🗢 📺 🐾 🗙 🕭 🕭

Witheridge

SS8014 🍺 *Mitre Inn*

Mitre Inn, *Two Moors Way, Witheridge, Tiverton, Devon, EX16 8AH.*
Large Victorian coaching inn.
Open: All Year (not Xmas/New Year)
01884 861263 Mr & Mrs Parsons
D: £18–£25 **S:** £20–£27
Beds: 3F 1D 5T **Baths:** 1 En 3 Sh
🛇 🅿 (5) 🗢 🐾 🗙 🕭 🕭 cc

Woodbury

SY0187 🍺 *Malsters Arms, White Hart, Green Door*

Greenacre, *Couches Lane, Woodbury, Exeter, EX5 1HL.*
Secluded, comfortable country accommodation near village. Large stream-bordered gardens.
Open: All Year (not Xmas)
01395 233037 Mrs Price
Fax: 01395 233574
D: £15–£18 **S:** £21–£24
Beds: 1D 2T **Baths:** 2 En 1 Pr
🛇 🅿 (5) 📺 🐾 🕭 🕭

Cottles Farm, *Woodbury, Exeter, Devon, EX5 1ED.*
Thatched farmhouse 10 mins from M5. Wonderful views, peaceful surroundings.
Open: All Year (not Xmas)
01395 232547 Mrs Brown
D: £18–£20 **S:** £20–£23
Beds: 1F 1D 1T **Baths:** 2 En 1 Pr
🅿 (3) 🗢 📺 🕭

Woodleigh

SX7448

Yeo Farm, *Topsham Bridge, Woodleigh, Kingsbridge, Devon, TQ7 4DR.*
C14th Farm house in 86 acres of woods and pasture mile of riverbank.
Open: All Year
01548 550586 Mrs Smith
yeomary@members.shines.net
D: £20–£25 **S:** £20–£25
Beds: 1T **Baths:** 1 En
🅿 (2) 🗢 📺 🕭 🕭

Woolacombe

SS4543 🍺 *Jubilee Inn, Chichester Arms, Red Barn, Stables, Golden Hind, The Mill*

Ossaborough House, *Woolacombe, Devon, EX34 7HJ.*
Open: All Year
Grades: ETC 3 Diamond
01271 870297 Mr & Mrs Day
D: £21–£25 **S:** £21–£25
Beds: 2F 2T 2D **Baths:** 5 En 1 Pr
🛇 🅿 (8) 🗢 📺 🐾 🕭 🕭
Escape to our lovely C17th country house originating in the days of Saxon England - rustic beams. Thick stone walls, inglenook fireplaces, candlelit dinners. All rooms sympathetically restored. Explore rolling hills, rugged cliffs, picturesque villages, stunning golden beaches and secluded coves.

Camberley, *Beach Road, Woolacombe, Devon, EX34 7AA.*
Large Victorian house with views to sea and NT land. Use of indoor pool.
Open: All Year (not Xmas)
Grades: ETC 3 Diamond
01271 870231 Mr & Mrs Riley
camberley@tesco.net
D: £20–£25 **S:** £19–£24
Beds: 3F 3D 1T **Baths:** 6 En 1 Pr
🛇 🅿 (6) 📺 🕭 🕭 cc

Barton Lea, *Beach Road, Woolacombe, Devon, EX34 7BT.*
Warm welcome, sea views, big breakfast menu, close to Coastal Foot Path.
Open: Easter to Oct
01271 870928 Mrs Vickery
D: £15.50–£20 **S:** £20–£25
Beds: 1F 1D 1T **Baths:** 3 En
🛇 🅿 (7) 🗢 📺 🕭 🕭

Sunny Nook, *Beach Road, Woolacombe, Devon, EX34 7AA.*
Delightful home in lovely situation, wonderful views and excellent breakfasts. No smoking throughout.
Open: All Year (not Xmas)
01271 870964 Mr Fenn
D: £18–£23 **S:** £25–£30
Beds: 1F 1D 1T **Baths:** 2 En 1 Pr
🛇 (8) 🅿 (5) 🗢 🗙 🕭 🕭

Clyst House, *Rockfield Road, Woolacombe, Devon, EX34 7DH.*
Friendly, comfortable guest house close blue flag beach. Delicious English breakfast. Beautiful walking area.
Open: Mar to Nov
01271 870220 Mrs Braund
D: £20–£22 **S:** £20–£22
Beds: 1F 1D 1T **Baths:** 1 Sh
🛇 (7) 🅿 🗢 📺 🕭 🕭

Woolsery (Woolfardisworthy)

SS3321 🍺 *Farmers Arms, Hart Inn, Manor Inn*

Stroxworthy Farm, *Woolsery, Bideford, Devon, EX39 5QB.*
Delightful farmhouse, working dairy farm 4 miles from Clovelly.
Open: Easter to Oct
01237 431333 Mrs Beck
D: £20 **S:** £20
Beds: 1F 2D 1S **Baths:** 3 En 1 Pr
🛇 🅿 (10) 📺 🕭

Yelverton

SX5267 🍺 *Drakes Manor, Rock Inn*

Overcombe Hotel, *Old Station Road, Horrabridge, Yelverton, Devon, PL20 7RA.*
Open: All Year
01822 853501 GH & G Wright
D: £22–£22.50 **S:** £22–£28
Beds: 2F 5D 3T 1S **Baths:** 10 Pr 1 Sh
🛇 🅿 (10) 📺 🐾 🗙 🕭 &
Enjoy beautiful views across the Walkham Valley towards High Tor. Situated within the Dartmoor National Park between Plymouth and Tavistock. Garden. Home cooked food. Ideal for walking, cycling, visiting National Trust properties and the coasts of Devon and Cornwall.

The Rosemont Guest House,
Greenbank Terrace, Yelverton, Devon,
PL20 6DR.
Open: All Year (not Xmas)
Grades: ETC 3 Diamond
01822 852175 Mr & Mrs Eastaugh
b&b@rosemontgh.fsnet.co.uk
D: £21–£22 **S:** £21–£32
Beds: 1F 3D 2T 1S **Baths:** 7 En
⌖ ▣ (5) ⅏ ⊠ ⋔ ▥ ▣ ♨ cc
Overlooking moorland village green
within the glorious Dartmoor National
Park. Historic Plymouth, Tavistock,
Buckland Abbey, Garden House and
Lydford Gorge all nearby. Excellent free
range breakfast using local produce.
Pubs, restaurants and other amenities
within village.

Stokehill Farmhouse, *Yelverton,*
Devon, PL20 6EW.
Open: All Year (not Xmas/New Year)
01822 853791 Mrs Gozzard
D: £22.50–£25 **S:** £27–£30
Beds: 1T 2D **Baths:** 1Ensuite 1 Pr
⌖ (10) ▣ ⅏ ⊠ ▥ ▣ ♨
Beautiful country house set in lovely
grounds in a quiet, rural setting. Large
bedrooms and bathrooms richly
furnished with stunning views across
rolling countryside. On the edge of the
Dartmoor National Park but close to
Plymouth and the coast.

Knightstone Tea Rooms, *Crapstone*
Road, Yelverton, Devon, PL20 6BT.
Quiet, secluded, of historic interest,
overlooking moors. Ideal for sightseeing.
Open: All Year
Grades: ETC 2 Diamond
01822 853679 Mrs Hayes
D: £17.50 **S:** £17.50
Beds: 1F 1T 1S **Baths:** 1 Sh
⌖ ▣ (20) ⅏ ⊠ ✕ ▥ ▣ ♨ cc

Rettery Bank, *Harrowbeer Lane,*
Yelverton, Devon, PL20 6EA.
Quiet house with wonderful views,
comfortable beds, jacuzzi, English
breakfast.
Open: All Year (not Xmas)
01822 855088 (also fax)
Ms Leavey
bandt@leavey.fsbusiness.co.uk
D: £20–£25 **S:** £16–£20
Beds: 1D 1T **Baths:** 1 En 1 Sh
⌖ (5) ▣ (2) ⊠ ✕ ▥ ▣ ♨

BATHROOMS
Pr - Private
Sh - Shared
En - Ensuite

Yeoford

SX7898   🍺 Mare & Foal

Warrens Farm, *The Village, Yeoford,*
Crediton, Devon, EX17 5JD.
C16th Devon longhouse. Antique
furniture. Good meals. Prime touring
position.
Open: All Year
01363 84304 (also fax)
W Brimacombe Nelissen
D: £18 **S:** £20
Beds: 1F 2D **Baths:** 2 En
⌖ ▣ (4) ⊠ ✕ ▥ ▣ ♨

Yettington

SY0585   🍺 Sir Walter Raleigh, Rolle Arms

Lufflands, *Yettington, Budleigh*
Salterton, Devon, EX9 7BP.
Comfortable C17th farmhouse in rural
location.
Open: All Year
Grades: ETC 4 Diamond, AA 4 Diamond
01395 568422
Mrs Goode
Fax: 01395 568810
lufflands@compuserve.com
D: £20–£22 **S:** £20–£27
Beds: 1F 1D 1S
Baths: 1 En 1 Pr
⌖ ▣ (10) ⅏ ⊠ ⋔ ▥ ▣ ♨

Dorset

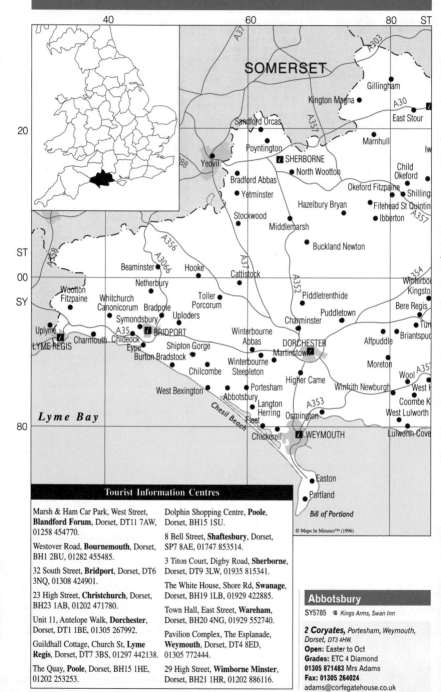

SOMERSET

Gillingham

Kington Magna ●

A30

East Stour

Sandford Orcas ●

Poyntington ●

Marnhull

SHERBORNE

North Wootton ●

Child Okeford

Bradford Abbas ●

Okeford Fitzpaine ●

Shilling

Yetminster ●

Hazelbury Bryan ●

Fifehead St Quintin

Stockwood ●

Ibberton ●

Middlemarsh ●

Buckland Newton ●

Beaminster ●   Hooke ●   Cattistock ●

Winterbo

Netherbury

Piddletrenthide ●

Kingsto

Wootton Fitzpaine

Toller Porcorum

Puddletown ●

Bere Regis

Whitchurch Canonicorum   Bradpole

Uploders

Charminster ●

Symondsbury

A35

Uplyme ●

BRIDPORT

Winterbourne Abbas

DORCHESTER

Affpuddle ●

Briantspud

LYME REGIS   Charmouth   Chideock

Shipton Gorge

Martinstown

Eype

Burton Bradstock

Winterbourne Steepleton

Moreton ●

Chilcombe

Wool

West H

West Bexington ●

Portesham ●

Higher Came ●

Winfrith Newburgh ●

Abbotsbury ●

Langton Herring

Coombe K

Lyme Bay

Chesil Beach

Fleet ●

Osmington ●

West Lulworth

Chickerell ●

WEYMOUTH

Lulworth Cove

Easton ●

Portland ●

Bill of Portland

© Maps In Minutes™ (1996)

Tourist Information Centres

Marsh & Ham Car Park, West Street, **Blandford Forum**, Dorset, DT11 7AW, 01258 454770.

Westover Road, **Bournemouth**, Dorset, BH1 2BU, 01282 455485.

32 South Street, **Bridport**, Dorset, DT6 3NQ, 01308 424901.

23 High Street, **Christchurch**, Dorset, BH23 1AB, 01202 471780.

Unit 11, Antelope Walk, **Dorchester**, Dorset, DT1 1BE, 01305 267992.

Guildhall Cottage, Church St, **Lyme Regis**, Dorset, DT7 3BS, 01297 442138.

The Quay, **Poole**, Dorset, BH15 1HE, 01202 253253.

Dolphin Shopping Centre, **Poole**, Dorset, BH15 1SU.

8 Bell Street, **Shaftesbury**, Dorset, SP7 8AE, 01747 853514.

3 Titon Court, Digby Road, **Sherborne**, Dorset, DT9 3LW, 01935 815341.

The White House, Shore Rd, **Swanage**, Dorset, BH19 1LB, 01929 422885.

Town Hall, East Street, **Wareham**, Dorset, BH20 4NG, 01929 552740.

Pavilion Complex, The Esplanade, **Weymouth**, Dorset, DT4 8ED, 01305 772444.

29 High Street, **Wimborne Minster**, Dorset, BH21 1HR, 01202 886116.

Abbotsbury

SY5785   🍴 Kings Arms, Swan Inn

2 Coryates, *Portesham, Weymouth, Dorset, DT3 4HW.*
Open: Easter to Oct
Grades: ETC 4 Diamond
01305 871483 Mrs Adams
Fax: 01305 264024
adams@corfegatehouse.co.uk

Affpuddle

SY8093   ◖ *Moreton Arms, Martyrs Inn*

Appletrees, *Affpuddle, Dorchester, Dorset, DT2 7HH.*
Traditional cottage, Hardy, Martyrs', T E Lawrence/museums all close.
Open: Easter to Sept
01929 471300 (also fax)
Mr Howell
gar@garethhowell.net
D: £15–£17 **S:** £15–£17
Beds: 2F 2T **Baths:** 1 Sh
🛏 (1) 🅿 (2) ⅍ 📺 🛖 ✕ ▦ ♨ ⚓

Alderholt

SU1212   ◖ *Churchill Arms*

Hillbury, *2 Fir Tree Hill, Camel Green, Alderholt, Fordingbridge, Hants, SP6 3AY.*
Large modern bungalow in peaceful surroundings. Warm welcome and comfortable.
Open: All Year
Grades: ETC 3 Diamond
01425 652582 Mrs Sillence
Fax: 01425 657587
D: £18–£20 **S:** £18–£20
Beds: 1F 1T 1S **Baths:** 1 Pr 1 Sh
🛏 🅿 (4) ⅍ 📺 ▦, 📹 ⚓

Quorum, *18 Broomfeld Drive, Alderholt, Fordingbridge, Hants, SP6 3HY.*
Modern bungalow, New Forest area, convenient Salisbury and South Coast.
Open: All Year (not Xmas)
Grades: AA 4 Diamond
01425 656735 Mr & Mrs Gatherer
D: £20–£22
Beds: 1D 1T **Baths:** 1 En 1 Pr
🛏 (5) 🅿 (3) ⅍ 📺 ▦, 📹 ⚓

Merrimead, *12 Station Road, Alderholt, Fordingbridge, Hants, SP6 3RB.*
Prize winning cook in village home with lovely garden.
Open: All Year (not Xmas)
Grades: ETC 4 Diamond
01425 657544 Fax: 01425 650400
merrimead@ic24.net
D: £18–£23 **S:** £20–£26
Beds: 1D 1T **Baths:** 1 En 1 Pr
🛏 🅿 (3) ⅍ 📺 ▦, 📹 ⚓

Ashley Heath

SU1205   ◖ *Old Barn Farm*

Lion's Hill Farm, *Ashley Heath, Ringwood, Hants, BH24 2EX.*
Open: All Year
Grades: ETC 2 Diamond
01425 472115
Mr & Mrs Hodges
D: £20–£25 **S:** £25–£30
Beds: 1F 1T 1D
Baths: 1 Pr 1 Sh
🛏 🅿 (6) 📺 🛖 ✕ ▦, 📹 ❋ ♨ ⚓
Traditional Victorian Farmhouse with uninterrupted views over forest and farmland. Direct access to forest trail way for cycling horse riding, walking. Stabling for horses and other pets welcome. Guests' heated swimming pool. Close to country park, Bournemouth and New Forest. AGA cooked breakfasts.

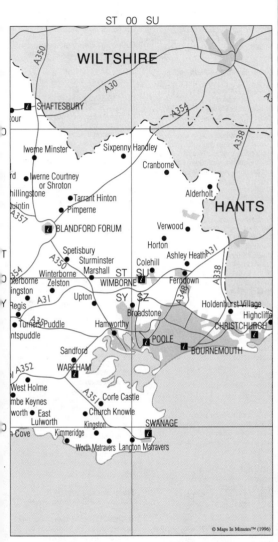

ST   OO   SU

WILTSHIRE

A350 · A30 · A354 · A338
SHAFTESBURY
tour
Iwerne Minster · Sixpenny Handley
Cranborne
rd · Iwerne Courtney or Shroton
hillingstone · Tarrant Hinton
bintin · Pimperne
Alderholt
HANTS
A357
BLANDFORD FORUM
Verwood
Spetisbury · Horton
Sturminster Marshall · Ashley Heath A31
terborne · Winterborne Zelston · Colehill
Y · ingston · A31 · Upton · ST SU
Regis · WIMBORNE · Ferndown
A348 · A338
Holdenhurst Village
Broadstone · Highcliffe
Turners Puddle · Hamworthy · CHRISTCHURCH
ntspuddle · POOLE
Sandford · BOURNEMOUTH
A352 · WAREHAM
A351
West Holme
mbe Keynes · Corfe Castle
worth · East Lulworth · Church Knowle
Cove · Kimmeridge · Kingston · SWANAGE
Worth Matravers · Langton Matravers

© Maps In Minutes™ (1996)

D: £20–£25 **S:** £35
Beds: 1F 1T 1D **Baths:** 3 En
🛏 (4) 🅿 (3) ⅍ 📺 ▦, ⚓
A Victorian house of character and charm peacefully situated in the Waddon Valley near the beautiful West Dorset coastline. Friendly welcome, every comfort and a delightful secluded garden awaits you. easy access Dorchester, Weymouth and the Ancient village of Abbotsbury.

Swan Lodge, *Abbotsbury, Weymouth, Dorset, DT3 4JL.*
Comfortable modern rooms with tea and coffee facilities and colour TVs.
Open: All Year
Grades: ETC 3 Diamond
01305 871249 (also fax) Mr Roper
D: £22–£28 **S:** £30–£45
Beds: 3D **Baths:** 3 En
🛏 🅿 📺 🛖 ✕ ▦, 📹 ⚓ cc

Beaminster

ST4701   ◖ *Bridge House, Fox, Greyhound, Pickwick's*

Beam Cottage, 16 North Street, *Beaminster, Dorset, DT8 3DZ.*
Open: All Year (not Xmas)
01308 863639 Mrs Standeven
D: £25–£30 **S:** £30–£35
Beds: 1F 1D 2T **Baths:** 2 En 1 Pr
⛌ 🅿 (3) 📺 🛉 ✕ 🎠 ⚲
Very attractive Grade II Listed cottage in delightful secluded garden. Also available pretty twin bedded garden cottage with all facilities. All rooms have own sitting room .

The Walnuts, 2 Prout Street, *Beaminster, Dorset, DT8 3AY.*
Listed building situated just off town square. Very comfortable establishment.
Open: All Year
Grades: ETC 4 Diamond
01308 862211 C Pieles'z
D: £24–£27.50 **S:** £28–£35
Beds: 2D 1T **Baths:** 2 En 1 Pr
⛌ (8) 🅿 (3) ⚵ 🎠 📺 ⚲

Kitwhistle Farm, *Beaminster Down, Beaminster, Dorset, DT8 3SG.*
Quiet location, downland dairy farm. All facilities on ground floor.
Open: Easter to Oct
Grades: ETC 3 Diamond
01308 862458 (also fax)
Mrs Hasell
D: £18–£22 **S:** £22–£25
Beds: 1F **Baths:** 1 En
⛌ 🅿 ⚵ 📺 ⚲

Jenny Wrens, 1 Hogshill Street, *Beaminster, Dorset, DT8 3AE.*
Part of C17th tearoom in charming small Dorset town.
Open: All Year
01308 862814 Fax: 01308 861191
D: £24 **S:** £28–£44
Beds: 2D 1T **Baths:** 3 En
⛌ (12) ⚵ 🎠 📺 ⚲

Bere Regis

SY8494   ◖ *Drax Arms*

Appletree Cottage, 12 Sitterton, Bere *Regis, Wareham, Dorset, BH20 7HU.*
Open: All Year (not Xmas/New Year)
01929 471686 Mrs Wilson
D: £20 **S:** £22
Beds: 1T 1D **Baths:** 1 Sh
⛌ (10) ⚵ 🎠 📺 ⚲
Charming 17th Century thatched cottage with roses and honeysuckle around the door. Low beamed lounge with inglenook and wood-burner. Centrally placed, in Hardy Country, to enjoy Dorset's beautiful coast, countryside and resorts. 20 minutes from Lulworth Cove and Durdle Door.

B&B owners may vary rates - be sure to check when booking

Planning a longer stay? Always ask for any special rates

Blandford Forum

ST8806   ◖ *Greyhound, Charlton Inn, Langton Arms*

Lower Bryanston Farm, Blandford *Forum, Dorset, DT11 0LS.*
Open: All Year (not Xmas)
01258 452009 (also fax)
D: £20–£25 **S:** £25–£30
Beds: 1F 1T 3D **Baths:** 1 En 1 Pr 1 Sh
⛌ (10) ⚵ 📺 ⚲
Attractive farmhouse set in extensive grounds. Spacious bedrooms with comfortable beds and beautiful views. Full English breakfast. Guest sitting room and garden where children can play. Ten minute walk to the Georgian town of Blandford Forum and centrally located to discover Dorset.

Fortune House, 19 Bayfran Way, *Blandford Forum, Dorset, DT11 7RZ.*
Easy walking distance of town and local places of interest.
Open: All Year
01258 455154 Ms Billam
D: £17 **S:** £17
Beds: 1D 2T 1S **Baths:** 2 Sh
⛌ 🅿 (2) 📺 ✕ 🎠 ⚲ ✳

South Pasture, St Leonards Avenue, *Blandford Forum, Dorset, DT11 7PD.*
Peaceful location close to town centre. Natural therapies available.
Open: All Year (not Xmas/New Year)
01258 452804 Mrs Busst
southpasture@aol.com
D: £20–£25 **S:** £20–£25
Beds: 1T **Baths:** 1 Pr
🅿 📺 ✕ 🎠 ⚲

Park Lodge Bungalow, Whitecliff Mill *Street, Blandford Forum, Dorset, DT11 7BN.*
Comfortable, refurbished bungalow, quiet surroundings, pleasant gardens. Close town centre.
Open: All Year
01258 452834 Mrs Atkins
jamesatkins@ukonline.co.uk
D: £18–£22 **S:** £20–£25
Beds: 1D 1T **Baths:** 1 En 1 Pr
🅿 (2) ⚵ 🎠 📺 🎠 ⚲ 🅖 ♿

8 Park Road, Blandford Forum, Dorset, *DT11 7BX.*
Character Victorian house. Close to town centre. Attractive, secluded garden.
Open: Feb to Oct
01258 453809 D: £17–£25 **S:** £17–£25
Beds: 1T 1D **Baths:** 1 En 1 Sh
⛌ (10) ⚵ 🛉 ✕ 🎠 📺 ⚲

6 Courtney Close, Blandford Forum, *Dorset, DT11 8RD.*
Quiet, peaceful, with views of Hampledon Hall. Excellent walks nearby.
Open: All Year (not Xmas)
01258 860056 Mrs Elly
D: £20–£25 **S:** £–£25
Beds: 2F 1D 1T 1S **Baths:** 1 Pr
🅿 (5) ⚵ ✕ 🎠 📺 ⚲

Bournemouth

SZ0891   ◖ *Neptune, Westbourne, Spyglass & Kettle, Durley Inn, Moon In The Square, Seagull, Commodore, Inn On The Park, Goat & Tricycle, Riverside Inn, Edward's Bar, Lynton Court, Hungry Man, Royal Exeter, Jumping Jacks*

Balincourt Hotel, 58 Christchurch *Road, Bournemouth, Dorset, BH1 3PF.*
Open: All Year
Grades: AA 4 Diamond
01202 552962 Mr & Mrs Gandolfi
D: £25–£30 **S:** £30–£45
Beds: 5D 5T 2S **Baths:** 12 En 1 Sh
⛌ 🅿 (11) ⚵ 📺 ✕ 🎠 ⚲ ✳ ⚲ cc
An elegant Victorian residence with luxury spacious rooms. Somewhere you can be sure of a warm welcome and personal attention. The hotel has a non-smoking policy. Minimum age of 16. Close to the seafront and town centre.

Chilterns Hotel, 44 Westby Road, *Bournemouth, Dorset, BH5 1HD.*
Open: Apr to Sept
01202 396539 (also fax)
Mr Whitney
bwhit@tinyworld.co.uk
D: £20–£25 **S:** fr £18.50
Beds: 3F 8D 4T 2S **Baths:** 9 En 1 Pr 7 Sh
⛌ 🅿 (10) 📺 ✕ 🎠 ⚲
Excellent location. Few minutes to pier, glorious golden sandy beaches, wooded cliff top walks, shopping precinct, T/Operators. Comfortable, welcoming. Highly recommended for short or long stay. Level walking, AMPLE PARKING. Parties welcome.

Cransley Hotel, 11 Knyveton Road, *East Cliff, Bournemouth, Dorset, BH2 3QG.*
Open: All Year
Grades: ETC 3 Diamond, AA 3 Diamond
01202 290067 Mr Goodwin
Fax: 01202 292977
info@cransley.com
D: £23–£27 **S:** £27–£40
Beds: 4T 5D 2S **Baths:** 10 En 1 Pr
⛌ (8) ⚵ 📺 🎠 ⚲ cc
A comfortable and elegant house for non smokers, set in a quiet pine avenue. Close to the town centre and beach. Conveniently placed for all major road and rail links. As seen on ITV's 'Dream Town'.

Tenby House Hotel, 23 Pinecliffe, *Southbourne, Bournemouth, Dorset, BH6 3PY.*
Delightful, Edwardian-style private hotel. superbly located for shops, pubs & restaurant. **Open:** Jan to Dec
01202 423696 Mrs Rudland
D: £17–£22 **S:** £17–£22
Beds: 2F 3D 3T 2S **Baths:** 4 En 3 Sh
⛌ (2) 🅿 (5) ⚵ 🛉 ✕ 🎠 📺 ⚲

Cremona Hotel, 61 St Michaels Road, *West Cliff, Bournemouth, Dorset, BH2 5DP.*
A small family-run hotel in the Town Centre and near sea.
Open: All Year
01202 290035 P Littlewort
Fax: 01202 297177
Enquiries@cremona.co.uk
D: £16–£25 **S:** £20–£35
Beds: 3F 2T 4D **Baths:** 7 En 2 Sh
⛌ 📺 🛉 🎠 ⚲ cc

Shady Nook Guest House, *3 Upper Terrace Road, Bournemouth, Dorset, BH2 5NW.*
Town centre guest house near beach & entertainment. Excellent food and service.
Open: All Year (not Xmas)
01202 551557 Mr Holdaway
D: £17–£24 **S:** £20–£26
Beds: 2F 3D 2T 1S **Baths:** 5 En 1 Sh
🛇 🅿 (4) 🅣 ⼍ ✕ 📖 🖂 🖤 🖕

Shoreline Hotel, *7 Pinecliffe Avenue, Southbourne, Bournemouth, BH6 3PY.*
Close to new Forest, Beaulieu Motor Museum, Salisbury Wilton House.
Open: Easter to Dec
Grades: ETC 4 Diamond
01202 429654 (also fax)
D: £13–£21 **S:** £13–£24
Beds: 2F 4D 2T 2S **Baths:** 5 En 2 Sh
🛇 (5) 🅿 (5) 🅣 ⼍ 📖 🖤 ✻ 🖕

St Michaels Friendly Guest House, *42 St Michaels Road, Westcliffe, Bournemouth, Dorset, BH2 5DY.*
Home cooking. Five minutes walk to town or sea and international conference centre.
Open: All Year
01202 557386 (also fax)
Mrs Davies
D: fr £16 **S:** fr £16
Beds: 1F 2D 2T 1S **Baths:** 2 Sh
🛇 🅣 ⼍ ✕ 📖 🖤 ✻ 🖕

Sirena Hotel, *20 Knole Road, Bournemouth, Dorset, BH1 4DQ.*
Small family hotel, near Boscombe gardens few min from sea/shops.
Open: All Year
01202 394877 Miss Williams
D: £16–£20 **S:** £14–£16
Beds: 2F 3D 2T 2S **Baths:** 2 En 2 Sh
🛇 (5) 🅿 ⼍ 🅣 ⼍ 🖤 🖕

Alum Chine Hotel, *33 Studland Road, Bournemouth, Dorset, BH4 8HZ.*
Open: All Year
01202 761193 Mr & Mrs Lait
alum.chine.hotel@ukgateway.net
D: £18–£22 **S:** £18–£22
Beds: 4F 2D 1T 2S **Baths:** 6 En 1 Sh
🛇 🅿 (4) ⼤ 🅣 ✕ 📖 🖤 ✻ 🖕 cc
Comfortable, friendly licensed hotel, offering delicious home-cooked food, facing wooded Alum Chine. 500 yds from clean, sandy beach. 20 mins walk along promenade to Bournemouth - cinemas, shops and theatres. Within easy reach of New Forest, Poole and much more.

West Cliff Sands Hotel, *9 Priory Road, West Cliff, Bournemouth, Dorset, BH2 5DF.*
Open: All Year
01202 557013 (also fax)
Mr & Mrs Pannell
D: £23–£30 **S:** £35–£45
Beds: 5F 11D **Baths:** 16 En
🛇 🅿 (16) 🅣 ⼍ 📖 🖤 🖕 cc
A quality detached reasonably priced hotel set in a prime position on the popular west cliff. Two minutes walk to pier, theatres, Bournemouth International Conference and Leisure Centre, and many pubs and restaurants. Five minutes walk to town centre.

Highclere Hotel, *15 Burnaby Road, Bournemouth, Dorset, BH4 8JF.*
Edwardian house hotel only 4 minutes from safe sandy beaches.
Open: Easter to Oct
Grades: ETC 3 Diamond, AA 3 Diamond
01202 761350 Mr & Mrs Baldwin
Fax: 01202 767110
daveril@highclerehotel.freeserve.co.uk
D: £22–£25 **S:** £22–£25
Beds: 4F 1T 4D **Baths:** 9 En
🛇 (3) 🅿 (5) 🅣 ⼍ 📖 🖕 cc

Audmore Hotel, *3 Cecil Road, Boscombe, Bournemouth, Dorset, BH5 1DU.*
Friendly family-run licensed hotel near beach/shop. Many ensuites.
Open: All Year (not Xmas/New Year)
Grades: ETC 3 Diamond
01202 395166 Mrs Lane
D: £17–£22 **S:** £17–£22
Beds: 5F 2D 1T 2S **Baths:** 6 En 3 Sh
🛇 🅿 (4) ⼤ ✕ 📖 🖤 🖕

Victoria, *120 Parkwood Road, Southbourne, Bournemouth, Dorset, BH5 2BN.*
A friendly, comfortable private house near beach, shops and buses.
Open: May to Oct
01202 423179 Mrs Rising
D: £13–£13.50 **S:** £13–£13.50
Beds: 1D 1T **Baths:** 1 Sh
🛇 (4) 🅿 (2) 🅣 📖 🖤 🖕

Fircroft Hotel, *Owls Road, Boscombe, Bournemouth, BH5 1AE.*
Friendly family hotel close sea and shops (cycle friendly). Free entry to health club.
Open: All Year
Grades: ETC 2 Diamond, AA 2 Star, RAC 2 Star
01202 309771 D: £22–£30 **S:** £22–£30
Beds: 14F 12D 18T 6S
🛇 🅿 📖 ⼍ ✕ 📖 🖤 ✻ 🖕 cc

Ardene Hotel, *12 Glen Road, Boscombe, Bournemouth, Dorset, BH5 1HR.*
Friendly hotel situated close to beach and nightlife.
Open: Easter to Sep
Grades: ETC 3 Diamond
01202 394928 (also fax)
Miss Griffiths
ardenehotel@talk21.com
D: £17.50–£24 **S:** £17.50–£21.50
Beds: 3F 2D 4T 4S **Baths:** 6 En 3 Sh
🛇 🅿 (5) 🅣 ⼍ ✕ 📖 🖕

Mayfield Guest House, *Knyveton Gardens, 46 Frances Road, Bournemouth, Dorset, BH1 3SA.*
Friendly guest house opposite Knyveton Gardens. Central sea, shops, rail, coach.
Open: Jan to Nov
Grades: ETC 4 Diamond
01202 551839 (also fax)
Mrs Barling
accom@may-field.co.uk
D: £18–£22 **S:** £18–£22
Beds: 1F 5D 1T 1S **Baths:** 7 En 1 Pr
🛇 (5) 🅿 (5) 🅣 ✕ 📖 🖤 🖕

Bramdean Hotel, *30 Westbourne Park Road, Westbourne, Bournemouth, Dorset, BH4 8HG.*
Bramdean, full English breakfast, comfortable family rooms - some ensuite.
Open: All Year (not Xmas/New Year)
01202 764095 Mr Marshall
D: £17–£22 **S:** £18–£22
Beds: 5F 1S **Baths:** 3 En 1 Sh
🛇 (4) 🅿 (5) 🅣 🖤 📖 🖕

Stella Maris Guest House, *88 Southbourne Road, Southbourne, Bournemouth, Dorset, BH6 3QQ.*
Friendly guesthouse. Few minutes level walk to amenities. OAP discounts.
Open: All Year
01202 426874 Mrs Starling
info@stellamaris.free-online.co.uk
D: £15–£20 **S:** £14–£28.50
Beds: 2F 5D 1T **Baths:** 6 Pr
🛇 🅿 (6) 🅣 ⼍ ✕ 📖 🖤 ✻ 🖕

Kingsley Hotel, *20 Glen Road, Boscombe, Bournemouth, Dorset, BH5 1HR.*
Small, quality, smoke free hotel, close to sandy beaches and shops.
Open: Easter to Sept
01202 398683 Mr & Mrs Smith
Fax: 0870 1672820
enq@kingsleyhotel.co.uk
D: £20–£25 **S:** £20–£25
Beds: 3F 5D 1T 1S **Baths:** 10 En
🛇 (5) 🅿 (6) ⼤ ✕ 📖 🖤 🖕 cc

Moordown, *1031 Wimborne Road, Bournemouth, Dorset, BH9 2BX.*
3 miles from Bournemouth near shops and bus route.
Open: All Year (not Xmas)
01202 527419 Miss Barton
D: £25–£30 **S:** £15–£20
Beds: 2D 1S **Baths:** 1 Sh
🅿 ⼤ 🅣 📖

Sandelheath Hotel, *1 Knyveton Road, Bournemouth, Dorset, BH1 3QF.*
Situated in an avenue of pine trees, convenient for beaches, local attractions and town centre.
Open: All Year (not Xmas)
01202 555428 Mrs Buick
derek_buick@hotmail.com
D: £20–£27.50 **S:** £23.50–£27.50
Beds: 1F 2D 2T 3S **Baths:** 6 En 2 Sh
🛇 (3) 🅿 (7) 🅣 📖 🖤 🖕

Woodside Hotel, *29 Southern Road, Southbourne, Bournemouth, Dorset, BH6 3SR.*
Family-run licensed hotel in quiet road, three minutes' level walk Blue Flag beach, shops.
Open: All Year
01202 427213 Mr & Mrs Eslick
D: £15–£20 **S:** £15–£20
Beds: 1F 5D 2T 1S **Baths:** 4 En 2 Pr 2 Sh
🛇 🅿 (5) 🅣 ✕ 📖 🖤 ✻ 🖕 cc

Sunnydene Hotel, *11 Spencer Road, Bournemouth, Dorset, BH1 3TE.*
In a quiet park area opposite a colourful display of trees and shrubs.
Open: Jun to Oct
01202 552281 **D:** £17–£23 **S:** £17
Beds: 1F 5D 2T 2S **Baths:** 7 En 1 Sh
🛇 🅿 (5) 🅣 ✕ 📖 🖕

The Cottage Hotel, 12 Southern Road, Southbourne, Bournemouth, Dorset, BH6 3SR.
Select family-run private hotel; beach and New Forest nearby.
Open: Feb to Nov
01202 422764 Mr Halliwell
Fax: 01202 381442
ron+val@jvhalliwell.force9.co.uk
D: £23–£24.50 **S:** £29.50–£31
Beds: 2F 2D 2T **Baths:** 4 En 2 Pr
⌕ (8) 🅿 (8) ⅄ 📺 ✕ 🎟 🖥 ⅃ ♨

Bradford Abbas

ST5814   🍺 Rose & Crown

Heartsease Cottage, North Street, Bradford Abbas, Sherborne, Dorset, DT9 6SA.
Delightful Dorset village cottage. Idyllic garden, conservatory, themed bedrooms.
Open: All Year
Grades: ETC 5 Diamond
01935 475480 (also fax)
Mr & Mrs Dann
D: £20–£27 **S:** £20–£29
Beds: 1D 2T **Baths:** 1 En 1 Pr
⌕ (8) 🅿 (4) 📺 🖥 🅥 ♨

Bradpole

SY4894

New House Farm, Mangerton Lane, Bradpole, Bridport, Dorset, DT6 3SE.
Country farmhouse near sea, fossils, coastal path, coarse fishing lake.
Open: All Year (not Xmas)
01308 422884 (also fax) Mrs Greening
D: £18–£22 **S:** £20–£25
Beds: 2F **Baths:** 2 En
⌕ 🅿 (6) ⅄ ✕ 🖥 🅥 ♨

Briantspuddle

SY8193

Longacre Barn, The Old Dairy, Briantspuddle, Dorchester, Dorset, DT2 7HT.
Longacre Barn is a unique and very interesting barn conversion offering luxury accommodation. **Open:** All Year
01929 472531 Mrs Wenham
celia@longacre-barn.freeserve.co.uk
D: £20–£27.50 **S:** £20–£30
Beds: 2D 2T **Baths:** 1 En 1 Sh
⌕ 🅿 (5) ⅄ 📺 🖥 🅥 ♨ cc

Bridport

SY4693   🍺 Crown Inn, The Uploaders, The Bull, Hardy's, Tiger Inn, Woodhay

Britmead House, West Bay Road, Bridport, Dorset, DT6 4EG.
Open: All Year
Grades: ETC 4 Diamond, AA 4 Diamond
01308 422941 Mr Hardy
Fax: 01308 422516
britmead@talk21.com
D: £22–£31 **S:** £26–£40
Beds: 2F 3D 2T **Baths:** 7 En
⌕ 🅿 (8) 📺 ★ ✕ 🖥 🅥 ♨ cc
Situated between Bridport and West Bay Harbour with its beaches, golf course, walks, Chesil Beach and the Dorset Coast Path. All rooms have colour TV, mini bar, tea and coffee making facilities. South-facing lounge and dining room overlooking gardens. Private parking.

The Old Dairy House, Walditch, Bridport, Dorset, DT6 4LB.
Open: All Year
01308 458021 Mrs Long
D: £20 **S:** £20
Beds: 1D 1T **Baths:** 1 Sh
🅿 (4) ⅄ 📺 🖥 🅥 ♨
A friendly welcome to relax in this peaceful corner of West Dorset. Enjoy full English breakfast. Guests' TV lounge with log fire. Gardens, abundant wildlife. Rural/coastal walks. 18-hole golf 2 miles. Good selection country pubs nearby. Adults only.

Green Lane House, Bridport, Dorset, DT6 4LH.
Welcoming, spacious home in own grounds. 1.5 miles from coast.
Open: All Year (not Xmas/New Year)
01308 422619 (also fax)
Mrs Prideaux
D: £20 **S:** £20
Beds: 1T 1D **Baths:** 2 En
⌕ 🅿 (5) ⅄ 📺 ★ ✕ 🖥 🅥 ♨

Saxlingham House, West Road, Symondsbury, Bridport, Dorset, DT6 6AA.
Extensive country views many local attractions warm friendly welcome.
Open: Easter to September
01308 423629 Mr & Mrs Nicholls
D: £15–£17 **S:** £15–£17
Beds: 1T 2D **Baths:** 3 En
🅿 ⅄ 📺 ♨

Broadstone

SZ0095   🍺 Dorset Soldier, Lamb's Green Inn, Stepping Stones, Corkers, Yachtsman, Crown Hotel, Shah Of Persia, Red Lion, Grasshopper, Conjurer's Half Crown, Coventry Arms

Ashdell, 85 Dunyeats Road, Broadstone, Poole, Dorset, BH18 8AF.
Central, comfortable, secluded. Breakfast/EM choice. Historic countryside/beaches, short breaks.
Open: All Year (not Xmas)
Grades: ETC 2 Diamond
01202 692032 Mrs Critchley
ian@ashdell.fsnet.co.uk
D: £16–£19 **S:** £19–£21
Beds: 1F 1D 1T 1S **Baths:** 1 Sh
⌕ (5) 🅿 (3) ★ ✕ 🖥 🅥 ♨

Tarven, Corfe Lodge Road, Broadstone, Dorset, BH18 9NF.
Quiet woodland location near Poole/Wimborne. Ample parking. Warm welcome.
Open: All Year (not Xmas/New Year)
Grades: ETC 3 Diamond
01202 694338 Mrs Browning
D: £16–£17 **S:** £16–£17
Beds: 1D 2S **Baths:** 2 Sh
⌕ (4) 🅿 (6) ⅄ 📺 ✕ 🖥 🅥 ♨

'Bless This Nest', 40 Dunyeats Road, Broadstone, Dorset, BH18 8AH.
Victorian cottage with pretty garden. 5-10 minutes from Poole/harbour/docks /ferries. **Open:** All Year
01202 778443 Mrs Churchill
janet@blessthisnest.freeserve.co.uk
D: £18–£20 **S:** £20–£22
Beds: 1D 1T 1S **Baths:** 1 Sh
⌕ (6) 🅿 (2) ⅄ 📺 🖥 🅥 ♨

Buckland Newton

ST6805   🍺 Piddle Inn, Thimble, Brace Of Pheasants

Whiteways Farmhouse Accommodation, Bookham Farm, Buckland Newton, Dorchester, Dorset, DT2 7RP.
Open: All Year (not Xmas/New Year)
Grades: ETC 4 Diamond
01300 345511 (also fax)
bookhamfarm@netscapeonline.co.uk
D: £20–£25 **S:** £20–£25
Beds: 1F 1S **Baths:** 1 En 1 Pr
⌕ 🅿 (3) ⅄ 📺 🖥 ♨
A warm welcome awaits you at the hamstone and flint farmhouse. Situated at the head of the Blackmore Vale, the rooms enjoy panoramic views over unspoilt countryside. Excellent walks including The Wessex Way and Hardy Trail. 30 minutes from sea.

Holyleas House, Buckland Newton, Dorchester, Dorset, DT2 7DP.
Open: All Year (not Xmas/New Year)
Grades: ETC 4 Diamond Sliver Award
01300 345214 Mrs Bunkall
Fax: 01305 264488
D: £22.50–£25 **S:** £25–£35
Beds: 1T 1D 1S
Baths: 1 En 2 Pr
⌕ 🅿 (6) ⅄ 📺 ★ ✕ 🖥 🅥 ♨
The family labrador will welcome you to this typical period country house set in 1/2 acre lovely garden. Rooms are beautifully decorated with antique furniture and enjoy fine views. Relax in the guests sitting room with log fire burning in winter.

Rew Cottage, Buckland Newton, Dorchester, DT2 7DN.
Thomas Hardy country, easy reach Dorchester, Sherborne, Salisbury, Lyme Regis, sea.
Open: Jan to Dec
Grades: ETC 4 Diamond
01300 345467 (also fax)
Mrs McCarthy
D: £20–£25 **S:** £29–£35
Beds: 1D 1T 1S **Baths:** 2 Pr
⌕ 🅿 (6) 📺 ★ 🖥 🅥 ♨

Burton Bradstock

SY4889

Burton Cliff Hotel, Cliff Road, Burton Bradstock, Bridport, Dorset, DT6 4RB.
Open: All Year
Grades: ETC 3 Diamond
01308 897205 Mr Hoare
Fax: 01308 898111
D: £21–£39 **S:** £24.50–£36
Beds: 8T 7D 3S
Baths: 12 En 12 Pr 3 Sh
⌕ 🅿 (40) ⅄ 📺 ★ ✕ 🖥 🅥 ♨ ⅏ cc
Situated on the cliff top with superb sea views and surrounded by National Trust countryside. Many guest rooms overlook the beach/sea. Excellent home cooking bought to you by our team of friendly and enthusiastic staff. Private off-road parking.

Cattistock

SY5999

Sandhills Cottage, *Sandhills, Cattistock, Dorchester, DT2 0HQ.*
Open: All Year
Grades: ETC 4 Diamond
01300 321146 Mr & Mrs Roca
Fax: 01300 321146
m.vroca@lineone.net
D: £22–£24 **S:** £25–£28
Beds: 2T 1D **Baths:** 3 En
📺 (12) 🅿 (8) ⊬ 📺 🛏 🖳 🖢
Sandhills cottage lies in a rural hamlet within ten minutes walk the village of Cattistock has a shop/ P.O., pub and a beautiful church. Sandhills offers superb scenery and good walking, some of Dorset's finest beaches are within easy driving distance.

Charminster

SY6892 ⚅ *Inn For All Seasons, Junction Hotel, Old Ship, Trumpet Major, Bakers Arms*

Slades Farm, *North Street, Charminster, Dorchester, Dorset, DT2 9QZ.*
Superb accommodation and every comfort in recently converted barn.
Open: All Year
Grades: ETC 4 Diamond
01305 265614 (also fax)
Mr & Mrs Woods
D: £18–£25 **S:** £30–£35
Beds: 1F 2D **Baths:** 3 En
📺 🅿 (8) ⊬ 📺 🛏 🖳 🖢

Charmouth

SY3693 ⚅ *Five Bells, Ship Inn*

Cardsmill Farm, *Whitchurch Canonicorum, Bridport, Dorset, DT6 6RP.*
Comfortable farmhouse on working family farm 3 miles from coast.
Open: All year (not Xmas)
Grades: ETC 3 Diamond
01297 489375 (also fax)
Mrs Johnson
cardsmill@aol.com
D: £18–£24 **S:** £19–£23
Beds: 1F 1D 1S **Baths:** 2 En
📺 🅿 (6) 📺 🛏 🖳 🖤 🖢

Stonebarrow Manor, *Stonebarrow Lane, Charmouth, Dorset, DT6 6RA.*
C16th house in 2 acres. Beach, fossils, great walking country.
Open: All Year (not Xmas/New Year)
01297 560212 Mike & Sue Bomford
Fax: 01297 560234
bomfords@hotmail.com
D: £25 **S:** £25
Beds: 4F 4D 3T 2S **Baths:** 11 En 1 Sh
📺 (6) 🅿 (15) ⊬ 📺 🛏 🖳 🖤 🖢

Hensleigh Hotel, *Lower Sea Lane, Charmouth, Bridport, Dorset, DT6 6LW.*
Comfort and hospitality, 300 metres from beach and cliff walks.
Open: Feb to Nov
01297 560830 (also fax)
Mr & Mrs Davis
D: £24–£30 **S:** £24–£45
Beds: 1F 2D 5T 2S **Baths:** 10 En
📺 🅿 (20) ⊬ 📺 🛏 🗙 🖳 🖤 🖢 cc

Chickerell

SY6480 ⚅ *White Hart, Lodmore Inn, Pulpit, Waterloo, Turk's Head*

Stonebank, *14 West Street, Chickerell, Weymouth, Dorset, DT3 4DY.*
Charming C17th former farmhouse ideally situated for exploring coast and country.
Open: Apr to Sep
Grades: ETC 5 Diamond
01305 760120 Mrs Westcott
Fax: 01305 760871
stw@stonebank-chickerell.co.uk
D: £22.50–£25 **S:** £35
Beds: 2D **Baths:** 2 En
🅿 (2) ⊬ 📺 🖳 🖢

Chideock

SY4292 ⚅ *George Inn, All in the Clock House, Anchor*

Warren House B&B, *Chideock, Bridport, Dorset, DT6 6JW.*
Open: All Year (not Xmas)
Grades: ETC 4 Diamond, AA 4 Diamond
01297 489704 (also fax)
Mr & Mrs Tweddle
D: £22–£25 **S:** £27–£30
Beds: 2F 1D 1T **Baths:** 4 En
📺 🅿 (7) ⊬ 📺 🖳 🖢
Grade II Listed C17th thatched house, high quality, comfortable spacious rooms. Friendly informal atmosphere. Area of Outstanding Natural Beauty with Coastal Path and beach within walking distance. Close to all local amenities. Intercity rail lines at Axminster or Dorchester.

Chideock House Hotel, *Main St, Chideock, Bridport, Dorset, DT6 6JN.*
Open: All Year
Grades: ETC 2 Star, AA 2 Star
01297 489242 Mr Dunn
Fax: 01297 489184
anna@chideockhousehotel.com
D: £27.50–£42.50 **S:** £50–£80
Beds: 9D **Baths:** 8 En 1 Pr
📺 (15) 🅿 🛏 🗙 🖳 🖤 🖢 cc
Ten minute walk to the sea and coastal path with stunning scenery. 'Harbour Lights' filmed locally. Abbots Swannery, Mapperton Gardens and Athelhampton House all nearby. Stunning food in candle lit restaurant. Close to Lyme Regis & Charmouth. Weymouth 20 mins.

Betchworth House, *Chideock, Bridport, Dorset, DT6 6JW.*
Open: All Year
Grades: ETC 4 Diamond, AA 4 Diamond, RAC 4 Diamond
01297 489478 Jill & John Lodge
Fax: 01297 489932
D: £22–£25 **S:** £27–£30
Beds: 1F 2D 2T **Baths:** 3 En 2 Pr
📺 (10) 🅿 (6) ⊬ 📺 🖳 🖤 🖢 cc
Very friendly C17th guesthouse has been refurbished to a very high standard. Each room is well equipped with thoughtful extras such as tissues, toiletries, hairdryer. renowned Dorset cream teas. Attractive cottage garden. Private parking. Sea 3/4 mile. Pubs nearby.

Frogmore Farm, *Chideock, Bridport, Dorset, DT6 6HT.*
C17th farmhouse overlooking Lyme Bay. Adjoining South West Coast Path.
Open: All Year
01308 456159 Mrs Norman
D: £16–£20 **S:** £20–£23
Beds: 1F 1D 1T 1S **Baths:** 2 En 2 Pr
📺 (8) 🅿 (6) ⊬ 📺 🛏 🗙 🖳 🖤 🖢

Chimneys Guest House, *Main Street, Chideock, Bridport, Dorset, DT6 6JH.*
Warm welcome, comfortable bedrooms, guest lounge & dining room. Private parking.
Open: All Year (not Xmas)
Grades: RAC 4 Diamond
01297 489368 D Backhouse & J M Backhouse
D: £22.50–£25 **S:** £25
Beds: 1F 1T 3D **Baths:** 4 En
📺 🅿 (5) ⊬ 📺 🛏 🖳 🖢

Chilcombe

SY5291 ⚅ *The Crown*

Rudge Farm, *Chilcombe, Bridport, Dorset, DT6 4NF.*
Open: All Year (not Xmas)
Grades: ETC 4 Star
01308 482630 Ms Diment
Fax: 01308 482635
stilwell@rudgefarm.co.uk
D: £25–£27 **S:** £24–£26
Beds: 1F 2D 1T
Baths: 4 En
📺 🅿 (4) ⊬ 📺 🖳 🖤 🖢 cc
Peacefully situated in the beautiful Bride Valley just 2 and a half miles from the sea and overlooking lakes in our wild flower meadow. Large, comfortable rooms with far-reaching views. Tranquil walled garden filled with the scent of roses, honeysuckle and jasmine.

Child Okeford

ST8312 ⚅ *Cricketers' Arms*

Bartley House, *Upper Street, Child Okeford, Blandford Forum, Dorset, DT11 8EF.*
Beautiful, spacious Victorian house in quiet village location. Great breakfasts!
Open: All Year
01258 860420 Mrs Langley
D: £17.50–£20 **S:** £20–£25
Beds: 2F 1D 1T **Baths:** 2 En 1 Pr
📺 🅿 (6) 📺 🛏 🖳 🖤 🖢

Christchurch

SZ1693 ⚅ *Fisherman's Haunt, Woolpack, Lamb Inn, Three Tuns, Globe Inn, Cat & Fiddle, Centurion, Rising Sun, Ship In Distress*

Chalkwood, *45 Barrak Road, Christchurch, Dorset, BH23 1PA.*
Large Victorian comfortable family home. Children under twelve sharing parents' room half price.
Open: All Year (not Xmas)
01202 474527
Mrs Chalk
D: £16–£18 **S:** £16–£18
Beds: 2F 1D 1T 1S **Baths:** 3 En 1 Sh
📺 🅿 (5) 📺 🗙 🖳 🖢

Beverly Glen, *1 Stuart Road, Highcliffe, Christchurch, Dorset, BH23 5JS.*
5 mins walk to seafront, shops, restaurants, etc. 10 mins car to New Forest.
Open: All Year (not Xmas)
Grades: ETC 4 Diamond
01425 273811 Mr Welch
D: £20–£30 **S:** £22–£30
Beds: 1F 3D 1T 1S **Baths:** 6 En
⌂ (6) 🅿 📺 ⛥ 🛍 Ⅴ ⬩ cc

Bure Farmhouse, *107 Bure Lane, Friar's Cliff, Christchurch, Dorset, BH23 4DN.*
Edwardian farmhouse, beautiful, peaceful surroundings, sea and New Forest.
Open: All Year
Grades: ETC 3 Diamond
01425 275498 Mrs Erhardt
D: £18–£23 **S:** £20–£25
Beds: 2D 1T **Baths:** 3 En
⌂ (4) 🅿 (4) ⛥ 📺 🛍 Ⅴ ⬩

Holfleet Cottage, *2 Bockhampton Road, Winkton, Christchurch, Dorset, BH23 7AE.*
Comfortable, quiet, rural cottage close to sea and New Forest.
Open: Apr to Sep
01425 672560 Mrs Snelling
john@holfleet.freeserve.co.uk
D: £17 **S:** fr £17
Beds: 1S 2T **Baths:** 1 Pr
⌂ 🅿 (4) ⛥ 📺 🛍 ⬩

Ivy Lea, *120 Stony Lane, Burton, Christchurch, Dorset, BH23 7LD.*
Chalet bungalow near town, forest, rivers, beaches. Friendly cosy atmosphere.
Open: All Year (not Xmas)
01202 499517 Mrs Sandison
D: £17.50–£20 **S:** £25
Beds: 1F 2D 1T **Baths:** 1 Sh
⌂ 🅿 (4) ⛥ 📺 🛍 Ⅴ ⬩

Salmons Reach Guest House, *28 Stanpit, Christchurch, Dorset, BH23 3LZ.*
Situated between Mudeford and Christchurch. Near Bournemouth and New Forest.
Open: All Year
01202 477315 D: £17.50–£25 **S:** £18–£25
Beds: 2F 3D 2T 1S **Baths:** 2 En 2 Sh
⌂ 🅿 📺 ⛥ 🛍 ✸ ⬩

Church Knowle

SY9381　⚑ *New Inn*

Bradle Farmhouse, *Church Knowle, Corfe Castle, Wareham, Dorset, BH20 5NU.*
Relax and unwind in our picturesque farmhouse in the heart of Purbeck.
Open: All Year (not Xmas)
Grades: ETC 4 Diamond
01929 480712 Mrs Hole
Fax: 01929 481144
hole.bradle@farmersweekly.net
D: £21–£23 **S:** £25–£35
Beds: 2D 1T **Baths:** 3 En
⌂ (5) 🅿 (3) 📺 🛍 Ⅴ ⬩

Planning a longer stay? Always ask for any special rates

Colehill

SU0201　⚑ *Stocks Inn*

Rosewell, *110 Lonnen Road, Colehill, Wimborne, BH21 7AY.*
Friendly family home in quiet area. Wimborne, 2 miles. Children welcome.
Open: All Year (not Xmas)
01202 849806 Mrs Tolman
Fax: 01202 881918
D: £22–£25
Beds: 1F 1D **Baths:** 1 En 1 Pr
⌂ 🅿 (4) ⛥ 📺 🛍 Ⅴ ⬩

Coombe Keynes

SY8484　⚑ *Castle Inn*

Highfield Guest House, *Coombe Keynes, Wool, Wareham, Dorset, BH20 5PS.*
Family home amongst thatched cottages, hamlet five minutes, Lulworth Cove.
Open: All Year (not Xmas)
01929 463208 (also fax)
Mr & Mrs Mitchell
j.mitchell@coombekeynes.freeserve.co.uk
D: £21–£22.50
Beds: 3D **Baths:** 2 En 1 Pr
⌂ 🅿 (4) ⛥ 📺 🛍 Ⅴ ⬩

Corfe Castle

SY9682　⚑ *Castle Inn, New Inn, Scot Arms*

Knitson Old Farm House, *Corfe Castle, Wareham, Dorset, BH20 5JB.*
Open: Easter to Oct
01929 422836 Mrs Helfer
mark@knitson.freeserve.co.uk
D: £19–£22 **S:** £20–£22
Beds: 1F 1D 1S **Baths:** 2 Sh
⌂ 🅿 (4) 📺 ✕ Ⅴ ⬩
C16th farmhouse, 3 miles from Corfe, 1 from Swanage. Ridgeway and footpaths in all directions. Plantsman's garden, long views, whole food in season, wood stove, carpeted comfortable rooms, traditional breakfasts, years of experience, featured in the Best of British.

Bradle Farmhouse, *Church Knowle, Corfe Castle, Wareham, Dorset, BH20 5NU.*
Relax and unwind in our picturesque farmhouse in the heart of Purbeck.
Open: All Year (not Xmas)
Grades: ETC 4 Diamond
01929 480712
Mrs Hole
Fax: 01929 481144
hole.bradle@farmersweekly.net
D: £21–£23 **S:** £25–£35
Beds: 2D 1T **Baths:** 3 En
⌂ (5) 🅿 (3) 📺 🛍 Ⅴ ⬩

Tilia House, *115 East Street, Corfe Castle, Wareham, Dorset, BH20 5EG.*
Bedrooms with fires, handbasins. Home made bread, menu choice.
Open: All Year
01929 480043
Mrs Hayward
lesh@corfe-castle.demon.co.uk
D: £14.30–£20 **S:** £28.60–£40
Beds: 1T 1D **Baths:** 1 Sh
🅿 (2) ⛥ 📺 Ⅴ ⬩

Cranborne

SU0513

La Fosse Restaurant, *London House, The Square, Cranborne, Wimborne, Dorset, BH21 5PR.*
Small, family run restaurant with rooms, super food, comfortable accommodation.
Open: All Year
Grades: ETC 3 Diamond
01725 517604 Mr La Fosse
Fax: 01725 517778
D: £32.50–£35 **S:** £35–£37.50
Beds: 2D 1T **Baths:** 3 En
⌂ (10) ⛥ 📺 ✕ 🛍 Ⅴ ⬩ cc

Dorchester

SY6890　⚑ *Inn For All Seasons, Junction Hotel, Old Ship, Trumpet Major, Bakers Arms*

Churchview Guest House, *Winterbourne Abbas, Dorchester, Dorset, DT2 9LS.*
Open: All Year (not Xmas)
Grades: ETC 3 Diamond
01305 889296 (also fax)
Mr Deller
stay@churchview.co.uk
D: £22–£29 **S:** £22–£32
Beds: 1F 4D 3T 1S **Baths:** 7 En 1 Sh
⌂ (5) 🅿 (10) ⛥ 📺 ⛥ ✕ 🛍 Ⅴ ⬩ cc
Delightful C17th village guest house near Dorchester offers comfort, delicious breakfasts, home-cooked evening meals. 9 character bedrooms, period dining room, two relaxing lounges and bar. Your hosts will give every assistance on local information to ensure a memorable stay.

Slades Farm, *North Street, Charminster, Dorchester, Dorset, DT2 9QZ.*
Open: All Year
Grades: ETC 4 Diamond
01305 265614 (also fax)
Mr & Mrs Woods
D: £21–£25 **S:** £30–£35
Beds: 1F 2D **Baths:** 3 En
⌂ 🅿 (8) ⛥ 📺 ⛥ 🛍 ⬩
Superb accommodation and every comfort in recently converted barn. Village location, 2 miles from Dorchester in heart of Thomas Hardy country. 1.5 acres of garden, paddock with River Cerne at end. Own poultry.

Maumbury Cottage, *9 Maumbury Road, Dorchester, Dorset, DT1 1QW.*
Homely accommodation, Thomas Hardy country, local produce, central for museums, records office, buses & railway.
Open: All Year
01305 266726 D: £17–£18 **S:** £17–£18
Beds: 1D 1T 1S **Baths:** 1 Sh
🅿 (3) ⛥ 📺 🛍 ⬩

Maiden Castle Farm, *Dorchester, Dorset, DT2 9PR.*
Victorian farmhouse on large working farm 1m Dorchester, 7m Weymouth.
Open: All Year
Grades: ETC 4 Diamond, Silver Award
01305 262356 Mrs Hoskin
Fax: 01305 251085
D: £25 **S:** £25
Beds: 1F 2D 1T 2S **Baths:** 3 En 1 Pr
⌂ 🅿 (10) 📺 ⛥ 🛍 Ⅴ ⬩

Tarkaville, *30 Shaston Crescent,*
Dorchester, DT1 2EB.
Superb comfortable modern house.
Quiet, close to town, friendly welcome.
Open: All Year (not Xmas)
Grades: ETC 4 Diamond
01305 266253 Mrs Otter
D: £16–£20 **S:** £16–£35
Beds: 1D 1T 1S **Baths:** 1 Sh
🛇 🅿 (3) ⊬ 📺 🛒 🖫 ♿

East Lulworth

SY8682

Botany Farm House, *East Lulworth,*
Wareham, Dorset, BH20 5QH.
Atmospheric country living, flowers,
birds, animals, tranquil location. Warmest
welcome.
Open: All Year (not Xmas)
01929 400427 Mrs Hemsley
hemsleys@lineone.net
D: £20 **S:** £25
Beds: 2D 1T **Baths:** 2 En 1 Pr
🛇 🅿 (4) 📺 ⛨ ✕ 🛒 🖫 ♿

East Stour

ST7922 🍺 *Crown Inn*

Aysgarth, *Back Street, East Stour,*
Gillingham, Dorset, SP8 5JY.
Ground floor accommodation. Good
touring centre. Discount 3 night stay.
Open: All Year (not Xmas)
Grades: ETC 4 Diamond
01747 838351 Mrs Dowding
aysgarth@lineone.net
D: £17.50–£19 **S:** £20–£22
Beds: 1T 2D **Baths:** 2 En 1Private
🛇 🅿 (3) ⊬ 🛒 ♿

Easton

SY6971 🍺 *New Inn*

Ambleside, *Reforne Close, Easton,*
Portland, Dorset, DT5 2AL.
Friendly comfortable accommodation,
secluded gardens. Close to coastal paths.
Open: All Year (not Xmas)
01305 822149
Mrs Comben
D: £15–£18 **S:** fr £15
Beds: 1F 1T **Baths:** 1 Pr
🛇 🅿 (2) ⊬ 📺 🛒 🖫 ♿

Eype

SY4491

Eypes Mouth Country Hotel, *Eype,*
Bridport, Dorset, DT6 6AL.
Open: All Year
Grades: ETC Two star
01308 423300 Ms Tye
Fax: 01308 420033
D: £29.50–£38
S: £29.50–£38
Beds: 18F 3T 13D 2S **Baths:** 18 En
🅿 📺 ⛨ ✕ 🛒 🖫 ♿ ⚘ ♿ cc
Situated in a secret spot down a leafy
lane, just a five minute walk from the sea.
Restaurant with views over Lyme Bay.
Smugglers Cellar Bar serving bar snacks
both lunch time and evening, with patio
overlooking the sea.

BEDROOMS
F - Family
D - Double
T - Twin
S - Single

Ferndown

SU0700 🍺 *Tap & Railway, Smugglers' Haunt,*
Pure Drop

Pennington Copse, *11 Denewood*
Road, West Moors, Ferndown, Dorset,
BH22 0LX.
Quiet Edwardian house, 5 min walk to
village pubs and restaurants.
Open: All Year (not Xmas)
01202 894667 Mrs Hedley
D: £18–£20 **S:** £25–£30
Beds: 2D **Baths:** 1 Sh
🅿 ⊬ 📺 🛒 ♿

73 Beaufoys Avenue, *Ferndown,*
Dorset, BH22 9RN.
Large house in woodland garden.
Open: All Year (not Xmas)
01202 876729 Mrs Davies
D: £20–£22 **S:** £18–£20
Beds: 1D 1T **Baths:** 1 En 1 Pr 1 Sh
🛇 🅿 (6) 📺 ✕ 🛒 🖫 ♿

Fifehead St Quintin

ST7710 🍺 *The Bull*

Lower Fifehead Farm, *Fifehead St*
Quintin, Sturminster Newton, Dorset,
DT10 2AP.
Beautiful listed farmhouse situated
countryside, warm welcome.
Open: All Year
01258 817335 (also fax) Mrs Miller
D: £17.50–£25 **S:** £20–£25
Beds: 2D 1T **Baths:** 2 En 1 Pr
🛇 🅿 (4) 📺 🛒 🖫 ♿

Fleet

SY6380 🍺 *Turks Head*

Highfield, *Fleet, Weymouth, Dorset,*
DT3 4EB.
Ideal location, beautiful countryside,
excellent accommodation, wonderful
walks, relaxation.
Open: All Year (not Xmas)
Grades: ETC 4 Diamond, Silver
01305 776822 Mrs Weeden
highfield.fleet@lineone.net
D: £22–£25
Beds: 1F 1D 1T **Baths:** 3 En
🛇 🅿 (4) ⊬ 📺 🛒 🖫 ♿

Gillingham

ST8026 🍺 *Dolphin, Red Lion*

Bugley Court Farm, *Gillingham,*
Dorset, SP8 5RA.
Peaceful location with wonderful views in
comfortable family home.
Open: All Year
01747 823242 Mrs Lewis
D: £18
Beds: 1F 1T **Baths:** 1Private
🅿 (2) ⊬ 📺 🛒 ♿

Hamworthy

SY9991 🍺 *The Yachtsman*

53 Branksea Avenue, *Hamworthy,*
Poole, Dorset, BH15 4DP.
Select accommodation for those seeking
something special. Large bedroom/
lounge. Magnificent harbour views.
Open: All Year
01202 673419 Mrs Wadham
Fax: 01202 667260
johnrenate@lineone.net
D: £23–£27.50 **S:** £28–£37
Beds: 1D 1T
Baths: 2 En
🛇 🅿 (3) ⊬ 📺 🛒 🖫 ♿

Hazelbury Bryan

ST7408 🍺 *The European Inn*

The Old Malthouse, *Droop, Hazelbury*
Bryan, Sturminster Newton, Dorset, DT10
2ED.
Open: All Year
01258 817735 Mr Bleathman
D: £18–£20 **S:** £20–£25
Beds: 1F 2D **Baths:** 1 En
Relaxed romantic short breaks, C17th
Malthouse renowned for its peaceful rural
location and traditional hospitality.
Spacious comfortable rooms, ensuite
master bedroom with four poster. Guest
lounge with inglenook fireplace. Stunning
views over the Blackmore Vale. Pets
welcome.

Highcliffe

SZ2094 🍺 *The Globe, Hinton Oak*

The White House, *428 Lymington*
Road, Highcliffe, Christchurch, Dorset,
BH23 5HF.
Beautiful Victorian house. 5 min walk
beach, shops, restaurants. Short drive
New Forest.
Open: All Year (not Xmas/New Year)
Grades: ETC 4 Diamond, AA 4 Diamond
01425 271279
F G White
Fax: 01425 276900
thewhitehouse@themail.co.uk
D: £22–£25 **S:** £25–£35
Beds: 6F 2T 3D 1S **Baths:** 5 En 5 Pr 1 Sh
🛇 🅿 ⊬ 📺 🛒 ♿ cc

Higher Came

SY6987 🍺 *Black Dog Broadmayne*

Higher Came Farmhouse, *Higher*
Came, Dorchester, Dorset, DT2 8NR.
Open: All Year
01305 268908 (also fax)
Mrs Bowden
highercame@eurolink.ltd.net
D: £21–£27 **S:** £23–£32
Beds: 1F 2D
Baths: 1 En 2 Pr
🛇 🅿 (4) 📺 ⛨ 🛒 🖫 ♿ ⚘ ♿ cc
Beautiful 17th Century Farmhouse
nesting at the foot of the Ridgeway in the
heart of Hardy country. Spacious rooms,
lovely gardens, great breakfast, relaxing
atmosphere. Close to Maiden castle,
Dorchester and the spectacular Dorset
coastline; discover and explore.

Holdenhurst Village

SZ1395　🏮 *Strouden Park*

Magdalen Cottage, *17 Holdenhurst Village, Holdenhurst, Bournemouth, Dorset, BH8 0EE.*
Open: All Year (not Xmas)
01202 395582 Mrs Bowring
D: £18–£22 **S:** £24–£28
Beds: 2T **Baths:** 1 Shared
🅿 (2) 📺 🏠 🛗 ♿
Charming C17th Grade II Listed thatched cottage with wealth of character, beams, inglenook. Overlooking quiet village green within easy reach of Bournemouth. 4 miles Christchurch, New Forest and beautiful Dorset coastline. Excellent fishing. River Stour 3 minutes walk and Avon Royalty 3 miles.

Hooke

ST5300　🏮 *Winyards Gap Inn, Talbot Inn*

Watermeadow House, *Bridge Farm, Hooke, Beaminster, Dorset, DT8 3PD.*
Open: Easter to Oct
Grades: ETC 4 Diamond, Silver Award, AA 4 Diamond
01308 862619 (also fax)
Mrs Wallbridge
enquiries@watermeadowhouse.co.uk
D: £22–£24 **S:** £24–£28
Beds: 1F 1D **Baths:** 1 En 1 Pr
🛏 🅿 (4) ⌘ 📺 ✕ 🛗 Ⅴ ♿
Watermeadow house, part of a working dairy farm, is a large Georgian style house on the edge of small village of Hooke. Breakfast is served in a sun lounge and the River Hooke meanders close by the garden. A warm welcome awaits you.

Horton

SU0307　🏮 *Horton Inn*

Treetops, *Wigbeth, Horton, Wimborne, Dorset, BH21 7JH.*
Rural, chalet bungalow, lovely views. Light airy rooms, large garden.
Open: All Year
01258 840147 Mr Purchase
treetops.bandb@virgin.net
D: £18 **S:** £20
Beds: 1T 1D **Baths:** 2 En
🛏 🅿 (3) ⌘ 📺 🏠 🛗 ♿

Ibberton

ST7807　🏮 *Crown Inn*

Manor House Farm, *Ibberton, Blandford Forum, Dorset, DT11 0EN.*
C16th comfortable farmhouse; also working dairy and sheep farm.
Open: All Year
01258 817349 Mrs Old
D: £14–£18 **S:** £16–£18
Beds: 2D 1T **Baths:** 2 En 1 Sh
🛏 🅿 (3) ⌘ 📺 🏠 🛗 ♿

B&B owners may vary rates - be sure to check when booking

Iwerne Courtney or Shroton

ST8512　🏮 *Cricketers*

Lattemere, *Frog Lane, Iwerne Courtney or Shroton, Blandford Forum, Dorset, DT11 8QL.*
Comfortable welcoming home in quiet picturesque village. outstanding countryside walks. **Open:** All Year
01258 860115 Mrs Wright
D: £20–£22 **S:** £20–£25
Beds: 1D 1T **Baths:** 1 En 1 Pr
🛏 🅿 (3) ⌘ 📺 🛗 Ⅴ ♿

Foxhangers, *4 Old Mill Cottages, Iwerne Courtney or Shroton, Blandford Forum, Dorset, DT11 8TW.*
Modern cottage in quiet and peaceful village. Excellent breakfast.
Open: All Year (not Xmas)
01258 861049 Mrs Moss
Fax: 01258 860785
jane_moss@talk21.com
D: £20 **S:** £25
Beds: 1D **Baths:** 1 En
🅿 (1) ⌘ 📺 ✕ 🛗 ♿

Iwerne Minster

ST8614　🏮 *Talbot Hotel*

The Talbot Hotel, *Blandford Road, Iwerne Minster, Blandford Forum, Dorset, DT11 8QN.*
Country Inn offering comfortable rooms, good food, ale, affordable prices.
Open: All Year
01747 811269 Mr & Mrs Richardson
D: £13.75–£19.25 **S:** £15–£35
Beds: 2F 2D 1T 1S **Baths:** 2 En 2 Sh
🛏 🅿 (30) 📺 ✕ 🛗 Ⅴ ♿

Kimmeridge

SY9179　🏮 *Seven Taps, New Inn*

Kimmeridge Farmhouse,
Kimmeridge, Wareham, Dorset, BH20 5PE.
Picturesque farmhouse with views of Kimmeridge Bay - spacious and attractively furnished ensuite bedrooms.
Open: All Year (not Xmas)
Grades: ETC 4 Diamond
01929 480990 Mrs Hole
D: £22–£23 **S:** £25–£35
Beds: 2D 1T **Baths:** 3 En
🛏 (10) 🅿 (3) ⌘ 📺 ✕ 🛗 Ⅴ ♿

Kingston (Swanage)

SY9579　🏮 *Fox*

Kingston Country Courtyard,
Greystone Court, Kingston (Corfe Castle), Wareham, Dorset, BH20 5LR.
Open: All Year (not Xmas/New Year)
Grades: ETC 4 Diamond
01929 481066 Mrs Fry **Fax:** 01929 481256
annfry@kingstoncountrycourtyard.co.uk
D: £24–£35 **S:** £26–£35
Beds: 1T 4D 2S **Baths:** 7 En
🅿 (20) ⌘ 📺 Ⅴ ♿ 🐾
Character guest rooms in a courtyard setting. Magnificent views of Corfe Castle from our gardens where peacocks roam. Close to coastal path for walkers or ideal base for touring Dorset. Beaches or shops & theatres within easy reach by car.

Kington Magna

ST7623　🏮 *Stapleton Arms*

Kington Manor Farm, *Church Hill, Kington Magna, Gillingham, Dorset, SP8 5EG.*
Attractive farmhouse. Peaceful, pretty village overlooking Blackmore Vale. Heated pool. **Open:** All Year (not Xmas)
Grades: ETC 4 Diamond
01747 838371 (also fax) Mrs Gosney
D: fr £22 **S:** fr £24
Beds: 1F 1D 1T **Baths:** All Pr
🛏 🅿 ⌘ 📺 🏠 🛗 Ⅴ ♿

Langton Herring

SY6182　🏮 *Elm Tree Inn*

East Cottage Bed & Breakfast,
Langton Herring, Weymouth, Dorset, DT3 4HZ.
Comfortable, idyllic coastal location, spacious farm cottage, famous Chesil Beach. **Open:** All Year
01305 871627 A W Freeman
bedandbreakfast@eastcottage1.freeserve.co.uk
D: £22–£24 **S:** £22–£24
Beds: 1F 2D 1T **Baths:** 2 En 1 Pr 1 Sh
🛏 🅿 (4) ⌘ 📺 🏠 🛗 Ⅴ ❀ ♿ ♿

Langton Matravers

SY9978　🏮 *Kings Arms, Ship Inn*

Maycroft, *Old Malthouse Lane, Langton Matravers, Swanage, Dorset, BH19 3JA.*
Comfortable Victorian home, close to Coastal Path. Recommended by Which?.
Open: Mar to Oct
01929 424305 (also fax) Mrs Bjorkstrand
janet.bjorkstrand@btinternet.com
D: £17–£19 **S:** £22–£25
Beds: 1D 1T **Baths:** 1 Sh
🛏 (3) 🅿 (4) 📺 🛗 Ⅴ ♿

Lulworth Cove

SY8279　🏮 *Castle Inn, Lulworth Cove Hotel*

Mill House Hotel, *Lulworth Cove, West Lulworth, Wareham, Dorset, BH20 5RQ.*
Open: Feb to Dec
01929 400404 Mr Payne
Fax: 01929 400508
dukepayne@hotmail.com
D: £25–£40 **S:** £35–£40
Beds: 2F 6D 1T **Baths:** 9 En
🛏 🅿 (9) 📺 ✕ 🛗 Ⅴ ♿ cc
Julian & Jenny Payne welcome you to their nine bedroom, country house-style hotel in the heart of Lulworth Cove, opposite the duck pond and 150 yards from the water's edge. Fantastic walks, beaches, golf, horse-riding, sightseeing all locally. Licensed bar & tea rooms.

Shirley Hotel, *West Lulworth, Wareham, Dorset, BH20 5RL.*
Magnificent coastal path & inland walks from hotel. Family-run serving delicious food. **Open:** Feb to Nov
01929 400358 Tony Williams
Fax: 01929 400167
durdle@aol.com
D: £33.50–£44 **S:** £33.50–£59
Beds: 2F 8D 4T 1S **Baths:** 15 En
🛏 🅿 (22) 📺 🏠 ✕ 🛗 Ⅴ ♿ cc

Lyme Regis

SY3392 🍴 *Dorset Hotel, Pilot Boat, Victoria, Volunteer*

Hillsett, *Haye Lane, Lyme Regis, Dorset, DT7 3NG.*
Open: All Year (not Xmas/New Year)
01297 445 259 (also fax)
Mr Thompson
pat.thompson@bigfoot.com
D: £20–£25 **S:** £20–£25
Beds: 1F 1D **Baths:** 1 En 1 Sh
📺 (8) 🅿 (7) 🗹 🖤 ₤
Lovely modern family home set in beautiful surroundings overlooking Lym valley, Golden Cap & Lyme Bay. 15 minutes walk to centre of famous Lyme Regis, Cobb Harbour & beach. Private car park, heated open air pool, sauna and pool table.

Lydwell House, *Lyme Road , Uplyme, Lyme Regis, Dorset, DT7 3TJ.*
Open: All Year
Grades: ETC 3 Diamond
01297 443522 Mr Brittain
D: £23–£27 **S:** £23–£27
Beds: 2F 1D 1T 1S **Baths:** 5 En
📺 🅿 (7) 🗶 🖤 🗶 🖤 ₤ cc
A pre-Victorian house set within 0.75 acre of Victorian gardens including ponds, folly and rare plants. The rooms are spacious, comfortable and well equipped with televisions, telephones, tea making and all ensuite. The food is home cooked.

Tudor House Hotel, *3/5 Church Street, Lyme Regis, Dorset, DT7 3BS.*
Open: All Year (not Xmas/New Year)
Grades: ETC 3 Diamond
01297 442472 Mr Ray
D: £24–£49 **S:** £28–£38
Beds: 9F 5D 1T 1S **Baths:** 14 En 2 Pr
📺 🅿 (15) 🗹 🖤 🍴 🗶 🖤 🖤
A historic Elizabethan house, circa 1580, one minutes level walk to the sea in the centre of Old Lyme Regis. Part plaster ceiling designed by Sir Walter Raleigh. Cellar bar with original well. Parking. www.thetudorhouse.co.uk.

Charnwood Guest House, *21 Woodmead Road, Lyme Regis, Dorset, DT7 3AD.*
Open: All Year **Grades:** ETC 3 Diamond
01297 445281 Mr Bradbury
charnwood@lymeregis62.freeserve.co.uk
D: £19–£24 **S:** £19–£24
Beds: 1F 4D 2T 1S **Baths:** 6 En 1 Sh
📺 (5) 🅿 (7) 🗹 🖤 🖤 🖤 ₤ cc
1910 style house with balcony. Scenic river walk to town (5 mins) past pubs, restaurants etc. Quiet, safe, easy access to walking, fossiling and beach. Discounts for 3 plus nights midweek Sun-Thurs. Clean, friendly, personally run with hearty breakfast.

Mayflower Cottage, *39 Sherborne Lane, Lyme Regis, Dorset, DT7 3NY.*
Quiet, traffic-free. Secluded garden. Town centre, Free parking nearby.
Open: All Year (not Xmas)
01297 445930 Mr Snowsill
D: £20–£25 **S:** fr £25
Beds: 1F 1D 1T **Baths:** 3 En
📺 🅿 (3) 🗹 🖤 🖤 ₤

The Old Monmouth Hotel, *12 Church Street, Lyme Regis, Dorset, DT7 3BS.*
C17th building, centrally situated for beaches, harbour and all amenities.
Open: All Year (not Xmas)
01297 442456 Mr & Mrs Brown
Fax: 01297 443577
oldmonhotel@btinternet.com
D: £19–£22 **S:** £26–£30
Beds: 1F 4D 1T **Baths:** 5 En 1 Sh
📺 🗹 🗶 🖤 🖤 🖤 ₤ cc

The Red House, *Sidmouth Road, Lyme Regis, Dorset, DT7 3ES.*
Elegant house with wonderful views Eastwards beyond Golden Cap.
Open: Easter to Nov
Grades: ETC 4 Diamond
01297 442055 (also fax) Mr & Mrs Norman
red.house@virgin.net
D: £22–£27 **S:** £33–£40
Beds: 1D 2T **Baths:** 3 En
📺 (8) 🅿 (3) 🗹 🖤 🖤 ₤ cc

Marnhull

ST7718 🍴 *Crown Inn, The Bull, The Blackmore Vale*

Moorcourt Farm, *Moorside, Marnhull, Sturminster Newton, Dorset, DT10 1HH.*
Friendly, welcoming, happy farmhouse. Central touring. Ginormous breakfast menu. **Open:** Easter to Oct
01258 820271 (also fax) Mrs Martin
D: £16–£17 **S:** £16–£17
Beds: 2D 1T **Baths:** 2 Sh
📺 (10) 🅿 (6) 🗹 🖤 ₤

Martinstown

SY6488 🍴 *Brewer's Arms*

The Old Post Office, *Martinstown, Dorchester, Dorset, DT2 9LF.*
Good rural base in small village.
Open: All Year
01305 889254 (also fax) Mrs Rootham
D: £17.50–£25 **S:** £–£25
Beds: 1D 2T **Baths:** 1 Sh
📺 🅿 (3) 🖤 🍴 🗶 🖤 🖤 ₤

Old Brewery House, *Martinstown, Dorchester, DT2 9JR.*
Charming old house in village. Excellent for exploring Hardy's Wessex.
Open: Easter to Sep
01305 889198 Mrs Cooke **Fax: 01305 889802**
D: £14–£19.50 **S:** £14–£19.50
Beds: 1D 1T **Baths:** 1 Sh
📺 🅿 (2) 🗹 🖤 🖤 🖤 ₤

Middlemarsh

ST6706 🍴 *White Horse, Royal Oak*

White Horse Farm, *Middlemarsh, Sherborne, Dorset, DT9 5QN.*
Open: All Year (not Xmas/New Year)
01963 210222 Mr & Mrs Wilding
enquiries@whitehorsefarm.co.uk
D: £20–£25 **S:** £24–£28
Beds: 1S 1D 1T **Baths:** 3 En
📺 🅿 (10) 🖤 🖤 🖤 ₤
Set in beautiful Thomas Hardy country, within easy reach of the south coast. Friendly, comfortable, family run B&B with private conservatory/lounge and dining room in quiet location. Ideal for touring. Patio, gardens, paddock and duck pond. Every comfort. Inn 100 yards.

Moreton

SY8089

Frampton Arms, *Moreton, Dorchester, Dorset, DT2 8BB.*
Traditional country pub with two bars, two restaurants and function room.
Open: All Year (not Xmas)
01305 852253 Mr Paulson
Fax: 01305 854586
D: £20–£25 **S:** £30–£35
Beds: 1F 2D **Baths:** 2 En, 1 Sh
📺 🅿 (40) 🗹 🖤 🖤 ₤ cc

Netherbury

SY4699 🍴 *Hare and Hounds*

Southview, *Whitecross, Netherbury, Bridport, Dorset, DT6 5NH.*
Detached country cottage, lovely views and gardens in picturesque village.
Open: All Year
Grades: ETC 3 Diamond
01308 488471 Mr Kennedy
D: £22.50–£25 **S:** £22.50–£25
Beds: 1T 2D **Baths:** 1 En 1 Sh
📺 (5) 🅿 (4) 🗹 🖤 🍴 🗶 🖤 ₤

North Wootton

ST6514 🍴 *Three Elms*

Stoneleigh Barn, *North Wootton, Sherbourne, Dorset, DT9 5JW.*
Beautiful stone barn close to Sherborne. A special place.
Open: All Year (not Xmas/New Year)
Grades: ETC 4 Diamond, Silver Award
01935 815964 Mrs Chant
stoneleigh@ic24.net
D: £23–£25 **S:** £30–£37.50
Beds: 1F 1D **Baths:** 1 En 1 Pr
📺 (6) 🅿 (4) 🗹 🖤 🖤 ₤

Okeford Fitzpaine

ST8010 🍴 *Royal Oak*

Etheridge Farm, *Darknoll Lane, Okeford Fitzpaine, Blandford Forum, Dorset, DT11 0RP.*
In the heart of the Blackmore Vale, close to Lulworth.
Open: Feb to Dec
01258 860037 Ms Thorne
D: fr £17
Beds: 1F 1T 1D **Baths:** 2 Sh
📺 🅿 🖤 ₤

Osmington

SY7283 🍴 *Sunray Hotel*

Rosedale, *Church Lane, Osmington, Weymouth, Dorset, DT3 6EW.*
Very attractive cottage. Large, comfortable rooms, warm friendly atmosphere. **Open:** Mar to Oct
Grades: ETC 2 Diamond
01305 832056 Mrs Legg
D: £16–£17 **S:** £18–£19
Beds: 1D 1T **Baths:** 1 En 1 Pr
📺 (5) 🅿 (3) 🖤 🖤 ₤

Planning a longer stay? Always ask for any special rates

Rosthwaite, *Church Lane, Osmington,*
Weymouth, Dorset, DT3 6EW.
Bungalow set in picturesque village,
comfortable beds and excellent
breakfasts. **Open:** All Year
01305 833621 Ms Leigh
D: £15–£17 **S:** £15–£20
Beds: 1D 1T **Baths:** 1 Sh
🛇 🅿 (2) ⅍ 🆅 🛍 🆅 ⚓

Upton Farm, *Ringstead, Dorchester,*
Dorset, DT2 8NE.
Historic barn conversion short stroll to
secluded beach, 3 acres garden
Open: Easter to Oct **Grades:** ETC 5 Star
01305 853970 (also fax) Mr & Mrs Davies
D: £29 **S:** £30–£35
Beds: 2D
🛇 (6) 🅿 (6) ⅍ 🆅 🛍 ✿ ⚓ ᕕ

Piddletrenthide

SY7099 🍺 *Piddle Inn, Poachers' Inn*

Poachers Inn, *Piddletrenthide,*
Dorchester, Dorset, DT2 7QX.
Country inn, set in the heart of the lovely
Piddle Valley. All rooms en suite.
Open: All Year
01300 348358 D Fox **Fax: 01300 348153**
D: £27.50 **S:** £35
Beds: 1F 15D 2T **Baths:** 18 En
🛇 🅿 (40) 🆅 ᕁ ✕ 🛍 🆅 ⚓ cc

Pimperne

ST9008 🍺 *Farquharson Arms*

The Old Bakery, *Church Road,*
Pimperne, Blandford Forum, Dorset,
DT11 8UB.
A warm welcome awaits, in this former
shop and bakery. **Open:** All Year
01258 455173 P J Tanner
D: £12.50–£15 **S:** £15–£20
Beds: 1T 1D 1S **Baths:** 2 Sh
🛇 (3) 🅿 (2) ⅍ ᕁ ✕ 🛍

Poole

SZ0191 🍺 *Lamb's Green Inn, Stepping Stones,*
Corkers, Yachtsman, Crown Hotel, Shah Of Persia,
Red Lion, Grasshopper, Conjurer's Half Crown, St
Peters Finger

Sarnia Cherie, *375 Blandford Road ,*
Hamworthy, Poole, Dorset, BH15 4JL.
Open: All Year (not Xmas)
Grades: ETC 4 Diamond, AA 4 Diamond
01202 679470 (also fax) C Collier
D: £20–£22.50 **S:** £25–£30
Beds: 2D 1T **Baths:** 3 En
🛇 🅿 (3) 🆅 ᕁ 🛍 🆅 ⚓
A charming house. A warm welcome
offering excellent bed & breakfast only 5
mins to town centre, beach and Poole
Quay (ferry terminal to Channel Islands). Ideal
central location for exploring Dorset's
wonderful coastline.

Highways Bed & Breakfast, *29*
Fernside Road, Poole, Dorset, BH15 2QU.
1920's house, very comfortable. Fire
hygiene certificate, all ensuite & parking.
Open: All Year **Grades:** ETC 3 Diamond
01202 677060 Mr & Mrs Bailey
D: £20–£22.50 **S:** £20–£25
Beds: 4D 1T **Baths:** 5 En
🛇 🅿 (6) 🆅 ✕ 🛍 🆅 ⚓

Ashdell, *85 Dunyeats Road, Broadstone,*
Poole, Dorset, BH18 8AF.
Central, comfortable, secluded.
Breakfast/EM choice. Historic
countryside/beaches, short breaks.
Open: All Year (not Xmas)
Grades: ETC 2 Diamond
01202 692032 Mrs Critchley
ian@ashdell.fsnet.co.uk
D: £16–£19 **S:** £19–£21
Beds: 1F 1D 1T 1S **Baths:** 1 Sh
🛇 (5) 🅿 (3) ᕁ ✕ 🛍 🆅 ⚓

Southern Comfort Guest House,
192 Bournemouth Road, Poole, Dorset,
BH14 9HZ.
Open: All Year
01202 722250 (also fax)
Mrs Richmond
pam@scomfort.fsnet.co.uk
D: £20–£25 **S:** £35–£45
Beds: 1F 3D 1T **Baths:** 4 Pr 1 Sh
🛇 🅿 (6) ⅍ ✕ 🛍 🆅 ⚓ cc
Midway between Poole and Bournemouth
main A35. Clean family run, most rooms
ensuite. Car parking guests sitting patio.
non-smoking throughout. TV, tea & Coffee
in all rooms. Beach hut hire available.
Beaches about 2 miles away.

Melbury Guest House, *101 Parkstone*
Road, Poole, Dorset, BH15 2NZ.
Comfortable Edwardian home opposite
Poole Park, near beaches, ferries, town.
Open: All Year
01202 749015 Mrs Lloyd
D: £16–£20 **S:** £16–£20
Beds: 1F 1D 1T 1S **Baths:** 2 Sh
🛇 (5) 🅿 (4) ⅍ 🆅 🛍 ⚓

31 Chaddesley Glen, Canford
Cliffs, *Poole, Dorset, BH13 7PB.*
Vegetarian B&B, beautiful harbour views,
quiet, peaceful, 1 minute walk to sandy
beach.
Open: All Year (not Xmas)
01202 700037 Mr Mills
D: £20–£22 **S:** £20–£30
Beds: 1F 11D **Baths:** 1 En 1 Sh
🛇 🅿 (2) ⅍ ᕁ ✕ 🛍 🆅 ⚓

Tideway, *Beach Road, Upton, Poole,*
Dorset, BH16 5NA.
Please look at our website for further
detail & pictures -
www.maidinessex.com/tideway.
Open: All Year (not Xmas)
01202 621293 (also fax)
Mr & Mrs Yates
tidewaybb@aol.com
D: £20–£25 **S:** £23–£25
Beds: 1D 1T **Baths:** 1 Sh
🛇 🅿 (3) ⅍ ✕ 🛍 ⚓

Seacourt Guest House, *249*
Blandford Road, Hamworthy, Poole,
Dorset, BH15 4AZ.
Comfortable surroundings. Friendly
atmosphere. Warm welcome.
Open: All Year
Grades: AA 3 Diamond
01202 674995 (also fax)
Ms Hewitt
D: £20 **S:** £30–£40
Beds: 1F 2D 2T **Baths:** 5 En
🛇 🅿 (3) 🆅 ᕁ 🛍 ⚓ ᕕ

South Rising Guest House, *86*
Parkstone Road, Poole, Dorset, BH15 2QE.
Well appointed, homely atmosphere,
close to town centre and beaches.
Open: All Year (not Xmas/New Year)
Grades: ETC 3 Diamond
01202 240766 Mr Keller
D: £20–£25 **S:** £20–£25
Beds: 3F 3D **Baths:** 4 En 2 Sh
🛇 (5) 🅿 (6) ⅍ 🆅 🛍 ⚓

Fleetwater Guest House, *161*
Longfleet Road, Poole, Dorset, BH15 2HS.
Family-run guest house, close to Poole
Park and Lakes, town centre.
Open: All Year (not Xmas/New Year)
Grades: ETC 3 Diamond
01202 682509 Mr Hewitt
D: £22.50–£23 **S:** £25–£30
Beds: 1F 2D 1T **Baths:** 4 En
🛇 🅿 (4) 🆅 ᕁ ✕ 🛍 ⚓

Vernon, *96 Blandford Road, Beacon Hill,*
Poole, Dorset, BH16 6AD.
Modern bungalow, lovely front garden.
Ideally situated for touring Dorset.
Open: All Year
Grades: ETC 2 Diamond
01202 625185 Mr Rendell
D: £15–£16 **S:** £20–£22
Beds: 2D 1T **Baths:** 3 En
🛇 🅿 (4) 🆅 ᕁ ✕ 🛍 🆅 ⚓ ᕕ

Portesham

SY6085 🍺 *Kings Arms*

Lavender Cottage, *9 Malthouse*
Meadow, Portesham, Weymouth, Dorset,
DT3 4NS.
Lovely scenery, quiet location,
birdwatchers' and walkers' paradise,
hearty breakfast.
Open: All Year (not Xmas)
01305 871924 Mrs Haine
D: £17.50 **S:** £17.50
Beds: 1D 1T **Baths:** 1 Sh
⅍ 🆅 🛍 ⚓

The Old Fountain, *36 Front Street,*
Portesham, Weymouth, Dorset, DT3 4ET.
Former public house opposite village
duck pond, owner WCTB guide.
Open: All Year (not Xmas)
01305 871278 (also fax)
Ms Martin
D: £18–£20 **S:** £20–£25
Beds: 1D 1T **Baths:** 1 Sh
🛇 🆅 🛍 🆅 ⚓

Portland

SY6874 🍺 *Clifton Hotel*

The Old Vicarage, *Grove Road,*
Portland, Dorset, DT5 1DB.
Portland stone Victorian vicarage.
Comfortable rooms, good food, friendly
atmosphere.
Open: All Year (not Xmas/New Year)
01305 824117
Carolyn Robb
mccormicksmith@oldvicarage.fsnet.co.uk
D: £20–£25 **S:** £22–£28
Beds: 1F 1T 1D **Baths:** 3 En
🅿 (3) 🆅 ᕁ 🛍 🆅 ⚓

BATHROOMS
Pr - Private
Sh - Shared
En - Ensuite

Poyntington

ST6420 ⬧ *Crown Inn*

Welgoer, *Poyntington, Sherborne, Dorset, DT9 4LF.*
Comfortable accommodation in quiet village near Sherborne. Ideal touring base. **Open:** All Year
Grades: ETC 3 Diamond
01963 220737 Mrs Neville
D: £20–£25 **S:** £20–£25
Beds: 1T 1D **Baths:** 1 En 1 Pr
⛲ (5) 🅿 (2) 🖵 🖩 🔟 🕹

Puddletown

SY7594 ⬧ *Prince Of Wales*

Zoar House, *Puddletown, Dorchester, Dorset, DT2 8SR.*
Victorian house. Garden, orchard, paddocks, Hardy's Cottage, Athelhampton, Forest nearby.
Open: All Year
01305 848498 Mrs Stephens
D: £15–£19 **S:** £16–£20
Beds: 1F 1D 1T **Baths:** 1 En 1 Sh
⛲ 🅿 (6) 🖵 🖩 🕯 🔟 🕹

Sandford

SY9289 ⬧ *Bakers Arms, The Sandford*

Foresters, *14 Keysworth Drive, Sandford, Wareham, Dorset, BH20 7BD.*
Modern spacious bungalow. Peaceful location. Wildlife garden, private off-road parking. Large breakfasts.
Open: All Year (not Xmas/New Year)
01929 556090 Mr Harris
foresters@keysworth14.freeserve.co.uk
D: £16.50–£20 **S:** £16.50–£22.50
Beds: 1T 1D 1S
🅿 (5) 🖵 🖩 🔟 🕹

Glen Ness, *1 The Merrows, Sandford, Wareham, Dorset, BH20 7AX.*
Spacious cedar/stone bungalow. Ideal touring base. Warm friendly welcome.
Open: All Year
01929 552313 Mrs Gegg
D: £16.50 **S:** £16.50
Beds: 3D 3S **Baths:** 1 Sh
⛲ 🅿 (4) 🖵 🖩 🕯 🗙 🖩 🔟 🕹

Sandford Orcas

ST6220 ⬧ *Mitre Inn*

The Alders, *Sandford Orcas, Sherborne, Dorset, DT9 4SB.*
Situated in unspoilt picturesque conservation village; sitting room with log fire in inglenook fireplace.
Open: All Year
01963 220666 Fax: 01963 220106
jonsue@btinternet.com
D: £22.50–£25 **S:** £35–£38
Beds: 1D 1T **Baths:** 2 Pr
⛲ 🅿 (4) 🖵 🖩 🕹

Shaftesbury

ST8622 ⬧ *Talbot, Two Brewers, Kings Arms, Mitre, Grove Arms, Rising Sun*

Charnwood Cottage, *Charlton, Shaftesbury, Dorset, SP7 9LZ.*
C17th thatched cottage with lovely garden. Good base for touring.
Open: All Year (not Xmas/New Year)
01747 828310 (also fax) Mr & Mrs Morgan
D: £18–£19 **S:** fr £20
Beds: 1T 1D **Baths:** 1 Sh
⛲ (5) 🅿 (2) 🖵 🕯 🖩

Ye Olde Wheelwrights, *Birdbush, Ludwell, Shaftesbury, Dorset, SP7 9NH.*
Accommodation in separate annexe. Children and families welcome. Hearty breakfast. **Open:** April to October
01747 828955 C Dieppe
charles@cdieppe.freeserve.co.uk
D: £17.50–£20 **S:** £20–£22
Beds: 1T 1D **Baths:** 1 Sh
⛲ 🅿 🖵 🖩 🕹

5 Ivy Cross, *Shaftesbury, Dorset, SP7 8DW.*
Victorian house within easy walk to town centre. **Open:** Easter to Oct
01747 853734 Mrs Keating
D: fr £18 **S:** fr £18
Beds: 1F 1D 1T 1S **Baths:** 1 Sh
⛲ 🅿 (4) 🖵 🖩 🕯 🖩 🔟

Maple Lodge, *Christys Lane, Shaftesbury, Dorset, SP7 8DL.*
Within 5 mins walk of shops, restaurants and famous Gold Hill.
Open: All Year (not Xmas/New Year)
01747 853945 Mr & Mrs Jameson
maplelodge@tesco.net
D: £18–£22 **S:** £20–£25
Beds: 1F 1T 1D **Baths:** 2 En 1 Pr
⛲ 🅿 (8) 🖵 🖩 🔟 🕹

Sherborne

ST6316 ⬧ *Queen's Arms, Mitre Inn, Crown Hotel, Half Moon, Britannia Inn, Kings Arms, Old Inn*

Britannia Inn, *Sherborne, Dorset, DT9 3EH.*
Listed building, town centre, 300 years old. **Open:** All Year
Grades: ETC 2 Diamond
01935 813300 Mr Blackmore
D: £20–£35 **S:** £20–£35
Beds: 2F 1D 2T 2S **Baths:** 1 En 3 Sh
⛲ 🅿 (6) 🖵 🖩 🕯 🗙 🖩 🔟 🕹 cc

Ashclose Farm, *Charlton Horethorne, Sherborne, Dorset, DT9 4PG.*
Open: All Year (not Xmas)
Grades: ETC 3 Diamond
01963 220360 Mr & Mrs Gooding
gooding@ashclosefarm.freeserve.co.uk
D: £18–£22 **S:** £18–£22
Beds: 1D 1T 1S **Baths:** 1 En 1 Sh
⛲ 🅿 (5) 🖵 🕯 🖩 🔟 🕹
Comfortable farmhouse, peaceful countryside, friendly welcome and relaxed atmosphere. Large lounge with colour TV, children welcome, large attractive garden and conservatory with super panoramic views, comfortably furnished bedrooms. Good central position for exploring this area.

Bridleways, *Oborne Road, Sherborne, Dorset, DT9 3RX.*
Open: All Year (not Xmas)
Grades: ETC 3 Diamond
01935 814716 (also fax)
Mr & Mrs Dimond
D: £18–£22 **S:** £20–£22
Beds: 1D 2T **Baths:** 1 En 1 Pr
⛲ 🅿 (5) 🖵 🕯 🖩 🔟 🕹
Comfortable house overlooking castle, 10 mins walk to historic town centre, station, with plenty of eating places, off road parking for 5 cars. Holiday cottages and horse riding available on premises. Situated 1/4 mile off A30.

Clatcombe Grange, *Bristol Road, Sherborne, Dorset, DT9 4RH.*
Charming Listed converted barn. elevated views, spacious house/garden, ample parking, peaceful and friendly.
Open: All Year
Grades: ETC Listed Highly Commended, AA 4 Diamond
01935 814355 D: £25 **S:** £30–£36
Beds: 1T 1D 1S **Baths:** 2 En 1 Pr
⛲ 🅿 🕯 🖵 🗙 🖩 🔟 🕹

Shillingstone

ST8211

The Willows Tea Rooms, *5 Blandford Road, Shillingstone, Blandford Forum, Dorset, DT11 0SG.*
C18th cottage & tearooms in beautiful countryside. Blandford 5 miles.
Open: Feb to Xmas
01258 861167 Mr & Mrs Auckland
Willows@kauckland.demon.co.uk
D: fr £17.50 **S:** fr £20
Beds: 1D **Baths:** 1 En
⛲ 🅿 (6) 🕯 🗙 🖩 🔟 🕹 ♿

Shipton Gorge

SY4991 ⬧ *New Inn*

Cairnhill, *Shipton Gorge, Bridport, DT6 4LL.*
Beautiful countryside, warm welcome. Comfortable, spacious rooms, heated indoor pool.
Open: Easter to Oct
Grades: ETC 5 Diamond, Gold Award
01308 898203 (also fax)
R W Waite
cairnhill@talk21.com
D: £25 **S:** £25–£30
Beds: 1D 1T 1S **Baths:** 2 En 1 Pr
⛲ (7) 🅿 🕯 🖵 🖩 🔟 🕹

Sixpenny Handley

ST9918 ⬧ *The Bull*

Town Farm Bungalow, *Sixpenny Handley, Salisbury, Wilts., SP5 5NT.*
Excellent friendly accomodation. Magnificent views and peaceful surrounding. Superb breakfasts.
Open: All Year
Grades: AA 3 Diamond
01725 552319 (also fax)
Mrs Inglis
D: £17.50–£20 **S:** £22.50–£35
Beds: 1T 2D **Baths:** 1 En 1 Sh
⛲ 🅿 (6) 🖵 🕯 🗙 🖩 🔟 🕹

Stockwood

ST5806   ◫ Chetnole Inn

Church Farm, Stockwood, Dorchester, Dorset, DT2 0NG.
Spoil yourself and stay on a traditional working dairy farm.
Open: All Year
01935 83221 Mrs House
Fax: 01935 83771
ruth@churchfarm.co.uk
D: £20–£25 **S:** £20–£35
Beds: 2D 1T **Baths:** 3 En
⌂ ▣ (3) ⊁ 📺 ▥ Ⅴ ♨

Sturminster Marshall

SY9499   ◫ Red Lion, Black Horse

Kilvey, 26b Churchill Close, Sturminster Marshall, Wimborne, Dorset, BH21 4BQ.
Modern bungalow in pretty village situated between Blandford and Wimborne.
Open: All Year (not Xmas/New Year)
01258 857057 Mrs Hopkins
D: £19.50–£21.50 **S:** £25–£28
Beds: 1D 1T **Baths:** 2 En
⌂ (10) ▣ (4) ⊁ 📺 🐾 ▥ Ⅴ ✻ ♨ &

Swanage

SZ0278   ◫ Black Swan, Crow's Nest, Red Lion, White Horse, Tawnys

Plum Tree Cottage, 60 Bell Street, Swanage, Dorset, BH19 2SB.
Comfortable rooms, generous breakfasts, in cosy old Purbeck stone cottage.
Open: All Year
01929 421601 (also fax) Mr & Mrs Howells
D: £22.50–£30 **S:** £30–£40
Beds: 3D **Baths:** 1 En 2 Pr
▣ (2) ⊁ 📺 🐾 ✕ ▥ Ⅴ ♨

Perfick Piece, Springfield Road, Swanage, Dorset, BH19 1HD.
Small family guest house in quiet cul-de-sac near shops, beach and steam railway.
Open: All Year
01929 423178 Fax: 01929 423558
perfick-piece@supanet.com
D: £14–£19 **S:** £16–£20
Beds: 1F 1T 1D **Baths:** 1 En 1 Pr 1 Sh
⌂ ▣ (3) 📺 🐾 ✕ ▥ Ⅴ ✻ ♨

Glenlee Hotel, 6 Cauldon Avenue, Swanage, Dorset, BH19 1PQ.
Friendly family run hotel in delightful position close to beach.
Open: March to October
Grades: ETC 3 Diamond
01929 425794 Mr Jones
Fax: 01929 421530
info@glenleehotel.co.uk
D: £21–£26 **S:** £31.50–£39
Beds: 2F 2T 3D **Baths:** 7 En
⌂ (3) ▣ (7) 📺 ✕ ▥ ♨ cc

Hermitage Guest House, 1 Manor Road, Swanage, Dorset, BH19 2BH.
Quiet central location; relaxed atmosphere, bay views. 2 mins beach, Coastal Path. **Open:** Easter to Nov
01929 423014 Mrs Pickering
D: £18.50–£19.50 **S:** £20
Beds: 4F 2D 1T **Baths:** 2 Sh
⌂ (5) ▣ (7) ⊁ 📺 🐾 ▥ Ⅴ ♨

Eversden Hotel, 5 Victoria Road, Swanage, Dorset, BH19 1HS.
Comfortable, friendly hotel, 2 minutes walk to the beach.
Open: All Year
Grades: AA 3 Diamond
01929 423276 Mr & Mrs Ford
Fax: 01929 427755
D: £18–£27 **S:** £20–£28
Beds: 5F 6D 1T 1S **Baths:** 10 En 2 Sh
⌂ ▣ (10) 📺 🐾 ✕ ▥ Ⅴ ♨ & cc

Pennyfarthings, 124 Kings Road West, Swanage, Dorset, BH19 1HS.
Attractively friendly house overlooking steam railway. Breakfast in conservatory.
Open: All Year (not Xmas/New Year)
01929 422256 Mr & Mrs Davison
chris@pennyfarthings.com
D: £18–£20 **S:** £20–£22
Beds: 2D 1T 1S **Baths:** 2 En 1 Sh
⌂ (6) ▣ (2) ⊁ 📺 🐾 ✕ ▥ Ⅴ ♨

Sydling St Nicholas

SY6399   ◫ The Greyhound, Red Lion

Lamperts Cottage, Sydling St Nicholas, Dorchester, Dorset, DT2 9NU.
Traditional C16th thatched cottage, stream at front, beams, inglenook, flagstones.
Open: All Year
Grades: AA 3 Diamond
01300 341659 Mr Wills
Fax: 01300 341699
mikywillis@f1racing.co
D: £21 **S:** £25
Beds: 1F 1D 1T **Baths:** 2 Sh
⌂ (8) ▣ (3) 📺 🐾 ▥ Ⅴ ♨ cc

Magiston Farm, Sydling St Nicholas, Dorchester, Dorset, DT2 9NR.
C16th farmhouse, 400 acre working farm, large garden. Very peaceful.
Open: All Year (not Xmas)
Grades: ETC 3 Diamond
01300 320295
Mrs Barraclough
D: fr £18.50 **S:** fr £18.50
Beds: 1D 3T 1S **Baths:** 1 Pr 1 Sh
⌂ (10) ▣ (12) 🐾 ✕ ▥ Ⅴ ♨ &

City Cottage, Sydling St Nicholas, Dorchester, Dorset, DT2 9NX.
Country cottage, comfortable and a warm welcome assured.
Open: All Year (not Xmas)
01300 341300 Mrs Wareham
D: fr £18 **S:** fr £18
Beds: 1D 1S **Baths:** 1 Sh
⌂ (12) ▣ (2) 📺 ▥

Symondsbury

SY4493

Saxlingham House, West Road, Symondsbury, Bridport, Dorset, DT6 6AA.
Extensive country views many local attractions warm friendly welcome.
Open: Easter to September
01308 423629
Mr & Mrs Nicholls
D: £15–£17 **S:** £15–£17
Beds: 1T 2D **Baths:** 3 En
▣ ⊁ ▥ ♨

Tarrant Hinton

ST9311   ◫ Langton Arms

Meadow House, Tarrant Hinton, Blandford Forum, Dorset, DT11 8JG.
Quiet farm house over looking countryside, excellent tourist base, home-produced breakfast
Open: All Year (not Xmas)
Grades: ETC 4 Diamond, Silver Award
01258 830498 (also fax)
Ms Webster
rose.web@virgin.net
D: £19–£25 **S:** £19–£25
Beds: 1F 1D 1S **Baths:** 2 Sh
⌂ ▣ (6) ⊁ 📺 ▥ ♨

Toller Porcorum

SY5698   ◫ Marquis of Lorne, Three Horseshoes, The Spyway, Askers Well

Colesmoor Farm, Toller Porcorum, Dorchester, Dorset, DT2 0DU.
Small family farm in quiet setting with excellent views.
Open: May to Feb
Grades: ETC 4 Diamond
01300 320812
Mrs Geddes
Fax: 01300 321402
geddes.colesmoor@eclipse.co.uk
D: £20 **S:** £25
Beds: 1D 1T **Baths:** 2 En
⌂ ▣ (4) ⊁ 📺 ▥ Ⅴ ♨ 3

The Kingcombe Centre, Toller Porcorum, Dorchester, Dorset, DT2 0EQ.
Study centre beside the River Hooke surrounded by nature reserve.
Open: All Year
Grades: ETC 2 diamond
01300 320684
Mr Spring
Fax: 01300 021409
nspring@kingombe-centre.demon.co.uk
D: £15–£20 **S:** £15–£20
Beds: 3F 3T 2D 3S **Baths:** 11 Sh
⌂ ▣ (20) ⊁ 📺 🐾 ✕ ▥ Ⅴ ♨ &

Turners Puddle

SY8393   ◫ Cork & Bottle

Coneygar, Turners Puddle, Dorchester, Dorset, DT2 7JA.
Country house in 6 acres of land. Beautiful garden and setting, near River Piddle.
Open: All year (not Xmas)
01929 471375
Mrs Roffey
D: £17.50–£20 **S:** £–£20
Beds: 2T **Baths:** 2 Pr
⌂ (6) ▣ (4) ⊁ 📺 🐾 ▥ Ⅴ ♨

BATHROOMS

Pr - Private

Sh - Shared

En - Ensuite

Uploders

SY5093 ❦ *Crown Inn*

Uploders Farm, Uploders, Bridport, Dorset, *DT6 4NZ.*
Quiet position. Ideal for touring. Beautiful countryside. Good English breakfast.
Open: Easter to Oct
Grades: ETC 3 Diamond
01308 423380 D: £18–£20
Beds: 1F 1D **Baths:** 2 En
♿ (7) 🅿 (3) ⌿ 📺 🛏 ♨ ⚓

Upton (Poole)

SY9793 ❦ *St Peters Finger*

Tideway, Beach Road, Upton, Poole, Dorset, *BH16 5NA.*
Please look at our website for further detail & pictures.
www.maidinessex.com/tideway
Open: All Year (not Xmas)
01202 621293 (also fax) Mr & Mrs Yates
tidewaybb@aol.com
D: £20–£25 **S:** £23–£25
Beds: 1D 1T **Baths:** 1 Sh
♿ 🅿 (3) ⌿ 📺 ✕ ♨ 🚫

Verwood

SU0808 ❦ *Monmouth Ash*

Pear Tree Cottage, 93 Ringwood Road, Verwood, Dorset, *BH31 7AD.*
Old cottage, 10 minutes to Bournemouth. Open all year.
Open: All Year
01202 826734 Mrs Marcantonio
D: fr £20 **S:** fr £15
Beds: 2T 1S 1D **Baths:** 1 En 1 Sh
♿ 🅿 (5) ⌿ 📺 🛏 ✕ ♨ 🚫 ⚓ ♨

Wareham

SY9287 ❦ *Kings Arms*

Ashcroft Bed & Breakfast, 64 Furzebrook Road, Wareham, Dorset, *BH20 5AX.*
Friendly comfortable good food convenient for bird watching and walking. **Open:** All Year (not Xmas)
01929 552392 Mrs Cake
Fax: 01929 552422
cake@ashcroft-b-and-b.freeserve.co.uk
D: £17–£21 **S:** £18–£25
Beds: 1F 1D 1T 1S **Baths:** 2 En 2 Pr
♿ (3) 🅿 (6) ⌿ 📺 🛏 ✕ ♨ 🚫 ⚓

Dorothea Bed & Breakfast, 10 Sandford Road, Wareham, Dorset, *BH20 4DH.*
1930s cottage style home. Close railway, buses. Lovely garden.
Open: All Year
01929 553869 Mrs Holland
sylvantel@madasafish.com
D: £18–£20 **S:** £18–£20
Beds: 1D 1T 2S **Baths:** 2 Pr 2 En
♿ 🅿 (4) ⌿ 📺 🛏 ♨ 🚫 ♨

All details shown are as supplied by B&B owners in Autumn 2000

Anglebury House

Anglebury House, 15/17 North Street, Wareham, *BH20 4AB.*
Beautiful C16th building comfortable and full of character. Lawrence of Arabia was a guest here and took coffee in our quaint coffee shop. Excellent cuisine in our restaurant and coffee shop. Warm, friendly welcome.
Open: All Year
01929 552988 D: £18–£30 **S:** £20–£35
Beds: 1F 4D 1T 1S **Baths:** 5 En 2 Pr
♿ (6) ⌿ 📺 🛏 ✕ ♨ 🚫 🚫

West Bexington

SY5387

The Manor Hotel, West Bexington, Dorchester, Dorset, *DT2 9DF.*
C16th manor house, 500 yards Chesil Beach. Jacobean oak panelling and flagstone floors.
Open: All Year
01308 897616
Fax: 01308 897035
themanorhotel@btconnect.com
D: £46.50–£50 **S:** £55.50–£60
Beds: 1F 8D 3T 1S **Baths:** 13 En
♿ 🅿 📺 ✕ ♨ 🚫 ♨ 🚫

West Holme

SY8885 ❦ *Weld Arms*

The Old Granary, West Holme Farm, West Holme, Wareham, Dorset, *BH20 6AQ.*
Excellent location for walking and bird watching in Purbeck area.
Open: All Year (not Xmas)
01929 552972
Mrs Goldsack
Fax: 01929 551616
D: £21–£26 **S:** £30
Beds: 2T **Baths:** 2 En
🅿 (4) ⌿ 📺 ♨ 🚫 ♨ ⚓ 🚫 3

West Lulworth

SY8280 ❦ *Castle Inn*

The Copse, School Lane, West Lulworth, Wareham, Dorset, *BH20 5SA.*
Open: All Year (not Xmas)
01929 400581 (also fax)
Mr & Mrs Johari
ulla.johari@tesco.net
D: £15–£17.50 **S:** £15–£17.50
Beds: 1D 1T 1S **Baths:** 1 Sh
♿ 🅿 (3) 📺 ♨ ♨
Detached house in picturesque coastal village. Quiet location overlooking field in Area of Outstanding Natural Beauty. Close to Lulworth Cove and beaches. Generous Continental breakfast.

West Down Farm, West Lulworth, Wareham, Dorset, *BH20 5RY.*
Beautiful coastal area. Outstanding views. Ideal riding, cycling and walking.
Open: All Year
01929 400308 (also fax)
Ms Weld
westdown farm@supanet. co.uk
D: £18–£20 **S:** £25–£30
Beds: 1T 1D **Baths:** 1 Sh
♿ 🅿 📺 🛏 ♨ 🚫 ♨

Gatton House

Gatton House , West Lulworth, Wareham, Dorset, *BH20 5RU.*
Picturesque guest house with spectacular views, near Lulworth Cove and coastal path.
Open: March to Oct
Grades: ETC 4 Diamond
01929 400252 (also fax)
Mr Dale
mike@gattonhouse.co.uk
D: £23–£35 **S:** £33–£45
Beds: 1F 1T 6D **Baths:** 8 En
♿ 🅿 (9) ⌿ 📺 🛏 ♨ 🚫 ♨ 🚫

Graybank Bed & Breakfast, Main Road, West Lulworth, Wareham, Dorset, *BH20 5RL.*
Purbeck stone-built Victorian house. Warm welcome, excellent breakfast menu.
Open: Feb to Nov
Grades: ETC 3 Diamond
01929 400256 Mr & Mrs Burrill
D: £17–£20 **S:** £17–£20
Beds: 2F 3D 1T 1S **Baths:** 3 Sh
♿ (4) 🅿 (7) ⌿ 📺 🛏 ♨ 🚫 ♨

Tewkesbury Cottage, 28 Main Road, West Lulworth, Wareham, Dorset, *BH20 5RL.*
c1600 thatched cottage 8 minutes walk to beach, coastal paths. Full English breakfast.
Open: All Year
01929 400561 (also fax)
Mrs Laing
D: £18–£20 **S:** £20–£25
Beds: 2D 1T 1S **Baths:** 1 En 2 Sh
♿ (12) 🅿 (6) 🛏 ♨ 🚫 ♨ ⚓

Elads Nevar Guest House, West Road, West Lulworth, Wareham, Dorset, *BH20 5RZ.*
Modern house with large bedroom. Large English or vegetarian breakfast.
Open: All Year (not Xmas/New Year)
01929 400467 Mrs Ravensdale
D: £16–£19
Beds: 1F 1D 1T **Baths:** 1 En 2 Sh
♿ (4) 🅿 (3) ⌿ 📺 🛏 ♨ 🚫 ♨

The Orchard, West Road, West Lulworth, Wareham, Dorset, *BH20 5RY.*
Peaceful off-road position, large garden.
Open: All Year (not Xmas/New Year)
01929 400592 Mr & Mrs Aldridge
theorchard@ic24.net
D: £18–£20
Beds: 2D 1T **Baths:** 3 En
♿ (5) 🅿 (3) ⌿ 📺 🛏 🚫 ♨

Weymouth

SY6779 ❦ *Dorthory Inn, White Hart, Lodmore Inn, Pulpit, Waterloo, Old Rooms, Excise House, Hog's Head, Hamiltons, Cork & Bottle, Sailors' Return*

Seaways, 5 Turton Street, Weymouth, Dorset, *DT4 7DU.*
Victorian building close to all amenities. Beach, Town and Parking.
Open: All Year (not Xmas/New Year)
01305 771646 Mr & Mrs Seward
seasew@supanet.com
D: £16 **S:** £16
Beds: 5D 1T 1S **Baths:** 2 Sh
♿ ⌿ 📺 ♨ 🚫 ♨

Esplanade Hotel, *141 The Esplanade, Weymouth, Dorset, DT4 7NJ.*
Seafront 1835 Georgian terrace hotel. Superior ensuite accommodation with car parking.
Open: Easter to Oct
Grades: AA 5 Diamond
01305 783129
Mr & Mrs Paul
D: £25–£35 **S:** £32–£35
Beds: 1F 7D 2T 1S **Baths:** 11 En
🛇 (6) 🅿 (9) ⊬ 📺 🎞 ⑭ ♨

Birchfields Hotel, *22 Abbotsbury Road, Weymouth, Dorset, DT4 0AE.*
Close to beach and town, short breaks welcome, ideal touring base.
Open: Easter to Oct
Grades: RAC 3 Diamond
01305 773255 (also fax)
Mr & Mrs Dutton
D: £20–£25 **S:** £16–£25
Beds: 2F 3D 2T 2S **Baths:** 3 En 7 Sh
🛇 🅿 (3) 📺 🎞 ⑭

Greenlands Guest House, *8 Waterloo Place, The Esplanade, Weymouth, Dorset, DT4 7PR.*
Family run guesthouse, on the sea front. Good wholesome breakfast.
Open: All Year (not Xmas)
01305 776368 (also fax)
Mr & Mrs Turbett
greenlands@kevandjackie.demon.co.uk
D: £15–£20
Beds: 2F 5D
🛇 🅿 (7) 📺 🎞 ⑭ ♨ cc

Kings Acre Hotel, *140 The Esplanade, Weymouth, Dorset, DT4 7NH.*
Open: Feb to Nov
Grades: ETC 4 Diamond
01305 782534 Mrs Mears
Fax: 01305 732354
D: £25–£35 **S:** £32.50–£40
Beds: 2F 7D 2T **Baths:** 10 En 1 Pr
🛇 🅿 (9) ⊬ 📺 × 🎞 ⑭ ♨ cc
Lovely, private run hotel in a grand Victorian terrace. offering friendly, courteous service, good food. Ideally located overlooking Weymouth's beach and bay and close to all amenities.

Hardwick House, *23 Hardwick Street, Weymouth, Dorset, DT4 7HU.*
Friendly guest house, mins from seafront and town centre.
Open: Jan to Nov
01305 784303 Mrs Austin
D: £15–£20 **S:** £15–£20
Beds: 2F 2T 3D 1S **Baths:** 3 En 1 Sh
🛇 🅿 📺 × ♨ ♨ cc

Hotel Fairhaven, *37 The Esplanade, Weymouth, Dorset, DT4 8DH.*
Beach front hotel, close town centre & harbour. 24 hour reception.
Open: Mar to Nov
Grades: RAC 2 Star
01305 760200 Mr Thwaite
Fax: 01305 760300
fairhaven@kingshotels.f9.co.uk
D: £30–£34 **S:** £32–£37
Beds: 12F 10D 50T 10S **Baths:** 82 En
🛇 🅿 (20) 📺 × ⑭ ♨ cc

SY3995   🍺 *Five Bells*

Cardsmill Farm, *Whitchurch Canonicorum, Bridport, Dorset, DT6 6RP.*
Comfortable farmhouse on working family farm 3 miles from coast.
Open: All year (not Xmas)
Grades: ETC 3 Diamond
01297 489375 (also fax) Mrs Johnson
cardsmill@aol.com
D: £18–£24 **S:** £19–£23
Beds: 1F 1D 1S **Baths:** 2 En
🛇 🅿 (6) 📺 🎞 ⑭ ♨

SU0100   🍺 *Rising Sun, Pudding & Pye, Stocks Inn, Dorners*

Turi, *21 Grove Road, Wimborne Minster, Dorset, BH21 1BN.*
Victorian house with garden, off main road between Minster and market.
Open: All Year
01202 884818 Mrs Joyner
joyturl@care4tree.net
D: £14–£16 **S:** £14–£16
Beds: 1F 1T **Baths:** 2 Sh
🛇 ⊬ 📺 🎞 ⑭ ♨

Moor Allerton, *Holtwood, Wimborne Minster, Dorset, BH21 7DU.*
Tranquillity amidst glorious countryside, beaches, New Forest. Warmest Christian welcome.
Open: All Year (not Xmas/New Year)
01258 840845 (also fax) Mrs Oliver
martinoliver1@talk21.com
D: £18–£23 **S:** £20–£24
Beds: 1T 1D 1S **Baths:** 2 Pr
🛇 🅿 📺 🍴 × 🎞 ⑭ ♨ ♨

Sunnysides, *18 Victoria Road, Wimborne Minster, Dorset, BH21 1EW.*
Warm, friendly, good touring centre close to town centre and eating places.
Open: All Year
01202 886953 Mrs Randall
D: £16 **S:** £16
Beds: 1D 1T **Baths:** 1 Sh
🛇 (5) 🅿 (2) ⊬ 📺 🎞 ⑭ ♨

Heatherlands, *13 Wimborne Road, Colehill, Wimborne Minster, Dorset, BH21 2RS.*
A large Victorian house where guests are treated as friends.
Open: All Year (not Xmas/New Year)
01202 882032 Mrs Gibbs
D: £17–£18 **S:** £17–£18
Beds: 2F 1D **Baths:** 1 Sh
🛇 🅿 ⊬ 📺 🍴 🎞 ⑭ ♨

SY8084   🍺 *Sailors Return*

The Manor House, *Winfrith Newburgh, Dorchester, Dorset, DT2 8JR.*
Historic manor house with luxury rooms near Lulworth Cove.
Open: All Year (not Xmas)
01305 854987 Mr & Mrs Smith
Fax: 01305 854988
jennie@dorsetcoastalcottages.com
D: £23–£25
Beds: 1F 1T **Baths:** 1 En 1 Pr
🛇 ⊬ 📺 🎞 ⑭ ♨

SY8697   🍺 *The Greyhound*

West Acres, *West Street, Winterbourne Kingston, Blandford Forum, Dorset, DT11 9AT.*
Quiet spacious rural bungalow, large garden, excellent walking/riding paths.
Open: All Year
01929 471293 Mrs Jenkins
D: £20 **S:** £23
Beds: 1F 1T 1D **Baths:** 1 En 1 Sh
🛇 (10) 🅿 (8) ⊬ 📺 × 🎞 ♨ ♿

SY8997

Brook Farm, *Winterborne Zelston, Blandford Forum, Dorset, DT11 9EU.*
In quiet pretty hamlet, comfortable farmhouse accommodation, river & farmland views. Numerous country inns locally.
Open: All Year (not Xmas)
Grades: ETC 3 Diamond
01929 459267 (also fax) Mrs Kerley
D: £17–£22 **S:** £22–£25
Beds: 2D 1T **Baths:** 2 En 1 Pr
🛇 (10) 🅿 ⊬ 📺 🎞 ⑭ ♨

SY6190

Churchview Guest House, *Winterbourne Abbas, Dorchester, Dorset, DT2 9LS.*
Delightful C17th village guest house near Dorchester offers comfort, delicious breakfasts.
Open: All Year (not Xmas)
Grades: ETC 3 Diamond
01305 889296 (also fax)
Mr Deller
stay@churchview.co.uk
D: £22–£29 **S:** £22–£32
Beds: 1F 4D 3T 1S **Baths:** 7 En 1 Sh
🛇 (5) 🅿 (10) ⊬ 📺 🍴 × 🎞 ⑭ ♨ cc

SY6289   🍺 *Coach and Horses, Brewers Arms*

The Old Rectory, *Winterbourne Steepleton, Dorchester, Dorset, DT2 9LG.*
Open: All Year
Grades: ETC 4 Diamond
01305 889468 M Tree
Fax: 01305 889737
trees@eurobell.co.uk
D: £23–£50
Beds: 3T **Baths:** 3 En
🛇 🅿 (6) ⊬ 📺 🎞 ⑭ ♨
Situated in a quiet hamlet in Hardy country. historic Dorchester 4 miles. Weymouth sandy beach 8 miles. Enjoy a peaceful night sleep, a copious English, vegetarian or continental breakfast. Superbly appointed lounge. Croquet lawn. Putting green. Local pub of walking distance.

All details shown are as supplied by B&B owners in Autumn 2000

Wool

SY8486   *Seven Stars, Ship Inn*

East Burton House, *East Burton, Wool, Wareham, Dorset, BH20 6HE.*
Relax and enjoy real food in our peaceful country house.
Open: All Year
01929 463857 Mrs Francis
Fax: 01929 463026
mikef@fdn.co.uk
D: £22–£23 **S:** £32–£36
Beds: 2D 1T **Baths:** 2 Sh
🛏 🅿 (6) ⊬ 📺 ▥ Ⅴ ♨

Long Coppice, *Bindon Lane, Wool, Wareham, Dorset, BH20 6AS.*
Bungalow in peaceful countryside a haven for wildlife and birds.
Open: All Year (not Xmas/New Year)
01929 463123 Ms Lowman
D: £20–£47 **S:** £25–£27
Beds: 1F 1T **Baths:** 2 Pr 1 Sh
🛏 🅿 ⊬ 📺 🛌 ▥ Ⅴ ♨

Fingle Bridge, *Duck Street, Wool, Wareham, Dorset, BH20 6DE.*
Warm welcome, good food in friendly family home.
Open: All Year
01929 462739
Mrs Baker
D: £20–£25 **S:** £18
Beds: 1F 1T 1D **Baths:** 1 En 1 Sh
🛏 🅿 (3) ⊬ 📺 ▥ Ⅴ ♨

Wootton Fitzpaine

SY3695   *Shave Cross Inn*

Higher Spence, *Wootton Fitzpaine, Charmouth, DT6 6DF.*
No street lights or proper road – instead peace, tranquillity, beautiful country & sea views.
Open: All Year (not Xmas)
01297 560556
D: £18–£20 **S:** £21–£23
Beds: 1F 1D **Baths:** 2 En
🛏 (3) 🅿 (3) ⊬ 📺 🛌 ♨

Worth Matravers

SY9777   *King's Arms, The Ship*

The Haven, *Worth Matravers, Swanage, Dorset, BH19 3LF.*
Friendly welcome to comfortable modern house with pleasant sea views.
Open: All Year
01929 439388 Mr & Mrs Taylor
D: £20–£25 **S:** £20–£25
Beds: 1D 1T **Baths:** 1 En 1 Pr
🛏 ⊬ 📺 🛌 ✕ ▥ ♨

Yetminster

ST5910

Manor Farm House, *High Street, Yetminster, Sherborne, Dorset, DT9 6LF.*
Open: All Year (not Xmas)
01935 872247 (also fax)
Mr & Mrs Partridge
D: £30–£35 **S:** £–£35
Beds: 2T 1D 1S **Baths:** 4 En
🅿 (20) ⊬ 📺 ✕ ▥ Ⅴ ♨ **cc**
Interesting manor farmhouse rebuilt in C17th, with many architectural features.

County Durham

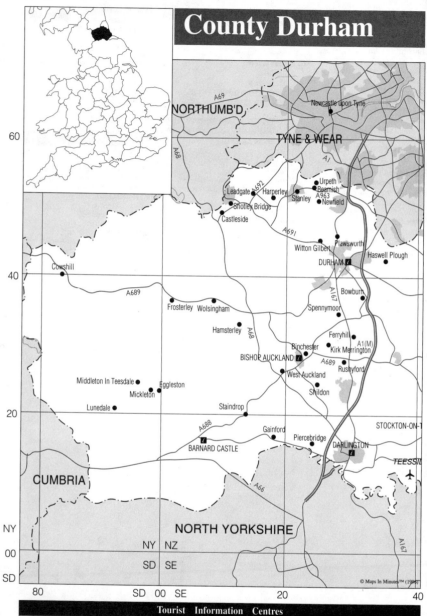

Tourist Information Centres

43 Galgate, **Barnard Castle**, County Durham, DL12 8EL, 01833 690909.

North of England Open Air Museum, **Beamish**, Stanley, County Durham, DH9 0RG, 0191 370 2533.

Town Hall, Market Place, **Bishop Auckland**, County Durham, DL14 7NP, 01388 604922.

4 West Row, **Darlington**, County Durham, DL1 5PL, 01325 388666.

Market Place, **Durham**, DH1 3NJ, 0191 384 3720.

Leisure Services Department, Civic Centre, Victoria Road, **Hartlepool**, County Durham, TS24 8AY, 01429 266522.

20 The Upper Chare, **Peterlee**, County Durham, SR8 5TE, 0191 586 4450.

Market Place, **Stanhope**, County Durham, DL13 2FJ, 01388 527650.

Theatre Yard, Off High Street, **Stockton-on-Tees**, TS18 1AT, 01642 393936.

Barnard Castle

NZ0516 🍺 *Old Well Inn, King's Head, Ancient Unicorn, Old Fields, The Bank, Redwell Inn, Fox & Hounds*

Old Well Inn, *21 The Bank, Barnard Castle, Co Durham, DL12 8PH.*
Open: All Year
Grades: ETC 3 Diamond, RAC 3 Diamond
01833 690130 Mrs Rabley
Fax: 01833 690140
reservations@oldwellinn.co.uk
D: £30–£35 **S:** £48–£57
Beds: 2F 6D 2T **Baths:** 10 En
🛏 ⅍ 📺 🍴 ✗ 📖 🎗 🛇 & cc
Recommended by the Times and Sunday Telegraph, this C17th tavern in Teesdale boasts spacious ensuite rooms, freshly prepared local produce, antique shops, museums, castles. Beautiful scenery, wonderful walks, river and reservoir fishing and riding.

West Roods Farm, *Boldron, Barnard Castle, Co Durham, DL12 9SW.*
Geordie welcome, kettle on the boil on arrival 5pm (1700 hrs).
Open: May to Oct
Grades: ETC 2 Diamond
01833 690116 Mrs Lowson
D: £20 **S:** £20–£25
Beds: 1F 1D 1S **Baths:** 2 En 1 Sh
🛏 (5) 🅿 (6) ⅍ 📺 📖 🎗

Cloud High, *Eggleston, Barnard Castle, Co Durham, DL12 0AU.*
Luxury hospitality, gourmet breakfasts, a delight. Come and be pampered!
Open: Easter to Nov
Grades: ETC 4 Diamond, Gold
01833 650644 Mr & Mrs Bell
D: £22–£24.50 **S:** £30
Beds: 2D 1T **Baths:** 3 En
🅿 (4) ⅍ 📺 📖 🛇 🎗

Spring Lodge, *Newgate, Barnard Castle, Co Durham, DL12 8NW.*
Regency villa built in 1825 standing in its own grounds.
Open: All Year (not Xmas)
01833 638110 (also fax)
Mrs Ormston
D: £20–£25 **S:** £25–£30
Beds: 1D 2T **Baths:** 2 En 1 Pr
🛏 🅿 (6) 📺 🍴 🛇 🎗

Beamish

NZ2253 🍺 *Beamish Mary Inn*

No Place House, *Beamish, Stanley, Co Durham, DH9 0QH.*
Converted co-operative store, close to Beamish Museum. Friendly warm welcome. **Open:** All Year
Grades: ETC 2 Diamond
0191 370 0891 Mrs Wood
D: £18.50–£20 **S:** £22–£25
Beds: 2D 1T **Baths:** 2 En 1 Sh
🛏 (3) 🅿 (5) 📺 🍴 📖 🛇 ❋ 🎗

The Coach House, *High Urpeth, Beamish, Stanley, Co Durham, DH9 0SE.*
Country hamlet location, near Durham City, Beamish, Metro Centre & A1(M).
Open: All Year
Grades: ETC 4 Diamond
0191 370 0309 Mrs Foreman
Fax: 0191 370 0046
coachhouse@foreman25.freeserve.co.uk
D: £20–£22.50 **S:** £25–£30
Beds: 1F 1T 1D **Baths:** 1 En 2 Pr
🛏 🅿 (6) 📺 🍴 ✗ 📖 🛇 🎗 cc

Binchester

NZ2031 🍺 *Top House*

Five Gables, *Binchester, Bishop Auckland, DL14 8AT.*
Victorian house in country, with gardens. 15 minutes from Durham.
Open: All Year (not Xmas/New Year)
Grades: ETC 3 Diamond
01388 608204
P.M.I Weston
Fax: 01388 663092
book.in@fivegables.co.uk
D: £22.50 **S:** £27.50
Beds: 1T 2D 1S **Baths:** 3 En 1 Pr
🛏 (5) 🅿 (2) ⅍ 📺 🍴 ✗ 📖 🛇 🎗

Bishop Auckland

NZ1928 🍺 *Pollards Inn*

Albion Cottage Guest House, *Albion Terrace, Bishop Auckland, Co Durham, DL14 6EL.*
Detached early Victorian house close to bus and train stations.
Open: All Year (not Xmas)
01388 602217
Miss Gordon
D: £18 **S:** £18
Beds: 1D 1T 2S **Baths:** 2 Sh
🅿 (6) 📺 📖 🎗

Bowburn

NZ3038 🍺 *Seven Stars*

Hill Rise Guest House, *13 Durham Road West, Bowburn, Co Durham, DH6 5AU.*
Excellent standard of accommodation in large ensuite rooms.
Open: All Year
Grades: ETC 4 Diamond
0191 377 0302 (also fax)
Mrs Bland
D: £20–£25 **S:** £20–£30
Beds: 3F 1D 1S **Baths:** 4 En
🛏 🅿 (4) ⅍ 📺 📖 🎗 cc

Castleside

NZ0849

Bee Cottage Farm, *Castleside, Consett, Co Durham, DH8 9HW.*
Ideally situated for Beamish Museum, Durham Cathedral, C2C cycle track and Metro Centre.
Open: All Year
01207 508224
Mrs Lawson
D: £22–£70 **S:** £28–£35
Beds: 4F 3D 2T 1S **Baths:** 5 En 2 Sh
🛏 🅿 (20) ⅍ 📺 🍴 ✗ 📖 🛇 ❋ 🎗

40

BATHROOMS
Pr - Private
Sh - Shared
En - Ensuite

B&B owners may vary
rates - be sure to check
when booking

© Maps In Minutes™ (1996)

Cowshill

NY8540   Cowshill Hotel

Low Cornriggs Farm, *Cowshill, Wearhead, Bishop Auckland, Co Durham, DL13 1AQ.*
Magnificent views, excellent farmhouse food and B&B between Alslow and Stanhope.
Open: All Year **Grades:** ETC 4 Diamond
01388 537600 Mrs Elliott **Fax:** 01388 537777
D: £20–£21 **S:** £25–£27
Beds: 1F 1D 1T **Baths:** 4 Pr
  (5)   (6)   cc

Darlington

NZ2814   The Bridge, Carlbury Arms, Car Vagio

Aberlady Guest Hotel, *51 Corporation Road, Darlington, Co Durham, DL3 6AD.*
Victorian house close to town centre, Railway Museum, cinema & restaurants.
Open: All Year (not Xmas)
Grades: ETC 1 Diamond
01325 461449 Mrs Chaplin
D: £14–£18 **S:** £14–£18
Beds: 2F 3T 2S **Baths:** 2 Sh
  (2)

Balmoral Guest House, *63 Woodland Road, Darlington, Co Durham, DL3 7BQ.*
Victorian Town house with individually decorated bedrooms close to centre.
Open: All Year (not Xmas/New Year)
Grades: ETC 3 Diamond
01325 461908 Mr Hawke
D: £18–£23 **S:** £22–£35
Beds: 3F 1D 1T 4S **Baths:** 4 Pr 2 Sh

Durham

NZ2742   Duke Of Wellington, Court Inn, Durham Light Infantryman, Court Inn, Port & Glass, Blacksmith's Arms, Newton Grange Inn, Seven Stars, Three Tuns, Travellers Rest

Castle View Guest House, *4 Crossgate, Durham, DH1 4PS.*
City centre Georgian guest house, close to castle and cathedral.
Open: All Year (not Xmas)
Grades: ETC 3 Diamond
0191 386 8852 (also fax) Mrs Williams
castle_view@hotmail.com
D: £26–£27.50 **S:** £40
Beds: 3D 2T 1S **Baths:** 6 En
  (2)   cc

The Pink House, *16 Gilesgate, Durham, DH1 1QW.*
Small Georgian house. Homely, central.
Open: All Year
0191 386 7039 Mrs Miles
D: £16 **S:** £17
Beds: 1F 1D **Baths:** 1 Sh

The Gilesgate Moor Hotel, *Teasdale Terrace, Gilesgate, Durham, DH1 2RN.*
Friendly family run pub offering attractive high quality accommodation.
Open: All Year (not Xmas)
Grades: ETC 3 Diamond
0191 386 6453 R Sutton
D: £18 **S:** £18
Beds: 1F 5T 1S **Baths:** 3 En 2 Sh
  (7)

26 St Johns Road, *Nevilles Cross, Durham, DH1 4NU.*
Late Victorian house. Good food, friendly welcome, quiet residential area.
Open: All Year (not Xmas)
0191 384 8329 Mrs Burton
D: £18 **S:** £21
Beds: 1D 1T **Baths:** 1 Sh

Lothlorien, *Front Street, Witton Gilbert, Durham, DH7 6SY.*
Comfortable period cottage just outside Durham on direct route to Hadrian's Wall.
Open: All Year (not Xmas)
Grades: ETC 3 Diamond
0191 371 0067 Mrs Milne
D: £19–£20 **S:** £19–£20
Beds: 1D 1T 1S **Baths:** 2 Sh
  (3)

Hill Rise Guest House, *13 Durham Road West, Bowburn, Durham, DH6 5AU.*
Excellent standard of accommodation in large ensuite rooms.
Open: All Year
Grades: ETC 4 Diamond
0191 377 0302 (also fax)
Mrs Bland
D: £20–£25 **S:** £20–£30
Beds: 3F 1D 1S **Baths:** 4 En
  (4)   cc

14 Gilesgate, *Durham, DH1 1QW.*
Central, spacious C18th town house with four poster beds and antiques.
Open: All Year (not Xmas)
Grades: ETC 2 Diamond
0191 384 6485 Mr Nimmins
Fax: 0191 386 5173
bb@nimmins.co.uk
D: £17–£20 **S:** £17–£20
Beds: 1F 1D 1T 1S **Baths:** 2 Sh
  (1)

Green Grove, *99 Gilesgate, Durham, DH1 1JA.*
Large Victorian town house 12 min walk from city centre.
Open: All Year (not Xmas)
Grades: ETC 3 Diamond
0191 384 4361 Mr Dockery
bill.dockery@amserve.net
D: £17.50–£25 **S:** £20–£35
Beds: 1F 2D 2T 2S **Baths:** 4 En 1 Sh
  (8)

Queens Head Hotel, *2-6 Sherburn Road, Gilesgate Moor, Durham, DH1 2JR.*
Comfortable, clean, friendly. Full breakfast. English, Cantonese food. 2 minutes A1. **Open:** All Year
0191 386 5649 P Collins
Fax: 0191 386 7451
D: £17.50–£27.50 **S:** £22
Beds: 2F 1D 2T 2S **Baths:** 2 Sh
  (7)   cc

9 Leazes Place, Claypath, *Durham, DH1 1RE.*
Situated in charming period cul-de-sac. Short walk from market place.
Open: Easter to Oct
0191 386 8479 Miss Thomas
D: £15 **S:** £15
Beds: 2T **Baths:** 1 Sh
  (3)   (1)

The Anchorage, *25 Langley Road, Newton Hall, Durham, DH1 5LR.*
Large detached family home with pretty gardens, 1 mile north of city centre, convenient for commercial and countryside. Spacious accommodation with guest lounge, double bed and bed settee. Guest book quotes - 'a haven'...'lovely room'...'brilliant food'...'thoughtful caring hosts'.
Open: All Year
Grades: ETC 3 Diamond
0191 386 2323 (also fax)
S E Percival
anchorageb@aol.com
D: £22.50 **S:** £25
Beds: 1F **Baths:** 1 En
  (1)

Eggleston

NZ0023   Moorcock Inn

Moorcock Inn, *Hill Top, Gordon Bank, Eggleston, Co Durham, DL12 0AU.*
Open: All Year
Grades: ETC 3 Diamond
01833 650395 Mr & Mrs Zacharias
Fax: 01833 650052
D: £32–£37 **S:** £20–£25
Beds: 6D 6S **Baths:** 4 En 3 Sh
  (30)   cc
Country inn with scenic views over Teesdale ideal for walking. Cosy ensuite bedrooms. Open log fire. Over fifty malt whiskeys, real ales. Excellent home cooked food using local Beef, pork, lamb, extensive fish monger. Dogs welcome.

Ferryhill

NZ2832   Ye Olde Fleece Inn

Elm Garth, *Mainsforth, Ferryhill, Co Durham, DL17 9AA.*
Open: All Year (not Xmas)
Grades: ETC 3 Diamond
01740 652676 Mr & Mrs Dobbing
elmgarth_bedandbreakfast@yahoo.com
D: £18–£20 **S:** £20–£22
Beds: 1F 1D **Baths:** 1 En 1 Pr
  (3)
Fine accommodation in superb countryside: C17th house, very quiet location and easy to get to a traditional farming village with views to the Cleveland Hills. Brochure, location map available, can post or fax.

Frosterley

NZ0237

High Laithe, *Hill End, Frosterley, Bishop Auckland, County Durham, DL13 2SX.*
Small working farm. Peacefully situated. Splendid views. Ideal touring, walking.
Open: All Year (not Xmas)
Grades: ETC 3 Diamond
01388 526421 Mr Moss
D: £18 **S:** £18
Beds: 1D 1S **Baths:** 1 Pr
  (5)   (2)

Planning a longer stay? Always ask for any special rates

Gainford

NZ1617

Queens Head Hotel, 11 Main Road, Gainford, Darlington, *DL2 3DZ.*
Inn/restaurant/bar meals. A67 between Darlington and Barnard Castle.
Open: All Year
01325 730958 Mrs Batty
D: £22.50 **S:** £35
Beds: 2F 1T 2D **Baths:** 5 En
🛏 🅿 (30) 📺 ⌕ ✕ ⽥ 🆅 ⚓ cc

Hamsterley

NZ1131   🍺 *Victoria Inn*

Dryderdale Hall, Hamsterley, Bishop Auckland, Co Durham, *DL13 3NR.*
Beautiful Victorian country house set in 19 acres of parkland with stream and ponds.
Open: All Year
01388 488494 D Morley
D: £25 **S:** fr £35
Beds: 1D 2T **Baths:** 3 En
🛏 🅿 (6) 📺 ✕ ⽥ 🆅 ⚓

Harperley

NZ1753   🍺 *Harperley Hotel*

Bushblades Farm, Harperley, Stanley, County Durham, *DH9 9UA.*
Georgian farmhouse, rural setting, close Beamish Museum and Durham City.
Open: All Year (not Xmas)
Grades: ETC 3 Diamond
01207 232722
Mrs Gibson
D: £17–£19.50 **S:** £20–£25
Beds: 2D 1T **Baths:** 1 En 2 Sh
🛏 (12) 🅿 (4) 📺 ⽥ ⚓ &

Haswell Plough

NZ3742

The Gables Hotel, Haswell Plough, Durham, *DH6 2EW.*
Small family run hotel 5 miles east of Durham city on the B1283.
Open: All Year
Grades: AA listed
0191 526 2982 (also fax)
Mr Milner
johnmgables@aol.com
D: £17.50–£28 **S:** £19–£30
Beds: 1F 2D 2T **Baths:** 2 Sh 3 En
🛏 🅿 (30) ⌣ 📺 ⌕ ✕ ⽥ 🆅 ⚓ & &

Kirk Merrington

NZ2631   🍺 *Fox and Hound*

Highview Country House, Kirk Merrington, Spennymoor, *DL16 7JT.*
Set in one acre panoramic country side, good pubs, safe parking, peaceful
Grades: ETC 3 Diamond
01388 811006 (also fax)
highview house@genie.co.uk
D: fr £23 **S:** fr £25
Beds: 1F 1T 4D 1S
Baths: 7 Ensuite
🛏 🅿 ⌣ 📺 ⌕ ✕ ⽥ 🆅 ⚓ &

Leadgate

NZ1251   🍺 *Jolly Droviers*

Low Brooms Farm, Consett, County Durham, *DH8 7SR.*
Farmhouse with panoramic view. Base for Durham. Newcastle C2C route.
Open: All Year (not Xmas/New Year)
Grades: ETC 2 Daimond
01207 500594 (also fax)
Mrs Turnbull
D: £18–£23 **S:** £19.50–£18.50
Beds: 1F 1T
🛏 🅿 ⌣ 📺 ⌕ ⽥ 🆅 ⚓

Lunedale

NY9221

Wemmergill Hall Farm, Lunedale, Middleton in Teesdale, Barnard Castle, County Durham, *DL12 0PA.*
Traditional farmhouse, views over Moorland and Reservoir. walkers/ birdwatchers paradise!
Open: Jan to Nov
Grades: ETC 3 Diamond
01833 640379 (also fax)
Mrs Stoddart
D: £18–£20 **S:** £20–£25
Beds: 1F 1D
🛏 (4) 🅿 (2) ⌣ ✕ ⚓

Mickleton

NY9623   🍺 *Blacksmiths Arms*

Pine Grove, Lowside, Mickleton, Barnard Castle, Co Durham, *DL12 0JQ.*
Situated on quiet back road with fine views of Teesdale.
Open: All Year (not Xmas)
Grades: ETC 3 Diamond
01833 640886 Mr & Mrs Gillings
chris@cgillings.freeserve.co.uk
D: £16–£18 **S:** £17–£19
Beds: 1F 1D 1T **Baths:** 1 Sh
🛏 🅿 (4) ⌣ 📺 ⌕ ⽥ 🆅 ⚓

Middleton in Teesdale

NY9425   🍺 *Kings Head, Talbot Hotel, Teesdale Hotel, Bridge Inn, Chatterbox,*

Brunswick House, 55 Market Place, Middleton in Teesdale, Barnard Castle, Co Durham, *DL12 0QH.*
Charming C18th guest house, excellent food. Many beautiful walks.
Open: All Year
Grades: ETC 4 Diamond, AA 4 Diamond
01833 640393 (also fax)
Mr & Mrs Milnes
enquiries@brunswickhouse.net
D: £20–£24 **S:** £22.50–£30
Beds: 3D 2T **Baths:** 5 En
🛏 🅿 (5) ⌣ 📺 ✕ ⽥ 🆅 ⚓ cc

Bluebell House, Market Place, Middleton in Teesdale, Barnard Castle, Co Durham, *DL12 0GG.*
Former inn, beautiful walks, good food, friendly family atmosphere guaranteed.
Open: All Year (not Xmas)
Grades: ETC 3 Diamond
01833 640584 Ms Northey
D: £16–£17 **S:** £21–£25
Beds: 2D 2T **Baths:** 3 En 1 Pr
🛏 🅿 (2) ⌣ 📺 ⌕ ⽥ 🆅 ⚓ &

RATES

D = Price range per person sharing in a double room
S = Price range for a single room

Kingsway Adventure Centre, Alston Road, Middleton in Teesdale, Barnard Castle, Co Durham, *DL12 0UU.*
A warm friendly family run outdoor activity centre.
Open: All Year (not Xmas/New Year)
01833 640881 Mr Hearn
Fax: 01833 640155
adam@kingswaycentre.co.uk
D: fr £13 **S:** fr £13
Beds: 3F 2T **Baths:** 2 En 2 Sh
🛏 🅿 (10) ⌣ ✕ ⽥ 🆅 ⚓ & &

Lonton South, Middleton in Teesdale, Barnard Castle, Co Durham, *DL12 0PL.*
Beautiful view. Farmhouse. Comfortable beds, good breakfast. Overlook garden.
Open: Mar to Oct
Grades: ETC 3 Diamond
01833 640409 Mrs Watson
D: £18–£20 **S:** £20–£24
Beds: 1D 1S **Baths:** 1 Sh
🛏 (9) 🅿 (6) ⌣ 📺 ⽥ ⚓

25 Bridge Street, Middleton in Teesdale, Barnard Castle, Co Durham, *DL12 0QB.*
Victorian private house.
Open: All Year
01833 640549 Mrs Sowerby
D: £20 **S:** £20
Beds: 1D 4T 1S **Baths:** 1 Sh
🛏 (12) 🅿 ⌣ 📺 ⌕ ⽥ 🆅 ⚓

Newfield

NZ2452   🍺 *Highwayman*

Malling House, 1 Oakdale Terrace, Newfield, Chester-le-Street, County Durham, *DH2 2SU.*
Heather, your host, has extensive knowledge of area and attractions.
Open: All Year
Grades: ETC 3 Diamond
0191 370 2571 Ms Rippon
Fax: 0191 370 1391
D: £36–£46 **S:** £20–£26
Beds: 1F 1T 1S
🛏 🅿 (3) 📺 ⽥ 🆅 ⚓

Piercebridge

NZ2015   🍺 *The Bridge, Carlbury Arms*

Holme House, Piercebridge, Darlington, Co Durham, *DL2 3SY.*
Attractive C18th farmhouse surrounded by beautiful countryside, spacious comfortable accommodation.
Open: All Year (not Xmas)
Grades: ETC 3 Diamond
01325 374280 (also fax)
Mrs Graham
graham@holmehouse22.freeserve.co.uk
D: £22.50–£25 **S:** £22.50–£30
Beds: 1F 1T **Baths:** 2 En
🛏 🅿 (4) 📺 ⽥ 🆅 ⚓

Plawsworth

NZ2647   *Traveller's Rest, Red Lion*

Lilac Cottage, Wheatley Well Lane, Plawsworth, Chester-le-Street, Co Durham, *DH2 3LD.*
Stone built Georgian cottage just off A167. Very conveniently situated for Durham city. **Open:** All Year (not Xmas)
Grades: ETC 2 Diamond
0191 371 2969 Mrs Prizeman
D: £17.50 **S:** £17.50
Beds: 1D 1T 1S **Baths:** 2 Sh
🄿 (2) ⌀ ⊡ ▥ ⊡ ♨

Rushyford

NZ2829

Garden House, Windlestone Park, Windlestone, Rushyford, Ferryhill, County Durham, *DL17 0LZ.*
House with stunning walled garden. Haven of peace and tranquillity.
Open: All Year **Grades:** ETC 4 Diamond
01388 720217 Ms Cattell
D: £20–£22 **S:** £25–£28
Beds: 1T 2D **Baths:** 2 En 1 Pr
🖙 🄿 ⌀ ⊡ ✕ ▥ ⊡ ♨ ⟨

Shildon

NZ2227   *Clive Hall*

101 Main Street, Shildon, Co Durham, *DL4 1AW.*
8 miles from Aim. Ample parking. Georgian mid terrace.
Open: All Year (not Xmas/New Year)
01388 772646 Mr Walton
D: £17 **S:** £17
Beds: 1F 1T 1D
🖙 🄿 (18) ⊡ ▥ ♨

Shotley Bridge

NZ0852   *Punchbowl, Manor House*

Crown & Crossed Swords Hotel, Shotley Bridge, Consett, Co Durham, *DH8 0NH.*
Historical country hotel and restaurant in small village. **Open:** All Year
01207 502006 Mrs Suddick
D: £18–£23 **S:** £20–£25
Beds: 2F 4D 3T 1S **Baths:** 4 En 2 Sh
🖙 🄿 (40) ⊡ ✕ ▥ ⊡ ♨ cc

Spennymoor

NZ2533   *Fox & Hounds, Half Moon, Thinford Inn, Shaftoes*

Idsley House, 4 Green Lane, Spennymoor, Co Durham, *DL16 6HD.*
Beautiful Victorian detached house, close Durham city, 6 miles south on A167/A688 junction. **Open:** All Year
Grades: ETC 4 Diamond
01388 814237 Mrs Dartnall
D: £24 **S:** £35–£38
Beds: 1F 2D 2T 1S **Baths:** 4 En 1 Pr
🖙 (5) 🄿 (8) ⌀ ⊡ ✕ ▥ ⊡ ♨ cc

RATES

D = Price range per person sharing in a double room

S = Price range for a single room

Ye Olde Station Guest House, 1 Whitworth Terrace, Spennymoor, Co Durham, *DL16 7LD.*
Family-run guest house.
Open: All Year
01388 814455 Mr Murrray
D: £14.50–£16 **S:** £15–£17
Beds: 2F 3T 2S **Baths:** 1 Pr 2 Sh
🖙 (1) 🄿 (8) ⊡ ▥ ♨

Staindrop

NZ1220   *Sun Inn, Brown Jug*

Malvern House, 7 Front Street, Staindrop, Darlington, Co Durham, *DL2 3LZ.*
Georgian town house, overlooking the green in conservation village.
Open: All Year
01833 660846 Mrs Gray
D: £18 **S:** £18
Beds: 2T **Baths:** 1 Sh
🖙 ⊡ ⊩ ▥ ♨

Stanley

NZ1952   *Harperley Hotel*

Bushblades Farm, Harperley, Stanley, County Durham, *DH9 9UA.*
Georgian farmhouse, rural setting, close Beamish Museum and Durham City.
Open: All Year (not Xmas)
Grades: ETC 3 Diamond
01207 232722 Mrs Gibson
D: £17–£19.50 **S:** £20–£25
Beds: 2D 1T **Baths:** 1 En 2 Sh
🖙 (12) 🄿 (4) ⊡ ▥ ♨ ⟨

Stillington

NZ3724   *The Hamilton*

Post Office House, Redmarshall Street, Stillington, Stockton-on-Tees, Cleveland, *TS21 1JS.*
Spacious modern rooms. Private entrance with own keys.
Open: All Year
01740 630301 (also fax)
harewood@tesco.net
D: £20 **S:** £25
Beds: 2D **Baths:** 2 En
⊡ ▥ ♨

B&B owners may vary rates - be sure to check when booking

Urpeth

NZ2554

The Coach House, High Urpeth, Beamish, Stanley, Co Durham, *DH9 0SE.*
Country hamlet location, near Durham City, Beamish, Metro Centre & A1(M).
Open: All Year
Grades: ETC 4 Diamond
0191 370 0309
Mrs Foreman
Fax: 0191 370 0046
coachhouse@foreman25.freeserve.co.uk
D: £20–£22.50 **S:** £25–£30
Beds: 1F 1T 1D **Baths:** 1 En 2 Pr
🖙 🄿 (6) ⊡ ✕ ▥ ⊡ ♨ cc

West Auckland

NZ1726   *Brown Jug, Evenwood Gate*

Country Style, Etherley Bank, West Auckland, Bishop Auckland, Co Durham, *DL14 0LG.*
All rooms are ground floor, each with separate entry from off road car park.
Open: All Year
01388 832679
Ms Walton
D: £17.50–£18.50 **S:** £20–£22
Beds: 1F 1D 1T 1S **Baths:** 4 En
🖙 (1) 🄿 (8) ⊡ ⊩ ♨

Witton Gilbert

NZ2346   *Travellers Rest*

Lothlorien, Front Street, Witton Gilbert, Durham, *DH7 6SY.*
Comfortable period cottage just outside Durham on direct route to Hadrian's Wall.
Open: All Year (not Xmas)
Grades: ETC 3 Diamond
0191 371 0067
Mrs Milne
D: £19–£20 **S:** £19–£20
Beds: 1D 1T 1S **Baths:** 2 Sh
🖙 🄿 (3) ⊡ ▥ ⊡ ♨

Wolsingham

NZ0737   *Bay Horse Hotel, Mill Race*

Bay Horse Hotel, Upper Town, Wolsingham, Bishop Auckland, Co Durham, *DL13 3EX.*
Traditional Dales hotel with home-cooked meals and cask-conditioned beers.
Open: All Year
01388 527220
Mrs Ellila
Fax: 01388 528721
D: £20–£22.50 **S:** £25
Beds: 4D 4T
Baths: 8 Pr 1 Sh
🖙 🄿 (20) ⌀ ⊡ ⊩ ✕ ⊡ ✿ ♨ cc

Planning a longer stay? Always ask for any special rates

Stilwell's National Trail Companion

46 Long Distance Footpaths
Where to Stay * Where to Eat

Other guides may show you where to walk, **Stilwell's National Trail Companion** shows your where to stay and eat. The perfect companion guide for the British Isles' famous national trails and long distance footpaths, Stilwell's make pre-planning your accommodation easy. It lists B&Bs, hostels, campsites and pubs - in the order they appear along the routes - and includes such vital information as maps, grid references and distance from the path; Tourist Board ratings; the availability of vehicle pick-up, drying facilities and packed lunches. So whether you walk a trail in stages at weekends or in one continuous journey, you'll never be stuck at the end of the day for a hot meal or a great place to sleep.

Enjoy the beauty and adventure of Britain's – and Ireland's – long distance trails with Stilwell's National Trail Companion.

Paths in England
Cleveland Way & Tabular Hills Link – Coast to Coast Path – Cotswald Way – Cumbria Way – Dales Way – Essex Way – Greensand Way – Hadrian's Wall – Heart of England Way – Hereward Way – Icknield Way – Macmillan Way – North Downs Way – Oxfordshire Way – Peddars Way and Norfolk Coastal Path – Pennine Way – Ribble Way – The Ridgeway – Shropshire Way – South Downs Way – South West Coast Path – Staffordshire Way – Tarka Trail – Thames Path – Two Moors Way - Vanguard Way - Viking Way – Wayfarer's Walk – Wealdway – Wessex Ridgeway – Wolds Way

Paths in Ireland
Beara Way – Dingle Way – Kerry Way – Ulster Way – Western Way – Wicklow Way

Paths in Scotland
Fife Coastal Walk – Southern Upland Way – Speyside Way – West Highland Way

Paths in Wales
Cambrian Way – Glyndwr's Way – Offa's Dyke Path – Pembrokeshire Coast Path – Wye Valley Walk

£9.95 from all good bookstores (ISBN 1-900861-25-9) or £10.95 (inc p&p) from Stilwell Publishing Ltd, 59 Charlotte Road, London EC2A 3QW (020 7739 7179)

Essex

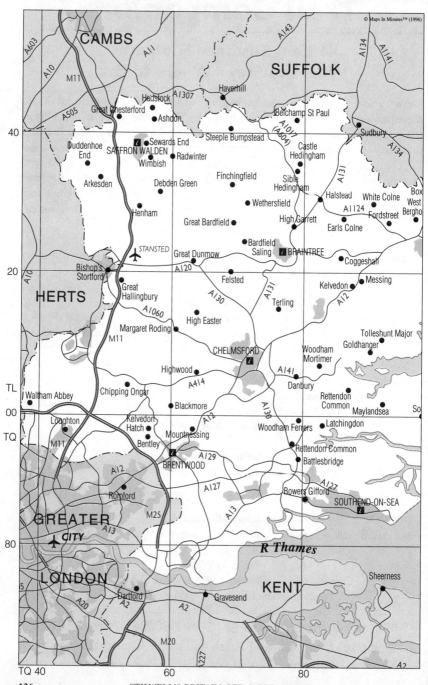

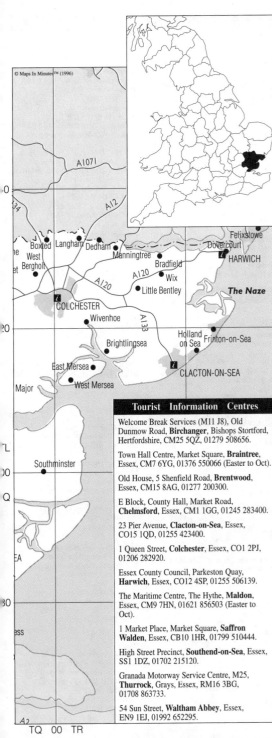

Arkesden

TL4834 🍺 *Axe & Compass*

Parsonage Farm, *Arkesden, Saffron Walden, Essex, CB11 4HB.*
Victorian farmhouse on arable farm in centre of award-winning village.
Open: All Year (not Xmas)
01799 550306 Mrs Forster
D: £17.50–£25 **S:** £25
Beds: 2D 1T **Baths:** 2 En 1 Sh
🛇 🅿 (5) ⊬ 📺 🛏 🕮 🗓 🛆

Ashdon

TL5842 🍺 *Rose & Crown*

Cobblers, *Bartow Road, Ashdon, Saffron Walden, Essex, CB10 2HR.*
Peaceful place, warm welcome, relaxing rooms, bountiful breakfasts, great garden!
Open: All Year (not Xmas)
Grades: ETC 4 Diamond
01799 584666 Mrs Slater
cobblers@ashdon2000.freeserve.co.uk
D: £20 **S:** £20–£25
Beds: 2D **Baths:** 1 En 1 Pr
🛇 (3) 🅿 (4) 📺 🕮 🗓 🛆

Bardfield Saling

TL6826 🍺 *White Hart*

Taborsfield, *Woolpits Road, Bardfield Saling, Braintree, Essex, CM7 5EA.*
Detached house, attractive rural setting.
Open: All Year
01371 850391 Mrs Smith
D: £16–£17.50 **S:** £16–£17
Beds: 1F 1D 1S **Baths:** 1 En 1 Sh
🛇 🅿 (8) ⊬ 📺 🛏 🕮 🗓 🛆

Battlesbridge

TQ7794 🍺 *The Barge, The Hawk*

The Cottages Guest House,
Beeches Road, Battlesbridge, Wickford, Essex, SS11 8TJ.
Rural, cosy, licensed guest house. Easy reach Southend, Chelmsford, Basildon. Licensed bar.
Open: All Year (not Xmas)
Grades: ETC 2 Diamond
01702 232105 Miss Carr
cottages200@totalise.co.uk
D: £17.50–£25 **S:** £20–£60
Beds: 1F 1D 3T 1S **Baths:** 3 En 1 Sh
🅿 (10) 📺 🛏 ✕ 🕮 🛆

Belchamp St Paul

TL7942 🍺 *Half Moon Inn*

The Plough, *Belchamp St Paul, Sudbury, Suffolk, CO10 7BT.*
Charming former pub. Peaceful village. Comfortable friendly atmosphere. Centrally located.
Open: All Year
Grades: ETC 4 Diamond, Silver
01787 278882 Mrs Stormont
chris.stormont@virgin.net
D: £20–£25 **S:** £20–£30
Beds: 1T 1D **Baths:** 2En
🛇 (6) 🅿 (4) ⊬ 📺 🕮 🗓 🛆

Tourist Information Centres

Welcome Break Services (M11 J8), Old Dunmow Road, **Birchanger**, Bishops Stortford, Hertfordshire, CM25 5QZ, 01279 508656.

Town Hall Centre, Market Square, **Braintree**, Essex, CM7 6YG, 01376 550066 (Easter to Oct).

Old House, 5 Shenfield Road, **Brentwood**, Essex, CM15 8AG, 01277 200300.

E Block, County Hall, Market Road, **Chelmsford**, Essex, CM1 1GG, 01245 283400.

23 Pier Avenue, **Clacton-on-Sea**, Essex, CO15 1QD, 01255 423400.

1 Queen Street, **Colchester**, Essex, CO1 2PJ, 01206 282920.

Essex County Council, Parkeston Quay, **Harwich**, Essex, CO12 4SP, 01255 506139.

The Maritime Centre, The Hythe, **Maldon**, Essex, CM9 7HN, 01621 856503 (Easter to Oct).

1 Market Place, Market Square, **Saffron Walden**, Essex, CB10 1HR, 01799 510444.

High Street Precinct, **Southend-on-Sea**, Essex, SS1 1DZ, 01702 215120.

Granada Motorway Service Centre, M25, **Thurrock**, Grays, Essex, RM16 3BG, 01708 863733.

54 Sun Street, **Waltham Abbey**, Essex, EN9 1EJ, 01992 652295.

Bentley

TQ5696

The Coach House, Mores Lane, Bentley, Brentwood, Essex, CM14 5PZ.
200-year-old coaching house in grounds of 1 acre.
Open: All Year (not Xmas/New Year)
01277 375015 S Mead
Fax: 01277 372954
sheilaghandroger@aol.com
D: £22–£25 **S:** £22–£25
⚡ 📺 🛏 🅥 ⚓

Blackmore

TL6001 🍺 *The Bull*

Little Lampetts, Hay Green Lane, Blackmore, Ingatestone, Essex, CM4 0QE.
Secluded period house; easy access to M25 mainline stations towns.
Open: All Year
01277 822030 Mrs Porter
littlelampetts@hotmail.com
D: £22.50–£25 **S:** £25–£27.50
Beds: 2T **Baths:** 1 Pr
📇 (5) ⚡ 📺 🛏 ✕ 🅥 ⚓

Bowers Gifford

TQ7588

38 Kelly Road, Bowers Gifford, Basildon, Essex, SS13 2HL.
Self contained apartment. Train to London 45 minutes. Country setting and views.
Open: All Year
Grades: ETC 3 Diamond
01268 726701 Ms Jenkinson
patricia.jenkinson@tesco.net
D: £28–£40 **S:** £22–£25
Beds: 2D
🦮 📇 (8) 📺 ✕ 🛏 🅥 ⚓ ⚓

Boxted

TL9933 🍺 *The Angel*

Round Hill House, Parsonage Hill, Boxted, Colchester, Essex, CO4 5ST.
Stands on a low hill overlooking pastures where cattle graze.
Open: All Year
Grades: ETC 4 Diamond
01206 272392 (also fax)
jermar@appleonline.net
D: £22.50–£26 **S:** £30–£35
Beds: 1F 1D 1T **Baths:** 2 En 1 Pr
🦮 📇 (6) 🐕 🛏 ✕ 🛏 🅥 ⚓

Bradfield

TM1430 🍺 *Village Maid*

Emsworth House, Ship Hill, Bradfield, Manningtree, Essex, CO11 2UP.
Set in a large beautiful garden with stunning views over the estuary.
Open: All Year
01255 870860 Mrs Linton
emsworthhouse@hotmail.com
D: £19–£25 **S:** £27–£36
Beds: 1F 2D 1T **Baths:** 1 En 2 Sh
🦮 📇 (10) 📺 🐕 🛏 🅥 ⚓

Braintree

TL7623

The Old House Guesthouse, 11 Bradford Street, Braintree, Essex, CM7 9AS.
Family-run, C16th guest house within walking distance town centre.
Open: All Year
01376 550457 Mrs Hughes
Fax: 01376 343863
old_house@talk21.com
D: £19–£30 **S:** £23–£30
Beds: 2F 5D 1T **Baths:** 6 Pr 2 Sh
🦮 📇 (10) ⚡ 📺 ✕ 🛏 🅥 ⚓ cc

Brightlingsea

TM0817 🍺 *Red Lion*

Paxton Dene, Church Road, Brightlingsea, Essex, CO7 0QT.
Spacious cottage-style accommodation, edge of historic Cinque Port Town.
Open: All Year
01206 304560 Mr & Mrs Reynolds
Fax: 01206 302877
D: £19–£21 **S:** £25–£29
Beds: 1F 1D 1T **Baths:** 3 En
🦮 📇 (4) ⚡ 📺 ✕ 🛏 🅥 ⚓

Castle Hedingham

TL7835 🍺 *The Bell, White Hart*

Fishers, 36 St James Street, Castle Hedingham, Halstead, Essex, CO9 3EW.
Peaceful stay overlooking lovely garden. Excellent for touring Essex/Suffolk border.
Open: All Year (not Xmas)
01787 460382 (also fax) Mrs Hutchings
D: £20–£25 **S:** £25–£30
Beds: 1T **Baths:** 1 Pr
🦮 (8) 📇 (1) ⚡ 📺 🛏 🅥 ⚓

Chelmsford

TL7006 🍺 *Black Bull, White Hart Pub, Springfield Arms*

Aquila B&B, 11 Daffodil Way, Springfield, Chelmsford, Essex, CM1 6XB.
B&B frequent buses to Chelmsford. London 35 Min by train.
Open: All Year
Grades: ETC 2 Diamond
01245 465274
D: £19.50–£24.50 **S:** £19.50–£24.50
Beds: 1D 1T 1S
📇 (3) 📺 🛏 🅥 ⚓ cc

Aarandale, 9 Roxwell Road, Chelmsford, Essex, CM1 2LY.
Large Victorian house close to Chelmsford town centre and park.
Open: All Year
01245 251713 (also fax)
Mrs Perera
aarandaleg@aol.com
D: £20–£22 **S:** £22–£32
Beds: 1F 1T 4S **Baths:** 1 En 1 Sh
📇 (6) 📺 ✕ 🛏 🅥 ⚓

B&B owners may vary
rates - be sure to check
when booking

Clacton-on-Sea

TM1715 🍺 *Nookes & Crannies*

The Hamelin Hotel, 20 Penfold Road, Clacton-on-Sea, Essex, CO15 1JN.
A Christian family-run hotel close to sea and shops. **Open:** All Year (not Xmas)
01255 474456 Mrs Baker
Fax: 01255 428053
healingch@aol.com
D: £16–£24 **S:** £20–£28
Beds: 3F 2D 2T 1S **Baths:** 3 En 1 Sh
🦮 📇 (3) ⚡ 📺 🐕 ✕ 🛏 🅥 ⚓ cc

Brunton House, 15 Carnarvon Road, Clacton-on-Sea, Essex, CO15 6PH.
In room substantial continental breakfast. Nice rooms for nice people.
Open: All Year (not Xmas/New Year)
01255 420431 Mrs Walton
D: £12.50–£20 **S:** £17.50–£35
Beds: 6D 1S **Baths:** 3 En 1 Sh
🦮 📇 (6) 📺 🛏 ⚓ 🦽

Coggeshall

TL8522 🍺 *Woolpack Inn*

White Heather Guest House, 19 Colchester Road, Coggeshall, Colchester, Essex, CO6 1RP.
Modern, family-run guest house, overlooking farmland.
Open: All Year (not Xmas)
01376 563004 Mrs Shaw
D: £22–£22.50 **S:** £22–£25
Beds: 2D 2S **Baths:** 2 En 1 Sh
📇 (8) ⚡ 📺 🛏 ⚓

Colchester

TL9925 🍺 *Forresters, George, Siege House, Red Lion, Roverstye, Peveril Hotel*

Salisbury Hotel, 112 Butt Road, Colchester, Essex, CO3 3DL.
Open: All Year **Grades:** AA 2 Diamond
01206 508508 Fax: 01206 797265
D: £25–£35 **S:** £30–£40
Beds: 2F 4T 3D 3S **Baths:** All En
🦮 📇 📺 ✕ 🛏 ⚓ cc
Situated in the historical garrison town of Colchester and within easy reach of 3 cathedral cities. Despite being in the centre of town this pub has a relaxed and informal atmosphere. The in-house bar and restaurant serve delicious and innovative meals

St John's Guest House, 330 Ipswich Road, Colchester, Essex, CO4 4ET.
Well situated close to town, convenient for A12 and A120 Harwich.
Open: All Year
01206 852288 Mrs Knight
D: £20–£25 **S:** £26–£45
Beds: 2F 2D 2T 2S **Baths:** 5 En 3 Sh
🦮 📇 (10) ⚡ 📺 🐕 🛏 🅥 ⚓ ⚓

11a Lincoln Way, Colchester, Essex, CO1 2RL.
Friendly, comfortable modern house in quiet residential area, five minutes' walk from town centre. **Open:** All Year
01206 867192 Mr & Mrs Edwards
Fax: 01206 799993
j.medwards@easicom.com
D: £18–£20 **S:** £18–£22
Beds: 1T 1S **Baths:** 1 Sh
🦮 (4) 📇 (1) ⚡ 📺 🐕 ✕ 🛏 🅥 ⚓

Peveril Hotel, *51 North Hill, Colchester, Essex, CO1 1PY.*
Town centre holiday accommodation. Superb food, near castle.
Open: All Year (not Xmas)
01206 574001 (also fax)
D: £27–£45 **S:** £27–£45
Beds: 4F 6D 2T 5S **Baths:** 6 En 4 Sh
🛏 🅿 (10) 📺 🍴 ✕ 🛋 Ⅴ ♿ **cc**

8 Broadmead Road, Parsons Heath, *Colchester, Essex, CO4 3HB.*
Friendly family home, quiet residential area. 10 mins bus/car from town centre.
Open: All Year
01206 861818 (also fax) Mr & Mrs Smith
brenda@btsmith.fsnet.co.uk
D: £18.50 **S:** £25
Beds: 1D **Baths:** 1 Sh
🅿 🛋 📺 ✕ 🛋 Ⅴ ♿

Danbury

TL7705 🍺 *The Bell, Griffin Inn, The Cricketers*

Southways, *Copt Hill, Danbury, Chelmsford, Essex, CM3 4NN.*
House with large attractive garden adjoining National Trust common land.
Open: All Year **Grades:** ETC 3 Diamond
01245 223428 Mrs Deavin
D: £19–£20 **S:** £20
Beds: 2T **Baths:** 1 Sh
🛏 🅿 (2) 📺 🍴 🛋 Ⅴ ♿

Debden Green

TL5732

Wigmores Farm, *Debden Green, Saffron Walden, Essex, CB11 3LX.*
Situated in beautiful open countryside near Thaxted and Saffron Walden.
Open: All Year (not Xmas)
01371 830050 Mr & Mrs Worth
D: £19–£24 **S:** £24
Beds: 1F 2D 1T **Baths:** 2 Sh
🛏 🅿 (10) 📺 🍴 ✕ 🛋 ♿

Dedham

TM0533 🍺 *Marlborough Head*

Mays Barn Farm, *Mays Lane, Dedham, Colchester, Essex, CO7 6EW.*
A Comfortable well-furnished old house with wonderful views of Dedham Vale.
Open: All Year
Grades: ETC 4 Diamond
01206 323191 Mrs Freeman
maysbarn@talk21.com
D: £20–£22 **S:** £25–£30
Beds: 1D 1T **Baths:** 1 En 1 Pr
🛏 (12) 🅿 (3) 🚭 📺 🛋 ♿

Dovercourt

TM2531 🍺 *Royal Oak Inn*

Dudley Guest House, *34 Cliff Road, Dovercourt, Harwich, Essex, CO12 3PP.*
Family-run Victorian house. Railway/buses short walk. Pubs, restaurants, shops, banks close by.
Open: All Year
Grades: ETC 2 Diamond
01255 504927 Mr Rackham
D: £14–£18 **S:** £18–£22
Beds: 1F 1D 1T 1S **Baths:** 1 En 2 Sh
🅿 🅿 (4) 🚭 📺 🛋 Ⅴ ♿

Duddenhoe End

TL4636 🍺 *Axe and Compass*

Rockells Farm, *Duddenhoe End, Saffron Walden, Essex, CB11 4UY.*
Georgian farmhouse with lake view.
Open: All Year (not Xmas/New Year)
Grades: ETC 4 Diamond
01763 838053 Mrs Westerhuis
D: £20–£25 **S:** £20–£25
Beds: 1F 1T 1S **Baths:** 3 En
🛏 🅿 (4) 📺 ✕ 🛋 ♿ ♿

Earls Colne

TL8528 🍺 *The Piazza*

Elm House, *14 Upper Holt Street, Earls Colne, Colchester, Essex, CO6 2PG.*
Fine, brick-built, small, Georgian family home in village.
Open: All Year (not Xmas)
01787 222197 Lady Larcom
D: £19–£25 **S:** £19–£25
Beds: 1F 1D 1T **Baths:** 1 En 1 Sh
🛏 🅿 (3) 📺 🍴 ✕ 🛋 Ⅴ ♿

Drum Inn, *21 High Street, Earls Colne, Colchester, Essex, CO6 2PA .*
Attractive village pub surrounded by beautiful Essex countryside walks.
Open: All Year
01787 222368
D: £22–£25.50
Beds: 3T **Baths:** 3 En
🛏 🅿 📺 🍴 ✕ 🛋 Ⅴ ♿ **cc**

East Mersea

TM0514 🍺 *Dog & Pheasant*

Bromans Farm, *East Mersea, Colchester, Essex, CO5 8UE.*
Grade II Listed C14th farmhouse, 5 minutes from sea - 9 miles Colchester.
Open: All Year
Grades: ETC 4 Diamond
01206 383235 (also fax)
Mrs Dence
D: £20–£25 **S:** £25–£30
Beds: 1D 1T 1S **Baths:** 2 Pr
🛏 🅿 (3) 🚭 📺 🍴 🛋 Ⅴ ♿

Felsted

TL6720 🍺 *Flitch Of Bacon, The Chequers, The Swan, Three Horseshoes*

Yarrow, *Felsted, Great Dunmow, Essex, CM6 3HD.*
Please see website www.yarrow.ic24.net
Open: All Year
01371 820878 (also fax)
Mr & Mrs Bellingham Smith
yarrow@ic24.net
D: fr £17 **S:** fr £18
Beds: 1D 1T 1S **Baths:** 1 En 1 Sh
🛏 🅿 (6) 🚭 📺 🛋 ♿

BATHROOMS

Pr - Private

Sh - Shared

En - Ensuite

Planning a longer stay? Always ask for any special rates

Fordstreet

TL9226 🍺 *Coopers Arms, Queen's Head, Shoulder of Mutton*

Old House, *Fordstreet, Aldham, Colchester, Essex, CO6 3PH.*
Fascinating Grade II Listed C14th hall house - oak beams, log fires, large garden.
Open: All Year
Grades: ETC 3 Diamond
01206 240456 (also fax)
Mrs Mitchell
D: £20–£25 **S:** fr £27.50
Beds: 1F 1T 1S **Baths:** 1 En 2 Pr
🛏 🅿 (6) 📺 🛋 ♿ **cc**

Frinton-on-Sea

TM2318 🍺 *Essex Skipper*

Russell Lodge, *47 Hadleigh Road, Frinton-on-Sea, Essex, CO13 9HQ.*
Home comfort and Edwardian elegance near seafront and town centre.
Open: All Year
01255 675935 J M Russell
D: £20 **S:** £20
Beds: 1T 1D 1S **Baths:** 1 En, 1 Sh
🛏 🅿 🚭 📺 🍴 🛋 ♿

Uplands Guest House, *41 Hadleigh Road, Frinton on Sea, Essex, CO13 9HQ.*
Quiet and comfortable. Just three minutes walk. Ample parking.
Open: All Year (not Xmas)
Grades: ETC 3 Diamond
01255 674889 Mrs Creates
D: £23–£28.50 **S:** £23–£37.50
Beds: 1D 3S 2T **Baths:** 4 En 2 Sh
🅿 (5) 🚭 ✕ 🛋 ♿

Goldhanger

TL9008 🍺 *Chequers Inn*

The Chequers Inn, *The Square, Goldhanger, Maldon, Essex, CM9 8AS.*
Central to Maldon, Chelmsford and Colchester.
Open: All Year
01621 788203 Mr Jones
Fax: 01621 788500
D: fr £17.50 **S:** fr £20
Beds: 1D 3T **Baths:** 1 Sh
🛏 🅿 (30) 📺 ✕ Ⅴ

Great Bardfield

TL6730 🍺 *The Vine*

Bucks House, *Vine Street, Great Bardfield, Braintree, Essex, CM7 4SR.*
Beautiful C16th house, great breakfasts, warm welcome. Conservation village centre.
Open: All Year (not Xmas)
01371 810519 Mrs Turner
Fax: 01371 811175
D: £20–£25 **S:** £25
Beds: 2D 1T **Baths:** 3 En 1 Pr
🛏 🚭 📺 🍴 🛋 ♿

Great Chesterford

TL5042   ◀ *The Plough*

White Gates, School Street, Great Chesterford, Saffron Walden, Essex, CB10 1PH.
C18th timber framed cottage in heart of historic village.
Open: All Year
Grades: ETC 4 Diamond
01799 530249 Mrs Mortimer
D: £19–£25 **S:** £23–£25
Beds: 1F 1T 1S **Baths:** 1 En 1 Sh
🛇 🅿 (3) ⁵⁄₄ 📺 🖳 🛒

Great Dunmow

TL6221   ◀ *Flitch of Bacon*

Homelye Farm, Homelye Chase, Braintree Road, Great Dunmow, Essex, CM6 3AW.
Good quality motel-style accommodation close to Stansted Airport.
Open: All Year
Grades: ETC 4 Diamond, AA 4 Diamond
01371 872127 Mrs Pickford
Fax: 01371 876428
homelye@supanet.com
D: fr £25 **S:** £25–£30
Beds: 1F 3D 2T 3S **Baths:** 9 En
🛇 🅿 (9) ⁵⁄₄ 🖳 🛒 cc

Great Hallingbury

TL5019   ◀ *Hop Poles, The George*

Yew Tree Farmhouse, Tilekiln Green, Great Hallingbury, Bishops Stortford, Herts, CM22 7TQ.
Family-run C17th farmhouse in 2 acres, close M11 & Stansted Airport.
Open: All Year (not Xmas)
01279 758875 (also fax)
D: £27.50–£45 **S:** £45–£65
Beds: 1F 1D 1T 1S **Baths:** 4 Pr
🛇 (5) 🅿 (10) ⁵⁄₄ 📺 🖳 �V 🛒

Hadstock

TL5544   ◀ *Kings Head*

Yardleys, Orchard Pightle, Hadstock, Cambridge, CB1 6PQ.
Open: All Year (not Xmas/New Year)
Grades: ETC 4 Diamond
01223 891822 (also fax)
Mrs Ludgate
yardleys@waitrose.com
D: £22–£25 **S:** £25–£32
Beds: 2T 1D **Baths:** 1 En 2 Pr
🛇 🅿 (5) ⁵⁄₄ 📺 🗙 🖳 �V 🛒 cc
Peace and quiet in pretty village only 20 minutes Cambridge, 10 minutes Saffron Walden. Warm welcome and excellent breakfasts in comfortable home with guest lounge, garden and conservatory. Convenient for M11, Duxford, Newmarket, Stansted and Harwich. E.M by arrangement or good local restaurants.

B&B owners may vary rates - be sure to check when booking

Halstead

TL8130   ◀ *The Bull*

Mill House, The Causeway, Halstead, Essex, CO9 1ET.
Listed town house in the market town, private parking, Brochure available.
Open: All Year (not Xmas)
Grades: ETC 4 Diamond
01787 474451 Mr & Mrs Stuckey
Fax: 01787 473893
stuckey@townsford.freeserve.co.uk
D: £24–£25 **S:** £30–£48
🛇 (12) 🅿 (18) ⁵⁄₄ 📺 🖳 �V 🛒 cc

The Woodman Inn, Colchester Road, Halstead, Essex, CO9 2DY.
Comfortable mock-Tudor public house.
Open: All Year
01787 476218 (also fax)
Mr Redsell
D: £18 **S:** £18
Beds: 1F 1D 1T 1S **Baths:** 1 Sh
🛇 🅿 (12) 📺 🗙 🖳 🛒

Harwich

TM2431   ◀ *The Royal Oak*

Tudor Rose, 124 Fronks Road, Dovercourt, Harwich, CO12 4EQ.
Harwich international port. Seafront, Railway 5 minutes. London 1 hour.
Open: May to Aug
01255 552398
janet@morgan-co12.freeserve.co.uk
D: £17.50 **S:** £20–£30
🛇 🅿 (2) ⁵⁄₄ 📺 🖳 �V 🛒

Henham

TL5428   ◀ *The Crown, The Cock*

Roblin, Carters Lane, Henham, Bishop's Stortford, Herts, CM22 6AQ.
Family home, large garden, lovely country village quiet setting.
Open: April to Nov
01279 850370 (also fax)
Mrs Burgess
D: £20 **S:** £22.50
Beds: 1D 1T **Baths:** 1 Sh
🛇 (8) ⁵⁄₄ 📺 🖳 🛒

Bacons Cottage, Crow Street, Henham, Bishops Stortford, Herts, CM22 6AG.
Thatched cottage in picturesque setting near Stansted Airport, charming village.
Open: All Year (not Xmas)
01279 850754 Mrs Philpot
D: £16–£18 **S:** £18–£22
Beds: 1D 1S **Baths:** 1 En
🅿 (1) ⁵⁄₄ 🖳 🛒

High Easter

TL6214

The Cock & Bell, The Street, High Easter, Chelmsford, Essex, CM1 4QW.
14th Century former Coaching Inn - operating as charming Guest House.
Open: All Year (not Xmas/New Year)
01245 231296 A Steel
D: £19.50–£24.50 **S:** £22.50–£27.50
Beds: 2D 1F 1S **Baths:** 2 En 1 Sh
🅿 📺 🗙 🖳 �V 🛒

High Garrett

TL7726

Hare & Hounds, High Garrett, Braintree, Essex, CM7 5NT.
A friendly welcome and hearty breakfast awaits all that stay at the Hare and Hounds.
Open: All Year
01376 324430 J Bowyer
D: £22–£50 **S:** £22–£50
Beds: 1F 1D 2T 1S **Baths:** 3 En 1 Sh
🛇 🅿 (20) 📺 🛏 🗙 🖳 �V 🛒 cc

Highwood

TL6404   ◀ *Bull*

Wards Farm, Loves Green, Highwood Road, Highwood, Chelmsford, Essex, CM1 3QJ.
Traditional oak beamed 16th century farmhouse, moated grounds, log fires.
Open: March to Dec
01245 248812 Mrs Barton
D: £22.50 **S:** £23–£25
Beds: 1T 1D
🛇 (101) 🅿 (8) 📺 🛏 🗙 🖳 �V 🛒

Holland-on-Sea

TM1915   ◀ *Kingscliffe Hotel, Oakwood Inn*

Devonia, 46 Brighton Road, Holland-on-Sea, Clacton-on-Sea, Essex, CO15 1SR.
Open: All Year
01255 812548 Mrs Davies
ray@davis2065.freeserve.co.uk
D: £16–£18 **S:** £20–£25
Beds: 1F 1T 1D **Baths:** 2 En 1 Pr
🛇 🅿 (2) ⁵⁄₄ 📺 🛏 🗙 🖳 �V 🛒 ᴅ
Detached bungalow in quiet location with off road parking. 200m from sandy beach, 5 minutes walk to Holland Haven Country Park and nearby country Inn. Clacton Pier 5 minutes by car. Ground floor ensuite rooms. Homely with good breakfasts.

Kingscliffe Hotel, Kings Parade, Holland-on-Sea, Clacton on Sea, Essex, CO15 5HT.
The premier hotel on the Tendring Peninsula. Superb clifftop views and assured comfort.
Open: All Year
01255 812343 J R Cottrell
Fax: 01255 812271
D: £33.50–£43.50 **S:** £56–£77
Beds: 10D 1T 3S **Baths:** 14 En
🛇 🅿 (70) ⁵⁄₄ 📺 🗙 🖳 �V ✳ 🛒 cc

Kelvedon

TL8518   ◀ *Sun Inn*

Highfields Farm, Kelvedon, Colchester, Essex, CO5 9BJ.
Farmhouse in quiet countryside location, convenient for A12 and London.
Open: All Year
Grades: ETC 3 Diamond
01376 570334 (also fax)
Mrs Bunting
D: £22 **S:** £22–£24
Beds: 1D 2T **Baths:** 2 En 1 Pr
🛇 🅿 (4) ⁵⁄₄ 📺 🛏 🖳 �V 🛒

Kelvedon Hatch

TQ5799   🍺 *Dog & Partridge, Eagle*

57 Great Fox Meadow, *Kelvedon Hatch, Brentwood, Essex, CM15 0AX.*
Homely friendly clean comfortable overlooking farmlands. 4 miles from Brentwood and Ongar.
Open: All Year (not Xmas)
01277 374659 Mrs Maguire
D: £16–£21 **S:** £16–£21
Beds: 1D 1S **Baths:** 1 Sh
🛇 (3) 🅿 (2) 🗶 📺 🎂 🕭

Langham

TM0233   🍺 *Shepherd & Dog*

Oak Apple Farm, *Greyhound Hill, Langham, Colchester, Essex, CO4 5QF.*
Comfortable farmhouse tastefully decorated with large attractive garden.
Open: All Year (not Xmas)
Grades: ETC 4 Diamond
01206 272234 Mrs Helliwell
rosie@oakapplefarm.fsnet.co.uk
D: fr £22 **S:** fr £22
Beds: 2T 1S **Baths:** 1 Sh
🛇 🅿 (6) 📺 🎂 📼 🕭

Latchingdon

TL8800   🍺 *Red Lion, Black Lion*

Neptune Cafe Motel, *Burnham Road, Latchingdon, Chelmsford, Essex, CM3 6EX.*
Open: All Year
Grades: ETC 2 Diamond, AA 2 Diamond
01621 740770 Mr Lloyd
D: fr £17.50 **S:** fr £25
Beds: 4F 4D 2T 10S **Baths:** 10 En 2 Pr 1 Sh
🛇 🅿 (40) 🗶 📺 🍴 🎂 📼 🕭 🕭 1
Cafe motel, luxury chalets adjoining. Close to boating and fishing areas, golfing and horse riding close by. Lovely rural setting with grand views.

Little Bentley

TM1125   🍺 *Bricklayers Arms*

Bentley Manor, *Little Bentley, Colchester, Essex, CO7 8SE.*
C15th manor house, close to Colchester, 15 mins port of Harwich.
Open: All Year
01206 250622 Mrs Dyson
Fax: 01206 251820
ngd@freenet.co.uk
D: £20–£22 **S:** £24–£26
Beds: 1F 1S 1T **Baths:** 2 En
🛇 🅿 🗶 📺 🎂 🕭

Loughton

TQ4396   🍺 *Plume & Feather, The Wheatsheaf*

9 Garden Way, *Loughton, Essex, IG10 2SF.*
Large private house situated on the edge of Epping Forest.
Open: All Year
Grades: ETC 3 Diamond
020 8508 6134 Mrs Thein
D: £18–£20 **S:** £20–£25
Beds: 1D 1T 1S **Baths:** 1 Sh
🛇 🅿 (3) 🗶 📺 🎂 🕭

Manningtree

TM1031   🍺 *Village Maid*

Dairy House Farm, *Bradfield Road, Wix, Manningtree, Essex, CO11 2SR.*
Spacious quality, rural accommodation. A really relaxing place to stay.
Open: All Year (not Xmas)
Grades: ETC 4 Diamond, Gold
01255 870322 Mrs Whitworth
Fax: 01255 870186
D: £18.50–£20 **S:** £26
Beds: 1D 2T **Baths:** 2 En 1 Pr
🛇 (12) 🅿 (4) 📺 🎂 📼 🕭

Margaret Roding

TL5912

Greys, *Ongar Road, Margaret Roding, Great Dunmow, Essex, CM6 1QR.*
Old beamed cottage, pleasantly situated amidst our farmland tiny village.
Open: All Year (not Xmas)
Grades: ETC 3 Diamond, AA 3 Diamond
01245 231509 Mrs Matthews
D: fr £22 **S:** fr £23
Beds: 2D 1T **Baths:** 1 Sh
🛇 (10) 🅿 (3) 🗶 📺 🎂

Maylandsea

TL9002   🍺 *Maryland Mill, Black Lion*

25 West Avenue, *Maylandsea, Chelmsford, Essex, CM3 6AE.*
Modern detached private residence, country views, few minutes to sailing facilities.
Open: All Year (not Xmas/New Year)
01621 740972 Mrs Clark
Fax: 01621 740945
D: £17–£19 **S:** £17–£19
Beds: 1D 1T **Baths:** 1 Pr
🛇 (3) 🅿 (5) 🗶 📺 🗶 🎂 🕭

Messing

TL8918

Crispin's, *The Street, Messing, Colchester, Essex, CO5 9TR.*
Candle-lit Elizabethan restaurant with beamed rooms, lounge and secluded garden.
Open: All Year
01621 815868 D: £24.75 **S:** £30
Beds: 1F 1D **Baths:** 2 En

Mountnessing

TQ6297   🍺 *George & Dragon, Prince of Wales, Plough*

Millers, *Thoby Lane, Mountnessing, Brentwood, Essex, CM15 0TD.*
Beautiful house and garden overlooking countryside close to A12, 10 mins M25.
Open: All Year
01277 354595 Mrs Stacey
D: £25 **S:** £30
Beds: 1F 2T **Baths:** 1 Pr
🛇 🅿 🗶 📺 🎂 🕭

Planning a longer stay? Always ask for any special rates

All details shown are as supplied by B&B owners in Autumn 2000

Radwinter

TL6037   🍺 *Plough Inn*

The Plough Inn, *Sampford Road, Radwinter, Saffron Walden, Essex, CB10 2TL.*
C17th village inn providing home-cooked food, fresh fish a speciality.
Open: All Year
01799 599222 Fax: 01799 599161
D: £25 **S:** £50
Beds: 2D 1T **Baths:** 3 Pr
🛇 🅿 (40) 🗶 📺 🍴 🗶 🎂 🕭 🕭 cc

Rettendon Common

TQ7796   🍺 *Bell, Wheatsheaf, Hawk*

Crossways, *Main Road, Rettendon Common, Chelmsford, Essex, CM3 8DY.*
Secluded home set well back from A130, dual carriageway.
Open: All Year (not Xmas)
Grades: ETC 3 Diamond
01245 400539 Mr Graham
Fax: 01245 400127
crossways@somnific.freeserve.co.uk
D: £20 **S:** £20–£25
Beds: 1T **Baths:** 1 Pr
🅿 (3) 🗶 📺 🍴 🎂 🕭 🕭 3

Saffron Walden

TL5438   🍺 *Crown, Eight Bells, Rose & Crown, White Hart*

Rowley Hill Lodge, *Little Walden Road, Saffron Walden, Essex, CB10 1UZ.*
C19th farm lodge thoughtfully enlarged. Both bedrooms with baths & power showers. **Open:** All Year (not Xmas)
Grades: ETC 4 Diamond
01799 525975 Mr & Mrs Haslam
Fax: 01799 516622
eh@clara.net
D: fr £24 **S:** fr £28
Beds: 1D 1T **Baths:** 2 Pr
🛇 🅿 (4) 📺 🎂 📼 🕭

Archway Guest House, *Church Street, Saffron Walden, Essex, CB10 1JW.*
Unique house decorated with antiques, toys and rock & pop memorabilia.
Open: All Year
Grades: ETC 4 Diamond
01799 501500 F Miles
D: £25–£30 **S:** £30–£40
Beds: 1F 2D 2T 1S **Baths:** 3 En 1 Pr 1 Sh
🛇 🅿 (3) 📺 🍴 🎂 📼 🕭

Ashleigh House, *7 Farmadine Grove, Saffron Walden, Essex, CB11 3DR.*
Pleasant house close to town centre. Comfortable rooms. Quiet location.
Open: All Year
Grades: ETC 4 Diamond
01799 513611 Mrs Gilder
deborah@annglider.fsnet.co.uk
D: £18–£19 **S:** £20–£24
Beds: 1D 1T 2S **Baths:** 1 Pr 1 Sh
🛇 (6) 🅿 (5) 🗶 📺 🎂 📼 🕭

Cobblers, *Bartow Road, Ashdon, Saffron Walden, Essex, CB10 2HR.*
Peaceful place, warm welcome, relaxing rooms, bountiful breakfasts, great garden!
Open: All Year (not Xmas)
Grades: ETC 4 Diamond
01799 584666 Mrs Slater
cobblers@ashdon2000.freeserve.co.uk
D: £20 **S:** £20–£25
Beds: 2D **Baths:** 1 En 1 Pr
♿ (3) 🅿 (4) 📺 ⛛ 🖤 🎲 👶

10 Victoria Avenue, *Saffron Walden, Essex, CB11 3AE.*
Detached house, one hundred years old. Lock up for bicycles. On street parking.
Open: All Year
Grades: ETC 2 Diamond
01799 525923 Mrs Gilder
D: £16 **S:** £16
Beds: 1T 3S **Baths:** 1 Sh
♿ ⛛ 📺 🖤 🎲 👶

Newdegate House, *Howlett End, Wimbish, Saffron Walden, Essex, CB10 2XW.*
Warm welcome, convenient for Duxford War Museum, Cambridge, Stansted Airport.
Open: All Year (not Xmas)
Grades: ETC 4 Diamond, Silver
01799 599748 (also fax)
Mr & Mrs Haigh
D: £17–£20 **S:** £24–£29.50
Beds: 1D 1T **Baths:** 1 En 1 Pr
♿ (10) 🅿 (10) ⛛ 📺 🖤 🎲 👶

1 Gunters Cottages, *Thaxted Road, Saffron Walden, Essex, CB10 2UT.*
Quiet comfortable accommodation. Indoor heated swimming pool. Friendly welcome.
Open: All Year (not Xmas)
01799 522091 Mrs Goddard
D: fr £19.50 **S:** fr £25
Beds: 1D **Baths:** 1 Pr
🅿 (4) ⛛ 📺 🖤 👶

TL5638   🏚 *The Plough*

Tipswains, *Cole End, Sewards End, Saffron Walden, Essex, CB10 2LJ.*
Beautiful Listed C17th thatched cottage situated in 1-acre garden surrounded by farmland. **Open:** All Year (not Xmas)
01799 523911 Mrs Dighton
D: £20–£25 **S:** £25–£28
Beds: 2D **Baths:** 2 Pr
♿ (1) 🅿 (5) ⛛ 📺 🖤 👶

TL7734   🏚 *Bell Castle, Wjite Horse*

Hedingham Antiques, *100 Swan Street, Sible Hedingham, Halstead, Essex, CO9 3HP.*
Victorian house and shop combined in centre of busy village.
Open: All Year (not Xmas)
Grades: ETC 3 Diamond
01787 460360 Mrs Patterson
Fax: 01787 469109
patriciapatterson@totalise.co.uk
D: £20 **S:** £22.50
Beds: 1D 2T **Baths:** 3 En
♿ 🅿 (4) 📺 🖤 🎲 👶

TQ8786   🏚 *Hamlet, Cricketers, Last Post*

Retreat Guest House, *12 Canewdon Road, Westcliff-on-Sea, Southend-on-Sea, Essex, SS0 7NE.*
Open: All Year **Grades:** ETC 3 Diamond
01702 348217 Mr & Mrs Bartholomew
Fax: 01702 391179
retreatguesthouse.co.uk@tinyworld.co.uk
D: £22.50–£25 **S:** £25–£40
Beds: 1F 5D 3T 4S **Baths:** 6 En 1 Pr 2 Sh
♿ 🅿 (7) 📺 ⛛ 🖤 🎲 👶
Quality accommodation, ideally situated in the quieter, more picturesque side of Southend. Close to the Cliff's Pavilion, Westcliff Station & near to the seafront leading to Southend's main attractions. Most rooms ensuite. Some to ground floor - Private secure parking.

Terrace Hotel, *8 Royal Terrace, Southend-on-Sea, Essex, SS1 1DY.*
Grade II Listed overlooking estuary. Close to high street and sea front.
Open: All Year
Grades: AA 3 Diamond, RAC 3 Diamond
01702 348143 (also fax) Mr & Mrs Beck
D: £17–£20 **S:** £20–£21
Beds: 2F 3D 1T 3S **Baths:** 2 En 3 Pr 6 Sh
♿ (3) 📺 🖤 🎲 👶

TQ9599

Saxegate Guest House, *44 North Street, Southminster, Essex, CM0 7DG.*
Victorian home within easy reach of Maldon and Burnham-on-Crouch.
Open: All Year **Grades:** ETC 3 Diamond
01621 773180 Mrs Battson
Fax: 01621 774116
D: £18–£25 **S:** £18–£25
Beds: 1F 2T 1D **Baths:** 2 En 1 Sh
♿ 🅿 (7) 📺 ✕ 🖤 🎲 👶 ♿

TL6841   🏚 *Fox & Hounds*

Yew Tree House, *15 Chapel Street, Steeple Bumpstead, Haverhill, Suffolk, CB9 7DQ.*
Victorian home offering superior accommodation, breakfast menu. Centre of village.
Open: All Year
Grades: ETC 3 Diamond
01440 730364 (also fax)
Mrs Stirling
D: £22 **S:** £25–£27
Beds: 1D 1T **Baths:** 2 En
♿ (2) 🅿 (2) 📺 ✕ 🖤 🎲 👶

TL7614   🏚 *Square & Compass*

Old Bakery, *Waltham Road, Terling, Chelmsford, Essex, CM3 2QR.*
Converted bakery in quiet unspoilt village on the Essex Way.
Open: All Year
Grades: ETC 4 Diamond
01245 233363 Mrs Lewis
D: £22.50–£25 **S:** £22.50–£25
Beds: 1T 1D **Baths:** 2 En
♿ (10) 🅿 (2) ⛛ 📺 🖤 👶 ♿

TL9011   🏚 *The Bell, The Compasses*

Wicks Manor Farm, *Witham Road, Tolleshunt Major, Maldon, Essex, CM9 8JU.*
Comfortable moated farmhouse with large garden near Blackwater Estuary. Working farm.
Open: All Year (not Xmas/New Year)
Grades: ETC 4 Diamond
01621 860629 (also fax)
Mrs Howie
D: £18 **S:** £20
Beds: 1D **Baths:** 1 Pr
♿ 🅿 ⛛ 🖤 📺 🎲 👶

TL3800   🏚 *The Volunteer*

Ivydene Cottage, *Woodgreen Road, Waltham Abbey, EN9 3SD.*
Historic town and surroundings, canals and local interests.
Open: All Year (not Xmas)
01992 716082 (also fax)
Mrs Oatham
D: £20–£35 **S:** £25
Beds: 2T 1D **Baths:** 2 En 2 Sh
🅿 (5) ⛛ 📺 ✕ 🖤 🎲 👶

TL9627   🏚 *Queens Head, White Hart, Treble Tile*

The Old Post House, *10 Colchester Road, West Bergholt, Colchester, Essex, CO6 3JG.*
Large Victorian private house, warm welcome, quiet secluded garden.
Open: All Year
Grades: ETC 3 Diamond
01206 240379 Mrs Brown
Fax: 01206 243301
D: £20–£25 **S:** fr £20
Beds: 1F 1D 1T **Baths:** 1 En 1 Sh
♿ (1) 🅿 (3) 📺 🖤 👶

TM0112   🏚 *Willow Lodge, Blackwater Hotel*

Hazel Oak, *28 Seaview Avenue, West Mersea, Colchester, Essex, CO5 8HE.*
A quiet residential family home, situated in tree-lined avenue leading to waterfront.
Open: All Year (not Xmas)
Grades: ETC 3 Diamond
01206 383030 (also fax)
Mrs Blackmore
ann.blackmore@btinternet.com
D: £22–£25 **S:** £25–£30
Beds: 1D 1T **Baths:** 1 En 1 Pr
♿ 🅿 (2) ⛛ 📺 🖤 🎲

Blackwater Hotel, *20-22 Church Road, West Mersea, Colchester, Essex, CO5 8QH.*
Ideal for sailing, fishing, birdwatching. Friendly informal atmosphere, excellent food.
Open: All Year (not Xmas)
01206 383338 M & D Warring
Fax: 01206 383038
blackwaterhotel@dial.pipex.com
D: £25–£30 **S:** £35–£50
Beds: 2F 4D 2T 1S **Baths:** 6 En 3 Pr
🅿 (6) ⛛ 📺 🖤 ✕ 🎲 👶 CC

Wethersfield

TL7131   *George, Dog Inn, Bull*

Spicers Farm, *Rotten End, Wethersfield, Braintree, Essex, CM7 4AL.*
Attractive farmhouse in tranquil surroundings, lovely views. Rooms ensuite.
Open: All Year (not Xmas)
Grades: ETC 4 Diamond, AA 4 Diamond
01371 851021 (also fax) Mrs Douse
spicers.farm@talk21.com
D: £18.50–£19.50 **S:** £26–£30
Beds: 1D 2T **Baths:** 3 Pr
🛏 🅿 (6) 🛏 📺 🛒 🛗 ☕

Brook Farm, *Wethersfield, Braintree, Essex, CM7 4BX.*
Beautiful historic farmhouse, spacious rooms, secure parking, warm welcome.
Open: All Year
01371 850284 Mrs Butler
D: £17.50 **S:** £17.50
Beds: 1F 1D 1T **Baths:** 2 Pr
🛏 🅿 (6) 🛏 📺 🛒 🛗 ✳ ☕

White Colne

TM8729

Larkswood, *32 Colchester Road, White Colne, Colchester, Essex, CO6 2PN.*
Pretty chalet bungalow in Colne Valley west of Colchester.
Open: All Year **Grades:** ETC 3 Diamond
01787 224362 Mr Fewster
D: £17.50–£19 **S:** £25
Beds: 1T **Baths:** 1 En
🅿 (2) 📺 🛗 ☕

Wimbish

TL5837   *White Hart*

Newdegate House, *Howlett End, Wimbish, Saffron Walden, Essex, CB10 2XW.*
Warm welcome, convenient for Duxford War Museum, Cambridge, Stansted Airport.
Open: All Year (not Xmas)
Grades: ETC 4 Diamond, Silver
01799 599748 (also fax)
Mr & Mrs Haigh
D: £17–£20 **S:** £24–£29.50
Beds: 1D 1T **Baths:** 1 En 1 Pr
🛏 (10) 🅿 (10) 🛏 📺 🛒 🛗 ☕

Wivenhoe

TM0421   *William Boosey, Black Buoy Pub*

2 Alma Street, *Wivenhoe, Colchester, Essex, CO7 9DL.*
Grade II Listed early Victorian house, close to River Colne.
Open: All Year (not Xmas)
01245 380705 Mrs Tritton
D: £21–£22.50 **S:** £21.50–£23
Beds: 1T 1S **Baths:** 1 Sh
🛏 (9) 🅿 (4) 📺 ✕ 🛒 🛗 ☕

BATHROOMS

Pr - Private

Sh - Shared

En - Ensuite

National Grid References are for villages, towns and cities – not for individual houses

Wix

TM1628   *Village Maid*

Dairy House Farm, *Bradfield Road, Wix, Manningtree, Essex, CO11 2SR.*
Spacious quality, rural accommodation. A really relaxing place to stay.
Open: All Year (not Xmas)
Grades: ETC 4 Diamond, Gold
01255 870322 Mrs Whitworth
Fax: 01255 870186
D: £18.50–£20 **S:** £26
Beds: 1D 2T **Baths:** 2 En 1 Pr
🛏 (12) 🅿 (4) 📺 🛒 🛗 ☕

Woodham Mortimer

TL8104   *Hurdlemakers' Arms*

Little Owls, *Post Office Road, Woodham Mortimer, Maldon, Essex, CM9 6ST.*
Open: All Year
Grades: ETC 3 Diamond
01245 224355 (also fax)
Mrs Bush
the.bushes@virgin.net
D: £20–£25 **S:** £25–£30
Beds: 1F 1T 1D **Baths:** 2 Sh
🛏 🅿 (10) 🛏 📺 🛏 ✕ 🛒 🛗 ☕
Panoramic views over surrounding countryside. Private indoor swimming pool.

Gloucestershire

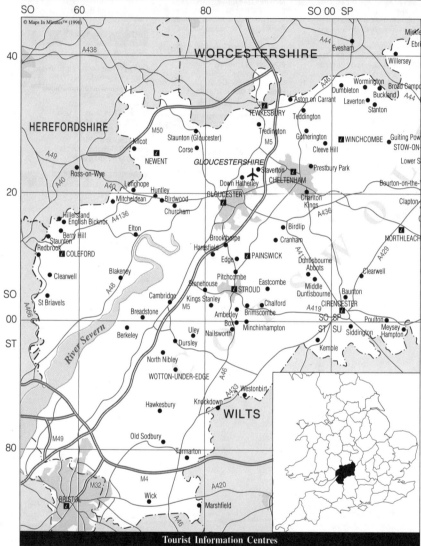

Tourist Information Centres

77 Promenade, **Cheltenham**, Glos, GL50 1PP, 01242 522878.

High Street, **Chipping Campden**, Glos, GL55 6AT, 01386 841206.

Corn Hall, Market Place, **Cirencester**, Glos, GL7 2NW, 01285 654180.

27 Market Place, **Coleford**, Glos, GL16 8AE, 01594 836307.

St Michaels Tower, The Cross, **Gloucester**, Glos, GL1 1PD, 01452 421188.

The Library, High Street, **Newent**, Glos, GL18 1AS, 01531 822145.

Cotswold Countryside Collection, **Northleach**, Glos, GL54 3JH, 01451 860715 (Easter to Oct).

The Library, Stroud Road, **Painswick**, Stroud, Glos, GL6 6DT, 01452 813552 (Easter to Oct).

Hollis House, The Square, **Stow-on-the-Wold**, Cheltenham, Glos, GL54 1AF, 01451 831082.

St Nicholas Church, St Nicholas Street, **Bristol**, BSI 1UE, 0117 926 0767

Subscription Rooms, George Street, **Stroud**, Glos, GL5 1AE, 01453 765768.

The Old Court House, 63 Long Street, **Tetbury**, Glos, GL8 8AA, 01666 503552 (Easter to Oct).

64 Barton Street, **Tewkesbury**, Glos, GL20 5PX, 01684 295027.

Town Hall, High Street, **Winchcombe**, Cheltenham, Glos, GL54 5LJ, 01242 602925 (Easter to Oct).

Amberley

SO8501 ◁ *The Black Horse, Amberley Inn*

High Tumps, *St. Chloe Green, Amberley, Stroud, Glos, GL5 5AR.*
Modest secluded family home offers bed and breakfast accommodation in self contained annexe.
Open: All Year
Grades: ETC 4 Diamond
01453 873584 Fax: 01453 873587
dakavic@high-tumps.freeserve.co.uk
D: £15–£17 **S:** £15–£17
Beds: 1T **Baths:** 1 En
�� 🏢 ♨

Aston Magna

SP1935 ◁ *Ebrington Arms*

Bran Mill Cottage, *Aston Magna, Moreton in Marsh, Glos, GL56 9QP.*
Small traditional B&B in peaceful Cotswold cottage. Friendly, welcoming, homely.
Open: All Year (not Xmas)
Grades: ETC 3 Diamond
01386 593517
enquiries@branmillcottage.co.uk
D: £16–£18 **S:** £19–£25
Beds: 1D 1T 1S **Baths:** 1 Pr 1 Sh
🢢 (14) 🅿 (3) ⼐ 🇹🇻 🏢 ♨

Aston on Carrant

SO9434 ◁ *Fox & Hounds*

Wisteria Cottage, *Aston on Carrant, Tewkesbury, Glos, GL20 8HL.*
Pretty rural hamlet, traditional country breakfast, excellent walking/touring area.
Open: Easter to Oct
01684 772357 Mrs Allen
D: £18–£20 **S:** £22–£25
Beds: 1D 1T **Baths:** 1 En 1 Pr
🢢 🅿 (3) ⼐ 🇹🇻 ♞ ♨

Baunton

SP0204 ◁ *Hare & Hounds*

Windrush, *Baunton, Cirencester, Glos, GL7 7BA.*
Detached house in large gardens. Beautiful views over Cotswold countryside.
Open: All Year (not Xmas)
01285 655942 (also fax)
S J Rees
D: £20–£25 **S:** £20–£30
Beds: 1F 1D 1T **Baths:** 1 En 1 Pr 1 Sh
🢢 🅿 (4) ⼐ 🇹🇻 🏢 🇻 ♨

Berkeley

ST6899 ◁ *Black Horse North Nibley, Stage Coach*

Pickwick Farm, *Berkeley, Glos, GL13 9EU.*
Ensuite annexe room overlooks large garden, views to Cotswolds, golf nearby.
Open: All Year (not Xmas)
Grades: ETC 3 Diamond
01453 810241
Mrs Jordan
pickwick@supanet.com
D: £18–£20 **S:** £18–£19
Beds: 1F 1D 1T **Baths:** 1 En 1 Sh
🢢 (2) 🅿 (4) ⼐ 🇹🇻 🏢 🇻 ♨

Berry Hill

SO5712 ◁ *Kings Head*

Westlands House, *20 Grove Road, Berry Hill, Coleford, Glos, GL16 8QY.*
Cottage close to forest walks, historic sites, outdoor pursuits.
Open: All Year (not Xmas)
01594 837143
Mrs Atherley
D: £15 **S:** £15
Beds: 1D 1T **Baths:** 1 Sh
🢢 🅿 (2) ⼐ ♞ 🏢 ♨

Birdlip

SO9214 ◁ *Air Balloon*

Beechmount, *Birdlip, Gloucester, GL4 8JH.*
Open: All Year
Grades: ETC 3 Diamond
01452 862262 (also fax)
Mrs Carter
thebeachmount@breathemail.net
D: £16–£21 **S:** £16–£32
Beds: 2F 2D 2T **Baths:** 2 En 2 Sh
🢢 🅿 (7) ⼐ 🇹🇻 ✕ 🏢 🇻 ♨ cc
Warm welcome in family-run guest house. Personal attention. Ideal centre for walking, touring.

Birdwood

SO7418 ◁ *Severn Bore*

Birdwood Villa Farm, *Main Road, Birdwood, Huntley, Gloucester, GL19 3EQ.*
Open: All Year
Grades: ETC 2 Diamond
01452 750451 M King
D: £20–£25 **S:** £21–£26
Beds: 1F 1D **Baths:** 2 En
🢢 🅿 (8) ⼐ 🇹🇻 ♞ 🏢 🇻 cc
115-year-old farmhouse on attractive arable farm with views of Cotswold and Forest of Dean. Plenty of local pubs for good quality food and drink. An ideal base for many attraction in the Cotswold and the Forest of Dean.

Blakeney

SO6706 ◁ *New Inn, Red Hart*

Viney Hill Country Guesthouse, *Blakeney, Glos, GL15 4LT.*
A period house set in the quiet Gloucestershire countryside.
Open: All Year **Grades:** ETC 4 Diamond
01594 516000 Mr Humphreys
Fax: 01594 516018
info@vineyhill.co.uk
D: £26–£32 **S:** fr £35
Beds: 4D 2T **Baths:** 6 En
🢢 🅿 (7) ⼐ 🇹🇻 ✕ 🏢 🇻 ✳ ♨ cc

Blockley

SP1634 ◁ *Great Western Inn, Crown Hotel*

Tudor House, *High Street, Blockley, Moreton in Marsh, Glos, GL56 9EX.*
Excellent walking, gardens to visit.
Open: All Year (not Xmas)
01386 700356 Mrs Thompson
D: £25–£30 **S:** £25–£30
Beds: 1D 1T **Baths:** 1 Sh
🢢 (10) 🅿 (2) ⼐ 🇹🇻 🏢 ♨

Arreton Guest House, *Station Road, Blockley, Moreton-in-Marsh, Glos, GL56 6DT.*
Open: All Year
Grades: ETC 4 Diamond, AA 4 Diamond
01386 701077 (also fax)
bandb@arreton.demon.co.uk
D: £20–£22 **S:** £28–£30
Beds: 1F 1D 1T **Baths:** 3 En
🢢 🅿 ⼐ 🇹🇻 🏢 🇻 ♨ ♨
Arreton is situated in the north Cotswold in the village of Blockley. Once famous in the 1700's for its silk trade, Arreton dates from 1600 being built of Mellow Cotswold stone.

Park Farm, *Blockley, Moreton in Marsh,*
Glos, GL56 9TA.
Beautiful old farmhouse, idyllic location,
easy walk village. Warm welcome.
Open: All Year
01386 700266 Mr & Mrs Dee
D: fr £17 **S:** fr £17
Beds: 1D 1T 2S **Baths:** 1 Sh
🛇 🅿 (6) ⚲ 📺 �🛉 Ⓥ ♨

The Malins, *21 Station Road, Blockley,*
Moreton In Marsh, Glos, GL56 9ED.
Attractive Cotswold stone house, many
facilities, friendly hosts.
Open: All Year
Grades: ETC 3 Diamond
01386 700402 (also fax)
Mrs Malin
D: fr £18 **S:** fr £25
Beds: 1D 2T **Baths:** 3 Pr
🛇 🅿 (5) ⚲ 📺 🛏 Ⓥ ❋ ♨

Bourton-on-the-Water

SP1620   ♠ *Plough, Kingsbridge Inn, Mouse*
Trap Inn, Coach & Horses, Duke of Wellington

Lansdowne House, *Lansdowne,*
Bourton-on-the-Water, Cheltenham, Glos,
GL54 2AT.
Tastefully furnished ensuite accom-
modation. Combination of old and
antique furniture.
Open: All Year (not Xmas)
Grades: ETC 4 Diamond
01451 820812 Mrs Garwood
Fax: 01451 822484
lansdowne-house@ukf.net
D: £17.50–£20 **S:** £30–£35
Beds: 1F 2D **Baths:** 3 En
🛇 🅿 (4) 📺 📖 Ⓥ ♨

6 Moore Road, *Bourton-on-the-Water,*
Cheltenham, Glos, GL54 2AZ.
Cotswold stone house, quiet road, yards
to village, peaceful garden.
Open: Feb to Dec
01451 820767 Mrs Mustoe
D: £19–£21 **S:** £20–£25
Beds: 1D 1T **Baths:** 1 En 1 Pr
🛇 (5) 🅿 (3) ⚲ 📺 🛏 📖 Ⓥ ♨

Holly House, *Station Road, Bourton-*
on-the-Water, Cheltenham, Glos, GL54 2ER.
Spacious Cotswold style house. Breakfast
in conservatory overlooking delightful
gardens.
Open: Feb to Oct
Grades: ETC 4 Diamond
01451 821302 Mr Stanfield
D: £20–£25 **S:** £28–£32
Beds: 2D 1T 1S **Baths:** 4 En
🛇 🅿 (6) ⚲ 📺 ✕ 📖 Ⓥ ♨

Lansdowne Villa Guest House,
Bourton-on-the-Water, Cheltenham, Glos,
GL54 2AR.
This large, detached Cotswold stone
house stands at the end of this beautiful
village.
Open: Feb to Dec
01451 820673 Mr & Mrs Harris
Fax: 01451 822099
D: fr £24 **S:** fr £32
Beds: 8D 2T 2S **Baths:** 12 En
🛇 🅿 (14) ⚲ 📺 ✕ 📖 ♨

Box

SO8600

Saint Giles, *Box, Minchinhampton,*
Stroud, Glos, GL6 9HE.
Attractive C18th Cotswold stone house;
delightful village, quiet, friendly, relaxing.
Open: All Year (not Xmas)
01453 832283
daphne_edwards@hotmail.com
D: fr £17.50 **S:** fr £20
Beds: 1D 1T **Baths:** 1 Pr 1 Sh
🛇 ⚲ 📺 ✕ 📖 Ⓥ ♨

Breadstone

SO7100   ♠ *Prince of Wales, Salmon Inn*

Green Acres Farm Guest House,
Breadstone, Berkeley, Glos, GL13 9HF.
Open: All Year
01453 810348 Ms Evans
Fax: 01453 810799
barbara@greenacresfarm.co.uk
D: £23.50–£26 **S:** £24.50–£26.50
Beds: 2T 2D 2S **Baths:** 6 En
🅿 ⚲ 📺 🛏 📖 ♨ cc
C12th Berkeley Castle. Gloucester
Waterway Museum, Docklands, wild fowl
and wetlands, Bath, Wales, Forest of
Dean, Cotswolds, Bristol. Tranquil setting
in large garden overlooking Welsh Hills
and Cotswolds. Full English breakfast.
Clean and comfortable our promise.

Brimscombe

SO8702   ♠ *Ship Inn*

Brandon Quarhouse, *Brimscombe,*
Chalford, Stroud, Glos, GL5 2RS.
Cotswold hillside house, pretty/
productive garden, exquisite walks, warm
welcome.
Open: All Year (not Xmas/New Year)
01453 883664 Mrs Clapham
D: £19 **S:** £16–£19
Beds: 1T 1S **Baths:** 1 En 1 Sh
🛇 (8) 🅿 (4) ⚲ 📺 🛏 ✕ 📖 Ⓥ ♨

Broad Campden

SP1537   ♠ *Bakers Arms*

Marnic House, *Broad Campden,*
Chipping Campden, Glos, GL55 6UR.
Comfortable, friendly and well furnished
family home. Peacefully situated, scenic
views.
Open: All Year (not Xmas/New Year)
Grades: ETC 4 Diamond, Gold, AA 4
Diamond
01386 840014 Mrs Rawlings
Fax: 01386 840441
marnic@zoom.co.uk
D: £22–£25 **S:** £38–£40
Beds: 2D 1T **Baths:** 2 En 1 Pr
🛇 (10) 🅿 (4) 📺 📖 Ⓥ ♨

Wyldlands, *Broad Campden, Chipping*
Campden, Glos, GL55 6UR.
Cotswold stone house with open views
over countryside in conservation village.
Open: All Year (not Xmas)
01386 840478 Mrs Wadey
Fax: 01386 849031
D: £22 **S:** £28
Beds: 1D 1T 1S **Baths:** 2 En 1 Pr
🛇 🅿 (4) ⚲ 📺 📖 Ⓥ ♨

Brockweir

SO5401   ♠ *Moon & Sixpence*

Honeyfield Farm, *Mill Hill, Brockweir,*
Chepstow, Monmouthshire, NP16 7NN.
Honeyfields Farm is situated on the
outskirts of the historic village of
Brockweir.
Open: All Year
01291 689859 Mr Murphy
D: £17–£21 **S:** £17–£26
Beds: 3T 1S **Baths:** 2 En 3 Sh
🛇 🅿 (6) ⚲ 📺 📖 Ⓥ ❋ ♨

Brookthorpe

SO8312   ♠ *Four Mile House*

Brookthorpe Lodge, *Stroud Road,*
Brookthorpe, Gloucester, GL4 0UQ.
Open: All Year
Grades: ETC 3 Diamond
01452 812645 Mr Bailey
enq@brookthorpelodge.demon.co.uk
D: £20–£27.50 **S:** £31–£33
Beds: 2F 2D 2T 3S **Baths:** 6 En 2 Pr 1 Sh
🛇 🅿 (15) 📺 ✕ 📖 Ⓥ ❋ ♨ ⚿
Licensed family-run three storey Georgian
house in lovely countryside at foot of
Cotswold escarpment, 4 miles from
Gloucester. Close to ski slope, horse
riding and golfing. Good walking country
- ideal base for Cotswolds, Gloucester
docks and cathedral. Separate smoking
area.

Buckland

SP0736   ♠ *Snowshill Arms*

Garretts Farm, *Buckland, Broadway,*
Worcs, WR12 7LY.
Friendly welcome awaits in peaceful
village, near all Cotswolds attractions.
Open: All Year (not Xmas)
01386 852091 (also fax)
Mrs Smith
mytton.smith@virgin.net
D: £20–£30 **S:** £22–£40
Beds: 1T **Baths:** 1 Pr
🛇 🅿 (2) ⚲ 📺 📖 ♨

Cambridge

SO7403   ♠ *Milton Arms, Haymakers, Master*
Mariner, George Inn, Black Bull, Granta Inn, Coach
& Horses, Green Man, Robin Hood, Clarendon
Arms, Free Press, Red Lion, Old Crown, Travellers
Rest, White Horse, The Grapes, Old Spring, The
Volunteer, Browns, Live & Let Live, The Rock,
Cambridge Blue, Crown

Hamden Guest House, *89 High*
Street, Cherry Hinton, Cambridge, CB1 9LU.
Open: All Year
Grades: AA 3 Diamond
01223 413263 Mr Casciano
Fax: 01223 245960
D: £22.50–£25 **S:** £28–£32
Beds: 1F 2D 1T 1S **Baths:** 5 En
🛇 (10) 🅿 (7) ⚲ 📺 📖 ♨ cc
High standard of bed & breakfast
accommodation. All rooms with ensuite
shower. Situated on the outskirts of
Cambridge, short distance from city
centre, approx. 2 miles. Frequent bus
service. Private car park. Local shops,
pubs, restaurants within walking
distance.

Chalford

SO8902 ◁ The Ram, Ragged Cot

Ashleigh House, Bussage, Chalford,
Stroud, Glos, GL6 8AZ.
Detatched house and attractive gardens
in peaceful hillside village location with
parking in grounds
Open: Mar to Nov
01453 883944 Mr Dunsford
Fax: 01453 886931
D: £21–£26 **S:** £28–£33
Beds: 3F 3D 3T **Baths:** 9 En
🛇 (8) ▣ (9) ⊬ 🖾 ✕ 🔲 ⩍

Beechcroft, Brownshill, Chalford,
Stroud, Glos, GL6 8AG.
Quietly situated Edwardian house. Home-
made bread and preserves. Good walking.
Open: All Year
01453 883422 Mrs Salt
D: £18–£22 **S:** £22–£25
Beds: 1D 1T **Baths:** 1 Pr
🛇 ▣ (3) ⊬ 🖾 ✕ 🔲 ⟨V⟩ ⩍

Charfield

ST7191 ◁ Pear Tree, Railway Tavern

Falcon Cottage, 15 Station Road,
Charfield, Wotton-under-Edge, Glos, GL12
8SY.
Convenient for M5, Bath, Bristol,
Cheltenham, Cotswolds, Cotswold Way.
Open: All Year (not Xmas)
Grades: ETC 4 Diamond
01453 843528 Mrs Haddrell
D: £20 **S:** £20
Beds: 2T **Baths:** 1 Sh
🛇 ▣ (2) ⊬ 🖾 🔲 ⟨V⟩ ⩍

Charlton Kings

SO9620 ◁ Ryeworth Inn, Reservoir Inn

Langett, London Road, Cheltenham,
Glos, GL54 4HG.
On Cotswold Way, adjoining large
woodland, super walks, large bungalow.
Open: All Year (not Xmas)
01242 820192 (also fax)
Mr Cox
cox@langett.freeserve.co.uk
D: £18–£20 **S:** £20–£23
Beds: 1D 1T **Baths:** 1 Sh
🛇 (5) ▣ (10) 🖾 🔲 ⟨V⟩ ⩍

Cheltenham

SO9422 ◁ Apple Tree, Bell, Plough, High
Roost, Royal Oak, Kings Arms, Rising Sun, Hewlett
Arms, Flynns, Sherborne Inn, Bentley's

Parkview, 4 Pittville Crescent,
Cheltenham, Glos, GL52 2QZ.
Regency house in Cheltenham - nicest
area. Cotswolds, Sudeley Castle,
Stratford are nearby.
Open: All Year
Grades: ETC 3 Diamond
01242 575567 Mrs Sparrey
jospa@tr250.freeserve.co.uk
D: £20–£25 **S:** £20–£25
Beds: 1F 1T 1S **Baths:** 2 En 2 Sh

Central Hotel, 7-9 Portland Street,
Cheltenham, Glos, GL52 2NZ.
Grade II Listed building in town centre,
one block from shops and Regent Arcade.
Open: All Year
Grades: ETC 3 Diamond
01242 582172 Mr Rouse
D: £22–£28.50 **S:** £27–£37
Beds: 2F 3D 5T 4S **Baths:** 6 En 2 Sh
🛇 ▣ (8) ⊬ 🖾 ✕ 🔲 ⩍ cc

Beaumont House Hotel,
Shurdington Road, Cheltenham, Glos, GL53
0JE.
Relaxed, friendly, peaceful, comfortable,
totally non smoking. Four poster rooms.
Garden.
Open: All Year (not Xmas/New Year)
Grades: ETC 4 Diamond, Silver, AA 4
Diamond, RAC 4 Diamond
01242 245986 Fax: 01242 520044
rocking.horse@virgin.net
D: £30–£40 **S:** £42–£56
Beds: 1F 3T 10D 2S **Baths:** 16 En
🛇 (10) ▣ (16) ⊬ 🖾 🔲 ⩍ cc

Clun House, 4 The Oaks, Up Hatherley,
Cheltenham, Glos, GL51 5TS.
Spacious, modern, quiet house; lounge
available, easy access M5.
Open: All Year (not Xmas)
01242 523255
Mrs Hyde
D: £16–£18 **S:** £16–£18
Beds: 1D 2S **Baths:** 1 Pr 1 Sh
🛇 (10) ▣ (5) ⊬ 🖾 🔲 ⩍

Heron Haye, Cleeve Hill, Cheltenham,
Glos, GL52 3PW.
Quiet location, 3 miles Cheltenham
Racecourse. Comfortable home. Full
English breakfast. Superb views.
Open: All Year
01242 672516 Mr Saunders
dick.whittamore@virgin.net
D: £22.50–£30 **S:** £25–£30
Beds: 2D 1S **Baths:** 1 Sh
▣ (4) ⊬ 🐾 🔲

Crossways Guest House, Oriel
Place, 57 Bath Road, Cheltenham, Glos,
GL53 7LH.
Fine Regency house in the centre of
Cheltenham.
Open: All Year
Grades: ETC 3 Diamond
01242 527683
Mr Lynch
Fax: 01242 577226
cross.ways@btinternet.com
D: £22–£25 **S:** £22–£25
Beds: 3F 1T 1D 1S **Baths:** 3 En 1 Sh
🛇 ⊬ 🖾 🐾 🔲 ⟨V⟩ ⩍ cc

Lonsdale House, Montpellier Drive,
Cheltenham, Glos, GL50 1TX.
Comfortable rooms in Regency house;
easy walk into town centre.
Open: All Year
01242 232379 (also fax)
Mr Mallinson
lonsdalehouse@hotmail.com
D: £20–£24 **S:** £20–£30
Beds: 3F 2D 1T 4S **Baths:** 3 En 2 Pr 2 Sh
🛇 ▣ (6) 🖾 🔲 ⩍ cc

St Michaels Guest House, 4
Montpellier Drive, Cheltenham, Glos, GL50
1TX.
Five minutes' walk from centre. Non
smoking, parking, highly commended.
Open: All Year (not Xmas)
01242 513587 (also fax)
Mrs Perkin
st_michaels_guesthouse@yahoo.com
D: £20–£25 **S:** £27–£45
Beds: 1F 2D 1T **Baths:** 3 En 1 Pr
🛇 ▣ (4) ⊬ 🖾 🔲 ⟨V⟩ ⩍ cc

Strayleaves, 282 Gloucester Road,
Cheltenham, Glos, GL51 7AG.
Conveniently situated for the railway
station and the town centre.
Open: All Year
01242 572303 (also fax)
Mr Andrews
D: £19–£22.50 **S:** £26–£30
Beds: 1F 1D 1T 1S **Baths:** 4 En
🛇 ▣ 🖾 🐾 ✕ 🔲 ⟨V⟩ ⩍

Chipping Campden

SP1539 ◁ Bakers' Arms, Volunteer Inn, King's
Arms, Butchers' Arms, Three Ways, Ebrington
Arms, Wheatsheaf Inn

Holly House, Ebrington, Chipping
Campden, Glos, GL55 6NL.
Open: All Year (not Xmas)
Grades: AA 4 Diamond
01386 593213
Mrs Hutsby
Fax: 01386 593181
D: £21–£24 **S:** £30–£40
Beds: 3F/D/T **Baths:** 3 En
🛇 ▣ (5) ⊬ 🖾 🔲 ⟨V⟩ ⩍
Situated in centre of picturesque
Cotswold village, 2 miles Chipping
Campden & Hidcote Gardens. 11 miles
Stratford, 20 miles Warwick. All rooms
spaciously appointed with Ensuite
facilities. lovely garden room at guest
disposition. Laundry, parking. Local pub
serves meals.

Marnic House, Broad Campden,
Chipping Campden, Glos, GL55 6UR.
Open: All Year (not Xmas/New Year)
Grades: ETC 4 Diamond, Gold, AA 4
Diamond
01386 840014
Mrs Rawlings
Fax: 01386 840441
marnic@zoom.co.uk
D: £22–£25 **S:** £38–£40
Beds: 2D 1T **Baths:** 2 En 1 Pr
🛇 (10) ▣ (4) 🖾 🔲 ⟨V⟩ ⩍
Comfortable, friendly and well furnished
family home. Peacefully situated, scenic
views. Ideal base for touring the
Cotswolds. Bedrooms have full facilities.
Non-smoking, private parking.

The Guest House, Lower High Street,
Chipping Campden, Glos, GL55 6DZ.
Period Cotswold stone cottage, easy
walking to local beauty spots and shops.
Open: Easter to Nov
01386 840163 Mrs Benfield
D: £19–£22 **S:** fr £25
Beds: 1D 1T **Baths:** 2 En
🖾 🐾 🔲 ⩍

Weston Park Farm, *Dovers Hill, Chipping Campden, Glos, GL55 6UW.*
Penod farmhouse in magnificent setting, adjacent NT, on small farm.
Open: All Year
01386 840835 Mr Whitehouse
D: £25 **S:** £25
Beds: 1F 1D **Baths:** 1 En
🛏 🅿 📺 ⬛ ☑ ☟

Catbrook House, *Catbrook, Chipping Campden, Glos, GL55 6DE.*
Quietly situated with lovely views over fields & meadows, only 10 mins walk town centre.
Open: All Year (not Xmas)
01386 841499 Mrs Klein
m.klein@virgin.net
D: £20.50–£24.50 **S:** £35–£44
Beds: 2D 1T **Baths:** 1 En 2 Pr
🛏 (9) 🅿 (3) ⬛ ☟

Churcham

SO7618   🍴 *Red Lion, Severn Bore*

Edgewood House, *Churcham, Gloucester, GL2 8AA.*
Large country house overlooking secluded gardens. Comfortable rooms , generous breakfasts.
Open: All Year (not Xmas)
Grades: AA 4 Diamond
01452 750232 D: £23–£25 **S:** £25–£35
Beds: 1F 1D 1T **Baths:** 2 En 1 Pr
🛏 (10) 🅿 (6) ⬛ 📺 ⬛ ☑ ☟

Cirencester

SP0202   🍴 *Plough, Golden Cross, Crown Of Crucis, Falcon, Wagon & Horses, Odd Fellows, Drillman, Talbot*

Sprucewood, *Elf Meadow, Poulton, Cirencester, Glos, GL7 5HQ.*
Quiet, homely, comfortable. Open views. Warm, friendly welcome awaits you.
Open: All Year (not Xmas)
Grades: ETC 4 Diamond
01285 851351 (also fax)
Mr & Mrs Walker
D: £16–£20 **S:** £22–£25
Beds: 1D 1T 1S **Baths:** 1 Sh
🛏 🅿 (4) ⬛ 📺 ⬛ ☑ ☟

Sunset, *Baunton Lane, Cirencester, Glos, GL7 2NQ.*
Quiet, small family house conveniently situated for touring the Cotswolds.
Open: Easter to Oct
Grades: ETC 3 Diamond
01285 654822 Mrs Castle
D: £16–£17 **S:** £16–£17
Beds: 1T 2S **Baths:** 1 Sh
🛏 (5) 🅿 (5) ⬛ 📺 ⬛ ☑ ☟

Chesil Rocks, *Baunton Lane, Cirencester, Glos, GL7 2LL.*
Pleasant friendly home, quiet lane. Access town & country walks.
Open: All Year (not Xmas)
Grades: ETC 3 Diamond
01285 655031 Mrs Clayton
D: £17 **S:** £17
Beds: 1T 2S **Baths:** 1 Sh
🛏 (2) 🅿 (2) ⬛ 📺 ⬛ ☑ ☟

The Ivy House, *2 Victoria Road, Cirencester, Glos, GL7 1EN.*
Imposing Victorian town centre residence. Bright, comfortable, high standard B&B. **Open:** All Year (not Xmas)
01285 656626 Mrs Marriot
D: £18–£22 **S:** £25–£35
Beds: 1F 3D **Baths:** 4 En
🛏 🅿 (5) ⬛ 📺 ⬛ ☑ ☟

Clonsilla Guest House, *7 Victoria Road, Cirencester, Glos, GL7 1EN.*
Five minutes from town centre.
Open: All Year
01285 652621 Mr Sullivan
D: £17–£25 **S:** £20–£30
Beds: 1F 2D 4T 1S **Baths:** 4 En 1 Sh
🛏 🅿 (5) 📺 ⬛ ☑ ☟

Clapton-on-the-Hill

SP1617   🍴 *Plough, Kingsbridge Inn, Mouse Trap Inn, Coach & Horses*

Farncombe, *Clapton-on-the-Hill, Bourton-on-the-Water, Cheltenham, Glos, GL54 2LG.*
Come and share our peace and tranquillity with superb views.
Open: All Year (not Xmas)
Grades: ETC 4 Diamond
01451 820120 (also fax) Mrs Wright
jwrightbb@aol.com
D: £20–£23 **S:** £25–£30
Beds: 2D 1T **Baths:** 1 En 2 Sh
🛏 🅿 (4) ⬛ 📺 ⬛ ☑ ☟

Upper Farm, *Clapton-on-the-Hill, Bourton-on-the-Water, Cheltenham, Glos, GL54 2LG.*
Period farmhouse, spectacular views warm welcome, superior accommodation, village location. **Open:** Feb to Dec
Grades: ETC 5 Diamond
01451 820453 Mrs Adams
Fax: 01451 810185
D: £20–£22.50 **S:** £25–£30
Beds: 1F 2D 1T **Baths:** 3 En 1 Sh
🛏 (6) 🅿 (6) ⬛ 📺 ⬛ ☟

Clearwell

SO5708   🍴 *Butchers Arms*

Scatterford Cottage, *The Butts, Clearwell, Coleford, Glos, GL16 8PW.*
On edge of pretty village overlooking open country. Private parking.
Open: All Year (not Xmas)
01594 835527 Mrs Simpson
D: £17.50 **S:** £20
Beds: 1D 1T **Baths:** 1 Sh
🛏 (10) 🅿 (4) ⬛ 📺 ☟ ⬛ ☟

Cleeve Hill

SO9826   🍴 *Apple Tree, Plough, High Roost, Royal Oak, Kings Arms, Rising Sun*

Heron Haye, *Cleeve Hill, Cheltenham, Glos, GL52 3PW.*
Quiet location, 3 miles Cheltenham Racecourse. Comfortable home. Full English breakfast. Superb views.
Open: All Year
01242 672516 Mr Saunders
dick.whittamore@virgin.net
D: £22.50–£30 **S:** £25–£30
Beds: 2D 1S **Baths:** 1 Sh
🅿 (4) ⬛ 📺 ☟ ⬛

Cleyne Hage, *Southam Lane, Cleeve Hill, Cheltenham, Glos, GL52 3NY.*
Views of Malverns, Cleeve Hill, Racecourse. 3 miles Cheltenham. Ideally situated walking, touring.
Open: All Year
01242 518569 Mrs Blankenspoor
Fax: 01242 238068
Laurina.Blankenspoor@screaming.net
D: fr £18 **S:** fr £20
Beds: 1F 1D 1T 1S **Baths:** 2 En 1 Pr 1 Sh
🛏 🅿 (8) ⬛ 📺 ☟ ⬛ ☟ ☟

Coleford

SO5710   🍴 *Montague Inn*

Marefold, *Gorsty Knoll, Milkwall, Coleford, Glos, GL16 7LR.*
Edge Forest nature reserve. Walkers, cyclists, birdwatchers paradise, village half a mile.
Open: All Year (not Xmas)
01594 833969 Mrs Webb
D: £16–£18 **S:** £16–£18
Beds: 1T 1S **Baths:** 1 Pr 1 Sh
🛏 🅿 (2) 📺 ☟ ⬛ ☑ ☟

Corse

SO7826   🍴 *The Swan*

Kilmorie, *Gloucester Road, Corse, Staunton, Gloucester, GL19 3RQ.*
Open: All Year (not Xmas)
Grades: ETC 3 Diamond
01452 840224 Ms Barnfield
D: £16–£20 **S:** £18–£20
Beds: 1F 2D 1T 1S **Baths:** 3 En 1 Pr 1 Sh
🛏 (5) 🅿 (8) 📺 ⬛ ✕ ⬛ ☑ ☟
Grade II Listed (c1848) smallholding, quality all ground floor accommodation, tea trays, toiletries, TVs all rooms, mainly ensuite; rural location, large garden to relax, watch birds, butterflies wildlife we encourage, meet our miniature goats, pony, hens. Ramble countryside footpaths, safe parking.

Cranham

SO8913   🍴 *Black Horse Inn*

Pound Cottage, *Cranham, Gloucester, GL4 8HP.*
Cotswold cottage in quiet village surrounded by countryside and woodlands.
Open: All Year (not Xmas)
01452 812581 Ms Dann
Fax: 01452 814380
ddann@globalnet.co.uk
D: £20 **S:** £25
Beds: 1D 1T **Baths:** 1 Sh
🛏 (2) 🅿 (1) ⬛ 📺 ⬛ ☑ ☟

Down Hatherley

SO8622   🍴 *Queens Head*

Frog Furlong Cottage, *Frog Furlong Lane, Down Hatherley, Gloucester, GL2 9QE.*
In the Green Belt, standing quietly alone, surrounded by fields.
Open: All Year (not Xmas/New Year)
01452 730430 (also fax)
Mrs Rooke
D: £20–£22 **S:** £25–£27
Beds: 1D 1T **Baths:** 1 En
🅿 (3) ⬛ 📺 ✕ ⬛ ☑ ☟

Dumbleton

SP0136   🍴 *Harvest Home*

Raymeadow Farm, *Dumbleton, Evesham, Worcs, WR11 6TR.*
Peaceful farmhouse nestling within the Cotswolds between Stratford/Cheltenham/Cirencester. **Open:** Mar to Oct
01242 621215 Ms Alvis
D: £20–£25 **S:** £20–£25
Beds: 1F 1T 1S **Baths:** 1 Sh
🛇 🅿 📺 🛍.

Duntisbourne Abbots

SO9608   🍴 *Five Mile House, Highwayman*

Dixs Barn, *Duntisbourne Abbots, Cirencester, Glos, GL7 7JN.*
Converted barn on family run farm on edge of village with magnificent views.
Open: All Year
01285 821249 Mrs Wilcox
D: £20–£25 **S:** £25–£30
Beds: 1D 1T **Baths:** 1 En 1 Pr
🛇 🅿 (8) 🛠 📺 🛏 ✕ 🛍. 🆅 🕭

Dursley

ST7698   🍴 *Old Bell*

Drakestone House, *Stinchcombe, Dursley, Glos, GL11 6AS.*
Open: Feb to Nov
01453 542140 (also fax)
Mr & Mrs St John Mildmay
D: £31.50–£36.50 **S:** £36.50
Beds: 1D 2T **Baths:** 1 Pr 1 Sh
🛇 🅿 (4) 🛠 📺 🛏 ✕ 🛍. 🆅 🕭
Drakestone is charming. An arts and crafts building with a large garden from the same period. Romantic and restful, the house sits on a wooded hillside with magnificent views. Nearby is Berkeley Castle, Slimbridge, Bath, Bristol and Cheltenham.

Stanthill House, *Uley Road, Dursley, Glos, GL11 4PF.*
Lovely Georgian town house; spacious rooms, comfortable beds, good food.
Open: All Year
01453 549037 Liz Gresko
D: £21–£23.50 **S:** £21–£23.50
Beds: 2D 1T **Baths:** 2 En 1 Pr
🛇 🅿 🛠 📺 🛏 🕭

Eastcombe

SO8804

Pretoria Villa, *Wells Road, Eastcombe, Stroud, Glos, GL6 7EE.*
Enjoy luxurious bed and breakfast in relaxed family country house.
Open: All Year (not Xmas)
Grades: ETC 4 Diamond
01452 770435 Mrs Solomon
D: £22 **S:** £25
Beds: 1D 1T 1S **Baths:** 1 En 1 Pr
🛇 🅿 (3) 🛠 📺 ✕ 🛍. 🆅 🕭

B&B owners may vary rates - be sure to check when booking

Ebrington

SP1840   🍴 *Ebrington Arms*

Holly House, *Ebrington, Chipping Campden, Glos, GL55 6NL.*
Situated in centre of picturesque Cotswold village, 2 miles Chipping Campden.
Open: All Year (not Xmas)
Grades: AA 4 Diamond
01386 593213 Mrs Hutsby
Fax: 01386 593181
D: £21–£24 **S:** £30–£40
Beds: 3F/D/T **Baths:** 3 En
🛇 🅿 (5) 🛠 📺 🛍. 🆅 🕭

Edge

SO8509   🍴 *Edgemoor Inn*

Wild Acre, *Back Edge Lane, Edge, Stroud, Glos, GL6 6PE.*
Rural location overlooking Painswick. Ideal base for touring the Cotswolds.
Open: Easter to Oct
Grades: ETC 3 Diamond
01452 813077 Mrs Sanders
D: £18–£20 **S:** £20–£22
Beds: 1D 1T **Baths:** 1 En 1 Sh
🛇 (3) 🅿 (3) 🛠 📺 🛍. 🕭 ઠ

Elton

SO6913   🍴 *Bowling Green*

Homestead Farm, *Main Street, Elton, Matlock, Derbyshire, DE4 2BW.*
Working farmhouse B&B in centre of village, all home comforts.
Open: All Year
01629 650359 Mrs Carson
D: £14.50 **S:** £14.50
Beds: 1D **Baths:** 1 En
🛇 🅿 (5) 📺 🛏 ✕ 🛍. 🆅 ✳ 🕭

English Bicknor

SO5815   🍴 *Dog & Muffler*

Dryslade Farm, *English Bicknor, Coleford, Glos, GL16 7PA.*
C18th farmhouse. Relaxed, friendly atmosphere. Forest walks and cycling.
Open: All Year
Grades: ETC 4 Diamond
01594 860259 (also fax)
Mrs Gwilliam
gwilliam@dryslade.freeserve.co.uk
D: £18–£22 **S:** £21–£25
Beds: 1F 1T 1D **Baths:** 2 En 1 Pr
🛇 🅿 (6) 🛠 📺 🛏 🛍. 🆅 🕭

Fairford

SP1500   🍴 *Bull Hotel*

Waiten Hill Farm, *Mill Lane, Fairford, Glos, GL7 4JG.*
Imposing C19th farmhouse overlooking River Coln and famous church.
Open: All Year
Grades: ETC 2 Diamond
01285 712652 (also fax)
Mrs Rymer
D: £17.50–£20 **S:** £20–£25
Beds: 1F 1D 1T **Baths:** 2 En
🛇 🅿 📺 🛏 🛍. 🆅 🕭

Gloucester

SO8318   🍴 *Beacon Hotel, King Edward, Linden Tree, Tall Ship, White Smiths*

Georgian Guest House, *85 Bristol Road, Gloucester, GL1 5SN.*
Part-Georgian terraced house, 15 minutes walk city centre.
Open: All Year
Grades: ETC 1 Diamond
01452 413286 (also fax)
J W Nash
D: £14.50–£16.50 **S:** £14.50–£15.50
Beds: 4F 3T 2S **Baths:** 5 En 1 Sh
🛇 🅿 (3) 📺 🛏 🛍. 🕭

Gemini Guest House, *83a Innsworth Lane, Longlevens, Gloucester, GL2 0TT.*
Friendly, family-run guest house, 2 miles from M5/jct 11.
Open: All Year (not Xmas/New Year)
01452 415849 Mrs Burby
D: £15–£18 **S:** £16–£18
Beds: 1F 1D 1S **Baths:** 1 Sh
🛇 (7) 🅿 (6) 🛠 📺 🛍. 🕭

The Chestnuts, *9 Brunswick Square, Gloucester, GL1 1UG.*
Located in Gloucester's finest Georgian square. Close shops, Cathedral Museum and docks.
Grades: ETC 4 Diamond
01452 330356 (also fax)
Mrs Champion
davidchampion1@compuserve.com
D: £21 **S:** £25
🛇 🅿 (1) 📺 ✕ 🛍. 🆅 🕭

Lower Green Farmhouse, *Haresfield, Stonehouse, Glos, GL10 3DS.*
C18th Listed Cotswold stone farmhouse with countryside views.
Open: All Year (not Xmas/New Year)
01452 728264 (also fax)
Mrs Reed
lowergreen@lineone.net
D: £18.50 **S:** £20
Beds: 1F 1T **Baths:** 2 Sh
🛇 🅿 (6) 📺 🛏 🛍. 🆅 🕭

Rotherfield House Hotel, *5 Horton Road, Gloucester, GL1 3PX.*
Immaculate, extended detached Victorian property. Friendly atmosphere, excellent choice food.
Open: All Year
01452 410500 Mr Eacott
D: £22–£25 **S:** £24–£36
Beds: 2F 3D 1T 7S **Baths:** 4 En 2 Pr
🛇 🅿 (9) 📺 🛏 ✕ 🛍. 🆅 ઠ cc

Gotherington

SO9629   🍴 *Royal Oak, Shutter Inn*

Pardon Hill Farm, *Prescott, Gotherington, Cheltenham, Glos, GL52 4RD.*
Modern, comfortable farmhouse, lovely views.
Open: All Year
Grades: ETC 3 Diamond, AA 3 Diamond
01242 672468 (also fax)
Mrs Newman
janet@pardonhillfarm.freeserve.co.uk
D: £22–£50 **S:** £27–£35
Beds: 1D 1T 1S **Baths:** 3 En
🛇 🅿 (6) 📺 🛏 🛍. 🆅 🕭

Moat Farm, Malleson Road, Gotherington, Cheltenham, Glos, GL52 4ET.
Situated in the heart of the Cotswolds between Cheltenham and Tewkesbury.
Open: All Year (not Xmas)
01242 672055 Mr & Mrs Tilley
Fax: 07050 665639
D: £18–£19 **S:** £18–£19
Beds: 2D 2T
🏠 🅿 📺 🍴 🛏 🗓 Ⓥ 🍷

Great Rissington

SP1917 🍴 Lamb Inn

Lower Farmhouse, Great Rissington, Bourton on the Water, Cheltenham, Glos, GL54 2LH.
Child friendly guest accommodation in converted barn by lovely Georgian home.
Open: All Year
01451 810163 Mr & Mrs Fleming
Fax: 01451 810187
D: £17.50–£22 **S:** £17.50–£25
Beds: 1D 1S **Baths:** 1 Pr
🏠 🅿 (3) 🗓 📺 🛏 🗓 Ⓥ 🍷

Guiting Power

SP0924

Halfway House, Kineton, Guiting Power, Cheltenham, Glos, GL54 5UG.
C17th inn close to all major Cotswold attractions large gardens.
Open: All Year
Grades: ETC 3 Diamond
01451 850344 Mr & Mrs Hamer
halfwayhs@aol.com
D: £30–£40 **S:** £30–£40
Beds: 3D 1T **Baths:** 4 En
🏠 📺 🛏 🗓 ✳ 🍷 cc

Haresfield

SO8110 🍴 Beacon Hotel

Lower Green Farmhouse, Haresfield, Stonehouse, Glos, GL10 3DS.
C18th Listed Cotswold stone farmhouse with countryside views.
Open: All Year (not Xmas/New Year)
01452 728264 (also fax)
Mrs Reed
lowergreen@lineone.net
D: £18.50 **S:** £20
Beds: 1F 1T **Baths:** 2 Sh
🏠 🅿 (6) 📺 🛏 🗓 Ⓥ 🍷

Hawkesbury

ST7686

Ivy Cottage, Inglestone Common, Hawkesbury, Badminton, GL9 1BX.
Comfortable cottage surrounded by ancient woodland on edge of Cotswolds.
Open: All Year (not Xmas/New Year)
01454 294237 Mrs Canner
D: £19–£20 **S:** £22–£25
Beds: 1F 1D 1T 1S **Baths:** 2 Sh
🏠 🅿 (3) 🗓 📺 🛏 ✕ 🗓 Ⓥ 🍷 ♿

National Grid References are for villages, towns and cities – not for individual houses

Hillersland

SO5714

Symonds Yat Rock Lodge, Hillersland, Coleford, Glouc, GL16 7NY.
Beautiful edge of forest location above the Wye Valley.
Open: Feb to Nov
01594 836191 **Fax:** 01594 836626
D: £22–£27 **S:** £36
Beds: 3F 1D 1T **Baths:** 5 En
🏠 🅿 📺 🛏 ✕ 🗓 Ⓥ 🍷 cc

Huntley

SO7219 🍴 Red Lion

Forest Gate, Huntley, Gloucester, GL19 3EU.
Large Victorian rectory ideal for visiting Royal Forest of Dean.
Open: All Year (not Xmas)
Grades: ETC 3 Diamond
01452 831192 (also fax)
Mr Blakemore
forest.gate@huntley-glos.demon.co.uk
D: £23–£26 **S:** £23–£26
Beds: 1F 1D 1S **Baths:** 1 En 1 Sh
🏠 🅿 (6) 🗓 📺 🗓 Ⓥ 🍷 cc

Kemble

ST9897 🍴 Wild Duck, Tavern Inn, Thames Head

Smerrill Barns, Kemble, Cirencester, Glos, GL7 6BW.
Open: All Year (not Xmas)
Grades: ETC 4 Diamond
01285 770907 Mrs Sopher
Fax: 01285 770706
D: fr £27.50 **S:** fr £45
Beds: 1F 5D 1T
Baths: 7 En 1 Sh
🏠 🅿 (8) 🗓 📺 🗓 Ⓥ 🍷
An ideal base for touring the Cotswolds or walking the Thames Path. An C18th converted barn, all rooms ensuite, guest lounge with log fires in winter, drinks licence. Will pick up from local rail station (Kemble). Traditional inns nearby.

Kilcot

SO6925 🍴 The Roadmaker

Cherry Grove B&B, Mill Lane, Kilcot, Newent, Glos, GL18 1NY.
Peaceful rural situation near Wye Valley, good cycling and walking.
Open: All Year (not Xmas)
01989 720126 Mr & Mrs Inwood
D: £15–£17 **S:** £16–£18
Beds: 1F 1D **Baths:** 1 Pr 1 Sh
🏠 (5) 🅿 (6) 🗓 📺 🗓 Ⓥ 🍷

Withyland Heights, Kilcot, Newent, Glos, GL18 1PG.
Farmhouse B&B accommodation on a working dairy farm set in beautiful unspoilt countryside.
Open: All Year
01989 720582
Fax: 01989 720238
D: £16–£23 **S:** £16–£23
Beds: 1D 1T **Baths:** 1 En 1 Pr
🏠 🅿 🗓 📺 🗓 Ⓥ 🍷

Kings Stanley

SO8103 🍴 Kings Head

Old Chapel House, Broad Street, Kings Stanley, Stonehouse, Glos, GL10 3PN.
Converted chapel on Cotswold Way overlooking escarpment.
Open: All Year (not Xmas)
01453 826289 Mrs Richards Hanna
D: £21.50 **S:** £20
Beds: 1F 1D 2T 1S **Baths:** 2 En 1 Sh
🏠 (5) 🅿 (4) 📺 ✕ 🗓 Ⓥ 🍷

Nurashell, Bath Road, Kings Stanley, Stonehouse, Glos, GL10 3JG.
Victorian house. Village centre. Shops and pubs close. Station 2 miles. Bus route.
Open: All Year
01453 823642 Mrs Rollins
D: fr £18 **S:** fr £18
Beds: 1D 1T **Baths:** 1 Sh
🏠 🅿 🗓 📺 🛏 🗓 🍷

Knockdown

ST8388 🍴 Holford Arms

Avenue Farm, Knockdown, Tetbury, Glos, GL8 8QY.
300-year-old farmhouse in farm adjoining Westonbirt Arboretum. Bath, Bristol & Gloucester within easy reach.
Open: All Year **Grades:** ETC 3 Diamond
01454 238207 Mrs King
Fax: 01454 238033
sonjames@breathemail.net
D: £20–£25 **S:** £25
Beds: 1F 1D 2T **Baths:** 2 En 1 Sh
🏠 🅿 (6) 🗓 📺 🗓 Ⓥ 🍷

Laverton

SP0735 🍴 Mount Inn

Gunners Orchard, Laverton, Broadway, Glos, WR12 7NA.
Comfortable private house in quiet and beautiful setting personal attention.
Open: All Year (not Xmas/New Year)
01386 584213 Mrs Stephenson
D: £18–£20 **S:** £25–£30
Beds: 1D 1T **Baths:** 1 Sh
🏠 (10) 🅿 (6) 🗓 📺 🛏 🗓 🍷

Lechlade

SU2199 🍴 Trout Inn, New Inn, Red Lion

Cambrai Lodge Guest House, Oak Street, Lechlade On Thames, Glos, GL7 3AY.
Modern comfortable house off the road. Ideal for touring Cotswolds.
Open: All Year
Grades: ETC 4 Diamond Silver Award
01367 253173 Mr Titchener
D: £23–£28 **S:** £28–£44
Beds: 1F 1D 1T 2S **Baths:** 2 En 1 Pr 1 Sh
🏠 🅿 (9) 🗓 📺 🛏 🗓 🍷

Apple Tree House, Buscot, Faringdon, Oxon, SN7 8DA.
Old property in National Trust village, 5 mins' walk River Thames, one acre garden. **Open:** All Year (not Xmas)
Grades: ETC 3 Diamond, AA 3 Diamond, RAC 3 Diamond
01367 252592 Mrs Reay emreay@aol.com
D: £18–£22 **S:** £23–£28
Beds: 2D 1T **Baths:** 1 En 2 Pr
🏠 🅿 (10) 🗓 📺 🛏 🗓 Ⓥ 🍷

The New Inn Hotel, *Market Square, Lechlade On Thames, Glos, GL7 3AB.*
C17th fully modernised coaching inn on River Thames in the Cotswold.
Open: All Year
01367 252296 Mr Sandhu
Fax: 01367 252315
info@newinnhotel.co.uk
D: £20–£32.50 **S:** £40–£55
Beds: 2F 10D 10T 4S **Baths:** 26 En
🄿 (40) ⅍ 🺾 ✕ 🔟 🖂 🗓 ✿ ♨

Longhope

SO6818 ◀ *Farmers Boy, Moody Cow*

The Old Farm, *Barrel Lane, Longhope, Glos, GL17 0LR.*
Open: All Year
Grades: ETC 4 Diamond
01452 830252 Mrs Rodger
Fax: 01452 830255
lucyr@avnet.co.uk
D: £16–£24.50 **S:** £24–£29
Beds: 2D 1T **Baths:** 3 En
🐾 (12) 🄿 (6) ⅍ � ✖ 🔟 🖂 🗓
Charming C16th farmhouse full of character, beams and fireplaces. Set in an idyllic rural location, within easy reach of the Cotswolds, Oxford, Cheltenham and Stratford. Royal Forest of Dean nearby. Excellent walking/cycling from the farm. Or just come to relax!

Lower Slaughter

SP1623 ◀ *Coach & Horses, Plough Inn*

Seymour House Farm, *Fosseway, Lower Slaughter, Bourton-on-the-Water, Cheltenham, Glos, GL54 2HW.*
Traditional Cotswold house on working small holding. Excellent touring centre.
Open: All Year
01451 820132 (also fax)
Mr & Mrs Hedges
D: £17.50–£20
Beds: 1F 1D
🐾 🄿 (6) ⅍ 🔟 🛏 🖂 ✿

Lakeside, *Fosseway, Lower Slaughter, Cheltenham, Glos, GL54 2EY.*
Comfortable home on edge of unspoilt village. One mile north of Bourton-on-the-Water on A429.
Open: All Year (not Xmas)
01451 821206 Mrs Goss
D: £16–£20 **S:** £20
Beds: 1F 1D **Baths:** 1 En 1 Pr
🐾 (4) 🄿 (5) ⅍ 🔟 🖂 ✿

Lower Swell

SP1725 ◀ *Golden Ball*

Golden Ball Inn, *Lower Swell, Stow-on-the-Wold, Glos, GL54 1LF.*
Delightful C17th village inn, genuine home-cooked food, friendly atmosphere, pets welcome.
Open: All Year
Grades: ETC 2 Diamond
01451 830247 A R Knowles
thegolden.ball@virgin.net
D: £22.50–£27.50 **S:** £30–£35
Beds: 3D 1T **Baths:** 4 En
🐾 (15) 🔟 🛏 ✕ 🖂 ✿ cc

Marshfield

ST7773 ◀ *Catherine Wheel*

Knowle Hill Farm, *Beeks Lane, Marshfield, Chippenham, Wilts, SN14 8BB.*
Farmhouse in beautiful, peaceful surroundings. 8 miles Bath, 5 miles M4 (J18).
Open: All Year (not Xmas)
01225 891503 Mrs Bond
D: £18–£20 **S:** £18–£20
Beds: 1F 1D 1T **Baths:** 1 En 1 Sh
🐾 🄿 (3) 🔟 🛏 ✕ 🖂 🗓 ✿

Meysey Hampton

SU1199 ◀ *Masons Arms*

The Masons Arms, *High Street, Meysey Hampton, Cirencester, Glos, GL7 5JT.*
Origins date C17th beside village green in award-winning village.
Open: All Year
Grades: ETC 3 Diamond, AA 3 Diamond
01285 850164 (also fax)
Mr O'Dell
jane@themasonsarms.freeserve.co.uk
D: £28–£32 **S:** £38–£42
Beds: 1F 5D 2T 1S **Baths:** 9 En
🐾 (3) 🄿 (4) 🔟 ✕ 🖂 🗓 ✿ cc

Mickleton

SP1643 ◀ *Bakers' Arms, Volunteer Inn, King's Arms, Butchers' Arms, Three Ways*

The Bank House, *Mickleton, Chipping Campden, Glos, GL55 6RX.*
Period house with tranquil old world garden in heart of historic village.
Open: All Year (not Xmas)
01386 438302 Mrs Billington
D: £21–£22.50 **S:** £30–£32
Beds: 1F 1D 2T **Baths:** 1 En 2 Pr
🐾 🄿 (3) ⅍ 🔟 🖂 ✿

Middle Duntisbourne

SO9806 ◀ *Five Mile, The Bell*

Manor Farm, *Middle Duntisbourne, Cirencester, Glos, GL7 7AR.*
Farmhouse set in beautiful Duntisbourne.
Open: All Year (not Xmas/New Year)
Grades: ETC 3 Diamond
01285 658145 Mrs Barton
Fax: 01285 641504
tina.barton@farming.co.uk
D: £20–£25 **S:** £40–£45
Beds: 1D 1T **Baths:** 1 En 1 Pr
🐾 (8) ⅍ 🔟 🛏 🖂 ✿

Minchinhampton

SO8600 ◀ *Old Lodge, Ram Inn, Halfway House, Britannia Inn*

Burleigh Farm, *Minchinhampton, Stroud, Glos, GL5 2PF.*
Attractive Cotswold stone farmhouse in 38 acres of parkland. Breathtaking views.
Open: All Year (not Xmas)
Grades: ETC 4 Diamond, Silver
01453 883112 (also fax)
Mr & Mrs Vines
D: £24–£28.50 **S:** fr £39
Beds: 2D 1T **Baths:** 1 En 1 Pr
🐾 (10) 🄿 (5) ⅍ 🔟 ✕ 🖂 ✿

Hunters Lodge, *Dr Browns Road, Minchinhampton, Stroud, Glos, GL6 9BT.*
Large Cotswold stone house adjoining NT land. Tourist guide available.
Open: All Year (not Xmas)
Grades: AA 4 Diamond
01453 883588 Mrs Helm
Fax: 01453 731449
D: £21–£24 **S:** fr £30
Beds: 2D 1T **Baths:** 1 En 2 Pr
🐾 🄿 (6) 🔟 🖂 ✿

Hyde Crest, *Cirencester Road, Minchinhampton, Stroud, Glos, GL6 8PE.*
Beautiful country house. All bedrooms have own patio into gardens.
Open: All Year
Grades: ETC 4 Diamond, AA 4 Diamond
01453 731631
100621.3266@compuserve.com
D: £22.50–£45 **S:** £25–£30
Beds: 2D 1T **Baths:** 3 En
🐾 (6) 🄿 (6) ⅍ 🔟 🛏 🖂 🗓 ✿ &

Mitcheldean

SO6618

Gunn Mill House, *Lower Spout Lane, Mitcheldean, Glos, GL17 0EA.*
The Andersons offer great hospitality and food in their Georgian home set in the 27,000 acres of the Royal Forest of Dean. Enjoy trips to Tintern Abbey, Gloucester and Hereford Cathedrals or walking, cycling, pony trekking through the forest.
Open: All Year
Grades: ETC 4 Diamond, Silver
01594 827577 (also fax)
info@gunnmillhouse.co.uk
D: £25–£40 **S:** £27.50–£45
Beds: 1F 5D 2T **Baths:** 8 En
🐾 🄿 (14) ⅍ 🔟 🛏 ✕ 🖂 🗓 ✿ cc

Moreton-in-Marsh

SP2032 ◀ *Black Bear, Redesdale Arms, Swan Inn, Farriers Arms, Inn Of The Marsh, Ebrington Arms, Fox & Hounds, Wellington, Farmers Arms*

Warwick House, *London Road, Moreton-in-Marsh, Glos, GL56 0HH.*
Open: All Year
Grades: ETC 3 Diamond
01608 650773 (also fax) Mr & Mrs Grant
charlie@warwickhousebnb.demon.co.uk
D: £17.50–£20 **S:** £20–£25
Beds: 1T 2D **Baths:** 2 En 1 Pr
🄿 (3) ⅍ 🔟 🖂 🗓 ✿ ✿
A perfect touring base for the Cotswolds. I will collect from bus or train station, or 5 minutes walk from train station on A44 towards Oxford. Facilities include washing/ironing, video player and phone. See website for more details including swimming pool.

Bran Mill Cottage, *Aston Magna, Moreton in Marsh, Glos, GL56 9QP.*
Small traditional B&B in peaceful Cotswold cottage. Friendly, welcoming, homely.
Open: All Year (not Xmas)
Grades: ETC 3 Diamond
01386 593517
enquiries@branmillcottage.co.uk
D: £16–£18 **S:** £19–£25
Beds: 1D 1T 1S **Baths:** 1 Pr 1 Sh
🐾 (14) 🄿 (3) ⅍ 🔟 🖂 🗓 ✿

Fourshires, Great Wolford Road, Moreton-in-Marsh, Glos, GL56 0PE.
Open: All Year (not Xmas)
Grades: ETC 4 Diamond
01608 651412 (also fax)
Mrs Affron
m1aff@aol.com
D: £20–£22 **S:** £25–£30
Beds: 2D 1T **Baths:** 2 En 1 Pr
🛇 (10) 🅿 (6) ⊬ 📺 🛲 🔓
Beautiful country house set in 3 acres of garden, 1 mile from Moreton-in-Marsh. Ideal centre to tour Cotswolds, Stratford-on-Avon etc. All rooms have colour TV and video, trouser-press, tea/coffee, hairdryers, cycle hire, excellent decor, first class welcome.

Roosters, Todenham, Moreton-in-Marsh, Glos, GL56 9PA.
Beautifully situated for exploring Cotswolds. Lovely C17th stone house. Lovely gardens.
Open: All Year (not Xmas)
Grades: ETC 4 Diamond
01608 650645 (also fax)
Ms Longmore
D: £23–£25 **S:** £25–£30
Beds: 1D 2T **Baths:** 2 En 1 Pr
🛇 🅿 (8) ⊬ 📺 🛏 ✗ 🛲 �V 🔓

Moreton House, High Street, Moreton-in-Marsh, Glos, GL56 0LQ.
100-year-old family-run guest house.
Open: All Year
01608 650747 Mr & Mrs Dempster
Fax: 01608 652747
moreton_house@msn.com
D: fr £21 **S:** fr £22
Beds: 1F 6D 2T 2S **Baths:** 7 Pr 4 Sh
🛇 🅿 (5) 📺 🛏 ✗ 🛲 �V ✿ 🔓

Rest Harrow, Evenlode Road, Moreton-in-Marsh, Glos, GL56 0NJ.
Large semi-detached house, extensive views. Country location, Stratford, Warwick accessible.
Open: All Year (not Xmas)
01608 650653 Mrs Miles
D: £15–£17 **S:** £16–£18
Beds: 1F **Baths:** 1 En
🛇 🅿 (3) ⊬ 📺 🛲 �V 🔓

New Farm Guest House, Dorn, Moreton-in-Marsh, Glos, GL56 9NS.
Old farmhouse spacious bedrooms, lovely four poster bedroom. Hot crispy bread.
Open: All Year
01608 650782 Mrs Righton
D: £18–£20 **S:** £20–£22
Beds: 2D 1T **Baths:** 3 En 1 Pr
🛇 (10) 🅿 (6) ⊬ 📺 🛲 �V 🔓

Nailsworth

ST8499   🍺 Rose & Crown, Egypt Mill, The George

The Vicarage, Nailsworth, Stroud, Glos, GL6 0BS.
Large, comfortable, quiet Victorian vicarage. Beautiful garden. Good breakfast.
Open: All Year
01453 832181 Mrs Strong
D: £23 **S:** fr £22
Beds: 1T 3S **Baths:** 1 Pr 1 Sh
🛇 (2) 🅿 (4) ⊬ 📺 🛏 🛲 🔓

Aaron Farm, Nympsfield Road, Nailsworth, Stroud, Glos, GL6 0ET.
Warm and friendly, central for walking and touring Cotswolds and Gloucestershire. **Open:** All Year
01453 833598 (also fax) Mrs Mulligan
aaronfarm@compuserve.com
D: £20–£21 **S:** £28–£30
Beds: 1D 2T **Baths:** 3 En
🛇 🅿 (5) ⊬ 📺 🛏 🛲 �V 🔓

Newent

SO7225   🍺 Beauchamp Arms, Kings Arms

The Old Winery, Welsh House Lane, Newent, Gloucestershire, GL18 1LR.
Comfortable, very attractive former winery, overlooking pretty countryside and vineyards. **Open:** All Year (not Xmas)
Grades: ETC 5 Diamond, Gold, AA 5 Diamond, RAC 5 Diamond
01531 890824 (also fax)
Mr & Mrs Kingham
D: £28–£32 **S:** £28–£32
Beds: 1T **Baths:** 1 En
🛇 🅿 (20) ⊬ 📺 ✗ 🛲 �V 🔓

Merton House, 7 Birches Lane, Newent, Gloucestershire, GL18 1DN.
Open: All Year
01531 820608 D: £17–£18 **S:** £22–£24
Beds: 2D **Baths:** 1 Sh
🅿 (4) ⊬ 📺 🛲 �V 🔓
Quiet rural location, good views, excellent walking, touring, local attractions.

North Nibley

ST7395   🍺 Black Horse

Nibley House, North Nibley, Dursley, Glos, GL11 6DL.
Magnificent Georgian manor house, centrepiece of 200-acre farm.
Open: All Year (not Xmas)
01453 543108 Mrs Eley
D: £22–£25 **S:** £22–£25
Beds: 1F 1D 1T **Baths:** 2 En 1 Pr
🛇 🅿 (12) ⊬ 📺 🛏 ✗ 🛲 �V 🔓

Northleach

SP1114   🍺 Plough Inn

Market House, The Square, Northleach, Cheltenham, Glos, GL54 3EJ.
400-year-old house in the heart of the Cotswolds. **Open:** Mar to Oct
01451 860557 Mr Eastman
D: fr £19 **S:** fr £22
Beds: 1D 1T 2S **Baths:** 1 Pr 1 Sh
🛇 (12) ⊬ 📺 🛲 �V 🔓

Old Sodbury

ST7581   🍺 Dog Inn, The Bell, Old Home

Dornden Guest House, Church Lane, Old Sodbury, Bristol, BS37 6NB.
Former vicarage, quietly situated, views to Welsh hills.
Open: All Year (not Xmas)
Grades: ETC 4 Diamond
01454 313325 Mrs Paz
Fax: 01454 312263
dorndenguesthouse@tinyworld.co.uk
D: £27–£30 **S:** £25–£40
Beds: 5F 2T 2S **Baths:** 6 En 2 Sh
🛇 🅿 (15) ⊬ 📺 🛏 ✗ 🛲 �V 🔓

1 The Green, Old Sodbury, Bristol, BS37 6LY.
Close M4 M5 ideal location for Cotswold Way, Bath and Bristol.
Open: All Year (not Xmas)
01454 314688 Mr & Mrs Rees
D: £22–£26 **S:** £22–£26
Beds: 2D 1T 3S **Baths:** 1 En 2 Sh
🅿 (4) ⊬ 📺 🛲 🔓

Painswick

SO8609   🍺 Black Horse, Royal Oak, Gither Bar, Falcon Inn, Edgemoor Inn

Thorne, Friday Street, Painswick, Stroud, Glos, GL6 6QJ.
Tudor merchants house with market hall pillars 'in situ' on Cotswolds Way.
Open: Easter to Nov
01452 812476 Mrs Blatchley
D: £23–£25 **S:** £25
Beds: 2T **Baths:** 2 Pr
🅿 📺 🛲 🔓

Castle Lodge, The Beacon, Painswick, Stroud, Glos, GL6 6TU.
Set high in woodland, adjacent golf. Trout fishing, riding nearby.
Open: All Year
Grades: ETC 4 Diamond, Silver
01452 813603 (also fax) Mrs Cooke
D: £26–£30 **S:** £30
Beds: 1F 1D 1T **Baths:** All En
🛇 🅿 ⊬ 📺 🛏 🛲 🔓

Wheatleys, Cotswold Mead, Painswick, Stroud, Glos, GL6 6XB.
Open: All Year (not Xmas)
Grades: ETC 5 Diamond, Gold
01452 812167 Mrs Burgess
Fax: 01452 814270
wheatleys@dial.pipex.com
D: fr £25 **S:** fr £35
Beds: 1D 1T **Baths:** 2 En
🛇 (10) 🅿 (4) ⊬ 📺 🛲 🔓
Set in a beautiful Cotswold village, Wheatley's offers a relaxing base to unwind. A particularly well-appointed suite with connecting sitting room. Guests have full use of the pleasant secluded garden (with croquet), and breakfast can be served on the terrace.

Upper Doreys Mill, Edge, Painswick, Stroud, Glos, GL6 6NF.
C18th cloth mill by stream. Old Beams and log fires. **Open:** All Year
01452 812459 Mrs Marden
sylvia@painswick.co.uk
D: £22–£25
Beds: 2D 1T **Baths:** 3 En
🛇 🅿 (4) ⊬ 📺 �V 🔓

Pitchcombe

SO8508   🍺 Edgemoor Inn

Gable End, Pitchcombe, Stroud, Glos, GL6 6LN.
C16th-17th house commands an elevated position overlooking Painswick Valley.
Open: All Year (not Xmas/New Year)
Grades: ETC 3 Diamond
01452 812166 Mrs Partridge
Fax: 01452 812719
D: £22.50 **S:** £30
Beds: 2D **Baths:** 2 En
🛇 (5) 🅿 (4) 🛲 🔓

Poulton

SP1001 ⫷ *Falcon Inn*

Sprucewood, *Elf Meadow, Poulton, Cirencester, Glos, GL7 5HQ.*
Quiet, homely, comfortable. Open views. Warm, friendly welcome awaits you.
Open: All Year (not Xmas)
Grades: ETC 4 Diamond
01285 851351 (also fax) Mr & Mrs Walker
D: £16–£20 **S:** £22–£25
Beds: 1D 1T 1S **Baths:** 1 Sh
🛇 🅿 (4) 🛏 📺 ▥ Ⅴ ᵻ

Prestbury Park

SO9524

Hunters Lodge, *Cheltenham Race Course, Prestbury Park, Cheltenham, Glos, GL50 4SH.*
Open: May to Sep
01242 513345 Ms Clark **Fax: 01242 527306**
D: fr £18.50 **S:** fr £21
Beds: 31F 31T 51S **Baths:** 18 Sh
🛇 🅿 📺 🛏 ✕ ▥ Ⅴ ᵻ ᵭ cc
Hunters lodge is a friendly hotel situated within the grounds of Cheltenham Racecourse - the home of national hunt racing. The hotel provides an ideal base for groups visiting Cheltenham and specialises in offering comfortable yet economic accommodation for families, coach parties, sports and cultural tours. Accommodation can be booked throughout the year except during race meetings when the hotel is closed to the public.

Redbrook

SO5310 ⫷ *Boat Inn, Fish'n'Game*

Tresco, *Redbrook, Monmouth, NP5 4LY.*
Beautiful Wye Valley riverside house, fishing, pony trekking, walking, canoeing.
Open: All Year
01600 712325 Mrs Evans
D: fr £16.50 **S:** fr £16.50
Beds: 1F 1D 1T 2S **Baths:** 2 Sh
🛇 🅿 📺 🛏 ✕ ▥ Ⅴ ✿ ᵻ ᵭ

Sherborne

SP1714 ⫷ *Old Inn, The Fox*

The Mead House, *Sherborne, Cheltenham, Gloucs, GL54 3DR.*
Charming C18th house in quiet valley. Warm welcome, comfort, exceptional breakfasts. **Open:** All Year (not Xmas)
01451 844239 Mrs Medill
D: £20–£25 **S:** £20–£25
Beds: 1D 1T **Baths:** 1 Pr
🛇 (12) 🅿 (2) 📺 🛏 ▥ Ⅴ ᵻ

Siddington

SU0399 ⫷ *The Greyhound*

Coleen B&B, *Ashton Road, Siddington, Cirencester, Glos, GL7 6HR.*
Choice accommodation in the Cotswolds. Pub with character 50 metres.
Open: All Year **Grades:** ETC 4 Diamond
01285 642203 Mrs Proctor
proprietor@coleen.co.uk
D: £20–£25 **S:** £30–£40
Beds: 2D 1T **Baths:** 1 En 1 Pr
🅿 (4) ⽶ 📺 ▥ Ⅴ ᵻ

St Briavels

SO5604 ⫷ *The George, The Crown*

Offas Mead, *The Fence, St Briavels, Lydney, Glos, GL15 6QG.*
Large country home on Offa's Dyke Path. Ensuite only.
Open: Easter to Oct
Grades: ETC 3 Star
01594 530229 (also fax) Mrs Lacey
D: £18–£20 **S:** £18–£20
Beds: 1D 2T **Baths:** 2 En 1 Pr
🛇 (10) 🅿 (6) ⽶ 📺 ▥ Ⅴ ᵻ

Woodcroft, *Lower Meend, St Briavels, Lydney, Glos, GL15 6RW.*
Enjoy badgers, bats & buzzards in the beautiful Wye Valley.
Open: All Year
01594 530083 Mrs Allen
b&b@woodcroft.freeserve.co.uk
D: £18–£20 **S:** £25
Beds: 2F 1T **Baths:** 3 En
🛇 (7) 🅿 📺 🛏 ▥ Ⅴ ᵻ ᵭ

Stanton

SP0634 ⫷ *The Mount Inn*

Shenberrow Hill, *Stanton, Broadway, Worcs, WR12 7NE.*
Charming house and cottage accommodation in beautiful unspoilt village. Unforgettable.
Open: All Year (not Xmas)
Grades: ETC 4 Diamond
01386 584468 (also fax) Mrs Neilan
D: £25–£27.50 **S:** fr £30
Beds: 1F 1D 1T **Baths:** 2 En 1 Pr
🛇 (5) 🅿 (5) 📺 🛏 ✕ ▥ Ⅴ ᵻ

Staunton (Coleford)

SO5412 ⫷ *White Horse Inn*

Graygill, *Staunton, Coleford, Glos, GL16 8PD.*
Quietly situated off A4136. Ideal for Forest of Dean, Wye Valley.
Open: All Year (not Xmas)
Grades: ETC 3 Diamond
01600 712536 Mrs Bond
D: fr £17.50 **S:** fr £17.50
Beds: 1D 1T **Baths:** 2 En
🛇 🅿 (4) 📺 🛏 ▥ ᵻ

Staunton (Gloucester)

SO7829 **Mayfield Cottage,** *Moat Lane, Staunton, Gloucester, GL19 3QA.*
C18th extended cottage, rural location, convenient Malverns and Gloucester. Home cooking.
Open: All Year (not Xmas/New Year)
01452 840673 Mrs Clayton
D: £18–£20 **S:** £18–£20
Beds: 1D 1T **Baths:** 2 En
🅿 (4) ⽶ 📺 🛏 ✕ ▥ Ⅴ ᵻ

B&B owners may vary rates - be sure to check when booking

Staverton

SO8823 ⫷ *The Pheasant, The House in the Tree*

Hope Orchard , *Gloucester Road, Staverton, Cheltenham, Glos, GL51 0TF.*
Attractive rooms overlooking old orchard and paddock. Picnic area available.
Open: All Year (not Xmas/New Year)
Grades: ETC 3 Diamond
01452 855556 Mrs Parker
Fax: 01452 530037
info@hopeorchard.com
D: £20–£45 **S:** £25–£30
Beds: 3F 3T 3D **Baths:** 8 En
🛇 🅿 (12) 📺 🛏 ▥ ᵻ ᵭ cc

Stonehouse

SO8005 ⫷ *Beacon Hotel, Ryford Lodge*

Tiled House Farm, *Oxlynch, Stonehouse, Glos, GL10 3DF.*
Open: All Year (not Xmas)
Grades: ETC 4 Diamond
01453 822363 Mrs Jeffery
nigel.jeffery@ukgateway.net
D: £19–£21 **S:** £19–£20
Beds: 1D 1T 1S **Baths:** 1 Pr 1 Sh
🛇 (10) 🅿 (2) ⽶ 📺 ▥ ᵻ
C16th black and white half-timbered farmhouse, with oak beams and Inglewood fireplace, Large garden. This a working Dairy Farm with pedigree Friesian cattle, situated at the edge of Cotswolds and towards Severn vale. close to Slimbridge, Painswick, Berkeley Castle.

Merton Lodge, *8 Ebley Road, Stonehouse, Glos, GL10 2LQ.*
Off road, large beautiful house and garden, lovely views, parking.
Open: All Year (not Xmas/New Year)
Grades: ETC 2 Diamond
01453 822018 Mrs Hodge
D: £19–£21 **S:** £19–£21
Beds: 3D **Baths:** 1 En 1 Sh
🛇 🅿 ⽶ 📺 🛏 ▥ Ⅴ

Stow-on-the-Wold

SP1826 ⫷ *Horse & Groom, Queens Head, Farmers Lodge, White Hart, King's Arms, Golden Ball, Fosse Manor Hotel*

Golden Ball Inn, *Lower Swell, Stow-on-the-Wold, Glos, GL54 1LF.*
Delightful C17th village inn, genuine home-cooked food, friendly atmosphere, pets welcome.
Open: All Year **Grades:** ETC 2 Diamond
01451 830247 A R Knowles
thegolden.ball@virgin.net
D: £22.50–£27.50 **S:** £30–£35
Beds: 3D 1T **Baths:** 4 En
🛇 🅿 (15) 📺 🛏 ✕ ▥ Ⅴ ᵻ cc

Corsham Field Farmhouse, *Bledington Road, Stow-on-the-Wold, Cheltenham, Glos, GL54 1JH.*
Homely farmhouse with breathtaking views, ideally situated for exploring Cotswolds. **Open:** All Year
Grades: ETC 3 Diamond, AA 3 Diamond
01451 831750 Mr Smith
D: £17.50–£22.50 **S:** £20–£25
Beds: 3F 2D 2T **Baths:** 5 En 1 Sh
🛇 🅿 (10) 📺 🛏 ▥ Ⅴ ᵻ

The Limes, *Evesham Road, Stow-on-the-Wold, Cheltenham, Glos, GL54 1EN.*
Large Victorian house, attractive garden. 4 minute walk to town, comfortable.
Open: All Year (not Xmas)
Grades: ETC 3 Diamond
01451 830034 Mr Keyte
D: £21.50 **S:** £25–£42
Beds: 1F 4D 2T **Baths:** 4 En 1 Pr
🛇 🅿 (5) 📺 🐾 🛆 📟 ♿

Fifield Cottage, *Fosse Lane, Stow-on-the-Wold, Cheltenham, Glos, GL54 1EH.*
Cottage: private road, peaceful situation. Close to town. Attractive garden.
Open: All Year (not Xmas)
01451 831056 Mrs Keyte
D: £19–£22 **S:** fr £23
Beds: 1F 1D 1T **Baths:** 2 En 1 Pr
🛇 🅿 (4) 📺 🐾 🛆 📟 ♿

South Hill Farmhouse, *Fosseway, Stow-on-the-Wold, Cheltenham, Glos, GL54 1JU.*
Listed Cotswold farmhouse. On-site parking, ideal for walkers.
Open: All Year
01451 831888 Mr & Mrs Cassie
Fax: 01451 832255
info@southhill.co.uk
D: fr £19
Beds: 1F 2D 2T 1S **Baths:** 1 Pr 5 En
🛇 🅿 (10) ⅙ 📺 🛆 ♿ ᴄᴄ

The Gate Lodge, *Stow Hill, Stow-on-the-Wold, Cheltenham, Glos, GL54 1JZ.*
Grade II Listed building; formerly gate lodge to Netherswell Manor.
Open: All Year (not Xmas)
Grades: ETC 4 Diamond
01451 832103 Mr & Mrs Feasey
D: £18–£20 **S:** £20–£25
Beds: 2D **Baths:** 2 En
🛇 🅿 (4) ⅙ 📺 🛆 ♿

Pear Tree Cottage, *High Street, Stow-on-the-Wold, Cheltenham, Glos, GL54 1DL.*
Period cottage with very relaxed atmosphere, convenient to town square.
Open: All Year
Grades: ETC 3 Diamond
01451 831210 Mr Henderson
peartreecottage@btinternet.com
D: £20–£25 **S:** £30–£35
Beds: 2D **Baths:** 2 En
🛇 (1) 🅿 (2) 📺 🛆 📟 ♿

Old Farmhouse Hotel, *Lower Swell, Stow-on-the-Wold, Cheltenham, Glos, GL54 1LF.*
C16th converted manor farm in quiet hamlet, 1 mile west of Stow.
Open: All Year
Freephone 0800 0561150 Mr Burger
Fax: 01451 870962
oldfarm@globalnet.co.uk
D: £20–£57.50 **S:** £30–£67.50
Beds: 3F 6D 3T **Baths:** 10 En 2 Sh
🛇 🅿 (25) 📺 🐾 🛆 ♿ ☀ ᴄᴄ

Please respect a B&B's wishes regarding children, animals and smoking

All details shown are as supplied by B&B owners in Autumn 2000

Stroud

SO8405   🍺 *Tipputs Inn, Imperial Hotel, Downfield Hotel, Clothiers' Arms, Vine Tree, British Oak*

The Downfield Hotel, *Cainscross Road, Stroud, Glos, GL5 4HN.*
Stunning views of the hills and valleys. An unforgettable holiday.
Open: All Year
Grades: ETC 3 Diamond, AA 3 Diamond, RAC 3 Diamond
01453 764496 Fax: 01453 753150
messenger@downfieldotel.demon.co.uk
D: £20–£27 **S:** £30–£45
Beds: 2F 9D 6T 4S **Baths:** 11 En 10 Sh
🛇 🅿 (25) ⅙ 📺 🐾 🛆 📟 ♿ ᴄᴄ

Clothiers Arms, *Bath Road, Stroud, Glos, GL5 3JJ.*
Open: All Year
Grades: ETC 3 Diamond
01453 763801 Mrs Close
Fax: 01453 757161
luciano@clothiersarms.demon.co.uk
D: £20–£33 **S:** £23–£35
Beds: 7F 3D 2T **Baths:** 6 En 1 Pr
🛇 🅿 (50) ⅙ 📺 🐾 🛆 📟 ♿ ᴄᴄ
The Clothiers Arms is within walking distance of Stroud town centre, trains and bus station. Ideal location for Bath, Cheltenham, Cirencester. We have large beer garden, children's play area, 50 seater restaurant and ample car parking facilities.

Cairngall Guest House, *65 Bisley Old Road, Stroud, Glos, GL5 1NF.*
Large elegant Victorian Listed house, elevated position with superb views.
Open: All Year (not Xmas)
01453 766689 Mr & Mrs Fabb
D: £23–£25 **S:** £23–£25
Beds: 2D 1T 1S **Baths:** 2 Sh
🛇 (10) 🅿 (6) ⅙ 📺 🛆 ♿

Court Farm, *Randwick, Stroud, Glos, GL6 6HH.*
C17th beamed Cotswold farmhouse, large garden, abundant wildlife, good views.
Open: All Year
01453 764210 Mr Taylor
D: £19–£20 **S:** £19–£20
Beds: 2F 1T **Baths:** 2 En 1 Sh
🛇 🅿 (6) ⅙ 📺 🐾 🛆 📟 ♿

Teddington

SO9633   🍺 *The Pheasant*

Bengrove Farm, *Bengrove, Teddington, Tewkesbury, Glos, GL20 8JB.*
C17th, Listed. Lovely views. Peaceful, timber/beamed attractive rooms.
Open: All Year (not Xmas)
01242 620332 Mrs Hopkins
Fax: 01242 620851
D: £17–£20 **S:** £20–£25
Beds: 3T **Baths:** 1 En 2 Sh
🛇 🅿 (10) ⅙ 📺 🐾 🛆 ♿

Tewkesbury

SO8933   🍺 *Black Bear, Woody's*

Hoo Farm, *Gloucester Road, Tewkesbury, Glos, GL20 7DD.*
Superior hospitality in beautiful farmhouse, six acre grounds in glorious countryside.
Open: All Year
01684 292185 (also fax)
Mrs Mitchell
hoofarm@ukonline.co.uk
D: fr £20 **S:** fr £20
Beds: 2T 1S **Baths:** 1 Pr 1 Sh
🛇 🅿 (10) ⅙ 📺 🐾 🛆 📟 ♿

Carrant Brook House, *Rope Walk, Tewkesbury, Glos, GL20 5DS.*
Victorian family home, two mins walk to all amenities, pool, theatre.
Open: All Year
Grades: ETC 3 Diamond
01684 290355 Mrs Bishop
anna@shail64.freeserve.co.uk
D: £25–£55 **S:** £27.50–£35
Beds: 1D 1T 1S **Baths:** 3 En
🛇 🅿 (4) ⅙ 📺 🛆 📟 ♿ ☀

Two, Back of Avon, *Riverside Walk, Tewkesbury, Glos, GL20 5BA.*
Lovely Queen Anne house, Grade II Listed, overlooking river.
Open: All Year
Grades: ETC 2 Diamond
01684 298935 Mr & Mrs Leach
D: £19–£22 **S:** £22–£25
Beds: 1F 1D 1T **Baths:** 2 En
🛇 🅿 ⅙ 📺 🐾 🛆 📟 ♿

Barton House Guesthouse, *5 Barton Road, Tewkesbury, Glos, GL20 5QG.*
Regency house close to town centre, Abbey, rivers and M5.
Open: All Year
01684 292049 M J Green
D: £18–£25 **S:** £25–£30
Beds: 2F 1T 1D **Baths:** 2 En 1 Sh
🛇 🅿 (4) 📺 ♿

Todenham

SP2336   🍺 *Farmers Arms*

Roosters, *Todenham, Moreton-in-Marsh, Glos, GL56 9PA.*
Beautifully situated for exploring Cotswolds. Lovely C17th stone house. Lovely gardens.
Open: All Year (not Xmas)
Grades: ETC 4 Diamond
01608 650645 (also fax)
Ms Longmore
D: £23–£25 **S:** £25–£30
Beds: 1D 2T **Baths:** 2 En 1 Pr
🛇 🅿 (8) ⅙ 📺 🐾 🛆 📟 ♿

Tormarton

ST7678   🍺 *The Portcullis*

Chestnut Farm, *Tormarton, Badminton, Glos, GL9 1HS.*
Small Georgian farmhouse.
Open: All Year
01454 218563 (also fax) Ms Cadei
D: £30–£40 **S:** £30–£40
Beds: 1F 4D 2T **Baths:** 7 Pr
🛇 🅿 (8) 📺 🐾 🛆 📟 ♿ ☀

The Portcullis, *Tormarton, Badminton, GL9 1HZ.*
Traditional ivy-clad inn and restaurant in pretty Cotswold village. **Open:** All Year (not Xmas)
01454 218263 Fax: 01454 218094
D: £20–£25 **S:** £28–£30
Beds: 1F 2D 4T **Baths:** 7 En
🛇 (6) 🅿 (40) 🗹 ✕ 🖳 🆅 🛊 cc

Tredington

SO9029 🍺 *The Shutter*

Gothic Farm, *Tredington, Tewkesbury, Glos, GL20 7BS.*
Friendly, comfortable, character farmhouse with wonderful views of the Cotswolds.
Open: All Year (not Xmas)
01684 293360 Mr Coleman
molliecoleman@aol.com
D: £18–£25 **S:** £20–£30
Beds: 1D 1T **Baths:** 1 Pr 2 Sh
🛇 (2) 🅿 (10) 🗲 🗹 🐾 ✕ 🖳 🆅 🛊 cc

Uley

ST7898 🍺 *Old Crown, Rose & Crown*

Hill House, *Crawley Hill, Uley, Dursley, Glos, GL11 5BH.*
Very warm welcome. Cotswold stone house, beautiful views, quiet location.
Open: All Year (not Xmas)
01453 860267 Mr & Mrs Kent
D: £18.50–£22 **S:** £17–£30
Beds: 1F 1D 1T 1S **Baths:** 2 En 1 Sh
🛇 🅿 (5) 🗲 🗹 ✕ 🖳 🆅 🛊

Westonbirt

ST8589 🍺 *Holford Arms*

Avenue Farm, *Knockdown, Tetbury, Glos, GL8 8QY.*
300-year-old farmhouse in farm adjoining Westonbirt Arboretum. Bath, Bristol & Gloucester within easy reach.
Open: All Year
Grades: ETC 3 Diamond
01454 238207 Mrs King
Fax: 01454 238033
sonjames@breathemail.net
D: £20–£25 **S:** £25
Beds: 1F 1D 2T **Baths:** 2 En 1 Sh
🛇 🅿 (6) 🗲 🗹 🖳 🆅 🛊

Wick

ST7072 🍺 *Rose & Crown*

Toghill House Farm, *Toghill, Wick, Bristol, BS15 5RT.*
Warm cosy farmhouse, formerly resting house for monks (4 miles Bath).
Open: All Year
01225 891261
Mrs Bishop
D: £23–£25 **S:** £29–£37
Beds: 2F 6D 3T **Baths:** 8 Pr
🛇 🅿 (20) 🗲 🗹 🐾 🖳 🆅 🛊 ♿

Willersey

SP1040

Lower Field Farm, *Willersey, Broadway, Worcs, WR12 5HF.*
Genuine farmhouse, comfort and hospitality on a mixed sheep and cereal farm. **Open:** All Year
01386 858273 J Hill
Fax: 01386 854608
info@lowerfield-farm.co.uk
D: £22.50–£25 **S:** £22.50–£25
Beds: 2F 1D **Baths:** 3 En
🛇 🅿 (6) 🗲 🗹 ✕ 🖳 🆅 ✿ 🛊

Winchcombe

SP0228 🍺 *Plaisterers Arms, Harvest Home, Hobnails, Pheasant, Royal Oak, White Hart, Corner Cupboards*

Ireley Grounds, *Barnhouse, Broadway Road, Winchcombe, Cheltenham, Glos, GL54 5NY.*
Open: All Year (not Xmas)
Grades: ETC 4 Diamond
01242 603736 Mr Wright
D: £22.50–£32.50 **S:** £22.50–£32.50
Beds: 1F 3D **Baths:** 4 En
🛇 🅿 (20) 🗲 🗹 🖳 🆅 🛊
IRELEY GROUNDS is a stunning Cotswold house in 6 acres of attractive gardens with magnificent views of the countryside and Great Western Railway. Relax in the lounge with its sofas and log fires. A function suite is available for up to 100 people.

The Homestead, *Smithy Lane, Greet, Winchcombe, Cheltenham, Glos, GL54 5BP.*
C16th country house in beautiful Cotswold countryside, local pub nearby.
Open: Feb to Nov
01242 603808 Mrs Bloom
D: £20–£22.50 **S:** £20–£30
Beds: 2F 2D **Baths:** 3 En 2 Pr 1 Sh
🛇 (6) 🅿 (4) 🗹 🐾 🖳 🛊

Ireley Farm, *Ireley Road, Winchcombe, Cheltenham, Glos, GL54 5PA.*
C18th Cotswold stone character farmhouse. Relaxed excellent breakfasts.
Open: Jan to Nov
01242 602445 Mrs Warmington
warmingtonmaggot@aol.com
D: £20–£25 **S:** £20–£25
Beds: 1F 1D 1T **Baths:** 2 En 1 Pr
🛇 🅿 🗹 ✕ 🆅 🛊

Manor Farm, *Winchcombe, Cheltenham, Glos, GL54 5BJ.*
Cotswold manor on family farm. S/c cottages, camping and caravan space on farm.
Open: All Year (not Xmas)
Grades: ETC 4 Diamond
01242 602423 (also fax)
Mr & Mrs Day
janet@dickandjanet.fsnet.co.uk
D: £25–£30 **S:** fr £30
Beds: 2D 1T **Baths:** 3 En
🛇 🅿 (20) 🗹 🖳 🛊

Blair House, *41 Gretton Road, Winchcombe, Cheltenham, Glos, GL54 5EG.*
Georgian house in historic town. Warm friendly welcome, excellent breakfasts.
Open: All Year
Grades: ETC 3 Diamond
01242 603626 Mrs Chisholm
Fax: 01242 604214
chrisssurv@aol.com
D: £20–£21 **S:** £22–£25
Beds: 1D 1T 2S **Baths:** 1 En 1 Sh
🛇 🅿 (1) 🗲 🗹 🖳 🆅 🛊

Sudeley Hill Farm, *Winchcombe, Cheltenham, Glos, GL54 5JB.*
Comfortably furnished C15th farmhouse.
Open: All Year (not Xmas)
Grades: ETC 4 Diamond, AA 4 Diamond
01242 602344 (also fax)
Mrs Scudamore
D: £22–£25 **S:** £30–£32
Beds: 1F 1D 1T **Baths:** 3 En
🛇 🅿 (10) 🗹 🖳 🆅 🛊

Gower House, *16 North Street, Winchcombe, Cheltenham, Glos, GL54 5LH.*
C18th town house near shops.
Open: All Year (not Xmas)
01242 602616 Mrs Simmonds
D: £20–£22.50 **S:** £30–£40
Beds: 1D 2T **Baths:** 3 En
🛇 🅿 (3) 🗹 🖳 🆅 🛊

Elms Farm, *Gretton, Winchcombe, Cheltenham, Glos, GL54 5HQ.*
Farmhouse set in peaceful location, close to places of interest.
Open: All Year (not Xmas)
Grades: ETC 4 Diamond
01242 620150 (also fax)
R Quilter
rose@elmfarm.demon.co.uk
D: £25–£30 **S:** £30–£35
Beds: 1F 1T **Baths:** 2 En
🛇 🅿 (4) 🗲 🗹 🐾 🖳 🛊

Wormington

SP0336 🍺 *Pheasant Inn*

Manor Farm, *Wormington, Broadway, Worcs, WR12 7NL.*
C16th listed Tudor farmhouse in quiet village near church. **Open:** All Year
01386 584302 Mrs Russell
mark@smith-russell.softnet.co.uk
D: £20–£22 **S:** £20–£30
Beds: 2D 1T **Baths:** 2 En 1 Pr
🛇 (5) 🅿 (4) 🗲 🗹 🖳 🛊

Wotton-under-Edge

ST7692 🍺 *Royal Oak*

Wotton Guest House, *31a Long Street, Wotton-under-Edge, Glos, GL12 7BX.*
C17th Manor house, superb food in adjoining coffee shop. **Open:** All Year
01453 843158 Mrs Nixon
Fax: 01453 842410
D: £24 **S:** £30
Beds: 1F 2D 2S **Baths:** 7 En
🛇 🅿 (12) 🗲 🗹 🐾 🖳 🛊

Greater Manchester & Merseyside

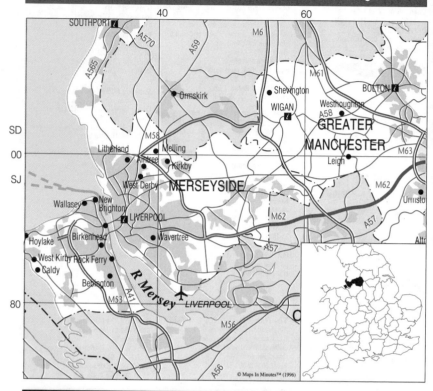

© Maps In Minutes™ (1996)

Tourist Information Centres

Stamford New Road, **Altrincham**, Cheshire, WA14 1EJ, 0161 912 5931.

32 Market Street, **Ashton-under-Lyne**, Lancs, OL6 6ER, 0161 343 4343.

Town Hall, Victoria Square, **Bolton**, Lancashire, BL1 1RU, 01204 334400.

Derby Hall, Market Street, **Bury**, Lancashire, BL9 0BN, 0161 705 5122.

6 Station Road, **Cheadle Hulme**, Cheshire, SK8 5AE, 0161 486 0283.

Town Hall Extension, Lloyd Street, **Manchester**, M60 2LA, 0161 234 3157 / 8.

International Arrivals Hall, Terminal 1, **Manchester Airport**, M90 3NY, 0161 436 3344.

International Arrivals Hall, Terminal 2, **Manchester Airport**, M90 4TU, 0161 489 6412.

11 Albion Street, **Oldham**, Lancs, OL1 3BD, 0161 627 1024.

The Clock Tower, Town Hall, **Rochdale**, Lancashire, OL16 1AB, 01706 356592.

Graylaw House, Chestergate, **Stockport**, Cheshire, SK1 1NG, 0161 474 3320 / 1.

High Street, Uppermill, **Uppermill**, Saddleworth, Lancashire, OL3 6HS, 01457 870336.

Trencherfield Mill, Wigan Pier, **Wigan**, Lancashire, WN3 4EL, 01942 825677.

MERSEYSIDE

Woodside Ferry Terminal, Woodside, **Birkenhead**, Merseyside, L41 1EQ, 0151 647 6780.

Merseyside Welcome Centre, Clayton Square Shopping Centre, **Liverpool**, Merseyside, L1 1QR, 0151 709 3631.

Atlantic Pavilion, Albert Dock, **Liverpool**, L3 4AA, 0151 708 8854.

112 Lord Street, **Southport**, Merseyside, PR8 1NY, 01704 533333.

Altrincham

SJ7687   🍺 *Old Mill, Hare and Hounds*

Acorn Of Oakmere, 6 Wingate Drive Timperley, Altrincham, Greater Manchester, WA15 7PX.
Open: All Year **Grades:** ETC 3 Diamond
0161 980 8391 Mrs Moore
oakmere6@cwctv.net
D: £25–£30 **S:** £25–£30
Beds: 1T 1S **Baths:** 1 En 1 Sh
🛇 🅿 (2) 🐾 🔟 📺 🅥 ♨
Warm comfortable family home, attractive walled garden. Relax with sunken spa bath. Easy access Trafford and Lowry centres, Manchester's shopping Theatres, Concert halls 20 minutes by Metro tram. Quality restaurants in Altrincham market town 1 mile. Close to M6, M60.

Belvedere Guest House, 58 Barrington Road, Altrincham, Cheshire, WA14 1HY.
Close to tram, restaurants, pubs. Manchester Airport 12 minutes away.
Open: All Year **0161 941 5996** Mr Kelly
Fax: **0161 929 6450**
D: fr £18 **S:** fr £20
Beds: 2F 1T **Baths:** 4 Pr
🛇 🅿 (5) 🔟 🍴 ✕ 📺 🅥 ♨ 👶 1

Bebington

SJ3383 🍺 *The Acorn*

Bebington Hotel, *24 Town Lane, Bebington, Wirral, Merseyside, L63 5JG.*
Open: All Year (not Xmas)
0151 645 0608 (also fax)
Mrs Vaghena
D: £20–£22.50 **S:** fr £25
Beds: 1F 5D 1T 8S
Baths: All En
🛇 🅿 (12) 🖾 🏋 ✕ 🛒 🖾 🗓 🛓
This professionally-run family hotel guarantees a warm welcome. All rooms of high standard, tastefully decorated, home from home comforts. Well-lit car park. Residents licence. Only five minutes from Bebington station and easy reach of Liverpool and Chester.

Birkenhead

SJ3088 🍺 *Mersey Clipper, Canarvon Castle*

Ashgrove Guest House, *14 Ashville Road, Claughton, Prenton, Birkenhead, Merseyside, CH43 8SA.*
Open: All Year
0151 653 3794 Mr Lupton
briory@barclays.net
D: £16–£18 **S:** £16–£20
Beds: 1F 2D 2T 2S
Baths: 1 En 3 Sh
🛇 🅿 (6) 🖾 🏋 ✕ 🛒 🖾 🗓 🛓
Friendly family-run establishment with musical ties, overlooking parkland. Main shopping area 1 mile . Mileage Liverpool 4 Chester 17 Southport 23 Blackpool 80. Games room. self catering from £14 per night/ £70 per week, per person.

Victoria House, *12 Shrewsbury Road, Oxton, Birkenhead, CH43 1UX.*
Victorian house. Large rooms, large gardens. 1 mile town centre.
Open: All Year
Grades: ETC 2 Diamond
0151 652 8379 D: £20–£22 **S:** £20–£22
Beds: 1F 2T 1D 1S **Baths:** 1 En 2 Sh
🛇 🅿 (6) ⅙ ✕ 🖾 ✕ 🛒 🖾 🗓 🛓

Bolton

SD7108 🍺 *Farmers' Arms*

Heyesleigh, *98 Castle Road, Bolton, Lancs, BL2 1JL.*
Situated off main A58. Bury Bolton Road. 7 mins' walk town centre.
Open: All Year (not Xmas)
01204 523647 Mrs Longworth
Fax: 07070 712838
D: £16–£18 **S:** £17–£22
Beds: 3F 2D 1T 3S **Baths:** 5 En 1 Sh
🛇 🖾 ✕ 🛒 🖾 🛓

Glengarry Guest House, *79 Bradford Street, Bolton, Lancs, BL2 1JY.*
Small, established, family run, 5 mins motorway & town centre.
Open: All Year (not Xmas)
01204 534299 Mrs Hope
D: £17–£18 **S:** £17–£18
Beds: 1F 1D 4T 1S **Baths:** 3 Sh
🛇 🅿 🖾 🖾 🏋 ✕ 🗓 🛓

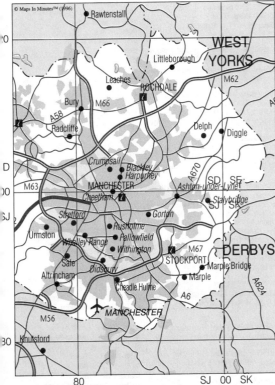

© Maps In Minutes™ (1996)

Ashton-under-Lyne

SJ9399 🍺 *Dog & Partridge, Hare & Hounds, King William*

Lynwood Hotel, *3 Richmond Street, Ashton-under-Lyne, Greater Manchester, OL6 7TX.*
Open: All Year
Grades: ETC 3 Diamond
0161 330 5358 (also fax)
Mrs Lindsay
D: £20–£24 **S:** £20–£24
Beds: 1F 1T 2S **Baths:** 2 En 1 Sh
🛇 🅿 🖾 🛒 🖾 🛓
A friendly family-run hotel in a quiet location, 5 mins from Ashton and Portland Basin. Manchester Airport 20 mins, convenient to motorways, Manchester, Gmex, Arena, Lowry centre, Velodrome Granada studios and Trafford Centre, also for Commonwealth Games. Pubs and restaurants close by. A warm welcome guaranteed

Planning a longer stay? Always ask for any special rates

King William IV Hotel, *Stamford Street West, Ashton-under-Lyne, Lancashire, OL6 7QU.*
Mainly for commercial traveller seeking good clean accommodation at reasonable rates. **Open:** All Year (not Xmas/New Year)
0161 339 6016 D: £15 **S:** £15
Beds: 5T 2D 1S **Baths:** 5 Pr
⅙ 🖾 ✕ 🛒 🖾 ✳ 🛓 cc

Linda Linney, *112 Cranbourne Road, Ashton-under-Lyne, OL7B 9BW.*
Private house, quiet area, 15 mins walk to town centre. **Open:** All Year
0161 330 7599 D: £15 **S:** fr £15
Beds: 1D 1T 1S **Baths:** 1 Sh
🛇 🅿 (2) 🖾 🛒 🛓

Welbeck House Hotel, *324 Katherine Street, Ashton-under-Lyne, OL6 7BD.*
Family-run hotel, close to motorway networks, warm welcome.
Open: All Year (not Xmas)
Grades: RAC 3 Diamond
0161 344 0751 J Warhurst
Fax: 0161 343 4278
welbeck5000@breathemail.net
D: £25–£28 **S:** £32–£38
Beds: 2F 2D 2T 4S **Baths:** 10 En
🛇 🅿 (15) 🖾 🏋 ✕ 🛒 🖾 🛓 cc

Bury

SD8010 🍺 *Sir Robert Peel*

Pennine View, 8 Hunstanton Drive, Brandlesholme, Bury, Greater Manchester, BL8 1EG.
Quiet, comfortable rooms, excellent breakfasts, convenient - city, town and country. **Open:** All Year
0161 763 1249 Mrs McKeon
D: £15 **S:** £20
Beds: 3D **Baths:** 1 Sh
🛇 ⓟ (3) 🚫 📺 🛏 ✕ 🏛 Ⓥ 🛔

Ashbury Guest House, 235 Rochdale Road, Bury, Greater Manchester, BL9 7BX.
Convenient for motorway network, metro into Manchester, East Lancs Railway.
Open: All Year
0161 762 9623 G Woodall
Fax: 0161 763 3887
D: £20–£22 **S:** £20–£25
Beds: 1D 1T 2S **Baths:** 1 En 1 Sh

Caldy

SJ2285 🍺 *Cottage Loaf*

Cheriton, 151 Caldy Road, Caldy, West Kirby, Wirral, CH48 1LP.
Beautiful country house set in 1 acre of gardens, situated in an exclusive area.
Open: All Year
0151 625 5271 (also fax) Mrs Smith
cheriton151@hotmail.com
D: £18–£20 **S:** £25–£27
Beds: 2T 1S **Baths:** 2 Sh
🛇 ⓟ (6) 📺 🛏 🏛 Ⓥ 🛔

Cheadle Hulme

SJ8786 🍺 *Red Lion, Hesketh Tavern, Church Inn, George & Dragon*

Spring Cottage, 60 Hulme Hall Road, Cheadle Hulme, Cheadle, Cheshire, SK8 6JZ.
Beautiful Victorian house adjacent to the C17th Hulme Hall. **Open:** All Year
Grades: ETC 3 Diamond
0161 485 1037 (also fax) Mr Stent
D: £27–£30 **S:** £20–£30
Beds: 2T 1S 1F **Baths:** 3 Pr 1 Sh
🛇 ⓟ (6) 📺 🛏 🏛 Ⓥ 🛔 cc

156 Queens Road, Cheadle Hulme, Cheadle, SK8 5HY.
Guided walks arranged (all levels). 10 mins Manchester Airport, Stockport.
Open: All Year
0161 485 2435 Mrs Burgess
D: £17–£20 **S:** £17–£20
Beds: 1D 2S **Baths:** 2 En
🛇 (10) ⓟ (4) 🚫 📺 🛏 🏛 🛔

Delph

SD9807 🍺 *Old Bell*

Old Bell Inn Hotel, Delph, Oldham, Lancs, OL3 5EG.
C18th coaching inn. Delightful bedrooms. Fine food and ales.
Open: All Year
01457 870130 Mr Grew
Fax: 01457 876597
D: £25–£35 **S:** £30–£35
Beds: 6D 1T 3S **Baths:** 9 En 1 Pr
🛇 ⓟ (25) 📺 🛏 ✕ 🏛 Ⓥ 🛔 cc

Globe Farm Guest House, Huddersfield Road, Standedge, Delph, Oldham, Lancashire, OL3 5LU.
Former coaching house converted into comfortable ensuite bed & breakfast.
Open: All Year (not Xmas)
01457 873040 (also fax)
D: fr £19.75 **S:** fr £25
Beds: 1F 5D 4T 4S **Baths:** 14 En
🛇 ⓟ (30) 📺 ✕ 🏛 🛔

Diggle

SE0008 🍺 *Diggle Hotel, Floating Light, Church Inn, Navigation Inn*

New Barn, Harrop Green Farm, Diggle, Oldham, Lancs, OL3 5LW.
Working farm, lovely views over Saddleworth villages. Close to Standedge Canal Tunnel. **Open:** All Year (not Xmas)
01457 873937 Mr Rhodes
D: £16–£17 **S:** £16–£18
Beds: 1F 1D 1T 1S **Baths:** 1 Pr 1 Sh
🛇 ⓟ (10) 📺 🛏 🏛 Ⓥ 🛔

Sunfield, Diglea, Diggle, Saddleworth, Oldham, Lancs, OL3 5LA.
Scenic Saddleworth Canal towpaths, walking, cycling, horse riding, its all here.
Open: All Year
01457 874030 Mr & Mrs Francis
Fax: 01457 810488
D: £15–£18 **S:** £20–£25
Beds: 1F 3D 2T 1S **Baths:** 7 En
🛇 ⓟ (8) 🚫 📺 🛏 🏛 Ⓥ ✳ 🛔 ♿

Hoylake

SJ2188 🍺 *Green Lodge, Wetherspoons, King's Gap*

Wirral Point Guest House, 37 Stanley Road, Hoylake, Wirral, Merseyside, CH47 1HN.
Large detached house beside Dee Estuary backing onto Royal Liverpool golf course.
Open: All Year (not Xmas)
0151 632 5121 Mr & Mrs Ellis-Jones
D: £18 **S:** £18
Beds: 1F 1D 1T **Baths:** 1 Pr 1 Sh
🛇 ⓟ (10) ✕ 🏛 Ⓥ 🛔 ♿

Kirkby

SJ4199

Greenbank Guest House, 193 Rowen Drive, Kirkby, Liverpool, Merseyside, L32 0SG.
Open: All Year (not Xmas/New Year)
0151 546 9971 (also fax)
D: £34–£38 **S:** £22–£25
Beds: 1D 1S **Baths:** 1 Sh
🛇 (10) ⓟ (2) 🚫 📺 ✕ 🏛 🛔
Small welcoming guest house. 5 minutes drive to Aintree Race Course, football ground, golf course and Knowsley Safari Park. Knowsley and Kirkby business areas easy access to A38, M57, 58 and 62 Motorways. Open aspect to rear of building. Private off road parking.

B&B owners may vary rates - be sure to check when booking

Leigh

SD6500 🍺 *Three Crowns*

Three Crowns, 188 Chapel Street, Leigh, Lancashire, WN7 2DW.
Three Crowns, Leigh, pub/restaurant open all year round.
Open: All Year
01942 673552 D: £15 **S:** £15
Beds: 1T 1S
🛇 ⓟ 📺 🏛 Ⓥ 🛔 cc

Litherland

SJ3498

Litherland Park, 34 Litherland Park, Litherland, Bootle, L21 9HP.
Victorian detached house, spacious lounge, three bedrooms. Warm welcome assured.
Open: All Year (not Xmas/New Year)
Grades: ETC 3 Diamond
0151 928 1085 B Harper
D: £19 **S:** £20
Beds: 2D 1S **Baths:** 2 Sh
ⓟ (4) 📺 ✕ 🏛 🛔

Littleborough

SD9316 🍺 *The Beach, Charlotte's*

Hollingworth Lake B&B, 164 Smithybridge Road, Hollingworth Lake, Littleborough, Lancashire, OL15 0DB.
Beautiful garden near Hollingworth Lake Country Park, walks, riding and restaurants nearby.
Open: All Year
Grades: ETC 4 Diamond, AA 4 Diamond, RAC 4 Diamond
01706 376583 Ms Wood
D: £15–£22.50 **S:** £25–£30
Beds: 1F 2D 1T 1S
Baths: All Rooms with En-suite
🛇 ⓟ (5) 🚫 📺 🛏 🏛 Ⓥ 🛔 ♿ cc 3

Swing Cottage Guest House, 31 Lakebank, Hollingworth Lake Country Park, Littleborough, Greater Manchester, OL15 0DQ.
'North West Best B&B' winner 2000 - beautiful countryside.
Open: All Year
Grades: ETC 4 Diamond
01706 379094
C Dean
Fax: 01706 379091
swingcottage@aol.com
D: £22.50 **S:** £35
Beds: 2F 1T **Baths:** 3 En
🛇 ⓟ 🚫 📺 ✕ 🏛 Ⓥ 🛔 cc

Waterside Inn, 1 Inghams Lane, Littleborough, Lancashire, OL15 0AY.
Situated on canal, 0.50 mile Hollingworth Lake, 1 min railway station.
Open: All Year
01706 376250
Mr Grindrod
D: £25–£40 **S:** £25–£40
Beds: 3F 1D **Baths:** 3 En
🛇 ⓟ (8) 📺 ✕ 🏛 Ⓥ 🛔

LIVERPOOL Central

SJ3490   *The Philharmonic, Cafe No.7*

Embassie Youth Hostel, *1 Falkner Square, Liverpool, L8 7NU.*
Town house in beautiful Georgian Falkner Square. Head towards Anglican cathedral, up Canning St.
Open: All Year
0151 707 1089 Mr Murphy
D: fr £12.50 **S:** £9.50–£11.50
Beds: 20S **Baths:** 5 Sh
(12) P TV

LIVERPOOL Wavertree

SJ3889

Holmeleigh Guest House, *93 Woodcroft Road, Wavertree, Liverpool, L15 2HG.*
Family-run continental breakfast only 2.50 miles from city centre.
Open: All Year
Grades: ETC 2 Diamond
0151 734 2216 (day) Mrs Bridge
Fax: 0151 291 9877
bridges01@cableinet.co.uk
D: £15–£25 **S:** £15–£30
Beds: 4T 2D 4S **Baths:** 6 En 1 Sh
TV

LIVERPOOL West Derby

SJ3993

Parkland Bed & Breakfast, *38 Coachman's Drive, Croxteth Park, Liverpool, L12 0HX.*
Quiet residential house in country park. 5 miles from city centre.
Open: All Year (not Xmas/New Year)
Grades: ETC 3 Diamond
0151 259 1417 R Todd
D: £20 **S:** £20
Beds: 1T 1D **Baths:** 1 Sh
(2) TV

MANCHESTER Blackley

SD8602   *Heaton Park*

Bentley Guest House, *64 Hill Lane, Blackley, Manchester, M9 6PF.*
A private homely semi-detached house, personal service, comfortable quality accommodation.
Open: All year
Grades: ETC 3 Diamond
0161 795 1116 R Kerassites
D: £15–£20 **S:** £18–£20
Beds: 2D 1S **Baths:** 1 En 1 Sh
(9) P (3) TV

MANCHESTER Cheetham

SD8400

New Central Hotel, *144-146 Heywood Street, Cheetham, Manchester, M8 7PD.*
Small, comfortable, friendly hotel.
Open: All Year
Grades: AA 1 Diamond, RAC 1 Diamond
0161 205 2169 (also fax)
Mrs Greenwood
newcentral@talk21.com
D: £16.50–£17.50 **S:** £18.50–£21.50
Beds: 1F 1D 2T 7S **Baths:** 5 Pr 2 Sh
(2) P (7) TV

MANCHESTER Crumpsall

SD8402   *Three Arrows*

Cleveland Lodge, *117 Cleveland Road, Crumpsall, Manchester, M8 4GX.*
Nearby Metrolink station, serves city centre and places of interest.
Open: All Year
0161 795 0007 (also fax)
A Musgrove
D: £17 **S:** £25
Beds: 2D 1S
TV

MANCHESTER Didsbury

SJ8491

Green Gables Guest House, *152 Barlow Moor Road, Didsbury, Manchester, M20 2UT.*
Warm, friendly guest house. Convenient for all Manchester attractions.
Open: All Year
0161 445 5365 Fax: 0161 445 5363
D: £18–£20 **S:** £18–£22
Beds: 6F 6T 6D 7S **Baths:** 1 En 6 Sh
(2) TV cc

MANCHESTER Fallowfield

SJ8593

Wilmslow Hotel, *356 Wilmslow Road, Fallowfield, Manchester, M14 6AB.*
Family run, helpful staff, pubs and restaurants 5 minutes walk.
Open: All Year
Grades: ETC 2 Diamond
0161 225 3030 Fax: 0161 257 2854
D: £16–£21 **S:** £19.95–£30.65
Beds: 4F 6T 9D 9S **Baths:** 14 En 3 Sh
P (10) TV cc

MANCHESTER Gorton

SJ8896   *The Windmill*

Clyde Mount Guest House, *866 Hyde Road, Debdale Park, Gorton, Manchester, M18 7LH.*
Large Victorian house overlooking park, friendly, comfortable, convenient city centre.
Open: All Year
0161 231 1515
clydemount.sw@amserve.net
D: £18 **S:** £18
Beds: 1F 3D 3T 3S **Baths:** 3 Sh
P (8) TV cc

MANCHESTER Harpurhey

SD8601

Harpers Hotel, *745 Rochdale Road, Harpurhey, Manchester, M9 5SB.*
Rooms ensuite. 2 miles city centre, Manchester Arena, Velodrome, 2002 Stadium.
Open: All Year
0161 203 5475 (also fax)
D: £22–£30 **S:** £32–£40
Beds: 13F **Baths:** 13 En
TV

MANCHESTER Rusholme

SJ8695

Elton Bank Hotel, *62 Platt Lane, Rusholme, Manchester, M14 5NE.*
The Elton Bank Hotel offers the ideal combination of a peaceful parkside setting.
Open: All Year
0161 224 6449 eltonbank@dial.pipex.com
D: £20–£23 **S:** £27–£34
Beds: 1F 2D 4T 3S **Baths:** 3 En 4 Sh
(16) TV cc

MANCHESTER Stretford

SJ8095   *Quadrant*

Greatstone Hotel, *843-845 Chester Road, Gorse Hill, Stretford, Manchester, M32 0RN.*
Family-run . Five minute walk Man. Utd Football Ground. **Open:** All Year
0161 865 1640 Mr Sill
D: £18–£20 **S:** £20–£22
Beds: 1F 5T 6D 12S **Baths:** 2 En 4 Pr 3 Sh
P (50) TV cc

MANCHESTER
Whalley Range

SJ8294

Polex Hotel, *70-78 Dudley Road, off Withington Road, Whalley Range, Manchester, M16 8DE.*
Hotel established 1964. 2 miles city centre, 1.5 miles Old Trafford, 3 miles airport. Near Manchester United and Manchester City football grounds, Old Trafford Cricket Ground. Continental breakfast, central heating, 4 languages spoken, convenient M60 and other motorways. **Open:** All Year
0161 881 4038 Mr Klocek
Fax: 0161 881 1567
D: £26–£30 **S:** fr £25
Beds: 2F 10D 24S **Baths:** 36 En
(6) P (24) TV cc

MANCHESTER Withington

SJ8592   *The Drop Inn*

The Drop Inn Hotel, *393 Wilmslow Road, Withington, Manchester, M20 4WA.*
Pub/Hotel separate buildings. Satellite television. Pool room. Very warm and cosy. **Open:** All Year
0161 286 1919 G Wood
Fax: 0161 286 8880
thedropinn@maileaseynet.co.uk
D: £25–£45 **S:** £25–£45
Beds: 15F 23T 7D 1S
P (50) TV cc

Marple

SJ9588   *The Midland, Romper, Sportsman's Arms*

The Pineapple Inn, *45 Market Street, Marple, Stockport, Cheshire, SK6 7AA.*
Friendly traditional inn.
Open: All Year (not Xmas)
0161 427 3935 Mrs Beecham
D: fr £18 **S:** fr £18
Beds: 2T **Baths:** 1 Sh
P (10) TV

Victoria Cottage, Hawk Green, Marple, Stockport, Cheshire, SK6 7HZ.
Charming historic cottage. Rural location, Cheshire/Derbyshire border. Access Manchester.
Open: All Year
0161 449 8830 Mrs Heller
D: £15–£20 **S:** £15–£23
Beds: 2D 1S **Baths:** 1 Pr 1 Sh
🛏 🅿 (6) 📺 🎿 ✕ 🔟 📺 🎿

Sinclair Lodge, 84 Strines Road, Marple, Stockport, SK6 7DU.
Modern bungalow, countryside setting, yet convenient for town and airport.
Open: All Year (not Xmas)
Grades: ETC 3 Diamond
0161 449 9435 (also fax) M Scott
mscott144@aol.com
D: £20–£28 **S:** £20–£25
Beds: 1D 1S **Baths:** 1 En
🛏 🅿 (6) ½ 📺 🔟 📺 🎿

Marple Bridge

SJ9689   🍺 Rock Tavern

Shire Cottage Farmhouse, Benches Lane, Marple Bridge, Stockport, Cheshire, SK6 5RY.
Home from home, peaceful, central for Peak District and Manchester.
Open: All Year
01457 866536 Mrs Sidebottom
D: £19–£22 **S:** £22–£24
Beds: 1F 1D 1T 1S **Baths:** 2 Pr 1 Sh
🛏 🅿 (5) 📺 🎿 🔟 📺 🎿 ⅙

New Brighton

SJ3093

Sherwood Guest House, 55 Wellington Road, New Brighton, Wallasey, Wirral, CH45 2ND.
Family run guest house close to train/bus station/ motorway.
Open: All Year (not Xmas/New Year)
Grades: ETC 3 Diamond
0151 639 5198 Mrs Breteton
frankbrereton@hotmail.com
D: £15–£18 **S:** £15–£18
Beds: 2F 3T **Baths:** 3 En 2 Sh
🛏 📺 🎿 ✕ 🔟 📺 🎿

Wellington House Hotel, 65 Wellington Road, New Brighton, Wirral, Merseyside, CH45 2NE.
Sea views, ground-floor rooms available. Bar, enclosed parking, CCTV.
Open: All Year (not Xmas)
0151 639 6594 (also fax)
Mr Edwards
D: £18–£22.50 **S:** £20–£25
Beds: 4F 2D 3T 2S **Baths:** 8 En 2 Sh
🛏 🅿 (14) 📺 🎿 ✕ 🔟 📺 ⅙ cc

RATES

D = Price range per person sharing in a double room

S = Price range for a single room

Radcliffe

SD7807

Hawthorn Hotel, 143 Stand Lane, Radcliffe, Manchester, M26 1JR.
Comfortable friendly family-run hotel, convenient Bury, Bolton, Manchester, near Metrolink.
Open: All Year (not Xmas)
0161 723 2706 (also fax) Mr Smith
D: £22.25–£24.75 **S:** £34.50–£39.50
Beds: 1F 5D 7T 1S **Baths:** 14 En
🛏 🅿 (9) 📺 🎿 ✕ 🔟 📺 🎿 cc

Rochdale

SD8913   🍺 Egerton Arms, Owd Bet's

Britannia Inn, 4 Lomax Street, Rochdale, Lancs, OL12 0DN.
Friendly local public house serving real ale, CAMRA listed.
Open: All Year
01706 646391 Mr Ainsworth
D: £13–£15 **S:** £15
Beds: 3T **Baths:** 1 Sh
📺 ✕ 🔟 🎿

Oulder Lodge, Oulder Drive, Bamford, Rochdale, Lancashire, OL11 5LB.
Beautiful house, quiet location, close to amenities, friendly experienced hosts.
Open: All Year
01706 631502 Mrs Hill
D: fr £18 **S:** fr £18
Beds: 1F 2D 1S **Baths:** 2 Sh
🛏 🅿 (12) 📺 🎿 ✕ 🔟 📺 🎿

Leaches Farm, Ashworth Valley, Rochdale, Lancs, OL11 5UN.
C17th Pennine farm. Wonderful views. Home from home.
Open: Jan to Dec
01706 641116 Mrs Neave
Fax: 01706 228520
D: £17–£19 **S:** £21–£26
Beds: 1D 1T 1S **Baths:** 1 Sh
🛏 (7) 🅿 (6) ½ 📺 🎿 🔟 📺 🎿

Sale

SJ7891   🍺 Little 'b', Kings Ransom

Brooklands Luxury Lodge, 208 Marsland Road, Sale, Cheshire, M33 3NE.
Open: All Year
Grades: AA 4 Diamond
0161 973 3283 Mr Bowker
Fax: 0161 282 0524
D: £24–£29 **S:** £26–£30
Beds: 2F 2D 1T 4S **Baths:** 5 En 2 Sh
🛏 (1) 🅿 (7) ½ 📺 ✕ 🔟 🎿 cc
Charming residence in beautiful garden. Free car park. 2 minutes to Metrolink tram, frequent service to airport and city (7 km). Shops, pubs, restaurants nearby. On A6144, 1 mile from M60 motorway (J6). Which? Good B&B guide. Jacuzzi.

Newjoy Guest House, 21 Poplar Grove, Sale, M33 3AX.
10 minutes walk, Sale, Metrolink. 15 minute drive, airport, Manchester.
Open: All Year (not Xmas)
0161 973 7125 (also fax) Mrs Pollard
D: £12.50–£15 **S:** £16–£18
Beds: 2T 2S **Baths:** 2 Sh
🛏 (2) 🅿 (6) 📺 🎿 🔟 🎿

Shevington

SD5408

Wilden, 11a Miles Lane, Shevington, Wigan, Lancashire, WN6 8EB.
Large bungalow. Secluded large gardens. 1 mile M6. Off road parking.
Open: All Year (not Xmas/New Year)
Grades: ETC 3 Diamond
01257 251516 D Axon
D: £17.50–£20 **S:** £17.50–£20
Beds: 1T 2D **Baths:** 1 En 1 Sh
🅿 (5) ½ 🔟 ✕ 🔟 🎿 ⅙ cc

Southport

SD3317   🍺 Cloisters, Wetherspoons, Windmill Inn

The Sidbrook Hotel, 14 Talbot Street, Southport, Lancashire, PR8 1HP.
Family run hotel close to town centre and amenities.
Open: All Year (not Xmas)
Grades: ETC 3 Diamond, AA 3 Diamond
01704 530608 (also fax)
Mrs Barker
sidbrookhotel@tesco.net
D: £19.50–£22.50 **S:** fr £28.50
Beds: 1F 5D 2T **Baths:** 8 En
🛏 🅿 (8) 📺 🔟 🎿 cc

Rosedale Hotel, 11 Talbot Street, Southport, Merseyside, PR8 1HP.
Friendly family run hotel close to all Southport's main attractions.
Open: All Year (not Xmas/New Year)
Grades: ETC 3 Diamond, AA 3 Diamond, RAC 3 Diamond
01704 530604 (also fax)
Mr & Mrs Beer
info@rosedalehotelsouthport.co.uk
D: £25–£27 **S:** £25–£27
Beds: 2F 2T 2D 3S **Baths:** 8 En 1 Pr
🛏 (2) 🅿 (6) 📺 🔟 🎿 cc

Waterford Hotel, 37 Leicester Street, Southport, Merseyside, PR9 0EX.
Quiet location overlooking lake. Central for shops and restaurants. Parking.
Open: March-Dec
Grades: ETC 4 Diamond
01704 530559 T Riley
D: £25–£30 **S:** £39–£45
Beds: 5F 1T 2D
🛏 🅿 📺 🔟 🎿 🔟 🎿 cc

The White Lodge, 12 Talbot Street, Southport, PR8 1HP.
Small select hotel offering high standards in food, cleanliness and service.
Open: All Year (not Xmas)
Grades: AA 3 Diamond, RAC 3 Diamond
01704 536320 (also fax)
Mr McKee
D: £22–£27 **S:** £22–£27
Beds: 2F 2D 4S **Baths:** 5 En 3 Sh
🛏 🅿 (6) ½ 📺 🔟 📺 🎿

Talbot, Portland Street, Southport, Lancashire, PR8 1LR.
A beautiful family-run hotel, close to town centre and promenade. **Open:** All Year
01704 533975 Fax: 01704 530126
D: £20–£25 **S:** £20–£25
Beds: 4F 15T 5S **Baths:** 2 En
🛏 🅿 (20) ½ 📺 🎿 ✕ 🔟 📺 ❋ 🎿

BATHROOMS
Pr - Private
Sh - Shared
En - Ensuite

Edendale Hotel, *83 Avondale Road, Southport, Lancashire, PR9 0NE.*
Victorian hotel, family-run, tranquil, spacious surroundings, excellent food.
Open: All Year
01704 530718 Fax: 01704 547299
D: £19.50–£21.50 **S:** £22.50–£27.50
Beds: 2F 3D 2T 1S **Baths:** 7 En 1 Pr
🐾 🅿 🗲 📺 🍴 ✕ 🛏 📶 🔥 cc

Stalybridge

SJ9698 🍺 *Roaches Lock*

Flushing Meadow, *293-295 Wakefield Road, Heyrod, Stalybridge, SK15 3BY.*
Countryside views, close to Stalybridge and Manchester. Warm welcome guaranteed. **Open:** All Year
0161 338 3125 (also fax)
J D Braithwaite
flushingmeadow@hotmail.com
D: £19–£22.50 **S:** £20–£22
Beds: 3D 2T 2S **Baths:** 2 En 2 Sh
🐾 🅿 (8) 📺 🛏 ✕ 📶 🔥

Stockport

SJ8990 🍺 *Red Lion*

Northumbria House, *35 Corbar Road, Stockport, Cheshire, SK2 6EP.*
Edwardian house, quiet location, beautiful garden, Heartbeat Award, Northumbrian hospitality.
Open: All Year (not Xmas)
0161 483 4000 Mrs Kennington
D: £18–£21 **S:** £20–£23
Beds: 1D 1T **Baths:** 1 Sh
🅿 (2) 🗲 📺 📶 🔥

Urmston

SJ7594 🍺 *Fox & Hounds*

Beech Cottage, *80 Bent Lanes, Davyhulme, Urmston, Manchester, M41 8WY.*
C16th cottage, large gardens near M60 and Trafford Centre.
Open: All Year (not Xmas)
0161 748 4649 Mr & Mrs Pollington
D: £16–£18 **S:** £18–£20
Beds: 1D **Baths:** 1 Pr
🅿 (1) 🗲 📺 📶 🔥

Wallasey

SJ2992 🍺 *The Lighthouse*

St Nicholas Vicarage, *22 Groveland Road, Wallasey, Merseyside, CH45 8JY.*
Homely vicarage very near seafront, quiet suburban surroundings, excellent breakfast.
Open: All Year
0151 639 3589 Mrs Bentley
D: £10–£12.50 **S:** £10–£12.50
Beds: 1F 1D 1T 1S **Baths:** 1 En 1 Sh
🐾 🅿 (2) 🗲 🛏 📶 🔥

West Kirby

SJ2086 🍺 *Moby Dick, Ring O' Bells, Hilbre Court, Surfers, Green Room*

Warren Cottage, *42 Caldy Road, West Kirby, Wirral, Merseyside, CH48 2HQ.*
Spectacular river views. Exceptional accommodation, close to Chester, Liverpool.
Open: All Year
0151 625 8740 Mrs Graves
Fax: 0151 625 4115
sue@warrencott.demon.co.uk
D: £20–£30 **S:** £25–£35
Beds: 1D 1F 1S **Baths:** 2 En 1 Sh
🐾 🅿 (2) 🗲 📺 📶 🔥

Planning a longer stay? Always ask for any special rates

National Grid References are for villages, towns and cities – not for individual houses

Maconachie Guest House, *1 Victoria Road, West Kirby, Wirral, Merseyside, CH48 3HL.*
Victorian house overlooking the Dee estuary. Manx kippers a breakfast speciality. **Open:** All Year
Grades: ETC 3 Diamond
0151 625 1915 Mrs Hicks
D: £18–£20 **S:** fr £25
Beds: 1D 1T **Baths:** 2 Pr
🐾 🅿 (1) 📺 📶 🔥 cc

Westhoughton

SD6506 🍺 *Masons Arms*

Daisy Hill Hotel, *3 Lower Leigh Road, Daisy Hill, Westhoughton, Bolton, BL5 2JP.*
Village pub close to motorway and train station, rooms, separate building to pub.
Open: All Year **Grades:** ETC 3 Star
01942 812096 J Nuttal
daisy.hill@cwcom.net
D: £17.50–£20 **S:** £25–£27.50
Beds: 2T 2S **Baths:** 4 Pr
🐾 🅿 📺 🛏 📶 🔥 cc

Wigan

SD5805

Hotel Bel-Air, *236 Wigan Lane, Wigan, Lancs, WN1 2NU.*
Family run hotel and restaurant close to Wigan centre and M6 motorway J27.
Open: All Year
Grades: AA 2 Star, RAC 2 Star
01942 241410 Mr Lacaille
Fax: 01942 243967
belair@hotelwigan.freeserve.co.uk
D: £22.50–£24.75 **S:** £35–£39.50
Beds: 11F **Baths:** 11 En
🐾 🅿 (12) 📺 ✕ 📶 🔥 🔥

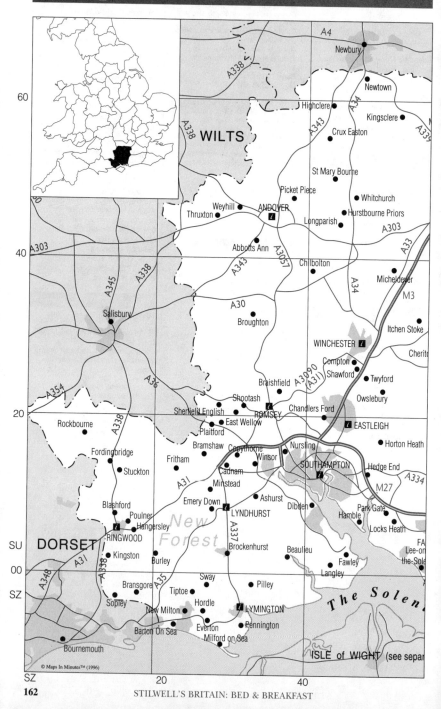

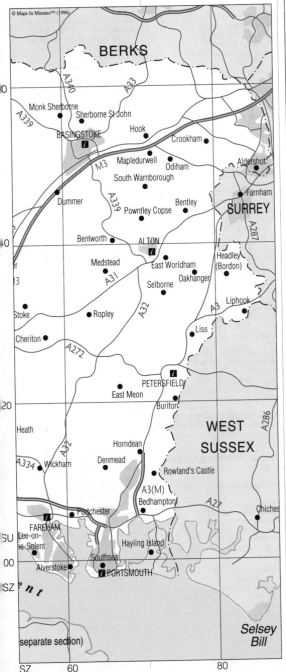

© Maps In Minutes™ (1996)

Tourist Information Centres

Military Museum, Queens Avenue, **Aldershot**, Hants, GU11 2LG, 01252 320968.

7 Cross & Pillory Lane, **Alton**, Hants, GU34 1HL, 01420 88448.

Bridge Street, **Andover**, Hants, SP10 1BL, 01264 324320.

Willis Museum, Old Town Hall, Market Place **Basingstoke**, Hants, RG21 1QD, 01256 817618.

Town Hall Centre, Leigh Road, **Eastleigh**, Hants, SO5 4DE, 01703 641261.

Westbury Manor, West Street, **Fareham**, Hants, PO16 0JJ, 01329 221342.

Gurkha Square, Fleet Road, **Fleet**, Hants, GU13 8BX, 01252 811151.

Salisbury Street, **Fordingbridge**, Hants, SP6 1AB, 01425 654560 (Easter to Oct).

Gosport Museum, Walpole Road, **Gosport**, Hampshire, PO12 1NS, 01705 522944.

1 Park Road South, **Havant**, Hants, PO9 1HA, 01705 480024.

Beachlands Seafront, **Hayling Island**, Hants, PO11 0AG, 01705 467111 (Easter to Oct).

Car Park behind Waitrose, St Thomas Street, **Lymington**, Hants, SO41 9NB, 01590 689000 (Easter to Oct).

New Forest Museum & Visitor Centre, Main Car Park, **Lyndhurst**, Hants, SO43 7NY, 01703 282269.

County Library, 27 The Square, **Petersfield**, Hants, GU32 3HH, 01730 268829.

102 Commercial Road, **Portsmouth**, Hants, PO1 1EJ, 01705 838382.

The Hard, **Portsmouth**, Hampshire, PO1 3QJ, 01705 826722.

Terminal Building, Portsmouth Ferryport, **Portsmouth**, Hampshire,01705 838635.

The Furlong, **Ringwood**, Hants, BH24 1AZ, 01425 470896 (Easter to Oct).

Bus Station Car Park, Broadwater Road, **Romsey**, Hants, SO51 8BF, 01794 512987.

M27 Services (Westbound), **Southampton**, SO16 8AW, 01703 730345.

9 Civic Centre Road, **Southampton**, SO14 7LP, 01703 221106.

Clarence Esplanade, **Southsea**, Portsmouth, Hampshire, PO5 3ST, 01705 832464 (Easter to Oct).

Guildhall, The Broadway, **Winchester**, Hants, SO23 9LJ, 01962 840500.

Abbotts Ann

SU3243   Black Swan, Poplar Farm Inn

Carinya Farm, Cattle Lane, Abbotts Ann, Andover, Hampshire, SP11 7DR.
Working stock farm, modern farmhouse with traditional values. Wildlife pond, large patio and conservatory.
Open: All Year
Grades: ETC 3 Diamond
01264 710269 D W Fergusson
carinya.farm@virginnet.co.uk
D: £20 **S:** £25
Beds: 1T 1D **Baths:** 2 En
P (4) ⊬ ⊡ ⊞ V ⚓

Virginia Lodge, Salisbury Road, Abbotts Ann, Andover, Hants, SP11 7NX.
Bungalow - welcome tea-tray, convenient Stonehenge, Thruxton, cathedrals ferries. Excellent breakfasts.
Open: All Year
01264 710713 Mrs Stuart
info@lakelandcottages.co.uk
D: £19–£21 **S:** £20–£30
Beds: 1D 2T 1S **Baths:** 1 En 1 Sh
⛼ (2) P (6) ⊬ ⊡ ⊞ V ⚓ ⅌

East Manor House, Abbotts Ann, Andover, Hampshire, SP11 8H.
An attractive 300 year old manor house with inglenooks, beams and a courtyard.
Open: All Year (not Xmas)
01264 710031 D Carden
eastmanor@tesco.net
D: £21–£23 **S:** £23–£25
Beds: 2D 1S **Baths:** 1 En
⛼ P (3) ⊬ ⊡ ⊞ ⚓

Aldershot

SU8750   Duke of York

12 Hillside Road, Aldershot, Hants, GU11 3NB.
Large Edwardian house, close to town centre and railway station.
Open: All Year
01252 330000 Mrs Burrage
D: £15 **S:** £25
Beds: 1D 1T **Baths:** 1 Sh
⊬ ⊡ ↑ ⊞ ⚓

The Duke of York, 248 Weybourne Road, Aldershot, Hants, GU11 3NF.
A friendly public house with 5 real ales & good food.
Open: All Year (not Xmas)
01252 321150 Mr Thomas
Fax: 01252 345684
D: £30–£43 **S:** £35–£43
Beds: 1D 3T **Baths:** 4 En
⛼ (5) P (8) ⊬ ⊡ ✕ ⊞ ⚓ cc

BEDROOMS
F - Family
D - Double
T - Twin
S - Single

Alton

SU7139   Sun Inn, French Horn, Three Horseshoes, New Inn, Red Lion

Walnut Tree Barn, Bentworth, Alton, Hampshire, GU34 5JT.
Open: All Year (not Xmas)
01420 561281 J Crawford
jackiecrawfor25@hotmail.com
D: £22–£25 **S:** £25–£30
Beds: 1D 1T **Baths:** 1 En 1 Pr
P (4) ⊬ ⊡ ⊞ ⚓
Recently converted detached barn in peaceful location on edge of charming village; overlooking open countryside. Lovely village pub opposite. Luxuriously appointed rooms, double also with sitting area and video. Alton, Jane Austen's house, Watercress Line 4 miles, Winchester 15 miles.

The Vicarage, East Worldham, Alton, Hants, GU34 3AS.
Warm, friendly peaceful country vicarage nearby serving excellent food.
Open: All Year (not Xmas/New Year)
Grades: ETC 2 Diamond
01420 82392 Mrs Bradford
Fax: 01420 82367
wenrose@bigfoot.com
D: £18–£20 **S:** £18–£20
Beds: 1D 1S 1T **Baths:** 2 Sh
⛼ (10) P (5) ⊬ ⊡ ↑ ⊞ ⚓

Alverstoke

SZ6098   Cocked Hat

Cherry Trees, 15 Linden Grove, Alverstoke, Gosport, PO12 2ED.
Close to harbour, beach, naval establishments; small, friendly, family run.
Open: All Year (not Xmas)
023 9252 1543 Fax: 023 9260 1887
lmgell@aol.com
D: £14–£16 **S:** £14–£16
Beds: 1F 1D 1T 1S **Baths:** 2 Sh
⊡ ⊞ ⚓

Andover

SU3645   Poplar Farm Inn, White Hart, Crook & Shears, Folly Inn

Salisbury Road Bed & Breakfast, 99 Salisbury Road, Andover, Hants, SP10 2LN.
Virtually self-contained ground floor with access to beautiful garden.
Open: All Year (not Xmas)
Grades: ETC 3 Diamond
01264 362638 Mrs Targett
D: £20–£25 **S:** £20–£30
Beds: 1F **Baths:** 1 Pr
⛼ P (2) ⊬ ⊡ ⊞ ⚓

Amarylan, 20 Junction Road, Andover, Hants, SP10 3QU.
Town centre location, minutes bus and train stations, churches, golf.
Open: All Year
Grades: ETC Listed
01264 355362 (also fax)
Mrs Daws
D: £20–£25 **S:** £20–£25
Beds: 1F 1T 1S **Baths:** 1 En 1 Sh
⛼ (8) P (4) ⊬ ⊡ ⊞ ⚓

Ashurst

SU3411   Happy Cheese

Kingswood Cottage, 10 Woodlands Road, Ashurst, Southampton, SO40 7AD.
Open: All Year
Grades: ETC 4 Diamond, Silver Award
023 8029 2582 Fax: 023 8029 3435
info@newforestaccommodation.co.uk
D: £20–£25 **S:** £25–£40
Beds: 2D **Baths:** 2 En
⛼ (8) P (3) ⊬ ⊡ ⊞ V ⚓
Quietly situated, picturesque cottage in park-like grounds opposite New Forest. Short walk to pubs and station;easy drive Beaulieu, Exbury Gardens and Lyndhurst. Bike hire and delivery arranged. Spacious, pretty, ensuite rooms with television, tea/coffee and hairdryers. Great breakfasts; warm welcome.

Granby Manor, 147 Lyndhurst Road, Ashurst, Southampton, SO40 7AW.
Friendly family Victorian home; large conservatory overlooking secluded garden.
Open: All Year
023 8029 2357 **D:** £17–£19 **S:** £20–£25
Beds: 1F 1T **Baths:** 1 En 1 Sh
⛼ P (6) ⊬ ⊡ ⊞ V ✱ ⚓

Barton on Sea

SZ2393   Rising Sun, The Rydal, Royal Oak, New Centurion

The Old Coastguard Hotel, 53 Marine Drive East, Barton on Sea, New Milton, Hants, BH25 7DX.
Magnificent views, lovely walking, overlooking needles/ I.O.W, Close to New Forest.
Open: All Year
Grades: ETC 3 Diamond
01425 612987 I S Philpott
Fax: 01425 612987
dp@theoldcoastguard.fsnet.co.uk
D: £23–£30 **S:** £33–£35
⛼ (12) P (10) ⊡ ↑ ✕ ⊞ V ⚓ ⅌ cc

Tower House, Christchurch Road, Barton on Sea, New Milton, Hants, DH25 6QQ.
Between New Forest and sea, spacious comfortable rooms. Comprehensive breakfast menu.
Open: All Year (not Xmas)
Grades: AA 5 Diamond
01425 629508 (also fax)
Mrs Steenhuis
bandb@towerhouse-newforest.co.uk
D: £20–£25 **S:** £20–£25
Beds: 2D 1T **Baths:** 3 En
⛼ (7) P (7) ⊬ ⊡ ⊞ V ⚓

Cleeve House, 58 Barton Court Avenue, Barton on Sea, New Milton, Hants, BH25 7HG.
Large character family home, close to sea, non-smoking house.
Open: All Year (not Xmas)
Grades: ETC 4 Diamond, AA 4 Diamond
01425 615211 (also fax)
Mrs Carter
D: £20–£23 **S:** £20
Beds: 1F 1D 1T 1S **Baths:** 2 En 1 Sh
⛼ P (8) ⊬ ⊡ ⊞ V ⚓

The Wight House, *41 Marine Drive East, Barton on Sea, New Milton, Isle of Wight, BH25 7DX.*
Beautiful cliff top house, great breakfasts, pretty ensuite bedrooms, swimming pool.
Open: All Year **Grades:** ETC 4 Diamond
01425 614008 D: £20–£25 **S:** £25–£30
Beds: 1T 2D **Baths:** 3 En
🛇 (8) 🅿 (4) ⊬ TV 🎹 🖾 ♨

Basingstoke

SU6352 🍺 *The Bounty, The Skewers*

The Carroll's Guesthouse, *104 Gershwin Road, Brighton Hill, Basingstoke, Hants, RG22 4HJ.*
Basing House; Cromwell battle, many other historical places around.
Open: All Year
01256 410024 Mr Carroll
D: £17.50–£18.50 **S:** £15.50–£17.50
Beds: 1F 2T 1S **Baths:** 1 Sh
🛇 (5) 🅿 (4) TV 🎹 ♨

Mrs Broad's Rowan B&B, *3 Roding Close, Riverdene, Basingstoke, Hampshire, RG21 4DU.*
Private house. Clean, comfortable. 10 mins walk town. Mons - Fridays No Cards/cheques accepted.
Open: All Year (not Xmas/New Year)
01256 321143 Mrs Broad
Fax: 01256 420828
D: fr £20 **S:** £–£25
Beds: 1T 1S **Baths:** 1 Sh
⊬ TV 🎹 ♨

3 Irwell Close, Riverdene, *Basingstoke, Hampshire, RG21 4DG.*
Informal theatrical atmosphere, short walk to town, restaurants, theatres.
Open: All Year
01256 325610 (also fax) Mr Bye
graham@ozuk.demon.co.uk
S: £15–£18
Beds: 1S **Baths:** 1 Sh
🅿 (1) ⊬ TV 🎹 ♨

Fordyce, *Hackwood Road, Basingstoke, Hants, RG21 3AF.*
Clean, comfortable and homely. Non-smoking, close to town centre.
Open: Jan to Dec
01256 468461 Mrs Cooke
D: £20 **S:** £20
Beds: 2D 1T **Baths:** 1 Pr 2 Sh
🛇 (8) 🅿 (4) ⊬ TV ★ 🎹 ♨

Beaulieu

SU3802 🍺 *Montagu Arms, Royal Oak, Turfcutters' Arms, Bridge Tavern*

Leygreem Farm House, *Lyndhurst Road, Beaulieu, Brockenhurst, Hants, SO42 7YP.*
Open: All Year (not Xmas)
Grades: ETC 3 Diamond
01590 612355 (also fax) Mr Helyer
D: £21–£23.50 **S:** £25–£30
Beds: 2D 1T **Baths:** 3 En
🅿 (6) ⊬ TV 🎹 🖾 ♨
Victorian farmhouse in rural setting 1 mile from Beaulieu village ideal for Motor Museum, Buckler's Yard, New Forest and Exbury Gardens. Mountain bikes available for guests' use. Off-road private parking. Discounts 3 days or more. A warm welcome assured.

2 Northern Cottages, *Beaulieu, Hants, SO42 7YE.*
Lovingly restored C18th cottage, centre of village overlooking 'Palace House'.
Open: All Year (not Xmas/New Year)
Grades: ETC 4 Diamond
01590 612127 (also fax) Mrs Hills
christine.hills@btinternet.com
D: £22.50–£25 **S:** £22.50–£25
Beds: 1D 1T **Baths:** 1 Sh
⊬ TV 🎹 🖾 ♨

The Rectory, *Palace Lane, Beaulieu, Brockenhurst, Hants, SO42 7YG.*
Large, comfortable house close to village and Motor Museum.
Open: All Year (not Xmas)
Grades: ETC 3 Diamond
01590 612242 (also fax) Mrs Abernethy
D: £22.50–£25 **S:** £25
Beds: 1D 1T 1S **Baths:** 1 En 1 Sh
🛇 (10) 🅿 (8) ⊬ TV 🎹 🖾 ♨

Old School House, *High Street, Beaulieu, Brockenhurst, Hants, SO42 7YD.*
Warm welcome in beautiful family home built in 1864 for schoolmaster.
Open: All Year (not Xmas)
Grades: ETC 4 Diamond
01590 612062 (also fax)
Mrs Edmondson
D: £22.50–£25 **S:** £35–£45
Beds: 1D 1T **Baths:** 1 Sh
🛇 🅿 (2) ⊬ TV 🎹 🖾 ♨

Bedhampton

SU7006 🍺 *The Ship*

High Towers, *14 Portsdown Hill Road, Bedhampton, Havant, Hants, PO9 3JY.*
Modern house with superb views of countryside and sea.
Open: All Year
Grades: ETC 3 Diamond
023 9247 1748 Mrs Boulton
D: £18–£22 **S:** £22–£26
Beds: 1D 1T 12S **Baths:** 4 En
🛇 (5) 🅿 (6) ⊬ TV 🎹 ♨

Bentley

SU7844 🍺 *Hen & Chicken, Jolly Farmer, Anchor, Prince Of Wales*

Pittersfield, *Hole Lane, Bentley, Farnham, Surrey, GU10 5LT.*
Period courtyard annexe in peaceful rural surroundings.
Open: All Year
Grades: ETC Listed, High Comm
01420 22414 (also fax)
Mrs Coulton
D: £25–£30 **S:** £25–£30
Beds: 3F 1T 1D 1S **Baths:** 2 En 2 Pr 1 Sh
🛇 🅿 (3) ⊬ TV × 🎹 🖾 ♨

Bentworth

SU6640 🍺 *Sun Inn, Star Inn*

Newmans Cottage, *Drury Lane, Bentworth, Alton, Hampshire, GU34 5RJ.*
C17th cottage of great character in lovely gardens overlooking countryside.
Open: All Year (not Xmas/New Year)
01420 563707 AdmiralD@aol.com
D: £20–£22.50 **S:** £25–£30
Beds: 1D **Baths:** 1 Pr
🅿 (2) ⊬ TV 🎹 🖾 ♨

Blashford

SU1507 🍺 *The Alice Lisle Inn*

Fraser House, *Salisbury Road, Blashford, Ringwood, Hants, BH24 3PB.*
Open: All Year
Grades: ETC 3 Diamond
01425 473958 (also fax)
fraserhouse@b.t.internet.com
D: £22.50 **S:** £30
Beds: 2T 2D **Baths:** 4 En
🅿 (6) ⊬ TV ★ 🎹 🖾 ♨ cc
Very comfortable accommodation. Easy access to New Forest and south coast beaches. Riding, fishing, watersports nearby. Guest lounge. Ideal weekend break. Discounts for weekly bookings.

Braishfield

SU3725 🍺 *Dog & Crook, Malthouse, Dukes Head*

Cranford Farm, *Rudd Lane, Braishfield, Romsey, Hants, SO51 0PY.*
Open: All Year
Grades: AA 4 Diamond
01794 368216 (also fax)
B J C Brooks
D: £22.50–£32.50 **S:** £35
Beds: 3F 1T 2D **Baths:** 6 En
TV ♨
Cranford Farm is a large secluded farmhouse set in 3 acres of farmland in the beautiful Test Valley. Just off A3057 between Braishfield and Michelmersh. All rooms are comfortably furnished with colour TV, tea and coffee. All ensuite.

Springwood, *Crook Hill, Braishfield, Romsey, Hants, SO51 0QB.*
Opposite Hillier gardens/arboretum. 2.50 acres includes copse. French spoken.
Open: All Year
01794 368134 Mrs Dickens
D: fr £16 **S:** fr £18
Beds: 1D **Baths:** 1 Pr
🅿 (4) ⊬ TV × 🎹 ♨

Bramshaw

SU2716 🍺 *Green Dragon*

Forge Cottage, *Stocks Cross, Bramshaw, Lyndhurst, SO43 7JB.*
Private rooms situated within the beautiful gardens of Listed cottage.
Open: All Year (not Xmas/New Year)
Grades: ETC 3 Diamond
023 8081 3873 Mr & Mrs Davies
idavies1@compuserve.com
D: £20–£25 **S:** £40
Beds: 2D
🛇 🅿 (3) ⊬ TV 🎹 ♨

Bransgore

SZ1998 🍺 *Three Tuns*

The Corner House, *Betsy Lane, Bransgore, Christchurch, Hants., BH23 8AQ.*
Family house, edge of village, close to forest and pub.
Open: All Year (not Xmas/New Year)
Grades: ETC 4 Diamond
01425 673201 J Stainland
D: £20 **S:** £22
Beds: 1F 1T **Baths:** 2 En
🛇 🅿 (3) ⊬ TV 🎹 ♨

Wiltshire House, *West Road, Bransgore, Christchurch, Dorset, BH23 8BD.*
Secluded Victorian house; New Forest, near sea. Four poster accommodation.
Open: All Year
01425 672450 Mr Hooper
D: £18–£24 **S:** £20–£26
Beds: 1F 1D **Baths:** 2 En
📷 🅿 (3) ⚡ 📺 📖 ♿

Brockenhurst

SU2902 🍺 *Snakecatcher, Red Lion, Rose & Crown, Foresters, Hobler Inn*

Seraya Guest House, *8 Grigg Lane, Brockenhurst, Hants, SO42 7RE.*
Open: All Year
Grades: AA 3 Diamond
01590 622426 Mrs Ward
edwin.ward@nationwideisp.net
D: £19–£25 **S:** fr £22
Beds: 2D 1T **Baths:** 1 Sh 1 En
📷 🅿 (4) ⚡ 📺 🐕 📖 🅅 ♿
Family run (non smoking) B&B in Brockenhurst, the heart of the new Forest. Easy access to M27. The waterloo - Bournemouth train serves Brockenhurst (1 hour, 20 minutes) We are in easy reach of Portsmouth, Stonehenge, Bournemouth and to isle of Wight.

Little Heathers, *13 Whitemoor Road, Brockenhurst, Hants, SO42 7QG.*
Friendly comfortable spacious bungalow, quiet location, 3 - 7 days special breaks.
Open: All Year
Grades: ETC 4 Diamond, Sliver Award
01590 623512 Mrs Harris
Fax: 01590 624255
little_heathers@hotmail.com
D: £22–£27
Beds: 1T 1D **Baths:** 2 En
📷 🅿 (5) ⚡ 📺 🐕 📖 🅅 ♿

Porthilly House, *Armstrong Road, Brockenhurst, Hants, SO42 7TA.*
Open: All Year
Grades: AA 5 Diamond
01590 623182 Mrs Brown
Fax: 01590 622178
sue@bandbnewforest.co.uk
D: £29–£32 **S:** £40–£50
Beds: 2D **Baths:** 2 En
📷 (8) 🅿 (4) ⚡ 📺 📖 🅅 ♿
Luxurious king size suites in lovely, spacious 1920's house in heart of New Forest . Five minutes' walk from Brockenhurst village. Peaceful no-through road adjoining forest. Delicious breakfasts in magnificent conservatory overlooking beautiful garden and large Swimming pool. Excellent pubs/restaurants. Mainline station.

Briardale, *11 Noel Close, Brockenhurst, Hants., SO42 7RP.*
Friendly comfortable home - quiet yet close to village + forest
Open: Feb to Dec
Grades: ETC 3 Diamond
01590 623946 (also fax)
Mrs Parkin
D: £21–£26 **S:** £32–£37
Beds: 2F 2D **Baths:** 2 En
🅿 (3) ⚡ 📺 ✕ 📖 🅅 ♿

Hilden, *Southampton Road, Boldre, Brockenhurst, Hampshire, SO41 8PT.*
Comfortable Edwardian house 50 yards open New Forest, 2.5m from sea.
Open: All Year
Grades: ETC 3 Diamond
01590 623682 Mrs Arnold-Brown
Fax: 01590 624444
D: £20–£25 **S:** £20–£35
Beds: 3F **Baths:** 3 En
📷 🅿 (6) 📺 🐕 📖 🅅 ❀ ♿

Oakmere Guest House, *North Weirs, Brockenhurst, Hants, SO42 7QA.*
Quiet situation on edge of village, with direct forest access.
Open: Easter to October
01590 622133 Mrs Williamson
D: £19 **S:** £25
Beds: 1T **Baths:** 1 En
📷 🅿 (2) ⚡ 📺 📖 ♿ ♿

Brookside Cottage, *Collyers Road, Brockenhurst, Hants, SO42 7SE.*
Picturesque cottage, secluded area. Golf, riding, famous gardens nearby.
Open: All Year (not Xmas)
Grades: ETC 3 Diamond
01590 623973 Mrs Branfoot
D: £27–£28 **S:** £27–£28
Beds: 1T 1S **Baths:** 1 Pr
📷 🅿 (2) ⚡ 📖 🅅 ♿

Caters Cottage, *Latchmoor, Brockenhurst, Hampshire, SO42 7UP.*
Uniquely secluded, 2 miles from village centre. The ideal hideaway.
Open: All Year (not Xmas)
01590 623225 D: £22–£25 **S:** £25–£26
Beds: 1D 1T 1S **Baths:** 1 Sh
📷 (8) 🅿 (6) ⚡ 📺 🐕 📖 🅅 ♿

Butts Lawn, *11 Careys Cottages, Brockenhurst, Hants, SO42 7TF.*
Attractive cottage in superb setting overlooking picturesque ford.
Open: All Year
01590 622276 D: £16–£22.50 **S:** £20
Beds: 1F 1D **Baths:** 1 Sh
🅿 (1) 🐕 📖

Broughton

SU3133 🍺 *Tally Ho!*

Kings, *Salisbury Road, Broughton, Stockbridge, SO20 8BY.*
Standing in half acre of garden, surrounded by open countryside.
Open: All Year (not Xmas/New Year)
01794 301458 Mrs Heather
D: £18 **S:** £18
Beds: 1T 1S **Baths:** 1 Pr
🅿 (3) ✕ 📖 🅅 ♿

The Old Plough, *High Street, Broughton, Stockbridge, Hampshire, SO20 8AE.*
Charming Grade II Listed cottage in centre of idyllic village.
Open: All Year (not Xmas)
01794 301598 Mrs Paul
paul_family@broughton26.freeserve.co.uk
D: fr £20 **S:** fr £25
Beds: 1D **Baths:** 1 Pr
📷 🅿 (1) ⚡ 📺 🐕 📖 🅅 ♿

Buriton

SU7320

Nursted Farm, *Buriton, Petersfield, Hants, GU31 5RW.*
Relax in the atmosphere of our 300 year old farmhouse.
Open: May to Feb
01730 264278 Mrs Bray
D: £18 **S:** £18
Beds: 3T **Baths:** 1 Pr 1 Sh
📷 🅿 📺 📖 🅅

Burley

SU2103 🍺 *White Buck Inn, Burley Inn*

Bay Tree House, *1 Clough Lane, Burley, Ringwood, Hants, BH24 4AE.*
Open: All Year (not Xmas)
Grades: ETC 3 Diamond
01425 403215 (also fax)
Mrs Allen
baytreehousebandb@burleyhants.freeserve.co.uk
D: £22.50–£25 **S:** £22.50–£25
Beds: 1F 1S **Baths:** 1 Sh
📷 🅿 (4) ⚡ 📺 📖 🅅 ♿
Friendly home in the New Forest. Large garden for guests, lovely walks, cycle hire, riding, fishing close by. Warm welcome, good English breakfast, home produce.

Charlwood, *Longmead Road, Burley, Ringwood, Hants, BH24 4BY.*
Country house. Lovely gardens, views, quiet, rural off main road.
Open: Feb to Nov
Grades: ETC 4 Diamond
01425 403242 Mrs Russell
D: £23–£26 **S:** £28–£30
Beds: 1D 1T **Baths:** 1 Sh
🅿 (3) ⚡ 📺 🐕 📖 🅅 ♿

Great Wells House, *Beechwood Lane, Burley, Ringwood, Hants, BH24 4AS.*
Beautiful period property in the heart of the New Forest.
Open: Feb to Nov
Grades: ETC 5 Diamond, Gold Award
01425 402302 (also fax)
Mrs Stewart
chrisstewart@compuserve.com
D: £25–£35 **S:** £30–£55
Beds: 3D **Baths:** 3 En
🅿 (10) ⚡ 📺 📖 🅅 ♿

Cadnam

SU2913 🍺 *Compass Inn*

Bushfriers, *Winsor Road, Winsor, Southampton, SO40 2HF.*
Forest cottage, peaceful surroundings, New Forest heritage area, highly rated breakfasts.
Open: All Year (not Xmas)
023 8081 2552 Mr & Mrs Wright
D: £19–£21 **S:** £23–£25
Beds: 1F **Baths:** 1 Pr
📷 🅿 (2) ⚡ 📺 🐕 📖 🅅 ♿

Planning a longer stay? Always ask for any special rates

Chandlers Ford

SU4320 *King Rufus, Gateway*

133 Bournemouth Road, *Chandlers Ford, Eastleigh, Hants, SO53 3HA.*
Comfortable accommodation, choice of breakfast. Easy access to M3/M27.
Open: All Year
Grades: ETC 3 Diamond
023 8025 4801 (also fax)
Mr Lanham
D: £20–£21 **S:** £20–£21
Beds: 1F 1S **Baths:** 1 Sh
🛋 🅿 (2) ⅍ 📺 ▥ 🕯

Blackbird Hill, *24 Ashbride Rise, Chandlers Ford, Eastleigh, Hampshire, SO53 1SA.*
Detached bungalow in quiet residential area. Easy access to M3 and M27.
Open: All Year (not Xmas)
023 8026 0398 D: £20–£22 **S:** £20–£22
Beds: 1D 1S **Baths:** 1 Sh
🛋 (5) 🅿 (1) ⅍ 🕇 ✕ ▥ 🕯

Cheriton

SU5828 *Flower Pots*

The Garden House, *Cheriton, Alresford, Hampshire, SO24 0QQ.*
Edge of pretty village. Tennis court. Near Cheriton Battle Field. Personal tour by arrangement
Open: All Year
01962 771352 Mrs Verney
Fax: 01962 771667
verney@standrewsball.co.uk
D: £20–£24 **S:** £20–£24
Beds: 2T 1D **Baths:** 1 Pr 1 Sh
🛋 🅿 (4) ⅍ 📺 ✕ ▥ 🔳 🕯 ₺

Chilbolton

SU3940 *Abbot's Mitre*

Uplands, *Drove Road, Chilbolton, Stockbridge, Hants, SO20 6AD.*
Lovely Test Valley, south of Andover. Bungalow, large garden, very quiet.
Open: All Year (not Xmas)
Grades: ETC 3 Diamond
01264 860650 (also fax)
Mrs Hayman-Joyce
june@haymanjoyce.freeserve.co.uk
D: £22.50 **S:** £26
Beds: 1S 2D **Baths:** 1 En 1 Sh
🛋 🅿 (5) ⅍ 📺 ▥ 🔳 ₺ ₺

The Rectory, *Chilbolton, Stockbridge, SO20 6BA.*
Large bungalow situated centrally near pub in beautiful village.
Open: All Year
01264 860258 (also fax)
Mrs Williams
errolw@compuserve.com
D: £20 **S:** £20–£25
Beds: 1F 1S **Baths:** 1 En 1 Pr
🛋 🅿 📺 🕇 ▥ 🔳 🕯 ₺

BATHROOMS
Pr - Private
Sh - Shared
En - Ensuite

Compton

SU4625 *Wykeham Arms, Old Forge, Bridge*

Old Orchard, *Compton Street, Compton, Winchester, Hants, SO21 2AT.*
Architect's unusual home in 1 acre garden. Quiet setting. Memorable breakfasts.
Open: All Year (not Xmas/New Year)
01962 712460 Mrs Case
D: £22.50–£24
Beds: 1T **Baths:** 1 Pr
🅿 (3) ⅍ 📺 ▥ 🕯

The Manor House, *Place Lane, Compton, Winchester, Hants, SO21 2BA.*
Very old house, acre of interesting garden, conservation area.
Open: All Year (not Xmas/New Year)
01962 712162 Mrs Neyroud
D: fr £15 **S:** fr £16
Beds: 1D **Baths:** 1 Sh
🅿 📺 ▥ 🕯

Copythorne

SU3115 *White Hart*

The Old Well Restaurant, *Romsey Road, Copythorne, Southampton, SO40 2PE.*
Beautiful rest/hotel on the edge of the New Forest.
Open: All Year
Grades: AA 3 Star, RAC 3 Diamond
023 8081 2321 Mrs Thompson
Fax: 023 8081 2158
D: £22.50–£30 **S:** £26–£35
Beds: 2F 5D **Baths:** 4 En 3 Sh
🛋 🅿 ⅍ 📺 🕇 ✕ ▥ 🔳 ₺ ₺ cc

Crookham

SU7952 *Chequers*

Orchard House, *Crondall Road, Crookham, Fleet, Hampshire, GU13 0SY.*
Comfortable period house. Large garden, rural surroundings, French & Italian spoken. **Open:** All Year (not Xmas)
Grades: ETC 2 Diamond
01252 850333 Mr & Mrs Longrigg
Fax: 01252 852553
D: £25 **S:** £25–£30
Beds: 1D 1T 1S **Baths:** 2 Pr
🛋 🅿 (8) 📺 ▥ 🔳 🕯

Crux Easton

SU4256 *Furze Bush*

Manor House, *Crux Easton, Newbury, Hants, RG20 9QF.*
Historic farmhouse in quiet village, lovely views, near Highclere Castle.
Open: All Year
01635 254314 Mrs O'Shaughnessy
Fax: 01635 254246
D: £20 **S:** £22.50–£25
Beds: 3T **Baths:** 2 Sh
🛋 🅿 (8) 📺 🕇 ✕ ▥ 🕯 ₺

Denmead

SU6511 *Bat & Ball*

Forest Gate, *Hambledon Road, Denmead, Waterlooville, Hants, PO7 6EX.*
Private Georgian house set in two acres of garden.
Open: All Year (not Xmas)
023 9225 5901 Mrs Cox
D: £20–£24 **S:** £24–£28
Beds: 2T **Baths:** 2 En
🛋 (10) 🅿 (4) ⅍ 📺 ✕ ▥ 🕯

Dibden

SU4008 *Pilgrim Inn*

Dale Farm Guest House, *Manor Road, Applemore Hill, Dibden, Southampton, SO45 5TJ.*
Olde world farmhouse with direct access to the New Forest, horse riding next door.
Open: All Year
023 8084 9632 Mrs Archdeacon
Fax: 023 8084 0285
D: fr £19.50 **S:** fr £25.50
Beds: 1F 1T 3D 1S **Baths:** 4 Pr 2 Sh
🛋 🅿 📺 ✕ ▥ 🔳 🕸 🕯

Dummer

SU5845 *Queen Inn, Sun Inn*

Oakdown Farm, *Dummer, Basingstoke, Hants, RG23 7LR.*
Secluded modern farm bungalow next to M3 J7 on Wayfarers walk.
Open: All Year
Grades: ETC 3 Diamond
01256 397218 Mrs Hutton
D: £17.50 **S:** £20
Beds: 1D 2T **Baths:** 1 Sh
🛋 (12) 🅿 (4) ⅍ 📺 ▥ 🔳 🕯

East Meon

SU6822 *Old George Inn, The Thomas Lord*

Drayton Cottage, *East Meon, Petersfield, Hants, GU32 1PW.*
Luxury country cottage; antiques and oak beams, overlooking glorious countryside.
Open: All Year
01730 823472 Mrs Rockett
D: £20–£23 **S:** £25
Beds: 1D 1T **Baths:** 1 En 1 Pr
🅿 (3) 📺 ▥ 🔳 🕯

Coombe Cross House & Stables, *Coombe Road, East Meon, Petersfield, Hants, GU32 1HQ.*
Early Georgian House on South Downs, beautiful views, tranquil setting.
Open: All Year (not Xmas)
01730 823298 Mrs Bulmer
Fax: 01730 823515
investor.focus@btinternet.com
D: fr £25 **S:** fr £30
Beds: 1D 2T 1S **Baths:** 2 Pr 1 Sh
🛋 (12) 🅿 (10) 📺 ▥ 🕯

East Wellow

SU3020   The Shoe

Roselea, Hamdown Crescent, East Wellow, Romsey, Hampshire, SO51 6BJ.
Quiet mainly ground floor accommodation, near New Forest and M27.
Open: All Year (not Xmas)
Grades: ETC 4 Diamond
01794 323262 Mr & Mrs Cossburn
pennyc@tcp.co.uk
D: £17.50 **S:** £20
Beds: 1D 1T 1S **Baths:** 2 En 1 Sh
🛏 (8) 🅿 (2) ⅏ ⅏ ⅏ ⅏ ⅏ ⅏

East Worldham

SU7438   Sun Inn, French Horn, Three Horseshoes, New Inn, Red Lion

The Vicarage, East Worldham, Alton, Hants, GU34 3AS.
Warm, friendly peaceful country vicarage nearby serving excellent food.
Open: All Year (not Xmas/New Year)
Grades: ETC 2 Diamond
01420 82392 Mrs Bradford
Fax: 01420 82367
wenrose@bigfoot.com
D: £18–£20 **S:** £18–£20
Beds: 1D 1S 1T **Baths:** 2 Sh
🛏 (10) 🅿 (5) ⅏ ⅏ ⅏ ⅏ ⅏ ⅏

Eastleigh

SU4519   Leigh Hotel, Cricketers' Arms, Harvester Restaurant

Twyford Lodge, 104-106 Twyford Road, Eastleigh, Hants, SO50 4HN.
Family-run, good food, good local amenities; Southampton Airport 10 mins.
Open: All Year (not Xmas)
023 8061 2245 D: £20 **S:** £20–£30
Beds: 2F 1D 6T 4S **Baths:** 1 Pr 3 Sh
🛏 🅿 (15) ⅏ ⅏ ⅏ ⅏

Emery Down

SU2808   New Forest Inn

Stable End Guest House, Mill Lane, Emery Down, Lyndhurst, Hants, SO43 7FJ.
Lovely forest views and usually ponies outside the gate.
Open: All Year
Grades: AA 3 Diamond
023 8028 2504 (also fax)
Mrs Dibben
dibbenfam@aol.com
D: £25–£30 **S:** £25–£30
Beds: 1D 1T **Baths:** 2 En
🛏 🅿 (4) ⅏ ⅏ ⅏ ⅏ ⅏ ⅏ ⅏ ⅏

Everton

SZ2994   The Crown

Efford Cottage, Milford Road, Everton, Lymington, Hants, SO41 0JD.
Friendly spacious Georgian cottage. Award-winning guest house. Four course multi-choice breakfast.
Open: All Year
01590 642315 Mrs Ellis
Fax: 01590 641030
D: £23–£26 **S:** fr £30
Beds: 1F 3D 1T **Baths:** 3 En
🛏 (14) 🅿 (4) ⅏ ⅏ ⅏ ⅏ ⅏ ⅏

Fareham

SU5606   The Seagull, The Cormorant

Beaulieu, 67 Portchester Road, Fareham, Hants, PO16 8AP.
Detached house, pleasant gardens, non-smoking, near golf club. M27 (J11) one mile.
Open: All Year
01329 232461 (also fax)
Mrs Wycherley
D: £18–£20 **S:** £18–£25
Beds: 1D 1T 1S **Baths:** 1 Sh
🛏 🅿 (3) ⅏ ⅏ ⅏ ⅏

Linden Lodge, 1 Hollam Close, Titchfield, Fareham, Hants, PO14 3DU.
Comfortably furnished ensuite room. TV, tea tray, microwave oven. Peaceful, large garden, ample parking. Suitable stopover for ferry ports at Portsmouth also Eastleigh Airport. 1.5 miles from the M27 - easy access. Many pubs and restaurants within walking distance.
Open: All Year
01329 845539 Mrs Macey
D: £16–£32 **S:** £16
Beds: 1F 1T **Baths:** 1 Sh 1 Pr
🛏 🅿 (3) ⅏ ⅏ ⅏ ✕ ⅏ ⅏

Fawley

SU4603   Bridge Tavern

Walcot House, Blackfield Road, Fawley, Southampton, SO45 1ED.
Home from home. Good location for touring the area.
Open: All Year
Grades: ETC 2 Diamond
023 8089 1344
Fax: 023 8089 0748
D: £18.50–£20 **S:** £19–£22
Beds: 1T 1D 5S **Baths:** 1 En 1 Sh
🛏 🅿 (13) ⅏ ⅏ ⅏ ⅏ ⅏ ⅏ ⅏ cc

Fordingbridge

SU1414   Churchill Arms

Hillbury, 2 Fir Tree Hill, Camel Green, Alderholt, Fordingbridge, Hants, SP6 3AY.
Large modern bungalow in peaceful surroundings. Warm welcome and comfortable.
Open: All Year
Grades: ETC 3 Diamond
01425 652582 Mrs Sillence
Fax: 01425 657587
D: £18–£20 **S:** £18–£20
Beds: 1F 1T 1S **Baths:** 1 Pr 1 Sh
🛏 🅿 (4) ⅏ ⅏ ⅏ ⅏ ⅏

Fritham

SU2314   Bell Inn, Lamb Inn, Nomansland, White Hart

Primrose Cottage, Fritham, Lyndhurst, Hants, SO43 7HH.
Victorian cottage, forest access. Your own lounge and bathroom. Garage. Discounts.
Open: Mar to Nov
023 8081 2272 Mr & Mrs Penfound
D: fr £20 **S:** fr £25
Beds: 1D/T **Baths:** 1 Pr
🛏 (8) 🅿 (1) ⅏ ⅏ ⅏ ⅏ ⅏

Fritham Farm, Fritham, Lyndhurst, Hants, SO43 7HH.
Lovely house on working farm. Wonderful walking/cycling. Quiet location.
Open: Feb to Oct
Grades: ETC 4 Diamond, AA 4 Diamond
023 8081 2333 (also fax) Mrs Hankinson
D: £20–£22 **S:** £25–£30
Beds: 1T 2D **Baths:** 3 En
🛏 (10) 🅿 (4) ⅏ ⅏ ⅏ ⅏ ⅏ ⅏

Hamble

SU4706   Whyte Hart

Honeysuckle, Flowers Close, Hamble, Southampton, Hants, SO31 4LU.
Bed and breakfast close to Hamble River, Marinas, pubs, yacht clubs.
Open: All Year (not Xmas)
023 8045 3209 (also fax)
D: £18–£20 **S:** £20–£25
Beds: 2D **Baths:** 1 Sh
🛏 (10) 🅿 (2) ⅏ ⅏ ⅏ ⅏ ⅏

Hangersley

SU1706   Alice Lisle

Dunain Farm, Hangersley, Ringwood, Hants, BH24 3JN.
Secluded bungalow, situated on high ground, 1.5 miles from Ringwood.
Open: Mar to Oct
01425 472611 Mrs Griffin
dunain@aol.com
D: £19–£20 **S:** £22–£24
Beds: 1F 1T 1D **Baths:** 1 Sh
🛏 🅿 (8) ⅏ ⅏ ⅏ ⅏

Hayling Island

SU7201   The Rose-in-June, Yew Tree, Ferry Boat, Barely Mow, Maypole, Ship, Inn on the Beach, Olive Leaf

The Old Vine, 67 Havant Road , Hayling Island, Hampshire, PO11 0PT.
Central location. Eat like a lion. Sleep like a baby. **Open:** All Year
023 9246 2543 Mrs Panagiotidis
gpanag67@aol.com
D: £18–£21 **S:** £20–£25
Beds: 3D **Baths:** 2 Pr
🛏 🅿 ⅏ ⅏ ⅏ ✕ ⅏ ⅏

Redwalls, 66 Staunton Avenue, Hayling Island, Hampshire, PO11 0EW.
Non-smoking superior, quiet accommodation close to the sea. Extensive breakfasts.
Open: All Year (not Xmas/New Year)
023 9246 6109 Mr & Mrs Grover
daphne@redwalls66.co.uk
D: £18–£20 **S:** £18–£20
Beds: 2T 1D **Baths:** 2 En 1 Pr
🅿 (4) ⅏ ⅏ ⅏ ⅏

Tide Reach, 214 Southwood Road, Hayling Island, Hants, PO11 9QQ.
Right on the beach! Sailors, surfers and anglers particularly welcome, landlubbers too. Which? recommended.
Open: All Year
Grades: ETC 3 Diamond
0800 970 1670 Colin & Guoying Huggins
Fax: 023 9246 7828
D: £15–£23 **S:** £15–£23
Beds: 1D 1T **Baths:** 1 Pr 1 Sh
🛏 (12) 🅿 (5) ⅏ ⅏ ⅏ ⅏ ⅏

Anns Cottage, *45 St Andrews Road, Hayling Island, Hants, PO11 9JN.*
Quiet location opposite open parkland. Good English breakfast, 100 yards seafront.
Open: All Year
023 9246 7048 Mrs Jay
D: £16–£20 **S:** £17–£20
Beds: 1F 1D 1T **Baths:** 1 En 1 Sh
🛏 🅿 (3) ⅏ 📺 🛒 Ⓥ ♨

Maidlings, *55 Staunton Avenue, Hayling Island, Hants, PO11 0EW.*
Delightful family home close to beach with a great breakfast.
Open: All Year (not Xmas/New Year)
023 9246 6357 Mrs Harper
D: £18–£25 **S:** £20–£25
Beds: 2D 1T
🛏 🅿 (3) ⅏ 📺 🛒

Broad Oak Hotel, *Copse Lane, Hayling Island, Hants, PO11 0QB.*
Peaceful country location just 500 yds from main road. Clean, comfortable.
Open: All Year (not Xmas)
023 9246 2333 Mrs Millins (managing)
tim@hay-isle.demon.co.uk
D: £27–£30 **S:** £30–£34
Beds: 2F 7D 2T 2S **Baths:** 13 En
🛏 🅿 (30) ⅏ 📺 🍴 ✕ 🛒 Ⓥ ♨ cc

Headley (Bordon)

SU8236 🍺 *Holly Bush, The Crown*

Heather Bank, *May Close, Headley, Bordon, Hants, GU35 8LR.*
Family house in quiet private lane surrounded by National Trust land.
Open: All Year
01428 712666 Mrs McBeath
D: £17.50 **S:** £18
Beds: 1D 2T 1S **Baths:** 1 Sh
🛏 🅿 (6) ⅏ 📺 🍴 ✕ 🛒 Ⓥ ♨

Hedge End

SU4912 🍺 *Horse & Jockey, Farmers Home*

Montana Guest House, *90 Lower Northam Road, Hedge End, Southampton, Hants, SO30 4FT.*
Friendly, comfortable, clean accommodation. Good breakfast. 5 minutes from M27.
Open: All Year (not Xmas)
01489 782797 Mr & Mrs Harbour
D: fr £19 **S:** fr £20
Beds: 1F 1D 2T 4S **Baths:** 3 En 2 Sh
🛏 🅿 (7) 📺 🍴 🛒 ♨

Highclere

SU4360 🍺 *Yew Tree Inn, Red House*

Highclere Farm, *Highclere, Newbury, Hampshire, RG20 9PY.*
Situated in designated Area of Outstanding Natural Beauty & close to Highclere Castle - Newbury Racecourse.
Open: All Year (not Xmas/New Year)
Grades: ETC 3 Diamond
01635 255013 Mrs Walsh
walshhighclere@newburyweb.com
D: fr £25 **S:** fr £40
Beds: 1F 1D **Baths:** 1 En
🛏 🅿 📺 🛒 Ⓥ ♨

Hook

SU7254 🍺 *The Falcon, Crooked Billet*

Cherry Lodge, *Reading Road, Hook, Basingstoke, Hants, RG27 9DB.*
Friendly family-run guest house in country surroundings.
Open: All Year (not Xmas/New Year)
Grades: AA 3 Diamond
01256 762532 (also fax)
Mrs Phillips
D: £32–£35 **S:** £32–£35
Beds: 2F 5T 4D 3S **Baths:** 14 En
🛏 (4) 🅿 (35) 📺 🍴 ✕ 🛒 ♨ & cc

Hordle

SZ2795 🍺 *Crown Inn, Royal Oak, Three Bells*

Spinney Cottage, *219 Everton Road, Hordle, Lymington, Hants, SO41 0HE.*
Welcome, charming, New Forest Home. Rural setting, superb breakfasts.
Open: Jan to Oct
Grades: ETC 4 Diamond, Silver Award
01590 644555 (also fax)
Mrs Blackwell
spinneycottage@aol.com
D: £22–£25 **S:** £22–£26
Beds: 2D 1S **Baths:** 2 Pr
🅿 (3) 📺 🍴 🛒 Ⓥ ♨

Horndean

SU7013 🍺 *Red Lion*

Rosedene, *63 Rosemary Way, Horndean, Waterlooville, Hants, PO8 9DQ.*
Attractive bungalow, heated indoor pool, quiet location near South Downs.
Open: All Year
Grades: ETC 4 Diamond
023 9261 5804 Mrs Batten
Fax: 023 9242 3948
pbbatt@aol.com
D: £17.50–£20 **S:** fr £25
Beds: 1D 1S **Baths:** 1 Sh
🛏 (5) 🅿 (4) ⅏ 📺 🛒 ♨

Horton Heath

SU4916 🍺 *Fox & Hounds*

Sandelwood, *Knowle Lane, Horton Heath, Eastleigh, Hants, SO50 7DZ.*
Quiet country house, extensive rural views. Friendly. Comfortable attractive rooms.
Open: All Year
023 8069 3726 Mrs Phipp
D: £44–£48 **S:** £22–£26
Beds: 1F 1D **Baths:** 2 En
🛏 🅿 (3) ⅏ 📺 🍴 🛒 Ⓥ ♨

Hurstbourne Priors

SU4346

The Hurstbourne, *Hurstbourne Priors, Whitchurch, Hants, RG28 7SE.*
Public house, offering good food and quality ales.
Open: All Year
01256 892000 Mr & Mrs Essen
Fax: 01256 895351
D: £20–£25 **S:** £25
Beds: 3F 2D 1T **Baths:** 1 Sh
🛏 🅿 📺 ✕ 🛒 Ⓥ ♨ cc

Itchen Stoke

SU5532

The Parsonage, *Itchen Stoke, Alresford, Hants, SO24 0QU.*
Modern house, quiet rural setting, very central for touring.
Open: All Year (not Xmas)
01962 732123 Mrs Pitt
D: £20 **S:** fr £20
Beds: 1T **Baths:** 1 Sh
🅿 (20) 🍴 🛒 Ⓥ ♨ & cc

Kingsclere

SU5258 🍺 *The Crown*

Cleremede, *Fox's Lane, Kingsclere, Newbury, Berks, RG20 5SL.*
Secluded house with beautiful garden very close to village centre.
Open: All Year
Grades: ETC 4 Diamond
01635 297298 Mrs Salm
Fax: 01635 299934
salm@cleremede.co.uk
D: £20–£25
Beds: 1D 2T **Baths:** 2 En 1 Pr
🛏 (10) 🅿 (6) ⅏ 📺 🍴 🛒 Ⓥ ♨

11 Hook Road, *Kingsclere, Newbury, Berkshire, RG20 5PD.*
Open: All Year
Grades: ETC 3 Diamond
01635 298861 (also fax)
Mr & Mrs Phillips
johnaphillips@barclays.net
D: £16.50 **S:** £20
Beds: 2T 1S **Baths:** 1 Sh
🛏 🅿 (5) ⅏ 📺 🍴 ✕ 🛒 Ⓥ ♨
Quiet, comfortable modern house in historic Kingsclere. Easy road access.

Kingston

SU1402 🍺 *Woolpack*

Greenacres Farmhouse, *Christchurch Road, Kingston, Ringwood, Hants, BH24 3BJ.*
Comfortable Victorian family home near New Forest and River Avon.
Open: All Year (not Xmas)
Grades: ETC 4 Diamond
01425 480945
Mrs Armstrong
D: fr £18 **S:** fr £20
Beds: 1D 2T **Baths:** 1 En 1 Sh
🛏 🅿 (5) ⅏ 📺 🛒 ♨

Langley

SU4400 🍺 *Langley Tavern*

Langley Village Restaurant & Guest House, *Lepe Road, Langley, Southampton, SO45 1XR.*
Close to Motor Museum, Beaulieu, Exbury Gardens and Calshot Castle.
Open: All Year (not Xmas)
023 8089 1667
Mrs McEvoy
alexismcevoy@tinyworld.co.uk
D: £19–£21 **S:** £19–£21
Beds: 1D 1T 2S **Baths:** 1 Sh
🛏 (12) 🅿 (8) 📺 🛒 Ⓥ ♨

Lee-on-the-Solent

SU5600   🍺 *Inn by the Sea*

Chester Lodge, *20 Chester Crescent, Lee-on-the-Solent, Gosport, Hampshire, PO13 9BH.*
Family-run, close to beach, sailing, naval establishments, historic ships.
Open: All Year (not Xmas)
023 9255 0894 Mrs Jeffery
D: £15–£17 **S:** £15–£17
Beds: 1F 1D 1T 1S **Baths:** 2 Sh
🛉 🅿 (6) 📺 🛢 ♨

Liphook

SU8431   🍺 *Black Fox, Rising Sun*

The Bailiffs Cottage, *Hollycombe, Liphook, Hants, GU30 7LR.*
Open: All Year
Grades: ETC 3 Diamond
01428 722171 (also fax)
Mrs Jenner
D: £21–£23 **S:** £21–£23
Beds: 1T 1S **Baths:** 1 Sh
🛉 🅿 (3) ⚡ 📺 🛢 📺 ♨
Welcoming, C18th cottage on borders of W Sussex, Hampshire & Surrey. 25 miles Chichester, Guildford, Portsmouth. Close to Hollycombe Steam Collection. Special rates regular 4 nights weekly at least 3 weeks. Varied breakfast menu in dining room. Very relaxing.

Liss

SU7827   🍺 *The Sun, Jolly Drover*

Glendale, *Hatch Lane, Rake, Liss, Hampshire, GU33 7NJ.*
Large family house in 4.50 acres, garden with tennis court set in country woodland.
Open: All Year (not Xmas)
01730 893451 Mrs Browse
Fax: 01730 892626
carol@cbrowse.fsnet.co.uk
D: £22.50–£25 **S:** £25–£30
Beds: 1D 1T 1S **Baths:** 1 En 1 Pr
🅿 ⚡ 📺 🛢 ♨

Locks Heath

SU5107   🍺 *Talisman, Jolly Farmer*

29 St John's Road, *Locks Heath, Southampton, SO31 6NE.*
Monday to Friday accomodation only. Easy access to local amenities.
Open: All year (not Xmas)
01489 573929 Mrs Taylor
S: £17–£20
Beds: 4S **Baths:** 1 Sh
🅿 (2) ⚡ 📺 ✕ 🛢 ♨

Longparish

SU4344   🍺 *Plough*

Yew Cottage, *Longparish, Andover, Hampshire, SP11 6OE.*
Cosy thatched cottage in beautiful village on the River Test.
Open: All Year
01264 720325 Mr & Mrs Lowry
yewcottage@ukgateway.net
D: £20–£25 **S:** £22.50–£27.50
Beds: 2T 1S **Baths:** 1 En 1 Sh
🛉 🅿 (3) ⚡ 📺 🛢 ♨

Lymington

SZ3295   🍺 *Wagon & Horses, Mayflower Hotel, Crown Inn, Fisherman's Rest, King's Head, Toll House, Chequers, Fisherman's Rest, Hare & Hounds, Ship*

Jevington, *47 Waterford Lane, Lymington, Hants, SO41 3PT.*
Open: All Year
01590 672148 (also fax)
Mr & Mrs Carruthers
D: £22–£25 **S:** £22–£35
Beds: 1F 1D 1T **Baths:** 3 En
🛉 (4) 🅿 (4) ⚡ 📺 🛉 🛢 📺 ♨
Situated in quite lane, comfortable family run B&B walking distance to local pubs.

Our Bench Guest House, *9 Lodge Road, Pennington, Lymington, Hants, SO41 8HH.*
Open: All Year (not Xmas)
Grades: ETC 4 Diamond
01590 673141 (also fax)
Mrs Lewis
ourbench@newforest.demon.co.uk
D: £22–£27.50 **S:** £22–£30
Beds: 1D 1T 1S **Baths:** 3 En
🛉 (14) 🅿 (6) ⚡ 📺 ✕ 🛢 📺 ♨ & **cc 3**
Large non-smoking bungalow between the forest and coast. Garden with heated indoor pool.

The Rowans, *76 Southampton Road, Lymington, Hants, SO41 9GZ.*
Open: All Year
Grades: ETC 4 Diamond
01590 672276 Mrs Baddock
Fax: 01590 688610
D: £20–£25 **S:** £20–£27
Beds: 3F 3D 3T
Baths: 3
🛉 (5) 🅿 (6) ⚡ 📺 🛢 📺 ♨
A delightful detached period house. Five minutes walk to high street. Ideal for marinas, IOW Ferry and New Forest. Beautiful ensuite rooms. Spacious residents dining room. Ample parking. A friendly atmosphere awaits you. Formerly owners of White Lyon, Lymington.

Admiral House, *3 Stanley Road, Lymington, Hants, SO41 3SJ.*
Comfortable accommodation near pubs, shops, coastal walk, marinas & forest.
Open: All Year
01590 674339
Mrs Wild
bill@wild27.freeserve.co.uk
D: £12–£14 **S:** £12–£14
Beds: 2F 1T **Baths:** 1 Sh
🛉 🅿 📺 🛉 🛢 📺 ♨

Monks Pool, *Waterford Lane, Lymington, Hants, SO41 3PS.*
Unique spacious home. Centre Lymington. Large, sunny garden, private lake.
Open: Jan to Dec
01590 678850 (also fax)
M C Otten
cam@monkspool.swinternet.co.uk
D: £20–£30 **S:** £25–£35
Beds: 2D 1T **Baths:** 2 En 1 Sh
🛉 🅿 (4) ⚡ 📺 🛉 🛢 📺 ♨

Albany House, *3 Highfield, Lymington, Hants, SO41 9GB.*
Elegant Regency, 1 minute to Town centre. Large garden, pleasant outlook.
Open: All Year (not Xmas)
01590 671900 Mrs Callagher
albany-house@hotmail.com
D: £28.50–£33 **S:** £45–£50
Beds: 1F 1D 1T **Baths:** 3 En
🛉 🅿 (7) 📺 🛉 ✕ 🛢 📺 ♨

The Borough Arms, *39 Avenue Road, Lymington, Hants, SO41 9GP.*
Family run pub near town centre. Warm and friendly welcome.
Open: All Year
01590 672814 D: fr £22.50 **S:** fr £22.50
Beds: 1D 1T **Baths:** 2 En
🛉 (3) 🅿 (30) 📺 🛉 ✕ 🛢 ♨

Hideaway, *Middle Common Road, Pennington, Lymington, Hants, SO41 8LE.*
Quiet chalet house. Private parking.
Open: All Year (not Xmas)
Grades: ETC Listed
01590 676974 Mrs Pickford
D: fr £18 **S:** fr £25
Beds: 1F 1D 1T **Baths:** 3 En
🛉 🅿 (3) ⚡ 📺 🛢 ♨

West Lodge, *40 Southampton Road, Lymington, Hants, SO41 9GG.*
Spacious Edwardian house, elegantly furnished, close to town centre, New Forest.
Open: All Year (not Xmas/New Year)
Grades: ETC 4 Diamond
01590 672237 Mrs Jeffcock
Fax: 01590 673592
D: £50–£60 **S:** £28–£30
Beds: 1D 1T 1S **Baths:** 2 Pr
🛉 🅿 (3) 📺 🛢 ♨

Jack In The Basket, *7 St Thomas Street, Lymington, Hants, SO41 9NA.*
C17th house in centre of Lymington; modern bedrooms. daytime restaurant.
Open: All Year
01590 673447 Mr & Mrs Carter
D: £17–£25 **S:** £20–£28
Beds: 1F 1D 1T **Baths:** 1 Pr 1 Sh
🛉 📺 🛉 ✕ 🛢 📺

Lyndhurst

SU2908   🍺 *Fox & Hounds, Crown, Mailman's Arms, Oak, Waterloo Arms, Mill House, Stirrup Fox & Hounds, Crown, Mailman's Arms, Oak, Waterloo Arms, Mill House, Stirrup*

Beechen House, *Clayhill, Lyndhurst, Hants., SO43 7DN.*
Open: All Year
Grades: ETC 3 Diamond
023 8028 3584 Mrs Marshall
D: £22–£25 **S:** £18–£20
Beds: 1F 1D 1S **Baths:** 1 En 1 Sh
🛉 (8) 🅿 (6) ⚡ 📺 🛉 🛢 📺 ♨
Private Victorian home, full English breakfast, non-smoking. Secure off-road private parking. Birthdays and anniversaries our speciality. Dogs welcome, comfortable walking distance to Lyndhurst village for excellent eating establishments. easy access at all times to forest for walking or cycling.

Lyndhurst House, *35 Romsey Road, Lyndhurst, Hants, SO43 7AR.*
Open: All Year (not Xmas)
Grades: ETC 4 Diamond, Silver, RAC 4 Diamond
023 8028 2230 Mr & Mrs Wood
bcjwood@lyndhouse.freeserve.co.uk
D: £22–£26
Beds: 1F 4D **Baths:** 5 En
⌂ (10) ▣ (5) ⌷ ▦ ◫ **cc**
In the heart of New Forest and conveniently situated for a complete range of activities. Lyndhurst House offers a comfortable and relaxed homely atmosphere. All ensuite and well equipped bedrooms, some with four posters. Excellent English or vegetarian breakfast.

The Penny Farthing Hotel, *Romsey Road, Lyndhurst, Hampshire, SO43 7AA.*
Open: All Year (not Xmas)
Grades: ETC 4 Diamond, AA 4 Diamond, RAC 4 Diamond
023 8028 4422 Mr & Mrs Saqui
Fax: 023 8028 4488
D: £25–£45 **S:** £35
Beds: 2F 9D 3T 1S
Baths: 10 En 1 Pr 2 Sh
⌂ ▣ (15) ▦ ⍦ ▦ ◫ ▴
Welcome to our cheerful small hotel, ideally situated in Lyndhurst village centre. We offer a variety of rooms mainly ensuite with colour TV, tea/coffee tray and telephones. There is a large car park and secure bike store. New Forest Visitor Centre 5 mins' walk.

The Laurels, *9 Wellands Road, Lyndhurst, Hants, SO43 7AB.*
Excellent accommodation, quiet, central, New Forest location, warm welcome guaranteed.
Open: All Year (not Xmas)
023 8028 2545
Mrs Kennard
kennard.laurels@virginnet.co.uk
D: £18–£20 **S:** fr £20
Beds: 1D/T **Baths:** 1 Pr
⌂ (8) ▣ (1) ⌷ ▦ ◫ ▴

Forest Cottage, *High Street, Lyndhurst, Hants, SO43 7BH.*
Charming 300-year-old cottage. Warm, comfortable and friendly.
Open: All Year
Grades: ETC 4 Diamond, Silver
023 8028 3461
Mrs Rowland
D: £20–£22 **S:** £20–£22
Beds: 1D 1T 1S **Baths:** 2 Sh
⌂ (14) ▣ (3) ⌷ ▦ ◫ ▴

Rose Cottage , *Chapel Lane, Lyndhurst, Hants, SO43 7FG.*
Charming C18th cottage, large peaceful garden and close to forest and village.
Open: All Year
Grades: ETC 4 Diamond
023 8028 3413 (also fax)
Mrs Dawson
cindy@rosecottageb-b.freeserve.co.uk
D: £21–£24 **S:** £25–£30
Beds: 1F 2D **Baths:** 1 En 1 Sh
⌂ ▣ (6) ⌷ ▦ ⍦ ✕ ▦ ◫ ▴

Whitemoor House Hotel,
Southampton Road, Lyndhurst, Hants, SO43 7BU.
Award-winning food. Log fires in winter. Beautiful gardens in summer.
Open: All Year (not Xmas)
Grades: AA 3 Diamond
023 8028 2186 Mr Barron
D: £20–£30 **S:** £20–£40
Beds: 2F 4D 2T **Baths:** 8 En
⌂ ▣ (12) ⌷ ▦ ⍦ ✕ ▦ ◫ **cc**

Clarendon Villa, *Gosport Lane, Lyndhurst, Hants, SO43 7BL.*
Victorian family house, village centre, breakfast served in your room.
Open: All Year (not Xmas)
Grades: AA 3 Diamond
023 8028 2803 M Preston
Fax: 023 8028 4303
clarendonvilla@i12.com
D: £22.50–£30 **S:** £25–£35
Beds: 1F 2D **Baths:** 3 En
⌂ ▣ (4) ⌷ ▦ ⍦ ▦ ◫ **cc**

Owl Cottage, *Clayhill, Lyndhurst, Hants, SO43 7DE.*
Off beaten track, direct access to forest - escape for a while.
Open: All Year
023 8028 3800 Mr & Mrs Lowe
D: £20 **S:** £20
Beds: 1D 1S **Baths:** 1 En
▣ (6) ⌷ ▦ ◫ ▴

SU6951 ⌂ *Fox & Goose, The Gamekeepers*

Eastside Coach House, *Frog Lane, Mapledurwell, Basingstoke, Hants, RG25 2LP.*
A unique very attractive property sitting in the bed of the Basingstoke Canal.
Open: All Year
01256 465559 (also fax)
Mr & Mrs Cashmore
eastside@breathmail.net
D: £20–£25 **S:** £25–£30
Beds: 2F 1D 4T 2S **Baths:** 3 En 1 Pr 2 Sh
⌂ ▣ (12) ⌷ ▦ ⍦ ▦ ◫ ▴ ₲

SU6537 ⌂ *Sun Inn, French Horn, Three Horseshoes, New Inn, Red Lion, Star*

Ramjaks, *High Street, Medstead, Alton, Hants, GU34 5LW.*
A family home set in large garden.
Open: All Year
01420 562601 Mrs Williams
ramjaks@btinternet.com
D: fr £16 **S:** fr £17
Beds: 1D 1T 1S **Baths:** 1 Sh
▣ (4) ⌷ ▦ ✕ ▦ ◫ ▴

Orchard View, *High Street, Medstead, Alton, Hants., GU34 5LN.*
Modern bungalow secluded ample parking central for touring bus route.
Open: All Year (not Xmas)
01420 562480 Mrs Westbrook
D: £16–£18 **S:** £16–£20
Beds: 1D 1T **Baths:** 1 En 1 Sh

SU5139 ⌂ *Half Moon, Spread Eagle*

Orchard Close, *The Highways, Micheldever, Winchester, Hampshire, SO21 3BP.*
Open: Easter to December
01962 774470 Mrs Holmes
D: £18–£20 **S:** £25–£30
Beds: 1T 2D **Baths:** 1 En 1 Sh
⌂ ▣ ⌷ ▦ ◫ ▴ ₲
Quiet spacious accommodation overlooking lawns and garden. 5 miles city centre.

SZ2891

Cherry Trees, *Lymington Road, Milford on Sea, Lymington, Hants, SO41 0QL.*
Open: All Year **Grades:** AA 4 Diamond
01590 643746 S Gadd
cherrytrees@beeb.net
D: £20–£25 **S:** £22–£35
Beds: 1F 1T 1D **Baths:** 2 En 1 Pr
⌂ ▣ ⌷ ▦ ⍦ ✕ ▦ ◫ ▴ ₲
Warm welcome assured at this lovely character retreat. Pretty rooms delightful garden. Easy walk to village and beach. Aromatherapy, beauty treatments, massage and Reiki offered. Delicious vegetarian, vegan or continental four-course breakfast. Brochure available. Also luxury self-catering for six.

SU2811 ⌂ *Trusty Servant, New Forest Inn*

Grove House, *Minstead, Lyndhurst, Hants, SO43 7GG.*
New Forest small holding. Excellent comfort, varied breakfast, superb walking/riding. **Open:** All Year
023 8081 3211 Mrs Dixon
D: £22–£25
Beds: 1T **Baths:** 1 Pr
⌂ ▣ ⌷ ▦ ⍦ ▦ ◫ ▴

Broad Oak Farm, *School Lane, Minstead, Lyndhurst, Hants, SO43 7GL.*
Quiet & friendly working farm in lovely setting; good English breakfast.
Open: Mar to Oct
023 8081 2627 D: £18 **S:** £20
Beds: 1F 1D **Baths:** 1 Sh
⌂ ▣ (2) ▦ ⍦ ▦ ▴

Holly Brae, *Lyndhurst Road, Minstead, Lyndhurst, Hants, SO43 7HA.*
Quiet, friendly, smallholding on to open forest, walking, good English breakfast.
Open: Easter to Oct
01703 812442 (also fax)
Mrs Glover
D: £18–£20 **S:** £18–£20
Beds: 1F 1T **Baths:** 1 Sh
▦ ◫

BATHROOMS
Pr - Private
Sh - Shared
En - Ensuite

Monk Sherborne

SU6056   ◀ *The Mole*

Manor Farm, *Monk Sherborne, Basingstoke, Hants, RG26 5HW.*
Traditional old farmhouse in a rural setting.
Open: All Year (not Xmas/New Year)
01256 850889 Mrs Dalgarno
D: £16 **S:** £20–£22
Beds: 1D 1F **Baths:** 1 Sh
🅿 (6) ⅍ 📺 ✕ 🛏 🛈

New Milton

SZ2395   ◀ *The Rydal, Walkford Inn*

Saint Ursula, *30 Hobart Road, New Milton, Hants, BH25 6EG.*
Ideal for New Forest/coast. Large comfortable house. Central. Disabled facilities.
Open: All Year
Grades: ETC 3 Diamond
01425 613515 Mrs Pearce
D: £20 **S:** £20
Beds: 1F 1D 2T 2S
Baths: 3 En 2 Pr 1 Sh
🛏 🅿 (4) ⅍ 📺 🛏 🛈 📺 ✿ 🛈 ⅋ 3

Newtown (Newbury)

SU4763   ◀ *Swan Inn, Carpenters Arms*

White Cottage, *Newtown, Newbury, Berks, RG20 9AP.*
Delightful semi-rural cottage on the edge of Watership Down.
Open: All Year (not Xmas)
Grades: ETC 3 Diamond
01635 43097 (also fax)
Mrs Meiklejohn
ellie@p-p-ifsnet.co.uk
D: £22–£25 **S:** £25–£30
Beds: 1D 1T 1S **Baths:** 1 Sh
🛏 (3) 🅿 ⅍ 📺 🛏 🛈 📺 🛈

Nursling

SU3716

Conifers, *6 Nursling Street Cottages, Nursling, Southampton, Hants, SO16 0XH.*
Attractive 1930s cottage. Comfortable beds. Family Garden. Country pubs nearby.
Open: All Year
023 8034 9491 (also fax)
Mrs Hinton
D: £18–£25 **S:** £18–£25
Beds: 1F 1D 1S **Baths:** 2 En
🛏 🅿 (2) ⅍ 📺 🛏 ✕ 🛈 📺 🛈

Oakhanger

SU7635   ◀ *Red Lion*

Ivanhoe, *Oakhanger, Bordon, Hants., GU35 9JG.*
Comfortable accommodation with rural views. Small village central for walking.
Open: All Year (not Xmas/New Year)
Grades: ETC 4 Diamond
01420 473464
Mrs Britton
D: fr £18 **S:** fr £25
Beds: 1T **Baths:** 1 Pr
🛏 🅿 (1) ⅍ 📺 🛏 🛈 📺 🛈

Odiham

SU7451

Newlands Farm, *Odiham, Hook, Hampshire, RG29 1JD.*
Period farmhouse working farm. Quiet. Basins rooms, home made bread, marmalade.
Open: All Year (not Xmas)
01256 702373 (also fax)
Mrs Saunders
mary.saunders@farming.co.uk
D: £15–£16 **S:** £15–£16
Beds: 2S 1D **Baths:** 2 Sh
🅿 (3) ⅍ 📺 🛈 🛈

Owslebury

SU5123   ◀ *Ship Inn*

Mays Farmhouse, *Longwood Dean, Owslebury, Winchester, Hants, SO21 1JS.*
Lovely C16th farmhouse, beautiful countryside; peaceful with good walks.
Open: All Year
01962 777486 Mrs Ashby
Fax: 01962 777747
rosalieashhby@maysfarm.fsnet,co,uk
D: £22.50–£25 **S:** £25–£30
Beds: 1F 1D 1T **Baths:** 3 Pr
🛏 (7) 🅿 (5) ⅍ 📺 🛏 🛈 📺 🛈 🛈

Park Gate

SU5108   ◀ *Tallishaw Inn, Talisman Inn*

60 Southampton Road, *Park Gate, Southampton, Hants., SO31 6AF.*
Quiet peaceful situation in lovely garden convenient to motorway.
Open: All Year (not Xmas/New Year)
Grades: ETC 2 Diamond
01489 573994 Mrs White
D: £18–£20 **S:** £18–£20
Beds: 1F 1S **Baths:** 1 Sh
🛏 🅿 (5) ⅍ 📺 🛏 🛈

Four Winds Guest House, *17 Station Road, Park Gate, Southampton, Hants., SO31 7GJ.*
Centrally situated, convenient for motorway, near to River Hamble sailing.
Open: All Year (not Xmas)
01489 584433 Mr & Mrs Yates
D: £20 **S:** £21–£25
Beds: 1F 2D 2T 1S **Baths:** 4 En 1 Sh
🛏 🅿 (6) 📺 🛏 🛈 🛈 cc

Pennington

SZ3194   ◀ *Hare & Hounds*

Our Bench Guest House, *9 Lodge Road, Pennington, Lymington, Hants, SO41 8HH.*
Large non-smoking bungalow between the forest and coast. Garden with heated indoor pool.
Open: All Year (not Xmas)
Grades: ETC 4 Diamond
01590 673141 (also fax)
Mrs Lewis
ourbench@newforest.demon.co.uk
D: £22–£27.50 **S:** £22–£30
Beds: 1D 1T 1S **Baths:** 3 En
🛏 (14) 🅿 (6) ⅍ 📺 ✕ 🛏 🛈 🛈 cc 3

Petersfield

SU7423   ◀ *Harrow Inn, Half Moon, Good Intent, Five Bells*

Heath Farmhouse, *Sussex Road, Petersfield, Hants, GU31 4HU.*
Georgian farmhouse, lovely views, large garden, quiet surroundings, near town.
Open: All Year **Grades:** ETC 3 Diamond
01730 264709 Mrs Scurfield
pruesc@waitrose.com
D: £18–£20 **S:** £20–£25
Beds: 1F 1D 1T **Baths:** 1 En 1 Sh
🛏 🅿 (5) ⅍ 📺 🛈 🛈 🛈

Heathside, *36 Heath Road East, Petersfield, Hants, GU31 4HR.*
Petersfield pretty market square and shops. 15 minutes walk across heath.
Open: All Year (not Xmas)
Grades: ETC 3 Diamond
01730 262337 Mrs Cafferata
D: £20–£25 **S:** £22–£25
Beds: 1T 2S **Baths:** 1 En 1 Pr 1 Sh
🅿 (3) ⅍ 📺 🛈 🛈

Ridgefield, *Station Road, Petersfield, Hants, GU32 3DE.*
Friendly family atmosphere, near town & station; Portsmouth ferries: 20 mins drive.
Open: All Year (not Xmas)
Grades: ETC 2 Diamond
01730 261402 Mrs West
ymcokw@hants.gov.uk
D: £20 **S:** £25–£30
Beds: 1D 2T **Baths:** 2 Sh
🛏 🅿 (4) ⅍ 📺 🛈 🛈 🛈

Beaumont, *22 Stafford Road, Petersfield, Hampshire, GU32 2JG.*
Warm welcome, comfortable beds, excellent breakfasts with home-made preserves. **Open:** All Year (not Xmas)
Grades: ETC 3 Diamond
01730 264744 (also fax) Mrs Bewes
david.bewes@btinternet.com
D: £20 **S:** £20–£25
Beds: 2T 1S **Baths:** 1 Sh
🛏 (12) 🅿 (2) ⅍ 📺 🛈 🛈

Picket Piece

SU3947   ◀ *Wyke Down Country Pub*

Cherry Trees, *Picket Piece, Andover, Hampshire, SP11 6LY.*
Family run in rural location, large garden and ample parking. **Open:** All Year
01264 334891 (also fax)
S Barnett
D: £20–£25 **S:** £20–£25
Beds: 1F 1T 1S **Baths:** 1 Sh
🅿 (4) ⅍ 📺 🛈

Pilley

SZ3499   ◀ *Fleur De Lys*

Mistletoe Cottage, *3 Jordans Lane, Pilley Bailey, Pilley, Lymington, Hampshire, SO41 5QW.*
Quiet New Forest hamlet. Convenient for Beaulieu and the coast.
Open: All Year
Grades: ETC 4 Diamond
01590 676361 **D:** £18–£25 **S:** £25–£35
Beds: 2D **Baths:** 2 En
🅿 (4) ⅍ 📺 🛈 🛈 🛈

Plaitford

SU2719   ⚓ *Shoe Inn, Red Rover*

Southernwood, *Plaitford Common, Salisbury Road, Plaitford, Romsey, Hants, SO51 6EE.*
Family home, edge of New Forest, ferries, Stonehenge, Romsey, Salisbury.
Open: All Year **Grades:** ETC 2 Diamond
01794 323255 Mrs Hocking
D: £35–£40 **S:** £35–£40
Beds: 1F 3D 1T **Baths:** 1 Pr 1 Sh
🐾 🅿 (4) 📺 🛏 📶 🗓 ♿

Pyesmead Farm, *Salisbury Road, Plaitford, Romsey, Hants, SO51 6EE.*
Farmhouse on family stock farm.
Open: All Year (not Xmas/New Year)
Grades: ETC 3 Diamond
01794 323386 (also fax) Mrs Pybus
pyesmead@talk21.com
D: £17–£20 **S:** £20–£25
Beds: 2D 1T **Baths:** 1 En 1 Pr
🐾 🅿 (10) ½ 📺 🛏 📶 ♿

Portchester

SU6105

Appletrees, *144 Castle Street, Portchester, Fareham, Hants, PO16 9QH.*
Near Portchester Castle, Port Solent Marina, Portsmouth ferries/maritime attractions. **Open:** All Year
023 9237 0376 Mrs Jones
D: £18–£22 **S:** £18–£25
Beds: 1T 1S **Baths:** 1 Pr 1 Sh
🅿 (2) ½ 📺 📶 ♿

Portsmouth

SU6501   ⚓ *Churchillian, Coastguard Tavern, Bold Forester, Eastney, Seafarers, Wetherspoons, Town House, Still & West, The Vaults, Touchdown, Rickshaws*

Bembell Court Hotel, *69 Festing Road, Southsea, Portsmouth, Hants, PO4 0NQ.*
Open: All Year
Grades: ETC 3 Diamond, AA 3 Diamond
023 9273 5915 Mr Irwin
Fax: 023 9275 6497
keith@bembell.freeserve.co.uk
D: £24.75–£27 **S:** £38–£40
Beds: 2F 4D 4T 3S **Baths:** 13 En
🐾 🅿 (10) 📺 ✕ 📶 🗓 ♿ cc
Friendly family hotel ideally situated for ferries. Single night and midweek bookings.

Hamilton House, *95 Victoria Road North, Southsea, Hants, PO5 1PS.*
Open: All Year
Grades: ETC 4 Diamond, AA 4 Diamond
023 9282 3502 (also fax)
Graham & Sandra Tubb
sandra@hamiltonhouse.co.uk
D: £20–£24 **S:** £25–£40
Beds: 3F 3D 2T 1S **Baths:** 5 En 2 Sh
🐾 ½ 📺 📶 🗓 ♿
Delightful Victorian town house B&B. Bright, modern rooms, many original features. Centrally located 5 mins by car from Historic Ships, Museums, University, City Centre/stations, Guildhall, Continental/I.O.W Ferry-ports & Gunwharf Quays. Breakfast served from 6.15 am for early travellers.

The Elms Guest House, *48 Victoria Road South, Southsea, Hants, PO5 2BT.*
Close to Naval Heritage Complex. Within walking distance of restaurants and seafront.
Open: All Year
Grades: ETC 3 Diamond, AA 3 Diamond
023 9282 3924 (also fax)
Mrs Erskine
theelmsgh@aol.com
D: £20–£22.50 **S:** £30–£45
Beds: 2F 1D 2T **Baths:** 5 En
🐾 (4) 🅿 (2) ½ 📺 📶 ♿ cc

Hillside Lodge, *1 Blake Road, Farlington, Portsmouth, Hants, PO6 1ET.*
House on hill slopes above Portsmouth. Continental ferries, etc, easily accessible.
Open: All Year
023 9237 2687 Mrs Wood
D: £18–£22 **S:** £18
Beds: 1D 1T 1S **Baths:** 1 En 1 Sh
🐾 🅿 📺 📶 ♿

Poulner

SU1606   ⚓ *White Buck*

The Old Cottage, *Cowpitts Lane, Poulner, Ringwood, Hants, BH24 3JX.*
Stunning views over the forest from our secluded C17th thatched and beamed cottage.
Open: All Year (not Xmas)
Grades: AA 4 Diamond
01425 477956 (also fax)
Mr Theobald
D: £22–£28
Beds: 1F 1D 1T **Baths:** 3 En
🐾 (8) 🅿 (4) ½ 📺 📶 ♿

Powntley Copse

SU7044   ⚓ *George Hotel, Chequers Inn*

Farthings, *Powntley Copse, Alton, Hampshire, GU34 4DL.*
Delightful family house in attractive woodland setting near South Warnborough.
Open: All Year (not Xmas/New Year)
01256 862427 Mrs Hare
Fax: 01256 862602
farthings@powntleycopse.net
D: £22–£25 **S:** £22–£25
Beds: 1T **Baths:** 1E
🐾 🅿 (6) ½ 📺 📶 ♿

Ringwood

SU1505   ⚓ *Alice Lysle, Old Beams, Fish Inn, Woolpack, White Hart, Woopack, Elm Tree, White Buck*

The Old Cottage, *Cowpitts Lane, Poulner, Ringwood, Hants, BH24 3JX.*
Open: All Year (not Xmas)
Grades: AA 4 Diamond
01425 477956 (also fax) Mr Theobald
D: £22–£28
Beds: 1F 1D 1T **Baths:** 3 En
🐾 (8) 🅿 (4) ½ 📺 📶 ♿
Stunning views over the forest from our secluded C17th thatched and beamed cottage. Superb luxurious ensuite bedrooms. Lounge with inglenook. Wonderful walking by Linford Brook and across the Forest . Riding, cycling . Ideal Burley, Ringwood, Salisbury and South Coast.

Greenacres Farmhouse, *Christchurch Road, Kingston, Ringwood, Hants, BH24 3BJ.*
Comfortable Victorian family home near New Forest and River Avon.
Open: All Year (not Xmas)
Grades: ETC 4 Diamond
01425 480945 Mrs Armstrong
D: fr £18 **S:** fr £20
Beds: 1D 2T **Baths:** 1 En 1 Sh
🐾 🅿 (5) ½ 📺 📶 ♿

Beau Cottage, *1 Hiltom Road, Ringwood, Hants, BH24 1PW.*
Quiet old modernised cottage. Comfortable and friendly. Good English breakfast.
Open: All Year (not Xmas)
Grades: ETC 3 Diamond
01425 461274 Mrs Willis
D: £17–£22 **S:** £17–£24
Beds: 1T 1D 1S **Baths:** 3 En
🐾 (12) 🅿 (5) ½ 📺 📶 🗓 ♿

The Nest, *10 Middle Lane, off School Lane, Ringwood, Hants, BH24 1LE.*
Lovely Victorian family home, ideal, quiet, convenient town centre position.
Open: All Year
Grades: AA 4 Diamond
01425 476724 Fax: 01425 467724
bb@ynixon.freeserve.co.uk
D: £19–£25 **S:** £20–£30
Beds: 2D 1T 1S **Baths:** 2 Sh
🐾 🅿 (6) ½ 📺 🛏 📶 🗓 ♿

Torre Avon, *21 Salisbury Road, Ringwood, Hants, BH24 1AS.*
Luxury accommodation, friendly hospitality, hearty breakfasts and the New Forest. **Open:** All Year (not Xmas)
Grades: ETC 4 Diamond
01425 472769 (also fax)
Mr & Mrs Edwards
b+b@torreavon.freeserve.co.uk
D: £18–£24 **S:** £25–£30
Beds: 1F 1D 1T **Baths:** 2 En 1 Pr
🐾 (8) 🅿 (4) ½ 📺 📶 🗓 ♿

Old Stacks, *154 Hightown Road, Ringwood, Hants, BH24 1NP.*
Warm welcome and home-from-home hospitality assured in delightful spacious bungalow.
Open: All Year (not Xmas)
01425 473840 Mrs Peck
D: £20–£22.50 **S:** £25–£30
Beds: 1D 1T **Baths:** 1 En 1 Pr
🐾 (12) 🅿 (4) ½ 📺 📶 🗓 ♿

A Secret Garden, *132 Kingfisher Way, Poulner, Ringwood, Hants, BH24 3LW.*
Friendly modern house with secluded exotic garden for guests' use.
Open: All Year (not Xmas)
01425 477563 (also fax) Mrs Richey
jennybandb@aol.com
D: fr £20 **S:** fr £20
Beds: 2D 1S **Baths:** 2 Sh
🅿 (3) ½ 📺 🛏 📶 🗓 ♿

Rockbourne

SU1118   ◀ *Rose & Thistle*

Shearings, Rockbourne, Fordingbridge,
Hants, SP6 3NA.
Open: Feb to Dec
01725 518256 Mr Watts
Fax: 01725 518255
D: £26–£30 **S:** £26–£30
Beds: 1D 1T 1S **Baths:** 3 Pr
⌂ (12) ▣ (5) ⊬ ▣ ▥ ♨
Stonehenge, Wilton House, Stourhead
Gardens, Beaulieu Motor Museum, Mary
Rose Mary Rose, Salisbury Cathedral to
name a few. C16th stunning timberland
thatched cottage set in a delightful
garden in a pretty village with Roman
Villa and picturesque old pub.

Romsey

SU3521   ◀ *Hatchet Inn, Fountain Inn, Parish,
Lantern, White Hart, Sun Inn*

Ranvilles Farm House, Salisbury
Road, Romsey, Hants, SO51 6DJ.
Historic C16th farmhouse - king beds,
antiques, peaceful and pretty garden.
Open: All Year (not Xmas)
Grades: ETC 3 Diamond
02380 814481
Mrs Hughes
D: £25–£35 **S:** £30–£40
Beds: 1F 2D 1T **Baths:** 4 En
⌂ ▣ (8) ⊬ ▣ ♞ ▥ ▣ ♨

Woodlands Guest House, Bunny
Lane, Sherfield English, Romsey, Hants,
SO51 6FT.
Woodlands Guest House is situated
in quiet country lane. Friendly
accommodation.
Open: All Year
01794 884840
Mrs Hayter
D: £15–£18 **S:** £15–£20
Beds: 1F 1D 1T **Baths:** 2 En 1 Sh
⌂ ▣ (4) ⊬ ▣ ✕ ▥ ▣ ♨

Chalet Guest House, 105 Botley
Road, Romsey, Hants, SO51 5RQ.
Small family run B&B approx. 1 mile from
Romsey Centre.
Open: All Year
Grades: ETC 3 Diamond
01794 517299 Mrs Male
b-and-b@the-chalet.freeserve.co.uk
D: £20 **S:** £25
Beds: 2F 1D **Baths:** 2 En 1 Sh
⌂ ▣ (4) ⊬ ▣ ▥ ▣ ♨

Ropley

SU6431   ◀ *The Ship*

Thickets, Swelling Hill, Ropley,
Alresford, Hants, SO24 0DA.
Comfortable house with two acre garden
in Jane Austen Country.
Open: All Year (not Xmas)
01962 772467 Mr & Mrs Lloyd-Evans
D: £22 **S:** £24
Beds: 2T **Baths:** 2 Pr
⌂ (10) ▣ (2) ⊬ ▣ ▥ ♨

Rowland's Castle

SU7310   ◀ *Staunton Arms*

Cripple Creek Guest House, 86
Whichers Gate Road, Rowland's Castle,
Hampshire, PO9 6BB.
In countryside, pub 7 minutes' walk, 2
miles M27.
Open: All Year
023 9241 2468 (also fax)
Mr & Mrs Harrod
D: £18–£24 **S:** £18–£24
Beds: 2D 1T **Baths:** 3 En
⌂ ▣ (6) ⊬ ▣ ▥ ▣ ♨ ♿

Selborne

SU7433

**Thatched Barn House, Grange
Farm,** Gracious Street, Selborne, Alton,
Hants., GU34 3JG.
Family home quietly situated in
wonderful countryside in famous village.
Open: All Year (not Xmas)
Grades: ETC 4 Diamond
01420 511007 Mrs Thompstone
Fax: 01420 511008
bobt@dircon.co.uk
D: £22.50–£25 **S:** fr £27
Beds: 1D 1T **Baths:** 1 Pr
▣ (2) ⊬ ▣ ▥ ▣

Shawford

SU4624   ◀ *The Otter*

Hazards, Fairfield Road, Shawford,
Winchester, SO21 2DA.
Rural area, convenient for Winchester,
New Forest and South Coast.
Open: All Year (not Xmas)
01962 713294 Mrs Staunton
D: £20–£22 **S:** £20–£22
Beds: 1D 1T **Baths:** 1 Sh
⌂ (3) ▣ (4) ⊬ ▣ ▥ ▣ ♨

Sherborne St John

SU6254   ◀ *The Swan*

Cranes Farmhouse, Sherborne St
John, Basingstoke, Hants, RG24 9LJ.
15th century spacious farmhouse set in
beautiful gardens with pond.
Open: All Year (not Xmas/New Year)
01256 850126 T J & L D Bell
Fax: 01256 851714
D: £25–£30 **S:** £22–£25
Beds: 1T 1D 1S **Baths:** 2 Pr
⌂ (8) ▣ (4) ⊬ ▣ ▥ ▣ ♨

Sherfield English

SU2922   ◀ *Hatchet Inn*

Woodlands Guest House, Bunny
Lane, Sherfield English, Romsey, Hants,
SO51 6FT.
Woodlands Guest House is situated in
quiet country lane. Friendly
accommodation.
Open: All Year
01794 884840 Mrs Hayter
D: £15–£18 **S:** £15–£20
Beds: 1F 1D 1T **Baths:** 2 En 1 Sh
⌂ ▣ (4) ⊬ ▣ ✕ ▥ ▣ ♨

Shootash

SU3222   ◀ *The Hatchet*

Kintail, Salisbury Road, Shootash,
Romsey, Hants, SO51 6GA.
Pleasant comfortable home midway
between Salisbury & Winchester
cathedrals. **Open:** All Year (not Xmas)
01794 513849 Ms Mansbridge
D: £17.50–£19 **S:** £23–£25
Beds: 1D 1T **Baths:** 1 En 1 Pr
▣ (6) ⊬ ▣ ▥ ♨

Sopley

SZ1697   ◀ *Woolpack*

Well Cottage, 15 Sopley, Christchurch,
Dorset, BH23 7AX.
Ideally situated between New Forest and
beach warm welcome assured.
Open: All Year (not Xmas)
01425 674668 Mrs Ramm
well.cottage@tesco.net
D: £18–£20 **S:** £18–£25
Beds: 1D 1T 1S **Baths:** 1 Sh
⌂ ▣ (3) ♞ ✕ ▥ ♨ cc

South Warnborough

SU7247   ◀ *Hoddington Arms*

Street Farm House, The Street, South
Warnborough, Basingstoke, Hants, RG29 1RS.
Charming Jacobean farmhouse in village
setting restored to offer extremely
comfortable accommodation.
Open: All Year **Grades:** ETC 4 Diamond
01256 862225 (also fax) Mrs Turner
wendy@streetfarmhouse.co.uk
D: £17–£25
Beds: 1F 2T **Baths:** 1 Pr 1 Sh
⌂ ▣ (9) ⊬ ▣ ▥ ▣ ♨

Southampton

SU4212   ◀ *Bellemoor Inn, Golden Lion, Manor
House, Peg and Parrot, Rat and Parrot*

Ashelee Lodge, 36 Atherley Road,
Shirley, Southampton, SO15 5DQ.
Open: All Year (not Xmas)
Grades: ETC 3 Diamond, AA 3 Diamond
023 8022 2095 (also fax) Mrs Ward
D: £18–£23 **S:** £20
Beds: 1F 1D 1T 1S **Baths:** 1 En 1 Sh
⌂ (4) ▣ (3) ⊬ ▣ ▥ ▣ ♨ cc
Homely guest house. Dip pool, garden,
cable TV lounge, home-cooking. Base for
historic areas Salisbury, Stonehenge,
New Forest. Easy reach Southampton
Docks, universities, station. 0.50 mile city.
Pat Ward proprietor.

Villa Capri, 50-52 Archers Road,
Southampton, SO15 2LU.
Open: All Year
Grades: ETC 3 Diamond
023 8063 2800 Mr Fantini & Mrs Tordo
Fax: 023 8063 0100
D: £25–£27 **S:** £27–£30
Beds: 17F 1T 7D 6S **Baths:** 17 En 2 Sh
⌂ (10) ▣ (14) ▣ ♞ ✕ ▥ ♨ cc
Two Victorian houses joint converted to a
guest house near the cricket ground.
Central, New Forest only 14 miles away,
near the mayflower theatre, the common
is nearby. The new Western Esplanade
Shopping centre is 5 minutes away.

Madeleine Guest House, 55 The Polygon, Southampton, SO15 2BP. Family-run, city centre, close to rail, coach, station, docks.
Open: All Year (not Xmas)
023 8033 3331 Mrs Gilligan
D: £15–£16.50 **S:** fr £15
Beds: 2F 1D 1T 2S **Baths:** 1 Sh
⌕ 🅿 (4) 📺 ⊁ ✕ 🆅 ⓚ

Pages Place Guest House, 14 Porchester Road, Southampton, SO19 2LD. Friendly, quiet, yet near town.
Open: All Year
023 8042 1275 (also fax)
Mrs Smith
D: £15–£17 **S:** £22–£24
Beds: 1D 1T 1S **Baths:** 1 Sh
⌕ ⅍ 📺 ✕ 🆅 ⓚ

Conifers, 6 Nursling Street Cottages, Nursling, Southampton, Hants, SO16 0XH. Attractive 1930s cottage. Comfortable beds. Family Garden. Country pubs nearby.
Open: All Year
023 8034 9491 (also fax)
Mrs Hinton
D: £18–£25 **S:** £18–£25
Beds: 1F 1D 1S **Baths:** 2 En
⌕ 🅿 (2) ⅍ 📺 ⊁ ✕ 🆅 ⓚ

Aavon Pennywell Guest House, 12 Howard Road, Southampton, Hants, SO15 5BP.
Clean, friendly. Situated close to central Southampton and train station.
Open: All Year (not Xmas)
023 8033 3886 Mrs Augar
D: £20–£22 **S:** £21–£23
Beds: 1F 2T 2D 5S **Baths:** 1 En 2 Sh
⌕ (0) 🅿 (9) 📺 ⊞ 🆅 ⓚ cc

Mayview Guest House, 30 The Polygon, Southampton, SO15 2BN. Family run, clean accommodation close railway city centre. Reasonable rates.
Open: All Year (not Xmas)
Grades: ETC 3 Diamond
023 8022 0907 (also fax)
D: £17.50–£23.50 **S:** £17.50–£25
Beds: 2F 1D 1T 3S **Baths:** 4 En 1 Pr 1 Sh
⌕ (4) 📺 ⊁ ✕ ⊞ ⓚ ⓚ cc

Madison House, 137 Hill Lane, Southampton, SO15 5AF.
Friendly, comfortable, family run Victorian establishment one mile from city.
Open: All Year (not Xmas/New Year)
Grades: ETC 3 Diamond
023 8033 3374 Mrs Foley
Fax: 023 8033 1209
foley@madisonhouse.co.uk
D: £18–£30 **S:** £18–£30
Beds: 1F 3D 4T 1S **Baths:** 3 En 2 Sh
⌕ 🅿 (5) ⅍ 📺 ⊞ 🆅 ⓚ cc

Banister House Hotel, Banister Road, Southampton, SO15 2JJ.
A friendly welcome assured in this central family-run hotel.
Open: All Year (not Xmas)
023 8022 1279 Mr Parkinson
D: £17–£19 **S:** £24.50–£28.50
Beds: 3F 4D 4T 12S **Baths:** 13 En 4 Sh
⌕ 🅿 (14) 📺 ⊁ ✕ ⊞ ⓚ cc

Alcantara Guest House, 20 Howard Road, Shirley, Southampton, Hants., SO15 5BN.
Attractive quality accommodation, centrally situated for all city amenities.
Open: All Year
023 8033 2966 Mr & Mrs Rose
Fax: 023 8049 6163
D: fr £19 **S:** fr £22.50
Beds: 1F 2D 2T 4S **Baths:** 3 Pr 1 Sh
⌕ (2) 🅿 (7) 📺 ⊞ 🆅 ⓚ cc

Southsea

SZ6598 ◀ Seafarers, Coastguard Tavern, Bold Forester, Wetherspoons, Town House, Still & West, Vaults, Touchdown, Rickshaws, Eastney Tavern

Bembell Court Hotel, 69 Festing Road, Southsea, Portsmouth, Hants, PO4 0NQ.
Friendly family hotel ideally situated for ferries. Single night and midweek bookings.
Open: All Year
Grades: ETC 3 Diamond, AA 3 Diamond
023 9273 5915 Mr Irwin
Fax: 023 9275 6497
keith@bembell.freeserve.co.uk
D: £24.75–£27 **S:** £38–£40
Beds: 2F 4D 4T 3S **Baths:** 13 En
⌕ 🅿 (10) 📺 ✕ ⊞ 🆅 ⓚ cc

Hamilton House, 95 Victoria Road North, Southsea, Hants, PO5 1PS.
Delightful Victorian town house B&B. Bright, modern rooms, many original features.
Open: All Year
Grades: ETC 4 Diamond, AA 4 Diamond
023 9282 3502 (also fax)
Graham & Sandra Tubb
sandra@hamiltonhouse.co.uk
D: £20–£24 **S:** £25–£40
Beds: 3F 3D 2T 1S **Baths:** 5 En 2 Sh
⌕ ⅍ 📺 ⊞ 🆅 ⓚ

The Festing Grove Guest House, 8 Festing Grove, Southsea, Hants, PO4 9QA.
Open: All Year
Grades: ETC 3 Diamond, AA 3 Diamond
023 9273 5239 Mr Newton
D: £16–£20 **S:** £19–£28
Beds: 3F 2T 1D **Baths:** 1 En 3 Sh
⅍ 📺 ⊞ 🆅 ⓚ cc
Situated in quieter area of Southsea yet within 3 walking minutes of seafront, we are an ideal base for visiting all the maritime attractions by walking, car or bus. Festing Grove offers beautifully decorated rooms with cleanliness and service to match.

The Elms Guest House, 48 Victoria Road South, Southsea, Hants, PO5 2BT.
Close to Naval Heritage Complex. Within walking distance of restaurants and seafront.
Open: All Year
Grades: ETC 3 Diamond, AA 3 Diamond
023 9282 3924 (also fax)
Mrs Erskine
theelmsgh@aol.com
D: £20–£22.50 **S:** £30–£45
Beds: 2F 1D 2T **Baths:** 5 En
⌕ (4) 🅿 (2) ⅍ 📺 ⊞ ⓚ cc

Norfolk Hotel, 25 Granada Road, Southsea, Hants, PO4 0RD.
Small friendly family-run. Close to seafront, convenient for ferries and local attractions. **Open:** All Year (not Xmas)
Grades: AA 3 Diamond
023 9282 4162 Mr Pilkington
D: £17–£21 **S:** £25
Beds: 2F 5D 2T 4S **Baths:** 12 En 1 Pr
⌕ 🅿 (9) 📺 ✕ ⊞ 🆅 ⓚ ⓚ cc

Victoria Court, 29 Victoria Road North, Southsea, Hants, PO5 1PL.
Open: All Year
Grades: ETC 3 Diamond
023 9282 277 Mr Johnson
stay@victoriacourt.co.uk
D: £17–£25 **S:** £20–£40
Beds: 2F 3T 1D **Baths:** 6 En
⌕ 📺 ⊁ ✕ ⊞ 🆅 ⓚ ⓚ
Central Portsmouth. Near main attractions and ferries. Motorway access and railways nearby. Your host not only experienced in running Victoria Court, sympathetically sees B&Bs through your eyes as a guest during charity cycle tours throughout Britain.

White House Hotel, 26 South Parade, Southsea, Hants, PO5 2JF.
Overlooking the Solent, most rooms seaview, Residents bar.
Open: All Year **Grades:** ETC 2 Star
023 9282 3709 L Keast
Fax: 023 9273 27859
D: £20–£25 **S:** £25–£35
Beds: 5F 5T 8D 1S **Baths:** 19 En
⌕ 📺 ✕ ⊞ 🆅 ⓚ cc

Oakleigh Guest House, 48 Festing Grove, Southsea, Hants, PO4 9QD.
Highly recommended, family-run guest house situated close to sea front.
Open: All Year
023 9281 2276 Mr Willett
D: £14.50–£17.50 **S:** £14.50–£25
Beds: 1F 3D 1T 2S **Baths:** 3 En 1 Sh
⌕ (2) 📺 ✕ ⊞ ⓚ

Woodville Hotel, 6 Florence Road, Southsea, Hants, PO5 2NE.
Comfortable family hotel with secure car park in central Southsea.
Open: All Year
023 9282 3409 Mr Chaffer
Fax: 023 9234 6089
woodvillehotel@cwcom.net
D: £17–£24 **S:** £22–£32
Beds: 2F 3D 2T 3S **Baths:** 10 Pr 1 Sh
⌕ 🅿 (12) ⅍ ✕ ⊞ 🆅 ⓚ

Lamorna Guest House, 23 Victoria Road South, Southsea, Hants, PO5 2BX.
Charming Victorian house, B&B only, ideally situated to all amenities.
Open: All Year
023 9281 1157 Mrs Barratt
D: £16–£20 **S:** £16–£20
Beds: 4F 1D 2T 1S **Baths:** 2 En
⌕ (5) 📺 ⊞ ⓚ

B&B owners may vary rates - be sure to check when booking

Glenroy Guest House, *28 Waverley Road, Southsea, Hants, PO5 2PW.*
Ideally situated within walking distance to most historical landmarks.
Open: All Year
023 9281 4922 Mrs Willis
D: £12–£18 **S:** £13–£18
Beds: 2F 2D 2T 2S
📷 🅿 📺 🍴 🛁 Ⅴ 🐾

Rydeview Hotel, *9 Western Parade, Southsea, Hants, PO5 3JF.*
14 bedroom guest house, open all year round, and overlooking the seafront and gardens.
Open: All Year (not Xmas)
023 9282 0865 (also fax)
derek.massey@telinco.co.uk
D: £17–£21 **S:** £17–£19
Beds: 5F 3D 3T 3S **Baths:** 9 En
📷 📺 🍴 🛁 Ⅴ 🐾 cc

Oakdale Guest House, *71 St Ronans Road, Southsea, Hants, PO4 0PP.*
Just 5 minutes' stroll from the seafront, South Parade Pier and the Canoe Lake.
Open: All Year
023 9273 7358 (also fax)
oakdale@btinternet.com
D: £19.50–£22 **S:** £24–£32
Beds: 2T 2D 2S **Baths:** 6 En
📷 (6) 📺 ✕ 🛁 Ⅴ 🐾 cc

Anne Boleyn Guest House, *33 Granada Road, Southsea, Hants, PO4 0RN.*
Happy seaside guest house 200 yards from beach. Bright spacious rooms. Year-round attractions.
Open: All Year
023 9273 1043
annieandlyndon@ukonline.co.uk
D: £16–£21 **S:** £18–£25
Beds: 2F 4D 1T 2S **Baths:** 3 Sh
📷 🅿 (10) ✂ 📺 🍴 🛁 Ⅴ 🐾

St Mary Bourne

SU4250

Coronation Arms, *St Mary Bourne, Andover, Hants, SP11 6AR.*
Traditional country pub in the heart of the beautiful Bourne Valley.
Open: All Year
01264 738432
davidpeartpeat32@supanet.com
D: £22 **S:** £22
Beds: 1F 1T 1D **Baths:** 1 En 1 Sh
📷 🅿 (20) 📺 🍴 ✕ 🛁 Ⅴ 🐾 cc

Stuckton

SU1613 🍺 *Three Lions, Forestors*

The Old Posthouse, *Stuckton Road, Stuckton, Fordingbridge, Hants, SP6 2HE.*
Open: All Year
01425 657477 Mrs Troy
Fax: 01425 657963
D: fr £18 **S:** fr £18
Beds: 1D 1T **Baths:** 2 Sh
📷 🅿 📺 🛁 Ⅴ 🐾
Comfortable detached house in New Forest village. 1/2 hour from Salisbury and Bournemouth. Good walking, horse riding and bird watching country. Excellent restaurant 2 mins walk. The home of a furniture maker and an artist.

Sway

SZ2798 🍺 *Hare & Hounds, White Rose, Gordleton Inn*

Squirrels, *Broadmead, Sway, Lymington, Hants, SO41 6DH.*
Secluded modern home. Tranquil setting. Forest, coast and Lymington town nearby.
Open: March to Dec
Grades: ETC 3 Diamond
01590 683163 Mrs Kilford
D: £19–£21 **S:** £25–£30
Beds: 1F 1D 1T 1S **Baths:** 1 En 1 Sh
📷 (8) 🅿 (8) ✂ 📺 🍴 🛁 Ⅴ 🐾 cc

Thruxton

SU2946 🍺 *The George, White Horse*

May Cottage, *Thruxton, Andover, Hampshire, SP11 8LZ.*
Open: All Year
Grades: ETC 4 Diamond, Silver, AA 4 Diamond, RAC 4 Diamond, Sparkling Diamond
01264 771241 Tom & Fiona Biddolph
Fax: 01264 771770
D: £25–£30
Beds: 1D 2T **Baths:** 2 En 1 Pr
📷 (8) 🅿 (4) ✂ 📺 🛁 Ⅴ 🐾
May Cottage dates back to 1740 and is situated in the heart of this picturesque tranquil village of Thruxton with old inn. Guests' own sitting/dining room and base for visiting ancient cities, stately homes and gardens just off A303. A non smoking establishment.

Tiptoe

SZ2597 🍺 *Rising Sun*

Acorn Palomino Shetland Pony Stud, *Brockhills Farm, Sway Road, Tiptoe, Lymington, Hants, SO41 6FQ.*
Warm welcome awaits guests in our 250-year-old cob farmhouse.
Open: All Year
01425 611280 (also fax)
Mr & Mrs Oakhill
brockhills.farm@virgin.net
D: £18–£20 **S:** £20
Beds: 1F 1D 1T **Baths:** 2 En 1 Pr
📷 🅿 (6) ✂ 📺 🍴 🛁 Ⅴ 🐾 ♿

Twyford

SU4824 🍺 *The Phoenix*

Twyford House, *Main Road, Twyford, Winchester, Hampshire, SO21 1NJ.*
Family home in Queen Anne House, Large grounds, Country walks.
Open: All Year (not Xmas/New Year)
01962 713114 Mrs Hawkes
D: fr £20 **S:** fr £20
Beds: 1F 1D **Baths:** 1 Pr 1Shared
📷 🅿 (3) ✂ 📺 🍴 🛁 🐾

Highfield Cottage, *Old Rectory Lane, Twyford, Winchester, Hampshire, SO21 1NS.*
Pretty country cottage with views, quietly situated, close to Winchester.
Open: All Year
01962 712921 C Rees
cjrees@estatesgazette.net
D: £17.50–£20 **S:** £17.50–£20
Beds: 1D 1T 1S **Baths:** 3 En
📷 🅿 (3) ✂ 📺 🍴 🛁 🐾

Weyhill

SU3146 🍺 *Weyhill Fair*

Juglans, *Red Post Lane, Weyhill, Andover, Hampshire, SP11 0PY.*
Large peaceful cottage garden good food/ale 5 minutes' walk.
Open: All Year
01264 772651 E Rotherham
D: £21–£25 **S:** £21–£25
Beds: 1D 1S **Baths:** 1 Sh
📷 (12) 🅿 (4) ✂ 📺 🛁 Ⅴ 🐾

Whitchurch

SU4647 🍺 *The Red House, Watership Down Inn*

Long Barrow House, *Cole Henley, Whitchurch, Hants, RG28 7QJ.*
Open: All Year
Grades: ETC 4 Diamond
01256 895980 Mrs Stevens
info@longbarrowhouse.co.uk
D: £20–£25 **S:** £25–£30
Beds: 1D 1T **Baths:** 2 En
📷 🅿 (20) ✂ 📺 🛁 🐾
Peaceful comfortable farmhouse on dairy farm in idyllic rural setting near Highclere Castle. Delightful cottage garden with thatched gazebo, charming rooms with lovely views, hearty English breakfast cooked on the Aga. Ample parking. Near Winchester, Salisbury, Stonehenge, New Forest.

Wickham

SU5711 🍺 *King's Head, Greens, Wickham*

Wickhaven, *23 School Road, Wickham, Fareham, Hants, PO17 5AA.*
Quality B&B in peaceful, friendly, comfortable house. Free tea/coffee.
Open: All Year (not Xmas)
01329 832457 Mrs Toogood
D: fr £18 **S:** fr £18
Beds: 1F 1D 1T 1S **Baths:** 1 Sh
📷 (12) 🅿 (2) ✂ 📺 🍴 🛁

The Willows, *Fareham Road, Wickham, Fareham, Hampshire, PO17 5BY.*
Close to twelve golf courses, sea and main cities/attractions.
Open: All Year (not Xmas)
01329 833742 (also fax)
Mr Barnatt
D: £17.50–£20 **S:** £17.50
Beds: 1F 3D 1S **Baths:** 2 Sh
📷 (6) 🅿 (10) 📺 🛁 🐾

Montrose, *Shirrell Heath, Wickham, Southampton, SO32 2HU.*
Attractive Victorian country house offering accommodation of a high standard in pleasant surroundings.
Open: All Year
01329 833345 (also fax)
Mrs Chivers
D: fr £22 **S:** fr £25
Beds: 2D 1T **Baths:** 1 Pr 1 Sh
🅿 (4) ✂ 📺 🛁 Ⅴ 🐾

National Grid References are for villages, towns and cities – not for individual houses

Winchester

SU4829 ◀ Roebuck Inn, Queen Inn, Bell Inn,
Wykeham Arms, White Horse, Stanmore Hotel, Cart
Horse, Plough

The Farrells, 5 Ranelagh Road,
Winchester, Hants, SO23 9TA.
Open: All Year (not Xmas) **Grades:** ETC 3 Diamond
01962 869555 (also fax)
Mr Farrell
thefarrells@easicom.com
D: £20–£25 **S:** £22
Beds: 1F 1D 1T 1S **Baths:** 1 En 1 Pr 2 Sh
⛵ (5) ⊬ 📺 🛏. 🏠
Turn of the century Victorian villa,
furnished in that style. We are close to
the Cathedral and like to share our love of
Winchester with our guests.

8 Salters Acres, Winchester, Hants,
SO22 5JW.
Detached family home in large gardens.
Breakfast in conservatory, easy access to
city centre.
Open: All Year (not Xmas/New Year)
01962 856112 Mr & Mrs Cater
accommodation@8salters.freeserve.co.uk
D: £19–£22.50 **S:** £25–£30
Beds: 1T 1D 1S **Baths:** 1 Pr 1 Sh
⛵ (8) 🄿 (8) ⊬ 📺 🛏. 🏠

Sycamores, 4 Bereweeke Close,
Winchester, Hants, SO22 6AR.
Convenient but peaceful location about 2
km north-west of city centre.
Open: All Year
Grades: ETC 3 Diamond
01962 867242 Mrs Edwards
Fax: 01962 620300
sycamores.b-and-b@virgin.net
D: £20
Beds: 2D 1T **Baths:** 3 Pr
🄿 (3) ⊬ 📺 🛏. 🏠

BATHROOMS

Pr - Private

Sh - Shared

En - Ensuite

---

85 Christchurch Road, Winchester,
Hants, SO23 9QY.
Comfortable detached Victorian family
house, convenient base for Hampshire
sightseeing.
Open: All Year **Grades:** ETC 4 Diamond
01962 868661 (also fax)
Mrs Fetherston-Dilke
fetherstondilke@x-stream.co.uk
D: £25–£26 **S:** £25–£30
Beds: 1D 1T 1S **Baths:** 2 En 1 Sh
⛵ 🄿 (3) ⊬ 📺 🛏. 🏠

St Margaret's, 3 St Michael's Road,
Winchester, Hampshire, SO23 9JE.
Comfortable rooms in Victorian house,
close to cathedral and colleges.
Open: All Year (not Xmas)
Grades: ETC 2 Diamond
01962 861450 Mrs Brett
D: £20–£21 **S:** £22
Beds: 1D 1T 2S **Baths:** 2 Sh
⛵ (4) 🄿 (1) ⊬ 📺 🛏. 🏠

Rocquaine, 19 Downside Road,
Winchester, SO22 5LT.
Spacious welcoming detached family
home in quiet residential area.
Open: All Year (not Xmas)
01962 861426 Mrs Quick
D: £18–£19 **S:** £20–£25
Beds: 1D 1T 1S **Baths:** 1 Sh
⛵ (8) 🄿 (4) ⊬ 📺 🛏. 🏠

32 Hyde Street, Winchester, Hants,
SO23 7DX.
Attractive C18th town house, close to city
centre.
Open: All Year (not Xmas/New Year)
01962 851621 Mrs Tisdall
D: £17–£18 **S:** £26
Beds: 1F 1D **Baths:** 1 Sh
⛵ ⊬ 📺 🛏. 🏠

Portland House Hotel, 63 Tower
Street, Winchester, Hants, SO23 8TA.
Quiet city centre location a few minutes
from major sites.
Open: All Year (not Xmas/New Year)
Grades: ETC 3 Diamond
01962 865195 Mr & Mrs Knight
D: £22.50–£55 **S:** £48
Beds: 1F 1T 2D **Baths:** 4 En
⛵ (5) 🄿 (5) 📺 🛏. 🏠

Shawlands, 46 Kilham Lane,
Winchester, Hants, SO22 5QD.
Attractive house on edge of Winchester in
quiet lane overlooking fields.
Open: All Year
01962 861166 (also fax)
Mrs Pollock
kathy@pollshaw.u-net.com
D: £19–£22.50 **S:** £27–£30
Beds: 2F 1D 2T **Baths:** 1 Pr 2 Sh
⛵ (5) 🄿 (4) ⊬ 📺 🛏 🛏. 🏠 👶 cc 3

The Lilacs, 1 Harestock Close, off
Andover Road North, Winchester, Hants,
SO22 6NP.
Attractive, Georgian-style family home.
Comfortable, clean and excellent cuisine.
Open: All Year (not Xmas)
01962 884122 Mrs Pell
richard@rbpell.freeserve.co.uk
D: £17.50–£18 **S:** £22–£25
Beds: 1D 1T **Baths:** 1 Sh
⛵ 🄿 (3) ⊬ 📺 🛏. 🏠

Giffard House Hotel, 50 Christchurch
Road, St Cross, Winchester, Hants,
SO23 9SU.
Comfortable Victorian house within ten
minutes' walk of the city centre.
Open: All Year
01962 852628 Fax: 01962 856722
D: £25–£35 **S:** £35–£45
Beds: 1F 6D 2T 5S **Baths:** 14 En
⛵ 🄿 (14) 📺 🛏. 🏠

Winsor

SU3114 ◀ Compass Inn

Bushfriers, Winsor Road, Winsor,
Southampton, SO40 2HF.
Forest cottage, peaceful surroundings,
New Forest heritage area, highly rated
breakfasts.
Open: All Year (not Xmas)
023 8081 2552 Mr & Mrs Wright
D: £19–£21 **S:** £23–£25
Beds: 1F **Baths:** 1 Pr
⛵ 🄿 (2) ⊬ 📺 🛏 🛏. 🏠

Herefordshire

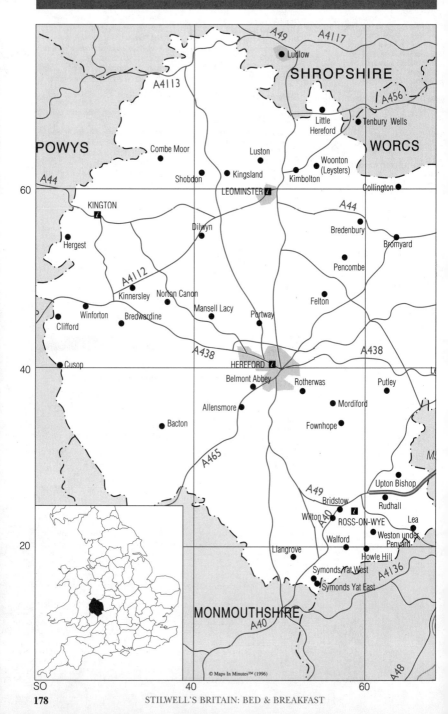

Tourist Information Centres

1 Rowberry Street, **Bromyard**,
Herefordshire, HR7 4DX,
01885 482341.

Queenswood Country Park, Dinmore
Hill, **Dinmore**, Queenswood,
Herefordshire, HR6 0PY, 01568 797842.

1 King Street, **Hereford**, HR4 9BW,
01432 268430.

1 Church Lane, **Ledbury**, Herefordshire,
HR8 1EA, 01531 636147.

1 Corn Square, **Leominster**,
Herefordshire, HR6 8LR, 01568 616460

20 Broad Street, **Ross-on-Wye**,
Herefordshire, HR9 7EA, 01989 562768

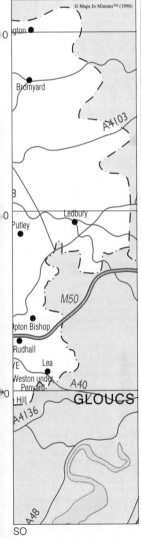
© Maps In Minutes™ (1996)

Allensmore

SO4635   🍺 *Three Horseshoes*

Holly House Farm, *Allensmore,
Hereford, HR2 9BH.*
Delightful family country farmhouse in
beautiful and peaceful open countryside.
Open: All Year (not Xmas)
01432 277294 Mrs Sinclair
Fax: 01432 261285
hollyhousefarm@aol.com
D: £20 **S:** £20
Beds: 1D 2T 1S **Baths:** 1 En 2 Pr 1 Sh
🛇 🅿 (30) 📺 🛏 🛋 🅅 ♨

Bacton

SO3632   🍺 *Temple Bar, Enyas Harold*

Pentwyn Cottage, *Bacton, Hereford,
HR2 0AP.*
An idyllic mature cottage garden 1.5
acres of winding paths, pool and stream.
Open: All Year (not Xmas)
01981 240508 (also fax)
Mrs Gunn
D: £15–£20 **S:** £17–£20
Beds: 1F 1D **Baths:** 1 En 1 Pr
🛇 🅿 (10) 📺 🛋 ♨

Belmont Abbey

SO4838

Hedley Lodge, *Belmont Abbey,
Hereford, HR2 9RZ.*
Open: All year
Grades: ETC 4 Diamond
01432 277475 Fax: 01432 277597
hedleylodge@aol.com
D: £24.50–£26 **S:** £29.50–£31.50
Beds: 1F 4D 12T **Baths:** 17 En
🛇 🅿 (200) 📺 ✕ 🛋 ♨ ♨ 🅬 cc
Superbly located on the edge of historic
Hereford and within the beautiful
grounds of Belmont Abbey, Hedley Lodge
offers a warm friendly welcome in its
comfortable modern guest house. Full
licensed restaurant open to all visitors.

Bredenbury

SO6056   🍺 *Barnaby Arms*

Red Hill Farm, *Bredenbury, Bromyard,
Herefordshire, HR7 4SY.*
C17th comfortable farmhouse, peaceful
countryside, panoramic views. Central for
Malvern, Hereford, Worcester.
Open: All Year (not Xmas)
Grades: ETC 2 Diamond
01885 483255 Mrs Evans
Fax: 01885 483535
D: £16–£17 **S:** £18–£20
Beds: 1F 1D 1T 1S **Baths:** 1 Sh
🛇 🅿 (10) 📺 🛏 ✕ 🛋 🅅 ♨

Munderfield Harold, *Bredenbury,
Bromyard, Herefordshire, HR7 4SZ.*
B&B and day fishing.
Open: Mar to Dec
01885 483231 Mrs Morgan
D: £14–£19 **S:** £14–£19
Beds: 1F 1D 1T
🛇 (7) 🅿 (10) 📺 🛏 🅅 ♨

Bredwardine

SO3344

Red Lion Hotel, *Bredwardine,
Hereford, HR3 6BU.*
Open: All Year
01981 500303 Fax: 01981 500400
D: £20–£29.50 **S:** £28–£40
Beds: 2F 5T 2D **Baths:** 9 En
🛇 🅿 (15) 📺 🛏 ✕ 🛋 🅅 ♨ cc
17th Century inn in the heart of the Wye
Valley. Warm friendly atmosphere, good
food. An ideal centre for relaxation and
touring. Private fishing on River Wye, golf
breaks. A peaceful haven in a busy world.
Discover the Wye Valley.

Bridstow

SO5824   🍺 *Red Lion*

Lavender Cottage, *Bridstow, Ross-on-
Wye, Herefordshire, HR9 6QB.*
Arrive as a guest, depart as a friend.
Open: All Year (not Xmas)
Grades: ETC 3 Diamond
01989 562836 Mrs Nash
Fax: 01989 762129
barbara_lavender@yahoo.co.uk
D: £17.50 **S:** fr £25
Beds: 1D 2T **Baths:** 2 En 1 Pr
🛇 (8) 🅿 (3) ⅙ 📺 ✕ 🛋 🅅 ♨

Bromyard

SO6554   🍺 *Bay Horse, Royal Oak*

Park House, *28 Sherford Street,
Bromyard, Herefordshire, HR7 4DL.*
Open: All Year
01885 482294 (also fax)
Mr Gardiner
parkhouse@callnetuk.com
D: £20–£25 **S:** £22.50–£30
Beds: 1F 1T 2D **Baths:** 3 En 1 Pr
🛇 🅿 (6) 📺 🛏 ✕ 🛋 🅅 ♨ 🅬 ♨ &
Enjoy the country without the crowds.
Walk to great walks, superb pubs and
really friendly people. Excellent base for
touring North Hertfordshire. Family
hospitality in very comfortable, character
property with view. Good parking, garage
for bikes. Children half price.

Clifford

SO2445   🍺 *Royal Oak, The Pandy*

Cottage Farm, *Middlewood, Clifford,
Hereford, HR3 5SX.*
Quiet location, birds, walking, working
farm, families welcome, good value.
Open: All Year (not Xmas)
Grades: ETC 3 Diamond
01497 831496 (also fax)
Mrs Jones
D: £17–£18 **S:** £18
Beds: 1F 1T **Baths:** 1 Sh
🛇 🅿 (4) ⅙ 🛋 ♨ &

BATHROOMS

Pr - Private

Sh - Shared

En - Ensuite

Collington

SO6460

Granary Licensed Restaurant,
Church House Farm, Collington,
Bromyard, Herefordshire, HR7 4NA.
All bedrooms ground floor in converted
barns with licensed restaurant.
Open: All Year
01885 410345 Mrs Maiden
Fax: 01885 410555
D: £20–£22 **S:** fr £22
Beds: 1D 4T **Baths:** 5 Pr
🛏 🅿 (40) 📺 🍴 ✕ 🛏 🖾 ₤ 🕭 1

Combe Moor

SO3663

Brick House Farm, Combe Moor,
Presteigne, Powys, LD8 2HY.
Comfortable farmhouse on small holding.
Beautiful countryside. Warm welcome.
memorable meals.
Open: All Year
Grades: ETC 2 Star
01544 267306 Mr & Mrs Johnstone
Fax: 01544 260601
dmfj@johnstone.kc3.co.uk
D: £17.50–£20 **S:** £20
Beds: 3D 1T 1S **Baths:** 2 Sh
🛏 🅿 (4) 📺 🍴 ✕ 🛏 🖾 ₤

Cusop

SO2341

Fernleigh, Hardwick Road, Cusop, Hay-
on-Wye, Hereford, HR3 5QX.
Quiet location walking distance of the
famous book town of Hay-on-Wye.
Open: Easter to Oct
01497 820459 Mr Hughes
D: £15–£19 **S:** £19
Beds: 2D 1S **Baths:** 1 En 1 Sh
🛏 🅿 (4) 乡 📺 ✕ 🛏 ₤

Dilwyn

SO4154

Bedford House, Dilwyn, Hereford,
HR4 8JJ.
Open: All Year (not Xmas/New Year)
01544 388260 Mrs Anthony
D: £18–£20 **S:** fr £20
Beds: 1F 1T 1D **Baths:** 1 En 1 Sh
🛏 🅿 (4) 📺 🍴 🛏 🖾 ₤
Small friendly farm offering excellent
accommodation, peace and quiet. one of
the loveliest unspoilt countries of
England. Do the Black and White Trail
Black Mountains. Malvern's - Ludlow.
Ross- also National Trust Properties
nearby. Beautiful gardens open.

Felton

SO5848   🍴 Three Horseshoes

Felton House, Felton, Hereford, HR1 3PH.
Country house of character in tranquil
gardens. Relax on arrival with
refreshments.
Open: All Year (not Xmas)
01432 820366 (also fax) Mr Roby
D: £23 **S:** £23
Beds: 2D 1T 1S **Baths:** 2 En 2 Pr
🛏 🅿 (6) 乡 📺 🍴 🛏 🖾 ₤

Fownhope

SO5834   🍴 Green Man

Pippins, Capler Lane, Fownhope,
Hereford, HR1 4PJ.
Comfortable spacious accommodation
with lovely views of River Wye and rolling
countryside.
Open: All Year (not Xmas/New Year)
01432 860677 Mrs Corby
D: £20–£22 **S:** £23–£25
Beds: 2T **Baths:** 1 Pr
🅿 (4) 乡 📺 🛏 🖾 ₤

Hereford

SO5140   🍴 Horse & Groom, Imperial, Moon,
Bay Horse

Sink Green Farm, Rotherwas,
Hereford, HR2 6LE.
Open: All Year (not Xmas)
Grades: ETC 4 Diamond
01432 870223 Mr Jones
sinkgreenfarm@.msn.com
D: £20 £25 **S:** £21–£25
Beds: 2D 1T **Baths:** 3 En
🛏 🅿 (10) 乡 📺 🛏 🖾 ₤
We welcome you to our 16th Century
Farmhouse set in the picturesque Wye
Valley, yet only 3 miles from Hereford.
Relax in our tastefully decorated, ensuite
rooms, one four poster, all having
tea/coffee facilities, colour TV and central
heating.

Cedar Guest House, 123 White Cross
Road, Hereford, HR4 0LS.
Open: All Year
Grades: ETC 3 Diamond
01432 267235 (also fax)
Mr & Mrs Williams
D: £18–£20 **S:** £24–£35
Beds: 2F 1T 2D **Baths:** 1 En 1 Sh
🛏 🅿 (8) 📺 ✕ 🛏 ₤
A family run former Victorian gentleman's
residence residence many original
features. Offering spacious, central
heated accommodation. All rooms have
colour television and tea and coffee
making facilities. Within easy walking
distance of Historic city centre of
Hereford.

Hopbine Hotel, Roman Road,
Hereford, HR1 1LE.
Family run hotel in own extensive
grounds. Modern furnishings and
facilities.
Open: All Year
Grades: ETC 2 Diamond
01432 268722 (also fax)
Mrs Horne
D: £20–£25 **S:** £25–£30
Beds: 4F 6D 6T 4S **Baths:** 18 En 2 Sh
🛏 🅿 (30) 📺 🍴 ✕ 🛏 🖾 ₤

Ancroft, 10 Cheviot Close, Kings Acre,
Hereford, HR4 0TF.
On the edge of city within easy reach of
beautiful countryside.
Open: All Year (not Xmas)
Grades: ETC 3 Diamond
01432 274394 Mrs Davies
D: £18.50 **S:** £17.50–£18.50
Beds: 1D 2S **Baths:** 1 Sh
🛏 (10) 🅿 (3) 乡 📺 🛏 🖾

Hergest

SO2753   🍴 The Harp, Royal Oak

Bucks Head House, Upper Hergest,
Hergest, Kington, Herefordshire, HR5 3EW.
Situated on south side of Hergest Ridge
and Offa's Dyke Path.
Open: All Year
01544 231063 Mrs Protheroe
D: £18–£20 **S:** £18–£20
Beds: 2F 2D 1T 1S **Baths:** 2 Sh
🛏 🅿 (6) 📺 🍴 ✕ 🛏 🖾 ₤

Howle Hill

SO6020   🍴 Crown Inn

Old Kilns, Howle Hill, Ross-on-Wye,
Herefordshire, HR9 5SP.
Open: All Year
Grades: AA 4 Diamond, RAC 4 Diamond,
Sparkling Award
01989 562051 (also fax) Mrs Smith
D: £15–£30
Beds: 1F 1T 2D **Baths:** 1 En 1 Pr 1 Sh
🛏 🅿 (8) 📺 🍴 ✕ 🛏 🖾 ✿ ₤ 🕭
Stay as our guests at our privately owned
country house set in a quiet village
location, with church and village inn.
Come and relax in front of our log fire and
let us do the work.

Kimbolton

SO5261

The Fieldhouse Farm, Bache Hill,
Kimbolton, Leominster, Herefordshire,
HR6 0EP.
Traditional farmhouse, oak beams, log
fires, wonderful views and delicious
breakfasts.
Open: Apr to Nov
Grades: ETC 3 Diamond
01568 614789 Mrs Franks
D: £19–£21 **S:** £20–£22
Beds: 1T **Baths:** 1 Pr
🛏 🅿 (4) 乡 📺 🍴 🖾 ₤

Kingsland

SO4461   🍴 Angel Inn

Holgate Farm, Kingsland, Leominster,
Herefordshire, HR6 9QS.
C17th farmhouse on working farm,
attractive bedrooms, delicious breakfasts.
Open: All Year (not Xmas)
01568 708275 Mrs Davies
D: £17–£18 **S:** £18
Beds: 1F 1T **Baths:** 1 Sh
🛏 🅿 (3) 乡 📺 🍴 🛏 🖾 ₤

Kington

SO2956   🍴 Harp, Swan Inn, Royal Oak, Queen's
Head, Sun

Dunfield Cottage, Kington,
Herefordshire, HR5 3NN.
Friendly, relaxed; lovely views;large
garden; log fires; H&C in bedrooms.
Open: All Year
01544 230632 (also fax)
Ms Green
robann@dunfieldcottage.kc3.co.uk
D: £16–£18 **S:** £16–£18
Beds: 1T 1D 1S **Baths:** 1 Sh
🛏 (10) 🅿 (6) 乡 📺 ✕ 🛏 🖾 ₤

Church House, *Church Road, Kington, Herefordshire, HR5 3AG.*
Large rooms with fine views in elegant Georgian family home.
Open: All Year (not Xmas)
01544 230534 Mrs Darwin
Fax: 01544 231100
darwin@kc3.co.uk
D: £20 **S:** £20–£30
Beds: 1D 1T **Baths:** 1 Sh
🛏 🅿 (2) ⅍ 🛏 🏢 🆅

Bollingham House, *Kington, Herefordshire, HR5 3LE.*
Period residence with glorious views. Gracious rooms. Delightful English garden.
Open: All Year
01544 327326 Mrs Grant
Fax: 01544 327880
bollhouse@bigfoot.com
D: £25–£28.50 **S:** fr £27.50
Beds: 2D 1T 1S **Baths:** 2 Pr
🛏 🅿 (10) ⅍ 🛏 🏢 🆅 ✕ 🏢 🆅 ♿

Cambridge Cottage, *19 Church Street, Kington, Herefordshire, HR5 3BE.*
C17th cottage; warm welcome, many return visits, comfortable beds, camping.
Open: All Year (not Xmas)
01544 231300 Mr & Mrs Hooton
gerry@kington.softnet.co.uk
D: £17.50 **S:** £17.50
Beds: 1F 1S **Baths:** 1 En 1 Sh
🛏 (3) 🅿 (2) ⅍ 🛏 🏢 🆅 ♿

Kinnersley

SO3449 🍺 *Royal George, Salutation*

Upper Newton Farmhouse, *Kinnersley, Hereford, HR3 6QB.*
C17th award-winning timbered farmhouse on working farm. Always a warm welcome.
Open: All Year
Grades: AA 4 Diamond
01544 327727 (also fax)
Mrs Taylor
enquiries@bordertrails.u-net.com
D: £25 **S:** £25
Beds: 2D 1T **Baths:** 3 Pr
🛏 🅿 (6) ⅍ 🛏 ✕ 🏢 🆅 ♿

Lea

SO6521

Lea House, *Lea, Ross-on-Wye, HR9 7JZ.*
Tastefully refurbished coaching inn, central for Wye valley/forest, Dean.
Open: All Year
Grades: ETC 4 Diamond
01989 750652 (also fax)
C Lerpiniere
leahouse@wyenet.co.uk
D: £18–£20 **S:** £22–£25
Beds: 2F 2T **Baths:** 2 En 1 Pr
🛏 🅿 (3) ⅍ 🛏 🏢 ✕ 🏢 🆅 ♿ cc

RATES

D = Price range per person sharing in a double room
S = Price range for a single room

Ledbury

SO7137

Leadon House Hotel, *Ross Road, Ledbury, Herefordshire, HR8 2LP.*
Open: All Year
Grades: ETC 2 Star
01531 631199 M H J Williams
Fax: 01531 631476
leadon.house@amserve.net
D: £25–£32 **S:** £34–£49
Beds: 2F 1T 2D 1S **Baths:** 6 En
🛏 🅿 (8) 🏢 🏢 🆅 ♿ ⅙ cc
Elegant Edwardian house in picturesque setting, approx. 1 mile from historic Ledbury convenient to Malvern hills, Wye Valley and Herefordshire's renowned black and white villages. Refurbished in period style with comfortable accommodation, attractive gardens. Good home cooked food. Restricted smoking.

Leominster

SO4959 🍺 *Stockton Cross, Rawtan, Bush Bank, Hop Pole Baron's Cross, Talbot Inn, Black Horse, Fountain*

Woonton Court Farm, *Woonton, Leysters, Leominster, Herefordshire, HR6 0HL.*
Comfortable Tudor farmhouse, own produce. Freedom to walk and enjoy wildlife. Rural peace.
Open: All Year (not Xmas)
Grades: AA 3 Diamond
01568 750232 (also fax)
Mrs Thomas
thomas.woontoncourt@farmersweekly.net
D: £20–£24 **S:** £22–£25
Beds: 1F 1D 1T **Baths:** 3 En
🛏 🅿 (3) 🏢 🏢 🆅 ♿

Rossendale Guest House, *46 Broad Street, Leominster, Herefordshire, HR6 8BS.*
Friendly traditional town centre establishment welcoming tourists and business visitors.
Open: All Year
Grades: ETC 3 Diamond
01568 612464 Mr Hosegood
D: £20–£25 **S:** £18–£22
Beds: 3D 2T 6S **Baths:** 1 En 1 Sh
🅿 (10) 🏢 ✕ 🏢 ♿

Copper Hall, *South Street, Leominster, Herefordshire, HR6 8JN.*
An attractive and comfortable C17th house with a warm welcome.
Open: All Year
Grades: ETC 4 Diamond
01568 611622 Mr & Mrs Crick
SCCrick@copperhall.freeserve.co.uk
D: £20–£22 **S:** £20–£25
Beds: 2D 2T **Baths:** 3 En 1 Pr
🛏 🅿 (4) 🏢 🛏 🏢 🆅 ♿

Highfield, *Newtown Ivington Road, Leominster, Herefordshire, HR6 8QD.*
Comfortable, friendly, spacious Edwardian house. Pleasant rural location, good views.
Open: Mar to Oct
01568 613216 Misses Fothergill
D: £18.50–£22 **S:** fr £18.50
Beds: 1D 2T **Baths:** 1 En 2 Pr
🅿 (3) ⅍ ✕ 🏢 🆅 ♿

Little Hereford

SO5568 🍺 *Temeside*

Haynall Villa, *Haynall Lane, Little Hereford, Ludlow, Shropshire, SY8 4BG.*
1820's farmhouse with original features, attractive garden in peaceful location.
Open: All Year (not Xmas/New Year)
Grades: AA 3 Diamond
01584 711589 (also fax)
Mrs Edwards
D: £18–£24 **S:** £18–£28
Beds: 1F 1D 1T **Baths:** 1 En 1 Sh
🛏 (6) 🅿 (3) ⅍ 🏢 🛏 ✕ 🏢 🆅 ♿

Llangrove

SO5219 🍺 *Royal Arms, New Inn*

Thatch Close, *Llangrove, Ross-on-Wye, Herefordshire, HR9 6EL.*
Secluded, quiet Georgian farmhouse, set in panoramic countryside, sympathetically modernised.
Open: All Year
Grades: ETC 3 Diamond
01989 770300 Mrs Drzymalski
edwards/drzymalski@virgin.net
D: £18–£20 **S:** £23–£26
Beds: 2D 1T **Baths:** 2 En 1 Pr
🛏 🅿 (8) ⅍ 🏢 🛏 ✕ 🏢 🆅 ♿

Luston

SO4863 🍺 *Maidenhead, Orleton The Balance*

Ladymeadow Farm, *Luston, Leominster, Herefordshire, HR6 0AS.*
Large, friendly, comfortable C17th farmhouse near two NT properties.
Open: Easter to Nov
Grades: ETC 3 Diamond
01568 780262 Mrs Ruell
D: £19–£22 **S:** £19–£22
Beds: 1F 1D 1S **Baths:** 1 En 1 Sh
🛏 🅿 (20) ⅍ 🏢 🏢 🆅 ♿

Mansell Lacy

SO4245 🍺 *Dog & Duck*

Apple Tree Cottage, *Mansell Lacy, Hereford, HR4 7HH.*
C15th cottage in a peaceful situation surrounded by fields.
Open: All Year
01981 590688 Mrs Barker
monica.barker@tesco.net
D: £17–£20 **S:** £17–£20
Beds: 1D 2T **Baths:** 1 Pr 1 Sh
🛏 (14) 🅿 (4) ⅍ 🏢 🏢 🆅 ♿

Mordiford

SO5737 🍺 *Yew Tree, Moon Inn*

Orchard Farm House, *Mordiford, Hereford, HR1 4EJ.*
C17th farmhouse overlooking beautiful Lugg Valley and Black Mountains.
Open: All Year (not Xmas)
01432 870253 Mrs James
Fax: 01432 851440
donphelps@donrye.freeserve.co.uk
D: £18–£18.50 **S:** £20–£21
Beds: 2D 1T **Baths:** 1 Pr 1 Sh
🛏 🅿 ⅍ 🏢 🛏 ✕ 🏢 🆅 ♿

Norton Canon

SO3847   ⊲ *Salutation Inn*

The Old Vicarage, Norton Canon,
Hereford, HR4 7BQ.
Impressive former vicarage situated in
delightful, peaceful surroundings.
Open: All Year (not Xmas/New Year)
01544 318146 Mrs Gallimore
D: £25 **S:** £25
Beds: 1T 1D 1S **Baths:** 2 En 1 Pr
🄿 (6) ⅙ ✕ 📺 📺 🕭

Pencombe

SO5952   ⊲ *Englands Gate, The Lamb*

Hennerwood Farm, Pencombe,
Bromyard, Herefordshire, HR7 4SL.
Traditional dairy farm, quiet position.
Panoramic views of beautiful
Herefordshire.
Open: Easter to Oct
01885 400245 (also fax)
Mrs Thomas
hennerwood@farming.co.uk
D: £20 **S:** £20
Beds: 1F 1D
🄿 (2) 🄿 ⅙ 📺 📺 🕭

Portway

SO4845   ⊲ *The Bay Horse*

Heron House, Canon Pyon Road,
Portway, Hereford, HR4 8NG.
Open: All Year
Grades: ETC 3 Diamond
01432 761111 R F Huckle
Fax: 01432 760603
bb.hereford@tesco.net
D: £19–£21 **S:** £16–£17.50
Beds: 1F 1D **Baths:** 1 En 1 Sh
🄿 (10) 🄿 (4) ⅙ 📺 ✕ 📺 ✻ 🕭
Relaxing house, near Hereford City, with
spacious rooms and country views. Full
English breakfast. Private off-road
parking. Suitable location for walking,
cycling, golf, Wye valley, Black and White
Trail and other country interests. Also
facilities for business guests.

Putley

SO6337   ⊲ *The Crown Inn, The Trumpet Inn*

The Coach House, Putley, Ledbury,
Herefordshire, HR8 2QP.
The Coach House is an eighteenth
century coaching stable set in gorgeous
Herefordshire.
Open: All Year
01531 670684 (also fax)
Mrs Born
wendyborn@putley-coachhouse.co.uk
D: £16–£17.50 **S:** £22–£25
Beds: 1T 2D 1S
🄿 ⅙ 📺 📺 🕭

BATHROOMS

Pr - Private

Sh - Shared

En - Ensuite

Ross-on-Wye

SO6024   ⊲ *Eagle, White Lion, Royal Arms, New
Inn, Prince of Wales, Slip, Western Cross, Moody
Cow*

Sunnymount Hotel, Ryefield Road,
Ross-on-Wye, Herefordshire, HR9 5LU.
Small, family-run hotel, quiet,
comfortable, excellent home-cooked
meals. **Open:** All Year
Grades: ETC 4 Diamond
01989 563880 Mr & Mrs Robertson
Fax: 01989 566251
sunnymount@tinyworld.co.uk
D: £20–£25 **S:** £20–£27
Beds: 4D 2T **Baths:** 2 En 1 Sh
🄿 🄿 (6) 📺 ✕ 📺 📺 🕭 cc

Thatch Close, Llangrove, Ross-on-Wye,
Herefordshire, HR9 6EL.
Secluded, quiet Georgian farmhouse, set
in panoramic countryside,
sympathetically modernised.
Open: All Year **Grades:** ETC 3 Diamond
01989 770300 Mrs Drzymalski
edwards/drzymalski@virgin.net
D: £18–£20 **S:** £23–£26
Beds: 2D 1T **Baths:** 2 En 1 Pr
🄿 🄿 (8) ⅙ 📺 ✇ ✕ 📺 📺 🕭

Rowan Lea, Ponts Hill, Ross-on-Wye,
Herefordshire, HR9 5SY.
Friendly, peaceful, detached dormer
bungalow. Lovely views, gardens, big
breakfast. **Open:** All Year
Grades: ETC 2 Diamond
01989 750693 Ms Griffiths
D: £15–£16 **S:** £15–£16
Beds: 1F 1D **Baths:** 1 Sh
🄿 (2) ⅙ 📺 📺 🕭

Benhall House, Wilton, Ross-on-Wye,
Herefordshire, HR9 6AG.
Open: All Year (not Xmas)
Grades: ETC 3 Diamond
01989 567420 (also fax) Mrs Beddows
D: £20 **S:** £25
Beds: 1F **Baths:** 1 En
🄿 🄿 (10) 📺 ✇ ✕ 📺 📺 🕭
Down a quiet cul-de-sac road on the edge
of Ross-on-Wye, we are within walking
distance of many excellent pubs and
restaurants. Wye valley walk is less than
half a mile and Symonds Yat and forest of
Dean in close proximity.

Broadlands, Ledbury Road, Ross-on-
Wye, Herefordshire, HR9 7BG.
Broadlands home from home. Good food,
warm welcome. **Open:** All Year
01989 563663 Mrs Ryder
D: £18–£19 **S:** £18–£20
Beds: 2D 2S **Baths:** 1 Sh
🄿 🄿 (6) 📺 📺 📺 🕭

Copperfield House, Copperfield,
Wilton Lane, Ross-on-Wye, Herefordshire,
HR9 6AH.
Spacious family home, river meadow
views, attractive bedrooms, residents
conservatory lounge.
Open: All Year **Grades:** ETC 4 Diamond
01989 764379 Mrs Brown
fran_brown@talk21.com
D: £19.50 **S:** £25
Beds: 1D 1T **Baths:** 1 Sh
🄿 🄿 (4) ⅙ 📺 ✇ 📺 📺 🕭

Lyndor, Hole-in-the-Wall, Ross-on-Wye,
Herefordshire, HR9 7JW.
Beautiful beamed country cottage in
picturesque surroundings overlooking
River Wye.
Open: All Year (not Xmas)
01989 563833 D: £16–£18 **S:** £18–£20
Beds: 1D 1T **Baths:** 1 Pr
🄿 (12) 🄿 ⅙ 📺 ✕ 📺 🕭

Welland House, Archenfield Road,
Ross-on-Wye, Herefordshire, HR9 5BA.
Large family house with attractive garden
within walking distance of town and open
countryside.
Open: All Year
01989 566500 (also fax)
Mrs Harries
wellandhouse@hotmail.com
D: £18–£20 **S:** £20–£23
Beds: 1D 1T **Baths:** 1 Sh
🄿 (5) 🄿 ⅙ 📺 📺 📺 🕭

Rotherwas

SO5338   ⊲ *The Moon*

Sink Green Farm, Rotherwas,
Hereford, HR2 6LE.
We welcome you to our C16th Farmhouse
set in the picturesque Wye Valley.
Open: All Year (not Xmas)
Grades: ETC 4 Diamond
01432 870223 Mr Jones
sinkgreenfarm@.msn.com
D: £20–£25 **S:** £21–£25
Beds: 2D 1T **Baths:** 3 En
🄿 🄿 (10) ⅙ 📺 ✇ 📺 📺 🕭

Rudhall

SO6225   ⊲ *Penny Farthing
Moody Cow*

Rudhall Farm, Rudhall, Ross-on-Wye,
Herefordshire, HR9 7TL.
Elegant country house. Warm welcome.
Aga cooked breakfasts. Highly
recommended by guests.
Open: All Year (not Xmas)
Grades: ETC 4 Diamond, Silver Award
01989 780240 Mrs Gammond
D: £25–£50 **S:** £25–£30
Beds: 2D **Baths:** 1 Pr 1 Sh
🄿 (10) ⅙ 📺 📺 📺 🕭

Shobdon

SO3961   ⊲ *Bateman Arms*

The Paddock, Shobdon, Leominster,
Herefordshire, HR6 9NQ.
Open: All Year (not Xmas)
Grades: ETC 4 Diamond, Gold Award, AA
4 Diamond
01568 708176 Mrs Womersley
Fax: 01568 708829
thepaddock@talk21.com
D: £20–£23 **S:** £30–£32
Beds: 4D 1T **Baths:** 5 En
🄿 🄿 (5) ⅙ 📺 ✕ 📺 📺 🕭
Delightful ground floor ensuite
accommodation, situated in the beautiful
border region between England and
Wales. Large garden and patio, delicious
home cooked food. Popular walking area,
local National Trust attractions.

Symonds Yat East

SO5616 🍺 *Three Crowns, Ye Hostelrie, Saracens Head Inn*

Rose Cottage, *Symonds Yat East, Ross-on-Wye, Herefordshire, HR9 6JL.*
Comfortable riverside accommodation with a touch of luxury.
Open: All Year **Grades:** ETC 3 Diamond
01600 890514 Mrs Whyberd
Fax: 01600 890498
D: £16.50–£24.50 **S:** £30–£35
Beds: 3D **Baths:** 2 En 1 Pr
🅿 (3) ⅙ 📺 ⽊ 🏬 Ⓥ 🎇

Symonds Yat West

SO5516 🍺 *Three Crowns*

Riversdale Lodge Hotel, *Symonds Yat West, Ross-on-Wye, Herefordshire, HR9 6BL.*
Family run country house hotel, Riverside setting overlooking Wye Rapids.
Open: Feb to Dec **Grades:** ETC 3 Diamond
01600 890445 Mr & Mrs Armsden
Fax: 01600 890443
info@riversdale.uk.com
D: £35 **S:** £50
Beds: 1F 1T 3D **Baths:** 5 En
🐕 (1) 🅿 (11) 📺 ⽊ ✕ 🏬 Ⓥ 🎇 🎇 cc

Upton Bishop

SO6427 🍺 *Moody Cow*

Bishop's Acre, *Upton Bishop, Ross-on-Wye, Herefordshire, HR9 7TT.*
Comfortable, spacious south-facing house. Guest rooms enjoy amazing views over large garden. **Open:** All Year (not Xmas)
01989 780318 (also fax) Mrs Stirrup
rstirrup@netlineuk.net
D: £20 **S:** £25
Beds: 1D 1T 1S **Baths:** 2 En 1 Sh
🐕 (3) 🅿 (3) ⅙ 📺 🏬 Ⓥ 🎇

Walford (Ross-on-Wye)

SO5820

The Inn on the Wye, *Kerne Bridge, Walford, Ross-on-Wye, Herefordshire, HR9 5QT.*
C18th coaching inn, fully restored (mid 90s), on banks of River Wye.
Open: All Year
01600 890872 Fax: 01600 890594
D: £24–£32.50 **S:** £36.50–£42.50
Beds: 8D 1T **Baths:** 9 En
🐕 🅿 📺 ⽊ ✕ 🏬 Ⓥ 🎇 🎇 cc

Weston under Penyard

SO6223 🍺 *Weston Cross*

Wharton Farm, *Weston under Penyard, Ross-on-Wye, Herefordshire, HR9 5SX.*
17th and 19th century farmhouse, near the forest of Dean and Wye valley.
Open: All Year (not Xmas)
Grades: ETC 3 Diamond
01989 750255 (also fax)
Mrs Savidge
D: £20–£22 **S:** £20–£25
Beds: 2D 1T **Baths:** 1 En 2 Pr
🐕 🅿 (5) 📺 🏬 Ⓥ 🎇

Wilton

SO5824 🍺 *White Lion*

Benhall House, *Wilton, Ross-on-Wye, Herefordshire, HR9 6AG.*
Down a quiet Cul-de-sac road on the edge of Ross-on-Wye.
Open: All Year (not Xmas)
Grades: ETC 3 Diamond
01989 567420 (also fax)
Mrs Beddows
D: £20 **S:** £25
Beds: 1F **Baths:** 1 En
🐕 🅿 (10) 📺 ⽊ ✕ 🏬 Ⓥ 🎇

Winforton

SO2947 🍺 *Rhydspence Inn.*

Winforton Court, *Winforton, Hereford, HR3 6EA.*
Romantic C16th manor house in beautiful Wye Valley, offering country house ambience.
Open: All Year (not Xmas)
01544 328498 (also fax)
Mrs Kingdon
D: £25–£34
S: fr £33.50
Beds: 3D **Baths:** 3 En
🐕 (10) 🅿 (8) ⅙ 📺 ⽊ Ⓥ 🎇

Woonton (Leysters)

SO5462 🍺 *The Fountain, Stockton Cross*

Woonton Court Farm, *Woonton, Leysters, Leominster, Herefordshire, HR6 0HL.*
Comfortable Tudor farmhouse, own produce. Freedom to walk and enjoy wildlife. Rural peace.
Open: All Year (not Xmas)
Grades: AA 3 Diamond
01568 750232 (also fax)
Mrs Thomas
thomas.woontoncourt@farmersweekly.net
D: £20–£24
S: £22–£25
Beds: 1F 1D 1T **Baths:** 3 En
🐕 🅿 (3) 📺 🏬 Ⓥ 🎇

B&B owners may vary rates - be sure to check when booking

Hertfordshire

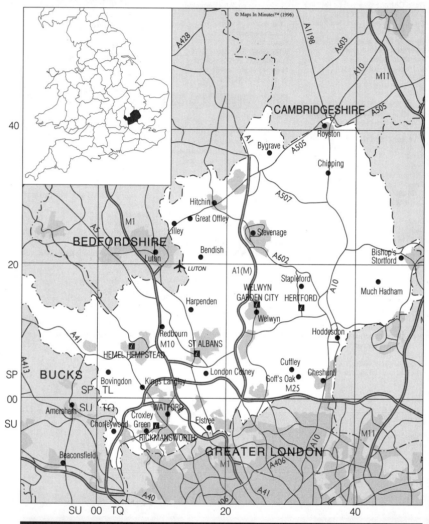

© Maps In Minutes™ (1996)

Bendish

TL1621 ◆ *Maidens Head*

Bendish House, *Bendish, Hitchin, Hertfordshire, SG4 8JA.*
Hilltop location, stunning views overlooking Mimram valley. Artists studio available.
Open: All Year (not Xmas)
01438 871519 Fax: 01438 871499
D: £20–£25 **S:** £20–£25
Beds: 1D 1T 1S
🛇 🅿 (6) ⊬ 📺 🗻 ⚲

Bishop's Stortford

TL4921 ◆ *Harvest Moon, Jades*

Pearse House Conference & Training Centre, *Parsonage Lane, Bishop's Stortford, Herts, CM23 5BQ.*
Victorian mansion housing excellent conference facilities and ensuite bedrooms.
Open: All Year (not Xmas/New Year)
Grades: AA 3 Diamond
01279 757400 D Doyle
Fax: 01279 506591
pearsehouse@route56.co.uk
D: £35–£40 **S:** £60–£70
Beds: 2F 5T 7D 23S **Baths:** 35 En 2 Pr
🛇 🅿 ⊬ 📺 ✕ 🗻 ⚲ ♨ cc

Broadleaf Guest House, *38 Broadleaf Avenue, Bishop's Stortford, Herts, CM23 4JY.*
Close to Stansted Airport; fast trains into London and Cambridge.
Open: All Year (not Xmas)
01279 835467 Mrs Cannon
paula@broadleaf63.freeserve.co.uk
D: £25 **S:** £25–£30
Beds: 1F 1D 1T **Baths:** 1 Pr
🛇 🅿 (2) ⊬ 📺 🐾 🗻 🇻 ⚲

Anglesey House, *16 Grailands, Bishop's Stortford, Herts, CM23 3RG.*
Delightful family home in a quiet area close to town. **Open:** All Year (not Xmas)
Grades: AA 4 Diamond
01279 653614 Mrs Windus
jeanwindus@breathemail.net
D: £22–£26 **S:** £30–£45
Beds: 1D 2T **Baths:** 1 En 1 Sh
🛇 (8) 🅿 (6) ⊬ 📺 🗻 🇻 ⚲

Bovingdon

TL0103 ◆ *Royal Oak*

Rose Farm, *Water Lane, Bovingdon, Hemel Hempstead, Herts, HP3 0NA.*
Country situated, newly-built farmhouse convenient M1, M25, trains, London.
Open: All Year (not Xmas)
01442 834529 Mrs Mills
D: £25 **S:** fr £35
Beds: 2T **Baths:** 2 En
🛇 (3) 🅿 (10) 📺 🗻 🇻 ⚲ &

RATES

D = Price range per person sharing in a double room
S = Price range for a single room

Bygrave

TL2636 ◆ *Bushel & Strike, Rose & Crown, Engine*

Bygrave B&B, *59 Ashwell Road, Bygrave, Baldock, Hertfordshire, SG7 5DY.*
Friendly family home, rural location. Guests' room, use of garden.
Open: All Year (not Xmas)
01462 894749 Mrs Spaul
D: £22–£25 **S:** £22–£25
Beds: 2D 2T 1S **Baths:** 2 En 1 Sh
🛇 🅿 (5) ⊬ 📺 🗻 🇻 ⚲

Cheshunt

TL3602

The Old Barn, *Goffs Lane, Cheshunt, EN7 5EP.*
C17th barn standing in 3 acres of park-like grounds, swimming pool, off-street parking.
Open: All Year
01992 620564 (also fax)
Mrs Russell
D: £30–£35 **S:** £30–£40
Beds: 1F 1D 1T 1S **Baths:** 1 En 1 Sh
🛇 🅿 (12) 📺 🐾 ✕ 🗻 🇻 ♨ ⚲ cc

Chipping

TL3532 ◆ *Countryman Inn*

Ashford Cottage, *Chipping, Buntingford, Herts, SG9 0PG.*
Elizabethan thatched cottage, acre of gardens, heavily timbered.
Open: All Year
01763 274163 Mr & Mrs Kenyon
Fax: 01763 271655
jefferyk@csma-netlink.co.uk
D: £22.50 **S:** £22.50
Beds: 1D 2S **Baths:** 1 Sh
🛇 🅿 (6) ⊬ 📺 ✕ 🗻 🇻 ⚲

Chorleywood

TQ0296 ◆ *Rose & Crown*

Kennels Cottage, *Common Road, Chorleywood, Herts, WD3 5LW.*
A quiet oasis. A mellow brick cottage. A warm welcome.
Open: All Year (not Xmas)
01923 282927 Mrs Smethurst
D: fr £22.50 **S:** fr £25
Beds: 2F 2S **Baths:** 1 Sh
🛇 🅿 (4) ⊬ 📺 🗻 🇻 ⚲

Croxley Green

TQ0695 ◆ *Coach & Horses, The Green, The Artichoke,*

Farthings, *Copthorne Road, Croxley Green, Rickmansworth, Hertfordshire, WD3 4AE.*
Situated in private road. Close to station and M25 Motorway.
Open: All Year (not Xmas/New Year)
01923 771431 Mrs Saunders
bazmau@barclays.net
D: £22.50 **S:** £22.50
Beds: 1T 2S **Baths:** 1 Sh
🛇 (6) 🅿 (6) ⊬ 📺 🗻 ⚲

Cuffley

TL3003 ◆ *Harvester*

Wutherings, *43 Colesdale, Cuffley, Potters Bar, Herts, EN6 4LQ.*
Unusual split-level bungalow, near London yet overlooking open country.
Open: All Year (not Xmas)
Grades: ETC 4 Diamond
01707 874545 Mrs Pettit
D: £18.50–£20 **S:** £18.50–£20
Beds: 1D 1S **Baths:** 1 Sh
🅿 (2) ⊬ 📺 🗻 🇻 ⚲

Elstree

TQ1795 ◆ *Waggon & Horses*

North Medburn Farm, *Watling Street, Elstree, Herts, WD6 3AA.*
Easy access to London.
Open: All Year (not Xmas)
020 8953 1522 Mrs Williams
D: £20–£25 **S:** £20–£25
Beds: 1F 3T 1S **Baths:** 1 En 1 Sh
🅿 (4) ⊬ 🗻

Goff's Oak

TL3203 ◆ *Wheelwrights*

329 Goffs Lane, *Goff's Oak, Cheshunt, Herts, EN7 5QH.*
Detached house close to countryside, walks drives, country pubs.
Open: All Year
01992 628524 (also fax) Mrs Morgan
D: £30–£32 **S:** £28–£30
Beds: 2F 3D 1T **Baths:** 6 En
🛇 🅿 (5) 📺 ✕ 🗻 🇻 ♨ ⚲

Great Offley

TL1426 ◆ *Red Lion, Green Man*

Church View, *Kings Walden Road, Great Offley, Hitchin, Herts, SG5 3DU.*
Comfortable home opposite village Church, convenient for Luton, Hitchin and Stevenage.
Open: All Year (not Xmas)
01462 768719 (also fax) Mr Maybury
D: £22.50–£25 **S:** £30–£35
Beds: 1D 1T **Baths:** 1 En 1 Pr
🛇 (10) 🅿 (2) ⊬ 📺 🗻 ⚲

Harpenden

TL1314 ◆ *Harrow, Fox, Harpenden Arms, Old Bell*

The Old Cottage, *417 Luton Road, Harpenden, Herts, AL5 3QE.*
Comfortable C18th cottage, convenient London and airports warm welcome.
Open: All Year (not Xmas)
01582 762257 Mr & Mrs Horn
D: £20 **S:** £20–£25
Beds: 1F 1D 1S **Baths:** 1 En
🛇 🅿 (3) 📺 ⚲

Milton Hotel, *25 Milton Road, Harpenden, Herts, AL5 5LA.*
Family run (Victorian house) business offering a warm welcome.
Open: All Year (not Xmas/New Year)
01582 762914 Mr Gray
D: £25 **S:** £40
Beds: 4D 1F **Baths:** 5 En
🛇 🅿 (8) 📺 🗻 ⚲ cc

Hemel Hempstead

TL0607   *The Bell, The Packhorse*

Southville Private Hotel, *9 Charles Street, Hemel Hempstead, Herts, HP1 1JH.*
Detached small hotel, near town centre. Car park. Near M1 and M25.
Open: All Year
01442 251387 Mr Davis
D: £20.56 **S:** £29.38
Beds: 2F 1D 6T 10S **Baths:** 6 Sh
🛏 🄿 (7) 🖾 🛏 🛒 🖵 🖩 ♿ CC

Hertford

TL3212   *The Greyhound, George & Dragon*

Bengeo Hall, *St Leonards Road, Hertford, Herts, SG14 3JN.*
C17th manor, peaceful, spacious, gracious. Friendly New Zealand hospitality. Something special.
Open: All Year (not Xmas)
01992 505897 Mrs Savory
Fax: 01992 503667
D: £25–£30 **S:** £30–£45
🛏 (10) 🄿 (20) ⌦ 🖾 ♿

Hitchin

TL1828

Firs Hotel, *83 Bedford Road, Hitchin, Herts, SG5 2TY.*
Comfortable hotel with relaxed informal atmosphere. Excellent rail/road links and car parking.
Open: All Year
Grades: RAC Star
01462 422322 M Girgenti
Fax: 01462 432051
enquiries@firshotel.co.uk
D: £26–£30 **S:** £37.50–£50
Beds: 3F 3D 8T 16S **Baths:** 30 En
🛏 🄿 (30) ⌦ 🖾 🛏 🛒 🖵 🖩 ♿ CC

Hoddesdon

TL3708

The Bell Inn, *Burford Street, Hoddesdon, Herts, EN11.*
Close to M25 and A10. Contractors welcome. Entertainment weekends.
Open: All Year
01992 463552 Mr & Mrs Corrigan
Fax: 01992 450400
D: £17–£22 **S:** £24
Beds: 7F 5T 3S **Baths:** 2 En 4 Sh
🛏 🖾 🛏 🛒 🖵 🖩 ♿ CC

Kings Langley

TL0702   *Bricklayers, Two Brewers, Eagle*

Woodcote House, *7 The Grove, Chipperfield Road, Kings Langley, Herts, WD4 9JF.*
Detached timber-framed house in acre of gardens.
Open: All Year (not Xmas)
Grades: ETC 3 Diamond
01923 262077 Mr & Mrs Leveridge
Fax: 01923 266198
leveridge@btinternet.com
D: £20–£24 **S:** £22–£26
Beds: 1D 1T 2S **Baths:** 4 En
🛏 (1) 🄿 (6) ⌦ 🖾 🛒 🖵 🖩 ♿

Lilley

TL1126   *Lilley Arms*

Lilley Arms, *West Street, Lilley, Luton, Beds, LU2 8LN.*
Early C18th coaching inn.
Open: All Year
01462 768371 Mrs Brown
D: £20–£30
Beds: 1F 1D 3T **Baths:** 3Ensuite 1 Sh
🛏 🄿 ⌦ 🖾 🛒 🖵 🖩 ♿ CC

London Colney

TL1804   *Colney Fox*

The Conifers, *42 Thamesdale, London Colney, St Albans, Herts, AL2 1TL.*
Modern detached house. Historic city of St Albans 3 miles.
Open: All Year
Grades: ETC 3 Diamond
01727 823622 D: £16.50–£19.50 **S:** £22–£25
Beds: 1D 1T 1S **Baths:** 1 Sh
🛏 (12) 🄿 ⌦ 🖾 🖵 🖩 ♿

Much Hadham

TL4219   *Hoops Inn, Jolly Wagonners, The Crown*

Sidehill House, *Perry Green, Much Hadham, Herts, SG10 6DS.*
C17th house, 4 acres of garden and wood in pretty village.
Open: All Year **Grades:** ETC 4 Diamond
01279 843167 Mrs Stephens
D: £23–£26 **S:** £25–£48
Beds: 2T **Baths:** 1 Pr 1 En
🛏 🄿 ⌦ 🖾 🖵 🖩 ♿

Redbourn

TL1012   *The Chequers, The Bull*

Broomsticks, *106 High Street, Redbourn, St Albans, Herts, AL3 7BD.*
Pretty Victorian cottage, attractive, well-maintained gardens, breakfasts a speciality. **Open:** All Year (not Xmas)
01582 792882 Mrs Simpson
D: £20 **S:** £20
Beds: 1T 1S **Baths:** 1 Sh
🛏 🄿 ⌦ 🖾 🛒 🖵 🛏

20 Cumberland Drive, *Redbourn, Herts, AL3 7PG.*
Comfortable quiet home in village; easy access to M1, London.
Open: All Year (not Xmas)
01582 794283 Mrs Tompkins
D: £18 **S:** £18
Beds: 1T 1S **Baths:** 1 Pr 1 Sh
🛏 (10) 🄿 ⌦ 🖾 🖵 🛏

Rickmansworth

TQ0494   *Red House, Fox & Hounds, Scotch Bridge Mill, Coach & Horses*

Tall Trees, *6 Swallow Close, Nightingale Road, Rickmansworth, Herts, WD3 2DZ.*
Situated in quiet cul-de-sac near underground station. Home-made bread and preserves. **Open:** All Year
01923 720069 Mrs Childerhouse
D: £22–£23 **S:** £22–£23
Beds: 1D 3S **Baths:** 1 Sh
🛏 (10) 🄿 (4) ⌦ 🖩 🖩 ♿

The Millwards Guest House, *30 Hazelwood Road, Croxley Green, Rickmansworth, Herts, WD3 3EB.*
Family run, pleasant canalside location. Convenient motorways, trains, motorways, business parks.
Open: All Year
01923 226666 Mrs Millward
Fax: 01923 252874
D: £19–£20 **S:** £22.50–£25
Beds: 2T **Baths:** 2 Sh
🛏 (2) 🄿 (2) ⌦ 🖾 🛏 🖩 🖩 ♿

Royston

TL3541   *Jockey Inn, White Bear Lodge, Green Man*

Jockey Inn, *31-33 Baldock Street, Royston, Herts, SG8 5BD.*
Traditional public house, real ales. Comfortable rooms - ensuite/cable TV. Hearty breakfast.
Open: All Year
01763 243377
D: £26.50–£28.50 **S:** £29.95–£34
Beds: 3T 1F **Baths:** 5 En
🛏 (8) 🄿 (5) 🖾 🛒 🖩 🖩 ♿

St Albans

TL1507   *King William IV, Mile End House, Robin Hood, Crown*

2 The Limes, Spencer Gate, *St Albans, Herts, AL1 4AT.*
A modern, comfortable home, quiet cul-de-sac, 10 mins town centre. Home-baked bread.
Open: All Year
Grades: ETC 3 Diamond
01727 831080 Mrs Mitchell
hunter.mitchell@virgin.net
D: £15 **S:** £20
Beds: 1T 1S **Baths:** 1 Sh
🛏 (3) 🄿 (2) ⌦ 🖾 🖩 🛏

76 Clarence Road, *St Albans, Herts, AL1 4NG.*
Spacious Edwardian house opposite park. Easy walking to trains (London)
Open: All Year (not Xmas/New Year)
Grades: ETC 4 Diamond
01727 864880 (also fax)
Mr & Mrs Leggatt
pat.leggatt@talk21.com
D: £23–£25 **S:** £26–£30
Beds: 1T 1S **Baths:** 1 Sh
🄿 (2) ⌦ 🖾 🖩 🖩 ♿

5 Cunningham Avenue, *St Albans, Herts, AL1 1JJ.*
Family home, quiet tree-lined avenue, half mile city centre.
Open: All Year (not Xmas)
Grades: ETC 3 Diamond
01727 857388 Mrs Cullingford
benita@cullingford.fsnet.co.uk
D: £18–£20 **S:** £18–£22
Beds: 1D 2T **Baths:** 1 En 1 Sh
🛏 🄿 (2) 🖾 🖩

National Grid References are for villages, towns and cities – not for individual houses

Stapleford

TL3116 🍴 *Papillon*

Little Pipers, *1 Church Lane, Stapleford, Hertford, Herts, SG14 3NB.*
Quiet riverside village location. Good transportation links to London.
Open: All Year
01992 589085 Mrs Lewis
D: £18–£25 **S:** £20–£30
Beds: 4D **Baths:** 1 En 1 Sh
🅿 (6) ⅍ 📺 🛏 ▥ ♨ ♿

Stevenage

TL2424

Abbington Hotel, *23 Hitchin Road, Stevenage, Herts, SG1 3BJ.*
Old town location. All ensuite, telephone, remote CTV, Hairdryer etc.
Open: All Year (not Xmas/New Year)
01438 315241 Fax: 01438 745043
abbington.hotel@virgin.net
D: £22.50–£28.75 **S:** £35–£52.50
Beds: 1F 2T 10D 7S **Baths:** 20 En
🛏 🅿 (24) ⅍ 📺 ✕ ▥ ♨ cc

Watford

TQ1097 🍴 *Red House, Coach & Horses, Yates Wine Lodge*

Grey's Bed & Breakfast, *1 Wellington Road, Watford, Herts, WD1 1QU.*
Ideally located for railway station, town centre and business parks.
Open: Jan to Dec
07990 956260 M-L Grey
Fax: 01923 492446
greysbnb@bigfoot.com
D: fr £22.50 **S:** fr £25
Beds: 2T 1S **Baths:** 2 Sh
🅿 (4) ⅍ 📺 ♨

The Millwards Guest House, *30 Hazelwood Road, Croxley Green, Rickmansworth, Herts, WD3 3EB.*
Family run, pleasant canalside location. Convenient motorways, trains, motorways, business parks.
Open: All Year
01923 226666 Mrs Millward
Fax: 01923 252874
D: £19–£20 **S:** £22.50–£25
Beds: 2T **Baths:** 2 Sh
🛏 (2) 🅿 (2) ⅍ 📺 🛏 ▥ ♨ ♿

33 Courtlands Drive, *Watford, Herts, WD1 3HU.*
Detached warm & friendly convenient London, Canal, Motorways M1 M25.
Open: All Year
01923 220531 Mrs Troughton
D: £19–£20 **S:** £20–£22
Beds: 2T 1S **Baths:** 1 Sh
🛏 (3) 🅿 (7) ⅍ 📺 🛏 ▥ ♨

Welwyn

TL2316 🍴 *Red Lion*

Christmas Cottage, *3 Ayot Green, Welwyn, Herts, AL6 9AB.*
Open: All Year
01707 321489 Mr & Mrs Sherriff
Fax: 01707 392659
janesherriff@tesco.net
D: £25–£30 **S:** £45–£55
Beds: 1D 1T 1S **Baths:** 2 En 1 Pr
🛏 🅿 (10) ⅍ 📺 🛏 ▥ ♨
Charming 300-year-old cottage on village green, comfortable bedrooms overlooking garden and swimming pool, close to Hatfield & Welwyn Garden City stations. Rich local interest including cathedral city of St Albans & Hatfield House.

RATES

D = Price range per person sharing in a double room
S = Price range for a single room

Welwyn Garden City

TL2413 🍴 *The Cottage, Sun Inn*

The Seven Bees, *76 Longcroft Lane, Welwyn Garden City, Herts, AL8 6EF.*
Peaceful detached house, beautiful garden, short walk to town centre.
Open: All Year (not Xmas)
01707 333602 Mrs Bunyan
D: £ **S:** fr £25
Beds: 1T 1S **Baths:** 1 Sh
🅿 (1) ⅍ 📺 ▥ ♨ ♨

73 Attimore Road, *Welwyn Garden City, Herts, AL8 6LG.*
Private house.
Open: All Year
01707 323868 (also fax)
Mrs Densham
tdalink@aol.com
D: £17.50–£20 **S:** £20–£25
Beds: 2D 2S **Baths:** 2 Sh
🅿 (6) ⅍ 📺 ▥ ♨

BEDROOMS
F - Family
D - Double
T - Twin
S - Single

Isle of Wight

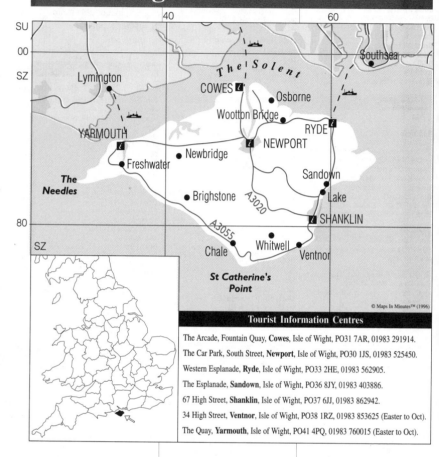

SU
00
SZ

40

Lymington

The Solent

COWES *i*
Osborne

Wootton Bridge

YARMOUTH
i

Freshwater

RYDE *i*
NEWPORT *i*

Newbridge

60

Southsea

The
Needles

The Needles

Brighstone

A3020

Sandown
Lake

SHANKLIN *i*

80

SZ

A3055

Chale

Whitwell
Ventnor

St Catherine's
Point

© Maps In Minutes™ (1996)

Tourist Information Centres

The Arcade, Fountain Quay, **Cowes**, Isle of Wight, PO31 7AR, 01983 291914.

The Car Park, South Street, **Newport**, Isle of Wight, PO30 1JS, 01983 525450.

Western Esplanade, **Ryde**, Isle of Wight, PO33 2HE, 01983 562905.

The Esplanade, **Sandown**, Isle of Wight, PO36 8JY, 01983 403886.

67 High Street, **Shanklin**, Isle of Wight, PO37 6JJ, 01983 862942.

34 High Street, **Ventnor**, Isle of Wight, PO38 1RZ, 01983 853625 (Easter to Oct).

The Quay, **Yarmouth**, Isle of Wight, PO41 4PQ, 01983 760015 (Easter to Oct).

Brighstone

SZ4382 Countryman Inn, Three Bishops, The Crown

Buddlebrook Guest House,
Moortown Lane, Brighstone, Newport, Isle of Wight, PO30 4AN.
Peaceful country guest house. Adults only. Non-smokers. Super breakfast.
Open: All Year
Grades: ETC 3 Diamond
01983 740381 (also fax)
Mr & Mrs Woodford
D: £20–£25 **S:** £22–£25
Beds: 2D 1T **Baths:** 3 En
P (3) ⅍ ⊡ ★ ▥ ♨

Planning a longer stay? Always ask for any special rates

Chale

SZ4877 Clarendon Hotel, Wight House

Cortina, Gotten Lane, Chale, Ventnor, Isle of Wight, PO38 2HQ.
Modern comfortable bungalow.
Open: All Year (not Xmas)
Grades: ETC 3 Diamond
01983 551292 Mrs Whittington
D: fr £17 **S:** fr £20
Beds: 1D 1T **Baths:** 1 Sh
P (6) ⅍ ⊡ ▥ ♨

RATES

D = Price range per person sharing in a double room

S = Price range for a single room

Cowes

SZ4996 Duke Of York, Anchor Inn

Gurnard Pines Holiday Village,
Cockleton Lane, Cowes, Isle of Wight, PO31 8QE.
Open: All Year
Grades: ETC 4 Star
01983 292395
Fax: 01983 299415
mail@pines.tcp.co.uk
D: £25–£40 **S:** £35–£50
Beds: 20F 30T 30D
Baths: 40 En 40 Pr
⅍ P (200) ⊡ ✕ ⊻ ♨ ⅊ cc
Countryside location close to the yachting haven of Cowes offering B&B accommodation in luxury pine lodges or bungalows. Facilities include first class restaurant, coffee shop, club and bars, heated pools, health suite, fitness complex, tennis courts, crazy golf and pétanque.

Halcyone Villa, *Grove Road, off Mill Hill Road, Cowes, Isle of Wight, PO31 7JP.*
Small friendly Victorian guest house situated near marinas and town.
Open: All Year
Grades: ETC 3 Diamond
01983 291334 Miss Fussell
sandra@halcyone.freeserve.co.uk
D: £17.50–£35 **S:** £17.50–£35
Beds: 1F 2D 2T 1S **Baths:** 1 En 1 Pr 1 Sh
⏰ 🅿 📺 ⋔ ▦ 🎗

Hillbrow Private Hotel, *Tuttons Hill, Cowes, Isle of Wight, PO31 8JA.*
Small friendly family run hotel rurally situated.
Open: All Year (not Xmas/New Year)
Grades: ETC 4 Diamond
01983 297240 (also fax)
Mr Mortlock
D: £20–£25 **S:** £20–£30
Beds: 1F 1D 2T 1S **Baths:** 3 En 1 Sh
⏰ 🅿 (5) 📺 ✕ ▦ 🎗

Green Bank, *54 Mill Hill Road, Cowes, Isle of Wight, PO31 7EG.*
Large friendly detached Victorian accommodation offering excellent facilities in Cowes, famous yachting centre.
Open: All Year (not Xmas)
01983 291928 (also fax)
Grant & Ellen Vincent
grant@cowes2000.freeserve.co.uk
D: £18–£25 **S:** £18–£25
Beds: 1F 2D **Baths:** 1 En 1 Pr 1 Sh
⏰ 🅿 ⅟ 📺 ▦ 🎗

Freshwater

SZ3486

Brookside Forge Hotel, *Brookside Road, Freshwater, Isle of Wight, PO40 9ER.*
Family run hotel, ideal for West Wight, walking and cycling.
Open: All Year (not Xmas)
01983 754644 Mr Chettle
D: £20–£21 **S:** £20–£21
Beds: 2F 2D 2T 1S **Baths:** 7 En
⏰ 🅿 (7) ⅟ 📺 ⋔ ✕ ▦ 🎗 cc

Lake

SZ5883 🍺 *Farmers Arms, Manor House*

Cliff Lodge, *13 Cliff Path, Lake, Isle of Wight, PO36 8PL.*
Large Edwardian house. Gardens lead to Sandown/Shanklin cliff path.
Open: Feb to Nov
Grades: ETC 3 Diamond
01983 402963 Mrs Grinstead
D: £15–£20 **S:** £15–£20
Beds: 2F 5D 1T **Baths:** 8 En
⏰ (2) 🅿 (8) 📺 ▦ 🎗

Pebblecombe Guest House, *48 Sandown Road, Lake, Sandown, Isle of Wight, PO36 9JT.*
Five minutes from coastal path, station, village and buses.
Open: All Year (not Xmas)
Grades: ETC 2 Diamond
01983 402609 (also fax)
Mr & Mrs Hallett
D: £13–£16 **S:** £13–£16
Beds: 2F 2D 1T 1S **Baths:** 3 En 2 Pr
⏰ 🅿 (6) ⅟ 📺 ✕ ▦ 🎗

Newbridge

SZ4187

Homestead Farm, *Newbridge, Yarmouth, Isle of Wight, PO41 0TZ.*
New wing of modern farmhouse.
Open: Jan to Dec
Grades: ETC 3 Diamond
01983 531270 Mrs Priddle
D: £20 **S:** £25
Beds: 1F 1T 1D 1S **Baths:** 2 En
⏰ 🅿 📺 ⋔ ▦ 🎗 &

Newport

SZ5089 🍺 *The George*

Magnolia House, *6 Cypress Road, Newport, Isle of Wight, PO30 1EY.*
Picturesque character house, secluded garden, large rooms, convenient for town.
Open: All Year **Grades:** ETC 4 Diamond
01983 529489 Mrs Brooks
magnoliaiw@aol.com
D: £19–£21 **S:** £22–£25
Beds: 1D 1S **Baths:** 2 En
🅿 (2) ⅟ 📺 ▦ 🎗 cc

Osborne

SZ5194 🍺 *Prince of Wales, Folly Inn*

The Doghouse, *Crossways Road, Osborne, East Cowes, Isle of Wight, PO32 6LJ.*
Somewhere special. Popular friendly comfortable ensuite rooms near Osborne House.
Open: All Year
Grades: ETC 4 Diamond
01983 293677 D: £20–£30 **S:** £30–£35
Beds: 1T 1D **Baths:** 2 En
🅿 (3) ⅟ 📺 ⋔ ▦ 🎗

Crossways House, *Crossways Road, Osborne, East Cowes, Isle of Wight, PO32 6LJ.*
Beautiful Victorian residence opposite Osborne House close to Cowes marinas.
Open: All Year
01983 298282 (also fax) Mrs Baldwin
D: £22.50–£30 **S:** £27.50–£35
Beds: 1F 3D 2T **Baths:** 5 Pr 1 Sh
⏰ 🅿 (10) 📺 ✕ ▦ 🎗

Ryde

SZ5992 🍺 *The Baywatch Marine, White Hart*

Seaward, *14 & 16 George Street, Ryde, Isle of Wight, PO33 2EW.*
Close to beach, ferry terminals, town centre and local amenities.
Open: All Year
Grades: ETC 2 Diamond
01983 563168 seaward@fsbdial.co.uk
D: £15–£22 **S:** £18–£24
Beds: 2F 1T 3D 1S **Baths:** 2 En 4 Sh
⏰ 📺 ✕ 🎗 &

Rowantrees, *63 Spencer Road, Ryde, Isle of Wight, PO33 3AF.*
Modern detached house,quiet rural setting, minutes from town centre+sea front.
Open: All Year (not Xmas/New Year)
01983 568081 D: £15–£16 **S:** £16
Beds: 1D/1F 2S **Baths:** 1 Sh + toilet
⏰ 🅿 (4) 📺 ⋔ ▦ 🎗

Brantoria, *44 St Thomas St, Ryde, Isle of Wight, PO33 2DL.*
Some rooms with sea view. One minute from beach. Close to ferry.
Open: All Year
01983 562724 Mrs Sims
D: £15–£16 **S:** £15–£16
Beds: 2F 2D 2T **Baths:** 2 Sh
⏰ 📺 ⋔ ✕ ▦ 🎗 &

Sandown

SZ5984 🍺 *Crab House, Longshoreman, Plough & Barleycorn, Culver Haven, Caulkhead, White Hart, Stag Inn, Manor House, Barnaby's*

The Iona Private Hotel, *44 Sandown Road, Sandown, Isle of Wight, PO36 9JT.*
Open: All Year
Grades: ETC 3 Diamond
01983 402741 (also fax)
Mr Joy & Nora Dempsey
lionahotel@netscapeonline.co.uk
D: £15–£19 **S:** £15–£19
Beds: 3F 4D 2T 3S
Baths: 4 Pr 2 Sh
⏰ 🅿 (6) 📺 ⋔ ✕ ▦ 🎗 ✽ 🎗 cc
'Home across the water' is the motto for our 3-Diamond rated guest house, a few minutes walk from a beautiful cliff path and sandy beach. We offer the warmest of welcomes, good home cooking, licensed bar, TV and refreshments in each room. Children welcome.

Hazelwood Hotel, *19 Carter Street, Sandown, Isle of Wight, PO36 8BL.*
Open: All Year
Grades: AA 3 Diamond
01983 402536 Mrs Wright
D: £18–£24 **S:** £20
Beds: 3F 1T 1D **Baths:** Sh
⏰ 🅿 (8) 📺 ⋔ ✕ 🎗 ✽ 🎗 &
Victorian hotel. near sea and nightclub. Home cooking, relaxed family atmosphere. Children's toys and rocking horse. All babies needs available/baby sitting by arrangement. Relaxing garden. Provide snacks, licensed bar. We enjoy small groups and cater for business peoples needs.

Montpelier Hotel, *Pier Street, Sandown, Isle of Wight, PO36 8JR.*
Situated in one of the finest positions in Sandown.
Open: All Year
Grades: ETC 3 Diamond
01983 403964 S Birks
Fax: 0709 2212734
still@montpelier-hotel.co.uk
D: £18–£25 **S:** £18–£25
Beds: 2F 1T 3D 1S **Baths:** 5 En 1 Pr
⏰ 📺 🎗 cc

Mount Brocas Guest House, *15 Beachfield Road, Sandown, Isle of Wight, PO36 8LT.*
Beach, pier, shops, buses, coastal walks. 2 minutes from Mount Brocas.
Open: All Year (not Xmas)
01983 406276
Mrs King
brocas@netguides.co.uk
D: £15–£20 **S:** £15–£20
Beds: 2F 3D 2T 1S
Baths: 4 En 2 Pr
⏰ ⅟ 📺 ⋔ ▦ 🎗

St Ninans Guest House, *19 Avenue Road, Sandown, Isle of Wight, PO36 8BN.*
1 minute to beach. Victorian guest house, family-run.
Open: Easter to Oct
Grades: ETC 3 Diamond
01983 462755 Mrs Ryan
D: £16–£17 **S:** £16–£17
Beds: 5F 4T 1D **Baths:** 1 En 3 Sh
☑ ⬛ ✕ ♨

Sands Hotel, *Seafront, Sandown, Isle of Wight, PO36 8AT.*
Fully licensed run hotel on Sandown's sandy sea front.
Open: All Year
Grades: ETC 1 Star
01983 402305 (also fax)
Mrs Hedges
sw@sands-hotel.co.uk
D: £22–£33 **S:** £22–£33
Beds: 8F 12D 6T 8S **Baths:** 34 En
☑ ⬛ (14) ⬛ ⬛ ✕ ⬛ ⬛ ♨ ♨ cc

Shanklin

SZ5881

Hambledon Hotel, *Queens Road, Shanklin, Isle of Wight, PO37 6AW.*
Open: All Year
Grades: ETC 2 Star, AA 2 Star, RAC 2 Star
01983 862403 Mr Sewell
D: £23–£26 **S:** £25
Beds: 4F 4D 1T 1S **Baths:** 10 En
☑ ⬛ (8) ☑ ✕ ⬛ ♨ ♨
Family licensed hotel offers genuine personal service. All bedrooms ensuite and tastefully decorated, full central heating, colour TV, radios, tea and coffee making facilities, choice of menu. Great position for town centre, beach and old village. Totally non-smoking.

Culham Lodge Hotel, *31 Landguard Manor Road, Shanklin, Isle of Wight, PO37 7HZ.*
Open: Feb to Dec
Grades: ETC 4 Diamond
01983 862880 (also fax) Mr Metcalf
metcalf@culham99.freeserve.co.uk
D: £23–£24 **S:** £22–£23
Beds: 4D 5T 1S **Baths:** 10 En
☑ (12) ⬛ (8) ☑ ✕ ⬛ ⬛ ♨ cc
This delightful small hotel perfect for breaks is well known for good value, with lovely gardens, heated swimming pool, conservatory. All rooms satellite TV, hairdryers, teamakers. Ferry-inclusive packages available. We can book your ferry and save you money.

Overstrand Hotel, *Howard Road, Shanklin, Isle of Wight, PO37 6HD.*
Open: Easter to Oct
Grades: ETC 2 Star
01983 862100 Mr & Mrs Vale
stillwell@overstrand-hotel.co.uk
D: £19–£30 **S:** £24–£35
Beds: 6F 3D 2T 2S **Baths:** 12 En 1 Pr
☑ ⬛ (20) ✕ ☑ ✕ ⬛ ⬛ ♨ ♨ cc
Building full of character. Beautiful sea views. Free parking, huge 3-acre garden. Free use of local leisure centre. Warm and friendly atmosphere. Excellent food - good value. Children most welcome. Resident proprietors in 27th year.

The Hazelwood , *14 Clarence Road, Shanklin, Isle of Wight, PO37 7BH.*
Friendly hotel, own grounds close to cliff path, station, town.
Open: All Year (not Xmas)
Grades: ETC 3 Diamond
01983 862824 (also fax) Mr & Mrs Tubbs
barbara.tubbs@thehazelwood.free-online.co.uk
D: £18–£20 **S:** £18–£20
Beds: 2F 3D 2T 1S **Baths:** 8 En
☑ (5) ⬛ (3) ⬛ ⬛ ✕ ⬛ ⬛ ♨ cc

Rosemere, *31 Queens Road, Shanklin, Isle of Wight, PO37 6DQ.*
Comfortable accommodation within easy reach of town/beaches/cliff walks.
Open: All Year (not Xmas/New Year)
01983 862930 (also fax)
Mrs Impey
D: £14.75–£18 **S:** £14.75–£18
Beds: 3D **Baths:** 3 En
☑ (5) ⬛ (4) ☑ ✕ ⬛ ⬛

Marlborough Hotel, *16 Queens Road, Shanklin, Isle of Wight, PO37 6AN.*
Family-run hotel set in its own grounds.
Open: All Year **Grades:** ETC 2 Star
01983 862588 (also fax) Mrs Floyd
D: £22–£28 **S:** £22–£28
Beds: 3F 7D 8T 2S **Baths:** 20 En
☑ ⬛ (20) ☑ ✕ ⬛ ⬛ ♨ ♨ ♨ cc

The Edgecliffe Hotel, *Clarence Gardens, Shanklin, Isle of Wight, PO37 6HA.*
Perfect location to explore the Island, relaxing, great food.
Open: All Year
01983 866199 Barry and Alsion O'Sullivan
Fax: 01983 868841
edgecliffe.hotel@nationwideisp.net
D: £19–£25 **S:** £19–£25
Beds: 10 F/D/T/S **Baths:** 9 En 1 Pr
☑ ✕ ☑ ✕ ⬛ ⬛ ♨ ♨

Ventnor

SZ5677   🍴 *Spyglass Inn, Mill Bay*

Picardie Hotel, *Esplanade, Ventnor, Isle of Wight, PO38 1JX.*
Welcoming small family hotel on sea front with fine walking, cycling.
Open: All Year
Grades: AA 3 Diamond
01983 852647 (also fax)
D: £25–£35 **S:** £30–£35
Beds: 3F 1T 4D 1S **Baths:** 5 En 4 Pr
☑ ☑ ✕ ⬛ ♨ ♨ ♨

Cornerways Hotel, *39 Medeira Road, Ventnor, Isle of Wight, PO38 1QS.*
Quiet location with magnificent views over sea and Downs.
Open: Mar to Oct
01983 852323 Mr Malcolm
D: £20–£25 **S:** £20–£35
Beds: 2F 3D 1T **Baths:** 6 En
☑ ⬛ (4) ✕ ☑ ⬛ ✕ ⬛ ⬛ ♨ cc

All details shown are as supplied by B&B owners in Autumn 2000

National Grid References are for villages, towns and cities – not for individual houses

---

The Brunswick Hotel, *Victoria Street, Ventnor, Isle of Wight, PO38 1ET.*
Three story detached house. Superb local walking and attractions.
Open: All Year (not Xmas)
Grades: ETC 3 Diamond
01983 852656 Mr Barker
graemebarker@aol.com
D: £20–£25
Beds: 2F 2D 1T **Baths:** 4 Pr 1 En
☑ ☑ ✕ ⬛ ⬛ ♨ ♨

Whitwell

SZ5277   🍴 *White Horse Inn*

The Old Rectory, *Ashknowle Lane, Whitwell, Ventnor, Isle of Wight, PO38 2PP.*
Victorian house in historic village. Luxury ensuite rooms. Large garden.
Open: All Year
01983 731242 Mr Thornton
Fax: 01983 731288
rectory@ukonline.co.uk
D: £25–£35 **S:** £30–£40
Beds: 1T 1D **Baths:** 2 En
⬛ (8) ✕ ☑ ⬛ ⬛ ♨

Wootton Bridge

SZ5491   🍴 *Fishbourne Inn, Woodmans Arms*

Briddlesford Lodge Farm, *Wootton Bridge, Ryde, Isle of Wight, PO33 4RY.*
Friendly family farm with 150 Guernsey Dairy herd. Good breakfasts.
Open: All Year (not Xmas/New Year)
01983 882239
Mrs Griffin
D: £20–£22 **S:** £20–£22
Beds: 1F 1D 1T **Baths:** 1 En1 Sh
☑ ⬛ (3) ☑ ⬛ ⬛ ⬛ ♨

Bridge House, *Kite Hill, Wootton Bridge, Ryde, Isle of Wight, PO33 4LA.*
Warm welcome and hearty breakfast with homemade preserves in Georgian Listed home.
Open: All Year (not Xmas)
01983 884163
D: £19–£20 **S:** £25–£35
Beds: 2D 1T
Baths: 1 En 2 Pr
☑ (9) ⬛ (3) ✕ ☑ ⬛ ⬛ ♨

Yarmouth

SZ3589   🍴 *New Inn*

Quinces, *Cranmore Avenue, Yarmouth, Isle of Wight, PO41 0XS.*
Delightful house in peaceful countryside. Attractive, comfortable rooms, beautiful garden.
Open: All Year (not Xmas)
01983 760080 Mrs Poulter
D: £20–£25 **S:** £20–£25
Beds: 1D 1T **Baths:** 1 Pr
☑ ⬛ (4) ✕ ☑ ⬛ ⬛ ♨

Isles of Scilly

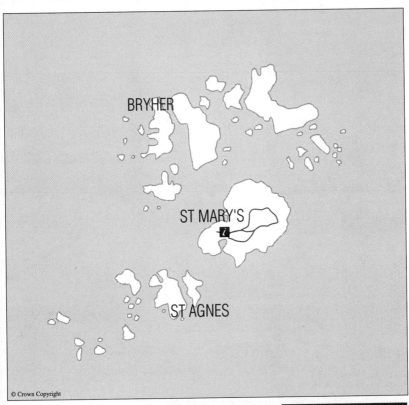

© Crown Copyright

SV8715   *Vine Cafe, Fraggle Rock*

Soleil d'Or, Bryher, Isles of Scilly, TR23 0PR.
Soleil d'Or, the perfect base to enjoy the tranquillity of Bryher.
Open: Easter to Oct
01720 422003 Mrs Street
D: £22–£26 **S:** £22–£40
Beds: 2D 1T **Baths:** 3 En
🛇 (3) 🖵 ✕ 🆚 🖳 ♨

St Agnes

SV8807

42 Covean Cottage, St Agnes, Isles of Scilly, TR22 0PL.
Attractive granite cottage set in subtropical garden.
Open: Easter to Nov
Grades: ETC 4 Diamond
01720 422620 (also fax) Mrs Sewell
D: £25–£35 **S:** £25–£35
Beds: 2D 2T **Baths:** 3 En 1 Sh
🛇 (9) 🖵 🕇 ✕ 🆚 ♨

St Mary's

SV9010   *Mermaid Inn, Bishop & Wolf, The Galey, Atlantic Inn*

Lyonnesse House, The Strand, St Mary's, Isles of Scilly, TR21 0PT.
Magnificent sea views and imaginative Aga cooked cuisine, great hospitality.
Open: Mar to Oct
Grades: ETC 3 Diamond
01720 422458 Mrs Woodcock
D: £25 **S:** £25
Beds: 1F 3D 3T 2S **Baths:** 5 Sh
🛇 (5) ⅍ 🆚 🖳 ♨

Tourist Information Centre

Porthcressa Bank, **St Mary's**, Isles of Scilly, TR21 0JY, 01720 422536.

Marine House, Church Street, Hugh Town, St Mary's, Isles of Scilly, TR21 0JT.
A very comfortable guest house, near harbour, beaches and shops.
Open: Easter to Sep
Grades: ETC 3 Diamond
01720 422966 Mrs Rowe
peggy@rowe55.freeserve.co.uk
D: £22–£25 **S:** £22–£25
Beds: 1D 1T 1S **Baths:** 1 En
🛇 (9) 🅿 ⅍ 🆚 🖳 ♨

Veronica Lodge, Garrison, St Mary's, Isles of Scilly, TR21 0LS.
Rooms with outstanding sea views; quiet location, 3 minutes from beach.
Open: Feb to Dec
01720 422585 **D:** £23 **S:** £23
Beds: 2D 1T **Baths:** 1 Sh
🛇 (14) 🆚 🖳 🖳 ♨

Kent

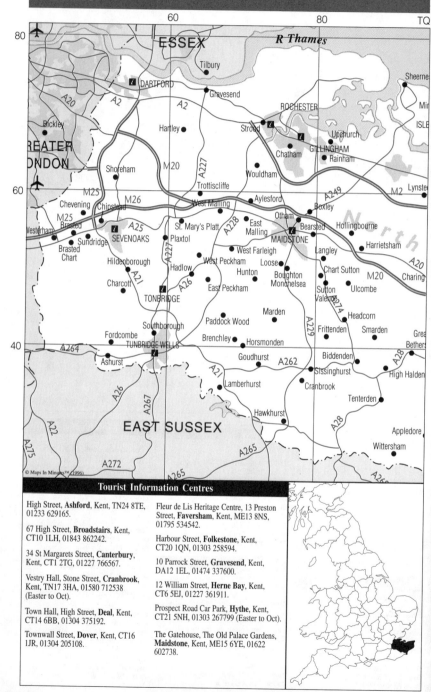

Tourist Information Centres

High Street, **Ashford**, Kent, TN24 8TE, 01233 629165.

67 High Street, **Broadstairs**, Kent, CT10 1LH, 01843 862242.

34 St Margarets Street, **Canterbury**, Kent, CT1 2TG, 01227 766567.

Vestry Hall, Stone Street, **Cranbrook**, Kent, TN17 3HA, 01580 712538 (Easter to Oct).

Town Hall, High Street, **Deal**, Kent, CT14 6BB, 01304 375192.

Townwall Street, **Dover**, Kent, CT16 1JR, 01304 205108.

Fleur de Lis Heritage Centre, 13 Preston Street, **Faversham**, Kent, ME13 8NS, 01795 534542.

Harbour Street, **Folkestone**, Kent, CT20 1QN, 01303 258594.

10 Parrock Street, **Gravesend**, Kent, DA12 1EL, 01474 337600.

12 William Street, **Herne Bay**, Kent, CT6 5EJ, 01227 361911.

Prospect Road Car Park, **Hythe**, Kent, CT21 5NH, 01303 267799 (Easter to Oct).

The Gatehouse, The Old Palace Gardens, **Maidstone**, Kent, ME15 6YE, 01622 602738.

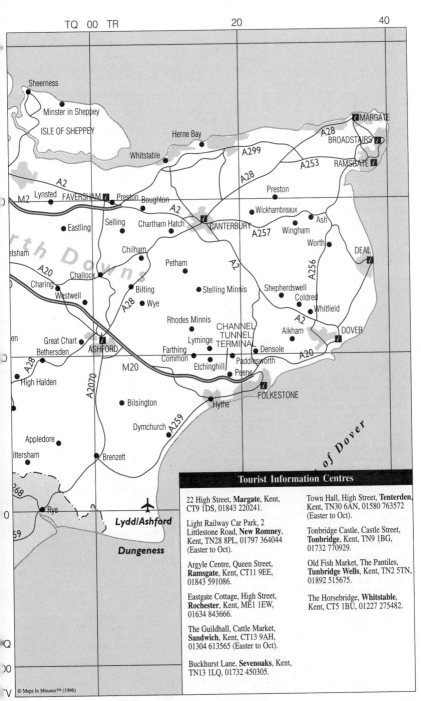

Tourist Information Centres

22 High Street, **Margate**, Kent,
CT9 1DS, 01843 220241.

Light Railway Car Park, 2
Littlestone Road, **New Romney**,
Kent, TN28 8PL, 01797 364044
(Easter to Oct).

Argyle Centre, Queen Street,
Ramsgate, Kent, CT11 9EE,
01843 591086.

Eastgate Cottage, High Street,
Rochester, Kent, ME1 1EW,
01634 843666.

The Guildhall, Cattle Market,
Sandwich, Kent, CT13 9AH,
01304 613565 (Easter to Oct).

Buckhurst Lane, **Sevenoaks**, Kent,
TN13 1LQ, 01732 450305.

Town Hall, High Street, **Tenterden**,
Kent, TN30 6AN, 01580 763572
(Easter to Oct).

Tonbridge Castle, Castle Street,
Tonbridge, Kent, TN9 1BG,
01732 770929.

Old Fish Market, The Pantiles,
Tunbridge Wells, Kent, TN2 5TN,
01892 515675.

The Horsebridge, **Whitstable**,
Kent, CT5 1BU, 01227 275482.

© Maps In Minutes™ (1996)

Alkham

TR2542   ◙ *Marquis Of Granby*

Owler Lodge, *Alkham Valley Road, Alkham, Dover, Kent, CT15 7DF.*
Lovely house in beautiful village for touring East Kent.
Open: All Year (not Xmas)
Grades: ETC 4 Diamond, Silver Award
01304 826375 Mrs Owler
Fax: 01304 829372
owlerlodge@aol.com
D: £21–£24 **S:** £35–£38
Beds: 1F 1D 1T **Baths:** 3 En
⛺ (5) ▣ (3) ⊬ ⊡ ⛏ ✕ ▥ ⚲

Appledore

TQ9529   ◙ *Black Lion, The Swan, The Bayleaves*

Park Farm Barn, *Appledore, Ashford, Kent, TN26 2AR.*
Quiet country location near Rye, Tenterden, the sea and channel ports.
Open: All Year (not Xmas)
Grades: ETC 3 Diamond
01233 758159 (also fax)
Mrs Thomas
D: £15–£20 **S:** £20
Beds: 1D 1T 1S **Baths:** 1 En 1 Sh
⛺ ▣ (4) ⊡ ✕ ▥ ⚲ ⚲

Ash (Sandwich)

TR2758   ◙ *Chequers Inn*

55 Guilton, *Ash, Canterbury, Kent, CT3 2HR.*
Open: All Year (not Xmas)
01304 812809 Mrs Smith
D: £16 **S:** fr £18
Beds: 2D **Baths:** 1 En
▣ (2) ⊬ ⊡ ✕ ⚲
Between Canterbury and Sandwich, Victorian cottage, log fires, Victorian type dining room with original features, cottage garden, ideal touring Kent nature reserves, wildlife park, historic buildings, wine trails, Dover ferries, Manston airport and coast within easy reach.

Ashford

TR0042   ◙ *Hare & Hounds, Pilgrims' Rest, Harvesters, Wetherspoons, Downtown Diner*

Warren Cottage Hotel, *136 The Street, Willesborough, Ashford, Kent, TN24 0NB.*
Open: All Year
Grades: ETC 3 Diamond
01233 621905 Mrs Jones
Fax: 01233 623400
general@warrencottage.co.uk
D: £25–£35 **S:** £20–£39.90
Beds: 1F 3D 1T 1S **Baths:** 6 En
⛺ ▣ (20) ⊬ ⊡ ⛏ ✕ ▥ ⚲ cc
17th Century hotel set in 2.50 acres. M20, Junction 10. All rooms ensuite. Car park CCTV security. Minutes to Ashford International Station and Channel Tunnel Ports.

Planning a longer stay? Always ask for any special rates

Heather House, *40 Burton Road, Kennington, Ashford, Kent, TN24 9DS.*
Open: All Year (not Xmas/New Year)
Grades: ETC 3 Diamond
01233 661826 Mrs Blackwell
Fax: 01233 635183
D: fr £20 **S:** fr £20
Beds: 1F 1D 1S **Baths:** 2 Sh
▣ ⊡ ⚲
Heather House offers a warm, friendly welcome in quiet residential area. Near Eurostar.

Quantock House, *Quantock Drive, Ashford, Kent, TN24 8QH.*
Quiet residential area. Easy walk to town centre. Comfortable and welcoming.
Open: All Year (not Xmas)
Grades: ETC 3 Diamond
01233 638921 Mr & Mrs Tucker
tuckers@quantockhouse.freeserve.co.uk
D: £19–£22 **S:** £20–£22
Beds: 1F 1D 1T 1S **Baths:** 3 En
⛺ (7) ▣ (3) ⊬ ⊡ ▥ ⚲

Mayflower House, *61 Magazine Road, Ashford, Kent, TN24 8NH.*
Friendly atmosphere, large garden. Close to town centre, international station.
Open: All Year (not Xmas)
Grades: ETC 3 Diamond
01233 621959 (also fax)
Mrs Simmons
D: £16.50–£17.50 **S:** £18–£20
Beds: 1D 2S **Baths:** 1 Sh
⛺ ⊡ ✕ ▥ ⚲ ⚲

Glenmoor, *Maidstone Road, Ashford, Kent, TN25 4NP.*
Victorian gamekeepers cottage close to international station and motorway.
Open: All Year (not Xmas/New Year)
Grades: ETC 3 Diamond
01233 634767 Mrs Rowlands
D: £17 **S:** £20
Beds: 2D 1T **Baths:** 1 Sh
⛺ (5) ▣ (3) ⊬ ⊡ ▥ ⚲

Ashford Guest House, *15 Canterbury Road, Ashford, Kent, TN24 8LE.*
Elegant Victorian building, spacious rooms, private parking, near town centre.
Open: All Year (not Xmas)
Grades: ETC 4 Diamond
01233 640460 Mrs Noel
Fax: 01233 626504
srcnoel@netcomuk.co.uk.
D: £20 **S:** £25
Beds: 2F 2D 2T **Baths:** 6 En
▣ (6) ⊬ ⊡ ▥ ⚲ cc

Vickys Guest House, *38 Park Road North, Ashford, Kent, TN24 8LY.*
Town centre, close to international station, Canterbury, Folkestone and Dover nearby.
Open: All Year
Grades: AA 2 Diamond
01233 631061 Mrs Ford
Fax: 01233 640420
vicky@ford27.freeserve.co.uk
D: £18–£21 **S:** £18–£21
Beds: 1F 1D 1S **Baths:** 2 Pr 1 Sh
⛺ ▣ ⊡ ⛏ ✕ ▥ ⚲ cc

2-4 Canterbury Road, *Ashford, Kent, TN24 8JX.*
Victorian semi-detached. 10 mins Eurostar station, 4 mins walk London coach stop.
Open: All Year (not Xmas/New Year)
01233 623030 (also fax)
Mr & Mrs Lavender
D: £19–£20 **S:** £20–£21
Beds: 2T 2S **Baths:** 1 Sh
⛺ (5) ▣ (4) ⊬ ⊡ ▥

Ashurst

TQ5138

Manor Court Farm, *Ashurst, Tunbridge Wells, Kent, TN3 9TB.*
Spacious Georgian farmhouse with lovely views. Working farm.
Open: All Year (not Xmas)
01892 740279 Mrs Soyke
D: £22–£24 **S:** £22–£30
Beds: 1D 2T **Baths:** 2 Sh
⛺ ▣ (10) ⊡ ⛏ ▥ ⊡

Aylesford

TQ7258   ◙ *Chequers*

Wickham Lodge, The Quay, *High Street, Aylesford, Kent, ME20 7AY.*
Open: All Year
Grades: ETC 4 Diamond, AA 4 Diamond, RAC 4 Diamond
01622 717267 Mrs Kelsey Bourne
Fax: 01622 792855
wickhamlodge@aol.com
D: £25–£27.50 **S:** £27.50
Beds: 1F 1D 1S
Baths: 2 En 1 Pr
⛺ ▣ (4) ⊬ ⊡ ⛏ ▥ ⊡ ⚲ cc
Fine Georgian house on the banks of the River Medway near the historic Aylesford Bridge. Lawns to river at the front with an old English walled garden to the rear. Recent refurbishment throughout the house.

The Guest House, *The Friars, Aylesford Priory, Aylesford, Kent, ME20 7BX.*
Open: All Year (not Xmas/New Year)
01622 717272 M Larcombe
Fax: 01622 715575
friarsreception@hotmail.com
D: £19–£24 **S:** £19–£24
Beds: 2F 1D
Baths: 2 Pr
⛺ ▣ (50) ⊬ ⊡ ✕ ▥ ⚲ cc
Picturesque priory home to a community of Carmelite Friars, founded in 1242. Come and enjoy the peaceful setting, the gardens, shops, pottery. The shrine and chapels house some wonderful modern works of art. Situated between Rochester and Maidstone, close to motorway.

Court Farm, *High Street, Aylesford, Maidstone, Kent, ME20 7AZ.*
Beams, four poster, spa, antiques, drawing room. Sorry, no children.
Open: All Year
01622 717293 (also fax)
Mrs Tucker
enquiries@courtfarm.com
D: fr £25 **S:** fr £25
Beds: 2D 1T 1S **Baths:** 3 En 1 Pr
▣ (6) ⊬ ⊡ ⛏ ✕ ▥ ⚲ cc

Bearsted

TQ7955 ◀ *White Horse*

The Hazels, *13 Yeoman Way, Bearsted, Maidstone, Kent, ME15 8PQ.*
Large, comfortable family home in quiet location, easy access M20 and A20.
Open: All Year
Grades: ETC 4 Diamond
01622 737943 Mr & Mrs Buse
dbuse@totalise.co.uk
D: £20–£25 **S:** £22–£25
Beds: 1T **Baths:** 1 En
🛇 (2) 🅿 ⅙ 📺 📖 🚶

Bethersden

TQ9240 ◀ *The Bull, The George, Royal Standard, Three Chimneys*

The Coach House, *Oakmead Farm, Bethersden, Ashford, Kent, TN26 0NB.*
Rural, well back of road in 5 acres gardens and paddocks.
Open: Mar to Oct
Grades: ETC 3 Diamond
01233 820583 (also fax)
B Broad
D: £19 **S:** £25
Beds: 1F 1D 1T **Baths:** 2 En 1 Pr
🛇 🅿 (10) 📺 ✕ 📖 🅥 🚶

Potters Farm, *Bethersden, Ashford, Kent, TN26 3JX.*
Lovely peaceful quiet annexe on delightful friendly farm.
Open: All Year
Grades: ETC 3 Diamond
01233 820341 Mr & Mrs Anderson
Fax: 01233 820469
ianmcanderson@cs.com
D: £18.75–£20 **S:** £20–£22
Beds: 2T **Baths:** 1 Pr
🛇 🅿 (6) ⅙ 📺 🐾 📖 🅥 🚶 ♿

Bethersden Old Barn, *The Old Barn , Bridge Farm, Bethersden, Ashford, Kent, TN26 3LE.*
200-year-old converted Kentish barn, close Sissinghurst, Tenterden, Rye, Leeds Castle, pretty Kentish villages.
Open: All Year
01233 820434 L Frisby
barn@ukpages-net
D: £24–£27.50 **S:** £27.50
Beds: 1D 1T **Baths:** 1 En 1 Pr
🛇 🅿 (3) ⅙ 📺 📖 🅥 🚶 cc

Bickley

TQ4269 ◀ *Chequers, Crown*

Glendevon House Hotel, *80 Southborough Road, Bickley, Bromley, Kent, BR1 2EN.*
3 Crown hotel near Bromley town centre. All rooms ensuite **Open:** All Year
Grades: ETC 3 Diamond, RAC 3 Diamond
020 8467 2183 D: £34 **S:** £35–£46
Beds: 4T 4D 2S 2F **Baths:** 12 En 1 Pr
🛇 (2) 🅿 (8) ⅙ 📺 ✕ 📖 🅥 ✳ 🚶 cc

B&B owners may vary rates - be sure to check when booking

Biddenden

TQ8438 ◀ *Red Lion, Three Chimneys*

Frogs Hole Oast, *Sissinghurst Road, Biddenden, Ashford, Kent, TN27 8LW.*
Listed oasthouse in 1.5 acres on farm adjacent Sissinghurst Castle.
Open: Easter to Oct
01580 291935 Mrs Hartley
hartley@frogsholeoast.freeserve.co.uk
D: £23–£26 **S:** £26–£35
Beds: 1D 2T **Baths:** 1 En 1 Pr 1 Sh
🛇 🅿 (5) 📺 📖 🅥 🚶

Drayton House Farm, *Stede Quarter, Biddenden, Ashford, Kent, TN27 8JQ.*
Small, working farm within easy reach of many tourist attractions.
Open: Apr to Oct
01580 291931 Mrs Lidgett
D: £13–£18 **S:** £26–£36
Beds: 3T **Baths:** 2 Sh
🛇 🅿 (5) 📺 📖

Bettmans Oast, *Hareplain Road, Biddenden, Ashford, Kent, TN27 8LJ.*
Converted barn and oasthouse in 10 acres countryside, near Sissinghurst Gardens. **Open:** All Year (not Xmas)
01580 291463 (also fax) Mrs Pickup
D: £22.50–£28 **S:** £35–£45
Beds: 2D 1T **Baths:** 2 En 1 Sh
🛇 (11) 🅿 (4) ⅙ 📺 📖 🅥 🚶 cc

Millfield, *Tenterden Road, Biddenden, Ashford, Kent, TN27 8BB.*
On edge of a pretty Wealden village with short walk to good local pub.
Open: Easter to Oct
01580 291542 Mrs Williams
Fax: 01580 291344
mjandbm@aol.com
D: £22–£26 **S:** £28–£32
Beds: 2T **Baths:** 2 En
🅿 (2) ⅙ 📺 📖 🚶

Bilsington

TR0434 ◀ *White Horse*

Willow Farm, *Stone Cross, Bilsington, Ashford, Kent, TN25 7JJ.*
Organic smallholding in rural setting. Home-made bread but no chintz.
Open: All Year (not Xmas)
Grades: ETC 2 Diamond
01233 721700 Mrs Hopper
renee@willow-farm.freeserve.co.uk
D: £18.50–£20 **S:** £20–£25
Beds: 1F 1D 1T 1S **Baths:** 1 Pr 1 Sh
🛇 🅿 (6) ⅙ 📺 ✕ 📖 🅥

Bilting

TR0449 ◀ *Tickled Trout*

The Old Farm House, *Soakham Farm, White Hill, Bilting, Ashford, Kent, TN25 4HB.*
Open: All Year (not Xmas)
01233 813509 Mrs Feakins
D: £16–£19 **S:** £18–£25
Beds: 1F 1D 1T
🛇 🅿 ⅙ 📺 📖 🅥 🚶
Set in beautiful rolling countryside on the North Downs Way, Soakham is a working farm and its location is ideal for walking or visiting many places in the South East. You are assured of a friendly welcome.

Boughton

TR0659 ◀ *Queen's Head, White Horse, Cock Inn, Albion*

Tenterden House, *209 The Street, Boughton, Faversham, Kent, ME13 9BL.*
Half acre garden in historic village with two pubs. **Open:** All Year
01227 751593 Mrs Latham
D: £20–£22 **S:** £30–£35
Beds: 1D 1T **Baths:** 2 En
🛇 🅿 (4) 📺 🚶

Boughton Monchelsea

TQ7651

Hideaway, *Heath Road, Boughton Monchelsea, Maidstone, Kent, ME17 4HN.*
Chalet bungalow edge of village. Pub meals one minute walk.
Open: Jan to Dec **Grades:** ETC 2 Star
01622 747453 (also fax) Mrs Knight
D: £16 **S:** £20
Beds: 1D **Baths:** 1 Pr
🛇 🅿 (2) 📺 🐾 📖 🅥 🚶

Boxley

TQ7757 ◀ *Kings Arms, The Bull*

Barn Cottage, *Harbourland, Boxley, Maidstone, Kent, ME14 3DN.*
Converted C16th barn convenient for motorways and Channel Tunnel.
Open: All Year (not Xmas)
01622 675891 Mrs Munson
D: £15–£20 **S:** £15–£20
Beds: 1D 1T **Baths:** 2 En
🛇 (5) 🅿 ⅙ 📺 ✕ 📖 🅥 🚶

Brasted

TQ4755 ◀ *The Bull*

Holmesdale House, *High Street, Brasted, Westerham, Kent, TN16 1HS.*
Delightful Victorian house (part C17th). Chartwell, Hever, Knole and Mainline Station. **Open:** All Year
01959 564834 (also fax) Mr Jinks
D: £20–£27.50 **S:** £30
Beds: 1F 3D 1T **Baths:** 3 En 1 Sh
🛇 🅿 (7) 📺 📖 🅥 🚶 ♿

Lodge House, *High Street, Brasted, Westerham, Kent, TN16 1HS.*
Character property, a short walk from popular village pubs. **Open:** All Year
01959 562195 Mr & Mrs Marshall
D: £20–£25 **S:** £25–£30
Beds: 1F 2D **Baths:** 1 En 1 Sh
🛇 🅿 (3) ⅙ 📺 📖 🅥 🚶

Brasted Chart

TQ4653 ◀ *The Bull, White Hart*

The Orchard House, *Brasted Chart, Westerham, Kent, TN16 1LR.*
Family home, quiet, rural surroundings, near Chartwell, Hever, Knole, Gatwick.
Open: All Year (not Xmas)
Grades: ETC 3 Diamond
01959 563702 Mrs Godsal
David.Godsal@tesco.net
D: fr £21 **S:** fr £22
Beds: 2T 1S **Baths:** 2 Sh
🛇 🅿 (4) ⅙ 📺 📖 ♿

Brenchley

TQ6741   🍺 *Castle Inn, Bull Inn*

Hononton Cottage, *Palmers Green Lane, Brenchley, Tonbridge, Kent, TN12 7BJ.*
Delightfully situated Listed home amidst close to Tunbridge Wells.
Open: All Year (not Xmas/New Year)
01892 722483 Mrs Marston
D: £23–£24 **S:** £30
Beds: 1T **Baths:** 1 Pr
🛇 🄿 (2) 📺 🛏 💭 💫 🛆 &

Fairmans Cottage, *Fairmans Road, Brenchley, Tonbridge, Kent, TN12 7JA.*
Charming C18th cottage in unspoilt countryside, surrounded by orchards.
Open: All Year (not Xmas)
01892 722379 D Taylor
Fax: 01892 724532
fairmans@clivet.co.uk
D: £19 **S:** £35
Beds: 1D 1S **Baths:** 1 Pr
🄿 (2) 🖊 📺 💭 🛓

Brenzett

TR0027

Fleur De Lis, *Brenzett, Romney Marsh, Kent, TN29 9UG.*
Set in the beautiful Romney Marsh. Best food for miles. **Open:** All Year
01797 344234 Fax: 01797 344669
D: £15–£20 **S:** £18–£20
Beds: 1F 2D 2T 2S **Baths:** 2 En 2 Sh
🛇 🄿 (20) 📺 ✕ 💭 🛓 &

Broadstairs

TR3967   🍺 *Prince Albert, Tartar Frigate*

Keston Court Hotel, *14 Ramsgate Road, Broadstairs, Kent, CT10 1PS.*
Pleasant hotel with hospitality to match, five mins' walk to town, beach, most amenities.
Open: All Year
01843 862401 Mr & Mrs McVicker
D: £16–£19 **S:** £16–£19
Beds: 5D 2T 1S **Baths:** 3 En 2 Sh
🄿 (8) 🖊 📺 💭 💫 🛓

Devonhurst Hotel, *Eastern Esplanade, Broadstairs, Kent, CT10 1DR.*
Overlooking sandy beach and English Channel. Residential licensed family-run.
Open: All Year
Grades: ETC 4 Diamond, AA 4 Diamond, RAC 4 Diamond
01843 863010 Mr & Mrs Payne
Fax: 01843 868940
info@devonhurst.co.uk
D: £26.50–£29.50 **S:** £29.50
Beds: 1F 7D **Baths:** 9 En
🛇 (5) 📺 ✕ 💭 💫 🛓 ❄ 🛓 cc

The Queens Hotel, *31 Queens Road, Broadstairs, Kent, CT10 1PG.*
Open: All Year
Grades: ETC 2 Diamond
01843 861727 Fax: 01843 600993
enquiries@queenshotel.org
D: £18–£22 **S:** £18 £25
Beds: 4D 2T 3S **Baths:** 5 En 2 Sh
🛇 📺 💭 🛓 cc
Warm and friendly family-run hotel. Ideally situated for beach.

Canterbury

TR1457   🍺 *King's Head, Bat & Ball, Thomas A Becket, Westgate Inn, Bishop's Finger, Old City, White Hart, Three Tuns, The Unicorn, The George, The Gravnille, White Horse, Wetherspoons*

Castle Court Guest House, *8 Castle Street, Canterbury, Kent, CT1 2QF.*
Open: All Year
Grades: ETC 2 Diamond
01227 463441 (also fax)
Mr Turner
guesthouse@castlecourt.fsnet.co.uk
D: £21–£26 **S:** £21–£24
Beds: 3F 2D 3T 1S **Baths:** 4 En 3 Sh
🛇 🄿 (3) 📺 🛏 💭 💫 🛓 cc
One of eight guesthouses within the city wall, dated 1836 a Listed Georgian building, close to cathedral. Colour TV all rooms, some ensuite. Friendly family house offering comfortable and clean accommodation. Just 2 minutes walk to shops, buses & trains.

Chaucer Lodge, *62 New Dover Road, Canterbury, Kent, CT1 3DT.*
Open: All Year
Grades: ETC 4 Diamond, AA 4 Diamond
01227 459141 (also fax)
Mr Wilson
wchaucerldg@aol.com
D: fr £20 **S:** fr £24
Beds: 2F 2T 3D 2S **Baths:** 9 En
🛇 🄿 (10) 🖊 📺 ✕ 💭 💫 ❄ 🛓
Family-run friendly guest house close to City Centre. Cathedral, Cricket Club and Hospitals. Colour TV, fridges, mini-bars and tea/coffee-making facilities in all rooms. Breakfast menu. High standard of cleanliness and service provided in a relaxed atmosphere. Secure off-road parking.

Clare Ellen Guest House, *9 Victoria Road, Canterbury, Kent, CT1 3SG.*
Open: All Year
Grades: ETC 4 Diamond, Silver Award, AA 4 Diamond, 2 Eggcups
01227 760205 Mrs Williams
Fax: 01227 784482
loraine.williams@clareellenguesthouse.co.uk
D: £24–£26 **S:** £26–£28
Beds: 1F 2D 2T 1S **Baths:** 6 En
🛇 🄿 (8) 📺 💭 💫 🛓
Large elegant ensuite rooms with TV, hairdryer, clock/radio and tea/coffee facilities. Full English breakfast. Vegetarian and special diets catered for on request. Six minutes' walk to town centre, bus and train station. Parking/garage available. Credit cards accepted.

Oriel Lodge, *3 Queens Avenue, Canterbury, Kent, CT2 8AY.*
Near city centre, private parking, lounge, log fire, afternoon tea.
Open: All Year
Grades: ETC 4 Diamond, Silver, AA 4 Diamond
01227 462845 (also fax)
Mr & Mrs Rishworth
info@oriel-lodge.co.uk
D: £22–£33 **S:** £26–£32
Beds: 1F 3D 1T 1S **Baths:** 2 En 2 Sh
🛇 (6) 🄿 (6) 📺 💭 🛓 cc

Abberley House, *115 Whitstable Road, Canterbury, Kent, CT2 8EF.*
Comfortable B&B in residential area close to centre. Warm welcome.
Open: All Year (not Xmas)
Grades: ETC 3 Diamond
01227 450265 Mr Allcorn
Fax: 01227 478626
D: £20–£23.50 **S:** £25
Beds: 2D 1T **Baths:** 1 En 1 Sh
🄿 (3) 🖊 📺 💭 💫 🛓

Abbey Lodge Guest House, *8 New Dover Road, Canterbury, Kent, CT1 3AP.*
Cathedral city centre 10 mins walk, Dover 20 mins ride. **Open:** All Year
01227 462878 Mrs Gardner
D: £17–£20 **S:** £20–£25
Beds: 1F 1T 1S **Baths:** 2 En 1 Sh
🛇 🄿 (16) 🖊 📺 🛏 💭 💫

Little Courtney Guest House, *5 Whitstable Road, St Dunstans, Canterbury, Kent, CT2 8DG.*
Open: All Year
01227 454207 Mrs Mercer
D: £17.50–£20 **S:** £20–£25
Beds: 2T 1S **Baths:** 1 Sh
🄿 (1) 🖊 📺 🛏 💭 🛓
A warm welcome awaits you at our small family run guest house, we are close to the town centre of Canterbury, University and Railway station. Ideal for destinations with the coast only a short drive away.

Cathedral Gate Hotel, *36 Burgate, Canterbury, Kent, CT1 2HA.*
Family-run medieval hotel next to Canterbury Cathedral. Warm welcome.
Open: All Year
Grades: ETC 3 Diamond, AA 3 Diamond
01227 464381 Mrs Jubber
Fax: 01227 462800
cgate@cgate.demon.co.uk
D: £22–£40.50 **S:** £23–£54
Beds: 5F 9D 7T 6S **Baths:** 12 En 3 Sh
🛇 📺 🛏 ✕ 💭 🛓 cc

London Guest House, *14 London Road, Canterbury, Kent, CT2 8LR.*
Recommended by Let's Go and Which? Good B&B guides.
Open: All Year **Grades:** ETC 3 Diamond
01227 765860 Mrs Cabrini
Fax: 01227 456721
londonguesthousecabnkz@supanet.com
D: £18–£22 **S:** fr £18
Beds: 1F 1D 2T 2S **Baths:** 2 Sh
🛇 📺 🛓

Milton House, *9 South Canterbury Road, Canterbury, Kent, CT1 3LH.*
Railway cricket ground cathedral 15 minutes walk. Dover 15 miles.
Open: All Year (not Xmas/New Year)
01227 765531 Mrs Wright
D: £15–£18 **S:** £20
Beds: 1D 1T **Baths:** 1 Sh
🄿 📺 🛏 💭 💫 🛓

Kingsmead House, *68 St Stephen's Road, Canterbury, Kent, CT2 7JF.*
Comfortable C17th home, quiet yet close to city centre. **Open:** All Year (not Xmas)
Grades: ETC 3 Diamond
01227 760132 J Clark
D: £22–£25
Beds: 2D 1T **Baths:** 3 En
🛇 (8) 🄿 (3) 📺 💭 🛓

Corner House, 113 Whitstable Road, Canterbury, Kent, CT2 8EF.
Pilgrim's first view of the cathedral! 2 minutes from the Corner House.
Open: All Year (not Xmas)
01227 761352 Prof McDonnell
Fax: 01227 761065
jean@unispacekent.co.uk
D: £19–£22.50 **S:** £25–£35
Beds: 1F 1T 1S **Baths:** 2 En 1 Sh
🛏 (10) ▣ (4) ▥ ▥ ♨

Acacia Lodge, 39 London Road, Canterbury, Kent, CT2 8LF.
Beautiful period house near centre, cathedral, station. Very friendly and clean.
Open: All Year
01227 769955 Mrs Cain
Fax: 01227 478960
michael.cain1@virgin.net
D: £17–£22 **S:** £20–£30
Beds: 2D 1T **Baths:** 3 Pr
🛏 ▣ (3) ⅄ ▥ ♁ ▥ ▥ ♨

Tudor House, 6 Best Lane, Canterbury, Kent, CT1 2JB.
Comfortable family guest house city centre, near cathedral and shops.
Open: All Year
01227 765650 D: £18–£23 **S:** £20–£35
Beds: 1F 4D 2T 1S **Baths:** 3 En 5 Sh
🛏 ▣ (2) ▥ ▥ ♨

Tanglewood Cottage, 40 London Road, Canterbury, Kent, CT2 8LF.
Converted farmworker's cottage close to A2/M2 slip road, convenient university and rail stations. **Open:** All Year (not Xmas)
01227 786806 D: £17–£21 **S:** fr £25
Beds: 2D 1T **Baths:** 2 En 1 Pr
▣ (4) ⅄ ▥ ▥ ♨

The Plantation, Iffin Lane, Canterbury, Kent, CT4 7BD.
Quiet, modern house in 5 acres, beautiful gardens, overlooking cathedral.
Open: All Year (not Xmas)
01227 472104 (also fax)
plantation@excite.co.uk
D: £19–£24 **S:** £25
Beds: 1D 1T **Baths:** 2 En
🛏 (5) ▣ (4) ⅄ ▥ ▥ ♨

Challock
TR0150 ⬤ Flying Horse

Hegdale Farm House, Hegdale Lane, Challock, Ashford, Kent, TN25 4BE.
16th century farmhouse, good food,relaxing atmosphere. Comfortable lounge and peaceful garden.
Open: All Year (not Xmas)
Grades: AA 3 Diamond
01233 740224 Mrs Baxter
D: £20–£22.50 **S:** £22.50
Beds: 1F 1D 1T **Baths:** 1 En 2 Sh
🛏 ▣ (8) ⅄ ▥ ▥ ♨

RATES

D = Price range per person sharing in a double room
S = Price range for a single room

Charcott
TQ5247 ⬤ The Greyhound

Charcott Farmhouse, Charcott, Leigh, Tonbridge, Kent, TN11 8LG.
Family home in glorious rural setting. home-made spread. Guests lounge.
Open: All Year (not Xmas/New Year)
Grades: ETC 4 Diamond, Sliver
01892 870024 Mr & Mrs Morris
Fax: 01892 870158
nicholasmorris@charcott.freeserve.co.uk
D: £45 **S:** £30
Beds: 3T **Baths:** 2 En 1 Pr
🛏 (5) ▣ (4) ⅄ ▥ ♁ ▥ ▥ ♨

Charing
TQ9549 ⬤ Rose & Crown, Royal Oak, Munday Bois

23 The Moat, Charing, Ashford, Kent, TN27 0JH.
On North Downs Way. Shops, buses, trains, London, Canterbury, Eurostar.
Open: Apr to Sep
01233 713141 Mrs Micklewright
D: £20 **S:** £25
Beds: 1T **Baths:** 1 En
🛏 ▣ (1) ⅄ ▥ ▥ ♨

Barnfield, Charing, Ashford, Kent, TN27 0BN.
Charming C15th farmhouse in superb location, overlooking lake and garden.
Open: All Year (not Xmas)
Grades: ETC 3 Diamond, AA 3 Q
01233 712421 (also fax)
Mrs Pym
D: £22–£24 **S:** £24–£28
Beds: 2D 1T 3S **Baths:** 1 Sh
🛏 ▣ (99) ⅄ ▥ ▥ ♨

Chart Sutton
TQ8049 ⬤ Lord Raglan

White House Farm, Green Lane, Chart Sutton, Maidstone, Kent, ME17 3ES.
C15th farmhouse, good home-cooking, near Leeds and Sissinghurst Castles and M20.
Open: All Year (not Xmas)
Grades: ETC 3 Diamond
01622 842490 (also fax)
Mrs Spain
D: £19–£22 **S:** fr £22
Beds: 2 D 1T **Baths:** 1 En 2 Pr
🛏 (8) ▣ (4) ⅄ ▥ ✕ ▥ ▥ ♨

Chartham Hatch
TR1056 ⬤ Chapter Arms

The Willows, Howfield Lane, Chartham Hatch, Canterbury, Kent, CT4 7HG.
Quiet country lane - garden for enthusiasts, 2 miles Canterbury.
Open: All Year
Grades: ETC 4 Diamond
01227 738442 (also fax)
Mrs Gough
thegoughs@hotmail.com
D: £23–£27
Beds: 1D 1T **Baths:** 2 Pr
🛏 (5) ▣ ⅄ ▥ ▥ ▥ ♨ ♿

Chatham
TQ7665 ⬤ Hollywood Bowl

Holmwood Hotel, 158 Maidstone Road, Chatham, Kent, ME4 6EN.
1900s converted house. Family-run, with large terraced & lawned gardens complete with mature trees.
Open: Feb to Dec
01634 842849 Mr Cheeseman
Fax: 01634 832905
D: £17.75–£18.25 **S:** £23–£24
Beds: 1F 1D 3T 6S **Baths:** 8 En 2 Sh
🛏 ▣ (16) ▥ ♁ ✕ ▥ ▥ ❋ ♨ ♿

Chevening
TQ4857 ⬤ Bricklayers Arms

Crossways House, Chevening Road, Chevening, Sevenoaks, Kent, TN14 6HF.
Beautiful Kentish Ragstone circa 1760 in 5 acres. Conferences welcome.
Open: All Year (not Xmas/New Year)
01732 456334 Mrs Weavers
Fax: 01732 452334
D: fr £25 **S:** fr £25
Beds: 4D **Baths:** 3 En 1 Pr
🛏 ▣ (4) ⅄ ▥ ▥ ♨

Chilham
TR0653 ⬤ White Horse, The George

Stour Valley House, Pilgrims Lane, Chilham, Canterbury, Kent, CT1 3RS.
Bedrooms with scenic views, all ensuite, hearty breakfast, evening meals.
Open: All Year (not Xmas)
01227 738991 (also fax)
Mrs Ely
fionaely@stourvalleyhouse.freeserve.co.uk
D: £25–£30 **S:** £20–£60
Beds: 1F 1D 1T **Baths:** 1 Sh
🛏 ▣ ⅄ ▥ ✕ ▥ ▥ ♨ ♿ cc

Chipstead
TQ4955 ⬤ George & Dragon

Sevenoaks Trimstone, 19 Sandilands, Chipstead, Sevenoaks, Kent, TN13 2SP.
Guest annexe for sole use of guests overlooking terrace and garden.
Open: All Year (not Xmas)
01732 456536 D: £15 **S:** £30
Beds: 2T **Baths:** 1 Pr
▣ (1) ⅄ ▥ ▥ ♨

Coldred
TR2746 ⬤ The Lydden Bell

Colret House, The Green, Coldred, Dover, Kent, CT15 5AP.
Open: All Year
Grades: ETC 4 Diamond
01304 830388 Mrs White
Fax: 01304 830348
D: £25–£30 **S:** £25–£30
Beds: 2F **Baths:** 2 En
🛏 ▣ (6) ⅄ ▥ ♁ ✕ ▥ ♨ ♿
Garden rooms in grounds of detached Edwardian property facing the village green of Coldred - twice recently voted the best kept village in Kent. Easy access from A2 - Canterbury/Sandwich/Dover all within 15 minutes drive. Ideal overnight stop for ferries/shuttle.

Cranbrook

TQ7736 ♨ Green Cross, Windmill Inn, White Horse, Star & Eagle, Bull Inn, Three Chimneys

The Hollies, *Old Angley Road, Cranbrook, Kent, TN17 2PN.*
Well-appointed comfortable bungalow, delightful garden, close to town centre & Sissinghurst Gardens.
Open: All Year (not Xmas)
01580 713106 Mrs Waddoup
D: £20 **S:** £20
Beds: 1F 1T 1S **Baths:** 1 En 1 Pr
🛏 🅿 (2) ⅍ 🅣 ♀ 🗙 �ⅲ 🔔 🕯 1

Cordons, *Round Green Lane, Colliers Green, Cranbrook, Kent, TN17 2NB.*
House in lovely garden off quiet wooded lane. Close to Sissinghurst.
Open: All Year
01580 211633 Mrs Johnstone
D: £18–£20 **S:** £20–£22
Beds: 1D 1T 1S **Baths:** 2 Pr
🅿 (4) ⅍ 🅣 �ⅲ 🅥 🔔

Hillview Cottage, *Starvenden Lane, Sissinghurst, Cranbrook, Kent, TN17 2AN.*
Total peace. Attractive, comfortable house close National Trust properties.
Open: All Year
Grades: ETC 3 Diamond
01580 712823 Mrs Lloyd Jones
rmlj@starlaine.freeserve.co.uk
D: £20–£30 **S:** £20–£30
Beds: 1D 1T **Baths:** 2 En 1 Pr
🛏 (6) 🅿 ⅍ 🅣 ♀ 🗙 �ⅲ 🅥 🔔

The Oast, *Hallwood Farm, Cranbrook, Kent, TN17 2SP.*
Traditional Kent, preserved, secluded, beamed oasthouse conversion on working farm. **Open:** Mar to Nov
01580 712416 (also fax)
hallwoodfarm@aol.com
D: £22.50
Beds: 1T 1D **Baths:** 2 En
🛏 (10) 🅿 (6) ⅍ �ⅲ 🔔

Dartford

TQ5273 ♨ Royal Victoria, Bull

Rosedene Guest House, *284-286 Lowfield Street, Dartford, Kent, DA1 1LH.*
On A225 near M25/M20 A20/A2 London 40 minutes Dover 1 hour.
Open: All Year
01322 277042 Mrs Rose
D: £18–£20 **S:** £25–£28
Beds: 1F 4T 1S **Baths:** 2 Sh
🛏 🅿 (4) 🅣 �ⅲ 🅥 🔔

Deal

TR3752 ♨ Prince Albert, Bowling Green Inn, The Sportsman, Three Compasses, Kings Head

The Roast House Lodge, *224 London Road, Deal, Kent, CT14 9PW.*
Lodge accommodation, garden and sunbathing patio. 1 mile Deal seafront, golf courses nearby.
Open: All Year
Grades: ETC 3 Diamond
01304 380824 M Stokes
D: £20–£25 **S:** £20–£25
Beds: 2F 1D 1T 1S **Baths:** 5 En
🛏 🅿 🅣 ♀ �ⅲ 🔔 🕯 cc

Sondes Lodge, *14 Sondes Road, Deal, Kent, CT14 7BW.*
Close to seafront, town, castles, golf courses. Warm welcome.
Open: All Year
Grades: ETC 4 Diamond, AA 4 Diamond
J Hulme
D: £22.50–£25 **S:** £25–£35
Beds: 2D 1T **Baths:** 3 En
🅣 �ⅲ 🔔 cc

The Prince Albert, *187-189 Middle Street, Deal, Kent, CT14 6LW.*
Family run inn located in conservation area, close to amenities and beach.
Open: All Year
01304 375425 Mr & Mrs Hopkin
Fax: 01304 369950
prince-albert-inn@deal-uk.freeserve.co.uk
D: £17–£25 **S:** £22–£30
Beds: 1F **Baths:** 1 En 1 Sh
🛏 🅣 🗙 �ⅲ 🅥 ✳ 🔔

Densole

TR2141

Garden Lodge, *324 Canterbury Road, Densole, Folkestone, Kent, CT18 7BB.*
Attractive family-run guest house, heated swimming pool, cream teas.
Open: All Year
01303 893147 (also fax) Mrs Cooper, MCFA
gardenlodge@tritonek.com
D: £25–£30 **S:** £25–£30
Beds: 1F 1D 1T 3S **Baths:** 4 En
🛏 🅿 (12) ⅍ 🅣 🗙 �ⅲ 🅥 🔔 🕯 cc 3

Dover

TR3141 ♨ Chequers Inn, Red Lion, Park Inn, Eight Bells, White Horse, Marquis of Granby, Lighthouse, The Britannia, The Plough, The Swingate

Owler Lodge, *Alkham Valley Road, Alkham, Dover, Kent, CT15 7DF.*
Lovely house in beautiful village for touring East Kent. **Open:** All Year (not Xmas)
Grades: ETC 4 Diamond, Silver Award
01304 826375 Mrs Owler
Fax: 01304 829372
owlerlodge@aol.com
D: £21–£24 **S:** £35–£38
Beds: 1F 1D 1T **Baths:** 3 En
🛏 (5) 🅿 (3) ⅍ 🅣 ♀ 🗙 �ⅲ 🔔

Hubert House, *9 Castle Hill Road, Dover, Kent, CT16 1QW.*
Comfortable Georgian house with parking; ideally situated for local attractions and ferries. **Open:** Nov to Sep
Grades: ETC 3 Diamond
01304 202253 Mr Hoynes
D: £20–£25 **S:** £28–£30
Beds: 2F 2D 2T 1S **Baths:** 7 En
🛏 🅿 (6) 🅣 �ⅲ 🔔 cc

Valjoy Guest House, *237 Folkestone Road, Dover, Kent, CT17 9SL.*
Victorian family house situated near rail, ferry and tunnel terminals.
Open: All Year (not Xmas)
01304 212160 Mr Bowes
D: £15–£20 **S:** £15–£20
Beds: 3F 1S **Baths:** 1 Sh
🛏 🅿 (5) 🅣 🗙 �ⅲ 🔔

Bleriot's , *Belper House, 47 Park Avenue, Dover, Kent, CT16 1HE.*
A Victorian residence with ensuite rooms and off-road parking.
Open: All Year (not Xmas)
Grades: ETC 2 Diamond
01304 211394 Mrs Casey
D: £18–£23 **S:** £20–£46
Beds: 2F 3D 2T 1S **Baths:** 6 En 2 Sh
🛏 🅿 (8) 🅣 �ⅲ 🔔 cc

Beulah House, *94 Crabble Hill, Dover, Kent, CT17 0SA.*
Welcome to this imposing award-winning guest house in 1 acre of magnificent topiaried gardens.
Open: All Year
Grades: AA 4 Diamond
01304 824615 Mrs Owen
Fax: 01304 828850
owen@beulahhouse94.freeserve.co.uk
D: £22–£25 **S:** £30–£35
Beds: 2F 4D 3T **Baths:** 9 En
🛏 🅿 ⅍ 🅣 �ⅲ 🔔 🕯 cc

Number One Guest House, *1 Castle Street, Dover, Kent, CT16 1QH.*
Georgian town house. All rooms ensuite. GARAGE PARKING. Port nearby
Open: All Year
Grades: AA 4 Diamond, RAC 4 Diamond Sparkling Award
01304 202007 Ms Reidy
Fax: 01304 214078
res@number1guesthouse.co.uk
D: £20–£25 **S:** £25–£30
Beds: 1F 2D 2T **Baths:** All Ensuite
🛏 🅿 (4) 🅣 �ⅲ 🅥 🔔

Blakes Of Dover, *52 Castle Street, Dover, Kent, CT16 1PJ.*
Blakes of Dover, restaurants, local fish, real ales, 52 whiskeys.
Open: All Year (not Xmas)
Grades: ETC 3 Star
01304 202194 (also fax)
J Toomey
j.j.t@btinternet.com
D: £27.50–£40 **S:** £27.50–£40
Beds: 2F 3D 2T **Baths:** 6 En
🛏 🅣 🗙 �ⅲ 🅥 🔔 🕯 cc

Talavera House, *275 Folkestone Road, Dover, Kent, CT17 9LL.*
Spacious late Victorian house close to stations, ferries, town centre.
Open: All Year
Grades: ETC 3 Diamond
01304 206794 J Hilton
Fax: 01304 207067
john-jan@talavera-house.freeserve.co.uk
D: £15–£22 **S:** £18–£25
Beds: 1F 1T 1D 1S **Baths:** 1 En 1 Sh
🛏 🅿 (3) 🅣 ♀ 🗙 �ⅲ 🅥 🔔 cc

Dover's Restover Bed & Breakfast, *69 Folkestone Road, Dover, Kent, CT17 9RZ.*
Highly recommended, beautifully refurbished ensuite rooms, centrally situated for all amenities.
Open: All Year
01304 206031 Mrs Adams
D: £15–£25 **S:** £18–£27
Beds: 1F 4D 1T **Baths:** 3 En 1 Sh
🛏 🅿 (3) 🅣 �ⅲ 🅥 🔔

Whitmore Guest House, 261
Folkestone Road, Dover, Kent, CT17 9LL.
Warm welcome at a highly recommended
family-run Victorian guest house.
Open: All Year (not Xmas)
01304 203080 Mr & Mrs Brunt
Fax: 01304 240110
whitmoredover@aol.com
D: £15–£22 **S:** £17–£25
Beds: 2F 1D 1T **Baths:** 2 En 1 Sh
🏠 🅿 (6) ⅙ 📺 �📷 📖 Ⅴ ⚓ **cc**

Dymchurch

TR1029 🍺 *Shepherd & Crook, Ship Inn, Ocean Inn*

Waterside Guest House, 15 Hythe
*Road, Dymchurch, Romney Marsh, Kent,
TN29 0LN.*
Open: All Year
Grades: ETC 4 Diamond, AA 4 Diamond,
RAC 4 Diamond, Sparkling Diamond
Award
01303 872253 Mrs Tinklin
water.side@cwcom.net
D: £18–£20 **S:** £20–£25
Beds: 1F 2D 2T **Baths:** 4 En 1 Sh
🏠 🅿 (7) 📺 ✕ 📖 Ⅴ ✿ ⚓
Cottage-style house offering comfortable
rooms, attractive gardens. Ideally situated
for Channel crossings and exploring Kent
and E Sussex. Experience the RH&D
railway or stroll along nearby beaches,
finally enjoying a drink or meal chosen
from our varied menu.

The Ship Inn, 118 High Street,
*Dymchurch, Romney Marsh, Kent, TN29
0LD.*
Family-run C15th inn on the South Coast
of Kent.
Open: All Year
Grades: ETC 2 Diamond
01303 872122 Mr Sharp
stilwells@theshipinn.co.uk
D: £19–£21 **S:** £19–£31
Beds: 4F 2D 2S **Baths:** 2 Sh
🏠 🅿 📺 ✕ 📖 Ⅴ ⚓

Dolly Plum Cottage, Burmarsh Road,
*Dymchurch, Romney Marsh, Kent, TN29
0JS.*
Edwardian cottage set in 1 acre pretty
gardens complete with sheep grazing in
orchard.
Open: All Year
01303 874558 Mrs Cowell
D: £23–£30 **S:** £23–£35
Beds: 1F 1D 1T **Baths:** 3 En
🏠 🅿 ⅙ 📺 ✕ 📖 Ⅴ ✿ ⚓ ♿

East Malling

TQ7057 🍺 *King & Queen*

Hawthorn Cottage, Easterfields, East
Malling, West Malling, Kent, ME19 6BE.
Quiet country setting ideally situated for
touring Kent, 3 miles M20 (J5).
Open: All Year (not Xmas)
01732 843805 (also fax)
Mrs Horvath
easterfields@talk21.com
D: £18 **S:** £18
Beds: 1T 1S **Baths:** 1 Pr
🏠 🅿 (3) ⅙ 📺 📖 Ⅴ ⚓

BATHROOMS

Pr - Private

Sh - Shared

En - Ensuite

East Peckham

TQ6648 🍺 *The Bush, Blackbird & Thrush*

Roydon Hall, off Seven Mile Lane, East
Peckham, Tonbridge, Kent, TN12 5NH.
Open: All Year (not Xmas/New Year)
Grades: ETC 3 Diamond
01622 812121 Mrs Bence
Fax: 01622 813959
roydonhall@btinternet.com
D: £17.50–£22.50 **S:** £21–£55
Beds: 4F 2D 6T 2S **Baths:** 7 En 1 Pr 5 Sh
🏠 🅿 ⅙ 📺 ✕ 📖 Ⅴ ⚓ **cc**
Very attractive 16th century manor in 10
acres of woodlands and gardens.
Peaceful atmosphere, magnificent views.
Comfortable rooms. Organic meals
available. Less than one hour from
central London, Dover and south coast.
Perfect for exploring historic towns and
beautiful houses and gardens of Kent and
Sussex.

Eastling

TQ9656 🍺 *Carpenters' Arms*

The Carpenters' Arms, The Street,
Eastling, Faversham, Kent, ME13 0AZ.
C14th inn, candlelit restaurant, adjoining
lodge, 30 mins Channel Ports.
Open: All Year (not Xmas/New Year)
01795 890234 Mrs O'Regan
Fax: 01795 890654
D: £24.75–£26 **S:** £41.50
Beds: 3D **Baths:** 3 En
🏠 (12) 🅿 (20) 📺 ✕ 📖 Ⅴ ⚓ **cc**

Etchinghill

TR1639 🍺 *New Inn*

One Step Beyond, Westfield Lane,
Etchinghill, Folkestone, Kent, CT18 8BT.
Modern house. Quiet village location, 4
mins from Channel Tunnel.
Open: All Year (not Xmas/New Year)
01303 862637 (also fax)
J Holden
johnosb@rdplus.net
D: £17.50–£20 **S:** £20–£22
Beds: 1D **Baths:** 1 En
⅙ 📺 📖 Ⅴ ⚓

Farthing Common

TR1340

Southfields, Farthing Common,
Lyminge, Folkestone, Kent, CT18 8DH.
Southfields is a family home on the North
Downs, with panoramic views.
Open: Mar to Oct
01303 862391 Ms Wadie
D: fr £20 **S:** fr £20
Beds: 1F 1S **Baths:** 1 Sh
🏠 🅿 (6) ⅙ 📺 ✕ 📖 Ⅴ ⚓

Faversham

TR0161 🍺 *White Lion, Rose & Crown,
Carpenters' Arms, Albion Tavern, The Phoenix, The
George*

Preston Lea, Canterbury Road,
Faversham, Kent, ME13 8XA.
Open: All Year **Grades:** ETC 4 Diamond,
Silver, AA 4 Diamond
01795 535266 Mr Turner
Fax: 01795 533388
preston.lea@which.net
D: £23–£26 **S:** £35
Beds: 1T 2D **Baths:** 2 En 1 Pr
🏠 🅿 (10) ⅙ 📺 📖 ⚓ **cc**
A warm welcome in this large elegant
house with unique architectural features
set in beautiful secluded gardens. The
sunny, spacious bedrooms furnished with
antiques offer every comfort. Afternoon
tea on arrival and delicious breakfast
grilled in the Aga, to order.

Owens Court Farm, Selling,
Faversham, Kent, ME13 9QN.
Open: All Year
01227 752247 (also fax) Mrs Higgs
D: £20 **S:** £20
Beds: 1F 1T 1S **Baths:** 2 Sh
🏠 🅿 (5) 📺 📖 Ⅴ ⚓
Owens Court is a peaceful Kentish
Georgian farmhouse on a fruit farm. A
quiet spot a mile off the M2. Near all
Channel ports. Large comfortable rooms.
Lovely Garden.

The Carpenters' Arms, The Street,
Eastling, Faversham, Kent, ME13 0AZ.
C14th inn, candlelit restaurant, adjoining
lodge, 30 mins Channel Ports.
Open: All Year (not Xmas/New Year)
01795 890234 Mrs O'Regan
Fax: 01795 890654
D: £24.75–£26 **S:** £41.50
Beds: 3D **Baths:** 3 En
🏠 (12) 🅿 (20) 📺 ✕ 📖 Ⅴ ⚓ **cc**

Tanners Cottage, 37 Tanner Street,
Faversham, Kent, ME13 7JP.
Attractive old cottage in quiet area of
lovely old market town.
Open: All Year (not Xmas)
01795 536698 M Jameson
D: £14–£15 **S:** £14–£15
Beds: 1D 1T **Baths:** 1 Sh
🏠 (5) ⅙ 📺 📖 ⚓ **cc**

March Cottage, 5 Preston Avenue,
Faversham, Kent, ME13 8NH.
Relaxed comfortable accommodation in
the medieval market town of Faversham.
Open: All Year **Grades:** ETC 3 Diamond
01795 536514 Mrs Moss
D: £21–£25 **S:** £25–£35
Beds: 1D 1T 1S **Baths:** 1 En 1 Pr 1 Sh
🏠 ⅙ 📺 📖 Ⅴ ⚓ ♿

Heronsmere, 19 Nobel Court,
Faversham, Kent, ME13 7SD.
Quiet location with attractive garden and
homely atmosphere.
Open: All Year (not Xmas)
01795 536767 Mrs Griffiths
keithf@griff16.freeserve.co.uk
D: £18.50–£21 **S:** £18.50–£21
Beds: 1D 1T **Baths:** 1 En 1 Pr
🏠 (3) ⅙ 📺 ✕ 📖 Ⅴ ⚓ ♿

Folkestone

TR2136   ⚓ *Ship Inn, Carpenters, New Inn, Castle Inn, Wetherspoons, Cat & Custard Pot*

Wycliffe Hotel, 63 Bouverie Road West, Folkestone, Kent, CT20 2RN.
Clean, comfortable, affordable accommodation near shuttle, Seacat, 15 minutes Dover Port. **Open:** All Year
01303 252186 (also fax)
Mr & Mrs Shorland
shorland@wycliffehotel.freeserve.co.uk
D: £18–£21 **S:** £18–£21
Beds: 2F 5D 4T 1S **Baths:** 1 Pr 2 Sh
🛏 🄿 (8) 🄫 🛏 ✕ 🎟 ❋ ≞

West Lodge, Peene, Folkestone, Kent, CT18 8BA.
Open: All Year (not Xmas)
01303 274762
john@gredley.freeserve.co.uk
D: £17.50 **S:** £25
Beds: 2F **Baths:** 1 Sh
🛏 🄿 (3) ⅍ 🄫 🛏 🎟 ≞
West Lodge is a Grade II Listed property set in 3 acres in quiet village yet only 10 minutes from Folkestone and the Channel Tunnel. Ideally situated for walkers being on the Pilgrims' Way and near the North Downs Way.

Seacliffe, 3 Wear Bay Road, Folkestone, Kent, CT19 6AT.
Homely comfortable family run very convenient for beach, port, tunnel.
Open: All Year (not Xmas)
01303 254592 Ms Foot
D: £16–£18 **S:** £16–£20
Beds: 1F 1D 1T **Baths:** 1 Sh
🛏 ⅍ 🄫 🎟 ≞

Rosa Villa Guest House, 237 Dover Road, Folkestone, Kent, CT19 6NH.
Friendly, family welcome. Good base for exploring Kent, excellent walking. Smoke free.
Open: All Year (not Xmas)
01303 251415 Mr Elcombe
rosavilla@supanet.com
D: £15–£20 **S:** £18–£24
Beds: 2F 2D 1T **Baths:** 1 Sh
🛏 ⅍ 🄫 🎟 ≞

Normandie Guest House, 39 Cheriton Road, Folkestone, Kent, CT20 1DD.
Small family run guest house near town centre.
Open: All Year (not Xmas/New Year)
01303 256233 Mrs Watts
D: £16–£17.50 **S:** £16–£17.50
Beds: 2F 1D 2T 1S **Baths:** 1 Sh
🛏 (4) 🄫 🎟 ≞

Frittenden

TQ8141   ⚓ *Windmill*

Tolehurst Barn, Knoxbridge, Cranbrook Road, Frittenden, Cranbrook, Kent, TN17 2BP.
Quiet, rural environment, near to many fine houses, castles & gardens.
Open: All Year (not Xmas/New Year)
Grades: ETC 4 Diamond
01580 714385 (also fax)
Mrs Tresilian
D: fr £20 **S:** fr £25
Beds: 1F 1T 1D **Baths:** 2 En 1 Pr
🛏 🄿 (4) ⅍ 🄫 🛏 ✕ 🎟 🎟 ≞

Gillingham

TQ7767   ⚓ *White Horse, Manor Farm, Queen's Head, The Bell, Spyglass & Kettle, Hungry Fox, The Star*

Ramsey House, 228a Barnsole Road, Gillingham, Kent, ME7 4JB.
Established 15 years. Friendly atmosphere, close A2, M2, Maritime museums, Kent.
Open: All Year
Grades: ETC 3 Diamond
01634 854193 Mrs Larssen
D: £16–£18 **S:** £20–£25
Beds: 1S 2T **Baths:** 1 En 1 Sh
🛏 (3) 🄿 (2) ⅍ 🄫 🎟 ≞

178 Bredhurst Road, Wigmore, Gillingham, Kent, ME8 0QX.
Large chalet bungalow 4 minutes M2.
Open: All Year
01634 233267 Mrs Penn
D: £16–£20 **S:** £16–£20
Beds: 1F 1T **Baths:** 2 En
🛏 🄿 (2) 🄫 🎟 ≞

Abigails, 17 The Maltings, Rainham, Gillingham, Kent, ME8 8JL.
Friendly service family establishment central location rural views water garden.
Open: All Year
01634 365427 Ms Penfold
D: £15 **S:** £15
Beds: 1F 1D 1S **Baths:** 2 En
🛏 🄿 (4) 🄫 🛏 ✕ 🎟 🎟 ≞

King Charles Hotel, Brompton Road, Gillingham, Kent, ME7 5QT.
Modern, family-run hotel, set in the heart of maritime Kent.
Open: All Year
01634 830303 Mr DeGiorgio
Fax: 01634 829430
enquiries@kingcharleshotel.co.uk
D: fr £20 **S:** fr £34
Beds: 20F 30D 30D 1S **Baths:** 81 En
🛏 🄿 ⅍ 🄫 🛏 ✕ 🎟 ❋ ≞ ৬ cc

Mayfield Guest House, 34 Kingswood Road, Gillingham, Kent, ME7 1DZ.
Victorian house with modern extension.
Open: All Year (not Xmas)
01634 852606 Mrs Sumner
D: £17.50 **S:** £20
Beds: 2F 2D 5T 1S **Baths:** 5 En 2 Sh
🛏 🄿 (5) 🄫 🎟 🎟 ≞ cc

Goudhurst

TQ7237   ⚓ *Green Cross Inn, Wild Duck*

West Winchet, Winchet Hill, Goudhurst, Cranbrook, Kent, TN11 1JX.
Open: All Year
01580 212024 Mrs Parker
D: £25–£35 **S:** £35–£40
Beds: 1D 1T **Baths:** 1 En 1 Pr
🛏 (5) 🄿 (5) ⅍ 🄫 🛏 🎟 🎟 ≞
Victorian mansion in parkland with 2 beautifully decorated rooms on ground floor with views over the gardens, each with TV etc. Magnificent drawing room for guest use. Ideal for touring Kent and East Sussex. near Sissinghurst, Scotney Castle.

Gravesend

TQ6574   ⚓ *Gravesend Boat*

48 Clipper Crescent, Riverview Park, Gravesend, Kent, DA12 4NN.
Comfortable bedrooms. Close to A2/ M2 frequent trains to London.
Open: All Year (not Xmas)
01474 365360 Mrs Jeeves
D: £17–£17.50 **S:** £17.50
Beds: 1T 1S **Baths:** 1 Sh
🛏 (3) 🄿 (1) ⅍ 🄫 🎟 ≞

Great Chart

TQ9842

Goldwell Manor, Great Chart, Ashford, Kent, TN23 3BY.
Historic C11th manor, quiet, secluded and comfortable with country views.
Open: All Year (not Xmas)
01233 631495 (also fax)
Mr Wynn-Green
D: £23–£28 **S:** £25–£35
Beds: 1F 2D 1T 1S **Baths:** 1 En 1 Pr 1 Sh
🛏 (1) 🄿 (10) 🄫 🛏 ✕ 🎟 🎟 ≞

Hadlow

TQ6350   ⚓ *Carpenters' Arms*

Dunsmore, Hadlow Park, Hadlow, Tonbridge, Kent, TN11 0HX.
Private park, quiet, own entrance to ground floor accommodation.
Open: All Year (not Xmas)
01732 850611 (also fax) Mrs Tubbs
D: £18–£20 **S:** £20–£25
Beds: 1T **Baths:** 1 Pr
🛏 🄿 🎟 ≞

Harrietsham

TQ8752   ⚓ *Dog & Bear*

Homestay, 14 Chippendayle Drive, Harrietsham, Maidstone, Kent, ME17 1AD.
Close to Leeds castle and ideally situated for exploring Kent.
Open: All Year (not Xmas/New Year)
Grades: ETC 3 Diamond
01622 858698 (also fax) Ms Beveridge
johnbtaylor@homestay14.freeserve.co.uk
D: £18–£20 **S:** £23–£24
Beds: 2 T
⅍ 🄫 ✕ 🎟 ≞

Hartley (Meopham)

TQ6067   ⚓ *Black Lion*

Dartford Kaye Cottage, 18 Old Downs, Hartley, Longfield, Kent, DA3 7AA.
Open: All Year (not Xmas)
Grades: ETC 4 Diamond
01474 702384 (also fax) Mrs Smith
b-b@kaye-cottage.freeserve.co.uk
D: £20–£35 **S:** £25–£30
Beds: 1F 2D 1T 1S **Baths:** 2 En 2 Sh
🛏 🄿 (5) ⅍ 🄫 🎟 ≞
Picturesque cottage. Excellent location A2, A20, M20, M25 Dartford crossing. Gravesend 5 minutes Brands Hatch. London golf club, Blue water shopping complex and Dartford crossing, BR Victoria 40 minutes. Friendly Accommodation. All rooms to high standard. Lovely gardens. Tennis court. quiet location.

Hawkhurst

TQ7630 🍺 *Oak & Ivy*

Southgate Little Fowlers, *Rye Road, Hawkhurst, Kent, TN18 5DA.*
C17th country house Kent/Sussex border. Amidst many N.T properties and gardens.
Open: Easter to Nov
Grades: ETC 4 Diamond
01580 752526 (also fax)
Mrs Woodard
susan.woodard@btinternet.com
D: £24–£30 **S:** £30–£40
Beds: 1T 1D **Baths:** 2 En
🛏 (10) 🅿 (4) ⌿ 📺 🛍 🖻 ♨

Headcorn

TQ8344 🍺 *The Hawksenbury, Shant Hotel, New Flying Horse*

Mistral, *3 Oxenturn Road, Wye, Ashford, Kent, TN25 5BH.*
Open: Jan to Dec
Grades: ETC 3 Diamond
01233 813011 Mr & Mrs Chapman
Fax: 01233813011
geoff@chapman.invictanet.co.uk
D: £25 **S:** £25
Beds: 1T 1S **Baths:** 1 Sh
🛏 🅿 (2) ⌿ 📺 🛍 🖻 ♨
Comfortable and well appointed house, mature garden, secluded but readily accessible to Wye village. Convenient for Ashford International Station, Canterbury, Dover, Leeds Castle, Sissinghurst, Stour Festival and Wye Downs.

Four Oaks, *Four Oaks Road, Headcorn, Ashford, Kent, TN27 9PB.*
Restored 500 year old farmhouse. Quiet location. Close Leeds Castle, Sissinghurst, Eurolink.
Open: All Year
Grades: ETC 3 Diamond, RAC 3 Diamond
01622 891224 Mrs Thick
Fax: 01622 890630
info@fouroaks.uk.com
D: £18–£20 **S:** £20–£25
Beds: 2F 1T **Baths:** 1 En 1 Sh
🛏 🅿 (4) ⌿ 📺 🐾 ✗ 🛍 🖻 ♨ cc

Herne Bay

TR1768 🍺 *The Plough, Huntsman and Horne*

'Hobbit Hole', *41a Pigeon Lane, Herne Bay, Kent, CT6 7ES.*
Open: All Year (not Xmas)
Grades: ETC 3 Diamond
01227 368155 (also fax) Mrs Herwin
hobhole@aol.com
D: £18–£20 **S:** £20–£26
Beds: 1F 1T 1D **Baths:** 1 En 1 Pr
🅿 (7) 📺 🛍 🖻 ♨
Hobbit's thaumaturgic atmosphere! Peaceful sleep on transcendental beds! Serves Bilbo Baggins's breakfasts! Private parking. Taverns just a short gallop away! One mile from the Saxon Walk fossil beach. is surrounded by lush Historic places interspersed with Inns and Haunts!

Planning a longer stay? Always ask for any special rates

High Halden

TQ8937 🍺 *The Chequers*

Draylands, *High Halden, Ashford, Kent, TN23 3JG.*
Secluded location in Garden of England. Bedrooms with extensive views over open farmland.
Open: All Year (not Xmas/New Year)
Grades: ETC 3 Diamond
01233 850048 (also fax)
Mrs Russell
sallyrussell30@hotmail.com
D: £23–£25 **S:** £27–£30
Beds: 2D **Baths:** 2 En
🅿 (3) ⌿ 📺 ✗ 🛍 🖻 ♨

11 The Martins, *High Halden, Ashford, Kent, TN26 3LD.*
Quiet rural modern house. Safe parking. Good food. Homely atmosphere.
Open: Mar to Nov
Grades: ETC 4 Diamond
01233 850013 Mr & Mrs Thorowgood
Fax: 01233 850549
bobandsandy@thorowgood.fsnet.co.uk
D: £22.50–£25 **S:** fr £27.50
Beds: 1F 1D 1T **Baths:** 1 En 1 Pr 1 Sh
🛏 (5) 🅿 (4) ⌿ 📺 🛍 ♨

Hildenborough

TQ5648 🍺 *The Cockhorse*

150 Tonbridge Road, *Hildenborough, Tonbridge, Kent, TN11 9HW.*
Warm friendly house. B245 between Tonbridge 2 miles; Sevenoaks, M25 10 mins.
Open: All Year (not Xmas)
01732 838894
Mrs Romney
D: £12.50–£34 **S:** £15–£18
Beds: 2T **Baths:** 1 Sh
🛏 🅿 (2) ⌿ 📺 🛍 ♨

Hollingbourne

TQ8455 🍺 *Windmill, Sugar Loaves, Dirty Habit*

The Limes, *53 Eyhorne Street, Hollingbourne, Maidstone, Kent, ME17 1TS.*
Peaceful C18th home, large walled garden and conservatory; nearby village pubs, Leeds Castle, M20.
Open: Feb to Dec
Grades: ETC 4 Diamond
01622 880554
Mrs Reed
Fax: 01622 880063
thelimes@btinternet.com
D: £20–£22.50 **S:** £25–£30
Beds: 1D 2S **Baths:** 1 Pr 1 Sh
🛏 (10) 🅿 (5) ⌿ 📺 🛍 ♨

Woodhouses, *49 Eyhorne Street, Hollingbourne, Maidstone, Kent, ME17 1TR.*
C17th interconnected cottages close to village pubs and Leeds Castle.
Open: All Year
Grades: ETC 4 Diamond
01622 880594 (also fax)
Mr & Mrs Woodhouse
D: £20 **S:** £22–£25
Beds: 3T **Baths:** 3 En
🛏 (10) 🅿 (3) ⌿ 📺 🛍 🖻 ♨

Horsmonden

TQ7040 🍺 *Gun & Spit Roast*

Forge House, *Brenchley Road, Horsmonden, Tonbridge, Kent, TN12 8DN.*
Friendly house, ideal touring base, washbasins in all bedrooms.
Open: All Year
01892 723584 Mrs Brett
D: £15–£17 **S:** £15–£17
Beds: 1D 1T 1S **Baths:** 1 Sh
🛏 🅿 (5) ⌿ 📺 🛍 🖻 ♨

Hunton

TQ7149 🍺 *The Bull, Walnut Tree*

The Woolhouse, *Grove Lane, Hunton, Maidstone, Kent, ME15 0SE.*
C17th Listed beamed converted barn, peaceful lovely atmosphere, antique furniture.
Open: All Year (not Xmas)
01622 820778 Mrs Wetton
Fax: 01622 820645
D: £25 **S:** £25
Beds: 4F 1D 2T 1S **Baths:** 3 En 1 Pr
🅿 (10) 📺 🐾 🛍 🖻 ♨

Wealden Hall House, *East Street, Hunton, Maidstone, Kent, ME15 0RB.*
Get away from it all - stay at Wealden Hall.
Open: Mar to Dec
01622 820246 Mrs Horrocks
D: £20–£23 **S:** £30
Beds: 3D **Baths:** 2 En 1 Pr
🛏 (12) 🅿 (4) ⌿ 📺 🛍 🖻 ♨

Hythe

TR1634 🍺 *White Hart*

Maccassil, *50 Marine Parade, Hythe, Kent, CT21 6AW.*
A warm and friendly B&B in an idyllic peaceful location.
Open: All Year
01303 261867 D: £18–£21 **S:** £20–£25
Beds: 1F 1D 1T **Baths:** 2 En 1 Sh
🛏 🅿 (3) ⌿ 📺 🛍 ♨ 🚿

Hill View, *4south Road, Hythe, Kent, CT21 6AR.*
Late Victorian house close to sea swimming pool and town.
Open: All Year (not Xmas)
01303 269783 Mrs Warbuton
beewarb@tesco.net
D: £16–£18 **S:** £18–£20
Beds: 1F 1T **Baths:** 1 Sh
🛏 (5) 📺 🛍 ♨

Lamberhurst

TQ6736 🍺 *Chequers Inn*

Chequers Oast, *Lamberhurst, Tunbridge Wells, Kent, TN3 8DB.*
Picturesque oast house in village centre. Ideal location for touring.
Open: Easter to Oct
01892 890579 Mrs Harrison
D: £20 **S:** £22
Beds: 1D 1T **Baths:** 1 En 1 Pr
🛏 (5) 🅿 (2) ⌿ 📺 🛍 🖻 ♨

Langley

TQ8051 🍺 *Crown, Horseshoes, Ten Bells*

Langley Oast, *Langley Park, Langley, Maidstone, Kent, ME17 3NQ.*
Luxuriously converted oast off A274 south of Maidstone in open countryside overlooking a lake.
Open: All Year (not Xmas)
Grades: AA 4 Diamond
01622 863523 (also fax)
Mrs Clifford
D: £22.50–£30 **S:** £25–£50
Beds: 1F 1D 2T 1S **Baths:** 2 En 1 Sh
🛏 (2) 🅿 (5) ⊁ 🖾 🎞 🖾 ♨

Loose

TQ7551 🍺 *Chequers*

Vale House, *Old Loose Hill, Loose, Maidstone, Kent, ME15 0BH.*
Vale House stands in a secluded garden in the pretty historic village of Loose.
Open: All Year (not Xmas)
Grades: ETC 3 Diamond
01622 743339 Mrs Gethin
Fax: 01622 743103
D: £20–£26 **S:** £20–£30
Beds: 2D 2T 1S **Baths:** 1 Pr 1 Sh
🛏 🅿 ⊁ 🖾 🎞 ♨

Lyminge

TR1541 🍺 *New Inn*

Southfields, *Farthing Common, Lyminge, Folkestone, Kent, CT18 8DH.*
Open: Mar to Oct
01303 862391 Ms Wadie
D: fr £20 **S:** fr £20
Beds: 1F 1T **Baths:** 1 Sh
🛏 🅿 (6) ⊁ 🖾 ✕ 🎞 🖾 ♨
Southfields is a family home on the North Downs, with panoramic views. Eight acres of pasture and a large garden are ideal for a peaceful break. Kent's historic towns and the Channel termini are within easy reach by car.

Lynsted

TQ9460 🍺 *Black Lion*

Forge Cottage, *Lynsted, Sittingbourne, Kent, ME9 0RH.*
Converted C17th century forge and cottage in picturesque village.
Open: All Year (not Xmas)
01795 521273 Mr Bage
Fax: 01795 521669
david.bage4@which.net
D: fr £15 **S:** £15–£20
Beds: 1F 1D 1T **Baths:** 2 Sh
🛏 (10) 🅿 ⊁ 🖾 🐾 🎞

RATES
D = Price range per person sharing in a double room
S = Price range for a single room

Maidstone

TQ7655 🍺 *The Chequers, The Plough, White House, Grangemoor Hotel, Muggleton's, Chiltern Hundreds, The Fountain, Fox & Goose, Crown & Horseshoes, Ten Bells*

Langley Oast, *Langley Park, Langley, Maidstone, Kent, ME17 3NQ.*
Open: All Year (not Xmas)
Grades: AA 4 Diamond
01622 863523 (also fax)
Mrs Clifford
D: £22.50–£30 **S:** £25–£50
Beds: 1F 1D 2T 1S **Baths:** 2 En 1 Sh
🛏 (2) 🅿 (5) ⊁ 🖾 🎞 🖾 ♨
Luxuriously converted oast off A274 south of Maidstone in open countryside overlooking a lake.

Grove House, *Grove Green Road, Weavering, Maidstone, Kent, ME14 5JT.*
Attractive front garden for guests to enjoy quiet peaceful surroundings.
Open: All Year
Grades: ETC 4 Diamond, AA 4 Diamond
01622 738441 S Costella
D: £22.50–£25 **S:** £25–£35
Beds: 1T 2D **Baths:** 1 En 1 Sh
🅿 (6) ⊁ 🖾 🎞 ♨ cc

Court Farm, *High Street, Aylesford, Maidstone, Kent, ME20 7AZ.*
Beams, four poster, spa, antiques, drawing room. Sorry, no children.
Open: All Year
01622 717293 (also fax)
Mrs Tucker
enquiries@courtfarm.com
D: fr £25 **S:** fr £25
Beds: 2D 1T 1S **Baths:** 3 En 1 Pr
🅿 (6) ⊁ 🖾 🐾 ✕ 🎞 🖾 ♨ cc

Wits End Guest House, *78 Bower Mount Road, Maidstone, Kent, ME16 8AT.*
Quiet Edwardian Licensed guest house, close to town centre.
Open: All Year
Grades: ETC 3 Diamond
01622 752684 Mrs King
Fax: 01622 688943
D: £22–£30 **S:** £23–£30
Beds: 2F 1D 2T 2S **Baths:** 4 En 2 Sh
🛏 🅿 (8) 🖾 🐾 🎞 🖾 ♨

Fairlawn, *Whiterock Place, Terrace Road, Maidstone, Kent, ME16 8HX.*
Bungalow in secluded garden. Ten minute walk town centre. Rail/bus links nearby.
Open: All Year (not Xmas/New Year)
Grades: ETC 2 Diamond, AA 2 Diamond, RAC 2 Diamond
01622 763642 (also fax)
Mrs Outlaw
D: £15–£17 **S:** £18–£24
Beds: 1D 1T 1S
🅿 (13) ⊁ 🖾 🐾 🎞 ♨ ⅗ 3

Emmaus, *622 Loose Road, Maidstone, Kent, ME15 9UW.*
Original post office, detached house, above Loose Valley. Guest lounge.
Open: All Year
01622 745745 Mrs Hodgson
D: £36–£40 **S:** £18–£20
Beds: 1T 2S **Baths:** 2 Sh
🛏 (5) 🖾 🎞 ♨

BATHROOMS
Pr - Private
Sh - Shared
En - Ensuite

10 Fant Lane, *Maidstone, Kent, ME16 8NL.*
Character cottage; colour TV, tea/coffee facilities, Close to railway station, M20, M2.
Open: All Year
01622 729883 Mrs Layton
D: £15–£20 **S:** £15–£25
Beds: 1F 1T 1S **Baths:** 1 Sh
🛏 🅿 (2) ⊁ 🖾 ✕ 🎞 🖾 ♨

51 Bower Mount Road, *Maidstone, Kent, ME16 8AX.*
Large, comfortable Edwardian. Semi-easy access town centre and motorway.
Open: All Year (not Xmas)
01622 762948 Mrs Haddow
sylviabnb@compuserve.com
D: £17–£18 **S:** £16–£18
Beds: 1F 1T 1S **Baths:** 1 Sh
🛏 (9) ⊁ 🖾 🎞 🖾 ♨

54 Mote Avenue, *Maidstone, Kent, ME15 7ST.*
Spacious home by Mote Park, convenient for town and countryside.
Open: All Year
01622 754016 Mrs Seager
D: £16–£17 **S:** £17–£18
Beds: 1D 1T **Baths:** 1 Sh
🛏 (12) 🅿 (2) ⊁ 🖾 🎞 🖾 ♨

Marden

TQ7444

Tanner House, *Tanner Farm, Goudhurst Road, Marden, Tonbridge, Kent, TN12 9ND.*
Open: All Year (not Xmas)
Grades: ETC 4 Diamond
01622 831214 Mrs Mannington
tannerfarm@compuserve.com
D: £20–£22.50 **S:** fr £30
Beds: 1D 2T **Baths:** 3 En
🛏 (5) 🅿 (3) ⊁ 🖾 ✕ 🎞 🖾 ♨ cc
A warm welcome awaits you at our comfortable Tudor Farmhouse and our quality touring caravan and camping park. Quality home - cooking using local produce and our own home-made jams and preserves. an ideal touring base or stopover.

Margate

TR3570 🍺 *Dog & Duck, The Wheatsheaf, Wig & Pen, The Belleview*

The Happy Dolphin, *11 Buenos Ayres, Margate, Kent, CT9 5AE.*
Victorian private guest house overlooking beach. CTV, radio/cassette, fridge, phone, iron, hairdryer.
Open: All Year
01843 296473 (also fax)
Ms Stratford
D: £15–£35 **S:** £20–£35
Beds: 4F 1D 1T 2S **Baths:** 6 En 2 Pr
🖾 🐾 ✕ 🎞 🖾 ♨ cc

Malvern Hotel, *Eastern Esplanade, Cliftonville, Margate, Kent, CT9 2HL.*
Open: All Year
01843 290192 (also fax)
D: £20–£22.50 **S:** £22.50–£30
Beds: 2F 5D 2T 1S **Baths:** 8 En 1 Sh
📺 🛏 ▦ ♨ cc
Small, sea front, close to indoor bowls, Winter Gardens, amenities etc. Canterbury, Dover and Folkestone (Channel Tunnel) within easy distance. All rooms TV, tea/coffee-making facilities. Dining room is non-smoking. Choice of menu. Visa, Switch and MasterCard telephone bookings accepted.

Somerville Hotel, *9 Canterbury Road, Margate, Kent, CT9 5AQ.*
Family-run hotel overlooking sea close to all amenities.
Open: All Year (not New Year)
01843 224401 Mr Hubbard
D: £15–£20 **S:** £20–£25
Beds: 1F 5D 2T 2S **Baths:** 2 En 2 Sh
📺 ▦ ✕ 🛏 ♨ ♨

Mentone Lodge, *5 Norfolk Road, Margate, Kent, CT9 2HU.*
A warm and friendly Victorian guest house, close to local attractions, shops and beach.
Open: All Year (not Xmas)
01843 292152 Mr & Mrs Clarke
mentone@libertysurf.co.uk
D: £17–£21 **S:** £17–£21
Beds: 1F 3D 1T 1S **Baths:** 4 En 1 Sh
📺 🛏 ▦ ♨

Carnforth, *103 Norfolk Road, Cliftonville, Margate, Kent, CT9 2HX.*
Small Victorian family run hotel. Comfortable licensed bar, pool table.
Open: All Year
Grades: ETC 3 Diamond
01843 292127 Mrs Heffer
carnforth-hotel@cwcom.net
D: £18–£20 **S:** £15–£16.50
Beds: 3F 2D 2S **Baths:** 5 En 1 Sh
📺 🛏 (3) 📺 🛏 ✕ ▦ ♨ ♨

Bay View Guest House, *12 Buenos Ayres, Margate, Kent, CT9 5AE.*
Large Victorian private guest house, overlooking sea. Two minutes BR stations.
Open: All Year (not Xmas)
01843 297188 Mr & Mrs Hughes
D: £12.50–£22.50 **S:** £15–£25
Beds: 3F 3D 1T 1S **Baths:** 3 Sh
📺 📺 ✕ ▦ ♨ ♨

Minster in Sheppey

TQ9573

Mia Crieff, *Mill Hill, Chequers Road, Minster in Sheppey, Sheerness, ME12 3QL.*
Detached house with large garden. comfortable accommodation and full breakfast.
Open: All Year (not Xmas)
Grades: ETC 4 Diamond
01795 870620 Mrs White
D: £19–£20 **S:** £23–£25
Beds: 3D **Baths:** 3 En
📺 📺 (5) 📺 ▦ ♨ ♨

BATHROOMS

Pr - Private

Sh - Shared

En - Ensuite

Otham

TQ7953   🍺 *The Plough*

Valley View Guest House, *Valley View, Greenhill, Otham, Maidstone, Kent, ME15 8RR.*
A large detached property, charmingly converted from a single storey barn and stable block.
Open: All Year
01622 862279 (also fax)
Mr Crouch
D: £20–£24 **S:** £25–£32
Beds: 2F 2D 2T 2S **Baths:** 6 En 2 Pr
📺 📺 (10) ✕ 📺 ▦ ♨ ♨ ♿

Paddlesworth

TR1940   🍺 *Cat & Custard Pot*

Pigeonwood House, *Arpinge, Folkestone, Kent, CT18 8AQ.*
Ancient homely farmhouse in beautiful downland spectacular views rural tranquillity.
Open: Apr to Oct
Grades: ETC 4 Diamond
01303 891111 Mr & Mrs Martin
Fax: 01303 891019
samandmary@aol.com
D: £20–£25 **S:** £25–£35
Beds: 1F 1D 1T **Baths:** 2 En 1 Pr
📺 (5) 📺 (5) ✕ 📺 ▦ ♨

Paddock Wood

TQ6744   🍺 *The Chequers*

Little Fowle Hall Oast, *Lucks Lane, Paddock Wood, Tonbridge, Kent, TN12 6PA.*
London: Train 1 Hour.
Open: All Year (not Xmas)
01892 832602 Mr Lumley
D: £20 **S:** £20
Beds: 1F 2T **Baths:** 1 En 1 Sh
📺 📺 (8) ✕ 📺 🛏 ▦ ♨

Peene

TR1837   🍺 *New Inn, Cat & Custard Pot*

West Lodge, *Peene, Folkestone, Kent, CT18 8BA.*
Grade II Listed property set in 3 acres in quiet village.
Open: All Year (not Xmas)
01303 274762
john@gredley.freeserve.co.uk
D: £17.50 **S:** £25
Beds: 2F **Baths:** 1 Sh
📺 📺 (3) ✕ 📺 🛏 ▦ ♨

National Grid References are for villages, towns and cities – not for individual houses

Petham

TR1351   🍺 *The Compasses, The Chequers*

South Wootton House, *Capel Lane, Petham, Canterbury, Kent, CT4 5RG.*
A beautiful farmhouse with conservatory set in extensive gardens, surrounded by fields and woodland.
Open: All Year (not Xmas/New Year)
01227 700643 F Mount
Fax: 01227 700613
D: £40–£45 **S:** £25–£30
Beds: 1F 1T **Baths:** 1 Pr
📺 📺 ✕ 📺 ▦ ♨

Upper Ansdore, *Duckpit Lane, Petham, Canterbury, Kent, CT4 5QB.*
Tudor farmhouse overlooking nature reserve; quiet, rural, Canterbury 15 mins.
Open: All Year
01227 700672 (also fax)
Mr & Mrs Linch
D: £21 **S:** £30–£35
Beds: 3F 1D 1T 1S **Baths:** 3 Pr
📺 (5) 📺 (5) ✕ 📺 ♨

Plaxtol

TQ6053   🍺 *Kentish Rifleman*

Periwick Place, *The Street, Plaxtol, Sevenoaks, Kent, TN15 0QF.*
Early Victorian village house surrounded by mature pretty garden (visitors welcome to use this).
Open: All Year (not Xmas)
01732 811024 Mrs Golding
D: £27 **S:** £27.50
Beds: 1D 1T **Baths:** 1 Sh
📺 (10) 📺 (4) ✕ 📺 ▦ ♨

Preston (Faversham)

TR0261

The Windmill Inn, *Canterbury Road, Preston, Faversham, ME13 8LT.*
Typical English pub, two bars, dining area, warm friendly welcome.
Open: All Year
Grades: ETC 2 Diamond
01795 536505 D: £22–£36 **S:** £18
Beds: 2T 2S **Baths:** 1 Sh
📺 📺 (8) 📺 ✕ 📺 ▦ ♨

Preston (Wingham)

TR2561

Forstal House, *The Forstal, Preston, Canterbury, Kent, CT3 1DT.*
Open: All Year (not Xmas)
01227 722282 Mrs Scott
Fax: 01227 722295
D: fr £20 **S:** fr £22
Beds: 1D 1T **Baths:** 1 En 1 Pr
📺 📺 (4) ✕ 📺 ▦ ♨ ♿
Secluded C18th country house near river and orchards. Beautiful walled garden with water features and heated swimming pool. Superb home grown produce in season. Comfortable TV room.

Planning a longer stay? Always ask for any special rates

Rainham

TQ8165   🍺 The Cricketers, Harvester, Beefeater

Irwin Grange, Meresborough Road, Rainham, Gillingham, Kent, ME8 8PN.
Farm house set in 13 acres, good view of River Medway.
Open: All Year (not Xmas)
01634 232801 Mrs Knight
D: £17.50 **S:** £20
Beds: 1F 2T **Baths:** 2 Sh
🛏 🅿 (10) 🔟 🎿 🖳 Ⅴ ♿

Ramsgate

TR3864   🍺 Churchill Tavern, Royal Harbour, Foy Boat, Anne's Party

The Royale Guest House, 7 Royal Road, Ramsgate, Kent, CT11 9LE.
Friendly, family-run guest house; close to all amenities.
Open: All Year
Grades: ETC 2 Diamond
01843 594712 (also fax)
Mrs Barry
D: £15–£18 **S:** £15–£20
Beds: 1F 2D 2T 4S **Baths:** 2 En 2 Sh
🛏 (2) 🔟 🎿 🖳 ♿

Glendevon Guest House, 8 Truro Road, Ramsgate , Kent, CT11 8BD.
Comfortable ensuite rooms with own well equipped kitchen/eating areas.
Open: All Year
Grades: ETC 3 Diamond
01843 570909 (also fax)
S & A Everix
glendevon@currantbun.com
D: £16–£20 **S:** £20–£24
Beds: 1F 2T 3D **Baths:** 6 En
🛏 (5) 🔟 🖳 ♿ cc

Spencer Court Hotel, 37 Spencer Square, Ramsgate, Kent, CT11 9LD.
Grade II Listed Regency hotel overlooking gardens, tennis courts & sea.
Open: All Year
01843 594582 Mr & Mrs Jordan
D: £17–£23 **S:** £20–£25
Beds: 2F 3D 2T 2S **Baths:** 4 En 2 Sh
🛏 🔟 🖳 Ⅴ ♿ cc

York House, 7 Augusta Road, Eastcliff, Ramsgate, Kent, CT11 8JP.
Homely guest house near sea and shops.
Open: All Year (not Xmas)
01843 596775 Mr & Mrs Rhodes
D: £15–£17 **S:** £15–£17
Beds: 2F 2D 1T 2S **Baths:** 1 En 2 Sh
🛏 🔟 🖳 Ⅴ ♿

The Royal Harbour Hotel, 8 Nelson Crescent, Ramsgate, Kent, CT11 9JF.
A beautiful Georgian town house in Ramsgate's best known historic garden crescent.
Open: All Year (not Xmas)
01843 584198 James Thomas
Fax: 01843 586759
royalharbour@talk21.com
D: £15–£25 **S:** £15–£30
Beds: 3F 4D 3T 2S **Baths:** 4 En 2 Sh
🛏 🔟 🎿 ♿

The Regency Hotel & School Of English, Royal Crescent, Ramsgate, Kent, CT11 9PE.
Friendly atmosphere with foreign students from all over the world.
Open: All Year
01843 591212 **Fax:** 01843 850035
regency.school@btinternet.com
D: £14–£19 **S:** £24–£34
Beds: 2F 1D 47T 26S **Baths:** 17 En 12 Sh
🛏 ✗ 🖳 cc

Rhodes Minnis

TR1443   🍺 George Inn, Kings Arms

Monsoon Lodge, Rhodes Minnis, Canterbury, Kent, CT4 6XX.
Family home, quiet, relaxing. Rural location between Folkestone and Canterbury.
Open: All Year (not Xmas/New Year)
Grades: ETC 3 Diamond
01303 863272 (also fax) Mrs Mills
D: £19–£25 **S:** £20–£25
Beds: 1F 1T 1D **Baths:** 3 En
🛏 🅿 (4) ½ 🔟 🖳 Ⅴ ♿ cc

Rochester

TQ7468   🍺 Royal Oak, King's Head, Waterman's Arms, Queen Charlotte, White Horse

Wouldham Court Farmhouse, 246 High Street, Wouldham, Rochester, Kent, ME1 3TY.
Beamed Grade II Listed farmhouse, inglenook fireplace, overlooking River Medway.
Open: All Year (not Xmas)
Grades: ETC 3 Diamond
01634 683271 (also fax)
Ms Parnell
wouldham.b-b@virgin.net
D: £22 **S:** £18–£22
Beds: 1F 1D 1S **Baths:** 2 Sh
🛏 🅿 (1) ½ 🔟 🎿 ✗ 🖳 Ⅴ ♿ cc

255 High Street, Rochester, Kent, ME1 1HQ.
Victorian family house near station. Antique four poster bed.
Open: All Year (not Xmas)
01634 842737 Mrs Thomas
D: £14–£16 **S:** £16–£25
Beds: 1F 1D 1T **Baths:** 1 Pr 1 Sh
🛏 🔟 ♿

St Ouen, 98 Borstal Road, Rochester, Kent, ME1 3BD.
Victorian house with comfortable rooms overlooking River Medway. Amenities close-by. **Open:** All Year (not Xmas)
01634 843528 Mrs Beggs
m.s.beggs@98borstal.freeserve.co.uk
D: £16–£20 **S:** £18–£20
Beds: 1D 1T 1S **Baths:** 1 Sh
🛏 ½ 🔟 🎿 🖳 ♿

St Martin, 104 Borstal Road, Rochester, Kent, ME1 3BD.
Comfortable Victorian home overlooking river, easy walk to city centre.
Open: All Year (not Xmas)
01634 848192 Mrs Colvin
icolvin@stmartin.freeserve.co.uk
D: £16–£18 **S:** £16–£18
Beds: 1D 2T **Baths:** 2 Sh
🛏 🔟 🎿 ✗ 🖳 Ⅴ ♿

52 Borstal Street, Rochester, Kent, ME1 3HL.
Comfortable Victorian Terraced house. Suitable for cat lovers. Smokers welcome.
Open: All Year
01634 812347 Ms Walker
D: £12.50 **S:** £20
Beds: 1D **Baths:** 1Sh
🅿 🔟 🖳 ♿

11 Ethelbert Road, Rochester, Kent, ME1 3EU.
Large family home 10 minutes walk from historic city centre.
Open: All Year (not Xmas)
01634 403740 Mrs Jenkinson
D: £18–£20 **S:** £20
Beds: 1D 1T
½ 🔟 🖳 ♿

Selling

TR0456   🍺 Rose & Crown, White Lion

Owens Court Farm, Selling, Faversham, Kent, ME13 9QN.
Owens Court is a peaceful Kentish Georgian farmhouse on a fruit farm.
Open: All Year
01227 752247 (also fax) Mrs Higgs
D: £20 **S:** £20
Beds: 1F 1T 1S **Baths:** 2 Sh
🛏 🅿 (5) 🔟 🖳 Ⅴ ♿

Sevenoaks

TQ5255   🍺 White Hart, The Chequers, Rose & Crown, The Bull

40 Robyns Way, Sevenoaks, Kent, TN13 3EB.
Quiet location, station 10 minutes walk. French spoken, self catering available.
Open: All Year
01732 452401 Mrs Ingram
valerie.ingram@centrenet.co.uk
D: £25–£28 **S:** £27–£30
Beds: 1F 1D 1T **Baths:** 2 En 1 Sh
🛏 🅿 (3) ½ 🔟 🖳 Ⅴ ♿ ♿

Green Tiles, 46 The Rise, Sevenoaks, Kent, TN13 1RJ.
Quiet annexe in lovely garden, own entrance, for 1-5 guests. **Open:** All Year
01732 451522 (also fax) Mrs Knoops
D: £20–£22 **S:** fr £30
Beds: 1F **Baths:** 1 En
🛏 🅿 (2) ½ 🔟 🖳 ♿

56 The Drive, Sevenoaks, Kent, TN13 3AF.
Lovely Edwardian house and garden close to station and town. Peaceful.
Open: All Year (not Xmas)
Grades: ETC 3 Diamond
01732 453236 Mrs Lloyd
jwlloydsks@aol.com
D: £19–£24.50 **S:** £22–£28
Beds: 2T 2S **Baths:** 2 Sh
🅿 (4) 🔟 ♿

Sevenoaks Star House, Star Hill, Sevenoaks, Kent, TN14 6HA.
Country house, large garden, stunning views. Near Sevenoaks and M25.
Open: All Year (not Xmas)
Grades: ETC 3 Diamond
01959 533109 **D:** £18–£20.50 **S:** £20–£22.50
Beds: 2T 1D **Baths:** 2 Pr
🛏 🅿 ½ 🔟 🖳 ♿

Planning a longer stay? Always ask for any special rates

Burley Lodge, *Rockdale Road , Sevenoaks, Kent, TN13 1JT.*
Beautiful Edwardian house situated in conservation area in a cul-de-sac off the High Street.
Open: All Year
01732 455761 Ms Latter
Fax: 01732 458178
D: £20 **S:** £27
Beds: 1F **Baths:** 1 En
🛏 🅿 📺 🍴 ✕ 🛁 Ⅴ 🌡

Sheerness
TQ9175

Victoriana Hotel, *103-109 Alma Road, Sheerness, Kent, ME12 2PD.*
Small, family-run hotel offering friendly welcome & service.
Open: All Year
01795 665555 Mr Taylor
Fax: 01795 580633
D: £16–£29 **S:** £17–£29
Beds: 2F 4D 8T 6S **Baths:** 9 En 3 Sh
🛏 🅿 (8) 📺 🍴 ✕ 🛁 Ⅴ 🌡 & cc

Shepherdswell
TR2547 🍺 *Crown Inn, The Bell*

Sunshine Cottage, *The Green, Mill Lane, Shepherdswell, Dover, Kent, CT15 7LQ.*
C17th cottage on village green, beautifully restored. Pretty garden/courtyard. **Open:** All Year
Grades: ETC 4 Diamond, Silver
01304 831359 Mrs Popple
D: £22–£25 **S:** £30–£35
Beds: 6F 5D 1T **Baths:** 4 En 2 Pr 4 Sh
🛏 🅿 (6) ⚡ 📺 ✕ 🛁 Ⅴ 🌡 & cc 1

Shoreham
TQ5261 🍺 *King's Arms*

Church House, *Church Street, Shoreham, Sevenoaks, Kent, TN14 7SB.*
Georgian house; large garden and tennis court in picturesque village.
Open: All Year (not Xmas/New Year)
Grades: ETC 4 Diamond, Silver Award
01959 522241 (also fax) Mrs Howie
www.heartofkent.org.uk
katehowie@compuserve.com
D: £22–£28 **S:** £30–£35
Beds: 3T **Baths:** 1 En 1 Sh
📺 🛁 Ⅴ 🌡 &

Sissinghurst
TQ7937 🍺 *Bull Inn, Three Chimneys*

Hillview Cottage, *Starvenden Lane, Sissinghurst, Cranbrook, Kent, TN17 2AN.*
Total peace. Attractive, comfortable house close National Trust properties.
Open: All Year
Grades: ETC 3 Diamond
01580 712823 Mrs Lloyd Jones
rmlj@starlaine.freeserve.co.uk
D: £20–£30 **S:** £20–£30
Beds: 1D 1T **Baths:** 2 En 1 Pr
🛏 (6) 🅿 ⚡ 📺 🍴 ✕ 🛁 Ⅴ 🌡

Smarden
TQ8842

Chequers Inn, *Smarden, Ashford, Kent, TN27 8QA.*
C14th village inn. Renowned for good food and ambience.
Open: All Year (not Xmas)
Grades: ETC 3 Diamond
01233 770217 Fax: 01233 770623
D: fr £25 **S:** fr £26
Beds: 1F 2T 2D 1S **Baths:** 3 En 2 Pr
🛏 🅿 (18) 📺 🍴 ✕ Ⅴ 🌡

Southborough
TQ5842 🍺 *George & Dragon, The Imperial*

10 Modest Corner, *Southborough, Tunbridge Wells, Kent, TN4 0LS.*
Situated in quiet, picturesque hamlet away from traffic, within easy reach of M25.
Open: All Year
01892 522450 Ms Leemhuis
annekel@talk21.com
D: £20–£22.50 **S:** £25–£30
Beds: 1D 2T **Baths:** 1 Pr 1 Sh
🛏 🅿 (2) ⚡ 📺 🍴 🛁 Ⅴ 🌡 &

St Mary's Platt
TQ6057 🍺 *Brickmakers' Arms*

Stone Cottage, *Maidstone Road, St Mary's Platt, Borough Green, Sevenoaks, Kent, TN15 8JH.*
Convenient M20/M25 and Brands Hatch. 40 minutes to London.
Open: All Year (not Xmas)
01732 883098 Mrs Record
D: £20 **S:** £20
Beds: 1F 1D **Baths:** 1 Sh
🛏 (3) 🅿 (10) ⚡ 📺 🛁 🌡

Stelling Minnis
TR1346 🍺 *Rose & Crown, Hop Pocket*

Bower Farm House, *Bossingham Road, Stelling Minnis, Canterbury, Kent, CT4 6BB.*
Open: All Year (not Xmas/New Year)
Grades: ETC 4 Diamond, Silver Award
01227 709430
book@bowerbb.freeserve.co.uk
D: £21–£23 **S:** £25–£30
Beds: 1T 1D **Baths:** 1 En 1 Pr
🛏 🅿 (5) 📺 🍴 🛁 Ⅴ 🌡
Breakfast on fresh bread and new laid eggs in a charming heavily beamed C17th Kentish farmhouse on the edge of a medieval common. Visit historic Canterbury, walk in the beautiful countryside or see Dover castle and the white cliffs.

Strood
TQ7268 🍺 *Sans Pareil*

3 Hillside Avenue, Frindsbury, *Strood, Rochester, ME2 3DB.*
Friendly family Victorian home in quiet road, close to amenities.
Open: All Year
01634 713642 Mrs Firmin
D: £15–£18 **S:** £15–£18
Beds: 1F 1T 1S **Baths:** 2 Sh
🛏 ⚡ 📺 🍴 ✕ 🛁 Ⅴ 🌡

Sundridge
TQ4855 🍺 *White Horse Inn*

The Red House, *Church Road, Sundridge, Sevenoaks, Kent, TN14 6EA.*
Queen Anne House in Beautiful gardens near Hever, Chartwell, London.
Open: All Year (not Xmas/New Year)
01959 565444 Mrs Belle
Fax: 01732 452312
balles@waitrose.com
D: £25 **S:** £25
Beds: 3D **Baths:** 1 En 1 Sh
🅿 (4) ⚡ 📺 🛁 🌡

Sutton Valence
TQ8149

The Queens Head, *High Street, Sutton Valence, Maidstone, Kent, ME17 3AG.*
Open: All Year
01622 843225 J Pilcher
Fax: 01622 842651
D: £22.50–£25 **S:** £22.50–£25
Beds: 2F 1T 1D **Baths:** 1 Sh
🛏 🅿 ⚡ 📺 🛁 🌡 & cc
Spectacular countryside views of Weald of Kent, built 1460 and features Oak Beams, Inglenook fireplace and low ceilings. Excellent home cooked food in countryside style. Award winning viewpoint Garden. historical village over 1000 years old with Castle Ruins.

Tenterden
TQ8833 🍺 *Eight Bells, The Chequers, White Lion, Lemon Tree*

The White Cottage, *London Beach, Tenterden, Kent, TN30 6SR.*
2 miles north of Tenterden on A28 road, rural position.
Open: All Year
Grades: ETC 3 Diamond
01233 850583
Mrs Matthews
D: £16.50–£18.50 **S:** £20–£22
Beds: 2D 1T **Baths:** 1 En 2 Sh
🛏 🅿 (3) ⚡ 📺 🍴 ✕ Ⅴ 🌡

Draylands, *High Halden, Ashford, Kent, TN23 3JG.*
Secluded location in Garden of England. Bedrooms with extensive views over open farmland.
Open: All Year (not Xmas/New Year)
Grades: ETC 3 Diamond
01233 850048 (also fax)
Mrs Russell
sallyrussell30@hotmail.com
D: £23–£25 **S:** £27–£30
Beds: 2D **Baths:** 2 En
🅿 (3) ⚡ 📺 ✕ 🛁 🌡

11 East Hill, *Tenterden, Kent, TN30 6RL.*
Happy family atmosphere in Victorian house. German spoken, quiet location.
Open: All Year
Grades: ETC 3 Diamond
01580 766805 (also fax)
Mrs Thompson
D: £18–£19 **S:** £20
Beds: 1D 1T 1S **Baths:** 1 Sh
🛏 🅿 (4) ⚡ 📺 🛁 Ⅴ 🌡

Tonbridge

TQ5946   *Kentish Rifleman, Chaser Inn*

Starvecrow Place, Starvecrow Hill, *Shipbourne Road, Tonbridge, Kent, TN11 9NL.*
Relaxed luxury accommodation set in delightful woodlands. Heated outdoor swimming pool. **Open:** All Year (not Xmas)
01732 356863 Mrs Batson
D: £19–£22 **S:** £30
Beds: 2D 1T **Baths:** 2 En 1 Pr
🛇 (13) 🅿 (6) ⌿ 📺 🗐 Ⅴ ♨

Trottiscliffe

TQ6460   *The Plough*

Bramble Park, *Church Lane, Trottiscliffe, West Malling, Kent, ME19 5EB.*
Secluded tranquil Victorian rectory in beautiful private parkland. Spacious comfortable. **Open:** All Year
01732 822397 Mrs Towler
D: £20 **S:** £20
Beds: 1F 1D 1S **Baths:** 1 Pr 2 Sh
🛇 🅿 (6) 📺 🗐.

Tunbridge Wells

TQ5839   *The Barn, Brecknock Arms, George & Dragon, Robin Hood*

Vale Royal Hotel, *54-57 London Road, Tunbridge Wells, Kent, TN1 1DS.*
Open: All Year **Grades:** ETC 3 Star
01892 525580 V Constantine
reservations@valeroyalhotel.co.uk
D: £32.50–£34.50 **S:** £45–£48
Beds: 2F 6D 6T 6S **Baths:** 20 En
🛇 🅿 (3) 📺 ♂ ✕ 🗐 Ⅴ ♨ cc
Situated in the lovely Spa Town, overlooking the common. All rooms undergone recent refurbishment and include direct dial telephones. Relax in the countryside, visit stately homes, formal gardens, close to M25 and Gatwick Airport.

Ford Cottage, *Linden Park Road, Tunbridge Wells, Kent, TN2 5QL.*
Open: Feb to Nov **Grades:** ETC 4 Diamond
01892 531419 Mrs Cusdin
FordCottage@tinyworld.co.uk
D: £21–£25
Beds: 3T **Baths:** 2 En 1 Pr
🛇 (5) 🅿 (5) ⌿ 📺 🗐 Ⅴ ♨ &
Picturesque and charming Victorian cottage, 3 mins walk to Pantiles, easy access to town centre and central station. Mainly ground floor accommodation, lovely garden, perfect base for exploring numerous castles, stately homes and gardens nearby.

Blundeston, *Eden Road, Tunbridge Wells, Kent, TN1 1TS.*
Open: All Year (not Xmas/New Year)
Grades: ETC 4 Diamond
01892 513030 Mrs Day
Fax: 01892 540255
D: £23–£26 **S:** £23–£26
Beds: 1T 1D **Baths:** 2 En
🛇 (9) 🅿 ⌿ 📺 ♂ 🗐 Ⅴ ♨
Beautiful period house in quiet secluded part of the old village area of Tunbridge Wells. Within five minutes walk of many restaurants the old High Street, Pantiles and railway station.

Ash Tree Cottage, *Eden Road, Tunbridge Wells, Kent, TN1 1TS.*
Delightful cottage-style house in a secluded private road, short walk to the famous Pantiles, the High Street, the station and many restaurants.
Open: All Year (not Xmas/New Year)
Grades: ETC 4 Diamond
01892 541317 Mrs Rogers
Fax: 01892 616770
D: £22.50–£25 **S:** £35–£42
Beds: 1D 1T **Baths:** 2 En
🛇 (9) 🅿 (4) ⌿ 📺 🗐 Ⅴ ♨ &

Hadleigh, *69 Sandown Park, Tunbridge Wells, Kent, TN2 4RT.*
Quiet house. Close to Tunbridge Wells. Kent-Sussex countryside.
Open: All Year **Grades:** ETC 3 Diamond
01892 822760 Mr & Mrs Gardiner
Fax: 01892 823170
D: £22 **S:** £22–£25
Beds: 2F 1T 1D **Baths:** 1 Sh
🛇 🅿 (2) ⌿ 📺 🗐 Ⅴ ♨

Ulcombe

TQ8448   *Who'd a' Thought It*

Bramley Knowle Farm, *Eastwood Road, Ulcombe, Maidstone, Kent, ME17 1ET.*
Modern farmhouse, 10 min (J8)M20, near Leeds castle.
Open: All Year (not Xmas)
Grades: ETC 3 Diamond
01622 858878 D Leat
Fax: 01622 851121
D: £19–£22 **S:** £18–£20
Beds: 2D 1S **Baths:** 1 En 1 Sh
🛇 (3) 🅿 (6) ⌿ 📺 🗐 Ⅴ ♨

Upchurch

TQ8467   *The Crown*

Suffield House, *The Street, Upchurch, Sittingbourne, Kent, ME9 7EU.*
Open: All Year (not Xmas)
Grades: ETC 4 Diamond
01634 230409
Mr & Mrs Newbery
D: £24 **S:** £24
Beds: 2D 1T
🛇 (10) 🅿 (10) ⌿ 📺 ✕ 🗐 Ⅴ ♨
Suffield House - a Victorian house set in the rural village of Upchurch, between Rainham and Sittingbourne. Easy access to historic Faversham, Rochester and the Saxon Shore Way. Village pub and golf course. Warm and friendly welcome and a superb breakfast.

West Farleigh

TQ7152   *The Bull*

St Helens Cottage, *St Helens Lane, West Farleigh, Maidstone, Kent, ME15 0JJ.*
200- year-old cottage, heavily beamed, inglenook fireplace. Set in 2 acres overlooking River Medway.
Open: All Year
01622 720263
Mr & Mrs Taylor
D: £17.50 **S:** £22
Beds: 1F 1D 1T **Baths:** 1 En 1 Pr
🛇 (1) 🅿 (20) 📺 ✕ 🗐 Ⅴ ✱ ♨

West Malling

TQ6757

Scott House, *37 High Street, West Malling, Maidstone, Kent, ME19 6QH.*
Open: All Year (not Xmas/New Year)
01732 841380 E G Smith
Fax: 01732 522367
mail@scott-house.co.uk
D: £34.50 **S:** £49
Beds: 1T 3D 1S **Baths:** 3 En 1 Sh
🛇 (10) ⌿ 📺 🗐 Ⅴ ♨ cc
Scott house is a grade II Georgian town house in the high street of West Malling, this is a family home from which we run an antique and interior business as well as offering Bed & Breakfast.

West Peckham

TQ6452   *Artichoke Inn, The Swan*

Adams Well Cottage, *Forge Lane, Gover Hill, West Peckham, Maidstone, ME18 5JR.*
Victorian county cottage, rural location, surrounded by half acre mature garden.
Open: All Year (not Xmas)
Grades: ETC 3 Diamond
01732 851729 (also fax)
Mr & Mrs Higgs
adamswell@msn.com
D: £20 **S:** £23–£28
Beds: 2D 1S **Baths:** 1 Sh
🛇 (8) 🅿 (3) ⌿ 📺 ♨

Westerham

TQ4454   *The Bull, White Hart*

Holmesdale House, *High Street, Brasted, Westerham, Kent, TN16 1HS.*
Delightful Victorian house (part C17th). Chartwell, Hever, Knole and Mainline Station.
Open: All Year
01959 564834 (also fax)
Mr Jinks
D: £20–£27.50 **S:** £30
Beds: 1F 3D 1T **Baths:** 3 En 1 Sh
🛇 🅿 (7) 📺 🗐 Ⅴ ♨ &

The Orchard House, *Brasted Chart, Westerham, Kent, TN16 1LR.*
Family home, quiet, rural surroundings, near Chartwell, Hever, Knole, Gatwick
Open: All Year (not Xmas)
Grades: ETC 3 Diamond
01959 563702 Mrs Godsal
David.Godsal@tesco.net
D: fr £21 **S:** fr £22
Beds: 2T 1S **Baths:** 2 Sh
🛇 🅿 (4) ⌿ 📺 🗐 &

Corner Cottage, *Toys Hill, Westerham, Kent, TN16 1PY.*
Attractive self contained accommodation in Laura Ashley fabrics. Spectacular panoramic views.
Open: All Year
Grades: ETC 4 Diamond, Silver Award
01732 750362 Mrs Olszowska
Fax: 01959 561911
olszowskiathome@jshmanco.com
D: £45–£50 **S:** £30–£35
Beds: 1F
🛇 🅿 (1) ⌿ 📺 🗐 Ⅴ ♨

Westwell

TQ9847   Royal Oak

Dean Court Farm, Challock Lane,
Westwell, Ashford, Kent, TN25 4NH.
Period rural farmhouse, central for
channel ports and touring Kent.
Open: All Year (not Xmas)
01233 712924 Mrs Lister
D: £20–£25 **S:** £20–£25
Beds: 1D 2T **Baths:** 1 Sh
⌂ ▣ (3) ▥ ⛬ ⚓

Whitfield

TR2945   Dover Castle

Rolles Court, Church Whitfield Road,
Whitfield, Dover, Kent, CT16 3HY.
Country home 3 miles Dover. Picturesque
gardens. Very friendly atmosphere.
Open: All Year
01304 8274871 Mrs Montgomery
Fax: 01304 827877
rollescourt@tesco.net
D: £25–£30 **S:** £25–£30
Beds: 1F 1T 1D **Baths:** 3 En
⌂ ▣ ⚓ ▥ ⛬ ✕ ▥ ✿ ⚓

Whitstable

TR1066   Rose in Bloom

The Cherry Garden, 62 Joy Lane,
Whitstable, CT5 4LT.
Open: All Year
Grades: ETC 3 Diamond
01227 266497 Mr & Mrs Harris
D: £19–£22.50 **S:** £25
Beds: 1D 1T 1S **Baths:** 2 En 1 Pr
⌂ ▣ (3) ⚓ ▥ ⛬ ▥ ⚓
Enjoy a warm welcome at The Cherry
Garden. Well furnished rooms, quiet and
comfortable. Excellent breakfast choice.
Large pretty garden. Close to coastal
footpath with easy walk to heritage town
and beach. On bus route and six miles to
Canterbury.

Wickhambreaux

TR2258   The Rose

The Old Stone House, The Green,
Wickhambreaux, Canterbury, Kent, CT3 1RQ.
Historic medieval house next to river and
picturesque village green.
Open: All Year
01227 728591 Mrs Knight
D: fr £20 **S:** fr £20
Beds: 1F 1D 1T 1S **Baths:** 2 Pr 2 Sh
⌂ ▣ (6) ⚓ ▥ ⛬ ⚓ ⚓ ⚓

Wingham

TR2357   Three Tuns

Twitham Court Farm, Staple Road,
Wingham, Canterbury, Kent, CT3 1LP.
Picturesque Victorian farmhouse in 2
acres of beautiful gardens with a friendly,
peaceful and relaxed atmosphere, quiet
and comfortable rooms with garden
views, and excellent breakfasts. The
ancient Cathedral City of Canterbury is 9
miles, 16 miles to Dover.
Open: All Year
01227 720265 M Duck & D Bowden
Fax: 01227 722177
flower@twitham.fsnet.co.uk
D: £17.50–£25 **S:** £20–£35
Beds: 1F 3D 1T **Baths:** 2 En 1 Sh
⌂ ▣ (8) ⚓ ▥ ⛬ ▥ ⚓

Wittersham

TQ8926   Ewe & Lamb, The Swan

Oxney Farm, Moons Green, Wittersham,
Tenterden, Kent, TN30 7PS.
Warm welcome from the 1998 Kent
Hospitality Award winner.
Open: All Year
01797 270558 Mrs Burnett
Fax: 01797 270958
oxneyf@globalnet.co.uk
D: £25–£30 **S:** £25–£30
Beds: 2D 1T **Baths:** 2 En 1 Pr
▣ (3) ⚓ ▥ ⛬ ▥ ⚓ cc

Worth

TR3355   St Crispin Inn

Ilex Cottage, Temple Way, Worth, Deal,
Kent, CT14 0DA.
Lovely secluded peaceful C18th house,
charming, well-appointed rooms, rural
views.
Open: All Year (not Xmas)
01304 617026 Mrs Stobie
Fax: 01304 620890
info@ilexcottage.co.uk
D: £20–£25 **S:** £25–£35
Beds: 1F 1D 1T **Baths:** 3 En
⌂ ▣ (6) ⚓ ▥ ✿ ⛬ ▥ ⚓

Wouldham

TQ7164   Watermans

Wouldham Court Farmhouse, 246
High Street, Wouldham, Rochester, Kent,
ME1 3TY.
Beamed Grade II Listed farmhouse,
inglenook fireplace, overlooking River
Medway.
Open: All Year (not Xmas)
Grades: ETC 3 Diamond
01634 683271 (also fax)
Ms Parnell
wouldham.b-b@virgin.net
D: £22 **S:** £18–£22
Beds: 1F 1D 1S **Baths:** 2 Sh
⌂ ▣ (1) ⚓ ▥ ✿ ✕ ⛬ ▥ ⚓ cc

Wye

TR0546   New Flying Horse

Selsfield, 46 Oxenturn Road, Wye,
Ashford, Kent, TN25 5AZ.
Ideal stop Channel Tunnel/ferries, North
Downs Way- Pilgrim's Way Sustrans.
Open: All Year
01233 812133 (also fax)
J & J Morris
D: fr £20 **S:** fr £25
Beds: 2T
▣ ⚓ ▥ ⛬ ⚓

Lancashire

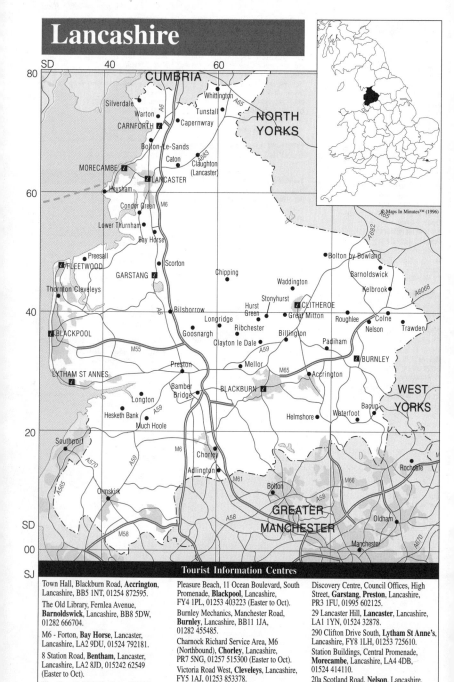

Tourist Information Centres

Town Hall, Blackburn Road, **Accrington**, Lancashire, BB5 1NT, 01254 872595.

The Old Library, Fernlea Avenue, **Barnoldswick**, Lancashire, BB8 5DW, 01282 666704.

M6 - Forton, **Bay Horse**, Lancaster, Lancashire, LA2 9DU, 01524 792181.

8 Station Road, **Bentham**, Lancaster, Lancashire, LA2 8JD, 015242 62549 (Easter to Oct).

King George's Hall, Northgate, **Blackburn**, Lancashire, BB2 1AA, 01254 53277.

1 Clifton Street, **Blackpool**, Lancashire, FY1 1LY, 01253 621623.

Pleasure Beach, 11 Ocean Boulevard, South Promenade, **Blackpool**, Lancashire, FY4 1PL, 01253 403223 (Easter to Oct).

Burnley Mechanics, Manchester Road, **Burnley**, Lancashire, BB11 1JA, 01282 455485.

Charnock Richard Service Area, M6 (Northbound), **Chorley**, Lancashire, PR7 5NG, 01257 515300 (Easter to Oct).

Victoria Road West, **Cleveleys**, Lancashire, FY5 1AJ, 01253 853378.

12-14 Market Place, **Clitheroe**, Lancashire, BB7 2DA, 01200 25566.

Ferry Office, Ferry Dock, The Esplanade, **Fleetwood**, Lancashire, FY7 6DN, 01253 773953.

Discovery Centre, Council Offices, High Street, **Garstang**, **Preston**, Lancashire, PR3 1FU, 01995 602125.

29 Lancaster Hill, **Lancaster**, Lancashire, LA1 1YN, 01524 32878.

290 Clifton Drive South, **Lytham St Anne's**, Lancashire, FY8 1LH, 01253 725610.

Station Buildings, Central Promenade, **Morecambe**, Lancashire, LA4 4DB, 01524 414110.

20a Scotland Road, **Nelson**, Lancashire, BB9 7UU, 01282 692890.

The Guildhall, Lancaster Road, **Preston**, Lancashire, PR1 1HT, 01772 253731.

41-45 Kay Street, **Rawtenstall**, Lancashire, BB4 7LS, 01706 226590.

Accrington

SD7528 ◄ The George

Wendys B&B, *139 Whalley Road, Accrington, Lancs, BB5 1BX.*
Friendly welcome; close to town centre and motorway networks.
Open: All Year
01254 871060 Mrs Walsh
D: £17.50–£18 **S:** £18
Beds: 2F 1T 1S **Baths:** 1 En 1 Sh
🛇 🅿 📺 ✕ 🛋 Ⅴ ♨

Adlington

SD6013 ◄ The Millstone

Briarfield House, *Bolton Road, Anderton, Adlington, Chorley, Lancs, PR6 9HW.*
In own grounds, beautiful views over open countryside. Private parking.
Open: All Year
01257 480105 Mrs Baldwin
brihouse@classicfm.net
D: fr £17.50 **S:** fr £20
Beds: 1D 2T **Baths:** 2 En 1 Pr
🛇 ⅟ 📺 🛋 Ⅴ ♨

Bacup

SD8622 ◄ Rose & Bowl, The Crown, Mario's

Pasture Bottom Farm, *Bacup, Lancs, OL13 0UZ.*
Comfortable farmhouse bed & breakfast in a quiet rural area on a working beef farm.
Open: All Year (not Xmas)
Grades: ETC 3 Diamond
01706 873790 (also fax)
A Isherwood
ha.isherwood@zen.co.uk
D: £15–£16 **S:** £15–£16
Beds: 1D 2T **Baths:** 2 En 1 Pr 1 Sh
🛇 🅿 (4) ⅟ 📺 🛉 ✕ 🛋 ♨

Bamber Bridge

SD5626 ◄ Hob Inn

Anvil Guest House, *321 Station Road, Bamber Bridge, Preston, Lancs, PR5 6EE.*
Comfortable, friendly, near Junct.M6, M61, M65. Central heating, TV lounge.
Open: All Year (not Xmas)
01772 339022
J C Arkwright
D: £13.50 **S:** £15
Beds: 2F 4D 3T **Baths:** 2 Sh
🛇 📺 🛋 ♨

Barnoldswick

SD8746 ◄ Fosters Arms, Fanny Grey, Milano's

Foster's House, *203 Gisburn Road, Barnoldswick, Lancs, BB18 5JU.*
A warm welcome awaits at our beautiful home from home.
Open: All Year
Grades: ETC 2 Diamond
01282 850718
Mr & Mrs Edwards
D: £20 **S:** £20
Beds: 2D 2T **Baths:** 3 En 1 Sh
🛇 🅿 (4) 📺 🛉 🛋 Ⅴ ♨ & cc

Bay Horse

SD4953 ◄ Bay Horse Hotel, Manor Inn

Stanley Lodge Farmhouse, *Cockerham Road, Bay Horse, Lancaster, Lancs., LA2 0HE.*
Rural area, Lancaster canal nearby. Lakes, Yorkshire Dales, golfing, horse riding nearby.
Open: All Year (not Xmas/New Year)
Grades: ETC 3 Diamond
01524 791863 D: £18–£20 **S:** £18–£20
Beds: 1F 2D **Baths:** 1 Sh
🛇 🅿 (4) 📺 🛉 🛋 Ⅴ ♨

Saltoke South, *Bay Horse, Galgate, Lancaster, LA2 0HL.*
A beautiful old stone family home set in open countryside.
Open: All Year (not Xmas)
01524 752313 G W Robin
grobin1@bayhorse21.freeserve.co.uk
D: £15–£20 **S:** fr £20
Beds: 1D 1T **Baths:** 1 Sh
🛇 🅿 (6) ⅟ 📺 🛉 🛋 Ⅴ ♨

Billington

SD7235

Rosebury, *51 Pasturelands Drive, Billington, Clitheroe, Lancs, BB7 9LW.*
Quality family accommodation, guest rooms overlook the beautiful Ribble Valley.
Open: All Year (not Xmas/New Year)
Grades: ETC 3 Diamond
01254 822658 C P Hamer
enquires@rosebury-guest-house.co.uk
D: £20–£22.50 **S:** £20–£22.50
Beds: 1F 1T **Baths:** 2 Sh
🛇 🅿 ⅟ 📺 🛉 ✕ 🛋 Ⅴ ♨

Bilsborrow

SD5139 ◄ Roebuck Inn

Olde Duncombe House, *Garstang Road, Bilsborrow, Preston, Lancs, PR3 0RE.*
Traditional cottage-style family run bed & breakfast offering a high standard of accommodation.
Open: All Year
01995 640336 Mr Bolton
bolton3@netlineuk.net
D: £22.50–£25 **S:** £35–£39.50
Beds: 1F 5D 1T 2S **Baths:** 9 En
🛇 🅿 (2) 📺 🛋 Ⅴ ♨ cc

Blackburn

SD6827 ◄ Boar's Head, Butlers' Arms

The Chimneys, *139 Preston New Road, Blackburn, Lancs, BB2 6BJ.*
Open: All Year (not Xmas/New Year)
01254 665026
D: £18–£20 **S:** £18–£25
Beds: 2F 4T 3D 2S
Baths: 2 En 3 Sh
🛇 🅿 (8) 📺 🛉 ✕ 🛋 Ⅴ ♨
Family run Victorian property, central location, within easy reach of the motorways, offering comfortable accommodation and friendly service. Spacious bedroom, guest lounge with open fire. Excellent home cooking. Private off-road parking.

Shalom, *531b Livesey Branch Road, Blackburn, BB2 5DF.*
Luxurious accommodation in uniquely styled home. Hospitality second to none.
Open: All Year
01254 209032 (also fax)
Mr Schofield
paul@shalomblackburn.co.uk
D: £22–£25 **S:** £22–£25
Beds: 1D 1T 1S **Baths:** 3 En
🛇 🅿 (4) ⅟ 📺 🛉 🛋 Ⅴ ♨ cc

Ellerbeck Guest House, *37 Wellington Street, St Johns, Blackburn, Lancs, BB1 8AF.*
Family-run hotel established 21 years. Quiet location close to town centre.
Open: All Year (not Xmas/New Year)
01254 261057
D: £16–£19 **S:** £20–£24
Beds: 3F 3D 2T 2S **Baths:** 7 Pr 3 Sh
🛇 🅿 (10) 📺 🛉 ✕ 🛋 Ⅴ ♨ & cc

Blackpool

SD3136 ◄ Yeadon Way, Counting House, The Washington, The Glyn, Edward's, Eating Inn, Royal Oak, Duke Of York, Hop Inn

The Arncliffe Hotel, *24 Osborne Road, South Shore, Blackpool, Lancs, FY4 1HJ.*
Open: Mar to Jan
Grades: ETC 3 Diamond
01253 345209 (also fax)
Mrs Wood
arncliffehotel@talk21.com
D: £13–£25 **S:** £13–£20
Beds: 1F 5D 1T 1S **Baths:** 5 En 1 Sh
🛇 🅿 (3) 📺 ✕ 🛋 Ⅴ ♨ ♨ cc
Small licensed, family-run hotel, catering for couples and families. Close to pleasure beach and promenade. Good healthy home cooking. Heartbeat Award for 7th year. Separate dining tables. Excellent choice on dinner menu. Comfortable beds with duvets.

The Carlis Private Hotel, *34 Charnley Road, Blackpool, Lancs, FY1 4PF.*
Open: All Year
01253 622586 (also fax)
Mrs Boyd
carlishotel@gofornet.co.uk
D: £13–£25 **S:** £16–£30
Beds: 5F 9D 3T 2S **Baths:** 12 En 7 Sh
🛇 📺 ✕ 🛋 Ⅴ ♨ cc
Licensed, good food and cleanliness assured. Central to beach, shops, shows, Tower and winter gardens. TV lounge, pool table. Hygiene certificate. Weekly rates from £68 B&B, e's extra. All rooms have tea/coffee making facilities, central heating, TV.

Fairway Hotel, *34/36 Hull Road, Blackpool, Lancs, FY1 4QB.*
Open: All Year
Grades: ETC 3 Diamond
01253 623777 Mr Hodges
Fax: 01253 753455
bookings@fairway.gb.com
D: £18–£20 **S:** £31–£33
Beds: 10F 8D **Baths:** 18 En
🛇 📺 ✕ 🛋 Ⅴ ♨ ♨ cc
Family-run licensed hotel, close to Tower, Winter Gardens, shops and night life. No hidden extras. Deposit refundable if not satisfied on arrival. New Year breaks a speciality.

St Ives Hotel, *10 King George Avenue, North Shore, Blackpool, Lancs, FY2 9SN.*
Open: All Year
01253 352122 (also fax)
Mrs Dempsey
D: £16–£20
Beds: 3F 4D 2T **Baths:** 5 En 4 Sh
🛇 (2) 🅿 (14) ⌇ 📺 ✕ 🛏 Ⅴ 🍴 ♣ ⚓ cc
A highly recommended hotel situated just off Queen's Promenade, within easy reach of all amenities, including golf course. Most rooms ensuite with tea/coffee making facilities and full central heating throughout. Excellent food and a high standard of cleanliness.

Granville Hotel, *12 Station Road, Blackpool, Lancashire, FY4 1BE.*
Close to pleasure beach, south pier, and all amenities etc.
Open: Easter to November
Grades: ETC 3 Diamond
01253 343012 Mr Taylor
Fax: 01253 408594
wilft@thegranvillehotel.co.uk
D: £18–£26 **S:** £19–£26
Beds: 5F 5D 2S **Baths:** 11 En 1 Pr
🛇 🅿 (2) 📺 ✕ 🛏 Ⅴ ♣ 🍴 cc

Clarron House, *22 Leopold Grove, Blackpool, Lancs, FY1 4LD.*
Clean and friendly, adjacent Winter Gardens, near theatres, shops, promenade.
Open: All Year
01253 623748
 Mr & Mrs O'Donnell
D: £13–£21 **S:** £16–£24
Beds: 3F 4D 1T **Baths:** 6 En 1 Sh
🛇 📺 ✕ 🛏 Ⅴ ♣ 🍴 cc

Westcliffe Private Hotel, *46 King Edward Avenue, Blackpool, FY2 9TA.*
Homely hotel in select area adjacent Queen's Promenade; comfort assured.
Open: All Year (not Xmas)
01253 352943 Mr Carter
D: £18–£22 **S:** £18–£22
Beds: 2D 2T 3S **Baths:** 8 Pr
🛇 (7) 📺 ✕ 🛏 Ⅴ 🍴

Regency Hotel, *50 Charnley Road, Blackpool, Lancs, FY1 4PE.*
Open: All Year (not Xmas/New Year)
01253 625186 (also fax)
Mr Wyers
regency.hotel@talk21.com
D: £14–£35 **S:** £20–£45
Beds: 8F 9D **Baths:** 14 En 2 Sh
🛇 (1) 🅿 (3) 📺 ✕ 🛏 Ⅴ 🍴 cc
The Regency is a family run Hotel ideally situated in the heart of Blackpool. Close to the shops, Tower, Wintergreens, Promenade and countless attractions. We offer a warm welcome to couples, families, OAPs and delegates, specialising in excellent home cooking.

Wescoe Private Hotel, *14 Dean Street, Blackpool, Lancs, FY4 1AU.*
Quality hotel near to sea front. Friendly welcome and cleanliness assured.
Open: All Year
01253 342772 Ms McClelland
wescoe@amserve.net
D: £15–£26 **S:** £15–£31
Beds: 4F 1T 5D **Baths:** 7 En 1 Sh
🛇 🅿 (4) 📺 🛏 ✕ 🛏 Ⅴ 🍴

Cherry Blossom Hotel, *2 Warley Road Corner, North Promenade, Blackpool, FY1 2JU.*
Open: All Year
01253 355533 Fax: 01253 355534
D: £17–£30 **S:** £17–£30
Beds: 4F 4D 6T 1S **Baths:** 15 En
🛇 🅿 (14) 📺 🛏 🍴 cc
Large Victorian house, overlooking Irish sea, converted into a 15 bedroom hotel with large public bar. Many rooms have spa baths, trouser press and hair dryers. Ornate ceiling plaster work old panelling and Victorian fireplaces are original features which have been retained.

Astoria Hotel, *118-120 Albert Road, Blackpool, Lancs, FY1 4PN.*
Excellent food and accommodation, all ensuite with satellite TV. Adjacent Winter Gardens, shops & theatres
Open: All Year
01253 621321 Fax: 01253 293203
astoria.hotel@cableinet.co.uk
D: £19–£29 **S:** £19–£29
Beds: 12F 13D 1T 2S **Baths:** 28 En
🛇 🅿 (4) 📺 ✕ 🛏 Ⅴ ♣ 🍴 cc

Sheron House, *21 Gynn Avenue, Blackpool, Lancs, FY1 4PN.*
In a word - 'Quality'. Good food, good company, comfortable bed!
Open: All Year (not Jan)
01253 354614 sheronhouse@amserve.net
D: £16.50–£22 **S:** £16.50–£27
Beds: 2F 1T 3D **Baths:** 6 En
🛇 ⌇ 📺 ✕ 🛏 Ⅴ ♣ 🍴 cc

The Blue Royale, *11 Charles Street, Blackpool, FY1 3HD.*
Small friendly guest house caters for all.
Open: All Year
01253 628107 D: £13–£20 **S:** £13–£20
Beds: 3F 4D 3T 1S **Baths:** 4 En 1 Pr
🛇 📺 ✕ 🛏 Ⅴ ♣ 🍴

The Marina, *30 Gynn Avenue, Blackpool, Lancs, FY1 2LD.*
Blackpool's little gem. Quieter area, close to the Prom.
Open: Easter to Nov
01253 352833 Mrs Lockhart
D: £13–£19 **S:** £13–£19
Beds: 2F 1T 1D **Baths:** 1 En 1 Sh
🛇 (5) 📺 🛏 ✕ 🛏 Ⅴ 🍴 cc

Thistledome Guest House, *67 Alexandra Road, Blackpool, FY1 6HW.*
Small, friendly. 2 mins promenade between North and South piers.
Open: Easter to Nov
01253 408787 Mrs Jackson
D: £12–£14 **S:** £12–£14
Beds: 2F 4D 2S **Baths:** 2 En 2 Sh
🛇 📺 Ⅴ 🍴

The Grosvenor View Hotel, *7-9 King Edward Avenue, Blackpool, Lancs, FY2 9TD.*
Family-run hotel in quiet area of Blackpool. Quiet relaxed atmosphere.
Open: All Year
01253 352851 Mr Jackson
grosvenor_view@yahoo.co.uk
D: £16–£23 **S:** £16–£23
Beds: 2F 8D 5T 2S **Baths:** 10 Pr 7 Sh
🛇 🅿 (12) ⌇ 📺 ✕ 🛏 Ⅴ ♣ 🍴 ♿ cc

Beachcomber Hotel, *78 Reads Avenue, Blackpool, FY1 4DE.*
Comfortable centrally situated hotel; all rooms ensuite, off road parking.
Open: All Year
Grades: ETC 3 Diamond
01253 621622 Mr & Mrs Mcphail
Fax: 01253 299254
beachcomber@euphony.net
D: £17–£22 **S:** £17–£22
Beds: 2F 4D 3T 1S **Baths:** 10 En
🛇 🅿 (10) 📺 ✕ 🛏 Ⅴ 🍴 cc

Summerville Guest House, *132 Albert Road, Blackpool, FY1 4PN.*
Small and friendly guest house in the centre of town.
Open: All Year (not Xmas)
01253 621300 Mr & Mrs Nichol
dave@summerville132.freeserve.co.uk
D: £13–£19 **S:** £13–£19
Beds: 3F 3D 1T 1S **Baths:** 1 En 1 Sh
🛇 🅿 (2) 📺 ✕ 🛏 Ⅴ 🍴

Windsor Hotel, *53 Dean Street, Blackpool, FY4 1BP.*
Convenient all major attractions. Satisfaction for the more discerning guest. **Open:** All Year
Grades: ETC 3 Diamond, AA 3 Diamond
01253 346886 (also fax)
hazel@windsorhotel.co.uk
D: £17–£24 **S:** £19–£26
Beds: 2F 7D 2T 1S **Baths:** 12 En
🛇 🅿 (8) ⌇ 📺 ✕ 🛏 Ⅴ 🍴 cc

Cresta Hotel, *85 Whithnell Road, Blackpool, FY4 1HE.*
Family-run, all ensuite hotel adjacent to the pleasure beach.
Open: All Year
0800 0745584 (also fax) J Snelson
john@cresta-hotel.com
D: £12–£20 **S:** £13–£22
Beds: 3F 5D 1T **Baths:** 8 En
🛇 🅿 (3) 📺 ✕ 🛏 Ⅴ 🍴 cc

Dale House, *16 Dale Street, Blackpool, FY1 6EE.*
Friendly house. Central location near sea front. Home cooked food, personal service.
Open: All Year
01253 620548 (also fax)
D: £15–£18 **S:** £15–£18
Beds: 2F 2D 1T **Baths:** 3 En 1 Pr 1 Sh
🛇 🅿 (3) 📺 🛏 ✕ 🛏 Ⅴ ♣ 🍴

The Tudor Rose Original, *5 Withnell Road, Blackpool, Lancs, FY4 1HF.*
Lovely small hotel. Licensed bar, large dining room/separate tables.
Open: All Year
01253 343485 Mrs Thompson
D: £18–£25 **S:** £18–£25
Beds: 8D 2T 1S **Baths:** 11 En
📺 ✕ 🛏 Ⅴ ♣ 🍴

Brentwood, *50 Egerton Road, Blackpool, Lancs, FY1 2NW.*
Spacious corner position, all rooms 1st floor, no back rooms.
Open: Easter to Nov
01253 623612 Mr & Mrs Bohannon
D: £14–£20.50
Beds: 2F 3D **Baths:** 5 En
🛇 (3) 🅿 (5) 📺 🛏 Ⅴ 🍴

Normoss House Hotel, *13 Reads Avenue, Blackpool, Lancs, FY1 4BW.*
Small friendly comfortable guest house catering for families, couples and senior citizens.
Open: Easter to Dec
01253 621137 (also fax)
Mrs Brown
john-lyn@normosshouse.freeserve.co.uk
D: £16–£21 **S:** £16–£31
Beds: 5F 4D 1T **Baths:** 10 En
⛻ 📺 ✕ Ⅲ ⚓ ❋ ⚲

Red Court Private Hotel, *4 Harrowside West, Blackpool, Lancs, FY4 1NW.*
Sea, garden views to south of pleasure beach.
Open: Easter to Nov
01253 341510 Mr & Mrs Murphy
D: £15–£22 **S:** £15–£22
Beds: 4F 9D 5T **Baths:** 10 En 2 Sh
⛻ 📇 (6) 📺 ❦ ✕ Ⅲ ⚓ ⚲ cc

Langworthy House Hotel, *5 Lonsdale Road, Blackpool, Lancs, FY1 6EE.*
Beautiful friendly guest house. Central location, licensed bar, families welcome.
Open: Jan to Nov
01253 345914 Roger & Maggie Holdoway
D: £10–£25 **S:** £15–£25
Beds: 5F 6D **Baths:** 5 En 1 Sh
⛻ ⚡ 📺 Ⅲ ⚓

Lonsdale Hotel, *25 Cocker Street, Blackpool, Lancs, FY1 2BZ.*
Small friendly hotel situated in a quiet area of North Shore.
Open: All Year (not Xmas)
01253 621628 Mr Lonsdale
D: £16–£26 **S:** £19–£29
Beds: 6D 3T 1S **Baths:** 10 En
📇 (6) 📺 Ⅲ ⚓ ⚲ cc

Wilmar , *42 Osborne Road, Blackpool, Lancs, FY4 1HQ.*
Pauline and Nigel offer you a warm welcome to our homely guest house.
Open: All Year (not Xmas)
01253 346229 Mrs Hyde
D: £17.50–£25 **S:** £17.50–£25
Beds: 5D 1T 1S **Baths:** 6 En 1 Pr
⛻ (12) 📺 ✕ Ⅲ ⚓ ⚲

Fairmont Private Hotel, *40 King Edward Avenue, Blackpool, Lancs, FY2 9TA.*
Small family-run hotel situated in select area of North Shore, off Queens Promenade.
Open: All Year
01253 351050 D: £16.50–£21.50 **S:** £16.50–£21.50
Beds: 4F 2D 4S **Baths:** 10 En
⛻ (2) 📺 ✕ Ⅲ ⚓ ⚲ cc

Gables Balmoral Hotel, *Balmoral Road, South Shore, Blackpool, Lancs, FY4 1HR.*
An exceptional 70 bedroomed hotel situated in a prime position, opposite Blackpool pleasure beach.
Open: All Year
01253 345432 Fax: 01253 406058
david_gables-balmoral@virgin.co.uk
D: £25–£39 **S:** £30–£50
Beds: 16F 24D 15T 13S
⛻ ⚡ 📺 ❦ ✕ Ⅲ ⚓ ❋ ⚲ ♿ cc

The Seymour Hotel, *30 Queens Promenade, Blackpool, Lancashire, FY2 9RN.*
Luxury beach front hotel, lift to all floors, car park, dancing and regular entertainment.
Open: All Year
01253 352789 Mr Arnett
seymour@hotel53.freeserve.co.uk
D: £22–£26 **S:** £24–£28
Beds: 1F 1D 3T **Baths:** 20 Pr
⛻ 📇 (10) ⚡ 📺 ❦ ✕ Ⅲ ⚓ ❋ ⚲ ♿ cc

Northlands Hotel, *31-33 Hornby Road, Blackpool, FY1 4QG.*
The Northlands Hotel is in the centre of Blackpool, close to the Winter Gardens.
Open: All Year
01253 625795 (also fax)
northlands.hotel@virgin.net
D: £17–£25 **S:** £17–£25
Beds: 5F 19D **Baths:** 21 En 2 Sh
⛻ 📺 ✕ Ⅲ ⚓ ❋ ⚲ cc

Bolton by Bowland

SD7849

Middle Flass Lodge, *Settle Road, Bolton by Bowland, Clitheroe, Yorkshire, BB7 4NY.*
Idyllic countryside location. Chef prepared cuisine. Cosy rooms. Friendly welcome.
Open: All Year
Grades: ETC 4 Diamond, AA 4 Diamond
01200 447259 Mrs Simpson
Fax: 01200 447300
D: £22–£30 **S:** £27–£35
Beds: 1F 2D 2T **Baths:** 5 En suite
⛻ 📇 (24) ⚡ ✕ Ⅲ ⚓ ⚲ cc

Bolton-le-Sands

SD4868 🍺 *Robin Hood, Railway Inn*

Row-Bar, *4 Whin Grove, Bolton-le-Sands, Carnforth, Lancs, LA5 8DD.*
Friendly family-run private home close to M6 and Lakes.
Open: All Year (not Xmas)
01524 735369 B Udall
D: £16 **S:** fr £20
Beds: 2D **Baths:** 2 En
⛻ 📇 (2) ⚡ 📺 Ⅲ ⚓ ⚲

Burnley

SD8332 🍺 *Red Rock, Bay Horse, Mama Mia at Crossways*

Windsor House, *71 Church Street, Padiham, Burnley, Lancs, BB12 8JH.*
Large family run Victorian house, with a huge Lancashire welcome.
Open: All Year (not Xmas)
Grades: ETC 2 Diamond
01282 773271 Mrs Stinton
D: £18 **S:** £18
Beds: 1D 3T 3S **Baths:** 1 Pr 3 Sh
⛻ (10) 📇 (8) ⚡ 📺 ✕ Ⅲ ⚓ ⚲

Planning a longer stay? Always ask for any special rates

Capernwray

SD5371

Capernwray House, *Capernwray, Carnforth, Lancs, LA6 1AE.*
Beautiful country house. Panoramic views. Tastefully decorated throughout. Close Lakes, Dales, Lancaster.
Open: All Year (not Xmas)
Grades: ETC 4 Diamond, Silver Award
01524 732363 (also fax)
Mrs Smith
thesmiths@capernwrayhouse.com
D: £21–£23 **S:** £30
Beds: 2D 1T 1S **Baths:** 3 En 1 Sh
⛻ (5) 📇 (8) ⚡ 📺 ✕ Ⅲ ⚓ ⚲ cc

Carnforth

SD4970 🍺 *Malt Shovel, George Washington, County Hotel*

Capernwray House, *Capernwray, Carnforth, Lancs, LA6 1AE.*
Open: All Year (not Xmas)
Grades: ETC 4 Diamond, Silver Award
01524 732363 (also fax)
Mrs Smith
thesmiths@capernwrayhouse.com
D: £21–£23 **S:** £30
Beds: 2D 1T 1S **Baths:** 3 En 1 Sh
⛻ (5) 📇 (8) ⚡ 📺 ✕ Ⅲ ⚓ ⚲ cc
Beautiful country house. Panoramic views. Tastefully decorated throughout. Close Lakes, Dales, Lancaster.

Cotestone Farm, *Sand Lane, Warton, Carnforth, Lancs, LA5 9NH.*
Near Leighton Moss RSPB Reserve, Lancaster/Morecambe, Lakes & Dales.
Open: All Year (not Xmas)
Grades: ETC 3 Diamond
01524 732418 G Close
D: £16 **S:** £17
Beds: 1F 1D 1T 1S **Baths:** 2 Sh
⛻ 📇 (4) 📺 ❦ Ⅲ ⚓ ⚲

Galley Hall Farm, *Shore Road, Carnforth, Lancashire, LA5 9HZ.*
C17th farm house, lovely coastal and Lakeland views and friendly welcome.
Open: All Year (not Xmas/New Year)
Grades: ETC 4 Diamond
01524 732544 V Casson
D: £18 **S:** £18
Beds: 1T 1D 1S **Baths:** 1 Sh
⚡ 📺 ❦ Ⅲ ⚓ ⚲

Caton

SD5364

Kilcredan, *14 Brookhouse Road, Caton, Lancaster, Lancashire, LA2 9QT.*
Friendly welcome set in the Lune Valley. Ideal for walking.
Open: All Year
Grades: ETC 1 Diamond
01524 770271 Miss Beattie
D: £18 **S:** £18
Beds: 1F 1D 1T 1S **Baths:** 1 En 1 Sh
⛻ 📇 (3) 📺 ❦ Ⅲ ⚓ ⚲

B&B owners may vary rates - be sure to check when booking

Chipping

SD6243

Carrside Farm, *Chipping, Preston, Lancs, PR3 2TS.*
Working sheep farm with hill views in the forest of Bowland.
Open: All Year
01995 61590 J Cowgill
D: £25–£30 **S:** £25–£30
Beds: 1D 1F 1S **Baths:** 2 En 1 Pr 1 Sh
🛇 (5) 🄿 (8) ⼴ �📺 🐾 🛋 🖤 👶

Chorley

SD5817   ⬥ *The Hartwood, Seaview Inn*

Crowtress Cottage Guest House,
190 Preston Road, Chorley, Lancashire, PR6 7AZ.
C18th country cottage complemented with Lancashire hospitality.
Open: All Year
Grades: ETC 3 Diamond
01257 269380 J Wrenall
D: £20–£30 **S:** fr £25
Beds: 1D 1T 1S **Baths:** 1 En 1 Sh

The Roost, *81 Pall Mall, Chorley, Lancs, PR7 3LT.*
Late Victorian, homely atmosphere. Five mins' walk market, town centre.
Open: All Year
01257 263856 Mr & Mrs Edelston
D: £18 **S:** £20
Beds: 1T **Baths:** 1 Sh
⼴ 📺 ✕ 🛋 👶

Claughton (Lancaster)

SD5666   ⬥ *Royal Oak*

Low House Farm, *Claughton, Lancaster, Lancs., LA2 9LA.*
Open: All Year (not Xmas/New Year)
Grades: ETC 3 Diamond
015242 21260
Mrs Harvey
shirley@lunevalley.freeserve.co.uk
D: £20 **S:** £20–£25
Beds: 1F 1D 1S
Baths: 1 En 1 Pr 1 Sh
🛇 🄿 (4) ⼴ 📺 🐾 🛋 🖤 👶
Enjoy a warm welcome on our working mixed dairy farm in the heart of the picturesque Lune Valley. Guest lounge and large garden. Ideal base for Lakes, Yorkshire Dales and N.W. Coast. M6 J34 6 miles.

Clayton Le Dale

SD6733   ⬥ *Royal Oak, The Traders*

2 Rose Cottage, *Longsight Road, Clayton le Dale, Blackburn, Lancs, BB1 9EX.*
Picturesque cottage, gateway to Ribble Valley. Comfortable, fully equipped rooms.
Open: All Year
01254 813223
M Adderley
Fax: 01254 813831
bbrose.cott@talk21.com
D: fr £19 **S:** fr £23
Beds: 1F 1D 3T **Baths:** 3 En 1 Pr
🛇 🄿 (4) 📺 🐾 🛋 🖤 👶 cc

Clitheroe

SD7441   ⬥ *Swan With Two Necks, Edisford Bridge Inn, Edisford Inn, Old Post House*

Selborne House, *Back Commons, Clitheroe, Lancs, BB7 2DX.*
Detached house on quiet lane giving peace and tranquillity. Excellent for walking, birdwatching, fishing.
Open: All Year
Grades: ETC 3 Diamond
01200 423571 (also fax)
J V Barnes
judithv.barnes@LineOne.net
D: £18.50–£20 **S:** £21–£22.50
Beds: 1F 2D 1T **Baths:** 4 En
🛇 (1) 🄿 (4) 📺 🐾 ✕ 🛋 🖤 👶

Brooklands, *9 Pendle Road, Clitheroe, Lancs, BB7 1JQ.*
A warm welcome. Detached comfortable Victorian home. Town centre nearby.
Open: All Year
Grades: ETC 3 Diamond
01200 422797 (also fax)
J Lord
kenandjean@tesco.net
D: £16–£19.50 **S:** £17–£22
Beds: 1D 2T **Baths:** 1 En 1 Sh
🛇 🄿 (5) 📺 🐾 🛋 🖤 👶 cc

Colne

SD8940   ⬥ *Hare & Hounds, White Bear*

Wickets, *148 Keighley Road, Colne, Lancs, BB8 0PJ.*
Edwardian family home overlooking open countryside, comfortable and attractive bedrooms.
Open: All Year (not Xmas)
Grades: ETC 4 Diamond
01282 862002 Mrs Etherington
Fax: 01282 859675
wickets@colne148.fsnet.co.uk
D: £18–£21 **S:** £18–£22
Beds: 1D 1T 1S **Baths:** 1 En 1 Pr 1 Sh
🛇 (11) 🄿 (1) ⼴ 📺 🛋 🖤 👶

Higher Wanless Farm, *Red Lane, Colne, Lancs, BB8 7JP.*
Beautifully situated, canalside, lovely walking, ideal for business people, Mill, shops etc.
Open: Jan to Nov
01282 865301 C Mitson
Fax: 01282 865823
wanlessfarm@bun.com
D: £20–£24 **S:** £20–£24
Beds: 1F 1T 1S **Baths:** 1 En 1 Sh
🛇 (3) 🄿 (4) 📺 🛋 🖤 👶

Conder Green

SD4656   ⬥ *The Stork*

Stork Hotel, *Conder Green, Lancaster, Lancashire, LA2 0AN.*
Traditional country inn 3 miles from Lancaster and close to Glasson Dock.
Open: All Year
Grades: ETC 3 Diamond
01524 751234 A Cragg
D: fr £20 **S:** fr £24.50
Beds: 1F 3D 3T 2S **Baths:** 9 Pr
🛇 (20) 📺 🐾 ✕ 🛋 🖤 👶

Fleetwood

SD3247

Chavock Guest House, *116 London Street, Fleetwood, Lancs, FY7 6EU.*
Licensed guest house.
Open: All Year (not Xmas/New Year)
01253 771196 (also fax)
Mr McEvoy
suemcevoy@justtalk21.com
D: £14–£19 **S:** £15–£20
Beds: 1F 2D 1S 1T **Baths:** 1 En
🛇 🄿 📺 🐾 ✕ 🛋 🖤 ❄ 👶

Garstang

SD4945   ⬥ *Royal Oak, Wheatsheaf Inn, The Flag, Th' Owd Tithe Barn, Crofters Hotel, Guy's Thatched Hamlet*

Sandbriggs, *Lancaster Road, Garstang, Preston, Lancs, PR3 1JA.*
Comfortable, convenient, secluded private house and gardens with secure parking.
Open: All Year
01995 603080 (also fax)
Mr Wilkinson
D: £15–£18 **S:** fr £15
Beds: 1D 2T **Baths:** 1 Pr 2 Sh
🛇 (4) 🄿 (10) 📺 🐾 🛋 👶

Calderbank Country Lodge,
Garstang, Preston, Lancs, PR3 1UL.
Calderbank restaurant and hotel. Small Georgian residence in the forest.
Open: All Year
01995 604384 B Jackson
D: £20 **S:** £20
Beds: 1T 1S **Baths:** 1 En
🛇 🄿 📺 ✕ 🛋 🖤 👶 cc

Guys Thatched Hamlet, *Canal Side, Garstang, Preston, Lancs, PR3 0RS.*
Thatched canalside inn and hotel with cricket ground, bowling green.
Open: All Year
01995 640010 R Wilkinson
Fax: 01995 640141
guysth@aol.com
D: fr £19 **S:** fr £38
Beds: 10F 11D 32T **Baths:** 53 Pr
🛇 🄿 📺 🐾 ✕ 🛋 🖤 👶 ♿

Ashdene, *Parkside Lane, A6, Garstang, Preston, Lancs, PR3 0JA.*
Family run detached house 6 miles from M6 J33-32.
Open: All Year
01995 602676 J Wrathall
D: £18–£20 **S:** £22–£25
Beds: 2D 1T **Baths:** 3 En
🛇 🄿 (5) 📺 🐾 🛋 👶

Goosnargh

SD5536   ⬥ *Green Man, The Grapes*

Isles Field Barn, *Syke House Lane, Goosnargh, Preston, Lancs, PR3 2EN.*
Spacious accommodation surrounded by beautiful countryside. Hearty breakfast, friendly welcome.
Open: All Year
01995 640398 Mr McHugh
D: £19 **S:** £19
Beds: 1F 1D 1T **Baths:** 3 En
🛇 🄿 (6) 📺 🛋 🖤 👶

1 Willow Grove, Goosnargh, Preston,
PR3 2DE.
Private house, village location, close to
M6, M55, Blackpool, Lancaster.
Open: All Year (not Xmas)
01772 865455 Mrs Dewhurst
D: £15 **S:** £15
Beds: 1D 1T 1S **Baths:** 1 Sh
🛏 🛇 🅟 📺 🛇 📖 🛇 🖺

Great Mitton

SD7138

Aspinall Arms Hotel, Great Mitton,
Clitheroe, Lancs, *BB7 9PQ.*
Originally the ferryman's house, the
Aspinall Arms dates back to coach and
horses times.
Open: All Year
01254 826223 Mr Morrell
michael@aspinall-arms.freeserve.co.uk
D: £22.50 **S:** £30
Beds: 2D 1S **Baths:** 3 En
🅟 (50) 📺 📖 🛇 🖺 cc

Helmshore

SD7821 🍺 White Horse

The Willows, 41 Cherrytree Way,
Helmshore, Rossendale, Lancs, *BB4 4JZ.*
The Willows - warm welcome awaits,
beautiful views, swimming pool.
Open: All Year (not Xmas)
Grades: ETC 4 Diamond
01706 212698 Mrs Tod
fred@mitchell1.btinternet.com
D: £18–£22
Beds: 2D **Baths:** 2 En
🛏 🅟 (2) 🛇 📺 📖 🖺

Hesketh Bank

SD4423

The Becconsall Hotel, 25 Station
Road, Hesketh Bank, Preston, *PR4 6SP.*
Friendly local pub restaurant in semi-rural
location.
Open: All Year
01772 815313 D: £17.50 **S:** £22.50
Beds: 3D
🅟 (20) 📺 ✕ 📖 🛇 🖺 cc

Heysham

SD4161 🍓 Strawberry Gardens

It'll Do, 15 Oxcliffe Road, Heysham,
Morecambe, Lancs., *LA3 1PR.*
Ideal for touring Lake District Heysham
Port. Lancaster M6.
Open: Jan to Dec
Grades: ETC 3 Diamond
01524 850763 Mrs Peter
D: fr £14 **S:** fr £15
Beds: 1T 1D **Baths:** 1 Sh
🛏 🅟 (4) 📺 🍴 📖 🖺

BATHROOMS

Pr - Private

Sh - Shared

En - Ensuite

Hurst Green

SD6838 🍺 The Shireburn

Shireburn Arms Hotel, Whalley Road,
Hurst Green, Clitheroe, Lancs, *BB6 9QJ.*
A warm friendly welcome, excellent inn
and restaurant, unrivalled views.
Open: All Year
Grades: ETC 2 Star, AA 2 Star
01254 826518 S J Alcock
Fax: 01254 826208
sales@shireburnarms.fsnet.co.uk
D: £32.50–£42.50 **S:** £45–£65
Beds: 1S 2F 12D 3T **Baths:** 18 En
🛏 🅟 (50) 🛇 📺 🍴 ✕ 📖 🛇 ✳ 🖺 🚿 cc

Lancaster

SD4761 🍺 White Cross, Boot & Shoe

Lancaster Town House, 11/12
Newton Terrace, Caton Road, Lancaster,
Lancashire, *LA1 3PB.*
Open: All Year
Grades: ETC 3 Diamond, AA 3 Diamond
01524 65527 Mrs Hedge-Holmes
hedge-holmes@talk21.com
D: £20–£25 **S:** £19–£25
Beds: 1F 3D 1T 3S **Baths:** All En
🛏 🅟 📺 📖 🛇 🖺 cc
Guest house on outskirts of historic
Lancaster, ideal for visiting coast, lakes
and Lune Valley. 1 mile from J34 on M6.
All rooms ensuite with text TV, radio-
alarms, hairdryers and hospitality trays.
Unrestricted off-road parking available
and secure for cycles/motor cycles.

Shakespeare Hotel, 96 St
Leonardgate, Lancaster, Lancs., *LA1 1NN.*
City centre multi-award-winning B&B.
Very special breakfasts.
Open: All Year (not Xmas)
01524 841041
B Sylvester
D: £20 **S:** £20–£30
Beds: 2F 3D 1T 2S **Baths:** 8 En
🛏 🅟 (3) 🛇 📺 📖 🛇 🖺

Longridge

SD6037 🍺 Alston Arms, White Bull, Heathcotes

14 Whittingham Road, Longridge,
Preston, Lancs, *PR3 2AA.*
Homely, hearty breakfasts, scenic area,
walking, sports, shopping, motorway
accessibility.
Open: All Year
01772 783992 D Morley
D: £18 **S:** £18
Beds: 1F 1T 1S **Baths:** 1 Sh
🛏 🅟 (4) 📺 📖 🛇 🖺

Jenkinsons Farmhouse, Longridge,
Alston, Preston, Lancs, *PR3 3BD.*
Set in idyllic countryside. Perfect
stopover from London to Scotland.
Open: All Year (not Xmas)
Grades: AA 4 Diamond
01772 782624
Mrs Ibison
D: fr £20 **S:** fr £23.50
Beds: 2D 3T 1S **Baths:** 4 Sh
🛏 (12) 🅟 (10) 🛇 📺 🍴 📖 🖺

Longton

SD4726 🍺 Rose & Crown, Midge Hall

Moorside Villa, Drumacre Lane West,
Longton, Preston, Lancs., *PR4 4SB.*
Comfortable and homely accommodation
close to M6 and M62, M65 access.
Open: All Year (not Xmas)
Grades: ETC 4 Diamond
01772 616612 D: £22–£27.50 **S:** £25–£30
Beds: 2D 1T **Baths:** 2 En
🅟 (6) 🛇 📺 📖 🛇 🖺

Willow Cottage, Longton Bypass,
Longton, Preston, Lancs, *PR4 4RA.*
Old cottage set in beautiful gardens and
countryside with its own horse stud farm.
Open: All Year
01772 617570 Mrs Caunce
D: £22–£25 **S:** £22–£25
Beds: 3D **Baths:** 1 En 1 Pr 2 Sh
🛏 🅟 (10) 📺 ✕ 📖 🖺

Lower Thurnham

SD4655

Thurnham Mill Hotel, Thurnham,
Lancaster, *LA2 0BD.*
Located in the heart of a picturesque and
historical area close to Lancaster.
Open: All Year
Grades: ETC 2 Star
01524 752852 Fax: 01524 752477
D: £27.25 **S:** £39.50
Beds: 6F 3D 8D **Baths:** 17 En
🛏 🅟 (80) 🛇 📺 🍴 ✕ 📖 🛇 🖺 🚿 cc

Lytham St Annes

SD3327 🍺 Salter's Wharf, The Fairhaven, The
Queensway, Brewers Fayre

Sea Croft Hotel, 5 Eastbank Road,
Lytham St Annes, Lancs, *FY8 1ND.*
A warm welcome in friendly, family-run
licensed hotel adjacent to promenade
and town centre.
Open: All Year (not Xmas)
01253 721806 (also fax)
Mr Taylor
D: £19–£20 **S:** £15–£21
Beds: 5F 1D 1T 2S **Baths:** 8 En 1 Sh
🛏 🅟 (5) 📺 ✕ 📖 🛇 🖺

Monarch Hotel, 29 St Annes Road
East, Lytham St Annes, Lancs, *FY8 1TA.*
Clean, comfortable hotel with great food,
licensed. Aromatherapy, reflexology
available.
Open: All Year (not Xmas)
Grades: ETC 3 Diamond
01253 720464 (also fax)
Mr Churchill
churchill@monarch91.freeserve.co.uk
D: £21–£25 **S:** £19–£25
Beds: 2F 2D 3T 3S **Baths:** 7 En 1 Pr
🛏 🅟 (8) 📺 ✕ 📖 🛇 🖺

Harcourt, 21 Richmond Road, Lytham St
Annes, Lancs, *FY8 1PE.*
Small private family hotel, town centre.
200 yds to beach and attractions.
Open: All Year
01253 722299 D: £16–£19 **S:** £16–£18
Beds: 3F 3D 1T 3S **Baths:** 5 En 5 Sh
🛏 🅟 (6) 📺 📖 🛇 🖺

Gaydon Hotel, *33 Derbe Road, Lytham St Annes, Lancs, FY8 1NJ.*
Beautifully maintained Victorian guest house. Very friendly welcome assured.
Open: All Year
01253 722082 Mrs Crichton
D: £16–£40 **S:** £16–£40
Beds: 2F 1D 1T 2S **Baths:** 3 En 1 Sh
🛏 ₽ (4) 📺 🔭 ✕ 🞖 📶 ♨ 🕭

Parkwater, *27-33 Fairhaven Road, Lytham St Annes, Lancs, FY8 1NN.*
Adjacent promenade sea front and pleasure island complex family hotel.
Open: All Year
01253 725106 Fax: 01253 720863
enquiries@parkwater.co.uk
D: £33–£35 **S:** £33–£35
Beds: 15F 12T 16D 7S **Baths:** 50 En
🛏 ₽ (30) 📺 🔭 ✕ 🞖 📶 ♨ 🕭 cc

Melrose Sandpiper Hotel, *37 South Promenade, Lytham St Annes, Lancs, FY8 1LS.*
Family run hotel, overlooking gardens and sea. Excellent food and accommodation. **Open:** Jan to Dec
01253 725117 (also fax) Mrs Bennet
melrose_sandpiper@tinyonline.co.uk
D: fr £25 **S:** £25–£32
Beds: 4F 12D 8S 4T **Baths:** 28 En
🛏 ₽ (15) ✔ 📺 🔭 ✕ 🞖 📶 ♨ 🕭 cc

Strathmore Hotel, *305 Clifton Drive South, Lytham St Annes, Lancs, FY8 1HN.*
Few minutes' walk promenade, swimming pool, pier, beaches St Annes' main shopping centre. **Open:** All Year
Grades: ETC 3 Diamond, AA 3 Diamond, RAC 3 Diamond
01253 725478 D: £19–£23 **S:** £19–£23
Beds: 4D 5T 1S **Baths:** 5 En 5 Sh
🛏 (9) ₽ (10) 📺 ✕ 🞖 ♨ 🕭

The Breverton Hotel, *64 Orchard Road, Lytham St Annes, Lancs, FY8 1PJ.*
Detached licensed family hotel, garden, conservatory, homely atmosphere children welcome.
Open: Mar to Nov
01253 726179 Mrs Mulholland
D: £18–£20 **S:** £18–£20
Beds: 8F 1T 2D **Baths:** 11 En 1 Sh
🛏 ₽ (5) 📺 🔭 ✕ 🞖 📶 🕭 🕭

Clifton Park Hotel, *299-301 Clifton Drive South, Lytham St Annes, Lancs, FY8 1HN.*
Now called Clifton Park Hotel, licensed, car park, parties welcome. Two minutes to beach.
Open: All Year
01253 725801 Mr Lord
Fax: 01253 725735
reservations@
cliftonparkhotel.freeserve.co.uk
D: £25–£38 **S:** £27–£40
Beds: 4F 13D 7T 2S **Baths:** 23 Pr 3 Sh
🛏 ₽ (10) 📺 ✕ 🞖 ♨ 🕭 cc

Aileena, *39 Derbe Road, Lytham St Annes, Lancs, FY8 1NJ.*
Lovely Victorian house, 40 yds from sea, warm welcome, excellent breakfasts.
Open: All Year (not Xmas)
01253 721897 D: £17–£18 **S:** £18–£19
Beds: 2F 3D 1T 2S **Baths:** 6 En 2 Sh
🛏 ₽ (4) 📺 🞖 🕭

SD6531 🍺 *Royal Oak, The Traders*

2 Rose Cottage, *Longsight Road, Clayton le Dale, Blackburn, Lancs, BB1 9EX.*
Picturesque cottage, gateway to Ribble Valley. Comfortable, fully equipped rooms.
Open: All Year
01254 813223 M Adderley
Fax: 01254 813831
bbrose.cott@talk21.com
D: fr £19 **S:** fr £23
Beds: 1F 1D 2T **Baths:** 3 En 1 Pr
🛏 ₽ (4) 📺 🔭 🞖 📺 🕭 cc

SD4364

Warwick Hotel, *394 Marine Road East, Morecambe, Lancs, LA4 5AN.*
Open: All Year (not Xmas/New Year)
Grades: ETC 4 Diamond RAC 4 Diamond, Sparkling Award
01524 418151 A & A Leach
Fax: 01524 427235
D: £23–£27 **S:** £25–£30
Beds: 3T 7D 3S **Baths:** 13 Pr
🛏 ₽ ✔ 📺 ✕ 🞖 📺 🕭
Non-smoking hotel overlooking bay and South Lakeland Hills, beyond ideal for discerning guest and over over 40's. A Victorian terraced property on the promenade. Only 30 minutes from the lakes and dales. Easy access to motorway, junction 34.

Harwood House Hotel, *1 Chatsworth Road, Westminster Road, Morecambe, Lancs, LA4 4JG.*
2 mins walk to seafront, licensed restaurant and residents' bar.
Open: All Year
01524 412845 J R Whitworth
Fax: 01524 409138
hhhotel@supanet.com
D: £15–£22 **S:** £15–£22
Beds: 1F 2T 6D 4S **Baths:** 2 En 1 Pr 2 Sh
🛏 (4) 📺 🔭 ✕ 🞖 📺 🕭

The Trevelyan , *27 Seaview Parade, West End Road, Morecambe, Lancs, LA4 4DJ.*
Comfortable guest house. Glorious Morecambe Bay. Ideal touring base.
Open: All Year
Grades: ETC 2 Diamond
01524 412013 G Catterall
thetrevelyan@supanet.com
D: £15–£17.50 **S:** £15
Beds: 2F 1T 4D 4S **Baths:** 1 En 4 Sh
🛏 ₽ 📺 ✕ 🞖 📺 🕭

SD4723 🍺 *Black Horse*

The Barn Guest House, *204 Liverpool Old Road, Much Hoole, Preston, Lancs., PR4 4QB.*
Semi rural location off the A59 between Preston and Southport.
Open: All Year (not Xmas/New Year)
Grades: ETC 3 Diamond
01772 612654 L Gabbott
D: £20–£22.50 **S:** £25–£27.50
Beds: 1F 1T 1S **Baths:** 2 Sh
🛏 ₽ (3) 📺 🔭 🞖 🕭

SD8637

Lovett House, *6 Howard Street, off Carr Road, Nelson, Lancs, BB9 7SZ.*
Extremely comfortable rooms; Delicious breakfasts - served late! Relaxing, friendly atmosphere.
Open: All Year
01282 697352 L A Helm
Fax: 02182 700186
lovetthouse@cwcom.net
D: £18.50–£24 **S:** £20.50–£26
Beds: 1F 1T **Baths:** 2 En 1 Sh
🛏 📺 ✕ 🞖 📺 🕭

SD4108 🍺 *Briars Hall Hotel, Ship Inn*

The Meadows, *New Sutch Farm, Sutch Lane, Ormskirk, Lancashire, L40 4BU.*
Beautiful C17th farmhouse. Ground floor guest rooms. Excellent breakfasts.
Open: All Year (not Xmas)
Grades: ETC 4 Diamond
01704 894048 D: fr £17.50 **S:** fr £19.50
Beds: 2D 1S **Baths:** 2 En 1 Pr
📺 📺 📺 🕭

SD7933 🍺 *Red Rock, Bay Horse, Mama Mia at Crossways*

Windsor House, *71 Church Street, Padiham, Burnley, Lancs, BB12 8JH.*
Large family run Victorian house, with a huge Lancashire welcome.
Open: All Year (not Xmas)
Grades: ETC 2 Diamond
01282 773271 Mrs Stinton
D: £18 **S:** £18
Beds: 1D 3T 3S **Baths:** 1 Pr 3 Sh
🛏 (10) ₽ (8) ✔ 📺 🞖 📺 🕭

SD3647 🍺 *Saracen's Head, Black Bull, Fernhill Pub, Bourne Arms*

Townfoot Cottage, *Back Lane, Preesall, Poulton le Fylde, Lancs., FY6 0NG.*
Country cottage, comfortable accommodation, good food, picturesque setting, relaxing break.
Open: All Year (not Xmas/New Year)
01253 812681 C Richards
D: £17–£19 **S:** £20–£25
Beds: 1F 1D **Baths:** 1 Sh
🛏 ₽ (3) ✔ 📺 📺 🕭

SD5329 🍺 *Welcome Tavern*

Stanley Guest House, *7 Stanley Terrace, Preston, PR1 8JE.*
Five minutes' walk to town centre, overlooking quiet bowling area.
Open: All Year
01772 253366 Fax: 01772 252802
stanley.guest.house@prestonlancs.freese
rve.co.uk
D: £16–£18 **S:** £20–£25
Beds: 3F 2D 2S **Baths:** 2 En 1 Sh
🛏 ₽ (5) 📺 🔭 ✕ 🞖 📺 🕭 cc

Ribchester

SD6435 🍺 *Hall's Arms, Punch Bowl, Black Bull, White Bull*

New House Farm, Preston Road, Ribchester, Preston, Lancs, PR3 3XL.
Old renovated farmhouse, rare breeds.
Open: All Year
01254 878954 J & R Bamber
D: £18–£22 **S:** £22–£25
Beds: 1F 1D 1T **Baths:** 3 En
🛇 (4) 🄿 (8) ⅙ 📺 🎟 🖤 🕯

Smithy Farm, Huntingdon Hall Lane, Dutton, Ribchester, Preston, Lancs, PR3 2ZT.
Unspoilt countryside 15 mins M6.
Friendly hospitality, children half price.
Open: Mar to Nov
01254 878250
M Jackson
D: £12.50 **S:** £18
Beds: 1F 1D 1T **Baths:** 1 Sh
🛇 🄿 📺 🦃 ✕ 🕯

Roughlee

SD8440 🍺 *Barley Mow, Harpers Inn*

Thorneyholme Farm Cottage,
Barley New Road, Roughlee, Burnley, Lancashire, BB12 9LH.
A warm welcome awaits you at this lovely Georgian farmhouse.
Open: All Year (not Xmas)
01282 612452 D: £20–£25 **S:** £20–£25
Beds: 1F 1D 1T 1S **Baths:** 2 En
🛇 🄿 ⅙ 📺 🖤 🕯 ♿

Scorton

SD5049

Woodacre Hall Farm, Scorton, Preston, Lancs, PR3 1BN.
Working farm built in the late 1600's, Home from Home.
Open: Easter to Nov
Grades: ETC 3 Diamond
01995 602253 (also fax) Ms Whitaker
D: £17–£19 **S:** £20–£22
Beds: 2D **Baths:** 1 En, 1 Pr
🄿 (4) 📺 🦃 ✕ 🕯

Silverdale

SD4675 🍺 *The Ship*

The Limes Village Guest House, 23 Stankelt Road, Silverdale, Carnforth, Lancs, LA5 0TF.
A lovely Victorian house. Very comfortable. Excellent food.
Open: All Year
01524 701454 (also fax)
Mrs Livesey
D: £20–£22
Beds: 1F 1D 1T **Baths:** 3 Pr
🛇 🄿 (3) ⅙ 📺 ✕ 🖤 🕯 ♿ 🕯

Stonyhurst

SD6939

Alden Cottage, Kemple End, Birdy Brow, Stonyhurst, Clitheroe, Lancashire, BB7 9QY.
Luxury accommodation in an idyllic C17th beamed cottage.
Open: All Year (not Xmas/New Year)
Grades: ETC 4 Diamond / Silver award
01254 826468 Mrs Carpenter
carpenter@aldencottage.f9.co.uk
D: £24.50 **S:** £25.50
Beds: 1T 2D **Baths:** 1 En 2 Pr
🄿 (3) ⅙ 📺 🖤 🕯

Thornton Cleveleys

SD3442

Beacholme Guest House, 38 Beach Road, Thornton-Cleveleys, Lancs, FY5 1EQ.
Small, friendly, non-smoking guest house, close to tramline and seashore.
Open: All Year
01253 855350 Ms Nicholson
beach_holme@hotmail.com
D: fr £15 **S:** fr £15
Beds: 2D 1T 2S **Baths:** 1 En 1 Sh
🛇 🄿 (2) ⅙ 📺 ✕ 🖤 🕯 ♿ ♿

Esperance Villa Guest House, 30 Ellerbeck Road, Thornton-Cleveleys, Lancs, FY5 1DH.
Family run hotel, close to shops, Blackpool and Fleetwood bingo and clubs.
Open: All Year (not Xmas/New Year)
01253 853513 Mrs Duckett
D: £15–£17 **S:** £15–£17
Beds: 1F 4D 1T 1S **Baths:** 2 Sh
🛇 🄿 (3) 📺 ✕ 🖤 🕯

Trawden

SD9138 🍺 *Sun Inn*

Middle Beardshaw Head Farm,
Trawden, Colne, Lancs, BB8 9PP.
C18th beamed farmhouse in picturesque setting of woodland, pools and meadows.
Open: All Year (not Xmas)
01282 865257 Mrs Mann
D: £18.50–£20 **S:** £18.50–£20
Beds: 1F 2D 3S **Baths:** 1 En 1 Sh
🛇 🄿 (10) 📺 ✕ 🖤 🕯

Tunstall

SD6073 🍺 *Lunesdale Arms*

Barnfield Farm, Tunstall, Kirkby Lonsdale, Carnforth, Lancs, LA6 2QP.
1702 family farmhouse on a 200 acre working farm. **Open:** All Year (not Xmas)
01542 74284 (also fax)
Mrs Stephenson
D: fr £16 **S:** fr £17.50
Beds: 1F/T 1D **Baths:** 2 Sh
🛇 🄿 ⅙ 📺 🖤 🕯

Waddington

SD7243 🍺 *Moorcock Inn, Duke of York*

Moorcock Inn, Slaidburn Road, Waddington, Clitheroe, Lancs, BB7 3AA.
A warm welcome awaits at this friendly country inn.
Open: All Year
Grades: ETC 2 Star
01200 422333 F M Fillary
D: £30–£35 **S:** £38–£42
Beds: 3D 8T **Baths:** 11 Pr
🛇 🄿 (150) 📺 🦃 ✕ 🖤 🕯 ♿ CC

Waddington Arms, Clitheroe Road, Waddington, Clitheroe, Lancs, BB7 3HP.
Traditional country inn, real beer, real food, real bedrooms.
Open: All Year
01200 423262 P Warburton
D: £25–£35 **S:** £35–£45
Beds: 4D 2T **Baths:** 6 En
🛇 🄿 (50) ⅙ 📺 🦃 ✕ 🖤 🕯 ✳ ♿ CC

Warton

SD5072 🍺 *Malt Shovel, George Washington*

Cotestone Farm, Sand Lane, Warton, Carnforth, Lancs, LA5 9NH.
Near Leighton Moss RSPB Reserve, Lancaster/Morecambe, Lakes & Dales.
Open: All Year (not Xmas)
Grades: ETC 3 Diamond
01524 732418 G Close
D: £16 **S:** £17
Beds: 1F 1D 1T 1S **Baths:** 2 Sh
🛇 🄿 (4) 📺 🦃 🖤 🕯

Waterfoot

SD8322

729 Bacup Road, Waterfoot, Rossendale, Lancs, BB4 7EU.
In the heart of the picturesque Rossendale Valley. Food everyday.
Open: All Year
01706 214493 P Stannard
Fax: 01706 215371
info@theroyal-hotel.co.uk
D: £23.50–£30 **S:** £25–£35
Beds: 1F 5D 2T 5S **Baths:** 13 En
🛇 🄿 (10) 📺 🦃 ✕ 🖤 🕯 CC

Whittington

SD6076 🍺 *Dragon's Head*

The Dragon's Head, Main Street, Whittington, Carnforth, LA6 2NY.
Small country pub in Lune valley 2 miles west of Kirkby Lonsdale B6254.
Open: All Year
015242 72383 D: £20–£25 **S:** £20–£25
Beds: 1F 1D 1S **Baths:** 1 Sh
🛇 (5) 🄿 (10) 📺 🦃 ✕ 🖤 🕯

Leicestershire

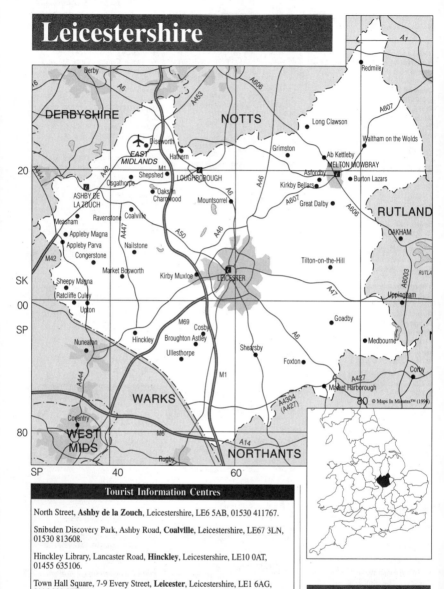

© Maps In Minutes™ (1996)

Ab Kettleby

SK7222 ◾ *Red Lion, The Anchor*

White Lodge Farm, *Nottingham Road, Ab Kettleby, Melton Mowbray, Leicestershire, LE14 3JB.*
Farm buildings tastefully converted into self-contained rooms overlooking garden.
Open: All Year
Grades: ETC 4 Diamond
01664 822286 Mrs Spencer
D: £19 **S:** £22
Beds: 1F 1D 1T **Baths:** 3 En
🐾 (9) 🅿 (4) ⚲ 📺 ▥ 🛏

Appleby Magna

SK3110   Black Horse

Ferne Cottage, 5 Black Horse Hill, Appleby Magna, Swadlincote, Derbyshire, DE12 7AQ.
Open: All Year (not Xmas)
Grades: ETC 3 Diamond
01530 271772 G A Bird
Fax: 01530 270652
D: £17–£25 **S:** £17–£25
Beds: 1F 1D 1T 1S **Baths:** 1 En 1 Sh
📺 🄿 (5) 📺 ⛨ 🛏 🏭, 📺 🎱
C18th beamed cottage. Homely, friendly, comfortable accommodation in the quiet historic village of Appleby Magna with off road parking. Half a mile from M42 (J11), 20 mins from NEC, Birmingham and East Midlands Airport. Lace making tuition by arrangement.

Appleby Parva

SK3109   Cock Inn

Elms Farm, Atherstone Road, Appleby Parva, Swadlincote, Leicestershire, DE12 7AG.
Pleasant farmhouse in rural position within 1.5 miles of M42.
Open: All Year (not Xmas)
Grades: ETC 3 Diamond
01530 270450 Ms Frisby
D: £20–£22 **S:** £20–£22
Beds: 1D 1T 1S **Baths:** 2 En 1 Pr
📺 (4) 🄿 (4) 📺 🏭, 📺 🎱

Asfordby

SK7019   Crown Inn

Amberley, 4 Church Lane, Asfordby, Melton Mowbray, Leics, LE14 3RU.
Beautiful riverside bungalow . idyllic floodlit lawns/gardens. Enjoy breakfast in garden room. **Open:** All Year
Grades: ETC 4 Diamond
01664 812314 B P Brotherhood
Fax: 01664 813740
doris@amberly.softnet.co.uk
D: £18.50–£22 **S:** £20–£25
Beds: 1T 1D 1S **Baths:** 2 En
📺 (14) 🄿 🎱 📺 🏭, 🎱 👶 🚿

Ashby de la Zouch

SK3516   Bull & Lion

The Bungalow, 10 Trinity Close, Ashby de la Zouch, Leics, LE65 2GQ.
Private family home in quiet cul-de-sac, easy access to motorways. **Open:** All Year
01530 560698 Mrs Chapman
D: £17.50–£18 **S:** £18
Beds: 1D 1T **Baths:** 1 Sh
📺 🄿 (3) 🎱 📺 🗙 🏭, 📺 🎱

Broughton Astley

SP5292   White Horse, Bull's Head

The Old Farm House, Old Mill Road, Broughton Astley, Leicester, Leics, LE9 6PQ.
Georgian farmhouse, quietly situated in well-serviced village. Good access M1 (J20/21), M69. **Open:** All Year (not Xmas)
01455 282254 Mrs Cornelius
D: £19–£23 **S:** £19–£23
Beds: 1D 2T 1S **Baths:** 2 Sh
🄿 (6) 🎱 📺 🏭, 📺 🎱

Coalville

SK4214   Robin Hood, The Plough

Church Lane Farm House, Ravenstone, Coalville, Leicester, LE67 2AE.
Open: All Year (not Xmas)
Grades: ETC 4 Diamond, AA 4 Diamond
01530 811299 Mrs Thorne
Fax: 01530 810536
aa.bnb.coalville@talk21.com
D: fr £22.50 **S:** fr £25
Beds: 2D 2T **Baths:** 4 En
📺 (15) 🄿 (6) 🎱 📺 🛏 🗙 📺 🎱
Queen Anne farmhouse, Ravenstone between M1 & A42. Interior designer & artist's home, antique furnishings throughout.

Cosby

SP5494   Bull's Head

The Vineries, Cosby, Leicester, LE9 1UL.
Open: All Year (not Xmas/New Year)
0116 2750817 Mrs Warren
D: £25–£27.50 **S:** £35
Beds: 2D 1S **Baths:** 3 En
📺 (16) 🄿 (8) 🎱 📺 🗙 🏭, 📺 🎱
Lovely period house in 1.5 acre gardens. All rooms tastefully furnished, overlooking gardens and countryside. Very peaceful and comfortable. Excellent accommodation with warm welcome, personal service and delicious breakfast. Easy access to motorway network. Ideal for business traveller and tourist.

Diseworth

SK4524   Bull & Swan

Lady Gate Nursery, 47 The Green, Diseworth, Derby, Derbyshire, DE74 2QN.
Close to airport, Donington Park Racing Circuit, exhibition centre, M1/M42.
Open: All Year (not Xmas)
01332 855263 (also fax) Mrs Bebbington
D: £18–£25 **S:** £20–£25
Beds: 1T 1D 1S **Baths:** 2 Sh
📺 (9) 🄿 (5) 🎱 📺 🏭, 🌸 🎱

Foxton

SP7089   Black Horse

The Old Manse, Swingbridge Street, Foxton, Market Harborough, Leics, LE16 7RH.
Period house in conservation village. Canals, locks, local inns nearby.
Open: All Year (not Xmas)
Grades: ETC 4 Diamond, Silver Award
01858 545456 Mrs Pickering
D: fr £22.50 **S:** fr £32
Beds: 3T/D **Baths:** 3 En
📺 🄿 (6) 🎱 📺 🏭, 🎱

Goadby

SP7598   Fox & Hounds

The Hollies, Goadby, Leicester, LE7 9EE.
Beautiful Listed house in quiet village in pretty Leicestershire countryside.
Open: All Year (not Xmas)
Grades: ETC 3 Diamond
0116 259 8301 Mrs Parr **Fax: 0116 259 8491**
holliesbb@aol.com
D: £22.50 **S:** £25
Beds: 1F 1D 1S **Baths:** 1 En 1 Sh
📺 (5) 🄿 (3) 🎱 📺 🛏 🏭, 🎱

Great Dalby

SK7414   Royal Oak

Dairy Farm, 8 Burrough End, Great Dalby, Melton Mowbray, Leics, LE14 2EW.
Working dairy farm 30 minutes from Leicester, Nottingham, 5 minutes Melton.
Open: All Year
Grades: ETC 3 Diamond
01664 562783 Mrs Parker
D: £18–£20 **S:** £20
Beds: 2D 1T **Baths:** 2 En 1 Pr
📺 🄿 (5) 📺 🛏 🏭, 📺 🎱

Glebe Farm, Nether End, Great Dalby, Melton Mowbray, Leics, LE14 2EY.
Comfortable farmhouse in pretty village. Generous breakfasts. Large garden.
Open: All Year
01664 561548 Mrs Byrne
D: £35–£38 **S:** £20–£22
Beds: 1F 1D **Baths:** 1 Sh
📺 (3) 📺 🛏 🗙 🏭, 📺 🎱

Grimston

SK6821   Black Horse

Gorse House, Main Street, Grimston, Melton Mowbray, Leicestershire, LE14 3BZ.
Open: All Year
Grades: ETC 4 Diamond
01664 813537 (also fax)
Mr & Mrs Cowdell
cowdell@gorsehouse.co.uk
D: £20–£25 **S:** £20–£25
Beds: 1F 1T 1D **Baths:** 2 En 1 Sh
📺 (12) 🄿 (4) 🎱 📺 🏭, 📺 🎱
Extended 17th Century cottage, well furnished attractive garden, in quiet conservation village. two miles from A46 convenient Leicester, Nottingham and East Midlands Airport. Good restaurant and pub within 100 yards. Beautiful countryside for walking, riding (stables available) and touring.

Hathern

SK5022   Anchor Inn, King's Arms

Leys Guest House, Loughborough Road, Hathern, Loughborough, Leics, LE12 5JB.
Situated in small village. Close to Derbyshire, Leicestershire and Nottinghamshire. **Open:** All Year
01509 844373 (also fax) Mrs Hudson
alanhudson@talk21.com
D: £17–£19 **S:** £17–£19
Beds: 2F 2T 2S **Baths:** 2 En 2 Sh
📺 🄿 (8) 📺 🛏 🏭, 📺 🎱 👶 cc

Hinckley

SP4294   Holywell Inn

The Guest House, 45 Priesthills Road, Hinckley, Leics, LE10 1AQ.
Edwardian period house set in quiet pleasant area of Hinckley.
Open: All Year (not Xmas)
Grades: ETC 3 Diamond
01455 619720 S Farmer
priest@hills45.freeserve.co.uk
D: £20 **S:** £22
Beds: 3T 1S **Baths:** 2 Sh 1 En
🎱 📺 🏭, 🎱

Hollycroft Hotel, 24 Hollycroft, Hinckley, Leics, LE10 0HG.
Small family run hotel. All rooms ensuite, private car park. **Open:** All Year
01455 637356 (also fax)
Mrs Hughes
jane.hughes@dtn.ntl.com
D: fr £22.50 **S:** fr £25
Beds: 2F 2D 1T **Baths:** 5 En
🛏 🅿 (10) 📺 🛏 ✕ 🛒 🔲 ⚫ ♨ ⚫ cc 1

Kirby Muxloe

SK5104   🍺 *Royal Oak*

Faith Cottage, 400 Ratby Lane, Kirby Muxloe, Leicester, Leics, LE9 9AQ.
Quaint spotlessly clean cottage type accommodation, easy access to M1.
Open: All Year (not Xmas)
0116 238 7435 Mrs Saunders
faithcottage@netscapeonline.co.uk
D: £18.50 **S:** £18.50–£20
Beds: 2T 1S **Baths:** 1 En 1 Pr
🛏 (7) 🅿 (6) 🌂 🛒 ⚫

Kirkby Bellars

SK7117   🍺 *Flying Childers*

Tole Cottage, 10 Main Street, Kirby Bellars, Melton Mowbray, Leicestershire, LE14 2EA.
Open: All Year
Grades: ETC 4 Diamond
01664 812932
michael@handjean.freeserve.co.uk
D: £20–£21 **S:** £25
Beds: 1F 1D 1S **Baths:** 1 En 1 Sh
🛏 (7) 🅿 (3) 🌂 🛒 🛒 🔲 ⚫
Situated in the picturesque Wreake Valley, a warm welcome awaits you. Charming, early C19th cottage with inspirational garden and rooms containing unique decorative effects. Excellent location for outdoor pursuits, business or leisurely breaks. Enjoy the relaxed atmosphere and peaceful surroundings.

Leicester

SK5804   🍺 *White Horse, Union Inn, Local Hero, Country House, The Huntsman, Braunstone Inn*

Craigleigh Hotel, 17-19 Westleigh Road, Leicester, LE3 0HH.
Open: All Year (not Xmas)
0116 254 6875 (also fax)
S T Pattison
D: £19–£22 **S:** £18–£28
Beds: 4D 3T 4S **Baths:** 8 En 2 Sh
📺 🛒 🔲 ⚫ cc
Victorian house, pleasant location, close to city and sports venues.

Aylestone Park Hotel, 69 Belvoir Drive, Leicester, LE2 8PB.
Quiet, comfortable hotel, particularly suited to the business man. Convenient location.
Open: All Year
0116 283 3637 (also fax)
Mr Davies
alex-f45@yahoo.com
D: £16–£20 **S:** £22–£28
Beds: 3T 2D 12S **Baths:** 7 En 11 Sh
🛏 (5) 🅿 (14) 📺 🛏 ✕ 🛒 ⚫

Long Clawson

SK7227

Elms Farm, 52 East End, Long Clawson, Melton Mowbray, Leics, LE14 4NG.
Warm comfortable old farmhouse village setting in Vale of Belvoir.
Open: All Year (not Xmas)
01664 822395 Mrs Whittard
Fax: 01664 823399
jwhittard@ukonline.co.uk
D: £17–£21 **S:** £18–£26
Beds: 1F 1D 1S **Baths:** 1 En 1 Sh
🛏 🅿 (4) 🌂 📺 ✕ 🛒 🔲 ⚫

Loughborough

SK5319   🍺 *Grand Central Hotel, Harvester, Boat Inn*

Charnwood Lodge Guest House, 136 Leicester Road, Loughborough, Leics, LE11 2AQ.
Spacious Victorian licensed guesthouse in quiet surroundings 5 mins town centre.
Open: All Year (not Xmas)
Grades: ETC 3 Diamond
01509 211120 Mrs Charwat
Fax: 01509 211121
charnwoodlodge@charwat.freeserve.co.uk
D: £20–£35 **S:** £30–£45
Beds: 2F 1T 4D 1S **Baths:** 6 En
🛏 🅿 (8) 📺 🛏 ✕ 🛒 🔲 ⚫ 🔲 cc

Peachnook Guest House, 154 Ashby Road, Loughborough, Leics, LE11 3AG.
Built around 1890, small and friendly guesthouse near all amenities.
Open: All Year **01509 264390** Ms Wood
D: £15–£30 **S:** £15–£30
Beds: 4F 2D 2T 1S
🛏 (5) 📺 🔲 ⚫

Meadow Guest House, 155 Meadow Lane, Loughborough, Leics, LE11 1JX.
Family-run guest house with hot and cold facilities, colour TV and parking.
Open: All Year **01509 217409**
naushad@naushad.freeserve.co.uk
D: £12.50–£15 **S:** £15–£17.50
Beds: 1F 1D 2T 1S **Baths:** 1 En 2 Sh
🛏 🅿 (5) 📺 ✕ 🛒 🔲 ⚫

New Life Guest House, 121 Ashby Road, Loughborough, Leics, LE11 3AB.
Beautiful Victorian villa, 5 mins to centre, university. Parking outside house.
Open: All Year
Grades: ETC 3 Diamond, welcome Host
01509 216699 Mrs Burnard
Fax: 01509 210020
jean@newlife-fp.co.uk
D: £14.50–£21 **S:** £14.50–£21
Beds: 1F 1T 2S **Baths:** 2 En 1 Sh
🛏 🌂 📺 🛒 🔲 ⚫ ♨ ⚫

Market Bosworth

SK4003

Bosworth Firs, Bosworth Road, Market Bosworth, Nuneaton, Warks, CV13 0DW.
Comfortable, clean, friendly. Home cooking, varied menu. Attractive décor, furnishings. **Open:** All Year
01455 290727 Mrs Christian
D: £20–£24 **S:** £20–£30
Beds: 2D 2T 2S **Baths:** 2 En 1 Pr 1 Sh
🛏 🅿 (6) 🌂 📺 ✕ 🛒 🔲 ⚫ ⚫

Measham

SK3312   🍺 *Belper Inn, Hollybush Inn, The Swan*

Measham House Farm, Gallows Lane, Measham, Swadlincote, Derbyshire, DE12 7HD.
Open: All Year (not Xmas)
Grades: ETC 4 Diamond
01530 270465 (also fax)
Mr Lovett
D: £21 **S:** £21
Beds: 1F 2T **Baths:** 3 En 1 Pr
🛏 🅿 (20) 🌂 📺 🛏 🛒 🔲 ⚫
Large Georgian farmhouse on 500 acre working farm close to the heart of the National Forest. Warm welcome, spacious garden, country walks, three ensuite bedrooms.

Laurels Guest House, 17 Ashby Road, Measham, Swadlincote, Derbyshire, DE12 7JR.
High class accommodation. Rural surroundings. Orchard, pond. Parking. Motorway access.
Open: All Year
Grades: ETC 3 Diamond
01530 272567 Mrs Evans
Fax: 01530 270466
evanslaurels@onetel.net.uk
D: £22–£25 **S:** £22–£25
Beds: 1D 2T **Baths:** 2 En 1 Pr
🛏 (1) 🅿 (8) 🌂 📺 🛒 ⚫

Medbourne

SP7993   🍺 *Nevill Arms*

Medbourne Grange, Nevill Holt, Medbourne, Market Harborough, Leics, LE16 8EF.
Comfortable farmhouse with breathtaking views; quiet location & heated pool.
Open: All Year (not Xmas)
01858 565249 Mrs Beaty
Fax: 01858 565257
D: £19–£22 **S:** £19–£25
Beds: 2D 1T **Baths:** 1 Sh 2 En
🛏 🅿 (6) 🌂 📺 ✕ 🛒 ⚫

Melton Mowbray

SK7519   🍺 *Crown Inn, Black Swan, Harborough Hotel, Royal Oak*

Dairy Farm, 8 Burrough End, Great Dalby, Melton Mowbray, Leics, LE14 2EW.
Working dairy farm 30 minutes from Leicester, Nottingham, 5 minutes Melton.
Open: All Year **Grades:** ETC 3 Diamond
01664 562783 Mrs Parker
D: £18–£20 **S:** £20
Beds: 2D 1T **Baths:** 2 En 1 Pr
🛏 🅿 (5) 📺 🛏 🛒 🔲 ⚫

Amberley, 4 Church Lane, Asfordby, Melton Mowbray, Leics, LE14 3RU.
Beautiful riverside bungalow. Idyllic floodlit lawns/gardens. Enjoy breakfast in garden room.
Open: All Year
Grades: ETC 4 Diamond
01664 812314 B P Brotherhood
Fax: 01664 813740
doris@amberly.softnet.co.uk
D: £18.50–£22 **S:** £20–£25
Beds: 1T 1D 1S **Baths:** 2 En
🛏 (14) 🅿 🌂 📺 🛒 ⚫ ⚫

The Noel Arms, *31 Burton Street, Melton Mowbray, Leics, LE13 1AE.*
Ensuite bed & breakfast. Real ale. Clean, friendly atmosphere. **Open:** All Year
01664 562363 Mrs Ling **D:** £17.50 **S:** £17.50
Beds: 2F 2T 2S **Baths:** 4 En
⛱ 🅿 📺 🍴 📶 ♨

Kirmel Guesthouse, *23/25 Mill Street, Melton Mowbray, Leics, LE13 1AY.*
Open: All Year
01664 564374 Ms Hardy
Beds: 2T 1S 1F 1D **Baths:** 1 Sh 1 En
⛱ 🅿 ⧖ 📺 🍴 ✕ 📶 ♨ ❋ ♨
Kirmel Guesthouse is a very clean and homely run family business offering first class accommodation at a very competitive price. Situated close to all amenities, shopping centre a few minutes walk away, within easy reach of sports and leisure facilities.

Beckmill Guest House, *44 Kings Road, Melton Mowbray, Leics, LE13 1QF.*
Victorian house near town centre.
Open: All Year **01664 852881** Mrs Blades
D: £19–£25 **S:** £19
Beds: 1F 2D 2T 1S **Baths:** 1 En 1 Sh
⛱ ⧖ 📺 🍴 📶 📶 ♨

Mountsorrel

SK5814   🍺 *Quorndon Fox*

Barley Loft Guest House, *33a Hawcliffe Road, Mountsorrel, Loughborough, Leics, LE12 7AQ.*
Open: All Year **01509 413514** Mrs Pegg
D: £17.50–£19 **S:** £18–£20
Beds: 2F 1D 1T 2S **Baths:** 2 En
⛱ 🅿 (12) 📺 🍴 📶 ♨ ♿
Spacious bungalow close to A6 between Leicester and Loughborough. Quiet, rural location, riverside walks, local historical attractions. Comfortable base for working away from home. Guests' fridge, microwave, toaster. Traditional hearty breakfast. Suitable for disabled. Excellent local supermarket, pubs, takeaways, restaurants,.

Nailstone

SK4107   🍺 *Nut & Squirrel*

Glebe Farm, *Rectory Lane, Nailstone, Nuneaton, Warks, CV13 0QQ.*
Comfortable farmhouse on working farm near Bosworth Battlefield and Mallory Park. **Open:** All Year (not Xmas)
01530 260318 Mrs Payne
D: £15 **S:** £15
Beds: 1D 1T 1S **Baths:** 2 Sh
⛱ 🅿 (5) ⧖ 📺 📶 ♨

Oaks in Charnwood

SK4716   🍺 *Ye Olde Bulls Head, Forrest Rock, Jolly Farmers*

Lubcloud Farm, *Charley Road, Oaks in Charnwood, Loughborough, Leics, LE12 9YA.*
Organic working dairy farm. Peaceful rural location on Charnwood Forest.
Open: All Year
01509 503204 Mr & Mrs Newcombe
Fax: 01509 651267
D: £20–£22 **S:** £22.50–£25
Beds: 1F 2D **Baths:** 3 En
⛱ 🅿 (10) ⧖ 📺 📶 ♨

St Josephs, *Abbey Road, Oaks in Charnwood, Coalville, Leics, LE67 4UA.*
Old country house where hosts welcome you to their home.
Open: Apr to Oct
01509 503943 Mrs Havers
m.havers@virginnet.co.uk
D: £19 **S:** £19
Beds: 2T 1S **Baths:** 1 Sh
⛱ 🅿 (3) ⧖ 📺 📶 📶 ♨

Osgathorpe

SK4219   🍺 *George & Dragon*

The Royal Oak Inn, *20 Main Street, Osgathorpe, Loughborough, Leics, LE12 9TA.*
High standard coaching inn in picturesque countryside. Secured parking.
Open: All Year
Grades: ETC 3 Diamond
01530 222443 V A Jacobs
D: £20–£22.50 **S:** £30–£35
Beds: 2T 1D **Baths:** 3 En
⛱ 🅿 (50) ⧖ 📺 📶 ♨ ♿

Ratcliffe Culey

SP3299   🍺 *Gate Inn*

Manor Farm, *Ratcliffe Culey, Atherstone, Warks, CV9 3NY.*
Victorian house located in small quiet friendly village in beautiful countryside.
Open: All Year
Grades: ETC 3 Diamond
01827 712269 Mrs Trivett
jane@ousbey.com
D: £17–£18 **S:** £20
Beds: 2D **Baths:** 1 Sh
⛱ 🅿 (2) ⧖ 📺 🍴 ✕ 📶 ♨ cc

Ravenstone

SK4013   🍺 *Robin Hood, The Plough*

Church Lane Farm House, *Ravenstone, Coalville, Leicester, LE67 2AE.*
Queen Anne farmhouse, Ravenstone between M1 & A42. Interior designer & artist's home, antique furnishings throughout. **Open:** All Year (not Xmas)
Grades: ETC 4 Diamond, AA 4 Diamond
01530 811299 Mrs Thorne
Fax: 01530 810536
aa.bnb.coalville@talk21.com
D: fr £22.50 **S:** fr £25
Beds: 2D 2T **Baths:** 4 En
⛱ (15) 🅿 (6) ⧖ 📺 🍴 ✕ 📶 ♨

Sheepy Magna

SK3201   🍺 *Black Horse*

Elmsdale, *Ratcliffe Lane, Sheepy Magna, Atherstone, Leicestershire, CV9 3QY.*
Open: All Year (not Xmas)
01827 718810 Mrs Calcott
D: £18 **S:** £18
Beds: 1F 2S **Baths:** 1 Sh
⛱ 🅿 (5) ⧖ 📺 🍴 📶 ♨
Modern family farmhouse set in 200 acres of farmland. River and pool fishing, clay pigeon shooting (by arrangement) country paths. A warm welcome awaits you. Well equipped rooms with extras.

Shepshed

SK4719

Croft Guesthouse, *21 Hall Croft, Shepshed , Loughborough, Leicestershire, LE12 9AN.*
Warm family atmosphere, spacious rooms, secure parking - motor bikes, cycles.
Open: All Year (not Xmas/New Year)
Grades: ETC 3 Diamond
01509 505657 Fax: 08700 522266
ray@croftguesthouse.demon.co.uk
D: £22–£25 **S:** £30–£35
Beds: 2F 3T 3D 2S **Baths:** 5 En 1 Sh
⛱ ⧖ 📺 📶 ♨ cc

Tilton on the Hill

SK7405   🍺 *Salisbury, Rose & Crown*

Knebworth House, *Loddington Lane, Launde, Tilton on the Hill, Leicester, Leics, LE7 9DE.*
Comfortable accommodation in secluded countryside. **Open:** All Year (not Xmas)
0116 259 7257 Mrs Setaycor
D: £15 **S:** fr £15
Beds: 1F 1T 1S **Baths:** 1 Sh
🅿 (10) 📺 📶 ♨

Ullesthorpe

SP5087   🍺 *The Swan*

Forge House, *College Street, Ullesthorpe, Lutterworth, Leics, LE17 5BU.*
Excellent accommodation with attractive gardens. Ideal for business and pleasure.
Open: All Year
01455 202454 (also fax)
s.silvester@virgin.net
D: fr £20 **S:** £20–£25
Beds: 1D 1T **Baths:** 1 En 1 Sh
⛱ (10) 🅿 (3) ⧖ 📺 📶 ♨

Upton

SP3699   🍺 *The Cock*

Sparkenhoe Farm, *Upton, Nuneaton, Warks, CV13 6JX.*
Open: All Year **01455 213203** Mrs Clarke
D: £25 **S:** £25–£30
Beds: 1D 2T **Baths:** 2 En 1 Pr
⛱ 🅿 (10) ⧖ 📺 🍴 📶 ♨
Beautiful Georgian farmhouse with fabulous countryside views. Large comfortable rooms recently refurbished to a high standard. Excellent pub and restaurant within 1 mile. Situated NEC - 20 minutes, B'ham Airport 20 minutes, Market Bosworth 5 minutes, Stratford upon Avon 40 minutes.

Waltham on the Wolds

SK8025   🍺 *Marquis of Granby, Royal Horseshoes*

Bryn Barn, *38 High Street, Waltham on the Wolds, Melton Mowbray, Leics, LE14 4AH.*
Charmingly converted stables & barn, original timber beams, picturesque conservation village in Vale of Belvoir.
Open: All Year (not Xmas)
Grades: AA 4 Diamond
01664 464783 Mr & Mrs Rowlands
D: £19–£21 **S:** £25–£28
Beds: 1F 2D 1T **Baths:** 2 En 2 Sh
⛱ 🅿 (4) ⧖ 📺 🍴 📶 ♨

Lincolnshire

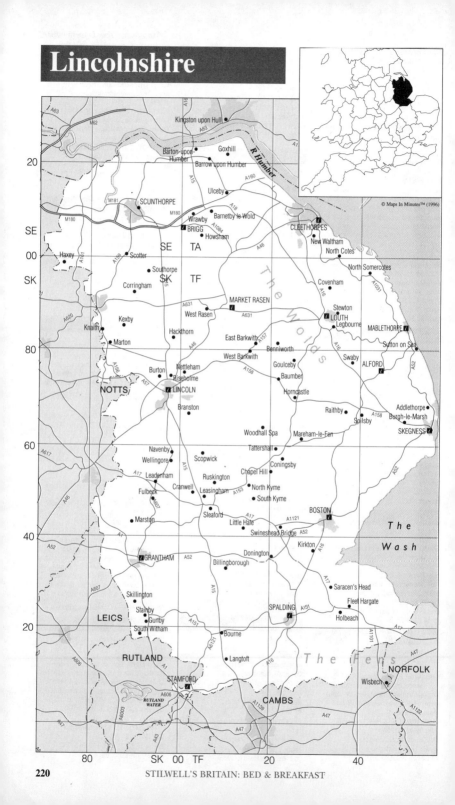

© Maps In Minutes™ (1996)

STILWELL'S BRITAIN: BED & BREAKFAST

Tourist Information Centres

The Manor House, West Street, **Alford**, Lincolnshire, LN13 9DJ, 01507 462143 (Easter to Oct).

Blackfriars Arts Centre, Spain Lane, **Boston**, Lincolnshire, PE21 6HP, 01205 356656.

The Buttercross, Marketplace, **Brigg**, North Lincs, DN20 8ER, 01652 657053.

42-43 Alexandra Road, **Cleethorpes**, N E Lincs, DN35 8LE, 01472 323111.

The Guildhall Centre, St Peter's Hill, **Grantham**, Lincolnshire, NG31 6PZ, 01476 406166.

National Fishing Heritage Centre, Alexandra Dock, **Grimsby**, N E Lincs, DN31 1UF, 01472 325932.

The Trinity Centre, Spilsby Road, **Horncastle**, Lincs, LN9 9AW, 01507 526636 (Easter to Oct).

Humberside International Airport, **Kirmington**, North Lincolnshire, DN39 6YH, 01652 688456.

9 Castle Hill, **Lincoln**, LN1 3AA, 01522 526450.

New Market Hall, Off Cornmarket, **Louth**, Lincolnshire, LN11 9NS, 01507 609289.

Dunes Family Entertainment Centre, Central Promenade, **Mablethorpe**, Lincolnshire, LN12 1RG, 01507 472496.

Cranwell Aviation Heritage Centre, Heath Farm, **North Rauceby**, Cranwell, Sleaford, Lincolnshire, NG34 8QR, 01529 488490 (Easter to Oct).

Embassy Centre, Grand Parade, **Skegness**, Lincolnshire, PE25 2UP, 01754 764821.

The Mill, Money's Yard, Carre Street, **Sleaford**, Lincolnshire, NG34 7TW, 01529 414294.

Ayscoughfee Hall, Churchgate, **Spalding**, Lincolnshire, PE11 2RA, 01775 725468.

Addlethorpe

TF5468

Lambourne House, Ashtree Court, Mill Lane, Addlethorpe, Skegness, Lincolnshire, PE25 1HW.
Just two miles from Skegness, set in the quiet greenery of Lincolnshire farmland.
Open: All Year (not Xmas)
01754 766527 (also fax)
D: £20–£25 **S:** £20–£30
Beds: 1D 2T **Baths:** 2 En 1 Pr
⌂ 🅿 🗡 📺 ✕ 🛏 📶 ♿

Alford

TF4575   *Half Moon, Anchor Inn*

Halton House, 50 East Street, Alford, Lincs, LN13 9EH.
Comfortable relaxing accommodation.
Open: All Year (not Xmas)
01507 462058 Mrs Mackey
D: fr £18 **S:** fr £19
Beds: 1D 1T **Baths:** 1 Sh
🅿 (3) 🗡 📺 🛏 ⚓

Barnetby le Wold

TA0509   *Station Hotel*

Holcombe Guest House, 34 Victoria Road, Barnetby le Wold, Lincs, DN38 6JR.
First class accommodation and a warm welcome awaits you.
Open: All Year
01652 680655 Mrs Vora
Fax: 01652 680841
holcombe.house@virgin.net
D: £16.25–£20 **S:** £20
Beds: 2F 1T 5S **Baths:** 4 Pr 2 Sh
⌂ 🅿 (7) 📺 🏃 ✕ 📶 📺 🛏 ♿ cc

Reginald House, 27 Queen Road, Barnetby le Wold, Lincolnshire, DN38 6JH.
Beautiful modern bungalow with newly-built first floor ensuite guest accommodation.
Open: All Year
01652 688566 Fax: 01652 688510
D: £17.50–£20 **S:** £22.50–£25
Beds: 1D 1T **Baths:** 2 En
🅿 (4) 🗡 📺 ✕ 📶 ⚓

Barrow upon Humber

TA0720   *Royal Oak*

Glebe Farm, Cross Street, Barrow upon Humber, Lincolnshire, DN18 5QD.
Spacious accommodation in village location. Superb for walking, cycling, sightseeing.
Open: All Year (not Xmas/New Year)
01469 531548 Mrs Styles
Fax: 01469 530034
glebe-farm@lineone.net
D: £19–£20 **S:** £16–£20
Beds: 1D 1S **Baths:** 1 Pr
⌂ (5) 🅿 (2) 🗡 📺 ⚓

Barton-upon-Humber

TA0321   *White Swan*

White Swan Hotel, Fleetgate, Barton-upon-Humber, Lincs, DN18 5QD.
Local friendly pub, pool, darts, doms etc.
Open: All Year (not Xmas)
01652 632459 D: £23.50 **S:** £30
Beds: 1D 3T **Baths:** 2 En 1 Sh
🅿 (10) 📺 ✕ 🛏 ⚓

Baumber

TF2274   *Coach & Horses*

Baumber Park, Baumber, Horncastle, Lincs, LN9 5NE.
Period farmhouse; bedrooms with fine views; gardens, walking, cycling, golf.
Open: All Year (not Xmas)
Grades: ETC 4 Diamond, highly Commended
01507 578235 Mrs Harrison
Fax: 01507 578417
D: £20–£25 **S:** £20–£30
Beds: 1D 1T **Baths:** 1 En 1 Pr
⌂ 🅿 (4) 📺 🏃 ✕ 🛏 ⚓

B&B owners may vary rates - be sure to check when booking

National Grid References are for villages, towns and cities – not for individual houses

Benniworth

TF2081

Glebe Farm, Church Lane, Benniworth, Market Rasen, Lincolnshire, LN8 6JP.
C18th Listed farmhouse in Lincolnshire Wolds. **Open:** All Year
Grades: ETC 4 Diamond
01507 313231 (also fax)
Mrs Selby
D: £22.50–£27 **S:** £25–£27
Beds: 1D 1T **Baths:** 2 En 1 Pr
🅿 (6) 🗡 📺 📶 📺 ❄ ⚓

Billingborough

TF1134   *Fortescue Arms*

St Boswells, 10 Vine Street, Billingborough, Sleaford, Lincs, NG34 0QE.
Old attractive house with attractive garden overlooked by village church.
Open: All Year
01529 240413 (also fax)
john.hockin@btinternet.com
D: £18–£20 **S:** £18–£20
Beds: 1D 2T **Baths:** 1 Sh
⌂ 🅿 (1) 📺 ✕ 📶 📺 ⚓

Boston

TF3344   *The Mill, White Hart, Four Crossroads, Red Cow, Good Barns, Cowbridge Inn*

The New England Hotel, Wide Bargate, Boston, Lincolnshire, PE21 6SH.
Open: All Year
Grades: ETC 3 Star, AA 3 Star
01205 365255 Mr Maund
D: £30.25–£36.25 **S:** £50–£62.50
Beds: 2F 5T 10D 8S **Baths:** 25 En
⌂ 🅿 📺 🏃 ✕ 📶 📺 ❄ ⚓ cc
The New England is a top quality hotel with restaurant, bar, residents' lounge, good secure parking. Located in the town centre, we are close to Boston Stump, the Maud Foster Windmill and only 1/2 hour drive from Skegness and Lincoln.

Lochiel Guest House, 69 Horncastle Road, Boston, Lincs, PE21 9HY.
Comfortable, friendly, picturesque waterside setting. Large garden. Working windmill view.
Open: All Year
01205 363628 Mr & Mrs Lynch
D: £18 **S:** £20
Beds: 1D 1T 1S **Baths:** 1 Sh
⌂ 🅿 (3) 🗡 📺 📶 📺 ⚓

90 Pilleys Lane, Boston, Lincs, PE21 9RB.
Comfortable, detached bungalow. Quiet. Close to Pilgrim Hospital. Lovely residential area.
Open: All Year
01205 360723 Mrs Claridge
D: £22–£36 **S:** £22–£36
Beds: 1T **Baths:** 1 Pr
⌂ (1) 🅿 🗡 📺 🏃 ✕ 📶 ❄ ⚓ ♿

Bourne

TF0920   Wishing Well

The Old Mill, 16 Victoria Place, Bourne, Lincs, PE10 9LJ.
Spacious family home where a warm and friendly welcome awaits.
Open: All Year (not Xmas/New Year)
01778 394893 Mr Davison
oldmill@bourne1.screaming.net
D: £15 **S:** £15
Beds: 2T **Baths:** 1 Sh
🛇 🅿 ⏁ 📺 🖳 ▥

Branston

TF0267   Mill Lodge

73 Station Road, Branston, Lincoln, Lincs., LN4 1LG.
Modern house, ground floor bedrooms. Attractive gardens. Quiet location, easy to find. Wonderful breakfasts.
Open: All Year
Grades: ETC 3 Diamond
01522 828658 M A Buckingham
D: £25 **S:** £25
Beds: 1T 1D **Baths:** 1 En 1 Pr
🛇 (5) 🅿 (4) ⏁ 📺 🐾 🖳 ▥ ▤

Brigg

TA0007   King William, Queen's Head, Arties Mill

The Woolpack Hotel, Market Place, Brigg, Lincs., DN20 8HA.
A Grade II Listed building and a fully licensed public house, with comfortable accommodation.
Open: All Year (not Xmas)
01652 655649 (also fax)
harry@woolpack488.freeserve.co.uk
D: £15–£20 **S:** £18–£25
Beds: 2F 3T 1S **Baths:** 2 En 1 Pr 1 Sh
🛇 🅿 (20) ⏁ 📺 ✕ 🖳 ▥ ▤

Hamsden Garth, Cadney Road, Howsham, Market Rasen, Lincolnshire, LN7 6LA.
High quality modern accommodation in rural setting. Convenient M18, Humberside Airport.
Open: All Year (not Xmas)
Grades: AA 3 Diamond
01652 678703 (also fax)
Mrs Robinson
gerald@hamsden.demon.co.uk
D: fr £15 **S:** fr £17
Beds: 1T 2S **Baths:** 1 En
🛇 🅿 (10) ⏁ 📺 🐾 🖳 ▥ ▤ ♿

Burgh le Marsh

TF5064   Ye Old Burgh Inn

The Old Mill, West End, Burgh le Marsh, Skegness, Lincs, PE24 5EA.
Tastefully converted windmill set in lovely countryside, near the coast.
Open: All Year (not Xmas)
01754 810081 (also fax)
Mr & Mrs Southward
oldmillburgh@talk21.com
D: £16–£26 **S:** £25–£30
Beds: 1F 1D 1T **Baths:** 2 En 1 Sh
🛇 🅿 (6) ⏁ 📺 🖳 ▤

Burton

SK9674   Pyewipe Inn

New Farm, Burton, Lincoln, Lincs, LN1 2RD.
328 acre working farm, open countryside, Lincoln Cathedral nearby.
Open: Easter to Nov
Grades: ETC 2 Diamond
01522 527326 Mrs Russon
D: £19 **S:** £22.50
Beds: 2T **Baths:** 1 Pr 1 Sh
🛇 (5) 🅿 (3) ⏁ 📺 ✕ 🖳 ▥ ▤ ♿

Chapel Hill

TF2054

The Crown Inn, Chapel Hill, Tattershall, Lincoln, LN4 4PX.
Ensuite rooms, varied menu, walks, fishing, boating, real ale, Entertainment.
Open: All Year
01526 342262 (also fax) Mr Harrington
barryharrington@hotmail.com
D: £18 **S:** £20
Beds: 1F 2T 1S
🛇 🅿 (15) ⏁ 📺 ✕ 🖳 ▤

Cleethorpes

TA3008   The Punchbowl, The Swashbuckle, Willow Hotel, Schubert's, The Ambassador, Sted's

Adelaide Hotel, 41 Isaacs Hill, Cleethorpes, Lincs, DN35 8JT.
Open: All Year
Grades: ETC 4 Diamond
01472 693594 Fax: 01472 329717
robert.callison@dtn.ntl.com
D: £15–£18.50 **S:** £16–£25
Beds: 2F 5T 4D 2S
Baths: 3 En 2 Sh
🛇 (3) 🅿 (4) 📺 🖳 ▥ ▤
Adelaide hotel is a small delightful family run hotel. This fine established has recently been awarded 4 Diamond by English tourist board. If you require superb accommodation, friendliness, cleanliness and good home quality cooked food. Look no further.

Alpine Guest House, 55 Clee Road, Cleethorpes, Lincs., DN35 8AD.
Welcoming comfortable accommodation at realistic prices.
Open: All Year (not Xmas)
Grades: ETC 3 Diamond
01472 690804 (also fax)
w.sanderson@ntlworld.com
D: £12.50–£14 **S:** £14–£16
Beds: 2F 1T 2S **Baths:** 2 Sh
🛇 (2) 🅿 (3) ⏁ 📺 🐾 ✕ 🖳 ▥ ▤

Hotel 77, 77 Kingsway, Cleethorpes, Lincs, DN35 0AB.
Situated near the leisure centre, boating lake and leisure park
Open: All Year (not Xmas/New Year)
01472 692035 Mr & Mrs Knox
Fax: 01472 692035
D: fr £19.50 **S:** fr £25
Beds: 3F 3T 4D 4S **Baths:** All En
🛇 🅿 📺 🐾 ✕ 🖳 ▥ ▤ cc

Lindenthorpe Guest House, 19 Grant Street, Cleethorpes, Lincs, DN35 8AT.
Comfortable accommodation, 5 minutes to rail station, sea front, attractions.
Open: All Year
01472 313005 Mrs Richardson
Fax: 01472 312070
lindenthorpe@fsbdial.co.uk
D: £12 **S:** £14
Beds: 1F 2T 2S **Baths:** 1 Sh
🛇 📺 ✕ 🖳 ▥ ▤

Gladson Guest House, 43 Isaacs Hill, Cleethorpes, Lincs, DN35 8LQ.
Licensed family guest house, personal attention. Close to seafront.
Open: All Year
01472 694858 Mrs Pearce
Fax: 01472 239642
gladson@tinyonline.co.uk
D: £13–£14 **S:** £15–£16
Beds: 2F 1D 2S
🛇 📺 ✕ 🖳 ▥ ▤

Holmhirst Hotel, 3 Alexandra Road, Cleethorpes, Lincs, DN35 8LQ.
Family-run seafront hotel. Good food a speciality.
Open: All Year (not Xmas)
Grades: AA 3 Diamond, RAC 3 Diamond
01472 692656 (also fax)
Mr Barrs
holmhirst@aol.com
D: £20 **S:** £18–£25
Beds: 1D 2T 5S **Baths:** 5 En 1 Sh
🛇 (3) 🅿 (5) 📺 ✕ 🖳 ▥ ▤ cc

Pelham View Guest House, 12 Isaacs Hill, Cleethorpes, Lincs, DN35 8JS.
A warm welcome awaits all guests to Pelham View Guest House.
Open: All Year (not Xmas)
01472 690781 Mr Sharpe
D: £13–£16 **S:** fr £14
Beds: 3F 1D 1T **Baths:** 1 Pr
🛇 📺 🐾 🖳 ▥ ✳ ▤

Aavon Court, 4 Isaacs Hill, Cleethorpes, Lincs, DN35 8JR.
Highly recommended, superbly furnished, clean, friendly, with excellent food. **Open:** All Year
01472 698706 Mrs Marriott
Fax: 01472 594853
janet@aavoncourtguesthouse.co.uk
D: £13–£20 **S:** £16–£25
Beds: 2F 4D 4T 6S **Baths:** 1 En 2 Pr 3 Sh
🛇 📺 🖳 ▥ ▤ ♿

Argyll Guest House, 25 Clee Road, Cleethorpes, Lincs, DN35 8AD.
A must for walks and photographers - everything you could want.
Open: All Year (not Xmas)
01472 692253 H R Wood
Fax: 01472 321729
harry@llbb.freeserve.co.uk
D: £13–£15 **S:** £13–£15
Beds: 2D 2T 2S **Baths:** 1 Sh
🛇 🅿 (4) 📺 🖳 ▤

National Grid References are for villages, towns and cities – not for individual houses

Tudor Terrace Guest House, *11 Bradford Avenue, Cleethorpes, Lincs, DN35 0BB.*
ETC and AA inspected, the perfect location for that well-earned break.
Open: All Year
01472 600800 Mrs Ross
Fax: 01472 501395
tudor.terrace@btinternet.com
D: £15–£18 **S:** £16–£23
Beds: 3D 1T 2S **Baths:** 4 En 1 Sh
⊁ 𝔓 (2) ⊬ 📺 🕇 ✕ 📖 Ⅴ ⚘ ♿ 3

Ginnie's, *27 Queens Parade, Cleethorpes, Lincs, DN35 0DF.*
A warm welcome awaits you at Ginnie's Guest House. 100% non-smoking guest house.
Open: All Year (not Xmas)
01472 694997 Mr Akrill
Fax: 01472 319799
D: £15 **S:** £15
Beds: 5D 1T 1S **Baths:** 8 En
⊁ (3) 𝔓 (2) ⊬ 📺 📖 Ⅴ ⚘ ♿

Clee House, *31-33 Clee Road, Cleethorpes, Lincs, DN35 8AD.*
Attractive Edwardian property set in own grounds only five minutes' walk Cleethorpes' main attractions.
Open: All Year
01472 200850 (also fax)
Mr Parker
clee.house@btinternet.com
D: £22.50–£30 **S:** £25–£35
Beds: 6F 3D 1T **Baths:** 9 En 1 Pr
⊁ 𝔓 (10) 📺 ✕ 📖 Ⅴ ⚘ ♿ cc

Coningsby

TF2258 🍺 White Bull

The White Bull, *High Street, Coningsby, Lincoln, Lincs, LN4 4RB.*
Open: All Year
01526 342439
Mr & Mrs Gordon
Fax: 01526 342818
thewhitebullconingsby@tinyworld.co.uk
D: £15–£19 **S:** £17–£22
Beds: 2D 2S **Baths:** 2 En 2 Sh
⊁ 𝔓 (35) ⊬ 📺 📖 Ⅴ ⚘
Friendly pub with real ale, riverside beer garden and large children's playground, children's certificate. Traditional home-made meals available everyday. Open all day - food served 11 am to 11 pm. 1 mile from the Battle of Britain Memorial Flight at RAF Coningsby.

Corringham

SK8791

The Beckett Arms, *25 High Street, Corringham, Gainsborough, Lincolnshire, DN21 5QP.*
Open: All Year
Grades: ETC 3 Diamond
01427 838201

D: £17–£20 **S:** £20–£24
Beds: 2F 1T 1D
Baths: 4 En
⊁ 𝔓 (30) 📺 🕇 ✕ 📖 Ⅴ ⚘ ♿ cc
Centrally located accomodation offering a warm welcome and home-cooked meals

Covenham

TF3394 🍺 Mill House, Fleece Inn

Driftwood, *Newbridge Lane, Covenham, Louth, Lincs, LN11 0PQ.*
Enjoy peace, comfort, good food and a lovely garden.
Open: All Year (not Xmas)
01507 363681 Mrs Shaw
D: £20 **S:** £20
Beds: 1D 1S **Baths:** 1 Pr
⊁ (5) 𝔓 (2) ⊬ 📺 📖 ⚘

Cranwell

TF0349

Byards Leap Cottage, *Cranwell, Sleaford, Lincs, NG34 8EY.*
Comfortable country cottage, beautiful garden, home cooking with home-grown produce. **Open:** All Year (not Xmas)
Grades: ETC 2 Diamond
01400 261537 Mrs Wood
lustacottage@supanet.com
D: fr £18 **S:** fr £18
Beds: 1D 1T **Baths:** 1 Sh
⊁ 𝔓 (6) ⊬ 📺 ✕ 📖 Ⅴ ⚘

Donington

TF2135 🍺 Black Swan

Cooks, *19 Quadring Road, Donington, Spalding, Lincs, PE11 4TB.*
Complete suite comprises double room, dressing area, separate shower room.
Open: All Year (not Xmas)
01775 820478 Mrs Silverton
D: £18 **S:** £22–£25
Beds: 2D 1T **Baths:** 1 En 1 Sh
𝔓 (4) ⊬ 📺 📖 ⚘

East Barkwith

TF1681 🍺 Crossroads Inn

The Grange, *Torrington Lane, East Barkwith, Market Rasen, Lincs, LN8 5RY.*
A beautiful Georgian farmhouse offering everything for a perfect break.
Open: All Year (not Xmas)
Grades: ETC 4 Diamond, Silver
01673 858670
sarahstamp@farmersweekly.net
D: fr £22 **S:** £25–£28
Beds: 2D **Baths:** 2 En
⊁ 𝔓 ⊬ 📺 📖 Ⅴ ⚘

Fleet Hargate

TF3925 🍺 The Bull, Rose & Crown

Willow Tea Rooms And B&b, *Old Main Road, Fleet Hargate, Spalding, Lincs, PE12 8LL.*
Open: All Year
01406 423112 D: £16–£18 **S:** £20–£22
Beds: 2F 3D 1T **Baths:** 5 En 1 Pr
⊁ 𝔓 (6) 📺 🕇 ✕ 📖 Ⅴ ⚘
Pretty English tea rooms renowned for good food. Comfortable accommodation.

All details shown are as supplied by B&B owners in Autumn 2000

Fulbeck

SK9450

Hare & Hounds, *The Green, Fulbeck, Grantham, Lincs, NG32 3JJ.*
C17th inn. Real ales, food all week. Patio garden. 10 mins A1.
Open: All Year
Grades: ETC 3 Diamond , AA 3 Diamond
01400 272090 A Nicholas
Fax: 01400 273663
D: £20–£27.50 **S:** £30–£40
Beds: 4D 2T 2F **Baths:** 8 En
⊁ 𝔓 ⊬ 📺 🕇 ✕ 📖 Ⅴ ⚘ cc

Goulceby

TF2579 🍺 Three Horseshoes

Holly House, *Watery Lane, Goulceby, Louth, Lincs, LN11 9UR.*
Open: All Year (not Xmas)
01507 343729 Mrs Lester
D: £15–£16 **S:** £15–£16
Beds: 1D 1T **Baths:** 1 Sh
𝔓 (2) 📺 ✕ 📖 Ⅴ ⚘
Quiet village location in Lincolnshire Wolds. Comfortable cottage set in large garden of interest to serious gardeners. Excellent cooked breakfast and comfortable beds, off road parking. French, Hebrew and German spoken. Antiques dealers welcome.

Goxhill

TA1021

Glengarth, *South End, Goxhill, Barrow-upon-Humber, Lincs, DN19 7LZ.*
Comfortable, modernised farmhouse, open fires, quiet location in beautiful countryside, warm welcome.
Open: All Year
01469 530991 (also fax)
Mrs Monro
D: £15–£16 **S:** £15–£16
Beds: 1D 1T **Baths:** 1 Pr 1 Sh
⊁ (2) 𝔓 (8) ⊬ 📺 🕇 ✕ 📖 Ⅴ ⚘ ⚘

Grantham

SK9136 🍺 Fox & Hounds, Tollemache Inn

Park Lodge Guest House, *87 Harrowby Road, Grantham, Lincolnshire, NG31 9ED.*
A Victorian town house decorated in the William Morris style.
Open: All Year (not Xmas)
01476 567330 (also fax)
Mr & Mrs Parkes
kath@parkes.org
D: fr £20 **S:** fr £24
Beds: 2D 1T 1S **Baths:** 2 En 1 Pr
⊁ (12) 𝔓 (7) ⊬ 📺 🕇 📖 Ⅴ ⚘

Church View, *12 North Parade, Grantham, Lincs., NG31 8AN.*
A well appointed Listed Georgian town house. Town centre location.
Open: All Year
01476 560815
Mr & Mrs Waldren
D: £15–£18 **S:** £17
Beds: 1D 1T 1S **Baths:** 2 En
⊁ (1) ⊬ ✕ 📖 Ⅴ ⚘

The Roost Guest House, 82
Harrowby Road, Grantham, Lincs,
NG31 9DS.
Large Victorian private house.
Open: All Year (not Xmas/New Year)
Grades: ETC 3 Diamond
01476 560719
Mr & Mrs Stobbs
Fax: 01476 563303
D: £16–£20 **S:** £17–£25
Beds: 2T 1D **Baths:** 2 En
🛏 🅿 (3) 🛇 📺 🏠 🗙 🛏 📺 ▪

The Five Bells, 79 Brook Street,
Grantham, Lincs, NG31 6RY.
Friendly town pub, quiet accommodation,
good beer, good food.
Open: All Year
01476 400555
Mr & Mrs Mills
steve@5bells.freeserve.co.uk
D: £16 **S:** £22
Beds: 3T 1D **Baths:** 4 En
🛏 📺 🏠 🗙 ▪

Gunby

SK9121 ◀ *Blue Dog*

Brook House, Gunby, Grantham, Lincs,
NG33 5LF.
Charming period stone house surrounded
by colourful walled garden.
Open: All Year (not Xmas)
01476 860010 (also fax)
Mrs Mayne
D: £18–£19 **S:** £18.50–£19.50
Beds: 3T **Baths:** 1 Pr
🛏 (10) 🅿 (4) 🛇 📺 📺 📺 ▪

Hackthorn

SK9982 ◀ *Cross Keys*

Honeyholes, South Farm, Hackthorn,
Lincoln, Lincs., LN2 3PW.
Relax in this stylish, friendly, Edwardian
farmhouse just 2 miles off A15.
Open: All Year (not Xmas)
01673 861868 (also fax)
Mrs Greenfield
dgreen8234@aol.com
D: £19–£22 **S:** £22
Beds: 2D 1T **Baths:** 1 En 1 Sh
🛏 (5) 🅿 (5) 🛇 📺 🏠 🗙 📺 📺 ▪

Haxey

SK7799

Duke William, Church Street, Haxey,
Doncaster, South Yorkshire, DN9 2HY.
18th century inn refurbished to provide
accommodation in a warm and friendly
atmosphere
Open: All Year
Grades: ETC 3 Diamond
01427 752210 (also fax)
D: £22.50 **S:** £32
Beds: 2T 4D
🛏 🅿 (36) 📺 📺 ▪ ▪ cc

Please respect a B&B's wishes
regarding children, animals
and smoking

Holbeach

TF3625 ◀ *Chequers Hotel*

Elloe Lodge, 37 Barrington Gate,
Holbeach, Spalding, Lincs, PE12 7LB.
Spacious house, old market town, close
pubs & restaurants. Snooker room,
drawing room, delightful gardens.
Open: All Year (not Xmas)
01406 423207 (also fax) Mrs Vasey
bandbholbeach@lineone.net
D: £19 **S:** £25
Beds: 3D **Baths:** 2 Pr
🛏 🅿 (10) 🛇 📺 🗙 📺 ▪ ▪

Cackle Hill House, Cackle Hill Lane,
Holbeach, Spalding, Lincs, PE12 8BS.
Spacious, comfortable, tastefully-
furnished farmhouse set in a rural
position. **Open:** All Year (not Xmas)
01406 426721 Mrs Biggadike
Fax: 01406 424659
D: £20–£22 **S:** £22–£24
Beds: 1D 2T **Baths:** 2 En 1 Pr
🛏 (10) 🅿 (5) 🛇 📺 🏠 📺 ▪

Barrington House, Barrington Gate,
Holbeach, Spalding, Lincs, PE12 7LB.
Spacious Georgian house 3 minutes walk
from pubs and restaurants.
Open: All Year
01406 425178 (also fax) Mrs Symonds
denni@barringtonhouse.co.uk
D: £25–£22.50 **S:** £23–£25
Beds: 2D 1T 1S **Baths:** 3 En 2 Pr
🛏 🅿 (4) 📺 🏠 📺 📺 ▪

Horncastle

TF2669 ◀ *Fighting Cocks*

Milestone Cottage, 42 North Street,
Horncastle, Lincs, LN9 5DX.
Comfortable, self contained
accommodation in Georgian town
cottage. Self catering option available.
Open: All Year
01507 522238 D: £20 **S:** £20
Beds: 1T **Baths:** 1 En
🛏 🅿 (2) 📺 🏠 📺 ▪

Colkirk House, Manor House Street,
Horncastle, Lincs, LN9 5HF.
Converted warehouse in the middle of a
small market town, quiet attractive
outlook. **Open:** All Year (not Xmas)
01507 527366 (also fax)
D: £16 **S:** £17
Beds: 1D 1T **Baths:** 1 Pr
🛏 🅿 (3) 📺 🏠 📺 ▪

Howsham

TA0403 ◀ *King William, Queen's Head*

Hamsden Garth, Cadney Road,
Howsham, Market Rasen, Lincolnshire,
LN7 6LA.
High quality modern accommodation in
rural setting. Convenient M18,
Humberside Airport.
Open: All Year (not Xmas)
Grades: AA 3 Diamond
01652 678703 (also fax) Mrs Robinson
gerald@hamsden.demon.co.uk
D: fr £15 **S:** fr £17
Beds: 1T 2S **Baths:** 1 En
🛏 🅿 (10) 🛇 📺 🏠 📺 📺 ▪ ▪

Kexby

SK8785 ◀ *Stag's Head, Cross Keys, Fox &*
Hounds

Kexby Grange, Kexby, Gainsborough,
Lincs, DN21 5PJ.
Victorian farmhouse in pleasant
countryside, convenient for Hemswell
antiques, Lincoln and Wolds.
Open: All Year (not Xmas)
Grades: ETC 3 Diamond
01427 788265 Mrs Edwardson
D: £16 **S:** £16
Beds: 1D 1S **Baths:** 1 Pr 1 Sh
🅿 (4) 🛇 📺 🗙 📺 📺 ▪

Kirton

TF3038 ◀ *Merry Monk*

Westfield House, 31 Willington Road,
Kirton, Boston, Lincs, PE20 1EP.
Victorian house in large village, 4 miles
from historic Boston
Open: All Year
01205 722221 Mrs Duff
D: £15 **S:** £15
Beds: 1F 1D 1S **Baths:** 1 Sh
🛏 🅿 (5) 📺 🏠 📺 ▪

The Nook, 45 Boston Road, Kirton,
Boston, Lincolnshire, PE20 1ES.
Farm cottage C1900, village location, 3
miles from historic Boston.
Open: All Year (not Xmas)
01205 723419 D: fr £16 **S:** fr £16
Beds: 1F 1S **Baths:** 1 Sh
🛇 📺 🗙 📺 📺 ▪

Langtoft

TF1212

Courtyard Cottage, 2 West End,
Langtoft, Peterborough, PE6 9LS.
A tastefully refurbished C18th stone
cottage providing a warm welcome.
Open: All Year
Grades: ETC 4 Diamond
01778 348354 (also fax)
david_tinegate@ic24.net
D: £22.50–£30 **S:** £30–£50
Beds: 1F 1D 1T **Baths:** 2 En 1 Pr
🛏 🛇 📺 🏠 🗙 📺 📺 ▪ 🅱

Leadenham

SK9552

George Hotel, High Street, Leadenham,
Lincoln, Lincs, LN5 0PP.
Open: All Year
Grades: ETC 3 Diamond
01400 272251
Mr Willgoose
Fax: 01400 272091
D: £14–£20 **S:** £20–£25
Beds: 1F 2D 2T 1S
Baths: 6 En
🛏 🅿 📺 🏠 🗙 📺 📺 ▪ 🅱 cc 1
The George at Leadenham is a small
country hotel just off the A17 midway
between Newark, Sleaford, Grantham,
Lincoln. Its homely atmosphere and
reputation for fine food makes it a haven
for the weary tourist and accessible
stopping place for businessmen.

Leasingham

TF0548 ◑ *Duke of Wellington*

Manor Farm, *Leasingham, Sleaford, Lincs, NG34 8JN.*
Two pleasant rooms overlooking large garden on working farm. Peaceful.
Open: All Year
01529 302671 Mrs Franks
Fax: 01529 414946
j.h.franks@amserve.net
D: £15–£17.50 **S:** £20
Beds: 2F **Baths:** 1 Sh
⛺ 🅿 📺 ⭐ 🛏 🖤

Legbourne

TF3684

Boothby House, *Legbourne, Louth, Lincolnshire, LN11 8LH.*
Situated at the edge of the picturesque Lincolnshire Wolds in a peaceful rural setting.
Open: All Year (not Xmas)
01507 601516 (also fax)
Mrs Wilson
boothbyhouse@freeuk.com
D: £18–£21 **S:** £18
Beds: 1D 1T 1S **Baths:** 1 En 1 Sh
⛺ 🅿 (4) 📺 ✕ 🖤 🛏 🖤

Lincoln

SK9771 ◑ *Lord Tennyson, Sun Inn, The Barge, Royal William, Horse & Groom, Burton Arms, Wig & Mitre*

Admiral Guest House, *16/18 Nelson Street, Lincoln, LN1 1PJ.*
Open: All Year (not Xmas)
Grades: RAC 3 Diamond
01522 544467 (also fax)
Mr Major
tony@admiral63.freeserve.co.uk
D: £18–£20 **S:** £–£22
Beds: 1F 3D 2T 3S **Baths:** 7 En 2 Pr
⛺ 🅿 (12) 📺 🛏 ✕ 🖤 🖤 🖤 & cc
Admiral Guest House, also known as Nelsons Cottages, situated just off main A57 close to city centre and Lincoln University, offering large floodlit car park, also close to Brayford pool, cathedral and castle and all amenities. All rooms ensuite and private bath.

Edward King House, *The Old Palace, Minster Yard, Lincoln, LN2 1PU.*
Open: All Year (not Xmas)
Grades: ETC 2 Diamond
01522 528778 Rev Adkins
Fax: 01522 527308
ekh@oden.org.uk
D: £18.50–£20.50 **S:** £19–£21
Beds: 1F 11T 5S **Baths:** 8 Sh
⛺ 🅿 (12) ⭐ 📺 🛏 🖤 🖤 cc
A former residence of the Bishops of Lincoln at the historic heart of the city and next to the cathedral and medieval old palace. We offer a peaceful haven with a secluded garden and superb views.

B&B owners may vary rates - be sure to check when booking

South Park Guest House, *11 South Park, Lincoln, LN5 8EN.*
Open: All Year (not Xmas/New Year)
01522 528243 Mr Bull
Fax: 01522 524603
D: £18–£26 **S:** £22–£25
Beds: 1F 2T 2D 1S **Baths:** 6 En
⛺ (1) 🅿 (6) 📺 ✕ 🖤 🖤
Fine Victorian detached house, recently refurbished to provide excellent quality accommodation, while maintaining many original features & character. Situated overlooking the South Common, only a short walk to shops, pubs, restaurants, city centre and tourist attractions. Ensuite rooms. Private parking.

Hamiltons Hotel, *2 Hamilton Road, St Catherines, Lincoln, LN5 8ED.*
Friendly family run hotel in a detached former Victorian home.
Open: All Year
01522 528243 June Bull
Fax: 01522 524603
D: £18–£20 **S:** £18–£25
Beds: 1F 3T 2D 3S **Baths:** 4 En 5 Sh
⛺ 🅿 (9) 📺 🛏 ✕ 🖤 🖤 ✿ 🖤

A B C Charisma Guest House, *126 Yarborough Road, Lincoln, LN1 1HP.*
Beautiful views overlooking Trent valley 10 minutes walk to tourist area.
Open: All Year
01522 543560 (also fax)
D: £20–£22.50 **S:** £20–£25
Beds: 1F 2T 6D 2S **Baths:** 3 En 4 Sh
⛺ (10) 🅿 (10) ⭐ 📺 🖤 🖤

Newport Guest House, *26-28 Newport, Lincoln, LN1 3DF.*
A high standard establishment 500 metres from historic city centre.
Open: All Year (not Xmas)
Grades: ETC 3 Diamond, AA 3 Diamond
01522 528590 Mr Clarke
Fax: 01522 544502
info@newportguesthouse.co.uk
D: £16–£20 **S:** £16–£28
Beds: 2D 5T 1S **Baths:** 5 En 2 Sh
⛺ (6) 🅿 (5) ⭐ 📺 🛏 🖤 🖤 &

The Old Rectory, *19 Newport, Lincoln, LN1 3DQ.*
Large Edwardian home near cathedral, castle, pubs and restaurants.
Open: All Year (not Xmas)
01522 514774 Mr Downes
D: £20 **S:** £20–£25
Beds: 2F 4D 1T 1S **Baths:** 5 En 1 Sh
⛺ 🅿 (8) ⭐ 📺 🖤 🖤 🖤

Westlyn House, *67 Carholme Road, Lincoln, LN1 1RT.*
Late Georgian house close to university, marina, cathedral, castle, city centre.
Open: All Year (not Xmas)
Grades: RAC 3 Diamond
01522 537468 (also fax)
Mrs Shelton
westlyn.bblincoln@easicom.com
D: £17.50–£20 **S:** £20–£25
Beds: 1F 1T 2D 1S **Baths:** 5 En
⛺ (3) 🅿 (4) ⭐ 📺 🛏 🖤 🖤 🖤

The Bakery Guest House, *26-28 Burton Road, Lincoln, LN1 3LB.*
Converted bakery only two minutes from Lincoln castle and cathedral.
Open: All Year
01522 576057 (also fax)
D: £20–£30 **S:** £25–£40
Beds: 1F 2D 1T **Baths:** 3 En 1 Pr
⛺ 📺 🛏 🖤 & cc

Elma Guest House, *14 Albion Crescent, off Long Leys Road, Lincoln, LN1 1EB.*
Quiet location, friendly family home with garden pond and willow tree.
Open: All Year
Grades: AA 2 Diamond
01522 529792 (also fax)
Mrs Guymer
ellen@elma-guesthouse.freeserve.co.uk
D: £17–£20 **S:** £17–£20
Beds: 1D 1T 1S **Baths:** 2 Sh
⛺ 🅿 (5) 📺 ✕ 🖤 🖤 🖤

Jaymar, *31 Newland Street West, Lincoln, LN1 1QQ.*
Close proximity to: city attractions, A46, A57. Early breakfasts available.
Open: All Year (not Xmas)
01522 532934 Mrs Ward
D: £15 **S:** £15
Beds: 1D 1S **Baths:** 1 Sh
⛺ ⭐ 📺 🛏 🖤

Ridgeways Guest House, *243 Burton Road, Lincoln, LN1 3UB.*
Situated uphill within easy walking distance to the historic heart of Lincoln.
Open: All Year
01522 546878 (also fax)
Mr Barnes
ridgeways@talk21.com
D: £17.50–£25 **S:** £20–£25
Beds: 2F 1D 1T **Baths:** 3 En 1 Pr
🅿 (6) ⭐ 📺 🛏 🖤 🖤 & cc

The Barbican Hotel, *11 St Marys Street, Lincoln, LN5 7EQ.*
Victorian Hotel. Refurbished. Opposite railway station. An ideal central location.
Open: All Year (not Xmas)
01522 543811 **D:** fr £26 **S:** £39
Beds: 5D 2T 5S **Baths:** 12 En
⛺ 📺 🛏 🖤 & cc

Eardleys Hotel, *21 Cross O'Cliff Hill, Lincoln, LN5 8PN.*
Homely hotel, overlooking parkland & golf course. Guest bar & parking.
Open: All Year
01522 523050 (also fax) Mr Hill
D: £17.50–£20 **S:** £20–£25
Beds: 2F 2D 1T 1S **Baths:** 2 En 2 Sh
⛺ 🅿 (10) 🛏 ✕ 🖤 🖤 🖤

Little Hale

TF1441 ◑ *Nag's Head*

Bywell, *20 Chapel Lane, Little Hale, Sleaford, Lincs, NG34 9BE.*
Bungalow backing onto farmland. Heckington Windmill & tea-room 1.5 miles.
Open: All Year
01529 460206 Mrs Downes
D: fr £17.50 **S:** £
Beds: 1D 1T **Baths:** 1 En 1 Sh
⛺ 🅿 (3) ⭐ 📺 ✕ 🖤 &

Louth

TF3387 🍺 *Masons' Arms, White Horse, Mill House, Fleece Inn, Whitehouse Inn*

Boothby House, *Legbourne, Louth, Lincolnshire, LN11 8LH.*
Open: All Year (not Xmas)
01507 601516 (also fax)
Mrs Wilson
boothbyhouse@freeuk.com
D: £18–£21 **S:** £18
Beds: 1D 1T 1S **Baths:** 1 En 1 Sh
🛇 🅿 (4) 📺 ✕ 🛏 🎱 ♨
Situated at the edge of the picturesque Lincolnshire Wolds in a peaceful rural setting.

Butterfield's Guest House, *63 Legbourne Road, Louth, Lincs, LN11 8ES.*
One mile from market town of Louth/Lincs Wolds.
Open: All Year
01507 606719 Mrs Butterfield
D: £18–£21.50 **S:** £20–£25
Beds: 1F 2D 2S **Baths:** 1 En 2 Sh
🛇 🅿 (7) ⅋ 📺 🛏 ✕ 🛏 🎱 ♨

Mablethorpe

TF5085

Park View Guest House, *48 Gibralter Road, Mablethorpe, Lincs, LN12 2AT.*
Open: All Year
01507 477267 (also fax)
Mr Dodds
D: £14–£16 **S:** £14–£16
Beds: 2F 1T 2D **Baths:** 1 En 2 Sh
🛇 🅿 (6) 📺 ✕ 🛏 🎱 ♨ ♿
Clean and comfortable licensed guest house with some ground floor bedrooms. Beside sandy beach and Queens Park, with lake, boating, bowling, crazy golf, children's play land and funfair. Free private parking, good home cooked food and optional evening meals.

Mareham le Fen

TF2761 🍺 *Royal Oak*

Barn Croft, *Main Street, Mareham le Fen, Boston, Lincs, PE22 7QJ.*
Ensuite facilities in rural setting. Ideal for coast, Lincoln, Boston.
Open: All Year
01507 568264 Mrs Shaw
D: £17 **S:** £20–£25
Beds: 2D 1T **Baths:** 2 En 1 Pr
🅿 (4) ⅋ 📺 🛏 🎱 ♨

Market Rasen

TF1089 🍺 *The Chase, Gordon Arms, White Swan*

Waveney Cottage Guest House, *Willingham Road, Market Rasen, Lincs, LN8 3DN.*
Small Tudor-style cottage. Ideal base for walking and cycling.
Open: All Year
Grades: ETC 3 Diamond
01673 843236 Mrs Bridger
D: fr £19.50 **S:** fr £21.50
Beds: 1D 2T **Baths:** 3 En
🛇 🅿 (6) ⅋ 📺 ✕ 🛏 ♨ ♨

White Swan Hotel, *29 Queen Street, Market Rasen, Lincs, LN8 3.*
Close to Racecourse, offering warm, friendly atmosphere.
Open: All Year
01673 843356 M Scuffam
martin-scuffam@hotmail.com
D: fr £17.50 **S:** fr £17.50
Beds: 1F 1D 2T 1S **Baths:** 1 Sh
🛇 🅿 (10) 📺 ✕ 🛏 🎱 ♨

Marston

SK8943

Thorold Arms, *Marston, Grantham, Lincs, NG32 2HH.*
Popular pub, good beer, home-cooked food, fresh vegetables, veggie meals too.
Open: All Year **Grades:** ETC 3 Diamond
01400 250899 Mr Bryan
Fax: 01400 251030
D: £29.50–£32.50 **S:** £27.50–£29.50
Beds: 1F 1D **Baths:** 2 En
🛇 (5) 🅿 (16) 📺 🛏 ✕ 🛏 ❄ 🎱 ♨ cc

Marton

SK8482

The Black Swan Guest House, *High St, Marton, Gainsborough, Lincolnshire, DN21 5AH.*
Open: All Year **Grades:** AA 4 Diamond
01427 718878 (also fax)
info@blackswan-marton.co.uk
D: £25–£30 **S:** £30
Beds: 2F 4D 1T 1S **Baths:** 8 En
🛇 🅿 (8) ⅋ 📺 ✕ 🛏 🎱 ❄ ♨ ♿ cc
A beautifully restored C18th coaching inn offering high quality ensuite accommodation. Much favoured stop for business travellers, British and international tourists and family groups. Excellent breakfasts in house, and superb choice of dinners only 5 minutes away. booking advisable.

Navenby

SK9858 🍺 *Marquis of Granby, King's Head*

The Barn, *North Lane, Navenby, Lincoln, LN5 0EH.*
Beautiful home adjacent walking. Convenient Air field - Trails, Lincoln, Grantham, Newark.
Open: All Year (not Xmas/New Year)
Grades: ETC 4 Diamond, Silver Award
01522 810318 (also fax) Mr & Mrs Gill
peter.sheila@thebarnnavenby.freeserve.c
o.uk
D: £17–£19 **S:** £25
Beds: 1F 1T **Baths:** 1 En 1Private
🛇 (7) 🅿 (6) ⅋ 📺 🛏 🎱 ♨

Nettleham

TF0075 🍺 *Black Horse*

9 Haymans Ghyll, *Nettleham, Lincoln, LN2 2PD.*
C18 cottage situated centre village, private lounge. Lincoln ten minutes.
Open: All Year (not Xmas/New Year)
01522 751812 (also fax)
Mr Dawkins
dawkins_net@talk21.com
D: £20–£22 **S:** £25–£30
Beds: 2D **Baths:** 1 En 1 Pr
⅋ 📺 🛏 🎱 ♨

New Waltham

TA2904

Peaks Top Farm, *Hewitts Avenue, New Waltham, Grimsby, DN36 4RS.*
Our converted barns offer stylish, comfortable accommodation, farmhouse breakfasts. **Open:** Mar to Dec
Grades: ETC 3 Diamond
01472 812941 lmclayton@tinyworld.co.uk
D: £18 **S:** £18–£25
Beds: 2F 1D 2S **Baths:** 5 En
🅿 (6) ⅋ 📺 🛏 ♨ ♿

North Cotes

TA3400

Fleece Inn, *Lock Road, North Cotes, Grimsby, Lincs, DN36 5UP.*
Relaxed beamed country inn, open fires, home cooked bar and restaurant meals served daily. **Open:** All Year (not Xmas)
01472 388233 **D:** £17–£20 **S:** £20
Beds: 1F 2T **Baths:** 1 Sh
🛇 🅿 📺 🛏 ♨

North Kyme

TF1552

Old Coach House Tea Rooms & Cafe, *Church Lane, North Kyme, Lincoln, LN4 4DJ.*
Beautifully refurbished old Georgian house offering warm and friendly welcome. **Open:** All Year
Grades: ETC 4 Diamond
01526 861465 Mr & Mrs Grice
Fax: 01526 861658
D: £18–£22 **S:** £18–£22
Beds: 3D 3T 1S **Baths:** 3 En
🛇 🅿 ⅋ 📺 ✕ 🛏 🎱 ❄ ♨

North Somercotes

TF4296 🍺 *Bay Horse, Traveller's Joy*

Pigeon Cottage, *Conisholme Road, North Somercotes, Louth, Lincolnshire, LN11 7PS.*
Open: All Year
Grades: ETC 2 Diamond
01507 359063 Ms Hills
D: £20–£22 **S:** £20–£22
Beds: 3F 1T 1D 1S **Baths:** 6 En
🛇 🅿 (6) 📺 🛏 ✕ 🛏 🎱 ♨ ♿
Fishing lake on site, Craft studio, pets area and 4 acres of playing field together make this modern accommodation suitable for all ages and tastes.

Raithby (Spilsby)

TF3767 🍺 *Red Lion*

Red Lion Inn, *Raithby, Spilsby, Lincs, PE23 4DS.*
Open: All Year
01790 753727 Mrs Smith
D: £19.50–£20 **S:** fr £28
Beds: 2D 1T **Baths:** 3 En
🛇 🅿 (20) 📺 🛏 ✕ 🛏 ♨ cc
Old world inn in centre of pretty Wolds village. Real ales, log fires in the winter, char grilled steaks, fish, home-made curries and Sunday roasts. Regular Lincoln coast buses. Pretty ensuite rooms. Great English breakfasts.

Riseholme

SK9775

Groveside Guest House, St Georges
Lane, Riseholme, Lincoln, LN2 2LQ.
Will situated for cathedral, castle,
showground and historic Uphill.
Open: All Year
01522 527997 Mrs Wallace
Fax: 01522 569525
bandb@gloria.force9.co.uk
D: £18–£20 **S:** £18
Beds: 2F 1T 1S **Baths:** 2 Sh
🛇 **P** (6) ⚡ 🔟 ✕ 🎨 📺 🛱

Ruskington

TF0851

Sunnyside Farm, Leasingham Lane,
Ruskington, Sleaford, Lincolnshire, NG34
9AH.
Perfectly located base for historic
centres, golf, walking,cycling. Horse
riding.
Open: All Year
01526 833010 D A Luke
D: £20–£22 **S:** £20–£22
Beds: 1F 1T **Baths:** 2 En
🛇 **P** 🔟 ♥ ✕ 🎨 🛱

Saracen's Head

TF3427   🍺 *The Chequers, Bull's Neck*

Pipewell Manor, Washaway Road,
Saracen's Head, Holbeach, Spalding, Lincs,
PE12 8AL.
Tastefully furnished rooms. Beautiful
grounds featuring a miniature railway.
Free use of cycles.
Open: All Year (not Xmas/New Year)
Grades: ETC 4 Diamond, AA 4 Diamond
01406 423119 (also fax)
Mrs Honnor
D: £44–£46 **S:** £30–£32
Beds: 2D 1T 1S **Baths:** 3 En 1 Pr
🛇 **P** (6) ⚡ 🔟 🎨 📺 🛱

Scopwick

TF0658   🍺 *Royal Oak*

The Millhouse, Heath Road, Scopwick,
Lincoln, Lincs, LN4 3JB.
Fine Georgian stone house set in
beautiful gardens amidst open
countryside. **Open:** All Year
Grades: ETC 4 Diamond
01526 321716 (also fax) Ms Gale
shirley.gale@farming.co.uk
D: £20–£25 **S:** £25–£28
Beds: 1T 2D **Baths:** 3 En
🛇 **P** (6) ⚡ 🔟 ♥ ✕ 🎨 🛱

Scotter

SE8800

Ivy Lodge Hotel, 4 Messingham Road,
Scotter, Gainsborough, Lincs, DN21 3UQ.
Family run, situated on A159 between
Gainsborough and Scunthorpe in a
picturesque village.
Open: All Year
01724 763723 Mrs Mewis
Fax: 01724 763770
D: £23.50 **S:** £27.50–£38
Beds: 1F 1D 1T 2S **Baths:** 5 En
🛇 **P** (8) 🔟 ♥ ✕ 🎨 📺 🛱

Scunthorpe

SE8910   🍺 *The Buccaneer*

Lindsey Hotel, 26-28 Normanby Road,
Scunthorpe, Lincs., DN15 6AL.
Central family run hotel on route between
Lincoln and York.
Open: All year
01724 844706 (also fax)
D: £14–£17 **S:** £17–£24
Beds: 2F 2D 3T 4S **Baths:** 3 En 3 Sh
🛇 (1) **P** (10) 🔟 ♥ 🎨 📺 🛱

Downs Guest House, 33 Deyne
Avenue, Scunthorpe, Lincs, DN15 7PZ.
Quiet location with all town centre
facilities on the doorstop.
Open: All Year
Grades: ETC 3 Diamond
01724 850710 Mr & Mrs Pickwell
Fax: 01724 330928
D: £16–£18 **S:** £19–£22
Beds: 3T 2D 2S **Baths:** 2 Sh
🛇 **P** (3) 🔟 ♥ ✕ 🎨 📺 🛱 ♿

Skegness

TF5663   🍺 *Marine Boathouse*

**The Tudor Lodge Licensed Guest
House,** 61 Drummond Road, Skegness,
Lincolnshire, PE25 3BB.
Open: All Year
01754 766487 M Lowe
D: £16–£18 **S:** £18–£20
Beds: 3F 2D 3T 1S
🛇 **P** (12) 🔟 ♥ ✕ 🎨 📺 🛱 ♿ **cc**
Tudor Lodge is within 5 min walk to
sands, bowling greens and town centre.
We offer 7 nights half board at £119.00, 4
nights £79.00 plus 3 night breaks at
£59.00. All rooms ensuite. Extra 10%
discount when playing full amount on
booking.

Mayfair Hotel, 10 Saxby Avenue,
Skegness, PE25 3JZ.
The Mayfair is well situated in quiet
location close to sea front/ town centre.
Open: All Year (not Xmas/New Year)
01754 764687 D: £14–£20 **S:** £14–£20
Beds: 1F 5T 2D **Baths:** 8 En
🛇 **P** (5) ⚡ 🔟 ♥ ✕ 🎨 📺 🛱 ♿

Craigside Hotel, 26 Scarborough
Avenue, Skegness, Lincs, PE25 2SY.
Family run hotel, close to seafront,
theatre and town centre.
Open: Easter to September
01754 763307 (also fax)
Mrs Milner
kenanddeb@craigside69.freeserve.co.uk
D: £20–£22 **S:** £20–£22
Beds: 5F 5D 3T 3S **Baths:** 12 En 1 Sh
🛇 **P** (10) 🔟 ✕ 🎨 📺 🛱 ♿ **cc**

**The Carlton Hotel and Holiday
Flats,** 70 Drummond Road, Skegness,
Lincs, PE25 3BR.
Well-positioned family hotel near to
seafront and town centre.
Open: All Year (not Xmas)
01754 765340 Fax: 0870 1115700
carltonhotel@yahoo.co.uk
D: £14–£19 **S:** £28–£38
Beds: 3F 4D 2T **Baths:** 4 En 4 Sh
🛇 (2) 🔟 🎨 🛱 **cc**

Hamewith, 12 Cecil Avenue, Skegness,
Lincs, PE25 2BX.
Small, centrally-positioned guest house,
handy all amenities.
Open: All Year
01754 766770 Mr Gunner
info@hamewith.freeserve.co.uk
D: £15–£20 **S:** £15–£20
Beds: 2F 3D 1T 1S **Baths:** 1 Sh
🛇 🔟 ♥ ✕ 🎨 📺 🛱 🛱

Clumber House Hotel, 17 Castleton
Boulevard, Skegness, Lincs, PE25 2TU.
Well appointed 1930's hotel with many of
the original features.
Open: All Year
01754 767552 Mr Moore
D: £22–£25 **S:** £22–£30
Beds: 3D 2T 2S **Baths:** 5 Pr 1 Sh
P (5) 🔟 ✕ 🎨 📺 🛱 🛱 ♿

Fairways, 1 Cavendish Road, Skegness,
Lincs, PE25 2QU.
Pleasant family-run guest house, close to
station, seafront town.
Open: All Year
01754 767556 D: £13–£15 **S:** £13–£15
Beds: 1F 4D 1T **Baths:** 2 Sh
🛇 **P** (5) 🔟 ✕ 📺 🛱

Scarborough House Hotel, 54 South
Parade, Skegness, Lincs, PE25 3HW.
Licensed, friendly, sea front hotel
overlooking Bowling Greens and boating
lakes. **Open:** All Year
01754 764453 Mr Ward
D: £15–£20 **S:** £18–£22
Beds: 3F 3D 1T 1S **Baths:** 4 En 1 Sh
🛇 (1) **P** (10) 🔟 ✕ 🛱 **cc**

Newhaven Guest House, 21
Sunningdale Drive, Skegness, Lincs,
PE25 1BB.
Come and unwind in our guest house
situated in a quiet area of Skegness.
Open: All Year
01754 762618 D: £13–£25 **S:** £13–£25
Beds: 2F 5D 1S **Baths:** 5 En 2 Sh
🛇 **P** (8) 🔟 ✕ 🎨 📺 🛱 🛱

Beachdene, 46 Scarborough Avenue,
Skegness, Lincs, PE25 2TA.
Two minutes to sea front amusements,
shopping, park, local amenities.
Open: Easter to Sep
01754 764409 D: £15–£20
Beds: 3F 3D 1T **Baths:** 4 En 3 Sh
🛇 **P** (5) 🔟 ✕ 🎨 📺 🛱

Skillington

SK8925   🍺 *Cross Swords*

Sproxton Lodge, Skillington,
Grantham, Lincs, NG33 5HJ.
Quiet family farm alongside Viking way.
Everyone welcome.
Open: All Year (not Xmas)
01476 860307 Mrs Whatton
D: £17–£18 **S:** £17–£18
Beds: 1F 1D 1S **Baths:** 1 En 1 Sh
🛇 (5) **P** (4) ⚡ 🔟 ✕ 🎨 📺 🛱

Planning a longer stay? Always
ask for any special rates

Sleaford

TF0645   *Jolly Scotchman, Duke of Wellington*

Anna Farmhouse, *Holdingham, Sleaford, Lincs, NG34 8NR.*
Open: All Year (not Xmas)
01529 307292 Mrs Wiles
D: £17–£19 **S:** £20–£22
Beds: 1F 1D 1T **Baths:** 2 Sh
🛏 🅿 (6) ⚲ 📺 ✕ Ⅴ ❋
Friendly atmosphere in C16/17th farmhouse. Ideal stop London Airports to Lincoln, York, Scotland. Large parking area in grounds, large English breakfast served after 7.00, Continental earlier. Standing back from A15 south, A15/A17, close to RAF Cranwell, Belvoir Castle, Belton House.

The Mallards Hotel, *6 Eastgate, Sleaford, Lincolnshire, NG34 7DJ.*
10 rooms, family hotel, riverside location, central Sleaford.
Open: All Year (not Xmas)
01529 413758 Mr & Mrs Smith
D: £25–£40 **S:** £25
Beds: 6T 2D 2S **Baths:** 10 En
🛏 🅿 📺 ✕ ▥ ⚱ cc

South Kyme

TF1749   *Hume Arms*

Hume Arms Hotel, *High Street, South Kyme, Lincoln, LN4 4AD.*
Home cooked food and traditional beers. Fishing lake. Caravans welcome.
Open: All Year
01526 861004 Mr Leggat
D: £15–£16 **S:** £20
Beds: 1D 1T **Baths:** 1 En 1 Sh
🛏 🅿 (20) 📺 ✕ ▥ ⚱ &

South Witham

SK9219   *Blue Cow*

Rose Cottage, *7 High Street, South Witham, Grantham, Lincs, NG33 5QB.*
C18th stone cottage in two acres midway between Stamford/Grantham/Rutland Water.
Open: All Year
01572 767757 Mrs Van Kimmenade
Fax: 01572 767199
bob@vankimmenade.freeserve.co.uk
D: £22.50–£25 **S:** £25
Beds: 1F 1D 1T 2S **Baths:** 3 En
🛏 🅿 (6) ⚲ 📺 ⊁ ✕ ▥ Ⅴ ⚱ &

Southorpe

SK8995   *Millstone Inn*

Midstone Farm House, *Midstone House, Southorpe, Stamford, Lincs, PE9 3BX.*
Beautiful stone Georgian house in quiet location. Meet George the pot bellied pig.
Open: All Year
Grades: ETC 4 Diamond
01780 740136 Mrs Harrison Smith
Fax: 01780 749294
midstonehouse@amserve.net
D: £25–£30 **S:** £25–£30
Beds: 1D 1T **Baths:** 1 En 1 Pr
🛏 🅿 ⚲ 📺 ⊁ ✕ ▥ Ⅴ ⚱

RATES

D = Price range per person sharing in a double room
S = Price range for a single room

Spalding

TF2422   *White Horse, Red Lion, Hungry Horse*

High Bridge House, *9 London Road, Spalding, Lincs, PE11 2TA.*
Situated along riverside next to Town Centre Georgian House Friendly.
Open: All Year (not Xmas/New Year)
01775 725810 Mrs Marshall
D: £38–£40 **S:** £19–£25
Beds: 2T 4S 6F **Baths:** 3 Sh
🛏 (10) 📺 ▥ ⚱

The Bull Inn, *Knight Street, Spalding, Lincs, PE11 3GA.*
Village pub/restaurant with rooms, close to Spalding, Lincs.
Open: All Year (not Xmas/New Year)
01775 723022 Ms Gardner
D: £15 **S:** £15
Beds: 1D 3T **Baths:** 1 Sh
🛏 🅿 📺 ✕ ▥ Ⅴ ⚱ cc

Spilsby

TF4066

Hethersett House, *3 The Terrace, Spilsby, Lincolnshire, PE23 5JR.*
Open: All Year
01790 752566 C M Morgan
D: fr £17.50 **S:** fr £17.50
Beds: 1T 2D **Baths:** 1 Sh
🛏 (10) ⚲ 📺 ▥ ⚱
Listed Georgian townhouse in small market town, antiques, log fires, walled garden, home-cooked food. Walk well-signed footpaths, cycle empty byroads, wonderful views of Wolds and Fens. Visit medieval churches, Lincoln Cathedral, Tennyson country, antique centres, markets and relax.

Stainby

SK9022   *Blue Cow*

The Old Blue Dog, *Colsterworth Road, Stainby, Grantham, Lincs, NG33 5QT.*
Beautiful stone residence in lovely rural countryside. Leicestershire/Lincolnshire border. **Open:** All Year
01476 861010 Mrs Jones
Fax: 01476 861645
fiona@thinkingstyles.co.uk
D: £25 **S:** £25
Beds: 1F 1D
🛏 🅿 (7) ⚲ ✦ ✕ ▥ Ⅴ ⚱

BATHROOMS

Pr - Private
Sh - Shared
En - Ensuite

Stamford

TF0207   *St Mary's Vaults, Hole in the Wall, The Bull, The Swan, The Dolphin, George Hotel, St Peters Inn, Green Man, Golden Pheasant*

Courtyard Cottage, *2 West End, Langtoft, Peterborough, PE6 9LS.*
Open: All Year
Grades: ETC 4 Diamond
01778 348354 (also fax)
david_tinegate@ic24.net
D: £22.50–£30 **S:** £30–£50
Beds: 1F 1D 1T **Baths:** 2 En 1 Pr
🛏 ⚲ 📺 ✕ ▥ Ⅴ ⚱ &
A tastefully refurbished C18th stone cottage providing a warm welcome, situated 50 yds west of the A15. It is double glazed and has central heating. All rooms have tea/coffee making facilities, colour TV and hairdryers; full English breakfast. No smoking.

Highfields, *31 Main Road, Collyweston, Stamford, Lincs, PE9 3PF.*
Detached black & white chalet house surrounded by fields.
Open: All Year
Grades: ETC Listed
01780 444339 Mrs Hindley
prhinkley@aol.com
D: £20–£21 **S:** £20–£21
Beds: 1D 1T 1S **Baths:** 1 En 1 Sh
🛏 (4) 🅿 (4) 📺 ✦ ✕ ▥ Ⅴ ⚱ &

Cringleford, *7 Exeter Gardens, Stamford, Stamford, Lincs, PE9 2RN.*
Comfortable house in residential area 0.50 mile from town centre.
Open: All Year (not Xmas)
01780 762136 Mrs Webster
D: £19–£22 **S:** £19–£22
Beds: 1D 1S **Baths:** 1 Pr
🅿 (2) 📺 ▥ Ⅴ ⚱

Birch House, *4 Lonsdale Road, Stamford, Lincs, PE9 2RW.*
Established well-presented family-run suburban house one mile from Stamford.
Open: All Year (not Xmas)
01780 754876 Mrs Headland
D: £18.50–£25 **S:** £18.50–£25
Beds: 2D 2S **Baths:** 1 Sh
🛏 (5) 🅿 (3) ⚲ 📺 ⚱

The Lincolnshire Poacher, *Broad Street, Stamford, Lincs, PE9 1PX.*
Historic converted brewery in the centre of Stamford.
Open: All Year
01780 764239 P Martin
D: fr £18 **S:** fr £18
Beds: 1F 2T 1S **Baths:** 1 Sh
🛏 (1) ⚲ 📺 ✦ ▥ Ⅴ ⚱

5 Rock Terrace, Scotgate, *Stamford, Lincs., PE9 2YJ.*
Early Victorian terraced house on edge of town centre, bedrooms are well furnished.
Open: All Year
01780 755475 Mrs Averdieck
D: £20–£27.50
Beds: 1D 1T **Baths:** 2 Pr
⚲ 📺 ▥ Ⅴ ⚱

Stewton

TF3586 ⚐ *Kay's Bar*

The Old Rectory, Stewton, Louth, Lincs, *LN11 8SF.*
An old rectory in peaceful garden. Come and see!
Open: All Year
01507 328063 ajp100@postmaster.co.uk
D: £22.50 **S:** £25
Beds: 2T 2D **Baths:** 3 En 1 Pr
⛄ 🅿 (6) 🔟 🐾 🛏 🖥 🆅 🛋

Sutton on Sea

TF5281

Walnut End, 53a Alford Road, Sutton on Sea, Mablethorpe, Lincs, *LN12 2HQ.*
Quiet location; 500 metres shops and beach. All rooms ground floor and ensuite.
Open: All Year (not Xmas)
01507 443451 (also fax)
Mrs Smith
D: £20–£22 **S:** £23–£25
Beds: 2D 1T **Baths:** 3 En
🅿 (6) ⅙ 🔟 🖥 🆅

Swaby

TF3876 ⚐ *Masingberd Arms*

Jasmine Cottage, Church Lane, Swaby, Alford, Lincolnshire, *LN13 0BQ.*
Peaceful village, excellent accommodation in an Area of Outstanding Natural Beauty.
Open: All Year (not Xmas/New Year)
01507 480283 (also fax)
P Fieldsend
fieldsend@btinternet.com
D: £19–£20 **S:** £24–£25
Beds: 1T 2D **Baths:** 2 En
🅿 (2) ⅙ 🔟 🖥 🛋 🚿

Swineshead Bridge

TF2242 ⚐ *Barge Hotel*

Boston Lodge, Browns Drove, Swineshead Bridge, Boston, Lincs, *PE20 3PX.*
Ideally situated for touring the Fens and South Lincolnshire.
Open: All Year (not Xmas)
Grades: AA 3 Diamond
01205 820983 S Humphreys
Fax: 01205 820512
info@bostonlodge.co.uk
D: £18 **S:** £22
Beds: 2F 3D 2T 2S **Baths:** 9 En
⛄ 🅿 (12) ⅙ 🔟 🐾 🖥 🆅 🛋 🚿 2

Tattershall

TF2158 ⚐ *Prattington Arms*

Lodge House, Market Place, Tattershall, Lincoln, Lincs, *LN4 4LQ.*
Clean comfortable accommodation. Close RAF Coningsby. Walking, Cycling, Angling, Golf.
Open: All Year
01526 342575 (also fax)
Mr Palethorpe
D: £14–£16 **S:** £13–£17
Beds: 1D 1T 2S **Baths:** 2 En 1 Sh
⛄ (1) 🅿 (3) ⅙ 🔟 🖥 🚿

Ulceby (Immingham)

TA1014 ⚐ *Brocklesby Ox*

Gillingham Rest, Spruce Lane, Ulceby, Lincolnshire, *DN39 6UL.*
Quiet extremely comfortable high class guest house situated 4 miles from Humberside International Airport.
Open: All Year
Grades: ETC 4 Diamond
01469 588427 Ms Connole
D: fr £20 **S:** fr £22
Beds: 2T 2S **Baths:** 2 Pr 1 Sh
⛄ 🅿 (12) 🔟 🖥 🚿 1

Wellingore

SK9856

Marquis of Granby, High Street, Wellingore, Lincoln, *LN5 0HW.*
Friendly village inn, midway between Lincoln, Grantham, Sleaford and Newark.
Open: All Year (not Xmas)
01522 810442
Mrs Justice
D: £20–£25 **S:** £22.50–£25
Beds: 1F 2D 4T
Baths: 6 En 1 Pr
⛄ 🅿 🔟 🐾 ✗ 🖥 🆅 🚿 cc

West Barkwith

TF1580

The Manor House, West Barkwith, Market Rasen, Lincs., *LN8 5LF.*
Beautiful C18th manor house overlooking extensive landscaped gardens and lake.
Open: All Year (not Xmas/New Year)
Grades: ETC 4 Diamond, Silver Award
01673 858253 (also fax)
J A Hobbins
D: £22.50 **S:** £25–£28
Beds: 1T 1D **Baths:** 2 En

West Rasen

TF0689 ⚐ *Bottle & Glass*

Chuck Hatch, Kingerby Road, West Rasen, Market Rasen, Lincs, *LN8 3NB.*
Superb facilities, hospitality, quiet country lakeside garden location, coarse fishing.
Open: All Year
Grades: AA 4 Diamond
01673 842947 (also fax)
D: £22.50–£27.50 **S:** £32.50–£40
Beds: 2D 2T **Baths:** 4 En
🅿 (4) ⅙ 🔟 🖥 🚿

Woodhall Spa

TF1963 ⚐ *The Mall, Abbey Lodge, Eagle Lodge*

Claremont Guest House, 9-11 Witham Road, Woodhall Spa, Lincs, *LN10 6RW.*
Friendly personal service in a traditional unspoilt Victorian guest house.
Open: All Year
Grades: ETC 2 Diamond
01526 352000 Mrs Brennan
D: £15–£20 **S:** £15–£20
Beds: 4F 2D 1T 3S **Baths:** 3 En 2 Sh
⛄ 🅿 (4) 🔟 🐾 🆅 🚿

Newlands Guest House, 56 Woodland Drive, Woodhall Spa, Lincs, *LN10 6YG.*
Open: All Year (not Xmas)
Grades: ETC 4 Diamond
01526 352881 D: £18–£20 **S:** £20
Beds: 1D 2T **Baths:** 2 En 1 Pr
⛄ 🅿 (8) ⅙ 🔟 🖥 🆅 🚿
Luxury accommodation in quiet tree-lined lane. Very convenient for village and international golf courses. Special aviation room and guest lounge. Very attractive gardens, excellent centre for visiting Lincolnshire.

Wrawby

TA0308 ⚐ *Black Horse*

Wish-u-well Guest House, Brigg Road, Wrawby, Brigg, Lincolnshire, *DN20 8RH.*
Modern bungalow in extensive private grounds. Country pub short walk.
Open: All Year
Grades: ETC 3 Diamond
01652 652301 (also fax)
Mrs Jobson
wishwell@talk21.com
D: £16–£17.50 **S:** £18–£20
Beds: 2D 1T **Baths:** 3 En
⛄ 🅿 (6) ⅙ 🔟 ✗ 🖥 ❄ 🚿 🚿

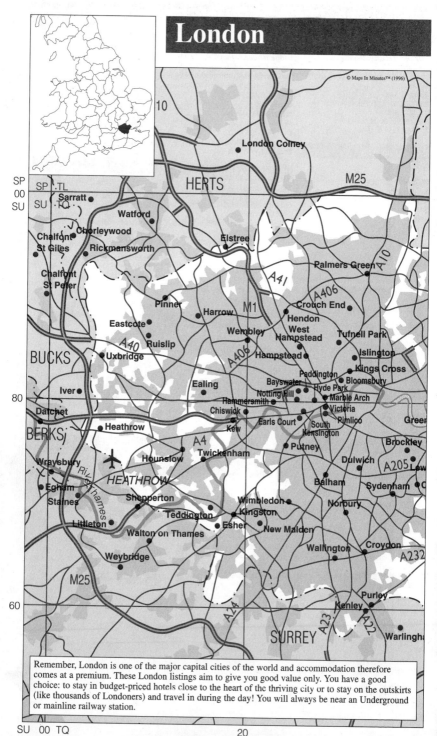

London

© Maps In Minutes™ (1996)

London Colney

HERTS

M25

SP
00
SU

SP TL
SU TQ

Sarratt
Watford
Chalfont
St Giles
Chorleywood
Rickmansworth
Elstree

Chalfont
St Peter

Palmers Green

A41

A406

A10

Pinner
Harrow
M1
Crouch End
Hendon
West
Hampstead
Tufnell Park

Eastcote
Ruislip
Wembley
Islington

BUCKS
Uxbridge
A40
A406
Hampstead
Kings Cross

Iver
Ealing
Paddington
Bloomsbury
Bayswater
Hyde Park
Notting Hill
Marble Arch
Hammersmith
Chiswick
Victoria
Earls Court
Pimlico
South
Kensington

80

Datchet

BERKS
Heathrow
Kew

Green

Brockley

Wraysbury
Hounslow
Twickenham
Putney
Dulwich
A205 Lew

Egham
HEATHROW
Belham
Sydenham

Staines
Shepperton
Wimbledon
Norbury

Littleton
Teddington
Kingston
Esher
New Malden

Walton on Thames
Wallington
Croydon

Weybridge
A232

M25

Purley

60
A24
Kenley
A23
A22
Warlingha

SURREY

Remember, London is one of the major capital cities of the world and accommodation therefore comes at a premium. These London listings aim to give you good value only. You have a good choice: to stay in budget-priced hotels close to the heart of the thriving city or to stay on the outskirts (like thousands of Londoners) and travel in during the day! You will always be near an Underground or mainline railway station.

Central Library, Townley Road, **Bexley**, Kent, DA6 7HJ, 020 8303 9052.

Hall Place, Bourne Road, **Bexley**, Kent, DA5 1PQ, 01322 558676 (Easter to Oct).

Katharine Street, **Croydon**, Surrey, CR9 1ET, 020 8253 1009 (Easter to Oct).

Tesco Store Car Park, Edgington Way, **Foots Cray**, Kent, DA14 5BN, 01322 614660 (Easter to Oct).

46 Greenwich Church Street, **Greenwich**, London, SE10 9BL, 020 8858 6376.

Central Hall, Mare Street, **Hackney**, London, E8 1HE, 020 8985 9055.

Thames Tower, Blacks Road, **Hammersmith**, London, W6 9EL, 020 8846 9000.

Civic Centre, Station Road, **Harrow**, Middlesex, HA1 2UJ, 020 8424 1103 / 2.

Heathrow 1,2 and 3 Underground Station, The Concourse, **Heathrow**, Middlesex, TW6 2JA, 020 7604 2890.

Terminal 3 Arrivals, Heathrow Airport, **Heathrow**, Middlesex, TW6 1AN, 0839 123456.

Central Library, 14 High Street, **Hillingdon**, Middlesex, UB8 1HD, 01895 250706.

24 The Treaty Centre, Hounslow High Street, **Hounslow**, Middlesex, TW3 1ES, 020 8583 2929.

Discover Islington Visitor Centre, 44 Duncan Street, **Islington**, London, N1 8BW, 020 7278 8787.

26 Grosvenor Gardens, **Kensington**, London, SW1W 0DU, 020 7604 2890.

The Market House, Market Place, **Kingston**, Surrey, KT1 1JS, 020 8547 5592.

Arrivals Hall, Waterloo International Station, **Lambeth**, London, SE1 7LT, 0839 123456.

Lewisham Library, 199-201 Lewisham High Street, **Lewisham**, London, SE13 6LG, 020 8297 8317.

Liverpool Street Underground Station, **London**, EC2M 7PN, 0839 123456.

Town Hall, High Road, **Redbridge**, Essex, IG1 1DD, 020 8478 3020.

Old Town Hall, Whittaker Avenue, **Richmond**, Surrey, TW9 1TP, 020 8940 9125.

Unit 4, Lower Level, Cotton's Centre, Middle Yard, **Southwark**, London, SE1 2QJ, 020 7403 8299.

107A Commercial Street, **Spitalfields**, London, E1 6BG, 020 7375 2549.

44 York Street, **Twickenham**, Middlesex, TW1 3BZ, 020 8891 1411.

Victoria Station Forecourt, **Victoria**, London, SW1V 1JU, 0839 123456.

Basement Services Arcade, Selfridges store, Oxford Street, **Westminster**, London, W1, 0839 123456.

British Travel Centre, Piccadilly Circus, **Westminster**, London.

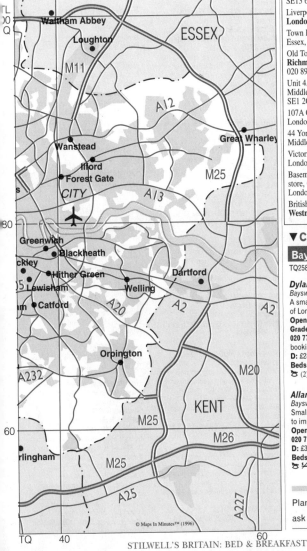

▼ CENTRAL LONDON

Bayswater

TQ2580

Dylan Hotel, 14 Devonshire Terrace, Bayswater, London, W2 3DW.
A small select hotel situated in the heart of London.
Open: All Year
Grades: ETC 2 Diamond RAC 2 Diamond
020 7723 3280 Fax: 020 7402 2443
bookings@dylan-hotel.com
D: £28–£38 **S:** £35–£52
Beds: 3F 5D 6T 4S **Baths:** 9 En 7 Sh
🛏 (2) ⌿ 📺 🖼 🖳 cc

Allandale Hotel, 3 Devonshire Terrace, Bayswater, London, W2 3DN.
Small, select family hotel quietly situated to impress you as being cared for.
Open: All Year
020 7723 8311 (also fax)
D: £30–£35 **S:** £45–£50
Beds: 5F 9D 4T 2S **Baths:** 20 En
🛏 ⌿ 📺 �🍴 ✕ 🖼 🖳 ❀ ⅙ cc 2

Planning a longer stay? Always ask for any special rates

Bloomsbury

TQ3082   🍺 *The Just So, The Goose, The Lamb*

Garth Hotel, 69 Gower Street, Bloomsbury, London, WC1E 6HJ.
Open: All Year
020 7636 5761 Mr Hoare
garth.hotel@virgin.net
D: £25–£40 **S:** £35–£48
Beds: 5F 5T 4D 3S **Baths:** 8 En 4 Sh
🛇 📺 🕭 ✕ 🕮 🛇 ✿ 🔥 **cc**
The hotel, in the heart of London, has a friendly, peaceful atmosphere with clean comfortable rooms. All seventeen rooms have central heating, colour TV., tea/coffee facilities & direct-dial telephones. It has recently been refurbished to a very high standard.

Mentone Hotel, 54-55 Cartwright Gardens, Bloomsbury, London, WC1H 9EL.
Open: All Year
Grades: AA 3 Diamond
020 7387 3927 Mr Tyner **Fax: 020 7388 4671**
mentonehotel@compuserve.com
D: £74–£79 **S:** £74–£79
Beds: 10F 10D 10T 10S **Baths:** All En
🛇 📺 🕭 🔥 **cc**
The Mentone Hotel has been established under present ownership for 25 years and has long been a popular choice with tourists, due to it's pleasant surrounding and central location. This Bed and Breakfast Hotel lies in the heart of Bloomsbury.

Acorn Hotel, 42 Tavistock Place, Bloomsbury, London, WC1H 9RE.
Listed building near Russell Square.
Open: All Year
020 7837 3077 Mr Grover
D: £30–£38 **S:** £48–£52
Beds: 1F 6D 4T 1S **Baths:** 4 Sh
📺 🕭 ✿

Earl's Court

TQ2578   🍺 *Prince of Teck, The Swan*

Merlyn Court Hotel, 2 Barkston Gardens, Earl's Court, London, SW5 0EN.
Open: All Year (not Xmas)
Grades: ETC 2 Diamond
020 7370 1640 Mr Ishani
Fax: 020 7370 4986
london@merlyncourt.demon.co.uk
D: £24–£35 **S:** £30–£60
Beds: 5F 4D 6T 4S **Baths:** 10 En 2 Pr
🛇 ✕ 🔥 🕮 🔥 **cc**
Easy connections to Heathrow, Gatwick and Motorways M4, M40, M1 and city centre.

Ramsees Hotel, 32-36 Hogarth Road, Earl's Court, London, SW5 0PU.
Open: All Year **Grades:** ETC 2 Diamond
020 7370 1445 Mr Younis
Fax: 020 7244 6835
ramsees@rasool.demon.co.uk
D: £23–£26 **S:** £33–£45
Beds: 15F 22D 11T 13S **Baths:** 47 En
🛇 📺 🕮 **cc**
The hotel is ideally located in fashionable Kensington close to the heart of the city. Within one minute's walk from Earls Court station which makes most major shopping areas of Knightsbridge, Oxford Street and Kensington within easy reach.

Rasool Court Hotel, 19-21 Penywern Road, Earl's Court, London, SW5 9TT.
Open: All Year **Grades:** ETC 1 Diamond
020 7373 8900 Mr Younis
Fax: 020 7244 6835
rasool@rasool.demon.co.uk
D: £23–£27 **S:** £33–£50
Beds: 8F 16D 8T 25S **Baths:** 35 En
🛇 📺 🕮 **cc**
The hotel is ideally located in fashionable Kensington close to the heart of the city. The tourist attractions of Buckingham Palace, the Tower of London and the museums are easily accessible. The immediate area itself has a variety of restaurants and shops for your convenience.

Oliver Plaza Hotel, 33 Trebovir Road, Earl's Court, London, SW5 9NE.
Open: All Year
020 7373 7183 Fax: 020 7244 6021
oliverplaza@capricornhotels.co.uk
D: £20–£35 **S:** £15–£25
Beds: 6F 20T 10D 2S **Baths:** 38 En
🅿 (3) 📺 🕮 🔥 **cc**
A nice value for money property in the heart of London. Good access to all public transport facilities and helpful staff to make your stay an enjoyable experience. Family run with emphasis on comfort.

Lord Jim Hotel, 23-25 Penywern Road, Earl's Court, London, SW5 9TT.
Attractive, well-appointed, moderately priced hotel close to city, airports, Earl's Court, Olympia. **Open:** All Year
Grades: ETC 2 Diamond
020 7370 6071 Mr Tayeb
Fax: 020 7373 8919
taher_tayeb@compuserve.com
D: £15–£30 **S:** £25–£50
Beds: 9F 16D 19T 9S **Baths:** 30 En 22 Sh
🛇 ✕ 📺 🕮 🔥 **cc**

Windsor House, 12 Penywern Road, Earl's Court, London, SW5 9ST.
Close to Earls Court/Olympia exhibition halls and South Kensington museums/Knightsbridge.
Open: All Year **Grades:** ETC 1 Diamond
020 7373 9087 Mr Wardle
Fax: 020 7385 2417
D: £20–£30 **S:** £28–£46
Beds: 6F 5D 5T 2S **Baths:** 12 En 5 Pr 1 Sh
🛇 📺 🕭 🕮 🔥

York House Hotel, 27-28 Philbeach Gardens, Earl's Court, London, SW5 9EA.
Excellent value efficiently run B&B in the heart of Kensington. **Open:** All Year
Grades: ETC 2 Diamond
020 7373 7519 Mr Idriss
Fax: 020 7370 4641 yorkhh@aol.com
D: £27–£37 **S:** £27–£37
Beds: 3F 3D 3T 14S **Baths:** 3 En 7 Sh
🛇 📺 🕮 **cc**

Flora Hotel, 11-13 Penywern Road, Earl's Court, London, SW5 9TT.
Depend on comfort for convenience and good value for money. **Open:** All Year
020 7373 6514 Mr Hirji **Fax: 020 7370 3639**
cihotel@aol.com
D: £40–£50 **S:** £55–£65
Beds: 4F 12D 24T 13S **Baths:** 53 En
🛇 📺 🕮 🔥 **cc**

Hyde Park

TQ2780   🍺 *Monkey Puzzle*

Classic Hotel, 92 Sussex Gardens, Hyde Park, London, W2 1UY.
Beautifully decorated, ideal for business, shopping, leisure. Paddington station close by.
Open: All Year
Grades: ETC 2 Diamond
020 7706 7776 Mrs Hassan
classichotel@compuserve.com
D: £30–£36 **S:** £45–£52
Beds: 3F 3D 4T 2S
🛇 🅿 (2) 📺 🕮 🔥 **cc**

Islington

TQ3184   🍺 *Camden Head, The York*

Kandara Guest House, 68 Ockendon Road, Islington, London, N1 3NW.
Open: All Year
Grades: ETC 3 Diamond
020 7226 5721 Mrs Harmon
Fax: 020 7226 3379
admin@kandara.co.uk
D: £24.50–£28 **S:** £39–£44
Beds: 3F 3D 1T 4S **Baths:** 5 Sh
🛇 ✕ 📺 🕮 🔥 **cc**
Small family-run guest house near the Angel, Islington. Free street parking and good public transport to the West End and City. All our bedrooms recently decorated and furnished. During 1999 we doubled the number of showers and toilets.

Kings Cross

TQ3083

A Fairway Hotel, 13-15 Argyle Street, Kings Cross, London, WC1H 8EJ.
Open: All Year
020 7278 8682 (also fax)
Mrs Caruana
fairway@cyberlobby.com
D: £19–£22 **S:** £28–£35
Beds: 7F 10T 10D 6S **Baths:** 3 En 8 Sh
🛇 📺 🕮 ✿ 🔥 **cc**
Comfortable family run B&B close to all major tourist attractions and shopping centres. Excellent transport links, direct lines from Heathrow and Gatwick Airports.

Marble Arch

TQ2881   🍺 *The Aristocrat*

Lincoln House Hotel, 33 Gloucester Place, Marylebone, London, W1U 8HY.
Open: All Year
Grades: ETC 2 Diamond
020 7486 7630 Mr Shariff
Fax: 020 7486 0166
reservations@lincoln-house-hotel.co.uk
D: £39–£45 **S:** £65–£69
Beds: 3F 7D 3T 9S **Baths:** 20 En 2 Sh
🛇 (2) 🕮 🔥 **cc**
Built in the days of King George III, this hotel offers Georgian charms and character. Ensuite rooms with modern comforts. Competitively priced. Located in London's West End, next to Oxford street shopping, close to Theatreland. Ideal for business or leisure.

Notting Hill

TQ2480

Manor Court Hotel, *7 Clanricarde Gardens, Notting Hill Gate, London, W2 4JJ.* Only a few minutes away from Kensington & Hyde Park.
Open: All Year
Grades: ETC 1 Diamond
020 7727 5407 Mr Zaidi
Fax: 020 7229 2875
D: £25–£30 **S:** £35–£45
Beds: 3F 9D 3T 5S **Baths:** 17 En 3 Sh
🛇 📺 ▥ cc

Paddington

TQ2681 ◀ *The Dickens, The Sawyer, Sussex Arms, Monkey Puzzle, The Swan, The Victoria*

Ruddimans Hotel, *160 Sussex Gardens, Paddington, London, W2 1UD.*
Open: All Year
Grades: ETC 2 Diamond
020 7723 1026 Mr Charalambols
Fax: 020 7262 2983
reservations@ruddimonshotel.co.uk
D: £25–£32 **S:** £35–£45
🛇 📶 📺 ▥ cc
A warm and friendly atmosphere with a bit of a difference. Excellent buffet English breakfast in our themed dining room.

Albro House Hotel, *155 Sussex Gardens, Paddington, London, W2 2RY.* Near Hyde Park, public transport. Ideal location. Comfortable rooms, all with TV.
Open: All Year
020 7724 2931
Mr Caruso
Fax: 020 7262 2278
joe@albrohotel.freeserve.co.uk
D: £28–£36 **S:** £38–£56
Beds: 4F 6D 6T 2S **Baths:** 18 En
🛇 (4) 📶 (1) ⋇ 📺 ▥ ♨

Barry House Hotel, *12 Sussex Place, Paddington, London, W2 2TP.* Central location. Comfortable ensuite rooms. Competitive rates and a lovely English breakfast.
Open: All Year
020 7723 7340 Mr Bhasin
Fax: 020 7723 9775
bh-hotel@bigfoot.com
D: £38–£40 **S:** £40–£41
Beds: 4F 3D 8T 4S **Baths:** 15 En 3 Sh
🛇 📺 ▥ ♨ cc

Pimlico

TQ2978 ◀ *Morpeth Arms*

Elizabeth House Hotel, *118 Warwick Way, Pimlico, London, SW1 4JB.* B&B close Victoria Station. Underground, BR, coach station. 24 hour reception.
Open: All Year
020 7630 0741
Mr Hussain
Fax: 020 7630 0740
D: £25–£30 **S:** £30–£35
Beds: 8F 13T 3D 11S **Baths:** 10 En
📺 ▥ cc

South Kensington

TQ2678 ◀ *Dryton Arms*

Swiss House Hotel, *171 Old Brompton Road, South Kensington, London, SW5 0AN.*
Open: All Year
Grades: ETC 3 Diamond, RAC 3 Diamond
020 7373 2769 Mr Vincenti
Fax: 020 7373 4983
recep@swiss-hh.demon.co.uk
D: £42.50–£49.50 **S:** £46–£65
Beds: 8F 11D 10T 4S **Baths:** 1 Sh
🛇 ⋇ 📶 ♜ ▥ cc
Excellent value for money has always been our motto. The hotel knows guests' priorities and aims to meet them all. Cleanliness, service with a smile, value and comfort come as standard. Best value in London award winner.

Victoria

TQ2878 ◀ *The Albert, Marquis Of Westminster, St George's Tavern, The Constitution, Princess Royal, The Chimes*

Edward House B&B, *5 St George's Drive, Victoria, London, SW1V 4DP.*
Open: All Year
020 7834 5207 Fax: 020 7976 5428
edwardhouse@hotmail.com
D: £30–£32.50 **S:** £37.50–£50
Beds: 21F 4D 8T **Baths:** 15 En 3 Pr 4 Sh
🛇 📶 📺 ▥ ♨
Conveniently situated, walking distance famous landmarks - Buckingham Palace, Westminster Abbey, Houses of Parliament, Trafalgar Square, Piccadilly Circus, Leicester Square, many more. Victoria rail, bus, tube and Victoria Coach Station, serving London and the whole country, just a few minutes away.

Stanley House Hotel, *19-21 Belgrave Road, Victoria, London, SW1V 1RB.*
Open: All Year
020 7834 5042 Mr Shah
Fax: 020 7834 8439
cmahotel@aol.com
D: £25–£31 **S:** £42–£52
Beds: 11F 25D 8T **Baths:** 11 En 26 Pr 6 Sh
🛇 📶 📺 ▥ cc
Stanley House Hotel, central location in elegant Belgravia, 4/5 minutes' walk from Victoria Transport complex for easy access to all famous sights and West End shopping and theatre. Spacious bedrooms having ensuite facilities. Prices inclusive of full English breakfast. Tea/coffee available 24 hours.

Alexander Hotel, *13 Belgrave Road, Victoria, London, SW1V 1RB.*
Open: All Year (not Xmas)
020 7834 9738 Mr Montagnani
Fax: 020 7630 9630
D: £22.50–£65 **S:** £30–£60
Beds: 3F 7D 2T 1S **Baths:** 13 En
🛇 📶 📺 ▥ cc
Clean, comfortable, affordable family run Bed & Breakfast situated in the centre of London. Within walking distance of London's tourist attractions, Victoria, Underground, bus station and Gatwick Express Airport Terminal only a 250 meter walk away.

Planning a longer stay? Always ask for any special rates

Marne Hotel, *34 Belgrave Road, Victoria, London, SW1V 1RG.* Comfortable family run B&B based in the heart of London.
Open: All Year
020 7834 5195 Mr Montagnani
Fax: 020 7976 6180
D: £21–£35 **S:** £35–£55
Beds: 3F 5D 1T 3S **Baths:** 8 En 1 Sh
🛇 📺 ▥ cc

Collin House, *104 Ebury Street, Victoria, London, SW1W 9QD.*
Open: All Year (not Xmas/New Year)
Grades: ETC 3 Diamond
020 7730 8031 (also fax)
Mr Thomas
D: £32.50–£40 **S:** £52–£60
Beds: 1F 5D 4T 3S **Baths:** 8 En 3 Sh
🛇 ⋇
Centrally located providing an ideal base for visiting London's many attractions. 5 minutes from Victoria Station & well-serviced by bus, underground & taxis. Comfortable beds, full breakfast, no smoking throughout.

Holly House Hotel, *20 Hugh Street, Victoria, London, SW1V 1RP.* Bed & breakfast in the heart of London. Affordable accommodation perfectly situated.
Open: All Year
020 7834 5671 Mr Jessa
Fax: 020 7233 5154
hhhotel@ukgateway.net
D: fr £20 **S:** fr £30
Beds: 2F 10D 7T 6S **Baths:** 11 En 7 Sh
🛇 📺 ▥ cc

St George's Hotel, *25 Belgrave Road, Victoria, London, SW1V 1RB.* Comfortable, clean, spacious bright rooms. Handy for Gatwick and Heathrow. Great central location.
Open: All Year
Grades: ETC 1 Diamond
020 7828 2061 Mr Zaidi
Fax: 020 7834 8439
cmahotel@aol.com
D: £25–£30 **S:** £30–£45
Beds: 4D 4T 2F 1S **Baths:** 3 En 8 Pr
🛇 ⋇ 📺 ▥

Melita House Hotel, *35 Charlwood Street, Victoria, London, SW1V 2DU.* Excellent location and value, extensive facilities for category, recommended.
Open: All Year
020 7828 0471
Mr Gabrielle
Fax: 020 7932 0988
reserve@melita.co.uk
D: £35–£40 **S:** £45–£60
Beds: 22F 10D 5T 7S **Baths:** 22 En
🛇 📶 ⋇ 📺 ▥ ♨ ❋ cc

Colliers Hotel, 97 Warwick Way,
Victoria, London, SW1V 1QL.
A clean budget priced family-run hotel
with a friendly atmosphere.
Open: All Year
020 7834 6931 Fax: 020 7834 8439
D: £22–£24 **S:** £34–£38
Beds: 2F 6T 7D 3S **Baths:** 2 En 5 Sh
🛇 📺 🏢 **cc**

Airways Hotel, 29-31 St Georges Drive,
Victoria, London, SW1V 4DG.
Located in London's central area of
Victoria, the Hotel is an elegant C19th
building. **Open:** All year
020 7834 0205 Mr Popat
Fax: 020 7932 0007
sales@airways-hotel.com
D: £40–£40 **S:** £50–£60
Beds: 40F 12D 8T 7S **Baths:** 40 En
🛇 🄿 ⤴ 📺 🏋 🏢 🛆 🕭 **cc**

▼ EAST LONDON

Forest Gate

TQ4085   🍺 Wetherspoons

Grangewood Lodge Hotel, 104 Clova
Road, Forest Gate, London, E7 9AF.
5 minute walk to Forest Gate station for
easy access to central London and
Docklands. **Open:** All Year
Grades: ETC 1 Diamond
020 8534 0637 Mr Downing
Fax: 020 8503 0941
grangewoodlodgehotel@talk21.com
D: £17.50–£22 **S:** £22–£40
Beds: 4F 1D 4T 9S **Baths:** 2 En 4 Sh
🛇 (10) 🄿 (2) 📺 🏢 🕭 **cc**

Ilford

TQ4486   🍺 Spoon of Ilford, Sefers Rest

Woodville Guest House, 10/12 Argyle
Road, Ilford, Essex, IG1 3BQ.
Open: All Year (not Xmas/New Year)
Grades: AA 3 Diamond, RAC 3 Diamond
020 8478 3779 Mrs Murray
Fax: 020 8478 6282
cassewoodville-guesthouse.co.uk
D: £20–£30 **S:** £30–£45
Beds: 3F 6T 4D 3S **Baths:** 5 En 2 Pr 5
Sh
🛇 🄿 (12) 📺 🏢 🕭
Private Family-run business for twenty-
five years. Extremely friendly, minutes
from shops and trains. City 20 minutes,
West End 30 to 40 minutes. Easy access
from M11 and M25. Children especially
welcome. Large patio and garden.

Wanstead

TQ4088

The Fosters, 71 Grosvenor Road,
Wanstead, London, E11 2ES.
Excellent accommodation, quiet,
welcoming, comfortable. Close to tube.
Unrestricted parking.
Open: All Year (not Xmas)
020 8530 6970 (also fax)
Mrs Foster
b&b@the-fosters71.freeserve.co.uk
D: £22–£25 **S:** £37.50–£45
Beds: 1F 1D 1T **Baths:** 2 En 1 Sh
🛇 ⤴ 🏢 🕭 **cc**

▼ NORTH LONDON

Crouch End

TQ3089

22 Trinder Road, (off Shaftesbury
Road), Crouch Hill, London, N19 4QU.
Quiet, rustic, terraced house near lively
bars, cafes, leafy area. Longer stays
negotiated.
Open: All Year
020 7686 4073 (also fax)
Ms Shrive
D: £17.50–£20 **S:** £20–£30
Beds: 1D 2S **Baths:** 2 Sh
🄿 📺 🏢

Mount View, 31 Mount View Road,
Crouch End, London, N4 4SS.
Near Finsbury Park Underground -
Piccadilly and Victoria lines. No smoking.
Parking.
Open: All Year
020 8340 9222 Mrs Hendrickx
Fax: 020 8342 8494
o_hendrickx@hotmail.com
D: £25–£30 **S:** £35–£50
Beds: 1D 1T **Baths:** 1 En
🛇 ⤴ 📺 🏢 🖂 **cc**

Hampstead

TQ2685   🍺 The Spaniards, Jack Straw's Castle

Dillons Hotel, 21 Belsize Park,
Hampstead, London, NW3 4DU.
Handy for central London - budget B&B
close Hampstead and Camden.
Open: All Year
Grades: ETC 1 Diamond
020 7794 3360 Mr Dillon
Fax: 020 7431 7900
desk@dillonshotel.com
D: £22.50–£27.50 **S:** £30–£40
Beds: 3F 5D 4T 1S **Baths:** 8 En 3 Sh
🛇 📺 🏢 **cc**

Hendon

TQ2389

Rilux House, 1 Lodge Road, Hendon,
London, NW4 4DD.
High standard,overlooking garden, quiet
and friendly.
Open: All Year
020 8203 0933 Mrs Weissman
rilux@compuserve.com
D: £30–£35 **S:** £35–£40
Beds: 1F 1D 1T 1S **Baths:** 1 En 1 Pr
🛇 🄿 (2) ⤴ 📺 🏢 🖂 🕭 🛆 1

Palmers Green

TQ3093

71 Berkshire Gardens, Palmers
Green, London, N13 6AA.
Private house with garden.
Open: All Year
020 8888 5573 Mr Clark
D: £18–£22 **S:** £18–£22
Beds: 1T **Baths:** 1 Sh

Planning a longer stay? Always
ask for any special rates

RATES

D = Price range per person
sharing in a double room
S = Price range for a
single room

Tufnell Park

TQ2986   🍺 Boston Bar, Lord Palmerston

Five Kings Guest House, 59 Anson
Road, Tufnell Park, London, N7 0AR.
Open: All Year
Grades: ETC 2 Diamond
020 7607 3996 Mr Poulacheris
Fax: 020 7609 5554
D: fr £19 **S:** £24–£28
Beds: 4F 3D 3T 6S **Baths:** 16 En 7 Pr 3 Sh
🛇 (4) 📺 🏢 🕭 **cc**
Five Kings is a family-run guest house in
a quiet residential area. Only 15 minutes
to Central London and tourist attractions.
Camden Lock, London Zoo, Kings Cross,
St Pancras station are only 2 miles away.
No parking restrictions in Anson Road.

Queens Hotel, 33 Anson Road, Tufnell
Park, London, N7 0RB.
Victorian building, 5 minutes walk to
Tufnell park station.
Open: All Year
020 7607 4725 Mr Stavrou
Fax: 020 7607 9725
queens@stavrouhotels.co.uk
D: £23–£27 **S:** £27–£34
Beds: 25 **Baths:** 25 En 13 Sh
🛇 🄿 (7) 📺 🏢 ✱ 🕭

West Hampstead

TQ2585

Charlotte Guest House, 195-197
Sumatra Road, West Hampstead, London,
NW6 1PF.
Access to the West End or City in 10-15
minutes.
Open: All Year
020 7794 6476 Mr Koch
Fax: 020 7431 3584
D: £20–£30 **S:** £30–£45
Beds: 2F 12D 12T 12S **Baths:** 14 En 6 Sh
🛇 📺 🏢 🕭 **cc**

▼ SOUTH LONDON

Balham

TQ2873   🍺 The Point

Milo Guest House, 52 Ritherdon
Road, Balham, London, SW17 8QG.
Victorian house in quiet residential area,
25 minutes from central London. Parking
facilities.
Open: All Year
020 8678 7123 Fax: 020 8678 7124
D: £15–£17.50 **S:** £12.50–£15
Beds: 2F 5T 2S **Baths:** 3 Sh
🄿 📺 🏢 🕭

National Grid References are for villages, towns and cities – not for individual houses

Blackheath

TQ3976 🍺 *Sun in the Sands, Royal Oak*

Numbernine Blackheath Ltd., *9 Charlton Road, Blackheath, London, SE3 7EU.*
Open: All Year **Grades:** ETC 4 Diamond
020 8858 4175 (also fax)
no9limited@hotmail.com
🛏 (5) 🅿 (4) ⊁ 📺 ✕ 🛆 🖳 ☺ **cc**
Number Nine is a friendly, non-smoking guest house located at The Royal Standard, within fifteen minutes walking distance of the historic town of Greenwich. This recently fully refurbished Victorian guest house provides warm, comfortable, safe, fully Fire Certificated surroundings.

135 Shooters Hill Road, *Blackheath, London, SE3 8UQ.*
Victorian family house/garden close central London, River Thames, Jubilee/DLR. lines. **Open:** All Year
020 8858 1420 P & J Poole
D: £25–£35 **S:** £25–£30
Beds: 1F 1D **Baths:** 2 En
🛏 🅿 (1) ⊁ 📺 🖳 ✿ ☺

Brockley

TQ3674 🍺 *la lanema*

Geoffrey Road B & B, *66 Geoffrey Road, Brockley, London, SE4 1NT.*
Friendly and relaxed Victorian family home in Brockley conservation area.
Open: All Year **Grades:** ETC 2 Diamond
020 8691 3887 (also fax) Ms Dechamps
b&bgeoffrey@woodin.u-net.com
D: £20–£22.50 **S:** £20–£25
Beds: 1T **Baths:** 1 Sh
🛏 ⊁ 📺 🖳 🛆 ☺

Catford

TQ3873 🍺 *Goose & Granite, Catford Ram*

Hazeldene Bed & Breakfast, *75 Brownhill Road (South Circular Road), Catford, London, SE6 2HF.*
Traditional English B&B, Victorian house. Greenwich 3 miles/ Zone 3.
Open: All Year
020 8697 2436 Fax: 020 8473 9601
hazeldene@zoo.co.uk
D: £20–£22.50 **S:** £20–£35
Beds: 1F 1D 2T 2S **Baths:** 1 En 2 Sh
🛏 (8) 🅿 (1) 📺 🖳 🛆 ☺

Croydon

TQ3265

Croydon Friendly Guest House, *16 St Peters Road, Croydon, CR0 1HD.*
Open: All Year
020 8680 4428 Mr Hasan
D: £20–£30 **S:** £25–£30
Beds: 1T 5S **Baths:** 2 En 2 Sh
🛏 (1) 🅿 (6) ⊁ 📺 ✕ 🖳 🛆 ☺
Large character full detached house enjoying a warm friendly atmosphere. Situated within easy walking distance of all train and bus services into Central London and al main amenities, restaurants, pubs and theatres in Croydon. Comfortable rooms, ample off road parking.

Dulwich

TQ3472 🍺 *Alleyn's Head, Crown, The Greyhound*

Diana Hotel, *88 Thurlow Park Road, West Dulwich, London, SE21 8HY.*
Comfortable hotel near Dulwich village, a pleasant London suburb. **Open:** All Year
020 8670 3250 Fax: 020 8761 8300
dihotel@aol.com
D: £25–£30 **S:** £30–£50
Beds: 1F 5T 5D 2S **Baths:** 4 En 2 Sh
🛏 🅿 📺 🖳 🛆

Greenwich

TQ3977 🍺 *Welcome Inn*

78 Vanbrugh Park, Blackheath, *Greenwich, London, SE3 7JQ.*
Lovely Victorian House. Blackheath/Greenwich. Own living room. bedrooms overlook beautiful garden.
Open: All Year
020 8858 0338 Mrs Mattey
Fax: 020 8444 6690
D: £20–£25 **S:** £25–£30
Beds: 1F 2T **Baths:** 1 En 1 Pr
🛏 🅿 (3) 📺 🖳 🛆

Greenwich Parkhouse Hotel, *1 & 2 Nevada Street, Greenwich, London, SE10 9JL.*
Small hotel, beautifully situated within World Heritage by gates of Royal Greenwich Park. **Open:** All Year
020 8305 1478 Mrs Bryan
D: £20–£25 **S:** £33
Beds: 21F **Baths:** 2 En 1 Pr 2 Sh
🛏 🅿 (8) ⊁ 📺 🖳 🛆

Dover House, *155 Shooters Hill, Greenwich, London, SE18 3HP.*
Victorian family house opposite famous Oxleas Wood, 8 miles Central London. Warm welcome awaits.
Open: All Year (not Xmas)
020 8856 9892 (also fax) Mrs Araniello
D: £20 **S:** £25
Beds: 2F 2T 2S **Baths:** 1 Sh
🛏 🅿 ⊁ 📺 🖳 🛆 ☺

Hither Green

TQ3974 🍺 *The Railway*

51 Manor Park, *Hither Green, London, SE13 5RA.*
Generous friendly Victorian house. 20 mins central London. Own kitchen.
Open: All Year
020 8318 6474 Mr McMurray
Fax: 020 8244 6690
mcmurray@dircon.co.uk
D: £18–£20 **S:** £20
Beds: 2T 1S **Baths:** 2 Sh
🛏 (10) 🅿 (2) 📺 🖳 🛆

13 Wellmeadow Road, *Hither Green, London, SE13 6SY.*
3 Minutes BR Station, 6 Minutes A2 to Dover or M25.
Open: All Year **Grades:** ETC 2 Diamond
020 8697 1398 Mrs Noonan
Fax: 020 8697 1398
D: £20 **S:** fr £18
Beds: 2F 2D **Baths:** 2 Sh
🛏 🅿 (2) ⊁ 📺 ✕ 🖳

Kenley

TQ3259 🍺 *Wattenden Arms*

Appledore, *6 Betula Close, Kenley, Surrey, CR8 5ET.*
Comfortable detached house in quiet wooded location. Near M25, Gatwick.
Open: All Year
Grades: ETC 3 Diamond
020 8668 4631 (also fax)
Mrs Wilmshurst
D: £22–£24 **S:** £25
Beds: 1D 1T 1S **Baths:** 1 Sh
🛏 (12) 🅿 (2) ⊁ 📺 🖳 🛆

Kingston

TQ1869 🍺 *The Mill, The Ram*

40 The Bittoms Kingston Upon, *Kingston, KT1 2AP.*
Very close to town centre & River Thames. Quiet location.
Open: All Year
020 8541 3171 Mrs Lefebvre
D: £22.50–£27.50 **S:** £25–£35
Beds: 1T 1D 1S **Baths:** 1 Sh
🛏 (4) 📺 ✕ 🖳 🛆

Lewisham

TQ3875 🍺 *The George, The Crown*

8 Yeats Close, Eliot Park, *Lewisham, London, SE13 7ET.*
Open: All Year
Grades: ETC 2 Diamond
020 8318 3421 (also fax)
Ms Hutton
D: £22.50–£25 **S:** £25
Beds: 1D 1T 1S **Baths:** 1 Sh
🛏 ⊁ 📺 🖳 🛆
Homely base in quiet tree-lined road convenient for Greenwich & Central London, only 5 minutes from the Heath yet easy access to the Dome, all bus, train, DLR connections.

Baileys, *77 Belmont Hill, Lewisham, London, SE13 5AX.*
Large, refurbished Victorian house near Greenwich and stations. Close to London.
Open: All Year
020 8852 7373 Mrs Bailey
Fax: 020 8473 7777
D: £20–£25 **S:** £20–£25
Beds: 1F 2T 1S **Baths:** 1 Sh
🛏 ⊁ 📺 ✕ 🖳 🛆

Manna House, *320 Hither Green Lane, Lewisham, London, SE13 6TS.*
Family home, convenient for millennium dome, Greenwich & central London.
Open: All Year
020 8461 5984 Mrs Rawlins
Fax: 020 8695 5316
mannahouse@aol.com
D: £20–£25 **S:** £25–£30
Beds: 1F 1D 1S **Baths:** 2 Sh
🛏 (5) 🅿 (2) ⊁ 📺 🖳 🛆 ☺ **cc**

RATES

D = Price range per person sharing in a double room
S = Price range for a single room

New Malden

TQ2167　◀ *The Fountain*

30 Presburg Road, *New Malden, Surrey, KT3 5AH.*
Open: All Year (not Xmas)
020 8949 4910 Mr & Mrs Evans
D: £22.50–£25 **S:** £25–£30
Beds: 1F 1D 1S **Baths:** 2 Sh
Easy 20 minute rail journey to Central London & to Hampton Court Palace (Annual July Flower Show); 10 minutes to Kingston-upon-Thames, Wimbledon (tennis), A3 road (1 minute away) gives access to Guildford, Wisley Gardens, Legoland, Windsor & M25.

Norbury

TQ3169　◀ *Moon Under Water*

The Konyots, *95 Pollards Hill South, Norbury, London, SW16 4LS.*
Located in a quiet residential area with a park nearby.
Open: All Year
Grades: ETC 1 Diamond
020 8764 0075 Mrs Konyot
D: fr £15 **S:** fr £15
Beds: 1F 1S **Baths:** 1 Sh

Orpington

TQ4565　◀ *Brewers Fayre*

20 The Avenue, *St Pauls Cray, Orpington, Kent, BR5 3DL.*
Open: All Year (not Xmas/New Year)
020 8300 1040 (also fax)
Mrs Tomkins
tomkinsbandb@
20theavenue.freeserve.co.uk
D: £21 **S:** £21–£25
Beds: 1D 1T 1S **Baths:** 1 Sh
Detached family house in cul-de-sac. Excellent full English breakfast. Good road and rail connections. 12 miles, Central London, A20 adjacent 3 miles J3 M25. Sidcup St Mary Cray for frequent trains to London.

Purley

TQ3161　◀ *Marine Bar, Foxley Hatchet, Toby Inn*

The Nook, *12 Grasmere Road, Purley, Surrey, CR8 1DU.*
Edwardian house, near to Purley station, small house with personal attention.
Open: 07/01/01 to 28/12/01
020 8660 1742 Mrs Andrews
D: £18–£20 **S:** £18–£20
Beds: 1D 2S **Baths:** 1 Sh

Putney

TQ2374

The Grange, *One Fanthorpe Street, Putney, London, SW15 1DZ.*
Open: All Year (not Xmas)
020 8785 7609 Mr & Mrs Taylor
Fax: 020 8789 5584
bbputney@btinternet.com
D: £24 **S:** £30
Beds: 1D 1T **Baths:** 1 En 1 Sh
A warm welcome awaits you to our comfortable family home, which is close to Thames, and convenient for bus, Underground and BR mainline. Evening meals by arrangement from £14. Bed and continental breakfast £24 - £30 per person per night.

Sydenham

TQ3471

97 Wiverton Road, *Sydenham, London, SE26 5JB.*
Open: All Year (not Xmas/New Year)
020 8778 8101 Dr & Mrs Tegner
henrytegner@sydenham2.demon.co.uk
D: £30–£40 **S:** £30–£40
Beds: 2T **Baths:** 1 Pr 1 Sh
We offer bed and breakfast accommodation in our charming Victorian home in south-east London. Quiet location, pretty garden, yet only 20 minutes from the West End by frequent train service. Private sitting room for guests.

Wallington

TQ2864　◀ *Whispering Moon*

17 Osmond Gardens, *Wallington, Surrey, SM6 8SX.*
Trains direct to London (33 mins), near Croydon, quiet road.
Open: All Year (not Xmas)
020 8647 1943 Mrs Dixon
Fax: 020 8715 6085
dixonguest@jennifer22.fsnet.co.uk
D: £23–£26 **S:** £25–£30
Beds: 1F 1D **Baths:** 1 En 1 Sh

Welling

TQ4675

De & Dees B&B, *91 Welling Way, Welling, Kent, DA16 2RW.*
Family home near Oxleas Woods. No smoking, very clean.
Open: All Year
020 8319 1592 (also fax)
Mrs Dalton
D: £20–£25 **S:** £20–£25
Beds: 1F 1T 1S **Baths:** 1 Pr

All details shown are as supplied by B&B owners in Autumn 2000

Wimbledon

TQ2471　◀ *Yates*

22 Mayfield Road, *Wimbledon, London, SW19 3NF.*
Artist's detached house. Warm welcome. Near BR, Underground, A3 & M25.
Open: All Year
Grades: ETC 2 Diamond
020 8543 2607 (also fax)
Mr & Mrs Daglish
daglish@gofornet.co.uk
D: fr £25 **S:** fr £25
Beds: 1D 1T **Baths:** 1 En 1 Pr

▼ WEST LONDON

Chiswick

TQ2078

Fouberts Hotel, *162-166 Chiswick High Road, Chiswick, London, W4 1PR.*
Family-run hotel, continental atmosphere.
Open: All Year
Grades: ETC 2 Star
020 8994 5202 Mr Lodico
D: £35–£40 **S:** £25–£27.50
Beds: 6F 6D 4T 16S **Baths:** 32 Pr

Ealing

TQ1780　◀ *Duffy's, The Townhouse*

68 Cleveland Road, *Ealing, London, W13 8AJ.*
Open: All Year
020 8991 5142 Mrs McHugh
Fax: 020 8998 2872
D: £26–£28 **S:** £28–£30
Beds: 2F 1D 1T 1S **Baths:** 1 En 2 Pr 1 Sh
Large luxury house overlooking parkland bright airy rooms friendly atmosphere, 30 mins to central London or Heathrow tea and coffee facilities hairdryers and colour TV supplied.

24 Barnfield Road, *Ealing, London, W5 1QT.*
Luxurious accommodation, friendly family home. very clean rooms, TV, coffee making.
Open: All Year
020 8998 2831 Ms Schmidt-Neill
Fax: 020 8621 0094
niceroom@aol.com
D: £20–£25 **S:** £25–£30
Beds: 1F 1T 1D 1S **Baths:** 2 Sh

Abbey Lodge Hotel, *51 Grange Park, Ealing, London, W5 3PR.*
Halfway between Heathrow and central London. Home from home atmosphere.
Open: All Year (not Xmas)
Grades: ETC 2 Diamond, RAC 2 Diamond
020 8567 7914 Mrs Grindrod
Fax: 020 8579 5350
enquiries@londonlodgehotels.com
D: £26–£28.50 **S:** fr £39
Beds: 3F 3D 1T 9S **Baths:** 16 En

Grange Lodge Hotel, *48/50 Grange Road, Ealing, London, W5 5BX.*
Home away from home - close to 3 Tube stations and lines.
Open: All Year (not Xmas)
Grades: ETC 3 Diamond, RAC 3 Diamond
020 8567 1049
enqiries@londonlodgehotels.com
D: £26–£28.50 **S:** £29–£45
Beds: 2F 3D 2T 7S **Baths:** 9 En 5 Sh
🛇 🅿 (7) 📺 🍴 📖 ♨ 🚺 cc

Eastcote
TQ1088

7 Eastfields, *Eastcote, Pinner, HA5 2SR.*
Access to places of interest, many excellent restaurants, transport nearby.
Open: All Year (not Xmas)
020 8429 1746 Mrs Mash
D: fr £23 **S:** fr £23
Beds: 2T **Baths:** 1 Sh
🍴 📺 📖 ♨

Hammersmith
TQ2279   ◖ *The Dove, Crabtree Tavern, William Morris*

67 Rannoch Road, *Hammersmith, London, W6 9SS.*
Open: All Year
020 7385 4904 Mr & Mrs Armanios
Fax: 020 7610 3235
D: £22 **S:** £32
Beds: 1F 1D 1T **Baths:** 1 Sh
🛇 🍴 📺 📖 🚺 ♨
Comfortable, central, Edwardian family home. Quiet, close river, pubs, restaurants. Great base for sightseeing/courses/business. Excellent transport facilities. Direct lines to theatres, shopping, Harrods, museums, Albert Hall, Earls Court/Olympia Exhibitions; Heathrow, Gatwick (Victoria), Eurostar. Children's reductions. Continental Breakfast.

Harrow
TQ1488   ◖ *The Apollo, Cumberland Hotel, Moon on the Hill*

Crescent Hotel, *58-60 Welldon Crescent, Harrow, Middx, HA1 1QR.*
Open: All Year **Grades:** ETC 3 Diamond
020 8863 5491 Mr Jivraj
Fax: 020 8427 5965
jivraj@crsnthtl.demon.co.uk
D: £27.50–£32.50 **S:** £40–£50
Beds: 2F 2D 4T 13S **Baths:** 18 En 3 Sh
🛇 🅿 (7) 📺 📖 🚺 ♨ cc
A modern, friendly hotel in a quiet crescent in the heart of Harrow, yet only a short drive to Wembley and the West End with Heathrow easily accessible. 21 rooms all ensuite, comfortable and well furnished, with colour TV, satellite, fridge, telephone and tea/coffee making facilities.

BEDROOMS
F - Family
D - Double
T - Twin
S - Single

Hindes Hotel, *8 Hindes Road, Harrow, Middx, HA1 1SJ.*
Owner-run business where we take pride in providing friendly personal service to our guests.
Open: All Year
020 8427 7468 Mr Ahluwalia
reception@hindeshotel.com
D: £27.50–£55 **S:** £37–£45
Beds: 4D 6T 4S **Baths:** 7 En 7 Sh
🛇 🅿 (25) 📺 ✕ 📖 ♨ ♨ cc

Central Hotel, *6 Hindes Road, Harrow, Middx, HA1 1SJ.*
Town centre guest house close to Heathrow, M1, M25, parking.
Open: All Year (not Xmas)
020 8427 0893 Mr Ryan
D: £24–£29 **S:** £35–£48
Beds: 3F 2D 4T 4S **Baths:** 5 En 3 Sh
🛇 🅿 (12) 📺 📖 ♨ cc

Heathrow
TQ0980   ◖ *Great Western*

Shepiston Lodge, *31 Shepiston Lane, Heathrow, Middx, UB3 1LJ.*
Character house near Heathrow.
Open: All Year
020 8573 0266 Mr Dhawan
Fax: 020 8569 2536
shepiston@aol.com
D: fr £24.75 **S:** fr £36.50
Beds: 2F 3D 11T 6S **Baths:** 22 En 1 Sh
🛇 🅿 (20) 🍴 📺 ✕ 📖 🚺 ♨ 🚹 cc

Hounslow
TQ1475   ◖ *The Bulstrode*

Lampton Guest House, *47 Lampton Road, Hounslow, Middx, TW3 1JG.*
Ideal for Heathrow airport and central London, stop over, superbly located.
Open: All Year **Grades:** ETC 3 Diamond
020 8570 0056 Fax: 020 8570 1220
D: £25–£30 **S:** £45–£60
Beds: 4F 4D 4T 8S **Baths:** 20 En 1 Pr 1 Sh
🛇 (3) 🅿 (10) 📺 📖 ♨ cc

Kew
TQ1876   ◖ *Coach & Horses, Kew Gardens Hotel, Ship*

Melbury, *33 Marksbury Avenue, Kew, Richmond, Surrey, TW9 4JE.*
Friendly and welcoming, refurbished private home, close to Richmond and Kew Gardens Underground.
Open: All Year
Grades: ETC 2 Diamond
020 8876 3930 (also fax)
Mrs Allen
D: £22.50–£27.50 **S:** £25–£35
Beds: 1T 1D 1F 1S **Baths:** 2 En 1 Sh
🛇 (2) 🅿 (1) 🍴 📺 ✕ 📖 ♨

179 Mortlake Road, *Kew, Richmond, Surrey, TW9 4AW.*
Georgian house close to Kew Gardens, PRO and Underground.
Open: All Year
Grades: ETC 3 Diamond
020 8876 0584 (also fax)
Mrs Butt
D: £25 **S:** fr £35
Beds: 1T **Baths:** 1 En
🅿 (5) 📺 🍴 📖 ♨

34 Forest Road, *Kew, Richmond, Surrey, TW9 3BZ.*
Open: All Year
020 8332 6289 (also fax) Mrs Royle
D: £20–£23 **S:** £22–£28
Beds: 1F 1D 1T
🛇 (12) 🍴 📺 📖 ♨
A comfortable Edwardian era family home. 5 minutes walk from Kew Gardens station, 35 mins to Westminster. 5 mins to Richmond, Kew Botanical Gardens and Public Records Office. Pleasant walks along Thames river bank. Good selection of pubs and restaurants nearby.

1 Chelwood Gardens, *Kew, Richmond, Surrey, TW9 4JG.*
Situated in quiet cul-de-sac. Friendly house near Kew Gardens Station.
Open: All Year
020 8876 8733 Mrs Gray
Fax: 020 8255 0171
mrsljgray@aol.com
D: £25–£27 **S:** £30
Beds: 4F 2T 2S **Baths:** 2 Sh
🛇 (5) 🅿 (6) 🍴 📺 📖 ♨

Pinner
TQ1189   ◖ *Queens Head*

Pinner Bed and Breakfast, *9 Cranbourne Drive, Pinner, Middx, HA5 1BX.*
1930s house in peaceful setting. Short walk to Pinner station.
Open: All Year (not Xmas)
020 8866 5308 J Mckee
D: £20–£25 **S:** £20–£25
Beds: 1D 1T **Baths:** 1 Sh
🛇 🅿 (3) 📺 📖 ♨

Goodmans, *11 Meadow Road, Pinner, Middx, HA5 1EB.*
Modern, comfortable, family home.
Open: All Year
020 8868 1074 Mrs Goodman
D: fr £15 **S:** fr £15
Beds: 2T **Baths:** 2 Sh
🛇 🅿 (2) 📖 ♨

Ruislip
TQ0987   ◖ *J J Moons*

2 Cornwall Road, *Ruislip, Middx, HA4 6RS.*
Small friendly private house. Short walk underground stations. Near M40/M25.
Open: All Year
01895 636676 (also fax) Mrs Glanvill
D: £20 **S:** £25
Beds: 1D 2S **Baths:** 1 Sh
🅿 (2) 🍴 📺 📖 🚺 ♨

Teddington
TQ1670   ◖ *Tide End Pub*

93 Langham Road, *Teddington, Middx, TW11 9HG.*
Sympathetically restored Edwardian house with original features and brass beds. **Open:** All Year (not Xmas)
020 8977 6962 Mrs Norris
lesleyanorris@aol
D: £22.50–£25 **S:** £30–£45
Beds: 1D 1T **Baths:** 1 Sh
🍴 📺 📖

Twickenham

TQ1573_   ◀ *Pope's Grotto*

11 Spencer Road, *Strawberry Hill, Twickenham, Middx, TW2 5TH.*
Stylish Edwardian house near Richmond and Hampton Court. Excellent transport, easy parking. **Open:** All Year
Grades: ETC 3 Diamond
020 8894 5271 Mrs Duff
D: £20–£25 **S:** £20–£25
Beds: 2D 1T **Baths:** 1 En 1 Sh
🛏 (12) �P ⊬ 📺 🎢.

Avalon Cottage, *50 Moor Mead Road, Twickenham, TW1 1JS.*
Avalon Cottage is a private Edwardian house beside a park and tennis courts.
Open: All Year **Grades:** ETC 3 Diamond
020 8744 2178 Mrs Thompson
Fax: 020 8891 2444
avalon@mead99.freeserve.co.uk
D: £25–£35 **S:** £30–£35
Beds: 1D 1S **Baths:** 1 En 1 Sh
🛏 (1) ⊬ 📺 🎢 ♿ **cc**

Uxbridge

TQ0583   ◀ *Load of Hay*

Cleveland Hotel, *4 Cleveland Road, Uxbridge, Middx, UB8 2DW.*
Open: All Year
01895 257618 Mrs Tindale
Fax: 01895 239710
D: £20–£22 **S:** £29–£36
Beds: 5F 3D 1T 5S **Baths:** 9 En 3 Sh
🛏 P (10) 📺 🎢 ♿ **cc**
Early Victorian detached property with modern extension. Convenient for central London and Heathrow. Close to several motorway routes. Near Brunel University and Hillingdon Hospital.

Hillbenn House, *235 Park Road, Uxbridge, Middx, UB8 1NS.*
10 Minutes from Heathrow Airport. 10 Minutes walk to tube station.
Open: All Year
01895 850787 Fax: 01895 814909
hillbenn.house@btinternet.com
D: £22.50–£25 **S:** £35–£40
Beds: 1F 3T 1S **Baths:** 5 En
P (4) ⊬ 📺 🎢. ♿

Spackman Guest House, *14 Hillingdon Road, Uxbridge, Middx, UB10 0AD.*
Listed house near town centre, Heathrow, M4, M40. English breakfast.
Open: All Year (not Xmas)
01895 237994 Mrs Spackman
Fax: 01895 234953
D: £20–£25 **S:** £25
Beds: 1D 1T 1S **Baths:** 1 Sh
🛏 P (3) 📺 🎢 🎢. 📺 ♿

Wembley

TQ1785   ◀ *The Blackbird*

Aaron (Wembley Park) Hotel, *8 Forty Lane, Wembley, Middx, HA9 9EB.*
Open: All Year
020 8904 6329 Mr Patel
Fax: 020 8385 0472
enquiries@aaronhotel.com
D: £22.50–£35 **S:** £29–£32
Beds: 6F 2D 1T 1S **Baths:** 9 En 1 Sh
🛏 P (11) 📺 🎢 ✕ 🎢. 📺 ✳ ♿
We are a small family-run hotel. We are within easy reach of the Wembley Stadium Arena, Conference Centre and exhibition halls. Park Royal, Harrow are close by. Wembley Park Tube Station is 10 minutes walk away, West End 20 minutes by tube.

RATES
D = Price range per person sharing in a double room
S = Price range for a single room

Elm Hotel, *1-7 Elm Road, Wembley, Middx, HA9 7JA.*
Open: All Year (not Xmas)
Grades: ETC 3 Diamond, RAC 3 Diamond
020 8902 1764 Mr Gosden
Fax: 020 8903 8365
info@elmhotel.co.uk
D: £32.50–£36 **S:** £48
Beds: 9F 7D 11T 6S **Baths:** 33 En
🛏 P (7) 📺 🎢 🎢. ♿ **cc**
Wembley Stadium, area and conference centre 1200 yds. Wembley central (main line and underground) 150 yards. M1 2.50 miles, Heathrow Airport 8 miles. Comfortable family run 33 bedroom hotel. Get into hot water with your wife, some double rooms have Jacuzzi, jet spa baths.

Adelphi Hotel, *4 Forty Lane, Wembley, Middlesex, HA9 9EB.*
Close to Wembley complex. Warm, friendly atmosphere. Free car park.
Open: All Year
Grades: ETC 3 Diamond, AA 3 Diamond, RAC 3 Diamond
020 8904 5629 Fax: 020 8904 5314
enquiry@adelphihotel.fsnet.co.uk
D: £22.50–£27.50 **S:** £35–£49
Beds: 2F 3T 5D 3S
Baths: 11 En 9 Pr 2 Sh
🛏 P 📺 🎢. ♿ **cc**

Stilwell's Britain Cycleway Companion

23 Long Distance Cycleways –
Where to Stay * Where to Eat

County Cycleways – Sustrans Routes

The first guide of its kind, **Stilwell's Britain Cycleway Companion** makes planning accommodation for your cycling trip easy. It lists B&Bs, hostels, campsites and pubs– in the order they appear along the selected cycleways – allowing the cyclist to book ahead. No more hunting for a room, a hot meal or a cold drink after a long day in the saddle. Stilwell's gives descriptions of the featured routes and includes such relevant information as maps, grid references and distance from route; Tourist Board ratings; and the availability of drying facilities and packed lunches. No matter which route – or part of a route – you decide to ride, let the **Cycleway Companion** show you where to sleep and eat.

As essential as your tyre pump – the perfect cycling companion: **Stilwell's Britain Cycleway Companion**.

Cycleways
Sustrans
Carlisle to Inverness – Clyde to Forth - Devon Coast to Coast -
Hull to Harwich – Kingfisher Cycle Trail - Lon Las Cymru – Sea to Sea (C2C)
– Severn and Thames – West Country Way – White Rose Cycle Route
County
Round Berkshire Cycle Route – Cheshire Cycleway – Cumbria Cycleway –
Essex Cycle Route – Icknield Way - Lancashire Cycleway –
Leicestershire County Cycleway – Oxfordshire Cycleway –
Reivers Cycle Route – South Downs Way - Surrey Cycleway –
Wiltshire Cycleway – Yorkshire Dales Cycleway

£9.95 from all good bookstores (ISBN 1-900861-26-7) or £10.95
(inc p&p) from Stilwell Publishing Ltd, 59 Charlotte Road, London
EC2A 3QW (020 7739 7179)

Norfolk

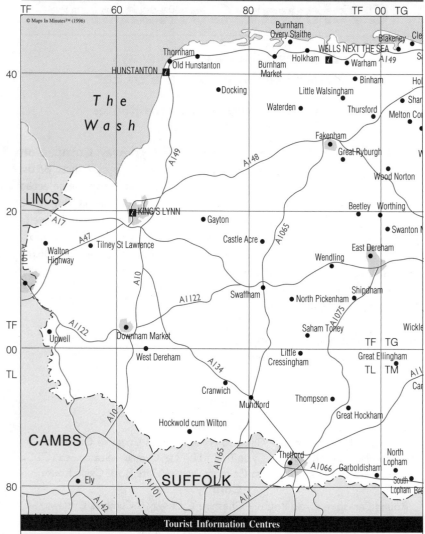

TF   60   80   TF   00   TG

© Maps In Minutes™ (1996)

Burnham Overy Staithe
Blakeney   Cle
Thornham
WELLS NEXT THE SEA
Old Hunstanton
Holkham
Warham   A149   S
HUNSTANTON
Burnham Market
40
Binham
Docking
Little Walsingham
Hol
Waterden
Thursford
Shar
Melton Co
The Wash
Fakenham
Great Ryburgh
W
Wood Norton
LINCS
A149
A148
Beetley   Worthing
KING'S LYNN
20
Swanton N
Gayton
A47
Castle Acre
A1065
East Dereham
Walton Highway
Tilney St Lawrence
Wendling
A10
Shipdham
Swaffham
North Pickenham
A1122
Saham Toney
A1075
Wickle
TF
00
Upwell
A1122
Downham Market
TF   TG
West Dereham
A134
Little Cressingham
Great Ellingham
TL
TL   TM
A1
A107
Cranwich
Car
Thompson
Mundford
Hockwold cum Wilton
Great Hockham
CAMBS
A1065
North Lopham
A1101
Thetford
A1066   Garboldisham
80
Ely
SUFFOLK
South Lopham Bra
A142
A11

Tourist Information Centres

Bus Station, Prince of Wales Road, **Cromer**, Norfolk, NR27 9HS, 01263 512497 (Easter to Oct).

Meres Mouth, Mere Street, **Diss**, Norfolk, IP22 3AG, 01379 650523 (Easter to Oct).

Red Lion House, Market Place, **Fakenham**, Norfolk, NR21 9BY, 01263 512497 (Easter to Oct).

Marine Parade, **Great Yarmouth**, Norfolk, NR30 2EJ, 01493 842195 (Easter to Oct).

Station Road, **Hoveton**, Norwich, NR12 8EU, 01603 782281 (Easter to Oct).

The Green, **Hunstanton**, Norfolk, PE36 5AH, 01485 532610.

The Old Gaol House, Saturday Market Place, **King's Lynn**, Norfolk, PE30 5DQ, 01553 763044.

Shirehall Museum, Common Place, **Little Walsingham**, Walsingham, Norfolk, NR22 6BP, 01328 820510

2a Station Road, **Mundesley**, Norwich, NR11 8JH, 01263 512497 (Easter to Oct).

The Guildhall, Gaol Hill, **Norwich**, NR2 1NF, 01603 666071.

The Staithe, **Ranworth**, Norwich, NR13 6HY, 01603 270453 (Easter to Oct).

Station Approach, **Sheringham**, Norfolk, NR26 8RA, 01263 512497 (Easter to Oct).

Staithe Street, **Wells-next-the-Sea**, Norfolk, NR23 1AN, 01263 512497 (Easter to Oct).

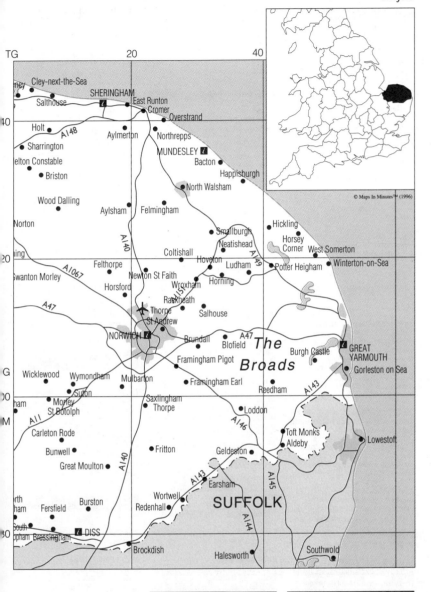

© Maps In Minutes™ (1996)

RATES

D = Price range per person sharing in a double room

S = Price range for a single room

Aldeby

TM4493 🍺 *Toft Lion, Waveney Inn, The Crown*

The Old Vicarage, *Rectory Road, Aldeby, Beccles, Suffolk, NR34 0BJ.*
Spacious old vicarage, tranquil 3 acre garden within open countryside.
Open: All Year (not Xmas)
Grades: ETC 3 Diamond
01502 678229
Mrs Butler
D: £17 **S:** £17
Beds: 3T **Baths:** 1 En 2 Pr
🛇 🅿 (3) ⚒ 📺 🛏 🛆

Aylmerton

TG1839 🍺 *Wheatsheaf*

Woodlands Guest House, *Holt Road, Aylmerton, Norwich, NR11 8AQ.*
Large family home. 3 acres lawned/wooded grounds. Surrounding open countryside.
Open: All Year (not Xmas/New Year)
01263 837480
Mrs Lee
D: £20–£26 **S:** £25–£40
Beds: 2F 2T 2D **Baths:** 3 En 1 Sh
🛇 🅿 (10) ⚒ 📺 🛏 ✕ 🛆 📺 🛆

Aylsham

TG1927   🍺 *Buckingham Arms, Saracen's Head, Green's, Ratcatchers'*

The Old Pump House, *Holman Road, Aylsham, Norwich, NR11 6BY.*
Open: All Year (not Xmas)
Grades: ETC 4 Diamond
01263 733789 (also fax)
Mr & Mrs Richardson
D: £20–£24 **S:** £18–£27
Beds: 1F 2D 2T 1S **Baths:** 4 En 1 Sh
🛇 🅿 (6) ⅙ 📺 🛉 ✕ 🖳 Ⅴ 🏊
Warm, welcoming Georgian farmhouse full of character and near to the Broads, Norwich, stately houses (Blickling Hall 1 mile) and the coast. Breakfasts freshly cooked to order in the pine-shuttered Red Room overlooking the peaceful garden.

Stone House, *20 Millgate, Aylsham, Norwich, NR11 6HX.*
1850 flint house, 1.5 miles narrow gauge railway. Coast, broads nearby.
Open: Easter to Oct
01263 734567 Ms Downes
D: £17.50–£20 **S:** £17.50–£20
Beds: 1S 1D 1T
🛇 (5) 🅿 (2) ⅙ 📺 ✕ 🖳 Ⅴ 🏊

Bacton

TG3433

Seacroft Private Hotel, *Coast Road, Bacton, Norwich, NR12 0HS.*
Beautiful sea view situation. Ideal for touring or beach. Personal supervision.
Open: All Year (not Xmas)
01692 650302 Fax: 01692 651511
D: £19.50–£26 **S:** £19.50–£26
Beds: 2F 3D 2T **Baths:** 7 En 2 Sh
🅿 (9) 📺 ✕ 🖳 Ⅴ 🏊 ⅙ cc

Beetley

TF9718   🍺 *Kings Head*

Shillingstone, *Church Road, Beetley, Dereham, Norfolk, NR20 4AA.*
Situated in Breckland area of Norfolk with own Flora and Fauna, Sandringham, NT properties.
Open: All Year
Grades: ETC 3 Diamond
01362 861099 Fax: 01362 869153
jeannepartridge@ ukgateway.net
D: £20–£22.50 **S:** £22
Beds: 1F 1D 1T **Baths:** 3 En
🛇 🅿 (6) ⅙ 📺 🛉 🖳 Ⅴ ✴ 🏊

Peacock House, *Peacock Lane, Beetley, Dereham, Norfolk, NR20 4DG.*
Lovely old farmhouse, rurally situated. Good home cooking and great hospitality.
Open: All Year
Grades: ETC 4 Diamond, Gold Award
01362 860371 Mrs Bell
PeackH@aol.com
D: £21–£22.50 **S:** £25–£27
Beds: 1F 1T 1D **Baths:** 3 En
🛇 🅿 (4) ⅙ 📺 🛉 ✕ 🖳 Ⅴ 🏊

Planning a longer stay? Always ask for any special rates

BATHROOMS
Pr - Private
Sh - Shared
En - Ensuite

Binham

TF9839   🍺 *Three Horseshoes*

Meadow House, *Walsingham Road, Binham, Fakenham, NR21 0BU.*
Traditional Norfolk house in quiet country location, 3m unspoilt North Norfolk Heritage Coastline.
Open: Mar to Oct
01328 830551 Mrs West
fieldhse21@aol.com
D: £18 **S:** £25
Beds: 2D
🅿 (3) ⅙ 📺 🖳 Ⅴ 🏊

Blakeney

TG0243   🍺 *Kings Arms, White Horse*

White Barn, *Back Lane, Blakeney, Norfolk, NR25 7NP.*
Delightful ensuite annexe with individual access near Blakeney Quay.
Open: All Year (not Xmas)
01263 741359 (also fax)
Mr & Mrs Millard
millard@clara.co.uk
D: £20 **S:** £25–£35
Beds: 1D 1T **Baths:** 2 En
🅿 (5) ⅙ 📺 🖳 Ⅴ 🏊

Dallinga, *71 Morston Road, Blakeney, Holt, Norfolk, NR25 7BD.*
Open: All Year
01263 740943 Mr & Mrs Ward
D: £18.75–£21.25
Beds: 1D 1T **Baths:** 2 En
🛇 (12) 🅿 (6) 📺 🖳 Ⅴ 🏊
4-5 minutes walk to Blakeney Quay. Excellent breakfast menu from local produce ad fish.

Blofield

TG3309   🍺 *Two Friends*

Aldwin, *Woodbastwick Road, Blofield, Norwich, NR13 4QH.*
Large detached bungalow convenient for Norwich and Broads. Norwich 7 miles.
Open: Easter to Oct
01603 713059 Mr Key
D: £15–£20 **S:** £16–£20
Beds: 1D 1T **Baths:** 1 Sh
🅿 (3) 🖳

Bressingham

TM0780   🍺 *Garden House*

Poplar Farm, *Fersfield Road, Bressingham, Diss, Norfolk, IP22 2AP.*
Quiet countryside, close Bloom's Gardens and steam museums, Norwich, Ipswich & coast.
Open: All Year (not Xmas)
01379 687261 Mrs Soar
D: £18.2–£20 **S:** £18.2–£20
Beds: 1D 1T 2S **Baths:** 1 En 2 Sh
🅿 (10) 📺 🖳 🏊

Briston

TG0632   🍺 *Duke's Head*

Hall Farm, *Mill Road, Briston, Melton Constable, Norfolk, NR24 2JF.*
Open: All Year (not Xmas/New Year)
01263 861055 Mr Lester & Ms R. Buley
markrl1000@aol.com
D: £20–£22.50
Beds: 2D **Baths:** 2 Pr
🅿 (6) ⅙ 📺 🛉 🖳 Ⅴ 🏊
'Warm welcome', 'Splendid breakfast', 'Amazing house'. Extracts from our visitors' book. Listed Tudor farmhouse full of period features, overlooking the village green. Aga-cooked breakfasts and olde worlde charm. (Beams/inglenooks) Spacious rooms. Holt 4 miles. Cley 8 miles.

Brockdish

TM2079   🍺 *Del A Pone Arms*

Grove Thorpe, *Grove Road, Brockdish, Diss, IP21 4JE.*
Country house built 1610 nestling in 9 acres private fishing lake beautiful grounds price from £25 pppn. All ensuite, open all year, grading 5 Diamond Gold - children over 12 yrs.
Open: Jan to Dec
01379 668305 Mr & Mrs Morrish
Fax: 01379 688305
D: £25–£32 **S:** £40
Beds: 1T 2D
🛇 (12) 🅿 (20) ⅙ 📺 ✕ 🖳 Ⅴ 🏊 ⅙ 🚹

Brundall

TG3208   🍺 *Shoulder Of Mutton*

Braydeston House, *The Street, Brundall, Norwich, NR13 5JY.*
Elegant house in wooded gardens only 10 minutes from Norwich.
Open: All Year (not Xmas/New Year)
Grades: ETC 3 Diamond
01603 713123 Mrs Knox
ann@braydeston.freeserve.co.uk
D: £22.50–£25 **S:** £25–£28
Beds: 2T **Baths:** 1 Pr 1 Sh
🛇 🅿 (2) 📺 🖳 Ⅴ 🏊

Bunwell

TM1293

The Cottage, *Rectory Lane, Bunwell, Norwich, Norfolk, NR16 1QU.*
Open: All Year
01953 789226 P M Jenkins
D: £17–£20 **S:** £28–£30
Beds: 1F 2D **Baths:** 3 En
🛇 🅿 (4) ⅙ 📺 🛉 ✕ 🖳 Ⅴ 🏊 ⅙
Picturesque C18th thatched cottage set in peaceful country gardens, easy access to many market towns and coast. All accommodation has private facilities of a very high standard. Home-cooked evening meals on request. Guest sitting room overlooks garden and fields.

National Grid References are for villages, towns and cities – not for individual houses

Burgh Castle

TG4804

Church Farm Free House, *Church Road, Burgh Castle, Great Yarmouth, Norfolk, NR31 9QG.*
Church Farm nestles beside Breydon Water where the rivers Waveney and Yare meet.
Open: All Year
01493 780251 Mr Snell
D: fr £18 **S:** fr £20
Beds: 2F 2D 1T 1S **Baths:** 4 En 2 Sh
🛇 🅿 🗶 📺 🗶 📖 🗓 ✿ ♨

Burnham Market

TF8342 ◁ *Host Arms*

Wood Lodge, *Millwood, Herrings Lane, Burnham Market, King's Lynn, Norfolk, PE31 8DP.*
Peaceful, luxurious coastal lodge.
Open: All Year (not Xmas)
Grades: ETC 4 Diamond
01328 730152 Mrs Leftley
Fax: 01328 730158
D: £27.50–£30 **S:** £35–£45
Beds: 1D 1T
🛇 (8) 🅿 🗶 📺 ♞ 📖 ☂

Burnham Overy Staithe

TF8444 ◁ *The Hero*

Domville Guest House, *Glebe Lane, Burnham Overy Staithe, Kings Lynn, Norfolk, PE31 8JQ.*
Quietly situated family-run guest house. Home cooking a speciality.
Open: All Year (not Xmas)
Grades: ETC 3 Diamond
01328 738298 (also fax)
Mrs Smith
D: £18–£23 **S:** £20–£25
Beds: 2T 3S 2D **Baths:** 4 En
🛇 (6) 🅿 (10) 🗶 📺 🗶 🗓 ☂

Burston

TM1383 ◁ *The Crown*

Rose Cottage, *Diss Road, Burston, Diss, IP22 3TP.*
Genuine C18th house in village centre on church green.
Open: All Year (not Xmas)
Grades: ETC 3 Diamond
01379 740602 (also fax) Mr Bromley
cyrilbrom@aol.com
D: £20–£25 **S:** £20–£25
Beds: 1D 2S **Baths:** 1 Sh
🗶 📺 ♞ 📖 ☂

Carleton Rode

TM1193 ◁ *King's Head, The Domino*

Upgate Farm, *Carleton Rode, Norwich, NR16 1NJ.*
Friendly homely accommodation offered in comfortable farmhouse set in rural location.
Open: All Year (not Xmas)
Grades: ETC 3 Diamond
01953 860300 (also fax)
Mr Wright
D: £17–£18 **S:** £17–£18
Beds: 1D 1T **Baths:** 1 Sh
🛇 🅿 (2) 🗶 📺 📖 ☂

Castle Acre

TF8115 ◁ *Castle Gate, George & Dragon, Ostrich Inn*

Willow Cottage Tea Rooms & B&B, *Stocks Green, Castle Acre, Kings Lynn, Norfolk, PE32 2AE.*
Open: All Year (not Xmas)
01760 755551 Mr Gray
Fax: 01760 755799
gv33@dial.pipex.com
D: £15–£18 **S:** £18–£20
Beds: 1F 2D 1T **Baths:** 1 Sh
🛇 🅿 (4) 🗶 📺 📖 🗓 ☂
Attractive beamed tea rooms and guest bedrooms, delicious home-cooked cakes, soups and puddings. Within walking distance of Cluniac Priory, Castle and River Nar. Ideal base for visiting local attractions in North and West Norfolk, warm friendly welcome.

Gemini House, *Pyes Lane, Castle Acre, Kings Lynn, Norfolk, PE32 2XB.*
Well-situated for all Norfolk sights.
Open: All Year
01760 755375 Mrs Clark
D: £15–£17.50 **S:** fr £15
Beds: 2D 2T **Baths:** 1 En 1 Sh
🛇 🅿 (4) 📺 ♞ 📖 ☂

Lodge Farm, *Castle Acre, Kings Lynn, Norfolk, PE32 2BS.*
Large comfortable farmhouse, gardens and paddocks, near Peddars Way.
Open: All Year (not Xmas)
Grades: ETC 4 Diamond, AA 4 Diamond
01760 755506 Mrs Coghill
coghill@lodgefarmcastleacre.co.uk
D: £23–£25 **S:** £23–£25
Beds: 3T **Baths:** 1 Pr 1 Sh
🛇 (5) 🅿 (6) 🗶 📺 📖 ☂

Cley-next-the-Sea

TG0443 ◁ *George & Dragon, Three Swallows*

Cley Windmill, *Cley-next-the-Sea, Holt, Norfolk, NR25 7NN.*
Historic windmill overlooking beautiful unspoilt Norfolk coastal marshes. Wonderfully atmospheric.
Open: All Year
01263 740209 (also fax)
Mr Bolam
D: £35–£49 **S:** £70
Beds: 4D 3T **Baths:** 7 Pr
🛇 🅿 (12) 📺 ♞ 🗶 📖 🗓 ☂ ♿ cc

Marshlands, *High Street, Cley-next-the-Sea, Holt, Norfolk, NR25 7RB.*
Victorian old town hall house, with warm and friendly atmosphere.
Open: All Year (not Xmas/New Year)
01263 740284 Mr & Mrs Kinsella
D: fr £16 **S:** fr £28
Beds: 1D 2T **Baths:** 2 En 1 Pr
🛇 (12) 🗶 📺 ♞ 📖 🗓 ☂

BEDROOMS
F - Family
D - Double
T - Twin
S - Single

Coltishall

TG2720 ◁ *Goat*

Broadgates, *1 Wroxham Road, Coltishall, Norwich, NR12 7DU.*
Comfortable accommodation in Broadland village.
Open: All Year (not Xmas)
Grades: ETC Listed
01603 737598 Mrs Dack
broad1gates@tesco.net
D: £21 **S:** £21
Beds: 1F 1T **Baths:** 1 En 1 Pr
🛇 🅿 (8) 🗶 📺 📖 🗓 ☂

Cranwich

TL7794

Old Bottle House, *Cranwich, Mundford, Thetford, Norfolk, IP26 5JL.*
Open: All Year
01842 878012 Mrs Ford
D: £20–£22 **S:** £20–£22
Beds: 1F 2T 1D **Baths:** 1 Sh
🛇 (5) 🅿 (10) 🗶 📺 🗶 📖 🗓 ☂
275 year old former coaching inn, on edge of Thetford Forest. Colour co-ordinated bedrooms with tea/coffee making facilities and colour TV. Delicious meals are served in the dining room, which has an inglenook fireplace. Warm friendly welcome.

Cromer

TG2142 ◁ *Red Lion*

Cambridge House, *Sea Front, East Cliff, Cromer, Norfolk, NR27 9HD.*
Superb uninterrupted sea views above the promenade and beach. Good touring base.
Open: All Year (not Xmas/New Year)
Grades: ETC 3 Diamond
01263 512085 Mrs Wass
D: £18–£25 **S:** £18–£25
Beds: 3F 1D 1S **Baths:** 3 En 1 Pr 1 Sh
🛇 🅿 (5) 🗶 📺 ♞ 🗶 📖 🗓 ☂

Crowmere Guest House, *4 Vicarage Road, Cromer, Norfolk, NR27 9DQ.*
Charming Victorian house. Situated conveniently for beach and town. Quiet location.
Open: Easter to Oct
Grades: AA 3 Diamond
01263 513056 Ms Marriott
D: £17–£20 **S:** £20–£40
Beds: 1F 2D 1T **Baths:** 4 En
🛇 🅿 (4) 🗶 📺 📖 🗓 ☂

Diss

TM1180 ◁ *White Horse, Red Lion, Saracen's Head*

Stenneth, *Airfield Road, Fersfield, Diss, Norfolk, IP22 2B .*
Open: All Year
Grades: ETC 4 Diamond
01379 688182 K Webb
Fax: 01379 688260
ken@strenneth.co.uk
D: £25–£35 **S:** £28–£50
Beds: 4D 2T 1S **Baths:** 7 En
🛇 🅿 (9) 🗶 📺 ♞ 📖 ☂ ♿ cc
Close to Bressingham Gardens. C17th with newer single storey courtyard wing.

Park Hotel, *29 Denmark Street, Diss,*
IP22 4LE.
Friendly run market town hotel, ideal for
touring Norfolk and Suffolk.
Open: All Year
Grades: ETC 2 Star
01379 642244 R Twigge
Fax: 01379 644218
park.hotel@btinternet.com
D: £27.50–£40 **S:** £25–£30
Beds: 2F 8D 4T 2S
⏰ ▣ ⊬ 🖵 ⊁ ✕ ▥ Ⅴ ❊ ♨ ⅋ ὣ cc

Docking

TF7637 ⚓ *Pilgrim's Reach, Railway Inn*

Jubilee Lodge, *Station Road, Docking,*
King's Lynn, Norfolk, PE31 8LS.
Comfortable Tudor style house. Pleasant
village between Fakenham and the
seaside resort of Hunstanton. Only 8
miles from Royal Estate at Sandringham
4 miles. Peddars Way, good centre for
bird watchers, easy access to a wide
range of facilities.
Open: All Year
Grades: ETC 3 Diamond
01485 518473 Mrs Howard
Fax: 01482 518473
D: £17.50 **S:** £17.50
Beds: 2D 1T **Baths:** 3 En
▣ (3) ⊬ 🖵 ✕ ▥ Ⅴ ὣ

The Homestead, *High Street, Docking,*
King's Lynn, Norfolk, PE31 8NH.
The Homestead stands in an acre of
grounds with views over open fields.
Open: All Year (not Xmas)
01485 518930 Mrs Firth
Fax: 01485 518940
ranthony.firth@btinternet.com
D: £21–£22.50 **S:** £20–£25
Beds: 1D 1T **Baths:** 1 En 1 Sh
▣ ⊬ 🖵 ▥ Ⅴ ὣ

Downham Market

TF6103 ⚓ *Crown Hotel*

The Dial House, *12 Railway Road,*
Downham Market, Norfolk, PE38 9EB.
Lovely old C18th family home. Good food
and home made bread.
Open: All Year
Grades: AA 4 Diamond
01366 388358 Mrs Murray
bookings@thedialhouse.co.uk
D: £17.50–£22.50 **S:** £25–£33
Beds: 1D 2T **Baths:** 2 En 1 Pr
▣ (6) ⊬ 🖵 ✕ ▥ Ⅴ ὣ

Earsham

TM3289 ⚓ *Black Swan*

Park Farm, *Harleston Road, Earsham,*
Bungay, Norfolk, NR35 2AQ.
Spacious farmhouse, unique hand
decoration, fantastic views with every
comfort.
Open: All Year
Grades: ETC 4 Diamond, Silver Award,
AA 4 Diamond
01986 892180 Mrs Watchorn
Fax: 01986 894796
watchorn_s@freenet.co.uk
D: £23–£35 **S:** £32–£46
Beds: 2D 1T **Baths:** 3 En
⏰ ▣ (10) ⊬ 🖵 ⊁ ✕ ▥ Ⅴ ὣ cc

Fakenham

TF9230

Yew Tree House, *2 East View,*
Hempton, Fakenham, Norfolk, NR21 7LW.
Open spaces, birdwatching area. Close to
Sandringham, North Norfolk Coast.
Open: All Year **01328 851450** Mr Beales
D: £15–£18 **S:** £15–£18
Beds: 1F 1D 1T 1S **Baths:** 1 Sh
⏰ (1) ▣ (5) ⊬ 🖵 ⊁ ✕ Ⅴ ὣ

Felmingham

TG2529 ⚓ *Crown Inn*

Larks Rise, *North Walsham Road,*
Felmingham, North Walsham, Norfolk,
NR28 0JU.
Open: Mar to Nov **Grades:** ETC 2 Diamond
01692 403173 Mrs Rudd
D: £14–£20 **S:** £16–£26
Beds: 1F 1D 1T **Baths:** 1 Pr 1 Sh
⏰ ▣ (2) 🖵 ✕ ▥ Ⅴ ὣ
Traditionally-built family home with half
acre secluded gardens in quiet rural area
full of wildlife and historical interest.
Superb centre for exploring North Norfolk
and the Broads. Close to Weavers Way
and Norfolk Coastal footpaths. Riding
and fishing nearby.

Felthorpe

TG1618 ⚓ *Red Lion, Parson Woodforde,*
Blacksmiths, Yeast & Feast, Ratcatchers, Marsham
Arms, Dog

Spinney Ridge, *Hall Lane, Felthorpe,*
Norwich, NR10 4BX.
Open: All Year (not Xmas)
01603 754833 Mr & Mrs Thompson
D: £18–£20 **S:** £18–£20
Beds: 2D 2T 1S **Baths:** 2 En 1 Sh
⏰ (1) ▣ (6) ⊬ 🖵 ▥ Ⅴ ὣ
Characterful quiet house in a wooded
rural setting with a warm and friendly
welcome and service 6 miles north of
Norwich off the A1149. Centre for North
Norfolk and the Broads convenient to
recommended restaurants. No smoking,
no dogs, please.

Lodge Farmhouse, *89 The Street,*
Felthorpe, Norwich, NR10 4BY.
Comfortable friendly family house, edge
of village location, good breakfast.
Open: All Year (not Xmas)
01603 754896 Mrs Howe
D: £15 **S:** £15
Beds: 1D 1T **Baths:** 1 Sh
⏰ ▣ (4) ⊬ 🖵 ▥ Ⅴ ὣ

Fersfield

TM0683 ⚓ *White Horse, Red Lion, Garden*
House

Stenneth, *Airfield Road, Fersfield, Diss,*
Norfolk, IP22 2B .
Close to Bressingham Gardens. C17th
with newer single storey courtyard wing.
Open: All Year **Grades:** ETC 4 Diamond
01379 688182 K Webb
Fax: 01379 688260
ken@strenneth.co.uk
D: £25–£35 **S:** £28–£50
Beds: 4D 2T 1S **Baths:** 7 En
⏰ ▣ (9) ⊬ 🖵 ⊁ ▥ ὣ ὣ cc

Flint Barn, Fenners Farm, *Fersfield,*
Diss, IP22 2AW.
Open: All Year (not Xmas/New Year)
01379 687794 Mr & Mrs Green
Joan.Green@tesco.net
D: £18–£19 **S:** £18–£20
Beds: 1F 1S **Baths:** 1 Sh
⏰ (10) ▣ (4) ⊬ 🖵 ▥.
Converted barn in rural setting of 2 acres.
Full English breakfast, Bressingham
Steam Museum and Blooms Gardens
nearby, Banham Zoo 7 miles. Norwich,
Bury, Thetford and Ipswich within 20
miles. National Trust properties within
easy reach, also Norfolk Broads.

Framingham Earl

TG2702 ⚓ *The Gull, Railway Tavern*

The Old Rectory, *Hall Road,*
Framingham Earl, Norwich, NR14 7SB.
Beautifully restored period family house
in large country garden.
Open: All Year (not Xmas)
Grades: ETC 4 Diamond, Silver Award
01508 493590 Mr & Mrs Wellings
Fax: 01508 495110
brucewellings@
drivedevice.freeserve.co.uk
D: £21–£25 **S:** £25–£28
Beds: 1D 1T **Baths:** 1 Sh
⏰ ▣ (4) ⊬ 🖵 ▥ Ⅴ ὣ

Framingham Pigot

TG2703 ⚓ *The Gull*

The Old Rectory, *Rectory Lane,*
Framingham Pigot, Norwich, NR14 7QQ.
Friendly comfortable Victorian Rectory.
Large garden. 10 mins Norwich centre.
Open: All Year (not Xmas)
01508 493082 Mrs Thurman
D: £21 **S:** £21
Beds: 1F 1D 1T **Baths:** 2 En 1 Sh
⏰ ▣ (6) ⊬ 🖵 ▥. ὣ

Fritton (Long Stratton)

TM2293 ⚓ *Waterside Inn*

Fritton Old Rectory, *Fritton, Long*
Stratton, Norwich, NR15 2QT.
Gracious country house in 4 acres of
serene gardens, on edge of conservation
village.
Open: All Year (not Xmas)
01508 498297 Mr & Mrs Bacon
D: £22–£23 **S:** £26–£30
Beds: 1D 2T **Baths:** 2 En 1 Sh
⏰ (8) ▣ (6) ⊬ 🖵 ▥. ὣ

Garboldisham

TM0081 ⚓ *The Fox, White Horse*

Ingleuk Lodge, *Hopton Road,*
Garboldisham, Diss, Norfolk, IP22 2RQ.
Pretty rural location with all rooms
overlooking partly wooded grounds.
Open: All Year
01953 681541 Mr & Mrs Stone
Fax: 01953 681638
D: £27.50 **S:** £33
Beds: 3D 3T 1S 1F **Baths:** 8 En
⏰ ▣ (15) 🖵 ⊁ ▥ ❊ ⅋ ὣ cc

Gayton

TF7219   ⚓ *Crown Gayton*

West Hall Farm, *Winch Road, Gayton, King's Lynn, Norfolk, PE32 1QP.*
Large farmhouse overlooking open countryside, close to wildlife hospital and Sandringham.
Open: All Year (not Xmas)
01553 636519 (also fax)
Mr Pooley
mike@westhallfarm.screaming.net
D: £16–£18 **S:** £20
Beds: 2D **Baths:** 2 Sh
🛪 🅿 (5) ⚡ �📺 🎞,

Geldeston

TM3992   ⚓ *The Wherry Inn*

Archway Cottage, *Geldeston, Beccles, Suffolk, NR34 0LB.*
Clean comfortable cottage with a warm welcome to all our guests.
Open: All Year
01508 518056 Mrs Dean
heatherarchwaycottage@redhotant.co.uk
D: £19 **S:** £25–£28
Beds: 2D **Baths:** 1 Sh
🛪 (2) 🅿 (2) ⚡ �📺 🎞, ��V 🛆

Gorleston on Sea

TG5204

The Ship Hotel, *71 Avondale Road, Gorleston On Sea, Great Yarmouth, NR31 6DJ.*
Victorian house yards from sea. Ideal for touring Norfolk
Open: All Year (not Xmas/New Year)
Grades: AA 2 Diamond
01493 662746 Fax: 01493 662746
grahambb@aol.com
D: £21–£27 **S:** £21–£30
Beds: 1F 1T 6D 1S **Baths:** 9 Ensuite
🛪 🅿 (5) �📺 ♍ ✕ �V 🛆 cc

Great Ellingham

TM0197   ⚓ *The Crown*

Home Cottage Farm, *Penhill Road, Great Ellingham, Attleborough, Norfolk, NR17 1LS.*
Spacious self-contained B&B accommodation at period farmhouse in rural seclusion.
Open: All Year
01953 483734 M Jacobs
royandmaureen@mail.com
D: £18–£20 **S:** £18–£20
Beds: 2T 1D 1S **Baths:** 1 Pr 1 Sh
🛪 🅿 (4) ⚡ �📺 🎞, �V 🛆

Cannells Farm, *Bow Street, Great Ellingham, Attleborough, Norfolk, NR17 1JA.*
C18th traditional Norfolk farmhouse overlooking open countryside. Quiet location.
Open: All Year (not Xmas/New Year)
01953 454133 (also fax)
Mrs Thomas
D: £18–£20 **S:** £18–£20
Beds: 1T 1D 1S **Baths:** 1 Sh
🛪 (8) 🅿 (8) ⚡ �📺 ✕ 🎞, �V 🛆

Great Hockham

TL9492

Manor Farm, *Vicarage Road, Great Hockham, Thetford, Norfolk, IP24 1PE.*
Escape to Manor Farm. Relax and unwind at this C16th refurbished farmhouse.
Open: All Year (not Xmas)
01953 498204 Mrs Thomas
D: £18–£24 **S:** £18–£21
Beds: 1D 1T 1S **Baths:** 1 En 1 Sh
🅿 (4) ⚡ �📺 ✕ 🎞, �V 🛆

Great Moulton

TM1690   ⚓ *Fox & Hounds*

Oakbrook, *Frith Way, Great Moulton, Norwich, NR15 2HE.*
Open: All Year
01379 677359 Mr Hawes
D: £16.50–£19 **S:** £16.50–£19
Beds: 1F 1T 2S
🛪 🅿 (8) ⚡ �📺 ✕ 🎞, �V ✿ 🛆 &
Very friendly reception. Food excellent, just like staying with old friends: Doris, Ted and Jackie Salisbury 'Very hospitable, helpful and friendly. Good location to get away from the busy city life, nice to get a good taste of beautiful Norfolk.

Great Ryburgh

TF9527

Highfield Farm, *Great Ryburgh, Fakenham, Norfolk, NR21 7AL.*
Beautiful large farmhouse, peaceful location, welcoming hosts.
Open: All Year (not Xmas)
01328 829249 Mrs Savory
Fax: 01328 829422
D: fr £20 **S:** fr £25
Beds: 1D 2T **Baths:** 1 En 1 Sh
🛪 (12) 🅿 (8) ⚡ �📺 ✕ 🎞, 🛆

Great Yarmouth

TG5207   ⚓ *Gallon Pot, Tudor Pie*

The Collingwood Hotel, *25/26 Princes Road, Great Yarmouth, NR30 2DG.*
Open: All Year
Grades: RAC 3 Diamond
01493 844398 (also fax)
Mr & Mrs Mills
D: £18–£25 **S:** £18–£20
Beds: 8F 3D 2T 6S **Baths:** 10 En 9 Sh
🛪 (10) �📺 �V 🎞, 🛆 cc
Princes Road is the best road for hotels. We are at the seafront and 100 yds from Britannia Pier and all the shows and amusements. Walking distance from main shops at the heart of the Norfolk Broads - no hills to walk up. Guest lounge, licensed bar.

RATES

D = Price range per person sharing in a double room

S = Price range for a single room

Sunshine Lodge Hotel, *73 Marine Parade, Great Yarmouth, Norfolk, NR30 2DQ.*
Open: All Year (not Xmas/New Year)
01493 842250 Mr Hughes
Fax: 01493 857521
john@sunshinelodge.freeserve.co.uk
D: £13–£25 **S:** £18–£30
Beds: 4F 7D **Baths:** 5 En 1 Sh
🛪 🅿 (1) ⚡ �📺 🎞, �V 🛆 cc
Close to major attractions, shops and restaurants. Most rooms have sea views, two have a balcony overlooking the sea. All rooms well appointed with tea/coffee making facilities and colour television with satellite. Bar with reduced price drinks (i.e. mostly £1.50).

Barnard House, *2 Barnard Crescent, Great Yarmouth, Norfolk, NR30 4DR.*
Delightful family home. Bedrooms overlooking gardens. Excellent Aga cooked breakfast.
Open: All Year (not Xmas/New Year)
Grades: ETC 4 Diamond, Silver Award, AA 4 Diamond
01493 855139 J Norris
Fax: 01493 843143
barnardhouse@btinternet.com
D: £22–£24 **S:** £25–£30
Beds: 1F 2D **Baths:** 2 En 1 Pr
🛪 🅿 (3) ⚡ �📺 ♍ ✕ 🎞, �V 🛆

Silverstone House, *29 Wellesley Road, Great Yarmouth, NR30 1EU.*
All rooms ensuite, residential bar, close to all amenities.
Open: All Year (not Xmas)
01493 844862 Mr Parker
D: £17.50 **S:** £17.50
Beds: 5F 5D **Baths:** 10 En
🛪 ⚡ ✕ 🎞, �V 🛆 cc

Strathclyde Guest House, *6 Paget Road, Great Yarmouth, NR30 2DN.*
24 hour bar/games room. 100 yards from sea front.
Open: All Year
01493 851596 Zoe Cook
strathclyde-yarmouth@hotmail.com
D: £13–£17 **S:** £12–£16
Beds: 2F 2T 2D 1S **Baths:** 1 En, 3 Sh
🛪 ♍ ✕ 🎞, 🛆

Britannia Guest House, *119 Wellesley Road, Great Yarmouth, NR30 2AP.*
Comfortable rooms, good breakfasts, close to beach, shops, restaurants, amusements.
Open: All Year
01493 856488 (also fax)
D: £13.50–£17 **S:** £13.50–£17
Beds: 1F 3D 1T 2S **Baths:** 1 En 1 Sh
🛪 (3) ⚡ �📺 �V 🛆

Holland House, *13 Apsley Road, Great Yarmouth, Norfolk, NR30 2HG.*
Friendly family run guest house, one minute from sea.
Open: All Year (not Xmas/New Year)
01493 859534 Mr & Mrs Simmons
D: £12–£15 **S:** £12–£15
Beds: 2F 4D 1S
🛪 ⚡ ✕ 🎞, �V 🛆

Norfolk Map page 240

Beaumont House, *52 Wellesley Road, Great Yarmouth, Norfolk, NR30 1EX.*
2 minutes from Yarmouth's golden beaches. 5 minutes from town.
Open: All Year (not Xmas/New Year)
01493 843957 (also fax) Mr Burch
hotel.beaumont@virgin.net
D: £16–£22 **S:** £16–£22
Beds: 2F 5D 1T 1S **Baths:** 2 Sh
🛏 (8) 🅿 🟤 📺 ✕ 🏠 Ⅴ 🔥 cc

Concorde Private Hotel, *84 North Denes Road, Great Yarmouth, Norfolk, NR30 4LW.*
Family-run hotel, close to the beach and waterways.
Open: All Year **Grades:** RAC 3 Diamond
01493 843709 (also fax) Mrs Sexton
concordeyarmouth@hotmail.com
D: £17.50–£22.50 **S:** £17.50–£22.50
Beds: 4F 1T 5D 1S **Baths:** 11 En
🛏 🅿 (8) 📺 🛏 ✕ 🏠 🌸 🔥 cc

Ryecroft, *91 North Denes Road, Great Yarmouth, Norfolk, NR30 4LW.*
Award winning. Licensed, guesthouse with private parking. Near the sea front.
Open: All Year
Grades: ETC 3 Diamond
01493 844015 Mr Van Kassel
Fax: 01493 856096
lee_van_kassel@compuserve.com
D: £15–£24 **S:** £15–£24
Beds: 3F 3D 1T 1S **Baths:** 4 En 1 Pr 1 Sh
🛏 🅿 (6) 📺 ✕ 🏠 🌸 🔥 cc

Happisburgh

TG3731

Cliff House Guest House and Tea Shop, *Beach Road, Happisburgh, Norwich, NR12 0PP.*
Comfortable Edwardian guest house and teashop on cliff top in attractive village.
Open: All Year (not Xmas)
Grades: ETC 3 Diamond
01692 650775 Ms Wrightson
D: £16 **S:** £16
Beds: 1D 1T 2S **Baths:** 2 Sh
🛏 🅿 (4) 🟤 📺 ✕ 🏠 Ⅴ 🔥

Hickling

TG4123 🍺 *Greyhound Inn*

Paddock Cottage, *Staithe Road, Hickling, Norwich, NR12 0YJ.*
Comfortable modern cottage, quiet location, close nature reserve, sailing, fishing.
Open: All Year (not Xmas)
01692 598259 Mrs Parry
D: £18 **S:** £20
Beds: 1F 1D 1T **Baths:** 1 En 2 Pr
🛏 🅿 (4) 📺 🛏 🏠 Ⅴ 🔥

Hockwold cum Wilton

TL7388 🍺 *New Inn, Red Lion*

Junipers, *18 South Street, Hockwold cum Wilton, Thetford, Norfolk, IP26 4JG.*
Village near Mildenhall, Thetford. Forest, fishing, touring, historic sites.
Open: All Year
01842 827370 Mrs Waddington
D: £20 **S:** £20
Beds: 2T 1S **Baths:** 2 Sh
🛏 🅿 (4) ✕ 📺 🛏 🏠 Ⅴ 🔥 ♿

Holkham

TF8943 🍺 *The Nelson*

Peterstone Cutting, *Peterstone, Holkham, Wells-next-the-Sea, Norfolk, NR23 1RR.*
Peterstone Cutting nestles in the old railway cutting, adjacent to Holkham Hall Parkland.
Open: All Year (not Xmas)
01328 730171 (also fax)
Mr & Mrs Platt
D: £18–£24 **S:** £30–£40
Beds: 4D 1T **Baths:** 1 En 1 Pr 1 Sh
🛏 🅿 (4) ✕ ✕ 🏠 Ⅴ 🔥 ♿

Holt

TG0739 🍺 *Kings Head*

Hempstead Hall, *Holt, Norfolk, NR25 6TN.*
Close to the North Norfolk coast and set in beautiful surroundings.
Open: All Year (not Xmas)
01263 712224 **D:** £20–£25
Beds: 1F 1D **Baths:** 1 En 1 Pr
🛏 (3) 📺 🏠 🔥

Horning

TG3417 🍺 *Ferry Inn, Swan Inn*

Keppelgate, *Upper Street, Horning, Norwich, NR12 8NG.*
Delightful rural Broadland views. Boating, fishing, windmills. Convenient for coast.
Open: All Year (not Xmas/New Year)
01692 630610 Mrs Freeman
D: £17–£18 **S:** £20
Beds: 1F 1D 1T **Baths:** 1 En 1 Sh
🛏 (2) 🅿 (3) 📺 🏠 Ⅴ 🔥 ♿

Horsey Corner

TG4523 🍺 *Nelson's Head*

The Old Chapel, *Horsey Corner, Great Yarmouth, Norfolk, NR29 4EH.*
Open: All Year
Grades: ETC 4 Diamond
01493 393498 Mr & Mrs Lewin
Fax: 01493 393444
D: £18–£22 **S:** £23–£33
Beds: 1F 1D 1T **Baths:** 3 En
🛏 🅿 (4) ✕ 📺 🛏 🏠 Ⅴ ♿ 3
Converted chapel offers ground floor accommodation in NT Area of Outstanding Beauty. A short walk from the wide sandy beach and Horsey Mere within easy reach of the Broads. Ideal for nature lovers. All rooms have countryside views.

Horsford

TG1916 🍺 *The Chequers, The Yeast And Feast Inn*

Church Farm Guest House, *Church Street, Horsford, Norwich, NR10 3DB.*
Modern comfortable farmhouse, large garden. **Open:** All Year
Grades: ETC 3 Diamond
01603 898020 Mrs Hinchley
Fax: 01603 891649
D: £25–£30 **S:** £25–£30
Beds: 2F 2D 2T **Baths:** 6 En 1 Sh
🛏 🅿 (20) 📺 🏠 Ⅴ 🔥 cc

Hoveton

TG3018 🍺 *Wroxham Riverside Hotel*

The Beehive, *Riverside Road, Hoveton, Norwich, NR12 8UD.*
Beautiful thatched riverside cottage overlooking River Bure and the Broads.
Open: All Year (not Xmas/New Year)
01603 784107 R J Wendrop
D: £20–£22 **S:** £25–£30
Beds: 1F 1T 2D **Baths:** 1 En 1 Sh
🛏 (15) 🅿 (7) ✕ 📺 ✕ 🏠 Ⅴ 🔥 cc

Hunstanton

TF6740 🍺 *Golden Lion, Marine Bar, Le Strange Arms, Ancient Mariner, Platters*

Kiama Cottage, *23 Austin Street, Hunstanton, Norfolk, PE36 6AN.*
Open: All year (not Xmas)
Grades: ETC 3 Diamond
01485 533615 Mr & Mrs Gardiner
D: £18–£25 **S:** £20–£25
Beds: 2F 2D **Baths:** 3 En 1 Pr
🛏 ✕ 📺 🏠 Ⅴ 🔥
A warm welcome awaits you at our Victorian-style cottage located in a quiet residential area and ideally situated for visiting Hunstanton attractions and West Norfolk generally. Hosts Neville & Beverley are well travelled and are sensitive to your needs.

Peacock House, *28 Park Road, Hunstanton, Norfolk, PE36 5BY.*
A large warm and comfortable Victorian house serving memorable breakfasts.
Open: All Year **Grades:** ETC 3 Diamond
01485 534551 Mrs Sandercock
D: £17.50–£24.50 **S:** £24–£30
Beds: 1F 1T 1D **Baths:** 3 En
🛏 (5) ✕ 📺 🏠 🌸 🔥

The Gables, *28 Austin Street, Hunstanton, PE36 6AW.*
Recently refurbished attractive Edwardian home retaining many original features.
Open: All Year
Grades: ETC 4 Diamond, AA 4 Diamond
01485 532514 Mrs Bamfield
D: £17–£23
Beds: 5F 1D 1T **Baths:** 5 En
🛏 ✕ 📺 ✕ 🏠 Ⅴ 🔥 cc

Rosamaly Guest House, *14 Glebe Avenue, Hunstanton, Norfolk, PE36 6BS.*
Warm, friendly atmosphere. Hearty breakfasts, tasty evening meals. Comfy ensuite bedrooms, quiet, convenient location.
Open: All Year (not Xmas)
Grades: ETC 3 Diamond
01485 534187 Mrs Duff Dick
D: £18–£23 **S:** £20–£25
Beds: 1F 3D 1T 1S **Baths:** 5 En
🛏 📺 🛏 ✕ 🏠 Ⅴ 🔥

Burleigh Hotel, *7 Cliff Terrace, Hunstanton, Norfolk, PE36 6DY.*
Victorian family-run hotel, close to sea front and gardens.
Open: All Year **Grades:** ETC 4 Diamond
01485 533080 Mr & Mrs Abos
D: £21–£25 **S:** £23–£25
Beds: 4F 4D 2T 1S **Baths:** 9 En 2 Pr
🛏 (5) 🅿 (7) 📺 ✕ 🏠 Ⅴ 🔥

King's Lynn

TF6120   🐦 *The Wildfowler*

The Old Rectory, *33 Goodwins Road, King's Lynn, Norfolk, PE30 5QX.*
Open: All Year
Grades: ETC 4 Diamond
01553 768544 C Faulkner
D: £21 **S:** £32
Beds: 2F 2T **Baths:** 4 En
🛇 📺 (5) ⅙ 📺 📺 🎍, 🔥
Elegant former rectory. Well-appointed, high quality ensuite accommodation. Guests have freedom of access at all times. Off street parking, storage for cycles, non-smoking, quietly situated, close to centre of historic attractive market town. Well-behaved pets welcome.

Maranatha Havana Guest House, *115 Gaywood Road, King's Lynn, Norfolk, PE30 2PU.*
Friendly family run. Special rates for children, groups catered for.
Open: All Year
Grades: ETC 2 Diamond
01553 774596 Mr Bastone
D: £15–£20 **S:** fr £20
Beds: 2F 2D 3T 2S **Baths:** 4 En 2 Sh
🛇 📇 (9) 📺 🎍 ✕ 📺 📺 🎍 ♿

Flints Hotel, *73 Norfolk Street, King's Lynn, Norfolk, PE30 1AD.*
Modern hotel.
Open: All Year
01553 769400 Mr Flint
D: fr £18 **S:** fr £18
Beds: 1F 1D 1T 1S
🛇 (1) 📇 (7) 📺 ✕ 📺 📺 ✳ 🎍

Little Cressingham

TF8700   🐦 *White Horse*

Sycamore House, *Little Cressingham, Thetford, Norfolk, IP25 6NE.*
Large country home, tranquil village, luxurious jacuzzi bathroom, numerous attractions. **Open:** All Year
01953 881887 (also fax) Mr Wittridge
D: £22 **S:** £22
Beds: 2D 1T 1S **Baths:** 1 En 1 Sh
🛇 📇 (10) 📺 📺 📺 🎍

Little Walsingham

TF9337 **St Davids House,** *Friday Market, Little Walsingham, Walsingham, Norfolk, NR22 6BY.*
Tudor house in medieval village; five miles from coast. **Open:** All Year
Grades: ETC 2 Diamond
01328 820633 Mrs Renshaw
D: £21–£24 **S:** £26–£30
Beds: 2F 1D 2T **Baths:** 2 En 2 Sh
🛇 📇 📺 🎍 ✕ 📺 ✳ 🎍

The Old Bakehouse, *33 High Street, Little Walsingham, Norfolk, NR22 6BZ.*
Restaurant with good food and attractive rooms in historic village.
Open: All Year (not Xmas)
01328 820454 Mrs Padley
chris@cpadley.freeserve.co.uk
D: £22.50 **S:** £27.50
Beds: 2D 1T **Baths:** 3 En
🛇 📺 🎍 ✕ 📺 📺 🎍

Loddon

TM3698   🐦 *Kings Head*

Poplar Farm, *Sisland, Loddon, Norwich, NR14 6EF.*
Working farm pigs, cows. Quiet, rural setting near Broads.
Open: All Year (not Xmas)
01508 520706 Mrs Hemmant
milly@hemmant.myhome.org.uk
D: £17–£25 **S:** £18–£25
Beds: 1F 1D 1T **Baths:** 1 En 1 Pr
🛇 📇 (4) ⅙ 📺 ✕ 📺 🎍

Ludham

TG3818   🐦 *Kings Arms*

Malthouse Farmhouse, *Malthouse Lane, Ludham, Norfolk, NR29 5QL.*
Pretty 1750s cottage, quiet location, 10 mins stroll to river/village/pub.
Open: All Year (not Xmas)
Grades: ETC 3 Diamond
01692 678747 (also fax)
Mrs Ferguson
lynn@fergs.demon.co.uk
D: £15.75–£20 **S:** £22.50–£30
Beds: 1F 1D
⅙

Melton Constable

TG0433   🐦 *J H Stracey*

Burgh Parva Hall, *Melton Constable, Norfolk, NR24 2PU.*
Listed C16th farmhouse with country views, near coast, large bedrooms.
Open: All Year
01263 862569 (also fax) Mrs Heal
judyheal@talk21.com
D: £18 **S:** £20
Beds: 1D 1T **Baths:** 1 Sh
🛇 📇 (4) 📺 🎍 ✕ 📺 📺 🎍

Morley St Botolph

TG0800   🐦 *Three Boars*

Home Farm, *Morley, St Botolph, Wymondham, Norfolk, NR18 9SU.*
Set in 4 acres of secluded grounds, 3 miles from 2 towns.
Open: All Year (not Xmas)
01953 602581 Mrs Morter
D: £18–£20 **S:** £18–£20
Beds: 1T 1D 1S **Baths:** 1 Sh
🛇 (5) 📇 (5) ⅙ 📺 📺 🎍

Mulbarton

TG1901   🐦 *World's End, Bird in Hand*

Richmond Lodge, *The Common, Mulbarton, Norwich, Norfolk, NR14 8JW.*
Open: All Year (not Xmas/New Year)
01508 570449 Mrs Freeman
Fax: 01508 570372
gillandpaul.freeman@ukgateway.net
D: £39.50–£41 **S:** £23.50–£25
Beds: 1F 3D 1S **Baths:** 2 En 2 Sh
🛇 📇 (20) ⅙ 📺 🎍 ✕ 📺 📺 🎍 ♿
Situated just 4 miles south of Norwich. Beautiful setting, games room, outdoor heated swimming pool, palm trees, barbecue area. TV in all rooms. Situated just off a 45 acre common & duck pond. Village has shop & pub. Golf, horse riding, excellent restaurants nearby.

Mundford

TL7993   🐦 *Crown Inn*

Treetops, *6 Swaffham Road, Mundford, Thetford, Norfolk, IP26 5HR.*
Comfortable bungalow on A1065. Guests own entrance, sitting/dining room.
Open: All Year (not Xmas/New Year)
01842 878557 Mrs Edmunds
Fax: 01842 879078
D: £18 **S:** £18
Beds: 1T 1D **Baths:** 1 En 1 Pr
📇 (8) 📺 📺 🎍

Neatishead

TG3420   🐦 *Taps Horning, White Horse*

Allens Farmhouse, *Three Hammer Common, Neatishead, Norwich, NR12 8XW.*
Open: All Year
01692 630080 Mr & Mrs Smerdon
D: £16–£20 **S:** £16
Beds: 2D 1T **Baths:** 1 En 1 Sh
🛇 📇 (3) ⅙ 📺 🎍 ✕ 📺 📺 🎍
Allens Farmhouse, built in the early 1700's was a working farm until early 1980's when it was extensively modernised. It has a large walled garden, landscaped to create a beautiful lawn surrounded by flower beds with the added attraction of a well, fish pond and orchard.

Newton St Faith

TG2117

Elm Farm Country House, *Horsham St Faith, Norwich, NR10 3HH.*
Country house in village of Horsham St Faith, 4 miles from Norwich.
Open: All Year
Grades: ETC 4 Diamond, AA 4 Diamond
01603 898366 Fax: 01603 897129
D: £26–£29 **S:** £31–£38
Beds: 2F 5T 4D 3S **Baths:** 14 En
🛇 📇 (20) 📺 📺 🎍 📺 💷 cc

North Lopham

TM0382   🐦 *Kings Head, White Horse*

Belgate, *The Street, North Lopham, Diss, Norfolk, IP22 2LR.*
Peaceful bungalow. Large secluded garden, benefit of own front door.
Open: All Year
01379 687346 Mrs Hogg
Fax: 01379 688439
D: £18 **S:** £18
Beds: 1T **Baths:** 1 En
🛇 (16) 📇 (2) ⅙ 📺 🎍 🎍

North Pickenham

TF8606   🐦 *Blue Lion*

Riverside House, *Meadow Lane, North Pickenham, Swaffham, Norfolk, PE37 8LE.*
Flintstone cottage by River Wissey, set in two acre garden.
Open: All Year (not Xmas)
01760 440219 Mrs Norris
D: £16 **S:** £16
Beds: 2T **Baths:** 1 Sh
🛇 📇 📺 🎍 📺 📺 🎍

North Walsham

TG2830   🚇 *Beechwood Hotel, Goat Inn, King's Arms*

Toll Barn, *Heath Rd, Norwich Road, North Walsham, Norfolk, NR28 0JB.*
Private lodges in a quiet rural setting, adjacent to grazing farmland with horses & sheep.
Open: All Year (not Xmas)
01692 403638 Fax: 01692 500993
nola@toll-barn.fsbusiness.co.uk
D: £18–£25 **S:** £25
Beds: 1F 1D 1T 1S **Baths:** 4 En
🐾 🅿 (6) ⚲ 📺 🛏 ⬛ ♿

Pine Trees, *45 Happisburgh Road, North Walsham, Norfolk, NR28 9HB.*
Lovely house, guest bedrooms overlooking garden with grass tennis court.
Open: All Year (not Xmas/New Year)
Grades: ETC 4 Diamond
01692 404213 (also fax)
Mrs Blaxell
D: £20 **S:** £20
Beds: 1T 1D **Baths:** 2 Sh
🐾 (10) 🅿 (2) ⚲ 📺 ⬛ 🛏

Green Ridges, *104 Cromer Road, North Walsham, Norfolk, NR28 0HE.*
Clean, friendly, modern comfortable ensuite accommodation.
Open: All Year (not Xmas)
01692 402448 Mrs Mitchell
D: £20–£25 **S:** £20–£25
Beds: 1F 1T **Baths:** 2 En
🐾 🅿 (5) 📺 🛏 ⬛ 🛏 🛏

Northrepps

TG2439

Shrublands Farm, *Northrepps, Cromer, Norfolk, NR27 0AA.*
Shrublands is a 300 acre family arable farm 2 miles south-east of Cromer.
Open: All Year (not Xmas)
01263 579297 (also fax)
Mrs Youngman
youngman@farming.co.uk
D: £21–£23 **S:** £25–£27
Beds: 1D 2T
🐾 🅿 (4) ⚲ 📺 ✕ ⬛ 🛏

Norwich

TG2308   🚇 *Coach & Horses, Pickwick, Black Horse, Tuns, Falcon, Town House*

Earlham Guest House, *147 Earlham Road, Norwich, NR2 3RG.*
Open: All Year (not Xmas)
Grades: ETC 4 Diamond, AA 4 Diamond
01603 454169 (also fax)
Mr & Mrs Wright
earlhamgh@hotmail.com
D: £20–£23 **S:** £22–£25
Beds: 1F 3D 1T 3S **Baths:** 2 En 2 Sh
🐾 (10) ⚲ 📺 ⬛ 🛏 🛏 cc
Susan & Derek Wright offer welcoming and friendly hospitality with comfortable modern facilities, close historic Norwich, University and Norfolk Broads. Vegetarian choices, personal keys. Short break rates available 1 Oct - 31 Mar. No smoking throughout. All cards welcome.

Arbor Linden Lodge, *Linden House, 557 Earlham Road, Norwich, NR4 7HW.*
Open: All Year **Grades:** ETC 4 Diamond
01603 451303 Mr Betts
Fax: 01603 250641
info@guesthouses.uk.com
D: £20–£25 **S:** £26–£35
Beds: 1F 1T 3D 1S **Baths:** 6 En
🐾 🅿 (10) ⚲ 📺 ⬛ 🛏 🛏 cc
Family run for quality and warmth of welcome. Secure parking. free parking near city centre. garden breakfast conservatory. Garden/play area. Convenient rivers, broads, UEA, Norwich and BUPA hospitals, Sports Park Olympic Centre, bus and fast food takeaway. refrigerator/microwave in guest lounge.

Beaufort Lodge, *62 Earlham Road, Norwich, NR2 3DF.*
Open: All Year (not Xmas/New Year)
Grades: AA 4 Diamond
01603 627928 (also fax) Mr Dobbins
D: £25 **S:** £35–£40
Beds: 3D 1S **Baths:** 3 En 1 Pr
🅿 ⚲ 📺 🛏
Spacious Victorian house with ample parking. Within easy walking distance of city centre. A short drive away are the Broads and the Coastal towns of Cromer and Sheringham. Inland there are many historic and interesting houses to visit including Sandringham.

Trebeigh House, *16 Brabazon Road, Hellesdon, Norwich, NR6 6SY.*
Warm welcome to quiet friendly house convenient city country airport.
Open: All Year (not Xmas)
01603 429056 Mrs Jope
Fax: 01603 414247
christine@trebeigh.madasafish.com
D: £18–£19 **S:** £18–£20
Beds: 1D 1T **Baths:** 1 Sh
🐾 🅿 (3) ⚲ 📺 ⬛ 🛏

Rosedale, *145 Earlham Road, Norwich, NR2 3RG.*
Comfortable, family-run guest house. Easy access to city, coast & university.
Open: All Year (not Xmas)
01603 453743 Mrs Curtis
Fax: 01603 259887
drcbac@aol.com
D: £19–£40 **S:** £18–£25
Beds: 2F 2T 2S **Baths:** 2 Sh
🐾 (4) ⚲ 📺 ⬛ 🛏 cc

Pine Lodge, *518 Earlham Road, Norwich, NR4 7HR.*
Distinctive, cheerful and comfortable accommodation between university and the city centre. **Open:** All Year
01603 504834 Mr & Mrs Tovell
tovell@tovell.fsnet.co.uk
D: £18–£20 **S:** £25
🅿 📺 ⬛ 🛏

Harvey House Guest House, *50 Harvey Lane, Norwich, NR7 0AQ.*
Comfy, no smoking with easy access to city and Broads. **Open:** All Year
Grades: ETC 3 Diamond
01603 436575 (also fax) G Pritchard
gareth.pritchard@which.net
D: £18–£21 **S:** £18–£25
Beds: 1F 1D 2T 1S **Baths:** 3 En 1 Pr 1 Sh
🐾 (3) 🅿 (6) ⚲ 📺 ⬛ 🛏 🛏

Butterfield Hotel, *4 Stracey Road, Norwich, NR1 1EZ.*
We offer warm, friendly welcome to ensure your stay is a happy one.
Open: All Year **Grades:** ETC Listed
01603 661008 L Ackhe Kamal
D: £20–£35 **S:** £20–£35
Beds: 4F 4T 6S 2D **Baths:** 2 En
🐾 🅿 (5) 📺 🛏 ✕ ⬛ ♣ 🛏 ♿

Potter Heigham

TG4119   🚇 *The Falgate, The Crown*

Hazelden, *Bridge Road, Potter Heigham, Great Yarmouth, NR29 5JB.*
Ideal for coast, Broads, nature reserve, walking, boating, cycling, fishing.
Open: All Year (not Xmas)
Grades: ETC 3 Diamond
01692 670511 Mr & Mrs Girling
D: £18–£20 **S:** £21–£25
Beds: 1D/F **Baths:** 1 En
🐾 🅿 (2) ⚲ 📺 🛏 ⬛ 📺

Rackheath

TG2813   🚇 *Green Man*

Barn Court, *Back Lane, Rackheath, Norwich, NR13 6NN.*
Spacious accommodation built around a courtyard. Ideal for exploring Norfolk.
Open: All Year (not Xmas)
Grades: ETC 3 Diamond
01603 782536 (also fax) Mrs Simpson
D: £18–£21 **S:** £20–£25
Beds: 2D 1T **Baths:** 1 En 2 Sh
🐾 🅿 (3) ⚲ 📺 🛏 ⬛ 📺 🛏 ♿

Manor Barn House, *Back Lane, Rackheath, Norwich, NR13 6NN.*
Traditional C17th Norfolk barn, exposed beams and cottage in garden.
Open: All Year **Grades:** ETC 3 Diamond
01603 783543 Mrs Lebbell
D: £21–£24 **S:** £21–£28
Beds: 3D 2T 1S **Baths:** 4 En 1 Pr
🐾 (5) 🅿 (6) ⚲ 📺 🛏 ⬛ 🛏 🛏

Redenhall

TM2684

Hill Farm, *Redenhall, Harleston, Norfolk, IP20 9QN.*
Farmhouse working arable and stock farm 1 mile from town.
Open: All Year (not Xmas)
01379 852289 (also fax) Mrs Renaut
D: fr £15 **S:** fr £15
Beds: 1F 1T
🐾 🅿 ⚲ 📺 🛏 ⬛

Reedham

TG4201   🚇 *Railway Tavern, Ferry Inn, Ship Inn, The Nelson*

Briars, *Riverside, Reedham, Norwich, NR13 3TF.*
This welcoming home has a wonderful location with a first floor residents lounge & balcony.
Open: All Year (not Xmas)
01493 700054 (also fax)
Mr Monk
D: £26 **S:** £37
Beds: 3D **Baths:** 3 En 1 Sh
🐾 (6) 🅿 (6) 📺 🛏 ✕ ⬛ 📺 🛏 cc

Saham Toney

TF8902   ⚓ *The Windmill*

The Croft, 69 Hills Road, Saham Toney,
Thetford, Norfolk, *IP25 7EW.*
Beautiful creeper covered Victorian
Farmhouse. Delightful garden, Quiet
position.
Open: All Year
01953 881372 Mrs Baldwin
D: £20–£22 **S:** £22–£24
Beds: 1T 1D **Baths:** 1 En 1 Sh
⛵ (12) 🅿 (4) ⚡ 📺 ▥, 🆅 🕯

Salhouse

TG3114   ⚓ *Bell Inn, Dun Cow*

Brooksbank, Lower Street, Salhouse,
Norwich, *NR13 6RW.*
C18th house Broadland village within
easy reach of Norfolk coast.
Open: All Year (not Xmas)
01603 720420 (also fax)
Mr & Mrs Coe
ray@brooksbanks.freeserve.co.uk
D: £18–£20 **S:** £25–£28
Beds: 2D 1T **Baths:** 3 En
🅿 (4) ⚡ 📺 🕯 ▥, 🕯

Salthouse

TG0843   **Cumfus Bottom,** Purdy St,
Salthouse, Holt, Norfolk, *NR25 7XA.*
Rooms set in country garden, only
minutes away from the beach and Heath
Lane.
Open: All Year
01263 741118 (also fax)
Mrs Holman
D: £20–£22.50 **S:** £20–£25
Beds: 1D 1T **Baths:** 2 En
⛵ 🅿 📺 🕯 ▥, 🕯

Saxlingham Thorpe

TM2197   ⚓ *Waterside Inn*

Foxhole Farm, Windy Lane, Foxhole,
Saxlingham Thorpe, Norwich, *NR15 1UG.*
Friendly welcome. Spacious farmhouse.
Comfortable bedrooms. Generous English
breakfasts.
Open: All Year (not Xmas)
Grades: ETC 4 Diamond, AA 4 Diamond
01508 499226 (also fax)
foxholefarm@hotmail.com
D: £18–£20 **S:** £20–£22
Beds: 1D 1T **Baths:** 2 En
⛵ (14) 🅿 (8) ⚡ 📺 ✕ ▥, 🆅 🕯

Sharrington

TG0336   ⚓ *Wiveton Bluebell*

Daubeney Hall , Sharrington, Melton
Constable, Norfolk, *NR24 2PQ.*
Attractive Listed farmhouse in quiet
village. Splendid breakfast. Warm
welcome.
Open: Easter to Oct
Grades: RAC 4 Diamond
01263 861412 N Ogier
ninaogier@hotmail.com
D: £20 **S:** £20–£25
Beds: 1T 2D **Baths:** 2 En 1 Pr
⚡ 📺 🕯 ▥, 🆅 🕯

Sheringham

TG1543   ⚓ *Two Lifeboats, Crown, Wyndham
Arms, Sherry & Ham, Lobster, Crown, Marmalade,
Red Lion*

Sheringham Lodge, 50 Cromer Road,
Sheringham, Norfolk, *NR26 8RS.*
Open: All Year
Grades: ETC 3 Diamond
01263 821954 Mr & Mrs Hare
shrilodge@ic24.net
D: £18–£21 **S:** £18–£21
Beds: 5F 1T 3D 1S **Baths:** 1 En 3 Pr 1 Sh
⛵ (5) 🅿 (6) ⚡ 📺 ▥, 🕯
Attractive guest house run by Gordon and
Jean Hare with ensuite facilities to most
rooms. Residents lounge with TV and
video. Very close to town centre, railway
station and bus stop. Discounts for senior
citizens.

The Melrose, 9 Holway Road,
Sheringham, Norfolk, *NR26 8HN.*
Open: All Year
01263 823299 J & S Parsonage
jsparsonage@btconnect.com
D: £20–£22 **S:** £20–£27
Beds: 1F 2D 1S **Baths:** 6 En
⛵ 🅿 📺 🕯 ✕ ▥, 🆅 🕯
We are in walking distance of rail and bus
stations, town centre and beach. Dine by
firelight in winter - we have a licensed
bar.

Whelk Coppers, Westcliff, Sheringham,
Norfolk, *NR26 8LD.*
Open: All Year (not Xmas/New Year)
01263 825771 S & P Foster
peter.foster@ic24.net
D: £17–£20 **S:** £17–£20
Beds: 1F 1D **Baths:** 1 En 1 Pr
⛵ 📺 🕯
Traditional English tea-rooms panelled in
Indian teak from old sailing ship, views
over sea front & golf course. All that can
be heard are the sounds of the sea yet
only 2 minutes walk from a wealth of
pubs, restaurants and interesting shops.

The Bay-Leaf Guest House, 10 St
Peters Road, Sheringham, Norfolk,
NR26 8QY.
Charming Victorian licensed guest house,
nestled between steam railway and sea.
Open: All Year
Grades: ETC 3 Diamond, AA 3 Diamond
01263 823779 Mr Pigott
D: £18–£22 **S:** £20–£25
Beds: 2F 3D 2T **Baths:** 7 En
⛵ 🅿 (4) 📺 ▥, 🆅 🕯 ♿

The Birches, 27 Holway Road,
Sheringham, Norfolk, *NR26 8HW.*
Open: April to Oct
Grades: AA 4 Diamond
01263 823550 Ms Pearce
D: £20–£25 **S:** £25
Beds: 1D 1T **Baths:** 2 En
⛵ (12) 🅿 (2) ⚡ 📺 ✕ ▥, 🆅 🕯
Small guest house conveniently situated
for town and sea front. Ideal centre for
touring North Norfolk. Attractions include
The North Norfolk Railway, National Trust
Properties, some of England's best bird
watching areas and award winning
beaches.

Canton House, 14 Cliff Road,
Sheringham, Norfolk, *NR26 8BJ.*
Warm welcome. Comfortable
surroundings. Excellent breakfast. Home
made bread.
Open: All Year (not Xmas/New Year)
01263 824861 Ms Rayment
chrissy@tooment.freeserve.co.uk
D: £20.50–£21 **S:** £20.50–£21
Beds: 1F 1T 1D **Baths:** 2 En 2 Sh
⛵ (1) 📺 🕯 ✕ ▥, 🆅 🕯

The Old Vicarage, Sheringham,
Norfolk, *NR26 8NH.*
Excellent accommodation, comfortable,
well-furnished bedsitting rooms. Superb
breakfasts. Quiet location.
Open: Mar to Nov
01263 822627 Mrs Lees
D: £25–£27 **S:** £28–£40
Beds: 1D 1T **Baths:** 3 En
⛵ (12) 🅿 (6) 📺 🕯 ✕ ▥, 🆅 🕯

Sans Souci, 19 Waterbank Road,
Sheringham, Norfolk, *NR26 8RB.*
A charming Victorian guest house, 3
minutes from all amenities.
Open: Easter to Oct
01263 824436 Mrs Majewski
D: £17–£20 **S:** £17–£20
Beds: 1D 1T 1S **Baths:** 1 Sh
⛵ 🅿 (3) ⚡ 📺 🕯 ▥, 🆅 🕯

Shipdham

TF9507

Pound Green Hotel, Pound Green
Lane, Shipham, Thetford, Norfolk, *IP2S 7LS.*
An acre of own grounds. Peaceful rural
setting.
Open: All Year
Grades: AA 2 Star
01362 820940 Mr Hales & Ms S Woods
Fax: 01362 821253
poundgreen@aol.com
D: £22.50–£25 **S:** £25–£35
Beds: 1F 8D 1S **Baths:** 8 En 2 Pr
⛵ 🅿 (50) ⚡ 📺 ✕ ▥, 🆅 ✳ 🕯 ♿ cc

Smallburgh

TG3324   ⚓ *The Crown*

Bramble House, Catts Common,
Smallburgh, Norfolk, *NR12 9NS.*
Friendliness and comfort guaranteed in
our large country house, in 1.5 acres
Open: All Year (not Xmas)
Grades: ETC 4 Diamond, Silver
01692 535069 (also fax) S Ross
bramblehouse@tesco.com
D: £22–£24 **S:** £30
Beds: 1F 1T 1S **Baths:** 4 En
⛵ 🅿 (4) ⚡ 📺 ✕ ▥, 🆅 🕯

South Lopham

TM0481   ⚓ *White Horse*

Malting Farm, Blo Norton Road, South
Lopham, Diss, Norfolk, *IP22 2HT.*
Elizabethan timber-framed farmhouse on
working farm. Patchwork & quilting.
Open: Jan to Dec
Grades: ETC 3 Diamond
01379 687201 Mrs Huggins
D: £21–£23 **S:** £25–£30
Beds: 1D 1T **Baths:** 1 En 1 Sh
⛵ 🅿 ⚡ ▥, 🆅 🕯

Swaffham

TF8109 ◀ *Red Lion, Horse & Groom, George Hotel*

Purbeck House, Whitsands Road, Swaffham, Norfolk, *PE37 7BJ.*
Family guest house. Warm welcome. Large garden. Full English breakfast.
Open: All Year
01760 721805 Mrs Webster
D: £18–£20 **S:** fr £20
Beds: 2F 2T 2S **Baths:** 1 En 2 Sh
🛇 🅿 (3) 📺 🍴 🛗 🖢

Swanton Morley

TG0217 ◀ *Darby's, Angel*

Kesmark House, Gooseberry Hill, Swanton Morley, Dereham, Norfolk, *NR20 4PP.*
Open: All Year (not Xmas/New Year)
01362 637663 Mr & Mrs Willis
Fax: 01362 637800
kesmark@netcomuk.co.uk
D: £17.50–£25 **S:** £25–£40
Beds: 1F 1T 2D **Baths:** 1 En 2 Pr
🛇 🅿 (3) ⅙ 📺 🍴 ✕ 🛗 🖂 🖢
Beautiful Listed house in 2 acres of wooded gardens. Perfect base for exploring Breckland's local attractions. Close to pubs, fishing. Easy reach North Coast (Holkham etc.), Norwich, Broads, Fakenham races. Elegantly furnished rooms, superb Aga-cooked breakfasts. S/C cottage also available.

Thetford

TL8783 ◀ *Black Horse, Anchor Hotel*

43 Magdalen Street, Thetford, Thetford, Norfolk, *IP24 2BP.*
House built in 1575 close to town centre.
Open: All Year (not Xmas/New Year)
01842 764564 Mrs Findlay
D: £36 **S:** £18
Beds: 2T 1S **Baths:** 1 Sh
🛇 🅿 (1) 📺 🛗 🖂 🖢

Thompson

TL9196 ◀ *Chequers*

College Farm, Thompson, Thetford, Norfolk, *IP24 1QG.*
Converted C14th college of priests; 3 acre garden, wonderful breakfasts.
Open: All Year
01953 483318 (also fax)
Mrs Garnier
D: £20 **S:** £20
Beds: 2D 1T **Baths:** 1 Pr 1 Sh 2 En
🛇 (7) 🅿 (10) 📺 🛗

The Thatched House, Pockthorpe Corner, Thompson, Thetford, Norfolk, *IP24 1PJ.*
16th Century, delightful village on the edge of the Brecklands.
Open: All Year
01953 483577 Mrs Mills
D: fr £20 **S:** fr £25
Beds: 1D 2T **Baths:** 2 Sh 1 Pr
🛇 (6) 🅿 (4) ⅙ 📺 🍴 ✕ 🛗 🖢 🔥

Thornham

TF7343 ◀ *King's Head, The Lifeboat, Titchwell Manor*

Orchard House, Thornham, Hunstanton, Norfolk, *PE36 6LY.*
Tucked away in large garden, centre of conservation village.
Open: All Year (not Xmas Day)
Grades: ETC 4 Diamond
01485 512259 Mrs Rutland
D: £22.50–£30 **S:** £35–£45
Beds: 2T 2D **Baths:** 3 En 1 Pr
🛇 (8) 🅿 (6) ⅙ 📺 🛗 🖢

Thorpe St Andrew

TG2609 ◀ *The Buck*

Raeburn, 83 Yarmouth Road, Thorpe St Andrew, Norwich, *NR7 0HE.*
2 miles Norwich centre, on bus route, opposite Thorpe Tare.
Open: All Year (not Xmas/New Year)
01603 439177 Mrs Hawkins
D: £18–£20 **S:** £18–£20
Beds: 1D 1T 1S **Baths:** 1 Sh
🅿 (4) 📺 🛗 🖂 🖢

Norwood House, 14 Stanmore Road, Thorpe St Andrew, Norwich, Norfolk, *NR7 0HB.*
Detached house with attractive garden in peaceful cul-de-sac, 2 miles from historic Norwich.
Open: All Year (not Xmas)
01603 433500 Mrs Simpson
D: £20–£22.50 **S:** £20–£22.50
Beds: 2D 1S **Baths:** 2 Sh
🛇 (10) 🅿 (4) 📺 🛗 🖢

Thursford

TF9734 ◀ *Chequers Inn, The Crawfish*

Old Coach House, Thursford, Fakenham, Norfolk, *NR21 0BD.*
Peaceful farmhouse. 8 m beautiful coastline. Suit birdwatchers and country lovers.
Open: All Year (not Xmas/New Year)
Grades: AA 3 Diamond
01328 878273 Mrs Green
D: £20–£28 **S:** £24–£28
Beds: 3T 1D **Baths:** 2 En 1 Sh
🛇 🅿 (6) 📺 🍴 ✕ 🛗 🖂 🖢

Tilney St Lawrence

TF5514 ◀ *Coach & Horses, Wildflower*

The Garden House, 27 Magdalen Road, Tilney St Lawrence, King's Lynn, Norfolk, *PE34 4QX.*
Open countryside, fishing, Sandringham House and Historic Lynn nearby.
Open: Easter to Oct
01945 880610 Mr & Mrs Swain
D: £16 **S:** £20
Beds: 1T 1D **Baths:** 1 En 1 Sh
🛇 🅿 (8) ⅙ 📺 🍴 🛗 🖢

B&B owners may vary
rates - be sure to check
when booking

Upwell

TF5002

Five Bells Inn, 1 New Road, Upwell, Wisbech, Cambs, *PE14 9AA.*
Attractive riverside village inn, comfortable rooms and award-winning restaurant. **Open:** All Year
Grades: AA 2 Star
01945 772222 Fax: 01945 774433
D: £20–£25 **S:** £25–£30
Beds: 1F 3D 3T **Baths:** 7 En
🛇 🅿 (20) ⅙ 📺 🍴 ✕ 🛗 🖂 🖢 cc

Walton Highway

TF4912 ◀ *King Of Hearts*

Homeleigh Guest House, Lynn Road, Walton Highway, Wisbech, Cambs, *PE14 7DE.*
Homeleigh Guest House built 1880s. All rooms ensuite. **Open:** All Year
01945 582356 Mrs Wiseman
Fax: 01945 587006
D: fr £20 **S:** fr £20
Beds: 2D 2T 2S **Baths:** 6 En
🛇 🅿 (6) 📺 🍴 ✕ 🛗 🖂 🖢 ⚘ 🔥 🖢 cc

Maple Lodge, Lynn Road, Walton Highway, Wisbech, Cambs, *PE14 7QE.*
Modern family home on outskirts of village, overlooking open fields.
Open: All Year
01945 461430 D: £18–£21 **S:** £18–£21
Beds: 2D 1T 1S **Baths:** 1 En 1 Sh
🛇 🅿 (5) ⅙ 📺 ✕ 🛗 🖂 🖢

Warham

TF9441 ◀ *Three Horseshoes*

The Three Horseshoes / The Old Post Office, 69 Bridge Street, Warham, Wells-next-the-Sea, Norfolk, *NR23 1NL.*
Dream country cottage adjoining award-winning village pub.
Open: All Year (not Xmas)
01328 710547 Mr Salmon
D: £24–£26 **S:** £24
Beds: 3D 1S **Baths:** 1 En 1 Sh
🛇 (14) 🅿 (10) ⅙ 📺 🍴 ✕ 🛗 🖂 🖢

Waterden

TF8836 ◀ *Ostrich Inn*

Old Rectory, Waterden, Walsingham, Norfolk, *NR22 6AT.*
Waterden rectory Holkham estate situated in peaceful rural surroundings.
Open: All Year
01328 823298 Mrs Pile
D: £20–£22 **S:** £20–£35
Beds: 1F 1T 2D **Baths:** 3 En
🛇 🅿 (4) 📺 🍴 🛗 🖂 ⚘ 🖢 🔥

Wells-next-the-Sea

TF9143 ◀ *Crown Hotel, The Edinburgh, Ark Royal, Lifeboat Inn, Three Horseshoes*

Greengates, Stiffkey Road, Wells-next-the-Sea, Norfolk, *NR23 1QB.*
C18th cottage with views over salt marsh to sea. **Open:** All Year (not Xmas)
01328 711040 Mrs Jarvis
D: £19–£23 **S:** £20–£25
Beds: 1D 1T **Baths:** 1 En 1 Pr 1 Sh
🅿 (2) ⅙ 📺 🛗 🖂 🖢

East House, East Quay, Wells-next-the-Sea, Norfolk, NR23 1LE.
Old house overlooking marsh, creeks and boats to distant sea.
Open: All Year (not Xmas)
01328 710408 Mrs Scott
D: £22.50 **S:** £26
Beds: 2T **Baths:** 2 En
⛄ (7) 🅿 (2) 🖼 📖 🎥 ₺

St Heliers Guest House, Station Road, Wells-next-the-Sea, Norfolk, NR23 1EA.
Central Georgian family house in secluded gardens with excellent breakfasts.
Open: 10 months
01328 710361 (also fax)
Mrs Kerr
st.heliers@btinternet.com
D: £16–£25 **S:** £18–£30
Beds: 1D 1T 1S **Baths:** 2 Sh 1 En
🅿 (4) ⚡ 🖼 📖 🎥 ₺

Wendling

TF9213

Greenbanks Country Hotel,
Wendling, Dereham, Norfolk, NR19 2AR.
Central touring, NT properties, private fishing, 5 ground floor suites. Meadow gardens.
Open: All Year
Grades: AA 4 Diamond
01362 687742 greenbanks@skynow.com
D: £28–£36 **S:** £36–£50
Beds: 3F 3T 2D **Baths:** 8 En
⛄ 🅿 🖼 🍴 ✗ 📖 🎥 ❋ ₺ & cc

West Dereham

TF6500 ⚓ Foldgate Inn

Bell Barn, Lime Kiln Road, West Dereham, King's Lynn, PE33 9RT.
Quality accommodation with rustic charm, quiet rural setting.
Open: All Year (not Xmas)
Grades: ETC 4 Diamond
01366 500762 (also fax)
Mrs Wood
chris@woodbarn.freeserve.co.uk
D: £20 **S:** £25
Beds: 1F 1D **Baths:** 1 En 1 Pr
⛄ 🅿 (4) 🖼 📖 🎥 ₺

West Somerton

TG4620 ⚓ The Lion, Fishermans Return

The White House Farm, The Street, West Somerton, Great Yarmouth, Norfolk, NR29 4EA.
Open: All Year (not Xmas)
Grades: ETC 3 Diamond
01493 393991 Mr Dobinson
prued@hotmail.com
D: £18–£20 **S:** £18–£20
Beds: 3D **Baths:** 1 En 1 Sh
⛄ 🅿 (4) ⚡ 🖼 📖 ₺
Welcoming, peaceful old farmhouse close to Broads (rowing dinghy) and lovely beach. Enjoyable walks and bike rides. Substantial breakfasts. Private ensuite bath or shower rooms. Comfortable bedrooms overlooking sunny walled garden. Guest lounge and conservatory for space and relaxation.

Wicklewood

TG0702

Witch Hazel, Church Lane, Wicklewood, Wymondham, NR18 9QH.
Peter and Eileen welcome you to Witch Hazel - a spacious detached house.
Open: All Year
Grades: ETC 4 Diamond
01953 602247 (also fax)
Mr & Mrs Blake
D: £20 **S:** £26
Beds: 3D **Baths:** 3 En
⛄ (15) 🅿 (3) ⚡ 🖼 ✗ 📖 🎥 ₺

Winterton-on-Sea

TG4919 ⚓ Fishermans Return

Tower Cottage, Black Street, Winterton-on-Sea, Great Yarmouth, Norfolk, NR29 4AP.
Pretty flint cottage. Excellent breakfast. Peaceful village with sandy beach.
Open: All Year (not Xmas)
01493 394053 (also fax)
Mr Webster
D: £18–£20 **S:** fr £20
Beds: 2D 1T **Baths:** 1 En 2 Pr
⛄ (8) 🅿 (3) 🖼 📖 ₺

Wood Dalling

TG0927 ⚓ Earl Arms

Westwood Barn, Crabgate Lane South, Wood Dalling, Norwich, NR11 6SW.
Outstanding accommodation, idyllic countryside location for Norwich, Broads, coastal resorts.
Open: All Year
01263 584108 Mrs Westwood
D: £23–£26 **S:** £32–£33
Beds: 2T **Baths:** 3 En
⛄ (12) 🅿 (6) ⚡ 🖼 ✗ 📖 🎥 ❋ ₺ &

Wood Norton

TG0127

Manor Farm, Wood Norton, Dereham, Norfolk, NR20 5BE.
A warm welcome awaits you at large grade II Listed farmhouse.
Open: All Year (not Xmas/New Year)
Grades: ETC 4 Diamond
01362 683231 Mrs Crowe
D: £20–£25
Beds: 1T 2D **Baths:** 2 En 1 Pr
⛄ (10) 🅿 (4) ⚡ 🖼 ✗ 📖 🎥 ₺

Worthing

TG0019 ⚓ Kings Head

Tannery House, Church Road, Worthing , Dereham, Norfolk, NR20 5HR.
Open: All Year (not Xmas/New Year)
01362 668202 Mr & Mrs Eve
george@eve.01.fsnet.co.uk
D: £22–£26 **S:** £24–£28
Beds: 1T 3D **Baths:** 2 En 1 Sh
⚡ 🖼 🍴 📖 ₺
Quietly situated C18th house in the heart of rural Norfolk. In unspoilt Hamlet convenient to the coast, Broads, Norwich and Sandringham. Beautiful riverside setting overlooking own well stocked fishing lake. Picturesque garden. 4 acres including water. Free fishing to guests.

Wortwell

TM2784

Rose Cottage, 62 High Road, Wortwell, Harleston, IP20 0EF.
Friendly proprietor, Otter Trust close by, 45 minutes from coast.
Open: All Year
01986 788174 Mrs Gaffney
D: £19–£22 **S:** £20–£25
Beds: 1D 1T **Baths:** 1 Sh
⛄ 🅿 (6) ⚡ 🖼 🍴 📖 ₺

Wroxham

TG3017 ⚓ The Bridge

Wroxham Park Lodge, 142 Norwich Road, Wroxham, Norwich, NR12 8SA.
Victorian house with garden, ideal touring Norfolk and the Broads.
Open: All Year
Grades: ETC 4 Diamond
01603 782991 K Jackman
D: £20–£23 **S:** £20–£26
Beds: 1F 1T 2D **Baths:** 4 En
⛄ 🅿 (4) 🖼 🍴 📖 ₺

Wymondham

TG1101 ⚓ Crossed Keys, White Horse, Three Boars, Pelican, Bird In Hand

Turret House, 27 Middleton Street, Wymondham, Norfolk, NR18 0AB.
Victorian town house of considerable character - close to historic abbey.
Open: All Year
01953 603462 (also fax)
Mrs Morgan
D: £20 **S:** £20
Beds: 1F 1T 1S **Baths:** 1 Sh
⛄ 🅿 (2) ⚡ 🖼 🍴 📖 🎥 ₺ cc

Witch Hazel, Church Lane, Wicklewood, Wymondham, NR18 9QH.
Open: All Year
Grades: ETC 4 Diamond
01953 602247 (also fax)
Mr & Mrs Blake
D: £20 **S:** £26
Beds: 3D **Baths:** 3 En
⛄ (15) 🅿 (3) ⚡ 🖼 ✗ 📖 🎥 ₺
Peter and Eileen welcome you to Witch Hazel - a spacious detached house in a peaceful rural environment with mature gardens in which to relax. All rooms ensuite. No smoking throughout. Ideal central touring base.

York House, Middleton Street, Wymondham, NR18 0AB.
Grade II Listed house in centre of Wymondham. Norwich 8 miles.
Open: All Year (not Xmas)
01953 606284 Ms Van Hattern
D: £20 **S:** £20
Beds: 1T
⛄ ⚡ 🖼 🍴 📖 ₺

Please respect a B&B's wishes regarding children, animals and smoking

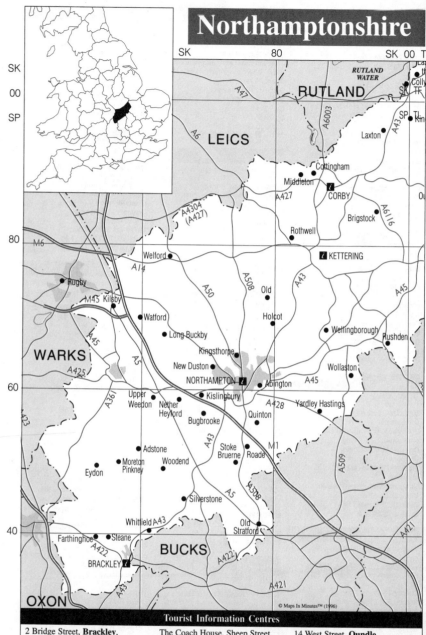

Northamptonshire

Tourist Information Centres

2 Bridge Street, **Brackley**,
Northamptonshire, NN13 5EP,
01280 700111.

Civic Centre, George Street, **Corby**,
Northamptonshire, NN17 1QB,
01536 402551.

Moot Hall, Market Square,
Daventry, Northamptonshire,
NN11 4BH, 01327 300277.

The Coach House, Sheep Street,
Kettering, Northamptonshire,
NN16 0AN,
01536 410266.

Mr Grant's House, 10 St Giles
Square, **Northampton**, NN1 1DA,
01604 622677.

14 West Street, **Oundle**,
Northamptonshire, PE8 4EF,
01832 274333.

Wellingborough Library, Pebble
Lane, **Wellingborough**,
Northamptonshire, NN8 1AS,
01933 225365.

Abington

SP7761 ⚜ *Pickering Phips*

Pembroke House, *36 Garrick Road, Abington, Northampton, NN1 5ND.*
Beautiful Victorian property, all facilities, near park, town and M1.
Open: Jan to Nov
01604 621858 Mr Thomas
D: £17–£19 **S:** £17.50–£19.50
Beds: 1D 1T 1S **Baths:** 1 Sh
🛇 ⵣ 📺 ⵂ ✕ 🛏 ♨

Adstone

SP5951 ⚜ *Royal Oak*

Manor Farm, *Adstone, Towcester, Northants, NN12 8DT.*
C17th stone farmhouse, tiny quiet village; ideal location for relaxation or exploring.
Open: All Year
01327 860284 Mrs Paton
Fax: 01327 860685
ross_mcintyre@msn.com
D: £20–£25 **S:** £20–£25
Beds: 1F 1D 1S **Baths:** 2 En 1 Pr
🛇 📱 ⵣ 📺 🛏 🛏 ⵂ ♨

Planning a longer stay? Always ask for any special rates

Barnwell

TL0484 ⚜ *Montagu Arms*

Lilford Lodge Farm, *Barnwell, Oundle, Peterborough, Northamptonshire, PE8 5SA.*
Open: All Year (not Xmas)
Grades: ETC 4 Diamond
01832 272230 (also fax)
Mrs Dijksterhuis
trudy@lilford-lodge.demon.co.uk
D: £18–£21 **S:** £18–£21
Beds: 1F 1D 2T 2S **Baths:** 6 En
🛇 📱 (20) ⵣ 📺 🛏 ⵂ 🛏
C19th farmhouse and adjoining barn recently converted. Set in the Nene Valley, 3 miles south of Oundle, 5 miles north of A14. Peterborough, Stamford, Kettering, Wellingborough and Corby are within easy reach. Coarse fishing available. Quiet, rural location.

Brackley

SP5837 ⚜ *The Fox*

Walltree House Farm, *Steane, Brackley, Northants, NN13 5NS.*
Central touring base. Comfortable warm converted stables. Ground floor bedrooms and cottages. Laundry.
Open: All Year (not Xmas)
01295 811235 Mrs Harrison
Fax: 01295 811147
D: £27.50–£37.50 **S:** £37.50–£40
Beds: 4F 2D 3T **Baths:** 7 En 3 Pr
🛇 📱 (15) ⵣ 📺 🛏 🛏 **cc**

Brigstock

SP9485

Bridge House, *3 Grafton Road, Brigstock, Kettering, Northants, NN14 3EY.*
Quiet modern home in pretty village. Warm welcome. Full breakfast.
Open: All Year (not Xmas)
01536 373297 D: £16.50–£18 **S:** £16.50–£18
Beds: 1T 1S **Baths:** 1 Sh
🛇 📱 (3) ⵣ 📺 ✕ 🛏 ♨

Bugbrooke

SP6757 ⚜ *Five Bells, The Wharf*

Cherry Tree Cottage, *26a Camphill, Bugbrooke, Northampton, NN7 3PH.*
Cleanliness, warm hospitality, hearty breakfast and pleasant surrounding are our speciality. **Open:** All Year
Grades: ETC 3 Diamond
01604 830929 Mrs Corben
D: £20–£25 **S:** £20–£25
Beds: 1T 1D **Baths:** 1 Sh
🛇 (2) 📱 (5) ⵣ 📺 🛏 ⵂ 🛏

Collyweston

SK9902

Highfields, *31 Main Road, Collyweston, Stamford, Lincs, PE9 3PF.*
Detached black & white chalet house surrounded by fields.
Open: All Year
Grades: ETC Listed
01780 444339 Mrs Hindley
prhinkley@aol.com
D: £20–£21 **S:** £20–£21
Beds: 1D 1T 1S **Baths:** 1 En 1 Sh
🛇 (4) 📱 (4) 🛏 🛏 ✕ 🛏 ⵂ 🛏 ♨

Corby

SP8889 ⚜ *Spread Eagle, Corby Candle, Oakley Hay, Game Bird*

Macallan Guest House, *18-20 Lundy Avenue, Corby, Northants, NN18 8BU.*
Near Rockingham Castle, Indy race track (opening Sept 2001).
Open: All Year
01536 261848 Mrs MacLeod
D: £15–£18 **S:** £15–£18
Beds: 1D 2T 3S **Baths:** 3 Sh
📱 (6) 📺 ✕ 🛏 ⵂ 🛏

65 Rockingham Road, *Corby, Northants, NN17 1AH.*
Detached modern bungalow.
Open: All Year
01536 262084 Mrs Haas
D: £12.50–£20 **S:** £15–£20
Beds: 1T 2S **Baths:** 1 Sh
🛇 (5) 📱 (1) ⵣ 📺 🛏 ⵂ 🛏 &

Cottingham

SP8490 ⚜ *Royal George, Spread Eagle*

Bancroft House, *34 Bancroft Road, Cottingham, Market Harborough, Leics, LE16 8XA.*
Friendly atmosphere. Quiet location. Huge breakfast if required. Access to garden.
Open: All Year (not Xmas/New Year)
01536 770799 Mrs Evans
judy@bancroft88.fsnet.co.uk
D: £16–£18 **S:** £16–£18
Beds: 1D 2S **Baths:** 1 Sh
🛇 (0) 📱 (6) ⵣ 📺 🛏 ⵂ 🛏

Easton-on-the-Hill

TF0004 ⚜ *Oak*

Hillcroft House, *25 High Street, Easton-on-the-Hill, Stamford, Lincs, PE9 3LN.*
Converted stone farmhouse, spacious grounds, quiet position in conservation village.
Open: All Year (not Xmas)
01780 755598 Mrs McCallum
D: £17.50–£20 **S:** £20–£22.50
Beds: 1D 2T **Baths:** 1 Pr 1 Sh
🛇 📱 (4) ⵣ 📺 🛏 🛏 ⵂ 🛏

Eydon

SP5450 ⚜ *Royal Oak*

Crockwell Farm, *Eydon, Daventry, Northants, NN11 3QA.*
Open: All Year
Grades: ETC 4 Diamond, Silver Award
01327 361358 J B Harper
Fax: 01327 361573
crockwellfarm@supanet.com
D: £25–£30 **S:** £30
Beds: 2F 2T 1D **Baths:** 4 En 1 Pr
🛇 📱 (6) 📺 🛏 🛏 🛏 **cc**
Individually furnished accommodation in beautiful C17th barns. All bedrooms have south facing views over open countryside. Accommodation benefits from excellent kitchen and sitting room facilities. Fantastic food served at our own village pub. Events catered for in vaulted hall.

Farthinghoe

SP5339 ✦ Fox Inn

Greenfield, Baker Street, Farthinghoe, Brackley, Northants, NN13 5PH.
Open: All Year (not Xmas)
Grades: ETC 4 Diamond
01295 712380 V Webb
Fax: 01295 710557
vivwebb@aol.com
D: £20–£25 **S:** £20–£25
Beds: 1D 1T **Baths:** 1 Pr
🛏 (8) 🅿 (2) ⚟ 📺 🛏 🖳 �📺 🌡
Post office, C16th church and pub are near our comfortable modern home. Silverstone race circuit, Canons Ashby, Sulgrave Manor, Oxford, Stratford, Warwick Castle and the Cotswolds are easily accessible. M40 (J11) London to Birmingham is 4 miles away.

Holcot

SP7969 ✦ White Swan

White Swan Inn, Main Street, Holcot, Northampton, NN6 9SP.
The atmosphere of a genuine country inn.
Open: All Year
01604 781263 (also fax) Mr Hodgson
white_swan_inn_holcot@compuserve.com
D: £20–£27.50 **S:** £20–£27.50
Beds: 1D 1T 2S **Baths:** 2 Sh
🛏 (5) 🅿 (10) 📺 ✕ 🖳 �📺 🌡

Kettering

SP8778 ✦ Star Inn, Beeswing, Goody's, Wayfarers, Earl Of Dalkeith

Pennels Guest House, 175 Beatrice Road, Kettering, Northants, NN16 9QR.
Quality accommodation, well-maintained, some ground-room bedrooms overlooking private garden, quiet area. **Open:** All Year
Grades: ETC 3 Diamond, AA 3 Diamond, RAC 3 Diamond
01536 481940 Mrs Green
Fax: 01536 410798
pennelsgh@aol.com
D: £20–£22 **S:** £22.50–£25
Beds: 1D 3T 3S **Baths:** 5 En 1 Sh
🛏 🅿 (6) ⚟ 📺 🛏 ✕ 🖳 �📺 🌡 ⅙ cc

Hawthorn House Private Hotel, 2 Hawthorn Road, Kettering, Northants, NN15 7HS.
Victorian town house private hotel. Hour train time to London.
Open: All Year **Grades:** ETC 3 Diamond
01536 482513 Mrs McQuade
Fax: 01536 513121
D: £20 **S:** £28
Beds: 1D 4T **Baths:** 3 En 2 Pr
🛏 🅿 (4) 📺 ✕ 🖳 🌡

Kilsby

SP5570 ✦ Red Lion, Hunt House, The George

The Hollies Farmhouse, Main Road, Kilsby, Rugby, Northamptonshire, CV23 8XR.
Comfortable farmhouse, conveniently central for leisure or business activities.
Open: All Year **Grades:** ETC 3 Diamond
01788 822629 Mrs Liddington
D: £20–£25 **S:** £25–£35
Beds: 2D 1T **Baths:** 1 En 1 Sh
🛏 🅿 (8) ⚟ 📺 🛏 🖳 🌡

King's Cliffe

TL0097 ✦ Cross Keys, Queens Head

19 West Street, King's Cliffe, Peterborough, Northamptonshire, PE8 6XB.
Open: All Year (not Xmas)
Grades: ETC 4 Diamond
01780 470365 J Dixon
Fax: 01780 470623
100537.156@compuserve.com
D: £20–£25 **S:** £25
Beds: 1S 1D 1T **Baths:** 3 Pr
🅿 (2) ⚟ 📺 ✕ 🖳 �📺 🌡
Grade II Listed 500 year old house, Beautiful walled garden, reputedly one of King johns Hunting lodges. Delicious dinners on request. Situated in attractive stone village near Stamford, central location for many stately homes and other historic attractions.

Freestone Lodge, Bridge Street, King's Cliffe, Peterborough, PE8 6XH.
Traditional stone house in countryside room overlook garden and stables.
Open: All Year
01780 470213 (also fax) Mr & Mrs Blunt
freesto@aol.com
D: £20–£25 **S:** £20–£25
Beds: 1F 2T **Baths:** 1 Sh
🛏 (8) 🅿 (6) 🛏 🖳 🌡

Kingsthorpe

SP7563

The Old Church Institute, Kingsthorpe Village, Northampton, NN2 6QB.
Tastefully converted detached Edwardian property, attractive gardens. Close Pubs/shops etc. **Open:** All Year
01604 715500 (also fax)
E Bergin
D: £20–£25 **S:** £20–£25
Beds: 2D 2T **Baths:** 2 En 1 Sh
⚟ 🖳 🌡

Kislingbury

SP6959 ✦ Old Red Lion

The Elms, Kislingbury, Northampton, NN7 4AH.
Victorian house overlooking our farm land. Close to Nene Way Walk.
Open: All Year
Grades: ETC 3 Diamond
01604 830326 Mrs Sanders
D: £19 **S:** £19
Beds: 1D 1T 1S 3F **Baths:** 1 Sh
🛏 🅿 (4) ⚟ 📺 🛏 ✕ 🖳 �📺 🌡

Laxton

SP9496 ✦ Queen's Head

The Old Vicarage, Laxton, Corby, Northants, NN17 3AT.
Delightful 'gothic' home, gardens; hamlet on borders Northants, Rutland, Lincs.
Open: All Year (not Xmas)
01780 450248 Mrs Hill-Brookes
Fax: 01780 450398
susan@marthahill.co.uk
D: £18.50–£19.50 **S:** £18.50–£19.50
Beds: 1F 1D 1T **Baths:** 2 Pr
🛏 🅿 (4) 📺 🛏 🖳 �📺 🌡 cc

Long Buckby

SP6267 ✦ Stag's Head

Murcott Mill, Murcott, Long Buckby, Northampton, NN6 7QR.
Beautifully situated Georgian Mill house, ideal for Althorp House & stopovers.
Open: All Year
01327 842236 Mrs Hart
Fax: 01327 844524
bhart6@compuserve.com
D: £20–£21 **S:** £20–£25
Beds: 1F 1D 2T **Baths:** 3 En
🛏 🅿 (10) 📺 🛏 ✕ 🖳 �📺 🌡

Middleton

SP8390 ✦ Red Lion

Valley View, 3 Camsdale Walk, Middleton, Market Harborough, Leics, LE16 8YR.
Elevated, stone-built house with panoramic views of the Welland Valley.
Open: All Year (not Xmas)
01536 770874 Mrs Randle
D: £17–£18 **S:** £18
Beds: 1D 1T **Baths:** 1 Sh
🛏 🅿 (2) ⚟ 📺 🖳 �📺 🌡

Moreton Pinkney

SP5749 ✦ Royal Oak, England's Rose, Star Inn, Three Conies

The Old Vicarage, Moreton Pinkney, Daventry, Northants, NN11 3SQ.
Comfortable, pretty C18th house with walled garden in rural village.
Open: All Year (not Xmas)
Grades: ETC 4 Diamond, Silver
01295 760057 (also fax)
Col & Mrs Eastwood
tim@tandjeastwood.fsnet.co.uk
D: £27.50–£30 **S:** £30–£35
Beds: 1D 1T **Baths:** 1 En 1 Pr
🛏 (7) 🅿 (3) ⚟ 📺 🛏 ✕ 🖳 🌡

England's Rose, Upper Green, Moreton Pinkney, Daventry, Northants, NN11 3SG.
C17th coaching inn. Open fires, A la carte restaurant four poster bedroom.
Open: All Year
Grades: ETC 3 Diamond, AA 3 Diamond
01295 760353 (also fax)
sheila@englandrose.freeserve.co.uk
D: £25–£50 **S:** £25–£50
Beds: 2F 3T 4D 1S **Baths:** 10 En
🛏 🅿 ⚟ 📺 🛏 ✕ 🖳 �📺 ⚘ 🌡 ⅙ cc

Nether Heyford

SP6658 ✦ Forrester's Arms

Heyford B&B, 27 Church Street, Nether Heyford, Northampton, NN7 3LH.
Lovely village, 1.5 miles M1 J16. Quiet, friendly and comfortable.
Open: All Year
Grades: ETC 2 Diamond
01327 340872 Mrs Clements
D: £16–£20 **S:** £20–£25
Beds: 3T 2S **Baths:** 2 En 1 Sh
🛏 🅿 (8) 📺 🖳 🌡

Northampton

SP7561 ◑ *White Elephant, Country Tavern, Porky's, Lumbertubs, Rose & Crown, White Hart, Dusty Fox, Abington*

Castilian House, *34 Park Avenue North, Northampton, NN3 2JE.*
Family-run, easy access to main routes, town centre amenities.
Open: All Year (not Xmas)
01604 712863 (also fax)
Mrs Smith
D: £19.50–£20 **S:** £19.50–£20
Beds: 2S **Baths:** 1 Sh
🛇 (14) 🖵 ✕ 🏛 Ⅴ ▲

Abington Town House, *Ardington Road, Abington Park, Northampton, NN1 5LP.*
Open: All Year (not Xmas/New Year)
01604 633128 Ms Brown
D: £20–£22.50 **S:** £20–£30
Beds: 1D 2T 1S **Baths:** 1 Pr 1 Sh
⅙ 🖵 ✕ 🏛 Ⅴ ▲
A traditional Edwardian house with a typically English atmosphere, operating on friendly Christian principles, with care and consideration for all our guests. Near to Northampton town centre and adjacent to delightful Abington Park.

Rowena, *569 Harlestone Road, New Duston, Northampton, NN5 6NX.*
Full of Victorian charm and character, close to city centre.
Open: All Year
Grades: ETC 4 Diamond
01604 755889 P Adcock
D: £22.50–£25 **S:** £22.50–£25
Beds: 1D 1T 1S **Baths:** 1 Sh
🅿 (3) ⅙ 🖵 🏛 ▲

Birchfields Guest House, *17 Hester Street, Northampton, NN2 6AP.*
Very comfortable friendly guest house.
Open: All Year (not Xmas)
01604 628199 Mrs Dickens
D: £15–£25 **S:** £16–£17
Beds: 2F 1D 2T 1S **Baths:** 2 Sh
🛇 ⅙ Ⅴ ✳

Old

SP7873 ◑ *White Horse*

Wold Farm, *Old, Northampton, NN6 9RJ.*
Anne and Bruce Engler welcome you to their C18th farmhouse on 250-acre farm.
Open: All Year
01604 781258 Mrs Engler
D: £25–£28 **S:** £30
Beds: 2D 1T 2S **Baths:** 5 En
🛇 🅿 (6) ⅙ 🖵 ♞ 🏛 ▲

Old Stratford

SP7741 ◑ *White Bear*

Furtho Manor Farm, *Old Stratford, Milton Keynes, Bucks, MK19 6BA.*
Dairy and arable farm, 10 mins to central Milton Keynes. **Open:** All Year (not Xmas)
01908 542139 (also fax)
Mrs Sansome
D: £20–£22 **S:** £20–£25
Beds: 1D 2T **Baths:** 2 Sh
🛇 🅿 (6) 🖵 🏛 Ⅴ ▲ ఉ

Oundle

TL0487 ◑ *The Ship Inn*

Ashworth House, *75 West Street, Oundle, Peterborough, Northamptonshire, PE8 4EJ.*
Open: All Year
Grades: ETC 3 Diamond
01832 275312 (also fax)
Mrs Crick
D: £20–£25 **S:** £25–£30
Beds: 1D 1T **Baths:** 2 En
🛇 (1) ⅙ 🖵 ✕ 🏛 Ⅴ ▲
Grade II Listed town house with attractive walled gardens, in historic Oundle, close to the town centre and amenities, country park and the famous public school. Very comfortable ensuite accommodation with colour TV. Imaginative, traditional Aga cooking.

Quinton

SP7754 ◑ *White Hart*

Quinton Green Farm, *Quinton, Northampton, NN7 2EG.*
C17th farmhouse on working farm near Northampton, M1 (J15) and Milton Keynes.
Open: All Year (not Xmas)
01604 863685 Mrs Turney
Fax: 01604 862230
D: £22.50–£25 **S:** £25–£27.50
Beds: 1D 1T 1S **Baths:** 3 En
🛇 🅿 (12) 🖵 ♞ 🏛 Ⅴ ▲

Roade

SP7652

Chapter House, *High Street, Roade, Brackley, Northants, NN13 5NS.*
Magnificent, converted, 3rd oldest Baptist chapel, large airy lounges.
Open: All Year
Grades: ETC 4 Diamond
01604 862523 Mr & Mrs Morgan
Fax: 01604 864117
D: fr £25 **S:** £29.50–£45
Beds: 1F 1D 1T **Baths:** 3 En
🛇 🅿 (10) ⅙ 🖵 ♞ 🏛 Ⅴ ▲ cc

Rothwell

SP8180

Rothwell House Hotel, *Bridge Street, Rothwell, Kettering, Northants, NN14 6JW.*
Open: All Year
01536 713000 Mr Cleary
Fax: 01536 713888
rothwell.house@virgin.net
D: £20–£30 **S:** £37–£49.50
Beds: 1F 5D 3T 11S **Baths:** 20 En
🛇 🅿 (10) ⅙ 🖵 ♞ ✕ 🏛 Ⅴ ▲ cc
A family run establishment offering a warm welcome. All rooms are ensuite with TV, telephone and tea/coffee making facilities. There is a fully licensed bar and a restaurant serving home cooked food. Contractors welcome.

All details shown are as supplied by B&B owners in Autumn 2000

Rushden

SP9666

The Old Rectory, *45 Rushden Road, Wymington, Rushden, Northants, NN10 9LN.*
A Victorian rectory set in 5.50 acres of private grounds. A warm welcome guaranteed. **Open:** All Year
01933 314486 Mrs Denton
Fax: 01933 411266
D: £18.50–£21 **S:** £17.50–£22
Beds: 2F 4D 2T 2S **Baths:** 6 En
🛇 🅿 (20) ⅙ 🖵 ✕ 🏛 Ⅴ ▲ ఉ

Silverstone

SP6644 ◑ *White Horse*

Silverthorpe Farm, *Abthorpe Road, Silverstone, Towcester, Northants, NN12 8TW.*
Spacious, family-run, rural bungalow, 1.5 miles Silverstone Circuit.
Open: All Year (not Xmas)
Grades: AA 3 Diamond
01327 858020 Mrs Branch
Fax: 01327 858406
D: £20–£23 **S:** £25
Beds: 1F 1D 1T 1S **Baths:** 2 Sh
🛇 🅿 (8) ⅙ 🖵 🏛 Ⅴ ▲ ఉ

Steane

SP5539 ◑ *The Fox*

Walltree House Farm, *Steane, Brackley, Northants, NN13 5NS.*
Central touring base. Comfortable warm converted stables. Ground floor bedrooms and cottages. Laundry.
Open: All Year (not Xmas)
01295 811235 Mrs Harrison
Fax: 01295 811147
D: £27.50–£37.50 **S:** £37.50–£40
Beds: 4F 2D 3T **Baths:** 7 En 3 Pr
🛇 🅿 (15) ⅙ 🖵 🏛 ▲ cc

Stoke Bruerne

SP7449 ◑ *Old Chapel, Boat Inn*

Beam End , *Stoke Park, Stoke Bruerne, Towcester, Northants, NN12 7RZ.*
Open: All Year (not Xmas)
Grades: ETC 4 Diamond, Silver Award
01604 864802 Ms Hart **Fax: 01604 864637**
beamend@bun.com
D: £25–£30 **S:** £25–£30
Beds: 2D 1T **Baths:** 1 En 1 Sh
🛇 🅿 (5) ⅙ 🖵 ✕ 🏛 Ⅴ ▲
Converted Victorian stable/barn with log fires, acre gardens. Mile-long private road. Quiet location. Perfect for holidaymakers and business stopovers alike. 5 miles to M1 (J15), convenient for Northampton and Milton Keynes, Silverstone circuit, Canal Centre, Althorpe House.

Waterways Cottage, *Stoke Bruerne, Towcester, Northants, NN12 7SD.*
Modernised and extended thatched cottage in centre of lively canalside village. **Open:** All Year (not Xmas)
01604 863865 (also fax) Mrs Cox
D: fr £15 **S:** fr £18
Beds: 1D 2T **Baths:** 1 En 1 Sh
🛇 🅿 (6) 🖵 ♞ 🏛 ▲

Upper Weedon

SP6258   🍺 *Globe Hotel, Cross Roads Hotel*

Mullions, *9 Oak Street, Upper Weedon, Northampton, NN7 4RQ.*
C17th stone cottage, quiet location. Fields view from back garden.
Open: All Year (not Xmas)
Grades: ETC 4 Diamond
01327 341439 (also fax)
Mrs Piercey
D: £19 **S:** £19
Beds: 1D **Baths:** 1 Pr
🅿 (2) ⊬ 📺 ✕ 🏛 ♨

Watford

SP6068   🍺 *Red Lion*

Pandock Cottage, *Watford, Northampton, NN6 7UE.*
Close to M1 (J18), spacious and traditionally furnished, rural - car essential.
Open: All Year (not Xmas)
Grades: ETC 4 Diamond
01788 823615 D: £20–£30 **S:** £20–£25
Beds: 3F 1D 1T 1S **Baths:** 2 En
🅿 (3) ⊬ 📺 🏛 ♨

Welford

SP6480   🍺 *Shoulder Of Mutton*

West End Farm, *5 West End, Welford, Northampton, NN6 6HJ.*
Comfortable 1848 farmhouse. Quiet village street. 2 miles A14/J1.
Open: All Year
Grades: ETC 4 Diamond
01858 575226 Mrs Bevin
bevin@uklynx.net
D: £16–£20 **S:** £18–£24
Beds: 1D 1T **Baths:** 1 Sh
👜 🅿 (2) ⊬ 📺 Ⓥ ♨

Planning a longer stay? Always ask for any special rates

Wellingborough

SP8967   🍺 *Nag's Head*

Duckmire, *1 Duck End Wallaston, Wellingborough, Northants, NN29 7SH.*
Old stone house full of character, accessible for Wellingborough, Northampton, Milton Keynes.
Open: All Year (not Xmas)
Grades: ETC 4 Diamond
01933 664249 (also fax)
Mrs Woodrow
kerry@foreverengland.freeserve.co.uk
D: £19–£20 **S:** £20
Beds: 1T **Baths:** 1 Pr
🅿 (2) ⊬ 📺 ✕ 🏛 ♨

Whitfield

SP6039   🍺 *The Sun*

Chestnut View, *Mill Road, Whitfield, Brackley, Northants, NN13 5TQ.*
Peaceful old cottage, beautiful rural views, near Silverstone, Oxford, Cotswolds.
Open: All Year
01280 850246 Mrs James
D: £22.50–£28 **S:** fr £22.50
Beds: 1T **Baths:** 1 Pr
👜 🅿 (2) 🍴 ✕ 🏛 Ⓥ ♨

RATES

D = Price range per person sharing in a double room

S = Price range for a single room

Wollaston

SP9162   🍺 *Nags Head Pub*

45 Eastfield Road, *Wollaston, Wellingborough, Northamptonshire, NN29 7RS.*
Open: All Year
01933 665266 Mr & Mrs Childs
eastfield.wollaston@21.com
D: £20–£25 **S:** £25–£30
Beds: 1F 1T **Baths:** 1 En 1 Pr
⊬ 📺 🏛 Ⓥ ♨
Friendly, helpful accommodation offering quality rooms and excellent breakfasts. Semi-detached Victorian house in village close to Northamptonshire/Bedfordshire border. Ideal base for Santa Pod Raceway, Nene Valley country path, annual International Waendel Walk and Summer Lees local nature reserve.

Woodend

SP6149   🍺 *The Star, Three Conies, Crown*

Christacorn House, *Main Street, Woodend, Towcester, Oxon, NN12 8RX.*
Period house in small rural village. Well furnished, private parking.
Open: All Year (not Xmas/New Year)
01327 860452 (also fax) Ms Manners
mannersfam@cs.com
D: £22.50–£25 **S:** £22.50–£25
Beds: 1S 2D 1T **Baths:** 2 Sh
👜 🅿 (6) ⊬ 📺 🍴 🏛 Ⓥ ♨

Yardley Hastings

SP8656   🍺 *Rose & Crown*

Dar Cottage, *Northampton Road, Yardley Hastings, Northampton, NN7 1EX.*
C16th cottage near Castle Ashby, Marquis of Northampton's house. **Open:** All Year
01604 696217 Mr Brooks
D: £19–£21 **S:** £19–£21
Beds: 2D 1T 1S **Baths:** 1 Pr 1 Sh
📺 🍴 🏛 ♨

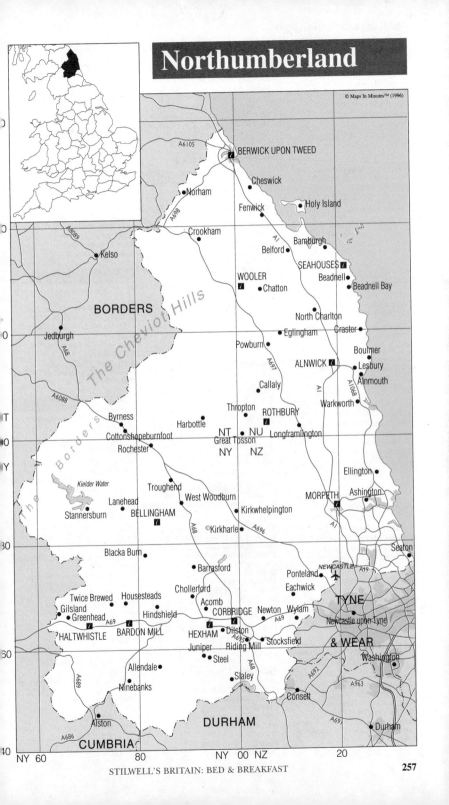

Northumberland

© Maps In Minutes™ (1996)

BERWICK UPON TWEED

Cheswick

Norham

Fenwick

Holy Island

Crookham

Bamburgh

Belford

SEAHOUSES

Kelso

WOOLER

Beadnell

Chatton

Beadnell Bay

BORDERS

The Cheviot Hills

North Charlton

Jedburgh

Egtingham

Craster

Powburn

Boulmer

ALNWICK

Lesbury

Callaly

Alnmouth

Thropton

ROTHBURY

Warkworth

Byrness

Harbottle

NT   NU

Longframlington

Cottonshopeburnfoot

Great Tosson

Rochester

NY   NZ

The Borders

Kielder Water

Ellington

Troughend

Ashington

Lanehead

West Woodburn

MORPETH

Stannersburn

BELLINGHAM

Kirkwhelpington

Kirkharle

Seaton

Blacka Burn

Barrasford

NEWCASTLE

Ponteland

Chollerford

Eachwick

Twice Brewed

Housesteads

Acomb

TYNE

Gilsland

Newton   Wylam

Greenhead

Hindshield

CORBRIDGE

Newcastle upon Tyne

HALTWHISTLE

BARDON MILL

HEXHAM

Dilston

Stocksfield

& WEAR

Juniper

Riding Mill

Washington

Allendale

Steel

Ninebanks

Slaley

Alston

Consett

DURHAM

Durham

CUMBRIA

NY 60   80   NY 00 NZ   20

Tourist Information Centres

Adderstone Services, **Adderstone**, Belford, Northumberland, NE70 7JU, 01668 213678.

The Shambles, **Alnwick**, Northumberland, NE66 1TN, 01665 510665.

Council Sub Offices, Dilston Terrace, **Amble-by-the-Sea**, Northumberland, NE65 0DT, 01665 712313 (Easter to Oct).

Main Street, **Bellingham**, Hexham, Northumberland, NE48 2BQ, 01434 220616.

Castlegate Car Park, **Berwick-upon-Tweed**, Northumberland, TD15 1JS, 01289 330733.

The Vicars Pele, Market Place, **Corbridge**, Northumberland, NE45 5AA, 01434 632815 (Easter to Oct).

Craster Car Park, **Craster**, Northumberland, NE66 3TW, 01665 576007 (Easter to Oct).

Church Hall, Main Street, **Haltwhistle**, Northumberland, NE49 9DP, 01434 322002.

The Manor Office, Hallgate, **Hexham**, Northumberland, NE46 1XD, 01434 605225.

The Chantry, Bridge Street, **Morpeth**, Northumberland, NE61 1PJ, 01670 511323.

Military Road, **Once Brewed**, Bardon Mill, Hexham, Northumberland, NE47 7AN, 01434 344396 (Easter to Oct).

Waterworld, Front Street, **Prudhoe**, Northumberland, NE42 5DQ, 01661 833144.

Church House, Church Street, **Rothbury**, Morpeth, Northumberland, NE65 7UP, 01669 620887 (Easter to Oct).

Car Park, Seafield Road, **Seahouses**, Northumberland, NE68 7SR, 01665 720884 (Easter to Oct).

Bus Station Car Park, High Street, **Wooler**, Northumberland, NE71 8LD, 01668 282123 (Easter to Oct).

Acomb

NY9366

Mariner's Cottage Hotel, *Fallowfield Dene Road, Acomb, Hexham, Northd, NE46 4RP.*
Open: All Year
01434 603666 Mrs Darling
D: £18–£20 **S:** £18–£20
Beds: 1F 1D 1T 2S **Baths:** 3 Pr 2 Sh
⌂ (5) **P** (60) 🖵 🍴 ✕ ▥ Ⅴ ♨
Hotel set in country, 3 miles from market town of Hexham & within easy reach of Hadrian's Wall, Kielder Water, Beamish Museum, Metro Shopping Centre.

Allendale

NY8355 🍺 *King's Head, Allendale Hotel*

Thornley House, *Allendale, Hexham, Northd, NE47 9NH.*
Beautiful country house in spacious grounds near Hadrian's Wall.
Open: All Year **Grades:** ETC 4 Diamond
01434 683255 Mr Finn
e.finn@ukonline.co.uk
D: £18.50–£19.50 **S:** £18.50–£19.50
Beds: 2D 1T **Baths:** 2 En 1 Pr
⌂ (9) **P** (4) 🖵 🍴 ✕ ▥ Ⅴ ♣ ♨

Alnmouth

NU2410 🍺 *Red Lion, The Saddle*

Hipsburn Farm, *Lesbury, Alnmouth, Alnwick, Northd, NE66 3PY.*
Open: Easter to Oct
Grades: ETC 4 Diamond
01665 830206 Ms Tulip
D: £20–£25 **S:** £20–£25
Beds: 2D 1T **Baths:** 3 En
P ⅔ 🖵 ▥ ♨
Large Georgian farmhouse, centrally located on heritage coastline, superb views over Aln Estuary. Ideally situated for golfers, walkers & bird watchers. Northumberland National Park offers a wonderful opportunity for those wishing to walk & explore also Farne Islands famous for colonies of seals & seabirds.

Beaches B&B, *56 Northumberland Street, Alnmouth, Northd, NE66 2RJ.*
Open: All Year
01665 830443 Mrs Hall
D: £18–£25 **S:** £18–£30
Beds: 1D 1T **Baths:** 2 En
⌂ 🖵 🍴 ✕ ▥ Ⅴ
Cosy oak beamed former granary, bright spacious bedrooms above popular BYO restaurant specialising in local seafood and game. Two minutes walk to beautiful beaches and only a short drive to many Castles and Museums.

Alnwick

NU1813 🍺 *The Plough, Shepherd's Rest, The Fleece*

The Georgian Guest House,
Hotspur Street, Alnwick, Northd, NE66 1QE.
Open: All Year **Grades:** ETC 2 Diamond
01665 602398 (also fax) Mr Gibb
georgianguesthouse@eggconnect.net
D: £15–£20 **S:** £20–£25
Beds: 2T 2D **Baths:** 4 En
⌂ **P** (3) ⅔ 🖵 🍴 ▥ Ⅴ
A friendly, family run stone guest house only yards from the 14th century Hotspur Tower, two minutes walk from the town centre and within 10 minutes walk of Alnwick Castle and its famous new gardens. Special 'short break' rates available.

Aydon House, *South Road, Alnwick, Northd, NE66 2NT.*
Comfortable and clean accommodation offered. Large private car park.
Open: Easter to Oct
Grades: ETC 3 Diamond
01665 602218 Mr Carroll
D: £17–£22 **S:** £17–£22
Beds: 2F 2D 2T 2S **Baths:** 8 En
⌂ **P** (9) 🖵 ▥ ♨

Charlton House, *2 Aydon Gardens, Alnwick, Northd, NE66 2NT.*
Charming Victorian town house. Breakfast choices include kippers and home-made pancakes.
Open: All Year (not Xmas)
01665 605185 Mrs Jones
charltonhouse@talk21.com
D: £20 **S:** £25–£35
Beds: 3D 1T 1S **Baths:** 5 Pr
P (6) ⅔ 🖵 ▥ Ⅴ ♨

Rooftops, *14 Blakelaw Road, Alnwick, Northd, NE66 1AZ.*
Spacious accommodation panoramic views. Friendly, hospitality tray with home baking, fresh fruit.
Open: Jan-Nov
Grades: ETC 4 Diamond, Silver
01665 604201 Mrs Blair
D: £18–£19
Beds: 1D **Baths:** 1 En
⌂ **P** (1) ⅔ 🖵 ▥ Ⅴ ♨

Ashington

NZ2787 🍺 *The Plough*

Hagg Farmhouse, *Ellington, Ashington, Northd, NE61 5JW.*
Old farmhouse, open aspect coast and country.
Open: All Year (not Xmas/New Year)
01670 860514 Mrs Nixon
D: £15–£18 **S:** £16–£20
Beds: 1F 1D 1T 1S **Baths:** 1 En 1 Pr 2 Sh
⌂ **P** (6) ⅔ 🖵 🍴 ▥ ♨

Bamburgh

NU1734 🍺 *Green House, Lord Crewe, Victoria Hotel, Miren Head*

Broome, *22 Ingram Road, Bamburgh, Northumberland, NE69 7BT.*
Peaceful location on edge of village - 5 mins walk to beach/castle.
Open: All Year (not Xmas/New Year)
Grades: ETC 4 Diamond
01668 214287 Ms Dixon
mdixon4394@aol.com
D: £25–£28 **S:** £30
Beds: 1T 1D **Baths:** 1 Sh
⌂ (12) **P** (2) ⅔ 🖵 ✕ ▥ Ⅴ ♨ ♿

Greengates, *34 Front Street, Bamburgh, Northumberland, NE69 7BJ.*
Castle views (100m away). Free range breakfast Cycle hire. **Open:** All Year
Grades: ETC 3 Diamond
01668 214535 Claire Sundin
bamburgh.sunset@talk21.com
D: £19.50–£35 **S:** £25–£45
Beds: 2T 1D **Baths:** 2 Pr 1 En
⌂ **P** ⅔ 🖵 🍴 ▥ Ⅴ ♨

Squirrel Cottage, *1 Friars Court, Bamburgh, Northd, NE69 7AE.*
Quality accommodation. Guest rooms with sea or castle views. Minutes from magnificent castle/beaches.
Open: Feb to Nov
01668 214494 Mrs Turnbull
shelaghturnbull@hotmail.com
D: £21–£25 **S:** fr £24
Beds: 2D 1T **Baths:** 2 En 1 Pr
⌂ (12) **P** (4) ⅔ 🖵 ▥ Ⅴ ♨

Hillside House, *25 Lucker Road, Bamburgh, Northumberland, NE69 7BS.*
Victorian terraced house, period features, central for beach, castle, countryside.
Open: Feb to Nov
01668 214218 Ms Gray
D: £22.50–£27.50 **S:** £30
Beds: 2D 1T **Baths:** 2 En 1 Pr
🛇 (9) ⏣ 📺 ▥ Ⓥ 🔥

Bardon Mill

NY7865

Carrsgate East, *Bardon Mill, Hexham, Northumberland, NE47 7EX.*
Relaxing, comfortable C17th home. Great views, good exploration base.
Open: Feb to Nov
Grades: ETC 4 Diamond
01434 344376 Mrs Armstrong
Fax: 01434 344011
lesley@armstrongrl.freeserve.co.uk
D: £23–£27 **S:** £25–£27
Beds: 2D **Baths:** 2 En
🅿 (6) ⏣ 📺 ▥ 🔥

Barrasford

NY9173

Elwood, *Barrasford, Hexham, Northd, NE48 4AN.*
Secluded Georgian country house with extensive grounds. Uninterrupted views.
Open: All Year
01434 681421 Mrs Towle
Fax: 01434 681026
elwood@northumbria.com
D: £15–£18 **S:** £15–£18
Beds: 1F 2D 2T 2S **Baths:** 2 En 1 Sh
🛇 (5) 🅿 (10) 📺 🍴 ✕ ▥ Ⓥ ✿ 🔥

Beadnell

NU2329

Beach Court, *Harbour Road, Beadnell, Northd, NE67 5BJ.*
Magnificent turreted beachside home offering an atmosphere of timeless tranquillity.
Open: All Year
Grades: ETC 5 Diamond
01665 720225 Mrs Field
Fax: 01665 721499
info@beachcourt.com
D: £29.50–£39.50 **S:** £44.50–£54.50
Beds: 2D 1T **Baths:** 3 Pr
🅿 (4) ⏣ 📺 🍴 ✕ ▥ Ⓥ ✿ 🔥

Beadnell Bay

NU2327 🍺 *Craster Alms*

Low Dover, *Harbour Road, Beadnell Bay, Chathill, Northd, NE67 5BJ.*
Open: All Year (not Xmas)
Grades: ETC 4 Diamond, Silver, AA 4 Diamond
01665 720291 (also fax)
Mrs Thompson
kathandbob@lowdover.co.uk
D: £26–£29
Beds: 1D 1T **Baths:** 2 En
🛇 (12) 🅿 (2) ⏣ 📺 ▥ Ⓥ ⅗ 🔥
Relax in comfort, ground floor suites, beautiful gardens, beach 50 metres.

National Grid References are for villages, towns and cities – not for individual houses

Belford

NU1033 🍺 *Black Swan, The Bluebell*

Rosebank, *5 Cragside Avenue, Belford, Northd, NE70 7NA.*
Open: Easter to Oct
01668 213762 (also fax)
Mrs Godtschaalk
D: £19–£23 **S:** £21–£25
Beds: 1F 1T **Baths:** 1 Sh
🛇 🅿 (2) ⏣ 📺 ▥ Ⓥ 🔥
Warm welcome to comfortable Dutch bungalow. Private parking and large garden. Lovely views. Ideal centre for visiting castles, stately homes, beautiful beaches, Holy Island and the Farne Islands (grey seals and puffins). Golf, swimming, walking, rock cli.

The Farmhouse Guest House, *24 West Street, Belford, Northumberland, NE70 7QE.*
Central village location quiet comfortable accommodation home cooking speciality.
Open: All Year (not Xmas)
Grades: ETC 3 Diamond
01668 213083 Mr & Mrs Wood
D: £17–£19.50 **S:** £22–£23.50
Beds: 1F 2D **Baths:** 1 En 2 Pr
🛇 🅿 (1) ⏣ 📺 ✕ ▥ Ⓥ 🔥

Oakwood House, *3 Cragside Avenue, Belford, Northumberland, NE70 7NA.*
A quality country-style home with panoramic views over open countryside.
Open: All Year
Grades: ETC 4 Diamond, Silver
01668 213303 Ms Allan
D: £21–£23 **S:** £26–£28
Beds: 2D 1T **Baths:** 2 En 1 Pr
🅿 (3) ⏣ 📺 ▥ Ⓥ 🔥

Bellingham

NY8383 🍺 *Rose & Crown, Cheviot Hotel*

Lyndale Guest House, *Bellingham, Hexham, Northd, NE48 2AW.*
Open: All Year (not Xmas)
Grades: ETC 4 Diamond
01434 220361 (also fax)
Mrs Gaskin
D: £23.50–£25 **S:** fr £23.50
Beds: 1F 2D 1T 1S **Baths:** 2 En 1 Pr 1 Sh
🛇 🅿 (5) ⏣ 📺 🍴 ✕ ▥ Ⓥ ⅗ cc
Tour the Borders, good walking, Hadrian's Wall, Pennine Way, Kielder Water or cycle the Reivers' Route. Relax in our walled garden. Sunlounge with panoramic views. Excellent dinners, choice of breakfasts, quality ground floor ensuites. Special discounts.

Please respect a B&B's wishes regarding children, animals and smoking

Berwick-upon-Tweed

NT9953 🍺 *Bluebell, Foxton's, Cobbled Yard, Barrels, Leaping Salmon, Elizabethan, The Plough, Meadow House, Salutation Inn, Rob Roy, White Swan, Magnus*

40 Ravensdowne, *Berwick-upon-Tweed, Northumberland, TD15 1DQ.*
Open: All Year (not Xmas)
Grades: ETC 4 Diamond
01289 306992 Mrs Muckle
petedot@dmuckle.freeserve.co.uk
D: £18–£25
Beds: 1F 2D 1T **Baths:** 4 En
🛇 ⏣ 📺 ▥ 🔥
A warm welcome awaits you, 3 luxury ensuite rooms furnished to a very high standard. Hearty breakfast including home cured bacon, free range eggs, real coffee. 1 minute to Elizabethan Walls. 2 minutes to town centre. Resident parking tickets supplied. No smoking.

The Friendly Hound, *Ford Common, Berwick-upon-Tweed, Northumberland, TD15 2QD.*
Open: All Year
Grades: ETC 4 Diamond
01289 388554 Mrs Maycock
friendlyhound.bb.@talk21.com
D: £21.50–£23 **S:** £21.50–£23
Beds: 1F 2D **Baths:** 3 En
🛇 🅿 (5) ⏣ 📺 ✕ ▥ Ⓥ 🔥
The Friendly Hound, recently sympathetically restored to create a welcoming home, offers comfortable accommodation, good food, super views and convenient quiet location for touring North Northumberland and the Scottish borders. Arrive as guests and leave as friends.

Rob Roy Pub & Restaurant, *Dock Road, Tweedmouth, Berwick-upon-Tweed, Northumberland, TD15 2BQ.*
Open: All Year (not Xmas)
Grades: ETC 3 Diamond
01289 306428 Mr Wilson
D: fr £23 **S:** fr £27
Beds: 1D 1T **Baths:** 2 En
📺 ✕ ▥ Ⓥ 🔥
Stone-built cosy riverside pub with open coal fire. Bar/restaurant menus offer fresh Northumbrian salmon and seafood, lobster, crab, oysters etc. 2 mins Berwick centre or sea front. Excellent situation to explore Northumberland. Twenty years with the Wilsons.

Cobbled Yard Hotel, *40 Walkergate, Berwick-upon-Tweed, Northumberland, TD15 1DJ.*
Open: All Year
Grades: ETC 3 Diamond
01289 308407 Ms Miller
Fax: 01289 330623
D: £25 **S:** £30
Beds: 3F 2D **Baths:** 5 En
🛇 🅿 ⏣ 🍴 ✕ ▥ Ⓥ 🔥 cc
Surrounded by Berwick's Elizabethan walls we are situated two minutes' walk from town centre, one minute from Barracks Museum, near golf course, beaches, sports complex. Family-run hotel. Food to cater to all tastes, pick up service from railway station.

6 North Road, Berwick-upon-Tweed, Northumberland, TD15 1PL.
Open: All Year (not Xmas)
Grades: ETC 4 Diamond
01289 308949 (also fax) Ms Booth
D: £17–£19
Beds: 1F 1D **Baths:** 1 Sh
🛇 ₱ ⌁ ⺃ ⺃ 🕮 ₂
Beautiful Edwardian house; spacious, comfortable rooms near town centre and railway station. Perfect for exploring the Northumberland coast and the Scottish borders. Private off road parking, non smoking.

Wallace Guest House, 1 Wallace Green, Berwick-upon-Tweed, Northumberland, TD15 1EB.
Open: Easter to Nov
Grades: ETC 3 Diamond
01289 306539 Mrs Hoggan
Fax: 01289 332617
wallaceguesthouse@yahoo.com
D: £22 **S:** £30
Beds: 1D 2T **Baths:** 1 Pr 2 En
🛇 ₱ (4) ⌁ ⺃ ✕ 🕮 ₂ ₂
Berwick -upon - Tweed, the forgotten jewel of the North. This ancient and historic town offers so much you will never get bored. There are many Castles and historic houses to visit in the area and also many Nature Reserves.

Dervaig Guest House, 1 North Road, Berwick-upon-Tweed, TD15 1PW.
Large Victorian guest house, close railway station/town, ample private parking. **Open:** All Year
Grades: ETC 4 Diamond, AA 4 Diamond
01289 307378 Mr Doyle
dervaig@btinternet.com
D: £20–£27 **S:** £25–£45
Beds: 1F 2D 2T **Baths:** 4 En 1 Pr
🛇 ₱ (8) ⺃ 🕮 ₂

The Old Vicarage Guest House, Church Road, Tweedmouth, Berwick-upon-Tweed, Northumberland, TD15 2AN.
Attractive C19th detached house, refurbished to highest standards. 10 minutes walk from town centre.
Open: All Year (not Xmas)
Grades: ETC 4 Diamond, AA 4 Diamond
01289 306909 Mrs Richardson
D: £17–£54 **S:** £17–£18
Beds: 1F 4D 1T 1S **Baths:** 4 En 1 Sh
🛇 ₱ (5) ⺃ 🕮 ₂ ₂

Bridge View, 14 Tweed Street, Berwick-upon-Tweed, Northumberland, TD15 1NG.
200 year old house overlooking Royal Border Bridge with splendid views.
Open: All Year
01289 308098 Mrs Weatherley
D: £20–£25 **S:** £25–£28
Beds: 1F **Baths:** 1 En
🛇 ₱ ⌁ ⺃ 🕮 ₂ ₂

Queens Head Hotel, 6 Sandgate, Berwick-upon-Tweed, TD15 1EP.
Family-run hotel situated in town centre near historic town walls.
Open: All Year
Grades: AA 1 Star, RAC 1 Star
01289 307852 Mr Kerr
Fax: 01289 307858
D: £35–£40 **S:** £35–£40
Beds: 2F 1D 1S **Baths:** 6 En
🛇 ⌁ ⺃ ⺃ ✕ 🕮 ₂ cc

3 Scotts Place, Berwick-upon-Tweed, Northd, TD15 1LQ.
Georgian town house near town centre and station. Residents parking permit available.
Open: All Year
01289 305323 Mrs Blaaser
scottsplace@btinternet.com
D: £18–£25 **S:** fr £25
Beds: 2D 1T **Baths:** 3 En
🛇 (7) ⺃ ⺃ ✕ 🕮 ₂

Meadow Hill Guest House, Duns Road, Berwick-upon-Tweed, Northumberland, TD15 1UB.
Enjoys spectacular views over River Tweed, Cheviots and coast to Holy Island.
Open: All Year
01289 306325 Mr Hall
D: £20–£35 **S:** £30–£50
Beds: 3F 1D 2T **Baths:** 6 En
🛇 ₱ (12) ⺃ ⺃ ✕ 🕮 ₂ ₂ 2

4 North Road, Berwick-upon-Tweed, TD15 1PL.
Beautifully furnished and decorated Edwardian house. Comfortable stay assured.
Open: Easter to Oct
01289 306146 (also fax)
Mrs Thornton
sandra@thorntonfour.freeserve.co.uk
D: £16–£19 **S:** £16–£19
Beds: 1D 1T 1S **Baths:** 1 Sh
🛇 (5) ₱ (3) ⌁ ⺃ 🕮 ₂

West Sunnyside House, Tweedmouth, Berwick-upon-Tweed, Northd, TD15 2QN.
C19th farmhouse 1.5 miles from town centre on the southern approach road.
Open: All Year
01289 305387 Ms Jamieson
D: £17 **S:** £22.50–£25
Beds: 1F 1T **Baths:** 1 Sh
🛇 ₱ (3) ⌁ ⺃ 🕮 ₂

NY8278 🍺 Battlesteads Hotel

Hetherington Farm, Blacka Burn, Wark, Hexham, Northd, NE48 3DR.
Traditional farmhouse in lovely countryside. Ideal walking, touring, warm welcome.
Open: Easter to Nov
01434 230260 Mrs Nichol
D: £18–£25 **S:** £18–£25
Beds: 4F 1D 1S **Baths:** 1 En 1 Pr 1 Sh
🛇 (10) ₱ (4) 🕮 ₂

NU2614

21 Boulmer Village, Alnwick, Northumberland, NE66 3BS.
Charming fisherman's cottage. Log fire. Beautiful views overlooking the sea.
Open: Mar to Nov
Grades: ETC 4 Diamond
01665 577262 M H Campbell
D: £20–£25 **S:** £20–£27
Beds: 2D **Baths:** 2 En 1 Pr
🛇 ₱ (5) ⌁ ⺃ 🕮 ₂ ₂

NT7602 🍺 Byrness Hotel, The Redesdale

Low Byrness Farm, Byrness, Otterburn, Newcastle-upon-Tyne, Northumberland, NE19 1TF.
150 year old house in the Northumberland national Park.
Open: All Year (not Xmas/New Year)
Grades: ETC 4 Diamond
01830 520648 Mrs Cranston
Fax: 01830 520733
pdq@globalnet.co.uk
D: £9–£10 **S:** £22–£28
Beds: 1F 3D **Baths:** 2 En 1 Sh
🛇 (12) ₱ (8) ⌁ ⺃ ✕ 🕮 ₂ ₂

NU0509

Callaly Cottage, Callaly, Whittingham, Alnwick, Northd, NE66 4TA.
Beautiful country house close to National Park and Heritage Coast.
Open: All Year
01665 574684 Ms Watson
callaly@alnwick.org.uk
D: £19–£20 **S:** £25
Beds: 2D 1T **Baths:** 3 En
⺃ ⺃ ✕ 🕮 ₂

NU0528 🍺 Percy Arms

The Old Manse, New Road, Chatton, Alnwick, Northumberland, NE66 5PU.
Beautiful Victorian Manse, NTB B&B of Year 1999 & 2000.
Open: All Year
Grades: ETC Five Diamond, Gold
01668 215343 C Brown
chattonbb@aol.com
D: £25–£30 **S:** £25–£45
Beds: 1T 1D **Baths:** 2 En
🛇 (10) ₱ (4) ⌁ ⺃ ⺃ 🕮 ₂ ₂ ₂

NU0246 🍺 White Swan

Ladythorne House, Cheswick, Berwick-upon-Tweed, TD15 2RU.
Beautiful Georgian country house, wonderful views, central rural location.
Open: All Year
Grades: ETC 3 Diamond
01289 387382 Mrs Parker
Fax: 01289 387073
valparker@
ladythorneguesthouse.freeserve.co.uk
D: £16–£17 **S:** £16–£17
Beds: 2F 2T 1D 1S **Baths:** 3 Sh
🛇 ₱ (8) ⌁ 🕮

NY9170 🍺 Hadrian Hotel, Crown Inn

Brunton Water Mill, Chollerford, Hexham, Northd, NE46 4EL.
Beautifully converted water mill on the doorstep of Brunton Turrett.
Open: All Year **Grades:** ETC 4 Diamond
01434 681002 Mrs Pesarra
pessara@bruntonmill.freeserve.co.uk
D: £24–£26 **S:** £40
Beds: 1D 1T **Baths:** 2 En 1 Sh
🛇 (12) ₱ (8) ⌁ ⺃ 🕮 ₂ ₂

Corbridge

NY9964 🍺 *Black Bull, The Angel, The Wheatsheaf*

The Hayes Guest House, *Newcastle Road, Corbridge, Northd, NE45 5LP.*
Large house in historic village with views over valley.
Open: All Year (not Xmas/New Year)
01434 632010 Mrs Matthews
mjctmatthews@talk21.com
D: £20–£25 **S:** £20–£25
Beds: 2F 1D 1T 1S **Baths:** 2 En 1 Sh
🛇 🅿 (12) 📺 🍴 ▥ 📋 ♨

Priorfield, *Hippingstones Lane, Corbridge, Northd, NE45 5JP.*
Elegantly furnished family house. Peaceful location. Whirlpool bath in double room.
Open: All Year
Grades: ETC 4 Diamond, AA 4 Diamond
01434 633179 (also fax)
Mrs Steenberg
D: £18–£25 **S:** £25–£32
Beds: 1D 1T **Baths:** 2 En
🛇 (5) 🅿 (2) ⊬ 📺 ▥ ♨

Dilston Mill, *Corbridge, Northumberland, NE45 5QZ.*
Historic converted mill. Private suite: sleeps 2-6. Beautiful riverside setting.
Open: All Year
Grades: ETC 4 Diamond
01434 633493 Mrs Ketelaar
Fax: 01434 633513
jan.ketelaar@virgin.net
D: £24–£26 **S:** £32–£35
Beds: 1F 1D **Baths:** 1 Pr
🛇 🅿 (3) ⊬ ▥ 📋 ♨

Cottonshopeburnfoot

NT7801 🍺 *Byrness Hotel, Redesdale Arms*

Border Forest Caravan Park, *Cottonshopeburnfoot, Otterburn, Newcastle-upon-Tyne, NE19 1TF.*
Attractive motel, chalet rooms situated in picturesque Kielder Forest Park.
Open: All Year (not Xmas)
01830 520259 Mr & Mrs Bell
D: £19 **S:** fr £21
Beds: 2F **Baths:** 2 En
🛇 (1) 🅿 (10) ⊬ 📺 🍴 ▥ 📋 ♨ ♿

Craster

NU2519 🍺 *Cottage Inn, Masons Arms, Jolly Fisherman*

Stonecroft, Dunstan, *Craster, Alnwick, Northd, NE66 3SZ.*
Friendly family home. Spacious comfortable. Rural. Hearty breakfasts. Wonderful coastline.
Open: All Year (not Xmas)
Grades: ETC 4 Diamond, Silver
01665 576433 Mrs Stafford
sally@stonestaff.freeserve.co.uk
D: £19
Beds: 2D **Baths:** 2 En
🛇 (1) 🅿 (4) ⊬ 📺 ▥ 📋 ♨

4 South Acres, *Craster, Alnwick, Northd, NE66 3TN.*
50 yards from seafront. Delightful beach . Quiet location. Central for local castles.
Open: All Year (not Xmas)
01665 576374 Mrs Lumsden
D: £17–£18
Beds: 1T 1D 1S
🛇 🅿 📺 🍴 ▥ 📋

Crookham

NT9138

The Coach House, *Crookham, Cornhill-on-Tweed, Northd, TD12 4TD.*
Spacious warm accommodation, excellent fresh food. Free afternoon tea.
Open: Easter to Oct
Grades: ETC 4 Diamond
01890 820293 Mrs Anderson
Fax: 01890 820284
thecoachhouse@englandmail.com
D: £25–£36 **S:** £25–£39
Beds: 2D 5T 2S **Baths:** 7 En
🛇 🅿 (15) 📺 🍴 ✗ ▥ 📋 ♨ ♿ cc 1

Dilston

NY9862 🍺 *Black Bull, The Angel*

Dilston Mill, *Corbridge, Northumberland, NE45 5QZ.*
Historic converted mill. Private suite: sleeps 2-6. Beautiful riverside setting.
Open: All Year
Grades: ETC 4 Diamond
01434 633493 Mrs Ketelaar
Fax: 01434 633513
jan.ketelaar@virgin.net
D: £24–£26 **S:** £32–£35
Beds: 1F 1T 1D **Baths:** 1 Pr
🛇 🅿 (3) ⊬ ▥ 📋 ♨

Eachwick

NZ1171 🍺 *Plough Inn, Robin Hood*

Hazel Cottage, *Eachwick, Newcastle-upon-Tyne, NE18 0BE.*
Traditional Northumbrian farmhouse in pretty rural area. Easy access Newcastle.
Open: All Year
Grades: ETC 4 Diamond
01661 852415 Fax: 01661 854797
hazelcottage@eastwick.fsbusiness.co.uk
D: £20 **S:** £25
Beds: 1T 1D
🅿 (4) ⊬ 📺 ✗ ▥ 📋 ♨ cc

Eglingham

NU1019

Ash Tree House, *The Terrace, Eglingham, Alnwick, Northd, NE66 2UA.*
Warm Northumbrian welcome in our lovely home between hills and coast.
Open: All Year
Grades: ETC 4 Diamond
01665 578533 Mrs Marks
D: £22 **S:** £27
Beds: 1D 1T **Baths:** 1 Sh
🅿 (3) ⊬ 📺 ✗ ▥ 📋

Planning a longer stay? Always ask for any special rates

BATHROOMS

Pr - Private

Sh - Shared

En - Ensuite

Ellington

NZ2791 🍺 *The Plough*

Hagg Farmhouse, *Ellington, Ashington, Northd, NE61 5JW.*
Old farmhouse, open aspect coast and country.
Open: All Year (not Xmas/New Year)
01670 860514
Mrs Nixon
D: £15–£18 **S:** £16–£20
Beds: 1F 1D 1T 1S
Baths: 1 En 1 Pr 2 Sh
🛇 🅿 (6) ⊬ 📺 ▥ 📋 ♨

Fenwick (Holy Island)

NU0640 **The Manor House,** *Fenwick, Berwick-on-Tweed, Northumberland, TD15 2PQ.*
Peaceful, magical, Northumbrian, easy-relaxed home, kid-free zone.
Open: Feb to Nov
Grades: ETC 3 Diamond
01289 381006 (also fax)
Ms Simpson & Ms S Leister
D: £21 **S:** £30
Beds: 1D 1T 1S **Baths:** 2 En 1 Pr
⊬ 📺 ✗ ▥ 📋 ♨

Cherry Trees, *Fenwick, Berwick-upon-Tweed, TD15 2PJ.*
Detached house, large comfortable bedrooms. Holy Island approx. 6 mils.
Open: May to Sep
01289 381437
D: £14–£15 **S:** £15–£16
Beds: 1F 1D 1T 1S
Baths: 2 Sh
🛇 🅿 (6) 📺 🍴 ✗ ▥ 📋 ♨

Gilsland

NY6366 🍺 *Samson Inn*

The Hill on the Wall, *Gilsland, Brampton, Cumbria, CA8 7DA.*
Fascinating Listed C16th 'fortified farmhouse' overlooking Hadrian's Wall.
Open: All Year
Grades: ETC 4 Diamond
016977 47214 (also fax)
Mr Swan
thehill@hadrians-wall.demon.co.uk
D: £20–£22 **S:** £25–£27
Beds: 2D 1T **Baths:** 3 En
🛇 🅿 ⊬ 📺 🍴 ✗ ▥ 📋 ♨

RATES

D = Price range per person sharing in a double room

S = Price range for a single room

Howard House Farm, Gilsland,
Carlisle, Cumbria, CA6 7AN.
Comfortable farmhouse on Roman wall.
Open: All Year
016977 47285
Mrs Woodmass
D: £19–£22 **S:** £19–£22
Beds: 1F 1D 1T **Baths:** 1 En 1 Sh
🛇 (5) 🅿 (4) ☑ 🐾 ✕ 🎟 🖷 ♿

Great Tosson

NU0200 ◙ Newcastle House, Queen's Head,
Three Wheat Heads

Tosson Tower Farm, Great Tosson,
Rothbury, Morpeth, Northd, NE65 7NW.
Spacious, warm, wonderful views,good
food, friendly welcome. Free fishing.
Open: All Year (not Xmas/New Year)
Grades: ETC 4 Diamond Sliver Award
01669 620228 (also fax)
Mrs Foggin
ann@tossontowerfarm.com
D: £22–£22.50 **S:** £30–£35
Beds: 1F 1D 1T **Baths:** 3 En
🛇 🅿 (4) ☑ 🐾 🖷 ♿

Greenhead

NY6665 ◙ Holmhead Bar

Holmhead Licensed Guest House,
Thirlwall Castle Farm, Hadrians Wall,
Greenhead, Brampton, CA8 7HY.
Enjoy fine food and hospitality with a
personal touch.
Open: All Year (not Xmas)
Grades: ETC 4 Diamond
016977 47402 (also fax)
Mr & Mrs Staff
Holmhead@hadrianswall.freeserve.co.uk
D: £28–£29 **S:** £37–£38
Beds: 1F 1D 2T **Baths:** 4 En
🛇 🅿 (4) ✓ ☑ ✕ 🖷 ☑ ✿ ♿ cc

Haltwhistle

NY7064 ◙ Spotted Cow, Manor House, Centre
Of Britain Hotel, Milecastle Inn

Manor House Hotel, Main Street,
Haltwhistle, Northd, NE49 0BS.
Open: All Year
01434 322588 R Nicholson
D: £15–£22 **S:** £20–£25
Beds: 1F 1D 4T **Baths:** 3 En 3 Sh
🛇 🅿 (4) ☑ ✕ 🖷 ☑ ♿ cc
Small hotel with busy public bar serving
good selection of real ales wines &
spirits. Very popular for meals at an
affordable price. Separate dining area
available away from bar. Hotel centrally
situated 2 miles from Hadrian's Wall.
Warm welcome from Kathleen and
Raymond Nicholson.

The Old School House, Fair Hill,
Haltwhistle, Northumberland, NE49 9EE.
Friendly welcome. Brilliant breakfast - no
need for lunch! Hadrian's Wall on
doorstep.
Open: All Year (not Xmas)
Grades: ETC 4 Diamond
01434 322595 (also fax)
Mrs O'Hagan
vera@oshouse.freeserve.co.uk
D: £18–£20 **S:** £25–£30
Beds: 2D 1T **Baths:** 3 Pr
🅿 (6) ✓ ☑ 🖷 ☑ ♿

Hall Meadows, Main Street,
Haltwhistle, Northd, NE49 0AZ.
Large comfortable C19th private house,
central for Hadrian's Wall.
Open: All Year (not Xmas)
Grades: ETC 3 Diamond
01434 321021 Mrs Humes
D: £17 **S:** £18
Beds: 1D 1T 1S **Baths:** 1 Sh
🛇 🅿 (3) ☑ 🖷 ♿

Ald White Craig Farm, Hadrian's Wall,
Shield Hill, Haltwhistle, Northd, NE49 9NW.
Snug old rambling single storey
farmhouse.
Open: Easter to Oct
01434 320565 (also fax)
Ms Laidlow
D: £21–£25 **S:** £28–£32
Beds: 1D 1T **Baths:** 2 En
🅿 (2) ✓ ☑ 🖷 ♿ ♿ cc

Harbottle

NT9304

The Byre Vegetarian B&B, Harbottle,
Morpeth, Northumberland, NE65 7DG.
Beautiful stone built byre conversion in
historic village with castle ruins.
Open: All Year **Grades:** ETC 4 Diamond
01669 650476 Mrs Srinivasan
rosemary@the-byre.co.uk
D: £18–£20 **S:** £18–£26
Beds: 1T 1D
🛇 🅿 (2) ✓ ☑ ✕ 🖷 ☑ ♿

Hexham

NY9364 ◙ Dipton Mill, Boatside Inn, Heart Of
All England, Rose & Crown, Angel

Rose & Crown Inn, Slaley, Hexham,
Northd, NE47 0AA.
Warm, friendly family-run inn, with good
wholesome home cooking. Meals served
daily.
Open: All Year
Grades: ETC 3 Diamond, AA 3 Diamond,
RAC 3 Diamond
01434 673263 Mr & Mrs Pascoe
Fax: 01434 673305
rosecrowninn@supanet.com
D: £22.50–£25 **S:** £27.50–£32.50
Beds: 2T 1S **Baths:** 3 En 3 Pr
🛇 (5) 🅿 (35) ✓ ☑ ✕ 🖷 ☑ ♿ cc

Burncrest Guest House, Burnland
Terrace, Hexham, Northd, NE46 3JT.
Spacious terraced house, home from
home, private car park.
Open: All Year
01434 605163 (also fax)
Mr Ellery
D: £20–£25 **S:** £20–£25
Beds: 3D **Baths:** 2 Sh
🛇 🅿 (3) ✓ ☑ 🖷 ♿

Old Red House Farm, Dipton Mill,
Hexham, NE46 1XY.
Superbly appointed C19th private stone
cottage in lovely rural location.
Open: Feb to Oct
Grades: ETC 4 Diamond
01434 604463 Mrs Bradley
susan.bradley@ukonline.co.uk
D: £23–£25 **S:** £30
Beds: 1T **Baths:** 1 Pr
🅿 (2) ✓ ☑ 🐾 🖷 ♿

East Peterel Field Farm, Yarridge
Road, Hexham, NE46 2JT.
Beautiful award winning manor house in
rolling countryside.
Open: All Year
01434 607209 Mrs Carr
Fax: 01434 601753
D: £25–£30 **S:** fr £35
Beds: 3D **Baths:** 2 En 1 Pr
🛇 (10) ☑ 🐾 ✕ 🖷 ☑ ♿

Kitty Frisk House, Corbridge Road,
Hexham, Northumberland, NE46 1UN.
Elegant Edwardian country house in
Hexham. Good base for touring.
Open: All Year
Grades: ETC 4 Diamond
01434 601533 (also fax)
A Humphrey
alan@kittyfriskhouse.co.uk
D: £24–£25 **S:** £32–£50
Beds: 1D 2T **Baths:** 2 En 1 Pr
🛇 🅿 (6) ✓ ☑ 🖷 ♿

Dukeslea, 32 Shaws Park, Hexham,
Northd, NE46 3BJ.
Comfortable, modern, detached family
home, overlooking golf course. Quiet
location.
Open: All Year (not Xmas)
01434 602947 (also fax)
Mrs Theobald
dukeslea@hotmail.com
D: £18–£20 **S:** £20–£26
Beds: 2D **Baths:** 2 En
🛇 (1) 🅿 (4) ✓ ☑ 🖷 ☑ ♿

West Close House, Hextol Terrace,
Hexham, Northd, NE46 2AD.
Charming, secluded detached 1920s villa.
Immaculately maintained.
Open: All Year
01434 603307 Patricia Graham-Tomlinson
D: £20–£26 **S:** £18–£21
Beds: 2D 2S **Baths:** 2 En 1 Sh
🛇 (12) 🅿 (4) ✓ ☑ 🖷 ☑ ♿

Topsy Turvy, 9 Leazes Lane, Hexham,
Northd, NE46 3BA.
As my guests say, 'Comfortable, colourful,
friendly and peaceful'.
Open: All Year
01434 603152 Ms McCormick
topsy.turvy@ukonline.co.uk
D: £19–£20 **S:** £25
Beds: 2D **Baths:** 2 En
🛇 🅿 (4) ✓ ☑ 🐾 🖷 ♿

Hindshield

NY8367

Hadrian Lodge Country Hotel,
Hindshield Moss, North Road, Haydon
Bridge, Hexham, Northumberland, NE47
6NF.
In tranquil rural location, set in open
pasture bordered by pine forest.
Open: All Year
Grades: ETC 3 Diamond
01434 688688 Mrs Murray
Fax: 01434 684867
hadrianlodge@hadrianswall.co.uk
D: £19.50–£24.50 **S:** £19.50–£24.50
Beds: 3F 4D 1T 1S **Baths:** 8 En 1 Pr
🛇 🅿 ☑ ✕ ☑ ♿ ♿ cc

Holy Island

NU1241

Open Gate, *Marygate, Holy Island, Berwick-upon-Tweed, TD15 2SD.*
450 years old. Quiet, Christian home. Centre of Holy Island.
Open: All Year
01289 389222 theopengate@bigfoot.com
D: £20.50–£22.50 **S:** £25–£27
Beds: 1T 3D **Baths:** 3 En
🅿 (5) 🌌✕ 🖵 Ⓥ ♿

Housesteads

NY7868 🍺 *Milecastle Inn*

Crindledykes Farm, *Housesteads, Bardon Mill, Hexham, Northd, NE47 7AF.*
Well-maintained C17th farmhouse, good food and a warm welcome.
Open: Easter to Nov
Grades: ETC 4 Diamond
01434 344316 Mrs Davidson
D: £17–£20 **S:** fr £20
Beds: 1D 1T **Baths:** 1 Sh
🌄 🅿 🌌 Ⓣ ✕ 🖵 ♿

Juniper

NY9358 🍺 *Dipton Mill*

Peth Head Cottage, *Juniper, Hexham, Northd, NE47 0LA.*
Traditional country cottage, Charming En suite Rooms, Pretty Garden.
Open: All Year (not Xmas)
01434 673286 Mrs Liddle
Fax: 01434 673038
113736.1113@compuserve.com
D: £20 **S:** £20
Beds: 2D **Baths:** 2 En
🌄 🅿 (2) 🌌 🖵 ♿

Kirkharle

NZ0182

Shieldhall, *Kirkharle, Morpeth, Northd, NE61 4AQ.*
The best accommodation in Northumberland with excellent home-cooked food.
Open: Easter to Nov
01830 540387 (also fax)
Mr Gay
D: £20–£30 **S:** £20–£50
Beds: 3D 3T 1S **Baths:** 6 En
🌄 (13) 🅿 (10) 🌌 Ⓣ 🍴 ✕ 🖵 Ⓥ ♿ cc

Kirkwhelpington

NY9984 🍺 *Bay Horse, Knowesgate Inn*

Cornhills, *Kirkwhelpington, Northumberland, NE19 2RE.*
Large Victorian farmhouse. Working farm, outstanding views in peaceful surroundings.
Open: All Year (not Xmas)
Grades: ETC 4 Diamond, Silver
01830 540232 Ms Thornton
Fax: 01830 540388
cornhills@farming.co.uk
D: £21–£23 **S:** £25–£30
Beds: 1D 2T **Baths:** 2 En 1 Pr
🌄 🅿 (10) 🌌 Ⓣ 🖵 ♿

Lanehead

NY7985 🍺 *The Holly Bush Inn*

Ivy Cottage, *Lanehead, Tarset, Hexham, Northumberland, NE48 1NT.*
200 year old cottage with stunning views over open countryside.
Open: All Year
Grades: ETC 3 Diamond
01434 240337 (also fax) Mrs Holland
john.holland@compag.com
D: £18–£20 **S:** £18–£20
Beds: 1T 1D **Baths:** 1 En 1 Sh
🌄 🅿 Ⓣ 🖵 ♿

Lesbury

NU2312 🍺 *The Mason Arms*

Hawkill Farmhouse, *Lesbury, Alnwick, Northumberland, NE66 3PG.*
Open: Feb to Nov
Grades: ETC 4 Diamond, Silver Award
01665 830380 Mrs Vickers
D: £20–£25 **S:** £25–£30
Beds: 2T 1D **Baths:** 3 En
🌄 🅿 (10) Ⓣ 🖵 ♿
Large traditional farmhouse set in extensive, secluded gardens, with magnificent views of the Aln valley mid way Alnwick/ Alnmouth. Ideal for beaches, castles and places of interest.

Longframlington

NU1300

The Lee Farm, *nr Rothbury, Longframlington, Morpeth, Northd, NE65 8JQ.*
Comfortable farmhouse with wonderful views, ideal base for touring Northumberland. **Open:** Mar to Nov
01665 570257 Mrs Aynsley
D: £18–£21 **S:** £25–£28
Beds: 1F 1D 1T **Baths:** 1 En 1 Sh
🌄 🅿 (4) 🌌 Ⓣ ✕ Ⓥ ❀

Morpeth

NZ2085 🍺 *Sun Inn*

Elder Cottage, *High Church, Morpeth, Northd, NE61 2QT.*
C18th century cottage with garden and sun room; easy access from A1.
Open: All Year (not Xmas)
Grades: ETC 4 Diamond
01670 517664 Mrs Cook
Fax: 01670 517644
cook@eldercot.freeserve.co.uk
D: £15–£17.50 **S:** £20–£25
Beds: 2D 1T **Baths:** 1 Sh
🌄 🅿 (3) 🌌 Ⓣ ✕ 🖵 Ⓥ ♿

Newton

NZ0364 🍺 *Robin Hood*

Crookhill Farm, *Newton, Stocksfield, Northd, NE43 7UX.*
Comfortable welcoming farmhouse ideal for exploring Hadrian's Wall.
Open: All Year
Grades: ETC 3 Diamond
01661 843117 Mrs Leech
Fax: 01661 844702
D: £20 **S:** £20
Beds: 1F 1T 1S **Baths:** 1 Sh
🌄 🅿 (4) 🌌 Ⓣ ✕ 🖵 Ⓥ ♿

Ninebanks

NY7853

Taylor Burn, *Ninebanks, Hexham, Northd, NE47 8DE.*
Large, comfortable farmhouse, excellent food warm welcome wonderful scenery.
Open: All Year
01434 345343 Mrs Ostler
mavis@taylorburn.freeserve.co.uk
D: £18 **S:** £18
Beds: 1D 1S 1T **Baths:** 1 Pr
🌄 (7) 🅿 (5) 🌌 Ⓣ 🍴 ✕ 🖵 Ⓥ ♿

Norham

NT9047 🍺 *Masons Arms*

Todlaw, *58 Castle Street, Norham, Berwick-upon-Tweed, TD15 2LQ.*
Lovely old village on Tweed; ideal for touring and fishing.
Open: All Year (not Xmas)
01289 382447 Mr Brown
D: £18–£20 **S:** £20–£22
Beds: 1D 1T **Baths:** 1 En 1 Sh
🌄 (7) 🅿 (3) 🌌 Ⓣ 🍴 ✕ 🖵 ♿

North Charlton

NU1623

North Charlton Farmhouse, *North Charlton, Chathill, Northumberland, NE66 5HP.*
Open: All Year
01665 579443 Ms Armstrong
Fax: 01665 579407
glenc99@aol.com
D: £25–£30 **S:** fr £35
Beds: 1T 2D **Baths:** 2 En 1 Pr
🌄 (12) 🅿 (10) 🌌 🖵 Ⓥ
A warm welcome awaits you in our newly restored beautifully furnished farmhouse, offering modern comfort in elegant surroundings. Ideally located for enjoying coast, castles Holy Island. Billingham only 10 minutes drive and a little further is Wooler, the gateway to the Cheviot Hills.

Ponteland

NZ1673 🍺 *Blackbird Inn, The Plough*

7 Collingwood Cottages, *Limestone Lane, Ponteland, Newcastle-upon-Tyne, NE20 0DD.*
Quiet informal home in countryside. Lovely views from rooms.
Open: All Year (not Xmas)
01661 825967 Mrs Baxter
D: £17.50 **S:** £20–£25
Beds: 1F 1D **Baths:** 1 Sh
🌄 🅿 (4) 🌌 Ⓣ 🍴 🖵 ♿

Powburn

NU0616 🍺 *Tankerville Arms*

Brandon White House, *Powburn, Alnwick, Northd, NE66 4JE.*
Comfortable rambling Grade II Listed farmhouse on mixed 500-acres in AONB.
Open: All Year
01665 578252 Mrs Dods
Fax: 01665 578630
D: £17 **S:** £17
Beds: 1F 1T **Baths:** 1 Sh
🌄 🅿 (8) 🌌 🍴 ✕ Ⓥ ♿

Riding Mill

NZ0161

Broomley Fell Farm, *Riding Mill, Northumberland, NE44 6AY.*
Warm welcome in cosy separate annexe, beams and log fire.
Open: All Year
Grades: ETC 3 Diamond
01434 682682 Ms Davies
Fax: 01434 682728
D: £20 **S:** £20–£25
Beds: 1F 1S **Baths:** 1 En 1 Pr
🛏 🅿 (6) 🖵 ✕ 🛋 🍴 cc

Rochester

NY8398 ◄ *The Dodger*

Redesdale Arms Hotel, *Rochester, Otterburn, Newcastle-upon-Tyne, NE19 1TA.*
Family-run 600-year-old coaching inn. Superb home cooking.
Open: All Year (not Xmas)
01830 520668 Mrs Wright
Fax: 01830 520063
redesdale@destination-england.co.uk
D: £28–£33 **S:** fr £36
Beds: 3F 3D 4T **Baths:** 10 En
🛏 🅿 (20) 🖵 🍴 ✕ 🛋 🍴 & cc 1

Rothbury

NU0501 ◄ *Queen's Head, Newcastle Hotel, Three Wheat Heads*

Silverton House, *Rothbury, Morpeth, Northumberland, NE65 7RJ.*
Open: All Year (not Xmas)
Grades: ETC 4 Diamond
01669 621395 Mrs Wallace
maggie.wallace1@virgin.net
D: £18–£19 **S:** £25–£38
Beds: 1D 1T
🛏 🅿 (2) ✔ 🖵 🍴 ✕ 🛋 🍴
Built in 1901 as a work house, now a comfortable home. Guest lounge with open fire. Home made bread and fresh local produce. Quiet, peaceful situation in beautiful countryside on outskirts of Rothbury. Good walking country. Central for touring Northumberland.

Wagtail Farm, *Rothbury, Morpeth, Northumberland, NE65 7PL.*
Comfortable bedrooms, good breakfasts, in a beautiful location.
Open: May to Oct
Grades: ETC 3 Diamond
01669 620367 Mrs Taylor
D: £16 **S:** £21
Beds: 2D **Baths:** 1 Sh
🛏 (12) 🅿 (2) ✔ 🖵 🛋 🍴

Tosson Tower Farm, *Great Tosson, Rothbury, Morpeth, Northd, NE65 7NW.*
Spacious, warm, wonderful views,good food, friendly welcome. Free fishing.
Open: All Year (not Xmas/New Year)
Grades: ETC 4 Diamond Sliver Award
01669 620228 (also fax)
Mrs Foggin
ann@tossontowerfarm.com
D: £22–£22.50 **S:** £30–£35
Beds: 1F 1D 1T **Baths:** 3 En
🛏 🅿 (4) 🖵 🍴 🛋 🍴

Silverton Lodge, *Silverton Lane, Rothbury, Morpeth, Northd, NE65 7RJ.*
Converted school. Countryside. Warm welcome. Home from home. Acclaimed cooking.
Open: Mar to Nov
Grades: ETC 4 Diamond, Sliver Award
01669 620144 Mrs Hewison
Fax: 01669 621920
silvertonlodge@virgin.net
D: £20–£23 **S:** £35–£40
Beds: 1D 1T **Baths:** 1 Pr 1 En
🛏 (10) 🅿 (4) ✔ 🖵 ✕ 🛋 🍴 🍴

Seahouses

NU2032 ◄ *Longstone House, Lodge, Links, Silks Bar*

Wyndgrove House, *156 Main Street, Seahouses, Northumberland, NE68 7HA.*
Family-run guesthouse. Ideal base for countryside, coast and Farne Islands.
Open: All Year
Grades: ETC 3 Diamond
01665 720658 Mr & Mrs Haile
D: £18–£25 **S:** £18–£23
Beds: 4F 2T 1D **Baths:** 2 En 3 Sh
🛏 🖵 🍴 🛋 🍴 cc

Slate Hall , *174 Main Street, Seahouses, Northd, NE68 7UA.*
Comfortable farmhouse with delicious breakfast. Horse riding available on site.
Open: All Year (not Xmas)
Grades: ETC 4 Diamond
01665 720320 Mr & Mrs Nicol
Fax: 01665 720199
ian@slatehall.freeserve.co.uk
D: £20–£25
Beds: 1F 1D **Baths:** 1 En 1 Pr
🛏 🅿 (2) ✔ 🖵 🍴 ✕ 🛋 🍴

Seaton Sluice

NZ3376 ◄ *Waterford Arms*

The Waterford Arms, *Collywell Bay Road, Seaton Sluice, Whitley Bay, NE26 4QZ.*
Very famous fish restaurant in a busy touristy area.
Open: All Year
Grades: ETC 2 Star
0191 237 0450
D: £22.95–£24.95 **S:** £30
Beds: 1F 2T 2D **Baths:** 5 En 2 Pr
🛏 🅿 (30) ✔ 🖵 🍴 ✕ 🛋 🍴 & cc 2

Slaley

NY9757 ◄ *Rose & Crown*

Rose & Crown Inn, *Slaley, Hexham, Northd, NE47 0AA.*
Warm, friendly family-run inn, with good wholesome home cooking. Meals served daily.
Open: All Year
Grades: ETC 3 Diamond, AA 3 Diamond, RAC 3 Diamond
01434 673263
Mr & Mrs Pascoe
Fax: 01434 673305
rosecrowninn@supanet.com
D: £22.50–£25 **S:** £22.50–£32.50
Beds: 2T 1S **Baths:** 3 En 3 Pr
🛏 (5) 🅿 (35) ✔ 🖵 ✕ 🛋 🍴 cc

Rye Hill Farm, *Slaley, Hexham, Northd, NE47 0AH.*
Open: All Year
Grades: ETC 4 Diamond
01434 673259 Mrs Courage
Fax: 01434 673259
enquiries@consult-courage.co.uk
D: £20 **S:** £25
Beds: 2F 3D 1T **Baths:** 6 En
🛏 🅿 (6) 🖵 🍴 ✕ 🛋 🍴 cc
Small friendly livestock farm. Gorgeous views all round. Pretty ensuite rooms in converted barn. We are noted for tasty evening meals (home cooked), friendly atmosphere and large bath towels. 5 miles south of Hexham.

Stannersburn

NY7287 ◄ *Pheasant Inn*

Spring Cottage, *Stannersburn, Hexham, Northumberland, NE48 1DD.*
1 mile Kielder Water. Warm welcome, good food, beautiful scenery.
Open: All Year (not Xmas)
Grades: ETC 3 Diamond
01434 240388 Mr & Mrs Ormesher
D: £18–£21 **S:** £18–£21
Beds: 1F 1D **Baths:** 2 En
🛏 🅿 🖵 🍴 🛋 🍴 &

Steel

NY9363 ◄ *Travellers Rest*

Dukesfield Hall Farm, *Steel, Hexham, Northumberland, NE46 1SH.*
Charming Grade II farmhouse. warm and friendly. Excellent facilities.
Open: All Year
Grades: ETC 3 Diamond
01434 673634 Mrs Swallow
cath@dukesfield.supanet.com
D: £20 **S:** £20
Beds: 1T 2D **Baths:** 3 En
🛏 🅿 (4) ✔ 🖵 🍴 🛋 🍴

Stocksfield

NZ0561 ◄ *The Wellington, Riding Mill*

Old Ridley Hall, *Stocksfield, Northd, NE43 7RU.*
Large private house. Listed. Quiet. Near Metro centre,Durham, Beamish.
Open: All Year (not Xmas)
Grades: ETC 3 Diamond
01661 842816 Mrs Aldridge
oldridleyhall@talk21.com
D: £19.50–£25 **S:** £19.50–£25
Beds: 1F 2T 1S **Baths:** 1 Pr 2 Sh
🛏 🅿 (14) ✔ 🖵 🍴 ✕ 🛋 🍴

Thropton

NU0202 ◄ *Cross Keys, Three Wheatheads*

Lorbottle, *West Steads, Thropton, Morpeth, Northd, NE65 7JT.*
Spacious farmhouse overlooking the Simonside Hills, Coquet Valley, Cheviot Hills. Rothbury 5 miles.
Open: May to Nov
Grades: ETC 3 Diamond
01665 574672 (also fax) Mrs Farr
helen.farr@farming.co.uk
D: £18–£19 **S:** £18–£25
Beds: 1D 1T 1S **Baths:** 1 Sh
🛏 🅿 (3) ✔ 🖵 🛋 🍴

Farm Cottage, *Thropton, Morpeth,*
Northumberland, NE65 7NA.
Olde worlde cottage with pretty country
gardens, exceptional evening meals.
Open: All Year (not Xmas)
Grades: ETC 4 Diamond, Silver Award
01669 620831 (also fax) Mrs Telford
jean@farmcottage44.fsnet.co.uk
D: £21–£22 **S:** £31–£32
Beds: 1F 2D 1T **Baths:** 4 En
🛇 (10) 🅿 (4) ⥼ 📺 ✕ 🍽 📋 ♨ cc

Troughend

NY8692 🍺 *Bay Horse*

Brown Rigg Cottage, *Troughend,*
Otterburn, Newcastle-upon-Tyne, NE19 1LG.
Wind and solar powered stone cottage.
Peacefully situated. Open countryside.
Open: All Year
01830 520541 Mrs Boon
davidn.boon@btinternet.com
D: £18–£20 **S:** £20
Beds: 1F 1D **Baths:** 1 Pr
🅿 (6) ⥼ 📺 🐾 ✕ 🍽 📋 ♨

Twice Brewed

NY7567

Saughy Rigg Farm, *Twice Brewed,*
Haltwhistle, Northumberland, NE49 9PT.
Near Hadrian's Wall, delicious food,
comfortable accommodation, children &
pets welcome. **Open:** All Year
Grades: ETC 3 Diamond
01434 344746 Ms McNulty
kathandbrad@aol.com
D: £15 **S:** £15
Beds: 1F 1T **Baths:** 1 En 1 Pr
🛇 🅿 📺 🐾 ✕ 🍽 📋 ♨ ♨

RATES

D = Price range per person
sharing in a double room
S = Price range for a
single room

Warkworth

NU2405 🍺 *Masons' Arms, Marina Arms*

Bide A While, *4 Beal Croft, Warkworth,*
Morpeth, Northd, NE65 0XL.
Full traditional breakfast served, good
base for touring historic Northumberland,
birdwatching, etc.
Open: All Year
01665 711753 Mrs Graham
D: £16–£19 **S:** £20–£23
Beds: 1F 1D **Baths:** 1 En 1 Sh
🛇 (2) 🅿 (3) ⥼ 📺 🐾 🍽 📋 ♨ ♨ ♿

West Woodburn

NY8887 🍺 *Bay Horse*

Yellow House Farm, *West Woodburn,*
Hexham, Northumberland, NE48 2RA.
Old farmhouse with all modern
conveniences, half hour from Hadrian's
Wall, Kielder Water. **Open:** All Year
Grades: ETC 3 Diamond
01434 270070 Ms Walton
D: £15–£19 **S:** £15–£20
Beds: 1F 1T 1D **Baths:** 3 En
🛇 🅿 (6) ⥼ 📺 🐾 🍽 📋 ♨

Wooler

NT9928 🍺 *Tankerville Arms, The Wheatsheaf,*
Ryecroft Hotel

Winton House, *39 Glendale Road,*
Wooler, Northumberland , NE71 6DL.
Charming Edwardian house, quietly
positioned, comfortable spacious rooms.
Walkers welcome. **Open:** Mar to Nov
01668 281362 Mr Gilbert
winton.house@virgin.net
D: £20–£22 **S:** £25–£27
Beds: 2D 1T **Baths:** 2 En 1 Sh
🛇 ⥼ 📺 🍽 ♨

Wylam

NZ1164

Wormald House, *Main Street, Wylam,*
Northd, NE41 8DN.
Very welcoming, pleasant country home
in attractive Tyne Valley village.
Open: All Year (not Xmas)
Grades: ETC 4 Diamond
01661 852529 (also fax)
Mr & Mrs Craven
D: £19.50–£21 **S:** £19.50–£21
Beds: 1D 1T **Baths:** 2 En
🛇 🅿 (3) ⥼ 📺 🍽 📋 ♨ cc

National Grid References are for
villages, towns and cities – not
for individual houses

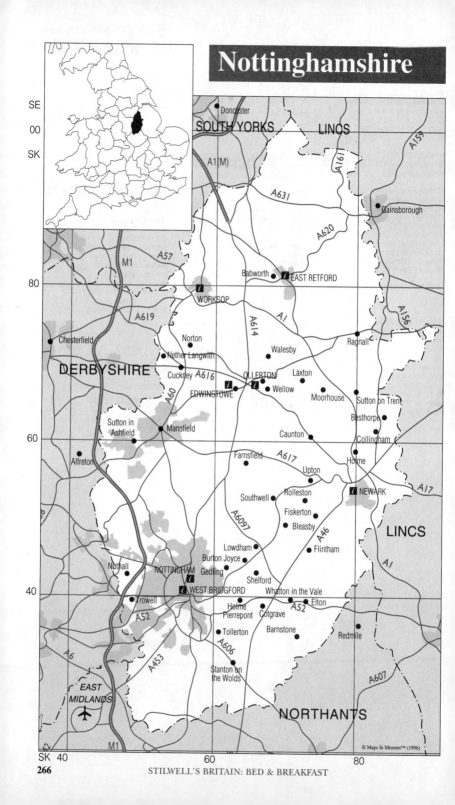

Nottinghamshire

STILWELL'S BRITAIN: BED & BREAKFAST

Tourist Information Centres

Amcott House Annexe, 40 Grove Street, **East Retford**, Nottinghamshire, DN22 6JU, 01777 860780.

Sherwood Forest Visitor Centre, **Edwinstowe**, Mansfield, Nottinghamshire, NG21 9HN, 01623 824490.

The Gilstrap Centre, Castlegate, **Newark**, Nottinghamshire, NG24 1BG, 01636 655765.

1-4 Smithy Row, **Nottingham**, NG1 2BY, 0115 915 5330.

Sherwood Heath, Ollerton Roundabout, **Ollerton**, Newark, Nottinghamshire, NG22 9DR, 01623 824545.

County Hall, Loughborough Road, **West Bridgford**, Nottingham, NG2 7QP, 0115 977 3558.

Worksop Library, Memorial Avenue, **Worksop**, Nottinghamshire, S80 2BP, 01909 501148.

Babworth

SK6880 🍺 *Crab & Mussel*

The Barns Country Guest House, Morton Farm, Babworth, Retford, Notts, DN22 8HA.
Rural setting close to A1 on pilgrim fathers trail.
Open: All Year (not Xmas)
Grades: ETC 4 Diamond
01777 706336 H R R Kay
Fax: 01777 709773
harry@thebarns.co.uk
D: £22–£26 **S:** £30–£33
Beds: 1F 5D **Baths:** 6 En
🛏 🅿 (6) ⅏ 🔟 🏢 ﹗ cc

Barnstone

SK7335

Barnstone Olde House, Barnstone, Nottingham, NG13 9JP.
Central for Newark, Grantham, Nottingham. Landscaped garden, rustic charm, beautiful view.
Open: All Year (not Xmas)
Grades: ETC 3 Diamond
01949 860456 (also fax) Mrs Baker
D: £20–£25 **S:** £22.50–£30
Beds: 2D 1T **Baths:** 2 En
🛏 🅿 (4) ⅏ 🔟 🏮 ✗ 🏢 🔟 ﹗

BATHROOMS

Pr - Private

Sh - Shared

En - Ensuite

Planning a longer stay? Always ask for any special rates

Besthorpe

SK8265

Lord Nelson Inn, Main Road, Besthorpe, Newark, Nottinghamshire, NG23 7HR.
C18th former coaching inn with excellent food reputation.
Open: All Year (not Xmas/New Year)
Grades: ETC 3 Diamond
01636 892265 D: £20 **S:** £25
Beds: 2T 1D 1S **Baths:** 1 En 1 Sh
🅿 (20) ⅏ ✗ 🏢 🔟 ﹗ cc

Bleasby

SK7149 🍺 *Red Lion, Coach & Horses*

Little Rudsey Farm, Bleasby, Nottingham, NG14 7FR.
Traditional farmhouse, rural setting. Robin Hood country. Newark,/Nottingham/Lincoln/Southwell easy reach.
Open: All Year (not Xmas/New Year)
01636 830249 Mrs Norman
D: £16 **S:** £16
Beds: 1F 1T **Baths:** 1 Sh
🛏 (4) 🅿 (3) 🔟 🏮 🏢 🔟 ﹗

Burton Joyce

SK6443 🍺 *The Wheatsheaf*

Willow House, 12 Willow Wong, Burton Joyce, Nottingham, NG14 5FD.
1850's house with Victorian charm. Beautiful riverbanks 2 minutes walk.
Open: All Year
0115 931 2070 Mrs Baker
D: £17.50 **S:** £16–£20
Beds: 1F 1D **Baths:** 1 Sh
🛏 🅿 🔟 🏮 🏢 🔟 ﹗

Caunton

SK7460 🍺 *The Beck, The Plough*

Knapthorpe Lodge, Hockerton Road, Caunton, Newark, Notts, NG23 6AZ.
Large farmhouse overlooking beautiful countryside. Comfortable & friendly.
Open: All Year
Grades: ETC 3 Diamond
01636 636262 Fax: 01636 636415
D: £20–£25 **S:** £25–£30
Beds: 1T 1D **Baths:** 1 En 1 Pr
🛏 🅿 (6) 🔟 ✗ 🏢 🔟 ﹗

Collingham

SK8361 🍺 *Kings Head*

Lime Tree Farm, Lunn Lane, Collingham, Newark, Notts, NG23 7LP.
Attractive, converted barn in quiet conservation area of village.
Open: All Year
Grades: ETC 4 Diamond
01636 892044 Mrs Glenny
D: £18–£20 **S:** £20–£25
Beds: 1D 2T **Baths:** 2 En 1 Pr
🛏 🅿 (6) 🔟 🏢 🔟 ﹗

Cotgrave

SK6435 🍺 *Rose & Crown*

Marl Pit Cottage, 28 Main Road, Cotgrave, Nottingham, NG12 3HN.
Quality cottage accommodation, semi-rural location, very comfortable and friendly. **Open:** All Year (not Xmas)
0115 989 4805 (also fax)
mp1@nascr.net
D: £20
Beds: 2D **Baths:** 1 Sh
🛏 🅿 (2) ⅏ 🔟 🏢 🔟 ﹗

Cuckney

SK5670

The Greendale Oak, High Croft, Cuckney, Mansfield, Notts, NG20 9NQ.
300 year old pub/restaurant near Sherwood Forest & the Dureries. **Open:** All Year
01623 844441 D: £37 **S:** £18.50
Beds: 1F 1T 1D 2S **Baths:** 2 Sh
🛏 🅿 (4) ⅏ 🔟 🏮 ✗ 🏢 🔟 ﹗ cc

East Retford

SK7080 🍺 *Gate Inn, Sherwood Ranger, Northern Inn*

The Black Boy, 14 Moorgate, East Retford, Notts, DN22 6RH.
Local pub, historic town, fishing, sightseeing, power stations, easy reach.
Open: Jan to Dec
01777 702758 Mrs Cliff
D: £15–£20 **S:** £15
Beds: 2T 1S **Baths:** 2 En 1 Pr 1 Sh
🛏 (8) 🅿 (12) 🔟 🏢 ﹗

Newcastle Arms Hotel, 37 Bridgegate, East Retford, Notts, DN22 7UX.
Friendly market town hotel; free house.
Open: All Year
01777 702446 Fax: 01777 703755
newcarms@globalnet.co.uk
D: £13–£16 **S:** £13–£16
Beds: 3F 4T 3S **Baths:** 4 En 2 Sh
🛏 🅿 🔟 ﹗

Edwinstowe

SK6266 🍺 *Black Swan, Maid Marion, Robin Hood*

Marion's Manor, Ollerton Road, Edwinstowe, Mansfield, Nottinghamshire, NG21 9QG.
Enjoy a break in the heart of Sherwood Forest staying with a real Marion.
Open: All Year
01623 822135 D: £18–£25 **S:** £22–£25
Beds: 1F 1D 1T **Baths:** 3 En
🛏 🅿 (4) ⅏ 🔟 🏮 🏢 🔟 ﹗

Robin Hood Farm, Rufford Road, Edwinstowe, Mansfield, Notts, NG21 9HX.
Open: All Year
01623 824367 robinhoodfarm@aol.com
D: £17.50–£20 **S:** £17.50–£20
Beds: 1F 1D 1T **Baths:** 1 Sh
🛏 🅿 (6) ⅏ 🔟 🏮 🏢 🔟 ﹗
Olde farmhouse in Robin Hood's village in Sherwood Forest. Close to Clumber & Rufford Country Parks, Centre Parcs and South Forest Leisure Complex. Easy access Nottingham and Lincoln. Set in extensive gardens, reductions for children and extra nights secure parking.

Elton

SK7738 ◀ *Maonr Arms*

Grange Farm, Sutton Lane, Elton,
Notts, NG13 9LA.
Splendid views over open countryside.
Belvoir castle and market towns nearby.
Open: All Year (not Xmas/New Year)
01949 850357 (also fax)
Mrs Tomlinson
D: £20
Beds: 1D **Baths:** 1 Pr
🅿 (4) ⅍ 📺 ▥ ♨

Farnsfield

SK6357 ◀ *The Plough*

Grange Cottage, Main Street,
Farnsfield, Newark, Notts, NG22 8EA.
Beautiful cottage, wonderful gardens,
village location in Robin Hood country.
Open: All Year
Grades: AA 3 Diamond
01623 882259 Mrs Kitchen
Fax: 01636 882259
jo@grange-cottage.co.uk
D: £22.50–£25 **S:** £22.50–£25
Beds: 3T **Baths:** 1 En 1 Sh
🐾 (2) 🅿 📺 ♈ ▥ ▣ ♨

Fiskerton

SK7351 ◀ *Bromley Arms*

The Three Firs, 21 Marlock Close,
Fiskerton, Southwell, Notts, NG25 0UB.
Modern detached corner residence in
quiet cul-de-sac with secluded garden.
Open: All Year (not Xmas)
01636 830060 (also fax)
Mr & Mrs Jakeman
three-firs@bushinternet.com
D: £17.50–£21.50 **S:** £19–£24
Beds: 2D 2S **Baths:** 1 En 1 Pr 1 Sh
🐾 (5) 🅿 (4) ⅍ 📺 ▥ ▣ ♨

Flintham

SK7445

The Boot & Shoe Inn, Main Street,
*Flintham, Newark, Nottinghamshire, NG23
5LA.*
Recently renovated family run pub in
quiet village.
Open: All Year (not Xmas/New Year)
Grades: ETC 3 Diamond
01636 525246 K M Butler
D: £24 **S:** £32
Beds: 1F 1T 2D 1S **Baths:** 5 En
🐾 🅿 (5) ⅍ 📺 ♈ ✕ ▥ ▣ ♨ cc

Holme

SK8059 ◀ *Lord Nelson*

Gothic Farmhouse, Main Street,
*Holme, Newark, Nottinghamshire, NG23
7RZ.*
Old farmhouse near old church close to
Trent River.
Open: All Year (not Xmas/New Year)
01636 640656 Mr & Mrs Oxford
D: £25–£50 **S:** £25
Beds: 2T **Baths:** 1 En 1 Sh
🅿 📺 ▥ ▣ ♨

Holme Pierrepont

SK6339 ◀ *Goose At Gamston*

Holme Grange Cottage, Adbolton
Lane, Holme Pierrepont, Nottingham, NG12
2LU.
Victorian cottage, 3 miles city, close to
National Water Sports Centre.
Open: All Year (not Xmas)
0115 981 0413
jean.colinwightman@talk21.com
D: £18–£20 **S:** £18–£20
Beds: 1F 1D 1T **Baths:** 1 En 1 Sh
🅿 (6) ⅍ 📺 ▥ ▣ ♨

Laxton

SK7267 ◀ *Dovecote Inn*

Manor Farm, Moorhouse Road, Laxton,
Newark, Notts, NG22 0NU.
Old comfortable farmhouse in medieval
village near to Sherwood Forest.
Open: All Year (not Xmas)
Grades: ETC 2 Diamond
01777 870417 Mrs Haigh
D: £16–£17 **S:** £17–£18
Beds: 2F 1D **Baths:** 1 Sh
🐾 🅿 (3) 📺 ♈ ▣ ♨

Lilac Farm, Laxton, Newark, Notts, NG22
0NX.
Laxton: last remaining open field village.
Heritage museum adjacent to Lilac Farm.
Open: All Year (not Xmas/New Year)
Grades: ETC 2 Diamond
01777 870376 (also fax) Mrs Rose
D: £18–£20 **S:** £18–£20
Beds: 1F 1D **Baths:** 1 Sh
🐾 🅿 (6) 📺 ♈ ✕ ▥ ▣ ♨

Lowdham

SK6746 ◀ *Worlds End*

Old School Mews, 64a Main Street,
Lowdham, Nottingham, NG14 7BE.
Spacious, interesting, historic converted
school house in Robin Hood country.
Open: All Year (not Xmas/New Year)
0115 966 4838 J A McLaughlin
D: £25–£40 **S:** £25–£40
Beds: 2T 1D **Baths:** 1 En 1 Pr
🅿 ⅍ 📺 ▥ ▣ ♨

Mansfield

SK5361 ◀ *Robin Hood, Jug & Glass, Greendale
Oak, White Gates, Black Bull*

Bridleways Guest House, Newlands
Farm Lane, Mansfield, Notts, NG19 0HU.
Bridgeways originally 2 late C18th farm
cottages retains many period features
inside. **Open:** Jan to Dec
01623 635725 D: £20–£25 **S:** £22.50–£25
Beds: 1F 2D 2T 1S **Baths:** 6 En
🐾 🅿 (20) ⅍ 📺 ✕ ▥ ♨ ♿

Parkhurst Guest House, 28
*Woodhouse Road, Mansfield, Notts, NG18
2AF.*
Friendly family-run guest house, walking
distance to Mansfield centre.
Open: All Year **Grades:** AA 3 Diamond
01623 627324 Fax: 01623 621855
philfletcher@parkhurst28.freeserve.co.uk
D: £17.50–£25
Beds: 3F 4D 2T 3S **Baths:** 5 En 1 Sh
🐾 🅿 (10) 📺 ▥ ▣ ✿ ♨

Moorhouse

SK7566 ◀ *The Old Plough*

Brecks Cottage, Green Lane,
Moorhouse, Newark, Notts, NG23 6LZ.
This beautifully renovated and extended
300-year-old cottage offers modern
comforts. **Open:** All Year (not Xmas)
01636 822445 Mrs Thomas
brecks@mcmail.com
D: £18 **S:** £18
Beds: 2D 1T **Baths:** 1 Pr 1 Sh
🐾 🅿 (3) ⅍ 📺 ♈ ▥ ▣ ♨

Nether Langwith

SK5370 ◀ *Jug & Glass*

Boon Hills Farm, Nether Langwith,
Mansfield, Notts, NG20 9JQ.
Comfortable stone farmhouse with large
garden on working farm. **Open:** Mar to Oct
01623 743862 Mrs Palmer
michael.palmer3@virgin.net
D: fr £17 **S:** fr £18
Beds: 2D 1T **Baths:** 1 Sh
🐾 🅿 (4) ⅍ 📺 ▥ ♨

Newark

SK7953 ◀ *Fox & Crown*

Aandacht, 54 Boundary Road, Newark-
on-Trent, Notts, NG24 4AL.
Friendly semi-detached house in
residential area. Newark Castle stands
over the River Trent. **Open:** Jan to Dec
01636 703321 Mrs Watkins
D: £12.50–£15 **S:** £12.50–£15
Beds: 1F 1S 1D **Baths:** 1 Sh
🐾 (4) 🅿 (3) 📺 ♈ ✕ ▥ ▣ ♨

Albert House, 76 Albert Street, Newark-
on-Trent, Notts, NG24 4BB.
Large private house. 5 mins from town
centre.
Open: All Year
01636 705525 (also fax)
Mr Hall
D: £18–£20 **S:** £19–£21
Beds: 1F 2T 2S
🐾 (12) 🅿 (6) ▥ ♨

The Boot & Shoe Inn, Main Street,
*Flintham, Newark, Nottinghamshire, NG23
5LA.*
Open: All Year (not Xmas/New Year)
Grades: ETC 3 Diamond
01636 525246 K M Butler
D: £24 **S:** £32
Beds: 1F 1T 2D 1S **Baths:** 5 En
🐾 🅿 (5) ⅍ 📺 ♈ ▥ ▣ ♨ cc
Recently renovated family run pub in
quiet village.

Norton

SK5772 ◀ *Greendale Oak*

Norton Grange Farm, Norton,
Cuckney, Mansfield, Notts, NG20 9LP.
Situated in beautiful village on edge of
Sherwood Forest.
Open: All Year (not Xmas)
Grades: ETC 2 Diamond
01623 842666 Mr Palmer
D: £18–£20 **S:** £20–£22
Beds: 1F 1D 1T **Baths:** 1 Sh
🐾 🅿 (4) 📺 ♈ ♨

Nottingham

SK5641   *The Larwood, Castle, Wolds, Willow Tree, Trent Bridge Inn, Lakeside, O'Riley's*

Talbot House Hotel, *18-20 Bridgford Road, West Bridgford, Nottingham, NG2 6AB.*
Open: All Year
0115 981 1123 Mr Brown
Fax: 0115 981 3545
jktalbot@netcomuk.co.uk
D: £25–£40 **S:** £25–£40
Beds: 6F 6D 6T 6S **Baths:** 20 En 4 Sh
🛏 🅿 (30) 🄣 ⛻ ✕ 🍴 🖤 🖳 **cc**
Central position. 1 mile Nottingham City Centre, national Ice Centre. Holme Pierrepont national Water Sports Centre and central TV studios. One minute walk Nottm. Forest & Notts. County football grounds. Opposite Trent Bridge Cricket Ground. Half Mile rail/bus station.

Gallery Hotel, *8-10 Radcliffe Road, West Bridgford, Nottingham, NG2 5FW.*
Old Victorian house family hotel. 11 years by Mr & Mrs Don Masson.
Open: All Year
Grades: ETC 3 Diamond, AA 3 Diamond
0115 981 3651 Mr & Mrs Masson
Fax: 0115 981 3732
D: £25 **S:** £26–£35
Beds: 3F 5D 4T 3S **Baths:** 15 En
🛏 (1) 🅿 (50) 🔀 🄣 🍴 🖳 🖤 &

Adams' Castle View Guest House, *85 Castle Boulevard, Nottingham, NG7 1FE.*
Comfortable city guest house, close to bus/railway stations, activities.
Open: All Year
Grades: ETC 3 Diamond
0115 950 0022 Mr Adams
D: £20–£23 **S:** £20–£23
Beds: 1D 1T 2S **Baths:** 4 En
🔀 🄣 🖳 🖤 &

The Willows, Tophouse Farm, *Lamin's Lane, , Arnold, Nottingham, NG5 8PH.*
Working farm near Sherwood forest. excellent neighbouring bar and restaurant.
Open: All Year (not Xmas/New Year)
0115 967 0089 A Lamin
lamin.tophousefarm@btinternet.com
D: £19–£20 **S:** £22–£25
Beds: 1T **Baths:** 1 En
🛏 🅿 (20) 🔀 🄣 🖤 &

Rushcliffe Guest House, *104 Radcliffe Road, West Bridgford, Nottingham, NG2 5HG.*
Comfortable rooms, quality evening meals, close to all amenities.
Open: All Year
0115 981 1413 Mrs Nurse
Fax: 0115 981 1416
D: £14–£16 **S:** £20
Beds: 1F 1D 3T **Baths:** 3 Sh
🛏 🅿 (5) 🄣 ⛻ ✕ 🖳 🖤 & &

All details shown are as supplied by B&B owners in Autumn 2000

9 Elm Bank, Mapperley Park, *Nottingham, NG3 5AJ.*
Family-run Victorian house in conservation area, 12 min walk to city centre. **Open:** All Year
0115 962 5493 (also fax)
Mr & Mrs Stewart
stewpot1a@aol.com
D: £20–£25 **S:** £20–£27
Beds: 1F 2D 2T 1S **Baths:** 3 En 3 Pr
🛏 (1) 🅿 (2) 🄣 ⛻ 🖳 🖤 ✻ & &

Nuthall

SK5144   *Three Ponds, The Queens Head*

Camelot, *22 Watnall Road, Nuthall, Nottingham, NG16 1DU.*
J(26), M1, Spacious family bungalow. Pleasant gardens. Frequent bus station.
Open: All Year
0115 938 2597 (also fax) Mr & Mrs Cains
D: £17–£20 **S:** £20–£22
Beds: 1F 1D **Baths:** 1 En 1 Sh
🛏 🅿 (2) 🔀 🄣 🖳 🖤 & &

Ollerton

SK6567

Ollerton House Hotel, *Wellow Road, Ollerton, Newark, Notts, NG22 9AP.*
Close to Robin Hood country and Rufford Park, Sherwood Forest. **Open:** All Year
01623 861017 D: £17.50–£19.50 **S:** £17.50–£19.50
Beds: 2F 1D 3S **Baths:** 2 Sh
🛏 🅿 (80) 🄣 ✕ 🖳 🖤 ✻ &

Ragnall

SK8073   *Bridge Inn*

Ragnall House, *Ragnall, Newark, Notts, NG22 0UR.*
Period residence in large grounds. Lincoln and Sherwood forest nearby.
Open: All Year **Grades:** ETC 3 Diamond
01777 228575 (also fax) Mrs Hatfield
D: £17–£20 **S:** £16–£18
Beds: 1F 1D 2T 1S **Baths:** 1 En 2 Pr 1 Sh
🛏 🅿 (7) 🄣 🖳 &

Rolleston

SK7452   *Crown, Full Moon*

Racecourse Farm, *Station Road, Rolleston, Newark, Notts, NG23 5SE.*
Two hundred year old cottage facing the village church.
Open: All Year
01636 812176 Mrs Lee
D: £22–£23 **S:** £25
Beds: 1T 1D **Baths:** 1 En 1 Sh
🛏 (14) 🅿 (4) 🔀 🄣 ✕ 🖳 🖤 &

Shelford

SK6642   *Tom Browns*

Fox Cottage , *Main Street, Shelford, Nottingham, NG12 1ED.*
Beautiful cottage in delightful gardens with country views, quiet village
Open: All Year
0115 933 5741 (also fax)
Mrs Lewis
D: £20 **S:** £25
Beds: 3D **Baths:** 3 En
🛏 🅿 (8) 🔀 🄣 ⛻ 🖳 🖤 &

Southwell

SK7053   *Full Moon*

The Three Firs, *21 Marlock Close, Fiskerton, Southwell, Notts, NG25 0UB.*
Open: All Year (not Xmas)
01636 830060 (also fax)
Mr & Mrs Jakeman
three-firs@bushinternet.com
D: £17.50–£21.50 **S:** £19–£24
Beds: 2D 2S **Baths:** 1 En 1 Pr 1 Sh
🛏 (5) 🅿 (4) 🔀 🄣 🖳 🖤 &
Modern detached corner residence in quiet cul-de-sac with secluded garden and sheltered patio within an historic Trentside village. Fishing, horse riding/racing, golf courses, dinghy sailing and waterskiing all within 4 miles. Conducted tours of Southwell Minster, Sherwood Forest and Newark.

Barn Lodge, *Duckers Cottage, Brinkley, Southwell, Notts, NG25 0TP.*
Converted barn in open countryside. . Railway station, race course, Southwell Minster nearby.
Open: All Year (not Xmas/New Year)
Grades: ETC 3 Diamond
01636 813435 Mrs Hanbury
barnlodge@hotmail.com
D: £40 **S:** £25
Beds: 1F 1D 1T **Baths:** 3 En
🛏 🅿 (3) 🄣 ⛻ 🖳 🖤 &

Stanton-on-the-Wolds

SK6330   *The Pullman*

Laurel Farm, *Browns Lane, Stanton-on-the-Wolds, Keyworth, Nottingham, NG12 5BL.*
Lovely old farmhouse, NGS garden. Spacious rooms, convenient attractions.
Open: All Year
Grades: ETC 3 Diamond
0115 937 3488 Mrs Moffat
Fax: 0115 937 6490
laurelfarm@yahoo.com
D: fr £22.50 **S:** £30
Beds: 2D 1T **Baths:** 2 En 1 Pr
🛏 🅿 (8) 🔀 🄣 ⛻ 🖳 🖤 & **cc**

Sutton in Ashfield

SK4958   *Fox & Crown*

Dalestorth Guest House, *Skegby Lane, Skegby, Sutton in Ashfield, Notts, NG17 3DH.*
Grade II Georgian Listed building. Clean, friendly accommodation hotel standards.
Open: All Year
01623 551110 Mr Jordan
Fax: 01623 442241
D: £15–£17.50 **S:** £16–£18
Beds: 2F 3D 3T 5S **Baths:** 8 Sh
🛏 🅿 (50) 🄣 🖳 & &

Sutton on Trent

SK7965   ◀ *The Memory Lane*

Woodbine Farmhouse, *1 Church Street, Sutton on Trent, Newark, Notts, NG23 6PD.*
Open: All Year (not Xmas)
01636 822549 Mrs Searle
Fax: 01636 821716
woodbinefarmhouse@cs.com
D: £18–£21 **S:** £20
Beds: 3D 1T 1S **Baths:** 1 En 3 Sh
⌂ 🅿 (5) ✓ ✕ 🛏 🎔 🗐 🛁
Heavily beamed farmhouse with original yard and buildings. Family home of Jennie Searle, water colourist and poet in quiet location on edge of conservation village yet close to A1. Aga cooking, pleasant walks along country lanes and by River Trent.

Tollerton

SK6134   ◀ *Griffin Inn, Plumtree*

Cherry Tree, *13 Lothain Road, Tollerton, Nottingham, NG12 4EH.*
Open: All Year
0115 937 5076 Ms Gaskell
D: £18–£19 **S:** £18–£20
Beds: 1T 1D 1S **Baths:** 2 Sh
⌂ 🅿 (4) ✓ 🎔 🗐 🛁 🛗
Peaceful and friendly family home in quiet cul-de-sac in village south east of Nottingham. Overlooks fields and guests are encouraged to use pretty garden. Easy access to many places of interest and M1. Home made bread and preserves.

Trowell

SK4839   ◀ *Festival Inn*

Church Farm Guest House, *1 Nottingham Road, Trowell, Nottingham, NG9 3PA.*
C17th former farmhouse.
Open: All Year (not Xmas)
0115 930 1637 Fax: 0115 930 6991
D: £20 **S:** £20
Beds: 1F 3D 2T 2S **Baths:** 2 Sh
⌂ 🅿 ✓ 🎔 🗐 🛁

Upton (Southwell)

SK7354   ◀ *French Horn*

The Wheelhouse, *Mill Lane, Upton, Newark, Notts, NG23 5SZ.*
Mill situated over river, views over all elevations, overlooks racecourse.
Open: All Year (not Xmas)
01636 813572 Mrs Scothern
D: £20 **S:** £20
Beds: 1F 1D 1S **Baths:** 1 En
⌂ 🅿 (6) ✓ 🎔

Planning a longer stay? Always ask for any special rates

Walesby

SK6870   ◀ *Carpenters Arms*

13 New Hill, *Walesby, Newark, Notts, NG22 9PB.*
1950 semi-detached house with large garden in a small village.
Open: All Year (not Xmas)
01623 863834 Mrs Marsh
D: fr £14 **S:** fr £14
Beds: 2D **Baths:** 1 Sh
⌂ (1) 🅿 (3) ✓ 🎔 🛏 🗐 🛁 🛗

West Bridgford

SK5836   ◀ *The Wolds, Willow Tree, Trent Bridge Inn, The Larwood, Nottingham Knight, Stratford Haven*

Gallery Hotel, *8-10 Radcliffe Road, West Bridgford, Nottingham, NG2 5FW.*
Old Victorian house family hotel. 11 years by Mr & Mrs Don Masson.
Open: All Year
Grades: ETC 3 Diamond, AA 3 Diamond
0115 981 3651 Mr & Mrs Masson
Fax: 0115 981 3732
D: £25 **S:** £26–£35
Beds: 3F 5D 4T 3S **Baths:** 15 En
⌂ (1) 🅿 (50) ✓ 🎔 🗐 🛁 🛗

Rushcliffe Guest House, *104 Radcliffe Road, West Bridgford, Nottingham, NG2 5HG.*
Comfortable rooms, quality evening meals, close to all amenities.
Open: All Year
0115 981 1413
Mrs Nurse
Fax: 0115 981 1416
D: £14–£16 **S:** £20
Beds: 1F 1D 3T **Baths:** 3 Sh
⌂ 🅿 (5) 🎔 🛏 ✕ 🗐 🛁 🛗

Balmoral Hotel, *55-57 Loughborough Road, West Bridgford, Nottingham, NG2 7LA.*
Family-run hotel, 1.5 miles from city centre, to Holme Pier Point International Water Sports Centre.
Open: All Year
Grades: AA 2 Star, RAC 2 Star
0800 952 2992
Mr Jarrett
Fax: 0115 955 2991
balmoralhotel55@hotmail.com
D: £25–£30 **S:** £25–£35
Beds: 2F 9D 16T 14S **Baths:** 39 Pr
⌂ 🅿 (30) 🎔 ✕ 🗐 🛁 🛗 cc

Acorn Hotel, *4 Radcliffe Road, West Bridgford, Nottingham, NG2 5FW.*
Detached Victorian building, next to Trent Bridge Cricket ground.
Open: All Year (not Xmas)
Grades: ETC 3 Diamond, AA 3 Diamond
0115 981 1297
Fax: 0115 981 7654
D: £22–£25 **S:** £30
Beds: 2F, 7T, 2D, 1S **Baths:** 12 En
⌂ 🅿 (12) ✓ 🎔 🗐 🛁 cc

Croft Hotel, *6-8 North Road, West Bridgford, Nottingham, NG7 7NH.*
Charming, quiet Victorian B&B, 1.5 miles from Nottingham city centre.
Open: All Year (not Xmas)
0115 981 2744 (also fax)
Mr & Mrs Kennedy
D: £18–£20 **S:** £20–£25
Beds: 3F 2D 3T 8S **Baths:** 5 Sh
⌂ 🅿 (12) 🎔 🛏 🗐 🛁 🛗

Grantham Hotel, *24-26 Radcliffe Road, West Bridgford, Nottingham, NG2 5FW.*
1 mile south of the city centre, 0.25 mile from Trent Bridge.
Open: All Year
0115 981 1373 Fax: 0115 981 8567
D: fr £22 **S:** fr £23
Beds: 3F 4T 2D 13S **Baths:** 15 En 2 Sh
⌂ (1) 🅿 (20) 🎔 🛏 ✕ 🗐 🛁 🛗 cc

Whatton in the Vale

SK7439   ◀ *Manor Arms*

The Dell, *Church Street, Whatton in the Vale, Nottingham, Notts., NG13 9EL.*
Conservation area residence. Guests private sitting rooms, swimming pool, snooker.
Open: All Year
Grades: ETC 4 Diamond
01949 850832 Mrs Fraser
D: £17.50–£19.50 **S:** £25–£27.50
Beds: 1F 1T 1D **Baths:** 1 En 1 Pr
⌂ 🅿 (3) ✓ 🎔 🗐 🛁 🛗

Worksop

SK5879   ◀ *Newcastle Arms*

Sherwood Guest House, *57 Carlton Road, Worksop, Notts, S80 1PP.*
Comfortable/friendly accommodation near railway station, Clumber Park, A1/M1.
Open: All Year
Grades: ETC 3 Diamond
01909 474209 Mr Wilkinson
D: £21–£23.50 **S:** £21–£26
Beds: 2F 4T 1S **Baths:** 2 En 2 Sh
⌂ 🅿 (1) ✓ 🎔 🛏 🗐 🛁 🛗

Dukeries Licensed Guest House, *29 Park Street, Worksop, Notts, S80 1HW.*
Small and friendly with quality accommodation. Licensed lounge/bar. Close A1/M1. **Open:** All Year
01909 476674
www.dukeries@supanet.com
D: £22.50–£25 **S:** £30–£35
Beds: 2T 2D 2S **Baths:** 6 En
⌂ 🅿 🎔 ✕ 🗐 🛁 🛗 cc

National Grid References are for villages, towns and cities – not for individual houses

Oxfordshire

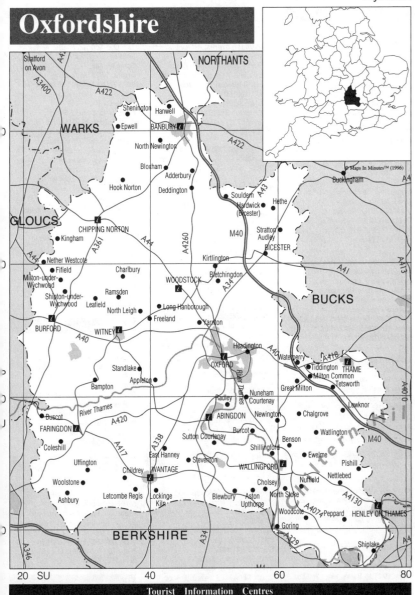

© Maps In Minutes™ (1996)

Tourist Information Centres

Abbey House, Abbey Close, **Abingdon**, Oxfordshire, OX14 3JD, 01235 522711.

Motorway Service Area (M40 J10), Northampton Road, **Ardley**, Bicester, Oxfordshire, OX6 9RD, 01869 345888.

Banbury Museum, 8 Horsefair, **Banbury**, Oxfordshire, OX16 0AA, 01295 259855.

Unit 6A, Bicester Village, Pingle Drive, **Bicester**, Oxfordshire, OX6 7WD, 01869 369055.

The Brewery, Sheep Street, **Burford**, Oxfordshire, OX8 4LP, 01993 823558.

5 Middle Row, **Chipping Norton**, Oxfordshire, OX7 5NJ, 01608 644379.

Car Park, Station Road, **Didcot**, Oxfordshire, 01235 813243.

The Pump House, 5 Market Place, **Faringdon**, Oxfordshire, SN7 7HL 01367 242191 (Easter to Oct).

Town Hall, Market Place, **Henley-on-Thames**, Oxfordshire, RG9 2AQ, 01491 578034 (Easter to Oct).

The Old School, Gloucester Green, **Oxford**, OX1 2DA, 01865 726871.

Town Hall, **Thame**, Oxfordshire, OX9 3DP, 01844 212834.

9 St Martin's Street, **Wallingford**, Oxfordshire, OX10 0AL, 01491 826972.

Vale & Downland Museum Centre, Church Street, **Wantage**, Oxon, OX12 8BL,   01235 760176.

Town Hall, Market Square, **Witney**, Oxfordshire, OX8 6AG, 01993 775802.

Hensington Rd, **Woodstock**, Oxfordshire, OX20 1JQ, 01993 813276 (Easter to Oct).

Abingdon

SU4997   ◀ *The Plough, The Parasol, The Ox, Boundary House, Wheatsheaf Inn, Pickled Newt*

Barrows End, *3 The Copse , Abingdon, Oxon, OX14 3YW.*
Modern chalet bungalow, peaceful setting. Easy access Oxford/Abingdon.
Open: All Year (not Xmas)
01235 523541 Mrs Harmsworth
DSHarm@tesco.net
D: £19–£20 **S:** £25
Beds: 3T **Baths:** 1 En 2 Pr
🅿 (3) ⅊ 📺 🛏 ♨

Acer House, *5 Kysbie Close, Abingdon, Oxon, OX14 1XZ.*
Quiet, safe neighbourhood - pleasant gardens. All rooms colour co-ordinated.
Open: All Year
01235 550579 Mrs Rhodes
D: £17–£18 **S:** £17–£22
Beds: 1D 1T 1S **Baths:** 1 Sh
🅿 (2) ⅊ 📺 🛏 ♨

The Old Vicarage, *17 Park Cresent, Abingdon, Oxon, OX14 1DF.*
Lovely Victorian vicarage in leafy conservation area. Breakfast in conservatory.
Open: All Year (not Xmas)
01235 522561 D: £20–£26 **S:** £25–£35
Beds: 1D 1T **Baths:** 1 En 1 Pr
🅿 (3) ⅊ 📺 🛏 ♨

Conifer Lodge, *1 The Copse, Abingdon, Oxon, OX14 3YW.*
Large modern family home overlooking a copse. Bus stop nearby.
Open: All Year (not Xmas)
01235 527158 Mrs Shaw
D: £22.50–£30 **S:** £25–£35
Beds: 1D 2S 1F **Baths:** 2 Pr 1 Sh
🐾 (5) 🅿 (7) ⅊ 📺 🛏 ♨

Adderbury

SP4735

Morgans Orchard Restaurant, *9 Twyford Gardens, Twyford, Adderbury, Banbury, Oxon, OX17 3JA.*
Award-winning French restaurant with quality B&B within rustic village location.
Open: All Year
01295 812047 Mr Morgan
morgarest@aol.com
D: £20–£25 **S:** £27.50–£40
Beds: 1D 2T 1S **Baths:** 1 En 1 Pr 3 Sh
🐾 🅿 (3) ⅊ 📺 🛏 ✗ 🛏 ♨ 📺 ♨ cc

Appleton

SP4401   ◀ *Eight Bells*

West Farm, *Eaton, Appleton, Abingdon, Oxon, OX13 5PR.*
Farm house, 6 miles west of Oxford. 5 miles Abingdon. Excellent touring centre.
Open: Easter to Oct
01865 862908 Mrs Gow
D: £22–£28 **S:** £22–£30
Beds: 1F 1D 1T 1S **Baths:** 1 Pr 1 Sh
🐾 🅿 (8) 📺 🛏 🛏 ♨

Ashbury

SU2685   ◀ *Rose and Crown*

The Village Stores, *Ashbury, Swindon, Wiltshire, SN6 8NA.*
Eighteen century thatched cottage/ village stores in pretty Downland village.
Open: All Year (not Xmas/New Year)
01793 710262 (also fax)
Mr & Mrs Schiff
D: £22.50–£30 **S:** £25–£30
Beds: 1F 1T 1D **Baths:** 1 En 1 Pr
🐾 🅿 ⅊ 📺 ✗ 📺

Aston Upthorpe

SU5585   ◀ *The Crown*

Middle Fell, *Moreton Road, Aston Upthorpe, Didcot, Oxon, OX11 9ER.*
Georgian village house, tastefully appointed. Secluded garden bordering Aston Stud.
Open: All Year (not Xmas)
Grades: ETC 4 Diamond
01235 850207 (also fax)
C Millin
D: £22.50–£25 **S:** £25–£35
Beds: 1F 1D 1T **Baths:** 3 En
🐾 (10) 🅿 (4) ⅊ 📺 🛏 ♨

Bampton

SP3103   ◀ *Talbot Hotel, Romany Inn*

Morar, *Weald Street, Bampton, Oxon, OX18 2HL.*
Wake to the mouthwatering smell of homemade bread baking.
Open: Mar to Dec
01993 850162 Ms Rouse
Fax: **01993 851738**
morar@cwcom.net
D: £22.50–£25 **S:** £22.50–£25
Beds: 2D 1T **Baths:** 2 En 1 Pr
🐾 (6) 🅿 (4) ⅊ 📺 🛏 📺 ♨ cc

Banbury

SP4540   ◀ *Swan Inn, Merto's*

Belmont Guest House, *34 Crouch Street, Banbury, Oxon, OX16 9PR.*
Family run Guest house close to all town amenities.
Open: All Year (not Xmas)
01295 262308 Mr Raby
Fax: **01295 275982**
D: £21–£24 **S:** £25–£35
Beds: 1F 2D 2T 3S **Baths:** 5 Pr 1 Sh
🐾 (10) 🅿 (6) ⅊ 📺 ✗ 🛏 📺 ♨ 🛏 cc

Benson

SU6191   ◀ *Three Horseshoes, Crown*

Fyfield Manor, *Brook Street, Benson, Wallingford, Oxon, OX10 6HA.*
Medieval dining room. Beautiful water gardens. Essentially a family house.
Open: All Year (not Xmas/New Year)
01491 835184 Mrs Brown
Fax: **01491 825635**
D: £25 **S:** £30
Beds: 1D 1T **Baths:** 2 En 1 Pr
🐾 (10) 🅿 (6) ⅊ 📺 🛏 📺 ♨

Bicester

SP5822   ◀ *The Bell, Red Lion*

The Old School, *Stratton Audley, Bicester, Oxon, OX6 9BJ.*
Open: All Year
Grades: ETC 2 Diamond
01869 277371 Mrs Wertheimer
sawertheimer@hotmail.com
D: £25–£35 **S:** £25–£30
Beds: 3T 1S **Baths:** 2 Sh
🐾 🅿 (6) 📺 🛏 🛏 📺 ♨ ✳
Interesting C17th house in pretty village. Pleasant garden with tennis court and croquet. Guests' own drawing room. Tea and home-make cakes on arrival. Village has charming thatched pub serving excellent meals. Very comfortable beds. Everyone sleeps well - so peaceful.

Home Farm House, *Middle Aston, Bicester, Oxon, OX25 5PX.*
Peaceful 17th Century farmhouse with stunning views and lovely garden.
Open: All Year
Grades: ETC 3 Diamond
01869 340666 Fax: 01869 347789
cparsons@telinco.co.uk
D: £25–£28 **S:** £25–£35
Beds: 1T 1D **Baths:** 1 En 1 Pr
🐾 (12) 🅿 (4) ⅊ 📺 🛏 ♨

Bletchingdon

SP5018

Stonehouse Farm, *Weston Road, Bletchingdon, Kidlington, Oxon, OX5 3EA.*
C17th farmhouse set in 560 acres 15 mins from Oxford.
Open: All Year (not Xmas/New Year)
Grades: ETC Commended
01869 350585 Mrs Hedges
D: £18–£22 **S:** £20–£24
Beds: 1F 1D 1T 1S **Baths:** 2 Sh
🐾 (12) 🅿 (6) ⅊ 📺 📺 ♨

Bloxham

SP4236   ◀ *Red Lion*

Brook Cottage, *Little Bridge Road, Bloxham, Banbury, Oxon, OX15 4PU.*
Warm welcome to C17th thatched cottage. Personal management by owner.
Open: All Year
01295 721089 D: £18.50 **S:** £18.50
Beds: 1D 1T 1S **Baths:** 1 En 1 Pr
🅿 (4) ⅊ 📺 🛏 ♨

Burcot

SU5695

Dinckley Court, *Burcot, Abingdon, Oxon, OX14 3DP.*
Beautiful Thames riverside coach house, offering luxury ensuite accommodation in 8 acre grounds.
Open: All Year
Grades: ETC 4 Diamond, AA 4 Diamond
01865 407763 Mrs Godfrey
annette@dinckleycourt.co.uk
D: £27.50–£32.50 **S:** £45–£55
Beds: 1D 4T **Baths:** 5 Pr
🐾 🅿 (20) ⅊ 📺 ✗ 🛏 📺 ♨ cc

Burford

SP2512 *Old Bull*

The Old Bell Foundry, *45 Witney Street, Burford, Oxon, OX18 4RX.*
Tranquil setting, a short distance from Burford High Street.
Open: All Year (not Xmas)
01993 822234 (also fax)
Ms Barguss
D: £24–£25
Beds: 1F **Baths:** 1 En
ॐ 🄿 (1) ⊬ 🄫 ▥ 🄥 🕭

Buscot

SU2397 *Trout Inn*

Apple Tree House, *Buscot, Faringdon, Oxon, SN7 8DA.*
Old property in National Trust village, 5 mins' walk River Thames, one acre garden.
Open: All Year (not Xmas)
Grades: ETC 3 Diamond, AA 3 Diamond, RAC 3 Diamond
01367 252592 Mrs Reay
emreay@aol.com
D: £18–£22 **S:** £23–£28
Beds: 2D 1T **Baths:** 1 En 2 Pr
ॐ 🄿 (10) ⊬ 🄫 ▥ 🄥 🕭

Chalgrove

SU6396 *Red Lion*

Cornerstones, *1 Cromwell Close, Chalgrove, Oxford, OX44 7SE.*
Pretty detached bungalow, situated just off B480 in charming Oxfordshire village.
Open: All Year
Grades: ETC 3 Diamond
01865 890298 D: £14.50 **S:** £23
Beds: 2T **Baths:** 1 Sh
ॐ (5) 🄿 (2) ⊬ 🄫 🎄 ▥ 🕭 ⅙

Charlbury

SP3619 *Bull Inn*

Banbury Hill Farm, *Enstone Road, Charlbury, Chipping Norton, Oxon, OX7 3JH.*
Situated on eastern edge of Cotswolds, overlooking the Evenlode Valley.
Open: All Year (not Xmas)
Grades: ETC 4 Diamond
01608 810314 Mrs Widdows
Fax: 01608 811891
D: £18–£25 **S:** £20–£35
Beds: 7F 2D 3T 1S **Baths:** 11 En 1 Sh
ॐ 🄿 (10) ⊬ 🄫 ▥ 🕭 ⅙ cc

Childrey

SU3587 *The Hatchett*

Ridgeway House, *West Street, Childrey, Wantage, Oxon, OX12 9UL.*
Luxury, countryside home in quiet Downland village near the Ridgeway.
Open: All Year
01235 751538 (also fax)
Mrs Roberts
robertsfamily@compuserve.com
D: £20–£22.50 **S:** £23–£29
Beds: 1F 1T 1S **Baths:** 2 En
ॐ 🄿 (5) ⊬ 🄫 ▥ 🄥 🕭

Chipping Norton

SP3126 *Blue Boar*

The Old Bakehouse, *50 West Street, Chipping Norton, Oxon, OX7 5ER.*
An old bakehouse, warm & friendly atmosphere, near town centre.
Open: All Year (not Xmas/New Year)
01608 643441 Mr & Mrs Cashmore
D: £22.50–£25 **S:** £35
Beds: 1F 1D **Baths:** 2 En
ॐ (8) 🄿 (2) ⊬ 🄫 ▥ 🕭

Cholsey

SU5886 *The Beetle and Wedge*

The Well Cottage, *Caps Lane, Cholsey, Wallingford, Oxon, OX10 9HQ.*
Delightful cottage with ensuite bedrooms in secluded garden flat. **Open:** All Year
01491 651959 J Alexander
Fax: 01491 651675
thewellcottage@talk21.com
D: £15–£25 **S:** £20–£30
Beds: 2T 1D **Baths:** 2 En 1 Pr

Deddington

SP4631 *The Unicorn*

Hill Barn, *Milton Gated Road, Deddington, Banbury, Oxon, OX15 0TS.*
Converted barn in open countryside, convenient for Oxford, Cotswolds, Warwick, Stratford. **Open:** All Year (not Xmas) **Grades:** ETC 2 Diamond
01869 338631 Mrs White
hillbarn-bb@supanet.com
D: £20–£25 **S:** £25–£27.50
Beds: 1F 1D 2T **Baths:** 1 En 1 Sh
ॐ 🄿 (6) 🄫 🎄 ▥ 🕭

Stonecrop Guest House, *Hempton Road, Deddington, Banbury, Oxon, OX15 0QH.*
Detached house close to places of interest. A warm welcome.
Open: All Year **Grades:** ETC 2 Diamond
01869 338335 Fax: 01869 338505
D: £16–£19 **S:** £16–£19
Beds: 1F 1D 1T 1S **Baths:** 2 Sh
ॐ (10) 🄿 (6) ▥ 🕭

East Hanney

SU4192

Bramley House, *Mill Orchard, East Hanney, Wantage, Oxon, OX12 0JH.*
Village near Berkshire Downs, Oxford, Cotswolds. Pubs, restaurant serve food.
Open: All Year (not Xmas)
01235 868314 D: £19–£20 **S:** £20–£22
Beds: 2D 1S **Baths:** 1 En 1 Sh
🄿 (3) ⊬ 🄫 ▥ 🄥 🕭

Epwell

SP3441 *The Bell*

Yarnhill Farm, *Shenington Road, Epwell, Banbury, Oxon, OX15 6JA.*
Peaceful farmhouse; ideally situated for Cotswolds, Stratford upon Avon, Oxford.
Open: All Year (not Xmas)
Grades: ETC 3 Diamond
01295 780250 D: £18–£25 **S:** £18–£25
Beds: 1D 1T 1S **Baths:** 1 Pr 1 Sh
ॐ (8) 🄿 (6) ⊬ 🄫 ▥ 🕭

Ewelme

SU6491 *Crown, Shepherds Hut*

Fords Farm, *Ewelme, Wallingford, Oxon, OX10 6HU.*
Picturesque setting in historic village. Warm, friendly atmosphere. Good views.
Open: All Year
Grades: ETC 4 Diamond
01491 839272 Miss Edwards
D: £24–£25 **S:** £30–£35
Beds: 1D 2T **Baths:** 1 Pr 1 Sh
🄿 (8) ⊬ 🄫 ▥ 🕭

May's Farm, *Turner's Court, Ewelme, Wallingford, Oxon, OX10 6QF.*
Working stock farm. Fabulous views, quiet location, good walking.
Open: All Year
01491 641294 Mrs Passmore
Fax: 01491 641697
mays.farm@tesco.net
D: £19–£22 **S:** £25–£30
Beds: 1F 1T 1S **Baths:** 1 En 1 Sh
ॐ 🄿 (4) ⊬ 🄫 ▥ 🕭

Faringdon

SU2895 *Fox & Hounds, The Plough*

Faringdon Hotel, *1 Market Place, Faringdon, Oxon, SN7 7HL.*
Open: All Year
Grades: ETC 3 Diamond, AA 2 Star, RAC 2 Star
01367 240536 Fax: 01367 243250
D: £30–£35 **S:** £45–£60
Beds: 3F 14D 1T 3S **Baths:** 20 En
ॐ 🄫 🎄 ✕ ▥ 🕭 cc
Situated near C12th parish church, on site of palace of Alfred the Great.

Portwell House Hotel, *Market Place, Faringdon, Oxon, SN7 7HU.*
Relax in the ancient market town of Faringdon within reach of the Cotswolds.
Open: All Year
Grades: ETC 1 Star
01367 240197 Mr Pakeman
Fax: 01367 244330
D: fr £25 **S:** fr £40
Beds: 2F 3D 2T 1S **Baths:** 8 En
ॐ (2) 🄿 (4) ⊬ 🄫 ✕ ▥ 🄥 ❋ 🕭 ⅙ cc

Fifield

SP2319 *Merrymouth Inn*

Merryfield, *High Street, Fifield, Chipping Norton, Oxon, OX7 6HL.*
Quiet and peaceful, an ideal centre for touring the Cotswolds.
Open: All Year (not Xmas)
Grades: ETC 3 Diamond
01993 830517 Mrs Palmer
jpmgtd@freeuk.com
D: £22.50–£25 **S:** £25–£30
Beds: 2T **Baths:** 1 En 1 Pr
🄿 (4) ⊬ 🄫 ▥ 🕭

BATHROOMS

Pr - Private

Sh - Shared

En - Ensuite

Freeland

SP4112   ◀ *Shepherd's Hall*

Shepherds Hall Inn, *Witney Road, Freeland, Witney, Oxon, OX8 8HQ.*
Open: All Year
Grades: ETC 2 Diamond
01993 881256 Mr Fyson
D: £22.50–£25 **S:** £25–£35
Beds: 1F 1D 2T 1S **Baths:** 5 En
⛄ 🅿 (50) 📺 ⵜ 🛏 ♨ cc
Attractive inn with excellent well-appointed accommodation. Wide selection of appetising meals available lunch times & evenings. Ideally situated for Oxford, Woodstock - Blenheim Palace - and Cotswolds. On A4095 Woodstock-Witney Road.

Wrestler's Mead, *35 Wroslyn Road, Freeland, Witney, Oxon, OX8 8HJ.*
Chalet bungalow. Quiet rural area. MasterCard and Visa accepted.
Open: All Year
01993 882003 (also fax)
Mrs Taphouse
D: fr £19 **S:** fr £17
Beds: 1F 1D 1S **Baths:** 2 En 1 Sh
⛄ 🅿 (3) 📺 ⵜ 🛏 ♨

Goring

SU6081   ◀ *Catherine Wheel, John Barleycorn, Miller Of Mansfield, Bull Inn, Perch & Pike*

The Catherine Wheel, *Station Road, Goring, Reading, Berks, RG8 9HB.*
Accommodation in a Victorian cottage in riverside village.
Open: All Year
01491 872379 Mrs Kerr
D: fr £20 **S:** fr £25
Beds: 2D 1T **Baths:** 2 Sh
⛄ ⵜ 📺 ✕ 🛏 ♨ cc

Great Milton

SP6302   ◀ *The Bull*

Colletts View, *Great Milton, Oxford, Oxfordshire, OX44 7YA.*
Set in lovely gardens, ground floor rooms, Oxford Chilterns close.
Open: All Year (not Xmas/New Year)
01844 278824 Mrs Hayes
sputnik@ukgateway.net
D: £18–£20 **S:** £20–£22
Beds: 2F 2T **Baths:** 1 Sh
⛄ (15) 🅿 (2) ⵜ 🛏 ♨

Hanwell

SP4344   ◀ *The Bell*

The Coach House, *Hanwell Castle, Hanwell, Banbury, Oxon, OX17 1HN.*
Part of C15th castle in 20 acre garden undergoing restoration.
Open: Apr to Oct
01295 730764 Mrs Taylor
D: £18–£25 **S:** £18–£25
Beds: 1F 1D 1T **Baths:** 3 En
⛄ (1) 🅿 (6) 📺 ⵜ 🛏 ♨ ♿

Hardwick (Bicester)

SP5729   ◀ *The Butchers Arms*

Sycamore House, *Church Lane, Hardwick, Bicester, Oxon, OX6 6SS.*
Newly built farmhouse in a secluded area in a small village.
Open: All Year (not Xmas/New Year)
01869 277984 Ms Curtis
D: £20–£25 **S:** £20–£25
Beds: 1T 1D 1S **Baths:** 1 Sh
⛄ (3) 🅿 (6) ⵜ 📺 🛏 ♨

Headington

SP5407   ◀ *White Horse, Cafe Noir*

All Seasons Guest House, *63 Windmill Road, Headington, Oxford, Oxfordshire, OX3 7BP.*
Comfortable guest house, non- smoking, parking, convenient airports and Brookes University.
Open: All Year
01865 742215 Mr & Mrs Melbye
Fax: 01865 432691
info@allseasons-oxford.com
D: £22.50–£31 **S:** £27–£45
Beds: 1T 3D 2S **Baths:** 4 En 1 Sh
⛄ (6) 🅿 (6) ⵜ 📺 🛏 ♨ cc

Sandfield House, *19 London Road, Headington, Oxford, OX3 7RE.*
Fine period house. Direct coaches to London, Heathrow & Gatwick.
Open: All Year (not Xmas)
Grades: ETC 4 Diamond
01865 762406 (also fax)
Mrs Anderson
stay@sandfield-guesthouse.co.uk
D: £29–£34 **S:** £30–£34
Beds: 2D 2S **Baths:** 3 En 1 Pr
⛄ (6) 🅿 (5) ⵜ 📺 🛏 ♨ cc

Henley-on-Thames

SU7682   ◀ *Anchor, Bottle & Glass, Golden Ball, Rose & Crown*

Ledard, *Rotherfield Road, Henley-on-Thames, Oxon, RG9 1NN.*
Elegant Victorian house and garden within easy reach of Henley.
Open: All Year (not Xmas)
01491 575611 Mrs Howard
alan.howard@iee.org
D: £20 **S:** £20
Beds: 1F 1D 1T **Baths:** 2 Pr
⛄ 🅿 (4) ⵜ 📺 🛏 ♨

Alftrudis, *8 Norman Avenue, Henley-on-Thames, Oxon, RG9 1SG.*
Victorian home, quiet cul-de-sac two minutes town centre station, river.
Open: All Year **Grades:** ETC 4 Diamond
01491 573099 Mrs Lambert
Fax: 01491 411747
b&b@alftrudis.fsnet.co.uk
D: £25–£30 **S:** £40–£50
Beds: 2D 1T **Baths:** 2 En 1 Pr
⛄ (8) 🅿 (2) ⵜ 📺 🛏 ♨

National Grid References are for villages, towns and cities – not for individual houses

4 Coldharbour Close, *Henley-on-Thames, Oxon, RG9 1QP.*
Large sunny bungalow in quiet location; secluded garden with patio.
Open: Easter to Nov
Grades: ETC 3 Diamond
01491 575297 (also fax)
Mrs Bower
jennybower@email.com
D: £24–£28 **S:** £27–£30
Beds: 1D 1T **Baths:** 1 Pr 1 En
⛄ 🅿 (3) ⵜ 📺 ✕ 🛏 ♨ ♿ ♨

Hethe

SP5829   ◀ *Whitmore Arms*

Manor Farm, *Hethe, Bicester, Oxfordshire, OX6 9ES.*
Between Oxford and Stratford. Charming stone Manor house in lovely village.
Open: All Year
Grades: ETC 4 Diamond
01869 277602 Mrs Reynolds
Fax: 01869 278376
D: £25–£30 **S:** £30–£35
Beds: 2D **Baths:** 1 En 1 Pr
⛄ 🅿 (2) ⵜ 📺 ✕ 🛏 ♨

Hook Norton

SP3533   ◀ *Sun Inn*

Symnel, *High St, Hook Norton, Banbury, Oxfordshire, OX15 5NH.*
Real ale brewery, pottery, Roll Right stones. Excellent restaurants wonderful countryside.
Open: All Year (not Xmas)
Grades: ETC 2 Diamond
01608 737547 Mrs Cornelius
cornelius@hooky13.freeserve.co.uk
D: £16 **S:** £16
Beds: 1D 2T **Baths:** 1 Sh
⛄ 🅿 ⵜ 📺 ✕ 🛏 ♨ ♨

Kingham

SP2524   ◀ *Kings Head*

The Old Stores, *Foscot, Kingham, Chipping Norton, Oxon, OX7 6RH.*
Charming Cotswold stone cottage in lovely rural location, 1.5 miles from Kingham.
Open: Mar to Nov
01608 659844 (also fax)
D: £18–£20 **S:** £22–£23
Beds: 1D **Baths:** 1 Pr
🅿 (2) ⵜ 📺 ♨

Kirtlington

SP4919   ◀ *Oxford Arms*

Two Turnpike Cottages, *Kirtlington, Oxford, OX5 3HB.*
Cotswold stone cottage with pretty gardens in village setting.
Open: All Year
01869 350706 Mrs Jones
margarethjones@hotmail.com
D: £21–£24 **S:** £25
Beds: 2D **Baths:** 1 Sh
⛄ 🅿 (2) ⵜ 📺 ⵜ 🛏 ♨

Leafield

SP3115 ◖ The Swan, The Maytime

Langley Farm, Leafield, Witney, Oxon,
OX8 5QD.
Working farm set in open country 3 miles
from Burford. **Open:** May to Oct
Grades: ETC 3 Diamond
01993 878686 Mrs Greves
gwengreves@farmline.com
D: £17.50–£20
Beds: 2D 1T **Baths:** 1 Pr 2 Sh
⛺ (8) ▣ (8) 🖵 🛏 🛒 🕭

Pond View, 10 Fairspear Road, Leafield,
Witney, Oxon, OX8 5NT.
Village location handy for visiting
Burford, Blenheim Palace and Oxford.
Open: All Year **Grades:** ETC 3 Diamond
01993 878133 Mrs Wiggins
D: £19–£21 **S:** £19–£21
Beds: 3D 2S **Baths:** 2 En 2 Sh
⛺ ▣ (4) 🖢 🖵 🛏 🛒 🕭

Letcombe Regis

SU3886 ◖ Greyhound, Lamb

Quince Cottage, Letcombe Regis,
Wantage, Oxon, OX12 9J.
Large thatched cottage, exposed beams,
near Ridgeway, warm family atmosphere.
Open: All Year
01235 763652 Mrs Boden
D: £21–£25 **S:** £25
Beds: 1T 1S **Baths:** 1 Pr
⛺ (1) ▣ (2) 🖢 🖵 🛒 🕭

Old Vicarage, Letcombe Regis,
Wantage, Oxon, OX12 9JP.
Delightful Victorian home, elegant
accommodation, near pub, pretty
downland village. **Open:** All Year (not
Xmas)
01235 765827 Mrs Barton
Fax: 020 8743 8740
hughb@thehogarth.co.uk
D: £22–£25 **S:** £22–£30
Beds: 1D 1T 1S **Baths:** 1 En 1 Sh
⛺ ▣ (2) 🖢 🖵 🛒

Lewknor

SU7197 ◖ Leathern Bottle

Moorcourt Cottage, Weston Road,
Lewknor, Watlington, Oxfordshire, OX9 5RU.
Beautiful C15th cottage, open views, very
quiet, friendly and comfortable.
Open: All Year
01844 351419 (also fax) Mrs Hodgson
D: £22.50 **S:** £30
Beds: 1T 1D **Baths:** 1 En 1 Pr
▣ (4) 🖵 🛒 🕭

Lockinge Kiln

SU4283

Lockinge Kiln Farm, The Ridgeway,
Lockinge Kiln, Wantage, Oxon, OX12 8PA.
Quiet comfortable farmhouse working
farm ideal walking riding cycling country.
Open: All Year (not Xmas)
01235 763308 (also fax) Mrs Cowan
stellacowan@hotmail.com
D: £19 **S:** £22
Beds: 1D 1T 1S **Baths:** 3 Sh
⛺ (10) ▣ (3) 🖢 🖵 🛒 🕭

Long Hanborough

SP4114 ◖ The Boot, Barnard's Gate, The Bell,
Hand In Shears, Cock Inn

Gorselands Hall, Boddington Lane,
North Leigh, Witney, Oxon, OX8 6PU.
Lovely old Cotswold stone farmhouse
with oak beams in delightful rural setting.
Open: All Year
Grades: ETC 3 Diamond, RAC 3 Diamond
01993 882292 Mr & Mrs Hamilton
Fax: 01993 883629
hamilton@gorselandshall.com
D: £22.50–£25 **S:** £30–£35
Beds: 4D 1T 1F **Baths:** 6 En
⛺ ▣ (6) 🖢 🖵 🛒 🗡 🛒 🖵 🕭 cc

Wynford House, 79 Main Road, Long
Hanborough, Near Woodstock, Oxon,
OX8 8BX.
Comfortable warm family house in
village. Good walks, local pubs.
Open: All Year (not Xmas)
01993 881402
Mrs Ellis
Fax: 01993 883661
D: £20–£23 **S:** £25–£40
Beds: 1F 1D 1T **Baths:** 1 En 1 Sh
⛺ ▣ 🖢 🖵 🛏 🗡 🛒 🖵 🕭

Milton Common

SP6503 ◖ The Bull

Byways, Old London Road, Milton
Common, Thame, Oxon, OX9 2JR.
A spacious bungalow, comfortable and
cosy, good views, with large garden.
Open: All Year
01844 279386 D: £23 **S:** £25
Beds: 2T **Baths:** 1 En 1 Pr
▣ (3) 🖢 🛒 🖵 🕭

Milton-under-Wychwood

SP2618 ◖ Quart Pot, Lamb Inn

Sunset House, Jubilee Lane, Milton-
under-Wychwood, Chipping Norton,
Oxfordshire, OX7 6EW.
Period Cotswold house, charming
bedrooms with ensuite private facilities.
Open: All Year
01993 830581
Mrs Durston
D: £23.50–£25 **S:** £27.50–£30
Beds: 2D 1T **Baths:** 2 En 1 Pr
⛺ (5) ▣ (3) 🖢 🖵 🛒 🖵 🕭

Nether Westcote

SP2220 ◖ Merrymouth Inn

Cotswold View Guest House,
Nether Westcote, Chipping Norton, Oxon,
OX7 6SD.
Open: All Year (not Xmas/New Year)
Grades: ETC 3 Diamond
01993 830699 Mr Gibson
info@cotswoldview-guesthouse.co.uk
D: £20–£25 **S:** £25–£30
Beds: 2D 2T 1S 2F **Baths:** 5 En 2 Pr
⛺ ▣ (8) 🖢 🖵 🛏 🗡 🛒 🖵 🕭 cc
We welcome you to Cotswold view
guesthouse, which we have built on the
site of my family's farmyard. In the
unspoilt and quiet village of Nether
Westcote. We offer luxury accomodation
and a hearty English breakfast.

Nettlebed

SU6986 ◖ Crown Inn

Park Corner Farm House, Nettlebed,
Henley-on-Thames, Oxon, RG9 6DX.
Queen Anne farmhouse in AONB
between Henley-on-Thames and Oxford.
Open: All Year (not Xmas/New Year)
01491 641450 Mrs Rutter
D: £22.50 **S:** £25
Beds: 2T 1S **Baths:** 1 Sh 1 Pr
⛺ ▣ (6) 🖢 🛏 🛒 🕭

Newington

SU6096 ◖ Six Bells

Ewe Farm, Newington, Wallingford,
Oxon, OX10 7AF.
Attractive farmhouse set in large garden
with lovely views of open countryside.
Open: All Year
01865 891236 (also fax)
Mrs Brown
D: £19–£22.50 **S:** £20–£25
Beds: 1D 2T 2S **Baths:** 2 En 1 Pr
▣ (4) 🖵 🛒 🕭

North Leigh

SP3812 ◖ Royal Oak, Sheppard Hall, Woodman

Elbie House, East End, North Leigh,
Witney, Oxon, OX8 6PZ.
C16th inn, located in quiet hamlet. Many
special touches not to be equalled
elsewhere! **Open:** All Year
Grades: ETC 4 Diamond
01993 880166 Mrs Buck
buck@elbiehouse.freeserve.co.uk
D: £22.50–£25 **S:** £30–£35
Beds: 2F **Baths:** 2 En
⛺ (7) ▣ (10) 🖢 🖵 🛒 🖵 🕭 ♿

North Leigh Guest House, 28
Common Road, North Leigh, Witney, Oxon,
OX8 6RA.
Clean friendly family home, guest own
suite. Evening meal available.
Open: All Year
Grades: ETC 4 Diamond
01993 881622 Mrs Perry
D: £22.50 **S:** £22.50
Beds: 1F 1T **Baths:** 2 En
⛺ ▣ (5) 🖢 🖵 🗡 🛒 🖵 🕭

The Leather Bottel Guest House,
East End, North Leigh, Witney, Oxon, OX8
3PX.
Ideally situated Blenheim Palace,
Cotswolds and Oxford. Follow signs to
Roman Villa off A4095.
Open: All Year
01993 882174 Mr Purcell
D: £20–£25 **S:** £30
Beds: 1F 1D 1T **Baths:** 3 En
⛺ (4) ▣ (4) 🖢 🖵 🗡 🛒 🕭

RATES

D = Price range per person
sharing in a double room
S = Price range for a
single room

BATHROOMS
Pr - Private
Sh - Shared
En - Ensuite

North Newington

SP4239 ⚐ *North Arms*

Broughton Grounds Farm, *North Newington, Banbury, Oxon, OX15 6AW.*
Open: All Year (not Xmas)
01295 730315 Margaret Taylor
broughtongrounds@hotmail.com
D: £16–£18 **S:** £16–£18
Beds: 1D 1T 1S **Baths:** 1 Sh
🛇 (2) 🅿 (3) ⚥ 📺 🛄
Enjoy warm hospitality & peaceful surroundings at our C17th stone farmhouse. A working family farm situated on the Broughton Castle estate with beautiful views & walks. New, very comfortable spacious accommodation, log fire in dining room, delicious breakfast & cream teas with home produce.

North Stoke

SU6186

Footpath Cottage, *The Street, North Stoke, Wallingford, Oxon, OX10 6BJ.*
Lovely old cottage, peaceful river village. Warm welcome, excellent food.
Open: All Year
01491 839763 Mrs Tanner
D: £19–£20 **S:** £20
Beds: 2D 1S **Baths:** 1 En 1 Sh
🛇 📺 🐾 ✗ 🛄 ⚥ 🛄

Nuffield

SU6687 ⚐ *The Crown*

The Rectory, *Nuffield, Henley-on-Thames, Oxon, RG9 5SN.*
Working Rectory on the ridgeway path at 700 feet; Aga breakfasts
Open: All Year
01491 641305 (also fax)
Mr Shearer
D: £15–£18 **S:** £18–£20
Beds: 1D 1T 1S **Baths:** 1 Pr
🛇 🅿 (4) ⚥ ✗ 🛄 ⚥

Nuneham Courtenay

SU5598 ⚐ *The Crown, Seven Stars*

The Old Bakery, *Nuneham Courtenay, Oxford, OX44 9NX.*
Open: All Year
01865 343585 maggie.howard@virgin.net
D: £25–£30 **S:** £30–£40
Beds: 1F 2T 1D **Baths:** 4 En
🛇 🅿 (10) ⚥ 📺 🐾 ✗ 🛄 ⚥ ❋ 🛄 ⚥ 🅲🅲
Beautifully renovated large Listed C18th country cottage on the outskirts of Oxford City (5 miles) . Nuneham Courtenay believed to be the oldest planted village in England. Lovely gardens. warm welcome, great breakfasts. Visit us once, you're sure to return.

Oxford

SP5106 ⚐ *Carpenters' Arms, Vine, Bear & Ragged Staff, Tree, Marsh Harrier, Prince of Wales, Trout Inn, Old Ale House, Radcliffe Arms, Eight Bells, Fox & Hounds, Boundary House, Ox, Cafe Noir, Squire Basset, Victoria Arms, Duke of Monmouth*

Green Gables, *326 Abingdon Road, Oxford, Oxfordshire, OX1 4TE.*
Open: All Year (not Xmas/New Year)
Grades: ETC 3 Diamond, AA 3 Diamond
01865 725870 Mr & Mrs Bhella
Fax: 01865 723115
green.gables@virgin.net
D: £25–£30 **S:** £32–£50
Beds: 3F 4D 1T 1S **Baths:** 7 En 1 Sh
🛇 (9) 📺 🛄 ⚥ 🛄 🛄 🅲🅲
Characterful detached Edwardian house shielded by trees. Bright spacious rooms with TV & beverage facilities. Ensuite rooms. 1.25 miles to city centre, on bus routes. Ample off-street parking. Direct line phones in rooms and disabled room available.

The Bungalow, *Cherwell Farm, Mill Lane, Old Marston, Oxford, OX3 0QF.*
Open: Mar to Oct
Grades: ETC 3 Diamond
01865 557171 Mrs Burdon
D: £21–£25 **S:** £25–£35
Beds: 2D 2T **Baths:** 2 En 1 Sh
🛇 (7) 🅿 (6) ⚥ 📺 🛄 ⚥ 🛄
Modern bungalow in five acres open countryside, no bus route. 3 miles to city centre.

Pine Castle Hotel, *290 Iffley Road, Oxford, OX4 4AE.*
Close to shops, launderette, post office. Frequent buses. River walks nearby.
Open: All Year (not Xmas)
Grades: ETC 4 Diamond, AA 4 Diamond
01865 241497 Mrs Morris
Fax: 01685 727230
stay@pinecastle.co.uk
D: £32.50–£37 **S:** £55–£60
Beds: 1F 5D 2T **Baths:** 8 En
🛇 🅿 (4) 📺 🛄 ⚥ 🛄

Gables Guest House, *6 Cumnor Hill, Oxford, Oxfordshire, OX2 9HA.*
Award winning detached house with beautiful garden. Close to city.
Open: All Year
Grades: ETC 4 Diamond , AA 4 Diamond
01865 862153 Mrs Tompkins
Fax: 01865 864054
stay@gables-oxford.co.uk
D: fr £22 **S:** fr £26
Beds: 2S 2D 2T **Baths:** 6 En
🛇 🅿 (6) ⚥ 📺 🛄 ⚥ 🛄

Highfield West, *188 Cumnor Hill, Oxford, OX2 9PJ.*
Comfortable home in residential area, heated outdoor pool in season.
Open: All Year (not Xmas)
Grades: ETC 3 Diamond
01865 863007 Mr & Mrs Mitchell
highfieldwest@email.msn.com
D: £22.50–£28.50 **S:** £26–£29
Beds: 1F 1D 1T 2S **Baths:** 3 En 1 Sh
🛇 🅿 (5) ⚥ 📺 🐾 🛄 ⚥ 🛄

Sportsview Guest House, *106-110 Abingdon Road, Oxford, OX1 4PX.*
Open: All Year (not Xmas)
Grades: ETC 3 Diamond
01865 244268 Mrs Saini
Fax: 01865 249270
D: £24–£30 **S:** £30–£50
Beds: 5F 6T 3D 6S **Baths:** 12 En 12 Pr 2 Sh
🛇 (4) 🅿 (11) ⚥ 📺 🛄 ⚥ 🅲🅲
Situated south of the city centre. A few minutes' walk takes you to the towpath and a very pleasant walk to the city & its famous landmarks. On a direct bus route, with easy access to railway & bus stations.

Acorn Guest House, *260 Iffley Road, Oxford, Oxfordshire, OX4 1SE.*
Modern comfort in Victorian house convenient for all local attractions.
Open: All Year (not Xmas/New Year)
Grades: ETC 2 Diamond, AA 2 Diamond, RAC 2 Diamond
01865 247998 Mrs Lewis
D: £24–£27 **S:** £26–£29
Beds: 5F 2D 1T 4S **Baths:** 1 En, 4 Sh
🛇 (9) 🅿 (11) 📺 🛄 ⚥ 🛄 🅲🅲

58 St John Street, *Oxford, OX1 2QR.*
Tall Victorian house central to all colleges, museums and theatres.
Open: All Year
01865 515454 Mrs Old
D: £18–£19 **S:** fr £18
Beds: 1F 1T 1S **Baths:** 2 En
🛇 (1) ⚥ 🛄

Sandfield House, *19 London Road, Headington, Oxford, OX3 7RE.*
Fine period house. Direct coaches to London, Heathrow & Gatwick.
Open: All Year (not Xmas)
Grades: ETC 4 Diamond
01865 762406 (also fax)
Mrs Anderson
stay@sandfield-guesthouse.co.uk
D: £29–£34 **S:** £30–£34
Beds: 2D 2S **Baths:** 3 En 1 Pr
🛇 (6) 🅿 (5) ⚥ 📺 🛄 ⚥ 🛄 🅲🅲

Chestnuts, *72 Cumnor Hill, Oxford, OX2 9HU.*
Country house in acre of garden, 1.5 miles from Oxford.
Open: All Year
Grades: ETC 3 Diamond
01865 863602 **D:** £21–£24 **S:** £24–£30
Beds: 1D 1T **Baths:** 1 En 1 Pr
🅿 ⚥ 🛄 ⚥

Milka's Guest House, *379 Iffley Road, Oxford, Oxon, OX4 4DP.*
Family run guest house situated close to Iffley village.
Open: All Year
Grades: ETC 3 Diamond
01865 778458 Fax: 01865 776477
milkas@dial.pipex.com
D: £22.50–£27.50 **S:** £25–£35
Beds: 2D 1S **Baths:** 1 En
🛇 (5) 🅿 (5) ⚥ 📺 🛄 ⚥ 🅲🅲

Planning a longer stay? Always ask for any special rates

Lakeside Guest House, *118 Abingdon Road, Oxford, Oxfordshire, OX1 4PZ.*
Edwardian house overlooking Thames. One mile Oxford. Next to park - swimming pool/tennis. **Open:** All Year
Grades: ETC 3 Diamond
01865 244725 (also fax) Mrs Shirley
daniela.shirley@btclick.com
D: £24–£30
Beds: 2F 3D 1T **Baths:** 3 En 3 Sh
ॐ 🄿 (6) ⅋ 🅅 ✕ 🗏 🆅 🕯

5 Galley Field, *Radley Road, Abingdon, Oxon, OX14 3RU.*
Detached house in quiet cul-de-sac, north of the Thames, Abingdon & A34.
Open: Easter to Oct
01235 521088 Mrs Bird
D: £16.50–£17.50 **S:** £23–£25
Beds: 2T 1S **Baths:** 2 Sh
ॐ (12) 🄿 (2) ⅋ 🅅 🗏 🕯

Peppard

SU7081 🍺 *Unicorn, Red Lion, Dog, Grouse & Claret*

Slaters Farm, *Peppard, Henley-on-Thames, Oxon, RG9 5JL.*
Quiet, friendly country house with lovely garden and tennis court.
Open: All Year (not Xmas)
Grades: ETC 3 Diamond, AA 3 Diamond
01491 628675 (also fax) Mrs Howden
D: fr £24 **S:** fr £28
Beds: 1D 2T **Baths:** 1 Pr 1 Sh
ॐ 🄿 (6) ⅋ 🅅 ✕ 🗏 🆅

Pennyford House, *Peppard, Henley-on-Thames, Oxon, RG9 5JE.*
Family home with dogs. Happy atmosphere. Nice garden. Local interests.
Open: All Year
01491 628272 (also fax)
Mrs Howden-Ferme
D: £25–£35 **S:** £30–£35
Beds: 1T 3D 1S **Baths:** 4 En 1 Pr
ॐ 🄿 (10) ⅋ 🐾 🗏 🕯

Pishill

SU7289 🍺 *The Crown*

Bank Farm, *Pishill, Henley-on-Thames, Oxon, RG9 6HJ.*
Quiet comfortable farmhouse, beautiful countryside. Convenient Oxford, London, Windsor.
Open: All Year (not Xmas)
Grades: ETC 2 Diamond
01491 638601 Mrs Lakey
bankfarm@compuserve.com
D: £23 **S:** £20–£23
Beds: 1F 1S **Baths:** 1 En 1 Sh
ॐ 🄿 (5) ⅋ 🅅 🐾 🗏 🕯

Orchard House, *Pishill, Henley-on-Thames, Oxfordshire, RG9 6HJ.*
Property in area outstanding natural Beauty surrounded by ancient Woodlands.
Open: All Year
01491 638351 (also fax)
Mrs Connolly
D: £25 **S:** £25
Beds: 2F 1D 1T **Baths:** 3 En 1 Pr
ॐ 🄿 ⅋ 🅅 🐾 ✕ 🗏 🕯

Radley

SU5298

Hollies, *8 New Road, Radley, Abingdon, Oxon, OX14 3AP.*
Rural small and friendly family B&B convenient for all attractions.
Open: All Year
01235 529552 D: £25 **S:** £25
Beds: 2T **Baths:** 1 Sh
ॐ 🄿 ⅋ 🅅 🐾 ✕ 🗏 🆅 🕯

Ramsden

SP3515 🍺 *Royal Oak*

Ann's Cottage, *Ramsden, Chipping Norton, Oxon, OX7 3AZ.*
Charming cottage with garden full of flowers. Excellent pub nearby.
Open: All Year
Grades: ETC 2 Diamond
01993 868592 Mrs Foxwood
D: fr £19 **S:** fr £19
Beds: 1T 1S **Baths:** 1 Pr
ॐ (10) 🄿 (2) ⅋ 🗏 🕯

Shenington

SP3742 🍺 *The Bell Inn*

Top Farm House, *Shenington, Banbury, Oxfordshire, OX15 6LZ.*
C18th Horton stone farmhouse set on the edge of village green.
Open: All Year (not Xmas/New Year)
Grades: ETC 3 Diamond
01295 670226 Fax: 01295 678170
m.coles2@ntlworld.com
D: £20–£25 **S:** £25–£30
Beds: 1T 2D **Baths:** 1 En 1 Sh
ॐ 🄿 (4) ⅋ 🅅 🗏 🕯

Shillingford

SU5992 🍺 *Six Bells*

Marsh House, *Court Drive, Shillingford, Wallingford, Oxon, OX10 7ER.*
Spacious house in quiet rural surroundings, next to the Thames Path and River Thames.
Open: All Year (not Xmas)
01865 858496 (also fax)
P Nickson
D: £20–£25 **S:** £20–£25
Beds: 1T 2S **Baths:** 2 En 1 Pr
ॐ (8) 🄿 (4) ⅋ 🅅 🗏 🕯

Shiplake

SU7678 🍺 *Baskerville Arms, White Hart*

The Knoll, *Crowsley Road, Shiplake, Henley-on-Thames, Oxfordshire, RG9 3JT.*
Comfortable private home beautifully restored by local craftsmen, extensive landscaped gardens.
Open: All Year (not Xmas)
0118 940 2705 (also fax)
Mr Green
milpops2@aol.com
D: £26–£27 **S:** £45
Beds: 1F 1D 1T **Baths:** 3 En
ॐ (12) 🄿 (6) ⅋ 🅅 🗏 🕯 &

Shipton-under-Wychwood

SP2717 🍺 *Red Horse, Lamb Inn, Crown Hotel*

Garden Cottage, *Fiddlers Hill, Shipton-under-Wychwood, Chipping Norton, Oxon, OX7 6DR.*
Attractive stone cottage, country views, quiet, ideal for exploring Cotswolds.
Open: All Year (not Xmas)
Grades: ETC 3 Diamond
01993 830640 C Worker
D: £15–£25 **S:** £25–£35
Beds: 1D 1T **Baths:** 2 En
ॐ (8) 🄿 (2) ⅋ 🅅 🗏 🕯

6 Courtlands Road, *Shipton-under-Wychwood, Chipping Norton, Oxon, OX7 6DF.*
Friendly, quiet, comfortable house/garden.
Open: All Year
01993 830551 Mr & Mrs Fletcher
j-jfletcher@which.net
D: £17.50–£22.50 **S:** £20–£25
Beds: 2D 1T **Baths:** 2 En 1 Pr
🄿 (3) ⅋ 🅅 🗏 🆅 🕯

Souldern

SP5231 🍺 *The Fox*

The Fox Inn, *Souldern, Bicester, Oxon, OX6 9JN.*
Stone inn, restaurant, beautiful village convenient for Oxford, Woodstock, Stratford and Warwick.
Open: All Year (not Xmas)
Grades: ETC 2 Diamond
01869 345284 Mr MacKay
Fax: 01869 345667
D: £20–£25 **S:** £28–£35
Beds: 3D 1T **Baths:** 2 En 1 Sh
ॐ 🄿 (6) 🅅 🐾 ✕ 🗏 🆅 🕯 cc

Standlake

SP3903 🍺 *The Bell*

Hawthorn Cottage, *The Downs, Standlake, Witney, Oxon, OX8 7SH.*
Elegant rooms in detached house, on edge of country village.
Open: All Year (not Xmas)
01865 300588 (also fax)
Mrs Peterson
D: £20–£22.50 **S:** £28–£38
Beds: 1D 1T **Baths:** 1 En 1 Pr
ॐ (3) 🄿 (3) ⅋ 🅅 🗏 🕯

Steventon

SU4691 🍺 *The Fox, The Cherry Tree*

Tethers End, *Abingdon Road, Steventon, Abingdon, Oxon, OX13 6RW.*
Open: All Year
01235 834015 Ms Miller
Fax: 01235 862990
peterdmiller@btinternet.com
D: £22–£25 **S:** £25–£28
Beds: 1F 1D **Baths:** 2 En
ॐ 🄿 ⅋ 🅅 🗏 🆅 🕯
Comfortable ground floor accommodation, situated on the edge of a peaceful village green. Ideally placed for visiting Oxford, Abingdon, Wantage, historic Ridgeway, Blenheim Palace and Didcot Railway Centre. Caroline and Peter Miller offer you a warm welcome.

Stratton Audley

SP6026 🍺 *Red Lion*

The Old School, Stratton Audley, Bicester, Oxon, OX6 9BJ.
Interesting C17th house in pretty village. Pleasant garden with tennis court and croquet. Guests' own drawing room. Tea and home-make cakes on arrival. Village has charming thatched pub serving excellent meals. Very comfortable beds. Everyone sleeps well - so peaceful.
Open: All Year
Grades: ETC 2 Diamond
01869 277371 Mrs Wertheimer
sawertheimer@hotmail.com
D: £25–£35 **S:** £25–£30
Beds: 3T 1S **Baths:** 2 Sh
🛏 🅿 (6) 📺 🛏 🛍 ⅏ ❀

Sutton Courtenay

SU5093 🍺 *George & Dragon, The Fish, The Swan*

Bekynton House, 7 The Green, Sutton Courtenay, Abingdon, Oxon, OX14 4AE.
Courthouse overlooking village green. Thames and 3 pubs - 5 minutes.
Open: All Year (not Xmas)
01235 848630 Ms Cornwall
Fax: 01235 848436
suecornwall@compuserve.com
D: £25–£28 **S:** £25–£28
Beds: 1D 2T 1S **Baths:** 2 Sh
🛏 🅿 (2) ⅏ 📺 🛍 ⅏ ❀

Tetsworth

SP6802 🍺 *Lion On The Green*

The Lion on the Green, 40 High Street, Tetsworth, Thame, Oxon, OX9 7AS.
Open: All Year
01844 281274 Mr Hodgkinson
D: £16.50–£20 **S:** £25–£30
Beds: 1F 2T **Baths:** 1 Sh
🛏 🅿 (20) 📺 🛏 ✕ 🛍 ⅏ cc
Privately owned country inn & restaurant right on the Oxfordshire Way. We specialise in top quality home-cooked food at affordable prices. Your pleasure is our business!

Little Acre, 4 High Street, Tetsworth, Thame, Oxon, OX9 7AT.
Open: All Year
01844 281423 (also fax) Ms Tanner
D: £18–£22.50 **S:** £25–£35
Beds: 1F 2D 2T **Baths:** 3 En 2 Sh
🛏 🅿 (5) 📺 🛍 ⅏ &
We offer a warm welcome, hearty breakfasts, comfy beds and beautiful gardens and fields to stroll in, with the dreaming spires of oxford and the Cotswolds on the doorstep, you'll never be short of activities to give your holiday a special touch.

RATES

D = Price range per person sharing in a double room

S = Price range for a single room

Thame

SP7005

Oakfield, Thame Park Road, Thame, Oxon, OX9 3PL.
Open: All Year (not Xmas)
Grades: ETC 4 Diamond
01844 213709 **D:** £20–£25 **S:** £–£27.50
Beds: 1D 2T **Baths:** 1 En 1 Sh
🛏 (8) 🅿 (6) ⅏ 📺 🛏 🛍 ⅏ &
We offer a warm welcome to our lovely farmhouse home, set in 25 acres of grounds - part of our larger 400 acre mixed farm. We have good food comfortable beds and a homely atmosphere. Out in the country, but only 10 minutes walk to town centre.

Field Farm, Rycote Lane, Thame, Oxon, OX9 2HQ.
Open: All Year (not Xmas)
Grades: ETC 3 Diamond
01844 215428 Mrs Quartly
D: £20 **S:** £25 **Beds:** 2D **Baths:** 2 En
🅿 ⅏ 📺 🛍 ⅏
Comfortable bungalow on working farm. Pretty garden, countryside views.

Tiddington

SP6504 🍺 *Fox Pub*

Albury Farm, Draycott, Tiddington, Thame, Oxon, OX9 2LX.
Peaceful open views in quiet location, clean, tidy, friendly. Close to river with private fishing. **Open:** All Year
01844 339740 (also fax) Mrs Ilbery
D: £20 **S:** £20
Beds: 1D 1T **Baths:** 1 Pr 1 Sh
🅿 (4) ⅏ 📺 ✕ 🛍 ⅏

Uffington

SU3089 🍺 *Fox & Hounds*

Norton House, Broad Street, Uffington, Faringdon, Oxon, SN7 7RA.
Friendly C18th family home in quiet, pretty village. **Open:** All Year (not Xmas)
01367 820230 (also fax) Mrs Oberman
106436.145@compuserve.com
D: £20–£21 **S:** £23–£26
Beds: 1F 1D 1S **Baths:** 2 Pr
🛏 🅿 (3) ⅏ 📺 🛏 🛍 ⅏

The Craven, Uffington, Faringdon, Oxon, SN7 7RD.
C17th thatched, beamed farmhouse/hotel. **Open:** All Year
01367 820449 Mrs Wadsworth
D: fr £20 **S:** fr £25
Beds: 1F 3D 2T 2S **Baths:** 2 Pr 2 Sh
🛏 🅿 (9) 📺 🛏 ✕ 🛍 ⅏ ❀ &

Wallingford

SU6089 🍺 *Shepherd's Hut, Six Bells, Bell, The Queens Head*

Little Gables, 166 Crowmarsh Hill, Wallingford, Oxford, OX10 8BG.
Delightfully large private house where a warm welcome awaits you. **Open:** All Year
Grades: ETC 3 Diamond
01491 837834 Mrs Reeves
Fax: 01491 834426 jill@stayingaway.com
D: £25–£35 **S:** £30–£35
Beds: 2F 2D 3T 1S **Baths:** 2 En 1 Pr
🛏 🅿 ⅏ 📺 🛍 ⅏ &

Munts Mill, Castle Lane, Wallingford, Oxfordshire, OX10 0BN.
Near town centre on edge of Chilterns - advance booking only.
Open: All Year (not Xmas)
01491 836654 Mrs Broster
S: £20–£25
Beds: 2S
⅏ 📺 🛍 ⅏

North Farm, Shillingford Hill, Wallingford, Oxon, OX10 8NB.
Quiet comfortable farmhouse on working farm, close to River Thames.
Open: All Year (not Xmas)
01865 858406 Mrs Warburton
Fax: 01865 858519
northfarm@compuserve.com
D: £24–£28 **S:** £28–£38
Beds: 2D 1T **Baths:** 1 En 2 Pr
🛏 (8) 🅿 (6) ⅏ 📺 🛍 ⅏

Wantage

SU4087

The Bell Inn, 38 Market Place, Wantage, Oxon, OX12 8AH.
C16th market town inn. Good beer and home-cooked food in warm friendly atmosphere.
Open: All Year
01235 763718 (also fax)
Mrs Williams
D: £22.50–£27.50 **S:** £20–£35
Beds: 2F 5D 4T 7S **Baths:** 11 En 2 Sh
🛏 📺 🛏 ✕ 🛍 ⅏ cc

Waterperry

SP6205

Holbeach, Worminghall Road, Waterperry, Oxford, OX33 1LF.
Private country home, good food, comfortable beds and friendly service.
Open: All Year (not Xmas)
01844 339623 **D:** £20 **S:** £20–£25
Beds: 1F 2D 1S **Baths:** 1 En 1 Pr 1 Sh
🛏 🅿 (6) 📺 🛏 ✕ 🛍 ⅏

Watlington

SU6894

Woodgate Orchard Cottage, Howe Road, Watlington, Oxon, OX9 5EL.
Open: All Year
01491 612675 (also fax)
R Roberts
mailbox@wochr.freeserve.co.uk
D: £25–£35 **S:** £30
Beds: 1F 1T 1D **Baths:** 1 En 1 Pr
🛏 🅿 (8) ⅏ 📺 🛍 ⅏
Warm welcome, countryside location, comfortable rooms, home-cooking, restful gardens, red kites gliding above. 500m off Ridgeway, convenient for Oxfordshire Way and Cycle Path, Chiltern Way, Thames Path and towns of Oxford, Henley, Reading, Windsor, Heathrow. Oxford Tube bus stop 2 miles away Lewknor - transport arrangements.

Planning a longer stay? Always ask for any special rates

Witney

SP3509 ◗ *Royal Oak, Court Inn, Lamb, Bird in Hand, Three Horse Shoes, Fleece*

Ann's Cottage, *Ramsden, Chipping Norton, Oxon, OX7 3AZ.*
Charming cottage with garden full of flowers. Excellent pub nearby.
Open: All Year
Grades: ETC 2 Diamond
01993 868592
Mrs Foxwood
D: fr £19 **S:** fr £19
Beds: 1T 1S **Baths:** 1 Pr
🛏 (10) ⓟ (2) ⌇ 📺 🏧 ⚓

The Witney Hotel, *7 Church Green, Witney, Oxon, OX8 6AZ.*
Open: All Year (not Xmas/New Year)
Grades: ETC 2 Diamond
01993 702137 Mrs McDermott
Fax: 01993 705337
D: fr £25 **S:** £30–£35
Beds: 2F 5D 2T 1S **Baths:** 10 En
🛏 📺 🏧 🍴 ⓥ ⚓ & cc
A small family-run B&B situated in a Listed building overlooking Historic Church Green and within a few minutes walk of local amenities clean and comfortable accommodation at reasonable prices.

Springhill Farm, *Cogges, Witney, Oxon, OX8 6UL.*
Open: All Year (not Xmas/New Year)
Grades: ETC 3 Diamond
01993 704919
Mrs Strainge
D: £19–£20 **S:** £20–£25
Beds: 1F 1D **Baths:** 2 En
🛏 ⓟ (4) ⌇ 📺 🏧 ⓥ ⚓
Working mixed farm situated a mile from Witney, overlooking the Windrush Valley. We offer a warm welcome in our old Cotswold stone farmhouse, with lovely views from comfortable ensuite rooms. Ideal for visiting Cogges Museum, Witney, Cotswolds, Blenheim and Oxford.

Field View, *Woodgreen, Witney, Oxon, OX8 6DE.*
Cotswold stone house set in 2 secluded acres.
Open: All Year (not Xmas/New Year)
Grades: ETC 4 Diamond Sliver Award
01993 705485 Mrs Simpson
jsimpson@netcomuk.co.uk
D: £24–£25 **S:** £30–£35
Beds: 1D 2T **Baths:** 3 En
ⓟ (6) ⌇ 📺 🏧 ⚓

Windrush House, *55 Crawley Road, Witney, Oxon, OX8 5HX.*
Comfortable home ideally situated for touring the Cotswolds and Oxford.
Open: All Year
Grades: ETC 3 Diamond
01993 774454
Mr & Mrs Curtis
Fax: 01993 709877
heraldic@compuserve.com
D: £25 **S:** £30
Beds: 1D 1T **Baths:** 2 Pr
ⓟ (6) ⌇ 📺 🏧 ⚓

Woodcote

SU6481 ◗ *Red Lion*

The Hedges, *South Stoke Road, Woodcote, Reading, Berks, RG8 0PL.*
Peaceful, rural situation, historic Area of Outstanding Natural Beauty.
Open: All Year (not Xmas)
Grades: ETC 3 Diamond
01491 680461 Mrs Howard-Allen
D: £17–£19 **S:** £17–£19
Beds: 2T 2S **Baths:** 1 Pr 1 Sh
🛏 ⓟ (4) 📺 🏧 🍴 ⚓

Woodstock

SP4416 ◗ *Woodstock Arms, Star, Boot, Barnard's Gate, Bell, Hand In Shears, Cock Inn, Kings Arms, Royal Oak, Black Prince, Sheppard Hall*

The Lawns, *2 Flemings Road, Woodstock, Oxon, OX20 1NA.*
Open: All Year
Grades: ETC 2 Diamond
01993 812599 (also fax)
Mr & Mrs Farrant
www.touristnetuk.com/wm/lawns
D: £19–£20 **S:** £25–£30
Beds: 1F 1T 1D 1S **Baths:** 1 Pr 1 Sh
🛏 ⓟ ⌇ 📺 🍴 🏧 ⚓ cc
Lovely homely accommodation. All guests welcomed as family. Attractive garden surroundings, real old English (eccentric) welcome. Just see the garden items (unusual). 5 minutes walk to town centre - probably one of the best (value for money) B+B accommodation in England. (Free car wash+laundry+gift) names in lights.

Gorselands Hall, *Boddington Lane, North Leigh, Witney, Oxon, OX8 6PU.*
Open: All Year
Grades: ETC 3 Diamond, RAC 3 Diamond
01993 882292 Mr & Mrs Hamilton
Fax: 01993 883629
hamilton@gorselandshall.com
D: £22.50–£25 **S:** £30–£35
Beds: 4D 1T 1F **Baths:** 6 En
🛏 ⓟ (6) ⌇ 📺 🍴 ✗ 🏧 ⓥ ⚓ cc
Lovely old Cotswold stone farmhouse with oak beams and flagstone floors in delightful rural setting. Large garden with tennis court. Ideal for Blenheim Palace, the Cotswolds and Oxford. Comfortable attractively furnished bedrooms with views of the garden or surrounding countryside.

Plane Tree House B&B, *48 Oxford Street, Woodstock, Oxon, OX20 1TT.*
Open: All Year (not Xmas)
01993 813075 Mrs Clark
D: £25–£35 **S:** £45–£70
Beds: 2D 1T **Baths:** 2 En 1 Pr
🛏 ⌇ 📺 🏧 ⓥ ⚓
A recently renovated Listed Cotswold stone house with exposed beams and open fires in Woodstock's historic town centre. Only minutes' walk from Blenheim Palace and excellent shops and restaurants. An ideal base for touring Oxford and The Cotswolds.

Hamilton House, *43 Hill Rise, Old Woodstock, Woodstock, Oxon, OX20 1AB.*
Open: All Year
01993 812206 (also fax)
Mrs Bradford
D: £20–£25 **S:** £30–£35
Beds: 1T 2D **Baths:** 3 En
🛏 ⓟ 📺 🏧 ⓥ ⚓ cc
Very widely acclaimed B&B. Offering unbeatable standards of cleanliness, service and hospitality. Almost every amenity available. Excellent location for beginning and ending your tour. Constantly revisited due unquestionably to the helpfulness and friendliness of Kay - your hostess.

Elbie House, *East End, North Leigh, Witney, Oxon, OX8 6PZ.*
C16th inn, located in quiet hamlet. Many special touches not to be equalled elsewhere!
Open: All Year
Grades: ETC 4 Diamond
01993 880166 Mrs Buck
buck@elbiehouse.freeserve.co.uk
D: £22.50–£25 **S:** £30–£35
Beds: 2F **Baths:** 2 En
🛏 (7) ⓟ (10) ⌇ 📺 🏧 ⓥ ⚓ 🎿 ⚓ &

Regent House, *Oxford Street, Woodstock, Oxon, OX20 1TQ.*
Large Georgian house situated in the centre of historic Wood stock.
Open: All Year
01993 811004 Mrs Gosling
D: £25–£30 **S:** £35–£45
Beds: 4D **Baths:** 4 En
🛏 ⓟ (3) ⌇ 📺 🏧 ⚓

Woolstone

SU2988 ◗ *White Horse*

Hickory House, *Woolstone, Faringdon, Oxon, SN7 7QL.*
Open: All Year (not Xmas)
01367 820303 Mr & Mrs Grist
Fax: 01367 820958
rlg@hickoryhouse.freeserve.co.uk
D: £19–£25 **S:** £21–£25
Beds: 2T **Baths:** 2 En
🛏 (12) ⓟ (2) ⌇ 📺 🏧 ⚓
Situated in a delightful picturesque village beneath the White Horse Hill near the Ridgeway, Hickory House offers comfortable accommodation in a recently built self-contained extension. Pub serving food is a minutes walk. Oxford, Bath and the Cotswolds are within easy driving distance.

Yarnton

SP4712 ◗ *Squire Bassett*

Kings Bridge Guest House, *Woodstock Road, Yarnton, Kidlington, Oxon, OX5 1PH.*
Ideally situated for Oxford and Blenheim Palace in Woodstock.
Open: All Year (not Xmas/New Year)
Grades: ETC 3 Diamond, AA 3 Diamond
01865 841748 Ms Shaw
Fax: 01865 370215
kings.bridge@talk21.com
D: £22.50–£30 **S:** £35–£50
Beds: 1F 2D 1T **Baths:** 4 En
🛏 ⓟ (6) ⌇ 📺 🏧 ⚓ cc

Rutland

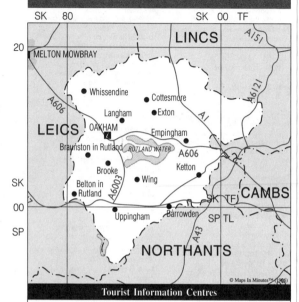

LINCS

MELTON MOWBRAY

- Whissendine
- Cottesmore
- Langham
- Exton
- OAKHAM
- Empingham
- Braunston in Rutland
- RUTLAND WATER
- A606
- Brooke
- Ketton
- Belton in Rutland
- Wing
- Uppingham
- Barrowden

LEICS

CAMBS

NORTHANTS

© Maps In Minutes™ (2005)

Tourist Information Centres

Sykes Lane, **Empingham**, Oakham, Rutland, LE15 8PX, 01780 460321 (Easter to Oct).

Oakham Library, Catmos Street, **Oakham**, Rutland, LE15 6HW, 01572 724329.

Barrowden

SK9500   Exeter Arms

Ashleigh House, 2 Wakerley Road, Barrowden, Oakham, Rutland, LE15 8EP.
Open: All Year (not Xmas/New Year)
01572 747398 Mrs Kennedy
Fax: 01572 747117
ashleighhouse@cwcom.net
D: £18.50–£25 **S:** £20–£35
Beds: 1T 2D **Baths:** 1 En 1 Pr 1 Sh
Ashleigh house is a stone built house built in 1971. It has been our home for the past 13 years. We have stunning views of the Wetland Valley and Rockingham forest. Barrowden is a beautiful Rutland village of approx 400 people

Exeter Arms, Barrowden, Oakham, Rutland, LE15 8EQ.
Open: All Year (not Xmas/New Year)
01572 747247
Mr & Mrs Blencowe
Fax: info@exeterarms.co.uk
D: £25–£35
S: £30–£35
Beds: 2T 1D
Baths: 3 En
CC
C17th village inn with C21st accommodation, overlooking Welland Valley, 10 minutes drive from Rutland Water. Food freshly-bought & cooked on daily basis. Cask-conditioned beer from our own brewery plus regularly-changing guests. Live music is a regular occurrence , & fortnightly folk-club.

31 Wakerley Road, Barrowden, Oakham, Rutland, LE15 8EP.
Rutland water, Welland Valley. Bungalow, garden, attractive conservation village.
Open: All Year (not Xmas/New Year)
01572 747455 Mr & Mrs Hennessy
D: £18–£20 **S:** £18–£28
Beds: 1F 1T 1D 1S **Baths:** 1 En 1 Sh
(8)

High House, Wakerley Road, Barrowden, Oakham, Rutland, LE15 8EP.
Small spacious country house with glorious views over the Welland Valley.
Open: All Year **01572 747354** Mrs Dawson
Fax: 01572 747194
pipdawson@aol.com
D: £19.50 **S:** £19.50
Beds: 2T 1D 1S **Baths:** 2 Pr or Sh
(6) (10)

Belton in Rutland

SK8101   Bewicke Arms, Fox Inn, Vaults, Sun Inn, Blue Ball, Noel's Arms, Salisbury Arms, Cuckoo

The Old Rectory, 4 New Road, Belton in Rutland, Oakham, Rutland, LE15 9LE.
Open: All Year **Grades:** RAC 3 Diamond
01572 717279 Mr Peach
Fax: 01572 717343
bb@stablemate.demon.co.uk
D: £16–£23 **S:** £16–£30
Beds: 2F 2D 3T 1S **Baths:** 5 En 1 Sh
(10) CC
Large country house & guest annexe in conservation village overlooking Eyebrook valley & rolling Rutland countryside. Comfortable/ varied selection of rooms, mostly ensuite,direct outside access. Real farmhouse or continental breakfast. Public house 100 yds. 10 minutes Rutland Water.

Planning a longer stay? Always ask for any special rates

College Farm, *College Farm Road, Belton in Rutland, Oakham, Rutland, LE15 9AF.*
Set in idyllic Rutland countryside. Ramblers and bird watchers paradise. 1 mile A47.
Open: All Year
01572 717440 Mrs Brown
patricia@collegefarm.freeserve.co.uk
D: £20 **S:** £20
Beds: 1T **Baths:** 1 Pr
⌂ 🅿 (4) ⊬ 📺 ⋔ 📖 ⚲

Braunston in Rutland

SK8306   🍺 *Old Plough*

Rutland Cottages, *5 Cedar Street, Braunston in Rutland, Oakham, Rutland, LE15 8QS.*
B&B with a difference! Guests have freedom of a cottage.
Open: All Year
01572 722049 John & Connie Beadman
Fax: 01572 770928
rbeadman@compuserve.com
D: £20–£25 **S:** £25–£30
Beds: 2D 2S **Baths:** 2 Pr
⌂ 🅿 (3) ⊬ 📺 📖 📺 ⚲

Brooke

SK8505   🍺 *Plough and Blue Ball*

The Old Rectory, *Brooke, Oakham, Rutland, LE15 8DE.*
Stone thatch cottage in quiet hamlet. Large garden, good walking area.
Open: All Year
01572 770558 (also fax)
Mrs Clemence
D: £20–£25 **S:** £20–£25
Beds: 1F 1T 1S **Baths:** 3 En
⌂ 🅿 (6) ⊬ ⋔ 📖 ⚲

Cottesmore

SK9013   🍺 *Sun Inn*

The Tithe Barn, *Clatterpot Lane, Cottesmore, Oakham, Rutland, LE15 7DW.*
Comfortable, spacious, ensuite rooms with a wealth of original features.
Open: All Year
Grades: ETC 3 Diamond
01572 813591 D: £18–£24 **S:** £20–£35
Beds: 2F 1D 1T **Baths:** 3 En 1 Pr
⌂ (1) 🅿 (6) ⊬ 📺 ⋔ 📖 📺 ✳ ⚲ cc

Empingham

SK9508   🍺 *White Horse*

Little Hoo, *Nook Lane, Empingham, Oakham, Rutland, LE15 8PT.*
C16th luxury cottage, 2 minutes from Rutland Water. Barn for drying clothes.
Open: All Year
01780 460293 Mr Coxhead
john@littlehoo.freeserve.co.uk
D: £22.50 **S:** £26
Beds: 1F 3T 1S **Baths:** 2 Pr
⌂ (2) 🅿 (10) ⊬ 📺 ⋔ ✕ 📖 ⚲

Exton

SK9211   🍺 *Fox & Hounds*

Fox & Hounds, *Exton, Oakham, Rutland, LE15 8AP.*
Country inn overlooking village green. 2 miles Rutland Water, half mile Bransdale Gardens.
Open: All Year (not Xmas/New Year)
Grades: ETC Listed
01572 812403 D Hillier
D: £20–£22 **S:** £22–£24
Beds: 1D 1T 1S
⌂ (8) 🅿 (20) ⋔ ✕ 📖 📺

Hall Farm, *Cottesmore Road, Exton, Oakham, Rutland, LE15 8AN.*
Close to Rutland Water and Geoff Hamiltons Barnsdale TV gardens.
Open: All Year (not Xmas)
Grades: ETC 3 Diamond
01572 812271 Mr & Mrs Williamson
D: £17.50–£22 **S:** £20–£24.50
Beds: 1F 1D 1T **Baths:** 1 En 2 Sh
⌂ 🅿 (6) ⊬ 📺 ⋔ 📖 ⚲

Ketton

SK9704   🍺 *Northwick Arms*

16 Northwick Road, *Ketton, Stamford, PE9 3SB.*
Split-level stone bungalow. Warm welcome. Between Rutland Water and Stamford.
Open: Feb to Nov
01780 721411 J Coyne
D: £16.50 **S:** £16.50
Beds: 1T 1S **Baths:** 1 Sh
🅿 (1) ⊬ 📺 📖 📺

All details shown are as supplied by B&B owners in Autumn 2000

Langham

SK8410   🍺 *Noel Angus*

Keighwood House, *The Range, Langham, Oakham, Rutland, LE15 7EB.*
Large, modern, detached house. 0.33 acre Nature gardens, picturesque village.
Open: All Year (not Xmas)
01572 755924 Mr McMorran
D: £25 **S:** £25
Beds: 1D 1T 2S **Baths:** 1 Sh
🅿 (3) ⊬ 📺 📖 ⚲

Oakham

SK8508   🍺 *Admiral Hornblower, Nicks, White Lion, Odd House, Whippen Inn*

Angel House, *20 Northgate, Oakham, Rutland, LE15 6QS.*
Unique Victorian house. Converted outbuildings. Secluded courtyard. Lounge, patio, fridge/freezer, microwave.
Open: All Year
01572 756153 Mrs Weight
D: £11–£17 **S:** £17–£24
Beds: 1D 2T **Baths:** 3 En
⌂ 🅿 📺 📺 ⚲

Uppingham

SP8699   🍺 *Vaults*

Boundary Farm B&B, *Glaston Road, Uppingham, Oakham, Rutland, LE15 9PX.*
Modern farmhouse in countryside. 5 mins easy walk into Uppingham.
Open: Easter to Dec
Grades: ETC 4 Diamond
01572 822354 (also fax) Mrs Scott
D: fr £21 **S:** fr £22
Beds: 1T 1D **Baths:** 2 En
⌂ 🅿 (3) ⊬ 📺 📖 ⚲

Wing

SK8903   🍺 *Kings Arms*

The Kings Arms Inn, *Top Street, Wing, Oakham, Rutland, LE15 8SE.*
Open: All Year
Grades: ETC 4 Diamond, AA 4 Diamond
01572 737634 Mr Hornsey
Fax: 01572 737255
enquiries@thekingsarms-wing.co.uk
D: £25–£50 **S:** £35–£70
Beds: 4F 4D 4T 8S **Baths:** All En
⌂ 🅿 (40) ⊬ 📺 ✕ 📖 📺 ✳ ⚲ cc
A 350-year-old family owned country inn. Peaceful village, plenty of character throughout. All rooms decorated and furnished to very high standard. Fresh cooked food, ideal base for walking/cycling/fishing/sailing. Rutland Water 2 miles.

Shropshire

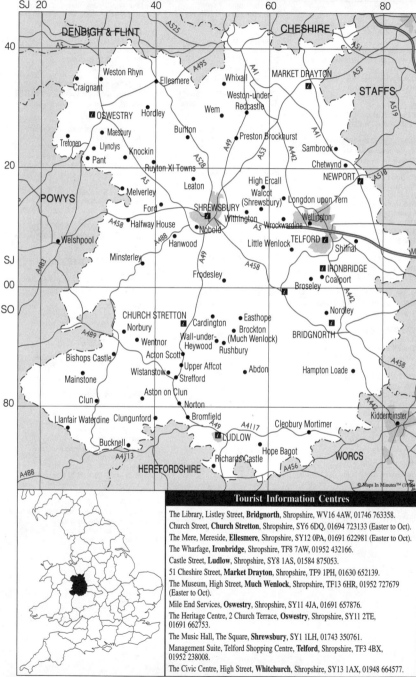

SJ 20   40   60   80

DENBIGH & FLINT

CHESHIRE

Weston Rhyn

Craignant

Ellesmere

Whixall

MARKET DRAYTON

STAFFS

Weston-under-Redcastle

OSWESTRY

Hordley

Wem

Maesbury

Burlton

Preston Brockhurst

Sambrook

Trefonen

Llynclys

Knockin

Chetwynd

Pant

Ruyton XI Towns

NEWPORT

POWYS

Melverley

Leaton

High Ercall

Ford

Walcot (Shrewsbury)

Longdon upon Tern

SHREWSBURY

Halfway House

Withington

Wellington

Welshpool

Hanwood

Nobold

Wroxwardine

TELFORD

Minsterley

Little Wenlock

Shifnal

Frodesley

IRONBRIDGE

Coalport

Broseley

CHURCH STRETTON

Easthope

Nordley

Norbury

Cardington

Brockton (Much Wenlock)

BRIDGNORTH

Wentnor

Wall-under-Heywood

Rushbury

Acton Scott

Bishops Castle

Upper Affcot

Abdon

Hampton Loade

Mainstone

Wistanstow

Strefford

Clun

Aston on Clun

Norton

Llanfair Waterdine

Clungunford

Bromfield

Cleobury Mortimer

Kidderminster

Bucknell

LUDLOW

Hope Bagot

WORCS

Richards Castle

HEREFORDSHIRE

© Maps In Minutes™ (19)

Tourist Information Centres

The Library, Listley Street, **Bridgnorth**, Shropshire, WV16 4AW, 01746 763358.

Church Street, **Church Stretton**, Shropshire, SY6 6DQ, 01694 723133 (Easter to Oct).

The Mere, Mereside, **Ellesmere**, Shropshire, SY12 0PA, 01691 622981 (Easter to Oct).

The Wharfage, **Ironbridge**, Shropshire, TF8 7AW, 01952 432166.

Castle Street, **Ludlow**, Shropshire, SY8 1AS, 01584 875053.

51 Cheshire Street, **Market Drayton**, Shropshire, TF9 1PH, 01630 652139.

The Museum, High Street, **Much Wenlock**, Shropshire, TF13 6HR, 01952 727679 (Easter to Oct).

Mile End Services, **Oswestry**, Shropshire, SY11 4JA, 01691 657876.

The Heritage Centre, 2 Church Terrace, **Oswestry**, Shropshire, SY11 2TE, 01691 662753.

The Music Hall, The Square, **Shrewsbury**, SY1 1LH, 01743 350761.

Management Suite, Telford Shopping Centre, **Telford**, Shropshire, TF3 4BX, 01952 238008.

The Civic Centre, High Street, **Whitchurch**, Shropshire, SY13 1AX, 01948 664577.

Abdon

SO5786   ◗ *Boyne Arms*

Earnstrey Hill House, *Abdon, Craven Arms, Shropshire, SY7 9HU.*
Open: All Year (not Xmas)
Grades: ETC 4 Diamond
01746 712579 Mrs Scurfield
Fax: 01746 712631
D: £25 **S:** fr £20
Beds: 1D 2T **Baths:** 1 En 2 Sh
🛇 🄿 ⅍ ✕ 🏢 ♨
Comfortable, warm, spacious family house 1200 ft up Brown Clee Hill. Superb views westwards towards Long Mynd and Wales. We keep horses, sheep, dogs, free-range hens on our 11 acres. Wonderful walking and riding. Experienced walking hosts will help plan/guide.

Spring Cottage, *Cockshutford Road, Abdon, Craven Arms, Shropshire, SY7 9HU.*
Magnificent hillside location, stunning views, relaxing friendly atmosphere, near Shropshire Way.
Open: All Year (not Xmas)
01746 712551 Mrs Langham
Fax: 01746 712001
D: £20–£27.50 **S:** £23–£30
Beds: 1D 1T 1S **Baths:** 2 En 1 Pr
🛇 (8) 🄿 (6) ⅍ 🖵 🐾 ✕ 🏢 Ⓥ ♨

Acton Scott

SO4589   ◗ *Station Inn*

Acton Scott Farm, *Acton Scott, Church Stretton, Shropshire, SY6 6QN.*
Lovely C17th old house in peaceful hamlet, good walking area.
Open: Feb to Oct
01694 781260 Mrs Jones
D: £19–£22 **S:** £20–£40
Beds: 1F 1D 1T **Baths:** 2 En 1 Pr
🛇 🄿 (6) ⅍ 🖵 🐾 🏢 Ⓥ ♨

Aston on Clun

SO3881   ◗ *Engine & Tender*

Millstream Cottage, *Aston on Clun, Craven Arms, Shropshire, SY7 8EP.*
Open: All Year **Grades:** ETC 3 Diamond
01588 660699 Miss Reeves
D: £22–£24 **S:** £22–£24
Beds: 1D 1T **Baths:** 1 Sh
🛇 🄿 (2) 🖵 🐾 🏢 Ⓥ ♨
A warm welcome awaits you in an attractive Grade II Listed cottage with six acres of private fields and woodland. Comfortable beds and good breakfast. An Area of Outstanding Natural Beauty, noted for walking, cycling and birdwatching.

Bishop's Castle

SO3288   ◗ *Castle Hotel, Boar's Head, Six Bells, Three Tuns*

Lower Broughton Farm, *Bishop's Castle, Shropshire, SY15 6SZ.*
Originally a medieval hall house, now a spacious and comfortable farmhouse.
Open: Feb to Dec
01588 638393 Mr & Mrs Bason
D: £17–£20 **S:** £20–£25
Beds: 2D 1T **Baths:** 1 En 1 Sh
🛇 🄿 (6) ⅍ 🖵 🐾 🏢 ♨

Bridgnorth

SO7193   ◗ *Shakespeare, Down Inn, Pheasant, Punch Bowl, Falcon Hotel, Parlors Hall Hotel, Poacher's Pocket*

Wyndene Guest House, *57 Innage Lane, Bridgnorth, Shropshire, WV16 4HS.*
Near to Severn Valley Railway, Ironbridge and Much Wenlock.
Open: All Year
Grades: AA 2 Diamond
01746 764369 Mrs Morse
wyndene@bridgnorth2000.freeserve.co.uk
D: £20–£22 **S:** £20–£21
Beds: 1D 1T 2S **Baths:** 1 En 1 Sh
🛇 🄿 (3) ⅍ 🖵 ✕ 🏢 Ⓥ ♨

Severn Hall, *Stanley Lane, Bridgnorth, Shropshire, WV16 4SR.*
Lovely half-timbered farmhouse on banks of the River Severn.
Open: All Year (not Xmas)
Grades: ETC 4 Diamond
01746 763241 Mrs Woolrich
D: £18–£30 **S:** £18–£25
Beds: 1D 1T **Baths:** 1 En 1 Pr
🛇 🄿 (6) ⅍ 🏢 ♨

The Golden Lion, *83 High Street, Bridgnorth, Shropshire, WV16 4DS.*
Fully licensed C17th inn on Bridgnorth's historic High Street, by the Northgate.
Open: All Year
01746 762016 (also fax)
Mr Watkins
D: £17.50–£21 **S:** £21.50–£27.50
Beds: 4F **Baths:** 1 En 2 Sh
🛇 🄿 (15) 🖵 🐾 ✕ 🏢 ♨

Brockton (Much Wenlock)

SO5793   ◗ *The Feathers*

Old Quarry Cottage, *Brockton, Much Wenlock, Shropshire, TF13 6JR.*
Lovely stone cottage set in the countryside. Close to Ironbridge, Wenlock Edge and Ludlow.
Open: All Year (not Xmas/New Year)
Grades: ETC 4 Diamond
01746 785596 Mrs Thorpe
nan@brockton.fsbusiness.co.uk
D: £20–£21 **S:** £30
Beds: 1T 1D **Baths:** 2 En
🄿 (2) ⅍ 🖵 🏢 Ⓥ ♨

Bromfield

SO4776   ◗ *The Cookhouse*

Bromfield Manor, *Bromfield, Ludlow, Shropshire, SY8 2JU.*
Stone-built Grade II Listed former rectory in one acre of gardens with delightful views.
Open: All Year (not Xmas)
01584 856536 (also fax)
C Mason
john.mason9@virgin.net
D: £25–£35 **S:** £35–£50
Beds: 1D 1T **Baths:** 2 Pr
🛇 (12) 🄿 (10) ⅍ 🖵 🏢 Ⓥ ♨

Planning a longer stay? Always ask for any special rates

Broseley

SJ6701   ◗ *The Lion, The Pheasant, Brewery Inn*

Lord Hill Guest House, *Duke Street, Broseley, Shropshire, TF12 5LU.*
Former public house, easy access to Ironbridge, Telford and museums.
Open: All Year
01952 884270 Mr McNally
D: £16–£20 **S:** £16–£20
Beds: 7F 1D 1T 2S **Baths:** 1 En 3 Pr 3 Sh
🛇 (6) 🄿 (9) 🖵 🐾 🏢 Ⓥ ♿

Bucknell

SO3573   ◗ *Baron Of Beef*

The Hall, *Bucknell, Shropshire, SY7 0AA.*
Explore the English/Welsh Borders. Escape life's hectic pace, relax into the friendly atmosphere.
Open: Mar to Nov
01547 530249 (also fax)
Mrs Price
D: £20–£22 **S:** £20–£22
Beds: 2D 1T **Baths:** 1 En 1 Sh
🛇 (7) 🄿 (4) ⅍ 🖵 ✕ 🏢 ♨

Burlton

SJ4526   ◗ *Burlton Inn*

The Grove, *Burlton, Shrewsbury, SY4 5SZ.*
Open: All Year
01939 270310 Mrs Martin
D: £17–£19 **S:** £20
Beds: 1T 1D **Baths:** 2 En 2 Pr
🛇 🄿 (4) ⅍ 🖵 🏢 ♨
Tucked away in Brother Cadfael country nine miles north of Shrewsbury. Imposing 'foursquare' sandstone farmhouse. Three-quarter acre grounds, handsome 'Vine wall' folly. Handy for Ironbridge, Powis Castle, Ellesmere College, Adcotes, PGL, Sleap Aerodrome and Sansaw Heath, fabulous breakfast.

Cardington

SO5095   ◗ *Royal Oak*

Grove Farm, *Cardington, Church Stretton, Shropshire, SY6 7JZ.*
Central to many places of interest, good home cooking. Recommended.
Open: All Year
Grades: ETC 2 Diamond
01694 771451 Mrs Pennington
D: £16–£18 **S:** £18–£20
Beds: 1F 1T **Baths:** 1 Sh
🛇 (10) 🄿 ⅍ 🖵 🐾

Chetwynd

SJ7321   ◗ *The Swan, The Lamb*

Lane End Farm, *Chester Road, Chetwynd, Newport, Shropshire, TF10 8BN.*
Friendly farmhouse in wonderful countryside. Large comfortable rooms. Delicious breakfasts.
Open: All Year
Grades: ETC 4 Diamond, Sliver
01952 550337 (also fax)
Mrs Park
D: £20 **S:** £25
Beds: 2D 1T **Baths:** 2 Pr 1 Sh
🛇 🄿 (5) 🖵 🐾 ✕ 🏢 Ⓥ ✿ ♨

Church Stretton

SO4593 🍺 *Plough Inn, Station Inn, Old Cobbler's*

Belvedere Guest House, Burway Road, Church Stretton, Shropshire, SY6 6DP.
Open: All Year (not Xmas)
Grades: ETC 4 Diamond, AA 4 Diamond, RAC 4 Diamond
01694 722232 (also fax)
Mr Rogers
belv@bigfoot.com
D: £25–£27 **S:** £25–£30
Beds: 3F 4D 2T 3S **Baths:** 6 En 3 Sh
🛏 🅿 (8) 🔟 📺 🍴 ✕ 🛋 ▦ 🗓 ⚓ **cc**
Beautiful rural surroundings, on the edge of 6,000 acres of National Trust hill country.

Gilberries Farm Cottage, Wall-under-Heywood, Church Stretton, Shropshire, SY6 7HZ.
Open: Easter to Nov
Grades: ETC 4 Diamond
01694 771400
Mrs Griffiths
Fax: 01694 771663
D: £19–£21 **S:** £22–£24
Beds: 1D 1T **Baths:** 1 En 1 Pr
🛏 (3) 🅿 (10) 🔟 ▦ 🗓 ⚓
Quoted as 'an oasis' - a haven of peace and tranquillity with views of the famous Wenlock Edge. Picturesque countryside, ideal for walking. A warm welcome awaits. Farmhouse breakfasts and rooms with views.

Old Rectory House, Burway Road, Church Stretton, Shropshire, SY6 6DW.
Georgian former Rectory. Lovely garden and view. Convenient Town/Hills.
Open: All Year
Grades: ETC 3 Diamond
01694 724462 Mr Smith
Fax: 01694 724799
D: £18–£25 **S:** £18–£25
Beds: 2D 1T **Baths:** 1 En 1 Sh
🛏 🅿 (4) 🔟 ✕ ▦ 🗓 ⚓

Highcliffe, Madeira Walk, Church Stretton, Shropshire, SY6 6JQ.
Panoramic views. Hills, town centre and station 10 minutes walk.
Open: All Year (not Xmas/New Year)
Grades: ETC 2 Diamond
01694 722908 Mr & Mrs Wren
D: £17 **S:** £17
Beds: 1F 1D 1S **Baths:** 1 Sh
🛏 ⅍ 🔟 ✕ 🗓 ⚓

Cleobury Mortimer

SO6775 🍺 *Sun & Slipper, Crown, Fountain*

Woodview, Mawley Oak, Cleobury Mortimer, Kidderminster, Shropshire, DY14 9BA.
Villa-style country residence in five acres, with indoor heated swimming pool.
Open: All Year
Grades: ETC 4 Diamond
01299 271422
Mrs Hale
D: £25
Beds: 1T 1D **Baths:** 2 En
🅿 (2) ⅍ 🔟 ⚓

2 Clematis Cottages, Hopton Bank, Cleobury Mortimer, Kidderminster, Worcs, DY14 0HF.
On slopes of Clee Hills between Ludlow and Cleobury Mortimer.
Open: All Year
01584 890807 (also fax)
Mrs Crowhurst
alaneadc@aol.com
D: £15–£18 **S:** £15–£18
Beds: 1F 2S **Baths:** 1 En
🛏 🅿 (2) 🔟 📺 ⚓ ♿

Clun

SO3080 🍺 *Sun Inn, White Horse, Castle Hotel, Three Tuns, Bishop's Castle*

The Old Stables And Saddlery, Crown House, Church Street, Clun, Craven Arms, Shropshire, SY7 8JW.
Superb self-contained Georgian stable conversion in lovely courtyard garden.
Open: All Year (not Xmas)
Grades: ETC 4 Diamond
01588 640780 Mrs Bailey & Mr R Maund
D: £20–£22.50 **S:** £22–£25
Beds: 1D 1T 1S **Baths:** 1 En 1 Pr 1 Sh
🛏 (8) 🅿 (2) ⅍ 🔟 ⅍ ▦ 🗓 ⚓

Llanhedric Farm, Clun, Craven Arms, Shropshire, SY7 8NG.
Tranquil country retreat - rooms overlooking beautiful views of Clun Valley.
Open: Easter to Nov
01588 640203 (also fax)
Mrs Jones
D: £18–£20 **S:** £18–£21
Beds: 1F 1D 1T **Baths:** 1 En 1 Sh
🛏 🅿 (5) ⅍ 🔟 ✕ ▦ 🗓 ⚓

Clun Farm, High Street, Clun, Craven Arms, Shropshire, SY7 8JB.
C16th double cruck character farmhouse in the heart of the village.
Open: All Year (not Xmas)
01588 640432 Mr & Mrs Whitfield
D: £18–£20 **S:** fr £18
Beds: 1F 1T 2S **Baths:** 1 En 1 Sh
🛏 🅿 (6) 🔟 ▦ 🗓

Clungunford

SO3978 🍺 *Engine & Tender*

North Barn, Abcott Manor, Clungunford, Craven Arms, Shropshire, SY7 0PX.
Perfect setting in South Shropshire hills - ideal walking, touring centre.
Open: All Year (not Xmas)
01588 660596 Mrs Mattison
D: £16.50–£17 **S:** £17.50–£18
Beds: 1D 2S **Baths:** 1 Pr
🛏 (6) 🅿 (4) ⅍ 🔟 ⅍ ✕ ▦ 🗓

Knock Hundred Cottage, Abcott, Clungunford, Craven Arms, Shropshire, SY7 0PX.
C16th Knock Hundred Cottage is situated in the scenic Clun Valley.
Open: All Year
01588 660594 (also fax)
Mrs Prytz
D: £22.50 **S:** £25
Beds: 1D 1T **Baths:** 1 En 1 Pr
🛏 (14) 🅿 (2) ⅍ 🔟 ✕ ▦ 🗓

Coalport

SJ6902 🍺 *Horse & Jockey*

Thorpe House, Coalport, Telford, Shropshire, TF8 7HP.
Riverside country house in beautiful Ironbridge Gorge, close to museums.
Open: All Year **Grades:** ETC 3 Diamond
01952 586789 (also fax) Mr Richards
D: £18–£22 **S:** £18–£30
Beds: 1F 2D 1S **Baths:** 2 En 1 Sh
🛏 🅿 (6) 🔟 ⅍ 🛋 ▦ 🗓 ⚓

Craignant

SJ2535 🍺 *Green inn*

The Quarry, Craignant, Selattyn, Oswestry, Shropshire, SY11 4LT.
Attractive farmhouse.
Open: Easter to October
01691 658674 Mrs Tomley
D: £16 **S:** £16
Beds: 1D 2S 3F **Baths:** 1 Sh
🛏 🅿 🔟 🔟 ⅍ ✕ ▦ 🗓 ⚓

Easthope

SO5695 🍺 *Wenlock Edge Inn, Longvine Arms*

Madam's Hill, Hill Top, Easthope, Much Wenlock, Shropshire, TF13 6DJ.
Once two weavers' cottages, Madams Hill nestles into Wenlock Edge, a designated AONB.
Open: All Year (not Xmas)
01746 785269 (also fax)
Mr & Mrs Bushell
D: £19–£20 **S:** £20–£22
Beds: 1D 1T **Baths:** 1 Sh
🛏 🅿 (2) ⅍ ⅍ 🛋 ▦ 🗓 ⚓

Ellesmere

SJ3934 🍺 *Black Lion, Trotting Mare, Queen's Head*

Mereside Farm, Ellesmere, Shropshire, SY12 0PA.
Open: All Year (not Xmas)
Grades: ETC 4 Diamond, Silver
01691 622404 (also fax)
Mrs Stokes
nicky@mereside.free-online.co.uk
D: £20 **S:** £20–£25
Beds: 1D 1T **Baths:** 1 En 1 Pr
🛏 🅿 (7) ⅍ 🔟 ⅍ 🛋 ▦ 🗓 ⚓
Happy friendly Atmosphere in C18th farmhouse situated between The Mere (lake) and canal. Delicious Aga breakfasts with renowned Home Made sausages. Comfy beds, beautiful garden, sitting room with log fire, many gardens/NT properties in the area. Enjoyed by all that stay.

The Grange, Grange Road, Ellesmere, Shropshire, SY12 9DE.
Peaceful Georgian country house in ten acres. Characterful and spacious.
Open: All Year (not Xmas)
Grades: ETC 3 Diamond
01691 623495 Mrs Ward-Allen
Fax: 01691 623227
rosie@thegrange.uk.com
D: £27.50–£30 **S:** £23–£29
Beds: 1F 4D 7T 4S **Baths:** 13 En 2 Sh
🛏 🅿 (15) ⅍ 🔟 ⚓ ♿

Hordley Hall, Hordley, Ellesmere,
Shropshire, SY12 9BB.
Large Georgian house, peaceful relaxed
atmosphere, overlooking gardens and
countryside.
Open: All Year
01691 622772 Mrs Rodenhurst
D: £20–£25 **S:** £20–£25
Beds: 2D 1T 1S **Baths:** 2 En 1 Sh
🛇 🅿 (6) ⅛ 🅢 🛏 ✕ 🎟 🔻 🖵 ♨

Ford

SJ4113 ◀ The Crossgates

Cardeston Park Farm, Ford,
Shrewsbury, Shropshire, SY5 9NH.
Large farm house set in peaceful
countryside close to Welsh border.
Open: All Year (not Xmas)
Grades: ETC 3 Diamond
01743 884265 (also fax)
Mrs Edwards
D: £17.50–£35 **S:** £17.50–£35
Beds: 2D 1T **Baths:** 2 En 1 Pr
🅿 (4) 🛏 🎟 ♿ cc

Frodesley

SJ5101 ◀ The Pound

Meadowlands, Lodge Lane, Frodesley,
Dorrington, Shrewsbury, Shropshire, SY5
7HD.
Open: All Year
Grades: ETC 3 Diamond
01694 731350 (also fax)
Ron & Jennie Repath
D: £18–£20 **S:** £20–£25
Beds: 2D 1T **Baths:** 2 En 1 Pr
🛇 🅿 (4) ⅛ 🅢 ✕ 🎟 🔻 🖵 ♨
Comfortable modern house set in eight
acres of accessible gardens, woodland
and paddocks. Quiet location in delightful
hamlet with panoramic views of Stretton
Hills. Large residents lounge, silent fridge
in guest rooms, brochure available, maps
and guides for loan.

Halfway House

SJ3411 ◀ Yockleton Arms, Halfway House

Brambleberry, Halfway House,
Shrewsbury, Shropshire, SY5 9DD.
Tastefully furnished house, lovely garden,
rooms overlooking beautiful Shropshire
countryside.
Open: All Year (not Xmas)
Grades: ETC 4 Diamond
01743 884762 Mrs Astbury
D: £15–£25 **S:** £17–£25
Beds: 1D 1T 1S **Baths:** 1 Sh
🛇 (8) 🅿 (6) ⅛ 🅢 ✕ 🎟 🔻 🖵 ♨

Hampton Loade

SO7486 ◀ King's Arms, Bull's Head

Hampton House, Hampton Loade,
Chelmarsh, Bridgnorth, Shropshire, WV16
6BN.
Intriguing C16th farmhouse with
inglenook fireplaces and a wealth of
beautiful oak beams.
Open: All Year
01746 861436 Ms Yeomans
D: £19.50–£20.50 **S:** £26–£27
Beds: 1T 2D **Baths:** 1 En 2 Pr
🅿 (6) ⅛ 🖵 ♨

Hanwood

SJ4409 ◀ Red Lion

The White House, Hanwood,
Shrewsbury, SY5 8LP.
C16th home with beautiful gardens and
river. Near Powis Castle, Ironbridge,
Chirk. **Open:** All Year
01743 860414 (also fax) Mrs Mitchell
mgm@whitehousehanwood.freeserve.co.
uk
D: £25–£30 **S:** £28–£45
Beds: 4D 1T 1S **Baths:** 3 En 1 Sh
🛇 (12) 🅿 (10) ⅛ 🅢 ✕ 🎟 🖵 ♨

High Ercall

SJ5917 ◀ Cleveland Arms, The Bulls Head

The Mill House, Shrewsbury Road,
High Ercall, Telford, Shropshire, TF6 6BE.
Grade II converted watermill on working
small holding and family home.
Open: All Year (not Xmas/New Year)
Grades: ETC 4 Diamond
01952 770394 Mrs Yates
mill-house@talk21.com
D: £15–£20 **S:** £25–£30
Beds: 1F 1D **Baths:** 1 Pr 1 Sh
🛇 🅿 (4) ⅛ 🎟 🛏 🖵 ♨

Hope Bagot

SO5874 ◀ Penny Black

Croft Cottage, Cumberley Lane, Hope
Bagot, Ludlow, Shropshire, SY8 3LJ.
Peace and quiet - brook, gardens,
badgers, honey, dogs and ducks!
Open: All Year (not Xmas)
Grades: ETC 3 Diamond
01584 890664 (also fax)
Mrs Hatchell
croft.cottage@virgin.net
D: £20–£21 **S:** £20–£23
Beds: 1D 1T **Baths:** 1 En 1 Pr
🛇 🅿 (4) ⅛ 🅢 🛏 ✕ 🎟 🔻 🖵 ♨ ♿

Hordley

SJ3830 ◀ Queen's Head

Hordley Hall, Hordley, Ellesmere,
Shropshire, SY12 9BB.
Large Georgian house, peaceful relaxed
atmosphere, overlooking gardens and
countryside.
Open: All Year
01691 622772 Mrs Rodenhurst
D: £20–£25 **S:** £20–£25
Beds: 2D 1T 1S **Baths:** 2 En 1 Sh
🛇 🅿 (6) ⅛ 🅢 🛏 ✕ 🎟 🔻 🖵 ♨

Ironbridge

SJ6703 ◀ Malthouse, Meadow Inn, Horse &
Jockey, Old Vaults, Moat House

Post Office House, 6 The Square,
Ironbridge, Telford, Shropshire, TF8 7AQ.
Comfortable C18th house overlooking
Iron Bridge. Central for museums.
Open: All Year
Grades: ETC 3 Diamond
01952 433201 Mrs Jones
Fax: 01952 433582
hunter@pohouse-ironbridge.fsnet.co.uk
D: £19–£22 **S:** £29–£34
Beds: 1F/T 2D **Baths:** 1 En 1 Sh
🛇 🅿 (2) 🎟 🛏 🎟 🔻 🖵 ♨

The Library House, 11 Severn Bank,
Ironbridge, Telford, Shropshire, TF8 7AN.
Grade II Listed building situated in a
quiet and pretty backwater.
Open: All Year (not Xmas)
01952 432299 Mr Maddocks
Fax: 01952 433967
libhouse@enta.net
D: £25–£27.50 **S:** £45
Beds: 1F 3D 1T 4S **Baths:** 3 En
🛇 (10) 🅿 ⅛ 🅢 🛏 🎟 🔻 🖵 ♨

Knockin

SJ3222 ◀ Bradford Arms

Top Farm House, Knockin, Oswestry,
Shropshire, SY10 8HN.
Open: All Year **Grades:** ETC 4 Diamond,
Silver Award, AA 4 Diamond
01691 682582 P Morrissey
Fax: 01691 682070
p.a.m@knockin.freeserve.co.uk
D: £22.50–£25 **S:** £27.50–£30
Beds: 1F 1T 1D **Baths:** 3 En
🛇 (12) 🅿 (6) 🅢 🛏 🎟 🖵 ♨
Lovely half timbered 16th century house
in attractive village. Comfortable and
pretty ensuite bedrooms. Large guest
drawing room with beams, grand piano
and log fires in winter. Dining room over
looking garden, hearty breakfasts,
friendly house, great atmosphere. Good
pub food in walking distance.

Leaton

SJ4618 ◀ The Boreatton Arms

The Old Vicarage, Leaton, Shrewsbury,
Shropshire, SY4 3AP.
Set in acres of grounds in beautiful open
countryside 4 miles from medieval
Shrewsbury. **Open:** All Year
Grades: ETC 4 Diamond
01939 290989 (also fax) Ms Mansell Jones
m-j@oldvicleaton.freeserve.co.uk
D: £20 **S:** £25
Beds: 1T 1D **Baths:** 2 En
🅿 (6) ⅛ 🅢 🎟 🖵 ♨

Little Wenlock

SJ6406 ◀ Huntsman Inn, Coalbrookdale Inn

Wenboro Cottage, Church Lane, Little
Wenlock, Telford, Shrops, TF6 5BB.
Pretty cottage set in peaceful village near
Ironbridge and Telford centre.
Open: All Year (not Xmas)
Grades: ETC 3 Diamond
01952 505573 Mrs Carter
rcarter@wenboro.freeserve.co.uk
D: £20–£22.50
Beds: 1D 1T **Baths:** 1 En 1 Pr
🛇 🅿 (2) 🎟 🖵 ♨

Llanfair Waterdine

SO2476 ◀ Lloyney Inn, Red Lion

The Mill, Lloyney, Llanfair Waterdine,
Knighton, Powys, LD7 1RG.
Wonderful countryside in the Teme Valley,
home cooking.
Open: All Year (not Xmas/New Year)
Grades: ETC 2 Star
01547 528049 (also fax) Mr & Mrs Davies
D: £20 **S:** £20
Beds: 2D 2T 1S **Baths:** 1 En 2 Pr 2 Sh
🛇 🅿 (6) ⅛ 🅢 🛏 ✕ 🎟 🔻 🖵 ♨ ♿ 2

Llynclys

SJ2823   🍺 *Lime Kiln*

Bridge House, Llynclys, Oswestry, SY10 8AE.
Lovely rooms. Beautiful views. Superb breakfasts. Comfort, quality and value.
Open: All Year (not Xmas/New Year)
Grades: ETC 4 Diamond
01691 830496 (also fax) Mr & Mrs Taylor
jenny@llynclys.freeserve.co.uk
D: £18.50–£22 **S:** £20–£25
Beds: 1T 1D **Baths:** 2 En
🛇 (5) 🅿 (4) ⊬ 📺 🕇 🛗 🖳 ♨

Longdon upon Tern

SJ6215   🍺 *Bucks Head*

Red House Farm, Longdon upon Tern, Wellington, Telford, Shropshire, TF6 6LE.
Open: All Year
01952 770245 Mrs Jones
rhf@virtual-shropshire.co.uk
D: £18–£25 **S:** £20–£25
Beds: 1F 1T 1D 1S **Baths:** 2 En 1 Sh
🛇 🅿 (4) 📺 🕇 🖳 ♨ ♨
Red House Farm is a late Victorian farmhouse with comfortable well furnished rooms. TV and drinks tray. Excellent breakfasts. Longdon-on-Tern is central for Shrewsbury, Telford, Ironbridge. Ideal for business or pleasure. Families welcome, 'home comforts with personal attention'.

Ludlow

SO5174   🍺 *Unicorn Inn, Charlton Arms, The Cookhouse, Church Inn*

Henwick House, Gravel Hill, Ludlow, Shropshire, SY8 1QU.
Open: Apr to Dec
Grades: ETC 3 Diamond
01584 873338 Mrs Cecil-Jones
D: £20 **S:** £18
Beds: 1D 2T 1S **Baths:** 2 En
🛇 🅿 (3) ⊬ 📺 🕇 🛗 ♨
Warm, comfortable Georgian coach house. Friendly, informal atmosphere, good traditional English breakfast. En suite Bedrooms, comfortable beds, TV, tea/coffee facilities and much more. Easy walking distances from town centre and local inns.

Bull Hotel, Bull Ring, Ludlow, Shropshire, SY8 1AD.
Centrally located inn with private parking, very comfortable guest rooms.
Open: All Year **Grades:** ETC 3 Diamond
01584 873611 Mr & Mrs Maile
Fax: 01584 873666
D: £22.50 **S:** £30
Beds: 1F 2D 1T **Baths:** 4 En
🛇 🅿 (6) 📺 🕇 🛗 ♨ cc

Hen & Chickens Guest House, 103 Old Street, Ludlow, Shropshire, SY8 1NU.
Characterful building, convenient location, near castle, interesting shops, excellent restaurants.
Open: All Year (not Xmas)
Grades: ETC 3 Diamond
01584 874318 Mrs Ross
sally@hen-and-chickens.co.uk
D: £20–£25 **S:** £20–£30
Beds: 2D 1T 2S **Baths:** 2 Sh 1 En
🛇 🅿 (6) ⊬ 📺 🕇 🛗 ♨ cc

Maesbury

SJ3026   🍺 *Navigation Inn, Queen's Head, Sweeny Hall*

Ashfield Farmhouse, Maesbury, Oswestry, Shrops, SY10 8JH.
Old roses and scarlet creepers ramble this C16th Border coach/farmhouse. A5 1 m.
Open: All Year
Grades: ETC 4 Diamond, Silver Award
01691 653589 (also fax)
Mrs Jones
D: £20–£25 **S:** £25–£30
Beds: 1F 1T 1D **Baths:** 2 En 1 Pr
🛇 🅿 (8) 📺 🕇 🛗 🖳 ♨

Mainstone

SO2787   🍺 *Sun Inn, White Horse, Castle Hotel, Three Tuns, Bishop's Castle*

New House Farm, Mainstone, Clun, Craven Arms, Shropshire, SY7 8NJ.
Peaceful, isolated C18th farmhouse, set high in Clun Hills near Welsh border.
Open: Easter to Oct
01588 638314 Mrs Ellison
D: £24–£25 **S:** £25–£28
Beds: 1F 1T **Baths:** 1 En 1 Pr
🅿 (6) ⊬ 📺 🕇 🛗 ♨

Market Drayton

SJ6734   🍺 *Stafford Court Hotel*

80 Rowan Road, Market Drayton, Shropshire, TF9 1RR.
Peaceful, hospitable. Home form home. Short walk to town centre.
Open: All Year (not Xmas/New Year)
Grades: ETC 4 Diamond
01630 655484 (also fax)
Mrs Russell
D: £19–£21 **S:** £20–£22
Beds: 1T **Baths:** 1 Pr
🅿 (1) ⊬ 📺 ✕ 🛗 ♨

Melverley

SJ3316   🍺 *Tontine Inn, Stables Inn*

Church House, Melverley, Oswestry, Shropshire, SY10 8PJ.
Beautiful setting next to River Vyrnwy by historic Melverley church.
Open: All Year (not Xmas)
Grades: ETC 3 Diamond
01691 682754 Mr & Mrs Sprackling
melverley@aol.com
D: £17–£20 **S:** fr £20
Beds: 1F 1D 1T **Baths:** 2 Pr
🛇 🅿 (3) ⊬ 📺 🕇 🛗 🖳

Minsterley

SJ3705

Cricklewood Cottage, Plox Green, Minsterley, Shrewsbury, Shropshire, SY5 0HT.
Delightful C18th country cottage, beautiful garden and tempting breakfast menu.
Open: All Year (not Xmas)
01743 791229 Mr & Mrs Costello
D: £22.50–£25 **S:** £22.50–£37.50
Beds: 2D 1T **Baths:** 3 En
🛇 (8) 🅿 (4) ⊬ 📺 🛗 ♨

Newport

SJ7418   🍺 *Swan, Lamb, Falcon*

Lane End Farm, Chester Road, Chetwynd, Newport, Shropshire, TF10 8BN.
Friendly farmhouse in wonderful countryside. Large comfortable rooms. Delicious breakfasts.
Open: All Year
Grades: ETC 4 Diamond, Silver
01952 550337 (also fax)
Mrs Park
D: £20 **S:** £25
Beds: 2D 1T **Baths:** 2 Pr 1 Sh
🛇 🅿 (5) 📺 🕇 ✕ 🛗 🖳 ♨ ♨

Sambrook Manor, Sambrook, Newport, Shropshire, TF10 8AL.
200-acre mixed farm. Old manor farmhouse built in 1702. Beautiful gardens.
Open: All Year (not Xmas)
Grades: ETC 3 Diamond
01952 550256 Mrs Mitchell
D: £18–£20 **S:** £18–£20
Beds: 2F 1D 1T **Baths:** 3 En 1 Sh
🛇 🅿 (5) ⊬ 📺 ✕ 🛗 ♨

Nobold

SJ4710   🍺 *Cygnets, New Inn*

The Day House, Nobold, Shrewsbury, Shropshire, SY5 8NL.
Delightful period farmhouse, extensive gardens, abundant wildlife, easy access Shrewsbury.
Open: All Year (not Xmas/New Year)
Grades: ETC 4 Diamond
01743 860212 (also fax)
Mrs Roberts
D: £23–£26 **S:** £25–£27
Beds: 1F 1T 1D **Baths:** 3 En
🛇 🅿 ⊬ 📺 🕇 🛗 🖳 ♨

Norbury

SO3592   🍺 *Sun Inn*

Suttocks Wood, Norbury, Bishops Castle, Shropshire, SY9 5EA.
Scandinavian house in a woodland setting near Long Mynd and Stiperstones.
Open: All Year
Grades: ETC 4 Diamond
01588 650433 Mrs Williams
Fax: 01588 650492
shuttockswood@barclays.net
D: £23–£26 **S:** £25–£28
Beds: 1D 2T **Baths:** 3 En
🛇 (12) 🅿 (8) ⊬ 📺 ✕ 🛗 🖳 ♨ cc

Nordley

SO6996   🍺 *Pheasant*

The Albynes, Nordley, Bridgnorth, Shropshire, WV16 4SX.
Beautiful country house peacefully set in Parkland. Guest rooms overlook gardens.
Open: All Year (not Xmas/New Year)
Grades: ETC 5 Diamond Sliver Award
01746 762261 Mrs Woolley
D: £20–£25 **S:** £25–£30
Beds: 1D 1T 1S **Baths:** 2 En 1 Pr
🛇 (5) 🅿 (10) ⊬ 📺 🛗 🖳 ♨

Norton (Craven Arms)

SO4581   🍴 *The Cookhouse*

The Firs, Norton, Craven Arms, Shropshire, SY7 9LS.
Open: All Year **Grades:** ETC 4 Diamond
01588 672511 (also fax)
Mrs Bebbington
thefirs@go2.co.uk
D: £20–£25 **S:** £20–£25
Beds: 1F 2D **Baths:** 2 En 1 Pr
🛇 🅿 (5) ⅍ 🖵 🛏 🎟, Ⅴ ♨
Victorian stone farmhouse standing in large garden with ample parking, magnificent views in Area of Outstanding Natural Beauty. Walking distance of Stokesay Castle, 6 miles to historic Ludlow, with its abundance of Michelin star restaurants. Horse and pony stabling available.

Oswestry

SJ2929   🍴 *Bradford Arms, Bear Hotel, Navigation Inn, Queen's Head, Sweeny Hall, Wynnstay Hotel*

Ashfield Farmhouse, Maesbury, Oswestry, Shrops, SY10 8JH.
Old roses and scarlet creepers ramble this C16th Border coach/farmhouse. A5 1m.
Open: All Year
Grades: ETC 4 Diamond, Silver Award
01691 653589 (also fax)
Mrs Jones
D: £20–£25 **S:** £25–£30
Beds: 1F 1T 1D **Baths:** 2 En 1 Pr
🛇 🅿 (8) 🖵 🛏 🎟, Ⅴ ♨

Ash Court, Weston Lane, Oswestry, Shropshire, SY11 2BB.
Beautiful C18th house with country style bedrooms overlooking Gardens and countryside.
Open: All Year
Grades: ETC 4 Diamond
01691 662921 J Edwards
edwards.ashcourt@virgin.net
D: £18–£20 **S:** £20–£23
Beds: 1T 1D **Baths:** 1 Sh
🛇 🅿 (2) ⅍ 🖵 🎟, Ⅴ ♨

Montrose, Weston Lane, Oswestry, Shropshire, SY11 2BG.
Comfortable Victorian house, easy walk into town. Good touring centre.
Open: All Year
Grades: ETC 2 Diamond
01691 652063 Mrs Leggatt
D: £15 **S:** £15–£18
Beds: 2T **Baths:** 1 Sh
🛇 🅿 (4) ⅍ 🖵 🎟, Ⅴ ♨

Pant

SJ2722

Three Firs, Pant, Oswestry, Shropshire, SY10 8LB.
Quiet homely countryside accommodation adjoining golf course, Welsh/English border.
Open: All Year
Grades: ETC 3 Diamond
01691 831375 three.firs@lineone.net
D: £18–£25 **S:** £18–£25
Beds: 2F 1D **Baths:** 2 En 1 Sh
🛇 🅿 (6) 🖵 🛏 🗙 🎟, Ⅴ ❋ ♨

Richards Castle

SO4969   🍴 *The Boot*

Longlands, Woodhouse Lane, Richards Castle, Ludlow, Shropshire, SY8 4EU.
Farmhouse in lovely rural landscape. Near historic Ludlow, Welsh Marches.
Open: Jan to Dec
01584 831636 Mrs Kemsley
D: £20–£22 **S:** £25
Beds: 1D 1T **Baths:** 1 En 1 Pr
🛇 🅿 (4) ⅍ 🖵 🛏 🗙 🎟, Ⅴ ♨

Rushbury

SO5191   🍴 *The Plough, Longville Arms, The Royal Oak*

The Coates, Rushbury, Church Stretton, Shropshire, SY6 7DZ.
C15th family farmhouse with tennis court, in beautiful peaceful countryside.
Open: February to November
Grades: ETC 2 Diamond
01694 771330 (also fax)
Mrs Madeley
D: £19–£22 **S:** £22–£25
Beds: 2T **Baths:** 1 En 1 Sh
🛇 🅿 (4) ⅍ 🛏 Ⅴ ♨

Ruyton-XI-Towns

SJ3922   🍴 *Talbot Inn*

Brownhill House, Brownhill, Ruyton-XI-Towns, Shrewsbury, SY4 1LR.
Old world standards, modern facilities and relaxed atmosphere in historic village.
Open: All Year
Grades: AA 3 Diamond
01939 261121 Yoland & Roger Brown
Fax: 01939 260626
brownhill@eleventowns.co.uk
D: £16.50–£22 **S:** £20–£25
Beds: 1D 1T 1S **Baths:** 3 En
🛇 🅿 (5) 🖵 🗙 🎟, Ⅴ ♨ cc

Sambrook

SJ7024   🍴 *Falcon Inn*

Sambrook Manor, Sambrook, Newport, Shropshire, TF10 8AL.
200-acre mixed farm. Old manor farmhouse built in 1702. Beautiful gardens.
Open: All Year (not Xmas)
Grades: ETC 3 Diamond
01952 550256 Mrs Mitchell
D: £18–£20 **S:** £18–£20
Beds: 2F 1D 1T **Baths:** 3 En 1 Sh
🛇 🅿 (5) ⅍ 🗙 🎟, ♨

Shifnal

SJ7407   🍴 *Old Bell*

Tree Tops, The Hem, Shifnal, Shropshire, TF11 9PS.
C18th cottage with friendly atmosphere, near Ironbridge, Cosford, Weston Park.
Open: All Year
01952 460566 Mrs Bell
julia@treetops.enta.net
D: fr £18 **S:** fr £20
Beds: 1D 1T 1S **Baths:** 1 Pr 1 Sh
🛇 (9) 🅿 (3) ⅍ 🖵 🛏 🎟, Ⅴ

Shrewsbury

SJ4912   🍴 *Talbot Inn, Boathouse Inn, Armory, Abbey Hotel, Dun Cow Inn, Lea Cross Inn, Bull, Three Fishes, Crown, New Inn, Cornhouse, Red Lion, Red Barn, Traitors' Gate, Old Bell, Severn Apprentice*

Brownhill House, Brownhill, Ruyton-XI-Towns, Shrewsbury, SY4 1LR.
Open: All Year
Grades: AA 3 Diamond
01939 261121 Yoland & Roger Brown
Fax: 01939 260626
brownhill@eleventowns.co.uk
D: £16.50–£22 **S:** £20–£25
Beds: 1D 1T 1S **Baths:** 3 En
🛇 🅿 (5) 🖵 🗙 🎟, Ⅴ ♨ cc
Old world standards, modern facilities and relaxed atmosphere in the historic village of Ruyton XI Towns. Unique 2 acre garden with beautiful views. Easy access - Ironbridge to Snowdonia, Chester to Ludlow. Good food using local/home grown produce. Local pubs in walking distance.

The Bancroft , 17 Coton Crescent, Shrewsbury, Shropshire, SY1 2NY.
Within easy walking distance of town centre and railway station.
Open: All Year (not Xmas)
Grades: ETC 3 Diamond
01743 231746 (also fax)
Mrs Oldham-Malcolm
bancroft01@aol.com
D: £16–£19 **S:** £18–£22
Beds: 1D 1T 2S **Baths:** 2 Sh
🛇 🅿 (4) ⅍ 🖵 🎟, Ⅴ ♨ cc

2 Lythwood Hall, Bayston Hill, Shrewsbury, Shropshire, SY3 0AD.
Quality accommodation in a comfortable spacious Georgian house.
Open: All Year
Grades: ETC 3 Diamond, AA 3 Diamond
07074 874747 Mr & Mrs Bottomley
Fax: 07074 874747
D: £20 **S:** £20
Beds: 1D 1T **Baths:** 1 Pr 1 Sh
🛇 🅿 (2) ⅍ 🖵 🗙 🎟, Ⅴ ♨

Castlecote Guest House, 77 Monkmoor Road, Shrewsbury, Shropshire, SY2 5AT.
Family-run, comfortable Victorian house, close to all amenities.
Open: All Year (not Xmas)
Grades: ETC 3 Diamond
01743 245473 Mrs Tench
D: £17.50–£22 **S:** £17.50–£22
Beds: 2F 4D 2T **Baths:** 1 En 2 Sh
🛇 🅿 (4) 🖵 🎟, Ⅴ ♨

The Stiperstones, 18 Coton Crescent, Coton Hill, Shrewsbury, SY1 2NZ.
Very comfortable, quality accommodation. High standard of cleanliness. Extensive facilities.
Open: All Year
Grades: ETC 3 Diamond, AA 3 Diamond
01743 246720 Mrs MacLeod
Fax: 01743 350303
stiperston@aol.com
D: £18.50–£20 **S:** £22.50
Beds: 1F 2D 1T 1S **Baths:** 4 Sh
🛇 🅿 (6) ⅍ 🖵 🎟, Ⅴ ♨

Avonlea, 33 Coton Crescent, Coton Hill, Shrewsbury, Shropshire, SY1 2NZ.
Open: Jan to Mid Dec
01743 359398 Mrs O'Keefe
D: £17–£19 **S:** £18–£20
Beds: 2T 1S **Baths:** 1 En 1 Sh
⊜ (11) 📺 🛍 Ⅴ ♨
Comfortable, attractive Edwardian town house. Ten minute walk from town centre, Railway, Bus stations, records and research library. Shrewsbury Castle, 'Brother Cadfael' trail. Town centre attractions of historical Shrewsbury. Quarry park, Dingle Agric show ground. Venue for flower show.

Meole Brace Hall, Meole Brace , Shrewsbury, Shropshire, SY3 9HF.
Beautiful house set in 3 acres yet close to town.
Open: All Year (not Xmas/New Year)
Grades: ETC 5 Diamond, Silver
01743 235566 Mrs Hathaway
Fax: 01743 236886
enquiries@meolebracehall.co.uk
D: £24.50–£28 **S:** £39–£46
Beds: 1T 2D **Baths:** 2 En 1 Pr
⊜ (12) 🅿 (12) ⚡ 📺 🛏 ✕ 🛍 Ⅴ ♨

Trevellion House, 1 Bradford Street, Shrewsbury, Shropshire, SY2 5DP.
Comfortable Victorian family-run guest house, Shrewsbury's attractions within easy walking distance.
Open: All Year **Grades:** ETC 3 Diamond
01743 249582 Ms Taplin
Fax: 01743 232096
marktaplin@
bradfordstreet.junglelink.co.uk
D: £17–£20 **S:** £17–£20
Beds: 2T 1D **Baths:** 1 Pr 1 Sh
⊜ 📺 🛏 🛍 Ⅴ ♨

Glynndene Park Terrace, Abbey Foregate, Shrewsbury, Shropshire, SY2 6BL.
A beautiful Victorian house opposite abbey and walking distance of town.
Open: All Year
01743 352488 (also fax) Mrs Arnold
D: £18–£20
Beds: 1D 2T **Baths:** 1 Sh
⊜ (9) ⚡ 📺 🛍 Ⅴ ♨

Berwyn House, 14 Holywell Street, Abbey Foregate, Shrewsbury, Shropshire, SY2 5DB.
A Victorian town house sited on the original C11th abbey courtyard, 8 minutes' walk from the centre of Shrewsbury, it is ideal if you are looking to discover traditional England from a 'home from home' guest house atmosphere. **Open:** All Year (not Xmas)
Grades: AA 2 Diamond
01743 354858 Mrs Simpson
Fax: 07970 502321
berwynguesthouse@amsl.freeserve.co.uk
D: £20–£26 **S:** £20–£28
Beds: 1F 1D 1T 1S **Baths:** 1 Sh
⊜ (1) 🅿 (1) ⚡ 📺 🛍 Ⅴ ♨

National Grid References are for villages, towns and cities – not for individual houses

Anton House, 1 Canon Street, Monkmoor, Shrewsbury, Shropshire, SY2 5HG.
Luxurious comfortable Victorian house, 10 minute stroll from town centre.
Open: All Year (not Xmas)
Grades: ETC 4 Diamond
01743 359275 Mrs Herbert
Fax: 01743 270168
antonhouse@supanet.com
D: £20 **S:** £25
Beds: 1F 1D 1T **Baths:** 2 Sh
⊜ (5) 🅿 (3) ⚡ 📺 🛍 ♨

Abbey Court House, 134 Abbey Foregate, Shrewsbury, Shropshire, SY2 6AU.
Abbey Court house situated close to many places of historical interest.
Open: All Year (not Xmas/New Year)
Grades: ETC 3 Diamond
01743 364416 Mrs Turnock
Fax: 01743 358559
D: £19–£23 **S:** £20–£30
Beds: 1F 3D 4T 2S **Baths:** 4 En 2 Sh
⊜ (10) 🅿 (10) 📺 Ⅴ ♨

Merevale House, 66 Ellesmere Road, Shrewsbury, SY1 2QP.
Lovely Victorian house, 10 minutes' walk to Shrewsbury railway and bus stations.
Open: All Year (not Xmas)
01743 243677 Mrs Spooner
D: £17 **S:** fr £16
Beds: 3D **Baths:** 1 Sh
⊜ 🅿 (3) 📺 🛍 ♨

Restawhile, 36 Coton Crescent, Shrewsbury, SY1 2NZ.
A warm welcome awaits you. Cosy rooms & good food.
Open: All Year
01743 240969 Mr & Mrs Cox
Fax: 01743 231841
Restawhile@breathemail.net
D: £18–£21 **S:** £25–£30
Beds: 2D 1T **Baths:** 3 En
🅿 (5) 📺 🛍 ♨

Strefford

SO4385 🚃 Plough Inn

Strefford Hall, Strefford, Craven Arms, Shropshire, SY7 8DE.
Spacious farmhouse in peaceful setting with panoramic views of Wenlock Edge.
Open: All Year (not Xmas)
01588 672383 Mrs Morgan
Fax: 01588 673855
D: £20–£21 **S:** £21–£28
Beds: 2D 1T **Baths:** 3 En
⊜ 🅿 (3) ⚡ 📺 ✕ 🛍 Ⅴ ♨

Telford

SJ6909 🚃 Coalbrookdale Inn, Red Lion, Swan, Buck's Head, Priors' Lodge, Station, Plough, Huntsman Inn

Wenboro Cottage, Church Lane, Little Wenlock, Telford, Shrops, TF6 5BB.
Pretty cottage set in peaceful village near Ironbridge and Telford centre.
Open: All Year (not Xmas)
Grades: ETC 3 Diamond
01952 505573 Mrs Carter
rcarter@wenboro.freeserve.co.uk
D: £20–£22.50
Beds: 1D 1T **Baths:** 1 En 1 Pr
⊜ 🅿 (2) 📺 🛍 ♨

Stone House, Shifnal Road, Priorslee, Telford, Shropshire, TF2 9NN.
A warm, friendly guest house with a large walled garden.
Open: All Year
Grades: ETC 4 Diamond
01952 290119 (also fax)
Mrs Silcock
dave@
stonehouseguesthouse.freeserve.co.uk
D: £20–£21 **S:** £26–£27
Beds: 1F 2D 2T **Baths:** 5 En
⊜ 🅿 (4) ⚡ 📺 ✕ 🛍 Ⅴ ♨

Trefonen

SJ2526

The Pentre, Trefonen, Oswestry, Shropshire, SY10 9EE.
Rural bliss, 16th century farmhouse, stunning views, dinner specialities.
Open: All Year (not Xmas/New Year)
Grades: AA 4 Diamond
01691 653952 Mr Gilbert
thepentre@micro-plus-web.net
D: £21 **S:** £29
Beds: 2F **Baths:** 2 En
⊜ 🅿 (10) ⚡ 🛏 ✕ 🛍 Ⅴ ✿ ♨

Upper Affcot

SO4486 🚃 Traveller's Rest

Travellers Rest Inn, Upper Affcot, Church Stretton, Shropshire, SY6 6RL.
Traditional inn with good food, real ale, good company.
Open: All Year (not Xmas)
Grades: ETC 3 Diamond, RAC 3 Diamond
01694 781275 Mr Allison
Fax: 01694 781555
reception@travellersrestinn.co.uk
D: £25 **S:** £30
Beds: 5D 2T 1S **Baths:** 8 En
⊜ 🅿 (30) 📺 🛏 ✕ 🛍 Ⅴ ♨ cc

Walcot (Shrewsbury)

SJ5911 🚃 Alscott Inn

Alscott Inn, Walcot, Wellington, Telford, Shropshire, TF6 5EQ.
Friendly, family run country inn. Home cooking, Beer garden.
Open: All Year (not Xmas/New Year)
Grades: ETC 2 Diamond
01952 248484 Ms Young
alscottinn@yahoo.co.uk
D: £16–£20 **S:** £20–£25
Beds: 2D 2T **Baths:** 2 En 1 Sh
⊜ 🅿 (40) 📺 🛏 ✕ 🛍 Ⅴ cc

Wall-under-Heywood

SO5192 🚃 Plough Inn

Gilberries Farm Cottage, Wall-under-Heywood, Church Stretton, Shropshire, SY6 7HZ.
Quoted as 'an oasis' - a haven of peace and tranquillity.
Open: Easter to Nov
Grades: ETC 4 Diamond
01694 771400 Mrs Griffiths
Fax: 01694 771663
D: £19–£21 **S:** £22–£24
Beds: 1D 1T **Baths:** 1 En 1 Pr
⊜ (3) 🅿 (10) 📺 🛍 Ⅴ ♨

Wellington

SJ6411   *Red Lion, Swan, Buck's Head, Cock*

The Paddock, *Arelston Manor, Arleston Lane, Wellington, Telford, Shropshire, TF1 2LT.*
Peaceful, individual, detached, modern but cottage-style house on the outskirts of Wellington.
Open: All Year (not Xmas)
01952 243311 (also fax)
Mrs Hanley
D: £28–£35 **S:** £26–£30
Beds: 2D 2S **Baths:** 2 En 1 Sh
ॐ ⊬ 🖵 ✕ 🎟 . 🖵 . ♨

Wem

SJ5129   *Raven, Bull & Dog, Old Post Office, Dicken Arms*

Forncet, *Soulton Road, Wem, Shrewsbury, Shropshire, SY4 5HR.*
Open: All Year (not Xmas)
Grades: ETC 2 Diamond
01939 232996 Mr & Mrs James
D: £17.50 **S:** £17.50
Beds: 1F 1T 1S **Baths:** 2 Sh
ॐ 🅿 (6) ⊬ 🖵 ✕ 🎟 . 🖵 . ♨
Forncet is a spacious Victorian house with attractively furnished rooms and a large well maintained garden. Enjoy good home cooking, the billiard room provides entertainment for the evenings and a large selection of videos and board games is also available.

Lowe Hall Farm, *The Lowe, Wem, Shrewsbury, Shropshire, SY4 5UE.*
Historically famous C16th farmhouse. Antique furnishings. Highest standard of accommodation gauranteed.
Open: All Year
01939 232236 Mrs Jones
bandb@lowehallfarm.demon.co.uk
D: £20 **S:** £22
Beds: 1F 1D 1T **Baths:** 2 En 1 Pr
ॐ 🅿 (6) ⊬ 🎟 . 🖵 . ♨

Wentnor

SO3892   *The Crown, Inn On The Green*

The Green Farm, *Wentnor, Bishops Castle, Shropshire, SY9 5EF.*
Situated in picturesque South Shropshire hills between Long Mynd and Stiperstones.
Open: All Year
01588 650394
Mrs Clements
D: £23–£24 **S:** £30
Beds: 1D **Baths:** 1 En
ॐ (9) 🅿 (3) ⊬ 🎟 . 🖵 . ♨

Weston Rhyn

SJ2835   *The Plough*

Rhoswiel Lodge, *Weston Rhyn, Oswestry, Shropshire, SY10 7TG.*
Victorian country house pleasantly situated beside Shropshire Union/Llangollen Canal.
Open: All Year (not Xmas)
01691 777609
Mrs Plunkett
Fax: 01691 774952
D: £16–£17.50 **S:** £18–£22
Beds: 1D 1T **Baths:** 1 En 1 Pr
ॐ 🅿 (2) ⊬ 🎟 . 🖵 . ♨

Weston-under-Redcastle

SJ5628   *Bear Inn*

Windmill Cottage Guest House,
Weston-under-Redcastle, Shrewsbury, Shropshire, SY4 5UX.
Next to Hawkstone golf follies. Ideal walkers, golfers, countryside lovers.
Open: Feb to Dec
Grades: ETC 3 Diamond
01939 200219 (also fax)
Mr & Mrs Trasatti
glt@windmillcottage.co.uk
D: fr £20 **S:** fr £30
Beds: 4T **Baths:** 4 En
ॐ (9) 🅿 (8) ⊬ 🎟 . 🖵 . ♨ &

Whitchurch

SJ5441   *Bull Dog*

Stoneleigh, *16 Sedgeford, Whitchurch, Shropshire, SY13 1EX.*
Home from home, comfortable beds, good breakfast, beautiful garden.
Open: All Year (not Xmas)
01948 664618
Mrs Gibson
D: £15 **S:** £15
Beds: 1D 1T 1S **Baths:** 2 Sh
ॐ 🅿 (3) 🎟 . ♨

Roden View, *Dobson's Bridge , Whixall, Whitchurch, Shropshire, SY13 2QL.*
Make yourselves at home and enjoy the comfort of our C17th country cottage.
Open: Feb to Dec
Grades: ETC 4 Diamond, Silver, RAC 4 Diamond, Sparkling
01948 710320 (also fax)
J James
D: £18 **S:** £18
Beds: 1D/F 1D 2T **Baths:** 4 En
ॐ 🅿 (8) 🎟 ✕ . 🖵 . ♨

Whixall

SJ5134

Roden View, *Dobson's Bridge , Whixall, Whitchurch, Shropshire, SY13 2QL.*
Make yourselves at home and enjoy the comfort of our C17th country cottage.
Open: Feb to Dec
Grades: ETC 4 Diamond, Silver Award RAC 4 Diamond, Sparkling Diamond
01948 710320 (also fax) J James
D: £18 **S:** £18
Beds: 1D/F 1D 2T **Baths:** 4 En
ॐ 🅿 (8) 🎟 ✕ . 🖵 . ♨

Wistanstow

SO4285   *Station Inn*

Leacroft, *Leamoor Common, Wistanstow, Craven Arms, Shropshire, SY7 8DN.*
Beautiful country home, between Wenlock Edge and the Long Mynd.
Open: All Year
01694 781556 (also fax) Mr & Mrs Maddock
sue@maddock.enta.net
D: £20–£22.50 **S:** £22.50–£25
Beds: 1T 1D **Baths:** 1 En 1 Pr
🅿 ⊬ 🎟 🛏 . ♨

Withington

SJ5712   *Corbet Arms, The Plough*

Garden Cottage, *Withington, Shrewsbury, Shropshire, SY4 4QA.*
Open: All Year (not Xmas)
Grades: ETC 3 Diamond
01743 709511 (also fax) Mrs Hopper
silvia.hopper@garden-cottage.fsnet.co.uk
D: £20–£22 **S:** £19–£30
Beds: 1D 1T 1S **Baths:** 1 En 1 Sh
ॐ 🅿 (6) ⊬ 🎟 . 🖵 . ♨
Delightful Grade II Listed country house of great charm and character, in quiet village setting, providing extra comfort. central for Shrewsbury, Attingham Park, Ironbridge, Wroxeter Roman city, plus many more attractions. Welcoming, friendly hosts. Discount short breaks. Snooker table. Brochure.

Wrockwardine

SJ6211   *The Plough*

Church Farm, *Wrockwardine, Wellington, Telford, Shropshire, TF6 5DG.*
Down a lime-tree avenue lies our superb situated C18th village farmhouse.
Open: All Year
01952 244917 (also fax) Mrs Savage
savage@churchfarm.freeserve.co.uk
D: £20–£26 **S:** £25–£36
Beds: 3D 3T **Baths:** 3 Pr 1 Sh
ॐ (5) 🅿 (20) 🎟 🛏 ✕ . 🖵 . ♨

Somerset

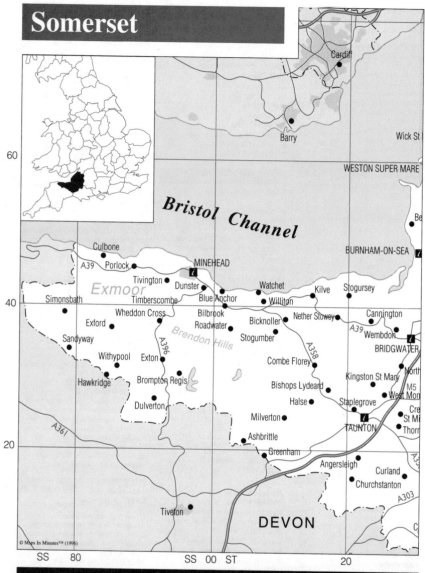

Tourist Information Centres

Somerset Visitor Centre, M5 South, Sedgemoor Services, **Axbridge**, Somerset, BS26 2UF, 01934 750833 (Easter to Oct).

Abbey Chambers, Abbey Church Yard, **Bath**, N E Somerset, BA1 1LY, 01225 477101.

Town Hall, High Street, **Bridgwater**, Somerset, TA6 3ES, 01278 427652 (Easter to Oct).

St Nicholas Church, St Nicholas Street, **Bristol**, BS1 1UE, 0117 926 0767.

Bristol Airport, North Somerset, BS19 3DY, 01275 474444.

South Esplanade, **Burnham-on-Sea**, Somerset, TA8 1BB, 01278 787852.

The Guildhall, Fore Street, **Chard**, Somerset, TA20 1PP, 01460 67463.

The Gorge, **Cheddar**, Somerset, BS27 3QE, 01934 744071 (Easter to Oct).

The Round Tower, Justice Lane, **Frome**, Somerset, BA11 1BB, 01373 467271.

The Tribunal, 9 High Street, **Glastonbury**, Somerset, BA6 9JJ, 01458 832954 (Easter to Oct).

Old Town Hall, **Midsomer Norton**, Bath, N E Somerset, BA3 2UG, 01761 412221.

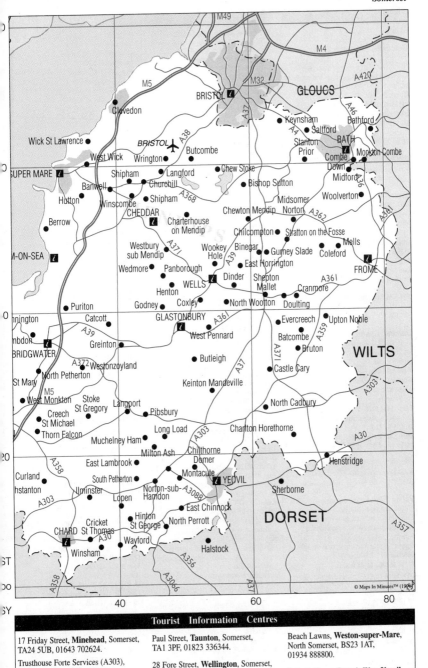

Tourist Information Centres

17 Friday Street, **Minehead**, Somerset, TA24 5UB, 01643 702624.

Trusthouse Forte Services (A303), **Podimore**, Yeovil, Somerset, BA22 8JG, 01935 841302 (Easter to Oct).

Gordano Services (M5 J19), **Portbury**, Bristol, BS20 9AX, 01275 375516.

Paul Street, **Taunton**, Somerset, TA1 3PF, 01823 336344.

28 Fore Street, **Wellington**, Somerset, TA21 8AQ, 01823 664747 (Easter to Oct).

Town Hall, Market Place, **Wells**, Somerset, BA5 2RB, 01749 672552.

Beach Lawns, **Weston-super-Mare**, North Somerset, BS23 1AT, 01934 888800.

Petter's House, Petter's Way, **Yeovil**, Somerset, BA20 1SH, 01935 471279.

Angersleigh

ST1918

Gatchells, *Angersleigh, Taunton, Somerset, TA3 7SY.*
Beautiful C15th thatched cottage with lovely gardens in a glorious and secluded setting.
Open: All Year
01823 421580 Mandy Watts
gatchells@somerweb.co.uk
D: £19–£23 **S:** £27
Beds: 1F 1D 1T **Baths:** 2 En 1 Pr
⌂ �ℙ Ⅳ ⋔ ✕ ☐ cc

Ashbrittle

ST0521   ⚐ *Globe Inn*

Lower Westcott Farm, *Ashbrittle, Wellington, Somerset, TA21 0HZ.*
Devon/ Somerset borders family farm, ideal Moors/ Coasts. Picturesque countryside.
Open: All Year (not Xmas)
01398 361296 Mrs Heard
D: £18–£20 **S:** £18–£20
Beds: 1F 1T **Baths:** 1 En 1 Pr
⌂ ℙ (4) ⅙ Ⅳ ✕ ☐ Ⅴ ⚑

Banwell

ST3959

Banwell Castle, *Banwell, Weston-super-Mare, Somerset, BS29 6NX.*
Victorian castle, outstanding views, still a family home.
Open: All Year
Grades: ETC 3 Diamond
01934 822263
Mr Parsons
Fax: 01934 823946
BanwellCastle@supanet.com
D: £25 **S:** £25
Beds: 4D **Baths:** 4 En
⌂ ℙ (40) Ⅳ ⋔ ☐ Ⅴ ⚑ cc

Batcombe

ST6837   ⚐ *Old Red Lion, Three Horseshoes*

Valley View Farm, *Batcombe, Shepton Mallet, Somerset, BA4 6AJ.*
Bungalow residence, extensive gardens, secluded, overlooking a picturesque valley.
Open: All Year (not Xmas/New Year)
Grades: ETC 3 Diamond
01749 850302 (also fax)
Mrs Mead
D: £20 **S:** £22
Beds: 1T 1D **Baths:** 1 En 1 Sh
⌂ ℙ ⅙ Ⅳ ⋔ ☐ Ⅴ ⚑

Batcombe Vale, *Batcombe, Shepton Mallet, Somerset, BA4 6BW.*
Own secluded valley of lakes and wild gardens. Wells-Longleat.
Open: Mar to Nov
01749 830246 (also fax)
Mrs Sage
donaldsage@compuserve.com
D: £18–£20 **S:** £20–£22
Beds: 1F 1T 1D
⌂ ℙ (6) ⅙ Ⅳ ⋔ ☐ ⚑

Bath

ST7464   ⚐ *Royal Oak, Dolphin, Wheelwrights Arms, Old Crown, Huntsman, George, Devonshire Arms, Sportsman, Waldergrave Arms, Bear, Park Tavern, Rose & Crown, Weston Walk, Boathouse, Lambridge Harvester, Green Park Station, Saracen's Head, Hop Pole*

Bailbrook Lodge, *35-37 London Road West, Bath, BA1 7HZ.*
Open: All Year
Grades: ETC 3 Diamond, AA 3 Diamond
01225 859090 Mrs Sexton
Fax: 01225 852299
hotel@bailbrooklodge.demon.co.uk
D: £30–£40 **S:** £39–£50
Beds: 4F 4D 4T **Baths:** 12 En
⌂ ℙ (14) ⅙ Ⅳ ✕ ☐ Ⅴ ⚑ cc
A warm welcome is assured at Bailbrook Lodge, an imposing Georgian House set in its own gardens. The elegant period bedrooms (some four posters) offer ensuite facilities, TV and hospitality trays. Private parking. 1.5 miles from Bath centre. Close to M4.

Sarnia, *19 Combe Park, Weston, Bath, BA1 3NR.*
Open: All Year (not Xmas/New Year)
Grades: AA 4 Diamond
01225 424159 Mr & Mrs Fradley
Fax: 01225 337689
D: £25–£32.50 **S:** £30–£40
Beds: 1F 1D 1T **Baths:** 2 En 1 Pr
⌂ ℙ (3) ⅙ Ⅳ ☐ Ⅴ ⚑ cc
Superb bed & breakfast in large Victorian home, easy reach of town centre. Spacious bedrooms, private facilities, newly decorated, attractively furnished. Breakfast in sunny dining room, English, Continental and vegetarian menus, home made jams, marmalades, comfortable lounge, secluded garden, private parking & children welcome.

The Manor House, *Monkton Combe, Bath, BA2 7HD.*
Open: All Year
Grades: ETC 3 Diamond
01225 723128 Mrs Hartley
Fax: 01225 722972
beth@manorhousebath.co.uk
D: £22.50–£35 **S:** £30–£35
Beds: 2F 5D 1T **Baths:** 8 En
⌂ ℙ (12) Ⅳ ⋔ ✕ ☐ Ⅴ ⚑ & 2
Restful rambling medieval manor by millstream in Area of Outstanding Natural Beauty. 2.50 miles from city. Occupied since 1262, the manor has spacious ensuite rooms with four-posters and suites. Breakfast 'til noon, champagne breakfast in bed. A 'British Ancient Monument'.

Koryu B&B, *7 Pulteney Gardens, Bath, Somerset, BA2 4HG.*
Open: All Year
01225 337642 (also fax) Mrs Shimizu
D: £22–£25 **S:** £22–£25
Beds: 1F 2D 2T 2S **Baths:** 5 En 2 Sh
⌂ ℙ (2) ⅙ Ⅳ ✕ ☐ ⚑
Completely renovated Victorian home run by a young Japanese lady, extremely clean, delicious breakfasts with wide menu, beautiful linens; a bright, cheerful and welcoming house. Abbey and Roman baths 5 mins, gorgeous Kennet and Avon canal 2 mins.

Wentworth House Hotel, *106 Bloomfield Road, Bath, BA2 2AP.*
Open: All Year **Grades:** AA 2 Star, RAC 4 Diamond Sparkling
01225 339193 Mrs Boyle
Fax: 01225 310460
stay@wentworthhouse.co.uk
D: £25–£47.50 **S:** £40–£60
Beds: 2F 12D 2T 2S **Baths:** 17 En 1 Pr
⌂ ⅙ ℙ (20) Ⅳ ✕ ☐ Ⅴ ⚑ cc
A Victorian mansion 15 minutes' walk from the city. Quiet location with large garden and car park. Heated swimming pool, licensed restaurant and cocktail bar. Golf and walks nearby. Lovely rooms, some with four-poster beds and conservatories.

Marlborough House, *1 Marlborough Lane, Bath, BA1 2NQ.*
Open: All Year
Grades: ETC 4 Diamond, AA 4 Diamond
01225 318175 L Dunlop
Fax: 01225 466127
mars@manque.dircon.co.uk
D: £32.50–£47.50 **S:** £45–£75
Beds: 2F 1T 3D 1S **Baths:** 7 En
⌂ ℙ ⅙ Ⅳ ⋔ ✕ ☐ Ⅴ ⚹ ⚑ cc
An enchanting Victorian small hotel in the heart of Georgian Bath, exquisitely furnished, but run in a friendly and informal style. Specialising in organic vegetarian world cuisine. Our central location, gorgeous rooms, and unique menu make Marlborough House truly special.

Cranleigh, *159 Newbridge Hill, Bath, Somerset, BA1 3PX.*
Open: All Year (not Xmas)
Grades: AA 4 Diamond
01225 310197 Mr Poole
Fax: 01225 423143
cranleigh@btinternet
D: £33–£40 **S:** £45–£55
Beds: 3F 2T 4D **Baths:** 8 En
⌂ (5) ℙ (5) ⅙ Ⅳ ☐ ⚑ cc
Charming Victorian house a short distance from the city centre. Spacious bedrooms, most with country views, offer comfort and quality. Imaginative breakfasts served in elegant dining room include fresh fruit salad and scrambled eggs with smoked salmon.

Dene Villa, *5 Newbridge Hill, Bath, BA1 3PW.*
Victorian family-run guest house, a warm welcome is assured. **Open:** All Year
01225 427676 Mrs Surry
Fax: 01225 482684
denevilla@yahoo.co.uk
D: £20–£22.50 **S:** £19–£22
Beds: 1F 1D 1T 1S **Baths:** 3 En
⌂ (3) ℙ (4) Ⅳ ☐ Ⅴ ⚑

Blairgowrie House, *55 Wellsway, Bath, BA2 4RT.*
Fine late Victorian Residence operating as a privately owned family-run guest house. **Open:** All Year
Grades: AA 4 Diamond
01225 332266 Mr Roberts
Fax: 01225 484535
blairgowrie.bath@ukgateway.net
D: £27.50–£30
Beds: 1T 2D **Baths:** 2 En 1 Pr
⌂ ℙ ⅙ Ⅳ ☐ Ⅴ ⚑ 3

The Old Red House, 37 *Newbridge Road, Bath,* BA1 3HE.
A romantic Victorian gingerbread house with stained glass windows, comfortable bedrooms, superbly cooked breakfasts.
Open: Mar to Dec
Grades: AA 3 Diamond
01225 330464 Fax: 01225 331661
oldredhouse@amserve.net
D: £22–£33 **S:** £30–£45
Beds: 1F 4D 1T 1S **Baths:** 3 En 1 Pr 1 Sh
♿ (4) **P** (4) ⅙ ▥ ✝ ▥ ▥ ⚓ **cc**

Pantiles, *Bathway, Chewton Mendip, Bath, Somerset,* BA3 4NS.
Delightful family home set in 2 acres of garden and paddock.
Open: All Year (not Xmas)
Grades: ETC 4 Diamond
01761 241519 Ms Hellard
Fax: 01761 241598
D: £19–£20 **S:** £21–£22
Beds: 1F 2T **Baths:** 2 En 1 Pr
♿ **P** (20) ⅙ ▥ ▥ ▥ ⚓

The Albany Guest House, 24 *Crescent Gardens, Bath,* BA1 2NB.
Open: All Year (not Xmas/New Year)
Grades: ETC 4 Diamond, Silver Award
01225 313339 Mrs Wotley
the_albany@lineone.net
D: £17–£25 **S:** £22–£25
Beds: 2D 1T 2S **Baths:** 1 En 1 Sh
♿ (5) **P** (3) ⅙ ▥ ▥ ⚓
Jan & Bryan assure you of a warm welcome to their Victorian home. Only five minutes walk to the city centre - Roman Baths, Abbey, Royal Crescent etc. Delicious English or vegetarian breakfast. Imaginatively decorated rooms and first class service.

3 Thomas Street, *Walcot, Bath, Somerset,* BA1 5NW.
Charming Georgian house convenient to all city amenities and shops.
Open: All Year (not Xmas)
Grades: ETC 3 Diamond
01225 789540 Ms Saunders
D: £20–£22.50 **S:** £20–£22.50
Beds: 2T **Baths:** 1 En 1 Sh
⅙ ▥ ▥ ▥ ⚓

Wellsway Guest House, 51 *Wellsway, Bath,* BA2 4RS.
Edwardian house near Alexandra Park. Easy walks to city centre.
Open: All Year
Grades: ETC 2 Diamond
01225 423434 Mrs Strong
D: £18–£20 **S:** £20
Beds: 1F 1D 1T 1S **Baths:** 4 Sh
♿ **P** (4) ▥ ✝ ▥ ▥

Flaxley Villa, 9 *Newbridge Hill, Bath,* BA1 3PW.
Comfortable Victorian house near Royal Crescent. 15 minute walk to centre.
Open: All Year
Grades: ETC 3 Diamond
01225 313237 Mrs Cooper
D: £20–£25 **S:** £18–£36
Beds: 3D 1T 1S **Baths:** 3 En
♿ **P** (5) ▥ ▥ ▥ ⚓

14 Raby Place, *Bathwick Hill, Bath, Somerset,* BA2 4EH.
Charming Georgian terraced house with beautiful interior rooms.
Open: All Year **Grades:** ETC 4 Diamond
01225 465120 Mrs Guy
Fax: 01225 465283
D: £22.50–£25 **S:** £25–£35
Beds: 1F 2D 1T 1S **Baths:** 3 En 2 Pr
♿ ⅙ ▥ ▥ ▥ ⚓

Forres House, 172 *Newbridge Road, Bath,* BA1 3LE.
A warm welcome, comfortable bed and big breakfast awaits you.
Open: All Year
Grades: ETC 3 Diamond
01225 427698 J Jones
clive.sampson@eke.co.uk
D: £20–£25 **S:** £30–£35
Beds: 2F 1T 2D **Baths:** 5 En
♿ **P** (5) ⅙ ▥ ▥ ▥ ⚓ **cc**

Cherry Tree Villa, 7 *Newbridge Hill, Bath, Somerset,* BA1 3PW.
Small friendly Victorian home 1 mile from city centre.
Open: All Year (not Xmas/New Year)
01225 331671 Ms Goddard
D: £18–£24 **S:** £20–£30
Beds: 1F 1D 1S **Baths:** 1 Sh
♿ (4) **P** ▥ ▥ ⚓

No 2 Crescent Gardens, *Upper Bristol Road, Bath,* BA1 2NA.
Beautiful B&B in the heart of Bath. Warm welcome.
Open: All Year (not Xmas/New Year)
Grades: ETC 4 Diamond
01225 331186 Mr Bez
D: £19–£25 **S:** £19–£25
Beds: 1F 3T 3D **Baths:** 3 En 1 Sh
⅙ ▥ ▥ ⚓

Grove Lodge, 11 *Lambridge , Bath,* BA1 6BJ.
Elegant, Georgian villa, large rooms with views.
Open: All Year (not Xmas/New Year)
01225 310860 I Miles
Fax: 01225 429630
grovelodge@bath24.fsnet.co.uk
D: £25–£30 **S:** £30–£35
Beds: 1F 1T 2D 1S **Baths:** 3 Pr
♿ (6) ▥ ▥ ▥ ⚓

Ashley House, 8 *Pulteney Gardens, Bath,* BA2 4HG.
Comfortable Victorian house level walk to attractions/ stations.
Open: All Year
Grades: ETC 3 Diamond
01225 425027 Mrs Pharo
D: £23–£33 **S:** £25–£30
Beds: 1F 4D 1T 1S **Baths:** 5 Pr 2 Sh
♿ ⅙ ▥ ▥ ▥ ⚓

Westerlea, 87 *Greenway Lane, Bath,* BA2 4LN.
Georgian style house, large gardens, friendly, ensuite accommodation, cars garaged. **Open:** All Year (not Xmas)
Grades: ETC 4 Diamond
01225 311543 (also fax)
westerle@netcomuk.co.uk
D: £27.50–£37.50 **S:** £45–£65
Beds: 2D **Baths:** 2 En
♿ (12) **P** (2) ⅙ ▥ ✝ ▥ ▥ ⚓ **cc**

Georgian Guest House, 34 *Henrietta Street, Bath,* BA2 6LR.
Grade I Listed town house, situated just 2 mins walk to city centre in a peaceful location. Enjoy your English/continental breakfast in our sunny dining room overlooking the garden. Winter breaks available. **Open:** All Year (not Xmas)
Grades: ETC 3 Diamond
01225 424103 Mr Kingwell
Fax: 01225 425279
georgian@georgian-house.co.uk
D: £30–£35 **S:** £30–£50
Beds: 7D 2T 2S **Baths:** 7 En 1 Sh
♿ ⅙ ▥ ▥ ⚓ **cc**

The Terrace Guest House, 3 *Pulteney Terrace, Bath,* BA2 4HJ.
Mid-terrace house, 7 minutes from city centre and railway station.
Open: All Year (not Xmas)
01225 316578 Mrs Gould
D: £16–£17.50 **S:** £18–£20
Beds: 1D 1T **Baths:** 1 Sh
♿ (6) ▥ ▥ ▥ ⚓

Bathford

ST7966 ⬟ *The Crown*

Bridge Cottage, *Northfield End, Ashley Road, Bathford, Bath,* BA1 7TT.
Pretty cottage with lovely gardens. Village location near Bath city.
Open: All Year (not Xmas)
01225 852399 Mrs Bright
D: £20–£27.50 **S:** £25–£40
Beds: 2D 1T **Baths:** 2 Pr
♿ **P** ⅙ ▥ ✝ ▥ ▥ ⚓

Garston Cottage, *Ashley Road, Bathford, Bath, N E Somerset,* BA1 7TT.
Country cottage, 2 miles from Bath, courtyard garden with jacuzzi.
Open: All Year
01225 852510 Ms Smart
Fax: 01225 852793
garstoncot@aol.com
D: £20–£25 **S:** £25–£30
Beds: 1F 1D 1T **Baths:** 3 En
♿ **P** (2) ⅙ ▥ ✝ ▥ ▥ ⚓ **cc**

Berrow

ST2952 ⬟ *Berrow Inn, Red Cow, Brean Down Inn*

Martins Hill Farmhouse, *Red Road, Berrow, Burnham-on-Sea, Somerset,* TA8 2RW.
Quiet farmhouse overlooking countryside. Golf course, sandy beach 1 mile.
Open: March to Oct
01278 751726 Mrs Davies
Fax: 01278 751230
D: £20–£22.50
Beds: 1F 1D 1T **Baths:** 1 En 1 Pr 1 Sh
♿ **P** (6) ⅙ ▥ ▥ ▥ ✤ ⚓ **cc**

Yew Tree House, *Hurn Lane, Berrow, Burnham-on-Sea, Somerset,* TA8 2QT.
A warm welcome to our refurbished part C17th house. **Open:** All Year (not Xmas)
Grades: ETC 4 Diamond, Silver
01278 751382 (also fax)
N J & G M Crewdson
D: £22 **S:** £22
Beds: 1F 1D 1T **Baths:** 3 En
♿ **P** (14) ⅙ ▥ ▥ ▥ ⚓

Bicknoller

ST1139   Bicknoller Inn

Quantock Moor Farm Cottage,
Bicknoller, Taunton, Somerset, TA4 4ER.
Peaceful surroundings. Foot of Quantock
Hills. Panoramic views. Ideal for
walking/touring
Open: All Year (not Xmas)
01984 656626 Mrs Seamons
quantock@operamail.com
D: £16 **S:** £16
Beds: 1D 1T 1S **Baths:** 1 Pr
⌂ ⓟ (3) 📺 🛏 ✕ 🖾 🗓 🛠

Bilbrook

ST0240   Dragon House Hotel

Steps Farmhouse, Bilbrook, Minehead,
Somerset, TA24 6HE.
Open: Feb to Nov
Grades: ETC 4 Diamond
01984 640974 Mr & Mrs James
stepsfarmhouse@fsbdial.co.uk
D: £20—£22 **S:** £25
Beds: 1F 1D 1T **Baths:** 3 En
⌂ ⓟ (6) 🖾 📺 🖾 🗓 🛠
Traditional C16th former farmhouse
situated near Dunster offering ensuite
bed and breakfast accommodation, in
barn conversions located in beautiful
secluded gardens with views towards
Exmoor; breakfasts are served in our cosy
dining room with oak beams and
inglenook fireplace.

Binegar

ST6149   Horse & Jockey, The George

Mansefield House, Old Rectory
Garden, Binegar, Bath, Somerset, BA3 4UG.
Open: All Year (not Xmas/New Year)
Grades: ETC 4 Diamond, Silver Award
01749 840568 Ms Anstey
Fax: 01749 840572
mansfieldhouse@aol.com
D: £25 **S:** £30
Beds: 2T 1D **Baths:** 2 En 1 Pr
ⓟ (4) 🖾 📺 🖾 🛠
Spacious detached house situated on
edge of Mendip Hills. Quiet village
location. Local inns nearby offering good
food. Easy access from Bristol (A37) or
Bath/Wells (B3139). City of Wells,
Shepton Mallet (Royal Bath and West
Show ground) within minutes drive.
Bath/Bristol 15 miles.

Bishop Sutton

ST5859   Ring Of Bells, Red Lion, Pony and
Trap

Centaur, Ham Lane, Bishop Sutton,
Bristol, BS39 5TZ.
Comfortable house, peaceful location,
within easy reach Bath, Bristol, Wells,
Cheddar.
Open: Mar to Oct
Grades: ETC 3 Diamond
01275 332321 Mrs Warden
D: £18—£19.50 **S:** £14—£20.50
Beds: 1F 1T 1S **Baths:** 1 En 2 Sh
⌂ ⓟ (4) 📺 🖾 🗓 🛠

Bishops Lydeard

ST1629   Lethbridge Arms

The Mount, 32 Mount Street, Bishops
Lydeard, Taunton, Somerset, TA4 3AN.
Open: All Year (not Xmas)
Grades: ETC 4 Diamond
01823 432208 Mr & Mrs Hinton
d.hinton@talk21.com
D: £20 **S:** £20—£25
Beds: 1D 3T **Baths:** 2 Sh
⌂ (2) ⓟ (4) 🖾 📺 🖾 🗓 🛠
A charming comfortable Georgian period
residence set in a picturesque village at
the foot of the Quantock Hills. Ideal
centre for walking, West Somerset Steam
Railway, Exmoor, Hestercombe Gardens,
Dunster Castle, North/South coasts. A
friendly relaxed atmosphere.

Blue Anchor

ST0343   Blue Anchor, Bay Hotel

Langbury Hotel, Blue Anchor,
Minehead, Somerset, TA24 6LB.
Small hotel. Sea views. 4 miles
Minehead, in quiet village.
Open: All Year (not Xmas)
Grades: ETC 3 Diamond, AA 3 Diamond
01643 821375 (also fax)
enquiries@langbury.co.uk
D: £21.50—£25 **S:** £21.50—£45
Beds: 1F 2D 2T **Baths:** 5 En
⌂ ⓟ (5) 📺 🛏 🖾 🗓 🛠 ♿ cc

Bridgwater

ST3037   Hope Inn, Tudor Hotel, Quantock
Gateway, Malt Shovel Inn, Kings Head

The Acorns, 61 Taunton Road,
Bridgwater, Somerset, TA6 3LP.
Open: All Year (not Xmas)
01278 445577
jillgraham@theacorns.fsbusiness.co.uk
D: £17.50—£20 **S:** £17.50—£20
Beds: 3F 2D 5T 3S **Baths:** 5 En 3 Sh
⌂ ⓟ (15) 📺 🛏 🖾 🛠
Jill and Ken offer welcoming and friendly
hospitality with modern facilities, good
breakfast, guest lounge. Large Victorian
house overlooking the Bridgwater and
Taunton Canal. 1.5 miles from M5. Ideal
for touring Somerset and Devon. Please
telephone for colour brochure anytime.

Ash-Wembdon Farm, Hollow Lane,
Wembdon, Bridgwater, Somerset, TA5 2BD.
Enjoy a refreshing and memorable stay at
our elegant yet homely farmhouse.
Open: All Year (not Xmas)
Grades: ETC 4 Diamond, Silver Award
01278 453097 Mrs Rowe
Fax: 01278 445856
mary.rowe@btinternet.com
D: £22—£25 **S:** £24—£28
Beds: 2D 1T **Baths:** 2 En 1 Pr
⌂ (10) ⓟ (4) 🖾 📺 🖾 🗓 🛠 cc

Please respect a B&B's wishes
regarding children, animals
and smoking

Admirals Rest Guest House, 5
Taunton Road, Bridgwater, Somerset,
TA6 3LW.
Elegant Victorian house, close to town
centre, children welcome.
Open: All Year
Grades: ETC 3 Diamond, AA 3 Diamond
01278 458580 (also fax)
Mrs Parker
sueparker@admiralsrest.freeserve.co.uk
D: £17—£22 **S:** £18—£24
Beds: 2F 1D 1T **Baths:** 3 En 1 Pr
⌂ ⓟ (5) 📺 ✕ 🖾 🗓 🛠

Brompton Regis

SS9431   George Inn

Bruneton House, Brompton Regis,
Dulverton, Somerset, TA22 9NN.
Open: All Year (not Xmas)
Grades: AA 2 Diamond
01398 371224 J Stringer
brunetonhouse@hotmail.com
D: £18—£20 **S:** £18—£20
Beds: 2D 1T **Baths:** 1 En 2 Pr
⌂ ⓟ (3) 📺 ✕ 🖾 🗓 🛠
Spacious C17th house with beautiful
garden overlooking the Pulham Valley.
Exmoor village location only 1 mile from
Wimbleball Lake, ideally situated for
North Devon and Somerset coastline.
Relaxed accommodation in comfortable
sunny rooms with easy access to country
pursuits amid stunning scenery.

Bruton

ST6834   Royal Oak

The Old Forge, 89 High Street, Bruton,
Somerset, BA10 0AL.
High-quality accommodation in Saxon
town. Surrounded by beautiful
countryside. **Open:** All Year (not Xmas)
01749 812585 (also fax) Mr Dunn
bb@levent.co.uk
D: £17.50—£20 **S:** £20—£25
Beds: 1D 1T **Baths:** 1 En 1 Sh
⌂ ⓟ (2) 🖾 📺 🖾 🗓 🛠

Burnham-on-Sea

ST3049   Dunstan House, Red Cow, Berrow
Inn

Priorsmead, 23 Rectory Road,
Burnham-on-Sea, Somerset, TA8 2BZ.
Edwardian family home, peaceful
gardens, swimming, quality
accommodation. Reduction three nights.
Open: All Year (not Xmas)
Grades: ETC 3 Diamond
01278 782116 (also fax) Mrs Alexander
PriorsMead@aol.com
D: £17—£18 **S:** £20
Beds: 1D 2T **Baths:** 2 En 1 Pr
⌂ (10) ⓟ (3) 🖾 📺 🖾 🛠

Somewhere House, 68 Berrow Road,
Burnham-on-Sea, Somerset, TA8 2EZ.
Victorian property within easy reach of
town centre, near golf course.
Open: All Year (not Xmas/New Year)
Grades: ETC 3 Diamond
01278 795236 Mr & Mrs Fellingham
di&allen@somewherehouse.co.uk
D: £16—£20 **S:** £22—£25
Beds: 2F 2T 2D **Baths:** 4 En 2 Sh
ⓟ (6) 🖾 📺 🖾 🗓 🛠 cc

Shalimar Guest House, *174 Berrow Road, Burnham-on-Sea, Somerset, TA8 2JE.*
Large detached bungalow near to golf course, beach, town and motorway J22.
Open: All Year
Grades: ETC 2 Diamond
01278 785898 Mrs Marriott
D: £14.95–£16.50 **S:** £14.95–£16.50
Beds: 2F 1D 1T **Baths:** 3 En 1 Sh
🛏 🅿 (5) 📺 🖤 ✕ 🛒 📋 🅥 ♨ ♿

Butcombe

ST4958 ◖ *Queen Adelaide*

Butcombe Farm, *Aldwick Lane, Butcombe, BS40 7UW.*
Open: All Year (not Xmas/New Year)
Grades: ETC 4 Diamond
01761 462380 Mr Harvey
Fax: 01761 462300
info@butcombe-farm.demon.co.uk
D: £20–£27 **S:** £30–£39
Beds: 2T 3D **Baths:** 5 En
🛏 🅿 🖤 📺 ✕ 🛒 📋 🅥 ♨ cc
Converted Fourteenth Century Manor house with character accommodation nestled at foot of Mendip hills. Glorious countryside. ideal for walking cycling, horse riding and fishing nearby at Blagdon Lake. Close to Bristol, Bath, Cheddar, Wells, Sedgemoor, Exmoor, Wye Valley and Cotswolds.

Butleigh

ST5233 ◖ *Rose & Portcullis*

Court Lodge, *Butleigh, Glastonbury, Somerset, BA6 8SA.*
Attractive modernised 1850 lodge. In picturesque garden, edge of Butleigh. 3 miles Glastonbury & Street.
Open: All Year (not Xmas)
01458 850575 Mrs Atkinson
D: fr £15.50 **S:** fr £14
Beds: 1D 1T 2S **Baths:** 2 En
🛏 🅿 🖤 📺 🖤 ✕ 🛒 🅥

Cannington

ST2539

Cannington College, *Cannington, Bridgwater, Somerset, TA5 2LS.*
Situated in the attractive village of Cannington near the Quantock Hills and the coast.
Open: Jul to Sep
01278 655200 Fax: 01278 655055
collinsa@cannington.ac.uk
D: £18.50–£25 **S:** £18.50–£25
Beds: 6T 63S **Baths:** 69 En
🅿 🖤 📺 ✕ 🛒 🅥 ♨

Castle Cary

ST6332 ◖ *George Hotel, Pilgrims Rest*

Orchard Farm, *Castle Cary, Somerset, BA7 7NY.*
Comfortable farmhouse in large gardens and quiet countryside.
Open: All Year **Grades:** ETC 3 Diamond
01963 350418 (also fax)
Mr & Mrs Boyer
boyeroj@talk21.com
D: £18–£24 **S:** £18–£24
Beds: 1F 1D **Baths:** 2 Pr
🛏 🅿 (4) 📺 🖤 ✕ 🛒 🅥 ♨ ♿

Catcott

ST3939 ◖ *King William, The Crown*

Honeysuckle, *King William Road, Catcott, Bridgwater, Somerset, TA7 9HV.*
Set in award-winning 'Britain in Bloom' village of Catcott, within easy reach mystic Glastonbury.
Open: All Year (not Xmas)
01278 722890 Mr & Mrs Scott
D: £16–£20 **S:** £18–£25
Beds: 1D 1T **Baths:** 1 En 1 Sh
🛏 (6) 🅿 (3) 🖤 📺 🛒 🅥 ♨

Chard

ST3208 ◖ *Hornsbury Mill, Happy Return, Windwhistle Inn, Cotley Inn*

Yew Tree Cottage, *Hornsbury Hill, Chard, Somerset, TA20 3DB.*
Open: All Year (not Xmas/New Year)
Grades: AA 4 Diamond
01460 64735 Viv & Phillip Hopkins
ytcottage@aol.com
D: £22.50 **S:** £30–£35
Beds: 1T 2D **Baths:** 3 En
🛏 (10) 🅿 (4) 🖤 📺 🛒 🅥 ♨
Equipped to a high standard with large ensuite bathrooms, Yew Tree Cottage (part mid-eighteenth century) offers a friendly welcome, peaceful surroundings, large mature gardens, and excellent position for reaching south coast resorts and north Somerset, Exmoor and Dartmoor.

Watermead Guest House, *83 High Street, Chard, Somerset, TA20 1QT.*
Charming Guest house, a warm welcome assured, large car park.
Open: All Year
Grades: AA 3 Diamond
01460 62834 Mr & Mrs Cole
Fax: 01460 67448
D: £45 **S:** £20–£30
Beds: 1F 3D 3T 3S **Baths:** 6 En 1 Sh
🛏 🅿 (12) 🖤 📺 🖤 🛒 🅥 ♨

Home Farm, *Hornsbury Hill, Chard, Somerset, TA20 3DX.*
We offer you a very warm welcome and comfortable stay in our family home.
Open: All Year
01460 63731 Mrs Walker
D: £18 **S:** £15–£18
Beds: 1D 1T 1S **Baths:** 1 Sh
🛏 🅿 (4) 🖤 📺 🖤 🛒

Charlton Horethorne

ST6623 ◖ *Mitre Inn, Britannia Inn, Kings Arms, Old Inn, Half Moon, Queens Arms*

Ashclose Farm, *Charlton Horethorne, Sherborne, Dorset, DT9 4PG.*
Comfortable farmhouse, peaceful countryside, friendly welcome and relaxed atmosphere.
Open: All Year (not Xmas)
Grades: ETC 3 Diamond
01963 220360 Mr & Mrs Gooding
gooding@ashclosefarm.freeserve.co.uk
D: £18–£22 **S:** £18–£22
Beds: 1D 1T 1S **Baths:** 1 En 1 Sh
🛏 🅿 (5) 🖤 📺 🖤 🛒 ♨

Charterhouse-on-Mendip

ST5055 ◖ *New Inn*

Warren Farm, *Charterhouse-on-Mendip, Blagdon, Bristol, BS40 7XR.*
1,000 acre sheep farm on the Mendips near Cheddar Gorge.
Open: Jan to Dec
01761 462674 Mrs Small
D: £17 **S:** £17
Beds: 1F 1D 1S **Baths:** 1 Sh
🛏 🅿 (20) 🖤 📺 🛒 🅥 ♨

Cheddar

ST4553 ◖ *Lamb Inn, Gardners Arms, Rodney Stolce, Bath Arms*

Constantine, *Lower New Road, Cheddar, Somerset, BS27 3DY.*
Open: All Year (not Xmas)
Grades: ETC 3 Diamond
01934 741339 Mr & Mrs Mitchell
D: £18–£20 **S:** £18–£20
Beds: 1F 1D 1S **Baths:** 1 Sh
🛏 🅿 (5) 🖤 📺 🖤 ✕ 🛒 🅥 ♨
Edge of Cheddar village with beautiful views of Cheddar Gorge and Mendips. Easy reach of Wells, Street and Glastonbury. Short distance to 2 motorway junctions, Bristol International Airport and Weston-super-Mare. Warm, friendly welcome, comfortable accommodation and good breakfast.

Southland House, *Upper New Road, Cheddar, Somerset, BS27 3DW.*
Excellent ensuite accommodation, outskirts of Cheddar Village, ideal touring centre.
Open: All Year (not Xmas)
01934 742189 Mrs Biggin
D: £18–£20 **S:** £20–£25
Beds: 1F 1T **Baths:** 2 En
🛏 (1) 🅿 (4) 🖤 📺 🛒 🅥 ♨

Tor Farm Guest House, *Nyland, Cheddar, Somerset, BS27 3UD.*
High quality farmhouse accommodation close to Bath, Wells, Glastonbury and Cheddar.
Open: All Year (not Xmas)
Grades: ETC 4 Diamond, AA 4 Diamond
01934 743710 Mrs Ladd
bcjbkj@aol.com
D: £17.50–£24 **S:** £25–£30
Beds: 1F 3D 2T 1S **Baths:** 5 En 2 Sh
🛏 🅿 (10) 🖤 📺 🛒 🅥 ♨ cc

Chew Stoke

ST5561 ◖ *Queens Arms, Stoke Inn*

Orchard House, *Bristol Road, Chew Stoke, Bristol, BS40 8UB.*
Family-run, 'home from home'.
Open: All Year
Grades: ETC 3 Diamond
01275 333143 Mrs Hollomon
Fax: 01275 333754
orchardhse@ukgateway.net
D: £20–£25 **S:** £20–£25
Beds: 1F 2D 3T 1S **Baths:** 5 En 1 Pr 1 Sh
🛏 🅿 (8) 📺 ✕ 🛒 🅥 ♨ cc

Dewdown Cottage, Nempnett
Thrubwell, Chew Stoke, Bristol, BS40 8YF.
Quiet ground floor room, views to
Mendips, 30 mins Bath, Cheddar.
Open: All Year
Grades: ETC 3 Diamond
01761 462917 Mrs Larter
dewdown@hotmail.com
D: £19–£20 **S:** £22–£24
Beds: 1F **Baths:** 1 En
⏰ (8) 🅿 (2) ⌿ 📺 ⼞ 🛏 �🍴 🖵 🖉

Chewton Mendip

ST5953 ⚑ *Waldergrave Arms, Kings Arms*

Franklyns Farm, Chewton Mendip,
Bath, Somerset, BA3 4NB.
Open: All Year
Grades: ETC 3 Diamond
01761 241372 (also fax)
Mrs Clothier
D: fr £20 **S:** fr £22.50
Beds: 2T 1D **Baths:** 2 En 1 Pr
⏰ 🅿 ⌿ 📺 🛏 🖵 🖉 ✿ 🖉
Cosy farmhouse in the heart of Mendip
Hills. Superb views in peaceful setting.
Large garden, with tennis. We offer
genuine hospitality and delicious
breakfast. Ideal touring for Bath, Wells,
Cheddar, Glastonbury, Longleat and the
coast.

Pantiles, Bathway, Chewton Mendip,
Bath, Somerset, BA3 4Ns.
Delightful family home set in 2 acres of
garden and paddock.
Open: All Year (not Xmas)
Grades: ETC 4 Diamond
01761 241519 Ms Hellard
Fax: 01761 241598
D: £19–£20 **S:** £21–£22
Beds: 1F 2T **Baths:** 2 En 1 Pr
⏰ 🅿 (20) ⌿ 📺 🛏 🖵 🖉 🖉

Chilcompton

ST6452 ⚑ *Somerset Wagon*

Pipers Pool, Wells Road, Chilcompton,
Bath, Somerset, BA3 4ET.
Friendly welcome, indoor pool, great food,
near Bath, Cheddar, Wells.
Open: All Year (not Xmas/New Year)
01761 233803 Mrs Sawyer
D: £20–£25 **S:** £25–£30
Beds: 1T 2D **Baths:** 1 En
⏰ 🅿 (6) ⌿ 📺 ✕ 🖵 🖉 🖉

Chilthorne Domer

ST5219 ⚑ *Carpenter Arms*

Jessops, Vagg Lane, Chilthorne Domer,
Yeovil, BA22 8RY.
Open: All Year (not Xmas/New Year)
01935 841097 (also fax)
Mr & Mrs White
D: £40–£48 **S:** £20–£25
Beds: 1T 1D 1S **Baths:** 1 En 1 Sh
⏰ 🅿 ⌿ 📺 🛏 🖵 🖉 🖉
New bungalow, Jessops, with panoramic
views,set in open countryside, one
ensuite with four-poster. Yeovil town just
5 minutes drive away. Short walk to the
local pubs (good food).

Churchill

ST4359 ⚑ *Nelsons Arms, Stag & Hounds*

Clumber Lodge, New Road, Churchill,
Winscombe, Somerset, BS25 5NW.
Open: All Year
Grades: ETC 3 Diamond
01934 852078 (also fax)
D: £15–£17 **S:** £16–£18
Beds: 2T **Baths:** 1 Sh
⏰ 🅿 (3) ⌿ 📺 🛏 🖵 🖉 🖉
Bungalow with pretty garden, situated at
the foot of Mendip Hills (Area of
Outstanding Natural Beauty). Ideal for
walking or touring West Country. 3 miles
Cheddar. Comfortable accommodation.
Personal, friendly service. Good food.

Churchstanton

ST1914

Pear Tree Cottage, Stapley,
Churchstanton, Taunton, Somerset, TA3
7QA.
Open: All Year
01823 601224 Mrs Parry
Fax: 01823 601224
colvin.parry@virgin.net
D: £15–£17 **S:** £24
Beds: 1F 1D 1S **Baths:** 1 En 1 Pr
⏰ 🅿 (4) ⌿ 📺 🛏 ✕ 🖵 🖉 🖉
Picturesque thatched cottage. Traditional
garden, croquet lawn plus 2.50 acres
arboretum. Idyllic tranquillity in beautiful
A0NB countryside. Central for touring
north/south coasts, Exmoor, Dartmoor,
Bath, Wells, Cheddar etc. Encircled by
many famous private/National Trust
Gardens. Stress-free paradise.

Clevedon

ST3971 ⚑ *Little Harp*

Maybank Guest House, 4 Jesmond
Road, Victoria Road, Clevedon, Somerset,
BS21 7SA.
Large Victorian commercial and family
guest house, some sea views.
Open: All Year (not Xmas)
01275 876387 Mr & Mrs Goulding
D: £17–£23 **S:** £17–£25
Beds: 3F 3D 3T 5S **Baths:** 5 En 3 Sh
⏰ 🅿 (8) 📺 🖵 🖉 🖉

Combe Down

ST7562 ⚑ *The Horseshoe*

The Glade, Shaft Road, Combe Down,
Bath, Somerset, BA2 7HP.
Open: All Year
Grades: ETC 3 Diamond
01225 833172 L Markham
theglade@uk2.net
D: £18–£27.50 **S:** £20–£30
Beds: 1F 1D **Baths:** 2 En
⏰ 🅿 (4) ⌿ 📺 🛏 🖵 🖉 🖉
Secluded sylvan retreat 1.5 miles from
Bath centre. Comfortable, spacious
accommodation in 1/2 acre natural
woodland garden. Complimentary home-
made cream tea on arrival. Ground floor
bedrooms, delicious free-range
breakfasts, 10% short break discounts.
Low season midweek breaks £18 pppn.
Peace.

Combe Florey

ST1531 ⚑ *Blue Ball, Rising Sun*

Combe Down Lodge, Combe Florey,
Taunton, Somerset, TA4 3JG.
Open: Easter to Sept
Grades: ETC 4 Diamond
01984 667379 Mrs Murdoch
D: £22–£25 **S:** £25–£27
Beds: 1D **Baths:** 1 En
🅿 (10) ⌿ 📺 ✕ 🖵 🖉 🖉
Originally a hunting lodge, set peacefully
in 30 acres of private ancient woodland.
Easy access to Taunton. M5 J25, Exmoor
and North Somerset coast. West
Somerset steam railway is nearby. Guests
are assured individual attention and high
quality cuisine.

Redlands House, Trebles Holford,
Combe Florey, Taunton, Somerset, TA4 3HA.
Open: All Year (not Xmas)
Grades: ETC 4 Diamond, AA 4 Diamond
01823 433159 B L Totman
redlandshouse@hotmail.com
D: £26.50 **S:** £28
Beds: 1D 1T **Baths:** 2 En
⏰ 🅿 (3) ⌿ 📺 🛏 🖵 🖉 🖉 ⚤ 3
A warm welcome awaits you at this
peaceful spot by the Quantock Hills.
Good location for touring, walking,
cycling or just enjoying the local scenery
and wildlife. Close to the restored West
Somerset Railway. Downstairs courtyard
room suitable for disabled.

Coxley

ST5343

Tynings House, Coxley, Wells,
Somerset, BA5 1RF.
Open: All Year (not Xmas/New Year)
Grades: AA 4 Diamond
01749 675368 (also fax)
Ms Parsons
b-and-b@tyningshouse.com
D: £25–£35 **S:** £35–£45
Beds: 1T 2D **Baths:** 3 En 3 Pr
🅿 (10) ⌿ 📺 🖵 🖉 🖉
Tynings House lies on the edge of a small
village in the heart of Somerset. It is
surrounded by 8 acres of Garden and
Meadow with beautiful views over
unspoilt countryside

Cranmore

ST6643 ⚑ *Poachers, Strode Arms*

Burnt House Farm, Waterlip,
Cranmore, Shepton Mallet, Somerset, BA4
4RN.
Plentiful choice breakfasts in refurbished
farmhouse. Relaxing hot hydro spa.
Welcome.
Open: All Year
Grades: ETC 4 Diamond, Silver Award
01749 880280 Mr Hoddinott
Fax: 01749 880004
D: £24 **S:** £30
Beds: 1F 1D 1T **Baths:** 1 En 2 Pr
⏰ (4) 🅿 (10) ⌿ 📺 🖵 🖉 🖉

Planning a longer stay? Always

ask for any special rates

Lynfield, Frome Road, Cranmore, Shepton Mallet, Somerset, BA4 4QQ.
Country house in large garden, close Bath and West show ground.
Open: All Year (not Xmas)
Grades: ETC 3 Diamond
01749 880600 Mrs Gilderthorp
rsgildo@aol.com
D: £20 **S:** £25
Beds: 1D 1T 1S **Baths:** 2 En 1 Sh
⛺ 🅿 (3) ⊬ 📺 🛏 🖤 👍 &

Creech St Michael

ST2625 ◁ Riverside Inn, Rising Sun

Creechbarn, Vicarage Lane, Creech St Michael, Taunton, TA3 5PP.
Converted longbarn in rural location. Quiet. 3 mins M5 J25.
Open: All Year (not Xmas/New Year)
Grades: AA 4 Diamond
01823 443955 H M Humphreys
Fax: 01823 443509
mick@somersite.co.uk
D: £20–£22 **S:** £20–£29
Beds: 1T 2D **Baths:** 1 En
⛺ 🅿 (4) 📺 🖤 🖤 👍

Cricket St Thomas

ST3708 ◁ Windwhistle Inn

The Firs, Crewkerne Road, Cricket St Thomas, Chard, Somerset, TA20 4BU.
Family home. Warm atmosphere. Beautiful Somerset, Devon, Dorset countryside views.
Open: All Year
01460 65646 Mrs Bright
D: £22.50 **S:** £22.50–£25
Beds: 2D 1T **Baths:** 1 En 2 Pr
⛺ 🅿 (8) ⊬ 📺 🖤 🖤 👍

Culbone

SS8448 ◁ Culbone Inn

Silcombe Farm, Culbone, Porlock, Minehead, Somerset, TA24 8JN.
Comfortable secluded Exmoor farmhouse overlooking sea in beautiful walking country.
Open: All Year (not Xmas)
01643 862248 Mrs Richards
D: £18–£20 **S:** £20
Beds: 1D 2T 1S **Baths:** 1 En 1 Sh
⛺ (4) 🅿 (6) 📺 🛏 ✕ 🖤 🖤 👍

Curland

ST2717 ◁ Square & Compass, Greyhound Inn

The Spinney, Curland, Taunton, Somerset, TA3 5SE.
Quality ensuite B&B with excellent evening meals (recommended). Convenient from M5 and A303.
Open: All Year
Grades: ETC 4 Diamond, AA 4 Diamond
01460 234362 (also fax)
Mr & Mrs Bartlett
bartlett.spinney@zetnet.co.uk
D: £22–£24 **S:** £30
Beds: 1F 1D 1T **Baths:** 3 En
⛺ 🅿 (6) ⊬ 📺 ✕ 🖤 🖤 👍

Dinder

ST5744 ◁ Slab House

Crapnell Farm, Dinder, Wells, Somerset, BA5 5HG.
Crapnell is peace and tranquillity when you stay in our C16th farmhouse.
Open: All Year
01749 342683 Mrs Keen
pamkeen@yahoo.com
D: £18–£25 **S:** £25–£30
Beds: 2D 2T **Baths:** 2 En 1 Sh
⛺ (5) 🅿 ⊬ 📺 🖤 🖤 👍

Doulting

ST6443

Temple House Farm, Doulting, Shepton Mallet, Somerset, BA4 4RQ.
Listed farmhouse, warm welcome, close to East Somerset Railway and many other attractions. **Open:** All Year
Grades: ETC 3 Diamond
01749 880294 Mrs Reakes
D: £42 **S:** £25
Beds: 1T 1D
⛺ (5) 🅿 (4) ⊬ 📺 ✕ 🖤 🖤 👍

Dulverton

SS9128 ◁ Tarr Farm Inn, Bridge, Lion Hotel, White Horse, Rock Inn, Badger's Holt, Lowtron Cross Inn

Exton House Hotel, Exton, Dulverton, Somerset, TA22 9JT.
Open: All Year **Grades:** ETC 4 Diamond
01643 851365 Mr & Mrs Glaister
Fax: 01643 851213
D: £25–£32.50 **S:** £32.50
Beds: 3F 4D 1T 1S **Baths:** 8 En 1 Pr
⛺ 🅿 (9) ⊬ 📺 🛏 ✕ 🖤 🖤 ❋ 👍 & cc
A small Family run Hotel set amidst wonderful scenery on the side of Exton valley, spacious, comfortable rooms, Delicious food, excellent wines, make Exton a delightful base to explore Exmoor and the surrounding countryside.

Highercombe Farm, Dulverton, Somerset, TA22 9PT.
Open: Mar to Nov
Grades: ETC 4 Diamond, Silver Award
01398 323616 (also fax) Mrs Humphrey
abgail@highercombe.demon.co.uk
D: fr £20 **S:** fr £28
Beds: 2D 1T **Baths:** 3 En
⛺ (6) 🅿 📺 🛏 ✕ 🖤 🖤 👍
On the very edge of expansive moorland, you will find our welcoming farmhouse home. All ensuite rooms beautifully co-ordinated, overlooking our 450 acres of working farm. Wonderful farmers' breakfasts, optional evening meals. A quiet and relaxing place to stay.

Springfield Farm, Ashwick Lane, Dulverton, Somerset, TA22 9QD.
Magnificent moorland/woodland views. 1.5 miles to Tarr Steps. Comfortable farmhouse with good food.
Open: Easter to Nov
Grades: ETC 4 Diamond
01398 323722 Mrs Vellacott
info@springfieldfarms.freeserve.co.uk
D: £20–£23 **S:** £25–£35
Beds: 2D 1T **Baths:** 2 En 1 Pr
⛺ (3) 🅿 ⊬ 📺 🛏 ✕ 🖤 🖤 👍

Winsbere House, 64 Battleton, Dulverton, Somerset, TA22 9HU.
Delightful private House. Lovely country views. Excellent Location touring Exmoor.
Open: All Year (not Xmas/New Year)
01398 323278 Mrs Rawle
D: £17–£23.50 **S:** £20
Beds: 1T 2D **Baths:** 2 En 1 Sh
⛺ (8) 🅿 (3) ⊬ 📺 🖤 👍

Threadneedle, East Anstey, Tiverton, Devon, EX16 9JH.
Open: All Year
Grades: ETC 3 Diamond
01398 341598 Mr & Mrs Webb
D: £23–£25 **S:** £23–£25
Beds: 1D 1T **Baths:** 2 En
⛺ 🅿 (10) ⊬ 📺 🖤 🖤 👍
Built in the style of a Devon Longhouse, set in three acres, close to Dulverton. Spacious well appointed rooms, central heating, comfortable ensuite accommodation, parking. Horses and dogs by arrangement. Generous breakfasts leave guest replete and ready to enjoy Exmoor.

Dunster

SS9943 ◁ Castle Hotel, Stags Head

Yarn Market Hotel, 25 - 31 High Street, Dunster, Minehead, Somerset, TA24 6SF.
Family run with a friendly, relaxed atmosphere. Quaint village setting.
Open: All Year
Grades: ETC 3 Star
01643 821425 A.J Brunt
Fax: 01643 821475
yarnmarket.hotel@virgin.net
D: £25–£45 **S:** £30–£40
Beds: 3F 4T 10D 3S **Baths:** 15 En
⛺ 🅿 ⊬ 📺 🛏 ✕ 🖤 🖤 ❋ 👍 cc

Conygar House, 2a The Ball, Dunster, Minehead, Somerset, TA24 6SD.
Quiet situation. Country views. Personal attention and excellent service guaranteed.
Open: Feb to Nov
Grades: ETC 4 Diamond Sliver Award
01643 821872 Mrs Bale
bale.dunster@virgin.net
D: £23–£25 **S:** £28–£30
Beds: 2D 1T **Baths:** 2 En 1 Sh
⛺ (4) ⊬ 📺 🖤 🖤 👍

East Chinnock

ST4913 ◁ Portman Arms, Royal George

The Gables Guest House, High Street, East Chinnock, Yeovil, Somerset, BA22 9DR.
Open: All Year (not Xmas/New Year)
01935 862237 (also fax)
L W J Jones
D: £18–£20 **S:** £18–£20
Beds: 1F 2T 2D **Baths:** 3 En
⛺ 🅿 (6) ⊬ 📺 ✕ 🖤 👍
300-year-old cottage on A30 between Yeovil and Crewkerne. Cream teas and home cooking. Evening meals and full English breakfast. Good touring centre.

East Horrington

ST5746 🍺 Fountain Inn, Wagon & Horses, Slabhouse Inn

Manor Farm, Old Frome Road, East Horrington, Wells, BA5 3DP.
Open: All Year **Grades:** AA 4 Diamond
01749 679832 Mrs Fridd
Fax: 01749 679849
fridd@fridd-wells.freeserve.co.uk
D: £25 **S:** £30
Beds: 2T **Baths:** 1 En 1 Pr
🛏 🅿 (3) 📺 🍴 ✕ 🏰 Ⅴ 🐾
Guaranteed warm welcome to our stunning 15th century Listed farmhouse. Abundant period features full of charm and every comfort. Spacious accommodation, relaxed atmosphere. Just miles from Wells and easy access Bath, Glastonbury, Cheddar.

East Lambrook

ST4318 🍺 Wyndham Arms, Royal Oak

East Lambrook Farm, East Lambrook, South Petherton, Somerset, TA13 5HH.
C17th Thatched farmhouse. Quiet, comfortable, excellent breakfasts, large garden, tennis. **Open:** All Year (not Xmas)
01460 240064 Mrs Eeles
D: £22–£24 **S:** £22–£24
Beds: 2D 1T **Baths:** 2 Pr
🛏 (3) 🅿 (3) ⊬ 📺 ✕ 🏰 🐾

Evercreech

ST6438

Crossdale Cottage, Pecking Mill, Evercreech, Shepton Mallet, Somerset, BA4 6PQ.
Recently renovated 280-year-old stone built former farmhouse conveniently close to Bath & West showground.
Open: All Year
01749 830293 D: £19–£23 **S:** £23–£26
Beds: 2D 2T 1S **Baths:** 2 En 2 Sh
🅿 (5) ⊬ 📺 🏰 Ⅴ 🐾

Exford

SS8538 🍺 White Horse

Court Farm, Exford, Minehead, Somerset, TA24 7LY.
Peaceful farmhouse at heart of Exmoor next to River Exe. **Open:** All Year (not Xmas)
01643 831207 (also fax)
Mr & Mrs Horstmann
beth@courtfarm.co.uk
D: £18 **S:** £18
Beds: 11T **Baths:** 1 Sh
🛏 🅿 ⊬ 📺 🏰 Ⅴ 🐾

Exton

SS9233 🍺 Badger's Holt, Lowtron Cross Inn

Exton House Hotel, Exton, Dulverton, Somerset, TA22 9JT.
A small Family run Hotel set amidst wonderful scenery on side of Exton valley.
Open: All Year **Grades:** ETC 4 Diamond
01643 851365 Mr & Mrs Glaister
Fax: 01643 851213
D: £25–£32.50 **S:** £32.50
Beds: 3F 4D 1T 1S **Baths:** 8 En 1 Pr
🛏 🅿 (9) ⊬ 📺 🍴 ✕ 🏰 Ⅴ ✤ 🐾 🐕 cc

Frome

ST7747 🍺 Royal Oak, Sun, Masons' Arms, Talbot

Wadbury House, Mells, Frome, Somerset, BA11 3PA.
Open: All Year **Grades:** ETC 3 Diamond
01373 812359 Mrs Brinkmann
sally.brinkmann@talk21.com
D: £25–£36 **S:** £28–£40
Beds: 1F 2T 1D **Baths:** 3 En 1 Pr
🛏 🅿 (10) 📺 🍴 ✕ 🏰 Ⅴ 🐾
An historic country house with galleried hall, surrounded by gardens and parkland affording complete peace and quiet. Magnificent views, elegant comfortable rooms, log fires in winter, home-produce and a warm welcome. Nearby to many places of interest. Outdoor heated pool.

Kensington Lodge Hotel, The Butts, Frome, Somerset, BA11 4AA.
Comfortable hotel fitness and leisure facilities near Bath, Longleat, Cheddar Caves.
Open: All Year
Grades: AA 2 Diamond
01373 463935 Mr Aryan
Fax: 01373 303570
irajaryan@aol.com
D: £25 **S:** £30–£40
Beds: 1F 2D 3T 1S **Baths:** 6 En
🛏 🅿 (40) 📺 🏰 ✤ 🐾

Higher West Barn Farm, Witham Friary, Frome, BA11 5HH.
Attractive barn conversion, friendly atmosphere, excellent home cooking, countryside location.
Open: All Year
Grades: ETC 4 Diamond, Silver
01749 850819 Mrs Harrison
ea.harrison@tesco.net
D: £25–£27.50 **S:** £30–£35
Beds: 2D 1T **Baths:** 1 En 2 Pr
🅿 (6) ⊬ 📺 ✕ 🏰 Ⅴ 🐾 🐕 3

Glastonbury

ST5039 🍺 Rose & Portcullis, Who'd A Thought It, Mitre, Camelot Inn, Pilgrim's Rest, Lion

Meadow Barn, Middlewick Farm, Wick Lane, Glastonbury, Somerset, BA6 8JW.
Open: All Year (not Xmas)
Grades: ETC 3 Diamond
01458 832351 (also fax)
Mrs Coles
D: £20.50–£22 **S:** £26–£30
Beds: 2D 1T 1F **Baths:** 3 Pr
🛏 🅿 📺 ✕ 🏰 Ⅴ 🐾 🐕
Tastefully converted barn, ground floor ensuite accommodation with olde worlde charm and country-style decor. Set in award-winning cottage gardens, apple orchards and meadows. Beautiful tranquil countryside. Meadow Barn has a luxury indoor heated swimming pool.

Lottisham Manor, Glastonbury, Somerset, BA6 8PF.
C16th manor house. Lovely garden. Hard tennis court. Perfect peace and comfort.
Open: All Year
01458 850205 Mrs Barker-Harland
D: £17.50–£20 **S:** £17.50
Beds: 1F 1D 1T 1S **Baths:** 2 Sh
🛏 🅿 (8) ⊬ 📺 🏰 Ⅴ 🐾

Pippin, 4 Ridgeway Gardens, Glastonbury, Somerset, BA6 8ER.
Every comfort in peaceful home opposite Chalice Hill. Short walk Tor/town
Open: All Year **Grades:** ETC 3 Diamond
01458 834262 Mrs Slater
daphneslaterpippinbb@talk21.com
D: £16–£18 **S:** £17–£20
Beds: 1D 1T **Baths:** 1 Sh
🛏 🅿 (2) 📺 🍴 🏰 Ⅴ 🐾

Hillclose, Street Road, Glastonbury, Somerset, BA6 9EG.
Warm friendly atmosphere, clean rooms, comfortable beds, full English breakfast.
Open: All Year (not Xmas)
01458 831040 (also fax)
Mr & Mrs Riddle
D: £16–£20 **S:** £25–£35
Beds: 1F 2D 1T **Baths:** 2 Sh
🅿 (4) 📺 🏰 🐾

Court Lodge, Butleigh, Glastonbury, Somerset, BA6 8SA.
Attractive modernised 1850 lodge. In picturesque garden, edge of Butleigh. 3 miles Glastonbury & Street.
Open: All Year (not Xmas)
01458 850575 Mrs Atkinson
D: fr £15.50 **S:** fr £14
Beds: 1D 1T 2S **Baths:** 2 En
🛏 🅿 ⊬ 📺 🍴 ✕ 🏰 Ⅴ

Little Orchard, Ashwell Lane, Glastonbury, Somerset, BA6 8BG.
Glastonbury, famous for historic Tor, King Arthur, abbey ruins and alternative centre.
Open: All Year
Grades: ETC 3 Diamond
01458 831620 Mrs Gifford
D: £16.50–£21 **S:** £17–£22
Beds: 1F 1D 1T 2S **Baths:** 2 Sh
🛏 🅿 ⊬ 📺 🍴 🏰 Ⅴ 🐾

Cradlebridge Farm, Glastonbury, Somerset, BA16 9SD.
Only by staying here will you appreciate the ambience.
Open: All Year
Grades: AA 4 Diamond, RAC 4 Diamond
01458 831827 Mrs Tinney
D: £22–£25 **S:** £30
Beds: 2F **Baths:** 2 Pr
🛏 (3) 🅿 (10) ⊬ 📺 🍴 🏰 Ⅴ 🐾 🐕

Shambhala Healing Centre, Coursing Batch, Glastonbury, Somerset, BA6 8BH.
Beautiful house, sacred site on side of the Tor. Healing, massage, great vegetarian food.
Open: All Year
01458 833081 I & A Nixon
Fax: 01458 831797
isisandargon@shambhala.co.uk
D: £20–£30 **S:** £20–£25
Beds: 3D 1T 1S **Baths:** 3 Sh
🛏 🅿 ⊬ 📺 ✕ 🏰 Ⅴ 🐾

Blake House, 3 Bove Town, Glastonbury, Somerset, BA6 8JE.
Lovely welcoming C17th Listed house built of stones from Glastonbury Abbey.
Open: All Year (not Xmas)
01458 831680 Mrs Hankins
D: £18–£20 **S:** £22.50–£25
Beds: 1D 1T **Baths:** 2 En
🅿 (2) ⊬ 📺 🏰 🐾

1 The Gables, Street Road,
Glastonbury, Somerset, BA6 9EG.
Tea/coffee all rooms. Shower and toilet
separate. 1 minute to town.
Open: Feb to Nov
01458 832519 Mrs Stott
D: fr £13
Beds: 2D 1F 1T **Baths:** 1 En 1 Sh
🛏 (8) 🅿 (4) 🕮 📺 🛎

Godney

ST4842 🍺 *Sheppey Inn*

Double Gate Farm, Godney, Wells,
Somerset, BA5 1RX.
Comfortable, friendly, award-winning
accommodation. Wonderful breakfasts -
lots to see and do.
Open: All Year (not Xmas/New Year)
Grades: ETC 4 Diamond, Gold, AA 4
Diamond, RAC 4 Diamond
01458 832217 Mrs Millard
Fax: 01458 835612
hilary@doublegate.demon.co.uk
D: fr £22.50 **S:** fr £30
Beds: 1F 4D 3T **Baths:** 8 En
🛏 🅿 (8) 🕮 📺 📺 🛎

Greenham

ST0720 🍺 *Globe Inn*

Greenham Hall, Greenham,
Wellington, Somerset, TA21 0JJ.
Impressive Victorian turreted house with
informal friendly atmosphere. Central
location in beautiful countryside.
Open: All Year
01823 672603 Mrs Ayre
Fax: 01823 672307
peterjayre@cs.com
D: £21 **S:** £27–£32
Beds: 1F 3D 2T 1S **Baths:** 4 En 1 Pr 2 Sh
🛏 🅿 (10) 📺 📺 🛎

Greinton

ST4136 🍺 *Pipers Inn*

West Town Farm, Greinton,
Bridgwater, Somerset, TA7 9BW.
A friendly atmosphere, a warm welcome
and a high standard of hospitality awaits
you.
Open: Mar to Sep
01458 210277 Mrs Hunt
D: £20–£24 **S:** £25–£29
Beds: 1D 1T **Baths:** 2 En
🛏 (3) 🅿 (4) 📺 🛎

Gurney Slade

ST6249 🍺 *Somerset Waggon, George Inn*

Lilac Cottage, Gurney Slade, Bath, BA3
4TT.
Charming C18th house in village location
between Bath and Wells.
Open: All Year
Grades: AA 2 Diamond
01749 840469 D: £15–£17 **S:** £15–£17
Beds: 1F 2D 1T **Baths:** 1 Sh
🛏 🅿 📺 🛎

Planning a longer stay? Always
ask for any special rates

Halse

ST1327

New Inn, Halse, Taunton, Somerset,
TA4 3AF.
Typical village inn, friendly atmosphere,
relax and enjoy excellent home cooked
fayre.
Open: All Year
Grades: ETC 3 Diamond
01823 432352 Ms Hayes
D: £18–£21 **S:** £20–£35
Beds: 2T 3D 5S **Baths:** 6 En 4 Sh
🅿 📺 🛎 cc

Hawkridge

SS8530

East Hollowcombe Farm,
Hawkridge, Dulverton, Somerset, TA22 9QL.
Working farm, beautiful scenery, ideal
stopover for Two Moors Way.
Open: Easter to Oct
01398 341622 H Floyd
D: £17–£18 **S:** £17–£18
Beds: 1F 1D 1S **Baths:** 1 Sh
🛏 🅿 (8) 📺 🛎

Henstridge

ST7219 🍺 *Virginia Ash, Fountain Inn*

Quiet Corner Farm, Henstridge,
Templecombe, Somerset, BA8 0RA.
Country house atmosphere with lovely
garden; imaginative breakfasts.
Recommended by 'Which?'.
Open: All Year
Grades: ETC 4 Diamond
01963 363045 (also fax)
Mrs Thompson
quietcorner.thompson@virgin.net
D: £21–£23 **S:** £25–£30
Beds: 1F 2D **Baths:** 1 En 1 Sh
🛏 🅿 (8) 📺 🛎

Henton

ST4945 🍺 *Pheasant Inn*

Rose Farm, Henton, Wells, Somerset,
BA5 1PD.
Lovely Georgian farmhouse with views of
Mendip Hills, large garden, orchard next
to river.
Open: Easter to Oct
01749 672908 Mrs Doherty
D: £19.50 **S:** £25
Beds: 1D 1T **Baths:** 1 En 1Pr
🛏 (5) 🅿 (4) 🛎 cc

Hinton St George

ST4212 🍺 *The Lord Poulett*

Rookwood, West Street, Hinton St
George, Somerset, TA17 8SA.
Comfortable accommodation in tranquil
setting Listed NGS Garden.
Open: All Year (not Xmas/New Year)
01460 73450 Mrs Hudspith
D: £18–£19 **S:** £18–£19
Beds: 2T **Baths:** 1 En 1 Sh
🛏 (10) 🅿 (2) 📺 🛎

Ludneymead, Hinton St George,
Somerset, TA17 8TD.
Family run farm close to many
attractions. Secluded, peaceful, open
views.
Open: Easter to Oct
01460 57145 Mrs Chapman
D: £19–£21
Beds: 1D **Baths:** 1 Pr
📺 ✕ 📺 🛎

Hutton

ST3458 🍺 *Old Inn*

Moorlands Country Guest House,
Hutton, Weston-super-Mare, Somerset,
BS24 9QH.
Fine Georgian house, extensive
landscaped gardens, village pub serves
meals.
Open: All Year
Grades: ETC 3 Diamond
01934 812283 (also fax)
Mr & Mrs Holt
D: £20–£25 **S:** £20–£30
Beds: 3F 2D 1T 1S **Baths:** 5 En 1 Sh
🛏 🅿 (7) 📺 🛎 cc 3

Ilminster

ST3614 🍺 *The Crown*

Hylands, 22 New Road, Ilminster,
Somerset, TA19 9AF.
Attractive Edwardian end of terrace, small
country/town family home.
Open: All Year (not Xmas)
01460 52560 Mrs Hayter
haytorbandb@talk21.com
D: £12.50 **S:** fr £15
Beds: 1D 1T **Baths:** 2 Sh
🛏 🅿 (2) 📺 🛎

Keinton Mandeville

ST5430

Stangray House, Church Street, ,
Keinton Mandeville, Somerton, Somerset,
TA11 6ER.
Family run country house in pleasant
rural surroundings. Garden. Parking.
Open: All Year
Grades: ETC 4 Diamond
01458 223984 Ms Bassett
dpm@euphmy.net
D: £18–£22.50 **S:** £20–£25
Beds: 1F 1T 1D **Baths:** 1 En 1 Sh
🛏 🅿 (6) 📺 ✕ 📺 🛎

Keynsham

ST6568 🍺 *The Talbot*

Fiorita, 91 Bath Road, Keynsham, Bristol,
BS31 1SR.
Warm welcome, comfortable family home
midway between Bristol and Bath.
Open: Jan to Dec
0117 986 3738 (also fax)
Mrs Poulter
D: £14.50–£16 **S:** £16–£18
Beds: 1D 1T **Baths:** 1 En 1 Sh
🛏 🅿 (4) 📺 🛎

Kilve

ST1443   *Hood Arms*

The Old Rectory, Kilve, Bridgwater, Somerset, TA5 1DZ.
Foot of Quantocks; scenic walking/touring, local beach, pub, comfortable.
Open: All Year (not Xmas)
Grades: ETC 3 Diamond
01278 741520 Chris & Jan Alder
oldrectorykilve@yahoo.co.uk
D: £22–£25 **S:** £20–£25
Beds: 1F 1D 1T **Baths:** 3 En
P (4) � ▼ ✦ ▥ ♿

Kingston St Mary

ST2229   *Swan Inn*

Lower Marsh Farm, Kingston St Mary, Taunton, Somerset, TA2 8AB.
Open: All Year
Grades: AA 3 Diamond
01823 451331 (also fax)
Mr & Mrs Gothard
mail@lowermarshfarm.co.uk
D: £22.50–£25 **S:** £25–£28
Beds: 1F 1T 1D **Baths:** 2 En 1 Pr
⊱ P ⊁ ▼ ✕ ▥ ♿
Only 10 mins M5 (J25). A warm welcome is assured at our tastefully refurbished farmhouse on a working farm overlooking the vale of Taunton, nestling at the foot of the Quantock Hills. Attractive ensuite rooms, dining room and gardens, with traditional home cooking breakfast

Langport

ST4126   *Old Forge Inn*

Spring View, Wagg Drove, Huish Episcopi, Langport, Somerset, TA10 9ER.
Open: All Year (not Xmas/New Year)
Grades: ETC 3 Diamond
01458 251215 Mrs Ruddock
ruddockspring@aol.com
D: £19–£21 **S:** £20–£30
Beds: 1T 2D **Baths:** 2 En 1 Pr
P (3) ⊁ ▼ ▥ ♿
Warm welcome, comfortable accommodation, full English breakfast, rural setting edge of 'Somerset Levels', close to Langport and Somerton, royal capital of ancient Wessex. Ideal for stopover, touring, walking, cycling and that longed for lazy, relaxing break. Bird watchers paradise.

Amberley, Long Load, Langport, Somerset, TA10 9LD.
Quality accommodation with far-reaching views on edge of Somerset Levels.
Open: All Year (not Xmas)
Grades: ETC 4 Diamond
01458 241542 Ms Jarvis
D: £17–£18 **S:** £17–£18
Beds: 1F 1T 1D **Baths:** 1 En 1 Sh
⊱ P (4) ⊁ ▼ ✦ ✕ ▥ Ⓥ ♿

Long Load

ST4623   *Bell Inn*

Fairlight, Martock Road, Long Load, Langport, Somerset, TA10 9LG.
Detached bungalow, magnificent views. 2.50 acre garden, orchard & plantation.
Open: All Year (not Xmas/New Year)
Grades: ETC 3 Diamond
01458 241323 Mrs Hook
D: £17.50–£18.50 **S:** £18.50–£19
Beds: 1D 1T **Baths:** 1 En 1 Pr
⊱ (10) P (6) ▼ ▥ ♿

Lopen

ST4214

Rathmore, Main St, Lopen, South Petherton, Somerset, TA13 5JU.
Pretty village house, comfortable, modern, in rolling countryside, pleasant views.
Open: All Year
01460 240279 Mrs Webster
D: £16–£18 **S:** £16
Beds: 2D 1S **Baths:** 1 Sh
⊱ (6) P (3) ⊁ ▼ ✦ ✕ ▥ Ⓥ ♿

Martock

ST4619   *Nag's Head, White Hart*

The Nags Head, East Street, Martock, Somerset, TA12 6NF.
Open: All Year
Grades: ETC 3 Diamond, Gold
01935 823432 Fax: 01935 824265
D: fr £25 **S:** fr £30
Beds: 1F **Baths:** 1 En
⊱ P (24) ⊁ ▼ ✦ ✕ ▥ Ⓥ ♿ CC
The Nags Head is a charming village pub which dates back over 150 years. A warm welcome and superb home cooking are a feature. Accommodation is a beautifully presented self contained flat in a converted barn. A perfect location for a romantic getaway.

Wychwood, 7 Bearley Road, Martock, Somerset, TA12 6PG.
One of the top 20 finalists for AA Landlady of the Year 1999.
Open: Mar to Nov
01935 825601 (also fax)
Mrs Turton
wychwood@dancefloor.demon.co.uk
D: £21–£23 **S:** £31–£33
Beds: 2D 1T **Baths:** 2 En 1 Pr
P (4) ⊁ ▼ ▥ Ⓥ ♿ CC

Mells

ST7249   *Talbot Inn*

Wadbury House, Mells, Frome, Somerset, BA11 3PA.
An historic country house with galleried hall, surrounded by gardens.
Open: All Year
Grades: ETC 3 Diamond
01373 812359 Mrs Brinkmann
sally.brinkmann@talk21.com
D: £25–£36 **S:** £28–£40
Beds: 1F 2T 1D **Baths:** 3 En 1 Pr
⊱ P (10) ✦ ✕ ▥ Ⓥ ♿

Midford

ST7560   *Hope Anchor*

Clearbrook Farm, Midford, Bath, Somerset, BA2 7DE.
Creaky old farmhouse with lovely views from all rooms. **Open:** All Year
01225 723227 Ms Cross
Fax: 01225 722860
D: £17–£19 **S:** £20–£25
Beds: 2D 1T **Baths:** 2 Sh
⊱ P (10) ⊁ ✦ ▼ ▥ ♿

Midsomer Norton

ST6554   *Fosseyway Country Club, White Post Inn*

Ellsworth, Fosseway, Midsomer Norton, Bath, Somerset, BA3 4AU.
Situated on the A367 on Somerset border 8 miles from city of Wells.
Open: All Year
01761 412305 (also fax) Mrs Gentle
accommodation@
ellsworth.fsbusiness.co.uk
D: £22–£25 **S:** £25–£35
Beds: 2F 2T 1D **Baths:** 3 En 1 Sh
⊱ (2) P (4) ⊁ ▼ ▥ Ⓥ ♿

Milton Ash

ST4621   *Bell Inn*

Bartletts Farm, Isle Brewers, Taunton, Somerset, TA3 6QN.
Between A303 and M5. Comfortable family accommodation where all are welcome including horses.
Open: All Year
01460 281423 Mr & Mrs Peach
sandjpeach@tesco.net
D: £18–£20 **S:** £18–£20
Beds: 3F **Baths:** 1 En 1 Sh
⊱ P ▼ ✕ Ⓥ ♿

Milverton

ST1225   *Fitzhead Inn*

Lovelynch Farm, Milverton, Taunton, Somerset, TA4 1NR.
Quiet C15th farm, good views. Easy access Exmoor. Good English breakfast. Antique furniture.
Open: All Year (not Xmas)
01823 400268 Mrs Loram
D: £17–£18 **S:** £20–£25
Beds: 1F 1D 1T 1S **Baths:** 2 Sh
⊱ P ⊁ ▼ ▥ Ⓥ ♿

Minehead

SS9646   *Queen's Head, Beach Hotel, York House*

1 Glenmore Road, Minehead, Somerset, TA24 5BQ.
Open: All Year
01643 706225 Mrs Sanders
D: £16.50–£18.50 **S:** £16.50
Beds: 1F 1D 1T 1S **Baths:** 2 En 1 Sh
⊱ (6) P (2) ⊁ ▼ ▥ Ⓥ ♿
A superior Victorian family-run guest house offering a friendly welcome and relaxing atmosphere, an excellent range of breakfasts including vegetarian. Number one is perfectly situated just back from the promenade with only a short level walk to local amenities.

Beaconwood Hotel, *Church Road, North Hill, Minehead, Somerset, TA24 5SB.*
Open: All Year
Grades: ETC 2 Star
01643 702032 (also fax)
Mr Roberts
beaconwood@madasafish.com
D: £30–£35 **S:** £33–£40
Beds: 2F 6D 6T **Baths:** 14 En
🛇 🅿 (25) 📺 🍴 ✕ 🛍 Ⅴ ♯ 🛓 cc
Edwardian country house hotel, set in 2 acres of terraced gardens with panoramic views of Exmoor area. With heated outdoor swimming pool & grass tennis court. 200 yards from South West Coast Path.

Rectory House Hotel, *Northfield Road, Minehead, TA24 5QH.*
Former rectory, magnificent hill and sea views. Putting green.
Open: All Year
Grades: RAC 2 Star
01643 702611 Mr Wilson
D: £30 **S:** £30
Beds: 3F 2D 2T **Baths:** 7 En
🛇 🅿 (8) 📺 🍴 ✕ Ⅴ 🛓 ♿ cc

Monkton Combe

ST7762 ◀ *Wheelwrights Arms*

The Manor House, *Monkton Combe, Bath, BA2 7HD.*
Restful rambling medieval manor by millstream in Area of Outstanding Natural Beauty. **Open:** All Year
Grades: ETC 3 Diamond
01225 723128 Mrs Hartley
Fax: 01225 722972
beth@manorhousebath.co.uk
D: £22.50–£35 **S:** £30–£35
Beds: 2F 5D 1T **Baths:** 8 En
🛇 🅿 (12) 📺 🍴 ✕ 🛍 🛓 ♿ ♨ 2

Montacute

ST4916 ◀ *Phelips Arms*

Mad Hatters Tea Rooms, *1 South Street, Montacute, Somerset, TA15 6XD.*
Listed Georgian property in picturesque village. Idyllic walks, Near NT properties.
Open: All Year **Grades:** ETC 3 Diamond
01935 823024 Mrs Hicken
D: £17.50–£21 **S:** £23–£29
Beds: 1D 1T 1S **Baths:** 1 Pr 2 En
🛇 ✁ 📺 Ⅴ 🛓

Muchelney Ham

ST4323 ◀ *Devonshire Arms*

Muchelney Ham Farm, *Muchelney Ham, Langport, Somerset, TA10 0DJ.*
Open: All Year
Grades: ETC 5 Diamond, Gold Award.
01458 250737 Mrs Woodborne
D: £25–£35 **S:** £25–£35
Beds: 1F 3D 2T 1S **Baths:** 6 En 1 Pr
🛇 (8) 🅿 (8) ✁ 📺 🛍 ♯ 🛓
B&B with country house atmosphere. Beautiful traditional Somerset farmhouse mainly C17th, tastefully furnished with period furniture, beams and inglenook. Situated on the Somerset levels with peaceful and relaxing garden. Ideal centre for touring many NT properties, air museum, golf and fishing. Somerset & Dorset coast 25 miles.

Nether Stowey

ST1839 ◀ *Ancient Mariner*

The Manse, *Lime Street, Nether Stowey, Bridgwater, Somerset, TA5 1NG.*
You will find a warm welcome and comfortable rooms at the Manse.
Open: All Year (not Xmas)
01278 732917 Mr Simmonds
D: £20 **S:** £25
Beds: 1D 1T **Baths:** 2 En
🅿 (4) ✁ 📺 🛍 🛓

North Cadbury

ST6327

Ashlea House, *High Street, North Cadbury, Yeovil, Somerset, BA22 7DP.*
1 km A303, centre village, highly commended service, accommodation, home cooking.
Open: All Year (not Xmas/New Year)
Grades: ETC 4 Diamond
01963 440891 Mr & Mrs Wade
ashlea@btinternet.com
D: £22–£25 **S:** £25–£27
Beds: 1T 1D **Baths:** 1 En 1 Pr
🅿 (2) ✁ 📺 ✕ 🛍 Ⅴ 🛓

North Perrott

ST4709

The Manor Arms, *North Perrott, Crewkerne, TA18 7SG.*
Open: All Year
Grades: ETC 3 Diamond, AA 3 Diamond
01460 72901 (also fax) Mr Gilmore
info@manorarmshotel.co.uk
D: £19–£24 **S:** £35–£38
Beds: 1F 5D 3T **Baths:** 9 En
🛇 🅿 (24) ✁ 📺 ✕ 🍴 🛍 Ⅴ 🛓 ♿ cc
A lovely 16th Century Listed Inn overlooking the village green offering a high standard of ensuite accommodation. Renowned and excellent home-made bar and restaurant meals. Stay for free on a gourmet break and pay only £25.00 for dinner and breakfast!

North Petherton

ST2832 ◀ *Maypole Inn*

Quantock View House, *Bridgwater Road, North Petherton, Bridgwater, Somerset, TA6 6PR.*
Central for Cheddar, Wells, Glastonbury, the Quantocks and the sea.
Open: All Year
Grades: ETC 3 Diamond, AA 3 Diamond
01278 663309 Mr & Mrs George
wendy@quantockview.freeserve.co.uk
D: £16–£20 **S:** £18–£24
Beds: 2F 1D 1T **Baths:** 3 En 1 Pr
🛇 🅿 (8) ✁ 📺 🍴 ✕ 🛍 ♯ 🛓 cc

Lower Clavelshay Farm, *North Petherton, Bridgwater, Somerset, TA6 6PJ.*
Buzzards, badgers and beautiful countryside surround our C17th farmhouse.
Open: March-Nov
01278 662347 (also fax)
Mrs Milverton
D: £20–£23 **S:** £23–£26
Beds: 1F 2D **Baths:** 2 En 1 Pr
🛇 🅿 (4) ✁ 📺 🍴 🛍 Ⅴ 🛓

North Wootton

ST5641 ◀ *Crossways Inn*

Riverside Grange, *Tanyard Lane, North Wootton, Wells, Somerset, BA4 4AE.*
A charming converted Tannery quietly situated on the River edge.
Open: All Year **Grades:** AA 5 Diamond
01749 890761 Mrs English
D: £19.50–£22 **S:** £25–£29
Beds: 1D 1T **Baths:** 2 Pr
🛇 🅿 (6) 📺 🍴 🛍 🛓

Norton-sub-Hamdon

ST4715 ◀ *Lord Nelson*

Courtfield, *Norton-sub-Hamdon, Stoke-sub-Hamdon, Somerset, TA14 6SG.*
Comfortable, relaxed, peaceful. Breakfast in conservatory? Special accommodation, beautiful gardens.
Open: All Year (not Xmas)
01935 881246 Mrs Constable
courtfield@hotmail.com
D: £25–£28 **S:** fr £38
Beds: 1D 1T **Baths:** 2 Pr
🛇 (8) 🅿 (4) 📺 🍴 ✕ 🛍 Ⅴ 🛓

Brook House, *Norton-sub-Hamdon, Stoke-sub-Hamdon, Somerset, TA14 6SR.*
Gracious Georgian family home in unspoilt quiet Hamstone village with pub providing good food. **Open:** Easter to Nov
Grades: ETC 4 Diamond, Silver
01935 881789 (also fax) Mr & Mrs Fisher
D: £25 **S:** £35
Beds: 1D 1T **Baths:** 2 Pr
🛇 (10) 🅿 (2) ✁ 📺 🛍 Ⅴ 🛓

Panborough

ST4745 ◀ *Panborough Inn*

Garden End Farm, *Panborough, Wells, Somerset, BA5 1PN.*
Working farm offering good B&B, central location for many attractions.
Open: Easter to Dec
01934 712414 Mrs Badman
D: £14–£15 **S:** £16
Beds: 1D 1T **Baths:** 1 Sh
🛇 🅿 (6) 📺 🛍 Ⅴ 🛓

Pibsbury

ST4326 ◀ *Lime Kiln*

All's Well, *Pibsbury, Langport, Somerset, TA10 9EG.*
On working farm between Yeovil and Taunton. Golf course/fishing/walks.
Open: All Year (not Xmas)
01458 241465 Mrs Crossman
D: £15–£17.50 **S:** £15–£17.50
Beds: 1F 1D 1T **Baths:** 1 En 1 Sh
🛇 🅿 (6) ✁ 📺 🛍 🛓

Porlock

SS8846 ◀ *Royal Oak, Ship Inn, Castle Hotel, Culbone Inn, Overstream Hotel*

Overstream Hotel, *Parsons Street, Porlock, Minehead, Somerset, TA24 8QJ.*
Situated in the centre of Porlock, between Exmoor and the sea. **Open:** Easter to Nov.
01643 862421 (also fax)
D: £21–£30 **S:** £30
Beds: 1F 2T 4D 2S **Baths:** 9 En
🛇 🅿 ✁ 📺 ✕ 🛍 Ⅴ 🛓

Leys, *The Ridge, Bossington Lane, Porlock, Minehead, Somerset, TA24 8HA.*
Beautiful family home, delightful garden, with magnificent views.
Open: All Year (not Xmas)
01643 862477 (also fax)
Mrs Stiles-Cox
D: £19 **S:** £19
Beds: 1D/T 2S **Baths:** 1 Sh
🛇 🅿 (4) ⅍ 📺 🛏 📖 ⅴ ⅃

Hurlstone, *Sparkhayes Lane, Porlock, Minehead, Somerset, TA24 8NE.*
Quiet house near village centre sea and moorland views.
Open: All Year (not Xmas)
01643 862650 Mrs Coombs
D: £18 **S:** £18
Beds: 1D 1T **Baths:** 1 Sh
🛇 🅿 🛏 ⅃

West Porlock House, *Country House Hotel, West Porlock, Porlock, Minehead, Somerset, TA24 8NX.*
Superbly set in beautiful woodland garden with magnificent sea views.
Open: Feb to Nov
Grades: ETC 4 Diamond
01643 862880 Mrs Dyer
D: £25.50–£27.50 **S:** fr £30
Beds: 1F 2D 2T **Baths:** 2 En 3 Pr
🛇 (6) 🅿 (8) ⅍ 📺 📖 ⅃ cc

Silcombe Farm, *Culbone, Porlock, Minehead, Somerset, TA24 8JN.*
Comfortable secluded Exmoor farmhouse overlooking sea in beautiful walking country.
Open: All Year (not Xmas)
01643 862248 Mrs Richards
D: £18–£20 **S:** £20
Beds: 1D 2T 1S **Baths:** 1 En 1 Sh
🛇 (4) 🅿 (6) 📺 🛏 ✕ 📖 ⅴ ⅃

Puriton

ST3241 🍺 *Puriton Inn*

Rockfield House, *Puriton Hill, Puriton, Bridgwater, Somerset, TA7 8AG.*
Just off M5 (J23). Good food and friendly atmosphere.
Open: All Year (not Xmas)
Grades: AA 3 Diamond
01278 683561 (also fax)
Mrs Pipkin
rockfieldhouse@talk21.com
D: £16–£20 **S:** £16
Beds: 1F 1D 1T 1S **Baths:** 2 En 1 Sh
🛇 🅿 (5) ⅍ 📺 ✕ 📖 ⅴ ⅃

Canns Farm, *Canns Lane, Puriton, Bridgwater, Somerset, TA7 8AY.*
C17th farmhouse village location easy access from M5.
Open: All Year (not Xmas)
Grades: ETC 3 Diamond
01278 684773 (also fax)
K Lewis
cannsfarm@minim.com
D: £16–£20 **S:** £18–£24
Beds: 1F 1T **Baths:** 1 En 1 Pr
🛇 🅿 (3) ⅍ 📺 🛏 ✕ 📖 ⅃ &

Planning a longer stay? Always ask for any special rates

Roadwater

ST0338 🍺 *Royal Oak*

Stamborough Farm, *Roadwater, Watchet, Somerset, TA23 0RW.*
Elegant Georgian farmhouse in a secluded valley but not isolated.
Open: All Year
01984 640258 Fax: 01984 641051
rileystamco@compuserve.com
D: £19.50–£21.50 **S:** £19.50–£21.50
Beds: 2D 1T **Baths:** 3 En
🛇 (5) 🅿 (8) 📺 ✕ 📖 ⅴ ⅃

Saltford

ST6866

Long Reach House Hotel, *321 Bath Road, Saltford, Bristol, BS31 1TJ.*
Gracious house standing in 2 acres midway between Bath and Bristol.
Open: All Year
Grades: ETC 2 Star
01225 400500 Fax: 01225 400700
lrhouse@aol.com
D: £22.50–£45 **S:** £45–£50
Beds: 2F 7T 7D 2S **Baths:** 18 En
🛇 🅿 ⅍ 📺 🛏 ✕ 📖 ❊ ⅴ & cc

Sandyway

SS7933

Barkham, *Sandy, Exmoor, Devon, EX36 3LU.*
Tucked away in hidden valley in the heart of Exmoor.
Open: All Year (not Xmas)
Grades: ETC 4 Diamond, AA 4 Diamond
01643 831370 (also fax)
Mrs Adie
adie.exmoor@btinternet.com
D: £23–£30
Beds: 2D 1T **Baths:** 1 En 1 Sh
🛇 (12) 🅿 (6) ⅍ 📺 ✕ 📖 ⅴ

Shepton Mallet

ST6143 🍺 *Poachers Rest, Strode Arms, Bull Terrier*

Burnt House Farm, *Waterlip, Cranmore, Shepton Mallet, Somerset, BA4 4RN.*
Plentiful choice breakfasts in refurbished farmhouse. Relaxing hot hydro spa. Welcome.
Open: All Year
Grades: ETC 4 Diamond, Silver Award
01749 880280 Mr Hoddinott
Fax: 01749 880004
D: £24 **S:** £30
Beds: 1F 1D 1T **Baths:** 1 En 2 Pr
🛇 (4) 🅿 (10) ⅍ 📺 📖 ⅴ ⅃

Park Farm House, *Forum Lane, Bowlish, Shepton Mallet, Somerset, BA4 5JL.*
Comfortable C17th house with peaceful garden and private off-road parking.
Open: All Year
01749 343673 Fax: 01749 345279
D: £17.50–£18.50 **S:** £17.50–£18.50
Beds: 2T 1D **Baths:** 1 En 2 Pr
🛇 🅿 (3) 📺 📖 ⅴ ⅃

Shipham

ST4457

Herongates, *Horseleaze Lane, Shipham, Winscombe, Somerset, BS25 1UQ.*
Noted for quality, peaceful location.
Open: All Year (not Xmas/New Year)
Grades: ETC 3 Diamond
01934 843280 Mrs Stickland
D: £15.50–£18.50 **S:** £15.50–£18.50
Beds: 2D 1T **Baths:** 2 En 1 Pr
🛇 🅿 (3) ⅍ 📺 ✕ 📖 ⅴ ⅃

Simonsbath

SS7739

Emmett's Grange Farm, *Simonsbath, Minehead, Somerset, TA24 7LD.*
Open: All Year (not Xmas/New Year)
01643 831138 (also fax)
T Barlow
D: £28–£35 **S:** £33–£40
Beds: 1T 2D
🛇 🅿 ⅍ 📺 🛏 ✕ 📖 ⅴ ⅃ cc
Emmett's Grange provides an oasis of friendly civilisation within its own 900 acres amidst the stunning wild and rugged Exmoor National Park. Luxurious B&B with moorland views. Guests own elegant drawing room. Gourmet food available and many local pubs. Fully licensed.

South Petherton

ST4316 🍺 *Brewer's Arms, Royal Oak, Poulet Arms*

Kings Pleasure, *24 Silver Street, South Petherton, Somerset, TA13 5BZ.*
Listed hamstone house, beautiful garden; in centre of conservation village.
Open: All Year
Grades: ETC 4 Diamond, Silver Award
01460 241747 Mr & Mrs Veit
n.veit@kingspleaure.fsnet.co.uk
D: fr £25 **S:** fr £35
Beds: 1D 1T **Baths:** 2 En
🛇 🅿 (2) ⅍ 📺 🛏 📖 ⅃

Watergore House, *Watergore, South Petherton, Somerset, TA13 5JQ.*
Picturesque old ham stone house with large garden just off A303.
Open: All Year (not Xmas)
01460 240677 (also fax)
Mr & Mrs Gordon
D: £20 **S:** fr £20
Beds: 2D 1T **Baths:** 2 Sh
🛇 (6) 🅿 (4) ⅍ 📺 📖 ⅃

Stanton Drew

ST5963 🍺 *Druids Arms*

Auden House, *Stanton Drew, Bristol, BS39 4DJ.*
Large modern house in attractive village, stone circles, historic toll house.
Open: All Year (not Xmas)
01275 332232 (also fax)
Mrs Smart
auden@iname.com
D: £15–£17.50 **S:** £17.50
Beds: 2F 1D 1T 1S **Baths:** 1 En
🛇 🅿 (6) ⅍ 📺 🛏 ✕ 📖 ⅴ ⅃

Valley Farm, *Sandy Lane, Stanton Drew, Bristol, BS39 4EL.*
Modern farmhouse, quiet location, old village with druid stones.
Open: All Year (not Xmas)
01275 332723 Mrs Keel
D: £19–£22 **S:** £20–£24
Beds: 1F 2D **Baths:** 3 En
🛏 🅿 (4) ⊬ 📺 📖 🎵 🖳 ♿

Stanton Prior

ST6762 🍺 *Wheatsheaf*

Poplar Farm, *Stanton Prior, Bath, BA2 9HX.*
Spacious C17th farmhouse. Family-run farm. Idyllic village setting.
Open: All Year **Grades:** ETC 3 Diamond, AA 3 Diamond
01761 470382 **(also fax)** Mrs Hardwick
poplarfarm@talk21.com
D: £20–£27 **S:** £20–£30
Beds: 1F 1D 1T **Baths:** 2 En
🛏 (4) 🅿 (6) ⊬ 📺 📖

Staplegrove

ST2126 🍺 *Cross Keys*

Yallands Farmhouse, *Staplegrove, Taunton, Somerset, TA2 6PZ.*
A warm welcome is assured at our beautiful C16th house.
Open: All Year **Grades:** ETC 4 Diamond
01823 278979 Mr & Mrs Kirk
Fax: 0870 284 9194
mail@yallands.co.uk
D: £26.50–£27.50 **S:** £29–£33
Beds: 1F 2D 1T 2S **Baths:** 6 En
🛏 🅿 (6) 📺 📖 🖳 ♿ cc

Stogumber

ST0937 🍺 *White Horse*

Chandlers House Guest House, *Stogumber, Taunton, Somerset, TA4 3LA.*
Listed period house with old walled garden in a beautiful conservation village.
Open: Easter to Oct
01984 656580 **D:** £20–£25 **S:** £20–£25
Beds: 2T 1S **Baths:** 1 En 1 Pr
🛏 (5) 🅿 (1) ⊬ 📺 🐾 📖

Stogursey

ST2042 🍺 *Penhale Round*

Acland Hood Arms, *11 High Street, Stogursey, Bridgewater, Somerset, TA5 1TB.*
C17th pub in picturesque village between M5 and Exmoor. **Open:** All Year (not Xmas)
01726 732489 Mrs Goulding
D: £17.50–£20 **S:** £20–£25
Beds: 2T 2D **Baths:** 4 En
🛏 (10) 🅿 (20) ⊬ 📺 ✕ 📖 ♿

Stoke St Gregory

ST3427 🍺 *Rose and Crown Inn*

Parsonage Farm, *Stoke St Gregory, Taunton, Somerset, TA3 6ET.*
Georgian farmhouse situated on the Somerset Levels. Working dairy farm.
Open: All Year (not Xmas/New Year)
01823 698205 Mrs House
D: £17–£20 **S:** £19–£23
Beds: 1F **Baths:** 1 Sh
🛏 🅿 (2) 📺 📖 ♿

Stratton-on-the-Fosse

ST6550 🍺 *Ring Of Roses*

Oval House, *Stratton-on-the-Fosse, Bath, Somerset, BA3 4RB.*
Charming C17th house on Mendip Hills between Bath and Wells. **Open:** All Year
01761 232183 **(also fax)** Mrs Mellotte
mellotte@clara.co.uk
D: £18 **S:** £20
Beds: 1T 1S **Baths:** 1 Sh
🛏 🅿 (5) 📺 🐾 📖 🖳 ♿

Taunton

ST2324 🍺 *Square & Compass, Greyhound Inn, Cross Keys, Pen & Quill, King's Arms, Old Inn, Merry Monk, Cavalier*

Yallands Farmhouse, *Staplegrove, Taunton, Somerset, TA2 6PZ.*
Open: All Year **Grades:** ETC 4 Diamond
01823 278979 Mr & Mrs Kirk
Fax: 0870 284 9194
mail@yallands.co.uk
D: £26.50–£27.50 **S:** £29–£33
Beds: 1F 2D 1T 2S **Baths:** 6 En
🛏 🅿 (6) 📺 📖 🖳 ♿ cc
A warm welcome is assured at our beautiful 16th century house. An oasis of 'old England' close to town centre yet unexpectedly peaceful and secluded. Comfortable, attractive ensuite rooms with ground floor room available. Out of season discounts. Phone for brochure.

The Old Mill, *Bishops Hull, Taunton, Somerset, TA1 5AB.*
Open: All Year (not Xmas)
01823 289732 **(also fax)**
Mr & Mrs Slipper
D: £22–£24 **S:** £30–£35
Beds: 2D **Baths:** 1 En 1 Pr
🅿 ⊬ 📺 📖 ♿
Grade II. Listed former Corn mill retaining many original workings and beamed ceilings, in lovely Riverside setting. A warm welcome awaits you, delightful bedrooms with Extensive Breakfast menu and large waterside Terrace. Exmoor and coast 35 minutes. packed lunches available.

Hillview Guest House, *Bishop's Hull, Taunton, Somerset, TA1 5EG.*
Spacious accommodation, warm and friendly atmosphere in attractive village near Taunton.
Open: All Year
Grades: ETC 3 Diamond
01823 275510 **(also fax)**
Mr Morgan
D: £17.50–£22.50 **S:** £17.50–£25
Beds: 2F 1D 1T 1S **Baths:** 2 En 3 Sh
🛏 🅿 (6) ⊬ 📺 🐾 📖 🖳 ♿ cc

Prockters Farm, *West Monkton, Taunton, Somerset, TA2 8QN.*
Beautiful C17th beamed farmhouse, large garden, 2 pubs easy walking.
Open: All Year
Grades: ETC 3 Diamond
01823 412269 **(also fax)**
Mrs Besley
info@scoot.co.uk
D: £21–£23 **S:** £21–£30
Beds: 2D 2T 2S 6F **Baths:** 2 En 2 Pr 2 Sh
🛏 🅿 (6) 📺 🐾 📖 🖳 ♿ cc

The Spinney, *Curland, Taunton, Somerset, TA3 5SE.*
Quality ensuite B&B with excellent evening meals (recommended). Convenient from M5 and A303.
Open: All Year
Grades: ETC 4 Diamond, AA 4 Diamond
01460 234362 **(also fax)**
Mr & Mrs Bartlett
bartlett.spinney@zetnet.co.uk
D: £22–£24 **S:** £30
Beds: 1F 1D 1T **Baths:** 3 En
🛏 🅿 (6) ⊬ 📺 ✕ 📖 🖳 ♿

Lower Farm, *Thorn Falcon, Taunton, Somerset, TA3 5NR.*
Picturesque 15th century thatched farmhouse, log fires, peaceful location, 3 miles Taunton.
Open: All Year (not Xmas)
Grades: AA 4 Diamond
01823 443549 **(also fax)**
Mrs Titman
lowerfarm@talk21.com
D: £23–£25 **S:** fr £30
Beds: 1F 1D 1T **Baths:** 1 En 1 Pr
🛏 🅿 (10) ⊬ 📺 ✕ 📖

Blorenge Guest House, *57 Staplegrove Road, Taunton, Somerset, TA1 1DL.*
We are situated within 10 mins of all Taunton's amenities.
Open: All Year
01823 283005 Mr Painter
D: £20–£35 **S:** £26–£40
Beds: 3F 9D 5T 7S **Baths:** 17 En 2 Sh
🛏 🅿 (18) 📺 🐾 ✕ 📖 🖳 ♿ cc

Thorn Falcon

ST2723

Lower Farm, *Thorn Falcon, Taunton, Somerset, TA3 5NR.*
Picturesque 15th century thatched farmhouse, log fires, peaceful location, 3 miles Taunton.
Open: All Year (not Xmas)
Grades: AA 4 Diamond
01823 443549 **(also fax)**
Mrs Titman
lowerfarm@talk21.com
D: £23–£25 **S:** fr £30
Beds: 1F 1D 1T **Baths:** 1 En 1 Pr
🛏 🅿 (10) ⊬ 📺 ✕ 📖

Timberscombe

SS9542 🍺 *Royal Oak*

Wellum, *Brook Street, Timberscombe, Minehead, Somerset, TA24 7TG.*
Lovely, spacious old house situated in Avil Valley, spectacular views.
Open: Mar to Nov
01643 841234 Mrs Kelsey
D: £16–£20 **S:** £16–£20
Beds: 1D 1T **Baths:** 1 Pr 1 Sh
🛏 📺 🐾 ✕ 📖 🖳 ♿

National Grid References are for villages, towns and cities – not for individual houses

Tivington

SS9345

Clements Cottage, *Tivington, Minehead, Somerset, TA24 8SU.*
Open: All Year
01643 703970
clementscottage@exmoorbandb.co.uk
D: £18.50–£20 **S:** £18.50–£20
Beds: 1F 1T 1D **Baths:** 1 En 1 Sh
🛇 🅿 (3) 📺 🍴 ✕ 🏠 📹 🔥
16th century cross-passage house with spectacular views of the Bristol Channel and the Dunkery Range. An excellent base to explore Exmoor with its beautiful scenery of rivers, streams, heather moorland, wooded valleys and dramatic coastline.

Upton Noble

ST7139   🍺 *Lamb Inn*

Kingston House, *Upton Noble, Shepton Mallet, Somerset, BA4 6BA.*
Quality accommodation with superb views across Witham Vale towards Alfred's Tower. **Open:** All Year (not Xmas)
01749 850805 (also fax) Mr Stroud
tim.r.stroud@rexam.co.uk
D: £18–£22 **S:** fr £18
Beds: 1D 2S **Baths:** 1 En 1 Pr
🛇 (3) 🅿 (3) 📺 ✕ 🏠 📹 🔥

Watchet

ST0643   🍺 *Star Inn*

Downfield House, *16 St Decuman's Road, Watchet, Somerset, TA23 0HR.*
Open: All Year **Grades:** ETC 2 Star, Silver Award, AA 2 Star
01984 631267 Fax: 01984 634369
D: £22–£27 **S:** £34–£39
Beds: 5D 2T **Baths:** 7 En
🛇 (12) 🅿 (15) ✂ 📺 🍴 ✕ 🏠 📹 🔥 cc
Spacious Victorian country house with converted and modernised coach house within a large garden in an elevated location. Views over the town and harbour from some rooms, comfortable lounge with open fire, chandeliered dining rooms, residents licence and totally non-smoking!

Esplanade House, *Watchet, Somerset, TA23 0AJ.*
Comfortable Georgian farmhouse, with pretty garden, in historic harbour setting.
Open: All Year (not Xmas/New Year)
Grades: ETC 3 Diamond
01984 633444 Mrs Fawcus
D: £18.50–£20 **S:** £23.50–£25
Beds: 1T 2D **Baths:** 2 En 1 Pr
🛇 (8) 🅿 (3) ✂ 📺 🍴 🏠 📹 🔥

Wayford

ST4006   🍺 *Windwistle Inn*

Manor Farm, *Wayford, Crewkerne, Somerset, TA18 8QL.*
Beautiful Victorian home in a peaceful location with undulating views.
Open: All Year **Grades:** AA 4 Diamond
01460 78865 Mr Emery
D: £22–£25 **S:** £22–£25
Beds: 2F 1T **Baths:** 3 En
🛇 🅿 (50) ✂ 📺 🏠 📹 🔥

Wedmore

ST4347   🍺 *The Gorge*

The George Hotel, *Church Street, Wedmore, Somerset, BS28 4AB.*
Open: All Year
01934 712124 Mr Hodge
Fax: 01934 712251
reception@thegeorgewedmore.co.uk
D: £17.50–£25 **S:** £20–£25
Beds: 2F 3D 3T **Baths:** 3 En 1 Sh
🛇 🅿 (30) ✂ 📺 🍴 ✕ 🏠 📹 🔥 cc
16th century coaching in set in centre of village in the heart of the Somerset levels and close to Cheddar, Wookey Hole, Wells and Glastonbury.

Wells

ST5445   🍺 *Burcott Inn, City Arms, Fountain Inn, Pheasant Inn, Sheppey Inn, City Arms, Wooley Hole Inn, Ring O' Bells, New Inn*

The Crown at Wells, *Market Place, Wells, Somerset, BA5 2RP.*
Open: All Year
Grades: ETC 3 Diamond
01749 673457 Sara Hodges
Fax: 01749 679792
reception@crownwells.demon.co.uk
D: £27.50–£30 **S:** fr £40
Beds: 4F 5D 4T 2S **Baths:** 15 En
🛇 🅿 (10) 📺 🍴 ✕ 🏠 📹 🔥 cc
The C15th Crown Inn is situated in the heart of Wells, within a stones throw of Wells Cathedral and moated Bishop's Palace. Delicious meals, snacks and refreshments available all day. We pride ourselves on a warm and friendly service.

Infield House, *36 Portway, Wells, Somerset, BA5 2BN.*
Open: All Year
Grades: AA 4 Diamond
01749 670989 infield@talk21.com
D: £21–£24.50 **S:** £31–£34.50
Beds: 2D 1T **Baths:** 3 En
🛇 (14) 🅿 (4) ✂ 📺 🍴 ✕ 🏠 📹 🔥 cc
Beautifully restored Victorian town house with period furnishing, portraits and decor. A short walk to city centre, cathedral and bishop's palace. Bountiful breakfasts, traditional English or vegetarian. Touring centre for Glastonbury, Cheddar, Bath or walking on Mendip hills. Evening meals by prior arrangement.

Broadleys, *21 Wells Road, Wookey Hole, Wells, Somerset, BA5 1DN.*
Open: All Year (not Xmas)
Grades: ETC 4 Diamond, Silver Award, AA 4 Diamond
01749 674746 (also fax)
Mrs Milton
broadleys@bobmilton.totalserve.co.uk
D: £18.50–£20 **S:** £25–£35
Beds: 3D **Baths:** 2 En 1 Pr
🛇 (10) 🅿 (4) ✂ 📺 📹 🔥
Large detached house situated between Wells and Wookey Hole with panoramic countryside views, quality accommodation includes guests' lounge featuring reading material, daily newspapers, videos and satellite television. Friendly well-travelled hosts, excellent parking, quick access to the West Mendip Way.

17 Priory Road, *Wells, Somerset, BA5 1SU.*
Large Victorian house. Homemade bread and preserves. Few mins' walk shops, cathedral, bus station.
Open: All Year (not Xmas)
01749 677300 Mrs Winter
D: £17.50 **S:** £17.50–£20
Beds: 3F 3S **Baths:** 2 Sh
🛇 🅿 (5) ✂ 📺 🏠 📹 🔥

Cadgwith House, *Hawkers Lane, Wells, Somerset, BA5 3JH.*
Delightfully furnished spacious family house, backing onto field. Beautiful bathrooms.
Open: All Year
Grades: ETC 4 Diamond
01749 677799 Mr & Mrs Pletts
D: £18–£20 **S:** £18–£25
Beds: 1F 1D 1T 1S **Baths:** 3 En 1 Pr
🛇 🅿 (3) 📺 🍴 🏠 📹 🔥

30 Mary Road, *Wells, Somerset, BA5 2NF.*
Open: Feb to Nov
Grades: ETC 3 Diamond
01749 674031 (also fax)
Mrs Bailey
triciabailey30@hotmail.com
D: £17.50–£18 **S:** £17.50–£18
Beds: 2D 2S **Baths:** 1 Sh
🛇 (3) 🅿 (5) 📺 🏠 📹 🔥
Small, friendly family home, approx. 10 minutes walk from city centre offering bright modern rooms and a choice of Breakfast.

Double Gate Farm, *Godney, Wells, Somerset, BA5 1RX.*
Comfortable, friendly, award-winning accommodation. Wonderful breakfasts - lots to see and do.
Open: All Year (not Xmas/New Year)
Grades: ETC 4 Diamond, Gold, AA 4 Diamond, RAC 4 Diamond
01458 832217 Mrs Millard
Fax: 01458 835612
hilary@doublegate.demon.co.uk
D: fr £22.50 **S:** fr £30
Beds: 1F 4D 3T **Baths:** 8 En
🛇 🅿 (8) ✂ 🏠 📹 🔥

Winsome House, *Portway, Wells, Somerset, BA5 2BE.*
1930 detached house in quiet cul-de-sac 2 mins from cathedral and city centre.
Open: All Year
Grades: ETC 3 Diamond
01749 679720 (also fax)
Mrs Lock
mikelock@mikelock.freeserve.co.uk
D: £18–£20 **S:** £20–£24
Beds: 1F 1D 1T **Baths:** 1 Sh
🅿 (3) ✂ ✕ 🏠 📹 🔥

The Limes, *29 Chamberlain Street, Wells, Somerset, BA5 2PQ.*
Beautifully restored Victorian town house in the centre of historic Wells.
Open: All Year (not Xmas)
01749 675716 Fax: 01749 674874
accommodation@thelimes.uk.com
D: £18–£20
Beds: 1D 1T
🛇 🅿 (2) ✂ 📺 🏠 📹 🔥 cc

Furlong House, *Lorne Place, St Thomas Street, Wells, Somerset, BA5 2XF.*
Georgian house, central Wells, walled gardens, very quiet, ample parking.
Open: All Year (not Xmas)
Grades: AA 4 Diamond
01749 674064 Mr Howard
howardwells@compuserve.com
D: £20–£23 **S:** £20–£42
Beds: 2D 1T **Baths:** 2 En 1 Sh
🛏 🅿 (4) ⊬ 📺 🎟 ☑ ♨

Birdwood House, *Bath Road, Wells, Somerset, BA5 3DH.*
Beautifully located on the edge of Mendips large Victorian gardens.
Open: All Year (not Xmas/New Year)
Grades: AA 2 Star
01749 679250 Mrs Crane
D: £18 **S:** £18
Beds: 2D 1S **Baths:** 1 Sh
🛏 (5) 🅿 (6) ⊬ 📺 🎟 ☑ ✳ ♨

Bekynton House, *7 St Thomas Street, Wells, Somerset, BA5 2UU.*
Three minutes from cathedral, a few more to city restaurants.
Open: All Year (not Xmas)
01749 672222 (also fax)
Mr & Mrs Gripper
desmond@bekynton.freeserve.co.uk
D: £23.50–£27 **S:** £25–£40
Beds: 1F 3D 2T **Baths:** 4 En 2 Pr
🛏 (7) 🅿 (6) ⊬ 📺 🎟 ♨ cc

Ancient Gate House Hotel, *Sadler Street, Wells, Somerset, BA5 2RR.*
Situated on the cathedral green, overlooking West front of cathedral.
Open: All Year
01749 672029 Mr Rossi
Fax: 01749 670319
info@ancientgatehouse.co.uk
D: £30–£35 **S:** £45–£50
Beds: 1F 6D 1T 1S **Baths:** 7 En 1 Sh
🛏 🅿 📺 🏠 ✗ 🎟 ☑ ♨ cc

Wembdon

ST2837 🍺 *Quantock Gateway, Malt Shovel*

Model Farm, *Perry Green, Wembdon, Bridgwater, Somerset, TA5 2BA.*
Between Quantocks and Levels. Comfortable Victorian farmhouse in peaceful rural setting.
Open: All Year (not Xmas/New Year)
Grades: ETC 4 Diamond, AA 4 Diamond
01278 433999 Mr & Mrs Wright
rmodelfarm@aol.com
D: £25–£30 **S:** £35
Beds: 1F 1D 1T **Baths:** 3 En
🛏 🅿 ⊬ 🎟 🏠 ✗ 🎟 ☑ ♨ cc

Ash-Wembdon Farm, *Hollow Lane, Wembdon, Bridgwater, Somerset, TA5 2BD.*
Enjoy a refreshing and memorable stay at our elegant yet homely farmhouse.
Open: All Year (not Xmas)
Grades: ETC 4 Diamond, Silver Award
01278 453097 Mrs Rowe
Fax: 01278 445856
mary.rowe@btinternet.com
D: £22–£25 **S:** £22–£28
Beds: 2D 1T **Baths:** 2 En 1 Pr
🛏 (10) 🅿 (4) ⊬ 📺 🎟 ☑ ♨ cc

West Monkton

ST2628 🍺 *Merry Monk*

Prockters Farm, *West Monkton, Taunton, Somerset, TA2 8QN.*
Beautiful C17th beamed farmhouse, large garden, 2 pubs easy walking.
Open: All Year **Grades:** ETC 3 Diamond
01823 412269 (also fax) Mrs Besley
info@scoot.co.uk
D: £21–£23 **S:** £21–£30
Beds: 2D 2T 2S 6F **Baths:** 2 En 2 Pr 2 Sh
🛏 🅿 (6) 📺 🏠 🎟 ☑ ♨ cc

West Pennard

ST5438 🍺 *Lion, Appletree*

The Lion at Pennard, *Glastonbury Road, West Pennard, Glastonbury, Somerset, BA6 8NH.*
Open: All Year **Grades:** ETC 3 Diamond
01458 832 941 Mr Moore
Fax: 01458 830 660
thelion@pennardfsbusiness.co.uk
D: £25–£35 **S:** £45–£50
Beds: 1F 2T 4D **Baths:** 7 En
🛏 🅿 📺 🎟 ✳ ♨ cc
15th Century coaching inn offering excellent ales, fine food and friendly atmosphere, with seven ensuite letting rooms in our converted barn. Open all year. Within easy reach of Wales, Glastonbury and Cheddar. Contact Les and Karen Moore.

Orchard House, *Church Lane, West Pennard, Glastonbury, Somerset, BA6 8NT.*
Grade II Listed by C15th church near open fields. **Open:** Easter to Sep
01458 832838 Mrs Sadler
D: £16.50 **S:** £16.50
Beds: 1F 1T 1D **Baths:** 1 Sh
🛏 🅿 (2) ⊬ 🏠 🎟 ☑ ♨

West Wick

ST3661

Orchard House, *Summer Lane, West Wick, Weston-super-Mare, Somerset, BS24 7TF.*
A luxury guest house close to M5 (J21).
Open: All Year
Grades: ETC 4 Diamond, Silver
01934 520948 (also fax)
D: £21–£27 **S:** £36–£49
Beds: 2D **Baths:** 2 En
🅿 (4) ⊬ 📺 ✗ 🎟 ♨

Westbury-sub-Mendip

ST5048 🍺 *Westbury Inn*

Lana Hollow Farm, *The Hollow, Westbury-sub-Mendip, Wells, Somerset, BA5 1HH.*
Open: All Year (not Xmas/New Year)
01749 870635 D: £20–£22 **S:** £22–£25
Beds: 1T 2D **Baths:** 3 En
🛏 🅿 ⊬ 📺 🎟 ☑ ♨
Modern farmhouse accommodation on working farm. Gently elevated site offering beautiful views over the moors and Somerset. Lovely comfortable family home. Breakfast room for sole guest use, breakfast served at separate tables. Full English breakfast and a varied menu. (Quiet location).

Weston-super-Mare

ST3261 🍺 *Old Thatched Cottage, Old Inn, Balmoral Hotel, Bobs Bar, Cabot Bar, Royal Hotel, Borough Arms*

Braeside Hotel, *2 Victoria Park, Weston-super-Mare, Somerset, BS23 2HZ.*
Open: All Year (not Xmas/New Year)
Grades: ETC 4 Diamond, AA 4 Diamond
01934 626642 (also fax)
Mr & Mrs Wallington
D: £25 **S:** £25
Beds: 1F 5D 1T 2S **Baths:** 9 En
🛏 📺 🏠 🎟 ☑ ♨
Fabulous views over Weston Bay; two minutes' walk from sandy beach. Quiet location. Directions: with sea on left, take first right after Winter Gardens, then first left into Lower Church Road. Victoria Park is on the right after the left hand bend.

Everley Villa, *35 Clevedon Road, Weston-Super-Mare, Somerset, BS23 1DB.*
Your comfort, our pleasure. Spacious accommodation, short walk beach, station.
Open: All Year
Grades: ETC Sliver Award
01934 643856 Mr & Mrs Howes
D: £20–£25 **S:** £20–£35
Beds: 2F 3D **Baths:** 2 En 1 Pr
🛏 🅿 ⊬ ✗ 🎟 ☑ ♨

Moorlands Country Guest House, *Hutton, Weston-super-Mare, Somerset, BS24 9QH.*
Fine Georgian house, extensive landscaped gardens, village pub serves meals.
Open: All Year
Grades: ETC 3 Diamond
01934 812283 (also fax)
Mr & Mrs Holt
D: £20–£25 **S:** £20–£30
Beds: 3F 2D 1T 1S **Baths:** 5 En 1 Sh
🛏 🅿 (7) 📺 🏠 🎟 ☑ ♨ cc 3

The Weston Rose, *2 Osborne Road, Weston-super-Mare, BS23 3EL.*
Open: All Year
01934 412690 Mrs Trueman
westonrose@beeb.net
D: £14–£19 **S:** £15–£23
Beds: 4F 3D 2T **Baths:** 4 En 2 Sh
🛏 🅿 (5) 📺 ✗ 🎟 ☑ ♨
Hearty traditional breakfasts - a feast for eye and stomach. our own prize winning preserves, yoghurts and fresh fruit always available. All rooms have fridges and hair dryers - most ceilings have fans. Our motto is 'Comfort is our concern', let us prove it!

Arilas, *78 Clevedon Road, Weston-super-Mare, Somerset, BS23 1DF.*
Family guest house close to beach, parks and local shops.
Open: All Year
01934 628283 Mrs Watkins
D: £15–£18 **S:** £15–£18
Beds: 1F 1D 1T 1S **Baths:** 1 En 2 Sh
🛏 📺 🏠 ✗ 🎟 ☑ ♨ ♿

Beverley Guest House, 11
Whitecross Road, Weston-super-Mare, Somerset, BS23 1EP.
Victorian style many original features. Close beach, town, railway station.
Open: All Year
Grades: AA 3 Diamond, Silver Award
01934 622956 Mrs Fry
D: £17–£21 **S:** £20–£25
Beds: 2F 1D 1T 1S **Baths:** 5 En
⛵ 📺 ✕ 🏠 📶 👤

Clifton Villa B&B, 11 Clifton Road,
Weston-super-Mare, Somerset, BS23 1BJ.
Bed and breakfast in family home, near town and beach.
Open: All Year (not Xmas)
01934 413243 Mr Weeks
D: £13–£17 **S:** £15–£20
Beds: 1F 1D 1T **Baths:** 2 En 1 Sh
✕ 📺 🏠 📶

Kenilworth B&B, 115 Locking Road,
Weston-super-Mare, Somerset, BS23 3ER.
Free tea/coffee making - Full English breakfast - Central heating - Car space.
Open: All Year (not Xmas)
01934 629398 Mrs Searle
D: £14–£16 **S:** £16–£20
Beds: 1F 3D 2T 1S **Baths:** 2 Sh
⛵ 🅿️ 📺 🏠 📶

Four Seasons Guest House, 103
Locking Road, Weston-super-Mare, Somerset, BS23 3EW.
Same proprietors since 1988. Featured 'Wish You Were Here'. Millennium discounts.
Open: All Year (not Xmas)
Grades: ETC 1 Diamond
01934 631124 J A Barcham
D: £14–£16 **S:** £14–£16
Beds: 2F 3D 1T 1S **Baths:** 3 Sh
⛵ (2) 🅿️ (2) 📺 🏠 👤

Vaynor, 346 Locking Road, Weston-super-Mare, Somerset, BS22 8PD.
Family-run guest house, many interesting attractions to visit for all ages.
Open: All Year (not Xmas/New Year)
01934 632332 Mrs Monk
Fax: 01934 418376
D: £14–£15 **S:** £14–£15
Beds: 1F 1T 1D
⛵ 🅿️ (3) 📺 🍴 ✕ 🏠 📶 👤

Orchard House, Summer Lane, West Wick, Weston-super-Mare, Somerset, BS24 7TF.
A luxury guest house close to M5 (J21).
Open: All Year
Grades: ETC 4 Diamond, Silver
01934 520948 (also fax)
D: £21–£27 **S:** £36–£49
Beds: 2D **Baths:** 2 En
🅿️ (4) ✕ 📺 ✕ 🏠 👤

Parasol, 49 Walliscote Road, Weston-super-Mare, BS23 1EE.
Easy reach of town, parks and sea front, ideal for touring.
Open: All Year
01934 636409 B & B Lewis
D: £17–£25 **S:** £20–£25
Beds: 4F 2D 2T **Baths:** 4 Pr
⛵ (3) 🅿️ (2) 📺 🏠 👤

Edelweiss Guest House, 24
Clevedon Road, Weston-super-Mare, North Somerset, BS23 1DG.
A friendly family-run guest house approx 150 yards from beach Tropicana and Sealife Centre.
Open: All Year (not Xmas)
01934 624705 Mr & Mrs Edgell
D: £16–£19 **S:** £16–£17
Beds: 2F 1D 1T 1S **Baths:** 4 En 1 Sh
⛵ ✕ ✕ 📺 📶 👤 ♿

Westonzoyland
ST3434   🍺 *Halfway Inn*

Phoenicia, 31 Liney Road,
Westonzoyland, Bridgwater, Somerset, TA7 0EU.
Private suite in modern detached house village location. comfortable beds.
Open: All Year
Grades: AA 3 Diamond
01278 691385 Mr & Mrs Pumfrey
Baths: 1 Pr
D: £21 **S:** £21
Beds: 1T 1D
⛵ (10) 🅿️ ✕ 📺 🏠 👤

Wheddon Cross
SS9238   🍺 *Rest & Be Thankful, Royal Oak, Raleigh Cross*

Triscombe Farm, Wheddon Cross,
Minehead, Somerset, TA24 7HA.
Open: All Year (not Xmas/New Year)
Grades: ETC 4 Diamond
01643 851227 (also fax)
Mrs Brinkley
D: £20–£30 **S:** £25–£40
Beds: 1T 2D **Baths:** 1 En 2 Pr
⛵ ✕ 📺 🏠 👤
Nestling in its own secluded valley with a stream cascading through the garden. You will receive a warm welcome at Triscombe Farm. An ideal base, close to coast and moorland in Exmoor National Park, to explore this beautiful area.

Little Quarme Farm, Wheddon Cross,
Exmoor, Minehead, Somerset, TA24 7EA.
C16th farmhouse, beautifully furnished & decorated. Outstanding, peaceful location, superb views.
Open: Mar to Nov
Grades: ETC 5 Diamond
01643 841249 (also fax)
Mrs Cody-Boutcher
106425.743@compuserve.com
D: £20–£23 **S:** £25–£30
Beds: 2D 1T **Baths:** 3 En
⛵ 🅿️ (6) ✕ 📺 ✕ 🏠 👤

Rest & Be Thankful Inn, Wheddon Cross, Exmoor, Minehead, Somerset, TA24 7DR.
Old coaching inn, ideal Exmoor location for walking and touring.
Open: All Year (not Xmas)
Grades: ETC 4 Diamond, Silver, AA 4 Diamond, RAC 4 Diamond
01643 841222 (also fax)
Mr Weaver
enquiries@restandbethankful.co.uk
D: £27–£30 **S:** £27–£30
Beds: 3D 1T 1S **Baths:** 5 En 1 Sh
⛵ (11) 🅿️ (30) ✕ 📺 ✕ 🏠 👤 cc

Wick St Lawrence
ST3665   🍺 *Full Quart*

Icleton Farm, Wick St Lawrence,
Weston-super-Mare, Somerset, BS22 7YJ.
C15th farmhouse 5 mins from M5 J21, ideal for touring West Country.
Open: All Year (not Xmas)
Grades: ETC 3 Diamond
01934 515704 Mrs Parsons
D: £17–£20 **S:** £17–£20
Beds: 1F 1D **Baths:** 1 Pr
⛵ (2) 🅿️ (2) 📺 🏠 📶 👤

Williton
ST0741   🍺 *Foresters' Arms Hotel*

Foresters Arms Hotel, 55 Long Street,
Williton, Taunton, Somerset, TA4 4QY.
C17th coaching inn on A39 between Quantock and Brendon Hills.
Open: All Year
01984 632508 Mr Goble
D: £17.50–£21 **S:** £18.50–£22
Beds: 2F 4D 1S **Baths:** 6 En 1 Sh
⛵ 🅿️ (20) 📺 🍴 ✕ 🏠 📶 ✳ 👤 ♿ cc

Winscombe
ST4056

Home Farm, Barton, Cheddar,
Winscombe, Somerset, BS25 1DX.
Open: All Year
Grades: ETC 4 Diamond, Silver
01934 842078 Mr & Mrs Marlow
info@homefarmcottages.co.uk
D: £22–£24 **S:** £22–£24
Beds: 2D
🅿️ (4) ✕ 📺 🍴 🏠 👤
The detached Bake House Suite - a delightful Listed building adjacent C15th farmhouse set in two acres. Private lounge, working inglenook fireplace, galleried bedroom and ensuite. A walkers' paradise directly from accommodation. Whirlpool/spa on site. Local country club membership available.

Winsham
ST3706   🍺 *Bell*

Court Farmhouse, Court Street,
Winsham, Chard, Somerset, TA20 4JE.
Within easy reach of the coastal resorts of West Dorset & East Devon.
Open: Feb to Nov
01460 30823 Mrs Sherrin
D: £25 **S:** £25
Beds: 1T **Baths:** 1 Pr
🅿️ 📺 🏠 👤

Withypool
SS8435   🍺 *Royal Oak*

The Old Rectory, Withypool,
Minehead, Somerset, TA24 7QP.
Pleasant view, comfortable beds and a good, hearty English breakfast.
Open: Easter to Oct
01643 831553 Mr Clatworthy
D: £16 **S:** £16
Beds: 1D 1T 1S **Baths:** 1 Sh
⛵ 🅿️ (4) ✕ 📺 🍴 🏠 📶 👤

Wookey Hole

ST5347   ◀ *Wooley Hole Inn, Ring O' Bells, New Inn*

Broadleys, *21 Wells Road, Wookey Hole, Wells, Somerset, BA5 1DN.*
Large detached house situated between Wells and Wookey Hole.
Open: All Year (not Xmas)
Grades: ETC 4 Diamond, Silver Award, AA 4 Diamond
01749 674746 (also fax) Mrs Milton
broadleys@bobmilton.totalserve.co.uk
D: £18.50–£20 **S:** £25–£35
Beds: 3D **Baths:** 2 En 1 Pr
🛏 (10) 🅿 (4) ⊬ 📺 🗄 Ⓥ ♨

Woolverton

ST7854   ◀ *Red Lion*

The Old School House, *Woolverton, Bath, Somerset, BA3 6RH.*
Homely accommodation. Converted Victorian school, 10 minutes south of Bath.
Open: All Year (not Xmas/New Year)
01373 830200 (also fax)
Peter & Mary Thornton
D: £20–£25 **S:** £25–£30
Beds: 1F 1T 2D **Baths:** 1 Sh
🛏 🅿 ⊬ 🗄 ♨

Wrington

ST4662   ◀ *White Hart*

Golden Lion Inn, *Wrington, Bristol, BS40 5LA.*
Weston-super-Mare, Mendips, Blagdon, Chew Lakes, Bristol, Clevedon within half-hour drive.
Open: All Year
01934 862205
Mr & Mrs Thorne
D: £18–£25 **S:** £20–£28
Beds: 2F 1D
Baths: 1 En 1 Sh
🛏 (6) 🅿 (3) 📺 ♨

Yeovil

ST5516   ◀ *Bell*

High Holborne, *188 Sherborne Road, Yeovil, Somerset, BA21 4HL.*
Good centre for touring Somerset and Dorset
Open: All Year
01935 421086 (also fax)
Mr Spencer
D: £16–£25 **S:** £16–£25
Beds: 1F 3T 2S **Baths:** 2 En
🛏 🅿 (8) 📺 🐾 🗄 ♨

Cartref, *10 Home Drive, Yeovil, Somerset, BA21 3AP.*
Warm, friendly, comfortable family home. Italian/Spanish spoken.
Open: All Year (not Xmas)
01935 421607 (also fax)
D: £16–£19 **S:** £17–£20
Beds: 1D 1T **Baths:** 1 Pr 1 Sh
🛏 🅿 (4) ⊬ 📺 🗄 Ⓥ ♨

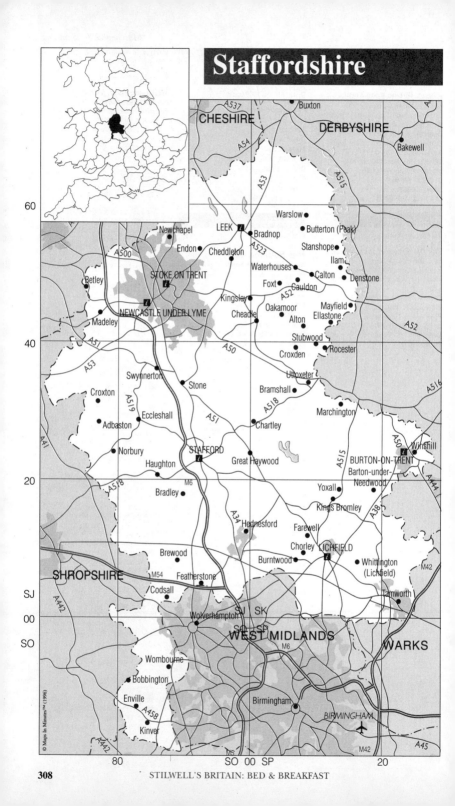

Staffordshire

Tourist Information Centres

Unit 40, Octagon Centre, New Street, **Burton upon Trent**, Staffs, DE14 3TN,
01283 516609.

Market Place, **Leek**, Staffs, ST13 5HH,
01538 483741.

Donegal House, Bore Street, **Lichfield**, Staffs, WS13 6NE,
01543 252109.

Area Reference Library, Ironmarket, **Newcastle-under-Lyme**, Staffs, ST5 1AT,
01782 297313.

The Ancient High House, Greengate Street, **Stafford**, Staffs, ST16 2JA,
01785 619136.

Potteries Shopping Centre, Quadrant Road, **Stoke-on-Trent**, Staffs, ST1 1RZ,
01782 236000.

Marmion House, Lichfield Street, **Tamworth**, Staffs, B79 7BZ,
01827 709581.

Adbaston

SJ7627 ◀ *Wharf Inn, Swan Inn*

Offley Grove Farm, *Adbaston, Eccleshall, Stafford, Staffordshire, ST20 0QB.*
You'll consider this a good find! Excellent breakfasts. Many guests return.
Open: All Year (not Xmas)
Grades: AA 3 Diamond, RAC 3 Diamond
01785 280205 (also fax)
Mrs Hiscoe James
accom@offleygrovefarm.freeserve.co.uk
D: £18.00–£22.00 **S:** £18.00–£22.00
Beds: 2D 1T **Baths:** 2 En

Alton

SK0742 ◀ *Blacksmiths' Arms*

Hillside Farm & Cottages, *Alton Road, Denstone, Uttoxeter, Staffs, ST14 5HG.*
Victorian farmhouse adjacent Alton Towers. Large gardens/orchard, views, cottages available.
Open: All year
Grades: ETC 3 Diamond
01889 590760 Mrs Johnson
D: £15.00–£18.00 **S:** £18.00–£20.00
Beds: 2F 1D 1T **Baths:** 2 En 2 Sh

Planning a longer stay? Always ask for any special rates

The Dale, *Alton, Stoke-on-Trent, Staffs, ST10 4BG.*
Ideal overnight base if visiting Alton Towers. Friendly family home.
Open: All Year (not Xmas)
Grades: ETC 4 Diamond
01538 702394 Mrs Burrows
thedalealton@talk21.com
D: £17.00 **S:** £22.00
Beds: 2T 1D **Baths:** 1 Sh

The Hawthorns, *8 Tythe Barn, Alton, Stoke-on-Trent, Staffs, ST10 4AZ.*
Home-from-home atmosphere. Alton Towers 1 mile. Peak District close by.
Open: All Year (not Xmas)
Grades: ETC 3 Diamond
01538 702197 Mrs Callear
Fax: 01538 703631
altonbb@aol.com
D: £17.50–£20.00 **S:** £22.00–£25.00
Beds: 1F 1D **Baths:** 1 Pr 1 Sh

Tythe Barn House, *Denstone Lane, Alton, Stoke-on-Trent, Staffs, ST10 4AX.*
C17th farmhouse cottage, one mile Alton Towers.
Open: All Year
01538 702852
Mrs Kilgallon
D: £15.00–£19.00 **S:** fr £20.00
Beds: 2F 3D **Baths:** 3 En 1 Sh

Rockhaven, *Smithy Bank, Alton, Stoke-on-Trent, Staffordshire, ST10 4AA.*
Modernised country home near Alton Towers, Potteries and Staffordshire Way.
Open: All Year (not Xmas)
01538 702066 Mrs Allen
D: £17.50–£25.00 **S:** £25.00
Beds: 1F 2D

Barton-under-Needwood

SK1818 ◀ *The Bell, Shoulder Of Lamb, Three Horseshoes*

Threeway Cottage, *2 Wales Lane, Barton-under-Needwood, Burton-upon-Trent, Staffs, DE13 8JF.*
1.25 miles off A38 in award winning village. C17th Listed charming beamed cottage.
Open: All Year
01283 713572
Mrs Jakeman
D: £20.00–£22.00 **S:** £20.00–£21.00
Beds: 1F 1T 1S **Baths:** 2 En 1 Pr

Betley

SJ7548 ◀ *Hand & Trumpet Inn, Swan Inn*

The White Cottage, *Main Road, Betley, Crewe, CW3 9BH.*
C16th cottage; tastefully decorated, peaceful gardens, excellent breakfasts.
Open: All Year (not Xmas)
01270 820218 Mrs Chisnall
D: £17.50 **S:** £25.00
Beds: 1T/F 1D 1S **Baths:** 1 Sh

Bobbington

SO8090 ◀ *Royal Oak, The Old Gate*

Whittmere Farm, *Bobbington, Stourbridge, West Midlands, DY7 5DX.*
Georgian Farmhouse on working Farm.
Open: All Year (not Xmas/New Year)
01384 221232 Mr & Mrs Snelson
D: £15.00–£20.00 **S:** £15.00–£20.00
Beds: 1F 1T **Baths:** 1 Sh

Bradley

SJ8717 ◀ *Red Lion, The Shropshire*

Littywood House, *Bradley, Stafford, Staffordshire, ST18 9DW.*
Littywood is a beautiful C14th manor house set in own grounds.
Open: All Year (not Xmas)
Grades: ETC 3 Diamond
01785 780234 Mrs Busby
Fax: 01785 780770
D: £20.00–£21.00 **S:** £25.00–£30.00
Beds: 1D 1T **Baths:** 1 En 1 Pr

Bradnop

SK0155

Middle Farm Guest House, *Apesford, Bradnop, Leek, Staffordshire, ST13 7EX.*
Old farmhouse converted to B&B. Ensuite rooms. Half-price children in family rooms.
Open: All Year
01538 382839 (also fax)
Ms Sheldon
D: £20.00–£25.00 **S:** £25.00–£30.00
Beds: 4F 2D 1T

Bramshall

SK0533 ◀ *Blythe Inn, Robin Hood*

West Lodge, *Bramshall, Uttoxeter, Staffs, ST14 5BG.*
Country house standing in a large secluded attractive garden, within easy reach of Stoke-on-Trent.
Open: All Year (not Xmas)
01889 568421
Mrs George
D: £18.00 **S:** £25.00
Beds: 2D 1T **Baths:** 1 En 1 Sh

Brewood

SJ8808 ◀ *The Royal Oak*

The Blackladies, *Brewood, Stafford, ST19 9BH.*
Grade II* Listed Tudor house set in 5 acres of gardens.
Open: All Year
Grades: ETC 5 Diamond Gold Award
01902 850210 Mrs Bywater
Fax: 01902 851782
D: £25.00–£32.50
S: £28.00–£35.00
Beds: 1F 1T 2D **Baths:** 3 En 1 Pr

Burntwood

SK0610   Nelson Chorley, Windmill, Star

Davoll's Cottage, 156 Woodhouses Road, Burntwood, Staffs, WS7 9EL.
Country cottage by woodland with easy access to Lichfield and the surrounding areas.
Open: All Year
Grades: ETC 3 Diamond
01543 671250 Mrs Chrisfield
D: £20.00–£22.00 **S:** £20.00–£25.00
Beds: 2T **Baths:** 1 En 1 Pr
⮁ ▣ (4) ⊁ ⬚ ⫟ ✕ ▦ ⬚ ⚲

Butterton

SK0756

Coxon Green Farm, Butterton, Leek, Staffordshire, ST13 7TA.
17th Century farmhouse in Peak District village overlooking Manifold Valley.
Open: All Year (not Xmas/New Year)
Grades: ETC 4 Diamond
01538 304221 Ms Tomkinson
D: £20.00–£22.00 **S:** £22.00–£25.00
Beds: 3D **Baths:** 3 En
▣ ⊁ ⬚ ▦ ⬚ ⚲

Calton

SK1050   Crown, Yew Tree

Broadhurst Farm, Calton, Waterhouses, Stoke-on-Trent, Staffs, ST10 3LQ.
Lovely farmhouse edge of Peak Park. Close to Alton Towers.
Open: Easter to Nov
Grades: ETC 3 Diamond
01538 308261 Mr & Mrs Mycock
D: £18.00–£20.00 **S:** £19.00–£22.00
Beds: 1F 1D **Baths:** 2 En
⮁ ▣ (14) ⬚ ⫟ ✕ ▦ ⬚ ⚲

Cauldon

SK0749

The Cross Inn & Restaurant, Cauldon Lowe, Cauldon, Waterhouses, Stoke on Trent, Staffordshire, ST10 3EX.
Warm welcoming inn set in heart of the Staffordshire countryside.
Open: All Year
Grades: ETC 3 Diamond
01538 308338 Mr Wilkinson
Fax: 01538 308767
106245.3615@compuserve.com
D: £20.00–£22.50 **S:** £20.00–£22.50
Beds: 2F 1T 4D 1S **Baths:** 8 En
⮁ ▣ ⊁ ⬚ ✕ ▦ ⚲ ♿ cc

Chartley

SK0028   Cock Inn

Mill Cottage B&B, Chartley, Stafford, Staffordshire, ST18 0LH.
Homely country cottage overlooking open countryside. A518 Stafford/Uttoxeter.
Open: All Year
Grades: ETC 2 Diamond
01889 271109 Ms Schuller
D: £13.50–£16.00 **S:** £17.50–£20.00
Beds: 1F 1D **Baths:** 1 Sh
⮁ ▣ (2) ⬚ ⫟ ▦ ⬚ ✳ ⚲

BATHROOMS
Pr - Private
Sh - Shared
En - Ensuite

Cheadle

SK0143   Talbot Inn, The Red Lion

Abbot's Haye, Cherry Lane, Cheadle, Stoke-on-Trent, Staffs, ST10 4QS.
Open: All Year (not Xmas/New Year)
01538 750645 Mr Piers-Leake
Fax: 01538 754951
abbots.haye@virgin.net
S: fr £25.00 **S:** fr £37.50
Beds: 4F 1D **Baths:** 5 En
⮁ ▣ (5) ⊁ ⬚ ✕ ▦ ⬚ ⚲ cc
Country guest house with Tudor roots. Quietly situated in six acres outside Cheadle. Four miles from Alton Towers with the Potteries and other Staffordshire attractions within easy reach. Comfortable beds, good breakfasts, beautiful gardens for guests to relax in.

Cheddleton

SJ9752   The Boat, Traveller's Rest

Hillcrest, 74 Folly Lane, Cheddleton, Leek, Staffordshire, ST13 7DA.
Country house idyllically situated overlooking countryside, good choice of breakfast.
Open: All Year (not Xmas/New Year)
01782 550483 j.a.coxon@talk21.com
D: £19.00–£22.00 **S:** £22.00–£25.00
Beds: 1T 2D **Baths:** 1 En 1 Pr
⮁ ▣ (4) ⊁ ⬚ ▦ ⬚ ⚲

Choir Cottage, Ostlers Lane, Cheddleton, Leek, Staffs, ST13 7HS.
17th Century cottage in quiet location. Ideal honeymoon or special anniversary treat.
Open: All Year (not Xmas)
Grades: ETC 5 Diamond, Gold Award, AA 5 Diamond
01538 360561 Mr & Mrs Sutcliffe
elaine.sutcliff@ic24
D: £27.50–£29.50 **S:** £35.00–£45.00
Beds: 1F 1D **Baths:** 2 En
⮁ (5) ▣ (6) ⊁ ✕ ▦ ⚲

Chorley

SK0710   The Windmill, Red Lion, Nelson

'Stone House' Farm, Farewell, Chorley, Lichfield, Staffs, WS13 8DS.
17th Century stone cottage surrounded by beautiful countryside. Peaceful hamlet.
Open: All Year
Grades: AA 4 Diamond
01543 682575 (also fax)
Mrs Cowell
D: £17.00–£22.00 **S:** £17.00–£24.00
Beds: 3D 1S **Baths:** 1 En 2 Sh
⮁ (5) ▣ ⊁ ⬚ ⫟ ▦ ⬚ ⚲ ♿

Codsall

SJ8703

Moors Farm & Country Restaurant, Chillington Lane, Codsall, Wolverhampton, Staffs, WV8 1QF.
Open: All Year
Grades: AA 3 Diamond, RAC 3 Diamond
01902 842330 Mrs Moreton
Fax: 01902 847878
enquiries@moorsfarm-hotel.co.uk
D: £22.50–£27.50 **S:** £30.00–£36.00
Beds: 1F 3D 2T 1S **Baths:** 4 En 2 Sh
⮁ (4) ▣ (20) ⊁ ⬚ ✕ ▦ ⬚ ⬚ ✳ ⚲ cc
A cosy farmhouse in a picturesque valley. Codsall Village 1 mile, Wolverhampton 5 miles. Bedrooms have lovely views and very good facilities. Mrs Moreton is an excellent cook; dinner served in the oak-beamed dining room accompanied by some wine from the bar is a must.

Croxden

SK0639   The Raddle

Woodhouse Farm, Nabb Lane, Croxden, Alton, Uttoxeter, Staffs, ST14 5JB.
Enchanting picture-book cottage standing on a quiet country lane close to many visitor attractions. **Open:** All Year
01889 507507 Fax: 01889 507282
ddeb@lineone.net
D: £19.00–£25.00 **S:** £29.00–£35.00
Beds: 1F 4D **Baths:** 5 En
▣ (6) ⊁ ⬚ ▦ ⬚ ⚲ cc

Croxton

SJ7831   Vernon Yonge

Glenwood, Croxton, Eccleshall, Staffordshire, ST21 6JA.
C16th Century framed cottage in small country village. **Open:** All Year
Grades: RAC 3 Diamond
01630 620238 Mr & Mrs Martin
D: £17.00–£19.00 **S:** £18.00–£20.00
Beds: 2T 1D **Baths:** 1 En
▣ (6) ⊁ ⬚ ⫟ ▦ ⬚ ⚲

Denstone

SK0940   Blacksmiths' Arms

Hillside Farm & Cottages, Alton Road, Denstone, Uttoxeter, Staffs, ST14 5HG.
Victorian farmhouse adjacent Alton Towers. Large gardens/orchard, views, cottages available.
Open: All year **Grades:** ETC 3 Diamond
01889 590760 Mrs Johnson
D: £15.00–£18.00 **S:** £18.00–£20.00
Beds: 2F 1D 1T **Baths:** 2 En 2 Sh
⮁ ▣ ⬚ ▦ ⬚ ⚲

Eccleshall

SJ8329

Wincote Farm, Wincote Lane, Eccleshall, Stafford, Staffordshire, ST21 6JE.
Exceptional country house on 100-acre mixed farm - a stay you will not forget.
Open: All Year
01785 850337 Mrs Norbury
Fax: 01785 850605
susannorbury@wincotefarm.freeserve.co.uk
D: £18.00–£26.00 **S:** £18.00–£20.00
Beds: 4F 2D 1T 1S **Baths:** 1 En 1 Sh
⮁ ▣ ⊁ ⬚ ✕ ▦ ⬚ ⚲

Ellastone

SK1143 🍺 *Royal Oak, Duncombe Arms*

Foxgloves, *Calwich Rise, Ellastone, Ashbourne, Derbyshire, DE6 2HE.*
Superbly restored barn accommodation and gardens in elevated situation, excellent views over Dove Valley.
Open: Mar to Nov
01335 324664 (also fax) Mr Smith
D: £20.00–£25.00 **S:** £22.00–£27.00
Beds: 1D **Baths:** 1 En 1 Pr
🛇 🅿 (8) ⅟ 📺 🎶 🔟 ☕

Endon

SJ9253 🍺 *The Plough, The Wheel*

The Hollies, *Clay Lake, Endon, Stoke-on-Trent, Staffs, ST9 9DD.*
Beautiful Victorian house, set in lovely garden, with country view.
Open: All Year (not Xmas)
Grades: ETC 3 Diamond
01782 503252 Mrs Hodgson
D: £18.00–£20.00 **S:** £22.00–£35.00
Beds: 1F 2D 2T **Baths:** 5 En
🛇 (2) 🅿 (5) ⅟ 📺 🎶 🔟 🅥 ☕

Reynolds Hey, *Park Lane, Endon, Stoke-on-Trent, Staffordshire, ST9 9JB.*
Set in rolling countryside, this modernised farmhouse offers comfortable and friendly accommodation.
Open: All Year (not Xmas)
Grades: ETC 3 Diamond
01782 502717 Mrs Weaver
D: £18.00–£20.00 **S:** £25.00
Beds: 1F 1D 1T **Baths:** 3 En
🛇 🅿 (3) ⅟ 📺 🎶 ✗ 🔟 🅥 ☕

Hollinhurst Farm, *Park Lane, Endon, Stoke on Trent, Staffs, ST9 9JB.*
Working farm; panoramic views close to Alton Towers, the Potteries.
Open: All Year **Grades:** ETC 4 Diamond
01782 502633 Mr Clowes
hjball@ukf.net
D: £18.00–£20.00 **S:** £18.00–£20.00
Beds: 1F 1D 1T **Baths:** 2 En 1 Pr
🛇 🅿 (5) ⅟ 📺 🎶 🔟 🅥 ✳ ☕ ♿

Enville

SO8287 🍺 *The Cat*

Morfe Hall, *Enville, Stourbridge, Staffs, DY7 5JU.*
Lovely old house surrounded by beautiful open country. **Open:** All Year
01384 877004 Mrs Hobbs
morfehall@hotmail.com
D: £25.00–£30.00 **S:** fr £25.00
Beds: 1D **Baths:** 1 En
🛇 🅿 (20) ⅟ 📺 🎶 ✗ 🔟 🅥 ☕

Farewell

SK0811 🍺 *The Nelson*

Little Pipe Farm, *Little Pipe Lane, Farewell, Lichfield, Staffs, WS13 8BS.*
Arable and beef working farm. C19th farmhouse superb views.
Open: All Year
01543 683066 Mrs Clewley
D: £16.00–£20.00 **S:** £18.00–£20.00
Beds: 1F 1D 1T **Baths:** 1 Sh
🛇 🅿 (10) 📺 ✗ 🔟 🅥 ☕

Featherstone

SJ9405

Featherstone Farm Hotel, *New Road, Featherstone, Wolverhampton, W Mids, WV10 7NW.*
Open: All Year
01902 725371 Fax: 01902 731741
D: £25.00–£35.00 **S:** £35.00–£45.00
Beds: 4D 2T 2S **Baths:** 4 En 2 Pr 2 Sh
🛇 (2) 🅿 ⅟ 📺 🎶 ✗ 🔟 🅥 ☕ ♿
Restaurant offering Indian cuisine, Rolls Royce available, half hour from NEC and NIA C17th complex.

Foxt

SK0348 🍺 *Fox and Goose*

Shaw Gate Farm, *Foxt, Stoke on Trent, Staffs, ST10 2HN.*
Overlooking Churnet Valley, Residents Bar, Near Alton Towers.
Open: All Year (not Xmas/New Year)
Grades: ETC 3 Diamond
01538 266590 (also fax)
Mr Morris
D: £20.00–£25.00 **S:** £30.00–£50.00
Beds: 2F 3D **Baths:** 5 En
🛇 🅿 ⅟ 📺 🔟 ☕ ✗ cc

Great Haywood

SK0023 🍺 *Hollybush Inn*

Common Farm Motel, *Pasturefields, Great Haywood, Stafford, ST18 0RB.*
Tastefully converted barns on a working farm with ample parking for larger vehicles.
Open: All Year (not Xmas)
01889 270209
Mrs Pickard
D: £16.25–£23.25 **S:** £17.00–£24.00
Beds: 3F 5D 2T 4S **Baths:** 12 En 1 Sh
🛇 (1) 🅿 (15) ⅟ 📺 🔟 🅥 ☕ ♿ cc

Haughton

SJ8620 🍺 *The Bell*

The Old School, *Newport Road, Haughton, Stafford, Staffordshire, ST18 9JH.*
Listed building (1841) in centre of attractive village close to Stafford.
Open: Easter to Oct
Grades: AA 3 Diamond
01785 780358 Mrs Jenks
info@theoldsc.co.uk
D: £19.00 **S:** £19.00
Beds: 1D 1T 1S **Baths:** 2 Sh
🛇 ⅟ 📺 🔟 🅥 ☕ ♿

Hednesford

SK0012 🍺 *Plough and Harrow*

York House Guest House, *34 Anglesey Street, Hednesford, Cannock, Staffs, WS12 5AA.*
Quiet, comfortable, spacious Edwardian house to accommodate worker or player.
Open: All Year
01543 422502 Ms Brown
D: £18.00 **S:** £26.00
Beds: 1F 4T 1D **Baths:** 2 En 1 Sh
🛇 🅿 (8) 🔟 🎶 🔟 🅥 ☕

Ilam

SK1350 🍺 *The Crown, The Forge*

Throwley Hall Farm, *Ilam, Ashbourne, Derbyshire, DE6 2BB.*
Large, rural Georgian farmhouse.
Open: All Year (not Xmas)
Grades: ETC 4 Diamond
01538 308202 Mrs Richardson
Fax: 01538 308243
throwleyhall@talk21.com
D: £22.00–£26.00 **S:** £22.00–£26.00
Beds: 2F 1T 1D **Baths:** 3 En 1 Pr
🛇 🅿 ⅟ 📺 🎶 🔟 🅥 ☕

King's Bromley

SK1216 🍺 *Royal Oak*

5 Manor Road, *King's Bromley, Burton-on-Trent, Staffs, DE13 7HZ.*
Early C19th manor cottage.
Open: All Year (not Xmas)
01543 472769 Mr & Mrs Hodges
b&b@torreavon.freeserve.co.uk
D: fr £15.00 **S:** fr £15.00
Beds: 1D 1T **Baths:** 1 Sh
🅿 (1) ⅟ 📺 🎶 ✗ 🔟 ☕

Kingsley

SK0046 🍺 *Linden Tree*

The Church Farm, *Holt Lane, Kingsley, Stoke on Trent, Staffs, ST10 2BA.*
VISITING ALTON TOWERS? RELAX AFTERWARDS IN OUR BEAUTIFUL PERIOD FARMHOUSE.
Open: All Year (not Xmas)
01538 754759 (also fax)
Mrs Clowes
D: £18.00–£20.00 **S:** £18.00–£22.00
Beds: 1F **Baths:** 1 En
🛇 🅿 (6) ⅟ 📺 🔟 ☕

Kinver

SO8483 🍺 *Vine Inn*

The Old Vicarage, *Vicarage Drive, Kinver, Stourbridge, W Mids, DY7 6HJ.*
Very quiet position near village and NT Rock House.
Open: All Year (not Xmas)
01384 872784 Mr & Mrs Harris
D: £20.00–£22.00 **S:** £20.00–£22.00
Beds: 2T 1S **Baths:** 1 En 1 Sh
🛇 🅿 (6) 📺 🎶 🔟 🅥 ☕

Leek

SJ9856 🍺 *The Abbey, Swan Hotel, Black Swan*

Beechfields, *Park Road, Leek, Staffordshire, ST13 8JS.*
Large Victorian house in spacious gardens. Delicious breakfast. Warm and relaxing.
Open: All Year (not Xmas)
Grades: ETC 4 Diamond
01538 372825 Mrs Rider
judith@beech-fields.fsnet.co.uk
D: £20.00 **S:** £25.00
Beds: 1F 2D **Baths:** 3 En
🛇 🅿 (4) ⅟ 📺 🎶 🔟 🅥 ☕

Birchalls (PF) Ltd, The Hatcheries, Church Lane, Mount Pleasant, Leek, Staffs, ST13 5ET.
Secluded position, adjacent to 26 acres local parklands, overlooking moorland areas. **Open:** All Year
01538 399552
D: £21.00–£25.00 **S:** £25.00–£29.00
Beds: 1F 1D 2T **Baths:** 6 Pr
⛺ (2) 🅿 (12) 📺 ⍩ ✕ 📖 👗

Warrington House, 108 Buxton Road, Leek, Staffs, ST13 6EJ.
Not posh! Clean, comfortable, happy, with plenty of good food. **Open:** All Year
01538 399566 Mr Whone
D: £15.00–£16.00 **S:** £17.00–£18.00
Beds: 1F 2T **Baths:** 1 Sh
⛺ 🅿 (1) 📺 ✕ 📖 ⍩ ❀ 👗

Lichfield

SK1109   The Boat, Three Tuns, The Greyhound, Little Barrow, Shoulder of Mutton, Pig & Truffle

Netherstowe House North, off Netherstowe Lane, Eastern Avenue, Lichfield, Staffs, WS13 6AY.
Grade II Listed Georgian building 3/4 mile from Lichfield city centre.
Open: All Year **Grades:** ETC 2 Diamond
01543 254631 Mrs Marshall
D: £19.00–£21.00 **S:** £21.00–£22.00
Beds: 1F 1T **Baths:** 1 Pr 1 Sh
⛺ (1) 🅿 (6) ⍐ 📺 📖 ⍩ ❀ 👗

Madeley

SJ7744

The Old Hall, Madeley, Crewe, Cheshire, CW3 9DX.
Timber-framed house of considerable character set in mature gardens.
Open: All Year (not Xmas)
01782 750209 Mrs Hugh
Fax: 01782 751040
ahugh@oldha11.freeserve.co.uk
D: £22.50–£30.00 **S:** £32.00–£45.00
Beds: 1F 1D 1T **Baths:** 1 En 1 Sh
⛺ (5) 🅿 (20) ⍐ 📺 ✕ 📖 ⍩ 👗

Marchington

SK1330   Dog & Partridge

Forest Hills, Moisty Lane, Marchington, Uttoxeter, Staffs, ST14 8JY.
Quiet Edwardian house enjoying views across River Dove Valley.
Open: All Year **Grades:** ETC 3 Diamond
01283 820447 Mrs Brassington
D: fr £21.00 **S:** fr £25.00
Beds: 3D 2T **Beds:** 5 En
⛺ (5) 🅿 (6) ⍐ 📺 ✕ 📖 ⍩ 👗

Mayfield

SK1546   Royal Oak

Dove House, Bridge Hill, Mayfield, Ashbourne, Derbyshire, DE6 2HN.
Large detached Victorian house close to Peak District and Alton Towers.
Open: All Year (not Xmas/New Year)
Grades: ETC 4 Diamond
01335 343329 Mrs Green
D: fr £20.00 **S:** fr £28.00
Beds: 1D **Baths:** 1 En
🅿 (1) 📺 ✕ 📖 ⍩ 👗

Newcastle-under-Lyme

SJ8546   Milehouse Inn, Polite Vicar, The Wulstan

Durlston Guest House, Kimberley Road (off A34), Newcastle-under-Lyme, Staffs, ST5 9EG.
Ten mins' walk from town centre, convenient for Alton Towers and Potteries. **Open:** All Year (not Xmas)
01782 611708 Mr & Mrs Stott
Fax: 01782 639770 durlston@cwcom.net
D: £17.50–£18.00 **S:** £20.00–£21.00
Beds: 2F 1D 1T 3S **Baths:** 2 Sh
⛺ ⍐ 📺 ⍩ 📖 ⍩ 💳 cc

Newchapel

SJ8654   Dog & Partridge, Packmoor

The Old Vicarage, Birchenwood Road, Newchapel, Stoke-on-Trent, Staffordshire, ST7 4QT.
Built 1848 in tranquil gardens. 10 minute M6. Rural retreat.
Open: All Year **Grades:** ETC 4 Diamond
01782 785270 Mrs Kent-Baguley
oldvicarageb&b@
birchenwood.freeserve.co.uk
D: £20.00–£25.00 **S:** £20.00–£25.00
Beds: 1F 1D 1S **Baths:** 2 En 1 Pr
⛺ (8) 🅿 (6) ⍐ 📺 ⍩ 📖 ⍩ 👗

Norbury

SJ7823   The Plough & Reform, The Woodweavers

Oulton House Farm, Norbury, Stafford, Staffordshire, ST20 0PG.
Visit our warm, comfortable Victorian farmhouse with marvellous countryside views. **Open:** All Year (not Xmas)
Grades: ETC 4 Diamond
01785 284264 (also fax)
Mrs Palmer
judy@palmerj.fsnet.co.uk
D: £22.50 **S:** £30.00
Beds: 2D 1T **Baths:** 3 En
⛺ 🅿 (3) 📺 📖 ⍩ 💳 cc

Oakamoor

SK0544   Cross Inn, Lord Nelson

Ribden Farm, Oakamoor, Stoke-on-Trent, Staffs, ST10 3BW.
Open: All Year (not Xmas)
Grades: ETC 4 Diamond, AA 4 Diamond, RAC 4 Diamond, Sparkling Diamond Award
01538 702830 Mrs Shaw
D: £20.00–£24.00 **S:** £30.00–£35.00
Beds: 5F 2D 1T **Baths:** 7 En 1 Pr
⛺ 🅿 (10) 📺 📖 👗 cc
Listed stone farmhouse (1748). Some rooms with four poster beds, all ensuite with TVs, clock radios and tea/coffee. Quiet countryside overlooking Weaver Hills, large gardens with safe off-road parking. Five minutes from Alton Towers.

National Grid References are for villages, towns and cities – not for individual houses

Rocester

SK1039   Red Lion

The Leeze Guest House, 63 High Street, Rocester, Uttoxeter, Staffs, ST14 5JU.
Friendly village location convenient for Potteries, Dales and Alton towers.
Open: All Year
Grades: ETC 3 Diamond, AA 3 Diamond
01889 591146 (also fax) Mr Venn
D: £20.00 **S:** £26.00
Beds: 2F 1D 2T **Baths:** 4 En 1 Pr
⛺ 🅿 (6) ⍩ ✕ 📖 ⍩ 👗

Stafford

SJ9223   Red Lion, Picture House, Sun Inn, Crown Inn, The Shropshire, The Radford, Bank Inn, Barley Mow

Bailey Hotel, 63 Lichfield Road, Stafford, Staffordshire, ST17 4LL.
Open: All Year (not Xmas)
Grades: ETC 3 Diamond
01785 214133 Mr & Mrs Ayres
Fax: 01785 227920
D: £18.00–£23.00 **S:** £21.50–£30.00
Beds: 1F 5D 3T 2S **Baths:** 4 En 2 Sh
⛺ 🅿 (11) 📺 ⍩ 📖 👗
Modern detached hotel, comfortably furnished, parking in own grounds.

Littlywood House, Bradley, Stafford, Staffordshire, ST18 9DW.
Littlywood is a beautiful C14th manor house set in own grounds.
Open: All Year (not Xmas)
Grades: ETC 3 Diamond
01785 780234 Mrs Busby
Fax: 01785 780770
D: £20.00–£21.00 **S:** £25.00–£30.00
Beds: 1D 1T **Baths:** 1 En 1 Pr
⛺ 🅿 (10) 📺 📖 👗

Cedarwood, 46 Weeping Cross, Stafford, Staffordshire, ST17 0DS.
Open: All Year (not Xmas)
Grades: ETC 4 Diamond, Silver Award
01785 662981 Mrs Welsby
D: £15.00–£18.00 **S:** £15.00–£18.00
Beds: 1D 1T 1S **Baths:** 2 Sh
⛺ (9) 🅿 (3) ⍐ 📺 📖 ⍩ 👗
Unusual detached bungalow in own grounds, excellent accommodation and hospitality.

Leonards Croft Hotel, 80 Lichfield Road, Stafford, Staffordshire, ST17 4LP.
Victorian house in award winning garden walking distance town centre.
Open: All Year (not Xmas/New Year)
Grades: AA 4 Diamond, RAC 4 Diamond
01785 223676 Mrs Johnson
D: £25.00–£30.00 **S:** £30.00–£35.00
Beds: 4F 3D 2T **Baths:** 4 En 4 Sh
⛺ 🅿 (10) ⍩ ✕ 📖 ⍩ 👗 cc

Vine Hotel, Salter Street, Stafford, Staffordshire, ST16 2JU.
This haven of your imagination is the Vine Hotel. **Open:** All Year
Grades: AA 2 Stars
01785 244112 Mr Austin
Fax: 01785 246612
D: £25.00–£26.00 **S:** £30.00–£40.00
Beds: 1F 10D 3T 10S **Baths:** 24 Pr 1 En
⛺ 🅿 (20) 📺 ✕ 📖 👗 cc

Stanshope

SK1254   ◀ *Watts Russell Arms*

Stanshope Hall, *Stanshope, Ashbourne, Derbyshire, DE6 2AD.*
Peace and quiet and lovely views over peak district hills.
Open: All Year (not Xmas)
01335 310278 Miss Chambers
Fax: 01335 310470
naomi@stanshope.demon.co.uk
D: £25.00–£40.00 **S:** £25.00–£40.00
Beds: 2D 1T **Baths:** 3 En
🛏 ▣ (3) 📺 🛒 🍽 ⱱ ⚓ **cc**

Stoke-on-Trent

SJ8747   ◀ *The Plough, The Wheel, Poachers Cottage*

The Hollies, *Clay Lake, Endon, Stoke-on-Trent, Staffs, ST9 9DD.*
Beautiful Victorian house, set in lovely garden, with country view.
Open: All Year (not Xmas)
Grades: ETC 3 Diamond
01782 503252 Mrs Hodgson
D: £18.00–£20.00 **S:** £22.00–£35.00
Beds: 1F 2D 2T **Baths:** 5 En
🛏 (2) ▣ (5) 🗡 📺 🛒 🍽 ⱱ ⚓

Reynolds Hey, *Park Lane, Endon, Stoke-on-Trent, Staffordshire, ST9 9JB.*
Open: All Year (not Xmas)
Grades: ETC 3 Diamond
01782 502717 Mrs Weaver
D: £18.00–£20.00 **S:** £25.00
Beds: 1F 1D 1T **Baths:** 3 En
🛏 ▣ (3) 🗡 📺 🛒 ✕ 🍽 ⱱ ⚓
Set in rolling countryside, this modernised farmhouse offers comfortable and friendly accommodation and a friendly atmosphere. Situated within a few miles of the world famous Doulton and Wedgwood potteries, Alton towers amusement park and the beautiful moors and dales of the Staffordshire Derbyshire borders.

The Old Dairy House, *Trentham Park, Stoke-on-Trent, Staffs, ST4 8AE.*
Listed half timbered house and gardens set in parkland. **Open:** All Year (not Xmas)
01782 641209 Mrs Moore
D: £20.00–£25.00 **S:** £30.00–£35.00
Beds: 2D **Baths:** 2 Pr
▣ (20) 📺 🛒 ✕ 🍽

Stone

SJ9034   ◀ *The Granvilles, The Star, George & Dragon*

Field House, *Stafford Road, Stone, Staffs, ST15 0HE.*
Open: All Year **Grades:** AA 3 Diamond
01785 605712 Mrs Busfield
D: £16.00–£18.00 **S:** £22.00–£26.00
Beds: 1F 1D 1T **Baths:** 1 En 1 Sh
🛏 ▣ (4) 🗡 📺 🍽 ⚓
Listed Georgian house offering charming spacious accommodation in warm, relaxed atmosphere, situated in beautiful grounds close to canal town centre and excellent choice of restaurants. Ideal for Wedgwood, Potteries, Shugborough, Alton Towers and the Peak District. Non-smoking bedrooms.

Lock House, *74 Newcastle Road, Stone, Staffs, ST15 8LB.*
Spacious accommodation in canal side house. Short walk to good restaurants.
Open: All Year (not Xmas/New Year)
Grades: ETC 4 Diamond
01785 811551 Mrs Heath
Fax: 01785 286587
mbd@fsdial.co.uk
D: £20.00–£22.00 **S:** £30.00–£32.00
Beds: 2D **Baths:** 2 En
🛏 ▣ (3) 🗡 📺 🛒 🍽 ⱱ ⚓

Stubwood

SK0939

Rowan Lodge, *Stubwood, Denstone, Uttoxeter, Staffordshire, ST14 5HU.*
A short drive to Alton Towers/Peak District.
Open: All Year (not Xmas/New Year)
Grades: ETC 4 Diamond
01889 590913 Mrs Warren
D: £17.00–£20.00 **S:** £18.00–£22.00
Beds: 1F 1D **Baths:** 2 En
🛏 ▣ (2) 🗡 📺 ✕ 🍽 ⚓

Swynnerton

SJ8535   ◀ *Fitzherbert Arms, Darlaston Inn*

Home Farm, *Swynnerton, Stone, Staffs, ST15 0RA.*
Elizabethan farmhouse, easy access to Alton towers and potteries.
Open: All Year
Grades: ETC 2 Diamond
01782 796241 Mrs Cope
homefarm@cope32.fsnet.co.uk
D: £17.50–£20.00 **S:** £17.50
Beds: 1F 3D 3T 3S **Baths:** 2 En 2 Pr 2 Sh
🛏 ▣ (10) 🛒 🍽 ✕ 🍽 ⱱ ⚓

Tamworth

SK2203

Victoria Court Hotel, *42 Victoria Road, Tamworth, Staffs, B79 7HU.*
Minutes from railway station and town centre. In-house Italian restaurant.
Open: All Year
01827 64698 Mrs Morlini
Fax: 01827 312368
victoriacourthotel@btinternet.com
D: £19.00–£27.50 **S:** £22.00–£38.00
Beds: 2F 1T 2D 4S **Baths:** 5 Pr 1 Sh
🛏 ▣ (20) 📺 ✕ 🍽 ⱱ ⚓ **cc**

Uttoxeter

SK0933

White Hart Hotel, *Carter Street, Uttoxeter, Staffs, ST14 8EU.*
Friendly, 16th century coaching inn, close to Alton towers.
Open: All Year
01889 562437 Mr Wood
Fax: 01889 565099
white.hart.hotel.104111@punchgroup.co.uk
D: £31.50–£63.00 **S:** £56.00
Beds: 3F 5T 11D 2S **Baths:** 21 En
🛏 ▣ (40) 🗡 📺 🛒 ✕ 🍽 ⱱ ⚓ **cc**

Warslow

SK0858

The Greyhound Inn, *Warslow, Buxton, Derbyshire, SK17 0JN.*
Cosy village pub, open fires, good home cooking, exceptionally friendly.
Open: All Year
01298 84249
Mr Mullarkey
D: £17.50 **S:** £17.50
Beds: 2D 2S **Baths:** 1 Sh
🛏 (10) ▣ (20) 🛒 ✕ 🍽 ⚓ **cc**

Waterhouses

SK0850   ◀ *Ye Olde Crown*

Lee House Farm, *Waterhouses, Stoke-on-Trent, Staffordshire, ST10 3HW.*
Lovely Georgian farmhouse village setting, close to the Manifold Valley.
Open: All Year
Grades: ETC 4 Diamond, AA 4 Diamond
01538 308439 Ms Little
D: £20.00–£25.00 **S:** £25.00–£30.00
Beds: 2D 1T **Baths:** 3 En
🛏 ▣ (4) 🗡 📺 🍽 ⱱ ⚓

Whittington (Lichfield)

SK1608   ◀ *The Dog*

Hawthorns House, *44a Church Street, Whittington, Lichfield, Staffs, WS14 9JX.*
Old Victorian house. 15 minutes Belfry and most motorways.
Open: All Year (not Xmas/New Year)
01543 432613
Mrs Christie
D: £38.00–£40.00
S: £19.00–£20.00
Beds: 2T 1D **Baths:** 1 Sh
🛏 ▣ 🗡 📺 ✕ 🍽 ⱱ ⚓

Winshill

SK2623   ◀ *Royal Oak*

Meadow View, *203 Newton Road, Winshill, Burton-upon-Trent, Staffs, DE15 0TU.*
Double-fronted house overlooking River Trent in attractive wooded garden.
Open: All Year (not Xmas)
Grades: ETC 3 Diamond
01283 564046
Mrs Hancox
D: £17.00 **S:** £17.00
Beds: 1T 1S **Baths:** 1 Pr
🛏 (10) ▣ (3) 🗡 📺 🛒 🍽 ⱱ ⚓

Wombourne

SO8792

24 Dinkinson Road, *Wombourne, Wolverhampton, W Mids, WV5 0NH.*
Central to many Midland attractions.
Open: All Year
01902 895614
Mrs Whitmore
D: fr £13.50 **S:** fr £13.50
Beds: 1T
🛏 ▣ 📺 🛒 ✕ 🍽

Suffolk

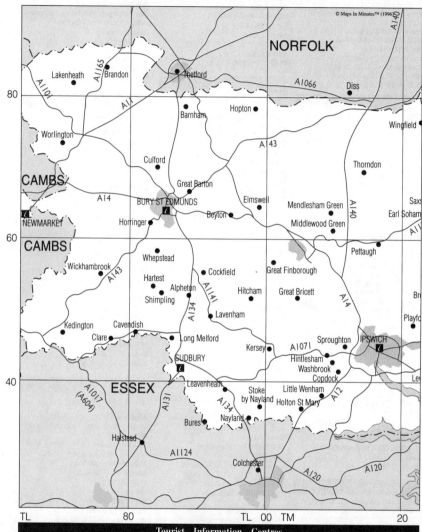

NORFOLK

CAMBS

CAMBS

ESSEX

Lakenheath • Brandon • Thetford • Diss
Worlington • Barnham • Hopton • Wingfield
Culford • A143 • Thorndon
Great Barton • Elmswell • Mendlesham Green • Saxs
BURY ST EDMUNDS • Beyton • Middlewood Green • Earl Soham
NEWMARKET • Horringer • Pettaugh
Whepstead • Cockfield • Great Finborough
Wickhambrook • Hartest • Hitcham • Great Bricett • Br
Shimpling • Alpheton • Lavenham • Playf
Kedington • Cavendish • Sproughton • IPSWICH
Clare • Long Melford • Kersey • A1071 • Hintlesham • Washbrook • Copdock • Le
SUDBURY • Leavenheath • Stoke by Nayland • Little Wenham • Holton St Mary
Bures • Nayland
Halstead • A1124
Colchester • A120

TL 80 TL 00 TM 20

Tourist Information Centres

The Cinema, High Street, **Aldeburgh**, Suffolk, IP15 5AU, 01728 453637 (Easter to Oct).

The Quay, Fen Lane, **Beccles**, Suffolk, NR34 9BH, 01502 713196 (Easter to Oct).

The Athenaeum, Angel Hill, **Bury St Edmunds**, Suffolk, IP33 1LY, 01284 764667.

Leisure Centre, Undercliff Road West, **Felixstowe**, Suffolk, IP11 8AB, 01394 276770.

Toppesfield Hall, **Hadleigh**, Ipswich, Suffolk, IP7 5DN, 01473 823778.

Town Hall, Princes Street, **Ipswich**, Suffolk, IP1 1BZ, 01473 258070.

Lady Street, **Lavenham**, Suffolk, CO10 9RA, 01787 248207 (Easter to Oct).

East Point Pavilion, Royal Plain, **Lowestoft**, Suffolk, NR33 0AP, 01502 523000 (Easter to Oct).

63 The Rookery, **Newmarket**, Suffolk, CB8 8HT, 01638 667200.

Town Hall, Market Place, **Southwold**, Suffolk, IP18 6EF, 01502 724729 (Easter to Oct).

Wilkes Way, **Stowmarket**, Suffolk, IP14 1DE, 01449 676800.

The Caravan, Station Road, **Sudbury**, Suffolk, CO10 6SS, 01787 881320 (Easter to Oct).

Station Buildings, **Woodbridge**, Suffolk, IP12 4AJ, 01394 382240.

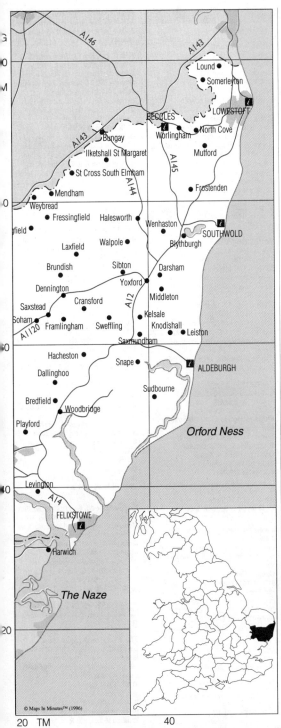

Aldeburgh

TM4656 🍺 *Railway Hotel, White Lion Hotel, Cross Keys, Mill Inn*

Faraway, *28 Linden Close, Aldeburgh, Suffolk, IP15 5JL.*
Quiet, being off main road, garden, car parking, dogs welcome.
Open: Easter to Nov
Grades: ETC 3 Diamond
01728 452571 Mrs Burrell
D: £18.00–£20.00 **S:** £18.00–£20.00
Beds: 1F 1T 1S **Baths:** 2 Sh
🛇 🅿 ⅍ 📺 🐾 🖤 ♥

Margarets, *50 Victoria Road, Aldeburgh, Suffolk, IP15 5EJ.*
Family-run Victorian house, sea and river 10 minutes walk.
Open: All Year (not Xmas/New Year)
Grades: ETC 3 Diamond
01728 453239 Mrs Testoni
D: £20.00 **S:** £25.00
Beds: 2D 1T **Baths:** 2 Sh
🛇 (10) ⅍ 📺 🖤 ♨

Worcester House, *1 Saxmundham Road, Aldeburgh, Suffolk, IP15 5JA.*
A large private house offering comfortable rooms, excellent breakfasts.
Open: All Year (not Xmas)
01728 453343 Mrs Stedman-Keeble
D: £20.00 **S:** £20.00
Beds: 1F 1D 1T 1S **Baths:** 1 Sh
🛇 🅿 (3) ⅍ 📺 🖤 ♥ ♨

Alpheton

TL8850 🍺 *Rose & Crown*

Amicus, *Old Bury Road, Alpheton, Sudbury, Suffolk, CO10 9BT.*
Just off A134 amid peaceful surroundings, ideal for garden lovers.
Open: All Year (not Xmas)
Grades: ETC 3 Diamond, Silver
01284 828579 Mrs Burcham
D: £17.50–£20.00 **S:** £20.00–£25.00
Beds: 1D 1T **Baths:** 2 Pr
🅿 (2) ⅍ 📺 🖤 🖤 ♨

Barnham

TL8779 🍺 *Grafton Arms, Dolphin*

East Farm, *Barnham, Thetford, Norfolk, IP24 2PB.*
Come & stay in large welcoming farmhouse and enjoy the farm countryside. **Open:** All Year (not Xmas)
Grades: ETC 4 Diamond
01842 890231 Mrs Heading
D: £20.00–£22.50 **S:** £23.00–£25.00
Beds: 1D 1T **Baths:** 2 En
🛇 🅿 (6) ⅍ 📺 🖤 ♨

Beccles

TM4289 🍺 *Bear & Bells*

Catherine House, *2 Ringsfield Road, Beccles, Suffolk, NR34 9PQ.*
Well furnished family home, excellent facilities, view over Waveney Valley.
Open: All Year **Grades:** ETC 4 Diamond
01502 716428 (also fax) Mrs Renilson
D: fr £20.00 **S:** fr £20.00
Beds: 3D **Baths:** 2 En 1 Pr
🛇 🅿 (4) 📺 🖤 🖤 ♨

Beyton

TL9363 ◆ *White Horse, Gardeners Arms*

Manorhouse, *The Green, Beyton, Bury St Edmunds, Suffolk, IP30 9AF.*
Open: All Year (not Xmas)
Grades: ETC 5 Diamond, Gold, AA 5 Diamond
01359 270960 Mrs Dewsbury
manorhouse@beyton.com
D: £24.00–£27.00 **S:** fr £38.00
Beds: 2D 2T **Baths:** 4 En
▷ (6) ⅍ ⊞ ⊞ ⅏ ▥
This C15th timbered longhouse overlooks 'the Green' in centre of pretty village with local hostelries. This is a place to relax and unwind. Large luxurious rooms, king-size beds. Choice of breakfasts at individual tables. 4 miles east of Bury St Edmunds.

Blythburgh

TM4475 ◆ *White Hart*

Little Thorbyns, *The Street, Blythburgh, Halesworth, Suffolk, IP19 9LS.*
Comfortable accommodation. Close to beaches, RSPB reserve, Southwold and East Anglia attractions. **Open:** All Year
01502 478664 (also fax) Mrs Harris
D: £20.00 **S:** £20.00–£40.00
Beds: 2T 2D 1S **Baths:** 3 En
▷ ▣ (8) ⅍ ⊞ ✕ ⅏ ▥ ⅃

Brandon

TL7886

Riverside Lodge, *78 High Street, Brandon, Suffolk, IP27 0AU.*
Home comforts abound. Charming Listed house with attractive riverside setting. Licensed bar. **Open:** All Year
01842 811236 Mrs Arnold
D: £15.00–£22.50 **S:** £17.50–£30.00
Beds: 3F 4D 3T **Baths:** 7 En 3 Sh
▷ ▣ (15) ⊞ ⅋ ✕ ⅏ ⅃ cc

Bredfield

TM2652 ◆ *Wilford Bridge Inn*

Moat Farmhouse, *Dallinghoo Road, Bredfield, Woodbridge, Suffolk, IP13 6BD.*
Open: Mar to Oct
Grades: ETC 3 Diamond
01473 737475 Mrs Downing
D: £17.00 **S:** £17.00
Beds: 1D 1T **Baths:** 1 Sh
▷ (1) ▣ (4) ⅍ ⊞ ⅏ ⅃
Ideal family home accommodation. Reductions for children. Self contained on ground floor, own sitting/TV room. Extensive gardens 1 mile from A12 close to heritage coast Ipswich 11 miles Woodbridge 3 miles and Aldeburgh Festival.

Moat Barn, *Bredfield, Woodbridge, Suffolk, IP13 6BD.*
Converted barn with original beams. Family atmosphere and tranquil surroundings. **Open:** All Year
Grades: ETC 3 Diamond
01473 737520 (also fax) Mr Allen
D: £19.50–£24.50 **S:** £29.00–£34.00
Beds: 1F 1D 1T **Baths:** 1 En 1 Sh
▷ ▣ (10) ⅍ ⊞ ⅏ ▥ ⅃

Brundish

TM2669 ◆ *Queen's Head*

Woodlands Farm, *Brundish, Woodbridge, Suffolk, IP13 8BP.*
Open: All Year (not Xmas/New Year)
Grades: AA 4 Diamond
01379 384444
Mrs Graham
woodlandsfarm@hotmail.com
D: £20.00–£22.50 **S:** £25.00–£27.50
Beds: 2D 1T **Baths:** 3 En
▷ (10) ▣ (6) ⅍ ⊞ ✕ ⅏ ▥ ⅃
Warm, friendly welcome assured at our comfortable cottage style farmhouse set in peaceful countryside near Framlingham. Ideal area for cycling/walking. Fishing available within easy walking distance. Excellent breakfasts using fresh local produce and free range eggs off the farm.

Bungay

TM3389

No 36, Fairfield Road, *Bungay, Suffolk, NR35 1RY.*
Open: All Year
01986 893897 Mr & Mrs Tate
heather.tate@talk21.com
D: £20.00–£22.00 **S:** £30.00–£35.00
Beds: 1D 1T **Baths:** 1 En 1 Pr
▷ ▣ (2) ⅍ ⊞ ✕ ⅏ ▥ ⅃
Comfortable family home overlooking open countryside. 10 minute walk to public indoor pool and to Bungay with its ancient castle, fine Georgian buildings, market place, butter cross and antiques. The River Waveney, Otter Trust, Aviation Museum, a short journey away.

Bures

TL9034 ◆ *Eight Bells, The Swan*

Queens House Guest House, *Church Square, Bures, Suffolk, CO8 5AB.*
Former C17th coaching inn in beautiful Stour Valley, Constable country.
Open: All Year (not Xmas)
01787 227760 Mr Arnold
Fax: 01787 227082
roger_arnold@hotmail.com
D: £24.00–£28.00 **S:** £28.00–£32.00
Beds: 1F 2D 2T **Baths:** 4 En 1 Pr
▷ ▣ (4) ⊞ ⅋ ✕ ⅏ ▥ ⅃ cc

Swan House, *Bridge Street, Bures, Suffolk, CO8 5AD.*
Great welcome awaits you at a beautiful, spacious, riverside home in the Stour Valley.
Open: All Year
01787 228098 (also fax)
Mrs Tweed
inga@itweed.freeserve.co.uk
D: £20.00–£22.00 **S:** £22.00–£25.00
Beds: 1F 1D 1S **Baths:** 2 Pr
▷ (1) ▣ (2) ⅍ ⊞ ⅏ ⅃

B&B owners may vary rates - be sure to check when booking

Bury St Edmunds

TL8564 ◆ *Hungry Horse, The Decanter, Masons Arms, Spread Eagle*

Kiln Farm, *Kiln Lane, Elmswell, Bury St Edmunds, Suffolk, IP30 9QR.*
Open: All Year
Grades: ETC 3 Diamond, AA 3 Diamond
01359 240442 Mrs Knights
barry-sue@kilnfarm.fsnet.co.uk
D: £20.00–£25.00 **S:** £25.00–£35.00
Beds: 1F 1D 1T 1S **Baths:** 4 En
▷ ▣ (10) ⊞ ⅋ ✕ ⅏ ▥ ⅃ ₺
Overlooking farmland and horse paddocks. Comfortable bedrooms are based courtyard style around a white bricked farmhouse. Good breakfasts served in cosy dining room. Good local pubs for dining out. Easy access to A14. Holiday cottage still available.

Oak Cottage, *54 Guildhall Street, Bury St Edmunds, Suffolk, IP33 1QF.*
Listed Tudor cottage, 2 mins from theatre, museums, shops, restaurants, cathedral, abbey, gardens. **Open:** All Year
01284 762745 (also fax) Sheila Keeley
D: £16.00–£26.50 **S:** £16.00–£20.00
Beds: 1F 1D 1T 1S **Baths:** 1 En 1 Pr 1 Sh
▷ ▣ (1) ⅍ ⊞ ⅋ ✕ ⅏ ▥ ⅃

Hilltop, *22 Bronyon Close, Bury St Edmunds, Suffolk, IP33 3XB.*
Home from Home. Quiet area. Ground floor bedroom, ensuite.
Open: All Year **Grades:** ETC 2 Diamond
01284 767066 Mrs Hanson
bandb@hilltop22br.freeserve.co.uk
D: £16.00–£20.00 **S:** £16.00–£25.00
Beds: 1F 1T 1S **Baths:** 1 Pr 1 Sh
▷ ▣ (2) ⅍ ⊞ ⅋ ✕ ⅏ ⅃

Ash Cottage, *59 Whiting Street, Bury St Edmunds, Suffolk, IP33 1NP.*
Listed Elizabethan town house in beautiful & ancient cathedral town.
Open: All Year
01284 755098 (also fax)
Mrs Barber-Lomax
D: fr £22.00 **S:** fr £30.00
Beds: 1D 1T **Baths:** 1 En 1 Pr
▷ ⅍ ⊞ ⅋ ⅏ ⅃ ▥ ❋ ₺

Copper Beech, *Grindle Gardens, Bury St Edmunds, Suffolk, IP33 2QG.*
Modern house, secluded location, close to town centre, trunk road network.
Open: All Year (not Xmas)
01284 767757 M Fallows
mfallows@mfallows.screaming.net
D: £18.00–£20.00 **S:** £20.00
Beds: 1D 1T **Baths:** 1 Sh
▣ (4) ⅍ ⊞ ⅏ ⅃

Cavendish

TL8046 ◆ *The Bull*

The Red House, *Stour Street, Cavendish, Sudbury, Suffolk, CO10 8BH.*
Be spoilt in beautiful, old house. Delightful garden, delicious breakfasts.
Open: All Year (not Xmas)
01787 280611 (also fax)
Mrs Theaker
D: £22.50–£25.00 **S:** fr £33.00
Beds: 2T **Baths:** 1 En 1 Pr
▷ ▣ (2) ⅍ ⊞ ⅏ ▥ ⅃

Clare

TL7645

Ship Stores, *22 Callis Street, Clare, Sudbury, Suffolk, CO10 8PX.*
Set in the beautiful small town of Clare, all rooms ensuite, breakfast to remember.
Open: All Year
Grades: ETC 3 Diamond, AA 3 Diamond
01787 277834 Mrs Bowles
shipclare@aol.com
D: £20.50–£23.00 **S:** £25.00–£41.00
Beds: 1F 3D 1T **Baths:** 5 En
🛏 🅿 (3) 🆃 ✕ 🎖 ♨ ♿ cc

Cockfield

TL9054 ◆ *Three Horseshoes, The Bull*

Craufurd House, *Cockfield, Bury St Edmunds, Suffolk, IP30 0HA.*
Self-contained unit in detached house.
Lavenham 4 miles, Bury St Edmunds 8 miles. **Open:** Easter to Oct
01284 828216 Mr & Mrs Bowen
D: fr £18.00 **S:** fr £20.00
Beds: 1D **Baths:** 1 Pr
🅿 (2) ⅏ 🆃 🎖 ♨

Copdock

TM1141 ◆ *The Brook*

Westhill, *Elm Lane, Copdock, Ipswich, Suffolk, IP8 3ET.*
Charming Georgian family home in pastoral setting. Gardens. Guestroom balcony. **Open:** All Year (not Xmas)
01473 730934 Mrs Winship
Fax: 01473 730259
alpheco@anglianet.co.uk
D: £19.00 **S:** £19.00
Beds: 2T 1S **Baths:** 1 Sh
🛏 (10) 🅿 (5) ⅏ 🆃 🎖 ♨

Cransford

TM3164 ◆ *White Horse, The Crown*

High House Farm, *Cransford, Near Franlingham, Woodbridge, Suffolk, IP13 9PD.*
Open: All Year
Grades: ETC 3 Diamond
01728 663461 Mrs Kindred
Fax: 01728 663409
D: fr £20.00 **S:** £25.00–£30.00
Beds: 1F 1D **Baths:** 1 En 1 Pr
🛏 🅿 (4) 🆃 🐾 🎖 ♨ ♨
Beautiful oak-beamed C15th farmhouse on family farm. Spacious and comfortable accommodation. Large family room with private bathroom. Double room ensuite. Inglenook fireplaces. Attractive Gardens. Quietly set. Ideal location to explore the heart of Rural Suffolk and the Heritage coast. Children welcome.

Culford

TL8369 ◆ *Woolpack, Linden Tree*

47 Benyon Gardens, *Culford, Bury St Edmunds, Suffolk, IP28 6EA.*
A modern bungalow overlooking fields and quietly situated.
Open: All Year (not Xmas/New Year)
01284 728763 Mrs Townsend
D: £16.00–£32.00 **S:** £18.00
🅿 (4) ⅏ 🆃 🎖

Dallinghoo

TM2655 ◆ *Three Horseshoes*

Old Rectory, *Dallinghoo, Woodbridge, Suffolk, IP13 0LA.*
Rare, restful, rural retreat, relaxing, remedial, regularly revisited, room service. **Open:** All Year (not Xmas)
Grades: ETC 3 Diamond
01473 737700 Mrs Quinlan
D: £16.00–£18.00
Beds: 1D 1T **Baths:** 1 Pr 1 Sh
🛏 🅿 (6) ⅏ 🎖 🆅

Darsham

TM4169 ◆ *The Fox*

Priory Farm, *Priory Lane, Darsham, Saxmundham, Suffolk, IP17 3QD.*
Open: Easter to Oct
Grades: ETC 3 Diamond
01728 668459 (also fax)
Mrs Bloomfield
D: £22.50–£30.00 **S:** £25.00–£35.00
Beds: 1D 1T **Baths:** 2 Pr
🛏 (12) 🅿 (2) ⅏ 🆃 🎖 🆅
Bed and breakfast in comfortable C17th farmhouse situated in peaceful countryside. Ideal base for exploring the Suffolk coast. All rooms with private facilities. Breakfast made with quality local specialities. Excellent pubs and restaurants nearby. Sorry no pets. Cycle hire available.

White House Farm, *Main Road, Darsham, Saxmundham, Suffolk, IP17 3PP.*
Period farmhouse. Extensive gardens.
Close Minsmere/Dunwich/Southwold. All facilities. **Open:** All Year
Grades: ETC 3 Diamond
01728 668632 Mrs Newman
D: £20.00–£27.50 **S:** £25.00–£35.00
Beds: 1T 2D **Baths:** 1 En 1 Sh
🛏 (5) 🅿 (20) ⅏ 🆃 🎖 ♨

Dennington

TM2867 ◆ *Queen's Head*

Fieldway, *Saxtead Road, Dennington, Woodbridge, Suffolk, IP13 8AP.*
Stylish house in quiet location facing village green. All rooms overlook beautiful garden.
Open: All Year (not Xmas)
Grades: ETC 4 Diamond
01728 638456 (also fax)
Mrs Turan
D: £20.00 **S:** £22.00
Beds: 1D 1T **Baths:** 1 Pr 1 Sh
🛏 (5) 🅿 (4) ⅏ 🆃 ✕ 🎖 ♨

Earl Soham

TM2363

Bridge House, *Earl Soham, Woodbridge, Suffolk, IP13 7RT.*
Beautiful C16th house. Warm welcome, good food; varied menu.
Open: All Year
Grades: ETC 4 Diamond, Siver Award
01728 685473/685289 J A Baker
DIBaker@care4free.net
D: £22.50–£25.00 **S:** £25.00
Beds: 1T 2D **Baths:** 3 En
🛏 (5) ⅏ 🆃 🎖 ♨ 🆅 ♨

Elmswell

TL9863 ◆ *Norton Dog*

Kiln Farm, *Kiln Lane, Elmswell, Bury St Edmunds, Suffolk, IP30 9QR.*
Overlooking farmland and horse paddocks. Comfortable bedrooms are based courtyard style. **Open:** All Year
Grades: ETC 3 Diamond, AA 3 Diamond
01359 240442 Mrs Knights
barry-sue@kilnfarm.fsnet.co.uk
D: £20.00–£25.00 **S:** £25.00–£35.00
Beds: 1F 1D 1T 1S **Baths:** 4 En
🛏 🅿 (10) 🆃 🐾 ✕ 🎖 🆅 ♨ ♿

Mulberry Farm, *Elmswell, Bury St Edmunds, Suffolk, IP30 9HG.*
Comfortable accommodation in peaceful setting with unspoilt views.
Open: All Year (not Xmas)
01359 244244 (also fax) Mr & Mrs Payne
woodside@talk21.com
D: £22.50–£25.00 **S:** £25.00–£27.00
Beds: 1F 1T **Baths:** 1 En 1 Pr
🛏 (5) 🅿 (10) ⅏ 🆃 🎖 🆅 ♨ ♿ 3

Felixstowe

TM3034

Iddesleigh Private Guest House,
11 Constable Road, Felixstowe, IP11 7HL.
We offer a cordial welcome in a friendly atmosphere. **Open:** All Year
01394 670546 Fax: 01394 273214
D: £16.50–£21.00 **S:** £17.50–£21.00
Beds: 2F 2T 2D 2S **Baths:** 1 En 1 Pr 2 Sh
🛏 🅿 (3) ⅏ 🆃 🐾 ✕ 🎖 ♨ ♨ ♿

Elm House, *32 Undercliff Road West, Felixstowe, Suffolk, IP11 8AJ.*
Detached, friendly, small guest house.
Open: All Year (not Xmas)
01394 282292 Mrs Nelmes
D: fr £15.00 **S:** fr £15.00
Beds: 1D 1T 1S **Baths:** 1 Sh
🅿 (3) ⅏ 🆃 🎖 🆅 ♨

Framlingham

TM2863 ◆ *The Crown, Queen's Head*

Shimmens Pightle, *Dennington Road, Framlingham, Woodbridge, Suffolk, IP13 9JT.*
Open: Easter to Nov
Grades: ETC 3 Diamond
01728 724036 Mrs Collett
D: £21.00–£22.00 **S:** £23.00–£25.00
Beds: 1D 2T **Baths:** 1 Sh
🛏 (8) 🅿 (5) ⅏ 🆃 🎖 🆅 ♨
Comfortable family home set in an acre of landscaped garden, overlooking fields. Within a mile of the historic castle town of Framlingham with its famous castle and church. Ground floor rooms with wash basins. Local cured bacon & home preserves. Guests lounge with TV.

Boundary Farm, *off Saxmundham Road, Framlingham, Woodbridge, Suffolk, IP13 9NU.*
C17th farmhouse, open countryside, ideal touring base. Brochure on request.
Open: All Year (not Xmas)
01728 723401 Mrs Cook
Fax: 01728 723877
D: £18.00–£25.00 **S:** £20.00–£25.00
Beds: 2D 1T **Baths:** 1 En 1 Sh
🛏 🅿 (4) 🆃 ✕ 🎖 🆅 ♨

Fressingfield

TM2677

Elm Lodge, *Chippenhall Green, Fressingfield, Eye, Suffolk, IP21 5SL.*
Victorian farmhouse on working farm, warm welcome guaranteed.
Open: Easter to Oct
01379 586249 Mrs Webster
D: £17.00–£21.00 **S:** £19.00–£23.00
Beds: 2D 1T **Baths:** 1 En 1 Sh
🛏 (9) 🅿 (3) 🛒 📺 🛏 ✗ 🆅 ♨

Frostenden

TM4781   🍺 *Angel Inn, Plough Inn*

Poplar Hall, *Frostenden Corner, Frostenden, Wangford, Suffolk, NR34 7JA.*
C16th haven of tranquillity set in lovely gardens and surrounded by countryside.
Open: All Year (not Xmas)
01502 578549 Mrs Garwood
D: £20.00–£26.00 **S:** £20.00–£36.00
Beds: 2D 1T **Baths:** 1 En 1 Sh
🛏 🅿 (6) 🛒 📺 🆅 ♨

Great Barton

TL8866   🍺 *Flying Fortress*

Cherry Trees, *Mount Road, Cattishall, Great Barton, Bury St Edmunds, Suffolk, IP31 2QU.*
Open: All Year (not Xmas)
01284 787501 Mrs Salmon
D: £19.00–£20.00 **S:** £24.00–£26.00
🛏 (4) 🅿 (5) 🛒 📺 ♨
Surrounded by lovely garden with fields beyond, yet only 2 miles from the centre of historic Bury St Edmunds. Comfortable beds and full English breakfast. Pub nearby for good meals.

Great Bricett

TM0350

Riverside Cottage, *The Street, Great Bricett, Ipswich, IP7 7DH.*
Charming and extremely comfortable ensuite rooms overlooking half acre garden.
Open: All Year (not Xmas)
Grades: ETC 4 Diamond
01473 658266 Mr Horne
chasmhorne@aol.com
D: £18.00–£22.00 **S:** £18.00–£22.00
Beds: 1D 1T **Baths:** 2 En
🛏 (1) 🅿 (3) 📺 ✗ 📺 🆅 ♨

Great Finborough

TM0157

Dairy Farmhouse, *Valley Lane, Great Finborough, Stowmarket, Suffolk, IP14 3BE.*
Open: All Year (not Xmas/New Year)
Grades: ETC 4 Diamond, Sliver Award
01449 615730 C Watson
D: £25.00–£30.00 **S:** £30.00–£35.00
Beds: 2D **Baths:** 1 Sh
🛏 🅿 (10) 🛒 📺 🛏 ✗ 📺 🆅 ♨
16th Century thatched farmhouse in 5 acres with delightful views. Open fires, beams and antiques, fresh flowers and lot of atmosphere in this beautiful home. Guests have own entrance and private use of sitting and dining room. Delicious suppers on request.

Hacheston

TM3059   🍺 *White Horse*

Cherry Tree House, *Hacheston, Woodbridge, Suffolk, IP13 0DR.*
Lovely countryside views, near to Framingham and Orford Castles and excellent golf courses.
Open: All Year
01728 746371 (also fax)
Mrs Hall
jcl@mcmail.com
D: £20.00–£22.00 **S:** £16.00–£25.00
Beds: 1F 2S **Baths:** 2 Sh
🛏 🅿 (3) 📺 ✗ 📺 🆅 ♨

Halesworth

TM3877   🍺 *White Hart, Rumburgh Buck, Huntsman & Hound*

Fen Way, *School Lane, Halesworth, Suffolk, IP19 8BW.*
Fen-way is set in its own 7 acres of meadowland.
Open: All Year
01986 873574 Mrs George
D: £18.00–£21.00 **S:** £20.00–£25.00
Beds: 2D 1T **Baths:** 1 En 1 Sh
🛏 (7) 🅿 (6) 📺 ✗ 📺 🆅 ♨

Rumburgh Farm, *Halesworth, Suffolk, IP19 0RU.*
Attractive C17th timber framed farmhouse on a mixed enterprise farm.
Open: All Year (not Xmas)
Grades: ETC 3 Diamond
01986 781351 (also fax)
binder@rumburghfarm.freeserve.co.uk
D: £16.50–£19.00 **S:** £21.00–£25.00
Beds: 1F 1D **Baths:** 2 En
🛏 (3) 📺 📺 ♨

Hartest

TL8352   🍺 *The Crown*

Giffords Hall, *Hartest, Bury St Edmunds, Suffolk, IP29 4EX.*
Lovely Georgian house set among vineyards, flower meadows and animals.
Open: All Year (not Xmas)
Grades: ETC 3 Diamond
01284 830464 Mr Kemp
inquiries@giffords.co.uk
D: £22.00–£25.00 **S:** £22.00–£25.00
Beds: 2T **Baths:** 3 En
🛏 🅿 (5) 🛒 📺 🛏 📺 🆅 ♨ cc

The Hatch, *Pilgrims Lane, Hartest, Bury St Edmunds, Suffolk, IP29 4ED.*
C15th thatched house in peaceful rural setting. Log fires, antiques and fine fabrics.
Open: All Year (not Xmas)
01284 830226 (also fax)
Mr & Mrs Oaten
D: £25.00–£30.00 **S:** fr £30.00
Beds: 1D 1T **Baths:** 2 En
🛏 (9) 🅿 (2) 🛒 📺 🛏 📺 ♨

All details shown are as supplied by B&B owners in Autumn 2000

Planning a longer stay? Always ask for any special rates

Hintlesham

TM0843   🍺 *The George*

College Farm, *Hintlesham, Ipswich, Suffolk, IP8 3NT.*
Peaceful 500-year-old farmhouse, close to Constable country and coast.
Open: Mid Jan to mid Dec
01473 652253 (also fax)
Mrs Bryce
bryce1@agripro.co.uk
D: £18.00–£22.00 **S:** £18.00–£26.00
Beds: 1D 1T 1S **Baths:** 1 En 1 Pr 1 Sh
🛏 (12) 🅿 (4) 🛒 📺 📺 🆅 ♨

Birch Farm, *Hintlesham, Ipswich, Suffolk, IP8 3NJ.*
Ensuite facilities with private kitchen/lounge/courtyard within idyllic farmhouse.
Open: All Year
01473 652249 Mrs Bryce
D: £20.00–£25.00 **S:** £25.00–£30.00
Beds: 2D 1S **Baths:** 2 En
🛏 🅿 (2) 📺 📺 🆅 ✽ ♨ ♿

Hitcham

TL9750   🍺 *White Horse*

Pansy Cottage, *The Causeway, Hitcham, Ipswich, Suffolk, Ip7 7NE.*
Pansy cottage is set in the heart of rolling countryside.
Open: All Year (not Xmas/New Year)
Grades: ETC 3 Diamond
01449 740858 R Edden
D: £18.00 **S:** £20.00
Beds: 1D 1S
🛏 🅿 🛒 📺 📺 ♨

Holton St Mary

TM0636   🍺 *King's Head, The Angel*

Stratford House, *Holton St Mary, Colchester, Essex, CO7 6NT.*
Luxury accommodation in Constable country; easy access for touring Suffolk & Essex.
Open: All Year (not Xmas)
Grades: ETC 4 Diamond
01206 298246 (also fax)
Mrs Selleck
D: £20.00 **S:** £20.00
Beds: 1D 1T 1S **Baths:** 1 Sh
🛏 (10) 🅿 (10) 🛒 📺 📺 ♨

Hopton

TL9978   🍺 *The Fox*

Holly Bank, *High Street, Hopton, Diss, IP22 2QX.*
Converted 1960s public house, guests' lounge, comfortable bedrooms. Sauna available at extra cost.
Open: All Year
01953 688147 (also fax)
Mr & Mrs Tomlinson
D: £17.50 **S:** £20.00
Beds: 1D 1T **Baths:** 1 Sh
🛏 🅿 (8) 🛒 📺 📺 ♨

Horringer

TL8261 🍺 *Beehive, Six Bells*

12 The Elms, *Horringer, Bury St Edmunds, Suffolk, IP29 5SE.*
Friendly modern house close to Ickworth National Trust House and Gardens.
Open: All Year
01284 735400 Ms Pemberton
D: £18.00–£20.00 **S:** £25.00–£40.00
Beds: 1D 1T 1S **Baths:** 1 Sh
🅿 (3) ⅍ 📺 📖 🎄

Ilketshall St Margaret

TM3585 🍺 *Rumburgh Buck*

Shoo-Devil Farmhouse, *Ilketshall St Margaret, Bungay, Suffolk, NR35 1QU.*
Enchanting thatched C16th farm house in secluded garden near St. Peters Brewery.
Open: All Year (not Xmas)
01986 781303 (also fax) Mrs Lewis
D: £18.50–£20.00 **S:** £20.00–£25.00
Beds: 1D 1T **Baths:** 2 En
🅿 (4) ⅍ 📺 ✕ 📖 📹 🎄

Ipswich

TM1644 🍺 *Royal George, The Westerfield, The Swan, The Greyhound, The Ram, The Railway, Beagle Inn, Talk of the Town*

Redholme, *52 Ivry Street, Ipswich, IP1 3QP.*
Open: All Year **Grades:** ETC 4 Diamond
01473 250018 (also fax)
Mr & Mrs McNeil
johnmcneil@
redholmeipswich.freeserve.co.uk
D: £20.25–£24.00 **S:** £25.20–£31.00
Beds: 1F 2D 2T 1S **Baths:** 5 En 1 Pr
🛏 🅿 (5) ⅍ 📺 📖 📹 🎄 🎄
Elegant Victorian house in large well maintained garden in quiet conservation area. 10 minutes' walk from town centre near Christchurch Park. Spacious bedrooms with complete bathrooms, we offer comfort in a friendly and helpful atmosphere. Good centre for visiting Suffolk.

Craigerne, *Cauldwell Avenue, Ipswich, Suffolk, IP4 4DZ.*
Large Victorian house, 3/4 acre pretty gardens. Friendly welcome.
Open: All Year (not Xmas)
01473 714061 Mrs Krotunas
D: fr £18.00 **S:** £18.00–£26.00
Beds: 1D 1T 2S **Baths:** 2 En 2 Sh
🅿 (6) 📺 📖 📹 🎄

Maple House, *114 Westerfield Road, Ipswich, Suffolk, IP4 2XW.*
Attractive house one mile to town centre; close to park. **Open:** All Year (not Xmas)
01473 253797 Mrs Seal
D: £25.00 **S:** £15.00
Beds: 2D 2S **Baths:** 2 En 1 Sh
🛏 🅿 (3) ⅍ 📺 ✕ 📖 🎄 🎄

Cliffden Guest House, *21 London Road, Ipswich, Suffolk, IP1 2EZ.*
Close to town centre. Full Sky TV Family run. **Open:** All Year
01473 252689 Mr Billington
Fax: 01473 252685
cliffden.hotel@virgin.net
D: £20.00–£30.00 **S:** £20.00–£30.00
Beds: 3F 1D 3T 8S **Baths:** 7 Pr 3 Sh
🛏 🅿 (5) 📺 ✕ 📖 🎄 🎄 cc

Stelvio Guest House, *Crane Hill, London Road, Ipswich, Suffolk, IP2 0SS.*
Red brick Edwardian house close to A12, A14 junction.
Open: All Year
01473 602982 Mr & Mrs Patrick
D: £20.00–£25.00 **S:** £21.00–£25.00
Beds: 1F 1T 1S **Baths:** 2 En 1 Pr
🛏 🅿 (10) ⅍ 📺 📖 📹 🎄

Sidegate Guest House, *121 Sidegate Lane, Ipswich, Suffolk, IP4 4JB.*
High quality ensuite rooms in beautiful house and gardens, family run.
Open: All Year
01473 728714 Mr & Mrs Marriott
Fax: 01473 728714 (phone first)
D: £20.00–£25.00 **S:** £27.00–£30.00
Beds: 1F 2D 1T **Baths:** 4 En
🛏 🅿 (5) ⅍ 📺 🎄 📖 📹 🎄

Kedington

TL7046 🍺 *White Horse*

Orchard House, *Mill Road, Kedington, Suffolk, CB9 7NN.*
A warm welcome awaits you at our comfortable modern home close to Stour Valley.
Open: All Year (not Xmas)
01440 713113 (also fax)
Mrs Osborne
D: £18.00–£22.00 **S:** £20.00–£25.00
Beds: 1D 2S **Baths:** 2 En 1 Sh
🛏 (8) 🅿 (6) ⅍ 📺 📖 🎄

Kelsale

TM3865 🍺 *Orgriffin Pub*

Touch Wood, *Main Road, Kelsale, Saxmundham, Suffolk, IP17 2NS.*
Quiet positioned house, convenient for Aldeburgh, Heritage coast and countryside.
Open: All Year (not Xmas/New Year)
01728 603214 Mrs Craddock
D: £18.50 **S:** £18.50
Beds: 2D **Baths:** 2 En
🛏 🅿 (2) ⅍ 📖 🎄

Mile Hill Barn, *Main Road, North Green, Kelsale, Saxmundham, Suffolk, IP17 2RG.*
Centrally located converted Suffolk oak barn, offering luxury ensuite accommodation.
Open: All Year
Grades: ETC 5 Diamond, Silver
01728 668519 Mr Covington
Richard@milehillbarn.freeserve.co.uk
D: £25.00–£35.00
Beds: 2D 1T **Baths:** 3 En
🅿 (20) ⅍ 📺 ✕ 📖 🎄

Kersey

TM0044 🍺 *The Bell*

Red House Farm, *Kersey, Ipswich, Suffolk, IP7 6EY.*
Comfortable farmhouse (c.1840).
Open: All Year
01787 210245 Mrs Alleston
D: fr £18.00 **S:** fr £20.00
Beds: 1D 1T **Baths:** 1 Pr 1 Sh
🅿 (4) 📺 🎄 ✕ 📖 📹 🎄 🎄

Knodishall

TM4261 🍺 *Butchers' Arms*

Sun Cottage, *Snape Road, Knodishall, Saxmundham, Suffolk, IP17 1UT.*
Warm, friendly welcome in pink washed cottage adjoining village common.
Open: Easter to Oct
Grades: ETC 4 Diamond
01728 833892 (also fax)
J Gadsby
suncottage@supanet.com
D: £20.00–£22.00 **S:** £24.00
Beds: 1T 1D **Baths:** 1 En
🅿 (3) ⅍ 📺 📖 🎄

Lakenheath

TL7182 🍺 *Bell Inn*

Bell Inn, *20 High Street, Lakenheath, Brandon, Suffolk, IP27 9DS.*
Old coaching house.
Open: All Year
01842 860308 (also fax)
C F Guy
D: £20.00–£45.00 **S:** £20.00–£30.00
Beds: 2F 1T 2D 1S **Baths:** 6 En
🛏 🅿 (20) 📺 🎄 ✕ 📖 📹 🎄 cc

Lavenham

TL9149 🍺 *The Angel, The Cock, The Greyhound, Great House*

Brett Farm, *The Common, Lavenham, Sudbury, Suffolk, CO10 9PG.*
Open: All Year (not Xmas/New Year)
Grades: ETC 4 Diamond
01787 248533 M Hussey
D: £22.50 **S:** £25.00
Beds: 1D 2T **Baths:** 2 En 1 Pr
🛏 🅿 ⅍ 📺 📖 📹 🎄
Riverside Bungalow in picturesque Countryside yet only 5 minutes walk from the centre of the Historic Village of Lavenham. Pretty comfortable bedrooms, full English breakfast, Romantic breakfast brought to your room for that special occasion. off road parking.

The Red House, *29 Bolton Street, Lavenham, Suffolk, CO10 9RG.*
Open: All Year (not Xmas)
Grades: ETC 4 Diamond
01787 248074 D Schofield
D: £25.00–£27.50 **S:** £40.00–£50.00
Beds: 1T 2D **Baths:** 3 En
🛏 (8) 🅿 (5) ⅍ 📺 🎄 ✕ 📖 🎄 🎄
In the heart of medieval Lavenham, The Red House is a comfortable friendly home. Attractively decorated bedrooms, pretty sitting room, sunny country garden to relax in, candlelit dinner by arrangement. The town has a wealth of timber-framed houses and a magnificent church.

Angel Gallery, *17 Market Place, Lavenham, Sudbury, Suffolk, CO10 9QZ.*
C15th Gallery in renowned market place with wonderful spacious rooms.
Open: All Year
Grades: ETC 4 Star
01787 248417 (also fax) Mrs Gibson
angel-gallery@gofornet.co.uk
D: fr £25.00 **S:** fr £35.00
Beds: 1D 2T **Baths:** 1 Sh
🅿 (3) ⅍ 📺 📖 📹 🎄 cc

Sunrise Cottage, *32 The Glebe, Lavenham, Sudbury, Suffolk, CO10 9SN.*
Luxurious/comfortable modern house in a quiet area near C15th church.
Open: All Year (not Xmas)
01787 248439 Maureen & Derek Allen
Deallen@tesco.net
D: £20.00 **S:** £25.00
Beds: 1D 2S **Baths:** 1 Sh
🛏 🄿 (3) 🍴 📺 🖥 🆅 ♿

Laxfield

TM2972 🍺 *King's Head, Royal Oak*

Watersmeet, *Framlingham Road, Laxfield, Woodbridge, Suffolk, IP13 8HD.*
Open: All Year (not Xmas/New Year)
Grades: ETC 4 Diamond
01986 798880 (also fax)
Mrs Jefferies
D: £20.00–£30.00 **S:** £25.00–£30.00
Beds: 1T 1D **Baths:** 2 Pr
🄿 (3) 🍴 📺 ✕ 🖥 🆅 ♿
Perfectly situated for exploring both the delightful coastal towns and charms of rural Suffolk. You are assured a warm welcome and extremely comfortable accommodation. Farmhouse breakfasts. Situated on the edge of a historic pretty village with museum, church and old inns.

Leiston

TM4462

White Horse Hotel, *Station Road, Leiston, Suffolk, IP16 4HD.*
Open: All Year
Grades: AA 1 Star, RAC 1 Star
01728 830694 Fax: 01728 833105
whihorse@globalnet.co.uk
D: £28.00 **S:** £35.00
Beds: 2F 5D 3T 3S **Baths:** 13 En
🛏 🄿 (14) 📺 ✝ ✕ 🖥 🆅 ✻ ♿ cc
The White Horse is ideally located to enjoy the many delights of the region including bird sanctuaries at Minsmere, Havergate and North Warren, golf at Thorpeness, Aldeburgh and Southwold, stately homes such as Heveningham and Framlingham Castle, Snape Maltings and the world-famous Aldeburgh Festival.

Levington

TM2339 🍺 *Ship Inn*

Lilac Cottage, *Levington Green, Levington, Ipswich, Suffolk, IP10 0LE.*
Pretty part-C18th cottage in peaceful village overlooking Orwell Estuary.
Open: All Year
01473 659509 D: £18.00–£20.00 **S:** £25.00
Beds: 2D **Baths:** 1 Pr/Shared
🛏 (12) 🄿 (2) 🖥 🆅 ♿

Little Wenham

TM0838 🍺 *The Case Is Altered*

Grove Farm House, *Little Wenham, Colchester, Essex, CO7 6QB.*
Relax and unwind in a very comfortable C15th farmhouse. Peaceful setting overlooking unspoilt countryside.
Open: All Year (not Xmas)
01473 310341 Mrs Collins
D: £18.00 **S:** £18.00
Beds: 1D 11T **Baths:** 1 Sh
🛏 (9) 🄿 (5) 🍴 ✕ 🖥 🆅 ♿

Long Melford

TL8645 🍺 *The Hare, Cock & Bell*

High Street Farm House, *Long Melford, Sudbury, Suffolk, CO10 9BD.*
Warm welcome 15th century beamed farmhouse pretty garden good food.
Open: All Year (not Xmas)
Grades: ETC 4 Diamond
01787 375765 (also fax) Mr Simmonds
anroy@lineone.net
D: £23.00–£26.00 **S:** £27.00–£35.00
Beds: 2D 1T 1S **Baths:** 2 En 2 Pr
🛏 (10) 🄿 (5) 🍴 📺 ✝ ✕ 🖥 🆅 ♿

Lound

TM5099 🍺 *Village Maid*

Hall Farm, *Jay Lane/Church Lane, Lound, Lowestoft, Norfolk, NR32 5LJ.*
Peaceful, traditional Suffolk farmhouse - spacious rooms, field views, huge breakfast. **Open:** Easter to Oct
Grades: ETC 4 Diamond
01502 730415 Ms Ashley
josephashley@compuserve.com
D: £18.00–£22.00 **S:** £18.00–£25.00
Beds: 1F 1D 2S **Baths:** 2 En 2 Sh
🛏 🄿 (6) 🍴 📺 ✝ 🖥 🆅 ♿

Lowestoft

TM5493 🍺 *Jolly Sailors, Churchills Bar, Hotel Hatfield*

The Jays Guest House, *14 Kirkley Cliff, Lowestoft, Suffolk, NR33 0BY.*
Licensed seafront guest house - for sensible rate, just phone for details.
Open: All Year
01502 561124 B Smith
D: £15.00–£20.00 **S:** £15.00–£20.00
Beds: 1F 2D 1T 2S **Baths:** 2 En 2 Sh
🛏 🄿 (6) 🍴 ✕ 🖥 ♿ cc

Kingfisher Guest House, *39 Marine Parade, Lowestoft, Suffolk, NR33 0QN.*
Centrally located sea front guest house, close to shops and amenities.
Open: All Year (not Xmas/New Year)
01502 582483 Mr & Mrs Davis
D: £15.00–£16.50 **S:** £16.00–£17.50
Beds: 2F 3T **Baths:** 1 Sh
🛏 🄿 (3) 📺 ✝ 🖥 ♿

Royal Court Hotel, *146 London Road South, Lowestoft, Suffolk, NR33 0AZ.*
The hotel at bed and breakfast prices; central position. **Open:** All Year
Grades: ETC 2 Diamond
01502 568901 (also fax)
D: £18.00–£20.00 **S:** £20.00–£25.00
Beds: 6F 1D 9T **Baths:** 18 En
🛏 🄿 (12) 📺 ✝ ✕ 🖥 🆅 ✻ ♿ & 2 cc

Wavecrest, *31 Marine Parade, Lowestoft, Suffolk, NR33 0QN.*
Warm welcoming family run B&B on sea front near all amenities.
Open: All Year (not Xmas/New Year)
Grades: AA 3 Diamond
01502 561268 (also fax)
Mrs Jackson
sue@wave-crest.freeserve.co.uk
D: £18.00–£22.00 **S:** £20.00–£25.00
Beds: 2F 3D **Baths:** 4 En 1 Pr
🛏 (3) 🄿 (1) 🍴 📺 🖥 ♿

Somerton Hotel, *Kirkley Cliff, Lowestoft, Suffolk, NR33 0BY.*
Relax by the sea in period furnished Victorian town house. Some rooms no smoking. **Open:** All Year (not Xmas)
01502 565665 Mr Crocker
Fax: 01502 501176
reception@somerton.screaming.net
D: £20.00–£22.50 **S:** £20.00
Beds: 2F 4D 2T 2S **Baths:** 5 En 1 Pr 2 Sh
🛏 🍴 📺 ✝ ✕ 🖥 🆅 ♿ cc

Fairways Guest House, *398 London Road South, Lowestoft, Suffolk, NR33 0BQ.*
Welcoming comfortable guest house - near beautiful beach (blue flag) and heritage coast. **Open:** All Year
01502 572659 Mrs Montali
amontali@netmatters.co.uk
D: £17.00–£25.00 **S:** £18.00–£23.00
Beds: 1F 3D 1T 2S **Baths:** 4 En 1 Pr 1 Sh
🛏 🄿 📺 ✝ ✕ 🖥 🆅 ♿ cc

The Willows Guest House, *49 Marine Parade, Lowestoft, Suffolk, NR33 0QN.*
Family-run guest house facing the award-winning South Beach.
Open: All Year (not Xmas)
01502 512561 Mr & Mrs Scott
D: £15.00–£20.00 **S:** £16.00–£18.00
Beds: 1F 2D 1T 2S **Baths:** 1 En 1 Pr 2 Sh
🛏 🄿 (2) 📺 ✕ 🖥 🆅 ♿

Mendham

TM2782 🍺 *Duke William, Black Swan*

Weston House Farm, *Mendham, Harleston, Norfolk, IP20 0PB.*
Attractive farmhouse, comfortably furnished, with large garden in peaceful rural setting. **Open:** Mar to Nov
Grades: ETC 3 Diamond, AA 3 Diamond
01986 782206 Mrs Holden
Fax: 01986 782414
holden@farmline.com
D: £18.00–£22.50 **S:** £22.50–£27.00
Beds: 2D 1T **Baths:** 3 En
🛏 🄿 (6) 🍴 📺 ✝ ✕ 🖥 🆅 ♿

Mendlesham Green

TM0963

Cherry Tree Farm, *Mendlesham Green, Mendlesham Green, Suffolk, IP14 5RQ.*
Open: All Year (not Xmas/New Year)
01449 766376 Mr Ridsdale
D: £25.00–£30.00 **S:** £35.00–£40.00
Beds: 3D **Baths:** 3 En
🄿 (3) 🍴 📺 ✕ 🖥
If you enjoy quality home cooking, with first rate ingredients, garden fresh vegetables and wine from the Suffolk Vineyards, then this is the place for you.

Middleton

TM4367 🍺 *Middleton Bell, The Ship*

Rose Villa, *The Street, Middleton, Saxmundham, Suffolk, IP17 3NJ.*
Private house, close to Minsmere.
Open: All Year
01728 648489 Mrs Crowden
D: fr £15.00 **S:** fr £15.00
Beds: 1D 1T **Baths:** 1 Sh
🄿 (3) 📺 🖥 ♿

Middlewood Green

TM0961 ◄ *The Crown*

The Bears House, *Mulberrytree Farm, Blacksmiths Lane, Middlewood Green, Stowmarket, Suffolk, IP14 5EU.*
B&B self-contained, converted barn sleeps 6. Indoor swimming pool.
Open: All Year
01449 711707 (also fax) Mr Beckett
D: £19.00–£21.00 **S:** £19.00–£21.00
ॐ 🅿 (5) 📺 🍴 🛏 ⬛ ♨ ♿

Mutford

TM4888 ◄ *Three Horseshoes*

Ash Farm, *Dairy Lane, Mutford, Beccles, Suffolk, NR34 7QJ.*
C16th farmhouse, quiet countryside, close to seaside (5 miles), warm welcome. **Open:** All Year
01502 476892 Mrs Warnes
D: £18.00–£20.00 **S:** £20.00
Beds: 1F **Baths:** 1 En
ॐ 🅿 (2) ✄ 📺 ⬛ ♨

Nayland

TL9734 ◄ *The Lion, White Hart*

Gladwins Farm, *Harpers Hill, Nayland, Colchester, Essex, CO6 4NU.*
Open: All Year (not Xmas)
Grades: ETC 4 Diamond
01206 262261 Mrs Dossor
Fax: 01206 263001
gladwinsfarm@compuserve.com
D: £28.00–£30.00 **S:** £25.00–£30.00
Beds: 2D 1S **Baths:** 2 En 1 Pr
ॐ (8) 🅿 (14) ✄ 📺 ✗ ⬛ ♨ ♿ cc
Traditional Suffolk farmhouse B&B with ensuite rooms, in 22 acres of beautiful rolling Constable country, or choose a self-catering cottage. Heated indoor pool, sauna, aromatherapy suite, hard tennis court, fishing lake, children's playground. Pets welcome. Colour brochure from resident owners.

Hill House, *Gravel Hill, Nayland, Colchester, Essex, CO6 4JB.*
C16th beamed hall house on edge of historic Constable village.
Open: All Year (not Xmas)
01206 262782 Mrs Heigham
D: £20.00–£26.00 **S:** £22.00–£25.00
Beds: 1D 1T 1S **Baths:** 1 En 2 Pr
ॐ (8) 🅿 (6) ✄ 📺 ⬛ ♨ ♿

Newmarket

TL6463 ◄ *Three Blackbirds, King's Head, Red Lion, White Lion, The Bushel*

17 Rous Road, *Newmarket, CB8 8DH.*
Open: All Year (not Xmas)
01638 667483 Mr & Mrs Crighton
crighton@rousnewmarket.freeserve.co.uk
D: £20.00–£25.00 **S:** £22.00–£25.00
Beds: 2T **Baths:** 1 Sh
ॐ ✄ 📺 ♨
We are a family home offering good basic accommodation, comfortable rooms and full English breakfasts. Centrally situated in town, ideal for racing enthusiasts and tourists alike. Midway between Cambridge and Bury St Edmunds. Connections to Ely and London.

Falmouth House, *Falmouth Avenue, Newmarket, Suffolk, CB8 0NB.*
Modern detached house; quiet location near town and race course.
Open: All Year (not Xmas)
01638 660409 Mrs Shaw
D: £22.50–£25.00 **S:** £30.00–£35.00
Beds: 1D 2T **Baths:** 1 Sh
🅿 (6) ✗ ⬛ ♨

North Cove

TM4689 ◄ *Three Horseshoes*

Fairfields Guest House, *Old Lowestoft Road, North Cove, Beccles, NR34 7PD.*
Open: All Year
01502 476261 Mrs Charalambous
D: £17.50–£19.00 **S:** fr £25.00
Beds: 2F 1T 2D **Baths:** 3 En 1 Sh
ॐ 🅿 (6) ✄ 📺 🍴 🛏 ⬛ ♨ ♿
Within easy reach of Norfolk Broads. 2 Miles Beccles, 10 miles, Norwich, 7 miles Lowestoft, 12 miles GT Yarmouth. Smoking allowed in lounge only. Private car park, walking distance to local pub with restaurant.

Playford

TM2147 ◄ *Admiral's Head, Falcon Inn*

Glenham, *Hill Farm Road, Playford, Ipswich, Suffolk, IP6 9DU.*
Situated in the Fynn valley. Warm welcome. Confirm e-mail by phone.
Open: All Year (not Xmas)
Grades: ETC 3 Diamond
01473 624939 Mr & Mrs Booker
glenham@tesco.net
D: £16.00–£25.00 **S:** £16.00–£20.00
Beds: 1F 1T 1S **Baths:** 1 Pr 1 Sh
ॐ 🅿 (3) ✄ 📺 🛏 ⬛ ♨

Saxmundham

TM3863 ◄ *The Griffin, Hedgehogs Restaurant*

Kiln Farm, *Kiln Lane, Benhall, Saxmundham, Suffolk, IP17 1HA.*
Cosy country home with inviting garden terrace and bountiful breakfasts.
Open: All Year
01728 603166 Mr Potter
comfort@kilnfarm33.freeserve.co.uk
D: £25.00 **S:** £–£35.00
Beds: 2T 1D **Baths:** 2 Sh
ॐ (5) 🅿 (4) 📺 🛏 ⬛

Saxtead

TM2525 ◄ *Old Mill House*

Ivy Farm, *The Green, Saxtead, Woodbridge, Suffolk, IP13 9QG.*
C19th farmhouse overlooking Saxtead Green and C18th windmill surrounded by 400 acres family farmland.
Open: All Year
01728 685621 (also fax)
S J Higgins
sarahiggins@skynow.net
D: £15.50–£22.00 **S:** £25.00
Beds: 1D 1T **Baths:** 2 En
ॐ 🅿 (6) ✄ 📺 🛏 ⬛ ♨ ♿

Shimpling

TL8551 ◄ *Rose & Crown*

Gannocks House, *Old Rectory Lane, Shimpling, Bury St Edmunds, Suffolk, IP29 4HG.*
Country house in quiet setting, rooms with luxury ensuite facilities/ fine furnishing.
Open: All Year
Grades: ETC 4 Diamond
01284 830499 (also fax)
gannocks-house@lineone.net
D: £22.50–£25.00 **S:** £25.00–£45.00
Beds: 1F 1D 1T **Baths:** 3 En
ॐ (8) 🅿 (5) ✄ 📺 ⬛ ♨ ♿

Sibton

TM3669 ◄ *The Griffin, Queen's Head*

Park Farm, *Sibton, Saxmundham, Suffolk, IP17 2LZ.*
Enjoy a friendly farmhouse welcome with your every comfort assured.
Open: All Year (not Xmas)
Grades: ETC 4 Diamond
01728 668324 M Gray
Fax: 01728 668564
margaret.gray@btinternet.com
D: £19.00–£22.00 **S:** £19.00–£22.00
Beds: 1D 2T **Baths:** 2 En 1 Pr
🅿 (6) ✄ ✗ ⬛ ♨ ♿

Sibton White Horse, *Halesworth Road, Sibton, Saxmundham, Suffolk, IP17 2JJ.*
C16th inn. 3 acres secluded grounds. 8 rooms with private facilities.
Open: All Year
01728 660337 Mr Dyke
pauldy@easynet.co.uk
D: £22.50 **S:** £27.00
Beds: 3D 2T 3S **Baths:** 7 En 1 Sh
ॐ 🅿 🛏 ✗ ⬛ ♨ ♿

Snape

TM3959 ◄ *Golden Key, The Crown, Plough & Sail*

Flemings Lodge, *Gromford Lane, Snape, Saxmundham, Suffolk, IP17 1RG.*
Very quiet lane, friendly welcome, hearty breakfasts in quality accommodation.
Open: All Year (not Xmas)
Grades: ETC 4 Diamond
01728 688502 (also fax)
Mrs Edwards
D: £20.00–£22.00 **S:** £28.00–£35.00
Beds: 1D 1T **Baths:** 1 Sh
🅿 (4) ✄ 📺 ⬛ ♨ ♿

Somerleyton

TM4897 ◄ *Duke's Head*

Dove Wood Cottage, *5 Station Cottages, Somerleyton, Lowestoft, Norfolk, NR32 5QN.*
Charming Edwardian cottage. Peaceful garden. Woodland walks, beautiful Broadland views.
Open: All Year (not Xmas/New Year)
01502 732627 Ms Spencer
D: fr £20.00 **S:** fr £22.00
Beds: 1F 1D **Baths:** 1 Pr 1 Sh
ॐ 🅿 (4) ✄ 📺 🛏 ⬛ ♨ ♿

Southwold

TM5076 ◖ *The Angel, The Plough, Lord Nelson, Swan, King's Head*

Victoria House, *9 Dunwich Road, Southwold, Suffolk, IP18 6LJ.*
Open: All Year **Grades:** ETC 4 Diamond
01502 722317 Mr & Mrs Henshaw
D: £22.50–£32.50 **S:** £22.50–£27.50
Beds: 1D 1T 1S **Baths:** 2 En 1 Pr
⑤ ▧ ⌧ ▥ 団 ▤
Situated close to beach and town centre of charming unique Southwold. Double room has half tester bed and balcony, with sea views. We pride ourselves in providing high standard comfortable accommodation with a hearty English breakfast to start your day.

Amber House, *North Parade, Southwold, Suffolk, IP18 6LT.*
Victorian seafront house, with magnificent views, comfortable and homely atmosphere. **Open:** All Year (not Xmas) **Grades:** ETC 3 Diamond
01502 723303 (also fax) Mrs Spring
spring@amberhouse.fsnet.co.uk
D: £25.00–£30.00 **S:** £35.00–£45.00
Beds: 1F 3D 1T **Baths:** 5 En
⑤ (5) ▧ ▥ 団 ▤

Northcliffe Guest House, *20 North Parade, Southwold, Suffolk, IP18 6LT.*
Charming Victorian terrace. Panoramic sea view, relaxed atmosphere, individually designed rooms, licensed.
Open: All Year **Grades:** ETC 4 Diamond
01502 724074 Mrs Henshaw
Fax: 01502 722218
D: £20.00–£30.00 **S:** £25.00–£45.00
Beds: 5D 1T 1S **Baths:** 5 En 1 Sh
⑤ ▧ ⌧ ✕ ▥ 団 ▤

No 21 North Parade, *21 North Parade, Southwold, Suffolk, IP18 6LT.*
Peace, tranquillity and stunning sea views overlooking Blue Flag Beach.
Open: All Year (not Xmas/New Year)
Grades: ETC 3 Diamond
01502 722573 richard.comrie@cw.com.net
D: £50.00–£65.00 **S:** £35.00
Beds: 1T 2D
▥ ▧ ▥ 団 ▤

No 3, Cautley Road, *Southwold, Suffolk, IP18 6DD.*
Edwardian family house; rooms ensuite, guest lounge and four poster.
Open: All Year (not Xmas)
01502 723611 Mr Collis
D: £20.00–£27.50 **S:** £20.00–£35.00
Beds: 1F 1D 1T **Baths:** 3 En

Sproughton

TM1244 ◖ *The George*

Finjaro Guest House, *Valley Farm Drive, Hadleigh Road, Sproughton, Ipswich, Suffolk, IP8 3EL.*
Deluxe accommodation 10 minutes from Ipswich, surrounded by open fields.
Open: All Year (not Xmas)
Grades: ETC 4 Diamond
01473 652581 Mrs Finbow
Fax: 01473 652139
D: £20.00–£23.00 **S:** £20.00
Beds: 1D 2S 1T **Baths:** 2 Sh
⑤ (3) ▧ ▥ ✕ ▥ 団 ▤

St Cross South Elmham

TM2983 ◖ *The Buck Inn*

South Elmham Hall, *St Cross South Elmham, Harleston, Suffolk, IP20 0PZ.*
Peaceful farmhouse, unspoilt views, wildlife, farm walks. 15 miles from coast.
Open: Easter to Dec
Grades: ETC 4 Diamond
01986 782526 Mrs Sanderson
Fax: 01986 782203
southelmham.co.uk
D: £22.50–£40.00 **S:** £30.00–£60.00
Beds: 2D 1T **Baths:** 3 En
▧ (3) ▥ ⌧ ▥ ▤ cc

Stoke-by-Nayland

TL9836 ◖ *The Angel*

Thorington Hall, *Stoke-by-Nayland, Colchester, Essex, CO6 4SS.*
Beautiful Seventeenth Century house belonging to the National Trust.
Open: Easter to Sep
01206 337329 Mrs Wollaston
D: £20.00–£22.00 **S:** £28.00
Beds: 1F 1D 1T 1S **Baths:** 1 Sh
▧ ▧ (4) ⌧ ▥

Ryegate House, *Stoke-by-Nayland, Colchester, Essex, CO6 4RA.*
In pleasant village setting. Warm Welcome, Fine Food, Restful Rooms.
Open: All Year (not Xmas)
01206 263679 Mr & Mrs Geater
D: £20.00–£24.00 **S:** £28.00–£34.00
Beds: 2D 1T **Baths:** 3 En
▧ (12) ▧ (5) ▥ ⌧ ▥ 団 ▤

Sudbourne

TM4153 ◖ *Kings Head, Jolly Sailor*

Long Meadow, *Gorse Lane, Sudbourne, Woodbridge, Suffolk, IP12 2BD.*
Comfortable, friendly, home from home, lovely garden, quiet rural location.
Open: All Year (not Xmas)
Grades: ETC 3 Diamond
01394 450269 Mrs Wood
D: £18.00–£20.00 **S:** £17.00–£19.00
Beds: 1D 1T 1S **Baths:** 1 Pr 1 Sh
▧ (12) ▧ (6) ▥ ⌧ ▥ 団 ▤

Sudbury

TL8741

The Old Bull Hotel, *Church Street, Ballingdon, Sudbury, Suffolk, CO10 6BL.*
C16th hotel & restaurant offering personal serice in a homely atmosphere.
Open: All Year
01787 374120 Mr Taylor
Fax: 01787 379044
D: £20.00–£27.00 **S:** £25.00–£38.00
Beds: 3F 5D 1T 1S **Baths:** 8 En 2 Sh
▧ ▧ ▥ ⌧ ▥ ▤ & cc

BEDROOMS
F - Family
D - Double
T - Twin
S - Single

Sweffling

TM3463 ◖ *Crown*

Wayside, *Glemham Road, Sweffling, Saxmundham, Suffolk, IP17 2QB.*
Comfortable accommodation on edge of village near Heritage coast attractions.
Open: All Year (not Xmas/New Year)
Grades: ETC 4 Diamond
01728 663256 M Wilkinson
D: £20.00–£22.00 **S:** £22.00–£25.00
Beds: 1T 1D **Baths:** 2 En
▧ (5) ▧ (4) ▥ ⌧ ▥

Thorndon

TM1369 ◖ *Four Horse Shoe*

Moat Farm, *Thorndon, Eye, Suffolk, IP23 7LX.*
Moat farm is an old Suffolk house in peaceful village.
Open: All Year (not Xmas/New Year)
Grades: ETC 4 Diamond
01379 678437 (also fax)
J & G Edgecombe
gerolde@clara.co.uk
D: £20.00–£23.00 **S:** £24.00–£28.00
Beds: 1F 2T 2D **Baths:** 2 En 1 Pr 1 Sh
▧ ▧ ▥ ⌧ ▥ 団 ▤

Walpole

TM3674 ◖ *Queen's Head*

The Old Vicarage, *Walpole, Halesworth, Suffolk, IP19 9AR.*
Spacious bedrooms, lovely views from every room.
Open: All Year
01986 784295 Mr Calver
D: £20.00–£25.00 **S:** £25.00–£30.00
Beds: 1T 1D **Baths:** 2 Pr
▧ ▧ (6) ▥ ⌧ ▥

Washbrook

TM1142 ◖ *Brook Inn*

High View, *Back Lane, Washbrook, Ipswich, Suffolk, IP8 3JA.*
Comfortable Edwardian house set in secluded garden. Quiet village location.
Open: All Year (not Xmas/New Year)
Grades: ETC 4 Diamond
01473 730494 Mrs Steward
graham.steward@pmail.net
D: £20.00–£22.00 **S:** £20.00–£22.00
Beds: 1T 1D 1S **Baths:** 1 Sh
▧ (12) ▧ (5) ▥ ⌧ ▥ 団 ▤

Stebbings, *Back Lane, Washbrook, Ipswich, IP8 3JA.*
Open: All Year (not Xmas)
Grades: ETC 4 Diamond
01473 730216 Mrs Fox
carolinefox@netscapeonline.co.uk
D: £16.00 **S:** £18.00
Beds: 2T
▧ ▧ (2) ▥ ⌧ ▥ ▤
Detached Georgian cottage; quiet village location, secure parking, mature pretty gardens & outbuildings. Full English breakfast with local produce. 3 miles Ipswich town centre. Ideally situated, Suffolk countryside & Constable country easy access A12, A14. Pets and children welcome. No smoking.

Wenhaston

TM4175   Queen's Head

The Old Vicarage, Wenhaton, Halesworth, Suffolk, *IP19 9EG.*
Period house in large grounds. Very peaceful, warm welcome assured.
Open: All Year **Grades:** ETC 4 Diamond
01502 478339 Mr & Mrs Heycock
Fax: 01502 478068
theycock@aol.com
D: £25.00–£30.00 **S:** £28.00–£33.00
Beds: 1T 2D **Baths:** 1 Pr 1 Sh
♿ (12) 🅿 (3) 📺 ▦ ☎

Weybread

TM2480

The Crown Inn, The Street, Weybread, Diss, Norfolk, *IP21 5TL.*
Traditional English pub. Excellent fishing. Countryside walks. Coastline driving distance. **Open:** All Year
01379 586710 L Rice
D: £25.00–£30.00 **S:** £25.00–£30.00
Beds: 1T 1D **Baths:** 2 En
🅿 (15) ⅋ 📺 ✕ ▦ 🆅 ☎

Whepstead

TL8357   White Horse

Folly House B&B, Folly Lane, Whepstead, Bury St Edmunds, *IP29 4TJ.*
Bed and Breakfast in the country, indoor pool. Excellent breakfasts.
Open: All Year (not Xmas)
01284 735207 L Lower
D: £20.00–£25.00 **S:** £25.00–£35.00
Beds: 1F 1D 1T **Baths:** 1 En 1 Sh
♿ 🅿 (10) ⅋ 📺 ✕ ▦ 🆅 ☎

Wickhambrook

TL7554   Cherry Tree

The Old Bakery, Off Mill Lane, Farley Green, Wickhambrook, Newmarket, Suffolk, *CB8 8PX.*
C17th house, quiet countryside, large rooms, comfortable beds, quality breakfasts. **Open:** All Year (not Xmas)
Grades: ETC 4 Diamond
01440 820852 (also fax) L Lambert
info@theoldbakery.freeserve.co.uk
D: £20.00–£22.50 **S:** £30.00–£35.00
Beds: 2D 1T **Baths:** 3 En
🅿 (4) ⅋ 📺 ✕ ▦ 🆅 ☎

Wingfield

TM2276   De la Pole Arms

Gables Farm, Wingfield, Diss, Norfolk, *IP21 5RH.*
Open: Jan to Dec
Grades: ETC 4 Diamond
01379 586355 (also fax)
Sue Harvey
sue.harvey@online.net
D: £20.00–£22.00 **S:** £22.50–£25.00
Beds: 1T 2D **Baths:** 3 En
♿ 🅿 (6) ⅋ 📺 ✖ ▦ ☎
Gables Farm is a heavily timbered 16th century moated farmhouse. All rooms are furnished to the highest standards. The comfortable bedrooms have colour TV, hospitality tray, hairdryer etc. Well-kept gardens are available for our guests to enjoy.

Woodbridge

TM2649   Coach & Horses

Dehen Lodge, Melton Road, Woodbridge, Suffolk, *IP12 1NH.*
Victorian house , large garden, stream, tennis court, riverside walk. Tidemill and town.
Open: All Year
Grades: ETC 3 Diamond
01394 382740 Mrs Schlee
D: £18.00–£20.00 **S:** £18.00–£20.00
Beds: 1D 1T 2S **Baths:** 2 Sh
♿ 🅿 (4) ⅋ 📺 ✖ ▦ ☎

Grove House Hotel, 39 Grove Road, Woodbridge, Suffolk, *IP12 4LG.*
A warm welcome awaits everyone at our newly extended and renovated hotel.
Open: All Year
01394 382202 grovehotel@btinternet.com
D: £25.00–£27.50 **S:** £25.00–£37.50
Beds: 1F 5D 3T 3S **Baths:** 11 En 1 Sh
♿ 🅿 (15) 📺 ✖ ✕ ▦ 🆅 ☎ ⅟ cc

RATES

D = Price range per person sharing in a double room
S = Price range for a single room

Worlingham

TM4490

Colville Arms Motel, Lowestoft Road, Worlingham , Beccles, Suffolk, *NR34 7EF.*
Village location close to Lowestoft, Norwich, Yarmouth, Broads, golf and fishing.
Open: All Year
01502 712571 (also fax)
P & N Brooks
pat@thecolvillearms.freeserve.co.uk
D: £22.50–£27.50 **S:** £32.50–£40.00
Beds: 4T 5D 2S **Baths:** 11 En
🅿 ✖ ✕ ▦ 🆅 ☎ cc

Worlington

TL6973   Walnut Tree

The Old Forge, Newmarket Road, Worlington, Bury St Edmunds, Suffolk, *IP28 8RZ.*
An attractive C18th cottage across road from pub near golf course.
Open: All Year (not Xmas/New Year)
01638 718014 Mrs Wilson
Fax: 01638 711616
D: £28.00–£40.00 **S:** £28.00
Beds: 1T **Baths:** 1 Pr
♿ 🅿 (2) ⅋ 📺 ▦ ☎

Yoxford

TM3968   The Griffin

The Old Mill House, Yoxford, Saxmundham, Suffolk, *IP17 3HE.*
Comfortable secluded Regency house. Peaceful grounds. Good food. Warm welcome.
Open: All Year
01728 668536 R J Draper
D: £17.50–£23.00 **S:** fr £20.00
Beds: 1F 1D **Baths:** 1 Pr
♿ 🅿 (6) ⅋ 📺 ✖ ✕ ▦ 🆅 ☎

Surrey

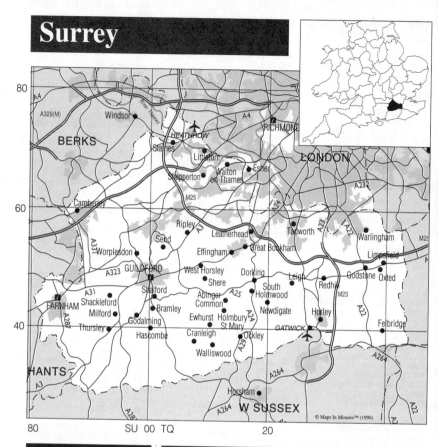

© Maps In Minutes™ (1996)

Tourist Information Centres

Motorway Services (M25 J5-6 eastbound), **Clacket Lane**, Westerham, Kent, TN16 2ER, 01959 565063.

Motorway Services (M25 J5-6 westbound), **Clacket Lane**, Westerham, Kent, TN16 2ER, 01959 565615.

Vernon House, 28 West Street, **Farnham**, Surrey, GU9 7BR, 01252 715109.

The Undercroft, 72 High Street, **Guildford**, Surrey, GU1 3HE, 01483 444333.

Abinger Common

TQ1145   🍺 *Plough Inn*

Park House Farm, *Leith Hill Road, Abinger Common, Dorking, Surrey, RH5 6LW.*
Open: All Year (not Xmas/New Year)
01306 730101 Mr & Mrs Wallis
Fax: 01306 730643
peterwallis@msn.com
D: £20.00–£30.00 **S:** £30.00–£50.00
Beds: 1T 2D **Baths:** 3 En
🛏 (12) 🅿 (10) ⅙ 📺 🛇 ♨
Set in 25 acres in an Area of Outstanding Natural Beauty, you are welcome to join us in a large spacious home which provides bright, tastefully decorated rooms, all with excellent views. Easy access to Gatwick and Heathrow.

RATES

D = Price range per person sharing in a double room
S = Price range for a single room

Bramley

TQ0044   🍺 *Jolly Farmer, Grantley Arms*

Beevers Farm, *Chinthurst Lane, Bramley, Guildford, Surrey, GU5 0DR.*
Peaceful surroundings, friendly atmosphere, own preserves, honey, eggs, nearby villages.
Open: Easter to Nov
Grades: ETC 3 Diamond
01483 898764 (also fax)
Mr Cook
D: £18.00–£25.00 **S:** fr £30.00
Beds: 1F 2T **Baths:** 1 Pr 1 Sh
🛏 🅿 (10) ⅙ 📺 🛇 ♨

Camberley

SU8860   🍺 *One Oak, Royal Standard*

Youlden Lodge, *12 Youlden Drive, Camberley, Surrey, GU15 1AL.*
Spacious Tudor-style private house. Ample private parking. Convenient M3.
Open: All Year
01276 61793 Mrs Bennie
D: £20.00–£25.00 **S:** £20.00–£25.00
Beds: 1D 1T 2S **Baths:** 2 Sh
🛏 🅿 (5) ⅙ 📺 🛇 ♨

11 Holly Avenue, Camberley, Surrey, GU16 5QX.
Detached house in peaceful, lightly wooded location 1½ miles Camberley and M.3.
Open: All Year (not Xmas/New Year)
01276 25406 Mrs Holland
D: £20.00 **S:** £17.50–£20.00
Beds: 1S 1T **Baths:** 2 Pr 1 Sh
🛇 (5) 🅿 (1) ⌨ �📺 🛏 🍴 ▥ Ⅴ 🛆

Loganberry Lodge, 6 Mytchett Road, Camberley, Surrey, GU14 6EZ.
Located close to M3 and Basingstoke Canal Centre. Car parking.
Open: All Year (not Xmas/New Year)
01252 544603
Mrs Wiltshire
D: £23.00–£25.00 **S:** £25.00–£28.00
Beds: 1D **Baths:** 1 En
🛇 🅿 (2) ⌨ ⏻ ✗ ▥ 🛆

Cranleigh

TQ0638

The White Hart Hotel, Ewhurst Road, Cranleigh, Surrey, GU6 7AE.
Listed coaching inn situated 8.5 miles south of Guildford.
Open: All Year
01483 268647 Mr Silver
Fax: 01483 267154
pasilver@netcomuk.co.uk
D: £24.00–£26.00 **S:** £38.00–£42.00
Beds: 1F 1S **Baths:** 12 En
🛇 ⏻ 🛏 ✗ ▥ Ⅴ 🛆 cc

Dorking

TQ1649 🍺 King's Arms, Old School House, King William, The Bush, Inn on the Green

The Waltons, 5 Rose Hill, Dorking, Surrey, RH4 2EG.
Listed house in conservation area. Beautiful views and friendly atmosphere
Open: All Year
01306 883127 (also fax)
Mrs Walton
thewaltons@rosehill5.demon.co.uk
D: £17.50–£20.00 **S:** £20.00–£32.50
Beds: 1F 1D 1T 1S **Baths:** 3 Sh
🛇 🅿 (3) ⌨ ⏻ 🛏 ✗ ▥ Ⅴ ❀ 🛆

Steyning Cottage, Horsham Road, South Holmwood, Dorking, Surrey, RH5 4NE.
Special rates for long term, including dinner. French spoken.
Open: All Year (not Xmas)
01306 888481 Mrs Treays
D: £18.00–£21.00 **S:** £18.00–£21.00
Beds: 1T 1S **Baths:** 1 Sh
🛇 🅿 (4) ⏻ 🛏 ✗ ▥

Shrub Hill, 3 Calvert Road, Dorking, Surrey, RH4 1LT.
Quiet comfortable family home with excellent views.
Open: All Year (not Xmas)
01306 885229 Mrs Scott Kerr
jackiesk@cwcom.net
D: £25.00–£26.00 **S:** fr £35.00
Beds: 1T 1S 1D **Baths:** 1 Sh 1 En
🛇 (8) 🅿 (2) ⌨ ⏻ 🛏 ▥ Ⅴ 🛆

Torridon Guest House, Longfield Road, Dorking, Surrey, RH4 3DF.
Large chalet bungalow - quiet location.
Open: All Year **Grades:** ETC 3 Diamond
01306 883724 Mrs Short
Fax: 01306 880759
D: £23.00–£24.00 **S:** £26.00–£28.00
Beds: 1D 1T 1S **Baths:** 1 Sh
🛇 🅿 (4) ⌨ ⏻ 🛏 ✗ ▥ Ⅴ 🛆 ♿

Effingham

TQ1153 🍺 Douglas Haig

Chalklands, Beech Avenue, Effingham, Surrey, KT24 5PJ.
Large detached house overlooking golf course. Good pub food nearby.
Open: All Year (not Xmas)
Grades: ETC 3 Diamond
01372 454936 Mrs Reilly
Fax: 01372 459569
rreilly@tecres.net
D: £22.00–£23.00 **S:** £30.00–£35.00
Beds: 1F 1D 1T **Baths:** 2 En 1 Pr
🛇 🅿 (8) ⌨ ⏻ 🛏 ✗ ▥ Ⅴ 🛆

Egham

TQ0071 🍺 Happy Man, The Beehive

The Old Parsonage, 2 Parsonage Road, Englefield Green, Egham, Surrey, TW20 0JW.
Georgian parsonage, traditionally furnished, old fashioned gardens. 30 minutes from London.
Open: All Year (not Xmas)
01784 436706 (also fax) Mr & Mrs Clark
D: £25.00–£40.00 **S:** £35.00–£55.00
Beds: 1F 2D 2T 1S **Baths:** 3 En 1 Sh
🛇 🅿 (6) ⌨ ⏻ 🛏 ✗ ▥ Ⅴ 🛆

Esher

TQ1464 🍺 The Swan

Lilac Cottage, 14 Greenways, Hinchley Wood, Esher, Surrey, KT10 0QD.
Luxury friendly family home convenient London, Hampton Court, Wisley, Sandown.
Open: All Year (not Xmas)
020 8398 7546 (also fax)
Mrs Evans
evans@greenways.demon.co.uk
D: £27.50–£30.00 **S:** £30.00–£35.00
Beds: 1D 1T **Baths:** 2 En
🛇 ⌨ ⏻ ▥ 🛆 cc

Ewhurst

TQ0940 🍺 The Windmill, Scarlett Arms, Bull's Head, The Parrot

High Edser, Shere Road, Ewhurst, Cranleigh, Surrey, GU6 7PQ.
Open: All Year (not Xmas)
Grades: ETC 3 Diamond
01483 278214 Mrs Franklin-Adams
Fax: 01483 278200
franklinadams@highedser.demon.co.uk
D: £27.50 **S:** £30.00–£35.00
Beds: 2D 1T **Baths:** 1 Sh
🛇 🅿 (6) ⌨ ⏻ 🛏 ▥ Ⅴ 🛆
C16th farmhouse in Area of Outstanding Natural Beauty, a beautiful setting for a restful break. We are close to many National Trust Properties and within easy reach of London. Gatwick/London airports are 30/45 minutes drive.

Malricks, The Street, Ewhurst, Cranleigh, Surrey, GU6 7RH.
Modern detached house, village location. Large attractive garden overlooking fields.
Open: All Year
01483 277575 Mrs Budgen
D: £19.00 **S:** £19.00
Beds: 1F 1T **Baths:** 1 En 1 Sh
🛇 🅿 (3) ⌨ ⏻ ▥ Ⅴ

Yard Farm, North Breache Road, Ewhurst, Cranleigh, Surrey, GU6 7SN.
Traditional C16th farmhouse in Surrey countryside surrounded by farmland.
Open: All Year (not Xmas)
01483 276649 (also fax)
Mrs Nutting
D: £22.50 **S:** £22.50–£25.00
Beds: 1D 2T 1S **Baths:** 2 En 1 Pr
🛇 (12) 🅿 (6) ⏻ 🛏 ▥ 🛆

Farnham

SU8446 🍺 Bat & Ball, The Cricketers, Hare & Hound, Cherry Tree, Prince Of Wales, The Anchor, Spotted Cow, Hen & Chicken, Jolly Farmer, Wellington's

Heath Lodge, 91a Shortheath Road, Farnham, Surrey, GU9 8SF.
Period house, quiet situation, Surrey/Hants border & Waterloo Station close by.
Open: All Year
01252 722918 Mrs Jones
gmjones33@aol.com
D: fr £22.50 **S:** fr £28.00
Beds: 2T **Baths:** 1 Sh
🛇 🅿 (4) ⌨ ⏻ ✗ ▥ Ⅴ ❀ 🛆

Pittersfield, Hole Lane, Bentley, Farnham, Surrey, GU10 5LT.
Period courtyard annexe in peaceful rural surroundings.
Open: All Year
Grades: ETC Listed, High Comm
01420 22414 (also fax)
Mrs Coulton
D: £25.00–£30.00 **S:** £25.00–£30.00
Beds: 3F 1T 1D 1S **Baths:** 2 En 2 Pr 1 Sh
🛇 🅿 (3) ⌨ ⏻ ✗ ▥ Ⅴ 🛆

Orchard House, 13 Applelands Close, Farnham, Surrey, GU10 4TL.
Visitors warmly welcomed at our quietly located home overlooking countryside.
Open: All Year (not Xmas)
01252 793813 Mrs Warburton
D: £18.00–£20.00 **S:** £18.00–£20.00
Beds: 1T 1S **Baths:** 1 Sh
🛇 🅿 (3) ⌨ ⏻ ▥ 🛆

Hawkridge, 20 Upper Old Park Lane, Farnham, Surrey, GU9 0AT.
Large house with lovely gardens in beautiful countryside.
Open: All Year
01252 722068 Mr & Mrs Ackland
chris.ackland@tesco.net
D: £20.00–£25.00 **S:** £20.00–£25.00
Beds: 1D 1T 1S **Baths:** 1 Sh
🛇 (10) 🅿 (6) ⌨ ⏻ ✗ ▥ Ⅴ 🛆

Felbridge

TQ3639

Toads Croak House, *30 Copthorne Road, Felbridge, East Grinstead, W Sussex, RH19 2NS.*
Beautiful Sussex cottage-style house, gardens. Gatwick parking. 17th independent year. **Open:** All Year
01342 328524 (also fax)
D: £18.50–£23.00 **S:** fr £24.00
Beds: 1F 1D 2T 1S **Baths:** 2 En 1 Sh
🛏 🄿 (7) ⅃ 🖤 🎞 ♨

Gatwick (Surrey side)

TQ2843 ◄ *Air Balloon, Ye Olde Six Bells, King's Head*

Melville Lodge Guest House, *15 Brighton Road, Gatwick, Horley, Surrey, RH6 7HH.*
Edwardian early 1900 house. Access to coach station and buses. **Open:** All Year
Grades: ETC 2 Diamond, RAC 2 Diamond
01293 784951 Mr & Mrs Brooks
Fax: 01293 785669
melvillelodge.guesthouse@tesco.net
D: £19.00–£22.50 **S:** £25.00–£35.00
Beds: 1F 3D 2T 1S **Baths:** 3 En 2 Sh
🛏 (1) 🄿 🖤 🐾 🎞 ♨ 🐕

Victoria Lodge Guest House, *161 Victoria Road, Horley, Surrey, RH6 7AS.*
Well-located for town centre, BR station,pubs, shops etc. families welcome.
Open: All Year
01293 432040 Mr & Mrs Robson
Fax: 01293 432042
prnrjr@globalnet.co.uk
D: £19.00–£25.00 **S:** £30.00–£48.00
Beds: 2F 2D 2S **Baths:** 2 En 2 Sh
🛏 🄿 (14) ⅃ 🖤 🎞 ♨ cc

Godalming

SU9643 ◄ *Inn on the Lake*

Sherwood, *Ashtead Lane, Godalming, Surrey, GU7 1SY.*
We have 4 cats and one Cavalier King Charles Spaniel - we welcome animal lovers. **Open:** All Year
01483 427545 (also fax)
Mr & Mrs Harrison
D: fr £22.50 **S:** fr £24.00
Beds: 1T 2S **Baths:** 1 Sh
🛏 (5) 🖤 🎞 ♨

Godstone

TQ3551 ◄ *Coach House*

Godstone Hotel, *The Green, Godstone, Surrey, RH9 8DT.*
Open: All Year
01883 742461 (also fax)
Mr Howe
D: fr £27.50 **S:** fr £39.00
Beds: 6D 2T **Baths:** 8 Pr
🛏 🄿 🖤 🐾 ✕ 🎞 🔘 ♨
C16th coaching house, original features, inglenook fireplaces. Our restaurant 'The Coach House' is renowned in the vicinity for superb cuisine at sensible prices - well worth a visit. Pre-booking is highly recommended. Our friendly staff look forward to welcoming you.

Great Bookham

TQ1354 ◄ *Windsor Castle, The Plough*

Selworthy, *310 Lower Road, Great Bookham, Leatherhead, Surrey, KT23 4DW.*
Attractive location overlooking Green Belt. Convenient, M25, Gatwick and Heathrow airports.
Open: All Year (not Xmas)
01372 453952 (also fax)
Mrs Kent
D: £19.00–£22.00 **S:** £23.00–£26.00
Beds: 1D 1T **Baths:** 1 Sh
🛏 (10) 🄿 (4) ⅃ 🖤 🎞

Guildford

SU9949 ◄ *King's Head, Jolly Farmer, Hare & Hounds, The Fox, White House, George Abbot, Grantley Arms*

Weybrook House, *113 Stoke Road, Guildford, Surrey, GU1 1ET.*
Quiet family B&B. A320 Near town centre/stations. Delicious breakfast.
Open: All Year (not Xmas)
01483 302394 Mr & Mrs Bourne
markmelb@hotmail.com
D: £20.00–£22.00 **S:** £28.00
Beds: 1F 1D 1S **Baths:** 2 Sh
🛏 🖤 🐾 🎞 ♨ cc

The Old Malt House, *Worplesdon, Guildford, Surrey, GU3 3PT.*
Old country house standing in extensive grounds with swimming pool.
Open: All Year
Grades: ETC 3 Diamond
01483 232152 Mrs Millar
D: £17.00–£18.00 **S:** £18.00–£25.00
Beds: 1T 2T **Baths:** 2 Sh
🛏 🄿 (6) 🖤 🎞 ♨

Atkinsons Guest House, *129 Stoke Road, Guildford, Surrey, GU1 1ET.*
Small comfortable family-run guest house close to town centre & all local amenities.
Open: All Year
01483 538260 Mrs Atkinson
D: £20.00–£22.50 **S:** £28.00–£45.00
Beds: 1D 1T 2S **Baths:** 2 En 1 Sh
🛏 (6) 🄿 (2) 🖤 🎞 ♨

Westbury Cottage, *Waterden Road, Guildford, Surrey, GU1 2AN.*
Cottage-style house in large secluded garden, 5 mins town centre, 2 mins station.
Open: All Year (not Xmas)
01483 822602 (also fax)
Mrs Smythe
D: £25.00 **S:** £30.00
Beds: 1D 2T **Baths:** 1 Sh
🛏 (6) 🄿 (3) ⅃ 🖤 🎞 ♨

Beevers Farm, *Chinthurst Lane, Bramley, Guildford, Surrey, GU5 0DR.*
Peaceful surroundings, friendly atmosphere, own preserves, honey, eggs, nearby villages.
Open: Easter to Nov
Grades: ETC 3 Diamond
01483 898764 (also fax)
Mr Cook
D: £18.00–£25.00 **S:** fr £30.00
Beds: 1F 2T **Baths:** 1 Pr 1 Sh
🛏 (10) ⅃ 🖤 🎞 ♨

25 The Chase, *Guildford, Surrey, GU2 5UA.*
10 minutes to town and station. Easy access to A3.
Open: All Year (not Xmas/New Year)
01483 569782 Mrs Ellis
D: £ **S:** £16.00
Beds: 2S
⅃ 🖤 🎞

2 Wodeland Avenue, *Guildford, GU2 4JX.*
Centrally located rooms with panorama. Friendly and modernised family home.
Open: All Year (not Xmas)
01483 451142 Mrs Hay
Fax: 01483 572980
rozanne.hay@talk21.com
D: £20.00–£22.00 **S:** £20.00–£25.00
Beds: 1D 1T **Baths:** 1 Pr 1 Sh
🛏 (3) 🄿 (3) ⅃ 🖤 🎞 🔘 ♨ 🐕

Quietways, *29 Liddington Hall Drive, Guildford, Surrey, GU3 3AE.*
Off A323, quiet cottage, end of cul-de-sac. Lounge, conservatory, pleasant garden.
Open: Jan to Nov
01483 232347 Mr White
D: fr £19.50 **S:** fr £25.00
Beds: 1D 1T **Baths:** 1 En 1 Pr
🄿 (2) ⅃ 🖤 🎞 ♨ 🐕

Hascombe

SU9939 ◄ *White Horse*

Hoe Farm, *Hoe Lane, Hascombe, Godalming, Surrey, GU8 4JQ.*
Elizabethan farmhouse in tranquil wooded valley, former retreat of Winston Churchill.
Open: All Year
01483 208222
Mrs Gordon
Fax: 01483 208538
D: £25.00–£30.00 **S:** £30.00
Beds: 1F 3D 3T 1S **Baths:** 3 Sh
🛏 (8) ⅃ 🖤 🐾 ✕ 🎞 🔘 ♨

Holmbury St Mary

TQ1144 ◄ *Royal Oak, Parrot Inn, The Volunteer, King's Head*

Bulmer Farm, *Holmbury St Mary, Dorking, Surrey, RH5 6LG.*
Quiet modernised C17th farmhouse/barn, large garden, picturesque village, self-catering.
Open: All Year
Grades: ETC 4 Diamond
01306 730210
Mrs Hill
D: £22.00–£24.00 **S:** £22.00–£35.00
Beds: 3D 5T **Baths:** 5 En 2 Sh
🛏 (12) 🄿 (12) ⅃ 🖤 🐾 🎞 🔘 ♨ 🐕 3

Planning a longer stay? Always ask for any special rates

Horley

TQ2843   Air Balloon, Ye Olde Six Bells, King's Head

Yew Tree, *31 Massetts Road, Horley, Surrey, RH6 7DQ.*
Tudor style house 1/2 acre gardens, close Gatwick Airport, near town centre.
Open: All Year
Grades: ETC 1 Diamond
01293 785855 (also fax)
Mr Stroud
D: £15.00–£20.00 **S:** £20.00–£25.00
Beds: 1F 2D 1T 2S **Baths:** 1 En 1 Sh
🛪 (2) ⱝ (10) 📺 🛏 ₤ cc

Victoria Lodge Guest House, *161 Victoria Road, Horley, Surrey, RH6 7AS.*
Well-located for town centre, BR station, pubs, shops etc. families welcome.
Open: All Year
01293 432040 Mr & Mrs Robson
Fax: 01293 432042
prnrjr@globalnet.co.uk
D: £19.00–£25.00 **S:** £30.00–£48.00
Beds: 2F 2D 2S **Baths:** 2 En 2 Sh
🛪 ⱝ (14) ⱳ 📺 🛏 ₤ cc

Prinsted Guest House, *Oldfield Road, Horley, Surrey, RH6 7EP.*
Spacious Victorian house in quiet situation ideal for Gatwick Airport.
Open: All Year (not Xmas)
Grades: ETC 4 Diamond, AA 3 Diamond, RAC 3 Diamond, Sparkling
01293 785233 Mrs Kendall
Fax: 01293 820624
D: £22.50–£23.50 **S:** £32.00
Beds: 2D 3T 2S **Baths:** 6 En 1 Pr
🛪 ⱝ (10) 📺 cc

Blackberry House, *8 Brighton Road, Horley, Surrey, RH6 7ES.*
Attractive house on the main A23. 5 mins' drive Gatwick airport.
Open: All Year (not Xmas)
01293 772447
D: £18.00–£20.00 **S:** £26.00–£30.00
Beds: 1D
ⱝ (4) ⱳ 📺 ₤

Logans Guest House, *93 Povey Cross Road, Horley, Surrey, RH6 0AE.*
Victorian garden setting, friendly hosts, holiday parking, really nice atmosphere.
Open: All Year
01293 783363 (also fax)
D: £20.00–£30.00 **S:** £20.00–£30.00
Beds: 2F 3D 4T 2S **Baths:** 3 En 1 Pr 2 Sh
🛪 ⱝ ⱳ 📺 🛏 ✗ ₤ ❋ ₤ ₤ cc

Gorse Cottage, *66 Balcombe Road, Horley, Surrey, RH6 9AY.*
Gatwick Airport 2 miles, pretty, detached house in residential area.
Open: All Year (not Xmas)
01293 784402 (also fax)
D: £17.50–£18.00
Beds: 1D 1T
ⱝ (2) ⱳ 🛏 ₤ ₤

Leatherhead

TQ1656   Windsor Castle, The Plough

Selworthy, *310 Lower Road, Great Bookham, Leatherhead, Surrey, KT23 4DW.*
Attractive location overlooking Green Belt. Convenient, M25, Gatwick and Heathrow airports.
Open: All Year (not Xmas)
01372 453952 (also fax)
Mrs Kent
D: £19.00–£22.00 **S:** £23.00–£26.00
Beds: 1D 1T **Baths:** 1 Sh
🛪 (10) ⱝ (4) ⱝ 📺 🛏 ₤

Leigh

TQ2246   The Plough

Barn Cottage, *Church Road, Leigh, Reigate, Surrey, RH2 8RF.*
Converted C17th barn, gardens with swimming pool, 100 yards from pub, 0.25 hr Gatwick.
Open: All Year
01306 611347 Mrs Comer
D: £25.00–£30.00 **S:** £35.00
Beds: 1D 1T **Baths:** 1 Sh
🛪 ⱝ (3) ⱝ 📺 🛏 ✗ ₤ ₤ ₤

Limpsfield

TQ4052   The George, The Crown, The Gurkha

Arawa, *58 Granville Road, Limpsfield, Oxted, Surrey, RH8 0BZ.*
Friendly, comfortable, welcoming. Lovely garden, excellent breakfast, good London trains.
Open: All Year
Grades: ETC 3 Diamond
01883 714104 (also fax)
D J Gibbs
david@arawa.co.uk
D: £18.00–£30.00 **S:** £18.00–£30.00
Beds: 1F 2T **Baths:** 1 En 1 Sh
🛪 ⱝ (3) ⱝ 📺 🛏 🛏 ₤ ₤ ₤ 3

Littleton

TQ0668   The Harrow

Old Manor House, *Squires Bridge Road, Littleton, Shepperton, Middx, TW17 0QG.*
Listed building dating from reign of Henry VII, set in 5 acres of garden.
Open: All Year
01932 571293 Mrs Bouwens
victor@oldmanorhouse.demon.co.uk
D: £25.00–£27.50 **S:** £30.00
Beds: 1D 1T 1S **Baths:** 1 En 1 Sh
🛪 (10) ⱝ (6) 📺 🛏 ₤ ₤

Milford

SU9442   The Star, Red Lion

Coturnix House, *Rake Lane, Milford, Godalming, Surrey, GU8 5AB.*
Modern house, family atmosphere, countryside position, easy access road/rail.
Open: All Year
01483 416897 Mr Bell
100523.1037@compuserve.com
D: £20.00 **S:** £20.00
Beds: 1D 1T 1S **Baths:** 1 Pr 1 Sh
🛪 (1) ⱝ (6) ⱝ 🛏 🛏 ₤ ₤

Newdigate

TQ1942   Six Bells, The Star, The Plough, Surrey Oaks, Six Bells

Sturtwood Farm, *Partridge Lane, Newdigate, Dorking, Surrey, RH5 5EE.*
Comfortable welcoming farmhouse in beautiful wooded countryside. Many historic properties nearby.
Open: All Year (not Xmas/New Year)
Grades: ETC 3 Diamond
01306 631308 Mrs MacKinnon
Fax: 01306 631908
D: £22.50–£25.00 **S:** £30.00–£35.00
Beds: 1T 1S 1D **Baths:** 1 En 1 Sh
🛪 ⱝ (6) ⱝ 📺 🛏 ✗ ₤ ₤ ₤

Ockley

TQ1439   Parrot Inn

Hazels, *Walliswood, Ockley, Dorking, Surrey, RH5 5PL.*
Separate suite. Superior accommodation. Beautiful gardens. Relaxed & peaceful. Convenient airports.
Open: All Year
01306 627228 Mrs Floud
susie.floud@ukgateway.net
D: £20.00–£25.00 **S:** £20.00–£30.00
Beds: 1F 1S **Baths:** 1 En 1 Sh
🛪 ⱝ (2) ⱝ 📺 🛏 ₤

Oxted

TQ3852   The Oxted, Old Bell, The Crown, The George, The Gurkha, Royal Oak

Pinehurst Grange Guest House, *East Hill (Part of A25), Oxted, Surrey, RH8 9AE.*
Comfortable Victorian ex-farmhouse with traditional service and relaxed friendly atmosphere.
Open: All Year (not Xmas/New Year)
01883 716413 Mr Rodgers
D: £21.00 **S:** £26.00
Beds: 1D 1T 1S **Baths:** 1 Sh
🛪 (5) ⱝ (3) ⱝ 📺 🛏 ₤ ₤

Meads, *23 Granville Road, Oxted, Surrey, RH8 0BX.*
Tudor style house on Kent/Surrey border station to London.
Open: All Year
Grades: ETC 4 Diamond
01883 730115 Mrs Holgate
Holgate@meads9.fsnet.co.uk
D: £25.00–£28.00 **S:** £28.00–£30.00
Beds: 1T 1D **Baths:** 1 En 1 Pr
🛪 ⱝ ⱝ 📺 🛏 ₤ ₤

Arawa, *58 Granville Road, Oxted, Surrey, RH8 0BZ.*
Friendly, comfortable, welcoming. Lovely garden, excellent breakfast, good London trains.
Open: All Year
Grades: ETC 3 Diamond
01883 714104 (also fax)
D J Gibbs
david@arawa.co.uk
D: £18.00–£30.00 **S:** £18.00–£30.00
Beds: 1F 2T **Baths:** 1 En 1 Sh
🛪 ⱝ (3) ⱝ 📺 🛏 🛏 ₤ ₤ ₤ 3

Old Forge House, *Merle Common, Oxted, Surrey, RH8 0JB.*
Welcoming family home in rural surroundings. Ten minutes from M25.
Open: All Year (not Xmas)
01883 715969 Mrs Mills
D: £18.00–£20.00 **S:** £18.00–£20.00
Beds: 1D 1T 1S **Baths:** 1 Sh
🏠 🄿 (4) 📺 🐾 ▥ cc

Redhill

TQ2750   🍺 *The Sun*

Lynwood Guest House, *50 London Road, Redhill, Surrey, RH1 1LN.*
Adjacent to a lovely park, within 6 minutes walking from railway station, town centre.
Open: All Year
Grades: AA 3 Diamond
01737 766894 Mrs Trozado
Fax: 01737 778253
lynwoodguesthouse@yahoo.co.uk
D: £25.00–£28.00 **S:** £32.00–£35.00
Beds: 4F 2D 1T 2S **Baths:** 3 En 6 Pr 1 Sh
🏠 🄿 (8) 📺 ▥ 🛁 cc

Ripley

TQ0456

The Half Moon, *High Street, Ripley, Woking, Surrey, GU23 6AN.*
Old world inn, all rooms colour TV, washbasins, tea/coffee.
Open: All Year
01483 224380 (also fax)
Mr Beale
D: £20.00 **S:** £40.00
Beds: 1D 6T **Baths:** 4 Pr 1 Sh
🏠 (7) 🄿 (20) 📺 ✕ ▥ 🛁

Send

TQ0255   🍺 *Onslow Arms*

Grantchester, *Boughton Hall Avenue, Send, Woking, Surrey, GU23 7DF.*
Open: All Year
01483 225383 Mrs Winterbourne
gary@hotpolmail.com
D: £22.00 **S:** £22.00–£25.00
Beds: 3T 2S **Baths:** 3 Sh
🏠 🄿 (9) ✎ 📺 ▥ 🛁
Attractive family house with large garden. 4 miles from Guildford, close to M25 and A3. Wisley Gardens and Clandon Park and golf courses nearby. Own transport recommended. Parking available. Long term stays very welcome.

Shackleford

SU9345

Seven Pines, *Shackleford Road, Shackleford, Godalming, Surrey, GU8 6AE.*
Charming, comfortable, country house in beautiful Surrey countryside. Convenient A3.
Open: All Year (not Xmas)
Grades: AA 3 Diamond
01483 425286 Mr & Mrs Hamilton
douglashamilton1@compuserve.com
D: £25.00–£30.00 **S:** £24.00–£30.00
Beds: 1F 1T **Baths:** 1 En 1 Sh
🏠 🄿 (6) ✎ 📺 ✕ ▥ 🛁

Shalford

TQ0046   🍺 *Sea Horse Pub*

The Laurels, *23 Dagden Road, Shalford, Guildford, Surrey, GU4 8DD.*
Quiet detached house. Direct access to footpaths. Near Guildford centre.
Open: All Year
01483 565753 Mrs Deeks
D: £20.00–£23.00 **S:** £22.00
Beds: 1T 1D
🏠 (6) 🄿 (5) ✎ 📺 🐾 ✕ ▥ 📺 🛁

Shepperton

TQ0767   🍺 *The Harrow, The Goat, The Bull*

91 Watersplash Road, *Shepperton, TW17 0EE.*
Olde worlde cottage with pretty bedrooms and old fashioned hospitality.
Open: All Year
01932 229987 (also fax) Mr Shaw
D: £19.00–£22.50 **S:** £25.00–£28.50
Beds: 2D 1T
🏠 ✎ 📺 ▥ 🛁

Shere

TQ0747   🍺 *White Horse, Prince of Wales*

Manor Cottage, *Shere, Guildford, Surrey, GU5 9JE.*
C16th cottage with old world garden, in centre of beautiful village.
Open: May to Sep
01483 202979 Mrs James
D: £20.00 **S:** £20.00
Beds: 1D 1S **Baths:** 1 Sh
🏠 (5) 🄿 ✎ 📺 🛁

Cherry Trees, *Gomshall, Shere, Guildford, Surrey, GU5 9HE.*
Quiet comfortable house, lovely garden, village foot of North Downs.
Open: All Year (not Xmas/New Year)
01483 202288 Mrs Warren
D: £–£25.00 **S:** £25.00–£30.00
Beds: 2D 3F 1S **Baths:** 2 En 1 Sh
🏠 🄿 (4) ✎ 📺 ▥ 📺 🛁 🚱

South Holmwood

TQ1745   🍺 *Inn on the Green*

Steyning Cottage, *Horsham Road, South Holmwood, Dorking, Surrey, RH5 4NE.*
Special rates for long term, including dinner. French spoken.
Open: All Year (not Xmas)
01306 888481 Mrs Treays
D: £18.00–£21.00 **S:** £18.00–£21.00
Beds: 1T 1S **Baths:** 1 Sh
🏠 🄿 (4) 📺 🐾 ✕ ▥

Staines

TQ0471   🍺 *Wheatsheaf, Pigeon*

The Penton, *39 Penton Road, Staines, Surrey, TW18 2JL.*
Open: All Year **01784 458787**
D: £20.00–£25.00 **S:** £20.00–£26.00
Beds: 4F 1D 1T 1S **Baths:** 2 En 1 Sh
🏠 🄿 (2) ✎ 📺 ▥ 📺 🌸 🛁
Homely character cottage close to River Thames, access to scenic walks and historic surroundings, 10 mins M25, 15 mins Heathrow, we provide a comfortable stay with an excellent breakfast.

Thursley

SU9039   🍺 *Three Horseshoes, The Star, White Hart, Pride of the Valley*

Hindhead Hill Farm, *Portsmouth Road, Thursley, Godalming, Surrey, GU8 6NN.*
Small Christian family farm. Our own free-range eggs for breakfast.
Open: All Year (not Xmas)
01428 684727 Mrs Roe
Fax: 01428 685004
D: £19.00 **S:** £20.00
Beds: 1F 1T **Baths:** 1 En 1 Pr
🏠 (5) 🄿 (4) ✎ 📺 ✕ ▥ 📺 🛁

Little Cowdray Farm, *Thursley, Godalming, Surrey, GU8 6QJ.*
Quiet peaceful situation, good walking area, edge of Devils Punch Bowl.
Open: All Year (not Xmas/New Year)
01428 605016 Mrs Goble
D: £31.00 **S:** £18.00
Beds: 1T **Baths:** 1 Sh
🄿 📺 🐾 ✕ ▥ 📺 🛁

Walliswood

TQ1137   🍺 *The Parrot*

Kerne Hus, *Walliswood Green Road, Walliswood, Dorking, Surrey, RH5 5RD.*
Open: All Year (not Xmas/New Year)
01306 627548 Mrs Seller
D: £22.00 **S:** £25.00
Beds: 1T 1D **Baths:** 1 Sh
🏠 (2) 🄿 (3) ✎ 📺 ▥ 🛁
1930's detached family home set in 1/2 acre of garden. Situated in small hamlet, west of Ockley and 7 miles north of Horsham. Interesting houses and gardens in Surrey and Sussex within easy reach and close to the Downs for walking.

Walton-on-Thames

TQ1066   🍺 *The Wellington, The Plough*

Beech Tree Lodge, *7 Rydens Avenue, Walton-on-Thames, Surrey, KT12 3JB.*
In quiet avenue, 10 mins BR station; close local shops.
Open: All Year
Grades: ETC 3 Diamond
01932 242738 Mrs Spiteri
Fax: 01932 886667
D: £20.00–£21.00 **S:** £22.00–£36.00
Beds: 1F 1T 1S **Baths:** 2 Sh
🏠 🄿 (8) ✎ 📺 🐾 ▥ 📺 🛁

Oak Tree Lodge, *11 Hersham Road, Walton-on-Thames, Surrey, KT12 1LQ.*
Mock Tudor family home near buses, railway station and airports.
Open: All Year (not Xmas)
01932 221907 Mrs Hall
D: £17.00–£20.00 **S:** £20.00–£22.00
Beds: 1D 1T 1S **Baths:** 1 Sh
🄿 (4) ✎ 📺 ▥ 🛁

National Grid References are for villages, towns and cities – not for individual houses

Warlingham

TQ3558   *White Lion, The Horseshoe*

Glenmore, *Southview Road, Warlingham, Surrey, CR6 9JE.*
Victorian House in the large grounds close to the countryside and London.
Open: All Year
01883 624530 Fax: 01883 624199
D: fr £17.50 **S:** fr £22.00
Beds: 2F 1T 2D **Baths:** 1 En 2 Sh
🛏 🅿 (6) ⌁ 📺 📖 🕯

West Horsley

TQ0752   *King William IV*

Brinford, *Off Shere Road, West Horsley, Leatherhead, KT24 6EJ.*
Comfortable modern house in peaceful rural location with panoramic views.
Open: All Year
01483 283636 Mrs Wiltshire
D: £20.00–£25.00 **S:** fr £25.00
Beds: 1D 1T 1S **Baths:** 1 En 1 Sh
🅿 (4) ⌁ 📺 📖 Ⓥ 🕯

Worplesdon

SU9753   *Cricketers, Hare & Hounds, The Fox*

The Old Malt House, *Worplesdon, Guildford, Surrey, GU3 3PT.*
Old country house standing in extensive grounds with swimming pool.
Open: All Year
Grades: ETC 3 Diamond
01483 232152 Mrs Millar
D: £17.00–£18.00 **S:** £18.00–£25.00
Beds: 1S 2T **Baths:** 2 Sh
🛏 🅿 (6) 📺 📖 🕯

East Sussex

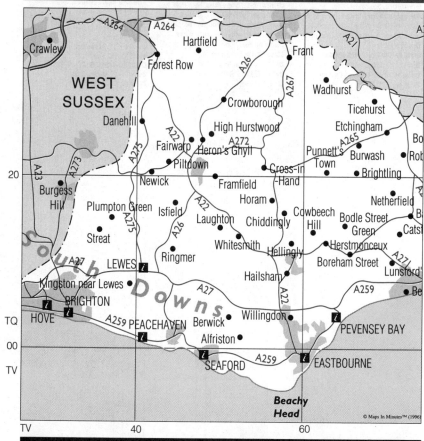

88 High Street, **Battle**, East
Sussex, TN33 0AQ,
01424 773721.

De La Warr Pavilion, Marina,
Bexhill-on-Sea, East Sussex,
TN40 1DP, 01424 732208.

10 Bartholomew Square,
Brighton, East Sussex,
BN1 1EQ, 01273 292599.

3 Cornfield Road, **Eastbourne**,
East Sussex, BN21 4QL,
01323 411400.

The Library, Western Road,
Hailsham, East Sussex,
BN27 3DN, 01323 840604.

4 Robertson Terrace, **Hastings**,
East Sussex, TN34 1EZ,
01424 781111.

Fishmarket, The Stade, **Hastings**,
East Sussex, TN34 1EZ,
01424 781111 (Easter to Oct).

King Alfred Leisure Centre,
Kingsway, **Hove**, East Sussex,
BN3 2WW, 01273 746100.

Church Road, **Hove**, East Sussex,
BN3 3BQ, 01273 292589.

187 High Street, **Lewes**, East
Sussex, BN7 2DE,
01273 483448.

Boship Roundabout (A22),
Lower Dicker, Hailsham, East
Sussex, BN27 4DP,
01323 442667.

Meridian Centre, Roderick
Avenue, **Peacehaven**, East
Sussex, BN10 8BB,
01273 582668.

Pevensey Castle, High Street,
Pevensey, East Sussex,
BN24 5LE,
01323 442667 (Easter to Oct).

The Heritage Centre, Strand
Quay, **Rye**, East Sussex,
TN31 7AY, 01797 226696.

Station Approach, **Seaford**, East
Sussex, BN25 2AR,
01323 897426.

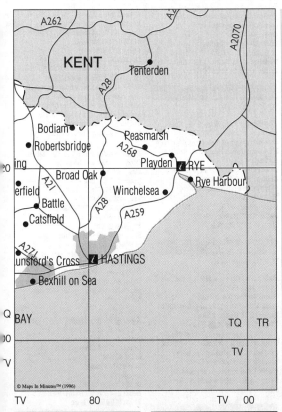

© Maps In Minutes™ (1996)

TV   80   TV   00

Alfriston

TQ5103 🍴 *Wingrove Inn, Ye Olde Smuggler's Inn, The George*

Meadowbank, *Sloe Lane, Alfriston, East Sussex, BN26 5UR.*
Open: All Year (not Xmas/New Year)
01323 870742 Mrs Petch
D: £20.00–£25.00 **S:** £30.00–£35.00
Beds: 1T 2D **Baths:** 1 En 2 Sh
🅿 (4) ⌖ 📺 🔥 🎖 📖 Ⓥ ♨ ₺
The beautiful private dwelling in tranquil setting, offers views of Cuckmere Valley and South Downs. only 3 minutes walk village centre. Ideal for walkers/cyclists. Private car park. Lovely gardens and conservatory in which to relax. Delicious English breakfast.

Dacres, *Alfriston, Polegate, East Sussex, BN26 5TP.*
Country cottage. Beautiful gardens. Near South Downs Way Glyndebourne, Seven Sisters. **Open:** All Year
01323 870447 Mrs Embry
D: £25.00 **S:** fr £40.00
Beds: 1T **Baths:** 1 Pr
🅿 (1) ⌖ 📺 📖 Ⓥ ₺ ₺

Battle

TQ7515 🍴 *Netherfield Arms, Black Horse, White Hart, King's Head*

Bell Cottage, *Vinehall Road, Robertsbridge, Battle, E Sussex, TN32 5JN.*
Open: All Year (not Xmas)
Grades: ETC 4 Diamond
01580 881164 Mrs Lowe
patricia.lowe@tesco.net
D: £20.00–£25.00 **S:** £25.00–£30.00
Beds: 1D 2T **Baths:** 1 En 1 Pr 1 Sh
🅿 (3) ⌖ 📺 📖 ₺ 3
C17th converted inn beamed throughout. Delightful gardens. Warm welcome assured. Comfortable accommodation, gourmet breakfasts with homemade preserves. Close to Battle, Hastings, Rye, Canterbury, Brighton, Sissinghurst Gardens within easy driving. UK B&B of the Year 1997.

B&B owners may vary
rates - be sure to check
when booking

Fox Hole Farm, *Kane Hythe Road, Battle, E Sussex, TN33 9QU.*
A restored country cottage; perfect place to relax and unwind.
Open: All Year
Grades: AA 4 Diamond
01424 772053 Mr Collins
Fax: 01424 773771
D: £24.50–£27.50 **S:** £29.00–£39.00
Beds: 3D **Baths:** 3 En
🅿 (6) ⌖ 📺 🔥 🎖 ✕ 📖 Ⓥ ₺ cc

Abbey View, *Caldbec Hill, Battle, East Sussex, TN33 0JS.*
Elegantly furnished accommodation overlooking beautiful Sussex countryside and Battle Abbey.
Open: All Year
Grades: ETC 4 Diamond
01424 775513 (also fax)
Mrs Whiteman
D: £25.00–£30.00 **S:** £30.00–£45.00
Beds: 2D 1T **Baths:** 2 En 1 Pr
♿ 🅿 (6) ⌖ 📺 ✕ 📖 Ⓥ ✿ ₺

Kelklands, *Off Chain Lane, Battle, East Sussex, TN33 0HG.*
Peaceful situation, short walk into town. No smoking, easy parking.
Open: All Year
Grades: ETC 3 Diamond
01424 773013
M Burgess
D: £20.00 **S:** £20.00
Beds: 1F 1T 1S **Baths:** 2 En 1 Sh
♿ (2) 🅿 (5) ⌖ 📺 📖 Ⓥ ₺

Farthings Farm, *Catsfield, Battle, East Sussex, TN33 9BA.*
Edwardian house on a 70-acre farm set half mile off the road.
Open: All Year (not Xmas)
Grades: ETC 4 Diamond, AA 4 Diamond
01424 773107
Mrs Rodgers
D: £25.00 **S:** £30.00
Beds: 2D 1T **Baths:** 2 Pr
♿ 🅿 (3) ⌖ 📺 ✕ 📖 ₺

East Sussex   Map page 330

Baytrees, 66 Hastings Road, Battle, East
Sussex, TN33 0TE.
Bungalow backing open countryside. 1
mile Battle, visit Battle Abbey and battle
ground.
Open: All Year (not Xmas)
01424 772764 Mrs Gammon
D: £17.50 **S:** £20.00
Beds: 1D 1T **Baths:** 2 En
⌂ ℗ (3) ½ 📺 ▥ 🖤 ♨

Berwick

TQ5104   ◀ Cricketers' Arms

Dawes House, Berwick, Polegate, E
Sussex, BN26 5QS.
Delightful period country home near
Alfriston in scenic Cuckmere valley.
Open: Feb to Nov
01323 871276 (also fax)
Mrs Wardroper
D: £22.50–£27.50 **S:** £25.00–£30.00
Beds: 1D 1T **Baths:** 1 En 1 Pr
⌂ ℗ (4) ½ 📺 ✕ ▥ ♨

Bexhill-on-Sea

TQ7308   ◀ The Wheatsheaf, King's Arms, The
Wilton, The Mermaid, Rose & Crown

Buenos Aires, 24 Albany Road, Bexhill-
on-Sea, E Sussex, TN40 1BZ.
Open: All Year
01424 212269 (also fax)
Mr & Mrs Robson
D: £17.50–£22.00 **S:** £19.00–£30.00
Beds: 1F 1D 1T 1S **Baths:** 1 En 2 Sh
⌂ (5) ½ 📺 ✕ ▥ 🖤 ❀ ♨
Well-established guest house offering a
high standard of comfortable
accommodation in a warm and friendly
atmosphere. Situated close to sea front
and town centre and De La Warr Pavilion,
offering both ensuite and standard
rooms.

Wakeford House, Potmans Lane,
Lunsford's Cross, Bexhill-on-Sea, E.
Sussex, TN39 5JL.
Edwardian-style house in country setting
with peaceful one acre garden.
Open: All Year
Grades: ETC 3 Diamond , AA 4 Diamond
01424 892013 Mrs Skinner
Fax: 01424 893978
keltie@globalnet.co.uk
D: £22.50–£25.00 **S:** £25.00–£30.00
Beds: 3F 1D 1S 1T **Baths:** 1 En 1 Sh
⌂ ℗ (5) 📺 ✝ ✕ ▥ 🖤 ♨

Manor Barn, Lunsford's Cross, Bexhill
on Sea, E. Sussex, TN39 5JJ.
Ensuite chalets, semi-rural setting on
A269, 3 miles sea.
Open: All Year
Grades: ETC 3 Diamond
01424 893018 (also fax)
Mrs Gillingham
D: £16.50–£18.00 **S:** £20.00–£24.00
Beds: 1F 1D 1T 1S **Baths:** 4 En
⌂ ℗ (6) ½ 📺 ▥ 🖤 ♨ &

National Grid References are for
villages, towns and cities – not
for individual houses

Bodiam

TQ7825   ◀ Curlew Inn

Elms Farm, Bodiam, Robertsbridge, E.
Sussex, TN32 5UU.
Bodiam Castle half mile. Farm horses,
cows, calves, dogs and cats.
Open: All Year
01580 830494 Mrs Parkes
D: fr £20.00 **S:** fr £20.00
Beds: 1F 1T 1S **Baths:** 1 En 1 Sh
⌂ ℗ (10) 📺 ✝ ✕ ▥ 🖤 ♨

Bodle Street Green

TQ6514   ◀ White Horse

The Stud Farm, Bodle Street Green,
Hailsham, E. Sussex, BN27 4RJ.
Comfortable farmhouse on working farm.
Situated between Heathfield, Hailsham,
Battle.
Open: All Year (not Xmas/New Year)
Grades: ETC 3 Diamond
01323 833201 (also fax)
Mr & Mrs Gentry
D: £20.00–£21.00 **S:** £22.00–£25.00
Beds: 1D 2T **Baths:** 1 Pr 1 Sh
℗ (3) ½ 📺 ✕ ▥ 🖤 ♨

Boreham Street

TQ6611   ◀ Ash Tree Inn

Baldocks, Boreham Street, Hailsham, E
Sussex, BN27 4SQ.
Open: All Year (not Xmas)
01323 832107 D: £20.00 **S:** £20.00–£30.00
Beds: 1D 1T **Baths:** 1 Sh
⌂ ℗ (2) ½ 📺 ✝ ✕ ▥ 🖤 ♨
A warm welcome awaits you at this part
C16th cottage in 1066 country with many
local walks. Situated 2 miles from
beautiful Herstmonceux Castle and
grounds and 5 miles from Pevensey
Castle - a good bird watching area
especially around the marshes.

Brightling

TQ6821   ◀ Jack Fullers, Swan Inn

Swallowfield Farm, Brightling,
Robertsbridge, East Sussex, TN32 5HB.
Elizabethan farmhouse and self-
contained cottage in thirty acres of
outstanding beauty.
Open: All Year
Grades: AA 4 Diamond
01424 838225 (also fax)
Mrs Page
rpage@hsfinancial.co.uk
D: £23.00–£25.00 **S:** £25.00
Beds: 1F 2T **Baths:** 2 En
⌂ ℗ (20) 📺 ✝ ✕ ▥ 🖤 ♨

3 Twelve Oak Cottages, Brightling,
Robertsbridge, East Sussex, TN32 5HS.
Self-contained, spacious accommodation
with beautiful views towards Darwell
reservoir.
Open: Easter to Nov
Grades: ETC 3 Diamond
01424 838263 Mrs Hinchey
D: £20.00 **S:** £20.00
Beds: 1D **Baths:** 1 En
⌂ ℗ (1) ½ 📺 ♨ &

Brighton

TQ3106   ◀ The Burlington, Hand In Hand, Lion
& Lobster, The Stag, Iron Duke, Samsons, Compton
Arms, Golden Girl, The Jesters

New Steine Hotel, 12a New Steine,
Brighton, E. Sussex, BN2 1PB.
Open: All Year **Grades:** AA 4 Diamond
01273 681546 Mr Guyat
Fax: 01273 679118
D: £20.00–£41.00 **S:** £25.00–£35.00
Beds: 2T 7D 2S **Baths:** 7 En 3 Sh
⌂ (12) 📺 ✕ ▥ 🖤 ♨ cc
With 4 Diamond, New Steine Hotel offers
high standard of service with personal
touch, room service menu. All bedrooms
are very spacious and individually
decorated. We are located in the heart of
Brighton, just minutes to Palace Pier.

Ambassador Hotel, 23 New Steine,
Brighton, E. Sussex, BN2 1PD.
Open: All Year (not Xmas)
Grades: ETC 4 Diamond
01273 676869 Mr Koullas
Fax: 01273 689988
D: £28.00–£38.00 **S:** £28.00–£38.00
Beds: 5F 5D 4T 6S **Baths:** 20 En
⌂ 📺 ▥ 🖤 cc
Situated in a seafront garden square,
excellent location from where you can
explore the sights, shops and
entertainments that Brighton has to offer
overlooking the sea and Palace Pier. You'll
enjoy our freshly cooked English or
vegetarian breakfast in our spacious
dining room.

Ainsley House Hotel, 28 New Steine,
Brighton, E. Sussex, BN2 1PQ.
Open: All Year (not Xmas)
Grades: ETC 4 Diamond, AA 4 Diamond
01273 605310 Mrs King
Fax: 01273 688604
ahhotel@fastnet.co.uk
D: £24.00–£39.00 **S:** £25.00–£35.00
Beds: 2F 4D 2T 3S **Baths:** 9 En 2 Sh
⌂ (5) ½ 📺 ▥ 🖤 ♨
Regency town house. Comfortable rooms.
Excellent breakfasts, warm welcome.

Brighton Marina House Hotel, 8
Charlotte Street, Brighton, E. Sussex, BN2
1AG.
Pivotally located, 2 minutes from beach,
10 minutes from the major attractions.
Open: All Year
Grades: ETC 3 Diamond, AA 3 Diamond,
RAC 3 Diamond
01273 605349 Mr Jung
Fax: 01273 679484
rooms@jungs.co.uk
D: £19.50–£89.00 **S:** £19.00–£45.00
Beds: 3F 7D 4T 3S **Baths:** 7 Pr 1 Sh
⌂ 📺 ✕ ▥ 🖤 ❀ ♨

Adastral Hotel, 8 Westbourne Villas,
Hove, E. Sussex, BN3 4GQ.
The Adastral hotel is a Victorian villa
situated 200 meters from the sea front.
Open: All Year
01273 888800 Mr Salanson
Fax: 01273 883839
adastral@mistral.co.uk
D: £41.00–£50.00 **S:** fr £44.00
Beds: 8S 2D 7T/F **Baths:** 11 En 3 Sh
⌂ ℗ (2) 📺 ✕ ▥ 🖤 ❀ ♨ & cc

Fyfield House, *26 New Steine, Brighton, E. Sussex, BN2 1PD.*
Welcoming, clean home from home with superb views of sea.
Open: All Year (not Xmas)
Grades: ETC 4 Diamond
01273 602770 (also fax)
Mr & Mrs Culpeck fyfield@aol.com
D: £20.00–£40.00 **S:** £20.00–£40.00
Beds: 1F 5D 1T 4S **Baths:** 6 En 1 Sh
⛄ 📺 ⁿ ✕ 🛏 Ⅴ 🍴 cc

Paskins Hotel, *19 Charlotte Street, Brighton, E. Sussex, BN2 1AG.*
Organic and natural food. Delicious traditional and vegetarian breakfasts. Stylish. **Open:** All Year
Grades: AA 4 Diamond
01273 601203 Fax: 01273 621973
Welcome@paskins.co.uk
D: £22.50–£45.00 **S:** £22.50–£35.00
Beds: 2F 10D 2T 6S **Baths:** 17 En 3 Sh
⛄ 📺 ⁿ ✕ 🛏 Ⅴ ✳ 🍴

Diana House, *25 St Georges Terrace, Brighton, E. Sussex, BN2 1JJ.*
Friendly run guest house. Close to seafront and town centre.
Open: All Year **Grades:** ETC 2 Diamond
01273 605797 Mrs Burgess
Fax: 01273 600533
diana@enterprise.net
D: £22.00–£25.00 **S:** £44.00–£50.00
Beds: 5F 5D 1S **Baths:** 9 En 2 Sh
⛄ 📺 🛏 🛏 Ⅴ 🍴 cc

Trouville Hotel, *11 New Steine, Brighton, E. Sussex, BN2 1PB.*
Listed Regency townhouse restored to high standard and situated in a seafront square. **Open:** Feb to Dec
Grades: AA 4 Diamond, RAC 4 Diamond
01273 697384 Mr Hansell
D: £25.00–£30.50 **S:** £25.00–£45.00
Beds: 2F 3D 1T 2S **Baths:** 6 Pr 1Shared
⛄ 🅿 📺 🛏 Ⅴ 🍴 cc

14 Roedean Way, *Brighton, East Sussex, BN2 5RJ.*
Situated above Brighton Marina. Stunning sea views. Quiet. Lovely garden.
Open: All Year (not Xmas/New Year)
01273 605369 Mrs Shepherd
rube@rshepherd.freeserve.co.uk
D: £20.00–£25.00 **S:** £20.00–£25.00
Beds: 1D 1S **Baths:** 2 Pr
🅿 (2) ✕ 📺 🛏 🍴

Market Inn, *1 Market Street, Brighton, East Sussex, BN1 1HH.*
Traditional inn, in the centre of Brighton's famous 'Lanes' area close to sea front.
Open: All Year
01273 329483 Fax: 01273 777227
marketinn@fsbdial.co.uk
D: £25.00–£30.00 **S:** £35.00–£45.00
Beds: 2D **Baths:** 2 En
📺 🛏 🍴 cc

Brighton Royal Hotel, *76 Grand Parade, Brighton, E. Sussex, BN2 2JA.*
Opposite Brighton's Royal Pavilion. Close to bars, clubs, shops, seafront
Open: All Year
01273 604182 (also fax)
D: £20.00–£80.00 **S:** £20.00–£45.00
Beds: 1F 1T 7D 1S **Baths:** 1 En 1 Pr 1 Sh
⛄ (6) 📺 🛏 ✳ cc

Brunswick Square Hotel, *11 Brunswick Square, Brighton, E. Sussex, BN3 1EH.*
All rooms ensuite, comfortable, bar, phone, satellite. Grade II Listed.
Open: All Year
Grades: ETC 2 Diamond
01273 205047 (also fax)
brunswick@brighton.co.uk
D: £30.00–£50.00 **S:** £45.00–£68.00
Beds: 7F 12D 2S **Baths:** 21 En
⛄ 📺 ✕ 🛏 Ⅴ ✳ 🍴 ♿ cc

Whitburn Lodge, *12 Montpelier Road, Brighton, E. Sussex, BN1 2LQ.*
Situated best part of Brighton. Thirty seconds seafront and town.
Open: All Year
01273 729005 (also fax)
Mrs Hurrell
D: £20.00–£23.00 **S:** £30.00–£46.00
Beds: 1F 2D 1T **Baths:** 2 Sh
⛄ (10) 🅿 📺 🛏 Ⅴ 🍴

Arlanda Hotel, *20 New Steine, Brighton, E. Sussex, BN2 1PD.*
We try to be the best private hotel in Brighton!
Open: All Year
Grades: ETC 4 Diamond, Silver Award, AA 4 Diamond, RAC 4 Diamond
01273 699300 Mr Mathews
Fax: 01273 600930
arlanda@brighton.co.uk
D: £28.00–£40.00 **S:** £28.00–£40.00
Beds: 5T 5D 5S **Baths:** 15 En
⛄ ✕ 📺 ✕ 🛏 Ⅴ 🍴 cc

Oriental Hotel, *9 Oriental Place, Brighton, E. Sussex, BN1 2LJ.*
Very friendly and relaxed hotel with contemporary decor, centrally located.
Open: All Year
01273 205050 Fax: 01273 821096
info@orientalhotel.co.uk
D: £15.00–£40.00 **S:** £15.00–£70.00
Beds: 8D 4S **Baths:** 8 En 2 Sh
⛄ 📺 🛏 🍴

Cavalaire Hotel, *34 Upper Rock Gardens, Brighton, E. Sussex, BN2 1QF.*
A fresh, clean, crisp ambience in stylish surroundings; perfect location.
Open: All Year
01273 696899 Mr Barritt
Fax: 01273 600504
cavalaire.hotel@virgin.net
D: £23.00–£40.00 **S:** £22.00–£40.00
Beds: 3F 3D 4T 1S **Baths:** 5 En 4 Pr 2 Sh
⛄ (5) 📺 🛏 🍴 cc

Broad Oak (Rye)

TQ8220 🍺 *Rainbow Trout, Peace & Plenty, The Mill*

Arndale Cottage, *Northiam Road, Broad Oak, Rye, E. Sussex, TN31 6EP.*
Charming period style country house surrounded by beautiful countryside.
Open: All Year (not Xmas/New Year)
Grades: ETC 4 Diamond
01424 882813 (also fax)
Mrs Smith
D: £20.00–£24.00 **S:** £30.00
Beds: 1F 1D 1T **Baths:** 3 En
⛄ 🅿 (6) ✕ 📺 🛏 🛏 🍴

Layces Bed & Breakfast, *Chitcombe Road, Broad Oak, Rye, E. Sussex, TN31 6EU.*
Overlooking large gardens and lovely Brede Valley. Pub/restaurant nearby.
Open: All Year
01424 882836 Mr Stephens
Fax: 01424 882281
stephens@layces.fsnet.co.uk
D: £19.00 **S:** £25.00
Beds: 2D 1T **Baths:** 2 En 1 Pr
⛄ (8) 🅿 (4) ✕ 📺 🛏 Ⅴ 🍴

Burwash

TQ6724 🍺 *The Wheel*

Woodlands Farm, *Heathfield Road, Burwash, Etchingham, E. Sussex, TN19 7LA.*
Comfortable, quiet, friendly C16th farmhouse, 0.25 mile off road.
Open: All Year
Grades: AA 2 Diamond
01435 882794 (also fax)
Mrs Sirrell
liz.sir@lineone.net
D: £20.00–£23.00 **S:** £20.00–£26.00
Beds: 2D 2T **Baths:** 1 En 2 Sh
⛄ 🅿 (6) ✕ 📺 ✕ 🛏 🍴 ✳ 🛏 ♿

Square Farm House, *Shrub Lane, Burwash, Etchingham, East Sussex, TN19 7BL.*
Edge of Burwash village C14th farmhouse, warm friendly atmosphere.
Open: All Year (not Xmas)
01435 882631 (also fax)
John & Liz Gullick
D: £15.00 **S:** £20.00
Beds: 1F 1D **Baths:** 1 Sh
⛄ 🅿 ✕ 📺 🛏 🍴

Catsfield

TQ7214

Farthings Farm, *Catsfield, Battle, East Sussex, TN33 9BA.*
Edwardian house on a 70-acre farm set half mile off the road.
Open: All Year (not Xmas)
Grades: ETC 4 Diamond, AA 4 Diamond
01424 773107 Mrs Rodgers
D: £25.00 **S:** £30.00
Beds: 2D 1T **Baths:** 2 Pr
⛄ 🅿 (3) ✕ 📺 ✕ 🛏 🍴

Chiddingly

TQ5414 🍺 *Six Bells*

Hale Farm House, *Chiddingly, Lewes, E Sussex, BN8 6HQ.*
Open: All Year
Grades: ETC 3 Diamond
01825 872619 (also fax)
Mrs Burrough
s.burrough@virgin.net
D: £18.00–£25.00 **S:** £18.00–£25.00
Beds: 1F 2T **Baths:** 1 En 1 Sh
⛄ 🅿 (3) ✕ 📺 🛏 ✕ 🛏 Ⅴ 🍴
Relax in spacious rooms of this 14th century Listed beamed farmhouse, situated on Weald Way over looking the South Downs, 12 miles from Eastbourne. Extensive gardens, meadows, woods, stream. Good walking, horse riding. Ponies available. Also Shakespeare and language courses.

Planning a longer stay? Always ask for any special rates

'Holmes Hill', Holmes Hill, Chiddingly, Lewes, E. Sussex, BN8 6JA.
Cosy, modernised, C18th cottage. Ideal for touring Glyndebourne, Eastbourne, Sussex Coast.
Open: All Year (not Xmas)
01825 872746 Mr & Mrs Farrier
D: £20.00 **S:** £25.00
Beds: 1D 1T **Baths:** 2 Pr
ॐ (3) **P** (3) ⚡ ☑ ▥ ☑ ♨

Cowbeech Hill

TQ6113 ◀ Merrie Harriers

Batchelors, Cowbeech Hill, Hailsham, E Sussex, BN27 4JB.
Close to Michelham Priory, Herstmonceux Castle, Eastbourne 12 miles.
Open: All Year
Grades: ETC 3 Diamond
01323 832215 Mrs Barrow
D: £22.50 **S:** fr £30.00
Beds: 1D 2T **Baths:** 1 En 1 Pr 2 Sh
ॐ (5) **P** (3) ⚡ ☑ ▥ ☑ ♨

Cross-in-Hand

TQ5521 ◀ Cross In Hand

Old Corner Cottage, Little London Road, Cross-in-Hand, Heathfield, E. Sussex, TN21 0LT.
Pretty cottage situated conveniently between Eastbourne and Tunbridge Wells.
Open: All Year
Grades: AA 4 Diamond
01435 863787 Mrs Brown
D: £19.50–£24.00 **S:** £25.00–£27.50
Beds: 2D 1T **Baths:** 3 En
ॐ **P** (10) ⚡ ☑ ♈ ▥ ☑ ♨

Crowborough

TQ5230 ◀ Boar's Head

Wareham Lodge, Boarshead, Crowborough, E Sussex, TN6 3HE.
Open: All Year (not Xmas)
Grades: ETC 4 Diamond
01892 653444 Mrs Collins
D: £21.00–£22.50 **S:** £25.00–£30.00
Beds: 2D **Baths:** 2 En
P (3) ⚡ ☑ ♈ ▥ ☑ ♨
Comfortable country house with beautiful one acre plantsman's garden.

Danehill

TQ4027 ◀ Rose & Crown, Coach & Horses

Sliders Farmhouse, Furners Green, Danehill, Uckfield, E. Sussex, TN22 3RT.
Picturesque C16th country house, peacefully situated down a country lane.
Open: All Year (not Xmas)
Grades: AA 4 Diamond
01825 790258 (also fax)
Mr Salmon
jean&davidsalmon@freeserve.co.uk
D: £22.00–£30.00 **S:** £34.00–£40.00
Beds: 1F 1D 1T **Baths:** 3 En
ॐ **P** (10) ☑ ▥ ☑ ♨

Tanyard House, Tanyard Lane, Danehill, Haywards Heath, W Sussex, RH17 7JW.
Charming home, close Ashdown Forest, Bluebell Railway, many famous gardens.
Open: All Year (not Xmas)
Grades: AA 4 Diamond
01825 740293 Mrs Macfarlane
D: £20.00–£25.00 **S:** £30.00–£40.00
Beds: 1D **Baths:** 1 Pr

Eastbourne

TQ5900 ◀ The Marine, Town House, Castle Inn, Lamb Inn, The Beach, The Waterfront, The Pilot, The Alexander

Heatherdene Hotel, 26-28 Elms Avenue, Eastbourne, E. Sussex, BN21 3DN.
Open: All Year
Grades: ETC 3 Diamond
01323 723598 (also fax)
Mrs Mockford
D: £17.00–£45.00 **S:** £16.00–£25.00
Beds: 1F 4D 8T 3S **Baths:** 6 En 3 Sh
ॐ ☑ ♈ ✕ ▥ ☑ ♨ ♣ ♨ 3
You will find good food and comfortable rooms at the Heatherdene. This family-run licensed hotel, set in a pleasant avenue, is close to the sea front and town centre. Train and coach stations are nearby, as are the theatres.

Innisfree House, 130a Royal Parade, Eastbourne, East Sussex, BN22 7JY.
Open: All Year (not Xmas)
01323 646777 (also fax)
Mrs Petrie
D: £19.00–£20.00 **S:** £25.00–£30.00
Beds: 1F 1D 1T **Baths:** 3 En
ॐ ⚡ ☑ ▥ ☑ ♨
Small family-run B&B on seafront, close to amenities, refurbished to high standards. Exclusive location with sea views, easy parking on road outside. Motorcycle storage. Stay a day or stay a week, your comfort & praise we aim to seek.

Ambleside Private Hotel, 24 Elms Avenue, Eastbourne, E. Sussex, BN21 3DN.
Open: All Year
01323 724991 Mr Pattenden
D: £18.00 **S:** £18.00–£25.00
Beds: 4D 4T 2S **Baths:** 2 Sh 2 En
☑ ♈ ✕ ▥ ♨
Situated on quiet avenue adjacent to seafront, pier, town centre, theatres, convenient for railway and coach stations. Short distance from South Downs Way, Wealdway. Colour TV in bedrooms. Compliant with environmental and fire regulations.

Camberley Hotel, 27-29 Elms Avenue, Eastbourne, E. Sussex, BN21 3DN.
Open: Mar to Oct
01323 723789
D: £18.00–£21.00 **S:** £18.00–£21.00
Beds: 4F 3D 3T 2S **Baths:** 7 En 2 Sh
ॐ **P** (3) ☑ ✕ ☑ ♨
Situated in a pleasant avenue close to town centre, sea front and all amenities. Licensed, ensuite, tea-making, colour TV in bedrooms. English breakfast.

The Manse, 7 Dittons Road, Eastbourne, East Sussex, BN21 1DW.
Open: All Year (not Xmas)
01323 737851 Mrs Walker
D: £15.00–£20.00 **S:** £20.00–£25.00
Beds: 1F 2T **Baths:** 2 En 1 Pr
ॐ (8) **P** (1) ⚡ ☑ ▥ ☑ ♨
Originally a Presbyterian manse, this character house is located in a quiet area yet within 5 minutes' walk of the town centre with its shops, restaurants and theatres. Seafront, South Downs, castles and Downland villages nearby.

Cherry Tree Hotel, 15 Silverdale Road, Eastbourne, E. Sussex, BN20 7AJ.
Award-winning family-run hotel, close to sea front, downlands and theatres.
Open: All Year
Grades: ETC 4 Diamond, Silver
01323 722406 Mr Henley
Fax: 01323 648838
anncherrytree@aol.com
D: £26.00–£33.00 **S:** £26.00–£33.00
Beds: 1F 3D 4T 2S **Baths:** 10 En
ॐ (7) ⚡ ✕ ▥ ☑ ♨ ♣ cc

Sheldon Hotel, 9-11 Burlington Place, Eastbourne, East Sussex, BN21 4AS.
Situated within a few minutes walk of sea front, theatres. Licensed.
Open: All Year
01323 724120 Fax: 01323 430406
gmeyer@sheldonhotel.fsbusiness.co.uk
D: £24.00–£27.00 **S:** £24.00–£27.00
Beds: 4F 6T 8D 6S **Baths:** 24 En
ॐ **P** ☑ ♈ ✕ ▥ ☑ ♨ ♣ cc

Southcroft Hotel, 15 South Cliff Avenue, Eastbourne, E. Sussex, BN20 7AH.
Friendly, family-run, non-smoking hotel. Close to Downs, sea and theatre.
Open: All Year
Grades: ETC 4 Diamond
01323 729071 Mrs Skriczka
southcroft@eastbourne34.freeserve.co.uk
D: £25.00–£28.00 **S:** £25.00–£28.00
Beds: 3D 2T 1S **Baths:** 6 En
⚡ ✕ ▥ ♨

Edelweiss Hotel, 10-12 Elms Avenue, Eastbourne, E. Sussex, BN21 3DN.
Central family-run Hotel just off seafront. Comfortable and welcoming.
Open: All Year
Grades: ETC 3 Diamond
01323 732071 (also fax)
Mr & Mrs Butler
peterbutler@fsbdial.co.uk
D: £16.00–£20.00 **S:** £16.00–£25.00
Beds: 1F 6D 5T 2S **Baths:** 3 En 4 Sh
ॐ ☑ ✕ ▥ ☑ ♨ ♣ cc

Cromwell Private Hotel, 23 Cavendish Place, Eastbourne, E. Sussex, BN21 3EJ.
Family run hotel in Victorian Town House (1851). Centrally located.
Open: Easter to Nov
Grades: ETC 4 Diamond
01323 725288 (also fax)
Mr & Mrs Millar
cromwell-hotel@lineone.net
D: £19.00–£24.00 **S:** £19.00–£23.00
Beds: 2F 3D 3T 3S **Baths:** 5 Pr 2 Sh
ॐ ✕ ▥ ☑ ♨ ♣ cc

Courtlands Hotel, *68 Royal Parade, Eastbourne, E. Sussex, BN22 7AQ.*
Seafront position, business/touring base.
Open: All Year
01323 721068
D: £20.00–£25.00 **S:** £20.00–£25.00
Beds: 3F 2D 1T 2S **Baths:** 3 En 1 Pr
🛇 🅿 (2) 📺 ✕ 📖 🛂 🔥

La Mer Guest House, *7 Marine Road, Eastbourne, E. Sussex, BN22 7AU.*
Just 50 yards from Eastbourne's beautiful seafront and beach easy access to South Downs
Open: May to Sep
01323 724926 Mrs Byrne
D: £18.00–£24.00 **S:** £18.00–£24.00
Beds: 2D 2T 2S **Baths:** 2 En
🛇 (14) 🅿 📺 📖 🛂 🔥

Channel View Hotel, *57 Royal Parade, Eastbourne, E. Sussex, BN22 7AQ.*
A friendly family-run seafront hotel situated opposite the Redoubt Gardens.
Open: All Year (not Xmas)
01323 736730 Fax: 01323 644299
D: £17.00–£22.00 **S:** £22.00–£32.00
Beds: 1F 2D 3T 2S **Baths:** 4 En 1 Sh
🛇 📺 🍴 ✕ 📖 🛂 🔥

Beachy Rise, *20 Beachy Head Road, Eastbourne, E. Sussex, BN20 7QN.*
In Meads village near Beachy Head and sea and university. Ensuite bedrooms.
Open: All Year
01323 639171
D: £22.00–£28.00 **S:** £25.00–£29.00
Beds: 1F 4D 1T **Baths:** 6 En
🛇 (1) 📺 📖 🛂 🔥

Downland Hotel, *37 Lewes Road, Eastbourne, East Sussex, BN21 2BU.*
Charming small hotel, ideally located for all main amenities and commercial centre.
Open: All Year
01323 732689 Fax: 01323 720321
D: £25.00–£37.50 **S:** £30.00–£40.00
Beds: 2F 7D 2T 1S **Baths:** 12 En
🅿 (9) 🛂 📺 ✕ 📖 🛂 ❀ 🔥 cc

Etchingham

TQ7126

King Johns Lodge, *Sheepstreet Lane, Etchingham, East Sussex, TN19 7AZ.*
Historic Listed house in 8 acres of garden and parkland. House dates from C14th
Open: All Year (not Xmas)
01580 819232 Fax: 01580 819562
D: £30.00–£35.00 **S:** £50.00–£55.00
Beds: 1F 3D 1T **Baths:** 2 En 3 Pr
🛇 (7) 🅿 (12) 📺 ✕ 📖 🔥

Fairwarp

TQ4626 🍺 *The Foresters*

Broom Cottage, *Browns Brook, Fairwarp, Uckfield, E Sussex, TN22 3BY.*
Victorian cottage in lovely garden on Ashdown Forest. Very peaceful.
Open: All Year
01825 712942 D: £20.00–£25.00 **S:** £25.00
Beds: 1D 1T Sh
🛇 🅿 🛂 📺 🍴 📖 🛂 🔥

Forest Row

TQ4234 🍺 *Checkers, Hatch Inn*

Woodcote, *Park Road, Forest Row, RH18 5BX.*
Friendly family home in private road adjacent to Ashdown Forest.
Open: All Year (not Xmas/New Year)
01342 822170 S Hillen
Fax: 01342 823134
shhillen@hotmail.com
D: £30.00–£60.00 **S:** £30.00–£60.00
Beds: 1T 1D **Baths:** 1 En
🅿 (2) 🛂 📖 🛂 🔥

Framfield

TQ4920

Beggars Barn, *Barn Lane, Framfield, Uckfield, E Sussex, TN22 5RX.*
Unique C18th converted barn with enchanting separate accommodation.
Open: All Year (not Xmas)
01825 890869 Fax: 01825 890868
cp@systematic-telecoms.co.uk
D: £20.00 **S:** £25.00
Beds: 1F 1D **Baths:** 1 En
🅿 (2) 📺 🍴 ✕ 🛂 🔥

Frant

TQ5935 🍺 *The George*

Melling, *The Green, Frant, Tunbridge Wells, E Sussex, TN3 9ED.*
Pretty house overlooks village green. Walkers welcome.
Open: All Year (not Xmas)
01892 750380 D: £20.00 **S:** £20.00
Beds: 1T **Baths:** 1 Sh
🛂 📖 🔥

Rowden House Farm, *Frant, Tunbridge Wells, Kent, TN3 9HS.*
Elizabethan farmhouse in 20 acres; Area of Outstanding Natural Beauty.
Open: Apr to Oct
01892 750259 Mrs Carrell
D: £22.50–£25.00 **S:** £22.00–£24.00
Beds: 1T 2S **Baths:** 1 Pr 1 Sh
🛇 (10) 🅿 (10) 🛂 📺 📖 🔥

Hailsham

TQ5809 🍺 *Merry Harriers*

Longleys Farm Cottage, *Harebeating Lane, Hailsham, E Sussex, BN27 1ER.*
Quiet country location near prime tourist attractions informal and friendly.
Open: All Year
Grades: ETC 3 Diamond
01323 841227 (also fax) J Hook
D: £18.00 **S:** £20.00–£25.00
Beds: 1F 1D 1T **Baths:** 2 En 1 Pr
🛇 🅿 (4) 🛂 📺 🍴 ✕ 📖 🔥

Windesworth, *Carters Corner, Hailsham, E Sussex, BN27 4HT.*
Comfortable family home in quiet location with lovely views.
Open: Apr to Nov
Grades: ETC 4 Diamond
01323 847178 Mr Toye
Fax: 01323 440696
D: £20.00–£24.00 **S:** £20.00–£24.00
Beds: 1D 1T **Baths:** 1 En 1 Sh
🛇 (1) 🅿 (3) 🛂 📺 📖 🛂 🔥

Hartfield

TQ4735 🍺 *Hay Wagon, Anchor Inn*

The Paddocks, *Chuck Hatch, Hartfield, East Sussex, TN7 4EX.*
In the Ashdown Forest, 0.25 mile from Pooh Sticks Bridge. Walkers and children welcome.
Open: All Year (not Xmas)
01892 770623 Ms McAll
D: £19.00 **S:** £19.00
Beds: 1D 1T 1S **Baths:** 1 Pr 1 Sh
🛇 🅿 🛂 📺 📖 🛂 🔥

Hastings

TQ8110 🍺 *Star Inn, Queen's Head, Plough Inn, The Admiral, The Cove, Royal Oak, Bo Peep, Churchill's*

Lansdowne Hotel, *1 Robertson Terrace, Hastings, E. Sussex, TN34 1JE.*
Open: All Year
Grades: ETC 2 Diamond
01424 429605
lansdowne.hotel@btinternet.com
D: £23.50–£28.50 **S:** £24.50–£31.00
Beds: 6F 15D 3T 4S **Baths:** 28 En 2 Sh
🛇 📺 ✕ 📖 🛂 ❀ 🔥 cc
Family run for 25 years; great value for money and very high standards. Extensive sea views, close to all the old and new town attractions. Out of season offers, senior citizens prices. Telephones in all rooms. Bar snacks and full menu available.

White Cottage, *Battery Hill, Hastings, E. Sussex, TN35 4AP.*
Open: Feb to Oct
Grades: AA 3 Diamond
01424 812528 Fax: 01424 812285
D: £22.50–£25.00 **S:** £22.50–£25.00
Beds: 1T 3D **Baths:** 3 En 1 Pr
🛇 (7) 🅿 (4) 🛂 📖 🔥
Set on the outskirts of the peaceful village of Fairlight, White Cottage is a cheerful, friendly, family run B&B featuring beautiful gardens providing far reaching channel views.

Westwood Farm, *Stonestile Lane, Hastings, E. Sussex, TN35 4PG.*
Working sheep farm, peaceful, rural. Outstanding views over Brede Valley.
Open: All Year (not Xmas)
Grades: ETC 3 Diamond
01424 751038 (also fax)
Mr York
york@westwood-farm.fsnet.co.uk
D: £18.00–£25.00 **S:** £22.00–£29.00
Beds: 1F 1D 1T **Baths:** 2 En 1 Pr
🛇 (5) 🅿 (8) 🛂 📺 📖 🛂 ♿

Grand Hotel, *Grand Parade, St Leonards On Sea, Hastings, E. Sussex, TN38 0DD.*
Seafront family hotel in heart of 1066 country.
Open: All Year
01424 428510 (also fax)
Mr & Mrs Mann
D: £18.00–£35.00 **S:** £24.00–£45.00
Beds: 3F 6D 4T 4S **Baths:** 3 En 4 Pr 12 Sh
🛇 🅿 🛂 📺 ✕ 📖 🛂 ❀ 🔥 ♿ 2

Millifont Guest House, 8/9
Cambridge Gardens, Hastings, E. Sussex,
TN3 1EH.
Centrally situated 15-bedroomed guest
house, lounge / games room.
Open: All Year (not Xmas)
Grades: ETC 3 Diamond
01424 425645 Mr Main
D: £15.00–£20.00 **S:** £15.00–£20.00
Beds: 3F 6D 2T 4S **Baths:** 2 En 1 Pr 4 Sh
🛇 🅿 📺 🛏 🖭 🖂 ♿

Emerydale, 6 King Edward Avenue,
Hastings, E. Sussex, TN34 2NQ.
Charming comfortable house near
Alexandra Park, town, sea front. Off A21.
Open: All Year (not Xmas)
Grades: ETC 4 Diamond
01424 437915
Mrs Emery
Fax: 01424 444124
D: £18.00–£20.00 **S:** £18.00–£22.00
Beds: 1D 1T 1S **Baths:** 1 En 1 Sh
🛇 (12) 📺 🖭 🖂

Cambridge Guest House, 18
Cambridge Gardens, Hastings, E. Sussex,
TN34 1EH.
Friendly, clean family guest house. 3
minutes walk to town centre
Open: All Year
Grades: ETC 4 Diamond
01424 712995
D: £16.00–£22.00 **S:** £14.00–£20.00
Beds: 1F 4T 1D 3S **Baths:** 3 En 2 Sh
🛇 🖂 📺 🛏 🖭 🖂 ♿

The Sherwood Guest House, 15
Grosvenor Crescent, St Leonards on Sea,
Hastings, E. Sussex, TN38 0AA.
Seafront guest house, with antique
furnishings.
Open: All Year (not Xmas)
Grades: ETC 3 Diamond
01424 433331 (also fax)
Mr Aldridge
D: £16.50–£25.00
Beds: 2F 4D 2T 2S **Baths:** 5 En 2 Sh
🛇 (5) 🖂 📺 🛏 ♿ cc

Marina Lodge Guest House, 123
Marina, St Leonards on Sea, Hastings, E.
Sussex, TN38 0BN.
Large seafront family guest house.
Open: All Year (not Xmas/New Year)
Grades: ETC 2 Diamond
01424 715067 Mrs Snell
Fax: 01424 716614
marina.lodge@dial.pipex.com
D: £15.00–£25.00 **S:** £15.00–£25.00
Beds: 3D 1F 2S **Baths:** 2 En 2 Sh
🛇 📺 🖭 🖂 ♿

Argyle Guest House, 32 Cambridge
Gardens, Hastings, E. Sussex, TN34 1EN.
The Argyle is centrally situated near rail,
bus and all amenities.
Open: All Year
Grades: AA 2 Diamond
01424 421294 Mr Jacob
Fax: 01424 722755
argyle.1066country@talk21.com
D: £30.00–£40.00 **S:** £15.00–£20.00
Beds: 8F 4D 2T 2S **Baths:** 3 En 2 Sh 3 Pr
🛇 (4) 📺 🖭 🖂 ♿ cc

The Pines, 50 Baldslow Road, Hastings,
E. Sussex, TN34 2EY.
Lovely Victorian house, quiet location, 15
minutes' walk to town centre.
Open: All Year (not Xmas)
01424 435838 (also fax)
Mrs Piper
D: £15.00–£18.00 **S:** £18.00–£20.00
Beds: 1F 2D 1T 1S **Baths:** 2 En 1 Sh
🛇 🖂 📺 🖭 🖂

Heathfield

TQ5821   🍺 *Cross In Hand, The Star, Prince of*
Wales

Old Corner Cottage, Little London
Road, Cross-in-Hand, Heathfield, E.
Sussex, TN21 0LT.
Pretty cottage situated conveniently
between Eastbourne and Tunbridge
Wells. **Open:** All Year
Grades: AA 4 Diamond
01435 863787 Mrs Brown
D: £19.50–£24.00 **S:** £25.00–£27.50
Beds: 2D 1T **Baths:** 3 En
🛇 🅿 (10) 🖂 📺 🛏 🖭 🖂 ♿

Spicers Cottage, 21 Cade Street,
Heathfield, E Sussex, TN21 9BS.
Old beamed cottage on the high Weald of
East Sussex.
Open: All Year
Grades: ETC 4 Diamond
01435 866363 Mr Gumbrell
spicersbb@cs.com
D: £20.00–£22.50 **S:** £20.00–£25.00
Beds: 1D 1T 1S **Baths:** 1 En 2 Pr
🛇 🅿 🖂 📺 ✕ 🖭 🖂 ♿ cc

Grove Hill House, Hellingly,
Hailsham, E Sussex, BN27 4HG.
Period farmhouse in beautiful quiet
setting in over 2 acres of grounds.
Open: All Year
01435 812440 (also fax)
Mrs Berthon
D: £19.00–£22.00 **S:** £25.00–£30.00
Beds: 1D 1T **Baths:** 1 En 1 Pr
🛇 🅿 (4) 🖂 ✕ 🖭

Hellingly

TQ5812   🍺 *Horse & Groom*

Grove Hill House, Hellingly,
Hailsham, E Sussex, BN27 4HG.
Period farmhouse in beautiful quiet
setting in over 2 acres of grounds.
Open: All Year
01435 812440 (also fax)
Mrs Berthon
D: £25.00–£22.00 **S:** £25.00–£30.00
Beds: 1D 1T **Baths:** 1 En 1 Pr
🛇 🅿 (4) 🖂 ✕ 🖭

Heron's Ghyll

TQ4826   🍺 *The Foresters*

Tanglewood, Oldlands Hall, Heron's
Ghyll, Uckfield, E Sussex, TN22 3DA.
Peaceful setting on Ashdown Forest.
Large pretty garden, warm welcome.
Open: All Year (not Xmas)
01825 712757 Mrs Clarke
D: £24.00 **S:** £25.00–£30.00
Beds: 2D 1T **Baths:** 1 Pr 1 Sh
🅿 (6) 🖂 📺 ✕ 🖭 🖂 ♿

Herstmonceux

TQ6312   🍺 *Brewer's Arms*

Sandhurst, Church Road,
Herstmonceux, Hailsham, E Sussex, BN27
1RG.
Large bungalow in countryside. Easy
access to village and coast.
Open: All Year (not Xmas)
Grades: ETC 4 Diamond
01323 833088
junerussell@compuserve.com
D: £20.00–£25.00 **S:** £20.00–£30.00
Beds: 2F 2D **Baths:** 3 En 1 Pr
🛇 🅿 (4) 🖂 📺 🖭 🖂

High Hurstwood

TQ4926   🍺 *Crown & Gate, Maypole Inn, White*
Hart

Chillies Granary, High Hurstwood,
Crowborough, E. Sussex, TN6 3TB.
Awarded 2nd place in 'B&B of the Year' by
SEETB.
Open: Mar to Dec
Grades: ETC 4 Diamond
01892 655560 (also fax)
Mr & Mrs Peck
D: £23.00–£27.00 **S:** £25.00–£45.00
Beds: 1F 1D 1T **Baths:** 2 En 1 Pr
🛇 🅿 (6) 🖂 📺 🖭 🖂 ✳ ♿

Tronning, Coombelands, Wittersham,
Rye, Kent, TN30 7NU.
Situated in quiet village between Rye and
Tenterden. Good touring area.
Open: All Year
Grades: AA 3 Diamond, RAC 3 Diamond
01797 207768 (also fax)
Mrs Brown
D: £20.00–£25.00 **S:** £20.00–£25.00
Beds: 1D 1T 1S **Baths:** 1 En 1 Sh
🛇 🅿 (4) 🖂 📺 🖭 🖂 ✳ ♿

Horam

TQ5717   🍺 *Brewer's Arms, Vines Cross*

Oak Mead Nursery, Horam,
Heathfield, E. Sussex, TN21 9ED.
Set in beautiful, quiet countryside, off
road parking, good breakfasts.
Open: Jan to Dec
Grades: ETC 3 Diamond
01435 812962 Mrs Curtis
D: £18.00 **S:** £18.00–£22.00
Beds: 1D 1T 1S **Baths:** 2 En 1 Pr
🛇 🅿 (4) 🖂 📺 🖭 🖂 ♿

Hove

TQ2805   🍺 *Iron Duke, Lion & Porter, Cooper's*
Cask

Adastral Hotel, 8 Westbourne Villas,
Hove, E. Sussex, BN3 4GQ.
The Adastral hotel is a Victorian villa
situated 200m from the seafront.
Open: All Year
01273 888800 Mr Salanson
Fax: 01273 883839
adastral@mistral.co.uk
D: £41.00–£50.00 **S:** fr £44.00
Beds: 8S 2D 7T/F **Baths:** 11 En 3 Sh
🛇 🅿 (2) 📺 🛏 ✕ 🖭 🖂 ♿ cc

Lichfield House, *30 Waterloo Street, Hove, E. Sussex, BN3 1AN.*
Town centre location, close to sea and night life.
Open: All Year **Grades:** ETC 3 Diamond
01273 777740 Mr Byrne
Fax: 01273 732970
feelgood@lichfieldhouse.freeserve.co.uk
D: £16.00–£35.00 **S:** £32.00–£80.00
Beds: 2F 5D 2T 1S **Baths:** 4 En 1 Pr 1 Sh
🛇 (2) 📺 ♥ ✕ ▥ 🗸 ᵻ

Isfield

TQ4517 🍺 *Halfway House, The Peacock*

Farm Place, *Isfield, Uckfield, E. Sussex, TN22 5TY.*
Peaceful attractive timbered country house, rural aspect, large garden, grass tennis court. **Open:** Mar to Nov
01825 750485 (also fax) Mrs Houchen
D: £22.00–£24.00 **S:** £20.00–£25.00
Beds: 1F 1D 1T 1S **Baths:** 1 En 1 Pr
🅿 (5) 🗲 📺 ▥ ᵻ

Kingston near Lewes

TQ3908 🍺 *The Juggs*

Settlands, *Wellgreen Lane, Kingston near Lewes, Lewes, E Sussex, BN7 3NP.*
Open: All Year (not Xmas)
Grades: ETC 4 Diamond
01273 472295 (also fax) Mrs Arlett
D: £20.00–£25.00 **S:** £25.00–£27.50
Beds: 1D 1T **Baths:** 2 Sh
🛇 🅿 (3) 🗲 📺 ▥ 🗸 ᵻ
Swedish timber-framed house in picturesque down land setting. Excellent walking, coast 6 miles. Friendly atmosphere, comfortable accommodation. Historic Lewes, Glyndebourne, ferries nearby.

Laughton

TQ5013 🍺 *The Cook, The Gun, The Bluebell, Lamb Inn*

Holly Cottage, *Lewes Road, Laughton, Lewes, E. Sussex, BN8 6BL.*
Charming C18th Listed country cottage.
Open: All Year **Grades:** ETC 4 Diamond
01323 811309 Mrs Clarke
Fax: 01323 811106
D: £23.00–£25.00 **S:** £30.00–£35.00
Beds: 1F 1T 1D **Baths:** 3 En
🛇 🅿 (3) 🗲 📺 ♥ ▥ ᵻ க

Lewes

TQ4110 🍺 *Royal Oak, Pelham Arms, Cock Inn, Steward's Enquiry, King's Head*

Sussex Country Accommodation, *Crink House, Barcombe Mills, Lewes, E. Sussex, BN8 5BJ.*
Open: All Year (not Xmas)
Grades: ETC 4 Diamond, Silver Award
01273 400625 Mrs Gaydon
D: £25.00–£30.00 **S:** £30.00–£40.00
Beds: 2D 1T **Baths:** 3 En
🛇 🅿 (10) 🗲 📺 ▥ 🗸 ᵻ
Victorian farmhouse with panoramic views. Welcoming rural family home, base for exploring Sussex with its wealth of walks and attractions, castles, country houses, gardens, museums. Within reach Brighton, Eastbourne, Glyndebourne - self catering also available.

Castle Banks Cottage, *4 Castle Banks, Lewes, E. Sussex, BN7 1UZ.*
Beamed cottage, pretty garden, quiet lane, close to castle, shops, restaurants.
Open: All Year (not Xmas)
01273 476291 (also fax)
Mrs Wigglesworth
awigglesworth@iname.com
D: £22.50 **S:** £22.50–£30.00
Beds: 1T 1S **Baths:** 1 Sh
🛇 📺 ▥ 🗸 ᵻ

Phoenix House, *23 Gundreda Road, Lewes, E. Sussex, BN7 1PT.*
Comfortable family home - quiet road - 5 minutes to town centre.
Open: All Year (not Xmas/New Year)
01273 473250 Mrs Greene
charg55@yahoo.com
D: £17.50–£22.50 **S:** £25.00
Beds: 1T 1D 1S **Baths:** 1 Pr 1 Sh
🛇 🅿 (2) 🗲 📺 ▥ 🗸 ᵻ

Normandy, *37 Houndean Rise, Lewes, East Sussex, BN7 1EQ.*
Comfortable room in large detached family house, additional bed available, overlooking South Downs.
Open: All Year (not Xmas)
01273 473853 (also fax) Mrs Kemp
lkemp@btinternet.com
D: £22.00–£25.00 **S:** £30.00–£35.00
Beds: 1D **Baths:** 1 Pr
🛇 🗲 📺 ▥ ᵻ

Lunsford's Cross

TQ7210 🍺 *King's Arms, Rose & Crown*

Wakeford House, *Potmans Lane, Lunsford's Cross, Bexhill-on-Sea, E. Sussex, TN39 5JL.*
Edwardian-style house in country setting with peaceful one acre garden.
Open: All Year
Grades: ETC 3 Diamond , AA 4 Diamond
01424 892013 Mrs Skinner
Fax: 01424 893978
keltie@globalnet.co.uk
D: £22.50–£25.00 **S:** £25.00–£30.00
Beds: 3F 1D 1S 1T **Baths:** 1 En 1 Sh
🛇 🅿 (5) 📺 ♥ ✕ ▥ 🗸 ᵻ

Manor Barn, *Lunsford's Cross, Bexhill on Sea, E. Sussex, TN39 5JJ.*
Ensuite chalets, semi-rural setting on A269, 3 miles sea.
Open: All Year **Grades:** ETC 3 Diamond
01424 893018 (also fax)
Mrs Gillingham
D: £16.50–£18.00 **S:** £20.00–£24.00
Beds: 1F 1D 1T 1S **Baths:** 4 En
🛇 🅿 (6) 🗲 📺 ▥ 🗸 ᵻ க

Marle Green

TQ5916 🍺 *Gun Inn*

Great Ivy Mill, *Horebeech Lane, Marle Green, Horam, East Sussex, TN21 9EA.*
Situated in peaceful countryside backing onto open fields, ideal for business or leisure. **Open:** All Year
01435 812393 Mr West
Fax: 01435 813486
greativymill@mistral.co.uk
D: £18.00 **S:** £18.00
Beds: 2D 2S **Baths:** 2 En 1 Pr
🛇 (8) 🅿 (4) 🗲 📺 ♥ ▥ ᵻ க cc

Netherfield

TQ7118 🍺 *Netherfield Arms, White Hart*

Roseneath, *Netherfield Road, Netherfield, Battle, E Sussex, TN33 9PY.*
Situated in an area of outstanding natural beauty-1066 country.
Open: All Year
01424 772953 Mrs Vane
roseneath00@mircosoft.com
D: £40.00–£60.00 **S:** £25.00–£30.00
Beds: 1T 2D **Baths:** 1 En 1 Sh
🛇 🅿 🗲 ♥ ▥ 🗸 ᵻ

Newick

TQ4121 🍺 *The Bull, Royal Oak, The Griffin*

Pinecroft, *Allington Road, Newick, Lewes, E Sussex, BN8 4NA.*
Easy reach of Lewes, Brighton, National Trust gardens and Gatwick.
Open: All Year
01825 723824 (also fax)
Mrs Thomas
diane.pinecroft@ic24.net
D: £36.00 **S:** £20.00
Beds: 1F 1T **Baths:** 1 Sh
🛇 🅿 (2) 🗲 📺 ▥ 🗸 ᵻ

Holly Lodge, *Oxbottom Lane, Newick, Lewes, E Sussex, BN8 4RA.*
Georgian family house in pretty garden on outskirts of village.
Open: All Year (not Xmas)
Grades: ETC 3 Diamond
01825 722738 Fax: 01825 723624
D: £22.50–£24.50 **S:** £25.00
Beds: 1F 2D 1T **Baths:** 1 En 1 Pr
🛇 🅿 (6) 🗲 📺 ▥ ᵻ

Firle Cottage, *High St, Newick, Lewes, East Sussex, BN8 4LT.*
Delightful cottage, close to village centre and Bluebell Railway.
Open: All Year
01825 722392 Mrs Hart
D: £18.00–£36.00 **S:** £18.00–£25.00
Beds: 2D 1T 1S **Baths:** 1 Pr 1 Sh
🛇 🅿 (4) 📺 ▥ ᵻ

Peasmarsh

TQ8723 🍺 *Horse & Cart, Cock Horse*

Kimbley Cottage, *Main Street, Peasmarsh, Rye, E. Sussex, TN31 6UL.*
Friendly country house. 5 minutes' drive to historic Rye, beaches 15 minutes.
Open: All Year (not Xmas)
01797 230514 Mrs Richards
D: £21.00–£22.00 **S:** £27.00
Beds: 3D **Baths:** 3 En
🛇 🅿 (4) 🗲 📺 ▥ 🗸 ᵻ

New House Farm, *Peasmarsh, Rye, E. Sussex, TN31 6TD.*
C17th farmhouse in beautiful countryside on working farm, quiet location.
Open: Apr to Oct
01797 230201 (also fax)
Mrs Ashby
D: £20.00–£25.00 **S:** £20.00–£25.00
Beds: 2D 1T **Baths:** 1 Pr 1 Sh
🛇 🅿 (10) 🗲 ᵻ

Busti, *Barnetts Hill, Peasmarsh, Rye, E. Sussex, TN31 6YJ.*
Comfortable, detached house near woodland; ideal touring Kent, East Sussex.
Open: Easter to Oct
01797 230408 (also fax)
Mrs Coote
hcoote@currantbun.com
D: £16.00–£17.00 **S:** £18.00–£25.00
Beds: 1D 1T **Baths:** 1 Sh
🛇 (12) ₽ (5) ⊬ 📺 🎞 🖾 ₺

Pevensey Bay

TQ6504   ◀ *Bay Hotel, The Moorings, The Castle*

Driftwood, *36 Eastbourne Road, Pevensey Bay, Pevensey, E. Sussex, BN24 6HJ.*
Comfortable home, village centre, beach 2 mins, BIG breakfast. Friendly!
Open: All Year
01323 768530 Ms McKeever
D: £16.00–£18.00 **S:** £20.00–£36.00
Beds: 1F 1D **Baths:** 1 Sh
🛇 (5) ₽ (3) ⊬ 📺 ✕ 🎞 🖾 ₺

Piltdown

TQ4422   ◀ *The Peacock*

Holly Farm, *Piltdown, Uckfield, E. Sussex, TN22 3XB.*
Comfortable Victorian house, near Bluebell Railway, Sheffield Park, Fletching, Buxted.
Open: All Year
01825 722592 (also fax)
Ms Mayes
D: fr £25.00 **S:** fr £25.00
Beds: 1F 2D **Baths:** 1 Pr 1 Sh
🛇 ₽ ⊬ 🎞 ₺

Playden

TQ9221   ◀ *Peace & Plenty*

The Corner House, *Peasmarsh Road, Playden, Rye, E. Sussex, TN31 7UL.*
Welcoming, comfortable guest house. Excellent accommodation one mile from Rye
Open: All Year
Grades: ETC 3 Diamond
01797 280439 richardturner5@virgin.net
D: £18.00–£20.00 **S:** £20.00–£25.00
Beds: 1F 1D 1T **Baths:** 1 Sh
🛇 ₽ (3) ⊬ 📺 ₺

Plumpton Green

TQ3616   ◀ *Winning Post*

Farthings, *Station Road, Plumpton Green, Lewes, E. Sussex, BN7 3BY.*
Relaxed, friendly atmosphere in village setting under South Downs.
Open: All Year (not Xmas)
01273 890415 Mrs Baker
D: £20.00–£25.00 **S:** £22.00–£30.00
Beds: 2D 1T **Baths:** 1 En 1 Sh
🛇 (11) ₽ (4) ⊬ 📺 🖤 ✕ 🎞 ₺

Planning a longer stay? Always ask for any special rates

Punnett's Town

TQ6320   ◀ *Three Cups*

Ringwood, *Forest Lane, Punnetts Town, Heathfield, E Sussex, TN21 9JA.*
Detached Victorian annexe situated in beautiful countryside; ideal walking, cycling. **Open:** Apr to Oct
Grades: ETC 4 Diamond
01435 830630 Mrs Batehup
D: fr £22.50 **S:** fr £30.00
Beds: 1T **Baths:** 1 En
₽ (2) 📺 🎞 ₺

Ringmer

TQ4412   ◀ *Green Man, Anchor Inn*

Gote Farm, *Gote Lane, Ringmer, Lewes, E. Sussex, BN8 5HX.*
Traditional Sussex farmhouse near Glyndebourne, Newhaven, Brighton and South Downs Way.
Open: All Year (not Xmas)
Grades: ETC 4 Diamond
01273 812303 (also fax) Mrs Craig
janecraig@ukgateway.net
D: £20.00 **S:** £25.00–£30.00
Beds: 1D 1T 1S **Baths:** 2 Sh
🛇 ₽ (4) ⊬ 📺 🎞 🖾 ₺

Robertsbridge

TQ7423   ◀ *Netherfield Arms, Black Horse, White Hart*

Bell Cottage, *Vinehall Road, Robertsbridge, Battle, E Sussex, TN32 5JN.*
C17th converted inn beamed throughout. Delightful gardens. Warm welcome assured. **Open:** All Year (not Xmas)
Grades: ETC 4 Diamond
01580 881164 Mrs Lowe
patricia.lowe@tesco.net
D: £20.00–£25.00 **S:** £25.00–£30.00
Beds: 1D 2T **Baths:** 1 En 1 Pr 1 Sh
₽ (3) ⊬ 📺 🎞 ₺ 3

Rye

TQ9120   ◀ *Horse & Cart, Queen's Head, The Landgate, Union Inn, Ypres Castle, The Standard*

Kimbley Cottage, *Main Street, Peasmarsh, Rye, E. Sussex, TN31 6UL.*
Open: All Year (not Xmas)
01797 230514 Mrs Richards
D: £21.00–£22.00 **S:** £27.00
Beds: 3D **Baths:** 3 En
🛇 ₽ (4) ⊬ 📺 🎞 🖾 ₺
Friendly country house. 5 minutes' drive to historic Rye, beaches 15 minutes.

The Rise, *82 Udimore Road, Rye, E. Sussex, TN31 7DY.*
Open: All Year (not Xmas/New Year)
Grades: ETC 4 Star, Silver Award
01797 222285 T E Francis
therise@bb-rye.freeserve.co.uk
D: £25.00–£30.00 **S:** £30.00–£35.00
Beds: 1T 3D
🛇 (1) ₽ (4) ⊬ 📺 🏸 🎞 ₺
Pleasant and comfortable house with terraced gardens, all bedrooms and dining room facing green fields to distant sea. Only eight minutes walk to the historical town centre complemented by numerous Inns and eating establishments. Enjoyable and well planned walks available.

The Old Vicarage, *66 Church Square, Rye, E. Sussex, TN31 7HF.*
Splendid Georgian house, peaceful & picturesque setting. Superb breakfast. Award hotel.
Open: All Year (not Xmas)
Grades: AA 5 Diamond, Premier
01797 222119 Mr Masters
Fax: 01797 227466
oldvicaragerye@tesco.net
D: £18.50–£37.00 **S:** £37.00–£58.00
Beds: 1F 3D 1T **Baths:** 5 En
🛇 (8) ₽ (5) ⊬ 📺 🎞 🖾 ₺

Aviemore Guest House, *28/30 Fishmarket Road, Rye, E. Sussex, TN31 7LP.*
Imposing Tudor style Victorian house, town centre 2 minute walk, situated on the A259.
Open: All Year (not Xmas)
Grades: ETC 3 Diamond
01797 223052 (also fax)
Mrs Keay
aviemore@lineone.net
D: £18.00–£22.50 **S:** £20.00
Beds: 4D 3T 1S **Baths:** 4 En 2 Sh
🛇 📺 ✕ 🎞 🖾 ₺ cc

Jeakes House, *Mermaid Street, Rye, E. Sussex, TN31 7ET.*
Award-winning C16th B&B hotel in cobbled old town-centre. Traditional elegance with modern amenities.
Open: All Year
Grades: ETC 5 Diamond, AA 5 Diamond, RAC 5 Diamond, Sparkling
01797 222828 (also fax)
Mrs Hadfield
jeakeshouse@btinternet.com
D: £28.50–£48.50 **S:** £29.50–£63.00
Beds: 2F 8D 1T 1S **Baths:** 9 En 1 Pr 2 Sh
🛇 (12) ₽ (20) 📺 🏸 🎞 🖾 ₺ cc

Little Saltcote, *22 Military Road, Rye, East Sussex, TN31 7NY.*
Genuine welcome in Edwardian family home, generous English /Vegetarian breakfasts.
Open: All Year (not Xmas)
Grades: ETC 3 Diamond, AA 3 Diamond
01797 223210 D Martin
Fax: 01797 224474
littlesaltcote.rye@virgin.net
D: £18.50–£23.50 **S:** £23.50–£28.00
Beds: 3F 2D **Baths:** 3 En 1 Sh
🛇 ₽ (3) 📺 🏸 ✕ 🎞 🖾 ₺

Culpeppers, *15 Love Lane, Rye, E. Sussex, TN31 7NE.*
5 minutes walk Rye in quiet position adjacent countryside. Parking.
Open: All Year (not Xmas)
Grades: ETC 4 Diamond
01797 224411 (also fax)
P Ciccone
peppersrye@aol.com
D: £24.00–£25.00 **S:** £23.00–£25.00
Beds: 1T 2S **Baths:** 1 En 1 Sh
🛇 ⊬ 📺 🎞 🖾 ₺

Western House, *113 Winchelsea Road, Rye, E. Sussex, TN31 7EL.*
Charming C18th Listed house and gardens. **Open:** All Year
01797 223419 Mrs Dellar
D: £20.00–£25.00 **S:** £25.00–£30.00
Beds: 2D 1T **Baths:** 3 En
🛇 (10) ₽ (3) 📺 🎞 ₺

Rye Harbour

TQ9319   *Inkerman Arms, William the Conqueror*

The Old Vicarage, *Rye Harbour, Rye, E. Sussex, TN31 7TT.*
Victorian former vicarage, quietly situated, antique furniture, open fires, sumptuous breakfasts, near sea.
Open: All Year
Grades: ETC 3 Diamond, AA 3 Diamond
01797 222088 Mr Bosher
D: fr £19.50 **S:** fr £22.50
Beds: 1D 1T **Baths:** 1 Sh
🛏 🅿 (2) 🚳 📺 🐕 🛍 📺 🕴

Seaford

TV4898   *White Lion*

Holmes Lodge, *72 Claremont Road, Seaford, East Sussex, BN25 2BJ.*
Open: All Year
Grades: ETC 3 Diamond
01323 898331 M D Parr
Fax: 01323 491346
holmes.lodge@freemail.co.uk
D: £19.00–£25.00 **S:** £20.00–£30.00
Beds: 3F 2D 1T 6S **Baths:** 1 Pr 2 Sh
🛏 🅿 (10) 🚳 📺 🛍 📺 ✳ 🕴
Sherlock Holmes theme. Convenient for Downs, walks/cycling, Cuckmere Haven, 7 sisters, Beachy Head, Newhaven Ferry. Beach/town/trains 300 metres, bus-stop outside, singles/groups welcome all year. Bar/restaurant adjacent. Free tea/coffee room into conservatory, large garden, sea views.

Silverdale, *21 Sutton Park Road, Seaford, E. Sussex, BN25 1RH.*
Family run town centre house hotel excellent value for money.
Open: All Year
Grades: AA 4 Diamond, RAC 4 Diamond
01323 491849
Mr Cowdrey
Fax: 01323 891131
silverdale@mistral.co.uk
D: £13.00–£28.00 **S:** £25.00–£45.00
Beds: 2F 6D **Baths:** 6 En 2 Sh
🛏 🅿 (5) 📺 🐕 ✕ 🛍 📺 🕴 ♿ 1 cc

Streat

TQ3515   *The Bull*

North Acres, *Streat, Hassocks, E. Sussex, BN6 8RX.*
Unique Victorian country house in tiny Hamlet near South Downs.
Open: All Year (not Xmas)
01273 890278 (also fax)
J & V Eastwood
eastwood_streat@yahoo.com
Beds: 2F 2T 1S **Baths:** 3 Sh
🛏 🅿 (20) 🚳 📺 🛍 🕴

Ticehurst

TQ6930   *Salehurst Halt*

Pashley Farm, *Pashley Road, Ticehurst, Wadhurst, East Sussex, TN5 7HE.*
Peaceful Victorian farmhouse with glorious views of the Sussex Weald.
Open: All Year (not Xmas/New Year)
01580 200362 Mrs Humphrey
Fax: 01580 200832
colina@pashleyfarm.co.uk
D: £40.00 **S:** £30.00
Beds: 1T 1D **Baths:** 1 Sh
🛏 🅿 (4) 🚳 📺 🐕 🛍

Wadhurst

TQ6431   *Best Beech Inn*

Kirkstone, *Mayfield Lane, Wadhurst, E. Sussex, TN5 6HX.*
Large Victorian house with fine views in rural East Sussex.
Open: All Year (not Xmas)
01892 783204 Mr & Mrs Inman
colininman@compuserve.com
D: £20.00–£22.00 **S:** £22.00–£25.00
Beds: 1F 1T **Baths:** 2 Sh
🛏 🅿 (4) 📺 🛍 🕴

Spring Cottage, *Best Beech Hill, Wadhurst, E. Sussex, TN5 6JH.*
Modern family house, split level. Close National Trust Properties - views!
Open: All Year (not Xmas)
Grades: ETC 3 Diamond
01892 783896 Ms Bones
Fax: 01892 784866
D: £18.00–£25.00 **S:** £25.00–£35.00
Beds: 1F 1D **Baths:** 1 En 1 Sh
🛏 🅿 (4) 📺 🛍 📺 🕴

Whitesmith

TQ5213   *Six Bells*

Whitesmith Barn, *Whitesmith, Lewes, E Sussex, BN8 6HA.*
Attractive barn, quiet lane off A22. Ideal Glyndebourne, Lewes, Eastbourne.
Open: All Year (not Xmas/New Year)
Grades: ETC 4 Diamond, Silver Award
01825 872867 Mrs Snelling
snellings@bun.com
D: £20.00–£22.50 **S:** £27.00–£28.00
Beds: 1D **Baths:** 1 En
🅿 (6) 🚳 📺 🛍 🕴

Willingdon

TQ5802   *Red Lion, The Wheatsheaf*

Butlers Gate, *24 Wish Hill, Willingdon, Eastbourne, BN20 9EX.*
Attractive room quiet family home Victorian brass bed sea views.
Open: All Year (not Xmas)
01323 509897 D: fr £20.00 **S:** fr £25.00
Beds: 1F **Baths:** 1 En
🛏 (6) 🅿 (2) 🚳 📺 🛍 📺 🕴

Winchelsea

TQ9017   *Bridge Inn, New Inn*

Strand House, *Tanyards Lane, Winchelsea, Rye, E. Sussex, TN36 4JT.*
Charming C15th B&B, beams, inglenooks, pretty gardens, lounge, licensed.
Open: All Year (not Xmas)
Grades: ETC 4 Diamond, AA 4 Diamond, RAC 4 Diamond, Sparkling Diamond
01797 226276 Mr & Mrs Woods
Fax: 01797 224806
D: £22.00–£32.00 **S:** £28.00–£34.00
Beds: 2F 7D 1T **Baths:** 9 En 1 Pr
🛏 (4) 🅿 (10) 🚳 ✕ 🛍 📺 🕴 cc

Cleveland Place, *Friars Road, Winchelsea, East Sussex, TN36 4ED.*
1850s house in ancient Cinque Port of Winchelsea, near Rye.
Open: Easter to Oct
01797 225358 Ms Cash
D: fr £26.00 **S:** fr £34.00
Beds: 2D **Baths:** 2 En
🛏 (12) 🅿 (3) 🚳 🐕 🛍 🕴

West Sussex

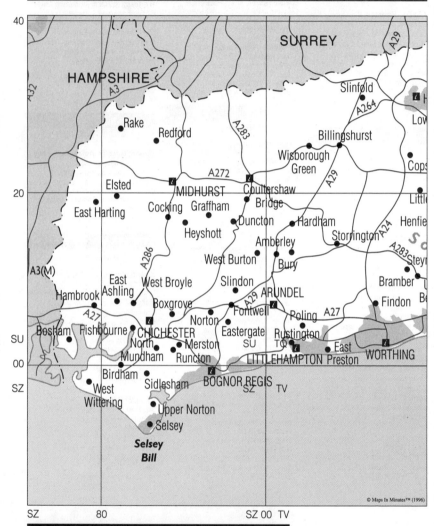

© Maps In Minutes™ (1996)

Tourist Information Centres

61 High Street, **Arundel**, West Sussex, BN18 9NJ, 01903 882419.

Belmont Street, **Bognor Regis**, West Sussex, PO21 1BJ, 01243 823140.

St Peter's Market, West Street, **Chichester**, West Sussex, PO19 1AH, 01243 775888.

Little Chef Complex, **Fontwell**, Arundel, West Sussex, BN18 0SD, 01243 543269.

International Arrivals, The Concourse, South Terminal, **Gatwick**, West Sussex, RH6 0NP, 01293 535353.

9 The Causeway, **Horsham**, West Sussex, RH12 1HE, 01403 211661.

Windmill Complex, Coastguard Road, **Littlehampton**, West Sussex, BN17 5LH, 01903 713480 (Easter to Oct).

North Street, **Midhurst**, West Sussex, GU29 9DW, 01730 817322.

Market Square, **Petworth**, West Sussex, GU28 0AF, 01798 343523.

Chapel Road, **Worthing**, West Sussex, BN11 1HL, 01903 210022.

Marine Parade, **Worthing**, West Sussex, BN11 3PX, 01903 210022 (Easter to Oct).

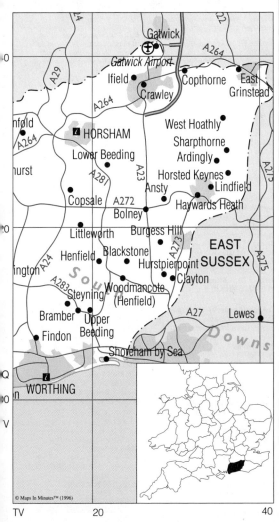

© Maps In Minutes™ (1996)

Ansty

TQ2823 ◀ *Green Cross*

Netherby, *Bolney Road, Ansty, Haywards Heath, W Sussex, RH17 5AW.*
Open: All Year
01444 455888 (also fax)
Mr & Mrs Gilbert
D: £19.00–£20.00 **S:** £20.00–£22.00
Beds: 2D 1T **Baths:** 1 Sh
⏰ 🄿 (6) ⊁ 🖵 🏰 🛏 🅥 ♨
Cosy Victorian detached country cottage on A272. 1.25 miles from A23, convenient for Gatwick Airport, Hickstead, Ardingly Showground, Brighton, Glyndebourne Opera, Bluebell Railway and National Trust Gardens. Firm beds, full English breakfast, sinks in all rooms, warm welcome.

Ardingly

TQ3429 ◀ *White Hart, Gardener's Arms*

Stonelands West Lodge, *Ardingly Road, West Hoathly, East Grinstead, West Sussex, RH19 4RA.*
Open: All Year
Grades: ETC 3 Diamond
01342 715372 Mrs Hutchings
D: £20.00–£35.00 **S:** £20.00–£25.00
Beds: 1T 1D 1S **Baths:** 1 En 1 Sh
⏰ 🄿 (2) ⊁ 🖵 🏰 🛏 ♨ &
Victorian lodge on B2028 between Turners Hill and Ardingly. Close Wakehurst Place, Ardingly Showground, Bluebell Railway. Convenient London, Brighton, Gatwick. Warm, friendly welcome. Comfortable beds. Single, double, twin rooms. Ground floor annexe with ensuite facilities. Full English breakfast. No smoking.

The Mount, *Little London, Ardingly, Haywards Heath, West Sussex, RH17 6TJ.*
Wakehurst Place, Bluebell Railway, SE Agricultural Showground, South Downs, Sheffield Park.
Open: All Year (not Xmas/New Year)
01444 892252 Dr Dale
Fax: 01444 892974
jwdale@ardingly.demon.co.uk
D: £20.00 **S:** £20.00
Beds: 2D 2S
⏰ 🄿 ⊁ 🏰 🛏 🅥 ♨

Arundel

TQ0106 ◀ *George & Dragon, Six Bells, The Spur, White Hart*

Medlar Cottage, *Poling, Arundel, W. Sussex, BN18 9PT.*
Attractive country home in quiet village location. Restful and relaxing.
Open: All Year (not Xmas)
Grades: ETC 3 Diamond
01903 883106 (also fax) Mr & Mrs Mercer
D: £20.00–£22.50 **S:** £20.00–£25.00
Beds: 2D 1T 1S **Baths:** 1 En 2 Sh
⏰ (2) 🄿 (3) ⊁ 🖵 🏰 🛏 🅥 ♨

B&B owners may vary
rates - be sure to check
when booking

Amberley

TQ0313 ◀ *The Sportsman, Black Horse*

Bacons, *Amberley, Arundel, W. Sussex, BN18 9NJ.*
Pretty old cottage in the heart of the village.
Open: All Year (not Xmas)
01798 831234 Mrs Jollands
D: fr £18.00 **S:** fr £18.00
Beds: 2T **Baths:** 1 Sh
⏰ 🏰 🛏

Woodybanks, *Crossgates, Amberley, Arundel, W. Sussex, BN18 9NR.*
Magnificent elevated views across the beautiful Wildbrooks, situated in picturesque historic Amberley.
Open: All Year
01798 831295
Mr & Mrs Hardy
D: £18.00 **S:** £20.00–£25.00
Beds: 1D 1T.
Baths: 1 Sh
⏰ 🄿 (2) ⊁ 🖵 🏰 🅥 ♨ &

Portreeves Acre, *The Causeway, Arundel, W. Sussex, BN18 9JL.*
3 minutes from station, castle and town centre.
Open: All Year (not Xmas/New Year)
01903 883277 Mr Rogers
D: £21.00–£23.00 **S:** £30.00–£35.00
Beds: 1F 1D 1T **Baths:** 2 En 1 Pr
☎ (12) ⯀ (6) �📺 🛏 🎵 ▥ ▦ ▮

Billingshurst

TQ0825

Groom Cottage, *Station Road, Billingshurst, W Sussex, RH14 9RF.*
Comfortable rooms. Five minutes from station and village. English breakfast.
Open: All Year (not Xmas/New Year)
01403 782285 Ms Gander
D: £20.00–£22.50 **S:** £25.00–£30.00
Beds: 2T **Baths:** 2 En
⯀ (2) ⯑ 📺 ▦ ▮

Birdham

SU8200   ⯐ *Crown & Anchor, The Bell*

The Red House, *Lock Lane, Birdham Pool, Birdham, Chichester, W Sussex, PO20 7BB.*
Open: All Year
Grades: ETC 4 Diamond
01243 512488 Mrs Groom
Fax: 01243 514563
susie.redhouse@ukonline.co.uk
D: £30.00–£35.00 **S:** £35.00–£40.00
Beds: 1T 1D **Baths:** 2 En
⯀ ⯑ 📺 🗙 ▦ ▮
Listed Georgian property with stunning views over Birdham Pool, providing a warm welcome and quiet location. Coastal walks on doorstep. Take a drink on the terrace, plan a night at the theatre, or wander round the marina. Sweet-scented walled garden.

Seldens, *Bell Lane, Birdham, Chichester, W. Sussex, PO20 7HY.*
Lovely, spacious secluded bungalow, large attractive gardens. 2 miles beach.
Open: All Year (not Xmas)
01243 512358 Mrs Hepburn
D: fr £25.00 **S:** fr £25.00
Beds: 1D 1S **Baths:** 1 En 1 Pr
⯀ (3) ⯑ 📺 ▦ ▮

Blackstone

TQ2416   ⯐ *The Plough*

Yeomans Hall, *Blackstone, Henfield, W Sussex, BN5 5TB.*
Medieval house with cottage garden. Conservation area in rural hamlet.
Open: All Year (not Xmas)
01273 494224 (also fax)
Mr Kerridge
stay@yeomanshall.fsnet.co.uk
D: £24.00–£27.50 **S:** £38.00–£40.00
Beds: 2D 1S **Baths:** 2 En
⯀ (2) ⯑ 📺 ▦ ▮

Planning a longer stay? Always ask for any special rates

Bognor Regis

SZ9398   ⯐ *Alexander Tavern, The George, Waverney Bar*

Jubilee Guest House, *Gloucester Road, Bognor Regis, W Sussex, PO21 1NU.*
Open: All Year (not Xmas/New Year)
Grades: ETC 3 Diamond, AA 3 Diamond
01243 863016 Fax: 01243 868017
jubileeguesthouse@breathmail.net
D: £18.00–£30.00 **S:** £18.00–£30.00
Beds: 3F 1D 2S **Baths:** 2 En 1 Sh
☎ ⯀ (4) 📺 ▦ ▮ cc
Family run business 75 yds from seafront and beach. An excellent position for access to shops, pubs and restaurants. Butlins family entertainment resort, and leisure centre close at hand. Within easy reach of Brighton, Arundel, Chichester, Portsmouth and South Downs

Regis Lodge, *Gloucester Road, Bognor Regis, W. Sussex, PO21 1NU.*
Attractive seaside guest house clean and comfortable throughout ideal base.
Open: All Year (not Xmas)
Grades: ETC 3 Diamond, AA 3 Diamond
01243 827110 (also fax) Mr Rider
frank@regislodge.fsbusiness.co.uk
D: £20.00–£30.00 **S:** fr £20.00
Beds: 3F 6D 3T **Baths:** 12 En
☎ (5) ⯀ (9) 📺 ▦ ▮

Selwood Lodge, *93 Victoria Drive, Bognor Regis, W. Sussex, PO21 2DZ.*
Friendly family hotel. Licensed bar. Games room. Garden. No restrictions.
Open: All Year
01243 865071 (also fax) Mrs Bodle
D: £17.00–£20.00 **S:** £20.00–£25.00
Beds: 2F 2D 1T **Baths:** 1 En 2 Sh
☎ ⯀ (3) 📺 🛏 🗙 ✿ ▮

Lorna Doone, *58 Sandymount Avenue, Bognor Regis, W. Sussex, PO22 9EP.*
Bungalow, max. 6 people. Residential area. University 5 mins by car.
Open: All Year **Grades:** ETC 4 Diamond
01243 822203 (also fax)
Mr & Mrs Robinson
joan@lornadoone.freeserve.co.uk
D: £19.00–£25.00 **S:** £19.00–£25.00
Beds: 2D 1T **Baths:** 2 En 1 Pr
⯀ (3) ⯑ 📺 ▦ ▮

The Old Priory, *80 North Bersted Street, Bognor Regis, W. Sussex, PO22 9AQ.*
Grade II Listed priory, restored back to a high specification.
Open: All Year
01243 863580 Mrs Collinson
Fax: 01243 826597
old.priory@mcmail.com
D: £22.00–£60.00 **S:** £25.00–£30.00
Beds: 3D 1S **Baths:** 2 En 1 Sh
☎ ⯀ 📺 🗙 ▦ ▮

Homestead Private Hotel, *90 Aldwick Road, Bognor Regis, West Sussex, PO21 2PD.*
Older style hotel, 100-years-old run by resident proprietors since 1978.
Open: All Year (not Xmas)
01243 823443 Mr Stickley
D: £16.00–£20.00 **S:** £16.00–£20.00
Beds: 2F 3D 3T 2S **Baths:** 3 En 2 Sh
☎ ⯀ (10) 📺 🗙 ▦ ▮

Bolney

TQ2623   ⯐ *Bolney Stage*

Butchers, *Ryecroft Road, Bolney, Haywards Heath, W Sussex, RH17 5PS.*
Comfortable bedroom with ensuite bathroom. Breakfast room overlooking landscaped gardens.
Open: All Year (not Xmas)
Grades: ETC 4 Diamond
01444 881503 Mrs Darby
D: £25.00–£27.50 **S:** £30.00–£35.00
Beds: 1D
☎ ⯀ (1) ⯑ 📺 ▦ ▮

Bosham

SU8004   ⯐ *The Swan, Berkeley Arms, Bosham Inn*

Barford, *Bosham Lane, Bosham, Chichester, W Sussex, PO18 8HL.*
Cottage style bungalow near Saxon church and quay, cycle-hire.
Open: All Year
Grades: ETC 3 Diamond
01243 573393 (also fax)
Mr & Mrs Flanagan
Tony@aflanagan.freeserve.co.uk
D: £18.00–£20.00 **S:** £25.00–£30.00
Beds: 2D 1T **Baths:** 1 Sh
☎ ⯀ (1) 📺 🛏 🗙 ▦ ▮

Good Hope, *Delling Lane, Old Bosham, Chichester, W. Sussex, PO18 8NR.*
Friendly comfortable ground floor accommodation in beautiful historic harbour village.
Open: All Year (not Xmas)
Grades: ETC 4 Diamond
01243 572487 Mrs Jones
Fax: 01243 530760
D: £22.50–£28.00 **S:** £25.00–£45.00
Beds: 1T **Baths:** 1 En
⯀ (2) ⯑ 📺 ▦ ▮

Vine Cottage, *3 Stream Close, Bosham, Chichester, W Sussex, PO18 8LP.*
Vine Cottage close to old Bosham.
Open: All Year
01243 572064 Mrs King
D: £18.50–£20.00 **S:** £18.50–£20.00
Beds: 2T **Baths:** 1 Sh
☎ ⯀ (2) 📺 🛏 🗙 ▦ ▮

Boxgrove

SU9006   ⯐ *Olde Cottage Inn, Anglesea Arms, Winterton Arms*

The Brufords, *66 The Street, Boxgrove, Chichester, W. Sussex, PO18 0EE.*
Quiet annexe with own entrance.
Open: All Year
01243 774085 Mrs Bruford
Fax: 01243 781235
brendan@jbjcoffey.freeserve.co.uk
D: £20.00–£25.00 **S:** £30.00–£40.00
Beds: 2D 1T **Baths:** 3 En
⯀ (4) ⯑ 📺 ▦ ▮

All details shown are as supplied by B&B owners in Autumn 2000

Bramber

TQ1810

Castle Hotel, *The Street, Bramber, Steyning, W. Sussex, BN44 3WE.*
Pretty village, spacious characterful romantic friendly inn.
Open: All Year
01903 812102
Mr & Mrs Mitchell
Fax: 01903 816711
D: £22.00–£30.00 **S:** £35.00–£40.00
Beds: 1F 6D 3T **Baths:** 10 En
🛇 🅿 (15) ⚡ 🔟 ✕ 🎹 🔻 ♨ CC

Burgess Hill

TQ3119 ◀ *Royal Oak, Top House, The Woolpack*

The Homestead, *Homestead Lane, Burgess Hill, West Sussex, RH15 0RQ.*
Open: All Year
Grades: ETC 4 Diamond
01444 246899 (also fax)
homestead@burgess-hill.co.uk
D: £22.50–£25.00 **S:** £22.50–£25.00
Beds: 2D 1T 1S **Baths:** 4 En
🛇 (12) 🅿 ⚡ 🔟 🎹 🔻 ♨ & CC
Peaceful home in 7.5 acres at end of private lane. Ground floor bedrooms with wheelchair access, Bluebell steam railway, Glyndebourne, South Downs Way, National Trust locations and gardens nearby. Railway station 1 km, Brighton, Gatwick, Lewes 15 mins. London 50 mins.

Roselands, *3 Upper St Johns Road, Burgess Hill, W Sussex, RH15 8HB.*
Large family home in cul-de-sac close to town centre and local park.
Open: All Year
01444 870491 A & V Tancred
D: £19.50 **S:** £20.00
Beds: 1T 1D 2S **Baths:** 2 Sh
🛇 🅿 (4) 🔟 🎹 🔻 ♨

49 Ferndale Road, *Burgess Hill, W Sussex, RH15 0EZ.*
Comfortable modern family home quiet location 10 mins train station.
Open: All Year (not Xmas)
01444 241778
Mrs Watson
padw@uk.packardbell.org
D: £17.50 **S:** £18.50
Beds: 2T **Baths:** 2 Sh
🅿 (2) ⚡ 🔟 🎹 ♨

Bury

TQ0113 ◀ *George & Dragon, The Swan*

Tanglewood, *Houghton Lane, Bury, Pulborough, W Sussex, RH20 1PD.*
Warm welcome in our comfortable home, with beautiful views of South Downs.
Open: All Year
01798 831606 (also fax)
Mrs House
D: £22.00–£25.00 **S:** £18.00–£20.00
Beds: 1D 1S **Baths:** 1 Sh
🅿 (3) 🔟 🎹 ❄ ♨

Pulborough Eedes Cottage, *Bignor Park Road, Bury Gate, Bury, Pulborough, W Sussex, RH20 1EZ.*
Quiet country house surrounded by farmland, very warm personal welcome.
Open: All Year (not Xmas)
Grades: ETC 4 Diamond
01798 831438 Fax: 01798 831942
D: £22.50–£25.00 **S:** £25.00–£30.00
Beds: 1D 2T **Baths:** 1 En 1 Sh
🛇 🅿 (10) 🔟 🎹 🔻 ♨ &

Harkaway, *8 Houghton Lane, Bury, Pulborough, W. Sussex, RH20 1PD.*
Quiet location beneath South Downs. Full English and vegetarian breakfast.
Open: All Year
01798 831843 Mrs Clark
D: £17.00–£19.00 **S:** £17.00–£19.00
Beds: 1D 2T **Baths:** 1 En 1 Sh
🛇 (6) 🅿 (3) ⚡ 🔟 🎹 🔻 ♨

Chichester

SU8604 ◀ *Gribble Inn, Nags Head, The Fountain, Old Cross, Selsey Inn, Crown & Anchor, Selsey Tram, Bull's Head, The Woolpack*

Abelands Barn, *Merston, Chichester, West Sussex, PO20 6DY.*
Open: All Year (not Xmas)
Grades: ETC 4 Diamond, Silver
01243 533826 Mr Richardson
Fax: 01243 555533
D: £25.00–£30.00
Beds: 1F 1D 1T **Baths:** 3 En
🛇 🅿 (5) 🔟 🎹 ♨ & CC
Traditional Sussex stone barn and annexe converted into a family home by present owners.

Hedgehogs, *45 Whyke Lane, Chichester, W. Sussex, PO19 2JT.*
Open: All Year
Grades: ETC 3 Diamond
01243 780022 Mrs Hosking
D: £17.00–£20.00 **S:** £23.00–£24.50
Beds: 2D 1S **Baths:** 2 Sh
🛇 🅿 (3) ⚡ 🔟 🎹 🔻 ♨
Non-smokers are offered a friendly welcome at our peaceful family home & secluded garden. Just a short walk from city centre, stations, theatre. Short bus ride from South Downs Way. Roman Palace & villa, open air & other museums, wild life reserves.

Marias, *47 Birdham Road, Chichester, W. Sussex, PO19 2TB.*
Delightful detached house with lovely garden. Private parking & security lighting. **Open:** All Year
01243 783452 Mrs O'Flinn
D: fr £22.00 **S:** fr £20.00
Beds: 1D 1T 1S **Baths:** 1 En 1 Sh
🅿 (5) ⚡ 🔟 🎹 ♨

Friary Close, Friary Lane, *Chichester, W Sussex, PO19 1UF.*
Grade II Listed Georgian house built astride the ancient city wall in central Chichester. **Open:** All Year
Grades: ETC 4 Diamond, Silver
01243 527294 Mr & Mrs Taylor
Fax: 01243 533876
friaryclose@argonet.co.uk
D: £25.00–£35.00 **S:** fr £35.00
Beds: 3T **Baths:** 3 En
🅿 (3) ⚡ 🔟 🎹 ♨ CC

Litten House, *148 St Pancras, Chichester, W. Sussex, PO19 1SH.*
Unexpectedly quiet Georgian house with garden, king-sized bed; city centre.
Open: All Year
Grades: ETC 3 Diamond
01243 774503 Mrs Steward
Fax: 01243 539187
victoria@littenho.demon.co.uk
D: £22.00–£30.00 **S:** £27.00–£35.00
Beds: 1F 1D 1T **Baths:** 2 Sh
🛇 ⚡ 🔟 🎹 ♨

Riverside Lodge, *7 Market Avenue, Chichester, W. Sussex, PO19 1JU.*
Traditional brick and flint house near city centre.
Open: All Year (not Xmas)
Grades: ETC 3 Diamond
01243 783164 Mrs Tregear
tregeardavid@hotmail.com
D: £22.00–£25.00 **S:** fr £25.00
Beds: 2D **Baths:** 2 En
🅿 (2) ⚡ 🎹 ♨

112 St Pancras, *Chichester, W Sussex, PO19 4LH.*
Listed Georgian town house, part converted brewery. Central Chichester.
Open: All Year
Grades: ETC 3 Diamond
01243 789872 Mrs Jaeger
Fax: 01243 789872
liz@jaegerl.freeserve.co.uk
D: £23.00–£25.00 **S:** £25.00
Beds: 2D 1S **Baths:** 1 En 1 Sh
⚡ 🔟 🎹 🔻 ♨

Cedar House, *8 Westmead Road, Chichester, W Sussex, PO19 3JD.*
Beautiful accommodation, close to city centre and many local attractions.
Open: All Year
Grades: ETC 4 Diamond, AA 4 Diamond
01243 787771 Mr & Mrs Woodcock
mel.judi@talk21.com
D: £20.00–£22.50 **S:** £18.00–£25.00
Beds: 2D 1T 1S **Baths:** 2 En 1 Sh
🅿 (5) ⚡ 🔟 🎹 🔻 ♨

Encore, *11 Clydesdale Avenue, Chichester, W. Sussex, PO19 2LW.*
Quiet comfortable town house, three minutes walk to city centre.
Open: All Year (not Xmas/New Year)
Grades: ETC 4 Diamond
01243 528271
Mr Rourke
D: £20.00–£25.00 **S:** £23.00–£40.00
Beds: 1D 1T **Baths:** 1 Sh
🅿 (2) ⚡ 🔟 🎹 ♨

The Bedford Hotel, *Southgate, Chichester, W. Sussex, PO19 1DP.*
Situated in central Chichester, ideal base to explore city's streets.
Open: All Year (not Xmas)
Grades: AA 2 Star
01243 785766 (also fax)
Mr & Mrs Winship
bedford@win-ship.demon.co.uk
D: £44.00–£45.00 **S:** £60.00–£75.00
Beds: 2F 7D 7T 4S **Baths:** 7 Pr 13 En
🛇 🅿 (8) ⚡ 🔟 🎹 ✕ 🎹 🔻 ♨ CC

Whyke Cottage, 17 Whyke Lane,
Chichester, W. Sussex, PO19 2JR.
Quiet city-centre self-contained flats, B&B
or self-catering. **Open:** All Year
01243 788767 Mr Hollis
D: £20.00–£27.50 **S:** fr £30.00
Beds: 1D 2T **Baths:** 2 Pr
🛏 🅿 (2) ½ 📺 �🖵 🐾

Clayton

TQ3014   🍺 Jack & Jill

Dower Cottage, Underhill Lane,
Clayton, Hassocks, W. Sussex, BN6 9PL.
Open: All Year (not Xmas)
01273 843363 Mrs Bailey
Fax: 01273 846503
andy@dowerbailey.freeserve.co.uk
D: £22.50–£30.00 **S:** £30.00–£50.00
Beds: 2F 2D 1T 1S **Baths:** 2 En 1 Sh
🛏 🅿 (8) ½ 📺 �🖵 🔽
Large country house in beautiful location
overlooking the Sussex Weald. Ideal for
walking, cycling, riding the South Downs
yet only 15 mins from Brighton for
nightlife. Library for guest use & colour
TVs in all rooms. Peace & quiet away
from city stress!

Cocking

SU8717   🍺 Bell Inn

Moonlight Cottage Tea Rooms,
Chichester Road, Cocking, Midhurst, W.
Sussex, GU29 0HN.
Warm welcome, pretty tea rooms/ garden.
comfortable bed, excellent breakfast.
Open: All Year **Grades:** ETC 3 Diamond
01730 813336 Mrs Longland
bedtime@moonlightcottage.net
D: £20.00–£23.00 **S:** £20.00–£23.00
Beds: 2D 1T **Baths:** 1 Sh
🛏 🅿 (5) �🖵 🔽 🐾

Copsale

TQ1724   🍺 The Bridge

Copsale Farm, Copsale, Horsham, W.
Sussex, RH13 6QU.
Open: All Year
01403 732237 Mrs Churcher
Fax: 01403 731114
D: £20.00 **S:** £20.00
Beds: 1F 2D **Baths:** 1 En 1 Sh
🛏 🅿 (7) ½ 📺 🐾 �🖵 🔽 🐾
Spacious C14th beamed farmhouse amid
37 acres. Rurally situated, easy access to
Horsham and main routes, Next to
Downs Link, Bridle Path. Walkers and
cyclists welcomed. Traditional English
breakfast (vegetarians welcome). Local
pub for evening meals. 0.75 hour
airport/seaport.

Copthorne

TQ3139   🍺 Cherry Tree, Duke's Head

Homesteads, 58 Church Lane,
Copthorne, Crawley, W Sussex, RH10 3QF.
Semi detached family home, warm
welcome. M23 5 mins, Gatwick 8 mins.
Open: All Year
01342 713221 Mrs Nixon
D: £20.00 **S:** £20.00
Beds: 2T
🛏 🅿 (2) ½ 📺 �🖵 🐾

Coultershaw Bridge

SU9618   🍺 Badgers Pub

The Old Railway Station,
Coultershaw Bridge, Petworth, W Sussex,
GU28 0JF.
Without doubt the most beautiful railway
station in Britain.
Open: All Year
Grades: ETC 5 Diamond, Silver Award
01798 342346 (also fax)
Mrs Rapley
mlr@old-station.co.uk
D: £32.00–£47.00 **S:** £40.00–£65.00
Beds: 1T 5D **Baths:** 6 En
🛏 (12) 🅿 (20) ½ 📺 ⛵ 🔽 🐾 👶 cc

Crawley

TQ2636   🍺 The Plough, Royal Oak, The Gate,
The Flight

Waterhall Country House,
Prestwood Lane, Ifield Wood, Ifield,
Crawley, W Sussex, RH11 0LA.
Open: All Year (not Xmas)
Grades: ETC 3 Diamond, RAC 3 Diamond
01293 520002 Mrs Dawson
Fax: 01293 539905
info@waterhall.co.uk
D: £22.50 **S:** £35.00
Beds: 4D 3T 1S 2F **Baths:** 10 En
🛏 (25) ½ 📺 ⛵ 🐾 cc
Attractive Country house set in 28 acres -
ideal for Gatwick bed & breakfast. All
rooms ensuite, with colour television and
tea/coffee making facilities. We provide a
warm and friendly welcome to all our
guests. Holiday parking available.

Duncton

SU9517   🍺 Cricketers

Drifters, Duncton, Petworth, W. Sussex,
GU28 0JZ.
Quiet comfortable country house - TV -
tea & coffee making facilities in rooms.
Open: All Year (not Xmas)
Grades: ETC 3 Diamond
01798 342706 Mrs Folkes
D: £20.00–£25.00 **S:** fr £25.00
Beds: 1D 2T 1S **Baths:** 1 En 1 Sh
🅿 (3) ½ 📺 ✕ ⛵ 🔽 🐾

East Ashling

SU8207   🍺 Horse & Groom

Englewood, East Ashling, Chichester,
W. Sussex, PO18 9AS.
Cottage style home in large garden.
Downland village in AONB.
Open: All Year (not Xmas)
Grades: ETC 4 Diamond
01243 575407 Mrs Jones
D: £22.50–£26.00 **S:** £33.00–£36.00
Beds: 2D **Baths:** 2 En
🅿 (4) ⛵ ✕ ⛵ 🔽 🐾

BEDROOMS

F - Family
D - Double
T - Twin
S - Single

East Grinstead

TQ3938   🍺 Dorset Arms, Bricklayers Arms, Star
Inn

Cranston House, Cranston Road, East
Grinstead, W. Sussex, RH19 3HW.
. Attractive large detached house in
residential area. Gatwick 15 minutes.
Open: All Year (not Xmas)
Grades: ETC 3 Diamond
01342 323609 (also fax)
Mr Linacre
accomodation@cranstonhouse.sereamin
g.net
D: £20.00–£40.00 **S:** £28.00–£40.00
Beds: 1F 1D 1T **Baths:** 1 En
🛏 (6) 🅿 (4) ½ 📺 🐾 ⛵ 🔽 🐾

Grinstead Lodge Guest House,
London Road, East Grinstead, W Sussex,
RH19 1QE.
Friendly family run with ample parking.
Open all year round.
Open: All Year
01342 317222 (also fax)
D: £22.00–£28.00 **S:** £20.00–£33.00
Beds: 1F 4T 2D 2S **Baths:** 7 En 1 Sh
🛏 🅿 (8) ⛵ 🐾 🔽 🐾 cc

Brentridge, 24 Portland Road, East
Grinstead, W. Sussex, RH19 4EA.
Beautiful garden, central and quiet. Close
to Gatwick, M25 & south coast.
Open: All Year (not Xmas)
01342 322004 Mrs Greenwood
Fax: 01342 324145
mgreenw145@aol.com
D: £18.00–£25.00 **S:** £25.00
Beds: 2D **Baths:** 1 En 1 Sh
🛏 🅿 (1) ½ 🐾 🔽

East Harting

SU7919   🍺 The Ship, Three Horseshoes, White
Hart

Oakwood, Eastfield Lane, East Harting,
Petersfield, Hampshire, GU31 5NF.
Foot of South Downs, beautiful
countryside, Chichester, Portsmouth easy
reach.
Open: All Year
01730 825245
Mrs Brightwell
D: £20.00–£22.50 **S:** £20.00–£25.00
Beds: 2T **Baths:** 2 Pr
🅿 ½ 📺 🐾 ✕ 🔽 🐾

East Preston

TQ0602   🍺 Fletchers Arms

Roselea Cottage, 2 Elm Avenue, East
Preston, Littlehampton, West Sussex, BN16
1HJ.
Charming cottage in quiet seaside village
near Goodwood, Arundel, Worthing.
Open: All Year
01903 786787
Mrs Bartram
Fax: 01903 770220
D: £17.50–£22.50 **S:** £20.00–£40.00
Beds: 2D 1T **Baths:** 1 En 1 Sh
🅿 (3) ½ 📺 🐾 🐾

Eastergate

SU9404   ◀ *The George, Wilkes Head*

Greenfields Farm, *Fontwell Avenue, Eastergate, Chichester, W. Sussex, PO20 6RU.*
Warm welcome, comfortable rooms, lovely gardens. Genuine home from home.
Open: All Year (not Xmas)
01243 542815 Mrs Bland
Fax: 01243 544662
d.bland@zetnet.co.uk
D: £16.00–£18.00 **S:** £18.00–£25.00
Beds: 1F 1D 1T **Baths:** 1 Sh
ॐ 🅿 (4) ⊬ 🆅 🈁 🛆

Downfields, *Level Mare Lane, Eastergate, Chichester, W Sussex, PO20 6SB.*
Open: All Year (not Xmas)
01243 542012 Mrs Cane
D: £18.00–£25.00 **S:** £20.00–£27.00
Beds: 1T **Baths:** 1 Pr
🅿 (4) ⊬ 🆅 🈁 🛆
Country house near Chichester, Arundel, Goodwood, Bognor Regis. Six miles from the coast, large garden.

Elsted

SU8119   ◀ *The Wheatsheaf, Half Moon, Bricklayers Arms, The Swan, The Elsted, Three Horseshoes*

Three, *Elsted, Midhurst, W Sussex, GU29 0JY.*
Oldest house in village (1520). Pub, cricket ground, church nearby. Warm welcome.
Open: Mar to Nov
01730 825065 Mrs Hill
Fax: 01730 825496
rh@rhill.ftech.co.uk
D: fr £25.00 **S:** fr £22.50
Beds: 1D 1T 1S **Baths:** 1 Pr 1 Sh

Findon

TQ1208   ◀ *The Gun, Findon Manor, Black Horse*

The Coach House, *41 High Street, Findon, Worthing, West Sussex, BN14 0SU.*
Village location in South Downs. Excellent walks/cycling. Close to coast.
Open: All Year
01903 873924 A Goble
D: £19.50–£22.00 **S:** £25.00–£27.50
Beds: 1F 1T 1D **Baths:** 3 En
ॐ 🅿 (3) 🆅 🍴 🈁 🛆

Findon Tower, *Cross Lane, Findon, Worthing, W Sussex, BN14 0UG.*
Elegant Edwardian country house, walking distance excellent village pubs/restaurants.
Open: All Year (not Xmas)
01903 873870 Mr & Mrs Smith
D: £25.00–£30.00 **S:** £30.00–£40.00
Beds: 2D 1T 1S **Baths:** 3 En
ॐ 🅿 (10) ⊬ 🈁 🛆

National Grid References are for villages, towns and cities – not for individual houses

Fishbourne

SU8304

Wilbury House, *Main Road, Fishbourne, Chichester, W Sussex, PO18 8AT.*
Attractive home close to Fishbourne Roman Palace, overlooking farmland, Bosham's picturesque harbour 1.5 miles.
Open: All Year (not Xmas)
Grades: ETC 4 Diamond, AA 4 Diamond
01243 572953 Mrs Penfold
Fax: 01243 574150
puffin01@globalnet.co.uk
D: £20.00–£25.00 **S:** £25.00–£35.00
Beds: 1F 1D 1T 1S **Baths:** 1 En 2 Sh
ॐ (5) 🅿 (4) ⊬ 🆅 🍴 🈁 🛆

Fontwell

SU9506   ◀ *The Spur*

Woodacre, *Arundel Road, Fontwell, Arundel, W Sussex, BN18 0SD.*
Set in beautiful garden surrounded by woodland. Everyone made welcome.
Open: All Year **Grades:** ETC 4 Diamond
01243 814301 Ms Richards
Fax: 01243 814344 wacrebb@aol.com
D: £20.00–£25.00 **S:** £20.00–£30.00
Beds: 1F 2T 1D **Baths:** 1 En 1 Pr 2 Sh
ॐ 🅿 (20) ⊬ 🆅 🍴 ✕ 🈁 🛆 cc

Gatwick

TQ2740   ◀ *The Plough, Royal Oak, The Gate, The Greyhound, Flight Tavern*

April Cottage, *10 Langley Lane, Ifield, Crawley, West Sussex, RH11 0NA.*
Warm & friendly 200-year-old house in quiet lane, near pubs, churches, station, shops. **Open:** All Year
01293 546222 Mrs Pedlow
Fax: 01293 518712
aprilcottage@networkclub.co.uk
D: £22.50–£25.00 **S:** £35.00
Beds: 1F 1D 2T **Baths:** 2 En 2 Sh
ॐ (6) 🅿 (8) ⊬ 🆅 🈁 🛆

Brooklyn Manor Hotel, *Bonnetts Lane, Gatwick, Crawley, W. Sussex, RH11 0NY.*
Ideal location for Gatwick overnight stopover. Courtesy transport & holiday parking.
Open: All Year (not Xmas)
Grades: ETC 3 Diamond
01293 546024 Mr Davis
Fax: 01293 510366
D: £19.50–£26.00 **S:** £32.00–£43.50
Beds: 3F 4D 3T 1S **Baths:** 4 En 3 Sh
ॐ 🅿 ⊬ 🆅 🈁 🛆 cc

Graffham

SU9217   ◀ *The Foresters, White Horse*

Brook Barn, *Selham Road, Graffham, Petworth, W Sussex, GU28 0PU.*
Open: All Year (not Xmas)
Grades: ETC 4 Diamond, Silver
01798 867356 Mr & Mrs Jollands
D: £25.00 **S:** £30.00
Beds: 1D **Baths:** 1 En
ॐ 🅿 (2) 🆅 🍴 🈁 🛆
Large double bedroom with ensuite bathroom, leads directly to own conservatory and secluded 2-acre garden. Close to South Downs Way, excellent pubs within walking distance, in quiet rural village in beautiful area of Sussex, ideal for a relaxing break.

Hambrook

SU7806   ◀ *Fox & Hounds*

Woodpeckers, *56 The Avenue, Hambrook, Chichester, W Sussex, PO18 8TY.*
Quiet, cosy bungalow, semi-rural area near Bosham, Chichester and Emsworth.
Open: All Year (not Xmas)
01243 573856 Mrs Ingram
D: £18.50 **S:** £25.00
Beds: 1D 1T **Baths:** 1 Pr 1 Sh
ॐ (5) 🅿 (2) ⊬ 🆅 🍴 🈁 🛆 🛆

Hardham

TQ0417   ◀ *Chequers*

Moseley's Barn, *London Road, Hardham, Pulborough, West Sussex, RH20 1LB.*
Grades: ETC 4 Diamond, Silver
01798 872912 (also fax) Mrs Newton
D: £22.50–£27.50 **S:** £30.00–£40.00
Beds: 1T 2D **Baths:** 2 En 1 Pr
ॐ (10) 🅿 ⊬ 🆅 🍴 🈁 🛆
Converted C17th barn with galleried beamed hall with panoramic views of South Downs. Conveniently placed for RSPB. Reserve, South Downs Way and also Arundel, Petworth, Chichester, Goodwood and coast. Also available one bedroomed stone cottage on B&B or self catering basis

Haywards Heath

TQ3324   ◀ *The Wheatsheaf, The Dolphin, Ardingly Inn*

Pinehurst, *Tylers Green, Haywards Heath, W. Sussex, RH16 4BW.*
Open: All Year
01444 456578 Mrs O'Riordan
D: £25.00–£35.00 **S:** £35.00–£40.00
Beds: 1D 2T **Baths:** 4 En
ॐ (8) 🅿 (4) ⊬ 🆅 🈁 🛆 ❄ 🛆 🛆
Beautiful oak-beamed country house set in over an acre of mature gardens backing onto nature reserve. Full English breakfast. Local to many Sussex Gardens & attractions. Walking distance to restaurants, pub.

12 Petlands Road, *Haywards Heath, W Sussex, RH16 4HH.*
Homely cottage atmosphere.
Open: All Year
01444 454473 Mrs Hartley
D: £21.00 **S:** £21.00
Beds: 1D 1T 1S **Baths:** 1 Sh
ॐ (1) ⊬ 🆅 🍴 🈁 🛆

Little Buntings, *32 Balcombe Road, Haywards Heath, W Sussex, RH16 1PF.*
Pleasant family house, attractive garden with parking space near station.
Open: All Year
01444 450161 Mrs Shephard
Su.sh@ic24.net
D: £19.00–£20.00 **S:** £20.00
Beds: 1D 1S **Baths:** 1 Shared
ॐ 🅿 (4) 🆅 🛆

Copyhold Hollow, *Copyhold Lane,*
Borde Hill, Haywards Heath, W Sussex,
RH16 1XU.
Warm welcome. Oak beamed C16th,
Inglenook countryside, garden, guests
lounge.
Open: All Year
Grades: ETC 4 Diamond
01444 413265 Mrs Druce
1@copyholdhollow.freeserve.co.uk
D: £27.50 **S:** £30.00–£50.00
Beds: 1D 1T 1S **Baths:** 3 En
🛇 🄿 (6) 📺 🕇 ✕ 🛏 🖂 ☑ 🛎

Henfield

TQ2116   🍺 *George Hotel, The Plough*

1 The Laurels, *Martyns Close, Henfield,*
West Sussex, BN5 9RQ.
Quiet village location. Easy access to
Brighton, Gatwick and many places of
interest.
Open: All Year
Grades: ETC 4 Diamond
01273 493518 Mr Harrington
D: £22.50–£30.00 **S:** £22.00–£30.00
Beds: 2D 1S **Baths:** 2 En 1 Sh
🛇 🄿 (3) 📺 🛏 ☑ 🛎

Leeches, *West End Lane, Henfield, W*
Sussex, BN5 9RG.
Rural Tudor farmhouse, river and country
walks. Heated swimming pool.
Open: All Year
01273 492495 Mrs Abbott
Fax: 01273 493000
D: £22.50–£25.00 **S:** £25.00
Beds: 1D 2T 2S **Baths:** 2 Pr 2 Sh
🛇 (5) 🄿 (6) 📺 🛏 🛎

Lyndhurst, *38 Broomfield Road,*
Henfield, West Sussex, BN5 9UA.
Elegant Victorian house, comfortable
spacious rooms, antique beds, cotton bed
linen. **Open:** All Year
01273 494054 Mrs Slingsby
Fax: 01273 491334
linda.Slingsby@ukgateway.net
D: £17.50–£20.00 **S:** £20.00–£27.50
Beds: 1F 1D 1T **Baths:** 3 Sh
🛇 🄿 (6) 🕊 📺 🕇 ✕ 🛏 🖂 ☑ 🛎

Heyshott

SU8917   🍺 *The Unicorn*

Little Hoyle, *Hoyle Lane, Heyshott,*
Midhurst, W Sussex, GU29 0DX.
Open: All Year (not Xmas)
Grades: ETC 4 Diamond
01798 867359 (also fax)
Mr & Mrs Ralph
D: £23.00–£26.00 **S:** £35.00
Beds: 1D **Baths:** 1 En
🛇 🄿 (2) 🕊 📺 🛏 ☑ 🛎
Comfortable, welcoming, peaceful, large
garden, splendid views to South Downs,
near Petworth, Goodwood, Chichester.

RATES

D = Price range per person
sharing in a double room
S = Price range for a
single room

Planning a longer stay? Always
ask for any special rates

Horsham

TQ1731   🍺 *Norfolk Arms*

The Larches, *28 Rusper Road,*
Horsham, West Sussex, RH12 4BD.
Friendly family house close to stations
and attractive town centre. Separate
visitors' entrance.
Open: All Year
01403 263392 Mrs Lane
D: £23.00–£25.00 **S:** £20.00–£25.00
Beds: 1F 2T 2S **Baths:** 2 En
🛇 🄿 (3) 📺 ✕ 🛏 🌼 🛎

Alton House, *29 Rusper Road,*
Horsham, W Sussex, RH12 4BA.
Open: All Year
01403 211825 Mrs Ashton
D: £22.50–£25.00 **S:** fr £35.00
Beds: 3D 1T **Baths:** 3 Pr 1 Sh
🛇 (1) 🄿 (4) 📺 🕇 🛏 🛎
15 Minutes Gatwick Airport Leonondslee
and Nymans Gardens, 35 minutes
Worthing and Brighton, easy access to
London 1 hour by train.

The Wirrals, *1 Downsview Road,*
Horsham, W Sussex, RH12 4PF.
Attractive detached home with a
welcoming atmosphere and comfortable
accommodation.
Open: All Year (not Xmas)
Grades: ETC 3 Diamond
01403 269400 (also fax) Mrs Archibald
p.archibald@lineone.net
D: £19.50 **S:** £22.00
Beds: 1D 1S **Baths:** 1 Sh
🄿 (2) 🕊 📺 🛏 🛎

Horsted Keynes

TQ3827   🍺 *Green Man, The Crown*

The Croft, *Lewes Road, Horsted Keynes,*
Haywards Heath, W Sussex, RH17 7DP.
Open: All Year
Grades: AA 3 Diamond
01825 790546 Mrs Ollif
D: £22.50–£25.00 **S:** £25.00–£30.00
Beds: 1T 1D **Baths:** 1 Sh
🛇 🄿 (4) 🕊 📺 🕇 ✕ 🛏 🖂 🛎
A warm welcome is assured in this
comfortable family house situated in a
quiet village location. Convenient for the
Bluebell Railway, SoE Showground,
Ardingly, Wakehurst Place, Sheffield Park
and the Ashdown Forest. The village also
boasts two excellent country pubs.

Hurstpierpoint

TQ2816   🍺 *The Pilgrim, The Goose*

Wickham Place, *Wickham Drive,*
Hurstpierpoint, Hassocks, W. Sussex, BN6
9AP.
Large house in a lovely village just off the
A23.
Open: All Year (not Xmas)
01273 832172 Mrs Moore
D: £22.50–£25.00 **S:** £30.00
Beds: 1D 2T **Baths:** 1 Sh
🛇 🄿 (5) 🕊 📺 🕇 🛏 ☑ 🛎

Ifield

TQ2537   🍺 *The Plough, Royal Oak, The Gate,*
The Flight

Waterhall Country House,
Prestwood Lane, Ifield Wood, Ifield,
Crawley, West Sussex, RH11 0LA.
Attractive Country house set in 28 acres -
ideal for Gatwick bed & breakfast.
Open: All Year (not Xmas)
Grades: ETC 3 Diamond, RAC 3 Diamond
01293 520002 Mrs Dawson
Fax: 01293 539905
info@waterhall.co.uk
D: £22.50 **S:** £35.00
Beds: 4D 3T 1S 2F **Baths:** 10 En
🛇 🄿 (25) 🕊 📺 🛏 🛎 cc

April Cottage, *10 Langley Lane, Ifield,*
Crawley, West Sussex, RH11 0NA.
Warm & friendly 200-year-old house in
quiet lane, near pubs, churches, station,
shops. **Open:** All Year
01293 546222 Mrs Pedlow
Fax: 01293 518712
aprilcottage@networkclub.co.uk
D: £22.50–£25.00 **S:** £35.00
Beds: 1F 1D 2T **Baths:** 2 En 2 Sh
🛇 (6) 🄿 (8) 🕊 📺 🛏 ☑ 🛎

Lindfield

TQ3425   🍺 *Gardeners' Arms, Bent Arms, Red*
Lion

2 Hickmans Close, *Lindfield,*
Haywards Heath, W Sussex, RH16 2PS.
Detached house, quiet, 5 minutes walk
picturesque village high street.
Open: All Year
01444 482006 Mr & Mrs Robinson
D: £15.00–£17.50 **S:** £20.00
Beds: 1D 1T **Baths:** 2 Sh
🛇 (6) 🄿 (2) 🕊 📺 🛏 🛎

Littleworth

TQ1920   🍺 *The Windmill*

Pound Cottage, *Mill Lane, Littleworth,*
Partridge Green, W. Sussex, RH13 8JU.
Comfortable detached country house,
warm welcome and good English
breakfasts. **Open:** All Year
Grades: ETC 3 Diamond
01403 710218 Mrs Brown
Fax: 01403 711337
poundcottagebb@amserve.net
D: £18.00–£20.00 **S:** £18.00–£20.00
Beds: 1D 1T 1S **Baths:** 1 Sh
🛇 🄿 (8) 🕊 📺 🛏 🛎

Lower Beeding

TQ2128   🍺 *Wheatsheaf Inn, Plummers Plain,*
Hare & Hounds, Royal Oak

Village Pantry, *Handcross Road,*
Plummers Plain, Lower Beeding,
Horsham, W Sussex, RH13 6NU.
Superb comfortable rooms, lovely garden,
close Gatwick, Horsham, Brighton,
Crawley. Warm welcome.
Open: All Year (not Xmas)
Grades: ETC 3 Diamond
01403 891319 (also fax) Mrs Jays
D: £20.00–£24.00 **S:** £26.00–£38.00
Beds: 1F 2D 1T 1S **Baths:** 3 En 1 Sh
🛇 🄿 (6) 🕊 📺 🛏 🖂 ☑ 🛎

The Old Posthouse, *Plummers Plain, Lower Beeding, Horsham, W. Sussex, RH13 6NU.*
Victorian, beautiful garden, close to Leonardslee, Nymans, Bluebell Railway, Horsham Brighton.
Open: All Year (not Xmas)
01403 891776 Dr Crisp
D: £20.00–£22.50 **S:** £21.00–£25.00
Beds: 1F 2D 1T 2S **Baths:** 3 En 1 Sh
📺 🅿 (6) 📺 ✕ 🃏 🖾 ⚓ **cc**

Merston

SU8902 🍺 *Gribble Inn*

Abelands Barn, *Merston, Chichester, West Sussex, PO20 6DY.*
Traditional Sussex stone barn and annexe converted into a family home by present owners. **Open:** All Year (not Xmas)
Grades: ETC 4 Diamond, Silver
01243 533826 Mr Richardson
Fax: 01243 555533
D: £25.00–£30.00
Beds: 1F 1D 1T **Baths:** 3 En
📺 🅿 (5) 📺 🖾 ⚓ 🃏 **cc**

Midhurst

SU8821 🍺 *The Wheatsheaf, Half Moon, Bricklayers Arms, The Swan, The Elsted, Three Horseshoes*

Oakhurst Cottage, *Carron Lane, Midhurst, W. Sussex, GU29 9LF.*
Beautiful cottage in lovely surroundings within easy reach of Midhurst amenities.
Open: All Year
Grades: ETC 3 Diamond
01730 813523
Mrs Whitmore Jones
D: £25.00–£30.00 **S:** £25.00–£30.00
Beds: 1D 1T 1S **Baths:** 1 En 1 Sh
📺 (4) 🅿 (2) 🃏 📺 🖾

Three, *Elsted, Midhurst, W Sussex, GU29 0JY.*
Oldest house in village (1520). Pub, cricket ground, church nearby. Warm welcome. **Open:** Mar to Nov
01730 825065 Mrs Hill
Fax: 01730 825496
rh@rhill.ftech.co.uk
D: fr £25.00 **S:** fr £22.50
Beds: 1D 1T 1S **Baths:** 1 Pr 1 Sh

The Crown Inn, *Edinburgh Square, Midhurst, W. Sussex, GU29 9NL.*
C16th character inn, real ales, log fires, home-cooked food.
Open: All Year
01730 813462 Mr Stevens
D: £17.50–£20.00 **S:** £20.00–£25.00
Beds: 1D 1T 1S **Baths:** 1 Sh
🃏 📺 🃏 ✕ 🖾 🖾 ⚓

Carrondune, *Carron Lane, Midhurst, W Sussex, GU29 9LD.*
Comfortable old family country house, quiet location, 5 mins town centre.
Open: Feb to Nov
01730 813558 Mrs Beck
D: £20.00–£25.00 **S:** £25.00–£30.00
Beds: 1D 1T **Baths:** 1 Sh
📺 (5) 🅿 (4) 📺 🖾 ⚓

North Mundham

SU8702 🍺 *Walnut Tree*

Enford Mead, *Post Office Lane, North Mundham, Chichester, W Sussex, PO20 6JY.*
Welcoming family house, quiet county village, convenient - Chichester, Goodwood coast. **Open:** All Year (not Xmas)
01243 783946 (also fax) Mrs Sampson
D: £19.00–£23.00 **S:** £19.00–£25.00
Beds: 2D **Baths:** 2 En
📺 🅿 (6) 🃏 📺 🖾 ⚓

Norton

SU9206 🍺 *Old Cottage Inn, The Newburgh*

Five Acres, *Norton Lane, Norton, Chichester, W. Sussex, PO20 6NH.*
Open: All Year (not Xmas/New Year)
01243 543294 Mrs Underwood
D: £22.50 **S:** £25.00
Beds: 1D 2T 2S **Baths:** 1 En 1 Pr 1 Sh
🅿 (6) 🃏 📺 🖾 🃏 ✤ ⚓ ⚓ ♿
Charming comfortable house, lovely gardens, really quiet location. Tranquil setting yet close to excellent pubs which serve evening meals. Guest TV lounge, beamed dining room, delicious breakfasts. Ample off street parking. Close to Chichester, Arundel and racecourses. No smoking.

Poling

TQ0404 🍺 *George & Dragon, Six Bells*

Medlar Cottage, *Poling, Arundel, W. Sussex, BN18 9PT.*
Attractive country home in quiet village location. Restful and relaxing.
Open: All Year (not Xmas)
Grades: ETC 3 Diamond
01903 883106 (also fax)
Mr & Mrs Mercer
D: £20.00–£22.50 **S:** £20.00–£25.00
Beds: 2D 1T 1S **Baths:** 1 En 2 Sh
📺 (2) 🅿 (3) 🃏 📺 🃏 🖾 🖾 ⚓

Rake

SU8027 🍺 *The Sun, Jolly Drover*

Glendale, *Hatch Lane, Rake, Liss, Hampshire, GU33 7NJ.*
Large family house in 4.5 acres, garden with tennis court set in country woodland. **Open:** All Year (not Xmas)
01730 893451 Mrs Browse
Fax: 01730 892626
carol@cbrowse.fsnet.co.uk
D: £22.50–£25.00 **S:** £25.00–£30.00
Beds: 1D 1T 1S **Baths:** 1 En 1 Pr
🅿 🃏 📺 🖾 ⚓

Redford

SU8625

Redford Cottage, *Redford, Midhurst, W Sussex, GU29 0QF.*
Warm welcome in old beamed cottage in quiet country location.
Open: All Year (not Xmas)
Grades: ETC 4 Diamond, AA 4 Diamond
01428 741242 (also fax)
C Angela
D: £30.00–£35.00 **S:** £35.00–£40.00
Beds: 1T 2D **Baths:** 3 En
🅿 (10) 🃏 📺 🖾 ⚓

Runcton

SU8801 🍺 *Walnut Tree*

Springdale Cottage, *Runcton, Chichester, W Sussex, PO20 6PS.*
Beautiful C18th cottage in delightful gardens down country lane.
Open: All Year
Grades: ETC 3 Diamond
01243 783912
Mr & Mrs Davey
D: £20.00–£25.00 **S:** £20.00–£25.00
Beds: 1F 1D 1S **Baths:** 1 En 1 Pr 1 Sh
📺 🅿 (6) 🃏 🖾 ⚓

Rustington

TQ0502 🍺 *Smugglers' Inn, The Windmill*

Kenmore Guest House, *Claigmar Road, Rustington, Littlehampton, W. Sussex, BN16 2NL.*
Open: All Year
Grades: ETC 4 Diamond, Silver Award, AA 4 Diamond
01903 784634 (also fax)
Mrs Dobbs
kenmoreguesthouse@amserve.net
D: £23.50–£26.00 **S:** £23.50–£26.00
Beds: 3F 3D 1T 1S **Baths:** 8 En
📺 🅿 (8) 🃏 📺 🃏 ✕ 🖾 🖾 ⚓ **cc**
Secluded Edwardian house in the heart of the village close to the sea. Ideal for historic towns, castles, cathedrals and stately homes. Comfortable accommodation with extras in room including fridges and hairdryers with nice touches like potpourri, tissues and face cloths.

Selsey

SZ8593 🍺 *Lifeboat Inn*

42 Kingsway, *Selsey, Chichester, W Sussex, PO20 0SY.*
Ground-floor apartment plus courtyard garden with waterfall and lighting.
Open: All Year
Grades: ETC 3 Diamond
01243 604711 (also fax)
Mr & Mrs Lucas
stephen.lucas2@virgin.net
D: £15.00–£25.00 **S:** £15.00–£25.00
Beds: 1F 1D **Baths:** 1 En
📺 🅿 (2) 📺 🖾 ⚓

Sharpthorne

TQ3732 🍺 *The Crown*

Saxons, *Horsted Lane, Sharpthorne, East Grinstead, W. Sussex, RH19 4HY.*
Detached country house, beautiful countryside. Near National Trust properties.
Open: All Year
01342 810821 Mrs Smith
excol@aol.com
D: £20.00–£25.00 **S:** £20.00–£25.00
Beds: 2D 1T **Baths:** 1 Sh 1 En
📺 🅿 (6) 🃏 📺 🖾 🖾 ⚓

B&B owners may vary rates - be sure to check when booking

Shoreham-by-Sea

TQ2205

The Crabtree, *6 Buckingham Road, Shoreham-by-Sea, W. Sussex, BN43 5UA.*
All rooms comfortably decorated. Close to sea front, station, local attractions.
Open: All Year
01273 463508 L B Dove
D: £17.50–£20.00 **S:** £20.00–£25.00
Beds: 2F 1T 1D **Baths:** 1 Sh
☼ ▣ (10) ⅄ ⊠ ⊁ ✕ Ⅲ ⓥ ▴

Sidlesham

SZ8597   ⚫ *Selsey Tram*

Bird Pond Nursery, *Selsey Road, Sidlesham, Chichester, W Sussex, PO20 7NF.*
Secluded bungalow, convenient Chichester, Goodwood, Pagham Harbour. Golf, sailing and beaches.
Open: All Year (not Xmas)
Grades: ETC 3 Diamond
01243 641212 (also fax)
Mrs Upstone
D: £20.00–£25.00 **S:** £20.00–£25.00
Beds: 1F 1S **Baths:** 1 En 1 Pr
▣ (6) ⅄ ⊠ ⊁ Ⅲ ⓥ ▴ ₺

Meadowview, *Jury Lane, Sidlesham, Chichester, W. Sussex, PO20 7PX.*
17 miles to Portsmouth and historic ships. All rooms ground floor, lovely garden views.
Open: All Year
01243 641316 Mrs Shepherd
D: £22.50–£25.00 **S:** £30.00–£50.00
Beds: 3D **Baths:** 3 En
▣ (4) ⊠ Ⅲ ⓥ ▴

Slindon

SU9608   ⚫ *Newburgh Arms*

Mill Lane House, *Mill Lane, Slindon, Arundel, W. Sussex, BN18 0RP.*
In peaceful village on South Downs, views to coast.
Open: All Year
Grades: ETC 3 Diamond
01243 814440 Mrs Fuente
Fax: 01243 814436
D: £22.50 **S:** £28.50
Beds: 2D 1T **Baths:** 3 En
☼ ▣ (7) ⊠ ⊁ ✕ Ⅲ ⓥ ▴ ₺ 3

Slinfold

TQ1131

Wendys Cottage, *Five Oaks Road, Slinfold, Horsham, West Sussex, RH13 7RQ.*
Farmhouse 3 miles from Horsham - ample parking. English breakfast.
Open: All Year
01403 782326 (also fax)
D: £20.00–£22.50 **S:** £25.00–£30.00
Beds: 1F 1T **Baths:** En
☼ ▣ ⅄ ⊠ ⊁ Ⅲ ▴

All details shown are as supplied by B&B owners in Autumn 2000

Steyning

TQ1711   ⚫ *Star Inn, The Fountain, The Chequers*

Wappingthorn Farmhouse, *Horsham Road, Steyning, West Sussex, BN44 3AA.*
Open: All Year
Grades: ETC 4 Diamond
01903 813236 Mr Shapland
arianne@wappingthorn.demon.co.uk
D: £20.00–£25.00 **S:** £27.50–£35.00
Beds: 1F 1T 1D 1S **Baths:** 4 En
☼ ▣ (8) ⅄ ⊠ Ⅲ
Traditional farmhouse, recently refurbished, set in 2 acres of gardens. Located within our family operated, 300 acre dairy farm. All rooms overlook fields and the South Downs. Includes breakfast. 10 miles Brighton. 8 miles Worthing. Steyning Village 1 mile.

5 Coxham Lane, *Steyning, W. Sussex, BN44 3LG.*
Comfortable house in quiet lane.
Open: All Year
01903 812286 Mrs Morrow
D: £16.00 **S:** £16.00
Beds: 2T 1S **Baths:** 1 Sh
▣ (3) ⊁ Ⅲ ⓥ ▴

Sheppenstrete House, *Sheep Pen Lane, Steyning, W. Sussex, BN44 3GP.*
Charming, comfortable period house, hidden just off High Street.
Open: All Year (not Xmas)
01903 813179 Mrs Wood
Fax: 01903 814400
valerie@mecservices.freeserve.co.uk
D: £25.00–£30.00 **S:** £25.00–£40.00
Beds: 1T 1S
▣ (1) ⅄ ⊠ ✕ Ⅲ ▴

Storrington

TQ0814   ⚫ *Anchor Inn, Old Forge, New Moon*

Willow Tree Cottage, *Washington Road, Storrington, Pulborough, W. Sussex, RH20 4AF.*
Welcoming, friendly, quiet. All rooms ensuite. Colour TV, tea-making facilities.
Open: All Year (not Xmas)
01903 740835 Mrs Smith
D: £20.00–£22.50 **S:** £25.00–£30.00
Beds: 2D 1T **Baths:** 3 Pr
☼ ▣ (10) ⅄ ⊠ ⊁ Ⅲ ⓥ ▴

No 1, Lime Chase (off Fryern Road), *Storrington, Pulborough, W. Sussex, RH20 4LX.*
Award winning luxury accommodation in secluded village setting. Restaurants close by. **Open:** All Year
Grades: ETC 5 Diamond, Gold
01903 740437 (also fax) Mrs Warton
fionawarton@limechase.co.uk
D: £32.50–£40.00 **S:** £45.00–£55.00
Beds: 1T 1D **Baths:** 1 En 1 Pr
☼ (10) ▣ (5) ⅄ ⊠ Ⅲ ⓥ ▴ ₺

Hampers End, *Rock Road, Storrington, Pulborough, W Sussex, RH20 3AF.*
Mike and Lorna Cheeseman welcome you to their lovely mellowed country house.
Open: All Year (not Xmas)
01903 742777 Fax: 01903 742776
D: £22.50–£27.50
Beds: 1F 2D 1T **Baths:** 3 En 1 Pr
☼ (10) ▣ (6) ⊠ Ⅲ ▴

Upper Beeding

TQ1910

The Rising Sun, *Upper Beeding, Steyning, W. Sussex, BN44 3TQ.*
Open: All Year (not Xmas)
01903 814424 Mr & Mrs Taylor-Mason
D: £17.00 **S:** £20.00
Beds: 2D 1T 2S **Baths:** 1 Sh
▣ (20) ⊠ ⊁ ✕ Ⅲ ⓥ ▴ cc
A delightful Georgian country inn, set amidst the South Downs. Tony & Sue offer a warm welcome, fine selection of real ales and traditional home-cooked food lunchtime and evenings. Comfortable rooms, all with wash basin. Renowned full English breakfast.

West Broyle

SU8406   ⚫ *Fox & Hound*

Primrose Cottage, *Old Broyle Road, West Broyle, Chichester, W. Sussex, PO19 3PR.*
Victorian house 1.75 miles Chichester close to theatre, Goodwood, countryside.
Open: All Year
Grades: ETC 3 Diamond
01243 788873 Mrs Brooks
D: £22.00–£28.00 **S:** £20.00–£44.00
Beds: 1T 1D 1S **Baths:** 2 Sh
▣ (4) ⅄ ⊠ Ⅲ ⓥ ▴

West Burton

SU9913   ⚫ *Squire & Groom*

Cokes Barn, *West Burton, Pulborough, W Sussex, RH20 1HD.*
Converted barn surrounded by beautiful NGS garden in peaceful hamlet.
Open: All Year (not Xmas)
Grades: ETC 4 Diamond
01798 831636 (also fax)
Mrs Azis
D: £20.00–£25.00 **S:** £20.00–£25.00
Beds: 2T 1S **Baths:** 1 Sh
▣ (3) ⅄ Ⅲ

West Hoathly

TQ3632   ⚫ *White Hart, Gardeners' Arms*

Stonelands West Lodge, *Ardingly Road, West Hoathly, East Grinstead, West Sussex, RH19 4RA.*
Victorian lodge on B2028 between Turners Hill and Ardingly. Close Wakehurst Place.
Open: All Year
Grades: ETC 3 Diamond
01342 715372 Mrs Hutchings
D: £20.00–£35.00 **S:** £20.00–£25.00
Beds: 1T 1D 1S **Baths:** 1 En 1 Sh
☼ ▣ (2) ⅄ ⊠ ⊁ Ⅲ ▴ ₺

BATHROOMS

Pr - Private

Sh - Shared

En - Ensuite

West Wittering

SZ7798

Home Farm House, *Elms Lane, West Wittering, Chichester, W Sussex, PO20 8LW.*
Open: All Year (not Xmas/New Year)
01243 514252 Mrs Morton
Fax: 01243 512804
peter-paddymorton@talk21.com
D: £25.00–£35.00 **S:** £25.00–£50.00
Beds: 1S 2D **Baths:** 1 En 1 Pr
🄿 (4) ⌇ 📺 ▥ ⚓
An elegant, spacious house, set in an attractive garden on a peaceful lane. Easy walking distance to West Wittering beach, Chichester Harbour and the National Trust's East Head sand dune spit. Excellent public houses and restaurants nearby. Chichester 10 minutes, Goodwood 15 minutes.

Wisborough Green

TQ0425 🍺 *Three Crowns*

Lower Sparr Farm, *Skiff Lane, Wisborough Green, W Sussex, RH14 0AA.*
Farmhouse set in quiet surroundings overlooking large garden and pastureland.
Open: All Year (not Xmas)
Grades: ETC 4 Diamond
01403 820465 Mrs Sclater
Fax: 01403 820678
sclater@lowersparrbb.f9.co.uk
D: £22.00 **S:** £25.00
Beds: 1D 1T 1S **Baths:** 2 Pr
🛏 🄿 (4) ⌇ 📺 ✕ ▥ ⚓

Woodmancote (Henfield)

TQ2314

The Tithe Barn, *Brighton Road, Woodmancote, Henfield, West Sussex, BN5 9ST.*
Woodmancote - West Sussex. Converted flint barn with views of South Downs.
Open: All Year
01273 492986 (also fax)
Mrs Warren
chriswarren@breathenet.com
D: £18.00–£25.00 **S:** £18.00–£25.00
Beds: 2T 1S **Baths:** 1 Sh
🛏 🄿 (3) ⌇ 📺 🐾 ▥ 🆅 ⚓

Worthing

TQ1303 🍺 *The Cricketers, Hare & Hounds*

Tudor Lodge, *25 Oxford Road, Worthing, W. Sussex, BN11 1XQ.*
Victorian house near amenities for warm welcome and excellent breakfast.
Open: All Year (not Xmas)
01903 234401 Mrs Colbourn
D: £18.00–£20.00 **S:** £18.00–£20.00
Beds: 1D 1T 1S **Baths:** 1 Sh
🛏 🄿 (2) ⌇ 📺 ▥ 🆅 ⚓

B&B owners may vary rates - be sure to check when booking

Merton Guest House, *96 Broadwater Road, Worthing, W Sussex, BN14 8AW.*
Friendly and attentive service with high standard accommodation.
Open: All Year
Grades: ETC 3 Diamond
01903 238222 (also fax)
Mr Smith
stay@mertonhouse.freeserve.co.uk
D: £24.00 **S:** £25.00–£30.00
Beds: 3D 1T 1S **Baths:** 5 En
🛏 (8) 🄿 (5) ⌇ 📺 ✕ ▥ 🆅 ⚓ ♿ cc

Manor Guest House, *100 Broadwater Road, Worthing, West Sussex, BN14 8AN.*
Detached cottage-style house. Ideally situated for business and pleasure.
Open: All Year
Grades: ETC 3 Diamond
01903 236028 Mr Emms
Fax: 01903 230404
stay@manorworthing.com
D: £20.00–£30.00 **S:** £20.00–£35.00
Beds: 2F 3D 1S **Baths:** 3 En 1 Sh
🛏 🄿 (8) ⌇ 📺 🐾 ▥ 🆅 ⚓ ♿ cc

RATES

D = Price range per person sharing in a double room
S = Price range for a single room

Teesside

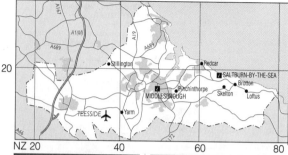

NZ 20   40   60   80

Brotton

NZ6820

The Arches Hotel, Birkbeck Low Farm, Brotton, Saltburn-by-the- Sea, TS12 2QX.
Open: All Year
01287 677512 Fax: 01287 677150
birkralysc@aol.com
D: £20.00–£30.00 **S:** £30.00–£35.00
Beds: 11F 5T 6D **Baths:** Pr
🅿 (20) ⌛ 📺 🔟 🐾 🔟 ♨ ⚓ cc
Beautiful coastal and golf course views, with the warmest welcome assured. Special terms for long stays. Log fires. Visit Whitby. Staithes, North York's steam railway.

Loftus

NZ7118

White Horse Inn, 73 High Street, Loftus, Saltburn-by-the- Sea, TS13 4HG.
Friendly village pub near to Yorkshire moors and seaside.
Open: All Year (not Xmas)
01287 640758 C Rowe
D: £15.00–£18.00 **S:** £15.00–£18.00
Beds: 2F 1T **Baths:** 1 En 1 Sh
🐾 🅿 (5) 📺 🐾 ✕ 🔟 🔟 ⚓

Middlesbrough

NZ5118 ⬤ Highfield

White House Hotel, 311 Marton Road, Middlesbrough, TS4 2HG.
Family run, close to centre, good English breakfast, car parking. **Open:** All Year
01642 244531
D: £15.00–£17.50 **S:** £18.50–£22.00
Beds: 2F 2D 6T 5S **Baths:** 4 En 3 Sh
🐾 📺 🐾 🔟 ⚓

Pinchinthorpe (Middlesbrough)

NZ5418

Pinchinthorpe Hotel, Pinchinthorpe, Guisborough, TS14 8HG.
In N Yorks National Park close to Heartbeat & Herriot Country
Open: All Year **Grades:** ETC 4 Diamond
01287 630200 (also fax) G Tinsley
D: £45.00–£65.00 **S:** £65.00–£85.00
Beds: 6D **Baths:** 6 En
🅿 📺 ✕ ⚓ ⚓ ♿

Redcar

NZ6124

The Kastle, 55/56 Newcomen Terrace, Redcar, Teesside, TS10 1DB.
Open: All Year
01642 489313
D: £10.00–£17.00 **S:** £10.00–£17.00
Beds: 3F 6T 6D 6S **Baths:** 6 En 5 Sh
🐾 🅿 (70) 📺 🐾 ✕ 🔟 ⚓ ♨ cc
Situated on the sea front opposite Redcar leisure centre and golf course. The Kastle is an ideal venue for visitors visiting Redcar, within easy reach of town centre and racecourse. Our prices include full English breakfast with use of the Knights bar and lounge.

A 2 Z, 71 Station Road, Redcar, TS10 1RD.
Near town centre, beach, racecourse, golf course and Yorkshire Moors.
Open: All Year (not Xmas)
01642 775533 Mrs Hodgin
D: £10.00–£12.00 **S:** £12.00–£13.00
Beds: 4T 2S **Baths:** 2 Sh
🐾 📺 🐾 ✕ 🔟 🔟 ⚓

Saltburn-by-the-Sea

NZ6722 ⬤ Holly Bush, Blacksmiths Arms, Ship, Lingdale

Runswick Bay Hotel, Runswick Bay, Saltburn-by-the-Sea, Cleveland, TS13 5HR.
In well-known village of Runswick Bay and within North York Moors National Park.
Open: All Year (not Xmas/New Year)
01947 841010
D: £22.50–£25.00 **S:** £25.00–£28.00
Beds: 1F 1T 4D **Baths:** 6 En
🐾 🅿 📺 🐾 ✕ 🔟 🔟 ⚓ cc

Westerlands Guest House, 27 East Parade, Skelton, Saltburn-by-the-Sea, N. Yorks, TS12 2BJ.
Large modern detached house, beautiful views sea/countryside, alongside Cleveland way long-distance path.
Open: Mar to Oct
01287 650690 Mr Bull
D: £15.00 **S:** £15.00
Beds: 6F 3D 3S **Baths:** 3 Pr
🐾 🅿 (5) ⌛ 📺 🐾 ✕ 🔟 🔟 ⚓

The Spa Hotel, Saltbank, Saltburn-by-the-Sea, Cleveland, TS12 1HH.
Our reputation is built on traditional quality accommodation and food.
Open: All Year
01287 622544 Mr Devnay
Fax: 01287 625870
spahotels@aol.com
D: £25.00 **S:** £35.00
Beds: 4F 20D 7T **Baths:** 31 En
🐾 🅿 (40) ⌛ 📺 🐾 ✕ 🔟 🔟 ♨ ⚓ ♿ cc

Skelton (Saltburn)

NZ6518 ⬤ Holly Bush Blacksmiths Arms, Ship, Lingdale Tavern

Westerlands Guest House, 27 East Parade, Skelton, Saltburn-by-the-Sea, N. Yorks, TS12 2BJ.
Large modern detached house, beautiful views sea-countryside, alongside Cleveland way long-distance path.
Open: Mar to Oct
01287 650690 Mr Bull
D: £15.00 **S:** £15.00
Beds: 6F 3D 3S **Baths:** 3 Pr
🐾 🅿 (5) ⌛ 📺 🐾 ✕ 🔟 🔟 ⚓

Stillington

NZ3724 ⬤ The Hamilton

Post Office House, Redmarshall Street, Stillington, Stockton-on-Tees, Cleveland, TS21 1JS.
Spacious modern rooms. Private entrance with own keys.
Open: All Year
01740 630301 (also fax)
harewood@tesco.net
D: £20.00 **S:** £25.00
Beds: 2D **Baths:** 2 En
📺 🔟 ⚓

Yarm

NZ4112 ⬤ Black Bull, New Cross Keys

2 Valley Close, Yarm, Cleveland, TS15 9SE.
Friendly, comfortable, modern, detached house in peaceful wooded surroundings.
Open: All Year (not Xmas)
01642 780633 Mrs Bond
D: £18.00–£25.00 **S:** £18.00–£25.00
Beds: 1T 2S 1D **Baths:** 1 En 1 Sh
🐾 (5) 🅿 (2) ⌛ 📺 🔟 🔟 ⚓

Tyne & Wear

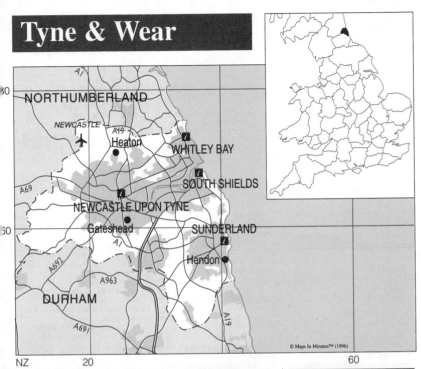

© Maps In Minutes™ (1996)

NZ   20   60

Tourist Information Centres

Central Library, Prince Consort Road, **Gateshead**, Tyne & Wear, NE8 4LN, 0191 477 3478.

Metrocentre Portcullis, 7 The Arcade, **Gateshead**, Tyne & Wear, NE11 9YL, 0191 460 6345.

Bede's World - The Museum, Church Bank, **Jarrow**, Tyne & Wear, NE32 3DY, 0191 489 2106.

Central Library, Princess Square, **Newcastle-upon-Tyne**, Tyne & Wear, NE99 1DX, 0191 261 0691.

Main Concourse, Central Station, **Newcastle-upon-Tyne**, NE1 5DL, 0191 230 0030.

Ferry Terminal, Tyne Commission Quay, **North Shields**, Tyne & Wear, NE29 6EN, 0191 257 9800 (Easter to Oct).

Museum & Art Gallery, Ocean Road, **South Shields**, Tyne & Wear, NE33 2HZ, 0191 454 6612.

Amphitheatre, Sea Road, **South Shields**, Tyne & Wear, NE33 2LD, 0191 455 7411 (Easter to Oct).

Unit 3, Crowtree Road, **Sunderland**, Tyne & Wear, SR1 3EL, 0191 553 2001.

Park Road, **Whitley Bay**, Tyne & Wear, NE26 1EJ, 0191 200 8535.

Newcastle Airport, **Woolsington**, Tyne & Wear, NE13 8BZ, 0191 214 4422.

Gateshead

NZ2561   🍺 *Nine Pins, The Victoria*

Cox Close House, Ravensworth, Gateshead, Tyne & Wear, NE11 0HQ.
Unique C16th. Secluded yet near city and tourist attractions. **Open:** All Year
0191 488 7827
johnpat@grayravensworth.freeserve.co.uk
D: £18.00–£22.00 **S:** £18.00–£22.00
Beds: 1F 1D 1T **Baths:** 1 En 1 Sh
🛉 🅿 ⊁ 📺 🛏 ✕ 🍽 🎦 🔥

Bellevue Guest House, 31-33 Belle Vue Bank, Low Fell, Gateshead, Tyne & Wear, NE9 6BQ.
Victorian terrace, centrally located for Metro Centre, Newcastle stadium, Beamish Museum. **Open:** All Year
0191 487 8805 Mr Wallace
D: £18.00–£20.00 **S:** £18.00–£28.00
Beds: 1F 1D 2T 2S **Baths:** 2 En 1 Sh
🛉 🅿 📺 ✕ 🍽 🎦 🔥 &

Hendon

NZ3956

Acorn Guest House, 10 Mowbray Road, Hendon, Sunderland, Tyne & Wear, SR2 8EN.
Situated near town centre Mowbray Park and all local amenities. **Open:** All Year
Grades: ETC 2 Diamond
0191 514 2170 A Morrison
theacornguesthouse@hotmail.com
D: £15.00 **S:** £16.00
Beds: 3F 5T 1D
🛉 🅿 (9) 📺 🛏 ✕ 🍽 🎦 🔥

Newcastle-upon-Tyne

NZ2564   🍺 *Prince of Wales*

Chirton House Hotel, 46 Clifton Road, Newcastle-upon-Tyne, NE4 6SH.
Victorian-style house, conviniently situated for city, airport, Northumberland and Durham. **Open:** All Year
0191 273 0407 (also fax) Mrs Turnbull
D: £18.00–£23.00 **S:** £26.00–£36.00
Beds: 3F 2D 3T 3S **Baths:** 6 En 5 Sh
🛉 🅿 📺 🛏 🍽 🎦 🔥

South Shields

NZ3666   🍺 *The Beacon, Harbour Lights, Sea Hotel*

Saraville Guest House, 103 Ocean Road, South Shields, Tyne & Wear, NE33 2JL.
Family-run & centrally located. Close to Metro **Open:** All Year
0191 454 1169 (also fax) Mrs Taylor
emma@saraville.freeserve.co.uk
D: fr £20.00 **S:** £25.00–£28.00
Beds: 1F 1D 1T 2S **Baths:** 3 En
🛉 (6) 🅿 ⊁ 📺 🎦 🔥

Marina Guest House, 32 Seaview Terrace, South Shields, Tyne & Wear, NE33 2NW.
Three storey Victorian house overlooking the park with panoramic sea views.
Open: All Year (not Xmas/New Year)
Grades: ETC 3 Diamond
0191 456 1998 Mrs Johnson
D: £19.00 **S:** £26.00
Beds: 2F 2T 2S **Baths:** 4 Pr 1 Sh
🛉 (3) ⊁ 📺 🍽 🎦 🔥

Dunlin Guest House, *11 Urfa Terrace, South Shields, Tyne & Wear, NE33 2ES.*
Friendly family run guest house in town centre/sea front area.
Open: All Year (not Xmas/New Year)
Grades: ETC 3 Diamond
0191 456 7442 Mrs Wilson
D: £16.00 **S:** £16.00–£23.00
Beds: 1F 2D 1T 2S **Baths:** 2 Sh
⌕ 🅿 (2) ⊬ 🖵 ⼍ ✕ ▥ ♥ ♨ ♿

Sea Crest Guest House, *34 Lawe Road, South Shields, Tyne & Wear, NE33 2EU.*
Centrally located, popular family run guest house overlooking paths and sea front.
Open: All Year
0191 427 1447 Mrs Stidolph
cat7781@hotmail.com
D: fr £17.00 **S:** fr £17.00
Beds: 3F 1T 2S 3D **Baths:** 2 Sh
⌕ 🅿 (2) ⊬ 🖵 ⼍ ▥ ♥ ♨

Sunderland

NZ3957

Braeside Guest House, *26 Western Hill, Beside University, Sunderland, Tyne & Wear, SR2 7PH.*
Open: Jan to Nov
Grades: ETC 2 Diamond
0191 565 4801 Fax: 0191 552 4198
george@the20thhole.co.uk
D: £15.00–£17.50 **S:** £18.00–£23.00
Beds: 2T 1D **Baths:** 1En 1Sh
⌕ (12) 🅿 🖵 ▥ ♨
Experience our unique theme rooms, hearty northern breakfasts. The delights of Sunderland indoor shopping mall, recently doubled in size and Northumbria's beautiful countryside. We arrange golf at the top courses and tennis coaching and matches at Puma international centre.

Whitley Bay

NZ3572 🍺 Berkeley Tavern, Fitzgeralds, The Station, The Avenue

Marlborough Hotel, *20-21 East Parade, Whitley Bay, NE26 1AP.*
Open: All Year (not Xmas)
Grades: ETC 4 Diamond, AA 4 Diamond
0191 251 3628 J A Thompson
Fax: 0191 252 5033
reception@marlborough-hotel.com
D: £28.00–£32.00 **S:** £22.00–£38.00
Beds: 4F 5D 3T 5S **Baths:** 14 En 1 Pr 2 Sh
⌕ (3) 🅿 (5) ⊬ 🖵 ✕ ▥ ♥ ♨ 3 **CC**
Traditional family hotel on the sea front overlooking the beach, about 5 minutes walk from the town centre and about 7 to 8 minutes walk from the Metro station. We have a 'no smoking' policy in all our bedrooms.

Metro Guest House, *26 Percy Road, Whitley Bay, NE26 2AX.*
Open: All Year
0191 253 0123 E Douglas
D: £14.00–£15.00 **S:** £14.00–£15.00
Beds: 2F 1T 2S **Baths:** 2 Sh
⌕ 🅿 (3) 🖵 ⼍ ✕ ▥ ♨
A comfortable and friendly guest house in the centre of Whitley Bay. Close to all amenities and sea front, adjacent to the Metro station for easy access to Newcastle, Eldon Square and the Metro Centre. Licensed.

Seacrest Hotel, *North Parade, Whitley Bay, NE26 1PA.*
Friendly family-run hotel, Restaurant & bar, 24 hour reception. **Open:** All Year
Grades: AA 2 Star, RAC 2 Star
0191 253 0140 (also fax)
karenmccallum@lbtclick.com
D: £27.50–£30.00 **S:** £30.00–£46.00
Beds: 4F 6D 3T 9S **Baths:** 22 En
⌕ 🅿 (4) ⊬ 🖵 ✕ ▥ ♥ ♨ **CC**

The Lindsay Guest House, *50 Victoria Avenue, Whitley Bay, Tyne & Wear, NE26 2BA.*
Small family-run guest house, overlooking tennis courts and bowling green.
Open: All Year
0191 252 7341 A Ward
Fax: 0191 257 0077
D: £20.00–£25.00 **S:** £25.00–£30.00
Beds: 4F 2D **Baths:** 4 En 2 Sh
⌕ 🅿 (3) 🖵 ⼍ ▥ ♨

The Ardrossan Guest House, *25 Oxford Street, Whitley Bay, Tyne & Wear, NE26 1AD.*
Open: All Year
0191 252 8628
A Middleton
D: fr £15.00
Beds: 1D 1T
🖵 ▥ ♨
Small guest house, conveniently situated, with a warm friendly atmosphere.

Cherrytree House, *35 Brook Street, Whitley Bay, Tyne & Wear, NE26 1AF.*
Edwardian town house near sea front in a quiet street.
Open: All Year
0191 251 4306 (also fax)
Mr Coleman
cherrytreehouse@cherrytreehouse.free-online.co.uk
D: £16.00–£22.00 **S:** £15.00–£35.00
Beds: 2D 1T 1S **Baths:** 3 En 1 Pr
⌕ 🅿 (1) 🖵 ⼍ ▥ ♨

National Grid References are for villages, towns and cities – not for individual houses

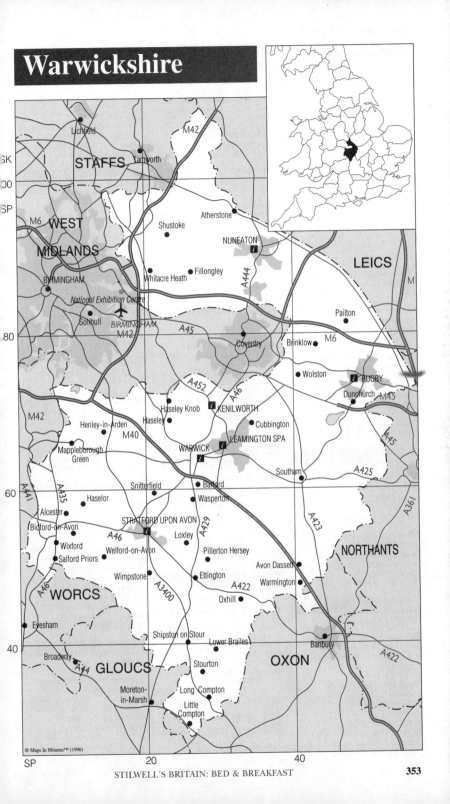

Warwickshire

© Maps In Minutes™ (1996)

Tourist Information Centres

The Library, 11 Smalley Place, **Kenilworth**, Warks, CV8 1QG, 01926 850708.

Jephson Lodge, Jephson Gardens, The Parade, **Leamington Spa**, Warks, CV32 4AB, 01926 311470.

Nuneaton Library, Church Street, **Nuneaton**, Warks, CV11 4DR, 01203 384027.

The Library, St Matthew's Street, **Rugby**, Warks, CV21 3BZ, 01788 534970.

Bridgefoot, **Stratford-upon-Avon**, Warks, CV37 6GW, 01789 293127.

The Court House, Jury Street, **Warwick**, Warks, CV34 4EW, 01926 492212.

Alcester

SP0857

Roebuck Inn, Birmingham Road, Alcester, Warks, B49 5QA.
Traditional country inn, non-smoking, restaurants, excellent food, beer, beds.
Open: All Year
01789 762410 Fax: 01789 765794
D: £22.50–£30.00 **S:** £35.00–£45.00
Beds: 1F 6D 4T **Baths:** 11 En
⏰ 🅿 ⅍ 📺 🐾 ✕ 🛏 Ⓥ ❋ 🍴 &

Atherstone

SP3197   ◗ Blue Lion, Red Lion

Abbey Farm, Merevale Lane, Atherstone, Warks, CV9 2LA.
Period farmhouse in attractive surroundings, by a lake, set in beautiful countryside.
Open: All Year (not Xmas)
01827 713119 Mrs Noble
merevale_abbey@msn.com
D: £20.00–£22.50 **S:** £22.50–£25.00
Beds: 2T **Baths:** 1 Sh
⏰ (8) 🅿 (3) ⅍ 📺 🛏 🍴

Avon Dassett

SP4150   ◗ Butchers' Arms, The Avon

Crandon House, Avon Dassett, Leamington Spa, Warks, CV33 0AA.
Luxury farmhouse accommodation, quiet location, superb views, extensive breakfast menu.
Open: All Year (not Xmas)
Grades: ETC 5 Diamond, Silver
01295 770652 Miss Lea
Fax: 01295 770632
crandonhouse@talk21.com
D: £20.00–£25.00 **S:** fr £30.00
Beds: 3D 2T **Baths:** 4 En 1 Pr
⏰ (8) 🅿 (8) 📺 🛏 🛍 Ⓥ 🍴 cc

Barford

SP2760   ◗ Granville Arms

Avonside Cottage, 1 High Street, Barford, Warwick, CV35 8BU.
C17th riverside cottage. Luxurious and spacious guest rooms. Delightful garden.
Open: All Year (not Xmas)
Grades: ETC 5 Diamond, Gold
01926 624779 D: £23.00–£27.00
Beds: 1D 1T **Baths:** 2 En
🅿 (4) ⅍ 📺 🛍 Ⓥ 🍴

Bidford-on-Avon

SP0952   ◗ Frog & Bullrush, Bull's Head

Fosbroke House, 4 High Street, Bidford-on-Avon, Alcester, Warks, B50 4BU.
Welcoming period house close to riverside walks and country pubs.
Open: Feb to Dec
Grades: ETC 4 Diamond
01789 772327 Mr & Mrs Newbury
D: £20.00–£25.00 **S:** £25.00–£30.00
Beds: 1F 2D 1T 1S **Baths:** 5 En
⏰ 🅿 (8) 📺 🐾 🛍 Ⓥ 🍴

Brinklow

SP4379

The White Lion, Broad Street, Brinklow, Rugby, Warks, CV23 0LN.
A warm welcome awaits you at our traditional country inn.
Open: All Year (not Xmas)
Grades: ETC 3 Diamond
01788 832579 Mr Yeend
brinklowlion@supanet.com
D: fr £20.00 **S:** fr £25.00
Beds: 1D 3T **Baths:** 4 En
⏰ 🅿 📺 ✕ 🛍 🍴 & ⅃

Cubbington

SP3468   ◗ King's Head

Bakers Cottage, 52/54 Queen Street, Cubbington, Leamington Spa, CV32 7NA.
C17th cottage. Ideal sightseeing base for Leamington Spa, Warwick, Stratford.
Open: All Year
Grades: ETC 4 Diamond
01926 772146 E Soden
D: £20.00–£23.00 **S:** £20.00–£25.00
Beds: 3T **Baths:** 2 En 1 Pr
⏰ 🅿 (4) ⅍ 📺 🐾 🛍 Ⓥ 🍴

Dunchurch

SP4871   ◗ Dun Cow

Toft Hill, Dunchurch, Rugby, Warks, CV22 6NR.
Country house situated on outskirts of picturesque village of Dunchurch.
Open: All Year **Grades:** ETC 4 Diamond
01788 810342 Mary Wells
D: £20.00 **S:** £20.00
Beds: 1F 1D 1S **Baths:** 1 Pr 1 Sh
⏰ 🅿 📺 🐾 🛍 🍴

All details shown are as supplied by B&B owners in Autumn 2000

Village Green Hotel, The Green, Dunchurch, Rugby, CV22 6NX.
Lovely, fully refurbished hotel. Historic, picturesque, award-winning old coaching village.
Open: All Year
01788 813434 Mrs Twigger
Fax: 01788 814714
villagegreenhotel.rugby@btinternet.com
D: £24.50–£35.00 **S:** £39.00–£54.00
Beds: 5D 1T 4S **Baths:** 10 En
⏰ 🅿 ⅍ 📺 🛍 Ⓥ 🍴 cc

Ettington

SP2648   ◗ Hounds Hill, The Bell, White Horse, Chequers Inn

Thornton Manor, Ettington, Stratford upon Avon, Warks, CV37 7PN.
Friendly welcome to working farm in quiet relaxing C16th home.
Open: Easter to Dec
01789 740210 Mrs Hutsby
D: £21.00–£25.00 **S:** £25.00–£30.00
Beds: 2D 1T **Baths:** 2 En 1 Pr
⏰ (5) 🅿 (4) ⅍ 📺 🛍 🍴

The Leys, 64 Banbury Road, Ettington, Stratford-upon-Avon, Warks, CV37 7SU.
Open: All Year (not Xmas/New Year)
01789 740365 (also fax)
Mrs Brewer
bobbrewer@beeb.net
D: £18.00–£20.00 **S:** £20.00–£25.00
Beds: 1D 1T **Baths:** 2 Pr
⏰ (10) 🅿 (2) ⅍ 📺 🛍 Ⓥ 🍴
Comfortable stylish family village home tastefully decorated. Guests bedrooms each have a private bathroom and overlook open farmland with distant countryside views. Excellent full English breakfast. ETC's 'Welcome Host'. Close to Chase Conference Centre, Stratford, Warwick Castle and Cotswolds.

Fillongley

SP2887   ◗ Manor House, Saracen's Head, Cottage Inn, Horse & Jockey, Weavers' Arms

Bourne Brooke Lodge, Mill Lane, Fillongley, Coventry, W Mids, CV7 8EE.
Peace and tranquillity, high standards of comfort and cleanliness, no smoking
Open: All Year
Grades: ETC 4 Diamond
01676 541898 (also fax)
Mrs Chamberlain
D: £20.00–£25.00 **S:** £20.00–£30.00
Beds: 1D 2T 1S **Baths:** 3 En
🅿 (6) ⅍ 📺 🛍 ❋ 🍴

Haseley

SP2268   ◗ Falcon Inn

Shrewley Pools Farm, Haseley, Warwick, CV35 7HB.
Glorious early C17th Listed farmhouse, beautiful 1 acre gardens. Working farm.
Open: All Year (not Xmas)
01926 484315 Mrs Dodd
D: £22.50–£30.00 **S:** £30.00–£35.00
Beds: 1F 1T **Baths:** 2 En
⏰ 🅿 (6) ⅍ 📺 ✕ Ⓥ 🍴

Haseley Knob

SP2371 ☖ *Fen End, The Falcon*

Croft Guest House, *The Croft, Haseley Knob, Warwick, CV35 7NL.*
Friendly family country guest house. Near Warwick, Coventry, Stratford, NEC/NAC.
Open: All Year (not Xmas)
Grades: ETC 4 Diamond, AA 4 Diamond, RAC 4 Diamond
01926 484447 (also fax)
Mr & Mrs Clapp
david@croftguesthouse.co.uk
D: £23.00–£25.00 **S:** £34.00
Beds: 2F 3D 3T 1S **Baths:** 7 En 2 Pr
☖ 🅿 (8) ⅍ 📺 🍴 📖 🎇 🍵 cc

Haselor

SP1257 ☖ *King's Head*

Walcote Farm, *Walcote, Haselor, Alcester, Warks, B49 6LY.*
Easy to find, our beautiful C16th listed oak-beamed farmhouse with inglenook firelaces.
Open: All Year (not Xmas)
01789 488264 (also fax)
Mr & Mrs Finnemore
john_finnemore@compuserve.com
D: £20.00–£23.00 **S:** £25.00–£30.00
Beds: 2D 1T **Baths:** 3 En
☖ 🅿 (6) ⅍ 📺 📖 🍵 🎇

Henley-in-Arden

SP1566 ☖ *Black Swan*

Holland Park Farm, *Buckley Green, Henley-in-Arden, Solihull, W Mids, B95 5QF.*
Open: All Year
01564 792625 (also fax)
Mrs Connolly
D: £22.00–£25.00 **S:** £25.00–£30.00
Beds: 2F **Baths:** 2 En
☖ 🅿 (4) 📺 🍴 📖 🍵 🎇
A Georgian style house set in centre of peaceful Farmland including the historic grounds of the mount and other interesting walks ideally situated in Shakespeare's country convenient to airport NEC NAC and Cotswolds closed on Christmas day H of E 3 stars.

Kenilworth

SP2872 ☖ *Clarendon Arms, The Anchor, Green Man*

Hollyhurst Guest House, *47 Priory Road, Kenilworth, Warks, CV8 1LL.*
Friendly, relaxed atmosphere in comfortable Victorian town house near centre.
Open: All Year (not Xmas)
Grades: AA 3 Diamond
01926 853882 Mr & Mrs Wheat
Fax: 01926 855211
admin@hollyhurstguesthouse.co.uk
D: £20.00–£22.50 **S:** £25.00–£30.00
Beds: 1F 2D 4T 1S **Baths:** 3 Pr 2 Sh
☖ 🅿 (9) ⅍ 📺 📖 🎇

Please respect a B&B's wishes regarding children, animals and smoking

Abbey Guest House, *41 Station Road, Kenilworth, Warks, CV8 1JD.*
Comfortable Victorian house, well equipped bedrooms, close to town centre.
Open: All Year (not Xmas)
Grades: ETC 4 Diamond
01926 512707 Mrs Jefferies
the-abbey@virgin.net
D: £22.50 **S:** £26.00
Beds: 3D 2T 2S **Baths:** 6 En 1 Pr
☖ 🅿 (2) ⅍ 📺 📖 🍵 🎇

The Cottage Inn, *36 Stoneleigh Road, Kenilworth, Warks, CV8 2GD.*
Friendly family-run free house - great traditional ales & fine wines. Real home-cooked specials.
Open: All Year
Grades: ETC 3 Diamond
01926 853900 Mr & Mrs English
Fax: 01926 856032
D: £18.00–£25.00 **S:** £30.00
Beds: 4D 2T **Baths:** 6 En
☖ 🅿 (20) 📺 📖 🍵 🎇 cc

Banner Hill Farm, *Rouncil Lane, Kenilworth, Warks, CV8 1NN.*
Homely Georgian farmhouse. Middle of nowhere. No distance from anywhere.
Open: All Year (not Xmas)
01926 852850 Mr Snelson
D: £16.00–£20.00 **S:** £16.00–£25.00
Beds: 1F 1D 2T 2S **Baths:** 3 En 1 Pr 2 Sh
☖ 🅿 (8) ⅍ 📺 🍴 ✗ 📖 🍵 🎇

Enderley Guest House, *20 Queens Road, Kenilworth, Warwickshire, CV8 1JQ.*
Friendly, homely, family run guest house close to town centre.
Open: All Year
Grades: ETC 4 Diamond
01926 855388
D: £22.00–£30.00 **S:** £27.00–£30.00
Beds: 1F 1T 2D 1S **Baths:** 5 En
🅿 (2) ⅍ 📺 📖 🍵 🎇

Victoria Lodge Hotel, *180 Warwick Road, Kenilworth, Warks, CV8 1HU.*
Built in 1850, completely refurbished, luxury accommodation, beautiful Victorian wall garden.
Open: All Year (not Xmas)
Grades: ETC 4 Diamond, AA 4 Diamond
01926 512020 Mr Woolcock
Fax: 01926 858703
info@victorialodgehotel.co.uk
D: fr £29.50 **S:** £40.00–£46.00
Beds: 6D 2T 1S **Baths:** 9 En
☖ (14) 🅿 (10) ⅍ 📺 📖 🎇 cc

Castle Laurels Hotel, *22 Castle Road, Kenilworth, Warks, CV8 1NG.*
Beautiful Victorian house opposite the castle in Kenilworth old town.
Open: All Year (not Xmas)
Grades: ETC 4 Diamond Sliver Award, AA 4 Diamond
01926 856179 N C Moore
Fax: 01926 854954
moores22@aol.com
D: £28.50 **S:** £36.00–£45.00
Beds: 5D 3T 3S **Baths:** 11 En
☖ 🅿 (12) ⅍ 📺 📖 🍵 🎇 cc

Howden House, *170 Warwick Road, Kenilworth, CV8 1HS.*
Comfortable home conveniently located for Warwick University, NAC, NEC, Airports.
Open: All Year (not Xmas)
Grades: ETC 2 Diamond
01926 850310 D: £18.00 **S:** £20.00
Beds: 1D 1T 2S
☖ 🅿 (1) ⅍ 📺 📖 🍵 🎇 🎇

The Quince House, *29 Moseley Road, Kenilworth, CV8 2AR.*
Comfortable accommodation close to NEC, 5 mins from NAC/M40.
Open: All Year
Grades: ETC 4 Diamond
01926 858652 Mrs Thomas
gomers@netlineuk.net
D: £22.00–£25.00 **S:** £25.00
Beds: 2T **Baths:** 2 En 1 Sh
☖ 🅿 (3) ⅍ 📺 🍴 📖 🍵 🎇

Ferndale Guest House, *45 Priory Road, Kenilworth, Warks, CV8 1LL.*
Delightfully furnished family-run guest house; all rooms en suite.
Open: All Year
01926 853214 Fax: 01926 858336
D: £20.00 **S:** £26.00–£30.00
Beds: 2F 2D 2T 2S **Baths:** 8 En
🅿 (7) ⅍ 📺 📖 🍵 cc

Leamington Spa

SP3165 ☖ *White Lion, King's Head, Rugby Tavern*

Hedley Villa Guest House, *31 Russell Terrace, Leamington Spa, Warks, CV31 1EZ.*
Friendly house within walking distance of railway station and town.
Open: All Year
Grades: ETC 3 Diamond
01926 424504 Mr Tocker & Mrs P Ashfield
Fax: 01926 745801
D: £19.00–£25.00 **S:** £25.00–£30.00
Beds: 2F 1T 1D 3S **Baths:** 1 En 4 Sh
☖ 📺 🍴 ✗ 📖 🍵 🎇 🎇

11 St Andrews Road, *Leamington Spa, Warks, CV32 7EU.*
Relax and enjoy our peaceful home. Special welcome. Delicious food.
Open: All Year (not Xmas)
01926 428864 Mrs Poultney
D: £15.00–£18.00
Beds: 1D 1T **Baths:** 1 En 1 Sh
🅿 (1) ⅍ 📺 ✗ 📖 🍵 🎇

Charnwood Guest House, *47 Avenue Road, Leamington Spa, Warks, CV31 3PF.*
Comfortable, informal atmosphere, close to town centre, also Warwick Castle.
Open: All Year (not Xmas)
Grades: ETC 3 Diamond
01926 831074 (also fax)
Mr Booth
D: £17.00–£18.00 **S:** £17.00–£25.00
Beds: 1F 2D 2T 1S **Baths:** 2 En 2 Sh
☖ 🅿 (6) 📺 🍴 ✗ 📖 🍵 🎇 cc

Milverton House Hotel, *1 Milverton Terrace, Leamington Spa, CV32 5BE.*
Attractive Victorian property within 5 mins walk of town centre.
Open: All Year
Grades: ETC 4 Diamond, AA 4 Diamond
01926 428335 (also fax)
D: £24.00–£30.00 **S:** £24.00–£45.00
Beds: 1F 5D 2T 2S **Baths:** 7 En 3 Sh
📺 (5) 🅿 (6) 📺 🍴 ⷠ ⯑ CC

Corkill, *27 Newbold Street, Leamington Spa, CV32 4HN.*
Regency town centre house. Quiet location, convenient for all facilities.
Open: All Year (not Xmas)
Grades: ETC 3 Diamond
01926 336303 Mrs Corkill
mrscorkill@aol.com
D: £20.00–£25.00 **S:** £25.00–£35.00
Beds: 1F 1D 1T **Baths:** 3 En
🅿 (2) ⯑ 📺 ⷠ 📺 ⯑

Eaton Court Hotel, *1-7 St Marks Road, Leamington Spa, Warks, CV32 6DL.*
Family owned hotel, excellent licensed restaurant. Close to Warwick Castle.
Open: All Year (not Xmas/New Year)
Grades: ETC 3 Star
01926 885848 (also fax)
Mr Gregory
info@eatoncourt.co.uk
D: £30.00–£40.00 **S:** £40.00–£60.00
Beds: 4F 12D 12T 8S **Baths:** 36 En
📺 🅿 (36) ⯑ 📺 🍴 ✕ 📺 ⯑ CC

Little Compton

SP2630   🍴 *Red Lion*

Rigside, *Little Compton, Moreton-in-Marsh, Glos, GL56 0RR.*
Lovely landscaped gardens backing onto farmland.
Open: All Year
Grades: AA 4 Diamond
01608 674128 (also fax) Ms Cox
rigside@lineone.net
D: £22.00–£23.00 **S:** £20.00–£22.00
Beds: 2D 1S 1T **Baths:** 2 En 1 Sh
📺 (9) 🅿 (6) 📺 📺 ⯑

Long Compton

SP2832

Tallet Barn, *Yerdley Farm, Long Compton, Shipston-on-Stour, Warks, CV36 5LH.*
Comfortable annexed rooms, a warm welcome and a quiet village location.
Open: All Year
Grades: ETC 4 Diamond
01608 684248 Mrs Richardson
Fax: 01068 684248
D: £20.00–£21.00 **S:** £25.00
Beds: 1D 1T **Baths:** 2 En
📺 (6) 🅿 (2) ⯑ 📺 ⯑ ⯑

Planning a longer stay? Always ask for any special rates

Lower Brailes

SP3139   🍴 *George Hotel, Gate Inn, Peacock*

The George Hotel, *High Street, Lower Brailes, Banbury, Oxon, OX15 5NU.*
Open: All Year
01608 685223 Fax: 01608 685916
D: £25.00–£60.00 **S:** £25.00–£60.00
Beds: 1F 8T 1D 1S **Baths:** 1 En 9 Pr 1 Sh
📺 (1) 🅿 (80) ⯑ 📺 🍴 ✕ ⯑ 📺 ⯑ ✳ ⯑ CC
A C12th inn, good, friendly public bar, large gardens with 'undercover' outside eating area. On Cotswolds near Stratford-on-Avon (14 miles). Well-kept local, off-road footways. Good centre to visit entire Cotswold area.

New House Farm, *Lower Brailes, Banbury, Oxon, OX15 5AD.*
New House farm is set between two villages in outstanding area of beauty.
Open: All Year (not Xmas)
Grades: AA 4 Diamond
01608 686239 Ms Taylor
Fax: 01608 686455
helen@brailes88.fsnet.co.uk
D: £18.00–£20.00 **S:** £20.00–£25.00
Beds: 2D 1T **Baths:** 2 En 1 Pr
📺 🅿 (10) 📺 🍴 ⯑ 📺 ⯑

Loxley

SP2552   🍴 *Fox Inn*

Elm Cottage, *Stratford Road, Loxley, Warks, CV35 9JW.*
Private house in open countryside. Stratford-upon-Avon 3 miles.
Open: All Year (not Xmas)
Grades: ETC 4 Diamond
01789 840609 Mrs Brocklehurst
D: £21.00 **S:** £25.00
Beds: 1D 1T 1S **Baths:** 1 Sh
📺 (10) 🅿 (6) ⯑ ⯑ ⯑

Mappleborough Green

SP0765   🍴 *The Dog*

The Woodlands, *Birmingham Road, Mappleborough Green, Studley, Warwickshire, B80 7DE.*
Comfortable family home, M42 4 miles. Convenient NEC and Shakespeare Country.
Open: All Year (not Xmas/New Year)
01527 852293 Mrs Johnson
Fax: 01527 852001
djohn2693@aol.com
D: £25.00 **S:** £25.00
Beds: 1T 1D **Baths:** 1 En 1 Pr
📺 (12) 🅿 (8) ⯑ 📺 📺 ⯑

Nuneaton

SP3691

La Tavola Calda, *68 & 70 Midland Road, Nuneaton, Warks, CV11 5DY.*
A family-run Italian restaurant and hotel. Handy for M69 - M6.
Open: All Year (not Xmas/New Year)
Grades: ETC 2 Diamond
024 7638 1303 Mr Emanuele
Fax: 024 7638 1816
D: £32.00–£35.00 **S:** £20.00–£25.00
Beds: 2F 5T 1S **Baths:** 8 En
📺 (5) 🅿 📺 ✕ 📺 ⯑ CC

Oxhill

SP3145   🍴 *Royal Oak*

Nolands Farm, *Oxhill, Warwick, CV35 0RJ.*
Situated in tranquil valley, annexed bedrooms, some ground floor, romantic four posters.
Open: All Year (not Xmas)
01926 640309 Mrs Hutsby
Fax: 01926 641662
nolandsfm@compuserve.com
D: £18.00–£24.00 **S:** £25.00–£40.00
Beds: 1F 6D 1S **Baths:** 10 En
📺 (7) 🅿 (10) ⯑ 📺 ✕ 📺 ⯑ CC

Pailton

SP4781   🍴 *White Lion*

White Lion Inn, *Coventry Road, Pailton, Rugby, Warks, CV23 0QD.*
C17th coaching inn recently modernised retaining all the olde world atmosphere.
Open: All Year
Grades: ETC 3 Diamond
01788 832359 (also fax)
Mr Brindley
D: £19.50–£24.50 **S:** £21.00–£31.00
Beds: 9D **Baths:** 5 En 2 Sh
📺 🅿 (60) ⯑ 📺 🍴 ✕ 📺 ⯑ ⯑ ⯑ CC

Pillerton Hersey

SP2948   🍴 *Royal Oak*

Docker's Barn Farm, *Oxhill Bridle Road, Pillerton Hersey, Warwick, CV35 0QB.*
Idyllically situated barn conversion surrounded by its own land.
Open: All Year (not Xmas)
01926 640475 Ms Howard
Fax: 01926 641747
jwhoward@cwcom.net
D: £21.00–£25.00 **S:** £28.00–£38.00
Beds: 1F 2D **Baths:** 3 En
📺 (8) 🅿 (6) ⯑ 📺 🍴 📺 ⯑ ⯑ ⯑

Rugby

SP5075   🍴 *Sheaf & Sickle, The Bull, Old Smithy*

Manor Farm, *Buckwell Lane, Clifton-upon-Dunsmore, Rugby, Warks, CV23 0BJ.*
Converted barn on working farm. Courtyard garden and patio area.
Open: All Year
01788 544016 (also fax)
Mrs Walters
D: £45.00–£50.00 **S:** £25.00–£30.00
Beds: 1D 1T 2S **Baths:** 4 En
📺 (12) 🅿 (6) ⯑ 📺 📺 ⯑

RATES

D = Price range per person sharing in a double room
S = Price range for a single room

BEDROOMS

F - Family
D - Double
T - Twin
S - Single

Lawford Hill Farm, *Lawford Heath Lane, Rugby, Warks, CV23 9HG.*
Come and relax in our spacious Georgian farmhouse & converted stables in a picturesque garden.
Open: All Year (not Xmas)
01788 542001 Mr & Mrs Moses
Fax: 01788 537880
lawford.hill@talk21.com
D: £22.00–£24.00 **S:** £26.00–£27.00
Beds: 3D 2T 1S **Baths:** 3 En 2 Sh
🛇 🅿 (12) 🛇 📺 🏃 🛒 ♨

Salford Priors

SP0751 🍺 *Blossom Valley Inn*

Orchard House, *Salford Priors, Evesham, Worcestershire, WR11 5UX.*
Ideally located for visiting Stratford-upon-Avon and Broadway. Overlooking C12th Norman village church.
Open: All Year
01789 773476 Ms Page
D: fr £17.50 **S:** fr £35.00
Beds: 2F 1D **Baths:** 3 Sh
🛇 (10) 🅿 (10) 🛇 📺 ♨

Shipston on Stour

SP2540 🍺 *The Horseshoe*

Shipston Guest House, *42 Church Street, Shipston-on-Stour, Warks, CV36 4AS.*
Charming C17th cottage in delightful country town of Shipston on Stour.
Open: All Year (not Xmas)
01608 661002 Mrs Roberts
Fax: 01608 664008
petelain@aol.com
D: £19.00 **S:** £35.00
Beds: 1F 1D 1T **Baths:** 2 En 1 Pr
🛇 🅿 (3) 🛇 📺 🏃 🛒 🍴 ♨ ♿

Shustoke

SP2290 🍺 *The Plough*

The Old Vicarage, *Shustoke, Coleshill, Birmingham, Warks, B46 2LA.*
Business at the NEC Birmingham, airport, walking the Heart of England Way.
Open: All Year (not Xmas)
01675 481331 (also fax)
Mrs Hawkins
D: £20.00 **S:** £20.00–£22.00
Beds: 3D **Baths:** 2 Sh
🛇 🅿 (6) 📺 ✕ 🛒 🍴 ♨

Snitterfield

SP2159 🍺 *Snitterfield Arms*

The Hill Cottage, *Kings Lane, Snitterfield, Stratford upon Avon, Warks, CV37 0QA.*
Country house in 1.5 acres and bluebell wood. Glorious views to Stratford (3 miles).
Open: All Year (not Xmas)
01789 731830 Mrs Waldron
Fax: 01789 730288
hilcott_bb@hotmail.com
D: £24.00–£25.00 **S:** fr £28.00
Beds: 1D 1T 1S **Baths:** 1 En 1 Sh
🛇 🅿 (4) 🛒 ♨

Southam

SP4162 🍺 *Old Mint, Bowling Green*

Briarwood, *34 Warwick Road, Southam, Leamington Spa, Warwickshire, CV47 0HN.*
Edwardian house on the outskirts of a small market town.
Open: All Year (not Xmas)
Grades: ETC 3 Diamond
01926 814756 Mrs Bishop
D: £20.00–£25.00 **S:** £20.00–£30.00
Beds: 1D 1S **Baths:** 2 En
🅿 (1) 🛇 📺 🛒 ♨

Stourton

SP2937 🍺 *Cherrington Arms*

Brook House, *Stourton, Shipston-on-Stour, Warwickshire, CV36 5HQ.*
Lovely old house, edge pretty Cotswold village. Ideal touring Stratford, Oxford, Cotswolds.
Open: All Year (not Xmas/New Year)
01608 686281 Mrs McDonald
graemedonald@msn.com
D: £22.00–£23.00 **S:** £27.00–£30.00
Beds: 1F 1D **Baths:** 1 En 1 Pr
🛇 (7) 🅿 (4) 📺 🛒 ♨

Stratford-upon-Avon

SP1955 🍺 *The Tramway, Old Thatch, Dirty Duck, The Lamplighter, The Garrick, Black Swan, Edward Moon, Salmon Tail*

Penshurst, *34 Evesham Place, Stratford-upon-Avon, Warks, CV37 6HT.*
Open: All Year
Grades: ETC 3 Diamond
01789 205259 Mrs Cauvin
Fax: 01789 295322
penshurst@cwcom.net
D: £15.00–£23.00 **S:** £17.00–£22.00
Beds: 2F 3D 1T 2S **Baths:** 4 En 1 Pr 3 Sh
🛇 📺 🛒 ♨ ♿ 2
A prettily refurbished Victorian town house 5 minutes' walk from centre. Totally non-smoking. Delicious breakfasts, either English or Continental, served from 7.00 am right up until 10.30 am. Excellent value for money. Brochure available.

Stretton House, *38 Grove Road, Stratford-upon-Avon, Warks, CV37 6PB.*
Open: All Year (not Xmas)
Grades: ETC 3 Diamond, AA 3 Diamond
01789 268647 (also fax) Mr Machin
skyblues@strettonhouse.co.uk
D: £15.00–£28.00 **S:** £22.00–£40.00
Beds: 1F 2D 3T 1S **Baths:** 4 En
🛇 (8) 🅿 (6) 🛇 📺 🏃 🛒 ♨ ♿
We've got a home from home where a warm and friendly welcome awaits you from Michael and Yvonne. Comfortable accommodation at reasonable prices. Ensuite and standard rooms. Best B&B Recommended, Stratford in Bloom Guest House 1997/98. Just 3 minutes' walk to town centre.

B&B owners may vary rates - be sure to check when booking

Minola Guest House, *25 Evesham Place, Stratford-upon-Avon, Warks, CV37 6HT.*
Open: All Year (not Xmas)
Grades: ETC 3 Diamond
01789 293573 Mr & Mrs Castelli
Fax: 01789 551625
D: £22.00–£25.00 **S:** £22.00–£35.00
Beds: 2D 1T 2S **Baths:** 4 Pr 1 Sh
🛇 🅿 (2) 🛇 📺 🛒 ♨
'Minola' is situated in the old town of Stratford, the theatres, being a major attraction, are within easy walking distance as is the town centre and the railway station. 'Minola' is a stopping point for the 'open air bus tour'.

Linhill Guest House, *35 Evesham Place, Stratford-upon-Avon, Warks, CV37 6HT.*
Open: All Year
Grades: ETC 3 Diamond
01789 292879 Ms Tallis
Fax: 01789 299691
linhill@free4all.co.uk
D: £15.00–£25.00 **S:** £15.00–£25.00
Beds: 2F 4D 4T 1S **Baths:** 3 En
🛇 🅿 🛇 ✕ 🛒 📺 ♨ ♿
A family run Victorian guest house situated 5 minutes from town centre. Choice of breakfasts excellent home cooked evening meals, baby-sitting at no extra cost.

Clomendy, *10 Broad Walk, Stratford-upon-Avon, Warwickshire, CV37 6HS.*
Small Victorian house, central, Rail/coach Guests met, Non smoking.
Open: All Year (not Xmas/New Year)
Grades: ETC 4 Diamond
01789 266957 Mr Jones
D: £20.00–£23.00 **S:** £30.00
Beds: 1T 1D 1S **Baths:** 2 En 1 Pr
🛇 (5) 🅿 (1) 🛇 📺 🛒 📺 ♨

Faviere, *127 Shipston Road, Stratford-upon-Avon, Warks, CV37 7LW.*
A ten minute walk will bring you to the Theatres and Town centre.
Open: All Year
Grades: ETC 4 Diamond
01789 293764 Mr & Mrs Martinez
Fax: 01789 269365
guestsfaviere@cwcom.net
D: £17.00–£24.00 **S:** £20.00–£25.00
Beds: 1F 1D/1T 1S **Baths:** 3 En 1 Pr
🛇 (0) 🅿 (5) 🛇 📺 🛒 📺 ♨

Broadlands Guest House, *23 Evesham Place, Stratford-upon-Avon, Warks, CV37 6HT.*
Relaxed and friendly atmosphere five minutes to town centre.
Open: All Year (not Xmas)
Grades: ETC 3 Diamond
01789 299181 Mr P Gray & Mr J L Worboys
Fax: 01789 551382
broadlands.com@virgin.net
D: £16.00–£28.00 **S:** £16.00–£28.00
Beds: 3D 1T 1S **Baths:** 5 En
🛇 (10) 🅿 (5) 📺 🛒 ♨

Planning a longer stay? Always ask for any special rates

Hampton Lodge, *38 Shipston Road, Stratford-upon-Avon, Warwickshire, CV37 7LP.*
Just minutes from RSC theatre - your ideal base in Stratford.
Open: All Year (not Xmas/New Year)
Grades: RAC 4 Diamond
01789 299374 (also fax)
Mr Brewerton
hamptonlodge@aol.com
D: £23.00–£30.00 **S:** £35.00–£45.00
Beds: 2F 5D **Baths:** 7 En
ⓢ ₽ (9) ⅍ ⓣⓥ ✕ ▥ Ⓥ ᵻ Ⓖ cc

The Dylan Guest House, *10 Evesham Place, Stratford-upon-Avon, Warks, CV37 6HT.*
Charming Victorian house, 5 minutes town centre, theatre and river.
Open: All Year (not Xmas)
Grades: ETC 3 Diamond, AA 3 Diamond
01789 204819 Mr Elmy
elmy@lineone.net
D: £23.00–£25.00 **S:** £24.00–£26.00
Beds: 1F 3D 1T 1S **Baths:** 5 En
ⓢ (5) ₽ (5) ⅍ ⓣⓥ ↑ ▥ Ⓥ ᵻ Ⓖ

Nandos, *18-19 Evesham Place, Stratford-upon-Avon, Warks, CV37 6HT.*
Close to Stratford Town Centre, Attractions and Theatre and Cotswolds.
Open: All Year
Grades: ETC 3 Diamond RAC 2 Diamond
01789 204907
Mrs Morris
D: £18.00–£24.00 **S:** £18.00–£40.00
Beds: 3F 13D 4T 3S **Baths:** 17 En 3 Sh
ⓢ ₽ (8) ⅍ ⓣⓥ ↑ ▥ Ⓥ ᵻ Ⓖ cc

Arrandale Guest House, *208 Evesham Road, Stratford-upon-Avon, Warks, CV37 9AS.*
Comfortable, double-glazed, family run. 15 min walk Shakespearean properties.
Open: All Year (not Xmas)
Grades: ETC 3 Diamond
01789 267112 Mrs Mellor
christopher@arrandale208.freeserve.co.uk
D: £15.50–£18.00 **S:** £25.00–£30.00
Beds: 2D 1T **Baths:** 2 En 1 Sh
₽ (3) ⓣⓥ ↑ ✕ ▥ ᵻ Ⓖ cc

Curtain Call, *142 Alcester Road, Stratford-upon-Avon, Warwickshire, CV37 9DR.*
Warm and welcoming. Ideal for town centre and Shakespeare houses.
Open: All Year
Grades: ETC 3 Diamond, AA 3 Diamond, RAC 3 Diamond
01789 267734 (also fax) J Purlan
curtaincall@btinternet.com
D: £20.00–£30.00 **S:** £20.00–£30.00
Beds: 1F 2D 1T 2S **Baths:** 4 En 1 Sh
ⓢ ₽ (6) ⅍ ⓣⓥ ✕ ▥ Ⓥ ᵻ Ⓖ cc

Hunters Moon Guest House, *150 Alcester Road, Stratford-upon-Avon, Warks, CV37 9DR.*
Modern, detached, run by Stratfordians.
Open: All Year (not Xmas)
Grades: AA 3 Diamond
01789 292888 (also fax) Mrs Austin
thehuntersmoon@compuserve.com
D: fr £18.00 **S:** fr £20.00
Beds: 2F 2D 1T 2S **Baths:** 7 Pr
ⓢ (2) ₽ (6) ⅍ ⓣⓥ ▥ ᵻ

Midway Guest House, *182 Evesham Road, Stratford-upon-Avon, Warks, CV37 9BS.*
Traditional, comfortable, nicely located for all attractions, town centre, race course.
Open: All Year (not Xmas/New Year)
Grades: ETC 4 Diamond
01789 204154 Mr Cornwell
D: £20.00–£23.00 **S:** £35.00–£40.00
Beds: 3D **Baths:** 3 En
ⓢ (7) ₽ (3) ⓣⓥ ▥ ᵻ

Parkfield Guest House, *3 Broad Walk, Stratford-upon-Avon, Warks, CV37 6HS.*
Elegant Victorian house, quiet central location. Wide breakfast choice.
Open: All Year
01789 293313 Mr Pettitt
parkfield@btinternet.com
D: £21.00–£23.00 **S:** £22.00–£23.00
Beds: 1F 4D 1T 1S **Baths:** 6 En 1 Pr
ⓢ (5) ₽ (7) ⅍ ⓣⓥ ▥ Ⓥ ᵻ cc

Hardwick House, *1 Avenue Road, Stratford-upon-Avon, Warks, CV37 6UY.*
Impressive Victorian building. Lovely quiet area.
Open: All Year
01789 204307 Mrs Wootton
Fax: 01789 296760
hardwick@waverider.co.uk
D: £20.00–£29.00 **S:** £32.00–£38.00
Beds: 2F 8D 2T 2S **Baths:** 14 En
ⓢ ₽ (10) ⅍ ⓣⓥ ▥ Ⓥ ᵻ cc

Courtland Hotel, *12 Guild Street, Stratford-upon-Avon, Warks, CV37 6RE.*
Large comfortable Georgian house, town centre, antique furniture, home preserves.
Open: All Year (not Xmas)
01789 292401 (also fax)
Mrs Johnson
bridget.johnson4@virgin.net
D: £20.00–£30.00 **S:** £25.00–£40.00
Beds: 2F 1D 2T 2S **Baths:** 3 En 2 Sh
ⓢ ₽ (3) ⓣⓥ ▥ Ⓥ

Acer House, *44 Albany Road, Stratford-upon-Avon, Warks, CV37 6PQ.*
Quality accommodation, quiet, near town centre, rooms overlook pleasant garden.
Open: All Year (not Xmas)
01789 204962 Mrs Hall
D: £16.00–£18.00 **S:** £17.00–£18.00
Beds: 1T 1S **Baths:** 1 Sh
ⓢ (4) ⅍ ⓣⓥ ▥ Ⓥ ᵻ

Green Haven, *217 Evesham Road, Stratford-upon-Avon, Warks, CV37 9AS.*
A home away from home & value for money.
Open: All Year (not Xmas)
01789 297874 Mr & Mrs Learmount
greenhaven@travelink.com
D: £18.00–£24.00 **S:** £20.00–£40.00
Beds: 1F 2D 2T **Baths:** 5 En
ⓢ ₽ (6) ⅍ ⓣⓥ ↑ ✕ ▥ Ⓥ ᵻ Ⓖ

BATHROOMS

Pr - Private

Sh - Shared

En - Ensuite

SP4147   ◀ *The Plough*

The Old Rectory, *Warmington, Banbury, Oxfordshire, OX17 1BU.*
Open: All Year (not Xmas)
01295 690531 Mrs Cockcroft
Fax: 01295 690526
sirwhcockcroft@clara.co.uk
D: £25.00–£30.00 **S:** fr £35.00
Beds: 2T 1D **Baths:** 3 En
₽ (3) ⅍ ⓣⓥ ▥ ᵻ
Beautiful C18th house with lovely garden on the green in idyllic peaceful village. Ideal for visiting Stratford-upon-Avon, Oxford, Warwick Castle, Blenheim Palace, the Cotswolds, Upton House and many gardens open to the public, among them Brook Cottage.

Pond Cottage, *The Green, Warmington, Banbury, Oxon, OX17 1BU.*
Picturesque Grade II Listed cottage, overlooking duckpond. 6 miles from M40 (J11/12).
Open: Feb to Nov
01295 690682 Mrs Viljoen
D: £20.00 **S:** £21.00–£30.00
Beds: 1D 1S **Baths:** 1 Sh
₽ (2) ⅍ ⓣⓥ ▥ ᵻ

The Glebe House, *Warmington, Banbury, Oxon, OX17 1BT.*
Farmhouse style offering a warm welcome, comfort and peace.
Open: Easter to Nov
01295 690642 (also fax)
Mrs Thornton
D: £20.00–£24.00 **S:** £20.00–£24.00
Beds: 2D 1T **Baths:** 2 En 1 Pr
ⓢ (5) ₽ (6) ⅍ ⓣⓥ ↑ ▥ ᵻ

SP2865   ◀ *Fen End, The Racehorse, Simple Simon, Millwright Arms, Lord Nelson, The Crown, The Falcon*

Ashburton Guest House, *74 Emscote Road, Warwick, CV34 5QG.*
Extremely high standard of accommodation and close to town centre.
Open: All Year (not Xmas)
Grades: ETC 3 Diamond
01926 401082 Mrs Whitelaw
Fax: 01926 419237
100534.444@compuserve.com
D: £20.00 **S:** £20.00–£25.00
Beds: 2F 1T 4S **Baths:** 4 En 1 Pr 2 Sh
ⓢ (1) ₽ (3) ⓣⓥ ↑ ▥ ᵻ cc

Croft Guest House, *The Croft, Haseley Knob, Warwick, CV35 7NL.*
Friendly family country guest house. Near Warwick, Coventry, Stratford, NEC/NAC.
Open: All Year (not Xmas)
Grades: ETC 4 Diamond, AA 4 Diamond, RAC 4 Diamond
01926 484447 (also fax)
Mr & Mrs Clapp
david@croftguesthouse.co.uk
D: £23.00–£25.00 **S:** £34.00
Beds: 2F 3D 3T 1S **Baths:** 7 En 2 Pr
ⓢ ₽ (8) ⅍ ⓣⓥ ↑ ▥ ᵻ Ⓖ cc

Chesterfields, *84 Emscote Road, Warwick, CV34 5QJ.*
The ideal location for Warwick Castle, Stratford and The Cotswolds.
Open: All Year (not Xmas)
01926 774864 Mr & Mrs Chapman
D: £17.50–£19.00 **S:** £18.00–£22.00
Beds: 2F 2D 1T 2S **Baths:** 1 Sh
🛏 🅿 (8) 📺 🛏️ 🎱 ♨

Austin Guest House, *96 Emscote Road, Warwick, CV34 5QJ.*
Black and white Victorian house, one mile from town centre and castle.
Open: All Year (not Xmas)
Grades: ETC 3 Diamond, AA 3 Diamond
01926 493583 Mr & Mrs Winter
Fax: 01926 493679
D: £18.00–£21.00 **S:** £18.00–£21.00
Beds: 2F 2D 2T 1S **Baths:** 5 En 1 Sh
🛏 🅿 (6) 📺 🛏️ 🎱 ♨ cc

Park House Guest House, *17 Emscote Road, Warwick, CV34 4PH.*
Victorian blue brick building on outskirts of Warwick. Family run.
Open: All Year (not Xmas)
Grades: ETC 3 Diamond
01926 494359 (also fax)
M Chaglayan
park.house@ntlworld.com
D: £17.50–£25.00 **S:** £20.00–£25.00
Beds: 1F 2D 2T 3S **Baths:** 8 En
📺 🛏️ 🎱 ♨

Wasperton

SP2659 🍺 *The Ferry*

Lower Rowley, *Wasperton, Warwick, CV35 8EB.*
Open: All Year
Grades: ETC 4 Diamond
01926 624937 Mrs Veasey
Fax: 01926 620053
lowerowley@uk.packardbell.org
D: £20.00–£22.50 **S:** £25.00–£35.00
Beds: 1T 1D **Baths:** 2 En
🛏 (8) 🅿 (2) ⅓ 📺 🛏️ 🎱 ♨
Lower Rowley - Country home enjoying glorious views backing onto River Avon. 4 miles Warwick, 6 miles Stratford-upon-Avon. Offering peace and quiet in tastefully furnished non-smoking ensuite accommodation. Easy access to NEC, NAC, ICC and The Cotswolds.

Welford-on-Avon

SP1451 🍺 *Bell Inn*

Springfields Farm, *Welford Road, Welford-on-Avon, Stratford upon Avon, Warks, CV37 8RA.*
Farmhouse - walk in Shakespeare's paths.
Open: All Year
Grades: ETC Listed
01789 720361 Mrs Reid
Fax: 01789 720885
enquiries@reidgroup.co.uk
D: £16.00–£20.00 **S:** £16.00
Beds: 1F 1D 2T 1S **Baths:** 1 En 1 Sh
🛏 (6) 🅿 (12) ⅓ 🛏️

One Acre Guest House, *Barton Road, Welford-on-Avon, Stratford upon Avon, Warks, CV37 8EZ.*
Pretty Shakespearean village 4 miles Stratford upon Avon, 6 miles Cotswolds.
Open: Mar to Nov
01789 750477 Ms Clifton
D: £20.00 **S:** £30.00
Beds: 3D
🛏 (12) 🅿 (3) ⅓ 📺 ✕ 🛏️ 🎱 ♨

Mullions, *Greenhill, Welford-on-Avon, Stratford-upon-Avon, Warks, CV37 8PP.*
Beautiful riverside country house in 5 acres with far-reaching views towards the Cotswolds.
Open: All Year (not Xmas)
01789 750413 Mrs Wheeler
Fax: 01789 751147
bandbpmw@aol.com
D: £21.00–£25.00 **S:** £31.00–£35.00
Beds: 2D **Baths:** 1 En 1 Pr
🅿 ⅓ 📺 🛏️ ♨

Whitacre Heath

SP2192 🍺 *Swan*

Heathland Farm, *Birmingham Road, Whitacre Heath, Coleshill, W Mids, B46 2ER.*
Comfortable quiet secluded farmhouse, outskirts of village, courtyard parking.
Open: All Year (not Xmas)
Grades: ETC 3 Diamond
01675 462129 Mr Barnes
D: £21.00–£22.00 **S:** £25.00–£28.00
Beds: 3T 2S **Baths:** 5 En 1 Pr
🅿 (10) 📺 🛏️ ♨

Wimpstone

SP2148 🍺 *Howard Arms*

Whitchurch Farm, *Wimpstone, Stratford upon Avon, Warks, CV37 8NS.*
Lovely Georgian farmhouse set in park-like surroundings, 4.5 miles south of Stratford-upon-Avon.
Open: All Year (not Xmas)
Grades: ETC 3 Diamond
01789 450275 (also fax)
Mrs James
D: £19.00–£20.50 **S:** £20.00–£22.00
Beds: 2D 1T **Baths:** 1 En
🛏 (0) 🅿 (3) ⅓ 📺 ✕ 🛏️ 🎱 ♨

Wixford

SP0854 🍺 *The Fish*

Orchard Lawns, *Wixford, Alcester, Warks, B49 6DA.*
Delightful house and grounds in small village, ideal touring centre.
Open: All Year (not Xmas)
Grades: ETC 4 Diamond, Silver
01789 772668 Mrs Kember
D: £20.00–£22.00 **S:** £20.00–£22.00
Beds: 1D 1T 1S **Baths:** 1 En 1 Sh
🛏 (5) 🅿 (6) ⅓ 📺 🛏 🛏️ 🎱

Wolston

SP4175 🍺 *Queen's Head, Red Lion, Half Moon, Royal Oak*

The Byre, *Lords Hill Farm, Wolston, Coventry, Warks, CV8 3GB.*
Homely hospitality, Food Hygiene Award 1998. 2 miles from Ryton Gardens.
Open: All Year (not Xmas)
Grades: ETC 4 Diamond, Silver Award
024 7654 2098 Mrs Gibbs
D: £22.00–£38.00 **S:** £22.00–£38.00
Beds: 2D 1T **Baths:** 1 En 1 Sh
🛏 (5) 🅿 (4) 📺 🛏️ ♨

Lords Hill Farm, *Coalpit Lane, Wolston, Coventry, Warks, CV8 3GB.*
Lovely views, very peaceful and private. Convenient for motorway network.
Open: All Year (not Xmas/New Year)
024 7654 4430 Mrs Gibbs
D: £25.00 **S:** £25.00
Beds: 1D **Baths:** 1 Pr
🅿 (2) ⅓ 📺 🛏️ ♨

West Midlands

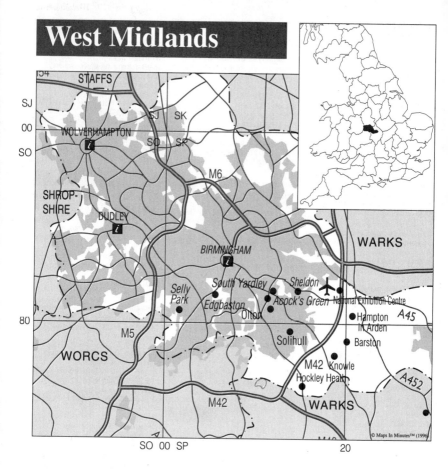

SO 00 SP   20

© Maps In Minutes™ (1996)

Barston

SP2078 🍺 Malt Shovel, Bull's Head

The Gatehouse, Barston Lane, Barston, Solihull, W Mids, B92 0JN. Large Victorian house - close to Junction 5 M42.
Open: All Year (not Xmas/New Year)
Grades: ETC 3 Diamond
01675 443274 (also fax) Mr Emmett
D: £20.00–£30.00 **S:** £20.00–£30.00
Beds: 1D 2T 3s **Baths:** 2 En 1 Sh
🐕 🅿 (20) 🛇 📺 🐾 🎇 🛗 🆅 🚱

BIRMINGHAM   Acock's

SP1183 🍺 Great Western, Westley Arms

Atholl Lodge, 16 Elmdon Road, Acock's Green, Birmingham, B27 6LH. Friendly guest house, convenient for NEC, airport, Birmingham, Solihull centres.
Open: All Year (not Xmas)
Grades: ETC 3 Diamond
0121 707 4417 (also fax) Mrs Davey
D: £18.00–£23.00 **S:** £23.00–£27.00
Beds: 1F 1D 1T 5S **Baths:** 2 En 4 Sh
🐕 🅿 (10) 📺 🐾 🛗 🚱

Greenway House Hotel, 978 Warwick Road, Acock's Green, Birmingham, B27 6QG. Small, privately run hotel, friendly service, very close to motorway network.
Open: All Year (not Xmas)
Grades: ETC 2 Diamond
0121 706 1361 (also fax)
D: £15.00–£18.00 **S:** £18.00–£25.00
Beds: 3F 3D 2T 6S **Baths:** 8 En 6 Sh
🐕 🅿 (18) 📺 🐾 ✕ 🛗 🆅 🚱

Ashdale House Hotel, 39 Broad Road, Acock's Green, Birmingham, B27 7UX. Victorian house overlooking park, near to airport, station, NEC and city centre.
Open: All Year
Grades: AA 3 Diamond
0121 706 3598 Mrs Read
Fax: 0121 707 2324
D: £20.00–£23.00 **S:** £22.00–£28.00
Beds: 2F 1D 6S **Baths:** 4 En 1 Pr 4 Sh
🐕 (1) 🅿 (4) 📺 🐾 🛗 🆅 🚱 cc

Planning a longer stay? Always ask for any special rates

Abberley, 51 Victoria Road, Acock's Green, Birmingham, B27 7YB. Comfortable Victorian house, quiet location.
Open: All Year (not Xmas)
0121 707 2950
Mrs Lendon
D: £22.00–£25.00 **S:** £24.00–£30.00
Beds: 2T 1D **Baths:** 1 En 1 Sh
🅿 (4) 📺 🛗 🆅 🚱

BIRMINGHAM Edgbaston

SP0584 🍺 Garden House

Woodville House, 39 Portland Road, Edgbaston, Birmingham, B16 9HN.
Open: All Year (not Xmas)
Grades: ETC 1 Diamond
0121 454 0274
Mr Desousa
Fax: 0121 454 5965
D: £17.00 **S:** fr £17.00
Beds: 2F 3D 5T 6S **Baths:** 4 En 3 Pr
🐕 🅿 (12) 📺 🐾 🛗 🚱
First class accommodation just one mile from city centre. All rooms colour TV, tea/coffee making facilities. Ensuite bedrooms available. Car parking. Full English breakfast.

Tourist Information Centres

Convention & Visitor Bureau, 2 City Arcade, **Birmingham**, West Midlands, B2 4TX, 0121 643 2514.

Convention & Visitor Bureau, National Exhibition Centre, **Birmingham**, West Midlands, B40 1NT, 0121 780 4321.

130 Colmore Row, **Birmingham**, B3 3AP, 0121 693 6300.

The Merry Hill Centre, Merry Hill, **Brierley Hill**, Dudley, West Midlands, DY5 1SY, 01384 481141.

Bayley Lane, **Coventry**, West Midlands, CV1 5RN, 01203 832303.

39 Churchill Shopping Centre, **Dudley**, West Midlands, DY2 7BL, 01384 812830.

Central Library, Horner Road, **Solihull**, West Midlands, B91 3RG, 0121 704 6130.

18 Queen Square, **Wolverhampton**, West Midlands, WV1 1TQ, 01902 556110.

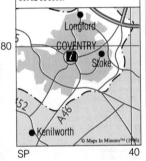

SP   40

Kennedy Guest House, *38 York Road, Edgbaston, Birmingham, B16 9JB.*
Large Victorian private house.
Open: All Year
0121 454 1284 Mr & Mrs Kennedy
Fax: 0121 454 3040
D: fr £20.00
Beds: 1F 4T 5S **Baths:** 2 Sh
⌂ 🄿 (3) 🖺 🏠 🛏 🎁 🖾 ♨

Cook House Hotel, *425 Hagley Road, Edgbaston, Birmingham, B17 8BL.*
Full of Victorian charm and character. Close to city centre. **Open:** All Year
0121 429 1916
D: £18.00–£22.00 **S:** £20.00–£30.00
Beds: 3F 5T 2D 3S **Baths:** 1 En 2 Pr 6 Sh
⌂ 🄿 (15) 🖺 🛏 🎁 🖾 ♨

BIRMINGHAM Selly Park

SP0582

Awentsbury Hotel, *21 Serpentine Road, Selly Park, Birmingham, B29 7HU.*
Victorian country house set in own gardens, close to Birmingham University.
Open: All Year **Grades:** AA 2 Diamond
0121 472 1258 (also fax) Mr Kerr
D: fr £24.00 **S:** fr £34.00
Beds: 1F 2D 8T 5S **Baths:** 6 Pr 2 Sh
⌂ 🄿 (12) 🖺 🛏 ✕ 🖾 🖾 ♨ ♿

BIRMINGHAM   Sheldon

SP1584   🍺 *The Wheatsheaf*

Elmdon Guest House, *2369 Coventry Road, Sheldon, Birmingham, B26 3PN.*
Friendly, family-run guest house close to NEC airport.
Open: Jan to Dec
0121 742 1626 (also fax) Mr Gardner
D: £22.50–£27.50 **S:** £28.00–£38.00
Beds: 1F 2D 2T 2S **Baths:** 7 En
⌂ (1) 🄿 (7) 🖺 🖾 🛏 ✕ 🎁 🖾 ♨ cc

BIRMINGHAM   South Yardley

SP1284   🍺 *Shooting Star*

Gables Nest, *1639 Coventry Road, South Yardley, Birmingham, B26 1DD.*
Friendly family-run guest house situated near to the National Exhibition Centre.
Open: All Year
Grades: ETC 3 Diamond, AA 3 Diamond, RAC 3 Diamond
0121 708 2712 M A Page
Fax: 0121 707 3396
D: £20.00–£25.00 **S:** £20.00–£30.00
Beds: 1F 3T 1S **Baths:** 4 En 1 Pr
⌂ 🄿 🖺 🛏 🎁 ♨

Coventry

SP3378   🍺 *Gatehouse Tavern, The Tollgate, The Vale, Bear Inn, White Lion, Royal Oak, Bull & Butcher, Three Tons, Browns*

Abigail Guest House, *39 St Patricks Road, Coventry, W Mids, CV1 2LP.*
Small, comfortable, convenient, city-centre, near NEC, NAC & universities.
Open: All Year (not Xmas)
Grades: ETC 3 Diamond
024 7622 1378 Mrs Ford
D: £18.50–£20.00 **S:** fr £18.50
Beds: 1F 1D 1T 3S **Baths:** 2 Sh
⌂ 🖺 🛏 🎁 ♨

Almar Lodge, *37 Mount Nod Way, Coventry, W Mids, CV5 7GY.*
Homely accommodation, quiet location, near NEC/NAC, A45, transport available.
Open: All Year (not Xmas)
024 7646 8841 Mrs Bastock
ag002a@netgates.co.uk
D: £16.00–£20.00 **S:** £16.00–£20.00
Beds: 1T 1S **Baths:** 1 En 1 Sh
⌂ 🄿 (2) 🖾 🖺 🎁 ♨

Gilcrist Guest House, *106 St James Lane, Coventry, W Mids, CV3 3GS.*
Accommodation near local motorways, Marconi, Jaguar, NEC and Peugeot.
Open: All Year (not Xmas)
024 7630 2001 Mrs Howes
D: £20.00–£22.00 **S:** £20.00–£22.00
Beds: 1T 1S **Baths:** 1 Sh
⌂ 🄿 (3) 🖾 🖺 🎁 🖾 ♨

Albany Guest House, *121 Holyhead Road, Coventry, W Mids, CV1 3AD.*
Located near city centre, NEC, NAC. Skating, cinema close by.
Open: All Year **Grades:** ETC 3 Diamond
024 7622 3601 (also fax) Mr Jones
D: £17.00–£18.00 **S:** £18.00–£20.00
Beds: 1F 3T 1S **Baths:** 2 Sh
⌂ (5) 🖾 🛏 ✕ 🎁 🖾 ♨

Chester House, *3 Chester Street, Coventry, W Mids, CV1 4DH.*
Large white building in Chester street, ten minute walk to town.
Open: All Year
Grades: ETC 3 Diamond
024 7622 3857 Mrs Saunders
chesterhouse@talk21.com
D: £17.00–£22.50 **S:** £17.00–£22.50
Beds: 1F 1S **Baths:** 1 En 1 Sh
⌂ 🖾 🛏 ✕ 🎁 🖾 ♨ ♿

Brookfields, *134 Butt Lane, Allesley, Coventry, W Mids, CV5 9FE.*
Well appointed, friendly. 6 mile NEC, 3 miles Coventry. Local amenities, semi-rural location.
Open: All Year (not New Year)
Grades: ETC 4 Diamond
024 7640 4866 Mrs Marson
Fax: 024 7640 2022
brookfieldscoventry@easicom.com
D: £24.00 **S:** £25.00–£28.00
Beds: 1D 1T 2S **Baths:** 4 En
⌂ (16) 🄿 (4) 🖾 ♨

Lodge Farm House, *Westwood Heath Road, Coventry, W Mids, CV4 8AA.*
Country house set in 2 acres of attractive gardens.
Open: All Year
Grades: ETC 4 Diamond
024 7646 6786 (also fax)
Mrs Hall
davidjohnhall@msn.com
D: £21.00–£22.00 **S:** £24.00–£25.00
Beds: 1D 1T 1S **Baths:** 2 En 1 Pr
⌂ (3) 🄿 (5) 🖾 🖾 ♨

Northanger House, *35 Westminster Road, Coventry, W Mids, CV1 3GB.*
Homely guest house close to NEC, NAC, railway station.
Open: All Year
024 7622 6780 Ms Beccham
D: £15.00–£17.00 **S:** £17.00–£18.00
Beds: 2F 1D 2T 4S **Baths:** 3 Pr
⌂ 🖾 ✕ 🎁 🖾 ♨

Abbrymar Guest House, *39a St Patricks Road, Coventry, W Mids, CV1 2LP.*
High standard good quality central to town and all amenities.
Open: All Year (not Xmas)
024 7622 5969 Mrs Broadbent
D: £17.00–£19.00 **S:** £22.00–£26.00
Beds: 1F 1D 3T 1S **Baths:** 2 Sh
⌂ 🄿 (5) 🖾 🛏 🎁 🖾 ♨

Fir Trees Hotel, *11 Eastern Green Road, Coventry, W Mids, CV5 7LG.*
Individually designed bedrooms with ensuite bathrooms. Heated outdoor swimming pool.
Open: All Year
024 7646 5746 Mrs Tonge
D: £18.00–£24.00 **S:** £18.00–£26.00
Beds: 1F 4D 3T 4S **Baths:** 5 En 4 Pr 2 Sh
⌂ 🄿 (12) 🖾 🛏 ✕ 🎁 🖾 ♨ ♿

B&B owners may vary rates - be sure to check when booking

Dudley

SO9390   🏚 *Park Inn*

Merdeka, *16 Dawlish Road, Woodsetton,
Dudley, W Mids, DY1 4LU.*
Detached residence 1 mile from Dudley
town centre; no smoking.
Open: All Year (not Xmas)
01902 884775 Mrs Green
D: fr £19.00 **S:** fr £19.00
Beds: 1T 1S **Baths:** 1 Sh
🛇 🅿 (3) ⊬ 🖾 📮 🛏 ✕ 🎟 🉐 👤

Hampton in Arden

SP2081   🏚 *Malt Shovel, Bull's Head*

The Cottage, *Kenilworth Road,
Hampton in Arden, Solihull, W Mids, B92
0LW.*
Excellent accommodation in a charming
cosy cottage close to the NEC.
Open: All Year (not Xmas)
Grades: ETC 3 Diamond, AA 3 Diamond,
RAC 3 Diamond
01675 442323 Mr Howles
Fax: 01675 443323
D: £20.00–£24.00 **S:** £28.00–£30.00
Beds: 2F 2D 1T 4S **Baths:** 8 En 1 Pr
🛇 🅿 (10) 🖾 🎟 👤🐾👤

The Hollies Guest House,
*Kenilworth Road, Hampton In Arden,
Solihull, W Mids, B92 0LW.*
Warm & welcoming. Excellent breakfast,
close NEC, Birmingham Airport/station.
Lounge, snacks available.
Open: All Year (not Xmas)
Grades: ETC 3 Diamond, AA 3 Diamond,
RAC 3 Diamond
01675 442681 Mr Hardwick
Fax: 01675 442941
m_hardwick@hotmail.com
D: £22.50–£25.00 **S:** £30.00–£40.00
Beds: 1F 5D 3T 1S **Baths:** 8 En
🛇 🅿 (12) 🖾 🛏 ✕ 🎟 👤👤

Hockley Heath

SP1573   🏚 *Bird In Hand, The Wharf*

Illshaw Heath Farm, *Kineton Lane,
Hockley Heath, Solihull, B94 6RX.*
Working farm close to NEC, Birmingham
airport and Shakespeare country.
Open: All Year (not Xmas)
Grades: ETC 4 Diamond
01564 782214 Ms Garner
D: £20.00–£22.50 **S:** £25.00–£30.00
Beds: 1D 4T **Baths:** 4 En 1 Pr
🛇 🅿 (8) 🖾 🎟 👤 🉐

Rose Cottage, *Stratford Road, Hockley
Heath, Solihull, B94 5NH.*
Central location, convenient for Stratford,
Warwick, Birmingham. Four pubs nearby.
Open: All Year (not Xmas)
01564 782936
D: £20.00–£25.00 **S:** £20.00–£25.00
Beds: 1D 5T **Baths:** 4 En 2 Sh
🛇 (5) 🅿 (6) ⊬ 🖾 🎟 👤

B&B owners may vary
rates - be sure to check
when booking

Boxtrees Farm, *Stratford Road, Hockley
Heath, Solihull, West Mids, B94 6EA.*
This C18th farmhouse has recently been
converted into superb accommodation.
Open: All Year
01564 782039 Mr Hiley
Fax: 01564 784661
b&b@boxtrees.co.uk
D: £22.50–£30.00 **S:** £45.00–£55.00
Beds: 1F 1D 2T **Baths:** 4 En
🛇 🅿 (50) ⊬ 🖾 🎟 👤 cc

Knowle

SP1876   🏚 *Black Boy, Heron's Nest, Wilson
Arms*

Ivy House, *Warwick Road, Knowle,
Solihull, W Mids, B93 0EB.*
Large rural country house.
Open: All Year
Grades: ETC 3 Diamond, AA 3 Diamond
01564 770247 Mr & Mrs Townsend
Fax: 01564 778063
@ivy-guest-house.freeserve.co.uk
D: £22.50–£30.00 **S:** £30.00–£45.00
Beds: 1F 2D 3T 2S **Baths:** 8 En
🛇 🅿 (20) ⊬ 🖾 🛏 🎟 👤 🉐 🉐

Achill House, *35 Hampton Road,
Knowle, Solihull, W. Mids, B93 0NR.*
Located in the historic village of Knowle
100 metres from the High Street.
Open: All Year
01564 774090 (also fax)
Mrs Liszewski
achill5@aol.com
D: £17.50–£25.00 **S:** £20.00–£28.00
Beds: 1F 2T 1D 1S **Baths:** 3 En 2 Sh
🛇 🅿 (6) 🖾 🎟 ✳ 👤 cc

Longford

SP3584

Chogan Bed & Breakfast, *33
Longford Road, Longford, Coventry,
Warwickshire, CV6 6DY.*
Old cottage style building, very moderate
accommodation, sky digital lounge.
Open: All Year
024 7666 1861 Fax: 024 7668 9733
D: £18.00–£25.00 **S:** £18.00–£25.00
Beds: 1F 3T 3S **Baths:** 2 En 2 Sh
🛇 🅿 🖾 ✕ 🎟 ✳ 👤 cc

Olton

SP1382   🏚 *Spread Eagle, Westley Hotel*

Abberose, *18 Victoria Road, Olton,
Birmingham, B27 7YA.*
Open: All Year (not Xmas/New Year)
0121 708 0867
D: £40.00–£46.00 **S:** £21.00–£28.00
Beds: 1F 2T 1D 2S **Baths:** 2 En 1 Pr 1 Sh
🛇 🅿 (4) ⊬ 🖾 🎟 👤 🉐
Comfortable, private detached home,
guest house. Convenient to Airport,
NEC,ICC,NIA. Public Transport, leisure
facilities plus various eating
establishments all within easy walking
distance. English or continental
breakfast. TV and tea /coffee facilities.
Non smokers please.

Warwick Court, *19 Old Warwick Road,
Olton, W Mids, B92 7JQ.*
Converted Edwardian property; spacious
accommodation with open fires.
Open: All Year
0121 707 6481 Fax: 0121 708 2093
D: £22.50–£27.50 **S:** £25.00–£42.00
Beds: 1F 2D 3T 4S **Baths:** 6 En 2 Pr
🛇 🅿 (10) ⊬ 🖾 ✕ 🎟 👤 cc

Solihull

SP1579   🏚 *Fats Cats, Red House, Shelley Barn,
The Bear*

Michaelmas House, *1159 Warwick
Road, Solihull, West Midlands, B91 3HQ.*
Open: All Year (not Xmas/New Year)
0121 705 1414 (also fax)
Mrs Horton
D: fr £25.00 **S:** £25.00–£30.00
Beds: 3F 1T 1D 1S **Baths:** 2 En 1 Pr 1 Sh
🛇 🅿 (6) ⊬ 🖾 ✕ 🎟 👤 🉐
An elegant Georgian style house with
mature gardens less than 1 mile from
Solihull town centre, just ten minutes
from Birmingham Airport and the
National Exhibition Centre, providing
luxury overnight accommodation for the
discerning traveller.

Bibury House, *Kenilworth Road,
Solihull, West Midlands, B92 0LR.*
Imposing refurbished country house 5
mins N.E.C and airport.
Open: All Year
01675 443518 (also fax)
A Hardwick
biburyhouse@aol.com
D: £22.00–£24.00 **S:** fr £28.00
Beds: 2F 3T 2D **Baths:** 7 En
🛇 🅿 (9) 🖾 🛏 🎟 👤 🉐

Acorn Guest House, *29 Links Drive,
Solihull, W Mids, B91 2DJ.*
Homely service in a quiet family house
overlooking golf course.
Open: All Year (not Xmas)
Grades: ETC 4 Diamond
0121 705 5241 Mrs Wood
acorn.wood@btinternet.com
D: £20.00–£25.00 **S:** £20.00–£25.00
Beds: 1D 2T 2S **Baths:** 1 En 1 Pr 1 Sh
🅿 (5) ⊬ 🖾 🎟 👤

Ravenhurst Guest House, *56 Lode
Lane, Solihull, W Mids, B91 2AW.*
Solihull centre, leisure centre, pubs,
restaurants, railway station on doorstep.
Open: All Year
Grades: ETC 3 Diamond
0121 705 5754 Mr Keppy
Fax: 0121 704 0717
D: £19.00–£24.00 **S:** £25.00–£40.00
Beds: 1F 2D 2T **Baths:** 2 En 3 Sh
🛇 🅿 (6) 🖾 🛏 🎟 👤 cc

Ammonds, *11 Clifton Crescent, Solihull,
W Mids, B91 3LG.*
Friendly, quiet, 5 mins Solihull. Near NEC,
Stratford, Warwick. Weekday let.
Open: All Year (not Xmas/New Year)
0121 704 9399 Mrs Hammond
D: fr £18.00 **S:** fr £19.00
Beds: 3S **Baths:** 1 Sh
🛇 (8) 🅿 (3) ⊬ 🖾 🎟 👤

The White House Hotel, *104 Olton Road, Solihull, W Mids, B90 3NN.*
Small, comfortable, quiet, business-style hotel near Solihull, NEC and Birmingham.
Open: All Year (not Xmas)
0121 745 3558 jeremymills@
thewhitehousehotel.freeserve.co.uk
D: £23.00–£25.00 **S:** £24.50–£26.50
Beds: 1F 2D 2T 3S **Baths:** 4 En
🅿 (8) 📺 ✕ 🏬 Ⓥ ⚓ cc

Stoke

SP3679 🍺 *Walsgrave Inn*

Avon Gables, *33 Avon Street, Stoke , Coventry, West Midlands, CV2 3GJ.*
Elegant Edwardian house, comfortable airy rooms.
Open: All Year (not Xmas/New Year)
024 7644 9521 Mrs Lewis
avongables_marion@yahoo.co.uk
D: £20.00–£25.00
Beds: 2T 1D **Baths:** 1 En 2 Sh
🐾 (2) 🅿 (3) ⚹ 📺 ✕ 🏬 Ⓥ ⚓

Wolverhampton

SO9198 🍺 *Golden Cup*

Wulfrun Hotel, *37 Pipers Row, Wolverhampton, W Mids, WV1 3JY.*
Small family hotel in town centre close to British Rail.
Open: All Year
01902 424017 Mr Perry
Fax: **01902 426656**
D: £19.00 **S:** £24.00
Beds: 2F 4D 3T 5S
🐾 🅿 (3) 📺 ✕ 🏬 Ⓥ cc

Fox Hotel International , *118 School Street, Wolverhampton, W Mids, WV3 0NR.*
Near town centre, Black Country Museum. Easy reach for shopping Merryhill Centre.
Open: All Year
01902 421680 Mr Kalirai
Fax: **01902 711654**
salesfoxhotel@co.uk
D: £29.00–£59.00 **S:** fr £25.00
Beds: 1F 6D 26S **Baths:** 33 En
🐾 🅿 ⚹ 📺 ✕ 🏬 Ⓥ ✳ ⚓ cc

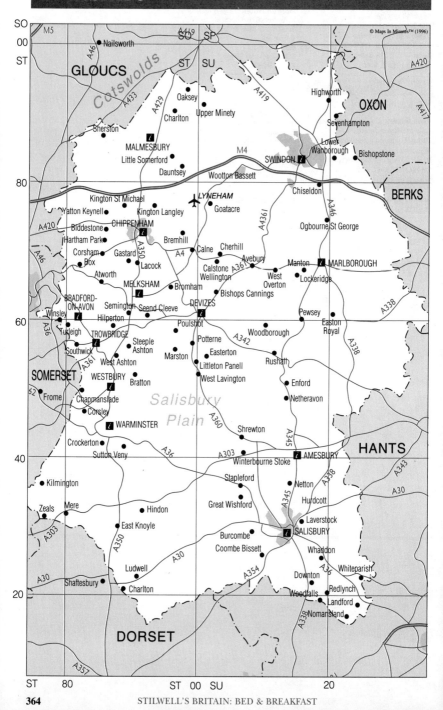

Amesbury

SU1541   New Inn, Rose and Crown

Catkin Lodge, 93 Countess Road, Amesbury, Salisbury, SP4 7AT.
The nearest B&B to Stonehenge. Friendly, comfortable and good value.
Open: All Year
Grades: AA 3 Diamond
01980 624810 Mr Grace
Fax: 01980622139
catkin@amesbury.in2home.co.uk
D: £19.00–£23.00 **S:** fr £18.00
Beds: 2F 1D 1T **Baths:** 1 En 1 Sh
🛏 (5) 🅿 (5) ⅍ 📺 🖳 🎱 🌡

Atworth

ST8665   Golden Fleece, White Hart

Kings Stile Cottage, 153 Bath Road, Atworth, Melksham, Wiltshire, SN12 8JR.
Cottage in village location. Convenient for Bath, Bradford-on-Avon, NT properties. Delicious breakfasts.
Open: All Year
01225 706202 (also fax)
Mr & Mrs Hughes
sean@kingstile.freeserve.co.uk
D: £18.00–£20.00 **S:** £20.00–£25.00
Beds: 1T 1D
🛏 🅿 (2) ⅍ 📺 🖳 🎱 🌡

Church Farm, Atworth, Melksham, Wilts, SN12 8JA.
Working dairy farm, large garden. Easy access Bath, Lacock, Bradford-on-Avon.
Open: Easter to Oct
01225 702215 Mrs Hole
churchfarm@tinyonline.co.uk
D: £17.50–£20.00 **S:** £20.00–£25.00
Beds: 1F 1D **Baths:** 1 Sh
🛏 🅿 (4) 📺 🎱 🌡

Avebury

SU1069   Waggon & Horses, Red Lion

6 Beckhampton Road, Avebury, Marlborough, Wilts, SN8 1QT.
Nearby Avebury Stone Circle, Ridgeway Walk, Silbury Hill, bus route.
Open: All Year (not Xmas)
01672 539588 Mrs Dixon
D: £16.00–£20.00 **S:** £25.00–£30.00
Beds: 1D 1T **Baths:** 1 Sh
🛏 🅿 (6) 📺 🖳 🌡

Biddestone

ST8673   White Horse

Home Place, Biddestone, Chippenham, Wiltshire, SN14 7DG.
End of farmhouse, on Village Green. Opposite Duck Pond.
Open: All Year
Grades: ETC 2 Diamond
01249 712928 Ms Hall
D: £15.00–£17.50 **S:** £15.00–£17.50
Beds: 1F 1T 1S **Baths:** 1 Sh
🛏 🅿 (2) ⅍ 📺 🖳 🌡

Planning a longer stay? Always ask for any special rates

Home Farm, Biddestone, Chippenham, Wilts, SN14 7DQ.
Listed C17th farmhouse working farm, picturesque village. Stroll to pubs.
Open: All Year (not Xmas)
01249 714475 Mr & Mrs Smith
Fax: 01249 701488
smith@homefarmb-b.freeserve.co.uk
D: £20.00–£22.50 **S:** £25.00–£30.00
Beds: 2F 1D **Baths:** 2 En 1 Pr
🛏 🅿 (4) ⅍ 📺 🖳 🎱 🌡

Bishopstone (Swindon)

SU2483   Royal Oak

Prebendal Farm, Bishopstone, Swindon, Wilts, SN6 8PT.
Farmhouse serving local organic produce, short walk to excellent pubs.
Open: All Year (not Xmas)
01793 790485 Mrs Selbourne
D: £25.00–£30.00 **S:** £25.00–£30.00
Beds: 2D 1T 1S **Baths:** 2 Sh
🛏 🅿 (12) 📺 🐾 ✗ 🖳 🎱 🌡

Box

ST8268   Swan

Owl House, Lower Kingsdown Road, Kingsdown, Box, Corsham, Wilts, SN13 8BB.
Situated 4 miles from Bath, offering spectacular views over the Avon Valley.
Open: All Year
Grades: AA 5 Diamond
01225 743883 A Venus
Fax: 01225 744450
venus@zetnet.co.uk
D: £25.00–£32.50 **S:** £25.00–£35.00
Beds: 1F 1D 1T 1S **Baths:** 3 En 1 Pr
🛏 (8) 🅿 (4) ⅍ 📺 🖳 🎱 🌡

Bradford-on-Avon

ST8261   Barge, Bear, Beehive, Cross Guns, Hop Pole, King's Arms, New Inn, Plough, Seven Stars, Three Horseshoes

Chard's Barn, Leigh Grove, Bradford-on-Avon, Wilts, BA15 2RF.
Open: All Year (not Xmas)
01225 863461
Mr & Mrs Stickney
stickney@chardsbarn.freeserve.co.uk
D: £20.00–£23.00 **S:** £20.00
Beds: 1D 1T 1S **Baths:** 2 En 1 Pr
🛏 🅿 (4) ⅍ 📺 🐾 🖳 🎱 🌡 ♿
Quiet C17th barn in unspoilt countryside with lovely gardens, view and walks. All ground floor, individually styled bedrooms, choice of breakfasts. Historic town and golf course, one mile. Close - Bath, Castle Combe, Longleat. Easy for Salisbury Plain and Stonehenge.

The Locks, 265 Trowbridge Road, Bradford-on-Avon, Wilts, BA15 1UA.
Adjoining canal tow path. Ideal walking/cycling 7/8 mile town centre.
Open: All Year
01225 863358
Mrs Benjamin
D: £17.50–£20.00 **S:** £20.00–£30.00
Beds: 1F 2T **Baths:** 1 En 1 Pr 1 Sh
🛏 (3) 🅿 (6) ⅍ 📺 🖳 🎱 🌡

Great Ashley Farm, *Ashley Lane, Bradford-on-Avon, Wilts, BA15 2PP.*
Delightful rooms. Great hospitality. Delicious breakfast. Colour brochure. Sliver award.
Open: All Year (not Xmas)
Grades: ETC 4 Diamond
01225 864563 (also fax) Mrs Rawlings
greatashleyfarm@farmersweekly.net
D: £20.00–£24.00 **S:** £25.00–£45.00
Beds: 1F 2D **Baths:** 3 En
🛇 🅿 🗶 📺 📖 🛈

Springfields, *182a Great Ashley, Bradford on Avon, Wilts, BA15 2PP.*
Unique ground-level ensuite double room with adjoining dining-room/lounge. Peaceful countryside setting.
Open: All Year
Grades: ETC 3 Diamond
01225 866125 Ms Rawlings
D: £20.00–£22.50 **S:** £30.00–£35.00
Beds: 1D **Baths:** 1En
🗶 📺 🗙 🛈 🛓

Serendipity, *19f Bradford Road, Winsley, Bradford-on-Avon, Wilts, BA15 2HW.*
Bungalow with beautiful gardens, badgers feeding nightly, ground floor room available.
Open: All Year
Grades: ETC 4 Diamond
01225 722380 Mrs Shepherd
Fax: 01225 723451
vanda.shepherd@tesco.net
D: £21.00–£22.50 **S:** £30.00–£40.00
Beds: 1F 1D 1S **Baths:** 3 En
🛇 🅿 (5) 🗶 📺 📖 🛈 🛓 🛓 3

Avonvilla, *Avoncliff, Bradford-on-Avon, Wilts, BA15 2HD.*
Superb canal and riverside setting. Free parking and fishing. Excellent walking.
Open: All Year
01225 863867 Mrs Mumford
mumford@avonvilla.fsnet.co.uk
D: £17.00 **S:** £20.00
Beds: 1D 1T 1S
🛇 (5) 🅿 🗶 📺 📖 🛈 🛓

Bratton

ST9152 🍺 *Duke*

The Duke Inn, *Melbourne Street, Bratton, Westbury, Wilts, BA13 4RW.*
Traditional oak-beamed village inn serving good fresh food, real ale.
Open: All Year
Grades: AA 2 Diamond
01380 830242 Mr Overend
Fax: 01380 831239
D: £22.50–£25.00 **S:** £25.00–£30.00
Beds: 2D 1T **Baths:** 2 Sh
🛇 (14) 🅿 (30) 🗶 📺 🗙 📖 🛈 ❄ 🛓 🛓 cc

Bremhill

ST9773 🍺 *George*

Lowbridge Farm, *Bremhill, Calne, Wilts, SN11 9HE.*
Old thatched farmhouse. Varied stock. Scenic views. Places to visit.
Open: All Year
01249 815889 Miss Sinden
D: £23.00 **S:** £23.00
Beds: 1F 1D 1T **Baths:** 1 Sh
🛇 🅿 (8) 🗶 📺 🗙 📖 🛈 🛓

Bromham

ST9665

Wayside, *Chittoe Heath, Bromham, Chippenham, Wilts, SN15 2EH.*
Situated in the heart of the Wiltshire countryside yet within easy distance of Bath. **Open:** All Year
01380 850458 (also fax) Mr Collins
andrew.imi@virgin.net
D: £22.50–£25.00 **S:** £25.00
Beds: 1F 1D 1T **Baths:** 2 En 1 Pr
🛇 🅿 (6) 🗶 📺 🍴 📖 🛓 🛓

Burcombe

SU0730 🍺 *Ship Inn*

Manor Farm, *Burcombe, Salisbury, Wilts, SP2 0EJ.*
Country location providing peace and comfort, with historical attractions nearby. **Open:** Mar to Dec
01722 742177 Mrs Combes
Fax: 01722 744600
D: £21.00–£22.50 **S:** £30.00–£35.00
Beds: 1D 1T **Baths:** 2 En
🛇 🅿 (4) 🗶 📺 📖 🛓

Calne

ST9971 🍺 *Black Horse*

Lower Sands Farm, *Low Lane, Calne, Wilts, SN11 8TR.*
Old farmhouse, v. quiet homely and friendly. Good breakfast, large garden.
Open: All Year (not Xmas)
Grades: ETC 1 Diamond
01249 812402 Mrs Henly
D: £17.00–£18.00 **S:** £17.00–£18.00
Beds: 1D 1T 1S **Baths:** 1 Sh
🅿 (10) 📺 📖 🛓

Calstone Wellington

SU0268 🍺 *White Horse*

Manor Farmhouse, *Calstone Wellington, Calne, Wiltshire, SN11 8PY.*
Open: All Year
Grades: ETC 4 Diamond, Silver Award
01249 816804 Mrs Maundell
Fax: 01249 817966
calstonebandb@farmersweekly.net
D: £27.50–£32.50 **S:** £30.00–£40.00
Beds: 2D **Baths:** 2 En
🛇 (12) 🅿 (2) 🗶 📺 🗙 📖 🛈 🛓
Unique, secluded downland location. Interesting house with genuine history and Victorian four poster. Spacious, comfortable, peaceful. Glorious views. Perfect for visiting many interesting places nearby. The warmest welcome, top quality accommodation, the relaxed atmosphere and good food await.

Chapmanslade

ST8348 🍺 *Three Horseshoes*

Spinney Farm, *Thoulstone, Chapmanslade, Westbury, Wilts, BA13 4AQ.*
In heart of Wiltshire countryside. Easy reach of Bath, Longleat.
Open: All Year
01373 832412 Mrs Hoskins
D: fr £19.00 **S:** fr £20.00
Beds: 1F 1D 1T **Baths:** 2 Sh
🛇 🅿 (8) 📺 🍴 🗙 📖 🛈 🛓

Charlton (Malmesbury)

ST9588 🍺 *Horse and Groom*

Stonehill Farm, *Charlton (Malmesbury), Malmesbury, Wilts, SN16 9DY.*
C15th farmhouse on dairy farm, warm welcome, delicious breakfasts.
Open: All Year **Grades:** ETC 4 Diamond
01666 823310 (also fax)
Mr & Mrs Edwards
D: £20.00–£25.00 **S:** £20.00–£27.00
Beds: 2D 1T **Baths:** 1 En 1 Sh
🛇 🅿 (3) 📺 🍴 📖 🛓

Charlton (Shaftesbury)

ST9022 🍺 *Grove Arms, Talbot*

Charnwood Cottage, *Charlton, Shaftesbury, Dorset, SP7 9LZ.*
C17th thatched cottage with lovely garden. Good base for touring.
Open: All Year (not Xmas/New Year)
01747 828310 (also fax)
Mr & Mrs Morgan
D: £18.00–£19.00 **S:** fr £20.00
Beds: 1T 1D **Baths:** 1 Sh
🛇 (5) 🅿 (2) 📺 🍴 📖

Cherhill

SU0370 🍺 *Black Horse*

Poachers Croft, *Yatesbury Hill, Cherhill, Calne, Wilts, SN11 8XY.*
Lovely country B&B below white horse. Area of Outstanding Natural Beauty.
Open: All Year **Grades:** ETC 3 Diamond
01249 812587 Mrs Trafford
D: £25.00–£30.00 **S:** fr £25.00
Beds: 1F
🛇 🅿 (6) 📺 🍴 📖 🛈 🛓 🛓

Chippenham

ST9173 🍺 *Biddestone Arms, Rowden Arms, Three Crowns, Wellesley Arms, White Horse*

Bramleys, *73 Marshfield Road, Chippenham, Wilts, SN15 1JR.*
Large Victorian house, Grade II Listed.
Open: All Year **Grades:** ETC 1 Diamond
01249 653770 Mrs Swatton
D: £18.00–£20.00 **S:** £17.00–£19.00
Beds: 1F 3T 1S **Baths:** 1 Pr 1 Sh
🛇 🅿 (4) 🗶 📺 📖 🛈 🛓

Frogwell House, *132 Hungerdown Lane, Chippenham, Wilts, SN14 0BD.*
Family-run C19th stone-built house providing comfortable accommodation.
Open: All Year **Grades:** ETC 4 Diamond
01249 650328 (also fax) Mrs Burgess
D: £19.00–£20.00 **S:** £25.00–£28.00
Beds: 1F 1D 2T 1S **Baths:** 2 En 1 Sh
🛇 🅿 (6) 🗶 📺 🍴 🗙 📖 🛈 🛓

Olivemead Farm, *Olivemead Lane, Dauntsey, Chippenham, Wilts, SN15 4JQ.*
Delightful C18th farmhouse, convenient M4, Bath, Cotswolds, Stonehenge.
Open: All Year (not Xmas)
Grades: ETC 2 Diamond
01666 510205 (also fax) Mrs Candy
olivemead@farming.co.uk
D: £20.00–£44.00 **S:** £20.00–£22.00
Beds: 1F 1D 1T **Baths:** 1 Sh
🛇 🅿 (6) 🗶 📺 🛓

Chiseldon

SU1879   🍺 *Patriots' Arms, Calley Arms*

Courtleigh House, *40 Draycott Road, Chiseldon, Swindon, Wilts, SN4 0LS.*
Large well-appointed country home; large garden with downland views.
Open: All Year (not Xmas)
Grades: ETC 3 Diamond
01793 740246 Ms Hibberd
rhib494369@aol.com
D: £18.50–£21.00 **S:** £22.00–£25.00
Beds: 2T 1S **Baths:** 1 En 1 Sh
🛇 **P** (3) ⌀ �📺 🛏. 🚿

Codford St Mary

ST9739   🍺 *Angel*

Glebe Cottage, *Church Lane, Codford St. Mary, Warminster, Wiltshire, BA12 0PJ.*
Open: All Year (not Xmas/New Year)
Grades: ETC 4 Diamond, Silver Award
01985 850565 Mrs Richardson-Aitken
Fax: 01985 850666
bobr-a@care4free.net
D: £25.00–£27.00 **S:** £25.00–£27.00
Beds: 1F 1T **Baths:** 2 Pr
🛇 (3) **P** (3) ⌀ 📺 🛏. 🚿
Glebe Cottage, a 250 year old former home of the Sexton, is situated in the attractive Wylye Valley. Close to Salisbury Plain and Anzac war graves. Convenient for Salisbury, Bath and Stonehenge.

Coombe Bissett

SU1026   🍺 *Fox & Goose, Yew Tree Inn, White Hart, Radnor Arms*

Swaynes Firs Farm, *Grimsdyke, Coombe Bissett, Salisbury, Wilts, SP5 5RF.*
Spacious farmhouse on working farm with horses, cattle, poultry, geese & duck ponds etc.
Open: All Year (not Xmas)
Grades: ETC 3 Diamond
01725 519240
Mr Shering
swaynes.firs@virgin.net
D: £20.00–£22.00 **S:** £25.00–£30.00
Beds: 1F 2T **Baths:** 3 En
🛇 **P** (6) 📺 🛏 🚿

Corsham

ST8670   🍺 *White Horse Inn, Hare & Hounds, Harp and Crown, George*

Heatherly Cottage, *Ladbrook Lane, Gastard, Corsham, Wilts, SN13 9PE.*
Open: All Year (not Xmas/New Year)
Grades: ETC 4 Diamond
01249 701402
Mrs Daniel
Fax: 01249 701412
ladbrook1@aol.com
D: £23.00–£25.00 **S:** £27.00–£30.00
Beds: 1T 2D **Baths:** 3 En
🛇 (10) **P** (8) ⌀ 📺 🛏. 📺 🚿
C17th cottage set in quiet location with large garden. Guests have separate wing of the house with their own entrance. Close to Bath, Lacock, Castle Combe, Avebury and Stonehenge. Ample space for parking and local pubs nearby for evening meals.

Thurlestone Lodge, *13 Prospect, Corsham, Wilts, SN13 9AD.*
Elegant Victorian home set in landscaped gardens, close to town centre.
Open: All Year (not Xmas/New Year)
01249 713397 Mrs Ogilvie-Robb
D: £21.00–£24.00 **S:** £30.00–£40.00
Beds: 1T 1D **Baths:** 1 En 1 Pr
🛇 **P** (5) ⌀ 🛏 🛏. 📺 🚿

Bellwood, *45 Pickwick, Corsham, Wilts, SN13 0HX.*
Charming 1708 cottage (adjacent to owners), pubs nearby, Bath 8 miles.
Open: All Year
01249 713434 Mrs Elliott
D: £20.00–£22.00 **S:** £22.00–£25.00
Beds: 2T 1S **Baths:** 1 Pr 1 Sh
🛇 (2) **P** (4) ⌀ 📺 🛏 🛏. 📺 ❀ 🚿

Corsley

ST8246   🍺 *Three Horseshoes*

Sturford Mead Farm, *Corsley, Warminster, Wilts, BA12 7QU.*
Farmhouse in Area of Outstanding Natural Beauty close to Longleat.
Open: All Year
Grades: ETC 4 Diamond, AA 4 Diamond
01373 832213 (also fax) Mrs Corp
lynn_sturford.bed@virgin.net
D: £22.00 **S:** £30.00–£28.00
Beds: 1D 2T **Baths:** 2 En 1 Pr
🛇 **P** (6) ⌀ 📺 🛏. 📺 🚿

Crockerton

ST8642   🍺 *Bath Arms*

Stoneyside, *PottersHill, Crockerton, Warminster, Wiltshire, BA12 8AS.*
Lovely peaceful bungalow, easy access, garden to relax in with lovely views of valley.
Open: All Year (not Xmas)
Grades: ETC 3 Diamond
01985 218149 Mrs Elkins
D: £20.00–£22.50 **S:** £25.00–£30.00
Beds: 1D 1T **Baths:** 1 En 1 Pr
🛇 **P** (2) ⌀ 📺 🛏. 🚿 🚿

Springfield House, *Crockerton, Warminster, Wilts, BA12 8AU.*
Beautiful country house - sunny, antique furnished, rooms overlook gardens to woodland.
Open: All Year
01985 213696 (also fax)
Mrs Singer
D: £28.00–£30.00 **S:** £38.00–£40.00
Beds: 2D 1T **Baths:** 2 En 1 Pr
🛇 (12) **P** (6) ⌀ 📺 ✕ 🛏. 📺 🚿 🚿

Dauntsey

ST9982   🍺 *Three Crowns, Wellesley Arms*

Olivemead Farm, *Olivemead Lane, Dauntsey, Chippenham, Wilts, SN15 4JQ.*
Delightful C18th farmhouse, convenient M4, Bath, Cotswolds, Stonehenge.
Open: All Year (not Xmas)
Grades: ETC 2 Diamond
01666 510205 (also fax)
Mrs Candy
olivemead@farming.co.uk
D: £20.00 **S:** £20.00–£22.00
Beds: 1F 1D 1T **Baths:** 1 Sh
🛇 **P** (6) ⌀ 📺 🛏 🚿

Devizes

SU0061   🍺 *Barge, Bell, Bridge, Bear, Black Swan, Churchill, George & Dragon, Royal Oak, Stage Post, Moonrakers, Elm Tree, Four Seasons, Owl*

Littleton Lodge, *Littleton Panell, Devizes, Wilts, SN10 4ES.*
Comfortable Victorian house. In conservation village, gardens, good pubs nearby. **Open:** All Year
Grades: ETC 4 Diamond, AA 4 Diamond
01380 813131 Mr & Mrs Linton
Fax: 01380 816969
stay@littletonlodge.co.uk
D: £22.50–£25.00 **S:** £30.00–£40.00
Beds: 2D 1T **Baths:** 3 En
🛇 **P** (5) ⌀ 📺 🛏. 📺 🚿 🚿 **cc**

Lower Foxhangers Farm, *Rowde, Devizes, Wilts, SN10 1SS.*
Open: May to Oct
Grades: ETC 3 Diamond
01380 828254 (also fax) Mr & Mrs Fletcher
sale@foxhangers.co.uk
D: £20.00–£22.00 **S:** £22.00–£25.00
Beds: 2D 1T **Baths:** 1 Pr 2 En
🛇 **P** (4) ⌀ 📺 🛏 📺 🚿
Relax with pleasant dreams in our rural retreat amid the Wiltshire countryside. Roam the canal towpaths and see the gaily painted narrow boats as they lazily glide through the rippling water or climb the unrivalled flight of Caen Hill Locks.

Eastcott Manor, *Easterton, Devizes, Wilts, SN10 4PL.*
Elizabethan manor house in own grounds. Tranquil location.
Open: All Year (not Xmas)
Grades: ETC 3 Diamond, AA 3 Diamond
01380 813313 Mrs Firth
D: £22.00–£25.00 **S:** £22.00–£25.00
Beds: 1D 1T 2S **Baths:** 2 En 2 Pr
🛇 **P** (20) 📺 🛏 ✕ 🚿

Craven House, *Station Road, Devizes, Wilts, SN10 1BZ.*
Victorian house 50 yards from centre for restaurants and pubs. **Open:** All Year
01380 723514 Mrs Shaw
D: fr £20.00 **S:** fr £20.00
Beds: 1F 1D 2T **Baths:** 2 En 1 Pr 1 Sh
🛇 📺 ✕ 🛏. 🚿

Blounts Court Farm, *Coxhill Lane, Potterne, Devizes, Wiltshire, SN10 5NQ.*
Traditional farmhouse set in 150 acres; beautiful rooms, homely atmosphere.
Open: All Year **Grades:** ETC 5 Diamond, Gold, AA 5 Diamond
01380 727180 Mr & Mrs Cary
D: £25.00 **S:** £32.00–£37.00
Beds: 1D 1T **Baths:** 2 En
🛇 (8) **P** (8) ⌀ 📺 🛏 🛏. 📺 🚿

Gate House, *Wick Lane, Devizes, Wilts, SN10 5DW.*
Large house and garden, not on main road. Bath/Salisbury 25 miles.
Open: All Year (not Xmas)
01380 725283 Mrs Stratton
Fax: 01380 722382
laura@gatehouse-b-and-b.freeserve.co.uk
D: £20.00 **S:** £22.50
Beds: 1D 1T 1S **Baths:** 1 En 1 Sh
P (6) ⌀ 📺 🛏. 📺 🚿

Asta, *66 Downlands Road, Devizes, Wilts, SN10 5EF.*
Comfortable, modern house in quiet road, 15 minutes from town centre.
Open: All Year
01380 722546 Mrs Milne-Day
D: fr £16.00 **S:** fr £16.00
Beds: 1D 2S **Baths:** 1 Sh
🛏 🅿 (2) 📺 ⛩ ✕ 🃏 🆅

Glenholme Guest House, *77 Nursteed Road, Devizes, Wilts, SN10 3AJ.*
Friendly, comfortable house. Warm welcome. Lovely historic town.
Open: All Year
01380 723187 Mrs Bishop
D: £18.00 **S:** £20.00
Beds: 1F 1T **Baths:** 1 Sh
🛏 🅿 📺 ⛩ ✕ 🃏 🆅 🖢

The Chestnuts, *Potterne Road, Devizes, Wiltshire, SN10 5DD.*
Good base for Bath, Salisbury, Stonehenge, Avebury and Kennet & Avon Canal.
Open: All Year (not Xmas)
01380 724532 Mrs Mortimer
D: £20.00–£25.00 **S:** £25.00
Beds: 1F 1T **Baths:** 2 En
🛏 🅿 (2) ⅍ 📺 🃏 🆅 🖢

Downton

SU1821   🍺 *White Horse*

The Warren, *15 High Street, Downton, Salisbury, Wilts, SP5 3PG.*
Grade II Listed, large garden. Close to New Forest and Stonehenge. Pretty village.
Open: All Year (not Xmas/New Year)
Grades: AA 4 Diamond
01725 510263 Mrs Baxter
D: £25.00 **S:** £38.00–£40.00
Beds: 2D 2T **Baths:** 2 Pr 2 En
🛏 (5) 🅿 (8) 📺 ⛩ 🃏 🆅 🖢

East Knoyle

ST8830   🍺 *Fox & Hounds*

Moors Farmhouse, *East Knoyle, Salisbury, Wilts, SP3 6BU.*
C17th farmhouse suite of large rooms. Naturally beautiful/interesting area.
Open: All Year (not Xmas)
01747 830385 Mrs Reading
john.reading@virgin.net
D: £25.00 **S:** £25.00
Beds: 1T **Baths:** 1 En
🛏 (8) 🅿 (2) 📺 🃏 🖢

Easterton

SU0255   🍺 *Royal Oak*

Eastcott Manor, *Easterton, Devizes, Wilts, SN10 4PL.*
Elizabethan manor house in own grounds. Tranquil location.
Open: All Year (not Xmas)
Grades: ETC 3 Diamond, AA 3 Diamond
01380 813313 Mrs Firth
D: £22.00–£25.00 **S:** £22.00–£25.00
Beds: 1D 1T 2S **Baths:** 2 En 2 Pr
🛏 🅿 (20) 📺 ⛩ ✕ 🖢

Easton Royal

SU2060   🍺 *Royal Oak, Three Horseshoes*

Folletts, *Easton Royal, Pewsey, Wilts, SN9 5LZ.*
Convenient for Kennet & Avon canal. Stonehenge and Avebury.
Open: All Year (not Xmas/New Year)
Grades: ETC 4 Diamond
01672 810619 (also fax)
Mrs Landless
margaretlandless@talk21.com
D: £22.50–£25.00 **S:** £30.00–£35.00
Beds: 2D 1T **Baths:** 3 En
🛏 🅿 (6) ⅍ 📺 ✕ 🃏 🆅 🖢

Enford

SU1351   🍺 *Swan Inn*

Enford House, *Enford, Pewsey, Wilts, SN9 6DJ.*
Salisbury Plain. River village, old rectory, beautiful garden, thatched wall.
Open: All Year (not Xmas)
Grades: ETC 3 Diamond
01980 670414 Mr Campbell
D: £18.00 **S:** £20.00
Beds: 1D 2T **Baths:** 2 Sh
🛏 🅿 (5) ⅍ 📺 ⛩ ✕ 🃏 🆅 🖢

Gastard

ST8868   🍺 *George*

Heatherly Cottage, *Ladbrook Lane, Gastard, Corsham, Wilts, SN13 9PE.*
C17th cottage set in quiet location with large garden. Guests have separate wing.
Open: All Year (not Xmas/New Year)
Grades: ETC 4 Diamond
01249 701402 Mrs Daniel
Fax: 01249 701412
ladbrook1@aol.com
D: £23.00–£25.00 **S:** £27.00–£30.00
Beds: 1T 2D **Baths:** 3 En
🛏 (10) 🅿 (8) ⅍ 📺 🃏 🆅 🖢

Goatacre

SU0177   🍺 *Duke*

Fenwicks, *Goatacre, Calne, Wilts, SN11 9HY.*
Delightful, secluded country home in idyllic grounds. High level of warmth and hospitality.
Open: All Year (not Xmas)
01249 760645 (also fax)
Mrs Fenwicks
D: £22.50–£25.00 **S:** £27.00–£30.00
Beds: 1F 1D 1T **Baths:** 3 Pr
🛏 (9) 🅿 (8) ⅍ 📺 ✕ 🃏 🆅

Great Wishford

SU0735   🍺 *Swan*

Wishford Farmhouse, *Great Wishford, Salisbury, Wilts, SP2 0NN.*
Good touring centre.
Open: All Year (not Xmas)
01722 790235 Mrs Thatcher
D: £15.00–£20.00 **S:** £16.00–£18.00
Beds: 2T 1S **Baths:** 1 En 1 Sh
🅿 (3) ⅍ 📺 🃏 🖢

Hartham Park

ST8672   🍺 *White Horse*

Church Farm, *Hartham Park, Corsham, Wiltshire, SN13 0PU.*
Cotswold farmhouse in rural location, stunning views, quiet and peaceful.
Open: All Year (not Xmas/New Year)
Grades: ETC 4 Diamond, AA 4 Diamond
01249 715180 Mrs Jones
Fax: 01249 715572
kmjbandb@aol.com
D: £20.00–£25.00 **S:** £20.00–£22.00
Beds: 1F 1D 1S **Baths:** 2 En 1 Pr
🛏 (1) 🅿 (6) ⅍ 📺 🃏 🆅 🖢

Highworth

SU2092   🍺 *Radnor, Carriers Arms*

Roves Farm, *Sevenhampton, Swindon, Wilts, SN6 7QG.*
Spacious comfortable quiet accommodation surrounded by beautiful countryside on a working farm.
Open: All Year
Grades: ETC 3 Diamond
01793 763939 (also fax)
joanna@rovesfarm.co.uk
D: £20.00–£22.00 **S:** £26.00–£27.00
Beds: 1F 1T **Baths:** 2 En
🛏 🅿 (4) ⅍ 📺 🃏 🆅 🖢

Hilperton

ST8759   🍺 *Lion and Fiddle*

62b Paxcroft Cottages, *Devizes Road, Hilperton, Trowbridge, Wiltshire, BA14 6JB.*
Lovely Garden with far reaching views overlooking the Wiltshire downs.
Open: All Year (not Xmas)
Grades: ETC 3 Diamond
01225 765838 S J Styles
D: £20.00–£22.00 **S:** £20.00–£22.00
Beds: 1F 1T 1D **Baths:** 2 En 1 Pr
🛏 🅿 (6) ⅍ 📺 ✕ 🃏 🆅 🖢

Hindon

ST9132

Chicklade Lodge, *Chicklade, Hindon, Salisbury, Wilts, SP3 5SU.*
Charming Victorian cottage. Under 2 hour drive from Heathrow.
Open: All Year
Grades: ETC Lamb Inn
01747 820389 Mrs Jerram
aud.jerram@virgin.net
D: £20.00 **S:** £25.00
Beds: 2T 1D **Baths:** 1 Sh
🛏 (5) 🅿 (4) ⅍ 📺 ⛩ ✕ 🃏 🆅 🖢

Hurdcott

SU1633   🍺 *Black Horse*

Holly House, *Hurdcott, Winterbourne Earls, Salisbury, Wiltshire, SP4 6HL.*
Village guest house short distance to Stonehenge and Salisbury Cathedral.
Open: All Year
01980 610813 (also fax)
Mrs Barrett
sheila@holly-house.co.uk
D: £18.00–£24.00 **S:** £20.00–£25.00
Beds: 2D 1T **Baths:** 2 En 1 Pr
🅿 (10) ⅍ 📺 🃏 🖢 **cc**

Kilmington

ST7736   *Spread Eagle*

The Red Lion Inn, *On B3092 (Mere to Frome road), Kilmington, Warminster, Wilts, BA12 6RP.*
Unspoilt 15th century traditional inn. Stourhead 1 mile. Comfortable beds, good breakfasts.
Open: All Year (not Xmas/New Year)
01985 844263 Mr Gibbs
D: £17.50 **S:** £25.00
Beds: 1D 1T **Baths:** 1 Sh
 (4) P (25) ✔ ✝ Ⅲ Ⓥ ♿

Kington Langley

ST9277   *Hit or Miss*

Finnygook, *Days Lane, Kington Langley, Chippenham, Wilts, SN15 5PA.*
Open: All Year (not Xmas/New Year)
01249 750411 Mrs Weston
Fax: 01249 750526
D: £18.50–£25.00 **S:** £18.50–£30.00
Beds: 2T 2D 1S **Baths:** 1 Pr 1 Sh
P (4) ✔ ℡ Ⅲ Ⓥ ♿
Quiet family home set in secluded garden with views over open countryside. On edge of beautiful village. 1 mile from M4 Junction 17. Ideally placed for touring the South Cotswolds and Wiltshire Downs. 1 hour from Bath, Bristol, Chichester or Salisbury.

Kington St Michael

ST8977

The Jolly Huntsman Inn, *Kington St Michael, Chippenham, Wilts, SN14 6JB.*
Very friendly country pub, lots of local amenities. Easily accessible.
Open: All Year
01249 750305 Mr Lawrence
Fax: 01249 750182
D: £30.00 **S:** £45.00
Beds: 3F 3D **Baths:** 6 En
 P (15) ✔ ℡ ✝ ✕ Ⅲ Ⓥ ♿ cc

Lacock

ST9168   *George, Red Lion, Carpenters' Arms, Angel*

The Old Rectory, *Lacock, Chippenham, Wilts, SN15 2JZ.*
Open: All Year
Grades: ETC 4 Diamond
01249 730335 Mrs Sexton
Fax: 01249 730166
elaine@oldrectorylacock.freeserve.co.uk
D: £22.50–£25.00 **S:** £25.00–£27.50
Beds: 1F 1D 1T **Baths:** 3 En
 P (6) ✔ ℡ ✝ Ⅲ ♿
Superb Gothic Victorian architecture, set in 8 acres of grounds and gardens, many original features and 4 poster beds. Excellent pubs a stroll away in famous Lacock location for tourists and businessmen, M4 (J17), close by. Bath 12 miles, London 2 hours. Recomm in 'Off the Beaten Track'.

Planning a longer stay? Always ask for any special rates

Lacock Pottery, *The Tan Yard, Lacock, Chippenham, Wilts, SN15 2LB.*
Beautiful, comfortable, working pottery, medieval village.
Open: All Year (not Xmas/New Year)
Grades: ETC 4 Diamond
01249 730266 Mrs McDowell
Fax: 01249 730948
simone@lacockbedandbreakfast.com
D: £29.50–£39.50 **S:** £37.00–£59.00
Beds: 1T 2D **Baths:** 1 En 1 Sh 1 Pr
 P (6) ✔ ℡ ✝ Ⅲ Ⓥ ♿ cc

Landford

SU2619   *Lamb*

Springfields, *Lyndhurst Road, Landford, Salisbury, Wilts, SP5 2AS.*
Friendly hospitality close to New Forest, Salisbury, Southampton. Lovely rooms.
Open: All Year **Grades:** AA 4 Diamond
01794 390093 (also fax) Mrs Westlake
springfields_bb@libertysurf.co.uk
D: £17.00–£20.00 **S:** £25.00
Beds: 2D 1S **Baths:** 2 Sh
 P (6) ✔ ℡ ✝ Ⅲ ♿

Laverstock

SU1530

The Twitterings, *73 Church Street, Laverstock, Salisbury, Wiltshire, SP11QZ.*
Quiet location. Comfortable self contained rooms. English breakfast a speciality.
Open: All Year (not Xmas/New Year)
Grades: ETC 3 Diamond
01722 321760 Mrs Henly
D: £20.00 **S:** £20.00–£25.00
Beds: 1T 1D **Baths:** 2 En
 P (4) ✔ ℡ Ⅲ Ⓥ ♿ ♿

Little Somerford

ST9684   *Three Crowns*

Lovett Farm, *Little Somerford, Nr Malmesbury, Chippenham, Wilts, SN15 5BP.*
Open: All Year
Grades: ETC 4 Diamond, AA 4 Diamond
01666 823268 (also fax) Mrs Barnes
lovetts_farm@hotmail.com
D: £23.00–£25.00 **S:** £25.00–£30.00
Beds: 1D 1T **Baths:** 2 En
 (3) P (5) ✔ ℡ Ⅲ ♿
Delightful farmhouse on working farm with beautiful views from the attractive ensuite bedrooms. Enjoy a hearty breakfast in our cosy dining room/lounge. Close to Malmesbury, England's oldest borough. Convenient M4, Bath, Cotswolds and Stonehenge. Excellent food pubs nearby.

Littleton Panell

ST9954   *Stage Post, Owl*

Littleton Lodge, *Littleton Panell, Devizes, Wilts, SN10 4ES.*
Comfortable Victorian house. In conservation village, gardens, good pubs nearby. **Open:** All Year
Grades: ETC 4 Diamond, AA 4 Diamond
01380 813131 Mr & Mrs Linton
Fax: 01380 816969
stay@littletonlodge.co.uk
D: £22.50–£25.00 **S:** £30.00–£40.00
Beds: 2D 1T **Baths:** 3 En
 P (5) ✔ ℡ Ⅲ Ⓥ ♿ ♿ cc

Lockeridge

SU1467   *Who'd A Thought It*

The Taffrail, *Back Lane, Lockeridge, Marlborough, Wilts, SN8 4ED.*
Great welcome, comfort, tranquillity. Delightful modern home and lovely garden.
Open: Jan to Nov
01672 861266 (also fax)
Mrs Spencer
spencer.taffrail@ukgateway.net
D: £17.50 **S:** £20.00
Beds: 1D 1T 1S **Baths:** 1 Sh
 (8) P (3) ✔ ℡ Ⅲ

Lower Wanborough

SU2083

Iris Cottage, *Bury Croft, Lower Wanborough, Swindon, Wilts, SN4 0AP.*
Very comfortable village cottage. Swindon 4 miles. Near Ridgeway Path.
Open: All Year (not Xmas)
01793 790591 Mrs Rosier
D: £19.00 **S:** £20.00
Beds: 2S **Baths:** 1 Sh
P (2) ✔ ℡ Ⅲ

Ludwell

ST9122   *Rising Sun*

Ye Olde Wheelwrights, *Birdbush, Ludwell, Shaftesbury, Dorset, SP7 9NH.*
Accommodation in separate annexe. Children and families welcome. Hearty breakfast. **Open:** April to October
01747 828955 C Dieppe
charles@cdieppe.freeserve.co.uk
D: £17.50–£20.00 **S:** £20.00–£22.00
Beds: 1T 1D **Baths:** 1 Sh
 P ✔ ℡ ♿

Malmesbury

ST9387   *Plough Inn, Wheatsheaf Inn, Old Inn, White Horse, Smoking Dog, Whole Hog, Horse & Groom*

Bremilham House, *Bremilham Road, Malmesbury, Wilts, SN16 0DQ.*
Open: All Year (not Xmas)
Grades: ETC 3 Diamond
01666 822680 Mrs Ball
D: £17.50 **S:** £20.00
Beds: 2D 1T **Baths:** 2 Sh
 P (3) ✔ ℡ ✝ Ⅲ ♿
Delightful Edwardian cottage set in a mature walled garden in a quiet location on the edge of historic Malmesbury, England's oldest borough. The town, dominated by a stunning Norman Abbey, is central for Bath, Cheltenham, Salisbury and the glorious Cotswolds.

Stonehill Farm, *Charlton (Malmesbury), Malmesbury, Wilts, SN16 9DY.*
C15th farmhouse on dairy farm, warm welcome, delicious breakfasts.
Open: All Year
Grades: ETC 4 Diamond
01666 823310 (also fax)
Mr & Mrs Edwards
D: £20.00–£25.00 **S:** £20.00–£27.00
Beds: 2D 1T **Baths:** 1 En 1 Sh
 P (3) ℡ ✝ Ⅲ ♿

Manton

SU1768   ◆ Oddfellows Arms

Sunrise Farm, Manton, Marlborough,
Wilts, SN8 4HL.
Peacefully located approximately 1 mile
from Marlborough. Friendly, comfortable,
relaxing atmosphere. **Open:** March to Oct
Grades: ETC 3 Diamond
01672 512878 (also fax) Mrs Couzens
D: £19.00–£20.00 **S:** £19.00–£25.00
Beds: 1D 2T **Baths:** 2 Pr
🛇 (14) 🅿 (3) 🗲 📺 🛏 📖 Ⅴ ♨

Marlborough

SU1869   ◆ Bear, Roebuck, Sun, Oddfellows
Arms

Browns Farm, Marlborough, Wilts, SN8
4ND.
Peaceful farmhouse on edge of
Savernake Forest. Overlooking open
farmland. **Open:** All Year
01672 515129 Mrs Crockford
crockford@farming.co.uk
D: £16.00–£20.00 **S:** £20.00–£25.00
Beds: 1F 1T 2D **Baths:** 1 En 1 Sh
🛇 🅿 (6) 🗲 📺 🛏 📖 Ⅴ ♨

Beam End, 67 George Lane,
Marlborough, Wilts, SN8 4BY.
Peaceful detached house, every comfort,
good centre for touring Wiltshire.
Open: All Year (not Xmas)
Grades: ETC 3 Diamond
01672 515048 (also fax)
Mrs Drew
drew@beamend.co.uk
D: £20.00–£27.50 **S:** £20.00–£30.00
Beds: 1T 2S **Baths:** 1 En 1 Sh
🅿 (3) 🗲 📺 📖 ♨

54 George Lane, Marlborough,
Wiltshire, SN8 4BY.
Near town centre. Detached house -
Large garden. Non smokers only.
Open: All Year (not Xmas/New Year)
01672 512579 Mr & Mrs Young
D: fr £17.00 **S:** fr £17.00
Beds: 1T 2S **Baths:** 1 Sh
🅿 (3) 🗲 📖 Ⅴ ♨

West View, Barnfield, Marlborough,
Wiltshire, SN8 2AX.
Delightful peaceful, rural home, close to
town. Ideal walkers, cyclists.
Open: All Year
Grades: ETC 3 Diamond
01672 515583 Fax: 01672 519014
maggiestewart@euphony.net
D: £20.00–£25.00 **S:** £35.00–£45.00
Beds: 1F 3D **Baths:** 2 Pr 1 Sh
🛇 🅿 (3) 🗲 📺 🛏 ✕ 📖 Ⅴ ♨ &

Sunrise Farm, Manton, Marlborough,
Wilts, SN8 4HL.
Peacefully located approximately 1 mile
from Marlborough. Friendly, comfortable,
relaxing atmosphere.
Open: March to Oct
Grades: ETC 3 Diamond
01672 512878 (also fax)
Mrs Couzens
D: £19.00–£20.00 **S:** £19.00–£25.00
Beds: 1D 2T **Baths:** 2 Pr
🛇 (14) 🅿 (3) 🗲 📺 📖 Ⅴ ♨

Cartref, 63 George Lane, Marlborough,
Wilts, SN8 4BY.
Family home near town centre. Ideal for
Avebury, Savernake, Wiltshire Downs.
Open: All Year (not Xmas)
01672 512771 Mrs Harrison
cartref@themail.co.uk
D: £18.00 **S:** £20.00
Beds: 1F 1D 1T **Baths:** 1 Sh
🛇 (6) 🅿 (2) 🛏 📖 Ⅴ

Marston

ST9657   ◆ Rose & Crown

Home Farm, Close Lane, Marston,
Devizes, Wilts, SN10 5SN.
C15th Wiltshire long house. Quiet rural
setting, 20 minutes from Stonehenge.
Open: All Year (not Xmas)
01380 725484 Mrs Reardon
D: £20.00–£23.00 **S:** £23.00–£27.00
Beds: 1D 1T **Baths:** 2 En
🛇 🅿 (6) 🗲 📺 📖 Ⅴ ♨

Melksham

ST9063   ◆ Kings Arms, Barge Inn, West End
Inn

Craycroft, 402 The Spa, Spa Road,
Melksham, Wilts, SN12 6QL.
Georgian Spa house, Grade II Listed,
offering a warm welcome, comfortable
accommodation. **Open:** All Year
01225 707984 Mrs Pavey
D: £16.00–£20.00 **S:** £17.00–£21.00
Beds: 1F 1D 1S **Baths:** 2 En 1 Sh
🛇 🅿 (6) 🗲 📺 🛏 📖 Ⅴ ♨

Mere

ST8132   ◆ Talbot Inn, Butt of Sherry, Old Ship

Norwood House, Mere, Warminster,
Wilts, BA12 6LA.
Large ground floor room with French
windows onto pleasant garden.
Open: All Year
01747 860992 (also fax) Mrs Tillbrook
home@tillbrooks.freeserve.co.uk
D: £18.00 **S:** £22.00
Beds: 1F 1T **Baths:** 1 En
🛇 🅿 (3) 📺 🛏 📖 ♨ &

Downleaze, North Street, Mere,
Warminster, Wilts, BA12 6HH.
Comfortable red brick house, quiet, close
to town centre. Warm welcome.
Stourhead - two miles.
Open: All Year (not Xmas/New Year)
Grades: ETC 2 Diamond
01747 860876 Mrs Lampard
D: £16.00–£18.00 **S:** £17.50–£20.00
Beds: 1D 1T **Baths:** 2 En
🛇 (5) 🅿 (6) 🗲 📺 📖 Ⅴ ♨

Netheravon

SU1549   ◆ Dog and Gun

Paddock House, High Street,
Netheravon, Salisbury, Wiltshire, SP4 9QP.
Comfortable village house in Netheravon.
Close to Stonehenge and Avebury.
Open: All Year (not Xmas/New Year)
Grades: ETC 3 Diamond
01980 670401 (also fax) Mrs Davis
D: £18.00–£20.00 **S:** £18.00–£20.00
Beds: 1T 1D **Baths:** 1 En 1 Sh
🛇 (3) 🅿 (2) 🗲 📺 📖 Ⅴ ♨

Netton

SU1336   ◆ Bridge, Black Horse

The Old Bakery, Netton, Salisbury,
Wilts, SP4 6AW.
The Old Bakery is a pleasantly
modernised former village bakery in the
Woodford Valley.
Open: All Year (not Xmas)
Grades: ETC 3 Diamond
01722 782351 Mrs Dunlop
valahen@aol.com
D: £18.00–£20.00 **S:** £20.00–£25.00
Beds: 1D 1T 1S **Baths:** 2 En 1 Pr
🛇 (5) 🅿 (3) 📺 📖 ♨

Thorntons, Netton, Salisbury, Wilts, SP4
6AW.
Tranquil village convenient for Salisbury
and Stonehenge. Home cooking a
speciality. **Open:** All Year (not Xmas)
01722 782535 (also fax) Mrs Bridger
D: £18.00–£20.00 **S:** £20.00–£25.00
Beds: 1F 1D 1S **Baths:** 2 Sh
🛇 (5) 🅿 🗲 📺 📖 Ⅴ ♨ &

Avonbank, Netton, Salisbury, Wilts, SP4
6AW.
Open: All Year (not Xmas)
Grades: ETC 3 Diamond
01722 782331 Mrs Vincent
vincent@netton.freeserve.co.uk
D: £16.00–£20.00 **S:** £20.00–£25.00
Beds: 3F 2T 1D **Baths:** 1 En 1 Sh
🛇 🅿 (3) 🗲 📺 ✕ 📖 Ⅴ ♨ &
Comfortable modern house with very
pretty garden overlooking water meadow
and River Avon. Guests sitting room.
good breakfast with home-made
marmalade and jams. Baby sitting by
arrangement. It is possible to obtain day
fishing license.

Nomansland

SU2517   ◆ Lamb

Clovenway House, Forest Road,
Nomansland, Sailsbury, Wiltshire, SP5 2BN.
Country house, garden overlook New
Forest, close - village pub, restaurant.
Open: All Year
Grades: AA 4 Diamond
01794 390620 (also fax) Mrs Fryer
D: £18.00–£22.00 **S:** £20.00–£30.00
Beds: 1F 1T 1D **Baths:** 1 En 2 Pr
🛇 (5) 🅿 (4) 🗲 📺 🛏 📖 Ⅴ ♨

Oaksey

ST9993

Manby's Farm, Oaksey, Malmesbury,
Wiltshire, SN16 9SA.
Open: All Year
Grades: ETC 4 Diamond, Commended,
AA 4 Diamond
01666 577399 Mr Shewry-Fitzgerald
Fax: 01666 577241
D: £20.00–£23.00 **S:** £25.00–£35.00
Beds: 1F 1T 1D **Baths:** 3 En
🛇 (3) 🅿 🗲 📺 ✕ 📖 Ⅴ ♨ & cc
A warm welcome awaits guests at our
farmhouse, situation on the Wilts/Glos
border. Bright, cheerful rooms, ground &
first floor, adaptable accommodation.
Relax over breakfast in our elegant dining
room. Ideal location for visiting Bath,
Cotswolds, Oxford. Wheelchair friendly.

All details shown are as
supplied by B&B owners in
Autumn 2000

Ogbourne St George

SU1974 🍺 *Old Crown*

The Old Crown, *Marlborough Road,
Ogbourne St George, Marlborough, Wilts,
SN8 1SQ.*
Close to historic Marlborough. Covered
well in restaurant.
Open: All Year (not Xmas/New Year)
01672 841445 Mr & Mrs Shaw
Fax: 01672 841056
info@theinnwiththewell.com
D: £20.00–£30.00 **S:** £35.00–£45.00
Beds: 2T **Baths:** 2 Pr
🛏 🅿 (15) ⅍ 🗹 � ✕ 🍽 🖳 🎇 🐾 **cc**

Pewsey

SU1660 🍺 *French Horn*

Old Dairy House, *Sharcott, Pewsey,
Wilts, SN9 5PA.*
Thatched dairy house in four acres.
Pewsey 1 mile. **Open:** All Year
Grades: ETC 4 Diamond
01672 562287
Mr & Mrs Stone
old.dairy@virgin.net
D: £30.00 **S:** £35.00

Potterne

ST9958 🍺 *George & Dragon*

Blounts Court Farm, *Coxhill Lane,
Potterne, Devizes, Wiltshire, SN10 5NQ.*
Traditional farmhouse set in 150 acres;
beautiful rooms, homely atmosphere.
Open: All Year
Grades: ETC 5 Diamond, Gold, AA 5
Diamond
01380 727180
Mr & Mrs Cary
D: £25.00 **S:** £32.00–£37.00
Beds: 1D 1T **Baths:** 2 En
🛏 (8) 🅿 ⅍ 🗹 🏇 🍽 🖳 🎇 🐾

Poulshot

ST9659 🍺 *Raven*

Poulshot Lodge Farm, *Poulshot,
Devizes, Wilts, SN10 1RQ.*
Picturesque farmhouse in Poulshot;
centrally situated for exploring historic
Wiltshire. **Open:** All Year (not Xmas)
01380 828255 Mr & Mrs Hues
D: £19.00–£20.00 **S:** £20.00–£22.00
Beds: 2T **Baths:** 1 Sh
🛏 (5) 🅿 (2) ⅍ 🗹 🍽 🖳 🎇

Townsend Farmhouse, *Poulshot,
Devizes, Wilts, SN10 1SD.*
Large, comfortable farmhouse on
outskirts of village in central Wiltshire.
Open: All Year
01380 828221 (also fax) Mrs Young
mg.boo@virgin.net
D: £16.00–£20.00 **S:** £16.00–£18.00
Beds: 2D 1T **Baths:** 1 Sh
🛏 (4) 🅿 (3) 🗹 🏇 🖳 🎇

Higher Green Farm, *Poulshot,
Devizes, Wilts, SN10 4RW.*
Peaceful C17th timbered farmhouse,
facing village green, inn nearby.
Open: Easter to Nov
01380 828355 Mrs Nixon
D: £18.00 **S:** £18.00
Beds: 1D 1T 2S **Baths:** 2 Sh
🛏 🅿 (6) ⅍ 🗹 🏇 🍽 🖳 🎇

Redlynch

SU2021 🍺 *Kings Head, Apple Tree*

Yew Tree Cottage, *Grove Lane,
Redlynch, Salisbury, Wilts, SP5 2NR.*
Open: All Year
01725 511730 Mr & Mrs Churchill
D: £18.00–£20.00 **S:** £18.00–£20.00
Beds: 1D 1T 1S **Baths:** 1 Sh
🛏 🅿 (6) ⅍ 🗹 🍽 🖳 🎇
Spacious country house in large garden
overlooking Paddock. In pretty New
Forest Village, Redlynch, near Salisbury
Cathedral city. welcoming, comfortable,
relaxing, good breakfasts, guests lounge.
Superb for quiet walking, cycling, forest,
downland, riding, golf, fishing. Ideal
exploration base.

Saddlers, *Princes Hill, Redlynch,
Salisbury, Wilts, SP5 2HF.*
Pretty cottage in New Forest Heritage
area. Salisbury 7 miles.
Open: All Year (not Xmas/New Year)
Grades: ETC 4 Diamond
01725 510571 (also fax)
Mrs Sanders
annesbandb@saddlers.org.uk
D: £16.50–£20.00 **S:** £20.00
Beds: 1D 1T **Baths:** 1 Sh
🛏 🅿 (2) ⅍ 🗹 🏇 🖳 🎇

Rushall

SU1256 🍺 *Swan, Charlton Cat*

Little Thatch, *Rushall, Pewsey, Wilts,
SN9 6EN.*
A picturesque thatched house with a
beautiful garden in heart of Wiltshire
countryside.
Open: All Year
Grades: ETC 3 Diamond
01980 635282 (also fax)
Mrs Newton
D: £21.50 **S:** £25.00
Beds: 1T **Baths:** 1 En
🅿 (2) ⅍ 🖳 🎇

Salisbury

SU1430 🍺 *Avon Brewery, Barford Inn, Bell Inn,
Castle Inn, Fox & Goose, George & Dragon, Grey
Fisher, Haunch Of Venison, Hogs Head, Markest
Inn, Radnor Arms, Ship, White Hart, White Horse,
Wyndham Arms Yew Tree*

Swaynes Firs Farm, *Grimsdyke,
Coombe Bissett, Salisbury, Wilts, SP5 5RF.*
Spacious farmhouse on working farm
with horses, cattle, poultry, geese & duck
ponds etc.
Open: All Year (not Xmas)
Grades: ETC 3 Diamond
01725 519240 Mr Shering
swaynes.firs@virgin.net
D: £20.00–£22.00 **S:** £25.00–£30.00
Beds: 1F 2T **Baths:** 3 En
🛏 🅿 (6) 🗹 🏇 🖳 🎇

The Old Rectory B&B, *Belle Vue
Road, Salisbury, Wiltshire, SP1 3YE.*
Open: All Year
Grades: ETC 4 Diamond
01722 502702 Ms Smith
Fax: 01722 501135
stay@theoldrectory.co.uk
D: £18.00–£27.00 **S:** £20.00–£40.00
Beds: 2T 1D **Baths:** 2 En 1 Pr
🛏 (10) 🅿 (1) ⅍ 🗹 🍽 🖳 🎇
Welcoming Victorian home, nestled in
rich green English garden on a quiet
street. Offering warm hospitality, bright
airy bedrooms, quiet breakfast/sitting
room with picture window and open fire.
Short walk to city centre. Perfect for a
quiet comfortable stay.

Weaver's Cottage, *37 Bedwin Street,
Salisbury, Wilts, SP1 3UT.*
C15th city centre cottage, cosy, oak-
beamed, 2 minutes market square & bus
station.
Open: All Year (not Xmas)
01722 341812 Mrs Bunce
D: £15.00–£20.00 **S:** £23.00–£25.00
Beds: 1F 1D **Baths:** 1 Sh
🗹 🖳 🎇

Hayburn Wyke Guest House, *72
Castle Road, Salisbury, Wilts, SP1 3RL.*
Open: All Year
Grades: AA 3 Diamond, RAC 3 Diamond
01722 412627 Mrs Curnow
hayburn.wyke@tinyonline.co.uk
D: £20.00–£25.00 **S:** £29.00–£48.00
Beds: 2F 3D 2T **Baths:** 4 En 3 Sh
🛏 🅿 (7) 🗹 🖳 🎇 🐾 **cc**
A family run friendly guest house,
Hayburn Wyke is a fine Victorian house,
situated by Victoria Park, half a mile
riverside walk from Salisbury Cathedral
and city centre. Many places to visit
locally, including Stonehenge, Wilton
House and Old Sarum.

Websters, *11 Hartington Road,
Salisbury, Wilts, SP2 7LG.*
Set on the end of a delightfully colourful
terrace with sumptuous choices for
breakfast.
Open: All Year
Grades: ETC 4 Diamond, Silver, RAC 4
Diamond, Sparkling
01722 339779 (also fax)
Mrs Webb
websters.salis@eclipse.co.uk
D: £19.00–£21.00
S: £30.00–£34.00
Beds: 1D 2T 2S **Baths:** 5 En
🛏 (12) 🅿 (5) 🗹 ✕ 🖳 🎇 🐾 1 **cc**

The White Horse Hotel, *38 Castle
Street, Salisbury, Wilts, SP1 1BN.*
Open: All Year
01722 327844 Fax: 01722 336226
D: £35.00–£50.00 **S:** £27.00–£35.00
Beds: 2F 3T 4D
Baths: 1 En 2 Sh
🛏 🅿 (9) 🗹 ✕ 🖳 🎇 **cc**
Traditional pub/ Inn offering a beautiful
Cathedral view and only 10 minutes walk.
Off side parking. Comfortable rooms.
Home cooked pub food. Friendly
welcoming service.

Wyndham Park Lodge, *51 Wyndham Road, Salisbury, Wilts, SP1 3AB.*
Large Victorian house, close to city centre. Friendly family-run establishment.
Open: All Year
Grades: ETC 4 Diamond
01722 416517 Fax: 01722 328851
wyndham@wyndham51.freeserve.co.uk
D: £19.00–£21.00 **S:** £26.00–£32.00
Beds: 1F 1T 1D 1S **Baths:** 4 En
⌂ ▣ (3) 📺 🗚 Ⓥ ⚲

Byways House, *31 Fowlers Road, Salisbury, Wilts, SP1 2QP.*
Attractive Victorian House, quiet, parking. Fowlers Road opposite youth hostel.
Open: All Year (not Xmas/New Year)
Grades: ETC 3 Diamond
01722 328364 Mr & Mrs Arthey
Fax: 01722 322146
byways@bed-breakfast-salisbury.co.uk
D: £22.50–£39.00 **S:** £30.00–£60.00
Beds: 3F 7T 7D 4S **Baths:** 19 En 1 Sh
⌂ ▣ (15) 🗚 📺 🍴 🗚 ⚲ ♿ **cc**

Cricket Field House Hotel, *Wilton Road, Salisbury, Wilts, SP2 7NS.*
All rooms ensuite. Ample car parking. Beautiful garden.
Open: All Year (not Xmas)
Grades: AA 4 Diamond
01722 322595 (also fax)
Mrs James
D: £30.00–£35.00 **S:** £40.00–£45.00
Beds: 1F 7D 3T 3S **Baths:** 14 En
▣ (14) 🗚 📺 ✕ 🗚 Ⓥ ⚲ ♿

Farthings, *9 Swaynes Close, Wyndham Road, Salisbury, Wilts, SP1 3AE.*
Comfortable old house in quiet street near city centre.
Open: All Year
Grades: ETC 3 Diamond
01722 330749 (also fax)
Mrs Rodwell
farthings@shammer.freeserve.co.uk
D: £20.00–£25.00 **S:** fr £20.00
Beds: 1D 1T 2S **Baths:** 2 En 1 Sh
▣ (1) 🗚 📺 🗚 ⚲

Richburn Guest House, *25 Estcourt Road, Salisbury, Wilts, SP1 3AP.*
Building over 150 years old - 5 mins walk city centre,10 minutes Cathedral.
Open: All Year (not Xmas/New Year)
Grades: ETC 3 Diamond
01722 325189 (also fax)
Mrs West
D: £18.00–£30.00 **S:** £20.00–£40.00
Beds: 1F 1D 1T 1S **Baths:** 4 En
⌂ (10) ▣ (5) 🗚 📺 🍴 ✕ 🗚 ⚲

Castlewood Guest House, *45 Castle Road, Salisbury, Wilts, SP1 3RH.*
Large Edwardian house tastefully restored throughout, pleasant 10 mins' riverside walk city centre.
Open: All Year
Grades: ETC 3 Diamond
01722 324809 Mrs Feltham
Fax: 01722 421494
D: £20.00–£22.50 **S:** £20.00–£25.00
Beds: 3F 1D 1T 1S **Baths:** 3 En 2 Sh
⌂ ▣ (4) 🗚 📺 🍴 ✕ ⚲

The Old Bakery, *35 Bedwin Street, Salisbury, Wilts, SP1 3UT.*
C15th house, cosy oak-beamed bedrooms, city centre location. Room only rates also available.
Open: All Year (not Xmas)
Grades: ETC 2 Diamond
01722 320100 Mrs Bunce
D: £19.00–£26.00 **S:** £23.00–£26.00
Beds: 1F 1D 1T 1S **Baths:** 2 En 1 Sh
⌂ 📺 🗚 ⚲

48 Wyndham Road, *Salisbury, Wilts, SP1 3AB.*
Edwardian home, tastefully restored and furnished with antiques, close to city centre, quiet area.
Open: All Year (not Xmas)
01722 327757 Mrs Jukes
D: £17.00–£20.00 **S:** fr £20.00
Beds: 2D 1T **Baths:** 1 En 1 Sh
⌂ 🗚 📺 🗚 ⚲

Gerrans House, *91 Castle Road, Salisbury, Wilts, SP1 3RW.*
Comfortable detached house, private facilities and secure parking.
Open: Easter to Nov
01722 334394 Mrs Robins
Fax: 01722 332508
D: £20.00–£23.00 **S:** £30.00–£35.00
Beds: 1D 1T **Baths:** ? Fn
⌂ (7) ▣ (2) 🗚 📺 🗚 ⚲

Leenas Guest House, *50 Castle Road, Salisbury, Wilts, SP1 3RL.*
Friendly family-run guest house. Pretty bedrooms and delightful public areas.
Open: All Year
01722 335419 (also fax)
Mrs Street
D: £21.00–£24.00 **S:** £22.00–£36.00
Beds: 1F 2D 2T 1S **Baths:** 5 En 1 Sh
⌂ ▣ (6) 📺 🗚 ⚲

ST9261   🍺 *Barge Inn*

Rew Farm, *Seend Cleeve, Melksham, Wiltshire, SN12 6PS.*
Working dairy farm. Few minutes walk to Kennet and Avon Canal.
Open: All Year (not Xmas/New Year)
Grades: ETC 3 Diamond
01380 828289 A Newman
D: £20.00 **S:** £25.00
Beds: 1T
⌂ ▣ (2) 🗚 📺 🗚 Ⓥ ⚲

ST8960   🍺 *Linnet, Somerset Arms, Lamb on the Strand*

New House Farm, *Littleton, Semington, Trowbridge, Wilts, BA14 6LF.*
Victorian former farmhouse, open countryside, lovely gardens, good touring centre.
Open: All Year
Grades: ETC 3 Diamond
01380 870349 Mrs Ball
D: £20.00 **S:** £25.00
Beds: 2D 1T **Baths:** 3 En
⌂ ▣ (10) 🗚 📺 ✕ 🗚 ⚲ ♿

Brook House, *Semington, Trowbridge, Wilts, BA14 6JR.*
Georgian house, large grounds. Convenient for Bath, Stonehenge and canal.
Open: Feb to Nov
01380 870232 Mrs Bruges
Fax: 01380 871431
D: £19.00–£25.00 **S:** £25.00
Beds: 1F 1D 1T **Baths:** 1 En 1 Sh
⌂ ▣ 🗚 🗚 🍴 🗚 ⚲

SU2090   🍺 *Radnor, Carriers Arms*

Roves Farm, *Sevenhampton, Swindon, Wilts, SN6 7QG.*
Spacious comfortable quiet accommodation surrounded by beautiful countryside on a working farm.
Open: All Year
Grades: ETC 3 Diamond
01793 763939 (also fax)
joanna@rovesfarm.co.uk
D: £20.00–£22.00 **S:** £26.00–£27.00
Beds: 1F 1T **Baths:** 2 En
⌂ ▣ (4) 🗚 📺 🗚 Ⓥ ⚲

ST8586   🍺 *Rattlebone Inn, Carpenters Arms*

Widleys Farm, *Sherston, Malmesbury, Wilts, SN16 0PY.*
200-year-old farmhouse. Peaceful and quiet. Log fires in season. Working farm.
Open: All Year (not Xmas)
Grades: ETC 3 Diamond
01666 840213 Mrs Hibbard
Fax: 01666 840156
D: £20.00–£25.00 **S:** £20.00–£25.00
Beds: 1F 1D 1T **Baths:** 1 En 1 Sh
⌂ ▣ (6) 📺 🗚 ⚲

SU0644   🍺 *George*

Maddington House, *Shrewton, Salisbury, Wilts, SP3 4JD.*
Beautiful Listed C17th house, three miles from Stonehenge.
Open: All Year (not Xmas)
01980 620406 (also fax)
Mrs Robothan
D: £20.00–£25.00 **S:** fr £25.00
Beds: 1F 1D 1T **Baths:** 2 En 1 Pr
⌂ ▣ (4) 🗚 📺 🗚 Ⓥ ⚲

SU0737   🍺 *Swan Inn*

Elm Tree Cottage, *Stapleford, Salisbury, Wilts, SP3 4LH.*
Light airy rooms with conservatory or large garden for relaxation.
Open: Easter to Oct
01722 790507 Mrs Sykes
jan.sykes@virgin.net
D: £22.50–£25.00 **S:** fr £22.00
Beds: 1F 2D **Baths:** 3 Pr
⌂ ▣ (3) 📺 🍴 🗚 Ⓥ ⚲

Planning a longer stay? Always ask for any special rates

Steeple Ashton

ST9056

Spiers Piece Farm, Steeple Ashton, Trowbridge, Wilts, BA14 6HG.
Fantastic views, spacious garden and farmhouse, peace in countryside location.
Open: Feb to Nov
01380 870266 (also fax)
Ms Awdry
D: £16.50–£18.00 **S:** £17.00–£19.00
Beds: 2D 1T **Baths:** 2 Sh
🛏 (1) 🅿 (10) 🔟 🛏 🎢 🔟 🅥 ⚘

Sutton Veny

ST9041 🍺 Angel

The Beeches Farm, Deverill Road, Sutton Veny, Warminster, BA12 7BY.
Many animals, lovely views, adaptable relaxed atmosphere, Longleat 10 mins.
Open: All Year
01985 840796 (also fax)
Mrs Ridout
D: £17.50–£20.00 **S:** £20.00–£25.00
Beds: 1F **Baths:** 1 En
🛏 🅿 (5) ⅍ 🔟 🛏 🗙 🅥 ⚘

Swindon

SU1685 🍺 Kingsdown, Regent Hotel, Savoy, Wheatsheaf

Bradford Guest House, 40 Devizes Road, Old Town, Swindon, Wilts, SN1 4BG.
Small friendly guest house.
Open: All Year (not Xmas/New Year)
01793 642427 Ms McCalla
Fax: 01793 430381
sam@smccalla.freeserve.co.uk
D: £21.00–£24.00 **S:** £27.00–£33.00
Beds: 2T 4D 2S **Baths:** 8 En
🛏 🅿 (8) ⅍ 🔟 🕮 ⚘ **cc**

Abalone Guest House, 7 Sheppard Street, Swindon, Wilts, SN1 7DB.
Town centre location, close to bus and train stations.
Open: All Year
01793 521285 J Strudwick
D: £15.00 **S:** £15.00
Beds: 4F 1D 2T 2S **Baths:** 4 En 1 Sh
🛏 🔟 🕮 ⚘

L'Hotel Du Nord, 100 Country Road, Swindon, SN1 2EP.
Centrally situated family-run business, comfortable room with sat TV, convenient for all town facilities.
Open: All Year
01793 491120 D: £19.00 **S:** £19.50
Beds: 2D 1T 1S **Baths:** 3 En 1 Sh
🛏 (3) 🅿 (4) 🔟 🗙 🕮 ⚘ **cc**

Royston Hotel, 34 Victoria Road, Old Town, Swindon, SN1 3AS.
A charmingly refurbished Victorian town house with a friendly atmosphere.
Open: All Year
01793 522990 Fax: 01793 522991
royston.hotel@easynet.co.uk
D: £17.50–£25.00 **S:** £20.00–£50.00
Beds: 3F 5D 4T 4S **Baths:** 6 En 2 Pr 4 Sh
🛏 🅿 (6) ⅍ 🔟 🛏 🗙 🕮 🅥 ⚘ **cc**

Trowbridge

ST8557 🍺 Lion and Fiddle, Hungerford Arms

62b Paxcroft Cottages, Devizes Road, Hilperton, Trowbridge, Wiltshire, BA14 6JB.
Lovely Garden with far reaching views overlooking the Wiltshire downs.
Open: All Year (not Xmas)
Grades: ETC 3 Diamond
01225 765838 S J Styles
D: £20.00–£22.00 **S:** £20.00–£22.00
Beds: 1F 1T 1D **Baths:** 2 En 1 Pr
🛏 🅿 (6) ⅍ 🔟 🗙 🕮 🅥 ⚘

44 Wingfield Road, Trowbridge, Wilts, BA14 9ED.
Fine Victorian house. 'Home from Home'.
Open: All Year
01225 761455 Mr & Mrs Dobbin
D: fr £20.00 **S:** fr £20.00
Beds: 1F 1D 1T 1S
🛏 🔟 🛏 🗙 🕮 🅥 ⚘ ⚘

Turleigh

ST8060 🍺 Seven Stars

Draycot, Cottles Lane, Turleigh, Bradford on Avon, Wiltshire, BA15 2HJ.
Warm welcome, Peaceful location, Lovely views, Guests sitting room and garden.
Open: All Year (not Xmas/New Year)
01225 863198 Mrs Slingsby
masdraycot@hotmail.com
D: £22.00–£25.00 **S:** £22.00–£30.00
Beds: 1T 1D **Baths:** 2 En
🅿 (3) ⅍ 🔟 🕮 ⚘

Upper Minety

SU0091 🍺 Plough

Flisteridge Cottage, Flisteridge Road, Upper Minety, Malmesbury, Wilts, SN16 9PS.
Country hospitality, quiet seclusion, delicious breakfasts, pretty rooms, large garden. **Open:** All Year
01666 860343 Mrs Toop-Rose
D: £19.00–£22.00 **S:** £19.00–£30.00
Beds: 2D 1T **Baths:** 1 Pr 1 Sh
🛏 (14) 🅿 (4) ⅍ 🔟 🗙 🕮 🅥 ⚘

Warminster

ST8745 🍺 Old Bell

Belmont, 9 Boreham Road, Warminster, BA12 9JP.
Open: All Year
Grades: ETC 4 Diamond
01985 212799 (also fax)
Mrs Monkcom
monkcom@freeuk.com
D: £17.00–£20.00 **S:** £16.00–£25.00
Beds: 2D **Baths:** 1 Sh
🛏 (5) 🅿 (6) ⅍ 🔟 🕮 🅥 ⚘
Well-situated for town, spacious rooms, friendly welcome, good facilities.

Farmers Hotel, 1 Silver Street, Warminster, Wilts, BA12 8PS.
Comfortable family hotel Listed C17th Grade II building.
Open: All Year
01985 213815 (also fax)
Mr Brandani
D: £16.00–£17.50 **S:** £17.00–£25.00
Beds: 4F 5D 2T 10S **Baths:** 13 En 3 Sh
🛏 🅿 (5) 🔟 🛏 🗙 🕮 🅥 ⚘ **cc**

West Ashton

ST8755 🍺 Longs Arms, Hungry Horse

Water Gardens, 131 Yarnbrook Road, West Ashton, Trowbridge, Wiltshire, BA14 6AF.
Detached bungalow, large gardens ideally situated for Bath and Area.
Open: All Year (not Xmas)
Grades: AA 3 Diamond
01225 752045 Mrs Heard
lucy@heard28.freeserve.co.uk
D: fr £18.00
Beds: 1F 1D 1T **Baths:** All En
🅿 (3) ⅍ 🔟 🛏 🗙 🕮 🅥 ⚘

West Lavington

SU0052 🍺 Bridge

Parsonage House, West Lavington, Devizes, Wilts, SN10 4LT.
Welcoming relaxed family home in peaceful surroundings overlooking the church.
Open: All Year (not Xmas/New Year)
01380 813345 Mrs West
D: £20.00–£25.00 **S:** £25.00–£30.00
Beds: 1D 1T **Baths:** 1 Sh
🛏 🅿 (3) ⅍ 🔟 🗙 🕮 🅥 ⚘

The Stage Post, 9 High Street, West Lavington, Devizes, Wilts, SN10 4HQ.
Traditional country inn close to edge of Salisbury Plain, oak-beamed conservatory restaurant.
Open: All Year
01380 813392 Mr & Mrs Irwin
Fax: 01380 818539
stagepost@hotmail.com
D: £25.00–£35.00 **S:** £35.00–£40.00
Beds: 1F 5D 1T 2S **Baths:** 9 En
🛏 🅿 (35) 🔟 🗙 🕮 ⚘ **cc**

West Overton

SU1268 🍺 Bell, Wagon & Horses

Cairncot, West Overton, Marlborough, Wilts, SN8 4ER.
Situated between Avebury and Marlborough, Cairncot offers comfortable accommodation with superb country views.
Open: All Year
Grades: ETC 3 Diamond
01672 861617 Mrs Leigh
aaw@comms-audit.co.uk
D: £20.00–£25.00 **S:** £20.00
Beds: 1D 1S **Baths:** 1 Sh
🛏 🅿 (6) ⅍ 🔟 🛏 🕮 🅥 ⚘

Westbury

ST8650 🍺 Full Moon

Brokerswood House, Brokerswood, Westbury, Wilts, BA13 4EH.
Situated in front of 80 acres of woodland, open to the public.
Open: All Year (not Xmas)
01373 823428 Mrs Phillips
D: £15.00–£18.00 **S:** £15.00–£18.00
Beds: 3F 1D 1T 1S **Baths:** 1 En 1 Pr 1 Sh
🛏 (1) 🅿 (6) ⅍ 🔟 🛏 🅥 ⚘

Whaddon

SU1926

Three Crows Inn, *Old Southampton Road, Whaddon, Salisbury, Wiltshire, SP5 3HB.*
Quiet country inn, oak beams, home cooked food, country walks.
Open: All Year (not Xmas/New Year)
Grades: ETC 3 Diamond
01722 710211 (also fax)
Ms Sutton
lsu4210600@aol.com
D: £36.00–£48.50 **S:** £18.00–£25.00
Beds: 2T 2D **Baths:** 2 En 2 Sh
⌂ 🅿 ⅙ 📺 🏋 ✕ 🛏 🎱 🐾 cc

Whiteparish

SU2524

Newton Farmhouse, *Southampton Road, Whiteparish, Salisbury, Wilts, SP5 2QL.*
Historic C16th farmhouse, close to New Forest, Salisbury & Stonehenge.
Open: All Year
Grades: ETC 5 Diamond, Silver Award, AA 5 Diamond
01794 884416
Mr & Mrs Lanham
Fax: 01794 884416
enquiries@newtonfarmhouse.co.uk
D: £19.00–£25.00 **S:** £25.00–£30.00
Beds: 3F 2T 3D **Baths:** 8 En
⌂ 🅿 (10) ⅙ 📺 ✕ 🛏 🎱 🐾 🎱

Winsley

ST7961   🍽 *Seven Stars*

Conifers, *4 King Alfred Way, Winsley, Bradford-on-Avon, Wilts, BA15 2NG.*
Quiet area, pleasant outlook, friendly atmosphere, convenient Bath, lovely walks.
Open: All Year
Grades: ETC 2 Diamond
01225 722482 Mrs Kettley
D: £17.00–£18.00 **S:** £18.00–£20.00
Beds: 1T 1D **Baths:** 1 Sh
⌂ 🅿 ⅙ 📺 🏋 🛏 🎱

3 Corners, *Cottles Lane, Winsley, Bradford-on-Avon, Wilts, BA15 2HJ.*
House in quiet village edge location, attractive rooms and gardens.
Open: All Year (not Xmas)
01225 865380 Mrs Cole
sandra@turleigh.freeserve.co.uk
D: £22.50–£25.00 **S:** £26.00–£30.00
Beds: 1F 1D **Baths:** 1 En 1 Pr
⌂ 🅿 (4) ⅙ 📺 ✕ 🛏 🎱 🎱

Serendipity

Serendipity, *19f Bradford Road, Winsley, Bradford-on-Avon, Wilts, BA15 2HW.*
Bungalow with beautiful gardens, badgers feeding nightly, ground floor room available.
Open: All Year
Grades: ETC 4 Diamond
01225 722380
Mrs Shepherd
Fax: 01225 723451
vanda.shepherd@tesco.net
D: £21.00–£22.50 **S:** £30.00–£40.00
Beds: 1F 1D 1S **Baths:** 3 En
⌂ 🅿 (5) ⅙ 📺 🛏 🎱 ❋ 🎱 🐾 3

Winterbourne Stoke

SU0741   🍽 *Boot Inn*

Scotland Lodge, *Winterbourne Stoke, Salisbury, SP3 4TF.*
Spacious comfortable rooms, easy access. Good touring centre. Personal service.
Open: All Year
Grades: ETC 4 Diamond, AA 4 Diamond
01980 620943
Mrs Singleton
Fax: 01980 621403
scotland.lodge@virginnet.co.uk
D: £17.50–£27.50 **S:** £25.00–£30.00
Beds: 1F 2T 1D **Baths:** 4 En
⌂ 🅿 ⅙ 📺 🛏 🎱 🎱

Woodborough

SU1159   🍽 *Barge Inn, Seven Stars*

St Cross, *Woodborough, Pewsey, Wilts, SN9 5PL.*
Pewsey Vale - heart of crop circles, beautiful countryside, Kennet & Avon Canal 8 mins' walk.
Open: All Year
01672 851346 (also fax)
Mrs Gore
D: £25.00–£35.00
Beds: 1D 1T **Baths:** 1 Sh
⌂ (6) 🅿 (1) ⅙ 📺 🏋 🎱

Well Cottage, *Honey Street, Woodborough, Pewsey, Wilts, SN9 5PS.*
Warm welcome awaits at our picturesque cottage. Amidst outstanding countryside.
Open: All Year
Grades: ETC 3 Diamond
01672 851577
Mrs Trowbridge
b.trowbridgewellcottage@yahoo.com
D: £18.00–£23.00 **S:** £28.00–£36.00
Beds: 2D 1T **Baths:** 3 En
⌂ 🅿 (4) ⅙ 📺 🏋 ✕ 🛏 🎱 🎱

Woodfalls

SU1920   🍽 *Appletree Inn*

Vale View Farm, *Slab Lane, Woodfalls, Salisbury, Wilts, SP5 2NE.*
Modern attractive farmhouse close to New Forest . Good touring area.
Open: All Year
01725 512116 Mrs Barker
D: £20.00–£22.00 **S:** fr £15.00
Beds: 1D 1T 1S **Baths:** 2 Pr 1 Sh
⌂ (10) 🅿 (4) ⅙ 🛏 🎱

Wootton Bassett

SU0683   🍽 *The George*

The Hollies, *Greenhill Hook, Wootton Bassett, Swindon, SN4 8EH.*
Beautiful countryside, large garden, Swindon 15 mins, Cotswold water parks 20 mins.
Open: All Year (not Xmas)
01793 770795
D: £16.00–£18.00 **S:** £18.00–£19.50
Beds: 2D 1T 1S **Baths:** 2 Sh
⌂ (3) 🅿 (4) ⅙ 📺 🛏 🎱

Yatton Keynell

ST8676   🍽 *Bell Inn, Salutation Inn*

Oakfield Farm, *Easton Piercy Lane, Yatton Keynell, Chippenham, Wilts, SN14 6JU.*
Cotswold stone farmhouse in open countryside. Ideal for Cotswolds, Bath, Stonehenge.
Open: Mar to Oct
01249 782355 Mrs Read
Fax: 01249 783458
D: £20.00–£22.50 **S:** £25.00–£30.00
Beds: 2D 1T **Baths:** 1 En 1 Sh
⌂ 🅿 (8) ⅙ 📺 🛏 🎱 🎱

Zeals

ST7731   🍽 *White Lion*

Cornerways Cottage, *Zeals, Longcross, Warminster, Wilts, BA12 6LL.*
Open: All Year
Grades: ETC 4 Diamond
01747 840477 (also fax)
Mr & Mrs Snook
D: £19.00–£21.00 **S:** £25.00
Beds: 2D 1T **Baths:** 2 En 1 Pr
⌂ (8) 🅿 (6) ⅙ 📺 ✕ 🛏 🎱 🎱
Cornerways is a C18th cottage offering a high standard of accommodation with a lovely 'cottagey' feel, complemented by excellent breakfasts in the old dining room. Stourhead 2 miles, Longleat 4 miles, Bath/Salisbury 25 miles.

Worcestershire

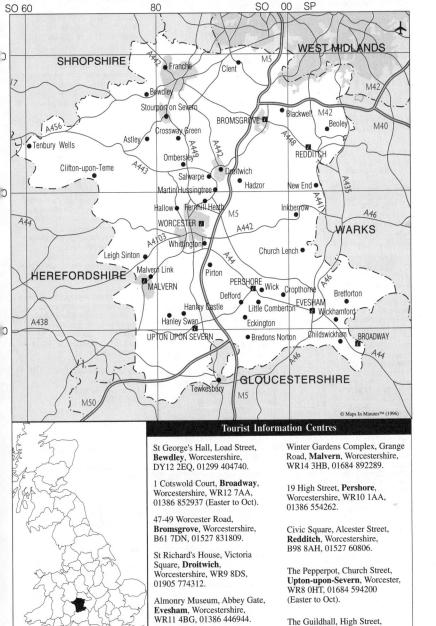

SO 60   80   SO 00 SP

SHROPSHIRE
WEST MIDLANDS
Franche
Clent
M5
Bewdley
M42
Stourport on Severn
Blackwell M42
Beoley
M40
BROMSGROVE
A456
Crossway Green
A448
REDDITCH
Astley
Tenbury Wells
Ombersley
Clifton-upon-Teme
A443
Droitwich
Salwarpe
Martin Hussingtree
Hadzor
New End
A435
Hallow Fernhill Heath
Inkberrow
A46
WORCESTER
M5
A442
WARKS
A4103
Whittington
Church Lench
A44
Leigh Sinton
HEREFORDSHIRE
Malvern Link
Pirton
A46
MALVERN
PERSHORE Wick Cropthorne
Defford
Bretforton
A438
Hanley Castle
Little Comberton
EVESHAM
Hanley Swan
Wickhamford
Eckington
UPTON UPON SEVERN
Bredons Norton
Childswickham
BROADWAY
A44
A46
Tewkesbury M5
GLOUCESTERSHIRE

© Maps In Minutes™ (1996)

M50

Tourist Information Centres

St George's Hall, Load Street, **Bewdley**, Worcestershire, DY12 2EQ, 01299 404740.

1 Cotswold Court, **Broadway**, Worcestershire, WR12 7AA, 01386 852937 (Easter to Oct).

47-49 Worcester Road, **Bromsgrove**, Worcestershire, B61 7DN, 01527 831809.

St Richard's House, Victoria Square, **Droitwich**, Worcestershire, WR9 8DS, 01905 774312.

Almonry Museum, Abbey Gate, **Evesham**, Worcestershire, WR11 4BG, 01386 446944.

Severn Valley Railway Station, Comberton Hill, **Kidderminster**, Worcestershire, DY10 1QX, 01562 829400 (Easter to Oct).

Winter Gardens Complex, Grange Road, **Malvern**, Worcestershire, WR14 3HB, 01684 892289.

19 High Street, **Pershore**, Worcestershire, WR10 1AA, 01386 554262.

Civic Square, Alcester Street, **Redditch**, Worcestershire, B98 8AH, 01527 60806.

The Pepperpot, Church Street, **Upton-upon-Severn**, Worcester, WR8 0HT, 01684 594200 (Easter to Oct).

The Guildhall, High Street, **Worcester**, WR1 2EY, 01905 726311.

Astley

SO7868   🍺 *Red Lion, New Inn*

Woodhampton House, *Weather Lane, Astley, Stourport-on-Severn, Worcestershire, DY13 0SF.*
Set in rural Worcestershire, delightful coach house. Always warm welcome.
Open: All Year (not Xmas/New Year)
Grades: ETC 3 Diamond
01299 826510 Mrs Knight
Fax: 01299 827059
pete-a@sally-a.freeserve.co.uk
D: £22.50–£25.00 **S:** £25.00–£30.00
Beds: 1F 1T 1D 1S **Baths:** 2 En
🐾 🅿 (3) ⊬ 🖰 🏲 🛏 🖮 🎔 ♨ 🕭

Beoley

SP0669

Windmill Hill, *Cherry Pit Lane, Beoley, Redditch, Worcs, B98 9DH.*
C15th-style house and cottage annexe in 11 acres.
Open: All Year (not Xmas)
01527 62284 Mr & Mrs Cotton
Fax: 01527 64476
macotton@tinyonline.co.uk
D: £20.00–£25.00 **S:** £20.00–£25.00
Beds: 1D 1T 2S **Baths:** 1 En 3 Sh
🐾 (1) 🅿 (8) ⊬ 🖰 🛏 🖮 🕭 ♨ 🚻

Bewdley

SO7875   🍺 *Colliers' Arms, Bellman's Cross, James's, Pack Horse*

Lightmarsh Farm, *Crundalls Lane, Bewdley, Worcs, DY12 1NE.*
Elevated position, outstanding views, peaceful location. Comfortable accommodation, quality breakfasts.
Open: All Year (not Xmas/New Year)
Grades: ETC 4 Diamond
01299 404027 Mrs Grainger
D: £22.50 **S:** £30.00
Beds: 1D 1T **Baths:** 1 En 1 Pr
🐾 (10) 🅿 (6) 🖰 🖮 🎔 🕭

Bank House, *14 Lower Park, Bewdley, Worcs, DY12 2DP.*
Warm family atmosphere, superb breakfasts, close to town centre / countryside / river.
Open: All Year (not Xmas)
Grades: AA 3 Diamond
01299 402652 (also fax)
Mrs Nightingale
D: £20.00 **S:** £20.00
Beds: 1F 1T 1S **Baths:** 2 Sh
🐾 🅿 (2) ⊬ 🖰 🖮 🎔 🕭

Tarn B&B, *Long Bank, Bewdley, Worcs, DY12 2QT.*
Unusual House in Acres of Gardens, fields with spectacular views.
Open: Feb to Nov
01299 402243 T Beves
D: £19.00–£21.00 **S:** £23.00–£25.00
Beds: 2T 2S **Baths:** 3 Sh
🐾 🅿 (6) ⊬ 🖰 🖮 🎔

Planning a longer stay? Always ask for any special rates

Blackwell

SO9972

Rosa Lodge, *38 Station Road, Blackwell, Bromsgrove, B60 1PZ.*
Open: All Year
Grades: AA 4 Diamond
0121 445 5440 (also fax)
D: £25.00 **S:** £30.00
Beds: 2D 1T 1S **Baths:** 3 En 1 Pr
🐾 (15) 🅿 (6) ⊬ 🖰 🏲 🛏 🖮 🎔 ♨ 🕭 🚻
Country village house in Blackwell, near Bromsgrove. Tastefully renovated 1989, all ensuite bedrooms are beautifully furnished with many luxuries. Superb food in Edwardian style dining room, 1.5 miles from motorway complex of M42, M5 and M40. Easy access NEC, Birmingham, Stratford, Warwick.

Bredons Norton

SO9339   🍺 *Fox and Hound*

Round Bank House, *Lampitt Lane, Bredons Norton, Tewkesbury, Glos, GL20 7HB.*
Beautiful views and countryside very peaceful homely and comfortable.
Open: All Year (not Xmas/New Year)
Grades: ETC 3 Diamond
01684 772983 Mr & Mrs Thornton
Fax: 01684 773035
D: £37.00–£40.00 **S:** £23.00–£25.00
Beds: 1T 1D **Baths:** 1 En
🐾 🅿 🖰 🖮 🕭

Bretforton

SP0943   🍺 *Wheatsheaf*

The Pond House, *Lower Fields, Weston Road, Bretforton, Evesham, Worcs, WR11 5QA.*
Accommodation in the Cotswolds. Friendly relaxed atmosphere. Perfect base gardens, historical sites, castles.
Open: All Year (not Xmas)
01386 831687 Mrs Payne
Fax: 01386 831558
anne@pondhousebnb.freeserve.co.uk
D: £24.00–£28.00 **S:** £38.00–£46.00
Beds: 2D 2T **Baths:** 4 En
🐾 (8) 🅿 (10) ⊬ 🖰 🖮 🎔 🕭

Broadway

SP0937   🍺 *Crown & Trumpet, Horse & Hounds, Sandy Arms, Fox & Trumpet, Childswickham Arms, Pheasant, Swan Hotel, Bell Inn, Fleece, Olivers*

Crown & Trumpet Inn, *Church Street, Broadway, Worcs, WR12 7AE.*
Open: All Year
Grades: ETC 3 Diamond
01386 853202 Mr Scott
Fax: 01386 834650
ascott@cotswoldholidays.co.uk
D: fr £24.00
Beds: 3D 1T **Baths:** 4 En
🐾 🅿 (6) 🏲 ✕ 🖮 🎔 🕭
C17th Cotswold inn in picturesque village (also on the Cotswold Way). With log fires and oak beams, the Inn specialises in homemade local & seasonal dishes. Ideal base for touring & walking.
http://www.cotswoldholidays.co.uk.

Southwold House, *Station Road, Broadway, Worcs, WR12 7DE.*
Open: All Year
Grades: ETC 4 Diamond, AA 4 Diamond
01386 853681 Mrs Smiles
Fax: 01386 854610
D: £24.00–£25.00 **S:** £25.00–£27.00
Beds: 1F 4D 2T 1S **Baths:** 7 En
🐾 🅿 (8) ⊬ 🖰 🏲 🖮 🎔 🕭 🚻 cc
We invite you to our spacious and tastefully decorated Edwardian house situated in one of the Cotswolds most picturesque villages. We are 4 minutes walk from pubs, restaurants and Cotswold Way. Stately houses and gardens abound. Stratford-upon-Avon 22 minutes.

Brook House, *Station Road, Broadway, Worcs, WR12 7DE.*
Open: All Year (not Xmas)
01386 852313 Mr & Mrs Thomas
D: £20.00–£26.00 **S:** £20.00–£40.00
Beds: 2F 2D 1T 1S **Baths:** 3 En 1 Pr 1 Sh
🐾 🅿 (6) 🖰 🏲 🖮 🎔 🕭
Traditional Victorian house with large rooms, overlooking fields, hills and gardens. Five minutes walk from the village centre. Brookhouse is an ideal centre for exploring Cotswold villages gardens, wildlife centres. With golf courses, fishing river trips and horseriding nearby. Reductions for three or more nights.

Whiteacres Guest House, *Station Road, Broadway, Worcs, WR12 7DE.*
Tastefully decorated Victorian house, two rooms having four poster beds.
Open: All Year (not Xmas)
Grades: ETC 4 Diamond, AA 4 Diamond
01386 852320
Mr Allen
whiteacres@btinternet.com
D: £25.00–£27.50
Beds: 4D 1T **Baths:** 5 En
🅿 (8) ⊬ 🖰 🖮 🕭

Quantocks, *Evesham Road, Broadway, Worcs, WR12 7PA.*
Large detached house in 3 acres with superb views of Cleeve/Bredon/Malvern hills.
Open: March to November
01386 853378
Mr & Mrs Stephens
quantocks_broadway@yahoo.co.uk
D: £22.50–£25.00 **S:** £30.00–£35.00
Beds: 1F 1T **Baths:** 2 En
🐾 🅿 ⊬ 🖰 🖮 🎔 🕭 🚻

Windrush House, *Station Road, Broadway, Worcs, WR12 7DE.*
Elegant Edwardian detached house located near Broadway village green.
Open: All Year
Grades: ETC 4 Diamond, AA 4 Diamond, RAC 4 Diamond
01386 853577
Susan & Richard Pinder
Fax: 01386 853790
richard@broadway-windrush.co.uk
D: £25.00–£30.00 **S:** £25.00–£40.00
Beds: 3D 2T **Baths:** 5 En
🐾 🅿 (6) ⊬ 🖰 🏲 ✕ 🖮 🎔 🕭 ♨ 🕭

The Driffold Guest House, Murcot
Turn, A44, Broadway, Worcs, WR13 7HT.
Country house,large rear garden, near
Broadway. Friendly, welcoming
atmosphere.
Open: All Year
01386 830825 (also fax)
Mr Reohorn and Mrs B Byrne
cotswoldbb@x-stream.co.uk
D: £20.00–£30.00 **S:** £20.00
Beds: 1F 1D 1T 3S **Baths:** 2 En 1 Sh
🛇 (3) 🖫 (10) ⅍ 🖻 ⊁ 🛏 🎟 ✿ 🏃

Olive Branch Guest House, 78 High
Street, Broadway, Worcs, WR12 7AJ.
Family-run C16th Grade II Listed guest
house on Cotswold Way.
Open: All Year
01386 853440
Mr Talboys
Fax: 01386 859070
clive@theolivebranch.u-net.com
D: £23.50–£30.00 **S:** £35.00–£50.00
Beds: 2F 3D 2T 1S **Baths:** 7 En 1 Pr
🛇 🖫 (8) ⅍ 🖻 🎟 🖫 🏃 cc

Pathlow House, 82 High Street,
Broadway, Worcs, WR12 7AJ.
Beautiful Cotswold stone house, with
separate small cottage built in 1720s.
Open: All Year
01386 853444 (also fax)
Mr Green
pathlow@aol.com
D: £17.50–£25.00 **S:** £25.00–£45.00
Beds: 2F 5D 1T **Baths:** 6 En 2 Sh
🛇 🖫 (8) ⅍ 🖻 🛏 ⊁ 🖫 ✿ 🏃 cc

Bromsgrove

SO9570 🍴 Wildmoor Oak, Golden Cross,
Shoulder Of Mutton, Handbury Turn, Talbot

Bea's Lodge, 245 Pennine Road,
Bromsgrove, Worcs, B61 0TG.
Modern house in quiet area, convenient
for M5, M6, M40, M42.
Open: All Year
Grades: ETC 2 Diamond
01527 877613 Mrs Lodge
D: fr £20.00 **S:** fr £20.00
Beds: 1T 1S **Baths:** 1 Sh
🛇 (3) 🖫 (2) ⅍ 🖻 ⊁ 🎟 🏃

Woodcote Farm, Kidderminster Road,
Bromsgrove, Worcs, B61 9EA.
Attractive C18th farmhouse with moated
garden on organic working farm.
Open: All Year
01562 777795 Mrs Prichard
Fax: 01562 777024
D: £20.00–£22.00 **S:** £25.00–£27.50
Beds: 1F 1D 1T **Baths:** 3 En 1 Sh
🛇 🖫 (10) ⅍ 🖻 🛏 🎟 🖫 🏃 ㅊ

Korners, 1 Willow Close, Bromsgrove,
Worcs, B61 8RG.
Walking distance from town, opposite
Saunders Park.
Open: All Year (not Xmas)
01527 832832 Mrs Hunt
D: £20.00–£25.00 **S:** £25.00
Beds: 2T 1S **Baths:** 1 Pr
🛇 🖫 (3) 🖻 🎟 🏃

Childswickham

SP0738

Mount Pleasant Farm,
Childswickham, Broadway, Worcs, WR12
7HZ.
Working farm three miles from Broadway.
Very quiet accommodation, excellent
views.
Open: All Year
Grades: ETC 4 Diamond, AA 4 Diamond,
RAC 4 Diamond
01386 853424 Mrs Perry
D: £23.00–£25.00 **S:** fr £30.00
Beds: 2D 1T 1S **Baths:** 4 Pr
🛇 (5) 🖫 (10) ⅍ 🖻 🎟 🏃

Church Lench

SP0251 🍴 Flyford Arms

Hill Barn Orchard, Evesham Road,
Church Lench, Evesham, Worcs, WR11 4UB.
Stylish house and garden, trout lakes all
in 50 acres.
Open: Easter to Oct
01386 871035 (also fax)
Mr & Mrs Badger
D: fr £25.00 **S:** £40.00
Beds: 2T **Baths:** 2 En
🛇 (6) 🖫 (6) ⅍ 🖻 🛏 ⊁ 🎟 🖫 🏃 ㅊ

Clent

SO9279 🍴 Fountain Inn, French Hen

St Elisabeths Cottage, Woodman
Lane, Clent, Stourbridge, W Mids, DY9 9PX.
Large country cottage close to motorway
links. Excellent pubs nearby.
Open: All Year
Grades: ETC 4 Diamond
01562 883883 Mrs Blankstone
Fax: 01562 885034
D: £26.00–£30.00 **S:** £28.00–£30.00
Beds: 2D 1T **Baths:** 3 En
🖫 (6) ⅍ 🖻 🛏 ⊁ 🎟

Clifton upon Teme

SO7161 🍴 Lion Inn

Pitlands Farm, Clifton upon Teme,
Worcester, WR6 6DX.
C15th farmhouse near Rivers Teme and
Severn, Worcestershire Way.
Open: Mar to Nov
01886 812220 (also fax)
Mrs Mann
D: £20.00–£22.00 **S:** £20.00–£22.00
Beds: 1F 2T **Baths:** 2 En 1 Pr
🛇 (2) 🖫 (10) ⅍ 🎟 🏃

Cropthorne

SO9944 🍴 New Inn

Cedars Guest House, Evesham Road,
Cropthorne, Pershore, Worcs, WR10 3JU.
Ideal for touring Cotswolds, Malverns,
Stratford-upon-Avon & Cheltenham.
Open: All Year
01386 860219 Mrs Ward
cedarsguesthouse@ukonline.co.uk
D: £18.00–£22.00 **S:** £18.00–£25.00
Beds: 1F 2D 2T **Baths:** 3 En 2 Sh
🛇 🖫 (6) ⅍ 🖻 🎟 🖫 🏃

Crossway Green

SO8468 🍴 Crown, Sandys

Yew Tree House, Norchard, Crossway
Green, Stourport on Severn, DY13 9SN.
Open: All Year
Grades: ETC 4 Diamond
01299 250921 Mrs Knight
paul@knightp.swinternet.co.uk
D: fr £25.00 **S:** fr £25.00
Beds: 1F 2T 2D **Baths:** 5 En
🛇 🖫 🖻 🛏 ⊁ 🎟 🖫 🏃
Built in 1754, stepping over the threshold
is a fascinating mix of elegance and
atmosphere. Peacefully tucked away but
convenient to all motorways systems and
sightseeing. Splendid breakfasts
provided, weather permitting served in
beautiful gardens. Tennis court on site by
arrangement.

Defford

SO9143 🍴 Defford Arms

Brook Cottages, Upton Road, Defford,
Worcester, WR8 9BA.
Brook Cottages, 3 miles outside market
town of Pershore set in acre of gardens.
Open: All Year
01386 750229 (also fax)
Mrs Martin
brook_cottages@tesco.net
D: £19.50–£40.00 **S:** £22.50–£40.00
Beds: 1D 1T 1S **Baths:** 2 Sh
🛇 🖫 (5) ⅍ 🖻 🎟 🖫 🏃

Droitwich

SO8963 🍴 Castle, Chequers

Temple Broughton Farm, Broughton
Green, Droitwich, WR9 7EF.
Listed Manor House,elegantly furnished,
Spectacular views with tennis court.
Open: All Year (not Xmas/New Year)
Grades: ETC 4 Diamond, Gold
01905 391456 Mrs Lawson
Fax: 01905 391515
D: £25.00–£27.50 **S:** £30.00–£35.00
Beds: 1T 3D **Baths:** 3 En 1 Sh
🖫 (6) ⅍ 🖻 🎟 🏃

Foxbrook, 238a Worcester Road,
Droitwich, Worcs, WR9 8AY.
Relaxed friendly atmosphere. Close to
motorway, town, centre and bus route.
Open: All Year (not Xmas)
01905 772414 Mrs Turner
D: £17.00–£20.00 **S:** £17.00–£30.00
Beds: 2D 1T 1S **Baths:** 1 En 2 Pr 1 Sh
🖫 (4) ⅍ 🎟 🖫 🏃

Eckington

SO9241 🍴 Bell, Anchor

The Bell Inn, Church Street, Eckington,
Pershore, WR10 3AN.
Country pub restaurant at base of historic
Bredon Hill between Tewkesbury &
Pershore.
Open: All Year
01386 750205 Mrs Livingstone
the_bell_uk@hotmail.com
D: £25.00–£30.00 **S:** £27.50–£35.00
Beds: 1F 2D 1T **Baths:** 4 En
🛇 🖫 🖻 🛏 ⊁ 🎟 🖫 🏃 cc

Evesham

SP0343   ⬛ *Bell, Anchor, Royal Oak, Crown, Strawberry Fields, Fish & Anchor, Witherspoons*

6 Fountain Gardens, *Waterside, Evesham, Worcs, WR11 6JY.*
Evesham town house, non-smoking, friendly, comfortable beds, good food.
Open: All Year
01386 47384 (also fax)
Mrs Roberts
sheila.roberts@care4free.net
D: £15.00–£17.00 **S:** £15.00–£17.00
Beds: 1D 1S **Baths:** 1 Sh
🅿 (4) ⅋ 📺 ✕ 🛒 Ⅴ ✿

Anglers View, *90 Albert Road, Evesham, Worcs, WR11 4LA.*
5 minutes form town/bus stations and River Avon.
Open: All Year
01386 442141 S Tomkotwicz
sarahbandb2000atyahoo.co.uk
D: £17.50–£30.00 **S:** £20.00–£35.00
Beds: 1F 3T **Baths:** 1 Pr 2 Sh
🐾 🅿 (2) ⅋ 📺 ✕ 🛒 🟦 🛒

26 Greenhill, *Evesham, Worcs, WR11 4LP.*
Sudely Castle, Ragley Hall, Stratford-upon-Avon. All within 14 miles.
Open: All Year
01386 40560 Mr & Mrs Barrett
D: £15.00–£25.00 **S:** £25.00–£50.00
Beds: 1F 1D 1T **Baths:** 2 Pr 1 Sh
🐾 🅿 (3) 📺 🛒 Ⅴ ✕ ⅋

Fircroft, *84 Greenhill, Evesham, Worcs, WR11 4NH.*
Elegant house in attractive gardens with relaxed and friendly atmosphere.
Open: Easter to Oct
01386 45828 Ms Greenwood
D: £18.00–£22.00 **S:** fr £25.00
Beds: 1F 1T **Baths:** 1 En
🐾 🅿 (6) ⅋ 📺 🛒 🛒

Park View Hotel, *Waterside, Evesham, Worcs, WR11 6BS.*
Friendly family-run riverside hotel tour the Cotswolds and Shakespeare country.
Open: All Year (not Xmas)
01386 442639 Mr & Mrs Spires
mike.spires@btinternet.com
D: £19.00–£21.00 **S:** £21.00–£24.00
Beds: 6D 10T 10S **Baths:** 7 Sh
🐾 🅿 (30) 📺 🛒 ✕ Ⅴ cc

Bowers Hill Farm, *Bowers Hill, Willersey, Evesham, Worcs, WR11 5HG.*
Secluded & peaceful location with tree-lined drive & large garden. Clean & comfortable.
Open: All Year
01386 834585 Ms Bent
Fax: 01386 830234
sarah@bowershillfarm.com
D: £22.50–£25.00 **S:** £30.00–£35.00
Beds: 1F 1D 1T **Baths:** 2 En 1 Pr
🐾 🅿 (5) ⅋ 📺 🛒 🛒 Ⅴ ✿ 🛒

B&B owners may vary rates - be sure to check when booking

Fernhill Heath

SO8659   ⬛ *White Hart*

Heathside, *Droitwich Road, Fernhill Heath, Worcester, WR3 7UA.*
Victorian house extension, high standards, gardens, conservatory, car park; licensed.
01905 458245 (also fax) Mr Lewis
D: £20.00–£25.00 **S:** £25.00–£29.00
Beds: 1D 3T 5S **Baths:** 6 En 3 Sh
🐾 🅿 (13) ⅋ 📺 🛒 🛒 🛒 cc

Franche

SO8178   ⬛ *The Bellmans Cross*

Hollies Farm Cottage, *Franche, Kidderminster, Worcestershire, DY11 5RW.*
Country cottage. Peaceful location just off the beaten track.
Open: All Year (not Xmas/New Year)
Grades: ETC 4 Diamond
01562 745677 Mrs Glover
Fax: 01562 824580
pete@top-floor.fsbusiness.co.uk
D: £20.00–£22.00 **S:** £22.00–£24.00
Beds: 1T 1D **Baths:** 1 En 1 Pr
🐾 🅿 ⅋ 📺 🛒 🛒 Ⅴ 🛒

Hadzor

SO9162   ⬛ *The Eagle and the Sun*

Hadzor Court, *Hadzor, Droitwich, Worcs, WR9 7DR.*
Open: All Year (not Xmas)
01905 794401 / 0966 512755 Mrs Brooks
Fax: 01905 794636
jbbrooks_hadzor@hotmail.com
D: £20.00 **S:** £25.00–£30.00
Beds: 1D 1T **Baths:** 2 En
🅿 ⅋ 📺 ✕ 🛒 Ⅴ 🛒
Listed farmhouse in historic hamlet . Wonderful character, antiques, countryside, sun-terrace, business and meeting facilities, cellar bar, country weddings. 40 mins Stratford upon Avon, 25 mins Worcester, 40 mins Birmingham Airport, NEC.

Hallow

SO8258   ⬛ *Wagon Wheel, Hunter's Lodge*

Ivy Cottage, *Sinton Green, Hallow, Worcester, WR2 6NP.*
Charming cottage in quiet village, four miles from Worcester centre.
Open: Mar to Oct **Grades:** ETC 4 Diamond
01905 641123 Mrs Rendle
D: £21.00 **S:** £25.00–£30.00
Beds: 1D 1T 1S **Baths:** 1 En 1 Pr
🐾 🅿 (4) ⅋ 📺 🛒 🛒 Ⅴ 🛒

Hanley Castle

SO8341   ⬛ *Railway Inn, Plough & Harrow, Swan*

The Chestnuts, *Gilberts End, Hanley Castle, Worcester, Worcs, WR8 0AS.*
Delightful family home with a relaxed welcoming atmosphere in a tranquil setting. **Open:** All Year
Grades: ETC 4 Diamond, AA 4 Diamond
01684 311219 Ms Parker
D: £20.00–£25.00 **S:** £20.00–£30.00
Beds: 1F 1T 1D **Baths:** 3 En
🐾 🅿 ⅋ 📺 🛒 Ⅴ 🛒

Four Hedges,

The Rhydd, Hanley Castle, Malvern, Worcester, WR8 0AD.
Friendly family house, spacious garden. Three Counties Showground 4 miles.
Open: All Year (not Xmas)
Grades: AA 2 Diamond
01684 310405 (also fax)
Mrs Cooper
fredgies@aol.com
D: £15.00–£17.00 **S:** £15.00–£17.00
Beds: 1D 1T 2S **Baths:** 1 En 1 Sh
🐾 🅿 (5) ⅋ 📺 🛒 🛒

Hanley Swan

SO8143   ⬛ *Swan Inn*

Pyndar Lodge, *Roberts End, Hanley Swan, Worcester, WR8 0DN.*
Elegant, spacious, homely accommodation in a beautiful English village.
Open: All Year (not Xmas)
01684 310716 Ms Thompson
wat@itsystems.co.uk
D: £22.00–£30.00 **S:** £30.00–£35.00
Beds: 2D 1T **Baths:** 3 En
🐾 🅿 (6) ⅋ 📺 🛒 Ⅴ 🛒

Yew Tree House, *Hanley Swan, Worcester, WR8 0DN.*
Attractive Georgian house in picturesque village at the foot of the Malvern Hills.
Open: All Year (not Xmas)
01684 310736 Mr Young
Fax: 01684 311709
yewtreehs@aol.com
D: £20.00–£25.00 **S:** £28.00–£32.00
Beds: 2D 1T **Baths:** 3 En
🐾 🅿 (6) ⅋ 📺 🛒 Ⅴ 🛒 ♿

Inkberrow

SP0057   ⬛ *Bull's Head*

Perrymill Farm, *Little Inkberrow, Inkberrow, Worcester, WR7 4JQ.*
Attractive Georgian farmhouse set in rural Worcestershire - family run.
Open: All Year
Grades: ETC 3 Diamond
01386 792177 Mrs Alexander
Fax: 01386 793449
alexander@estatesgazette.net
D: fr £25.00 **S:** fr £25.00
Beds: 1T 1D 1S **Baths:** 1 Sh
🐾 🅿 (8) 📺 🛒 ✕ 🛒 Ⅴ 🛒

Leigh Sinton

SO7750   ⬛ *Red Lion*

Chirkenhill, *Leigh Sinton, Malvern, Worcs, WR13 5DE.*
Beautiful farmhouse with extensive views. Arkley House in ITV's Noah's Ark series.
Open: All Year
01886 832205 Mrs Wenden
D: £20.00 **S:** £25.00
Beds: 2D 1T **Baths:** 3 Pr
🐾 🅿 (6) 📺 🛒 🛒

All details shown are as supplied by B&B owners in Autumn 2000

Little Comberton

SO9643   ◀ *Old Mill*

Byeways, *Pershore Road, Little Comberton, Pershore, Worcs, WR10 3EW.*
Countryside location centrally situated for visiting Stratford, Broadway, Cheltenham, Oxford.
Open: Jan to Nov
Grades: ETC 3 Diamond
01386 710203 (also fax) G Wright
D: £16.00–£20.00 **S:** £18.00–£20.00
Beds: 1F

Malvern

SO7846   ◀ *Bluebell Inn, Red Lion, Hawthorn Inn*

Nether Green Farm, *Ridge Way Cross, Malvern, Worcs, WR13 5JS.*
5 Miles to Spa Town of Malvern and the Malvern hills for great walking.
Open: All Year (not Xmas)
01886 880387 Mrs Orford
D: £16.00 **S:** £16.00
Beds: 1D 1T 1S **Baths:** 1 Sh
🐾 🅿 (3) 🍴 ▥ 🎱 ♿

Priory Holme, *18 Avenue Road, Malvern, Worcs, WR14 3AR.*
Victorian family home situated in tree lined avenue: walking distance town centre & station.
Open: All Year
Grades: ETC 4 Diamond
01684 568455 Mrs Emuss
D: £25.00–£28.00 **S:** £25.00–£32.00
Beds: 1F 1D 1T 1S **Baths:** 4 En 1 Pr 1 Sh
🐾 🅿 (4) ⊬ ▥ 🍴 ✕ ▥ ♿

Kylemore, *30 Avenue Road, Malvern, Worcs, WR14 3BJ.*
Large Victorian house standing in 0.33 acre.
Open: All Year (not Xmas)
01684 563753 Mrs Bell
D: £15.00–£16.00 **S:** £15.00–£16.00
Beds: 2D 1T 1S **Baths:** 1 Sh
🐾 🅿 (4) ▥ 🍴 ♿

The Mill House, *16 Clarence Road, Malvern, Worcs, WR14 3EH.*
Quiet but central to Gt Malvern station, fitness centre, theatres.
Open: All Year (not Xmas)
01684 562345 (also fax)
Mrs Coates
whinray@aol.com
D: £20.00–£25.00 **S:** £30.00
Beds: 2D 1T **Baths:** 1 En 1 Sh
🅿 (6) ⊬ ▥ 🎱 ▥ ♿

Malvern Link

SO7847   ◀ *Swan, Scallywags, Bluebell, Red Lion, Hawthorn Inn*

Rathlin, *1 Carlton Road, Malvern Link, Worcs, WR14 1HH.*
A private family home offering friendly bed and breakfast accommodation.
Open: All Year
Grades: ETC 4 Diamond
01684 572491 Mrs Guiver
D: £18.00–£22.00 **S:** £18.00–£22.00
Beds: 1T 2D **Baths:** 1 En 2 Sh
🅿 (1) ⊬ ▥ 🍴 🎱 ▥ ♿

Edgeworth, *4 Carlton Road, Malvern Link, Worcs, WR14 1HH.*
Edwardian family home near station and access to hill walks.
Open: All Year
Grades: ETC 3 Diamond
01684 572565
Mrs Garland
susan.garland@talk21.com
D: £18.00–£20.00 **S:** £19.00–£22.00
Beds: 1D 2S **Baths:** 1 Sh
🐾 🅿 (2) ⊬ ▥ 🍴 🎱 ▥ ♿

Hillside, *113 Worcester Road, Malvern Link, Malvern, Worcs, WR14 1ER.*
Victorian residence close to town centre and hills, overlooking the common.
Open: All Year
01684 565287 (also fax)
Mrs Bambury
D: £20.00–£22.50 **S:** £27.50–£30.00
Beds: 2D 1T **Baths:** 2 En 1 Pr
🐾 (11) ▥ 🎱 ▥ ♿

Martin Hussingtree

SO8860   ◀ *Bull*

Knoll Farm, *Ladywood Road, Martin Hussingtree, Worcester, Worcs., WR3 7SY.*
Open: All Year
01905 455565
Mrs Griggs
aligriggs@hotmail.com
D: £20.00–£30.00 **S:** £25.00–£30.00
Beds: 1T 2D **Baths:** 2 En 1 Sh
🐾 🅿 (10) ▥ 🍴 ♿
The house is set in a rural location with wonderful views towards Abberley and Malvern Hills. Comfortable rooms, full English breakfast and a warm welcome. Between the historic towns of Worcester and Droitwich. Close to M5, off-road parking.

New End

SP0460   ◀ *Wheelbarrow Castle*

Delaware House, *162 The Ridgeway, New End, Astwood Bank, Redditch, Worcestershire, B96 6NJ.*
Modern house in quiet location, 4 miles Redditch.
Open: All Year (not Xmas)
01527 892852 Mr Neale
D: £15.00 **S:** £15.00
Beds: 1D 1S **Baths:** 2 En
🅿 (2) ⊬ ▥ 🎱

Ombersley

SO8463   ◀ *King's Arms, Crown & Sandys*

Greenlands, *Uphampton, Ombersley, Droitwich, Worcs, WR9 0JP.*
C16th picturesque house. Peaceful conservation hamlet. Character bedrooms. Every comfort.
Open: All Year
Grades: ETC 4 Diamond
01905 620873
Mrs Crossland
xlandgreenlands@onetel.net.uk
D: £18.00–£25.00 **S:** £30.00–£40.00
Beds: 2D 1T 1S **Baths:** 1 En 2 Sh
🐾 🅿 (6) ⊬ ▥ 🍴 🎱 ▥ ♿

Pershore

SO9445   ◀ *Old Mill, Defford Arms, Brandy Cask*

Besford Bridge House, *Besford Bridge, Pershore, Worcs, WR10 2AD.*
Georgian farmhouse in rural location just two miles from Pershore.
Open: All Year (not Xmas/New Year)
01386 553117 Mrs Dodwell
sallydodwell@classicfm.net
D: £18.00–£24.00 **S:** £20.00–£24.00
Beds: 2D **Baths:** 1 Sh
🅿 (2) ⊬ ▥ ✕ 🎱 ▥ ♿

AyrtonHouse, *6 Bridge Street, Pershore, Worcs, WR10 1AT.*
Listed town house in centre of Pershore. Ideal touring base.
Open: All Year
01386 556449 Mr Brighton
Fax: 01386 555660
D: £20.00–£25.00 **S:** £20.00–£30.00
Beds: 1D 2T **Baths:** 1 Sh
🐾 (5) 🅿 (1) ⊬ ▥ 🎱 ▥ ♿

The Barn, *Pensham Hill House, Pensham Hill, Pershore, Worcs, WR10 3HA.*
Superior ground floor accommodation in a C19th barn conversion.
Open: All Year
01386 555270 Mrs Horton
Fax: 01386 552894
D: £25.00–£30.00 **S:** £32.50–£37.50
Beds: 2D 1T **Baths:** 3 En
🅿 (6) ⊬ ▥ 🎱 ♿

Pirton

SO8747   ◀ *Fruiterers' Arms*

The Old Smithy, *Pirton, Worcester, WR8 9EJ.*
C17th century black and white country house quiet location near M5 motorway.
Open: All Year (not Xmas)
Grades: ETC 4 Diamond
01905 820482 Mrs Wynn
welcome@TheOldSmithy.co.uk
D: £19.00–£21.00 **S:** £25.00–£27.00
Beds: 1D 1T **Baths:** 1 Pr 1 Sh
🅿 (6) ⊬ ▥ ✕ 🎱 ▥ ♿ cc

Redditch

SP0368

Oakland, *64 Ledbury Close, Matchborough East, Redditch, Worcs, B98 0BS.*
Detached family home with easy access to Warwick, Stratford, motorway network.
Open: All Year
01527 524764 Mr & Mrs Lewis
D: £20.00–£25.00
Beds: 1D **Baths:** 1 En
🅿 (3) ▥ 🎱 ▥ ♿

Walcote, *Dagnell End Road, Bordesley, Redditch, Worcs, B98 9BH.*
Comfortable country home, three miles to M42, opposite golf course.
Open: All Year (not Xmas/New Year)
01527 68784 Mrs Smith
D: £17.50 **S:** £17.50
Beds: 2T 1S **Baths:** 1 Sh
🐾 (1) 🅿 (7) ▥ ✕ 🎱 ▥ ♿

Salwarpe

SO8762 ◆ White Hart

Middleton Grange, Ladywood Road, Salwarpe, Droitwich Spa, Worcestershire, WR9 5PA.
Open: All Year **Grades:** ETC 4 Diamond
01905 451678 S Harrison
Fax: 01905 453978
salli@middletongrange.demon.co.uk
D: £25.00–£30.00 **S:** £25.00–£30.00
Beds: 2T 3D **Baths:** 4 En 1 Pr
🛌 🅿 (8) 🖂 📺 🍴 🎱 🔊 🔽 ♿
C18th farmhouse set in picturesque gardens in rural location. Full of character and charm. Only 4 minutes Droitwich and 10 Worcester. Luxurious accommodation, excellent service in a friendly and relaxed environment. 6 minutes M5 Motorway.

Stoulton

SO9050 ◆ Plough & Harrow

Caldewell, Stoulton, Worcester, WR7 4RL.
Georgian mansion in parkland setting with animals and miniature railway.
Open: All Year (not Xmas)
Grades: ETC 3 Diamond
01905 840894 (also fax) Mrs Booth
sheila@caldewell.demon.co.uk
D: £20.00–£22.50 **S:** £23.00–£27.00
Beds: 3D 1T **Baths:** 2 En 2 Sh
🛌 🅿 (6) 🖂 📺 🍴 🎱 🔽 ♿

Stourport-on-Severn

SO8171 ◆ Bird In Hand, Black Star

Baldwin House, 8 Lichfield Street, Stourport-on-Severn, Worcs, DY13 9EU.
Grade II Listed Georgian town house, close to historic canal basins.
Open: All Year
Grades: ETC 4 Diamond
01299 877221 (also fax) Mrs Barclay
balwinhousebb@aol.com
D: £20.00–£25.00 **S:** £22.50–£30.00
Beds: 2F 4D 2T 2S **Baths:** 7 En 1 Sh
🛌 🖂 📺 🍴 ✕ 🔽 ♿

Tenbury Wells

SO5967 ◆ Fountain Inn

Redgate House, Bromyard Road, Tenbury Wells, Worcs, WR15 8BS.
Large Victorian private house.
Open: All Year (not Xmas)
01584 810574 Mrs Picton
D: £17.50–£18.50 **S:** £17.50–£18.50
Beds: 2T **Baths:** 1 En 1 Pr
🅿 (2) 🖂 ♿

Upton-upon-Severn

SO8540 ◆ Plough & Harrow, Swan, King's Head, Drum & Monkey, Anchor, Hunters

Four Hedges, The Rhydd, Hanley Castle, Malvern, Worcester, WR8 0AD.
Friendly family house, spacious garden. Three Counties Showground 4 miles.
Open: All Year (not Xmas)
Grades: AA 2 Diamond
01684 310405 (also fax) Mrs Cooper
fredgies@aol.com
D: £15.00–£17.00 **S:** £15.00–£17.00
Beds: 1D 1T 2S **Baths:** 1 En 1 Sh
🛌 🅿 (5) 🖂 📺 🍴 ♿

Lockeridge Farm, Upton-upon-Severn, Worcester, WR8 0RP.
Comfortable accommodation, all rooms showers, ensuite. Friendly service, visitor satisfaction. **Open:** All Year (not Xmas)
01684 592193 Mrs Albert
frank@albert85.freeserve.co.uk
D: £15.00–£17.00 **S:** £20.00–£22.00
Beds: 2F 1T **Baths:** 1 Sh
🛌 🅿 (4) 📺 🍴 ✕ 🔽 ♿

Tiltridge Farm & Vineyard, Upper Hook Road, Upton-upon-Severn, Worcester, WR8 0SA.
Attractive farmhouse with vineyards between River Severn and Malvern Hills.
Open: All Year (not Xmas/New Year)
Grades: ETC 4 Diamond
01684 592906 Fax: 01684 594142
elgarwine@aol.com
D: £20.00–£23.00 **S:** £25.00–£30.00
Beds: 1T 2D **Baths:** 3 En
🛌 🅿 (10) 🖂 📺 🍴 🎱 🔽 ♿

Jasmin, 21 School Lane, Upton-upon-Severn, Worcester, WR8 0LD.
Modern comfortable bungalow in quiet road in town. 3 miles to M50/M5.
Open: All Year
01684 593569 Mrs Leighton
D: £18.00–£21.00 **S:** £20.00–£25.00
Beds: 1D 1T **Baths:** 1 Sh
🛌 🅿 (10) 🅿 (2) 🖂 📺 🍴 🎱 ♿

Whittington

SO8753 ◆ Retreat, Plough & Harrow, Fruiterers' Arms, Swan

Woodview, High Park, Whittington, Worcester, WR5 2RS.
Comfortable friendly accommodation set in 10 acres garden, donkey paddocks.
Open: All Year (not Xmas)
01905 351893 Mrs Wheeler
betty.wheeler@talk21.com
D: £19.00–£22.00 **S:** £20.00–£25.00
Beds: 2D 2T **Baths:** 1 En 2 Sh
🛌 🅿 (4) 🖂 📺 🍴 🔽 ♿

Wick

SO9545

6 Hopney Cottage, Wick, Pershore, Worcs, WR10 3JT.
Spacious cottage providing a friendly atmosphere, comfortable bedrooms with views. **Open:** All year (not Xmas)
01386 556341 (also fax)
Mrs Shakespeare
hopneycottage@hotmail.com
D: £18.00–£25.00 **S:** £18.00
Beds: 2D 2T 1S **Baths:** 1 En 1 Sh
🅿 (10) 🖂 📺 ♿

RATES

D = Price range per person sharing in a double room
S = Price range for a single room

Wickhamford

SP0642 ◆ Childswickham Inn

Avonwood, 30 Pitchers Hill, Wickhamford, Evesham, Worcestershire, WR11 6RT.
High standard of furnishings and decor. 3 miles from Broadway.
Open: All Year (not Xmas/New Year)
Grades: ETC 4 Diamond, Silver Award
01386 834271 (also fax) Ms Morgan
D: £19.50 **S:** £19.50–£26.00
Beds: 1T 2D **Baths:** 3 En
🛌 (12) 🅿 (8) 🖂 📺 🍴 🎱 ♿

Worcester

SO8555 ◆ Bull, Kings Arms, Cross Keys, Retreat, Plough & Harrow, Fruiterers' Arms, Swan, Talbot

The Old Smithy, Pirton, Worcester, WR8 9EJ.
C17th century black and white country house quiet location near M5 motorway.
Open: All Year (not Xmas)
Grades: ETC 4 Diamond
01905 820482 Mrs Wynn
welcome@TheOldSmithy.co.uk
D: £19.00–£21.00 **S:** £25.00–£27.00
Beds: 1D 1T **Baths:** 1 Pr 1 Sh
🅿 (6) 🖂 📺 ✕ 🎱 🔽 ♿ cc

Woodview, High Park, Whittington, Worcester, WR5 2RS.
Comfortable friendly accommodation set in 10 acres garden, donkey paddocks.
Open: All Year (not Xmas)
01905 351893 Mrs Wheeler
betty.wheeler@talk21.com
D: £19.00–£22.00 **S:** £20.00–£25.00
Beds: 2D 2T **Baths:** 1 En 2 Sh
🛌 🅿 (4) 🖂 📺 🍴 🎱 ♿

Oaklands B&B, Grange Lane, Claines, Worcester, WR3 7RR.
Peaceful, rural outlook, yet easy access Worcester city, Stratford, Cotswolds.
Open: All Year (not Xmas)
Grades: ETC 4 Diamond
01905 458871 Mrs Gadd
Fax: 01905 759362
D: £25.00–£30.00 **S:** £30.00
Beds: 1F 1D 1T 1S **Baths:** 4 En
🛌 🅿 (6) 📺 🍴 ✕ 🎱 cc

Beacon Lodge, 84 Victoria Avenue, Worcester, WR5 1ED.
Quiet, private house. Convenient to M5, J7.
Open: All Year (not Xmas)
01905 763098 Mr & Mrs Baldock
D: £15.00–£21.00 **S:** £16.00–£22.00
Beds: 2T 1S **Baths:** 1 En 1 Sh
🖂 📺 🎱 🔽 ♿

Wyatt Guest House, 40 Barbourne Road, Worcester, WR1 1HU.
Small family-run guest house, near city centre, racecourse, cathedral.
Open: All Year (not Xmas)
01905 26311 (also fax)
Mr & Mrs Neale
wyatt.guest@virginnet.co.uk
D: £20.00–£22.00 **S:** £22.00–£35.00
Beds: 3F 2D 2T 1S **Baths:** 7 Pr
🛌 📺 🍴 🎱 ♿

Stilwell's Ireland: Bed & Breakfast 2000

Think of Ireland and you think of that world famous Irish hospitality. The warmth of the welcome is as much a part of this great island as are the wild and beautiful landscapes, the traditional folk music and the Guinness. Everywhere you go, town or country, North or South, you can't escape it. There are few better ways of experiencing this renowned hospitality, when traveling through Ireland, than by staying at one of the country's many Bed & Breakfasts. And there's no better way of choosing a convenient and desirable B&B than by consulting **Stilwell's Ireland: Bed & Breakfast 2001**.

Stilwell's Ireland: Bed & Breakfast 2001 contains over 1,400 entries – private houses, country halls, farms, cottages, inns, small hotels and guest houses – listed by county, in both Northern Ireland and the Republic of Ireland. Each entry includes room rates, facilities, Tourist Board grades or notices of approval and a brief description of the B&B, its location and surroundings. The average charge per person per night is £18. The listings also provide the names of local pubs and restaurants which serve food in the evening. As with all Stilwell B&B guides, Stilwell's Ireland has maps, listings of Tourist Information Offices and air, rail, bus and ferry information.

Treat yourself to some Irish hospitality with **Stilwell's Ireland: Bed & Breakfast 2001**.

£6.95 from all good bookstores (ISBN 1-900861-24-0) or £7.95 (inc p&p) from Stilwell Publishing Ltd, 59 Charlotte Road, London EC2A 3QW (020 7739 7179)

East Yorkshire

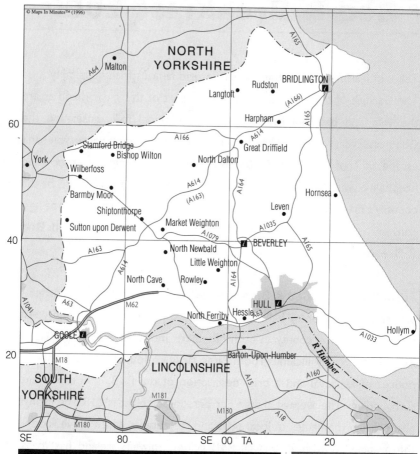

© Maps In Minutes™ (1996)

Tourist Information Centres

The Guildhall, Register Square, **Beverley**, East Yorkshire, HU17 9AU, 01482 867430.

25 Prince Street, **Bridlington**, East Yorkshire, YO15 2NP, 01262 673474.

North Bank Viewing Area, Ferriby Road, **Hessle**, Hull, HU13 0LN, 01482 640852.

68 High Street, **Holme-on-Spalding-Moor**, York, YO4 4AA, 01430 860479.

75 Newbegin, **Hornsea**, East Yorkshire, HU18 1PA, 01964 536404 (Easter to Oct).

75-76 Carr Lane, **Hull**, HU1 3RQ, 01482 223559.

Central Library, Albion Street, **Hull**, HU1 3TF, 01482 223344.

King George Dock, Hedon Road, **Hull**, HU9 5PR, 01482 702118.

Pier Towers, **Withernsea**, East Yorkshire, HU19 2JS, 01964 615683.

Barmby Moor

SE7748 ◀ *Wellington Oak*

Alder Carr House, *York Road, Barmby Moor, York, YO42 4HU.*
Georgian style house set in 10 acres. Well positioned for historic Beverley and coast.
Open: All Year (not Xmas)
01759 380566 Mrs Steel
D: £17.00–£20.00 **S:** £20.00–£22.00
Beds: 1F 2D **Baths:** 2 En 1 Pr
⊬ ▣ (10) ▥ ▦ ▟

B&B owners may vary
rates - be sure to check
when booking

Beverley

TA0440 ❦ Rose & Crown, Mokescroft Inn, Hayride, Queens Head

Number One, 1 Woodlands, Beverley, E. Yorks, HU17 8BT.
Victorian house, home cooking, open fires, library, lovely gardens.
Open: All Year
01482 862752 Mrs King
neilandsarah@mansle.karoo.co.uk
D: £18.00–£22.00 **S:** £19.50–£29.00
Beds: 1D 1T 1S **Baths:** 1 En 1 Sh
🛏 🅿 (1) ⅃ 🅅 🛏 ✕ 🎱 🆅 🕹

Eastgate Guest House, 7 Eastgate, Beverley, E. Yorks, HU17 0DR.
Family-run Victorian guest house close to Beverley Minster and army museum.
Open: All Year (not Xmas)
01482 868464 Ms Anderson
Fax: 01482 871899
D: £15.00–£25.00 **S:** £20.00–£35.00
Beds: 7F 3D 3T 5S **Baths:** 7 Pr 3 Sh
🛏 🅅 🛏 🎱 🆅

Bishop Wilton

SE7955

High Belthorpe, Bishop Wilton, York, YO42 1SB.
Large comfortable farmhouse in peaceful setting with wonderful views, private fishing. **Open:** All Year (not Xmas)
Grades: ETC 3 Diamond
01759 368238 M Hamdan
keebyah@netscapeonline.co.uk
D: fr £17.63 **S:** fr £20.00
Beds: 1F 1D
🛏 🅿 🅅 ✕ 🎱 🆅 🕹

Bridlington

TA1867 ❦ Sea Blrd, Ship, Southcliff Hotel, Martonian

Grantlea Guest House, 2 South Street, Bridlington, E Yorks, YO15 3BY.
Open: All Year (not Xmas)
01262 400190 M J Odey
D: £15.00–£16.00 **S:** £15.00–£16.00
Beds: 2D 2T 2S **Baths:** 3 En 1 Sh
🛏 🅅 ✕ 🎱 🆅 🕹
Grantlea guest house is situated on the south side of Bridlington, 1 minute from the beach and Spa Theatre. 2 minutes from the harbour and town centre. Ideal for walking, fishing and golf as well as beach holidays. All rooms have colour TVs and tea/coffee making facilities.

Richmond Guest House, 9 The Crescent, Bridlington, E Yorks, YO15 2NX.
Welcoming bed and breakfast looking out over the sea **Open:** All Year (not Xmas)
01262 674366 J Brewer
D: £19.00–£24.00 **S:** £20.00–£22.00
Beds: 5F 2T 3D 1S **Baths:** 2 En 2 Sh
🛏 🅿 (4) ⅃ 🅅 🕹

Gables Private Hotel, 16 Landsdowne Road, Bridlington, YO15 2QS.
Prime location, 50 yards from promenade, close to all amenities.
Open: Easter to Oct
01262 672516
D: £15.00–£16.00 **S:** £15.00–£16.00
Beds: 1F 1T 1D 1S **Baths:** 2 Sh
🛏 🅿 (3) 🅅 🛏 ✕ 🎱 🕹

Seawind's Guest House, 48 Horsforth Avenue, Bridlington, E Yorks, YO15 3DF.
Quiet location, close to beach, town centre and Spa theatre.
Open: All Year
01262 676330 M J Chambers
seawinds@btinternet.com
D: £16.00–£18.00 **S:** £20.00–£25.00
Beds: 1T 4D 1S **Baths:** 1 En 2 Sh
🅿 (4) 🅅 🎱 🕹

Longleigh B&B, 12 Swanland Avenue, Bridlington, E. Yorks, YO15 2HH.
Quiet location, 4 minutes from town and seafront.
Open: All Year
01262 676234
D: £16.00–£18.00 **S:** £16.00–£17.00
Beds: 1T 2D 1S
🅅 🎱 🕹

Winston House Hotel, South Street, Bridlington, E. Yorks, YO15 3BY.
Small friendly seaside hotel. Come and be spoiled.
Open: All Year
Grades: ETC 3 Diamond
01262 670216 (also fax)
Mr & Mrs Botham
D: £19.00–£22.00 **S:** £19.00–£23.00
Beds: 1F 6D 1T 3S **Baths:** 11 Pr
🛏 🅅 ✕ 🎱 🆅 ❀ 🕹 cc

Thiswilldo Guest House, 31 St Hilda Street, Bridlington, E. Yorks, YO15 3EE.
Close to beach, harbour, rail/coach station. Cleanliness and good food assured.
Open: All Year
01262 678270 D: fr £13.00 **S:** fr £13.00
Beds: 2F 2D 1T 1S **Baths:** 1 Sh
🛏 🅅 ✕ 🎱 🆅 ❀ 🕹

Waverley Hotel, 105 Cardigan Road, Bridlington, E. Yorks, YO15 3LP.
Family run. Situated in quiet residential area. 2 minutes South Beach.
Open: All Year
01262 671040
Mrs Britton
waverley.hotel@
bridlington.world.online.co.uk
D: £19.00–£20.00 **S:** £27.00–£28.00
Beds: 3F 1T 1D **Baths:** 5 En
🛏 (1) 🅿 (3) 🅅 ✕ 🎱 🆅 ❀ 🕹

Springfield Private Hotel, 12 Trinity Road, Bridlington, E. Yorks, YO15 2EY.
Family run guesthouse, good home cooking a speciality, Ensuite available.
Open: All Year
01262 672896 Mrs Newsome
D: fr £15.00 **S:** fr £15.00
Beds: 2F 2D 1T 2S **Baths:** 2 Sh 4 En
🛏 🅅 ✕ 🎱 🆅 ❀ 🕹

Ashford Private Hotel, 94 Trinity Road, Bridlington, E. Yorks, YO15 2HF.
The Ashford Private Hotel is a small, family-run, warm and friendly guest house.
Open: All Year (not Xmas)
01262 675849 Mrs Porritt
D: £18.00–£20.00 **S:** fr £20.00
Beds: 3F 2D 1T **Baths:** 5 En 1 Pr
🛏 🅿 🅅 🛏 🎱 🕹

Goole

SE7423

Briarcroft Hotel, 49-51 Clifton Gardens, Goole, East Yorkshire, DN14 6AR.
Comfortable, friendly, pleasant hotel - licensed.
Open: All Year
01405 763024 (also fax)
Mr Ramsdale
D: fr £20.00 **S:** fr £24.00
Beds: 2F 6D 4T 5S **Baths:** 10 Pr 6 Sh
🛏 🅿 (6) ⅃ 🅅 🛏 ✕ 🎱 🆅 🕹

Clifton Hotel, 155 Boothferry Road, Goole, DN14 6AL.
Comfortable hotel, delightfully upgraded with much care & thought.
Open: All Year (not Xmas)
01405 761336
Mr Hope
Fax: 01405 762350
D: £24.00–£26.00 **S:** £29.75–£44.00
Beds: 1F 3D 1T 4S **Baths:** 8 En 1 Pr
🛏 🅿 (9) 🅅 🛏 🎱 🆅 🕹

Great Driffield

TA0257

The Wold Cottage, Wold Newton, Driffield, E Yorks, YO25 0HL.
Award-winning spacious C18th farmhouse away from roads. Ideal for Bampton cliffs and historic house.
Open: All Year
Grades: ETC 4 Diamond, Silver, AA 5 Diamond
01262 470696 (also fax)
Mrs Gray
woldcott@wold-newton.freeserve.co.uk
D: £24.00–£30.00 **S:** £25.00–£30.00
Beds: 2D 1T **Baths:** 3 En
🛏 🅿 (10) ⅃ 🅅 ✕ 🎱 🆅 🕹 cc

Harpham

TA0961

St Quintins Arms Inn, Main Street, Harpham, Driffield, E. Yorks, YO25 4QY.
Comfortable family run inn with garden providing good meals and ales.
Open: All Year (not Xmas/New Year)
Grades: ETC 4 Diamond
01262 490329 (also fax)
Mr Curtis
D: £19.00–£23.00 **S:** £28.50
Beds: 1F 1T 2D **Baths:** 4 En
🛏 🅿 (50) 🅅 🛏 ✕ 🎱 🆅 🕹 cc

Hessle

TA0326 ❦ Country Park Inn, The Hase

Redcliffe House, Redcliffe Road, Hessle, E Yorks, HU13 0HA.
Beautifully appointed, riverside location close to Humber Bridge, Hull, Beverley.
Open: All Year
01482 648655
S Skiba
D: £20.00 **S:** £20.00–£35.00
Beds: 2D 2T 1S
Baths: 4 En 1 Sh
🛏 🅿 (6) 🅅 🎱 🆅 🕹

Hollym

TA3425

Plough Inn, *Northside Road, Hollym, Withernsea, E Yorks, HU19 2RS.*
Relaxed friendly atmosphere, open coal fires, large beer garden.
Open: All Year
01964 612049 Mr Robinson
D: £16.00–£20.00 **S:** £20.00
Beds: 1F 4T **Baths:** 3 En
⌖ 🅿 (20) 📺 ✕ 📖 ▾ ≜

Hornsea

TA2047   ◀ *Marine Hotel, The Odd Place*

Southfield Guest House, *61 Eastgate, Hornsea, E. Yorks, HU18 1NB.*
Homely Victorian house near the sea. Stairlift for semi-disabled.
Open: All Year
01964 534961 Mr Hornby
D: £14.00–£16.00 **S:** £14.00
Beds: 1F 2D 1T 1S **Baths:** 1 En 1 Sh
⌖ 🅿 (2) 📺 ✝ ✕ 📖 ▾ ≜

Hull

TA0929   ◀ *Hanorth Arms, The Zoological*

Allandra Hotel, *5 Park Avenue, Hull, HU5 3FN.*
Open: All Year
Grades: ETC 2 Diamond
01482 493349
Fax: 01482 492680
D: £19.50 **S:** £26.00
Beds: 2F 1T 7D **Baths:** 10 En
⌖ 🅿 (5) 📺 ✝ ✕ 📖 ▾ ≜ cc
Charming Victorian town house hotel, family run, close to all amenities. Delightfully situated, convenient universities and town centre opposite pleasant parking. All rooms ensuite.

Beck House , *628 Beverley High Road, Hull, HU6 7LL.*
Traditional town house, B&B, fine accommodation, close to university etc.
Open: All Year
01482 445468 Mrs Aylwin
D: £19.00–£22.00 **S:** £19.00–£22.00
Beds: 3D 3S **Baths:** 1 En 1 Sh
⌖ 🅿 (4) 📺 📖 ≜ cc

The Tree Guest House, *132 Sunny Bank, Spring Bank West, Hull, HU3 1LE.*
Close to the city centre and universities. Special rates available.
Open: All Year
01482 448822
Fax: 01482 442911
D: fr £17.00 **S:** £10.00–£24.00
Beds: 1F 3D 3S **Baths:** 3 En 2 Sh
⌖ 🅿 📺 ✝ 📖 ≜ ♿

Marlborough Hotel, *232 Spring Bank, Hull, HU3 1LU.*
Family run, near city centre.
Open: All Year
01482 224479 (also fax)
Mr Norman
D: fr £17.00 **S:** fr £17.00
Beds: 2 F 2D 7T 5S **Baths:** 3 Sh
⌖ 🅿 (10) 📺 ✝ ✕ 📖

Langtoft

TA0166

The Ship Inn, *Scarborough Road, Langtoft, Driffield, East Yorks, YO25 3TH.*
17th Century coaching Inn, guest rooms overlooking Wolds rolling countryside.
Open: All Year
Grades: ETC 3 Diamond
01377 267243
D: £19.95–£21.95 **S:** £29.50–£31.50
Beds: 2T 2D 2S
⌖ 🅿 ✂ 📺 ✕ 📖 ▾ ✳ ≜ ♿ cc

Leven

TA1144

New Inn, *44 South Street, Leven, Beverley, HU17 5NZ.*
Old Georgian coaching house adjacent to rural canal - fishing allowed.
Open: All Year
Grades: AA 2 Diamond
01964 542223 P T Oliver
D: £17.50 **S:** £23.00
Beds: 1F 3D 1T 1S **Baths:** 6 En
⌖ 🅿 (50) 📺 ✝ ✕ 📖 ▾ cc

Little Weighton

SE9933   ◀ *Black Horse*

Rosedale B&b, *9 Skidby Road, Little Weighton, Cottingham, E Yorks, HU20 3UY.*
Bungalow accommodation set in large beautiful garden at the foot of the Yorkshire Wolds.
Open: All Year
01482 846074 I Wilkinson
D: £15.00 **S:** £20.00
Beds: 1F 2T **Baths:** 1 En 1 Sh
⌖ 🅿 (6) 📺 ✝ 📖 ▾ ≜

Market Weighton

SE8741   **The Gables,** *38 Londesborough Road, Market Weighton, York, YO43 3HS.*
Friendly, comfortable, quiet country house.
Open: All Year (not Xmas)
01430 872255 Mr & Mrs Reeson
D: fr £16.00 **S:** fr £16.00
Beds: 1D 1T 1S **Baths:** 1 Sh
⌖ 🅿 (5) 📺 ✝ 📖 ≜

North Cave

SE8932   ◀ *White Hart*

Albion House, *18 Westgate, North Cave, Brough, E Yorks, HU15 2NJ.*
Warm welcome in pleasant family home decorated in Victorian style.
Open: All Year
Grades: ETC 2 Diamond
01430 422958
D: £15.00–£20.00 **S:** £15.00–£20.00
Beds: 1F 1D 1S **Baths:** 1 En 1 Sh
⌖ 🅿 (6) ✂ 📺 ✝ ✕ 📖 ▾ ≜ ♿

All details shown are as supplied by B&B owners in Autumn 2000

North Dalton

SE9352   ◀ *The Star*

Garth House, *Main Street, Thwing, Driffield, E Yorks, YO25 3DY.*
Open: All Year (not Xmas)
01262 470843 (also fax)
Mr Dell
D: £20.00 **S:** £20.00
Beds: 2D **Baths:** 1 En 1 Sh
⌖ 🅿 (1) ✂ 📺 ▾ ≜
Situated in a quiet rural Yorkshire Wolds village, only 8 miles from Bridlington and within easy reach of York, Beverley and the North Yorkshire Moors, a warm welcome invites you to get off the beaten track, explore and relax.

North Ferriby

SE9826

B&B at 103, *103 Ferriby High Road, North Ferriby, East Yorks, HU14 3LA.*
Comfortable house, large garden, overlooking river near Humber Bridge and Hull. **Open:** All Year
Grades: ETC 3 Diamond
01482 633637 Mrs Simpson
simpson.103@usa.net
D: £15.00 **S:** £15.00
Beds: 1D 1T 1S **Baths:** 1 Sh
⌖ (7) 🅿 (2) ✂ 📺 ✝ ✕ 📖 ▾ ≜

North Newbald

SE9136

The Gnu Inn, *The Green, North Newbald, York, YO43 4SA.*
Traditional country inn in picturesque surroundings; good for walkers and cyclists.
Open: All Year
Grades: ETC 3 Diamond
01430 827799
D: £20.00–£30.00 **S:** £20.00–£30.00
Beds: 1F 1D 1T **Baths:** 3 En
⌖ 🅿 (25) ✂ 📺 ✕ 📖 ▾ ≜ cc

Rowley

SE9832

Rowley Manor Hotel, *Rowley, Little Weighton, Cottingham, E. Yorks, HU20 3XR.*
Situated in 35 acres of gardens & lawns, farmland.
Open: All Year
Grades: AA 2 Stars, RAC 2 Stars
01482 848248 Fax: 01482 849900
info@rowleymanir.com
D: £55.00–£95.00 **S:** £55.00–£70.00
Beds: 3T 10D 3S **Baths:** 16 En
⌖ 🅿 (50) ✂ 📺 ✝ ✕ 📖 ▾ ✳ ≜ cc

Rudston

TA0966

Bosville Arms, *High Street, Rudston, Driffield, East Yorkshire, YO25 4UB.*
Quality country retreat in historic Yorkshire village near east coast.
Open: All Year **Grades:** ETC 3 Diamond
01262 420259 (also fax)
hogan@bosville.freeserve.co.uk
D: £24.95–£28.75 **S:** £29.95–£34.95
Beds: 3T 3D
⌖ 🅿 (40) 📺 ✕ 📖 ▾ ✳ ≜ cc

Shiptonthorpe

SE8543 ◀ *Crown, Black Horse, Ship*

Robeanne House Farm & Stables,
Driffield Lane, Shiptonthorpe, York, YO43 3PW.
Open: All Year
01430 873312 (also fax) Mrs Wilson
robert@robeannefreeserve.co.uk
D: £20.00–£40.00 **S:** £20.00–£25.00
Beds: 3F 2D 1T **Baths:** 6 En
ॐ ▣ (10) ☑ ☊ ✕ ▥ ☑ ✿ ➳ cc
Comfortable family house,large spacious
rooms countryside views. Good food
warm welcome, within easy reach of York,
the Yorkshire coast Moors and Dales.
Local walking, Gliding, Racing Castle
Howard and much more.

Stamford Bridge

SE7155 ◀ *Goldcup Inn*

High Catton Grange, *Stamford Bridge, York, YO41 1EP.*
Open: All Year (not Xmas/New Year)
Grades: ETC 4 Diamond
01759 371374 (also fax) Ms Foster
D: £19.00–£23.00 **S:** £28.00–£35.00
Beds: 1F 1D **Baths:** 1 En 1 Pr
ॐ ▣ (6) ☑ ☊ ▥ ☑ ➳
A warm welcome awaits you at this C18th
farmhouse in peaceful rural location.
With ample parking, only 7 miles from
historic York. Bedrooms are prettily
furnished with colour TV. Cosy lounge,
elegant dining room, good English
breakfasts. Also self catering cottage
available.

RATES

D = Price range per person
sharing in a double room
S = Price range for a
single room

Sutton upon Derwent

SE7046

Sutton Arms, *Main Street, Sutton upon Derwent, York, YO41 4BT.*
Village pub. Warm, friendly, atmosphere.
Entertainment, bar & restaurant meals.
Open: All Year
01904 608477 Fax: 01904 607585
D: £17.50–£20.00 **S:** £17.50–£20.00
Beds: 1D 1T 1S **Baths:** 1 En 1 Sh
▣ (30) ⊬ ☑ ✕ ▥ ☑ ➳ cc

Wilberfoss

SE7351 ◀ *Gold Cup*

Cuckoo Nest Farm, *Wilberfoss, York, YO41 5NL.*
Red brick traditional house, park and ride
nearby for York.
Open: All Year (not Xmas)
Grades: ETC 3 Diamond
01759 380365 J M Liversidge
D: £20.00–£25.00 **S:** fr £23.00
Beds: 1T 1D **Baths:** 1 Pr
ॐ ▣ ⊬ ☑ ▥ ➳

Withernsea

TA3427 ◀ *Northfield, Bounty*

Vista Mar Guest House, *48 Promenade, Withernsea, E. Yorks, HU19 2DW.*
Seafront location, residents lounge,
central for all amenities.
Open: All Year
01964 612858 Mr & Mrs Hirst
D: £13.00–£16.00 **S:** £15.00–£20.00
Beds: 1F 1D 2T 3S **Baths:** 2 En 2 Sh
ॐ ☑ ☊ ▥ ➳

Take 5 Guest House, *5 Young Street, Withernsea, E. Yorks, HU19 2DX.*
Small and friendly coastal accom-
modation.
Open: All Year
01964 613716
Mrs Redfearn
D: £13.00 **S:** £13.00
Beds: 1F 2D 1T 1S **Baths:** 2 Sh
ॐ ☑ ☊ ▥ ➳

St Hilda Guest House, *40 The Promenade, Withernsea, E. Yorks, HU19 2DW.*
Victorian house, superb sea views. Two
minutes from town centre.
Open: All Year (not Xmas)
01964 612483 (also fax)
sthilda@aol.com
D: £12.50–£12.00
S: £12.50–£12.00
Beds: 2D 1T 2S
Baths: 1 En 1 Sh
ॐ ☑ ▥ ➳

North Yorkshire

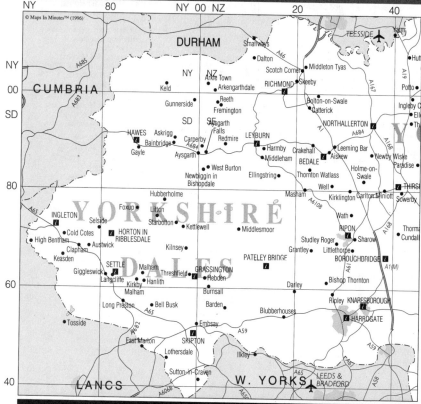

Tourist Information Centres

Bedale Hall, **Bedale**, N.Yorks, DL8 1AA, 01677 424604 (Easter to Oct).

Fishergate, **Boroughbridge**, York, YO5 9AL, 01423 323373 (Easter to Oct).

The Moors Centre, Danby Lodge, Lodge Lane, **Danby**, Whitby, N.Yorks, YO21 2NB, 01287 660654 (Easter to Oct).

Chapel Lane, **Easingwold**, York, YO6 3AE, 01347 821530 (Easter to Oct).

John Street, **Filey**, N.Yorks, YO14 9DW, 01723 512204 (Easter to Oct).

National Park Centre, Hebden Road, **Grassington**, Skipton, N.Yorks, BD23 5LB, 01756 752774 (Easter to Oct).

High Green Car Park, **Great Ayton**, Middlesborough, TS9 6BJ, 01642 722835 (Easter to Oct).

Fountain Street, **Guisborough**, Cleveland, TS14 6QF, 01287 633801.

Royal Baths Assembly Rooms, Crescent Road, **Harrogate**, N.Yorks, HG1 2RR, 01423 537300.

Dales Countryside Museum, Station Yard, **Hawes**, N.Yorks, DL8 3NT, 01969 667450 (Easter to Oct).

Town Hall, Market Place, **Helmsley**, York, YO6 5BL, 01439 770173 (Easter to Oct).

Pen-y-ghent Cafe, **Horton-in-Ribblesdale**, Settle, N.Yorks, BD24 0HE, 01729 860333.

Community Centre Car Park, **Ingleton**, Carnforth, Lancashire, LA6 3HJ, 015242 41049 (Easter to Oct).

35 Market Place, **Knaresborough**, N.Yorks, HG5 8AL, 01423 866886 (Easter to Oct).

Thornborough Hall, **Leyburn**, N.Yorks, DL8 5AD, 01969 623069.

The Old Town Hall, Market Place, **Malton**, N. Yorks, YO17 0LH, 01653 600048 (Easter to Oct).

51 Corporation Road, **Middlesbrough**, TS1 1LT, 01642 243425.

The Applegarth Car Park, **Northallerton**, N.Yorks, DL7 8LZ, 01609 776864.

14 High St, **Pateley Bridge**, Harrogate, N.Yorks, HG3 5AP, 01423 711147 (Easter to Oct).

Eastgate Car Park, **Pickering**, N.Yorks, YO18 7DP, 01751 473791.

3 Dundas Street, **Redcar**, Cleveland, TS10 3AD, 01642 471921.

Friary Gardens, Victoria Road, **Richmond**, N.Yorks, DL10 4AJ, 01748 850252.

Minster Road, **Ripon**, N.Yorks, HG4 1LT, 01765 604625 (Easter to Oct).

3 Station Buildings, Station Square, **Saltburn-by-the-Sea**, Cleveland, TS12 1AQ, 01287 622422.

Unit 3, Pavilion House, Valley Bridge Road, **Scarborough**, N.Yorks, YO11 1UY, 01723 373333.

Pavilion Service Area, A1, **Scotch Corner**, Richmond, N.Yorks, DL10 6PQ, 01325 377677 (Easter to Oct).

Park St, **Selby**, N.Yorks, YO8 0AA, 01757 703263.

Town Hall, Cheapside, **Settle**, N.Yorks, BD24 9EJ, 01729 825192.

Old Town Hall, Sheep Street, **Skipton**, N.Yorks, BD23 1JH, 01756 792809.

Sutton Bank Visitor Centre, **Sutton Bank**, Thirsk, N.Yorks, YO7 2EK, 01845 597426 (Easter to Oct).

14 Kirkgate, **Thirsk**, N.Yorks, YO7 1PQ, 01845 522755.

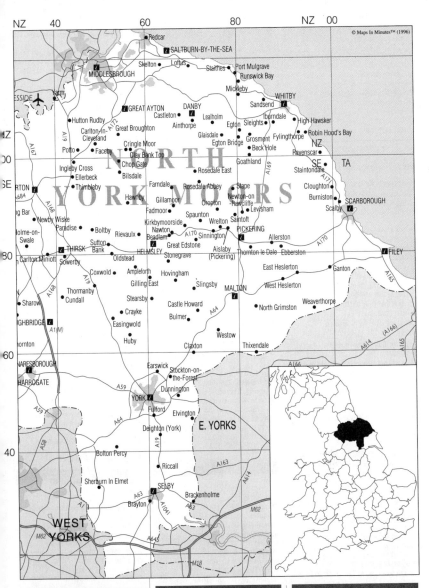

© Maps In Minutes™ (1996)

Redcar

SALTBURN-BY-THE-SEA

Skelton Loftus Staithes Port Mulgrave
MIDDLESBROUGH Runswick Bay
Mickleby
ESSIDE Nunthorpe Sandsend WHITBY
GREAT AYTON DANBY
Hutton Rudby Castleton Lealholm Iburndale High Hawsker
Carlton-in- Great Broughton Ainthorpe Egton Sleights
Cleveland Glaisdale Grosmont Robin Hood's Bay
Potto Facety Cringle Moor Egton Bridge Fylingthorpe NZ
Ingleby Cross Clay Bank Top Beck Hole Ravenscar SE TA
Ellerbeck Chop Gate Goathland Staintondale
NORTH Rosedale East Cloughton
Thimbleby Farndale Rosedale Abbey Stape Burniston
YORK MOORS Newton-on- SCARBOROUGH
g Bar Hawnby Gillamoor Cropton Rawcliffe Scalby
Newby Wiske Fadmoor Levisham
Holme-on- Paradise Boltby Spaunton Wrelton Saintoft FILEY
Swale Rievaulx Kirkbymoorside PICKERING
Nawton Allerston
THIRSK Beadlam Sinnington Thornton le Dale Ebberston
Carlton Miniott Sutton Great Edstone Aislaby
Sowerby Bank Stonegrave (Pickering) East Heslerton Ganton
Oldstead HELMSLEY
Coxwold Ampleforth Hovingham West Heslerton
Thormanby Gilling East Slingsby MALTON
GHBRIDGE Cundall Stearsby Castle Howard North Grimston Weaverthorpe
Sharow Crayke Bulmer
Easingwold Westow
Huby Thixendale
Claxton
NARESBOROUGH Earswick Stockton-on-
HARROGATE the-Forest
Dunnington
YORK E. YORKS
Fulford
Elvington
Deighton (York)
Bolton Percy
Riccall
Sherburn In Elmet SELBY Brackenholme
Brayton
WEST YORKS

Tourist Information Centres

Langborne Road, **Whitby**, N.Yorks,
YO21 1YN, 01947 602674.

De Grey Rooms, Exhibition Square,
York, YO1 2HB, 01904 621756.

Outer Concourse, York Railway Station,
York, YO2 2AY, 01904 621756.

6 Rougier St, **York**, YO2 1JA,
01904 620557.

Ainthorpe

NZ7008   *Fox & Hounds*

Rowantree Farm, *Ainthorpe, Danby,
Whitby, N. Yorks, YO21 2LE.*
Situated in the heart of the North
Yorkshire Moors, with panoramic
moorland views.
Open: All Year (not Xmas/New Year)
Grades: ETC 3 Diamond
01287 660396 Mrs Tindall
krbsatindall@aol.com
D: £17.00–£18.00 **S:** £17.00–£18.00
Beds: 1F 1T **Baths:** 2 Sh

Aiskew

SE2789   *Fox & Hounds, Green Dragon*

Bobbie's B&B, *XVII Century Cottage,
Aiskew, Bedale, N. Yorks, DL8 1DD.*
Grade II Listed C17th cottage with pretty
old cottage gardens.
Open: All Year (not Xmas)
01677 423385
Ms Bauer
D: £17.00–£18.00
S: £19.00–£25.00
Beds: 1D 2T **Baths:** 2 Sh

Aislaby (Pickering)

SE7785   ◧ *Blacksmiths' Arms*

Blacksmiths Arms, *Aislaby, Pickering, N. Yorks, YO18 8PE.*
Former oak beamed Blacksmiths, excellent cuisine, comfortable rooms, friendly atmosphere.
Open: All Year (not Xmas)
Grades: ETC 3 Diamond
01751 472182 Mrs Bullock
blacksmitharms@easicom.com
D: £20.00–£25.00 **S:** £20.00–£25.00
Beds: 1F 3D 1T 1S **Baths:** 3 Pr 2 Sh
⛄ 🅿 (20) 📺 🏃 ✕ 🏢 🖤 🕊 ᄒ cc

Ampleforth

SE5878   ◧ *Abbey In, White Horse, White Swan, Wombwell Arms, Rydale Lodge*

Carr House Farm, *Shallowdale, Ampleforth, York, YO62 4ED.*
Idyllic C16th farmhouse, romantic 4 poster bedrooms, internationally recommended, Heartbeat countryside.
Open: All Year (not Xmas)
Grades: ETC 3 Diamond
01347 868526 Mrs Lupton
D: fr £20.00 **S:** fr £20.00
Beds: 3D **Baths:** 3 En
⛄ (7) 🅿 (5) ⅄ 📺 ✕ 🏢 🖤 🕊

Spring Cottage, *Ampleforth, York, YO62 4DA.*
Magnificent views over Ryedale; close to Heartbeat and Herriot Country.
Open: All Year
Grades: ETC 3 Diamond
01439 788579 (also fax)
Mr Benson
D: £20.00–£22.00 **S:** £20.00–£22.00
Beds: 1F 1D **Baths:** 2 En
⛄ 🅿 (4) ⅄ 📺 🏃 ✕ 🏢 🖤 🕊

Arkengarthdale

NZ0002   ◧ *Buck Hotel, Great Britain*

The White House, *Arkle Town, Arkengarthdale, Richmond, N. Yorks, DL11 6RB.*
A 200-year-old former farmhouse offering ensuite accommodation, fine home cooking and off-road parking.
Open: Mar to Oct
01748 884088 Mrs Whitworth
Fax: 01748 884203
D: £18.50–£21.00 **S:** £26.00–£30.00
Beds: 2D 1T **Baths:** 2 Pr 1 Sh
⛄ (10) 🅿 (5) ⅄ 📺 ✕ 🏢 🖤

Arkle Town

◧ *Great Britain*

The Ghyll, *Arkle Town, Arkengarthdale, Richmond, DL11 6EU.*
Excellent accommodation with wonderful views of Arkengarthdale at this former farm house.
Open: All Year (not Xmas)
01748 884353 Mr & Mrs Good
Fax: 01748 884015
D: £19.00 **S:** £22.00
Beds: 2D 1T **Baths:** 3 En
⛄ (10) 🅿 (10) ⅄ 📺 🏃 🏢 🖤 🕊 cc

Askrigg

SD9491   ◧ *Kings Arms, Crown Inn, George & Dragon, Rose & Crown*

Milton House, *Askrigg, Leyburn, N. Yorks, DL8 3HJ.*
Lovely old Dales family home situated in Askrigg village in beautiful countryside.
Open: All Year (not Xmas)
Grades: ETC 3 Diamond
01969 650217 Mrs Percival
D: £19.00–£21.00 **S:** £25.00–£30.00
Beds: 3D **Baths:** 3 En
⛄ (10) 🅿 (3) ⅄ 📺 🏃 🏢 🖤 🕊

Thornsgill House, *Moor Road, Askrigg, Leyburn, N. Yorks, DL8 3HH.*
Situated in quiet corner in Askrigg, famous for 'All Creatures Great and Small'. **Open:** All Year
Grades: ETC 4 Diamond
01969 650617 Mrs Gilyeat **D:** £22.00
Beds: 1D 1T 1S **Baths:** 2 En 1 Pr
⛄ (10) 🅿 (3) ⅄ 📺 🏃 ✕ 🏢 🖤

Winville Hotel & Restaurant , *Main Street, Askrigg, Leyburn, N Yorks, DL8 3HG.*
C19th Georgian hotel in centre of Herriot village.
Open: All Year
01969 650515 Mr Buckle
Fax: 01969 650594
D: £24.00–£28.50 **S:** £24.00–£38.50
Beds: 4F 4D 2T **Baths:** 10 En
⛄ (18) 📺 🏃 ✕ 🏢 🖤 🕊 cc

Carr End House, *Countersett, Askrigg, Leyburn, North Yorkshire, DL8 3DE.*
Charming C17th country house. Idyllic situation, warm, comfortable. Excellent food. **Open:** All Year (not Xmas)
01969 650346 Mrs Belward
D: £20.00–£22.00 **S:** £20.00–£22.00
Beds: 1F 2D **Baths:** 2 En 1 Pr
⛄ 🅿 (7) ⅄ 📺 🏢 🖤 🕊

Austwick

SD7668

Dalesbridge, *Austwick, Settle, Lancaster, LA2 8AZ.*
Friendly relaxing ensuite B & B. Outstanding views and a great atmosphere. **Open:** All Year
Grades: ETC 3 Diamond
015242 51021 C MacDougall
info@dalesbridge.co.uk
D: £24.00 **S:** £29.00
Beds: 1F 3T 1D 1S **Baths:** 4 En 1 Sh
⛄ 🅿 (60) ⅄ 📺 🏃 ✕ 🏢 🖤 🕊 cc

Aysgarth

SE0088   ◧ *George & Dragon, Palmer Flatt Hotel*

Low Gill Farm, *Aysgarth, Leyburn, N. Yorks, DL8 3AL.*
Dairy and sheep farm. Peaceful surroundings, beautiful views of Wensleydale. **Open:** Feb to Oct
Grades: ETC 3 Diamond
01969 663554 Mrs Dinsdale
val-dinsdale@
cowgillfarm.fsbusiness.co.uk
D: £18.00–£20.00
Beds: 1F 1D **Baths:** 2 En
⛄ 🅿 (3) ⅄ 🏢 🖤 🕊

Thorngarth, *Home Farm, Aysgarth, Leyburn, N. Yorks, DL8 3AG.*
Modern bungalow close to Aysgarth Falls. good for touring. **Open:** Easter to October
01969 663519 Mrs Spence
D: £17.00–£20.00 **S:** £20.00
Beds: 2D **Baths:** 1 En 1 Pr
⛄ 🅿 (4) ⅄ 📺 🏢 🕊

Aysgarth Falls

SE0188

Wensleydale Farmhouse, *Aysgarth Falls, Leyburn, N. Yorks, DL8 3SR.*
Situated 300 yards from the famous Aysgarth Falls. Superb views.
Open: All Year
01969 663534 (also fax) Mr & Mrs O'Reilly
wensleyfar@aol.com
D: £22.00 **S:** £27.00
Beds: 1F 3D **Baths:** 3 En 1 Pr
⛄ (6) 🅿 (4) ⅄ 📺 🏢 🖤 🕊

Barden (Skipton)

SE0557

Little Gate Farm, *Drebley, Barden, Skipton, N Yorks, BD23 6AU.*
Open: Easter to Nov
01756 720200 D: £19.00 **S:** £19.00
Beds: 1F 1D 1T **Baths:** 1 Pr 1 Sh
⛄ 🅿 ⅄ 📺 🏢 🖤 🕊
Beautiful Grade I Listed C15th Dales farmhouse; all rooms look down the valley to the River Wharfe. We are a working sheep-rearing farm, breeding our own collies.

Howgill Lodge, *Barden, Skipton, N. Yorks, BD23 6DJ.*
Uninterrupted views over beautiful Wharfedale. Once experienced, you will return. **Open:** All Year (not Xmas)
01756 720655 Mrs Foster
D: £27.00–£30.00 **S:** £32.00–£35.00
Beds: 1F 2D 1T **Baths:** 4 En
⛄ 🅿 (10) 📺 ✕ 🏢 🖤 🕊 cc

Beadlam

SE6584

White Horse Inn, *Beadlam, Nawton, York, YO62 7SU.*
Handy for North Yorkshire Moors and coast. Warm and friendly, comfortable and good food. **Open:** All Year
01439 770627 Mr Rymer
D: £15.00 **S:** £15.00
Beds: 1D 1T 1S **Baths:** 1 Sh
⛄ 🅿 (6) 📺 🏃 🏢 🖤 🕊

Beck Hole

NZ8202   ◧ *Goathland Hotel*

Brookwood Farm, *Beck Hole, Goathland, Whitby, N. Yorks, YO22 5LE.*
Open: All Year (not Xmas/New Year)
01947 896402 B Fox
D: £18.00–£25.00 **S:** £20.00–£26.50
Beds: 2D **Baths:** 1 En 1 Sh
🅿 (4) ⅄ 📺 🏃 🏢 🖤 🕊
Beautifully situated in wooded Moorland Valley, set in 18 acres of ancient meadows to explore, 1 mile from Goathland, 10 from Whitby. Breakfast served in sunny conservatory overlooking flower Garden. Wood burning stove in the lounge, Quiet, private, classy country bedrooms.

Bedale

SE2688   🍺 *Black Swan, Castle Arms Fox & Hounds, Green Dragon, Swadale Arms, Plummers*

Stabann Georgian Bed & Breakfast, *16 North End, Bedale, North Yorkshire, DL8 1AB.*
Grade II Listed Georgian house, large comfortable rooms, good breakfast.
Open: March to Jan
Grades: ETC 4 Diamond
01677 424454 Mr Hall
D: £20.00–£22.00 **S:** £28.00
Beds: 1F 1D
🛇 🅿 (6) ⊁ 📺 🎍 🛇 👗 ᕵ

Hyperion House, *88 South End, Bedale, N. Yorks, DL8 2DS.*
Open: All Year (not Xmas/New Year)
01677 422334
Mrs Dean
dean.hyperion@tinyworld.co.uk
D: £20.00–£25.00 **S:** £25.00–£30.00
Beds: 2D 1T **Baths:** 1 En
🛇 (12) 🅿 (4) ⊁ 📺 🛇 👗
Beautiful house offering superb accommodation. Excellent Breakfasts a warm welcome from your hosts with Tea and sconces in the conservatory overlooking our lovely Garden with visiting Birds. Idyllic area for holidays in the lovely north Yorkshire. Good north - stop over.

Waggon And Horses, *20 Market Place, Bedale, N. Yorks, DL8 1EQ.*
Traditional cosy pub c1680 in attractive market town, selection of real ales, large bedrooms.
Open: All Year
01677 422747
Mr Young
D: £22.50–£25.00 **S:** £25.00–£30.00
Beds: 3F **Baths:** 3 En
🛇 🅿 (10) 📺 🎍 🛇 👗

Southfield, *96 South End, Bedale, N. Yorks, DL8 2DS.*
Now 'Which?' Recommended. One mile from A1. Ideal North-South stopover.
Open: All Year (not Xmas/New Year)
Grades: AA 3 Diamond, RAC 3 Diamond
01677 423510 Mrs Keighley
D: £22.00 **S:** £22.00
Beds: 1T 1S **Baths:** 1 Pr
🛇 🅿 (4) ⊁ 📺 🎍 🛇 👗

Bell Busk

SD9056   🍺 *Angel*

Tudor House, *Bell Busk, Skipton, N Yorks, BD23 4DT.*
Open: February to Mid-December
Grades: ETC 4 Diamond
01729 830301 (also fax)
Mr Hitchen
bellbusk.hitch@virgin.net
D: £25.00 **S:** £21.00–£35.00
Beds: 1T 3D 1S **Baths:** 4 En 1 Sh
🛇 🅿 (10) ⊁ 📺 ✕ 🛇 👗 cc
Formerly a Victorian railway station retaining its character and charm yet with modern amenities. Set in acre of attractive gardens with superb views over Malhamdale. Ideal base for walking, exploring, relaxing in the Yorkshire Dales. Discounts for longer stays.

Bilsdale

SE5692

Lockton House Farm, *Bilsdale, Helmsley, York, YO62 5NE.*
C16th farmhouse central location many places of interest. **Open:** Easter to Oct
01439 798303 Mrs Easton
D: £17.00 **S:** £17.00
Beds: 1F 1D 1T **Baths:** 1 Sh
🛇 🅿 (1) 📺 🎍 ✕ 🛇 👗

Bishop Thornton

SE2663   🍺 *Drovers Inn*

Raventofts Head House, *Watergate Road, Bishop Thornton, Harrogate, N. Yorks, HG3 3JZ.*
Comfortable C18th farmhouse with small beef herd and a gaggle of geese.
Open: All Year (not Xmas)
01765 620279 D: £16.00–£18.00 **S:** £20.00
Beds: 1F 1T 1S **Baths:** 1 En 1 Sh
🛇 🅿 (8) 📺 🛇 👗

Blubberhouses

SE1655   🍺 *Stone House*

Scaife Hall Farm, *Blubberhouses, Otley, N. Yorks, LS21 2PL.*
C19th farmhouse in tranquil rural location. Ideal base for walking & exploring the Dales.
Open: All Year (not Xmas)
01943 880354 Mrs Ryder
christine.a.ryde@btinternet.com
D: £23.00–£25.00 **S:** £30.00–£35.00
Beds: 2D 1T **Baths:** 3 En
🛇 (10) 🅿 (3) ⊁ 📺 🛇 👗

Boltby

SE4986   🍺 *Carpenters' Arms, Whitstoncliffe Hotel, Hambleton Inn*

Willow Tree Cottage, *Boltby, Thirsk, N. Yorkshire, YO7 2DY.*
Large luxurious room with kitchenette. Quiet hillside village, spectacular views.
Open: All Year (not Xmas)
01845 537406 S C E Townsend
Fax: 01845 537073
townsend.sce@virgin.net
D: £22.00–£30.00 **S:** £30.00–£38.00
Beds: 1F **Baths:** 1 En
🛇 (5) 🅿 (2) ⊁ 📺 🎍 ✕ 🛇 👗

Low Paradise Farm, *Boltby, Thirsk, N. Yorks, YO7 2HS.*
Warm welcome. Hill walking, cycling and Herriot Museum nearby.
Open: March to Nov
01845 537253 Mrs Todd
D: £17.00–£18.00 **S:** £20.00
Beds: 1D 2T **Baths:** 1 Sh
🛇 (6) 🅿 (7) ⊁ 📺 🎍 ✕ 🛇 👗

Town Pasture Farm, *Boltby, Thirsk, N. Yorks, YO7 2DY.*
Comfortable farmhouse in beautiful village, central for Yorkshire Dales.
Open: All Year (not Xmas)
Grades: ETC 3 Diamond
01845 537298 Mrs Fountain
D: £17.50–£19.50 **S:** £18.50–£20.00
Beds: 1F 1T **Baths:** 2 En
🛇 🅿 (3) 📺 🎍 ✕ 🛇 👗

Bolton Percy

SE5341   🍺 *Shoulder Of Mutton*

Beckside House, *Main Street, Bolton Percy, York, YO23 7AQ.*
Self contained ground floor accommodation in very peaceful village near York.
Open: All Year (not Xmas)
01904 744246 Mrs Rhodes
peter.rhodes@tesco.net
D: £17.50 **S:** £20.00
Beds: 1D **Baths:** 1 En
🅿 (1) ⊁ 📺 🎍 🛇 👗

Bolton-on-Swale

SE2599   🍺 *Farmers Arms*

School House, *Bolton-on-Swale, Richmond, N. Yorks, DL10 6AQ.*
Early C18th converted school house in delightful rural setting.
Open: Apr to Oct
01748 818532 Mrs Robinson
york.robinson@virgin.net
D: £20.00 **S:** £20.00
Beds: 2T **Baths:** 1 Sh
⊁ 📺 ✕ 🛇 👗

Boroughbridge

SE3966   🍺 *Black Bull*

Arncliffe, *Church Lane, Boroughbridge, York, YO51 9BA.*
Comfortable, private facilities, close to York and the Dales.
Open: All Year (not Xmas)
01423 322048
mth@arncliffe63.freeserve.co.uk
D: £19.00 **S:** £25.00
Beds: 1D **Baths:** 1 Pr
🅿 📺 🛇

Brackenholme

SE7030

Hagthorpe House, *Selby Road, Brackenholme, Selby, N. Yorks, YO8 6EL.*
Beautiful country house, large garden, tennis, golf, fishing nearby.
Open: All Year (not Xmas)
01757 638867 Mrs Jackson
hagthorpe@supanet.com
D: £16.00–£18.00 **S:** £18.00–£20.00
Beds: 1D 1T **Baths:** 1 Sh
🛇 🅿 (3) ⊁ 📺 🛇 👗

Brawby

SE7378   🍺 *Golden Lion*

Brawby Grange, *Brawby, Malton, N. Yorks, YO17 6PZ.*
Comfortable farmhouse quiet location, central heating, wash basins all rooms, TV in lounge.
Open: All Year (not Xmas)
01653 668245 Mrs Fairweather
D: £16.00 **S:** fr £16.00
Beds: 2D 1T **Baths:** 1 Sh
🛇 🅿 (10) 📺 🛇 👗

Planning a longer stay? Always ask for any special rates

Brayton

SE6030

West Cottage, *Mill Lane, Brayton, Selby, N. Yorks, YO8 9LB.*
Small family-run B&B set in a delightful cottage garden with grass tennis court.
Open: All Year
01757 213318 (also fax)
Mrs Fletcher
D: fr £20.00 **S:** fr £25.00
Beds: 1F 1T **Baths:** 2 En
ਠ (12) ◪ (5) ⊬ ⅏ ▥ ▣ ♨

Brotton

NZ6820

The Arches Hotel, *Birkbeck Low Farm, Brotton, Saltburn-by-the- Sea, TS12 2QX.*
Open: All Year
01287 677512 Fax: 01287 677150
birkralysc@aol.com
D: £20.00–£30.00 **S:** £30.00–£35.00
Beds: 11F 5T 6D **Baths:** Pr
▣ (20) ⊬ ⅏ ▥ ▣ ♨ cc
Beautiful coastal and golf course views, with the warmest welcome assured. Special terms for long stays - log fires - visit Whitby. Staithes, North York's steam railway.

Bulmer

SE6967   ◧ *Bay Horse*

Lower Barn, *Bulmer, Castle Howard, York, YO60 7ES.*
200 years old converted barn. Recommended by Which? Good B&B guide.
Open: All Year
01653 618575 Mrs Hall
Fax: 01653 618183
D: £17.00–£18.00 **S:** £18.00–£20.00
Beds: 1D 1T **Baths:** 2 Pr
ਠ (10) ◪ (10) ⊬ ⅏ ✕ ▥ ▣ ♨

Burniston

TA0192   ◧ *Three Jolly Sailors, Oakwheel*

Harmony Country Lodge, *Limestone Road, Burniston, Scarborough, N Yorks, YO13 0DG.*
Octagonal peaceful retreat with superb sea views and 360º panorama.
Open: All Year
Grades: ETC 4 Diamond
0800 2985840 Mr & Mrs Hewitt
harmonylodge@cwcom.net
D: £22.50–£25.50 **S:** £20.50–£30.00
Beds: 5D 1T 1S **Baths:** 4 En 3 Sh
ਠ (7) ◪ (10) ⊬ ⅏ ✝ ✕ ▥ ▣ ✿ ♨

Burnsall

SE0361   ◧ *Fountain*

Burnsall Manor House Hotel, *Burnsall, Skipton, N. Yorks, BD23 6BW.*
Comfortable, friendly, relaxed. Good food, ideal base for walking.
Open: All Year
01756 720231 (also fax)
Mr Lodge
manorhouse@burnsall.fsnet.co.uk
D: £24.50–£28.50 **S:** £24.50–£28.50
Beds: 5D 3T **Baths:** 5 En 1 Pr 2 Sh
ਠ ▣ (9) ⊬ ⅏ ✝ ✕ ▥ ▣ ✿ ♨

Holly Tree Farm, *Thorpe, Burnsall, Skipton, N. Yorks, BD23 6BJ.*
Quiet, homely Dales sheep farm.
Open: All Year (not Xmas)
01756 720604 Mrs Hall
D: £18.00–£20.00 **S:** £18.00–£20.00
Beds: 1D 1S **Baths:** 1 Sh
ਠ (5) ▣ (2) ⊬ ⅏ ▣ ♨

Carlton Miniott

SE3981   ◧ *Dog & Gun, Red House, Vale of York*

Carlton House Farm, *Carlton Miniott, Thirsk, N. Yorks, YO7 4NJ.*
Warm Yorkshire welcome awaits in comfortable home. Lovely gardens and lanes to walk. **Open:** All Year
01845 524139 Mrs Lee
D: £15.00–£20.00 **S:** fr £15.00
Beds: 2D **Baths:** 1 Sh
ਠ (10) ▣ (4) ⊬ ⅏ ▥

Grove Dene, *Carlton Miniott, Thirsk, N. Yorks, YO7 4NJ.*
Open: All Year
01845 524257 Mrs Corner
D: £16.00 **S:** £20.00
Beds: 1D **Baths:** 1 Sh
ਠ ▣ (6) ⊬ ⅏ ✝ ▥ ▣ ♨ ⅊
Very homely bungalow 2 miles west of Thirsk, quiet and lovely views of garden. Fishing nearby and friendly B&B.

Carlton-in-Coverdale

SE0684

Abbots Thorn, *Carlton-in-Coverdale, Leyburn, N. Yorks, DL8 4AY.*
Open: Jan to Dec
Grades: ETC 4 Diamond
01969 640620 Mrs Lashmar
abbots.thorn@virgin.net
D: £18.00–£25.00 **S:** fr £28.00
Beds: 1D 1T **Baths:** 2 En 1 Pr
ਠ (12) ⊬ ⅏ ✝ ✕ ▥ ▣ ♨
Relax and unwind at our comfortable traditional Yorkshire Dales home. Oak-beamed guest lounge with open fire on those chilly evenings. Indulge yourself in our fabulous dinners. Superb scenery, terrific touring, wonderful walking. All bedrooms have beautiful views over glorious Coverdale.

Carperby

SE0089   ◧ *King's Arms, Wheatsheaf*

Cross House, *Carperby, Leyburn, N Yorks, DL8 4DQ.*
Old farmhouse, near Aysgarth Falls, excellent walking centre. Quiet.
Open: All Year (not Xmas/New Year)
Grades: ETC 2 Diamond
01969 663457 Mrs Mason
D: £16.00–£20.00 **S:** £16.00–£20.00
Beds: 1T 1D **Baths:** 1 En 1 Pr
ਠ ▣ ⊬ ⅏ ▥ ▣ ♨

The Old Stables, *Carperby, Wensleydale, Leyburn, N. Yorks, DL8 4DA.*
Delightful converted stables; perfect walking, touring base. Heart of Wensleydale. **Open:** Easter to Oct
01969 663590 (also fax) Mrs Nicholson
D: £21.00–£23.00 **S:** £30.00–£32.00
Beds: 2D 1T **Baths:** 3 En
▣ (4) ⊬ ⅏ ▥ ♨

Castle Howard

SE7170   ◧ *Crown & Cushion*

High Gaterley Farm, *Castle Howard, York, YO60 7HT.*
Open: All Year
Grades: ETC 4 Diamond
01653 694636 (also fax)
Mrs Turner
relax@highgaterley.com
D: £19.00–£25.00 **S:** £25.00
Beds: 2D 1T 1S **Baths:** 1 En 1 Sh
ਠ ▣ (10) ⊬ ⅏ ✝ ✕ ▥ ▣ ♨
Within the parkland of the estate with magnificent views over the Howardian Hills.

Castleton

NZ6808   ◧ *Moorlands Hotel, Eskdale Hotel*

Greystones Bed & Breakfast, *30 High Street, Castleton, Whitby, N. Yorks, YO21 2DA.*
Betwixt sea and moor 'Greystones' makes the perfect resting place.
Open: All Year
Grades: ETC 3 Diamond
01287 660744 D Wedgwood
D: fr £15.00 **S:** fr £15.00
Beds: 3D **Baths:** 1 Pr 1 Sh
ਠ ⊬ ⅏ ▥ ▣ ♨

Crown End, *Castleton, Whitby, N Yorks, YO21 2HP.*
Modern bungalow beautiful views of moors and dales, village 1 mile.
Open: All Year (not Xmas)
Grades: ETC 4 Diamond
01287 660267 Mrs Liddell
D: £16.00–£18.00 **S:** £16.00–£18.00
Beds: 1D 1T 1S **Baths:** 1 En 1 Pr
ਠ (8) ▣ (4) ⊬ ⅏ ▥ ▣ ♨

Catterick

SE2497   ◧ *Fathers Arms*

Rose Cottage Guest House, *26 High Street, Catterick, Richmond, N. Yorks, DL10 7LJ.*
Small cosy stone-built guest house, midway London-Edinburgh.
Open: All Year (not Xmas)
Grades: ETC 3 Diamond, AA 3 Diamond
01748 811164 Mrs Archer
D: £18.50–£21.00 **S:** £22.00–£27.00
Beds: 1D 2T 1S **Baths:** 2 En 1 Sh
ਠ ▣ (4) ⅏ ✝ ✕ ▥ ♨

Chop Gate

SE5599   ◧ *Buck*

Hill End Farm, *Chop Gate, Bilsdale, Stokesley North Yorkshire, TS9 7JR.*
Open: Easter to Nov
Grades: ETC 3 Diamond
01439 798278 Mrs Johnson
D: £21.00 **S:** £25.00
Beds: 1F 1T **Baths:** 2 En
ਠ (5) ▣ (3) ⊬ ⅏ ✝ ✕ ▥ ♨
Recommended by Which? Good bed and breakfast guide. Hill End farm beautiful views down the valley of Bilsdale which is midway between the market towns of Helmsley and Stokesley. Near to Herriot Heartbeat and Captain Cook Country

Buck Inn Hotel, Chop Gate, Stokesley,
Middlesbrough, TS9 7JL.
Friendly inn with restaurant; splendid
views of Bilsdale Valley.
Open: All Year (not Xmas)
01642 778334 Mrs Stewart
harmonylodge@cwcom.net
D: £21.00–£24.00 **S:** £28.00–£32.00
Beds: 1F 1D 4T **Baths:** 6 Pr
⑁ 🅿 📺 ✕ 🞑 Ⓥ ♨

Clapham

SD7469　🍴 Goat Gap Inn

Arbutus Guest House, Riverside,
Clapham, Lancaster, LA2 8DS.
Situated in heart of village, overlooking
river. Excellent food and parking.
Open: All Year
Grades: ETC 4 Diamond, AA 4 Diamond
015242 51240 Mrs Cass
Fax: 015242 51197
info@arbutus.co.uk
D: £20.00–£26.00 **S:** £20.00–£36.00
Beds: 2F 1D 2T 1S **Baths:** 5 En 1 Pr
⑁ 🅿 (6) ⠹ 🐾 ✕ 🞑 Ⓥ ♣ ♨

Goat Gap Inn, Newby, Clapham,
Lancaster, LA2 8JB.
300 year old inn within sight of the Three
Peaks. **Open:** All Year
015242 41230 Mr & Mrs Robb-Cummings
Fax: 015242 41651
duncan@goatgap.demon.co.uk
D: fr £24.00 **S:** fr £35.00
Beds: 1F 4D 1T **Baths:** 4 En 2 Sh
⑁ 🅿 📺 🐾 ✕ 🞑 Ⓥ ♣ ♨ cc

Flying Horseshoe Hotel, Clapham,
Lancaster, LA2 8ES.
Friendly and family run. Great food and
drink. Free fishing. **Open:** All Year
Grades: ETC 2 Star
015242 51229 (also fax)
Mr & Mrs Perrow
alan@laughing-gravy.co.uk
D: £20.00–£25.00 **S:** £27.50–£32.50
Beds: 3F 3D 1T
⑁ 🅿 (50) 📺 🐾 ✕ 🞑 Ⓥ ♨ cc

Claxton

SE6960　🍴 Tanglewood

Claxton Hall Cottage, Malton Road,
Claxton, York, YO60 7RE.
Peaceful cottage, beams and log fires.
Home baked cake on arrival. Romantic
candlelit dinners on request.
Open: All Year **Grades:** ETC 4 Diamond
01904 468697 (also fax) Mrs Brough
claxcott@aol.com
D: £20.00–£27.50 **S:** £20.00–£27.50
Beds: 1T 2D **Baths:** 1 En 2 Sh
⑁ 🅿 (10) ⠹ 📺 ✕ 🞑 Ⓥ ♨ cc

Clay Bank Top

NZ5701

Maltkiln House, Clay Bank Top,
Bilsdale, Middlesbrough, TS9 7HZ.
Stone farmhouse in secluded moorland
location with magnificent views.
Licensed. **Open:** All Year
01642 778216 (also fax) Mr & Mrs Broad
D: £17.00–£18.50 **S:** £17.00–£18.50
Beds: 1D 2T **Baths:** 1 En 1 Sh
⑁ (8) 🅿 (3) ⠹ ✕ Ⓥ ♨

Cloughton

TA0094　🍴 Falcon

Gowland Farm, Gowland Lane,
Cloughton, Scarborough, N. Yorks,
YO13 0DU.
Warm, friendly, peaceful, beautiful views,
quiet, convenient
Whitby/Scarborough/coast.
Open: Easter to Sep
01723 870924 Mr Martin
D: £16.50–£18.00 **S:** £16.50–£18.00
Beds: 1D 1T 1S **Baths:** 1 Sh
⑁ (3) 🅿 (6) 📺 ✕ 🞑 Ⓥ

Cold Cotes

SD7171　🍴 Goat Gap Inn

Moorview, Cold Cotes, Clapham,
Lancaster, LA2 8HS.
Beautiful detached house, peaceful,
comfortable, wonderful views and great
breakfast. **Open:** All Year (not Xmas)
015242 42085 Mrs Lupton
D: £18.00–£20.00 **S:** £20.00–£24.00
Beds: 2D 1T **Baths:** 2 En 1 Sh
⑁ (1) 🅿 (3) 📺 🐾 🞑 Ⓥ ♨

Coxwold

SE5377　🍴 Abbey Inn, Black Swan, Fauconberg
Arms

Dale Croft, Main Street, Coxwold, York,
YO61 4AB.
Dale Croft is a C17th old worldly cottage;
large gardens.
Open: All Year (not Xmas/New Year)
01347 868356 Mr & Mrs Richardson
D: £17.00–£20.00 **S:** £18.50–£20.00
Beds: 1F 1D 1T **Baths:** 1 Sh
⑁ 🅿 (5) 📺 🐾 🞑 Ⓥ ♨

Crakehall

SE2489　🍴 Bay Horse, Boot & Shoe

Waterside, Glenaire, Great Crakehall,
Bedale, N. Yorks, DL8 1HS.
Open: All Year (not Xmas)
01677 422908 Mrs Smith
Fax: 01677 422280
D: £19.00–£22.00 **S:** £25.00
Beds: 1D 2T **Baths:** 2 En 1 Pr
⑁ (5) 🅿 (4) ⠹ 📺 🐾 ✕ 🞑 Ⓥ ♨
Country house in 1 acre garden, trout
stream. Bedrooms overlook garden to
waters' edge. Guest lounge and sun
lounge. Peace and tranquillity is the
hallmark of a stay at Waterside. Perfectly
situated between the Yorkshire Dales and
Moors in Herriot country.

Crayke

SE5670　🍴 Durham Ox

The Hermitage, Crayke, York, YO61 4TB.
Open: All Year
Grades: ETC 3 Diamond
01347 821635 Mr Moverley
D: £26.00–£27.00 **S:** £26.00–£27.00
Beds: 1D 2T **Baths:** 1 En 1 Sh
⑁ 🅿 (4) 📺 🞑 Ⓥ ♨
Located on edge of small pretty village,
stone-built house set in large garden;
quiet setting with magnificent view in
Area of Outstanding Natural Beauty,
handy for York North York Moors, Wolds
and Dales. Two miles from A19.

Cringle Moor

NZ5503　🍴 Buck Inn

Beakhills Farm, Cold Moor, Cringle
Moor, Chop Gate, Stokesley,
Middlesbrough, TS9 7JJ.
Cosy farmhouse on working farm.
Open: All Year
01642 778371 Mrs Cook
D: fr £16.00 **S:** fr £16.00
Beds: 1F 1T 1D
⑁ 🅿 📺 🐾 ✕ Ⓥ

Cropton

SE7589　🍴 New Inn

Burr Bank Cottage, Cropton,
Pickering, N. Yorks, YO18 8HL.
Open: All Year
Grades: ETC 5 Diamond, Gold Award
01751 417777 Ms Richardson
Fax: 01751 417789
bandb@burrbank.com
D: £27.00 **S:** £27.00
Beds: 1D 1T **Baths:** 2 En
⑁ (12) 🅿 (10) ⠹ 📺 ✕ 🞑 Ⓥ ♨
Peace and quiet in 80 acres. Walks, rides
and drives to coast, moors, dales, Wolds
and York all less than 45 minutes away.
Ensuite accommodation. Winner for
Yorkshire 'Guesthouse Accommodation of
the Year' 2000. Ground floor.

High Farm, Cropton, Pickering, N.
Yorks, YO18 8HL.
Lovely Victorian house, beautiful garden
overlooking National Parkland, home
baking.
Open: All Year
01751 417461 Mrs Feaster
Fax: 01751 473250
D: £20.00
Beds: 3D **Baths:** 3 En
⑁ (10) 🅿 (10) 📺 🞑 Ⓥ ♣ ♨ cc

Cundall

SE4272　🍴 Farmers' Inn

Lodge Farm, Cundall, York, YO61 2RN.
A Georgian farmhouse by River Swale
offering accommodation in own private
suite.
Open: Mar to Nov
01423 360203 (also fax)
Mrs Barker
D: £20.00–£25.00 **S:** £30.00–£36.00
Beds: 1D **Baths:** 1 En
⑁ (2) 🅿 (2) ⠹ ✕ 🞑 ♨

Dalton (Richmond)

NZ1108　🍴 Traveller's Rest

Stonesthrow, Dalton, Richmond, North
Yorkshire, DL11 7HS.
Quiet village between Richmond and
Barnard Castle. Close to Yorkshire Dales.
Open: All Year
Grades: ETC 3 Diamond
01833 621493 Mrs Lawson
D: £18.00 **S:** £18.00
Beds: 2D 1S **Baths:** 1 Sh
⑁ (8) 🅿 (3) ⠹ ✕ 🞑 Ⓥ ♨

Holmedale, *Dalton (Richmond),*
Richmond, N. Yorks, DL11 7HX.
Georgian house in quiet village midway
Richmond and Barnard Castle.
Open: All Year (not Xmas)
01833 621236 (also fax)
Mrs Brooks
D: £15.00–£18.00 **S:** £15.00–£18.00
Beds: 1D 1T **Baths:** 1 En 1 Sh

Danby

NZ7008   ◀ *Fox & Hounds, Duke Of Wellington,*
Moorlands Hotel, Shepherds' Hall

Holly Lodge Farm, *Danby Head,*
Danby, Whitby, N Yorks, YO21 2NW.
Open: Easter to Oct
01287 660469 Mrs Shirley
D: £18.00–£19.00 **S:** £18.00–£20.00
Beds: 1D 1T 1S **Baths:** 1 Pr
🐾 🅿 (4) ⊬ 📺 ✕ 📖 🕭 📺 🐾
Farmhouse with beautiful views over
Danby Dale near to Heartbeat and Herriot
country, Whitby, York and North Yorks
Steam Railway, offering high class
accommodation, lounge, separate dining
room, bathroom with bath and shower,
comfortable beds and good food.

Sycamore House, *Danby, Whitby, N.*
Yorks, YO21 2NW.
C17th farmhouse with stunning views.
Ideal area for walking/touring.
Open: All Year (not Xmas)
Grades: ETC 3 Diamond
01287 660125 Mr Lowson
Fax: 01287 669122
sycamore.danby@btinternet.com
D: fr £20.00 **S:** fr £20.00
Beds: 1F 1D 1T 1S **Baths:** 1 En 1 Sh
🐾 🅿 (6) ⊬ 📺 ✕ 📖 📺 ♨ cc

Botton Grove Farm, *Danby Head,*
Danby, Whitby, N. Yorks, YO21 2NH.
Large stone built farmhouse; excellent
views of Danby Dale; warm welcome.
Open: May to March
Grades: ETC 3 Diamond
01287 660284 Mrs Tait
judytait@bottongrove.freeserve.co.uk
D: £18.00 **S:** £18.00–£25.00
Beds: 1D 1T 2S **Baths:** 1 Sh
🐾 🅿 (3) 📺 📖 📺 ♨

Darley

SE2059   ◀ *Wellington Inn*

Brimham Guest House, *Silverdale*
Close, Darley, Harrogate, N. Yorks, HG3 2PQ.
Family-run guest house, set in beautiful
Gardens Winner of 1999 'Yorkshire In
Bloom' Competition.
Open: All Year (not Xmas)
Grades: ETC 4 Diamond
01423 780948 Mrs Barker
D: fr £15.00 **S:** fr £20.00
Beds: 2D 1T **Baths:** 3 En
🐾 (1) 🅿 (4) ⊬ 📺 📖 📺 ♨

BATHROOMS

Pr - Private

Sh - Shared

En - Ensuite

Deighton (York)

SE6244   ◀ *White Swan*

Grimston House, *Deighton, York,*
YO19 6HB.
Open: All Year
01904 728328 Fax: 01904 720093
D: £48.00–£50.00 **S:** £30.00–£32.00
Beds: 1F 1T 5D **Baths:** 5 En
🐾 🅿 📺 🕭 📖 ♨
Built in the 1930s, Grimston House is an
attractive place standing within a walled
garden. Easy reach of York and on good
bus route. Good local pub with bar meals.

Dunnington

SE6652   ◀ *Windmill Inn, Cross Keys*

Brookland House, *Hull Road,*
Dunnington, York, YO19 5LW.
Private detached house, country area.
Wholesome breakfast, home-made
preserves.
Open: Mar to Dec
01904 489548 Mrs Foster
D: £16.00–£18.00 **S:** £17.00–£19.00
Beds: 1D 1T 1S **Baths:** 1 Sh
🐾 (5) 🅿 (3) ⊬ 📺 📖 ♨

Moonlight Cottage, *8 Greencroft*
Court, Dunnington, York, YO19 5QJ.
Comfortable and quiet. Convenient to
York Moors, dales, castle, Howard Coast.
Open: All Year
01904 489369 (also fax)
Mrs McNab
D: £15.00–£17.00
Beds: 1D **Baths:** 1 En
🐾 🅿 (2) ⊬ 📺 📖 📺 ♨

Earswick

SE6257   ◀ *Four Alls*

The Lodge, *302 Strensall Rd, Earswick,*
York, YO32 9SW.
Spacious guest rooms. large gardens.
easily reached off A1237 ring road.
Open: All Year
01904 761387 (also fax)
Mrs Edmondson
the.lodge@talk21.com
D: fr £19.00 **S:** fr £20.00
Beds: 1F 1D 1T **Baths:** 2 En 1 Sh
🐾 🅿 (3) ⊬ 📺 📖 📺 ♨

Fairthorne, *356 Strenshall Road,*
Earswick, York, YO32 9SW.
Peaceful country setting, dormer
bungalow. 3 miles from York, easy reach
North Yorks Moors.
Open: Dec to Dec
Grades: ETC 3 Diamond
01904 768609 (also fax)
J W Harrison
D: £16.00–£20.00 **S:** £20.00
Beds: 1F 1D **Baths:** 1 En
🐾 🅿 (2) 📺 📖 ♨

Easingwold

SE5369   ◀ *Carlton, Falconberg*

Yeoman's Course House, *Thornton*
Hill, Easingwold, York, YO61 3PY.
Set in an elevated position overlooking
the beautiful vale of York.
Open: Easter to Oct
Grades: ETC 2 Diamond
01347 868126
Mr & Mrs Addy
Fax: 01347 868129
chris@yeomanscourse.fsnet.co.uk
D: £18.50–£19.50 **S:** £18.50–£19.50
Beds: 1T 2D
🐾 (12) 🅿 (8) ⊬ 📺 📖 ♨

Garbutts Ghyll, *Thornton Hill,*
Easingwold, York, YO61 3PZ.
Family-run B&B on a working farm in its
own valley with panoramic views.
Open: Easter to Nov
01347 868644 Mrs Glaister
Fax: 01347 868133
D: £20.00–£25.00 **S:** £18.00–£20.00
Beds: 1D 1T **Baths:** 1 En
🐾 🅿 ⊬ 📺 🕭 📖 📺 ♨

East Heslerton

SE9276   ◀ *Dawnay Arms*

Manor Farm, *East Heslerton, Malton,*
N. Yorks, YO17 8RN.
Central for touring York, North York Moors
and coastal attractions.
Open: Easter to Oct
01944 728268 Ms Lumley
holiday@dclumley.netscapeonline.co.uk
D: £17.50–£20.00 **S:** £17.50–£20.00
Beds: 2F **Baths:** 2 Pr
🐾 🅿 (4) ⊬ 📺 📖 📺 ♨

East Marton

SD9050   ◀ *Cross Keys*

Drumlins, *Heber Drive, East Marton,*
Skipton, North Yorkshire, BD23 3LS.
Open: All Year
Grades: ETC 4 Diamond
01282 843521
Ms Moran
D: £22.00 **S:** £26.00
Beds: 1F 1T 1D **Baths:** 3 En
🐾 🅿 ⊬ 📺 📖 ✕ 📖 📺 ♨
Drumlins is situated in a Quiet cul-de-
sac off the A59 open views and easy
access to the Dales, Pennine way, and the
market town of Skipton, ensuite facilities
with welcome tray, separate lounge and
dining room ample parking private
garden.

Sawley House, *East Marton, Skipton,*
N. Yorks, BD23 3LP.
C12th farmhouse - farm & stables by
canal on Pennine Way.
Open: All Year (not Xmas)
01282 843207
Mrs Pilling
sawleyhouse@pilling23.freeserve.co.uk
D: £20.00–£22.00 **S:** fr £22.00
Beds: 3T **Baths:** 2 Sh
🅿 (12) 📺 🕭 📺 ♨

Ebberston

SE8982 ◀ *Grapes, Foxholme Hotel*

Foxholm Hotel, *Ebberston, Scarborough, N. Yorks, YO13 9NJ.*
Peaceful, licensed ground floor rooms country inn in quiet picturesque village.
Open: All Year (not Xmas)
Grades: ETC 3 Diamond
01723 859550 (also fax)
Mrs Clyde
kay@foxholm.freeserve.co.uk
D: £25.50–£28.50 **S:** £30.50–£33.50
Beds: 2D 2T **Baths:** 4 En
🛇 🅿 (20) 🖾 🖾 🖈 ✕ 🗏 🕎 🛋 cc

Studley House, *67 Main Street, Ebberston, Scarborough, N. Yorks, YO13 9NR.*
Hearty rooms, hearty breakfast. Picturesque village. Central for all attractions.
Open: All Year (not Xmas/New Year)
Grades: ETC 3 Diamond
01723 859285 (also fax)
Mrs Hodgson
D: £20.00–£25.00 **S:** £25.00–£30.00
Beds: 1D 1T 1S **Baths:** 3 En
🛇 (10) 🅿 (3) ⅍ 🖾 🗏 🕎 🛋 cc

Egton

NZ8006 ◀ *Horseshoe, Wheatsheaf*

Flushing Meadow, *Egton, Whitby, N Yorks, YO21 1UA.*
Superb moorland views. Ideal base for Esk Valley and steam railway.
Open: All Year
Grades: ETC 3 Diamond
01947 895395 Mrs Johnson
flushing_meadow_egton@yahoo.co.uk
D: £15.00–£19.50 **S:** £15.00–£17.00
Beds: 1D 1T 1S **Baths:** 1 En 1 Sh
🅿 (3) ⅍ 🖾 🗏 🛋

Egton Bridge

NZ8005

Broom House, *Broom House Lane, Egton Bridge, Whitby, N Yorks, YO21 1XD.*
Broom House - an excellent place to stay. We provide comfortable ensuite rooms.
Open: All Year (not Xmas)
01947 895279 Mr & Mrs White
Fax: 01947 895657
david.white@broomhouse.egtonbridge.fr
eeserve.co.uk
D: £19.50 **S:** fr £25.00
Beds: 2F 2D 1T **Baths:** 5 En
🛇 🅿 (7) ⅍ 🖾 ✕ 🗏 🕎 🛋

Ellerbeck

SE4397 ◀ *Golden Lion, Kings Head*

Old Mill House, *Ellerbeck, Osmotherley, Northallerton, N. Yorks, DL6 2RY.*
Delightful C17th mill set central for walking touring North Yorkshire.
Open: Easter to November
01609 883466 Mrs Shepherd
D: £20.00–£25.00 **S:** £20.00–£25.00
Beds: 1T 2D **Baths:** 1 En 1 Sh
🅿 (4) ⅍ 🖾 🖈

Ellingstring

SE1684

Holybreen, *Ellingstring, Masham, Ripon, HG4 4PW.*
Good home cooking at this spacious C18th cottage.
Open: All Year
01677 460216 Mrs Wright
Fax: 01677 460106
anne.wright@virgin.net
D: £14.00–£15.00 **S:** £15.00–£16.00
Beds: 1F 1D **Baths:** 1 Sh
🛇 🅿 (2) 🖾 🖈 ✕ 🗏 🕎 🛋

Elvington

SE7047 ◀ *St Vincent Arms*

The Old Gate House, *Wheldrake Lane, Elvington, York, YO41 4AZ.*
Family-run B&B 7 miles from York, situated in open countryside.
Open: All Year (not Xmas)
01904 608225 Mrs Gatenby
D: £14.00 **S:** £14.00
Beds: 1F 4D 1T 2S **Baths:** 4 En 1 Sh
🛇 🅿 (10) 🖾 🖈 🗏 🕎 🛋 &

Embsay

SE0053 ◀ *Elmtree Inn, Mason Arms*

Bondcroft Farm, *Embsay, Skipton, N Yorks, BD23 6SF.*
Sheep and Beef farm, well known for trailing and breeding sheep dogs.
Open: All Year
Grades: ETC 4 Diamond
01756 793371 Ms Clarkson
bondcroftfarm@bondcroftfarm.yorks.net
D: £20.00–£22.50
Beds: 1T 2D **Baths:** 3 En
🛇 🅿 (6) ⅍ 🖾 🗏 🕎 cc

Faceby

NZ4903

Four Wynds, *Whorl Hill, Faceby, Middlesbrough, TS9 7BZ.*
Small holding in beautiful countryside. Located off A172 between Swainby/ Faceby.
Open: All Year
Grades: ETC 3 Diamond
01642 701315 Mr Barnfather
D: £18.00–£20.00 **S:** £18.00–£20.00
Beds: 1F 1D 1T **Baths:** 1 En 1 Sh
🛇 🅿 (8) 🖾 🖈 ✕ 🗏 🕎 🛋

Fadmoor

SE6789

Mount Pleasant, *Rudland, Fadmoor, York, YO62 7JJ.*
Friendly welcome. Ideal for walking, touring from moors. Brochure available.
Open: All Year (not Xmas)
Grades: ETC 3 Diamond
01751 431579 Mary Clarke
info@mountpleasantbedandbreakfast.co.uk
D: £15.00–£16.00 **S:** £15.00–£16.00
Beds: 1F 1T **Baths:** 1 Sh
🛇 🅿 (4) 🅿 (6) 🖾 ✕ 🗏 🕎 🛋

Farndale

SE6697 ◀ *Royal Oak, Crown, Plough*

Keysbeck Farm, *Farndale, Kirkbymoorside, York, YO62 6UZ.*
Old oak-beamed farmhouse.
Open: All Year
01751 433221 Mrs Featherstone
D: fr £14.00 **S:** fr £14.00
Beds: 1D 1T 1S **Baths:** 1 Sh
🛇 🅿 🖈 ✕ 🕎 🛋

Olive House Farm, *Farndale, Kirkbymoorside, York, YO60 7JY.*
Homely accommodation, working farm, Heartbeat country, abbey ruins & stately homes. **Open:** Easter to Oct
01751 433207 Mrs Blacklock
D: £12.50 **S:** £14.00
Beds: 2F
🛇 🅿 (4) 🖾 🖈

Filey

TA1180

The Gables, *2a Rutland Street, Filey, N Yorks, YO14 9JB.*
Open: All Year
Grades: ETC 3 Diamond
01723 514750 R & K Broome
D: £19.00–£23.00 **S:** £21.00–£28.00
Beds: 1F 2T 2D **Baths:** 5 En
🛇 🖾 🖈 🗏 🕎 🛋 🛋
Characteristic Edwardian guest house offering friendly accommodation, comfortable ensuite rooms, colour television, hospitality tray. Central to all amenities. Reductions for 3 people or more nights.

The Forge, *23 Rutland Street, Filey, N. Yorks, YO14 9JA.*
Edwardian townhouse. Small, friendly, non-smoking, good food.
Open: All Year (not Xmas/New Year)
01723 512379 M Appleyard
mikeforgefiley@aol.com
D: £17.50–£19.00 **S:** £22.50–£24.00
Beds: 1F 1T 2D **Baths:** 4 En 1 Pr
🛇 (3) 🅿 🖾 🖈 ✕ 🗏 🕎 🛋 🛋 cc

Foxup

SD8676 ◀ *Tennats Arms*

Bridge Farm, *Foxup, Arncliffe, Skipton, N. Yorks, BD23 5QP.*
Working Dales farm situated in Littondale (the forgotten valley).
Open: Easter to Oct
01756 770249 Mrs Lund
D: £15.00 **S:** £18.00
Beds: 1T 2D **Baths:** 1 Sh
🛇 🅿 (4) 🖾 🖈 🕎 🛋

Fremington

SE0499 ◀ *Bridge Inn, Kings Arms*

Broadlands, *Fremington, Richmond, DL11 6AW.*
Peaceful village setting 5 mins from Reeth, spectacular views, comfortable accommodation. **Open:** All Year
Grades: ETC 1 Diamond
01748 884297 (also fax) Mrs Rudez
D: £19.00 **S:** £27.00
Beds: 1D 1T 1S **Baths:** 1 Sh
🛇 (12) 🅿 (4) ⅍ 🖾 🖈 🗏 🛋 &

Fulford

SE6149   *Saddle, Plough*

The Old Registry, 12 Main Street,
Fulford, York, YO10 4PQ.
Family-run period house. Easy access to
York and University.
Open: All Year (not Xmas)
01904 628136 Mr Beckett
D: £17.00–£25.00 **S:** £17.00–£25.00
Beds: 2D 1T 2S **Baths:** 4 En
🛇 🅿 (6) ⅋ 📺 📖 🎖 cc

Alfreda Guest House, 61 Heslington
Lane, Fulford, York, YO10 4HN.
Edwardian residence, large grounds. Car
park security lighting/camera.
Open: All Year (not Xmas)
01904 631698 Mr Bentley
Fax: 01904 211215
D: £22.00–£27.00 **S:** £25.00–£50.00
Beds: 4F 3D 3T **Baths:** 8 En 2 Sh
🛇 🅿 📺 🐾 📖 🎖 cc

Fylingthorpe

NZ9404   *Fylingdales, Victoria*

Red House, Thorpe Lane, Fylingthorpe,
Whitby, North Yorkshire, YO22 4TH.
Large Victorian house and garden.
Panelled staircase and gallery. Beautiful
views.
Open: Easter to Oct
01947 880079 Mrs Collinson
D: £18.00–£22.50 **S:** £20.00–£25.00
Beds: 1T 2D **Baths:** 1 En 1 Sh
🅿 (3) 📺 🐾 📖 🎖

South View, Sledgates, Fylingthorpe,
Robin Hood's Bay, Whitby, N. Yorks,
YO22 4TZ.
Comfortable detached house. Sea &
country views. Touring area. Bed time
drink.
Open: Easter to Oct
01947 880025 Mrs Reynolds
D: £16.00–£18.00
Beds: 2D **Baths:** 1 Sh
🛇 (5) 🅿 (2) 📺 🐾

Low Farm, Fylingthorpe, Whitby, N
Yorks, YO22 4QF.
Open: May to Nov
01947 880366 (also fax)
Mrs Hodgson
D: £18.00–£21.00
Beds: 1F **Baths:** 1 En
🅿 (1) ⅋ 📺 📖 🎖
Imposing Georgian farmhouse built from
local stone, set in beautiful countryside
on our working farm, 1.5 miles from the
picturesque village of Robin Hood's Bay.
Safe off road parking. Superb views over
garden and beyond. Large breakfasts.
Genuine Yorkshire welcome.

Croft Farm, Fylingthorpe, Whitby, N.
Yorks, YO22 4PW.
All rooms have extensive views over the
sea, moors and countryside.
Open: Easter to Oct
Grades: ETC 4 Diamond
01947 880231 (also fax)
Mrs Featherstone
D: £22.00–£24.00 **S:** £22.00–£27.00
Beds: 2D 1S **Baths:** 2 En 1 Pr
🛇 (5) 🅿 (4) ⅋ 📺 📖 🎖

Ganton

SE9977   *Ganton Greyhound*

The Ganton Greyhound, Main Street,
Ganton, Scarborough, N Yorks, YO12 4NX.
Family and country inn/hotel, 9 miles
from coast.
Open: All Year (not Xmas)
01944 710116 T Bennet
Fax: 01944 710738
gantongreyhound@supanet.com
D: fr £25.00 **S:** fr £40.00
Beds: 6F 4D 6T 2S **Baths:** 16 En
🛇 🅿 (20) ⅋ 📺 ✕ 📖 🎖 🎖 cc

Gayle

SD8789   *Board, Fountain, Crown, White Hart*

Blackburn Farm/Trout Fishery,
Gayle, Hawes, N Yorks, DL8 3NX.
Idyllic location. Quiet, rural but within
walking distance of Hawes.
Open: Easter to Oct
Grades: ETC 3 Diamond
01969 667524 Ms Moore
D: £17.00–£18.00
Beds: 2D **Baths:** 1 En 1 Pr
🅿 (4) ⅋ 📺 🐾 📖 🎖

East House, Gayle, Hawes, N. Yorks,
DL8 3RZ.
Delightful house. Superb views, ideal
centre for touring the dales.
Open: Feb to Nov
Grades: ETC 4 Diamond
01969 667405 Mrs Ward
loraward@lineone.net
D: £18.00–£21.00 **S:** £18.00
Beds: 1T 1D 1S **Baths:** 1 En 1 Sh
🛇 🅿 ⅋ 📺 📖 🎖

Gayle Laithe, Gayle, Hawes, N. Yorks,
DL8 3RR.
Modern, comfortable, converted barn.
Ideal for touring, cycling and walking.
Open: Easter to Nov
01969 667397 Mrs McGregor
D: £16.00–£17.00 **S:** £16.00–£17.00
Beds: 1D 1T 1S **Baths:** 1 Sh
🛇 🅿 (2) 📖 🎖

Giggleswick

SD8164   *Black Horse, Hart's Head*

Yorkshire Dales Field Centre,
Holme Beck, Raines Road, Giggleswick,
Settle, N. Yorks, BD24 0AQ.
Excellent cooking - comfortable well-
appointed converted barn.
Open: All Year
01729 824180 (also fax)
Mrs Barbour
yi67@dial.pipex.com
D: £10.50 **S:** £10.50
Beds: 6F 2S **Baths:** 5 Sh
🛇 🅿 (7) ⅋ 🐾 ✕ 📖 🎖 ❋ 🎖

BEDROOMS

F - Family
D - Double
T - Twin
S - Single

Gillamoor

SE6889   *Royal Oak*

The Manor Farm, Gillamoor,
Kirkbymoorside, York, YO62 7HX.
Warm welcome, farmily farm, central
location for walking and cycling tours.
Open: All Year
01751 432695 (also fax)
Mrs Gibson
D: £17.00–£18.00 **S:** fr £20.00
Beds: 1F 2D 1T **Baths:** 2 En 1 Pr
🛇 🅿 (4) 📺 🐾 ✕ 🎖

Gilling East

SE6177   *Fairfax Arms*

Hall Farm, Gilling East, York, YO62 4JW.
Warm family welcome, fantastic views,
close to Moors, Helmsley, York.
Open: All Year (not Xmas)
Grades: ETC 3 Diamond
01439 788314 Virginia Collinson
virginia@collinson2.fsnet.co.uk
D: £18.00–£20.00 **S:** £15.00–£20.00
Beds: 1D **Baths:** 1 En
🛇 🅿 ⅋ 📺 📖 🎖 🎖 3

Glaisdale

NZ7603   *Angler's Rest, Moon & Sixpence,
Wheatsheaf*

Arncliffe Arms Hotel, Glaisdale,
Whitby, N. Yorks, YO21 2QL.
Open: All Year
01947 897209 (also fax) Mr Westwood
D: £15.00 **S:** £15.00
Beds: 2D 2T 1S **Baths:** 1 Sh
🛇 🅿 📺 🐾 ✕ 📖 🎖
Very friendly & comfortable
accommodation. A must for curry lovers,
romantic area along River Esk, close
Beggars Bridge. 1 min from railway
station. Entertainment if required. Car
park, Coast to Coast drop off/pick up
point.

Postgate Farm, Glaisdale, Whitby, N
Yorks, YO21 2PZ.
Open: All Year (not Xmas)
Grades: ETC 4 Diamond
01947 897353 (also fax) Mrs Thompson
j-m.thompson.bandb@talk21.com
D: £16.00–£21.00 **S:** £20.00–£30.00
Beds: 2D 1T **Baths:** 3 En
🛇 🅿 (4) ⅋ 📺 📖 🎖
C17th Listed farmhouse in beautiful Esk
Valley, a walkers' paradise. Whitby - 10
miles. Steam railway and 'Heartbeat
Country' - 5 miles. Guest kitchen, fridge
and microwave. Games room, laundry,
drying facilities. All ensuite with TV,
courtesy tray, hairdryer, clock-radio. Also
studio flat self catering.

Hollins Farm, Glaisdale, Whitby, N.
Yorks, YO21 2PZ.
Comfortable C16th farmhouse near
moors, 8 miles coast, wonderful scenery.
Open: All Year (not Xmas)
Grades: ETC 3 Diamond
01947 897516 Mrs Mortimer
D: fr £15.00
Beds: 3F 1D 2T **Baths:** 2 Sh
🛇 🅿 (6) 📺 🐾 📖 🎖 🎖

Egton Banks Farm, *Glaisdale, Whitby, N. Yorks, YO21 2QP.*
Lovely old farmhouse in secluded valley, pretty decor. Warm welcome.
Open: All Year (not Xmas/New Year)
Grades: ETC 4 Diamond
01947 897289 A Richardson
D: £16.00–£18.00 **S:** £17.00–£18.00
Beds: 1F 1T 1D **Baths:** 1 En 1 Sh
🛇 🅿 ⌇ 📺 ✕ 🎔, 🆅 ♨

Red House Farm, *Glaisdale, Whitby, N. Yorks, YO21 2PZ.*
Listed Georgian farmhouse, refurbished, but retaining original features.
Open: All Year
01947 897242 (also fax)
Mr Spashett
D: £22.50 **S:** £22.50–£30.00
Beds: 2D **Baths:** 1 En 1 Sh
🛇 🅿 (6) ⌇ 📺 🎔 ♨

Goathland

NZ8301 🍺 *Saltersgate Inn, Mallyan Spout*

Fairhaven Country Hotel, *The Common, Goathland, Whitby, N. Yorks, YO22 5AN.*
Edwardian country house, superb moorland views in centre of village.
Open: All Year
Grades: ETC 3 Diamond, AA 3 Diamond
01947 896361 Mr Ellis
D: £27.00–£35.00 **S:** £21.00–£35.00
Beds: 3F 2T 2D 2S **Baths:** 4 En 3 Sh
🛇 🅿 (9) ⌇ 📺 🎔 ✕ 🎔, 🆅 ♨ cc

The Beacon Country House, *Goathland, Whitby, N Yorks, YO22 5AN.*
Late Victorian country house in 1 acre grounds.
Open: All Year
Grades: ETC 4 Diamond
01947 896409 Mrs Katz
Fax: 01947 896431
stewartkatz@compuserve.com
D: £22.50–£25.00 **S:** £22.50
Beds: 1F 2T 2D **Baths:** 4 En 1 Pr
🛇 🅿 ⌇ 📺 🎔 ✕ 🎔, ♨ cc

1 The Orchards, *Goathland, Whitby, N. Yorks, YO22 5JU.*
Comfortable homely accommodation, good views, quiet situation in popular village.
Open: All Year (not Xmas)
01947 896300 Mrs Turford
D: £16.00–£20.00 **S:** £16.00–£20.00
Beds: 1D 1T **Baths:** 1 Sh
🅿 (2) ⌇ 📺 ♨

Grantley

SE2369 🍺 *Brawtley Arms*

St Georges Court, *Old Home Farm, Grantley, Ripon, N. Yorks, HG4 3EU.*
Peace & tranquillity - we are 200 yards from any road; beautifully situated.
Open: All Year
Grades: ETC 4 Diamond, AA 4 Diamond
01765 620618 Mrs Gordon
D: £22.50–£25.00
Beds: 1F 4D 1T **Baths:** 6 En
🛇 (2) 🅿 (12) ⌇ 📺 🎔, 🆅 ♨ & cc

Grassington

SE0064 🍺 *Black Horse, Devonshire, Old Hall, Foresters' Arms*

Mayfield Bed & Breakfast, *Low Mill Lane, Grassington, Skipton, N. Yorks, BD23 5BX.*
Beautiful Dales longhouse. Guest rooms overlook fells and river.
Open: All Year
01756 753052 Mr & Mrs Trewartha
suzanneatmayfield@talk21.com
D: £22.00–£25.00 **S:** £25.00
Beds: 1F 1D 1T **Baths:** 1 En 1 Sh
🛇 🅿 (5) ⌇ 🎔 🎔, 🆅 ♨ ♨

Town Head Guest House, *1 Low Lane, Grassington, Skipton, N. Yorks, BD23 5AU.*
Friendly guest house at the head of the village between cobbled streets and moors. **Open:** All Year (not Xmas)
01756 752811 Mrs Lister
D: £25.00 **S:** £30.00
Beds: 3D 1T **Baths:** 4 En
🅿 (3) ⌇ 📺 🎔, 🆅 ♨

Lythe End, *Wood Lane, Grassington, Skipton, N. Yorks, BD23 5DF.*
Modern stone detached house, stunning views, quiet village location.
Open: All Year (not Xmas)
01756 753196 Mrs Colley
colley@grassington.fsnet.co.uk
D: £22.00–£25.00 **S:** £30.00
Beds: 1F 1D **Baths:** 1 En 1 Pr
🛇 (12) 🅿 (2) ⌇ 📺, 🆅 ♨

Craiglands, *1 Brooklyn, Threshfield, Grassington, Skipton, BD23 5ER.*
Elegant Edwardian house offering quality accommodation and superb breakfasts.
Open: All Year (not Xmas)
Grades: ETC 4 Diamond
01756 752093 Mrs Wallace
craiglands@talk21.com
D: £21.00–£26.00 **S:** £25.00–£28.00
Beds: 2D 1T 1S **Baths:** 3 En 1 Pr
🅿 (3) ⌇ 📺 🎔, ♨ cc

Kirkfield, *Hebden Road, Grassington, Skipton, N. Yorks, BD23 5LJ.*
Large house in own gardens. Panoramic views of Wharfe Valley. **Open:** All Year
01756 752385 Mr Lockyer
D: £18.00–£25.00 **S:** £20.00
Beds: 3F 1T 1S **Baths:** 2 En 1 Pr 1 Sh
🛇 🅿 (8) ⌇ 📺 🎔 ✕ 🎔, 🆅

Burtree Cottage, *Hebden Road, Grassington, Skipton, N. Yorks, BD23 5LH.*
Old cottage, comfortable rooms, lovely garden. Ideal walking/touring centre.
Open: Mar to Oct
01756 752442 Mrs Marsden
D: £17.50
Beds: 1D 1T **Baths:** 1 Sh
🛇 (10) 🅿 (2) ⌇ 🎔, 🆅

Springroyd House, *8a Station Road, Grassington, Skipton, N. Yorks, BD23 5NQ.*
Conveniently situated, friendly family home. **Open:** All Year
01756 752473 Mrs Robertshaw
springroyd.house@btinternet.com
D: £18.00–£20.00 **S:** £20.00–£22.00
Beds: 1F 1D 1T **Baths:** 1 En 2 Sh
🛇 🅿 (3) ⌇ 🎔 🎔, 🆅 ♨

New Laithe House, *Wood Lane, Grassington, Skipton, N. Yorks, BD23 5LU.*
A converted barn situated in the picturesque village of Grassington.
Open: All year (not Xmas)
01756 752764 Mrs Chaney
new.laithehouse@virgin.net
D: £21.00–£24.00 **S:** £25.00–£40.00
Beds: 1F 4D 2T **Baths:** 4 En 1 Pr
🛇 🅿 (7) 📺 🎔, 🆅 ♨ &

Great Ayton

NZ5611 🍺 *Royal Oak, Buck Hotel*

The Wheelhouse, *Langbaugh Grange, Great Ayton, Middlesbrough, Cleveland, TS9 6QQ.*
Open: All Year
01642 724523 D: £17.00 **S:** £19.00
Beds: 1F 1D **Baths:** 2 Pr
🛇 🅿 (3) 📺 🎔 🎔, 🆅 ♨
Converted barn/mill in half acre gardens with open views to Cleveland Hills. Close to coast and several historic sites. e.g. Mount Grace Priory and Captain Cook attractions. Coast to Coast, Cleveland Way, long distance walks - 1 mile. Lifts available.

The Granary, *Langbaugh Grange, Great Ayton, Middlesbrough, TS9 6QQ.*
Attractive converted barn near Captain Cook village with beautiful garden and lovely views. **Open:** Mar to Dec
01642 723357 Ms Jones
helen@rgjones.fsnet.co.uk
D: £17.00 **S:** £17.00
Beds: 1D 1T **Baths:** 1 Pr
🛇 (3) 🅿 (2) ⌇ 📺 🎔, 🆅 ♨

Eskdale Cottage, *31 Newton Road, Great Ayton, Middlesbrough, TS9 6DT.*
Lovely Victorian cottage near North Yorkshire Moors, all amenities in bedrooms. **Open:** All Year (not Xmas)
01642 724306 Mrs Houghton
D: £14.00–£19.00 **S:** £16.00–£20.00
Beds: 2T **Baths:** 1 Sh
🛇 (2) 🅿 (2) ⌇ 📺 ✕ 🎔, 🆅 ♨

Great Broughton

NZ5406 🍺 *Bay Horse, Black Horse, Jet Miners, Wainstones Hotel*

Ingle Hill, *Ingleby Road, Great Broughton, North Yorks, TS9 7ER.*
Spectacular views North York Moors, warm welcome, transport to walks.
Open: All Year (not Xmas)
01642 712449 Mrs Sutcliffe
D: £17.50 **S:** £18.50
Beds: 1F 1D 2T **Baths:** 2 En 2 Sh
🛇 🅿 (4) ⌇ 📺 🎔 🎔, 🆅 ♨ cc

Great Edstone

SE7084 🍺 *Appletree Inn*

Cowldyke Farm, *Great Edstone, Kirkbymoorside, York, YO62 6PE.*
Family run working farm set in idyllic peaceful Yorkshire countryside.
Open: All Year (not Xmas)
Grades: ETC 3 Diamond
01751 431242 Mrs Benton
D: £20.00 **S:** fr £20.00
Beds: 1F 1D **Baths:** 2 En
🛇 (3) 🅿 (10) 📺 🎔, ♨

Grosmont

NZ8205 ◀ *Post Gate*

Eskdale, *Grosmont, Whitby, N. Yorks,*
YO22 5PT.
Detached Georgian house overlooking
Esk Valley, North York Moors NP.
Open: Easter to Nov
01947 895385 (also fax) Mrs Counsell
d_and_s_counsell@yahoo.co.uk
D: £17.00–£17.50 **S:** £17.00–£17.50
Beds: 2D 2S **Baths:** 1 Sh
🛏 🅿 (3) 📺 🛏 🛒 🕹

Gunnerside

SD9598 ◀ *Oxnop Hall*

Oxnop Hall, *Low Oxnop, Gunnerside,*
Richmond, N. Yorks, DL11 6JJ.
Oxnop Hall is in an environmentally
sensitive area. Stone walls and barns.
Open: All Year (not Xmas)
01748 886253 Mrs Porter
D: £24.00–£31.00 **S:** £24.00–£34.00
Beds: 1F 3D 1T 1S **Baths:** 6 Pr
🛏 (7) 🅿 (6) 🗲 📺 🛒 🕹

Hanlith

SD9061 ◀ *Buck*

Coachmans Cottage, *Hanlith,*
Malham, Skipton, N. Yorks, BD23 4BP.
17th Century cottage with beautiful view.
Every comfort. **Open:** Easter to Dec
01729 830538 Mrs Jenkins
coachmans@jenkins47.totalserve.co.uk
D: £23.00
Beds: 2D **Baths:** 2 En
🛏 (10) 🅿 (3) 📺 🛒 🕹

Harmby

SE1289

Sunnyridge, *Argill Farm, Harmby,*
Leyburn, DL8 5HQ.
A warm welcome awaits you at
Sunnyridge, a spacious bungalow amidst
beautiful countryside. **Open:** Easter to Jan
01969 622478 Mrs Richardson
D: £17.00–£23.00 **S:** £17.00–£23.00
Beds: 1F 1D **Baths:** 1 En 1 Sh
🛏 🅿 (2) 📺 🛏 🗶 🛒 🕹

Harrogate

SE3055 ◀ *Black Swan, Clard Beagle, Dragon,*
Edwards, Empress, Greyhound, Hales Bar, Hogs
Head, Knox Arms, Nelson, Old Bell, Queen's Head,
Pine Marten, Rat & Parrot, Smiths' Arms

Ashley House Hotel, *36-40 Franklin*
Road, Harrogate, N. Yorks, HG1 5EE.
Open: All Year
Grades: ETC 4 Diamond, AA 4 Diamond,
RAC 4 Diamond **01423 507474** Mr & Mrs
Thomas **Fax:** 01423 560858
ashleyhousehotel@btinternet.com
D: £29.75–£42.50 **S:** £39.50–£75.00
Beds: 2F 5D 6T 5S **Baths:** 18 En
🛏 🅿 (4) 📺 🛏 🛒 🕹 cc
High standard of accommodation at
reasonable prices. Friendly hotel aiming to
give you a memorable stay and value for
money. Delightful bar with extensive
collection of whiskies. Excellent
restaurants within walking distance. Tour
the Yorkshire Dales and Moors from our
convenient location in this lovely spa town.

Parnas Hotel, *98 Franklin Road,*
Harrogate, N. Yorks, HG1 5EN.
Open: All Year
Grades: ETC 4 Diamond
01423 564493 (also fax)
Mr & Mrs McKay
robert@parho.freeserve.co.uk
D: £24.00–£25.00 **S:** fr £28.00
Beds: 3F 2D 2T 2S **Baths:** 9 En
🛏 🅿 (8) 📺 🛏 🗶 🛒 🕹 🕹 cc
Warm welcome to family run licensed
hotel in pleasant garden. Easy walk to
town centre, Conference Centre, Valley
Gardens. Great touring base. York 0.5
hour. Close to Emmerdale, Heartbeat
country and dales. Stop over on your way
to Scotland.

Hollins House, *17 Hollins Road,*
Harrogate, N. Yorks, HG1 2JF.
Open: All Year
Grades: ETC 3 Diamond
01423 503646 (also fax)
Mr Hamblin
D: £21.00–£24.00 **S:** £28.00–£30.00
Beds: 3T 2D 1S **Baths:** 3 En 3 Sh
🛏 (5) 🗲 📺 🛒 🕹 cc
Clean, quiet spacious accommodation in
a warm and friendly family run Victorian
House. Excellent breakfasts with a wide
choice for any style of diet, cooked by
your host, Peter, who has been a chef for
many years. Free on-street parking.

The Coppice, *9 Studley Road,*
Harrogate, N. Yorks, HG1 5JU.
Open: All Year
Grades: ETC 3 Diamond
01423 569626
Mr Richardson
Fax: 01423 569005
D: £22.00–£24.00 **S:** £26.00–£38.00
Beds: 1F 1T 2D 1S **Baths:** 5 En
🛏 (5) 🗲 📺 🗶 🛒 🕹 cc
A high standard of comfortable
accommodation awaits you at the
Coppice, excellent food and a warm
friendly welcome. All rooms en suite.
Quietly situated. Ideal location to explore
the Dales, halfway between London and
Edinburgh. Ring now.

Spring Lodge, *22 Spring Mount,*
Harrogate, N. Yorks, HG1 2HX.
Centrally situated Edwardian town house
in a quiet cul-de-sac. Non-smoking.
Open: All Year (not Xmas)
Grades: ETC 3 Diamond
01423 506036 (also fax)
Mr Vinter
D: £18.00–£22.00 **S:** £19.00–£36.00
Beds: 1F 4D 1S **Baths:** 2 En 1 Sh
🛏 🅿 (1) 🗲 📺 🛒 🕹

The Alexander, *88 Franklin Road,*
Harrogate, N. Yorks, HG1 5EN.
Elegant friendly fully restored Victorian
residence close to the town centre.
Open: All Year
Grades: ETC 4 Diamond
01423 503348 Mrs Toole
Fax: 01423 540230
D: £24.00–£25.00 **S:** £24.00–£25.00
Beds: 3F 2D 2S **Baths:** 5 En 1 Sh
🛏 🗲 📺 🛒 🕹

Eton House, *3 Eton Terrace,*
Knareborough Road, Harrogate, N. Yorks,
HG2 7SU.
Our home was built in 1876 and stands
on the edge of the Stray.
Open: All Year (not Xmas)
Grades: ETC 3 Diamond
01423 886850 (also fax)
Mrs Wyatt
janbounds@aol.com
D: £20.00–£25.00 **S:** £20.00–£30.00
Beds: 2F 2D 2T 1S **Baths:** 4 En 2 Sh
🛏 🅿 (10) 📺 🛏 🛒 🕹

Alamah, *88 Kings Road, Harrogate, N.*
Yorks, HG1 5JX.
Delightful Victorian guest house, 100
yards Exhibition Centre, 5 mins' walk
town centre.
Open: All Year
Grades: ETC 3 Diamond
01423 502187 Mr Wilkinson
Fax: 01423 566115
D: £25.00 **S:** £27.00–£30.00
Beds: 1F 2T 2D 2S **Baths:** 6 En 1 Pr
🛏 🅿 (10) 📺 🛒 🕹

Staveleigh, *20 Ripon Road, Harrogate,*
HG1 2JJ.
Victorian house of architectural interest,
stained glass windows and hand carved
oak fireplace.
Open: All Year
Grades: ETC 4 Diamond, Silver Award
01423 524175 Ms Sutton
Fax: 01423 524178
enquiries@staveleigh.co.uk
D: £23.00–£26.00 **S:** £30.00–£48.00
Beds: 1F 1D 1T **Baths:** 2 En 1 Pr
🛏 🅿 (3) 🗲 📺 🛏 🗶 🛒 🕹 cc

2 Stray Lodge, *Trinity Road, Harrogate,*
N. Yorks, HG2 9AU.
For luxury accommodation, good
breakfasts, good views phone Harrogate
01423 501592.
Open: All Year (not Xmas)
01423 501592 Mrs Scales
D: fr £20.00 **S:** fr £30.00
Beds: 1F 1T **Baths:** 1 En 1 Pr
📺 🛒 🕹

Sherwood, *7 Studley Road, Harrogate,*
N. Yorks, HG1 5JU.
Centrally located near Harrogate town
centre, in a quiet tree-lined street.
Open: All Year
Grades: ETC 3 Diamond
01423 503033 C Grant
Fax: 01423 564659
sherwood@hotels.harrogate.com
D: £20.00–£25.00 **S:** £30.00–£50.00
Beds: 1T 4D 1S **Baths:** 4 En 1 Sh
📺 🗶 🛒 🕹 cc

Oakbrae Guest House, *3 Springfield*
Avenue, Harrogate, N. Yorks, HG1 2HR.
Centrally situated for all amenities, a
warm friendly welcome awaits you.
Open: Easter to
Grades: ETC 4 Diamond
01423 567682 (also fax)
D: £25.00 **S:** £30.00
Beds: 2T 3D 3S **Baths:** 7 En 1 Pr
🛏 (12) 🅿 (6) 📺 🛏 🛒 🕹

Planning a longer stay? Always ask for any special rates

April House, 3 Studley Road, Harrogate, N. Yorks, HG1 5JU.
Select accommodation, quiet location, ensuite, easy parking, non-smoking.
Open: All Year
Grades: AA 3 Diamond
01423 561879 Mrs Hayes
Fax: 01423 548149
david@april94.freeserve.co.uk
D: £25.00–£30.00 **S:** £25.00–£30.00
Beds: 3F 1D 1S **Baths:** 2 Pr
🛏 (2) 🖳 📺 🕇 🛏 🖳 👤

Acacia Lodge, 21 Ripon Road, Harrogate, N. Yorks, HG1 2JL.
Everything you would expect from somewhere 'Highly Commended'. Entirely non-smoking.
Open: All Year
Grades: AA 4 Diamond
01423 560752 Mr & Mrs Bateson
D: £27.00–£34.00 **S:** £40.00–£58.00
Beds: 2F 2T 2D **Baths:** 6 En
🛏 (10) 🖳 (7) 🖳 📺 🛏 🖳 👤 ❋ 👤

Barkers, 204 Kings Road, Harrogate, N. Yorks, HG1 5JG.
Homely accommodation in one of England's best kept small towns.
Open: All Year (not Xmas/New Year)
Grades: ETC 3 Diamond
01423 568494 Mr Barker
eebarberuk@yahoo.co.uk
D: £20.00–£25.00 **S:** £28.00–£30.00
Beds: 1F 1D 1S **Baths:** 1 En 1 Sh
🛏 🖳 (2) 🖳 📺 🖳 👤

Amadeus Hotel, 115 Franklin Road, Harrogate, North Yorkshire, HG1 5EN.
Comfortable, family-run, vegetarian, friendly Victorian guest house; central location.
Open: All Year (not Xmas)
01423 505151 (also fax)
Mrs Frankland
frankland@
theamadeushotel.totalserve.co.uk
D: £23.00–£30.00 **S:** £21.00–£26.00
Beds: 1F 2T 2S **Baths:** 5 En
🛏 🖳 🖳 📺 ✕ 🖳 🖳 👤

Park Gate Hotel, 61-63 Valley Drive, Harrogate, N. Yorks, HG2 0JW.
Overlooking famous Valley Gardens and only five minutes away from town centre.
Open: All Year (not Xmas)
01423 567010 Fax: 01423 504045
D: £25.00–£27.50 **S:** £23.00–£25.00
Beds: 6D 6T 4S **Baths:** 12 En 2 Sh
🛏 (2) 📺 🖳 🖳 👤 cc

Rheda House Hotel, 26 Kings Road, Harrogate, HG1 5JW.
Small family-run, licensed guest house. Ensuite and standard rooms available.
Open: All Year (not Xmas)
01423 568114 (also fax)
D: £18.00–£22.50 **S:** £18.00–£25.00
Beds: 1F 1D 1T 2S **Baths:** 2 En
🛏 📺 🛏 🖳 🖳 👤

Hawes

SD8789 🍺 White Hart, Herriot's Hotel, Board Hotel, Fountain, Stone House, Wensleydale Pantry

The Bungalow, Springbank, Hawes, N. Yorks, DL8 3NW.
Large bungalow, excellent views, quiet, off road parking.
Open: Easter to Oct
Grades: ETC 2 Diamond
01969 667209 Mrs Garnett
D: £18.00–£20.00
Beds: 2D 1T **Baths:** 2 En 1 Sh
🛏 (4) 🖳 📺 🛏 🖳 🖳 👤

Ebor House, Burtersett Road, Hawes, N. Yorks, DL8 3NT.
Family-run friendly and central. Off road parking and cycle store.
Open: All Year (not Xmas)
Grades: ETC 3 Diamond
01969 667337 (also fax)
Mrs Clark
gwen@eborhouse.freeserve.co.uk
D: £17.00–£20.00 **S:** £19.00–£25.00
Beds: 2D 1T **Baths:** 2 En 1 Sh
🛏 🖳 (5) 🖳 📺 🛏 🖳 🖳 👤

The Green Dragon Inn, Hardraw, Hawes, N. Yorks, DL8 3.
A 100' waterfall in spectacular back garden.
Open: All Year (not Xmas)
01969 667392 Mr Stead
D: £23.50–£27.50 **S:** £24.50–£28.50
Beds: 2F 8D 2T 4S **Baths:** 16 Pr
🛏 🖳 (30) 📺 🛏 ✕ 🖳 👤 cc

Overdales View, Simonstone, Hawes, N Yorks, DL8 3LY.
Friendly welcome. Lovely views, peaceful surroundings, comfortable beds good food.
Open: Easter to Oct
01969 667186 Mrs Sunter
D: £16.00–£18.00 **S:** £18.00–£20.00
Beds: 1F/T 1D 1S **Baths:** 1 Sh
🛏 🖳 (5) 🖳 📺 🖳 🖳 👤

Steppe Haugh Guest House, Townhead, Hawes, N. Yorks, DL8 3RH.
C17th house offering a wealth of character and atmosphere.
Open: All Year (not Xmas)
01969 667645 Mrs Grattan
D: £18.00–£26.00 **S:** £20.00–£23.00
Beds: 3D 1T 1S **Baths:** 5 En
🛏 (7) 🖳 (6) 🖳 📺 🛏 🖳 🖳 👤

Tarney Fors, Hawes, N. Yorks, DL8 3LS.
Grade II Listed ex-farmhouse, now a comfortable guest house, in beautiful setting.
Open: Easter to Nov
01969 667475 Mrs Harpley
D: £25.00–£28.00 **S:** £40.00–£45.00
Beds: 3D **Baths:** 2 En 1 Pr
🛏 (7) 🖳 (8) 🖳 📺 🖳 👤 cc

B&B owners may vary rates - be sure to check when booking

Hawnby

SE5489 🍺 Hawnby Hotel, Hare Inn

Laskill Farm, Hawnby, Helmsley, York, YO62 5NB.
Laskill Farm is built on a medieval site once belonging to Rievaulx Abbey.
Open: All Year
Grades: ETC 4 Diamond, AA 4 Diamond
01439 798268 Mrs Smith
Fax: 01439 798498
suesmith@laskillfarm.fsnet.co.uk
D: fr £27.50 **S:** fr £27.50
Beds: 3D 2T 1S **Baths:** 5 En 1 Pr
🛏 🖳 (20) 📺 🛏 ✕ 🖳 🖳 👤 👤 cc

Hebden

SE0263 🍺 Clarendon

Court Croft, Church Lane, Hebden, Skipton, BD23 5DX.
Open: All Year
Grades: ETC 2 Diamond
01756 753406 Mrs Kitching
D: fr £17.50 **S:** £17.50–£20.00
Beds: 2T **Baths:** 1 Sh
🛏 🖳 🛏 🛏 🖳 🖳 👤
Family farmhouse in quiet village close to the Dales Way.

Helmsley

SE6184 🍺 White Rose, Feathers, Black Swan, Crown, Tudor Rose, Hawnby Hotel, Royal Oak, Hare

Laskill Farm, Hawnby, Helmsley, York, YO62 5NB.
Open: All Year
Grades: ETC 4 Diamond, AA 4 Diamond
01439 798268 Mrs Smith
Fax: 01439 798498
suesmith@laskillfarm.fsnet.co.uk
D: fr £27.50 **S:** fr £27.50
Beds: 3D 2T 1S **Baths:** 5 En 1 Pr
🛏 🖳 (20) 📺 🛏 ✕ 🖳 🖳 👤 👤 cc
Laskill Farm is built on a medieval site once belonging to Rievaulx Abbey. Scenic beauty all around in one of England's finest National Parks. Lots to do and see, or simply enjoy peace and tranquillity in our lovely 1 acre walled garden. A walkers' paradise.

4 Ashdale Road, Helmsley, York, YO62 5DD.
Quiet private house 5 minutes from Market Square and shops.
Open: All Year (not Xmas)
01439 770375 Mrs Barton
D: £15.00–£16.00 **S:** fr £16.00
Beds: 1D 1S **Baths:** 1 Sh
🖳 (2) 🖳 📺 🛏 🖳 👤

14 Elmslac Road, Helmsley, York, YO62 5AP.
Quiet house 4 mins' walk from market square. Pleasant situation.
Open: All Year
01439 770287 Mrs Holding
D: £13.50–£14.50 **S:** fr £14.00
Beds: 1D **Baths:** 1 Pr
🛏 (12) 🖳 📺

Stilworth House, *1 Church Street,*
Helmsley, York, YO62 5AD.
Elegant rooms, beautiful location
overlooking castle, hearty breakfast,
warm welcome.
Open: All Year (not Xmas)
Grades: ETC 4 Diamond
01439 771072 Mrs Swift
D: £17.50–£27.50 **S:** £30.00–£40.00
Beds: 1F 2D 1T **Baths:** 3 Pr 1 Sh
🛇 🄿 (4) ⅌ 📺 📖 🖤 🛊

Buckingham House, *33 Bridge Street,*
Helmsley, York, YO62 5DX.
Comfortable Georgian town house. Warm
welcome and good food.
Open: All Year (not Xmas)
01439 770613 Mrs Wood
mw@goodwood@enta.net
D: £18.00–£23.00 **S:** £18.00–£27.00
Beds: 1D 1T 1S **Baths:** 1 En 1 Sh
🛇 🄿 (1) 📺 ⅜ 📖 🖤 🛊

High Bentham

SD6669   🍺 *Punch Bowl*

Fowgill Park Farm, *High Bentham,*
Lancaster, LA2 7AH.
Beamed farmhouse enjoying panoramic
views, close to caves and waterfalls.
Open: Easter to Oct
Grades: ETC 4 Diamond
015242 61630 Mrs Metcalfe
D: £19.00–£22.00
Beds: 1D 1T **Baths:** 2 En
🛇 🄿 (4) ⅌ 📺 ⅜ ✕ 📖 🛊

High Hawsker

NZ9207   🍺 *Hare & Hounds*

Old Blacksmiths Arms, *High*
Hawsker, Whitby, N. Yorks, YO22 4LH.
Originally first pub in village. Large
garden with pond.
Open: Easter to Oct
01947 880800 Mrs Stubbs
D: £18.00–£19.00 **S:** £21.00–£24.00
Beds: 1T 2D **Baths:** 2 Sh
🛇 (12) 🄿 (3) 📺 ⅜ 📖 🖤 🛊 ♿

Holme-on-Swale

SE3582   🍺 *Kings Arms*

Glen Free, *Holme-on-Swale, Thirsk, N*
Yorks, YO7 4JE.
Secluded cottage, one mile from A1. Ideal
for Herriot country and Dales.
Open: All Year (not Xmas)
01845 567331 Mrs Bailes
D: £16.00–£18.00 **S:** £16.00–£18.00
Beds: 1F 1D **Baths:** 1 Sh
🛇 🄿 (4) ⅌ 📺 ⅜ 📖 🛊 ♿

Horton-in-Ribblesdale

SD8072   🍺 *Crown, Golden Lion*

The Willows, *Horton-in-Ribblesdale,*
Settle, N. Yorks, BD24 0HT.
Large detached house, luxurious
bedrooms in lovely Yorkshire Dales.
Open: Easter to Sep
01729 860373 (also fax)
Mrs Barker
D: £20.00–£24.00 **S:** £20.00–£25.00
Beds: 1F 1D 1T **Baths:** 1 En 1 Pr 1 Sh
🛇 🄿 (5) 📺 ⅜ ✕ 📖 🖤 🛊

The Rowe House, *Horton-in-*
Ribblesdale, Settle, N. Yorks, BD24 0HT.
Distinctive Georgian country house in
half-acre grounds TV lounge.
Open: Mar to Oct
01729 860212 Mr & Mrs Lane
D: £18.00–£22.00 **S:** £22.00–£26.00
Beds: 2D 3T **Baths:** 3 En 2 Sh
🛇 (12) 🄿 (6) 📺 📖 🖤 🛊

Hubberholme

SD9278   🍺 *George Inn*

Church Farm, *Hubberholme, Skipton,*
N. Yorks, BD23 5JE.
Traditional C16th dales farmhouse on
working hill farm. Ideal for walking/
touring.
Open: All Year
Grades: ETC 4 Diamond
01756 760240 Mrs Huck
D: £20.00 **S:** £20.00
Beds: 2D 2T **Baths:** 1 En 1 Pr
🛇 🄿 ⅌ 📺 📖 🖤 🛊

Huby (Easingwold)

SE5665   🍺 *New Inn*

New Inn Motel, *Main Street, Huby,*
York, YO61 1HQ.
Open: All Year
Grades: AA 3 Diamond
01347 810219 Mrs Birkinshaw
D: £24.00–£25.00 **S:** £28.00–£35.00
Beds: 3F 2D 2T 1S **Baths:** 8 En
🛇 🄿 (8) 📺 ⅜ ✕ 📖 🖤 🛊
The village of Huby, 'twixt York and
Easingwold, is situated 9 miles north of
York between the A19 & B1363. Ideal base
for coast, Moors, Dales, Herriot &
Heartbeat country, off-road parking; all
rooms overlook garden, all individually
accessed.

Hutton Rudby

NZ4606   🍺 *Bay Horse*

Greenview, *13 Eastside, Hutton Rudby,*
Yarm, N Yorks, TS15 0DB.
Open: All Year
01642 701739 Mrs Ashton
D: £18.00 **S:** fr £18.00
Beds: 1D 1T **Baths:** 2 En
🛇 (3) ⅌ 📺 📖 🛊
Overlooking the village green at Hutton
Rudby, Greenview offers you a delightful
stay bordering the National Park in North
Yorkshire. Rooms have showers,
comfortable beds, with a hearty
breakfast. Ideal for Coast to Coast,
Cleveland Way and new cycle route.

Iburndale

NZ8707   🍺 *Plough*

8 Mill Lane, *Iburndale, Sleights, Whitby,*
N. Yorks, YO22 5DU.
Ideal for North York Moors, coast, North
Yorkshire steam trains.
Open: All Year (not Xmas)
01947 810009 (also fax)
Mrs Hebdon
D: £18.00–£23.00 **S:** £20.00–£23.00
Beds: 2D **Baths:** 1 En 1 Sh
🛇 🄿 (4) 📺 📖 🛊

Ingleby Cross

NZ4500   🍺 *Black Horse, Blue Bell*

North York Moors Adventure Ctr,
Park House, Ingleby Cross, Northallerton,
N. Yorks, DL6 3PE.
Park House, traditional sandstone
farmhouse set in The National Park.
Open: Easter to Oct
01609 882571 (also fax)
Mr Bennett
D: fr £15.00 **S:** fr £15.00
Beds: 3F 1D 3T **Baths:** 2 Sh
🛇 (1) 🄿 (20) 📺 ⅜ ✕ 📖 🖤 🛊

Blue Bell Inn, *Ingleby Cross,*
Northallerton, N. Yorks, DL6 3NF.
Family run, real ales, coal fire, quiet
annexed accommodation.
Open: All Year
01609 882272 Mrs Kinsella
D: £20.00 **S:** £20.00
Beds: 4F 1D 4T **Baths:** 5 En
🛇 (20) 📺 ✕ 📖 🛊

Ingleton

SD6973   🍺 *Bridge Hotel, Craven Heifer, Marton*
Arms, Wheatsheaf

The Dales Guest House, *Main*
Street, Ingleton, Carnforth, North
Yorkshire, LA6 3HH.
Open: All Year
015242 41401 P D Weaire
dalesgh@hotmail.com
D: £19.00–£22.00 **S:** £19.00–£22.00
Beds: 1T 3D 1S **Baths:** 5 En
🛇 ⅌ 📺 ⅜ ✕ 📖 🖤 cc
A friendly welcome, cosy rooms with
views and substantial home cooked
meals await you, an ideal base for
exploring the Dales, Forest of Bowland
and Lakes. Special price breaks are
available and various activities can be
arranged for small groups.

Springfield Country House Hotel,
Ingleton, Carnforth, Lancs, LA6 3HJ.
Open: All Year (not Xmas)
Grades: ETC 3 Diamond, RAC 3 Diamond
015242 41280 (also fax)
Mr Thornton
D: £23.00–£25.00 **S:** £23.00–£25.00
Beds: 1F 3D 1T **Baths:** 5 En 1 Pr
🛇 🄿 (12) ⅌ 📺 ⅜ ✕ 📖 🖤 🛊 cc
Detached Victorian villa; large garden at
rear running down to River Greta. Patio,
small pond & waterfall. Home grown
vegetables in season. Front garden with
patio and conservatory.

Bridge End Guest House, *Mill Lane,*
Ingleton, Carnforth, Lancs, LA6 3EP.
Georgian Listed building, riverside
location adjacent to Waterfalls Walk
entrance.
Open: All Year
Grades: ETC 3 Diamond
015242 41413 Mrs Garner
garner01@tinyworld.co.uk
D: £19.00–£22.00 **S:** fr £25.00
Beds: 3D **Baths:** 3 En
🛇 (8) 🄿 (8) 📺 ✕ 📖 🖤 🛊 cc

Thorngarth House, *Ingleton, Carnforth, North Yorkshire, LA6 3HN.*
Country house surrounded by green fields. Wonderful food, open fires.
Open: All Year
015242 41295 (also fax)
Mr Bradley
nick@thorngarth-hotel-ingleton.co.uk
D: £22.00–£35.00 **S:** £22.00–£35.00
Beds: 4D 1T **Baths:** 4 En 1 Pr
🅿 (5) ⅄ ⊡ ✕ 🆙 ⅋ ≛ cc

Riverside Lodge, *24 Main Street, Ingleton, Carnforth, LA6 3HJ.*
Splendid Victorian house, terraced gardens leading to river. Superb views.
Open: All Year (not Xmas)
Grades: ETC 3 Diamond, AA 3 Diamond
015242 41359 Mr & Mrs Foley
andrewa@foleya.fsnet.co.uk
D: £21.00–£24.00 **S:** £30.00
Beds: 7D 1T **Baths:** 8 En
🅲 🅿 (8) ⅄ ⊡ ✕ 🆙 ⅌ ≛ cc

Ingleborough View Guest House,
Main Street, Ingleton, Carnforth, Lancashire, LA6 3HH.
Lovely Victorian house with picturesque riverside location. excellent accommodation and food.
Open: All Year (not Xmas)
015242 41523 Mrs Brown
D: £19.00–£20.00 **S:** £25.00–£28.00
Beds: 1F 2D 1T **Baths:** 2 En 2 Pr
🅲 🅿 (6) ⊡ ⅋ 🆙 ⅌ ≛

Keasden

SD7266

Lythe Birks, *Keasden, Lancaster, LA2 8EZ.*
Converted barn in its own grounds overlooking three peaks.
Open: All Year
Grades: ETC 3 Diamond
015242 51688 Mrs Phinn
D: £19.50 **S:** £25.00
Beds: 2D 1T
🅲 🅿 ⅄ ⊡ ⅋ ✕ 🆙 ≛

Keld

NY8901 🍺 *Farmers' Arms*

Greenlands, *Keld, Richmond, DL11 6DY.*
Refurbished farmhouse amidst the peace and beauty of Upper Swaledale.
Open: All Year
01748 886576 Mrs Thompson
D: £19.50
Beds: 2D **Baths:** 2 En
🅿 (2) ⅄ ⊡ 🆙 ≛

Kettlewell

SD9772 🍺 *Queen's Head, Race Horses, King's Head, The Bluebell*

Lynburn, *Kettlewell, Skipton, N. Yorks, BD23 5RF.*
Well preserved property with well tended grounds. Peaceful surroundings.
Open: Mar to Oct
Grades: ETC 3 Diamond
01756 760803 Mrs Thornborrow
D: £19.00–£20.00 **S:** £25.00
Beds: 1D 1T **Baths:** 1 Sh
🅲 (12) 🅿 (2) ⊡ 🆙 ⅌ ≛

Langcliffe Country House,
Kettlewell, Skipton, N. Yorks, BD23 5RJ.
Open: All Year (not Xmas)
Grades: AA 4 Diamond, RAC 4 Diamond
01756 760243 Mr Elliott
D: £45.00–£50.00 **S:** £65.00–£70.00
Beds: 1F 2T 2D **Baths:** 5 Pr 1 En
🅲 🅿 ⅄ ⊡ ⅋ ✕ 🆙 ⅌ ≛ cc
Kettlewell in Upper Wharfedale. Traditional stone house with beautiful gardens. Ensuite bedrooms. Elegant lounge with log fire. Conservatory restaurant serving superb food in a panoramic setting.

Kilnsey

SD9767 🍺 *Tennant Arms*

Skirfare Bridge Dales Barn, *C/o Northcote, Kilnsey, Skipton, N. Yorks, BD23 5PT.*
Open: All Year
01756 752465 (also fax)
Mrs Foster
D: £8.00 **S:** £8.00
Beds: 5F 1T **Baths:** 3 Sh
🅲 🅿 (8) ✕ 🆙
Converted stone barn in beautiful limestone countryside of upper Wharfedale, ideally situated for outdoor activities. Centrally heated. 25 bunk beds, drying room, kitchen, common room, all inclusive. Catering by arrangement. Individuals or school groups. Off-road parking. No pets.

Kirkby Malham

SD8961 🍺 *Victoria*

Yeoman's Barn, *Kirkby Malham, Skipton, North Yorks, BD23 4BL.*
Open: All Year (not Xmas/New Year)
01729 830639
Mrs Turner
D: £20.00–£25.00 **S:** £25.00
Beds: 2D **Baths:** 2 En
🅲 (5) ⊡ 🆙 ⅌ ≛
Converted C17th barn, large oak beams, newly decorated bedrooms. Warm welcome, tea tray on arrival, open fire. Market towns of Skipton, Settle and Hawes all nearby. Malham Cove, Janets Foss and Gordale Scar - all suitable for the weekend walker.

Kirkbymoorside

SE6987 🍺 *George & Dragon, Kings Head*

Red Lion House, *Crown Square, Kirkbymoorside, York, YO62 6AY.*
Open: All Year (not Xmas)
Grades: ETC 4 Diamond
01751 431815
S & A Thompson
angela.thomson@red-lion-house.freeserve.co.uk
D: £20.00–£22.50 **S:** fr £25.00
Beds: 2D 1T **Baths:** 1 En 1 Sh
🅲 ⅄ ⊡ 🆙 ⅌ ≛
A lovely Georgian house, situated in a quiet square in the centre of this small market town. Perfect for exploring the North York Moors and coast. Spacious rooms, crisp cotton bedding and excellent breakfasts. Good local pubs for evening meals.

Sinnington Common Farm,
Kirkbymoorside, York, YO62 6NX.
Spacious ground floor accom, own outside entrance, fridges, panoramic views. **Open:** All Year (not Xmas)
01751 431719 (also fax) Mrs Wiles
felicity@scfarm.demon.co.uk
D: £18.00–£20.00 **S:** £23.00–£25.00
Beds: 1F 1D 1T **Baths:** 3 En
🅲 🅿 (6) ⊡ ⅋ ✕ 🆙 ⅌ ≛ ⅊

Kirklington

SE3181 🍺 *Midland Arms, Black Horse*

Upsland Farm, *Lime Lane, Well, Bedale, N. Yorks, DL8 2PA.*
Beautiful house in Herriot and Heartbeat Country.
Open: All Year (not Xmas)
Grades: ETC 4 Diamond, AA 5 Diamond
01845 567709 (also fax) Mrs Hodgson
upsland@Btinternet.com
D: £25.00 **S:** £35.00
Beds: 1T 2D **Baths:** 3 En
🅲 🅿 (4) ⅄ ⊡ ⅋ ✕ 🆙 ⅌ ≛

Knaresborough

SE3557 🍺 *Yorkshire Lass, Mother Shipton's Inn, World's End, Bay Horse*

The Hermitage, *10 Waterside, Knaresborough, N Yorks, HG5 9AZ.*
Peaceful, riverside guest house. Picturesque location, near train, bus, A1.
Open: All Year (not Xmas/New Year)
Grades: ETC 3 Diamond
01423 863349 Mr Smulders
D: £22.00 **S:** £23.00–£28.00
Beds: 2D 1S **Baths:** 1 Pr 1 Sh
⊡ ⅋ 🆙 ⅌ ≛

Newton House Hotel, *5/7 York Place, Knaresborough, N Yorks, HG5 0AD.*
Situated in picturesque Knaresborough, a C17th former coaching inn.
Open: All Year (not Xmas)
Grades: ETC 4 Diamond, AA 4 Diamond, RAC 4 Diamond
01423 863539 Mr & Mrs Elliott
Fax: 01423 869748
newtonhouse@btinternet.com
D: £27.50–£32.50 **S:** £35.00–£45.00
Beds: 2F 7D 2T 1S **Baths:** 11 En 1 Pr
🅲 🅿 (12) ⊡ ⅋ ✕ 🆙 ⅌ ⅊ ≛ cc

Kirkgate House, *17 Kirkgate, Knaresborough, N Yorks, HG5 8AD.*
Friendly,non smoking accommodation near the market place, bus and train station. **Open:** All Year
Grades: ETC 4 Diamond
01423 862704 (also fax) S F Giesen
D: £22.00 **S:** £26.00–£32.00
Beds: 2D 1T **Baths:** 3 En
🅿 (2) ⅄ ⊡ ✕ 🆙 ⅌ ≛

Goldsborough House Barn Flat,
Goldsborough, Knaresborough, N Yorks, HG5 8PS.
Situated on edge of the village within walking distance of the Bay Horse pub.
Open: All Year
01423 860300 Mrs Bailey
Fax: 01423 860301
D: £25.00 **S:** £30.00
Beds: 1T 1D **Baths:** 1 Sh
🅲 (10) 🅿 (4) ⊡ 🆙 ≛

Langcliffe

SD8264

Bowerley Hotel & Conference Centre, *Langcliffe, Settle, BD24 9LY.*
Country House Hotel in 3 acres, Bar, Restaurant warm welcome.
Open: All Year
Grades: ETC 2 Star
01729 823811 G Ralph
Fax: 01729 822317
bowerleyhotel@aol.com
D: £25.00–£29.00 **S:** £32.00–£39.00
Beds: 2F 8T 6D 2S **Baths:** 18 En
🛇 🅿 (50) ⍻ 🅣 🏋 ✕ 📖 🆅 🕭 ₺ cc

Lealholm

NZ7607   🍺 *Fox & Hound*

High Park Farm, *Lealholm, Whitby, YO21 2AQ.*
Peaceful location. 15 minutes from the coast many attractions close by.
Open: Easter to Oct
Grades: ETC 3 Diamond
01947 897416 Mrs Welford
D: £18.50 **S:** £23.50
Beds: 1D **Baths:** 1 En
🛇 (5) 🅿 (1) ⍻ 🅣 📖 🆅 ₺

Leeming Bar

SE2890

Little Holtby, *Leeming Bar, Northallerton, N. Yorks, DL7 9LH.*
Open: All Year (not Xmas)
Grades: ETC 4 Diamond
01609 748762 Mrs Hodgson
littleholtby@yahoo.co.uk
D: £22.50–£25.00 **S:** £25.00
Beds: 3D 1T **Baths:** 2 En 1 Pr 1 Sh
🛇 (10) 🅿 (10) ⍻ 🅣 ✕ 📖 🆅 ₺
Today's discerning traveller is looking for somewhere special, where the warmth of welcome will remain a treasured memory. All guest rooms have wonderful views - treat yourself to a really memorable stay.

Levisham

SE8390

Rectory Farmhouse, *Levisham, Pickering, N. Yorks, YO18 7NL.*
Open: All Year
Grades: ETC 4 Diamond
01751 460304 Mrs Holt
rectoryfarmhouse@barclays.net
D: £20.00–£25.00 **S:** £24.00
Beds: 2D 1T **Baths:** 3 En
🛇 🅿 (8) ⍻ 🅣 🏋 ✕ 📖 🆅 ₺
Picturesque village surrounded by beautiful scenery; excellent walking, horse riding or just relaxing. Central location for coast, city of York, quaint market towns, historic and stately homes. Comfortable and welcoming. Afternoon teas/home baking. Riding holiday with own horse.

All details shown are as supplied by B&B owners in Autumn 2000

National Grid References are for villages, towns and cities – not for individual houses

Littlethorpe

SE3269   🍺 *Masons' Arms*

Moor End Farm, *Knaresborough Road, Littlethorpe, Ripon, N. Yorks, HG4 3LU.*
Pleasantly situated. A friendly welcome and very comfortable accommodation.
Open: All Year (not Xmas)
Grades: ETC 3 Diamond
01765 677419 Mrs Spensley
pspensley@ukonline.co.uk
D: £18.50–£24.00 **S:** £28.00–£40.00
Beds: 2D 1T **Baths:** 2 En 1 Sh
🅿 (5) ⍻ 🅣 📖 ₺

Litton

SD9074   🍺 *Queen's Arms*

Park Bottom, *Litton, Skipton, BD23 5QJ.*
Peaceful setting, wonderful views, ideal for walking, Which? recommended.
Open: All Year (not Xmas)
01756 770235 Mr & Mrs Morgan
D: £25.00 **S:** £30.00
Beds: 1F 2D 1T **Baths:** 4 En
🛇 🅿 (5) 🏋 📖 🆅 ₺

Loftus

NZ7118

White Horse Inn, *73 High Street, Loftus, Saltburn-by-the- Sea, TS13 4HG.*
Friendly village pub near to Yorkshire moors and seaside.
Open: All Year (not Xmas)
01287 640758 C Rowe
D: £15.00–£18.00 **S:** £15.00–£18.00
Beds: 2F 1T **Baths:** 1 En 1 Sh
🛇 🅿 (5) 🅣 🏋 ✕ 📖 🆅 ₺

Long Preston

SD8358   🍺 *Maypole Inn*

Inglenook, *22 Main Street, Long Preston, Skipton, BD23 4PH.*
Traditional Mullion-windowed cottage, village setting, ideal for Dales exploration.
Open: All Year
01729 840511 Mrs Parton
D: £18.00–£20.00 **S:** £25.00–£30.00
Beds: 1F **Baths:** 1 Pr
🅿 (4) 🅣 🏋 📖 🆅 ₺

Lothersdale

SD9645   🍺 *Hare & Hounds*

Lynmouth, *Dale End, Lothersdale, Skipton, N Yorks, BD20 8EH.*
On path, pretty bungalow set in lovely grounds.
Open: All Year (not Xmas)
01535 632744 (also fax)
Mrs Foster
g.foster488@aol.com
D: £17.50 **S:** £17.50
Beds: 1F 1D 1T **Baths:** 3 En
🛇 🅿 (4) ⍻ 🅣 📖 🆅 ₺ 🕭

Malham

SD9062   🍺 *Listers, Buck Inn*

Eastwood Guest House, *Malham, Skipton, North Yorkshire, BD23 4DA.*
High quality bed and breakfast in central village location.
Open: All Year
01729 830409 R D Scott
D: £20.00–£25.00 **S:** £18.00–£30.00
Beds: 1F 1T 1D **Baths:** 3 En
🛇 ⍻ 🅣 📖 ₺

Malton

SE7871   🍺 *George, Old Lodge*

The Brow, *York Road, Malton, N. Yorks, YO17 0AX.*
Georgian House, garden, fantastic riverside views, private parking.
Open: All Year (not Xmas)
Grades: ETC 3 Diamond
01653 693402 Mrs Hopkinson
D: £18.00–£30.00 **S:** £18.00–£25.00
Beds: 1F 2D 1T 1S **Baths:** 3 En 1 Sh
🛇 🅿 (6) 🅣 🏋 📖 ₺

Suddabys Crown Hotel, *Wheelgate, Malton, N. Yorks, YO17 0HP.*
Former Georgian coaching inn in market town centre, close to all Ryedale attractions.
Open: All Year (not Xmas)
01653 692038 Mr & Mrs Suddaby
Fax: 01653 691812
D: £17.00–£30.00 **S:** £18.00–£40.00
Beds: 2F 2D 4T **Baths:** 2 En 2 Sh
🛇 🅿 (10) 🅣 📖 🆅 ₺

Masham

SE2280

Bank Villa, *Masham, Ripon, North Yorks, HG4 4DB.*
Open: All Year (not Xmas)
Grades: AA 4 Diamond
01765 689605 (also fax)
Lucy & Bobby Thomson
D: £20.00–£25.00 **S:** £30.00–£40.00
Beds: 1F 3D 2T **Baths:** 3 En 1 Pr
🛇 (5) ⍻ 🅣 ✕ 📖 🆅 ₺
Welcoming Grade II Listed home in 0.5 acre terraced gardens, 2 minutes' walk from Masham's unique market place, refurbished to a high standard with individually decorated ensuite bedrooms, 2 delightful lounges, ideal base for exploring the Dales and Herriot country.

Haregill Lodge, *Ellingstring, Masham, Ripon, North Yorkshire, HG4 4PW.*
C18th farmhouse. Excellent views, superb cooking. Ideal base for Dales/Moors.
Open: All Year (not Xmas)
Grades: ETC 4 Diamond
01677 460272 (also fax)
Ms Greensit
haregilllodge@freenet.co.uk
D: £20.00–£21.00 **S:** £21.00–£22.00
Beds: 2T 1D **Baths:** 2 En 1 Pr
🛇 🅿 (4) 🅣 🏋 📖 🆅 ₺

Mickleby

NZ8012   🍴 *Ellerby Hotel*

Northfield Farm, Mickleby, Saltburn-by-the-Sea, N Yorks, TS13 5NE.
Quiet, friendly, comfortable farmhouse. Open views, ideal situation for walking.
Open: Easter to Oct
01947 840343
Mrs Prudom
D: £15.00–£20.00 **S:** £18.00
Beds: 1F 1D 1T **Baths:** 1 En 1 Sh
🛏 🅿 ⅙ 📺 🎵 🅥 ♨

Middleham

SE1287   🍴 *Richard III*

Yore View, Leyburn Road, Middleham, Leyburn, DL8 4PL.
Former 1921 picture house situated 200 yards from Middleham centre.
Open: All Year
Grades: ETC 4 Diamond
01969 622987 Mrs Roper
D: £20.00–£25.00 **S:** £25.00–£30.00
Beds: 1F 2D **Baths:** 2 En 1 Pr
🛏 🅿 (5) ⅙ 📺 🐾 ✕ 🅥 ✱ ♨ cc

Middlesbrough

NZ5118   🍴 *Highfield*

White House Hotel, 311 Marton Road, Middlesbrough, TS4 2HG.
Family run, close to centre, good English breakfast, car parking.
Open: All Year
01642 244531
D: £15.00–£17.50 **S:** £18.50–£22.00
Beds: 2F 2D 6T 5S **Baths:** 4 En 3 Sh
🛏 📺 🐾 🖶 ♨

Middlesmoor

SE0874   🍴 *Crown*

Dovenor House, Middlesmoor, Harrogate, HG3 5ST.
Beautiful stone house on edge of village with unsurpassed views.
Open: All Year
Grades: ETC 2 Diamond
01423 755697 (also fax)
Mrs Thurland
D: £18.00 **S:** £18.00–£20.00
Beds: 2F 1T **Baths:** 1 Sh
🛏 🅿 (3) ⅙ 📺 🐾 🖶 🅥 ✱ ♨

Middleton Tyas

NZ2206   🍴 *Shoulder of Mutton*

Greencroft, Middleton Tyas, Richmond, DL10 6PE.
Friendly family home ideal for Dales, York and east coast.
Open: All Year
Grades: ETC 3 Diamond
01325 377392
Mrs Alsop
Fax: 01833 621423
greencroft@madasafish.com
D: £18.00–£20.00 **S:** £25.00
Beds: 1F 1T **Baths:** 2 En
🛏 🅿 (4) ⅙ 📺 🖶 ♨

Nawton

SE6584

Plumpton Court, High Street, Nawton, York, YO62 7TT.
Family-run guest house. Excellent food, cosy, licensed bar/lounge.
Open: All Year
01439 771223 (also fax)
Mr Braithwaite
plumptoncourt@ukgateway.net
D: £20.00–£25.00 **S:** £25.00–£33.50
Beds: 3T 4D **Baths:** 7 En
🛏 (12) 🅿 (8) ⅙ 📺 ✕ 🖶 🅥 ♨

Newbiggin in Bishopdale

SD9985

East Lane House, Newbiggin in Bishopdale, Leyburn, DL8 3TF.
Herriot country. Refurbished farmhouse in unspoilt Bishopdale. Open countryside yet easy access.
Open: All Year (not Xmas)
01969 663234 Mrs Smith
mick@bishopdale977.freeserve.co.uk
D: £20.00–£22.50 **S:** £25.00–£27.00
Beds: 1D 1T **Baths:** 2 En
🅿 (6) ⅙ 📺 🐾 ✕ 🖶 ♨

Newby Wiske

SE3688   🍴 *Black Swan*

Well House, Newby Wiske, Northallerton, N. Yorks, DL7 9EX.
Beautiful landscaped gardens of one acre. Ideal for touring Yorkshire.
Open: All Year
Grades: ETC 4 Diamond
01609 772253 (also fax)
Mrs Smith
D: £18.00–£25.00 **S:** £20.00–£25.00
Beds: 2D **Baths:** 2 En
🛏 🅿 (6) ⅙ 📺 🐾 ✕ 🖶 ♨

Newton-on-Rawcliffe

SE8190   🍴 *Horseshoe, White Swan*

Rawcliffe House Farm, Newton-on-Rawcliffe, Pickering, N. Yorks, YO18 8JA.
Charming ensuite ground floor rooms with every convenience. A warm welcome and excellent accommodation.
Open: Easter to Oct
Grades: ETC 4 Diamond
01751 473292
Mrs Ducat
Fax: 01751 473766
sheilarh@yahoo.com
D: £25.50–£28.50 **S:** £30.50–£33.50
Beds: 2D 1T **Baths:** 3 En
🛏 (8) 🅿 (10) 📺 ✕ 🖶 🅥 ♨ 👵 cc

Swan Cottage, Newton-on-Rawcliffe, Pickering, N. Yorks, YO18 8QA.
Picturesque tranquil Village, Quiet pub next door, Wide breakfast choice.
Open: All Year
Grades: ETC 3 Diamond
01751 472502
Mrs Heaton
D: £15.50–£16.50 **S:** £15.50–£16.50
Beds: 1D 1T 1S **Baths:** 1 Sh
🛏 🅿 (2) 📺 🐾 ✕ 🖶 🅥 ✱ ♨

Planning a longer stay? Always ask for any special rates

North Grimston

SE8467

Middleton Arms, North Grimston, Malton, N. Yorks, YO17 8AX.
Friendly country pub with excellent reputation for quality food and homely accommodation.
Open: All Year (not Xmas)
01944 768255 Mrs Grayston
Fax: 01944 768389
D: £20.00 **S:** fr £27.50
Beds: 2D 1T **Baths:** 1 Pr 1 Sh
🛏 🅿 📺 ✕ 🖶 🅥 ♨

Northallerton

SE3794   🍴 *Bassetts, Black Swan, Golden Lion, Pepper Mill, New Inn*

Porch House, 68 High Street, Northallerton, N. Yorks, DL7 8EG.
Built 1584 original fireplaces and beams between Yorkshire Dales and Moors.
Open: All year (not Xmas)
Grades: ETC 4 Diamond, Silver, AA 4 Diamond
01609 779831 J A Barrow
Fax: 01609 778603
D: £24.50–£26.00 **S:** £33.00–£35.00
Beds: 4D 2T **Baths:** 6 En
🛏 (12) 🅿 (6) ⅙ 📺 🖶 🅥 ♨

Honeypots, 4 Pennine View, Northallerton, DL7 8HP.
Well-recommended guest house (visitors love it!), decorated to an extremely high standard.
Open: All Year (not Xmas/New Year)
Grades: ETC Listed
01609 777264 val@lougnu.demon.co.uk
D: £18.00–£20.00 **S:** £18.00–£20.00
Beds: 1T **Baths:** 1P
🛏 (12) 🅿 (1) ⅙ 📺 ✕ 🖶 🅥 ♨

Alverton Guest House, 26 South Parade, Northallerton, N. Yorks, DL7 8SG.
Modernised Victorian town house convenient for all the county town facilities.
Open: All Year (not Xmas)
01609 776207 (also fax)
Mr Longley
D: £18.00–£19.50 **S:** £17.50–£24.00
Beds: 1F 1D 1T 2S **Baths:** 3 En 1 Sh
🛏 🅿 (4) 📺 🖶 ♨

Oldstead

SE5280   🍴 *Abbey Inn*

Oldstead Grange, Oldstead, York, YO61 4BJ.
Beautiful quiet situation amidst our fields, woods and valleys. Traditional C17th features.
Open: All Year
01347 868634 Mrs Banks
anne@yorkshireuk.com
D: £24.00–£27.50 **S:** £28.00–£32.00
Beds: 1F 1D 1T **Baths:** 3 En
🛏 🅿 (3) ⅙ 📺 🖶 🅥 ♨ cc

Paradise

SE4687

High Paradise Farm, *Boltby, Thirsk, N Yorks, YO7 2HT.*
Set between the forest and the moors in Herriot Country.
Open: All Year
Grades: ETC 3 Diamond
01845 537235 Mr & Mrs Skilbeck
Fax: 01845 537033
info@highparadise.co.uk
D: £20.00 **S:** £23.00
Beds: 1F 1T 1D **Baths:** 3 En
🛇 🅿 (1004) 🛏 ✕ 📺 🖤 🖷 🖕 cc

Pateley Bridge

SE1565   🔹 *Crown*

Dale View, *Old Church Lane, Pateley Bridge, Harrogate, N. Yorks, HG3 5LY.*
Comfortable rooms. Beautiful views over Yorkshire Dales. Private parking.
Open: All Year
01423 711506 kenjsimpson@yahoo.com
D: £16.50–£25.00 **S:** £16.50–£25.00
Beds: 1F 2D **Baths:** 2 En 1 Sh
🛇 🅿 (5) 📺 🖷 🖕

Greengarth, *Greenwood Road, Pateley Bridge, Harrogate, N. Yorks, HG3 5LR.*
Central detached bungalow in lovely Dales town. Ground floor rooms.
Open: All year (not Xmas)
01423 711688
Mrs Ravilious
D: £16.00–£20.00 **S:** fr £16.00
Beds: 2D 1T 1S **Baths:** 2 En 1 Sh
🛇 (5) 🅿 (4) 🖤 📺 🛏 🖷 🖕 🖧

Pickering

SE7984   🔹 *Black Swan, White Swan, Forest & Vale, School House, Bay Horse, Horseshoe, Black Bull, Beansheaf*

Heathcote Guest House, *100 Eastgate, Pickering, N. Yorks, YO18 7DW.*
Open: Feb to Dec
Grades: ETC 4 Diamond
01751 476991 (also fax)
Mrs Lovejoy
joanlovejoy@lineone.net
D: £19.50–£23.00 **S:** fr £24.00
Beds: 3D 2T **Baths:** 5 En
🅿 (5) 🖤 📺 ✕ 🖷 🖕 cc
Our beautiful Victorian house is ideally situated for exploring the North Yorkshire Moors, visiting historic Whitby or the fascinating city of York. We provide superb breakfasts & delicious evening meals in a lovely setting; an ideal place to relax.

Barker Stakes Farm, *Lendales Lane, Pickering, N Yorks, YO18 8EE.*
Superb location, excellent food, comfortable rooms Yorkshire welcome = fantastic holiday.
Open: All Year (not Xmas/New Year)
Grades: ETC 3 Diamond
01751 476759 Mrs Hardy
D: £18.00–£20.00 **S:** £18.00–£20.00
Beds: 1T 2D **Baths:** 1 Pr 1 Sh
🛇 (5) 🅿 (6) 📺 ✕ 🖷 🖤 🖕

BATHROOMS
Pr - Private
Sh - Shared
En - Ensuite

Rawcliffe House Farm, *Newton-on-Rawcliffe, Pickering, N. Yorks, YO18 8JA.*
Open: Easter to Oct
Grades: ETC 4 Diamond
01751 473292 Mrs Ducat
Fax: 01751 473766
sheilarh@yahoo.com
D: £25.50–£28.50 **S:** £30.50–£33.50
Beds: 2D 1T **Baths:** 3 En
🛇 (8) 🅿 (10) 📺 ✕ 🖷 🖤 🖕 🖧 cc
Charming ensuite ground floor rooms with every convenience. A warm welcome and excellent accommodation in idyllic and spectacular setting of North Yorkshire Moors, ideal location for walking or touring. Friendly atmosphere and good food. Peace & tranquillity. Highly recommended.

Clent House, *15 Burgate, Pickering, North Yorkshire, YO18 7AU.*
Late C18th house, comfortable ensuite bedrooms, close to town centre, castle, moors railway. **Open:** All Year (not Xmas)
Grades: ETC 3 Diamond
01751 477928 K & I Loveday
bb1315@swiftlink.pnc-uk.net
D: £20.00 **S:** £20.00–£25.00
Beds: 1F 1T 1D **Baths:** 3 En
🛇 🅿 (3) 🖤 📺 🖷 🖕

Kirkham Garth, *Whitby Road, Pickering, N. Yorks, YO18 7AT.*
Quiet, private, homely residence, Ideal for York , forests moors and coast.
Open: All Year (not Xmas)
01751 474931 Mrs Rayner
D: £20.00–£22.00
Beds: 1F 1D 1T **Baths:** 1 Sh
🛇 🅿 (3) 🖤 📺 🖷 🖕

The Huntsman Restaurant and Guest House, *Main Street, Wrelton, Pickering, N. Yorks, YO18 8PG.*
Open: All Year
Grades: ETC 3 Diamond
01751 472530 Mr Lower
howard@thehuntsman.freeserve.co.uk
D: £16.00–£24.00 **S:** £18.00–£26.00
Beds: 1T 2D **Baths:** 3 En
🛇 🅿 (2) 📺 🛏 🖤 🖷 🖤 ✳ 🖕 cc
Quiet village location, 2 1/2 miles West Pickering leading to Rosedale foot of Yorkshire Moors. Converted stone-built farmhouse, rustic character, beamed ceilings, garden/patio, car park, licensed bar, Carol's home cooking - special offer 3 for 2 short breaks - brochure.

Rosebank, *61 Ruffa Lane, Pickering, North Yorks, YO18 7HN.*
Victorian former farmhouse. Large Garden. Town centre 5 minutes walk.
Open: Easter to Oct 31st
Grades: ETC 3 Diamond
01751 472531 (also fax)
D: £17.00–£22.00 **S:** £30.00
Beds: 3D **Baths:** 3 En
🅿 (3) 🖤 📺 🖷 🖤 🖕

Vivers Mill, *Mill Lane, Pickering, N. Yorks, YO18 8DJ.*
Ancient watermill in peaceful surroundings, sympathetically restored, 8 minutes' walk from the market place.
Open: All Year
01751 473640 Mr Saul & Mrs S Baxter
viversmill@talk21.com
D: £18.00–£27.00 **S:** £18.00–£27.00
Beds: 1F 5D 2T 1S **Baths:** 6 En 1 Sh
🛇 (5) 🅿 (10) 🖤 📺 🖷 🖤 🖕

Grindale House, *123 Eastgate, Pickering, N. Yorks, YO18 7DW.*
C18th stone Georgian town house. Luxurious, ensuite rooms with antique furniture.
Open: All Year
01751 476636 Mrs Hornsby
hornsby@cwcom.net
D: £20.00–£24.00 **S:** £25.00–£27.00
Beds: 2D 1T **Baths:** 3 En
🛇 🅿 (6) 📺 🛏 🖷 🖤 🖕

Eden House, *120 Eastgate, Pickering, N. Yorks, YO18 7DW.*
Delightful old cottage ideal for touring gardens, town, county.
Open: All Year
01751 472289 (also fax)
Mr Smith
D: £20.00–£21.00 **S:** £30.00–£35.00
Beds: 2D 1T **Baths:** 3 En
🛇 🅿 (4) 📺 ✕ 🖷 🖤 🖕

Rose Folly, *112 Eastgate, Pickering, N. Yorks, YO18 7DW.*
Enjoy breakfast overlooking delightful cottage gaarden. Convenient for all amenities.
Open: Feb to Nov
01751 475057 Mrs Rowe
gail@rosefolly.freeserve.co.uk
D: £18.00–£22.00
Beds: 2D **Baths:** 2 En
🅿 (2) 🖤 📺 🖷 🖤 🖕

Lingfield, *Middleton Road, Pickering, YO18 8AL.*
Quiet location, yet only five minutes' walk to railway and historic market place.
Open: Easter to Sep
01751 473456 Ms Kelleher
D: £16.00 **S:** £16.00–£20.00
Beds: 1F 1T **Baths:** 1 Sh
🛇 📺 🛏 🖷 🖤 🖕

Pinchinthorpe (Middlesbrough)

NZ5418

Pinchinthorpe Hotel, *Pinchinthorpe, Guisborough, TS14 8HG.*
In N Yorks National Park close to Heartbeat & Herriot Country
Open: All Year
Grades: ETC 4 Diamond
01287 630200 (also fax)
G Tinsley
D: £45.00–£65.00 **S:** £65.00–£85.00
Beds: 6D **Baths:** 6 En
🅿 📺 ✕ 🖷 🖕 🖧

Potto

NZ4703

Dog & Gun Country Inn, *Potto, Northallerton, DL6 3HQ.*
Open: All Year
01642 700232
D: £20.00–£25.00 **S:** £25.00–£30.00
Beds: 2F 2T 2D **Baths:** 5 En
🛏 🅿 (30) 📺 ✕ 🛍 📶 ♨ cc
Traditional country inn situated beside North Yorkshire Moors National Park. Warm friendly welcome, excellent cuisine and accommodation. Ideal touring base close to Teesside, Darlington, Northallerton, Thirsk. Approximately 25 miles from Whitby, Durham City, Yorkshire Dales, City of York, Ripon, Harrogate.

Ravenscar

NZ9801　🍺 *Bryherstones Inn, Falcon*

Bide A While Guest House, *3 Loring Road, Ravenscar, Scarborough, N. Yorks, YO13 0LY.*
Open: All Year
Grades: ETC 3 Diamond
01723 870643 Mr & Mrs Leach
Fax: 01723 871577
D: £16.50–£21.50 **S:** £20.00
Beds: 1F 2D 1T **Baths:** 3 En 1 Pr
🛏 🅿 📺 ✕ 🛍 📶 ♨
Small family guest house offering home comforts, home cooking a speciality. Situated on the edge of North York Moors, ideal for touring or walking the Yorkshire Dales. 1 hours scenic drive to York 11 miles from Scarborough and Whitby 500 metres from the sea.

Smugglers Rock Country Guest House, *Ravenscar, Scarborough, N. Yorks, YO13 0ER.*
Former smuggling inn twixt Whitby and Scarborough, refurbished and restored.
Open: All Year (not Xmas)
Grades: ETC 3 Diamond, AA 3 Diamond
01723 870044 Mr & Mrs Gregson
D: £23.00–£25.00 **S:** £26.00–£28.00
Beds: 1F 4D 2T 1S **Baths:** 8 En
🛏 🅿 (12) ⅍ 📺 ✝ ✕ 🛍 ♨

Dunelm, *Raven Hall Road, Ravenscar, Scarborough, N. Yorks, YO13 0NA.*
Friendly, flexible B&B. Splendid view. Walkers especially welcome!
Open: All Year (not Xmas)
01723 870430 Jenny Bartlet
D: £16.00–£18.00 **S:** £16.00–£18.00
Beds: 1D 1T 1S **Baths:** 2 Sh
🛏 🅿 ⅍ 📺 ✝ ✕ 🛍 ♨

Redcar

NZ6124

A 2 Z, *71 Station Road, Redcar, TS10 1RD.*
Near town centre, beach, racecourse, golf course and Yorkshire Moors.
Open: All Year (not Xmas)
01642 775533 Mrs Hodgin
D: £10.00–£12.00 **S:** £12.00–£13.00
Beds: 4T 2S **Baths:** 2 Sh
🛏 📺 ✕ 🛍 ♨

The Kastle, *55/56 Newcomen Terrace, Redcar, Teesside, TS10 1DB.*
Open: All Year
01642 489313
D: £10.00–£17.00 **S:** £10.00–£17.00
Beds: 3F 6T 6D 6S **Baths:** 6 En 5 Sh
🛏 🅿 (70) 📺 ✝ ✕ 🛍 📶 ♨ cc
Situated on the sea front opposite Redcar leisure centre and golf course. The Kastle is an ideal venue for visitors visiting Redcar, within easy reach of town centre and racecourse. Our prices include full English breakfast with use of the Knights bar and lounge.

Redmire

SE0491　🍺 *Bolton Arms*

Briar House, *Redmire, Leyburn, North Yorkshire, DL8 4EH.*
Comfortable C18th farmhouse, 'James Herriot' country. Good walking, cycling, touring. **Open:** All Year
01969 622335 Mr & Mrs Patterson
D: £16.00–£18.00 **S:** £20.00–£22.00
Beds: 1F 1T 2D **Baths:** 3 Sh
🛏 🅿 (4) ⅍ 📺 🛍 ♨

Reeth

SE0399　🍺 *Kings Arms Hotel, Bridge Inn, Black Bull, Buck Hotel*

Elder Peak, *Arkengarthdale Road, Reeth, Richmond, N Yorks, DL11 6QX.*
Friendly welcome. Good food. Peaceful, beautiful views. Ideal walking, touring.
Open: Easter to Oct
Grades: ETC 3 Diamond
01748 884770 Mrs Peacock
D: £17.00 **S:** £17.00–£20.00
Beds: 1D 1T **Baths:** 1 Sh
🛏 (5) 🅿 (2) 📺 🛍 ♨

Arkle House, *Mill Lane, Reeth, Richmond, North Yorks, DL11 6SJ.*
Old Georgian house full of character located alongside Arkle Beck.
Open: All Year **Grades:** ETC 4 Diamond
01748 884815 enquiries@arklehouse.com
D: £20.00–£25.00 **S:** £25.00–£27.50
Beds: 1F 1D **Baths:** 2 En
🛏 🅿 (2) ⅍ 📺 🛍 ♨

2 Bridge Terrace, *Reeth, Richmond, N. Yorks, DL11 6TP.*
Dry - cured Gloucester old spot bacon,local bread, fresh fruit, yoghurt.
Open: Easter to Nov
Grades: ETC 1 Diamond
01748 884572 Mrs Davies
davidsizer@freenetname.co.uk
D: £16.50–£17.50 **S:** £20.00–£22.00
Beds: 1D 1T **Baths:** 1 Sh
🛏 ⅍ 🛍 📺

The Black Bull, *Reeth, Richmond, N. Yorks, DL11 6SZ.*
In Yorkshire Dales National Park. On Inn Way. **Open:** All Year
Grades: ETC 3 Diamond
01748 884213 (also fax)
Mrs Sykes
D: £20.00–£25.00 **S:** £20.00–£37.50
Beds: 1F 1T 7D **Baths:** 6 En 1 Pr 2 Sh
🛏 📺 ✝ ✕ 🛍 ♨ ✳ cc

Riccall

SE6237　🍺 *Grey Mare, Hare & Hounds, Drovers*

South Newlands Farm, *Selby Road, Riccall, York, YO19 6QR.*
Friendly people, comfortable beds, ample fresh cooked food. Well located.
Open: All Year
Grades: ETC 3 Diamond
01757 248203 Mrs Swann
Fax: 01757 249450
pswann3059@aol.com
D: £18.00–£20.00 **S:** £20.00–£22.00
Beds: 1F 1D 1T **Baths:** 2 En
🛏 (3) 🅿 ⅍ 📺 ✝ ✕ 🛍 📶 ♨ cc

Richmond

NZ1701　🍺 *Angel, Buck Hotel, Black Lion, Shoulder Of Mutton, Holly Hill, Turf Hotel*

Pottergate Guest House, *4 Pottergate, Richmond, N Yorks, DL10 4AB.*
Comfortable guest house, friendly service, excellent value for money.
Open: All Year
Grades: ETC 2 Diamond, AA 2 Diamond
01748 823826 Mrs Firby
D: £19.00 **S:** £20.00
Beds: 1F 3D 1T 2S **Baths:** 3 Sh
🛏 🅿 (3) ⅍ 📺 ✕ 🛍 📶 ♨

66 Frenchgate, *Richmond, DL10 7AG.*
Comfortable rooms in beautiful old house. Stunning views of Richmond.
Open: All Year (not Xmas)
01748 823421 Mrs Woodward
paul@66french.freeserve.co.uk
D: £20.00–£21.00 **S:** £25.00–£26.00
Beds: 2D 1T **Baths:** 2 En 1 Pr
🛏 📺 ✝ 🛍 ♨

Caldwell Lodge, *Gilling West, Richmond, N. Yorks, DL10 5JB.*
Friendly welcome. Pretty village. 1 mile Scotch Corner.
Open: Easter to Oct
01748 825468 Mrs Bolton
D: £18.00–£20.00 **S:** £20.00–£22.00
Beds: 1F 1D **Baths:** 1 Sh
🛏 🅿 (4) 📺 🛍 ♨

West Cottage, *Victoria Road, Richmond, N. Yorks, DL10 4AS.*
Large Georgian town house. Easy walk into Richmond market place.
Open: Easter to Oct
01748 824046 Mrs Gibson
kay.gibson@tesco.net
D: £22.00–£25.00 **S:** £30.00–£40.00
Beds: 1D 1T **Baths:** 2 Pr
🛏 (5) 🅿 (2) ⅍ 📺 🛍 ♨

Channel House, *8 Frenchgate, Richmond, N. Yorks, DL10 4JG.*
Georgian town house near castle, shops, restaurants. Warm friendly welcome.
Open: All Year
01748 823844 (also fax) Mrs Gould
D: £17.00–£19.00 **S:** £20.00–£25.00
Beds: 1F 1D **Baths:** 1 En 1 Sh
🛏 (3) ⅍ 📺 ✝ 🛍 ♨

Planning a longer stay? Always ask for any special rates

Planning a longer stay? Always ask for any special rates

Westwood House, *5 Newbiggin, Richmond, N. Yorks, DL10 4DR.*
Comfortable Georgian town house situated just off Richmond market square.
Open: All Year
01748 823453 Mr Walker
D: £17.00 **S:** £17.00
Beds: 1F 1D 1T **Baths:** 1 Sh
🛏 (7) ⅋ 📺 🛏 💷 📖 ⅃ ♨

Windsor House, *9 Castle Hill, Richmond, N. Yorks, DL10 4QP.*
Grade II Listed Georgian house with large rooms and washing facilities.
Open: All Year
01748 823285 (also fax)
Mrs Adams
D: £17.00–£20.00 **S:** £17.00–£20.00
Beds: 2F 5D 2T 1S **Baths:** 2 Sh
🛏 📺 🛏 ✕ 📖 💷 ♣ ♨

Victoria House, *49 Maison Dieu, Richmond, N Yorks, DL10 7AU.*
Gateway to beautiful Yorkshire Dales, countryside with scenic walks, many places of historic interest.
Open: All Year (not Xmas)
01748 824830 Mr & Mrs Tate
D: £18.00–£20.00 **S:** £18.00–£20.00
Beds: 2D 1T **Baths:** 3 En
🛏 ⅋ 📺 🛏 📖 ♨

Rievaulx

SE5785 🍺 *Hare, Swan*

Barn Close Farm, *Rievaulx, Helmsley, York, YO62 5LH.*
Barn close. Hill farm in valley of Rievaulx. Recommended in Telegraph.
Open: All Year
01439 798321 Mrs Milburn
D: £20.00–£25.00
Beds: 1F 1D **Baths:** 1 En 1 Pr
🛏 💷 (6) 📺 🛏 ✕ 📖 💷 ♨

Ripley

SE2860

Newton Hall, *Ripley, Harrogate, N. Yorks, HG3 3DZ.*
Close to Harrogate, Fountains Abbey, The Dales, Skipton, Bolton Abbey, York.
Open: All Year
01423 770166 Mrs Iveson
D: £20.00–£24.00 **S:** £30.00
Beds: 2D 1T **Baths:** 1 Sh
🛏 💷 ⅋ 📺 📖 💷 ♨

Slate Rigg Farm, *Birthwaite Lane, Ripley, Harrogate, N. Yorks, HG3 3JQ.*
Secluded working family farm with beautiful views of Lower Nidderdale.
Open: All Year (not Xmas/New Year)
Grades: ETC 3 Diamond
01423 770135 Mrs Bowes
D: £20.00–£22.50 **S:** £25.00–£30.00
Beds: 1F 1T **Baths:** 2 Sh
🛏 💷 (4) 📺 📖 💷 ♨

Ripon

SE3171 🍺 *Brawtley Arms, Countryman, Golden Lion, Black Bull, Grantley Arms, Sawley Arms, Masons' Arms, Water Rat*

St Georges Court, *Old Home Farm, Grantley, Ripon, N. Yorks, HG4 3EU.*
Open: All Year
Grades: ETC 4 Diamond, AA 4 Diamond
01765 620618 Mrs Gordon
D: £22.50–£25.00
Beds: 1F 4D 1T **Baths:** 6 En
🛏 (2) 💷 (12) ⅋ 📺 🛏 📖 💷 ♨ ♿ cc
Peace & tranquillity - we are 200 yards from any road; beautifully situated.

Beech House, *7 South Crescent, Ripon, N. Yorks, HG4 1SW.*
Ripon - Cathedral city of the Dales.
Open: All Year (not Xmas)
Grades: ETC 3 Diamond
01765 603294 (also fax) Mrs Darbyshire
D: £20.00–£24.00
Beds: 1D 1T 1S **Baths:** 2 En 1 Sh
🛏 💷 (4) 📺 📖 💷 ♨

Bishopton Grove House, *Ripon, N. Yorks, HG4 2QL.*
Large comfortable Georgian house near Fountains Abbey and River Laver.
Open: All Year
Grades: ETC 3 Diamond
01765 600888 Mrs Wimpress
wimpress@bronco.co.uk
D: £18.00–£20.00 **S:** £20.00–£25.00
Beds: 1F 1D 1T **Baths:** 2 En
🛏 💷 (3) 📺 🛏 ✕ 📖 💷 ♨

Middle Ridge, *42 Mallorie Park Drive, Ripon, HG4 2QF .*
Traditional,family owned, tastefully furnished, quiet, garden, conservatory, city outskirts. **Open:** Easter to Sep
Grades: ETC 4 Diamond
01765 690558 Mrs Parker
john@midrig.demon.co.uk
D: £18.00–£20.00 **S:** £25.00–£30.00
Beds: 1D 1T **Baths:** 1 Sh
🛏 💷 (3) 📺 📖 💷 ♨

Moor End Farm, *Knaresborough Road, Littlethorpe, Ripon, N. Yorks, HG4 3LU.*
Pleasantly situated. A friendly welcome and very comfortable accommodation.
Open: All Year (not Xmas)
Grades: ETC 3 Diamond
01765 677419 Mrs Spensley
pspensley@ukonline.co.uk
D: £18.50–£24.00 **S:** £28.00–£40.00
Beds: 2D 1T **Baths:** 2 En 1 Sh
💷 (5) ⅋ 📺 📖 ♨

Robin Hood's Bay

NZ9504 🍺 *Bay Hotel, Dolphin, Flyingdale Inn, Grosvenor, Victoria*

Glen-lyn, *Station Road, Robin Hood's Bay, Whitby, N Yorks, YO22 4RA.*
Open: All Year **01947 880391** Mrs Price
jmpglenlyn@aol-com
D: £20.00 **Beds:** 1T 1D **Baths:** 2 En
💷 ⅋ 📺 📖 💷 ♨ ♨
Come and sample the delights of Robin Hoods Bay and stay in a tastefully decorated, well appointed detached bungalow. You can relax in the large, well maintained, mature gardens with seating area around a with water feature.

Clarence Dene, *Station Road, Robin Hood Bay, Whitby, North Yorks, YO22 4RH.*
Open: All Year (also fax)
Mrs Howard
dhcdene@aol.com
D: £20.00
Beds: 1F 1T 3D **Baths:** 5 En
🛏 💷 ⅋ 📺 📖 💷 ♨
Situated above this historic village. Clarence Dene retains many original Art Nouveau features. the spacious bedrooms have been sympathetically decorated and furnished, all are clean. comfortable and well appointed with ensuite facilities.

The White Owl, *Station Road, Robin Hood's Bay, Whitby, N. Yorks, YO22 4RL.*
Interesting house and garden. Centre of village near cliff edge.
Open: All Year
01947 880879 Mr & Mrs Higgins
D: £20.00 **S:** £20.00
Beds: 1F 1D 1T 1S **Baths:** 4 En
🛏 💷 (3) 📺 🛏 ♣ ♨

Meadowfield, *Mount Pleasant North, Robin Hood's Bay, Whitby, N. Yorks, YO22 4RE.*
Refurbished Victorian house. Friendly, comfortable, plenty of food. Non-smoking.
Open: All Year (not Xmas)
01947 880564 Mrs Luker
D: £17.00–£19.50 **S:** £20.00–£24.00
Beds: 2D 1T 2S **Baths:** 1 En 1 Sh
⅋ 📺 💷 ♨

Rosegarth, *Thorpe Lane, Robin Hood's Bay, Whitby, N. Yorks, YO22 4RN.*
Friendly comfortable accommodation. Ideal centre touring and walking.
Open: Easter to Nov
01947 880578 Mrs Stubbs
D: £16.50–£17.00 **S:** fr £17.00
Beds: 1D 1T 1S **Baths:** 1 Sh
🛏 (9) 💷 (4) 📺 📖 ♨

Flask Inn, *Robin Hood's Bay, Fylingdales, Whitby, YO22 4QH.*
Friendly family-run coaching inn. Excellent food served lunchtimes and evenings.
Open: All year
01947 880305 G Allison
Fax: 01947 880592
flaskinn@aol.com
D: £22.00 **S:** fr £28.00
Beds: 3F 4D 4T 1S **Baths:** 12 En
🛏 💷 📺 ✕ 📖 💷 ♨ cc

Rosedale Abbey

SE7295 🍺 *Milburn Arms, White Horse*

Sevenford House, *Rosedale Abbey, Pickering, N. Yorks, YO18 8SE.*
Originally a vicarage & built from the stones of Rosedale Abbey.
Open: All Year (not Xmas)
01751 417283 Ms Sugars
Fax: 01751 417505
sevenford@aol.com
D: £22.50 **S:** £27.50
Beds: 1F 1D 1T **Baths:** 3 En
🛏 💷 (9) ⅋ 📺 📖 💷 ♨

Rosedale East

SE7197

Moordale House, Dale Head, Rosedale East, Pickering, N. Yorks, YO18 8RH.
In the heart of National Park. Spectacular views. Ideal touring, walking, cycling.
Open: All Year (not Xmas)
Grades: ETC 3 Diamond
01751 417219 Mrs Harrison
D: £21.00–£23.00 **S:** £26.00–£28.00
Beds: 1F 2T 2D
⛩ 🅿 (6) 📺 🐾 ✕ 🏛 �V ♿

Runswick Bay

NZ8016 ◨ Royal Hotel

Cockpit House, The Old Village, Runswick Bay, Saltburn-by-the-Sea, N Yorks, TS13 5HU.
Seafront position, near pub, beach, cafe, all sea views. **Open:** All Year
Grades: ETC 2 Diamond
01947 840504 Mrs Smith
D: fr £17.00
Beds: 1D 2T **Baths:** 1 Sh
⛩ (5) 📺 🐾 🏛 �V ♿

Saintoft

SE7989 ◨ Cropton New Inn

Beech Cottage, Saintoft, Pickering, North Yorkshire, YO18 8QQ.
Large garden property nestled amongst trees, a particularly beautiful area.
Open: All Year **Grades:** ETC 3 Star
01751 417625 P & E Bramley
D: £16.00–£18.00 **S:** £20.00–£24.00
Beds: 1F 1T **Baths:** 2 En
⛩ 🅿 (2) ✕ 📺 🐾 🏛 �V ♿

Saltburn-by-the-Sea

NZ6722 ◨ Holly Bush, Blacksmiths Arms, Ship, Lingdale Tavern

Runswick Bay Hotel, Runswick Bay, Saltburn-by-the-Sea, Cleveland, TS13 5HR.
In well-known village of Runswick Bay and within North York Moors National Park. **Open:** All Year (not Xmas/New Year)
01947 841010
D: £22.50–£25.00 **S:** £25.00–£28.00
Beds: 1F 1T 4D **Baths:** 6 En
⛩ 🅿 📺 🐾 ✕ 🏛 �V ♿ cc

The Spa Hotel, Saltbank, Saltburn-by-the-Sea, Cleveland, TS12 1HH.
Our reputation is built on traditional quality accommodation and food.
Open: All Year **01287 622544** Mr Devnay
Fax: 01287 625870 spahotels@aol.com
D: £25.00 **S:** £35.00
Beds: 4F 20D 7T **Baths:** 31 En
⛩ 🅿 (40) ✕ 📺 🐾 ✕ 🏛 �V ♿ ⚷ cc

Westerlands Guest House, 27 East Parade, Skelton, Saltburn-by-the-Sea, N. Yorks, TS12 2BJ.
Large modern detached house, beautiful views sea countryside, alongside Cleveland way long-distance path.
Open: Mar to Oct
01287 650690 Mr Bull
D: £15.00 **S:** £15.00
Beds: 6F 3D 3S **Baths:** 3 Pr
⛩ 🅿 (5) ✕ 📺 🐾 ✕ 🏛 �V ♿

Sandsend

NZ8612 ◨ Hart Inn, White Horse, Griffin

Estbek House, Sandsend, Whitby, N. Yorks, YO21 3SU.
Fully equipped designer bedrooms. Fresh food, licensed restaurant.
Open: All Year **Grades:** ETC 3 Diamond
01947 893424 (also fax) Mr Cooper
R.C.Hill@Onyxnet.co.uk
D: £29.50 **S:** £27.50–£39.50
Beds: 1F 2D 2T **Baths:** 4 En 1 Pr
⛩ 🅿 ✕ 📺 🐾 🏛 �V ♿ cc

Scarborough

TA0388 ◨ Cask, Copper Horse, Crescent, Highlander, Ivanhoe, Little Jack's Bar, Newlands Park, Oakwheel, Poacher's Pocket, Rosette Inn, Scalby Manor, Scarborough Arms, Three Jolly Sailors

Howdale Hotel, 121 Queens Parade, Scarborough, N. Yorks, YO12 7HU.
Comfortable hotel, panoramic sea views, memorable breakfasts, ten minutes town.
Open: Easter to Oct
01723 372696 (also fax) Mr & Mrs Abbott
D: £17.00–£22.00 **S:** £25.00–£26.50
Beds: 1F 11D 2T 1S **Baths:** 13 En 2 Sh
⛩ 🅿 (9) 📺 🐾 🏛 �V ♿ cc

Ryndle Court Hotel, 47 Northstead Manor Drive, Scarborough, N. Yorks, YO12 6AF.
Looking for high standards at reasonable rates? Call us now! **Open:** Feb to Nov
Grades: ETC 2 Star, RAC 2 Star
01723 375188 (also fax) Mr & Mrs Davies
enquiries@ryndlecourt.co.uk
D: £28.00–£30.00 **S:** £28.00–£38.00
Beds: 1F 6D 5T 2S **Baths:** 14 En
⛩ 🅿 (10) 📺 🐾 🏛 �V ♿ cc

Richmond Private Hotel, 135 Columbus Ravine, Scarborough, N. Yorks, YO12 7QZ.
Small, comfortable, family-run hotel. Friendly atmosphere, good home cooking.
Open: All Year
01723 362934 Mr & Mrs Shaw
D: £15.00–£18.00 **S:** £15.00–£18.00
Beds: 2F 4D 1T 1S **Baths:** 3 En 1 Sh
⛩ 📺 🐾 ✕ 🏛 �V ♿

Wheatcroft Lodge, 156 Filey Road, Scarborough, N. Yorks, YO11 3AA.
High standards at reasonable rates. RAC Sparkling Diamond Award.
Open: All Year (not Xmas)
Grades: RAC 3 Diamond
01723 374613 Mrs Batty
D: £21.50 **S:** £21.50
Beds: 4D 2T 1S **Baths:** 7 En
🅿 (10) ✕ 📺 🏛 �V ♿ cc

Red Lea Hotel, Prince Of Wales Terrace, Scarborough, N. Yorks, YO11 2AJ.
Traditional hotel with good facilities and expansive sea views.
Open: All Year
Grades: ETC 2 Star Hotel, RAC 2 Star
01723 362431 Mr & Mrs Lee
Fax: 01723 371230
redlea@globalnet.co.uk
D: £27.00–£36.00 **S:** £27.00–£36.00
Beds: 7F 16D 23T 22S **Baths:** 68 En
⛩ 📺 ✕ 🏛 �V ♿ ⚷ cc

Russell Hotel, 22 Ryndleside, Scarborough, N Yorks, YO12 6AD.
Open: All Year
01723 365453 Lyn Stanley & Glen Martin
D: £17.00–£20.00 **S:** £18.00–£21.00
Beds: 4F 2D 2T 2S **Baths:** 7 En
⛩ 🅿 (10) 📺 🐾 ✕ 🏛 �V ♿ ⚷ 2
Detached 10 bedroom hotel, overlooking Peasholm Glen. Convenient for all North Bay attractions, all bedrooms on 2 floors, 7 ensuite large bedrooms with TV and tea/coffee making facilities, private car parking.

Leeway Hotel, 71 Queens Parade, Scarborough, YO12 7HT.
A family run licensed hotel overlooking The North Bay and Castle.
Open: Easter to Nov
01723 374371 Mr Saville
leenay@supanet.com
D: £17.00–£20.00 **S:** £17.00–£18.00
Beds: 2F 5D 2S **Baths:** 6 En
⛩ 🅿 (6) ✕ 📺 ✕ 🏛 ♿

Fixton, Scarborough, N Yorks, YO11 3UD.
Rural location near coast, Moors, Wolds, warm welcome, secure parking.
Open: All Year (not Xmas)
01723 890272 (also fax)
Mrs Wheater
D: £18.00–£20.00 **S:** £18.00
Beds: 2F 2D 1S **Baths:** 2 En 1 Sh

Casablanca Hotel, 20 Ryndleside, Scarborough, N. Yorks, YO12 6AD.
Overlooking Peasholm Park. Comfortable accommodation.
Open: All Year
01723 362288 (also fax)
Mrs Akel
casablanca_hotel@hotmail.com
D: £21.00–£23.00 **S:** £23.00–£25.00
Beds: 5F 6D 1T 1S **Baths:** 13 En
⛩ 🅿 (12) 📺 🐾 ✕ 🏛 �V ♿

Wharncliffe Hotel, 26 Blenheim Terrace, Scarborough, N Yorks, YO12 7HD.
Overlooking beautiful North Bay. Central, licensed bar. Clean and comfortable.
Open: Easter to Oct
Grades: ETC 4 Diamond
01723 374635 Mr & Mrs Clarke-Irons
D: £22.00–£24.00 **S:** £26.00–£28.00
Beds: 2F 7D 3T **Baths:** 12 En
⛩ (2) 🅿 (1) 📺 ✕ 🏛 �V ♿

Interludes, 32 Princess Street, Scarborough, N. Yorks, YO11 1QR.
Warm friendly hotel. Close to all Scarborough attractions. No children.
Open: All Year (not Xmas/New Year)
Grades: AA 4 Diamond
01723 360513 Mr Grundy
Fax: 01723 368597
interludes@cwcom.net
D: £21.00–£28.00 **S:** £23.00–£33.00
Beds: 3D 2T **Baths:** 4 En 1 Sh
✕ 📺 ✕ 🏛 �V ♿ cc

All details shown are as supplied by B&B owners in Autumn 2000

Northcote Quality Serviced Holiday Suites, 114 Columbus Ravine,
Scarborough, N. Yorks, YO12 7QZ.
Well established modern semi-detached hotel. **Open:** March to Nov
01723 367758 C M Thompson
christina.m.thompson@talk21.com
D: £7.50–£25.00
Beds: 4F/D **Baths:** 9 Pr
🛇 🅿 (5) ⅟ 📺 ⊁ 🎗 🛒 Ⅴ ⅃

The Terrace Hotel, 69 Westborough,
Scarborough, N. Yorks, YO11 1TS.
Close Railway station, town centre and all Scarborough's many attractions.
Open: All Year (not Xmas/New Year)
01723 374937 Mr & Mrs Kirk
D: £16.00–£21.00 **S:** £16.00–£21.00
Beds: 3F 3D 1S **Baths:** 2 En 2 Sh
🛇 🅿 (4) 📺 🛒 ⅃

Derwent House Hotel, 6 Rutland
Terrace, Queens Parade, Scarborough, N. Yorks, YO12 7JB.
Located near Castle, town, theatres and all major attractions.
Open: All Year
01723 373880 Mr & Mrs Greenhough
D: £17.00–£24.00 **S:** £20.00–£30.00
Beds: 4F 12D 4T 2S **Baths:** 6 En 3 Sh
🛇 (5) ⅟ 📺 ⅹ 🛒 ⅃

Villa Marina Hotel, 59 Northstead
Manor Drive, Scarborough, N. Yorks, YO12 6AF.
Detached, quiet location overlooking Peasholm Park, close to north side attractions. **Open:** Easter to Oct
Grades: ETC 4 Diamond
01723 361088 Mr & Mrs Pearson
D: £22.00–£28.00
Beds: 2F 6D 2T **Baths:** 10 En
🛇 (5) 🅿 (9) ⅟ 📺 🛒 Ⅴ ⅃ cc

The Girvan Hotel, 61 Northstead
Manor Drive, Scarborough, N. Yorks, YO12 6AF.
Modern detached hotel close to Peasholm Park and North Bay.
Open: All Year
01723 364518 (also fax)
Mrs Hurrell
D: £15.00–£24.00 **S:** £20.00–£29.00
Beds: 4F 2D 4T 2S **Baths:** 12 En
🛇 🅿 (10) 📺 ⅀ 🎗 🛒 Ⅴ ✳ ⅃ ♿ cc

Hotel Fantasia, 157 North Marine
Road, Scarborough, N Yorks, YO12 7HU.
Family-run friendly hotel, licensed bar, close to sea front.
Open: All Year
01723 368357 Mr & Mrs Torr
sadie@hotelfantasia.freeserve.co.uk
D: £15.00–£17.00
Beds: 1F **Baths:** 3 En 1 Sh
🛇 (0) ⅟ 📺 🛒 ✳ ⅃

The Duke Of York Guest House, 1-
2 Merchants Row, Eastborough, Scarborough, N. Yorks, YO11 1NQ.
Georgian guesthouse overlooking Scarborough's seafront. Home cooking. Warm welcome.
Open: All Year
01723 373875 Mr Addis
D: £15.00–£17.50 **S:** £15.00–£17.50
Beds: 2F 6D 2T 2S **Baths:** 12 En
🛇 🅿 (7) ⅟ 📺 🛒 ⅃

Anatolia Hotel, 21 West Street,
Scarborough, N Yorks, YO11 2QR.
Select Victorian house of charm and character, good home cooking.
Open: May to Oct
Grades: ETC 3 Diamond
01723 360864 Mr & Mrs Simpson
pat@patsimpson.freeserve.co.uk
D: £18.00–£20.00 **S:** £18.00–£20.00
Beds: 2F 3D 2T 2S **Baths:** 9 En 1 Pr
🛇 (5) 🅿 ⅟ 📺 ⅹ 🛒 Ⅴ ⅃

Glenderry Non-Smoking Guest House, 26 The Dene, Scarborough, N.
Yorks, YO12 7NJ.
Small, select, family-run guest house, quiet residential area, ideally situated for Peasholm Park.
Open: All Year (not Xmas)
01723 362546 Mrs Dugdale
glenderry@aol.com
D: £15.00–£18.50 **S:** £15.00–£22.00
Beds: 3F 1D 1S **Baths:** 2 En 1 Sh
🛇 (4) ⅟ 📺 ⅹ 🛒 Ⅴ ⅃ cc

Meadow Court Hotel, Queens
Terrace, Scarborough, N. Yorks, YO12 7HJ.
Family-run licensed hotel.
Open: All Year
01723 360839 Mr Buckle
D: £13.00–£14.00 **S:** £13.00–£14.00
Beds: 2F 4D 2T 2S **Baths:** 2 Sh
🛇 🎗 🛒 ✳ ⅃

Brincliffe Edge Hotel, 105 Queens
Parade, Scarborough, N. Yorks, YO12 7HY.
Comfortable family-run hotel overlooking North Bay.
Open: Easter to Oct
01723 364834 Mr & Mrs Sutcliffe
D: £18.25–£22.00 **S:** £18.25–£22.00
Beds: 1F 8D 1T 1S **Baths:** 9 En 2 Sh
🛇 (2) 🅿 (7) 📺 ⅹ 🛒 Ⅴ ⅃

Stewart Hotel, St Nicholas Cliff,
Scarborough, N. Yorks, YO11 2ES.
Overlooking the South Bay, Georgian Grade II Listed hotel; good breakfast.
Open: All Year
01723 361095 Mr Pummell
don.pummell@onyxnet.co.uk
D: £20.00–£25.00 **S:** £20.00–£25.00
Beds: 3F 9D 2T **Baths:** 14 En
🛇 📺 🛒 Ⅴ ✳ ⅃ cc

Philamon, 108 North Marine Road,
Scarborough, N. Yorks, YO12 7JA.
Friendly guest house overlooking cricket ground. Convenient for golf and theatres.
Open: All Year
01723 373107 Mrs Hunter
D: £14.50–£18.00 **S:** £14.50–£18.00
Beds: 1F 3D 2T 2S **Baths:** 3 En 1 Sh
🛇 (2) 📺 🛒 Ⅴ ⅃

Roslen Guest House, 110 North
Marine Road, Scarborough, N. Yorks, YO12 7JA.
Licensed Victorian-style guest house close North Bay amenities and walking distance town centre.
Open: All Year (not Xmas)
01723 363492 Mr & Mrs Walker
Fax: 01723 507318
bill@roslen.freeserve.co.uk
D: £13.00–£15.00 **S:** £13.00–£15.00
Beds: 5F 3S **Baths:** 2 Sh
🛇 (3) 📺 ⅹ 🛒 Ⅴ ⅃

Gordon Hotel, 24 Ryndleside,
Scarborough, N. Yorks, YO12 6AD.
North Bay overlooking Peasholm Park. Comfortable licensed family-run hotel.
Open: All Year (not Xmas)
01723 362177 Mr Strickland
gordonhotel@tesco.net
D: £17.00–£22.00 **S:** £17.00–£22.00
Beds: 3F 1T 5D 1S **Baths:** 8 En 2 Pr
🛇 🅿 (7) 📺 🎗 🛒 Ⅴ ⅃

Thornhurst Hotel, 39 North Marine
Road, Scarborough, N. Yorks, YO12 7EY.
Licensed. Close to amenities. Moors walks 10 mins' ride away. **Open:** All Year
01723 372498 Mr Burpitt
D: £13.50–£17.00 **S:** £13.50–£15.00
Beds: 3F 4D 2T 2S **Baths:** 4 En 2 Sh
🛇 (1) 🅿 (9) 📺 🎗 ⅹ 🛒 ✳ ⅃

Scotch Corner
NZ2105

Vintage Hotel, Scotch Corner,
Richmond, N. Yorks, DL10 6NP.
Conveniently situated roadside inn on A66, only quarter mile from A1 at Scotch Corner. **Open:** All Year (not Xmas)
Grades: ETC 3 Diamond, AA 3 Diamond, RAC 3 Diamond
01748 824424 Mr & Mrs Fothergill
D: £19.00–£27.00 **S:** £23.50–£42.50
Beds: 3D 2T 3S **Baths:** 5 En 1 Sh
🛇 (7) 🅿 (40) 📺 ⅹ 🛒 Ⅴ ⅃ cc

Selby
SE6132 🚃 Londesborough, Grey Horse

Hazeldene Guest House, 32-34
Brook Street, Selby, N. Yorks, YO8 4AR.
Attractive period house, featuring spacious ensuite rooms, market town location. **Open:** All Year (not Xmas)
Grades: ETC 2 Diamond, AA 2 Diamond
01757 704809 Mr Leake
Fax: 01757 709300
hazeldene@breathemail.net
D: £18.00–£22.00 **S:** £21.00–£30.00
Beds: 3D 3T 2S **Baths:** 4 En 2 Sh
🛇 (12) 🅿 (5) ⅟ 📺 🛒 Ⅴ ⅃ cc

Selside
SD7875 🚃 Crown

South House Farm, Selside, Settle, N.
Yorks, BD24 0HU.
Comfortable farmhouse accommodation set in the centre of the Peaks.
Open: Easter to Oct
01729 860271 Ms Kenyon
D: £20.00 **S:** £20.00
Beds: 1F 2D 1T **Baths:** 1 En
🛇 (1) 🅿 (6) ⅟ 📺 🎗 🛒 ⅃

Settle
SD8163 🚃 Golden Lion, Crown, Royal Oak

Liverpool House, Chapel Square,
Settle, N. Yorks, BD24 9HR.
Situated in quiet area yet within 3 mins' walk town square. **Open:** All Year
Grades: AA 3 Diamond
01729 822247 Mr & Mrs Duerden
D: £19.00–£23.00 **S:** £19.00–£20.00
Beds: 4D 1T 2S **Baths:** 2 En 2 Sh
🛇 🅿 (8) ⅟ 📺 🛒 Ⅴ ⅃ cc

The Yorkshire Rose Guest House,
Duke Street, Settle, North Yorkshire,
BD24 9AW.
Comfortable family run establishment
close to town centre/station. Relax.
Open: All Year
Grades: ETC 3 Diamond, AA 3 Diamond
01729 822032
yorkshirerose@tinyonline.co.uk
D: £15.00–£23.50 **S:** £15.00–£23.50
Beds: 1F 1T 2D 1S **Baths:** 2 En 1 Sh
🛇 🅿 (6) ⌁ 📺 🛏 🖳 🔥 **CC**

The Oast Guest House, *5 Penyghent*
View, Church Street, Settle, N. Yorks,
BD24 9JJ.
High standards with a Yorkshire welcome
await you.
Open: All Year
01729 822989 (also fax)
Mr & Mrs King
king@oast2000.freeserve.co.uk
D: £18.50–£23.00 **S:** £15.50–£17.50
Beds: 1F 2D 2T 1S **Baths:** 3 En 3 Sh
🛇 🅿 (4) ⌁ 📺 ✕ 🖳 🔆 🔥

Sharow

SE3271

Half Moon Inn, *Sharow Lane, Sharow,*
Ripon, N. Yorks, HG4 5BP.
Quiet C18th country inn on outskirts of
historic Ripon.
Open: All Year (not Xmas/New Year)
Grades: ETC 3 Diamond
01765 600291 D: £20.00 **S:** £24.50
Beds: 1T 2D **Baths:** 3 En 1 Sh
🛇 🅿 (10) 📺 ✕ 🖳 🔥 **CC**

Sherburn in Elmet

SE4933   ◀ *Half Moon Inn, Red Bear*

Church Hill Guest House, *3 Church*
Hill, Sherburn in Elmet, Leeds, LS25 6AX.
Open: All Year
01977 681000 A Beattie
Fax: 01977 681333
D: £17.50–£20.00 **S:** £18.50–£25.00
Beds: 1D 2T 1S **Baths:** 3 Sh
🛇 🅿 (8) 📺 🛏 🖳 🔥 🔥 **CC**
The accommodation is a purpose-built
annexe joined to owners' house, all
recently refurbished to high standard.
Our register has many glowing
testimonials. Very easy to find and
extremely convenient for York, Dales,
Moors, Pennines. Relaxed, easygoing and
friendly.

Wheelgate Guest House, *7 Kirkgate,*
Sherburn in Elmet, Leeds, West Yorkshire,
LS25 6BH.
Olde worlde cottage-style house,
convenient for Leeds, York, Selby.
Open: All Year (not Xmas)
Grades: ETC 3 Diamond
01977 682231 (also fax)
Mrs Tomlinson
D: £18.00–£23.00 **S:** £21.00–£28.00
Beds: 1D 3T **Baths:** 1 En 2 Sh
🛇 (4) 🅿 (7) ⌁ 📺 🛏 ✕ 🖳 🔥

Planning a longer stay? Always
ask for any special rates

Sinnington

SE7486   ◀ *Fox & Hounds*

Green Lea, *Sinnington, York, YO62 6SH.*
Open: March to Oct
Grades: ETC 3 Diamond
01751 432008 Mr & Mrs Turnbull
D: £18.00–£22.50 **S:** £18.00–£22.50
Beds: 1F 1T 1D **Baths:** 2 En 1 Sh
🛇 (5) 🅿 (4) ⌁ 📺 ✕ 🖳 🔥
Large converted bungalow in lovely pretty
village off A170. Lovely garden to relax in.
Ground floor rooms, very clean and
comfortable. Ideal centre for the moors,
coast, York. Lots of visitor attractions for
all interests, walking area. Quiet and
homely.

Skeeby

NZ1903   ◀ *Travellers Rest*

The Old Chapel, *Richmond Road,*
Skeeby, Richmond, North Yorks, DL10 5DR.
Beautifully converted Victorian chapel
situated in small village near Richmond.
Open: All Year (not Xmas/New Year)
Grades: ETC 4 Diamond
01748 824170 H Allan
hazel@theoldchapel.fsnet.co.uk
D: £20.00 **S:** £25.00
Beds: 2D **Baths:** 2 En
🛇 🅿 (2) ⌁ 📺 🖳 🔥 🔥

Skelton (Saltburn)

NZ6518   ◀ *Holly Bush Blacksmiths Arms,*
Ship, Lingdale Tavern

Westerlands Guest House, *27 East*
Parade, Skelton, Saltburn-by-the-Sea, N.
Yorks, TS12 2BJ.
Large modern detached house, beautiful
views sea-countryside, alongside
Cleveland way long-distance path.
Open: Mar to Oct
01287 650690 Mr Bull
D: £15.00 **S:** £15.00
Beds: 6F 3D 3S **Baths:** 3 Pr
🛇 🅿 (5) ⌁ 📺 🛏 ✕ 🖳 🔥 🔥

Skipton

SD9851   ◀ *Craven Heifer, Sailor, Fleece, Elm*
Tree, Slaters' Arms, Wooley Sheep, Black Horse

Low Skibeden Farmhouse, *Skibeden*
Road, Skipton, N. Yorks, BD23 6AB.
C16th farmhouse with little luxuries and
fireside treats at no extra charge.
Open: All Year
Grades: ETC 3 Star, AA 4 Diamond
01756 793849 Mrs Simpson
Fax: 01756 793804
skibhols.yorksdales@talk21.com
D: £20.00–£24.00 **S:** £25.00–£38.00
Beds: 3F 1D 1T **Baths:** 4 En 1 Sh
🛇 (12) 🅿 (5) ⌁ 📺 🖳 🔥 **CC**

Dalesgate Lodge, *69 Gargrave Road,*
Skipton, N. Yorks, BD23 1QN.
Comfortable rooms, friendly welcome.
Special winter breaks available.
Open: All Year
Grades: ETC 4 Diamond
01756 790672 Mr & Mrs Mason
D: £17.50–£20.00 **S:** £20.00–£25.00
Beds: 2D/T 2S **Baths:** 4 En
🛇 🅿 (2) ⌁ 📺 🖳 🔥

Bourne House, *22 Upper Sackville*
Street, Skipton, N Yorks, BD23 2EB.
Edwardian townhouse, quiet location,
close to town centre, easy parking.
Open: All Year (not Xmas/New Year)
Grades: ETC 3 Diamond
01756 792633 Mr & Mrs Barton
Fax: 01756 701609
bournehouse@totalise.co.uk
D: £16.00–£18.00 **S:** £17.00–£25.00
Beds: 1T 2D 1S **Baths:** 1 En   2 Sh
🛇 (3) ⌁ 📺 🖳 🔥 **CC**

Craven Heifer Inn, *Grassington Road,*
Skipton, BD23 3LA.
Country inn set at the gateway to the
Yorkshire Dales.
Open: All Year
Grades: ETC 3 Diamond
01756 792521 P G Smith
Fax: 01756 794442
philandlynn@cravenheifer.co.uk
D: fr £22.50 **S:** fr £44.95
Beds: 2F 13D 3T 1S **Baths:** 16 En 3 Sh
🛇 🅿 (99) ⌁ 📺 ✕ 🖳 🔥 🔥 🔥 **3 CC**

Highfield Hotel, *58 Keighley Road,*
Skipton, N. Yorks, BD23 2NB.
All ensuite homely rooms. 5 mins town
centre. Great Dales location.
Open: All Year (not Xmas)
Grades: ETC 2 Star
01756 793182 (also fax)
D A Davis
D: £18.50–£19.50 **S:** £25.00–£35.00
Beds: 1T 7D 2S **Baths:** 10 En
🛇 🅿 🖳 ✕ 🖳 🔥 **CC**

The Barn, *Main Street, Skipton, BD23*
4ND.
Yorkshire Dales - Long Preston situated
on the A65 Keighley to Kendal road.
Open: All Year (not Xmas)
01729 840426 Mrs Fleming
D: £19.00–£21.50 **S:** £22.50–£25.00
Beds: 1F 1D **Baths:** 1 En 1 Sh
🛇 (2) 🅿 (5) ⌁ 📺 🛏 🖳 🔥

Sleights

NZ8607   ◀ *Plough*

Ryedale House, *154-8 Coach Road,*
Sleights, Whitby, N. Yorks, YO22 5EQ.
National Park country 3.5 miles Whitby.
Magnificent moor/dale/coastal scenery.
Open: April to Oct
Grades: ETC 4 Diamond
01947 810534 (also fax)
Mrs Beale
D: £19.50–£21.00 **S:** £17.00–£22.00
Beds: 2D 2S **Baths:** 2 En 1 Pr
🅿 (3) ⌁ 📺 🖳 🔥 **CC**

Slingsby

SE6975   ◀ *Royal Oak, Malt Shovel*

Beech Tree House Farm, *South*
Holme, Slingsby, York, YO62 4BA.
Working farm. Beautiful area between
York and Scarborough. Children
welcome.
Open: All Year (not Xmas)
Grades: ETC 3 Diamond
01653 628257 D: £18.00 **S:** £18.00
Beds: 2F 1D 1T **Baths:** 3 Pr
🛇 🅿 (6) ✕ 🖳 📺

Planning a longer stay? Always
ask for any special rates

Smallways

NZ1111

A66 Motel, *Smallways, Richmond,
North Yorkshire, DL11 7QW.*
Not your usual motel at all! Converted
farmhouse, family-run for two
generations. **Open:** All year
01833 627334 (also fax) Mr Leonard
a66MOTEL@barnard-castle.co.uk
D: £20.00–£25.00 **S:** £22.00–£27.00
Beds: 2D 4S **Baths:** 6 En
🛇 🅿 (50) 📺 ➤ ✕ 📖 Ⅴ ዼ ৬ cc

Sowerby

SE4281

The Old Manor House, *27 Front
Street, Sowerby, Thirsk, N. Yorks, YO7 1JQ.*
Restored C15th manor house. Guest
suites overlooking gardens or village
green. **Open:** All Year (not Xmas)
01845 526642 Mr Jackson
Fax: 01845 526568
D: fr £20.00 **S:** fr £35.00
Beds: 1F 1D **Baths:** 2 En
🛇 🅿 ⅙ 📺 📖 ዼ

Spaunton

SE7289   ⬛ *Blacksmiths Arms*

Holywell House, *Spaunton Bank Foot,
Spaunton, Appleton Le Moors, York,
YO62 6TR.*
C18th beamed cottage with large garden.
Open: All Year (not Xmas/New Year)
Grades: ETC 4 Diamond
01751 417624 Mrs Makepeace
D: £36.00 **S:** £18.00
Beds: 1D 1T 1S
🛇 (5) 🅿 (4) ⅙ 📺 ➤ 📖 Ⅴ ዼ

Staintondale

SE9998   ⬛ *Falcon*

Island House, *Island Farm,
Staintondale, Scarborough, N Yorks,
YO13 0EB.*
Space, tranquillity, relaxation, tennis,
snooker, on organic farm. Beautiful
countryside. **Open:** Easter to Nov
Grades: ETC 4 Diamond
01723 870249 M Clarke
maryattheisland@tinyworld.co.uk
D: £20.00–£25.00 **S:** £25.00–£27.00
Beds: 1T 2D **Baths:** 3 En
🛇 🅿 (6) ⅙ 📺 ➤ 📖 Ⅴ ዼ

Tofta Farm, *Staintondale, Scarborough,
N. Yorks, YO13 0EB.*
Beautiful modernised farmhouse in 1.5
acres landscaped gardens.
Open: All Year (not Xmas/New Year)
01723 870298 Mrs Dobson
D: £16.00–£22.00 **S:** £20.00
Beds: 1F 3D **Baths:** 1 En 1 Sh
🛇 🅿 📺 ✕ 📖 Ⅴ ዼ

Staithes

NZ7718   ⬛ *Fox & Hounds, Royal George*

Brooklyn, *Brown's Terrace, Staithes,
Saltburn-by-the-Sea, TS13 5BG.*
Sea-captains's house, central, but quiet,
in picturesque fishing village.
Open: All Year (not Xmas)
01947 841396 Ms Heald
D: £18.50 **S:** £18.50
Beds: 1T 2D **Baths:** 2 Sh
🛇 📺 ➤ 📖 Ⅴ ዼ

Springfields, *42 Staithes Lane, Staithes,
Saltburn-by-the-Sea, N Yorks, TS13 5AD.*
Victorian house with countryside views.
Lounge available. In National Park.
Open: All Year
Grades: ETC 3 Diamond
01947 841011 Mrs Verrill
D: £15.00 **S:** £15.00
Beds: 1D 1S **Baths:** 1 En 1 Sh
🅿 (1) ⅙ 📺 📖 ዼ

Black Lion Hotel, *High Street,
Staithes, Saltburn-by-the-Sea, N Yorks,
TS13 5BQ.*
Georgian coaching inn. Short breaks.
Open fires. Picturesque fishing village.
Open: All Year
01947 841132 Mr Stead
D: £22.50–£25.00 **S:** £22.50–£30.00
Beds: 4F 4D 1S **Baths:** 9 En
🛇 🅿 📺 ➤ ✕ Ⅴ ዼ

Stape

SE7993   ⬛ *Horseshoe Inn*

Seavy Slack Farm, *Stape, Pickering, N.
Yorks, YO18 8HZ.*
Comfortable farmhouse on a working
farm serving good food.
Open: All Year (not Xmas)
Grades: ETC 3 Diamond
01751 473131
Mrs Barrett
D: £20.00–£25.00 **S:** £25.00
Beds: 1T 2D **Baths:** 3 En
🛇 (5) 🅿 (6) 📺 ➤ ✕ 📖 Ⅴ ዼ

Starbotton

SD9574   ⬛ *Fox*

Fox & Hounds Inn, *Starbotton,
Skipton, N. Yorks, BD23 5HY.*
Traditional cosy Dales inn.
Open: Mar to Dec
01756 760269
Mr & Mrs McFadyen
Fax: 01756 760862
hilarymcfadyen@supanet.com
D: £27.50 **S:** £35.00
Beds: 1D 1T
🅿 (12) ⅙ 📺 ➤ ✕ 📖 Ⅴ ዼ cc

RATES

D = Price range per person
sharing in a double room
S = Price range for a
single room

Stearsby

SE6172   ⬛ *Abbey Inn, Durham Ox, Fauconberg
Arms, New Inn, Rose & Crown, White Bear, White
Dog, White Swan, Wombwell Arms*

The Granary, *Stearsby, Brandsby, York,
YO61 4SA.*
Open: All Year (not Xmas/New Year)
Grades: ETC 4 Diamond
01347 888652 (also fax) Mr & Mrs Turl
robertturl@thegranary.org.uk
D: £22.00–£25.00 **S:** £25.00–£30.00
Beds: 3D **Baths:** 3 En
🛇 🅿 (6) ⅙ 📺 ➤ 📖 ዼ
A converted C18th granary set in
beautiful 1-acre garden located in quiet
Yorkshire hamlet, nestling in the
Howardian Hills (only 5 miles from Castle
Howard) but only 12 miles from the
historic city of York.

Stockton-on-the-Forest

SE6555   ⬛ *Fox Inn*

Orillia House, *89 The Village, Stockton-
on-the-Forest, York, YO32 9UP.*
Comfortable sympathetically renovated
300-year-old farmhouse in village
location. **Open:** All Year
01904 400600 Mr Cundall
Fax: 01904 400101
orilla@globalnet.co.uk
D: £19.00–£21.00 **S:** £24.00–£26.00
Beds: 2F 3D 2T **Baths:** 7 Pr
🛇 🅿 (20) ⅙ 📺 📖 Ⅴ ዼ ৬

Stonegrave

SE6578   ⬛ *Malt Shovel*

Manor Cottage, *Stonegrave , York,
YO62 4LJ.*
Quiet friendly home offering comfortable
spacious accommodation and peaceful
garden. **Open:** All Year (not Xmas/New
Year) **Grades:** ETC 4 Diamond
01653 628599 Trudy Visser
gideon.v@virgin.net
D: £17.50–£20.00 **S:** £20.00–£25.00
Beds: 2T **Baths:** 2 En
🅿 (4) ⅙ 📺 📖 Ⅴ ዼ

Studley Roger

SE2870   ⬛ *Sawley Arms Sawley*

The Wheelhouse, *2 Parklands, Studley
Roger, Ripon, HG4 3AY.*
Renovated mmill next to Studley Royal
Oak Park and Fountains Abbey.
Open: All Year (not Xmas)
01765 604508 J Burton itis@itis.slv.co.uk
D: £23.00–£25.00
Beds: 1D **Baths:** 1 En
🛇 (8) 🅿 (4) ⅙ 📺 📖 Ⅴ ዼ

Sutton Bank

SE5182   ⬛ *Hambleton Inn, Hare Inn*

Cote Faw, *Hambleton Cottages, Sutton
Bank, Thirsk, N. Yorks, YO7 2EZ.*
Comfortable cottage in National Park,
central for visiting North Yorkshire.
Open: All Year (not Xmas)
01845 597363 Mrs Jeffray
D: £16.00–£17.00 **S:** £16.00–£17.00
Beds: 1F 1D 1S **Baths:** 1 Sh
🛇 🅿 (3) 📺 📖 Ⅴ ዼ

High House Farm, *Sutton Bank, Thirsk, N. Yorks, YO7 2HA.*
Family-run dairy farm set in open countryside in a tranquil part of W Yorks.
Open: Easter to Nov
01845 597557 Mrs Hope
D: £20.00–£25.00 **S:** £22.00–£26.00
Beds: 1F 1D **Baths:** 1 Sh
🛇 🅿 (6) 📺 ✕ 🏛 Ⅴ ♿

Sutton-in-Craven

SE0043

Ravenshill, *Holme Lane, Sutton-in-Craven, Keighley, W. Yorks, BD20 7LN.*
Attached house opposite village park. Warm welcome in family home.
Open: All Year (not Xmas)
01535 633276 (also fax)
Mrs Barwick-Nicholson
oftours@cwcom.net
D: £18.00–£20.00 **S:** £18.00–£20.00
Beds: 1D 1T 1S **Baths:** 1 Sh
🛇 (12) 🅿 (2) ✁ 📺 ✕ 🏛 Ⅴ ♿

Thimbleby

SE4495   ◖ *Golden Lion*

Stonehaven, *Thimbleby, Osmotherly, Northallerton, DL6 3PY.*
Comfortable farmhouse, super view, lovely walks, good beds and good food.
Open: Easter to Nov
Grades: ETC 3 Diamond
01609 883689 Mrs Shepherd
D: £18.00–£20.00 **S:** £20.00–£22.00
Beds: 1D 1T **Baths:** 1 Pr
🛇 (1) 🅿 (3) ✁ 📺 🏛 Ⅴ ♿ cc

Thirsk

SE4282   ◖ *Hambleton Inn, Hare Inn, Dog & Gun, Carpenters' Arms, Whitstoncliffe Hotel, Old Oak Tree, Golden Fleece, Darrowby Inn, Black Swan, Carpenters' Arms, Sheppards Table, George*

Town Pasture Farm, *Boltby, Thirsk, N. Yorks, YO7 2DY.*
Comfortable farmhouse in beautiful village, central for Yorkshire Dales.
Open: All Year (not Xmas)
Grades: ETC 3 Diamond
01845 537298 Mrs Fountain
D: £17.50–£19.50 **S:** £18.50–£20.00
Beds: 1F 1T **Baths:** 2 En
🛇 🅿 (3) 📺 ✕ 🏛 Ⅴ ♿

8a The Conifers, Ingramgate,
Thirsk, N. Yorks, YO7 1DD.
Beautiful Dower House built in 1850. 5 mins walk from market place.
Open: Jan to Dec
01845 522179 Mrs Lee
D: £15.00 **S:** £15.00
Beds: 1F 1D 1S **Baths:** 1 Sh
🛇 🅿 (3) 📺 🍴 🏛 ♿

Lavender House, *27 Kirkgate, Thirsk, N. Yorks, YO7 1PL.*
Base for touring Dales and Moors, next door to James Herriot Centre.
Open: All Year (not Xmas)
01845 522224 Mrs Dodds
D: £17.00 **S:** £17.00–£20.00
Beds: 2F 1S **Baths:** 2 Sh
🛇 🅿 (3) ✁ 📺 🏛 Ⅴ ♿

Station House, *Station Road, Thirsk, N. Yorks, YO7 4LS.*
Old station master's house retaining character of railways. Ideal base for touring Dales & Moors.
Open: Easter to Oct
01845 522063 Mrs Jones
D: fr £17.00 **S:** fr £21.00
Beds: 1F 1D **Baths:** 2 En
🛇 🅿 (6) ✁ 📺 🍴 🏛 Ⅴ ♿

Laburnham House, *31 Topcliff Rd, Thirsk, N. Yorks, YO7 1RX.*
Spacious detached house, tastefully furnished with antiques and in the traditional manner. **Open:** Easter to Nov
01845 524120 Mrs Ogleby
D: £19.00–£21.00 **S:** £25.00–£35.00
Beds: 1F 1D 1T **Baths:** 2 En 1 Pr
🛇 (5) 🅿 (3) ✁ 📺 🏛 ♿

Hambleton House, *78 St James Green, Thirsk, N Yorks, YO7 1AJ.*
Restored Victorian house (though parts date back to 1683) overlooking the green.
Open: Easter to Oct
01845 525532 Mr & Mrs Boumer
hambletonh@aol.com
D: £16.00–£20.00 **S:** £18.00–£25.00
Beds: 2D 1T **Baths:** 2 En 1 Pr
🛇 (10) 🅿 ✁ 📺 🏛 Ⅴ ♿

Thixendale

SE8461   ◖ *Cross Keys*

Manor Farm, *Thixendale, Malton, N. Yorks, YO17 9TG.*
Working farm. Private spacious accommodation, overlooking pretty garden. Substantial breakfasts.
Open: All Year (not Xmas/New Year)
01377 288315 (also fax) Mrs Brader
D: £20.00 **S:** £20.00
Beds: 2F 1D 1T 1S **Baths:** 1 Pr
🛇 🅿 ✁ 📺 ✕ 🏛 Ⅴ ♿

Thormanby

SE4974   ◖ *Carlton Inn*

The Old Rectory, *Thormanby, Easingwold, York, YO61 4NN.*
Early C18th Listed rectory in the heart of Yorkshire. **Open:** All Year (not Xmas)
01845 501417 Mrs Ritchie
D: £16.00–£18.00 **S:** £18.00
Beds: 1F 1D 1T **Baths:** 2 En 1 Sh
🛇 🅿 (6) 📺 🍴 🏛 Ⅴ ♿

Thornton le Dale

SE8382   ◖ *Buck, Hall, New Inn*

Nabgate, *Wilton Road, Thornton le Dale, Pickering, N. Yorks, YO18 7QP.*
Open: All Year
Grades: ETC 4 Diamond
01751 474279 Mrs Pickering
D: £18.00–£20.00 **S:** £18.00–£20.00
Beds: 2D 1T **Baths:** 3 En
🛇 🅿 (4) 📺 🍴 🏛 Ⅴ ♿
Situated on the edge of beautiful Thornton le Dale, in TV's heartbeat country, this clean and friendly home offers excellent Yorkshire breakfasts. Central for Moors, Coast, Steam railway, York, Castle Howard and Dalby forest. Garden for guest to relax in. Own keys.

Tangalwood, *Roxby Road, Thornton le Dale, Pickering, N. Yorks, YO18 7SX.*
Friendly comfortable accommodation, quietly situated. Ideal for York, Moors, Coast.
Open: Easter to Oct
Grades: ETC 3 Diamond
01751 474688 Mrs Wardell
D: £16.00–£19.00 **S:** £20.00–£25.00
Beds: 1D 1T **Baths:** 1 En 1 Sh
🛇 (7) 🅿 (2) 📺 🍴 🏛 Ⅴ ♿

Thornton Watlass

SE2385

Buck Inn, *Thornton Watlass, Ripon, N. Yorks, HG4 4AH.*
Open: All Year (not Xmas)
Grades: ETC 1 Star, AA 1 Star
01677 422461 Mr & Mrs Fox
Fax: 01677 422447
D: £26.00–£30.00 **S:** £32.00–£38.00
Beds: 1F 3D 2T 1S **Baths:** 5 En 1 Sh
🛇 🅿 (20) 📺 🍴 ✕ 🏛 Ⅴ ♿ ♿ cc
Delightful country inn overlooking the cricket green in a quiet village just five minutes from the A1. Relax in our comfortable bedrooms, enjoy our superb home-cooked food and drink from our selection of five real ales. Large secluded garden with children's playground.

Threshfield

SD9863   ◖ *Old Hall, Foresters*

Grisedale Farm, *Threshfield, Skipton, N Yorks, BD23 5NT.*
Friendly traditional Dales farmhouse near Grassington with beautiful rural location.
Open: All Year (not Xmas/New Year)
01756 752516 Mrs Kitching
janette.kitching@tesco.net
D: £15.00–£18.00 **S:** £20.00
Beds: 1T 1D **Baths:** 1 Sh
🛇 🅿 (2) 📺 🍴 🏛 ♿

Bridge End Farm, *Threshfield, Skipton, N Yorks, BD23 5NH.*
Aga cooking, large garden, fishing, snooker and music rooms.
Open: All Year (not Xmas)
01756 752463 Mrs Thompson
D: £22.00–£26.00 **S:** £23.00–£27.00
Beds: 1F 1D 1T 4S **Baths:** 6 En
🛇 🅿 (8) ✁ 📺 ✕ 🏛 Ⅴ ♿

Wath

SE3277

George Inn Hotel, *Wath, Ripon, N. Yorks, HG4 5EN.*
Friendly country inn set in picturesque village.
Open: All Year
01765 640202 (also fax)
D: £48.00–£55.00 **S:** £29.50–£32.50
Beds: 2F 1T 3D **Baths:** 6 En
🛇 🅿 ✁ 📺 🍴 ✕ 🏛 Ⅴ ♿ cc

All details shown are as
supplied by B&B owners in
Autumn 2000

Weaverthorpe

SE9670   Star Inn

The Star Inn, Weaverthorpe, Malton, N.
Yorks, YO17 8EY.
Country Inn, quiet locality fine food,
Traditional Ales and open log fires.
Open: All Year
Grades: ETC 3 Diamond
01944 738273 Mr Richardson
starinn@quista.net
D: £20.00–£26.00 **S:** £20.00–£26.00
Beds: 1F 1D 1T **Baths:** 3 En
⌂ (5) 🅿 (30) 📺 ✕ ▥ Ⓥ ♨ cc

Well

SE2682   Midland Arms, Black Horse

Upsland Farm, Lime Lane, Well, Bedale,
N. Yorks, DL8 2PA.
Beautiful house in Herriot and Heartbeat
Country.
Open: All Year (not Xmas)
Grades: ETC 4 Diamond, AA 5 Diamond
01845 567709 (also fax)
Mrs Hodgson
upsland@Btinternet.com
D: £25.00 **S:** £35.00
Beds: 1T 2D **Baths:** 3 En
⌂ 🅿 (4) ⌿ 📺 ✱ ✕ ▥ Ⓥ ♨

Rowan Rise, Mill Lane, Well, Bedale, N
Yorks, DL8 2RX.
Comfortable accommodation in
picturesque village between Yorkshire
Dales and Moors.
Open: All Year (not Xmas)
01677 470394
Mrs Welham
jill@welham.freeserve.co.uk
D: £15.00 **S:** £16.00
Beds: 1D 1T **Baths:** 1 Sh
⌂ (4) 🅿 (2) ♨ ▥ ♨

West Burton

SE0186

Grange House, Walden Head, West
Burton, Leyburn, DL8 4LF.
Choose how you spend your day - take to
the hills or take breakfast in bed.
Open: All Year (not Xmas)
01969 663641 (also fax)
Mrs Mort
D: £21.00–£25.00 **S:** £21.00
Beds: 1D 1T 1S **Baths:** 1 En 1 Pr
⌂ (12) 🅿 (3) 📺 ✕ ▥ Ⓥ ♨

West Heslerton

SE9176   Dawney Arms

The Old Rectory, West Heslerton,
Malton, North Yorkshire, YO17 8RE.
B&B in fine Georgian house set in 2 acres
of garden.
Open: All Year (not Xmas/New Year)
Grades: ETC 4 Diamond
01944 728285
Mr & Mrs Hillas
6hillas@netlineuk.net
D: £19.00–£21.00
S: £19.00–£21.00
Beds: 1F 1T 1D **Baths:** 3 En
⌂ 🅿 (10) ⌿ 📺 ✱ ▥ Ⓥ ♨ ☖ cc

Westow

SE7565   Blacksmiths Arms

Woodhouse Farm, Westow, York,
YO60 7LL.
Beautiful peaceful traditional farmhouse
with views. Home-made bread etc.
Open: May to Nov
01653 618378 (also fax)
Mrs Wardle
woodhousefarm@farmersweekly.net
D: £17.50–£20.00 **S:** £17.50–£20.00
Beds: 1F 1D **Baths:** 1 En 1 Sh
⌂ 🅿 (6) 📺 ▥ Ⓥ ♨

Whitby

NZ8910   Plough, Granby, Shepherd's Purse,
White House, Dolphin

Ryedale House, 154-8 Coach Road,
Sleights, Whitby, N. Yorks, YO22 5EQ.
Open: April to Oct **Grades:** ETC 4 Diamond
01947 810534 (also fax) Mrs Beale
D: £19.50–£21.00 **S:** £17.00–£22.00
Beds: 2D 2S **Baths:** 2 En 1 Pr
🅿 (3) ⌿ 📺 ▥ Ⓥ ♨ cc
National Park country 3.5 miles Whitby.
Magnificent moor/dale/coastal scenery.
Relaxing house for non-smokers, high
standard, private facilities with many
extras. Gardens, beautiful views, extensive
traditional/vegetarian breakfasts. Regret
no pets. Illustrated brochure with
pleasure. Min booking 2 nights.

Kirklands Hotel, 17 Abbey Terrace,
Whitby, North Yorkshire, YO21 3HQ.
Open: Feb to Nov
01947 603868 (also fax)
Mr Halton
D: £24.00 **S:** £35.00
Beds: 6F 3D 2T 1S **Baths:** 6 En 3 Pr 3 Sh
⌂ 📺 ✱ ▥ Ⓥ ♨
The Kirkland's is privately run, close to all
amenities, comfortable rooms (en suite)
some with private bathrooms, TVs, coffee
and tea faculties, an excellent breakfast.
Pets and schools welcome, easy access
to the North Yorks. Moors and villages
and other major Tourist attractions.

Arches Guest House, 8 Havelock
Place, Hudson Street, Whitby, YO21 3ER.
Open: All Year
01947 601880 Mr Brew
dickruthbrew@aol.com
D: £20.00–£22.00 **S:** £25.00–£32.00
Beds: 3F 3D 2T 6D **Baths:** 8 En 1 Pr 2 Sh
⌂ ⌿ 📺 ✱ ▥ Ⓥ ♨ ☖ cc
Friendly, family run guesthouse, where a
warm welcome and a large breakfast is
always assured. The ideal base for
experiencing the old world charms of this
historic seaside town, exploring the
beautiful North Yorkshire Moors or
walking the Cleveland Way.

Rosslyn Guest House, 11 Abbey
Terrace, Whitby, YO21 3HQ.
Quality accommodation at affordable
prices, close to harbourside and
moorlands.
Open: All Year (not Xmas)
01947 604086 (also fax) A Briers
D: £16.50–£18.50 **S:** £20.00
Beds: 2F 2D 1T 1S **Baths:** 5 En 1 Pr
⌂ 🅿 (2) 📺 ✕ ▥ ♨

Seaview Guest House, 5 East
Crescent, Whitby, N Yorks, YO21 3HD.
Open: All Year (not Xmas/New Year)
Grades: ETC 3 Diamond
01947 604462 L Boettger
cview@supanet.com
D: £19.00–£22.00 **S:** £19.00–£21.00
Beds: 1F 5D 2S **Baths:** 6 En 1 Sh
⌂ 📺 ✱ ▥ Ⓥ ♨
Family run guest house with high
standard of cleanliness. Close to beach
and town. Breakfast freshly cooked form
menu. Beautiful views of sea and abbey.

Falcon Guest House, 29 Falcon
Terrace, Whitby, N. Yorks, YO21 1EH.
Quiet private house near centre. Sunny
breakfast room, organic produce.
Open: All Year
01947 603507 Mr Lyth
D: £18.00 **S:** £20.00
Beds: 2F **Baths:** 1 Sh
⌂ ⌿ 📺 Ⓥ ♨

Havelock Guest House, 30 Hudson
Street, Whitby, YO21 3ED.
Conveniently situated for the spa, beach,
harbour and shops. Sauna available.
Open: All Year (not Xmas)
01947 602295 (also fax)
M J Ryder
D: £17.00–£19.50 **S:** £17.00
Beds: 2F 5D 1T 5S **Baths:** 7 En 2 Sh
⌂ 📺 ▥ Ⓥ ♨

Haven Guest House, 4 East Crescent,
Whitby, N. Yorks, YO21 3HD.
Comfortable friendly guest house with
sea views. Comprehensive breakfast
menu.
Open: Easter to Oct
01947 603842
Mrs Smith
D: £18.00–£24.00 **S:** £21.00–£23.00
Beds: 1F 5D 2S **Baths:** 5 En 1 Sh
⌂ (5) 📺 ▥ ♨

Arundel House Hotel, Bagdale,
Whitby, North Yorkshire, YO21 1QJ.
Manor house near town centre, private
parking, restaurant & bar.
Open: All Year
01947 603645 (also fax)
arundel_house@hotmail.com
D: £20.00–£25.00 **S:** £25.00–£35.00
Beds: 3F 5D 2T 1S **Baths:** 11 En
⌂ 🅿 (7) 📺 ✱ ✕ ▥ Ⓥ ✳ ♨ cc

Wrelton

SE7686

**The Huntsman Restaurant and
Guest House,** Main Street, Wrelton,
Pickering, N. Yorks, YO18 8PG.
Quiet village location, leading to
Rosedale foot of Yorkshire Moors.
Open: All Year
Grades: ETC 3 Diamond
01751 472530
Mr Lower
howard@thehuntsman.freeserve.co.uk
D: £16.00–£24.00
S: £18.00–£26.00
Beds: 1T 2D **Baths:** 3 En
⌂ 🅿 (2) 📺 ✱ ✕ ▥ Ⓥ ✳ ♨ cc

Yarm

NZ4112 ◆ Black Bull, New Cross Keys

2 Valley Close, Yarm, Cleveland, TS15 9SE.
Friendly, comfortable, modern, detached house in peaceful wooded surroundings.
Open: All Year (not Xmas)
01642 780633 Mrs Bond
D: £18.00–£25.00 **S:** £18.00–£25.00
Beds: 1T 2S 1D **Baths:** 1 En 1 Sh
⊃ (5) ▣ (2) ⊬ ⛨ ▥ Ⅴ ⚓

York

SE5951 ◆ Bootham Tavern, Churchill's, Cross Keys, Doormouse, Elliott's, Exhibition, Four Alls, Gimcrack, Golden Slipper, Grange Hotel, Haxby Court, Hole In The Wall, Mason's Arms, Ye Olde Punch Bowl, Plough, Plunkett's, Royal Oak, Rubicon, Shoulder Of Mutton, Tankard, Tom Cobley's, Wagon & Horses, Walnut Tree, Windmill, York Arms

The Hazelwood, 24-25 Portland Street, Gillygate, York, YO31 7EH.
Open: All Year
Grades: ETC 4 Diamond, AA 4 Diamond, RAC 4 Diamond
01904 626548 I A McNabb
Fax: 01904 628032
D: £32.50–£45.00 **S:** £35.00–£80.00
Beds: 2F 8D 3T 1S **Baths:** 14 En
⊃ (8) ▣ (10) ⊬ ⛨ ▥ Ⅴ ⚓ cc
Situated in the very heart of York in an extremely quiet residential area only 400 yards from York Minster & with its own car park, an elegant Victorian townhouse with individually styled ensuite bedrooms. Wide choice of quality breakfasts including vegetarian and croissants and Danish pastries. Non-smoking.

Holly Lodge, 206 Fulford Road, York, YO10 4DD.
Open: All Year
Grades: ETC 4 Diamond, AA 4 Diamond, RAC 4 Diamond
01904 646005 Mr Gallagher
D: £29.00–£34.00 **S:** £48.00–£58.00
Beds: 1F 3D 1T **Baths:** 5 En 5 Pr
⊃ (7) ▣ ⊬ ⛨ ▥ Ⅴ ⚓ cc
Ideally located 10 mins' riverside walk from the centre, convenient for all York's amenities. This fine Georgian building, with comfortable rooms, walled garden and car park, offers a warm welcome. Booking recommended. Located on A19,1.5 miles towards the city from A19/A64 intersection.

Ascot House, 80 East Parade, Heworth, York, YO31 7YH.
Open: All Year (not Xmas)
Grades: ETC 4 Diamond
01904 426826 Mrs Wood
Fax: 01904 431077
J&K@ascot-house-york.demon.co.uk
D: £21.00–£25.00 **S:** £20.00–£24.00
Beds: 3F 8D 3T 1S **Baths:** 12 En 1 Pr 1 Sh
⊃ ▣ (14) ⛨ ⊬ ▥ ⚓ cc
A family-run Victorian villa, built in 1869, with rooms of character and many four-poster or canopy beds. Superb English breakfasts. Fifteen minutes' walk to Jorvik Viking Centre, Castle Museum or York Minster. Residential licence, sauna, private enclosed car park.

Midway House Hotel, 145 Fulford Road, York, YO10 4HG.
Open: All Year
Grades: ETC 3 Diamond
01904 659272 (also fax)
P G Armitage
D: £18.00–£33.00 **S:** £18.00–£35.00
Beds: 4F 8D 1T 1S **Baths:** 12 En 2 Sh
⊃ ▣ (14) ⊬ ⛨ ▥ Ⅴ ⚓ cc
Built in 1897, an elegant late-Victorian detached villa close to the city centre, university and minutes from York's bypass. We are totally non-smoking with an informal, friendly atmosphere. Large on-site private garden & secluded gardens.

Feversham Lodge International Guest House, 1 Feversham Crescent, York, YO31 8HQ.
Open: All Year
Grades: ETC 3 Diamond
01904 623882 (also fax)
Mr & Mrs Lutyens-Humfrey
feversham@lutyens.freeserve.co.uk
D: £20.00–£32.00 **S:** fr £25.00
Beds: 2F 5D 2T 1S **Baths:** 7 En 1 Pr 2 Sh
⊃ ▣ (9) ⊬ ⛨ ▥ ❈ ⚓ cc
A former C19th Methodist manse with lovely En suite rooms, including 'Laura Ashley' style honeymoon room with four poster or canopy bed; still retains characteristic original features. York Minster views; fresh home cooked delicious breakfast served. Winter short breaks OK. Japanese/Chinese/Italian/French spoken.

Nunmill House, 85 Bishopthorpe Road, York, YO23 1NX.
Open: Feb to Nov
Grades: ETC 4 Diamond, AA 4 Diamond
01904 634047
Mr & Mrs Whitbourn-Hammond
Fax: 01904 655879
b&b@nunmill.co.uk
D: £25.00–£30.00
S: fr £45.00
Beds: 1F 6D 1T
Baths: 7 En 1 Pr
⊃ ▣ (6) ⊬ ⛨ ▥ Ⅴ ⚓
Splendid Victorian house, lovingly furnished & smoke-free, for those looking for comfortable yet affordable accommodation. Easy walk to all attractions. SAE for brochure.

Bowen House, 4 Gladstone Street, Huntington Road, York, YO31 8RF.
Open: All Year (not Xmas)
Grades: ETC 3 Diamond
01904 636881
Mrs Wood
Fax: 01904 338700
info@bowenhouse.co.uk
D: £18.50–£24.00
S: £23.00–£28.00
Beds: 1F 2D 1T 1S
Baths: 2 En 1 Sh
⊃ ▣ (4) ⊬ ⛨ ▸ ▥ ⚓ cc
Small, family-run, Victorian guest house with period furnishings throughout. Excellent traditional and vegetarian breakfasts with free-range eggs and home made preserves. Short stroll to York city centre. Private car park. Non smoking in all rooms. Brochure available.

Wold View House Hotel, 171-175 Haxby Road, York, YO31 8JL.
Open: All Year (not Xmas/New Year)
01904 632061 (also fax)
Mr & Mrs Wheeldon
D: £19.00–£26.00 **S:** £19.00–£26.00
Beds: 2F 2T 10D 3S **Baths:** 17 En
⊃ ▣ (1) ⛨ × ▥ Ⅴ ⚓
Turn of the century hotel, tea and coffee facilities, clock radio alarms, all ensuite, cosy licensed bar, evening meals available, 15 minutes walk York Minster. Handy for touring Moors and East Coast. Near Sustrans cycle track.

Barrington House, 15 Nunthorpe Avenue, York, YO23 1PF.
Lovely guesthouse near city centre, racecourse, station, theatres, parking.
Open: All Year (not Xmas/New Year)
Grades: ETC 3 Diamond
01904 634539
D: £17.00–£22.00 **S:** £17.00–£22.00
Beds: 2F 2T 2D 1S **Baths:** 7 En
⊃ ⛨ ▥ ⚓ ⚓ & cc

Cumbria House, 2 Vyner Street, Haxby Road, York, YO31 8HS.
Beautifully decorated family-run guest house. Private car park. Ideal for city centre & all attractions.
Open: All Year
Grades: ETC 3 Diamond, AA 3 Diamond
01904 636817 Mrs Clark
reservation@
cumbriahouse.freeserve.co.uk
D: £19.00–£25.00 **S:** £20.00–£25.00
Beds: 2F 2D 1T 1S **Baths:** 2 En 4 Sh
⊃ ▣ (5) ⛨ ▥ Ⅴ ⚓ cc

Grange Lodge, 52 Bootham Crescent, Bootham, York, YO30 7AH.
Lovely family run guest house.
Open: All Year **Grades:** ETC 1 Diamond
01904 621137 Mrs Robinson
grangeldg@aol.com
D: £16.00–£22.00 **S:** £18.00–£20.00
Beds: 2F 3D 1T 1S **Baths:** 1 En 5 Pr 2 Sh
⊃ ⛨ × ▥ Ⅴ

Ashbourne House, 139 Fulford Road, York, YO10 4HG.
Friendly family run Victorian establishment. Providing the highest of standards.
Open: All Year (not Xmas/New Year)
Grades: ETC 4 Diamond, AA 4 Diamond, RAC 4 Diamond
01904 639912 Mr & Mrs Minns
Fax: 01904 631332
ashbourneh@aol.com
D: £20.00–£30.00 **S:** £34.00–£40.00
Beds: 2F 2T 3D **Baths:** 6 En 1 Pr
⊃ ▣ (6) ⊬ ⛨ ▥ Ⅴ ⚓ cc

St Raphael Guest House, 44 Queen Annes Road, Bootham, York, YO30 7AF.
Family-run mock Tudor guest house, tastefully decorated.
Open: All Year
Grades: ETC 2 Diamond, AA 2 Diamond, RAC 2 Diamond
01904 645028 Mrs Foster
Fax: 01904 658788
straphael2000@yahoo.co.uk
D: £19.00–£25.00 **S:** fr £21.00
Beds: 3F 2D 1T 2S **Baths:** All En
⊃ ▣ (2) ⛨ ▸ ▥ ⚓ cc

Ivy House Farm, *Kexby, York, YO41 5LQ.*
C19th farmhouse, central for York, East
Coast, Dales, Herriot country.
Open: All Year (not Xmas)
Grades: AA 3 Diamond, RAC 3 Diamond
01904 489368 Mrs Daniel
D: £16.00–£20.00 **S:** £20.00–£22.00
Beds: 1F 1D 1T 1S **Baths:** 2 En 1 Sh
⏰ ℙ (10) 📺 ▥ Ⅴ ⚲

Ivy House Farm, *Kexby, York, YO41 5LQ.*
C19th farmhouse, central for York, East
Coast, Dales, Herriot country.
Open: All Year (not Xmas)
Grades: AA 3 Diamond, RAC 3 Diamond
01904 489368 Mrs Daniel
D: £16.00–£20.00 **S:** £20.00–£22.00
Beds: 1F 1D 1T 1S **Baths:** 2 En 1 Sh
⏰ ℙ (10) 📺 ▥ Ⅴ ⚲

Park View Guest House, *34
Grosvenor Terrace, Bootham, York,
YO30 7AG.*
Victorian town house close to centre.
Front rooms have views of Minister.
Open: All Year (not Xmas)
Grades: ETC 3 Diamond
01904 620437 (also fax) Mrs Ashton
park_view@talk21.com
D: £22.00–£25.00 **S:** £25.00–£30.00
Beds: 1F 3D 2T 1S **Baths:** 5 En 1 Pr
⏰ ⚲ 📺 ▥ Ⅴ ⚲

Bay Tree Guest House, *92
Bishopthorpe Road, York, YO23 1JS.*
Tastefully decorated Victorian town
house, ten minutes walk from attractions.
Open: all year (not Xmas)
Grades: ETC 3 Diamond
01904 659462 (also fax) Mr Ridley
d.ridley.baytree@ondigital.co.uk
D: £21.00–£24.00 **S:** £22.00
Beds: 1F 1D 1T 2S **Baths:** 2 En 1 Sh
⏰ (1) ⚲ 📺 ▥ Ⅴ ⚲

Georgian Guest House, *35 Bootham,
York, YO30 7BT.*
Quality city centre accommodation with
car park. **Open:** All Year (not Xmas)
Grades: ETC 3 Diamond, AA 3 Diamond,
RAC 3 Diamond
01904 622874 Mr Semple
Fax: 01904 635379
georgian.house@virgin.net
D: £18.00–£28.00 **S:** £18.00–£35.00
Beds: 2F 7D 2T 2S **Baths:** 11 En 2 Sh
⏰ (5) ℙ (8) ⚲ 📺 ▥ Ⅴ ⚲ CC

Cornmill Lodge, *120 Haxby Road, York,
YO31 8JP.*
Vegetarian/vegan guest house. 15 mins'
walk York Minster. **Open:** All Year
Grades: ETC 3 Diamond, AA 3 Diamond
01904 620566 (also fax) Mrs Williams
cornmillyork@aol.com
D: £20.00–£26.00 **S:** £20.00–£26.00
Beds: 2D 1T/F 1S **Baths:** 3 En 1 Pr
⏰ ℙ (4) ⚲ 📺 ▥ Ⅴ ⚲ CC

Newton Guest House, *Neville Street,
Haxby Road, York, YO31 8NP.*
Few minutes walk from city. Friendly
family run. Non smoking.
Open: All Year (not Xmas)
Grades: ETC 3 Diamond
01904 635627 Mrs Tindall
D: £19.00–£22.00 **S:** £20.00–£25.00
Beds: 1F 2D 1T 1S **Baths:** 4 En 1 Pr
⏰ ℙ (5) ⚲ 📺 ▥ Ⅴ ⚲

Kismet Guest House, *147 Haxby
Road, York, YO31 8JW.*
Comfortable Victorian residence, peaceful
location. Excellent views of the
surrounding fells. **Open:** All Year
01904 621056 B Chamberlain & N
Summers
kismetguesthouse@yahoo.com
D: £25.00–£30.00 **S:** £20.00–£25.00
Beds: 1F 1T 4D **Baths:** 1S
⏰ ℙ (6) ⚲ 📺 ✕ ▥ ⚲

Heworth Court Hotel, *76 Heworth
Green, York, YO31 7TQ.*
Established recommended hotel. Ample
parking, York Minster within 1 mile
Open: All Year **Grades:** ETC 2 Star, AA 2
Star, RAC 2 Star
01904 425156 Mr Smith
hotel@heworth.co.uk
D: £30.00–£52.50 **S:** £46.00–£65.00
Beds: 2F 5T 10D 8S **Baths:** 25 En
⏰ ℙ (25) ⚲ 📺 ✕ ▥ Ⅴ ✳ ⚲ CC

Chimney's Bed and Breakfast, *18
Bootham Cresent, York, YO30 7AH.*
Beautiful olde-worlde house, 5 minutes
walk from York Minster/ city walls.
Open: All Year **Grades:** ETC 3 Diamond
01904 644334
D: £18.00–£25.00 **S:** £18.00–£25.00
Beds: 2T 2D 1S
⏰ (10) ⚲ 📺 ▥ Ⅴ ⚹

Northholme Guest House, *114
Shipton Road, York, YO30 5RN.*
Open: All Year (not Xmas)
Grades: ETC 3 Diamond
01904 639132 J L Liddle
g.liddle@tesco.net
D: £14.50–£19.00 **S:** £17.00–£24.00
Beds: 1F 1D 2T 1S **Baths:** 3 En 1 Sh
⏰ ℙ (4) ⚲ 📺 ▥ Ⅴ ⚲
Our family run detached home, in a semi-
rural setting, is convenient for York city
centre and the ring road. We have
comfortable, spacious, ensuite rooms
with colour TV and welcome tray. Private
parking.

Bishopgarth Guest House, *3
Southlands Road, Bishopthorpe Road,
York, YO23 1NP.*
Open: All Year (not Xmas/New Year)
Grades: ETC 3 Diamond
01904 635220 Mrs Spreckley
D: £15.00–£23.00 **S:** £20.00–£46.00
Beds: 2F 2D 1T **Baths:** 5 En 2 Sh
⏰ ⚲ 📺 ✕ ▥ Ⅴ ⚲ CC
In a quiet Victorian terrace, just ten
minutes pleasant walk from York's
historic heart, Bishopgarth offers comfort,
cleanliness, excellent home cooking
(evening meals available in the winter),
unfailing courtesy and a warm Yorkshire
welcome from the locally born resident
owners.

Fairthorne, *356 Strenshall Road,
Earswick, York, YO32 9SW.*
Peaceful country setting, dormer
bungalow. 3 miles from York, easy reach
North Yorks Moors. **Open:** Dec to Dec
Grades: ETC 3 Diamond
01904 768609 (also fax) J W Harrison
D: £16.00–£20.00 **S:** £20.00
Beds: 1F 1D **Baths:** 1 En
⏰ ℙ (2) 📺 ▥ ⚲

Sagar B&B The Bungalow, *Kexby,
York, YO41 5LA.*
A modern bungalow, four miles east of
York on A1079.
Open: All Year (not Xmas)
01759 380247 Mrs Sagar
D: £18.00 **S:** £20.00
Beds: 1D 1T **Baths:** 2 En
⏰ ℙ (2) 📺 ▥ Ⅴ ⚲

The Bentley Hotel, *25 Grosvenor
Terrace, Bootham, York, YO30 7AG.*
Victorian town house overlooking York
Minster with personal attention and
home-from-home hospitality.
Open: Feb to Dec
Grades: ETC 4 Diamond
01904 644313 (also fax)
Mr Lefebve
p.a.lefebve@tecco.net
D: £20.00–£27.00 **S:** £25.00–£30.00
Beds: 3D 1T 2S **Baths:** 4 En 1 Sh
⏰ (10) ℙ (1) ⚲ 📺 ▥ ⚲

Abbeyfields Guest House, *19
Bootham Terrace, York, YO30 7DH.*
Lovely Listed Victorian guest house 5
minutes walk from city centre.
Open: Feb to Jan
Grades: ETC 3 Diamond
01904 636471 (also fax)
Mr Martin
info@abbeyfields.co.uk
D: £24.00–£26.00 **S:** £30.00–£33.00
Beds: 5D 1T 3S **Baths:** 8 En 1 Pr
⏰ (12) ℙ (4) ⚲ 📺 ▥ Ⅴ ⚲

The Racecourse Centre, *Tadcaster
Road, York, YO24 1QG.*
Superior budget accommodation for
groups only. Minimum of 10 people.
Open: All Year
01904 636553 Mr Patmore
Fax: 01904 612815
info@racecoursecentre.co.uk
D: £17.50–£19.50 **S:** £17.50–£24.50
Beds: 23F 12T 8S **Baths:** 7 Sh
⏰ ℙ (40) 📺 ✕ ▥ Ⅴ ⚹

Chelmsford Place Guest House, *85
Fulford Road, York, YO10 4BD.*
Victorian house, 300 yards from river, 5
mins walk to centre.
Open: All Year
Grades: ETC 3 Diamond
01904 624491
D: £17.00–£24.00 **S:** £17.00–£38.00
Beds: 2F 3D 2T 1S **Baths:** 6 En 1 Sh
⏰ ℙ ▥ Ⅴ ⚲ CC

Ashbury Hotel, *103 The Mount, York,
YO24 1AX.*
Elegant refurbished Victorian townhouse,
close to city centre. Ensuite facilities.
Open: All Year (not Xmas)
Grades: ETC 3 Diamond
01904 647339 (also fax)
Mrs Richardson
ashbury@talk21.com
D: £20.00–£27.50 **S:** £15.00–£25.00
Beds: 1F 3D 1T **Baths:** 5 Pr
⏰ ℙ ⚲ 📺 ▥ ⚲ CC

Planning a longer stay? Always
ask for any special rates

York Lodge Guest House, *64 Bootham Crescent, Bootham, York, YO30 7AH.*
Comfortable, relaxing accommodation, friendly service.
Open: All Year
01904 654289 Mr Moore
D: £20.00–£22.00 **S:** £20.00
Beds: 2F 3D 2T 1S **Baths:** 4 En 2 Sh
⌂ 📺 🛏 📖 Ⓥ ♨

City Guest House, *68 Monkgate, York, YO31 7PF.*
Five minutes' walk to Minster, car park, excellent value.
Open: All Year (not Xmas)
01904 622483
Mr & Mrs Robinson
D: £20.00–£27.00 **S:** £20.00–£27.00
Beds: 1F 4D 1T 1S **Baths:** 6 En 1 Pr
⌂ (5) 🅿 (5) ✂ 📺 📖 Ⓥ ♨ **cc**

Dairy Guest House, *3 Scarcroft Road, York, YO23 1ND.*
Beautiful appointed Victoria house.
Tasteful in many ways!
Open: Feb to Dec
01904 639367 Mr Hunt
D: £20.00–£25.00 **S:** £30.00–£40.00
Beds: 2F 2D 1T **Baths:** 2 Pr 1 Sh
⌂ ✂ 📺 🛏 📖 Ⓥ ♨ ♿

Dalescroft Guest House, *10 Southlands Road, Bishopthorpe Road, York, YO23 1NP.*
Warm welcome in family-run guest house, 10 mins from city & race course.
Open: All Year
01904 626801
Mrs Blower
D: £14.00–£22.00 **S:** £15.00–£20.00
Beds: 1F 2D 2T 1S **Baths:** 2 En 1 Pr
⌂ ✂ 📺 🛏 ✕ 📖 Ⓥ ♨

The Beckett, *58 Bootham Crescent, Bootham, York, YO30 7AH.*
Large Victorian house in city centre near Minster. Great breakfast.
Open: All Year
01904 644728 Mrs Brown
Fax: 01904 639915
abrownyork@aol.com
D: £25.00–£27.50 **S:** £23.00–£26.00
Beds: 1F 3D 2T 1S **Baths:** 5 En 1 Pr 1 Sh
⌂ 🅿 ✂ 📺 📖 Ⓥ ♨ **cc**

The Hollies, *141 Fulford Road, York, YO10 4HG.*
Distinctive Edwardian residence, recently refurbished to provide quality accommodation.
Open: All Year
01904 634279 Mrs Wise
Fax: 01904 625435
hollies.guest@cwcom.net
D: £18.00–£28.00 **S:** £18.00–£27.00
Beds: 1F 3D 1S **Baths:** 3 En 2 Sh
⌂ (5) 🅿 (5) ✂ 📺 📖 Ⓥ ♨ ♿ **cc**

Foss Bank Guest House, *16 Huntington Road, York, YO31 8RB.*
Small family-run Victorian house, 5 minutes walk from York Minster.
Open: Feb to Dec
01904 635548 D: £17.00–£20.00 **S:** £18.50–£22.00
Beds: 3D 1T 2S **Baths:** 2 En 2 Sh
⌂ 🅿 (5) ✂ 📺 🛏 📖 Ⓥ ♨

Gables Guest House, *50 Bootham Crescent, York, YO30 7AH.*
Valerie Lapworth extends a warm welcome to our home & historic city.
Open: All Year
01904 624381 (also fax)
D: £18.00–£27.00 **S:** £18.00–£28.00
Beds: 1F 2D 2T 1S **Baths:** 4 En 2 Sh
⌂ 🅿 📺 🛏 ✕ 📖 Ⓥ ♣ ♨

Bank House, *9 Southlands Road, York, YO23 1NP.*
5 minutes' walk to the city centre.
Comfortable Victorian house. Race course nearby.
Open: All Year
01904 627803 Mr Farrell
D: £16.00–£22.00 **S:** fr £20.00
Beds: 7F 2D 2T 3S **Baths:** 1 En 7 Pr 7 Sh
⌂ ✂ 📺 🛏 ✕ 📖 ♣ ♨

Bronte Guesthouse, *22 Grosvenor Terrace, Bootham, York, YO30 7AG.*
Family-run Victorian guest house, quietly but conveniently situated from the historic centre.
Open: All Year (not Xmas)
01904 621066 Fax: 01904 653434
100754.300@compuserve.com
D: £23.00–£30.00 **S:** £25.00–£35.00
Beds: 1F 1D 1T 2S **Baths:** 5 En
⌂ 🅿 (1) 📺 📖 Ⓥ ♨

Victoria Villa, *72 Heslington Road, York, YO10 5AU.*
The Victorian villa guest house is a beautiful Victorian town house.
Open: All Year
01904 631647
D: £15.00–£20.00 **S:** £16.00–£25.00
Beds: 1F 3D 1T 1S **Baths:** 2 Sh
⌂ 🅿 (1) 📺 🛏 📖 Ⓥ ♨

Tower Guest House, *2 Feversham Crescent, Wiggington Road, York, YO31 8HQ.*
Friendly family-run guest house, 10 mins walk to city centre, full English breakfast.
Open: All Year
01904 655571 toweryork@aol.com
D: £20.00–£25.00 **S:** £22.00–£30.00
Beds: 1F 3D 1T 1S **Baths:** 6 En
⌂ 🅿 (6) ✂ 📺 ✕ 📖 Ⓥ ♨ **cc**

South Yorkshire

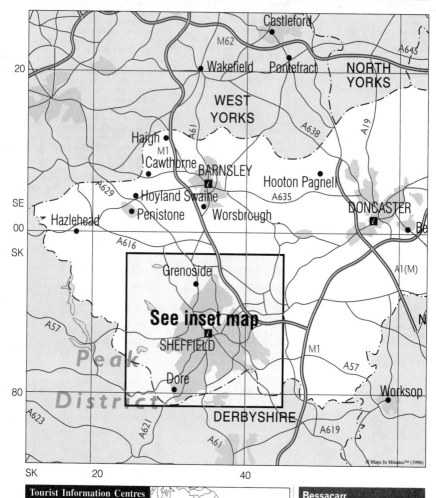

Tourist Information Centres

56 Eldon Street, **Barnsley**,
S.Yorks, S70 2JL, 01226 206757.

Central Library, Waterdale,
Doncaster, S.Yorks, DN1 3JE,
01302 734309.

Central Library, Walker Place,
Rotherham, S.Yorks, S65 1JH,
01709 823611.

Town Hall Extension, Union
Street, **Sheffield**, S1 2HH,
0114 273 4671 / 2.

Bessacarr

SE6101 🍽 *Hare and Tortoise, Punch' Hotel*

10 Saxton Avenue, *Bessacarr,*
Doncaster, South Yorkshire, DN4 7AX.
Open: All Year
01302 535578 A Gibbs
D: £18.00–£22.00 **S:** £22.50–£27.50
Beds: 2T 1D 1S **Baths:** 1 En 1 Sh
🅿 (2) ⌿ 📺 ✕ 🏢 Ⅴ 🍴
Friendly 1930 house, quiet, leafy
residential area. Near Dome, Racecourse.

All details shown are as
supplied by B&B owners in
Autumn 2000

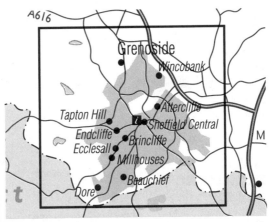

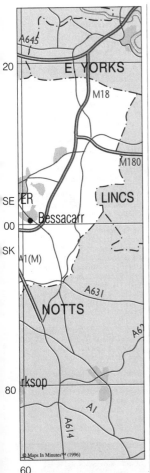

60

Cawthorne

SE2807   🍺 *Spencer Arms*

The Old Vicarage, *Cawthorne,*
Barnsley, S. Yorks, S75 4HW.
Luxurious accommodation in Georgian
vicarage, award-winning village.
Open: All Year (not Xmas)
01226 790063 Mr & Mrs Dorman
D: £25.00 **S:** £20.00–£25.00
Beds: 1F 1D 1T 1S **Baths:** 3 En 2 Pr 1 Sh
🛏 🅿 (5) ⚡ 📺 🔥 ✕ 🎱 �🅥 🛁

National Grid References are for

villages, towns and cities – not

for individual houses

Doncaster

SE5702   🍺 *Cumberland*

Earlesmere Guest House, *84 Thorne*
Road, Doncaster, S. Yorks, DN2 5BL.
Comfortable family-run guest house,
minutes from racecourse to town centre,
leisure centre.
Open: All Year
01302 368532
Mrs Barnes
D: £16.00–£20.00 **S:** £18.00–£25.00
Beds: 2F 1D 1T **Baths:** 1 En 1 Sh
🛏 🅿 (7) 📺 🔥 🎱 ⅴ 🛁

Dore

SK3181   🍺 *Hare & Hounds*

Critchleys, *6 Causeway Head Road,*
Dore, Sheffield, S17 3DJ.
A modern guest house near city and
country. Friendly, clean, excellent food
Open: All Year
0114 236 4328 (also fax)
Mr Critchleys
D: £17.50–£22.50
S: £25.00–£35.00
Beds: 1F 3D 3T 2S **Baths:** 5 En 3 Sh
🛏 (9) 🅿 (4) ⚡ 📺 🔥 🎱 ⅴ 🛁 & cc

Grenoside

SK3393   🍺 *Red Lion*

Middleton Green Farm, *Cinder Hill*
Lane, Grenoside, Sheffield, S35 8NH.
Luxurious C17th farm house. Your home
away from home.
Open: All Year
0114 245 3279 (also fax)
Ms Mennell
D: £22.00–£25.00 **S:** £30.00
Beds: 1D 2T 1S **Baths:** 3 Pr
🛏 🅿 (10) ⚡ 📺 🔥 🎱 ⅴ 🛁

Haigh

SE2912   🍺 *Old Post Office*

Old Haigh Cottage, *36 Jebb Lane,*
Haigh, Barnsley, South Yorkshire, S75 4BU.
Picturesque cottage in quiet lane next to
Yorkshire Sculpture Park.
Open: All Year
01924 830456
G Lees
geoff@twbooks.co.uk
D: £17.00–£18.50 **S:** £19.00–£20.50
Beds: 1F 1T 1D **Baths:** 1 Sh

Hazlehead

SE1800   🍺 *Dog & Partridge, Chase*

Delmont Grange, *Flouch, Hazlehead,*
Sheffield, S36 4HH.
Moorland views near 'Summer Wine'
country. Penistone market town.
Open: All Year
01226 767279
Mrs Cuss
nancuss@lineone.net
D: £22.50 **S:** £22.50
Beds: 1F 1T 1D **Baths:** 2 En
🛏 🅿 (8) ⅴ ✕ 🎱 ⅴ 🛁 &

Hooton Pagnell

SE4808

Rock Farm, *Hooton Pagnell, Doncaster,*
S. Yorks, DN5 7BT.
Traditional stone farmhouse in
picturesque village 2m NW of A1.
Open: All Year
Grades: ETC 3 Diamond
01977 642200 (also fax)
Mrs Harrison
D: £–£20.00 **S:** £18.00–£20.00
Beds: 1F 1D 1S **Baths:** 1 En1 Sh
🛏 🅿 (6) ⚡ 📺 🎱 🛁

Hoyland Swaine

SE2604   *Lord Nelson*

Fell House, *354 Barnsley Road, Hoylandswaine, Sheffield, S36 7HD.*
1830's cottage. Beautiful views, private suite to relax in comfort.
Open: All Year (not Xmas)
01226 790937 Ms Sykes
D: £18.00 **S:** £23.00
Beds: 1F **Baths:** 1 En
🛏 🅿 (2) 📺 🛏 📖 Ⅵ 🕭

Penistone

SE2403   *Fox House*

Millhouse Guest Centre, *Carr House Farm, Royd Lane, Penistone, Sheffield, S36 9NY.*
Converted barn in summer wine country overlooking open countryside.
Open: All Year (not Xmas)
01226 762917 Mr Worboys
mgc@wworboys.freeserve.co.uk
D: £12.50 **S:** £15.00
Beds: 1F 1D 1T **Baths:** 2 Sh
🛏 🅿 (4) ⚲ 📺 📖 🕭

Old Vicarage Guest House & Tea Rooms, *Shrewsbury Road, Penistone, Sheffield, S36 6DY.*
Situated in centre of Penistone, close to Pennine Way Trail.
Open: All Year
01226 376607 Mr Storer
Fax: 01226 766521
enquires@old vicarage.co.uk
D: £25.00–£55.00 **S:** £25.00–£45.00
Beds: 2F 4D 4S **Baths:** 5 En 5 Sh
🛏 🅿 (10) 📺 📖 🕭 ♿ cc

SHEFFIELD   Attercliffe

SK3788

Swan Hotel, *756 Attercliffe Road, Sheffield, S9 3RQ.*
Family-run hotel, close Sheffield city centre, next to Don Valley Stadium and Sheffield Arena.
Open: All Year
0114 244 7978 Fax: 0114 242 4928
swansheffield@btinternet.com
D: £17.50–£24.00 **S:** £25.00–£35.00
Beds: 4F 4D 4T 1S **Baths:** 10 En 3 Sh
🛏 🅿 (15) ⚲ 📺 🛏 📖 Ⅵ 🕭 cc

SHEFFIELD   Beauchief

SK3381   *Robin Hood, Millhouses, Waggon & Horses, White Swan*

Ashford, *44 Westwick Crescent, Beauchief, Sheffield, S8 7DH.*
Pleasant suburban home. Friendly, quiet, convenient, peak district city sports.
Open: All Year
Grades: ETC 3 Diamond
0114 237 5900 Mrs Sutton-Harvey
D: £18.00–£22.00 **S:** £18.00–£24.00
Beds: 1D 1T 1S/D **Baths:** 2 En 1Shared
🛏 (7) 🅿 (2) ⚲ 📺 ✕ 📖 🕭 ♿

SHEFFIELD   Brincliffe

SK3385   *Balter Tavern, Priory, Fox, Wagon & Horses, Robin Hood, Cross Pool*

Peace Guest House, *92 Brocco Bank, Hunters Bar, Sheffield, S11 8RS.*
B&B close to centre, university, hospitals. Friendly comfortable family run
Open: All Year
Grades: ETC 2 Diamond
0114 268 5110 Mr Manavi
D: £18.00–£40.00 **S:** £22.00–£27.00
Beds: 1F 2D 2T 3S **Baths:** 2 En 1 Pr 1 Sh
🛏 🅿 (6) ⚲ 📺 ✕ 📖 Ⅵ ✿ 🕭 cc

Hardwick House, *18 Hardwick Crescent, Sheffield, S11 8WB.*
Victorian house. Aga cooked breakfast. Free range eggs, own hens.
Open: All Year (not Xmas)
0114 266 1509
C.E Lennox
peter@lennox01.freeserve.co.uk
D: £21.00 **S:** £24.50
Beds: 1T, 2D **Baths:** 3 En,
🛏 🅿 (1) ⚲ 📺 📖 🕭

SHEFFIELD   Central

SK3586   *Robin Hood, Wagon & Horses, Millhouses, Priory, Fox, Cross Pool Tavern, Nag's Head*

Beech House, *44 Broomgrove Road, Sheffield, S10 2NA.*
Large homely Victorian house, close to universities, hospitals, Peak District.
Open: All Year (not Xmas)
0114 266 2537
Miss Boler
D: £19.50 **S:** £22.00
Beds: 1F 3D 3T 1S **Baths:** 2 Sh
🛏 (12) 🅿 (4) 📺 📖 Ⅵ 🕭

SHEFFIELD   Ecclesall

SK3284   *Prince Of Wales, Old Library, Cherry Tree, Robin Hood*

Hillside, *28 Sunningdale Mount, Ecclesall, Sheffield, S11 9HA.*
Your comfort is our interest. Quiet, modern, welcoming, close buses and town (2.5 miles).
Open: All Year
0114 262 0833
Mrs Whitehead
D: fr £19.00 **S:** fr £19.00
🛏 (1) 🅿 (2) ⚲ 📺 📖 🕭

Gulliver Bed & Breakfast, *167 Ecclesall Road South, Sheffield, S11 9PN.*
Victorian house in top residential area, near Peak District.
Open: All Year
0114 262 0729
Mrs Gulliver
D: £16.00 **S:** £16.00
Beds: 1D 1T 1S **Baths:** 1 Sh
🛏 (2) 🅿 (3) 📺 🛏 📖 Ⅵ

SHEFFIELD   Endcliffe

SK3286

Nini's Guest House, *41 Endcliffe Rise Road, Sheffield, S11 8RU.*
Family-run, offering a friendly and welcoming atmosphere. **Open:** All Year
0114 266 9114 A Kocura
D: £20.00 **S:** £22.00
Beds: 1D 2T 1S
🛏 (3) ⚲ 📺 🛏 📖 Ⅵ 🕭

SHEFFIELD   Millhouses

SK3283   *Robin Hood*

Tyndale, *164 Millhouses Lane, Sheffield, S7 2HE.*
Warm welcome awaits at clean, comfortable home in pleasant south-west of Sheffield. **Open:** All Year
0114 236 1660 Mr & Mrs Wilmshurst
D: £19.00 **S:** £19.00
Beds: 1F 1D 1S **Baths:** 1 Sh
🛏 (3) ⚲ 📺 🛏 📖 Ⅵ 🕭

SHEFFIELD   Tapton Hill

SK3286   *Crosspool Tavern*

St Pellegrino Hotel, *2 Oak Park, Sheffield, S10 5SD.*
Friendly, family-run hotel. Situated near to the centre of Sheffield.
Open: All Year **Grades:** ETC 2 Diamond
0114 268 1953 A Lawera
Fax: 0114 266 0151
D: £25.00–£35.00 **S:** £24.00–£35.00
Beds: 5F 2D 3T 4S **Baths:** 1 En 5 Pr 3 Sh
🛏 🅿 (20) ⚲ 📺 ✕ 📖 Ⅵ

SHEFFIELD   Wincobank

SK3891   *Robin Hood, Wagon & Horses, Priory, Fox, Cross Pool Tavern, Crown Inn*

Crown Inn, *21 Meadow Hall Road, Sheffield, South Yorkshire, S9 1BS.*
Modern family-run inn. **Open:** All Year
0114 243 1319 Mr Layne
D: fr £20.00 **S:** fr £20.00
Beds: 4T 1S
🛏 (8) 🅿 (8) 📺 ✕ 📖 🕭

Worsbrough

SE3503   *Button Mill*

The Button Mill Inn, *Park Road, Worsbrough, Barnsley, South Yorkshire, S70 5LJ.*
Open: All Year (not Xmas)
01226 282639 (also fax) Mr Loftus
D: fr £22.50 **S:** fr £25.00
Beds: 1F 1D 3T 2S **Baths:** 7 Pr
🛏 (14) 🅿 (60) ⚲ ✕ 📖 Ⅵ 🕭 ♿ cc
Olde Worlde Inn opposite Worsborough Country Park and Mill. Fishing reservoir and public walkways in walking distance. Comfortable rooms with televisions. Good food cooked fresh. Large menu to choose from. Vegetarian meals. Large wine list. Good selection of cask beers.

Stilwell's Britain: Hostels & Camping 2001

It's a great new idea! Hostels, camping barns, bunk houses **and** camping sites all in one user-friendly book. From now on, campers, tourers, backpackers, clubs and groups – anyone looking for low-cost and group accommodation – can find the right place to sleep for the right price by consulting the right guide – **Stilwell's Britain: Hostels & Camping 2001**.

Listings in **Stilwell's Britain: Hostels & Camping 2001** are arranged geographically by country, county and location throughout England, Scotland and Wales. Each entry includes tariffs, facilities, opening times and a brief description of the premise, it's location and surroundings. Many are accompanied by a picture of the site. The average charge per person per night is £8. As wi`th all Stilwell guides, the book contains local maps, grid references and listings of Tourist Information Centres. There's air, rail, bus and ferry information, too.

Whether you're traveling alone or in a group, you can plan your trip with a minimum of fuss with **Stilwell's Britain: Hostels & Camping 2001**.

£6.95 from all good bookstores (ISBN 1-900861-20-8) or £7.95 (inc p&p) from Stilwell Publishing Ltd, 59 Charlotte Road, London EC2A 3QW (020 7739-7179)

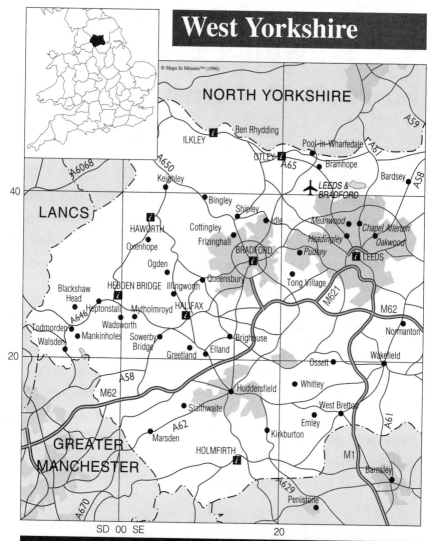

West Yorkshire

© Maps In Minutes™ (1996)

NORTH YORKSHIRE

ILKLEY · Ben Rhydding
Pool-in-Wharfedale
OTLEY · Bramhope
A65
Bardsey
Keighley
LEEDS &
BRADFORD
40 · Bingley
Shipley
LANCS · Idle
Meanwood · Chapel Allerton
HAWORTH · Cottingley · Headingley · Oakwood
Oxenhope · Frizinghall · Pudsey · LEEDS
BRADFORD
Ogden
HEBDEN BRIDGE · Illingworth · Queensbury · Tong Village
Blackshaw · M621
Head · M62
Heptonstall · Mytholmroyd · HALIFAX
Todmorden · Wadsworth · Normanton
Walsden · Mankinholes · Sowerby · Brighouse
Bridge · Elland
Greetland
20 · Ossett · Wakefield
M62 · A58
Huddersfield · Whitley
Slaithwaite · West Bretton
Emley · A61
A62 · Kirkburton
Marsden · M1
GREATER · HOLMFIRTH
MANCHESTER · Barnsley
A670 · A629
Penistone

SD 00 SE   20

Tourist Information Centres

National Museum of Photography, Film & TV,
Princes View, **Bradford**, W.Yorks, BD5 0TR,
01274 753678.

2 Victoria Road, Saltaire Village, **Bradford**,
BD18 3LA, 01274 774993.

Piece Hall, **Halifax**, W.Yorks, HX1 1RE,
01422 368725.

2-4 West Lane, **Haworth**, Keighley, W.Yorks,
BD22 8EF, 01535 642329.

1 Bridge Gate, **Hebden Bridge**, W.Yorks,
HX7 8EX, 01422 843831.

3-5 Albion Street, **Huddersfield**, W.Yorks,
HD1 2NW, 01484 223200.

Station Road, **Ilkley**, W.Yorks, LS29 8HA,
01943 602319.

Regional Travel Centre, City Station, **Leeds**,
LS1 1PL, 0113 242 5242.

Council Offices, 8 Boroughgate, **Otley**, W.Yorks,
LS21 3AH, 0113 247 7707.

15 Burnley Road, **Todmorden**, OL14 7BU,
01706 818181.

Town Hall, Wood Street, **Wakefield**, W.Yorks, WF1
2HQ, 01924 305000 / 1.

Council Offices, 24 Westgate, **Wetherby**, W.Yorks,
LS22 4NL, 01937 582706.

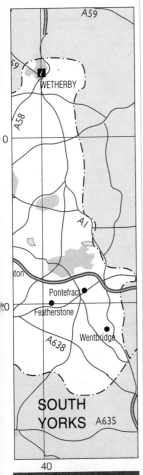

A59

WETHERBY

A58

0

A1

ton

Pontefrac

Featherstone

Wentbridge

A638

**SOUTH
YORKS** A635

40

Bardsey

SE3643 🍺 *Bingley Arms*

Gables B&B, *Mill Lane, Bardsey, Leeds, West Yorkshire, LS17 9AN.*
Open: All Year (not Xmas)
01937 574163 Mr & Mrs Gregory
D: £20.00–£24.00 **S:** £22.00–£27.00
Beds: 3D 1T 2S **Baths:** 1 En 2 Sh
🛏 🅿 (6) ⅒ 📺 🛉 🎟 🖲 🕯
Distinctive detached family home, in half acre gardens, offers friendly hospitality for any visitors to North Leeds, immediately adjacent extensive nature reserve, country walks. 4 miles Harewood House. 4 miles Wetherby. 4 miles several premier W Yorks golf courses.

Planning a longer stay? Always ask for any special rates

Ben Rhydding

SE1347

1 Tivoli Place, *Ben Rhydding, Ilkley, West Yorkshire, LS29 8SU.*
Conveniently situated in the lovely town of Ilkley. Easy walking distance to station, moor. **Open:** All Year
01934 609483 Fax: 01943 600320
D: £25.00 **S:** £30.00
Beds: 1F 2D 1T **Baths:** 3 En 1 Pr
⅒ 📺 🖲 🗙 🖦 🖲 🕸 🕯 cc

Bingley

SE1139 🍺 *Fishermans, Sun, Victoria*

March Cote Farm, *Woodside Avenue, Cottingley, Bingley, W. Yorks, BD16 1UB.*
A friendly welcome awaits you in our fully modernised farmhouse. **Open:** All Year
01274 487433 Mrs Warin **Fax: 01274 488153**
jeanwarin@nevisuk.net
D: £20.00–£25.00 **S:** £22.00–£25.00
Beds: 1F 2D **Baths:** 2 En 1 Pr
🛏 🅿 (6) 📺 🗙 🖦 🖲 🕯

Ashley End, *22 Ashley Road, off Ashfield Crescent, Bingley, W. Yorks, BD16 1DZ.*
Quiet, private house 5 miles Bradford; near main bus routes.
Open: All Year (not Xmas)
Grades: ETC 3 Diamond
01274 569679 Mrs Robertson
D: £18.00–£19.00 **S:** £18.00–£19.00
Beds: 1T 2S **Baths:** 1 Sh
🛏 (4) ⅒ 📺 🖦 🖲 🕯

Blackshaw Head

SD9527 🍺 *Shoulder Of Mutton, Sportsman, New Delight*

Badger Fields Farm, *Badger Lane, Blackshaw Head, Hebden Bridge, W. Yorks, HX7 7JX.*
Amidst beautiful gardens, spectacular views, 2 miles from Hebden Bridge.
Open: All Year **Grades:** ETC 3 Diamond
01422 845161 Mrs Whitaker
D: £19.00–£20.00 **S:** £20.00–£22.00
Beds: 1F 1D **Baths:** 1 Sh
🛏 🅿 (3) ⅒ 📺 🛉 🖦 🖲 🕯 🕭

Higher Earnshaw, *Blackshaw Head, Hebden Bridge, W. Yorks, HX7 7JB.*
Family smallholding, comfortable old farmhouse in lovely countryside. Warm welcome.
Open: All Year (not Xmas/New Year)
01422 844111 Mr & Mrs Redmond
D: £20.00 **S:** £21.00
Beds: 1F 1D 1S **Baths:** 1 Sh
🛏 🅿 (4) ⅒ 📺 🛉 🖦 🕯

Bradford

SE1632 🍺 *Brown Cow, Westleigh Hotel*

Carnoustie, *8 Park Grove, Bradford, W. Yorks, BD9 4JY.*
Detached Victorian house near Lister park and University Management centre.
Open: All Year **Grades:** ETC 3 Diamond
01274 490561 (also fax) Mr Sugden
D: £19.00–£21.00 **S:** £25.00–£27.00
Beds: 1D 1T 1S **Baths:** 3 En
🛏 🅿 (1) 📺 🖦 🖲 🕯

Prince of Wales, *91 Harrogate Road, Eccleshill, Bradford, West Yorkshire, BD2 3ES.*
Warm friendly pub 10 mins from Bradford, 15 mins Leeds, 10 mins Leeds-Bradford Airport.
Open: All Year
01274 638729 Mr Peat
D: £15.00–£25.00 **S:** £15.00–£25.00
Beds: 1F 3D 3T 1S **Baths:** 4 En 4 Sh
🛏 (1) 🅿 (30) 📺 🛉 🗙 🖦 🖲 🕯 🕭 cc

Ivy Guest House, *3 Melbourne Place, Bradford, W. Yorks, BD5 0HZ.*
Victorian house close to university, town, theatres & National Museum of Film, Photography & Television.
Open: All Year
Grades: ETC 2 Diamond
01274 727060 Mr Baggio
Fax: 01274 306347
101524,3725@compuserve.com
D: £17.00 **S:** £20.00
Beds: 3D 3T 2S **Baths:** 3 Sh
🛏 🅿 (10) 📺 🗙 🖦 🖲 🕯 cc

New Beehive Inn, *Westgate, Bradford, W. Yorks, BD1 3AA.*
Unique Edwardian traditional gaslit inn, centrally situated, good value.
Open: All Year
01274 721784 Mr Wagstaff
D: £19.00–£22.00 **S:** £22.00–£28.00
Beds: 3F 4D 4T 2S **Baths:** 9 En
🛏 🅿 (14) ⅒ 📺 🛉 🗙 🖦 🖲 🕯 cc

Bramhope

SE2543 🍺 *White Hart*

The Cottages, *Moor Road, Bramhope, Leeds, LS16 9HH.*
Old cottages, furnished to a high standard, fringe of village.
Open: All Year (not Xmas)
Grades: ETC 4 Diamond Silver
0113 284 2754 Mrs Adams
D: £23.00 **S:** £35.00
Beds: 4D 1T **Baths:** 5 En
🛏 (10) 🅿 (5) ⅒ 📺 🖦 🕯

Brighouse

SE1423

Lane Head Hotel, *2 Brighouse Wood Lane, Brighouse, Huddersfield, HD6 2AL.*
A renovated C17th coaching inn retaining many original features. **Open:** All Year
01484 714108 Mr & Mrs Mccue
Fax: 01484 380540
D: £20.00–£23.50 **S:** £29.38–£35.25
Beds: 10D 4T **Baths:** 14 En
🛏 🅿 ⅒ 📺 🛉 🗙 🖦 🖲 🕯 cc

Cottingley

SE1137 🍺 *Sun Inn, Victoria*

March Cote Farm, *Woodside Avenue, Cottingley, Bingley, W. Yorks, BD16 1UB.*
A friendly welcome awaits you in our fully modernised farmhouse. **Open:** All Year
01274 487433 Mrs Warin
Fax: 01274 488153
jeanwarin@nevisuk.net
D: £20.00–£25.00 **S:** £22.00–£25.00
Beds: 1F 2D **Baths:** 2 En 1 Pr
🛏 🅿 (6) 📺 🗙 🖦 🖲 🕯

Elland

SE1121

Pinfold Guest House, *Dewsbury Road, Elland, West Yorkshire, HX5 9JU.*
Recently refurbished Victorian coaching inn. warm and homely atmosphere.
Open: All Year
01422 372645 Mr & Mrs Parr
parr-pinfold@lineone.net
D: £19.00 **S:** £26.00
Beds: 1F 1D 2T 3S **Baths:** 7 En
🛏 🅿 (10) 📺 ✕ 🎗 🗊 ❋ 🛎

Emley

SE2413 🍺 *Green Dragon, White Horse, Three Acres*

Thorncliffe Farmhouse, *Thorncliffe Lane, Emley, Huddersfield, West Yorkshire, HD8 9RS.*
Rural C18th stone farmhouse on Kirklees Way. Close M1 (J38).
Open: All Year (not Xmas)
Grades: ETC 3 Diamond
01924 848277 Mrs Judd
D: £17.50–£20.00 **S:** £19.50–£25.00
Beds: 2T **Baths:** 2 En 1 Pr
🅿 (4) 📺 ✕ 🗊 🛎 ♿

Featherstone

SE4219 🍺 *Sun Inn*

Rolands Croft Guest House,
Rolands Croft, Featherstone, Pontefract, W Yorks, WF7 6ED.
A barn conversion overlooking fields & next to pub with meals at great prices.
Open: All Year
Grades: ETC 2 Star
01977 790802 Mr Sutton
D: £39.00–£44.00 **S:** £27.00
Beds: 1F 2T 1D 1S
🛏 🅿 ✗ 📺 🎗 🗊 ❋ 🛎 ♿ cc

Frizinghall

SE1435

Park Grove Hotel, *28 Park Grove, Frizinghall, Bradford, BD9 4JY.*
Quietly positioned, Victorian style, situated 2 minutes from city centre.
Open: All Year
Grades: ETC 2 Star, AA 2 Star
01274 543444 Mr Singh
Fax: **01274 495619**
enquiry@parkgrovehotel.co.uk
D: £25.00–£30.00 **S:** £40.00–£47.00
Beds: 2F 9D 2T 2S **Baths:** 15 En
🛏 🅿 (9) 📺 🗊 🗊 ❋ 🛎 cc

Greetland

SE0821 🍺 *Sportsmans Inn, Griffin Inn*

Crawstone Knowl Farm, *Rochdale Road, Greetland, Halifax, W. Yorks, HX4 8PX.*
Large comfortable Pennine farmhouse, convenient for Halifax Huddersfield and Dales.
Open: All Year
Grades: ETC 3 Diamond
01422 370470 Mrs Shackleton
D: £16.00–£20.00 **S:** £16.00–£20.00
Beds: 1F 1D 1T **Baths:** 3 En
🛏 🅿 (7) 🎗 📺 🎗 ✕ 🗊 🛎

Winchester, *4 Minster Close, Greetland, Halifax, West Yorkshire, HX4 8QW.*
Scenic views overlooking golf course. Private parking near Calderdale Way.
Open: All year
01422 377005 Mrs Wadsworth
D: £16.00–£20.00
Beds: 1D 2T **Baths:** 1 En 1 Sh
🛏 (3) 🅿 (3) 🎗 📺 🗊 🛎

Halifax

SE0925 🍺 *Stafford Arms*

Heathleigh Guest House, *124 Skircoat Road, Halifax, West Yorkshire, HX1 2RE.*
A beautiful Victorian house offering a warm welcome, comfortable beds and a delicious breakfast.
Open: All Year **Grades:** ETC 3 Diamond
01422 323957 Ms Eccles
D: £20.00 **S:** £20.00–£25.00
Beds: 1F 1D 2S **Baths:** 2 En 1 Pr 1 Sh
🛏 🅿 (2) 🎗 📺 🗊 🛎

The Rockhollow, *5 Causeway Foot, Ogden, Halifax, HX2 8XX.*
Open: All Year (not Xmas)
Grades: ETC 3 Diamond
01422 248049 (also fax) Mr Dennis
the-rockhollow@dial.pipex.com
D: £17.50 **S:** £17.50
Beds: 1D 1T 1S **Baths:** 1 En 1 Sh
🛏 🅿 (6) 📺 ✕ 🗊 🛎 cc
Set in open countryside, close to Halifax, Haworth, Bradford and Leeds. We offer spacious. well-appointed rooms, superb breakfasts. Very close to delightful walks round Ogden water, Yorkshire dales and York 1.5 hours away.

Field House, *Staups Lane, Stump Cross, Halifax, West Yorkshire, HX3 6XW.*
Charming Listed country farmhouse in the picturesque Shibden Valley.
Open: All Year (not Xmas/New Year)
Grades: ETC 4 Diamond
01422 355457 Mr Taylor
stayatfieldhouse@yahoo.co.uk
D: £20.00–£25.00 **S:** £25.00–£30.00
Beds: 2T 1D **Baths:** 2 En 1 Pr
🛏 (3) 🅿 (6) 🎗 📺 🎗 🗊 🛎 cc

Haworth

SE0337 🍺 *Silent Inn*

The Old Registry, *4 Main Street, Haworth, Keighley, West Yorkshire, BD22 8DA.*
Victorian guesthouse, where courtesy and charm extend, four poster beds, ensuite rooms. **Open:** All Year
01535 646503 Mrs Herdman
D: £18.00–£25.00 **S:** £18.00–£30.00
Beds: 1F 3T 5D 1S **Baths:** 9 En 1 Pr
🅿 🎗 📺 ✕ 🗊 ❋ 🛎 cc

Kershaw House, *90 West Lane, Haworth, Keighley, West Yorkshire, BD22 8EN.*
Situated on the edge of the moors, in the heart of Bronte country.
Open: All Year (not Xmas)
Grades: ETC 4 Diamond
01535 642074
kershawhouse.guesthouse@talk21.com
D: £20.00 **S:** £25.00
Beds: 1T 2D 1S **Baths:** 3 En 1 Pr
🅿 (4) 🎗 📺 🗊 🛎

Hebden Bridge

SD9927 🍺 *Stubbing Wharf, White Lion, White Swan, Hinchliffe Arms, Shoulder Of Mutton, Sportsman*

Myrtle Grove, *Old Les Road, Hebden Bridge, West Yorkshire, HX7 8HL.*
Open: All Year
01422 846078 Mrs Audsley
D: £20.00–£30.00 **S:** £25.00–£35.00
Beds: 1F 1D **Baths:** 1 En 1 Sh
🛏 🅿 (1) 🎗 📺 🎗 🗊 ❋ 🛎
Homely stone cottage overlooking Hebden Bridge with scenic views of the Calder Valley. Self contained, ensuite comfortable double room. CH, TV, tea coffee facilities, non smoking. Vegetarian food a speciality. Perfect location for walking and relaxing.

8 Birchcliffe (off Sandy Gate),
Hebden Bridge, West Yorkshire, HX7 8JA.
Stone cottage, close town centre, overlooking Calderdale valley. Continental breakfast.
Open: All Year
Grades: ETC 3 Diamond
01422 844777 Ms Handley
D: fr £15.00
Beds: 1D **Baths:** 1 En
🅿 (1) 📺 🗊 🛎 ♿

1 Primrose Terrace, *Hebden Bridge, W. Yorks, HX7 6HN.*
Pleasant Canal side location. In easy reach of town centre.
Open: All Year
Grades: ETC 2 Diamond
01422 844747 Ms McNamee
D: £–£32.00 **S:** £–£16.00
Beds: 1D 1S **Baths:** 1 Sh
🅿 (1) 📺 🗊 🛎

Higher Earnshaw, *Blackshaw Head, Hebden Bridge, W. Yorks, HX7 7JB.*
Family smallholding, comfortable old farmhouse in lovely countryside. Warm welcome.
Open: All Year (not Xmas/New Year)
01422 844117 Mr & Mrs Redmond
D: £20.00 **S:** £21.00
Beds: 1F 1D 1S **Baths:** 1 Sh
🛏 🅿 (4) 🎗 📺 🎗 🗊 🛎

Hebden Lodge Hotel, *6-10 New Road, Hebden Bridge, West Yorkshire, HX7 8AD.*
In the centre of Hebden Bridge overlooking the marina.
Open: All Year
01422 845272
D: £25.00–£35.00 **S:** £25.00–£45.00
Beds: 1F 7D 4T 2S **Baths:** 14 En
🛏 🎗 📺 🎗 ✕ 🗊 🛎 ❋ 🛎 cc

Hinchliffe Arms, *Cragg Vale, Hebden Bridge, HX7 5TA.*
Warm welcome in the idyllic valley of Cragg Vale.
Open: All Year
01422 883256 (also fax)
phil.chaplin@ukonline.co.uk
D: £20.00–£27.00 **S:** £30.00–£36.00
Beds: 3D **Baths:** 3 En
🅿 (30) 🎗 📺 ✕ 🗊 🛎 cc

Heptonstall

SD9728

Poppyfields House, *29 Slack Top, Heptonstall, Hebden Bridge, West Yorkshire, HX7 7HA.*
Open: All Year
Grades: ETC 3 Diamond
01422 843636 Mrs Simpson
Fax: 01422 845621
D: £19.00–£22.00 **S:** £22.00–£25.00
Beds: 1F 1D **Baths:** 2 En
🛇 🅿 (4) ⚡ �📺 🍴 🏵 Ⅲ. Ⓥ 🛁
Pennine house set amidst the dramatic hills of Calderdale. Wooded valley's, tumbling streams and Pennine Calderdale Way's close by. First class warm hospitality, friendly atmosphere, high standard of comfort, hearty breakfasts. Easy access by bus-rail-car-foot.

Holmfirth

SE1408 🍺 *Victoria Inn, Royal Oak, Old Bridge*

Holme Castle Country Hotel,
Holme Village, Holmfirth, Huddersfield, W. Yorks, HD7 1QG.
Open: All Year
Grades: AA 4 Diamond
01484 680680 Ms Hayfield
Fax: 01484 686764
jill.hayfield@virgin.net
D: £27.50–£37.50 **S:** £35.00–£55.00
Beds: 1F 2T 4D 1S **Baths:** 5 Pr 1 Sh
🛇 🅿 (12) ⚡ 📺 ╳ Ⅲ. Ⓥ 🛁 cc
Unusual mill house in Peak Park. 8 unique bedrooms, splendid views. Oak panelling, antiques, open fires. Hospitality, delicious fresh food, world wines. 'Room with a view' gallery cafe. Meetings, celebrations, midweek offers. Established 1983. A6024 2.5 miles SW Holmfirth.

Springfield House, *95 Huddersfield Road, Holmfirth, Huddersfield, W. Yorks, HD7 1JA.*
Victorian house on bus route in 'Last of the Summer Wine' town.
Open: All Year
Grades: ETC 3 Diamond
01484 683031 (also fax)
Mr Brook
ann_brook@hotmail.com
D: £16.00–£18.50 **S:** £21.00–£24.00
Beds: 2F 1D 1T **Baths:** 2 En 1 Sh
🛇 🅿 (2) ⚡ 📺 🍴 Ⅲ. Ⓥ 🛁

Valley Guest House, *97 Huddersfield Road, Holmfirth, Huddersfield, W. Yorks, HD7 1JA.*
Comfortable warm spacious Georgian residence, near M1 and M62 network.
Open: All Year
01484 681361 Mr & Mrs Kilner
D: £17.00–£19.00 **S:** £23.00–£26.00
Beds: 1F 1D 1T **Baths:** 2 En 1 Sh
🛇 🅿 (3) ⚡ 📺 Ⅲ. Ⓥ 🛁

National Grid References are for villages, towns and cities – not for individual houses

Huddersfield

SE1416

Ashfield Hotel, *93 New North Road, Huddersfield, HD1 5ND.*
Family business - friendly atmosphere with great food and Sky TV.
Open: All Year (not Xmas)
01484 425916 Mrs Ockenden
Fax: 01484 537029
D: £17.00–£25.00 **S:** £20.00–£35.00
Beds: 5F 5D 2T 8S **Baths:** 9 En 3 Sh
🛇 🅿 📺 🍴 ╳ Ⅲ. Ⓥ 🛁 cc

Idle

SE1737 🍺 *Hitching Post*

Glengarry Guest House, *175 Albion Road, Idle, Bradford, W. Yorks, BD10 9QP.*
Within easy reach of Bronte land/ Moors/ Industrial Heritage/ TVs 'Emmerdale'.
Open: All Year
01274 613781 Mr Swain
D: £14.50–£15.00 **S:** £16.00–£16.50
Beds: 2T 1S **Baths:** 2 Sh
🛇 (5) 📺 Ⅲ. 🛁

Ilkley

SE1147 🍺 *Riverside, Rose & Crown, Wharfedale Gate, Sailor, Crescent*

63 Skipton Road, *Ilkley, W. Yorks, LS29 9BH.*
Imposing stone detached house, gardens and ground-floor ensuite bedrooms.
Open: All Year **Grades:** ETC 2 Diamond
01943 817542 Mrs Roberts
D: £18.00–£20.00 **S:** £25.00
Beds: 2D 1T **Baths:** 2 En 1 Sh
🛇 🅿 (5) ⚡ 📺 🍴 Ⅲ. Ⓥ 🛁 cc

Archway Cottage, *24 Skipton Road, Ilkley, W. Yorks, LS29 9EP.*
Beautiful Victorian cottage in central Ilkley with outstanding moorland views.
Open: All Year **Grades:** ETC 3 Diamond
01943 603399 Mrs Green
D: £17.50–£20.00 **S:** £20.00–£25.00
Beds: 1F 2D 1T **Baths:** 1 En 2 Sh
🛇 🅿 (2) 📺 🍴 Ⅲ. Ⓥ 🛁

The Grove Hotel, *66 The Grove, Ilkley, W. Yorks, LS29 9PA.*
Delightful Victorian hotel in lovely surroundings, personally run by owners.
Open: All Year (not Xmas)
01943 600298 Mr & Mrs Thompson
Fax: 01943 817426
D: £29.50–£32.00 **S:** £42.00–£45.00
Beds: 2F 2D 2T **Baths:** 6 En 1 Sh
🛇 (5) 🅿 (5) 📺 Ⅲ. 🛁 cc

Illingworth

SE0728 🍺 *Bradshaw Tavern, Queen's Head*

The Elms, *Keighley Road, Illingworth, Halifax, W. Yorks, HX2 8HT.*
Detached Victorian house set in three quarter acre walled garden.
Open: All Year (not Xmas)
Grades: ETC 3 Diamond
01422 244430 Mrs Davis-Crowther
sylvia@theelms.force9.co.uk
D: £20.00–£22.00 **S:** £21.00–£23.00
Beds: 1F 1D 2S **Baths:** 3 En 1 Pr
🛇 🅿 (6) 📺 🍴 ╳ Ⅲ. Ⓥ 🛁

Keighley

SE0541

Currer Laithe Farm, *Moss Carr Road, Long Lee, Keighley, W. Yorks, BD21 4SL.*
Open: All Year (not Xmas)
01535 604387 Miss Brown
D: £14.50 **S:** £14.50
Beds: 2F 1D 3T **Baths:** 3 En 3 Pr 1 Sh
🛇 🅿 (10) 📺 ╳ 🛁 ♿
C16th, working, Pennine hill farm in Bronte Country. Splendid views of Airedale, Ilkley Moor, Ingleborough. Traditional fare. Guests returning for twenty years. Groups welcome. Excellent base for Haworth, Dales, museums, abbeys, markets, mill shops. Inglenook fireplace, beams and mullions.

Kirkburton

SE1912 🍺 *Dartmouth Arms*

Manor Mill Cottage, *21 Linfit Lane, Kirkburton, Huddersfield, West Yorkshire, HD8 0TY.*
Warm welcoming cottage twixt Huddersfield and Wakefield in rural peaceful countryside.
Open: All Year **Grades:** ETC 3 Diamond
01484 604109 Ms Askham
D: £16.00–£18.00 **S:** £16.00–£18.00
Beds: 1D 1T **Baths:** 1 En 1 Sh
🛇 (5) 🅿 (3) ⚡ 📺 🍴 Ⅲ. Ⓥ 🛁

LEEDS   Chapel Allerton

SE3037

Highbank Hotel & Restaurant, *83 Harehills Lane, Leeds, LS7 4HA.*
Convenient, affordable, comfortable, traditional hotel with modern facilities and secure car park. **Open:** All Year
Grades: ETC 3 Diamond, AA 3 Diamond
0870 7414 225 Mr Thomas
Fax: 0870 7414 227
info@highbankhotel.co.uk
D: £17.78–£25.00 **S:** £20.00–£39.50
Beds: 4F 4D 5T 8S **Baths:** 8 En 3 Sh
🛇 🅿 (30) ⚡ 📺 ╳ Ⅲ. Ⓥ ✳ 🛁 ♿ cc

LEEDS   Headingley

SE2836 🍺 *White Hart, Vesper Gate, Queens, Regent, Nag's Head, Old Red Lion, Wrens, Deer Park, Lawnswood Arms, White House*

Number 23, *23 St Chad's Rise, Far Headingley, Leeds, West Yorkshire, LS6 3QE.*
Quiet cul-de-sac overlooking church grounds. Easy access to public transport.
Open: All Year (not Xmas/New Year)
Grades: ETC 3 Diamond
0113 275 7825 Mr & Mrs Sheldrake
D: £17.50 **S:** £16.50–£17.50
Beds: 1T 4S **Baths:** 1 Sh
🛇 🅿 (2) ⚡ 📺 ╳ Ⅲ. Ⓥ 🛁

Saint Michaels Tower Hotel, *5 St Michaels Villas, Cardigan Road, Leeds, West Yorkshire, LS6 3AF.*
Licensed hotel, 1.5 mile from city centre. Near Headingley Cricket Ground.
Open: All Year **Grades:** ETC 3 Diamond
0113 275 5557 Mr Dervish
Fax: 0113 230 7491
D: £18.00–£20.50 **S:** £19.00–£21.50
Beds: 2F 7D 6T 7S **Baths:** 12 Pr 4 Sh
🛇 🅿 (20) ⚡ 📺 ╳ Ⅲ. Ⓥ 🛁 cc

RATES

D = Price range per person sharing in a double room
S = Price range for a single room

---

17 Cottage Road , Headingley, Leeds, West Yorkshire, LS6 4DD.
Late Georgian stone house ideal for universities and Headingley grounds.
Open: All Year (not Xmas)
0113 275 5575
Mr & Mrs Hood
D: £18.00 **S:** £18.00
Beds: 1T 2S
🛇 🅿 ⑃ 📺 🛏 💷 👤

LEEDS   Meanwood

SE2837   ⚓ *True Briton*

Aragon Hotel, 250 Stainbeck Lane, Leeds, LS7 2PS.
Large Victorian house set in large gardens, quiet and non smoking.
Open: All Year (not Xmas)
Grades: ETC 2 Star, AA 2 Star
0113 275 9306
R & D Woodward
Fax: 0113 275 7166
D: £24.90–£26.50 **S:** £39.90–£43.90 .
Beds: 2F 6D 2T 2S **Baths:** 12 En
🛇 🅿 (20) ⑃ 📺 ✕ 🔲 💷 👤 cc

The Ascot Grange Hotel, 126-130 Otley Road, Headingley, Leeds, LS16 5JX.
Recently refurbished, 2 miles from city centre, 1 mile from universities.
Open: All Year
Grades: ETC 2 Star
0113 293 4444
Fax: 0113 293 5555
D: £24.50–£43.00 **S:** £37.00–£43.00
Beds: 3F 11D 3T 6S **Baths:** 23 Pr
🛇 🅿 ⑃ 📺 ✕ 🔲 👤 & cc

LEEDS   Oakwood

SE3236   ⚓ *White Hart, Vesper Gate, Queens, Regent, Nag's Head, Old Red Lion,Wrens, Deer Park, Lawnswood Arms, White House*

Merevale Hotel, 16 Wetherby Road, Oakwood, Leeds, West Yorkshire, LS8 2QD.
Privately owned hotel offering friendly professional service. Elegant public rooms retain many period features.
Open: All Year (not Xmas)
0113 265 8933
Mr & Mrs Knight
Fax: 0113 2658933
D: £19.00–£24.00 **S:** £24.00–£37.00
Beds: 1F 3D 3T 5S
Baths: 7 En 2 Sh
🛇 (3) 🅿 (9) ⑃ 📺 🔲 👤 cc

B&B owners may vary rates - be sure to check when booking

Mankinholes

SD9623   ⚓ *Top Brink*

Cross Farm, Mankinholes, Todmorden, West Yorkshire, OL14 7JQ.
400 year old stone Pennine farmhouse and barn with hillside views.
Open: All Year **Grades:** ETC 4 Diamond
01706 813481 Mrs Hancock
D: £19.50 **S:** £19.50
Beds: 2T 2D **Baths:** 3 Pr
🛇 🅿 (4) ⑃ 📺 ✕ 🔲 💷 👤

Marsden

SE0411   ⚓ *White House, Olive Branch, Coach & Horses, Carriage House*

Throstle Nest Cottage, 3 Old Mount Road, Marsden, Huddersfield, West Yorkshire, HD7 6DU.
Olde Worlde C17th country cottage in beautiful Colne Valley. Close to all amenities. **Open:** All Year (not Xmas)
Grades: ETC 3 Diamond
01484 846371 (also fax)
Ms Hayes
throstle-nest@faxvia.net
D: £15.00–£20.00 **S:** £18.00–£20.00
Beds: 1F 1T **Baths:** 1 Sh
🛇 (2) 🅿 (3) 📺 🛏 🔲 💷 👤

Forest Farm, Mount Road, Marsden, Huddersfield, W. Yorks, HD7 6NN.
Come as a guest, leave as a friend.
Open: All Year (not Xmas)
01484 842687 (also fax)
Mr & Mrs Fussey
D: £16.00–£18.00 **S:** £16.00–£18.00
Beds: 1F 1D 1T **Baths:** 2 Sh
🛇 🅿 (6) 📺 🛏 ✕ 🔲 💷

Pear Tree Cottage, 18 Grange Avenue, Marsden, Huddersfield, West Yorkshire, HD7 6AQ.
Recommended by walkers and cyclists. Canal, station and village nearby.
Open: All Year (not Xmas/New Year)
01484 847518 (also fax)
Mr & Mrs Goodall
john@jgoodall.fsnet.co.uk
D: £16.00 **S:** £16.00
Beds: 1F 1S **Baths:** 2 Sh
🛇 ⑃ 📺 🛏 ✕ 🔲 💷

Steep Farm, Meltham Road, Marsden, Huddersfield, West Yorkshire, HD7 5JZ.
Lovely house and gardens. Pennine views, friendly welcome, great breakfasts.
Open: All Year
01484 846801 Mr Clark
D: £16.00 **S:** £16.00
Beds: 1D 1T 1S **Baths:** 1 En 1 Sh
🛇 🅿 (2) ⑃ 📺 🛏 ✕ 🔲 💷 👤

Mytholmroyd

SE0126   ⚓ *Shoulder Of Mutton*

Reedacres, Mytholmroyd, Hebden Bridge, W. Yorks, HX7 5DQ.
Homely, modern detached house with large garden, adjacent to Rochdale Canal.
Open: All Year (not Xmas)
01422 884423 Mr & Mrs Boggis
D: £18.00–£20.00 **S:** £20.00–£25.00
Beds: 2D **Baths:** 1 En 1 Sh
🛇 🅿 (4) 📺 🔲

Southfield

Southfield, Burnley Road, Mytholmroyd, Hebden Bridge, HX7 5PD.
Large Victorian family home set amidst large gardens overlooking the River Calder. **Open:** All Year (not Xmas)
01422 883007 (also fax)
philip@fieldsouth.freeserve.co.uk
D: £25.00 **S:** £35.00
Beds: 2D **Baths:** 2 En
🛇 🅿 (14) 📺 ✕ 🔲 👤

Ogden

SE0631

The Rockhollow, 5 Causeway Foot, Ogden, Halifax, HX2 8XX.
Set in open countryside, close to Halifax, Haworth, Bradford and Leeds.
Open: All Year (not Xmas)
Grades: ETC 3 Diamond
01422 248049 (also fax) Mr Dennis
the-rockhollow@dial.pipex.com
D: £17.50 **S:** £17.50
Beds: 1D 1T 1S **Baths:** 1 En 1 Sh
🛇 🅿 (6) 📺 ✕ 🔲 💷 👤 cc

Ossett

SE2820   ⚓ *Crown*

Crown Cottage, 18 Horbury Road, Ossett, W. Yorks, WF5 0BN.
Public house. **Open:** All Year
01924 272495 Mrs Jones
D: £18.00 **S:** £18.00
Beds: 1F 2D 2T 2S **Baths:** 2 Sh
🛇 🅿 (20) 📺 🛏 ✕ 🔲 💷 👤

Otley

SE2045   ⚓ *Bells of Otley*

18 Harecroft Road, Otley, W. Yorks, LS21 2BQ.
Quiet, friendly, private residence near River Wharfe and all amenities.
Open: All Year
01943 463643 Mrs Mandy
D: £17.00 **S:** £17.00
Beds: 1T 2S **Baths:** 2 Sh
🛇 🅿 (2) ⑃ 📺 🛏 🔲 👤

Oxenhope

SE0335   ⚓ *Three Sisters*

Springfield Guest House, Shaw Lane, Oxenhope, Keighley, W. Yorks, BD22 9QL.
Large Victorian Residence set in large well kept grounds. **Open:** All Year
01535 643951 Mrs Hargreaves
Fax: 01535 644672 best_bb_uk@msm.com
D: £25.00 **S:** £22.50–£25.00
Beds: 1F 3D 1T 3S **Baths:** 2 En 2 Sh
🛇 🅿 (6) 📺 🛏 ✕ 🔲 💷 👤

Pontefract

SE4521   ⚓ *Carlton Hotel*

Tudor Guest House, 18 Tudor Close, Pontefract, W. Yorks, WF8 4NJ.
Private house, residential area, near to town centre and racecourse.
Open: All Year (not Xmas)
01977 701007 Mrs Kilby
D: £17.50–£18.00 **S:** £25.00–£27.00
Beds: 2D **Baths:** 2 En 2 Pr
🛇 🅿 (2) 📺 🔲 👤

Pool-in-Wharfedale

SE2445 ⊿ *White Hart, Pool Inn, Half Moon Inn*

Rawson Garth, *Pool Bank Farm, Pool-in-Wharfedale, Otley, W. Yorks, LS21 1EU.*
Attractively converted coach house, open country views in heart of Emmerdale country.
Open: All Year (not Xmas)
Grades: ETC 3 Diamond
0113 284 3221 Mrs Waterhouse
D: £20.00 **S:** £30.00
Beds: 2D 1T **Baths:** 2 En 1 Pr
🛏 (12) 🅿 (4) ⊬ 📺 🎞 ≟ cc

Pudsey

SE2233

Heatherlea House, *105 Littlemoor Road, Pudsey, Leeds, West Yorkshire, LS28 8AP.*
Tastefully furnished, friendly, award-winning gardens. Near motorways, airport, Dales.
Open: All Year
Grades: ETC 3 Diamond
0113 257 4397 Mr & Mrs Barton
D: £17.00 **S:** £20.00–£24.00
Beds: 1T 1S
🛏 🅿 (2) ⊬ 📺 ✕ 🎞 🆅 ≟

Queensbury

SE1030 ⊿ *Ma Jones', Raggalds*

Mountain Hall, *Brighouse & Denholme Road, Queensbury, Bradford, W. Yorks, BD13 1LH.*
Former mill owners social institute. Situated 1200' overlooking Bradford-dale. Rural area.
Open: All Year (not Xmas)
01274 816258 Mrs Ledgard
Fax: 01274 884001
D: £20.00–£25.00 **S:** £20.00–£25.00
Beds: 3T 5D 5S **Baths:** 9 En 1 Sh
🛏 (16) 🅿 (10) ⊬ 📺 🎞 ✕ 🎞 🆅 ≟ cc

Sowerby Bridge

SE0523 ⊿ *Triangle Inn, Milbank*

The Dene, *Triangle, Sowerby Bridge, W Yorks, HX6 3EA.*
Georgian stone house in walled garden with wooded valley views. **Open:** July to April **Grades:** ETC 4 Diamond
01422 823562 Mr & Mrs Noble
noble@thedene-triangle.freeserve.co.uk
D: £22.50 **S:** £25.00
Beds: 1F 1T 1D **Baths:** 3 En
🅿 (4) ⊬ 📺 🎞 🆅 ≟

Stanbury

SE0137 ⊿ *Old Silent Inn, Friendly Inn, Wuthering Heights Inn*

Wuthering Heights Inn, *26 Main Street, Stanbury, Keighley, W. Yorks, BD22 0HB.*
Warm & friendly country pub, excellent food and traditional ales. **Open:** All Year
01535 643332 Mrs Mitchell
D: £17.00 **S:** £17.00
Beds: 1F 1D 1T 1S **Baths:** 2 Sh
🛏 🅿 (20) ⊬ 📺 🎞 ✕ 🎞 🆅 ≟

Ponden House, *Stanbury, Haworth, Keighley, W. Yorks, BD22 0HR.*
Bronte country, relax in tranquil historic setting, enjoy panoramic views of moors and reservoir. **Open:** All Year (not Xmas)
01535 644154 Mrs Taylor
D: £22.00 **S:** £22.00–£30.00
Beds: 1F 1D 1T 1S **Baths:** 1 En 2 Pr 2 Sh
🛏 🅿 🎞 ✕ 🎞 🆅 ≟

Todmorden

SD9424 ⊿ *Rose & Crown*

The Berghof Hotel, *Cross Stone Road, Todmorden, W. Yorks, OL14 8RQ.*
Authentic Austrian hotel and restaurant, function suite and conference facilities.
Open: All Year
01706 812966 (also fax) Mrs Brandstatter
berghof@tinyworld.co.uk
D: £27.50–£35.00 **S:** £42.50–£55.00
Beds: 5D 2T **Baths:** 7 En
🛏 🅿 (40) 📺 🎞 ✕ 🎞 🆅 ❄ ≟ cc

Cherry Tree Cottage, *Woodhouse Road, Todmorden, W. Yorks, OL14 5RJ.*
C17th detached country cottage nestling amidst lovely Pennine countryside.
Open: All Year (not Xmas)
Grades: ETC 4 Diamond
01706 817492 Mrs Butterworth
D: £16.00–£24.50 **S:** fr £16.00
Beds: 1F 1D 1T 1S **Baths:** 3 En 1 Pr 1 Sh
🛏 🅿 📺 🎞 ✕ 🎞 🆅 ≟

Wadsworth

SE0126 ⊿ *Hare & Hounds*

Hare & Hounds, *Wadsworth, Hebden Bridge, HX7 8TN.*
A family run country pub, ensuite bedrooms, Good Beer Guide.
Open: All Year **Grades:** ETC 3 Diamond
01422 842671 (also fax)
S Greenwood
D: £22.50–£25.00 **S:** £35.00–£40.00
Beds: 4D **Baths:** 4 En
🅿 (25) ⊬ 📺 ✕ 🎞 ≟

Wakefield

SE3220 ⊿ *British Oak*

Stanley View Guesthouse, *226/228 Stanley Road, Wakefield, W. Yorks, WF1 4AE.*
Close to city centre and motorway network M1/M62.
Open: All Year **Grades:** AA 3 Diamond
01924 376803 Mr Heppinstall
Fax: 01924 369123
D: £18.00–£54.00 **S:** £27.00–£54.00
Beds: 4F 10T 5D 2S **Baths:** 17 En 2 Pr
🛏 🅿 (10) ⊬ 📺 🎞 ✕ 🎞 🆅 ≟ cc

Walsden

SD9322 ⊿ *Bird I'th Hand*

Highstones Guest House, *Lane Bottom, Walsden, Todmorden, West Yorkshire, OL14 6TY.*
Large house set in half an acre with lovely views over open countryside.
Open: All Year **Grades:** ETC 2 Diamond
01706 816534 Mrs Pegg
D: £17.00 **S:** £17.00
Beds: 2D 1S **Baths:** 2 Sh
🛏 🅿 (3) ⊬ 📺 🎞 ✕ 🎞

Wentbridge

SE4817 ⊿ *Blue Bell Inn*

Bridge Guest House, *Wentbridge, Pontefract, W. Yorks, WF8 3JJ.*
Picturesque village close A1 & M62 with a friendly welcome.
Open: All Year
01977 620314
D: £21.00–£25.00 **S:** £21.00–£25.00
Beds: 4T 2D 1S **Baths:** 2 En 2 Sh
🛏 🅿 (8) 📺 🎞 ✕ 🎞 🆅 ≟ ♿

West Bretton

SE2813 ⊿ *Black Bull, British Oak*

Birch Laithes Farm, *Bretton Lane, West Bretton, Wakefield, W. Yorks, WF4 4LF.*
C18th house in countryside, 4 miles from Wakeland.
Open: All Year (not Xmas/New Year)
Grades: ETC 2 Diamond
01924 252129 Mrs Hoyland
D: £18.00–£20.00 **S:** £18.00–£20.00
Beds: 1F 1T 1D **Baths:** 2 Sh
🛏 (3) 🅿 📺 🎞 🆅 ≟

Wetherby

SE4048 ⊿ *Angel, Swan & Talbot, Old Red Lion, Wrens, Korks Winebar, Deer Park, Lawnswood Arms*

14 Woodhill View, *Wetherby, W. Yorks, LS22 4PP.*
Quiet Residential area near to town centre.
Open: All Year
Grades: ETC 2 Diamond
01937 581200 Mr Green
D: £18.00 **S:** £27.50
Beds: 1D 1T **Baths:** 1 Sh
🛏 🅿 (3) ⊬ 📺 🎞 ≟ cc

The Coach House, *North Grove Approach, Wetherby, West Yorkshire, LS22 7GA.*
C19th coach house very tranquil with own entrance. **Open:** All Year
Grades: ETC 4 Diamond
01937 586100 (also fax) Mrs Hobson
D: £15.99–£40.00 **S:** £15.99–£45.00
Beds: 1F **Baths:** 1 En
🛏 (1) 🅿 (4) ⊬ 📺 🎞 ✕ 🎞 🆅 ≟ ♿

Whitley

SE2217 ⊿ *Woolpack Country Inn*

The Woolpack Country Inn, *Whitley Road, Whitley, Dewsbury, West Yorkshire, WF12 0LZ.*
Charming country inn equidistant from Huddersfield, Wakefield & Dewsbury.
Open: All Year **Grades:** ETC 3 Star
01924 499999 (also fax) V Barraclough
enquiries@woolpackhotel.co.uk
D: £27.50 **S:** £44.50
Beds: 5T 6D **Baths:** 11 En
🛏 🅿 (80) ⊬ 📺 ✕ 🎞 🆅 ≟ ♿ cc

B&B owners may vary rates - be sure to check when booking

Isle of Man

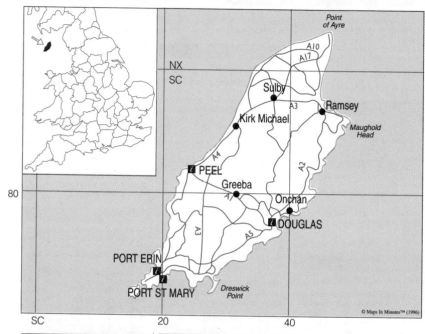

© Maps In Minutes™ (1996)

Tourist Information Centres

Airport Information Desk, Ronaldsway, **Ballasalla**, Isle of Man, IM9 2AS, 01624 821600.

Commissioners Office, Civic Centre, Farrants Way, **Castletown**, Isle of Man, IM9 1NR, 01624 825005.

The Old Grammar School, The Car Park, **Castletown**, Isle of Man, 01624 648000, (Easter to Oct).

Sea Terminal, **Douglas**, Isle of Man, IM1 2RH, 01624 686766.

Old Fire House, Mines Road, **Laxey**, Douglas, Isle of Man, IM4 7NJ, 01624 862007 (Easter to Oct).

Village Commissioners, Public Library, 61-69 Main Road, **Onchan**, Douglas, Isle of Man, IM3 1AJ, 01624 621228.

Commissioners Office, Town Hall, Derby Road, **Peel**, Isle of Man, IM5 1HH, 01624 842341.

Commissioners Office, Station Road, **Port Erin**, Isle of Man, IM9 6AE, 01624 832298.

Commissioners Office, Town Hall, **Port St Mary**, Isle of Man, IM9 5DA, 01624 832101.

Rushen Parish Commissioners, Clerk's Office, Hillside, Cronk Road, **Port St Mary**, Isle of Man, IM9 5AT, 01624 834501.

The Library, Town Hall, **Ramsey**, Isle of Man, IM8 1AB, 01624 817025.

Douglas

SC3875 ◀ *Casey's, Queen's, Horse & Plough, The Sefton*

All Seasons Hotel, *Broadway, Douglas, Isle of Man, IM2 3HX.*
Low cost travel arranged. Indoor heated pool. Ideal central location.
Open: All Year
Grades: AA 3 Diamond
01624 676323 (also fax)
Mr & Mrs Hanson
D: £17.50–£21.50 **S:** £17.50–£26.00
Beds: 3D 1T 2S **Baths:** 4 En 1 Sh
🏧 ✕ 📺 🍴 ♿ CC

The Devonian, *Broadway, Douglas, IM2 4EN.*
Victorian croft house on A9. Suitable for stop over to Oakney.
Open: All Year
01624 674676 (also fax)
D: £20.00–£25.00 **S:** £24.00–£27.00
Beds: 4S 6T **Baths:** 6 En 2 Sh
⚥ 📺 ✕ 📺 ♿

Rangemore, *12 Derby Square, Douglas, Isle of Man, IM1 3LS.*
Quiet Victorian garden, square, central, easy parking, relaxing and comfortable.
Open: All Year (not Xmas)
01624 674892 Mrs Quirk
Fax: 01624 671113
D: £14.00–£19.00 **S:** £15.00–£23.00
Beds: 1F 4D 3T 2S **Baths:** 5 En 3 Sh
🏧 (5) 📺 🍴 ✕ 📺 💷 ♿

Mitre Hotel, *Central Promenade, Douglas, Isle of Man, IM2 4LT.*
Large Victorian house overlooking the beach on Douglas Promenade.
Open: Easter to Oct
01624 629232 (also fax)
Mr & Mrs Lowry
mitre@mcb.net
D: £22.00–£30.00 **S:** £27.00
Beds: 3F 4D 6T **Baths:** 12 En
📺 ✕ 📺 💷

Castlemount Hotel, *4 Empire Terrace, Douglas, Isle of Man, IM2 4LE.*
Family-run hotel.
Open: Easter to Nov
01624 676448 Mr McFerran
D: £13.00–£16.00 **S:** £13.00–£16.00
Beds: 6F 2D 2T **Baths:** 8 En
🏧 📺 🍴 ✕ 📺 💷

Avalon, *10 Woodville Terrace, Douglas, Isle of Man, IM2 4HB.*
A warm, friendly guest house, very quiet, sunny position.
Open: All Year
01624 612844 Fax: 01624 628020
iomhotel@advsys.co.uk
D: £12.00–£18.00 **S:** £12.00–£18.00
Beds: 3F 4D 1T 4S **Baths:** 3 En 2 Sh

Planning a longer stay? Always ask for any special rates

Glenroy

SC4083 ◁ *Brown's*

The Greaves, *Ramsey Road, Laxey, Isle of Man, IM4 7PD.*
Homely guest house, good home cooking using local home-grown produce.
Open: All Year (not Xmas)
Grades: IOMTB Approved
01624 861500 Mrs Quirk
D: £17.00–£25.00 **S:** £17.00–£25.00
Beds: 2D 2S **Baths:** 1En 1Sh
🄿 📺 ✕

Greeba

SC3080 ◁ *Farmers Arms, Hawthorn Inn*

Kerrow Garrow Farm, *Greeba, St Johns, Isle of Man, IM4 3LG.*
Kerrow Garrow is a dairy farm with a homely atmosphere. **Open:** Easter to Oct
01624 801871 Mrs Jackson
Fax: 01624 801543
D: £18.00–£22.00 **S:** £18.00–£22.00
Beds: 1F 1D **Baths:** 1 En 1 Pr
🄲 🄿 (2) ⅍ 📺 🐾 🖥 🔌

Kirk Michael

SC3190 ◁ *Marine Hotel*

Lyngarth, *Station Road, Kirk Michael, Isle of Man, IM6 1HB.*
Open: Jan to Dec
01624 878607 E & M Collister
D: £16.00–£22.00 **S:** £22.00–£25.00
Beds: 3T **Baths:** 1 En 1 Sh
🄿 ⅍ 📺 🖥
Large secluded garden with patio/barbecue. We have wonderful views of Kirk Michael Mountains where the sun rises are unbelievable. Why not enjoy a peaceful and relaxing holiday away from stress of everyday life and go home feeling great.

Ramblin, *32 Murrays Road, Douglas, Isle of Man, IM2 3HP.*
Friendly B&B near all amenities. Hikers and bikers welcome. **Open:** All Year
Grades: IOMTB Listed, Comm
01624 610484 Mrs Conning
D: £18.00–£20.00 **S:** £18.00–£20.00
Beds: 1D 1T **Baths:** En
🄿 (1) ⅍ 📺 🐾 ✕ 🖥 🔌 🔌

Onchan

SC3978 ◁ *The Max, King Edward's Boy, Molly's Kitchen*

Banks Howe, *23 The Fairway, Onchan, Douglas, Isle of Man, IM3 2EG.*
Fully refurbished dormer bungalow set in attractive garden with pool.
Open: All Year
01624 661660 Mr & Mrs Leventhorpe
D: £24.00–£26.00 **S:** £29.00–£31.00
Beds: 1D 2T **Baths:** 2 En 1 Pr
🄲 (10) 🄿 (3) 📺 ✕ 🖥 🔌 ⅙

Mullen Beg, *Little Mill, Onchan, Douglas, Isle of Man, IM4 5BD.*
Open: All Year
01624 624495 (also fax)
Mr Ward
D: £21.00 **S:** £24.00
Beds: 1F 1D **Baths:** 2 En
🄲 (3) 🄿 (6) ⅍ 📺 ✕ 🖥 🔌 🔌
A beautiful country house set in tranquil surroundings overlooking glen and stream. One acre garden, sun patio, private parking. Manx farmhouse kitchen with home-cooking, conservatory, TV, tea/coffee making facilities, evening meal on request. 5 mins from Douglas.

Peel

SC2484 ◁ *Faraghers, Creek Inn, Waterfall Hotel, Ballacallin House*

The Merchant's House, *18 Castle Street, Peel, IM5 1AN.*
Georgian merchant's house, conservation area, comfortable rooms with TV, radio.
Open: All Year
Grades: IOMTB Listed, High Comm
01624 842541 (also fax)
jslater@enterprise.net
D: £18.00–£23.00 **S:** £23.00–£28.00
Beds: 2D **Baths:** 1 En 1 Sh
🄲 ⅍ 📺 🖥 🔌 🔌

Port Erin

SC1969 ◁ *Bradda Glen, Falcons Nest*

Regent House, *The Promenade, Port Erin, Isle of Man, IM9 6LE.*
Family-run guest house in beautiful seaside location.
Open: All Year
01624 833454 (also fax)
Mrs McGiffin
D: £22.50–£23.50 **S:** £25.00–£26.00
Beds: 2F 3D 2T 2S **Baths:** 7 En 2 Sh
🄲 🄿 ⅍ 📺 ✕ 🖥 🔌 🔌

Port Erin Hotels, *The Promenade, Port Erin, Isle of Man, IM9 6LH.*
Comfortable hotels overlooking beautiful Port Erin Bay with heavenly sunsets.
Open: Feb to Nov
Grades: RAC 3 Star
01624 833558 Mrs Gowing
Fax: 01624 835402
enq@porterinhotels.com
D: £25.00–£36.00 **S:** £25.00–£43.50
Beds: 42F 32D 36T 19S **Baths:** 129 En
🄲 🄿 (99) 📺 ✕ 🖥 🔌 ⅙ cc

The Anchorage, *Athol Park, Port Erin, Isle of Man, IM9 6EX.*
Visitors' lounge - TV, video, CD. Tasty home cooking. Coeliac diets catered for.
Open: All Year (not Xmas)
01624 832355 (also fax)
Mrs Cain
anchorage@enterprise-plc.com
D: £18.00–£21.00 **S:** £18.00–£21.00
Beds: 2F 2D 1T 3S **Baths:** 3 En 2 Sh
🄲 📺 ✕ 🖥 🔌 🔌

Port St Mary

SC2067 ◁ *Station Hotel*

Mallmore, *The Promenade, Port St Mary, Isle Of Man, IM9 5DE.*
Spacious Victorian terrace house above sandy beach with outstanding views across bay and harbour.
Open: All Year (not Xmas)
01624 836048 (also fax)
J Galjaardt
D: £13.50–£27.00
S: £20.25–£40.50
Beds: 6F 3T 2D 11S **Baths:** 2 En 8 Sh
🄲 ⅍ 📺 🐾 ✕ 🖥 🔌

Ramsey

SC4594

Stanleyville Guest House, *Stanley Mount West, Ramsey, Isle of Man, IM8 1LR.*
Minutes from all amenities, only yards away from seaside.
Open: All Year (not Xmas)
01624 814420
Mr & Mrs Gillings
D: £17.00 **S:** £17.00
Beds: 1F 2D 2T 3S **Baths:** 1 Sh
🄲 🄿 (6) 📺 🐾 ✕ 🖥 🔌

Thorncliffe Guest House, *Ballure Road, Ramsey, Isle of Man, IM8 1NE.*
Comfortable family run house on outskirts of Ramsey.
Open: All Year (not Xmas)
01624 813885 Mrs Dent
D: £18.00 **S:** £18.00
Beds: 1F 2D 2T 2S **Baths:** 2 Sh
🄲 📺 🐾 🖥 🔌 🔌

Sulby

SC3894 ◁ *Sulby Glen Hotel*

Ballacowell, *Cooilbane, Sulby, Isle of Man, IM7 2HR.*
Manx cottage near village pub and shop. Bikes/ hikers welcome.
Open: All Year
01624 897773 (also fax)
Ms Bedey
majbedey@ballacowell.co.uk
D: £20.00–£25.00 **S:** £25.00–£27.00
Beds: 2D **Baths:** 2 En
🄲 (7) 🄿 ⅍ 📺 🖥 🔌

Sulby Glen Hotel, *Main Road, Sulby, Isle of Man, IM7 2HR.*
Tradition country inn with uninterrupted views of glens; pub of the year.
Open: All Year
Grades: IOMTB 2 Star
01624 897240 (also fax)
Mrs Sayle
sulbyglenhotel@advsys.co.uk
D: £25.00–£27.00
Beds: 4D 4T 2S **Baths:** 4 En 2 Pr 7 Sh
🄲 🄿 📺 ✕ 🖥 🔌 ⅙ cc

Aberdeenshire & Moray

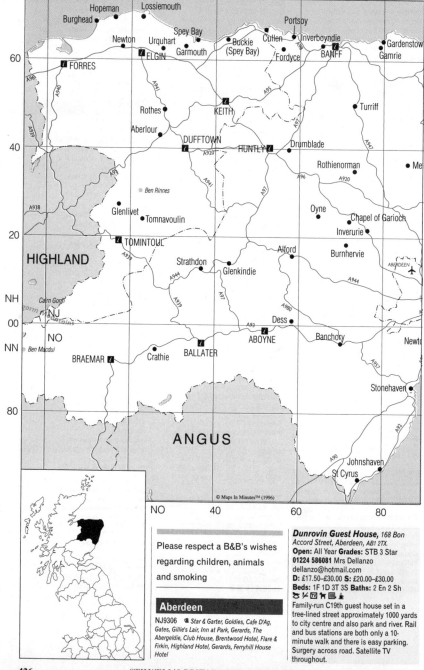

Aberdeen

NJ9306 ♨ *Star & Garter, Goldies, Cafe D'Ag, Gates, Gillie's Lair, Inn at Park, Gerards, The Abergeldie, Club House, Brentwood Hotel, Flare & Firkin, Highland Hotel, Gerards, Ferryhill House Hotel*

Dunrovin Guest House, *168 Bon Accord Street, Aberdeen, AB1 2TX.*
Open: All Year **Grades:** STB 3 Star
01224 586081 Mrs Dellanzo
dellanzo@hotmail.com
D: £17.50–£30.00 **S:** £20.00–£30.00
Beds: 1F 1D 3T 3S **Baths:** 2 En 2 Sh
🛏 🍽 📺 🎱 🛍 🚼
Family-run C19th guest house set in a tree-lined street approximately 1000 yards to city centre and also park and river. Rail and bus stations are both only a 10-minute walk and there is easy parking. Surgery across road. Satellite TV throughout.

Tourist Information Centres

St Nicholas House, Broad Street, **Aberdeen**, AB9 1GZ, 01224 632727.

Railway Museum, Station Yard, **Alford**, Aberdeenshire, AB33 8AD, 01975 562052 (Easter to Oct).

Station Square, **Ballaters**, Aberdeenshire, AB35 5QB, 01339 755306 (Easter to Oct).

Bridge Street, Banchory, Kincardineshire AB35 55X, 01330 822000.

Collie Lodge, Low Street, **Banff**, Banffshire, AB45 1AU, 01261 812419 (Easter to Oct).

The Mews, Mar Road, **Braemar**, Ballater, Aberdeenshire, AB35, 01339 741600 (Easter to Oct).

Car Park, **Crathie**, Ballater, Aberdeenshire, AB35 5TT, 01339 742414 (Easter to Oct).

The Clock Tower, The Square, **Dufftown**, Keith, Banffshire, AB55 4AD, 01340 820501 (Easter to Oct).

17 High Street, **Elgin**, Moray, IV30 1EE, 01343 542666.

116 High Street, **Forres**, Moray, IV36 0PH, 01309 672938 (Easter to Oct).

3 Saltoun Square, **Fraserburgh**, Aberdeenshire, AB43 5DB, 01346 518315 (Easter to Oct).

9A The Square, **Huntly**, Aberdeenshire, AB54 5AE, 01466 792255 (Easter to Oct).

18 High Street, **Inverurie**, Aberdeenshire, AB54 5AE, 01467 625800 (Easter to Oct).

66 Allardice Street, **Stonehaven**, Kincardineshire, AB3 2AA, 01569 762806 (Easter to Oct).

The Square, **Tomintoul**, Ballindalloch, Banffshire, AB37 9ET, 01807 580285 (Easter to Oct).

Roselodge Guest House, 3
Springbank Terrace, Aberdeen, AB11 6LS.
Quiet city centre location, convenient for all amenities. Private parking.
Open: All Year (not Xmas)
Grades: STB 2 Star
01224 586794 (also fax)
Mrs Wink
marywink@roseguest.freeserve.co.uk
D: £15.00–£18.00 **S:** £18.00–£20.00
Beds: 3F 2T 1S **Baths:** 2 Sh
🛇 🄿 (3) 📺 🛏 Ⓥ 🔥

Aberdeen Springbank Guest House, 6 *Springbank Terrace, Aberdeen, AB11 6LS.*
Comfortable family-run Victorian terraced house, non-smoking, 5 minutes from city centre.
Open: All Year
Grades: STB 2 Star
01224 592048 (also fax)
Mr & Mrs Robertson
D: £16.00–£20.00 **S:** £21.00–£26.00
Beds: 3F 4D 3T 4S **Baths:** 12 En 4 Sh
🛇 🚭 📺 🛏 Ⓥ 🔥

The Ferndale Private Hotel, 62 *Bon-Accord Street, Aberdeen, AB11 6EL.*
City centre, easy walk to station, shopping, clubs, etc.
Open: All Year (not Xmas/New Year)
01224 584835 A Noble
Fax: 01224 584724
ferndale@elbon.u-net.com
D: £17.00–£20.00 **S:** £20.00–£25.00
Beds: 7F 2T 2S **Baths:** 6 Sh
🛇 🄿 (4) 📺 Ⓥ 🔥 cc

Crown Private Hotel, 10 *Spring Bank Terrace, Aberdeen, AB1 2LS.*
Small, central, family-run private hotel.
Open: All Year
Grades: STB 2 Star
01224 586842 Mr Buthlay
Fax: 01224 573787
crown_hotel@yahoo.co.uk
D: £18.00–£22.00 **S:** £16.00–£28.00
Beds: 2F 2D 2T 3S **Baths:** 7 En 1 Sh
🛇 📺 🛏 Ⓥ 🔥

Cairnvale B&B, 5 *Cairnvale Crescent, Kincorth, Aberdeen, AB1 5JB.*
Homely accommodation. Personal attention. Easy access to Royal Deeside, city centre.
Open: All Year
Grades: STB 3 Star
01224 874163 (also fax)
Mrs Miller
D: £15.00–£18.00 **S:** £16.00–£18.00
Beds: 1D 1S 3F
🚭 📺 🛏 🔥

St Elmo, 64 *Hilton Drive, Aberdeen, AB24 4NP.*
Traditional granite family home, near historic university and city centre.
Open: All Year
Grades: STB 3 Star
01224 483065 Mrs Watt
stelmobandb@aol.com
D: £16.00–£17.00 **S:** £20.00–£24.00
Beds: 1D 2T **Baths:** 1 Sh
🛇 (1) 🄿 (2) 🚭 📺 🛏 🔥

Aaran Central Guest House, 27 *Jasmine Terrace, Aberdeen, AB24 5LA.*
By beach, Links Golf Course, fitness/swimming complex, city centre.
Open: All Year
01224 641410 G Reid
D: £14.00–£17.00 **S:** £16.00–£20.00
Beds: 2F 1D 5T 4S **Baths:** 3 Sh
🛇 (12) 🚭 📺 🛏 ❄ 🔥

Roselea Private Hotel, 12 *Springbank Terrace, Aberdeen, AB11 6LS.*
Friendly family-run hotel in city centre of Aberdeen.
Open: All Year
Grades: STB 2 Star GH
01224 583060 (also fax)
candfmoore@roseleahotel.demon.co.uk
D: £16.00–£20.00 **S:** £21.00–£27.00
Beds: 2F 3D 1T **Baths:** 1 En 2 Sh
🛇 🚭 📺 🛏 Ⓥ 🔥 cc

Beeches Private Hotel, 193 *Great Western Road, Aberdeen, AB10 6PS.*
Victoria detached property residential area close to the city centre.
Open: All Year (not Xmas)
Grades: STB 3 Star
01224 586413 Mr Sandison
Fax: 01224 596919
beeches-hotel@talk21.com
D: £18.00–£22.50 **S:** £22.00–£32.00
Beds: 2F 3D 2T 3S **Baths:** 7 En 2 Sh
🄿 (13) 🚭 📺 🛏 🔥 cc

Corner House Hotel, *385 Great Western Road, Aberdeen, AB1 6NY.*
Elegant West End hotel, offering good food with friendly service.
Open: All Year (not Xmas/New Year)
Grades: STB 3 Star, AA 3 Diamond
01224 313063 (also fax)
Mrs Heras
cornerhouse.hotel@virgin.net
D: £25.00–£30.00 **S:** £38.00–£48.00
Beds: 2F 6D 3T 6S **Baths:** 17 En
🛏 🄿 (8) 📺 🏧 ✕ 📖 🎄 🕎 cc

The Noble Guest House, *376 Great Western Road, Aberdeen, AB10 6PH.*
Family-run guest house, convenient for city centre and Deeside.
Open: All Year
Grades: STB 3 Star
01224 313678 H Noble
Fax: 01224 326981
D: £20.00–£27.00 **S:** £20.00–£27.00
Beds: 1F 1D 3S **Baths:** 3 En 2 Sh
🛏 🄿 (3) 📺 ✕ 📖 🕎 cc

Bon Accord Guest House, *162 Bon Accord Street, Aberdeen, AB1 2TX.*
Family-run, quiet, central. Bus-rail-ferry terminals, shopping, museums.
Open: All Year (not Xmas/New Year)
01224 594764 (also fax)
lorraine@bonaccordguesthouse.fsnet.co.uk
D: £16.00–£20.00 **S:** £20.00–£30.00
Beds: 3F 2T 1D 4S **Baths:** 2 En 2 Pr 6 Sh
🛏 🄿 (2) 🕎 📺 📖 🕎 🎄

Arden Guest House, *61 Dee Street, Aberdeen, AB1 2EE.*
3 Star STB Guesthouse in the heart of the city centre.
Open: All Year (not Xmas/New Year)
Grades: STB 3 Star
01224 580700 (also fax)
Mr Kelly
ann@ardenguesthouse.co.uk
D: £20.00–£24.00 **S:** £25.00–£40.00
Beds: 1F 2D 3T 5S **Baths:** 2 En 4 Sh
🛏 📺 📖 🕎 🎄 cc

Jurayne Guest House, *272 Holburn Street, Aberdeen, AB1 6DD.*
Friendly guest house. Close to town, park and pubs.
Open: All Year
01224 575601 Mr Ingram
D: £18.00–£20.00 **S:** £20.00–£22.00
Beds: 1F 2T 2S 2D **Baths:** 2 Sh
🛏 (3) 📺 🏧 📖 🎄 🕎

Adelphi Guest House, *8 Whinhill Road, Aberdeen, AB11 7XH.*
Family-run guest house, close to Duthie Park city centre.
Open: All Year
Grades: STB 3 Star
01224 583078 Fax: 01224 585434
stay@adelphiguesthouse.com
D: £17.50–£20.00 **S:** £22.50–£27.50
Beds: 3F 1D 1T 1S **Baths:** 3 En 1 Sh
🛏 📺 🏧 📖 🕎 🎄 cc

Planning a longer stay? Always ask for any special rates

81 Leggart Avenue, *Aberdeen, AB12 5UP.*
Open: All Year **Grades:** STB 2 Star
01224 872898 Mr & Mrs McIlraith
D: fr £17.50 **S:** fr £25.00
Beds: 1T **Baths:** 1 Pr
🛏 (7) 🄿 (1) 🕎 📺 📖 🎄
Convenient Royal, Deeside, Stonehaven, Altens, Tullos. Private parking, non-smoking.

Stewart Lodge Guest House, *89 Bon Accord Street, Aberdeen, AB11 6ED.*
Centrally situated, family-run, clean and friendly, near local amenities.
Open: All Year
01224 573823 (also fax)
Mrs Wann
D: £15.00–£19.00 **S:** £20.00–£23.00
Beds: 1F 3T 3S **Baths:** 3 Sh
🛏 🄿 (3) 📺 🏧 📖 🎄 cc

Haven Guest House, *62 Albergeldie Road, Aberdeen, AB1 6EN.*
Victorian house, quiet location. Warm, friendly atmosphere with personal attention. **Open:** All Year (not Xmas)
01224 585659 Mrs Hay
Fax: 01224 585672
albert.hay@tjrp.net
D: £14.00–£25.00 **S:** £16.00–£20.00
Beds: 1F 1D 2T 1S **Baths:** 2 Sh
🛏 🕎 📺 🏧 📖 🕎 🎄

Butler's Islander Guest House, *122 Crown Street, Aberdeen, AB11 6HJ.*
Comfortable central Georgian town house convenient for all transport.
Open: All Year (not Xmas)
01224 212411 (also fax)
Mr Butler
bookings@butlerigh.demon.co.uk
D: £18.00–£22.00 **S:** £25.00–£35.00
Beds: 3D 3T 1S **Baths:** 2 En 2 Sh
🛏 🕎 📺 📖 🕎 🎄 cc

Lillian Cottage, *442 King Street, Aberdeen, AB2 3BS.*
Situated only 15 min walk from Aberdeen centre. Very comfortable accommodation.
Open: All Year
01224 636947 (also fax)
lilliancottage.demon.co.uk
D: £18.00–£25.00 **S:** £23.00–£30.00
Beds: 1F 2D 1T 2S **Baths:** 1 En 2 Sh
🛏 🄿 (6) 🕎 📺 🏧 📖 🕎 🎄 cc

The Angel Islington Guesthouse, *191 Bon Accord Street, Aberdeen, AB1 2UA.*
Centrally located family-run business with satellite television in all rooms.
Open: All Year
01224 587043
D: £18.00–£22.50 **S:** £20.00–£30.00
Beds: 4F 3D 2T 2S **Baths:** All En
🛏 🄿 (1) 🕎 📺 🏧 📖 🕎

Roselynd House, *27 Kings Gate, Aberdeen, AB15 4EL.*
Elegant Victoria town house, situated in the West End, 20 mins' walk city centre.
Open: All Year
01224 640942 Mrs Neyedli
roselynd27@aol.com
D: fr £17.00 **S:** fr £23.00
Beds: 1F 2D 1T 1S **Baths:** 3 En 1 Sh
🄿 (3) 🕎 📺 📖 🕎 🎄

BATHROOMS
Pr - Private
Sh - Shared
En - Ensuite

Aberlour

NJ2642 🍺 *Aberlour Hotel*

83 High Street, *Aberlour, Banffshire, AB38 9QB.*
The heart of a village famous for whisky and shortbread.
Open: All Year
01340 871000 Miss Gammack
ruth@resolute.fsnet.co.uk
D: £15.00–£16.00 **S:** £15.00–£16.00
Beds: 1T 2D **Baths:** 2 Sh
🛏 🄿 (2) 🕎 📺 📖 🕎 🎄 cc

Aboyne

NO5298 🍺 *Boat Inn*

Struan Hall, *Ballater Road, Aboyne, Aberdeenshire, AB34 5HY.*
We are quietly situated in 2 acres of woodland garden.
Open: 1st Mar to 31st Oct
Grades: STB 5 Star
013398 87241 (also fax)
Mrs Ingham
struanhall@zetnet.co.uk
D: £26.00–£28.50 **S:** £26.00–£34.00
Beds: 1D 2T 1S **Baths:** 3 En 1 Pr
🛏 (7) 🄿 (6) 🕎 📺 🏧 📖 🕎 🎄 cc

Birkwood Lodge, *Gordon Crescent, Aboyne, Aberdeenshire, AB34 5HJ.*
Beautiful Victorian home. Large garden, quiet situation, centre small village.
Open: April to Oct
Grades: STB 4 Star
013398 86347 (also fax)
Mrs Thorburn
D: £27.50 **S:** £30.00–£35.00
Beds: 1D 2T **Baths:** 2 En 1 Pr
🛏 (6) 🄿 🕎 📺 ✕ 📖 🕎 🎄

Charleston Hotel, *Aboyne, Aberdeenshire, AB34 5HY.*
Warm welcome to breathtaking scenery near Balmoral Castle. Innumerable outdoor activities.
Open: All Year
013398 86475 Fax: 013398 86473
D: £23.00 **S:** £25.00
Beds: 1F 4T 2D 1S **Baths:** 5 En 2 Sh
🛏 🄿 (40) 📺 🏧 ✕ 📖 🕎 ❋ 🎄 🕎

Alford

NJ5716 🍺 *Vale Hotel, Forbes Arms*

Bydand B&B, *18 Balfour Road, Alford, Aberdeenshire, AB33 8NF.*
Family home. Warm, friendly welcome. Quiet location near village centre.
Open: All Year
Grades: STB 3 Star
01975 563613 Mrs Jack
D: £18.00–£20.00 **S:** £18.00–£20.00
Beds: 1D 1T **Baths:** 2 En
🛏 🕎 📺 📖 🎄

Ballater

NO3695   *Alexandra Hotel, Highlander, Glen Lui, Auld Kirk*

Morvada Guest House, *Braemar Road, Ballater, Aberdeenshire, AB35 5RL.*
Open: All Year (not Xmas)
Grades: STB 3 Star
013397 56334 (also fax)
Mr Campbell
morvada@aol.com
D: £19.00–£22.00 **S:** £20.00–£25.00
Beds: 5D 1T **Baths:** 6 En
🄿 (6) ⌧ ☒ 📺 🍴 🛏 ⬛ ⚓ cc
Allan and Thea Campbell welcome you to this lovely Victorian villa set in the beautiful village of Ballater. Excellent rooms, quality breakfasts, and a prime location for fine restaurants, Balmoral Castle, the Cairngorm Mountains, the Whisky and Castle Trails.

Deeside Hotel, *Braemar Road, Ballater, Aberdeenshire, AB35 5RQ.*
Open: Feb to Dec
Grades: STB 3 Star
013397 55420
Mr Brooker
Fax: 013397 55357
deesidehotel@talk21.com
D: £22.00–£26.00 **S:** £25.00–£30.00
Beds: 1F 4D 4T **Baths:** 9 Pr
☒ 🄿 (15) 📺 🍴 ✗ ⬛ ☒ ⚓ & cc
Victorian granite villa in quiet location with large informal garden. Attractive dining, conservatory and bar areas. Relaxed breakfast and dinner times. Good central base for touring NE Scotland's many varied visitor attractions. 2 Ground floor bedrooms. Taste of Scotland.

Dee Valley, *26 Viewfield Road, Ballater, Aberdeenshire, AB35 5RD.*
Large detached Victorian house. Quiet location. Stair lift. Beautiful countryside.
Open: Apr to Nov
Grades: STB 2 Star
013397 55408 (also fax)
Mrs Gray
D: £17.00–£20.00 **S:** £22.00–£25.00
Beds: 2F 1D 1T **Baths:** 1 En 2 Sh
☒ (1) 🄿 (3) ⌧ 📺 ⬛ ⚓

Inverdeen House B&B, *Bridge Square, Ballater, Aberdeenshire, AB35 5QJ.*
Enjoy the warm welcome excellent beds (2 king-size) and generous world class breakfast menu.
Open: All Year
013397 55759
Mr & Mrs Munroe
D: £22.50–£25.00 **S:** £25.00–£50.00
Beds: 1F 2D **Baths:** 2 Sh
☒ 🄿 (3) ⌧ 📺 ⬛ ⚓ & cc

Celicall, *3 Braemar Road, Ballater, Aberdeenshire, AB35 5RL.*
Family-run. Central Royal Deeside village. Patio garden front and rear.
Open: Easter to Oct
01339 755699
Mrs Cowie
D: £17.00–£20.00 **S:** fr £25.00
Beds: 2D 2T **Baths:** 4 En
🄿 (4) ⬛ ⚓

Morven Lodge, *29 Braemar Road, Ballater, Aberdeenshire, AB35 5RQ.*
Fine Victorian house in renowned village, close to all amenities.
Open: May to Sep
013397 55373 Mrs Henchie
D: £17.50–£18.00 **S:** fr £18.00
Beds: 1F 1D 1T **Baths:** 1 Pr 2 Sh
☒ (2) 🄿 (5) 📺 🍴 ⬛ ☒ ⚓

Banchory

NO7095   *Burnett Arms, Scott Skinners*

Dorena, *Strachan, Banchory, Kincardineshire, AB31 6NL.*
Open: All Year (not Xmas/New Year)
Grades: STB 4 Star
01330 822540 (also fax) D Mutch
D: £20.00 **S:** £25.00–£30.00
Beds: 1T 2D **Baths:** 3 En
🄿 (4) ⌧ 📺 ⬛ ☒ ⚓
Dorena is a modern bungalow with panoramic views over the river Feugh hills and woodlands. Visit castles, historic buildings, gardens and distilleries, and the breath taking scenery of Royal Deeside. You are assured of a very warm welcome from Doreen and Bill.

Wester Durris Cottage, *Banchory, Kincardineshire, AB31 3BQ.*
Homely accommodation near castle country, Deeside, welcome tea on arrival.
Open: Easter to Oct
01330 844638 Mrs Leslie
D: £16.00–£18.00 **S:** £20.00
Beds: 1F 1T **Baths:** 1 Sh
☒ (1) 🄿 (4) ⌧ 📺 ⬛ ⚓

Banff

NJ6864   *Banff Springs, Banff Links, County Hotel*

Clayfolds Farm, *Banff, AB45 3UD.*
Warm, comfortable accommodation on working farm. 3 miles from Banff.
Open: Easter to Sep
01261 821288 Mrs Eddison
clayfolds@farming.co.uk
D: fr £15.00 **S:** fr £15.00
Beds: 1F 1D 1S **Baths:** 1 Sh
☒ (2) 🄿 (4) 📺 ✗ ⬛ ⚓

Links Cottage, *Inverboyndie, Banff, AB45 2JJ.*
Picturesque seaside cottage; comfortable and relaxing. Explore this spectacular coastline. **Open:** Easter to Nov
Grades: STB 4 Star
01261 812223 (also fax)
Mrs Buchan
D: £24.00 **S:** £30.00–£44.00
Beds: 2D 1T **Baths:** 3 En
🄿 (6) ⌧ 📺 ⬛ ☒ ⚓ &

The Trinity And Alvah Manse, *21 Castle Street, Banff, AB45 1DH.*
Trinity Manse is restored and tastefully decorated to highest standards.
Open: All Year (not Xmas)
Grades: STB 3 Star
01261 812244 (also fax)
Ms Grant
oldmanse@tesco.net
D: £18.00–£20.00 **S:** £18.00–£23.00
Beds: 1D 1T **Baths:** 1 En 2 Pr
☒ ⌧ 📺 ⬛ ☒ ⚓

Braemar

NO1491   *Fife Arms, Braemar Lodge, Invercould Hotel*

Morningside, *Kindrochit Drive, Braemar, Ballater, Aberdeenshire, AB35 5YQ.*
Cosy house, ideal for walks, skiing and cycling. Meals on request.
Open: Jan to Oct
013397 41370 Mrs McKellar
D: £16.00–£20.00 **S:** £18.00–£20.00
Beds: 1D 1T **Baths:** 1 Sh
☒ 🄿 (3) ⌧ 📺 ✗ ⬛

Balnellan House, *Braemar, Aberdeenshire, AB35 5YQ.*
A charming renovated Victorian family home offering traditional Scottish hospitality. **Open:** All Year (not Xmas)
013397 41474 Mrs Sharp
balnellan@hotmail.com
D: £22.00 **S:** £25.00–£30.00
Beds: 2D 1T **Baths:** 3 En
☒ (1) 🄿 (4) ⌧ 📺 🍴 ✗ ⬛ ☒

Schiehallion House, *Glenshee Road, Braemar, Ballater, Aberdeenshire, AB35 5YQ.*
Hearty breakfasts. Friendly courteous service. Private parking. Village centre 500m. **Open:** Dec to Oct
Grades: STB 3 Star
013397 41679 Mrs Heyes
D: £18.00–£22.00 **S:** £19.00–£21.00
Beds: 2F 3T 3D 1S **Baths:** 5 En 1 Sh
☒ 🄿 (9) ⌧ 📺 🍴 ✗ ⬛ ☒ ❀ ⚓ & cc

Buckie (Spey Bay)

NJ4165

Cluny Hotel, *2 High Street, Buckie, Banffshire, AB56 1AL.*
Family-run,centrally located hotel overlooking the Moray Firth
Open: All Year **Grades:** STB 3 Star
01542 832922
D: £22.00–£28.00 **S:** £26.00–£28.00
Beds: 1F 2D 2T 1S **Baths:** 6 En
☒ 🄿 (40) 📺 🍴 ✗ ⬛ ☒ ⚓ cc

Burghead

NJ1169

Norland, *26 Grary Street, Burghead, Elgin, Moray, IV30 2UJ.*
Modern bungalow overlooking Burghead Bay and miles of golden sands.
Open: All Year (not Xmas)
01343 835212 Mrs Smith
D: fr £15.00 **S:** fr £15.00
Beds: 1F 1D 2T **Baths:** 2 Sh
☒ 🄿 ⌧ 📺 🍴 ✗ ⬛ ☒ ⚓ &

Burnhervie

NJ7219

Broadsea, *Burnhervie, Inverurie, Aberdeenshire, AB51 5LB.*
Homely accommodation on a working family farm. Good home cooking, quiet rural location. **Open:** All Year
Grades: STB 3 Star
01467 681386 Mrs Harper
elizharber@broadsea99.freeserve.co.uk
D: £19.00–£21.00 **S:** £22.00–£26.00
Beds: 1F **Baths:** 1 En
☒ 🄿 ⌧ 📺 🍴 ✗ ⬛ ☒ ⚓ &

Chapel of Garioch

NJ7124

Kirkton Park Bed And Breakfast, 5
*Kirkton Park, Chapel of Garioch, Inverurie,
AB51 5HF.*
Open: All Year (not Xmas/New Year)
01467 681281 kirkton-park@msn.com
D: £16.00–£22.00 **S:** £16.00–£22.00
Beds: 2T **Baths:** 1 En 1 Pr
🛇 🅿 (4) ⊬ 🆅 ✕ 🆖 ☷
Convenient for whiskey/ Castle trails-
close to Bennachie. Good views.

Crathie

NO2695

Inver Hotel, *Crathie, Ballater,
Aberdeenshire, AB35 5UL.*
Historic coaching inn dating from 1760,
only 50 yards from the river Dee.
Open: All Year
013397 42345 Mr Mathieson
Fax: 013397 42009
D: £15.00–£30.00 **S:** £20.00–£35.00
Beds: 1F 5D 3S **Baths:** 9 En
🛇 🅿 (30) 🆅 🅗 ✕ 🆖 🏵 ☷ cc

Cullen

NJ5167 🍴 *Royal Oak, Waverley Hotel, Three
Kings, Grant Arms*

The Elms Guest House, *2 Seafield
Place, Cullen, Buckie, Banffshire, AB56 2UU.*
Open: All Year
01542 841271 (also fax)
Mr Welford
D: £16.00–£20.00 **S:** £16.00–£20.00
Beds: 1F 2D 2T 1S **Baths:** 1 En 1 Pr 1 Sh
🛇 🅿 (4) 🆅 🅗 ✕ 🆖 🆅 ☷ ☇
Family run guest house offering very
comfortable accommodation. Close to
Speyside Way, coastal walks and cycle
trails, Whisky Trail & Castle Trail. Fishing,
sailing, horse riding. 10 golf courses in 18
mile radius.

Torrach, *147 Seatown, Cullen, Buckie,
Banffshire, AB56 4SL.*
Traditional house, near beach and golf
course. Warm friendly atmosphere.
Open: Easter to Oct
Grades: STB 3 Star
01542 840724 Mrs Mair
D: £16.00 **S:** £18.00
Beds: 1F 1D **Baths:** 1 Sh
🛇 🅿 (2) 🆅 🅗 🆖 🆅 ☷

Waverley Hotel, *12 Blantyre Street,
Cullen, Buckie, Banffshire, AB56 4RP.*
Situated near excellent golf courses. Also
Whisky and Castle Trails.
Open: All Year
01542 840210 Mrs Finnie
D: £16.00 **S:** £16.00
Beds: 3F 2T 2S **Baths:** 2 Sh
🛇 🅿 (5) 🆅 ✕ 🆖 🆅 ☷

B&B owners may vary
rates - be sure to check
when booking

Dess

NJ5700 🍴 *Gordon Arms, Boat Inn, Kincardine
O'Neill*

Newton of Drumgesk, *Dess, Aboyne,
Aberdeenshire, AB34 5BL.*
Comfortable quiet, typical Scottish
farmhouse in own acreage. Cot/high
chair available. **Open:** Mar to Oct
013398 86203 (also fax)
Mrs Selwyn Bailey crogerbailey@cs.com
D: £19.50–£25.00 **S:** £19.50–£25.00
Beds: 1T 1D **Baths:** 1 En
🛇 🅿 (6) ⊬ 🆅 🅗 🆖 ☷

Drumblade

NJ5840

Annandale House, *Drumblade,
Huntly, AB54 6EN.*
Beautifully furnished early Victorian
Manse, idyllic location. Ideal for touring.
Open: Mar to Jan **Grades:** STB 4 Star
01466 740233 (also fax) Ms Staunton
susan.staunton@virgin.net
D: £20.00–£27.50 **S:** £20.00–£25.00
Beds: 1T 2D 1S **Baths:** 4 En
🅿 (4) ⊬ 🆅 🅗 ✕ 🆖 🆅 ☷ cc

Dufftown

NJ3240 🍴 *Glenfiddich, Fife Arms, Masons'
Arms, Croft Inn, Commercial Hotel*

Davaar, *Church Street, Dufftown, Keith,
Banffshire, AB55 4AR.*
Nice Victorian house. Some guest rooms
overlooking garden at rear.
Open: All Year (not Xmas/New Year)
Grades: STB 3 Star
01340 820464 Mrs Macmillan
D: £16.00–£18.00 **S:** £25.00–£30.00
Beds: 1T 2D **Baths:** 2 En 1 Sh
🛇 🆅 ✕ 🆖 🆅 ☷

Errolbank, *134 Fife Street, Dufftown,
Keith, Banffshire, AB55 4DP.*
Friendly local hosts. Scottish breakfasts
our speciality. On Whisky Trail.
Open: All Year
01340 820229 Mrs Smart
D: £–£15.00 **S:** £15.50–£16.00
Beds: 3F 1D 1S **Baths:** 1 Sh
🛇 🅿 (5) 🆅 🅗 ✕ 🆖 🆅 ☷

Fife Arms Hotel, *2 The Square,
Dufftown, Keith, Banffshire, AB55 4AD.*
Small, modern town centre hotel. Steaks -
beef & ostrich our speciality.
Open: All Year
Grades: STB 1 Star, AA 3 Diamond
01340 820220 Mr Widdowson
Fax: 01340 821137
D: £20.00–£25.00 **S:** £22.00–£27.00
Beds: 2F 4T **Baths:** 6 En
🛇 (1) 🅿 (6) 🆅 🅗 ✕ 🆖 🆅 ☷ ☇ cc

Nashville, *8a Balvenie Street, Dufftown,
Keith, Banffshire, AB55 4AB.*
Relaxed family-run B&B. Whisky Trail -
yards from Glenfiddich Distillery.
Speyside Way close by. **Open:** All Year
01340 820553 (also fax) Mrs Morrison
nashville@dufftown72.freeserve.co.uk
D: £14.00–£16.00 **S:** £18.00–£20.00
Beds: 1F 1D 1T **Baths:** 1 Sh
🛇 🅿 (2) 🆅 🅗 🆖 ☷

Gowanbrae, *19 Church Street,
Dufftown, Keith, Banffshire, AB55 4AR.*
Beautiful Edwardian town house,
tastefully decorated and modernised.
Open: All Year (not Xmas)
01340 820461 (also fax)
Mr & Mrs Donald
gowanbrae@breathemail.net
D: £18.00–£20.00 **S:** £22.00–£24.00
Beds: 1F 2D 1T **Baths:** 4 En
🛇 🆅 🅗 🆖 ☷

Elgin

NJ2162 🍴 *Laichmoray Hotel, Ashvale, Tor
House, Royal, Abbey Court, Crooked Inn*

Foresters House, *Newton, Elgin,
Moray, IV30 8XW.*
Situated on B9013, 3 miles west of Elgin,
near sandy beaches and Whisky Trail.
Open: All Year **Grades:** STB 3 Star
01343 552862 Mrs Goodwin
goodwin@forestershouse.fsnet.co.uk
D: fr £15.00 **S:** fr £17.00
Beds: 2F **Baths:** 1 Sh
🛇 🅿 (2) 🆅 🅗 🆖 🆅 ☷

Woodlea, *38 Academy Street, Elgin,
Moray, IV30 1LR.*
Detached villa with garden. Near city
centre and railway station.
Open: All Year
01343 547114 Mrs Mckenzie
muriel@woodlea18.freeserve.co.uk
D: £15.00–£18.00 **S:** £15.00–£18.00
Beds: 1F 2T **Baths:** 1 En 1 Sh
🛇 🅿 (4) ⊬ 🆅 🅗 🆖 ☷

Ardgowan, *37 Duff Avenue, Elgin,
Moray, IV30 1QS.*
Welcome to our home - a non-smokers
delight. Freshly maintained quality
accommodation.
Open: Feb to Nov
01343 541993 (also fax)
Mrs McGowan
NonSmokersHaven@tinyworld.co.uk
D: £18.00–£22.00 **S:** £20.00–£30.00
Beds: 1D 1T **Baths:** 1 En 1 Pr
🅿 (2) ⊬ 🆅 🆖 ☷ ☇

Ellon

NJ9530 🍴 *Casa Salvatori, Buchan Hotel,
Station Hotel*

58 Station Road, *Ellon, Aberdeenshire,
AB4 9AL.*
Victorian house in town centre near
Whisky /Castle Trail, cycle routes.
Open: All Year (not Xmas)
01358 720263 Mrs Thomson
D: £16.00–£18.00 **S:** £18.00–£23.00
Beds: 2T **Baths:** 1 Sh
🅿 (4) ⊬ 🆅 🆖 🆅 ☷

Station Hotel, *Station Brae, Ellon,
Aberdeenshire, AB4 9BD.*
Family run hotel in quiet part of Ellon.
Ample parking.
Open: All Year
Grades: STB 2 Star
01358 720209 Mrs Keith
Fax: 01358 722855
stathotel@aol.com
D: £22.50–£25.00 **S:** £20.00–£35.00
Beds: 3F 3D 1T 1S **Baths:** 8 En
🛇 🅿 (40) 🆅 🅗 ✕ 🆖 🆅 ☷ cc

Cadha-Beag, *14 Turnishaw Hill, Ellon, Aberdeenshire, AB41 8BB.*
Quiet bungalow. Central to Castle and Whisky Trails. Golf.
Open: All Year (not Xmas)
01358 722383 Mrs Stevenson
D: £17.00–£17.50 **S:** £17.00–£17.50
Beds: 1T 1S **Baths:** 1 Sh
⚲ 📺 🖾 ♨

Fordyce

NJ5563

Academy House, *School Road, Fordyce, Portsoy, Banffshire, AB45 2SJ.*
Tastefully decorated and furnished country house. Paintings and pottery throughout. **Open:** All Year
Grades: STB 4 Star
01261 842743 Mrs Leith
academy_house@hotmail.com
D: £20.00–£24.00 **S:** £25.00–£27.00
Beds: 1D 1T **Baths:** 1 En 1 Sh
🐾 🅿 (5) 📺 🍴 ✕ 🖾 🖂 ♨

Forres

NJ0358 🍺 *Mossett Tavern, Crown & Anchor, Chimes, Kimberley*

Morven, *Caroline Street, Forres, Moray, IV36 0AN.*
Beautiful house, centre town location. Warm, friendly atmosphere. Private parking. Brochure available.
Open: All Year **Grades:** STB 3 Star
01309 673788 (also fax)
Mrs MacDonald
morven2@globalnet.co.uk
D: £18.00–£20.00 **S:** £18.00–£20.00
Beds: 1F 3T 1S **Baths:** 1 Pr 2 Sh
🐾 🅿 (5) ⚲ 📺 🍴 🖾 🖂 ♨

Mayfield Guest House, *Victoria Road, Forres, Moray, IV36 3BN.*
Centrally located with spacious rooms and quiet relaxed atmosphere, with restricted smoking areas.
Open: All Year (not Xmas)
Grades: STB 4 Star
01309 676931 W Hercus
bill-hercus@
mayfieldghouse.freeserve.co.uk
D: £17.00–£20.00 **S:** £25.00–£30.00
Beds: 1D 2T **Baths:** 2 En 1 Pr
🅿 (4) ⚲ 📺 🖾 ♨ cc

Milton of Grange Farm, *Forres, Moray, IV36 0TR.*
Working arable farm. 1 mile from Forres, close to picturesque Findhorn village.
Open: All Year (not Xmas)
Grades: STB 4 Star
01309 676360 (also fax)
Mrs Massie
hildamassie@aol.com
D: £18.00–£25.00 **S:** £20.00–£25.00
Beds: 1F 1D 1T **Baths:** 3 En
🐾 🅿 (4) ⚲ 📺 🖾 ♨

Heather Lodge, *Tytler Street, Forres, Moray, IV36 0EL.*
Situated in quiet area near town.
Open: All Year (not Xmas)
01309 672377 Mr Ross
D: £15.00–£20.00 **S:** £15.00–£20.00
Beds: 1F 1D 2T 3S **Baths:** 8 Pr
🅿 (12) 📺 🍴 🖾 ♨

Gamrie

NJ7965

Roughwards, *Gamrie, Gardenstown, Banff, AB45 3HA.*
Warm comfortable former farmhouse, walking, bird watching, near scenic Gardenstown, Crovie.
Open: All Year (not Xmas)
01261 851758 Mrs Hawick
hawick@btinternet.com
D: £15.00–£17.00 **S:** £15.00–£18.00
Beds: 1D 1T **Baths:** 1 Sh
🐾 (2) 🅿 (3) 📺 🍴 ✕ 🖾 🖂 ♨ 1

Gardenstown

NJ8064 🍺 *Knowes Hotel*

Bankhead Croft, *Gamrie, Banff, Aberdeenshire & Moray, AB45 3HN.*
Modern country cottage, offering high standards of comfort in tranquil surroundings.
Open: All Year
Grades: STB 3 Stars
01261 851584 (also fax)
Mrs Smith
lucinda@bankheadcroft.freeserve.co.uk
D: £15.00–£18.00 **S:** £18.00–£20.00
Beds: 1F 1D 1T **Baths:** 1 Pr
🐾 🅿 (6) ⚲ 📺 🍴 ✕ 🖾 🖂 ✿ ♨

Garmouth

NJ3364 🍺 *Garmouth Hotel*

Rowan Cottage, *Station Road, Garmouth, Fochabers, Moray, IV32 7LZ.*
C18th cottage & garden in rural village at Spey estuary.
Open: Jan to Nov
01343 870267 Mrs Bingham
Fax: 01343 870621
patricia@pbingham.fsnet.co.uk
D: £15.00 **S:** £15.00–£17.00
Beds: 1D 1T **Baths:** 1 Sh
🐾 🅿 (4) ⚲ 📺 🖾 ♨

Glenkindie

NJ4313

The Smiddy House, *Glenkindie, Alford, Aberdeenshire, AB33 8SS.*
Comfortable house with spacious garden, ideal touring base, home cooking.
Open: All Year (not Xmas)
019756 41216 Mrs Jones
D: £16.00–£17.00 **S:** £16.00–£20.00
Beds: 1D 1T **Baths:** 2 En
🐾 🅿 (6) ⚲ 📺 🍴 ✕ 🖾 🖂 ♨

Glenlivet

NJ1929 🍺 *Croft Inn*

Craighed, *Glenlivet, Ballindalloch, Banffshire, AB37 9DR.*
Traditional country house, overlooking beautiful heather hills, pine trees and stream.
Open: All Year (not Xmas)
Grades: STB 3 Star
01807 590436 R Wilson
D: £16.00–£18.00 **S:** £16.00–£18.00
Beds: 1T 1D
🅿 (4) ⚲ 📺 ✕ 🖾 🖂 cc

Hopeman

NJ1469 🍺 *Station Hotel*

Millseat, *Inverugie Road, Hopeman, Elgin, Moray, IV30 2SX.*
Comfortable self-contained suite, wonderful coastline, sports, wildlife, castles, whisky.
Open: All Year
01343 830097 Mrs Brooks
D: £14.00–£22.00 **S:** £18.00–£25.00
Beds: 1D 2S **Baths:** 1 En
🐾 🅿 (4) ⚲ 📺 🍴 🖾 🖂 ♨ ♿

Huntly

NJ5240 🍺 *Huntly Hotel, Gordons Arms*

Greenmount, *43 Gordon Street, Huntly, Aberdeenshire, AB54 8EQ.*
Family-run Georgian house. Excellent base for touring NE Scotland.
Open: All Year (not Xmas)
Grades: STB 3 Star
01466 792482 Mr Manson
D: £16.00–£19.00 **S:** £16.00–£25.00
Beds: 2F 4T 2S **Baths:** 4 En 1 Pr 1 Sh
🐾 🅿 (6) ⚲ 📺 ✕ 🖾 ♨

Dunedin Guest House, *17 Bogie Street, Huntly, Aberdeenshire, AB54 5DX.*
Dunedin guesthouse. A few minutes walk from town centre. All room ensuite.
Open: All Year
01466 794162 Mrs Keith
dunedin.guesthouse.@btinternet.uk
D: £18.50–£23.00 **S:** £18.50–£23.00
Beds: 6F 1D 4T **Baths:** 6 En
🐾 🅿 (8) ⚲ 📺 🖾 ♨

Strathlene, *Macdonald Street, Huntly, Aberdeenshire, AB54 8EW.*
Granite house near town centre and railway station. Warm welcome.
Open: All Year (not Xmas)
Grades: STB 3 Star
01466 792664 Mrs Ingram
D: £15.00–£17.50 **S:** £15.00–£16.00
Beds: 1D 1T 1S **Baths:** 1 En 1 Sh
⚲ 📺 🖾 ♨

Southview, *Victoria Road, Huntly, Aberdeenshire, AB56 5AH.*
Private house, close to town centre, convenient, castle and whisky trails.
Open: All Year
01466 792456 Mrs Thomson
D: £15.00 **S:** £16.00
Beds: 1F 2D 1T **Baths:** 2 Sh
🐾 🅿 (3) 📺 🍴 🖾 ✿ ♨

Inverboyndie

NJ6664 🍺 *Banff Links Hotel*

Links Cottage, *Inverboyndie, Banff, AB45 2JJ.*
Picturesque seaside cottage; comfortable and relaxing. Explore this spectacular coastline.
Open: Easter to Nov
Grades: STB 4 Star
01261 812223 (also fax)
Mrs Buchan
D: £24.00 **S:** £30.00–£44.00
Beds: 2D 1T **Baths:** 3 En
🅿 (6) ⚲ 📺 🖾 🖂 ♨ ♿

Inverurie

NJ7721   **◀** *Bugles*

Kingsgait, *3 St. Andrews Gardens, Inverurie, Aberdeenshire, AB51 3XT.*
Friendly family run establishment close to town centre.
Open: All Year
Grades: STB 2 Star
01467 620431 (also fax)
Mrs Christie
muriel@mchrstie25.freeserve.co.uk
D: £18.00–£23.00 **S:** £18.00–£23.00
Beds: 2T 1S **Baths:** 1 En 1 Sh
🛏 (2) 🄿 (3) 🗡 📺 🍴 🖳 🖤 🚲

Broadsea, *Burnhervie, Inverurie, Aberdeenshire, AB51 5LB.*
Homely accommodation on a working family farm. Good home cooking, quiet rural location.
Open: All Year
Grades: STB 3 Star
01467 681386 Mrs Harper
elizharber@broadsea99.freeserve.co.uk
D: £19.00–£21.00 **S:** £22.00–£26.00
Beds: 1F **Baths:** 1 En
🛏 🄿 🗡 📺 🍴 🗡 🖳 🖤 🚲 ♿

Glenburnie Guest House, *Blackhall Road, Inverurie, Aberdeenshire, AB51 9JE.*
Ideal for touring castle trail/ archaeological sites in area. Near town centre.
Open: All Year
Grades: STB Listed, Comm
01467 623044 Mrs Christie
D: £15.00–£17.00 **S:** £19.00–£20.00
Beds: 1D 5T 1D **Baths:** 2 Sh
🛏 🄿 (3) 🗡 📺 🍴 🖳 🚲

Johnshaven

NO7966   **◀** *Anchor Hotel*

Ellington, *Station Place, Johnshaven, Montrose, DD10 0JD.*
Comfortable modern family home in old fishing village. Ground-floor twin room.
Open: All Year (not Xmas)
Grades: STB 4 Star
01561 362756 Mrs Gibson
ellington13@supanet.com
D: £18.00–£20.00 **S:** £20.00
Beds: 1T 1D **Baths:** 2 En
🄿 (2) 📺 🍴 🖳 🚲

Keith

NJ4250   **◀** *Crown, Royal Hotel*

The Haughs, *Keith, Banffshire, AB55 6QN.*
Large comfortable farmhouse. Lovely view from dining room over rolling countryside.
Open: Easter to Oct
Grades: STB 3 Star GH, AA 4 Diamond
01542 882238 (also fax)
Mrs Jackson
jiwjackson@aol.com
D: £18.00–£21.00 **S:** £22.00–£25.00
Beds: 1F 2D 1T **Baths:** 3 En 1 Pr
🛏 (2) 🄿 (6) 📺 🗡 🖳 🚲

Lossiemouth

NJ2370   **◀** *Skerrybrae, Laverockbank, Lossie Inn*

Moray View, *1 Seatown Road, Lossiemouth, Moray, IV31 6JL.*
Open: All Year (not Xmas)
Grades: STB 3 Star
01343 813915 Mrs MacKenzie
D: fr £17.00 **S:** £21.00–£25.00
Beds: 2D 1T **Baths:** 2 Sh
🛏 🗡 📺 🖳 🚲
Moray View is over 350 years old. All rooms have sea views overlooking the Moray Firth. Many of the original beams are still intact. Close to the harbour and shops and sandy beaches.

Skerryhill, *63 Dunbar Street, Lossiemouth, Moray, IV31 6AN.*
Near beaches and golf course. Convenient for Castle & Whisky Trails.
Open: All Year
01343 813035 Mrs Stewart
D: £16.00–£18.00 **S:** fr £17.00
Beds: 1F 2D 1T **Baths:** 1 Sh
🛏 🄿 📺 🍴 🖳 🚲

Laburnum, *54 Queen Street, Lossiemouth, Moray, IV31 6PR.*
Family run home close to all amenities, including Beaches. **Open:** All Year
01343 813482 (also fax) Mrs Stephen
wistep@tinyworld.co.uk
D: £16.00–£20.00 **S:** £17.00–£20.00
Beds: 1F 1S 1D **Baths:** 1 En 1 Pr 1 Sh
🛏 🄿 (2) 📺 🍴 🖳 🚲

Lossiemouth House, *33 Clifton Road, Lossiemouth, Moray, IV31 6DP.*
Interesting house picturesque garden pleasant relaxed retreat friendly family atmosphere. **Open:** All Year
Grades: STB 3 Star, AA 3 Diamond
01343 813397 (also fax) Ms Reddy
frances@lossiehouse.freeserve.co.uk
D: £15.00–£18.00 **S:** £18.00–£23.00
Beds: 2F 1D 1T **Baths:** 2 En 1 Pr 1 Sh
🛏 🄿 (5) 🗡 📺 🖳 🖤 🚲

Maud

NJ9248   **◀** *Brucklay Arms*

Pond View, *Brucklay, Maud, Peterhead, AB42 4QW.*
Quiet house with panoramic view close to the National Cycle Route.
Open: All Year **Grades:** STB 3 Star
01771 613675 J & M Hepburn
Fax: 01771 613353
mhepburn@lineone.net
D: £20.00 **S:** £22.00–£25.00
Beds: 1T 1D
🄿 (4) 🗡 📺 🖳

Methlick

NJ8537   **◀** *Gight House Hotel, Ythanview Hotel*

Sunnybrae Farm, *Gight, Methlick, Ellon, Aberdeenshire, AB41 7JA.*
Traditional farmhouse; comfort in a peaceful location with lovely views.
Open: All Year
01651 806456 Mrs Staff
D: £17.00–£20.00 **S:** £17.00–£20.00
Beds: 1D 1T 1S **Baths:** 2 En
🛏 🄿 📺 🍴 🖳 🚲

Newton (Elgin)

NJ1663

5 Forrestry Cottages, *Newton , Elgin, IV30 8XP.*
Family home - providing warm, clean rooms. Lounge for relaxing with a TV.
Open: All Year
Grades: STB 2 Star
01343 546702 Ms Whyte
D: £14.00 **S:** £14.00
Beds: 1T 1D **Baths:** 1 Sh
🛏 🄿 (2) 📺 🗡 🍴 🖳 🖤 🚲

Newtonhill

NO9193   **◀** *The Quoiters*

3 Greystone Place, *Newtonhill, Stonehaven, Kincardineshire, AB39 3UL.*
Beautiful coastal village within easy reach Aberdeen and Royal Deeside.
Open: All Year (not Xmas)
Grades: STB 2 Star
01569 730391 (also fax)
Mrs Allen
patsbb@talk21.com
D: £15.00–£17.00 **S:** £15.00–£18.00
Beds: 1F 1T **Baths:** 2 Sh
🛏 🄿 (2) 📺 🍴 🗡 🖳 🖤 🚲

Oyne

NJ6625   **◀** *Cottage Inn*

Old Westhall, *Oyne, Insch, AB52 6QU.*
Friendly family B&B. Old coaching Inn at the foot Bennachie.
Open: All Year
Grades: STB 3 Star
01464 851474 P H West
taphwest@aol.com
D: £17.50–£20.00 **S:** £20.00–£25.00
Beds: 1D **Baths:** 1 Pr
🛏 🄿 (4) 🗡 📺 🗡 🖳 🚲

Peterhead

NK1346

Carrick Guest House, *16 Merchant Street, Peterhead, Aberdeenshire, AB42 1DU.*
Comfortable accommodation, centrally situated 2 minutes' walk from main shopping centre, harbour.
Open: All Year
01779 470610 (also fax)
Mrs Mroczek
D: £20.00–£25.00 **S:** £20.00–£25.00
Beds: 2F 3T 1S **Baths:** 6 En
🛏 🄿 (4) 📺 🍴 🖳 🖤 🚲

Portsoy

NJ5866

The Boyne Hotel, *2 North High Street, Portsoy, Banff, Aberdeenshire & Moray, AB45 2PA.*
Family run hotel situated 100 yards from C17th harbour.
Open: All Year
Grades: STB 2 Star
01261 842242 Mr Christie
enquiries@boynehotel.co.uk
D: £20.00–£25.00 **S:** £20.00–£25.00
Beds: 4D 4T 4S **Baths:** 12 En
🛏 🄿 📺 🍴 🗡 🖳 🖤 ✳ 🚲 cc

Rothes

NJ2749 ◖ *Seafield Arms, Eastbank Hotel*

Seafield Arms Hotel, *73 New Street, Rothes, Charlestown of Aberlour, Banffshire, AB38 7BJ.*
Small family hotel friendly atmosphere. Excellent homecooked meals, fully licensed. **Open:** All Year
01340 831587 Fax: 01340 831892
olga@seafieldarmshotel.demon.co.uk
D: £18.00–£20.00 **S:** £18.00–£20.00
Beds: 1F 1D 1T 2S **Baths:** 1 Sh
🛏 🅿 (8) 🗲 🛏 ✕ 🏢 🔟 ♿ cc

Rothienorman

NJ7235 ◖ *Rothie Inn*

Rothie Inn, *Main Street, Rothienorman, Inverurie, Aberdeenshire, AB51 8UD.*
Family-run village inn in the heart of castle country.
Open: All Year (not Xmas)
Grades: STB 3 Star
01651 821206 (also fax) Miss Thomson
rothieinn@accom90.freeserve.co.uk
D: £20.00–£25.00 **S:** £25.00–£30.00
Beds: 1F 1D 1T **Baths:** 3 En
🛏 🅿 (20) 🗲 🔟 🛏 ✕ 🏢 🔟 ♿ cc

Spey Bay

NJ3565 ◖ *Spey Bay Hotel*

31 The Muir, Bogmoor, *Spey Bay, Fochabers, IV32 7PN.*
1 Mile from Spey estuary, sighting of dolphins, seals osprey.
Open: All Year
01343 820196 J Philpott
D: £15.00–£16.00 **S:** £15.00–£16.00
Beds: 2D
🛏 🅿 🗲 🔟 ✕ 🏢 🔟 ♿

Stonehaven

NO8786 ◖ *Ship Inn, Creel Inn, County Hotel, Belvedere Hotel, Marine, St Leonard's Hotel*

Glencairn, *9 Dunnottar Avenue, Stonehaven, AB39 2JD.*
Open: All Year
01569 762612 M Sangster
maureen.sangster@virgin.net
D: £18.00–£20.00 **S:** £20.00–£22.00
Beds: 1T 1D 1S **Baths:** 2 En 1 Pr
🛏 🅿 (5) 🔟 🏢 ♿
Coastal location close to open air swimming pool and picturesque fishing harbour. Magnificent Dunnottar Castle one kilometre away. Recently refurbished to a high standard, all rooms have satellite TV and video and tea and coffee. Four poster available. Ensuite.

Arduthie House, *Ann Street, Stonehaven, Kincardineshire, AB3 2DA.*
Elegant detached Victorian guest house with attractive garden, central Stonehaven.
Open: All Year (not Xmas)
Grades: STB 4 Star GH, AA 4 Diamond
01569 762381 Mrs Marr
Fax: 01569 766366
arduthie@talk21.com
D: £24.00–£26.00 **S:** fr £18.00
Beds: 1F 2D 2T 1S **Baths:** 5 En 1 Pr
🛏 🔟 ✕ 🏢 🔟 ♿

Sirdhana, *11 Urie Crescent, Stonehaven, Kincardineshire, AB39 2DY.*
Victorian town house 5 minutes from centre and beach quiet area.
Open: Easter to Sep **Grades:** STB 4 Star
01569 763011
sirdhana.stonehaven@virgin.net
D: £20.00
Beds: 1D 1T **Baths:** 2 En
🅿 (2) 🗲 🔟 🏢 ♿

Beachgate House, *Beachgate Lane, Stonehaven, Kincardineshire, AB39 2BD.*
Beach front location, private parking, nice walks, central for all amenities.
Open: All Year (not Xmas)
Grades: STB 4 Star
01569 763155 (also fax) Mrs Malcolm
bill@beachgate13.freeserve.co.uk
D: £20.00 **S:** £22.00–£30.00
Beds: 2D 1T **Baths:** 2 En 1 Pr
🅿 (4) 🗲 🔟 🏢 🔟 ♿

4 Urie Crescent, *Stonehaven, Kincardineshire, AB3 2DY.*
Granite-built family house, close to town, station and beach.
Open: All Year **Grades:** STB 2 Star
01569 762220 Ms Ling
D: £16.00–£18.00 **S:** £18.00–£20.00
Beds: 1F 1D 1S **Baths:** 1 Sh
🛏 🅿 🗲 🔟 🛏 ♿

Dunnottar Mains Farm, *Stonehaven, Kincardineshire, AB3 2TL.*
Friendly farmhouse with sea views. Across road from Dunnottar Castle.
Open: Easter to Nov **Grades:** STB 4 Star
01569 762621 (also fax) Mrs Duguid
dunottar@escosse.net
D: £20.00 **S:** £22.00
Beds: 2D **Baths:** 1 En 1 Pr
🛏 (2) 🅿 🗲 🔟 🏢 🔟 ♿

Strathdon

NJ3512 ◖ *Glenkindie Arms, Crofters Inn*

Buchaam Farm, *Strathdon, Aberdeenshire, AB36 8TN.*
Open: May to Oct **Grades:** STB 3 Star
019756 51238 (also fax) Mrs Ogg
e.ogg@talk21.com
D: £16.00 **S:** £16.00
Beds: 1F 1D 1T **Baths:** 2 Sh
🛏 🅿 (3) 🔟 🏢
Enjoy Scottish hospitality on our 600 acre family-run farm in an area of unspoilt beauty, ideal for walkers and nature lovers. On Castle Trail and Highland Tourist Route. Central for touring Donside, Royal Deeside and Speyside. Free fishing.

Tomintoul

NJ1618 ◖ *Glenavon Hotel, Richmond Arms*

Bracam House, *32 Main Street, Tomintoul, Ballindalloch, AB37 9EX.*
Enjoy a warm welcome to the Highlands from the Camerons. **Open:** All Year
Grades: STB 3 Star
01807 580278 (also fax)
Mr & Mrs Cameron
camerontomintoul@compuserve.com
D: £15.00–£16.00 **S:** £15.00–£16.00
Beds: 1D 1T 1S **Baths:** 1 En 1 Sh
🛏 🅿 (2) 🗲 🔟 🛏 🏢 🔟 ♿

Croughly Farm, *Tomintoul, Ballindalloch, Banffshire, AB37 9EN.*
Farmhouse with breathtaking views of Cairngorm mountains. overlooking River Conglas.
Open: May to Oct
Grades: STB 2 Stars
01807 580476 (also fax)
Mrs Shearer
johnannecroughly@tinyworld.co.uk
D: £16.00–£18.00 **S:** £18.00–£20.00
Beds: 1F 1D **Baths:** 1 Pr 1 En
🛏 🅿 (3) 🔟 🛏 🏢 ♿

Findron Farm, *Braemar Road, Tomintoul, Ballindalloch, Banffshire, AB37 9ER.*
Situated in the Castle and Distillery area.
Open: All Year (not Xmas/New Year)
Grades: STB 3 Star
01807 580382 (also fax) Mrs Turner
elmaturner@talk21.com
D: £15.00–£17.00 **S:** £15.00–£17.00
Beds: 1F 1D 1T **Baths:** 2 En 1 Pr
🛏 🅿 🔟 🛏 ✕ 🏢 🔟 ✿ ♿

Tomnavoulin

NJ2126

Roadside Cottage, *Tomnavoulin, Glenlivet, Ballindalloch, Banffshire, AB37 9JL.*
Warm welcome, cool prices. Total customer care in glorious countryside.
Open: All Year (not Xmas)
Grades: STB 3 Star, AA 3 Diamond
01807 590486 (also fax) Mrs Marks
D: £16.00–£18.00 **S:** £16.00–£18.00
Beds: 1F 1D 1S **Baths:** 2 Sh
🛏 🅿 (4) 🔟 🛏 ✕ 🏢 🔟 ♿

Turriff

NJ7250

Lower Plaidy, *Turriff, Aberdeenshire, AB53 5RJ.*
A certificate of excellence ensures a warm welcome and individual attention.
Open: All Year (not Xmas)
01888 551679 Mr & Mrs Daley
lowplaidy@aol.com
D: £18.00–£22.00 **S:** £18.00–£22.00
Beds: 1D 1T 1S **Baths:** 1 Sh
🛏 🅿 (6) 🗲 🔟 🛏 ✕ 🏢 🔟 ♿

Urquhart

NJ2862

The Old Church of Urquhart, *Parrandier, Meft Road, Urquhart, Elgin, IV30 8NH.*
Distinctly different place to explore Malt Whisky Country, sea and Highlands.
Open: All Year
Grades: STB 4 Star
01343 843063 (also fax)
A Peter
D: £18.00–£27.50 **S:** £23.00–£28.00
Beds: 1F 2T 1D **Baths:** 2 En 1 Pr
🛏 🅿 (5) 🔟 🛏 ✕ 🏢 ♿ cc

Planning a longer stay? Always ask for any special rates

Angus

80

ABERDEENSHIRE & MORAY

Edzell

Glenisla

Cortachy ●   Aberlemno   Montrose
60   ● KIRRIEMUIR   ● Finavon
Airlie
●   Roundyhill   A932
PERTHSHIRE & KINROSS   FORFAR
Glamis
ARBROATH
40   Monikie   Elliot
Broughty Ferry   CARNOUSTIE
DUNDEE   Monifieth
DUNDEE
Firth of Tay   FIFE

© Maps In Minutes™ (1996)

NO   40   60   80

Tourist Information Centres

Market Place, **Arbroath**, Angus, DD11 1HR, 01241 872609.

St Ninian's Place, **Brechin**, Angus, DD9 7AH, 01356 623050 (Easter to Oct).

The Library, 1, High Street, **Carnoustie**, Angus, DD7 6AG, 01241 852258 (Easter to Oct).

4 City Square, **Dundee**, Angus, DD1 3BA, 01382 434664.

The Library, West High Street, **Forfar**, Angus, DD8 1AA, 01307 467876 (Easter to Oct).

Bank Street, **Kirriemuir**, Angus, DD8 4BE, 01575 574097 (Easter to Oct).

The Library, 214 High Street, **Montrose**, Angus, DD10 8PJ, 01674 672000 (Easter to Oct).

Airlie

NO3150

The Brae Of Airlie Farmhouse, *The Kirkton of Airlie, Airlie, Kirriemuir, Angus, DD8 5NJ.*
Fabulous, relaxing views. Large garden, facilities variable. Telephone for brochures.
Open: All Year **Grades:** STB 3 Star
01575 530293 (also fax) M Gardyne
mamie.gardyne@tesco.net
D: £20.00 **S:** £20.00
Beds: 2T **Baths:** 1 En 1 Sh
🅿 (4) ✕ 🕮 Ⅴ ♨ &

All details shown are as supplied by B&B owners in Autumn 2000

Arbroath

NO6441   🍺 *Old Brewhouse*

Inverpark Hotel, *42 Millgate Loan, Arbroath, Angus, DD11 1PQ.*
Small, family-owned hotel renowned and rewarded for quality food.
Open: All Year
Grades: STB 1 Star
01241 873378
Mr McIntosh
Fax: 01241 874730
D: £17.50–£27.50 **S:** £22.50–£27.50
Beds: 1F 1D 2T 2S **Baths:** 5 En 1 Pr 1 Sh
🛏 🅿 (20) 📺 ✕ 🕮 Ⅴ ♨ & cc

Planning a longer stay? Always ask for any special rates

Scurdy Guest House, 33 Marketgate, Arbroath, Angus, DD11 1AU.
Enjoy friendly warm hospitality and superb breakfast menu.
Open: All Year
01241 872417 (also fax)
Mr & Mrs Henderson
D: £15.00–£25.00 **S:** £15.00–£30.00
Beds: 3F 2D 4T **Baths:** 4 En 1 Pr 4 Sh
🏠 🄿 (4) 📺 ✕ 🗔 🖵 🎦 **cc**

Niaroo, 6 Alexandra Place, Arbroath, Angus, DD11 2BQ.
Lovely old Victorian villa overlooking sea. Tastefully decorated, smoke free.
Open: All Year (not Xmas)
01241 875660 Mrs Birse
D: fr £14.00 **S:** fr £15.00
Beds: 2F 1D 1T **Baths:** 1 Pr 2 Sh
🏠 🄿 ⊬ 📺 🎦 🖵 ♿

Hilltop, St Vigeans, Arbroath, Angus, DD11 4RD.
Pleasantly situated in large gardens. First class accommodation and warm hospitality guaranteed. **Open:** All Year
01241 873200 Mrs Osborne
D: £20.00–£27.50 **S:** £22.50–£27.50
Beds: 1F 1D 1T **Baths:** 2 Pr 1 Sh
🄿 (4) 📺 🎦 ✕ 🗔 🖵 ♿

Broughty Ferry

NO4630 ⚓ Ship Inn, Ferry Inn, Woodlands Hotel

Dawmara Guest House, 54 Monifieth Road, Broughty Ferry, Dundee, DD5 2RX.
House is 400 metres from beach and main shopping area.
Open: All Year **Grades:** STB 3 Star
01382 477951 Mrs Trainer
D: £20.00 **S:** £20.00
Beds: 2F 2D 2T 2S **Baths:** 3 En 2 Pr 1 Sh
🏠 (1) 🄿 ⊬ 📺 🖵 🖵 ✳ ♿ 3

Invergarth, 79 Camphill Road, Broughty Ferry, Dundee, DD5 2NA.
Family run in quiet area, close to beach and centre. **Open:** All Year (not Xmas)
Grades: STB 3 Star
01382 736278 Mrs Oakley
jill@oakley79.freeserve.co.uk
D: £17.00–£23.00 **S:** £18.00–£25.00
Beds: 1F 1T **Baths:** 2 Sh
🏠 🄿 (3) ⊬ 📺 🖵 🎦

Mossburn, 363 King Street, Broughty Ferry, Dundee, Angus, DD5 2HA.
Beautiful Victorian house in lovely Broughty Ferry. Many interesting craft shops.
Open: All Year (not Xmas)
01382 477331 Mrs Young
D: £16.00–£18.00 **S:** £20.00
Beds: 1D 1T **Baths:** 2 Sh
🏠 🄿 (2) 📺 🎦 🖵 🎦

Homebank, 9 Ellislea Road, Broughty Ferry, Dundee, DD5 1JH.
Splendid Victorian mansion house set in beautiful walled gardens in a select area.
Open: All Year
01382 477481 (also fax)
Mrs Moore
D: £22.50–£25.00 **S:** £25.00–£35.00
Beds: 2T 2 Single **Baths:** 2 En 2 Sh
🄿 (5) ⊬ 📺 🖵 🎦

Carnoustie

NO5634 ⚓ Cairds Hotel, Kinloch Arms

16 Links Parade, Carnoustie, Angus, DD7 7JE.
Stone built villa overlooking 18th fairway of championship golf course.
Open: All Year
01241 852381 (also fax)
Bill & Mary Brand
billbrand@dechmont16.freeserve.co.uk
D: £18.00 **S:** £18.00
Beds: 1D 1T 1S **Baths:** 1 Sh
🄿 ⊬ 📺 🖵 🎦

Park House, Park Avenue, Carnoustie, Angus, DD7 7JA.
Victorian house, three minutes from championship golf course, sea views.
Open: All Year (not Xmas)
Grades: STB 4 Star, AA 4 Diamond
01241 852101 (also fax) R Reyner
parkhouse@bbcarnoustie.fsnet.co.uk
D: £25.00 **S:** £25.00
Beds: 1D 1T 2S
🄿 (3) ⊬ 📺 🖵 🎦 🖵 **cc**

The Two Bs, 13 Queen Street, Carnoustie, Angus, DD7 7AX.
Established B&B, 2 minutes town centre, 5 minutes golf course.
Open: All Year
Grades: STB 3 Star
01241 852745 Mrs Burgess
Fax: 01241 410493
thetwobs@hotmail.com
D: £20.00 **S:** £20.00
Beds: 2D 1T **Baths:** 2 En 1 Pr
🏠 🄿 (2) 📺 🎦 ✕ 🗔 🎦

Cortachy

NO3959 ⚓ Drovers Inn, Memus

Muirhouses Farm, Cortachy, Kirriemuir, Angus, DD8 4QG.
Beautiful farmhouse in extensive mature garden on busy farm.
Open: All Year (not Xmas/New Year)
Grades: STB 3 Star
01575 573128 (also fax)
Mrs McLaren
sem8455@aol.com
D: £20.00 **S:** £20.00
Beds: 1F 1D 1S **Baths:** 1 Pr 1 Sh
🏠 🄿 (4) ⊬ 📺 🖵 🎦

Dundee

NO3632 ⚓ Old Bank Bar, Boar's Rock, Laings Bar, Roseangle, Royal Arch, Russells, Raffles, Hogs Head, Park Hotel, Antonio's,Craigtay Hotel, Ship

Ardmoy, 359 Arbroath Road, Dundee, Angus, DD4 7SQ.
Open: All Year
Grades: STB 3 Star
01382 453249 Mrs Taylor
taylord@sol.co.uk
D: £18.00–£25.00 **S:** £18.00–£25.00
Beds: 1F 1D 1T 1S **Baths:** 2 En 1 Sh
🏠 (5) 🄿 (4) ⊬ 📺 🎦 ✕ 🗔 🖵 🎦
Ardmoy is a family run lovely house, overlooking the River Tay. Near city centre, Discovery Point and Broughty Ferry where there are pubs and places to eat on every corner. Mrs Taylor has been serving lovely breakfasts for over 40 years.

Elm Lodge, 49 Seafield Road, Dundee, Angus, DD1 4NW.
Large Victorian Listed family home. Rooms with river view.
Open: Jan to Dec
Grades: STB 2 Star
01382 228402 Mrs McDowall
D: £18.00–£25.00 **S:** £18.00–£25.00
Beds: 1D 1T 1S **Baths:** 1 Sh
🄿 (4) 📺 🎦 🖵 🎦 🎦

Ash Villa, 216 Arbroath Road, Dundee, Angus, DD4 7RZ.
Home from home. Jim and Jay are waiting for you.
Open: All Year
Grades: STB 3 Star
01382 450831 Mrs Hill
D: fr £18.00 **S:** £18.00–£21.00
Beds: 1F 1T 1S **Baths:** 1 Sh 1 Pr
🏠 🄿 (4) ⊬ 📺 🎦 🖵 🎦

Errolbank Guest House, 9 Dalgleish Road, Dundee, Angus, DD4 7JN.
Spacious detached Victorian house. Family-run. 1.5 miles city centre.
Open: All Year (not Xmas)
Grades: STB 3 Star
01382 462118 (also fax)
Mr Wilson
D: £22.00–£24.00 **S:** £26.00–£30.00
Beds: 2D 3T 1S **Baths:** 5 En 1 Pr
🏠 🄿 (6) ⊬ 📺 🎦 🖵 🎦 ♿

Aberlaw Guest House, 230 Broughty Ferry Road, Dundee, Angus, DD4 7JP.
Victorian house overlooking River Tay. Warm welcome from Bruce & Beryl Tyrie.
Open: All Year (not Xmas/New Year)
Grades: STB 3 Star
01382 456929 (also fax)
Mr Tyrie
D: £20.00–£30.00 **S:** £16.00–£30.00
Beds: 1T 2D 2S **Baths:** 1 En 1 Sh
🏠 (12) 🄿 (6) ⊬ 📺 🎦 🖵 🎦

Craigtay Hotel, 101 Broughty Ferry Road, Tayside, Dundee, Angus, DD4 6JE.
Third generation family run hotel. Golfing and theatre breaks arranged.
Open: All Year **Grades:** STB 2 Star
01382 451142
Mr Carson
Fax: 01382 452940
paulshure@aol.uk
D: £24.50–£35.00 **S:** £36.00–£50.00
Beds: 2F 5D 8T 3S **Baths:** 18 En
🏠 🄿 (28) 📺 🎦 ✕ 🗔 🖵 🎦 **cc**

Cloisterbank, 8 Coupar Angus Road, Dundee, Angus, DD2 3HN.
Family run friendly accommodation. Near Country Park 5 minutes to 5 golf courses.
Open: All Year **Grades:** STB 1 Star
01382 622181 Mr Black
D: £16.00–£18.00 **S:** £18.50–£25.00
Beds: 1F 5T 1S **Baths:** 2 Sh 1 En
🏠 🄿 (5) 📺 🎦 ✕ 🗔 🖵 🎦

St Leonards Guest House, 22 Albany Terrace, Dundee, Angus, DD3 6HR.
Beautiful central town house. Highest rooms overlooking gardens and river.
Open: All Year
01382 227146 Ms Dunbar
D: £16.00–£18.00 **S:** fr £25.00
Beds: 1F 2D 2T **Baths:** 2 Sh
🏠 🄿 (2) 📺 🎦 ✳ 🎦

Edzell

NO6068 ◄ *Glenesk Hotel, Panmure Hotel, Luck Inn*

Inchcape, High Street, Edzell, Brechin, Angus, *DD9 7TF.*
Late Victorian house in pretty village.
Open: All Year
01356 647266 Mrs McMurray
D: £16.00–£18.00 **S:** £18.00–£20.00
Beds: 1F 1T 1S **Baths:** 3 En
⛾ 🅿 (2) ⊁ 📺 🍖 🛏 🏠 ♿

Elliot

NO6139

Five Gables House, Elliot, Arbroath, Angus, *DD11 2PE.*
Former clubhouse overlooking 18-hole golf course, panoramic views of coast at breakfast.
Open: All Year
01241 871632 Fax: 01241 873615
fivegableshouse@yahoo.com
D: £15.00–£25.00 **S:** £20.00–£25.00
Beds: 1F 1D 1T **Baths:** 3 En
⛾ 🅿 (20) 📺 🍖 🛏 ♿ 🐾 cc

Finavon

NO4957

Finavon Farmhouse, Finavon, Forfar, Angus, *DD8 3PX.*
Located within secluded grounds renowned for quality food and hospitality.
Open: Feb to Oct **Grades:** STB 4 Star
01307 850269 Mrs Rome
Fax: 01307 850380
jlr@finfarm.freeserve.co.uk
D: £21.00–£22.00 **S:** £21.00–£27.00
Beds: 2D 1T **Baths:** 3 En
⛾ 🅿 (7) 📺 🍖 🗙 🛏 📺 ♿

Forfar

NO4550 ◄ *Castle Club, Plough Inn*

Wemyss Farm, Montrose Road, Forfar, Angus, *DD8 2TB.*
190 acre mixed farm situated 2.5 miles along with a wide variety of animals.
Open: All Year
Grades: STB 3 Star
01307 462887 (also fax) Mrs Lindsay
wemyssfarm@hotmail.com
D: £17.00–£18.00 **S:** £20.00–£21.00
Beds: 1F 1D **Baths:** 2 Sh
⛾ 🅿 (6) 📺 🍖 🗙 🛏 📺 ✳ ♿ cc

Abbotsford B & B, 39 Westfield Crescent, Forfar, Angus, *DD8 1EG.*
Family run B&B close to Queen Mum's Ancestral Home.
Open: All Year (not Xmas)
01307 462830 Ms Humphries
abbotsfordbnb@aol.com
D: fr £16.00 **S:** fr £32.00
Beds: 1D 2T 1F **Baths:** 2 En 1 Sh
⛾ 🅿 (4) ⊁ 📺 🍖 🗙 🛏 📺 ♿ 🐾

B&B owners may vary rates - be sure to check when booking

Glamis

NO3846 ◄ *Strathmore Arms*

Arndean, Linross, Glamis, Forfar, Angus, *DD8 1QN.*
Close to Glamis Castle and in ideal walking country.
Open: All Year (not Xmas)
Grades: STB 2 Star
01307 840535 Mrs Ruffhead
arndean@btinternet.com
D: £16.00 **S:** £16.00–£20.00
Beds: 2T **Baths:** 1 Sh
🅿 (3) 📺 🍖 🛏 📺 ♿ ♿

Hatton Of Ogilvy, Glamis, Forfar, Angus, *DD8 1UH.*
Warm welcome awaits at family farm near Glamis Castle and tranquil Angus glens.
Open: Apr to Oct
Grades: STB 4 Star
01307 840229 (also fax)
Mrs Jarron
D: £20.00–£22.00 **S:** £25.00
Beds: 1T **Baths:** 1 En
⊁ 📺 ♿ ♿

Glenisla

NO2160

The Kirkside House Hotel, 11 Conigre Close, Glenisla, Blairgowrie, Perthshire, *PH11 8PH.*
Open: All Year
01575 582313
Janice Appleby & Tony Willis
D: £22.50 **S:** £22.50
Beds: 1F 3D 1S **Baths:** 3 En 1 Sh
⛾ 🅿 (50) 📺 🍖 🗙 🛏 📺 ♿ ✳ ♿ cc
Standing in its own 1.5 acres of garden the Kirkside overlooks the upper River Isla and offers peace, tranquillity, good food and friendly service. Ideal for touring the Central Highlands. Opportunities for hill walking, skiing, fishing, stalking and bird watching.

Kirriemuir

NO3853 ◄ *Glenisla Hotel, Lochside Lodge, Thrums Hotel, Woodville Inn, Park Tavern, Hooks*

Crepto, Kinnordy Place, Kirriemuir, Forfar, Angus, *DD8 4JW.*
10 minutes walk from town centre. Friendly, warm welcome. Comfortable.
Open: All Year
Grades: STB 2 Star
01575 572746 Mrs Lindsay
D: £22.00–£25.00 **S:** £22.00–£25.00
Beds: 1D 1T 1S **Baths:** 2 Sh
⛾ 🅿 (3) ⊁ 📺 🛏 ♿

Airlie Arms Hotel, St Malcolm's Wynd, Kirriemuir, Angus, *DD8 4HB.*
Traditional hotel. Listed building, completely refurbished to a high level of comfort.
Open: All Year
Grades: STB 2 Star
01575 572847 (also fax)
Mrs Graham
D: £25.00–£28.00 **S:** £28.00
Beds: 3F 7T **Baths:** 10 En
⛾ 🅿 (6) ⊁ 📺 🍖 🗙 🛏 📺 ♿ ✳ ♿ 🐾 cc

Woodlands, 2 Lisden Gardens, Kirriemuir, Angus, *DD8 4DW.*
Large, modern bungalow with panoramic views over Strathmore Valley, gateway to the Glens. **Open:** All Year (not Xmas)
Grades: STB 4 Star
01575 572582 Mrs Sillence
D: £22.00 **S:** £22.00
Beds: 1D 1T 1S **Baths:** 1 Sh
⛾ 🅿 (8) ⊁ 📺 🍖 🗙 🛏 📺 ♿

Letham

NO5248 ◄ *Letham Hotel*

Whinney-Knowe, 8 Dundee Street, Letham, Forfar, Angus, *DD8 2PQ.*
Large semi-detached villa in friendly rural surroundings. Guests lounge.
Open: All Year **Grades:** STB 3 Star
01307 818288 E Mann
D: £18.00–£20.00 **S:** £20.00–£25.00
Beds: 1T 2D **Baths:** 1 En 1 Sh
⛾ 🅿 (4) 📺 🍖 🛏 ♿

Monifieth

NO4932 ◄ *Royal Hotel*

49 Panmure Street, Monifieth, Dundee, Angus, *DD5 4EG.*
Cottage, comfortable beds, good breakfasts. Very near three golf courses.
Open: All Year
01382 535051 Mrs Merchant
Fax: 01382 535205 GeoMerchant@aol.com
D: £18.00–£20.00 **S:** £20.00
Beds: 1T **Baths:** 1 En
⛾ (12) 🅿 (4) ⊁ 📺 📺

Monikie

NO4938 ◄ *Craigton Coach*

Lindford House, 8 West Hillhead Road, Monikie, Angus, *DD5 3QS.*
Deluxe accommodation overlooking country park and close to local amenities.
Open: All Year (not Xmas)
Grades: STB 3 Star B&B
01382 370314 (also fax) M Milton
D: £18.00–£25.00 **S:** £20.00–£25.00
Beds: 2F 1D **Baths:** 2 Pr
⛾ 🅿 (6) 📺 🛏 📺 ♿

Montrose

NO7157 ◄ *Ferry Den Inn*

Byeways, 11 Rossie Terrace, Ferryden, Montrose, Angus, *DD10 9RX.*
Very comfortable, home from home. Turn sharp right past pub.
Open: All Year (not Xmas/New Year)
01674 678510 Mrs Docherty
D: £15.00 **S:** £20.00
Beds: 2D 1T **Baths:** 1 En 2 Pr
🅿 (3) ⊁ 📺 🍖 🗙 🛏 📺 ♿

Roundyhill

NO3750 ◄ *Strathmore Arms*

The Tollhouse, Roundyhill, Glamis, Angus, *DD8 1QE.*
Enjoy Scottish hospitality and Kiwi informality. C18th tollhouse totally renovated. **Open:** All Year (not Xmas)
01307 840436 Fax: 01307 840762
D: £22.00 **S:** £27.00
Beds: 2D 1T **Baths:** 2 En 1 Pr
🅿 (4) ⊁ 📺 🛏 📺 ♿

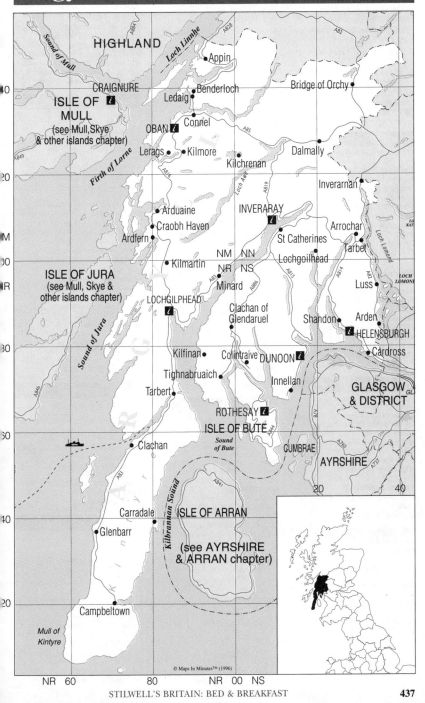

Tourist Information Centres

Ardgartan, Arrochar, Argyll,
01301 702432 (Easter to Oct).

Ballachulish, Argyll, PA39 4HP,
01855 811296 (Easter to Oct).

Mackinnon House, The Pier, **Campbeltown,**
Argyll, PA28 6SQ, 01586 552056.

7 Alexandra Parade, **Dunoon,** Argyll,
PA23 8AB, 01369 703785.

The Clock Tower, **Helensburgh,**
Dunbartonshire, G84 7DD, 01436 672642
(Easter to Oct).

Front Street, **Inveraray,** Argyll, PA32 8UY,
01499 302063.

Kilchoan, Acharacle, Argyll, PH36 4LH,
01972 510222 (Easter to Oct).

Lochnell Street, **Lochgilphead,** Argyll,
PA31 8JN, 01546 602344 (Easter to Oct).

Boswell House, Argyll Square, **Oban,** Argyll,
PA34 4AT, 01631 563122.

15 Victoria Street, **Rothesay,** Isle of Bute,
PA20 0AJ, 01700 502151.

Harbour Street, **Tarbert,** Argyll, PA29 6UD,
01880 820429 (Easter to Oct).

Main Street, **Tarbet,** Arrochar,
Dunbartonshire, G83 7DD, 01301 702260
(Easter to Oct).

Appin

NM9346   🕮 *Duror Hotel, Pierhouse Hotel*

Lurignish Farm, Appin, Argyll, *PA38 4BN.*
Traditional lochside hill farm, good home-
cooking, golf, boating, riding nearby.
Open: May-Sept
Grades: STB 2 Star
01631 730365 Mrs Macleod
lurignish@amserve.net
D: £16.00–£18.50 **S:** £16.50–£19.00
Beds: 1F 1D **Baths:** 1 Sh
🛇 🅿 (4) ⅙ 📺 🛏 ✕ 🛆 Ⅴ ₤

Rhngarbh Croft, Appin, Argyll, *PA38
4BA.*
Tranquil lochside croft in beautiful
wooded countryside. Good local food.
Open: All Year
Grades: STB 4 Star
01631 730309 Fax: 01631 730577
welcome@cheesemaking.co.uk
D: £24.00 **S:** £34.00
Beds: 1D 1T **Baths:** 1 En 1 Pr
🛇 🅿 ⅙ 📺 🛏 ✕ 🛆 Ⅴ ₤ ċ CC

Arden

NS3684

Polnaberoch, Arden, Luss, Alexandria,
Dunbartonshire, G83 8RQ.
Charming country cottage in lovely
gardens with beautiful surrounding
views.
Open: Easter to Nov
01389 850615 (also fax)
Mrs McNair
maclomond@sol.co.uk
D: £23.00–£27.00 **S:** £35.00–£40.00
Beds: 1D 1T **Baths:** 2 En
🅿 (3) ⅙ 📺 ✕ 🛆 ₤

Ardfern

NM8004   🕮 *Galley Of Lorne, Creels*

Lunga, Ardfern, Lochgilphead, Argyll,
PA31 8QR.
C17th estate Mansion overlooks islands &
Firth of Lorne. 3,000 acre private coastal
estate.
Open: All Year
Grades: STB 1 Star B&B
01852 500237 Mr Lindsay-MacDougall
Fax: 01852 500639
colin@lunga.demon.co.uk
D: £19.00–£22.00 **S:** fr £18.00
Beds: 1F 2D 1T 1S **Baths:** 4 Pr 1 Sh
🛇 🅿 📺 🛏 ✕ Ⅴ ₤

Tigh An Innis, Ardlarach Road, Ardfern,
Lochgilphead, Argyll, *PA31 8QN.*
Beautiful modern bungalow set near the
shores of Loch Craignish.
Open: All Year (not Xmas/New Year)
01852 500682 Mrs Wylie
joan.wylie@tesco.net
D: £18.50–£20.00 **S:** £18.50–£20.00
Beds: 1T 2D **Baths:** 3 En
🛇 🅿 (3) ⅙ 📺 🛆 Ⅴ ₤ ċ

Arduaine

NM8010   🕮 *Lord of the Isles*

Asknish Cottage, Arduaine, Oban,
Argyll, *PA34 4XQ.*
Open: All Year
01852 200247 Miss Campbell
D: £16.50–£17.50 **S:** £17.00–£22.00
Beds: 2D 1T **Baths:** 1 Sh
🛇 🅿 (3) ⅙ 📺 🛏 🛆 Ⅴ ₤
Halfway between Oban & Lochgilphead.
Warm welcome in hillside cottage
overlooking islands Jura to Luing, ideal
base for island hopping, Arduaine
Gardens, 0.5 miles. Boat trips, birds,
castles, walking, etc. nearby. Wild garden,
tame owner.

Arrochar

NN2904   🕮 *Loch Long Hotel, Callum's Bar,
Inverberg Inn*

Ferry Cottage, Ardmay, Arrochar,
Dunbartonshire, G83 7AH.
Open: All Year (not Xmas)
Grades: STB 2 Star
01301 702428 Mrs Bennetton
Fax: 01301 702729
CaroleBennetton@aol.com
D: £17.50–£23.50 **S:** £22.00–£35.00
Beds: 1F 2D 1T **Baths:** 3 En 1 Sh
🛇 (2) 🅿 (6) ⅙ 📺 ✕ 🛆 ₤ ċ CC
Originally the ferryman's cottage some
100 years ago, has now been fully
refurbished into our family home.
Elevated views overlooking Loch Long
and the Cobbler, 5 mins from Loch
Lomond. All rooms ensuite. Credit cards
accepted, tea/coffee, TV. We are a non-
smoking establishment.

BATHROOMS

Pr - Private

Sh - Shared

En - Ensuite

Seabank, Main Road, Arrochar, G83 7AG.
Open: All Year **Grades:** STB 2 Star
01301 702555 S Smillie
D: £16.00–£20.00 **S:** £20.00–£28.00
Beds: 1F 1D 1T
🛇 (8) 🅿 (6) Ⅴ 🛏 🛆 Ⅴ ₤
Lovely old house, beautiful views Loch
and Arrochar Alps. Great base hill-
walking, touring, fishing. Loch Lomond 2
miles, Glasgow 40 miles, historic Stirling
1.5 hours' drive. Walking distance village
pub - great food, reasonably priced, warm
welcome from Sam and Kathleen.

Benderloch

NM9038

Hawthorn, Benderloch, Oban, Argyll,
PA37 1QS.
Open: All Year
Grades: STB 3 Star
01631 720452 Mrs Currie
D: £18.00–£22.00 **S:** £25.00–£30.00
Beds: 1F 1D 1T **Baths:** 2 En 1 Pr
🅿 (5) 📺 ✕ 🛆 Ⅴ ₤ ċ CC
A warm welcome awaits you in this
delightful bungalow situated in 20 acres
of farming land. All rooms ensuite,
peaceful accommodation. 9 miles from
Oban, the main ferry terminal for the
islands. Ideal base for touring. Also beach
nearby and family restaurant 50 yds.

Rowantree Cottage, Keil Farm,
Benderloch, Oban, Argyll, *PA37 1QP.*
Peaceful, picturesque location, forest, hill
walks, trails and beach nearby.
Open: Easter to Oct
Grades: STB 3 Star
01631 720433 Mrs Golding
alan&margiealdwell@email.msn.com
D: £14.00–£16.50 **S:** £19.00–£21.50
Beds: 1F 1D 1T **Baths:** 1 Sh
🛇 🅿 (4) ⅙ 📺 🛏 ✕ 🛆 Ⅴ ₤

Bridge of Orchy

NN2939   🕮 *Bridge Of Orchy Hotel*

Glen Orchy Farm, Glen Orchy, Bridge
of Orchy, Argyll, *PA33 1BD.*
Remote sheep farm. Enjoy wildlife,
birdwatching, walking, climbing amongst
beautiful scenery. **Open:** Mar to Nov
01838 200221 Mrs MacLennan
Fax: 01838 200231
D: £16.00–£18.00 **S:** £16.00–£18.00
Beds: 2F **Baths:** 1 Sh
🛇 🅿 📺 ✕ 🛆 ₤

BUTE   Rothesay

NS0864   🕮 *Black Bull, Ardmory House,
Kettledrum*

Battery Lodge, 25 Battery Place,
Rothesay, Isle of Bute, PA20 9DU.
Open: All Year
01700 502169 M Leyden
D: £20.00–£22.00 **S:** £18.00–£20.00
Beds: 2F 1T 4D 1S **Baths:** 4 En 2 Pr 1 Sh
🛇 🅿 (7) 📺 ✕ 🛆 Ⅴ ₤ ċ
Built in 1865, Battery Lodge is a splendid
mid-Victorian enjoying spectacular views
across Rothesay Bay to the Argyllshire
Hills. Your hosts Martin and Lorraine offer
attractive bedrooms, most with ensuite
facilities, plus warm Scottish hospitality
with beautiful home cooking.

Alamein House Hotel, *28 Battery Place, Rothesay, Isle of Bute, PA20 9DU.*
Magnificent views from seafront bedrooms. Yachting, fishing, riding, cycling closeby.
Open: All Year
01700 502395 J F Hutchings
D: £19.00–£21.00 **S:** £20.00–£22.00
Beds: 1F 3T 3D **Baths:** 3 En 1 Pr 2 Sh
⏰ 🅿 (5) 📺 🛏 🎗 🖩 💟 🛴 🚶

The Commodore, *12 Battery Place, Rothesay, Isle of Bute, PA20 9DP.*
Fully modernised sea front guest house, family run, 'Which?' recommended.
Open: All Year
Grades: STB 3 Star
01700 502178 Mr Spear
Fax: 01700 503492
spearcommodere@aol.com
D: £18.00–£25.00 **S:** £25.00–£35.00
Beds: 2T 4D **Baths:** 6 En
⏰ 🅿 📺 🛏 🎗 🖩 💟 🛴

Avion, *16 Argyle Place, Rothesay, Isle of Bute, PA20 0BA.*
Warm, friendly, family seafront home. Breakfast to diet for.
Open: All Year
01700 505897 (also fax)
A Smith
avion@compuserve.com
D: £17.00–£22.00 **S:** £17.00–£20.00
Beds: 1F 1T 1S **Baths:** 2 En 1 Pr
⏰ 📺 🛏 🖩 💟 🛴

Campbeltown

NR7220 🏨 *Ardshiel Hotel*

Homestone Farm, *Campbeltown, Argyll, PA28 6RL.*
Wonderfully, peaceful location on working farm/riding centre. Excellent food.
Open: Easter to Oct
01586 552437 L McArthur
lorna@relaxscotland.com
D: £15.00–£17.50 **S:** £15.00–£17.50
Beds: 3D 2S **Baths:** 3 En 1 Sh
🅿 (10) 📺 ✕ 🛴

Sandiway, *Fort Argyll Road, Low Askomil, Campbeltown, Argyll, PA28 6SN.*
Warm welcome at modern bungalow on edge of town (lochside).
Open: All Year (not Xmas)
Grades: STB 3 Star
01586 552280 Mrs Bell
106751.1276@compuserve.com
D: £18.00–£20.00 **S:** £23.00–£25.00
Beds: 2T **Baths:** 1 Pr 1 Sh
⏰ (6) 🅿 (5) 🎗 📺 ✕ 🖩 💟 🛴 🚶

Bellfield Farm, *High Askomil, Campbeltown, Argyll, PA28 6EN.*
Comfortable farmhouse overlooking Campbeltown and loch; convenient to local amenities.
Open: All Year
01586 552646 (also fax)
Mrs McLean
D: £15.00–£17.00 **S:** £15.00–£17.00
Beds: 2T 1S **Baths:** 1 Sh
⏰ (4) 📺 🛏 ✕ 🖩 🛴

Cardross

NS3477 🏨 *Muirholm*

Glengate Cottage, *Main Road, Cardross, Dumbarton, G82 5NZ.*
Picturesque village. Minutes from Helensburgh seaside town. NTS. Properties and golf nearby.
Open: Easter to Oct **Grades:** STB 2 Star
01389 841737 Miss Mackie
D: £19.00–£21.00 **S:** £17.00
Beds: 2D 1S **Baths:** 1 Pr 1 Sh
🅿 (2) 🎗 📺 🖩 🛴

Kirkton House, *Darleith Road, Cardross, Argyll & Bute, G82 5EZ.*
Old farmstead hotel. Tranquil setting. Clyde views. Wine and dine.
Open: Feb to Nov **Grades:** STB 4 Star, AA 5 Diamond, RAC 5 Diamond
01389 841951 Mr & Mrs Macdonald
Fax: 01389 841868 stil@kirktonhouse.com
D: £30.50–£35.00 **S:** £40.50–£45.00
Beds: 4F 2T **Baths:** 6 En
⏰ 🅿 (12) 📺 🛏 ✕ 🖩 💟 🛴 🚶 cc

Carradale

NR8138 🏨 *Carradale Hotel, Ashbank Hotel*

The Mains Farm, *Carradale, Campbeltown, Argyll, PA28 6QG.*
Traditional, comfortable farmhouse near beach, forest walks, fishing, golf, wildlife.
Open: Easter to Oct
01583 431216 Mrs MacCormick
D: £16.50–£17.00 **S:** £16.50–£17.00
Beds: 1F 1D 1S **Baths:** 1 Sh
⏰ 🅿 (3) 🎗 📺 🛏 🛴

Ashbank Hotel, *Carradale, Campbeltown, Argyll, PA28 6RY.*
Centre of fishing village. Sea views, adjacent to golf course. **Open:** Easter to Oct
01583 431650 Mrs Cook
D: £21.00–£24.50 **S:** £23.00–£24.50
Beds: 1D 2T 1S **Baths:** 3 En 1 Pr
⏰ (1) 🅿 (5) 📺 🛏 ✕ 🖩 💟 🛴

Clachan (Kintyre)

NR7655

The Old Smithy, *Clachan, Tarbert, Argyll, PA29 6XL.*
Highland hospitality rated excellent by returning guests; home-baking at bedtime. **Open:** All Year (not Xmas)
01880 740635 Mrs Moller
moller_kintyre@tesco.net
D: £15.00–£16.00 **S:** £16.00–£17.00
Beds: 1D 1T **Baths:** 1 Sh
⏰ 🅿 (2) 🎗 📺 🖩 💟 🛴 🚶 cc

Clachan of Glendaruel

NS0083

Glendaruel Hotel, *Clachan of Glendaruel, Colintraive, Argyll, PA22 3AA.*
Charming family run hotel. Ideal for fishing, touring, walking etc.
Open: All Year (not Xmas)
Grades: STB 2 Star
01369 820274 Fax: 01369 820317
info@glendaruel-hotel.com
D: £30.00–£35.00 **S:** £35.00–£40.00
Beds: 3T 2D 1S **Baths:** 6 En
🅿 (10) 📺 🛏 ✕ 🖩 💟 🛴 cc

Colintraive

NS0374

Colintraive Hotel, *Colintraive, Argyll, PA22 3AS.*
Former Victorian hunting lodge - comfortable and informal family run hotel.
Open: All Year
Grades: STB 2 Star
01700 841207
Mr Williamson
kyleshotel@aol.com
D: £22.00–£28.00 **S:** £26.00–£30.00
Beds: 1F 1D 1T **Baths:** 4 Pr
⏰ 🅿 📺 🛏 ✕ 🖩 💟 🛴

Connel

NM9133 🏨 *Falls of Lora Hotel, Dunstafanage Arms*

Rosebank, *Connel, Oban, Argyll, PA37 1PA.*
Open: May to Sep
Grades: STB 1 Star
01631 710316
R L MacKechnie
D: £14.00–£16.00 **S:** £15.00–£17.00
Beds: 1D 1T 1S **Baths:** 1 Sh
⏰ 📺 🛏 🛴
Family house in quiet situation in Connel village overlooking Loch Etive, 5 miles from Oban. Excellent touring centre, large garden at rear. Home made preserves a speciality. Hand-knitted articles for sale. A warm welcome to home and overseas visitors.

Falls Of Lora Hotel, *Connel Ferry, Connel, Oban, Argyll, PA37 1PB.*
Warm, friendly atmosphere, accommodation to suit everyone, excellent food.
Open: Feb to Dec
Grades: STB 2 Star, AA 2 Star, RAC 2 Star
01631 710483 (also fax)
Miss Innes
D: £19.50–£55.50 **S:** £29.50–£53.50
Beds: 4F 6D 14T 6S **Baths:** 30 En
⏰ 🅿 (40) 📺 🛏 ✕ 🖩 💟 🛴 🚶 cc

Ronebhal Guest House, *Connel, Oban, Argyll, PA37 1PJ.*
Beautiful Victorian villa, speculator sea views. Highest standards and comfort.
Open: All Year (not Xmas/New Year)
Grades: STB 4 Star, AA 4 Diamond, RAC 4 Diamond Sparkling
01631 710310 (also fax)
Mr & Mrs Strachen
ronebhal@btinternet.com
D: £19.00–£28.50 **S:** £18.00–£45.00
Beds: 1F 3D 1T 1S **Baths:** 4 En 2 Pr
⏰ (6) 🅿 (6) 🎗 📺 🖩 💟 🛴 🚶 cc

Ach Na Craig, *Grosvenor Crescent, Connel, Oban, Argyll, PA37 1PQ.*
Modern house in woodland glade, all rooms ground floor.
Open: Easter to Oct
Grades: STB 2 Star
01631 710588 Mrs Craig
D: £18.00–£19.00 **S:** £25.00–£29.00
Beds: 1D 2T **Baths:** 3 En
🅿 (3) 🎗 📺 🛏 ✕ 🖩 💟 🛴 🚶

Craobh Haven

NM7907 ◄ *Loch Melfort, Galley Of Lorne*

Buidhe Lodge, *Craobh Haven, Lochgilphead, Argyll, PA31 8UA.*
Open: All Year (not Xmas)
Grades: STB 3 Star
01852 500291 Mr & Mrs Twinn
D: £23.00–£26.00 **S:** £33.00
Beds: 2D 4T **Baths:** 6 Pr
🛇 🅿 (8) 🅃 🍴 ✕ 🛏 🖿 🆅 🍲 ♿
Swiss-style lodge located on shores of Loch Shuna (20 miles from Oban). Near Arduaine NT Gardens and Historic Kilmartin Valley. Walk, ride or sail in spectacular West Coast scenery and return to our lodge to relax, enjoy good food and company.

Lunga, *Ardfern, Lochgilphead, Argyll, PA31 8QR.*
C17th estate mansion overlooks islands & Firth of Lorne. 3,000 acre private coastal estate. **Open:** All Year
Grades: STB 1 Star B&B
01852 500231 Mr Lindsay-MacDougall
Fax: 01852 500639
colin@lunga.demon.co.uk
D: £19.00–£22.00 **S:** fr £18.00
Beds: 1F 2D 1T 1S **Baths:** 4 Pr 1 Sh
🛇 🅿 🅃 🍴 ✕ 🖿 🆅 🍲

Dalmally

NN1626 ◄ *Glen Orchy Lodge*

Orchy Bank Guest House, *Dalmally, Argyll, PA33 1AS.*
Victorian house on the bank of the River Orchy.
Open: All Year
Grades: STB 2 Star GH
01838 200370 Mr Burke
D: £17.00–£20.00 **S:** £25.00–£28.00
Beds: 2F 2D 2T 2S **Baths:** 4 Sh
🛇 🅿 (8) 🅃 🍴 🖿 🆅 🍲

Craig Villa Guest House, *Dalmally, Argyll, PA33 1AX.*
Restored farmhouse set amidst breathtaking mountain scenery. All private suites. **Open:** Easter to Oct
01838 200255 (also fax)
Mr Cressey
D: £19.00–£23.00 **S:** fr £25.00
Beds: 2F 2D 2T **Baths:** 6 En
🛇 (1) 🅿 (10) 🅃 ✕ 🖿 🍲

Dunoon

NS1776 ◄ *Royal Marine Hotel, Hunters Quay*

Moncrieff, *133 Alexandra Parade, Dunoon, Argyll, PA23 8AW.*
Open: All Year
Grades: STB 2 Star Disabled facilities
01369 707945 (also fax)
Mrs Peel
willypeel@aol.com
D: £16.00–£20.00 **S:** £19.00–£25.00
Beds: 1T 2D **Baths:** 1 En 2 Sh
🛇 🅃 🍴 🖿 🆅 🍲 ♿
Family Tudor style home, panoramic sea views, private gardens, wheelchair users catered for. Perfect for walking or cycling in the Argyll Forest Park. Breathtaking drives over mountains and through sleepy glens. Daily sea cruises during the season

Lyall Cliff Hotel, *Alexandra Parade, East Bay, Dunoon, Argyll, PA23 8AW.*
Beautifully situated family-run seafront hotel. 3 ground floor rooms.
Open: Jan to Oct
Grades: STB 3 Star, AA 1 Star
01369 702041 (also fax) Mr & Mrs Norris
lyallcliff@talk21.com
D: £20.00–£30.00 **S:** £22.00–£35.00
Beds: 2F 4D 4T **Baths:** 10 En
🛇 🅿 (10) 🍴 🍴 ✕ 🖿 🆅 🍲 ♿ cc

Craigieburn Hotel, *Alexandra Parade, East Bay, Dunoon, Argyll, PA23 8AN.*
Friendly family-run private hotel with superb sea views.
Open: All Year (not Xmas)
Grades: STB 2 Star
01369 702048 Mrs Hutchinson
dangle@globalnet.co.uk
D: £16.00–£20.00 **S:** £16.00–£20.00
Beds: 3F 2D 2T 2S **Baths:** 3 Sh
🛇 🅿 (5) 🅃 🍴 ✕ 🖿 🍲

Milton Tower Hotel, *West Bay, Dunoon, Argyll, PA23 7LD.*
Small 3 Star family-run hotel with emphasis on home-cooked meals.
Open: All Year (not Xmas)
01369 705785 (also fax) Mr Fagan
miltontower@ic24.net
D: £18.00–£22.50 **S:** £18.00–£22.50
Beds: 2F 4D 1T 1S **Baths:** 7 En 1 Pr
🛇 🅿 (9) 🅃 ✕ 🖿 🆅 🍲 cc

Glenbarr

NR6736

Arnicle House, *Glenbarr, Tarbert, Argyll, PA29 6UZ.*
Beautiful country house situated on working farm and equitation centre.
Open: All Year
01583 421208 (also fax) Mrs McArthur
D: £16.00–£20.00 **S:** £20.00
Beds: 1D 2T **Baths:** 1 En 2 Sh
🛇 🅿 (6) 🅃 🖿 🆅 🍲

Helensburgh

NS2982 ◄ *Ardencaple Hotel, Toby, Commodore, Pinewood, Uppercrust*

County Lodge Hotel, *Old Luss Road, Helensburgh, Dunbartonshire, G84 7BH.*
Open: All Year
01436 672034 Fax: 01436 672033
D: fr £20.00 **S:** fr £20.00
Beds: 1F 3D 7T 1S **Baths:** 8 En 2 Sh
🛇 🅿 🅃 🍴 ✕ 🖿 🆅 🍲 cc
Saviour traditional Scottish hospitality at our family-run inn style hotel. Ideal location for Loch Lomond, Trossachs, Clyde area or for weekends away. Cosy lounge bar with log fire, entertainment every weekend. Brochure available, short break discount.

Drumfork Farm, *Helensburgh, G84 7JY.*
Working farm with friendly family, 20 minutes from Loch Lomond.
Open: All Year (not Xmas/New Year)
01436 672329 (also fax)
Mrs Howie
drumforkfm@aol.com
D: £20.00–£25.00 **S:** £30.00–£40.00
Beds: 2T 1D **Baths:** 3 En
🛇 🅿 (4) ✁ 🅃 🖿 🆅 🍲 ♿ cc

Ravenswood, *32 Suffolk Street, Helensburgh, Dunbartonshire, G84 9PA.*
Member walkers and cyclists scheme - Sliver Green Tourism Award.
Open: All year
Grades: STB 3 Star
01436 672112 (also fax)
Mrs Richards
ravenswood@breathemail.net
D: £25.00–£40.00 **S:** £25.00–£50.00
Beds: 2D 1T 1S **Baths:** 2 En 1 Pr 1 Sh
🛇 🅿 (4) ✁ 🆅 ✕ 🖿 🍲

Yetholm, *103 East Princes Street, Helensburgh, Dunbartonshire, G84 7DN.*
Open: All Year (not Xmas)
Grades: STB 3 Star
01436 673271 Mrs Mackenzie
D: £18.00–£22.00 **S:** £20.00–£22.00
Beds: 1D 1T **Baths:** 1 Pr 1 En
🛇 (5) 🅿 (3) ✁ 🅃 🖿 🆅 🍲
Convenient for an afternoon visit to 'Hill House' - Rennie Mackintosh. 10 mins drive to Loch Lomond. Good base for golf, sailing or touring Trossachs, or day trips to Glasgow, Oban, Inveraray.

Eastbank, *10 Hanover Street, Helensburgh, Dunbartonshire, G84 7AW.*
Upper flat of Victorian house 30 minutes from Glasgow airport.
Open: All Year (not Xmas)
Grades: STB 3 Star B&B
01436 673665 (also fax)
Mrs Ross
dorothy-ross@breathemail.net
D: £18.00–£23.00 **S:** £18.00–£20.00
Beds: 1F 1T 1S **Baths:** 1 En 1 Sh
🛇 (3) 🅿 (4) 🅃 🖿 🆅 🍲 cc

Arran View, *32 Barclay Drive, Helensburgh, Dunbartonshire, G84 9RA.*
Panoramic sea views, Convenient NT Hill House, Loch Lomond, golf.
Open: All Year
Grades: STB 4 Star
01436 673713 Mr & Mrs Sanders
Fax: 01436 672595
arranview@btinternet.com
D: £19.00–£22.00 **S:** £20.00–£25.00
Beds: 1D 1T 2S **Baths:** 2 En 1 Pr 1 Sh
🅿 (5) ✁ 🅃 🖿 🆅 🍲

28 Macleod Drive, *Helensburgh, Dunbartonshire, G84 9QS.*
Stunning views near Loch Lomond, Golf, walking and the Highlands.
Open: June to Sept
Grades: STB 3 Star
01436 675206 Mr & Mrs Calder
g.calder@talk21.com
D: £17.00–£19.00 **S:** £18.00–£20.00
Beds: 1F 1T 1S **Baths:** 2 Sh
🛇 🅿 (3) ✁ 🅃 🖿 🆅 🍲

4 Redclyffe Gardens, *Helensburgh, Dunbartonshire, G84 9JJ.*
Modern family home; sea views, quiet cul-de-sac, adjacent Mackintosh hill house.
Open: All Year (not Xmas)
Grades: STB 3 Star
01436 677688 (also fax)
Mrs Weston
dweston440@aol.com
D: £21.00–£24.00 **S:** £25.00–£30.00
Beds: 1D 1T **Baths:** 1 Pr 1 En
🛇 🅿 (3) ✁ 🅃 🖿 🆅 🍲

Garemount Lodge, Shandon,
Helensburgh, G84 8NP.
Delightful lochside home; large garden;
convenient Loch Lomond, Glasgow,
Highlands.
Open: All Year (not Xmas)
Grades: STB 3 Star
01436 820780 (also fax)
Mrs Cowie
nickcowie@compuserve.com
D: £20.00–£23.00 **S:** £28.00–£36.00
Beds: 1F 1D **Baths:** 1 En 1 Pr
🛏 🅿 (4) ⅍ 📺 🐾 💷 🖥 🎂

Maybank, 185 East Clde Street,
Helensburgh, Dunbartonshire, G84 7AG.
Attractive, early Victorian home in a level
location.
Open: All Year
Grades: STB 3 Star
01436 672865
Mrs Barella
D: £18.00 **S:** £22.00
Beds: 1F 1D 1T 1S **Baths:** 2 Pr
🛏 🅿 📺 🐾 💷 🖥 🎂 👓

Bonniebrae, 80 Sinclair Street,
Helensburgh, Dunbartonshire, G84 8TU.
Stone-built cottage, private garden. 2
mins walk town centre, 10 mins drive
Loch Lomond.
Open: All Year
Grades: STB 2 Star
01436 671469
Mrs Kirkpatrick
D: £20.00 **S:** £20.00
Beds: 2F **Baths:** En
🛏 🅿 (3) ⅍ 💷 🎂

Thorndean, 64 Colquhoun Street,
Helensburgh, Dunbartonshire, G84 9NF.
Warm, spacious Victorian home. 3 nights
for price of 2 in off season.
Open: All Year
01436 674922 Mrs Urquhart
Fax: 01436 679913
theurquharts@sol.co.uk
D: £22.00–£26.00 **S:** £22.00–£36.00
Beds: 1F 1D 1T **Baths:** 2 En 1 Pr
🛏 🅿 (8) ⅍ 📺 💷 🖥 cc

Greenpark, Charlotte Street,
Helensburgh, Dunbartonshire, G84 7ST.
Grade B Listed Art Deco villa set in one
acre of park-like grounds.
Open: Apr to Oct
01436 671545 (also fax)
Mrs McNeil
jmcneil@greenpark.swinternet.co.uk
D: £21.00–£24.00
Beds: 1D 1T **Baths:** 1 En 1 Pr
🅿 (3) 📺 🐾 💷 🎂

Lethamhill, 20 West Dhuhill Drive,
Helensburgh, Dunbartonshire, G84 9AW.
Delightful villa designed by John Burnet
in 1911. Furnished with antiques and
memorabilia.
Open: All Year (not Xmas)
01436 676016 (also fax)
Mrs Johnston
D: £25.00–£30.00 **S:** £35.00–£45.00
Beds: 2D 1T **Baths:** 3 En
🛏 🅿 (10) ⅍ 📺 💷 🖥 🎂

Innellan

NS1469 🍺 Osborne, Braemar

Ashgrove Guest House, Wyndham
Road, Innellan, Dunoon, Argyll, PA23 7SH.
Mid-19th century country house in
peaceful location, outstanding views.
Open: All Year (not Xmas)
01369 830306 Ms Kohls
Fax: 01369 830776
kohlsm@netcomuk.co.uk
D: £20.00–£23.00 **S:** £20.00–£23.00
Beds: 1F 1D 1T **Baths:** 3 En
🛏 📺 🐾 💷 🖥 🎂

Inveraray

NN0908 🍺 George Hotel, Fernpoint Hotel

Claonairigh House, Bridge of
Douglas, Inveraray, Argyll, PA32 8XT.
Open: All Year (not Xmas)
Grades: STB 3 Star
01499 302160 Fax: 01499 302774
fiona&argyll-scotland.demon.co.uk
D: £16.00–£22.00 **S:** £16.00–£25.00
Beds: 1D 2T **Baths:** 1 En 2 Sh
🛏 🅿 (8) ⅍ 📺 🗡 💷 🖥 🎂
A historic country house ideally situated
for access to the Argyll countryside and
coast. Nearby attractions include horse
riding, cycling, boat hide, golfing, fishing
and walking we can offer excellent
breakfast, beautiful rooms and a warm
welcome.

The Old Rectory, Inveraray, Argyll,
PA32 8UH.
Family-run Georgian house overlooking
Loch Fyne.
Open: All Year (not Xmas)
01499 302280 Mrs Maclaren
D: £15.00–£20.00 **S:** £15.00–£20.00
Beds: 4F 3D 1T 1S **Baths:** 3 Sh
🛏 (3) 🅿 (9) ⅍ 📺 💷 🖥

Creag Dhubh, Inveraray, Argyll, PA32 8XF.
Family-run bed and breakfast, superbly
situated by Loch Fyne.
Open: Feb to Nov
01499 302430 Mrs MacLugash
creagdhubh@freeuk.com
D: £20.00–£25.00
Beds: 1F 3D 1T **Baths:** 5 En
🛏 🅿 (6) ⅍ 📺 💷 🖥 🎂

Inverarnan

NN3118 🍺 Stagger Inn, Drovers Inn

Rose Cottage, Inverarnan, Glen
Falloch, Arrochar, Dunbartonshire, G83 7DX.
Renovated C18th cottage on West
Highland Way near Loch Lomond.
Open: All Year (not Xmas)
01301 704255 Mr and Mrs Fletcher
D: £19.00–£23.00
Beds: 1F 2T **Baths:** 1 En 1 Sh
🛏 🅿 (2) ⅍ 🗡 💷 🎂

All details shown are as
supplied by B&B owners in
Autumn 2000

Kilchrenan

NN0322 🍺 Kilchrenan Inn, Trade Winds

Innisfree, Kilchrenan, Taynuilt, Argyll,
PA35 1HG.
Wonderful scenery, modern croft house,
quiet, Oban 19 miles, popular destination.
Open: Easter to Sep
01866 833352 Mrs Wright
D: fr £18.00 **S:** fr £18.00
Beds: 1D 1T **Baths:** 2 Sh
🛏 🅿 (4) 📺 💷

Kilfinan

NR9378 🍺 Kilfinan Hotel

Auchnaskeoch Farm House,
Kilfinan, Tighnabruaich, Argyll, PA21 2ER.
Enjoy unspoiled countryside and
magnificent scenery; a warm Scottish
welcome awaits you. **Open:** All Year (not
Xmas) **Grades:** STB 3 Star
01700 811397 Mrs Mackay
Fax: 01700 811799
D: £17.50–£20.00 **S:** £18.00–£21.00
Beds: 1D **Baths:** 1 En
🅿 (1) 📺 ✕ 💷 🖥 🎂

Kilmartin

NR8398

Dunchragaig House, Kilmartin,
Lochgilphead, Argyll, PA31 8RG.
Comfortable detached home in large
garden, opposite historic standing stones.
Open: All Year (Not Xmas)
01546 605209 Mrs Norman
Fax: 01546 605300 dunchraig@aol.com
D: £18.00–£22.00
Beds: 1F 2D 2T **Baths:** 5 En
🛏 🅿 (6) ⅍ 📺 🐾 ✕ 💷 🖥 cc

Kilmore

NM8825 🍺 Barn Bar

Invercairn, Musdale Road, Kilmore,
Oban, Argyll, PA34 4XX.
Open: Easter to Oct
Grades: STB 4 Star
01631 770301 (also fax) Mrs MacPherson
invercairn.kilmore@virgin.net
D: £20.00–£25.00 **S:** £25.00–£30.00
Beds: 2D 1T **Baths:** 3 En
🅿 (4) ⅍ 📺 💷 🖥 🎂
Beautiful spot, only 10 minute drive from
Oban town centre. Wonderful base for
seeing the splendours of Argyll and the
Isles. Oban, a busy port and local centre,
offers visitors daily excursions to Mull
and Iona. Good food,warm West Highland
hospitality.

Ledaig

NM9037 🍺 Hawthorn Cottage

An Struan, Ledaig, Oban, Argyll, PA37 1QS.
Large modern bungalow in the
picturesque village of Benderloch, 7 miles
north of Oban. **Open:** All Year (not Xmas)
Grades: STB 3 Star
01631 720301 Mrs Knowles
Fax: 01631 720734
frankwop@btinternet.com
D: £18.00–£20.00 **S:** £20.00–£25.00
Beds: 2D 1T **Baths:** 1 En 1 Sh
🛏 🅿 ⅍ 📺 🐾 ✕ 💷 🖥 👓

Planning a longer stay? Always ask for any special rates

Lerags

NM8424

Lerags House, Lerags, Oban, Argyll, *PA34 4SE.*
Enchanting country house in mature gardens on Loch Feochan shore.
Open: Easter to Oct
Grades: STB 3 Star, AA 4 Diamond
01631 563381 N A Hill
Fax: 01631 563381
leragshouse@supanet.com
D: £22.50–£30.00 **S:** £22.50–£30.00
Beds: 4D 2T 1S **Baths:** 7 En
⛱ (12) 🅿 (7) ⚲ 📺 ✕ 🛏 📖 📹 🍴

Lochgilphead

NR8687   ⚑ *Stag Hotel, Victoria Hotel*

Corbiere, Achnabreac, Lochgilphead, Argyll, *PA31 8SG.*
Open: All Year (not Xmas/New Year)
Grades: STB 3 Star
01546 602764 Mrs Sinclair
D: £16.50–£17.50 **S:** £20.00
Beds: 1T 1D **Baths:** 2 Sh
⛱ 🅿 📺 🛏 🛢 📹 🍴
Bedrooms are spacious, comfortable, thoughtfully equipped. Peaceful, rural location. Uninterrupted views over meadows towards Crinan Canal and hills beyond. Convenient for exploring historic mid-Argyll, Kintyre Peninsula and Inner Isles. Looking forward to welcoming you.

Empire Travel Lodge, Union Street, Lochgilphead, Argyll, *PA31 8JS.*
Former cinema converted to create quality travel lodge.
Open: All Year (not Xmas)
Grades: STB 3 Star
01546 602381 Mr Haysom
Fax: 01546 606606
D: £23.00 **S:** £23.00
Beds: 2F 5D 2T **Baths:** 9 En
⛱ 🅿 (9) 📺 🛏 📹 🍴 🚃 1 cc

Kilmory House, Paterson Street, Lochgilphead, Argyll, *PA31 8JP.*
Lovely house & gardens situated lochside. Most rooms with loch views.
Open: All Year
Grades: STB 2 Star
01546 603658 Mr Moore
D: £16.50–£22.00 **S:** fr £20.00
Beds: 3D 3T **Baths:** 2 En 2 Pr 2 Sh
⛱ (10) 🅿 (16) ⚲ 📺 ✕ 🛏 📹 🍴 cc

The Argyll Hotel, Lochnell Street, Lochgilphead, Argyll, *PA31 8JN.*
Friendly village centre inn, quality restaurant, bar and value accommodation.
Open: All Year
01546 602221 Mr Smith
Fax: 01546 603576
argyll.hotel@btclick.com
D: £19.00–£25.00 **S:** £19.00–£25.00
Beds: 4D 4T 4S **Baths:** 6 En 2 Sh
⛱ 🅿 (4) 📺 🛏 ✕ 🛢 📹 🍴 cc

Luss

NS3592   ⚑ *Colquhoun Arms*

Shantron Farm, Shantron Cottage, Luss, Alexandria, Dunbartonshire, *G83 8RH.*
5000-acre farm with spectacular views of Loch and surrounding area.
Open: Mar to Nov
Grades: STB 3 Star
01389 850231 (also fax)
Mrs Lennox
rjlennox@shantron.u-net.com
D: £22.00–£30.00 **S:** £25.00–£30.00
Beds: 1F 1D 1T **Baths:** 3 En
⛱ 🅿 (3) 📺 📹 🍴 cc

Doune of Glen Douglas Farm, Luss, Loch Lomond, Alexandria, Argyll & Bute, *G83 8PD.*
Open: Easter to Oct
Grades: STB 4 Star
01301 702312 Mrs Robertson
Fax: 01301 702916
pjrobertson@glendouglas.u-net.com
D: £22.00–£30.00 **S:** £25.00–£35.00
Beds: 2D 1T **Baths:** 1 En 2 Sh
⛱ 🅿 📺 📹 🛏 📖 📹 🍴 cc
Remote working hill sheep farm set in 6000 acres hills above Loch Lomond, where a warm welcome awaits you. You can enjoy home cooking and home made preserves and eggs from our own hens before hill walking or observing the sheep and Highland cattle.

Blairglas, Luss, Alexandria, Dunbartonshire, *G83 8RG.*
Between Luss and Cameron house 25 mins from Glasgow airport.
Open: All Year (not Xmas)
Grades: STB 3 Star
01389 850278 (also fax)
Mrs Buchanan
D: £18.00–£23.00
Beds: 1F 1D 1T **Baths:** 3 En
⛱ 🅿 📺 🛏 ✕ 📖 🍴 ♿

The Corries, Inverbeg, Luss, Alexandria, Dunbartonshire, *G83 8PD.*
Beautiful easily accessible rural location. Panoramic views of Loch Lomond.
Open: All Year (not Xmas)
Grades: STB 3 Star
01436 860275 Mrs Carruthers
the_corries@hotmail.com
D: £20.00–£25.00 **S:** £25.00–£35.00
Beds: 1F 1D 1T **Baths:** 3 En
🅿 (4) ⚲ 🛏 📖 🍴 cc

Minard

NR9896   ⚑ *Lochgair Hotel*

Minard Castle, Minard, Inveraray, Argyll, *PA32 8YB.*
Warm welcome in our nineteenth-century castle beside Loch Fyne.
Open: April to Oct
Grades: STB 4 Star
01546 886272 (also fax)
Mr Gayre
reinoldgayre@bizonline.co.uk
D: £30.00–£40.00 **S:** £30.00–£40.00
Beds: 1F 2T **Baths:** 3 En
⛱ 🅿 (6) ⚲ 📺 🛏 📖 📹 🍴 cc

Oban

NM8630   ⚑ *Oban Inn, Aulays Bar, Kelvin Hotel, Lorne, Soroba House, Barn Bar, Kings Knoll, Donellys, Rowantree Hotel, Step Inn*

Thelwillows, Glenslellgh Road, Oban, Argyll, *PA34 4PP.*
Open: All Year (not Xmas/New Year)
01631 566240 D F Coates
Fax: 01631 566783
enquiries@obanaccommodation.com
D: £20.00–£25.00 **S:** £20.00–£25.00
Beds: 1T 1D **Baths:** 2 En
🅿 (4) ⚲ 📺 🛏 📹 🍴
Also self catering £15- £17.50 per person nightly. Large garden, private road, idyllic wooded country hillside, tree preservation area overlooking pleasant mile walk to town, golf course, hills gateway to the islands. Ferry 1 mile. Bicycles/ scooters available.

Harbour View Guest House, Shore Street, Oban, Argyll, *PA34 4LQ.*
Centrally situated town house.
Open: All Year (not Xmas)
Grades: STB 1 Star
01631 563462 Mrs McDougall
D: £15.00–£17.00
Beds: 2F 1D 1T **Baths:** 2 Sh
⛱ 📺 🛏 📹 🍴

The Torrans, Drummore Road, Oban, Argyll, *PA34 4JL.*
Detached bungalow overlooking Oban in pleasant peaceful residential area. Private parking.
Open: All Year
Grades: STB 3 Star
01631 565342 Mrs Calderwood
D: fr £16.00 **S:** fr £20.00
Beds: 1T 2D **Baths:** 2 En 1 Pr
⛱ 🅿 (3) 📺 🛏 📖 🍴

Glenara Guest House, Rockfield Road, Oban, Argyll, *PA34 5DQ.*
Open: Feb to Nov
Grades: STB 4 Star
01631 563172 Mrs Bingham
Fax: 01631 571125
glenara_oban@hotmail.com
D: £21.00–£27.00 **S:** £25.00–£35.00
Beds: 1F/T 3D **Baths:** 4 En
⛱ (12) 🅿 (5) ⚲ 📺 🛏 📹 🍴
We offer to our guests a quality of room, breakfast & welcome which will ensure your return. Centrally situated, sea views, off-street parking. Individually furnished rooms with king-sized beds reflecting Dorothy's commitment to quality. Glenara is a no-smoking guest house.

Alltavona, Corran Esplanade, Oban, Argyll, *PA34 5AQ.*
Open: Feb to Nov
01631 565067 (also fax)
Ms Harris
carol@alltavona.co.uk
D: £20.00–£33.00 **S:** £20.00–£55.00
Beds: 1F 5D 2T
⛱ (5) 🅿 ⚲ 📺 🛏 📹 🍴
Alltavona - a Victorian villa lying on Oban's esplanade. Visitors arriving at Alltavona for the first time are immediately aware that it is a house of outstanding quality, where no effort has been spared. Outstanding views of Oban Bay and surrounding islands.

Dana Villa, Dunollie Road, Oban, Argyll, PA34 5PJ.
Scottish hospitality, family run. Close to all amenities and waterfront.
Open: All Year
01631 564063 Mrs Payne
ednacp@aol.com
D: fr £15.00 **S:** fr £20.00
Beds: 2F 2D 3T 1S **Baths:** 3 En 1 Pr 2 Sh
⌒ 📺 ⊁ ✕ ▥ 💷 ⬩

Feorlin, Longsdale Road, Oban, Argyll, PA34 5DZ.
Open: Mar to Nov
Grades: STB 3 Star
01631 562930 Mrs Campbell
Fax: 01631 564199
campbellsmith@btinternet.com
D: £17.50–£20.00 **S:** £27.50
Beds: 1F **Baths:** 1 En
⌒ 🅿 (2) ⊁ 📺 ▥ 💷 ⬩
A warm welcome and traditional Scottish hospitality awaits you at Feorlin, a charming bungalow less than 8 mins walk from town and leisure sports complex. Great breakfasts with fresh produce, free range eggs, home made jams and marmalade.

Elmbank Guest House, Croft Road, Oban, Argyll, PA34 5JN.
Situated in quiet residential area. Large garden, 1 mile to station/ pier.
Open: Easter to Oct
01631 562545
Mrs Douglas
D: £16.00–£20.00 **S:** £16.00–£20.00
Beds: 4D 2T 1S **Baths:** 2 En 2 Sh
🅿 ▥ 💷 ⬩

Thornlea, Laurel Road, Oban, Argyll, PA34 5EA.
Small private bungalow in quiet residential area, 10 min from town centre.
Open: Easter to Sep
01631 562792 Mrs Millar
D: fr £13.50 **S:** £–£13.50
Beds: 1D 1S
⌒ 🅿 (2) 📺 ⊁ ▥ ⬩

Glenview, Soroba Road, Oban, Argyll, PA34 4JF.
Warm friendly welcome, good breakfasts, close to all travel terminals.
Open: All Year
01631 562267 Mrs Stewart
D: £15.00–£17.50 **S:** £16.00–£17.50
Beds: 2F 2T **Baths:** 1 Sh
⌒ 🅿 (6) 📺 ⊁ ▥ 💷 ⬩

Ardenlee, Pulpit Hill, Oban, Argyll, PA34.
Comfortable bungalow close to viewpoint over Oban Bay.
Open: Easter to Oct
Grades: STB 2 Star
01631 564255 Mrs Campbell
D: £16.00–£19.50
Beds: 2D 1T **Baths:** 3 En
🅿 (3) ⊁ 📺 ⊁ ▥ ⬩

Glenvista, Mossfield Avenue, Oban, Argyll, PA34 4EL.
Semi-detached villa, pleasant location, very comfortable, good Scottish breakfast.
Open: Easter to Sep
Grades: STB 2 Star
01631 563557
Mrs Carter
D: £16.00–£17.50
Beds: 2D **Baths:** 1 Sh
🅿 (1) ⊁ 📺 ▥ 💷 ⬩

Carradale, Glenmore Road, Oban, Argyll, PA34 4ND.
10 minutes walk from ferries, bus and train station, town centre.
Open: May to Oct
Grades: STB 3 Star
01631 564827
Mrs Thompson
fkthompson@talk21.com
D: £16.00–£19.00
Beds: 2D **Baths:** 2 En
🅿 (2) ⊁ 📺 ▥ ⬩

Lancaster Hotel, Esplanade, Oban, Argyll, PA34 5AD.
Seafront family hotel, fully licensed, adequate parking with leisure facilities.
Open: All Year
Grades: STB 2 Star, AA 2 Star, RAC 2 Star
01631 562587 (also fax)
Mrs Ramage
john@lancasterhotel.fresserve.co.uk
D: fr £24.50 **S:** fr £27.80
Beds: 3F 5D 10T 7S **Baths:** 24 En 4 Sh
⌒ 🅿 (20) 📺 ⊁ ✕ ▥ 💷 ⬩ cc

Kildonan, Mossfield Avenue, Oban, Argyll, PA34 4EL.
Small friendly guest house in quiet area near to golf courses.
Open: All Year (not Xmas)
01631 565872 Ms Barbour
D: £15.00

Shandon

NS2586 ⬩ Ardencaple Hotel

Garemount Lodge, Shandon, Helensburgh, G84 8NP.
Delightful lochside home; large garden; convenient Loch Lomond, Glasgow, Highlands.
Open: All Year (not Xmas)
Grades: STB 3 Star
01436 820780 (also fax)
Mrs Cowie
nickcowie@compuserve.com
D: £20.00–£23.00 **S:** £28.00–£36.00
Beds: 1F 1D **Baths:** 1 En 1 Pr
⌒ 🅿 (4) ⊁ 📺 ⊁ ▥ 💷 ⬩

St Catherines

NN1207 ⬩ Creggans Inn

Arnish Cottage Christian Guest House, Poll Bay, St Catherines, Cairndow, Argyll, PA25 8BA.
Idyllically situated on the shores of Loch Fyne.
Open: All Year (not Xmas)
01499 302405 (also fax) Mr Mercer
D: £25.00 **S:** £25.00
Beds: 2D 1T **Baths:** 3 En
⌒ (14) 🅿 (3) ⊁ 📺 ▥ ⬩

Tarbert (Kintyre)

NR8668 ⬩ Callums Bar, Tarbot Hotel, West Loch

Kintarbert Lodge, Kilberry Road, Tarbert, Argyll, PA29 6XX.
Open: Apr to Oct
Grades: STB 3 Star
01880 820237 Mrs Chainey
Fax: 01880 821149
bdchainey@aol.com
D: £18.00–£20.00 **S:** £18.00–£20.00
Beds: 1F 2T **Baths:** 2 En 1 Pr
⌒ 🅿 📺 ⊁ ▥ 💷 ⬩ & cc
Former farm house, 200 ft above West Loch Tarbert with panoramic views. Outside play area for children. 3 miles from Tarbert and 7,10 miles from Islay, Arran ferries. A quiet place to relax from the stresses of daily life.

Tarbet

NN3104 **Corner Stone,** 7 Ballyhennan Cresent, Tarbet, Arrochar, G83 7DB.
Beautiful stone built house, overlooking Loch Lomond's, breathtaking Mountains.
Open: All Year **Grades:** STB 3 Stars
01301 702592 Mr & Mrs McKinley
s.mckinley@talk21.com
D: £16.00–£18.00 **S:** £20.00–£25.00
Beds: 1T 1F **Baths:** 1 Sh
⌒ 🅿 ⊁ 📺 ▥ 💷

Lochview, Tarbet, Arrochar, Dunbartonshire, G83 7DD.
Clean, comfortable, friendly welcome in 200-year-old Georgian house.
Open: All Year (not Xmas)
Grades: STB 1 Star
01301 702200 Mrs Fairfield
D: £15.00–£17.00 **S:** £20.00
Beds: 1F 1D 1T **Baths:** 1 Sh
⌒ 🅿 📺 ⊁ ▥ ⬩ &

Tighnabruaich

NR9773 ⬩ Royal Hotel

Ferguslie, Seafront, Tighnabruaich, Argyll, PA21 2BE.
Superior Victorian villa, on sea front, with landscaped garden. Quality throughout.
Open: Easter to Oct **Grades:** STB 3 Star
01700 811414 Mrs McLachlan
D: £17.00 **S:** £18.00
Beds: 2D **Baths:** 1 Sh
🅿 (3) ⊁ 📺 ▥ 💷 ⬩

Ayrshire & Arran

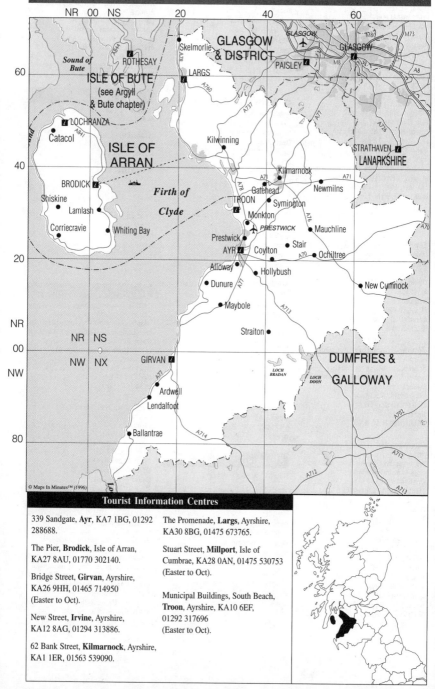

Tourist Information Centres

339 Sandgate, **Ayr**, KA7 1BG, 01292 288688.

The Pier, **Brodick**, Isle of Arran, KA27 8AU, 01770 302140.

Bridge Street, **Girvan**, Ayrshire, KA26 9HH, 01465 714950 (Easter to Oct).

New Street, **Irvine**, Ayrshire, KA12 8AG, 01294 313886.

62 Bank Street, **Kilmarnock**, Ayrshire, KA1 1ER, 01563 539090.

The Promenade, **Largs**, Ayrshire, KA30 8BG, 01475 673765.

Stuart Street, **Millport**, Isle of Cumbrae, KA28 0AN, 01475 530753 (Easter to Oct).

Municipal Buildings, South Beach, **Troon**, Ayrshire, KA10 6EF, 01292 317696 (Easter to Oct).

Alloway

NS3318

Garth Madryn, 71 Maybole Road,
Alloway, Ayr, KA7 4TB.
Alloway is a quiet residential area of Ayr
within easy reach of the town.
Open: All Year
01292 443346 Mrs MacKie
D: £16.00–£17.00 **S:** £16.00–£17.00
Beds: 2T **Baths:** 2 En

Ardwell

NX1693

Ardwell Farm, Ardwell, Girvan,
Ayrshire, KA26 0HP.
Picturesque farmhouse with rooms
overlooking the Firth of Clyde.
Open: All Year
Grades: STB 2 Star
01465 713389 Mrs Melville
D: £14.00–£15.00 **S:** £14.00–£16.00
Beds: 2T 1D **Baths:** 1 Sh
🛇 🅿 (3) ⅍ 📺 ⊀ 🎟 🖤 ⚓

ARRAN   Brodick

NS0136   🍺 Pirates Cove, Ormidale Bar, Brodick
Bar, Duncan's Bar, Arran Hotel, Ingledene Hotel

Kingsley Hotel, Brodick, Isle of Arran,
KA27 8AJ.
Open: Easter to Sep
01770 302226 kingsleyhotel@connectfree
D: £29.00–£29.50 **S:** £29.00–£29.50
Beds: 2F 6D 11T 8S **Baths:** 27 En
🛇 🅿 (30) 📺 ⊀ 🎟 🖤 ⚓ cc
Situated on Brodick seafront, overlooking
the Arran hills, Kingsley is one of Arran's
well known hotels with a reputation for
warm welcome, good food and relaxing
friendly atmosphere. Golf and family
packages a speciality, with our small
indoor heated swimming pool adding to
the experience.

Sunnyside, Kings Cross, Brodick, Isle of
Arran, KA27 8RG.
Open: All year (not Xmas)
Grades: STB 2 Star
01770 700422
D: £17.50–£20.00 **S:** £18.50–£24.00
Beds: 1D 1T/S **Baths:** 1 En 1 Pr
🛇 ⅍ 📺 ⊀ 🎟 🖤 ⚓ cc
Private entrance to comfortably furnished
double ensuite room with superb view
across the Clyde. Also one Twin/single
room having private facilities. Deck and
secluded sun trap garden. A haven for
peace and tranquillity. Private parking. 8
1/2 miles south Brodick.

Rosaburn Lodge, Brodick, Isle of
Arran, KA27 8DP.
Open: All Year
01770 302383
D: £24.00–£27.50 **S:** £24.00–£27.50
Beds: 1T 2D **Baths:** 3 En
🛇 🅿 ⅍ 📺 ⊀ 🎟 🖤 ⚓ ⚓
The lodge stands on the beautiful banks
of river Rosa within 2 acres of private
landscaped gardens. An ideal location for
hill walking golf cycling or relaxing on
this wonderful island. A warm welcome
awaits you from Paul and Leen.

Tigh Na Mara, Seafront, Brodick, Isle of
Arran, KA27 8AJ.
Beautifully situated on seafront
overlooking the mountains and Brodick
Bay. **Open:** All Year
Grades: STB 2 Star
01770 302538 Terry & Leslie Dunleavy
Fax: 01770 302546
arran.tighnamara@btinternet.com
D: £20.00–£24.00 **S:** £20.00–£24.00
Beds: 2F 5D 2T **Baths:** 2 En 3 Sh
🛇 (4) 🅿 (2) 📺 🎟 🖤 ⚓ ⚓ cc

ARRAN   Catacol

NR9149

Catacol Bay Hotel, Catacol, Brodick,
Isle of Arran, KA27 8HN.
Open: All Year (not Xmas)
01770 830231 Mr Ashcroft
Fax: 01770 830350
davecatbay@lineone.net
D: £20.00–£25.00 **S:** £20.00–£25.00
Beds: 3F 1D 1T 1S **Baths:** 2 Sh
🛇 (30) 📺 ⊀ 🎟 🖤 ⚓ cc
Small friendly fully licensed hotel
nestling in hills at the picturesque north
end of Arran situated on the seashore
overlooking the Kilbrannan Sound &
Kintyre. Self-catering bungalow also
available - sleeps 7.

ARRAN   Corriecravie

NR9223   🍺 Lagg Inn

Rosebank, Corriecravie, Brodick, Isle of
Arran, KA27 8PD.
Locally owned; ideal for walking, golf,
birdwatching and relaxing.
Open: All Year (not Xmas)
Grades: STB 2 Star
01770 870228 (also fax) Mrs Adamson
D: £17.00–£18.00 **S:** £17.00–£18.00
Beds: 1F 1D 1T 1S **Baths:** 1 En 1 Sh
🛇 🅿 📺 ⊀ 🎟 🖤 ⚓

ARRAN   Lamlash

NS0230   🍺 Drift Inn, Breadalbane

Westfield Guest House, Lamlash,
Brodick, Isle of Arran, KA27 8NN.
Typical island house, close to the sea,
overlooking Holy Isle. **Open:** All Year
01770 600428 Mrs Sloan
D: £16.00–£18.00 **S:** £16.00–£18.00
Beds: 2D 1T 2S **Baths:** 2 Sh
🛇 🅿 (6) ⅍ 📺 🎟 🖤 ⚓

ARRAN   Lochranza

NR9349

Butt Lodge Country House Hotel,
Lochranza, Brodick, Isle of Arran, KA27 8JF.
Open: Feb to Aug **Grades:** STB 4 Star
01770 830240 Fax: 01770 830211
butt.lodge@virgin.net
D: £25.00–£40.00 **S:** £25.00–£48.00
Beds: 5F 1D 1T 3S **Baths:** 1 Pr
🛇 🅿 ⅍ 📺 ⊀ 🎟 🖤 ⚓ ⚓
Beautiful 4 star family-run hotel, with
residential licence. Standing in 2 acres of
gardens with an abundance of wildlife,
nestling under the hills at the head of the
sea loch. Log fires, all rooms ensuite.
Private off-road parking. We are
renowned for our cuisine and fine dining.

Caber Feidh, Lochranza, Brodick, Isle of
Arran, KA27 8HL.
Caberfeidh is situated on the shores of
Lochranza on the Isle of Arran.
Open: All Year
01770 830255 (also fax)
Mrs Griffin
D: £22.50–£25.00 **S:** £20.00
Beds: 2D 1T 1S **Baths:** 1 En 1 Sh
🅿 (5) ⅍ 📺 🎟 ⚓

ARRAN   Shiskine

NR9129   🍺 Black Waterfoot Hotel

Croftlea, Shiskine, Brodick, Isle of Arran,
KA27 8EN.
Comfortable house with garden. Quiet
location 2 miles beach/golf course.
Open: All Year **Grades:** STB 2 Star
01770 860259 Mrs Henderson
D: £18.00–£20.00 **S:** £25.00
Beds: 2D 3T **Baths:** 3 En 1 Sh
🅿 (5) ⅍ 📺 ⊀ 🎟 🖤

ARRAN   Whiting Bay

NS0425   🍺 Burlington Hotel, Trafalgar,
Kiscadale Hotel, The Cameronia, The Shurrig

Argentine House Hotel, Whiting Bay,
Brodick, Isle of Arran, KA27 8PZ.
Swiss owners, superb views over Clyde,
first class cooking. Licensed.
Open: Mar to Jan
01770 700662 info@argentinearran.co.uk
D: £20.00–£32.00 **S:** £24.00–£50.00
Beds: 4D 1T **Baths:** 5 En
🛇 🅿 (6) 📺 ⊀ 🎟 🖤 ⚓ ⚓ cc

Ayr

NS3422   🍺 Tam O'Shanter, Kylestrome Hotel,
Finlay's Bar, Burrofield's Bar, Carrick Lodge,
Durward Hotel, Hollybush Inn, Balgarth,
Littlejohns

Inverlea Guest House, 42 Carrick
Road, Ayr, KA7 2RB.
Open: All Year
01292 266756 (also fax)
Mr & Mrs Bryson
D: £15.00–£20.00 **S:** £18.00–£25.00
Beds: 3F 2D 2T 1S **Baths:** 3 En 2 Pr 3 Sh
🛇 🅿 (5) 📺 🎟 🖤 ⚓
Family-run Victorian guest house which
has ensured personal attention for 15
years. Few minutes walk from beach and
town centre. Burns Cottage and 7 golf
courses nearby. Large enclosed car park
at rear of house.

Belmont Guest House, 15 Park
Circus, Ayr, KA7 2DJ.
Open: All Year (not Xmas)
Grades: STB 2 Star, AA 3 Diamonds
01292 265588 Mr Hillhouse
Fax: 01292 290303
belmontguesthouse@btinternet.com
D: £20.00–£22.00 **S:** fr £24.00
Beds: 2F 2D 1T **Baths:** 5 En
🛇 🅿 (5) 📺 ⊀ 🎟 🖤 ⚓ ⚓
Try a breath of fresh 'Ayr'. Warm,
comfortable hospitality assured in this
Victorian town house, situated in a quiet
residential area within easy walking
distance of the town centre and beach.
Ground floor bedrooms available.
Glasgow (Prestwick) Airport 6 miles.
Green Tourism Silver Award.

Kilkerran, 15 Prestwick Road, Ayr,
KA8 8LD.
Friendly family-run guest house on main
A74 Ayr - Prestwick route.
Open: All Year
Grades: STB 2 Star
01292 266477 Ms Ferguson
margaret@kilkerran-gh.demon.co.uk
D: £16.00–£20.00 **S:** £16.00–£20.00
Beds: 3F 2D 2T 2S **Baths:** 2 En 1 Pr 3 Sh
🛏 🄿 (10) 📺 ⼎ ✕ 🗔 📺 ✵ 🚼 ♿

Finlayson Arms Hotel, Coylton, Ayr,
KA6 6JT.
Superbly located for golfing holiday, with
over 30 courses, nearby including
Turnberry and Troon.
Open: All Year (not Xmas/New Year)
01292 570298
D: £22.50–£27.50 **S:** £25.00–£35.00
Beds: 1F 7T **Baths:** 8 En
🛏 🄿 (12) ⼎ 📺 ✕ 🗔 🚼 ♿ cc

Deanbank, 44 Ashgrove Street, Ayr,
KA7 3BG.
Convenient for Town centre, Station,Golf
and Burns Country.
Open: All Year (not Xmas)
Grades: STB 4 Star
01292 263745 Ms Wilson
D: £18.00–£20.00 **S:** £20.00–£25.00
Beds: 1F 1T **Baths:** 1 Sh
🛏 (1) ⼎ 📺 🗔 📺 🚼

Sunnyside, 26 Dunure Road, Doonfoot,
Ayr, *KA7 4HR.*
Close to Burns Cottage, Brig O'Doon;
spacious rooms; family welcome.
Open: All Year (not Xmas)
Grades: STB 3 Star
01292 441234 (also fax)
Mrs Malcolm
D: £20.00–£22.00 **S:** £26.00–£28.00
Beds: 2F **Baths:** 2 En
🛏 🄿 (4) ⼎ 📺 🗔 📺 🚼

Ferguslea, 98 New Road, Ayr, *KA8 8JG.*
Family run, good food, traditional Scottish
hospitality.
Open: All Year (not Xmas/New Year)
Grades: STB 2 Star
01292 268551 Mrs Campbell
D: £14.00–£16.00 **S:** £14.00–£16.00
Beds: 2T 1S **Baths:** 2 Sh
🛏 🄿 (3) 📺 ⼎ 🗔 🚼

Tramore Guest House, 17 Eglinton
Terrace, Ayr, *KA7 1JJ.*
In C12th old fort area, 2 mins from town
centre. **Open:** All Year
Grades: STB 3 Star
01292 266019 (also fax) E R Tumilty
D: £17.00–£18.00 **S:** £17.00–£19.00
Beds: 1D 2T **Baths:** 2 Sh
🛏 📺 ⼎ ✕ 🗔 📺 🚼

Langley Bank Guest House, 39
Carrick Road, Ayr, *KA7 2RD.*
A well appointed Victorian house.
Centrally situated, see website.
Open: All Year
Grades: STB 3 Star
01292 264246 Mr & Mrs Mitchell
Fax: 01292 282628
D: £15.00–£25.00 **S:** £20.00–£45.00
Beds: 1F 3D 2T **Baths:** 4 Pr 1 En
🛏 🄿 (4) 📺 🗔 🚼 cc

Dunedin, 10 Montgomerie Terrace, Ayr,
KA7 1JL.
Comfortable family home from home.
Open: Easter to Sept
Grades: STB 2 Star
01292 261224 Mrs Grant
D: £18.00–£19.00 **S:** £36.00–£46.00
Beds: 1F 1D **Baths:** 2 En
🛏 🄿 (2) ⼎ 📺 🗔

Windsor Hotel, 6 Alloway Place, Ayr,
KA7 2AA.
Town house hotel within 15 min drive of
14 golf courses.
Open: All Year (not Xmas)
Grades: STB 2 Star, AA 3 Diamond
01292 264689 Mrs Hamilton
D: £22.00–£25.00 **S:** £22.00–£35.00
Beds: 4F 3D 1T 2S **Baths:** 7 En 1 Pr 1 Sh
🛏 ⼎ 📺 ✕ 🗔 📺 🚼 cc

Town Hotel, 9-11 Barns Street, Ayr,
KA7 1XB.
Family run hotel, close to town centre and
10 local golf courses.
Open: All Year
01292 267595
D: £20.00–£25.00 **S:** £20.00–£25.00
Beds: 3F 1D 14T **Baths:** 18 En
🛏 (1) 🄿 (1) 📺 ⼎ ✕ 🗔 ✵ 🚼 ♿

The Dunn Thing Guest House, 13
Park Circus, Ayr, *KA7 2DJ.*
Victorian House in quiet street near town
centre.
Open: All Year
01292 284531 Mrs Dunn
thedunnthing@compuserve.com
D: £17.00–£20.00 **S:** £18.00–£22.00
Beds: 2D 1T **Baths:** 3 En
🛏 📺 ⼎ 🗔 📺 🚼

Iona, 27 St Leonards Road, Ayr, *KA7 2PS.*
Welcome to Iona for comfortable rooms
and full Scottish breakfast.
Open: Feb to Nov
01292 269541 (also fax)
Mr & Mrs Gibson
iona.guesthouse@tesco.net
D: £17.00–£20.00 **S:** £17.00–£20.00
Beds: 1D 1T 2S **Baths:** 2 En 1 Sh
🛏 🄿 (3) 📺 ⼎ 🗔 📺 🚼

Failte, 9 Prestwick Road, Ayr, *KA8 8LD.*
Situated on the main road for Glasgow, 10
mins from Prestwick International
Airport.
Open: All Year (not Xmas)
01292 265282 (also fax)
Mrs Jennifer Thomson
wthomson9@netscapeonline.co.uk
D: £19.00–£22.00 **S:** £19.00–£22.00
Beds: 1D 1T **Baths:** 1 En 1 Pr
🛏 🄿 📺 🗔 📺 🚼

Monaco Guest House, 41 Seafield
Drive, Ayr, *KA7 4BJ.*
Comfortable family-run B&B in quiet
seafront location with superb panoramic
views.
Open: Easter to Oct
01292 264295 J Lennon
D: £19.00–£24.00 **S:** £20.00–£24.00
Beds: 1D 1T 1S **Baths:** 1 En 1 Sh
🄿 (6) ⼎ 📺 🗔 📺 🚼

NX0982   ⚓ Kings Arms, Royal Hotel

Orchard Lea, 14 Main Street, Ballantrae,
Girvan, Ayrshire, *KA26 0NB.*
Comfortable house offers superb
breakfast. Quiet coastal village, ferries
nearby. **Open:** All Year (not Xmas)
01465 831509 Mr & Mrs Ward
D: £15.00 **S:** £15.00
Beds: 2D 1T **Baths:** 1 Sh
🛏 🄿 (12) ⼎ 📺 ⼎ 🗔 ✵ 🚼

Ardstinchar Cottage, 81 Main Street,
Ballantrae, Girvan, Ayrshire, *KA26 0NA.*
Beautiful cottage in magnificent
countryside.
Open: All Year (not Xmas/New Year)
01465 831343 Mrs Drummond
D: £16.00–£20.00 **S:** £20.00–£25.00
Beds: 2D 1T **Baths:** 1 Sh
🛏 🄿 (3) 📺 🗔 📺 ✵ 🚼

Laggan Farm, Ballantrae, Girvan,
Ayrshire, *KA26 0JZ.*
Comfortable Georgian House on dairy
farm close to Ayrshire Coast.
Open: Easter to Oct **Grades:** STB 3 Star
01465 831402 Mrs McKinley
j&r@lagganfm.freeserve.co.uk
D: £16.00–£19.00 **S:** £18.00–£21.00
Beds: 1F 1D 1T **Baths:** 1 En 2 Sh
🛏 🄿 ⼎ 📺 ⼎ ✕ 🗔 🚼

The Haven, 75 Main Street, Ballantrae,
Girvan, Ayrshire, *KA26 0NA.*
Delightful coastal village bungalow.
Superb breakfasts. Ferries nearby.
Panoramic views. **Open:** All Year
01465 831306 (also fax) Mrs Sloan
D: £18.00–£21.00 **S:** £20.00–£27.00
Beds: 1F 1T **Baths:** 2 Pr
🛏 (3) 🄿 (2) ⼎ 📺 📺 🚼

NS3232   ⚓ Tower Hotel

Fordell, 43 Beach Road, Barassie, Troon,
KA10 6SU.
Open: All Year (not Xmas/New Year)
Grades: STB 3 Stars
01292 313224 Mrs Mathieson
Fax: 01292 312141
morag@fordell.junglelink.co.uk
D: £18.00–£20.00 **S:** £20.00–£25.00
Beds: 1F 2T **Baths:** 2 Sh
⼎ 📺 ⼎ 🗔 📺 🚼
Relax in this Victorian House overlooking
the sea or use as a base to visit Ayrshire's
famed golf courses or many other
attractions. comfortable rooms, good
breakfasts, secure parking for cycles or
motor bikes. A warm welcome awaits

NX2382   ⚓ Galloway Hotel

14 Main Street, Barrhill, Girvan,
Ayrshire, *KA26 0PQ.*
Comfortable , homely in small village.
Central for local beauty spots.
Open: All Year
01465 821344 Mrs Hegarty
D: £15.00–£18.00 **S:** £18.00
Beds: 1F **Baths:** 1 Pr 1 Sh
🛏 ⼎ 📺 ⼎ ✕ 🗔 🚼

Blair Farm, *Barrhill, Girvan, Ayrshire,*
KA26 0RD.
Beautiful farmhouse, lovely views. Enjoy
peace, comfort & friendly hospitality.
Open: Easter to Nov
Grades: STB 4 Star
01465 821247 Mrs Hughes
D: £20.00–£22.00 **S:** £25.00
Beds: 1D 1T **Baths:** 1 En 1 Pr
🛇 🄿 📺 ⊁ ✕ 🎢 🛓

Beith

NS3553 ⬛ *Parrafin Lamp*

Townend of Shuterflat Farm, *Beith,*
Ayrshire, KA15 2LW.
Comfortable farmhouse, warm welcome,
15 minutes Glasgow Airport and city
centre.
Open: All Year
01505 502342 Mrs Lamont
D: £17.50 **S:** £17.50
Beds: 1T 2D **Baths:** 1 Sh
🛇 🄿 (4) 📺 ⊁ 🎢 🛓

Coylton

NS4219 ⬛ *The Kyle Hotel, The Finlayson Arms*

The Kyle Hotel, *Main Street, Coylton,*
Ayr, KA6 6JW.
Close to many Ayrshire top golf courses
and Ayr Racecourse.
Open: All Year
01292 570312 Mr Finlayson
Fax: 01292 571493
D: £22.50–£25.00 **S:** £22.50–£25.00
Beds: 3F 1T **Baths:** 2 En 1 Sh
🛇 📺 ⊁ ✕ 🎢 🛓 ⚡ cc

Dunure

NS2515 ⬛ *Anchorage*

Cruachan, *38 Station Road, Dunure, Ayr,*
KA7 4LL.
Magnificent views to Arran; close to
harbour and castle park.
Open: Apr to Oct
Grades: STB 4 Star
01292 500494 Mr Evans
Fax: 01292 500266
dnevans@lineone.net
D: £20.00–£25.00 **S:** £20.00–£30.00
Beds: 1D 1T **Baths:** 1 En 1 Pr
🄿 (4) ⊁ 📺 🎢 🛓

Gatehead

NS3936

Muirhouse Farm, *Gatehead,*
Kilmarnock, Ayrshire, KA2 0BT.
Comfortable farmhouse. Convenient to
town.
Open: All Year (not Xmas)
01563 523975 (also fax)
Mrs Love
D: £16.00–£20.00 **S:** £17.00–£20.00
Beds: 1F 1D 1T **Baths:** 2 En 1 Pr
🛇 🄿 (6) 📺 🎢 🎢 🖲 🛓

National Grid References are for
villages, towns and cities – not
for individual houses

Girvan

NX1897 ⬛ *Southfield Hotel, Aisa Graig Hotel,*
Roxy Bar

Hotel Westcliffe, *15-16 Louisa Drive,*
Girvan, Ayrshire, KA26 9AH.
Family run hotel on sea front, all rooms
ensuite. Spa/steam room.
Open: All Year
Grades: STB 2 Star
01465 712128 (also fax)
Mrs Jardine
D: £23.00–£26.00 **S:** £24.00–£28.00
Beds: 6F 5D 8T 1S **Baths:** 24 En
🛇 🄿 (6) 📺 ✕ 🎢 ✳ 🛓 🖲 cc

Thistleneuk Guest House, *19 Louisa*
Drive, Girvan, Ayrshire, KA26 9AH.
Victorian terrace, original features
overlooking Ailsa Craig. Local shops
nearby.
Open: Easter to Oct
Grades: STB 2 Star
01465 712137 (also fax)
Mr & Mrs Lacey
reservations@thistleneuk.freeserve.co.uk
D: £23.00 **S:** £23.00–£31.00
Beds: 2F 2D 2T 1S **Baths:** 7 En
🛇 (2) 📺 ✕ 🎢 🖲 🛓

Hollybush

NS3914 ⬛ *Hollybush Inn*

Malcolmston Farm, *Hollybush, Ayr,*
KA6 6EZ.
Farmhouse on A713 near Ayr, (near
Turnberry and Troon).
Open: Easter to Nov
01292 560238 Mrs Drummond
D: £16.00–£18.00 **S:** £16.00–£18.00
Beds: 1F 2D **Baths:** 1 En 2 Sh
🛇 🄿 (4) 📺 🎢 🎢 🛓 ♿

Kilmarnock

NS4238 ⬛ *Cochrane Inn, Wheatsheaf, Kings*
Arms, The Gathering, Ellerslie Inn

Hillhouse Farm, *Grassyards Road,*
Kilmarnock, Ayrshire, KA3 6HG.
Open: All Year
Grades: STB 4 Star
01563 523370 Mrs Howie
D: £18.00–£21.00 **S:** £18.00–£21.00
Beds: 3F 1T **Baths:** 2 En
🛇 🄿 (8) 📺 🎢 🎢 🖲 🛓
The Howie family extend a warm
welcome to their working dairy farm.
Large bedrooms with superb views over
garden and Ayrshire countryside. Central
location for coast, golf, fishing, Glasgow
and Prestwick Airports. Real farmhouse
breakfast, home baking for supper.

Tamarind, *24 Arran Avenue, Kilmarnock,*
Ayrshire, KA3 1TP.
Large ranch-style bungalow on one level.
Located at end of quiet tree-lined avenue.
Open: All Year
Grades: STB 3 Star
01563 571788 Mrs Turner
james@tamarind25.freeserve.co.uk
D: £17.50–£20.00 **S:** £25.00–£30.00
Beds: 1F 2T 1S **Baths:** 4 En
🛇 🄿 (4) ⊁ 📺 🎢 🛓 ⚡ cc

Burnside Hotel, 18 London Road,

Kilmarnock, Ayrshire, KA3 7AQ.
Friendly relaxed atmosphere, civilised,
comfortable, a touch of class.
Open: All Year
01563 522952 Mr & Mrs Dye
Fax: 01563 573381
D: £22.00–£28.00 **S:** £22.00–£30.00
Beds: 1F 3D 3T 3S **Baths:** 5 En 2 Pr 2 Sh
🛇 (8) 🄿 (10) ⊁ 📺 ✕ 🎢 🖲 ⚡ cc

Lindene, *1 Grange Terrace, Kilmarnock,*
KA1 2JR.
Central location, road network easily
accessible, warm hospitality, tasteful
accommodation.
Open: All Year (not Xmas)
01563 532772 Mrs Lindsay
D: £18.00–£20.00 **S:** £20.00–£22.00
Beds: 1T **Baths:** 1 Pr
🄿 (2) ⊁ 🎢 🖲 🛓

Kilwinning

NS3043 ⬛ *Blair Inn, Claremont Hotel*

Claremont Guest House, *27*
Howgate, Kilwinning, Ayrshire, KA13 6EW.
Friendly family B&B close to town centre
and public transport.
Open: All Year (not Xmas)
01294 553905 Mrs Filby
D: £17.00–£20.00 **S:** £17.00–£20.00
Beds: 1F 1S **Baths:** 2 Sh
🛇 🄿 (10) ⊁ 📺 🎢

Tarcoola, *Montgreenan, Kilwinning,*
Ayrshire, KA13 7QZ.
Attractive country setting convenient for
Arran ferry and Ayrshire golf.
Open: All Year
01294 850379 Mrs Melville
Fax: 01294 850249
bill_melville@hotmail.com
D: £16.00–£18.00 **S:** £16.00
Beds: 1T **Baths:** 1 Pr
🛇 (8) 🄿 (2) ⊁ 📺 🎢 🎢 🛓

Largs

NS2059 ⬛ *George, Morris's, Regattas, Haylie*
Hotel, Inverkip Hotel, Brisbane House, Flannigans

South Whittleburn Farm, *Brisbane*
Glen, Largs, Ayrshire, KA30 8SN.
Superb farmhouse accommodation,
enormous, delicious breakfasts. Warm,
friendly hospitality, highly recommended.
Open: All Year (not Xmas)
Grades: STB 4 Star, AA 4 Diamond
01475 675881 Mrs Watson
Fax: 01475 675080
D: fr £20.00 **S:** fr £20.00
Beds: 1F 1D 1T **Baths:** 3 En
🛇 🄿 (10) ⊁ 📺 🎢 🖲 🛓

Belmont House, *2 Broomfield Place,*
Largs, Ayrshire, KA30 8DR.
Interesting old waterfront house.
Spacious rooms. Views of Islands and
Highlands.
Open: All Year
01475 676264 Mr & Mrs Clarke
belmont.house@i12.com
D: £20.00–£25.00 **S:** £20.00–£25.00
Beds: 2D 1T **Baths:** 1 En 2 Pr
🛇 (4) 🄿 (2) 🎢 🎢 🖲 🛓

Stonehaven Guest House, *8 Netherpark Crescent, Largs, KA30 8QB.*
Open: All Year (not Xmas)
Grades: STB 4 Star
01475 673319 Mr Martin
stonehaven.martin@virgin.net
D: £20.00–£25.00 **S:** £18.00–£23.00
Beds: 1D 1T 1S **Baths:** 1 En 1 Sh
Situated in an elevated position with magnificent views over the bay to the Isles of Cumbrae, Arran, Bute and Ailsa Craig with Routenburn Golf Course and The Clyde. Muirsheil regional park at the rear. high Standards and personal attention given to all.

Rutland Guest House, *22 Charles Street, Largs, Ayrshire, KA30 8HJ.*
Comfortable, family-run guest house. 1 minute walk to view panoramic sites of Arran.
Open: All Year
Grades: STB 2 Star
01475 675642 Mrs Russell
rutland@22largs.freeserve.co.uk
D: £17.00–£18.00 **S:** £18.00–£20.00
Beds: 3F 1D 1T **Baths:** 1 En 1 Pr 2 Sh

Inverie, *16 Charles Street, Largs, Ayrshire, KA30 8HJ.*
Attractive comfortable home, warm hospitality, Scottish breakfast, central, adjacent to sea.
Open: All Year (not Xmas/New Year)
01475 675903 Mrs MacLeod
D: £17.00–£18.00 **S:** £17.00–£18.00
Beds: 1D 1T 1S **Baths:** 1 Sh
(3)

Carlton Guest House, *10 Aubery Crescent, Largs, KA30 8PR.*
Situated on the promenade with panoramic views of the Firth of Clyde.
Open: All Year (not Xmas)
01475 672313 Mr Thorpe
Fax: 01475 676128
carlton.guesthouse@usa.net
D: £18.00–£24.00 **S:** £18.00
Beds: 1F 1D 2T 1S **Baths:** 1 En 2 Sh
(7) **cc**

Broom Lodge, *5 Broomfield Place, Largs, KA30 8DR.*
Substantial property occupying one of the best seafront locations in Largs.
Open: All Year (not Xmas)
01475 674290 S Mills
D: £18.00–£20.00 **S:** £18.00–£20.00
Beds: 1F 1D 1S **Baths:** 2 Sh
(3)

Lendalfoot

NX1389

The Smiddy, *Lendalfoot, Girvan, KA26 0JF.*
Make yourself at home in comfortable home with panoramic views.
Open: May to Sep
01465 891204 Mrs Bell
D: £14.00 **S:** fr £14.00
Beds: 1D 1T **Baths:** 1 Sh

Mauchline

NS4927 *Maxwood Inn, Stair Inn*

Treborane, *Dykefield Farm, Mauchline, Ayrshire, KA5 6EY.*
This is a new cottage on farm; friendly atmosphere.
Open: All Year
Grades: STB 2 Star
01290 550328 Ms Smith
D: £12.00–£15.00
Beds: 2F **Baths:** 1 En 1 Sh

Ardwell, *103 Loudoun Street, Mauchline, KA5 5BH.*
Beautiful rooms, near centre of historic village. Great golf locally.
Open: All Year
01290 552987 Mrs Houston
D: £15.00–£17.00 **S:** £17.00–£19.00
Beds: 2F **Baths:** 2 En
(2)

Dykefield Farm, *Mauchline, KA5 6EY.*
Farmhouse B&B with friendly, family atmosphere. Private lounge for guests.
Open: All Year
Grades: STB 1 Star
01290 553170 Mrs Smith
D: £12.00 **S:** £12.00
Beds: 2F **Baths:** 1 Sh
(3)

Maybole

NS2909 *Welltrees Inn*

Homelea, *62 Culzean Road, Maybole, Ayrshire, KA19 8AH.*
Homelea is a spacious red sandstone Victorian family home, retaining many original features.
Open: Easter to Oct
Grades: STB 3 Star
01655 882736 Mrs McKellar
Fax: 01655 883557
gilmour_mck@msn.com
D: £17.50–£18.50 **S:** £20.00–£22.00
Beds: 1F 1T 1S **Baths:** 2 Sh
(3)

Garpin Farm, *Crosshill, Maybole, Ayrshire, KA19 7PX.*
Comfortable family farmhouse in beautiful Ayrshire countryside. Home baking.
Open: All Year
01655 740214 Mrs Young
D: £18.00–£20.00 **S:** £21.00–£20.00
Beds: 1F 1T 1D **Baths:** 1 Sh

Nether Culzean Farm, *Maybole, KA19 7JQ.*
Beautiful Listed C18th farmhouse, spacious and comfortable. Near Culzean Castle, beaches, golf courses.
Open: Easter to Oct
01655 882269 Mrs Blythe
D: £15.00–£17.00 **S:** £15.00–£17.00
Beds: 2F **Baths:** 1 Pr
(2)

Monkton

NS3627 *Wheatsheaf, North Beach Hotel*

Crookside Farm, *Kerrix Road, Monkton, Prestwick, Ayrshire, KA9 2QU.*
Comfortable farmhouse central heating throughout, ideal for golfing, close to airport.
Open: All Year (not Xmas)
01563 830266 Mrs Gault
D: fr £12.00 **S:** fr £12.00
Beds: 1F 1D **Baths:** 1 Sh

New Cumnock

NS6113

Low Polquheys Farm, *New Cumnock, Cumnock, Ayrshire, KA18 4NX.*
Modern farmhouse, very friendly and central.
Open: Easter to Oct
01290 338307 Mrs Caldwell
marjorie@low-polquheys.freeserve.co.uk
D: £13.00–£15.00 **S:** £15.00
Beds: 1F 1T 1S **Baths:** 1 Sh
(2)

Newmilns

NS5237 *Wee Train*

Whatriggs Farm, *Newmilns, Ayrshire, KA16 9LJ.*
Family-run 700-acre farm, with golf and family attractions nearby.
Open: All Year (not Xmas)
Grades: STB 2 Star
01560 700279 Mrs Mitchell
whatriggs@farming.co.uk
D: £15.00–£17.50 **S:** £15.00–£17.50
Beds: 2F **Baths:** 1 Sh
(6)

Ochiltree

NS5121 *Stair Inn*

Laigh Tareg Farm, *Ochiltree, Cymnock, KA18 2RL.*
Modern working dairy farm traditional farmhouse of great character with a warm family welcome.
Open: Easter to Oct
Grades: STB 2 Star
01290 700242 (also fax)
Mrs Watson
D: £18.00–£20.00 **S:** £18.00–£22.00
Beds: 2F **Baths:** 1 Pr 1 Sh
(1)

Prestwick

NS3425 *North Beach Hotel, Golf Inn, Carlton Hotel*

Knox Bed & Breakfast, *105 Ayr Road, Prestwick, Ayrshire, KA9 1TN.*
Superb accommodation, homely welcome, excellent value, close to all amenities, airport and Centrum Arena.
Open: All Year (not Xmas)
01292 478808 Mrs Wardrope
knox-bed-breakfast@talk21.com
D: £15.00–£18.00 **S:** £16.00–£20.00
Beds: 1D 1T 1S **Baths:** 1 Sh
(2) (4)

Skelmorlie

NS1967

Balvonie Conference & Holiday Centre, *Halketburn Road, Skelmorlie, Ayrshire, PA17 5BP.*
Tudor style manor house, for a perfect conference/retreat or holiday.
Open: All Year (not Xmas)
01475 520122 Fax: 01475 522668
D: £17.00 **S:** fr £17.00
Beds: 2F 1D 16T 1S **Baths:** 17 En 3 Pr
🐾 🄿 (17) 🗶 📺 ✕ 🛏 🆅 ⚓ &

Stair

NS4423

Stair Inn, *Stair, Mauchline, KA5 5HW.*
Conservation area. Guest rooms of a very high standard. **Open:** All Year
01292 591562 Mr Boyd
Fax: 01292 591650
D: £22.50–£25.00 **S:** £35.00–£39.00
Beds: 2F 3T 1D **Baths:** 6 En
🗶 📺 ✕ 🛏 🆅 ⚓ cc

Straiton

NS3804   🍺 *Black Bull*

Three Thorns Farm, *Straiton, Maybole, Ayrshire, KA19 7QR.*
Good wholesome food, scenic views, C18th farmhouse, Culzean and Blairguham Castles nearby.
Open: All Year
01655 770221 (also fax) Mrs Henry
D: £20.00 **S:** £22.00–£25.00
Beds: 1F 2D 1T **Baths:** 2 En 2 Pr
🐾 🄿 (10) 📺 🛏 🛏 🆅 ⚓ &

Symington

NS3831   🍺 *Wheatsheaf Inn*

Muirhouse Farm, *Symington, Kilmarnock, Ayrshire, KA1 5PA.*
Traditional comfortable farmhouse, excellent food, near golf, leisure, equestrian centre.
Open: All Year
Grades: STB 2 Star
01563 830218 Mrs Howie
D: £18.00–£20.00 **S:** £20.00
Beds: 1D 1T
Baths: 1 Sh
🐾 🄿 (20) 📺 🛏 🆅 ⚓

Troon

NS3230   🍺 *Old Loans Inn, Lookout, Wheatsheaf, South Beach Hotel, Anchorage, Towers*

The Cherries, *50 Ottoline Drive, Troon, Ayrshire, KA10 7AW.*
Beautiful quiet home on golf course near beaches and restaurants.
Open: All Year
Grades: STB 3 Star
01292 313312 Mrs Tweedie
Fax: 01292 319007
thecherries50@hotmail.com
D: £20.00–£24.00
S: £20.00–£25.00
Beds: 1F 1T 1S
Baths: 1 En 1 Pr 1 Sh
🐾 🄿 (5) 🗶 📺 🛏 🛏 🆅 ⚓

Planning a longer stay? Always ask for any special rates

Rosedale, *9 Firth Road, Barassie, Troon, KA10 6TF.*
Quiet seafront location - ideal for Sea Cat ferry to Ireland.
Open: All Year (not Xmas)
Grades: STB 2 Star
01292 314371
Mrs Risk
hmrisk@hotmail.com
D: £20.00 **S:** £20.00
Beds: 1D 1T 1S
🐾 (5) 🗶 📺 🛏 🆅 ⚓

Mossgiel, *56 Bentinck Drive, Troon, KA10 6Y.*
5 minutes from beach, 10 minutes' walk from golf courses.
Open: All Year
Grades: STB 2 Star
01292 314937 (also fax)
Mrs Rankin
mossgiel@aol.com
D: £19.00–£22.00 **S:** £22.00–£25.00
Beds: 1F 1D 1T **Baths:** 3 En
🐾 🄿 (3) 📺 🛏 🆅 ✳ ⚓ &

The Beeches, *63 Ottoline Drive, Troon, KA10 7AN.*
Bright spacious house,wooded gardens. Every amenity, beaches, golf, marina.
Open: All Year
Grades: STB 2 Star
01292 314180
D: £16.00–£18.00
S: £18.00–£20.00
Beds: 1D 1T 1S **Baths:** 2 Pr
🐾 🄿 (4) 🗶 📺 🛏 🆅 ⚓

Borders

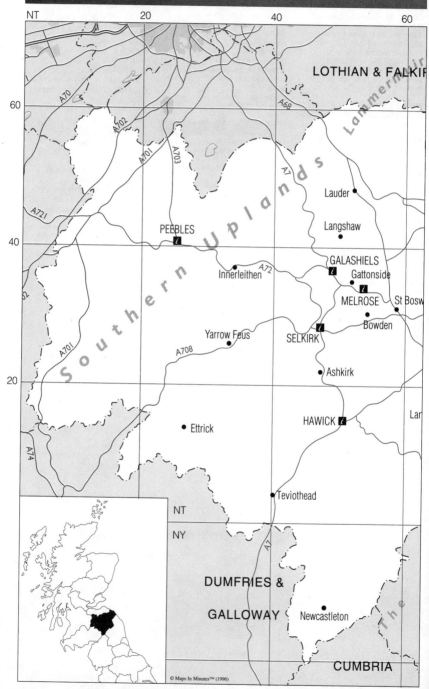

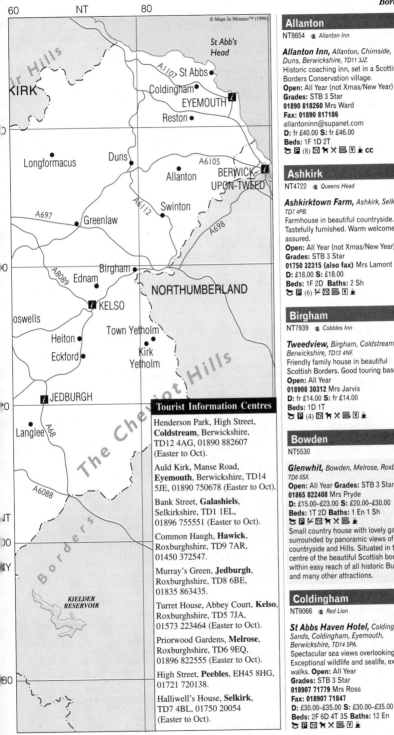

Allanton

NT8654   ⚐ *Allanton Inn*

Allanton Inn, Allanton, Chirnside,
Duns, Berwickshire, TD11 3JZ.
Historic coaching inn, set in a Scottish
Borders Conservation village.
Open: All Year (not Xmas/New Year)
Grades: STB 3 Star
01890 818260 Mrs Ward
Fax: 01890 817186
allantoninn@supanet.com
D: fr £40.00 **S:** fr £46.00
Beds: 1F 1D 2T
⛼ 🅿 (8) 📺 ⛺ ✕ 🛏 Ⓥ ♨ cc

Ashkirk

NT4722   ⚐ *Queens Head*

Ashkirktown Farm, Ashkirk, Selkirk,
TD7 4PB.
Farmhouse in beautiful countryside.
Tastefully furnished. Warm welcome
assured.
Open: All Year (not Xmas/New Year)
Grades: STB 3 Star
01750 32315 (also fax) Mrs Lamont
D: £18.00 **S:** £18.00
Beds: 1F 2D **Baths:** 2 Sh
⛼ 🅿 (6) ⅙ 📺 🛏 Ⓥ ♨

Birgham

NT7939   ⚐ *Cobbles Inn*

Tweedview, Birgham, Coldstream,
Berwickshire, TD12 4NF.
Friendly family house in beautiful
Scottish Borders. Good touring base.
Open: All Year
018908 30312 Mrs Jarvis
D: fr £14.00 **S:** fr £14.00
Beds: 1D 1T
⛼ 🅿 (4) 📺 ⛺ ✕ 🛏 Ⓥ ♨

Bowden

NT5530

Glenwhit, Bowden, Melrose, Roxburgh,
TD6 0SX.
Open: All Year **Grades:** STB 3 Star
01865 822408 Mrs Pryde
D: £15.00–£23.00 **S:** £20.00–£30.00
Beds: 1T 2D **Baths:** 1 En 1 Sh
⛼ 🅿 ⅙ 📺 ⛺ ✕ 🛏 ♨
Small country house with lovely garden,
surrounded by panoramic views of
countryside and Hills. Situated in the
centre of the beautiful Scottish borders,
within easy reach of all historic Buildings
and many other attractions.

Coldingham

NT9066   ⚐ *Red Lion*

St Abbs Haven Hotel, Coldingham
Sands, Coldingham, Eyemouth,
Berwickshire, TD14 5PA.
Spectacular sea views overlooking bay.
Exceptional wildlife and sealife, excellent
walks. **Open:** All Year
Grades: STB 3 Star
018907 71779 Mrs Ross
Fax: 018907 71847
D: £30.00–£35.00 **S:** £30.00–£35.00
Beds: 2F 6D 4T 3S **Baths:** 12 En
⛼ 🅿 📺 ⛺ ✕ 🛏 Ⓥ ♨

Tourist Information Centres

Henderson Park, High Street,
Coldstream, Berwickshire,
TD12 4AG, 01890 882607
(Easter to Oct).

Auld Kirk, Manse Road,
Eyemouth, Berwickshire, TD14
5JE, 01890 750678 (Easter to Oct).

Bank Street, **Galashiels**,
Selkirkshire, TD1 1EL,
01896 755551 (Easter to Oct).

Common Haugh, **Hawick**,
Roxburghshire, TD9 7AR,
01450 372547.

Murray's Green, **Jedburgh**,
Roxburghshire, TD8 6BE,
01835 863435.

Turret House, Abbey Court, **Kelso**,
Roxburghshire, TD5 7JA,
01573 223464 (Easter to Oct).

Priorwood Gardens, **Melrose**,
Roxburghshire, TD6 9EQ,
01896 822555 (Easter to Oct).

High Street, **Peebles**, EH45 8HG,
01721 720138.

Halliwell's House, **Selkirk**,
TD7 4BL, 01750 20054
(Easter to Oct).

Cul-na-Sithe, *Coldingham Bay, Coldingham, Eyemouth, Berwickshire, TD14 5PA.*
Near St Abbs fishing village and nature reserve, overlooking Coldingham Sands.
Open: Feb to Nov
018907 71565 (also fax)
Mr Paterson
culnasithe@clara.co.uk
D: £23.00–£26.50
Beds: 2D 1T **Baths:** 3 En
🖼 (3) ⚊ 📺 🖫 ✕ 🍴 �V ⚊ CC

Duns

NT7854   🍺 *Barniken House, Black Ball, Wheatsheaf, Allanton Inn*

St Albans, *Clouds, Duns, Berwickshire, TD11 3BB.*
Georgian manse, with period furnishings, overlooking small town.
Open: All Year (not Xmas/New Year)
Grades: STB 4 Star
01361 883285 Fax: 01361 884534
st_albans@email.msn.com
D: £19.50–£25.00 **S:** £22.00–£30.00
Beds: 2D/T 2S **Baths:** 2 Sh
🖼 (12) 📺 🍴 🖫 �V ⚊ CC

Kirkside House, *Bonkyl, Duns, Berwickshire, TD11 3RJ.*
Comfortable early Victorian house situated in a peaceful, rural location.
Open: All Year (not Xmas)
01361 884340 (also fax)
Mrs Taylor
D: £21.50 **S:** £21.50
Beds: 1T 1D **Baths:** 1 Pr 1 Sh
🖼 (12) 🖼 (2) ⚊ ✕ 🍴 🖫 �V ⚊

Eckford

NT7126

The Old Joiners Cottage, *Eckford, Kelso, Roxburghshire, TD5 8LG.*
Charming Borders style cottage with picturesque views over rolling countryside.
Open: All Year
Grades: STB 3 Star
01835 850323 (also fax)
Mr Butterfield
joiners.cottage@virgin.net
D: £18.00–£21.00 **S:** £21.00–£30.00
🖼 (3) ⚊ 📺 🍴 ✕ 🍴 🖫 �V ⚊ CC

Ednam

NT7337

Clifton Hill Farm, *Ednam, Kelso, Roxburghshire, TD5 7QE.*
Plumbraes Barn is in beautiful border countryside with a lovely riverside walk.
Open: All Year
01573 225028 Mrs Stewart
Fax: 01573 226416
archie@sol.co.uk
D: £22.50–£23.50 **S:** £30.00–£32.00
Beds: 2F 2D 2T **Baths:** 2 En 2 Pr
🖼 🖼 📺 ✕ 🍴 🖫 🌸 ⚊ ♿ CC

Planning a longer stay? Always ask for any special rates

Ettrick

NT2714   🍺 *Cross Keys*

West Deloraine Farm, *Ettrick, Selkirk, TD7 5HR.*
1000 acre farm situated in James Hogg and Sir Walter Scott country.
Open: Easter to Oct
01750 62207 Mrs Bernard
D: £16.00 **S:** £16.00
Beds: 1T 2D **Baths:** 2 Sh
🐾 🖼 📺 🍴

Galashiels

NT4936   🍺 *Kings Hotel, Woodlands Hotel, Cobbles Inn, Thistle Inn, Herges Bistro, Abbotsford Arms, Hunters Hall*

Watson Lodge, *15 Bridge Street, Galashiels, Selkirkshire, TD1 1SW.*
Open: All Year
01896 750551 Mrs Reid
D: £16.00–£20.00 **S:** £18.00–£20.00
Beds: 2T 1D **Baths:** 3 En
🐾 🖼 ⚊ 📺 🍴 🖫 �V ⚊
Centrally situated B&B; all guest rooms overlook quiet back garden. Bright comfortable rooms - all ensuite. Shopping, golf, fishing, walks, historic landmarks all at hand. Perfect location for touring all the borders. Good food close by. A friendly welcome awaits.

Island House, *65 Island Street, Galashiels, Selkirkshire, TD1 1PA.*
Comfortable family home. Town centre. Ideally situated for touring the Borders.
Open: All Year
Grades: AA 3 Diamond
01896 752649 Mr Brown
D: £15.00–£18.00 **S:** £15.00–£20.00
Beds: 1D 2T **Baths:** 2 En 1 Sh
🐾 🖼 (2) ⚊ 📺 🍴 🖫 ⚊

Ettrickvale, *33 Abbotsford Road, Galashiels, Selkirkshire, TD1 3HW.*
Warm, comfortable bungalow, ideally situated for touring Borders & Edinburgh.
Open: All Year (not Xmas)
Grades: STB 2 Star
01896 755224 Mrs Field
D: £16.00 **S:** £20.00
Beds: 1D 2T **Baths:** 2 Sh
🐾 🖼 (3) 📺 🍴 ✕ 🍴 🖫 �V ⚊ ♿ 3

Kings Hotel, *Galashiels, Selkirkshire, TD1 3AN.*
Situated in the town centre of busy market town of Galashiels.
Open: All Year (not Xmas)
Grades: STB 2 Star, AA 2 Star
01896 755497 (also fax)
Mr MacDonald
kingshotel@talk21.com
D: £25.00–£36.00 **S:** £35.00–£46.00
Beds: 1F 1D 4T 1S **Baths:** 7 Pr
🐾 (1) 🖼 (6) ⚊ 📺 🖫 �V ⚊ CC

Keranalt, *3 Bridge Street, Galashiels, Selkirkshire, TD1 1SW.*
Centrally situated double glazed homely welcome.
Open: All Year (not Xmas/New Year)
01896 754859 Mrs Lowe
D: £16.00 **S:** £16.00
Beds: 3T **Baths:** 2 Sh
🐾 📺 ✕ 🍴 🖫 �V ⚊

Abbotsford Arms Hotel, *Stirling Street, Galashiels, Selkirkshire, TD1 1BY.*
Centrally situated, family run; serving good food all day.
Open: All Year (not Xmas/New Year)
01896 752517
Fax: 01896 750744
cscott2517@aol.com
D: £29.00–£30.00
S: £38.00–£40.00
Beds: 4F 3D 5T 2S **Baths:** 14 En
🐾 🖼 (10) 📺 ✕ 🍴 🖫 �V ⚊ CC

Gattonside

NT5435   🍺 *Marmions*

Fauhope House, *Fauhope, Gattonside, Melrose, Roxburghshire, TD6 9LU.*
An Edwardian house looking over the river Tweed to Melrose Abbey.
Open: All Year
Grades: STB 4 Star
01896 823184 (also fax)
Mrs Robson
D: £25.00 **S:** £32.00
Beds: 2T 1D **Baths:** 3 En
🖼 ⚊ 🍴 🖫 ⚊ CC

Greenlaw

NT7146   🍺 *Blackadder, Cross Keys*

Bridgend House, *West High Street, Greenlaw, Duns, Berwickshire, TD10 6XA.*
Built 1816 with trout fishing in pretty riverside garden.
Open: All Year
Grades: STB 2 Star
01361 810270 (also fax)
Mrs Carruthers
aproposdes@fsbdial.co.uk
D: £18.00–£20.00 **S:** £24.00
Beds: 1F 1D 2T **Baths:** 3 En 1 Pr
🐾 🖼 (4) ⚊ 📺 🍴 ✕ 🍴 🖫 �V ⚊

Hawick

NT5015   🍺 *Cross Keys, Mansfield House, Buccleuch Hotel, Elm House*

Wiltonburn Farm, *Hawick, Roxburghshire, TD9 7LL.*
Delightful setting on hill farm with designer cashmere knitwear shop.
Open: All Year (not Xmas)
Grades: STB 3 Star
01450 372414
Mrs Shell
Fax: 01450 378098
shell@wiltonburnfarm.u-net.com
D: fr £20.00 **S:** fr £20.00
Beds: 1F 1D 1T **Baths:** 1 En 1 Pr 1 Sh
🐾 🖼 (6) ⚊ 📺 🍴 ✕ 🍴 🖫 �V ⚊ CC

Ellistrin, *6 Fenwick Park, Hawick, Roxburghshire, TD9 9PA.*
Welcoming family home in quiet area, close to all amenities.
Open: Easter to Oct
Grades: STB 3 Star
01450 374216 Mrs Smith
Fax: 01450 373619
ellistrin@compuserve.com
D: £18.00 **S:** £18.00
Beds: 2D 1T **Baths:** 3 En
🐾 🖼 (3) 📺 🍴 🖫 �V ⚊

Oakwood House, *Buccleuch Road,*
Hawick, Roxburghshire, TD9 0EH.
Victorian sandstone villa overlooking
bowling greens. Convenient
cashmere/knitwear outlets.
Open: All Year (not Xmas/New Year)
Grades: STB 3 Star
01450 372814 Mr & Mrs Richards
D: £19.00–£20.00 **S:** £22.00–£25.00
Beds: 2D 1T **Baths:** 2 En 1 Pr
🛇 🄿 (5) ⊁ 📺 🛒 Ⅵ ♨

Kirkton Farmhouse, *Hawick,*
Roxburghshire, TD9 8QJ.
Warm, friendly welcome. Open log fire,
private loch fishing, home cooking.
Open: All Year
01450 372421 Mrs Bell
bell.kirton@virgin.net
D: £15.00 **S:** £15.00
Beds: 2D 1T **Baths:** 1 Sh
🛇 🄿 (6) 📺 🛒 ✕ 🛒 Ⅵ ♨

Hillview, *Weensland Road, Hawick,*
Roxburghshire, TD9 9NP.
Warm friendly welcome guaranted. Close
to town centre; handy for golf, fishing,
walking & cycling.
Open: All Year (not Xmas)
01450 374100 Mrs Allan
D: £14.00–£15.00 **S:** £14.00–£15.00
Beds: 1D 1T 1S **Baths:** 1 Sh
🛇 ⊁ 📺 🛒 🛒 ♨

Heiton

NT7130 🍺 *Queens Head Hotel*

Goldilands, *Roxburgh Road, Heiton,*
Kelso, TD5 8TP.
New bungalow, 2 miles from Kelso,
adjacent to golf course.
Open: All Year
01573 450671 **(also fax)** Mrs Brotherston
jimbroth@aol.com
D: £20.00 **S:** £25.00
Beds: 2T 1D **Baths:** 3 En
🛇 (2) 🄿 (3) ⊁ 📺 🛒 🛒 ✳ ♨ ♿

Innerleithen

NT3336 🍺 *St Ronan's Hotel, Traquair Arms*

Caddon View Guest House, *14 Pirn*
Road, Innerleithen, Peebles-shire, EH44
6HH.
Open: All Year (not Xmas)
Grades: STB 4 Star
01896 830208 Mr & Mrs Djelili
caddonview@aol.com
D: £24.00–£30.00 **S:** £35.00–£40.00
Beds: 1F 3D 2T **Baths:** 6 En
🛇 🄿 (5) ⊁ 📺 🛒 ✕ 🛒 Ⅵ ✳ ♨ cc
Charming Victorian family house by the
River Tweed, ideally situated for walking,
fishing, touring or just relaxing. All rooms
individually designed and equipped to
make you feel at home. French restaurant
and sauna available.

St Ronan's Hotel, *High Street,*
Innerleithen, Peebles-shire, EH44 6HF.
Traditional 1823 coaching inn serving
good home-cooking and real ales all day.
Open: All Year
01896 831487 cath.st.ronans@virgin.net
D: £20.00–£25.00 **S:** fr £25.00
Beds: 2F 2D 2T **Baths:** 5 En 1 Pr
🛇 🄿 (25) 🛒 ✕ 🛒 Ⅵ ♨ ♿ cc

Jedburgh

NT6520 🍺 *Royal Hotel, Simply Scottish,*
Pheasant Inn, Forresters

Riverview, *Newmill Farm, Jedburgh,*
Roxburghshire, TD8 6TH.
Spacious modern villa overlooking River
Jed with country views.
Open: April to Oct **Grades:** STB 3 Star
01835 862145 Mrs Kinghorn
D: £18.00–£20.00 **S:** £23.00
Beds: 1T 2D **Baths:** 3 En
🄿 (4) 📺 🛒 ♨

Edgerston Rink Smithy, *Jedburgh,*
Roxburghshire, TD8 6PP.
Open: All Year **Grades:** STB 3 Star
01835 840328 Mr & Mrs Smart
royglen.rink@btinternet.com
D: £16.00–£18.00 **S:** £23.00
Beds: 2D **Baths:** 1 Sh
🛇 (12) 🄿 (4) 🛒 ✕ 🛒 ♨
Converted smithy overlooking the Cheviot
Hills backing on to natural woodland.
Very private facilities of a superior
standard. Warm welcome assured.
Private visitors lounge with TV, music
centre etc. Rural location alongside A68,
7 miles south of Jedburgh.

Hundalee House, *Jedburgh,*
Roxburghshire, TD8 6PA.
Open: Mar to Nov
01835 863011 **(also fax)**
Mrs Whittaker
sheila.whittaker@btinternet.com
D: £20.00–£23.00 **S:** £25.00–£35.00
Beds: 1F 3D 1T **Baths:** 4 En 1 Pr
🛇 (5) 🄿 (10) ⊁ 📺 🛒 Ⅵ ♨
Large Victorian private house.

Froylehurst, *The Friars, Jedburgh,*
Roxburghshire, TD8 6BN.
Detached Victorian house in large
garden. Spacious guest rooms, 2 mins
town centre.
Open: Mar to Nov
Grades: STB 4 Star
01835 862477 **(also fax)**
Mrs Irvine
D: £15.50–£18.00 **S:** £20.00–£25.00
Beds: 2F 1D 1T **Baths:** 2 Sh
🛇 (5) 🄿 (5) 📺 🛒 Ⅵ ♨

Ferniehirst Mill Lodge, *Jedburgh,*
Roxburghshire, TD8 6PQ.
Modern guest house in peaceful setting,
country lovers' paradise.
Open: All Year
Grades: STB 1 Star, AA 3 Diamond, RAC
3 Diamond
01835 863279 Mr Swanston
ferniemill@aol.com
D: £23.00 **S:** £23.00
Beds: 1F 3D 4T 1S **Baths:** 9 En 1 Sh
🛇 🄿 (10) 📺 🛒 🛒 Ⅵ ♨ cc

15 Hartrigge Crescent, *Jedburgh,*
Roxburghshire, TD8 6HT.
Comfortable family house, within short
distance of town centre.
Open: All Year
Grades: STB 2 Star
01835 862738 Mrs Crone
D: fr £15.50 **S:** fr £18.00
Beds: 1D 1T **Baths:** 1 Sh
🛇 (1) 🄿 (5) 📺 🛒 Ⅵ ♨

Craigowen, *30 High Street, Jedburgh,*
Roxburghshire, TD8 6AG.
Centrally located family home. A great
welcome. Real home from home.
Open: All Year (not Xmas)
01835 862604 Mrs Campbell
D: £16.00–£17.50 **S:** £17.00–£18.50
Beds: 1F 1T **Baths:** 2 Pr
🛇 🄿 (3) 📺 🛒 🛒 ♨

Willow Court, *The Friars, Jedburgh,*
Roxburghshire, TD8 6BN.
Modern, professionally-run guest house.
Lovely views over Jedburgh, two mins'
walk town centre.
Open: All Year (not Xmas)
01835 863702 Mr McGovern
Fax: 01835 864601
D: £18.00–£22.00 **S:** £27.00–£36.00
Beds: 1F 2D 1T **Baths:** 3 En 1 Pr
🛇 🄿 (5) 📺 🛒 🛒 Ⅵ ♨ ♿

Kenmore Bank , *Oxnam Road,*
Jedburgh, Roxburghshire, TD8 6JJ.
Charming, family run, just off A68.
Panoramic views over Abbey, ensuite.
Open: All Year
01835 862369 Mr Muller
joanne@diadembooks.com
D: £19.00–£23.00 **S:** £25.00–£43.00
Beds: 2F 2D 2T **Baths:** 6 En
🛇 🄿 (5) 🛒 ♨ cc

Maple Bank, *3 Smiths Wynd, Jedburgh,*
Roxburghshire, TD8 6DH.
Large town centre period house, easy
access restaurants, shops, buses.
Open: All Year
01835 862051 Mrs Booth
ann@maplebank1.demon.co.uk
D: £14.00–£15.00 **S:** £15.00–£28.00
Beds: 1F 1D **Baths:** 2 Sh
🛇 🄿 (2) 📺 🛒 🛒 Ⅵ ♨

Kelso

NT7234 🍺 *Black Swan, Border Hotel, Cobbles*
Inn, Plough Hotel, Queen's Head, Wagon & Horses

Craignethan House, *Jedburgh Road,*
Kelso, Roxburghshire, TD5 8AZ.
Open: All Year
Grades: STB 3 Star
01573 224818 Mrs McDonald
D: £18.50 **S:** fr £18.50
Beds: 2D 1T **Baths:** 1 Pr 1 Sh
🛇 🄿 (6) 📺 🛒 🛒 Ⅵ ♨ ♿ 3
Comfortable welcoming family home with
relaxed informal atmosphere. Breakfast
to suit all tastes and times. Afternoon tea,
tea/coffee in evening, home baking,
attractive garden, breathtaking
panoramic views of Kelso/Tweed Valley to
Floors Castle from all bedrooms. Scottish
Border Abbeys, Floors Castle, Tweed
Valley, Walter Scott country.

Lochside, *Town Yetholm, Kelso,*
Roxburghshire, TD5 8PD.
Victorian country house. Peaceful,
spacious, ensuite bedrooms. Beautiful
countryside.
Open: Apr to Oct
Grades: STB 3 Star B&B
01573 420349 Mrs Hurst
D: £20.00–£22.50 **S:** £22.50
Beds: 1D 1T **Baths:** 2 En
🛇 (2) 🄿 (2) ⊁ 📺 🛒 🛒 ♨

Duncan House, Chalkheugh Terrace, Kelso, Roxburghshire, TD5 7DX.

Georgian riverside house, spectacular views river & castle. 2 mins to centre town.

Open: All Year (not Xmas)
01573 225682 Mrs Robertson
D: £15.00–£17.00 **S:** £20.00–£30.00
Beds: 3F 1D **Baths:** 3 En 3 Pr 1 Sh
⌂ ▣ (6) ☎ ⅋ ⊞ ⌕ Ⅷ Ⓥ ⚊ ⅋

Bellevue House, Bowmont Street, Kelso, Roxburghshire, TD5 7DZ.

Ideally located for fishing, golfing, sightseeing, race course, town centre.

Open: All Year (not Xmas)
01573 224588 Mr & Mrs Thompson
D: £22.00–£25.00 **S:** £25.00–£35.00
Beds: 3D 3T **Baths:** 6 En
⌂ ▣ (7) ⅋ ⊞ ⌕ Ⅷ Ⓥ ⚊ cc

Kirk Yetholm

NT8228   🍺 Border Hotel, Cobbles Inn, Plough Hotel

Valleydene, High Street, Kirk Yetholm, Kelso, Roxburghshire, TD5 8PH.

Traditional Scottish welcome. Log fire. Comfortable rooms with excellent views.

Open: All Year
01573 420286 Mrs Campbell
D: £22.00 **S:** £25.00–£30.00
Beds: 2T 1D **Baths:** 2 En 1 Pr
⌂ (12) ▣ (4) ⊞ ⌕ ✕ Ⅷ Ⓥ ⚊

Blunty's Mill, Kirk Yetholm, Kelso, Roxburghshire, TD5 6PG.

Fabulous rural location set in 6 acres. Friendly welcome guaranteed.

Open: All Year
Grades: STB 2 Star
01573 420288 Mrs Brooker
gail_rowan@hotmail.com
D: £20.00–£30.00
Beds: 2T **Baths:** 1 Sh
⌂ ▣ (10) ⊞ ⌕ ✕ Ⓥ ⚊ ⅋ ⅃

Spring Valley, The Green, Kirk Yetholm, Roxburghshire, TD5 8PQ.

C18th house with superb views, situated in conservation village.

Open: All Year (not Xmas)
Grades: STB 3 Star
01573 420253 Mrs Ogilvie
D: £20.00–£22.00 **S:** £–£27.00
Beds: 1D 1T **Baths:** 2 Pr
⌂ (1) ▣ (3) ⅋ ⊞ ⌕ Ⅷ ⚊

Langlee

NT6417   🍺 The Pheasant, Simply Scottish

The Spinney, Langlee, Jedburgh, Roxburghshire, TD8 6PB.

Spacious house in main house and in nearby pine cabins.

Open: Mar to Nov
Grades: STB 4 Star, AA 5 Diamond
01835 863525 Mrs Fry
Fax: 01835 864883
thespinney@btinternet.com
D: £21.00–£23.00
Beds: 2D 1T 3F **Baths:** 5 En 1 Pr
⌂ ▣ (6) ⅋ ⊞ ⌕ Ⅷ Ⓥ ⚊ cc

Langshaw

NT5139

Over Langshaw Farm, Langshaw, Galashiels, Selkirkshire, TD1 2PE.

Welcoming family farm superb location in unspoilt border countryside.

Open: All Year **Grades:** STB 2 Star
01896 860244 Mrs Bergius
D: £20.00–£22.00 **S:** £25.00
Beds: 1F 1D **Baths:** 1 En 1 Pr 1 Sh
⌂ ▣ (3) ⅋ ⊞ ⌕ ✕ Ⅷ Ⓥ ⚊ ⅋

Lauder

NT5247   🍺 Lauderdale Hotel, Eagle Hotel, Black Bull Hotel

The Grange, 6 Edinburgh Road, Lauder, Berwickshire, TD2 6TW.

Open: All Year (not Xmas)
Grades: STB 3 Star, AA 3 Diamond
01578 722649 (also fax)
Tricia and Peter Gilardi
D: £17.00–£20.00 **S:** £18.00–£20.00
Beds: 1D 2T **Baths:** 1 Sh
⌂ ▣ (3) ⅋ ⊞ ⌕ Ⅷ Ⓥ ⚊

A peaceful haven from which to explore the tranquil Scottish and English borders, yet less than an hour's drive from Edinburgh. Overlooking the rolling Lammermuir Hills and on the Southern Upland Way, an ideal base for walking, cycling or relaxing.

Longformacus

NT6957

Eildon Cottage, Longformacus, Duns, Berwickshire, TD11 3NX.

Leave crowds behind set in beautiful rolling Lammermuir Hill Village.

Open: All Year (not Xmas/New Year)
01361 890230 Mrs Amos
D: £20.00–£25.00 **S:** £20.00–£25.00
Beds: 1F 1T 1D **Baths:** 2 En 1 Pr
▣ (3) ⊞ ⌕ ✕ Ⅷ Ⓥ ⚊

Kintra Ha, Gifford Road, Longformacus, Duns, Berwickshire, TD11 3NZ.

Recently converted, detached property. Edinburgh 50 mins. Access to rural pursuits. **Open:** All Year
Grades: STB 3 Star
01361 890660 (also fax) Mrs Lamb
lamb@kintrastell.co.uk
D: £–£20.00 **S:** £–£25.00
Beds: 1D 1T **Baths:** 2 En
⅋ ⊞ ⌕ ✕ Ⅷ Ⓥ ⚊ ⅃

Melrose

NT5433   🍺 Buccleuch Arms, Burts Hotel, Marmions

Fauhope House, Fauhope, Gattonside, Melrose, Roxburghshire, TD6 9LU.

Open: All Year **Grades:** STB 4 Star
01896 823184 (also fax) Mrs Robson
D: £25.00 **S:** £32.00
Beds: 2T 1D **Baths:** 3 En
▣ ⅋ ⌕ Ⅷ ⚊ cc

An Edwardian house looking over the river Tweed to Melrose Abbey and the Eildon hills. Fanhope within its spacious grounds offers seclusion with easy access to Melrose, shops and restaurants, golf courses, salmon fishing.

Old Abbey School House, Waverley Road, Melrose, Roxburghshire, TD6 9SH.

Charming old school house with character. Large bedrooms, restful atmosphere.

Open: March to November
01896 823432 Mrs O'Neill
D: £17.00–£21.00 **S:** £20.00–£25.00
Beds: 1T 2D **Baths:** 1 Pr 1 Sh
⌂ ▣ (5) ⅋ ⊞ ⌕ Ⅷ Ⓥ ⚊

Rivendell, The Croft, St Boswells, Melrose, TD6 0AE.

Open: All Year (not Xmas/New Year)
Grades: STB 4 Star
01835 822498 Mrs Mitchell
LizRivBB@cs.com
D: £18.00–£22.50 **S:** £25.00–£30.00
Beds: 2D 1T **Baths:** 2 En 1 Pr
▣ (3) ⅋ ⊞ ⌕ Ⅷ ⚊

Relax in our spacious family Victorian home overlooking Scotland's largest village green. Ideal central Scottish Borders location. Only 10 minutes from Kelso, Melrose, Jedburgh - Edinburgh one hour. River Tweed, Dryburgh Abbey & golf club all within easy walking distance.

Braidwood, Buccleuch Street, Melrose, Roxburghshire, TD6 9LD.

A Victorian town house situated a stones throw away from Melrose Abbey.

Open: All Year
Grades: STB 3 Star
01896 822488 Mrs Graham
D: £20.00–£24.00 **S:** £25.00
Beds: 3D 1F **Baths:** 2 En 2 Pr
⌂ ▣ ⅋ ⊞ ⌕ Ⅷ Ⓥ ⚊ ⅋

Newcastleton

NY4887   🍺 Bailey Mill

Bailey Mill, Bailey, Newcastleton, Roxburghshire, TD9 0TR.

Remote 18th century grain mill by river. Ideal retreat, jacuzzi, pony trekking

Open: All Year
016977 48617 Mrs Copeland
Fax: 016977 48074
D: £20.00–£25.00 **S:** £22.00–£28.00
Beds: 4F 6T 3D 4S **Baths:** 6 En 4 Pr 6 Sh
⌂ ▣ ⅋ ⌕ Ⅷ Ⓥ ⅋ ⚊ ⅃ cc

Peebles

NT2540   🍺 The Crown

Lyne Farmhouse, Lyne Farm, Peebles, EH45 8NR.

Open: All Year (not Xmas)
Grades: STB 2 Star
01721 740255 (also fax)
Mrs Waddell
awaddell@farming.co.uk
D: £18.00–£20.00 **S:** £20.00
Beds: 2D 1T **Baths:** 2 Sh
⌂ ▣ ⊞ ⌕ Ⅷ ⚊

Beautiful Georgian farmhouse, with tastefully decorated rooms overlooking scenic Stobo Valley. Walled garden plus hill-walking, picnic areas and major Roman fort all on farm. Ideally placed for Edinburgh and picturesque town of Peebles, plus Border towns and historic houses.

Reston

NT8862

Stoneshiel Hall, *Reston, Eyemouth, Berwickshire, TD14 5LU.*
Open: All Year (not Xmas/New Year)
01890 761267
Mr & Mrs Olley
D: fr £24.00 **S:** fr £24.00
Beds: 1T 1D **Baths:** 2 Pr
⑃ ⊞ (25) ⌇ ⊠ ✕ ▥ ⊻
A warm welcome awaits you at this historic mansion, set in extensive grounds and gardens overlooking beautiful Borders countryside. Traditionally furnished, the accommodation is spacious with an aura of stately splendour, where the emphasis is on flexibility and personal service.

Selkirk

NT4728 ⬤ *Queen's Head, Plough Inn, Cross Keys Inn, County Hotel*

Ivy Bank, *Hillside Terrace, Selkirk, TD7 2LT.*
Set back from A7 with fine views over hills beyond.
Open: Easter to Dec
Grades: STB 2 Star
01750 21270
Mrs MacKenzie
nettamackenzie@
ivybankselkirk.freeserve.co.uk
D: £17.50–£18.00 **S:** £18.00
Beds: 1D 1T 1S **Baths:** 2 En 1 Pr 1 Sh
⑃ ⊞ (4) ⊠ ✿ ▥ ⊻ ♨ cc

St Abbs

NT9167 ⬤ *St Abbs Haven, Anchor*

Castle Rock Guest House, *Murrayfield, St Abbs, Eyemouth, Berwickshire, TD14 5PP.*
Victorian house with superb views over sea and rocks.
Open: Feb to Nov
Grades: STB 3 Star
018907 71715
Mrs Wood
Fax: 018907 71520
boowood@compuserve.com
D: £23.00–£25.00 **S:** £23.00–£25.00
Beds: 1F 1D 1T 1S **Baths:** 4 En
⑃ ⊞ (4) ⌇ ⊠ ✿ ✕ ▥ ⊻ ♨ cc

7 Murrayfield, *St Abbs, Eyemouth, Berwickshire, TD14 5PP.*
Former fisherman's cottage in quiet village, close to beach/ harbour.
Open: All Year **Grades:** STB 3 Star
018907 71468 Mrs Wilson
D: £16.50–£19.00 **S:** £21.50–£24.00
Beds: 1F 1D **Baths:** 1 En 1 Sh
⑃ ⌇ ⊠ ✿ ▥.

St Boswells

NT5930 ⬤ *Buccleuch Arms Hotel*

Rivendell, *The Croft, St Boswells, Melrose, TD6 0AE.*
Relax in our spacious family Victorian home overlooking Scotland's largest village green.
Open: All Year (not Xmas/New Year)
Grades: STB 4 Star
01835 822498 Mrs Mitchell
LizRivBB@cs.com
D: £18.00–£22.50 **S:** £25.00–£30.00
Beds: 2D 1T **Baths:** 2 En 1 Pr
⊞ (3) ⌇ ⊠ ▥. ♨

Swinton

NT8347 ⬤ *Wheatsheaf Hotel*

Three to Six The Green, *Swinton, Duns, Berwickshire, TD11 3JQ.*
Comfortable ensuite accommodation in quiet village. Guest rooms overlook garden. **Open:** All Year
Grades: STB 3 Star
01890 860322 L Robertson
D: £20.00–£22.00 **S:** £26.00–£27.50
Beds: 1T 1D **Baths:** 2 En
⑃ (5) ⊞ (2) ⌇ ⊠ ▥. ⊻ ♨

Teviothead

NT4004

The Quiet Garden, *Hislop , Teviothead, Hawick, Roxburghshire, TD9 0PS.*
Open: Easter to Oct **Grades:** STB 3 Star
01450 850310 (also fax) Mrs Armitage
D: £16.00–£18.00 **S:** £16.00–£18.00
Beds: 1T 1D **Baths:** 1 Sh 1 Pr
⑃ ⊞ (2) ⌇ ⊠ ✕ ▥. ⊻ ♨ ♿
Small privately run, eco-friendly B&B with ground floor accommodation. 1 acre garden with organic vegetables, free range hens and ducks. Superb location for bird watchers, botanists and walkers. Quiet private position on border hill farm. 3 miles from A7. Need own transport.

RATES

D = Price range per person sharing in a double room
S = Price range for a single room

Town Yetholm

NT8127 ⬤ *Border Hotel, Cobbles Inn, Plough Hotel*

Lochside, *Town Yetholm, Kelso, Roxburghshire, TD5 8PD.*
Victorian country house. Peaceful, spacious, ensuite bedrooms. Beautiful countryside.
Open: Apr to Oct
Grades: STB 3 Star B&B
01573 420349 Mrs Hurst
D: £20.00–£22.50 **S:** £22.50
Beds: 1D 1T **Baths:** 2 En
⑃ (2) ⊞ (2) ⌇ ⊠ ✿ ▥. ♨

Blunty's Mill, *Kirk Yetholm, Kelso, Roxburghshire, TD5 6PG.*
Fabulous rural location set in 6 acres. Friendly welcome guaranteed.
Open: All Year
Grades: STB 2 Star
01573 420288
Mrs Brooker
gail_rowan@hotmail.com
D: £22.00–£30.00
Beds: 2T **Baths:** 1 Sh
⑃ ⊞ (10) ⊠ ✿ ✕ ❋ ♨ ♿

Yarrow Feus

NT3426 ⬤ *Cross Keys*

Ladhope Farm, *Yarrow Feus, Yarrow Valley, Selkirk, TD7 5NE.*
Beautiful farmhouse, log fires, very peaceful. Ideal for hunting, touring.
Open: Easter to Oct
01750 82216 Mrs Turnbull
anne@scottish.borders.com
D: £18.00–£20.00 **S:** £20.00–£22.00
Beds: 1F 1D **Baths:** 1 Sh
⑃ ⊞ (4) ⊠ ✿ ✕ ⊻ ♨

Dumfries & Galloway

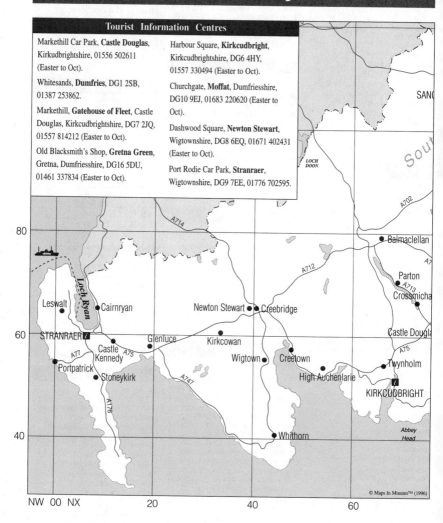

Tourist Information Centres

Markethill Car Park, **Castle Douglas**, Kirkbrightshire, 01556 502611 (Easter to Oct).

Whitesands, **Dumfries**, DG1 2SB, 01387 253862.

Markethill, **Gatehouse of Fleet**, Castle Douglas, Kirkcudbrightshire, DG7 2JQ, 01557 814212 (Easter to Oct).

Old Blacksmith's Shop, **Gretna Green**, Gretna, Dumfriesshire, DG16 5DU, 01461 337834 (Easter to Oct).

Harbour Square, **Kirkcudbright**, Kirkcudbrightshire, DG6 4HY, 01557 330494 (Easter to Oct).

Churchgate, **Moffat**, Dumfriesshire, DG10 9EJ, 01683 220620 (Easter to Oct).

Dashwood Square, **Newton Stewart**, Wigtownshire, DG8 6EQ, 01671 402431 (Easter to Oct).

Port Rodie Car Park, **Stranraer**, Wigtownshire, DG9 7EE, 01776 702595.

Annan

NY1966   Queensbury Arms

The Old Rectory Guest House, 12 St Johns Road, Annan, Dumfriesshire, DG12 6AW.
Open: All Year
01461 202029 (also fax)
J Buchanan & J Alexander
old-rectory-guest1@supanet.com

D: £22.00–£25.00 **S:** £22.00–£25.00
Beds: 2F 2D 1T 1S **Baths:** 5 En 1 Pr
⛄ (4) ▯ (6) ⅙ ▦ ♔ ✕ ▦ ▦ ❀ ♨
Charming C19th manse in the centre of Annan, 7 miles from famous wedding town Gretna, be assured of warm welcome, ensuite bedrooms, great Scottish breakfasts, home cooking, licensed, main Euro & Irish routes. Walkers, cyclist, small wedding parties welcome. Smoking lounge available.

Milnfield Farm, Low Road, Annan, Dumfriesshire, DG12 5QP.
Working farm, riverside walks, large garden; ideal for touring base.
Open: All Year (not Xmas)
Grades: STB 2 Star
01461 201811 R Robinson
D: £16.00–£18.00 **S:** £16.00–£18.00
Beds: 1F 1D
⛄ ▯ ⅙ ▦ ♔ ▦ ♨

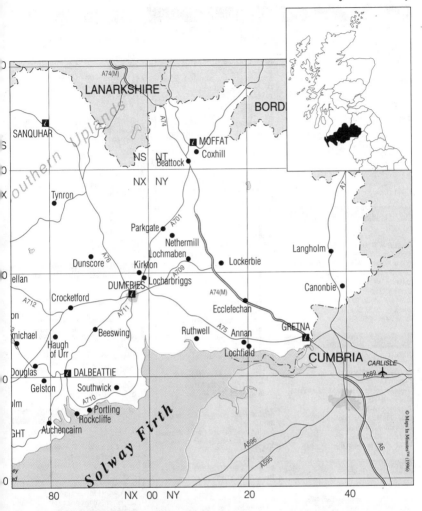

© Maps in Minutes™ (1996)

80   NX   00   NY   20   40

Auchencairn

NX7951 🍺 *Glenisle Inn, Old Smugglers Inn*

Torbay, *Blue Hill, Auchencairn, Castle Douglas, DG7 1QW.*
Open: Easter to Oct
Grades: STB 5 Star
01556 640180
J T Cannon
Fax: 01556 640228
cannontorbay@aol.com
D: £25.00 **S:** £30.00
Beds: 1T 1D
Baths: 2 En
🅿 ⅃ 📺 ▥ 🕭
Enjoy the tranquillity of the unspoilt countryside and relax in the tastefully furnished rooms. Wonderful views across the Solway. Lovely walks. Follow Heritage Trail for castles and abbeys. Coast 1 mile. Excellent pub in village - 0.5 mile.

The Rossan, *Auchencairn, Castle Douglas, Kirkcudbrightshire, DG7 1QR.*
Georgian style house 1869. Large secluded garden - bird watchers paradise. Resident owls. **Open:** All Year
Grades: STB 2 Star
01556 640269 Mrs Bardsley
Fax: 01556 640278
bardsley@rossan.freeserve.co.uk
D: £15.00 **S:** £20.00
Beds: 3D **Baths:** 2 Sh
🅿 (4) ⅃ 📺 ⛰ ✗ ▥ 🅈 ❋ 🕭

BATHROOMS

Pr - Private

Sh - Shared

En - Ensuite

Gallowa House, *The Square, Auchencairn, Castle Douglas, Kirkcudbrightshire, DG7 1QT.*
Families welcomed. Ideally situated for touring South West Scotland.
Open: All Year (not Xmas/New Year)
Grades: STB 3 Star
01556 640234 (also fax) J Smith
smith@gallowahouse.freeserve.co.uk
D: £16.00 **S:** £20.00 **Beds:** 1F 1D **Baths:** 1 Sh
🏖 ⅃ 📺 ▥ 🅈 🕭

Burnside House, *23 Main Street, Auchencairn, Castle Douglas, Kirkcudbrightshire, DG7 1QU.*
Friendly atmosphere with a good breakfast and comfortable rooms.
Open: All Year (not Xmas)
01556 640283 Mrs Norcross
bev-jade@supanet.com
D: £15.00 **S:** £15.00
Beds: 2F **Baths:** 1 En 1 Pr
🏖 🅿 (1) 📺 ⛰ ▥ 🅈 🕭

Balmaclellan

NX6579 ⚓ Lochinvar Hotel

High Park, Balmaclellan, Castle
Douglas, Kirkcudbrightshire, DG7 3PT.
Open: Easter to Oct
Grades: STB 2 Star
01644 420298 (also fax)
Mrs Shaw
high.park@farming.co.uk
D: £16.00–£17.00 **S:** £16.00–£17.00
Beds: 2D 1T **Baths:** 1 Sh
🛇 🅿 (4) ⅋ 📺 🍴 ✕ 🏠 Ⅴ 🎿 ⅙
A warm welcome awaits you at our
comfortable farmhouse by Loch Ken.
Double bedroom and bathroom on
ground floor, double and twin bedrooms
and toilet upstairs. All have tea/coffee
facilities, wash basins and TV.
Comfortable lounge. Brochure available.

Beattock

NT0802

Middlegill, Beattock, Moffat,
Dumfriesshire, DG10 9SW.
Manor farmhouse, 4 miles from Moffat.
Deer, peacocks, lovely walks.
Open: All year (not Xmas)
01683 300612 Mr Ramsden
D: £15.00–£19.00 **S:** £15.00–£19.00
Beds: 2F 2D 3S **Baths:** 2 Sh
🛇 ⅋ 📺 🍴 🏠 Ⅴ 🎿

Beeswing

NX8969

Locharthur House, Beeswing,
Dumfries, DG2 8JG.
Georgian house in beautiful countryside.
Open: All Year
Grades: STB 2 Star
01387 760235 Mrs Schooling
D: £18.00–£20.00 **S:** £20.00–£22.00
Beds: 1F 1D **Baths:** 2 En
🛇 🅿 (6) 📺 🍴 ✕ 🏠 Ⅴ 🎿

Cairnryan

NX0668

Albannach, Loch Ryan, Cairnryan,
Stranraer, Wigtownshire, DG9 8QX.
Victorian manse on the shores of Loch
Ryan, ideally situated for ferries to
Ireland.
Open: All Year
01581 200624 Mrs Craig
D: £19.00 **S:** £19.00
Beds: 1F 1D 1T 1S **Baths:** 4 En
🛇 🅿 (10) 📺 🍴 ✕ 🏠 Ⅴ 🎿

Canonbie

NY3876 ⚓ Cross Keys Hotel, Riverside Inn

Meadow View, Watch Hill Road,
Canonbie, DG14 0TF.
A warm Scottish welcome assured in this
friendly home.
Open: Easter to Oct
Grades: STB 3 Star
013873 71786 Mrs Bell
D: £17.50 **S:** £20.00
Beds: 1F 1D **Baths:** 2 En
🛇 🅿 (3) ⅋ 📺 🏠 🎿

Castle Douglas

NX7662 ⚓ Old Smugglers, King's Arms, Laurie
Arms, Douglas Arms, Grapes, Imperial Hotel,
Thistle Inn

Rose Cottage Guest House,
Gelston, Castle Douglas,
Kirkcudbrightshire, DG7 1SH.
Open: All Year (not Xmas)
Grades: STB 3 Star
01556 502513 (also fax)
Mr Steele
D: £18.00–£20.50 **S:** £18.00
Beds: 2D 3T 1S **Baths:** 1 En 2 Sh
🛇 🅿 (10) 📺 🍴 🏠 Ⅴ 🎿
Quiet country guest house in small
village, 2.5 miles from Castle Douglas.

Smithy House, The Buchan, Castle
Douglas, Kirkcudbrightshire, DG7 1TH.
Comfortable Galloway cottage
overlooking Carlingwark Loch. Central for
exploring Galloway.
Open: All Year (not Xmas/New Year)
Grades: STB 4 Star
01556 503841 Mrs Carcas
enquiries@smithyhouse.co.uk
D: £20.00–£27.50 **S:** £30.00–£35.00
Beds: 1T 2D **Baths:** 2 En 1 Pr
🅿 (4) ⅋ 📺 🏠 Ⅴ 🎿 cc

Airds Farm, Crossmichael, Castle
Douglas, Kirkcudbrightshire, DG7 3BG.
Scenic views over Loch Ken and the
Galloway Hills.
Open: All Year
Grades: STB 3 Star
01556 670418 (also fax) Mrs Keith
tricia@airds.com
D: £18.00–£23.00 **S:** £23.00–£27.00
Beds: 1F 1T 2D 1S **Baths:** 2 En 1 Sh
🛇 🅿 (6) ⅋ 📺 🍴 🏠 Ⅴ 🎿

Milton Park Farm, Castle Douglas,
DG7 3JJ.
A warm welcome and good food awaits
you in this comfortable farmhouse.
Open: Easter to Oct
01556 660212 Mrs Muir
D: £18.00–£20.00 **S:** £18.00–£20.00
Beds: 2D 1T **Baths:** 2 Sh
🛇 (9) 🅿 (4) 📺 🏠 🎿

Craigadam, Castle Douglas,
Kirkcudbrightshire, DG7 3HV.
Elegant country house within working
farm. Antique furnishings, log fires and
friendly atmosphere.
Open: All Year (not Xmas)
01556 650233 (also fax)
Mrs Pickup
inquiry@craigadam.com
D: £23.00 **S:** £28.00
Beds: 1F 2D 4T **Baths:** 3 Pr
🛇 🅿 (10) 📺 🍴 ✕ 🏠 🎿 cc

Imperial Hotel, King Street, Castle
Douglas, Kirkcudbrightshire, DG7 1AA.
Former coaching inn and Listed building.
All rooms ensuite. Warm friendly
welcome.
Open: All Year (not Xmas)
01556 502086 Fax: 01556 503009
david@thegolfhotel.co.uk
D: £27.00–£29.00 **S:** £35.00–£45.00
Beds: 5D 5T 2S **Baths:** 12 En
🛇 🅿 (20) 📺 🍴 ✕ 🏠 Ⅴ 🎿 cc

Dalcroy, 24 Abercromby Road, Castle
Douglas, Kirkcudbrightshire, DG7 1BA.
A warm Scottish welcome assured in this
long established spacious detached
house.
Open: May to Oct
01556 502674 Mrs Coates
ashley@academy67.freeserve.co.uk
D: £16.50–£17.50 **S:** £13.00
Beds: 1D 1T **Baths:** 1 Sh
🅿 (3) ⅋ 📺 🍴 🏠 🎿

Castle Kennedy

NX1160

Chlenry Farmhouse, Castle Kennedy,
Stranraer, Wigtownshire, DG9 8SL.
Situated in a private glen in the heart of
Galloway, comfortable old farmhouse.
Open: All Year (not Xmas)
01776 705316 Mrs Wolseley Brinton
Fax: 01776 889488
brinton@aol.com
D: fr £26.00 **S:** fr £30.00
Beds: 1D 1T **Baths:** 1 Pr 1 Sh
🛇 🅿 (4) ⅋ 📺 🍴 ✕ 🏠 Ⅴ 🎿

Coxhill

NT0904

Coxhill Farm, Old Carlisle Road, Coxhill,
Moffat, Dumfriesshire, DG10 9QN.
Stylish farmhouse set in 70 acres,
outstanding views, private parking.
Open: All Year (not Xmas/New Year)
Grades: STB 4 Star
01683 220471 Mrs Long
Fax: 01683 220871
D: £22.50 **S:** £30.00
Beds: 1D 1T **Baths:** 2 En
🛇 🅿 ⅋ 📺 ✕ 🏠 Ⅴ 🎿

Creebridge

NX4165

Villa Cree, Creebridge, Newton Stewart,
Wigtownshire, DG8 6NR.
Quiet riverside family house, excellent for
walking, wildlife, touring or business.
Open: All Year (not Xmas)
01671 403914 Mr Rankin
sad_rankin@tinyonline.co.uk
D: £18.00–£20.00 **S:** £18.00–£20.00
Beds: 2D 1T 1S **Baths:** 1 En 1 Pr
🛇 🅿 (3) ⅋ 📺 🏠 Ⅴ 🎿

Creetown

NX4758 ⚓ Barholm Arms

Wal-d-mar, Mill Street, Creetown,
Newton Stewart, Wigtownshire, DG8 7JN.
Open: All Year (not Xmas)
01671 820369 M Lockett
Fax: 01671 820266
howie@thebogue.freeserve.co.uk
D: £16.00 **S:** £16.00
Beds: 1D 1S **Baths:** 1 Sh
🛇 🅿 (3) 📺 🍴 🏠 Ⅴ 🎿 ⅙
Modern bungalow in quiet village
location, ideal base for touring, walking,
golf, etc. Comfortable beds, good
breakfasts, private off-road parking, warm
Scottish welcome assured. Situated
between Dumfries and Stranraer on the
Cree estuary.

Crocketford

NX8372

Henderland Farm, *Crocketford Road, Crocketford or Ninemile Bar, Dumfries, DG2 8QD.*
Substantial farmhouse, comfortably furnished with views of lovely open countryside.
Open: All Year (not Xmas)
Grades: STB 3 Star
01387 730270 Mrs Smyth
D: £17.00–£18.00 **S:** £18.00–£20.00
Beds: 1F 1D 1T **Baths:** 3 En
🛇 🅿 (4) 📺 🛏 ✕ 🍴 📖 ☑ ♨

Crossmichael

NX7366 🍺 *King's Arms, Imperial Hotel, Thistle Inn*

Culgruff House Hotel, *Crossmichael, Castle Douglas, Kirkcudbrightshire, DG7 3BB.*
Victorian baronial mansion, own grounds, overlooking loch, village, Galloway Hills.
Open: All Year
01556 670230 Mr Grayson
D: £17.50–£27.50 **S:** £20.00–£27.50
Beds: 4F 4D 7T 2S **Baths:** 4 En 4 Sh
🛇 🅿 (40) 📺 🛏 ✕ 🍴 📖 ☑ ♨ cc

Airds Farm, *Crossmichael, Castle Douglas, Kirkcudbrightshire, DG7 3BG.*
Scenic views over Loch Ken and the Galloway Hills.
Open: All Year
Grades: STB 3 Star
01556 670418 (also fax)
Mrs Keith
tricia@airds.com
D: £18.00–£23.00 **S:** £23.00–£27.00
Beds: 1F 1T 2D 1S **Baths:** 2 En 1 Sh
🛇 🅿 (6) ⅙ 📺 🛏 🍴 ♨

Deeside, *42 Main Street, Crossmichael, Castle Douglas, Kirkcudbrightshire, DG7 3AU.*
Friendly welcome and good breakfast. In Galloway.
Open: All Year (not Xmas/New Year)
Grades: STB 3 Star
01556 670239 Mrs Cowan
D: £17.00 **S:** £20.00
Beds: 1F 1D 1S **Baths:** 1 Sh
🛇 🅿 (2) ⅙ 📺 🛏 ✕ 🍴 ☑ ♨

Dalbeattie

NX8361

Belle Vue, *Port Road, Dalbeattie, Kirkcudbrightshire, DG5 4AZ.*
Beautiful granite house on the edge of Dalbeattie, facing the Galloway Hills.
Open: All Year (not Xmas)
01556 611833 Mrs Lock
Snraajj@bellevuebandb.freeserve.co.uk
D: £18.00–£22.00 **S:** £22.50–£25.00
Beds: 1F 1D 1T **Baths:** 1 En 2 Pr
🛇 🅿 (8) ⅙ 📺 ✕ 🍴 ☑ ♨ &

Planning a longer stay? Always ask for any special rates

13 Maxwell Park, *Dalbeattie, Kirkcudbrightshire, DG5 4LR.*
Family run house close to beach, fishing, golf and walks. **Open:** All Year
01556 610830 Mrs Tattersfield
D: £18.00–£21.00 **S:** £20.00–£25.00
Beds: 2D 1T **Baths:** 1 En 1 Sh
🛇 🅿 (3) ⅙ 📺 📖 ☑ ✳

Dumfries

NX9776 🍺 *Hill Hotel, Auldgirth Inn, Station Hotel, Courtyard, Rat & Carrot, Queensbury, Waverley Bar, Aberdour Hotel*

Hazeldean Guest House, *4 Moffat Road, Dumfries, DG1 1NJ.*
4 star Victorian villa. Non-smoking. Parking. Near town centre.
Open: All Year (not Xmas)
Grades: STB 4 Star
01387 266178 (also fax)
Mr & Mrs Harper
D: fr £20.00 **S:** £25.00–£28.00
Beds: 2F 2D 2T 1S **Baths:** 6 En
🛇 🅿 (8) ⅙ 📺 ✕ 🍴 ☑ ♨ & cc

Fernwood, *4 Casslands, Dumfries, DG2 7NS.*
Victorian sandstone villa, close to golf course and town centre.
Open: All Year (not Xmas)
Grades: STB 3 Star
01387 253701 (also fax) Mrs Vaughan
pamelavaughan@yahoo.com
D: £17.50–£18.50 **S:** £17.50
Beds: 1F 1D 2S **Baths:** 2 Sh
🛇 🅿 (6) ⅙ 📺 📖 ♨

Wallamhill House, *Kirkton, Dumfries, DG1 1SL.*
Country house, beautiful views, spacious rooms, leisure suite, safe parking.
Open: All Year (not Xmas)
Grades: STB 4 stars
01387 248249 (also fax) Mrs Hood
wallamhill@aol.com
D: £19.00–£22.00 **S:** £22.00–£28.00
Beds: 1F 2D 1T **Baths:** 4 En
🛇 🅿 (8) ⅙ 📺 📖 ☑ ♨ cc

30 Hardthorn Avenue, *Dumfries, DG2 9JA.*
Open: Easter to Oct
Grades: STB 2 Star B&B
01387 253502 (also fax) Ms Sloan
anniesbandb@aol.com
D: £16.00–£18.00 **S:** £23.00–£25.00
Beds: 1D 1T **Baths:** 1 Sh
🅿 (2) ⅙ 📺 📖 ♨
A warm Scottish welcome awaits you at No 30, a non-smoking private house with car parking in quiet residential area. Easy access from Dumfries bypass (A75) and less than a mile from town centre. Ideal base to explore SW Scotland.

Henderland Farm, *Crocketford Road, Crocketford or Ninemile Bar, Dumfries, DG2 8QD.*
Substantial farmhouse, comfortably furnished with views of lovely open countryside.
Open: All Year (not Xmas)
Grades: STB 3 Star
01387 730270 Mrs Smyth
D: £17.00–£18.00 **S:** £18.00–£20.00
Beds: 1F 1D 1T **Baths:** 3 En
🛇 🅿 (4) 📺 🛏 ✕ 🍴 📖 ☑ ♨

Lindean, *50 Rae Street, Dumfries, DG1 1JE.*
Town centre house in quiet residential area, near railway station.
Open: All Year **Grades:** STB 3 Star
01387 251888 Mrs Stein
D: £18.00–£20.00 **S:** £25.00
Beds: 2T 1D **Baths:** 2 En 1 Pr
🛇 🅿 ⅙ 📺 📖 ☑ ♨

Brackenbridge, *67 New Abbey Road, Dumfries, DG2 7JY.*
Brackenridge bed and breakfast, walking distance into the town centre and all local attractions.
Open: All Year
Grades: STB 3 Star, AA 3 Diamond
01387 263962 Mr & Mrs Thomson
D: £18.50–£25.00 **S:** £20.00
Beds: 3F 3T 1D 1S **Baths:** 2 En 1 Pr
🛇 🅿 📺 ✕ 🍴 ☑ ♨

Waverley Guest House, *21 St Mary's Street, Dumfries, DG1 1HB.*
5 minutes from town centre, across from Railway station. On main road.
Open: All Year
01387 254080 F Meikle- Latta
Fax: 01387 254848
southwest.lumber@virgin.net
D: £14.50–£20.00 **S:** £14.50–£24.00
Beds: 5F 3T 1D 5S **Baths:** 6 En
🛇 📺 🛏 ☑ ♨ cc

Cairndoon, *14 Newall Terrace, Dumfries, DG1 1LW.*
Elegant 1880 town house, graciously quiet. Warm and friendly welcome.
Open: All Year
01387 256991 Mrs Stevenson
stevenson.george@talk21.com
D: £20.00–£24.00 **S:** £21.00–£25.00
Beds: 2T 1S **Baths:** 2 En 1 Pr 1 Sh
🛇 🅿 (1) ⅙ 📺 📖 ☑ ✳ ♨

The Knock Guest House, *1 Lockerbie Road, Dumfries, DG1 3AP.*
Warm welcome. Convenient for golfing, fishing, touring. Cyclists welcome.
Open: All Year **Grades:** STB 1 Star
01387 253487 Mr Sutherland
D: £16.00–£16.50 **S:** £16.00–£16.50
Beds: 3F 1D 1T 1S
🛇 🅿 (1) 📺 🛏 ✕ 🍴 ☑ ♨

Franklea Guest House, *Castle Douglas Road, Dumfries, DG2 8PP.*
Bungalow 1 mile from Dumfries; ideal for golf next door, hill walking, Galloway park. **Open:** Easter to Nov
Grades: STB 3 Star
01387 253004 Mrs Wild
Fax: 01387 259301
D: £18.00–£20.00 **S:** £20.00–£22.00
Beds: 1F 1D **Baths:** 2 En
🛇 (5) 🅿 (5) 📺 🛏 ✕ 🍴 ☑ ♨ &

Fulwood Hotel, *Lovers Walk, Dumfries, DG1 1LX.*
Beautiful Victorian house opposite railway station in the heart of Burns country.
Open: All Year (not Xmas)
01387 252262 / 0411 260246
Fax: 01387 252262
D: £17.00–£21.00 **S:** £20.00–£30.00
Beds: 1F 2D 2T 1S **Baths:** 3 En 1 Pr 1 Sh
⅙ 📺 📖 ☑ ♨

Dunscore

NX8684   ⬤ *Craigdarroch Arms, George Hotel*

Boreland Farm, Dunscore, Dumfries,
DG2 0XA.
Organic farm in beautiful countryside by
the River Cairn.
Open: All Year
01387 820287 Mr & Mrs Barnes
barnes@borelandfarm.co.uk
D: £16.00 **S:** £17.00–£18.00
Beds: 1F 1D **Baths:** 2 En
⬤ ⬤ (10) ⚥ 📺 🛏 🔲 ⬤ ⬤

Low Kirkbride Farmhouse,
Dunscore, Dumfries, *DG2 0SP.*
Warm, comfortable farmhouse set amid
beautiful countryside, lovely views from
every room.
Open: All Year (not Xmas)
01387 820258 (also fax)
Mrs Kirk
D: £16.00–£18.00 **S:** £16.00–£18.00
Beds: 1D 1T **Baths:** 2 En
⬤ (8) ⬤ (4) 📺 🔲 ⬤

Ecclefechan

NY1974   ⬤ *Cressfield Hotel*

Carlyle House, Ecclefechan, Lockerbie,
Dumfriesshire, *DG11 3DG.*
C18th house in small village.
Open: All Year (not Xmas/New Year)
Grades: STB 1 Star
01576 300322 (also fax)
Mrs Martin
D: £14.00 **S:** £14.00
Beds: 1F 1T 1S **Baths:** 2 Sh
⬤ ⬤ (6) 📺 🛏 🔲 ⬤

2 Garthwaite Place, High Street,
Ecclefechan, Lockerbie, Dumfriesshire,
DG11 3DF.
Above average accommodation, just off
A74/M6. Home from home.
Open: All Year
01576 300846 Mrs Arbuckle
D: £15.00–£17.50 **S:** £20.00–£22.50
Beds: 2T **Baths:** 1 Sh
⬤ 📺 🛏 ✕ 🔲 ⬤

Gelston

NX7658   ⬤ *Old Smugglers, Kings Arms*

Rose Cottage Guest House,
Gelston, Castle Douglas,
Kirkcudbrightshire, *DG7 1SH.*
Quiet country guest house in small
village, 2.5 miles from Castle Douglas.
Open: All Year (not Xmas)
Grades: STB 3 Star
01556 502513 (also fax)
Mr Steele
D: £18.00–£20.50 **S:** £18.00
Beds: 2D 3T 1S **Baths:** 1 En 2 Sh
⬤ ⬤ (10) 📺 🛏 ✕ 🔲 ⬤

RATES

D = Price range per person
sharing in a double room
S = Price range for a
single room

Glenluce

NX1957   ⬤ *Kelvin House, Crown Hotel,
Inglenook Rest*

Bankfield Farm, Glenluce, Newton
Stewart, Wigtownshire, *DG8 0JF.*
Large spacious farmhouse on the
outskirts of quiet country village.
Open: All Year **Grades:** STB 2 Star
01581 300281 (also fax) Mrs Stewart
D: fr £17.00 **S:** fr £20.00
Beds: 1F 1D 1T **Baths:** 2 En 1 Pr
⬤ 📺 🔲 ⬤

Rowantree Guest House, 38 Main
Street, Glenluce, Newton Stewart,
Wigtownshire, *DG8 0PS.*
Clean and tidy family run, central to all
amenities.
Open: All Year
Grades: STB 2 Star
01581 300244 Mr Thomas
Fax: 01581 300366
D: £15.50–£18.00 **S:** £17.00–£24.00
Beds: 2F 2D 1T **Baths:** 2 En 1 Pr
⬤ ⬤ (8) 📺 🛏 ✕ 🔲 ⬤ ✿ ⬤ ⬤

Gretna

NY3167   ⬤ *Solway Lodge*

The Braids, Annan Road, Gretna,
Dumfriesshire, *DG16 5DQ.*
Open: All Year
01461 337409 (also fax)
Mrs Copeland
D: £16.00–£18.00 **S:** £25.00–£28.00
Beds: 2T **Baths:** 1 Sh
⬤ ⬤ (2) 📺 🔲 ⬤

Small friendly family B&B in bungalow
inside the entrance to our (BGHP Grade
4) caravan park. Open all year. Gretna
marriage centre, golf, Sunday market.
Good area for birdwatching in winter
months. Advice on fishing in the area.

Haugh of Urr

NX8066   ⬤ *The Grapes, Laurie Arms*

Corbieton Cottage, Haugh of Urr,
Castle Douglas, Kirkcudbrightshire, *DG7
3JJ.*
Charming country cottage, lovely views,
good food and a warm welcome.
Open: Feb to Dec
01556 660413 Mr Jones
ann&don@corbieton.demon.co.uk
D: £16.00–£18.00 **S:** £17.00–£18.00
Beds: 1D 1T **Baths:** 1 Sh
⬤ (2) ⚥ 📺 ✕ 🔲 ⬤

High Auchenlarie

NX5353

High Auchenlarie Farmhouse, High
Auchenlarie, Gatehouse of Fleet, Castle
Douglas, Kirkcudbrightshire, *DG7 2HB.*
Traditional farmhouse overlooking fleet,
Wigtown Bay, Isle of Man. Superb
location.
Open: Feb to Dec
Grades: STB 3 Star
01557 840231 (also fax)
Mrs Johnstone
D: £22.00–£26.00 **S:** £30.00–£36.00
Beds: 1F 1T 1D **Baths:** 3 En
⬤ ⬤ (4) ⚥ 📺 ✕ 🔲 ⬤

Kirkcowan

NX3261   ⬤ *Bladnoch Inn*

Tarff House, Kirkcowan, Newton
Stewart, Wigtownshire, *DG8 0HW.*
Victorian house set in 1 acre of garden,
within 5 miles good eating places.
Open: All Year
01671 830312 Mrs McGeoch
sandra@tarffhouse.ndo.co.uk
D: £15.00 **S:** £15.00
Beds: 1D 1T **Baths:** 2 Pr
⬤ ⬤ (4) 📺 🛏 🔲 ⬤ cc

Kirkcudbright

NX6850   ⬤ *Selkirk Arms*

Number 3 B&B, 3 High Street,
Kirkcudbright, *DG6 4JZ.*
Open: All Year
Grades: STB 3 Star
01557 330881 Miriam Baker
ham_wwk@hotmail.com
D: £22.50–£25.00 **S:** £25.00–£30.00
Beds: 2T 1D **Baths:** 2 En 1 Pr
⬤ ⚥ 📺 🔲 ⬤ ✿ ⬤

A 'B' Listed Georgian townhouse with a
C17th dining area and elegant guest
drawing room. No 3 is opposite the
National Trust for Scotland's Broughton
House and behind MacLellans Castle at
the end of Kirkcudbright's historic old
High Street.

Benutium, 2 Rossway Road,
Kirkcudbright, *DG6 4BS.*
Excellent quality. Ensuite bedroom and
private lounge/dining room. Magnificent
views.
Open: All Year
Grades: STB 4 Star
01557 330788
Mr & Mrs Garroch-Mackay
eileen.malcolm@benutium.freeserve.co.uk
D: £18.00–£24.00 **S:** £25.00
Beds: 1D 1T **Baths:** 1Pr 1Sh
⬤ (2) ⚥ 🔲 ⬤ ⬤

Baytree House, 110 High Street,
Kirkcudbright, *DG6 4JQ.*
Georgian town house in artist colony near
harbour, private parking.
Open: All Year
Grades: STB 4 Star, AA 5 Diamond
01557 330824 (also fax)
baytree@currantbun.com
D: fr £27.00 **S:** fr £27.00
Beds: 1D 2T **Baths:** 3 En

Kirkton

NX9782   ⬤ *Auldgirth Inn*

Wallamhill House, Kirkton, Dumfries,
DG1 1SL.
Country house, beautiful views, spacious
rooms, leisure suite, safe parking.
Open: All Year (not Xmas)
Grades: STB 4 stars
01387 248249 (also fax)
Mrs Hood
wallamhill@aol.com
D: £19.00–£22.00 **S:** £22.00–£28.00
Beds: 1F 2D 1T **Baths:** 4 En
⬤ ⬤ (8) ⚥ 📺 🔲 ⬤ ⬤ cc

Langholm

NY3684 ◀ *Reivers Rest, Cross Keys*

Burnfoot House, *Westerkirk, Langholm, Dumfriesshire, DG13 0NG.*
Spacious country home set in quiet and beautiful Eskdale Valley.
Open: March to Jan
Grades: STB 3 Star
01387 370611 Mr & Mrs Laverack
Fax: 01387 370616
sg.laverack@burnft.co.uk
D: £24.00 **S:** £27.00
Beds: 1T 3D **Baths:** 3 En 1 Pr
🛏 ⅄ 📺 🛏 🖳 📶 🔆 cc

Esk Brae, *Langholm, Dumfriesshire, DG13 0DP.*
Quiet bungalow, near town and river. Comfortable with good food.
Open: Mar to Oct
013873 80377 Mrs Geddes
D: £17.00 **S:** £17.00
Beds: 1D 1T **Baths:** 1 Sh
📶 (2) ⅄ 📺 🛏 🖳 📶 🔆 ♿

Leswalt

NX0163 ◀ *The Crown, Dunskey Golf Hotel*

Windyridge, *Auchnotteroch, Leswalt, Stranraer, Wigtownshire, DG9 0XL.*
Set in rolling countryside between Stranraer and Portpatrick 10 mins all ferries.
Open: All Year (not Xmas)
Grades: STB 1 Star
01776 870280 (also fax)
Mrs Rushworth
rushworth@windyridge96.fsnet.co.uk
D: fr £15.00 **S:** fr £15.00
Beds: 1D 1T **Baths:** 1 Sh
🛏 📶 (3) 📺 🛏 🖳 🔆

Locharbriggs

NX9980 ◀ *Hill Hotel, Auldgirth Inn, Station Hotel, The Courtyard*

Southpark Guest House, *Quarry Road, Locharbriggs, Dumfries, DG1 1QG.*
Peaceful edge of town location. Easy access from all major routes.
Open: All Year
01387 711188 (also fax)
Mr Maxwell
ewan@emaxwell.freeserve.co.uk
D: £17.00–£18.00 **S:** £17.00–£23.00
Beds: 1F 1D 1T 1S **Baths:** 2 En 2 Pr
🛏 📶 (15) ⅄ 📺 🖳 🔆 cc

Lochfield

NY2066 ◀ *Rat & Carrot*

20 Hardthorn Road, *Lochfield, Dumfries, DG2 9JQ.*
Comfortable accommodation in family home. Full Scottish breakfast. Warm welcome.
Open: Mar to Oct
01387 264415 Mrs Cherrington
pcherrington@hotmail.com
D: £15.00 **S:** £20.00
Beds: 1D **Baths:** 1 Pr
🛏 📶 (1) ⅄ 📺 🖳 🔆

Lochmaben

NY0882 ◀ *Crown*

Smallrigg, *Lochmaben, Lockerbie, DG11 1JH.*
Open: All Year (not Xmas/New Year)
Grades: STB 3 Star
01387 810462 Janet Newbould
jnewbould@ukgateway.net
D: £15.00 **S:** £18.00
Beds: 1T 1D **Baths:** 1 En 1 Pr
🛏 📶 (4) ⅄ 📺 🛏 🖳 📶 🔆
Smallrigg, only ten minutes drive from motorway network, is a small working dairy farm. Smallrigg's situation enjoys extensive views of surrounding countryside in an area suited to cycling, walking, fishing, and is approximately half mile from Lochmaben Golf Course.

Ardbeg Cottage, *19 Castle Street, Lochmaben, Lockerbie, Dumfriesshire, DG11 1NY.*
Open: Feb to Dec
Grades: STB 3 Star
01387 811855 (also fax)
Mr & Mrs Neilson
bill@neilson.net
D: fr £18.00 **S:** fr £18.00
Beds: 1D 1T **Baths:** 2 En
⅄ 📺 🛏 🖳 🔆 ♿ 3
Quiet, comfortable, friendly ground floor B&B in centre of village just 4 miles from A74 at Lockerbie. Ideal centre for exploring beautiful south-west Scotland.

Magdalene House, *Bruce Street, Lochmaben, Lockerbie, DG11 1PD.*
An elegant and comfortable home in historic village built around lochs.
Open: All Year
01387 810439 (also fax)
Lady Hillhouse
D: £20.00–£28.00 **S:** £25.00–£33.00
Beds: 1F 1T 1D
🛏 📶 (4) ⅄ 📺 🛏 🖳 📶 ❄ 🔆 cc

Lockerbie

NY1381 ◀ *Kings Arms, Somerton Hotel*

Rosehill Guest House, *9 Carlisle Road, Lockerbie, Dumfriesshire, DG11 2DR.*
Victorian sandstone house (1871). Half-acre garden. Easy access M74.
Open: All Year (not Xmas)
Grades: STB 3 Star, AA 4 Diamond
01576 202378 R A & G D Callander
D: £20.00 **S:** £20.00–£25.00
Beds: 1F 1D 2T 1S **Baths:** 3 En 2 Pr
🛏 📶 (5) 🛏 🖳 📶 🔆

Ravenshill House Hotel, *Dumfries Road, Lockerbie, Dumfriesshire, DG11 2EF.*
Large Victorian house, good food, quiet location, gardens, private car park.
Open: All Year
Grades: STB 2 Star, AA 1 Star
01576 202882 (also fax)
Ms Tindal
ravenshillhouse.hotel@virgin.net
D: £22.00–£25.00 **S:** £35.00
Beds: 2F 3D 3T **Baths:** 7 En 1 Pr
🛏 📶 (30) 📺 🛏 🖳 🔆 cc

Kings Arms Hotel

Kings Arms Hotel, *29 High Street, Lockerbie, DG11 2JL.*
C16th former coaching inn; cosy barn log fires. **Open:** All Year
Grades: STB 2 Star, AA 2 Star
01576 202410 (also fax) Mr Spence
D: £30.00 **S:** £35.00–£40.00
Beds: 3F 4D 2T 5S
🛏 📶 (10) ⅄ 📺 🛏 🖳 🔆 cc

The Elms, *Dumfries Road, Lockerbie, Dumfriesshire, DG11 2EF.*
Comfortable detached house. Friendly personal welcome. Private parking
Open: Mar to Nov **Grades:** STB 4 Star
01576 203898 (also fax) Mrs Rae
theelms@gofornet.co.uk
D: £19.00–£22.00 **S:** £22.00–£25.00
Beds: 1D 1T **Baths:** 2 En
🛏 (12) 📶 (2) ⅄ 📺 🖳 🔆

Corrie Lodge Country House, *Lockerbie, Dumfriesshire, DG11 2NG.*
B&B in lovely country house. Hunting, shooting, fishing. Golf course nearby.
Open: All Year **Grades:** STB 3 Star
01576 710237 Mr & Mrs Spence
D: £20.00 **S:** £20.00
Beds: 2D 1T 1S **Baths:** 2 Pr
📶 (6) ⅄ 📺 🛏 🖳 📶 🔆

Moffat

NT0805 ◀ *Black Bull, Allanton House, Star Hotel*

Woodhead Farm, *Moffat, Dumfriesshire, DG10 9LU.*
Open: All Year **Grades:** STB 4 Star
01683 220225 Mrs Jackson
D: £24.00–£26.00 **S:** £26.00–£30.00
Beds: 1D 2T **Baths:** 3 En
🛏 📶 (3) ⅄ 📺 🛏 🖳 📶 🔆
Luxuriously appointed farmhouse breakfast served in large conservatory, overlooking mature garden and surrounding hills. Working sheep farm. Ample safe parking. 2 miles from spa town of Moffat. All bedrooms have panoramic views.

Morlich House, *Ballplay Road, Moffat, Dumfriesshire, DG10 9JU.*
Open: Feb to Nov
01683 220589 Mrs Wells
Fax: 01683 221032
morlich.house@ndirect.co.uk
D: £20.00–£23.00 **S:** £20.00–£33.00
Beds: 2F 1D 1T 1S **Baths:** 4 En 1 Pr
🛏 📶 (6) ⅄ 📺 🛏 🖳 📶 🔆 cc
A superb Victorian country house set in quiet elevated grounds overlooking town.

Kirkland House, *Well Road, Moffat, Dumfriesshire, DG10 9AR.*
Listed former manse with many interesting features, set in peaceful gardens.
Open: All Year
Grades: STB 3 Star
01683 221133 (also fax)
Mr Watkins
Derekwatkins@
Kirklandhouse.freeserve.co.uk
D: £18.00–£20.00 **S:** fr £18.00
Beds: 1F 1T 1D **Baths:** 2 En 1 Pr
📶 (6) ⅄ 📺 🖳 📶 🔆

Waterside, Moffat, Dumfriesshire, DG10 9LF.
Open: Easter to Oct
01683 220092 Mrs Edwards
D: £19.00–£21.00 **S:** £21.00
Beds: 2D 2T **Baths:** 1 Pr 1 Sh
🛇 🅿 (4) ⌿ 📺 🎹 🛵
Large country house set in 12 acres of woodland garden with private stretch of river. The house is tastefully decorated throughout. We have a dog and cat, donkeys, peafowl, ducks, geese and hens. Ideal for walking, fishing, golf and bird watching.

Hartfell House, Hartfell Crescent, Moffat, Dumfriesshire, DG10 9AL.
Splendid Victorian manor house in peaceful location.
Open: All Year (not Xmas/New Year)
Grades: STB 4 Star, AA 4 Diamond
01683 220153 Mrs White
robert.white@virgin.net
D: £23.00 **S:** £25.00
Beds: 2F 4D 1T 1S **Baths:** 7 En 1 Sh
🛇 🅿 (8) 📺 🎇 ✕ 🎹 🖿 🛵

Morag, 19 Old Carlisle Road, Moffat, Dumfriesshire, DG10 9QJ.
Beautiful quiet location in charming town near Southern Upland Way.
Open: All Year
Grades: STB 3 Star
01683 220690 Mr & Mrs Taylor
D: £16.00–£18.00 **S:** £18.00–£19.00
Beds: 1D 1T 1S **Baths:** 1 Sh
🛇 (10) 🅿 (5) ⌿ 📺 🎇 ✕ 🎹 🖿 🛵

Ericstane, Moffat, Dumfriesshire, DG10 9LT.
Working hill farm in a peaceful valley. Moffat 4 miles.
Open: All Year
Grades: STB 3 Star
01683 220127 Mr Jackson
D: fr £20.00 **S:** fr £25.00
Beds: 1D 1S **Baths:** 2 En
🛇 (8) 🅿 📺 🖿 🛵

Allanton Hotel, 21-22 High Street, Moffat, Dumfriesshire, DG10 9HL.
Small inn in the scenic town of Moffat. Home cooking.
Open: All Year
01683 220343 Mr Kennedy
Fax: 01683 220914
D: £22.00–£30.00 **S:** £24.00–£32.00
Beds: 1F 2T 3D 1 S **Baths:** 2 En 6 Pr 1 Sh
🛇 ⌿ 📺 🎇 ✕ 🎹 🖿 🛵 cc

Wellview Hotel, Ballplay Road, Moffat, Dumfriesshire, DG10 9JU.
Excellent centre to explore Borders.
Open: All Year
Grades: STB 4 Star
01683 220184 (also fax)
Mr Schuckardt
info@wellview.co.uk
D: £36.00–£50.00 **S:** £53.00–£63.00
Beds: 4D 2T **Baths:** 6 En
🛇 🅿 (8) ⌿ 📺 🎇 ✕ 🎹 🖿 🛵 cc

Planning a longer stay? Always
ask for any special rates

Coxhill Farm, Old Carlisle Road, Coxhill, Moffat, Dumfriesshire, DG10 9QN.
Stylish farmhouse set in 70 acres, outstanding views, private parking.
Open: All Year (not Xmas/New Year)
Grades: STB 4 Star
01683 220471 Mrs Long
Fax: 01683 220871
D: £22.50 **S:** £30.00
Beds: 1D 1T **Baths:** 2 En
🛇 🅿 ⌿ 📺 ✕ 🎹 🖿 🛵

Stratford House, Academy Road, Moffat, Dumfriesshire, DG10 9HR.
Family-run B&B, 2 minutes from town centre. Off-road parking.
Open: All Year (not Xmas)
01683 220297 Mrs Forrester
D: £18.00–£20.00 **S:** £20.00–£25.00
Beds: 1F 2T **Baths:** 2 En 1 Pr
🛇 (10) 🅿 (2) 📺 🎇 🎹 🖿 🛵

Hazel Bank, Academy Road, Moffat, Dumfriesshire, DG10 9HP.
Welcome to Hazel Bank. A warm and personal welcome awaits all our guests.
Open: All Year
01683 220294 Mrs Watson
D: £17.00–£20.00 **S:** £23.00–£25.00
Beds: 1F 1D **Baths:** 1 En 1 Sh
🛇 📺 🎇 🖿 🛵 🖿 ♿

Merkland House, Buccleuch Place, Moffat, Dumfriesshire, DG10 9AN.
Spacious early Victorian house set in tranquil woodland gardens.
Open: All Year (not Xmas)
01683 220957 Mr & Mrs Tavener
D: £17.50–£22.00 **S:** £17.50–£22.00
Beds: 2F 2D 1T 1S **Baths:** 5 En 1 Pr
🛇 🅿 (8) 📺 🎇 ✕ 🎹 🖿 🛵 ♿

Nineoaks, Reid Street, Moffat, DG10 9JE.
Large spacious family bungalow situated in 3 acres with paddocks and horse.
Open: Easter to Nov
01683 220658 Mrs Jones
D: fr £17.00 **S:** fr £18.00
Beds: 1F 1D 1S **Baths:** 1 En 1 Pr
🅿 (3) ⌿ 📺 🖿 🛵

Marvig Guest House, Academy Road, Moffat, Dumfriesshire, DG10 9HW.
Hello! Welcome to Marvig, a renovated Victorian guest house offering personal attention.
Open: All Year (not Xmas)
01683 220628 (also fax)
Mr Muirhead
marvig.moffat@tesco.net
D: £18.00–£20.00 **S:** £20.00–£25.00
Beds: 1F 2D 2T 1S **Baths:** 2 En 2 Sh
🛇 🅿 (4) ⌿ 📺 🖿 🛵

NY0487 ⚓ Balcastle

Lochrigghead Farmhouse,
Nethermill, Parkgate, Dumfries, DG1 3NG.
Farmhouse, picturesque surroundings. Good food, hospitality. Ideal for touring Scotland.
Open: All Year
01387 860381 Mrs Burgoyne
D: £17.00 **S:** £17.00
Beds: 3F 1D 1T 1S **Baths:** 2 En 1 Pr 1 Sh
🛇 🅿 (10) 📺 🎇 ✕ 🎹 🖿 🛵 ✳ 🛵

NX4065

Rowallan House, Corsbie Road, Newton Stewart, DG8 6JB.
Visit our website - www.rowallan.co.uk - see what our guests say about Rowallan.
Open: All Year **Grades:** STB 4 Star
01671 402520 Mrs Henderson
rowallan@sol.co.uk
D: £27.00–£30.00 **S:** £27.00–£40.00
Beds: 2D 2T **Baths:** 4 En
🛇 (10) 🅿 (6) ⌿ 📺 🖿 🛵

Kilwarlin, Corvisel Road, Newton Stewart, Wigtownshire, DG8 6LN.
Victorian house, beautiful garden, central location, home-baking, golf, fishing.
Open: Easter to Oct
01671 403047 Mrs Dickson
D: £16.50 **S:** £16.50
Beds: 1F 1D 1S **Baths:** 1 Sh
🛇 (3) 🅿 (3) 📺 🖿 🛵

Eskdale, Princess Avenue, Newton Stewart, DG8 6ES.
Attractive detached house, very quiet residential area, 5 mins' walk town centre.
Open: All Year
01671 404195 Mrs Smith
D: £16.00–£18.00 **S:** £16.00–£20.00
Beds: 1D 1T 1S **Baths:** 1 Pr 1 Sh
🅿 (4) ⌿ 📺 🖿 🛵

NY0288 ⚓ Balcastle

Lochrigghead Farmhouse,
Nethermill, Parkgate, Dumfries, DG1 3NG.
Farmhouse, picturesque surroundings. Good food, hospitality. Ideal for touring Scotland.
Open: All Year
01387 860381 Mrs Burgoyne
D: £17.00 **S:** £17.00
Beds: 3F 1D 1T 1S **Baths:** 2 En 1 Pr 1 Sh
🛇 🅿 (10) 📺 🎇 ✕ 🎹 🖿 🛵 ✳ 🛵

NX6970 ⚓ Welcome Tavern

Drumrash Farm, Parton, Castle Douglas, Kirkcudbrightshire, DG7 3NF.
Traditional farmhouse, 300 yards from working farm. Superb views over Loch Ken.
Open: All Year
Grades: STB 2 Star
01644 470274 Mrs Cruikshank
D: £14.00–£16.00 **S:** £15.00–£18.00
Beds: 2F 1D **Baths:** 1 En 2 Sh
🛇 🅿 (6) ⌿ 📺 🎇 ✕ 🎹 🖿 🛵

NX8854 ⚓ The Anchor

Braemar, Portling, Dalbeattie, Kirkcudbrightshire, DG5 4PZ.
Welcome to Braemar, a charming friendly Victorian villa in picturesque Portling.
Open: May to Oct
01556 630414 (also fax)
Mrs Dennis
D: £19.00–£21.00 **S:** £25.00
Beds: 2D 1T **Baths:** 1 En 1 Sh
🅿 (3) ⌿ 📺 🎇 🎹 🖿 🛵

Portpatrick

NW9954 ◀ *Campbells, Mount Stewart, Downshire, Crown*

Melvin Lodge Guest House, South Crescent, Portpatrick, Stranraer, Wigtownshire, DG9 8LE.
Very comfortable, friendly house starting southern upland way.
Open: All Year **Grades:** STB 2 Star GH
01776 810238 Mr & Mrs Pinder
D: £20.00–£23.00 **S:** £20.00–£23.00
Beds: 4F 3D 1T 2S **Baths:** 5 En 1 Sh
⛺ 🅿 (8) ⽅ �📺 ⽤ 🍴 ⑭ �V ♨ cc

Torrs Warren Hotel, Stoneykirk, Portpatrick, Stranraer, Wigtownshire, DG9 9DH.
Delightful former manse set in peaceful countryside location. Warm welcome.
Open: All Year **Grades:** STB 2 Star
01776 830298 Mrs Camlin
Fax: 01776 830204
torrswarren@btinternet.com
D: £24.00 **S:** £28.00
Beds: 2F 2T 2D 2S **Baths:** 8 En
⛺ 🅿 (30) ⑭ ✕ ⑭ ⑭ ♨ 🍴 cc

Rickwood Private Hotel, Portpatrick, Stranraer, Wigtownshire, DG9 8TD.
Large Victorian house in acre of garden south facing overlooking village and sea.
Open: Mar to Oct
01776 810270
D: £21.50–£22.50 **S:** £21.50–£22.50
Beds: 1F 2D 2T **Baths:** 4 En 1 Pr
🅿 (5) ⑭ 🍴 ✕ ⑭ 🍴 cc

Mansewood, Dean Place, Portpatrick, Stranraer, Wigtownshire, DG9 8TX.
Quiet central location. Lovely views over putting green towards harbour.
Open: All Year (not Xmas)
01776 810256 Mrs Anderson
D: £18.00–£20.00 **S:** fr £20.00
Beds: 1D 2T **Baths:** 2 En 1 Sh
⛺ 🅿 (5) ⑭ ⑭ 🍴 🅖

Rockcliffe

NX8453 ◀ *Anchor Hotel*

The Cottage, 1 Barcloy Mill, Rockcliffe, Dalbeattie, Kirkcudbrightshire, DG5 4QL.
Quiet cottage in central village guest rooms overlooking garden and coast.
Open: All Year (not Xmas/New Year)
Grades: STB 3 Star
01556 630460 Mrs Bailey
elizabeth-bailey@rockcliffe-bandb.freeserve.co.uk
D: £17.50–£18.50 **S:** £23.00–£25.00
Beds: 1T 1D **Baths:** 1 En 1 Sh
⛺ 🅿 ⽅ ⑭ ✕ ⑭ 🍴

Ruthwell

NY0967

Kirkland Country House Hotel, Ruthwell, Dumfries, Borders, DG1 4NP.
Small country house hotel offering good food and friendly service.
Open: All Year **Grades:** STB 3 Star
01387 870284 Mrs Coatsworth
kirklands@hotel72.freeserve.co.uk
D: £25.00–£27.00 **S:** £35.00–£45.00
Beds: 1F 2T 3D **Baths:** 6 En
⛺ 🅿 (12) ⑭ ✕ ⑭ 🍴 🅖 **3 cc**

Sanquhar

NS7809 ◀ *Blackaddie Hotel*

4 Barons Court, Sanquhar, Dumfriesshire, DG4 6EB.
Comfortable self-contained flat. Ideal fishing, walking, golf and touring.
Open: All Year (not Xmas)
01659 50361 Mrs Clark
D: £17.00 **S:** £17.00
Beds: 1F 1D **Baths:** 2 En
🍴 ✕ ⑭ 🍴 🅖 cc

Penhurst, Townhead Street, Sanquhar, Dumfriesshire, DG4 6DA.
Family run bed and breakfast. Excellent home cooking.
Open: All Year
Grades: STB Listed, Comm
01659 50751 (also fax)
Mrs McDowall
D: £15.00 **S:** £15.00
Beds: 1F 1D 1T **Baths:** 1 Sh
⛺ ⑭ 🍴 ✕ ⑭ 🍴 🅖

Southwick

NX9357

Boreland of Southwick, Southwick, Dumfries, DG2 8AN.
Warm and friendly welcome awaits you on the beautiful Solway Coast.
Open: All Year
Grades: STB 4 Star
01387 780225 Mrs Dodd
boreland.southwic@virgin.net
D: £20.00–£25.00 **S:** £20.00–£25.00
Beds: 1T 2D **Baths:** 3 En
⛺ 🅿 ⽅ ⑭ ✕ ⑭ 🍴 ♨ cc

Stoneykirk

NX0853

Torrs Warren Hotel, Stoneykirk, Portpatrick, Stranraer, Wigtownshire, DG9 9DH.
Delightful former manse set in peaceful countryside location. Warm welcome.
Open: All Year
Grades: STB 2 Star
01776 830298 Mrs Camlin
Fax: 01776 830204
torrswarren@btinternet.com
D: £24.00 **S:** £28.00
Beds: 2F 2T 2D 2S **Baths:** 8 En
⛺ 🅿 (30) ⑭ ✕ ⑭ ⑭ ♨ 🍴 cc

Stranraer

NX0560 ◀ *Crown Inn, Harbour House, Swan Inn, Marine House, L'Aperitif, Dunskey Golf Hotel*

Windyridge, Auchnotteroch, Leswalt, Stranraer, Wigtownshire, DG9 0XL.
Set in rolling countryside between Stranraer and Portpatrick 10 mins all ferries.
Open: All Year (not Xmas)
Grades: STB 1 Star
01776 870280 (also fax)
Mrs Rushworth
rushworth@windyridge96.fsnet.co.uk
D: fr £15.00 **S:** fr £15.00
Beds: 1D 1T **Baths:** 1 Sh
⛺ 🅿 (3) ⑭ 🍴 ⑭ 🍴

Planning a longer stay? Always ask for any special rates

Neptune's Rest, 25 Agnew Crescent, Stranraer, Wigtownshire, DG9 7JZ.
Open: All Year
Grades: STB 2 Star
01776 704729 Mr McClymont
D: £15.00–£20.00 **S:** £16.00–£22.00
Beds: 2F 2D 1T 1S **Baths:** 3 En 2 Sh
⛺ ⑭ ✕ ⑭ ♨ 🍴 cc
Neptune's Rest overlooks Agnew Park with its boating lake and miniature railway, situated on the shores of Loch Ryan with its busy ferry routes. All bedrooms are pleasantly decorated & co-ordinated. You are assured of a warm welcome in this family-run guest house.

Windyridge Villa, 5 Royal Crescent, Stranraer, DG9 8HB.
Overlooking Loch Ryan. Convenient for ferry terminal and railway station.
Open: All Year (not Xmas/New Year)
Grades: STB 4 Star, AA 4 Diamond
01776 889900 (also fax)
Mrs Kelly
windyridge_villa@hotmail.com
D: £20.00–£22.00 **S:** £25.00–£28.00
Beds: 1T 1D **Baths:** 2 En
⛺ 🅿 (3) ⽅ ⑭ 🍴 ⑭ 🍴

Ivy House, London Road, Stranraer, DG9 8ER.
Lovely old town house, situated at the foot of Loch Ryan.
Open: All Year
Grades: STB 2 Star
01776 704176 Mr & Mrs Mcmillan
gregormcmillan@hotmail.com
D: £16.00–£19.00 **S:** £18.00–£25.00
Beds: 1F 1D 1T **Baths:** 2 En 1 Pr
⛺ 🅿 (10) ⑭ 🍴 🍴 ⑭ 🍴

Lorenza, 2 Birnam Place, Station Street, Stranraer, Wigtownshire, DG9 7HN.
Terraced house, central located, close to ferries, trains & buses.
Open: Jan to Dec
01776 703935 Mrs Jameson
D: £17.00 **S:** £15.00
Beds: 2D 1T **Baths:** 2 En 1 Sh
🅿 (4) ⑭ 🍴 🅖

Fernlea Guest House, Lewis Street, Stranraer, Wigtownshire, DG9 7AQ.
Friendly guest house, close to town centre and all ferries.
Open: All Year (not Xmas)
01776 703037 Mrs Drysdale
fernlea@tinyworld.co.uk
D: £16.00–£20.00 **S:** £23.00–£28.00
Beds: 2D 1T **Baths:** 3 En
⛺ 🅿 (5) ⽅ ⑭ 🍴 🍴

Jan Da Mar, 1 Ivy Place, London Road, Stranraer, Wigtownshire, DG9 8ER.
Updated Georgian town house with many original features.
Open: All Year
01776 706194 Mrs Bewley
bewley@tinyonline.co.uk
D: £16.00–£20.00 **S:** £18.00
Beds: 3F 3T 2S **Baths:** 2 En 2 Sh
⛺ 🅿 ⑭ 🍴 ⑭ 🍴

Abonny House, 10 Academy Street, Stranraer, Wigtownshire, DG9 7DR.
Warm friendly welcome awaits you at this family run B&B, day or night.
Open: All Year (not Xmas)
01776 706313 Mrs Harvey
D: £22.00–£24.00 **S:** £18.00–£30.00
Beds: 1F 1D 1T 1S **Baths:** 2 En 1 Sh
⛵ ⅍ 📺 ⵒ ✕ ▥ ⌕

Rawer Cottage, South Glenstockadale, Stranraer, DG9 8TS.
Former farm cottage, remote, peaceful yet only 10 mins from ferries to Northern Ireland.
Open: All Year
01776 810328 (also fax)
Mrs Ross
rawer@freenet.co.uk
D: £15.00–£18.00 **S:** £15.00–£18.00
Beds: 1F 1D 1T **Baths:** 1 Sh
⛵ 🅿 (4) 📺 ⵒ ✕ ⌕

Torthorwald

NY0378 ⬛ Four Crowns, The Manor Country House

Branetrigg Farm, Torthorwald, Dumfries, DG1 3QB.
Farmhouse with panoramic views; ideal for touring, cycling, fishing and golfing.
Open: Easter to Nov
Grades: STB 3 Star
01387 750650 Mrs Huston
D: £16.00–£18.00 **S:** £–£18.00
Beds: 1F 1D **Baths:** 1 Sh
📺 ▥

B&B owners may vary rates - be sure to check when booking

Twynholm

NX6654 ⬛ Murray Arms

Barbey Farm, Twynholm, Kirkcudbright, Kirkcudbrightshire, DG6 4PN.
Farmhouse accommodation with beautiful gardens in quiet rural area.
Open: Easter to Sep
01557 860229 Miss Service
D: £14.00 **S:** £14.00
Beds: 1F 1T
⛵ 🅿 (2) 📺 ⵒ ⌕

Tynron

NX8193 ⬛ Craigdarroch Arms

Dalmakerran, Tynron, Thornhill, Dumfriesshire, DG3 4LA.
Country house in 36 acres of pasture and woodland. Warm, friendly atmosphere.
Open: All Year (not Xmas)
01848 200379 (also fax) M Newbould
maryn@dalmakerran.freeserve.co.uk
D: £18.00–£20.00 **S:** £20.00
Beds: 1F 1D 1T 1S **Baths:** 1 En 1 Sh
⛵ 🅿 📺 ⵒ ▥ 📺 ⌕

Whithorn

NX4440 ⬛ Queen's Arms

Slan A Stigh, 34 George Street, Whithorn, Dumfries & Galloway, DG8 8NZ.
Open: All Year
01988 500699 Mr Burford
alexburford@supanet.com
D: £20.00 **S:** £20.00
Beds: 1F 2D **Baths:** 1 Sh
⛵ 🅿 (2) ⅍ 📺 ✕ ▥ 📺 ⌕
Slan A Stigh is a 1700 Georgian townhouse in historic Whithorn, site of the Whithorn Dig, The earliest Christian in Scotland. We are close to sea with good fishing in sea, loch, rivers. Ideal walking and cycling country.

Belmont, St John Street, Whithorn, Newton Stewart, Wigtownshire, DG8 8PG.
Visit nearby gardens, Whithorn, St Ninian's cave, many beautiful walks.
Open: All Year
01988 500890 (also fax) Mrs Fleming
D: £18.00–£21.00 **S:** £18.00–£21.00
Beds: 1D 1T 1S **Baths:** 1 Pr 1 Sh
⛵ (12) 🅿 (8) ⅍ 📺 ⵒ ✕ ▥ 📺 ⌕

Wigtown

NX4355 ⬛ Bladnoch Inn, Fordbank Hotel

Glaisnock House, 20 South Main Street, Wigtown, Wigtownshire, DG8 9EH.
Set in the heart of Scotland's book town with licensed restaurant.
Open: All Year (not Xmas)
Grades: STB 2 Star
01988 402249 (also fax) Mr & Mrs Cairns
cairns@glaisnock1.freeserve.co.uk
D: £17.50–£18.50 **S:** £18.50–£19.50
Beds: 2F 1T 1S **Baths:** 2 En 1 Pr 1 Sh
⛵ 📺 ⵒ ▥ 📺 ⌕ cc

Craigmount Guest House, High Street, Wigtown, Wigtownshire, DG8 9EQ.
Welcoming licensed family run home with space to relax. Safe, off-road parking. **Open:** All Year
01988 402291 / 0800 980 4510 Mrs Taylor
D: £17.00–£20.00 **S:** £17.00–£20.00
Beds: 2F 1D 1T 1S **Baths:** 2 En 1 Sh
⛵ 🅿 (10) 📺 ⵒ ✕ ▥ 📺 ⌕

The Old Coach House, 34 Bladnoch, Wigtown, Newton Stewart, DG8 9AB.
Grade C listed. Overlooking river. 35 minutes Stranraer ferry. Home baking. Brochure. **Open:** All Year
01988 402316 Mrs Key
D: £18.50–£20.00 **S:** £21.00
Beds: 1F 1T **Baths:** 2 En
⛵ 🅿 (5) 📺 ⵒ ✕ ▥ 📺 ✻ ⌕

Stilwell's Ireland: Bed & Breakfast 2000

Think of Ireland and you think of that world famous Irish hospitality. The warmth of the welcome is as much a part of this great island as are the wild and beautiful landscapes, the traditional folk music and the Guinness. Everywhere you go, town or country, North or South, you can't escape it. There are few better ways of experiencing this renowned hospitality, when traveling through Ireland, than by staying at one of the country's many Bed & Breakfasts. And there's no better way of choosing a convenient and desirable B&B than by consulting **Stilwell's Ireland: Bed & Breakfast 2001**.

Stilwell's Ireland: Bed & Breakfast 2001 contains over 1,400 entries – private houses, country halls, farms, cottages, inns, small hotels and guest houses – listed by county, in both Northern Ireland and the Republic of Ireland. Each entry includes room rates, facilities, Tourist Board grades or notices of approval and a brief description of the B&B, its location and surroundings. The average charge per person per night is £18. The listings also provide the names of local pubs and restaurants which serve food in the evening. As with all Stilwell B&B guides, Stilwell's Ireland has maps, listings of Tourist Information Offices and air, rail, bus and ferry information.

Treat yourself to some Irish hospitality with **Stilwell's Ireland: Bed & Breakfast 2001**.

£6.95 from all good bookstores (ISBN 1-900861-24-0) or £7.95 (inc p&p) from Stilwell Publishing Ltd, 59 Charlotte Road, London EC2A 3QW (020 7739 7179)

Fife

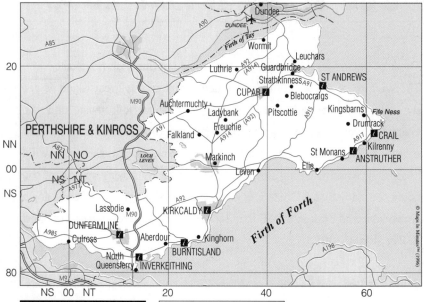

Tourist Information Centres

Scottish Fisheries Museum, **Anstruther**, Fife, KY10 3DQ, 01333 311073 (Easter to Oct).

Marketgate Museum & Heritage Centre, **Crail**, Anstruther, Fife, KY10 3TL, 01333 450869 (Easter to Oct).

Abbot House, Maygate, **Dunfermline**, Fife, KY12 7NH, 01383 720999 (Easter to Oct).

19 Whyte's Causeway, **Kirkcaldy**, Fife, KY1 1XF, 01592 267775.

South Street, **Leven**, Fife, KY8 4NU, 01592 267775.

Queensferry Lodge Hotel, **North Queensferry**, Inverkeithing, Fife, KY11 1JH, 01383 417759.

78 South Street, **St Andrews**, Fife, KY16 9JT, 01334 472021.

Aberdour

NT1985   🏚 *Aberdour Hotel*

Aberdour Hotel, *38 High Street, Aberdour, Burntisland, Fife, KY3 0SW.*
Friendly village inn, traditional cooking, real ales, Edinburgh half hour car/rail.
Open: All Year
Grades: STB 3 Star, AA 2 Star
01383 860325
Mr Thomson
Fax: 01383 860808
reception@aberdourhotel.co.uk
D: £25.00–£30.00 **S:** £35.00–£45.00
Beds: 4F 7D 5T **Baths:** 16 En
🐾 🅿 (8) 🔟 ⓧ ✖ 🎗 🖾, Ⅶ 🛋 ⚓ 1 **cc**

Anstruther

NO5603   🏚 *Crow's Nest, Salutation, Haven Restaurant, Dreel Tavern, Cellar*

Harefield Cottage, *Carvenom, Anstruther, Fife, KY10 3JU.*
Open: Easter to Oct **Grades:** STB 3 Star
01333 310346 Mrs Robinson
D: £20.00–£21.50 **S:** fr £24.00
Beds: 1T 1D **Baths:** 1 Pr 1 Sh
🅿 (4) 🔟 🎗 🖾, Ⅶ
Large, stone built, single storey cottage, large garden. All rooms have extensive view over fields and woods to firth of forth with May Island and Bass Rock. Private parking. Very Peaceful. Quiet location, one and half miles from town centre.

Royal Hotel, *20 Rodger Street, Anstruther, Fife, KY10 3HU.*
Family-run hotel, 100 yards seashore. Small harbour, sea trips to May Island Bird Sanctuary. **Open:** All Year
01333 310581 Mr Cook
D: £18.00–£22.00 **S:** fr £18.00
Beds: 1F 4T 4D 2S **Baths:** 1 En
🛏 🔟 🎗 🖾, Ⅶ 🛋

The Sheiling, *32 Glenogil Gardens, Anstruther, Fife, KY10 3ET.*
Pretty white bungalow, ground floor bedrooms overlook garden. Harbour 200m. **Open:** Easter to Sept
Grades: STB 3 Star
01333 310697 Mrs Ritchie
D: £16.00–£22.00 **S:** £22.00
Beds: 2D **Baths:** 1 Sh 1 Pr
🅿 (2) ⚡ 🔟 ✖ 🖾, Ⅶ 🛋 ⚓

The Hermitage, *Ladywalk, Anstruther, Fife, KY10 3EX.*
Home from Home, Quiet situation near Harbour, Superb walled Garden.
Open: All Year
Grades: STB 4 Star, AA 4 Diamonds
01333 310909 Mrs McDonald
Fax: 01333 311505
b&b@thehermitage.co.uk
D: £20.00–£30.00 **S:** £25.00–£30.00
Beds: 3D 1T **Baths:** 2 Sh
🕭 🅿 (4) ⅊ 📺 ✕ 🕮 Ⅴ ⅃ cc

Auchtermuchty

NO2311

Forest Hills Hotel, *High Street, Auchtermuchty, Cupar, Fife, KY14 7DP.*
Old inn situated in village square, surrounded by rolling countryside.
Open: All Year
01337 828318 (also fax)
Mr Van Beuskom
lomond.foresthotels@dtn.ntl.com
D: £25.00–£42.00 **S:** £37.00–£42.00
Beds: 2F 4D 2T 2S **Baths:** 8 Pr 1 Sh
🕭 📺 🕇 ✕ 🕮 Ⅴ ⅃

Blebocraigs

NO4215 ⅏ *Pitscottie Inn*

Torridon, *16 Main Street, Blebocraigs, Cupar, Fife, KY15 5UF.*
In quiet country village by St Andrews. Lovely views. Friendly.
Open: All Year
Grades: STB 3 Star
01334 850766 (also fax)
Mrs Grice
tonyw@gricet.freeserve.co.uk
D: £18.00–£21.00 **S:** £23.00–£26.00
Beds: 1T 1D **Baths:** 1 En 1 Pr
🕭 (10) 🅿 (6) ⅊ 📺 🕇 🕮 ⅃

Burntisland

NT2386 ⅏ *Kingswood Hotel, Inchview Hotel*

148a Kinghorn Road, *Burntisland, Fife, KY3 9JU.*
Panoramic views over River Forth, golf courses and water sports nearby.
Open: All Year
01592 872266 (also fax)
Mrs Redford
c148m@aol.com
D: £20.00–£25.00 **S:** £25.00–£30.00
Beds: 1F 1D **Baths:** 2 En
🕭 🅿 (2) 📺 🕇 🕮 Ⅴ ⅃

Crail

NO6107 ⅏ *Marine Hotel, East Neuk Hotel, Balcomie Hotel*

Woodlands Guest House, *Balcomie Road, Crail, Anstruther, Fife, KY10 5TN.*
Detached villa, superb views, beach half a minute, St Andrews 10 mins, golf courses.
Open: Feb to Dec
01333 450147 Mrs Wood
rachelwoodlandsbb@easicom.com
D: £18.00–£19.00 **S:** £20.00–£21.00
Beds: 1F 2D **Baths:** 2 Sh
🕭 (2) 🅿 (10) ⅊ 📺 🕇 🕮 ⅃ ⅂

Caiplie House, *53 High Street, Crail, Anstruther, Fife, KY10 3RA.*
Friendly, informal guest house. Taste of Scotland member.
Open: Feb to Nov
01333 450564 (also fax)
Mr & Mrs Strachan
caipliehouse@talk21.com
D: £17.00–£24.00 **S:** £18.00–£22.00
Beds: 1F 4D 1T 1S **Baths:** 3 En 1 Pr 2 Sh
🕭 🅿 (3) 📺 🕇 ✕ 🕮 Ⅴ ⅃

Culross

NS9886

Dundonald Arms Hotel, *Mid Causeway, Culross, Dunfermline, Fife, KY12 8HS.*
C16th time warp riverside village; white cottages, cobbled causeways.
Open: All Year
01383 882443 Mrs Finlayson
Fax: 01383 881137
D: £20.00–£30.00 **S:** £30.00–£40.00
Beds: 7F 3D 2T **Baths:** 7 En 7 Pr
🕭 🅿 (30) 📺 ✕ 🕮 Ⅴ ⅃ cc

Cupar

NO3714 ⅏ *Springfield Tavern, Ceres Inn, Eden House Hotel, St Michaels Inn, Guardbridge Hotel, Dairsie Inn, Dolls House*

Todhall House, *off A91, Cupar, Fife, KY15 4RQ.*
Welcoming country house near St Andrews - come explore the Kingdom of Fife.
Open: Mar to Oct
01334 656344 Mrs Donald
Fax: 01334 650791
todhallhouse@ukgateway.net
D: £25.00–£32.00 **S:** £30.00–£38.00
Beds: 2D 1T **Baths:** 3 En
🕭 (10) 🅿 (5) ⅊ 📺 ✕ 🕮 Ⅴ ⅃

Drumrack

NO5408 ⅏ *Cambo Arms, Kings Barns*

Drumrack Farm, *Drumrack, St Andrews, Fife, KY16 8QQ.*
Open: All Year (not Xmas)
01333 310520 Mrs Watson
D: £16.00 **S:** £16.00
Beds: 1D 1T 1S **Baths:** 1 Sh
🕭 🅿 (5) ⅊ 📺 ✕ Ⅴ ⅃
Situated 6 miles south of St Andrews on the B9131, a family-run farm of 350 acres with sheep and cattle. House and garden have fine views over River Forth. Ideally placed for golf, beaches and many places of interest.

Dunfermline

NT1087 ⅏ *Roadhouse, Saline Hotel, St Margaret's Hotel*

Broomfield Guest House, *1 Bloomfield Drive, Dunfermline, Fife, KY12 7DZ.*
Large Victorian house, near golf course, swimming pool and town centre.
Open: All Year (not Xmas/New Year)
01383 732498 Mrs Taylor
D: £19.00–£25.00 **S:** £16.00–£20.00
Beds: 1F 2D 1T 2S **Baths:** 5 En 1 Pr
🕭 🅿 (7) 📺 🕮 Ⅴ ⅃ ⅂

Bowleys Farm, *Roscobie, Dunfermline, Fife, KY12 0SG.*
Sample Scottish hospitality at its best! (30 minutes from Edinburgh).
Open: Feb to Dec
Grades: STB 3 Star
01383 721056 Mrs Fotheringham
bowleysfarm@hotmail.com
D: £18.00–£22.00 **S:** fr £25.00
Beds: 2F **Baths:** 1 En 1 Sh
🕭 🅿 (6) ⅊ 📺 🕇 ✕ 🕮 Ⅴ ⅃

Pitreavie Guest House, *3 Aberdour Road, Dunfermline, Fife, KY12 4PB.*
Family-run guest house on bus route to Edinburgh, well-appointed rooms.
Open: All Year
01383 724244 (also fax)
Mr & Mrs Walker
pitreavie@aol.com
D: £19.00–£21.00 **S:** £21.00–£25.00
Beds: 1F 1D 2T 2S **Baths:** 3 Sh
🕭 🅿 (6) ⅊ 📺 🕇 ✕ 🕮 Ⅴ ✳ ⅃ cc

Elie

NO4900 ⅏ *Ship Inn, The Toft*

Millford House, *19 High Street, Elie, Leven, Fife, KY9 1BY.*
Large Georgian house in peaceful seaside village. Golf, tennis, sailing.
Open: All Year
Grades: STB 2 Star
01333 330567 Mr Cowan
millfordhouse@netscapeonline.co.uk
D: £17.50–£20.00 **S:** £20.00–£25.00
Beds: 2D 1T
🕭 📺 🕮 Ⅴ ⅃ ⅂

Falkland

NO2507 ⅏ *Warbecks*

Templelands Farm, *Falkland, Cupar, Fife, KY15 7DE.*
Panoramic views, National Trust Properties nearby - Abundance of golf courses.
Open: Easter to Oct
Grades: STB 2 Star
01337 857383 Ms McGregor
D: £15.00 **S:** £15.00–£18.00
Beds: 1F 1D 1S **Baths:** 2 Sh
🕭 🅿 (3) ⅊ 📺 🕮 ⅃

Freuchie

NO2806

Lomond Hills Hotel, *Parliament Square, Freuchie, Cupar, Fife, KY7 7EY.*
Comfortable coaching inn, candle-lit restaurant and leisure centre.
Open: All Year
01337 857329 (also fax)
lomond.foresthotels@dtn.ntl.com
D: £27.50–£39.00 **S:** £40.00–£54.00
Beds: 4F 11D 7T 2S **Baths:** 24 En
🕭 🅿 ⅊ 📺 🕇 ✕ 🕮 Ⅴ ⅃

BEDROOMS
F - Family
D - Double
T - Twin
S - Single

Guardbridge

NO4519 Guardbridge Hotel

The Larches, 7 River Terrace,
Guardbridge, St Andrews, Fife, KY16 0XA.
Large, comfortable memorial hall.
Wonderful food. Fully ensuite/private
rooms. **Open:** All Year
01334 838008 (also fax) Mrs Mayner
thelarches@aol.com
D: £18.00–£28.00 **S:** £22.00–£32.00
Beds: 2D 1T **Baths:** 2 En 1 Pr
🛇 🅿 (4) ⌇ 📺 🍴 🛏 💷 🆅

Inverkeithing

NT1382

The Roods, 16 Bannerman Avenue,
Inverkeithing, Fife, KY11 1NG.
Award winning B&B set in quiet gardens
close to costal path
Open: All Year
Grades: STB 3 Stars, AA 4 Diamonds
01383 415049 (also fax) Mrs Marley
bookings@theroods.com
D: £20.00–£25.00 **S:** £20.00–£25.00
Beds: 1D 1T 1F **Baths:** 3 En
🛇 🅿 ⌇ 📺 ✕ 💷 🆅 ♿ cc

Kinghorn

NT2687 The Bay

Craigo-Er, 45 Pettycur Road, Kinghorn,
Fife, KY3 9RN.
Victorian house, panoramic sea views,
direct regular Edinburgh rail links.
Open: All Year
01592 890527 Mrs Thomson
D: £19.00 **S:** £19.00
Beds: 1D 2T **Baths:** 2 Sh
🛇 🅿 (1) 📺 🍴 🛏 💷 ♿

Kingsbarns

NO5912 Cambo Arms Hotel

Kingsbarns Bed & Breakfast, 3
Main Street, Kingsbarns, St Andrews, Fife,
KY16 8SL.
Warm, friendly, comfortable B&B in
picturesque coastal village. Golf courses
nearby.
Open: Apr to Oct
Grades: STB 4 Star
01334 880234 Mrs Hay
hay@itek-uk.com
D: £22.00–£25.00 **S:** fr £22.00
Beds: 2D 1T **Baths:** 3 En
🛇 🅿 (2) 📺 💷 🆅 ♿

Kirkcaldy

NT2791 Kingswood, Victoria, Wheatsheaf,
Mullins

Crawford Hall, 2 Kinghorn Road,
Kirkcaldy, Fife, KY1 1SU.
Open: All Year (not Xmas)
01592 262658 Mrs Crawford
D: £17.00–£19.00 **S:** £17.00–£19.00
Beds: 1F 1T **Baths:** 1 Sh
🛇 🅿 (4) 📺 🍴 ✕ 💷 ♿ &
Large, rambling old C19th house, once
local manse, set in lovely gardens. 2
minutes from beach, 10 minute walk to
town centre, bus/railway stations.
Comfortable rooms, hearty breakfast,
handy for golfers, near St Andrews.

Cameron House, 44 Glebe Park,
Kirkcaldy, Fife, KY1 1BL.
Quiet, friendly, good food central for
Edinburgh, Perth, St Andrews.
Open: All Year (not Xmas)
Grades: STB 2 Star B&B
01592 264531 Mrs Nicol
D: £15.00 **S:** £15.00–£17.00
Beds: 1F 1D **Baths:** 1 Sh
🛇 (1) ⌇ 📺 🍴 ✕ 💷 🆅

Castleview, 17 Dysart Road, Kirkcaldy,
Fife, KY1 2AY.
Situated on Fife coast near M90, within
reach Edinburgh, Perth, Dundee.
Open: All Year (not Xmas)
Grades: STB 1 Star B&B
01592 269275 Mrs Dick
D: £16.00–£17.00 **S:** £16.00–£17.00
Beds: 1F 2T **Baths:** 1 Sh
🛇 🅿 📺 🍴 ✕ 💷 🆅 ♿

Invertiel Guest House, 21 Pratt
Street, Kirkcaldy, Fife, KY1 1RZ.
Quality accommodation where you can
come & go as you please.
Open: All Year
01592 264849 Mrs Duffy
Fax: 01592 592440
invertiel@fife.ac.uk
D: £20.00–£25.00 **S:** £25.00–£50.00
Beds: 2F 1D 1T 1S **Baths:** 1 En 1 Sh
🛇 🅿 (7) 📺 ✕ 💷 🆅 ♿

Cherrydene, 44 Bennochy Road,
Kirkcaldy, Fife, KY2 5RB.
Victorian house retaining many original
features. Situated 5 minutes from bus
and rail stations.
Open: All Year
01592 202147 Mrs Nicol
Fax: 01592 644618
D: £16.00–£25.00 **S:** £22.00–£35.00
Beds: 1F 1D 1S **Baths:** 2 En 1 Sh
🛇 🅿 (3) 📺 🍴 ✕ 💷 🆅 ♿

Arboretum, 20 Southerton Road,
Kirkcaldy, Fife, KY2 5NB.
Extended bungalow - quiet area courtyard
for private parking, overlooking park.
Open: All Year
01592 643673 Mrs Duncan
D: £17.00–£20.00 **S:** £18.00–£22.00
Beds: 2D 1T **Baths:** 2 En 1 Pr
🛇 (8) 🅿 (6) 📺 🍴 🛏 💷 🆅 ♿

Dunedin House, 25 Townsend Place,
Kirkcaldy, Fife, KY1 1HB.
Excellent accommodation, central
location. Superb breakfast, private
parking, 35 mins Edinburgh & St
Andrews.
Open: All Year
01592 203874 Mr & Mrs Duffy
Fax: 01592 265274
info@dunedin-house.co.uk
D: £20.00–£22.00 **S:** £25.00–£28.00
Beds: 1F 1D 1S **Baths:** 1 Sh
🛇 🅿 (5) ⌇ 📺 ✕ 💷 🆅 ♿

National Grid References are for

villages, towns and cities – not

for individual houses

Ladybank

NO3009

Redlands Country Lodge, Pitlessie
Road, Ladybank, Cupar, Fife, KY15 7SH.
An attractive country cottage and pine
lodge, surrounded by trees and fields.
Open: Feb to Nov
01337 831091 (also fax)
Jim & Dorothy McGregor
D: £24.00 **S:** £24.00–£30.00
Beds: 2D 2T **Baths:** 4 En
🛇 🅿 (6) ⌇ 📺 🍴 ✕ 💷 🆅 ♿ cc

Lassodie

NT1292 Halfway House

Loch Fitty Cottage, Lassodie,
Dunfermline, Fife, KY12 0SP.
Enjoy the comfort of a family home, in
rural setting.
Open: All Year
Grades: STB 2 Star
01383 831081 Mr Woolley
n.woolley@btinternet.com
D: £18.00–£20.00 **S:** £18.00–£20.00
Beds: 1F 1D **Baths:** 1 En 1 Pr
🛇 🅿 (4) 📺 🍴 💷 🆅 ♿

Leuchars

NO4521 St Michaels Inn

Pinewood Country House, Tayport
Road, St Michaels, Leuchars, St Andrews,
Fife, KY16 0DU.
A quiet wooded area setting ideal for
short breaks or golfing holidays.
Open: All Year (not Xmas/New Year)
Grades: STB 3 Star
01334 839860 Mr Bedwell
Fax: 01334 839868
accommodation@pinewoodhouse.com
D: £22.00–£25.00 **S:** £32.00–£44.00
Beds: 2T 3D **Baths:** 4 En 1 Pr
📺 🍴 ✕ 💷 🆅 ♿ cc

Pitlethie Farm, Leuchars, St Andrews,
Fife, KY16 0DP.
Attractive comfortable farmhouse set in
open farmland.
Open: All Year (not Xmas)
01334 838649 Mrs Black
Fax: 01334 839281
D: £25.00 **S:** £26.50
Beds: 2T, 1S
🛇 ⌇ 📺

Leven

NO3800 Burns Tavern, Fettykil Fox

Duniface Farm, Windygates, Leven,
Fife, KY8 5RH.
Charming C19th farmhouse - comfortable
& welcoming, hearty breakfasts, ideal
touring base.
Open: All Year
01333 350272 (also fax)
Mrs Hamilton
auderymhamilton@tinyworld.co.uk
D: £15.00–£17.00 **S:** £15.00–£20.00
Beds: 1D 1F **Baths:** 1 Sh
🛇 🅿 ⌇ 📺 💷 🆅 ♿

Luthrie

NO3319 🗣 *Fernie Castle*

Easter Kinsleith, *Luthrie, Cupar, Fife, KY15 4NR.*
Gaplair is ideally situated for touring East and Central Scotland.
Open: Feb to Nov
Grades: STB 3 Star
01337 870363 Mr Rieu-Clarke
gapplair@compuserve.com
D: £18.00–£20.00 **S:** £18.00–£20.00
Beds: 1F 1D **Baths:** 2 En
🛇 (6) 🄿 (2) ⊬ 🗹 🍴 🎟 ⚲ cc

Markinch

NO2901 🗣 *Town House, Laurel Bank Hotel*

Wester Markinch Cottage, *Balbirnie Estate, Markinch, Glenrothes, Fife, KY7 6JN.*
Extended Victorian cottage, convenient for Edinburgh, Glasgow and St Andrews.
Open: All Year (not Xmas/New Year)
01592 756719 (also fax)
Ms Tjeransen
D: £18.00–£25.00 **S:** fr £16.00
Beds: 1D 2S 1T **Baths:** 1 En 1 Sh
🛇 🄿 (4) 🗹 🍴 🎟 🖂 ⚲

Shythrum Farm, *Markinch, Glenrothes, Fife, KY7 6HB.*
Peaceful farmhouse. Markinch 1 mile golfers haven, excellent touring base.
Open: Mar to Oct
Grades: STB 2 Stars
01592 758372 Mrs Craig
D: £19.00 **S:** £19.00
Beds: 1F 1T **Baths:** 1 En 1 Pr
🛇 🄿 (3) 🗹 🎟 🖂 ⚲

North Queensferry

NT1380 🗣 *Ferry Bridge Hotel, Albert Hotel*

Fourteen Falls, *Chapel Place, North Queensferry, Inverkeithing, Fife, KY11 1JT.*
C18th cottage under Forth Bridge, enclosed garden, emphasis on hospitality.
Open: All Year
01383 412749 (also fax)
Mrs Evans
b&b@fourteen-falls.in2home.co.uk
D: £22.00 **S:** £22.00
Beds: 1T **Baths:** 1 Sh
🄿 (3) ⊬ 🗹 🍴 ✕ 🎟 🖂 ⚲

Pitscottie

NO4113 🗣 *Pitscottie Inn*

Rockmount Cottage, *Dura Den Road, Pitscottie, Cupar, Fife, KY15 5TG.*
Open: All Year (not Xmas/New Year)
Grades: STB 3 Star
01334 828164 Mrs Reid
annmreid@rockmount1.freeserve.co.uk
D: £18.00–£25.00 **S:** £18.00–£25.00
Beds: 1F 1D 1S **Baths:** 1 Pr 2 Sh
🛇 🄿 (3) ⊬ 🗹 🎟 🖂 ⚲ 3
Lovely nineteenth century cottage tastefully modernised to a high standard just 7 miles from St. Andrews. Beautiful bedrooms with colour TV, tea, coffee and home baking. Good breakfasts and private parking. Children welcome and non smoking throughout.

St Andrews

NO5116 🗣 *Tavern, Pitscottie Inn, Guardbridge Hotel, Dolls House, Strathkinness Tavern, Cambo, Playfairs, Russell Hotel*

The Paddock, *Sunnyside, Strathkinness, St Andrews, KY16 9XP.*
Open: All Year (not Xmas/New Year)
Grades: STB 4 Stars
01334 850888 Mrs Taylor
Fax: 01334 850870
thepaddock@btinternet.com
D: £20.00–£26.00 **S:** £25.00–£40.00
Beds: 1T 2D
🄿 (8) 🗹 🎟 ⚲
Quality En suite accommodation in a modern residence with outstanding country views. Positioned in a secluded spot. Ample private parking . Guests may use the conservatory overlooking the gardens. St Andrews 2 miles.

Edenside House, *Edenside, St Andrews, Fife, KY16 9SQ.*
Pre 1775 farmhouse,2.5 miles from St Andrews. Parking guaranteed.
Open: All Year (not Xmas)
Grades: STB 3 Star, AA 3 Diamond
01334 838108 Douglas & Yvonne Reid
Fax: 01334 838493
yreid19154@aol.com
D: £20.00–£27.00 **S:** £32.00–£38.00
Beds: 1F 2D 5T **Baths:** 8 En
🛇 🄿 (10) ⊬ 🗹 🍴 🎟 🖂 ⚲ ⚲ cc

Cairnsden B&B, *2 King Street, St Andrews, Fife, KY16 8JQ.*
Comfortable family house, 7 mins town centre, early breakfasts for golfers.
Open: All Year (not Xmas)
Grades: STB 2 Star
01334 476326 Mrs Allan
Fax: 01334 840355
D: £16.00–£20.00 **S:** £18.00–£22.00
Beds: 1D 1T **Baths:** 1 Sh
🄿 (1) ⊬ 🗹 🍴 🎟 🖂 ⚲

Coppercantie, *8 Lawhead Road West, St Andrews, Fife, KY16 9NE.*
A warm welcome awaits in the home of Scottish historian.
Open: All Year (not Xmas)
Grades: STB 4 Star
01334 476544 Mrs Dobson
Fax: 01334 470322
f.dobson@zetnet.co.uk
D: £18.00–£24.00 **S:** £34.00–£40.00
Beds: 1F 1D 1T **Baths:** 1 En 2 Sh
🛇 (9) 🄿 🗹 🎟 ⚲ cc

23 Kilrymont Road, *St Andrews, Fife, KY16 8DE.*
Detached home, harbour area, East Sands, 10 mins famous golf course.
Open: April-Dec
01334 477946 Mrs Kier
mkier@talk21.com
D: £17.00–£19.00 **S:** £17.00–£20.00
Beds: 1D 1S
🛇 (7) 🄿 (1) ⊬ 🗹 🎟 ⚲ ⚲

Planning a longer stay? Always ask for any special rates

12 Newmill Gardens, *St Andrews, Fife, KY16 8RY.*
Spacious, bright room. Tranquil area. Conveniently situated.
Open: All Year (not Xmas/New Year)
Grades: STB 3 Star
01334 474552 (also fax)
Mrs Irvine
D: £18.00–£20.00 **S:** £20.00–£22.00
Beds: 1D **Baths:** 1 Pr
🄿 (1) ⊬ 🗹 🎟 🖂 ⚲

Amberside Guest House, *4 Murray Park, St Andrews, Fife, KY16 9AW.*
Amberside has become well known for its wonderful breakfast and lovely warm welcome.
Open: All Year
Grades: STB 3 Star, AA 3 Diamond
01334 474644 (also fax)
Mr Carney
amberside@talk21.com
D: £18.00–£28.00 **S:** £35.00–£45.00
Beds: 1F 2D 2T 1S **Baths:** 1 Pr
🛇 🄿 🗹 🍴 🎟 🖂 ✻ ⚲ cc

Spinkstown Farmhouse, *St Andrews, Fife, KY16 8PN.*
Two miles from St Andrews on A917.
Open: All Year (not Xmas)
01334 473475 (also fax) Mrs Duncan
D: £20.00 **S:** £25.00
Beds: 2D 1T **Baths:** 3 Pr
🄿 (4) ⊬ 🗹 🎟 🖂 ⚲

Ardmore, *1 Drumcarrow Road, St Andrews, Fife, KY16 8SE.*
Comfortable, non-smoking, family bungalow in quiet residential area opposite Botanical Gardens.
Open: Jan to Nov
01334 474574 Mrs Methven
D: £16.00–£18.00
Beds: 2D
🄿 (2) ⊬ 🗹 🎟 🖂 🗹

Whitecroft Guest Lodges, *33 Strathkinness High Road, St Andrews, Fife, KY16 9UA.*
Whitecroft has modern ensuite rooms with parking, private entrances.
Open: All Year
01334 474448 (also fax)
Mr & Mrs Horn
whitecroft@tesco.net
D: £22.00–£27.00 **S:** £30.00–£35.00
Beds: 3F 2D 1T **Baths:** 5 En
🛇 🄿 (5) ⊬ 🗹 🍴 🎟 ⚲ cc

St Monans

NO5201   🍴 *Mayview Hotel, Cabin Bar*

Inverforth, *20 Braehead, St Monans, Fife, KY10 2AN.*
Comfortable homely accommodation, home baking. Seaview, near St Andrews golf.
Open: Jun to Oct
Grades: STB 2 Star B&B
01333 730205
Miss Aitken
D: £17.50–£18.00
S: £17.50–£18.00
Beds: 1D 2T **Baths:** 1 Sh
📺 (8) 🚳 📺 🏬

Strathkinness

NO4616

Brig-A-Doon, *6 High Road, Strathkinness, St Andrews, Fife, KY16 9XY.*
Open: Easter to October
01334 850268 Mrs Watson
D: £20.00–£25.00 **S:** £25.00
Beds: 1T 1D **Baths:** 1 En 1 Pr
📺 (5) 🅿 (2) 🚳 📺 🏬
Brig-A-Doon was one time a Toll House. Panoramic views over St Andrews Bay and Tay Estuary. Very handy for local golf courses. Dundee, Perth within easy distance. Hospitality tray in bedrooms with extras. Wake up to a good Scottish breakfast.

Wormit

NO3925   🍴 *Sandford Country House Hotel*

Newton Farm, *Wormit, Newport-on-Tay, Fife, DD6 8RL.*
Traditional farmhouse overlooking our own trout loch, fly fishing, quad biking.
Open: Easter to Oct
Grades: STB 2 Star
01382 540125
K Crawford
Fax: 01382 542513
ghcrawford@ukonline.co.uk
D: £17.00
Beds: 1F 2T **Baths:** 1 Sh
📺 🅿 (8) 🚳 📺 🐾 ♨

Stilwell's Britain: Hostels & Camping 2001

It's a great new idea! Hostels, camping barns, bunk houses **and** camping sites all in one user-friendly book. From now on, campers, tourers, backpackers, clubs and groups – anyone looking for low-cost and group accommodation – can find the right place to sleep for the right price by consulting the right guide – **Stilwell's Britain: Hostels & Camping 2001**.

Listings in **Stilwell's Britain: Hostels & Camping 2001** are arranged geographically by country, county and location throughout England, Scotland and Wales. Each entry includes tariffs, facilities, opening times and a brief description of the premise, it's location and surroundings. Many are accompanied by a picture of the site. The average charge per person per night is £8. As wi`th all Stilwell guides, the book contains local maps, grid references and listings of Tourist Information Centres. There's air, rail, bus and ferry information, too.

Whether you're traveling alone or in a group, you can plan your trip with a minimum of fuss with **Stilwell's Britain: Hostels & Camping 2001**.

£6.95 from all good bookstores (ISBN 1-900861-20-8) or £7.95
(inc p&p) from Stilwell Publishing Ltd, 59 Charlotte Road,
London EC2A 3QW (020 7739-7179)

Glasgow & District

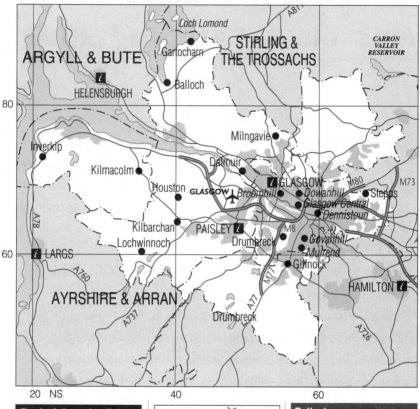

80

60

20 NS   40   60

RATES
D = Price range per person
sharing in a double room
S = Price range for a
single room

Balloch

NS3982 ◖ *Roundabout Inn, Balloch Hotel,
Corries, Stables, Clachan Inn*

Glyndale, *6 McKenzie Drive, Lomond
Road Estate, Balloch, Alexandria,
Dunbartonshire, G83 8HL.*
Easy access to Loch Lomond, Glasgow
Airport, public transport.
Open: All Year (not Xmas)
Grades: STB 3 Star B&B
01389 758238 Mrs Ross
glyndale_b_and_b@tinyworld.co.uk
D: £16.50–£17.50 **S:** £20.00
Beds: 1D 1T **Baths:** 1 Sh
ᴥ ₪ (2) ⠀⃠ ⃝ ⑂ 🍴 ▥ ⑂ ⭥

Anchorage Guest House, *Balloch
Road, Balloch, Alexandria, Dunbartonshire,
G83 8SS.*
Situated on the banks of Loch Lomond.
Ideal base for touring, fishing, sailing &
walking. **Open:** All Year
Grades: STB 1 Star
01389 753336 Mr Bowman
D: £18.00–£25.00
Beds: 1F 2D 4T **Baths:** 5 En 2 Sh
ᴥ (1) ₪ (6) ▣ 🍴 ✕ ▥ ⑂ ⚡ ♨ ⚹ 3

Dumbain Farm, Balloch, Alexandria,
Dunbartonshire, G83 8DS.
Newly converted byre on working farm.
Aga cooked breakfast. Homemade
raspberry jam.
Open: All Year
Grades: STB 3 Star
01389 752263 Mrs Watson
D: £20.00–£22.00 **S:** £18.00–£25.00
Beds: 1F 1T 1D **Baths:** 3 En
🛇 🅿 (5) 📺 🛏 📖 Ⅴ 🌢

Gowanlea Guest House, Drymen
Road, Balloch, Alexandria, Dunbartonshire,
G83 8HS.
Open: All Year (not Xmas/New Year)
Grades: STB 4 Star
01389 752456 Mrs Campbell
Fax: 01389 710543
gowanlea@aol.com
D: £19.00–£23.00 **S:** £22.00–£30.00
Beds: 1T 3D **Baths:** 4 En
🛇 🅿 (4) 🌢 📺 📖 Ⅴ 🌢 CC
Warm welcome awaits you at Campbell's
award winning family run guest house
B&B. Superior accommodation, excellent
hospitality. Ideal touring base.

Heathpete, 24 Balloch Road, Balloch,
Alexandria, Dunbartonshire, G83 8LE.
Superb hospitality offered in luxurious
accommodation central to all amenities.
Open: All Year
Grades: STB 3 Star
01389 752195 Mrs Hamill
sheathpete@aol.com
D: £12.00–£25.00 **S:** £18.00–£25.00
Beds: 2F 2D **Baths:** 4 En
🛇 🅿 (5) 📺 🛏 📖 Ⅴ 🌢 ⅅ

Auchry, 24 Boturich Drive, Balloch,
Alexandria, Dunbartonshire, G83 8JP.
Set in quiet cul de sac; walking distance
to Loch Lomond.
Open: All Year (not Xmas/New Year)
Grades: STB 3 Star
01389 753208 Mrs McIntosh
auchry@ic24.net
D: £17.00–£19.00 **S:** £18.00–£20.00
Beds: 1D 1S **Baths:** 1 En 1 Sh
🅿 (4) 🌢 📺 📖 🌢 CC

7 Carrochan Crescent, Balloch,
Alexandria, Dunbartonshire, G83 8PX.
A warm welcome awaits you; ideally
situated for touring etc.
Open: Easter to Oct
Grades: STB 3 Star
01389 750078 Mrs Campbell
D: £16.00 **S:** £18.00
Beds: 2D **Baths:** 1 Sh
🛇 🅿 (2) 📺 📖 Ⅴ 🌢

Gartocharn

NS4286   🏚 Hungry Monk, Clachan Inn

Mardella Farm, Old School Road,
Gartocharn, Loch Lomond, Alexandria,
Dunbartonshire, G83 8SD.
Friendly, welcoming, homely atmosphere.
Come and meet the quackers (ducks)!
Open: All Year
Grades: AA 4 Diamond
01389 830428 Mrs MacDonell
D: £18.50–£22.00 **S:** £31.00–£37.00
Beds: 1F 1D 1T **Baths:** 1 En 1 Sh
🛇 🅿 (4) 🌢 📺 🛏 📖 🌢❋🌢

Giffnock

NS5658   🏚 Orchard Park

Forres Guest House, 10 Forres
Avenue, Giffnock, Glasgow, G46 6LJ.
Located in quiet south side suburbs. 5
minutes from city centre.
Open: All Year (not Xmas)
Grades: STB 3 Star
0141 638 5554 Mrs Davies
Fax: 0141 571 9301
june@10forres.freeserve.co.uk
D: £18.00–£20.00 **S:** £18.00–£20.00
Beds: 2D
🅿 (4) 📺 📖 🌢

GLASGOW   Broomhill

NS5467   🏚 Air Organic, Bellahoustow Hotel,
Dino's, Dorsey's, Garfield House, Highlanders Park,
Mitchell's, Orchard Park, Pablo's, Park Bar,
Stravaigan's, Snaffil Bit

Lochgilvie House, 117 Randolph Road,
Broomhill, Glasgow, G11 7DS.
Open: All Year
Grades: STB 3 Star
0141 357 1593 Mrs Ogilvie
Fax: 0141 334 5828
reservations@lochgilvie.demon.co.uk
D: £25.00–£30.00 **S:** £25.00–£35.00
Beds: 1F 2D 3T **Baths:** 4 En
🛇 (10) 🅿 🌢 📺 📖 Ⅴ 🌢
Luxurious Victorian town house situated
in Glasgow's prestigious West End,
adjacent to rail station, beside the art
galleries, university, SECC, convenient for
International Airport.

Park House, 13 Victoria Park Gardens
South, Glasgow, G11 7BX.
Magnificent Victorian residence
overlooking private parkland in quiet
residential area.
Open: All Year
Grades: STB 4 Star
0141 339 1559 Mrs Hallam
Fax: 0141 576 0915
richardanddi.parkhouse.glasgow@dial.pi
pex.com
D: £25.00–£27.50 **S:** £32.00–£37.50
Beds: 2D 1T **Baths:** 2 En 1 Pr
🛇 🅿 (3) 📺 ✕ 📖 Ⅴ 🌢 CC

GLASGOW   Central

NS5865   🏚 Dorsey's, Park Bar, Mitchell's,
Stravaigan's, Orchard Park, Bellahoustow Hotel,
Garfield House, Highlanders Park, Snaffil Bit

Kirkland House, 42 St Vincent
Crescent, Glasgow, G3 8NG.
Open: All Year
Grades: STB 3 Star
0141 248 3458 Mrs Divers
Fax: 0141 221 5174
admin@kirkland.gispnet.com
D: £27.00–£30.00 **S:** £27.00–£30.00
Beds: 3D 2T 2S **Baths:** 6 En 2 Sh
🛇 (1) 🌢 📺 📖 🌢
City centre guest house with excellent
rooms on beautiful Victorian Crescent in
Finnieston (Glasgow's 'little Chelsea').
Short walk to Scottish Exhibition Centre,
Museum/Art Gallery, Kelvingrove Park
and all West End facilities. Glasgow
airport 10 minutes, member of the Harry
James society.

Kelvingrove Hotel, 944 Sauchiehall
Street, Glasgow, G3 7TH.
Open: All Year (not Xmas)
Grades: STB 2 Star
0141 339 5011 Mr Wills
Fax: 0141 339 6566
kelvingrove.hotel@business.ntl.com
D: £24.00–£29.00 **S:** £33.00–£38.00
Beds: 8D 4T 4F **Baths:** 10 En
🛇 🅿 (20) 🌢 📺 🛏 ✕ 📖 Ⅴ 🌢 CC
Centrally located family-run hotel, set in
Glasgow's fashionable West End. Close to
pubs, clubs, art galleries, museums,
University, shops, rail and bus links - all
within walking distance.

Adelaide's, 209 Bath Street, Glasgow,
G2 4HZ.
Central location, close to all major
attractions of revitalised city.
Open: All Year (not Xmas/New Year)
Grades: STB 2 Star
0141 248 4970 A R Meiklejohn
Fax: 0141 226 4247
info@adelaides.freeserve.co.uk
D: £25.00–£28.00 **S:** £35.00–£45.00
Beds: 2F 2T 2D 2S **Baths:** 6 En 2 Sh
🛇 🌢 📺 🌢 CC

Number Thirty Six, 36 St Vincent
Crescent, Glasgow, G3 8NG.
Situated in a Georgian terrace on the
edge of Glasgow city centre.
Open: All Year (not Xmas)
0141 248 2086 Mrs MacKay
Fax: 0141 221 1477
admin@no36.gisp.net
D: £25.00–£30.00 **S:** £30.00–£35.00
Beds: 4D 2T **Baths:** 4 En 2 Pr
🌢 📺 📖 🌢

GLASGOW   Dalmuir

NS4970   🏚 Radnor Park Hotel, Whiskey Joes

13 Southview, Dalmuir, Clydebank,
Dunbartonshire, G81 3LA.
Semi- villa: near Station/ Glasgow
Airport. Tourist board highly commended.
Open: All Year
0141 952 7007 Mrs McCay
D: £15.00–£18.00 **S:** £18.00–£20.00
Beds: 1T 1D 1S **Baths:** 1 En 1 Sh
🅿 (1) 🌢 📺 📖

GLASGOW   Dennistoun

NS6065   🏚 Fire Station Resturant, Dorsey's,
Park Bar, Mitchell's, Stravaigan's, Orchard Park,
Bellahoustow Hotel, Garfield House, Highlanders
Park, Snaffil Bit

Seton Guest House, 6 Seton Terrace,
Glasgow, G31 2HU.
Warm and friendly welcome assured. Five
minutes from city centre.
Open: All Year (not Xmas)
Grades: STB 2 Star
0141 556 7654 Mr Passway
Fax: 0141 402 3655
passway@seton.prestel.co.uk
D: £16.00–£17.00 **S:** £17.00–£18.00
Beds: 4F 2D 1T 1S **Baths:** 3 Sh
🛇 📺 🛏 📖 Ⅴ 🌢

Rosewood Guest House, 4 Seton
Terrace, Glasgow, G31 2HU.
Victorian House near City Centre, close to
many city attractions.
Open: All Year
Grades: STB 2 Stars
0141 550 1500 Ms Turner
Fax: 01555 393876
rosewoodguesthouse@hotmail.com
D: £17.00–£20.00 **S:** £19.00–£22.00
Beds: 3F 2T 1D 2S **Baths:** 3 Sh
🛏 🅿 📺 🛉 🏛 Ⓥ ♣ cc

GLASGOW   Dowanhill

NS5667   ⚓ Orchard Park Hotel, Bellahoustow
Hotel

The Terrace House Hotel, 14
Belhaven Terrace, Glasgow, G12 0TG.
Open: All Year
Grades: STB 2 Star
0141 337 3377 (also fax)
Mrs Black
admin@the-terrace.fsnet.co.uk
D: £29.00–£39.00 **S:** £49.00–£65.00
Beds: 4F 3D 5T 1S **Baths:** 12 En 1 Pr
🛏 ⅘ 📺 🛉 ✕ 🏛 Ⓥ ♣ cc
'B' Listed terraced townhouse, built circa
1860, boasting fine period features, such
as ornate cornices, wall friezes and
columned entrance. well connected to
transport links to city centre, Glasgow
Airport and Loch Lomond. A friendly
welcome awaits you.

GLASGOW   Drumbreck

NS5663   ⚓ Sherbrock Castle

Glasgow Guest House, 56 Dumbreck
Road, Glasgow, G41 5NP.
Turn of the century, red sandstone house,
antique decoration, friendly welcome.
Open: All Year
Grades: STB 3 Star
0141 427 0129
Mr Bristow
brian.muir@ukonline.co.uk
D: fr £20.00 **S:** fr £25.00
Beds: 3D 3T 1S 1F **Baths:** 8 En
🛏 🅿 (2) 📺 🛉 🏛 ♣ ♿ cc

GLASGOW   Govanhill

NS5862

Dunkeld Hotel, 10-12 Queens Drive,
Glasgow, G42 8BS.
Open: All Year
Grades: STB 2 Star, RAC 1 Star
0141 424 0160
P Martin
Fax: 0141 423 4437
dunkeldhot@aol.com
D: £22.00–£29.95 **S:** £30.00–£44.95
Beds: 4F 8T 11D 4S **Baths:** 21 En 6 Sh
🛏 🅿 (10) ⅘ 📺 🛉 ✕ 🏛 Ⓥ ♣ cc
Set in one of Glasgow's premier
conservation streets overlooking Queen's
Park. Elegant Victorian villa has bar,
restaurant, comfortable rooms with
satellite TV/tea/coffee
facilities/hairdryers/ironing boards &
mostly ensuite. Private parking. Near
Hampden National Stadium/Burrell
Collection.

BATHROOMS
Pr - Private
Sh - Shared
En - Ensuite

GLASGOW   Muirend

NS5760

16 Bogton Avenue, Muirend, Glasgow,
G44 3JJ.
Quiet red sandstone terraced private
house adjacent station, 12 mins city
centre.
Open: All Year (not Xmas)
0141 637 4402 (also fax)
Mrs Paterson
apaterson@gofornet.co.uk
D: £20.00 **S:** £22.00
Beds: 1D 2S **Baths:** 2 Sh
🅿 (2) ⅘ 📺 ✕ 🏛 Ⓥ ♣

Inverkip

NS2072

The Foresters, Station Road, Inverkip,
Greenock, Renfrewshire, PA16 0AY.
Charming Victorian villa in conservation
village. Five minutes walk to Scotland's
premier marina.
Open: All Year (not Xmas)
01475 521433 (also fax)
Mrs Wallace
forestershouse@msn.com
D: £22.00–£26.00 **S:** £20.00–£31.00
Beds: 1D 2T **Baths:** 3 En
🅿 (2) ⅘ 🛉 🏛 Ⓥ ♣ cc

Kilbarchan

NS4063   ⚓ Trust Inn

Gladstone Farmhouse, Burntshields
Road, Kilbarchan, Johnstone,
Renfrewshire, PA10 2PB.
Quiet countryside, 10 minutes Glasgow
airport on direct route.
Open: All Year
01505 702579 (also fax)
Mrs Douglas
D: £18.00 **S:** £20.00
Beds: 1F 1D 1T **Baths:** 1 Sh
🛏 🅿 (6) 📺 🛉 ✕ 🏛 Ⓥ ♣ ♿

Kilmacolm

NS3669   ⚓ Pullman

Margaret's Mill Farm, High Greenock
Road, Kilmacolm, Renfrewshire, PA13 4TG.
200-year-old farmhouse set in beautiful
valley. Comfortable spacious bedrooms
with colour TV.
Open: All Year
01505 873716
Mrs Henderson
D: £15.00–£18.00 **S:** £15.00–£18.00
Beds: 1F 1D 1T
🛏 🅿 (8) ⅘ 📺 ❄ ♣

All details shown are as
supplied by B&B owners in
Autumn 2000

Lochwinnoch

NS3559   ⚓ Mossend Hotel, Gateside Inn,
Brown Bull

Garnock Lodge, Lochwinnoch,
Renfrewshire, PA12 4JT.
Open: All Year
Grades: STB 4 Star , AA 4 Diamond
01505 503680 (also fax)
Mr & Mrs McMeechan
garnocklodge@cwcom.net
D: £18.00–£21.00 **S:** £25.00–£30.00
Beds: 1D 2T 1S **Baths:** 2 En 1 Sh
🛏 🅿 (4) 📺 🛉 ✕ 🏛 Ⓥ ♣ cc
A warm welcome awaits you at detached
house in rural situation easy access to
Glasgow Airport via main route also Loch
Lomond and Ayrshire coast, walking,
fishing, golf, cycling and bird watching,
home baking log fires, ensuite, off road
parking.

East Lochhead, Largs Road,
Lochwinnoch, Renfrewshire, PA12 4DX.
Beautifully restored farmhouse. Loch
views, gardens. Taste of Scotland.
Open: All Year
Grades: STB 4 Star, AA 5 Diamond,
Premier selected
01505 842610 (also fax)
Mrs Anderson
winnoch@aol.com
D: £30.00–£32.50 **S:** £30.00–£35.00
Beds: 1T 2D **Baths:** 3 En
🛏 🅿 (6) ⅘ 📺 🛉 ✕ 🏛 Ⓥ ♣ ♿ cc

Milngavie

NS5574   ⚓ Allander Bar, Cross Keys

13 Craigdhu Avenue, Milngavie,
Glasgow, G62 6DX.
Very comfortable family house where a
warm welcome is assured.
Open: Mar to Oct
Grades: STB 3 Star
0141 956 3439 Mrs Ogilvie
D: £18.00 **S:** £20.00–£25.00
Beds: 1F 1T
🛏 🅿 (4) ⅘ 📺 🛉 🏛 Ⓥ ♣

Westview, 1 Dougalston Gardens South,
Milngavie, Glasgow, G62 6HS.
Modern detached, unique, comfortable,
convenient to West Highland Way.
Open: All Year
0141 956 5973 Mr & Mrs McColl
D: £20.00 **S:** £24.00
Beds: 1F 1D 1T **Baths:** 3 En
🛏 🅿 (6) ⅘ Ⓥ ♣

RATES
D = Price range per person
sharing in a double room
S = Price range for a
single room

Paisley

NS4863　◀ *Lord Lounsdale, Paraffin Lamp*

Accara Guest House, *75 Maxwellton Road, Paisley, Renfrewshire, PA1 2RB.*
Grade II Listed building close to airport, museum, university, hospital.
Open: All Year
Grades: STB 2 Star
0141 887 7604 Mrs Stevens
Fax: 0141 887 1589
D: £20.00 **S:** £25.00
Beds: 1F 1T 1S **Baths:** 2 Sh
🛏 (4) ⏸ 📺 🛒 Ⓥ ♨ cc

Planning a longer stay? Always ask for any special rates

All details shown are as supplied by B&B owners in Autumn 2000

Myfarrclan Guest House, *146 Corsebar Road, Paisley, Renfrewshire, PA2 9NA.*
Nestling in leafy suburb of Paisley, lovingly restored bungalow offering many thoughtful extras.
Open: All Year
0141 884 8285 Mr & Mrs Farr
Fax: 0141 581 1566
myfarrclan_qwest@compuserve.com
D: £32.50–£35.00 **S:** £40.00–£60.00
Beds: 2D 1T **Baths:** 2 En 1 Pr
🛏 🅿 (2) ⏸ 📺 ✕ 🛒 Ⓥ ❀ ♨

Stepps

NS6668　◀ *Dorsey's, Park Bar, Mitchell's, Stravaigan's, Orchard Park, Bellahoustow Hotel, Garfield House, Highlanders Park, Snaffil Bit*

Avenue End B&B, *21 West Avenue, Stepps, Glasgow, G33 6ES.*
Open: All Year
Grades: STB 3 Star B&B
0141 779 1990 Mrs Wells
Fax: 0141 779 1990
avenueend@aol.com
D: £20.00–£25.00 **S:** £25.00–£27.50
Beds: 1F 1D 1S **Baths:** 2 En 1 Pr
🛏 🅿 (2) ⏸ 📺 🛒 Ⓥ ♨
Self built family home situated down quiet tree-lined lane. Glasgow east off A80, main route to Stirling (Braveheart Country) and the North. Easy commuting by public or own transport. M8 Exit 12. Home from home - warm welcome assured.

Highland

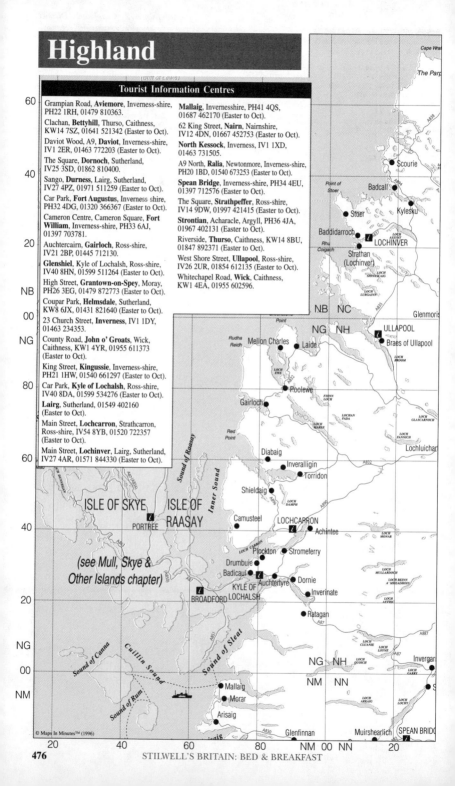

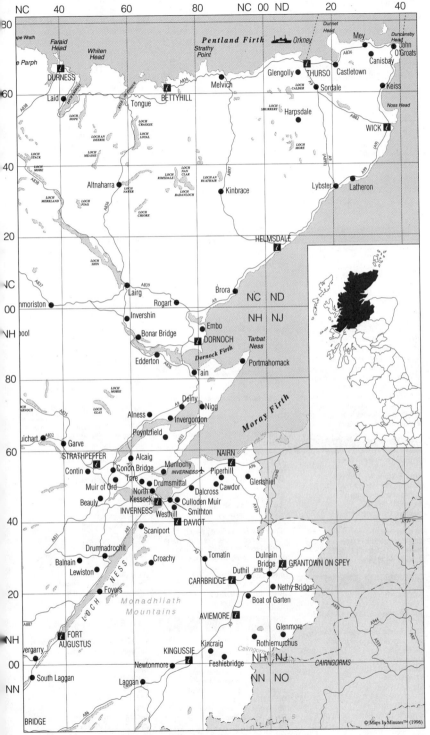

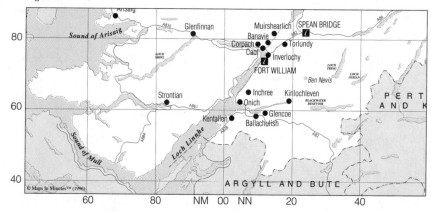

Achintee

NG9441   *Carron Restaurant, Strathcarron Hotel*

The Shieling, *Achintee, Strathcarron, Ross-shire, IV54 8YX.*
Open: All Year
01520 722364
Mrs Levy
jlevyshieling@talk21.com
D: £18.00–£20.00 **S:** £17.00
Beds: 2T 1S **Baths:** 1 En 1 Sh
Comfortable, homely, croft cottage, tastefully extended and modernised, only minutes from Strathcarron Railway station, surrounded by spectacular scenery; a central base for many leisure activities, particularly hill waking and climbing, and for day trips to such places as Skye and Inverewe Gardens.

Alcaig

NH5657   *Mallard, Cottage Bar*

Dun Eistein, *Alcaig, Conon Bridge, Dingwall, Ross-shire, IV7 8HS.*
Highland country cottage.
Open: May to Oct
Grades: STB 4 Star
01349 862210
Mrs Morrison
D: £18.50–£19.50 **S:** £24.00
Beds: 1F 1D **Baths:** 1 En 1 Pr

Alness

NH6569

An Laimhrig, *82 Obsdale Park, Alness, IV17 0TR.*
Modern detached house ideal touring centre, cyclists stopover for John O' Groats.
Open: All Year
Grades: STB 3 Star
01349 882016
Ms MacDonald
D: £17.00–£22.00
S: £18.00–£25.00
Beds: 1F 2T 1D **Baths:** 2 En 1 Sh

Altnaharra

NC5635

1 Macleod Crescent, *Altnaharra, Lairg, Sutherland, IV27 4UG.*
Hamlet pop. 31 nestling between 2 Munros, Ben Klebrig & Ben Hope, ideal base hillwalking. **Open:** Easter to
Grades: STB 3 Star
01549 411258 Mrs Barrie
D: fr £18.00 **S:** fr £23.00
Beds: 1F 2T **Baths:** 3 En

Ardelve

NG8727   *Loch Duich Hotel*

Caberfeidh House, *Ardelve, Kyle of Lochalsh, IV40 8DY.*
Beautiful lochside house with superb views of Eilean Donan Castle.
Open: All Year (not Xmas/New Year)
Grades: STB 2 Star
01599 555293 Mr Newton
D: £18.00–£22.00 **S:** £25.00–£30.00
Beds: 2T 3D 1S **Baths:** 2 En 1 Sh

Arisaig

NM6586   *Old Library*

Cnoc Na Faire Hotel, *Back of Keppoch, Arisaig, Inverness-shire, PH39 4NS.*
Family hotel overlooking Skye, sandy beaches. 9-hole golf course nearby.
Open: Mar to Oct
01687 450249 Miss MacDonald
D: £20.00–£25.00 **S:** £20.00–£35.00
Beds: 3D 2T 2S **Baths:** 2 En 1 Sh

Arnisdale

NG8410   *Glenelg Inn*

Corran, *Arnisdale, Kyle of Lochalsh, Ross-shire, IV40 8JJ.*
House is situated in small village surrounded by massive mountains overlooking Loch Horn. **Open:** All Year
01599 522336 Mrs Nash
D: £13.00–£16.00 **S:** £13.00–£16.00
Beds: 1F 1S **Baths:** 1 Sh

Auchtertyre

NG8328

Caladh Solas, *Auchtertyre, Kyle of Lochalsh, Ross-shire, IV40 8EG.*
Open: All Year (not Xmas)
Grades: STB 3 Star
01599 566317 Mrs Knowles
knowles@caladhsolas.freeserve.co.uk
D: £16.00–£22.00 **S:** £16.00–£30.00
Beds: 1D 1T 1S **Baths:** 1 En 1 Sh
Quality bed and breakfast with a warm welcome guaranteed. Set amid spectacular scenery, an ideal location for exploring Skye and the highlands. An experience you will want to repeat.

Aviemore

NH8912   *Glenmore Lodge, Cairngorm Hotel, Old Bridge Inn, Mackenzie's, WInking Owl*

Cairngorm Guest House, *Grampian Road, Aviemore, Inverness-shire, PH22 1RP.*
Open: Easter to Easter
01479 810630 (also fax)
Mrs Conn
conns@lineone.net
D: £18.00–£25.00
S: £20.00–£28.00
Beds: 1F 5D 3T
Baths: 9 En
Experience a real Scottish welcome. Have coffee with us on arrival. Relax in our guest lounge in front of a real fire with views of the Cairngorm mountains. Handy for train/bus. Two minutes walk to the centre. 24 hour access to rooms.

Cairn Eilrig, *Glenmore, Aviemore, Inverness-shire, PH22 1QU.*
Highland welcome. Secluded bungalow in Glenmore forest park panoramic views.
Open: All Year
Grades: STB 3 Star
01479 861223
Mrs Ferguson
D: £17.00–£18.00
S: £17.00–£20.00
Beds: 1F 1T **Baths:** 1 Sh

Ravenscraig Guest House,
Aviemore, Inverness-shire, PH22 1RP.
Central village location. Ideal for
exploring highlands or just relaxing.
Open: All Year
Grades: STB 2 Star GH, AA 3 Diamond,
RAC 3 Diamond
01479 810278 Mr & Mrs Gatenby
Fax: 01479 812742
ravenscrg@aol.com
D: £18.00–£24.00 **S:** £18.00–£24.00
Beds: 2F 5D 4T 1S **Baths:** 12 En
🛇 🅿 (16) 🖵 🕻 🛍 🛦 cc

Rowan Tree Country Hotel, Loch
Alvie, Aviemore, Inverness-shire, PH22 1QB.
C17th Coaching Inn. Characterful
bedrooms. Comfortable lounges. A warm
welcome. **Open:** All Year
Grades: STB 3 Star
01479 810207 (also fax)
enquires@rowantreehotel.com
D: £26.50–£31.50 **S:** £36.50–£41.50
Beds: 2F 3T 4D 1S **Baths:** 10 En 1 Sh
🛇 (12) 🅿 🖵 🕻 🗙 🛍 🗓 ✻ 🛦 cc

Eriskay, Craig-na-gower, Aviemore,
Inverness-shire, PH22 1RW.
Quietly situated warm and comfortable
house good base for touring.
Open: All Year **Grades:** STB 4 Star
01479 810717 Fax: 01479 812312
eriskay@cali.co.uk
D: £17.00–£20.00 **S:** £22.00–£26.00
Beds: 2D 1T **Baths:** 3 En
🅿 (4) 🖵 🛍 🗓 🛦

Dunroamin, Craig Gower Avenue,
Aviemore, Inverness-shire, PH22 1RN.
Comfortable, friendly, family-run home.
Rooms tasteful and spacious.
Open: All Year **Grades:** STB 2 Star
01479 810698 (also fax)
Mrs Sheffield
D: £16.00–£25.00 **S:** £20.00–£40.00
Beds: 2F 2D **Baths:** 3 En 1 Pr
🛇 🅿 (4) 🗠 🖵 🛍 🗓 ✻ 🛦

Waverley, 35 Strathspey Avenue,
Aviemore, Inverness-shire, PH22 1SN.
Modern comfortable bungalow in quiet
area. **Open:** All Year (not Xmas)
01479 811226 Mrs Fraser
maggie.fraser@talk21.com
D: £17.00–£20.00 **S:** £20.00–£25.00
Beds: 1D 1T **Baths:** 1 En 1 Pr
🛇 (8) 🗠 🛍 🗓 🛦 👤

Ardlogie Guest House, Dalfaber
Road, Aviemore, Inverness-shire, PH22 1PU.
Centre of Aviemore views over River Spey
to Cairngorm Mountains.
Open: All Year
Grades: STB 2 Star
01479 810747 D: £17.00 **S:** £17.00
Beds: 4D 1T **Baths:** 5 En
🛇 🅿 (3) 🖵 🕻 🛍 🛦 cc

Ryvoan, Grampian Road, Aviemore,
Inverness-shire, PH22 1RY.
Beautiful modern bungalow with patio
overlooking the Cairngorms situated at
north end of village.
Open: Dec to Oct
01479 810805 Mrs Cristall
D: £16.00 **S:** £18.00
Beds: 1T 1D **Baths:** 2 En
🅿 (3) 🖵 🕻 🛍 🛦

Badachro

NG7773 🍴 Badachro Inn

Lochside, Aird Road, Badachro, Gairloch,
Wester Ross, IV21 2AB.
Open: All Year
Grades: STB 3 Star
01445 741295 Mrs Foster
D: £21.00–£22.00
Beds: 1F 1D **Baths:** 2 En
🛇 🅿 🗠 🖵 🛍 🛦
All rooms face south across beautiful
sheltered Badachro Bay with its many
boats to the Torridon Mountains and the
village with its unique Inn serving
excellent food. Large sized bedrooms
with large superior bathrooms. Exclusive
situation with immediate shoreline
access.

Badcall (Scourie)

NC1542 🍴 Scourie Hotel, Anchorage Rest

Mountain View, Upper Badcall,
Scourie, Lairg, Sutherland, IV27 4TH.
All rooms overlooking beautiful Badcall
Bay. Near village, bird sanctuary.
Open: All Year
01971 502343 Mrs Macleod
olivmcl@aol.com
D: £15.50 **S:** £25.00
Beds: 1F 1T 1D **Baths:** 2 Sh
🛇 🅿 (3) 🖵 🗙 🛦

Baddidarroch

NC0822

Veyatie, 66 Baddidarroch, Lochinver,
Lairg, Sutherland, IV27 4LP.
Veyatie is a modern bungalow situated in
a beautiful, peaceful setting.
Open: All Year (not Xmas)
Grades: STB 4 Star
01571 844424 Mrs Chapman
veyatie@baddid.freeserve.co.uk
D: £20.00–£25.00 **S:** £30.00–£50.00
Beds: 2D 1T **Baths:** 2 En 1 Pr
🅿 (3) 🗠 🖵 🕻 🛍 🛦

Ballachulish

NN0858 🍴 Glencoe Hotel, Laroch Bar

Fern Villa Guest House, Loanfern,
Ballachulish, Argyll, PH49 4JE.
Open: All Year
Grades: STB 3 Star, AA 4 Diamond
01855 811393 Mr Chandler
Fax: 01855 811727
fernvilla@aol.com
D: £20.00–£22.00 **S:** £25.00–£27.00
Beds: 3D 2T **Baths:** 5 En
🛇 🅿 (5) 🗠 🖵 🗙 🛍 🗓 🛦
A warm welcome awaits you in this
beautifully upgraded Victorian house. The
village is surrounded by the spectacular
lochs & mountains of Glencoe. Natural
cooking of Scotland forms the basis of
our home made dinner menus. Non-
smoking.

Planning a longer stay? Always
ask for any special rates

Lyn Leven Guest House, West
Laroch, Ballachulish, Argyll, PA39 4JP.
Very warm Highland welcome in modern
comfortable family-run award-winning
guest house.
Open: All Year
Grades: STB 4 Star, AA 4 Diamond, RAC
4 Diamond
01855 811392 Mrs Macleod
Fax: 01855 811600
D: £20.00–£25.00 **S:** £25.00–£30.00
Beds: 4F 4D 4T **Baths:** 12 En
🛇 🅿 (10) 🖵 🕻 🗙 🛍 🗓 🛦 cc

Riverside House, Ballachulish, Argyll,
PH49 4JE.
Spacious rooms in modern house
overlooking river mountains and loch.
Open: Easter to Oct
Grades: STB 3 Star
01855 811473 Mrs Watt
D: £16.00–£20.00 **S:** £18.00–£22.00
Beds: 2D 1T **Baths:** 1 En 1 Sh
🛇 (2) 🅿 (4) 🗠 🖵 🛍 🛦

Inverlaroch, Albert Road, Ballachulish,
Argyll, PH49 4JR.
Modern, comfortable, spacious, homely
bungalow. Excellent for walking and
climbing.
Open: All Year (not Xmas)
01855 811726 Mrs Castles
inverlaroch@talk21.com
D: £17.00–£21.00 **S:** £34.00–£42.00
Beds: 1F 1D 1T **Baths:** 3 En
🛇 (3) 🅿 (5) 🗠 🖵 🛍 🛦

Tigh Ard, Brecklet, Ballachulish, Argyll,
PA39 4JG.
Lovely family bungalow panoramic view,
private parking.
Open: Easter to Sep
01855 811328 Mrs Dow
D: £16.00
Beds: 1D 1T **Baths:** 2 Sh
🅿 (2) 🗠 🖵 🛍

Balnain

NH4430

Glenurquhart House Hotel, Balnain,
Drumnadrochit, Inverness, IV63 6TJ.
In a scenic location between Loch Ness
and Glen Affric.
Open: Mar to Dec
Grades: STB 3 Star
01456 476234 C Hughes
D: £25.00–£35.00 **S:** £25.00–£40.00
Beds: 2F 2D 2T 2S **Baths:** 6 En 1 Sh
🛇 🅿 (8) 🖵 🗙 🛍 🗓 🛦 cc

Banavie

NN1177 🍴 Moorings Hotel, Lochy Bar

Rushfield House, Tomonie, Banavie,
Fort William, Inverness-shire, PH33 7LX.
Modern house with excellent views of
Ben Nevis situated 3 miles from Fort
William.
Open: Mar to Oct
Grades: STB 3 Star
01397 772063 Ms Corbett
rushbb0063@aol.com
D: £18.00–£25.00
Beds: 2F 1D **Baths:** 3 En
🛇 🅿 (3) 🗠 🖵 🛍 🗓 🛦

New House, *Shenghan Bridge, Banavie, Fort William, Inverness-shire, PH33 7PB.*
Open: March to Nov
01397 772228 Miss Ross
shenghan-
chalets@fortwilliam59.freeserve.co.uk
D: £18.00–£20.00 **S:** £18.00
Beds: 1T 1D **Baths:** 2 En
🛇 ⅃ 📺 ⏰ ✕ 📖 🖳 CC
Stunning views to Ben Nevis and Anoch Moe. Friendly family atmosphere. Situated on the banks of the Caledonian Canal. Converted barn restaurant adjacent to the Bed & Breakfast.

Grianan, *4 Lochiel Crescent, Banavie, Fort William, Inverness-shire, PH33 7LZ.*
Situated by Caledonian Canal. Fine views towards Ben Nevis.
Open: May to Sept
Grades: STB 3 Star
01397 772659 Mrs Maclean
imacleangrianan@hotmail.com
D: £15.00–£17.00 **S:** £18.00–£23.50
Beds: 1D 1F
🛇 (5) 🅿 (3) 🖳 ⏰ 📖 🖳 ♿ 🖳

Quaich Cottage, *Upper Banavie, Banavie, Fort William, Inverness-shire, PH33 7LX.*
Modern home on an elevated rural site. Spacious accommodation and a warm welcome.
Open: All Year (not Xmas)
01397 772799 (also fax)
D: £17.00–£20.00 **S:** £25.00–£35.00
Beds: 1F 1D 1T **Baths:** 3 En
🛇 (8) 🅿 (3) 📺 📖 🖳 🖳

Beauly

NH5246 🛏 *Old Arms Hotel, North Kessock Hotel, Moorings Hotel, Achilty Hotel*

Hillview Park, *Muir of Ord, Ross-shire, IV6 7XS.*
Rural situation, adjacent to golf course. Ground floor bungalow.
Open: Easter to Oct
Grades: STB 3 Star
01463 870787 Mrs Peterkin
D: £17.00–£19.00 **S:** £18.00–£20.00
Beds: 1F 1D 1T **Baths:** 3 En
🅿 (3) ⅃ 📺 📖 🖳

Bettyhill

NC7061

Shenley, *Bettyhill, Thurso, Caithness, KW14 7SS.*
Ideal centre for touring North Highlands, river and sandy beaches.
Open: Easter to Oct
01641 521421 Mrs Allan
D: £12.50–£18.00 **S:** £12.50–£18.00
Beds: 2T 1S **Baths:** 2 Sh
🛇 (5) 🅿 📺 ⏰ ✕ 📖 🖳

RATES

D = Price range per person sharing in a double room
S = Price range for a single room

Boat of Garten

NH9418 🛏 *Boat, Craigard Hotel, Heatherbank, Lisi's*

The Old Ferrymans House, *Boat of Garten, Inverness-shire, PH24 3BY.*
Open: All Year
01479 831370 (also fax) Ms Matthews
D: fr £19.50 **S:** fr £19.50
Beds: 1T 1D 2S **Baths:** 2 Sh
🛇 🅿 (4) ⅃ ⏰ ✕ 📖 🖳 🖳
Which? Recommended former ferryman's house, just across River Spey from village, welcoming, homely, comfortable. Sitting room with wood stove, many books, no TV. No set breakfast times, home-cooked meals with Highland specialities. Numerous walks, beautiful Strathspey countryside and Cairngorm mountains, castles, distilleries.

Avingormack Guest House, *Boat of Garten, Inverness-shire, PH24 3BT.*
Breathtaking views of the mountains, award winning food - just perfect.
Open: All Year **Grades:** STB 3 Star
01479 831614 Mrs Ferguson
avin.gormack@ukgateway.net
D: £19.00–£22.00 **S:** fr £19.50
Beds: 1F 2D 1T **Baths:** 2 En 1 Sh
🛇 🅿 (6) ⅃ 📺 📖 🖳 🖳 CC

Chapelton Steading, *Boat Of Garten, Inverness-shire, PH24 3BU.*
Spacious rural retreat. Charming garden with views of Cairngorm Mountains.
Open: March to Nov **Grades:** STB 4 Star
01479 831327 Mrs Smyth
chapelton@btinternet.com
D: £21.00–£22.00 **S:** £23.00–£25.00
Beds: 2T 1D **Baths:** 3 En
🛇 (10) 🅿 (4) ⅃ 📺 🖳

Heathbank - The Victorian House, *Drumuillie Road, Boat of Garten, Inverness-shire, PH24 3BD.*
Beautiful of character, house full of curiosities; each bedroom different in style and atmosphere. **Open:** All Year
01479 831234 Mr Burge
quirky@heathbank32.freeserve.co.uk
D: £25.00–£35.00 **S:** £30.00–£50.00
Beds: 5D 2T **Baths:** 7 En
🛇 (8) 🅿 (8) ⅃ ✕ 📖 🖳 🖳

Glen Sanda, *Street Of Kincardine, Boat of Garten, Inverness-shire, PH24 3BY.*
Modern bungalow, rural setting, near RSPB and all sporting amenities.
Open: All Year
01479 831494 Mrs Lyons
D: £20.00–£22.00 **S:** £20.00–£24.00
Beds: 2D 1T **Baths:** 3 En
🅿 (3) ⅃ 📺 📖 🖳

Mountain Innovations, *Fraoch Lodge, Deshar Road, Boat of Garten, Invernesshire, PH24 3BN.*
Fully equipped drying room, mountain weather forecasts. No restrictive meal times. **Open:** All Year
01479 831331 (also fax)
Mr Bateman
info@scotmountain.co.uk
D: £9.00–£15.50 **S:** £9.00–£15.50
Beds: 3F 3T **Baths:** 3 Sh
🛇 🅿 (12) ⅃ ⏰ 📖 🖳 🖳

Bonar Bridge

NH6191 🛏 *Dornoch Bridge Inn, Lady Ross, The Dunroamin*

Kyle House, *Dornoch Road, Bonar Bridge, Ardgay, Sutherland, IV24 3EB.*
Superb old Scottish house offering excellent accommodation. Ideal touring base.
Open: Feb to Nov
Grades: AA 3 Diamond, RAC 3 Diamond
01863 766360 (also fax)
Mrs Thomson
kyle.hse.@talk21.com
D: £19.00–£22.00 **S:** £24.00
Beds: 2F 1D 2T 1S **Baths:** 3 En 1 Sh
🛇 (4) 🅿 (6) ⅃ 📺 📖 🖳

Braes of Ullapool

NH1493 🛏 *Argyll Hotel*

Blawearie, *16 Corry Heights, Braes of Ullapool, Ullapool, Ross-shire, IV26 2SZ.*
Modern detached house with spectacular lochside views and warm hospitality.
Open: May to Sep
01854 612790 Mrs Clark
D: £16.00–£18.00 **S:** £16.00–£18.00
Beds: 1D 1T 1S **Baths:** 2 Sh
🛇 🅿 (3) ⅃ 📺 📖 🖳 🖳

Brora

NC9004 🛏 *Royal Marine Hotel, Links Hotel, Sutherland Arms*

Non Smokers Haven, *Tigh Fada, 18 Golf Road, Brora, Sutherland, KW9 6QS.*
Top quality welcoming home. Also self-catering, prime seaside location.
Open: All Year (not Xmas/New Year)
Grades: STB 4 Star
01408 621332 (also fax)
Mr & Mrs Clarkson
D: fr £18.00 **S:** fr £20.00
Beds: 1D 2T **Baths:** 1 En 2 Pr
🛇 (5) 🅿 (6) ⅃ 📺 📖 🖳

Glenaveron, *Golf Road, Brora, Sutherland, KW9 6QS.*
Open: All Year
Grades: STB 4 Star, AA 4 Diamond
01408 621601 (also fax)
Mr Fortune
glenaveron@hotmail.com
D: £24.00–£28.00 **S:** £28.00–£34.00
Beds: 1F 1D 1T **Baths:** 3 En
🛇 🅿 ⅃ 📺 📖 🖳 🖳 2 CC
A luxurious Edwardian house in mature gardens close to Brora golf club and beaches. Only a 25 minute drive to the famous Royal Dornoch golf club. Ideal base for touring the Highlands and Orkney. Non smoking. Friendly family home.

Ar Dachaidh, *Badnellan, Brora, Sutherland, KW9 6NQ.*
Traditional croft house, quiet crofting area, ideal golf, fishing, touring.
Open: Mar to Nov
Grades: STB 2 Star
01408 621658 (also fax)
Ms MacDonald
badnellan@madasafish.com
D: £17.00 **S:** £17.00
Beds: 1D 1T 1S **Baths:** 1 Sh
🛇 (12) 🅿 (3) 📺 ⏰ ✕ 📖 🖳 🖳

Sutherland Arms Hotel, Brora,
Sutherland, KW9 6NX.
Comfortable, traditional, family-run inn,
located village centre, on A9 route.
Open: All Year
01408 621209 Mr Munro
D: £19.00–£27.00 **S:** £19.00–£27.00
Beds: 2F 2D 2T 4S **Baths:** 2 En 1 Sh
🛏 🄿 (4) 🖂 🍴 ✕ 🛋 Ⓥ 🛢

Camusteel

NG7042 🍴 Applecross Inn, Flower Tunnel

Raon Mor, Camusteel, Applecross,
Strathcarron, Ross-shire, IV54 8LT.
Modern croft house wonderful views.
Ideal for hill walking and wildlife.
Open: May to Oct
01520 744260 Mrs Thompson
D: £14.50–£15.00
Beds: 2D 1T **Baths:** 1 Sh
🛏 🄿 (3) 🖂 🛋 Ⓥ

Canisbay

ND3472

Bencorragh House, Upper Gills,
Canisbay, John o' Groats, Wick, Caithness,
KW1 4YB.
Working croft. Panoramic views across
Pentland Firth near seasonal Orkney
ferry.
Open: Mar to Oct
Grades: STB 3 Star, AA 3 Diamond
01955 611449 (also fax)
Mrs Barton
D: £20.00–£21.00 **S:** £23.00–£25.00
Beds: 1F 2D 1T **Baths:** 4 En
🛏 (5) 🄿 (6) 🗶 🖂 🍴 ✕ 🛋 Ⓥ 🛢 CC

Caol

NN1076 🍴 Lochy Bar

Connamara, 27 Camaghael Road, Caol,
Fort William, PH33 7HU.
The front of the house faces Ben Nevis,
back looks onto Caledonian Canal.
Open: All Year
Grades: STB 2 Star
01397 702901 Mrs Mcginlay
Fax: 01397 700566
e.mcginlay@amserve.net
D: £17.00–£18.00 **S:** £20.00–£25.00
Beds: 2F
🛏 🄿 🗶 Ⓥ 🛢

Carrbridge

NH9022 🍴 Cairn Hotel, Rowanlea, Struan
Hotel

Cairn Hotel, Main Road, Carrbridge,
Inverness-shire, PH23 3AS.
Open: All Year (not Xmas)
Grades: STB 3 Star
01479 841212 Mr Kirk
Fax: 01479 841362
cairn.carrbridge@talk21.com
D: £19.00–£22.00 **S:** £19.00–£26.00
Beds: 2F 2D 1T 2S **Baths:** 4 En 1 Sh
🛏 🄿 (15) 🖂 🛢 CC
Enjoy the country pub atmosphere; log
fire, malt whiskies, real ales and
affordable food in this family-owned
village centre hotel close to the historic
bridge. A perfect base for touring
Cairngorms, Loch Ness, Whisky Trail and
beyond.

Carrmoor Guest House, Carr Road,
Carrbridge, Inverness-shire, PH23 3AD.
Licensed, family-run, warm welcome.
Popular restaurant, chef proprietor.
Open: All Year
Grades: STB 3 Star, AA 4 Diamond
01479 841244 (also fax) Mrs Stitt
christine@carrmoorguesthouse.co.uk
D: £19.50–£21.50 **S:** £22.00
Beds: 1F 3D 2T **Baths:** 6 En
🛏 🄿 (6) 🖂 🍴 ✕ 🛋 Ⓥ ❋ 🛢 CC

Craigellachie House, Main Street,
Carrbridge, Inverness-shire, PH23 3AS.
Traditional house in centre of small
Highland village on main tourist routes.
Open: All Year
Grades: STB 3 Star GH
01479 841641 Mrs Pedersen
e.pedersen@talk21.com
D: £16.00–£19.00 **S:** £16.00–£25.00
Beds: 2F 2D 2T 1S **Baths:** 3 En 2 Sh
🛏 🄿 (8) 🗶 🖂 ✕ 🛋 Ⓥ 🛢 CC

Pine Ridge, Carrbridge, Inverness-shire,
PH23 3AA.
Pine Ridge is a beautiful 100 year old
home. **Open:** All Year
01479 841646 Mrs Weston
jane.weston@tesco.net
D: £16.00–£20.00 **S:** £16.00–£25.00
Beds: 1F 1D 1T **Baths:** 1 En 1 Sh
🛏 🄿 (6) 🗶 🖂 🛋 🛢

Castletown (Thurso)

ND1967 🍴 Northern Sands Hotel

Greenland House, Main Street,
Castletown, Thurso, Caithness, KW14 8TU.
Greenland Guest House is a Victorian
period house, restored retaining many
original features.
Open: All Year (not Xmas)
01847 821694 (also fax)
Y Pollard
dgpolla@aol.com
D: £16.00–£20.00 **S:** £20.00–£25.00
Beds: 3D 2T **Baths:** 3 En 2 Sh
🛏 🄿 🗶 🖂 🛋 Ⓥ 🛢

Cawdor

NH8449 🍴 Cawdor Tavern

Dallaschyle, Cawdor, Nairn, IV12 5XS.
A gardener's delight. Only birds and
wildlife disturb the peace.
Open: All Year
01667 493422 Mrs MacLeod
Fax: 01667 493638
bookings@dallaschyle.fsnet.co.uk
D: £17.00 **S:** £25.00–£20.00
Beds: 1F 1D 1S **Baths:** 2 Sh
🛏 (2) 🄿 (4) 🗶 🖂 🛋 🛢 ් CC

Conon Bridge

NH5455 🍴 Conon Bridge Hotel

Conon Bridge Hotel, Conon Bridge,
Dingwall, Ross-shire, IV7 8HD.
Charming Scottish Highland inn offering
excellent comfort & fresh traditional food.
Open: All Year
01349 861500 Mr Jack
D: £17.50–£20.00 **S:** £21.00–£23.00
Beds: 1F 5D 2T 5S
🛏 🄿 (20) 🖂 🍴 ✕ 🛋 Ⓥ 🛢 CC

Contin

NH4555 🍴 Achilty Hotel

Millbrae, Contin, Strathpeffer, Ross-
shire, IV14 9EB.
Traditional highland house, 100 years
old,relax in peace, watch wildlife, feel
welcome.
Open: All Year
01997 421368
Mrs Redfern
D: £13.50–£15.00 **S:** £20.00
Beds: 1F 1D **Baths:** 1 Sh
🛏 🄿 (4) 🖂 🍴 🛋 Ⓥ 🛢

Corpach

NN0976 🍴 Lochy Bar, Mooring Hotel

Ben Nevis View, Corpach, Fort William,
Inverness-shire, PH33 7JH.
Modern, comfortable house, 5 minutes by
car from Fort William.
Open: Mar to Oct
Grades: STB 3 Star
01397 772131 Mrs Mooney
D: £18.00–£20.00 **S:** £20.00–£25.00
Beds: 1F 1D **Baths:** 2 En
🄿 (4) 🗶 🖂 🛋 🛢

The Neuk, Corpach, Fort William,
Inverness-shire, PH33 7LR.
Modern, privately run, home cooking.
Views over Ben Nevis. Private garden.
Open: All Year (not Xmas)
Grades: STB 2 Star
01397 772244 Mrs McCallum
D: £18.00–£24.00 **S:** £27.00–£36.00
Beds: 2F 1D 1T **Baths:** 4 En
🛏 🄿 (6) 🗶 🖂 🍴 ✕ 🛋 Ⓥ 🛢

Heston, Corpach, Fort William,
Inverness-shire, PH33 7LT.
Comfortable house with excellent views
on road to the Isles.
Open: March - November
Grades: STB 2 Star
01397 772425 Mrs Wynne
D: £18.00–£20.00 **S:** £22.00
Beds: 1F 1D 1T **Baths:** 2 En
🛏 (3) 🄿 (3) 🗶 🖂 🍴 🛋 🛢

Croachy

NH6427 🍴 Dores Inn

The Old Parsonage, Croachy,
Inverness, IV2 6UE.
Our family-run guest house offers
superior accommodation. Ensuite rooms,
lounge and large garden room.
Open: All Year
01808 521441 (also fax)
Isabell Steel
D: £17.50–£25.00 **S:** £20.00–£27.00
Beds: 3D **Baths:** 2 En 1 Pr
🛏 🄿 (6) 🖂 🍴 🛋 🛢 CC

Culloden Moor

NH7345   Cawdor Tavern, Culloden Moor Inn

Westhill House, *Westhill, Inverness, IV1 5BP.*
Open: Easter to Oct
Grades: STB 2 Star
01463 793225 Mrs Honnor
Fax: 01463 792503
janethon@piccolopress.demon.co.uk
D: £18.00–£20.00 **S:** £16.00–£18.00
Beds: 1F 1T 1S **Baths:** 2 En 1 Sh
Spacious, comfortable family home in lovely garden amidst trees, wildlife and glorious views. One mile Culloden Battlefield, three miles Inverness. Perfect for touring Highlands.

Culdoich Farm, *Culloden Muir, Inverness, IV2 5EL.*
Old farmhouse in peaceful surroundings. Good farmhouse cooking.
Open: May to Oct
Grades: STB 3 Star
01463 790268 Mrs Alexander
D: £17.00 **S:** £34.00
Beds: 1F 1T/D **Baths:** 1 Sh

King of Clubs, *Tigh-Na-Ceard, Culloden Moor, Inverness, IV2 5EE.*
A warm, friendly welcome awaits you at King of Clubs. Central to all amenities.
Open: All Year
01463 790476 (also fax)
V P Fraser
jimfraser@kingofclubs.demon.co.uk
D: £17.00–£19.00 **S:** £17.00–£19.00
Beds: 1F 1D 1T 1S **Baths:** 2 En 1 Sh

Dalcross

NH7748   Gun Lodge

Easter Dalziel Farm, *Dalcross, Inverness, IV2 7JL.*
Lovely Victorian farmhouse home on a working stock/arable farm.
Open: All Year (not Xmas/New Year)
01667 462213 (also fax)
Mrs Pottie
D: £17.00–£20.00 **S:** £20.00–£28.00
Beds: 2D 1T **Baths:** 2 Sh
cc

Daviot

NH7239   Deerstalker, Tomatin Inn

Torguish House, *Daviot, Inverness, IV2 5XQ.*
Former manse set in quiet rural area, childhood home of late author Alistair McLean.
Open: All Year
01463 772208 Mr & Mrs Allan
Fax: 01463 772308
amallan@torguish.com
D: £16.00–£22.00 **S:** £20.00–£25.00
Beds: 3F 3D 1T **Baths:** 5 En 2 Pr

Delny

NH7372   Johnnny Foxes

Under Beechwood, *Delny, Kilmvir Easter, , Ross-shire, IV18 ONW.*
Open: Feb to Nov
01862 842685
Mrs Horn
D: £16.00–£17.00 **S:** £16.00–£17.00
Beds: 1F 1T 1D 1S **Baths:** 1 Sh
Overlooking Cromarty Firth offering Traditional and friendly accommodation with good cooking and baking. Babies free. Children from 3 yrs sharing half price. Ideal for touring north and west coasts. Excellent fishing, hill walking, dolphin sea trips. Beautiful beaches.

Diabaig

NG7960

Ben Bhraggie, *Diabaig, Torridon, Achnasheen, Ross-shire, IV22 2HE.*
Comfortable homely cottage - fishing and hill walkers paradise.
Open: Easter to Nov
01445 790268 Mrs Ross
D: £14.00 **S:** £14.00
Beds: 1D 1T

Dornie

NG8826

Castle View, *Upper Ardelve, Dornie, Kyle of Lochalsh, Ross-shire, IV40 8EY.*
Outstanding views across Loch Alsh to Eilean Donan, Loch Duich, Five Sisters of Kintail.
Open: Easter to Oct
01599 555453 (also fax)
Ms McClelland
castleview@j-c-m.freeserve.co.uk
D: fr £20.00
Beds: 2D 1T **Baths:** 3 En

Dornoch

NH8089   Ragle Hotel, Castle Hotel, Sutherland House, Mallin House, Eagle Hotel, Grannie's Heiland Hame

Achandean Bungalow, *The Meadows, Dornoch, Sutherland, IV25 3SF.*
Open: Easter to Oct
Grades: AA 3 Diamond
01862 810413 (also fax)
Mrs Hellier
bhellier@lineone.net
D: £18.00–£22.00
Beds: 2D 1T **Baths:** 2 En 1 Pr
Audrey & Basil Hellier welcome you to our lovely home. Secluded, central position. Tastefully decorated ensuite bedrooms with every comfort. Ideal disabled and OAPs. Weekly rates. Reductions OAPs. Superb touring, walks, beach, golf, birdwatching, countryside, relaxation. Private parking. EM available.

Amalfi, *River Street, Dornoch, Sutherland, IV25 3LY.*
Modern comfortable house alongside golf course. Award winning beach 300m. friendly highland hospitality.
Open: All Year (not Xmas/New Year)
Grades: STB 3 Star
01862 810015 Mrs MacKay
mackay.amalfi@talk21.com
D: £18.00–£21.00 **S:** £20.00–£33.00
Beds: 1F 1T **Baths:** 2 En

Corven, *Station Road, Embo, Dornoch, Sutherland, IV25 3PR.*
Detached bungalow with panoramic views. Ideal base for touring North Scotland.
Open: Feb to Nov
Grades: STB 2 Star
01862 810128 Mrs Fraser
D: fr £16.00 **S:** fr £18.00
Beds: 2D 1T **Baths:** 1 En 1 Sh

Tordarroch, *Castle Street, Dornoch, Sutherland, IV25 3SN.*
Traditional stone built house set within walled gardens, ensuring peace & quiet.
Open: Easter to Oct
Grades: STB 3 Star
01862 810855 Mrs Matherson
D: £19.00–£21.00 **S:** £19.00–£21.00
Beds: 1D 1T 1S **Baths:** 1 En 1 Pr 1 Sh

Rosslyn Villa, *Castle Street, Dornoch, Sutherland, IV25 3SR.*
Comfortable ensuite rooms (non-smoking). Beautiful scenery, beach, golf and wildlife.
Open: All Year
01862 810237 Mr Miles
D: £15.00–£19.00 **S:** £15.00–£19.00
Beds: 1D 1T 1S **Baths:** 2 En 1 Pr

Parfour, *Rowan Crescent, Dornoch, Sutherland, IV25 4SF.*
3 mins Royal Dornoch, 5 mins sandy beach. Modern home.
Open: All Year
01862 810955 (also fax)
Mrs Young
D: fr £20.00
Beds: 2F 1T **Baths:** 3 Pr

Drumbuie

NG7731   Plockton Inn, Plockton Hotel, Off The Rails, Old School House, Tingle Creek Hotel

Glenmarvin, *Drumbuie, Kyle of Lochalsh, Ross-shire, IV40 8BD.*
Modern crofthouse in picturesque village between Plockton and Kyle of Lochalsh.
Open: All Year
01599 544380 (also fax)
Mrs Finlayson
D: £18.00
Beds: 1F 1T **Baths:** 2 En

Drumnadrochit

NH5030 ⚐ *Fiddlers, Hunters Bar, Drumnadrochit Hotel*

Ferness Cottage, *Lewiston, Drumnadrochit, Inverness, IV3 6UW.*
200 year old cottage within walking distance of Loch Ness.
Open: Easter to Oct
Grades: STB 3 Star
01456 450564 Mrs Campbell
ferness@freezone.co.uk
D: £18.00–£25.00 **S:** £20.00–£30.00
Beds: 1F 1T 2D **Baths:** 4 En

Westwood, *Lower Balmacaan, Drumnadrochit, Inverness, IV63 6WU.*
Comfortable bungalow near Loch Ness. Ideal walking and touring base.
Open: All Year
Grades: STB 3 Star B&B
01456 450826 (also fax)
S Silke
sandra@westwoodbb.freeserve.co.uk
D: £17.00–£21.00 **S:** fr £20.00
Beds: 1D 1T 1S **Baths:** 2 En 1 Sh
🛏 (8) 🅿 (4) ⚲ ♁ ✕ 🛏 📺 🖤 cc

Glen Rowan House, *West Lewiston, Drumnadrochit, Inverness, IV63 6UW.*
Very comfortable riverside village house near Urquhart Castle, Monster Exhibition.
Open: All Year (not Xmas)
01456 450235 Mrs Harrod
Fax: 01456 450817
glenrowan@loch-ness.demon.co.uk
D: £16.00–£25.00 **S:** £25.00–£42.00
Beds: 1D 2T **Baths:** 3 Pr
🛏 🅿 ⚲ 📺 ✕ 🛏 🖤 ♿

Twin Birches, *Milton, Drumnadrochit, IV63 6UA.*
Homely, good breakfast, comfortable rooms. Loch Ness, Urquhart Castle nearby.
Open: All Year (not Xmas/New Year)
01456 450359 Mrs Seeburg
D: £15.00–£16.00 **S:** £17.50–£18.00
Beds: 1T 1D
🅿 (3) ⚲ 📺 🛏

Bridgend House, *The Green, Drumnadrochit, Inverness, IV63 6TX.*
Highland home overlooking village green. Comfortable rooms. Imaginative evening meals.
Open: Feb to Dec
Grades: STB 3 Star
01456 450865 (also fax)
Mrs Luffman
D: £18.00–£22.00 **S:** £18.00–£20.00
Beds: 1F/T 1D 1S **Baths:** 1 En 1 Sh
🛏 (10) 🅿 (5) ⚲ 📺 ♁ ✕ 🖤 🛏

Gillyflowers, *Drumnadrochit, Inverness, IV63 6UJ.*
Renovated C18th farmhouse in beautiful rural setting.
Open: All Year
Grades: STB 3 Star
01456 450641 (also fax)
J Benzie
gillyflowers@cali.co.uk
D: £14.00–£18.00 **S:** £20.00–£28.00
Beds: 2D 1T **Baths:** 1 En 1 Sh
🛏 (7) 🅿 (3) ⚲ 📺 🛏 🖤 🛏

Drumsmittal

NH6449 ⚐ *North Kessock Hotel*

Culbin Drumsmittal Croft, *Drumsmittal, North Kessock, Inverness, IV1 3XF.*
Open: All Year (not Xmas)
Grades: STB 2 Star
01463 731455 (also fax)
Mrs Ross
ian-eliz@rossculbin.freeserve.co.uk
D: £15.00–£18.00
Beds: 1F 1T 1D **Baths:** 1 Pr 1 Sh
🛏 🅿 (4) ⚲ 📺 🖤 🛏
Situated on a Highland working croft. Set in beautiful countryside and making the Ideal touring base for seeing the Scottish Highlands and Island's. Offers - Moray Firth, Dolphins, Red Kites, wildlife park, riding centre stb. Good pubs + restaurants + night clubs + theatres

Dulnain Bridge

NH9924 ⚐ *Skye of Curr Hotel, Strathspey Hotel*

Broomlands, *Dulnain Bridge, Grantown-on-Spey, Moray, PH26 3LT.*
Open: Easter to Sept 30th
01479 851255 Mrs Noble
ernest@noble56.fsnet.co.uk
D: £16.00–£17.00 **S:** £16.00–£20.00
Beds: 1F 1D 1S **Baths:** 1 Sh
🛏 🅿 (4) 📺 ♁ ✕ 🛏
A Traditional Scottish house in a quiet village. Ideal centre for touring the highlands. Close to Cairngorm Mountains, walks, distilleries. Several good golf courses. Fishing and bird watching.

Auchendean Lodge, *Dulnain Bridge, Grantown-on-Spey, Moray, PH26 3LU.*
A popular and friendly country house hotel in a sensational setting.
Open: All Year
Grades: STB 4 Star
01479 851347 (also fax)
Mr Kirk
hotel@auchendean.com
D: £35.00–£47.00 **S:** £37.00–£58.00
Beds: 1F 1T 2D 1S **Baths:** 5 En
🛏 🅿 (8) 📺 ♁ ✕ 🛏 🖤 ♣ 🛏 ♿ cc

Durness

NC4067 ⚐ *Parkill Hotel, Smoo Cave Hotel, Sango Sands*

Glengolly House, *Durine, Durness, Lairg, Sutherland, IV27 4PN.*
Open: All Year
01971 511255 (also fax)
Mr Mackay
D: £16.00–£18.00
S: £18.00–£20.00
Beds: 1F, 1T,1D **Baths:** 1 En 1 Pr 1 Sh
🛏 🅿 (4) ⚲ 📺 🖤 🛏
Prepare to be enchanted by spectacular sunsets and breathtaking scenery. Come and stay at a traditional croft where you can watch Border Collies at work or listen to the corncrake. Enjoy outdoor pursuits in an area steeped in history.

Port Na Con House, *Loch Eriboll, Lairg, Sutherland, IV27 4UN.*
Open: All Year
Grades: AA 4 Diamond
01971 511367 (also fax)
Mrs Black
portnacon70@hotmail.com
D: £19.00–£20.00 **S:** £27.00–£28.00
Beds: 1F 2D 1T **Baths:** 1 En 1 Pr 1 Sh
🛏 🅿 (4) ⚲ ♁ ✕ 🛏 🖤 cc
Former customs house, sited on the shore of Loch Eriboll. All rooms overlook the sea and our raised conservatory offers magnificent views to Ben Hope (the most far Northerly Munro) and Ben Loyal. We have a restricted Licence.

Puffin Cottage, *Durness, Lairg, Sutherland, IV27 4PN.*
Close to the village with spectacular sea and country views.
Open: Easter to Oct
Grades: STB 3 Star
01971 511208 (also fax)
Mrs Frazer
puffincottage@aol.com
D: £17.00–£21.00 **S:** £25.00–£30.00
Beds: 2D **Baths:** 1 En 1 Sh
🅿 (2) ⚲ 📺 🛏

Duthil

NH9324

The Pines Country House, *Duthil, Carrbridge, Inverness-shire, PH23 3ND.*
Relax and enjoy our Highland hospitality. Set in mature woodlands where nature comes alive.
Open: All Year
01479 841220 Mrs Benge
thepines@dbenge.freeserve.co.uk
D: £19.00–£20.00 **S:** £21.50–£22.50
Beds: 1F 2D 1T **Baths:** 4 En
🛏 🅿 ⚲ 📺 ♁ ✕ 🛏 🖤 ♣ 🛏

Embo

NH8193 ⚐ *Grannie's Heiland Hame*

Corven, *Station Road, Embo, Dornoch, Sutherland, IV25 3PR.*
Detached bungalow with panoramic views. Ideal base for touring North Scotland.
Open: Feb to Nov
Grades: STB 2 Star
01862 810128 Mrs Fraser
D: fr £16.00 **S:** fr £18.00
Beds: 2D 1T **Baths:** 1 En 1 Sh
🛏 (10) 🅿 (4) ⚲ 📺 ♁ 🛏 🖤 🛏 ♿

Feshiebridge

NH8504

Balcraggan House, *Feshiebridge, Kincraig, Kingussie, Inverness-shire, PH21 1NG.*
Wonderful setting where wildlife, walks and cycle routes abound.
Open: All Year
01540 651488 Mrs Gillies
D: £25.00 **S:** £30.00–£35.00
Beds: 1D 1T **Baths:** 2 En
🛏 (10) 🅿 (3) ⚲ 📺 ✕ 🛏 🖤 🛏

Fort Augustus

NH3709 ◀ Lock Inn, Lovat Arms, Bothy

Lorien House, Station Road, Fort Augustus, Inverness-shire, PH32 4AY.
Open: All Year
Grades: STB 2 Star
01320 366736 E Dickie
Fax: 01320 366263
lorienhouse@aol.com
D: £20.00–£25.00 **S:** £25.00–£30.00
Beds: 3D 2T **Baths:** 2 En
🄿 (2) ⅏ 📺 🖩 Ⓥ ♨
Excellent full Scottish, Continental or fresh fruits breakfasts. Central for sightseeing Inverness, Ben Nevis, Isle of Skye, Aonach Mor skiing. Great pubs and restaurants nearby.

Caledonian Hotel, Fort Augustus, Inverness-shire, PH32 4BQ.
Typical small highland hotel centrally positioned for exploring Scotland.
Open: Easter to Oct.
Grades: STB 2 Star
01320 366256 J M MacLellan
Fax: 0870 284 1287
hotel-scotland.co.uk
D: £20.00–£30.00 **S:** £25.00–£35.00
Beds: 3F 3T 5D **Baths:** 7 En 2 Sh
🖰 (10) 🄿 (20) ⅏ 📺 ✕ 🖩 Ⓥ ♨ cc

Tigh Na Mairi, Canalside, Fort Augustus, Inverness-shire, PH32 4BA.
Stunning views all rooms ideal for Nessie hunting very welcoming.
Open: Easter to Oct
Grades: STB 2 Star
01320 366766 (also fax)
S V Callcutt
D: £11.00–£22.00 **S:** £14.00–£30.00
Beds: 2D 1T **Baths:** 1 Sh
🖰 (8) 🄿 (2) ⅏ 📺 🖩 Ⓥ ♨

Old Pier House, Fort Augustus, Inverness-shire, PH32 4BX.
Highland farmhouse in beautiful location beside loch Ness, riding boats.
Open: Easter to Nov
01320 366418 Mrs MacKenzie
D: £20.00–£35.00 **S:** £20.00–£30.00
Beds: 1F 2D 1T **Baths:** 4 En
🖰 (7) 🄿 (10) ⅏ 📺 🖩 Ⓥ ♨ cc

Fort William

NN1073 ◀ Moorings Hotel, Lochy Bar, Nevis Bank Hotel, Glen Nevis Rest, Gate Beag, Pat's Bar, Grogg & Gruel, Ben Nevis Rest, West End

Glenlochy Guest House, Nevis Bridge, Fort William, Inverness-shire, PH33 6PF.
Open: All Year
Grades: STB 3 Star, AA 3 Diamond
01397 702909 Mrs MacBeth
D: fr £17.00
Beds: 1F 4D 5T **Baths:** 8 En 1 Sh
🖰 (14) 📺 🖩 ♨ ♨
Situated 0.5 mile north of Fort William town centre, close to Ben Nevis. The famous West Highland walk ends at our guest house grounds. 8 of 10 bedrooms are ensuite. Large private car park.

Alltonside, Achintore Road, Fort William, Inverness-shire, PH33 6RW.
Open: All Year
Grades: STB 3 Star
01397 703542 (also fax)
Mrs Allton
altonside@aol.com
D: fr £16.00 **S:** fr £20.00
Beds: 1F 3D 2T **Baths:** 6 Pr
🖰 (8) 📺 🍴 🖩 Ⓥ ♨
Alltonside guest house commands magnificent views over Loch Linnhe to the hills beyond. Being close to the town of Fort William and Ben Nevis makes it an ideal base for sightseeing and visiting the many beautiful places in the Highlands.

Rushfield House, Tomonie, Banavie, Fort William, Inverness-shire, PH33 7LX.
Modern house with excellent views of Ben Nevis situated 3 miles from Fort William.
Open: Mar to Oct
Grades: STB 3 Star
01397 772063 Ms Corbett
rushbb0063@aol.com
D: £18.00–£25.00
Beds: 2F 1D **Baths:** 3 En
🖰 🄿 (3) ⅏ 📺 🖩 Ⓥ ♨

Ben Nevis View, Corpach, Fort William, Inverness-shire, PH33 7JH.
Open: Mar to Oct
Grades: STB 3 Star
01397 772131 Mrs Mooney
D: £18.00–£20.00 **S:** £20.00–£25.00
Beds: 1F 1D **Baths:** 2 En
🄿 (4) ⅏ 📺 🖩 ♨
Modern, comfortable house, 5 minutes by car from Fort William.

Ossian's Hotel, High Street, Fort William, Inverness-shire, PH33 6DH.
Open: All Year
01397 700857 J Wallace
Fax: 01397 701030
ossiansfw@aol.com
D: £16.00–£25.00 **S:** £18.00–£32.00
Beds: 10F 10D 10T 5S **Baths:** 32 En 3 Sh
🖰 🄿 📺 🍴 ✕ 🖩 Ⓥ ♨
Accommodation, food and drink for the budget traveller. Ideal town centre location. Couple of minutes walk from railway or bus. Warm, friendly and relaxed atmosphere.

11 Castle Drive, Lochyside, Fort William, PH33 7NR.
Open: All Year
Grades: STB 3 Star
01397 702659 Mrs Grant
D: £16.00–£18.00 **S:** £20.00–£24.00
Beds: 1T 1D **Baths:** 1 Sh
🖰 🄿 (2) ⅏ 📺 ✕ 🖩 Ⓥ ❀ ♨
Quiet residential area near castle. Views to Ben Nevis. Ideal base for walking, climbing, skiing. Intimate family home with cosy log fire in lounge when you can be assured of a warm and friendly welcome. Breakfast is the best in the west.

Planning a longer stay? Always ask for any special rates

Ferndale, Tomacharrich, Torlundy, Fort William, PH33 6SP.
Open: All Year **Grades:** STB 3 Star
01397 703593 Mrs Riley
D: £15.00–£20.00
Beds: 1F 2D **Baths:** 2 En 1 Pr
🖰 🄿 (6) ⅏ 📺 🍴 🖩 Ⓥ ♨
Large bungalow in beautiful country setting, with wonderful views of Ben Nevis and Nevis Range Ski Slope. Ideal base for walking, cycling, skiing and touring. Pony trekking, trout fishing and golfing all nearby. Breakfast served in conservatory. Nearest B&B to skiing.

Melantee, Achintore Road, Fort William, Inverness-shire, PH33 6RW.
Comfortable bungalow overlooking Loch Linnhe and the Ardgour hills.
Open: All Year (not Xmas)
Grades: STB 2 Star
01397 705329 Mrs Cook
Fax: 01397 700453
D: £15.50–£16.00 **S:** £15.50–£16.00
Beds: 1F 1D 1T 1S **Baths:** 2 Sh
🖰 (5) 🄿 (6) 📺 🖩 Ⓥ ♨

Glen Shiel Guest House, Achintore Road, Fort William, Inverness-shire, PH33 6RW.
Lochside location, panoramic views. Large car park. Tea makers, colour TV in all rooms. **Open:** Easter to Oct
Grades: STB 2 Star
01397 702271
D: £17.00–£20.00
Beds: 1F 3D 1T **Baths:** 3 En 1 Pr 1 Sh
🖰 (8) 🄿 (7) ⅏ 📺 🖩 Ⓥ ♨

Stronchreggan View Guest House, Achintore Road, Fort William, Inverness-shire, PH33 6RW.
Our house overlooks Loch Linnhe with views to Ardgour Hills.
Open: Easter to Oct
Grades: STB 3 Star GH
01397 704644 (also fax)
patricia@apmac.freeserve.co.uk
D: £19.00–£24.00
Beds: 5D 2T **Baths:** 5 En 2 Pr
🖰 (8) 🄿 (7) ⅏ 📺 ✕ 🖩 Ⓥ ♨

Abrach, 4 Caithness Place, Fort William, Inverness-shire, PH33 6JP.
Modern house in elevated position overlooking Loch Linnhe.
Open: All Year (not Xmas)
Grades: STB 3 Star
01397 702535 Mr & Mrs Moore
Fax: 01397 705629
cmoore3050@aol.com
D: £17.50–£23.00 **S:** £20.00–£30.00
Beds: 1D 1T 1S **Baths:** 2 En 1 Pr 1 Sh
🖰 🄿 (6) ⅏ 📺 🖩 Ⓥ ♨ cc

Distillery House, Nevis Bridge, North Road, Fort William, Inverness-shire, PH33 6LR.
Well-run guest house, ideally situated at end of Glen Nevis and West Highland Way. **Open:** All Year
Grades: STB 4 Star, AA 4 Diamond, RAC 4 Diamond, Sparkling Award
01397 700103 Mr MacPherson
Fax: 01397 702980 disthouse@aol.com
D: £20.00–£36.00 **S:** £22.00–£38.00
Beds: 1F 3D 1T 1S **Baths:** 7 En
🖰 🄿 (12) ⅏ 📺 🍴 🖩 ♨ cc

Rhu Mhor Guest House, *Alma Road,*
Fort William, Inverness-shire, PH33 6BP.
Old fashioned in acre of wild and
enchanting garden.
Open: Easter to Oct
Grades: STB 2 Star
01397 702213 Mr MacPherson
ian@rhumhor.co.uk
D: £16.00–£24.00 **S:** £17.00–£44.00
Beds: 1F 3D 1T 2S **Baths:** 2 Sh 4 En
⛄ (1) 🅿 (7) 📺 🍴 ✕ 🛏 📖 🖤 ♿ cc

Innseagan House Hotel, *Highland*
Holidays Scotland Ltd, Achintore Road,
Fort William, Inverness-shire, PH33 6RW.
In its own grounds overlooking Loch
Linnhe only 1.5 miles from Fort William.
Open: Easter to Oct
Grades: STB 3 Star Hotel
01397 702452 Mr Maclean
Fax: 01397 702606
frontdesk@innseagan-holidays.com
D: fr £22.50 **S:** fr £30.00
Beds: 14D 8T 2S **Baths:** 23 En 1 Pr
🅿 📺 ✕ 📖 🖤 cc

Stobahn, *Fassifern Road, Fort William,*
Inverness-shire, PH33 6BD.
Guest rooms overlooking Loch Linnhe.
Just off High Street.
Open: All Year
Grades: STB 2 Star
01397 702790 (also fax)
boggi@supanet.com
D: £15.00–£20.00 **S:** £18.00–£23.00
Beds: 1F 1T 2D **Baths:** 2 En 2 Sh
⛄ 🅿 📺 🛏 ✕ 📖 🖤 ♿ cc

Voringfoss, *5 Stirling Place, Fort*
William, Inverness-shire, PH33 6UW.
Experience the best of the highland
hospitality in a quiet situation.
Open: All Year
Grades: STB 4 Star
01397 704062 Mr & Mrs Fraser
D: £20.00–£26.00 **S:** £20.00–£26.00
Beds: 2D 1T **Baths:** 3 En
🅿 (4) 📺 📖 🖤 cc

19 Lundy Road, *Inverlochy, Fort*
William, Inverness-shire, PH33 6NY.
Family-run B&B. Views of Ben Nevis,
passing steam trains.
Open: All Year
Grades: STB 2 Star
01397 704918 Mrs Campbell
acampbell@talk21.com
D: £13.00–£17.00 **S:** £15.00–£20.00
Beds: 2F **Baths:** 1 Sh
⛄ 🅿 (2) 📺 🛏 ✕ 📖 🖤 ♿

Balcarres, *Seafield Gardens, Fort*
William, Inverness-shire, PH33 6RJ.
Beautiful villa in quiet location panoramic
views town centre 1 mile.
Open: All Year
01397 702377 Mrs Cameron
Fax: 01397 702232
balcarres@btinternet.com
D: £18.00–£25.00 **S:** fr £25.00
Beds: 1F 1D 1T **Baths:** 3 En
⛄ 🅿 (5) 🌾 📺 📖 🖤 ♿

Lochview Guest House,
Heathercroft, Argyll Terrace, Fort William,
Inverness-shire, PH33 6RE.
Quiet location on hillside above town,
with superb views.
Open: May to Sep
01397 703149 (also fax) Mrs Kirk
info@lochview.co.uk
D: £22.00–£27.00 **S:** £26.00–£32.00
Beds: 5D 2T 1S **Baths:** 5 En
🅿 (8) 🌾 📺 📖 ♿

Dorlin, *Cameron Road, Fort William,*
Inverness-shire, PH33 6LJ.
Modern bungalow, situated 200 yards
from town centre, near pubs and
restaurants. **Open:** All Year (not Xmas)
01397 702016 Mrs Macdonald
D: £18.00–£20.00 **S:** £20.00–£25.00
Beds: 2D **Baths:** 2 En
🅿 (2) 🌾 📺 🛏 📖 ♿

Foyers
NH4920 🍴 Foyers Hotel

Intake House, *Foyers, Inverness, IV2*
6YA.
Overlooking the River Foyers near the
famous Falls of Foyers.
Open: Easter to Nov
Grades: STB 4 Star
01456 486258 Mrs Grant
Fax: 01456 486258
D: £15.00–£18.00 **S:** £20.00–£25.00
Beds: 1T 2D **Baths:** 1 En 1 Sh
⛄ (14) 🅿 (5) 🌾 📺 📖 ♿

Gairloch
NG8076 🍴 Myrtle Bank Hotel, Gairloch Sands
Hotel, Old Inn, Millcroft Hotel

Croit Mo Sheanair, *29 Strath,*
Gairloch, Ross-shire, IV21 2DA.
Relax in our cosy family home; hand
decorated throughout with stencilling &
original artworks.
Open: Easter to Oct
Grades: STB 3 Star
01445 712389 L Bennett-Mackenzie
D: £15.00–£22.00
Beds: 1D 1T **Baths:** 1 En 1 Sh
⛄ 🅿 (3) 🌾 📺 📖 ♿

The Mountain Restaurant &
Lodge, *Strath Square, Gairloch, Ross-*
shire, IV21 2BX.
Unique informal coffee shop/restaurant.
Lochside sun terrace, views across water
to Torridon Mountains.
Open: Apr to Oct, Dec to Jan
01445 712316 (also fax)
Mr Rudge
D: £18.00–£29.95 **S:** £29.00–£59.90
Beds: 2D 1T **Baths:** 3 En
⛄ 🅿 (3) 📺 🛏 ✕ 📖 🖤 ❄ ♿ cc

Kerrysdale House, *Gairloch, Ross-*
shire, IV21 2AL.
A friendly welcome awaits you in our
warm comfortable house.
Open: Feb to Nov
01445 712292 (also fax)
Mrs MacRae
mac.kerr@btinternet.com
D: £18.00–£23.00 **S:** £18.00–£25.00
Beds: 2D 1T **Baths:** 2 En 1 Pr
⛄ 🅿 (3) 🌾 📺 🛏 ✕ 📖 🖤 ♿

Horisdale House, *Strath, Gairloch,*
Ross-shire, IV21 2DA.
Beautifully situated amidst spectacular
coastal scenery overlooking sea and
mountains.
Open: All Year (not Xmas)
01445 712151 (also fax)
Helen Morris
D: £17.00–£23.00 **S:** £18.00–£20.00
Beds: 1F 2D 1T 2S **Baths:** 2 En 1 Pr 2 Sh
⛄ 🅿 (8) 🌾 📺 🛏 📖 🖤 ♿

13 Strath, *Gairloch, Ross-shire, IV21 2BX.*
Good views, good varied breakfast, quiet.
Open: Easter to Oct
01445 712085 Mrs Gibson
louisegibson@cali.co.uk
D: £14.00–£16.00 **S:** £14.00–£16.00
Beds: 2D 1S **Baths:** 1 En 1 Sh
⛄ 🅿 (3) 📺 📖 🖤 ♿

Garve
NH3961 🍴 Garve Hotel, Inchbae Lodge Hotel,
Achilty Hotel

The Old Manse, *Garve, Ross-shire, IV23*
2PX.
Former manse c1860 set in quiet location
amidst beautiful scenery.
Open: All Year (not Xmas)
Grades: AA 3 Diamond
01997 414201 (also fax)
Mr & Mrs Hollingdale
D: £16.00–£17.00 **S:** £16.00–£17.00
Beds: 2D 1T **Baths:** 1 En 1 Sh
⛄ (10) 🅿 (6) 🌾 📖 ♿

Birch Cottage, *Station Road, Garve,*
Ross-shire, IV23 2PS.
Traditional Highland cottage, modernised
to a very high standard.
Open: Feb to Nov
Grades: STB 4 Star
01997 414237 (also fax)
Mrs Hayton
D: £15.00–£18.00 **S:** £17.00–£18.00
Beds: 2D 1T **Baths:** 3 En
⛄ (3) 🅿 (4) 🌾 📺 🛏 📖 🖤 ♿

Glencoe
NN1058 🍴 Glencoe Hotel, Clachaid Inn

Scorrybreac Guest House, *Glencoe,*
Ballachulish, Argyll, PH49 4HT.
Comfortable, secluded, overlooking Loch
Leven. All rooms on ground floor.
Open: 26 Dec to Oct
Grades: STB 3 Star , AA 3 Diamond
01855 811354 (also fax)
Mr Mortimer
john@scorrybreac.freeserve.co.uk
D: £16.00 **S:** fr £17.00
Beds: 3D 3T **Baths:** 5 En 1 Pr
⛄ 🅿 (8) 🌾 📺 🛏 ✕ 📖 🖤 ♿ cc

Dunire Guest House, *Glencoe,*
Ballachulish, Argyll, PA39 4HS.
Family run set in large garden.
Open: All Year (not Xmas)
01855 811305 Mrs Cameron
D: £16.00–£22.00
Beds: 33D 2T **Baths:** 5 En
⛄ 🅿 (8) 📺 🛏 📖 ❄ ♿

Glenfinnan

NM8980

Craigag Lodge Guest House,
Glenfinnan, Inverness-shire, PH37 4LT.
Victorian shooting lodge among superb
mountain scenery. Ideal walking/ wildlife
Open: Easter to Oct
01397 722240 Mr & Mrs Scott
D: £15.00–£20.00 **S:** fr £18.00
Beds: 1F 1D 1T **Baths:** 1 Sh
⌂ (9) ⊞ (4) ⊬ ⊡ Ⅷ ✕ Ⅴ ♨ ⅙

Glengolly

ND1066 ⊲ Pentland Hotel

Shinval, *Glengolly, Thurso, Caithness,*
KW14 7XN
Modern house with large garden. Four
miles from Orkney ferry.
Open: Jan to Dec
01847 894306 Mrs Sinclair
Fax: 01847 890711
mary@shinval.swinternet.co.uk
D: fr £15.00 **S:** fr £15.00
Beds: 1F 1D 1T **Baths:** 1 En 2 Sh
⌂ ⊞ (4) ⊡ Ⅷ Ⅷ Ⅴ ⅙

Glenmore

NH9809 ⊲ Glenmore Lodge, Cairngorm Hotel

Cairn Eilrig, *Glenmore, Aviemore,*
Inverness-shire, PH22 1QU.
Highland welcome. Secluded bungalow
in Glenmore forest park panoramic views.
Open: All Year
Grades: STB 3 Star
01479 861223 Mrs Ferguson
D: £17.00–£18.00 **S:** £17.00–£20.00
Beds: 1F 1T **Baths:** 1 Sh
⌂ ⊞ (2) ⊡ Ⅷ Ⅷ Ⅴ ⅙

Glenmoriston

NH2912 ⊲ Glenmoriston Arms Hotel

Burnside Guest House, *Bhlaraidh,*
Glenmoriston, Inverness, IV63 7YH.
Open: Mar to Nov
Grades: STB 2 Star
01320 351269 (also fax)
Mr & Mrs Lowe
D: £16.00–£17.50 **S:** £16.00–£17.50
Beds: 2D 1T 1S **Baths:** 2 Sh
⌂ ⊞ (5) ⊬ ⊡ Ⅷ ✕ Ⅷ Ⅴ ⅙
A comfortable family home situated in a
forested mountain area of Glenmoriston.
Burnside is on the A887 road to the Isles,
just 3 miles from Invermoriston and Loch
Ness. Comfortable beds, good breakfast ,
excellent hospitality, private off road
parking.

Glenshiel

NH9753

10 MacInnes Place, *Glenshiel, Kyle of*
Lochalsh, Ross-shire, IV40 8HX.
Beautiful view overlooking Loch Duich
and mountains. Ideal for hillwalkers.
Open: All Year (not Xmas)
01599 511384 (also fax)
L Macrae
D: £16.00–£20.00 **S:** £18.00–£20.00
Beds: 1F 1D 1T **Baths:** 1 En 1 Pr 1 Sh
⌂ ⊡ Ⅷ ✕ Ⅷ Ⅴ ⅙

Grantown-on-Spey

NJ0327 ⊲ Tyree House, Ben Mhorh, Garth
Hotel, Strathspey Hotel, Craggan Mill

Strathallan House, *Grant Road,*
Grantown-on-Spey, Moray, PH26 3LD.
Open: Easter to Oct
Grades: STB 3 Star GH
01479 872165 (also fax)
Mr Pearson
D: £18.00–£24.00
S: £18.00–£24.00
Beds: 3D 2T 1F **Baths:** 5 En 1 Pr
⌂ (7) ⊞ (6) ⊬ ⊡ ✕ Ⅷ Ⅴ ♨ ⅙ CC
Charming Victorian home, many original
features, offers first class accommodation
in spacious ensuite bedrooms,
comfortable 4 poster and king-size beds
available. Freshly cooked breakfasts with
wide choice. A warm welcome to all
guests. No single supplement.

Garden Park Guest House,
Woodside Avenue, Grantown-on-Spey,
Moray, PH26 3JN.
Charming Victorian guest house set in
lovely gardens in malt whisky country.
Open: Mar to Oct
Grades: STB 4 Star, AA 4 Diamond, RAC
4 Diamond
01479 873235
Mr Pattinson
D: £21.00–£24.00
Beds: 3D 2T **Baths:** 5 En
⌂ (12) ⊞ (8) ⊡ ✕ Ⅷ ⅙

Gaich Farm, *Grantown-on-Spey, Moray,*
PH26 3NT.
Beautiful working farmhouse overlooking
Cairngorms, comfortable beds, good
breakfast.
Open: May to Sept
01479 851381 Mrs Laing
Fax: 01479 851 381
gaich@tinyworld.co.uk
D: £16.00–£17.00 **S:** £16.00–£17.00
Beds: 1T 1D **Baths:** 1S
⌂ ⊞ Ⅷ Ⅷ ✕ Ⅷ ⅙

Firhall Guest House, *Grant Road,*
Grantown-on-Spey, Moray, PH26 3LD.
Beautiful Victorian house set in the heart
of Scottish Highlands.
Open: All Year (not Xmas)
Grades: STB 3 Star GH
01479 873097 (also fax)
Mr Salmon
firhall@cs.com
D: £17.00–£24.00 **S:** £17.00–£30.00
Beds: 3F 1D 1T 1S **Baths:** 3 En 1 Pr 1 Sh
⌂ ⊞ (8) ⊬ ⊡ Ⅷ Ⅴ ⅙

Ravenscourt House Hotel, *Seafield*
Avenue, Grantown-on-Spey, Moray,
PH26 3JG.
Victorian manse set in beautiful gardens
within walking distance of River Spey.
Open: All Year
Grades: RAC 5 Diamond
01479 872286 Mr & Mrs Lockey
Fax: 01479 873260
D: £30.00–£35.00 **S:** £35.00–£40.00
Beds: 2F 3D 2T 1S **Baths:** 9 En 2 Sh
⌂ ⊞ (8) ⊬ ⊡ ✕ Ⅷ Ⅴ ⅙ ⅙

Kinross Guest House, *Woodside*
Avenue, Grantown-on-Spey, Moray,
PH26 3JR.
Attractive Victorian villa in peaceful
southside of charming Highland town.
Open: All Year
01479 872042
Mr Milne
Fax: 01479 873504
milne@kinrosshouse.freeserve.co.uk
D: £20.00–£29.00 **S:** £21.00–£32.00
Beds: 2F 1D 2T 2S **Baths:** 5 En 2 Pr
⌂ (14) ⊞ (4) ⊬ ⊡ ✕ Ⅷ Ⅴ ♨ ⅙ ⅙ 3 CC

Harpsdale

ND1356 ⊲ Ulbster Arms

The Bungalow, *Bachmore Farm,*
Harpsdale, Halkirk, Caithness, KW12 6UN.
Modern comfortable friendly farmhouse.
Open: october
01847 841216
Mr & Mrs Waters
D: £18.00 **S:** £20.00
Beds: 1F 1D 1T **Baths:** 3 En
⌂ ⊞ ⊬ ⊡ ✕ Ⅷ Ⅴ ⅙

Helmsdale

ND0215 ⊲ Bannock Burn, Belgrave Arms

The Old Manse, *Stittenham Road,*
Helmsdale, Sutherland, KW8 6JG.
Beautiful Village settings,Garden, Access
to Salmon River, Fishing arranged.
Open: All Year
01431 821597 Mrs Goodridge
D: £18.00–£20.00 **S:** £18.00–£20.00
Beds: 1F 2T **Baths:** 1 En 1 Pr 1 Sh
⌂ ⊞ (4) ⊬ ⊡ ✕ Ⅷ Ⅴ ⅙

Broomhill House, *Helmsdale,*
Sutherland, KW8 6JS.
Comfortable crofthouse, panoramic
seaview.
Open: Apr to Oct
01431 821259 (also fax)
Mrs Blance
D: £18.00–£21.00 **S:** £25.00–£28.00
Beds: 1D 1T **Baths:** 2 En
⊞ (3) ⊡ Ⅷ ✕ Ⅷ Ⅴ ⅙

Kerloch, *67 Dunrobin Street, Helmsdale,*
Sutherland, KW8 6JX.
Superb view of the Harbour and Moray
Firth.
Open: All Year
01431 821396 Mrs Smith
D: £14.00 **S:** £14.00
Beds: 1F 1T 1S **Baths:** 2 Sh
⌂ ⊡ Ⅷ Ⅷ Ⅴ ⅙

Inchree

NN0263 ⊲ Four Seasons

Foresters Bungalow, *Inchree, Onich,*
Fort William, Inverness-shire, PH33 6SE.
Swedish-type bungalow in rural setting
by Glenrigh Forest.
Open: Easter to Oct
01855 821285 Mrs Maclean
D: £14.00–£16.00 **S:** £15.00–£20.00
Beds: 1F 2T **Baths:** 1 Sh
⌂ (2) ⊞ (4) ⊡ Ⅷ ✕ Ⅷ ⅙

Inveralligin

NG8457   Ben Damph, Tigh-an-eilean

Heather Cliff, Inveralligin, Torridon, Achnasheen, Ross-shire, IV22 2HB.
Enjoy magnificent North West Highlands scenery. Walk, climb or just relax.
Open: Easter to Oct
01445 791256 Mrs Rose
D: £15.00 **S:** £15.00
Beds: 1F 1D 1S **Baths:** 1 Sh
🖭 (4) 🖿 ♿

Invergarry

NH3001   Invergarry Hotel, Glengarry Castle Hotel, Lock Inn

Lundie View Guest House, Invergarry, Inverness-shire, PH35 4HN.
Open: All Year **Grades:** STB 4 Star
01809 501291 (also fax)
Mr & Mrs Girdwood
lundieview@talk21.com
D: £18.00–£24.00 **S:** £20.00–£28.00
Beds: 2D 2D 1T **Baths:** 4 En 1 Pr
🖻 🖭 (10) ✠ 🖵 🖮 ✗ 🖿 🖩 ❋ ♿ & cc
Set in heart of Great Glen near to Loch Ness Ben Nevis and much more. Ideal base for touring the Highlands. Excellent hospitality. Home cooked meals. We are licensed, so relax with a drink and enjoy the peace and tranquillity.

Lilac Cottage, South Laggan, Invergarry, Inverness-shire, PH34 4EA.
Comfortable accommodation,warm welcome in the heart of the great Glen.
Open: All Year **Grades:** STB 3 Star
01809 501410 Mrs Jamieson
lilac.cottage@virgin.net
D: £13.00–£16.00 **S:** £13.00–£20.00
Beds: 2D 1T **Baths:** 1 Sh
🖻 🖭 (4) 🖵 ✗ 🖿 ♿

Ardgarry Farm, Faichem, Invergarry, Inverness-shire, PH35 4HG.
Comfortable Accommodation, warm welcome, ideal for touring, beautiful forest walks. **Open:** Easter to October
01809 501226 Mr Wilson
Fax: 01809 501307
ardgarry.farm@lineone.net
D: £14.00–£15.00
Beds: 1F 2T 1D **Baths:** 2 Sh
🖺 (5) 🖻 (5) 🖵 🖮 ✗ 🖿 🖩 ♿

Invergarry Hotel, Invergarry, Inverness-shire, PH35 4HJ.
Great location for touring Scottish Highlands - access Loch Ness, Ben Nevis, Isle of Skye.
Open: All Year (not Xmas)
01809 501206 Mr MacCallum
Fax: 01809 501400 hotel@invergarry.net
D: £25.00–£36.00 **S:** £30.00–£41.00
Beds: 1F 5D 3T 1S **Baths:** 10 En
🖺 🖻 (20) 🖵 🖮 ✗ 🖿 🖩 ♿

Ardfriseal, Mandally Road, Invergarry, Inverness-shire, PH35 4HR.
Scenic views overlooking River Garry. Ideal base for touring W Highlands.
Open: Easter to Nov
01809 501281 Mrs Fraser
D: £15.00–£16.00 **S:** £15.00–£17.00
Beds: 2D 1T **Baths:** 1 Sh
🖻 (6) 🖿 🖩 ♿ &

Invergordon

NH7168   Foxes Hotel, Marine Hotel

Craigaron, 17 Saltburn, Invergordon, Ross-shire, IV18 0JX.
Ground floor bedrooms (some seafront), good breakfast, friendly, value for money.
Open: All Year (not Xmas/New Year)
Grades: STB 3 Star
01349 853640 Mrs Brown
Fax: 01349 853619
jobrown@craigaron.freeserve.co.uk
D: £18.00–£22.00 **S:** £20.00–£22.00
Beds: 4T 1S **Baths:** 2 En 1 Sh
🖻 (6) 🖵 🖮 🖿 ♿

Inverinate

NG9221   Dornie Hotel, Clachan, Loch Duich Hotel, Kintail Lodge Hotel

Foresters Bungalow, Inverinate, Kyle of Lochalsh, Ross-shire, IV40 8HE.
Shores of Loch Duich on main A87, with superb views of the Kintail Mountains.
Open: Easter to Oct
01599 511329 Mrs MacIntosh
Fax: 01599 511407
Donald.MacIntosh@tesco.net
D: £17.50–£20.00
Beds: 1D 1T **Baths:** 1 En 1 Pr
🖺 🖻 (2) 🖵 🖿 ♿ cc

Cruechan, 5 Glebe Road, Inverinate, Glenshiel, Kyle of Lochalsh, Ross-shire, IV40 8HD.
Seafront location, looking towards Mam Ratagan and Five Sisters of Kintail.
Open: All Year
01599 511328 (also fax)
Mrs Fraser
D: £16.00–£18.00 **S:** £18.00–£20.00
Beds: 2F **Baths:** 1 Sh
🖺 🖵 🖮 🖿 ♿

Mo Dhachaidh, Inverinate, Kyle of Lochalsh, Ross-shire, IV40 8HB.
Modern house with magnificent views overlooking Loch Duich and Kintail mountains.
Open: All Year (not Xmas)
01599 511351 (also fax)
Mrs Croy
croy-irenwick@currantbun.com
D: £16.00–£20.00 **S:** £16.00–£20.00
Beds: 1F 1D 1T 1S **Baths:** 1 En 1 Sh
🖺 🖻 (4) ✠ 🖮 🖿 ♿

Inverlochy

NN1174

19 Lundy Road, Inverlochy, Fort William, Inverness-shire, PH33 6NY.
Family-run B&B. Views of Ben Nevis, passing steam trains.
Open: All Year
Grades: STB 2 Star
01397 704918 Mrs Campbell
acampbell@talk21.com
D: £13.00–£17.00 **S:** £15.00–£20.00
Beds: 2F **Baths:** 1 Sh
🖺 🖻 (2) 🖵 🖮 ✗ 🖿 🖩 ♿

Inverness

NH6645   Beaufort Hotel, Castle, Cawdor Tavern, Craigmonie Hotel, Finlay's, Girvans,, Harlequin, Heathmount Hotel, Johnny Foxs', Kilcoy Arms, Loch Ness House, Mairten Lodge, No 27 Pub, Redcliffe, Waterfront

Eskdale Guest House, 41 Greig Street, Inverness, IV3 5PX.
Open: All Year (not Xmas)
Grades: STB 3 Star
01463 240933 (also fax)
Mrs Mazurek
eskdale.guesthouse@lineone.net
D: £16.00–£25.00 **S:** £22.00–£25.00
Beds: 2F 2D 1T 1S **Baths:** 3 En 1 Sh
🖺 🖻 (5) ✠ 🖵 🖿 ♿
Situated in the heart of Inverness only 5 minutes from bus/rail stations, this impeccably run guest house offers all the comforts of home and a warm Highland welcome. Private parking, discounts for stays over 3 days. Please phone Vera & Alex.

Pitfaranne, 57 Crown Street, Inverness, IV2 3AY.
Open: All Year
Grades: STB 3 Star
01463 239338 Gwen & Jim Morrison
D: £16.00–£20.00 **S:** £18.00–£26.00
Beds: 1F 2D 4T **Baths:** 1 En 1 Pr 2 Sh
🖺 🖻 (5) 🖵 🖮 🖿 🖩 ♿
5 minutes from town centre/rail/bus stations. Find true Highland hospitality in friendly relaxed atmosphere of 100-year-old town house in quiet location. Private showers in all cosy guest rooms. Daily room service. Extensive varied menu. Full Highland breakfast our speciality.

Strathmhor Guest House, 99 Kenneth Street, Inverness, IV3 5QQ.
Open: All Year
Grades: STB 2 Star
01463 235397 Mr & Mrs Reid
D: £20.00–£25.00 **S:** £18.00–£25.00
Beds: 2D 2T 1S **Baths:** 2 En 1 Pr 1 Sh
🖺 🖻 (5) 🖵 🖮 🖿 🖩 ♿
Warm welcome awaits at refurbished Victorian home. Comfortable bedrooms and good food. 10 minutes walk into town centre, theatres, restaurants, leisure centre; golf course and fishing nearby. Easy access for all traffic off A9.

Torridon Guest House, 59 Kenneth Street, Inverness, IV3 5PZ.
Open: All Year
Grades: STB 3 Star B&B
01463 236449 (also fax)
Mrs Stenhouse
louise@torridon59.freeserve.co.uk
D: fr £17.00
Beds: 3F **Baths:** 2 En 1 Pr
🖺 🖻 (4) 🖵 🖮 🖿 🖩 ♿
Comfortable, family-run house, 5 minutes from town centre, good food, good beds, and a warm welcome assured.

B&B owners may vary rates - be sure to check when booking

30 Culduthel Road, *Inverness, IV2 4AP.*
Open: All Year
01463 717181 Mrs Dunnett
Fax: 01463 717188
puffinexpress@cs.com
D: £12.50–£15.00 **S:** £18.00–£22.00
Beds: 1D 1T **Baths:** 1 En 1 Pr
⏱ (5) 🅿 (4) 🖵 🛉 ✕ 🕮 ☒ 🌢 ♿
1930's bungalow set in large garden,
pleasant to relax in on summer evenings.
Central heating. Lounge with open fire
which you may have to share with a cat.
Your hosts are both qualified local guides.

Fiveways Bed & Breakfast, *Tore,*
Muir of Ord, Ross-shire, IV6 7RY.
TV all rooms, guest lounge, spacious
parking, welcome always assured.
Open: Jun to Oct
Grades: STB 2 Star B&B
01463 811408 Mrs MacKenzie
D: fr £15.00 **S:** fr £17.00
Beds: 1F 1D 1T **Baths:** 1 En 2 Sh
⏱ 🅿 🖵 🛉 🕮 ☒ 🌢

Roseneath Guest House, *39 Greig*
Street, Inverness, IV3 5PX.
Open: All Year
Grades: STB 3 Star
01463 220201 (also fax)
Mr Morrison
roseneath@lineone.net
D: £15.00–£25.00
Beds: 3F 1T 2D **Baths:** 5 En 1 Pr
⏱ (7) 🅿 (3) 🖵 🕮 🌢 cc
Over 100 year old building in centre
location 200 yards from River Ness and
Greig Street Bridge. Only 5 minutes to
town centre and all tourist excursions.
Recently refurbished to very high
standards.

Loanfern Guest House, *4*
Glenurquhart Road, Inverness, IV3 5NU.
Victorian house with character. 10
minutes walk from town centre.
Open: All Year (not Xmas/New Year)
Grades: STB 3 Star
01463 221660 (also fax)
Mrs Campbell
D: £16.00–£22.00 **S:** £18.00–£23.00
Beds: 1F 2T 2D **Baths:** 1 En 2 Sh
⏱ 🅿 (4) 🖗 🖵 ☒ 🌢

Melness Guest House, *8 Old*
Edinburgh Road, Inverness, IV2 3HF.
Charming, award-winning guest house
close to town centre.
Open: All Year
Grades: STB 3 Star
01463 220963 Fax: 01463 717037
melness@joyce86.freeserve.co.uk
D: £20.00–£26.00 **S:** £25.00–£40.00
Beds: 1F 1T 1D **Baths:** 1 En 1 Sh
🅿 (3) 🖗 🖵 🕮 ☒ cc

Edenview, *26 Ness Bank, Inverness,*
IV2 4SF.
Comfortable friendly Victorian home on
River Ness within 5 minutes town, 7 miles
airport.
Open: Mar to Oct
Grades: STB 3 Star
01463 234397 Mrs Fraser
Fax: 01463 222742
D: £20.00–£24.00 **S:** £22.00–£28.00
Beds: 1F 1D 1T **Baths:** 2 En 1 Pr
⏱ (4) 🖵 🕮 ☒ 🌢

The Tilt, *26 Old Perth Road, Inverness,*
IV2 3UT.
Family home convenient for A9. Ideal
touring base. **Open:** All Year (not Xmas)
01463 225352 (also fax) Mrs Fiddes
D: fr £15.00 **S:** fr £17.00
Beds: 1F 1D 1T 1S **Baths:** 1 Sh
🅿 (4) 🖗 🖵 🕮 ☒

Abb Cottage, *11 Douglas Row,*
Inverness, IV1 1RE.
Central, quiet, riverside Listed terraced
cottage. Easy access public transport.
Open: Feb to Dec
01463 233486 Miss Storrar
D: £16.00–£18.00 **S:** £18.00–£25.00
Beds: 3T **Baths:** 1 Sh
⏱ (12) 🅿 (2) 🖗 🖵 ✕ 🕮 ☒ 🌢 ♿

Winmar House Hotel, *Kenneth*
Street, Inverness, IV3 5QG.
Full Scottish breakfast and friendly
welcome. Ample parking.
Open: All Year (not Xmas)
01463 239328 (also fax) Mrs Maclellan
winmarguesthouse@innerness ll.freeserve
.co.uk
D: £16.00–£22.00 **S:** £16.00–£22.00
Beds: 1D 6T 3S **Baths:** 1 En 4 Pr 2 Sh
⏱ 🅿 (10) 🖗 🖵 🛉 🕮 🌢 ♿ cc

MacGregor's, *36 Ardconnel Street,*
Inverness, IV2 3EX.
We are situated minutes from River Ness,
shops and castle.
Open: All Year (not Xmas/New Year)
01463 238357 Mrs MacGregor
james@seafieldorms.orknet.co.uk
D: £14.00–£18.00 **S:** £15.00–£20.00
Beds: 1F 3D 1T 3S **Baths:** 2 En 3 Sh
🖵 🛉 🕮 🌢

Hazeldean House, *125 Lochalsh Road,*
Inverness, IV3 5QS.
Friendly Highland welcome. Only 10 mins'
walk to town centre.
Open: All Year **Grades:** STB 3 Star
01463 241338 Mr Stuart
Fax: 01463 236387
D: £14.00–£20.00 **S:** £16.00–£22.00
Beds: 2F 4D 3T 2S **Baths:** 3 En 2 Sh
⏱ 🅿 (6) 🖗 🖵 🛉 🕮 🌢

101 Kenneth Street, *Inverness, IV3 5QQ.*
Ideal base for day trips to North Highland
and Islands.
Open: All Year
Grades: STB 2 Star
01463 237224 Mrs Reid
Fax: 01463 712249
D: £16.00–£20.00 **S:** £20.00–£25.00
Beds: 2F 2D 1T 1S **Baths:** 1 En 1 Pr 2 Sh
⏱ 🅿 (6) 🖗 🖵 🕮 ☒ 🌢 ♿ cc

Strathisla, *42 Charles Street, Inverness,*
IV2 3AH.
2 minutes' walk to high street. 5 mins to
rail and bus stations.
Open: All Year (not Xmas)
Grades: STB 3 Star
01463 235657 (also fax)
Mr & Mrs Lewthwaite
strathislabb@talk21.com
D: £15.00–£18.00 **S:** £16.00–£20.00
Beds: 1D 1T 2S **Baths:** 1 Sh
⏱ (8) 🅿 (2) 🖗 🖵 ✕ 🕮 ☒ 🌢

Ivybank Guest House, *28 Old*
Edinburgh Road, Inverness, IV2 3HJ.
Georgian home, near town centre and
with parking.
Open: All Year
Grades: STB 4 Star
01463 232796 (also fax)
Mrs Cameron
ivybank@talk21.com
D: £20.00–£27.50 **S:** £20.00–£55.00
Beds: 1F 4D 2T 5S **Baths:** 3 En 1 Pr 2 Sh
⏱ 🅿 🖗 🛉 🕮 ☒ ✳ 🌢 cc

5 Muirfield Gardens, *Inverness, IV2*
4HF.
Quiet residential area 15 mins walk to
town centre. All rooms on ground floor.
Open: Easter to Dec
Grades: STB 3 Star
01463 238114 Mrs MacDonald
D: £17.00–£20.00 **S:** £18.00–£20.00
Beds: 2D 1T **Baths:** 2 Sh
🅿 (3) 🖵 🕮 🌢

6 Broadstone Park, *Inverness, IV2 3LA.*
Family-run B&B. Victorian house 10 mins
town centre, bus and railway station.
Open: All Year (not Xmas)
Grades: STB 2 Star
01463 221506 Mrs Mackinnon
D: £20.00–£25.00 **S:** £21.00–£25.00
Beds: 1F 1D 1T 1S **Baths:** 2 En 1 Pr
⏱ (5) 🅿 (3) 🖗 🖵 ☒ 🌢

Lyndon, *50 Telford Street, Inverness, IV3*
5LE.
A warm and friendly welcome awaits you
at the Lyndon.
Open: All Year (not Xmas)
Grades: STB 3 Star
01463 232551 D Smith
donnas@tesco.net
D: £15.00–£22.00 **S:** £30.00–£40.00
Beds: 4F 1D 1T **Baths:** 6 En
⏱ 🅿 (6) 🖵 🛉 🕮 🌢 ♿ cc

Taigh Na Teile, *6 Island Bank Road,*
Inverness, IV2 4SY.
Overlooking the River Ness, this
beautifully appointed Victorian-style
house.
Open: All Year (not Xmas)
Grades: STB 4 Star
01463 222842 Mr & Mrs Menzies
Fax: 01463 226844
jenny@omn.co.uk
D: £20.00 **S:** £25.00–£30.00
Beds: 1D 2T **Baths:** All En
🅿 (4) 🖗 🖵 🕮 🌢

St Anns House, *37 Harrowden Road,*
Inverness, IV3 5QN.
Friendly, small, clean, family-run hotel, 10
minutes' walk from town centre, bus &
rail stations.
Open: Mar to Oct
01463 236157 (also fax)
Mr Wilson
stannshous@aol.com
D: £22.00–£24.00 **S:** £20.00–£30.00
Beds: 1F 2D 2T 1S **Baths:** 5 En 1 Pr
⏱ 🅿 (4) 🖗 🖵 🕮 ☒ 🌢

Hawthorn Lodge House, 15 Fairfield Road, Inverness, IV3 5QA.
The real taste of Scotland at Hawthorn Lodge.
Open: All Year
01463 715516 Mrs Davidson
Fax: 01463 221578
hawthorn@roamin.demon.co.uk
D: £20.00–£26.00 **S:** £20.00–£26.00
Beds: 2F 1D 1T **Baths:** 3 En 1 Sh
☒ 🅿 (6) ⚡ 📺 🎍 🛏 🖤 ♣ 👶 **cc**

Tanera, 8 Fairfield Road, Inverness, IV3 5QA.
Warm, comfortable house, close to River Ness, theatre and all amenities.
Open: All Year
01463 230037 (also fax)
Mrs Geddes
D: £18.00–£25.00 **S:** £20.00–£30.00
Beds: 2D 1T **Baths:** 2 En 1 Pr 1 Sh
☒ (10) 🅿 (3) ⚡ 📺 🛏 🖤 👶

Crown Hotel, 19 Ardconnel Street, Inverness, IV2 3EU.
Clean, warm, friendly. Excellent breakfast, four minutes from the station.
Open: All Year (not Xmas)
01463 231135 (also fax)
crownhotel@aol.com
D: £17.00–£20.00 **S:** £17.00–£25.00
Beds: 2F 2D 1T 2S **Baths:** 3 En 2 Sh
☒ 📺 🖤 👶 **cc**

Clach Mhuilinn, 7 Harris Road, Inverness, IV2 3LS.
Comfortable no smoking B&B with luxury, charming ensuite bedrooms.
Open: Easter to Oct
01463 237059 Mrs Elmslie
Fax: 01463 242092
still@ness.co.uk
D: £24.00–£27.50 **S:** £35.00–£40.00
Beds: 1D 1T **Baths:** 2 En
☒ (10) 🅿 (3) ⚡ 📺 🖤 👶 **cc**

Ivanhoe Guest House, 68 Lochalsh Road, Inverness, IV3 6HW.
Family-run, 10 mins' walk town centre. 'Highland Hospitality'.
Open: All Year (not Xmas)
01463 223020 (also fax)
Sandy Crerer
D: £16.00–£18.00 **S:** £16.00–£18.00
Beds: 2F 1T 2S **Baths:** 2 En 3 Sh
☒ (5) ⚡ 📺 🖤 👶

Kendon, 9 Old Mill Lane, Inverness, IV2 3XP.
Family bungalow in peaceful location with large garden and private parking.
Open: Apr to Oct
01463 238215 Mrs Kennedy
microflexsoftware@compuserve.com
D: £21.00–£25.00
Beds: 2D 1T **Baths:** 3 En
🅿 (4) ⚡ 📺 🖤 👶

Hebrides, 120a Glenurquhart Road, Inverness, IV3 5TD.
Quality graded B&B offering high standards, no smoking, private parking.
Open: All Year
01463 220062 Mrs MacDonald
D: £18.00–£25.00
Beds: 2D 1T **Baths:** 2 En
☒ (3) ⚡ 📺 🖤 👶

East Dene, 6 Ballifeary Road, Inverness, IV3 5PJ.
Near Eden Court Theatre.
Open: All Year
01463 232976 (also fax)
Mrs Greig
dgreig@nildram.co.uk
D: £22.00–£27.00 **S:** £29.00–£35.00
Beds: 3D 1T **Baths:** 3 En
🅿 (4) 📺 🛏 🖤 🖤 👶

Carbisdale, 43 Charles Street, Inverness, IV2 3AH.
Victorian family home, central location, ideal base for touring highlands.
Open: All Year
01463 225689 (also fax)
Mrs Chisholm
D: £16.00–£18.00 **S:** £20.00–£25.00
Beds: 2D 1T **Baths:** 2 Sh
📺 🖤 🖤 👶

Cambeth Lodge, 49 Fairfield Road, Inverness, IV3 5QP.
Comfortable detached Victorian house. Warm Scottish welcome assured.
Open: All Year (not Xmas)
01463 231764 Mrs Carson-Duff
D: £17.00–£20.00
Beds: 2D 1T **Baths:** 1 En 1 Pr 1 Sh
☒ 🅿 (5) ⚡ 📺 🖤 🖤 👶

Abbotsford, 7 Fairfield Road, Inverness, IV3 5QA.
Comfortable friendly home, centrally situated, 2 mins town centre.
Open: All Year (not Xmas)
01463 715377 Mr Griffin
D: £16.00–£20.00 **S:** £18.00–£25.00
Beds: 1F 1D **Baths:** 2 En
☒ (12) 🅿 (1) 📺 🖤 👶

Kinkell House, 11 Old Edinburgh Road, Inverness, IV2 3HF.
Traditional Georgian family home full of charm and character. Spacious rooms, tastefully decorated.
Open: All Year
01463 235243 Fax: 01463 225255
clare@kinkell.freeserve.co.uk
D: £18.00–£46.00 **S:** £20.00–£24.00
Beds: 4F 1D 1S **Baths:** 3 En 2 Sh
🅿 (8) 📺 🛏 🖤 👶 **cc**

Charden Villa, 11 Fairfield Road, Inverness, IV3 5QA.
Warm comfortable family-run house situated 10 mins' walk town centre.
Open: All Year
01463 222403 Mrs Munro
D: £18.00–£20.00 **S:** £22.00–£25.00
Beds: 4F, 3T or 1D **Baths:** 2 En, 1 Sh
☒ 📺 🖤 🖤 👶 ♣ 👶

Invershin

NH5796 ⚓ *Invershin Hotel*

Birkenshaw, Invershin, Lairg, Sutherland, IV27 4ET.
Modern house in woodland setting. Peaceful surroundings, self-contained entrance.
Open: May to CT
01549 421226 Mrs Alford
D: £15.00–£16.00 **S:** £15.00–£16.00
Beds: 2T **Baths:** 1 En 1 Pr
☒ (10) 🅿 (4) ⚡ 📺 🛏 🖤 👶

Invershin Hotel, Invershin, Lairg, Sutherland, IV27 4ET.
Old Drovers Inn overlooking Kyle of Sutherland, centrally situated for visiting coasts. **Open:** Apr to Nov
01549 421202 Fax: 01549 421212
D: £23.50–£25.00 **S:** £25.00–£27.50
Beds: 1F 4D 3T 2S **Baths:** 10 En
🅿 (30) 📺 ✖ 👶

John O' Groats

ND3773 ⚓ *John O' Groats House, Castle Arms*

Seaview Hotel, John o' Groats, Wick, Caithness, KW1 4YR.
Scenic seaside location. Family owned, five minutes from Orkney ferry.
Open: All Year **Grades:** STB 1 Star
01955 611220 (also fax) Mr Mowat
D: £14.50–£25.00 **S:** £20.00–£35.00
Beds: 3F 3D 2T 1S **Baths:** 5 En 2 Sh
☒ 🅿 (20) 📺 🛏 ✖ 🖤 🖤 👶

Bencorragh House, Upper Gills, Canisbay, John o' Groats, Wick, Caithness, KW1 4YB.
Working croft. Panoramic views across Pentland Firth near seasonal Orkney ferry. **Open:** Mar to Oct
Grades: STB 3 Star, AA 3 Diamond
01955 611449 (also fax) Mrs Barton
D: £20.00–£21.00 **S:** £23.00–£25.00
Beds: 1F 2D 1T **Baths:** 4 En
☒ (5) 🅿 (6) ⚡ 📺 🛏 ✖ 🖤 👶 **cc**

Post Office House, Canisbay, John o' Groats, Wick, Caithness, KW1 4YH.
100-year-old stone-built house in tranquil village of Canisbay, close John o' Groats, ferry. **Open:** Apr to Sep
01955 611213 (also fax) Mrs Manson
john-o-groats@ukf.net
D: £21.00–£23.00 **S:** £22.00–£25.00
Beds: 2D 1T **Baths:** 1 En 2 Sh
☒ (12) 🅿 (4) 📺 🖤 👶

Keiss

ND3461 **Links View,** Keiss, Wick, Caithness, KW1 4XG.
Attractive B&B overlooking Sinclair bay. 10 minutes from Orkney ferry.
Open: All Year
01955 631376 Mrs Brooks
D: £14.00–£15.00 **S:** fr £12.50
Beds: 1F 1D 1T **Baths:** 1 En 1 Sh
☒ 🅿 (8) ⚡ 📺 ✖

Kentallen

NN0157

Ardsheal House, Kentallen, Appin, Argyll, PA38 4BX.
Open: All Year
Grades: STB 4 Star, AA 5 Diamond
01631 740227 N V C Sutherland
Fax: 01631 740342
info@ardsheal.co.uk
D: £45.00 **S:** £45.00
Beds: 1F 2T 4D 1S **Baths:** 8 En
☒ 🅿 🛏 ✖ 🖤 🖤 👶 **cc**
Spectacularly situated on the shores of Loch Linnhe, standing in some 800 acres of woodlands, fields and gardens, this historic mansion is furnished with family antiques and pictures. Ideal for climbing, walking and touring or for the use of the full size billiards table.

Kinbrace

NC8632

Tigh achen Echan, *Kinbrace,*
Sutherland, KW11 6UB.
Natural stone-built house. View of river
and distant hills.
Open: All Year
01431 831207
Mrs MacKenzie
D: fr £15.00 **S:** fr £15.00
Beds: 2F **Baths:** 1 Sh
🛏 🅿 📺 ✕ 🛏 Ⅴ 🕯

Kincraig

NH8305   🍴 *Kith & Kin Inn, Ossian Hotel*

Ossian Hotel, *Kincraig, Kingussie,*
Inverness-shire, PH21 1QD.
Built in 1880's lochside village.
Magnificent mountain views.
Open: Feb to Dec
Grades: STB 2 Star
01540 651242
Mrs Rainbow
Fax: 01540 651633
ossian@kincraig.com
D: £20.00–£31.00 **S:** £20.00–£31.00
Beds: 2F 3D 2T 2S **Baths:** 8 En 1 Pr
🛏 🅿 (20) ⅍ 📺 🛏 ✕ 🛏 Ⅴ 🕯 cc

Balcraggan House, *Feshiebridge,*
Kincraig, Kingussie, Inverness-shire, PH21
1NG.
Wonderful setting where wildlife, walks
and cycle routes abound.
Open: All Year
01540 651488 Mrs Gillies
D: £25.00 **S:** £30.00–£35.00
Beds: 1D 1T **Baths:** 2 En
🛏 (10) 🅿 (3) ⅍ 📺 ✕ 🛏 Ⅴ 🕯

Braeriach Guest House, *Kincraig,*
Kingussie, Inverness-shire, PH21 1QA.
Beautiful riverside country house.
Spacious comfortable rooms with
incredible views.
Open: All Year
01540 651369 Mrs Johnson
D: £20.00–£25.00 **S:** £20.00–£25.00
Beds: 2D 2T **Baths:** 3 En 1 Pr
🛏 🅿 (4) 📺 🛏 ✕ 🛏 ❀ 🕯

Kirkbeag, *Milehead, Kincraig,*
Kingussie, Inverness-shire, PH21 1ND.
Freindly family B&B in converted C19th
church. Quiet country location.
Open: All Year
01540 651298 (also fax)
Mrs Paisley
D: £16.50–£17.50 **S:** £20.00–£23.00
Beds: 1D 1T **Baths:** 2 Sh
🛏 🅿 (6) 📺 ✕ 🛏 Ⅴ 🕯

Insh House, *Kincraig, Kingussie,*
Inverness-shire, PH21 1NU.
Friendly family guest house in splendid
rural location near loch & mountains.
Open: All Year (not Xmas)
01540 651377 Nick & Patsy Thompson
inshhouse@btinternet.com
D: £17.00–£20.00 **S:** £17.00–£20.00
Beds: 1F 1D 1T 2S **Baths:** 2 En 1 Sh
🛏 🅿 ⅍ 📺 🛏 ✕ 🛏 Ⅴ 🕯

Kingussie

NH7500   🍴 *Scot House Hotel, Tipsy Laird,*
Osprey Hotel

The Osprey Hotel, *Kingussie,*
Inverness-shire, PH21 1EN.
Open: All Year
Grades: STB 3 Star Hotel, AA 2 Star
01540 661510 (also fax)
Mr & Mrs Burrow
aileen@ospreyhotel.co.uk
D: £24.00–£30.00 **S:** £24.00–£30.00
Beds: 3D 3T 2S **Baths:** 8 En
🛏 🅿 📺 🛏 ✕ 🛏 Ⅴ 🕯 ⅙ cc
Small hotel in area of outstanding beauty,
offering a warm welcome, ensuite
accommodation and award-winning food.
Aileen & Robert hold AA food rosettes
and are members of the 'taste of
Scotland'. Ideal base for touring, walking,
golf, fishing, stb.

Arden House, *Newtonmore Road,*
Kingussie, Inverness-shire, PH21 1HE.
Excellent food and accommodation,
delightful centrally situated Victorian
villa.
Open: All Year
Grades: STB 3 Star GH
01540 661369 (also fax)
Mrs Spry
ardenhouse@compuserve.com
D: £18.00–£22.00 **S:** £18.00–£22.00
Beds: 2F 2D 1T 1S **Baths:** 3 En 3 Sh
🛏 (1) 🅿 (7) ⅍ 📺 🛏 ✕ 🛏 Ⅴ 🕯 ⅙ 2 cc

The Hermitage, *Spey Street,*
Kingussie, Inverness-shire, PH21 1HN.
Warm Highland welcome in heart of
Badenoch & Strathspey. Excellent touring
base.
Open: All Year (not Xmas)
Grades: STB 4 Star
01540 662137 Mr Taylor
Fax: 01540 662177
thehermitage@clara.net
D: £21.00–£23.00 **S:** £26.00–£28.00
Beds: 1F 1T 3D **Baths:** 5 En
🛏 🅿 📺 🛏 ✕ 🛏 Ⅴ 🕯 cc

St Helens, *Ardbroilach Road, Kingussie,*
Inverness-shire, PH21 1JX.
Built 100 years ago, St Helens is an
elegant Victorian villa.
Open: All Year
Grades: STB 4 Star
01540 661430 Mrs Jarratt
sthelens@talk21.com
D: fr £20.00 **S:** fr £38.00
Beds: 1D 1T **Baths:** 1 En 1 Pr
🛏 (12) 🅿 (3) ⅍ 📺 🛏 Ⅴ 🕯

Ruthven Farmhouse, *Kingussie,*
Inverness-shire, PH21 1NR.
Spacious farmhouse set amidst an acre
of landscaped grounds.
Open: All Year
Grades: STB 3 Star
01540 661226 Mr Morris
D: £18.00–£20.00 **S:** £18.00–£20.00
Beds: 2D 1T **Baths:** 1 En 2 Pr
🛏 (10) 🅿 (3) ⅍ 📺 🛏 Ⅴ ❀ 🕯

Dunmhor House, *67 High Street,*
Kingussie, Inverness-shire, PH21 1HX.
Centrally situated for numerous
attractions in beautiful scenic Highland
village. **Open:** All Year
01540 661809 (also fax)
D: £16.00–£18.00 **S:** £16.00–£20.00
Beds: 2F 2D 1S **Baths:** 2 Sh
🛏 🅿 (5) 📺 ✕ 🛏 Ⅴ 🕯

Bhuna Monadh, *85 High Street,*
Kingussie, Inverness-shire, PH21 1HX.
Listed building in scenic area with many
outdoor activities. **Open:** All Year
01540 661186 Ms Gibson
Fax: 01540 661186
enquiries@bhunamonadh.demon.co.uk
D: £15.00–£20.00 **S:** £20.00–£25.00
Beds: 1D 1T **Baths:** 2 En
🛏 🅿 (3) ⅍ 📺 🛏 🕯

Greystones, *Acres Road, Kingussie,*
Inverness-shire, PH21 1LA.
Victorian family home, pleasantly
secluded, a five-minute walk from
Kingussie. **Open:** All Year (not Xmas)
01540 661052 Mr & Mrs Johnstone
Fax: 01540 662162
greystones@lineone.net
D: £18.50 **S:** £18.50
Beds: 1F 1D 1T 1S **Baths:** 1 Pr 2 Sh
🛏 🅿 (6) ⅍ 📺 ✕ 🛏 Ⅴ 🕯 cc

Rowan House, *Homewood,*
Newtonmore Road, Kingussie, Inverness-
shire, PH21 1HD.
Quiet hillside position; outstanding views
of Spey Valley and mountains.
Open: All Year (not Xmas)
01540 662153 Ms Smiter
D: £17.00–£22.00 **S:** £17.00–£20.00
Beds: 1D 2T **Baths:** 1 En 2 Pr
🛏 (2) 🅿 (3) ⅍ 📺 🛏 🛏 🕯

Homewood Lodge, *Kingussie,*
Inverness-shire, PH21 1HD.
Homewood Lodge, a beautifully
decorated Victorian house set in mature
gardens.
Open: All Year
01540 661507 J Anderson
homewood-lodge@freeserve.co.uk
D: fr £15.00 **S:** fr £15.00
Beds: 1F 1T 2D **Baths:** 4 En
🛏 (6) ⅍ 📺 ✕ 🛏 Ⅴ ❀ 🕯

Kinlochleven

NN1861   🍴 *Tailrace Inn, Macdonald Hotel,*
Osprey Hotel

Macdonald Hotel and Camp Site,
Fort William Road, Kinlochleven, Argyll,
PH50 4QL.
Open: Mar to Dec
Grades: STB 3 Star
01855 831539 Mr & Mrs Reece
Fax: 01855 831416
martin@macdonaldhotel.demon.co.uk
D: £24.00–£32.00 **S:** £24.00–£44.00
Beds: 1F 4D 5T **Baths:** 10 En
🛏 🅿 (20) 📺 🛏 ✕ 🛏 Ⅴ 🕯 ❀ cc
A modern hotel in Highland-style on the
shore of Loch Leven. Superb views of the
loch and surrounding mountains. Only 25
metres from West Highland Way. The
walkers' bar provides an informal
atmosphere and a wide selection of bar
meals.

Edencoille, *Garbhien Road, Kinlochleven, Argyll, PA40 4SE.*
Friendly, comfortable B&B. Home cooking our speciality. Family run.
Open: All Year
Grades: STB 3 Star
01855 831358 (also fax)
Mrs Robertson
D: £18.00–£22.00 **S:** £26.00–£34.00
Beds: 2F 1D 2T **Baths:** 2 Sh 2 En
🛇 🅿 (5) 🅃 ✕ 🖵 🎔 ❋ 🎄

Hermon, *Kinlochleven, Argyll, PH50 4RA.*
Spacious bungalow in village surrounded by hills on West Highland way.
Open: Easter to Sep
01855 831383 Miss MacAngus
D: £16.00–£18.00 **S:** £18.00–£25.00
Beds: 1D 2T **Baths:** 1 En 1 Sh
🛇 🅿 (6) 🅃 🎔 🖵 🎄

Gharaidh Mhor, *15 Locheilde Road, Kinlochleven, Argyll, PA40 4RH.*
Small, family-run B&B, warm welcome, hearty breakfast.
Open: Easter to Oct
01855 831521 Mrs Fyfe
maureen@mpfyfe.freeserve.co.uk
D: £16.00 **S:** fr £21.00
Beds: 2T **Baths:** 1 Sh
🛇 ⅍ 🅃 🎔 🖵 🎄

Kyle of Lochalsh

NG7627 🍷 *Glenelg Inn, Off The Rails Restaurant*

Kyle Hotel, *Main Street, Kyle of Lochalsh, Ross-shire, IV40 6AB.*
Open: All Year
Grades: STB 3 Star
01599 534204 Fax: 01599 534932
thekylehotel@btinternet.com
D: £25.00–£47.00 **S:** £25.00–£47.00
Beds: 14T 8D 9S **Baths:** 31 En
🛇 🅿 ⅍ 🅃 ✕ 🖵 ❋ 🎄 cc
By the main crossing to the Isle of Skye via bridge and 200 metres from railway station. Kyle hotel offers a warm welcome. Experience superb local cuisine in our charming restaurant or enjoy a great value for money bar meal.

Tigh-a-Cladach, *Badicaul, Kyle of Lochalsh, Ross-shire, IV40 8BB.*
Open: Mar to Nov
01599 534891 (also fax)
Mrs Matheson
D: £16.00–£17.50 **S:** £16.00–£17.50
Beds: 1T 2D 1S **Baths:** 2 Sh
🛇 🅿 (5) 🅃 🎔 🖵 🎄
Situated between Kyle of Lochalsh and Plockton with superb views overlooking the Isle of Skye, all rooms with sea view. Guests can relax in the large garden or in the lounge and watch the seals play. Hotels and restaurants nearby for meals.

Marabhaig, *7 Coullindune, Glenelg, Kyle of Lochalsh, Ross-shire, IV40 8JU.*
Marabhaig - Situated on the shore of Glenelg Bay. Fantastic views.
Open: All Year
Grades: STB 3 Diamond
01599 522327 Mrs Cameron
D: £19.00–£21.00 **S:** £21.00–£23.00
Beds: 2T 3D **Baths:** 3 En 2 Sh
🅿 (6) ⅍ 🅃 ✕ 🖵 🎄 1

Ashgrove, *Balmacara Square, Kyle of Lochalsh, Ross-shire, IV40 8DJ.*
Very central West Highland location for touring and walking, including hill climbing.
Open: All Year
01599 566259 Mrs Gordon
D: £16.50–£20.00
Beds: 2D 1T **Baths:** 2 En 1 Pr
🛇 🅿 (3) 🅃 🎔 🖵 🎄

Achomraich, *Main Street, Kyle of Lochalsh, Ross-shire, IV40 8DA.*
Friendly family comfortable home. Parking, guest sitting room, Scottish breakfast.
Open: Easter to Oct
01599 534210 Mrs Murchison
D: £15.00–£17.00 **S:** £15.00–£17.00
Beds: 2D 1T **Baths:** 2 Sh
🛇 (3) 🅿 (4) 🅃 🎔 🖵

Kylesku

NC2233

Newton Lodge, *Kylesku, Lairg, Sutherland, IV27 4HW.*
Lovely new small hotel overlooking seal colony - spectacular scenery.
Open: Easter to Oct
01971 502070 (also fax)
Mr & Mrs Brauer
newtonlge@aol.com
D: £28.00–£30.00
Beds: 4D 3T **Baths:** 7 En
🅿 (10) ⅍ 🅃 ✕ 🖵 🎄 cc

Laggan (Newtonmore)

NN6194

Gaskmore House Hotel, *Laggan, Newtonmore, Inverness-shire, PH20 1BS.*
Set in heart of the Highlands a wonderful place just to be.
Open: Easter to Oct
Grades: STB 3 Star
01528 544250 (also fax)
gaskmorehouse@aol.com
D: £25.00–£45.00 **S:** £30.00–£50.00
Beds: 12T 12D 1S **Baths:** 25 En
🛇 🅿 ⅍ 🅃 ✕ 🖵 🎄 cc

Laid

NC4159

Rowan House, *90 Laid, Laid, Altnaharra, Lairg, Sutherland, IV27 4UN.*
Open: All Year
Grades: STB 1 Star
01971 511347 (also fax)
Mr MacLellan
shm@capetech.co.uk
D: £14.00–£19.00
S: £15.00–£20.00
Beds: 1F 2D 1T 1S **Baths:** 1 En 2 Sh
🛇 🅿 🅃 ✕ 🖵 🎄 cc
Set in a spectacular setting with uninterrupted views across Loch Eriboll to Ben Hope, Rowan House is in a private position on a 20 acre croft within 400m of the shore line. Launching facilities for diver, compressor nearby.

Laide

NG8992 🍷 *Aultbea Hotel, Ocean View Hotel*

Cul Na Mara Guest House, *Catalina Slipway, Sand passage, Laide, Achnasheen, Ross-shire, IV22 2ND.*
Open: All Year (not Xmas/New Year)
Grades: STB 3 Star
01445 731295
Mr Hart
Fax: 01445 731570
billhart@dircon.co.uk
D: £21.00 **S:** £31.00
Beds: 1F 1D **Baths:** 2 En
🛇 (5) 🅿 (4) 🅃 🎔 ✕ 🖵 🎄
A stay at 'Cul Na Mara' (Gaelic - Song of the Sea) is an enjoyable experience with superior Bed & Breakfast accommodation. Guest rooms fully ensuite complete with colour television - private dining room.

Lairg

NC5806 🍷 *Pitentrail Inn*

Muirness, *97 Lower Toroboll, Lairg, Sutherland, IV27 4DH.*
Comfortable croft house, superb open views. Central for day trips, close to railway.
Open: All Year
01549 402489
Mrs Grey
D: £16.00–£18.00 **S:** fr £18.00
Beds: 2D 1T **Baths:** 1 Pr 1 Sh
🛇 (2) 🅿 ⅍ 🅃 ✕ 🖵

Carnbren, *Lairg, Sutherland, IV27 4AY.*
Ideal centre for touring the North and West Highlands.
Open: Apr to Oct
01549 402259 Mrs MacKenzie
D: £16.50–£17.50
Beds: 1D 2T **Baths:** 1 En 2 Pr
🛇 🅿 (3) 🅃 🎔 🖵

Latheron

ND1933 🍷 *Latheroncoheel Hotel*

Tacher, *Latheron, Caithness, KW5 6DX.*
On A895 (Thurso). Modern, comfortable farmhouse.
Open: May to Oct
Grades: STB 3 Star
01593 741313 Mrs Falconer
D: £16.00–£18.00 **S:** £16.00–£20.00
Beds: 1F 1D 1T **Baths:** 1 En 1 Sh 1 Pr
🛇 🅿 (8) ⅍ 🅃 🎔 ✕ 🖵 🎄

Lewiston

NH5029 🍷 *Hunters Restaurant*

Woodlands, *East Lewiston, Drumnadrochit, Inverness, IV63 6UL.*
Family home, warm Scottish welcome awaits you. Central for touring.
Open: All Year (not Xmas)
Grades: STB 4 Star, AA 4 Diamond
01456 450356 Mr & Mrs Drysdale
Fax: 01456 450199
drysdale@woodlandsbandb.fsnet.co.uk
D: £18.00–£20.00
Beds: 2D 1T **Baths:** 3 En
🛇 🅿 (3) 🅃 ✕ 🖵 🎄 cc

Planning a longer stay? Always ask for any special rates

Lochcarron

NG8939   🍴 *Lochcarron Hotel, Rockvilla Hotel*

Aultsigh, Croft Road, Lochcarron, Strathcarron, Ross-shire, IV54 8YA.
Spectacular views over Loch Carron. Ideal base for climbing or touring.
Open: All Year
01520 722558 Ms Innes
moyra.innes@talk21.com
D: £16.00–£18.00 **S:** £18.00
Beds: 1F 1D 1T **Baths:** 2 Sh
🛏 🅿 (6) ⅍ 🔟 📮 🕭 🕹 ♿

Lochinver

NC0922

Veyatie, 66 Baddidarroch, Lochinver, Lairg, Sutherland, IV27 4LP.
Open: All Year (not Xmas)
Grades: STB 4 Star
01571 844424 Mrs Chapman
veyatie@baddid.freeserve.co.uk
D: £20.00–£25.00 **S:** £30.00–£50.00
Beds: 2D 1T **Baths:** 2 En 1 Pr
🅿 (3) ⅍ 🔟 📮 🕭
Veyatie is a modern bungalow situated in a beautiful, peaceful setting where our conservatory offers spectacular views over Lochinver bay to mountains beyond. Our bedrooms have many extra refinements for your comfort and the guests' lounge has fascinating character.

Suilven, Badnaban, Lochinver, Lairg, Sutherland, IV27 4LR.
3 miles from Lochinver, off Achiltibuie Road. Sea angling available.
Open: All Year (not Xmas/New Year)
01571 844358 Mrs Brown
D: £17.00 **S:** £22.00
Beds: 1T 1D **Baths:** 1 Sh
🅿 (2) 🔟 🕭 🕹 📮 🕭

Caisteal Liath, 74 Baddidarroch, Lochinver, Lairg, Sutherland, IV27 4LP.
Privately set overlooking Lochinver Bay, with spectacular sea/mountain views.
Open: Easter to Dec
01571 844457 (also fax)
Mrs MacLeod
caisteal_liath@compuserve.com
D: £25.00–£27.50 **S:** £35.00–£40.00
Beds: 1D 1T **Baths:** 2 En
🅿 (2) ⅍ 🔟 📮 🅅 🕭 CC

Lochluichart

NH3263

4 Mossford Cottages, Lochluichart, Garve, IV232QA.
Spectacular view across loch. Friendly informal atmosphere. Central touring position.
Open: All Year (not Xmas/New Year)
Grades: STB 3 Star
01997 414334 Mr & Mrs Doyle
D: £15.00–£18.00 **S:** £15.00–£18.00
Beds: 1F 1T 1D 1S **Baths:** 2 En 1 Pr 1 Sh
🛏 ⅍ 🕹 🗙 🕭 🕭

Lybster (Wick)

ND2435

Reisgill House, Lybster, Caithness, KW3 6BT.
Country house in quiet location. Traditional Scottish cooking our speciality.
Open: All Year (not Xmas/New Year)
Grades: STB 3 Star
01593 721212 (also fax) Ms Harper
helen@reisgill-house.com
D: fr £18.00 **S:** fr £18.00
Beds: 1F 2T 2D 1S **Baths:** 5 En 1 Pr
🛏 🅿 (6) ⅍ 🔟 🕹 🗙 🕭 🅅 🕭 CC

Mallaig

NM6/96   🍴 *Arisaig Hotel, Chlachain Bar, Cabin, Marine Hotel, Cornerstone Rest*

Spring Bank Guest House, East Bay, Mallaig, Inverness-shire, PH41 4QF.
Open: All Year (not Xmas/New Year)
01687 462459 (also fax) Mr Smith
j.t.smith0@talk21.com
D: £16.00–£17.00 **S:** £16.00–£17.00
Beds: 1F 2D 3T 2S **Baths:** 3 Sh
🛏 🔟 🕹 🗙 🕭 🅅 🕭 CC
Spring Bank is a traditional Highland house, situated overlooking the harbour and ferry terminals to Skye, the small Isles and Knoydart. Mallaig is at the end of the world famous West Highland Line and is ideal for walking and touring.

Rockcliffe, East Bay, Mallaig, Inverness-shire, PH41 4QF.
Quality accommodation overlooking bay. Trains, ferries and restaurants very close.
Open: Easter to Oct
01687 462484 Mrs Henderson
D: £16.00–£17.00 **S:** £17.00–£18.00
Beds: 2D 1S **Baths:** 2 Sh
🅿 (2) ⅍ 🔟 🕭 🅅 🕭

The Anchorage, Gillies Park, Mallaig, Inverness-shire, PH41 4QS.
Yards from station and ferry terminal.
Open: All Year (not Xmas/New Year)
Grades: STB 2 Star
01687 462454 (also fax)
Mrs Summers
anchoragemallaig@talk21.com
D: £18.00–£20.00 **S:** £18.00–£20.00
Beds: 1F 1D 1T 1S **Baths:** 4 En
🛏 ⅍ 🔟 🕭 🅅 🕭

The Moorings, Mallaig, Inverness-shire, PH41 4QS.
2 mins from railway station, ferry terminal; overlooking harbour.
Open: All Year (not Xmas)
01687 462225 M & J Carty
D: £13.00–£16.00 **S:** £15.00–£18.00
Beds: 1F 2D 2T 2S **Baths:** 5 En
🛏 🅿 (3) ⅍ 🔟 🕹 🕭 🕭

Glencross Stables, Morar, Mallaig, Inverness-shire, PH40 4PD.
Attractive Victorian farmhouse, close sandy beaches, fishing, golfing, island cruises. **Open:** All Year (not Xmas)
01687 450362 Mrs Millingan
Fax: **01687 450325**
D: £13.00 **S:** £18.00
Beds: 1T **Baths:** 1 En
🅿 (1) ⅍ 🕭 🕭

Mellon Charles

NG8491

Tranquillity, 21 Mellon Charles, Aultbea, Achnasheen, Ross-shire, IV22 2JN.
Comfortable home in quiet location with wonderful mountain views.
Open: All Year (not Xmas)
Grades: STB 3 Star
01445 731241 (also fax) Mr & Mrs Bond
D: £20.00 **S:** £20.00–£30.00
Beds: 1F 1D 1S **Baths:** 2 En 1 Pr
🛏 🅿 ⅍ 🔟 🗙 🅅 🕭

Coveview, Mellon Charles, Aultbea, Achnasheen, Ross-shire, IV22 2JL.
Quiet, comfortable bed and breakfast or self catering in the highlands of Scotland.
Open: All Year
01445 731351 Mrs MacRae
D: £16.00–£18.00 **S:** £18.00–£20.00
Beds: 1F 1D 1S **Baths:** 1 Pr 1 Sh
🅿 🔟 🕹 🕭 🅅

Melvich

NC8865   🍴 *Melvich Hotel*

Sheiling Guest House, Melvich, Thurso, Caithness, KW14 7YJ.
Fantastic views. Great warmth and comfort. Superb breakfasts. Visit Orkney.
Open: Apr to Oct
01641 531256 (also fax)
Mrs Campbell
thesheilling@btinternet.com
D: £22.00–£25.00 **S:** £30.00–£35.00
Beds: 2D 1T **Baths:** 3 En
🛏 🅿 (4) ⅍ 🔟 🕹 🕭 🅅 🕭

Melvich Hotel, Melvich, Thurso, Caithness, KW14 7YJ.
Former coaching inn - an oasis from the stresses of urban living.
Open: All Year (not Xmas)
01641 531206 Fax: **01641 531347**
melvichtl@aol.com
D: £20.00–£25.00 **S:** £30.00–£35.00
Beds: 4D 8T 2S **Baths:** 14 En
🛏 🅿 (8) 🔟 🗙 🕭 🅅 🕭 CC

Mey

ND2772

The Hawthorns, Mey, Thurso, Caithness, KW14 8XL.
Large country house set in own grounds with large private off-road car park.
Open: All Year
01847 851710 (also fax) Mrs MacKay
hawthorns-support@btinternet.com
D: fr £20.00 **S:** fr £25.00
Beds: 3D **Baths:** 3 En
🛏 🅿 (6) 🔟 🕹 🗙 🅅 🕭

RATES
D = Price range per person sharing in a double room
S = Price range for a single room

Morar

NM6793 ◀ Morar Hotel, Marine Hotel, Cabin Hotel

Sunset, *Morar, Mallaig, Inverness-shire, PH40 4PA.*
Family-run guest house, sea views, Thai food our speciality.
Open: All Year (not Xmas)
01687 462259 Mrs Clulow
Fax: 01687 460085
sunsetgh@aol.com
D: £12.50–£18.00 **S:** £12.50–£18.00
Beds: 1F 1D 1T **Baths:** 1 En 1 Sh
🐾 (2) 🅿 (6) ⊁ 📺 ✕ 🕮 📺 ⅙

Glengorm, *Morar, Mallaig, Inverness-shire, PH40 4PA.*
In Morar Village. Silversand beaches nearby. Ferry to Skye 2 miles.
Open: All Year
Grades: STB 2 Star
01687 462165 Mrs Stewart
glengormmorar@talk21.com
D: £15.00–£16.00
Beds: 1D 1T **Baths:** 1 Sh
🅿 (4) 📺 🕮 🕮 📺 ⅙

Sandholm Bed & Breakfast, *Morar, Mallaig, Inverness-shire, PH40 4PA.*
Sandholm overlooks Morar Bay and Islands of Eigg and Rum.
Open: All Year
01687 462592 (also fax)
Ms McEachen
sandholm@zetnet.co.uk
D: £12.00–£18.00 **S:** £15.00–£30.00
Beds: 2F 1D **Baths:** 1 En 1 Sh
🐾 🅿 (6) ⊁ 📺 🕮 📺 ⅙ cc

Muir of Ord

NH5250 ◀ Old Arms Hotel, North Kessock Hotel, Moorings Hotel, Achilty Hotel

Birchgrove, *Arcan, Muir of Ord, Ross-shire, IV6 7UL.*
Comfortable country house in quiet area. Guest rooms overlooking garden.
Open: All Year (not Xmas)
01997 433245 Mrs Bell
Fax: 01997 433304
D: £15.00–£16.50 **S:** £16.00–£17.00
Beds: 1F 1D 1T **Baths:** 1 En 1 Sh
🐾 🅿 (3) 📺 🕮 ⅙

Hillview Park, *Muir of Ord, Ross-shire, IV6 7XS.*
Rural situation, adjacent to golf course. Ground floor bungalow.
Open: Easter to Oct
Grades: STB 3 Star
01463 870787 Mrs Peterkin
D: £17.00–£19.00 **S:** £18.00–£20.00
Beds: 1F 1D 1T **Baths:** 3 En
🅿 (3) ⊁ 📺 🕮 ⅙

Dungrianach, *Corry Road, Muir of Ord, Ross-shire, IV6 7TN.*
Secluded rural setting in idyllic situation - peaceful and quiet.
Open: May to Sep
01463 870316 Mrs MacKenzie
D: £15.00 **S:** £15.00
Beds: 1D **Baths:** 1 Pr
🐾 (8) 🅿 (4) ⊁ 📺 ✕ ⅙

Blairdhu Farmhouse, *Muir of Ord, Ross-shire, IV6 7RT.*
Relax in pleasant country surroundings. An ideal base for touring.
Open: All Year
01463 870536 Mrs Morrison
D: £15.00 **S:** £20.00
Beds: 1F 1D 1S **Baths:** 2 Sh
🅿 📺 🕪 ✕ 🕮 📺 ⅙ ⅙

Muirshearlich

NN1380 ◀ Moorings Hotel

Strone Farm, *Muirshearlich, Banavie, Fort William, Inverness-shire, PH33 7PB.*
Rural setting, panoramic views Ben Nevis, Caledonian Canal. Traditional food.
Open: Feb to Nov
Grades: STB 3 Star
01397 712773 (also fax)
Mrs Cameron
D: £18.00–£20.00 **S:** £23.00–£25.00
Beds: 2D 1T
🐾 🅿 (3) 📺 ✕ 🕮 ⅙

Munlochy

NH6453

Craigiehowe, *3 Forestry House, Munlochy, Ross-shire, IV8 8NH.*
Quiet cul de sac near to all services.
Open: All Year (not Xmas)
01463 811402 Mrs Munro
D: £14.00–£16.00 **S:** £14.00–£16.00
Beds: 1F 1D
🐾 🅿 ⊁ 📺 🕮 ⅙

Nairn

NH8856 ◀ Havelock Hotel, Longhouse, Claymore Hotel, Links Hotel, Lothian Hotel, Newton Hotel, Argdour Hotel, Marine Hotel

Fonthill, *King Street, Nairn, IV12 4NP.*
Beautiful detached villa, central location, views on website.
Open: All Year
01667 455996 Mrs O'Grady
fonthill@classicfm.net
D: £18.00–£22.00 **S:** £18.00–£22.00
Beds: 1F 2D **Baths:** 1 En, 1 Pr, 1 Sh
🐾 🅿 (6) ⊁ 📺 🕪 ✕ 🕮 📺 ✼ ⅙

Redburn, *Queen Street, Nairn, IV12 4AA.*
Extremely attractive Victorian Villa, quiet location, close to all amenities.
Open: Easter to Oct
Grades: STB 3 Star
01667 452238 Mr & Mrs Clucas
clucas@redburnvilla.fsnet.co.uk
D: £17.00–£20.00 **S:** £17.00–£20.00
Beds: 1D 1T 1S **Baths:** 2 Sh
🐾 🅿 (4) ⊁ 📺 🕮 📺 ⅙

Durham House, *4 Academy Street, Nairn, IV12 4RJ.*
Elegant Victorian villa near beaches, golf, castles and historic sites.
Open: All Year (not Xmas)
Grades: STB 3 Star
01667 452345 (also fax)
P J Hudson
durhamhouse@nairn34.freeserve.co.uk
D: £18.00–£22.00 **S:** £16.00–£18.00
Beds: 1F 1D 1T 1S **Baths:** 2 En 1 Pr 1 Sh
🐾 🅿 (4) ⊁ 📺 🕪 ✕ 🕮 📺 ⅙ cc

Glenshiel, *Pier Road, Sandbank, Argyll, PA23 8QH.*
Elegant Victorian villa in secluded beautiful garden. Loch and mountain views.
Open: Easter to Oct
01369 701202 Mrs Galliard
ann@galliard.freeserve.co.uk
D: £20.00–£25.00 **S:** £25.00–£30.00
Beds: 1D 1T **Baths:** 2 Pr
🐾 🅿 (20) ⊁ 📺 🕪 🕮 📺 ⅙ ⅙

Bracadale House, *Albert Street, Nairn, Inverness-shire, IV12 4HF.*
A Victorian villa situated in the championship golfing, seaside town.
Open: Mar to Oct
Grades: STB 4 Star
01667 452547 H M MacLeod
bracadale_house@hotmail.com
D: £20.00–£22.00 **S:** £20.00–£25.00
Beds: 1T 2D **Baths:** 2 En 1 Pr
🐾 (13) 🅿 (3) ⊁ 📺 🕪 ✕ 🕮 📺 ⅙

Coel Mara, *Links Place, Nairn, IV12 4NH.*
Panoramic view of the Moray Firth, 200 yards from beach.
Open: All Year (not Xmas/New Year)
Grades: STB 4 Star
01667 452495 Mrs Mackintosh
Fax: 01667 451531
ceolmara15@aol.com
D: £20.00–£25.00 **S:** £20.00–£25.00
Beds: 1F 1D 1S **Baths:** 3 En
🐾 🅿 ⊁ 📺 🕪 🕮 📺 ⅙ cc

Ardgour Hotel, *Seafield Street, Nairn, IV12 4HN.*
'Home from home' excellent value.
Open: All Year
01667 454230 Mr Dunlop
D: £25.00–£30.00 **S:** £22.00–£35.00
Beds: 3F 2D 3T 2S **Baths:** 8 En 2 Pr
🐾 🅿 (12) 📺 🕪 ✕ 🕮 📺 ⅙

Lothian House Hotel, *Crescent Road, Nairn, IV12 4NBJ.*
Family run-hotel, licensed restaurant, sea views, ensuite rooms, all facilities. Off-road parking. Centrally situated.
Open: All Year
01667 453555
D: £18.00–£25.00 **S:** £19.00–£28.00
Beds: 1F 2D 2T 2S **Baths:** 2 Pr 2 Sh
🐾 🅿 (8) 📺 🕪 ✕ 🕮 📺 ⅙ cc

Nethy Bridge

NJ0020 ◀ Strathspey Hotel, The Mountview, Heatherbridge Hotel

Aspen Lodge, *Nethy Bridge, Inverness-shire, PH25 3DA.*
Warm welcome and memorable breakfast in heart of picturesque village.
Open: All Year (not Xmas)
Grades: STB 3 Star B&B
01479 821042 Mrs Renton
linda@aspenlodge.fsnet.co.uk
D: fr £19.00 **S:** fr £25.00
Beds: 1D 1T **Baths:** 1 En 1 Pr
🐾 (1) ⊁ 📺 🕮 📺 ⅙

Planning a longer stay? Always ask for any special rates

Newtonmore

NN7199   ⚐ *Braeriach Hotel, Glen Hotel, Ballavile Sport Hotel*

The Pines, *Station Road, Newtonmore, Inverness-shire, PH20 1AR.*
Open: Jan to Oct
01540 673271 Mr Walker
Fax: 01540 673882
D: £20.00–£25.00 **S:** £20.00–£25.00
Beds: 2D 2T 2S **Baths:** 6 En
🛏 (12) 🅿 (5) ⵣ 📺 ⵡ ✕ 🗐 ⵡ cc
Comfortable Edwardian house with river valley and mountain views. Peaceful wooded gardens rich in bird and wildlife. Conveniently located for public transport, touring, walking, cycling, golf, Cairngorm Mountains and RSPB reserves. Please phone for colour brochure.

Alder Lodge Guest House, *Glen Road, Newtonmore, Inverness-shire, PH20 1EA.*
Beautiful house, quiet situation, 0.25 mile from the shops and hotels.
Open: All Year
01540 673376 Mr Stewart
D: £15.00 **S:** £15.00
Beds: 2 T 2D **Baths:** 1 Sh
🛏 🅿 (6) ⵡ ✕ 🗐 ⵡ

Nigg

NH8071   ⚐ *Nigg Ferry Hotel*

Carse of Bayfield, *Nigg, Tain, Ross-shire, IV19 1QW.*
Overlooking Cromarty Firth on Pictish Trail. Walking, sandy beaches, golf courses & birdwatching nearby.
Open: All Year (not Xmas)
Grades: STB 3 Star
01862 863230 (also fax)
Mrs Campbell
D: £16.00–£18.00 **S:** £16.00–£18.00
Beds: 1D 1T **Baths:** 1 Sh
🛏 🅿 (6) ⵣ 📺 ⵡ ✕ 🗐 ⵡ

North Kessock

NH6548   ⚐ *North Kessock Hotel, Munlochy Hotel*

The Rowans, *Bogallan, North Kessock, Inverness, Highland, IV1 3XE.*
Open: All Year (not Xmas/New Year)
01463 731428 Mrs Davidson
ruth.davidson@ntlworld.com
D: £15.00–£17.50 **S:** £18.00–£20.00
Beds: 3D **Baths:** 2 En 1 Pr
ⵣ 📺 🗐 ⵡ
The Rowans is a modern family run bungalow on the outskirts of Inverness in area of scenic beauty known as the Black Isle. Ideal base for touring highlands - Loch Ness, Cairngorm Mountains, dolphin watch, golf courses, beaches, Culloden Battlefield close by.

37 Drumsmittal Road, *North Kessock, Inverness, IV1 3JU.*
Warm welcome awaits in comfortable bungalow. Ideal for touring Highlands.
Open: All Year **Grades:** STB 3 Star
01463 731777 Mrs Bonthrone
norah@kessock.fsnet.co.uk
D: £16.00–£18.00 **S:** £16.00–£18.00
Beds: 1D 1S **Baths:** 1 Sh
🅿 (2) ⵣ 📺 🗐 ⵡ

Helen's B&B, *8 Bellfield Drive, North Kessock, Inverness, IV1 3XT.*
Modern house overlooking Beauly Firth where dolphins can be viewed.
Open: Easter to Oct
Grades: STB 2 Star
01463 731317 H C Robertson
D: £16.00–£18.00 **S:** £17.00–£20.00
Beds: 1D 2T **Baths:** 1 Pr 1 Sh
🅿 (4) ⵣ 📺 🗐

Onich

NN0261

Camus House, *Lochside Lodge, Onich, Fort William, Inverness-shire, PH33 6RY.*
Beautiful Victorian country house in outstanding location between Fort William - Glencoe.
Open: Feb to Nov
Grades: STB 3 Star
01855 821200 Fax: 01855 821 200
young@camushouse.freeserve.co.uk
D: £23.50–£30.00 **S:** £27.50–£35.00
Beds: 2F 2T 3D **Baths:** 6 En 1 Sh
🛏 🅿 ⵣ 📺 ✕ 🗐 ⵡ cc

Piperhill

NH8651   ⚐ *Cawdor Tavern*

Colonsay, *Piperhill Cawdor, Cawdor, Nairn, IV12 5SD.*
Open: All Year (not Xmas/New Year)
01667 404305 Mrs Murray
dmmm16592@aol.com
D: £15.00 **S:** £18.00
Beds: 1F 1D **Baths:** 2 Sh
🛏 🅿 (3) ⵣ 📺 🗐 ⵡ
Beautiful new traditionally built detached house set in rural area close to Inverness, Nairn, Cawdor castle and Culloden battlefield, Golf and Fishing close by. Comfortable beds, tastefully decorated rooms and good Scottish breakfasts and evening tea, private off road parking.

Plockton

NG8033   ⚐ *Plockton Inn, Plockton Hotel, Off The Rails, Old School House, Tingle Creek Hotel*

Plockton Hotel, *Harbour Street, Plockton, Ross-shire, IV52 8TN.*
Waterfront inn in traditional row of stone houses, picturesque NT village of Plockton.
Open: All Year
01599 544274 Mrs Pearson
Fax: 01599 544475
D: £27.50–£35.00 **S:** £32.50–£40.00
Beds: 9D 4T 1S **Baths:** 13 En 1 Pr
🛏 ⵣ 📺 ✕ 🗐 ⵡ 3 cc

Tomacs, *Frithard, Plockton, Ross-shire, IV52 8TQ.*
Lovely views over Loch Carron & Applecross Hills; easy parking.
Open: All Year
01599 544321 Mrs Jones
D: £16.00–£20.00 **S:** fr £18.00
Beds: 2D 1T **Baths:** 1 En 1 Pr 1 Sh
🛏 🅿 📺 ⵡ 🗐 ⵡ

Planning a longer stay? Always ask for any special rates

The Sheiling, *Plockton, Ross-shire, IV52 8TL.*
Comfortable family home situated on a peninsula in the picturesque conservation village. **Open:** Easter to Oct
01599 544282 Mrs Macdonald
JANE@Sheiling282.freeserve.co.uk
D: £18.00–£22.00
Beds: 2D 1T **Baths:** 1 En 1 Sh
🛏 (12) 🅿 (3) 📺 🗐

Nessun Dorma, *Plockton, Ross-shire, IV52 8TF.*
Attractive, modern house, own grounds, close quiet road 10 mins' walk railway station. **Open:** All Year
01599 544235 Mr & Mrs Coe
gill@ecosse.net
D: £16.00 £18.00 **S:** £16.00–£20.00
Beds: 1D
🛏 🅿 (6) 📺 ⵡ 🗐 ⵡ

Creag Liath, *Achnandarach, Plockton, Ross-shire, IV52 8TY.*
Peaceful and quiet. Extensive information provided for local walking and touring Isle of Skye.
Open: Easter to Oct
01599 544341 (also fax)
N Campbell
D: £20.00–£23.00
Beds: 1D 1T
🅿 (4) ⵣ 📺 🗐 ⵡ

Poolewe

NG8580   ⚐ *Poolewe Hotel*

Creagan, *Poolewe, Ross-shire, IV22 2LD.*
Quiet country house in highland village. Private off-road parking, good breakfasts with home-baking.
Open: Mar to Oct
01445 781424 (also fax)
Mrs MacKenzie
D: £18.00 **S:** £25.00
Beds: 2D 1T **Baths:** 2 En 1 Pr
🛏 🅿 (4) ⵣ 📺 🗐 cc

Corriness Guest House, *Poolewe, Achnasheen, Ross-shire, IV22 2JU.*
Cherished Edwardian villa by Inverewe Gardens and Loch Ewe.
Open: Easter to Oct
01445 781262 Mrs Rowley
Fax: 01445 781263
D: £23.00–£25.00
Beds: 3T 2D **Baths:** 5 En
🛏 (10) 🅿 (10) ⵣ 📺 ✕ 🗐 ⵡ cc

Portmahomack

NH9184   ⚐ *Oyster Catcher Restaurant*

Wentworth House , *Tarbatness Road, Portmahomack, Tain, Ross-shire, IV20 1YB.*
Open: All Year
01862 871897 Mrs Elliott
monicaelliott@wentworth39.demon.co.uk
D: £20.00–£22.50 **S:** £25.00
Beds: 3T **Baths:** 1 En 2 Sh
🛏 🅿 (6) ⵣ 📺 ⵡ 🗐 ⵡ
Historic former manse beside golf course, overlooking the Dornoch Firth, home of the bottle-nosed dolphins. Portmahomack is the only West-facing village on East coast, next to Pictish archaeological site (largest in Europe) currently under excavation by York University.

Poyntzfield

NH7064 ◀ *Royal Hotel*

Newfield, Newhall Bridge, Poyntzfield, Dingwall, Ross-shire, IV7 8LQ.
Open: All Year
Grades: STB 4 Star
01381 610333 Mrs Munro
Fax: 01381 610325
jean.munro@tesco.net
D: £18.00–£25.00 **S:** £18.00–£24.00
Beds: 1F 1D 1S **Baths:** 1 En 2 Sh
⌂ (1) 🅿 (6) ⊁ 📺 ▥ 🛲
Newfield is a modernised traditional Scottish house set in 2 acres of mature gardens, situated 0.25 mile from Udale Bay Bird Sanctuary, 6 miles from Cromarty and 17 miles from Inverness. Ideal for touring the Highlands of Scotland.

Ratagan

NG9119

3 MacInnes Place, Ratagan, Glenshiel, Kyle of Lochalsh, Ross-shire, IV40 8HX.
Nestling at foot of Mam Ratagan overlooking Loch Duich and Five Sisters of Kintail.
Open: Easter to Oct
01599 511365 Mrs Aldam
D: £15.00–£18.00 **S:** £18.00–£20.00
Beds: 1F 1D 2T **Baths:** 3 En 1 Sh
⌂ 📺 ♈ ✕ ▥ 🆅 🛲

Rogart

NC7303 ◀ *Pittentrail Inn*

Benview, Lower Morness, Rogart, Sutherland, IV28 3XG.
Traditional country farmhouse offering peace and quiet, comfort, good food.
Open: Easter to Oct
01408 641222 Mrs Corbett
D: £15.00–£15.50 **S:** £16.00
Beds: 1T 1S 2D **Baths:** 2 Sh
⌂ (12) 🅿 ⊁ 📺 ♈ ✕ ▥ 🆅 🛲

Tigh Na Fuaran, Pitfure, Rogart, Sutherland, IV28 3UA.
Modern bungalow large garden golfing fishing walking ideal touring base.
Open: Easter to Oct
Grades: STB 3 Star
01408 641224 (also fax)
Mrs Colquhoun
D: £16.00–£18.00 **S:** £16.00–£18.00
Beds: 1D 1T **Baths:** 1 Sh
⌂ (5) 🅿 (3) 📺 ♈ ▥ 🛲

Rothiemurchus

NH9308 ◀ *Skiing Doo*

English Charlies, Rothiemurchus, Aviemore, Inverness-shire, PH22 1QP.
Lovely quiet family home rural setting with south-facing aspect.
Open: All Year (not Xmas)
01479 810837 (also fax)
Mrs Weir
penspots@btinternet.com
D: £16.00–£18.00 **S:** £18.00–£19.00
Beds: 1T 2S **Baths:** 2 Sh
⌂ (4) 🅿 (4) ⊁ 📺 ♈ ✕ ▥ 🆅 🛲 ⑂

B&B owners may vary rates - be sure to check when booking

Scaniport

NH6239 ◀ *Dores Inn*

Ballindarroch, Aldourie, Inverness, IV2 6EL.
Open: All Year
01463 751348 Mrs Parsons
Fax: 01463 751372
ali.phil@cwcom.net
D: £20.00–£30.00 **S:** £20.00–£30.00
Beds: 1F 1D 1T 1S **Baths:** 1 Pr 2 Sh
⌂ (8) 📺 ♈ ▥ 🆅 🛲
Situated ten minutes south of Inverness (B862), Ballindarroch is a unique Victorian country house in ten acres of woodland gardens, furnished with period pieces, hand painted Chinese wallpaper in drawing room. A warm and friendly house run on very informal lines.

Scourie

NC1544 ◀ *Scourie Hotel*

Minch View, Scouriemore, Scourie, Lairg, Sutherland, IV27 4TG.
Modern comfortable croft house. Home cooking. Outstanding views and hospitality.
Open: Easter to Oct
01971 502010 Mrs MacDonald
D: fr £16.00 **S:** fr £16.00
Beds: 2D 1T **Baths:** 2 Sh
⌂ 🅿 ⊁ 📺 ♈ ✕ ▥ 🆅

Fasgadh, Scourie, Lairg, Sutherland, IV27 4TG.
Beautiful views of Scourie, near to restaurant and Scourie Hotel.
Open: Easter to Oct
Grades: STB 3 Star
01971 502402 Mrs Mackay
sandra@scouriemore.co.uk
D: £17.00–£18.00 **S:** £18.00–£20.00
Beds: 1D 1T **Baths:** 2 En
⌂ (3) 📺 ♈ ✕ ▥ 🆅 🛲

Badcall Stoerview, Scourie, Lairg, Sutherland, IV27 4TH.
Every room with its own spectacular view of Badcall Islands and mountains.
Open: Easter to Oct
01971 502411 (also fax)
Mrs MacKay
D: fr £15.00 **S:** £20.00–£25.00
Beds: 1F 1D **Baths:** 1 Sh
⌂ 🅿 (4) 📺 ✕ ▥ 🆅 🛲 ♿

RATES
D = Price range per person sharing in a double room
S = Price range for a single room

NG8153 ◀ *Tigh An Cilan Hotel*

Tigh Fada, 117 Doireaonar, Shieldaig, Strathcarron, Ross-shire, IV54 8XH.
Family home on working croft, magnificent scenery.
Open: Feb to Nov
Grades: STB 2 Star
01520 755248 (also fax)
Mrs Calcott
D: £14.50–£15.50 **S:** £16.00–£18.00
Beds: 1F 1D 1T **Baths:** 2 Sh
⌂ 🅿 (3) 📺 ✕ ▥ 🆅 cc

Smithton

NH7145

3a Resaurie, Smithton, Inverness, IV2 7NH.
Open: All Year
01463 791714 Mrs Mansfield
mbmansfield@uk2net
D: £17.00–£21.00 **S:** £17.00–£21.00
Beds: 2D 1T **Baths:** 1 En 1 Sh
⌂ (3) ⊁ 📺 ♈ ✕ ▥ 🆅 🛲
Quiet residential area 3 miles east of Inverness. Public transport nearby. GB National Cycle Route 7 passes door. Adjacent to Farmland. Views to Moray Firth, Ben Wyvis and Ross-shire Hills. Home baking, high tea, Evening meals. A CHRISTIAN HOME.

Sordale

ND1461 ◀ *Ulbster Arms*

Sordale House, Sordale, Halkirk, Caithness, KW12 6XB.
C19th farmhouse, oak-beamed bedrooms, beautiful views overlooking River Thurso.
Open: All Year (not Xmas)
01847 831270 Mrs Rodgers
Fax: 01847 831971
peter.pj.rodgers@talk21.com
D: £16.00–£18.00 **S:** £18.00–£21.00
Beds: 1D 1T **Baths:** 2 Sh
⌂ 🅿 (4) ⊁ 📺 ✕ ▥ 🆅 🛲

South Laggan

NN2996

Forest Lodge, South Laggan, Invergarry, Inverness-shire, PH34 4EA.
Open: All Year (not Xmas/New Year)
Grades: STB 3 Star, AA 3 Diamond
01809 501219 Mr & Mrs Shearer
Fax: 01809 501476
info@flgh.co.uk
D: £17.00–£22.00 **S:** £24.00–£29.00
Beds: 2F 2T 3D **Baths:** 6 En 1 Pr
⌂ (10) ⊁ 📺 ✕ ▥ 🆅 🛲 cc
Ian and Janet Shearer offer friendly hospitality, pleasant en-suite accommodation, and home cooking in their rurally set home close to the Great Glen Way. Walking or touring, Forest Lodge is the perfect stopover.

All details shown are as supplied by B&B owners in Autumn 2000

Spean Bridge

NN2281   ◀ *Smiddy House, Spean Bridge Hotel, Aonach Mor Hotel*

Dreamweavers, *Earendil, Spean Bridge, PH34 4EQ.*
Traditional Scottish hospitality and cuisine amidst stunning Highland scenery.
Open: All Year
Grades: STB 2 Star
01397 712548 H Maclean
helen@dreamweavers.co.uk
D: £15.00–£20.00 **S:** £15.00–£20.00
Beds: 1F 1T 1D **Baths:** 1 En 2 Pr
🛇 🅿 (5) ⅏ �📺 ㅋ ✕ 🕮 Ⅵ ♿ 3

Coire Glas Guest House, *Spean Bridge, Inverness-shire, PH34 4EU.*
Spectacular views of Grey Corries. Ideal base for climbing / touring.
Open: All Year (not Xmas)
Grades: STB 2 Star, AA 3 Diamond
01397 712272 (also fax)
Mrs MacFarlane
enquiry@coireglas.co.uk
D: £14.50–£19.50 **S:** £14.50–£25.00
Beds: 2F 4D 4T 1S **Baths:** 8 En 3 Sh
🛇 🅿 (11) 📺 ✕ 🕮 ♿ cc

Coinachan Guest House, *Gairlochy Road, Spean Bridge, Inverness-shire, PH34 4EG.*
Open: All Year (not Xmas)
Grades: STB 4 Star
01397 712417 (also fax)
H C Hoare
D: £20.00–£25.00 **S:** £20.00–£35.00
Beds: 2D 1T **Baths:** 3 En
🅿 📺 ✕ 🕮 ♿
Enjoy a relaxing informal stay in a tastefully modernised C17th highland home offering a high standard of comfort and attention to detail. Privately situated overlooking mountains and moorland, carefully prepared 4 course dinner. Perfect touring base, special 7 day rates.

Corriechoille Lodge, *Spean Bridge, Inverness-shire, PH34 4EY.*
C18th lodge; stunning highland location, home cooked food, drinks licence.
Open: Mar to Oct
Grades: STB 4 Star GH, AA 4 Diamond
01397 712002 Mr & Mrs Swabey
enquiry@corriechoille.com
D: £20.00–£27.00
Beds: 2F 2D 1T **Baths:** 5 En
🛇 (7) 🅿 (6) ⅏ 📺 ✕ 🕮 Ⅵ ♿ cc

Tirindrish House, *Spean Bridge, Inverness-shire, PH34 4EU.*
Large, comfortable, historic highland house in 15-acre secluded garden.
Open: Jan to Oct
01397 712398 Mrs Wilson
Fax: 01397 712595
pj1@compuserve.com
D: £17.00–£20.00 **S:** £17.00–£28.00
Beds: 1F 1D 1T **Baths:** 1 En 2 Pr
🛇 🅿 (4) 📺 ㅋ ✕ 🕮 ♿

Planning a longer stay? Always ask for any special rates

Stoer

NC0328   ◀ *Riverside*

Stoer Villa, *Stoer, Lairg, Sutherland, IV27 4JE.*
Victorian villa near Atlantic, sandy beaches, hill walkers and anglers paradise.
Open: All Year (not Xmas/New Year)
01571 855305 Mrs Spykers
D: £15.00–£17.00 **S:** £15.00–£17.00
Beds: 1D 1T **Baths:** 1 Sh
🛇 🅿 (5) 📺 ✕ 🕮

Cruachan Guest House, *Stoer, Lochinver, Lairg, Sutherland, IV27 4JE.*
Friendly licensed accommodation. Beautiful beaches and mountains nearby.
Open: Apr to Oct
01571 855303 Miss Gould
D: £17.50–£20.00 **S:** £17.50–£20.00
Beds: 1D 2T 1S **Baths:** 1 Pr 1 Sh
🛇 🅿 (4) 📺 ㅋ ✕ 🕮 ♿

Strathan (Lochinver)

NC0821

Glenview , *Strathan, Lochinver, Lairg, Sutherland, IV27 4LR.*
Peaceful location, 100 yards off minor road, easy parking. 'Home from home'.
Open: March to Oct
01571 844324 Mrs Palmer
jand1@nascr.net
D: £17.00–£18.00 **S:** £16.00–£20.00
Beds: 1T 2D 2S **Baths:** 2 Sh
🛇 (14) 🅿 (6) ⅏ 📺 ✕ 🕮 ♿

Strathpeffer

NH4858   ◀ *Richmond Hotel, Brunstane Hotel, Holly Lodge Hotel*

Scoraig, *8 Kinnettas Square, Strathpeffer, Ross-shire, IV14 9BD.*
Quiet location in Victorian village ideal base for touring Highlands.
Open: All Year (not Xmas)
Grades: STB 3 Star
01997 421847 Mrs MacDonald
macdonald@kinnettas.freeserve.co.uk
D: £15.00–£17.00 **S:** £15.00–£20.00
Beds: 1F 1D 1T 1S **Baths:** 1 En 1 Sh
🛇 🅿 (6) 📺 ✕ 🕮 ♿

Burnhill, *Strathpeffer, Ross-shire, IV14 9DH.*
Victorian house situated at entrance to a former spa village.
Open: Easter to Oct
01997 421292 Mrs Watt
D: £14.00–£18.00 **S:** £18.00
Beds: 1F 1T 1D **Baths:** 1 En 1 Sh
🛇 🅿 ⅏ 📺 ♿

Inver Lodge, *Strathpeffer, Ross-shire, IV14 9DH.*
Late Victorian house,large garden, home baking/cooking. Highland hospitality, warm welcome.
Open: March to Dec
Grades: STB 3 Star, AA 3 Diamond
01997 421392 Mrs Derbyshire
debyshire@inverlg.fsnet.co.uk
D: £16.00–£17.00 **S:** £22.00–£25.00
Beds: 1F 1T
🛇 🅿 ⅏ 📺 ㅋ ✕ 🕮 Ⅵ ♿ cc

Craigvar

Craigvar, *The Square, Strathpeffer, Ross-shire, IV14 9DL.*
Beautifully situated luxury accommodation in unique Highland Victorian spa village.
Open: All Year (not Xmas/New Year)
Grades: STB 4 Star, AA 5 Diamond
01997 421622 (also fax)
Mrs Scott
craigvar@talk21.com
D: £20.00–£27.00 **S:** £24.00–£31.00
Beds: 1T 1D 1S **Baths:** 3 En
🅿 (4) ⅏ 📺 🕮 Ⅵ ♿ cc

Stromeferry

NG8634

Maple Lodge, *Stromeferry, Ross-shire, IV53 8UP.*
Detached house in secluded Glen. Mountain views all rooms.
Open: All Year
Grades: STB 2 Star
01599 577276 Mrs McDermott
jim@maple-lodge.co.uk
D: £16.00–£20.00 **S:** £16.00–£20.00
Beds: 1F 1T **Baths:** 1 En 1 Pr
🛇 🅿 (2) 📺 ㅋ ✕ 🕮 Ⅵ ♿

Strontian

NM8161   ◀ *Strothian Hotel, Benview Hotel*

Carm Cottage, *Monument Park, Strontian, Acharacle, Argyll, PH36 4HZ.*
Ideal stop for visiting Mull and smaller Isles, plus touring around Ardnamurchan.
Open: April to Oct
01967 402268 Mrs Macnaughton
Fax: 01967 402095
D: £16.00–£19.00
Beds: 3F 1T 2D **Baths:** 1 En 1 Sh
🛇 🅿 (3) 📺 ㅋ ✕ 🕮 ♿

Tain (Dornoch Firth)

NH7881   ◀ *Morangie House Hotel, Royal Hotel, Carnegie Lodge Hotel*

Carringtons, *Morangie Road, Tain, Ross-shire, IV19 1PY.*
Large Victorian house facing sea. Suitable stopover for Orkney Isles.
Open: All Year (not Xmas)
Grades: STB 3 Star
01862 892635 (also fax)
Mrs Roberts
mollie1@btinternet,com
D: £16.00–£18.00 **S:** £20.00–£25.00
Beds: 2F 1D **Baths:** 2 En
🛇 🅿 (6) 📺 ㅋ 🕮 Ⅵ ♿

Golf View Guest House, *13 Knockbreck Road, Tain, Ross-shire, IV19 1BN.*
Secluded Victorian House, overlooking Tain Golf Course and Dornoch Firth.
Open: Feb to Nov
Grades: STB 4 Star, AA 4 Diamond
01862 892856 Mrs Ross
Fax: 01862 892172
golfview@btinternet.com
D: £20.00–£25.00 **S:** £25.00–£40.00
Beds: 1F 1D 3T **Baths:** 3 En 1 Sh
🛇 (5) 🅿 (7) ⅏ 🕮 Ⅵ ♿ cc

Northfield, *23 Moss Road, Tain, Ross-shire, IV19 1HH.*
One mile from Glenmorangie Distillery, Tain golf course and museum.
Open: Jan to Nov
Grades: STB 3 Star
01862 894087 Mrs McLean
may-mclean@northfield23.fsnet.co.uk
D: £16.00–£19.00 **S:** £16.00–£25.00
Beds: 1D 1T 1S **Baths:** 2 En 1 Pr
🛇 (3) 🅿 (3) ⊬ 📺 🛍 Ⅴ ♨

Heatherdale, *2 Well Street, Tain, Ross-shire, IV19 1HJ.*
Centrally situated for travelling north and west. Golf, fishing, shooting.
Open: All Year (not Xmas/New Year)
01862 894340 Mrs Fraser
D: £18.00–£20.00 **S:** £25.00–£30.00
Beds: 1D 1T 1F **Baths:** 2 En 1 Pr
🛇 (3) ⊬ 📺 🛍 Ⅴ ♨

ND1168 🍴 *Halladale Inn, Melvich Hotel, Pentland Hotel, Northern Sands Hotel, Viking Bowl, Upper Deck*

Tigh na Clash, *Melvich, Thurso, Caithness, KW14 7YJ.*
Modern building. Country views. Ideally situated for touring north coast.
Open: Easter to October
Grades: STB 3 Star, AA 4 Diamond
01641 531262 (also fax)
Mrs Ritchie
tignaclash@mywebpage.net
D: £21.50–£23.00 **S:** £21.50–£23.00
Beds: 1F 2T 3D 2S **Baths:** 7 En 1 Pr
🅿 (8) 📺 🛍 ♨ cc

3 Ravenshill Road, *Thurso, Caithness, KW14 7PX.*
Open: May to Sep
Grades: STB 2 Star
01847 894801 Mrs Milne
D: £16.00 **S:** £17.00
Beds: 1D 1T **Baths:** 1 Sh
🛇 ⊬ 📺 🐾 🛍 Ⅴ ♨
Situated in mainland Britain's most northerly town. Comfortable family home, comfortable beds, substantial Scots breakfast, wonderful views of Orkney Islands. Spectacular sea and hill scenery. Access by road and rail.

9 Couper Street, *Thurso, Caithness, KW14 8AR.*
Friendly welcome, close to ferry to Orkney, beach and Train station.
Open: Jan to Dec
Grades: STB 2 Star
01847 894529 Mrs Oag
D: £15.00 **S:** £15.00
Beds: 1D 1T 2S **Baths:** 1 Sh
🛇 ⊬ 📺 🐾 🛍 Ⅴ ♨

Shinval, *Glengolly, Thurso, Caithness, KW14 7XN.*
Modern house with large garden. Four miles from Orkney ferry.
Open: Jan to Dec
01847 894306 Mrs Sinclair
Fax: 01847 890711
mary@shinval.swinternet.co.uk
D: fr £15.00 **S:** fr £15.00
Beds: 1F 1D 1T **Baths:** 1 En 2 Sh
🛇 🅿 (4) 📺 🐾 🛍 Ⅴ ♨ ⅙

Garth House, *Castletown, Thurso, Caithness, KW14 8SL.*
Garth house is 280 years old, overlooking Britain's most Northerly point.
Open: All Year
Grades: STB 4 Star
01847 821429 Mr & Mrs Garfield
paul.garfield@tesco.net
D: £20.00–£25.00 **S:** £20.00–£25.00
Beds: 1D 1T **Baths:** 1 En 1 Pr
🅿 (3) ⊬ 🐾 🛍 Ⅴ ♨

Ivordene, *Janetstown, Thurso, Caithness, KW14 7XF.*
Modern, comfortable farmhouse.
Open: All Year (not Xmas)
01847 894760 Mrs MacIvor
D: £15.00 **S:** £15.00
Beds: 1F 1D 2T 1S **Baths:** 2 Sh
🛇 🅿 (6) ⊬ 📺 🐾 🛍 ♨ ⅙

1 Granville Crescent, *Thurso, Caithness, KW14 7NP.*
Bungalow with beautiful views. Easy reach of station and Scrabster ferry terminal
Open: All Year (not Xmas)
01847 892993 (also fax)
Mrs Murray
D: fr £16.00
Beds: 2T **Baths:** 1 En 1 Pr
🛇 🅿 (2) ⊬ 📺 🐾 🛍 ♨ ⅙

Straven, *Haimer, Thurso, Caithness, KW14 8YN.*
Situated in countryside 1 mile Thurso, panoramic view of Caithness.
Open: All Year
01847 893850 Mrs Paul
francis-gordon.paul@virgin.net
D: £18.00–£20.00 **S:** £18.00–£22.00
Beds: 2 En
🅿 (4) ⊬ 📺 🛍 Ⅴ ♨ ⅙

NH8029 🍴 *Tomatin Inn*

Millcroft, *Old Mill Road, Tomatin, Inverness, IV13 7YN.*
1850 modernised crofthouse in quiet village. Ideal base for touring.
Open: All Year
Grades: AA 4 Diamond
01808 511405
Mrs Leitch
margaret_tomatin@hotmail.com
D: £18.00 **S:** £20.00–£25.00
Beds: 1D 1F **Baths:** 1 En 1 Pr
🛇 🅿 (3) 📺 🐾 🛍 Ⅴ

NC5956 🍴 *Craggan Hotel*

77 Dalcharn, *Tongue, Lairg, Sutherland, IV27 4XU.*
Croft cottage set in quiet valley. Families welcome. Phone for brochure.
Open: All Year
Grades: STB 2 Star
01847 611251 Mrs MacIntosh
D: £13.00–£15.00 **S:** £15.00
Beds: 1F 1D 1T 1S **Baths:** 1 En 1 Sh
🛇 🅿 (5) ⊬ 📺 ✕ 🛍 Ⅴ ✿ ♨ ⅙

Planning a longer stay? Always ask for any special rates

Strathtongue Old Manse, *Tongue, Lairg, Sutherland, IV27 4XR.*
Attractive Victorian Highland manse. Woodland setting. Beautiful beach, spectacular views.
Open: All Year (not Xmas/New Year)
01847 611252- Mrs MacKay
Fax: 01847 611252
D: £18.00–£20.00 **S:** £20.00–£25.00
Beds: 2D 1T **Baths:** 1 En 2 Pr
🛇 🅿 ⊬ 📺 🐾 ✕ 🛍 Ⅴ ♨

NH6052 🍴 *Kilcoy Arms*

Fiveways Bed & Breakfast, *Tore, Muir of Ord, Ross-shire, IV6 7RY.*
TV all rooms, guest lounge, spacious parking, welcome always assured.
Open: Jun to Oct
Grades: STB 2 Star B&B
01463 811408 Mrs MacKenzie
D: fr £15.00 **S:** fr £17.00
Beds: 1F 1D 1T **Baths:** 1 En 2 Sh
🛇 🅿 📺 🐾 🛍 Ⅴ ♨

NN1476 🍴 *Ben Nevis Restaurant*

Ferndale, *Tomacharrich, Torlundy, Fort William, PH33 6SP.*
Large bungalow in beautiful country setting, with wonderful views of Ben Nevis.
Open: All Year
Grades: STB 3 Star
01397 703593 Mrs Riley
D: £15.00–£20.00
Beds: 1F 2D **Baths:** 2 En 1 Pr
🛇 🅿 (6) ⊬ 📺 🐾 🛍 Ⅴ ♨

NG9056 🍴 *Ben Damph Bar, Tigh-an-eilean*

Annat Lodge, *Annat, Torridon, Achnasheen, Ross-shire, IV22 2EU.*
200-year-old cottage with antique furniture, set in lovely cottage garden.
Open: Easter to Nov
01445 791200 Mrs Wilson
D: £16.50–£18.50 **S:** fr £14.00
Beds: 1F 1T **Baths:** 1 En 1 Sh
🛇 🅿 (4) ⊬ 🐾 🛍 Ⅴ ♨

NH1294 🍴 *Argyll Hotel, Morefield Hotel, Arch Inn, Ferryboat Inn*

Broombank Bungalow, *Castle Terrace, Ullapool, IV26 2XD.*
A warm welcome awaits. Panoramic views over Loch Broom and Summer Isles
Open: All Year
Grades: STB 3 Star
01854 612247 Mrs Couper
shirley.couper@tesco.net
D: £17.50–£20.00
Beds: 1T 2D **Baths:** All En
🅿 (3) ⊬ 📺 🐾 🛍 ♨

Thornlea, 2 Morefield Crescent, *Ullapool, IV26 2XN.*
Comfortable accommodation in pleasant surroundings on outskirts of Ullapool.
Open: Easter to Sept **Grades:** STB 2 Star
01854 612944 Mrs Harvey
gjharvey@supanet.com
D: £14.00–£18.00 **S:** £15.00–£20.00
Beds: 1T 2D **Baths:** 1 En 1 Pr 1 Sh
⌂ (5) 🅿 (3) ⅙ 📺 ✹ ✕ 🛏 🖳 Ⓥ ⚲

3 Castle Terrace, *Ullapool, Ross-shire, IV26 2XD.*
Overlooking Summer Isles. Pretty rooms, home-made jams, vegetarian speciality. Some French/German spoken.
Open: Easter to Oct
Grades: STB 3 Star
01854 612409
Mrs Browne
D: £16.00–£19.00 **S:** £17.00–£18.00
Beds: 1D 1T 1S **Baths:** 1 En 1 Sh
🅿 (2) ⅙ 📺 🛏 🖳 Ⓥ

Oakworth, *Riverside Terrace, Ullapool, Ross-shire, IV26 2TE.*
Modern detached bungalow in the centre of Ullapool. **Open:** All Year
Grades: STB 3 Star
01854 612290 Mrs Downey
oakworth@ecosse.net
D: £15.00–£19.00
Beds: 3D **Baths:** 3 En
⌂ (12) 🅿 (3) ⅙ 📺 🛏 🖳 ⚲

The Sheiling Guest House, *Garve Road, Ullapool, Ross-shire, IV26 2SX.*
Purpose built guest house in one acre private grounds. Trout fishing free.
Open: All Year (not Xmas)
Grades: STB 4 Star, AA 4 Star
01854 612947 Mr MacKenzie
Fax: 01854 612 947
D: £23.00–£26.00 **S:** £23.00–£50.00
Beds: 4D 2T **Baths:** 6 En
🅿 (6) ⅙ 📺 🖳 Ⓥ ⚲

Ferry Boat Inn, *Shore Street, Ullapool, Ross-shire, IV26 2UJ.*
Superb views over Loch Broom, good home-cooked meals and a friendly relaxed bar atmosphere.
Open: All Year (not Xmas)
01854 612366 Mr & Mrs Smith
Fax: 01854 613266
ferryboat.inn@virgin.net
D: £25.00–£34.00 **S:** £27.00–£36.00
Beds: 1F 3T 4D 1S **Baths:** 9 En
⌂ 🛏 ✕ 🖳 Ⓥ ⚲

Westhill

NH7144   ◀ *Snow Goose, Cawdor Tavern*

Easter Muckovie Farm House, *Westhill, Inverness, IV2 5BN.*
Open: All Year **Grades:** STB 3 Star
01463 791556 J H MacLellan
dot.westhill@virgin.co.uk
D: £18.00–£20.00 **S:** £25.00
Beds: 2F **Baths:** 1 En 1 Pr
⌂ 🅿 (5) ⅙ 📺 🛏 ✕ 🖳 Ⓥ ⚲
Original farmhouse modernised set in a rural location overlooking Inverness town, Moray & Beauly Firth with Sutherland & Ross-shire Hills in background. Culloden Battlefield, Cawdor Castle & Clava Cairns nearby. Excellent Scottish breakfast provided in comfortable dining room.

Bayview, *Westhill, Culloden Moor, Inverness, IV2 5BP.*
Open: Easter to Oct **Grades:** STB 3 Star
01463 790386 (also fax) Mrs Campbell
bayviewguesthouse@btinternet.com
D: £18.00–£22.00 **S:** £20.00–£25.00
Beds: 1T 2D **Baths:** 2 En 1 Pr
🅿 (3) ⅙ 📺 🛏 ✕ 🖳 ⚲
Modern two storey house situated in 1/2 acre landscaped garden. Beautiful views to Ross-shire hills, Moray Firth and Inverness. 20 mins from Dalcross Airport. 1/2 mile from the famous Culloden Battlefield, 3 miles from Clava Cairns. Choice of breakfast, fresh produce used.

Wick

ND3650   ◀ *Carter's, Mackay's, Silver Darlings*

The Clachan, *South Rd, Wick, Caithness, KW1 5NJ.*
Family-run perfect for exploring the North and Orkney Islands.
Open: All Year (not Xmas)
Grades: STB 4 Star, AA 4 Diamond
01955 605384 Mrs Bremner
enquiry@theclachan.co.uk
D: £25.00–£25.00 **S:** £25.00–£30.00
Beds: 2D 1T **Baths:** 3 En
⌂ (12) 🅿 (4) ⅙ 📺 🖳 ⚲

Quayside, 25 Harbour Quay, Wick, Caithness, KW1 5EP.
Open: All Year
Grades: STB 2 Star
01955 603229 (also fax)
Mr Turner
quaysidewick@compuserve.com
D: £14.50–£19.50 **S:** £18.00–£28.00
Beds: 2F 2D 1T 2S **Baths:** 2 En 2 Sh
🅿 (4) ⅙ 📺 🖳 Ⓥ ⚲
We provide comfortable accommodation within a relaxed atmosphere, overlooking a traditional harbour front. For motoring and motorcycle enthusiasts, we provide a warm welcome, secure parking and simple but adequate repair facilities. Advice on daily sightseeing runs is available for all guests.

Macmillar House, 7 Tolbooth Lane, Wick, Caithness, KW1 4ND.
Old house built around end of 17th Century. 6 minutes railway station & bus station.
Open: All Year
01955 602120 Mrs Coghill
Fax: 01955 805667
sammy.777@btinternet.com
D: £20.00–£22.00 **S:** £20.00–£22.00
Beds: 1F 1D 1T 1S **Baths:** 3 En 1 Sh
⌂ 🅿 (3) 📺 🛏 🖳 Ⓥ ⚲

Stilwell's Britain Cycleway Companion

23 Long Distance Cycleways – Where to Stay * Where to Eat

County Cycleways – Sustrans Routes

The first guide of its kind, **Stilwell's Britain Cycleway Companion** makes planning accommodation for your cycling trip easy. It lists B&Bs, hostels, campsites and pubs– in the order they appear along the selected cycleways – allowing the cyclist to book ahead. No more hunting for a room, a hot meal or a cold drink after a long day in the saddle. Stilwell's gives descriptions of the featured routes and includes such relevant information as maps, grid references and distance from route; Tourist Board ratings; and the availability of drying facilities and packed lunches. No matter which route – or part of a route – you decide to ride, let the **Cycleway Companion** show you where to sleep and eat.

As essential as your tyre pump – the perfect cycling companion: **Stilwell's Britain Cycleway Companion**.

Cycleways

Sustrans
Carlisle to Inverness – Clyde to Forth - Devon Coast to Coast - Hull to Harwich – Kingfisher Cycle Trail - Lon Las Cymru – Sea to Sea (C2C) – Severn and Thames – West Country Way – White Rose Cycle Route

County
Round Berkshire Cycle Route – Cheshire Cycleway – Cumbria Cycleway – Essex Cycle Route – Icknield Way - Lancashire Cycleway – Leicestershire County Cycleway – Oxfordshire Cycleway – Reivers Cycle Route – South Downs Way - Surrey Cycleway – Wiltshire Cycleway – Yorkshire Dales Cycleway

---

£9.95 from all good bookstores (ISBN 1-900861-26-7) or £10.95 (inc p&p) from Stilwell Publishing Ltd, 59 Charlotte Road, London EC2A 3QW (020 7739 7179)

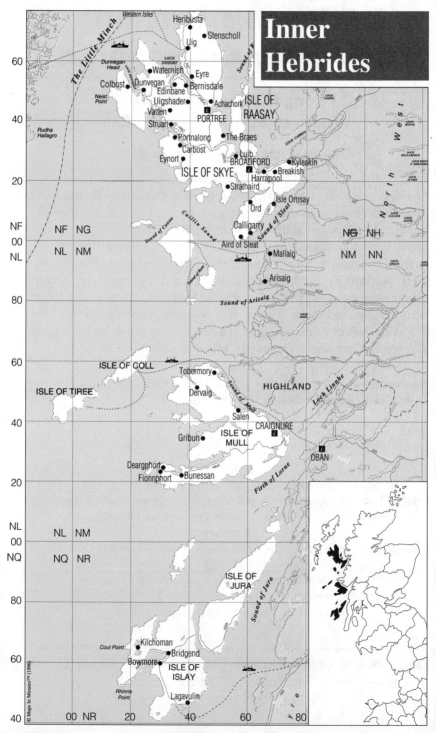

Inner Hebrides

STILWELL'S BRITAIN: BED & BREAKFAST

Tourist Information Centres

The Square, **Bowmore**, Isle of Islay, PA43 7JH, 01496 810254.

Car Park, **Broadford**, Isle of Skye, IV49 9AB, 01471 822361 (Easter to Oct).

The Pierhead, **Craignure**, Isle of Mull, PA65 6AY, 01680 812377.

Dunvegan, Isle of Skye, 01470 521581.

Meall House, **Portree**, Isle of Skye, IV51 9BZ, 01478 612137.

Main Street, **Tobermory**, Isle of Mull, PA75 6NU, 01688 302182 (Easter to Oct).

Ferry Terminal, **Uig**, Isle of Skye, 01470 542404 (Easter to Oct).

COLL — Isle of Coll

NM1955

Garden House, *Isle of Coll, PA78 6TB.*
Isolated comfortable farmhouse in middle of bird reserve. Unwind on holiday.
Open: Oct
01879 230374 (also fax) Mrs Graham
D: £18.00–£20.00 **S:** £24.00–£26.00
Beds: 1D 1T **Baths:** 1 Sh
🄿 (10) ⅏ 🅃 ✕ 🎟 🛆

ISLAY — Bowmore

NR3159

Lochside Hotel, *Shore Street, Bowmore, Isle of Islay, PA43 7LB.*
Excellent value accommodation, food and whisky! **Open:** All Year
01496 810244 Mrs Birse
birse@lochsidehotel.co.uk
D: fr £20.00 **S:** fr £20.00
Beds: 1F 1D 1T 5S **Baths:** 8 En
🄲 🅃 🛏 ✕ 🎟 🅅 🛆

ISLAY — Bridgend

NR3361

2 Mulindry Cottages, *Bridgend, Isle of Islay, PA44 7PZ.*
Open: All Year **Grades:** STB 3 Star B&B
01496 810397 Mrs Macfarlane
Fax: 01469 810397
D: £18.00 **S:** £20.00
Beds: 1T **Baths:** 1 Sh
🄲 ⅏ 🅃 🎟 🅅 🛆 ⅌ 3
Comfortable accommodation in family home. All on ground floor. Good breakfast provided, quiet scenic area with views to surrounding hills and iron age fort. Ideal location for walking, bird watching and fishing.

ISLAY — Lagavulin

NR4045 ◁ *Machrie Hotel*

Tigh Na Suil, *Lagavulin, Port Ellen, Isle of Islay, PA42 7DX.*
Peaceful village location. Close to distilleries. A warm welcome always
Open: Jan to Dec
01496 302483 (also fax) Mrs Bowness
D: £20.00–£22.00 **S:** £22.00–£30.00
Beds: 1T 2D **Baths:** 3 En
🄲 (5) ⅏ 🅃 🎟 🅅 🛆

MULL — Bunessan

NM3821

Ardness House, *Tiraghoil, Bunessan, Isle of Mull, PA67 6DU.*
Family-run B&B near Iona, Staffa, beaches, outstanding sea views.
Open: Easter to Oct
Grades: STB 3 Star
01681 700260 (also fax)
Messrs MacNeill
ardness@supanet.com
D: £18.00–£22.00
Beds: 2D 1T **Baths:** 3 En
🄲 🄿 (3) ⅏ ✕ 🎟 🅅 ✳

MULL — Craignure

NM7136 ◁ *Craignure Inn, Ceilidh Place*

Linnhe View, *Craignure, Isle of Mull, PA65 6AY.*
Comfortable ex-manse built 1850 overlooking Loch Linnhe with view of Ben Nevis.
Open: All Year
01680 812427 (also fax)
Mr & Mrs Roberts
D: £20.00–£25.00 **S:** £20.00–£25.00
Beds: 2D 1T **Baths:** 2 Sh
🄲 🄿 (4) 🅃 🛏 🎟 🅅 🛆

MULL — Deargphort

NM3025 ◁ *Red Bay Cottage*

Red Bay Cottage, *Deargphort, Fionnphort, Isle of Mull, PA66 6BP.*
Isolated, modernised home with restaurant. Ideal for Mull, Iona, Staffa.
Open: All Year (not Jan 1)
01681 700396 Mr Wagstaff
D: £16.50 **S:** £16.50
Beds: 1D 2T **Baths:** 3 Sh
🄲 🄿 (10) 🛏 ✕ 🎟 🅅 🛆

MULL — Dervaig

NM4352 ◁ *Ardbeg House,Bellachroy Hotel*

Kengharair Farm, *Dervaig, Isle of Mull, PA75 6QR.*
Victorian farmhouse on hillside overlooking glen and river beautiful scenery.
Open: Easter to
01688 400251 (also fax)
Mrs Caskie
D: £16.00–£17.00 **S:** £16.00–£18.00
Beds: 1F 2T **Baths:** 1 Sh
🄲 🄿 (4) 🅃 🅅 🛆

Antium Farm, *Dervaig, Tobermory, Isle of Mull, PA75 6QW.*
Traditional working farm. Many attractions including sightings of sea eagles.
Open: Easter to Oct
01688 400230 Mrs Boa
D: £18.00–£19.00
Beds: 2F **Baths:** 1 Sh
🄲 (1) 🄿 (2) 🅃 🎟 🅅 🛆

Planning a longer stay? Always ask for any special rates

Ardbeg House Hotel, *Dervaig, Tobermory, Isle of Mull, PA75 6QJ.*
Large Victorian picturesque village restaurant, licensed.
Open: All Year
01688 400254 (also fax)
Mr Shilling
D: fr £22.00 **S:** fr £22.00
Beds: 2F 2D 2T 1S **Baths:** 5 Pr 2 Sh
🄲 🄿 (10) 🛏 ✕ 🎟 🅅 ✳ 🛆 🛆

MULL — Fionnphort

NM3023 ◁ *Keel Row*

Caol-Ithe, *Fionnphort, Isle of Mull, PA66 6BL.*
Open: All Year (not Xmas/New Year)
01681 700375 (also fax)
Mrs Dickson
mary@caol-ithe.demon.co.uk
D: £20.00–£22.00 **S:** £20.00–£22.00
Beds: 1T 2D **Baths:** 2 En 1 Sh
🄲 🄿 ⅏ 🅃 🛏 🎟 🛆
Warm, spacious bungalow. A highland hospitality awaits you. Private car parking. 5 minutes walk to ferry for Iona and Staffa. Ideal location for bird watching, hill walking and relaxation. White, sandy beaches within walking distance

Staffa House, *Fionnphort, Isle of Mull, PA66 6BL.*
Open: Marc to Oct
Grades: STB 3 Star
01681 700677 (also fax)
D: £20.00–£25.00 **S:** £25.00–£44.00
Beds: 2T 1D **Baths:** 3 En
🄲 🄿 (5) ⅏ 🅃 🛏 ✕ 🎟 🅅 🛆 cc
Full of antiques and individual touches which set Staffa House apart from similar establishments. 2 minutes walk Iona/Staffa (Fingals Cave) ferries. Conservatory dining room full of floral extravaganza. Ideal for dinner watching Hebridean sunset and views of Iona and Abbey.

Bruach Mhor, *Fionnphort, Isle of Mull, PA66 6BL.*
Near Iona/Staffa ferries. Beautiful coastline, walking, wildlife. Vegetarian cooking.
Open: All Year (not Xmas)
01681 700276 (also fax)
Mrs Heald
heather@bruachmhor.ndo.co.uk
D: £16.00–£18.00 **S:** £16.00
Beds: 1F 1D 1T 1S **Baths:** 1 En 1 Sh
🄲 🄿 (4) 🅃 ✕ 🎟 🅅 🛆

MULL — Gribun

NM4534 ◁ *Salen Hotel*

Derryguaig, *Gribun, Isle of Mull, PA68 6EJ.*
Situated bottom Ben More overlooking Loch na Keal. Ideal walking, cycling, wildlife.
Open: All Year
01680 300363
R & A MacKenzie
D: £18.00–£20.00 **S:** £18.00–£20.00
Beds: 1T 2D **Baths:** 2 Sh
🄲 🄿 (4) ⅏ 🅃 🎟 🛆

MULL   Salen

NM5743   ☜ Oban Inn, Aulays Bar, Kelvin Hotel,
Soroba House, Barn Bar, Kings Knoll, Studio
Restaurant

Corriemar House, Esplanade, Oban,
Argyll, PA34 5AQ.
Open: All Year
Grades: STB 3 Star, AA 3 Diamond, RAC
3 Diamond
01631 562476
A Russell
Fax: 01631 564339
corriemar@tinyworld.co.uk
D: £18.00–£38.00 **S:** £20.00–£35.00
Beds: 2F 6D 4T 2S **Baths:** 12 En 2 Pr
🛏 🅿 (10) ⅋ 🖵 ✕ 🛒 Ⅴ ♨ 🌣 cc
Large Victorian house in prime location
on Oban's seafront. Ideal for use as a
base for touring local islands and loch or
just relax and watch the sun setting over
Oban Bay.

MULL   Tobermory

NM5055   ☜ Western Isles Hotel, Macdonald
Arms, Highland Cottage

Harbour Heights, Western Road,
Tobermory, Isle of Mull, PA75 6PR.
Open: Easter to 31/10/
Grades: STB 3 Star
01688 302430 (also fax)
Mr Stojak
D: £22.50–£25.00 **S:** £25.00–£30.00
Beds: 2T 4D **Baths:** 6 En
🛏 🅿 (20) ⅋ 🖵 🛏 🛒 Ⅴ ♨ 🌣
Recently refurbished with attention to
comfort and style. Lounge themed in
burgundy with Persian rugs, deep soft
sofas and log fire. Bedrooms in heavy
pine furniture and green tartan
furnishings. Guest rooms overlook garden
with views of sea and gardens.

Tobermory Hotel, 53 Main Street,
Tobermory, Isle of Mull, PA75 6NT.
Open: All Year (not Xmas)
Grades: STB 3 Star
01688 302091
Mr Stevens
Fax: 01688 302254
tobhotel@tinyworld.co.uk
D: £35.00–£45.00 **S:** £39.00–£90.00
Beds: 2F 8D 4T **Baths:** 15 En 1 Pr
🛏 🖵 🛏 ✕ 🛒 Ⅴ ♨ cc
Set on the waterfront of picturesque
Tobermory's Bay, a beautiful sixteen room
hotel, all private facilities with two ground
floor rooms. A great variety of delicious
meals and drinks from our cosy Water's
Edge restaurant. A warm welcome
guaranteed.

The Cedars, Dervaig Road, Tobermory,
Isle of Mull, PA75 6PY.
Detached bungalow, separate B&B
facilities, set in wooded garden.
Open: All Year (not Xmas)
Grades: STB 2 Star
01688 302096
Mr Bettley
D: £15.00–£16.00 **S:** £16.00–£20.00
Beds: 1D 1T **Baths:** 1 Sh
🛏 🅿 (4) 🛒 Ⅴ ♨

Harbour House, Main Street,
Tobermory, Isle of Mull, PA75 6NU.
Family-run guest house overlooking
Tobermory Bay.
Open: All Year (not Xmas)
01688 302209 Mrs MacLean
Fax: 01688 302750
harbourhou@aol.com
D: £19.50–£22.00 **S:** £19.50–£44.00
Beds: 2F 3D 2T 2S **Baths:** 5 En 2 Sh
🛏 🅿 (10) 🖵 🛏 🛒 ♨ 🌣 cc

2 Victoria Street, Tobermory, Isle of
Mull, PA75 6PH.
On-street parking, 5 minutes from shops
and harbour.
Open: All Year (not Xmas)
01688 302263 (also fax)
Mrs Harper
D: £14.00–£16.00 **S:** £15.00–£18.00
Beds: 1D 1T **Baths:** 1 Sh
🛏 🖵 Ⅴ ♨

Derwent House, Raeric Road,
Tobermory, Isle of Mull, PA75 6PU.
Detached house overlooking Tobermory
Bay and the Sound of Mull.
Open: Feb to Nov
01688 302420 (also fax)
D: £19.00–£20.00 **S:** £25.00
 Baths: 1 En 1 Pr 1 Sh
🛏 🅿 (4) ⅋ 🖵 🛏 🛒 Ⅴ ♨

SKYE   Achachork

NG4745   ☜ Cuillin Hills Hotel

Creag An Fhithich, 10 Achachork,
Achachork, Portree, Isle of Skye, IV51 9HT.
Modern farmhouse with panoramic views,
situated 2 miles north of Portree.
Open: Easter to Nov
01478 612213 (also fax)
Mrs MacDonald
D: fr £16.50 **S:** fr £16.50
Beds: 1F 1D 1T 1S **Baths:** 1 En 2 Sh
🛏 🅿 (6) 🖵 🛒 Ⅴ ♨

Myrtlebank, Achachork, Portree, Isle of
Skye, IV51 9HT.
Modern croft house overlooking Portree.
Panoramic view towards Cuillin
Mountains.
Open: May-Aug
01478 612597 (also fax)
Mrs Gilmour
skye.gilmour@lineone.net
D: fr £16.00 **S:** fr £16.00
Beds: 2F 1D 1S **Baths:** 2 En 1 Sh
🛏 🅿 (5) 🖵 🛏 Ⅴ ♨

Jacamar, 5 Achachork Road, Achachork,
Portree, Isle of Skye, IV51 9HT.
Country Bungalow overlooks Portree and
Cuillins. Excellent cooking Scottish
breakfast.
Open: All Year
01478 612274
Mrs Thorpe
Fax: 01478 611191
normal.pat@jacamar.idps.co.uk
D: £14.00–£19.00 **S:** £15.00–£19.00
Beds: 3F 1D 1S
🛏 🅿 ⅋ 🖵 ✕ 🛒 Ⅴ ♨

SKYE   Aird of Sleat

NG5900   ☜ Ardvasar Hotel

The Old School House, Aird of Sleat,
Ardvasar, Isle of Skye, IV45 8RN.
Open: Mar to Oct
Grades: STB 2 Star
01471 844218
Mrs Newman
D: £19.50–£24.00 **S:** £19.50–£24.00
Beds: 1D 1T 1S **Baths:** 1 Sh
🛏 (12) 🅿 (6) ⅋ 🖵 🛒 ♨
Old school house idyllically situated 30
yards from shore. Panoramic views of
mainland mountains across the sea.
Otters, dolphins, seals and whales seen
from windows. Buzzards, eagles, other
birds of prey and wild orchids in the area.
Armadale Ferry 4 miles.

SKYE   Bernisdale

NG4050

Rubislaw, 34 Bernisdale, Bernisdale,
Skeabost Bridge, Portree, Isle of Skye, IV51
9NS.
Crofthouse with all rooms on ground
level in a quiet lochside village.
Open: Easter to Oct
01470 532212 (also fax)
E M Macdonald
ettamacdonald@hotmail.com
D: £16.00–£22.00
Beds: 2D 1T **Baths:** 2 En 1 Sh
🅿 (4) 🖵 🛏 ✕ 🛒 Ⅴ ♨

SKYE   Breakish

NG6623   ☜ Crofters Kitchen, Claymore,
Rendezvous

Ashfield , Breakish, Isle of Skye, IV42 9PY.
Comfortable accommodation, overlooking
sea and mountains. Short walk to beach.
Open: Easter to Oct
Grades: STB 3 Star
01471 822301
Mrs Clarke
D: £16.00–£20.00 **S:** £18.00–£20.00
Beds: 2D **Baths:** 1 En 1 Sh
⅋ 🖵 🛒 Ⅴ

Fernlea, Breakish, Isle of Skye, IV42 8PY.
Large modern house with excellent sea
and mountain views.
Open: Easter to Oct
Grades: STB 3 Star
01471 822107
Mrs Harrison
D: £19.00–£24.00 **S:** £20.00–£26.00
Beds: 2D 1T **Baths:** 3 En
🛏 🅿 (4) ⅋ 🖵 🛒 Ⅴ ♨

Strathgorm, 15 Upper Breakish,
Breakish, Isle of Skye, IV42 9PY.
Spacious modern house overlooking sea.
Open: Feb to Dec
Grades: STB 4 Star
01471 822508 (also fax)
Mrs Graham
strathgorm@yahoo.com
D: £18.00–£22.00 **S:** £22.00–£25.00
Beds: 1F 1D 1T **Baths:** 2 En 1 Pr
🛏 🅿 (6) ⅋ 🖵 🛒 Ⅴ ♨

Shiloh, *Breakish, Isle of Skye, IV42 8PY.*
Modern style bungalow set in own
mature garden screened from main road
by trees.
Open: Easter to Sep
Grades: STB 3 Star
01471 822346 Mrs MacInnes
D: £18.00–£20.00
Beds: 1F 1D 1T **Baths:** 3 En
🛇 🅿 (10) 📺 🛏 🛋 Ⅴ ♨

Hazelwood, *5 Lower Breakish, Breakish,
Isle of Skye, IV42 8QA.*
Croft house on working croft . 1 mile off
main road, beside sea.
Open: Easter to Oct
01471 822431 Mrs Munro
D: £15.00–£17.50 **S:** £18.00–£20.50
Beds: 1F 1T **Baths:** 1 Sh
🛇 🅿 (3) 📺 Ⅴ

SKYE   Broadford

NG6423   🍺 *Claymore, Dunollie Hotel*

Millbrae House, *Broadford, Isle of
Skye, IV49 9AE.*
Open: Feb to Nov
01471 822310 (also fax)
P & V Tordoff
D: £16.00–£22.00 **S:** £16.00–£23.00
Beds: 2D 1T 1S **Baths:** 3 Pr 1 Sh
🗡 📺 🛋 Ⅴ ♨
A refurbished croft house looking to the
sea and hills. Bedrooms have private
facilities with tea/coffee trays. Non-
smoking. Antiques. Many foreign
languages spoken. Packed lunches. Help
with walking/driving tours gladly given.
Very friendly.

Tigh Na Mara, *Lower Harrapool,
Broadford, Isle of Skye, IV49 9AQ.*
Open: May to Oct
Grades: STB 2 Star
01471 822475 Mrs Scott
D: £16.00–£18.00
Beds: 1F **Baths:** 1 Pr
🛇 (1) 🅿 🗡 📺 ♨
150 year old traditional croft house in
quiet position a few yards from the sea.
Varied wildlife. Family room comprising
double and single bed plus good sized
bunks. Private sitting and bathrooms.
French and Italian spoken. TV and toys.
Restaurants nearby.

Ashgrove, *11 Black Park, Broadford, Isle
of Skye, IV49 9DE.*
Open: All Year
Grades: STB 3 Star
01471 822327 (also fax)
Mrs Flstbher
D: £18.00–£20.00
Beds: 2D 1T **Baths:** 2 En 1 Pr
🛇 (2) 🅿 (4) 🛏 🛋 ♨
Comfortable accommodation in
bungalow situated within walking
distance of hotels and restaurant and
other amenities. A warm welcome and a
full Scottish breakfast.

Planning a longer stay? Always
ask for any special rates

Caberfeidh, *1 Lower Harrapool,
Broadford, Isle of Skye, IV49 9AQ.*
Modern bungalow with spectacular
views. Sea shore location. Warm welcome
assured.
Open: All Year (not Xmas/New Year)
Grades: STB 3 Star
01471 822664 Mrs MacKenzie
D: £20.00–£23.00
Beds: 3D **Baths:** 3 En
🅿 (4) 🗡 🛏 🛋 Ⅴ ♨

The Skye Picture House, *Ard Dorch,
Broadford, Isle of Skye, IV49 9AJ.*
Comfortable lochside accommodation
with panoramic views. Wildlife abounds.
Home cooking. **Open:** All Year
Grades: STB 3 Star
01471 822531 (also fax) Mrs Terry
holidays@skyepicturehouse.co.uk
D: £20.00–£25.00 **S:** £20.00–£25.00
Beds: 1F 2D 1T 2S **Baths:** 2 En 2 Sh
🛇 🅿 🗡 📺 🛏 ✕ 🛋 Ⅴ ♨ cc

Swordale House, *Swordale, Broadford,
Isle of Skye, IV49 9AS.*
Hebridean island hospitality at its best,
comfort in a friendly and relaxing
atmosphere.
Open: Mar to Nov
01471 822272 (also fax) Mrs Christie
D: £18.00–£24.00 **S:** £25.00–£35.00
Beds: 3D **Baths:** 2 En 1 Pr
🛇 🅿 (3) 🗡 🛋 Ⅴ ♨ cc

SKYE   Calligarry

NG6203

1/2 10 Calligarry, *Calligarry, Ardvasar,
Isle of Skye, IV45 8RY.*
Overlooking the Sound of Sleat to the
mountains of Knoydart.
Open: Easter to Oct
01471 844312 Mr & Mrs Fraser
D: £15.00 **S:** £12.00
Beds: 1D 1T 1S **Baths:** 1 Sh
🅿 (5) 🗡 📺 🛋 ♨ ⅏

SKYE   Camustianavaig

NG5139   🍺 *Isles Hotel*

An Airigh Shamradh, *1/2 of 8
Camustianavaig, Camustianavaig, Portree,
Isle of Skye, IV51 9LQ.*
Outstanding sea views over
Camustianavaig Bay to the Cuillin Hills.
Open: All Year
Grades: STB 4 Star
01478 650224 (also fax)
Mrs Smith
D: fr £20.00
Beds: 1T 1D **Baths:** 2 En
🅿 (4) 📺 🛋 ♨

SKYE   Carbost (Drynoch)

NG3731   🍺 *Old Inn*

The Old Inn, *Carbost, Isle of Skye, IV47
8SR.*
On the shores of Loch Harport, the inn
provides an ideal setting for hillwalking.
Open: All Year
01478 640205 Mrs Morrison
D: £22.00–£24.50 **S:** £22.00–£24.50
Beds: 1F 2D 2T 1S **Baths:** 6 En
🛇 🅿 (25) 🗡 📺 🛏 ✕ 🛋 Ⅴ ♨ cc

SKYE   Colbost

NG2148   🍺 *Old School House*

An Cala, *1 Colbost, Colbost, Isle of Skye,
IV55 8ZT.*
Open: All Year (not Xmas)
01470 511393 Mrs Bohndorf
B&B@ancala.co.uk
D: £18.00 **S:** £21.50
Beds: 1T **Baths:** 1 Pr
🛇 🅿 📺 🛏 🛋 Ⅴ
Modern bungalow overlooking Loch
Dunvegan, 'The Three Chimneys' award-
winning restaurant and a folk museum
only 300 metres away. Dunvegan Castle
and many other man-made and natural
attractions within 10 mile radius and the
beauty of the island everywhere.

SKYE   Dunvegan

NG2547   🍺 *Dunvegan Hotel, Macleod Tables,
Three Chimneys, Chimes*

6 Altavaid, *Harlosh, Dunvegan, Isle of
Skye, IV55 8WA.*
Modern house, small garden, open
countryside. Loch Bracadale, MacLeods
Tables, Dunvegan Castle.
Open: Easter to Oct
Grades: STB 2 Star
01470 521704 Mrs Ewbank
D: £18.00–£20.00 **S:** £18.00–£20.00
Beds: 1F 1T **Baths:** 2 En
🅿 (2) 📺 🛋 Ⅴ ♨

Sea View, *3 Herebost, Vatten,
Dunvegan, Isle of Skye, Isle of Skye, IV55
8GZ.*
Modern bungalow with sea views, near
the famous Dunvegan castle.
Open: Easter to Oct
Grades: STB 3 Star
01470 521705 Mrs Campbell
D: £16.00–£17.50
Beds: 1D 1T **Baths:** 1 En 1 Pr
🅿 (2) 🗡 🛋 ♨

6 Castle Crescent, *Dunvegan, Isle of
Skye, IV55 8WE.*
Highland hospitality close to castle shops
and restaurants.
Open: All Year **Grades:** STB 3 Star
01470 521407 Mrs Stirling
D: £16.00–£17.00 **S:** £18.00–£20.00
Beds: 1F 1T **Baths:** 1 Sh
🛇 (1) 🅿 (2) 🗡 📺 🛏 🛋 Ⅴ ♨

Tigh-na-Mara, *2-3 Caroy, Dunvegan,
Isle of Skye, IV56 8FQ.*
HIghland welcome. View hills and Loch
Caroy. Dunvegan Castle nearby.
Open: All Year
01470 572338 (also fax)
Mrs Cleghorn-Redhead
nanted@tesco.net
D: £15.00 **S:** £15.00
Beds: 1D 2T **Baths:** 1 Sh
🛇 🅿 (5) 📺 🛏 🛋 Ⅴ ⌘ ♨

Herebost, *Dunvegan, Isle of Skye, IV55
8SZ.*
Views of sea & mountain 2 miles from
Dunvegan Castle. **Open:** Easter to Oct
01470 521255 Mrs MacDonald
D: £17.00–£19.00 **S:** £22.00–£24.00
Beds: 2D **Baths:** 1 En 1 Pr
🛇 🅿 (6) 🗡 📺 🛏 🛋 Ⅴ ♨

An Airidh, *6 Roag, Dunvegan, Isle of Skye, IV55 8ZA.*
Very comfortable and welcoming modern house, 4 miles Dunvegan, home of famous castle.
Open: All Year
01470 521738 Mrs Montgomery
Fax: 01470 521600
chrissiemontgomery@dial.pipex.com
D: £18.00–£22.00
Beds: 1F 1D **Baths:** 2 En
🛏 (2) 🅿 (4) 📺 🎗 💷 🖤 ₤

SKYE   Edinbane

NG3451   🍺 *Edinbane Hotel, Lodge Hotel*

Eileen Dubh, *Edinbane, Portree, Isle of Skye, IV51 9PW.*
Modern bungalow B&B establishment, situated in North West Skye.
Open: Oct
01470 582218 Mrs Cumming
D: £16.00–£18.00 **S:** £16.00–£18.00
Beds: 1F 1D **Baths:** 1 Sh
🛏 (8) 🅿 (3) ⅍ 📺 🎗 🗡 💷 🖤 ₤ ₺ 🐾 cc

SKYE   Eynort

NG3826   🍺 *Old Inn*

The Blue Lobster, *Glen Eynort, Isle of Skye, IV47 8SG.*
Walkers haven: Secluded, relaxed, in forest, by sea-loch and eagles!
Open: All Year
01478 640320 Mr Van der Vliet
bluelobster_grula@yahoo.com
D: £18.00 **S:** £23.00
Beds: 1D 2T
🛏 🅿 (4) 📺 🎗 🗡 💷 🖤

SKYE   Eyre

NG4153   🍺 *Skeabost House Hotel*

Cruinn Bheinn, *4 Eyre, Snizort, Portree, Isle of Skye, IV51 9XB.*
Open: Easter to Oct
Grades: STB 4 Star B&B
01470 532459 Mrs Gordon
D: £17.00–£22.00
Beds: 2D 1T **Baths:** 3 En
🛏 🅿 (3) ⅍ 📺 💷 ₤
Large modern crofthouse situated ten minutes' drive from Portree. We offer true highland hospitality with luxury accommodation and a friendly attentive service. Set in a beautiful tranquil location overlooking Loch Snizort and outer Hebrides and ideal base for exploring Skye.

SKYE   Harrapool

NG6522   🍺 *The Claymore*

The Sheiling, *2 Lower Harrapool, Broadford, Isle of Skye, IV49 9AQ.*
Open: All Year (not Xmas)
01471 822533 Mr & Mrs Shearer
D: £14.00–£20.00 **S:** £14.00–£20.00
Beds: 1F 1T 1D 1S **Baths:** 1 En 1 Sh
🛏 ⅍ 📺 🎗 💷 🖤 ₤
A lovely old traditional Skye house where a friendly Scottish welcome and a good breakfast is always assured. An ideal base for touring Skye, close to Broadford village. The area has beautiful views over Broadford bay to the mountains beyond.

SKYE   Heribusta

NG4070   🍺 *Flodigarry*

1 Heribusta, *Kilmuir, Portree, Isle of Skye, IV51 9YX.*
Open: Easter to Sep
01470 552341 Mrs Beaton
alanbeaton@yahoo.com
D: £13.00–£15.00 **S:** £14.00–£15.00
Beds: 2D 2S **Baths:** 2 Sh
🛏 🅿 📺 🎗 💷 ₤
Panoramic sea views towards Outer Hebrides. Set in a peaceful rural community with unrestricted views over unspoilt countryside. Superb base for quiet outdoor holiday with good walks in the vicinity. Excellent fishing, bird watching, sea life, archaeology and historic interest.

SKYE   Kilmuir (Uig)

NG3870

Whitewave Activities, *19 Lincro, Kilmuir, Portree, Isle of Skye, IV51 9YN.*
Imagine a cross between an outdoor centre, an inn and a ceilidh place.
Open: All Year
01470 542414 (also fax)
J White
info@white-wave.co.uk
D: £16.00–£18.00 **S:** £16.00–£18.00
Beds: 4F **Baths:** 1 En 2 Sh
🛏 🅿 (8) ⅍ 🎗 🗡 💷 ₺ 1 cc

SKYE   Kyleakin

NG7526   🍺 *Crofters Kitchen*

Blairdhu House, *Kyle Farm Rd, Kyleakin, Isle of Skye, IV41 8PR.*
Open: All Year
Grades: STB 4 Star
01599 534760
Ms Scott
Fax: 01599 534623
blairdhuskye@compuserve.com
D: fr £20.00
Beds: 1F 1D 1T **Baths:** 3 En
🛏 🅿 (6) ⅍ 📺 🎗 💷 🖤 ₤ ₺ cc
Beautifully situated house with panoramic views. All rooms are ensuite with TV, radio, hairdryers, tea/coffee making facilities. Guests also have their own lounge, excellent breakfast with a choice menu, private parking, 2 minutes walk from Skye Bridge.

West Haven, *Kyleakin, Isle of Skye, IV41 8PH.*
This house is one hundred years old it used to be a shepherd's house.
Open: Easter to Oct
01599 534476 Mrs MacAskill
D: £18.00 **S:** £18.00–£18.20
Beds: 1D 1T 1S **Baths:** 1 Sh
🛏 🅿 (6) 📺 🎗 💷 🖤 ₤

16 Kyleside, *Kyleakin, Isle of Skye, IV41 8PW.*
A warm, friendly Highland welcome awaits you at our guest house.
Open: All Year
01599 534468 Mrs Maclennan
D: £16.00–£20.00 **S:** £16.00–£20.00
Beds: 3D 1T 1S **Baths:** 1 En 2 Pr 2 Sh
🛏 🅿 📺 🎗 🗡 💷 🖤 🐾 ₤

17 Kyleside, *Kyleakin, Isle of Skye, IV41 8PW.*
A warm welcome awaits you at our family-run bed and breakfast situated on seafront.
Open: All Year
01599 534197 Mrs Macrae
D: £18.00–£19.00 **S:** £18.00–£19.00
Beds: 1D 1S **Baths:** 1 Pr 1 Sh
🛏 🅿 📺 🎗 💷 ₤

SKYE   Luib

NG5627

Luib House, *Luib, Broadford, Isle of Skye, IV49 9AN.*
Open: All Year
Grades: STB Scouser Lodge Hotel, Claymore Restaurant
01471 822724 Mrs Dobson
D: £18.00–£19.00 **S:** £25.00
Beds: 2D 1T **Baths:** 2 En 1 Pr
🛏 🅿 📺 🎗 🗡 💷 ₤
Luib House - Our home is your home and make full use of the guest lounge, with maps, books, games for the children. Make a snack or meal in guests kitchen! Breakfast an experience not to be missed.

SKYE   Ord

NG6213

Fiordhem, *Ord, Sleat, Isle of Skye, IV44 8RN.*
Fiordhem, our home, is a unique stone cottage idyllically situated 20 feet from lochside.
Open: Easter to Oct
01471 855226 Mrs La Trobe
D: £22.00–£26.00
Beds: 2D 1T **Baths:** 3 En
🅿 (5) ⅍ 📺 🗡 💷 ₤ cc

SKYE   Portnalong

NG3434   🍺 *Taigh Ailean*

Taigh Ailean Hotel, *Portnalong, Carbost, Isle of Skye, IV47 8SL.*
Superb lochside location with sea and mountain views.
Open: All Year
01478 640271 (also fax)
Mr & Mrs Anslow
call@taighaileanhotel.demon.co.uk
D: £20.00–£25.00 **S:** fr £28.00
Beds: 2F 2D 1T **Baths:** 3 Pr
🛏 🅿 (6) ⅍ 📺 🎗 🗡 💷 🖤 🐾 cc

SKYE   Portree

NG4843   🍺 *Bosville Hotel, Ishes Inn, Cuillin Hills Hotel, Skeabost House Hotel, Portree House*

Creag An Fhithich, *10 Achachork, Achachork, Portree, Isle of Skye, IV51 9HT.*
Open: Easter to Nov
01478 612213 (also fax)
Mrs MacDonald
D: fr £16.50 **S:** fr £16.50
Beds: 1D 1T 1S **Baths:** 1 En 2 Sh
🛏 🅿 (6) 📺 💷 🖤 ₤
Modern farmhouse with panoramic views, situated 2 miles north of Portree on A855 Staffin Road. Ideal for touring North and West of Island. TV lounge for guests use, full Scottish breakfast. Warm welcome.

Myrtlebank, *Achachork, Portree, Isle of Skye, IV51 9HT.*
Modern croft house overlooking Portree. Panoramic view towards Cuillin Mountains. **Open:** May-Aug
01478 612597 (also fax) Mrs Gilmour
skye.gilmour@lineone.net
D: fr £16.00 **S:** fr £16.00
Beds: 2F 1D 1S **Baths:** 2 En 1 Sh
🛇 🅿 (5) 📺 🗢 📖 🖫 👗

12 Stormyhill Road, *Portree, Isle of Skye, IV51 9DY.*
Centrally located in Portree village, within five minutes walking distance to shop, restaurants. **Open:** All Year
01478 613165 Mrs Nicolson
audrey-nicolson3@yahoo.co.uk
D: £17.50–£20.00 **S:** £20.00–£25.00
Beds: 1F 1T 2D **Baths:** 1 Pr 1 Sh
🛇 🅿 (3) 🗲 📺 📖 👗

Cnoc Iain, *3 Sluggans, Portree, Isle of Skye, IV51 9EQ.*
Modern home with friendly atmosphere; good Scottish breakfast, panoramic views. **Open:** Mar to Oct
Grades: STB 3 Star
01478 612143 Mrs MacSween
D: £19.00–£25.00 **S:** £30.00–£42.00
Beds: 2D 1T **Baths:** 3 En
🛇 🅿 (3) 📺 🗢 📖 🖫 👗

Glendale, *2 Carn Dearg Place, Portree, Isle of Skye, IV51 9PZ.*
Friendly family home, single guests welcome. Central for touring Skye.
Open: All Year
Grades: STB 3 Star
01478 613149 (also fax)
Mrs Algie
D: £20.00–£30.00 **S:** £25.00–£35.00
Beds: 2T 1D 1S **Baths:** 2 En 2 Sh
🛇 🅿 (3) 🗲 📺 📖 🖫 👗 ♿

brenitote, *9 Martin Crescent, Portree, Isle of Skye, IV51 9DW.*
Family B&B 5 mins walk from Portree village. Sun lounge and ensuite facilities.
Open: All Year **Grades:** STB 3 Star
01478 612808 Mrs Matheson
D: £16.00–£18.00
Beds: 1T 1D **Baths:** 2 En
🅿 📺 📖 🖫 👗

12 Fraser Crescent, *Portree, Isle of Skye, IV51 9PH.*
Family-run Bed & Breakfast, offering clean, comfortable accommodation, 5 mins from bus.
Open: Apr to Oct
Grades: STB 3 Star
01478 612529 Mr Speed
D: £19.00–£20.00 **S:** £19.00–£20.00
Beds: 1T 1D **Baths:** 1 Pr
🅿 (2) 📺 🗢 📖 🖫 👗

Easdale Bridge Road, *Portree, Isle of Skye, IV51 9ER.*
Centrally situated bungalow with view of Cuillins and warm welcome.
Open: Easter to Oct
Grades: STB 2 Star
01478 613244 Mrs Macdonald
D: £20.00–£25.00 **S:** £25.00–£30.00
Beds: 2D **Baths:** 2 En
🛇 🅿 (2) 📺 📖 🖫 👗

Givendale Guest House, *Heron Place, Portree, Isle of Skye, IV51 9EU.*
Quiet location outstanding views quality food and accommodation.
Open: Easter to Oct
Grades: STB 3 Star GH
01478 612183 Mrs Rayner
trevor@givendale7.freeserve.co.uk
D: £20.00–£25.00 **S:** £25.00–£35.00
Beds: 2D 2T **Baths:** 2 En 1 Sh
🛇 🅿 (6) 🗲 📺 📖 🖫 👗 cc

9 Stormyhill Road, *Portree, Isle of Skye, IV51 9DY.*
In quiet location 3 minutes walk from village centre and harbour.
Open: All Year
Grades: STB 3 Star
01478 613332 S Campbell
sandra_campbell_B_B@yahoo.co.uk
D: £18.00–£25.00 **S:** £20.00–£28.00
Beds: 3D **Baths:** 3 En
🅿 (3) 📺 🗢 📖 🖫 👗

Larch Grove, *Treaslane, Portree, Isle of Skye, IV51 9NX.*
Larch Grove offers you your own private suite - sitting room, double bedroom, bathroom.
Open: Easter to October
01470 582212 Mrs Aitken
D: £20.00–£25.00
Beds: 1D **Baths:** 1 En
🅿 🗲 📺 📖 👗

NG4867 🏠 *Glenview Inn, Flodigarry Hotel, Columba, Oystercatcher*

Gracelands, *5 Glasphein, Staffin, Portree, Isle of Skye, IV51 9LZ.*
Fantastic sea and hill views. Boat/fishing trips. Hill walking.
Open: Apr to Nov
01470 562313 Mrs Nicolson
D: £15.00–£16.00 **S:** £15.00–£16.00
Beds: 1F 2D 1T 1S **Baths:** 2 Sh
🛇 (4) 🅿 (3) 📺 📖 👗

Tigh Cilmartin, *Staffin, Portree, Isle of Skye, IV51 9JS.*
Comfortable bedrooms with mountain view. Good breakfasts with home-made bread and home-grown produce.
Open: All Year
01470 562331 Mrs Poole
D: £15.00–£19.00 **S:** £15.00–£25.00
Beds: 1F 1D 1T **Baths:** 1 En 1 Sh
🛇 🅿 (6) 📺 🗢 🗡 📖 👗

2 Glasphein, *Staffin, Portree, Isle of Skye, IV51 9JZ.*
Quiet, traditional, croft house with spectacular views.
Open: Easter to Oct
01470 562268 Mrs Macdonald
D: fr £14.00 **S:** fr £14.00
Beds: 1F 1T **Baths:** 1 Sh
🛇 (1) 🅿 (2) 📺 📖 👗

━━━━━━━━━━━━━━━━━

National Grid References are for villages, towns and cities – not for individual houses

NG4868 🏠 *Flodigarry Hotel, Glenview Inn*

Quiraing Lodge, *Stenscholl, Staffin, Portree, Isle of Skye, IV51 9JS.*
Victorian hunting lodge. Dramatically situated in acre of garden. Quiet, seaside location.
Open: All Year
01470 562330 Mr Gardener
D: £21.00 **S:** £21.00–£30.00
Beds: 1F 4T 2D 1S **Baths:** 3 Sh
🛇 🅿 (10) 🗲 🗡 📖 🖫 👗

Achtalean, *Stenscholl, Staffin, Portree, Isle of Skye, IV51 9JS.*
Working croft, views over sea & the Quinag. Home baking and a cosy peat fire.
Open: Easter to Oct
01470 562723 Mrs Gillies
achtalean.b.b@talk21.com
D: £16.00–£18.00
Beds: 1F 1D 1T **Baths:** 1 En 1 Sh
🛇 🅿 (6) 🗲 📺 🗡 📖 🖫 👗

NG5317 🏠 *The Hayloft*

Strathaird House, *Strathaird, Broadford, Isle of Skye, IV49 9AX.*
Open: Easter to Sep
Grades: STB 1 Star GH
01471 866269 Mr Kubale
Fax: 01471 866320
straithairdhouse.skye.co.uk
D: £25.00–£30.00 **S:** £25.00–£30.00
Beds: 4F 1D 2S **Baths:** 1 En 1 Pr 3 Sh
🛇 🅿 (6) 🗢 📖 👗 cc
Family-run guest house above Kilmarie Bay on the Elgol Road. Ideal for walks to Camasunary Bay, Blaven, the Cuillins, seashore exploring & boat trips to Loch Coruisk. Rambling house with glorious views. Licensed 'Hayloft Restaurant', fireside library, drying room & garden.

NG3438 🏠 *Munro Tables, Ullinish Lodge Hotel*

Ard-Bhealaidh, *Balgown, Struan, Isle of Skye, IV56 8FA.*
Scenic lochside view, and a warm Highland welcome, await all who stay.
Open: Easter to Oct
Grades: STB 3 Star
01470 572334 (also fax)
Mr MacKay
ard-bhealaidh@uk-bedandbreakfasts.com
D: fr £16.00 **S:** fr £16.00
Beds: 1F 1D 1S **Baths:** 1 En 1 Sh
🛇 🅿 (5) 📺 🗢 👗

Glenside, *4 Totarder , Struan, Isle of Skye, IV56 8FW.*
Situated on working croft in lovely valley. Warm welcome assured.
Open: Easter to Oct
Grades: STB 3 Star
01470 572253 Mrs MacCusbic
D: £17.00–£20.00 **S:** £20.00–£22.00
Beds: 1D 1T **Baths:** 1 En 1 Pr
🛇 (12) 🅿 (3) 🗲 🖫 ❀ cc

The Anchorage, 9 Eabost West, Struan,
Isle of Skye, IV56 8FE.
Modern comfortable bungalow with
panoramic sea and mountain views.
Open: All Year
Grades: STB 3 Star
01470 572206 Mrs Campbell
eabost@aol.com
D: £18.00–£20.00 **S:** £20.00
Beds: 2D 1T **Baths:** 2 En 1 Pr
❄ 🄿 (3) 📺 ⊁ ✕ 🖾 🖵 ⚓ CC

Seaforth, Coillore, Struan, Isle of Skye,
IV56 8FX.
Comfortable accommodation with
panoramic views, ideally situated for
touring.
Open: Oct
01470 572230 Mrs Mackinnon
D: £17.00–£19.00
Beds: 1D 2T **Baths:** 2 Sh
❄ 🄿 (4) 📺 🖾 ⚓

SKYE The Braes
NG5234 ◗ Portree House

Tianavaig, Camustianavaig, The Braes,
Portree, Isle of Skye, IV51 9LQ.
A pretty rural seashore location
magnificent sea and mountain views.
Open: All Year (not Xmas)
Grades: STB 3 Star
01478 650325 Mrs Corry
D: £17.50–£20.00 **S:** £17.50–£20.00
Beds: 2D **Baths:** 1 En 1 Pr
❄ 🄿 (2) ⊁ 📺 ⊁ 🖾 ⚓

Cnoc Donn, Achnahanaid, The Braes,
Portree, Isle of Skye, IV51 9LH.
Located on a working croft lovely sea and
mountain views.
Open: All Year (not Xmas)
01478 650327 Mrs Macpherson
D: £17.50 **S:** £17.50
Beds: 2D **Baths:** 1 Sh
❄ 🄿 (2) ⊁ 📺 🖾 ⚓

B&B owners may vary
rates - be sure to check
when booking

SKYE Uig (Uig Bay)
NG3963

Ard-na-mara, 11 Idrigill, Uig, Portree,
Isle of Skye, IV51 9XU.
Modern bungalow in a quiet location with
half acre garden. **Open:** All Year
01470 542281 Fax: 01470 542289
D: £18.00–£25.00
Beds: 3D 1F **Baths:** 4 En
❄ (14) 🄿 (4) 📺 ⊁ 🖾 ⚓

13 Earlish, Uig, Portree, Isle of Skye, IV51
9XL.
Comfortable modern house on working
croft. Extensive views over Loch Snizort
to Black Cuillins. **Open:** All Year
01470 542361 (also fax)
Mr & Mrs Pritcard
D: £14.00–£16.00 **S:** £14.00–£16.00
Beds: 2D 1T **Baths:** 2 Sh
❄ 🄿 (5) ⊁ 📺 ⊁ ✕ 🖾 🖵 ✳ ⚓

Idrigill House, Uig, Portree, Isle of
Skye, IV51 9XU.
Comfortable modern house in a quiet
location overlooking Uig Bay.
Open: All Year (not Xmas)
01470 542398 Mr & Mrs Watkins
Fax: 01470 542447
sue@idrigill.co.uk
D: £16.00–£24.00 **S:** £16.00–£24.00
Beds: 2D 1T 1S **Baths:** 1 En 2 Pr 1 Sh
🄿 (5) ⊁ 📺 ⊁ 🖾 ⚓

SKYE Uigshader
NG4346

Torwood, 1 Peiness, Uigshader, Portree,
Isle of Skye, IV51 9LW.
Open: Easter to Oct
Grades: STB 3 Star
01470 532479 Mrs Gillies
anne@selma.co.uk
D: £16.00–£20.00
Beds: 1F 1D 1T **Baths:** 2 En 1 Pr
❄ (1) 🄿 (4) ⊁ 📺 🖾 🖵
Torwood is a modern home offering
warm, comfortable accommodation
situated in the countryside yet only 10
minutes from Portree. An ideal base for
touring or relaxing. Pony trekking, golf &
fishing nearby. A warm highland welcome
awaits you.

SKYE Vatten
NG2843 ◗ Dunvegan Hotel

Sea View, 3 Herebost, Vatten, Dunvegan,
Isle of Skye, Isle Of Skye, IV55 8GZ.
Modern bungalow with sea views, near
the famous Dunvegan castle.
Open: Easter to Oct
Grades: STB 3 Star
01470 521705 Mrs Campbell
D: £16.00–£17.50
Beds: 1D 1T **Baths:** 1 En 1 Pr
🄿 (2) ⊁ 📺 🖾 ⚓

SKYE Waternish
NG2658 ◗ Lochbay Rest, Stein Inn

Lusta Cottage, 11-12 Lochbay,
Waternish, Isle of Skye, IV55 8GD.
Modern cottage set in 18 acre croft with
waterfalls to shore of Loch Bay.
Open: May to Oct
Grades: STB 3 Star
01470 592263 Mrs Smith
lustacottage@supanet.com
D: £20.00 **S:** £20.00
Beds: 1D 1T **Baths:** 1 En 1 Pr
🄿 (8) ⊁ 📺 🖾 ⚓

34 Lochbay, Waternish, Isle of Skye, IV55
8GD.
Newly built croft house with spectacular
views to Outer Hebrides.
Open: Easter to Oct
01470 592372 Mrs Broughton
D: £20.00–£25.00 **S:** £25.00–£27.00
Beds: 1D 1T **Baths:** 2 En
❄ (10) 🄿 (4) ⊁ 📺 ⊁ 🖾 ⚓

Planning a longer stay? Always
ask for any special rates

Stilwell's National Trail Companion

46 Long Distance Footpaths
Where to Stay * Where to Eat

Other guides may show you where to walk, **Stilwell's National Trail Companion** shows your where to stay and eat. The perfect companion guide for the British Isles' famous national trails and long distance footpaths, Stilwell's make pre-planning your accommodation easy. It lists B&Bs, hostels, campsites and pubs - in the order they appear along the routes - and includes such vital information as maps, grid references and distance from the path; Tourist Board ratings; the availability of vehicle pick-up, drying facilities and packed lunches. So whether you walk a trail in stages at weekends or in one continuous journey, you'll never be stuck at the end of the day for a hot meal or a great place to sleep.

Enjoy the beauty and adventure of Britain's – and Ireland's – long distance trails with Stilwell's National Trail Companion.

Paths in England
Cleveland Way & Tabular Hills Link – Coast to Coast Path – Cotswald Way – Cumbria Way – Dales Way – Essex Way – Greensand Way – Hadrian's Wall – Heart of England Way – Hereward Way – Icknield Way – Macmillan Way – North Downs Way – Oxfordshire Way – Peddars Way and Norfolk Coastal Path – Pennine Way – Ribble Way – The Ridgeway – Shropshire Way – South Downs Way – South West Coast Path – Staffordshire Way – Tarka Trail – Thames Path – Two Moors Way - Vanguard Way - Viking Way – Wayfarer's Walk – Wealdway – Wessex Ridgeway – Wolds Way

Paths in Ireland
Beara Way – Dingle Way – Kerry Way – Ulster Way – Western Way – Wicklow Way

Paths in Scotland
Fife Coastal Walk – Southern Upland Way – Speyside Way – West Highland Way

Paths in Wales
Cambrian Way – Glyndwr's Way – Offa's Dyke Path – Pembrokeshire Coast Path – Wye Valley Walk

---

£9.95 from all good bookstores (ISBN 1-900861-25-9) or £10.95 (inc p&p) from Stilwell Publishing Ltd, 59 Charlotte Road, London EC2A 3QW (020 7739 7179)

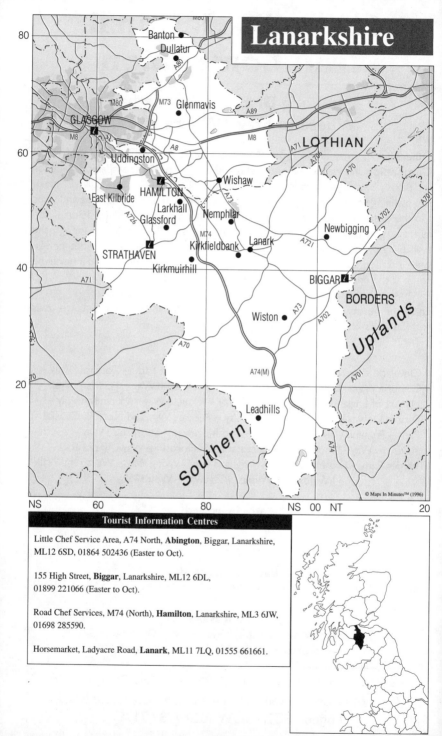

Lanarkshire

STILWELL'S BRITAIN: BED & BREAKFAST

Tourist Information Centres

Little Chef Service Area, A74 North, **Abington**, Biggar, Lanarkshire, ML12 6SD, 01864 502436 (Easter to Oct).

155 High Street, **Biggar**, Lanarkshire, ML12 6DL, 01899 221066 (Easter to Oct).

Road Chef Services, M74 (North), **Hamilton**, Lanarkshire, ML3 6JW, 01698 285590.

Horsemarket, Ladyacre Road, **Lanark**, ML11 7LQ, 01555 661661.

© Maps In Minutes™ (1996)

Banton

NS7579 🍺 *Swan Inn, Coachman Hotel*

Auchenrivoch Farm, *Banton, Kilsyth, Glasgow, G65 0OZ.*
Beautifully situated, south facing farmhouse. Large garden and views of Kelvin Valley. **Open:** All Year
01236 822113 Mrs Henderson
D: £18.00–£21.00 **S:** £20.00–£22.00
Beds: 2T
🛏 🅿 📺 🛏 🖼 Ⓥ ♨

Biggar

NT0437 🍺 *Elphinstone Hotel*

Lindsaylands, *Biggar, Lanarkshire, ML12 6EQ.*
Beautiful country house, peaceful setting, local touring, Edinburgh/Glasgow borders. **Open:** Easter to Nov
Grades: STB 4 Star
01899 220033 Mrs Stott **Fax: 01899 221009**
elspeth@lindsaylands.co.uk
D: £24.00–£28.00 **S:** £28.00–£30.00
Beds: 2D 1T **Baths:** 2 En 1 Pr
🛏 🅿 (8) 📺 ✕ 🖼 Ⓥ ♨

Cultershogle, *12 Langvout Gate, Biggar, Lanarkshire, ML12 6UF.*
Beautiful outlook from very comfortable bungalow; quiet location, home cooking.
Open: All Year (not Xmas)
01899 221702 Mr & Mrs Tennant
D: £18.00–£19.00 **S:** £20.00
Beds: 2T **Baths:** 2 En
🛏 🅿 (3) 🗶 📺 🛏 🖼 ♨

Cormiston Cottage, *Cormiston Road, Biggar, ML12 6NS.*
Open: All Year
Grades: STB 3 Star
01899 220 200 Mrs Wales
Fax: 0131 440 0272
jwales4453@aol.com
D: £20.00–£25.00 **S:** £25.00–£30.00
Beds: 1F 1T **Baths:** 1 En
🛏 (3) 🅿 (2) 📺 ✕ 🖼 Ⓥ ♨ 🔥
Delightful country cottage with beautiful views over the fields and hills beyond. The accommodation is on one floor and offers guests complete privacy. Spacious twin bedded room with En suite facilities. There are bunk beds in the adjoining offering family accommodation.

Woodgill, *12 Edinburgh Road, Biggar, Lanarkshire, ML12 6AX.*
Friendly and welcoming family home in historic country town.
Open: Easter to Oct
01899 220324 Mrs Brown
D: fr £18.00 **S:** fr £16.00
Beds: 1D 1T 1S **Baths:** 1 Sh
🛏 🅿 (4) 🗶 📺 🖼 Ⓥ ♨

BEDROOMS
F - Family
D - Double
T - Twin
S - Single

Dullatur

NS7476 🍺 *Castlecarry House Hotel, Craigmarloch Inn*

Dullatur House, *Dullatur, Glasgow, G68 0AW.*
Georgian mansion house circa 1740.
Open: All Year
01236 738855 (also fax) Mrs Moore
mooread@global.com
D: £19.50–£23.50 **S:** £21.50–£25.00
Beds: 1F 2T **Baths:** 2 En 1 Pr
🛏 🅿 (4) 📺 🛏 ✕ 🖼 Ⓥ ♨

East Kilbride

NS6354 🍺 *Kingsgate Still, Torrance Hotel, Calderwood Inn*

11 Markethill Road, The Village, *East Kilbride, Glasgow, G74 4AA.*
1920s detached sandstone house close to old village with great location.
Open: All Year (not Xmas)
01355 231547 (also fax)
Mrs Gibb
D: fr £17.50 **S:** fr £22.50
Beds: 4T **Baths:** 2 Sh
🛏 🅿 📺 🛏 ✕ 🖼 Ⓥ ♨

Glassford

NS7247 🍺 *Glassford Inn*

Avonlea, *46 Millar Street, Glassford, Strathaven, Lanarkshire, ML10 6TD.*
Comfortable homely accommodation country village near M74 junction 8. Rear garden.
Open: Jan to Nov
Grades: STB 3 Star, AA 2 Diamond
01357 521748 Miss Rankin
D: £18.00–£20.00 **S:** £22.00–£25.00
Beds: 2T **Baths:** 1 Sh
🛏 (7) 🗶 📺 🖼 ♨

Glenmavis

NS7567 🍺 *Kirkstyle Inn*

Rowan Lodge, *23 Condorrat Road, Glenmavis, Airdrie, Lanarkshire, ML6 0NS.*
Excellent bungalow accommodation opposite village church. Ideal for touring.
Open: All Year
Grades: STB 3 Star
01236 753934 june@rowanlodge.co.uk
D: £20.00–£30.00 **S:** £20.00–£30.00
Beds: 1T 1D 1S **Baths:** 3 En
🅿 (4) 🗶 📺 🖼 Ⓥ ♨ cc

Hamilton

NS7255 🍺 *Gults Bar, Harveys Bar, Hamilton Town Hotel*

57 Townhill Road, *Hamilton, Lanarkshire, ML3 9RH.*
Family house country view to rear, 5 minutes from M74.
Open: All Year (not Xmas)
01698 824174 Mrs Reddy
Fax: 01698 327018
p.j.reddy.ltd@cableinet.co.uk
D: £16.00–£18.00 **S:** £16.00–£18.00
Beds: 2T **Baths:** 2 Sh
🛏 (2) 🅿 (2) 📺 🖼 ♨

Glenmhor House, *6 Bent Road,*
Hamilton, Lanarkshire, ML3 6QB.
Traditional sandstone villa in quiet & central location. Recommended worldwide.
Open: All Year
01698 423293 Ms McCabe
D: £17.00 **S:** £18.00–£20.00
Beds: 1F 1T 1S **Baths:** 2 Sh
🛏 🅿 (3) 📺 🛏 🖼 Ⓥ ♨

Kirkfieldbank

NS8643 🍺 *The Tavern, Lovejoys*

Brig End B&B, *231 Riverside Road, Kirkfieldbank, Lanark, ML11 9JJ.*
Picturesque overlooking River Clyde between two bridges on Clyde walkway.
Open: All Year
01555 663855 Mrs Rankin
D: £18.00–£19.00 **S:** £19.00–£20.00
Beds: 2T **Baths:** 1 En 1 Pr
🛏 🅿 (3) 🗶 📺 ✕ 🖼 Ⓥ ♨

Kirkmuirhill

NS7943 🍺 *The Poachers*

Dykecroft Farm, *Kirkmuirhill, Lesmahagow, Lanark, ML11 0JQ.*
Convenient for Glasgow and airports. Tea-making facilities. Good breakfast.
Open: All Year
01555 892226 Mrs McInally
D: £18.50–£20.00 **S:** £20.00–£22.00
Beds: 2D 1T **Baths:** 2 Sh
🛏 🅿 (4) 📺 🛏 🖼 Ⓥ ♨ 🔥 1

Lanark

NS8843 🍺 *Crown Tavern, Lovejoys*

Roselea, *9 Cleghorn Road, Lanark, ML11 7QT.*
Edwardian House, original features. Close to New Lanark. Golf, fishing, riding and genealogy.
Open: All Year
Grades: STB 3 Star
01555 662540 Mrs Allen
margaretallen2@tesco.net
D: £18.00–£20.00 **S:** £17.00–£26.00
Beds: 1F 1D 1S **Baths:** 1 En 1 Sh
🛏 🅿 (2) 📺 🛏 🖼 Ⓥ ♣ ♨

5 Hardacres, *Lanark, ML11 7QP.*
Home form Home. Well-appointed bungalow, 25 miles Edinburgh-Glasgow.
Open: All Year (not Xmas)
Grades: STB 3 Star
01555 661002 Mrs Buchanan
D: £16.00–£18.00 **S:** £17.00–£18.00
Beds: 2D 1T **Baths:** 1 En 1 Sh
🅿 (1) 🗶 📺 🖼 ♨

Larkhall

NS7650

Shawlands Roadhouse Hotel, *Ayr Road, Canderside Toll, Larkhall, Lanarkshire, ML9 2TZ.*
Small family-run hotel.
Open: All Year
01698 791111 Mr Dowling
D: £16.80–£30.00 **S:** £24.80–£45.00
Beds: 1F 4D 16T 1S **Baths:** 22 En
🛏 🅿 (10) 🗶 📺 ✕ 🖼 Ⓥ ♣ ♨ 🔥 cc

Leadhills

NS8815 ◀ *Colebrook Arms, Hopetown Arms*

Meadowfoot Cottage, *Gowanbank, Leadhills, Biggar, Lanarkshire, ML12 6YB.*
Open: All Year (not Xmas)
Grades: STB 3 Star
01659 74369 Mrs Ledger
enquiries@meadowfootcottage.co.uk
D: £18.50–£20.00 **S:** £20.00–£25.00
Beds: 1F 1T **Baths:** 1 En 1 Sh
🛏 🅿 (4) ⅓ 🖵 ✕ 🎞 🖫 🛓
Blending history and modern amenities with the warmest welcome and delicious home cooking makes your stay a real highlight. Ideal for hill walking, Southern Upland Way, gold-panning, visiting Museum of Lead mining, Edinburgh, Glasgow, the beautiful Clyde Valley. Peaceful stopover just six miles from M74.

Newbigging

NT0145

Nestlers Hotel, *Newbigging, Lanark, ML11 8NA.*
Small intimate family run hotel in rural South Lanarkshire.
Open: All Year **Grades:** STB 2 Star
01555 840680 Mr Anderson
nestlers@hotel98.freeserve.co.uk
D: £23.50–£27.50 **S:** £28.50–£35.00
Beds: 1F 2T 1D **Baths:** 4 En
🛏 🅿 (9) ⅓ 🖵 ✽ ✕ 🎞 🖫 🛓 cc

Strathaven

NS7044 ◀ *Glassford Inn, Waterside, Strathaven Hotel*

Avonlea, *46 Millar Street, Glassford, Strathaven, Lanarkshire, ML10 6TD.*
Comfortable homely accommodation country village near M74 junction 8. Rear garden.
Open: Jan to Nov
Grades: STB 3 Star, AA 2 Diamond
01357 521748 Miss Rankin
D: £18.00–£20.00 **S:** £22.00–£25.00
Beds: 2T **Baths:** 1 Sh
🛏 (7) ⅓ 🖵 🎞 🛓

Kypemhor, *West Kype Farm, Strathaven, Lanarkshire, ML10 6PR.*
Bungalow with scenic rural views, 3 miles from busy market town.
Open: All Year
Grades: STB 2 Star
01357 529831 Mrs Anderson
D: £17.00–£20.00 **S:** £18.00–£22.00
Beds: 1D 1T **Baths:** 1 Sh
🛏 🅿 (12) 🖵 ✽ ✕ 🎞 🖫 🛓 🛓

Haroldslea, *3 Kirkhill Road, Strathaven, Lanarkshire, ML10 6HN.*
Modern detached villa with garden in quiet residential area near village centre.
Open: All Year (not Xmas/New Year)
Grades: STB Listed, Approv
01357 520617 Mrs Goodwillie
D: £20.00 **S:** £20.00
Beds: 1F 1D **Baths:** 2 Sh
🛏 🅿 (2) ⅓ 🖵 ✽ 🎞 🖫 🛓

Uddingston

NS6960 ◀ *Windmill, Redstones*

Phoenix Lodge Guest House, *4 Girdons Way, Uddingston, Glasgow, G71 7ED.*
Open: All Year **Grades:** STB 2 Star
01698 815296 Mr Boyce
Fax: 01698 267567
D: £19.00–£22.00 **S:** £23.00–£25.00
Beds: 6F 1T 1D **Baths:** 3 En 2 Sh
🛏 🅿 (8) 🖵 ✽ ✕ 🎞 ✳ 🛓 cc
Modern building, close to motorways north & south, rail station, lots of tourist attractions locally, walks, close to swimming pool, tenpin bowling, cinemas, parks, gymnasium, lots of pubs, clubs, various eating places, e.g. Indian, Italian, Chinese. Close to Glasgow Zoo.

BATHROOMS
Pr - Private
Sh - Shared
En - Ensuite

RATES
D = Price range per person sharing in a double room
S = Price range for a single room

Northcote Guest House, *2 Holmbrae Avenue, Uddingston, Glasgow, G71 6AL.*
Large Victorian private house, quiet locality. Easily accessible.
Open: All Year (not Xmas)
01698 813319 (also fax)
Mrs Meggs
meggs@accanet.com
D: £16.00–£17.00 **S:** £16.00–£17.00
Beds: 1F 1D 1S **Baths:** 1 Sh
🛏 🅿 (3) 🖵 🎞 🖫

Wishaw

NS7954 ◀ *Chardonnay*

The Mill House, *Garrion Bridge, Wishaw, Lanarkshire, ML2 0RR.*
Mill House, built 1907 with delightful garden, comfortable warm home.
Open: All Year
01698 881166 Mrs Pinkerton
Fax: 01698 886874
alanphotog@aol.com
D: £15.00–£18.00 **S:** £22.50–£27.50
Beds: 1F 1D 1T **Baths:** 1 En 1 Sh
🅿 (6) ⅓ 🖵 🎞 🛓

Wiston

NS9532

Wiston Place, *Wiston, Biggar, Lanarkshire, ML12 6HT.*
Peaceful homely C17th farmhouse; cottages available (4 Crowns).
Open: All Year (not Xmas)
01899 850235 Mrs McCaskie
D: £14.00–£16.00 **S:** £14.00–£16.00
Beds: 1F **Baths:** 1 Sh
🛏 🅿 🖵 ✽ 🎞 🛓

Stilwell's Ireland:
Bed & Breakfast 2000

Think of Ireland and you think of that world famous Irish hospitality. The warmth of the welcome is as much a part of this great island as are the wild and beautiful landscapes, the traditional folk music and the Guinness. Everywhere you go, town or country, North or South, you can't escape it. There are few better ways of experiencing this renowned hospitality, when traveling through Ireland, than by staying at one of the country's many Bed & Breakfasts. And there's no better way of choosing a convenient and desirable B&B than by consulting **Stilwell's Ireland: Bed & Breakfast 2001**.

Stilwell's Ireland: Bed & Breakfast 2001 contains over 1,400 entries — private houses, country halls, farms, cottages, inns, small hotels and guest houses — listed by county, in both Northern Ireland and the Republic of Ireland. Each entry includes room rates, facilities, Tourist Board grades or notices of approval and a brief description of the B&B, its location and surroundings. The average charge per person per night is £18. The listings also provide the names of local pubs and restaurants which serve food in the evening. As with all Stilwell B&B guides, Stilwell's Ireland has maps, listings of Tourist Information Offices and air, rail, bus and ferry information.

Treat yourself to some Irish hospitality with **Stilwell's Ireland: Bed & Breakfast 2001**.

£6.95 from all good bookstores (ISBN 1-900861-24-0) or £7.95 (inc p&p) from Stilwell Publishing Ltd, 59 Charlotte Road, London EC2A 3QW (020 7739 7179)

Lothian & Falkirk

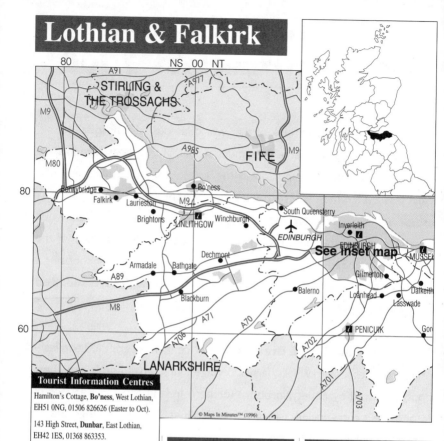

© Maps In Minutes™ (1996)

Tourist Information Centres

Hamilton's Cottage, **Bo'ness**, West Lothian, EH51 0NG, 01506 826626 (Easter to Oct).

143 High Street, **Dunbar**, East Lothian, EH42 1ES, 01368 863353.

3 Princes Street, **Edinburgh**, EH2 2AN, 0131 473 3800.

2-4 Glebe Street, **Falkirk**, FK1 1HX, 01324 620244.

Burgh Halls, The Cross, **Linlithgow**, West Lothian, EH49 7AH, 01506 844600.

Scottish Mining Museum, Lady Victoria Colliery, **Newtongrange**, Lothian, 0131 663 4262 (Easter to Oct).

Quality Street, **North Berwick**, East Lothian, EH39 4HJ, 01620 892197.

Granada Service Area, A1, **Old Craighall**, Musselburgh, East Lothian, EH21 8RE, 0131 653 6172.

Eastfield Industrial Estate, **Penicuik**, Midlothian, EH26 8HB, 01968 673846 (Easter to Oct).

Edinburgh Airport, **Turnhouse**, Edinburgh, 0131 473 3800.

Armadale

NS9368

Tarrareoch Farm, *Armadale, Bathgate, W Lothian, EH48 3BJ.*
C17th farmhouse all on one level. Midway Edinburgh/Glasgow. Beautiful countryside.
Open: All Year
Grades: STB 3 Star
01501 730404 (also fax)
Mrs Gibb
D: £16.00–£20.00 **S:** £20.00–£26.00
Beds: 1F 2T **Baths:** 1 En 1 Sh
🛇 🅿 (10) 📺 🐾 🛋 Ⓥ 🛢

Balerno

NT1666 🍴 *Tanners, Kestrel*

Newmills Cottage, *472 Lanark Road West, Balerno, EH14 5AE.*
Delightful house set in own grounds with ample private off-road parking.
Open: All Year
Grades: STB 4 Star, AA 4 Diamond
0131 449 4300 (also fax)
Mrs Linn
newmillscottage@blueyonder.co.uk
D: £20.00–£27.50 **S:** £25.00–£35.00
Beds: 2T **Baths:** 1 En 1 Pr
🅿 🏋 📺 🛋 Ⓥ 🛢

Bathgate

NS9769 🍴 *Kaim Park*

Hillview, *35 The Green, Bathgate, W Lothian, EH48 4DA.*
Quality and friendly accommodation with spectacular views of West Lothian.
Open: All Year (not Xmas)
Grades: STB 2 Star
01506 654830 (also fax)
Mrs Connell
D: £15.00–£16.00 **S:** £20.00–£22.00
Beds: 1F 1T **Baths:** 1 Sh
🛇 🏋 📺 🐾 🛋 Ⓥ 🛢

Blackburn

NS9865

Cruachan Guest House, *78 East Main Street, Blackburn, Bathgate, West Lothian, EH47 7QS.*
Relaxed, friendly, high-quality. Airport nearby, rail service to Edinburgh.
Open: All Year (not Xmas)
Grades: STB 3 Star
01506 655221 Mr Harkins
Fax: 01506 652395
cruachan.bb@virgin.net
D: £20.00–£23.00 **S:** £25.00–£30.00
Beds: 1F 3D **Baths:** 3 En 1 Pr
🛇 🅿 (5) 🏋 📺 🛋 Ⓥ 🛢

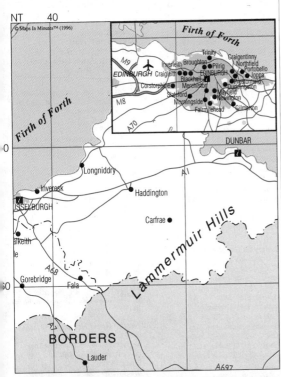

NT 40

© Maps In Minutes™ (1996)

Dalkeith

NT3467 ⚓ *Justinlees Inn, County Hotel*

Belmont, *47 Eskbank Road, Dalkeith, Midlothian, EH22 3BH.*
Spacious Victorian family house with lovely large garden.
Open: All Year (not Xmas/New Year)
0131 663 8676 (also fax)
Mrs Jarvis
D: £21.00–£23.00 **S:** £25.00–£30.00
Beds: 2D 1T **Baths:** 1 En 2 Sh
🛏 🅿 (8) ⅙ 📺 🛏 📖 Ⓥ cc

Dechmont

NT0370 ⚓ *Beecraigs Restaurant*

Bankhead Farm, *Dechmont, Broxburn, EH52 6NB.*
Panoramic views of beautiful countryside yet easy access to Edinburgh airport.
Open: All Year (not Xmas)
Grades: STB 3 Star
01506 811209 H Warnock
Fax: 07970 691318
bankheadbb@aol.com
D: £20.00–£25.00 **S:** £25.00–£35.00
Beds: 2F 2D 1T 2S **Baths:** 7 En
🛏 🅿 ⅙ 📺 📖 Ⓥ 👍 cc

Dunbar

NT6779 ⚓ *Craig En Gelt, Bayswell Hotel, Hillside Hotel, Starfish Restaurant*

Overcliffe Guest House, *11 Bayswell Park, Dunbar, E Lothian, EH42 1AE.*
Family-run, perfect for touring East Lothian's golf courses beaches.
Open: All Year
Grades: STB 2 Star, AA 3 Diamond
01368 864004 Mrs Bower
Fax: 01368 865995
overcliffe@aol.com
D: £20.00–£35.00 **S:** £25.00–£35.00
Beds: 3F 2T **Baths:** 3 En 2 Sh
🛏 (1) 🅿 (2) ⅙ 📺 🛏 📖 👍

Cruachan Guest House, *East Links Road, Dunbar, E Lothian, EH42 1LT.*
125 year old spacious roomed, family home on beach.
Open: All Year
Grades: STB 2 Star
01368 863006 Mr & Mrs McVicar
D: £20.00–£28.00 **S:** £20.00
Beds: 2F 1D 1T 1S **Baths:** 2 En 1 Pr
🛏 🅿 (5) 📺 🛏 ✕ 📖 Ⓥ 👍 ♿

Battleblent Hotel, *West Barns, Dunbar, E Lothian, EH42 1TS.*
Elevated castle- like country house hotel facing the Belhaven Bay.
Open: All Year
01368 862234 (also fax)
Mr Ferguson
battleblent. dunbar@tinyworld.co.uk
D: £25.00–£35.00 **S:** £25.00–£35.00
Beds: 1F 1D 3T 2S **Baths:** 7 En 1 Pr
🛏 🅿 (20) 📺 🛏 ✕ 📖 Ⓥ 👍 cc

Planning a longer stay? Always ask for any special rates

Bo'ness

NS9981 ⚓ *Richmond Park Hotel*

Haypark, *28 Grange Terrace, Bo'ness, EH51 9DS.*
Attractive stone built house overlooking the Forth, convenient for Edinburgh and Stirling.
Open: May to September
Grades: STB 2 Star
01506 823193 (also fax)
Mrs Croxford
D: £20.00–£25.00 **S:** £25.00
Beds: 1T 1D **Baths:** 1 Sh
⅙ 📺 📖 👍

Bonnybridge

NS8380 ⚓ *Castrechery House*

Bandominie Farm, *Walton Road, Bonnybridge, Stirlingshire, FK4 2HP.*
Farmhouse friendly atmosphere. 2 miles from A80, Castle Cary, B816.
Open: All Year (not Xmas/New Year)
Grades: STB 2 Star
01324 840284 Mrs Forrester
D: £17.00–£18.00 **S:** £17.00–£18.00
Beds: 1D 1T 1S **Baths:** 1 Sh
🛏 🅿 (3) ⅙ 📺 📖 👍

Brightons

NS9377 ⚓ *Whyteside Hotel*

Chez Nous, *Sunnyside Road, Brightons, Falkirk, FK2 0SA.*
Detached property with large car park equidistant Edinburgh-Glasgow, convenient for M9, M8.
Open: All Year (not Xmas)
01324 712836 (also fax)
Mr & Mrs Hunter
D: £18.00–£25.00 **S:** £18.00–£25.00
Beds: 2D 2T 2S **Baths:** 1 En 2 Sh
🛏 (9) 🅿 (8) ⅙ 📺 📖 Ⓥ 👍

Carfrae

NT5769 ⚓ *Goblin Ha Hotel, Tweedale Arms Hotel*

Carfrae Farm, *Carfrae, Haddington, E Lothian, EH41 4LP.*
Peaceful farmhouse overlooking lovely gardens. Edinburgh, The Borders, Golf nearby. **Open:** Apr to Oct
Grades: STB 4 Star
01620 830242 Mrs Gibson
Fax: 01620 830320
dgcarfrae@aol.com
D: £25.00–£27.00 **S:** £35.00–£40.00
Beds: 2D 1T **Baths:** 2 En 1 Pr
🛏 (10) 🅿 (6) ⅙ 📺 🛏 👍

EDINBURGH   Blackhall

NT2174

Sandilands House, *25 Queensferry Road, Edinburgh, EH4 3HB.*
1930's bungalow with many art deco features. Near Murrayfield Stadium.
Open: All Year
Grades: STB 4 Star
0131 332 2057 Mrs Sandilands
Fax: 0131 315 4476
D: £20.00–£34.00 **S:** £25.00–£45.00
Beds: 1F 1D 1T **Baths:** 3 En
🛏 🅿 ⚲ 📺 ▥ Ⓥ ♨ CC

EDINBURGH   Broughton

NT2575   🍴 *Clarmont Bar*

Ben Cruachan, *17 Mcdonald Road, Edinburgh, EH7 4LX.*
Open: April to Oct
Grades: STB 3 Star
0131 556 3709 N Stark
D: £25.00–£35.00
Beds: 1F 1T 1D **Baths:** 3 En
🛏 (10) 🅿 ⚲ 📺 ▥ Ⓥ ♨
Be assured of a very warm welcome at our family-run centrally situated guesthouse within walking distance of all main attractions. Bedrooms are fully equipped with your every comfort in mind. Excellent breakfast served. Free street parking.

Elas Guest House, *10 Claremont Crescent, Edinburgh, EH7 4HX.*
Georgian house, central Edinburgh. Free street parking. Traditional Scottish breakfasts. Groups - families welcome.
Open: All Year
Grades: STB 2 Star
0131 556 1929 Mrs Elas
D: £20.00–£30.00 **S:** £20.00–£30.00
Beds: 3F 2D 2T 1S **Baths:** 8 En
🛏 📺 🍴 ✕ ▥ Ⓥ ♨

Brodies Guest House, *22 East Claremont Street, Edinburgh, EH7 4JP.*
A warm Scottish welcome awaits you at our Victorian town house.
Open: All Year (not Xmas)
0131 556 4032 Mrs Olbert
Fax: 0131 556 9739
rose.olbert@saqnet.co.uk
D: £22.00–£35.00 **S:** £22.00–£30.00
Beds: 1F 1D 1T 1S **Baths:** 2 Pr 1 Sh
🛏 📺 ▥ Ⓥ ♨

EDINBURGH   Central

NT2573   🍴 *Golf Tavern, Bennets Bar, Minto Hotel, Navaar Hotel, Allison Hotel, Seahaven Hotel*

Rothesay Hotel, *8 Rothesay Place, Edinburgh, EH3 7SL.*
Heart of Edinburgh's Georgian new town in the city centre, short walk Princes Street.
Open: All Year
Grades: STB 2 Star, AA 3 Diamond
0131 225 4125 Mr Borland
info@rothesay-hotel.demon.co.uk
D: £25.00–£45.00 **S:** £38.00–£65.00
Beds: 2F 4D 18T 12S **Baths:** 36 Pr
🛏 📺 🍴 ✕ ♨ &

Averon Guest House, *44 Gilmore Place, Edinburgh, EH3 9NQ.*
Open: All Year
Grades: STB 1 Star, AA 2 Diamond, RAC 3 Diamond
0131 229 9932 Mr Cran
D: £18.00–£38.00 **S:** £25.00–£38.00
Beds: 2F 2D 3T 1S **Baths:** 6 Pr
🛏 🅿 (10) 📺 ▥ ♨ & CC
Fully restored Georgian town house, built in 1770. Central Edinburgh with car park. Standard and ensuite rooms available. STB, AA, RAC, Les Routiers recommended. 10 minute walk to Castle and Princes Street.

6 Dean Park Crescent, *Edinburgh, EH4 1PN.*
Warm friendly home. Large rooms. 10 mins walk to centre.
Open: Easter to Oct
Grades: STB 3 Star B&B
0131 332 5017 Mrs Kirkland
kirkland.b&b@cableinet.co.uk
D: £22.00–£29.00 **S:** £40.00–£55.00
Beds: 1F 1D 1T **Baths:** 1 En 1 Pr 1 Sh
🛏 ⚲ 📺 ▥ Ⓥ ♨ &

Amaryllis Guest House, *21 Upper Gilmore Place, Edinburgh, EH3 9NL.*
Warm, comfortable, friendly, central all attractions. Walkable but quietly situated.
Open: All Year (not Xmas)
Grades: STB 2 Star
0131 229 3293 (also fax)
L Melrose
ghamaryllis@aol.com
D: £18.00–£30.00 **S:** £25.00–£40.00
Beds: 3F 1D 1T **Baths:** 4 En 1 Pr
🛏 (10) 🅿 (2) 📺 ▥ ♨ CC

17 Hope Park Terrace, *Edinburgh, EH8 9LZ.*
Fifteen minutes' walk city centre. H&C in bedrooms.
Open: All Year
Grades: STB 1 Star
0131 667 7963 Mrs Frackelton
D: £25.00 **S:** £25.00
Beds: 2D **Baths:** 1 Sh
🛏 (10) ⚲ ▥ ♨

28 London Street, *Edinburgh, EH3 6NA.*
Central Georgian 1st flat 5 minutes walk from station.
Open: Easter to Oct
Grades: STB 2 Star
0131 556 4641 Mr & Mrs Campbell
D: £18.00–£25.00 **S:** £20.00–£27.00
Beds: 1F 1T 1D 1S **Baths:** 3 Sh
🛏 (5) 🅿 (1) 📺 ▥

Ailsa Craig Hotel, *24 Royal Terrace, Edinburgh, EH7 5AH.*
Elegant city centre Georgian town house hotel. Walking distance major attractions.
Open: All Year
Grades: STB 3 Star
0131 556 1022 Fax: 0131 556 6055
ailsacraighotel@ednet.co.uk
D: £25.00–£45.00 **S:** £25.00–£60.00
Beds: 5F 5D 3T 4S **Baths:** 14 En 1 Pr 2 Sh
🛏 📺 ✕ ▥ Ⓥ ♨ CC

Castle Park Guest House, *75 Gilmore Place, Edinburgh, EH3 9NU.*
Charming Victorian guest house ideally situated close to King Theatre & city centre.
Open: All Year
Grades: STB 2 Star
0131 229 1215 Fax: 0131 229 1223
D: £17.50–£25.00 **S:** £17.50–£22.50
Beds: 1F 4D 1T 2S **Baths:** 4 En 2 Sh
🛏 🅿 (4) 📺 🍴 ▥ ♨ CC

37 Howe Street, *Edinburgh, EH3 6TF.*
Listed building the the heart of Edinburgh in historic New Town.
Open: Easter to Oct
Grades: STB 2 Star
0131 557 3487 (also fax)
Mrs Collie
D: £20.00
Beds: 1D **Baths:** 1 Sh
📺 ▥ Ⓥ ♨ &

Aries Guest House, *5 Upper Gilmore Place, Edinburgh, EH3 9NW.*
Small central friendly ,all attractions walkable. TV, tea in rooms.
Open: All Year (not Xmas)
0131 229 4669 Mrs Robertson
D: £17.00–£28.00 **S:** £25.00–£35.00
Beds: 1F 2D 2T **Baths:** 2 Sh
🛏 📺 🍴 ▥ ♨ & CC

EDINBURGH Corstorphine

NT1972

Zetland Guest House, *186 St Johns Road, Edinburgh, EH12 8SG.*
A splendid Victorian house situated on the west side of Edinburgh.
Open: All Year
Grades: STB 3 Star GH, AA 4 Diamond
0131 334 3898 (also fax)
Mr Stein
zetland@dial.pipex.com
D: £20.00–£27.50 **S:** £20.00–£50.00
Beds: 1F 2D 4T 1S **Baths:** 4 En 2 Sh
🛏 🅿 (7) 📺 ▥ ♨

EDINBURGH Craigentinny

NT2974

Glenfarrer House, *36 Farrer Terrace, Edinburgh, EH7 6SG.*
Chalet bungalow close to excellent bus services. City centre 2 miles.
Open: Easter to Oct
0131 669 1265 Mrs Smith
D: fr £21.00 **S:** fr £17.00
Beds: 1D 1T 2S **Baths:** 2 En 1 Sh
🅿 (2) ⚲ 📺 ▥ Ⓥ ♨

EDINBURGH   Craigleith

NT2374

St Bernards Guest House, *22 St Bernards Crescent, Edinburgh, EH4 1NS.*
Victorian town house. 15 minute walk from city centre. Quiet location.
Open: All Year
0131 332 2339 Mr & Mrs Alsop
D: £22.50–£30.00 **S:** £25.00–£30.00
Beds: 3D 4T 1S **Baths:** 4 En 2 Sh
⚲ 📺 ▥ Ⓥ ♨

EDINBURGH Duddingston

NT2973 ◆ *Sheeps Heid Inn*

Sure & Steadfast, 76 Milton Road
West, Duddingston, Edinburgh, EH15 1QV.
Open: Easter to Sep
Grades: STB 3 Star B&B
0131 657 1189 Mr & Mrs Taylor
a_t_taylor@ednet.co.uk
D: £16.50–£22.00 **S:** £20.00–£44.00
Beds: 2D 1T **Baths:** 3 Sh
ᗡ 🅿 (3) ⌿ 🅦 ▥ 🆅 ≟ cc
Small, family-run 3 star B&B situated
about 2 miles from the city centre. The
property is located on the main bus route
and can be easily reached by taxi or bus
from the railway station or airport.

EDINBURGH Fairmilehead

NT2468 ◆ *Steading*

Valhalla, 35 Comiston View, Edinburgh,
EH10 6LP.
Modern detached property; quiet; golf, full
breakfast. Warm welcome guaranteed.
Open: All Year **Grades:** STB 2 Star
0131 445 5354 Mrs Stevenson-Renwick
D: £20.00–£32.00 **S:** £25.00–£35.00
Beds: 1D 1T 1S **Baths:** 2 En 1 Pr
ᗡ 🅿 (2) ⌿ 🅦 ▥ 🆅 ≟

EDINBURGH Gilmerton

NT2968

Emerald Guest House, 3 Drum
Street, Gilmerton, Edinburgh, EH17 8QQ.
Victorian villa situated on bus route to
city centre. **Open:** All Year (not
Xmas/New Year) **Grades:** STB 2 Star
0131 664 5918 Mrs O'Connor
D: £20.00–£31.00 **S:** £35.00
Beds: 1F 2T 2D **Baths:** 3 En 1 Sh
ᗡ (4) 🅿 (5) 🅦 ✕ ▥ 🆅 ≟

EDINBURGH Inverleith

NT2475 ◆ *Golf Tavern, Bennets Bar, Tapas Ole,
Minto Hotel, Navaar Hotel, Allison Hotel, Grannies
Attic, Seahaven Hotel*

The Innerleith Hotel, 5 Inverleith
Terrace, Edinburgh, EH3 5NS.
Licensed Victorian Hotel, city centre,
adjacent botanic gardens, groups
accepted. **Open:** All Year (not Xmas)
0131 556 2745 Mr & Mrs Case
Fax: 0131 557 0433
hotel@inverleith.freeserve.co.uk
D: £25.00–£50.00 **S:** £30.00–£50.00
Beds: 2F 2D 2T 2S **Baths:** 8 En
ᗡ ⌿ 🅦 ⵊ ✕ ▥ 🆅 ≟ cc

EDINBURGH Joppa

NT3173 ◆ *Bedford House Hotel*

Joppa Turrets Guest House, 1
Lower Joppa, Beach End of Morton Street,
Edinburgh, EH15 2ER.
Quiet, fine sea views, sandy beach,
unrestricted parking, frequent buses, 3.5
miles to city. **Open:** All Year (not Xmas)
0131 669 5806 (also fax)
Mr & Mrs Stanley
stanley@joppaturrets.demon.co.uk
D: £18.00–£35.00 **S:** £18.00–£35.00
Beds: 1F 4D **Baths:** 3 En 2 Sh
ᗡ (3) ⌿ 🅦 ▥ ≟

Buchanan Guest House, 97 Joppa
Road, Edinburgh, EH15 9HB.
Comfortable friendly family-run guest
house overlooking beach and Firth of
Forth.
Open: All Year (not Xmas)
0131 657 4117
Mr Buchanan
Fax: 0131 669 9353
buchananhouse@bigfoot.com
D: £18.00–£25.00 **S:** £18.00–£25.00
Beds: 1F 1D 2T **Baths:** 1 En 2 Sh
ᗡ 🅦 ▥ 🆅 ≟ cc

EDINBURGH Mayfield

NT2672 ◆ *Braidburn Inn, Leasley, La Campana,
Old Bell Inn*

The International, 37 Mayfield
Gardens, Edinburgh, EH9 2BX.
Open: All Year
Grades: STB 4 Star, AA 4 Diamond
0131 667 2511
Mrs Niven
Fax: 0131 667 1112
intergh@easynet.co.uk
D: £20.00–£40.00 **S:** £25.00–£45.00
Beds: 2F 2D 2T 3S **Baths:** 9 Pr
ᗡ 🅦 ▥ 🆅 ✳ ≟ ♿
An attractive stone built Victorian house
situated 1.5 miles south of Princes Street.
Lying on main bus route, access to city
centre is easy. The decor is outstanding,
some rooms enjoy magnificent views
across to the extinct Arthur's Seat
Volcano. Direct dial telephones.

Hopetoun Guest House, 15 Mayfield
Road, Edinburgh, EH9 2NG.
Open: All Year (not Xmas)
Grades: STB 3 Star
0131 667 7691
Mrs Mitchell
Fax: 0131 466 1691
hopetoun@aol.com
D: £20.00–£27.00 **S:** £25.00–£40.00
Beds: 1F 1D 1T **Baths:** 1 En 1 Pr 1 Sh
ᗡ 🅿 (2) ⌿ 🅦 ▥ 🆅 ≟ cc
Completely non-smoking. Small, friendly,
family-run guest house, close to
Edinburgh University. Excellent bus
service. Royal Mile/Castle 25 mins, on
foot. Personal attention in a relaxed,
informal atmosphere. Good choice of
breakfast. Owner a fund of local
information! Which? Books B&B Guide.

Lauderville Guest House, 52
Mayfield Road, Edinburgh, EH9 2NH.
Open: All Year
Grades: STB 4 Star
0131 667 7788
Mrs Marriott
Fax: 0131 667 2636
res@laudervilleguesthouse.co.uk
D: £25.00–£40.00 **S:** £28.00–£48.00
Beds: 1F 6D 2T 1S **Baths:** 10 En
ᗡ 🅿 (6) ⌿ 🅦 ✕ ▥ 🆅 ≟ cc
Restored Victorian town house minutes
from the city sights, Royal Mile, Castle,
Princes St. Elegant non-smoking
bedrooms and excellent breakfast awaits,
with varied menu including vegetarian.
Secluded garden and secure car park.
Traditional Pubs and quality Restaurants
nearby.

Ivy Guest House, 7 Mayfield Gardens,
Edinburgh, EH9 2AX.
Open: All Year
Grades: STB 3 Star, AA 3 Diamond, RAC
4 Diamond
0131 667 3411 Mr Green
Fax: 0131 620 1422
don@ivyguesthouse.com
D: £17.00–£35.00 **S:** £17.00–£65.00
Beds: 2F 3D 2T 1S **Baths:** 6 En 2 Pr
ᗡ 🅿 (7) 🅦 ⵊ ▥ ≟
Quiet, family-run Victorian villa guest
house, many local restaurants, close to
all Edinburgh's major cultural attractions,
golf courses, Commonwealth swimming
pool and university. A hearty Scottish
breakfast and a warm welcome is
assured.

Glenalmond Guest House, 25
Mayfield Gardens, Edinburgh, EH9 2BX.
Open: All Year (not Xmas)
Grades: STB 4 Star
0131 668 2392 (also fax)
Mr & Mrs Fraser
glen@almond25.freeserve.co.uk
D: £20.00–£35.00 **S:** £25.00–£40.00
Beds: 3F 4D 2T 1S **Baths:** 10 En
ᗡ (5) 🅦 ▥ 🆅 ≟ ♿
Deb & Dave warmly welcome you to their
superb accommodation. Ground, four
poster, en-suite rooms available. Close to
Waverley Station. Varied breakfast served
daily with home-made scones.

Lorne Villa Guest House, 9 East
Mayfield, Edinburgh, EH9 1SD.
Festival city residence, serving fine
Scottish cuisine with Scottish hospitality.
Open: All Year
Grades: STB 3 Star
0131 667 7159 (also fax)
Mr McCulloch
lornevilla@cableinet.co.uk
D: £18.00–£32.00 **S:** £18.00–£32.00
Beds: 1F 2D 3T 1S **Baths:** 3 En 1 Pr 3 Sh
ᗡ 🅿 (6) 🅦 ⵊ ✕ ▥ 🆅 ≟

Ben Doran Guest House, 11
Mayfield Gardens, Edinburgh , EH9 2AX.
Beautiful refurbished Georgian house.
Elegant, cosy, comfortable, central.
Family run hotel.
Open: All Year
Grades: STB 4 Star, AA 4 Diamond, RAC
4 Diamond, Sparkling Award
0131 667 8488 Dr Labaki
Fax: 0131 667 0076
info@bendoran.com
D: £25.00–£60.00 **S:** £25.00–£60.00
Beds: 4F 3D 2T 1S **Baths:** 6 En 4 Sh
ᗡ 🅿 (17) ⌿ 🅦 ✕ ▥ 🆅 ≟ cc

Crion Guest House, 33 Minto Street,
Edinburgh, EH9 2BT.
Family run guest house near city centre.
Most tourist attractions.
Open: All Year
Grades: STB Approv
0131 667 2708 Fax: 0131 662 1946
w.cheape@gilmourhouse.freeserve.co.uk
D: £20.00–£27.00 **S:** £20.00–£27.00
Beds: 1D 2T 1S **Baths:** 1 Sh
ᗡ 🅿 (2) 🅦 ▥ 🆅 ✳ ≟ cc

Tania Guest House, 19 Minto Street,
Edinburgh, EH9 1RQ.
Comfortable Georgian guest house, very
good bus route, Italian spoken.
Open: All Year (not Xmas)
Grades: STB 1 Star
0131 667 4144 Mrs Roscilli
D: £18.00–£25.00 **S:** £20.00–£27.50
Beds: 3F 1D 1T 1S **Baths:** 2 En
🛇 🅿 📺 ⏹ Ⅴ ♨

Parklands Guest House, 20 Mayfield
Gardens, Edinburgh, EH9 2BZ.
Comfortable well maintained Victorian
guest house near city centre.
Open: All Year
Grades: STB 3 Star, AA 3 Diamond
0131 667 7184 Mr Drummond
Fax: 0131 667 2011
parklands_guesthouse@yahoo.com
D: £22.00–£30.00 **S:** £25.00–£40.00
Beds: 1F 2D 2T 1S **Baths:** 5 En 1 Pr
🛇 🅿 (1) 📺 ⏹ Ⅴ ♨

Sylvern Guest House, 22 West
Mayfield, Edinburgh, EH9 1TQ.
Situated near the city centre. Good bus
routes, car park.
Open: All Year
Grades: STB 2 Star
0131 667 1241 (also fax)
Mr & Mrs Livornese
D: £17.00–£24.00
Beds: 2F 2T 2D **Baths:** 4 En 2 Sh
🛇 🅿 (8) ⌿ 📺 ⏹ ♨

Fairholme Guest House, 13 Moston
Terrace, Edinburgh, EH9 2DE.
Nestled away from noisy traffic, yet only
1.5 miles from Castle.
Open: All Year
Grades: STB 3 Star
0131 667 8645 Mrs Blows
Fax: 0131 668 2435
stilwell@fairholme.co.uk
D: £23.00–£35.00 **S:** £25.00–£40.00
Beds: 1F 1D 1T 1S **Baths:** 3 En 1 Pr
🛇 🅿 (1) ⌿ 📺 ⅏ ⏹ Ⅴ ♨ cc

St Conan's Guest House, 30 Minto
Street, Edinburgh, EH9 1SB.
A handsome, stone-built, Listed, end-
terrace Georgian town house on three
floors.
Open: All Year
0131 667 8393 (also fax)
Mr Bryce
st.conans@virgin.net
D: £20.00–£27.00 **S:** £20.00–£30.00
Beds: 3F 1D 3T **Baths:** 1 En 4 Pr 1 Sh
🛇 🅿 (7) 📺 ⅏ ⏹ Ⅴ ♨

Classic Guest House, 50 Mayfield
Road, Edinburgh, EH9 2NH.
Friendly, family-run Victorian house,
totally non-smoking. Personal service,
Scottish hospitality.
Open: All Year
0131 667 5847 Mrs Mail
Fax: 0131 662 1016
info@classichouse.demon.co.uk
D: £20.00–£30.00 **S:** £20.00–£40.00
Beds: 7F 1D 1T 3S **Baths:** 7 En
🛇 (3) 🅿 ⌿ 📺 ⏹ Ⅴ ♨ ♨ & cc

Abcorn Guest House, 4 Mayfield
Gardens, Edinburgh, EH9 2BU.
Detached Victorian villa, one mile from
Edinburgh city centre.
Open: All Year
0131 667 6548 abcorn@btinternet.com
D: £25.00–£35.00 **S:** £25.00–£35.00
Beds: 2F 2D 2T 1S **Baths:** 7 En
🛇 🅿 (6) 📺 ⏹ Ⅴ ♨ cc

Kingsway Guest House, 5 East
Mayfield, Edinburgh, EH9 1SD.
Warm, friendly, terraced Victorian villa
quietly situated near Castle & Princes
Street.
Open: All Year
0131 667 5029 Mrs Macdonald
Fax: 0131 662 4635
kingsway.guest.house@tinyworld.co.uk
D: £18.00–£35.00 **S:** £25.00–£35.00
Beds: 2F 2D 2T 1S **Baths:** 4 En 1 Pr 1 Sh
🅿 📺 ⅏ ⏹ Ⅴ ♨ cc

EDINBURGH   Merchiston

NT2472   🍴 Allison Hotel, Backstage Bistro,
Belfry, Bennets Bar, Cafe Royal, Grannies Attic,
Kings Wark, March Hall Hotel, Minto Hotel,
Navaar House, Railto Restaurant, Seahaven Hotel,
Suffolk Hall Hotel, Tatlers Golf Tavern, Tapas Ole

Villa Nina Guest House, 39
Leamington Terrace, Edinburgh, EH10 4JS.
Open: All Year (not Xmas/New Year)
Grades: STB 1 Star
0131 229 2644 (also fax)
Mr Cecco
villanina@amserve.net
D: £18.00–£24.00
Beds: 1F 2D 2T **Baths:** 2 Sh
🅿 📺 ⅏ ⏹ Ⅴ ♨
Very comfortable Victorian terrace house
situated in quiet residential part of city
yet 15 minutes' walk Princes Street,
Castle, theatres. TV in all rooms. Private
showers. Full cooked breakfast.

Granville Guest House, 13 Granville
Terrace, Edinburgh, EH10 4PQ.
Open: All Year (not Xmas)
Grades: STB 1 Star
0131 229 1676 B Oussellam
Fax: 0131 227 4633
granvilleguesthouse@tinyworld.co.uk
D: £19.00–£30.00 **S:** £20.00–£30.00
Beds: 2F 1T 3D 1S **Baths:** 2 En 2 Sh
🛇 🅿 (2) ⌿ 📺 ⅏ ♨
A family run guest house situated
centrally in Edinburgh, all local amenities
are nearby - not to mention the Kings
Theatre and a newly built leisure
complex. We are around a ten minute
walk from the city centre and the historic
Edinburgh Castle.

Nova Hotel, 5 Bruntsfield Crescent,
Edinburgh, EH10 4EZ.
Victorian, city centre, quiet area, free
parking, fully licensed, all rooms ensuite.
Lovely views.
Open: All Year
Grades: STB 3 Star
0131 447 6437 Mr McBride
Fax: 0131 452 8126 (preferred for
bookings)
jamie@scotland-hotels.demon.co.uk
D: £25.00–£55.00 **S:** £35.00–£70.00
Beds: 6F 2D 2T 2S **Baths:** 13 En
🛇 🅿 ⌿ 📺 ⅏ × ⏹ Ⅴ ♨ 1 cc

Leamington Guest House, 57
Leamington Terrace, Edinburgh, EH10 4JS.
Elegant Victorian town house close to city
centre. Warm welcome assured.
Open: All Year
Grades: STB 3 Star, AA 3 Diamond
0131 228 3879 Ms Stewart
Fax: 0131 221 1022
lemgh@globalnet.co.uk
D: £25.00–£40.00 **S:** £25.00–£40.00
Beds: 3F 2D 1T 2S **Baths:** 4 En 2 Sh
🛇 ⌿ 📺 ⅏ ⏹ Ⅴ ♨ cc

Kariba Guest House, 10 Granville
Terrace, Edinburgh, EH10 4BQ.
Victorian townhouse 15 minutes walk to
city centre. Private parking.
Open: All Year
Grades: AA 2 Diamond, RAC 2 Diamond
0131 229 3773 Mrs Holligan
Fax: 0131 229 4968
karibaguesthouse@hotmail.com
D: £18.00–£28.00 **S:** £25.00–£50.00
Beds: 2F 4D 3T **Baths:** 2 En
🛇 (1) 📺 ⅏ ⏹ Ⅴ ♨ & cc

EDINBURGH   Morningside

NT2471   🍴 Montpeliers

Dunedin, 21-23 Colinton Road,
Edinburgh, EH10 5DR.
Victorian terraced villa, furnished in
period-style. Princess street, 15 mins.
Open: All Year (not Xmas)
0131 447 0679 Mr Fortune
Fax: 0131 446 9358
h.fort10560@aol.com
D: £20.00–£30.00 **S:** £20.00–£30.00
Beds: 4F 2D 1T 2S **Baths:** 6 En 1 Pr 2 Sh
🛇 ⌿ 📺 ⅏ ♨ & cc

Sandeman House, 33 Colinton Road,
Edinburgh, EH10 5DR.
Non-smoking Victorian family home,
conveniently situated, unrestricted street
parking.
Open: All Year (not Xmas)
0131 447 8080 (also fax)
Ms Sandeman
D: £28.00–£36.00 **S:** £25.00–£45.00
Beds: 1D 1T 1S **Baths:** 3 Pr
🛇 ⌿ 📺 ⅏ Ⅴ ♨

EDINBURGH   Newington

NT2671   🍴 Old Bell Inn, Suffolk Hall Hotel,
Cragg, Braidburn Inn

Rowan Guest House, 13 Glenorchy
Terrace, Edinburgh, EH9 2DQ.
Open: All Year (not Xmas)
Grades: STB 3 Star, AA 3 Diamond
0131 667 2463 (also fax)
Mr & Mrs Vidler
rowanhouse@hotmail.com
D: £23.00–£32.00 **S:** £24.00–£29.00
Beds: 1F 3D 2T 3S **Baths:** 3 En 3 Sh
🛇 🅿 (2) 📺 ⅏ ♨ cc
Comfortable Victorian home in quiet,
leafy, conservation area, a mile and a half
from city centre, castle and Royal Mile.
Delicious breakfast, including porridge
and freshly baked scones. A warm
welcome and personal service from Alan
and Angela. Free parking.

Ascot Guest House, *98 Dalkeith Road, Edinburgh, EH16 5AF.*
Comfortable family run guest house close to all attractions.
Open: All Year
0131 667 1500 J Williams
ascotedinburgh@btinternet.com
D: £18.00–£30.00 **S:** £20.00–£40.00
Beds: 2F 2T 2D 1S **Baths:** 2 En 2 Pr 2 Sh
🛇 (10) 🅿 (3) 📺 📶 🛒 🖭 ⚓

Gifford House, *103 Dalkeith Road, Edinburgh, EH16 5AJ.*
Elegant Victorian house. Superior rooms with Edinburgh's attractions within easy reach.
Open: All Year
Grades: STB 4 Star
0131 667 4688 (also fax)
Mrs Dow
giffordhotel@btinternet.com
D: £20.00–£38.00 **S:** £23.00–£50.00
Beds: 2F 2D 2T 1S **Baths:** 7 En
🛇 🗡 📺 🏠 📶 🖭 ❋ ⚓ cc

17 Crawfurd Road, *Edinburgh, EH16 5PQ.*
Victorian family home, friendly welcome - easy access to city centre.
Open: May to Sep
Grades: STB 2 Star
0131 667 1191 Ms Simpson
D: £17.50–£25.00 **S:** £17.50–£25.00
Beds: 1D 1T 1S **Baths:** 2 Sh
🛇 🅿 (1) 🗡 📺 📶 ⚓

Kingsley Guest House, *30 Craigmillar Park, Edinburgh, EH16 5PS.*
Friendly family run house on excellent bus route for sightseeing.
Open: All Year
Grades: STB 3 Star, AA 3 Diamond
0131 667 8439 (also fax)
D: £20.00–£35.00 **S:** £25.00–£40.00
Beds: 1F 2T 3D **Baths:** 3 En 2 Pr
🛇 (3) 🅿 (5) 🗡 📺 📶 🖭 ⚓

7 Crawfurd Road, Newington, *Edinburgh, EH16 5PQ.*
Beautiful centrally located house. Guest rooms overlook well-maintained gardens.
Open: Easter to Oct
0131 667 2283 Mrs McLean
i_mclean@msn.com
D: £19.00–£25.00 **S:** £22.00–£25.00
Beds: 1F 1T 1S **Baths:** 1 Sh
🗡 📺 📶

NT2973 🍺 *Golf Tavern, Bennets Bar, Tapas Ole, Minto Hotel, Navaar Hotel, Allison Hotel, Grannies Attic, Seahaven Hotel*

Brae Guest House, *119 Willowbrae Road, Edinburgh, EH8 7HN.*
Friendly guest house. Meadowbank - Holyrood Palace, on main bus route.
Open: All Year
Grades: STB 3 Star, AA 3 Diamond
0131 661 0170 Mrs Walker
baeguesthouse@tinyworld.co.uk
D: £18.00–£40.00 **S:** £18.00–£40.00
Beds: 1F 1T 1D 1S **Baths:** 3 En 1 Pr
🛇 📺 🏠 📶 🖭 ⚓

NT2675 🍺 *Oyster Bar*

Claymore Guest House, *68 Pilrig Street, Edinburgh, EH6 5AS.*
Warm, welcoming, personally run, centrally situated, close to all attractions.
Open: All Year (not Xmas)
Grades: STB 2 Star GH
0131 554 2500 (also fax) Mrs Dorrian
D: £18.00–£30.00 **S:** fr £22.00
Beds: 2F 2D 2T **Baths:** 3 En 1 Pr 2 Sh
🛇 🗡 📺 🏠 📶 🖭 ⚓

Sunnyside Guest House, *13 Pilrig Street, Edinburgh, EH6 5AN.*
Beautiful Georgian family-run guest house. An easy atmosphere and ample breakfast. **Open:** All Year (not Xmas)
Grades: STB 2 Star
0131 553 2084 Mr Wheelaghan
sunnyside.guesthouse@talk21.com
D: £17.00–£30.00 **S:** £17.00–£30.00
Beds: 2F 4D 2T 1S **Baths:** 4 En 1 Pr 1 Sh
🛇 🅿 🗡 📺 📶 🖭 ⚓

Glenburn Guest House, *22 Pilrig Street, Edinburgh, EH6 5AJ.*
Clean, welcoming, budget accommodation. 15 minutes from the city centre. **Open:** All Year (not Xmas)
0131 554 9818 (also fax) Mrs McVeigh
glenburn@lineone.net
D: £19.00–£26.00 **S:** £20.00–£36.00
Beds: 3F 3D 4T 3S **Baths:** 1 En 6 Sh
📺 📶 ⚓

Balmoral Guest House, *32 Pilrig Street, Edinburgh, EH6 5AL.*
Excellent location for city centre, Leith Port and Royal Yacht 'Britannia'.
Open: All Year (not Xmas)
0131 554 1857 Fax: 0131 553 5712
mpimbert@aol.com
D: £17.00–£30.00 **S:** £25.00
Beds: 1F 2D 2T **Baths:** 1 En 2 Sh
🛇 🅿 🗡 📺 📶 ⚓

NT3074 🍺 *Peacock Inn*

Hopebank, *33 Hope Lane North, Portobello, Edinburgh, EH15 2PZ.*
Open: Easter to Oct
0131 657 1149 Ms Williamson
D: fr £20.00 **S:** fr £20.00
Beds: 2D 1T **Baths:** 3 Pr 1 Sh
🛇 🅿 🗡 📺 📶 🖭 ⚓
Victorian terraced Villa, Two minutes Sea - Beautiful Promenade, 20 minutes city centre, good break. Scottish Hospitality inexpensive Bus service to centre. Non smoking, showers ensuite, Tv in all rooms. Many golf courses Nearby, Good touring centre.

Cruachan, *6 Pittville Street, Edinburgh, EH15 2BY.*
Elegant Georgian villa adjacent to beach, promenade, city centre 2.5 miles. Good parking.
Open: Easter to Oct
Grades: STB 2 Star B&B
0131 669 2195 Mrs Thom
D: £20.00–£22.00 **S:** £19.00–£21.00
Beds: 2D 1T 1S **Baths:** 2 Sh
🛇 (12) 🅿 (3) 🗡 📺 🏠 🖭 ⚓

NT2771 🍺 *Golf Tavern, Bennets Bar, Tapas Ole, Minto Hotel, Navaar Hotel, Allison Hotel, Grannies Attic, Seahaven Hotel, Hotel Ceilidhonia*

Airdenair, *29 Kilmaurs Road, Edinburgh, EH16 5DB.*
Fabulous views of Edinburgh. Recently refurbished, family run. Quiet location
Open: All Year
Grades: STB 3 Star
0131 668 2336 Mrs Mclennan
airdenair@tinyonline.co.uk
D: £22.00–£30.00 **S:** £30.00–£40.00
Beds: 2T 2D 2S **Baths:** 5 En
🅿 🗡 📺 📶 🖭 ⚓ cc

Cameron Toll Guest House, *299 Dalkeith Road, Edinburgh, EH16 5JX.*
Eco-friendly family guest house on A7, 10 minutes from city centre.
Open: All Year
Grades: STB 4 Star
0131 667 2950 M Deans
Fax: 0131 662 1987
stil@edinburghguesthouse.co.uk
D: £20.00–£35.00 **S:** £25.00–£37.00
Beds: 3F 2T 3D 3S **Baths:** 10 En 1 Pr
🛇 🅿 (4) 🗡 📺 ✕ 📶 🖭 ⚓ ♿ cc

NT2271 🍺 *Dell Inn, Tickled Trout*

13 Moat Street, *Edinburgh, EH14 1PE.*
Comfortable accommodation, colour TV, each room.
Open: Easter to Mar
Grades: STB 2 Star
0131 443 8266 Mrs Hume
D: £15.00–£20.00 **S:** £18.00–£20.00
Beds: 1D 1T
🛇 🅿 📺 📶 🖭 ⚓

Doocote House, *15 Moat Street, Edinburgh, EH14 1PE.*
Victorian terraced house 2 miles from city centre unrestricted parking.
Open: All Year
Grades: STB 2 Star
0131 443 5455 Mr Manson
D: £18.00–£20.00 **S:** £20.00–£30.00
Beds: 1F 1D 1T **Baths:** 2 Sh
🛇 🅿 📺 🏠 📶 ⚓

NT2476 🍺 *Peacock Inn*

Falcon Crest, *70 South Trinity Road, Edinburgh, EH5 3NX.*
Victorian family home, 2 miles north of Edinburgh Castle.
Open: All Year (not Xmas)
Grades: STB 1 Star
0131 552 5294 Mrs Clark
D: £15.00–£26.00 **S:** £16.00–£26.00
Beds: 1F 2D 2T 1S **Baths:** 3 En 2 Sh
🛇 🅿 (2) 🗡 📺 🏠 ✕ 📶 🖭 ⚓ cc

B&B owners may vary rates - be sure to check when booking

Fala

NT4361   ⬧ *Juniper Lea Hotel*

Fala Hall Farm, *Fala, Pathhead, Midlothian, EH37 5SZ.*
Secluded C16th farmhouse on working farm, 15 miles from Edinburgh.
Open: All Year (not Xmas)
01875 833249 (also fax)
Mrs Lothian
H.Lothian@farming.co.uk
D: £16.00–£20.00 **S:** £20.00–£24.00
Beds: 1F 1D **Baths:** 1 Sh
⌂ 🅟 (3) 📺 🍴 🛏 📶 Ⓥ ⚗

Falkirk

NS8680   ⬧ *Copper Top*

Denecroft, *8 Lochgreen Road, Falkirk, FK1 5NJ.*
1.5 miles from town centre, near railway station and hospital.
Open: All Year
01324 629258 (also fax)
Mrs Stewart
D: £22.00–£26.00 **S:** £25.00–£30.00
Beds: 2T 1D 1S **Baths:** 3 En 1 Sh
🅟 (6) ⌿ 📺 📶 ⚗ cc

Gorebridge

NT3460   ⬧ *Coronation Inn*

Ivory House, *14 Vogrie Road, Gorebridge, EH23 4HH.*
Secluded Victorian house, 10 miles Edinburgh. Ideal base Borders/Coast.
Open: All Year
Grades: STB 4 Star
01875 820755 Mrs Maton
ivory.house@talk21.com
D: £25.00–£35.00 **S:** £27.50–£40.00
Beds: 1F 1D 1T **Baths:** 3 En
⌂ 🅟 (6) ⌿ 📺 📶 Ⓥ ⚗ & cc

Haddington

NT5173   ⬧ *George Hotel, Waterside Hotel, Plough Inn, Goblin Ha', Tweedale Arms*

28 Market Street, *Haddington, E Lothian, EH41 3JE.*
Open: All Year
Grades: STB 3 Star
01620 822465 Mrs Hamilton
Fax: 01620 825613
D: £20.00–£26.00 **S:** £18.00–£22.00
Beds: 1F 1D 2T 1S **Baths:** 2 En 1 Pr 2 Sh
⌂ ⌿ 📺 📶 Ⓥ ⚗
Victorian building in centre of picturesque Haddington on Edinburgh (17 miles) bus route. Ideal base for golf. Walkers and cyclists welcome. Meals available within walking distance.

Eaglescairnie Mains, *Haddington, E Lothian, EH41 4HN.*
Superb farmhouse with wonderful views over conservation award-winning farm.
Open: All Year (not Xmas)
Grades: STB 4 Star
01620 810491 (also fax)
Mrs Williams
williams.eagles@btinternet.com
D: £20.00–£27.00 **S:** £25.00–£35.00
Beds: 1D 1T 2S **Baths:** 2 En 1 Sh
⌂ 🅟 (6) ⌿ 📺 🍴 🛏 📶 ⚗ cc

The Farmhouse, *Upper Bolton, Haddington, EH41 4HW.*
A warm welcome awaits you at our traditional farm house.
Open: All Year (not Xmas)
Grades: STB 3 Star
01620 810476 Mrs Clark
boltontoad@yahoo.co.uk
D: £17.00–£20.00 **S:** fr £18.00
Beds: 1D 1T **Baths:** 1 Sh
⌂ 🅟 (4) 🛏 📶 ⚗

Inveresk

NT3572   ⬧ *Dolphin*

Delta House, *16 Carberry Road, Inveresk, Musselburgh, E Lothian, EH21 7TN.*
A beautiful Victorian house 7 miles east of central Edinburgh overlooking fields.
Open: All Year (not Xmas)
Grades: STB 3 Star
0131 665 2107 (also fax)
D: £20.00–£27.50 **S:** £30.00–£50.00
Beds: 1F 3D **Baths:** 2 En 1 Pr
⌂ (5) 🅟 (3) ⌿ 📺 📶 Ⓥ ⚗

Lasswade

NT3266   ⬧ *Countryside Inn*

Gorton House, *Lasswade, Midlothian, EH18 1EH.*
Converted stables, beautiful rural location, Edinburgh centre 9 miles.
Open: All Year (not Xmas)
0131 440 4332 Mr & Mrs Young
Fax: 0131 440 1779
D: £23.00–£27.00 **S:** £20.00
Beds: 1F 1T **Baths:** 1 Sh
⌂ 🅟 (2) 📺 🍴 📶 ⚗

Laurieston

NS9079   ⬧ *Lawries, Beancross Restaurant*

Oaklands, *32 Polmont Road, Laurieston, Falkirk, FK2 9QT.*
Open: All Year (not Xmas)
Grades: STB 4 Star
01324 610671 (also fax) Mrs Fattori
b-and-b@oaklands.ndirect.co.uk
D: £25.00–£35.00 **S:** £35.00
Beds: 1D 2T **Baths:** 3 En
⌂ 🅟 (4) ⌿ 📺 📶 Ⓥ ⚗ cc
Edwardian house, 1.5 miles Falkirk, situated 5 mins M9 (J5), taking you to Edinburgh (east), Glasgow, Stirling (west). 20 mins by road to Edinburgh Airport. Near 2 mainline rail stations, frequent service to Edinburgh/Glasgow (approx 20 mins each way).

Linlithgow

NS9977   ⬧ *Blackness Inn, Bridge Inn, Four Marys, Torphichin Inn*

Woodcockdale Farm, *Lanark Road, Linlithgow, W Lothian, EH49 6QE.*
Look no further. Easy access to airport, Edinburgh, Stirling. Phone now.
Open: All Year
01506 842088 (also fax) Mrs Erskine
arn-guest-house@euphony.net
D: £18.00–£20.00
Beds: 3F 2D 1T 1S **Baths:** 4 En 1 Pr 2 Sh
⌂ 🅟 ⌿ 📺 🛏 📶 Ⓥ ⚗ &

Wester William Craigs, *Linlithgow, W Lothian, EH49 6QF.*
Modern country house, quiet location, 2 miles from historic Linlithgow.
Open: All Year (not Xmas/New Year)
01506 845470 Mrs Millar
Fax: 01506 876166
info@craiglodges.freeserve.co.uk
D: £20.00–£22.50 **S:** £20.00–£25.00
Beds: 1D 1T **Baths:** 1 En 1 Pr
🅟 ⌿ 📺 📶 Ⓥ ⚗

Loanhead

NT2765   ⬧ *Countryside Inn*

Aaron Glen, *7 Nivensknowe Road, Loanhead, Edinburgh, EH20 9AU.*
Hotel quality accommodation at B&B prices.
Open: All Year
Grades: STB 3 Star, AA 3 Star
0131 440 1293 Mrs Davidson
Fax: 0131 440 2155
aaronglen1@aol.com
D: £20.00–£30.00 **S:** £25.00–£60.00
Beds: 1F 3D 1T **Baths:** 5 En
⌂ 🅟 (8) ⌿ 📺 🍴 🛏 📶 Ⓥ ⚗ & 3 cc

Inveravon House Hotel, *9 Inveravon Road, Loanhead, Midlothian, EH20 9EF.*
Large Victorian house.
Open: All Year
0131 440 0124 Mr Potter
D: £20.00–£25.00 **S:** £25.00
Beds: 5F 5D 1T 3S **Baths:** 13 En
⌂ 🅟 (20) 📺 🍴 ✕ 📶 Ⓥ ✲ ⚗ & cc

Longniddry

NT4476   ⬧ *Longniddry Inn*

13 Glassel Park Road, *Longniddry, EH32 0NY.*
20 minutes by train to Edinburgh. Easy access to golf courses.
Open: Easter to Sep
Grades: STB 3 Star
01875 852333 Mrs Morrison
D: £18.00–£20.00 **S:** £25.00
Beds: 1D 1T **Baths:** 2 Pr
⌂ (8) 🅟 (2) ⌿ 📺 📶 ⚗

The Spinney, *Old School Lane, Longniddry, E Lothian, EH32 0NQ.*
Bungalow, secluded position, near shops, bus and train to Edinburgh.
Open: Feb to Nov
Grades: STB 2 Star
01875 853325 Mr & Mrs Playfair
D: £18.00–£20.00 **S:** £20.00–£22.00
Beds: 2D 1T **Baths:** 1 En 1 Sh
⌂ 🅟 (3) ⌿ 📺 📶 Ⓥ ⚗

Musselburgh

NT3573   ⬧ *Musselburgh, Volunteer Arms, Woodside Hotel, Foreman's, Ravelston House Hotel, The Burgh*

18 Woodside Gardens, *Musselburgh, Midlothian, EH21 7LJ.*
Quiet bungalow, easy access Edinburgh, seaside, countryside and golf parking.
Open: All Year
Grades: STB 2 Star
0131 665 3170 Mrs Aitken
D: £17.00–£19.00 **S:** £17.00–£19.00
Beds: 1F 1D 1T **Baths:** 2 Sh
⌂ 🅟 (4) 📺 🍴 📶 Ⓥ ⚗ &

Craigesk, *10 Albert Terrace,*
Musselburgh, Midlothian, EH21 7LR.
Terraced villa overlooking golf and
racecourse. Bus/railway close by.
Open: All Year
Grades: STB 2 Star
0131 665 3344 (also fax)
Miss Mitchell
D: fr £17.00 **S:** fr £18.00
Beds: 2F 1D 1T 1S **Baths:** 2 Sh
🛏 🄿 (4) 📺 🛏 📖 Ⅴ 🎄

Eildon B&B, *109 Newbigging Road,*
Musselburgh, EH21 7AS.
Georgian townhouse. Frequent buses to
city centre(20 minutes). Parking.
Open: All Year
Grades: STB 3 Star
0131 665 3981 Mrs Roache
eve@stayinscotland.net
D: £16.00–£25.00 **S:** £25.00–£35.00
Beds: 1F 1D 1T **Baths:** 1 En 1 Sh
🎄 📺 📖 🎄 cc

Arden House, *26 Linkfield Road,*
Musselburgh, Midlothian, EH21 7LL.
A warm and friendly welcome awaits you
at Arden House. **Open:** All Year
Grades: STB 4 Star, AA 4 Diamond
0131 665 0663 (also fax)
Mr Pringle
ardenhouse@talk21.com
D: £18.00–£27.00 **S:** £25.00–£35.00
Beds: 2F 3T 2D **Baths:** 4 En 2 Sh
🛏 🎄 📺 🛏 📖 Ⅴ ❋ 🎄 cc

Inveresk House, *3 Inveresk Village,*
Musselburgh, Midlothian, EH21 7UA.
Historic mansion house in idyllic
conservation village. 7 miles Edinburgh.
Open: All Year
0131 665 5855 Mrs Chute
Fax: 0131 665 0578
chute.inveresk@btinternet.com
D: £30.00–£40.00 **S:** £35.00–£40.00
Beds: 1F 1D 1T **Baths:** 2 En 1 Pr
🛏 🄿 (10) 🎄 📺 🛏 📖 Ⅴ 🎄 cc

5 Craighall Terrace, *Musselburgh,*
Midlothian, EH21 7PL.
Detached bungalow near A199. Good bus
service, railway station nearby.
Open: Easter to Oct
0131 665 4294 Mrs Dixon
D: £12.00–£18.00 **S:** £20.00
Beds: 1D **Baths:** 1 Sh
🛏 (4) 🄿 (2) 🎄 🎄

17 Windsor Park, *Musselburgh,*
Midlothian, EH21 7QL.
Personally run B&B, quiet location twenty
mins from city centre.
Open: All Year
0131 665 2194 (also fax) Mr Wilson
mary@windsorpark.demon.co.uk
D: £25.00 **S:** £20.00–£30.00
Beds: 3D 1S **Baths:** 1 En 2 Sh
🛏 🄿 (2) 📺 🛏 📖 Ⅴ 🎄

23 Linkfield Road, *Musselburgh,*
Midlothian, EH21 7LQ.
Comfortable family house, overlooking
golf and racecourse. 20 mins bus service
to Edinburgh. **Open:** All Year
0131 665 7436 Mrs McGowan
D: £18.00–£20.00 **S:** £20.00–£25.00
Beds: 1F 1D **Baths:** 1 Sh
🎄 🎄 📺 📖 Ⅴ 🎄

North Berwick

NT5585 🛏 *Blenheim House Hotel, Castle Inn,*
Dalrymple Hotel,Nether Abbey Hotel, Pointgarry
Hotel, Tantallon Inn

Troon, *Dirleton Road, North Berwick, E*
Lothian, EH39 5DF.
Comfortable pleasant bungalow, large
garden. Outskirts of town, coastal view.
Open: Apr to Oct
Grades: STB 3 Star
01620 893555 Mrs Dixon
D: £16.00–£25.00
Beds: 1D **Baths:** 1 En
🄿 (1) 🎄 📺 📖 Ⅴ 🎄

The Belhaven Hotel, *28 Westgate,*
North Berwick, E Lothian, EH39 4AH.
Overlooking golf course and sea;
convenient for town centre and railway
station.
Open: Dec to Oct
Grades: STB 2 Star Hotel
01620 893009 M Free
D: £19.00–£26.00 **S:** £20.00–£35.00
Beds: 2F 5T 2S **Baths:** 5 En 4 Sh
🛏 (9) 📺 ✕ 📖 Ⅴ 🎄

Golf Hotel, *34 Dirleton Avenue, North*
Berwick, E Lothian, EH39 4BH.
Family run hotel in seaside town close to
golf courses.
Open: All Year
Grades: STB 1 Star
01620 892202 Mr Searle
Fax: 01620 892290
D: £26.00–£65.00 **S:** £26.00–£50.00
Beds: 5F 1D 3T 2S **Baths:** 10 Pr 1 Sh
🛏 🄿 (20) 🎄 📺 ✕ 📖 Ⅴ 🎄 ♿

Beehive Cottage, *12 Kingston, North*
Berwick, EH39 5JE.
Country cottage, own entrance, lovely
garden, views, homemade honey/jams.
Open: Apr to Oct
Grades: STB 3 Star
01620 894785 Mrs Fife
D: £20.00–£24.00 **S:** £25.00–£27.00
Beds: 1D **Baths:** 1 En
🛏 🄿 (1) 🎄 📺 🛏 📖 Ⅴ 🎄

The Studio, *Grange Road, North*
Berwick, E Lothian, EH39 4QT.
Converted Artists studio within pretty
walled garden. Quiet peaceful location.
Open: All Year
01620 895150 Mrs Ramsay
Fax: 01620 895120
johnvramsay@compuserve.com
D: £25.00–£30.00 **S:** £30.00–£37.50
Beds: 2D 1T **Baths:** 2 En 1 Pr
🄿 (2) 🎄 📺 📖 Ⅴ 🎄 ♿

Pathhead

NT3964 🛏 *Forresters*

The Old Farm House, *47 Main Street,*
Pathhead, Midlothian, EH37 5PZ.
Comfortable, C Listed B&B. 12 miles
south of Edinburgh on the A68.
Open: All Year
01875 320100 Mr Reid
Fax: 01875 320501
oldfarmhouse@tinyworld.co.uk
D: £16.00–£18.00 **S:** £20.00–£25.00
Beds: 1F 1T 1D **Baths:** 2 En 1 Pr
🛏 🄿 (3) 📺 🛏 📖 🎄 cc

Penicuik

NT2360 🛏 *Howgate*

Loanstone House, *Loanstone,*
Penicuik, EH26 8PH.
Open: Easter to Oct
Grades: STB 3 Star
01968 672449 Mrs Patch
the.patches@btinternet.com
D: £17.50 **S:** £20.00
Beds: 1D **Baths:** 1 Sh
🛏 🄿 (2) 🎄 📺 📖 🎄
A Victorian family house in peaceful
country surroundings.

South Queensferry

NT1277

Priory Lodge, *8 The Loan, South*
Queensferry, EH30 9NS.
Beautiful guest house in a tranquil
village, twenty minutes from Edinburgh.
Open: All Year (not Xmas)
Grades: STB 4 Star, AA 4 Diamond
0131 331 4345 (also fax)
C C Lamb
calmyn@aol.com
D: £25.00–£30.00 **S:** £35.00–£50.00
Beds: 3F 1D 1T **Baths:** 5 En
🛏 🄿 🎄 📺 📖 Ⅴ 🎄 cc

Stoneyburn

NS9762 🛏 *Croftmalloch Inn*

Eisenach, *1 Cannop Crescent,*
Stoneyburn, Bathgate, W Lothian, EH47 8EF.
Large detached countryside villa.
Open: All Year
01501 762659 Mrs Gray
cagray@eisenach.demon.co.uk
D: fr £15.00 **S:** fr £20.00
Beds: 1F 1D 1T 1S **Baths:** 1 Pr
🛏 🄿 (3) 🎄 📺 ✕ 📖 Ⅴ

Uphall

NT0572 🛏 *Beefeater*

20 Houston Mains Holdings,
Uphall, Broxburn, EH52 6PA.
Charming guest house eleven miles from
Edinburgh. Railway link nearby.
Open: All Year
Grades: ETC 3 Star
01506 854044 Mr Fisher
Fax: 01506 855118
michaelfisher@cmgh.freeserve.co.uk
D: £23–£25 **S:** £35–£37
Beds: 1F 1T 4D **Baths:** 6 En
🛏 🄿 🎄 📺 📖 🎄 ♿ cc

Winchburgh

NT0875

Turnlea, *123 Main Street, Winchburgh,*
Broxburn, EH52 6QP.
All bedrooms refurbished 1999.
Edinburgh 12 miles, airport 6 miles and
Linlithgow 6 miles.
Open: All Year (not Xmas)
Grades: STB 3 Star B&B
01506 890124 R W Redwood
royturnlea@hotmail.com
D: £22.00–£25.00 **S:** £25.00–£30.00
Beds: 1D 2T **Baths:** 3 En
🛏 🄿 (3) 🎄 📺 📖 🎄 cc

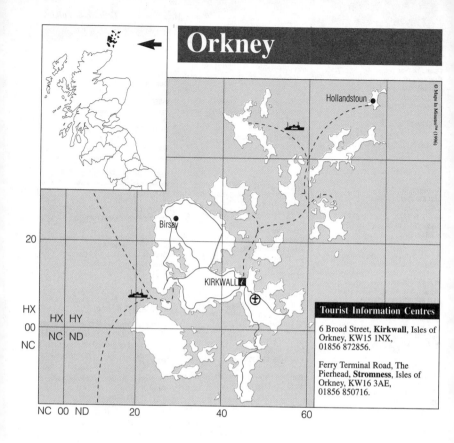

Hollandstoun

Birsay

KIRKWALL

20

HX
00
NC

HX HY

NC ND

NC 00 ND   20   40   60

Tourist Information Centres

6 Broad Street, **Kirkwall**, Isles of Orkney, KW15 1NX, 01856 872856.

Ferry Terminal Road, The Pierhead, **Stromness**, Isles of Orkney, KW16 3AE, 01856 850716.

MAINLAND   Birsay

HY2527 ⚓ *Barony Hotel, Smithfield Hotel, Merkister Hotel*

Heatherlea, *Birsay, Orkney, KW17 2LR.*
Modern bungalow overlooking trout-fishing loch, wild birds, numerous archaeological sites.
Open: Easter to Oct
Grades: STB 1 Star
01856 721382 (also fax)
Mrs Balderstone
D: £17.00 **S:** fr £17.00
Beds: 1D 1T **Baths:** 1 Sh
🛏 (6) 🅿 (2) ⚲ 📺 🛋.

Primrose Cottage, *Birsay, Orkney, KW17 2NB.*
Quiet country cottage overlooking Marwick Bay. Close RSPB reserves, the Loons and Marwick Head.
Open: All Year (not Xmas)
01856 721384 (also fax)
Mrs Clouston
D: £14.50–£19.00 **S:** £14.50–£19.00
Beds: 1D 1T 1S **Baths:** 2 En 1 Sh
🛏 🅿 (4) ⚲ 📺 ✕ 🛋 🔲 🍷 ⚱

MAINLAND   Kirkwall

HY4510 ⚓ *Queen's Hotel, Royal Hotel, West End Hotel*

7 Matches Square, *Kirkwall, Orkney, KW15 1AU.*
Personally run neighbouring houses. Centrally situated, shops, buses, ferries nearby.
Open: All Year
Grades: STB 1 Star
01856 872440
Mrs Parkins
D: £15.00–£17.00
S: £16.00–£18.00
Beds: 2T 1D 2S **Baths:** 1 En 2 Sh
🛏 🅿 (2) 📺 🐾 🛋 🔲 ⚱

Elderwood, *4 Park Loan, Kirkwall, Orkney, KW15 1PU.*
Modern bungalow in quiet cul-de-sac.
Open: All Year
01856 872657
Mrs Omand
D: £15.00 **S:** £15.00
Beds: 1D 1T **Baths:** 2 Sh
🅿 (2) ⚲ 📺 🛋 ⚱

Polrudden Guest House, *Peerie Sea Loan, Kirkwall, Orkney, KW15 1UH.*
Peaceful location, ten minutes walk from town centre. Stunning view.
Open: All Year (not Xmas)
Grades: STB 3 Star
01856 874761
Mrs Thornton
Fax: 01856 870950
linda@scapaflow.com
D: fr £22.00 **S:** fr £30.00
Beds: 2F 5T
Baths: 7 En
🛏 🅿 (7) 📺 ✕ 🛋 🔲 ⚱ cc

Lav'rockha Guest House, *Inganess Road, Kirkwall, Orkney, KW15 1SP.*
Superior accommodation at an affordable price, Finalist - 1999 Orkney Food awards.
Open: All Year
Grades: STB 4 Star
01856 876103 (also fax)
J Webster
lavrockha@orkney.com
D: £20.00–£24.00 **S:** £24.00–£30.00
Beds: 1F 2T 2D
Baths: 5 En
🛏 🅿 ⚲ 📺 🐾 ✕ 🛋 🔲 ✳ ⚱ ♿ cc

Shearwood, *Muddiesdale Road off Pickaquoy Road, Kirkwall, Orkney, KW15 1RR.*
Quiet country location, 10 mins walk town centre. Wonderful archaeology nearby.
Open: All Year
Grades: STB 2 Star
01856 873494 Mrs Braun
D: £15.00–£17.00 **S:** £17.00
Beds: 2T 1D **Baths:** 2 Sh
⛅ (12) 🅿 ⅃ 📺 🛏 ▥ Ⅴ ≜ ♿

Leikanger, *Old Scapa Road, Kirkwall, Orkney, KW15 1BB.*
15 minutes walk from centre of Kirkwall house on outskirts of town.
Open: All Year (not Xmas/New Year)
Grades: STB Listed, Comm
01856 872006 Mr & Mrs Linklater
D: £15.00–£16.00 **S:** £16.00–£17.00
Beds: 1D 1T 1S **Baths:** 2 Sh
⛅ 🅿 (2) 📺 🛏 ▥ Ⅴ ≜

MAINLAND   Sandwick

HY2519 ⚭ *Smithfield Hotel*

Netherstove, *Sandwick, Stromness, Orkney, KW16 3LS.*
Farmhouse B&B, overlooking the Bay of Skaill. Near Skara - Bare.
Open: Easter to Nov
Grades: STB 3 Star
01856 841625 (also fax)
Mrs Poke
ann.poke@virgin.net
D: £16.00–£18.50 **S:** £16.00–£18.50
Beds: 1D 1T **Baths:** 2 Sh
⛅ 🅿 ⅃ 📺 ✕ ▥ Ⅴ ≜

MAINLAND   Stromness

HY2509 ⚭ *Ferry Inn*

Lindisfarne, *Stromness, Orkney, KW16 3LL.*
Open: Jan to Dec
Grades: STB 3 Star
01856 850828 Mrs Worthington
Fax: 01856 850805
eprworthington@hotmail.com
D: £20.00–£22.00
Beds: 1F 4T **Baths:** 5 En
🅿 📺 ▥ Ⅴ ≜
Modern detached house, set in a elevated rural location, overlooking the town of Stromness views of Scapa Flow, the island of Gramsay, Hoy Hills and the island of Hoy also Stromness harbour.

Miller's House and Harbourside Guest House, *John Street, Stromness, Orkney, KW16 3AD.*
Breakfast in the oldest house in Stromness (1716). Centrally situated.
Open: Easter to Nov
Grades: STB 3 Star
01856 851969 Mrs Dennison
Fax: 01856 851967
millershouse@orkney.com
D: £20.00 **S:** £25.00
Beds: 4F 2D 2T **Baths:** 13 Pr 1 Sh
⛅ 🅿 ⅃ 📺 🛏 ✕ ▥ Ⅴ ≜

Planning a longer stay? Always ask for any special rates

BATHROOMS
Pr - Private
Sh - Shared
En - Ensuite

Oakleigh Hotel, *76 Victoria Street, Stromness, Orkney, KW16 3BS.*
Small family-run guest house.
Open: All Year (not Xmas)
Grades: STB 2 Star
01856 850447 Ms Woodford
D: £20.00–£25.00 **S:** £20.00–£25.00
Beds: 2D 4T **Baths:** 6 En
⛅ 🅿 (1) 📺 🛏 ✕ ▥ Ⅴ ≜

NORTH RONALDSAY
Hollandstoun

HY7553

North Ronaldsay Bird Observatory, *North Ronaldsay, Orkney, KW17 2BE.*
Comfortable island guest accommodation. Solar and wind powered.
Open: All Year (not Xmas/New Year)
Grades: STB 2 Star
01857 633200 A E Duncan
Fax: 01857 633207
alison@nrbo.prestel.co.uk
D: fr £18.00 **S:** fr £23.00
Beds: 2D 2T **Baths:** 4 En
⛅ 🅿 ⅃ 📺 ✕ ▥ Ⅴ ≜ ♿ 2 cc

Perthshire & Kinross

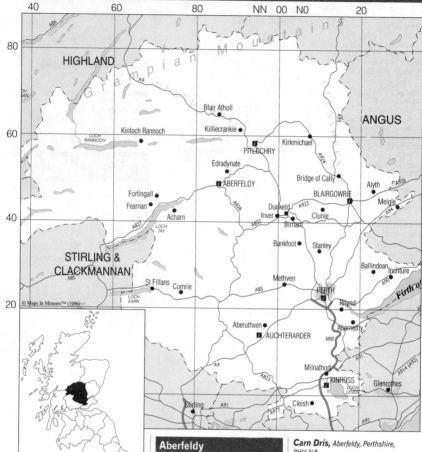

Tourist Information Centres

The Square, **Aberfeldy**, Perthshire, PH15 2DD, 01887 820276.

90 High Street, **Auchterarder**, Perthshire, PH3 1BJ, 01764 663450.

26 Wellmeadow, **Blairgowrie**, Perthshire, PH10 6AS, 01250 872960.

Town Hall, High Street, **Crieff**, Perthshire, PH7 3HU, 01764 652578.

The Cross, **Dunkeld**, Perthshire, PH8 0AN, 01350 727688.

Caithness Glass Car Park, A9 Western City By-pass, **Inveralmond**, Perth, 01738 638481.

Kinross Service Area, Junction 6, M90, **Kinross**, KY13 7BE, 01577 863680.

45 High Street, **Perth**, PH1 5TJ, 01738 450600.

22 Atholl Street, **Pitlochry**, Perthshire, PH16 5BX, 01796 472215.

Aberfeldy

NN8549 ⚓ *Black Watch, Aileen Chraggan Hotel, Coshieville Hotel*

Ardtornish, *Kenmore Street, Aberfeldy, PH15 2BL.*
In beautiful friendly Highland Perthshire with walking, golf, cycling, water sports and more. **Open:** All Year (not Xmas/New Year) **Grades:** STB 3 Star
01887 820629 Mrs Ross
ardtornish@talk21.com
D: £16.00–£19.00 **S:** £16.00–£19.00
Beds: 1D 1T 1D/F **Baths:** 1 En 1 Sh
🅿 (3) ⚡ 📺 🛏 🍽 📋

Tomvale, *Tom of Cluny Farm, Aberfeldy, Perthshire, PH15 2JT.*
Modern farmhouse with outstanding views of the Upper Tay Valley.
Open: All Year (not Xmas)
01887 820171 (also fax) Mrs Kennedy
dken301762@aol.com
D: fr £17.00 **S:** fr £18.00
Beds: 1F 1D **Baths:** 1 Sh
🐕 🅿 📺 🛏 ✕ 🍽 📋 🔥

Carn Dris, *Aberfeldy, Perthshire, PH15 2LB.*
Large Edwardian private house, ex manse, overlooking Aberfeldy golf course. **Open:** Easter to Oct
01887 820250 Mrs Bell Campbell
D: £20.00–£25.00 **S:** £20.00–£25.00
Beds: 2D 1T **Baths:** 1 En 1 Sh
🐕 (10) 🅿 (4) 📺 🛏 🍽

Novar, *2 Home Street, Aberfeldy, Perthshire, PH15 2AJ.*
Novar is a comfortable stone house near golf course; good walks.
Open: All Year (not Xmas)
01887 820779 Mrs Malcolm
D: £17.00–£19.00 **S:** £25.00
Beds: 1F 1D 1T **Baths:** 2 En 5 Pr 1 Sh
🐕 🅿 (3) ⚡ 📺 🛏 🍽 📋 🔥 ♿

National Grid References are for villages, towns and cities – not for individual houses

Abernethy

NO1816

Gattaway Farm, Abernethy, Perth,
Perthshire & Kinross, PH2 9LQ.
Large Georgian/Victorian farmhouse;
excellent views, excellent food.
Recommended.
Open: All Year
Grades: STB 3 Star
01738 850746 Mrs Dawson
Fax: 01738 850925
tarduff@aol.com
D: £19.00–£20.00 **S:** £20.00–£25.00
Beds: 2D 1T **Baths:** 3 En
🛇 🅿 (4) ⅍ 🎇 🏧 🗙 🎞 Ⅶ ♿ 🔥 1

Aberuthven

NN9815 ◫ Kirkstyle Inn

Craiginver, Aberuthven, Auchterarder,
PH3 1HE.
Open: April to Oct
Grades: STB 3 Star
01764 662411 J M Smith
jms@craiginver.freeserve.co.uk
D: £18.50–£19.50 **S:** £19.50–£20.50
Beds: 2T **Baths:** 1 En 1 Pr
🅿 (8) ⅍ 🎇 🏧 Ⅶ 🔥
Grade C Listed Victorian former manse
(rectory) set in large garden with views
over the earn valley towards the Ochils.
Ample private off-street parking.
comfortable beds and good Scottish
breakfasts. Easy access to the main cities
of Scotland.

Acharn

NN7543 ◫ Croft-na-caber Hotel

12 Ballinlaggan, Acharn, Aberfeldy,
Perthshire, PH15 2HT.
Warm welcome awaits in quiet lochside
village of Acharn, surrounded by beautiful
scenery.
Open: All Year
01887 830409 Mrs Spiers
BandB.acharn@virgin.net
D: £16.00 **S:** £16.00
Beds: 1T 1S **Baths:** 1 Sh
🛇 🅿 (2) ⅍ 🎇 🗙 🎞 Ⅶ ✿ 🔥

Alyth

NO2448 ◫ Lands of Loyal Hotel, Drummacree
Oven Bistro

Mona Gowan , 3 Strathmore Terrace,
Alyth, Blairgowrie, Perthshire, PH11 8DP.
Open: All Year (not Xmas/New Year)
Grades: STB 4 Star
01828 632489 (also fax)
lynne@monagowan.freeserve.co.uk
D: £20.00–£22.50 **S:** £20.00–£22.50
Beds: 1T 1D 1F **Baths:** 3 En
🛇 🅿 (3) ⅍ 🎇 🏧 Ⅶ 🔥
Fine detached Victorian Villa with
traditional coach house. Quietly situated
at the foot of Glen Isla and North of
historical Alyth. All bedrooms and sun
lounge are south facing with superb
uninterrupted views over large tiered
gardens, the Vale of Strathmore and the
Sidlaw Hills.

Auchterarder

NN9412 ◫ Golf Inn, Collearn Hotel, Cairn
Lodge, Cafe Cento

Nether Coul, Auchterarder, Perthshire,
PH3 1ET.
Substantial renovated cottage in rural
location.
Open: All Year
Grades: STB 3 Star
01764 663119 (also fax)
Mr & Mrs Robertson
nethercoul@talk21.com
D: £17.00–£19.00 **S:** £20.00–£25.00
Beds: 1F 1T **Baths:** 2 Pr
🛇 🅿 (5) ⅍ 🎇 🏧 🗙 🎞 Ⅶ 🔥

The Auld Nick, 89 The Feus,
Auchterarder, Perthshire, PH3 1DG.
Recently renovated former town police
station, located on main street.
Open: All Year (not Xmas)
Grades: STB 3 Star
01764 662916 (also fax)
auldnick.langtoon@virgin.net
D: £20.00–£25.00 **S:** £16.00–£20.00
Beds: 1F 1D 1T 1S **Baths:** 3 En 1 Sh
🛇 🅿 (4) ⅍ 🎇 🏧 🎞 Ⅶ 🔥

10 The Grove, Collearn,
Auchterarder, Perthshire, PH3 1PT.
Private house in quiet estate with off-
street parking.
Open: Jan to Dec
Grades: STB 2 Star
01764 662036 Mrs McFarlane
D: £17.50–£18.50 **S:** £18.00–£20.00
Beds: 1T **Baths:** 1 Sh
🛇 (3) 🅿 (1) ⅍ 🎇 🏧 🎞 Ⅶ 🔥 ♿

Ballindean

NO2529

The Orchard, Easter Ballindean,
Inchture, Perth, PH14 9QS.
Characterful cottage in lovely rural
setting. Magnificent views. Sunny
conservatory. **Open:** April to Oct
Grades: STB 3 Star
01828 686318 J.D Burrowes
theorchard@exl.co.uk
D: £22.00 **S:** £25.00–£27.00
Beds: 1T 2D **Baths:** 2 En 1 Pr
🛇 🅿 (4) ⅍ 🎇 🏧 🎞 Ⅶ 🔥 ♿

Balloch

NO2828 ◫ Inchture Hotel

Old School House, Main Street,
Inchture, Perth, PH14 9RN.
Listed old school house.
Open: All Year (not Xmas/New Year)
01828 686275 Mrs Howard
D: fr £17.00 **S:** fr £17.00
Beds: 2D 1T **Baths:** 1 En 1 Pr
🛇 🅿 (1) 🎇 🏧 🎞 Ⅶ 🔥

RATES

D = Price range per person
sharing in a double room

S = Price range for a
single room

Bankfoot

NO0635 ◫ Spiral Restaurant

Blair House, Main Street, Bankfoot,
Perth, PH1 4AB.
Gateway to Highlands. Ideal touring spot,
golfing, fishing, castles.
Open: All Year
Grades: STB 2 Star
01738 787338 (also fax)
Mrs McKay
D: £18.00 **S:** fr £22.50
Beds: 2D 1T **Baths:** 2 En 1 Pr
🛇 🅿 (3) Ⅶ 🎇 🎞 🔥

Birnam

NO0341 ◫ Birnam Hotel, Atholl Arms

The Waterbury Guest House,
Murthly Terrace, Birnam, Dunkeld,
Perthshire, PH8 0BG.
Listed Victorian home with modern
comforts next to Beatrix Potter garden.
Open: All Year
01350 727324 Mrs Neil
bneil@waterbury.demon.co.uk
D: £18.00–£22.00 **S:** £18.00–£22.00
Beds: 2F 3D 1T 2S **Baths:** 6 En 1 Sh
🛇 🅿 (4) Ⅶ 🎇 🗙 🎞 Ⅶ 🔥 cc

Blair Atholl

NN8764 ◫ Tilt Hotel, The Roundhouse

Dalgreine, off St Andrews Crescent,
Blair Atholl, Pitlochry, Perthshire, PH18 5SX.
Attractive comfortable guest house, set in
beautiful surroundings near Blair Castle.
Open: All Year
Grades: STB 3 Star, AA 4 Diamond
01796 481276 Mr & Mrs Pywell & Mrs F
Hardie
D: £16.00–£20.00 **S:** £17.00–£20.00
Beds: 1F 2D 2T 1S **Baths:** 2 En 1 Pr 1 Sh
🛇 🅿 (6) ⅍ 🎇 🗙 🎞 Ⅶ 🔥

Blairgowrie

NO1745 ◫ Angus Hotel Bar, Brig O'Blair,
Burrelton Park Inn, Victoria Hotel, Woodside Inn

The Laurels Guest House, Golf
Course Road, Rosemount, Blairgowrie,
Perthshire, PH10 6LH.
Open: Jan to Dec **Grades:** STB 3 Star
01250 874920 (also fax)
Mr & Mrs McPherson
D: £19.50–£20.00 **S:** £20.00–£30.00
Beds: 2D 3T 1S **Baths:** 4 En
🛇 🅿 (8) ⅍ 🎇 🗙 🎞 🔥 cc
Converted C18th farmhouse. First class
cooking, licensed. Our bedrooms are very
well-equipped with power showers in
ensuite rooms and bathroom.

Ridgeway, Wester Essendy, Blairgowrie,
Perthshire, PH10 6RA.
Bungalow overlooking loch and hills.
Friendly, comfortable accommodation,
large garden.
Open: All Year (not Xmas)
Grades: STB 3 Star
01250 884734 Mrs Mathews
Fax: 01250 884735
pam.mathews@btinternet.com
D: £22.00 **S:** £22.00
Beds: 1D 1T **Baths:** 2 En
🛇 🅿 (8) ⅍ Ⅶ 🎞 🔥

Garfield House, *Perth Road,*
Blairgowrie, Perthshire, PH10 6ED.
Attractive detached Victorian house.
Quiet and comfortable with lovely homely
atmosphere.
Open: Jan to Dec
Grades: STB 3 Star
01250 872999 Mrs Safsaf
D: £17.00–£20.00 **S:** £17.00–£20.00
Beds: 1D 1T 1S **Baths:** 2 En 1 Pr
🛏 🅿 (4) 🗠 📺 🛏 ⛬

Eildon Bank, *Perth Road, Blairgowrie,*
Perthshire, PH10 6ED.
Victorian detached house. Shops,
walking, ski-ing available in area.
Open: All Year (not Xmas)
Grades: STB 3 Star
01250 873648 (also fax)
Mrs Murray
D: £16.00–£18.00 **S:** £20.00–£22.00
Beds: 2D 1T
🛏 🅿 (4) 📺 🛏 ⛬

Bridge of Cally

NO1351 🍴 *Bridge Of Cully Hotel, The Corriefodly*

Bridge Of Cally Hotel, *Bridge of*
Cally, Blairgowrie, Perthshire, PH10 7JJ.
Small family hotel. Cooking award. Walk
over 2000 acres.
Open: All Year (not Xmas)
Grades: STB 2 Star
01250 886231 Mr McCosh
D: £20.00–£27.50 **S:** £20.00–£27.50
Beds: 1F 3D 4T 1S **Baths:** 7 En 2 Pr
🛏 🅿 📺 🛏 ✕ 🖿 📺 ⛬

Cleish

NT0998 🍴 *Tormaukin Inn, Balgeddie Toll*

Mawmill House, *Cleish, Kinross, KY13*
7LN.
Open: Easter to Oct
01577 850249 Mrs Whitehead
andrewmawmill@tinyworld.co.uk
D: fr £20.00 **S:** fr £25.00
Beds: 2D 1S **Baths:** 1 Pr
🛏 🅿 (4) 🗠 📺 🖿 📺 ⛬
Peaceful spacious C18th farmhouse in
the Cleish Valley. Convenient for
Edinburgh, Perth, St Andrews, Stirling &
routes to the Highlands. Private sitting
room. Traditional breakfast. Warmest
welcome. Perfect base for walking,
fishing, golf & sightseeing.

Clunie

NO1043

Bankhead, *Clunie, Blairgowrie,*
Perthshire, PH10 6SG.
Quiet house on small farm, golfing,
fishing, walking nearby.
Open: All Year
Grades: STB 3 Star
01250 884281 (also fax)
Mrs Wightman
ian@iwwightman.freeserve.co.uk
D: £18.00 **S:** £20.00–£21.00
Beds: 1F 1T **Baths:** 2 En
🛏 🅿 (3) 🗠 📺 🛏 ✕ 🖿 📺 ⛬

Comrie

NN7722 🍴 *Comrie Hotel, Royal Hotel, Deil's Cauldron, Achray House*

St Margarets, *Braco Road, Comrie,*
Crieff, Perthshire, PH6 2HP.
Attractive Victorian family house, good
fishing, golfing, walking, horse riding.
Open: Mar to Nov
Grades: STB 3 Star B&B
01764 670413 Mr & Mrs Paterson
D: £17.00–£20.00 **S:** £17.00–£20.00
Beds: 1D 2T **Baths:** 1 En 1 Sh
🛏 (3) 🅿 (4) 🗠 📺 🛏 📺 ⛬ ♿

Millersfield, *Dalginross, Comrie, Crieff,*
Perthshire, PH6 2HE.
Modern centrally heated bungalow.
Peaceful location, attractive garden and
warm welcome.
Open: All Year (not Xmas/New Year)
01764 670073 Mrs Rae
D: £19.00–£20.00 **S:** £19.00–£20.00
Beds: 1D 1T
🛏 (12) 🅿 (3) 🗠 📺 🖿 📺 ⛬ ♿

Crieff

NN8621 🍴 *Oakbank, Glenturret Distillery, Arouthie Hotel, Locke's Acre*

Merlindale, *Perth Road, Crieff, PH7 3EQ.*
Open: Feb to Dec **Grades:** STB 4 Star
01764 655205 (also fax)
Mr & Mrs Clifford
merlin.dale@virgin.net
D: £22.50–£27.00 **S:** £25.00–£35.00
Beds: 1F 1T **Baths:** 2 En
🛏 🅿 🗠 📺 ✕ 🖿 ⛬
Luxury Georgian house, all bedrooms
ensuite with tea/coffee making facilities.
We have a Jacuzzi bath, garden, ample
off-road parking, satellite television, and
extensive library. Cordon Bleu cooking is
our speciality. A warm welcome awaits
you in this non-smoking house.

Somerton House, *Turret Bank, Crieff,*
Perthshire, PH7 4JN.
Quietly situated in own grounds, large
detached modern private house.
Open: All Year (not Xmas)
01764 653513 Mrs Sloan
Fax: 01764 655028
katie@turretbank7.freeserve.co.uk
D: £15.00–£19.00 **S:** £19.00–£23.00
Beds: 1F 1D 1T **Baths:** 3 En
🛏 🅿 (6) 🗠 📺 🛏 🖿 📺 ⛬

5 Duchlage Terrace, *Crieff, Perthshire,*
PH7 3AS.
Peaceful and gracious rooms, superb
food, magnificent scenery, golf and
fishing. **Open:** All Year
01764 653516 (also fax)
Ms Coutts
D: £18.00–£20.00 **S:** £20.00–£25.00
Beds: 1F 1T **Baths:** 1 En 1 Pr
🛏 (2) 🅿 (2) 🗠 📺 🛏 ✕ 🖿 📺 ⛬

11 Galloway Crescent, *Crieff, PH7 4LG.*
Bungalow in quiet location close to
public parks and distillery.
Open: Easter to Oct
01764 655276 Mrs Cooper
D: £15.00–£18.00 **S:** £15.00–£18.00
Beds: 1T 1S
🅿 (2) 🗠 📺 🖿 ⛬

Dunkeld

NO0243

Taybank Hotel, *Tay Terrace, Dunkeld,*
Perthshire, PH8 0AQ.
Friendly music bar, spontaneous
sessions, beautiful location, tasteful
rooms.
Open: All Year
01350 727340 Mr Close
Fax: 01350 728606
admin@dunkeld.co.uk
D: £17.50 **S:** £17.50–£22.50
Beds: 2F 1T 1D 1S **Baths:** 2 Sh
🛏 🅿 ✕ cc

Edradynate

NN8852

Lurgan Farm, *Edradynate, Aberfeldy,*
Perthshire, PH15 2JX.
Traditional working farm, with stunning
views over the Tay Valley.
Open: All Year (not Xmas)
01887 840451 Mrs Kennedy
D: £17.00–£22.00 **S:** £17.00–£22.00
Beds: 1F **Baths:** 1 En
🛏 🅿 🗠 📺 🛏 🖿 📺 ⛬

Fearnan

NN7244

Tigh An Loan Hotel, *Fearnan,*
Aberfeldy, Perthshire, PH15 2PF.
Old inn built in C19th; beautifully situated
overlooking Loch Tay.
Open: Easter to Oct
Grades: STB 1 Star
01887 830249 Mr Kelloe
D: £29.00–£31.00 **S:** £29.00–£31.00
Beds: 1F 3S **Baths:** 3 En 2 Sh
🛏 🅿 (25) 📺 🛏 ✕ 🖿 ⛬ cc

Fortingall

NN7347 🍴 *Fortingall Hotel*

Kinnighallen Farm, *Duneaves Road,*
Fortingall, Aberfeldy, Perthshire, PH15 2LR.
Come and have a relaxing stay in this
sleepy, rural backwater where wildlife
abounds.
Open: May to Oct
Grades: STB 1 Star
01887 830619 Mrs Kininmonth
a.kininmonth@talk21.com
D: £15.00 **S:** £15.00
Beds: 1D 1T 1S **Baths:** 1 Sh
🛏 (2) 🅿 (5) 🛏 🖿 📺

Inver

NO0142 🍴 *Taybank, Macleans*

3 Knockard Road, *Pitlochry,*
Perthshire, PH16 5JE.
Birthplace of C18th Fiddler. Large
secluded garden. Open views.
Open: Easter to Oct
01796 472157 Mr & Mrs Gardiner
D: £14.00–£15.00
Beds: 1T 1D **Baths:** 1 Sh
🅿 (3) 📺 🖿 ⛬

Killiecrankie

NN9162   Killiecrankie Hotel

Tighdornie, Killiecrankie, Pitlochry,
Perthshire, PH16 5LR.
Modern house in historic Killiecrankie.
2.5 miles from Blair Castle.
Open: All Year
Grades: STB 3 Star
01796 473276 (also fax)
Mrs Sanderson
tigh-dornie@btinternet.com
D: £22.00–£24.00 **S:** £27.00
Beds: 1T 2D **Baths:** 3 En
(12) P (4) TV V

Kinloch Rannoch

NN6658

Dunalastair Hotel, Kinloch Rannoch,
Pitlochry, Perthshire, PH16 5PW.
Open: All Year
Grades: STB 3 Star, AA 2 Star
01882 632323 Paul Edwards
Fax: 01882 632371
reservations@dunalastair.co.uk
D: £27.50 **S:** £27.50
Beds: 2F 10D 10T 1S **Baths:** 25 En
P X V cc
Romantically situated in the heart of
Highland Perthshire, Dunalastair is a
C18th former shooting lodge, now a
wonderful hotel with luxurious rooms.
Cosy lounge and baronial dining areas.
Perfect base for exploring Scotland. This
is a genuine discount, come and see for
yourself.

Bunrannoch House, Kinloch
Rannoch, Pitlochry, Perthshire, PH16 5QB.
Lovely country house, beautiful views,
open fires. Warm welcome and excellent
food.
Open: All Year (not Xmas/New Year)
Grades: STB 2 Star
01882 632407 (also fax)
Mrs Skeaping
bun.house@tesco.net
D: £22.00–£24.00 **S:** £22.00–£24.00
Beds: 2F 3D 2T **Baths:** 5 Pr 2 Sh
P (10) X V cc

Kinross

NO1102   Carlin Maggies

Lochleven Inn, 6 Swansacre, Kinross,
Fife, KY13 7TE.
Local friendly inn (public bar).
Open: All Year
01577 864185 Mr McGregor
D: £18.00 **S:** £18.00
Beds: 1F 1T 1D **Baths:** 2 Pr
P (2) TV X V

The Roxburghe Guest House, 126
High Street, Kinross, Fife, KY13 8DA.
Family-run guest house. Ideal base in the
heart of Scotland, for fishing.
Open: All Year
01577 862498 Mrs Robertson
D: £16.00–£18.00 **S:** £16.00–£18.00
Beds: 2F 1D 2T **Baths:** 2 Sh
P (5) TV X V

Kirkmichael

NO0860   Strathardle Inn, Log Cabin Hotel

Curran House, Kirkmichael,
Blairgowrie, Perthshire, PH10 7NA.
Traditional Scottish house. Log fire.
Home baking on arrival.
Open: Jan to Sept
Grades: STB 4 Star
01250 881229 Mr & Mrs Van der Veldt
Fax: 01250 881448
a.m.vanderveldt@tesco.net
D: £18.00–£36.00
Beds: 2D 1T **Baths:** 1 Pr 1 Sh
P TV V

Meigle

NO2844   Belmount Arms

Loanhead House, Dundee Road,
Meigle, Blairgowrie, PH12 8SF.
Superb accommodation and food in edge
of castle estate location.
Open: All Year (not Xmas/New Year)
Grades: STB 4 Star
01828 640358 Mr Taylor
Fax: 0870 1329749
gill@loanheadhouse.co.uk
D: £20.00–£24.00 **S:** £20.00–£28.00
Beds: 1D 1T **Baths:** 1 En 1 Pr
P (4) TV V

Cardean Water Mill, Meigle,
Blairgowrie, Perthshire, PH12 8RB.
An 1840 watermill offers peace, free
fishing and beautiful gardens.
Open: All Year
01828 640633 Mr Wares
Fax: 01828 640741
D: £20.00 **S:** £20.00
Beds: 1T **Baths:** 1 Pr
P (2) TV

Methven

NO0226   Almondbank

Lismore, 1 Rorrie Terrace, Methven,
Perth, PH1 3PL.
Traditional Scottish hospitality in friendly
family home. Ideal touring base, 5 miles
from Perth.
Open: All Year
01738 840441 (also fax)
Mr Comrie
D: £14.50–£15.50 **S:** £17.50–£25.00
Beds: 1T 1D
(8) P (2) TV V cc

Milnathort

NO1204   Balgeddie Toll, Lamond Inn, Thistle
Hotel

Hattonburn Farmhouse, Milnathort,
Kinross, Fife, KY13 0SA.
Modernised C19th sandstone farmhouse,
close by M90. Edinburgh 35 mins, Perth
15 mins.
Open: All Year (not Xmas)
01577 862362 Mrs Todrick
D: £20.00–£25.00 **S:** £20.00–£25.00
Beds: 1D 1T **Baths:** 2 Pr
(8) P TV X V

Perth

NO1123   Isle Of Skye Hotel, Huntingtower
Hotel, Letham Farmhouse Hotel,Lovat Hotel,
Moncrieff Hotel, Paco's, Royal George Hotel, Silver
Broom, Wheel

Huntingtower House, Crieff Road,
Perth, PH1 3JJ.
Open: Feb to Dec
Grades: STB 3 Star
01738 624681
Mrs Lindsay
dlindsay@btinternet.com
D: £18.00–£21.00 **S:** £18.00–£21.00
Beds: 1D 2T **Baths:** 1 Pr 1 Sh
(11) P (3) TV V
Situated on the western outskirts of
Perth, this charming country house with
large, secluded garden nestles beside
historic Huntingtower Castle. There is
easy access to Perth & all main routes
throughout Scotland. A friendly welcome
& delicious breakfast are assured.

Aberdeen Guest House, Pitcullen
Crescent, Perth, PH2 7HT.
Beautiful Victorian house where comfort
and care is paramount.
Open: All Year
Grades: STB 4 Star
01738 633183 (also fax)
Mrs Buchan
buchan@aberdeenguesthouse.fsnet.co.uk
D: £18.00–£22.00 **S:** £18.00–£25.00
Beds: 2D 1T **Baths:** 1 En 2 Sh
P (4) TV V

Beeches, 2 Comely Bank, Perth, PH2
7HU.
Home from home Victorian house.
Friendly, relaxing, check web details!
Open: All Year
Grades: STB 3 Star
01738 624486 Mrs Smith
Fax: 01738 643382
enquiries@beeches-guest-house.co.uk
D: £18.00–£20.00 **S:** £18.00–£20.00
Beds: 1D 1T 2S **Baths:** 4 En
P (4) TV X cc

Dunallan Guest House, 10 Pitcullen
Crescent, Perth, PH2 7HT.
Well-appointed Victorian villa within
walking distance Perth City Centre.
Open: All Year
Grades: STB 3 Star
01738 622551 (also fax)
Mrs Brown
D: £20.00–£22.00 **S:** £21.50–£23.00
Beds: 1F 1D 2T 3S **Baths:** 7 En
P (7) TV X V cc

Arisaig Guest House, 4 Pitcullen
Crescent, Perth, Perthshire & Kinross, PH2
7HT.
Late-Victorian family run guest house
situated on the A94.
Open: All Year
Grades: STB 4 Star
01738 628240 (also fax)
Stewart & Wilma Bousie
reservations@arsaig.demon.co.uk
D: £20.00–£22.50 **S:** £25.00–£30.00
Beds: 1F 2D 1T 1S **Baths:** 5 En
P (5) TV cc

The Darroch Guest House, 9
Pitcullen Crescent, Perth, PH2 7HT.
Victorian semi, friendly relaxed
atmosphere, ideal base for touring.
Open: All Year **Grades:** STB 2 Star
01738 636893 (also fax) Mr & Mrs Hirst
D: £16.00–£21.00 **S:** £16.00–£25.00
Beds: 1F 1D 2T 2S **Baths:** 3 En 1 Sh
🛇 🅿 (8) 🔟 🟊 ✕ 🖿 🖳 ♨

Parkview Guest House, 22 Marshall
Place, Perth, PH2 8AG.
Listed Georgian town house. Very central,
overlooking park. **Open:** All Year
01738 620297 (also fax) Mr Farquharson
fiona.farquharson@btinternet.com
D: £16.00–£19.00 **S:** £18.00–£20.00
Beds: 4F 1T **Baths:** 3 En 1 Sh
🛇 🅿 (4) 🔟 🟊 🖿 🖳 ♨

Comely Bank Cottage, 19 Pitcullen
Cres, Perth, Perthshire, PH2 7HT.
Enjoy true Scottish hospitality in
comfortable family home, 10 minutes
walk city centre.
Open: All Year (not Xmas)
Grades: STB 3 Star
01738 631118 Mrs Marshall
Fax: 01738 571245
comelybankcott@hotmail.com
D: £18.00–£22.00 **S:** £22.00–£30.00
Beds: 1F 1D 1T **Baths:** 2 En 1 Pr
🛇 🅿 (3) 🔟 🟊 🖿 🖳 ♨ cc

Brae Lodge, 140 Glasgow Road, Perth,
PH2 0LX.
Small and friendly with lots of advice on
locality/ tours.
Open: All Year (not Xmas/New Year)
01738 624915 Mr Muir
D: £16.00–£18.00 **S:** £20.00–£25.00
Beds: 2F 1D **Baths:** 2 Sh
🛇 🅿 (2) ✌ 🔟 🟊 🖿 ♨

Heidl Guest House, 43 York Place,
Perth, Perthshire & Kinross, PH2 8EH.
Family run, central location, close to bus
and railway stations.
Open: All Year (not Xmas/New Year)
Grades: STB 2 Star
01738 635031 Mr & Mrs McMahon
Fax: 01738 643710
B&B@heidl.co.uk
D: £15.00–£22.00 **S:** £18.00–£26.00
Beds: 1F 2D 3T 2S **Baths:** 1 Pr 2 Sh
🛇 🅿 (3) 🔟 🟊 🖿 ♨

Creswick Guest House, 86 Dundee
Road, Perth, PH2 7BA.
Enjoy a 10 minute walk by beautiful
riverside to city centre.
Open: All Year (not Xmas)
01738 625896 Mrs Wilson
D: £17.00–£22.00 **S:** £25.00–£30.00
Beds: 2D 1T **Baths:** 2 En 1 Pr
🅿 (4) ✌ 🔟 🟊 ✕ 🖿 🖳 ♨

The Gables Guest House, 24
Dunkeld Road, Perth, PH1 5RW.
Ideal touring base. Traditionally home-
cooked meals by arrangement.
Open: All Year
01738 624717 (also fax) Mrs Tucker
gablesgh@aol.com
D: £20.00–£25.00 **S:** £21.00–£26.00
Beds: 2F 1D 1T 4S **Baths:** 4 En 1 Sh
🛇 🅿 (7) 🔟 🟊 ✕ 🖿 🖳 ♨

Abercrombie, 85 Glasglow Road, Perth,
PH2 0PQ.
Beautiful Victorian town house near rail
and bus station.
Open: All Year (not Xmas)
01738 444728 Mrs Dewar
D: £22.00–£27.00 **S:** £22.00–£27.00
Beds: 1D 1T 2S **Baths:** 3 En 1 Pr
🛇 (2) 🅿 (4) ✌ 🔟 🖿 🖳 ♨ ♨ ♿

Fern Villa, 41 Glasgow Road, Perth, PH2
0PE.
Friendly welcome, close to swimming, ice
rink, bus and train.
Open: All Year (not Xmas)
01738 637650 Mr & Mrs Kelly
D: £18.00–£20.00 **S:** £19.00–£21.00
Beds: 1F 1D 1S **Baths:** 3 En
🛇 🅿 (6) ✌ 🔟 🖿 🖳 ♨

Pitlochry

NN9458 🍴 *Acarsaid Hotel, Pine Trees Hotel,
Atholl Arms Hotel, Old Smithy, Old Armoury, Port-
na-Craig Inn, Moulin Hotel, Westlands, Mill,
McKay's, Ballinling Inn*

Auchlatt Steading, Kinnaird, Pitlochry,
Perthshire, PH16 5JL.
Open: Easter to Nov
01796 472661
Miss Elkins
Fax: 01796 472661
D: £17.00 **S:** £17.00
Beds: 1T 1D **Baths:** All En
🅿 (2) ✌ 🔟 🟊 🖿
Newly converted Scottish barn
comfortable beds and a good honest
breakfast overlooking Pitlochry and
surrounding beautiful countryside close
Edradour and Scotland smallest distillery
good hill walking and fishing, also the
theatre and much historic interest.

Atholl Villa, 29 Atholl Road, Pitlochry,
Perthshire, PH16 5BX.
Open: All Year
Grades: STB 3 Star
01796 473820
Mrs Bruce
atholluilla@aol.com
D: £17.50–£25.00 **S:** £17.50–£25.00
Beds: 3F 2T 2D **Baths:** 7 En
🛇 🅿 (10) ✌ 🔟 🟊 ✕ 🖿 🖳 ♨ ♨ ♿ cc
This 10 bedroom Victorian detached
stone house of typical highland
construction, built 150 years ago is
situated right at the edge of town, close
to rail and bus stations, an abundance of
restaurants, shops and the most famous
Festival Theatre

Wellwood House, West Moulin Road,
Pitlochry, Perthshire, PH16 5EA.
Open: March to Nov
Grades: STB 2 Star, AA 3 Diamond
01796 474288 Ms Herd
Fax: 01796 474299
wellwood@ukonline.co.uk
D: £19.50–£25.00 **S:** £25.00–£35.00
Beds: 1F 5D 4T **Baths:** 8 En 2 Sh
🛇 🅿 (25) 🔟 🟊 🖿 ♨
The Wellwood is a Victorian mansion
house set in 2 acres of splendid gardens,
yet only a 5 minute walk from town
centre, comfortable rooms, glorious
views, secure open car park.

Balrobin Hotel, Higher Oakfield,
Pitlochry, Perthshire, PH16 5HT.
Quality accommodation with panoramic
views at affordable prices.
Open: Apr to Oct
Grades: STB 3 Star, AA 2 Star,
RAC 2 Star
01796 472901 Mr Hohman
Fax: 01796 474200
info@balrobin.co.uk
D: £25.00–£33.00 **S:** £25.00–£39.00
Beds: 1F 10D 3T 1S **Baths:** 15 En
🛇 (5) 🅿 (15) ✌ 🔟 🟊 ✕ 🖿 🖳 ♨ cc

Easter Dunfallandy Country
House B&B, Pitlochry, Perthshire, PH16
5NA.
Beautifully presented country house with
fine views and gourmet breakfast.
Open: All Year (not Xmas/New Year)
Grades: STB 4 Star
01796 474128 Mr Mathieson
Fax: 01796 473994
sue@dunfallandy.co.uk
D: fr £28.00 **S:** fr £38.00
Beds: 1D 2T **Baths:** 3 En
🛇 (12) 🅿 (6) ✌ 🔟 🖿 🖳

Pooltiel, Lettoch Road, Pitlochry, PH16
5AZ.
Quiet scenic location in Perthshire
Highlands with panoramic views.
Open: Easter to Oct
Grades: STB 3 Star
01796 472184 Mrs Sandison
ajs@pooltiel.freeserve.co.uk
D: £17.00–£18.00 **S:** £17.00–£18.00
Beds: 1F 1T 1D **Baths:** 1 Sh
🛇 🅿 ✌ 🔟 🟊 🖿 ♨

Lynedoch, 9 Lettoch Terrace, Pitlochry,
Perthshire, PH16 5BA.
Open: Easter to Oct
01796 472119 Mrs WIlliamson
iwilliamson@talk21.com
D: £16.00–£18.00 **S:** £16.00–£18.00
Beds: 2D 1T **Baths:** 2 Sh
🅿 (3) ✌ 🔟 🟊 🖿
Stone-built semi-detached villa in
beautiful Highland Perthshire, ideally
situated for walking, golf, fishing stb.
Close by are hydroelectric dam, fish
ladder, world famous festival theatre, and
whisky distilleries. Views of Ben Vrackie
and the Fonab Hills.

8 Darach Road, Pitlochry, Perthshire,
PH16 5HR.
Semi detached house. Hill walking,
Theatre, various walks, central to cities.
Open: All Year (not Xmas/New Year)
01796 472074 Mrs Weyda-Wernick
weydawernick@aol.com
D: £15.00 **S:** fr £18.00
Beds: 1D **Baths:** 2 Sh
🛇 🅿 (2) 🔟 🟊 🖿 🖳

Carra Beag Guest House, 16
*Toberargan Road, Pitlochry, Perthshire,
PH16 5HG.*
Magnificent views; central location;
breakfast cooked to order; period
features.
Open: All Year **Grades:** STB 3 Star
01796 472835 (also fax) Mr Stone
D: £13.00–£23.00 **S:** £13.00–£23.00
Beds: 2F 3D 3T 2S **Baths:** 9 Pr 1 Sh
🛇 🅿 (9) ✌ 🔟 🟊 ✕ 🖿 🖳 ♨ ♨

Ferrymans Cottage, *Port-na-Craig, Pitlochry, Perthshire, PH16 5ND.*
Cosy riverside cottage below festival theatre or stroll into town.
Open: Easter to Nov
Grades: STB 3 Star
01796 473681 (also fax)
Mrs Sanderson
D: £19.00–£24.00
Beds: 2F **Baths:** 1 Pr 1 En
⌂ ▣ (6) ⊬ ▥ ▥ ▣ ▴

Rhynd

NO1520 ◖ *Baiglie Inn*

Fingask Farm , *Rhynd, Perth, Perthshire & Kinross, PH2 8QF.*
Spacious accommodation in well-appointed farmhouse in a peaceful part of central Perthshire.
Open: Easter to Oct
Grades: STB 4 Star
01738 812220 Mrs Stirrat
Fax: 01738 813325
libby@agstirrat.sol.co.uk
D: £19.00–£21.00 **S:** £19.00–£21.00
Beds: 1D 1T 1S **Baths:** 2 Pr
⌂ (10) ▣ (3) ⊬ ▥ ✕ ▥ ▴ cc

St Fillans

NN6924

Earngrove Cottage, *St Fillans, Crieff, Perthshire, PH6 2ND.*
Modernised traditional cottage amidst mountain loch scenery; golfing, hillwalking, fishing. **Open:** Mar to Nov
01764 685224 (also fax) Mrs Ross
D: £15.00 **S:** £18.00–£20.00
Beds: 2T **Baths:** 2 Sh
▣ (4) ⊬ ▥ ▼ ✕ ▥ ▣ ▴

Stanley

NO1133 ◖ *The Spiral*

Beechlea, *Stanley, Perth, Perthshire, PH1 4PS.*
Luxury comfortable B&B, beautiful quiet countryside, excellent location off A9.
Open: All Year (not Xmas)
Grades: STB 4 Star
01738 828715 Mrs Lindsay
chaslizlin@aol.com
D: £20.00–£27.00 **S:** £25.00–£27.00
Beds: 1F 1D 1T **Baths:** 3 En
⌂ (10) ▣ (6) ⊬ ▥ ▥ ▴ cc

The Linn, *3 Duchess Street, Stanley, Perth, PH1 4NF.*
Friendly hosts; rooms prettily furnished and decorated for your comfort.
Open: All Year (not Xmas)
01738 828293 Mrs Lundie
D: £20.00 **S:** £25.00–£30.00
Beds: 2F 1T **Baths:** 2 En 1 Pr
⌂ ▣ (20) ▥ ✕ ▥ ▣ ▴

Shetland

Tourist Information Centre

Market Cross, **Lerwick**, Shetland
Islands, ZE1 0JP, 01595 693434·

YELL

MAINLAND

Papa Stour

LERWICK
Scalloway • Gulberwick

Scousburgh •

FAIR ISLE

© Maps In Minutes™ (1996)

MAINLAND — Lerwick

HU4741   ◀ Candlestick Maker, Queen's Hotel,
Lerwick Hotel

Breiview, 43 Kantersted Road, Lerwick,
Shetland, ZE1 0RJ.
Friendly modern accommodation in quiet
location overlooks bay and Bressay.
Open: All Year (not Xmas/New Year)
Grades: STB 3 Star
01595 695956 Mr Glaser
Fax: 01595 365956
D: £25.00–£30.00 **S:** £30.00–£35.00
Beds: 1F 2D 3T **Baths:** 6 En
🛇 🅿 (6) 📺 ✕ 🛏 ⓥ ♨

Woosung, 43 St Olaf Street, Lerwick,
Shetland, ZE1 0EN.
Central, close to all amenities - street
parking. **Open:** All Year
01595 693687 Mrs Conroy
D: £17.00 **S:** £20.00
Beds: 3T 1S **Baths:** 2 Sh
🛇 📺 🍴 ✕ 🛏 ⓥ ♨

Whinrig, 12 Burgh Road, Lerwick,
Shetland, ZE1 0LB.
Private bungalow centrally heated neat
community centre museum town parks.
Open: Jan to Dec
01595 693554 Mrs Gifford
c.gifford@btinternet.com
D: £19.00–£20.00 **S:** £20.00
Beds: 3F 1D 1T **Baths:** 1 En 1 Pr
🅿 (3) ✍ 📺 🛏 ⓥ ♨ ♿ 3

MAINLAND — Scalloway

HU4039

Broch Guest House, Scalloway,
Lerwick, Shetland, ZE1 0UP.
Comfortable guest house.
Open: All Year (not Xmas)
01595 880767 Mrs Young
D: fr £17.00 **S:** fr £19.00
Beds: 3D **Baths:** 3 En
🛇 🅿 (3) 📺 🛏 ⓥ ♨

FAIR ISLE — Fair Isle

HZ2271

Upper Leogh, Fair Isle, Shetland, ZE2 9JU.
Working croft, hand spinning
demonstration/ tuition available. Local
crafts nearby.
Open: All Year **Grades:** STB 2 Star
01595 760248 Mrs Coull
kathleen.coull@lineone.net
D: £20.00–£22.00 **S:** £20.00–£22.00
Beds: 1T 1D 1S
🛇 🅿 (3) ✍ 📺 ✕ ⓥ ♨

MAINLAND — Gulberwick

HU4438

Virdafjell, Shurton Brae, Gulberwick,
Shetland, ZE2 9TX.
Peaceful Nordic home overlooking bay.
Walks, ponies, bird watching, good
touring base. **Open:** All Year
Grades: STB 3 Star
01595 694336 Mrs Stove
Fax: 01595 696252 d.stove@talk21.com
D: £20.00–£25.00 **S:** £22.00–£30.00
Beds: 2T 1D **Baths:** 1 En 1 Sh
🛇 🅿 (6) ✍ 📺 ✕ 🛏 ⓥ ♨

MAINLAND Scousburgh
HU3717

Spiggie Lodge, *Scousburgh, Shetland, ZE2 9JE.*
Overlooking Spiggie Loch and bird reserve. Ten minutes Sumburgh Airport.
Open: All Year
Grades: STB 2 Star
01950 460563 Mr Wilkins
nina.wilkins@zetnet.co.uk
D: £20.00–£22.00 **S:** £18.00–£20.00
Beds: 1T 1D 1S **Baths:** 2 En 1 Sh
🛇 🅿 (6) ⊬ ⊡ ✕ ▥ Ⅴ ♨

PAPA STOUR Papa Stour
HU1660

Northouse, *Papa Stour, Shetland, ZE2 9PW.*
Working island croft, marine conservation area, spectacular coastline, recreation/sitting room.
Open: All Year
01595 873238 Mrs Holt-Brook
D: £18.00–£19.00 **S:** £18.00–£20.00
Beds: 1F 1D 1T 1S **Baths:** 1 En 1 Sh
🛇 ⊬ ⊡ 🐾 ✕ ▥ Ⅴ ♨

Stirling & the Trossachs

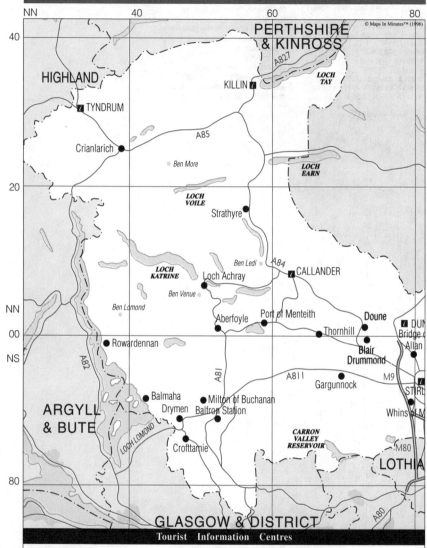

Tourist Information Centres

Main Street, **Aberfoyle**, Stirling,
FK8 3UG, 01877 382352
(Easter to Oct).

West Stirling Street, **Alva**,
Clackmannanshire, FK12 5EN,
01259 769696.

Rob Roy & Trossachs Visitor
Centre, Ancaster Square,
Callander, Perthshire,
FK17 8AD, 01877 330342.

Drymen Library, **Drymen**,
Glasgow, G63 0AA, 01360 660068
(Easter to Oct).

Stirling Road, **Dunblane**,
Perthshire, FK15 9EY,
01786 824428 (Easter to Oct).

Main Street, **Killin**, Perthshire,
FK21 8UH, 01567 820254
(Easter to Oct).

41 Dumbarton Road, **Stirling**,
FK8 2QJ, 01786 475019.

Royal Stirling Visitor Centre, The
Esplanade, **Stirling**,
01786 479901.

Motorway Service Area
(M9/M80 J9), **Stirling**,
01786 814111 (Easter to Oct).

Main Street, **Tyndrum**, Crianlarich,
Perthshire, FK20 8RY,
01838 400246 (Easter to Oct).

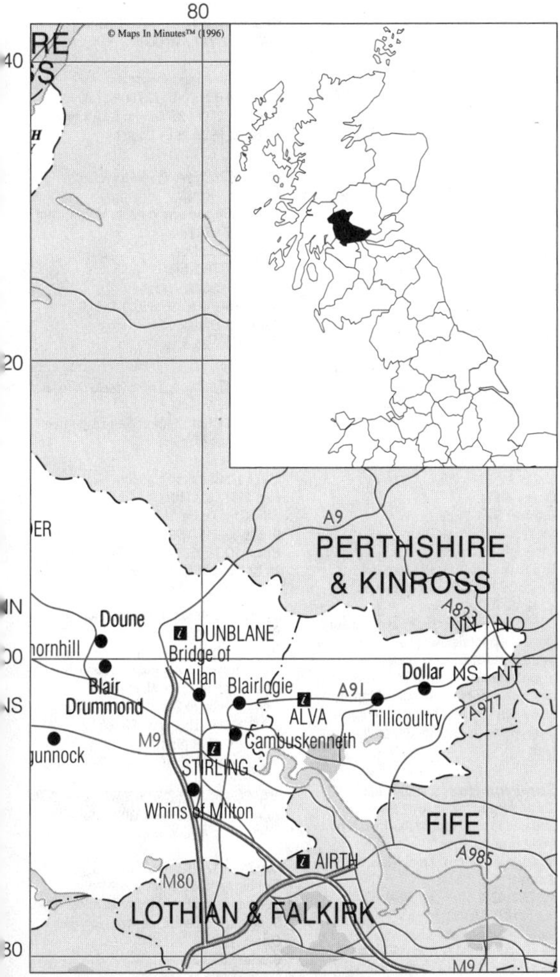

© Maps In Minutes™ (1996)

Alva

NS8897

Johnstone Arms Hotel, *48 Stirling Street, Alva, Clackmannanshire, FK12 5EA.*
100-year-old coaching house extensively refurbished, nestling at the foot of the Ochil Hills.
Open: All Year
01259 762884 Mr Cairns
D: £18.00–£20.00 **S:** £18.00–£20.00
Beds: 1F 2T 3S **Baths:** 2 En 1 Sh
🛏 (14) � (8) ⊁ 📺 ✕ 🏛 Ⅴ ✿ 🏌

Balfron Station

NS5289 🍴 *Clachan, Pottery*

Easter Balfunning Farm, *Drymen, Glasgow, G63 0NF.*
A warm welcome awaits you in our attractive farmhouse idyllically situated.
Open: All Year
Grades: STB 3 Star
01360 440755 Ms Black
D: £18.00–£21.00 **S:** £21.00–£27.00
Beds: 1D 1F **Baths:** 1 Pr 1 En
🛏 � (4) ⊁ 📺 🏌 🏛 Ⅴ 🏌 &

Balmaha

NS4290 🍴 *Oak Tree, Clachan Inn*

Critreoch, *Rowardennan Road, Balmaha, Glasgow, G63 0AW.*
Family home quiet location beautiful view over garden to Loch.
Open: May to Sept
Grades: STB 3 Star
01360 870309 Mrs MacLuskie
D: £20.00–£22.00 **S:** £25.00–£30.00
Beds: 1D 1T **Baths:** 1 En 1 Pr
ㄹ (6) ⊁ 📺 🏌 🏛 Ⅴ 🏌

Mar Achlais, *Milton of Buchanan, Balmaha, Glasgow, G63 0JE.*
Rural setting near Loch Lomond. Excellent touring centre for Scotland.
Open: All Year (not Xmas)
Grades: STB 3 Star
01360 870300 Mr Nichols
Fax: 01360 870444
marachlais@dial.pipex.com
D: £18.50 **S:** £23.50–£28.50
Beds: 1F 1D **Baths:** 2 En
🛏 ㄹ (2) 📺 🏌 ✕ 🏛 Ⅴ 🏌 cc

Conic View Cottage, *Balmaha, Glasgow, G63 0JQ.*
Beautifully situated near Loch Lomond and the West Highland Way, surrounded by forest walks. **Open:** Mar to Nov
01360 870297 Mrs Cronin
jenny@balmaha32.freeserve.co.uk
D: £15.00–£20.00 **S:** £18.00–£20.00
Beds: 1D 1S **Baths:** 1 Sh
ㄹ (2) ⊁ 📺 🏛 Ⅴ 🏌

Dunleen, *Balmaha, Glasgow, G63 0JE.*
Ranch-style house. Warm welcome, lovely garden, trout , east side of Loch Lomond. 'Which?' recommended.
Open: May to Oct
Grades: STB 4 Star
01360 870274 Mrs MacFadyen
D: £19.00–£20.00 **S:** fr £25.00
Beds: 1D 1T **Baths:** 1 Sh
🛏 ㄹ (4) ⊁ 📺 🏛 Ⅴ 🏌

Aberfoyle

NN5200 🍴 *Black Bull, Byre, Old Coach House, Inverard Hotel, Forth Inn*

Creag Ard House B&B, *Aberfoyle, Stirling, FK8 3TQ.*
A beautiful Victorian house with extensive and colourful gardens, set in magnificent scenery.
Open: All Year
Grades: STB 4 Star
01877 382297
Mrs Wilson
creag-ard@tinyonline.co.uk
D: £27.00–£40.00
S: £35.00–£70.00
Beds: 4D 2T **Baths:** 6 En
🛏 ㄹ (7) ⊁ 🏌 ✕ 🏛 Ⅴ 🏌 cc

Mayfield, *Main Street, Aberfoyle, Stirling, FK8 3UQ.*
Large Victorian private house in centre of Aberfoyle. **Open:** All Year (not Xmas/New Year) **Grades:** STB Listed, Comm
01877 382845 Mrs Oldham
D: £18.50–£22.00 **S:** £20.00–£25.00
Beds: 2D 1T 1S **Baths:** 3 En 1 Pr
🛏 ㄹ (4) 📺 🏌 🏛 Ⅴ &

Oak Royal Guest House, *Aberfoyle, Stirling, FK8 3UX.*
Beautiful Trossachs countryside. Ideal base for touring & outdoor enthusiasts.
Open: All Year
01877 382633 (also fax)
D: £20.00–£22.50 **S:** £25.00–£30.00
Beds: 2D 1T **Baths:** 2 En 1 Sh
🛏 ㄹ (6) ⊁ 📺 🏌 🏛 Ⅴ 🏌

Blair Drummond

NS7299   **⌖** *Cross Keys Hotel*

The Linns, *Kirk Lane, Blair Drummond, Stirling, FK9 4AN.*
Traditional cottage set in an exclusive rural location surrounded by hills & woodland. **Open:** All Year (not Xmas)
01786 841679 (also fax) Mr Darby
info@thelinns.co.uk
D: fr £18.50 **S:** fr £32.00
Beds: 1F 2D 1T **Baths:** 2 En
⌂ (2) **P** (7) **✉ ⌖ ✕ ▥ Ⅴ ♿ & cc**

Blairlogie

NS8296   **⌖** *Sword Hotel*

Blairmains Farm, *Manor Loan, Blairlogie, Stirling, FK9 5QA.*
Traditional stone farmhouse. working farm, beautiful country location. Warm Welcome. **Open:** All Year (not Xmas/New Year) **Grades:** STB 2 Star
01259 761338 Mrs Logan
D: £18.00–£20.00 **S:** £20.00–£23.00
Beds: 2T 1D **Baths:** 1 Sh
⌂ P ⅙ ✉ ▥ Ⅴ ♿

Bridge of Allan

NS7997   **⌖** *Old Bridge, Westerton Arms*

Lorraine, *10 Chalton Road, Bridge of Allan, Stirling, FK9 4DX.*
Listed building, off main road, lovely views, good walking country
Open: All Year (not Xmas)
01786 832042 B Holliday
Fax: 01786 831066
101567.2041@compuserve.com
D: £17.00–£18.00 **S:** £17.00–£25.00
Beds: 1D 1T 1S **Baths:** 1 Sh
⌂ P (4) **⅙ ✉ ▥ Ⅴ ♿**

Callander

NN6307   **⌖** *Abbotsford Lodge Hotel, Myrtle Inn, Crags Hotel, Bracklin Fall, Bridge End, Byre*

Arden House , *Bracklinn Road, Callander, Perthshire, FK17 8EQ.*
Open: Easter to Nov
01877 330235 (also fax)
Mr Mitchell & Mr W Jackson
D: £27.50–£30.00 **S:** fr £30.00
Beds: 3D 2T 1S **Baths:** 6 En
⌂ (14) **P** (6) **⅙ ✉ ▥ ♿ cc**
Tranquillity in the Trossachs. Peaceful Victorian country house with stunning views. Home of BBC TVs 'Dr Finlay's Case book'. Comfortable, Elegant Ensuite rooms with TV, tea/coffee and many thoughtful touches. Few minutes walk to village. Generous Breakfasts and genuine hospitality.

Campfield Cottage, *138 Main Street, Callander, Perthshire, FK17 8BG.*
Open: All Year (not Xmas/New Year)
01877 330597 Mrs Hunter
D: £18.00 **S:** £18.00
Beds: 2D 1T 1S **Baths:** 1 Sh
⌂ P ⅙ ✉ ⌖ ▥ Ⅴ ♿
Charming C18th cottage in the heart of Callander, down a quiet lane, for a good nights sleep. Highly recommended by people from all over the world, colour TVs in double rooms, washing facilities, tea/coffee, visitors lounge, conservatory, parking.

Glengarry Hotel, *Stirling Road, Callander, Perthshire, FK17 8DA.*
Open: All Year
01877 330216 info@glengarryhotel.com
D: £22.00–£25.00
Beds: 3F 1D **Baths:** 4 En
⌂ P (15) **✉ ⌖ ✕ ▥ Ⅴ ♿**
Family-run hotel in its own grounds in the picturesque town of Callander where the Lowlands meet the Highlands. Large comfortable bedrooms. A warm welcome, a hearty breakfast, traditional home-cooked evening meals. Easy access.

Riverview House, *Leny Road, Callander, Perthshire, FK17 8AL.*
Open: All Year (not Xmas)
Grades: STB 3 Star
01877 330635 Mr Little
auldtoll@netscapeonline.co.uk
D: £21.00–£22.00 **S:** £22.00–£24.00
Beds: 3D 2T 1S **Baths:** 5 En
P (6) **⅙ ✉ ✕ ▥ Ⅴ ♿**
Attractive, stone-built villa in own grounds within easy walking of town centre and cycle/pathway. Good home cooking. We also offer self catering cottages in beautiful Trossachs area.

Linley Guest House, *139 Main Street, Callander, Perthshire, FK17 8BH.*
Open: All Year
Grades: STB 3 Star
01877 330087 M McQuilton
linley_guesthouse@tinyworld.co.uk
D: £16.00–£18.50 **S:** £20.00–£25.00
Beds: 1F 1T 3D **Baths:** 2 En 2 Sh
⌂ P (4) **✉ ▥ Ⅴ ♿**
Comfortable Victorian terraced house close to Callander busy centre. Ideal for overnight stop/touring base for the magnificent scenery of the Trossachs renowned for hill walking, fishing, cycling and water sports. Stirling 25 minutes drive, Glasgow and Edinburgh only 1 hour.

Burnt Inn House, *Brig o' Turk, Callander, Perthshire, FK17 8HT.*
Situated in the heart of the Trossachs. Quiet rural location.
Open: All Year (not Xmas/New Year)
Grades: STB 3 Star
01877 376212 Mrs Trzebiatowski
Fax: 01877 376233
burntinnhouse@aol.com
D: £20.00–£25.00 **S:** £20.00–£25.00
Beds: 2T 1D **Baths:** 3 En
⌂ (12) **P** (3) **▥ ♿**

East Mains House, *Bridgend, Callander, Perthshire, FK17 8AG.*
C18th mansion house, mature garden.
Open: All Year **Grades:** STB 3 Star
01877 330535 (also fax)
Ms Alexander
east.mains@tesco.net
D: £22.00–£24.00 **S:** £29.00
Beds: 2F 4D **Baths:** 4 En
⌂ P (6) **⅙ ✉ ⌖ ▥ Ⅴ ♿ ♿ cc**

National Grid References are for villages, towns and cities – not for individual houses

Brook Linn Country House, *Callander, Perthshire, FK17 8AU.*
Lovely comfortable Victorian house with magnificent views and personal attention.
Open: Easter to Oct
Grades: STB 4 Star, AA 4 Diamond
01877 330103 (also fax)
Mrs House
derek@blinn.freeserve.co.uk
D: £23.00–£27.00 **S:** £23.00–£27.00
Beds: 1F 2D 2T 2S **Baths:** 6 En 1 Pr
⌂ P (8) **⅙ ✉ ⌖ ▥ Ⅴ ♿ cc**

White Cottage, *Bracklinn Road, Callander, FK17 8EQ.*
Situated in one acre garden. Magnificent views of Ben Ledi.
Open: Apr to Nov
Grades: STB 3 Star
01877 330896 Mrs Hughes
D: £17.50–£19.00 **S:** £22.00–£25.00
Beds: 2D **Baths:** 1 Sh
P (3) **⅙ ✉ ▥ Ⅴ ♿**

Roslin Cottage, *Lagrannoch, Callander, Perthshire, FK17 8LE.*
Beautiful C18th stone cottage & garden on outskirts of town.
Open: All Year
01877 330638 Mrs Ferguson
Fax: 01877 331448
alifer@msn.com
D: £15.50–£16.00 **S:** £18.50
Beds: 1D 1T 2S **Baths:** 1 Sh
⌂ P ✉ ⌖ ✕ ▥ Ⅴ ♿ ♿

Lamorna, *Ancaster Road, Callander, Perthshire, FK17 8JJ.*
Detached bungalow, panoramic views of Callander and surrounding countryside, quiet location, close all amenities.
Open: Easter to Oct
01877 330868 D: £18.00–£20.00
Beds: 1D 1T **Baths:** 1 Sh
P (2) **⅙ ✉ ▥ Ⅴ ♿**

Cambuskenneth

NS8094   **⌖** *Abbey Inn*

Carseview, *16 Ladysneuk Road, Cambuskenneth, Stirling, FK9 5NF.*
Quiet conservation village, 15 mins' walk Stirling town centre, panoramic views.
Open: All Year
Grades: STB 3 Star
01786 462235 (also fax)
Mr & Mrs Seaton
D: £18.00 **S:** £18.00–£20.00
Beds: 2T 1S **Baths:** 1 Sh
⌂ P (34) **⅙ ✉ ⌖ ✕ ▥ Ⅴ ♿ cc**

Crianlarich

NN3825   **⌖** *Ben More, Rod & Reel*

Ben More Lodge Hotel, *Crianlarich, Perthshire, FK20 8QS.*
Family-run lodge hotel with spectacular setting beneath Ben More.
Open: All Year
01838 300210 Mr Goodale
Fax: 01838 300218
john@ben-more.demon.co.uk
D: fr £25.00 **S:** fr £28.00
Beds: 2F 8D 1T **Baths:** 11 En
⌂ P ✉ ⌖ ✕ ▥ Ⅴ ♿ &

Craigbank Guest House, *Crianlarich, Perthshire, FK20 8QS.*
Situated one hour's drive from Glen Coe, Loch Lomond, the Trossachs.
Open: All Year (not Xmas)
01838 300279 Mr Flockhart
D: £17.00–£19.00 **S:** £25.00
Beds: 2F 1D 3T **Baths:** 2 En 2 Sh
(6)

Tigh-na Struith, *Crianlarich, Perthshire, FK20 8RU.*
90-year-old guest house surrounded by hills nestling by the river.
Open: Mar to Nov
01838 300235 Mr & Mrs Chisholm
Fax: 01838 300268
chisholm-crianlarich@gofornet.co.uk
D: £16.00–£22.00 **S:** £20.00–£30.00
Beds: 2F 3D 1T **Baths:** 1 En 2 Sh
(6)

The Lodge House, *Crianlarich, Perthshire, FK20 8RU.*
Superbly located guest house, magnificent views of Crianlarich hills.
Open: All Year
Grades: STB 4 Star, AA 4 Diamond
01838 300276 Mr Gaughan
admin@lodgehouse.co.uk
D: £25.00–£30.00 **S:** £35.00–£45.00
Beds: 1F 3D 2T **Baths:** 6 En
(10) cc

Croftamie

NS4786 *Clachan Inn, Wayfarers*

Croftburn, *Croftamie, Drymen, Glasgow, G63 0HA.*
Former gamekeeper's cottage in one acre of beautiful gardens overlooking Strathendrick Valley & Campsie Fells.
Open: All Year
Grades: STB 3 Star, AA 4 Diamond
01360 660796 Mrs Reid
Fax: 01360 661005
johnreid@croftbarn.fsnet.co.uk
D: £18.00–£22.00 **S:** £20.00–£25.00
Beds: 2D 1T **Baths:** 2 En 1 Pr
(12) (20) cc

Dollar

NS9597

Strathallan Hotel, *Chapel Place, Dollar, Clackmannanshire, FK14 7DW.*
Stylish accommodation in fully licensed inn with creative home cooking.
Open: All Year
01259 742205 Mr Green **Fax: 01259 743720**
nrgstrath@aol.com
D: £20.00–£25.00 **S:** £35.00–£45.00
Beds: 2D 1T **Baths:** 1 En 1 Sh
(20) cc

Doune

NN7301 *Red Lion Hotel, Highland Hotel, Crown Hotel*

The Red Lion Hotel, *Balkerach Street, Doune, FK16 6DF.*
Old hotel (1692), family-run business, 30 mins Edinburgh and Glasgow. Backpackers £8.50.
Open: All Year
01786 842066 D: £18.00–£20.00
Beds: 3D **Baths:** 1 En 1 Sh

Planning a longer stay? Always ask for any special rates

Inverardoch Mains Farm, *Doune, Perthshire, FK15 9NZ.*
Traditional farmhouse on working farm with panoramic views.
Open: Mar to Nov
01786 841268 Mrs Anderson
D: £20.00–£22.00 **S:** £22.00–£25.00
Beds: 1F 1D 1T **Baths:** 2 Pr 1 Sh
(6)

Drymen

NS4788 *Buchanan Arms, Clachan Inn, Pottery, Wayfarers, Winnock Hotel*

Green Shadows, *Buchanan Castle Estate, Drymen, Glasgow, G63 0HX.*
Open: All year (not Xmas)
01360 660289 Mrs Goodwin
D: £21.00 **S:** £24.00
Beds: 1F 1D 1S **Baths:** 2 Sh
(8)
Warm, friendly welcome in a beautiful country house with spectacular views over golf course and the Lomond Hills. Buchanan Castle to the rear. 1 mile from Drymen Centre, 2 miles from Loch Lomond. Glasgow Airport 40 mins away.

Easter Balfunning Farm, *Drymen, Glasgow, G63 0NF.*
Open: All Year
Grades: STB 3 Star
01360 440755 Ms Black
D: £18.00–£21.00 **S:** £21.00–£27.00
Beds: 1D 1F **Baths:** 1 Pr 1 En
(4)
A warm welcome awaits you in our attractive farmhouse idyllically situated with panoramic views of the Campsie Fells. Guest rooms look onto the garden towards the Campsies. Comfortable beds and excellent breakfasts. Convenient for Loch Lomond, Stirling and the Trossachs.

Croftburn, *Croftamie, Drymen, Glasgow, G63 0HA.*
Former gamekeeper's cottage in one acre of beautiful gardens overlooking Strathendrick Valley & Campsie Fells.
Open: All Year
Grades: STB 3 Star, AA 4 Diamond
01360 660796 Mrs Reid
Fax: 01360 661005
johnreid@croftbarn.fsnet.co.uk
D: £18.00–£22.00 **S:** £20.00–£25.00
Beds: 2D 1T **Baths:** 2 En 1 Pr
(12) (20) cc

Easter Drumquhassle Farm, *Gartness Road, Drymen, Glasgow, G63 0DN.*
Traditional farmhouse, beautiful views, home cooking, excellent base on the West Highland Way.
Open: All Year
Grades: STB 3 Star, AA 3 Diamond
01360 660893 Mrs Cross
Fax: 01360 660282
juliamacx@aol.com
D: £18.00–£25.00 **S:** £25.00–£30.00
Beds: 1F 1D 1T **Baths:** 3 En
(10)

Ceardach, *Gartness Road, Drymen, Glasgow, G63 0BH.*
Open: All Year (not Xmas)
01360 660596 (also fax)
Mrs Robb
D: £18.00–£20.00 **S:** £18.00–£20.00
Beds: 1D 1T **Baths:** 1 Sh
(1) (3)
250 year old Coach house. Situated near the shores of Loch Lomond large garden. Good home cooking, a warm and friendly welcome awaits you.

Glenava, *Stirling Road, Drymen, Glasgow, G63 0AA.*
A Warm welcome, stunning scenery, comfortable rooms, lovely local Walks.
Open: Easter to Oct
Grades: STB 3 Star
01360 660491 Ms Fraser
D: £18.00–£20.00 **S:** £30.00
Beds: 1D 1T **Baths:** 1 Sh
(4)

17 Stirling Road, *Drymen, Glasgow, G63 0BW.*
Family home in village near West Highland Way; lovely garden.
Open: All Year
01360 660273 (also fax)
Mrs Lander
david_lander@lineone.net
D: £15.00–£18.00 **S:** £18.00–£23.00
Beds: 1F 1T **Baths:** 1 Sh
(1)

Dunblane

NN7801 *Westlands Bar*

Mossgiel, *Doune Road, Dunblane, Perthshire, FK15 9ND.*
Charming well-equipped countryside house offering guests a comfortable relaxing holiday.
Open: March to October
01786 824325 Mrs Bennett
judy@mossgiel.com
D: £20.00–£22.00 **S:** £25.00
Beds: 2T 1D **Baths:** 2 En 1 Pr
(5)

Gargunnock

NS7094 *Gargunnock Inn*

East Lodge, *Leckie, Gargunnock, Stirling, FK8 3BN.*
Open: All Year (not Xmas)
Grades: STB 3 Star
01786 860605 Mrs Currie
janc123456@aol.com
D: £20.00–£22.00 **S:** £25.00–£28.00
Beds: 1D 1T **Baths:** 1 Pr 1 Sh
(3) 1
C19th lodge house tastefully extended. In attractive woodland setting. Ideal base to visit Edinburgh, Glasgow, Loch Lomond and Trossachs. 'Comfortable, peaceful and elegant'.

All details shown are as supplied by B&B owners in Autumn 2000

Killin

NN5732   ◖ *Bridge Of Lochay, Coach House, Killin Hotel, Shutters*

Falls of Dochart Cottage, *Killin, Perthshire, FK21 8SW.*
Open: All Year (not Xmas)
Grades: STB 2 Star
01567 820363 Mr & Mrs Mudd
D: £16.00–£17.00 **S:** fr £17.00
Beds: 1D 1T 1S **Baths:** 2 Sh
☺ (1) ⓟ (4) ⥀ ⓣⱴ ⴲ ⅏ ⅏ ⓥ
C17th cottage, overlooking the falls and river - home cooking - comfortable and friendly atmosphere. Open all year: central to magnificent mountain area - renowned for hill walking.

Main Street, *Killin, Perthshire, FK21 8TP.*
Open: All Year **Grades:** STB 2 Star
01567 820296 Mr & Mrs Garnier
Fax: 01567 820647
killinhotel@btinternet.com
D: £19.00–£35.00 **S:** £19.00–£35.00
Beds: 3F 6T 17D 6S **Baths:** 32 En
☺ ⓟ (20) ⥀ ⓣⱴ ⴲ ⅏ ⅏ ⓥ ⅏ ⅏ cc
The setting is magnificent, overlooking the river Lochay, we have a bistro restaurant specialising in home cooked dishes, all rooms are ensuite, lounge bar with stock of malt Whiskies. A friendly welcome from the owners guaranteed.

Allt Fulieach, *Maragowan, Killin, Perthshire, FK21 8TN.*
Comfortable, modern house at the head of Loch Tay. **Open:** All Year
01567 820962 Mr Judd
D: £19.00 **S:** £19.00
Beds: 2T 1D **Baths:** 3 En
☺ ⓟ (4) ⥀ ⓣⱴ ⅏ ⅏

The Coach House Hotel, *Lochay Road, Killin, Perthshire, FK21 8TN.*
Family-run hotel surrounded by mountains overlooking the river.
Open: All Year
01567 820349 (also fax)
D: £20.00–£26.00 **S:** £20.00–£26.00
Beds: 1F 1D 2T **Baths:** 2 En 2 Sh
☺ ⓟ (40) ⥀ ⓣⱴ ⅏ ⓥ ⅏ cc

Drumfinn House, *Manse Road, Killin, Perthshire, FK21 8UY.*
Warm, friendly country house in the centre of the highland village of Killin.
Open: All Year (not Xmas)
01567 820900 (also fax) Mrs Semple
drumfinnhouse@beeb.net
D: £16.00–£20.00
Beds: 1F 3D 2T **Baths:** 3 En 1 Sh
☺ (12) ⓟ (6) ⥀ ⓣⱴ ⴲ ⅏ ⅏

Loch Achray

NN5106

Glenbruach Country House, *Loch Achray, Trossachs, Callander, Perthshire, FK17 8HX.*
Open: All Year
01877 376216 (also fax) Mrs Lindsay
D: £22.00–£25.00 **S:** £22.00–£25.00
Beds: 2D 1T **Baths:** 2 En 1 Pr
☺ (12) ⓟ (3) ⥀ ⴲ ⅏ ⓣⱴ ⅏ ⓥ ⅏
Unique country mansion in the heart of Rob Roy country. All rooms with Loch views. Interesting interior design and collections in this Scots-owned home.

Milton of Buchanan

NS4490

Mar Achlais, *Milton of Buchanan, Balmaha, Glasgow, G63 0JE.*
Rural setting near Loch Lomond. Excellent touring centre for Scotland.
Open: All Year (not Xmas)
Grades: STB 3 Star
01360 870300 Mr Nichols
Fax: 01360 870444
marachlais@dial.pipex.com
D: £18.50 **S:** £23.50–£28.50
Beds: 1F 1D **Baths:** 2 En
☺ ⓟ ⓣⱴ ⴲ ⅏ ⓥ ⅏ cc

Ochtertyre

NS7497   ◖ *Leonardo's*

Broadford House, *Ochtertyre, Stirling, FK9 4UN.*
Open: Easter to Oct
Grades: STB 3 Star
01786 464674 Mrs Littlejohn
Fax: 01786 463256
simonlittlejohn@compuserve.com
D: £20.00–£23.00
Beds: 1T 1D **Baths:** 1 En 1 Pr
⥀ ⓣⱴ ⅏ ⅏
Lovely country house set in 2.5 acres of garden, adorned with 300 year old oak trees. Enjoy the character and tranquillity of this home in the country, yet only 5 minutes from the centre of Stirling.

Port of Menteith

NN5801   ◖ *Crown Hotel, Cross Keys*

Collymoon Pendicle, *Port of Menteith, Perthshire, FK8 3JY.*
Rural location beside river, good home cooking, assured warm welcome.
Open: Easter to Oct
01360 850222 Mrs Tough
106773,3050@compuserve.com
D: £16.00–£18.00 **S:** £20.00–£22.00
Beds: 1F 1D **Baths:** 1 Sh
☺ (5) ⓟ (4) ⴲ ⅏ ⅏

Rowardennan

NS3598

Anchorage Cottage, *Rowardennan, Drymen, Glasgow, G63 0AW.*
Open: Easter to Oct
01360 870394 (also fax)
D: £26.00–£30.00 **S:** £36.00–£40.00
Beds: 2T 1D **Baths:** 2 En 1 Pr
ⓟ (6) ⥀ ⓣⱴ ⅏ ⅏
Welcome to our family home on the eastern shore of Loch Lomond. Our accommodation is of the highest standards. The house commands unique magnificent views over the loch and islands to Luss on the western shore. Situated on the west Highland way.

BATHROOMS

Pr - Private

Sh - Shared

En - Ensuite

Stirling

NS7993   ◖ *Abbey Inn, Birds & Bees, Hog's Head, Hollybank, Porters, Silver Tassie, Terraces Hotel, Whistlebinkies*

Woodside Guest House, *4 Back Walk, Stirling, FK8 2QA.*
Open: All Year
01786 475470 Mr Drummond
D: fr £16.00 **S:** fr £18.00
Beds: 1F 3D 2T 1S **Baths:** 2 En 2 Pr 2 Sh
☺ ⓟ ⥀ ⓣⱴ ⴲ ⅏ ⓥ ⅏
Beautifully situated on the old historic Wall of Stirling. Modern, comfortable, friendly, central to all amenities. Five minutes' walk from rail and bus stations. All rooms have private showers.

Anderson House, *8 Melville Terrace, Stirling, FK8 2NE.*
Open: All Year (not Xmas)
Grades: STB 3 Star
01786 465185 Mrs Piggott
D: £22.00–£24.00 **S:** £25.00–£30.00
Beds: 1F 1T 1D 1S **Baths:** 3 En 1 Sh
☺ ⓟ (5) ⥀ ⓣⱴ ⅏ ⅏
Welcome to our 200 year old Georgian home within 2 minutes walk of historic Stirling. Large, bright rooms, antique furnishings, refurbished ensuites, a friendly atmosphere and and a great Scottish breakfast will make your stay a memorable one.

27 King Street, *Stirling, FK8 1DN.*
Comfortable Edwardian town house, convenient bus/rail stations, town centre.
Open: All Year
Grades: STB 2 Star
01786 471082 (also fax)
Mr & Mrs Macgregor
jennifer@sruighlea.demon.co.uk
D: £16.00–£20.00 **S:** £20.00 £25.00
Beds: 1F 1D 1T **Baths:** 2 Pr
☺ (2) ⥀ ⓣⱴ ⅏ ⓥ ⅏

12 Princes Street, *Stirling, FK8 1HQ.*
Central for Stirling. Near to Castle and Wallace's monument.
Open: All Year
01786 479228 (also fax) Mrs Cairns
D: £18.00–£20.00 **S:** £18.00–£20.00
Beds: 1D 1T 2S **Baths:** 2 En 2 Sh
☺ (3) ⓟ ⥀ ⓣⱴ ⴲ ⴲ ⅏ ⓥ ⅏

Tiroran, *45 Douglas Terrace, Stirling, FK7 9LW.*
Open: Easter to Oct **Grades:** STB 4 Star
01786 464655 Mrs Thomson
D: £18.00–£19.00
Beds: 1D 1T **Baths:** 1 Sh
☺ (9) ⓟ (2) ⥀ ⓣⱴ ⅏ ⓥ ⅏
Agnes ensures a warm Scottish welcome to Tiroran. A modern house situated in quiet residential area close to Kings Park Golf Course. Five minutes drive to town centre, railway station, castle and historic old town. Best B&B Tourist Award Winner.

16 Riverside Drive, *Stirling, FK8 1XF.*
Our small family home in quiet area near to town.
Open: All Year
01786 461105 Mrs Miller
D: £13.50–£14.50 **S:** £13.50–£14.00
Beds: 2S **Baths:** 1 Sh
⥀ ⓣⱴ ⅏ ⅏

Ravenscroft, *21 Clarendon Place, Stirling, FK8 2QW.*
Beautiful Victorian house in conservation area, views over to castle.
Open: All Year (not Xmas)
Grades: STB 4 Star
01786 473815 Mr & Mrs Dunbar
Fax: 01786 450990
dunbar@ravenscroft3.freeserve.co.uk
D: fr £23.50 **S:** fr £35.00
Beds: 1D 1T **Baths:** 1 En 1 Pr
🅿 (2) ⌿ 📺 🗐 Ⅴ ♨

Linden Guest House, *22 Linden Avenue, Stirling, FK7 7PQ.*
Situated in a tree-lined avenue only few minutes' walk to town centre.
Open: All Year **Grades:** STB 2 Star
01786 448850 (also fax)
Miss McGuinness
D: £18.00–£20.00 **S:** £19.00–£21.00
Beds: 2F 1D 1T **Baths:** 1 Sh
🗑 🅿 (2) 📺 ♀ ✕ 🗐 Ⅴ ♨

Barnsdale House, *19 Barnsdale Road, St Ninians, Stirling, FK7 0PT.*
Comfortable Victorian villa. Convenient base for touring central Scotland.
Open: All Year **Grades:** STB 3 Star
01786 461729 (also fax) Mrs Pain
barnsdalehouse@painstirling.freeserve.c
o.uk
D: £16.00–£18.00 **S:** £20.00–£25.00
Beds: 1F 1D **Baths:** 1 En 1 Pr
🗑 🅿 (3) ⌿ ✕ 🗐 Ⅴ ♨

Hopeton, *28 Linden Avenue, Stirling, FK7 7PQ.*
Ground floor flat of large detached stone building surrounded by attractive gardens. **Open:** All Year
01786 473418 Mrs McDonald
D: £18.00 **S:** fr £20.00
Beds: 1F 1D 1T **Baths:** 1 Pr 1 Sh
🗑 🅿 📺 ♀ 🗐 ♨ &

Wellgreen Guest House, *8 Pit Terrace, Stirling, FK8 2EZ.*
Family-run guest house close to town centre & all its amenities.
Open: All Year
01786 472675 Mrs Mcphail
D: £18.00 **S:** £18.00
Beds: 2F 1T 1S **Baths:** 2 Sh
🗑 🅿 ⌿ 📺 ♀ 🗐 Ⅴ ♨

Kerann, *110 Causewayhead Road, Stirling, FK9 5HJ.*
A warm welcome and excellent breakfast await you. **Open:** All Year
Grades: STB 3 Star
01786 462432 (also fax) Mrs Paterson
bookings@kerann.ndirect.co.uk
D: £19.00–£21.00
Beds: 1D 2T **Baths:** 3 En
🅿 (6) ⌿ 📺 🗐 Ⅴ ♨

Allandale, *98 Causewayhead Road, Stirling, FK9 5HJ.*
Warm, friendly family home.
Open: All Year
01786 465643 Mr & Mrs McLaren
D: £17.00–£18.00
Beds: 1F 1T **Baths:** 1 Sh
🅿 (2) ⌿ 📺 🗐 Ⅴ ♨

Strathyre

NN5617　🍺 *Strathyre Inn, Ben Shian Hotel*

Coire Buidhe, *Strathyre, Callander, Perthshire, FK18 8NA.*
Family Bed and Breakfast, centrally located for Stirling, Trossachs.
Open: All Year (not Xmas)
01877 384288 Mr & Mrs Reid
coire.buidhe@talk21.com
D: £18.00–£20.00 **S:** £17.00–£20.00
Beds: 3F 1D 1T 1S **Baths:** 1 Pr 3 Sh
🗑 🅿 (6) ⌿ 📺 ♀ 🗐 Ⅴ ♨

Dochfour, *Strathyre, Callander, FK18 8NA.*
Award-winning B&B in scenic glen, specialising in being the best!
Open: All Year
Grades: STB 3 Star
01877 384256 (also fax)
Mr & Mrs Ffinch
tony.ffinch@tesco.net
D: £18.00–£20.00 **S:** £23.00–£26.00
Beds: 2D 1T **Baths:** 2 En 1 Pr
🗑 🅿 (6) 📺 ✕ 🗐 Ⅴ ♨ ♨ cc

Rosebank House, *Strathyre, Callander, Perthshire, FK18 8NA.*
Rosebank house is a fine example of Victorian architecture.
Open: Mar to Dec
01877 384208 Mr & Mrs Moor
Fax: 01877 384201
D: £18.00–£20.00 **S:** £18.00–£25.00
Beds: 1F 2D 1T 1S **Baths:** 2 En 1 Pr
🗑 🅿 (3) ⌿ 📺 ♀ ✕ 🗐 Ⅴ ♨ ♨ cc

Thornhill

NS6699　🍺 *Lion & Unicorn, Crown Hotel*

The Granary, *West Moss Side, Thornhill, Stirling, FK8 3QJ.*
Open: All Year (not Xmas)
Grades: STB 4 Star
01786 850310 Mrs Cumming
D: £20.00–£22.00 **S:** £25.00
Beds: 2D 1S **Baths:** 2 En 1 Sh
🗑 🅿 (6) ⌿ 📺 🗐 Ⅴ ♨ ♨ &
Recently converted granary. Rooms overlooking gardens with spectacular views. Luxury ground floor suite (with log fire). Walk in the beautiful Trossachs or relax by the lochs. 10 miles west of Stirling. Fast half hourly train to Edinburgh.

Cairnsaigh, *Doig Street, Thornhill, Stirling, FK8 3PZ.*
Spacious modern bungalow 10 miles west of Stirling and 6 miles south of Callander.
Open: All Year
01786 850413 (also fax)
Mr & Mrs Boswell
boswell@cairnsaigh.freeserve.co.uk
D: £24.00–£27.50
Beds: 2D 1T **Baths:** 3 En
🗑 🅿 (3) ⌿ 📺 ♀ ✕ 🗐 Ⅴ ♨ ♨ & cc

Tillicoultry

NS9197

Wyvis, *70 Stirling Street, Tillicoultry, Clackmannanshire, FK13 6EA.*
Converted mill worker's cottage with views to the Ochil Hills.
Open: All Year (not Xmas/New Year)
Grades: STB 4 Star
01259 751513
Mrs Goddard
terrygoddard@netscapeonline.co.uk
D: £21.00–£28.00 **S:** £25.00–£28.00
Beds: 1T 1D **Baths:** 1 Pr 1 En
🗑 ⌿ 📺 ♀ ✕ 🗐 Ⅴ ♨

Tyndrum

NN3330

Glengarry Guest House, *Tyndrum, Crianlarich, Perthshire, FK20 8RY.*
Ideal base for touring and outdoor activities. Scottish welcome awaits.
Open: All Year
Grades: STB 2 Star
01838 400224
Mr & Mrs Mailer
glengarry@altavista.net
D: £18.00–£22.00 **S:** £25.00
Beds: 1F 1T 1D **Baths:** 2 En 1 Pr
🗑 (2) 🅿 (4) ⌿ ♀ ✕ 🗐 Ⅴ ♨

Whins of Milton

NS7990　🍺 *Holly Bank Hotel*

Whinwell Cottage, *171 Glasgow Road, Whins of Milton, Stirling, FK7 0LH.*
Immaculate, comfortable, accommodation, close to many tourist attractions and amenities.
Open: All Year
01786 818166
D: £18.00–£22.00
S: £20.00–£30.00
Beds: 1F 1T 1D **Baths:** 1 Sh
🗑 🅿 ⌿ 📺 🗐 Ⅴ ♨

Planning a longer stay? Always ask for any special rates

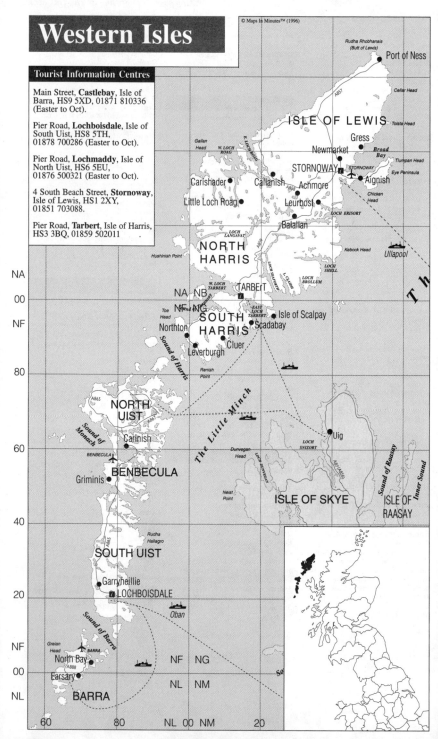

Western Isles

© Maps In Minutes™ (1996)

Tourist Information Centres

Main Street, **Castlebay**, Isle of Barra, HS9 5XD, 01871 810336 (Easter to Oct).

Pier Road, **Lochboisdale**, Isle of South Uist, HS8 5TH, 01878 700286 (Easter to Oct).

Pier Road, **Lochmaddy**, Isle of North Uist, HS6 5EU, 01876 500321 (Easter to Oct).

4 South Beach Street, **Stornoway**, Isle of Lewis, HS1 2XY, 01851 703088.

Pier Road, **Tarbert**, Isle of Harris, HS3 3BQ, 01859 502011

Rudha Rhobhanais
(Butt of Lewis)
Port of Ness

Cellar Head

ISLE OF LEWIS

Tolsta Head

Gress

Gailan Head
W. LOCH ROAG
E. LOCH ROAG

Newmarket
Broad Bay

STORNOWAY
STORNOWAY
Trumpan Head

Carishader
Callanish
Achmore
Aignish
Eye Peninsula

Little Loch Roag
Leurbost
Chicken Head

Balallan
LOCH ERISORT

LOCH LANGAVAT

Hushinish Point

NORTH HARRIS

LOCH SHELL

Kebock Head

LOCH SEAFORTH
L. CLAIDH
LOCH BROLLUM

Ullapool

NA

00

NF

NA NB
Sound of Harris
NF NG
Toe Head

W. LOCH TARBERT
TARBErT

SOUTH HARRIS
EAST LOCH TARBERT
Isle of Scalpay
Scadabay

Northton
Cluer
Leverburgh

80

Renish Point

NORTH UIST
A865
A867

Sound of Monach

Carinish

The Little Minch

Uig

Dunvegan Head
LOCH SNIZORT

60

BENBECULA

BENBECULA
Griminis

Neist Point

ISLE OF SKYE

Sound of Raasay
Inner Sound
ISLE OF RAASAY

40

Rudha Hallagro

SOUTH UIST

20

Garryheillie
LOCHBOISDALE

Oban

NF

00

Sound of Barra

Greian Head
BARRA
North Bay
A888
Earsary

NF NG

NL

BARRA
NL NM

NL 00 NM

60   80   NL 00 NM   20

The Little Minch

T h

Th

BARRA — Earsary

NL7099   *Craigard Hotel*

Gearadhmor, *123 Craigston, Earsary, Castlebay, Isle of Barra, HS9 5XS.*
Beautiful surroundings. Home cooking a speciality. Traditional Highland hospitality. **Open:** All Year
Grades: STB 3 Star
01871 810688 Mrs Maclean
archie.b.maclean@tesco.net
D: £15.00–£18.00 **S:** £15.00–£20.00
Beds: 2F 2T **Baths:** 1 En 3 Sh
� P (6) ▨ � ✕ ▥ Ⓥ ♿

BARRA — North Bay

NF7203   *Castlebay Hotel*

Northbay House, *Balnabodach, North Bay, Castlebay, Isle of Barra, HS9 5UT.*
Attractive former school with comfortable and spacious accommodation. Warm hospitality.
Open: All Year (not Xmas/New Year)
Grades: STB 4 Star
01871 890255 (also fax) Mrs Savory
northbayhouse@isleofbarra.com
D: £22.00–£26.00 **S:** £22.00–£26.00
Beds: 1T 1D **Baths:** 2 En
P (4) ⅟ ▨ ▥ ♿ 1

BENBECULA — Griminis

NF7851

Creag Liath, *15 Griminis, Griminish, Isle of Benbecula, HS7 5QA.*
Rural working croft, ideal for birdwatching, fishing, cycling and beachcombing. **Open:** All Year
01870 602992 Mrs MacDonald
creagliath@aol.com
D: £25.00 **S:** £25.00
Beds: 2F 1T 1D **Baths:** 2 En 2 Pr
⌣ P (5) ▨ ♣ ✕ ▥ Ⓥ ✻ ♿

HARRIS — Cluer

NG1490

Mount Cameron, *2 Cluer, Cluer, Isle of Harris, HS3 3EP.*
Open: All Year **Grades:** STB 3 Star
01859 530356 Mr Mackinnon
calmac2c@aol.com
D: £15.00–£20.00 **S:** £20.00
Beds: 2D **Baths:** 1 En 1 Pr 1 Sh
⌣ P ⅟ ▨ ♿
Mount Cameron is a seven apartment house. Situated within the scenic Bays of Harris. From the lounge and surrounding exterior of the house there are unparalleled views of the local bay across the Minch to Wester Ross and Skye.

HARRIS — Isle of Scalpay

NG2395   *Harris Hotel*

Seafield, *Isle of Scalpay, Isle of Harris, HS4 3XZ.*
Fantastic sea views, homely atmosphere. Free boat trip for two night stay.
Open: Easter to Nov **Grades:** STB 2 Star
01859 540250 Mrs Cunningham
roddy@mjg.sol.uk
D: £16.00–£18.00 **S:** £20.00–£22.00
Beds: 1F 2D **Baths:** 2 Sh
⌣ P (4) ⅟ ▨ ✕ ▥ ♿

HARRIS — Leverburgh

NG0186

Garryknowe, *Ferry Road, Leverburgh, Isle of Harris, HS5 3UA.*
Georgian house, scenic views. Good home-cooking. A home from home.
Open: Easter to Oct
01895 520246 Mrs MacKenzie
D: £16.00–£18.00 **S:** £20.00–£25.00
Beds: 3F 2D 1T **Baths:** 1 En 1 Sh
⌣ P (1) ▨ ♣ ▥ Ⓥ ♿

HARRIS — Northton

NF9989

39 Taobh Tuath, *Northton, Harris, HS3 3JA.*
Access to lovely secluded beaches. Dinner served from 6-8.
Open: Mar to Oct
01859 520228 Mrs Morrison
D: £18.00 **S:** £18.00
Beds: 1F 1D 1T **Baths:** 2 Sh
⌣ (1) P (6) ▨ ♣ ✕ ▥ Ⓥ

HARRIS — Scadabay

NG1792

Hillhead, *Scadabay, Harris, HS3 3ED.*
Hillhead set in beautiful peaceful surroundings, loch & sea fishing is available.
Open: Easter to Nov
01859 511226 Mrs MacLeod
D: £16.00–£17.00 **S:** £16.00
Beds: 1F 1D 1T **Baths:** 1 En 2 Pr 1 Sh
⌣ (4) P (4) ⅟ ▨ ♣ ✕ ▥ Ⓥ ♿

HARRIS — Tarbert

NB1500   *Harris Hotel*

Avalon, *12 West Side, Tarbert, Isle of Harris, HS3 3BG.*
Magnificent views, 3/4 mile ferry terminal. Excellent base for touring Lewes & Hams.
Open: All Year
Grades: STB 4 Star
01859 502334 Mrs Morrison
info@avalonguesthouse.co.uk
D: £20.00
Beds: 2T 1D **Baths:** 2 En 1 Pr
⌣ P (4) ⅟ ▨ ♣ ✕ ▥ Ⓥ ♿

Tigh Na Mara, *Tarbert, Harris, Isle of Harris, HS3 3DB.*
Beautiful location, magnificent sea views, hearty meals, near ferry terminal.
Open: All Year
01859 502270 Mrs Morrison
tighnamara@tarbert-harris.freeserve.co.uk
D: £16.00–£18.00 **S:** £16.00
Beds: 1F 1T 1S **Baths:** 1 En 1 Sh
⌣ P (3) ⅟ ▨ ✕ ▥ Ⓥ ♿ cc

All details shown are as supplied by B&B owners in Autumn 2000

LEWIS — Achmore

NB3128

Cleascro House, *Achmore, Isle of Lewis, Western Isles, HS2 9DU.*
Open: All Year (not Xmas/New Year)
Grades: STB 4 Star
01851 860302 (also fax) Mrs Murray
donnamurray@compuserve.com
D: £21.00–£25.00 **S:** £21.00–£25.00
Beds: 1T 2D **Baths:** 3 En
⌣ P ▨ ♣ ♣ ✕ ▥ Ⓥ ♿
Ideal location for touring Lewis and Harris with superb views of Uig and Harris hills. We are within easy reach of ferries, Callanish Stones and many places of interest. Superior accommodation and excellent cuisine. Featured in 'Which' good B&B guide.

LEWIS — Aignish

NB4832

Ceol-Na-Mara, *1a, Aignish, Point, Isle of Lewis, Western Isles, HS2 0PB.*
Family home, very comfortable and welcoming, rural area near Stornaway.
Open: All Year
01851 870339 (also fax) Ms MacDonald
lesmacd@globalnet.co.uk
D: £17.00–£19.00 **S:** £19.00–£21.00
Beds: 1F 1D 1T **Baths:** 1 Pr 1 Sh
⌣ P (3) ⅟ ▨ ♣ ✕ ▥ Ⓥ ♿

LEWIS — Balallan

NB2920

Clearview, *44 Balallan, Balallan, Isle of Lewis, HS2 9PT.*
Modern house, peaceful elevated location giving panoramic views. Walkers/cyclists welcome.
Open: All Year (not Xmas/New Year)
Grades: STB 3 Star
01851 830472 Mr & Mrs Mackay
D: £18.00–£20.00 **S:** £18.00–£20.00
Beds: 1T 2D **Baths:** 2 En 1 Pr
⌣ P (6) ⅟ ▨ ✕ ▥ ♿

LEWIS — Callanish

NB2133

Eshcol Guest House, *21 Breascleit, Callanish, Isle of Lewis, Western Isles, HS2 9ED.*
Modern guest house, Callanish Stones 2 miles. Featured in Which? B&B.
Open: All Year (not Xmas)
01851 621357 Mrs MacArthur
donlewis@madasafish.com
D: £29.00–£31.00 **S:** £39.00–£41.00
Beds: 1D 2T **Baths:** 2 En 1 Pr
⌣ (8) P (10) ⅟ ▨ ♣ ✕ ▥ Ⓥ ♿

LEWIS — Carishader

NB0933

1 Cairisiadar, *Carishader, Uig, Isle of Lewis, HS2 9ER.*
Comfortable crofthouse, traditional cooking, sea views, walks, friendly atmosphere. **Open:** All Year
01851 672239 Mrs MacKay
D: fr £16.00 **S:** fr £16.00
Beds: 1D 1T **Baths:** 1 Sh
P (3) ▨ ✕ ▥ Ⓥ

LEWIS Gress

NB4941

Caladh, 44 Gress, Isle of Lewis, Western Isles, HS2 0NB.
All rooms look overlook River and the sea, Even a talking Parrot.
Open: All Year
Grades: STB 3 Star
01851 820743 Mrs Evans
Eve@caladh.fsbusiness.co.uk
D: £17.00–£19.00 **S:** £18.00–£20.00
Beds: 2T **Baths:** 2 En
❄ (0) ⊞ (4) ⧖ 📺 ✕ ▥ 🖥 ❀ 🕯

LEWIS Leurbost

NB3725

Glen House, 77 Liurbost, Leurbost, Lochs, Isle of Lewis, HS2 9NL.
Quiet country residence overlooking scenic sea loch, offering high standard of food and accommodation.
Open: All Year
Grades: STB 2 Star
01851 860241
Mrs Reid
glenhouse@talk21.com
D: £19.00 **S:** £20.00
Beds: 2F 1D 1T **Baths:** 2 En 1 Pr
❄ (5) ⊞ ⧖ 📺 🕆 ✕ ▥ 🖥 🕯 ♿

LEWIS Little Loch Roag

NB1326

Scaliscro Lodge, Little Loch Roag, Isle of Lewis, HS2 9EL.
Private and secluded family run inn in spectacular sea front setting.
Open: 15/04/2001 to 31/10/2001
01851 672325
Mr MacKenzie
Fax: 01851 672393
jimmy.mackenzie@easynet.co.uk
D: £18.75–£27.50 **S:** £22.50–£27.50
Beds: 1F 3T 3D 1S **Baths:** 3 En 3 Pr
❄ ⊞ (20) 📺 🕆 ✕ ▥ 🕯 cc

RATES

D = Price range per person sharing in a double room
S = Price range for a single room

LEWIS Newmarket

NB4235

Lathamor, Bakers Road, Newmarket, Isle of Lewis, HS2 0EA.
Spacious family home, ideal for children, relaxed atmosphere, evening meals.
Open: All Year
01851 706093 (also fax)
Mrs Ferguson
D: £18.00 **S:** £14.00–£18.00
Beds: 1F 1D 1T **Baths:** 1 Pr 14 Sh
❄ ⊞ (4) ⧖ 📺 🕆 ✕ ▥ 🖥 🕯 cc

LEWIS Port of Ness

NB5363

Cliff House, Port of Ness, Isle of Lewis, HS2 0XA.
Cliff house situated above sandy beach and harbour.
Open: Easter to Oct
01851 810278 Mrs Morrison
D: £18.00–£20.00 **S:** £18.00–£20.00
Beds: 1D 2T **Baths:** 1 Sh
❄ (5) ⊞ (4) 📺 🕆 ✕ ▥ 🖥 🕯

LEWIS Stornoway

NB4232 🍴 Crown Hotel, Caledonia Hotel, Seaforth Hotel, County Hotel

Dunroamin, 18 Plantation Road, Stornoway, Isle of Lewis, HS1 2JS.
Centrally located Victorian Town House, warm welcome assured, Hearty breakfasts.
Open: All Year
01851 704578 Mrs MacLeod
Fax: 01851 170578
D: £17.00–£20.00 **S:** £18.00–£25.00
Beds: 3F 1D 1S **Baths:** 1 En 1 Sh
❄ 📺 🕆 ✕ ▥ 🖥 🕯

NORTH UIST Carinish

NF8259 🍴 Carinish Inn, Westford Inn, Langash Lodge

8 Cnoc Cuidehein, Carinish, Lochmaddy, Isle of North Uist, HS6 5HW.
A warm welcome and good food awaits you in our comfortable home.
Open: Easter to Nov
01876 580635 Mrs MacDonald
D: £15.00–£16.00 **S:** fr £19.00
Beds: 1F 1D 1T **Baths:** 1 Pr 1 Sh
❄ (5) ⊞ (5) 📺 🕆 ▥ 🖥 🕯

National Grid References are for villages, towns and cities – not for individual houses

SOUTH UIST Garryheillie

NF7522 🍴 Borrodale Hotel, Lochboisdale Hotel

Clan Ranald, 247 Gearraidh Sheile, Garryheillie, Lochboisdale, Isle of South Uist, HS8 5SX.
Working Croft 3 miles form ferry will collect form terminal.
Open: April to end Dec
Grades: STB 3 Star
01878 700263 Mr & Mrs MacDonald
D: £23.00 **S:** £23.00
Beds: 1T 1D 1S **Baths:** 3 En
❄ ⊞ 📺 🕆 ✕ ▥ 🖥 🕯

The Shieling, 238 Gearraidh Sheile, Garryheillie, Lochboisdale, Isle of South Uist, HS8 5SX.
Modern croft house, walking and birdwatching. Situated near main road.
Open: Easter to Oct
01878 700504 Mrs Peteranna
D: £18.00–£20.00 **S:** £20.00–£25.00
Beds: 1D 2T **Baths:** 3 En 1 Sh
❄ (12) ⊞ (6) ⧖ 📺 ✕ ▥ 🖥 🕯

SOUTH UIST Lochboisdale

NF7919

Riverside, Lochboisdale, Isle of South Uist, HS8 5TN.
Riverside house on working croft near mountains and fishing lochs.
Open: Easter to Oct
01878 700250 Mrs MacLellan
anne@muir10.freeserve.co.uk
D: £14.00–£18.00 **S:** £10.00–£18.00
Beds: 1F 1T 1S **Baths:** 2 Sh
⊞ (4) ⧖ 📺 ▥ 🕯

Bayview, Lochboisdale, Isle of South Uist, HS8 5TH.
Adjacent to Lochboisdale ferry terminal and overlooking the Minch.
Open: All Year
01878 700329 Mrs MacLellan
D: £18.00–£20.00
Beds: 1D 1T **Baths:** 1 En 1 Sh
❄ ⊞ ⧖ 📺 ✕ ▥ 🖥 ❀ 🕯

Stilwell's Britain: Hostels & Camping 2001

It's a great new idea! Hostels, camping barns, bunk houses **and** camping sites all in one user-friendly book. From now on, campers, tourers, backpackers, clubs and groups – anyone looking for low-cost and group accommodation – can find the right place to sleep for the right price by consulting the right guide – **Stilwell's Britain: Hostels & Camping 2001**.

Listings in **Stilwell's Britain: Hostels & Camping 2001** are arranged geographically by country, county and location throughout England, Scotland and Wales. Each entry includes tariffs, facilities, opening times and a brief description of the premise, it's location and surroundings. Many are accompanied by a picture of the site. The average charge per person per night is £8. As wi`th all Stilwell guides, the book contains local maps, grid references and listings of Tourist Information Centres. There's air, rail, bus and ferry information, too.

Whether you're traveling alone or in a group, you can plan your trip with a minimum of fuss with **Stilwell's Britain: Hostels & Camping 2001**.

£6.95 from all good bookstores (ISBN 1-900861-20-8) or £7.95 (inc p&p) from Stilwell Publishing Ltd, 59 Charlotte Road, London EC2A 3QW (020 7739-7179)

Anglesey

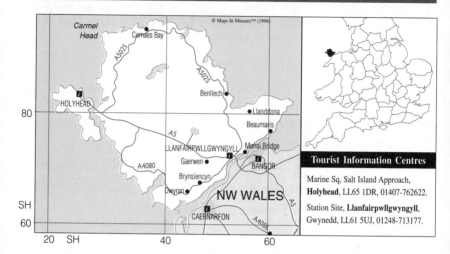

Tourist Information Centres

Marine Sq, Salt Island Approach, **Holyhead**, LL65 1DR, 01407-762622.

Station Site, **Llanfairpwllgwyngyll**, Gwynedd, LL61 5UJ, 01248-713177.

Beaumaris

SH6076 ◀ Sailors Return, Henllys Hall, Liverpool Arms, Tavern Rhyd

Mor Awel, Beaumaris, Anglesey, LL58 8NP. Victorian house, village rural location, nice walks, off road parking, evening meal. Licensed. **Open:** All Year (not Xmas) **Grades:** WTB 3 Star
01248 490930
Mr Thomas
Fax: 01248 490826 mor-awel@zetnet.co.uk
D: £20.00 **S:** £30.00
Beds: 2D 1T 1S **Baths:** 1 En 2 Sh
⌂ 🅿 (4) ⅙ 📺 🐕 🏢

Benllech

SH5182 ◀ Bay Court Hotel, Ship

Bay Court Hotel, Beach Road, Benllech, Tyn-y-Gongl, Anglesey, LL74 8SW. 200 yds from sandy beach. Nearby riding, golf, fishing. Handy Snowdonia National Park, ferries. **Open:** All Year
Grades: WTB 2 Star, AA 3 Diamond, RAC 3 Diamond
01248 852573 Mr Threfall
Fax: 01248 852606
D: £23.00–£28.00 **S:** £23.00–£28.00
Beds: 4F 10D 3T 5S **Baths:** 10 En 3 Sh
⌂ 🅿 (50) 📺 🐕 ✗ 🏢 🆅 ⚓ cc

Golden Sands Hotel, Benllech, Tyn-y-Gongl, Anglesey, LL74 8SP. Modern, overlooking beach.
Open: All Year
01248 852384 Mrs Littlemore
D: £18.50–£25.00 **S:** £20.00–£30.00
Beds: 4F 4D 2T 1S **Baths:** 11 Pr
⌂ 🅿 ⅙ 📺 🐕 ✗ 🏢 🆅 ❋ ⚓ 🐾 1

Brynsiencyn

SH4867 ◀ Penrhos Arms

Fron Guest House, Brynsiencyn, Llanfairpwllgwyngyll, Anglesey, LL61 6TX. Traditional high class accommodation with magnificent views of Snowdonia.
Open: Easter to Sept 30
Grades: WTB 3 Star
01248 430310 (also fax)
Mr Geldard
D: £16.00–£17.50 **S:** £16.50–£18.00
Beds: 3D **Baths:** 1 En 1 Sh
🅿 (4) ⅙ 📺 🏢 🆅 ⚓

Cemaes Bay

SH3694 ◀ Stag Inn

Woburn Hill Hotel, High Street, Cemaes Bay, Anglesey, LL67 0HU. Homely hotel in old fishing village serving local seafood dishes. Bar/Rest Menus.
Open: All Year
Grades: WTB 2 Star
01407 711388 Mrs Potter
Fax: 01407 711190
woburnhill@hushmail.com
D: £22.50–£25.00 **S:** £30.00–£40.00
Beds: 5D 2T 1S **Baths:** 5 En 1 Sh
🅿 (10) 📺 🏢 🆅 ❋ ⚓

RATES

D = Price range per person sharing in a double room

S = Price range for a single room

Many rates vary according to season – the lowest are shown here

Dwyran

SH4466

Tal-y-Foel, Dwyran, Llanfairpwllgwyngyll, LL61 6LQ.
Open: All Year (not Xmas/New Year)
Grades: WTB 4 Star
01248 430377 Fax: 01248 430977
hutchings@talyfoel.u-net.com
D: £25.00 **S:** £25.00–£30.00
Beds: 2F 2T **Baths:** 4 En
⌂ 🅿 📺 🐕 🏢 🆅 ⚓ & cc
Isle of Anglesey, spectacular waterfront location overlooking Snowdonia. Wales Tourist Board 4 star farm B&B, Taste of Wales and Welcome Host awards, en-suite bedrooms, some whirlpool baths. Many facilities, birdwatching, walking, fishing. Friendly BHS Riding Centre, horse livery, riding courses.

Gaerwen

SH4771 ◀ Penrhos Arms, Sailors Return

Benlas, Llandaniel, Gaerwen, Anglesey, LL60 6HB.
Pretty cottage, quiet country road, superb views to Snowdonia.
Open: Easter to Oct
01248 421543 Mrs Taylor
D: £18.00–£20.00 **S:** £20.00
Beds: 2D **Baths:** 1 Sh
⌂ 🅿 (3) ⅙ 🐕 🏢 ⚓

Holyhead

SH2482 ◀ *Valley Hotel, Boat House, Kings Arms, Crown*

Wavecrest, *93 Newry Road, Holyhead, Anglesey, LL65 1HU.*
Ideal ferry stopover for Ireland; close to the South Stack.
Open: All Year (not Xmas)
Grades: WTB 3 Star, AA 3 Diamond
01407 763637 Mr Hiltunen
Fax: 01407 764862 cwavecrest@aol.com
D: £16.00–£20.00 **S:** £18.00–£20.00
Beds: 3F 1D 1S **Baths:** 2 En 1 Pr 1 Sh
🛏 🅿 (4) 🗱 📺 🦮 ✕ 🎩 Ⓥ ♨

Bryn Awel, *Edmund Street, Holyhead, Anglesey, LL65 1SA.*
Victorian house. 10 minutes town, 10 minutes ferries. Home cooking.
Open: All Year **Grades:** WTB 2 Star
01407 762948 Mrs Jones
D: £15.50–£16.00 **S:** £18.00–£20.00
Beds: 1F 1D 1T 1S
🛏 🅿 (6) 📺 🦮 ✕ 🎩 ♨

Monravon Guest House, *Port-y-felin Road, Holyhead, Anglesey, LL65 1PL.*
Family-run B&B, 3 minutes to ferry/train terminals. Adjacent to park & beach.
Open: All Year (not Xmas)
Grades: WTB 3 Star GH
01407 762944 (also fax)
len@monravon.co.uk
D: £15.00–£18.50
Beds: 3F 3D 3T **Baths:** 9 En
🅿 🗱 📺 🎩 ♨ & cc

Hendre, *Porth y Felin Road, Holyhead, Anglesey, LL65 1AH.*
Large detached house in its own grounds facing park. All rooms individually designed. **Open:** All Year
01407 762929 (also fax)
rita@yr-hendre.freeserve.co.uk
D: £20.00–£22.50 **S:** £25.00–£30.00
Beds: 2D 1T **Baths:** 3 En
🛏 🅿 (6) 🗱 📺 🦮 ✕ 🎩 ♨

Roselea, *26 Holborn Road, Holyhead, Anglesey, LL65 2AT.*
Homely family-run B&B - warm welcome guaranteed to our visitors. 2 mins from ferries.
Open: All Year (not Xmas)
01407 764391 (also fax)
Mrs Foxley
D: £16.00–£20.00 **S:** fr £20.00
Beds: 1D 1T **Baths:** 1 Sh
🛏 🗱 📺 🎩 Ⓥ ♨

Tasma, *31 Walthew Avenue, Holyhead, Anglesey, LL65 1AG.*
Comfortable accommodation. Conveniently situated for ferries, railway, beaches and shops.
Open: All Year (not Xmas)
01407 762291 Mrs Jones
tasma_99@yahoo.com
D: £17.00 **S:** £20.00–£17.00
Beds: 2F **Baths:** 2 Sh
🛏 🅿 (1) 🗱 📺 ✕ 🎩 Ⓥ ♨

Llanddona

SH5779 ◀ *Bulls Head*

Tyn Pistyll, *Beach Road, Llanddona, Beaumaris, Anglesey, LL58 8UN.*
A beautiful quiet country residence with rooms overlooking the sea.
Open: Easter to Oct
01248 811224 (also fax)
Mrs Peacock
hpea200@aol.com
D: £24.00–£25.00 **S:** £26.00–£27.00
Beds: 1F 1D 1S **Baths:** 1 En 1 Pr
🛏 (5) 🅿 (4) 🗱 📺 🦮 🎩 Ⓥ ♨

BATHROOMS

Pr - Private

Sh - Shared

En - Ensuite

Maenaddwyn

SH4584 ◀ *Water Edge*

Tre-Wyn, *Maenaddwyn, Llangefni, LL71 8AE.*
A warm welcome. Comfortable accommodation and central to Anglesey's attractions.
Open: All Year (not Xmas/New Year)
Grades: WTB 4 Star, AA 4 Diamond
01248 470874 Ms Brown
Fax: 01248 470875
nia@trewyn.fsnet.co.uk
D: £20.00–£22.50 **S:** £25.00–£27.00
Beds: 1F 2T **Baths:** 3 En
🛏 🗱 📺 🎩 Ⓥ ♨

Menai Bridge

SH5572 ◀ *Penrhos Arms*

Wern Farm Guest House, *Pentraeth Road, Menai Bridge, Anglesey, LL59 5RR.*
Great hospitality. Hearty breakfasts and everything you could possibly need for a relaxing holiday.
Open: Feb to Nov
01248 712421 (also fax)
Mr & Mrs Brayshaw
brayshaw_wernfarm@compuserve.com
D: £21.00–£27.00 **S:** £25.00–£50.00
Beds: 2F 1T **Baths:** 1 En 1 Sh
🛏 🅿 🗱 📺 🎩 Ⓥ ♨

Valley

SH2979

Valley Hotel, *London Road, Valley, Holyhead, LL65 3DU.*
Superior ensuite accommodation and pub situated 4 miles from ferry.
Open: All Year
Grades: RAC 3 Diamond
01407 740203 K Snape
Fax: 01407 740686
valleyhotel@tinyworld.co
D: £25.00–£49.50 **S:** £37.50
Beds: 2F 9T 4D 5S **Baths:** 18 En 1 Sh
🛏 🅿 (40) 📺 🦮 ✕ 🎩 Ⓥ ♨ cc

Carmarthenshire

Tourist Information Centres

Lammas Street, **Carmarthen**, Dyfed, SA31 3AQ, 01267-231557.

Central Car Park, Broad Street, **Llandovery**, Dyfed, SA20 0AR, 01550-720693, (Easter to Oct).

Public Library, Vaughn St, **Llannelli**, SA15 3AS, 01554 772020

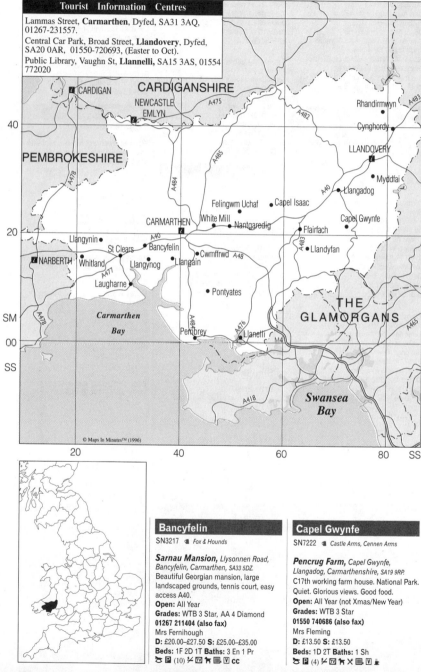

© Maps In Minutes™ (1996)

Bancyfelin

SN3217   Fox & Hounds

Sarnau Mansion, Llysonnen Road, Bancyfelin, Carmarthen, SA33 5DZ. Beautiful Georgian mansion, large landscaped grounds, tennis court, easy access A40.
Open: All Year
Grades: WTB 3 Star, AA 4 Diamond
01267 211404 (also fax)
Mrs Fernihough
D: £20.00–£27.50 **S:** £25.00–£35.00
Beds: 1F 2D 1T **Baths:** 3 En 1 Pr
🌣 🄿 (10) ⚡ 📺 🖤 🛏 ▦ Ⅴ cc

Capel Gwynfe

SN7222   Castle Arms, Cennen Arms

Pencrug Farm, Capel Gwynfe, Llangadog, Carmarthenshire, SA19 9RP. C17th working farm house. National Park. Quiet. Glorious views. Good food.
Open: All Year (not Xmas/New Year)
Grades: WTB 3 Star
01550 740686 (also fax)
Mrs Fleming
D: £13.50 **S:** £13.50
Beds: 1D 2T **Baths:** 1 Sh
🌣 🄿 (4) ⚡ 📺 🛏 ✕ ▦ Ⅴ ♨

Capel Isaac

SN5827   *Nag's Head, Cottage Inn*

The Manse, *Capel Isaac, Llandeilo, SA19 7TN.*
Peaceful organic farm, beautiful area, many attractions, castles, Aberglasney's historic gardens.
Open: All Year
Grades: WTB 2 Star
01558 668873 (also fax)
Mr & Mrs Smith
D: £16.00 **S:** £16.00
Beds: 1D 1T 1S **Baths:** 2 Pr 1 Sh
🅿 (6) ⅙ 📺 ✕ 🛏 💷 🖤 &

Carmarthen

SN4120   *Drovers Arms, Fox & Hounds, White Mill, Hamiltons, Branneys*

Meiros Hall Guest House, *2 Waterloo Terrace, Carmarthen, SA31 1DG.*
Open: All Year (not Xmas/New Year)
01267 222708 J D C Lewis
D: £17.00 **S:** £17.00
Beds: 1F 1T 1D 1S **Baths:** 1 Sh
🅱 ⅙ 📺 🛏 💷 🖤 &
Homely guest house minutes walk from the centre of quaint market county town of Carmarthen. Ideally located for sandy beaches and coves and Wales' National Parks. Ideal stopover for Irish Channel crossing. Tastefully decorated rooms with vanity units. Traditional cooked breakfast.

Plas Farm, *Llangynog, Carmarthenshire, SA33 5DB.*
Working farm. Spacious farmhouse. Quiet location. Ideal touring base.
Open: All Year
Grades: WTB 3 Star Farm
01267 211492 (also fax)
Mrs Thomas
D: £18.00–£20.00 **S:** £20.00–£25.00
Beds: 1F 1D 1T **Baths:** 2 En 1 Pr
🅱 🅿 (4) ⅙ 📺 🛏 💷 & & 3

Sarnau Mansion, *Llysonnen Road, Bancyfelin, Carmarthen, SA33 5DZ.*
Beautiful Georgian mansion, large landscaped grounds, tennis court, easy access A40.
Open: All Year
Grades: WTB 3 Star, AA 4 Diamond
01267 211404 (also fax)
Mrs Fernihough
D: £20.00–£27.50 **S:** £25.00–£35.00
Beds: 1F 2D 1T **Baths:** 3 En 1 Pr
🅱 🅿 (10) ⅙ 📺 🛏 💷 🖤 cc

Y Dderwen Fach, *98 Priory Street, Carmarthen, SA31 1NB.*
C17th town house of character. Convenient for shops, beaches, countryside.
Open: All Year (not Xmas)
Grades: WTB 2 Star GH
01267 234193 Mr & Mrs Bowyer
Fax: 01267 235766
D: £15.00–£17.50 **S:** £15.00–£21.50
Beds: 1D 1T 2S **Baths:** 2 En 1 Sh
🅱 (5) 📺 ✕ 💷 🖤 &

53 Parcmaen Street, *Carmarthen, SA31 3DR.*
Terraced house, walking distance town centre, bus/train stations, parking.
Open: All Year
Grades: WTB 1 Star
01267 238260 Mrs Jones
D: £14.00–£15.00 **S:** £15.00
Beds: 1D 1T
🅱 ⅙ 📺 💷 🖤 &

Trebersed Farmhouse, *Travellers Rest, St Peters, Carmarthen, SA31 3RR.*
Relax in peaceful countryside staying on friendly working dairy farm.
Open: All Year (not Xmas)
Grades: WTB 3 Star Farm
01267 238182 Mrs Jones
Fax: 01267 223633
trebersed.farm@farmline.com
D: £20.00 **S:** £25.00
Beds: 1F 1D 1T **Baths:** 3 En
🅱 🅿 (6) ⅙ 📺 🛏 💷 & cc

Cwmffrwd

SN4217   *Black Lion*

Llety'r Haul, *Bolahaul Road, Cwmffrwd, Carmarthen, SA31 2LW.*
Dormer bungalow on farm with lawned area, 1 mile off A484 on Bolahaul Road.
Open: All Year
01267 235493 Mr & Mrs Lewis
D: £15.00–£20.00 **S:** £20.00
Beds: 1F 1D 1T **Baths:** 3 En
🅱 🅿 (6) 📺 🛏 💷 &

Cynghordy

SN8040

Llanerchindda Farm, *Cynghordy, Llandovery, Carmarthenshire, SA20 0NB.*
Very comfortable farmhouse; views high over Towy Valley & Brecons. Log fires, underfloor heating, library.
Open: All Year (not Xmas)
01550 750274 Mr Bointon
Fax: 01550 750300
nick@cambrianway.com
D: £24.00 **S:** £24.00
Beds: 2F 4D 2T 1S **Baths:** 9 En
🅱 (14) 📺 🛏 ✕ 💷 🖤 & 2

Felingwm

SN5124   *Plough Inn*

Dolau Guest House, *Felingwm Isaf, Nantgaredig, Carmarthen, SA32 7PB.*
Attractive rural riverside location. Luxury accommodation, near botanic gardens.
Open: All Year **Grades:** WTB 4 Star GH
01267 290464 Mr Bright
dolau_felingwmisaf@yahoo.co.uk
D: £18.00–£25.00 **S:** £21.00–£25.00
Beds: 1F 1D 1T **Baths:** 2 En 1 Pr
🅱 🅿 (6) ⅙ 📺 ✕ 💷 🖤 &

Alltygolau Uchaf, *Felingwm, Carmarthen, SA32 7BB.*
A peaceful, tranquil garden of 2 acres surrounds this Georgian stone-walled farmhouse.
Open: All Year (not Xmas/New Year)
01267 290455 Dr Rouse
D: £17.50–£25.00 **S:** £17.50–£27.00
Beds: 2D 1T **Baths:** 1 En 2 Pr 1 Sh
🅱 🅿 (3) ⅙ 📺 🛏 💷 🖤 & 3

Ffairfach

SN6221   *Torbay Inn*

Tycefn Tregib, *Ffairfach, Llandeilo, Carmarthenshire, SA19 6TD.*
Converted barn, comfortable roms, peaceful wooded grounds, village, station, nearby.
Open: All Year
01558 823942 Mrs Evans
D: £19.00 **S:** £19.00–£25.00
Beds: 1F 1D 1T **Baths:** 2 En 1 Pr
🅱 🅿 (6) ⅙ 📺 💷 🖤 &

Laugharne

SN3010   *Under Milk Wood, Portreeve*

Swan Cottage, *20 Gosport St, Laugharne, Carmarthen, SA33 4SZ.*
Open: All Year
Grades: WTB 3 Star B&B
01994 427409 Mrs Brown
rob.erts@talk21.com
D: £18.00–£20.00 **S:** £18.00–£25.00
Beds: 1D **Baths:** 1 En
🅱 🅿 (1) ⅙ 📺 💷 🖤 ✳ &
Lovely stone cottage, one room only on ground floor, guaranteeing personal attention and excellent breakfasts. Tranquil landscaped garden offering views of castle, estuary & Dylan's Boat House with many local walks connecting with Pembrokeshire coastal path. Parking adjacent to cottage.

Castle House, *Market Lane, Laugharne, Carmarthen, SA33 4SA.*
Beautiful Georgian house with gardens overlooking the estuary and castle.
Open: All Year
01994 427616 Mrs Mitchell
charles@laugharne.co.uk
D: £25.00–£35.00 **S:** £30.00–£35.00
Beds: 1F 2D **Baths:** 2 En 1 Pr
🅱 🅿 (3) 📺 🖤 &

Llanboidy

SN2123   *Sporting Chance*

Castell Pigyn Farm, *Llanboidy, Whitland, Carmarthenshire, SA34 0LJ.*
Situated on a peaceful hilltop with fabulous views in all directions.
Open: Easter to Oct
Grades: WTB 3 Star
01994 448391 Mrs Davies
Fax: 01994 448755
D: £22.00 **S:** £27.00
Beds: 1F 1D 1T **Baths:** 2 En 1 Pr
🅱 🅿 📺 ✕ 💷 🖤 &

Llanddowror

SN2514   *The Rectory*

West Wood House, *Llanddowror, Carmarthen, SA33 4HL.*
Village not isolated, near Carmarthen, en-route Irish Ferries & Tenby.
Open: All Year
Grades: WTB 3 Star
01994 230512 (also fax)
Mrs Davies
D: £18.00–£20.00 **S:** £20.00–£25.00
Beds: 2D 1S **Baths:** 1 En 1 Sh
🅱 🅿 (4) ⅙ 📺 💷 🖤 &

Llandovery

SN7634 🍺 *King's Head, Castle, Drovers, Blue Bell, Lord Rhys*

Cwm Rhuddan Mansion, *Llandovery, Carmarthenshire, SA20 0DX.*
Open: All Year
Grades: WTB 4 Star
01550 721414 Mrs Wheadon
D: £25.00–£30.00 **S:** fr £30.00
Beds: 2F 1D **Baths:** 3 En
🛏 🅿 (10) 📺 🍴 🛏 💷 Ⅴ ♨
A unique French chateau-style mansion with original features, antique furnishings. Landscaped gardens with panoramic view of Towey Valley and Black Mountains. Relax in the elegant period lounge and large character bedrooms with open fires, garaging for special vehicles plus new large recreational room.

Llwyncelyn Guest House,
Llandovery, Carmarthenshire, SA20 0EP.
Charming stone-built house. Edge of town. Railway station 5 mins.
Open: All Year (not Xmas)
Grades: WTB 2 Star, AA 3 Diamond
01550 720566 Mr Griffiths
D: £18.50 **S:** £21.00–£25.00
Beds: 2D 2T 1S **Baths:** 2 Sh
🅿 (12) 📺 💷 ♨

Pencerrig, *New Road, Llandovery, SA20 0EA.*
Open: All Year
Grades: WTB 2 Star
01550 721259 **D:** £19.00 **S:** £19.00
Beds: 1D 1T 1S **Baths:** 2 En 1 Pr
🅿 (1) ⅚ 📺 💷 Ⅴ ♨
A Victorian house situated at the edge of town. Local shops, pubs, restaurants are 5 minutes walk away. Railway station nearby. The immediate area has plenty of walks to offer and birdwatching (the famous red kite).

Llandyfan

SN6417 🍺 *Cennen Arms*

Bryncoch Farm, *Llandyfan, Ammanford, SA18 2TY.*
Beautiful 200-year-old farmhouse overlooking Amman valley. Large gardens - farm not worked anymore.
Open: All Year
01269 850480 Fax: 01269 850888
bryncoch@tesco.net
D: £15.00–£18.00 **S:** £18.00–£20.00
Beds: 1F 1D 1T **Baths:** 3 En
🛏 🅿 (20) ⅚ 📺 🍴 💷 Ⅴ ♨

Llanelli

SN5000 🍺 *Greenfield Inn*

Southmead Guest House, *72 Queen Victoria Road, Llanelli, SA15 2TH.*
Southmead Guest house, ensuite rooms, car park, town centre.
Open: All Year (not Xmas)
Grades: WTB 2 Star, RAC 2 Diamond
01554 758588 R Fouracre
D: £15.00–£20.00 **S:** £15.00–£20.00
Beds: 1F 2D 2T 2S **Baths:** 4 En 2 Sh

Awel-Y-Mor, *86 Queen Victoria Road, Llanelli, SA15 2TH.*
Friendly-run, modern, well suited in Llanelli town centre.
Open: All Year
Grades: WTB 1 Star
01554 755357 (also fax)
Mr Hughes
D: £15.00–£17.50
S: £18.00–£20.00
Beds: 13F 7D 3T 3S **Baths:** 8 En 8 Pr 5 Sh
🛏 🅿 (12) 📺 🍴 ✕ 💷 ♨ 🕭

Llangadog

SN7028 🍺 *Castle Hotel*

Cynyll Farm, *Llangadog, Carmarthenshire, SA19 9BB.*
Comfortable C17th farmhouse. Excellent home cooking. Overlooks Black Mountains.
Open: All Year (not Xmas/New Year)
Grades: WTB 2 Star
01550 777316 (also fax)
Mrs Dare
D: £17.00 **S:** £17.00
Beds: 1F 1D **Baths:** 1 En 1 Pr
🛏 🅿 📺 ✕ Ⅴ ♨

Llangain

SN3815 🍺 *Tafarn Pantydderwen*

Brynderwen, *School Lane, Llangain, Carmarthen, SA33 5AE.*
Family-run B&B, quiet village setting. Comfortable rooms, convenient coast, countryside & Irish ferries.
Open: All Year (not Xmas)
Grades: WTB 3 Star
01267 241403 M Davies
D: £20.00–£24.00 **S:** £18.00–£24.00
Beds: 1D 1T 1S **Baths:** 2 En 1 Sh
🛏 🅿 (4) ⅚ 📺 💷 ♨

Llangynin

SN2519

Coedllys Uchaf, *Llangynin, Carmarthen, Carmarthenshire, SA33 4JY.*
Nestling in a beautiful valley. Our rooms are large, beautifully furnished and very comfortable.
Open: All Year (not Xmas)
01994 231455 Fax: 01994 231441
D: £25.00–£30.00
Beds: 1F 2D **Baths:** 1 En 1 Pr
🅿 (10) ⅚ 📺 🍴 ✕ ♨

Llangynog

SN3316 🍺 *Fox & Hounds*

Plas Farm, *Llangynog, Carmarthenshire, SA33 5DB.*
Working farm. Spacious farmhouse. Quiet location. Ideal touring base.
Open: All Year
Grades: WTB 3 Star Farm
01267 211492 (also fax)
Mrs Thomas
D: £18.00–£20.00 **S:** £20.00–£25.00
Beds: 1F 1D 1T **Baths:** 2 En 1 Pr
🛏 🅿 (4) ⅚ 📺 🍴 💷 ♨ 🕭 3

Myddfai

SN7730 🍺 *Plough Inn*

Erwlas, *Myddfai, Llandovery, Carmarthenshire, SA20 0JB.*
Modern, comfortable bungalow, quiet location, magnificent countryside. Ideal walking area.
Open: All Year (not Xmas)
01550 720797 Mrs Holloway
D: £13.50 **S:** £13.50
Beds: 1D 1T **Baths:** 1 Sh
🛏 🅿 (3) ⅚ 📺 🍴 ✕ 💷 Ⅴ

Nantgaredig

SN4921

Cothi Bridge Hotel, *Nantgaredig, Carmarthen, SA32 7NG.*
Overlooking River Cothi, centrally located for touring, en route to Ireland.
Open: All Year
01267 290251 Mrs Jones
Fax: 01267 290156
cothibridgehotel@compuserve.com
D: £25.00–£29.50 **S:** fr £35.00
Beds: 1F 6D 3T 2S **Baths:** 1 En 1 Pr
🛏 🅿 (30) ⅚ 📺 🍴 ✕ 💷 Ⅴ ♨ 🕭 cc

Newcastle Emlyn

SN3040 🍺 *White Hart*

Maes Y Derw Guest House,
Newcastle Emlyn, Carmarthenshire, SA38 9RD.
Delightful Edwardian house set in mature grounds overlooking the river Teifi.
Open: All Year
01239 710860 (also fax)
Mrs Davies
D: £18.00–£20.00 **S:** £25.00–£30.00
Beds: 1F 1D 1T **Baths:** 1 En 2 Pr
🛏 🅿 (8) 📺 🍴 ✕ 💷 Ⅴ ♨ cc

Pembrey

SN4201 🍺 *Ship Aground*

Four Seasons Guest House, *62 Gwscwm Road, Pembrey, Burry Port, Dyfed, SA16 0YU.*
A friendly guest house with ground floor accommodation available.
Open: All Year
Grades: WTB 3 Star
01554 833367 (also fax)
D: £18.00–£20.00 **S:** £22.00–£27.00
Beds: 1F 3T 1D **Baths:** 2 En 1 Sh
🛏 🅿 (10) ⅚ 📺 💷 ♨

Pontyates

SN4708 🍺 *Prince Of Wales, Square & Compass*

Glynfach Farm, *Pontyates, Llanelli, SA15 5TG.*
Warm welcome to our organic small holding. Creative breakfasts, coast and country.
Open: All Year (not Xmas)
Grades: WTB 3 Star
01269 861290 (also fax)
J Pearce
D: £18.00 **S:** £18.00
Beds: 1D 2T **Baths:** 1 Pr
🛏 🅿 ⅚ 📺 🍴 💷 Ⅴ ♨

Rhandirmwyn

SN7843

Bwlch-Y-Ffin, *Rhandirmwyn,*
Llandovery, Carmarthenshire, SA20 0PG.
Comfortable farmhouse with incredible
views across a tranquil wooded valley.
Open: All Year (not Xmas)
01550 760311 (also fax)
Mr & Mrs Williams
bppaw@aol.com
D: £16.50 **S:** fr £16.50
Beds: 1D 2T **Baths:** 1 Sh
ⓢ 🅿 ⼳ 🐈 ✕ 🖳 Ⓥ ♨

St Clears

SN2716 ◁ *White Lion*

Glascoed, *St Clears, Carmarthen,*
SA33 4AY.
Georgian farmhouse, spacious
comfortable rooms convenient for Ireland
ferry crossings.
Open: Easter to Oct
01994 231260
Mrs Griffiths
D: £18.00 **S:** £20.00
Beds: 1F 1D **Baths:** 1 Pr 1 Sh
ⓢ 🅿 (4) 📺 🖳 ♨

White Mill

SN4621 ◁ *White Mill*

Penrhiw Farm Guest House, *White*
Mill, Carmarthen, SA32 7ET.
Open: All Year **Grades:** WTB 2 Star
01267 290260 Mrs Jones
D: £20.00 **S:** £25.00
Beds: 2D **Baths:** 1 En 1 Pr
ⓢ 🅿 (10) 📺 🖳 ♨
Situated 1/4 mile off the A40 at Whitemill.
3 miles from Carmarthen. Peaceful
surroundings overlooking the Towy Valley
and surrounded by rolling hills. Ideally
situated for National Botanic Garden of
Wales, Aberglasney and touring West
Wales.

Whitland

SN2016 ◁ *Blue Boar*

Fforest Farm, *Whitland,*
Carmarthenshire, SA34 0LS.
Farm set in Taf Valley near coast.
Beautiful walks, fishing available
Open: All Year (not Xmas/New Year)
01994 240066 Mrs Windsor
D: £18.00 **S:** £18.00
Beds: 2F **Baths:** 2 En
🅿 ⼳ 📺 🖳

Ceredigion

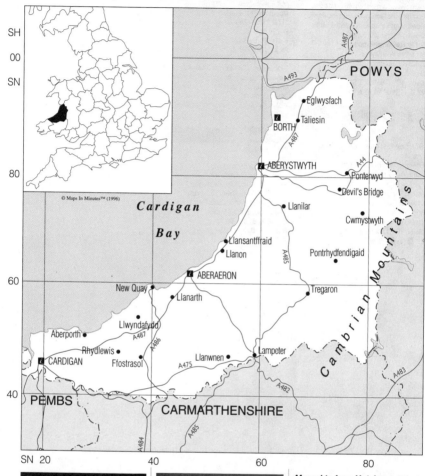

Tourist Information Centres

The Quay, **Aberaeron**, SA46 OBT,
01545 570602

Terrace Road, **Aberystwyth**,
SY23 2AG, 01970-612125.

High St, **Borth**, SY24 5HY,
01970-871174, (Easter to Oct).

Theatr Mwldan, Bath House Road,
Cardigan, SA43 2JY,
01239-613230.

Church St **New Quay**, SA45 9NZ,
01545-560865,
(Easter to Oct).

Market Hall, **Newcastle Emlyn**,
SA38 9AE,
01239-711333, (Easter to Oct).

The Square, **Tregaron**, SY25 6JN
01974 298248

Aberaeron

SN4562   🍺 *Harbourmaster Hotel, Royal Oak,
Prince Of Wales*

Arosfa, *Harbourside, Aberaeron,
Ceredigion, SA46 0BU.*
Harbourside. Superb Welsh breakfast
with highest AA Grade for 2001.
Open: All Year
Grades: WTB 3 Star, AA 4 Diamond
01545 570120 Mr Griffiths
arosfabandb@aol.com
D: £18.00–£25.00 **S:** £20.00–£30.00
Beds: 1F 2D 1T **Baths:** 4 En 1 Pr
🐾 (6) ▣ (4) ⌿ 📺 ▥ ♥ ▣ �&

Planning a longer stay? Always
ask for any special rates

Monachty Arms Hotel, *Market Street,
Aberaeron, Ceredigion, SA46 0AS.*
Centrally situated friendly family-run
hotel.
Open: All Year
01545 570389 Mr Howells
Fax: 01545 570596
D: £19.00–£22.00 **S:** £24.00–£28.00
Beds: 3F 3D 2S **Baths:** 5 En
🐾 ▣ (4) 📺 ⚲ ▥ ♨ ᴄᴄ

Llys Aeron Guest House, *Lampeter
Road, Aberaeron, Ceredigion, SA46 0ED.*
Enjoy the gracious rooms of this
impressive Georgian house.
Open: All Year
01545 570276 Mrs Mace
simon@mace115.freeserve.co.uk
D: £25.00 **S:** £25.00–£35.00
Beds: 1D 2T **Baths:** 3 En
🐾 ▣ (8) ⌿ 📺 ⚲ ▥ ▣ ♨

Hazeldene Guest House, *South Road, Aberaeron, SA46 0DP.*
Jackie and John Lewis offer you a warm, distinctively Welsh welcome to Hazeldene.
Open: Easter to Oct
01545 570652 Fax: 01545 571012
hazeldeneaberaeron@tesco.net
D: £19.00–£25.00 **S:** £22.00–£28.00
Beds: 2D 1T **Baths:** 3 En
🅿 (5) ⏏ 📺 ✕ 🖬 Ⓥ ⬤ CC

Aberporth
SN2651

Highcliffe Hotel, *School Road, Aberporth, Cardigan, SA43 2DA.*
Unspoilt sandy coves, bar, restaurant, waterfalls, dolphins. Kids/pets welcome.
Open: All Year
Grades: WTB 2 Star, AA 2 Star
01239 810534 (also fax)
Mr Conway
D: £24.75–£28.90 **S:** £32.40–£37.80
Beds: 4F 6D 4T 1S **Baths:** 14 En 1 Sh
⛵ 🅿 (18) 📺 ✕ 🖬 Ⓥ ❈ ⬤ CC

Aberystwyth
SN5881 ⬤ *Rhydypennau Inn, Welsh Black*

Garreg Lwyd Guest House, *Bow Street, Aberystwyth, Ceredigion, SY24 5BE.*
On A487. Private parking. Excellent breakfast. Television lounge. Tea & coffee facilities, snacks available.
Open: All Year (not Xmas)
Grades: WTB 2 Star
01970 828830 Mrs Edwards
D: £16.50–£19.00 **S:** £18.00–£20.00
Beds: 1F 2D 1T 1S **Baths:** 2 Sh
⛵ 🅿 (6) 📺 ✕ 🖬 Ⓥ ⬤

Marine Hotel, *Marine Terrace, Aberystwyth, Cardiganshire, SY23 2BX.*
Idyllic countryside setting new luxury guest house. Set in peaceful surroundings.
Open: Jan to Dec
Grades: WTB 3 Star, AA 4 Diamond
08000 190020 Mrs Evans
Fax: 01970 617435
D: £20.00–£35.00 **S:** £25.00–£35.00
Beds: 7F 14D 13T 5S **Baths:** 10 En
⛵ (1) 🅿 (12) 📺 ✕ 🖬 Ⓥ ❈ ⬤ & CC

Talbot Hotel, *Market Street, Aberystwyth, Ceredigion, SY23 1DL.*
Newly refurbished hotel, town centre location, conference room. Close to sea front. **Open:** All Year
01970 612575 E T Davies
Fax: 01970 412575
D: £18.00–£30.00 **S:** £25.00–£30.00
Beds: 5F 8T 5D **Baths:** 18 En
⛵ 📺 ✕ 🖬 ❈ CC

Yr Hafod, *1 South Marine Terrace, Aberystwyth, Ceredigion, SY23 1JX.*
'An excellent little bed and breakfast' - Lonely Planet guide to Britain.
Open: All Year (not Xmas/New Year)
Grades: WTB 3 Star, AA 4 Diamond
01970 617579 Mr Evans
Fax: 01970 636835
D: £20.00–£25.00 **S:** £20.00–£45.00
Beds: 4D 1T 2S **Baths:** 3 En 2 Sh
⛵ 🅿 (1) ⏏ 📺 🖬 Ⓥ ⬤

Sinclair Guest House, *43 Portland Street, Aberystwyth, Ceredigion, SY23 2DX.*
Immaculate relaxing accommodation with complementary standard of service, centrally situated.
Open: All Year (not Xmas)
01970 615158 (also fax)
Mr & Mrs Ward
D: £22.50–£24.00 **S:** £30.00
Beds: 1D 2T **Baths:** 3 En
⏏ 📺 🖬 Ⓥ ⬤

Borth
SN6089 ⬤ *Hafren Railway Hotel, Victorian Inn*

Glanmor Hotel, *High Street, Borth, Ceredigion, SY24 5JP.*
Small friendly seaside hotel close to golf course.
Open: All Year
Grades: WTB 1 Star
01970 871689 Mr Elliot
D: £21.00 **S:** £21.00
Beds: 3F 2D 1T 1S **Baths:** 2 En 2 Sh
⛵ 🅿 (6) 📺 ✕ 🖬 Ⓥ ⬤

Maesteg Guest House, *High Street, Borth, Ceredigion, SY24 5JP.*
Comfortable, friendly sea front B&B - 2 minutes to village. Aberystwyth 7 miles.
Open: Easter to Oct
01970 871928 Mrs Fiorentino
D: £16.00–£18.00 **S:** fr £16.00
Beds: 1F 1D 1T 1S **Baths:** 1 Sh
⛵ ⏏ 📺 🖬 Ⓥ ⬤

Cardigan
SN1746 ⬤ *Eagle, Ship*

Brynhyfryd Guest House, *Gwbert Road, Cardigan, SA43 1AE.*
2 miles Cardigan Bay; 6 minutes walk to town centre.
Open: All Year
Grades: WTB 3 Star, AA 3 Diamond, RAC 3 Diamond
01239 612861 (also fax)
Mrs Arcus
g.arcus@btinternet.com
D: £18.00–£20.00 **S:** £18.00–£25.00
Beds: 1F 3D 1T 2S **Baths:** 3 En 2 Pr
⛵ (5) ⏏ ✕ 🖬 Ⓥ ⬤

Maes-A-Mor, *Park Place, Gwbert Road, Cardigan, SA43 1AE.*
Centrally situated opposite the park. Ideal for coast and central Wales.
Open: All Year
01239 614929 (also fax)
Mr Jones
maesamor@jejones.demon.co.uk
D: £16.00–£18.00 **S:** fr £18.00
Beds: 1D 2T **Baths:** 3 En
⛵ (8) 🅿 (3) ⏏ 📺 🖬 ⬤

Plas Y Wern, *Tanygroes, Cardigan, SA43 2JP.*
Peaceful country farm house with beautiful sea views over Cardigan Bay.
Open: All Year (not Xmas)
01239 811506 (also fax)
Mrs Morgan
D: £17.00–£18.00 **S:** £20.00–£22.00
Beds: 1D 1T **Baths:** 2 En
🅿 ⏏ 📺 ✕ 🖬 Ⓥ ⬤

Cwmystwyth
SN7874 ⬤ *Miners' Arms*

Tainewyddion Uchaf, *Cwmystwyth, Aberystwyth, Ceredigion, SY23 4AF.*
Situated at over 1000 ft. Panoramic views overlooking the Ystwyth Valley.
Open: Easter to End Oct
01974 282672 Mrs Liford
D: £15.00–£18.00 **S:** £15.00–£18.00
Beds: 1T 1D 1S **Baths:** 1 En 1 Sh
⏏ ✕ 🖬 Ⓥ

Hafod Lodge, *Cwmystwyth, Aberystwyth, Ceredigion, SY23 4AD.*
Picturesque, peaceful location, ideal for touring river valleys, lakes, mountains and coast.
Open: All Year
01974 282247 Mr & Mrs Davis
D: £18.50–£24.00 **S:** £18.50–£24.00
Beds: 1D 1T **Baths:** 1 En 1 Pr
🅿 (6) ⏏ 📺 🐾 🖬 Ⓥ ⬤

Devil's Bridge
SN7376 ⬤ *Hafway Inn*

Mount Pleasant, *Devil's Bridge, Aberystwyth, Ceredigion, SY23 4QY.*
Lose the crowds amidst stunning scenery where red kites soar.
Open: All Year (not Xmas)
01970 890219 Mr & Mrs Connell
Fax: 01970 890239
D: £21.00–£23.00 **S:** £21.00–£29.00
Beds: 2D 2T **Baths:** 3 En 1 Pr
⛵ (12) 🅿 (4) ⏏ 📺 ✕ 🖬 Ⓥ ⬤

Eglwys Fach
SN6896

Tyglyneiddwen, *Eglwysfach, Machynlleth, Powys, SY20 8SX.*
Open: All Year (not Xmas)
Grades: WTB 2 Star
01654 781348
Mrs Greenwood
edna@aber.ac.uk
D: £18.00–£21.00 **S:** £18.00–£25.00
Beds: 2F 2D 1S **Baths:** 1 En 1 Sh
⛵ 🅿 (6) ⏏ 📺 🐾 ✕ Ⓥ ⬤
Characterful Victorian house with open fires. A warm welcome with excellent home cooking. Non-smoking, situated in the beautiful Dovey Valley near Ynyshir RSPB reserve and the Centre for Alternative Technology. Good walking country direct from the house.

Ffostrasol
SN3747 ⬤ *Ffostrasol Arms*

Plas Cerdin, *Ffostrasol, Llandysul, Ceredigion, SA44 4TA.*
Large modern split level house. Secluded position with breath taking views.
Open: All Year
Grades: AA 4 Diamond
01239 851329 (also fax)
Mrs Hicks
D: £19.00–£20.00 **S:** £20.00–£24.00
Beds: 1F 1D 1T **Baths:** 3 En
⛵ (3) 🅿 (4) 📺 🐾 ✕ 🖬 ⬤

Lampeter

SN5848   🍴 *Grannell Hotel, King's Head, Castle Hotel, Ram Inn*

Pantycelyn Guest House,
Llanwnnen, Lampeter, Ceredigion, SA48 7LW.
Warm welcome. Home cooking. Good holiday base. More at www.pantycelyn.co.uk.
Open: Feb to Oct
Grades: WTB 3 Star GH
01570 434455 (also fax)
Mrs Jenkins
HuwAnnJ@aol.com
D: £20.00–£22.00 **S:** £20.00–£22.00
Beds: 1D 1T 1S **Baths:** 3 En
🅿 (4) ⅍ 📺 🛉 ✕ 📖 🍽 ♨

Penlanmedd, *Llanfair Road, Lampeter, Ceredigion, SA48 8JZ.*
Open: All Year (not Xmas)
Grades: WTB 3 Star
01570 493438 (also fax)
Mrs Coombes
penlanmedd@coombes-e.freeserve.co.uk
D: £19.00–£20.00
Beds: 1F 1D 1T **Baths:** 3 En
🛏 🅿 (20) ⅍ ✕ 📖 📺 ♨
Come and be spoiled in our secluded C18th farmhouse with glorious views down the tranquil River Teifi valley to the mountains. We are just 0.5 hour from the coast. We offer good food, log fires and happy holidays.

Haulfan, *6 Station Terrace, Lampeter, Ceredigion, SA48 7HH.*
Central town position, near university, nature reserve and sea.
Open: Jan to Dec
Grades: WTB 3 Star, AA 3 Diamond
01570 422718
Mrs Williams
D: £17.00–£19.00 **S:** £17.00–£20.00
Beds: 1F 1D 1S **Baths:** 1 En 1 Sh
🛏 📺 🛉 📖 📺 ♨

Llanarth

SN4257

Beechwood, *Llanarth, Ceredigion, SA47 0RE.*
Friendly family run bed and breakfast in a quiet village.
Open: Easter to Sep
Grades: WTB 2 Star
01545 580280
Mrs Evans
D: fr £14.00 **S:** fr £16.00
Beds: 2F 1T **Baths:** 3 En
🛏 🅿 ⅍ 📺 🛉 📖 📺 ♨

Llanilar

SN6275   🍴 *Falcon Inn*

Glynwern Guest House, *Llanilar, Aberystwyth, Ceredigion, SY23 4NY.*
Picturesque riverside house - free fishing, beautiful views, golf, wildlife
Open: All Year (not Xmas/New Year)
Grades: WTB 2 Star
01603 782193
Miss Evans
D: £22.00 **S:** £22.00
Beds: 1T 2D **Baths:** 1 En
🅿 (2) ⅍ 📺 ✕ 📖 📺

Llanon

SN5166   🍴 *White Swan, Central Hotel*

The Barn House, *Llanon, Aberystwyth, Ceredigion, SY23 5LZ.*
Converted barn in landscaped gardens, sea views, aromatherapy, reflexology available.
Open: All Year
Grades: WTB 2 Star
01974 202581 Mrs Rees
D: £18.00–£25.00 **S:** £18.00–£25.00
Beds: 1F 1T 2S **Baths:** 1 En 1 Pr 1 Sh
🛏 🅿 (6) ⅍ 📺 🛉 📖 📺 ♨ ♨

Llansantffraid

SN5167

The Haven, *Winllan Road, Llansantffraid, Powys, SY22 6TR.*
Detached bungalow, Shropshire-Powys border, with panoramic views.
Open: All Year
Grades: WTB 3 Star
01691 828101 Mrs Wilde
D: £17.00–£19.00 **S:** £20.00–£21.00
Beds: 1F 1T **Baths:** 1 En 1 Pr
🅿 (4) ⅍ ✕ 📖 📺 ♨ ♨ ⅙ 1

Llanwnnen

SN5347   🍴 *Grannell Hotel*

Pantycelyn Guest House,
Llanwnnen, Lampeter, Ceredigion, SA48 7LW.
Warm welcome. Home cooking. Good holiday base. More at www.pantycelyn.co.uk.
Open: Feb to Oct
Grades: WTB 3 Star GH
01570 434455 (also fax) Mrs Jenkins
HuwAnnJ@aol.com
D: £20.00–£22.00 **S:** £20.00–£22.00
Beds: 1D 1T 1S **Baths:** 3 En
🅿 (4) ⅍ 📺 🛉 ✕ 📖 ♨

Llwyndafydd

SN3755   🍴 *Crown Inn*

Ty Hen Farm Hotel Cottages &,
Leisure Centre, Llwyndafydd, Llandysull, Ceredigion, SA44 6BZ.
Working sheep farm with private indoor pool and fitness room.
Open: Feb to Nov
01545 560346 (also fax) Mr Kelly
tyhen@ouvip.com
D: £25.50–£29.00 **S:** £25.50–£29.00
Beds: 1D 1T **Baths:** 2 Pr
🛏 🅿 (20) ⅍ 📺 🛉 ✕ 📖 ♨ ♨ ⅙ cc

New Quay

SN3859

Brynarfor Hotel, *New Road, New Quay, Ceredigion, SA45 9SB.*
Homely Victorian House, overlooking beaches, sea and superb Mountain views.
Open: Mar to Oct
Grades: WTB 2 Star, AA 3 Diamond, RAC 3 Diamond
01545 560358 Mr Jewess
Fax: 01545 561204
enquiries@brynarfor.co.uk
D: £28.00–£32.00 **S:** £25.00–£35.00
Beds: 3F 2D 1T **Baths:** 7 En
🛏 🅿 (10) 📺 ✕ 📖 📺 ♨ ⅙ cc

Ponterwyd

SN7480

The George Borrow Hotel,
Ponterwyd, Aberystwyth, Ceredigion, SY23 3AD.
Open: All Year (not Xmas)
01970 890230 Mr & Mrs Wall
Fax: 01970 890587
georgeborrow@clara.net
D: fr £25.00 **S:** fr £25.00
Beds: 2F 3D 2T 2S **Baths:** 9 En
🛏 🅿 (40) 📺 🛉 ✕ 📖 📺 ♨ cc
Famous old hotel set in beautiful countryside, overlooking Eagle Falls and the Rheidol Gorge. 3 miles Devils Bridge, 12 miles Aberystwyth. An ideal centre to explore mid-Wales. Good fishing, birdwatching and walking. Home made food and fine beer, log fires and a friendly welcome.

Pontrhydfendigaid

SN7366

Red Lion Hotel, *Pontrhydfendigaid, Ystrad Meurig, Ceredigion, SY25 6BH.*
Friendly riverside country pub/inn with caravan/camping facilities.
Open: All Year
01974 831232 Mr Earey
stearey@hotmail.com
D: fr £18.50 **S:** fr £18.50
Beds: 1F 1T 2D **Baths:** 4 En
🛏 🅿 (50) ⅍ 📺 🛉 ✕ 📖 📺 ♨ ♨

Rhydlewis

SN3447

Rhydlewis House, *Rhydlewis, Llandysul, Ceredigion, SA44 5PE.*
Open: All Year (not Xmas)
Grades: WTB 3 Star
01239 851748 (also fax)
Ms Russill
D: £20.00–£22.00 **S:** £20.00–£22.00
Beds: 1T 1D 1S **Baths:** 2 En 1 Pr
🛏 🅿 (3) ⅍ 📺 📖 📺 ♨
Stay at this exceptional guest house, once a venue for drovers. Experience a warm welcome, comfort, style and good locally produced food. Cardiganshire is Wales's hidden treasure with stunning scenery, castles, crafts, gardens and the heritage coast of Cardigan Bay. Self-catering cottage also available.

Nant Y Brenni, *Rhydlewis, Llandysul, Ceredigion, SA44 5SN.*
IBC farmhouse in peaceful location. great views, beaches 4 miles.
Open: All Year (not Xmas)
Grades: WTB 3 Star
01239 851368 S E Phillips
Fax: 01239 851891
sue@philpad.demon.co.uk
D: £20.00–£22.00 **S:** £19.00–£22.00
Beds: 1D 1T 1S **Baths:** 2 Sh
🛏 🅿 📺 🛉 ✕ 📖 ♨

National Grid References are for villages, towns and cities – not for individual houses

Taliesin

SN6591   *Wildfowler*

Free Trade Hall, *Taliesin, Machynlleth, Powys, SY20 8JH.*
Comfortable and welcoming, large garden, coastal views, interesting old shop.
Open: All Year (not Xmas)
Grades: WTB 3 Star
01970 832368 (also fax) Ms Regan
info@freetradehall.co.uk
D: £18.00–£20.00 **S:** £20.00–£23.00
Beds: 1F 2D **Baths:** 1 En 1 Sh
⌾ ▣ (3) ⅃ ⊡ ▦ Ⓥ ♨

Planning a longer stay? Always ask for any special rates

Tregaron

SN6759   *Talbot Hotel*

Lluest Guest House, *Lampeter Road, Tregaron, Ceredigion, SY25 6HG.*
Open: All Year (not Xmas)
Grades: WTB 3 Star
01974 298936 (also fax)
Mrs Bull
lluest@supanet.com
D: £16.00–£19.50
S: £16.00–£19.50
Beds: 2D 1T 1S **Baths:** 1 En 1 Sh
⌾ ▣ (5) ⅃ ⊡ ⼞ ✕ ▦ Ⓥ ♨
Large Victorian house, rambling gardens at the foot of The Cambrian Mountains. Good for birdwatching, walking, cycling and fishing. Within easy reach of coast, lakes and rivers. Off-street parking. Beautiful scenery abounds.

Talbot Hotel, *The Square, Tregaron, Ceredigion, SY25 6JL.*
Olde worlde comfortable family atmosphere, good food and real ales.
Open: All Year (not Xmas)
Grades: RAC 1 Star
01974 298208 Mr Williams
Fax: 01974 299059
talbothotel@btinternet.com
D: £21.00–£27.50 **S:** £25.00–£35.00
Beds: 1F 3D 8T 1S **Baths:** 10 En 5 Pr
⌾ ▣ (10) ⊡ ⼞ ✕ ▦ Ⓥ ♨ cc

Fro Villa, *Doldre, Tregaron, Ceredigion, SY25 6JZ.*
Traditional stone cottage, only five minutes' walk from village centre.
Open: All Year (not Xmas)
01974 298817 Mrs Whiting
D: fr £14.00 **S:** fr £15.00
Beds: 1D 1T **Baths:** 1 Sh
⌾ ⅃ ⊡ ✕ ▦ Ⓥ ♨

Denbigh & Flint

```
SH 00   SJ        20              40
```

Tourist Information Centres

Autolodge, Gateway Services (A55), **Ewloe**, Deeside, CH7 6HE, 01244 541597.

Town Hall, Castle Street, **Llangollen**, Denbighshire, LL20 5PD, 01978 860828.

Library, Museum & Art Gallery, Earl Road, **Mold**, Flintshire, CH7 1AP, 01352 759331.

Town Hall, Wellington Road, **Rhyl**, Flintshire, LL18 1BB, 01745 355068.

Ruthin Craft Centre, Park Road, **Ruthin**, Denbighshire, LL15 1BB, 01824 23992.

Lambpit Street, **Wrexham**, LL11 1AY, 01978 292015.

Bangor-on-Dee

SJ3742   ◖ Royal Oak

Fraser Cottage, High Street, Bangor-on-Dee, Wrexham, LL13 0AU.
Pure vegetarian B&B in Welsh Borderlands; rural village, informal atmosphere. **Open:** All Year
01978 781068 (also fax) Ms Knowles
101357.2201@compuserve.com
D: £15.00–£19.00 **S:** £15.00–£19.00
Beds: 2D 1T **Baths:** 3 En
♿ **P** (3) ⊬ ☑ ★ ▥ Ⓥ ❋ ♨

Bodelwyddan

SJ0075   ◖ Ty Fry

17 Cilgant Eglwys Wen,
Bodelwyddan, Rhyl, Denbighshire, LL18 5US.
Quiet bungalow located five miles from Rhyl, convenient for A55.
Open: All Year (not Xmas)
Grades: WTB 1 Star
01745 583221 Mrs Cox
D: £14.00–£18.50 **S:** £14.00–£16.00
Beds: 1D 1S **Baths:** 1 Sh
♿ (6) **P** (2) ⊬ ☑ ▥ ♨ ♿

Bodfari

SJ0970

Fron Haul, Sodom, Bodfari, Denbigh, LL16 4DY.
A oasis of calm and taste overlooking the vale of Clwyd.
Open: Jan to Dec **Grades:** WTB 3 Star
01745 710301 (also fax) Mrs Edwards
fronhaul@pantglasbodfari.freeserve.co.uk
D: £20.00–£25.00 **S:** £25.00
Beds: 1F 1D 1T 1S **Baths:** 1 En 2 Sh
♿ **P** (12) ⊬ ☑ ★ ✕ ▥ Ⓥ ❋ ♨

Bontuchel

SJ0857

Pantglas Ganol, Bontuchel, Ruthin, LL15 2BS.
Stay in this beautiful and peaceful location, enjoy the wildlife.
Open: All Year (not Xmas/New Year)
Grades: WTB 3 Star
01824 710639 (also fax)
Mrs Wilkinson
D: £20.00–£21.00 **S:** £21.00–£22.00
Beds: 1F 1T 1D **Baths:** 1 En 1 Pr
♿ **P** ☑ ★ ✕ ▥ ♨

Bwlchgwyn

SJ2653 ◁ *Moors*

Mountain View Farm, *Llanarmon Road, Bwlchgwyn, Wrexham, LL11 5YP.*
Excellent for Wrexham, Chester, Llangollen, Ruthin. Friendly, homely. Vegetarian speciality.
Open: All Year
01978 754432
D: £18.00–£25.00 **S:** £18.00–£25.00
Beds: 2T 1D **Baths:** 2 En 1 Pr
⌂ 𝗣 (8) ⅊ �📺 ⴕ ✕ 🏛 Ⅴ ⸚

Caerwys

SJ1272 ◁ *Pwllgwyn, Cherry Pie*

Plas Penucha, *Caerwys, Mold, Flintshire, CH7 5BH.*
Peaceful countryside, comfortable farmhouse with large gardens overlooking the Clwydian Hills.
Open: All Year
Grades: WTB 3 Star
01352 720210 Mrs Price
Fax: 01352 720881
D: £21.00–£25.00 **S:** £21.00–£25.00
Beds: 2D 2T **Baths:** 2 En 1 Pr 1 Sh
⌂ 𝗣 ⅊ �📺 ⴕ ✕ 🏛 Ⅴ ⸚

Chirk

SJ2837 ◁ *Waterside, Hand, Club House*

Sun Cottage, *Pentre, Chirk, Wrexham, LL14 5AW.*
Welcoming character cottage, 1723. Spectacular woodland views over river valley.
Open: All Year (not Xmas)
01691 774542 Mrs Little
little@suncottage-bb.freeserve.co.uk
D: £17.00 **S:** £17.00
Beds: 2F 1S **Baths:** 2 Sh
⌂ (10) 𝗣 (3) ⅊ �📺 🏛 Ⅴ ⸚

Pedlar Corner B & B, *Colliery Road, Chirk, Wrexham, LL14 5PB.*
Charming Edwardian cottage, beautiful garden, gorgeous breakfast, old fashioned hospitality.
Open: All Year (not Xmas/New Year)
Grades: WTB 2 Star
01691 772903 Mrs Berry
D: £17.00 **S:** £17.00
Beds: 2T **Baths:** 1 Sh
⌂ 𝗣 (3) ⅊ 🏛 Ⅴ ⸚

Clawdd-newydd

SJ0852

Bryn Coch, *Clawdd-newydd, Ruthin, LL15 2NA.*
Working farm near Clocaenog Forest overlooking Vale of Clwyd. Croeso!
Open: Easter to 31/10/00
Grades: WTB 2 Star
01824 750603 (also fax)
Mrs Jones
gaenorjones@hotmail.com
D: £17.00–£22.00 **S:** £18.00–£22.00
Beds: 2F **Baths:** 1 Sh
⌂ 𝗣 ⅊ �📺 ⴕ ✕ 🏛 Ⅴ ⸚

Corwen

SJ0743 ◁ *Grouse, Owain Glyndwr, Crown, Red Dragon*

Corwen Court Private Hotel, *London Road, Corwen, Denbighshire, LL21 0DP.*
Converted old police station/courthouse; six cells, now single bedrooms.
Open: Mar to Nov
01490 412854 Mr & Mrs Buckland
D: fr £16.50 **S:** fr £16.00
Beds: 4D 6S **Baths:** 4 En 2 Sh
⌂ (3) 𝗣 (6) ⴕ ✕ 🏛

Powys Country House , *Corwen, LL21 9EG.*
Beautiful, peaceful holiday location. 3 acres of well-tended gardens including a grass tennis court.
Open: All Year
01490 412367 Mr & Mrs Carnie
powyshouse@aol.com
D: £20.00–£25.00 **S:** £24.00–£25.00
Beds: 3F 1T 1D **Baths:** 5 En
⌂ (3) 𝗣 (10) 📺 ✕ 🏛 Ⅴ ⸚

Cynwyd

SJ0541

Pen y Bont Fawr, *Cynwyd, Corwen, LL21 0ET.*
Open: All Year **Grades:** WTB 3 Star
01490 412663 Mr Wivell
D: £15.00 **S:** £15.00
Beds: 1T 2D **Baths:** 2 En 1 Sh
⌂ 𝗣 (5) ⅊ �📺 🏛 Ⅴ ⸚
Situated in the Edeyrnion Valley, close to the Berwyn Mountains on the outskirts of Cynwyd Village near Corwen, Llangollen, Bala, Betws-y-Coed and Snowdonia, are nearby. Ideal for walking, cycling, fishing, and horse riding. Water sports in Bala. All rooms having mountain views.

Denbigh

SJ0566 ◁ *Gatherings, Bull*

Cayo Guest House, *74 Vale Street, Denbigh, LL16 3BW.*
Centrally situated town house. Ideal for viewing N. Wales. Pickup from Bodfari (Offa's Dyke).
Open: All Year (not Xmas/New Year)
Grades: WTB 2 Star, AA 3 Diamond, RAC 3 Diamond
01745 812686 Mrs MacCormack
D: £18.00–£19.00 **S:** £18.00–£19.00
Beds: 2D 3T 1S **Baths:** 3 En 1 Pr 1 Sh
⌂ ⅊ �📺 ⴕ ✕ 🏛 Ⅴ ⸚ cc

Flint

SJ2472 ◁ *Red Lion, Halfway House*

Oakenholt Farm, *Chester Road, Flint, Flintshire, CH6 5SU.*
Set in a beautiful location, convenient for touring Chester, North Wales and Liverpool.
Open: All Year
Grades: WTB 2 Star
01352 733264 Mrs Hulme
jenny@oakenholt.freeserve.co.uk
D: £20.00–£22.00 **S:** £25.00–£27.00
Beds: 1F 1D 1T 1S **Baths:** 4 En
⌂ 𝗣 ⅊ �📺 ✕ 🏛 Ⅴ ⸚

Froncysyllte

SJ2740 ◁ *Telford*

Argoed Farm, *Froncysyllte, Llangollen, Clwyd, LL20 7RH.*
Old farmhouse, beamed ceilings, inglenook fireplace in dining room.
Open: All Year
Grades: WTB 3 Star
01691 772367 Mrs Landon
llangollen@argoedfm.freeserve.co.uk
D: £20.00–£22.00 **S:** £20.00–£22.00
Beds: 1F 1D 1T 1S **Baths:** 4 En
⌂ 𝗣 (6) ⅊ �📺 ⴕ ✕ 🏛 Ⅴ ❋ ⸚

Garth

SJ2542 **Gwernydd Farm,** *Garth, Llangollen, LL20 7UR.*
Working farm, extensive views south, tastefully decorated, private parking.
Open: All Year (not Xmas)
Grades: WTB 3 Star
01978 820122 (also fax)
Mrs Morris
joan.morris@amserve
D: £17.00–£18.00 **S:** £17.00–£18.00
Beds: 2F **Baths:** 1 Sh
⌂ 𝗣 (4) ⅊ �📺 ⴕ ✕ 🏛 Ⅴ ⸚

Glyn Ceiriog

SJ2038

Pant Farm, *Glyn Ceiriog, Llangollen, LL20 7BY.*
Spectacular views, walking, riding on the doorstep, ideal touring base.
Open: All Year (not Xmas)
Grades: WTB 3 Star
01691 718534 (also fax)
Mrs Tomlinson
chris@pantfarmholidays.com
D: £19.00 **S:** fr £19.00
Beds: 2D 1S **Baths:** 2 En
⌂ 𝗣 (6) ⅊ ⴕ ⴕ ✕ 🏛 Ⅴ ⸚

Golden Pheasant Hotel, *Glyn Ceiriog, Llangollen, LL20 7BB.*
C18th country hotel/traditional inn in unspoilt valley. 15 minutes main road. Well-stocked bar.
Open: All Year
01691 718281 Mrs Lawson
Fax: 01691 718479
D: £29.50–£40.00 **S:** £35.00–£45.00
Beds: 3F 7D 6T 2S **Baths:** 19 En
⌂ 𝗣 ⅊ ⴕ ✕ 🏛 Ⅴ ❋ ⸚

Gwernymynydd

SJ2162 ◁ *Swan*

Rhos-y-gadfa, *4 Paddock Way, Ruthin Road, Gwernymynydd, Mold, Flintshire, CH7 5LA.*
All ensuite rooms, panoramic views, near all tourist attractions.
Open: All Year
01352 752339 Mrs Hughes
D: £18.00 **S:** £23.00
Beds: 1F 1D 1T **Baths:** 3 En
⌂ 𝗣 (10) ⅊ ⴕ 🏛 Ⅴ ⸚

Planning a longer stay? Always ask for any special rates

Hawarden

SJ3165   🍺 *Glynne Arms, Fox & Grapes*

The Coach House, Hawarden, Deeside, CH5 3DH.
A converted coach house 5 miles from Chester. Ideal for touring N. Wales.
Open: All Year (not Xmas/New Year)
01244 532328 (also fax) Mrs Jacks
D: £22.50 **S:** £25.00
Beds: 2D 2S **Baths:** 1 Sh
🐕 (12) 🄿 (4) 📺 🛍 🖦

St Deiniol's Library, Church Lane, Hawarden, Deeside, CH5 3DF.
William Gladstone's library, Grade I Listed, building set in own grounds.
Open: All Year (not Xmas)
Grades: WTB 3 Star
01244 532350 G P Morris
Fax: 01244 520643
deiniol.vistors@btinternet.com
D: £20.00 **S:** £20.00–£21.50
Beds: 7D 10T 16S **Baths:** 9 Sh
🄿 (20) ⊬ 📺 ✕ 🛍 🖦 CC

Higher Kinnerton

SJ3261   🍺 *Royal Oak, Swan Inn, Red Lion*

Green Cottage, Higher Kinnerton, Chester, CH4 9BZ.
6 miles from historic Chester, relaxing atmosphere, good food, in a Welsh rural setting. **Open:** All Year
Grades: WTB 3 Star
01244 660137 Mrs Milner
D: fr £19.00 **S:** £23.00–£24.00
Beds: 1D 1T **Baths:** 1 Pr
🐕 🄿 ⊬ 📺 🛍 🖦

Holywell

SJ1875   🍺 *Royal Oak, Halfway House*

Greenhill Farm, Bryn Celyn, Holywell, Denbigh & Flint, CH8 7QF.
16th Century timber framed farmhouse with 'old world' charm.
Open: Feb to Nov
Grades: WTB 2 Star, AA 3 Diamond
01352 713270 Mr & Mrs Jones
mary@greenhillfarm.fsnet.co.uk
D: £18.50–£20.50
Beds: 2F 1D 1T **Baths:** 2 En 2 Sh
🐕 🄿 (6) 📺 ✕ 🛍 🖦 🖦

Bryn Hedydd, Berthengam, Holywell, Flintshire, CH8 9BZ.
Grade II Listed oak-beamed Welsh long cottage in own secluded grounds in country village. **Open:** All Year (not Xmas)
01745 561552 Mrs Burgoyne
D: £15.00–£17.00 **S:** £15.00–£17.00
Beds: 1F 1T **Baths:** 1 Pr 1 Sh
🐕 (3) 🄿 (6) 📺 ✕ 🛍 🖦 & 🖦

Llandegla

SJ1952   🍺 *Crown Hotel, Plough Inn*

Raven Farm, Llandegla, Wrexham, Nr Denbighshire, LL11 3AW.
Converted C15th drover's inn/farm.
Open: Easter to Oct
01978 790224 Mrs Surrey
D: £16.50–£17.00 **S:** £16.50–£17.00
Beds: 2F 1D 2T 1S **Baths:** 1 En 1 Sh
🐕 (10) 🄿 (8) ⊬ 📺 🛍 🖦

Saith Daran Farm, Llandegla, Wrexham, LL11 3BA.
Friendly farmhouse B&B, beautiful scenery, ideal for touring in Wales.
Open: Mar to Oct
01978 790685 Mrs Thompson
D: £18.00 **S:** £18.00
Beds: 1D 1T **Baths:** 2 Pr
🐕 (5) 🄿 (4) 📺 🛍 🖦

Llandrillo

SJ0337   🍺 *Berwyn, Dudley Arms Hotel*

Y Llwyn Guest House, Llandrillo, Corwen, LL21 0ST.
Open: All Year
Grades: WTB 3 Star
01490 440455 Mrs Jones
aeron@yllwyn39.freeserve.co.uk
D: £20.00–£22.00 **S:** £–£26.00
Beds: 1D 1T **Baths:** 1 En 1 Pr
🐕 🄿 (3) 📺 ✕ 🛍 🖦 📺
Enjoy beautiful views of Berwyn Mountains from your bedroom, restaurants in walking distance; peaceful surroundings. Home-made bread and jams. Expect to be pampered, you will be welcomed with tea and welsh cakes in our beautiful flower garden.

Llanferres

SJ1860   🍺 *Druid Inn*

The White House, Rectory Lane, Llanferres, Mold, Denbighshire, CH7 5SR.
Victorian rectory with recently converted stables set in conservation area.
Open: All Year
01352 810259 rarmst@hotmail.com
D: £19.00–£22.00 **S:** £23.00–£25.00
Beds: 2D 1T **Baths:** 3 Pr
🐕 🄿 (6) 📺 🛍 🖦

Llanfwrog

SJ1157   🍺 *Ye Olde Crosse Keyes*

Firgrove, Llanfwrog, Ruthin, Denbighshire, LL15 2LL.
A Listed Georgian country house, set within 1.5 acres of mature and beautiful gardens.
Open: Feb to Nov
01824 702677 (also fax)
anna@firgrove.fsnet.co.uk
D: £20.00–£28.00 **S:** £25.00–£30.00
Beds: 2D **Baths:** 1 En 1 Sh
🄿 (3) ⊬ 📺 ✕ 🛍 🖦 CC

Llangollen

SJ2141   🍺 *Telford, Waterside Bar, Hand Hotel*

River Lodge, Mill Street, Llangollen, Clwyd, LL20 7UH.
Open: Feb to Dec
01978 869019 Mr Byrne
Fax: 01978 861841
chainbridge@hotmail.com
D: £15.00–£35.00 **S:** £15.00–£35.00
Beds: 4F 7D 7T **Baths:** 18 En
🐕 (30) ✕ 📺 🛍 & CC
On the banks of the River Dee, River Lodge is Llangollen's newest motel lodge, just 5 mins walk from the town centre, attractions, bars and restaurants. All rooms have a river/mountain view and full ensuite facilities.

Cloud Hill, Pentre , Chirk, Wrexham, LL14 5AN.
1972 Daily Mail House of the Year. Villa style open plan.
Open: All Year (not Xmas/New Year)
01691 773359 Mr Sutcliffe
orders@cloudhill.sagehost.co.uk
D: £18.00–£20.00 **S:** £18.00–£25.00
Beds: 3T 1D **Baths:** 2 En 1 Sh
🐕 (10) 🄿 (6) 📺 ✕ 🛍 🖦

Bryn Meirion, Abbey Road, Llangollen, Clwyd, LL20 8EF.
Edwardian house overlooking Dee, canal, steam railway and surrounding hills.
Open: All Year
Grades: WTB 3 Star
01978 861911 Mrs Hurle
jhurle@globalnet.co.uk
D: £20.00–£22.00 **S:** £24.00–£35.00
Beds: 1F 1D 1S **Baths:** 2 En 1 Pr
🐕 🄿 (4) ⊬ 📺 ✕ 🛍 📺 🖦

Hillcrest Guest House, Hill Street, Llangollen, Denbighshire, LL20 8EU.
Beautiful Victorian house, quiet area of Llangollen, a few minutes from the A5.
Open: All Year (not Xmas)
01978 860208 (also fax)
Mrs Lloyd
colin@hillcrest.llangollen.freeserve.co.uk
D: £21.00–£23.00 **S:** £35.00–£42.00
Beds: 2F 3D 2T **Baths:** 7 En
🐕 🄿 (10) ⊬ 📺 ✕ 🛍 📺 🖦

The Grange, Grange Road, Llangollen, Denbighshire, LL20 8AP.
Attractive country house in town with secluded 2-acre garden.
Open: All Year (not Xmas)
01978 860366 Mrs Evans
D: £20.00 **S:** fr £25.00
Beds: 1F 1D 1T **Baths:** 3 En
🐕 🄿 (3) ⊬ 📺 🛍 📺 🖦

Llangynhafal

SJ1263   🍺 *Golden Lion*

Esgairllygain (The Old Barn), Llangynhafal, Ruthin, Denbighshire, LL15 1RT.
Converted stone barn. Delightful views. Convenient Chester, North Wales, Snowdonia, Llangollen & coast.
Open: All Year (not Xmas)
01824 704047 (also fax)
Mrs Henderson
D: £18.50 **S:** £18.50–£21.00
Beds: 1F 1D **Baths:** 2 En
🐕 🄿 (2) ⊬ 📺 🛍 📺 🖦

Llantysilio

SJ1943   🍺 *Britannia Inn, Horseshoe Pass*

Hendy Isa, Llantysilio, Llangollen, Denbighshire, LL20 8DE.
Hendy Isa is a spacious rural property with pretty gardens.
Open: Jan to Dec
Grades: WTB 3 Star
01978 861232 (also fax)
Mr Jefferys
hendyisa@aol.com
D: £18.00–£20.00 **S:** £20.00–£25.00
Beds: 4F **Baths:** 4 Pr
🐕 🄿 (6) ⊬ 📺 🛍 📺 🖦

Lloc

SJ1376

Misty Waters Country Lodge Hotel, Lloc, Holywell, CH8 8RG.
Country lodge set in peaceful area with a friendly atmosphere.
Open: All Year
01352 720497 (also fax)
Mrs Hughes
D: £20.00 **S:** £30.00
Beds: 1F 4D **Baths:** 5 En
🛇 🄿 🛇 📺 ✕ 🖿 🛇 🛓 ♿

Maeshafn

SJ2061 🍺 Druid Inn

Hafan Deg, Maeshafn, Mold, Flintshire, CH7 5LU.
Open: All Year
Grades: WTB 3 Star
01352 810465 (also fax)
Mrs Scruton
dave@hafandeg.co.uk
D: £20.00 **S:** £20.00
Beds: 1F 1T 1D 1S **Baths:** 1 En 2 Pr 1 Sh
🛇 🄿 (4) 🛇 📺 🍴 🖿 🛓
A comfortable country home surrounded by woods and hills. Relax on patio or gallery, enjoy home-baked bread for breakfast in the open beamed dining hall with wood burning stove and slate floor. Explore market towns, Roman Chester, castles, mountains.

Marchwiel

SJ3547 🍺 Red Lion

Rose Lynn Cottage, Cock Bank, Marchwiel, Wrexham, LL13 0SU.
Quiet rural position near National Trust (Erddig Chirk), excellent food.
Open: All Year (not Xmas)
01978 780071 Mrs McDermott
D: £20.00–£22.00 **S:** £20.00–£22.00
Beds: 1T **Baths:** 1 En
🄿 (4) 🛇 📺 🖿 🛓

Mold

SJ2363 🍺 Bryn Awel Hotel, Belvedere

Heulwen, Maes Bodlonfa, Mold, Flintshire, CH7 1DR.
Spacious well-furnished rooms. Quiet, convenient town centre. Friendly - nothing too much trouble.
Open: All Year (not Xmas)
Grades: WTB 3 Star B&B, AA 3 Diamond
01352 758785 Mrs Hollywell
D: £19.00 **S:** £18.00–£25.00
Beds: 1F 1S **Baths:** 2 Pr
🛇 🄿 (3) 🛇 📺 🖿 🛇 🛓

Northop Hall

SJ2667 🍺 Black Lion

Brookside House, Northop Hall, Mold, Flintshire, CH7 6HR.
Relax enjoy the hospitality of our beautifully refurbished Welsh cottage.
Open: All Year (not Xmas)
01244 821146 Mrs Whale
christine@brooksidehouse.fsnet.co.uk
D: £18.00–£21.00 **S:** £24.00–£28.00
Beds: 1F 1D 1T **Baths:** 1 En 1 Pr 1 Sh
🛇 🄿 🛇 📺 🖿 🛇 🛓

Penley

SJ4140 🍺 Hanmer Arms

Bridge House, Penley, Wrexham, LL13 0LY.
Comfortable house, idyllic setting, open views. Landscaped gardens with stream.
Open: All Year (not Xmas)
Grades: WTB 3 Star
01978 710763 Mr & Mrs Clarke
D: £16.00–£18.00 **S:** £18.00–£20.00
Beds: 1D 2T **Baths:** 2 Sh
🛇 🄿 🛇 📺 🍴 ✕ 🖿 🛇 🛓

Pentre

SJ2940 🍺 Waterside Bar, Hand Hotel

Pentre Cottage, Pentre, Chirk, Wrexham, Flintshire, LL14 5AW.
Beautiful Welsh cottage with friendly Lancashire welcome; dog-lovers paradise.
Open: All Year (not Xmas)
01691 774265 Mrs Vant
vant@pentrecott.freeserve.co.uk
D: fr £16.00 **S:** £16.00–£18.00
Beds: 1D 1T **Baths:** 1 Pr 1 Sh
🄿 (3) 📺 🍴 ✕ 🖿 🛇 🛓

Cloud Hill, Pentre , Chirk, Wrexham, LL14 5AN.
1972 Daily Mail House of the Year. Villa style open plan.
Open: All Year (not Xmas/New Year)
01691 773359 Mr Sutcliffe
orders@cloudhill.sagehost.co.uk
D: £18.00–£20.00 **S:** £18.00–£25.00
Beds: 3T 1D **Baths:** 2 En 1 Sh
🛇 (10) 🄿 (6) 📺 ✕ 🖿 🛇 🛓

Prestatyn

SJ0682 🍺 Red Lion

Roughsedge House, 26/28 Marine Road, Prestatyn, Denbighshire, LL19 7HG.
Victorian guest house, excellent breakfast. Walkers welcome, Friendly atmosphere.
Open: All Year
Grades: WTB 1 Star
01745 887359 Mrs Kubler
Fax: 01745 852883
roughsedge@ykubler.fsnet,co,uk
D: £16.00–£20.00 **S:** £16.00–£25.00
Beds: 2F 4D 2T 2S **Baths:** 3 Pr 3 Sh
🛇 🄿 (3) 🛇 ✕ 🖿 🛇 🛓 cc

Traeth Ganol Hotel, 41 Beach Road West, Prestatyn, Denbighshire, LL19 7LL.
Luxury well-appointed seafront location.
Open: All Year
Grades: WTB 3 Star, AA 2 Star
01745 853594 Mr & Mrs Groves
Fax: 01745 886687
hotel@dnetw.co.uk
D: £28.00–£31.00 **S:** £39.00–£54.00
Beds: 6F 1D 1T 1S **Baths:** 9 En
🛇 🄿 (9) 🛇 📺 ✕ 🖿 🛇 ✻ 🛓 ♿ 1 cc

B&B owners may vary
rates - be sure to check
when booking

Rhyl

SJ0181 🍺 Grange, Boswells

The Kensington Hotel, 17 East Parade, Rhyl, LL18 3AG.
Open: All Year (not Xmas/New Year)
Grades: WTB 2 Star
01745 331868 (also fax)
Mr Dawson
D: £20.00–£34.00 **S:** £25.00–£35.00
Beds: 10F 4T 10D 10S **Baths:** 10 En 10 Pr
🛇 🄿 🖿 🛇 🛓 cc
Traditional Victorian bay property, now a family run hotel. Situated in a prominent position on the sea front. Quiet and close to the shops, clean beaches and amenities very clean warm and friendly. Exceptional Breakfast. perfect base for touring North Wales.

Links Guest House, 20 Beechwood Road, Rhyl, LL18 3EU.
Victorian house, East Parade beach, ground floor available. Bargain breaks.
Open: All Year
Grades: WTB 3 Star
01745 344381 (also fax)
Mrs Mariner
thelinksgh@cwcom.net
D: £15.00–£18.00 **S:** £16.00–£22.00
Beds: 3F 4D 2S **Baths:** 6 En 1 Pr
🛇 (5) 🛇 ✕ 🖿 🛓 cc

Snowdon House, 46 River Street, Rhyl, LL18 1PT.
Small family run guest house,adjacent to promenade, very central.
Open: All Year
Grades: WTB 1 Star
01745 331786 (also fax)
Mrs Roberts
D: £12.50–£16.00 **S:** £13.00–£17.00
Beds: 3F 1D 2T 2S **Baths:** 2 Sh
🛇 🄿 (3) 📺 🍴 ✕ 🖿 🛇 ✻ 🛓

Normaz Guest House, 19 Aquarium Street, Rhyl, LL18 1PG.
Comfortable great value guest house, near everything, loads to do.
Open: Easter to Oct
01745 334761 Mrs Harper
D: £15.00 **S:** £15.00
Beds: 2F 2D 1T 1S **Baths:** 1 Sh
🛇 📺 ✕ 🖿 🛇 🛓

Rossett

SJ3657 🍺 Boat House

Corner House Farm, Parkside, Rossett, Wrexham, LL12 0BW.
9 luxury holiday houses and apartments suitable for meetings, family gatherings, lovely rural location.
Open: All Year
Grades: WTB 5 Star
01829 270452 Mrs Coop
Fax: 01829 271260
D: £19.00–£26.00 **S:** fr £23.00
Beds: 1D 1T 1S **Baths:** 3 En
🛇 🄿 (14) 📺 🍴 ✕ 🖿 🛇 🛓 ♿ 3

Ruthin

SJ1258 ◖ *Golden Lion, Ye Olde Anchor*

Tyn-y-caeau Farmhouse, *Llanrhydd, Ruthin, Denbighshire, LL15 2US.*
Idyllic escape in orchard setting in 5 acres of farmland. Ruthin 1 mile.
Open: Mar to Nov
Grades: WTB 3 Star
01824 703883 Mrs Douglas
adder.black@lineone.net
D: £19.50 **S:** £19.50
Beds: 3F 2D 1T **Baths:** 1 En 1 Pr
⌂ ⊞ (5) ⌿ ⊞ ⊞ ⚲ cc

Trevor

SJ2742 ◖ *Telford*

Oaklands, *Trevor, Llangollen, Denbighshire, LL20 7TG.*
Charming Victorian house with lovely gardens in beautiful Vale of Llangollen.
Open: All Year (not Xmas)
01978 820152 Mrs Dennis
D: £16.00–£20.00 **S:** £18.00–£23.00
Beds: 1F 1D 2T **Baths:** 2 Sh
⌂ ⊞ (8) ⊞ ⊞ ⚲

Wrexham

SJ3350 ◖ *Fox & Hounds, Squire Yorke, Ffrwd*

The Windings, *Cea Penty Road, Wrexham, LL12 9TH.*
Delightful rural setting. Ideal base for Chester, North Wales, Wrexham.
Open: All Year
01978 720503 Mrs Rooks
Fax: 01978 757372
windings@enterprise.net
D: fr £20.00 **S:** fr £20.00
Beds: 1T 2D **Baths:** 1 Sh
⊞ (10) ⌿ ⊞ ⚲

Littleton, *24 Bersham Road, Wrexham, LL13 7UP.*
Quiet family B&B. Comfortable accommodation. Excellent breakfast, (home from home).
Open: All Year (not Xmas/New Year)
Grades: WTB 1 Star
01978 352867 Mrs Evans
Fax: 01978 352970
littletonb&b@talk21.com
D: £15.50–£17.00 **S:** £15.50–£17.00
Beds: 1F 1S **Baths:** 1 Sh
⌂ (10) ⌿ ⊞ ⊞ ⊞ ⚲

Plas Eyton, *Wrexham, LL13 0YD.*
Easily accessible large Victorian 3 acre smallholding in own private grounds.
Open: All Year
01978 820642 Mrs Davies
D: £14.00–£16.00 **S:** £14.00–£16.00
Beds: 1F 1D 1T 2S **Baths:** 2 En
⌂ ⊞ (10) ⌿ ⊞ ⊞ ⊞ ⚲

Stilwell's Britain Cycleway Companion

23 Long Distance Cycleways – Where to Stay * Where to Eat

County Cycleways – Sustrans Routes

The first guide of its kind, **Stilwell's Britain Cycleway Companion** makes planning accommodation for your cycling trip easy. It lists B&Bs, hostels, campsites and pubs– in the order they appear along the selected cycleways – allowing the cyclist to book ahead. No more hunting for a room, a hot meal or a cold drink after a long day in the saddle. Stilwell's gives descriptions of the featured routes and includes such relevant information as maps, grid references and distance from route; Tourist Board ratings; and the availability of drying facilities and packed lunches. No matter which route – or part of a route – you decide to ride, let the **Cycleway Companion** show you where to sleep and eat.

As essential as your tyre pump – the perfect cycling companion: **Stilwell's Britain Cycleway Companion.**

Cycleways

Sustrans

Carlisle to Inverness – Clyde to Forth - Devon Coast to Coast - Hull to Harwich – Kingfisher Cycle Trail - Lon Las Cymru – Sea to Sea (C2C) – Severn and Thames – West Country Way – White Rose Cycle Route

County

Round Berkshire Cycle Route – Cheshire Cycleway – Cumbria Cycleway – Essex Cycle Route – Icknield Way - Lancashire Cycleway – Leicestershire County Cycleway – Oxfordshire Cycleway – Reivers Cycle Route – South Downs Way - Surrey Cycleway – Wiltshire Cycleway – Yorkshire Dales Cycleway

---

£9.95 from all good bookstores (ISBN 1-900861-26-7) or £10.95 (inc p&p) from Stilwell Publishing Ltd, 59 Charlotte Road, London EC2A 3QW (020 7739 7179)

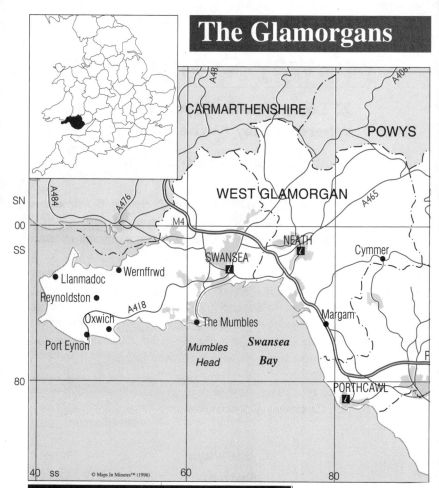

The Glamorgans

CARMARTHENSHIRE

POWYS

WEST GLAMORGAN

SN

00

SS

NEATH

SWANSEA

Cymmer

Llanmadoc   Wernffrwd

Reynoldston

Oxwich

Port Eynon

The Mumbles

Margam

Mumbles Head

Swansea Bay

80

PORTHCAWL

40   SS   © Maps In Minutes™ (1996)   60   80

Barry

ST1067   *Ship Inn*

Anglesea Guest House, *9 Romilly Road, Barry, S Glam, CF62 6AZ.* Small, late-Victorian guest house, near beaches and transport services. **Open:** All Year (not Xmas) **01446 749660** Mr Griffith **D:** £15.00–£16.00 **S:** £15.00–£16.00 **Beds:** 1F 1T 1S **Baths:** 1 Sh ⛄ (5) ⊬ ⦿ ▥ ⛭

RATES

D = Price range per person sharing in a double room

S = Price range for a single room

The Cottage Guest House, *Pwll y Pant, Caerphilly, Mid Glam, CF83 3HW.*
300 year old Cottage. Castles, coastline, mountains nearby. Warm welcome.
Open: All Year
Grades: WTB 3 Star, AA 3 Diamond
029 2086 9160 Mr Giles
thecottage@tesco.net
D: £17.00–£20.00 **S:** £26.00–£29.00
Beds: 3T **Baths:** 2 En 1 Pr
🛏 🅿 (5) 🏸 📺 🛢 🅥 🌰

Cardiff

ST1677 ⭐ *Beverley, Clifton Hotel, Halfway Hotel, Hayes Court, Poachers' Lodge, Robin Hood*

Rambler Court Hotel, *188 Cathedral Road, Pontcanna, Cardiff, S Glam, CF11 9JE.*
Open: All Year
Grades: WTB 2 Star
029 2022 1187 (also fax)
Mrs Cronin
D: £17.00–£20.00 **S:** £17.00–£25.00
Beds: 3F 3D 1T 3S **Baths:** 4 En 5 Sh
🛏 🅿 (4) 📺 🛢 🌰
Friendly family-run hotel, ideally situated in a tree-lined conservation area, close to all of the city's main attractions, 10 minutes' walk to the city centre and Millennium Stadium. Good local restaurants & pubs.

Preste Gaarden Hotel, *181 Cathedral Road, Pontcanna, Cardiff, S Glam, CF11 9PN.*
Highly recommended, modernised ex-Norwegian consulate offering olde-worlde charm.
Open: All Year (not Xmas)
Grades: WTB 2 Star Hotel
029 2022 8607 Mrs Nicholls
Fax: 029 2037 4805
cardiff.hotel@btinternet.com
D: £18.00–£22.00 **S:** £22.00–£27.00
Beds: 1F 2D 3T 4S **Baths:** 7 En 3 Pr
🛏 🅿 (3) 📺 🛢 🅥 🌰

Austins, *11 Coldstream Terrace, City Centre, Cardiff, CF11 6LJ.*
In the centre of the city 300 yards from Cardiff Castle.
Open: All Year
Grades: WTB 2 Star
029 2037 7148
Mr Hopkins
Fax: 029 2037 7158
austins@hotelcardiff.com
D: £17.50–£19.50 **S:** £20.00–£27.50
Beds: 1F 5T 5S **Baths:** 4 En 2 Sh
🛏 📺 🏸 🛢 🌰 cc

Annedd Lon Guest House, *157-159 Cathedral Road, Cardiff, S Glam, CF1 9PL.*
Centrally located guest house in elegant conservation area. Non smoking throughout.
Open: All Year (not Xmas/New Year)
Grades: AA 4 Daimond
029 2022 3349
Mrs Tucker
Fax: 029 2064 0885
D: £20.00–£22.50 **S:** £18.00–£30.00
Beds: 2F 1D 2T 1S **Baths:** 2 En 2 Sh
🛏 🅿 (7) 🏸 📺 🛢 🅥 🌰 cc

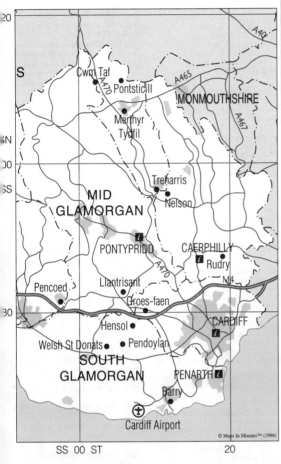

SS 00 ST   20

© Maps In Minutes™ (1996)

Caerphilly

ST1586 ⭐ *Cedar Tree, Traveller's Rest, The Moat, Black Cock, Kings Arms, Rudry Hotel, Maenllyod Inn*

The Coach House, *2 Twyn Sych, Rudry, Caerphilly, CF83 3EF.*
Open: All Year **Grades:** WTB 1 Star
029 2088 4772 (also fax) Mr Davis
D: £17.00–£20.00 **S:** £17.00–£25.00
Beds: 2F 1D 3T 4S **Baths:** 1 En 2 Pr 3 Sh
🛏 🅿 📺 🏸 🛢 🌰
Located in the heart of the country. 6 miles Cardiff or Newport, 3 miles Caerphilly Castle and town, half hour drive to the coast. Recreation centres within 10 minutes drive providing swimming, golf. Bowls and all indoor sporting activities.

Lugano Guest House, *Hillside Mountain Road, Caerphilly, Mid Glamorgan, CF83 1HN.*
Open: All Year (not Xmas)
Grades: WTB 3 Star, Highly Commended
029 2085 2672
ndowson@freeserve.co.uk
D: £16.50–£17.50
S: £22.50–£25.00
Beds: 1D 2T **Baths:** 3 En
🛏 (1) 🅿 (2) 🏸 📺 🛢 🌰
Charming character house, residents' own private garden and entrance. Upstairs bedrooms overlooking Caerphilly Castle, all rooms ensuite. Minutes' walk to town centre, castle, train and bus stations for regular services to the capital, Cardiff. Warm friendly welcome assured. No smoking.

Georgian Hotel, 179 Cathedral Road, Pontcanna, Cardiff, S Glam, CF1 9PL.
All rooms tastefully restored to today's standards, each having a colour television.
Open: All Year (not Xmas)
029 2023 2594 Mr Menin
D: £20.00–£27.50 **S:** £27.50–£35.00
Beds: 1F 2D 3T 2S **Baths:** 8 En
⌂ ⊠ ▦ ⚓

Cwm Taf

SO0013

Llwyn-On Guest House, Cwm Taf, Merthyr Tydfil, Mid Glam, CF48 2HT.
Brecon Beacons National Park, overlooking Llwyn Onn Reservoir and woodlands.
Open: All Year (not Xmas/New Year)
Grades: WTB 3 Star, AA 5 Diamond
01685 384384 Mrs Evans
Fax: 01685 359310
D: £25.00 **S:** £20.00–£25.00
Beds: 1D 1T 1S **Baths:** 3 En
⌂ ▣ (4) � ⊠ ✕ ▦ ⚓ cc

Cymmer (Glyncorrwg)

SS8695

Bryn Teg House, 9 Craig-y-fan, Cymmer, Port Talbot, SA13 3LN.
Mountains, biking, cycleways, country walks and fishing in country park.
Open: All Year (not Xmas)
Grades: WTB 2 Star B&B
01639 851820 (also fax)
D: £16.00 **S:** £16.00
Beds: 1D 2T **Baths:** 1 Sh
⌂ ⊠ ✝ ✕ ▦ ⚓ ⚓

Groes-faen

ST0680   ◀ Dynevor Arms

Smokey Cottage Guest House, Groes-Faen, Pontyclun, CF72 8NG.
Family-run guest house offering very best in accommodation, rural location but close Cardiff M4.
Open: All Year
Grades: WTB 3 Star
029 2089 1173 (also fax)
smokeycot@talk21.com
D: £20.00–£25.00 **S:** £20.00–£25.00
Beds: 1F 2T **Baths:** 3 En
⌂ ▣ ダ ⊠ ▦ ⚓

Hensol

ST0478   ◀ Castell Mynach

Llanerch Vineyard, Hensol, Pendoylan, Vale of Glamorgan, CF72 8JU.
One of Wales' 'Great Little Places', most ensuite rooms overlook largest vineyard in Wales.
Open: All Year (not Xmas)
01443 225877 Fax: 01443 225546
llanerch@cariadwines.demon.co.uk
D: £24.00–£30.00 **S:** £38.00–£50.00
Beds: 2D 2T **Baths:** 4 En
⌂ (8) ▣ (20) ダ ⊠ ▦ ⚓ cc

Llanmadoc

SS4493   ◀ Britannia Inn, King Arthur

Tallizmand, Llanmadoc, Gower, Swansea, W Glam, SA3 1DE.
Tastefully furnished ensuites. Coastal & inland walks, quiet sandy beaches.
Open: All Year (not Xmas)
Grades: WTB 3 Star
01792 386373 Mrs Main
D: £18.00–£21.00 **S:** £21.00–£25.00
Beds: 1D 2T **Baths:** 1 En 2 Pr
⌂ ▣ (5) ⊠ ✝ ▦ ⓥ ⚓

Britannia Inn, Llanmadoc, Gower, Swansea, W Glam, SA3 1DB.
Open: All Year (not Xmas/New Year)
Grades: WTB 2 Star
01792 386624 Mr Downie
mikdow@freeuk.com
D: £25.00 **S:** £32.50
Beds: 1F 1T 3D **Baths:** 5 En
⌂ ▣ (50) ⊠ ✕ ▦ ⓥ ⚓ cc
C18th family owned country inn close to Burry Inley and nature reserve. Excellent walking. Magnificent quiet beaches. Pub has beer garden with small menagerie. Extensive food menu and cask conditioned ales.

Llantrisant

ST0483

The Black Prince Hotel, Llantrisant Industrial Estate, Llantrisant, Pontyclun, Mid Glam, CF72 8LF.
Friendly, family-run pub. Informal atmosphere but guaranteed a welcome.
Open: All Year
01443 227723 Mr Long
Fax: 01443 228655
D: £27.00–£30.00 **S:** £27.00–£30.00
Beds: 37F **Baths:** 37 En
⌂ ▣ (100) ダ ⊠ ✝ ✕ ▦ ⓥ ✹ ⚓ ⚓ cc

Margam

SS7887

Ty'N-Y-Caeau, Margam, Port Talbot, W Glam, SA13 2NW.
Original vicarage for Margam Abbey since C17th, in walled gardens.
Open: Feb to Nov **Grades:** WTB 2 Star
01639 883897 Mrs Gaen
D: £22.00–£25.00 **S:** £25.00–£27.00
Beds: 1F 2D 4T **Baths:** 6 En 1 Pr
⌂ (2) ▣ (8) ダ ⊠ ✝ ✕ ▦ ⚓ ⚓

Merthyr Tydfil

SO0506   ◀ Mountain Ash, Brunswick, White Horse

Brynawel Guest House, Queens Road, Merthyr Tydfil, Mid Glam, CF47 0HD.
Open: All Year **Grades:** WTB 3 Star
01685 722573 Mrs Johnson
D: £23.00 **S:** £28.00
Beds: 1D 2T **Baths:** 3 En
⌂ ▣ (5) ダ ⊠ ▦ ⓥ ⚓
Large Victorian house, tastefully furnished, adjoining parks, family home, friendly atmosphere. Ensuite rooms, TV tea/coffee. Non-smoking, 10 mins Brecon Beacons National Park. Excellent Welsh breakfast. Ideal location for walkers, cyclists, business or quiet break.

Maes Y Coed, Park Terrace, Pontmorlais West, Merthyr Tydfil, Mid Glam, CF47 8UT.
Open: All Year
01685 722246 (also fax)
Mr Davies
D: £16.00–£18.00 **S:** £18.00–£22.00
Beds: 4F 5T 1S **Baths:** 4 En
⌂ ▣ (4) ⊠ ✝ ✕ ▦ ⚓
Large comfortable house on edge of Brecon Beacons in 1/4 acre of gardens. Edging the Taff Trail. Friendly welcome, good home cooked breakfast, evening meals. Ideal for golfing, fishing, walking and all outdoors pursuits.

Neath

SS7497   ◀ Crown & Sceptre, Highlander

Victoria Guest House, 10 Victoria Gardens, Neath, W Glam, SA11 3BE.
Victorian house close to town centre and beautiful Victorian gardens.
Open: All Year (not Xmas/New Year)
01639 636233 Mr & Mrs Riando
D: £15.00–£17.50 **S:** £16.00–£18.00
Beds: 1D 1T 2S **Baths:** 2 Sh
⌂ ▣ ダ ⊠ ✕ ▦ ⓥ ⚓

Nelson

ST1195   ◀ Railway Inn, Cross Inn

Fairmead, 24 Gelligaer Road, Treharris, Nelson, Mid Glam, CF46 6DN.
A small family run quiet haven, offering a warm welcome.
Open: All Year
Grades: WTB 4 Star
01443 411174 Mrs Kedward
Fax: 01443 411430
fairmeadhouse@aol.com
D: £21.50–£35.00 **S:** £27.50–£35.00
Beds: 2D 1T **Baths:** 2 En 1 Pr
⌂ ▣ (5) ダ ⊠ ✝ ✕ ▦ ⓥ ⚓

Oxwich

SS4986   ◀ King Arthur Hotel, Oxwich Bay Hotel, Paddys Bar

Little Haven Guesl House, Oxwich, Swansea, W Glam, SA3 1LS.
Open: Jan to Nov
Grades: WTB 1 Star
01792 390940 Mrs Lewis
D: £17.00 **S:** £19.00
Beds: 1F 2D 1T **Baths:** 1 En 1 Sh
⌂ ▣ (16) ⊠ ▦ ⚓
We offer B&B in the beautiful village of Oxwich, with the beach close by. Oxwich is in the centre of Gower, so it is the ideal place for a walking holiday.

Woodside Guest House, Oxwich, Gower, Swansea, W Glam, SA3 1LS.
Converted cottage, ensuite facilities. Near beach and coastal path.
Open: All Year
01792 390791 Mr Workman
D: £20.00–£26.00 **S:** £30.00–£45.00
Beds: 1F 3D 1T **Baths:** 4 En 1 Pr
⌂ ▣ (6) ⊠ ▦ ⓥ ⚓

Penarth

ST1871 🍺 *Railway Pub*

Alandale Guest House, *17 Plymouth Road, Penarth, S Glam, CF64 3DA.*
Open: All Year
Grades: WTB 1 Star, Commended
029 2070 9226 Mr Crothers
D: £25.00–£28.00 **S:** £20.00–£25.00
🛏 🅿 📺 🛉 🖩 ♨ ♿ cc
The family run Alandale Guesthouse is 5 minutes from the sea front. Cardiff Bay is 10 minutes by car and Cardiff is 10 minutes by train from Penarth station. Ideal guesthouse for holidays, work or short breaks.

Pencoed

SS9581 🍺 *Cafe Petit*

Chatterton Arms, *2 Hendre Road, Pencoed, Bridgend, Mid Glam, CF35 5NW.*
Busy public house in middle of village. Entertainment Fri/Sat. **Open:** All Year
01656 860293 Mrs Grant
D: £25.00–£30.00 **S:** £15.00–£20.00
Beds: 3T **Baths:** 2 En 1 Sh
🅿 (10) 📺 🖩 ♿

Pendoylan

ST0576 🍺 *Castell Mynach*

Llanerch Vineyard, *Hensol, Pendoylan, Vale of Glamorgan, CF72 8JU.*
One of Wales' 'Great Little Places', most ensuite rooms overlook largest vineyard in Wales.
Open: All Year (not Xmas)
01443 225877 Fax: 01443 225546
llanerch@cariadwines.demon.co.uk
D: £24.00–£30.00 **S:** £38.00–£50.00
Beds: 2D 2T **Baths:** 4 En
🛏 (8) 🅿 (20) ⅙ 📺 🖩 ♿ cc

Pontsticill

SO0511 🍺 *Butcher's Arms*

Butchers Arms, *Pontsticill, Merthyr Tydfil, CF48 2UE.*
Set in the beautiful surroundings of the Brecon Beacons National Park.
Open: All Year
01685 723544 Fax: 01685 388820
butchersarms@currantbun.com
D: £18.50–£22.50
Beds: 2D 1T **Baths:** 3 En
🛏 (1) 🅿 (20) ⅙ 📺 ✕ 🖩 ♿ cc

Pontypridd

ST0789 🍺 *Market Tavern*

Market Tavern Hotel, *Market Street, Pontypridd, Mid Glam, CF37 2ST.*
Open: All Year (not Xmas)
01443 485331 Mr John
Fax: 01443 491403
D: £19.00–£20.00 **S:** £28.00–£30.00
Beds: 4D 3T 4S **Baths:** 11 En
🛏 📺 🖩 ♿ ♿ cc
All bedrooms ensuite and delightfully furnished. Tavern bar offers good range of ales, wines and food. Chilli Pepper Cocktail Bar & Strads Nightclub are open late Friday & Saturday evenings. Centrally located. Ideal base for Cardiff & the Valleys.

Porthcawl

SS8277 🍺 *Rose & Crown, Royal Oak, Prince Of Wales, Farmers' Arms*

Rockybank Guest House, *15 De Breos Drive, Porthcawl, Mid Glam, CF36 3JP.*
First guest house off M4 J37. Quiet area, private parking, golf.
Open: All Year (not Xmas)
Grades: WTB 3 Star
01656 785823 (also fax)
Mrs Lewis
rockybank@totalise.co.uk
D: £21.00–£23.00 **S:** £25.00–£26.00
Beds: 1F 1D 1T **Baths:** 3 En
🛏 🅿 (6) ⅙ 📺 🖩 ♿ ♿

Rossett Guest House, *1 Esplanade Avenue, Porthcawl, CF36 3YS.*
Friendly sea side home situated on heritage coastline. Easy access surrounding areas.
Open: All Year (not Xmas)
Grades: WTB 2 Star
01656 771664 D: £15.00–£20.00
Beds: 1F **Baths:** 2 En 1 Sh
🛏 (1) 🅿 (2) 📺 🛉 ✕ 🖩 ♿ ♿

Haven Guest House, *50 New Road, Porthcawl, Mid Glam, CF36 5DN.*
Family-run guest house close to sea, beach, bowling, tennis, park, main shopping street.
Open: All Year
01656 788706 Mrs Seage
D: £18.00–£19.00 **S:** £17.00–£22.00
Beds: 3F 1D 1S **Baths:** 4 En 1 Sh
🛏 📺 ✕ 🖩 ♿ ♿

Reynoldston

SS4890 🍺 *King Arthur Hotel*

Greenways, *Hills Farm, Reynoldston, Swansea, W Glam, SA3 1AE.*
Reynoldston is central to beautiful Tower Bays, Three Cliffs, Rhossili.
Open: Easter to Nov
Grades: WTB 2 Star
01792 390125 Mrs John
D: £18.00–£20.00 **S:** £20.00–£25.00
Beds: 2D 1T
🛏 (5) 🅿 (3) 📺 🛉 🖩 ♿ cc

Rudry

ST1886 🍺 *Rudry Hotel, Maenllloyd Inn*

The Coach House, *2 Twyn Sych, Rudry, Caerphilly, CF83 3EF.*
Located in the heart of the country. 6 miles Cardiff or Newport.
Open: All Year
Grades: WTB 1 Star
029 2088 4772 (also fax)
Mr Davis
D: £17.00–£20.00 **S:** £17.00–£25.00
Beds: 2F 1D 3T 4S **Baths:** 1 En 2 Pr 3 Sh
🛏 🅿 📺 🛉 🖩 ♿

All details shown are as supplied by B&B owners in Autumn 2000

Swansea

SS6592 🍺 *Abertawe, Brynmor, Cross, George, Pilot, West Cross, Wig & Pen*

Rock Villa Guest House, *1 George Bank, The Mumbles, Swansea, W Glam, SA3 4EQ.*
Open: All Year (not Xmas/New Year)
Grades: RAC 3 Diamond
01792 366794 Mrs Thomas
D: £19.00–£23.00 **S:** £22.00–£32.00
Beds: 1F 2T 2D 1S **Baths:** 3 En 2 Sh
🛏 (3) 🅿 📺 🛉 🖩 📺 ♿
Family-run, friendly guest house. Beautiful view of Swansea Bay. Within walking distance of beach, bowling green, tennis courts and shops. Ideal for water skiing, surfing or sailing.

Mirador Guest House, *14 Mirador Crescent, Uplands, Swansea, W Glam, SA2 0QX.*
Proximity to university, beaches, Dylan Thomas trail, Gower, city centre and buses.
Open: All Year
Grades: WTB 2 Star GH
01792 466976 Mr Anderson
D: £20.00–£24.00 **S:** £20.00–£22.00
Beds: 1F 2D 1T 1S **Baths:** 3 En 2 Sh
🛏 📺 🛉 ✕ 🖩 📺 ♿

Tregare Hotel, *9 Sketty Road, Uplands, Swansea, W Glam, SA2 0EU.*
Friendly comfortable licensed hotel on main A4118 to the Gower.
Open: All Year (not Xmas/New Year)
Grades: WTB 2 Star
01792 470608 (also fax)
tregare.hotel@swig-online.co.uk
D: £22.00–£23.00 **S:** £22.00–£27.00
Beds: 2F 2D 7S **Baths:** 10 En 1 Sh
🛏 (8) ⅙ 📺 🖩 ♿ cc

Jezreel Guest House, *168 Bishopston Road, Swansea, W Glam, SA3 3EX.*
Beautiful Gower, beaches and countryside. Warm welcome from friendly hosts.
Open: All Year (not Xmas/New Year)
01792 232744 Mrs Jones
D: £16.00–£17.00 **S:** £17.00
Beds: 2D 1T **Baths:** 1 Sh
🛏 (1) 🅿 (4) ⅙ 📺 🖩 ♿

The Lyndale, *324 Oystermouth Road, Swansea, W Glam, SA1 3UJ.*
Seafront. Central to city amenities. Ideal base for exploring Gower.
Open: All Year (not Xmas)
01792 653882 Ms Williams
D: £14.00–£17.00 **S:** £15.00–£18.00
Beds: 1F 1D 3T 1S **Baths:** 2 Sh
🛏 (5) 🅿 📺 🛉 🖩 ♿

Osprey Guest House, *244 Oystermouth Road, Swansea, W Glam, SA1 3UH.*
Sea front - nearest city centre.
Open: All Year (not Xmas)
01792 642369 Mrs Ellis
D: fr £14.00 **S:** fr £15.00
Beds: 5F 3T 2S **Baths:** 3 Sh
🛏 🅿 📺 ✕ 🖩 📺 ♿

The Bayswater Hotel, 322
Oystermouth Road, Swansea, W Glam,
SA1 3UJ.
Comfortable, homely guest house
overlooking Swansea Bay. All rooms have
CTV.
Open: All Year (not Xmas)
01792 655301 Mr Ahern
Fax: 01792 643463
D: £13.00–£20.00 **S:** £18.00–£25.00
Beds: 1F 3D 1T 1S **Baths:** 2 En 1 Sh
🛏 ⊁ ⊡ ⛺ 🎍 Ⅲ, Ⅴ ♨ cc

Harlton Guest House, 89 King
Edward Road, Brynmill, Swansea, W Glam,
SA1 4LU.
Close to city centre with friendly and
pleasant accommodation.
Open: All Year
01792 466938 Mr Drinning
D: £12.00–£14.00 **S:** £12.00–£14.00
Beds: 2T 5S **Baths:** 1 Sh
🛏 ⊡ Ⅲ, ♨

The Oyster Hotel, 262 Oystermouth
Road, Swansea, W Glam, SA1 3UH.
Situated on the sea front, viewing the
Mumbles. Friendly, family-run licensed
hotel.
Open: All Year (not Xmas)
01792 654345 Mrs Peppard
D: £15.00–£19.00 **S:** £18.00–£19.00
Beds: 1F 4D 1T 2S **Baths:** 3 En 1 Sh
🛏 ⊡ 🎍 ✗ Ⅲ, Ⅴ ♨ cc

Planning a longer stay? Always

ask for any special rates

The Mumbles

SS6187   ⬤ Pilot, George, West Cross Inn

Rock Villa Guest House, 1 George
Bank, The Mumbles, Swansea, W Glam,
SA3 4EQ.
Family-run, friendly guest house.
Beautiful view of Swansea Bay.
Open: All Year (not Xmas/New Year)
Grades: RAC 3 Diamond
01792 366794 Mrs Thomas
D: £19.00–£23.00 **S:** £22.00–£32.00
Beds: 1F 2T 2D 1S **Baths:** 3 En 2 Sh
🛏 (3) 🅿 ⊡ 🎍 Ⅲ, Ⅴ ♨

The Coast House, 708 Mumbles Road,
The Mumbles, Swansea, W Glam, SA3 4EH.
Family-run - rooms with sea views -
ensuite - close to University, Gower, Cork
Ferry. **Open:** All Year (not Xmas)
01792 368702 Mrs Clarke
thecoasthouse@aol.com
D: £20.00–£24.00 **S:** £19.00–£25.00
Beds: 2F 3D 1S **Baths:** 5 En 1 Sh
🛏 🅿 ⊡ 🎍 Ⅲ, Ⅴ ♨

Treharris

ST0997   ⬤ Railway Inn, Cross Inn

Fairmead, 24 Gelligaer Road, Treharris,
Nelson, Mid Glam, CF46 6DN.
A small family run quiet haven, offering a
warm welcome.
Open: All Year **Grades:** WTB 4 Star
01443 411174 Mrs Kedward
Fax: 01443 411430
fairmeadhouse@aol.com
D: £21.50–£35.00 **S:** £27.50–£35.00
Beds: 2D 1T **Baths:** 2 En 1 Pr
🛏 🅿 (5) ⊁ ⊡ 🎍 ✗ Ⅲ, Ⅴ ♨

Welsh St Donats

ST0275   ⬤ Farmers Arms

Bryn-y-Ddafad, Welsh St Donats,
Cowbridge, CF71 7ST.
Open: All Year (not Xmas)
Grades: WTB 3 Star
01446 774451
Mrs Jenkins junejenkins@bydd.co.uk
D: £20.00–£22.50
S: £20.00–£30.00
Beds: 2D 2S
Baths: 1 En 1 Pr 1 Sh
🛏 (10) 🅿 (5) ⊁ ⊡ ✗ Ⅲ, Ⅴ ♨
Surrounded by panoramic views and a
network of footpaths, a spacious,
secluded comfortable country guest
house. First floor residents lounge with
balcony overlooking private garden and
sun lounge below. Generous breakfast
menu, vegetarian and special diet
options. A warm welcome assured.

Wernffrwd

SS5193   ⬤ North Gower Hotel, King Arthur

Aberlogin Fawr Farm, New Road,
Wernffrwd, Gower, Swansea, W Glam,
SA4 3TY.
Non-smoking, studio flat in beautiful
Welsh longhouse. Magnificent views.
Open: All Year
Grades: WTB 3 Star Farm
01792 850041
Mrs Rees
D: £25.00
Beds: 1D **Baths:** 1 En
🅿 ⊁ ⊡ Ⅲ, Ⅴ ❋ ♨ ♿

Stilwell's National Trail Companion

46 Long Distance Footpaths
Where to Stay * Where to Eat

Other guides may show you where to walk, **Stilwell's National Trail Companion** shows your where to stay and eat. The perfect companion guide for the British Isles' famous national trails and long distance footpaths, Stilwell's make pre-planning your accommodation easy. It lists B&Bs, hostels, campsites and pubs - in the order they appear along the routes - and includes such vital information as maps, grid references and distance from the path; Tourist Board ratings; the availability of vehicle pick-up, drying facilities and packed lunches. So whether you walk a trail in stages at weekends or in one continuous journey, you'll never be stuck at the end of the day for a hot meal or a great place to sleep.

Enjoy the beauty and adventure of Britain's – and Ireland's – long distance trails with Stilwell's National Trail Companion.

Paths in England
Cleveland Way & Tabular Hills Link – Coast to Coast Path – Cotswald Way – Cumbria Way – Dales Way – Essex Way – Greensand Way – Hadrian's Wall – Heart of England Way – Hereward Way – Icknield Way – Macmillan Way – North Downs Way – Oxfordshire Way – Peddars Way and Norfolk Coastal Path – Pennine Way – Ribble Way – The Ridgeway – Shropshire Way – South Downs Way – South West Coast Path – Staffordshire Way – Tarka Trail – Thames Path – Two Moors Way - Vanguard Way - Viking Way – Wayfarer's Walk – Wealdway – Wessex Ridgeway – Wolds Way

Paths in Ireland
Beara Way – Dingle Way – Kerry Way – Ulster Way – Western Way – Wicklow Way

Paths in Scotland
Fife Coastal Walk – Southern Upland Way – Speyside Way – West Highland Way

Paths in Wales
Cambrian Way – Glyndwr's Way – Offa's Dyke Path – Pembrokeshire Coast Path – Wye Valley Walk

£9.95 from all good bookstores (ISBN 1-900861-25-9) or £10.95 (inc p&p) from Stilwell Publishing Ltd, 59 Charlotte Road, London EC2A 3QW (020 7739 7179)

Monmouthshire

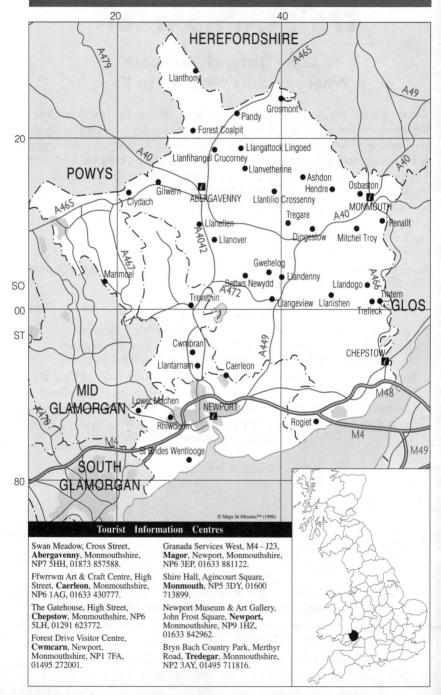

© Maps In Minutes™ (1996)

Tourist Information Centres

Swan Meadow, Cross Street,
Abergavenny, Monmouthshire,
NP7 5HH, 01873 857588.

Ffwrrwm Art & Craft Centre, High
Street, **Caerleon**, Monmouthshire,
NP6 1AG, 01633 430777.

The Gatehouse, High Street,
Chepstow, Monmouthshire, NP6
5LH, 01291 623772.

Forest Drive Visitor Centre,
Cwmcarn, Newport,
Monmouthshire, NP1 7FA,
01495 272001.

Granada Services West, M4 - J23,
Magor, Newport, Monmouthshire,
NP6 3EP, 01633 881122.

Shire Hall, Agincourt Square,
Monmouth, NP5 3DY, 01600
713899.

Newport Museum & Art Gallery,
John Frost Square, **Newport,**
Monmouthshire, NP9 1HZ,
01633 842962.

Bryn Bach Country Park, Merthyr
Road, **Tredegar**, Monmouthshire,
NP2 3AY, 01495 711816.

Abergavenny

SO2914 ◀ *King's Arms, Crown Inn, Old Mitre, Lamb & Flag, Walnut Tree, Bear Hotel, Nant-y-fyn, Red Hart*

The Wenallt, Gilwern, Abergavenny, Monmouthshire, NP7 0HP.
Open: All Year
Grades: WTB 3 Star
01873 830694
Mr Harris
D: £19.50–£26.00 **S:** £24.00–£28.00
Beds: 1F 6D 2T 6S **Baths:** 1 En 6 Pr
🛏 🅿 (20) ⅍ 📺 🍴 ✕ 🛍 🎦 ♨
C16th Welsh longhouse in 50 acres in Brecon Beacons National Park.

Pentre Court, Brecon Road, Abergavenny, NP7 9ND.
Open: All Year
Grades: WTB 2 Star
01873 853545
Mrs Candler
judith@pentrecourt.com
D: £18.00–£24.00 **S:** £18.00–£30.00
Beds: 3D **Baths:** 3 En
🛏 🅿 📺 ✕ 🛍 🎦 ♨
Spacious, welcoming Georgian house with open fires, set in 3 acres of pretty stream side interestingly stocked gardens/paddock, spring bulbs, shrubs and roses, with wonderful views over the Usk valley. Just inside the National Park beside footpath to River Usk and Sugarloaf Mountain.

Tyn-y-bryn, Deriside, Abergavenny, Monmouthshire, NP7 7HT.
Magnificent views, a homely atmosphere. Comfortable accommodation & warm welcome.
Open: All Year
Grades: WTB 3 Star Farm
01873 856682 (also fax)
Ms Belcham
cbelcham@care4free.net
D: fr £20.00 **S:** fr £25.00
Beds: 1F 1T 1D **Baths:** 2 En
🅿 (6) 📺 🍴 ✕ 🛍 🎦 ♨

Pentre House, Brecon Road, Abergavenny, Monmouthshire, NP7 7EW.
Charming small Georgian award-winning country house in wonderful gardens.
Open: All Year (not Xmas)
Grades: WTB 3 Star
01873 853435
Mrs Reardon-Smith
Fax: 01873 852321
Treardonsm@aol.com
D: £17.00–£18.00 **S:** £20.00–£25.00
Beds: 1F 1D 1T **Baths:** 2 Sh
🛏 🅿 (6) 📺 🍴 ✕ 🛍 🎦 ♨

Ty`r Morwydd House, Pen-y-Pound, Abergavenny, Monmouthshire, NP7 5UD.
Quality group accommodation, conferences, training etc. Advance bookings only.
Open: All Year (not Xmas/New Year)
Grades: WTB 3 Star
01873 855959 Mrs Senior
Fax: 01873 855443
tyrmorwydd@aol.com
D: £16.50 **S:** £16.50
Beds: 2F 18T 29S
🛏 🅿 (25) ⅍ 📺 🍴 ✕ 🛍 🎦 ♨

The Guest House & Mansel Restaurant, 2 Oxford Street, Abergavenny, Monmouthshire, NP7 5RP.
Near bus, railway station, town; excellent accommodation, choice of breakfast.
Open: Mar to Dec
01873 854823 Mrs Cook
D: £16.00–£19.00 **S:** £19.50–£27.00
Beds: 3F 6D 6T 2S **Baths:** 3 Sh
🛏 (6) 🅿 (10) 📺 ✕ 🛍 ♨

Maes Glas, Monmouth Road, Abergavenny, NP7 9SP.
Maes Glas is a detached bungalow, within easy walking distance of town centre. **Open:** All Year
01873 854494 (also fax) Mrs Haynes
maesglasbb@optusnet.com.au
D: £17.50–£20.00 **S:** £17.50–£20.00
Beds: 1F 1D
🛏 🅿 ⅍ 📺 ✕ 🛍 ♨ ♿

Bettws Newydd

SO3605 ◀ *Black Bear*

Thornbury Farm, Bettws Newydd, Usk, Monmouthshire, NP5 1JY.
Family Farm. Warm welcome, beautiful views, attractions - Castles, golf, walks.
Open: All Year (not Xmas/New Year)
01873 880598 Mrs Jones
D: £20.00 **S:** £22.00
Beds: 1T 2D **Baths:** 1 Sh
🛏 🅿 ⅍ 📺 🛍 🎦 ♨

Caerleon

ST3390 ◀ *Bell Inn*

Great House, Isca Road, Old Village, Caerleon, NP18 1QG.
Open: All Year (not Xmas)
Grades: WTB 3 Star
01633 420216 Mrs Price **Fax:** 01633 423492
price.greathouse@tesco.net
D: £25.00–£30.00 **S:** £30.00–£32.50
Beds: 2T 1S **Baths:** 1 En 1 Sh
🛏 (10) 🅿 (2) ⅍ 📺 ✕ 🛍 🎦 ♨
C16th, Grade II Listed, delightful village home with garden to river. Comfortable, pretty rooms and very warm welcome. 1.5 miles to M4. Good en route stop for Ireland and West Wales.

Chepstow

ST5393 ◀ *White Lion, Coach & Horses, Cross Keys*

Lower Hardwick House, Mount Pleasant, Chepstow, Monmouthshire, NP16 5PT.
Beautiful Georgian house, walled garden. Free car parking for duration walk.
Open: All Year
01291 622162 Mrs Grassby
D: £15.50–£18.00 **S:** £18.00–£25.00
Beds: 1F 1D 1T 1S **Baths:** 2 Pr 1 Sh
🛏 🅿 (12) 📺 🛍 🎦 ♨

The Old Course Hotel, Newport Road, Chepstow, Gwent, NP16 5PR.
Modern hotel, convenient for the Wye Valley, Chepstow races and more.
Open: All Year **Grades:** AA 3 Star
01291 626261 Fax: 01291 626263
D: £28.75–£32.25 **S:** £47.00–£53.00
Beds: 4F 10D 7T 10S **Baths:** 31 En
🛏 🅿 (180) 📺 🍴 ✕ 🛍 ♨ ♿ cc

The First Hurdle, 9-10 Upper Church St, Chepstow, Gwent, NP16 5EX.
Enjoy comfortable,ensuite accommodation. Centrally situated, family owned B&B. **Open:** Easter to Nov
01291 622189 Mrs Westwood
Fax: 01291 628421
D: £23.00–£25.00 **S:** £25.00–£27.50
Beds: 2D 2T 1S **Baths:** 5 En
⅍ 📺 🛍 🎦 ♨

Langcroft, 71 St Kingsmark Avenue, Chepstow, Monmouthshire, NP6 5LY.
Modern family friendly home. Town centre, four minutes' walk. **Open:** All Year
01291 625569 (also fax) Mrs Langdale
D: £18.00–£20.00 **S:** £20.00
Beds: 1D 1T 1S **Baths:** 1 Sh
🛏 🅿 (2) 📺 🍴 🛍 🎦 ♨

Clydach

SO2213

Rock & Fountain Hotel, Clydach, Abergavenny, NP7 0LL.
Family run hotel within the Brecon Beacons National Park.
Open: All Year **Grades:** WTB 3 Star
01873 830393 Fax: 01873 730393
archer@rockandfountain.fsnet.co.uk
D: £23.00–£28.00 **S:** £29.50–£33.00
Beds: 3F 1T 2D **Baths:** 6 En
🛏 🅿 (20) 📺 ✕ 🛍 🎦 ♨ cc

Cwmbran

ST2894 ◀ *Greenhouse, Red Lion*

Springfields, 371 Llantarnam Road, Llantarnam, Cwmbran, Monmouthshire, NP44 3BN.
Large welcoming Victorian home, family run for 27 years, Joan Graham.
Open: All Year
01633 482509 Mrs Graham
D: £15.75–£18.00 **S:** £15.75–£19.00
Beds: 2F 4D 3T **Baths:** 6 En 6 Pr 2 Sh
🛏 🅿 (16) 📺 🍴 🛍 🎦 ♨

Dingestow

SO4510 ◀ *Cripple Creek Inn*

Lower Pen-y-Clawdd Farm, Dingestow, Monmouth, NP5 4BG.
Very attractive house on working farm, rooms overlook landscaped gardens.
Open: March to Nov
Grades: WTB 2 Star
01600 740223 Mrs Bayliss
D: £18.00–£20.00 **S:** £20.00
Beds: 1F 1T **Baths:** 1 Sh
🛏 (1) 🅿 (10) ⅍ 📺 🍴 🛍 🎦 ♨

Forest Coalpit

SO2821 ◀ *Old Crown*

New Inn Farm, Forest Coalpit, Abergavenny, Monmouthshire, NP7 7LT.
Peaceful, welcoming mountain farmhouse. Superb views. Walking from the door. **Open:** All Year (not Xmas)
Grades: WTB 3 Star
01873 890466 (also fax) J Bull
newinn.farm@virgin.net
D: £20.00 **S:** £20.00
Beds: 1F 1D 1T **Baths:** 1 En 2 Pr
🛏 🅿 (10) ⅍ 📺 🍴 🛍 🎦 ♨ ♿

Gilwern

SO2414

The Wenallt, Gilwern, Abergavenny, Monmouthshire, NP7 0HP.
C16th Welsh longhouse in 50 acres in Brecon Beacons National Park.
Open: All Year
Grades: WTB 3 Star
01873 830694 Mr Harris
D: £19.50–£26.00 **S:** £24.00–£28.00
Beds: 1F 6D 2T 6S **Baths:** 1 En 6 Pr
🛇 🅿 (20) ⚡ 📺 🕇 ✕ 🏛 🅥 🛉

Grosmont

SO4024   ◀ Angel

Lawns Farm, Grosmont, Abergavenny, Monmouthshire, NP7 8ES.
Beautiful C17th farmhouse set in unspoilt countryside. 'A real gem!'.
Open: Feb to Nov
Grades: WTB 3 Star
01981 240298 Mr & Mrs Ferneyhough
Fax: 01981 241275
edna@ferneyhough8.freeserve.co.uk
D: £20.00–£24.00 **S:** £25.00
Beds: 2D 1T **Baths:** 2 En 1 Sh
🛇 🅿 ⚡ 📺 🏛 🅥 🛉

Gwehelog

SO3804   ◀ Hall

Ty-Gwyn Farm, Gwehelog, Usk, Monmouthshire, NP5 1RG.
Quiet countryside location with magnificent views, surrounded by secluded lawns.
Open: All Year (not Xmas)
01291 672878 (also fax)
Mr & Mrs Arnett
D: £19.00–£20.00 **S:** £25.00–£30.00
Beds: 2D 1T **Baths:** 2 En 1 Pr
🛇 (5) 🅿 ⚡ 📺 🏛 🛉

Hendre

SO4614   ◀ Halfway House

The Hendre Farmhouse, Hendre, Monmouth, NP25 4DJ.
Picturesque farmhouse, ideal base for walking, golfing, fishing, exploring Monmouthshire.
Open: All Year (not Xmas)
01600 740484 (also fax)
Mrs Baker
D: £22.00–£25.00 **S:** £25.00
Beds: 1F 1D 4T 2S **Baths:** 2 En 1 Pr 2 Sh
🛇 🅿 (10) ⚡ 📺 🕇 ✕ 🏛 🅥 🛉

Llandenny

SO4004   ◀ All Seasons

The Peargoed, Llandenny, Usk, Monmouthshire, NP5 1DH.
£15 pppn. Peargoed Farmhouse, Llandenny, Usk, Mon. 01291 690233.
Open: Easter to Oct
01291 690233 K M James
D: £15.00 **S:** £15.00
Beds: 1D 1S **Baths:** 1 Pr
🛇 (8) 🅿 (2) ⚡ 📺 🛉

Llandogo

SO5204   ◀ Old Farmhouse

Lugano, Llandogo, Monmouth, Monmouthshire, NP5 4TL.
Luxury accommodation, beautiful landscaped gardens, picturesque village location. **Open:** All Year (not Xmas)
01594 530496 Mrs Townsend
Fax: 01594 530956
D: £16.00–£19.50 **S:** £20.00
Beds: 2D 1T 1S **Baths:** 1 En 1 Sh
🛇 🅿 (4) ⚡ 📺 🏛 🅥 🛉

Llanellen

SO3010   ◀ Goose & Cuckoo

Yew Tree Farm, Llanellen, Abergavenny, NP7 9LB.
Exceptional self contained accommodation on secluded farm with far reaching views.
Open: April to October
Grades: WTB 2 Star
01873 854307 (also fax) Mr & Mrs Rose
D: £20.00 **S:** £25.00
Beds: 1F **Baths:** 1 En
🛇 🅿 (2) ⚡ 📺 🕇 🅥 🛉

Llanfihangel Crucorney

SO3221   ◀ Skirrid Inn

Pen-y-dre Farm, Llanfihangel Crucorney, Abergavenny, Gwent, NP7 8DT.
Open: All Year
01873 890246 (also fax) Mrs Jones
D: £20.00–£22.00 **S:** £20.00–£25.00
Beds: 2D 1D/F **Baths:** 2 En 1 Pr
🛇 🅿 (6) 📺 🕇 🏛 🅥 🛉 cc
We can promise you a warm welcome and hearty breakfast in our C17th farmhouse, situated in the picturesque village of Llanfihangel Crucorney. Ideal base for walking, sightseeing, pony trekking, golfing or just relaxing. Plenty of excellent places to eat.

Llangattock Lingoed

SO3620

Hunter's Moon Inn, Llangattock Lingoed, Abergavenny, Monmouthshire, NP7 8RR.
Beautiful C13th inn, away from it all location at foot of the Skirrid Mountain.
Open: All Year
01873 821499 Mr Evans
Fax: 01873 821411
D: £26.00–£32.00 **S:** £38.00–£41.00
Beds: 4D **Baths:** 4 En
🅿 (40) ⚡ 📺 ✕ 🏛 ✻ 🛉 cc

Llangeview

SO3900

The Rat Trap, Chepstow Road, Llangeview, Usk, Monmouthshire, NP5 1EY.
In the beautiful setting of the Vale of Usk (adjacent to the Wye Valley).
Open: All Year
01291 673288 Mr & Mrs Rabaiotti
Fax: 01291 673305
bookings@rattraphotel.co.uk
D: £29.50–£34.50 **S:** £20.00–£24.00
Beds: 1F 5D 5T 1S **Baths:** 12 En
🛇 (2) 🅿 (50) 📺 🕇 🏛 🅥 🛉 🕭 cc

National Grid References are for villages, towns and cities – not for individual houses

Llanishen

SO4702

Llanishen House, Llanishen, Chepstow, Gwent, NP16 6QS.
Secluded country house with magnificent grounds and panoramic views.
Open: All Year
01600 860700 Mrs Harmston
dharmston@llewellin7.freeserve.co.uk
D: £20.00–£30.00 **S:** £25.00–£30.00
Beds: 1F 2D **Baths:** 1 En 1 Pr 1 Sh
🛇 🅿 (4) ⚡ 📺 🏛 🛉

Llanover

SO3107   ◀ Goose & Cuckoo, Horseshoe, Star Inn

Ty Byrgwm, Upper Llanover, Abergavenny, NP7 9EP.
18th century cottage/barn, 26 acres in national park meadows/woodlands
Open: All Year
Grades: WTB 2 Star
01873 880725 Mrs Bloomfield
D: £22.50 **S:** £22.00
Beds: 1D 2S **Baths:** 2 En 1 Pr
🛇 (2) 🅿 (3) ⚡ 📺 🕇 ✕ 🏛 🛉

Llantarnam

ST3093   ◀ Greenhouse, Red Lion

Springfields, 371 Llantarnam Road, Llantarnam, Cwmbran, Monmouthshire, NP44 3BN.
Large welcoming Victorian home, family run for 27 years, Joan Graham.
Open: All Year
01633 482509 Mrs Graham
D: £15.75–£18.00 **S:** £15.75–£19.00
Beds: 2F 4D 3T **Baths:** 6 En 6 Pr 2 Sh
🛇 🅿 (16) 📺 🕇 🏛 🅥 🛉

Llanthony

SO2827

The Half Moon, Llanthony, Abergavenny, Monmouthshire, NP7 7NN.
C17th, beautiful countryside. Serves good food and real ales.
Open: All Year (not Xmas)
01873 890611 Mrs Smith
D: £20.00–£22.00 **S:** £22.00–£25.00
Beds: 2F 4D 2T 1S **Baths:** 2 Sh
🛇 🅿 (8) 📺 🕇 ✕ 🏛 🅥 🛉

Llantilio Crossenny

SO3914   ◀ King's Arms, Three Salmon

Treloyvan Farm, Llantilio Crossenny, Abergavenny, Monmouthshire, NP7 8UE.
Warm welcome, beautiful rural farmhouse, lovely views, guest rooms with showers. **Open:** Easter to Nov
01600 780478 Mrs Watkins
D: £15.00–£18.00 **S:** £18.00–£22.00
Beds: 1F 1T **Baths:** 1 Sh
🛇 🅿 ⚡ 📺 🕇 ✕ 🏛 🅥 🛉

Llanvetherine

SO3617 ⚓ *King's Arms*

Great Tre-Rhew Farm, *Llanvetherine, Abergavenny, Monmouthshire, NP7 8RA.*
Warm welcome on a Welsh working farm. Peaceful, rural & friendly.
Open: All Year (not Xmas)
Grades: WTB 2 Star
01873 821268 Ms Beavan
D: £17.50–£20.00 **S:** £17.50–£20.00
Beds: 1F 2D 1T 1S **Baths:** 2 Sh
🛏 🅿 📺 🛉 🗡 ⬛ Ⅴ ⚫

Llanvihangel Crucorney

SO3220 ⚓ *Crown Inn, Skirrid Inn*

Penyclawdd Farm, *Llanvihangel Crucorney, Abergavenny, Monmouthshire, NP7 7LB.*
Beef/sheep farm, very large garden. Easy reach Abergavenny, Hereford, Cardiff, Hay-on-Wye.
Open: All Year
Grades: WTB 3 Star, AA 3 Diamond
01873 890591 (also fax)
Mrs Davies
D: £20.00–£22.00 **S:** £20.00–£22.00
Beds: 2F **Baths:** 1 Sh
🛏 🅿 ⤢ 📺 🛉 🗡 ⬛ Ⅴ ✤ ⚫

The Skirrid Mountain Inn,
Llanvihangel Crucorney, Abergavenny, Monmouthshire, NP7 8DH.
An historic country inn of unique character. Wales' oldest inn.
Open: All Year
01873 890258 Miss Grant
D: £34.50–£39.50 **S:** £34.50–£39.50
Beds: 2D
🛏 🅿 ⤢ 📺 🛉 🗡 ⬛ Ⅴ ⚫

Lower Machen

ST2287 ⚓ *Hollybush Inn*

The Forge, *Lower Machen, Newport, NP1 8UU.*
Warm welcome, ideal for walking in forests or on mountains.
Open: All Year (not Xmas/New Year)
Grades: WTB listed comm
01633 440226 Mrs Jones
D: £16.50–£18.00 **S:** £18.00–£20.00
Beds: 1F 1D 1T **Baths:** 1 Sh
🛏 🅿 (3) 📺 🛉 ⬛ Ⅴ ⚫

Manmoel

SO1703 ⚓ *Travellers Rest*

Wyrloed Lodge, *Manmoel, Blackwood, Gwent, NP12 0RW.*
Victorian style home in mountain hamlet. Pub, views, peaceful, walking, touring, home cooking.
Open: All Year (not Xmas/New Year)
Grades: WTB 3 Star
01495 371198 (also fax) Mrs James
D: £20.00 **S:** £20.00
Beds: 1F 2D 1T **Baths:** 4 En
🛏 🅿 (6) ⤢ 📺 🛉 🗡 ⬛ Ⅴ ⚫

Planning a longer stay? Always ask for any special rates

Mitchel Troy

SO4910 ⚓ *The Cockett*

Church Farm Guest House, *Mitchel Troy, Monmouth, NP25 4HZ.*
C16th character (former) farmhouse set in large garden with stream.
Open: All Year (not Xmas)
Grades: WTB 2 Star GH, AA 3 Diamond
01600 712176 Mrs Ringer
D: £20.00–£23.50 **S:** £20.00–£23.00
Beds: 2F 3D 2T 1S **Baths:** 6 En 1 Sh
🛏 🅿 (12) ⤢ 📺 🛉 🗡 ⬛ Ⅴ ⚫

Monmouth

SO5012 ⚓ *Kings Head, Gate House, Vine Tree, Green Dragon, Punch House, Royal Oak, Robin Hood, Riverside Inn, French Horn*

Wye Avon, *New Dixton Road, Monmouth, NP5 3PR.*
Large, interesting stone-built Victorian house. A family home.
Open: All Year (not Xmas)
01600 713322 Mrs Cantrell
D: £16.00 **S:** £16.00–£21.00
Beds: 1F 1D 1S **Baths:** 1 Sh
🛏 🅿 ⤢ ⬛

Riverside Hotel, *Cinderhill Street, Monmouth, NP25 5EY.*
Outstanding converted C17th coaching inn.
Open: All Year
Grades: WTB 2 Star, AA 2 Star
01600 715577 Mr Dodd
Fax: 01600 712668
D: £25.00–£34.00 **S:** £40.00–£48.00
Beds: 2F 6D 9T **Baths:** 17 En
🛏 (1) 🅿 (25) ⤢ 📺 🛉 🗡 ⬛ ✤ ⚫ ⚫ cc

Burton House, *St James Square, Monmouth, NP5 3DN.*
Georgian town house, restaurants and shops nearby, good touring base.
Open: All Year (not Xmas)
01600 714958 Mrs Banfield
D: £18.00 **S:** £22.00
Beds: 1F 1D 1T **Baths:** 1 Sh
🅿 (3) 📺 ⬛ ⚫ cc

Offa's Bed & Breakfast, *37 Brook Estate, Monmouth, NP5 3AN.*
Situated in beautiful Wye Valley on Offa's Dyke Path, friendly and comfortable B&B.
Open: Easter to 30 Sept
01600 716934 Mr Ruston & Ms A West
rruston@surfaid.org
D: £17.50 **S:** £19.00
Beds: 1D 1T **Baths:** 1 Pr 1 Sh
🛏 🅿 (3) ⤢ 📺 🛉 ⬛ Ⅴ ⚫ ⚫

Newport

ST3188 ⚓ *Church House, Elm Tree, Rock & Fountain, Six Bells, Rhiwderin*

Pentre Tai Farm, *Rhiwderin, Newport, Monmouthshire, NP10 9RQ.*
Peaceful Welsh sheep farm in castle country close to M4.
Open: Feb to Nov **Grades:** WTB 2 Star
01633 893284 (also fax) Mrs Proctor
stay@pentretai.f9.co.uk
D: £19.00–£20.00 **S:** £24.00–£25.00
Beds: 1F 1D 1T **Baths:** 2 En 1 Sh
🛏 🅿 (4) ⤢ 📺 ⬛ ⚫

Chapel Guest House, *Church Road, St Brides Wentlooge, Newport, Monmouthshire, NP10 8SN.*
Comfortable accommodation in converted chapel situated between Newport and Cardiff.
Open: All Year
Grades: WTB 3 Star
01633 681018 Mr Bushell
Fax: 01633 681431
D: £19.00–£22.00 **S:** £23.00–£25.00
Beds: 1F 1D 1T 1S **Baths:** 4 En
🛏 🅿 (10) ⤢ 📺 🛉 ⬛ Ⅴ ⚫

The West Usk Lighthouse,
Lighthouse Road, St Brides Wentlooge, Newport, Monmouthshire, NP1 9SF.
Super B&B in real lighthouse, with water & four poster beds.
Open: All Year
Grades: WTB 2 Star B&B
01633 810126 Mr & Mrs Sheahan
Lighthouse1@tesco.net
D: £40.00 **S:** £50.00–£60.00
Beds: 1F 2D **Baths:** 3 En
🛏 🅿 (10) ⤢ 📺 🛉 ⬛ ⚫

Knoll Guest House, *145 Stow Hill, Newport, Monmouthshire, NP9 4FZ.*
Centrally located, Victorian style guesthouse. Refurbished 2000 to excellent standard.
Open: All Year
Grades: WTB 2 Star
01633 263557 Fax: 01633 212168
D: £22.00–£22.50 **S:** £35.00
Beds: 2F 2D 2T 2S **Baths:** 5 En 4 Pr 2 Sh
🛏 (1) 🅿 (4) ⤢ 📺 🛉 🗡 ⬛ Ⅴ ⚫ cc

Osbaston

SO5014

Caseta Alta, *15 Toynbee Close, Osbaston, Monmouth, NP25 3NU.*
Comfortable house. Glorious views of Monnow Valley. Good food and base for touring.
Open: All Year (not Xmas)
01600 713023 Mrs Allcock
D: £17.00–£21.00 **S:** £25.00–£30.00
Beds: 1D 1T 1S **Baths:** 1 En 1 Sh
🛏 (2) 🅿 (2) ⤢ 📺 🗡 ⬛ Ⅴ ⚫

Pandy

SO3322 ⚓ *Lancaster Arms, Pandy Inn, Park Hotel, Skirrid Inn, Offa's Tavern*

Old Castle Court Farm, *Pandy, Abergavenny, Monmouthshire, NP7 7PH.*
C13th farmhouse near Offa's Dyke path and River Monnow.
Open: Feb to Nov **Grades:** WTB 1 Star
01873 890285 Mrs Probert
D: £15.00 **S:** £16.00
Beds: 1F 1D 1T **Baths:** 3 En 3 Pr
🛏 🅿 (10) 📺 🛉 Ⅴ ⚫

Brynhonddu, *Pandy, Abergavenny, Monmouthshire, NP7 7PD.*
Large C16th-C19th country house in great location. **Open:** All Year (not Xmas)
Grades: WTB 2 Star
01873 890535 Mrs White
kdwhite@clara.net
D: £16.00–£20.00 **S:** £18.00
Beds: 1F 1D 1T **Baths:** 1 Sh 1 En
🛏 (5) 🅿 (6) 📺 🛉 ⬛ ⚫

RATES

D = Price range per person sharing in a double room

S = Price range for a single room

Lancaster Arms, Pandy, Abergavenny, Monmouthshire, NP7 8DW.
Country pub on Offa's Dyke path, edge of Black Mountains.
Open: All Year
Grades: WTB 2 Star
01873 890699 (also fax)
Mr & Mrs Lyon
slyon@waitrose.com
D: £20.00 **S:** £22.00
Beds: 2T **Baths:** 2 Pr
🛇 🅿 (10) 📺 🏲 ✕ 🛒 🔽 ♨ ₤

Penallt

SO5210   ◙ *Boat Inn*

Cherry Orchard Farm, Lone Lane, Penallt, Monmouth, NP5 4AJ.
Small C18th working farm situated in Lower Wye Valley.
Open: All Year (not Xmas)
01600 714416 Mrs Beale
Fax: 01600 714447
D: £18.00 **S:** £18.00
Beds: 2D **Baths:** 1 Sh
🛇 🅿 (4) 🗶 📺 🏲 ✕ 🛒 🔽 ✿ ₤

The Bush, Penallt, Monmouth, NP5 4SE.
C17th stone building in idyllic walking country.
Open: All Year
01600 772765 Mr & Mrs Boycott
Fax: 01600 860236
D: £22.50–£27.50 **S:** £27.50
Beds: 1F 3D 2T **Baths:** 6 En
🛇 🅿 🗶 📺 ✕ 🛒 ₤ cc

Rhiwderin

ST2687   ◙ *Rhiwderin*

Pentre Tai Farm, Rhiwderin, Newport, Monmouthshire, NP10 9RQ.
Peaceful Welsh sheep farm in castle country close to M4.
Open: Feb to Nov
Grades: WTB 2 Star
01633 893284 (also fax) Mrs Proctor
stay@pentretai.f9.co.uk
D: £19.00–£20.00 **S:** £24.00–£25.00
Beds: 1F 1D 1T **Baths:** 2 En 1 Sh
🛇 🅿 (4) 🗶 📺 🛒 ₤

Rogiet

ST4687   ◙ *Wheatsheaf*

Court Farm, Rogiet, Newport, Gwent, NP26 3UR.
Comfortable farmhouse near Usk, Chepstow and Wye Valley. Cardiff 16 miles, Bristol 17 miles.
Open: All Year
Grades: WTB 3 Star
01633 880232 S Anstey
D: £20.00–£25.00 **S:** £20.00–£25.00
Beds: 2F 2T **Baths:** 2 En 1 Pr
🛇 🅿 (10) 🗶 📺 🏲 🛒 🔽 ₤

St Brides Wentlooge

ST2982   ◙ *Church House Inn, Elm Tree, Rock & Fountain*

Chapel Guest House, Church Road, St Brides Wentlooge, Newport, Monmouthshire, NP10 8SN.
Comfortable accommodation in converted chapel situated between Newport and Cardiff.
Open: All Year **Grades:** WTB 3 Star
01633 681018 Mr Bushell
Fax: 01633 681431
D: £19.00–£22.00 **S:** £23.00–£25.00
Beds: 1F 1D 1T 1S **Baths:** 4 En
🛇 🅿 (10) 🗶 📺 🏲 🛒 🔽 ₤

The West Usk Lighthouse,
Lighthouse Road, St Brides Wentlooge, Newport, Monmouthshire, NP1 9SF.
Super B&B in real lighthouse, with water & four poster beds. **Open:** All Year
Grades: WTB 2 Star B&B
01633 810126 Mr & Mrs Sheahan
Lighthouse1@tesco.net
D: £40.00 **S:** £50.00–£60.00
Beds: 1F 2D **Baths:** 3 En
🛇 🅿 (10) 🗶 📺 🏲 🛒 ₤

Tintern

SO5300   ◙ *Moon & Sixpence, Wye Valley Hotel, Royal George Hotel*

Highfield House, Chapel Hill, Tintern, Chepstow, Monmouthshire, NP6 6TF.
Open: All Year
Grades: WTB 3 Diamond, AA 5 Diamond
01291 689838
  Mr McCaffery
Fax: 01291 689890
D: £24.50–£29.50 **S:** £30.00–£37.50
Beds: 2F 1D **Baths:** 2 En 1 Pr
🛇 🅿 (10) 📺 🏲 ✕ 🛒 🔽 ♨ ₤
Nestled into the hillside surrounded by forest above Tintern Abbey, this remarkable house offers wondrous views of the Wye Valley. Close Offa's Dyke on the Tintern Trail. Noted for Mediterranean cuisine served under candlelight. Log fires, very warm welcome.

Rose Cottage, The Chase, Woolaston, Glos, GL15 6PT.
Open: All Year **Grades:** WTB 3 Star
01291 689691 Mrs Dunbar
rosecottage@breathemail.net
D: £22.50 **S:** £45.00
Beds: 1T **Baths:** 1 En
🗶 📺 ✕ 🛒 🔽 ₤
Self contained small converted barn, peaceful location. Private off-road parking. Evening meals a speciality using own organic produce. On edge of Royal Forest of Dean close to Chepstow, Monmouth and Ross on Wye. Historic castles at Chepstow and St. Briavels.

Holmleigh, Monmouth Road, Tintern, Chepstow, Monmouthshire, NP6 6SG.
Beautiful old house overlooking the river Wye. **Open:** All Year
01291 689521 Mr & Mrs Mark
D: £15.50 **S:** £15.50
Beds: 2D 1T 1S **Baths:** 1 Sh
🛇 🅿 (3) 📺 🛒 ₤

The Old Rectory, Tintern, Chepstow, Monmouthshire, NP16 6SG.
Comfortable accommodation overlooking beautiful River Wye. Warm welcome, log fires, good cooking.
Open: All Year
01291 689519 Mrs Taylor
Fax: 01291 689939
D: £17.00–£20.00 **S:** £22.00–£27.50
Beds: 1F 2D 1T **Baths:** 1 En 1 Pr 1 Sh
🛇 🅿 (3) 🗶 📺 🏲 ✕ 🛒 🔽 ₤

Valley House, Raglan Road, Tintern, Chepstow, Monmouthshire, NP6 6TH.
C18th detached house in picturesque valley.
Open: All Year (not Xmas)
01291 689652 Mr & Mrs Howe
Fax: 01291 689805
petehowe@compuserve.com
D: £21.00 **S:** £30.00
Beds: 2D 1T **Baths:** 3 En
🅿 🗶 📺 🏲 🛒 🔽 ₤

Tregare

SO4110

Court Robert, Tregare, Raglan, Monmouthshire, NP5 2BZ.
Peaceful C16th home, log fires, antique furnishings, spacious comfortable bedrooms.
Open: All Year
01291 690709 (also fax)
Ms Paxton
courtrobert@virgin.net
D: £17.00 **S:** fr £19.00
Beds: 2F **Baths:** 1 Sh
🛇 🅿 (10) 📺 ✕ 🛒 🔽 ♿ cc

Trelleck

SO4901   ◙ *Lion Inn*

Hollytree House, Trelleck, Monmouth, NP25 4PA.
A Wye Valley rural village setting with pub and restaurant.
Open: All Year
01600 860181 Mr & Mrs Peckham
gerald.peckham@btclick.com
D: £19.50–£21.50 **S:** £20.50–£22.50
Beds: 1F 1T **Baths:** 1 Pr 1 Sh
🛇 (3) 🅿 (3) 🗶 📺 🏲 ✕ 🛒 ₤

Trevethin

SO2801   ◙ *The Horseshoe*

Ty'r Ywen Farm, Lasgarn Lane, Trevethin, Pontypool, Monmouthshire, NP4 8TT.
Remote C16th farmhouse in National Park. Magnificent views. Four poster beds.
Open: All Year (not Xmas)
01495 785200 (also fax)
Mrs Armitage
susan.armitage@virgin.net
D: £20.00–£28.00 **S:** £20.00–£56.00
Beds: 3D 1T **Baths:** 4 En
🛇 (14) 🅿 (10) 🗶 📺 🏲 ✕ 🛒 🔽 ₤ cc

Planning a longer stay? Always ask for any special rates

Stilwell's Ireland: Bed & Breakfast 2000

Think of Ireland and you think of that world famous Irish hospitality. The warmth of the welcome is as much a part of this great island as are the wild and beautiful landscapes, the traditional folk music and the Guinness. Everywhere you go, town or country, North or South, you can't escape it. There are few better ways of experiencing this renowned hospitality, when traveling through Ireland, than by staying at one of the country's many Bed & Breakfasts. And there's no better way of choosing a convenient and desirable B&B than by consulting **Stilwell's Ireland: Bed & Breakfast 2001**.

Stilwell's Ireland: Bed & Breakfast 2001 contains over 1,400 entries – private houses, country halls, farms, cottages, inns, small hotels and guest houses – listed by county, in both Northern Ireland and the Republic of Ireland. Each entry includes room rates, facilities, Tourist Board grades or notices of approval and a brief description of the B&B, its location and surroundings. The average charge per person per night is £18. The listings also provide the names of local pubs and restaurants which serve food in the evening. As with all Stilwell B&B guides, Stilwell's Ireland has maps, listings of Tourist Information Offices and air, rail, bus and ferry information.

Treat yourself to some Irish hospitality with **Stilwell's Ireland: Bed & Breakfast 2001**.

£6.95 from all good bookstores (ISBN 1-900861-24-0) or £7.95 (inc p&p) from Stilwell Publishing Ltd, 59 Charlotte Road, London EC2A 3QW (020 7739 7179)

North West Wales

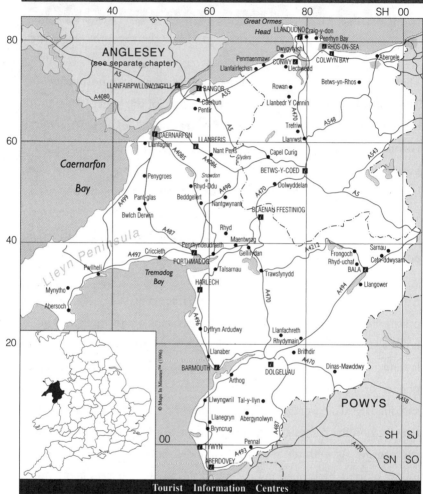

SH 00

ANGLESEY
(see separate chapter)

LLANFAIRPWLLGWYNGYLL 🚾

Great Ormes Head LLANDUDNO Craig-y-don
Penrhyn Bay
🚾 RHOS-ON-SEA
Dwygyfylchi
Penmaenmawr CONWY 🚾 COLWYN BAY Abergele
Llanfairfechan Llechwedd
BANGOR Rowan Betws-yn-Rhos
Caerhun
Pentir Llanbedr Y Cennin

CAERNARFON Trefriw
Llanfaglan LLANBERIS Llanrwst
Nant Peris Capel Curig
Glyders
Penygroes Snowdon BETWS-Y-COED
Rhyd-Ddu
Caernarfon Pant-glas Beddgelert Nantgwynant Dolwyddelan
Bay Bwlch Derwin
BLAENAU FFESTINIOG
Rhyd
Maentwrog
Criccieth Penrhyndeudraeth Sarnau
Lleyn Peninsula Gellilydan Frongoch Cefn-ddwysarn
PORTHMADOG Rhyd-uchaf BALA
Pwllheli Talsarnau Trawsfynydd Llangower
Tremadog
Bay HARLECH
Mynytho
Abersoch Dyffryn Ardudwy Llanfachreth
Rhydymain
Llanaber Brithdir
BARMOUTH Dinas-Mawddwy
DOLGELLAU
Arthog
POWYS
Llwyngwril Tal-y-llyn
Llanegryn Abergynolwyn
Bryncrug Pennal
TYWYN SH SJ
ABERDOVEY SN SO

© Maps In Minutes™ (1996)

Tourist Information Centres

The Wharf Gardens, **Aberdovey**, Gwynedd, LL35 0ED, 01654 767321 (Easter to Oct).

High Street, **Bala**, Gwynedd, LL23 7NH, 01678 521021.

The Old Library, Station Road, **Barmouth**, Gwynedd, LL42 1LU, 01341 280787 (Easter to Oct)

Royal Oak Stables, **Betws-y-Coed**, Gwynedd, LL24 0AH, 01690 710426.

Isallt, High Street, **Blaenau Ffestiniog**, Gwynedd, LL41 3HD, 01766 830360 (Easter to Oct).

Oriel Pendeitsh, Castle Street, **Caernarfon**, Gwynedd, LL55 2PB, 01286 672232.

40 Station Road, **Colwyn Bay**, LL29 8BU, 01492 530478.

Conwy Castle Visitor Centre, **Conwy**, Gwynedd, LL32 8AY, 01492 592248 (Easter to Oct).

Craft Centre, **Corris**, Machynlleth, Powys, SY20 9SP, 01654 761244.

Eldon Square, **Dolgellau**, Gwynedd, LL40 1PU, 01341 422888.

Gwyddfor House, High Street, **Harlech**, Gwynedd, LL46 2YA, 01766 780658 (Easter to Oct).

Amgueddfaír Gogledd, **Llanberis**, Gwynedd, LL55 4UR, 01286 870765.

Little Chef Services, A55/A5, **Llandegai**, Bangor, Gwynedd, LL57 7BG, 01248 352786.

1-2 Chapel Street, **Llandudno**, Gwynedd, LL30 2YU, 01492 876413.

High Street, **Porthmadog**, Gwynedd, LL49 9LP, 01766 512981.

The Promenade, **Rhos-on-Sea**, Colwyn Bay, LL29 8HH, 01492 548778 (Easter to Oct).

High Street, **Tywyn**, Gwynedd, LL36 9AD, 01654 710070 (Easter to Oct).

Aberdovey

SN6196   🍺 *Penhelig Arms*

Preswylfa , *Balkan Hill, Aberdovey, LL35 0LE.*
Detached Period House with Garden, private parking and stunning views.
Open: All Year
Grades: WTB 3 Star
01654 767239 Mrs Billingham
Fax: 01654 767983
preswylfa@cwcom.net
D: £25.00–£30.00 **S:** £30.00–£60.00
Beds: 2D 1T **Baths:** 3 En
🛏 (10) ❒ (3) ⌘ ❒ ❒ ⛾ ✕ ▥ ⛝ ✿ ♨

Bodfor Hotel, *Sea Front, Aberdovey, LL35 0EA.*
Open: All Year
Grades: WTB 2 Star
01654 767475 Mr Evans
Fax: 01654 767679
davidevans@bodforhotel.co.uk
D: £20.00–£29.50 **S:** £20.00–£29.50
Beds: 1F 6D 5T 4S **Baths:** 10 En 2 Pr 4 Sh
🛏 ❒ ❒ ⛾ ✕ ▥ ⛝ ⛝
Two star family run sea front hotel, on the main promenade, overlooking the sandy beach and Dovey Estuary. Superb restaurant with A la Carte menu, serving mouth watering dishes under the management of the highly rated local chef Rob Lomax.

Rossa Guest House, *Penrhos, Aberdovey, LL35 0NR.*
Family-run guest house. Home from Home. Golf, bowling on doorstep.
Open: Mar to Oct
Grades: WTB 2 Star
01654 767545 Mr Rowley
D: £18.50–£19.50 **S:** £19.00–£20.00
Beds: 2T 3D **Baths:** 5 En
🛏 (10) ❒ (5) ❒ ⛾ ▥ ⛝ ⛝

One Trefeddian Bank, *Aberdovey, LL35 0RU.*
Comfortable Edwardian house, elevated site, panoramic views over Cardigan Bay.
Open: Mar to Oct
Grades: WTB 3 Star
01654 767487 Mrs Jones
D: £15.00 **S:** £15.00
Beds: 2D 1T **Baths:** 1 Sh
🛏 ❒ (3) ⌘ ❒ ✕ ▥ ⛝ ⛝

Post Guest House, *Aberdovey Post Office, Aberdovey, Gwynedd, LL35 0EA.*
Friendly, tastefully furnished guest house, enjoying magnificent views. Central position.
Open: Feb to Nov
Grades: WTB 3 Star
01654 767201
D: £19.00–£20.00 **S:** £25.00–£35.00
Beds: 1F 1D **Baths:** 2 En

BATHROOMS

Pr - Private

Sh - Shared

En - Ensuite

Abergele

SH9477   🍺 *Ygwindy*

Dolhyfryd Lodge Hotel, *Rhuddlan Road, Abergele, LL22 7HL.*
Purpose built modern building, own key access, ideal location for all North Wales resorts.
Open: All Year
01745 826505 Mrs Beattie
Fax: 01745 827402
D: £18.00–£22.25 **S:** fr £27.00
Beds: 1F 2D 5T 2S **Baths:** 10 Pr
🛏 ❒ (20) ❒ ▥ ⛝ ⛝

Abergynolwyn

SH6706   🍺 *Hen Siop Cwrt, Railway Hotel, Riverside Inn*

Eisteddfa, *Abergynolwyn, Tywyn, LL36 9UP.*
Newly built bungalow, suitable for disabled in wheelchair, overlooking Tal-y-llyn Railway. **Open:** Mar to Nov
01654 782385 Mrs Pugh
Fax: 01654 782228
D: £20.00–£24.00 **S:** £20.00–£25.00
Beds: 2D 1T **Baths:** 2 En 1 Pr
🛏 ❒ ❒ ⛾ ✕ ▥ ⛝ ⛝

Riverside House, *Abergynolwyn, Tywyn, LL36 9YR.*
Victorian former quarry master's house, set in riverside gardens Magnificent views. **Open:** All Year
Grades: WTB 2 Star B&B
01654 782235 (also fax)Ron Bott
ronbott@talyllyn.freeserve.co.uk
D: £18.00–£20.00 **S:** £20.00–£30.00
Beds: 1F 3D 1S **Baths:** 1 En 1 Sh
🛏 ❒ (6) ⌘ ❒ ⛾ ✕ ▥ ⛝ ✿ ⛝

Abersoch

SH3128

Angorfa Guest House, *Lon Sarn Bach, Abersoch, Pwllheli, LL53 7EB.*
Newly decorated bedrooms, superb breakfast, great beaches, scenery, walks and activities. **Open:** All Year (not Xmas)
01758 712967 (also fax) Mrs Stanworth
D: £19.00–£25.00 **S:** £22.00–£30.00
Beds: 1F 2D 1T **Baths:** 2 Pr 2 Sh
🛏 ❒ (4) ⌘ ❒ ✕ ▥ ⛝ ⛝

Arthog

SH6414   🍺 *Fairbourne Hotel*

Graig Wen Guest House, *Arthog, LL39 1BQ.*
Open: All Year
Grades: WTB 2 Star
01341 250900 Mrs Ameson
Fax: 01341 250482
graig-wen@supanet.com
D: £17.00–£19.00 **S:** £18.00–£24.00
Beds: 1F 4D 1T 1S **Baths:** 3 En 2 Sh
🛏 (4) ❒ (20) ⌘ ❒ ✕ ▥ ⛝ ⛝ ♨ ⋒ 2
In 42 acres of woodland leading to Mawddach Estuary. Spectacular view of mountains, estuary, sea from house. Ideal for ramblers, cyclists, climbers, bird watchers. Cader Mountain, lakes, beaches, pony trekking, golf course, fishing, stream trains nearby. Disabled welcome.

Bala

SH9235   🍺 *Bryn Tirion, Eagles, Plas Yn Dre*

Frondderw Guest House, *Stryd-Y-Fron, Bala, Gwynedd, LL23 7YD.*
16th century mansion. Superb views Berwyn Mountains, Bala Lake, Snowdonia National Park.
Open: Mar to Nov
Grades: WTB 2 Star, AA 3 Diamond
01678 520301 Mr Jones
info@thefron.co.uk
D: £20.00–£25.00 **S:** £24.00–£36.00
Beds: 2F 2D 2T 1S **Baths:** 5 En 2 Sh
🛏 ❒ (8) ⌘ ❒ ▥ ⛝ ⛝

Melin Meloch (Water Mill) Guest House, *Llanfor, Bala, Gwynedd, LL23 7DP.*
Open: All Year
Grades: WTB 3 Star
01678 520101 B M Gunn
theoldmill@mac.com
D: £20.00–£25.00 **S:** £36.00–£42.00
Beds: 1F 3D 2T 2S **Baths:** 4 En 2 Pr 1 Sh
🛏 (4) ❒ (10) ⌘ ❒ ⛾ ✕ ▥ ⛝ ⛝ ♨
One of the most picturesque buildings and water gardens in this area. Featured on the TV holiday programme. Pretty accommodation in millers cottage and granary (with own front doors). Close to lake and white water rafting and fishing.

Traian, *95 Tegid Street, Bala, Gwynedd, LL23 7BW.*
Leisure centre with all facilities and High Tegid Railway and Steam Trains.
Open: All Year (not Xmas)
Grades: WTB 2 Star
01678 520059 Mrs Jones
D: £14.00–£17.00 **S:** £16.00–£18.00
Beds: 1F 1D 1T **Baths:** 1 Sh
🛏 ⌘ ❒ ▥ ⛝

Trem Aran House, *1 Glannau Tegid Tegid St, Bala, Gwynedd, LL23 7DZ.*
A chalet style detached house which has car park maintained to a good standard.
Open: Jan to dec **Grades:** WTB 1 Star
01678 520848 Mrs Jones
D: £16.50–£18.00 **S:** £16.50–£18.00
Beds: 1F 1T 1D **Baths:** 2 En
🛏 ❒ (4) ❒ ⛾ ✕ ▥ ⛝ ⛝ ✿ ⛝ ⛝

Plas Gower, *Llangower, Bala, LL23 7BY.*
A warm welcome in an old stone house, beautiful views over Bala Lake, mountains. **Open:** All Year (not Xmas)
Grades: WTB 4 Star
01678 520431 (also fax) Mrs Foreman
olwen@plasgower.com
D: £19.50–£21.00 **S:** £20.00–£22.00
Beds: 1D 1T **Baths:** 1 En 1 Pr
🛏 ❒ (4) ⌘ ❒ ▥ ⛝ ⛝

Bangor

SH5771   🍺 *Old Glan, Fat Cats*

Goetre Isaf Farmhouse, *Caernarfon Road, Bangor, LL57 4DB.*
Listed in Red Book - Eat well in Wales. Extensive garden. **Open:** All Year
Grades: AA 3 Diamond, RAC 3 Diamond
01248 364541 (also fax) Mr Whowell
wer@fredw.com
D: £16.50–£20.00 **S:** £18.50–£40.00
Beds: 1D 2T **Baths:** 1 En 1 Sh
🛏 ❒ (12) ⌘ ❒ ⛾ ✕ ▥ ⛝

B&B owners may vary
rates - be sure to check
when booking

Eryl Mor Hotel, *2 Upper Garth Road,*
Bangor, LL57 2SR.
Stunning views, comfortable rooms. Good
food and fully licensed!
Open: All Year
01248 353789 Mr Williams
Fax: 01248 354042
D: £19.00–£24.00 **S:** £22.00–£35.00
Beds: 4F 9D 6T 5S **Baths:** 16 Pr 8 Sh
🛇 🅿 (11) ⊬ 📺 ⌇ 🗙 🖿 Ⅴ ⚓

The Guest House, *32 Glynne Road,*
Bangor, LL57 1AN.
Very central. Light, airy rooms, large
choice of good food.
Open: All Year (not Xmas)
01248 352113 Mrs Roberts
D: fr £14.00 **S:** fr £14.00
Beds: 2D 2S **Baths:** 1 Sh
⊬ 📺 🖿 Ⅴ ⚓

Barmouth

SH6115 ❹ *Last Inn*

Wavecrest Hotel, *8 Marine Parade,*
Barmouth, North West Wales, LL42 1NA.
Welcoming and relaxing Which? B&B.
Excellent food, wine and whiskey.
Open: Easter to Oct
Grades: WTB 3 Star, AA 2 Star
01341 280330 (also fax)
Mr & Mrs Jarman
thewavecrest@talk21.com
D: £18.00–£27.00 **S:** £22.00–£37.00
Beds: 2F 3D 2T 2S **Baths:** 8 En 1 Pr
🛇 🅿 (2) ⊬ 📺 ⌇ 🗙 🖿 Ⅴ ⚓

The Gables, *Fford Mynach, Barmouth,*
Gwynedd, LL42 1RL.
Victorian house of character lovely
position near mountains - warm welcome.
Open: Easter to Nov
Grades: WTB 2 Star
01341 280553 Mr & Mrs Lewis
D: £18.00–£20.00 **S:** £18.00–£20.00
Beds: 1F 2D 1S **Baths:** 2 En 1 Sh
🛇 🅿 (4) ⊬ 📺 ⌇ 🗙 🖿 Ⅴ ⚓

Lawrenny Lodge Hotel, *Barmouth,*
LL42 1SU.
Small quiet family run hotel. Views over
harbour and estuary.
Open: Mar to Nov
Grades: WTB 2 Star
01341 280466 Mr Barber
Fax: 01341 281551
D: £22.00–£32.00 **S:** £32.00
Beds: 1F 4D 2T 1S **Baths:** 7 En 1 Sh
🛇 🅿 (9) 📺 ⌇ 🗙 🖿 Ⅴ ⚓ cc

The Sandpiper, *7 Marine Parade,*
Barmouth, LL42 1NA.
Sea front accommodation close to
station. Parking outside.
Open: Easter to Oct
Grades: WTB 2 Star
01341 280318 Mr & Mrs Palmer
D: £14.50–£21.00 **S:** £15.50–£17.00
Beds: 2F 7D 3S **Baths:** 6 Pr 2 Sh
🛇 🅿 📺 🖿 ⚓ ⬥ 3

Min Y Mor Hotel, *Marine Promenade,*
Barmouth, North West Wales, LL42 1HW.
Family run hotel, friendly atmosphere, in
a good central position.
Open: All Year
Grades: WTB 2 Star
01341 280555 Mr Atkins
Fax: 01341 280468
minymor@globalnet.co.uk
D: £52.00–£60.00 **S:** £52.00–£65.00
Beds: 8F 6D 8T 3S **Baths:** All En
🛇 🅿 (70) 📺 ⌇ 🗙 🖿 Ⅴ ❄ ⚓ cc

Tal-Y-Don Hotel, *High Street,*
Barmouth, LL42 1DL.
Families welcome. Home cooking, bar
meals and good beer.
Open: All Year (not Xmas)
01341 280508 Mrs Davies
D: £17.00–£20.00 **S:** £20.00–£25.00
Beds: 2F 4D 2T **Baths:** 4 En 2 Sh
🛇 🅿 ⊬ 📺 🗙 🖿 Ⅴ ⚓ cc

Endeavour Guest House, *Marine*
Parade, Barmouth, LL42 1NA.
Sea front location, beach 75 yards,
railway station 150 yards.
Open: All Year (not Xmas)
01341 280271 Mr & Mrs Every
D: £16.00–£20.00 **S:** £16.00
Beds: 7F 1S **Baths:** 4 En 1 Sh
🛇 (3) 🅿 (3) 📺 🖿 ⚓

Beddgelert

SH5948

Plas Colwyn Guest House,
Beddgelert, Caernarfon, LL55 4UY.
Comfortable C17th house, centre of
village, river and mountain views.
Open: All Year (not Xmas)
Grades: WTB 2 Star
01766 890458 Mrs Osmond
plascolwyn@hotmail.com
D: £18.00–£21.00 **S:** £18.00–£34.00
Beds: 2F 2D 1T 1S **Baths:** 3 En 3 Sh
🛇 🅿 (6) ⊬ 📺 ⌇ 🗙 🖿 Ⅴ ⚓ cc

Betws-y-Coed

SH7956 ❹ *Pont y Pair, Three Gables, Riverside,*
Royal Oak, Stables, Glen Aber Hotel, Fairy Falls
Hotel, Cross Keys, Ty Gwyn

Coed-y-Fron, *Vicarage Road, Betws-y-*
Coed, LL24 0AD.
Open: All Year
Grades: WTB 3 Star GH, AA 4 Diamond
01690 710365 Mr & Mrs Mills
mike&beth@coedyfron.enterprise-plc.com
D: £17.00–£22.00 **S:** £17.00–£20.00
Beds: 1F 3D 2T 1S **Baths:** 3 En 2 Sh
🛇 (2) 🅿 (3) 📺 ⌇ 🖿 Ⅴ ⚓ cc
Our lovely Victorian house & garden is in
the middle of the village & enjoys a
peaceful elevated location with superb
outlook over Betws-y-Coed, premier
touring centre of Snowdonia. Hearty
breakfasts & a warm welcome awaits
from your hosts Mike & Beth.

All details shown are as
supplied by B&B owners in
Autumn 2000

Fairy Glen Hotel, *Betws-y-Coed,*
LL24 0SH.
Open: Mar to Oct
Grades: WTB 2 Star, AA 1 Star
01690 710269 (also fax)
Mr & Mrs Youe
D: £21.00–£24.00 **S:** £21.00–£36.00
Beds: 2F 3D 2T 1S **Baths:** 6 En 1 Pr 1 Sh
🛇 🅿 (10) 📺 ⌇ 🗙 🖿 Ⅴ ⚓ cc
Family run 300-year-old small hotel,
overlooking River Conwy in the
Snowdonia National Park amongst
mountains & forest. Private car park and
licensed bar. Warm, friendly welcome
with fresh home-cooked meals from local
produce.

Cwmanog Isaf Farm, *Betws-y-Coed,*
LL24 0SL.
Open: All Year **Grades:** WTB 3 Star
01690 710225 (also fax) Mrs Hughes
D: £18.50–£19.50 **S:** £23.00
Beds: 1F 2D **Baths:** 3 En
🛇 (14) 🅿 (3) ⊬ 📺 🗙 🖿 Ⅴ ⚓
Nestling in spectacular scenery of the
Snowdonia National Park, this traditional
Welsh farmhouse enjoys a peaceful
homely atmosphere, comfortable beds,
unforgettable cuisine - situated on a
small working farm only 1 mile from the
picturesque village of Betws-y-Coed,
peace and tranquillity awaits.

Fron Heulog Country House,
Betws-y-Coed, LL24 0BL.
Open: All Year **Grades:** WTB 3 Star
01690 710736 Jean & Peter Whittingham
Fax: 01690 710920
jean&peter@fronheulog.co.uk
D: £20.00–£28.00
Beds: 2D 1T **Baths:** 3 En
🅿 ⊬ 📺 🖿 ⚓
Welcome to an elegant Victorian stone-
built home in peaceful wooded riverside
scenery. Excellent modern
accommodation - comfort, warmth, style.
Ideal Snowdonia location - tour, walk,
relax. Enjoy hosts' personal hospitality
and local knowledge. "Which?"
recommended. A5road; B5106 Pont y
Pair; left; 150 yards.

Royal Oak Farmhouse, *Betws-y-*
Coed, LL24 0AH.
Open: All Year (not Xmas)
Grades: WTB 3 Star
01690 710427 Mrs Houghton
D: £18.00–£20.00 **S:** £20.00–£25.00
Beds: 2D 1T **Baths:** 1 En 2 Sh
🛇 (10) 🅿 📺 🖿 Ⅴ ⚓
Part C13th water mill on beautiful
meander of River Llugwg. Golf course
adjacent, Fishing available from grounds,
secluded, but only 3 minutes walk from
village centre.

Park Hill Hotel, *Llanrwst Road, Betws-*
y-Coed, LL24 0HD.
Informal family-run hotel: fully cooked
breakfast; excellent views; heated
swimming-pool. **Open:** All Year
Grades: WTB 3 Star, AA 2 Star, RAC 2
Star
01690 710540 (also fax)
parkhill.hotel@virgin.net
D: £27.50–£29.00 **S:** £35.00–£45.00
Beds: 1F 5D 4T **Baths:** 9 En
🅿 (10) 📺 🗙 🖿 Ⅴ ⚓ cc

Royal Oak Farm Cottage, Betws-y-Coed, LL24 0AH.
Picturesque C17 farmhouse in a quiet riverside setting.
Open: All Year (not Xmas)
01690 710760 Mrs Houghton
D: £18.00–£20.00 **S:** £20.00–£24.00
Beds: 2D 1T **Baths:** 3 Pr
🅿 (4) ⅍ 🗠 🛏 📺 Ⅷ 🖪 ♨

Bryn Llewelyn Non-Smokers'
Guest House, Holyhead Road, Betws-y-Coed, LL24 0BN.
Attractive Victorian guest house. Village centre, ample private car park.
Open: All Year
Grades: WTB 2 Star, AA 2 Diamond
01690 710601 (also fax)
Mr Parker
D: £17.00–£29.50 **S:** £19.50–£27.50
Beds: 2F 3D 1T 1S **Baths:** 4 En 3 Sh
🛏 (2) 🅿 (9) ⅍ 📺 🛏 📺 Ⅷ 🖪 ♨

Riverside, Betws-y-Coed, LL24 0BN.
Centrally located in centre of village, comfortable accommodation and a superb restaurant.
Open: All Year
Grades: WTB 3 Star
01690 710650 (also fax)
riverside4u@talk21.com
D: £17.00–£22.00 **S:** £18.00–£22.00
Beds: 2D 2T **Baths:** 1 En 1 Pr 1 Sh
🛏 (10) ⅍ 📺 Ⅷ 🖪 ♨ cc

Aberconwy House, Llanrwst Road, Betws-y-Coed, North West Wales, LL24 0HD.
Victorian guest house, elevated position overlooking the picturesque Snowdonia National Park.
Open: All Year
Grades: WTB 4Star
01690 710202
Mr Jones
Fax: 01690 710800
aberconwy@betws-y-coed.co.uk
D: £22.00–£50.00 **S:** £22.00–£50.00
Beds: 1F 3T 4D **Baths:** 8 En
🛏 (8) 🅿 (10) ⅍ 📺 🛏 Ⅷ 🖪 ♨ ♨ cc

Bryn-y-Gwynt, Holyhead Road, Betws-y-Coed, North West Wales, LL24 0BN.
Warm welcome awaits you at our impeccably maintained non-smoking B&B.
Open: All Year (not Xmas)
01690 710502 (also fax)
Mrs Melling
stil@bryn-y-gwynt.clara.co.uk
D: £18.00–£21.50 **S:** £20.00–£21.50
Beds: 3D 1S **Baths:** 2 En 1 Sh
🅿 (3) ⅍ 📺 Ⅷ Ⅴ ♨

Rose Hill, Betws-y-Coed, Gwynedd, LL24 0HD.
Small & homely bed and breakfast, exceptional views, private parking.
Open: All Year
01690 710455
Mrs Cooke
mmcooke@ibm.net
D: £16.00–£25.00 **S:** £17.50–£27.00
Beds: 2D 1T **Baths:** 2 En 1 Pr
🛏 (3) 🅿 (6) 📺 Ⅷ Ⅴ ♨

BEDROOMS
F - Family
D - Double
T - Twin
S - Single

Betws-yn-Rhos
SH9073

Wheatsheaf Inn, Betws-yn-Rhos, Abergele, LL22 8AW.
Olde worlde C17th inn in award-winning village.
Open: All Year
Grades: WTB 2 Star Inn
01492 680218 D: £22.00 **S:** £26.00
Beds: 1F 2D 1S **Baths:** 4 En
🛏 (1) 🅿 (3) ⅍ 📺 🛏 ✕ Ⅷ Ⅴ ♨ cc

Blaenau Ffestiniog
SH7045 🍷 Grapes, Queen's Hotel

Bryn Elltyd, Tanygrisiau, Blaenau Ffestiniog, Gwynedd, LL41 3TW.
Mountain views: in an acre of peaceful grounds. Guided walking available.
Open: All Year
Grades: WTB 2 Star
01766 831356 (also fax)
Mr & Mrs Cole
bob6annie9@aol.com
D: fr £17.50 **S:** fr £17.50
Beds: 3T 1D **Baths:** 4 En
🛏 🅿 (4) 📺 🛏 Ⅷ Ⅴ ✽ ♨ ♿

Cae'r Blaidd Country House, Llan Ffestiniog, Blaenau Ffestiniog, Gwynedd, LL41 4PH.
Secluded tranquil refurbished Victorian country house with panoramic mountain views.
Open: All Year
Grades: WTB 4 Star
01766 762765 (also fax)
D: £25.00–£27.50 **S:** £25.00–£27.50
Beds: 1F 1D 1T **Baths:** 2 En 1 Pr
🛏 🅿 (6) ⅍ 📺 ✕ Ⅷ Ⅴ ♨

Afallon Guest House, Manod Road, Blaenau Ffestiniog, LL41 4AE.
Situated in Snowdonia National Park. Clean homely accommodation with Welsh breakfast.
Open: All Year (not Xmas)
Grades: WTB 3 Star
01766 830468 Mrs Griffiths
D: £15.00–£18.00 **S:** £15.00–£18.00
Beds: 1D 1T 1S **Baths:** 1 Sh
🛏 🅿 (4) ⅍ 📺 🛏 ✕ Ⅷ Ⅴ ♨

The Don Guest House, High Street, Blaenau Ffestiniog, LL41 3AX.
Victorian town house with breathtaking mountain views. Friendly welcome assured.
Open: All Year (not Xmas/New Year)
01766 830403 (also fax)
Mr Cotton
D: £14.00–£18.00 **S:** £15.00–£20.00
Beds: 3D 2T 1S **Baths:** 2 En 1 Sh
🛏 🅿 (2) 📺 ✕ Ⅷ Ⅴ ♨

Brithdir
SH7618

Llwyn Talcen, Brithdir, Dolgellau, LL40 2RY.
Open: Easter to Oct
Grades: WTB 1 Star
01341 450276 Mrs Griffiths
D: £18.00–£20.00 **S:** £18.00–£20.00
Beds: 1D 1S **Baths:** 1 En 1 Sh
🛏 (3) 🅿 (3) 📺 🛏 ✕ Ⅷ Ⅴ ♨
Enjoy a holiday/short break at our country house in rhododendron gardens.
Mountains on doorstep, yet close to spectacular Mawddach estuary. Ideal for walking, cycle trails, Wales little trains.
Log fires, delicious evening dinners. Croeso cynnes; warm welcome.

Bryncrug
SH6003

Peniarth Arms, Bryncrug, Tywyn, Gwynedd, LL36 9PY.
Cosy village inn Cader Idris. Tal-y-llyn railway nearby. Beautiful scenery.
Open: All Year (not Xmas/New Year)
Grades: WTB 3 Star
01654 711505 Mrs Mountford
Fax: 01654 712169
D: £17.00–£20.00 **S:** £18.00–£25.00
Beds: 4D **Baths:** 4 En
🛏 (1) 🅿 📺 ✕ Ⅴ ♨ cc

Dolgoch Falls Hotel, Dolgoch, Bryncrug, Tywyn, Gwynedd, LL36 9UW.
One of Wales' most comfortable family-run hotels, at foot of magnificent waterfalls and ravine.
Open: Mar to Dec
01654 782258 Mr Lycett
Fax: 01654 782209
D: £25.00–£30.00 **S:** fr £25.00
Beds: 3D 2T 1S **Baths:** 4 En 1 Sh
🛏 (12) 🅿 (50) 📺 🛏 ✕ Ⅷ Ⅴ ♨ cc

Caerhun (Bangor)
SH5769

Penhower Bed & Breakfast,
Caerhun, Bangor, Gwynedd, LL57 4DT.
Open: All Year (not Xmas)
Grades: WTB 4 Star
01248 362427 Mr Farrar
D: £18.00–£20.00 **S:** £20.00–£23.00
Beds: 1D 2T **Baths:** 3 En
🛏 🅿 (10) ⅍ 📺 🛏 ✕ Ⅷ Ⅴ ♨
A single-storey, stone built house in a peaceful setting with panoramic views of Snowdonia and Anglesey. Within easy reach of Bangor, an ideal centre for touring, de luxe accommodation, acclaimed home-cooking, brochure and photograph available on request.

RATES
D = Price range per person sharing in a double room
S = Price range for a single room

Caernarfon

SH4862 ◀ *Black Boy, Harp Inn, Newborough Arms*

The White House, *Llanfaglan, Caernarfon, LL54 5RA.*
Quiet, isolated country house. Magnificent views to mountains and sea.
Open: Mar to Nov **Grades:** WTB 3 Star
01286 673003 Mr Bayles
rwbayles@sjms.co.uk
D: £19.50–£21.50 **S:** fr £25.50
Beds: 2D 2T **Baths:** 3 En 1 Pr
🛏 🅿 (8) 📺 📫 🎮 🍴

Menai View Guest House & Restaurant, *North Road, Caernarfon, North Wales, LL55 1BD.*
Close to Caernarfon Castle, overlooking Menai Straights . Lounge/bar and restaurant. Spa-bath.
Open: All Year (not Xmas/New Year)
Grades: WTB 3 Star, AA 3 Diamond
01286 674602 (also fax)
menaiview@walesuk4.freeserve.co.uk
D: £17.50–£22.50 **S:** £22.50–£27.00
Beds: 3F 2T 4D **Baths:** All En
🛏 📺 📫 ✕ 🎮 🍴 ♿ cc

Prince of Wales Hotel, *Bangor Street, Caernarfon, LL55 1AR.*
Town location, perfect stopover en-route for Ireland's ferries or exploring Snowdonia. **Open:** All Year (not Xmas)
Grades: WTB 2 Star
01286 673367 Ms Parry **Fax:** 01286 676610
princeofwaleshotel@gofornet.co.uk
D: £19.00–£32.00 **S:** £19.00–£32.00
Beds: 2F 8D 7T 4S **Baths:** 19 En 2 Sh
🛏 🅿 (6) 📺 📫 ✕ 🎮 🍴 cc

Marianfa, *St David's Road, Caernarfon, Gwynedd, LL55 1EL.*
Ideal base touring Snowdonia, Llyn Peninsula, Anglesey, Llandudno, Conwy valley. **Open:** All Year
Grades: WTB 3 Star
01286 675589 Mrs Ashcroft
Fax: 01286 673689
D: £16.00–£22.00 **S:** £17.00–£25.00
Beds: 2F 1D 1T 1S **Baths:** 4 En 1 Pr
🛏 (10) 🅿 (5) 🎮 📺 🎮 🍴

Cadnant Valley Caravan Park, *Llanberis Road, Caernarfon, Gwynedd, LL55 2DF.*
Clean comfortable and friendly house, 0.25 mile from Caernarfon town.
Open: Easter to Sep
01286 673196 Mrs Noon
D: £15.00 **S:** £15.00
Beds: 1D 1T **Baths:** 1 Sh
🅿 (4) 📺 🎮 🍴

Capel Curig

SH7258 ◀ *Cobdens, Bryn Tyrch Hotel, Tyn y Coed*

Bryn Glo Cafe, *Capel Curig, Betws-y-Coed, LL24 0DT.*
Warm welcome and clean, comfortable accommodation in small family business.
Open: All Year **Grades:** WTB 2 Star B&B
01690 720215 Mrs Evans
D: fr £17.50 **S:** fr £18.00
Beds: 1D 1T 1S **Baths:** 1 Pr 1 Sh
🅿 (10) 🎮 🍴

Llugwy Guest House, *Capel Curig, Betws-y-Coed, LL24 0ES.*
Warm welcome, hearty breakfast, forest and mountain scenery. easily located.
Open: All Year
01690 720218 Mrs Cousins
D: £17.50–£18.50 **S:** £19.50–£21.50
Beds: 2D 1T 1S **Baths:** 2 Sh
🛏 🅿 (4) 🎮 📺 📫 ✕ 🎮 🍴 cc

Can-yr-Afon, *Capel Curig, Betwys-y-Coed, LL24 0DR.*
Situated in the heart of Snowdonia, near the famous Swallow Falls.
Open: All Year (not Xmas/New Year)
01690 720375 Mrs Berry
D: £18.00
Beds: 1F 1T 1D **Baths:** 2 Pr
🛏 (10) 🅿 (5) 🎮 📺 🎮 🍴 ♿

Capel Garmon

SH8155 ◀ *White Horse*

Llannerch Goch C17th Country House, *Capel Garmon, Betws-Y-Coed, North Wales, LL26 0RL.*
Peaceful 2 miles from picturesque Betws-y-Coed, clear views of the Snowdonia Mountain Range.
Open: All Year (not Xmas)
Grades: WTB 4 Star
01690 710261 Eirian Ifan
eirianifan@talk21.com
D: £20.00–£25.00 **S:** £25.00–£28.00
Beds: 3D **Baths:** 3 En
🛏 (8) 🅿 (3) 🎮 📺 🎮 🍴

White Horse Inn, *Capel Garmon, Llanrwst, Gwynedd, LL26 0RW.*
Charming unique 400-year-old inn perched on hill in heart of Snowdonia National Park. **Open:** all year
01690 710271 (also fax)Mrs Bower
white-horse-inn@betws-y-coed.co.uk
D: £24.00–£28.00 **S:** £30.00
Beds: 5D 1T **Baths:** 6 En
🛏 (12) 🅿 (20) 🎮 📺 📫 ✕ 🎮 🍴 ♦ ♿ cc

Cefn-ddwysarn

SH9638 ◀ *Bryn Tirion, Plas Yn Dre*

Erw Feurig Guest House, *Cefn-ddwysarn, Bala, Gwynedd, LL23 7LL.*
Farm guest house with magnificent views.
Open: All Year (not Xmas)
01678 530262 (also fax)
D: £18.00–£22.00 **S:** £16.00–£25.00
Beds: 2F 1D 1T 1S **Baths:** 2 En 1 Pr 1 Sh
🅿 (4) 🎮 📺 🎮 🍴

Colwyn Bay

SH8479 ◀ *Lodge, Rhos Fynach, Semaphore, Taylors, Toad Hall, White Lion*

Llysfaen House, *58 Llysfaen Road, Colwyn Bay, LL29 9HB.*
Magnificent sea views. Lovely house. Warm welcome. Good home cooking. Cleanliness assured.
Open: All Year
Grades: WTB 2 Star
01492 517859 Mr & Mrs Hooker
views@compuserve.com
D: £17.50 **S:** £17.50
Beds: 1F 1D 1S **Baths:** 1 Sh
🛏 🅿 (2) 🎮 📺 📫 ✕ 🎮 🍴

St Margaret's Hotel, *Princes Drive, Colwyn Bay, LL29 8RP.*
Open: All Year
01492 532718
stmargarets@hotelcb.fsnet.co.uk
D: £20.00–£24.00 **S:** £20.00–£24.00
Beds: 1F 5D 2T 2S **Baths:** 10 En
🛏 🅿 (10) 📺 📫 🎮 🍴 🎮 🍴 cc
Recommended by Which? Good Bed & Breakfast Guide. We are dedicated to the well-being of our guests. We provide excellent food and comfortable bedrooms with all the modern facilities expected from a first class establishment. A particularly pleasant place to stay.

Edelweiss Hotel, *Lawson Road, Colwyn Bay, LL29 8HD.*
C19th house, wooded garden, a slice of countryside by the sea.
Open: All Year
Grades: WTB 2 Star
01492 532314 Mr Baker
Fax: 01492 534707
D: £21.00 **S:** £21.00
Beds: 4F 10T 10D 3S **Baths:** 27 En
🛏 (25) 🎮 📺 ✕ 🎮 🍴 ♿ cc

Holly Tree Guest House, *11 Marine Road, Colwyn Bay, LL29 8PH.*
Friendly comfortable Victorian house. Modern facilities. Central to everywhere. Parking.
Open: All Year (not Xmas)
Grades: WTB 2 Star , AA 2 Diamond
01492 533254 Mr Ross
Fax: 01492 532332
ross@nationwideisp.net
D: £20.00 **S:** £25.00
Beds: 2F 4D 3T **Baths:** 9 En
🛏 🅿 (12) 🎮 🍴 🎮 🍴 cc

Marine Hotel, *West Promenade, Colwyn Bay, LL28 4BP.*
Superbly situated seafront hotel offering spacious comfortable ensuite accommodation.
Open: Easter to Oct
Grades: WTB 3 Star, AA 2 Star
01492 530295 Mr & Mrs Owen
resrvations@marinehotel.co.uk
D: £23.00–£24.00 **S:** £24.00–£29.00
Beds: 1F 6D 4T 3S **Baths:** 12 En 2 Pr
🛏 🅿 (10) 🎮 📺 📫 🎮 🍴 🎮 cc

Grosvenor Hotel, *106-108 Abergele Road, Colwyn Bay, LL29 7PS.*
Victorian Welsh stone hotel, offering spacious comfortable accommodation (licensed bar).
Open: All Year
Grades: WTB Listed
01492 530798 Mr Toombs
Fax: 01492 531586
D: £17.90–£20.00 **S:** £17.90–£20.00
Beds: 4F 2D 4T 7S **Baths:** 2 En 4 Sh
🛏 (14) 📺 📫 ✕ 🎮 🍴 ♦ ♿ cc

RATES

D = Price range per person sharing in a double room
S = Price range for a single room

Conwy

SH7777 ⬥ Mulberry, Fairy Glen, Tal y Cafn, Y
Groes, George & Dragon

Glan Heulog Guest House, Llanrwst
Road, Conwy, LL32 8LT.
Open: All Year
Grades: WTB 2 Star GH, AA 3 Diamond
01492 593845 Mr & Mrs Watson-Jones
D: £15.00–£20.00 **S:** £18.00–£24.00
Beds: 2F 2D 2T **Baths:** 5 En 1 Pr
⯅ 🄿 (7) ⬥ ⊡ 🛏 ✕ ▥ 🖾 ♨ **CC**
Warm welcome, comfortable beds and a
hearty breakfast in a fine Victorian house
situated in an elevated position with far-
reaching views to Snowdonia. Short walk
to castle. Centrally situated for
Snowdonia and all major attractions. Off-
road parking, garden.

Bryn Derwen, Woodlands, Conwy,
LL32 8LT.
Warm welcome to a gracious Victorian
home with panoramic views.
Open: All Year
Grades: WTB 3 Star, AA 3 Diamond
01492 596134 Mr & Mrs Smith
D: £18.00–£20.00 **S:** £18.00–£25.00
Beds: 1F 2D 3T **Baths:** 6 En
⯅ 🄿 (8) ⬥ ⊡ 🛏 ▥ 🖾 ✿ ♨

Fishermore, Llanrwst Road, Conwy, LL32
8HP.
Rural setting close to historic town, N.T.
gardens and mountains
Open: Easter to Oct
Grades: WTB 2 Star
01492 592891
Mrs Dyer
dyers@tesco.net
D: £17.00–£19.00
Beds: 1T 2D **Baths:** 2 En 1 Pr
🄿 (5) ⬥ ⊡ ▥ 🖾 ♨

Craig-y-don

SH7981

Hotel Carmen, 4 Carmen Sylva Road,
Craig-y-don, Llandudno, LL30 1LZ.
Hotel Carmen is situated in the quieter
part with easy parking. Excellent cuisine.
Open: Easter to Oct
Grades: WTB 2 Star
01492 876361
Mr Newberry
peter1@plynch-greatxscape.net
D: £20.00–£23.00 **S:** £23.50–£25.00
Beds: 2F 9D 3T **Baths:** 16 En
⯅ (9) ⬥ ⊡ ✕ ▥ 🖾 ✿ ♨

Criccieth

SH4938 ⬥ Poachers, Prince Of Wales, Moelwyn

Mor Heli Guest House, Min Y Mor,
Criccieth, LL52 0EF.
Open: All Year (not Xmas)
01766 522802 Fax: 01766 522878
D: fr £18.00 **S:** fr £18.00
Beds: 2F 2D 1T **Baths:** 5 Pr
⯅ 🄿 ⊡ 🛏 ✕ 🖾 ♨
Situated on sea front overlooking 100
miles of coastline. All bedrooms sea
views, full ensuite facilities, colour TV
and hospitality trays. Recommended by
guests since 1972.

Bron Rhiw Hotel, Caernarfon Road,
Criccieth, LL52 0AP.
Cosy, comfortable non-smoking hotel; a
truly warm welcome awaits you.
Open: Mar to Nov
Grades: WTB 2 Star Hotel
01766 522257 Ms Woodhouse & Ms S C
Williams
D: £20.00–£22.50 **S:** £20.00–£22.50
Beds: 7D 1T 1F **Baths:** 7 En 2 Pr
⯅ 🄿 (4) ⬥ ⊡ 🛏 ✕ ▥ 🖾 ♨ **CC**

Min y Gaer Hotel, Porthmadog Road,
Criccieth, North West Wales, LL52 0HP.
Comfortable hotel with delightful coastal
views. Ideal for touring Snowdonia.
Open: Easter to Oct
Grades: WTB 2 Star Hotel, AA 4
Diamond, RAC 4 Diamond
01766 522151 Fax: 01766 523540
info@minygaerhotel.co.uk
D: £22.00–£25.00 **S:** £22.00
Beds: 3F 4D 2T 1S **Baths:** 10 En
⯅ 🄿 (12) ⬥ ⊡ 🛏 ▥ 🖾 ♨ **CC**

Craig y Mor Guest House, West
Parade, Criccieth, LL52 0EN.
Tastefully upgraded Victorian house
overlooking sea into Tremadoc Bay.
Open: Mar to Oct
Grades: WTB 3 Star GH
01766 522830 Mr Williamson
enquiries@craig-y-mor-
bandb.freeserve.co.uk
D: £20.00–£21.00 **S:** fr £20.00
Beds: 4F 2D **Baths:** 6 En
⯅ 🄿 (6) ⊡ 🛏 ▥ ♨

Muriau, Criccieth, North West Wales,
LL52 0RS.
C17th gentleman's residence, secluded
garden.
Open: Mar to Oct
01766 522337 Mrs Neville
joybar@muriau.freeserve.co.uk
D: £16.50–£21.00 **S:** £16.50–£21.00
Beds: 3D 2T **Baths:** 3 En 1 Sh
⯅ (12) 🄿 (6) ⬥ ⊡ ✕ ▥ 🖾 ♨

Y Rhoslyn, 8 Marine Terrace, Criccieth,
North West Wales, LL52 0EF.
Comfortable seafront guest house in
unspoilt seaside town, close to beach,
castle.
Open: Feb to Nov
01766 522685 pete@rhoslyn.demon.co.uk
D: £13.50–£18.00 **S:** £16.00–£25.00
Beds: 2F 2D 1T 1S **Baths:** 2 En 1 Sh
⯅ ⬥ ⊡ 🛏 ✕ ▥ ♨

Dinas-Mawddwy

SH8514 ⬥ Dolbrodmaeth Inn

The Red Lion Inn, Dinas-Mawddwy,
Machynlleth, Powys, SY20 9JA.
Centuries-old traditional inn. In heart of
village amid scenic beauty of southern
Snowdonia.
Open: All Year (not Xmas)
Grades: WTB 1 Star
01650 531247 (also fax)
Mr Jenkins
llewcoch@yahoo.co.uk
D: £20.00–£25.00 **S:** £20.00–£25.00
Beds: 3F 1D 1T 1S **Baths:** 3 En
⯅ 🄿 (30) ⊡ 🛏 ✕ ▥ 🖾 ♨

Dolgellau

SH7217 ⬥ Cross Foxes, Dylanwad Da, George,
Royal Ship, Ivy House, Unicorn

Maesneuadd Farm, Llanfachreth,
Dolgellau, LL40 2DH.
Open: All Year
Grades: WTB 3 Star
01341 450256 Mrs Smith
D: £18.00–£22.00 **S:** fr £22.00
Beds: 1F 1T 1D **Baths:** 3 En
⯅ (3) 🄿 (6) ⬥ ⊡ 🛏 ▥ 🖾 ♨
Situated in a peaceful Area of
Outstanding Natural Beauty, our 200 year
old farmhouse offers excellent
accommodation in a friendly relaxing
atmosphere. We are surrounded by
gardens, flower meadow and woodland
with streams and waterfalls and have
breathtaking mountain views.

Ivy House, Finsbury Square, Dolgellau,
North West Wales, LL40 1RF.
Attractive country town guest house,
good home-made food.
Open: All Year
Grades: WTB 2 Star GH, AA 3 Diamond
01341 422535 Mrs Bamford
Fax: 01341 422689
ivy.hse.dolgellau@ic24.net
D: £18.50–£24.50 **S:** £23.00–£33.00
Beds: 1F 3D 2T **Baths:** 3 En 2 Sh
⯅ ⊡ 🛏 ✕ ▥ 🖾 ♨ **CC**

Tanyfron, Arran Road, Dolgellau, North
West Wales, LL40 2AA.
Modernised, former stone farmhouse,
beautiful views. Wales in Bloom Winners
1999.
Open: Feb to Nov
Grades: WTB 3 Star
01341 422638 Mrs Rowlands
Fax: 01341 421251
tanyfron@tesco.net
D: £20.00–£22.00
Beds: 1D 2T **Baths:** 3 En
⯅ (5) 🄿 (6) ⬥ ⊡ 🖾 ♨

Arosfyr Farm, Penycefn Road,
Dolgellau, North West Wales, LL40 2YP.
Homely friendly, farmhouse, flower,
gardens, mountainous, views, self-
catering available.
Open: All Year
Grades: WTB 2 Star
01341 422355 Mrs Skeel Jones
D: £15.00–£16.50 **S:** fr £18.00
Beds: 1F 1D 1T **Baths:** 2 Sh
⯅ 🄿 (4) ⊡ 🛏 ▥ 🖾 ♨

Glyn Farm House, Dolgellau, LL40 1YA.
Bedrooms with views, riverside path to
Dolgellau, near organised bicycle track.
Open: Mar to Nov
Grades: WTB 1 Star
01341 422286 Mrs Price
Fax: 01341 422105
D: £16.00–£20.00 **S:** £14.00–£20.00
Beds: 1D 1T **Baths:** 1 En 1 Sh
⯅ 🄿 (6) ⊡ 🛏 ▥ 🖾 ♨

Planning a longer stay? Always
ask for any special rates

Aber Cottage, Smithfield Street, Dolgellau, Gwynedd, LL40 1DE.
Cosy market town stone cottage (1811) foot of Cader - comfortable welcoming hospitality.
Open: All Year
01341 422460 Mrs Mullin
gmullini@compuserve.com
D: £18.00–£20.00 **S:** £18.50–£25.00
Beds: 1F 2D 1T 2S **Baths:** 2 En 1 Pr 2 Sh
🛇 (5) 🅿 (6) 🔟 🛏 📖 🗑 ★

Esgair Wen Newydd, Garreg Feurig, Llanfachreth Road, Dolgellau, LL40 2YA.
Bungalow, mountain views, very quiet. Friendly relaxed atmosphere. High standards.
Open: Feb to Nov
Grades: WTB 3 Star
01341 423952 Mrs Westwood
D: fr £18.00 **S:** fr £20.00
Beds: 2D 1T **Baths:** 1 Sh
🛇 (3) 🅿 (3) ⚡ 🔟 ✗ 📖 🗑 ★

Penbryn Croft, Cader Road, Dolgellau, LL40 1RN.
Open: All Year (not Xmas)
01341 422815
Ms Dunne
D: £20.00–£24.00
Beds: 4T 2D **Baths:** 2 Sh
🛇 ⚡ 🔟 ✗ 📖 🗑 ★
Situated at the foot of Cader Idris 200 yards from Dolgellau town centre recently refurbished but still retaining some original features including oak staircase and mosaic tiled floors. up to 12 people can be accommodated and a warm welcome assured.

Gwelafon, Caedeintur, Dolgellau, Gwynedd, North Wales, LL40 2YS.
Beautiful, high-standard, spacious house. Panoramic views of town and mountains.
Open: March to Oct
Grades: WTB 3 Star
01341 422634
Mrs Roberts
D: £20.00–£25.00 **S:** £17.00–£20.00
Beds: 1D 2S **Baths:** 1 En 1 Sh
🛇 (7) 🅿 (3) ⚡ 🔟 📖 🗑 ★

Bryn Yr Odyn Guest House,
Maescaled, Dolgellau, LL40 1UG.
Secluded C17th longhouse, 1/2 mile town centre, tour/walking guidance.
Open: All Year
01341 423470 Mr Jones
D: fr £17.00 **S:** fr £20.00
Beds: 1D 2T **Baths:** 2 Sh
🛇 🅿 (3) ⚡ 🔟 🛏 📖 🗑 ★

Dolwyddelan

SH7352 ◀ Gwydyr, Ellens Castle Hotel

Bryn Tirion Farm, Dolwyddelan, LL25 0JD.
C12th Dolwyddelan Castle, 100 yards on the farm, picturesque Lledr Valley.
Open: All Year (not Xmas/New Year)
Grades: WTB 2 Star
01690 750366 Mrs Price
D: £23.00–£25.00 **S:** £23.00–£25.00
Beds: 1F 1D 1T **Baths:** 2 En 1 Pr
🛇 🅿 ⚡ 🔟 📖 🗑 ★

Dwygyfylchi

SH7377

Caerlyr Hall Hotel, Conwy Old Road, Dwygyfylchi, Penmaenmawr, LL34 6SW.
Country house set in natural amphitheatre with sea and mountain views.
Open: All Year
Grades: WTB 3 Star
01492 623518 Mr & Mrs Warner
D: £25.00–£28.00 **S:** £25.00–£28.00
Beds: 5F 1D 3T **Baths:** 8 En 1 Pr
🛇 🅿 (12) 🔟 🛏 📖 🗑 cc

Dyffryn Ardudwy

SH5822 ◀ Hel y Bryn

Parc yr Onnen, Dyffryn Ardudwy, Gwynedd, LL44 2DU.
Rural setting; superb sea and mountain views by peaceful lane.
Open: All Year
Grades: WTB 3 Star
01341 247033 Mr & Mrs Bethell
D: £18.00–£20.00 **S:** £20.00
Beds: 1D 1T **Baths:** 2 En
🛇 🅿 (3) ⚡ 🔟 🛏 ✗ 📖 🗑 ★

The Old Farmhouse, Tyddyn Du, Dyffryn Ardudwy, Gwynedd, LL44 2DW.
Secluded luxury farmhouse; heated pool and hot spa; informal, friendly atmosphere.
Open: All Year
Grades: WTB 3 Star
01341 242711 M B Tibbetts
Fax: 01341 247881
duk572@aol.com
D: £16.66–£25.00 **S:** £10.00–£30.00
Beds: 1F 2D 2T **Baths:** 5 En
🛇 (5) 🅿 (10) ⚡ 🔟 🛏 ✗ 📖 🗑 ✹ ★

Ystumgwern Hall Farm, Dyffryn Ardudwy, LL44 2DD.
C16th luxury farmhouse, barn conversion.
Open: All Year
Grades: WTB 4 Star
01341 247249 (also fax)
Mrs Williams
jane@ystumgwern.co.uk
D: £25.00–£26.00
Beds: 3F 1D 1T **Baths:** 5 En
🛇 🅿 ⚡ 🔟 🛏 📖 🗑 ✹ ★ 3

Friog

SH6112 ◀ Fairbourne

Einion House, Friog, Fairbourne, North West Wales, LL38 2NX.
Lovely old house in marvellous walking country. Good home cooking.
Open: All Year (not Xmas/New Year)
Grades: WTB 2 Star
01341 250644 Mr Waterhouse
enquiries@einionhouse.freeserve.co.uk
D: £20.50 **S:** £22.00–£27.50
Beds: 4D 1T 1S **Baths:** 4 En 2 Pr
🛇 🔟 🛏 ✗ 📖 🗑 ★

All details shown are as supplied by B&B owners in Autumn 2000

Frongoch

SH9039 ◀ Plas Yn Dre

Rhydydefaid Farm, Frongoch, Bala, Gwynedd, LL23 7NT.
Traditional Welsh farmhouse, rural location for touring Snowdonia National Park.
Open: All Year (not Xmas)
01678 520456 (also fax)
Mrs Davies
D: £18.00–£19.00 **S:** £18.00–£19.00
Beds: 1F 1D 1T **Baths:** 2 En
🛇 🅿 (3) ⚡ 📖 🗑 ★

Gellilydan

SH6839 ◀ Bryn Arms

Tyddyn Du Farm, Gellilydan, Blaenau Ffestiniog, Gwynedd, LL41 4RB.
Enchanting C17th farmhouse; deluxe barn suites with jacuzzi, patio window, gardens etc.
Open: All Year (not Xmas)
01766 590281 Mrs Williams
info@tyddyndu.co.uk
D: £20.00–£28.00
Beds: 3F 1D **Baths:** 3 Pr 2 Sh
🛇 🅿 (8) ⚡ 🔟 🛏 ✗ 📖 🗑 ★ 🚲 3 cc

Glan-yr-afon (Fron-goch)

SH9040 ◀ Goat

The Old Post Office, Glan-yr-afon, Corwen, Gwynedd, LL21 0HB.
Open: All Year
Grades: WTB 3 Star
01490 460231 (also fax)
H J Jennings
D: £18.00–£19.50 **S:** £16.00–£19.50
Beds: 1F 1D 1T 1S **Baths:** 2 En 1 Sh
🛇 🅿 🔟 ✗ 📖 🗑 ★
Relax in a warm and friendly atmosphere. Situated on the A494, 7 miles from Bala Lake. Ideal for exploring Snowdonia, North and mid Wales. Colour TV and beverage tray in all rooms. Guest lounge. Incorporating North Wales' only dedicated Teddy Bear Shop.

Harlech

SH5831 ◀ Lion, Victoria

Tyddyn Y Gwynt, Harlech, LL46 2TH.
Perfect setting for peaceful holidays; warm welcome, tourist attractions, mountain scenery, beaches. Car essential.
Open: All Year
Grades: WTB 2 Star
01766 780298 Mrs Jones
D: £16.00 **S:** £16.00–£18.00
Beds: 1F 1D 1T 1S **Baths:** 1 Sh
🛇 🅿 (8) 🔟 🛏 📖 ★

Lion Hotel, Harlech, LL46 2SG.
2 bars & restaurant. Double rooms ensuite.
Open: All Year
01766 780731 Mr Morris
D: fr £22.00 **S:** fr £34.00
Beds: 3D 1T 2S **Baths:** 5 En 1 Pr
🅿 (3) 🔟 🛏 ✗ 📖 🗑 ★

Gwrach Ynys Country Guest House, Ynys, Talsarnau, North West Wales, LL47 6TS.
Open: March to Nov
Grades: WTB 4 Star, AA 4 Diamond
01766 780742 Mrs Williams
Fax: 01766 781199
gwynfor@btinternet.com
D: £23.00–£28.00 **S:** £30.00–£35.00
Beds: 2F 2D 2T 1S **Baths:** 6 En
🛇 🅿 (8) ⊬ 🗹 🖔 ✕ 🏛 🗸 ⚭
Edwardian country house set in a tranquil rural setting close to the sea and mountains in Snowdonia National Park. High quality, comfortable, non smoking accommodation and good food. Ideally located for walking, bird watching, golf and exploring the numerous castles, railways and attractions.

Maes yr Hebog, Heol y Bryn, Harlech, Gwynedd, LL46 2TU.
Quality bungalow accommodation, great food, spectacular views, mountains and coast.
Open: Easter to Oct
Grades: WTB 5 Star
01776 780885 Mr & Mrs Clark
D: £20.00–£24.00 **S:** £32.00–£42.00
Beds: 2D **Baths:** 2 En
🅿 (2) ⊬ 🗹 ✕ 🏛 ⚭

Castle Cottage Restaurant with Rooms, Pen Llech, Harlech, LL46 2YL.
Cosy restaurant with rooms, personal services.
Open: All Year
Grades: WTB 3 Star, AA 4 Diamond, RAC 4 Diamond
01766 780479 (also fax)
Mr Roberts
gh.robert@talk21.com
D: fr £31.00 **S:** fr £40.00
Beds: 3D 1T 2S **Baths:** 4 Pr 2 Sh
🛇 ⊬ 🗹 🖔 ✕ 🏛 ⚭ ⚭ cc

Godre'R Graig, Fford Newydd, Harlech, Gwynedd, LL46 2UD.
A gracious Edwardian house nestling at the foot of Harlech Castle.
Open: All Year (not Xmas)
01766 780905 (also fax)
Mr Lynch
mslynch@dialstart.net
D: £16.00–£18.00 **S:** £16.00–£25.00
Beds: 2F 4D 2T 1S **Baths:** 4 Sh
🛇 🅿 (8) 🗹 🖔 ✕ 🏛 ⚭ ⚭

Llanaber

SH6017

Llwyndu Farmhouse, Llanaber, Barmouth, Gwynedd, LL42 1RR.
C16th Llwyndu nestles in a spectacular location with panoramic views over Cardigan Bay.
Open: All Year (not Xmas)
01341 280144 Mrs Thompson
intouch@llwyndu-farmhouse.co.uk
D: £27.50–£32.00 **S:** £27.50–£32.00
Beds: 2F 4D 1T **Baths:** 7 En
🛇 🅿 (10) ⊬ 🗹 🖔 ✕ 🏛 ⚭ cc

Planning a longer stay? Always ask for any special rates

Llanbedr-y-cennin

SH7569

Waen Newydd, Llanbedr-y-Cennin, Conwy, Gwynedd, LL32 8UR.
Open: All Year
01492 660527 Fax: 01492 660155
jeffries@fsnet.co.uk
D: £20.00 **S:** £25.00
Beds: 1T **Baths:** 1 En
⊬ 🏛 ⚭
Secluded 19th century farmhouse. Spacious grounds high above village in open countryside. Superb views. Twin En suite bedroom, lounge own dining room, central heating, log burning stove, tea / coffee facilities. Ideal base for touring, walking and bird watching. Open all year.

Llanberis

SH5760 🛏 Padarn Lane Hotel, Royal Victoria, Gwynedd Hotel, Black Boy, Harp Inn, Newborough Arms

Beech Bank Guest House, High Street, Llanberis, Caernarfon, LL55 4EN.
Open: All Year (not Xmas)
01286 870414 Mrs Watson
D: £16.00 **S:** £17.00
Beds: 1F 2D 1T **Baths:** 1 Sh
🅿 (6) 🏛 ⚭
Situated at quiet end of village, overlooking lakes & mountains. Walking distance to Snowdon Mountain Railway. All rooms H&C and CH.

Mount Pleasant Hotel, High Street, Llanberis, Caernarfon, LL55 4HA.
Friendly, family-run, foot of Snowdon. Cosy bar, real ale. **Open:** All Year
Grades: WTB 1 Star
01286 870395 (also fax) Mrs Waterton
mph@waterton.org.uk
D: £16.00–£20.00 **S:** £16.00–£25.00
Beds: 2F 3D 1T 2S **Baths:** 1 En 2 Sh
🛇 🅿 (8) 🖔 ✕ 🏛 🗸 ⚭

Marteg, High Street, Llanberis, Caernarfon, Gwynedd, LL55 4HA.
Within walking distance of Snowdon mountain railway and all amenities.
Open: Easter to Dec
Grades: WTB 3 Star B&B
01286 870207 Mr & Mrs Torr
carol@marteg.freeserve.co.uk
D: £20.00–£22.00 **S:** £20.00–£22.00
Beds: 2D 1T **Baths:** 3 En
🅿 (4) ⊬ 🗹 🏛 🗸 ⚭

Glyn Afon , High Street, Llanberis, Caernarfon, LL55 4HA.
Family-run centrally situated close to mount Snowdon/ railway/ attractions.
Open: All Year **Grades:** WTB 2 Star
01286 872528 (also fax) Mrs Litton
glynafon.llanberis@virgin.net
D: £16.00–£18.00 **S:** £17.00–£18.00
Beds: 1F 4D 3T **Baths:** 2 En 2 Sh
🛇 🅿 (4) 🗹 🖔 ✕ 🏛 🗸 ⚭

Idan House, High Street, Llanberis, Caernarfon, LL55 4EN.
Idan House is in the heart of Snowdonia. Ideal for mountains and lakes.
Open: All Year
01286 870673 Mrs Roberts
D: £12.50–£15.00 **S:** £15.00
Beds: 1F 2D 2T 2S **Baths:** 1 Sh
🛇 🗹 🖔 🏛 ⚭

B&B owners may vary rates - be sure to check when booking

Llandudno

SH7881 🛏 Queens Arms, King's Head, Albert, Washington, Toby Tavern, Craigside

Hotel Carmen, 4 Carmen Sylva Road, Craig-y-don, Llandudno, LL30 1LZ.
Open: Easter to Oct
Grades: WTB 2 Star
01492 876361 Mr Newberry
peter1@plynch-greatxscape.net
D: £20.00–£23.00 **S:** £23.50–£25.00
Beds: 2F 9D 3T **Baths:** 16 En
🛇 (9) 🏛 🖔 ⚭
Hotel Carmen is situated in the quieter part with easy parking. Excellent cuisine.

Craiglands, 7 Carmen Sylva Road, Craig-y-don, Llandudno, LL30 1LZ.
Open: Easter to Nov
01492 875090 Mrs Mullin
D: £20.00–£25.00 **S:** £25.00
Beds: 2T 4D **Baths:** 6 En
🗹 ✕ 🏛 🗸 ⚭
A beautiful Victorian guesthouse close to the Promenade, lovely rooms all ensuite. Delicious breakfasts, dinner optional. A short drive to Snowdonia National Park with its beautiful mountains, lakes, walks, magical scenery and National Trust Properties and Gardens.

Fernbank, 9 Chapel Street, Llandudno, LL30 2SY.
Friendly family-run guest house in a town centre location. **Open:** All Year (not Xmas)
Grades: WTB 1 Star GH
01492 877251 jim42@lineone.net
D: £11.50–£13.50 **S:** fr £11.50
Beds: 3F 2D 3T 1S **Baths:** 3 En 3 Sh
🛇 🗹 ✕ 🏛 🗸 ⚭ ⚭ 3

Lympley Lodge, Colwyn Road , Craigside, Llandudno, North West Wales, LL30 3AL.
Open: All Year (not Xmas/New Year)
Grades: WTB 4 Star
01492 549304 Mrs Richards
patricia@lympleylodge.co.uk
D: £25.00–£27.50 **S:** £30.00–£32.50
Beds: 1T 2D **Baths:** 2 En 1 Pr
🛇 (12) 🅿 (5) 🗹 🏛 🗸 ⚭
Beautiful Victorian House with sea views, overlooking the sweep of Llandudno Bay. Elegant rooms with antique furnishings. Lympley Lodge is the perfect place to stay when exploring the beauty of North Wales.

Ty Glandwr, 42 St Mary's Road, Llandudno, Gwynedd, LL30 2UE.
Elegant Edwardian town house, convenient public transport, theatre, castles, Snowdonia.
Open: All Year (not Xmas/New Year)
Grades: WTB 3 Star
01492 871802 Mrs Beesley
tyglandwr@talk21.com
D: £19.00–£25.00 **S:** £22.00–£25.00
Beds: 1T 2D 1S **Baths:** 3 En 1 Pr
⊬ 🗹 🏛 🗸 ⚭

Karden Hotel, 16 Charlton Street, Llandudno, LL30 2AA.
Very pleasant and comfortable accommodation, vegetarian and allergy diets available.
Open: All Year
Grades: WTB 2 Star RAC 1 Diamond
01492 879347 Mr Roberts
D: £14.00–£16.50 **S:** £14.00–£16.50
Beds: 4F 4D 2S **Baths:** 4 En 2 Sh
🛇 📺 ✗ 🖿 ⓥ ✿ ♿

Cadnant Hotel, 38 Lloyd Street, Llandudno, LL30 2YG.
Small family run homely hotel, licensed bar, Clean and comfortable.
Open: All Year
01492 877832 Mr & Mrs Brown
D: £18.00 **S:** £18.00–£23.00
Beds: 1F 1T 6D **Baths:** 7 En 1 Pr
🛇 📺 ✗ 🖿 ⓥ ♿

Westdale Hotel, 37 Abbey Road, Llandudno, LL30 2EH.
Friendly, family-run hotel, six minutes walk to town centre.
Open: Feb to Oct
Grades: WTB 2 Star
01492 877996 (also fax)
D: £18.00–£21.50 **S:** £18.00–£21.50
Beds: 5F 4D 1T 2S **Baths:** 3 En 2 Sh
🛇 🅿 (4) 📺 ✗ 🖿 ⓥ ♿

Oakwood B&B, 21 St Davids Road, Llandudno, North West Wales, LL30 2UH.
Close to all amenities - beautiful tree-lined garden area.
Open: All Year
01492 879208 (also fax)
Mrs Cockburn
johndee@cockburn85.freeserve.co.uk
D: £18.00–£18.50 **S:** £18.00–£18.50
Beds: 2F 3D 1T 1S **Baths:** 6 En
📺 🖿 ⓥ ✿ ♿

St Hilary Hotel, Promenade, Llandudno, LL30 1BG.
A well-appointed promenade hotel, providing excellent accommodation.
Open: Mar to Oct
01492 875551 Mr Probert
Fax: 07079 003883
info@sthilaryhotel.co.uk
D: £16.50–£25.00 **S:** £32.50–£45.00
Beds: 2F 7D 2T **Baths:** 9 En 2 Sh
🛇 📺 🖿 ⓥ ♿ cc

White Lodge Hotel, Central Promenade, Llandudno, LL30 1AT.
Victorian sea front luxury hotel (all rooms ensuite) near theatre/conference centre.
Open: Easter to Oct
01492 877713 Mr Rigby
D: £26.00–£27.50 **S:** £39.00–£41.25
Beds: 2F 6D 4T **Baths:** 12 Pr
🛇 (5) 🅿 (12) 📺 🖿 ⓥ ♿

Cliffbury Hotel, 34 St Davids Road, Llandudno, LL30 2UH.
Non-smokers' haven in delightful homely surroundings.
Open: All Year
01492 877224 (also fax) Mr Horton
cliffbury@lineone.net
D: £18.50–£21.50 **S:** £24.00–£28.00
Beds: 2F 3D 2T 1S **Baths:** 6 En 1 Pr
🛇 🅿 (3) ✔ 📺 ✗ 🖿 ⓥ ♿ ✿ ♿

Bryn Y Bia Lodge Hotel, Craigside, Llandudno, LL30 3AS.
A little gem - charming spacious Victorian house - Bryn y Bia (Magpie Hill).
Open: Feb to Nov
01492 549644 (also fax) Mr Grimwood
carol@brynybia.demon.co.uk
D: £26.00–£34.00 **S:** £31.00–£35.00
Beds: 1F 7D 3T 1S **Baths:** 12 En
🛇 🅿 (12) 📺 ✗ 🖿 ⓥ ♿ cc

The Grafton Hotel, Promenade, Craig y Don, Llandudno, North West Wales, LL30 1BG.
Only 5 minutes' walk from North Wales Theatre & Conference Centre.
Open: All Year (not Xmas/New Year)
Grades: WTB 3 Star
01492 876814 Derek Griffiths
Fax: 01492 879073
derek@thegraftonhotel.com
D: £20.00–£28.00 **S:** £22.00–£28.00
Beds: 2F 10D 5T 5S **Baths:** 23 Pr
🛇 🅿 (12) 📺 ✗ 🖿 ⓥ ♿ ♨

Hollybank Guest House, 9 St Davids Place, Llandudno, LL30 2UG.
Quietly situated Edwardian house close to town centre. Excellent breakfasts.
Open: All Year (not Xmas)
01492 878521 M R Emberton
Fax: 0870 0549854
mike@hollybank-gh.demon.co.uk
D: £15.00–£24.00 **S:** £20.00–£30.00
Beds: 2F 2D 2T **Baths:** 6 En
🛇 🅿 (3) 📺 ✗ 🖿 ⓥ ♿

Bodnant Guest House, 39 St Marys Road, Llandudno, LL30 2UE.
Peaceful, flat location. Shopping centre and seafront short walking distance.
Open: All Year (not Xmas)
01492 876936
D: £18.00–£19.00 **S:** £18.00–£20.00
Beds: 2D 1T 1S **Baths:** 4 En
🅿 (1) ✔ ✗ 🖿 ⓥ ♿

Cedar Lodge Guest House, 7 Deganwy Avenue, Llandudno, LL30 2YB.
Family-run guest house, highly recommended. Centrally situated, close to shops and beach.
Open: Easter to Oct
01492 877730 D: £19.00–£21.00 **S:** £26.00–£28.00
Beds: 2D 4T 1S **Baths:** 6 En 1 Pr
🅿 (5) 📺 ✗ 🖿 ⓥ ♿ cc

Heatherdale, 30 St David's Road, Llandudno, LL30 2UL.
Set on a quiet tree-lined road with views to the Great Orme and Snowdonia.
Open: all year (not Xmas)
01492 877362
heatherdale@btinternet.com
D: £19.00–£21.00 **S:** £20.00–£22.00
Beds: 2F 3D 1T 1S **Baths:** 2 En 4 Pr
🛇 ✔ 📺 🖿 ♿

All details shown are as supplied by B&B owners in Autumn 2000

Llanegryn

SH6005

Cefn Coch Country Guest House, Llanegryn, Tywyn, LL36 9SD.
Open: Mar to Oct
Grades: WTB 3 Star
01654 712193 (also fax)
Mrs Sylvester
david@cefncoch.force9.co.uk
D: £22.00–£24.00 **S:** £22.00–£29.00
Beds: 2D 3T **Baths:** 3 En 2 Sh
🛇 (14) 🅿 (11) ✔ 📺 ✗ 🖿 ⓥ ♿
Cefn Coch, a former coaching inn, enjoys a beautiful garden with spectacular views over Dysynni Valley. An outstanding area for bird watching, walking, cycling, golfing. Fresh flowers, excellent cooking and good wine make for an enjoyable holiday in peaceful surroundings.

Llanfachreth

SH7522 🍴 *Ship, Tyn y Groes, Sospan*

Maesneuadd Farm, Llanfachreth, Dolgellau, LL40 2DH.
200-year-old farmhouse situated in a peaceful Area of Outstanding Natural Beauty. **Open:** All Year
Grades: WTB 3 Star
01341 450256 Mrs Smith
D: £18.00–£22.00 **S:** fr £22.00
Beds: 1F 1T 1D **Baths:** 3 En
🛇 (3) 🅿 (6) ✔ 📺 ✗ 🖿 ⓥ ♿

Heulwen, Llanfachreth, Dolgellau, North West Wales, LL40 2UT.
Large, comfortable, modern bungalow with panoramic views of the mountains.
Open: Feb to Nov
01341 423085 (also fax) Mrs Watts
watts@heulwen.freeserve.co.uk
D: £18.00–£19.00 **S:** £20.00–£21.00
Beds: 2D 1T **Baths:** 2 En 1 Sh
🛇 🅿 (5) ✔ 📺 ✗ 🖿 ♿ ♿

Llanfaglan

SH4760 🍴 *The Harp*

The White House, Llanfaglan, Caernarfon, LL54 5RA.
Quiet, isolated country house. Magnificent views to mountains and sea.
Open: Mar to Nov **Grades:** WTB 3 Star
01286 673003 Mr Bayles
rwbayles@sjms.co.uk
D: £19.50–£21.50 **S:** fr £25.50
Beds: 2D 2T **Baths:** 3 En 1 Pr
🛇 🅿 (8) ✗ 🖿 ♿

Llanfairfechan

SH6874 🍴 *Split Willow*

Rhiwiau Riding Centre, Llanfairfechan, LL33 0EH.
Magnificent views of mountains & sea; riding & walking.
Open: All Year (not Xmas)
Grades: WTB 2 Star
01248 680094 Mrs Hill
Fax: 01248 681143
rhiwiau@aol.com
D: £15.00–£16.50 **S:** £15.00–£16.50
Beds: 1F 1D 4T 1S **Baths:** 3 Sh
🛇 🅿 (12) ✔ 📺 ✗ 🖿 ⓥ ♿

Llanfor

SH9336 ◀ *Plas-Yn-Dre*

Melin Meloch (Water Mill) Guest House, *Llanfor, Bala, Gwynedd, LL23 7DP.*
One of the most picturesque buildings and water gardens in this area.
Open: All Year
Grades: WTB 3 Star
01678 520101 B M Gunn
theoldmill@mac.com
D: £20.00–£25.00 **S:** £36.00–£42.00
Beds: 1F 3D 2T 2S **Baths:** 4 En 2 Pr 1 Sh
🛇 (4) 🅿 (10) ⅔ 🅣 🕇 ✕ 🕮 🅥 🕹 &

Llangower

SH9032 ◀ *Plas Yn Dre*

Plas Gower, *Llangower, Bala, LL23 7BY.*
A warm welcome in an old stone house, beautiful views over Bala Lake, mountains.
Open: All Year (not Xmas)
Grades: WTB 4 Star
01678 520431 (also fax)
Mrs Foreman
olwen@plasgower.com
D: £19.50–£21.00 **S:** £20.00–£22.00
Beds: 1D 1T **Baths:** 1 En 1 Pr
🛇 🅿 (4) ⅔ 🅣 🕮 🅥 🕹

Llangwnnadl

SH2033 ◀ *Lion, Penrhyn Arms, Mill, Penybont*

Carrog Farm, *Llangwnnadl, Pwllheli, Gwynedd, LL53 7NL.*
Set in beautiful farmland with the sea visible across fields.
Open: Easter to Oct
Grades: WTB 3 Star Farm
01758 770694 Mrs Thomas
D: £18.00–£20.00 **S:** £18.00–£20.00
Beds: 3F 1T 1D 1S **Baths:** 2 Sh
🅣 ✕ 🕮 🕹

Llanrwst

SH7961 ◀ *Amser Da, Fairy Falls Hotel, Y Dolydd*

Argoed Guest House, *Trefriw, Betws-y-Coed, LL27 0TX.*
Comfortable old-fashioned house. Beautiful views of Conwy Valley. Easy access to mountains and coast.
Open: All Year
Grades: WTB 3 Star GH
01492 640091 Mr & Mrs Booth
Fax: 01492 642222
kath.argoed@btinternet.com
D: £18.50–£25.00 **S:** £18.50–£25.00
Beds: 1F 2D 1T 1S **Baths:** 1 En 1 Pr 1 Sh
🛇 🅿 (5) 🅣 🕮 ✕ 🕮 🕹

Nant-Y-Glyn Isaf, *Llanrwst, Gwynedd, LL26 0NN.*
Working farm. Spacious, well-appointed rooms. Magnificent views, quiet location.
Open: All Year
Grades: WTB 3 Star
01492 640327 (also fax)
Mrs Evans
maievans@farmwales.co.uk
D: £19.50–£25.00
Beds: 1F 1D 1T **Baths:** 3 En
🛇 (8) 🅿 ⅔ 🅣 🕮 🅥 🕹

Argoed, *Llwyn Brith, Betws-y-Coed Road, Llanrwst, North Wales, LL26 0HH.*
Family run guest house central to Snowdonia and North Wales coast.
Open: All Year (not Xmas)
01492 640628 Mrs Jones
D: £19.50 **S:** £22.00
Beds: 3D **Baths:** 3 En
🅿 ⅔ 🅣 🕮 🕹

Llansannan

SH9366 ◀ *Saracen's Head*

Cleiriach, *Llansannan, Denbigh, Conwy, LL16 5LW.*
Beautiful scenery, off the beaten track. Quiet and peaceful location.
Open: All Year (not Xmas/New Year)
01745 870695 Mrs Williams
katycleiriach@aol.com
D: £10.00 **S:** £12.00
Beds: 1T 1D **Baths:** 1 Sh
🛇 🅿 (2) ⅔ 🅣 🕇 ✕ 🕮 🅥 🕹

Llanuwchllyn

SH8730 ◀ *Eagles*

Eifionydd, *Llanuwchllyn, Bala, LL23 7UB.*
Beautiful location; warm welcome. Enjoy your vacation in well-appointed rooms.
Open: Easter to Oct
Grades: WTB 4 Star
01678 540622 (also fax) Mr & Mrs Murray
eifionydd@ntlworld.com
D: £20.00–£22.00 **S:** £25.00–£27.00
Beds: 1F 1T 1D **Baths:** 3 En
🛇 🅿 ⅔ 🅣 🕮 🅥 🕹

Llanycil

SH9134 ◀ *Plas-yn-Dre*

Abercelyn Guest House, *Llanycil, Bala, Gwynedd, LL23 7YF.*
Georgian residence set in landscaped gardens overlooking Bala lake.
Open: All Year (not Xmas/New Year)
Grades: WTB 3 Star
01678 521109 Mrs Hind
D: £22.50–£26.50 **S:** £25.00–£28.00
Beds: 2F 1T 1D **Baths:** 2 En 1 Pr
🛇 🅿 (4) ⅔ 🅣 🅥 🕹 cc

Llechwedd

SH7676 ◀ *Tal-y-Cafn*

Henllys Farm, *Llechwedd, Conwy, Gwynedd, LL32 8DJ.*
Situated in beautiful countryside 1.5 miles from historic Conwy with its castle.
Open: Easter to Nov
Grades: WTB 3 Star Farm
01492 593269 C Roberts
D: £18.00–£20.00 **S:** £18.00–£20.00
Beds: 1F 1D **Baths:** 2 En
🛇 🅿 ⅔ ✕ 🕮 🕹

Berthlwyd Hall, *Llechwedd, Conwy, Gwynedd, LL32 8DQ.*
Magnificent Victorian manor. Luxury accommodation, award winning food. 1.5 miles Conwy Castle. **Open:** All Year
01492 592409 Fax: 01492 592290
griffin-properties@virgin.net
D: £22.50–£40.00 **S:** £45.00
Beds: 1F 2D 1T 1S **Baths:** 5 En
🛇 🅿 🅣 🕇 ✕ 🕮 🅥 🕹 cc

Llwyngwril

SH5909 ◀ *Garthangarhad*

Bryn Y Mor Guest House, *Fairbourne Road, Llwyngwril, LL37 2JQ.*
Victorian house overlooking sea.
Open: Easter to Nov
01341 250043 R & J Webb
ron@fsmail.net
D: £18.00
Beds: 1F 1D 1T **Baths:** 3 En
🛇 🅿 (6) ⅔ 🅣 🕇 🕮 🅥 🕹

Maentwrog

SH6640 ◀ *Grapes*

The Old Rectory Hotel, *Maentwrog, Blaenau Ffestiniog, LL41 4HN.*
Main house/budget annexe, 3 acre garden. Informal, peaceful.
Open: All Year (not Xmas)
01766 590305 (also fax) Ms Herbert
D: £22.50–£32.50 **S:** £30.00–£45.00
Beds: 2F 6D 2T **Baths:** 10 En
🛇 🅿 🅥 🕇 ✕ 🕮 🅥 🕹

Mynytho

SH3030 ◀ *Glyn Y Weddw*

Paradwys, *Mynytho, Pwllheli, Gwynedd, LL53 7SA.*
Bungalow with panoramic sea and mountain views, peaceful; brochure available. **Open:** All Year
01758 740876 Mrs Roberts
D: £19.00
Beds: 1D **Baths:** 1 Pr
🅿 (1) ⅔ 🅣 🕮

Nant Peris

SH6058 ◀ *Vaynol Arms*

Tyn y Ffynnon, *Nant Peris, Caernarfon, Gwynedd, LL55 4UH.*
Beautiful spacious cottage set in 2 acres below Llanberis pass.
Open: All Year (not Xmas/New Year)
Grades: WTB 4 Star
01286 871723 Mrs Kelly
D: £18.00–£20.00 **S:** £20.00–£22.00
Beds: 1F 1T 2D **Baths:** 1 Pr 1 Sh
🛇 🅿 (6) 🅣 🕇 🕮

Snowdon House, *3 Gwastadnant, Nant Peris, Caernarfon, LL55 4UL.*
Comfortable beds, good breakfast and friendly welcome in magnificent scenery.
Open: All Year
01286 870356 Mr Cumberton
113441.1536@compuserve.com
D: £15.00–£17.50 **S:** £15.00–£17.50
Beds: 3D 1T 1S **Baths:** 1 Sh
🛇 🅿 (12) ⅔ 🕮 🅥 🕹

Nantgwynant

SH6250

Pen-Y-Gwryd Hotel, *Nantgwynant, Caernarfon, LL55 4NT.*
Famous mountain inn, heart of Snowdonia. Associated with Lord Hunt's Everest team (1953).
Open: March to Nov
01286 870211 Mrs Pullee
D: £23.00–£28.00 **S:** £33.00–£38.00
Beds: 16F 6T 9D 1S **Baths:** 5 En 5 Pr 5 Sh
🛇 🅿 (30) 🕇 ✕ 🕮 🅥 &

Pant-glas

SH4747

Hen Ysgol Old School Pant-glas,
Bwlch Derwin, Pant-glas,
Garndolbenmaen, LL51 9EQ.
Beautiful mid-C19th Welsh not country
school. Perfectly situated for the
attractions of Snowdonia.
Open: All year **Grades:** WTB 2 Star
01286 660701 T J Gibbins
oldschoolpantglas@talk21.com
D: £17.00–£20.00 **S:** £20.00–£25.00
Beds: 2F 1D 1T **Baths:** 1 En 1 Sh
🛇 🄿 (6) ⊬ 📺 ⓧ ⏵ 💻 🖼 ♨ ㅎ

Penmaenmawr

SH7176   🍺 New Legend

Bodlwyfan, Conwy Road,
Penmaenmawr, LL34 6BL.
Beautiful Victorian house, overlooking the
sea and mountains in quiet location.
Open: All Year
01492 623506 Mr Anderton
Bodlwyfan@totalise.co.uk
D: £17.50–£20.00 **S:** £18.00–£21.00
Beds: 1F 3T 2D 1S **Baths:** 2 Sh
🛇 🄿 (6) 📺 ⓧ ⏵ 💻 🖼 ♨ ㅎ

Pennal

SH6900

Marchlyn, Aberdovey Road, Pennal,
Machynlleth, SY20 9YS.
Quiet location near Aberdovey on a
Welsh-speaking working farm.
Open: All Year
Grades: WTB 2 Star
01654 702018
D: £17.00–£20.00
S: £17.00–£20.00
Beds: 1F 4D 1T 1S **Baths:** 2 En 1 Pr

Penrhyn Bay

SH8281

Awelfor Guest House, 74 Llandudno
Road, Penrhyn Bay, Llandudno, LL30 3HA.
Immaculately presented, close to all
amenities. Completely non smoking
establishment.
Open: All Year
Grades: WTB 3 Star
01492 549373
i+s@awelfor.freeserve.co.uk
D: £20.00–£23.00
Beds: 6D **Baths:** 6 Pr
🄿 ⊬ 📺 ⓧ 💻 ♨

Penrhyndeudraeth

SH6139

Wenallt, Penrhyndeudraeth, Gwynedd,
LL48 6PW.
Award winning guest house near
Portmeirion. Lovely views. Ideal touring
base.
Open: All Year (not Xmas/New Year)
Grades: WTB 3 Star
01766 770321 (also fax)
G Cooper
gh@wenalt.globalnet.co.uk
D: £22.00–£25.00 **S:** £27.00–£30.00
Beds: 1T 2D **Baths:** 1 En
🄿 (3) ⊬ 📺 ⓧ 💻 🖼 ♨ CC

Pentir

SH5667   🍺 Yaynol Arms

Rainbow Court Guest House,
Village Square, Pentir, Bangor, LL57 4UY.
1999 award-winning guest
house/restaurant. Mountains, attractions,
peace, friendly.
Open: All Year (not Xmas)
01248 353099 (also fax)
Mrs Lorrimer Riley
rainbow@marketite.co.uk
D: £16.00–£20.00 **S:** £16.00–£27.00
Beds: 1F 1D 1T 1S **Baths:** 1 En 1 Pr 1 Sh
🛇 🄿 (3) ⊬ 📺 ⓧ 💻 ♨ CC

Penygroes

SH4753   🍺 Bryn Eisteddfod

Lleuar Fawr, Penygroes, Caernarfon,
Gwynedd, LL54 6PB.
Peaceful location, substantial farmhouse
breakfast, comfortable bedrooms. Warm
Welsh welcome.
Open: All Year (not Xmas)
Grades: WTB 3 Star
01286 660268 (also fax) Mrs Lloyd Jones
user@lleuarfawr.fsnet.co.uk
D: £18.00–£20.00 **S:** £25.00
Beds: 1D 1T **Baths:** 2 En
🛇 🄿 ⊬ 📺 ⏵ 💻 ♨

Porthmadog

SH5638   🍺 Ship

35 Madog Street, Porthmadog,
LL49 9BU.
Modern terraced house.
Open: All Year (not Xmas)
01766 512843 Mrs Skellern
D: £14.00–£15.00 **S:** £14.00–£15.00
Beds: 1F 1D 1T 1S **Baths:** 2 Sh
🛇 (3) 📺 ⏵ 💻 ♨

Llwyn Derw, Morfa Bychan Road,
Porthmadog, LL49 9UR.
Period house, own grounds, town centre
1 km, beach 2 km. Open: Easter to Oct
01766 513869 john-parry@lineone.net
D: £18.00–£23.00 **S:** £21.00–£26.00
Beds: 1F 1D **Baths:** 1 En
🛇 (3) 🄿 (3) ⊬ 📺 💻

Pwllheli

SH3735   🍺 Victoria

Rhosydd, 26 Glan Cymerau, Pwllheli,
Gwynedd, LL53 5PU.
Detached bungalow, outskirts Pwllheli.
Near beach, leisure centre, golf marina.
Open: All Year
01758 612956 S Williams
helen@rhosydd.freeserve.co.uk
D: £15.00–£17.50 **S:** £15.00–£17.50
Beds: 1T 1D **Baths:** 1 En 1 Sh
🛇 🄿 ⊬ 📺 ⏵ ⓧ 💻 🖼 ♨ ㅎ

Llys Gwyrfai Guest House, 14 West
End Parade, Pwllheli, LL53 5PN.
Comfortable, friendly, welcome to our
home. Seafront, golf, Marina nearby.
Open: All Year (not Xmas)
01758 614877 (also fax) Mrs Thomas
D: fr £16.00 **S:** fr £17.00
Beds: 2D 1T **Baths:** 3 En
🛇 📺 ⏵ ⓧ 💻 🖼 ♨

Yoke House Farm, Pwllheli, LL53 5TY.
Listed Georgian farmhouse on dairy farm.
Peaceful location.
Open: Easter to Oct **Grades:** WTB 3 Star
01758 612621
annven@iocous.freeserve.co.uk
D: £20.00–£22.50 **S:** £22.50–£23.00
Beds: 1D 1T **Baths:** 1 Sh
🛇 (10) 🄿 (5) ⊬ 📺 💻 ♨

Rhos-on-Sea

SH8381   🍺 Ship, Queen's Head

Sunnyside, 146 Dinerth Road, Rhos-on-
Sea, Colwyn Bay, LL28 4YF.
Central for beaches, mountains, situated
between Llandudno and Colwyn Bay.
Open: All Year
01492 544048 Mrs Pryce
D: £29.00 **S:** £14.50–£29.00
Beds: 2F 1D 1T **Baths:** 1 Sh
🛇 🄿 ⊬ 📺 💻

Sunnydowns Hotel, 66 Abbey Road,
Rhos-on-Sea, Colwyn Bay, LL28 4NU.
Situated in a quiet area of Rhos, only 2
minutes walk to the beach.
Open: All Year
01492 544256 Mr Willington
Fax: 01492 543223
D: £25.00–£29.00 **S:** £30.00–£34.00
Beds: 3F 5D 5T 2S **Baths:** 15 En
🛇 🄿 (10) 📺 ⏵ ⓧ 💻 🖼 ♨ ㅎ

Whitehall Hotel, Cayley Promenade,
Rhos-on-Sea, Colwyn Bay, LL28 4EP.
A small select seaside village just
between Colwyn Bay & Llandudno on
lovely Cayley Promenade.
Open: Mar to Nov
01492 547296 Fax: 01492 543160
D: £22.50–£25.00 **S:** £22.50–£25.00
Beds: 2F 7D 3T **Baths:** 12 En
🛇 📺 ⏵ ⓧ 💻 🖼 ♨

Rhyd

SH6341   🍺 Brondanw Arms

Bodlondeb Farm, Rhyd,
Penrhyndeudraeth, LL48 6ST.
In small rural hamlet near Ffestiniog
Railway, Porthmeirion, mountains and
beaches.
Open: Easter to Oct
Grades: WTB 2 Star
01766 770640
bodlondeb.rhyd@virginnet.co.uk
D: £17.50–£19.50 **S:** £17.50–£19.50
Beds: 1T 2D
🛇 🄿 (2) ⊬ 📺 ⓧ 💻

Rhyd-Ddu

SH5652

Ffridd Isaf, Rhyd-Ddu, Caernarfon, LL54
6TN.
Open: All Year
01766 890452 Mrs Kent
D: £15.00 **S:** £15.00
Beds: 1T 1D **Baths:** 1 Sh
🄿 ⊬ ⓧ 💻 📺
Restored C16th Grade II farmhouse,
beneath Snowdon. Magnificent views, log
fires, good food, muddy boots no
problem, secure parking. Last house
before the summit on the Rhyd Ddu path.
Come and get away from it all.

Rhyd-uchaf

SH9037

Brynmelyn Farm, *Rhyd-uchaf, Bala, Gwynedd, LL23 7SD.*
1.5 miles from Bala Lake, beautiful scenic home from home.
Open: All Year
01678 520376 Mr & Mrs Edwards
D: £15.00–£16.00 **S:** £16.00–£17.00
Beds: 2D 1T 1S **Baths:** 2 Sh
🛏 (6) 🆃 ✕ 🖾 ❀ 🛎 cc

Rhydymain

SH7921

Rhaeadr Wnion, *Rhydymain, Dolgellau, LL40 2AH.*
Victorian house in 3 acres of gardens in beautiful Snowdonia.
Open: All Year
Grades: WTB 3 Star
01341 450249 Mrs Perkins
D: £17.00–£19.00 **S:** £17.00–£19.00
Beds: 2D 2T **Baths:** 2 En 1 Sh
🛏 🄿 (5) 🆃 ♔ ✕ 🖾 🆅 🛎

Rowen

SH7571 ◑ *Princes Arms, Groes*

Bulkeley Mill, *Rowen, Conwy, Gwynedd, LL32 8TS.*
Open: All Year
Grades: WTB 4 Star
01492 650481 Mrs Seville
SKenseville@cs.com
D: £26.00–£28.00
Beds: 1F 1D **Baths:** 2 En
🛏 🄿 🆃 🖾 🆅 🛎
Bulkeley Mill is situated in Rowen, one of the most picturesque villages in the Conwy Valley. The mill wheel has been renovated and the mill buildings converted to living accommodation in 1993/94, including the waterwheel. Unique property in gardens that offer complete peace and tranquillity.

Gwern Borter Holiday Farm, *Rowen, Conwy, LL32 8YL.*
You'll love it here! Manor house set in 11 acres of beautiful grounds.
Open: All Year (not Xmas)
01492 650460 (also fax)
Mr Powell
mail@snowdoniaholidays.co.uk
D: £23.00–£28.00 **S:** fr £26.00
Beds: 1F 2D **Baths:** 3 En 1 Sh
🛏 🄿 (18) 🆃 ♔ ✕ 🖾 🆅

Coed Lyn, *Barkers Lane, Rowen, Conwy, Gwynedd, LL32 8YL.*
Old gamekeeper's cottage with lovely gardens and stunning views of Welsh mountains. **Open:** Easter to Oct
01492 650469/ 0589 084111
D: £17.00–£20.00 **S:** fr £25.00
Beds: 1F 2D 1T **Baths:** 2 En 1 Pr
🛏 🄿 (3) 🆃 ♔ 🖾 🆅 🛎

Tal-y-llyn

SH7109 ◑ *Railway*

Rhosgadlas, *Tal-y-llyn, Tywyn, North West Wales, LL36 9AJ.*
Tastefully converted barn overlooking beautiful Tal-y-llyn lake. Traditional Welsh hospitality.
Open: Feb to Nov
Grades: WTB 3 Star
01654 761462 (also fax)
Mrs Bebb
rh.bebb@virgin.net
D: £20.00–£25.00 **S:** £22.00–£25.00
Beds: 1T 2D **Baths:** 2 En 1 Pr
🄿 (6) ⚥ ✕ 🖾 🆅 🛎

Talsarnau

SH6135

Estuary Motel Y Traeth, *Talsarnau, LL47 6TA.*
Snowdonia National Park, near Portmeirion. All modern ground floor rooms.
Open: All Year
Grades: WTB 3 Star, AA 2 Star
01766 771155 Mr King
D: £16.50–£24.50 **S:** £34.50
Beds: 1F 5D 4T **Baths:** 10 En
🛏 (16) 🄿 (30) 🆃 ♔ ✕ 🖾 🆅 ❀ 🛎 🦽 cc

Trawsfynydd

SH7035

Old Mill Farmhouse, *Fron Oleu Farm, Trawsfynydd, Blaenau Ffestiniog, LL41 4UN.*
Olde Worlde charm, wonderful scenery, friendly animals, large good breakfasts.
Open: All Year
Grades: WTB 3 Star Farm
01766 540397 (also fax)
Miss Roberts & Mrs P Osborne
penmar@oldmillfarm.spacomputers.com
D: £20.00–£25.00 **S:** £20.00–£25.00
Beds: 2F 3D 2T **Baths:** 7 En
🛏 🄿 (10) ⚥ 🆃 ♔ ✕ 🖾 🆅 ❀ 🛎 🦽

Trefriw

SH7863 ◑ *Fairy Falls Hotel*

Craig y Felin, *Trefriw, Betws-y-Coed, LL27 0RJ.*
Beautiful peaceful location. Panoramic views. Close to lakes and mountains.
Open: All Year
Grades: WTB 3 Star
01492 640868
gordon@couperg.freeserve.co.uk
D: £20.00–£23.00 **S:** £30.00–£32.00
Beds: 1F 1T 1D 1S **Baths:** 2 En 1 Pr 1 Sh
🛏 🄿 (5) ⚥ 🆃 ♔ 🖾 🆅 🛎

Planning a longer stay? Always ask for any special rates

Hafod Country Hotel, *Trefriw, Conwy, LL27 0RQ.*

Open: Feb to Jan
Grades: WTB 3 Star, AA 2 Star
01492 640029 Fax: 01492 641351
hafod@breathemail.net
D: £27.50–£40.00 **S:** £32.00–£47.50
Beds: 4D 2T **Baths:** 6 En
🛏 🄿 (12) ⚥ 🆃 ♔ ✕ 🖾 🆅 ❀ 🛎 cc
Converted farmhouse on edge of village nestling into heavily wooded foothills of Snowdonia, overlooks Conwy valley. Furnished with many antiques, own grounds, exceptional meals, licensed. Beautiful lakes nearby. Ideal for walkers, fishermen, touring north Wales or a relaxing short break.

Argoed Guest House, *Trefriw, Betws-y-Coed, LL27 0TX.*
Comfortable old-fashioned house. Beautiful views of Conwy Valley. Easy access to mountains and coast.
Open: All Year **Grades:** WTB 3 Star GH
01492 640091 Mr & Mrs Booth
Fax: 01492 642222
kath.argoed@btinternet.com
D: £18.50–£25.00 **S:** £18.50–£25.00
Beds: 1F 2D 1T 1S **Baths:** 1 En 1 Pr 1 Sh
🛏 🄿 (5) 🆃 ♔ ✕ 🖾 🆅 🛎

Tremadog

SH5640

Ty Newydd Guest House, *30 Dublin Street, Tremadog, Porthmadog, Gwynedd, LL49 9RH.*
Close to the Ffestiniog Railway, Porthmeirion and many other attractions.
Open: All Year (not Xmas/New Year)
Grades: WTB 2 Star
01766 512553 johnjulieo@aol.com
D: £18.50–£21.00 **S:** £28.50–£31.00
Beds: 1F 1T 2D **Baths:** 1 Sh
🛏 🄿 (6) 🆃 ♔ 🖾 🛎

Tywyn (Aberdovey)

SH5800 ◑ *Peniarth Arms, Tredegar Arms*

Hendy Farm, *Tywyn, LL36 9RU.*
Comfortable farmhouse near farm and beach. Own halt on Talyllyn railway.
Open: Easter to Oct
Grades: WTB 3 Star Farm
01654 710457 (also fax) Mrs Lloyd-Jones
jones@farmline.com
D: £18.00–£24.00 **S:** £22.00–£27.00
Beds: 2D 1T **Baths:** 2 En 1 Pr
🛏 🄿 ⚥ ♔ 🖾 🆅 🛎

Greenfield Hotel & Restaurant, *High Street, Tywyn, LL36 9AD.*
Small friendly licensed hotel. Close Talyllyn Steam and Main Railway.
Open: Feb to Dec
01654 710354 (also fax) Mrs Jenkins
D: £16.00–£18.50 **S:** £17.00–£19.50
Beds: 2F 3D 3T **Baths:** 6 Pr 1 Sh
🛏 🆃 ✕ 🖾 🆅 🛎

Pembrokeshire

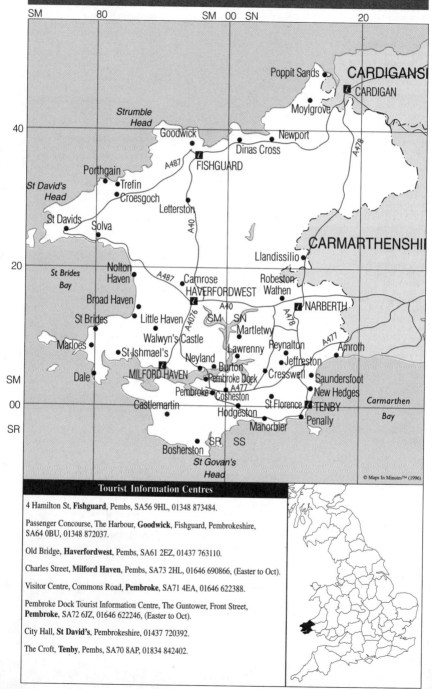

© Maps In Minutes™ (1996)

Tourist Information Centres

4 Hamilton St, **Fishguard**, Pembs, SA56 9HL, 01348 873484.

Passenger Concourse, The Harbour, **Goodwick**, Fishguard, Pembrokeshire, SA64 0BU, 01348 872037.

Old Bridge, **Haverfordwest**, Pembs, SA61 2EZ, 01437 763110.

Charles Street, **Milford Haven**, Pembs, SA73 2HL, 01646 690866, (Easter to Oct).

Visitor Centre, Commons Road, **Pembroke**, SA71 4EA, 01646 622388.

Pembroke Dock Tourist Information Centre, The Guntower, Front Street, **Pembroke**, SA72 6JZ, 01646 622246, (Easter to Oct).

City Hall, **St David's**, Pembrokeshire, 01437 720392.

The Croft, **Tenby**, Pembs, SA70 8AP, 01834 842402.

Amroth

SN1607 🍺 *Amroth Arms, Temple Bar*

Ashdale Guest House, *Amroth, Narberth, Pembs, SA67 8NA.*
Well situated for:- Beaches, theme parks, Dylan Thomas, Irish ferries.
Open: Easter to Nov
01834 813853 (also fax)
Mrs Williamson
D: £15.00–£16.00 **S:** £15.00–£16.00
Beds: 2F 1T 2D 1S **Baths:** 2 Sh
🛇 🅿 (6) 🔟 🎦 ✕ 🎬 🆅 🕯 ᴧ

Beach Haven Guest House,
Amroth, Narberth, SA67 8NG.
Quiet picturesque location, magnificent sea views, transfers available.
Open: All Year (not Xmas)
Grades: WTB 2 Star
01834 813310 Mr Rickards
D: £15.00–£17.00 **S:** £15.00–£17.00
Beds: 2D 1T 1S **Baths:** 2 En 2 Sh
🛇 (5) 🅿 🔟 🎦 ✕ 🆅 🕯

Bosherston

SR9694 🍺 *St Govan's Inn*

Trefalen Farm, *Bosherston, Pembroke, SA71 5DR.*
Idyllic coastal location. Wholehearted welcome in C17th farmhouse. Peace. Animals.
Open: All Year
Grades: WTB 2 Star
01646 661643 Mr & Mrs Giardelli
Fax: 01646 661626
trefalen@aol.com
D: £19.00 **S:** £22.50
Beds: 1S 1T 1D **Baths:** 2 Sh
🛇 🅿 🛏 🔟 🎦 ✕ 🎬 🕯

Cornerstones, *Bosherston, Pembroke, SA71 5DN.*
Immaculately contained accommodation. Half mile Broadhaven Beach and coastal path.
Open: All Year (not Xmas/New Year)
01646 661660 Mrs James
D: £20.00–£21.00 **S:** £25.00
Beds: 1T 1F **Baths:** 1 En 1 Pr
🛇 🅿 (4) 🛏 🔟 🎦 🎬 🆅 🕯

Broad Haven

SM8613 🍺 *Swan, Galleon, Royal, Nest*

Lion Rock, *Broad Haven, Haverfordwest, Pembs, SA62 3JP.*
Open: All Year (not Xmas/New Year)
Grades: WTB 3 Star
01437 781645 Mrs Main
Fax: 01437 781203
lion.rock@btinternet.com
D: £20.00–£30.00 **S:** £20.00–£25.00
Beds: 1T 2D 2S **Baths:** 3 En 2 Pr
🛇 (7) 🅿 (8) 🛏 🔟 🎦 ✕ 🎬 🆅 🕯
Stunning quiet cliff top position in Pembrokeshire Coast National Park. Single storey house. Views over ST. Brides Bay and Skomer Island. Owner Access to coast path. Warm welcome, help and information on local walks, beaches and watersports. Not to be missed.

Anchor Guesthouse, The Sea Front, *Broad Haven, Haverfordwest, Pembs, SA62 3JN.*
Opposite sandy beach with magnificent sea views. Adjacent cafe, shop restaurant. Coastal Path.
Open: All Year
Grades: WTB 2 Star
01437 781051 Mrs Morgan
Fax: 01437 781050
D: £17.50–£27.00 **S:** £17.50–£27.00
Beds: 8 **Baths:** 8 En
🛇 🅿 🔟 🎬 🆅 🕯

Burton

SM9805

Beggars Reach Hotel, *Burton, Milford Haven, Pembs, SA73 1PD.*
Open: All Year
01646 600700 W Smallman
Fax: 01646 600560
D: fr £26.25 **S:** fr £32.50
Beds: 3F 1T 6D 2S **Baths:** 12 En
🅿 (25) 🗶 🔟 🎦 ✕ 🎬 🆅 ❄ 🕯 cc
Quiet country house hotel. Ideal base for exploring Pembrokeshire.

Camrose

SM9219 🍺 *Rising Sun*

The Fold, Cleddau Lodge, *Camrose, Haverfordwest, Pembrokeshire, SA62 6HY.*
Converted C17th farmhouse, gardens, woodlands, river with otters, view of Preseli.
Open: Easter to Oct
Grades: WTB 2 Star
01437 710640 Mrs Brookman
Fax: 01437 710663
cleddau.lodge@btinternet.com
D: £15.00–£18.50 **S:** £18.50
Beds: 1D **Baths:** 1 Pr
🛇 🅿 (10) 🔟 🎬 🆅 🕯

Castlemartin

SR9198

Chapel Farm, *Castlemartin, Pembroke, Pembrokeshire, SA71 5HW.*
Large comfortable farmhouse overlooking sea, offers relaxing holidays to unwind.
Open: All Year
Grades: WTB 3 Star
01646 661312 (also fax)
Mrs Smith
chapelfarm@aol.com
D: £20.00–£22.00 **S:** £25.00–£27.00
Beds: 1F 1T **Baths:** 1 En 1 Pr
🛇 🅿 (10) 🔟 🎦 🎬 🆅 🕯

Cosheston

SN0003

Poyerston Farm, *Cosheston, Pembroke, SA72 4SJ.*
Charming Victorian farmhouse on a working farm. All ensuite bedrooms, some ground floor.
Open: All Year
01646 651347 (also fax)
Mrs Lewis
D: £20.00–£25.00 **S:** £25.00–£30.00
Beds: 2F 2D 1T **Baths:** 5 En
🛇 (4) 🅿 (12) 🗶 🔟 ✕ 🎬 🕯 ᴧ

Cresswell

SN0506 🍺 *Carew Inn*

Cresswell House, *Cresswell Quay, Kilgetty, Pembs, SA68 0TE.*
Beautiful riverside Georgian house. Guest rooms overlook waterside.
Open: All Year
01646 651435 Mr Wright
phil@creswellhouse.co.uk
D: £22.50–£25.00 **S:** £27.50
Beds: 1T 2D **Baths:** 2 En 1 Pr
🅿 ✕ 🎬 🕯

Croesgoch

SM8230 🍺 *Sloop, Square & Compass*

Bank House Farm, *Abereiddy Road, Croesgoch, Haverfordwest, Pembs, SA62 6XZ.*
Picturesque sea views on Country Road between Croesgoch and Abereiddy.
Open: All Year (not Xmas)
Grades: WTB 2 Star
01348 831305 Mrs Lloyd
D: £15.00–£18.00 **S:** fr £18.00
Beds: 1D 1T **Baths:** 1 Sh
🛇 🅿 🔟 🎦 ✕ 🎬 🕯

Maes y Ffynnon, *Penygroes, Croesgoch, Haverfordwest, Pembs, SA62 5JN.*
Modern large bungalow, private grounds; ideal base for walking or touring.
Open: Mar to Oct **Grades:** WTB 2 Star
01348 831319 Mrs Evans
D: fr £16.50 **S:** fr £18.50
Beds: 1F 1T **Baths:** 2 En
🛇 🅿 (4) 🔟 🛏 🎬 🆅 🕯

Dale

SM8005

The Post House Hotel, *Dale, Haverfordwest, Pembs, SA62 3RE.*
Open: closed feb
01646 636201
Mr & Mrs Riley
posthousedale@talk21.com
D: £24.00–£27.50 **S:** £26.00
Beds: 2T 2D 1S **Baths:** 5 En
🅿 (6) 🔟 ✕ 🎬 🆅 🕯
Licensed hotel, ensuite bedrooms, plus suite of rooms, TV Lounge, Conservatory. Residents evening meals, local produce, fresh fish. (vegetarians catered for). 100 yards from bay, sailing, windsurfing, walking just off the Pembrokeshire coast path. Close to offshore bird islands, Skomer, Skokholm and Grassholm.

Dinas Cross

SN0039 🍺 *Llwyngwair Arms, Ship Aground*

Fron Isaf Farm, *Dinas Cross, Newport, Pembs, SA42 0SW.*
Peaceful sheep farm with panoramic views of sea and hills.
Open: Apr to Oct
Grades: WTB 3 Star Farm
01348 811339 Mr & Mrs Urwin
claire.len@cwcom.net
D: £22.00 **S:** £25.00
Beds: 1F 1T **Baths:** 1 Sh
🛇 (3) 🅿 (5) 🔟 🛏 🎬 🆅 🕯

Fishguard

SM9537   Cartref Hotel, Farmhouse Kitchen, Ferryboat, Glendower, Hope & Anchor, Old Coach House, Rose & Crown, Royal Oak

The Beach House, Fishguard Harbour, Fishguard, Pembs, SA64 0DH.
Seafront guest house on Fishguard Harbour (village location).
Open: All Year
Grades: WTB 1 Star GH
01348 872085 Mrs Wagstaff
D: £13.50–£18.00 **S:** £13.50–£18.00
Beds: 2F 2D 2T 2S **Baths:** 2 En 3 Pr 1 Sh
🛏 🅿 (5) 📺 🍴 🛢 V ♨ cc

Cartref Hotel, 13-19 High Street, Fishguard, Pembs, SA65 9AW.
Friendly renovated hotel. Excellent family accommodation. Free garage. Open 24 hours.
Open: All Year
Grades: WTB 2 Star, AA 2 Star
01348 872430 Mrs Bjorkquist
Fax: 01348 873664
cartref@themail.co.uk
D: £24.00–£27.00 **S:** £32.00–£36.00
Beds: 2F 2D 2T 4S **Baths:** 10 En
🛏 🅿 (3) 📺 🍴 ✕ 🛢 V ♨ cc

Stanley House, Quay Road, Goodwick, Fishguard, Pembs, SA64 0BS.
Overlooking Fishguard, ferry terminal and bay and Preseli Hills beyond.
Open: All Year
Grades: WTB 2 Star, AA 3 Diamond
01348 873024 Mr Hendrie
D: £16.50–£19.50 **S:** £19.50
Beds: 2F 2D 2T 1S **Baths:** 1 En 1 Pr 2 Sh
🛏 🅿 (3) 📺 🍴 🛢 V ♨ cc

Inglewood, 13 Vergam Terrace, Fishguard, Pembs, SA65 9DD.
Comfortable terraced accommodation. One mile from Fishguard to Rosslare Ferries.
Open: Jan to Dec
01348 873475 Mrs Lewis
D: £16.00 **S:** £18.00–£20.00
Beds: 1D 1T
🛏 (12) 🅿 📺 🛢 V ♨

Cri'r Wylan, Pen Wallis, Fishguard, Pembs, SA65 9HR.
Relax in homely atmosphere - detached house - private parking. Superb views.
Open: All Year (not Xmas/New Year)
Grades: WTB 3 Star
01348 873398 Mrs Nicholas
D: £18.00–£20.00 **S:** £30.00
Beds: 1D 1T 1S **Baths:** 1 Sh
🛏 🅿 (4) ✂ 📺 🛢 V ♨

Coach House Cottage, Glendower Square, Goodwick, Fishguard, Pembs, SA64 0DH.
Stone built Pembrokeshire cottage, convenient for coastal path / Irish ferry.
Open: All Year (not Xmas/New Year)
01348 873660 Mrs Maxwell-Jones
lizmaxwell@aol.com
D: £15.00 **S:** £20.00
Beds: 1T **Baths:** 1 Sh
🛏 🅿 ✂ 📺 🍴 ✕ 🛢 V ♨

Goodwick

SM9438   Farmhouse Kitchen, Ferryboat Inn

Ivybridge, Drim Mill, Dyffryn, Goodwick, Fishguard, Pembs, SA64 0FT.
Open: All Year (not Xmas)
Grades: WTB 2 Star GH
01348 875366 Mrs Davies
Fax: 01348 872338
ivybridge@cwcom.net
D: £20.50–£24.50 **S:** fr £23.50
Beds: 4F 4D 2T 1S **Baths:** 4 En 2 Pr
🛏 🅿 (12) 📺 🍴 ✕ 🛢 V ♨ cc
Friendly family-run guest house. Ensuite rooms with colour TV and hot drinks tray. Good home cooking, heated indoor pool, licensed, vegetarians welcome. Ample off-road parking. 2 minutes ferry port. Early/late visitors welcome.

Stanley House, Quay Road, Goodwick, Fishguard, Pembs, SA64 0BS.
Overlooking Fishguard, ferry terminal and bay and Preseli Hills beyond.
Open: All Year
Grades: WTB 2 Star, AA 3 Diamond
01348 873024 Mr Hendrie
D: £16.50–£19.50 **S:** £19.50
Beds: 2F 2D 2T 1S **Baths:** 1 En 1 Pr 2 Sh
🛏 🅿 (3) 📺 🍴 🛢 V ♨ cc

Haverfordwest

SM9515   Artramont Arms, Stonemasons, George, Rising Sun

The Fold, Cleddau Lodge, Camrose, Haverfordwest, Pembrokeshire, SA62 6HY.
Converted C17th farmhouse, gardens, woodlands, river with otters, view of Preseli.
Open: Easter to Oct
Grades: WTB 2 Star
01437 710640 Mrs Brookman
Fax: 01437 710663
cleddau.lodge@btinternet.com
D: £15.00–£18.50 **S:** £18.50
Beds: 1D **Baths:** 1 Pr
🛏 🅿 (10) 📺 🛢 V ♨

Greenways, Shoals Hook Lane, Haverfordwest, Pembs, SA61 2XN.
Quiet retreat. The best in the west find peace in our heaven,.
Open: All Year
Grades: WTB 2 Star
01437 762345 Mr Tuson
Fax: 01437 769190
keith2sam@aol.co.uk
D: £20.00–£25.00 **S:** £20.00–£25.00
Beds: 1F 3D 3T 4S **Baths:** 3 En 1 Sh
🛏 🅿 📺 🍴 ✕ 🛢 V ♨ ♨

College Guest House, 93 Hill Street, Haverfordwest, Pembs, SA61 1QX.
Friendly welcome, spacious rooms, good 'Welsh' breakfast, smoking rooms available.
Open: All Year (not Xmas/New Year)
Grades: WTB 2 Star
01437 763710 (also fax)
Mr Gerson
D: £20.00–£23.00 **S:** £22.00–£25.00
Beds: 1D 5T 2S 1F **Baths:** 9 En
🛏 🅿 (30) ✂ 📺 🛢 V ♨ cc

Cuckoo Mill, Pelcomb Bridge, St Davids Road, Haverfordwest, Pembs, SA62 6EA.
Central Pembrokeshire. Quietly situated. Excellent food. Genuine welcome. Unrestricted access.
Open: All Year
Grades: WTB 3 Star
01437 762139 Mrs Davies
D: £20.00–£25.00 **S:** £20.00–£25.00
Beds: 1F 2D 1T **Baths:** 2 Sh
🛏 🅿 (4) 📺 🍴 ✕ 🛢 V ♨ ♨ ⚘

Penrhiwllan Old Rectory, Well Lane, Prendergast, Haverfordwest, Pembs, SA61 2PL.
Beautiful detached country setting in town. Ideal base for touring Pembrokeshire.
Open: All Year
01437 769049 Mrs Walker
D: £18.00–£21.00 **S:** £18.00–£21.00
Beds: 1F 2D **Baths:** 1 Pr 2 Sh
🛏 🅿 (6) ✂ 📺 🛢 V ♨

Crofty, Croes Goch, Haverfordwest, Pembs, SA62 5JT.
Crofty Guest House, situated in quiet village with comfortable rooms and good breakfast.
Open: All Year
01348 831441 Mrs Rees
D: £16.00–£19.00 **S:** £18.00
Beds: 4F 1D 1T **Baths:** 2 En 1 Pr
🛏 🅿 (6) 📺 🍴 🛢 V ♨

Hodgeston

SS0399   Freshwater East Inn

Rosedene, Hodgeston, Freshwater East, Pembroke, SA71 5JU.
Adjacent village green, memorable meals, licensed. Old fashioned courtesy, affordable luxury.
Open: All Year (not Xmas)
01646 672586 Mrs Fallon
eileen@rosedene85.freeserve.co.uk
D: £20.00–£25.00 **S:** £30.00–£35.00
Beds: 1F 3D 2T **Baths:** 7 En
🛏 🅿 (7) ✂ 📺 🛢 V ♨ ⚘ 1 cc

Jeffreston

SN0806   Jeffreyston Inn

Jeffreyston Grange, Jeffreyston, Kilgetty, Pembs, SA68 0RE.
Open: All Year (not Xmas)
01646 650159 Mr & Mrs Hesslegrave
Fax: 01646 651124
D: £18.00–£20.00 **S:** £18.00–£20.00
Beds: 1D 2T **Baths:** 2 En 1 Pr
🛏 🅿 (4) ✂ 📺 🛢 V ♨
A 'grand' name, but warm, friendly, cosy and comfortable peacefully located opposite the ancient parish church. Beautiful Pembrokeshire Coast, Daugleddau Waterway, castles, countryside. Enjoy them all and at the end of the day, let our home wrap itself around you.

Planning a longer stay? Always ask for any special rates

Lawrenny

SN0106

Knowles Farm, Lawrenny, Kilgetty, Pembs, SA68 0PX.
Lovely south-facing farmhouse, surrounded by the upper reaches of the Milford Haven estuary.
Open: Easter to Oct
01834 891221 V Lort-Phillips
Fax: 01834 891344
owenlp@globalnet.co.uk
D: £17.00–£23.00 **S:** £22.00–£30.00
Beds: 2D 2T **Baths:** 3 En 1 Pr
⏰ 🅿 (12) ⌇ 📺 🍴 ✕ 🏠 🖫 🖂 🖳 ♨

Letterston

SM9329 ⚓ Somethings Cooking

Heathfield, Mathry Road, Letterston, Haverfordwest, Pembs, SA62 5EG.
Georgian country house, ideally situated to explore all Pembrokeshire's treasures.
Open: Easter to Nov
01348 840263 (also fax)
Mrs Rees
angelica.tees@virgin.net
D: £20.00–£22.00 **S:** £25.00–£30.00
Beds: 2D 1T **Baths:** 2 En 1 Pr
⏰ 🅿 (10) ⌇ 📺 🍴 ✕ 🏠 🖂 🖳 ♨

Little Haven

SM8512 ⚓ Swan

The Bower Farm, Little Haven, Haverfordwest, Pembs, SA62 3TY.
Friendly farmhouse, fantastic sea views.
Open: All Year
Grades: WTB 3 Star Farm
01437 781554 Mr Birt-Llewellin
bowerfarm@lineone.net
D: £20.00–£27.00 **S:** £25.00–£30.00
Beds: 2F 1D 1T 1S **Baths:** 5 En
⏰ 🅿 (10) 📺 🍴 ✕ 🏠 🖳 ♨

Whitegates, Settlands Hill, Little Haven, Haverfordwest, Pembs, SA62 3LA.
Open: All Year (not Xmas)
01437 781386 (also fax)
Mr & Mrs Llewellin
D: £22.00–£27.00 **S:** £30.00–£35.00
Beds: 1F 4D 1T **Baths:** 4 En 2 Pr
⏰ 🅿 📺 🍴 ✕ 🏠 🖳 ❄ ♨ cc
Overlooking the sea and lovely fishing village, general good eating places within easy walking distance, lovely garden and conservatory bar overlooking sea. Fishing, wind surfing, horse riding and golf nearby, also Bird islands and wild flowers.

Llandissilio

SN1221 ⚓ Bush Inn

Plas-y-Brodyr, Rhydwilym, Llandissilio, Clynderwen, Pembs, SA66 7QH.
Peaceful farmhouse in unspoilt valley. Ideal base for exploring Pembrokeshire and West Wales. **Open:** Mar to Nov
Grades: WTB 4 Star Farm
01437 563771 Mrs Pogson
Fax: 01437 563294
janet@farmhols.freeserve.co.uk
D: £20.00–£22.00 **S:** £25.00–£27.00
Beds: 2D **Baths:** 1 En 1 Pr
⏰ (6) 🅿 (4) ⌇ 📺 ✕ 🏠 🖳 ♨

Manorbier

SS0697 ⚓ Lydstep Tavern, Castle Inn

Fernley Lodge, Manorbier, Tenby, Pembs, SA70 7TH.
Victorian house in heart of beautiful coastal village.
Open: All Year (not Xmas)
01834 871226 Mrs Cowper
fernleylodge@yahoo.com
D: £20.00–£25.00 **S:** £20.00–£25.00
Beds: 1F 1D **Baths:** 2 Pr
⏰ (2) 🅿 (7) ⌇ 📺 🍴 🏠 ♨ ⅙

The Old Vicarage, Manorbier, Tenby, Pembs, SA70 7TN.
Victorian Gothic old vicarage. Sandy beaches and stunning walking.
Open: All Year
01834 871452 (also fax)
Mrs McHugh
oldvic@moanorbier-tenby.fsnet.co.uk
D: £22.50–£27.50
Beds: 1D 1T **Baths:** 2 En
⏰ 🅿 ⌇ 📺 🏠 🖳 ♨

Marloes

SM7908 ⚓ Lobster Pot

Foxdale, Glebe Lane, Marloes, Haverfordwest, Pembs, SA62 3AX.
Set in the heart of the Pembrokeshire Coast National Park. Close to cliff path.
Open: All Year
Grades: WTB 3 Star
01646 636243 Mrs Roddam-King
foxdale.guest.house@totalise.co.uk
D: £18.00–£25.00 **S:** £23.00–£30.00
Beds: 2D 1T **Baths:** 2 En 1 Pr
🅿 (6) 📺 🍴 ✕ 🏠 🖳 ♨

Martletwy

SN0310

The Peacock Tea Garden, Hoarstone House, Martletwy, Narberth, Pembs, SA67 8AZ.
A country house situated in its own grounds amidst the tranquil countryside of mid-Pembrokeshire.
Open: Easter to Sept
Grades: WTB 3 Star
01834 891707 (also fax)
Mrs Mooney
peacock@jpmarketing.co.uk
D: £20.50–£27.50 **S:** £25.50–£32.50
Beds: 1D 1T **Baths:** 1 En 1 Pr
⏰ 🅿 (8) ⌇ 📺 ✕ 🏠 🖳 ♨

Milford Haven

SM9005 ⚓ Lord Nelson

Kings Arms, Hakin Point, Milford Haven, Pembs, SA73 3DG.
Public house, home cooking. Near marina, railway station. All rooms sea view.
Open: All Year (not Xmas)
01646 693478 Mrs Hutchings
D: £25.00–£30.00 **S:** £15.00
Beds: 2F 4T **Baths:** 3 En
⏰ 🅿 📺 ✕ 🖳 ♨

Planning a longer stay? Always ask for any special rates

Moylegrove

SN1144 ⚓ Eagle Inn

Trewidwal, Moylegrove, Cardigan, Pembrokeshire, SA43 3BY.
Beautiful farmhouse. Extensive grounds. Outstanding coastal and hill views. Peace.
Open: All Year (not Xmas/New Year)
01239 881651 Mr & Mrs Bloss
alan.bloss@btinternet.com
D: £15.00–£18.00 **S:** £18.00–£22.00
Beds: 1F 1D 1S **Baths:** 1 En 1 Sh
⏰ 🅿 (4) ⌇ 📺 🍴 🏠 🖳 ♨

The Old Vicarage, Moylgrove, Cardigan, Pembrokeshire, SA43 3BN.
Edwardian country house, large lawned garden and glorious sea view.
Open: Mar to Nov
Grades: WTB 4 Star
01239 881231 Patricia & David Phillips
Fax: 01239 881341
stay@old-vic.co.uk
D: £24.00–£28.00 **S:** £26.00–£38.00
Beds: 1T 2D **Baths:** 3 En
🅿 (5) ⌇ 📺 ✕ 🖳 ♨

Narberth

SN1014 ⚓ Angel

Great Canaston Farm, Robeston Wathen, Narberth, Pembrokeshire, SA67 8DE.
River and woodland walks surround comfortable/ spacious farmhouse. Breakfasts a speciality.
Open: All Year (not Xmas/New Year)
01437 541254 (also fax)
Mrs Lewis
eleanor2@tesco.net
D: £18.00–£23.00 **S:** £25.00
Beds: 2F **Baths:** 1 Sh
⏰ 🅿 (5) ⌇ 📺 ✕ 🏠 🖳 ♨

Timberlands, Princes Gate, Narberth, Pembs, SA67 8TF.
Views of Preseli Mountains, open fields at the back.
Open: Easter to Oct
01834 860688 Mrs Williams
D: £17.00–£18.00 **S:** £17.00–£20.00
Beds: 3F 2D 1T **Baths:** 3 En
⏰ (3) 🅿 (4) 📺 🏠 ⅙

New Hedges

SN1302

Pen Mar Guest House, New Hedges, Tenby, Pembs, SA70 8TL.
Friendly, comfortable, family-run hotel (Tenby 1 mile; Saundersfoot 1 1/2 miles) Rooms ensuite.
Open: All Year (not Xmas/New Year)
Grades: WTB 2 Star, RAC 3 Diamond
01834 842435 Mr Hurton
penmarhotel@jhurton.freeserve.co.uk
D: £18.00–£25.00 **S:** £23.50–£30.00
Beds: 2F 2T 6D **Baths:** 6 En 4 Sh
⏰ 🅿 (12) 📺 ✕ 🏠 🖳 ❄ ♨ cc

Newport

SN0539 🍺 *Golden Lion, Llwyngwair Arms, Royal Oak, Castle Hotel*

Llysmeddyg Guest House, *East Street, Newport, Pembrokeshire, SA42 0SY.*
Listed Georgian house and Mews flat and Mountain bike hire.
Open: All Year (not Xmas)
Grades: WTB 3 Star
01239 820008 Ian & Penny Ross
penny@ipross.freeserve.co.uk
D: £22.00–£24.00 **S:** £25.00–£35.00
Beds: 1F 1D 2T 1S **Baths:** 2 En 1 Sh
🛇 🅿 (5) ⊬ 📺 ✕ 🛏 Ⅴ ♨

Neyland

SM9605 🍺 *Oddfellows Arms*

Y Ffynnon, *45 Honeyborough Road, Neyland, Milford Haven, Pembs, SA73 1RF.*
Comfortable private house, friendly welcome. Irish ferry by prior arrangement.
Open: All Year (not Xmas)
01646 601369 Mr Hawley
D: £15.00 **S:** £15.00
Beds: 1D 1T 1S **Baths:** 1 Sh
🅿 (1) 📺 🛏 ♨

Nolton Haven

SM8618 🍺 *Mariners Inn*

Nolton Haven Farm House, *Nolton Haven, Haverfordwest, Pembs, SA62 4NH.*
Beachside farmhouse, working farm. 75 yards village inn, quiet, good walks.
Open: All Year (not Xmas)
Grades: WTB 2 Star
01437 710263 (also fax) Mr Canton
stilbb@noltonhaven.com
D: fr £15.00 **S:** fr £15.00
Beds: 3F 2D 1T 1S **Baths:** 2 Pr 4 Sh
🛇 🅿 (20) 📺 ✝ 🛏 Ⅴ

Pembroke

SM9801 🍺 *Dial Inn, Freshwater East Inn, Waterman's Arms, Old Cross, Saws Inn*

Merton Place House, *3 East Back, Pembroke, SA71 4HL.*
Open: All Year **Grades:** WTB 2 Star
01646 684796 Mrs Pearce
D: £15.00–£17.50 **S:** £17.50–£20.00
Beds: 2D 2T 1S **Baths:** 1 Sh
🛇 📺 🛏 ♨
Lovely old Victorian merchants' house, walled gardens at rear, with medieval features in lower Burgage. Small, pretty bedrooms. Two twin rooms and double so only six guests taken. Full of books and pictures. Centre of Pembroke, close castle, buses and trains.

High Noon Guest House, *Lower Lamphey Road, Pembroke, Pembrokeshire, SA71 4AB.*
Ensuites, comfortable and friendly. Delicious breakfasts, near castle, coastline, Irish ferry.
Open: All Year (not Xmas)
01646 683736 (also fax) Mr Barnikel
info@highnoon.co.uk
D: £16.50–£21.50 **S:** £18.50–£26.50
Beds: 2F 3D 1T 3S **Baths:** 5 En 2 Sh
🛇 🅿 (10) 📺 ✝ ✕ 🛏 Ⅴ ♨ cc

Pembroke Dock

SM9603 🍺 *Brewery Inn*

The Old Rectory, *Cosheston, Pembroke Dock, Pembroke, SA72 4UJ.*
Large former rectory in 2 acre gardens.
Open: All Year (not Xmas)
Grades: WTB 1 Star
01646 684960 Mrs Bailey
D: £17.50–£20.00 **S:** £17.50–£20.00
Beds: 1F 1D 2T 1S **Baths:** 2 Sh
🛇 🅿 (4) 📺 ✝ 🛏 ♨

Penally

SS1199 🍺 *Cross, Crown, Lydstep*

Giltar Grove Country House, *Penally, Tenby, Pembs, SA70 7RY.*
Open: All Year
Grades: WTB 3 Star, AA 4 Diamond
01834 871568 Ms Diment
giltarbnb@aol.com
D: £20.00–£25.00 **S:** £20.00–£25.00
Beds: 1F 3D 1T 1S **Baths:** 4 En 1 Pr 1 Sh
🛇 🅿 (10) ⊬ 📺 🛏 Ⅴ ♨
Late Victorian Welsh country house, totally refurbished with charm and character retained. Peaceful location, near unspoilt beaches and castles. Great walks, wildlife and scenery right outside the door - coastal path just 3 mins away. All bedrooms ensuite, 2 with four-posters.

Brambles Lodge, *Penally, Tenby, Pembs, SA70 7QE.*
Detached guest house in picturesque coastal village only 1.5m Tenby.
Open: Feb to Oct **Grades:** WTB 3 Star
01834 842393 Mrs Nightingale
nightingales@easicom.com
D: £16.00–£23.00 **S:** £18.00–£20.00
Beds: 1F 2T 4D 1S **Baths:** 6 En 1 Sh
🛇 (6) 🅿 (9) 📺 ✝ ✕ Ⅴ ♨

Crossing Cottage, *Penally, Tenby, Pembs, SA70 7PP.*
Secluded house, village outskirts, overlooks golf links, sandy beach nearby.
Open: All Year (not Xmas)
01834 842291 Mr & Mrs Watts
D: £15.00 **S:** £15.00
Beds: 1F 1D 1T **Baths:** 1 Sh
🛇 🅿 (6) ⊬ 📺 🛏 ♨

Poppit Sands

SN1548 🍺 *Webley Hotel*

Glan-y-Mor, *Poppit Sands, St Dogmaels, Cardigan, Pembs, SA43 3LP.*
Ex-farmhouse with sea view.
Open: All Year (not Xmas/New Year)
01239 612329 Mrs Sharp
D: £15.00 **S:** £15.00
Beds: 1D **Baths:** 1 Sh
🛇 🅿 📺 ✝ 🛏 Ⅴ ♨

BEDROOMS
F - Family
D - Double
T - Twin
S - Single

Porthgain

SM8132 🍺 *Sloop*

Ynys Barry Country Hotel, *Porthgain, Haverfordwest, Pembs, SA62 5BH.*
Open: All Year
01348 831180 Fax: 01348 831800
ynysbarry@adl.com
D: £18.00–£25.00 **S:** £18.00–£25.00
Beds: 4F 4T 6D **Baths:** 14 En
🛇 🅿 (200) 📺 ✝ ✕ 🛏 Ⅴ ♨ cc
Coastal hotel situated in the National Park. Close to coastal path and the beaches of Abereiddy and Traeth-Llyfn, and the unspoilt harbourside village of Porthgain. Ideal walking and holiday centre. Self-catering cottages also available, fully licensed bar and restaurant.

Reynalton

SN0908 🍺 *Boar's Head*

Carne Mountain Farm, *Reynalton, Kilgetty, Pembs, SA68 0PD.*
A warm welcome awaits you at our lovely 200-year-old farmhouse.
Open: All Year (not Xmas)
01834 860546 Mrs Holgate
D: £16.00–£17.50 **S:** £17.50–£18.50
Beds: 2F **Baths:** 1 Sh
🛇 🅿 (6) ⊬ 📺 ✝ 🛏 Ⅴ ♨

Robeston Wathen

SN0815 🍺 *Bush, Bridge*

Highland Grange Farm, *Robeston Wathen, Narberth, Pembs, SA67 8EP.*
Excellent central location on A40. Scenic countryside, bordering National Park.
Open: All Year
01834 860952 (also fax) Ms James
naomi.highland.grange@ukgateway.net
D: £15.00–£22.00 **S:** £18.00–£25.00
Beds: 2F 1D 1T 2S **Baths:** 2 En 2 Sh
🛇 🅿 (6) 📺 ✕ 🛏 Ⅴ ♨ ♿

Saundersfoot

SN1304

Cwmwennol Country House, *Swallowtree Woods, Saundersfoot, Pembs, SA69 9DE.*
Set in woodland, 3 mins walk beach. Log fire in bar, badgers in garden.
Open: All Year **Grades:** WTB 2 Star
01834 813430 (also fax) Mr Smiles
cwmwennol@lineone.net
D: £23.00–£25.00 **S:** £28.00–£30.00
Beds: 2F 7D 2T 2S **Baths:** 13 En
🛇 (4) 🅿 (50) ⊬ 📺 ✝ ✕ 🛏 Ⅴ ♨ cc

Solva

SM8024 🍺 *Royal George*

Pendinas, *St Brides View, Solva, Haverfordwest, Pembs, SA62 6TB.*
Glorious sea views from all rooms, good food, warm welcome.
Open: Easter to Oct
Grades: WTB 3 Star
01437 721283 Ms Davies
pendinas.solva@talk21.com
D: £20.00–£22.00 **S:** £25.00
Beds: 2D 1T **Baths:** 1 Sh
🅿 (3) ⊬ 📺 🛏 Ⅴ ♨

St Brides

SM8010 ◖ *Foxes, Lobster Pot, Hasguard Caravan*

Fopston Farm, *St Brides, Haverfordwest, Pembs, SA62 3AW.*
Open: Easter to October
Grades: WTB 2 Star
01646 636271 (also fax)
Mrs Price
D: £22.00–£25.00 **S:** £28.00–£31.00
Beds: 1F 2T 1D **Baths:** 1 En 2 Sh
⏦ 🅿 (6) ⊬ 📺 🎍 ▥, 🖤 ♿
Fopston is a working farm of 282 acres. An arable and beef enterprise, it is C17th with spacious and interesting features. For that quiet retreat to refresh the body and soul Fopston awaits you. Beautiful scenery, lovely safe beaches.

St Davids

SM7525 ◖ *Farmers Arms, Sloop*

Ramsey House, *Lower Moor, St Davids, Haverfordwest, Pembs, SA62 6RP.*
Open: All Year (not Xmas)
Grades: WTB 4 Star GH, AA 4 Diamond, RAC 4 Diamond
01437 720321 Mr & Mrs Thompson
Fax: 01437 720025
D: £29.00–£32.00 **S:** £29.00–£64.00
Beds: 4D 3T **Baths:** 6 En 1 Pr
🅿 (8) ⊬ 📺 🎍 ♈ ▥, 🖤 ♿ cc
Superior non-smoking 4 Star guest house exclusively for adults. Convenient location for cathedral and Coast Path. Award-winning dinners/wines with Welsh emphasis. Licensed bar and friendly relaxed hospitality completes your enjoyment. Dinner B&B £44-£48 pppn, £264-£288 weekly.

Pen Albro Guest House, *18 Goat Street, St Davids, Haverfordwest, Pembs, SA62 6RF.*
Cathedral 150 yards, coastal path 0.25 hr, pub next door.
Open: All Year
Grades: WTB 1 Star
01437 721865 D: £14.50 **S:** fr £14.50
Beds: 1D 1T 1S
📺 🎍 ✕ 🖤,

Ty Olaf, *Mount Gardens, St Davids, Pembs, SA62 6BS.*
Quiet bungalow, within reach of cathedral, restaurants, coast path, beaches.
Open: All Year
Grades: WTB 3 Star
01437 720885 (also fax)
Mrs Liggitt
rona.liggitt@which.net
D: £16.00–£18.00 **S:** £16.00–£18.00
Beds: 1F 1D 1T 1S **Baths:** 1 Sh
🅿 (3) ⊬ 📺 ▥, 🖤 ♿

Y Gorlan, *77 Nun Street, St Davids, Haverfordwest, Pembs, SA62 6NU.*
Close to cathedral, coastal path, beaches and golf course.
Open: All Year
01437 720837 Mr Bohlen
Fax: 01437 721148
D: £22.50–£27.00 **S:** £25.00–£27.00
Beds: 1F 2D 1T 1S **Baths:** 5 En
⏦ 🅿 (2) 📺 ✕ 🖤,

Y Glennydd Hotel, *51 Nun Street, St Davids, Haverfordwest, Pembs, SA62 6NU.*
Comfortable Victorian property - most rooms ensuite, popular licensed bistro.
Open: Feb to Oct
01437 720576 Mrs Foster
D: £17.50–£21.00 **S:** £18.50–£25.00
Beds: 4F 4D 2S **Baths:** 8 En 2 Sh
⏦ 📺 ✕ 🖤,

Penberi Cottage, *St Davids, Haverfordwest, SA62 6QL.*
Listed old village shop 1.5 miles from beautiful harbour village of Solva.
Open: All Year
01437 720528 (also fax)
gordon@chapchoc.demon.co.uk
D: £18.00 **S:** £25.00
Beds: 1T
🅿 (1) ⊬ 📺 🎍 ✕ 🖤, ♿ 3

St Florence

SN0801 ◖ *Sun Inn*

Grove Farmhouse, *St Florence, Tenby, Pembs, SA70 8LZ.*
C17th Listed farmhouse in centre of village of St. Florence.
Open: Apr to Oct
01834 871730 (also fax) Mrs Paice
rpaice@cwcom.net
D: £18.50
Beds: 1D **Baths:** 1 Pr
🅿 (1) ⊬ 📺 🖤, 🖤 ♿

St Ishmael's

SM8307 ◖ *Brook Inn*

Skerryback Farmhouse, *Sandy Haven, St Ishmael's, Haverfordwest, Pembs, SA62 3DN.*
Welcoming C18th farmhouse, adjoining coastal path, relaxed atmosphere, tea/coffee on arrival.
Open: March to November
Grades: WTB 3 Star
01646 636598 Mrs Williams
Fax: 01646 636595
williams@farmersweekly.net
D: £20.00–£25.00 **S:** £20.00–£24.00
Beds: 1D 1T 1S **Baths:** 1 Sh
⏦ 🅿 ⊬ 📺 ✕ 🖤, 🖤 ♿

Bicton Farm, *Bicton, St Ishmael's, Haverfordwest, Pembs, SA62 3DN.*
Warm welcome in comfortable farmhouse; attention to individual requirements. **Open:** Easter to Oct
01646 636215 Mrs Llewellyn
D: £19.00–£21.00 **S:** £19.00–£21.00
Beds: 3F 2D 1T **Baths:** 2 En 1 Sh
⏦ 🅿 ⊬ 📺 🎍 ▥,

Tenby

SN1300 ◖ *Coach & Horses, Five Arches, Normandie Hotel, Pig & Puffin*

Glenthorne Guesthouse, *9 Deer Park, Tenby, Pembs, SA70 7LE.*
Situated 250 metres from Tenby's beautiful beaches and coast path.
Open: All Year (not Xmas)
Grades: WTB 2 Star
01834 842300 Mr & Mrs Lapham
D: £14.00–£20.00 **S:** £14.00–£20.00
Beds: 2F 5D 1T 1S **Baths:** 5 En 1 Pr 3 Sh
⏦ 🅿 (5) 📺 🎍 ✕ 🖤, 🖤 ♿

Clarence House Hotel, *Esplanade, Tenby, Pembs, SA70 7DU.*
Seafront location. Superb coastal views. Close to all amenities.
Open: Feb to Dec
Grades: WTB 2 Star, AA 3 Diamond
01834 844371 Mr Phillips
Fax: 01834 844372
clarencehotel@freeuk.com
D: £14.00–£47.00 **S:** £16.00–£47.00
Beds: 25D 25T 18S **Baths:** 68 Pr
⊬ 📺 🎍 ♈ ▥, 🖤 ♿

Ripley St Marys Hotel, *St Marys Street, Tenby, Pembs, SA70 7HN.*
Central Floral Hotel, 75 yards from Sea Front, Private Garage Parking.
Open: Easter to Oct
Grades: WTB 2 Star Hotel, AA 3 Diamond, RAC 3 Diamond
01834 842837 (also fax)
Mr Mace
D: £25.00–£28.00 **S:** £25.00–£29.00
Beds: 3F 4D 3T 2S **Baths:** 8 En 3 Sh
⏦ 🅿 (12) 📺 🎍 ▥, 🖤

Pen Mar Guest House, *New Hedges, Tenby, Pembs, SA70 8TL.*
Open: All Year (not Xmas/New Year)
Grades: WTB 2 Star RAC 3 Diamond
01834 842435 Mr Hurton
penmarhotel@jhurton.freeserve.co.uk
D: £18.00–£25.00 **S:** £23.50–£30.00
Beds: 2F 2T 6D **Baths:** 6 En 4 Sh
⏦ 🅿 (12) 📺 ✕ 🖤, 🖤 ♿ cc
Friendly, comfortable, family-run hotel (Tenby 1 mile; Saundersfoot 1 1/2 miles) Rooms ensuite, TVs, sea views and Waterwynch Bay a short walk. Licensed restaurant, well-stocked bar, excellent British and Continental cuisine. Private car parking. Reductions for children.

St Oswalds Guest House, *Picton Terrace, Tenby, Pembs, SA70 7DR.*
Fifty yards beach, Town two minutes, Ensuite rooms, Private parking.
Open: April to October
01834 842130 (also fax) Mr Nichols
D: £17.00–£25.00
Beds: 7D 4F **Baths:** 11 En
⏦ (2) 🅿 (10) 📺 🖤,

Glenholme, *Picton Terrace, Tenby, Pembs, SA70 7DR.*
Comfortable warm and friendly atmosphere with delicious home made hearty meals. **Open:** All Year
Grades: WTB 2 Star
01834 843909 (also fax) Ms Milward
sandra.glenholme@talk21.com
D: £15.50–£22.50 **S:** £20.00–£25.00
Beds: 1F 3D 2T 1S **Baths:** 8 En
⏦ (10) ⊬ 📺 🎍 ✕ 🖤, 🖤 ♿

Hammonds Park Hotel, *Narberth Road, Tenby, SA70 8HT.*
10 minutes walk from seafront, Most rooms newly built last year.
Open: All Year
Grades: WTB 2 Star, AA 2 Star
01834 842696 Mr Draper
Fax: 01834 844295
bryndraper@compuserve.com
D: £19.00–£28.00 **S:** £21.00–£44.00
Beds: 6F 4D 3T **Baths:** 13 En
⏦ 🅿 (16) 📺 🖤, ♿ cc

Ivy Bank, Harding Street, Tenby, Pembs,
SA70 7LL.
Tenby's only 4 star guest house situated
in quiet town centre street.
Open: All Year
Grades: WTB 4 Star
01834 842311 Mrs Cromack
Fax: 01834 849053
trybanktenby@btinternet.com
D: £19.00–£25.00
S: £24.00–£30.00
Beds: 2F 3D 1T **Baths:** 5 En
🛏 ⅙ 📺 ✕ 🛒 🕯

Lyndale Guest House, Warren Street,
Tenby, Pembs, SA70 7JX.
Smart, friendly, family-run guest house
offering high standard accommodation.
Open: All Year (not Xmas)
01834 842836 Mrs Percival
D: £15.00–£19.00 **S:** £15.00–£19.00
Beds: 2D 2T 1S **Baths:** 5 En
🛏 (4) ⅙ 📺 🛒 🛈 🕯

Trefin

SM8332 ⬗ Square & Compass, Sloop, Ship

Maes y Ffynnon, Penygroes,
Croesgoch, Haverfordwest, Pembs,
SA62 5JN.
Modern large bungalow, private grounds;
ideal base for walking or touring.
Open: Mar to Oct **Grades:** WTB 2 Star
01348 831319 Mrs Evans
D: fr £16.50 **S:** fr £18.50
Beds: 1F 1T **Baths:** 2 En
🛏 📶 (4) ⅙ 📺 🐾 🛒 🛈 🕯

**The Old Court House Vegetarian
Guest House,** Trefin, Haverfordwest,
SA62 5AX.
Cosy cottage close to spectacular coastal
path; excellent vegetarian food.
Open: All Year **Grades:** WTB 3 Star
01348 837095 L Brodie
D: £21.50–£23.50 **S:** £21.50–£23.50
Beds: 2D 1T **Baths:** 2 En
🛏 (5) 📶 (2) ⅙ 📺 ✕ 🛒 🛈 🕯

Walwyns Castle

SM8711 ⬗ Masons Arms, Welcome Traveller

Barley Villa Farm House, Walwyns
Castle, Haverfordwest, Pembs, SA62 3EB.
Spacious modern farmhouse in scenic
countryside. Warm welcome awaits you.
Open: Easter to Nov
Grades: WTB 3 Star
01437 781254
Mrs Davies
barley-villa@pfh.co.uk
D: £18.00–£22.00 **S:** £21.00–£25.00
Beds: 2D 1T **Baths:** 2 En 1 Sh
🛏 (10) 📶 (4) ⅙ 📺 ✕ 🛒 🛈 🕯

All details shown are as
supplied by B&B owners in
Autumn 2000

Stilwell's Britain:
Hostels & Camping 2001

It's a great new idea! Hostels, camping barns, bunk houses **and** camping sites all in one user-friendly book. From now on, campers, tourers, backpackers, clubs and groups – anyone looking for low-cost and group accommodation – can find the right place to sleep for the right price by consulting the right guide – **Stilwell's Britain: Hostels & Camping 2001**.

Listings in **Stilwell's Britain: Hostels & Camping 2001** are arranged geographically by country, county and location throughout England, Scotland and Wales. Each entry includes tariffs, facilities, opening times and a brief description of the premise, it's location and surroundings. Many are accompanied by a picture of the site. The average charge per person per night is £8. As wi`th all Stilwell guides, the book contains local maps, grid references and listings of Tourist Information Centres. There's air, rail, bus and ferry information, too.

Whether you're traveling alone or in a group, you can plan your trip with a minimum of fuss with **Stilwell's Britain: Hostels & Camping 2001**.

£6.95 from all good bookstores (ISBN 1-900861-20-8) or £7.95 (inc p&p) from Stilwell Publishing Ltd, 59 Charlotte Road, London EC2A 3QW (020 7739-7179)

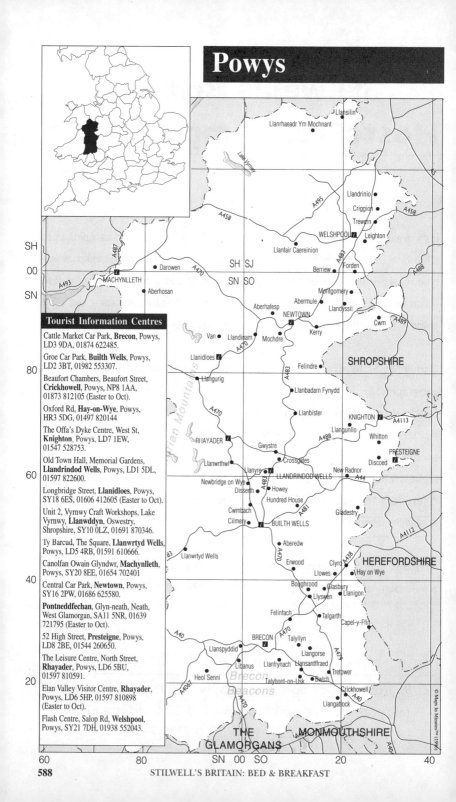

Powys

Tourist Information Centres

Cattle Market Car Park, **Brecon**, Powys, LD3 9DA, 01874 622485.

Groe Car Park, **Builth Wells**, Powys, LD2 3BT, 01982 553307.

Beaufort Chambers, Beaufort Street, **Crickhowell**, Powys, NP8 1AA, 01873 812105 (Easter to Oct).

Oxford Rd, **Hay-on-Wye**, Powys, HR3 5DG, 01497 820144

The Offa's Dyke Centre, West St, **Knighton**, Powys, LD7 1EW, 01547 528753.

Old Town Hall, Memorial Gardens, **Llandrindod Wells**, Powys, LD1 5DL, 01597 822600.

Longbridge Street, **Llanidloes**, Powys, SY18 6ES, 01606 412605 (Easter to Oct).

Unit 2, Vyrnwy Craft Workshops, Lake Vyrnwy, **Llanwddyn**, Oswestry, Shropshire, SY10 0LZ, 01691 870346.

Ty Barcud, The Square, **Llanwrtyd Wells**, Powys, LD5 4RB, 01591 610666.

Canolfan Owain Glyndwr, **Machynlleth**, Powys, SY20 8EE, 01654 702401

Central Car Park, **Newtown**, Powys, SY16 2PW, 01686 625580.

Pontneddfechan, Glyn-neath, Neath, West Glamorgan, SA11 5NR, 01639 721795 (Easter to Oct).

52 High Street, **Presteigne**, Powys, LD8 2BE, 01544 260650.

The Leisure Centre, North Street, **Rhayader**, Powys, LD6 5BU, 01597 810591.

Elan Valley Visitor Centre, **Rhayader**, Powys, LD6 5HP, 01597 810898 (Easter to Oct).

Flash Centre, Salop Rd, **Welshpool**, Powys, SY21 7DH, 01938 552043.

Aberedw

SO0847   Seven Stars

Court Farm, *Aberedw, Builth Wells, Powys, LD2 3UP.*
Strictly non-smoking, peaceful, picturesque. Hill-walking, birds and wildlife in abundance.
Open: Easter to Nov
01982 560277 Mr Davies
D: £17.00–£19.00 **S:** £18.00–£20.00
Beds: 2D 1S **Baths:** 1 En 1 Pr 1 Sh
⅏ 📺 🖳 Ⓥ ♨

Aberhafesp

SO0692   Talkhouse, Lion Hotel

Dyffryn Farm, *Aberhafesp, Newtown, Powys, SY16 3JD.*
5 Star accommodation on organic hill farm - walks and nature reserve nearby.
Open: All Year (not Xmas)
Grades: WTB 4 Star Farm, AA 5 Diamond
01686 688817 Mr & Mrs Jones
Fax: 01686 688324 dave&sue@clara.net
D: £24.00–£25.00 **S:** £24.00–£25.00
Beds: 1F 1D 1T **Baths:** 3 En
⅏ 📺 🖳 Ⓥ ♨

Aberhosan

SN8097   Star Inn

Bacheiddon Farm, *Aberhosan, Machynlleth, Powys, SY20 8SG.*
Working farm. Ideal walking, touring area. Close RSPB and MWT.
Open: May to Oct
01654 702229 Mrs Lewis
D: £18.00–£20.00 **S:** £20.00–£25.00
Beds: 3D **Baths:** 3 En
⅏ 🄿 📺 ♨

Abermule

SO1694

Dolforwyn Hall Hotel, *Abermule, Montgomery, Powys, SY15 6JG.*
Open: All Year **Grades:** WTB 3 Star
01686 630221 K Galvin
Fax: 01686 630360
enquiries@dolforwyn.co.uk
D: £30.00 **S:** £39.50–£45.00
Beds: 1F 2T 3D 2S **Baths:** 8 En
⅏ 🄿 (30) ⅍ 📺 🖳 Ⓥ ♨ cc
Picturesque country hotel with comfortable en-suite rooms overlooking the Severn Valley. Traditional country cooking using mainly fresh local and home-grown produce. An ideal base for visiting Dolforwyn, Montgomery and Powis Castles and the surrounding area.

Berriew

SJ1800   Horseshoes, Talbot Hotel, Red Lion

Plasdwpa Farm, *Berriew, Welshpool, Powys, SY21 8PS.*
Magnificent Mountain setting in this very comfortable farmhouse, very tranquil.
Open: March to November
Grades: WTB 3 Star
01686 640298 (also fax) Mrs Hughes
plas@care4free.net
D: £15.00–£16.00 **S:** £18.00–£20.00
Beds: 1F 1D 1T **Baths:** 1 Sh
⅏ 🄿 (4) ⅍ 📺 ✕ Ⓥ ♨

Boughrood

SO1339   Bridgend Inn, Griffin Inn

Balangia, *Station Road, Boughrood, Brecon, Powys, LD3 0YF.*
On the Wye Valley walk. Homely welcome given to all.
Open: Easter to Oct
01874 754453 Mrs Brown
D: £16.00–£17.00 **S:** £16.00–£34.00
Beds: 1D 1T 1S **Baths:** 1 Sh
⅏ 🄿 ⅍ 📺 ✕ 🖳 Ⓥ ♨ ♿

Upper Middle Road, *Boughrood, Brecon, Powys, LD3 0BX.*
Quietly situated, 180-year-old cottage, mountains, panorama, homely atmosphere.
Open: All Year (not Xmas)
01874 754407
Mrs Kelleher
karen@middleroad.free-online.co.uk
D: £17.00 **S:** £17.00–£25.00
Beds: 1D 1T **Baths:** 1 En 1 Pr
⅏ 🄿 (3) ⅍ 📺 ✕ 🖳 ♨

Brecon

SO0428   Bentley's, Clarence, Camden Arms, Castle, George, Lion, Three Horseshoes, Red Lion, Traveller's Rest, Tai 'R' Bull

Lansdowne Hotel, *39 The Watton, Brecon, Powys, LD3 7EG.*
Open: All Year
Grades: WTB 2 Star, AA 2 Star
01874 623321 Mrs Mulley
Fax: 01874 610438
reception@lansdownehotel.co.uk
D: £23.50–£25.00 **S:** £27.50–£30.00
Beds: 2F 5D 2T **Baths:** 9 Pr
📺 ✕ 🖳 Ⓥ ♨ cc
Our warm and friendly family-run hotel and restaurant is located in the centre of Brecon. You can enjoy comfortable accommodation and delicious freshly prepared food in our fully licensed restaurant. The perfect location for touring the beautiful National Park.

Ashgrove, *Llanspyddid, Brecon, Powys, LD3 8PB.*
Open: Mar to Sept
Grades: WTB 2 Star
01874 622833 Mr Wakeham
ashgrove@btclick.com
D: £15.00–£16.00 **S:** £15.00–£16.00
Beds: 1D 2T **Baths:** 2 Sh
🄿 (5) ⅍ 📺 🖳 Ⓥ ♨
This spacious old dower house is situated 2 miles from Brecon. Warm, relaxed, informal atmosphere. Close proximity to the Beacon Beacons and Black Mountains. Walkers/cyclists welcome. Excellent home cooking - 'Blas ar Gymru'/'Taste of Wales' awarded.

RATES

D = Price range per person sharing in a double room

S = Price range for a single room

Beacons Accommodation and Restaurant, *16 Bridge Street, Brecon, Powys, LD3 8AH.*
Open: All Year (not Xmas)
Grades: WTB 3 Star GH, AA 3 Diamond, RAC 3 Diamond
01874 623339 (also fax)
Mr & Mrs Jackson
beacons@brecon.co.uk
D: £18.00–£29.50 **S:** fr £20.00
Beds: 6F 4D 3T 1S **Baths:** 11 En 1 Sh
⅏ 🄿 (14) ⅍ 📺 🍴 ✕ 🖳 Ⓥ ♨ ♿ cc
Recently restored Georgian town house offering a variety of well appointed standard en-suite and luxury period rooms. A candlelit restaurant serves fine food and wines (5 nights). There is a cosy cellar bar and a restful lounge, private car park and a secure bike store.

Pen-y-Bryn House, *Llangorse, Brecon, LD3 7UG.*
Open: All Year (not Xmas)
Grades: WTB 4 Star
01874 658606 Mrs Thomas
Fax: 01874 658215
jumt@pen-y-bryn79.freeserve.co.uk
D: £20.00 **S:** £25.00
Beds: 1F 1T 1D **Baths:** 2 En 1 Pr
⅏ 🄿 ⅍ 📺 ✕ 🖳 Ⓥ ♨
Situated in the Brecon Beacons National Park, overlooking Llangorse Lake, with large gardens and mountains beyond. Also, we have nearby our own activity centre which offers riding, climbing indoor and out (best indoor climbing in Britain) and so much more.

Flag & Castle Guest House, *11 Orchard Street, Llanfaes, Brecon, Powys, LD3 8AN.*
Family run guest house near to town centre and National Park.
Open: All Year
Grades: WTB 3 Star
01874 625860 Mr & Mrs Richards
D: £20.00–£25.00 **S:** £25.00
Beds: 2T 1D **Baths:** 3 En
⅏ 🄿 ⅍ 📺 🍴 🖳 Ⓥ ✽ ♨

Tir Bach Guest House, *13 Alexandra Road, Brecon, Powys, LD3 7PD.*
Panoramic view of Brecon Beacons. Quiet road near town centre.
Open: All Year (not Xmas)
Grades: WTB 2 Star
01874 624551 Mrs Thomas
D: £18.00–£19.00 **S:** £25.00–£30.00
Beds: 1F 1D 1T **Baths:** 1 Sh
⅏ 📺 🍴 🖳 ♨

Brecon Canal Guest House, *Canal Bank, The Watton, Brecon, Powys, LD3 7HG.*
Open: Feb to Nov
Grades: WTB 2 Star
01874 623464 Fax: 01874 610930
brecanal@brecon112.freeserve.co.uk
D: £17.00–£20.00 **S:** £17.00
Beds: 1D 2T 1S **Baths:** 2 En
🄿 (6) 📺 🖳 Ⓥ ♨
Small, friendly, cottage-style guest house, situated adjacent to the Brecon canal close to new theatre. Quiet, semi-rural position, yet only 5 minutes walk from town centre. All rooms have TV, tea/coffee, some ensuite. Private parking.

Canal Bridge B&B, 1 Gasworks Lane, Brecon, LD3 7HA.
Spacious and comfortable B&B close to historic town centre, museums, theatre, River Usk.
Open: Mar to Nov
Grades: WTB 3 Star
01874 611088 Ms Lake
janet-lake@care4free.net
D: £18.00–£20.00 **S:** £20.00–£25.00
Beds: 1F 3D 1T 1S **Baths:** 4 En 2 Pr
🛇 (5) 🅿 (6) ⊁ 📺 🎹 ⱱ ♨ cc

Tir Bach, Libanus, Brecon, Powys, LD3 8NE.
Beautiful C17th Welsh Longhouse in Brecon Beacons National Park.
Open: All Year (not Xmas)
Grades: WTB 3 Star
01874 625675
Mrs Norris
Fax: 01874 611198
norris.tirbach@talk21.com
D: £20.00 **S:** £23.00–£25.00
Beds: 1T 2D **Baths:** 2 En 1 Pr
🛇 (12) 🅿 (6) ⊁ 📺 🎹 ⱱ ♨

County House, 100 The Struet, Brecon, LD3 7LS.
C18th Georgian Grade II Listed town house - served as judge's lodgings for 150 years.
Open: All Year
Grades: WTB 4 Star
01874 625844 (also fax)
Mr Cope
countyhouse@ukworld.net
D: £27.50 **S:** £37.50
Beds: 2D 1T **Baths:** 3 En
🛇 🅿 (6) 📺 🎹 ♨ 🎹 ⱱ ♨

Brynawel Guest House, 13 Cradoc Road, Brecon, LD3 9LH.
Impressive Victorian residence. Beautiful views, ensuites, TVs, drinks facilities.
Open: All Year (not Xmas)
Grades: WTB 3 Star
01874 624363 (also fax)
P Rogers
brynawel@hotmail.com
D: £20.00–£25.00 **S:** £20.00–£25.00
Beds: 2D 1T **Baths:** 3 En
🛇 (6) 🅿 (5) 📺 🎹 ♨ 🎹 ⱱ ♨

Glanyrafon, 1 The Promenade, Kensington, Brecon, Powys, LD3 9AY.
Riverside Edwardian house, view of Beacons, near town centre.
Open: Easter to Oct
01874 623302 (also fax)
Mrs Roberts
D: £17.50–£19.00 **S:** £20.00–£22.00
Beds: 2D 1T **Baths:** 2 Sh
🛇 (11) 🅿 (3) ⊁ 📺 🎹 ⱱ ♨

Blaencar Farm, Sennybridge, Brecon, Powys, LD3 8HA.
Tastefully restored farmhouse on working family farm. Quality ensuite accommodation in peaceful, accessible location.
Open: Easter to Nov
01874 636610
D: £20.00–£22.00 **S:** £24.00
Beds: 2D 1T **Baths:** 3 En
🅿 ⊁ 📺 🎹 ⱱ ♨

Builth Wells

SO0350   *Prince Llewelyn, Llanelwedd Arms, Greyhound*

Dollynwydd Farm, Builth Wells, Powys, LD2 3RZ.
Open: All Year (not Xmas)
Grades: WTB 2 Star
01982 553660 (also fax)
Mrs Williams
D: £18.00–£20.00 **S:** £18.00–£20.00
Beds: 1D 2T 2S **Baths:** 1 En 2 Sh
🛇 (14) 🅿 (6) ⊁ 📺 ✕ 🎹
C17th farmhouse lying beneath Eppynt Hills. Superb area for walking, bird-watching within easy distance, Brecon Beacons, Elan Valley, Hay-on-Wye, bookshops, very comfortable in quiet area, ample parking, lockup garage for bikes. 1 mile Builth Wells, B4520 first left down farm lane.

The Cedar Guest House, Hay Road, Builth Wells, Powys, LD2 3AR.
Built 1880, on A470 backing Wye Valley with good views, good food, parking.
Open: All Year
Grades: WTB 2 Star
01982 553356 Mr Morris
D: £18.00–£20.00 **S:** £27.50–£30.00
Beds: 1F 1D 3T 2S **Baths:** 5 En 2 Sh
🛇 🅿 (10) ⊁ 📺 🎹 ✕ 🎹 ⱱ ♨ cc

Rhydfelin, Cwmbach, Builth Wells, Powys, LD2 3RT.
1725 cosy stone guest house, restaurant, bar and tea garden.
Open: All Year (not Xmas)
Grades: WTB 3 Star
01982 552493 E M Moyes
liz@rhydfelinguesthouse.freeserve.co.uk
D: £19.00–£22.00 **S:** £26.00–£44.00
Beds: 1F 2D 1T **Baths:** 1 En 2 Sh
🛇 🅿 (12) ⊁ 📺 🎹 ✕ 🎹 ⱱ ♨

Woodlands, Hay Road, Builth Wells, Powys, LD2 3BP.
Impressive Edwardian house, with ensuite facilities with secluded parking.
Open: All Year (not Xmas)
Grades: AA 4 Diamond
01982 552354 (also fax) Mrs Nicholls
HeskethN@aol.com
D: £18.00–£20.00 **S:** £22.00–£25.00
Beds: 4T **Baths:** 4 En
🅿 (4) ⊁ 📺 🎹 ♨ 🎹

The Owls, 40 High Street, Builth Wells, Powys, LD2 3AB.
Convenient High Street location, close to showground, owls everywhere.
Open: All Year
01982 552518 Mrs Turner
Fax: 01982 553867
D: £14.00–£16.50 **S:** £14.00–£25.00
Beds: 1F 2D 1T 1S **Baths:** 5 En 1 Pr
🛇 🅿 (8) 📺 ✕ 🎹 ⱱ ♨

Bron Wye, Church Street, Builth Wells, Powys, LD2 3BS.
Christian family-run guest house. Overlooking River Wye.
Open: All Year
01982 553587 Mr & Mrs Wiltshire
D: £17.00 **S:** £17.00
Beds: 1F 2D 1T 2S **Baths:** 6 En
🛇 🅿 (7) ⊁ 📺 🎹 🎹 ♨

Bwlch

SO1421   *Traveller's Rest*

Upper Talybryn Farm, Bwlch, Brecon, Powys, LD3.
Authentically renovated C15 Welsh longhouse incorporating all the old features. **Open:** Apr to Nov
01874 676492 talybryn@cwcom.net
D: £17.50–£22.00 **S:** £20.00–£22.00
Beds: 1F 2D **Baths:** 2 En 1 Sh
🅿 (20) ⊁ 📺 🎹 🎹 ♨

Capel-y-ffin

SO2531

The Grange, Capel-y-Ffin, Abergavenny, NP7 7NP.
Small Victorian guest house situated in the beautiful Black Mountains.
Open: Easter to Nov
Grades: WTB 1 Star
01873 890215 Mrs Griffiths
Fax: 01873 890157
D: £22.50–£23.00 **S:** £22.50–£23.00
Beds: 1F 1D 1T 1S **Baths:** 3 En
🛇 (6) 🅿 (10) 📺 🎹 ✕ 🎹 ⱱ ♨ ♿

Cilmery

SO0051   *Prince Llewelyn*

Halcyon House, Cilmery, Builth Wells, Powys, LD2 3NU.
Jacuzzi, snooker, views, hospitality, inn; cows, sheep; self-catering, camping.
Open: All Year
01982 552838 Mr Johnson
Fax: 01982 551090 deejay1010@aol.com
D: £16.00–£20.00 **S:** £18.00–£22.00
Beds: 2F 1S **Baths:** 2 Sh
🛇 🅿 (7) 📺 🎹 ✕ 🎹 ⱱ ♨ ♿ cc

Clyro

SO2143   *Baskerville Arms*

Tump Farm, Clyro, Hay-on-Wye, Hereford, HR3 6JY.
Comfortable farmhouse accommodation, overlooking Wye Valley, near Hay -on-Wye. Substantial breakfasts.
Open: All Year
01497 820912 Mrs Francis
jafrancis20@hotmail.com
D: £12.50–£15.00 **S:** £14.00–£16.50
Beds: 1T 1D **Baths:** 1 Sh
🅿 (4) 📺 🎹 ♨

Crickhowell

SO2118   *Bear, Bell, Dragon's Head, Vinetree*

Castell Corryn, Llangenny, Crickhowell, Powys, NP8 1HE.
Open: All Year (not Xmas/New Year)
Grades: WTB 3 Star
01873 810327 (also fax) Mr Harris
113114.2610@compuserve.com
D: £20.00–£25.00 **S:** £25.00–£30.00
Beds: 2T 1D **Baths:** 2 En 1 Pr
🛇 🅿 (6) 📺 🎹 ⱱ ♨
Situated above the Usk Valley within the Brecon Beacons National Park. Outstanding views, beautiful restful gardens. Children welcome, special diets available. All rooms ensuite, colour TV, tea making facilities, hair dryer. Homely welcome.

Glangrwyney Court, *Crickhowell, Powys, NP8 1ES.*
Georgian mansion in 4 acres of established gardens surrounded by parkland.
Open: All Year
01873 811288 C R Jackson
Fax: 01873 810317
glangrwyne@aol.com
D: £22.50–£27.50 **S:** £30.00–£55.00
Beds: 1F 2T 2D **Baths:** 4 En 1 Pr
⌂ ▣ (10) ⊬ ⊡ ⊀ ✕ ▥ ⚘ ♨ ﹠

White Hall, *Glangrwyney, Crickhowell, Powys, NP8 1EW.*
Comfortable Georgian house next to restaurant, close to Black Mountains.
Open: All Year (not Xmas)
Grades: WTB 1 Star
01873 811155 Ms Llewelyn
Fax: 01873 840178
pllewelyn@white-hall.freeserve.co.uk
D: £15.00–£20.00 **S:** £20.00–£25.00
Beds: 1F 2D 1S **Baths:** 2 En 1 Sh
⌂ ▣ (3) ⊬ ⊡ ⊀ ▥ ⊻ ﹠

Bluebell Inn, *Glangrwyney, Crickhowell, Powys, NP8 1EH.*
C17th former coaching inn. Excellent food and ensuite accommodation.
Open: All Year
Grades: WTB 2 Star Inn
01873 810247 Mrs Grist
Fax: 01873 812155
bluebellinn@barclays.net
D: £25.00–£35.00 **S:** £30.00
Beds: 1F 1D 2T 1S **Baths:** 5 En
⌂ ▣ (20) ⊡ ✕ ▥ ⊻ ﹠ cc

Criggion

SJ2915 ◀ *Admiral Rodney, Bradford Arms*

Brimford House, *Criggion, Shrewsbury, SY5 9AU.*
Open: All Year
Grades: WTB 3 Star, AA 4 Diamond
01938 570235 Mrs Dawson
brimford.house@virginnet.co.uk
D: £20.00–£25.00 **S:** £20.00–£30.00
Beds: 1T 2D **Baths:** 2 En 1 Sh
⌂ ▣ (4) ⊡ ⊀ ▥ ⊻ ﹠
Elegant Georgian farmhouse in tranquil scenic surroundings between Breidden Hills and River Severn (fishing available). Large comfortable bedrooms. Breakfasts with home-made preserves and farmhouse eggs. Pub 3 minutes walk. Situated between Shrewsbury and Welshpool, ideal for touring Shropshire/Welsh border.

Crossgates

SO0864 ◀ *Builders Arms, Greenway Manor*

Guidfa House, *Crossgates, Llandrindod Wells, Powys, LD1 6RF.*
Stylish Georgian house offering comfort, good food and a relaxing atmosphere.
Open: All Year
Grades: WTB 4 Diamond, AA 4 Diamond, RAC 4 Diamond
01597 851241 Mr Millan
Fax: 01597 851875
guidfa@globalnet.co.uk
D: £26.50 **S:** £31.50
Beds: 2D 3T 1S **Baths:** 5 Pr 2 Sh
▣ (10) ⊬ ⊡ ✕ ▥ ⚘ ⊻ ﹠ ﹨ cc

Planning a longer stay? Always ask for any special rates

Cwm

SO2590 ◀ *Dragon Hotel, Castle Hotel*

The Drewin Farm, *Cwm, Church Stoke, Montgomery, Powys, SY15 6TW.*
C17th farmhouse with panoramic views. Offa's Dyke footpath on doorstep.
Open: Easter to Oct
01588 620325 (also fax)
Mrs Richards
ceinwen@drewin.freeserve.co.uk
D: £20.00–£21.00 **S:** £22.00
Beds: 1F 1T **Baths:** 2 En
⌂ ▣ (6) ⊬ ⊡ ⊀ ✕ ▥ ⊻ ﹠

Cwmbach (Builth Wells)

SO0254

Rhydfelin, *Cwmbach, Builth Wells, Powys, LD2 3RT.*
1725 cosy stone guest house, restaurant, bar and tea garden.
Open: All Year (not Xmas)
Grades: WTB 3 Star
01982 552493 E M Moyes
liz@rhydfelinguesthouse.freeserve.co.uk
D: £19.00–£22.00 **S:** £26.00–£44.00
Beds: 1F 2D 1T **Baths:** 1 En 2 Sh
⌂ ▣ (12) ⊬ ⊡ ⊀ ✕ ▥ ⊻ ﹠

Darowen

SH8201

Cefn Farm, *Darowen, Machynlleth, Powys, SY20 8NS.*
Unsurpassable views, good walking. Half hour drive seaside. Open fire, personal service.
Open: All Year
01650 511336 Mr Lloyd
D: £20.00 **S:** £20.00
Beds: 1F 1D
⌂ ▣ (3) ⊬ ⊡ ⊀ ▥ ⊻ ﹠ ﹨

Discoed

SO2764 ◀ *Crown, Royal Oak*

Gumma Farm, *Discoed, Presteigne, Powys, LD8 2NP.*
Old farm house set in 350 acres tastefully furnished with antiques.
Open: Easter to Oct
01547 560243 Mrs Owens
D: £16.00–£21.00 **S:** £16.00–£17.00
Beds: 1D 1T 1S **Baths:** 1 En 1 Sh
⌂ ▣ ⊡ ⊀ ✕ ⊻ ﹠

Disserth

SO0358 ◀ *Drover's Arms*

Disserth Mill, *Disserth, Builth Wells, Powys, LD2 3TN.*
A sun trap by a stream.
Open: Easter to Oct
01982 553217 Mrs Worts
D: £17.00–£20.00 **S:** £18.00–£20.00
Beds: 1T 1S **Baths:** 1 En
⌂ ▣ (4) ⊡ ⊀ ▥ ﹠

Erwood

SO0942 ◀ *Erwood Inn, Wheelwrights' Arms*

Hafod-y-Gareg, *Erwood, Builth Wells, Powys, LD2 3TQ.*
Open: All Year (not Xmas)
01982 560400 Mrs McKay
D: £13.50–£17.50 **S:** £13.50–£17.50
Beds: 1F 2D 1T **Baths:** 3 En
⌂ ▣ (6) ⊡ ⊀ ✕ ▥ ⊻ ﹠
Secluded medieval farmhouse in idyllic Welsh hillside locality. Tranquillity personified, a stress free retreat. Rooms overlooking pasture and woodland. Walk the Wye Valley or ancient bridleways. Equidistant from Hay-on-Wye, Brecon Beacons, Builth Wells. The perfect getaway.

Trericket Mill Vegetarian Guesthouse, *Erwood, Builth Wells, Powys, LD2 3TQ.*
Listed C19th watermill in Wye Valley, friendly and informal.
Open: All Year (not Xmas)
Grades: WTB 2 Star GH
01982 560312 Mr Legge
Fax: 01982 560768
D: £14.00–£21.00 **S:** fr £16.00
Beds: 2F 2D 2T **Baths:** 4 En 2 Sh
⌂ ▣ (8) ⊡ ✕ ▥ ⊻ ﹠

The Old Vicarage, *Erwood, Builth Wells, Powys, LD2 3DZ.*
An old vicarage with a difference! with wonderful views over countryside.
Open: All Year
Grades: WTB 3 Star
01982 560680 Mrs Williams
D: £15.50–£16.00 **S:** £16.00–£17.00
Beds: 1F 1D 1T **Baths:** 1 Sh
⌂ (1) ▣ ⊡ ⊀ ✕ ▥ ⊻ ⚘ ﹠

Orchard Cottage, *Erwood, Builth Wells, Powys, LD2 3EZ.*
C18th tastefully modernised Welsh stone cottage. Gardens overlooking river.
Open: All Year (not Xmas)
01982 560600 Mr & Mrs Prior
D: £17.00–£19.50 **S:** £20.00
Beds: 1F 1D 1T **Baths:** 1 En 1 Sh
⌂ ▣ (6) ⊡ ▥ ⊻ ﹠

Felindre

SO1681

Trevland, *Felindre, Knighton, Powys, LD7 1YL.*
Quiet border village . Warm welcome offered to all.
Open: All Year
01547 510211 Mrs Edwards
marion@trevland.freeserve.co.uk
D: £16.50–£17.50 **S:** £16.50–£17.50
Beds: 1F 1D 1T **Baths:** 3 En
⌂ ▣ (5) ⊡ ⊀ ✕ ▥ ⊻ ⚘ ﹠ ﹨

All details shown are as supplied by B&B owners in Autumn 2000

Felinfach

SO0933 ◈ *Griffin Inn, Old Ford Inn, Plough & Harrow*

Plough & Harrow Inn, *Felinfach, Brecon, Powys, LD3 0UB.*
Village inn offering comfortable ensuite accommodation, located 4 miles north of Brecon. **Open:** All Year
01874 622709 Ms Warren
cydsue@compuserve.com
D: £18.00–£20.00 **S:** £25.00
Beds: 1F 1D 1T **Baths:** 2 En 1 Pr
🛇 🅿 (20) 📺 🛏 ✕ 🛍 Ⓥ 🌢 🕭 **cc**

Forden

SJ2200 ◈ *Railway Inn, Cock Hotel*

Church House, *Forden, Welshpool, Powys, SY21 8NE.*
Georgian house, near Powis Castle and Welshpool Light Railway. Large garden.
Open: All Year (not Xmas/New Year)
01938 580353 Mrs Bright
D: £17.50 **S:** £17.50
Beds: 1F 1D 1T **Baths:** 1 Pr 1 Sh
🛇 🅿 ⅍ 📺 ✕ 🛍 Ⓥ 🌢

Heath Cottage, *Forden, Welshpool, Powys, SY21 8LX.*
Absolute peace, spectacular views and our own free range eggs.
Open: Easter to Oct
01938 580453 Mrs Payne
Fax: 01938 580543
D: £18.00–£20.00 **S:** £20.00–£25.00
Beds: 1F 1D 1S **Baths:** 3 En
🛇 🅿 (4) ⅍ 📺 🛍 Ⓥ 🌢

Gladestry

SO2355 ◈ *Royal Oak*

Offa's Dyke Lodge, *Gladestry, Kington, Herefordshire, HR5 3NR.*
Luxury accommodation, spectacular views, fine cooking, the perfect relaxing break. **Open:** All Year
Grades: WTB 4 Star
01544 370341 Steve Wright
Fax: 01544 370342 odl@offtec.ltd.uk
D: £25.00–£27.00 **S:** £33.00–£35.00
Beds: 1D 2T **Baths:** 2 En 1 Pr
🛇 🅿 (10) ⅍ 📺 ✕ 🛍 🌢 🕭 ♿ 3

Wain Wen, *Gladestry, Kington, Herefordshire, HR5 3NT.*
Comfortable farmhouse on working farm amid unspoilt Border country.
Open: Apr to Oct
01544 370226 Mrs Lloyd
D: £16.00 **S:** £16.00
Beds: 1D 1T **Baths:** 2 Sh
🛇 (8) 🅿 (4) ✕ Ⓥ 🌢

Glasbury

SO1739

Maes-Mawr, *Glasbury, Hereford, HR3 5ND.*
10 mins off A438 on a farm in countryside. Panoramic views of Black Mountains. **Open:** Easter to Nov
01497 847008
D: £15.00–£17.00 **S:** £16.00–£18.00
Beds: 1F 2D 1T **Baths:** 1 Sh
🛇 🅿 (5) 📺 🛏 🛍 Ⓥ 🌢 .

Gwystre

SO0665 ◈ *Gwystre Inn*

Gwystre Inn, *Gwystre, Llandrindod Wells, Powys, LD1 6RN.*
Friendly Georgian inn, beautiful rural location, river, gardens, near Elan Valley.
Open: All Year
01597 851650 Mr & Mrs Sherwood
D: £18.00–£27.50 **S:** £18.00–£35.00
Beds: 1F 2T **Baths:** 3 En
🛇 🅿 (20) 📺 🛏 ✕ 🛍 🌢

Hay-on-Wye

SO2242 ◈ *Swan Hotel, Old Black Lion, Hollybush Inn, Kilvert Court*

Tinto House, *Broad Street, Hay-on-Wye, Hereford, HR3 5DB.*
Open: All Year (not Xmas)
Grades: WTB 3 Star, AA 4 Diamond
01497 820590 Mr Evans
Fax: 01497 821058
D: fr £22.50 **S:** fr £30.00
Beds: 1F 2D 1T **Baths:** 4 En
🛇 🅿 (2) ⅍ 📺 🛍 Ⓥ 🌢
Comfortable Grade II Listed Georgian town house in the centre of famous book town of Hay-on-Wye, which has a large garden overlooking the River Wye and Radnorshire Hills.

Fernleigh, *Hardwick Road, Cusop, Hay-on-Wye, Hereford, HR3 5QX.*
Quiet location walking distance of the famous book town of Hay-on-Wye.
Open: Easter to Oct
01497 820459 Mr Hughes
D: £15.00–£19.00 **S:** £19.00
Beds: 2D 1S **Baths:** 1 En 1 Sh
🛇 🅿 (4) ⅍ 📺 ✕ 🛍 Ⓥ 🌢

The Bear, *Bear Street, Hay-on-Wye, Hereford, HR3 5AN.*
Charming comfortable 16th century house in centre of Hay-on-Wye.
Open: All Year
01497 821302 J Field
Fax: 01497 820506
thebear@jonfield.clara.net
D: £22.00–£27.00
Beds: 2D 1T **Baths:** 2 En 1 Sh
🅿 (4) ⅍ 📺 🛏 🛍 Ⓥ 🌢

Rest for the Tired, *6 Broad Street, Hay-on-Wye, Hereford, HR3 5DB.*
16th century building with modern comforts hearty breakfasts a warm welcome.
Open: All Year
01497 820550 Ms Fellowes
D: £18.00 **S:** £18.00
Beds: 2D 1T **Baths:** 3 En
🛇 🅿 (4) ⅍ 📺 🛍 🌢 **cc**

The Old Post Office, *Llanigon, Hay-on-Wye, Hereford, HR3 5QA.*
A very special find in Black Mountains, superb vegetarian breakfast.
Open: All Year
Grades: WTB 3 Star GH
01497 820008 Mrs Webb
D: £17.00–£25.00 **S:** £20.00–£45.00
Beds: 1F 1D 1T **Baths:** 2 En 1 Sh
🛇 🅿 (3) ⅍ 📺 🛏 🛍 Ⓥ 🌢

La Fosse Guest House, *Oxford Road, Hay-on-Wye, Hereford, HR3 5AJ.*
Make your holiday! Stay once and you'll be back. **Open:** All Year
01497 820613 Mr Crook
annabel@crook5.freeserve.co.uk
D: £20.00
Beds: 4D 1T **Baths:** 5 En
🛇 (9) 🅿 (5) ⅍ 📺 🛏 🛍 Ⓥ 🌢 **cc**

Belmont House, *Hay-on-Wye, Hereford, HR3 5DA.*
1700 coaching house with large bedrooms, with antique furniture and things. **Open:** All Year
01497 820718 (also fax) Mr Gwynne
D: £16.00–£20.00 **S:** £20.00
Beds: 2F 2T 2D 1S **Baths:** 2 En 5 Pr 1 Sh
🛇 🅿 (10) 📺 🛏 🛍 Ⓥ 🌢 ♯ 🌢

Lansdowne, *Cusop, Hay-on-Wye, Hereford, HR3 5RF.*
Victorian house, pretty garden, beautiful views, elegant spacious ensuite bedrooms. Quiet. **Open:** Feb-Nov
01497 820125 Mr Flack
D: £17.00–£18.00 **S:** £23.00–£36.00
Beds: 1D 1T **Baths:** 2 En
🛇 🅿 (3) ⅍ 📺 🛍 Ⓥ 🌢 ♿

Brookfield Guest House, *Brook Street, Hay-on-Wye, Hereford, HR3 5BQ.*
C16th Listed building in historic Hay-on-Wye. Atmosphere in this little market town is remarkable. **Open:** All Year
01497 820518 Mrs Price
Fax: 01497 821818
brookfieldguesthouse@btinternet.com
D: fr £18.00 **S:** fr £18.00
Beds: 2F 3D 3T **Baths:** 2 En 2 Sh
🛇 (6) 🅿 (4) 📺 🛍 Ⓥ 🌢

The Kingfisher, *Newport Street, Hay-on-Wye, Hereford, HR3 5BE.*
Hay on Wye - book town. Kingfisher House is renowned for friendly atmosphere. **Open:** All Year
01497 820448
D: £15.00–£20.00 **S:** £15.00–£20.00
Beds: 1F 2D 2T 2S **Baths:** 2 En 3 Sh
🛇 🅿 (8) 📺 🛏 ✕ 🛍 Ⓥ 🌢

Heol Senni

SN9223 ◈ *Lion*

Maeswalter, *Heol Senni, Brecon, Powys, LD3 8SU.*
300- year-old farmhouse situated in the picturesque Senni valley. **Open:** All Year
Grades: WTB 2 Star, AA 3 Diamond, RAC 3 Diamond
01874 636629 Mrs Mayo
D: £18.00–£19.50 **S:** £20.00–£25.00
Beds: 1F 1D 1T **Baths:** 1 En 2 Sh
🛇 (1) 🅿 (8) ⅍ 📺 🛏 🛍 Ⓥ 🌢

Neuadd, *Heol Senni, Brecon, Powys, LD3 8SU.*
Tranquil surroundings on working farm. Ideal location for walkers. Within Brecon Beacons National Park.
Open: May to Nov
01874 636258 (also fax)
Mrs Morgan
D: £18.00 **S:** £15.00
Beds: 1D 1S **Baths:** 1 Pr
🛇 🅿 ⅍ 📺 🛍 🌢

Howey

SO0558 ◆ *Three Wells, Drover's Arms, Ty Gwyn, Royal Oak, Stables*

Holly Farm, *Howey, Llandrindod Wells, Powys, LD1 5PP.*
Comfortable old farmhouse, dates back to Tudor times, bedrooms have lovely views of countryside.
Open: All Year (not Xmas)
Grades: WTB 3 Star Farm, AA 4 Diamond
01597 822402 Mrs Jones
D: £20.00–£25.00 **S:** £24.00–£26.00
Beds: 1F 2D 2T **Baths:** 3 En 2 Sh
⌂ ▣ (6) 🖵 ✕ ▥ Ⓥ ♨

The Three Wells Farm, *Chapel Road, Howey, Llandrindod Wells, Powys, LD1 5PB.*
Three Wells is a hidden gem in the heart of Wales.
Open: All Year
Grades: AA 4 Diamond
01597 824427 Mr Roobottom
Fax: 01597 822484
welcome@three-wells.co.uk
D: £19.00–£28.00 **S:** £25.00–£30.00
Beds: 8D 5T 1S **Baths:** 14 En
⌂ (8) ▣ (4) ✗ 🖵 ▥ Ⓥ ♨ cc

Hundred House

SO1154

Gaer Farm, *Hundred House, Llandrindod Wells, Powys, LD1 5RU.*
Converted stone timber barn with panoramic views of surrounding mountains.
Open: All Year (not Xmas)
Grades: WTB 2 Star
01982 570208 (also fax)
Mrs Harley
relax@gaerfarm.co.uk
D: £18.00–£25.00
Beds: 2F 1S **Baths:** 3 En
⌂ ▣ ✗ 🖵 ✕ ▥ Ⓥ ♨ ♿ 3

Kerry

SO1489 ◆ *Kerry Lamb, Dolfor Inn*

Greenfields, *Kerry, Newtown, Powys, SY16 4LH.*
Comfortable guest house, good food, warm welcome.
Open: All Year (not Xmas)
Grades: WTB 2 Star
01686 670596 Mrs Madeley
Fax: 01686 670354
D: £18.00–£20.00 **S:** £18.00–£22.00
Beds: 1F 1D 1T 1S **Baths:** 3 En
⌂ (4) ▣ (6) ✗ 🖵 ♈ ✕ ▥ Ⓥ ♨ cc

Knighton

SO2872 ◆ *Hundred House, George & Dragon, Horse & Jockey*

Westwood, *Presteigne Road, Knighton, Powys, LD7 1HY.*
Welcome to our detached Victorian home. Quiet town location; spacious, comfortable accommodation.
Open: All Year
01547 520317 Mrs Sharratt
sharrat@westwood.freeserve.co.uk
D: £17.00 **S:** £17.00
Beds: 1F 1D 1S **Baths:** 1 En 1 Sh
⌂ ▣ (4) ✗ 🖵 ✕ ▥ ♨

Pilleth Court, *Whitton, Knighton, Powys, LD7 1NP.*
16th century house in historic location offering quality accommodation.
Open: All Year (not Xmas)
01547 560272 (also fax)
Mrs Hood
D: fr £18.00 **S:** fr £20.00
Beds: 1F 2D 1T **Baths:** 1 En 1 Sh
⌂ (9) ▣ (6) 🖵 ✕ ▥ ♨

Offas Dyke House, *4 High Street, Knighton , Powys, LD7 1AT.*
Warm friendly B&B situated in the heart of Knighton.
Open: All Year
Grades: WTB 2 Star
01547 528634 (also fax)
S Ashe
D: £16.00 **S:** £16.00
Beds: 2T 3D 1S **Baths:** 3 Sh
⌂ ▣ (4) ✗ 🖵 ♈ ✕ ▥ Ⓥ ♨

The Fleece House, *Market Street, Knighton, Powys, LD7 1BB.*
Attractive decorated quality accommodation in converted C18th coaching inn.
Open: All Year
Grades: WTB 3 Star GH
01547 520168 Mrs Simmons
D: £20.00–£28.00 **S:** £23.00–£35.00
Beds: 6T **Baths:** 2 En 2 Sh
▣ ✗ 🖵 ▥ ♨

15 Mill Green, *Knighton, Powys, LD7 1EE.*
Welcoming colourful old cottage with secluded garden and private courtyard.
Open: Easter to Oct
01547 520075 Mrs Stothert
D: £14.00–£15.00 **S:** £14.00–£15.00
Beds: 1D 1T **Baths:** 1 En 1 Sh
⌂ ▣ (1) ✗ 🖵 ♈ ▥ ♨ ♿

Larkspur, *Larkey Lane, Knighton, Powys, LD7 1DN.*
Quiet location overlooking town centre and castle site.
Open: All Year
01547 528764 Mrs Heard
larkspur@knighton-wales.co.uk
D: £15.00 **S:** £15.00
Beds: 1D 1T **Baths:** 1 Pr
⌂ (1) ▣ ✗ 🖵 ▥ Ⓥ ♨

Leighton

SJ2305 ◆ *Talbot*

Orchard House, *Leighton, Welshpool, Powys, SY21 8HN.*
Friendly welcome and all comforts of home, good breakfast.
Open: All Year
01938 553624 (also fax)
Mrs Pearce
pearce@orchardhouse.softnet.co.uk
D: £18.00–£22.00 **S:** £18.00–£25.00
Beds: 2D 1T **Baths:** 3 En
⌂ ▣ 🖵 ♈ ▥ ♨ ♿

Planning a longer stay? Always ask for any special rates

Libanus

SN9925 ◆ *Tair Bull*

Tair Bull Inn, *Libanus, Brecon, Powys, LD3 8EL.*
Small friendly inn 3 miles out of Brecon market town. Beautiful scenery and walks.
Open: All Year
01874 625849 Mrs Williams
D: £21.00 **S:** £25.00–£42.00
Beds: 1F 3D 1T **Baths:** 5 En
⌂ ▣ (4) ✗ 🖵 ✕ ▥ Ⓥ ♨ cc

Llanbadarn Fynydd

SO0977 ◆ *New Inn*

Hillside Lodge Guesthouse,
Llanbadarn Fynydd, Llandrindod Wells, Powys, LD1 6TU.
Open: Jan to Dec
Grades: WTB 3 Star
01597 840364 Mr & Mrs Ainsworth
D: £20.00 **S:** £25.00
Beds: 2F 1T **Baths:** 3 En
⌂ ▣ (6) ✗ 🖵 ♈ ✕ ▥ Ⓥ ♨
On the edge of the village of Llanbadarn Fynydd. Half a mile from the main road standing on the hillside in private gardens overlooking the Ithon Valley. Private snooker room, full size table.

Llanbister

SO1073 ◆ *Lion*

The Lion, *Llanbister, Llandrindod Wells, Powys, LD1 6TN.*
Friendly local pub in beautiful countryside of unspoilt mid-Wales.
Open: All Year
01597 840244 Mrs Thomas
D: £18.00–£25.00 **S:** £18.00–£25.00
Beds: 1F **Baths:** 3 En 1 Pr
⌂ ▣ (4) 🖵 ♈ ✕ ▥ Ⓥ ♨

Llandinam

SO0288 ◆ *Lion Hotel, Red Lion*

Trewythen, *Llandinam, Powys, SY17 5BQ.*
Situated in scenic surroundings and ideal for touring Lakes and Wales.
Open: Easter to Nov
Grades: WTB 3 Star
01686 688444 (also fax)
Mrs Davies
D: £22.00–£24.00 **S:** £25.00–£30.00
Beds: 1F 1D **Baths:** 2 En
⌂ ▣ ✗ 🖵 ✕ ▥ Ⓥ ♨

Llandrindod Wells

SO0561 ◆ *Bell Inn, Builders Arms, Greenway Manor, Llanerch Inn, Three Wells, Drovers Arms*

Highbury Farm, *Llanyre, Llandrindod Wells, Powys, LD1 6EA.*
Peaceful location with short farm trail. Laundry room. Excellent food.
Open: Mar to Nov
Grades: WTB 3 Star
01597 822716 (also fax)
Mrs Evans
D: £18.00–£21.00 **S:** £21.00–£24.00
Beds: 1F 2D **Baths:** 2 En 1 Pr
⌂ (1) ▣ (3) ✗ 🖵 ▥ Ⓥ ♨

Planning a longer stay? Always ask for any special rates

Greenglades, Llanyre, Llandrindod Wells, Powys, LD1 6EA.
Beautiful country house in tranquil setting near village inn.
Open: All Year (not Xmas)
Grades: WTB 4 Star
01597 822950 E J Jones
D: £18.00–£22.00 **S:** £20.00–£24.00
Beds: 1F 1D 1T **Baths:** 2 En
😃 🅿 (3) ⚲ 🖾 🅏 🍴 🎺 🝗, 🆅 🍷

Greylands, High Street, Llandrindod Wells, Powys, LD1 6AG.
Handsome Victorian townhouse. Surrounded by beautiful countryside. Secure cycle storage.
Open: All Year
01597 822253 Mrs MacDonald
greylands@csma-netlink.co.uk
D: £16.00–£19.00 **S:** £17.00–£20.00
Beds: 1F 2D 1T 3S **Baths:** 6 En 1 Sh
😃 🅿 (5) 🝗 🎺 ✕ 🝗, 🆅 🍷 cc

Builders Arms, Crossgates, Llandrindod Wells, Powys, LD1 6RB.
Family run village inn. Garden, patio, large car park.
Open: All Year
Grades: WTB 2 Star
01597 851235 **D:** £17.50 **S:** £19.50
Beds: 1D 1T **Baths:** 1 En
😃 🅿 🖾 🝗 ✕ 🝗, 🍷

Guidfa House, Crossgates, Llandrindod Wells, Powys, LD1 6RF.
Stylish Georgian house offering comfort, good food and a relaxing atmosphere.
Open: All Year
Grades: WTB 4 Diamond, AA 4 Diamond, RAC 4 Diamond
01597 851241 Mr Millan
Fax: 01597 851875
guidfa@globalnet.co.uk
D: £26.50 **S:** £31.50
Beds: 2D 3T 1S **Baths:** 5 Pr 2 Sh
🅿 (10) 🝗 🖾 🆅 🝗, 🆅 ✳ 🍷 cc

Charis, Pentrosfa, Llandrindod Wells, Powys, LD1 5NG.
Edwardian house on edge of Llandrindod Wells in quiet residential road.
Open: All Year (not Xmas)
01597 824732 (also fax)
Mrs Gimson
iforpat.gimson@care4free.net
D: £17.00–£19.00 **S:** fr £25.00
Beds: 1F 2D 1T **Baths:** 2 En 1 Pr
😃 🅿 (3) 🝗 🖾 🎺 🝗, 🆅 🍷

Drovers Arms, Llandrindod Wells, Powys, LD1 5PT.
Quiet location, owner run, great food, own beer, real fire.
Open: All Year (not Xmas/New Year)
Grades: WTB 2 Star
01597 822508 Mrs Day
Fax: 01597 822711
info@drovers-arms.co.uk
D: £20.00–£25.00 **S:** £30.00
Beds: 2D 1T **Baths:** 3 En
😃 (8) 🅿 (3) 🝗 ✕ 🝗, 🆅 🍷

Llandrinio

SJ2817   🍺 *Punch Bowl*

Haimwood, Llandrinio, Llanymynech, Powys, SY22 6SQ.
C18th guesthouse. Beautiful rural situation and views. River Severn.
Open: All Year
01691 830764 (also fax) Mrs Nixon
D: £18.00–£23.00 **S:** £18.00–£28.00
Beds: 1D 2T **Baths:** 1 En 1 Sh
😃 🅿 (6) 🖾 ✕ 🆅 🍷

Llandyssil

SO1995

The Dingle, Cwmkinin, Llandyssil, Montgomery, Powys, SY15 6HH.
Converted barn. Private peaceful valley, running stream, wildlife. Garaging.
Open: All Year
01686 668838 Mrs Nicholson
D: £15.00 **S:** £15.00
Beds: 1F 1D 1S **Baths:** 1 Sh
😃 (8) 🅿 (6) 🝗 🖾 🝗, 🆅 ✳ 🍷 🍴 🍷

Llanfair Caereinion

SJ1006   🍺 *Goat, Stumble Inn, Nag's Head*

Cwm Llwynog, Llanfair Caereinion, Welshpool, Powys, SY21 0HF.
Easy reach Powis Castle, steam railway, garden with unusual plants.
Open: All Year (not Xmas)
Grades: WTB 3 Star Farm, AA 4 Diamond
01938 810791 (also fax)
Ms Cornes
D: fr £20.00 **S:** fr £20.00
Beds: 2D 1T **Baths:** 2 Pr 1 Sh
😃 🅿 🝗 🖾 🎺 ✕ 🝗, 🆅 🍷

Madogs Wells, Llanfair Caereinion, Welshpool, Powys, SY21 0DE.
Beautiful valley, watch bird life from your breakfast table. Astronomy holidays.
Open: All Year (not Xmas)
Grades: WTB 2 Star
01938 810446 (also fax) Mrs Reed
D: £17.00 **S:** £17.00
Beds: 1F 1D **Baths:** 1 Sh
😃 🅿 (5) 🝗 🖾 🎺 🝗, 🍷

Plas Bryn Penarth, Llanfair Caereinion, Welshpool, Powys, SY21 0BZ.
Large country home, mature grounds. Spectacular views of Berwyn Mountains.
Open: All Year (not Xmas)
Grades: WTB 4 Star
01938 810535 (also fax)
D: £20.00–£25.00 **S:** £20.00–£30.00
Beds: 1F 2D 1T 1S **Baths:** 4 En
🅿 (10) 🖾 🎺 🝗, 🆅 🍷

Llanfrynach

SO0725   🍺 *White Swan*

Llanbrynean Farm, Llanfrynach, Brecon, Powys, LD3 7BQ.
Beautiful countryside, traditional family farmhouse, ideal location for Brecon Beacons. **Open:** Easter to Nov
Grades: WTB 2 Star
01874 665222 Mrs Harpur
D: £19.00–£21.00 **S:** £20.00–£25.00
Beds: 1F 1D 1T **Baths:** 2 En 1 Pr
😃 🅿 (8) 🝗 🖾 🝗, 🆅 🍷

Llangattock

SO2117   🍺 *Vinetree, Bear, Dragon*

Ty Croeso Hotel, Dardy, Llangattock, Crickhowell, Powys, NP8 1PU.
Welsh stone building situated on hillside in Brecon Beacons National Park.
Open: All Year
01873 810573 Mr Moore
tycroeso@ty-croeso-hotel.freeserve.co.uk
D: £27.50–£32.50 **S:** £35.00
Beds: 4D 2T 2S **Baths:** 8 En
😃 (1) 🅿 (20) 🖾 🎺 ✕ 🝗, 🆅 🍷 cc

The Old Six Bells, Llangattock, Crickhowell, NP8 1PH.
Grade II Listed house in small village, 10 minutes' walking distance from Crickhowell.
Open: All Year (not Xmas)
01873 811965 (also fax)
Richard & Jane Reardon Smith
D: £19.00–£25.00
Beds: 1D 1T
😃 (2) 🅿 (2) 🝗 🖾 🝗, 🆅 🍷

Llangorse

SO1327   🍺 *Red Lion*

Shiwa, Llangorse, Brecon, Powys, LD3 7UG.
Open: All Year (not Xmas)
01874 658631 Mrs Gray
D: £20.00–£25.00 **S:** £20.00–£30.00
Beds: 2F 1D **Baths:** 3 En
😃 🅿 (5) 🝗 🖾 🝗, 🆅 🍷 cc
Overlooking Llangorse Lake but in a village location, 'Shiwa' offers comfortable accommodation in the activities centre of the Brecon Beacons. The African decor and memorabilia make it a special place for those on whom Africa has cast its spell!

Llangunllo

SO2171   🍺 *Castle, Horse & Jockey, Hundred House*

Cefnsuran Farm, Llangunllo, Knighton, Powys, LD7 1SL.
Open: All Year (not Xmas/New Year)
Grades: WTB 3 Star
01547 550219 Mrs Morgan
Fax: 01547 550348
cefn@suran.freeserve.co.uk
D: £20.00–£22.50 **S:** £20.00–£25.00
Beds: 1F 1D 1T **Baths:** 1 En 1 Pr
😃 🅿 (10) 🝗 🖾 ✕ 🝗, 🆅 🍷
Set in beautiful location for a peaceful, interesting and private holiday. Guests are welcome to stroll around gardens, waymarked farm trails and woodlands. Pools with abundant wildlife - flyfishing possible. Games room with fullsize snooker table. Self-catering available.

Rhiwlas, Llangunllo Halt, Llangunllo, Knighton, Powys, LD7 1SY.
The farm which is mainly stock producing includes a section of the Glyndwr's Way.
Open: Easter to Oct
01547 550256 Mrs Deakins
D: fr £15.50 **S:** £16.00–£16.50
Beds: 2D **Baths:** 1 Sh
😃 🅿 🖾 ✕ 🝗,

Llangurig

SN9079   ◆ *Black Lion, Blue Bell*

The Old Vicarage Guest House,
Llangurig, Llanidloes, Powys, SY18 6RN.
Open: Mar to Nov
Grades: WTB 2 Star
01686 440280 (also fax)
M Hartley
a0048805@infotrade.co.uk
D: £18.00–£22.00 **S:** £25.00
Beds: 1F 2D 1T **Baths:** 4 En
♿ (5) 🅿 (6) 🖵 ⴕ ✕ ⵑ 🆅 ⅃
The Old Vicarage is a charming Victorian
House situated in Llangurig, 1000 ft
above sea level, the highest village in
Wales. Ideal for visiting the mountains
and valleys of Central Wales. Good
walking/bird watching (Red Kite
Country). Warm welcome guaranteed.

Llanidloes

SN9584   ◆ *Unicorn*

Lloyds, *Cambrian Place, Llanidloes,
Powys, SY18 6BX.*
Long-established Victorian hotel in centre
of attractive market town.
Open: Mar to Jan
Grades: WTB 2 Star
01686 412284 Mr Lines
Fax: 01686 412666
D: £25.00 **S:** £19.00–£33.00
Beds: 3D 2T 4S **Baths:** 6 En 1 Sh
♿ 🖵 ✕ ⵑ 🆅 ⅃

Llanigon

SO2139   ◆ *Black Lion*

The Old Post Office, *Llanigon, Hay-
on-Wye, Hereford, HR3 5QA.*
A very special find in Black Mountains,
superb vegetarian breakfast.
Open: All Year **Grades:** WTB 3 Star GH
01497 820008 Mrs Webb
D: £17.00–£25.00 **S:** £20.00–£45.00
Beds: 1F 1D 1T **Baths:** 2 En 1 Sh
♿ 🅿 (3) ⵂ 🖵 ⴕ ⵑ 🆅 ⅃

Llwynbrain, *Llanigon, Hay-on-Wye,
Hereford, HR3 5QF.*
Warm, friendly family farmhouse with
views of Black Mountains.
Open: All Year (not Xmas)
01497 847266
sascha@gibbonsfarm/freeserve.co.uk
D: £18.00–£25.00 **S:** £18.00–£25.00
Beds: 2F 1S **Baths:** 1 Sh
♿ 🅿 (6) 🖵 ⴕ ⵑ 🆅 ⅃

Llanrhaeadr-ym-Mochnant

SJ1226   ◆ *Wynnstay Hotel*

Eirianfa, *Waterfull Road, Llanrhaeadr-ym-
Mochnant, Oswestry, Shropshire, SY10 0JX.*
Overlooking the village and the Tanat
Valley, we offer comfortable warm
accommodation.
Open: All Year (not Xmas)
Grades: WTB 1 Star
01691 780507 Phil Common & Cathy
Laceby
eirianfa@yahoo.com
D: £17.50–£20.00 **S:** £25.00–£35.00
Beds: 1F 1D **Baths:** 1 Sh
♿ 🅿 (3) ⵂ ⴕ ⵑ 🆅 ⅃

Llansantffraed

SO1223   ◆ *Traveller's Rest*

The Allt, *Llansantffraed, Talybont-on-
Usk, Brecon, Powys, LD3 7YF.*
C18th farmhouse overlooking River Usk
with magnificent mountain views.
Open: All Year (not Xmas)
01874 676310 Mrs Hamill-Keays
sh.k@virgin.net
D: £15.00–£16.50 **S:** £12.00–£15.00
Beds: 1F 1D 1S **Baths:** 1 Sh
♿ 🅿 (6) 🖵 ⴕ ✕ ⵑ 🆅 ⅃

Llansilin

SJ2028   ◆ *Wynnstay*

Lloran Ganol, *Llansilin, Oswestry,
Shropshire, SY10 7QX.*
Dairy and sheep working farm set in its
own Welsh valley.
Open: All Year
Grades: WTB 3 Star
01691 791287 Mrs Jones
D: fr £15.00 **S:** fr £15.00
Beds: 1D 1T 1S **Baths:** 2 Sh
♿ 🅿 ⵂ 🖵 ✕ ⵑ ⅃

Llanspyddid

SO0028

Ashgrove, *Llanspyddid, Brecon, Powys,
LD3 8PB.*
This spacious old dower house is situated
2 miles from Brecon.
Open: Mar to Sept
Grades: WTB 2 Star
01874 622833 Mr Wakeham
ashgrove@btclick.com
D: £15.00–£16.00 **S:** £15.00–£16.00
Beds: 1D 2T **Baths:** 2 Sh
🅿 (5) ⵂ ✕ ⵑ 🆅 ⅃

Llanwrthwl

SN9763   ◆ *Vulcan Arms*

Dyffryn Farm, *Llanwrthwl, Llandrindod
Wells, Powys, LD1 6NU.*
Idyllically situated above the Upper Wye
valley, near the Elan Lakes.
Open: Mar to Oct
01597 811017 Mrs Tyler
Fax: 01597 810609
dyffrymfm@cs.com
D: £20.00–£22.00 **S:** £20.00–£22.00
Beds: 1D 1T 1S **Baths:** 1 En 1 Pr 1 Sh
♿ (5) 🅿 (6) ⵂ 🖵 ⴕ ✕ 🆅 ⅃

Llanwrtyd Wells

SN8746   ◆ *Stonecroft Inn, New Inn*

Oakfield House, *Dol-y-coed Road,
Llanwrtyd Wells, LD5 4RA.*
Comfortable Edwardian house in Britain's
smallest town. Red kite country.
Open: Easter to Oct
Grades: WTB 3 Star
01591 610605
oakfieldbandb@hotmail.com
D: £19.00 **S:** £19.00–£22.00
Beds: 1D 1T 1S **Baths:** 2 Sh
♿ (5) 🅿 (1) ⵂ 🖵 ⵑ 🆅 ⅃

Carlton House Hotel, *Dolycoed Road,
Llanwrtyd Wells, Powys, LD5 4SN.*
Edwardian restaurant with rooms.
Excellent dining, comfortable rooms,
warm welcome.
Open: All Year (not Xmas)
01591 610248 Dr Gilchrist
Fax: 01591 610242
D: £30.00–£35.00 **S:** £30.00–£40.00
Beds: 1F 4D 1T 1S **Baths:** 5 En 2 Pr
♿ 🖵 ⴕ ✕ ⵑ 🆅 ⅃ cc

Haulwen, *Beulah Road, Llanwrtyd Wells,
Powys, LD5 4RF.*
Small & friendly,comfortable rooms,
hairdryers, toiletries, robes, electric radio
alarms in rooms.
Open: All Year
01591 610449 (also fax)
haulwenbb@dsfgs.globalnet.co.uk
D: £15.00–£20.00 **S:** £15.00–£20.00
Beds: 1D 1S **Baths:** 1 Sh
ⵂ ⴕ ⵑ ⅃ ♿

Llanyre

SO0462   ◆ *Bell Inn*

Highbury Farm, *Llanyre, Llandrindod
Wells, Powys, LD1 6EA.*
Peaceful location with short farm trail.
Laundry room. Excellent food.
Open: Mar to Nov **Grades:** WTB 3 Star
01597 822716 (also fax) Mrs Evans
D: £18.00–£21.00 **S:** £21.00–£24.00
Beds: 1F 2D **Baths:** 2 En 1 Pr
♿ (1) 🅿 (3) ⵂ 🖵 ✕ ⵑ 🆅 ⅃

Greenglades, *Llanyre, Llandrindod
Wells, Powys, LD1 6EA.*
Beautiful country house in tranquil
setting near village inn.
Open: All Year (not Xmas)
Grades: WTB 4 Star
01597 822950 E J Jones
D: £18.00–£22.00 **S:** £20.00–£24.00
Beds: 1F 1D 1T **Baths:** 2 En
♿ 🅿 (3) ⵂ 🖵 ⵑ 🆅 ⅃

Llowes

SO1942   ◆ *Maesllwch Arms*

Ty-Bach, *Llowes, Glasbury, HR3 5JE.*
Ornamental ponds, woodland garden,
breathtaking views, abundant wildlife,
birds. Friendly.
Open: All Year (not Xmas/New Year)
Grades: WTB 3 Star
01497 847759 J M Bradfield
Fax: 01497 847940
charles.bradfield@farmline.com
D: £22.50–£25.00 **S:** £30.00–£40.00
Beds: 1D **Baths:** 2 Pr
♿ (5) 🅿 (5) 🖵 ✕ ⵑ ⅃

Llyswen

SO1337   ◆ *Griffin Inn*

Lower Rhydness Bungalow,
Llyswen, Brecon, Powys, LD3 0AZ.
Very comfortable centrally-heated
bungalow, working farm, views into
valley. **Open:** Easter to Dec
01874 754264 Mrs Williams
D: fr £16.00 **S:** fr £16.00
Beds: 1D 1T 1S **Baths:** 1 Sh
♿ (3) 🖵 ⴕ ✕ ⵑ ⅃ ♿

Machynlleth

SH7400   ◆ *White Lion, Black Lion, Glyndwyr Hotel, White Horse, Wynnastay, Skinner's Arms*

Maenllwyd, *Newtown Road, Machynlleth, Powys, SY20 8EY.*
Home from home, within walking distance all amenities, safe parking.
Open: All Year (not Xmas)
Grades: WTB 3 Star GH, AA 3 Diamond
01654 702928 (also fax)
Mr Vince
nigel@maenllwyd.co.uk
D: £19.00–£22.00 **S:** £25.00
Beds: 1F 4D 3T **Baths:** 8 En
🛇 🅿 (10) ⊬ 📺 🎟 📖 Ⓥ ♨ cc

Talbontdrain, *Uwchygarreg, Machynlleth, Powys, SY20 8RR.*
Open: All Year (not Xmas/New Year)
01654 702192 Ms Matthews
talbontdrain@btclick.com
D: £19.00–£21.00 **S:** £16.00–£19.00
Beds: 1D 1T 2S **Baths:** 1 Pr 1 Sh
🛇 🅿 (4) ⊬ 📺 ✕ 📖 Ⓥ ♨
Friendly family B&B. We like having children here and are flexible about sleeping arrangements - there's even a barn for adventurous kids! We have dogs, cats and chickens, rivers, mountains and seaside not far away. Safe playing space and fantastic food.

Wynnstay Arms Hotel, *Maengwyn Street, Machynlleth, Powys, SY20 8AE.*
Old coaching inn, in heart of historic market town, in stunning Dovey Valley.
Open: All Year
Grades: AA 2 Star, RAC 2 Star
01654 702941 Mr Dark
Fax: 01654 703884
info@wynnstay-hotel.com
D: £35.00–£48.00 **S:** fr £45.00
Beds: 3F 9D 5T 6S **Baths:** 23 En
🛇 🅿 (36) ⊬ 📺 ✕ 📖 Ⓥ ♨ cc

Cwmdylluan Forge, *Machynlleth, Powys, SY20 8RZ.*
Modern riverside bungalow, rooms overlook lovely garden and river.
Open: All Year **Grades:** WTB 3 Star
01654 702684 M N Hughes
Fax: 01654 700133
D: £15.50–£17.50 **S:** £16.50–£18.00
Beds: 1D 1T 1S **Baths:** 2 Pr 2 Sh
🛇 (5) 🅿 (5) 📺 ✕ 📖 Ⓥ ♨ 🔥 ♨

Gwelfryn, *6 Green Fields, Machynlleth, Powys, SY20 8DR.*
Quiet but central, fantastic breakfasts, near all tourist attractions.
Open: Easter to Oct
Grades: WTB 2 Star
01654 702532 bb@gwelfryn.co.uk
D: £17.00–£19.50 **S:** fr £17.00
Beds: 1D 1T 1S **Baths:** 1 En 1 Pr
🛇 ⊬ 📺 🔥 📖 Ⓥ ♨

Awelon, *Heol Powys, Machynlleth, Powys, SY20 8AY.*
Centrally situated, small, comfortable private house. Warm welcome.
Open: All Year (not Xmas)
01654 702047 Ms Williams
D: £16.00–£17.00 **S:** £16.00–£17.50
Beds: 1T 1S **Baths:** 1 Sh
🛇 (2) ⊬ 🔥 📖 Ⓥ

Milebrook

SO3072

Milebrook House Hotel, *Milebrook, Knighton, Powys., LD7 1LT.*
Dower House once the retreat of Emperor Haile Selassie.
Open: All Year
Grades: WTB 3 Star, AA 2 Star
01547 528632 Fax: 01547 520509
hotel@milebrook.kc3
D: £37.75–£41.75 **S:** £51.00–£55.00
Beds: 3T 7D **Baths:** 10 En
🛇 (8) 🅿 (30) ⊬ 📺 ✕ 📖 Ⓥ ♨ 🔥 ♨ cc

Mochdre

SO0788   ◆ *Dolan Inn*

Llettyderyn, *Mochdre, Newtown, Powys, SY16 4JY.*
Traditional hospitality in a restored farmhouse, One ground floor room.
Open: All Year
Grades: WTB 3 Star Farm
01686 626131 Mrs Jandrell
D: £20.00–£22.00 **S:** £25.00–£27.00
Beds: 2D 1T **Baths:** 3 En
🛇 🅿 📺 ✕ 📖 Ⓥ ♨

Montgomery

SO2296   ◆ *Cottage, Dragon*

The Manor House, *Pool Road, Montgomery, Powys, SY15 6QY.*
Former house of correction, friendly welcome, private house.
Open: All Year
01686 668736 Mrs Williams
D: £16.00 **S:** £16.00
Beds: 1D 1T 1S **Baths:** 1 En 1 Pr
🛇 🅿 (2) 📺 🔥 📖 Ⓥ ♨

Little Brompton Farm, *Montgomery, Powys, SY15 6HY.*
Working C17th farm on Offa's Dyke. Superior quality for the discerning.
Open: All Year
01686 668371 (also fax)
Mrs Bright
D: £19.00–£20.00 **S:** £20.00–£22.00
Beds: 1F 1D 1T **Baths:** 2 En 1 Pr
🛇 🅿 ⊬ 📺 🔥 📖 Ⓥ ♨ ♨

New Radnor

SO2160   ◆ *Red Lion*

Bache Farm, *New Radnor, Presteigne, Powys, LD8 2TG.*
C17th farmhouse in beautiful unspoilt countryside amidst the Welsh Marches.
Open: All Year (not Xmas)
Grades: WTB 2 Star Farm
01544 350680 Mrs Hardwick
D: £18.00–£19.50 **S:** £22.00–£25.00
Beds: 2D 1T **Baths:** 1 Sh
🛇 🅿 ⊬ 📺 🔥 ✕ 📖 Ⓥ ♨

BATHROOMS

Pr - Private

Sh - Shared

En - Ensuite

Newbridge on Wye

SO0158

Lluest Newydd, *Llysdinam, Newbridge on Wye, Llandrindod Wells, Powys, LD1 6ND.*
Luxury remote farmhouse. Ideal for walking and birdwatching. Elan Valley close by.
Open: All Year
Grades: WTB 4 Star, AA 4 Diamond
01597 860435 (also fax)
Mrs Burton
lluestnewydd@talk21.com
D: £18.00–£22.00 **S:** £22.00–£26.00
Beds: 1F 1T 2D **Baths:** 2 En 1 Pr
🛇 🅿 (6) 📺 ✕ 📖 Ⓥ ♨ 🔥

Newtown

SO1191   ◆ *Kerry Lamb, Dolfor Inn*

Plas Canol Guest House, *New Road, Newtown, Powys, SY16 1AS.*
Detached house, comfortable beds, white cotton sheets, fresh flowers in bedrooms. Brochure available.
Open: All Year
Grades: WTB 3 Star B&B
01686 625598 Mrs Burd
D: £18.00–£20.00 **S:** £18.00–£26.00
Beds: 1F 1D 1T **Baths:** 2 En 1 Sh
🅿 (3) ⊬ 📺 📖 Ⓥ ♨

Greenfields, *Kerry, Newtown, Powys, SY16 4LH.*
Comfortable guest house, good food, warm welcome.
Open: All Year (not Xmas)
Grades: WTB 2 Star
01686 670596 Mrs Madeley
Fax: 01686 670354
D: £18.00–£20.00 **S:** £18.00–£22.00
Beds: 1F 1D 1T 1S **Baths:** 3 En
🛇 (4) 🅿 (6) ⊬ 📺 🔥 ✕ 📖 Ⓥ ♨ cc

Pen-Y-Gelli Country Guest House, *Wern-Ddu Lane, Newtown, Powys, SY16 3AH.*
Country guest house with swimming pool gardens and conservatory dining room.
Open: All Year
01686 628292 (also fax)
Mrs Hawkins
valerie.hawkins@virgin.net
D: £19.50–£20.00 **S:** £22.50–£25.00
Beds: 1F 1D 1T **Baths:** 3 En
🛇 🅿 (6) ⊬ 📺 ✕ 📖 Ⓥ ♨ 🔥 3

Pontsticill

SO0611   ◆ *Butcher's Arms*

Station House, *Pontsticill, Merthyr Tydfil, CF48 2UP.*
Open: All Year
01685 377798 Mrs Hills
Fax: 01685 384854
D: £22.50–£25.50 **S:** £22.50–£25.50
Beds: 1F **Baths:** 1 Pr
🛇 🅿 (3) ⊬ 📺 📖 Ⓥ ♨
Comfortable and carefully converted former railway station signal box. The property is on the edge of a reservoir with spectacular view across the water to the Brecon Beacons. The Brecon Mountain Railway and Taff Cycle Trail are adjacent.

Rhayader

SN9768 🐾 *Bear's Head, Crown, Triangle*

Liverpool House, East House, Rhayader, Powys, LD6 5EA.
Open: All Year (not Xmas)
Grades: WTB 2 Star
01597 810706 Mrs Griffiths
Fax: 01597 810964
ann@liverpoolhouse.net
D: £15.50–£17.00 **S:** £18.00–£22.00
Beds: 2F 5D 1S **Baths:** 7 En 1 Sh
🛏 🅿 (8) 🖵 🐾 🎵 ▥ ♨ cc
Excellent accommodation either in main house or annexe. Very close to the beautiful Elan Valley Reservoirs in an area suitable for bird watching, walking, cycling. Ideally central for touring Mid Wales. Groups Welcome. Cream teas, Welsh teas and snacks available.

Brynafon Country House Hotel, South Street, Rhayader, Powys, LD6 5BL.
Open: All Year
Grades: WTB 3 Star, AA 2 Star
01597 810735 Mrs Collins
Fax: 01597 810111
info@brynafon.co.uk.
D: £18.00–£40.00 **S:** fr £35.00
Beds: 1F 11D 4T **Baths:** 16 En
🛏 🅿 ⅍ ▥ 🐾 🐾 ✕ ▥ ▥ ♨ 🕭
A former Victorian workhouse built in 1876, this impressive building is now a comfortable, relaxed, family-run Hotel. Set amid glorious hills and mountains near Rhayader and the beautiful Elan Valley with a rare 'Red Kite' feeding centre next door.

Brynteg, East Street, Rhayader, Powys, LD6 5EA.
Comfortable Edwardian guest house, overlooking hills and gardens.
Open: All Year (not Xmas)
Grades: WTB 3 Star B & B
01597 810052 Mrs Lawrence
brynteg@hotmail.com
D: £16.50–£17.00 **S:** £16.00–£17.00
Beds: 2D 1T 1S **Baths:** 3 En 1 Pr
🛏 🅿 (4) 🖵 ▥ ♨

Beili Neuadd, Rhayader, Powys, LD6 5NS.
Award-winning accommodation in farmhouse - secluded position with stunning views.
Open: All Year (not Xmas)
Grades: WTB 4 Star
01597 810211 (also fax)
Mrs Edwards
ann-carl@thebeili.freeserve.co.uk
D: £21.00–£23.00 **S:** fr £21.00
Beds: 2D 1T 1S **Baths:** 2 En 2 Pr
🛏 (8) 🅿 🖵 🐾 🎵 ▥ ♨ 🕭

The Horseshoe Guest House, Church Street, Rhayader, Powys, LD6 5AT.
'Country Style' decor, conservatory with fig and grape vines.
Open: All Year (not Xmas)
Grades: WTB 3 Star GH
01597 810982 (also fax)
Mrs Stubbs
horseshoe@easicom.com
D: £18.00–£19.00 **S:** £18.00
Beds: 2D 1T 1S **Baths:** 2 En 1 Sh
🛏 🅿 (6) 🖵 🐾 ✕ ▥ ♨

Downfield Farm, Rhayader, Powys, LD6 5PA.
Beautifully situated, surrounded by hills and lakes. Also, Red Kite country.
Open: Mar to Oct
Grades: WTB 2 Star
01597 810394 Mrs Price
D: £17.00–£18.00 **S:** £18.00–£19.00
Beds: 2D 1T **Baths:** 2 Sh
🛏 🅿 (10) 🖵 🐾 🎵 ♨

Gigrin Farm, South Street, Rhayader, Powys, LD6 5BL.
Superb views; working farm, nature trail, feeding red kites everyday.
Open: All Year
01597 810243 Mrs Powell
Fax: 01597 810357
accomm@gigrin.co.uk
D: £16.00–£17.50 **S:** £17.50–£20.00
Beds: 2D **Baths:** 1 Sh
🛏 (5) 🅿 (3) ⅍ 🖵 ▥ ♨

Bryncoed, Dark Lane, Rhayader, Powys, LD6 5DA.
Victorian house set in 1/3 acre, originally built for local doctor.
Open: All Year
01597 811082 d.izzard@which.net
D: £14.50–£20.00 **S:** £15.00–£21.00
Beds: 3F 2D 2T **Baths:** 1 En 2 Pr 1 Sh
🛏 🅿 (4) ⅍ 🖵 🐾 ✕ ▥ ▥ ♨ 🕭 cc

Talgarth

SO1533 🐾 *Mason's Arms, Castle Inn*

The Olde Masons Arms Hotel, Hay Road, Talgarth, Brecon, Powys, LD3 0BB.
C16th hotel with country cottage ambience. Ideal for walking amidst Black Mountains & Brecon Beacons.
Open: All Year
Grades: WTB 3 Star
01874 711688 C J Evans
D: £26.50–£29.50 **S:** £29.50–£32.50
Beds: 2F 2D 1T 2S **Baths:** 7 En
🛏 🅿 (10) 🖵 🐾 ✕ ▥ ▥ ♨ cc

Castle Inn, Pengenffordd, Talgarth, Brecon, Powys, LD3 0EP.
Traditional country inn with the Brecon Beacons national park.
Open: All Year (not Xmas)
01874 711353 Mr Mountjoy
castlepen@aol.com
D: £20.00–£23.00 **S:** £20.00–£31.00
Beds: 1F 2D 1T 1S **Baths:** 2 En 1 Sh
🛏 🅿 (50) 🖵 ✕ ▥ ▥ ♨ cc

Talybont-on-Usk

SO1122 🐾 *Traveller's Rest*

Llanddety Hall Farm, Talybont-on-Usk, Brecon, Powys, LD3 7YR.
C17th Listed farmhouse in Brecon Beacons National Park, beautiful views.
Open: All Year (not Xmas)
Grades: WTB 3 Star Farm, AA 4 Diamond
01874 676415 Mrs Atkins
D: £22.00–£26.00 **S:** £25.00–£26.00
Beds: 2D 1T **Baths:** 2 En 1 Pr
🛏 (12) 🅿 (5) ⅍ 🖵 ✕ ▥ ♨

Talyllyn

SO1027 🐾 *Red Lion, White Swan, Castle*

Glascwm, Talyllyn, Brecon, Powys, LD3 7SY.
Tranquil rural setting, close to the Brecon Beacons and Llangorse Lake.
Open: All Year (not Xmas)
Grades: WTB 3 Star
01874 658659 J C King
Fax: 01874 658649
cathkin@lineone.net
D: £22.00
Beds: 1F 1D 1T **Baths:** 3 En
🛏 🅿 (4) ⅍ 🖵 ▥ ♨ ▥

Tretower

SO1821 🐾 *Farmers Arms*

The Firs, Tretower, Crickhowell, Powys, NP8 1RF.
Charming country house situated in a secluded position of Tredtower village.
Open: All Year
Grades: WTB 3 Star
01874 730780 (also fax)
Mrs Eckley
D: £19.00–£23.00 **S:** £25.00
Beds: 1F 3D 1T **Baths:** 2 En 2 Pr 2 Sh
🛏 🅿 (10) 🖵 🐾 ▥ ▥ ♨ 🕭 🕭

Trewern

SJ2711

Greenbank, Criggan Lane, Trewern, Welshpool, Powys, SY21 8EE.
Peaceful, rural, central for Wales and Borders. Welshpool 5 miles.
Open: All Year
Grades: WTB 2 Star
01938 570319 Mrs Hamer
Fax: 01938 570719
D: £17.00–£19.00 **S:** £17.00–£19.00
Beds: 1F 1T 1D **Baths:** 1 En 1 Sh
🛏 🅿 (3) 🖵 🐾 ✕ ▥ ♨

Van

SN9587 🐾 *Star Inn, Red Lion*

Esgairmaen, Van, Llanidloes, Powys, SY18 6NT.
Comfortable farmhouse in unspoilt countryside, ideal for waking and bird watching.
Open: Easter to Oct
01686 430272
D: £17.00–£19.00 **S:** £17.00–£19.00
Beds: 1F 1D **Baths:** 2 En
🛏 (1) 🅿 (4) ⅍ 🖵 🐾 ✕ ▥ ♨

Welshpool

SJ2207 🐾 *Green Dragon, Horseshoe, King's Head, Railway, Red Lion, Royal Oak, Star Inn, Talbot*

Tynllwyn Farm, Welshpool, Powys, SY21 9BW.
Visitor's remark - 'Nearest place to Heaven'. Friendly, quiet, wonderful views.
Open: All Year (not Xmas)
Grades: WTB 3 Star, AA 3 Star
01938 553175 Mrs Emberton
Fax: 01938 553996
D: £15.50–£18.00 **S:** £17.50–£22.00
Beds: 3F 1D 1T 1S **Baths:** 3 En 2 Sh
🛏 🅿 (10) 🖵 ▥ ♨

Meithrinfa, Forden, Welshpool, Powys, SY21 8RT.
Open: Easter to Nov **Grades:** WTB 3 Star
01938 580458 Mrs Hughes
D: £18.00–£20.00 **S:** £20.00–£22.00
Beds: 1F 1T **Baths:** 2 En
⌾ ℙ (3) ✗ ⊤⊻ ✕ 📖 ☂ ⌂
Meithrinfa is a large bungalow set in its own grounds, in an elevated position, overlooking the Severn Valley. Only 2 miles from market town of Welshpool and Powys Castle, Llanfair and W/pool steam railway canal barges, riding school, golf, lakes and mountains.

Lower Trelydan, Guilsfield, Welshpool, Powys, SY21 9PH.
Award-winning black-and-white farmhouse, ensuite, licensed bar, evening meals, Welshpool 2 miles.
Open: All Year (not Xmas/New Year)
Grades: WTB 4 Star, AA 4 Diamond
01938 553105 (also fax) Mrs Jones
stay@lowertrelydan.com
D: £24.00–£25.00 **S:** £25.00–£28.00
Beds: 1F 1D 1T **Baths:** 3 En
⌾ ℙ ⊤⊻ ✕ 📖 ☂ ✿ ☂

Tresi-Aur, Brookfield Road, Welshpool, Powys, SY21 7PZ.
Detached family home offers friendly hospitality conveniently situated to town.
Open: Jan to Nov
Grades: WTB 2 Star
01938 552430
Mrs Davies
D: £16.00–£18.00
S: £16.00–£18.00
Beds: 1F 1D 1T 1S **Baths:** 1 Pr
⌾ ℙ (2) ✗ ⊤⊻ 📖 ⊻ ☂

Hafren Guest House, 38 Salop Road, Welshpool, Powys, SY21 7EA.
Georgian house with medieval links in 'Gateway to Mid-Wales' town.
Open: All Year (not Xmas)
01938 554112
Ms Shaw
kuldip@caberwal.freeserve.com
D: £16.00–£18.00
S: £18.00–£20.00
Beds: 1F 1D 1T **Baths:** 1 En 1 Sh
⌾ ℙ (3) ⊤⊻ ⊁ ✕ 📖 ⊻ ☂

Dysserth Hall, Powis Castle, Welshpool, Powys, SY21 8RQ.
Comfortable, friendly, Listed manor home in peaceful countryside, superb view.
Open: Easter to Nov
01938 552153 (also fax)
Mrs Marriott
D: £21.00–£22.50
S: £21.00–£25.00
Beds: 1D 2T 1S
Baths: 2 Pr 1 Sh
⌾ (8) ℙ (12) ✗ ⊤⊻ 📖 ☂

Whitton

SO2767 ◀ Hundred House

Pilleth Court, Whitton, Knighton, Powys, LD7 1NP.
16th century house in historic location offering quality accommodation.
Open: All Year (not Xmas)
01547 560272 (also fax)
Mrs Hood
D: fr £18.00 **S:** fr £20.00
Beds: 1F 2D 1T **Baths:** 1 En 1 Sh
⌾ (9) ℙ (6) ⊤⊻ ✕ 📖 ☂

Stilwell's Britain Cycleway Companion

23 Long Distance Cycleways –
Where to Stay * Where to Eat

County Cycleways – Sustrans Routes

The first guide of its kind, **Stilwell's Britain Cycleway Companion** makes planning accommodation for your cycling trip easy. It lists B&Bs, hostels, campsites and pubs– in the order they appear along the selected cycleways – allowing the cyclist to book ahead. No more hunting for a room, a hot meal or a cold drink after a long day in the saddle. Stilwell's gives descriptions of the featured routes and includes such relevant information as maps, grid references and distance from route; Tourist Board ratings; and the availability of drying facilities and packed lunches. No matter which route – or part of a route – you decide to ride, let the **Cycleway Companion** show you where to sleep and eat.

As essential as your tyre pump – the perfect cycling companion: **Stilwell's Britain Cycleway Companion**.

Cycleways

Sustrans

Carlisle to Inverness – Clyde to Forth - Devon Coast to Coast -
Hull to Harwich – Kingfisher Cycle Trail - Lon Las Cymru – Sea to Sea (C2C)
– Severn and Thames – West Country Way – White Rose Cycle Route

County

Round Berkshire Cycle Route – Cheshire Cycleway – Cumbria Cycleway –
Essex Cycle Route – Icknield Way - Lancashire Cycleway –
Leicestershire County Cycleway – Oxfordshire Cycleway –
Reivers Cycle Route – South Downs Way - Surrey Cycleway –
Wiltshire Cycleway – Yorkshire Dales Cycleway

£9.95 from all good bookstores (ISBN 1-900861-26-7) or £10.95 (inc p&p) from Stilwell Publishing Ltd, 59 Charlotte Road, London EC2A 3QW (020 7739 7179)

Location Index

The cities, towns, villages and hamlets listed in this index all have entries in STILWELL'S: BRITAIN BED & BREAKFAST under their respective regional heading. If there is no listing for the place you wish to stay in, the section map for that particular region will show you somewhere else to stay close by.

C

Index

NOT LISTED IN STILWELL'S?

Do you know of a B&B that should be listed in these pages, but isn't? Use this form to recommend the B&B, telling us briefly why you think it merits inclusion.

I nominate the following B&B for inclusion in next year's edition of Stilwell's *Britain: Bed & Breakfast.*

B&B Owner's Name . . . .

B&B Address . . . .

. . . .

. . . .

B&B Tel No . . . .

Reasons for Nomination . . . .

. . . .

. . . .

. . . .

Nominated by . . . .

Nominee's Address . . . .

. . . .

. . . .

Please send this form to:
**Britain: B&B, Stilwell Publishing Ltd, The Courtyard,
59 Charlotte Road, Shoreditch, London, EC2A 3QW.**

ORDER A COPY FOR A FRIEND OR COLLEAGUE

Yes, I wish to order the following title/s :

___ **Stilwell's Britain: Bed & Breakfast 2001**
@ £11.95 (inc. £2 p&p)

___ **Stilwell's Ireland: Bed & Breakfast 2001**
@ £7.95 (inc. £1 p&p)

___ **Stilwell's National Trail Companion**
@ £10.95 (inc. £1 p&p)

___ **Stilwell's Cycleway Companion**
@ £10.95 (inc. £1 p&p)

Sterling or EC currency cheques only please, made payable to Stilwell Publishing Ltd. Please send me my copy within 21 days of receipt of this order.

Name . . . .

Address . . . .

. . . .

Postcode . . . .

Tel No . . . .

Please send this order form, accompanied by your payment, to:
**Copy Sales, Stilwell Publishing Ltd, The Courtyard,
59 Charlotte Road, Shoreditch, London, EC2A 3QW.**

Please debit my credit/payment card (Visa/Mastercard only).

Card No . . . .   Expiry date ___ / ___ / ___

Signature . . . .

If different from above please state card-holder name exactly as it appears on the card, followed by card-holder address.

NOT LISTED IN STILWELL'S?

Do you know of a B&B that should be listed in these pages, but isn't? Use this form to recommend the B&B, telling us briefly why you think it merits inclusion.

I nominate the following B&B for inclusion in next year's edition of Stilwell's *Britain: Bed & Breakfast.*

B&B Owner's Name . . . .

B&B Address . . . .

. . . .

. . . .

B&B Tel No . . . .

Reasons for Nomination . . . .

. . . .

. . . .

. . . .

Nominated by . . . .

Nominee's Address . . . .

. . . .

. . . .

Please send this form to:
**Britain: B&B, Stilwell Publishing Ltd, The Courtyard,
59 Charlotte Road, Shoreditch, London, EC2A 3QW.**

ORDER A COPY FOR A FRIEND OR COLLEAGUE

Yes, I wish to order the following title/s :

___ **Stilwell's Britain: Bed & Breakfast 2001**
@ £11.95 (inc. £2 p&p)

___ **Stilwell's Ireland: Bed & Breakfast 2001**
@ £7.95 (inc. £1 p&p)

___ **Stilwell's National Trail Companion**
@ £10.95 (inc. £1 p&p)

___ **Stilwell's Cycleway Companion**
@ £10.95 (inc. £1 p&p)

Sterling or EC currency cheques only please, made payable to Stilwell Publishing Ltd. Please send me my copy within 21 days of receipt of this order.

Name . . . .

Address . . . .

. . . .

Postcode . . . .

Tel No . . . .

Please send this order form, accompanied by your payment, to:
Copy Sales, Stilwell Publishing Ltd, The Courtyard, 59 Charlotte Road, Shoreditch, London, EC2A 3QW.

Please debit my credit/payment card (Visa/Mastercard only).

Card No . . . .   Expiry date ___ / ___ / ___

Signature . . . .

If different from above please state card-holder name exactly as it appears on the card, followed by card-holder address.

NOT LISTED IN STILWELL'S?

Do you know of a B&B that should be listed in these pages, but isn't? Use this form to recommend the B&B, telling us briefly why you think it merits inclusion.

I nominate the following B&B for inclusion in next year's edition of Stilwell's *Britain: Bed & Breakfast.*

B&B Owner's Name . . . .

B&B Address . . . .

. . . .

. . . .

B&B Tel No . . . .

Reasons for Nomination . . . .

. . . .

. . . .

. . . .

Nominated by . . . .

Nominee's Address . . . .

. . . .

. . . .

Please send this form to:
**Britain: B&B, Stilwell Publishing Ltd, The Courtyard,
59 Charlotte Road, Shoreditch, London, EC2A 3QW.**

ORDER A COPY FOR A FRIEND OR COLLEAGUE

Yes, I wish to order the following title/s :

___ **Stilwell's Britain: Bed & Breakfast 2001**
@ £11.95 (inc. £2 p&p)

___ **Stilwell's Ireland: Bed & Breakfast 2001**
@ £7.95 (inc. £1 p&p)

___ **Stilwell's National Trail Companion**
@ £10.95 (inc. £1 p&p)

___ **Stilwell's Cycleway Companion**
@ £10.95 (inc. £1 p&p)

Sterling or EC currency cheques only please, made payable to Stilwell Publishing Ltd. Please send me my copy within 21 days of receipt of this order.

Name . . . .

Address . . . .

. . . .

Postcode . . . .

Tel No . . . .

Please send this order form, accompanied by your payment, to:
Copy Sales, Stilwell Publishing Ltd, The Courtyard, 59 Charlotte Road, Shoreditch, London, EC2A 3QW.

Please debit my credit/payment card (Visa/Mastercard only).

Card No . . . .   Expiry date ___ / ___ / ___

Signature . . . .

If different from above please state card-holder name exactly as it appears on the card, followed by card-holder address.

Aubin Imprimeur
LIGUGÉ, POITIERS

Achevé d'imprimer en décembre 2000
N° d'impression L 60954
Dépôt légal décembre 2000
Imprimé en France

STILWELL'S

KEY TO ENTRIES

🐾 Children welcome (from age shown in brackets, if specified)

🅿 Off-street car parking (number of places shown in brackets)

🚭 No smoking

📺 Television (either in every room or in a TV lounge)

🐕 Pets accepted (by prior arrangement)

✕ Evening meal available (by prior arrangement)

Ⓥ Special diets catered for (by prior arrangement - please check with owner to see if your particular requirements are catered for)

▥ Central heating throughout

♿ Suitable for disabled people (please check with owner to see what level of disability is provided for)

♿2 Gradings of the Tourist Boards' national accessibility scheme: category 1 (highest) means accessible to wheelchair user travelling independently; 2 means accessible to wheelchair user travelling with assistance; 3 means accessible to person with limited mobility able to walk a few paces/up maximum three steps

❄ Christmas breaks a speciality

☕ Coffee/tea making facilities

cc Credit cards accepted

Use the **National Grid** reference with Ordnance Survey maps and any atlas that uses the British National Grid. The letters refer to a 100 kilometre grid square. The first two numbers refer to a North/South grid line and the last two numbers refer to an East/West grid line. The grid reference indicates their intersection point.

The **location heading** – every hamlet, village, town and city listed in this directory is represented on the local county map at the head of each section.

Local pubs – these are the names of nearby pubs that serve food in the evening, as suggested by local B&Bs.

Penny Hassett

PH2096 🍺 *Cat & Fiddle, The Bull*

The Old Rectory, *Main Street, Penny Hassett, Borchester, Borsetshire, BC2 3QT.*
C18th former rectory, lovely garden. Convenient for countryside and Borchester.
Open: All Year
Grades: ETC 3 Diamond
01676 512480 Mrs Grundy
Fax: 01676 512481
oldrectory@aol.com
D: £18.00-£20.00 **S:** £20.00-£23.00
Beds: 1F 1D 1T **Baths:** 1 En 1 Pr 1 Sh
🐾 🅿 (5) 🚭 📺 ✕ ▥ Ⓥ ❄ ☕ ♿ cc

Bedrooms
F = Family
D = Double
T = Twin
S = Single

Bathrooms
En = Ensuite
Pr = Private
Sh = Shared

D: **Price range** *per person* sharing in a *double room.*
S: **Price range** for a single person in a room.

Grades – The English Tourism Council (**ETC**) grades B&Bs for quality in Diamonds (**1 Diamond** to **5 Diamond**, highest) and hotels in Stars (**1 Star** to **5 Star**). The Jersey Tourist Board (**JTB**) uses the same system. Scottish and Welsh Tourist Board (**STB** and **WTB**) grades have two parts: the Star rating is for quality (**1 Star** to **5 Star**, highest), the other part designates the type of establishment, e.g. B&B, Guest House (**GH**), Country House (**CH**) etc. Isle of Man Tourist Board (**IOMTB**) grades have two parts: the range of facilities provided is represented by 'Listed' to 1 through 5 Crowns (**Cr**); there is also a general quality grading such as Approved (**Approv**) or Commended (**Comm**). The Guernsey Tourist Board (**GTB**) rates B&Bs for quality as Grade A (higher) or B. Ask at Tourist Information Centres for further information on these systems. The Automobile Association (**AA**) and Royal Automobile Club (**RAC**) both use, throughout the British–Irish Isles, the same system of Diamonds and Stars as the English Tourism Council.